Y0-DWN-140

VIRGINIA CRIMINAL LAW AND MOTOR VEHICLE HANDBOOK

including
Legislative Highlights and
Legal Guidelines

2001

(Includes enactments of the 2000 Regular Legislative Session through May 19, 2000)

GOULD PUBLICATIONS
of Florida, Inc.

Published by
GOULD PUBLICATIONS OF FLORIDA, INC.
1333 North U.S. Hwy. 17–92
Longwood, FL 32750–3724
(800) 717–7917
World Wide Web—http://www.gouldlaw.com
E–mail—info@gouldlaw.com

ISBN 1-882476-01-8

Every attempt has been made to ensure the accuracy and the completeness of the law contained herein. No express or implied guarantees or warranties are made.

Since laws change very often and vary from jurisdiction to jurisdiction, it is very important to check the timeliness and applicability of the laws contained herein.

FOREWORD

The material presented herewith in convenient form is the **Virginia Criminal Law and Motor Vehicle Handbook**, as currently amended to include enactments of the 2000 Regular Legislative Session through Chapter 1073 (May 19, 2000). All changes have been incorporated in text, and effective dates have been added where applicable. Also included are Legislative Highlights, Legal Guidelines, and a comprehensive index.

This handbook contains the following:

1) Title 18.2 – Crimes and Offenses Generally *(complete title)*

2) Title 19.2 – Criminal Procedure *(complete title)*

3) Title 46.2 – Motor Vehicles *(complete title)*

4) Title 52 – Police (State) *(complete title)*

5) Title 54.1, Chapter 34 – Drug Control Act *(complete chapter)*

6) Selected related statutes.

A complete, up-to-date, integrated index is also included.

Please note that the Virginia Code Commission may promulgate changes to the 1999 legislation through its authority stated in §9-77.10, which is as follows:

> The Commission may correct unmistakable printer's errors, misspellings and other unmistakable errors in the statutes as incorporated into the Code of Virginia, and may make consequential changes in the titles of officers and agencies, and other purely consequential changes made necessary by the use in the statutes of titles, terminology and references, or other language no longer appropriate.
>
> The Commission may renumber, rename, and rearrange any Code of Virginia titles, chapters, articles, and sections in the statutes adopted, and make corresponding changes in lists of chapter, article, and section headings, catchlines, and tables, when, in the judgment of the Commission, it is necessary because of any disturbance or interruption of orderly or consecutive arrangement.
>
> The Commission may correct unmistakable errors in cross-references to Code of Virginia sections and may change cross-references to Code of Virginia sections which have become outdated or incorrect due to subsequent amendment to, revision, or repeal of the sections to which reference is made.
>
> The Commission may omit from the statutes incorporated into the Code of Virginia provisions which, in the judgment of the Commission, are inappropriate in a code, such as emergency clauses, clauses providing for specific nonrecurring appropriations and general repealing clauses.

At the end of this book is Gould's handy ***Quick Find Locator***™ which will help you find the law you need.

Annual editions will incorporate changes as enacted. Please return the "IMPORTANT" subscription card at the front of this volume to ensure that you are notified when the latest changes are available.

Comments from users of this book and ways to improve its use would be appreciated by the publisher.

*This product is also available on **CD-ROM** as **Virginia Criminal and Motor Vehicle Laws DiskLaw**™. For details on how to obtain the laws you need and enforce for use on a single computer or on a network, please contact the publisher.*

This page intentionally left blank.

2000 Legislative Changes to the VIRGINIA CRIMINAL LAW AND MOTOR VEHICLE HANDBOOK

Section	Change	Bill No.	Chapter	Effective Date
2.1-116.05	Amend	SB 732	947	7/1/2000
2.1-116.05	Amend	HB 1177	1006	7/1/2000
2.1-124	Amend	HB 1362	239	7/1/2000
2.1-133.7	Amend	HB 77	314	7/1/2000
2.1-133.7:1	Amend	SB 415	616	7/1/2000
2.1-342.01	Amend	HB 690	66	7/1/2000
2.1-342.01	Amend	HB 1165	237	7/1/2000
2.1-342.01	Amend	SB 359	382	7/1/2000
2.1-342.01	Amend	HB 438	400	7/1/2000
2.1-342.01	Amend	HB 1187	430	7/1/2000
2.1-342.01	Amend	HB 1005	583	7/1/2000
2.1-342.01	Amend	HB 1304	589	7/1/2000
2.1-342.01	Amend	SB 390	592	7/1/2000
2.1-342.01	Amend	SB 552	594	7/1/2000
2.1-342.01	Amend	SB 479	618	7/1/2000
2.1-342.01	Amend	SB 441	657	7/1/2000
2.1-342.01	Amend	HB 1471	720	7/1/2000
2.1-342.01	Amend	HB 1295	932	7/1/2000
2.1-342.01	Amend	HB 1327	933	7/1/2000
2.1-342.01	Amend	SB 732	947	7/1/2000
2.1-342.01	Amend	HB 1177	1006	7/1/2000
2.1-342.01	Amend	SB 148	1064	7/1/2000
2.1-342.2	Amend	HB 445	227	7/1/2000
2.1-343	Amend	HB 445	227	7/1/2000
2.1-343.2	Amend	HB 1295	932	7/1/2000
2.1-344	Amend	SB 359	382	7/1/2000
2.1-344	Amend	HB 438	400	7/1/2000
2.1-344	Amend	HB 1471	720	7/1/2000
2.1-344	Amend	SB 148	1064	7/1/2000
2.1-639.14	Amend	HB 636	317	7/1/2000
3.1-796.93:1	Amend	HB 638	11	7/1/2000
3.1-796.93:1	Amend	SB 440	727	7/1/2000
3.1-796.96	Amend	HB 1514	1010	7/1/2001
3.1-796.120	Amend	HB 1514	1010	7/1/2001
4.1-100	Amend	SB 591	786	7/1/2000
4.1-100	Amend	SB 771	1037	7/1/2000
4.1-100	Amend	HB 1093	1052	7/1/2000
4.1-105	Amend	HB 1387	880	7/1/2000
4.1-105	Amend	SB 653	901	7/1/2000
4.1-201	Amend	SB 591	786	7/1/2000
4.1-305	Amend	HB 991	325	7/1/2000
4.1-325	Amend	SB 457	780	7/1/2000
6.1-112	Amend	SB 251	56	7/1/2000
8.01-225	Amend	HB 1049	928	7/1/2000
8.01-225	Amend	SB 148	1064	7/1/2000
8.01-226	Amend	HB 616	962	7/1/2000

(continued)

2000 Legislative Changes to the VIRGINIA CRIMINAL LAW AND MOTOR VEHICLE HANDBOOK

(Continued)

Section	*Change*	*Bill No.*	*Chapter*	*Effective Date*
8.01-310	Amend	HB 780	579	7/1/2000
prec. 9-173.21	New	HB 391	519	Pending
9-173.21	New	HB 391	519	Pending
9-183.2	Amend	HB 479	26	7/1/2000
9-183.3	Amend	HB 479	26	7/1/2000
15.2-1512.2	New	SB 755	791	7/1/2000
15.2-1702	Amend	HB 841	298	7/1/2000
15.2-1747	Amend	SB 293	772	7/1/2001
16.1-241	Amend	SB 685	830	7/1/2000
16.1-243	Amend	SB 685	830	7/1/2000
16.1-244	Amend	SB 475	781	7/1/2000
16.1-248.1	Amend	HB 567	836	7/1/2000
16.1-251	Amend	SB 447	385	7/1/2000
16.1-252	Amend	SB 447	385	7/1/2000
16.1-253.1	Amend	HB 511	34	7/1/2000
16.1-253.1	Amend	SB 353	654	7/1/2000
16.1-262	Amend	SB 685	830	7/1/2000
16.1-265	Amend	HB 1213	813	7/1/2000
16.1-272	Amend	HB 275	793	7/1/2000
16.1-272.1	New	HB 849	418	7/1/2000
16.1-273	Amend	SB 153	1020	7/1/2000
16.1-273	Amend	HB 383	1041	7/1/2000
16.1-278.7	Amend	HB 295	954	7/1/2000
16.1-278.7	Amend	SB 150	981	7/1/2000
16.1-278.7	Amend	SB 344	988	7/1/2000
16.1-278.8	Amend	HB 295	954	7/1/2000
16.1-278.8	Amend	SB 66	978	7/1/2000
16.1-278.8	Amend	SB 150	981	7/1/2000
16.1-278.8	Amend	SB 344	988	7/1/2000
16.1-278.8	Amend	SB 153	1020	7/1/2000
16.1-278.8	Amend	HB 383	1041	7/1/2000
16.1-278.8:01	New	SB 153	1020	7/1/2000
16.1-278.8:01	New	HB 383	1041	7/1/2000
16.1-278.9	Amend	HB 490	835	7/1/2000
16.1-279.1	Amend	HB 511	34	7/1/2000
16.1-279.1	Amend	SB 353	654	7/1/2000
16.1-284.1	Amend	SB 66	978	7/1/2002
16.1-285	Amend	HB 295	954	7/1/2000
16.1-285	Amend	SB 150	981	7/1/2000
16.1-285	Amend	SB 344	988	7/1/2000
16.1-299	Amend	HB 1206	431	7/1/2000
16.1-301	Amend	SB 312	211	7/1/2000
16.1-302.1	Amend	SB 348	339	7/1/2000
16.1-309.1	Amend	SB 361	563	7/1/2000
16.1-309.1	Amend	HB 673	603	7/1/2000
16.1-309.3	Amend	SB 345	195	7/1/2000

(continued)

2000 Legislative Changes to the VIRGINIA CRIMINAL LAW AND MOTOR VEHICLE HANDBOOK

(Continued)

Section	*Change*	*Bill No.*	*Chapter*	*Effective Date*
16.1-309.3	Amend	HB 948	806	7/1/2000
16.1-309.5	Amend	SB 196	562	7/1/2000
16.1-309.5	Amend	HB 387	601	7/1/2000
16.1-356	Amend	SB 301	337	7/1/2000
16.1-358	Amend	SB 520	216	7/1/2000
16.1-361	Amend	SB 301	337	7/1/2000
18.2-10	Amend	HB 978	361	7/1/2000
18.2-10	Amend	SB 125	767	7/1/2000
18.2-10	Amend	SB 197	770	7/1/2000
18.2-11	Amend	SB 197	770	7/1/2000
18.2-36.1	Amend	HB 355	956	7/1/2000
18.2-36.1	Amend	SB 183	982	7/1/2000
prec. 18.2-46.1	New	SB 143	332	7/1/2000
18.2-46.1 to 18.2-46.3	New	SB 143	332	7/1/2000
18.2-51.4	Amend	HB 355	956	7/1/2000
18.2-51.4	Amend	SB 183	982	7/1/2000
18.2-57	Amend	HB 297	288	7/1/2000
18.2-57	Amend	HB 1229	682	7/1/2000
18.2-57.01	New	HB 437	350	7/1/2000
18.2-57.3	Amend	HB 202	1040	7/1/2000
18.2-64.2	Amend	HB 202	1040	7/1/2000
18.2-67.4	Amend	HB 169	832	7/1/2000
18.2-67.4	Amend	HB 202	1040	7/1/2000
18.2-67.4:1	New	HB 141	831	7/1/2000
18.2-67.5:2	Amend	SB 176	333	7/1/2000
18.2-85	Amend	HB 198	951	7/1/2000
18.2-85	Amend	SB 202	1065	1/1/2001
18.2-152.2	Amend	HB 526	627	7/1/2000
18.2-152.7:1	New	HB 1524	849	7/1/2000
18.2-174.1	Amend	HB 616	962	7/1/2000
18.2-186.3	New	HB 373	349	7/1/2000
18.2-248	Amend	SB 153	1020	7/1/2000
18.2-248	Amend	HB 383	1041	7/1/2000
18.2-248.01	Amend	SB 153	1020	7/1/2000
18.2-248.01	Amend	HB 383	1041	7/1/2000
18.2-248.1	Amend	SB 199	819	7/1/2000
18.2-248.1	Amend	SB 153	1020	7/1/2000
18.2-248.1	Amend	HB 383	1041	7/1/2000
18.2-248.5	Amend	SB 153	1020	7/1/2000
18.2-248.5	Amend	HB 383	1041	7/1/2000
18.2-251	Amend	SB 153	1020	7/1/2000
18.2-251	Amend	HB 383	1041	7/1/2000
18.2-251.01	Amend	SB 153	1020	7/1/2000
18.2-251.01	Amend	HB 383	1041	7/1/2000
18.2-251.3	New	HB 280	348	7/1/2000

(continued)

2000 Legislative Changes to the VIRGINIA CRIMINAL LAW AND MOTOR VEHICLE HANDBOOK

(Continued)

Section	*Change*	*Bill No.*	*Chapter*	*Effective Date*
18.2-252	Amend	SB 153	1020	7/1/2000
18.2-252	Amend	HB 383	1041	7/1/2000
18.2-254	Amend	SB 153	1020	7/1/2000
18.2-254	Amend	HB 383	1041	7/1/2000
18.2-255	Amend	SB 153	1020	7/1/2000
18.2-255	Amend	HB 383	1041	7/1/2000
18.2-255.2	Amend	SB 153	1020	7/1/2000
18.2-255.2	Amend	HB 383	1041	7/1/2000
18.2-259.1	Amend	HB 991	325	7/1/2000
18.2-270	Amend	SB 525	784	7/1/2000
18.2-270	Amend	HB 355	956	7/1/2000
18.2-270	Amend	HB 386	958	10/1/2000
18.2-270	Amend	SB 149	980	10/1/2000
18.2-270	Amend	SB 183	982	7/1/2000
18.2-270.1	Amend	HB 386	958	10/1/2000
18.2-270.1	Amend	SB 149	980	10/1/2000
18.2-270.2	Amend	SB 535	341	7/1/2000
18.2-270.2	Amend	HB 1131	362	7/1/2000
18.2-271	Amend	HB 355	956	7/1/2000
18.2-271	Amend	SB 183	982	7/1/2000
18.2-271.1	Amend	HB 386	958	10/1/2000
18.2-271.1	Amend	HB 1102	970	7/1/2000
18.2-271.1	Amend	SB 149	980	10/1/2000
18.2-308.2:3	New	HB 309	794	7/1/2000
18.2-340.17	Amend	HB 1163	639	7/1/2000
18.2-340.20	Amend	HB 811	1000	7/1/2000
18.2-340.33	Amend	HB 811	1000	7/1/2000
18.2-369	Amend	HB 378	796	7/1/2000
18.2-370	Amend	SB 176	333	7/1/2000
18.2-370.2	New	SB 197	770	7/1/2000
18.2-371.2	Amend	HB 1461	883	7/1/2000
18.2-371.3	Amend	HB 1108	842	7/1/2000
18.2-373	Amend	HB 1492	1009	7/1/2000
18.2-391	Amend	HB 1492	1009	7/1/2000
18.2-426	Amend	HB 616	962	7/1/2000
18.2-465.1	Amend	HB 717	295	7/1/2000
18.2-473.1	Amend	HB 78	286	7/1/2000
19.2-11.01	Amend	SB 211	272	7/1/2000
19.2-11.01	Amend	SB 663	827	7/1/2000
19.2-56	Amend	SB 524	783	7/1/2000
19.2-72	Amend	HB 820	170	7/1/2000
19.2-120	Amend	HB 424	797	7/1/2000
19.2-123	Amend	HB 1533	885	7/1/2000
19.2-123	Amend	SB 153	1020	7/1/2000
19.2-123	Amend	HB 383	1041	7/1/2000
19.2-143	Amend	HB 1533	885	7/1/2000

(continued)

2000 Legislative Changes to the VIRGINIA CRIMINAL LAW AND MOTOR VEHICLE HANDBOOK

(Continued)

Section	*Change*	*Bill No.*	*Chapter*	*Effective Date*
19.2-152.4:1	New	HB 202	1040	7/1/2000
19.2-163	Amend	HB 1312	436	Pending
19.2-163	Amend	SB 481	448	Pending
19.2-165.1	Amend	HB 671	292	7/1/2000
19.2-169.3	Amend	SB 261	1024	7/1/2000
19.2-174.1	Amend	SB 261	1024	7/1/2000
19.2-187	Amend	SB 262	336	7/1/2000
19.2-215.1	Amend	HB 744	359	7/1/2000
19.2-245.1	Amend	HB 1156	327	7/1/2000
19.2-264.4	Amend	HB 705	838	7/1/2000
19.2-265.01	Amend	SB 348	339	7/1/2000
19.2-295.2	Amend	SB 125	767	7/1/2000
19.2-299.2	Amend	HB 386	958	10/1/2000
19.2-299.2	Amend	SB 149	980	10/1/2000
19.2-299.2	Amend	HB 202	1040	7/1/2000
19.2-303.3	Amend	HB 202	1040	7/1/2000
19.2-303.4	Amend	SB 62	186	7/1/2000
19.2-305.1	Amend	SB 330	775	7/1/2000
19.2-310.5	Amend	SB 619	284	7/1/2000
19.2-311	Amend	HB 95	668	7/1/2000
19.2-311	Amend	SB 168	690	7/1/2000
19.2-313 to 19.2-316	Amend	HB 95	668	7/1/2000
19.2-313 to 19.2-316	Amend	SB 168	690	7/1/2000
19.2-316.1	Amend	SB 188	769	7/1/2000
19.2-316.2	Amend	SB 329	338	7/1/2000
19.2-316.3	Amend	SB 329	338	7/1/2000
19.2-368.7	Amend	HB 1395	455	7/1/2000
19.2-368.11:1	Amend	HB 1397	847	7/1/2000
19.2-390.1	Amend	SB 279	250	7/1/2000
19.2-392.02	New	SB 603	860	1/1/2001
22.1-254	Amend	HB 1468	184	7/1/2000
23-232	Amend	HB 1471	720	7/1/2000
27-34.2:1	Amend	HB 1030	39	7/1/2000
27-34.2:1	Amend	SB 567	390	7/1/2000
29.1-301	Amend	SB 750	110	3/17/2000
29.1-301	Amend	HB 1277	142	3/17/2000
29.1-310.1	New	HB 664	12	7/1/2000
29.1-335	Amend	HB 896	132	7/1/2000
29.1-521	Amend	HB 675	13	7/1/2000
29.1-529	Amend	HB 100	6	7/1/2000
29.1-531	Amend	HB 502	403	7/1/2000
29.1-531	Amend	SB 395	447	7/1/2000
33.1-46.2	Amend	HB 793	322	4/3/2000
33.1-346	Amend	SB 317	20	7/1/2000

(continued)

2000 Legislative Changes to the VIRGINIA CRIMINAL LAW AND MOTOR VEHICLE HANDBOOK

(Continued)

Section	*Change*	*Bill No.*	*Chapter*	*Effective Date*
33.1-351	Amend	HB 1223	432	7/1/2000
33.1-351	Amend	SB 522	449	7/1/2000
33.1-369	Amend	HB 1091	140	7/1/2000
33.1-370	Amend	HB 1223	432	7/1/2000
33.1-370	Amend	SB 522	449	7/1/2000
33.1-375.1	Amend	HB 642	672	7/1/2000
44-146.13 to 44-146.17	Amend	HB 1352	309	7/1/2000
44-146.18 to 44-146.19	Amend	HB 1352	309	7/1/2000
44-146.20	Amend	HB 1352	309	7/1/2000
44-146.20	Amend	HB 1338	437	7/1/2000
44-146.21	Amend	HB 1352	309	7/1/2000
44-146.22	Amend	HB 1352	309	7/1/2000
44-146.24	Amend	HB 1352	309	7/1/2000
44-146.26 to 44-146.28	Amend	HB 1352	309	7/1/2000
44-146.28	Amend	SB 245	1023	7/1/2000
44-146.30	Amend	HB 1352	309	7/1/2000
46.2-209.1	New	HB 550	87	7/1/2000
46.2-209.1	New	HB 777	92	7/1/2000
46.2-209.1	New	HB 999	235	7/1/2000
46.2-209.1	New	SB 756	257	7/1/2000
46.2-212.1	Amend	HB 640	122	7/1/2000
46.2-224	Amend	HB 1181	141	7/1/2000
46.2-301	Amend	HB 355	956	7/1/2000
46.2-301	Amend	SB 183	982	7/1/2000
46.2-324.1	New	HB 1430	685	7/1/2000
46.2-328	Amend	HB 1465	269	7/1/2000
46.2-335	Amend	HB 1436	686	7/1/2000
46.2-341.28	Amend	HB 386	958	10/1/2000
46.2-341.28	Amend	SB 149	980	10/1/2000
46.2-342	Amend	HB 1090	810	7/1/2000
46.2-357	Amend	HB 355	956	7/1/2000
46.2-357	Amend	SB 183	982	7/1/2000
46.2-361	Amend	HB 19	792	7/1/2000
46.2-389	Amend	HB 355	956	7/1/2000
46.2-389	Amend	HB 564	959	7/1/2000
46.2-389	Amend	SB 183	982	7/1/2000
46.2-389	Amend	SB 292	985	7/1/2000
46.2-391	Amend	SB 3	243	7/1/2000
46.2-391	Amend	HB 355	956	7/1/2000
46.2-391	Amend	HB 386	958	10/1/2000
46.2-391	Amend	HB 564	959	7/1/2000
46.2-391	Amend	SB 149	980	10/1/2000
46.2-391	Amend	SB 183	982	7/1/2000

(continued)

2000 Legislative Changes to the VIRGINIA CRIMINAL LAW AND MOTOR VEHICLE HANDBOOK

(Continued)

Section	*Change*	*Bill No.*	*Chapter*	*Effective Date*
46.2-391	Amend	SB 292	985	7/1/2000
46.2-392	Amend	SB 649	342	7/1/2000
46.2-394	Amend	HB 355	956	7/1/2000
46.2-394	Amend	SB 183	982	7/1/2000
46.2-395	Amend	HB 355	956	7/1/2000
46.2-395	Amend	SB 183	982	7/1/2000
46.2-411.1	New	HB 564	959	7/1/2000
46.2-411.1	New	SB 292	985	7/1/2000
46.2-604	Amend	HB 57	667	7/1/2000
46.2-639	Amend	SB 404	71	7/1/2000
46.2-651	Amend	HB 1375	144	7/1/2000
46.2-665	Amend	HB 674	318	7/1/2000
46.2-667	Amend	HB 674	318	7/1/2000
46.2-692	Amend	HB 780	579	7/1/2000
46.2-712	Amend	HB 1002	133	7/1/2000
46.2-716	Amend	HB 56	258	7/1/2000
46.2-726	Amend	HB 658	126	7/1/2000
46.2-730	Amend	HB 441	259	7/1/2000
46.2-743	Amend	HB 10	75	7/1/2000
46.2-743	Amend	SB 123	190	7/1/2000
46.2-746.4	Amend	HB 10	75	7/1/2000
46.2-746.4	Amend	HB 27	111	7/1/2000
46.2-746.4:1	Repeal	SB 34	766	7/1/2000
46.2-746.4:2	New	HB 1422	145	7/1/2000
46.2-746.4:2	New	SB 34	766	7/1/2000
46.2-746.6:1	Repeal	HB 10	75	7/1/2000
46.2-746.6:1	Repeal	SB 34	766	7/1/2000
46.2-746.6:2	New	SB 34	766	7/1/2000
46.2-746.7	Amend	HB 10	75	7/1/2000
46.2-746.8	Amend	HB 10	75	7/1/2000
46.2-746.8:1	Amend	HB 1421	267	7/1/2000
46.2-746.9	Amend	HB 1457	148	7/1/2000
46.2-748.1	Repeal	HB 10	75	7/1/2000
46.2-749.2:3 to 46.2-749.2:6	Repeal	HB 10	75	7/1/2000
46.2-749.3	Amend	SB 530	729	1/1/2001
46.2-749.3	Amend	HB 1275	758	1/1/2001
46.2-749.7:1	Repeal	HB 10	75	7/1/2000
46.2-749.11	Repeal	HB 10	75	7/1/2000
46.2-749.19	Amend	SB 413	107	7/1/2000
46.2-749.32	New	SB 18	44	7/1/2000
46.2-749.32	New	HB 39	76	7/1/2000
46.2-749.32	New	HB 126	78	7/1/2000
46.2-749.32	New	HB 261	80	7/1/2000
46.2-749.32	New	HB 429	81	7/1/2000
46.2-749.32	New	HB 514	85	7/1/2000

(continued)

2000 Legislative Changes to the VIRGINIA CRIMINAL LAW AND MOTOR VEHICLE HANDBOOK

(Continued)

Section	*Change*	*Bill No.*	*Chapter*	*Effective Date*
46.2-749.32	New	HB 643	124	7/1/2000
46.2-749.32	New	HB 666	127	7/1/2000
46.2-749.32	New	HB 1371	143	7/1/2000
46.2-749.32	New	HB 1435	146	7/1/2000
46.2-749.32	New	HB 1516	150	7/1/2000
46.2-749.32	New	SB 122	189	7/1/2000
46.2-749.32	New	HB 396	226	7/1/2000
46.2-749.32	New	HB 722	319	7/1/2000
46.2-749.32 to 46.2-749.34	New	SB 34	766	7/1/2000
46.2-752	Amend	HB 1096	303	7/1/2000
46.2-803.1	Amend	SB 377	60	7/1/2000
46.2-803.1	Amend	HB 1186	306	7/1/2000
46.2-803.1	Amend	HB 544	407	7/1/2000
46.2-817	Amend	HB 533	315	7/1/2000
46.2-819.2	New	SB 530	729	1/1/2001
46.2-819.2	New	HB 1275	758	1/1/2001
46.2-828.1	New	SB 227	274	7/1/2000
46.2-833	Amend	HB 487	834	7/1/2000
46.2-833.01	Amend	HB 356	575	7/1/2000
46.2-869	Amend	SB 461	340	7/1/2000
46.2-873.1	New	HB 860	262	7/1/2000
46.2-882	Amend	HB 566	354	7/1/2000
46.2-882	Amend	HB 729	357	7/1/2000
46.2-882	Amend	HB 164	365	7/1/2000
46.2-920	Amend	HB 626	120	7/1/2000
46.2-924	Amend	HB 932	323	7/1/2000
46.2-1001	Amend	SB 360	59	7/1/2000
46.2-1001	Amend	HB 69	112	7/1/2000
46.2-1014	Amend	SB 247	54	7/1/2000
46.2-1014	Amend	HB 432	63	7/1/2000
46.2-1025	Amend	HB 501	84	7/1/2000
46.2-1025	Amend	HB 627	121	7/1/2000
46.2-1025	Amend	SB 309	278	7/1/2000
46.2-1095	Amend	SB 751	736	7/1/2000
46.2-1142	Amend	HB 1345	265	7/1/2000
46.2-1142.1	Amend	HB 1345	265	7/1/2000
46.2-1149	Amend	HB 707	129	7/1/2000
46.2-1156.1	New	SB 751	736	7/1/2000
46.2-1176	Amend	HB 1522	311	7/1/2000
46.2-1222.1	New	SB 474	72	7/1/2000
46.2-1222.1	New	HB 1466	270	7/1/2000
46.2-1313	Amend	SB 60	48	7/1/2000
46.2-1508	Amend	HB 1299	180	7/1/2000
46.2-1508.1	Amend	HB 1299	180	7/1/2000
46.2-1519	Amend	HB 1299	180	7/1/2000

(continued)

2000 Legislative Changes to the VIRGINIA CRIMINAL LAW AND MOTOR VEHICLE HANDBOOK

(Continued)

Section	*Change*	*Bill No.*	*Chapter*	*Effective Date*
46.2-1527.1	Amend	HB 1299	180	7/1/2000
46.2-1529	Amend	HB 676	128	7/1/2000
46.2-1530	Amend	HB 436	116	7/1/2000
46.2-1531	Amend	HB 1299	180	7/1/2000
46.2-1573	Amend	SB 407	106	7/1/2000
46.2-1600	Amend	HB 641	123	7/1/2000
46.2-1600	Amend	HB 999	235	7/1/2000
46.2-1600	Amend	SB 756	257	7/1/2000
46.2-1602.1	Amend	HB 999	235	7/1/2000
46.2-1602.1	Amend	SB 756	257	7/1/2000
46.2-1603	Amend	HB 999	235	7/1/2000
46.2-1603	Amend	SB 756	257	7/1/2000
46.2-1608	Amend	HB 641	123	7/1/2000
46.2-1705	Amend	HB 1256	179	7/1/2000
46.2-1908	Amend	HB 1299	180	7/1/2000
46.2-1908.1	New	HB 1299	180	7/1/2000
46.2-1919	Amend	HB 1299	180	7/1/2000
46.2-1929	Amend	HB 676	128	7/1/2000
46.2-1930	Amend	HB 436	116	7/1/2000
46.2-1931	Amend	HB 1299	180	7/1/2000
46.2-1982	Amend	SB 407	106	7/1/2000
46.2-1992.6	Amend	HB 1299	180	7/1/2000
46.2-1992.6:1	New	HB 1299	180	7/1/2000
46.2-1992.17	Amend	HB 1299	180	7/1/2000
46.2-1992.22	Amend	HB 676	128	7/1/2000
46.2-1992.23	Amend	HB 436	116	7/1/2000
46.2-1992.24	Amend	HB 1299	180	7/1/2000
46.2-1992.75	Amend	SB 407	106	7/1/2000
46.2-1993.6	Amend	HB 1299	180	7/1/2000
46.2-1993.6:1	New	HB 1299	180	7/1/2000
46.2-1993.17	Amend	HB 1299	180	7/1/2000
46.2-1993.22	Amend	HB 676	128	7/1/2000
46.2-1993.23	Amend	HB 436	116	7/1/2000
46.2-1993.24	Amend	HB 1299	180	7/1/2000
46.2-1993.73	Amend	SB 407	106	7/1/2000
51.1-205	Amend	HB 690	66	7/1/2000
51.1-205	Amend	SB 441	657	7/1/2000
51.1-205	Amend	HB 135	911	7/1/2000
51.1-206	Amend	HB 135	911	7/1/2000
51.1-216	Amend	HB 690	66	7/1/2000
51.1-216	Amend	SB 441	657	7/1/2000
51.1-216 to 51.1-218	Amend	HB 135	911	7/1/2000
52-1	Amend	SB 45	560	7/1/2000
52-1	Amend	HB 285	600	7/1/2000
52-4.3	Amend	SB 45	560	7/1/2000

(continued)

2000 Legislative Changes to the VIRGINIA CRIMINAL LAW AND MOTOR VEHICLE HANDBOOK

(Continued)

Section	*Change*	*Bill No.*	*Chapter*	*Effective Date*
52-4.3	Amend	HB 285	600	7/1/2000
52-8.1:1	New	SB 45	560	7/1/2000
52-8.1:1	New	HB 285	600	7/1/2000
52-36	Amend	HB 716	526	7/1/2000
53.1-131	Amend	HB 1004	423	7/1/2000
53.1-131.2	Amend	HB 1004	423	7/1/2000
53.1-132	Amend	HB 1004	423	7/1/2000
53.1-150	Amend	HB 202	1040	7/1/2000
53.1-161	Amend	SB 125	767	7/1/2000
53.1-162	Amend	SB 125	767	7/1/2000
54.1-2400.4	New	HB 677	578	7/1/2000
54.1-2902	Amend	HB 1469	688	7/1/2000
54.1-2903	Amend	HB 1469	688	7/1/2000
54.1-2988	Amend	HB 1367	590	7/1/2000
54.1-2988	Amend	SB 677	598	7/1/2000
54.1-2990	Amend	HB 1367	590	7/1/2000
54.1-2990	Amend	SB 677	598	7/1/2000
54.1-3303	Amend	HB 1437	882	7/1/2000
54.1-3303	Amend	HB 818	924	7/1/2000
54.1-3401	Amend	SB 679	861	7/1/2000
54.1-3401	Amend	HB 1341	878	7/1/2000
54.1-3401	Amend	HB 1477	935	4/9/2000
54.1-3408	Amend	HB 1013	135	7/1/2000
54.1-3408	Amend	HB 988	498	1/1/2001
54.1-3408	Amend	SB 679	861	7/1/2000
54.1-3408	Amend	HB 1391	881	7/1/2000
54.1-3408	Amend	HB 1477	935	4/9/2000
54.1-3408.01	New	HB 1013	135	7/1/2000
54.1-3408.01	New	HB 1341	878	7/1/2000
54.1-3410.1	New	SB 679	861	7/1/2000
54.1-3421	Amend	HB 1013	135	7/1/2000
54.1-3434	Amend	HB 1013	135	7/1/2000
54.1-3434.1	Amend	HB 1437	882	7/1/2000
54.1-3446	Amend	HB 280	348	7/1/2000
54.1-3448	Amend	HB 1013	135	7/1/2000
54.1-3450	Amend	HB 1013	135	7/1/2000
54.1-3450	Amend	HB 280	348	7/1/2000
54.1-3452	Amend	HB 1013	135	7/1/2000
prec. 58.1-1032	New	HB 1387	880	7/1/2000
prec. 58.1-1032	New	SB 653	901	7/1/2000
58.1-1032	New	HB 1387	880	7/1/2000
58.1-1032	New	SB 653	901	7/1/2000
58.1-1033	New	HB 1387	880	7/1/2000
58.1-1033	New	SB 653	901	7/1/2000
58.1-1037	New	HB 1387	880	7/1/2000
58.1-1037	New	SB 653	901	7/1/2000

(continued)

2000 Legislative Changes to the VIRGINIA CRIMINAL LAW AND MOTOR VEHICLE HANDBOOK

(Continued)

Section	*Change*	*Bill No.*	*Chapter*	*Effective Date*
prec. 58.1-2289	New	SB 530	729	1/1/2001
prec. 58.1-2289	New	HB 1275	758	1/1/2001
58.1-2289	New	SB 530	729	1/1/2001
58.1-2289	New	HB 1275	758	1/1/2001
prec. 58.1-2290	New	SB 530	729	1/1/2001
prec. 58.1-2290	New	HB 1275	758	1/1/2001
58.1-2290	New	SB 530	729	1/1/2001
58.1-2290	New	HB 1275	758	1/1/2001
58.1-2701	Amend	SB 530	729	1/1/2001
58.1-2701	Amend	HB 1275	758	1/1/2001
58.1-2702	Amend	SB 530	729	1/1/2001
58.1-2702	Amend	HB 1275	758	1/1/2001
59.1-148.3	Amend	SB 660	391	7/1/2000
63.1-248.2	Amend	HB 1360	500	7/1/2000
63.1-248.2:1	New	HB 1360	500	7/1/2000
63.1-248.3	Amend	HB 1360	500	7/1/2000
63.1-248.4	Amend	HB 1360	500	7/1/2000
63.1-248.5:1	Amend	HB 1360	500	7/1/2000
63.1-248.6	Amend	HB 1360	500	7/1/2000
63.1-248.6	Amend	SB 259	854	7/1/2000
63.1-248.6:01	New	HB 1360	500	7/1/2000
63.1-248.6:02	New	HB 1360	500	7/1/2000
63.1-248.6:2	Amend	HB 1360	500	7/1/2000
63.1-248.7	Amend	HB 1360	500	7/1/2000
63.1-248.7:1	Amend	HB 1360	500	7/1/2000
63.1-248.8	Amend	HB 865	95	7/1/2000
63.1-248.8	Amend	SB 691	734	7/1/2000
63.1-248.8	Amend	HB 935	805	7/1/2000
63.1-248.10	Amend	HB 1360	500	7/1/2000
63.1-248.13	Amend	HB 1360	500	7/1/2000
63.1-248.18	Amend	HB 1359	482	7/1/2000
63.1-248.18	Repeal	HB 1360	500	7/1/2000
63.1-248.19	New	HB 1360	500	7/1/2000

This page intentionally left blank.

HIGHLIGHTS OF THE 2000 VIRGINIA LEGISLATIVE SESSION

ABUSE/NEGLECT

Defined

"Abuse" of an incapacitated adult is "knowing and willful" conduct that causes physical injury or pain, or "knowing and willful" use of restraint as punishment, for convenience or as a substitute for treatment. (§18.2-369)

ARREST

Warrants

A sheriff or deputy may execute an arrest warrant throughout the county in which he serves and in any city surrounded thereby. (§19.2-72)

ASSAULT

Law-Enforcement Officers

It is a Class 2 misdemeanor to knowingly project a beam or point of light from a laser, laser gunsight or device that simulates a laser at a law-enforcement officer. (§18.2-57.01)

Teachers

"Simple assault" or "assault and battery" does not include a teacher's use of incidental or reasonable contact to maintain order and control, or reasonable and necessary force to prevent a student from hurting himself or others or destroying property, or to obtain a weapon or controlled substance that is upon a student's person or within his control. (§18.2-57)

COMPUTER CRIMES

Harassment by Computer

The offense of harassment by computer is created. (§18.2-371.2)

CRIMES AGAINST CHILDREN

Offenses Prohibiting Proximity to Children

Every adult convicted of an offense prohibiting proximity to children occurring after July 1, 2000, shall, as part of his sentence, be forever prohibited from loitering within 100 feet of any premises which he knows or has reason to know is a primary, secondary or high school; violation is a Class 6 felony. (§18.2-10)

DRUGS

Penalties

Any person who knowingly manufactures, sells, distributes or possesses with intent to distribute gamma-butyrolactone or 1, 4-butanediol, when intended for human consumption, is guilty of a Class 3 felony. (§18.2-251.3)

FRAUD

Identity Fraud

The offense of identity fraud is created. (§18.2-186.3)

GANGS

Criminal Gang Activity

If a member of a criminal street gang engages in a criminal act for the benefit of, at the direction of or in association with the gang, it is a Class 5 felony. (Violation of this section is a separate, distinct offense from the predicate crime.) If the member is over 18 years of age and knows or has reason to know that another member of the gang is a juvenile, it is a Class 4 felony. (§18.2-46.2)

A person over 18 years of age who solicits, invites, recruits or encourages a juvenile to actively participate in or become a member of a criminal street gang is guilty of a Class 6 felony. (§18.2-46.3)

JUVENILES

Penalties

The death penalty may not be imposed if the offender was less than 16 years of age at the time of the offense. (§18.2-10)

Release of Records

Law-enforcement agencies may release to the public records of juveniles, 14 years of age and older, charged with various violent crimes, including malicious wounding, abduction, robbery, carjacking, rape and forcible sodomy. (§16.1-301)

LAW-ENFORCEMENT OFFICERS

Benefits

The beneficiary of any law-enforcement officer or firefighter killed in the line of duty receives $75,000. (§2.1-133.7)

Fire Marshals

A local fire marshal, if authorized by the governing body of the locality which appointed him, has the same police powers as a sheriff or police officer with regard to offenses involving hazardous materials. (§27-34.2)

MOTOR VEHICLES

Emergency Vehicles

When operating under emergency conditions, an emergency vehicle may pass or overtake a stopped or slow-moving vehicle by going to the left of the vehicle either in a no-passing zone or by crossing the highway center line. (§46.2-920)

Equipment Violations

No colored glass, colored plastic or any other type of covering shall be placed, mounted or installed on or over any license plate if such covering in any way alters or obscures the alpha-numeric information or color of the license plate; no insignia, emblem or trailer hitch or coupling shall be mounted in such a way as to hide or obscure any portion of any license plate or render any position of it illegible. (§46.2-716)

Motorcycles may be equipped with one or more auxiliary brake lights of a type approved by the Superintendent of the Department of State Police. (§46.2-1014)

Registration

Unregistered agricultural vehicles may be operated along a highway to and from a refuse disposal facility for the purpose of disposing of garbage generated on a farm, and, for a distance of no more than 30 miles, for the purpose of obtaining seeds, fertilizers, chemicals or animal feed, and returning. (§46.2-665)

The Department of Motor Vehicles may issue permanent license plates without decals and a month and year of expiration to taxicabs. (§46.2-712).

Speed Limits

The maximum speed limit on a nonsurface treated highway is 35 m.p.h. (§46.2-873.1)

Traffic Infractions

A person who drives off from a filling station without paying for fuel is liable for a civil penalty not to exceed $100 and may have their license suspended for 30 days. (§46.2-749.3)

The requirement that commercial vehicles travel in one of the two right-most lanes on interstate highways does not apply to Interstate 295. (§46.2-803.1)

It is an affirmative defense to the charge of disregarding a signal by a law-enforcement officer to stop that the driver reasonably believed that he was being pursued by a person other than a law-enforcement officer. (§46.2-817)

A driver who intentionally impedes or disrupts a funeral procession is guilty of a traffic infraction. (§46.2-828.1)

A driver may be detained for failure to obey a traffic light when the officer is in uniform, displays his badge, and either observed the violation himself or received a radio message from another officer who observed the violation and furnished the license number or other positive identification of the vehicle. (§46.2-833)

No person under 16 years of age shall be transported in the rear cargo area of a pickup truck on the highways of Virginia, unless part of an organized parade or travelling from one parcel of land to another in connection with farming operations. (§46.2-1156.1)

OBSCENITY

Defined

"Obscene items" include any obscene writing, picture or similar visual representation, or sound recording, stored in an electronic or other medium retrievable in a perceivable form. (§18.2-373)

Distribution to Juveniles

Internet service providers are not responsible if a person uses their service to distribute obscene items to a juvenile. (§18.2-373)

SEARCH AND SEIZURE

Warrants

During the execution of a search warrant, no person other than the executing officers, the owners and occupants of the place to be searched (when permitted by the officer in charge) and persons designated by the officer in charge to assist or provide expertise may be present. (§19.2-56)

SEXUAL BATTERY

Infected Sexual Battery

Any person who, knowing that he is infected with HIV, syphilis or hepatitis B, engages in sexual conduct with the intention to transmit the infection to another person is guilty of a Class 6 felony. (§18.2-67.4)

TOBACCO

Sale or Distribution to Minors

It is illegal to sell or distribute "bidis" (products containing tobacco wrapped in a temburi leaf or tendu leaf) to persons under 18 years of age. (§18.2-371.2)

VIRGINIA CRIMINAL LAW AND MOTOR VEHICLE HANDBOOK

TABLE OF CONTENTS

Page

CODE OF VIRGINIA

TITLE 18.2 – CRIMES AND OFFENSES GENERALLY

TITLE 19.2 – CRIMINAL PROCEDURE

Table of Contents
(Continued)

TITLE 46.2 – MOTOR VEHICLES

Subtitle I – General Provisions; Department of Motor Vehicles

Subtitle II – Titling, Registration and Licensure

Subtitle III – Operation

Subtitle IV – Dealers, Commercial Driver Training Schools, and Scrappage Program

Subtitle V – Motor Carriers

TITLE 52 – POLICE (STATE)

Table of Contents
(Continued)

Table of Contents
(Continued)

Table of Contents
(Continued)

Chapter *Page*

Table of Contents
(Continued)

Table of Contents
(Continued)

Chapter *Page*

Subtitle III – Professions and Occupations Regulated by Boards Within the Department of Health Professions

Subtitle V – Occupations Regulated by Local Governing Bodies

TITLE 56 – PUBLIC SERVICE COMPANIES

TITLE 58.1 – TAXATION

Subtitle I – Taxes Administered by the Department of Taxation

Subtitle II – Taxes Administered by Other Agencies

Subtitle IV – Other Sources of State Revenue

TITLE 59.1 – TRADE AND COMMERCE

TITLE 60.2 – UNEMPLOYMENT COMPENSATION

Table of Contents
(Continued)

VIRGINIA LEGAL GUIDELINES

Editor's Note: This is a general overview of criminal procedure law. It should be used to achieve understanding of basic principles, but is not to be relied upon for guidance in a specific application. It is not to be used as a substitute for the opinion or advice of the appropriate legal counsel for the reader's department. To the extent possible, the information is current. However, very recent statutory and case law developments may not be covered.

I. INTRODUCTION

The Bill of Rights to the Federal Constitution, and corresponding provisions in each State's Constitution, provide citizens with certain fundamental safeguards from intrusive governmental conduct. Particularly relevant to situations involving a criminal suspect or defendant are the Fourth, Fifth, Sixth and, to a lesser extent, the Fourteenth Amendments. As a preliminary matter, the reader should note that the Federal Bill of Rights, as ultimately interpreted by the Supreme Court, guarantees U.S. citizens enumerated fundamental freedoms and provides the constitutionally required minimum levels of protection. Under the principles of federalism, state courts are free, in interpreting their respective state constitutions, to afford greater protection to state citizens. In many instances, the language in a state constitution mirrors the federal provision, and state courts hold that the right granted by the state constitution is to be construed the same as that granted by the Federal Constitution. See *Lowe v. Commonwealth*, 321 S.E.2d 273 (Va. 1984) (Article I, §10 of the Virginia Constitution provides "substantially the same" protections as the federal Fourth Amendment).

The Fourth Amendment guarantees the people the right to be secure in their persons, houses, papers and effects against unreasonable searches and seizures. This amendment also provides that no search or arrest warrants shall be issued, except those based on probable cause and which particularly describe both the place to be searched and the person or things to be seized.

The equivalent to the Fourth Amendment in the Virginia Constitution is Article I, §10, "General Warrants of search or seizure prohibited." This section provides that general warrants "without any evidence of fact furnished previously to the issuance, or which do not designate any specific thing or person to be seized, or do not particularly describe the offense claimed to have been committed" are prohibited. As mentioned above, this section provides "substantially this same" protections as the federal Fourth Amendment.

The Fifth Amendment provides (in pertinent part) that no person shall be compelled to be a witness against oneself in a criminal case. The Supreme Court has also found that an integral part of an accused's right to be free from compelled incrimination, is a judicially created right to have counsel present, and a right to refuse to answer questions during a custodial interrogation, even though the Constitution does not specifically provide such a safeguard.

The Sixth Amendment provides that a defendant in a criminal case, and a suspect in a criminal investigation, when the investigation focused on him or her or has reached a critical stage, shall enjoy the right to counsel to aid in his or her defense.

The Fifth and Fourteenth Amendments provide that no person shall be deprived of life, liberty or property without the due process of law. In the context of the rights of an accused, or a criminal suspect, this provision has been construed as offering protection against certain fundamentally unfair governmental conduct, particularly the use of suggestive, prejudicial or discriminatory identification procedures.

The ramifications of constitutional violations impact not only a law enforcement officers' efforts to enforce the law and obtain the conviction of criminal offenders, but also may lead to monetary sanctions against individual officers and the particular department employing them. Evidence seized in violation of the foregoing principles (whether it is physical evidence, e.g., contraband, or testimonial evidence, e.g., a statement or confession) generally cannot be introduced into evidence in any subsequent trial. The evidence will be excluded by the operation of a doctrine known as the exclusionary rule. The mechanism by which the use of evidence is denied to prosecutors is called suppression. Moreover, officers who violate a person's constitutional rights may be civilly liable to that person in monetary damages. Officers, or the municipalities for which they work, when they act in a manner inconsistent with their lawful authority, may also be held accountable for such damages.

II. DETENTION AND ARREST

A. Levels of Encounters

When reviewing the legality of police interactions with citizens, courts initially assess the nature and extent of the contact. To aid in this analysis, interactions, or encounters, are divided into three conceptual categories. First, there are encounters of a consensual nature. This has sometimes been called the "common law right to inquire." This is a right to ask a question, enjoyed by all citizens, whether they work in law enforcement or not.

Occupying the next tier of encounters are interactions of a more intrusive character. These are encounters commonly called detentions, investigatory stops or *Terry* stops. The justifications offered by law enforcement for this more forceful contact must be based on facts that are specific and articulable, and lead to a rational inference or a reasonable suspicion that criminal activity is being undertaken.

The final level of encounter is a formal arrest. To justify this action, law enforcement officials must possess a higher degree of suspicion, i.e., "probable cause" to believe that a crime is being, or has been, perpetrated and that a specific person committed it.

This initial categorization of encounters is essential to a determination of the rights of the individual. If the encounter was consensual, the Constitution is not implicated, because no seizure of a person, within the meaning of the Fourth Amendment, has taken place. However, if the encounter rises to the level of a detention or a full scale arrest, then that person has been seized, and law enforcement conduct will be judged according to the standards of the Fourth Amendment. The person seized can then avail himself or herself of the Amendment's protections.

B. Consensual Encounters – Right of Inquiry

The basic premise underlying a consensual encounter is that it is voluntary. Such an encounter is an interaction based on consent and is terminable by either party. Law enforcement officers do not infringe on a citizen's Fourth Amendment rights by merely approaching him or her at random in a public place in order to ask a few questions, as long as a reasonable person would understand that he or she could refuse to cooperate and excuse themselves from the exchange, if they choose to do so. Simply identifying oneself as an officer or asking for someone's name and identification is not an unreasonable intrusion or a seizure within the meaning of the Fourth Amendment. Courts reason that merely asking a few further questions, without more, does not constitute a seizure of the person. *Washington v. Commonwealth*, 509 S.E.2d 512 (Va. Ct. App. 1999). This is an important distinction, if the person has not been constitutionally seized, then the Fourth Amendment is not implicated and no constitutional violation can occur. A constitutional seizure occurs when the officer, by means of physical force, coercion or show of authority, has in some way restrained the freedom of a citizen, so that a reasonable person in the suspect's position would no longer feel as though he or she were free to leave. *Parker v. Commonwealth*, 496 S.E.2d 47 (Va. 1998); *Washington v. Commonwealth*, supra. Detentions and arrests are viewed as seizures of a person. These actions are reviewed under the Fourth Amendment's reasonableness standard and are subject to constitutional controls.

The objective test in a consensual encounter is whether a reasonable person would think that he or she were free to go. The following are suggestions for the law enforcement officer to establish a consensual encounter: (i) ask the citizen: May I talk to you? Can I have a minute of your time? Do you mind if I search you for drugs? Would you mind showing me what's in your hand? May I look in your purse/luggage? or (ii) simply walk up to a citizen in a public place and start a conversation.

The courts will probably rule that what the officer thought was a consensual encounter was in fact a detention if one or more of the following occur: (i) the officer displays a weapon; (ii) the officer uses a harsh, accusatorial tone of voice; (iii) the officer orders the citizen to do something, e.g., "Stop", "Open your hands", "Don't move", "Stay right there" or "Come over here"; (iv) the officer blocks the individual's path with a police vehicle or officer(s); (v) the individual is told he or she is a suspect; (vi) the officer physically touches the individual; (vii) the individual's property (driver's license, airline ticket or other personal property belonging to the individual) is retained. See *Parker v. Commonwealth*, supra.

For example, in *Langston v. Commonwealth*, 504 S.E.2d 380 (Va. Ct. App. 1998), three Richmond officer were on uniformed bicycle patrol in the 700 block of West Clay Street, a known drug "hot spot," when they saw defendant standing with a group in the yard of an abandoned house posted with a "No Trespassing" sign. When defendant saw the officers, he walked away down an alley. All three officers followed defendant down the alley, "where they peppered him with questions regarding his identity and destination." When defendant finally stopped and turned to face the officers, they surrounded him, two in front, one behind him, and blocked his path with their bikes. At this point, defendant was seized.

See also *Goodwin v. Commonwealth*, 398 S.E.2d 690 (Va. Ct. App. 1990), where defendant was seized when, as he was walking down the sidewalk, a patrol car stopped next to him and the officers inside told him that they wanted to pat him down. Compare with *Moss v. Commonwealth*, 373 S.E.2d 170 (Va. Ct. App. 1988), where a uniformed officer "jumped out" from behind some bushes in a private yard as defendant and his companions approached, then shined his flashlight directly on defendant. The officer later admitted at trial that his flashlight was "bright and has an effect of blinding the other parties, which stuns them." Defendant was seized.

Contrast with *Commonwealth v. Satchell*, 422 S.E.2d 412 (Va. Ct. App. 1992), where, in the mid-afternoon, defendant, who had been standing and talking to two other men on a corner in a high-crime area of Richmond, walked up to a stoop outside the door of a residence with his hand clinched. A lone, plain clothes officer with no visible weapons walked up to defendant and asked, "What's in your hand, pal?" The officer did not command defendant to show him, or use a threatening tone. Defendant was not seized.

Often an officer will approach a person in a public place (i.e. airport, bus station, train, plane or bus, etc.) An officer needs no reasonable suspicion to ask questions, or ask for a person's identification, as long as a reasonable person would understand that he or she could refuse to cooperate. *Florida v. Bostick*, 501 U.S. 429 (1991).

See *Greene v. Commonwealth*, 440 S.E.2d 138 (Va. Ct. App. 1994). Defendant arrived at Norfolk International Airport from New York, a "source city" for illegal narcotics; he had an "unnatural bulge" in the crotch of his pants, "maybe the size of a tennis ball." Therefore, "Drug Interdiction Team" agents decided they would try to learn a little more about him. An agent, dressed in street clothes with no visible weapon, approached defendant and, while standing five to six feet to his side, asked, "Excuse me, sir, can I talk with you?" The agent did not touch or threaten defendant, and when defendant asked to use the phone, the agent moved out of his way. Defendant was not seized.

Note: All traffic stops of moving vehicles are seizures of the person within the meaning of the Fourth Amendment, and must be supported by reasonable suspicion. *Ramos v. Commonwealth*, 516 S.E.2d 737 (Va. Ct. App. 1999).

Note: It is important for the law enforcement officer to remember that in a consensual encounter the citizen waives his Fourth and Fifth Amendment rights. The officer does not have to give the citizen *Miranda* warnings or Fourth Amendment rights. Once an arrest is made, or there is a detention, the person must be advised of his or her *Miranda* rights if the officer plans on questioning the person in custody.

C. Detentions and Investigatory Stops

The next conceptual category in the hierarchy of encounters are interactions that courts refer to as investigatory stops, temporary detentions or *Terry* stops. The U.S. Supreme Court articulated the standard officers require as a justification for this more intrusive action in *Terry v. Ohio*, 392 U.S. 1 (1968). The Court held that when an officer observes specific and articulable events which give rise to a reasonable suspicion that illegal activity may be underway then the officer is justified in detaining and questioning the individual. The requisite suspicion must derive from facts and inferences from those facts. Such suspicions cannot lead to a mere hunch that something is amiss. More is needed. The facts producing the officer's suspicions must be objectively reasonable at the time, taking into account all of the circumstances attendant to the encounter. Note that the observations made by the officer to justify a *Terry* stop need not be as convincing as information which would create "probable cause" for arrest.

In the *Terry* case the Court also held that when a law enforcement officer has a reasonable suspicion that illegal activity may be under way and the suspect has been detained, the officer is entitled to conduct a limited pat-down, or frisk, of the outer garments of the detainee to determine whether the suspect is armed or possesses an item that could be used to harm the officer. The requirements for, and the parameters of, this limited search are discussed below. The legal standard for the stop is the reasonable suspicion to believe the detainee is somehow engaged in unlawful activity. The legal standard for the frisk, unlike the stop, relates to fear that the suspect is armed with a deadly weapon.

1. Reasonable Suspicion.

a. In General. The level of doubt needed to permit this more intrusive type of encounter (i.e., a *Terry* stop) is phrased as "reasonable suspicion of criminal activity." This suspicion must be reasonable to a judge or jury looking at the encounter in hindsight, not suspicion that was subjectively reasonable to the officer at the time. To ascertain if the suspicion was, in fact, reasonable, one must look to all the circumstances surrounding the encounter. The facts known by the officer are relevant here (e.g., the suspect was arrested for burglary two months ago or an all-points bulletin just came out for a murder only two blocks away), as well as his or her observations (e.g., the suspect was stumbling or slurring words or seemed nervous when the officer spoke to him) and experience (e.g., "I've been a cop for fifteen years and I know what a drug deal looks like."). When taken together these elements must coalesce and point to a conclusion that a circumspect, judicious person would come to, namely, that some form of criminal endeavor was afoot. The facts given to support the suspicion must be detailed. The officer must be able to state them in a clear and concise fashion. A mere intuition or instinctive feeling, standing alone, is insufficient. Facts are needed to bolster the conclusion that the suspicion was reasonable. Assuming there was adequate justification for the stop, the means of investigation employed must be reasonably related to the suspicion created. Moreover, the detention must last no longer than reasonably necessary to dispel or confirm the suspicion (15 to 30 minutes is the time frame courts seem to routinely permit, although substantially longer detentions have been upheld, and shorter ones have been found excessive).

Note: If the officers do not have a justification for making the initial stop (i.e., at least a reasonable suspicion that criminal activity is underway), everything that may happen afterwards (e.g., guns or drugs are found) will be of no consequence. Any evidence that might have been used against the suspect becomes tainted by the police misconduct and will be suppressed as the result, or fruit, of an unconstitutional detention. This is known as the exclusionary rule.

b. Factors To Consider. For the professional officer, an important point to note is that an individual fact or observation, alone, may be as consistent with innocuous, perfectly lawful conduct and activities, as it is with criminal enterprise. Courts consistently look at the combination of several different observations, each of which when isolated may appear innocent, but when taken together would lead to a reasonable impression that illegal activities are taking place.

Investigatory stops are routinely conducted in a variety of factual settings. The process of detaining and questioning a person is not limited to an "on-the-street" scenario, where an officer detains and questions a pedestrian. Investigatory stops are permissible in situations involving vehicles and motorists as well. An officer may briefly detain and question the driver or passengers of a vehicle if he has a reasonable suspicion that the occupants are involved in criminal activity. Following a lawful stop an officer may, as a matter of course, order the driver and any passengers to step out of the vehicle, even without any particularized suspicion that the vehicle occupants are armed or may otherwise pose a threat to the officer.

c. Investigatory Stops. The police may briefly detain and question a person upon a reasonable suspicion, short of probable cause for arrest, that the person is involved in criminal activity. What is, or is not, reasonable suspicion depends on balancing, weighing and meshing a variety of factors, taking into account the particular factual setting with which an officer is confronted. Some factors commonly cited by courts when determining the existence or absence of reasonable suspicion are as follows:

(1) A prior criminal record does not create a reasonable suspicion that there is current criminal activity. However, if that knowledge is coupled with other concrete facts or observations, an officer may rely on the combination to create a reasonable suspicion of present criminal activity.

(2) An officer's awareness that a crime was recently committed in the vicinity is a pertinent consideration. Standing alone, however, this knowledge does not create a reasonable suspicion that an individual who happens to be in that area, a short time later, was the perpetrator.

(3) A suspect's presence in a high-crime area, or an area known for drug trafficking, standing alone, is not a basis for reasonable suspicion. But a suspect's presence in such an area is an articulable fact. Coupled with other more solid observations, such presence can create reasonable suspicion that the suspect is engaged in the unlawful activity for which the neighborhood is known.

(4) Evasive conduct, furtive gestures, concealing or attempting to conceal one's identity are criteria an officer may weigh in assessing if his suspicion is reasonable. However, each individual observation, without more, will not create a reasonable suspicion of criminal endeavor.

(5) The time of day or night in which the individual is observed is relevant. However, merely being out in public at a late hour, without more, will not justify a stop.

(6) Information given to an officer by a third party, an informant, is generally insufficient by itself to create reasonable suspicion. However, when this information is corroborated by officers through independent investigation, or there is extraneous evidence that the informant is reliable and truthful, reasonable suspicion may be based on the tip. An officer may rely on a flyer or bulletin, describing a suspect and disseminated by another law enforcement agency, for a source of reasonable suspicion. The officer relying on the bulletin does not have to demonstrate personal knowledge of the facts necessary to justify the stop. However, the party issuing the bulletin or flyer must have facts in his or her possession which would support a finding of reasonable suspicion. Moreover, the scope of the stop made by the officer relying on the bulletin may be no more intrusive than the issuing agency would have been justified in conducting.

d. Legality of a Stop. A determination that an officer possessed reasonable suspicion, justifying a detention, is only the first step in determining the legality of a stop. A reviewing court will ask initially if the officer's action was justified at its inception, and secondly whether it was reasonably related in scope to the circumstances which justified the interference in the first place. An examination of the scope of the stop addresses the following: (i) the length of the detention, and (ii) the methods employed during the stop. The duration of, and methods employed during the stop must be tailored to serve the purpose of confirming or alleviating the officer's suspicions. If those concerns are confirmed, and an officer's observations during the detention create probable cause, an arrest may be made. If the suspicions are dispelled, then the suspect should be let go. The detention must be sufficiently limited in temporal duration to satisfy the conditions of an investigative seizure. The nature of the questioning and level of force employed during the detention must be similarly limited. Even though the initial stop was

 Zv

justified, if the detention exceeds the scope authorized by its justification, i.e., "reasonable suspicion of criminal activity," it will be deemed an illegal stop, and any incriminating evidence found thereafter will not be admissible in court.

e. Justification of a Detention.

(1) Flight. A suspect's flight, when confronted with police presence, may give the officer reasonable suspicion to pursue and detain the suspect. Note, however, that not all conduct which merely avoids contact with law enforcement is considered flight from law enforcement.

See *Illinois v. Wardlow*, __ U.S. __ (No. 98-1036 Jan. 12, 2000). Two uniformed officers were in the last car of a four car police caravan that converged on an area of Chicago known for heavy narcotics trafficking, in order to investigate drug transactions. The officers observed defendant, who was standing next to a building holding an opaque bag, look at the police caravan, then run in the opposite direction. Given the character of the area and defendant's headlong flight ("the consummate act of evasion"), the officers had reasonable suspicion to stop him.

Compare with *White v. Commonwealth*, 492 S.E.2d 451 (Va. Ct. App. 1997). Officers were patrolling in Lynchburg at around 9:15 p.m. on a mid- December night, when they saw 10 or 15 males gathered in a semi-circle in a vacant lot, standing next to a Cadillac. As the officers approached the group, they heard someone shout "5-0", a street term for police. The entire group of men ran, leaving the Cadillac with its engine running and a door wide open. Police chased the men to the back of a nearby house, where they found defendant sitting on the back steps of the residence; this struck the officers as highly unusual, given the time of year and late hour. This strange behavior, given that the officers had just seen a group of men flee, justified an investigatory stop and frisk of defendant.

But see *Ewell v. Commonwealth*, 491 S.E.2d 721 (Va. Ct. App. 1997). An off-duty Virginia Beach officer was working as a security guard at an apartment complex. Late one night, at around 12:30 a.m., he saw defendant's Oldsmobile parked next to an apartment which was a suspected site of narcotics activity. Officer was familiar with most of the complex's residents and their vehicles, but he did not recognize this car. When officer approached in his marked vehicle, the Oldsmobile drove off. Officer saw defendant's face, but did not recognize him. Nevertheless, these observations alone were not enough to suggest criminal activity, so there was no reasonable suspicion for a stop.

(2) High-Crime Area. Presence in a high-crime area, when coupled with observations of suspicious activity, can create reasonable suspicion.

See, e.g., *Parker v. Commonwealth*, 496 S.E.2d 47 (Va. 1998). A Richmond officer was on patrol in the public housing development known a Creighton Court. Officer had made numerous drug arrests in and around this development, and "personally considered that area to be an open-air drug market." On Creighton Road, he saw a group of young men (including defendant) standing around a Cadillac with its trunk open. As the marked patrol car drew near, the men immediately shut the trunk and dispersed. Defendant placed an item in the waistband of his shorts as he walked away down Creighton. Officer then began to drive down Creighton, staying parallel to defendant, who was about 20 feet away on the sidewalk. When defendant noticed the car following him, he turned around and began walking back the other way. Officer had reasonable suspicion to stop defendant for questioning.

Compare with *Buck v. Commonwealth*, 456 S.E.2d 534 (Va. Ct. App. 1995). Plain clothes Arlington County officers were patrolling in a high-crime area where drug sales were known to frequently occur. They observed defendant standing on a corner talking with a "group of guys"; when the officers' unmarked car passed, the group dispersed. The officers circled the block, and when they returned, defendant had moved down the block and was talking with another group. Once again, when the officers passed, this second group dispersed. The officers again drove around the block; on their third pass through the area, they saw defendant sitting in the back seat of a car. As the officers neared, the car drove off. About three or four minutes later, the car returned and dropped defendant off about a block away from where he had been picked up. One of the officers would later testify that "smarter dealers" would only conduct drug transactions in cars, often driving around the block while doing so. After defendant got out of the car, an officer approached him on foot and identified himself. Defendant placed his closed fist to his mouth, then ran. The conduct the officers observed, when combined with the character of the surrounding neighborhood, established reasonable suspicion for a stop.

In *U.S. v. Edmonds*, 948 F. Supp. 562 (E.D. Va. 1996), aff'd, 149 F.3d 1171 (4th Cir.), cert. denied, 119 S. Ct. 257 (1998), an Arlington County officer was on patrol in Crystal City, an area which had experienced a recent rise in auto thefts. At about 10:30 p.m., he saw two men near a car parked on a grassy strip along South Eades Street, behind a parking garage. This was a clearly marked "No Parking" zone. One man was inside the car, while the other, defendant, was standing just outside the open door. This is primarily a commercial area, so it was dark and deserted at that late hour. When defendant saw the officer's patrol car, he began to walk away, slinging a large duffle bag over his shoulder as he went. The officer recognized this as the kind of bag auto thieves often conceal their tools in. As the officer drew closer, defendant began walking more quickly. The officer reasonably believed defendant was involved in auto theft or a related crime, so he validly stopped him.

But see *Goodwin v. Commonwealth*, 398 S.E.2d 690 (Va. Ct. App. 1990). Defendant was walking down the 1100 block of St. James Street in Richmond. a high-crime area where the officers on patrol had made numerous arrests. It was a cold, late December night, and defendant had on a bulky winter coat. When defendant saw the officers' patrol car, he "jammed" his hand into a pocket of the coat. The officers did not see any item in defendant's hand or in his pocket. Defendant did not flee or attempt to avoid the officers, but continued to walk toward the patrol car, then walked right past. Nor had the officers received a tip or other information suggesting defendant was involved in criminal activity. The Court concluded that the officers did not have a reasonable suspicion to stop and frisk defendant; his behavior was equally consistent with innocent activity as with criminal.

Compare with *Riley v. Commonwealth*, 412 S.E.2d 724 (Va. Ct. App. 1992). Officer saw defendant exit a vehicle along Dundee Street, near the corner of Midlothian Turnpike, another high-crime area of Richmond. Defendant turned his back to the officer and made a motion toward his waistband, then closed the door to the vehicle. The officer never saw any illegal object; defendant could have been tucking in his shirt or engaged in any number of other legitimate activities. Officer had no prior knowledge of defendant or any possible criminal activities on his part. The general character of the neighborhood alone was not enough to establish reasonable suspicion.

(3) Officer's Experience. Officers are entitled to rely on their own knowledge and experience in forming reasonable suspicion. Knowledge of an earlier crime in the area, coupled with observation of suspicious conduct, can justify a detention.

See *Ford v. Commonwealth*, 503 S.E.2d 803 (Va. Ct. App. 1998). A detective saw defendant walking with two women in the parking lot of the Cloverleaf shopping mall.

Defendant was carrying a white plastic bag. As the trio approached the wooded area on the east side of the lot, defendant looked over his shoulder several times, then separated from the women and entered the woods. He returned a minute or two later, without the bag, and the three entered the mall. The detective then entered the woods himself, and, within ten seconds, he found a white plastic bag hidden beneath two old, discarded mattresses. It was the only bag in the area similar to the one defendant had been carrying. Inside were five "rolled up" pieces of women's clothing, with the store tags still attached; however, there was no receipt or sales slip in the bag. Thirty to forty-five minutes later, when defendant exited the mall, the detective had reasonable suspicion to stop and question him about his apparent shoplifting.

In *Nelson v. Commonwealth*, 485 S.E.2d 673 (Va. Ct. App. 1997), two Newport News officers were dispatched to investigate a possible burglary in progress at 210 Nina Court. When they arrived on the scene, they were met by a neighbor who told them she had observed a black female in a black skirt and multi-colored top leaving 210 Nina Court and walking down Colony Road. She added that she knew the residents of that house were away, and that she had never seen this person at the residence before. The officers drove down Colony Road, and soon saw defendant, who was dressed as the neighbor had described. She was carrying an eight-inch straightened piece of coat hanger, which she laid on the curb as the officers approached. Defendant "was agitated and sweating profusely." When asked for identification, she said she had none. When asked her destination, she said she was walking to her home in Courthouse Green; however, as the officers pointed out, she had been walking in the opposite direction. After this, defendant's statements became "increasingly confusing and inconsistent, as she attempted to explain her actions to the officers." The officers had a particularized and objective basis for believing that defendant may have been involved in criminal activity, and therefore were justified in detaining her. (In addition, because burglary is a felony that clearly has the potential for violence, a pat down for weapons was also justified).

In *Thomas v. Commonwealth*, 434 S.E.2d 319 (Va. Ct. App. 1993), on reh'g, 444 S.E.2d 275 (1994), a Norfolk officer received a call at around 5 a.m. reporting a stabbing at a nearby location. While checking the area, the officer saw defendant coming around from the back side of a motel less than a block from the crime scene, which was unusual, given that there were "no rooms back there." Defendant matched the reported description of the assailant, and was the only person the officer saw on the street. The officer had reasonable suspicion to detain defendant in order to question him regarding the stabbing.

See also *Jackson v. Commonwealth*, 470 S.E.2d 138 (Va. Ct. App. 1996). In the early morning hours, a Richmond officer working off-duty in a high-crime neighborhood saw "muzzle flash" and heard "several shots [fired] from handguns." He looked over to the area where the shots seemed to have originated, and saw a group of seven or eight individuals. Officer had reasonable suspicion to stop and pat down each of these men.

In *Jones v. Commonwealth*, 484 S.E.2d 125 (Va. Ct. App. 1997), two Gloucester County officers were travelling in an unmarked Ford Bronco, when a car driven by defendant pulled up alongside them. The front seat passenger motioned to the rear seat passengers, after which they all stared at the officers; one of the men gestured as if shooting a gun. The car then took position immediately behind and to the right of the Bronco; it remained in this position even as the officers sped up to 70 m.p.h., slowed to 50 m.p.h., and stopped at a red light. One officer would later testify it seemed as if defendant was trying to ensure that his car "was always at an advantage to [their] vehicle." Three weeks earlier, a confidential-informant had told the officers that there was a "contract" out on them, in retaliation for a prior arrest. Several other informants had confirmed this story; one reported that money had already been paid for this purpose. One of the officers thought that defendant looked like one of the men arrested in that incident. When the officers entered York County, they obtained assistance from local county officers. These officers had reasonable suspicion to stop defendant, based on the passengers' gestures, the prior reported threats on the officers' lives, and his own erratic driving.

In *Lowery v. Commonwealth*, 388 S.E.2d 265 (Va. Ct. App. 1990), officer saw defendant driving northbound on Interstate 95 in a car with Florida license plates. A particular letter on the plates indicated that the car was a rental; the officer checked DMV records and learned that the car was owned by Alpha Auto Leasing. Because the officer knew that local leasing agencies (unlike the larger national agencies) often prohibit lessees from taking vehicles out of state, he reasonably believed that defendant was involved in criminal activity, and made a valid investigatory stop.

(4) Tips. Information provided by someone outside the circles of law enforcement may provide sufficient justification for a stop if it carries with it sufficient indicia of reliability. Factors that bolster the reliability of information may include: the reliability and reputation of the person providing the tip; corroboration of the details contained in the tip by independent police work; and the extent to which any information provided by the informant has proved to be accurate or useful in the past.

See, e.g., *O'Toole v. Commonwealth*, 458 S.W.2d 595 (Va. Ct. App. 1995), on reh'g, 467 S.E.2d 819 (1996). A reliable informant, whose previous tips had resulted in arrests and convictions for cocaine violations, told a Virginia Beach detective that he had been in defendant's apartment, and that an unnamed person in the apartment told him that defendant was "making the rounds," delivering cocaine in a Ford Bronco with Virginia license plates "CHUXX." The informant added that defendant was being accompanied by a black male known as "Junie," who was about five-foot-five and 150 pounds. The detective knew "Junie" was the nickname of Thomas Lee White, an individual he had previously arrested for a firearms violation. Thirty to forty minutes later, the detective saw the described Bronco, with White at the wheel. He had reasonable suspicion for an investigatory stop.

But see *Beckner v. Commonwealth*, 425 S.E.2d 530 (Va. Ct. App. 1993). A citizen pulled up behind a police cruiser, then flashed his lights to get the officer's attention. When the officer pulled over, the driver pulled along side, and said that there was a white female driving a 1966 Chevy without a license at a nearby gas station. Although this face-to-face confrontation provided some indicia of the tipster's reliability, nothing he said established his basis of knowledge. He did not tell the officer *how* he knew that the woman's license was suspended. Therefore, the tip did not establish reasonable suspicion for a stop.

(5) Anonymous Tips. An anonymous tip, if corroborated by other observations and supported by indicia of reliability, can create reasonable suspicion.

See, e.g., *Alabama v. White*, 496 U.S. 325 (1990). Police received an anonymous tip that defendant would leave a specific unit of an apartment building, and then, carrying a brown briefcase filled with cocaine, would travel in her brown Plymouth station wagon, which had a broken taillight, to a specific motel. Police watched the apartment complex, and saw a brown Plymouth wagon with a broken taillight. They then watched defendant exit the specified apartment, empty-handed, get into the car and drive directly toward the motel. Even though not every detail in the tip turned out to be totally correct, the partial corroboration by police alone provided reasonable suspicion for a stop.

See also *Gregory v. State*, 468 S.E.2d 117 (Va. Ct. App. 1996). At approximately 2 a.m., an anonymous tip to Richmond police stated that an individual "was standing out in the roadway" in the 1700 block of Carlyle Avenue "flagging motorists down to ask them if they wanted to buy drugs." The tipster described this dealer as a black male, dressed in a green sweat jacket with a green hooded jacket underneath, dark jeans, and tennis shoes, and provided the make and color of his vehicle. Two minutes after hearing a radio report regarding this tip, an officer approached the 1700 block of Carlyle. He knew this to be an area where police "always receive complaints of drug dealing." He saw defendant, a black male dressed as the tip had described, sitting in a matching vehicle. As the officer approached, defendant looked in his direction and became "slightly agitated"; he then began to walk away from his vehicle, looking over his shoulder as went. Defendant's furtive conduct and the officer's immediate verification of the many details the informant provided sufficiently corroborated the tip so that the officer had reasonable suspicion to stop and frisk defendant.

In *U.S. v. Perrin*, 45 F.3d 869 (4th Cir. 1995), cert. denied, 515 U.S. 1126 (1996), an anonymous call to York County police stated that "Charles Odell" (the defendant's first and middle names) was selling crack cocaine in the laundromat of the Yorktown Square Apartments, a known high-crime area. Three days later, the police received a second anonymous call; this caller alleged that "Charlie Red" (defendant's street name) was selling crack outside Building 4 of the same apartment complex. The officer was familiar with both the defendant and the character of the neighborhood where he was allegedly dealing; within an hour of the second call, officer drove by Building 4, where he saw defendant standing outside, drinking a beer. The fact that the officer received two calls within three days, both of which offered detailed descriptions of defendant's activities, combined with his own knowledge and observations to establish reasonable suspicion for a stop.

In *Bulatko v. Commonwealth*, 428 S.E.2d 306 (Va. Ct. App. 1993), an anonymous caller to the Chief of the Mount Jackson Police Department identified defendant by name, gave the color and license plate number of his Dodge, and stated that he was driving toward Mount Jackson without a license. A records check revealed that defendant was a habitual offender, and that the plate number the caller had given conformed to a car of the model and color he alleged. This sufficiently corroborated the tip, so that when, 45 minutes later, the Chief saw defendant's Dodge driving into town, he had reasonable suspicion for a stop.

But see *Hardy v. Commonwealth*, 399 S.E.2d 27 (Va. Ct. App. 1990). An anonymous caller to Richmond police stated that Kenneth Hardy (the defendant) was walking north on Hull Street dressed in a black coat with a white fur collar and a black fur hat; the unidentified caller went on the say that defendant was armed and had cocaine in his hat. Soon after receiving this tip, an officer, who knew defendant, saw him walking on Hull, wearing the described outfit. The Court found that the officer did not have reasonable suspicion for a stop. The tip provided nothing more than innocent details which any casual observer could have given; there were no predictions of defendant's future behavior, and no wealth of detail which would reveal the caller had an "inner-knowledge" of defendant's activities. The reliability of the tip could not be established.

Contrast with *Scott v. Commonwealth*, 560 S.E.2d 610 (Va. Ct. App. 1995). An anonymous tip stated that a light-complexioned black male in a white T-shirt, black shorts and Nikes with no socks, was brandishing a gun in a laundromat. An officer was only one block away, and arrived at the laundromat about one minute later. He saw defendant, who matched the description exactly, walking out. The Court found that, in this case, the officer's "immediate confirmation" of several details in the tip, when combined with the possibility of imminent danger to the public, justified a stop and frisk of defendant.

(6) "Erratic" Driving. Driving in an erratic manner in and of itself justifies a stop. Officers do not violate the Fourth Amendment by stopping and questioning someone who just committed a traffic violation in the officer's presence. Moreover, routine traffic infractions, even minor ones, can provide the requisite reasonable suspicion to stop a vehicle.

See, e.g., *U.S. v. Sakyi*, 160 F.3d 164 (4th Cir. 1998) (valid stop for a non-functioning brake light); *Reittinger v. Commonwealth*, 514 S.E.2d 775 (Va. Ct. App. 1999) (valid stop for a broken headlight); *Freeman v. Commonwealth*, 460 S.E.2d 261 (Va. Ct. App. 1995) (reasonable suspicion for a stop when defendant was driving in the center lane of a freeway 10 to 15 m.p.h. below the posted speed limited, and weaved within his own lane three or four times over the course of two miles).

But see *Neal v. Commonwealth*, 498 S.E.2d 422 (Va. Ct. App. 1998) ("An isolated instance of mild weaving within a lane is not sufficiently erratic to justify an investigatory stop[,]" although "repeated weaving within a lane provides sufficient reasonable and articulable suspicion to justify an investigatory stop.").

(7) Drug Courier Profiles. Profiles of drug couriers are relied on by officers to identify potential suspects. Generally, a match to the profile alone does not create reasonable suspicion to detain the suspect. The officer must observe other conduct or circumstances that sufficiently heighten his suspicion. Often, undercover officers will survey airport or bus terminals for individuals matching a certain profile. Factors utilized in compiling this profile may include: (i) a journey that originated in a source city for narcotics, or a short round trip, with a brief stay in such a city; (ii) the suspect carrying a hard-sided suitcase; (iii) the suspect appearing nervous when questioned; (iv) tickets that were paid for in cash; (v) the suspect providing inconsistent or wavering answers to inquiries; (vi) furtive movements (e.g., glancing over one's shoulder, not making eye contact, etc.). See *U.S. v. Sokolow*, 490 U.S. 1 (1989).

In *Williams v. Commonwealth*, 463 S.E.2d 679 (Va. Ct. App. 1995), police surveillance revealed that defendant made same day round-trips from Newport News to New York City twice in the course of a week. Officers knew New York to be a major source city for drugs. Defendant paid cash for his tickets – more specifically, he paid with used five, ten and twenty- dollar bills. He also used a different name on each trip. When defendant returned from his second trip, officers approached him in the hope of initiating a consensual interview. When they asked if he would speak with them, he replied, "no," then gave a "head fake" and ran. Reasonable suspicion existed to stop defendant and detain him for questioning.

Compare with *Wechsler v. Commonwealth*, 455 S.E.2d 744 (Va. Ct. App. 1995). A DEA agent assigned to the Dallas/Fort Worth airport notified agents at Washington National Airport to watch for an individual known as "Brian Wechsler" (the defendant). Wechsler was flying to Washington National from Tucson, by way of Dallas, and had reserved a one-way ticket just one hour before take-off, then arrived mere minutes before take-off, paying for his ticket in cash. He had checked two bags, but was carrying another two bags, and a person matching Wechsler's description had been seen walking around the Dallas airport "acting very nervous." Two agents waited at Washington National for Wechsler's scheduled flight to arrive; defendant was on board, and when he deplaned, he looked "right at" the agents, then "put his head down very quickly." Defendant waited in the baggage claim area for about five minutes; however, he then made eye contact with the agents, after which he attempted to make a phone call then left to get a taxi, without claiming any bags. The agents approached defendant outside by the cab stand, and initiated a consensual interview. Defendant claimed that he threw his ticket away in Arizona, and that he had not checked any bags nor just used the phone. He then consented to a search of his (carry-on) bags, where the agents found his ticket with two baggage check claim tickets attached, catching defendant in his lie. At this point, the agents had reasonable suspicion to detain defendant until the bags he checked (still circling the conveyor belt inside) could be sniffed by a drug dog.

In a typical scenario, a suspect matching the profile is approached by officers and asked a few questions. Often, a threshold issue in such cases is the nature of the questioning. If the encounter is consensual, then no Fourth Amendment concerns arise. If, however, the officers' suspicions are aroused and a more aggressive investigatory posture is assumed, the encounter may escalate into a *Terry* type detention, and the scope of the encounter must conform to constitutional guidelines. The method employed by investigating officers should be of the least intrusive means reasonably necessary to verify or dispel the officer's suspicion in a short period of time. Although the initial stop may be justified, it may become so protracted, exceeding a time limit that the officer would reasonably need to confirm or dispel his or her suspicions about possible trafficking activity, that it becomes unreasonable. To pass constitutional muster, a detention not only must be justified at its inception, but also must be reasonably related in scope to the circumstances that justified it in the first instance.

If, and when, such an encounter progresses into a full-blown detention, another frequently adjudicated question involves the seizure of a suspect's luggage, purse, handbag or other personal item. The general rule is that officers may effect a temporary seizure if they have reasonable suspicion that the luggage contains contraband. The seizure must be brief, and related in duration to dispelling any suspicion about what the luggage contains. Frequently, the luggage is subjected to a sniff-test (by a dog trained to recognize, by smell, the presence of narcotics or other drugs) or officers try to obtain consent to search the luggage. In such cases, a distinction must be drawn between detaining and actually opening and searching a container. Although police may temporarily detain a container based upon reasonable suspicion, they generally may not open it without a warrant, or some recognized exception to the warrant requirement.

(8) Roadblocks and Checkpoints. Roadblocks and checkpoints are used to make temporary stops. Municipal, county and state law enforcement divisions set up road blocks and check points for a variety of reasons: checking the validity of driver's license and registration; determining if the vehicle meets safety inspection minimums; deciding if the car has the necessary municipal parking permit; etc. Used with increasing frequency are checkpoints employed to apprehend intoxicated drivers.

What is at issue in these scenarios? Checkpoints involve a constitutional detention, a seizure of a person, without any level of particular, individualized doubt, i.e., reasonable suspicion or probable cause. Since there is no focused suspicion on an individual, rather than assessing the existence or absence of probable cause or reasonable suspicion, when the use of a roadblock is challenged, courts will examine police conduct and the circumstances of the stop and determine if the checkpoint is a reasonable intrusion, and therefore justifiable, under the Fourth Amendment. In the context of sobriety checkpoints, this reasonableness determination involves an analysis of three factors: (i) the magnitude of a state's interest in preventing accidents caused by intoxicated drivers; (ii) the extent to which the checkpoint advances that goal; and (iii) the measure of intrusion on an individual's privacy, both objectively, as perceived by the reviewing court, and subjectively, as the motorist may perceive the intrusion.

The U.S. Supreme Court applied these factors to determine the constitutionality of a sobriety checkpoint in *Michigan Dept. of State Police v. Sitz*, 496 U.S. 444 (1990). Here, Michigan implemented a program where checkpoints would be set up at predetermined sites along state roads. All drivers passing through would be stopped and checked for obvious signs of intoxication. If such indications were detected, the motorist would be taken out of the flow of traffic and an officer would check his or her license and registration. If warranted, the officer would conduct field sobriety tests. All other motorists would continue unimpeded after the initial screening. The check lasted 75 minutes, during which 126 vehicles passed through. The average delay was 25 seconds. Three motorists were detained on suspicion of intoxication, and two were arrested. The Court held that this checkpoint passed constitutional muster. Citing the aforementioned factors, the Court found that:

(a) Michigan had a substantial interest in eliminating drunken driving, noting that "no one can seriously dispute the magnitude of the drunken driving problem [or the] State's interest in eradicating it."

(b) This checkpoint advanced the state's interest in curbing the drunk driving problem, noting that the use of a permissible checkpoint is but one of many reasonable alternatives to remedying the problem, and "the choice among such reasonable alternatives remains with the governmental officials who have a unique understanding" of the problem and the resources available to combat it.

(c) The intrusion, both objective and subjective, was slight, pointing out the brevity (25 seconds) of the average encounter. The Court also noted that any subjective intrusion, such as making a motorist fearful or annoyed, was diminished by the fact that motorists could plainly see all vehicles were being stopped.

The Virginia Courts have upheld checkpoints under similar reasoning. They have consistently ruled that Virginia has a substantial interest in protecting its motorists, passengers, and pedestrians from unsafe drivers; therefore, the stops are reasonable. However, the checkpoint must be based on specific, objective facts, or it must be carried out pursuant to a plan embodying explicit, neutral limitations on the conduct of the officers. The Court will look at factors such as the length of the stop, the nature of the questions, whether adequate warning was provided, and whether the stops were made in a systematic, non-random fashion. *Simmons v. Commonwealth*, 371 S.E.2d 7 (Va. Ct. App. 1988).

In *Brown v. Commonwealth*, 454 S.E.2d 758 (Va. Ct. App. 1995), state troopers were operating a sobriety checkpoint in Saluda County pursuant to a memo issued by the Department of State Police. This memo explicitly stated that the checkpoint could be moved from its specified location to a second specified location only if "safety considerations prevent checkpoint operations at the intended location." However, the troopers chose to move the checkpoint solely because traffic was light at the original location and they were making few arrests. The checkpoint set up at the second location was illegal, because the troopers failed to comply with the administrative guidelines.

Compare with *Hall v. Commonwealth*, 406 S.E.2d 674 (Va. Ct. App. 1991). A memo issued by the Virginia State Police designated 54 locations in Accomack County where "checking details" could be set up. Troopers would be ordered by their supervisors to set up a checkpoint at the beginning of the week; however, the troopers themselves would choose the exact time during the week to conduct the checkpoint (subject to the two-hour time limit set in the memo) and which of the 54 approved sites at which to locate it. The Court found that the discretion this method provided troopers was too broad, and was thus likely to lead to abuse. Therefore, a checkpoint set up under these guidelines was illegal.

Contrast with *Crouch v. Commonwealth*, 494 S.E.2d 144 (Va. Ct. App. 1997). A state trooper received an assignment at the start of his work week to set up a traffic checking detail some time during the week, though no date or time was specified. His supervisor directed him to set up the checkpoint at the intersection of Routes 29 and 211; therefore, the trooper had no discretion as to location. In addition, once he selected a time, the trooper was required to obtain approval from a supervisor who was not part of the detail before he began stopping vehicles, which further limited his discretion. In addition, the Court noted the need to evaluate weather conditions and determine the availability of other officers provided a reasonable basis for this procedure. Furthermore, the trooper stopped all vehicles, and operated the checkpoint for one hour, so it complied with State Police Guidelines. The trooper did not have "unbridled discretion" in deciding when and where to begin stopping cars, and, therefore, the checkpoint he set up was valid.

See also *Price v. Commonwealth*, 483 S.E.2d 496 (Va. Ct. App. 1997). At a roadblock, the driver of a car was ordered not to drive after police discovered that his driver's license had been suspended with notice. Defendant, who was the only passenger in the car, then told the police that she was willing to drive his car away for him. Because defendant did not have her license with her, the police contacted a dispatcher to check her DMV record's from a computer to see if she was truly licensed to drive. While searching defendant's DMV records, the police computer also checked its data base of outstanding warrants and discovered an outstanding warrant for defendant's arrest. Defendant was arrested and heroin was found on her purse during a search incident to the arrest. The warrant check of defendant was performed in accordance with the roadblock plan, so that her arrest was proper and the heroin could be used as evidence against her.

A vehicle may be detained at a roadblock no longer than the brief period that is necessary to perform the activities authorized in the roadblock plan unless the officers develop reasonable suspicion that the motorist is unlicensed, the vehicle is not registered or there is some other violation of the law. *Gilpin v. Commonwealth*, 493 S.E.2d 393 (Va. Ct. App. 1997).

Note: Evasive maneuvers seemingly intended to avoid a roadblock may also establish reasonable suspicion for a stop. See *Bailey v. Commonwealth*, 508 S.E.2d 889 (Va. Ct. App. 1999). State troopers were conducting a roadblock at the intersection of Routes 606 and 674 in Henry County; traffic was "light." A knoll just north of the checkpoint blocked it from the view of southbound drivers, who could not see it until they reached the top of the knoll. When defendant's vehicle reached the top of the knoll, it stopped suddenly, then eased into the driveway of a private residence 50 to 75 yards before the roadblock. Defendant drove slowly, as if hesitant about stopping at the residence, and the whole time he kept looking at the troopers. When defendant got out of his car, the troopers were justified in stopping him and asking to see his license.

Compare with *Thomas v. Commonwealth*, 480 S.E.2d 135 (Va. Ct. App. 1997). Henrico County officers set up a roadblock where the exit ramp from Interstate 64 joins Nine Mile Road. Defendant's pick-up truck proceeded up the exit ramp, but then stopped on the shoulder of the road 30 yards before the roadblock. Defendant (the driver) and his passenger both then exited the truck. The troopers were justified in approaching defendant and requesting his driver's license.

(9) "Pretext" Stop. Pretext stop cases typically involve officers who have a hunch that the driver or passenger of a car is committing a given crime, e.g., possession of narcotics. However, nothing they have observed rises to the level of reasonable suspicion necessary to stop the car. The police then observe the motorist commit a minor traffic violation, and use this infraction, "the claimed pretext," to stop the vehicle and pursue a more intrusive line of investigation. In the adjudicated cases, the pretext stop search typically leads to the discovery of contraband wholly unrelated to the reason for the stop. In *Whren v. United States*, 517 U.S. 806 (1996), the U.S. Supreme Court held that "Ulterior motives do not invalidate police conduct that is justified on the basis of probable cause to believe a violation of the law has occurred." The true motivating factor behind the stop is irrelevant. As long as there is probable cause to believe the rules of the road have been violated, a detention under such circumstances is lawful. A suspect may not claim that he or she was illegally detained merely because an officer had a hunch that a different, more serious crime was being committed, although the officer lacked proof for that proposition and intended to find evidence of that crime during the stop. If there is an objectively valid reason for the stop, even one involving a minor traffic infraction, subjective intentions are irrelevant. The Court did note that a stop motivated by an intent to single out members of a suspect class, such as race, would, however, be impermissible.

2. Search Incident to a Detention. During an investigatory detention, an officer may come to reasonably believe that the persons with whom he is dealing may be armed and presently dangerous, and where nothing in the encounter serves to dispel his reasonable fear for his own or another's safety, he is entitled to conduct a carefully limited search of the outer clothing to discover weapons which might be used to assault him. *Terry v. Ohio*, 392 U.S. 1 (1968); *Harrel v. Commonwealth*, 517 S.E.2d 256 (Va. Ct. App. 1991).

See, e.g., *Logan v. Commonwealth*, 512 S.E.2d 160 (Va. Ct. App. 1999). Officer stopped a small, two-door car for lack of an inspection sticker. When he approached the car, he immediately saw a 9mm handgun in the middle of the dashboard. The car's four young passengers "all seemed kind of nervous." All four were ordered out of the vehicle; once out, though, they kept putting their hands in their pockets, had a hard time remaining stationary, and continually made eye contact with one another. Officer had reasonable suspicion to pat down all four young men.

But see *Stanley v. Commonwealth*, 433 S.E.2d 512 (Va. Ct. App. 1993) (a pat-down was not justified when defendant had a bulge in his front pants pocket caused by 28 folded bills and a small packet with a "tiny amount" of cocaine, as the officer could not reasonably have believed that this small bulge was a hidden weapon).

The scope of the search must be strictly limited, so that the officer seeks only items which could be used to harm him or her. See *Harris v. Commonwealth*, 400 S.E.2d 191 (Va. 1991). While validly frisking defendant, officer found a film canister in his pocket. When he asked what was in it, defendant replied, "Film." Officer opened it anyway, and discovered cocaine. The Court suppressed this evidence, because the officer should have ended his search once he determined that defendant was unarmed. The film canister obviously did not conceal a weapon, and the officer had only a hunch that it contained contraband.

If a weapon is found, the officer may seize the item, and retain it, if its possession is unlawful. If the officer determines that the suspect is not armed, the purpose of the frisk is satisfied and the probing can proceed no further. However, if in the frisking procedure an object is detected, in a pocket or under clothing, that is clearly not a weapon, but rather, and just as obviously, contraband, the item may be seized. The rule here is that officers conducting a *Terry* frisk are entitled to seize any items whose contour, shape or mass make its identity immediately apparent as contraband. The officer must be able to instantly tell the item is contraband, without resorting to further manipulation of the item. This corollary is sometimes called the "plain feel" doctrine. *Minnesota v. Dickerson*, 508 U.S. 366 (1993).

Minnesota v. Dickerson, supra, set out the three requirements for "Plain Feel". First, the officer must be lawfully in the touching area. Second, the officer must have some independent constitutional justification for placing his hands on the person or property in question. Third, upon touching the area the officer must, through the process of touching, garner probable cause to believe the object which he or she is touching constitutes evidence of crime, or contraband. The probable cause must be reasonably contemporaneous with the initial touching. Any evidence obtained as a result of an illegal pat down or frisk is inadmissible under the "Exclusionary Rule". *Minnesota v. Dickerson*, supra.

See, e.g., *U.S. v. Swann*, 149 F.3d 271 (4th Cir. 1998). Officer was investigating the recent theft of a wallet in an office building, when he encountered defendant and his companion stepping off an elevator; both men matched descriptions given by witnesses. The men seemed "edgy", and when officer said he needed to speak with them, one of the men tried to circle around and get behind him. This justified a frisk. Officer felt an object in defendant's left sock that he could not identify; it was "kind of abnormal, and it felt kind of hard." Officer then removed what turned out to be a stack of five stolen credit cards. Even though officer did not know what the object was when he removed it, this seizure was justified. The object's hardness and shape suggested that it could be a weapon. In addition, its location – in defendant's sock – also aroused the officer's suspicions; defendant had pockets where he would normally be expected to store small items, implying that he was attempting to conceal the object.

Compare with *James v. Commonwealth*, 473 S.E.2d 90 (Va. Ct. App. 1996). Defendant was a passenger in a car; the driver of the car was arrested on an outstanding felony warrant. After the driver was asked to step out of the vehicle, defendant began "making gestures" with his hands, and leaned down to the right so that officers could only see one of his hands. When told to put his hands on the dashboard, he did so, but only for a few seconds. He was then told repeatedly to get out of the car; he finally did so, but appeared "jittery." The officers had reasonable suspicion to pat defendant down. The searching officer felt a hard object, about three inches long, in defendant's pocket; he reasonably believed this was a weapon, and validly removed what turned out to be a glass crack pipe.

The safety concerns that underlie the *Terry* exception have relevance not only to detentions on the street or in a public place, but also to the detention of automobile drivers and passengers as well. The U.S. Supreme Court has noted that "roadside encounters between police and suspects are especially hazardous, and danger may arise from the possible presence of weapons in the area surrounding a suspect." Thus, the search of the passenger compartment of an automobile, limited to those areas in which a weapon may be placed or hidden, is permissible if the police officer possesses a reasonable belief based on specific and articulable facts which, taken together with the rational inferences from those facts, reasonably warrant the officer to believe that the suspect is dangerous and the suspect may gain immediate control of weapons. *Michigan v. Long*, 463 U.S. 1032 (1983); *U.S. v. Sakyi*, 160 F.3d 164 (4th Cir. 1998). The search must be limited in scope to the area which the defendant can reach easily, sometimes called the "zone within the wingspan," or "grabbable area." A *Terry* search of an automobile will generally not be allowed, however, if the stop was made solely to issue a traffic citation. *Knowles v. Iowa*, 525 U.S. 113 (1998).

In *U.S. v. Sakyi*, supra, defendant was stopped for a nonfunctioning brake light. When he opened the glove compartment to retrieve his registration, officer saw a box of Phillies Blunt cigars. Officer knew this brand of cigars was commonly employed by marijuana users to roll marijuana cigarettes. "Almost all the time" the officer had come into contact with Phillies Blunts – a total of several hundred cases – "there had also been evidence of marijuana." Therefore, officer had a reasonable suspicion that there were drugs in the car, and, given the "indisputable nexus between drugs and guns" and the lack of any evidence allaying his safety concerns, had reasonable suspicion to search the passenger compartment of defendant's car for weapons.

Note: Similarly, for safety reasons, following a lawful stop an officer may, as a matter of course, order the driver and any passengers to step out of the vehicle. *Pennsylvania v. Mimms*, 434 U.S. 106 (1977); *Maryland v. Wilson*, 519 U.S. 408 (1997); *Harris v. Commonwealth*, 500 S.E.2d 257 (Va. Ct. App. 1998).

The U.S. Supreme Court has expanded the coverage of the officer safety rationale supporting *Terry* and its progeny, and permitted a warrantless search of a residential arrest scene, creating a doctrine known as a protective sweep. The extent of the sweep is limited to a brief cursory visual inspection of the premises. The Court reasoned that it is reasonable for officers to safeguard themselves by insuring that no others are present who could injure them. It is important to note this is not a general crime scene exception to the warrant requirement but rather a doctrine that may be used to justify a warrantless search in particularized circumstances. A sweep is permissible "when the searching officer possesses a reasonable belief based on specific and articulable facts that the area to be swept harbors an individual posing a danger to those on the arrest scene." *Maryland v. Buie*, 494 U.S. 325 (1990).

3. Reasonable Suspicion and Probable Cause. The facts and observations divulged during an investigatory detention may lead to "probable cause" to arrest the person detained. However, the officer must possess facts sufficient to support crossing the threshold between mere reasonable suspicion to detain and question, and full probable cause to arrest, before the latter action may be taken. If the investigating officer does not yet possess facts sufficient to create probable cause to believe the detainee has committed a crime, yet restrains the liberty of the detainee in a manner consistent with a formal arrest, the detention, even if initially lawful, becomes illegal. For example, transporting a suspect involuntarily to a stationhouse for further questioning, without probable cause to link him with a crime, violates the detainee's Fourth Amendment rights. This more intrusive step in the investigatory process requires probable cause and cannot be justified on reasonable suspicion alone. Courts look to the extent of the restriction on an individual's freedom and movement, to determine if the restraint is more consistent with a detention, or a full-blown arrest. For example, although the use of handcuffs on a suspect is a "hallmark" of a formal arrest and is

generally considered a watershed, where a temporary detention becomes an arrest, a suspect nonetheless may be handcuffed or similarly restrained during a temporary detention, if the circumstances warrant.

One of the most common pitfalls in the area of reasonable suspicions and probable cause is the timing of an officer's arrest. In his or her zeal, an officer frequently acts prematurely and, as a result, nullifies what might have been a valid arrest. Thus, an officer may have grounds to approach an individual to question him or her and may even have reason to stop a person in order to obtain information. Certain officers, based on a "hunch" or a "gut feeling" that the individual is "dirty", will search or arrest the individual before they legally have grounds to do so. Many officers feel that the results of the search will justify the police activity. However, the courts have made it quite clear that a bad arrest or a bad search cannot be salvaged or corrected by what the officer recovers from the suspect.

Therefore an officer must proceed with care when approaching an individual on the street or in a car. The officer may only intrude upon the individual's privacy to the extent permitted. The officer can only act in relation to the information he or she possesses at that time. If the information he or she possesses does not constitute probable cause to arrest, the officer must not act prematurely and cannot take the person into custody. A law enforcement officer should proceed with questioning, surveillance or other appropriate police work which can culminate into probable cause.

4. Detention and Seizure of Property. Persons and vehicles are not the only potential subjects of a temporary detention. Officers may temporarily seize and detain items of personal property when they possess a reasonable suspicion that the property is connected with criminal activity. The detention must last no longer than reasonably necessary for the purpose of determining if the item is in fact linked to a criminal endeavor. If a brief investigation reveals that it is not, then the property should be returned to the owner. The Fourth Amendment protects property as well as privacy. *Soldal v. Cook County*, 506 U.S. 538 (1992). Therefore, similar to the seizure of an individual, "seizures of property are subject to Fourth Amendment scrutiny". *Soldal*, supra. This is true even when no search within the meaning of the Amendment has taken place. *Soldal*, supra.

Property is detained most often when the police wish to detain luggage, or a package, to search it for drugs. Often there is a slight delay to obtain a drug-sniffing dog. Items also may be held to search for weapons, explosive material or other contraband. Although in many cases the police will not need full probable cause for the detention of the property, in all cases the police will need some type of objective justification.

A detention of property may be deemed more reasonable if the police allow the owner of the object to leave. The police should then arrange a way to get the detained item back to that individual if their suspicions turn out to be baseless.

A "seizure" of property occurs when "there is some meaningful interference with an individual's possessory interests in that property." *U.S. v. Jacobsen*, 466 U.S. 109 (1984).

Note: In *U.S. v. Bond*, __ U.S. __ (No. 98-9349 Apr. 17, 2000), the Court held that warrantless "squeezing" or other physical manipulation by police of luggage in the overhead compartment of a vehicle or other publicly accessible space – as opposed to mere visual inspection – violates the Fourth Amendment. Although passengers must expect some "casual contact" with their bags by other passengers, they also have a reasonable expectation that their privacy will not be invaded by the other passengers feeling their bags in an exploratory manner.

D. Exclusionary Rule

1. Judicially Created. The exclusionary rule is a judicially created doctrine designed to protect those rights embodied in the Fourth Amendment. *Mapp v. Ohio*, 367 U.S. 643 (1961).

2. Application. The exclusionary rule is applicable only to constitutional violations by governmental action. A violation of privacy by an individual who is not an agent of the government is not a constitutional violation; therefore, the exclusionary rule will not apply to such intrusions. See *U.S. v. Jacobsen*, 466 U.S. 109 (1984).

3. Purpose. The federal exclusionary rule serves as a deterrence to unlawful police conduct. *U.S. v. Leon*, 468 U.S. 897 (1984).

E. Probable Cause

1. In General. In a pre-trial, investigatory context, probable cause is the highest constitutional degree of suspicion (in a trial, or guilt phase context, the "beyond a reasonable doubt" standard would be an even higher level of skepticism, bordering on certainty of guilt). Probable cause does not mean that the arrestee actually committed the suspected crime, or that the officer possesses enough proof to convict the suspect at a trial, or even that he will go to trial for the alleged offense. It does mean that at the time of the arrest, a person of reasonable caution, in the position of the officer, taking into account his experience, knowledge and observations, would believe that a crime has been or is being committed. *Taylor v. Commonwealth*, 284 S.E.2d 833 (Va. 1981); *Yancey v. Commonwealth*, 518 S.E.2d 325 (Va. Ct. App. 1999). When probable cause determinations, whether made by a magistrate or an officer in the field, are challenged, the outcome will often depend on the presence or absence of one seemingly insignificant factor. As with factors used in a reasonable suspicion analysis, when an isolated factor is viewed alone, it may seem trivial. When analyzed with all of the other circumstances surrounding the arrest, it may lead a reviewing court to conclude the conduct was reasonable, and that the challenged arrest was based on probable cause.

In a warrantless arrest situation a police officer will be making the initial probable cause determination. Since probable cause is a somewhat nebulous concept, courts have tried to provide guidance. The U.S. Supreme Court has stated that "[i]n determining probable cause, evidence required to establish guilt is not necessary, but on the other hand, good faith on the part of the arresting officers is not enough, and probable cause exists if the facts and circumstances known to the officer warrant a prudent man in believing that the offense has been committed." *Henry v. United States*, 361 U.S. 98 (1959).

2. Legal Definition. Probable cause is a standard of proof greater than that of reasonable suspicion needed for a detention. It does not rise to the level of proof needed to obtain a conviction. Probable cause to arrest may exist (as determined later by a reviewing court) even if the arresting officer subjectively did not believe he had sufficient facts to constitute probable cause, so long as the objective standard is met. An arrest may be effectuated pursuant to a validly executed warrant, or without, so long as probable cause exists.

The highest (most invasive) level of contact a law enforcement officer may have with a citizen is "probable cause to arrest." An officer may make a warrantless arrest if he or she has probable cause. Probable cause is the officer's knowledge of facts and circumstances based on reasonable, trustworthy information sufficient to warrant a prudent person to believe that the suspect has committed an offense. *Porterfield v. Lott*, 156 F.3d 563 (4th Cir. 1998).

"Probable cause or reasonable cause" means that an officer need not have information which excludes every conceivable possibility of innocence. Probable cause depends upon probabilities, not certainties. Thus, it must appear to the officer that it is at least more probable than not that a crime has taken place, and that the one arrested is its perpetrator. Conduct equally compatible with guilt or innocence will not constitute probable cause.

The subsequent determination of the guilt or innocence of the person arrested does not determine the legality of the arrest.

Because probable cause depends on the facts of each case, probable cause may or may not be found in certain instances.

3. Cautions To Observe (Warrantless Arrest). As every citizen knows, our society is overrun with drugs. Many people rely on the police to fight this "war" against drug activity. The police officer must resist the temptation to use whatever means possible in fighting this "war". Courts will not tolerate a violation of constitutional rights merely because it occurs in the fight against drugs.

Thus, while an exchange of money for a glassine envelope, tinfoil packet or small vial with white powder will constitute probable cause for an arrest in most cases, not every exchange will permit an arrest. An officer may feel that if he or she sees an exchange for any object, the courts will back him or her up should he or she make an arrest. This is not so. An officer must still have reason to believe that he or she is observing a sale of drugs. Should the officer observe an exchange of an object he or she cannot see, the officer should not move in to make an arrest, unless there are other factors which make it probable that drugs are being transferred.

The officer cannot use the "high-crime area" factor as a crutch to make the arrest. Most geographical areas today can be considered high-crime areas, and that fact, in and of itself, will not turn an improper arrest for drugs into a valid arrest. An officer may feel that he or she knows from his or her past experience that the individual has no other reason to be in this area except to buy or sell drugs. However, that fact by itself will not be enough probable cause to justify an arrest.

If a suspect flees, that fact may not, by itself, be a reason to pursue and make an arrest. It is usually the fact that the perpetrator flees, in addition to other factors, that will give rise to probable cause. For example, if the perpetrator drops property which appears to be stolen, or a motorist throws property out the window, those factors in combination with flight can result in probable cause. See *California v. Hodari*, 499 U.S. 621(1991), where a fleeing suspect in a high-crime area ran after being approached by officers, and threw away his cocaine. The U.S. Supreme Court held that when the defendant had not been arrested or seized through any use of physical force or show of authority and where the individual did not acquiesce or submit to any authority, the cocaine is admissible as evidence against the suspect.

4. Identification of Suspect Required. An officer must be sure that the description of a suspect is sufficiently detailed before he or she can effectuate an arrest. If the description is too vague or general, the officer should refrain from making the mistake of arresting the suspect prematurely. Instead he or she should ask the suspect certain questions or keep the suspect under surveillance. Obviously, if those procedures are not practical, the officer should use common sense and take reasonable steps to keep the suspect under observation.

The victim is the best source of identification of a suspect. The courts will assume that the victim is reliable and obviously knows what he or she is talking about. Unless a police officer has reason not to believe a victim (i.e., if he or she exhibits emotional or mental problems), the officer can rely on the victim for sufficient identification and probable cause to make an arrest, without having to verify the information.

A police officer can also rely on a citizen who is not the victim of a crime, to provide information which will constitute probable cause to make an arrest. While the courts have also found this type of citizen to be trustworthy, an officer must still verify that the citizen knows what he or she is talking about. This is known as the citizen's "basis of knowledge."

Occasionally a victim will tell a police officer that he or she is not absolutely certain of an identification or that a person only looks like the perpetrator of the crime. This information is usually insufficient to provide an officer with probable cause. However, probable cause will exist if the victim picks out a suspect's photograph.

5. Informant. When a police officer relies upon a confidential informant for information, there are certain points which the officer must keep in mind. Before the courts will find probable cause based on the informant's information, the officer must be sure that the tip is reliable. Two important components of this determination include whether the informant is both "credible" and has a "basis of knowledge."

In order to establish an informant's "credibility", an officer should determine the following: (i) whether the informant came forward in the past with accurate information; (ii) whether the informant is making a declaration against his or her penal interest; (iii) whether the officer can confirm details of the informant's story; (iv) whether the informant is an ordinary citizen who provides information solely to help solve a crime or prevent a future crime.

In order to establish an informant's "basis of knowledge", the officer must consider the following: (i) whether the informant spoke from personal knowledge; (ii) whether the officer observed conduct directly involving the criminal activity about which the informant gave information.

If, under the totality of the circumstances – including the informant's "credibility" and "basis of knowledge" – the reliability of the tip can be established by the officer, probable cause for an arrest will exist.

See, e.g., *Jefferson v. Commonwealth*, 497 S.E.2d 474 (Va. Ct. App. 1998). At around 6 p.m., a Henrico County officer received information from a known informant (who was seeking help on a misdemeanor charge by cooperating) stating that three people were selling drugs in front of 101 Virginia Avenue, "at the corner of Second and Virginia." The informant identified one of the men as Kenny "Boo" Jefferson (the defendant), a black male, five-foot-ten or eleven, with a thin build, two gold teeth and short cropped hair, wearing a gray shirt, jeans and gold chains around his neck. The informant went on to say that he had seen defendant exchange money for crack cocaine several times. After this call, the officer called a second informant, whom he had known for approximately three or four months and worked with "maybe a dozen times." This second informant had provided information leading to several arrests, although no convictions as of the date of this incident. Following the officer's instructions, this informant went by the corner "to see what was going on." At around 6:30 p.m., he reported back that there were indeed three individuals selling cocaine outside 101 Virginia Avenue, one of whom was defendant; he had directly seen defendant complete at least one drug sale. His description of defendant matched the one given by the first informant. Officer then had probable cause for a warrantless arrest of defendant.

6. Other Basis for Probable Cause. When a police officer relies on information from fellow police officers or from official police sources, he or she is entitled to assume that the "sending" officer has "probable cause" and that the information is reliable and accurate. However, an officer should also realize that if he or she acts on information which has become stale or outdated before the arrest (i.e., an outdated arrest warrant, parole warrant, stolen car report, etc.), the arrest will be voided by the courts. Note that a failure to make a diligent search for the defendant when acting on a warrant can invalidate an arrest.

"Probable cause" can come from a variety of sources. A police officer can obtain information from a defendant's accomplice. An officer can utilize fingerprints at the scene of a crime or even information from a conversation heard through a wall to obtain the necessary information for an arrest.

F. Arrest

1. Defined. The most invasive level of encounter a law enforcement officer may have with a citizen is the formal arrest. Courts look to a variety of factors to determine whether an arrest has taken place, or whether a temporary detention has escalated into a formal arrest. Criteria employed in this evaluation include: (i) whether the initial encounter was consensual; (ii) the duration or scope of the encounter, not only regarding the length of the detention, but also with respect to the degree of intrusiveness; (iii) an officer's statement that an individual is not free to leave, and what a reasonable suspect in a similar situation would believe regarding his liberty; (iv) whether the officer in some way restrained the suspect, and the nature and extent of that restraint; (v) the level of physical force threatened or employed; (vi) whether weapons or dogs were used to restrain, coerce or intimidate the suspect; (vii) the number of officers conducting the stop, and the nature of their questioning; (viii) whether or not the individual was transported to another location; (ix) whether the encounter took place in public view, or in a private or secluded area.

Note: Handcuffing alone does not render every seizure an arrest *U.S. v. Crittendon*, 883 F.2d 326 (4th Cir. 1989). Similarly, drawing a gun and frisking an individual does not necessarily make an encounter an arrest. *Wells v. Commonwealth*, 371 S.E.2d 19 (1988).

For purposes of constitutional analysis, as with a *Terry* detention, when a suspect is formally arrested, he has been seized for Fourth Amendment purposes, thus calling constitutional protections into play. However, unlike the limited intrusion imposed during a *Terry* stop, an arrest imposes the greatest restraint on an individual's liberty short of incarceration, and a higher level of skepticism – probable cause – must be demonstrated.

2. Warrantless Arrests

a. In Public Places. The majority rule, and the common law rule is that an officer is permitted to make a warrantless arrest in a public place for a misdemeanor or felony committed in his or her presence, as well as for a felony not committed in his or her presence, if the officer has probable cause to believe a felony has been committed, and the arrestee committed it. *Florida v. White*, 526 U.S. 559 (1999); *Armstrong v. Commonwealth*, 510 S.E.2d 247 (Va. Ct. App. 1999).

A warrantless arrest for a misdemeanor is generally subject to the requirement that the offense be committed in the presence of the officer. *Thompson v. Commonwealth*, 390 S.E.2d 198 (Va. Ct. App. 1990). However, by statute, Virginia allows warrantless arrests to be made for certain specified misdemeanors, notably shoplifting, carrying a weapon onto school property, brandishing a firearm, assault and battery (including domestic violence), destruction of property and theft of a vehicle. Also, the presence requirement is waived if both the officer and the person to be arrested are present at the scene of a vehicular accident, or a medical facility where a person has been transported following an accident. Such an arrest must follow a "reasonable complaint" from an observer of the misdemeanor. (See Virginia Code §19.2-81.)

Note: A third party report of a misdemeanor not committed in the arresting officer's presence, even if from a fellow officer, will not justify a warrantless arrest. *Penn v. Commonwealth*, 412 S.E.2d 189 (Va. Ct. App. 1991), aff'd, 420 S.E.2d 713 (Va. 1992). However, an arrest for a misdemeanor committed outside the presence of the officer will be valid if the officer received a radio message from his department or another law enforcement agency within the Commonwealth stating that an arrest warrant for the offense is on file. *Archer v. Commonwealth*, 492 S.E.2d 826 (Va. Ct. App. 1997).

As long as an officer has probable cause, he or she may make a warrantless arrest in a public place, even if he or she had time to first obtain a warrant.

b. Justification for a Warrantless Arrest. Statements made by a co- offender or accomplice can lead to probable cause for the arrest of his or her partner, when such a statement is against the maker's penal interest, or is corroborated by the police through their own independent line of investigation. When the statement given implicates the maker in wrongdoing, courts may attach greater weight to it. It is sometimes said that statements against penal interest carry their own indicia of reliability because it is unlikely and unnatural for persons to falsely incriminate themselves.

Information that comes from a source outside of law enforcement circles, from private citizens or police informers, may demonstrate facts sufficient to establish probable cause. To determine if an informant's tip supports a probable cause finding, courts will employ a totality of the circumstances analysis and examine all of the attendant factors, including the veracity and reliability of the informant, and the basis of the informant's knowledge. No one aspect of the tip or information, or the person giving it, is determinative on the issue of probable cause, but rather the sum of all the circumstances concerning the tip and the person making it must be examined (see discussion of Informants under Search and Seizure, below).

In *Stephenson v. Commonwealth*, 443 S.E.2d 173 (Va. Ct. App. 1994), a Newport News officer received a call from a citizen who lived in the 700 block of 32d Street. The citizen had previously complained of two black males "selling" on the 600 and 700 blocks, and the officer had told him to call back when the subjects returned. This citizen was not paid by or connected with the police, but had provided information which proved accurate in the past. In this call, the citizen stated that a black male in a white T- shirt, blue jeans and a brown hat was selling cocaine out of a two-door gray Datsun with specified plates. As the officer approached the area, the citizen called him back on his cell phone and stated that the dealer had just gone from the 700 block of 32d Street to the 600 block. The officer hung up just as he was rounding the corner onto the 600 block, and his headlights shined right on defendant, who matched the caller's description. A man standing with defendant immediately ran. Officer had probable cause to arrest defendant.

Flight, nervousness or evasive maneuvers when confronted with police presence, although not sufficient to create probable cause when standing alone, may create probable cause for arrest if it is coupled with a suspicion centering on the suspect.

See *Greene v. Commonwealth*, 440 S.E.2d 138 (Va. Ct. App. 1994). Defendant arrived at Norfolk International Airport from New York, a city considered "one of the primary sources for narcotics"; he had an "unnatural bulge" in the crotch of his pants, "maybe the size of a tennis ball." A plain clothes Drug Interdiction Team agent approached defendant and initiated a consensual interview; in addition to repeated complaints that his rights were being violated, defendant stated that he had not just arrived from La Guardia, even though surveillance had seen him deplane. Defendant then stated he wished to use the phone, and the agent stepped out of his way. Defendant did walk to a phone about ten to fifteen feet away, and pick up the receiver; however, when the agent was distracted by a conversation with a fellow agent, defendant slammed the phone down and ran for the restroom. The agent looked up and saw some type of white material hidden in the unzipped area of defendant's crotch. The agent caught up with defendant in a restroom stall, where defendant had dropped to his knees and was furiously trying to shove something into the commode with one hand, and flushing with the other. The agent had probable cause to arrest defendant. (The cocaine defendant had flushed was later recovered from the sewer).

Compare with *U.S. v. Rabinowitz*, 991 F. Supp. 760 (W.D. Va. 1998). Police were conducting surveillance of several marijuana fields they had discovered in a wooded area of Albemarle County. Defendant arrived in this area, carrying a backpack, and began to make his way down a path leading to one of the fields. He kept looking around cautiously, as if he realized the local foliage had been disturbed. When he was within 30 yards of the field, officers revealed and identified themselves. Defendant turned, dropped his backpack and ran. Police had probable cause to arrest him.

In *Farmer v. Commonwealth*, 462 S.E.2d 564 (Va. Ct. App. 1995), a Lynchburg officer received a dispatch relaying a tip from an unidentified citizen caller. The caller reported that she suspected a black male in a camouflage jacket and jeans was selling drugs in the 2800 block of Lorraine Street. She saw defendant flag down several cars, spend a short time talking with them, then return to the sidewalk. The officer knew this area to be "one of the prime illicit drug distribution sites" in the city. He arrived at the 2800 block of Lorraine approximately five minutes after receiving the dispatch, and saw defendant, dressed as described, standing on the passenger side of a pick-up truck. When he looked up and saw the marked police cruiser, he turned away and began to walk down Front Street. When the officer called out to him, defendant turned and looked at the officer, then took off running. With the officer in pursuit, defendant jumped a fence, then tried unsuccessfully to enter a locked house. At one point, defendant reached into his pockets as if trying to get rid of something. Finally, a back-up officer tackled defendant as he ran into a wooded area. Defendant's flight – in conjunction with the earlier tip and the high-crime area he was found in – established probable cause for his arrest.

Police are entitled to rely on facts garnered by those with whom they work. When more than one officer is working on a particular case, a reviewing court will take into account all of the information known to all of the officers on the case (not just the information known to the one who made the arrest), to determine if there was probable cause to arrest. This is known as the fellow officer rule. Probable cause may rest upon the collective knowledge of police where there is some degree of communication among them, rather than solely on the information possessed by the officer who made the arrest. If probable cause is possessed by one officer, and he communicates to a second officer, then that second officer may arrest although he does not have independent probable cause.

See *Armstrong v. Commonwealth*, 510 S.E.2d 247 (Va. Ct. App. 1999). An Alexandria officer was in a high-crime area watching for drug violations from a concealed location, 25 to 50 feet above street level; she had approximately 2000 hours of experience, and had seen crack cocaine at least 500 times. Using 20x80 binoculars, she saw defendant walking down the street with two women. When defendant was less than 100 feet away from her, he lifted his right hand in front of his body and opened his palm, exposing a "small, unpackaged, off-white, rock-like object, slightly smaller than a pencil eraser, which [the officer] believed to be a rock of crack cocaine." After looking at the rock for several seconds, defendant returned his hand to his side and got into a car with the two women. The officer radioed her observations to another officer on the ground, who then had probable cause to arrest defendant.

Facts officers turn up through their own investigations, or by their own observations, can form the basis of probable cause.

See *Parker v. Commonwealth*, 496 S.E.2d 47 (Va. 1998). Officer was patrolling near the Creighton Court housing development in Richmond, a high- drug area. Defendant was standing with a group of men around a Cadillac with an open trunk; when the men saw the marked patrol car, they shut the trunk and dispersed. As defendant walked away, he place something in the waistband of his basketball shorts. After defendant switched directions in an apparent attempt to avoid the officer, he was stopped. Defendant's shorts were made of a thin, white, "mesh" material, and officer could see a pink object between defendant's undergarments and his skin. Officer knew from his experience with drug arrests that dealers often hide their stash in their crotch area, and that pink baggies are commonly used to package crack cocaine. He asked defendant whether there was anything in his shorts; defendant said there was not, then grabbed his basketball shorts and boxers "and started, in very exaggerated motions, pulling them to the side, up and down shaking them in and out[,]" in an apparent effort to keep the pink object from falling out. Officer had probable cause to arrest, and validly seized the pink object (which, of course, proved to be crack) incident to that arrest.

If the officer actually observes someone committing an offense, then there is probable cause to make an arrest. Even if the officer does not witness the actual acts that constitute the offense, circumstantial evidence may create probable cause to believe the crime has been committed.

See *Moss v. Commonwealth*, 516 S.E.2d 246 (Va. Ct. App. 1999), defendant was parked at a Lynchburg gas station when a police investigator walked up to his vehicle and initiated a consensual conversation. While talking with defendant, the investigator noticed a "brown, hand-rolled marijuana cigarette laying in the ashtray in plain view between the driver's seat and the front passenger seat of the vehicle." He recognized the illegal nature of the cigarette from his training and experience. This observation provided probable cause to arrest defendant.

Compare with *Powell v. Commonwealth*, 497 S.E.2d 899 (Va. Ct. App. 1998). Three Lynchburg officers were on patrol in an area known as an open air drug market. They observed defendant and two other men sitting on a 18-inch-high wall, facing the street with their backs to a parking lot. The men were seated about three feet apart from one another. Upon seeing the officers, defendant placed his left hand, which was clinched in a fist, behind his back, keeping it close to his body; when he returned the hand to his side, it was no longer clinched. Neither of the other two men made any hand motions. When the officers pulled over, defendant stood up and began to walk away. One of the officers looked behind the wall and found a brown paper bag of crack cocaine, six to twelve inches directly behind the place where defendant had been sitting. The officers then had probable cause to arrest defendant for possession of cocaine.

In *Troncoso v. Commonwealth* 407 S.E.2d 349 (Va. Ct. App. 1991), officer was on patrol when he saw a car with flashing lights stopped illegally in the roadway next to a parked Trans Am. He returned a short time later, and while the illegally stopped car was now gone, the Trans Am remained. The car's three occupants quickly ducked down. When the officer pulled up behind the car, all three exited the vehicle in a "real hurry." The officer then activated his high-beams and spotlight; defendant, who was by the driver's side door, stopped, while the other two walked away quickly. Defendant became fidgety and began to sweat profusely; officer noticed a large bulge near his stomach area. At this point, officer had reasonable suspicion for a stop; he also performed a pat-down, and felt that the bulge was caused by a soft substance in a plastic bag. However, since he could not be sure it was contraband, he did not seize it, but instead went to his car to call for back- up. When he returned, he saw a bag of marijuana just under the Trans Am, next to where defendant was standing. Officer knew that the bag had not been there when he went to his car just moments before. Therefore, he had probable cause to arrest defendant for possession of marijuana.

c. Warrantless Arrest at a Residence. A distinction must be drawn between a warrantless arrest made in a public place, and one made in a residence. Historically, the home has enjoyed nearly sacrosanct status in American and English common law. Courts have long held that the home's threshold should not be crossed without significant justification. As a consequence of this long standing judicial respect for the integrity and privacy of the home, courts have held that in the absence of exigent circumstances or consent (see below), a law enforcement official may not make a warrantless entry into a person's home (or the curtilage of the home) to effect his arrest. *Jefferson v. Commonwealth*, 497 S.E.2d 474 (Va. Ct. App. 1998). Note, however, that a suspect cannot avoid a lawful warrantless public arrest already set in motion by retreating into his or her home.

The requirement of a warrant for an in-home arrest applies as well to the arrest of a suspect in the home of a third party, where the arrestee is an overnight guest, or in a motel or hotel room where the suspect has set up a temporary residence. See *Archer v. Commonwealth*, 492 S.E.2d 826 (Va. Ct. App. 1997). For similar reasons, if the police are to search in the home of a third party for a suspect, for whose arrest they already have a warrant, they must obtain a search warrant before entering the third party's home, absent exigent circumstances or consent. *Steagald v. United States*, 451 U.S. 204 (1981).

The possession of an arrest warrant provides officers with the authority to arrest an individual within his or her own home, and limited authority to enter the dwelling for that purpose. Possession of an arrest warrant may not adequately protect the privacy interests of a third party. The result of these rules is that if a suspect is to be arrested in a residence, a warrant must be obtained first, or the state will be forced to show that exigent circumstances or another applicable exception justified the otherwise illegal entry. If this burden is not met the arrest will be quashed. Any evidence the state hopes to use as a result of the arrest may be suppressed.

Note: If the officers in fact have probable cause to arrest, a confession obtained after a warrantless entry to effect the arrest, or other evidence found outside the home, is not necessarily inadmissible at trial.

d. Exceptions to the Warrant Requirement for Residence Arrest.

(1) Exigent Circumstances. Generally, exigent circumstances are explained as those surrounding a fast moving, often tense series of events, which call for quick and decisive law enforcement action. These are factors which allow law enforcement agents to conduct a warrantless arrest, based on probable cause, when there exists an urgent need for official action and time to secure a warrant is not available. Factors considered in determining if exigent circumstances are present include (*Dorman v. United States*, 435 F.2d 385 (D.C. Cir. 1970)): (i) if the offense was violent in nature; (ii) a reasonable belief the suspect is armed; (iii) the level of certainty that the suspect committed the offense; (iv) the level of certainty that the suspect is in the building; (v) evidence indicating that the suspect is a flight risk; (vi) the time of day; (vii) the level of force officers need to obtain entry to the premises.

The police generally must be unable to obtain a warrant in the time necessary to meet and defuse the situation, or at the very least, contacting a magistrate must be extremely impractical (e.g., late hour, remote location). In such situations, the requirement of a warrant may be excused. The presence of these extreme circumstances mandate the compelling need for quick activity and make warrantless in-home arrests reasonable within the meaning of the Fourth Amendment. If such circumstances were not present, a warrant would be required. Often cited examples of the risks created when officers hesitate in making a warrantless in-home arrest and instead seek to obtain a warrant before acting include: the risk of injury or death to officers or bystanders, the destruction or concealment of valuable evidence, or that the suspect may flee and elude capture.

A police officer can enter a premises without a warrant to protect individuals in distress, to assist victims of crimes that have just occurred, or to investigate suspicious signs of impending danger. In *People v. Mitchell*, 39 NY2d 173, 383 NYS2d 246 (1976), the Court held that there are three basic requirements for such action: (i) the police must have reasonable cause to believe that there is an emergency at hand and an immediate need for their assistance for the protection of life or property; (ii) the search must not be primarily motivated by an intent to arrest and seize evidence; and (iii) there must be some reasonable basis to associate the emergency with the area or property to be searched. Once the police respond and enter a premises pursuant to this exigency, they have the right to "restore or maintain the status quo during the emergency to control the dangerous or dynamic situation." This right enables the officer to take a number of intrusive actions ranging from a command to halt to a seizure of an individual. During the investigation of an emergency situation, the police may search for weapons to protect themselves and others and may look for injured or missing persons.

(2) Hot Pursuit. Hot pursuit can be thought of as a specific application of the general exigent circumstances exception. In *Warden v. Hayden*, 387 U.S. 294 (1967), the U.S. Supreme Court held that if police were in hot pursuit of a fleeing suspect, they were entitled to make a warrantless entry to effectuate the arrest if they had probable cause to believe the suspect committed a felony, and they believed he entered a specific dwelling. However, in *Welsh v. Wisconsin*, 466 U.S. 740 (1984), the Court held this exception was almost always inapplicable when the suspect committed a misdemeanor, traffic offense, or other non-jailable or minor infraction. To justify a warrantless in-home arrest based on this exception, the state must generally demonstrate that (i) the pursuit was undertaken immediately after the crime, (i.e., it was "hot"); and (ii) there was a continuity of pursuit from the crime to the place of arrest.

(3) Consent. A third exception to the warrant requirement for an in-home arrest comes into play when police officers are first given permission to enter the premises and then arrest a suspect inside. Valid consent to enter may be given by the owner, or one entitled to possession of the premises, or one with common control or joint access to the premises for most purposes. Valid consent is that which is given voluntarily (i.e., in the absence of overbearing conduct on the part of the law enforcement officials seeking permission). Consent may be either actually given, or implied from conduct or acts. The validity, or voluntariness, of consent is determined by examining all of the facts and circumstances surrounding the encounter.

3. Arrests Pursuant to Warrant. The essential difference between arrests with a warrant, and those without, involves where a person may be arrested. When acting pursuant to a warrant, police are entitled to arrest a suspect anywhere. This is not so, absent exigent circumstances, in the case of a warrantless arrest. Another distinction is that in a situation where an arrest is made with a warrant, the existence of probable cause is determined by a neutral and detached magistrate, who places his or her independent judgment between a perhaps overzealous law enforcement officials and the citizenry. In a situation where an arrest is made without a warrant, probable cause is determined by the officer in the field.

Note: An officer making an arrest with a warrant, or serving a summons, must give a copy to the accused. This is mainly for the purpose of defense. If the arresting officer does not have a copy, then the officer should present a copy to the accused as soon a possible. (Virginia Code §19.2-75.)

a. Delay in Making Arrest. A criminal suspect has no constitutional right to be arrested. There is no requirement that once law enforcement possesses probable cause to arrest, they do so immediately. However, a gap between the commission of the offense, or the time law enforcement becomes aware of it, and the arrest may be so protracted that it violates the Due Process clause of the Fourteenth Amendment. Although the Sixth Amendment guarantees a defendant the right to a speedy trial, it does not guarantee the right to a speedy arrest. However, an inordinate delay between the time a crime is committed and the time a defendant is arrested or indicted may violate Due Process guarantees. To prevail on such a claim, a defendant must show that (i) the delay caused actual and substantial prejudice to the defendant; and (ii) the delay was the product of deliberate action or inaction by law enforcement in order to gain a tactical advantage.

To demonstrate prejudice the defendant must show that real and tangible harm was done to his defense. The mere passage of time, and its effects, is not sufficient. The fact that "memories will dim, witnesses become inaccessible, and evidence will be lost" during the gap is inadequate to demonstrate the defendant cannot receive a fair trial and insufficient to show a Due Process violation. *U.S. v. Marion*, 404 U.S. 307 (1971).

b. Knock and Announce Rule.. When executing an arrest warrant, law enforcement officers should knock on the door of a residence or business, announce their purpose and authority, and give the occupants a reasonable opportunity to answer before forcing their way inside. *U.S. v. Grogins*, 163 F.3d 795 (4th Cir. 1998). However, there is no constitutional mandate that an officer must knock and announce his office and purpose before entering a dwelling in every instance. In situations where exigent circumstances are present, an unannounced entry may be reasonable (e.g., presence of weapons that may put officers at peril, the destruction of evidence, etc.). "A no- knock entry is justified when the police have a reasonable suspicion that knocking and announcing their presence, under the particular circumstances, would be dangerous or futile, or that it would inhibit the effective investigation of the crime." *Richards v. Wisconsin*, 520 U.S. 385 (1997). Police are not required to possess the higher standard of probable cause to believe that exigent circumstances exist, but only the less stringent standard of reasonable suspicion. The failure to knock and announce is not a per se constitutional violation. There are no rigid rules to determine when an unannounced entry will be excused. The constitutionality of the entry will be judged on the particular facts and circumstances of each case. However, the failure to knock and announce may render an entry unreasonable, and therefore unconstitutional, when there is no showing of exigent circumstances which justify the failure to first knock.

c. Use of Force To Effect Arrest. The general rule is that reasonable force may be used to place a suspect under arrest. The permissible quantum of force employed varies from situation to situation. A reasonable level of force in one context, may be unreasonable in another, and vice versa. Regardless the essential principle remains that the force used must be reasonable under the particular circumstances surrounding the arrest. The analysis applied by courts to determine the reasonableness of an officer's actions, focuses on the police conduct, viewed objectively, in light of the circumstances confronting the officers at the time, without regard to their subjective intent or motivation. Factors a court will weigh include the severity of the crime at issue, whether the suspect posed an immediate threat to the officers or others, and whether the suspect was actively resisting arrest or attempting to evade arrest by flight. *Lowery v. Stovall*, 92 F.3d 219 (4th Cir. 1996). The ultimate inquiry is whether a reasonable officer, confronted with the same circumstances, would have reacted in the same way.

In some situations, the use of deadly force is reasonable, within the meaning of the Fourth Amendment. Deadly force does not mean force that necessarily results in the death of the suspect, but rather a level of force that is reasonably likely to cause death or serious bodily injury. The U.S. Supreme Court has described the circumstances under which the use of deadly force may be reasonable for purposes of Fourth Amendment analysis, and therefore permissible. In *Tennessee v. Garner*, 471 U.S. 1 (1985), the Court stated "Where the officer has probable cause to believe that the suspect poses a threat of serious physical harm, either to the officer or to others, it is not constitutionally unreasonable to prevent escape by using deadly force." Thus, if the suspect threatens the officer with a weapon or there is probable cause to believe that he has committed a crime involving the "infliction or threatened infliction of serious physical harm", the use of deadly force is permissible. If the officer does not have probable cause to believe the above, reasonable, non-deadly force must be used to effect the arrest.

The rule in *Garner* is not applicable to a situation involving an arrest by a private person because private citizens are not bound by the Fourth Amendment. Similar principles apply, however, to the use of force employed by a private individual to effect an arrest, although any potential excessive force claim would be premised on state law tort principles, rather than on a theory involving the deprivation of constitutional rights.

G. Procedure After Arrest

When an individual is the subject of a warrantless arrest, he or she is entitled to a prompt judicial determination of probable cause to arrest (if he or she has been arrested pursuant to a warrant, a judge has already made a probable cause determination as a prerequisite to issuing the warrant). A prompt determination means that judicial hearing must be held as soon as is reasonably feasible. However, a finding must be made within 48 hours of the arrest. *County of Riverside v. McLaughlin*, 500 U.S. 44 (1991). A hearing provided within 48 hours may violate the promptness requirement if the arrested individual can prove that the probable cause determination was delayed in an unreasonable manner. Examples of unreasonable delays are ones for the purpose of gathering additional evidence against the defendant, or motivated by ill will toward the defendant. The judicial probable cause determination, may be combined with other proceedings, like an arraignment. If the state fails to provide a determination within this 48-hour window, the burden of proof shifts to the government to demonstrate the existence of an emergency or other extraordinary circumstances justifying the delay.

Note: The government cannot justify the failure to provide a determination within 48 hours on the basis of an intervening weekend (e.g., a person arrested on Thursday not given a hearing until Monday).

After making an arrest based on a warrant, the arresting officer must bring the accused before a judicial officer. This should be done as quickly as possible. The judicial officer shall immediately conduct a bail hearing and either admit the accused to bail or commit him to jail. In misdemeanors, the judge may, with the consent of the accused and the Commonwealth, proceed to trial. The judge must be a judge of the court with proper jurisdiction (Virginia Code §19.2-80.)

III. CRIMINAL LIABILITY

In order for criminal liability to attach, a person must engage in a course of conduct during which two factors coincide: a voluntary act committed by the accused and a culpable mental state, existing at the time of the act, e.g., negligently, recklessly, knowingly, intentionally or maliciously. Conduct is intentional when it is the actor's conscious objective to engage in that conduct. Conduct is knowing when the actor is aware that there is a high probability that he or she is engaging in that conduct. Conduct is reckless when the actor evinces a plain, conscious and unjustifiable disregard of harm, and that disregard involves a substantial deviation from acceptable standards. An act may, in some instances, be an omission to perform a duty that the law imposes. There are certain offenses that do not require a mental state coinciding with an act to create criminal liability; the act alone, regardless of the state of mind of the defendant when he committed the act, is sufficient to constitute the completed crime. These are called strict liability crimes.

IV. SEARCH AND SEIZURE

The Fourth Amendment mandates that citizens shall be free from unreasonable searches and seizures. What type of governmental conduct is deemed unreasonable, and therefore unconstitutional, is determined by the particular facts and circumstances of each case. However, some hard and fast rules do provide guidance. First and foremost among these is the core principle that all searches, unless conducted pursuant to a warrant, are per se unreasonable, therefore unconstitutional. *McCary v. Commonwealth*, 321 S.E.2d 637 (Va. 1984). There are, however, certain well crafted exceptions to the warrant requirement, permitting warrantless searches when the requirements of the relevant exception are met. These are discussed below.

A. The Warrant

The Fourth Amendment requires that a search warrant be issued by a magistrate or judge who must, after receiving an oath or affirmation from the warrant applicant, make an independent, neutral and detached determination whether probable cause exists to believe that particularly described property will be found at a particular place.

When applying for a warrant, an officer must present an affidavit which contains the facts that support a "probable cause" finding. The warrant, and the affidavit or testimony on which it is based must be legally sufficient. The warrant, and the affidavit that supports the warrant must contain facts that show a crime was committed, and facts that indicate why evidence will be found in a given place. Cursory assertions and bare-bones allegations will not support a warrant.

A criminal defendant may challenge the validity of a warrant, or the sufficiency of an affidavit, on constitutional grounds, or may allege the warrant does not fulfill the requirements of the warrant statute. A constitutional challenge would, for example, involve assertions that the facts as alleged do not establish "probable cause", or that the warrant did not "particularly" describe the place to be searched, et al., as required by the Fourth Amendment. A statutory challenge would involve allegations that the procedures required by the statute were not complied with.

Note: If the defendant shows that a search warrant contains false statements made by the affiant either knowingly or with reckless disregard for the truth, then the remaining information in the affidavit must independently establish probable cause, or else the warrant will be invalid. *Williams v. Commonwealth*, 496 S.E.2d 113 (Va. Ct. App. 1998).

B. Neutral and Detached Magistrate

The warrant must be issued by a removed, impartial judge. This requirement is premised on the notion "that a warrant authorized by a neutral and detached judicial officer is a more reliable safeguard against improper searches than the hurried judgment of a law enforcement officer engaged in the often competitive enterprise of ferreting out crime." *Lo-Ji Sales Inc. v. New York*, 442 U.S. 319 (1979). In *Lo-Ji*, the warrant was invalid when the magistrate who issued it went along on the raid he had authorized, and determined only when he saw certain materials what was obscene, and therefore what was to be seized. Similarly, where a warrant was issued by the state Attorney General, who was also actively involved in the investigation, and later prosecuted the case at trial, the initial probable cause determination was patently improper, for it was not made by an impartial and remote observer. *Coolidge v. New Hampshire*, 403 U.S. 443 (1971). To ensure the requisite neutrality, the issuing judge must not play a role in the investigation or the search itself.

C. Probable Cause Required – Justification for Issuance of a Warrant

The probable cause standard for issuance of a search warrant is essentially the same as that for arrest, the difference being that police must have probable cause to believe that a crime has been committed, and they can find certain evidence in a certain place. *Turner v. Commonwealth*, 420 S.E.2d 235 (Va. Ct. App. 1992). When making a probable cause determination, the issuing magistrate is entitled to consider all the circumstances surrounding an alleged crime, i.e., "the totality of the circumstances." There has to be, however, more than mere conjecture involved. Facts, real and demonstrable, must back up the allegations and assertions. Positive proof of illegal endeavor, and the location of incriminating evidence, is not required, but rather a showing that there is a probability of criminal activity, and proof thereof in a specific location. The facts relied upon by the magistrate must be contained within the four corners of the affidavit.

Three specific concepts, regarding sources of information, or the nature and quality of the information itself, pose special problems for courts when ascertaining the existence of probable cause: (i) the use of third party informants, rather than direct observation or personal knowledge; (ii) the facts relied upon may be too old or no longer accurate (staleness); (iii) the facts relied upon establish that a crime may take place, and evidence of that crime may be found in a certain place in the future, but not at present (anticipatory warrants).

1. Informants. Rarely do law enforcement officers rely on their own direct observations to provide the underlying facts supporting a warrant. In many, if not most cases, a third party will provide documentation of a crime's commission, and detail where evidence or contraband can be found. To determine if an informant's tip supports a probable cause finding, courts will employ a totality of the circumstances analysis and examine all of the attendant factors, including the veracity and reliability of the informant, and the basis of the informant's knowledge, as well as the extent to which that information can be or has been corroborated and verified. *Illinois v. Gates*, 462 U.S. 213 (1983); *Lester v. Commonwealth*, 518 S.E.2d 318 (Va. Ct. App. 1999).

No one aspect of the tip or information, or the person giving it, is determinative on the issue of probable cause. A question regarding the informant's veracity may be compensated for by strong evidence confirming the way in which the informant obtained his information, or verification that the facts he or she relayed are accurate, or some other factors indicating his reliability. *Polston v. Commonwealth*, 485 S.E.2d 632 (Va. Ct. App. 1997), aff'd, 498 S.E.2d 924 (Va. 1998). Even so, some broad generalizations may be made. Generally, the information provided by a non-confidential informant will be given greater deference than that provided by a confidential informant, who asks that his or her identity be kept secret. Courts reason that if someone is willing to expose themselves to public scrutiny, then the information they pass on is likely more reliable than information given by someone who is reluctant to associate their identity with the tip.

Information given by a witness to, or victim of a crime is likely to be perceived as more trustworthy than information given anonymously, or even by a known police informant. Generally, if other factors point to the conclusion that a witness's or victim's tip is reliable (i.e., some corroboration), and there is no evidence that calls his or her motives for giving information into question, there will not be an inquiry into that informants credibility or veracity. *Lester v. Commonwealth*, supra. Moreover, witness and victim informers have not had the opportunity to build up a reputation for giving solid information to the authorities, and they have had no reason to. There is no past conduct by which to gauge their propensity for honesty. Witness and victim informers generally have nothing to gain by giving information to police, other than the satisfaction of knowing they may help solve a crime, or prevent the commission of another.

A distinction may also be drawn between an anonymous tip, and a tip provided by an identified informant, or one with whom police have previously worked. A court may give more credence to an informant known to police, especially if he has provided solid information in the past. When the identity of the informant is known, there may be some basis for determining how the tipster came about his or her information. Rarely will an anonymous, uncorroborated tip form the basis of probable cause or reasonable suspicion. However, independent corroboration, on the part of officers working the case, may sufficiently bolster the tip, and if the information is sufficiently confirmed, create probable cause.

Statements against an informant's penal interest, i.e. which implicate him or herself in a crime, also carry a presumption of reliability, because courts reason it is unlikely and unnatural for a person to falsely incriminate themselves.

Regardless of who provides the information, the court will ultimately employ the same analysis, examining the totality of the circumstances; the informant's reputation for truthfulness, his or her dependability, and the circumstances under which he or she obtained the information.

See, e.g., *Lester v. Commonwealth*, supra. A concerned citizen came forward to police and stated that defendant was a thief who sold stolen property; he added that defendant had offered to sell him jewelry and a rifle engraved with the name "Katharina Bergdoll." An officer checked police records and learned that Ms. Bergdoll had in fact reported a burglary four days earlier, in which jewelry and a rifle had been taken. The officer who spoke with the informant knew him to be a long-time resident in the community, gainfully employed, who had never been arrested and who attended church on a regular basis; his only reason for remaining anonymous was fear of retribution. In addition, two other officers had received tips indicating that a white male known as "Paul" (defendant's first name) was selling stolen goods from the boarding house where defendant lived. Under the totality of circumstances, probable cause was established for a warrant to search defendant's residence.

Compare with *West v. Commonwealth*, 432 S.E.2d 730 (Va. Ct. App. 1993). A confidential-informant (C-I) told a Gloucester County deputy that a little over a week before, defendant had bragged to him about the 30 pounds of bacon and "boatload" of cigarettes he had taken from stores he had broken into, saying that any time the C-I needed these things, he should come by defendant's house and pick some up. The C-I also stated that defendant had mentioned taking a cash drawer, as well. This C-I was a county resident, and had given information to the deputy on two prior occasions, resulting in two misdemeanor arrests. In addition, the deputy knew of two break-ins under investigation where large amounts of bacon and cigarettes had been taken. The deputy had probable cause for a warrant to search defendant's house.

In *Boyd v. Commonwealth*, 402 S.E.2d 914 (Va. Ct. App. 1991), a C- I contacted Henrico County police and stated that, three days before, he had personally seen cocaine packaged for sale and scales for that purpose in defendant's Henrico residence at 1218 Wilkinson Road in Henrico. Although Henrico County police did not know this C-I's true name, an officer from another jurisdiction with whom the C-I had originally spoken did, and the affiant-officer from Henrico County was given a phone number and fictitious name with which he contacted the C-I. The affiant-officer averred that this C- I was a "concerned citizen" who had been a resident of Richmond for a year, held a substantial job and had no criminal record. He also averred that the C-I was familiar with cocaine based on past personal use. Moreover, by checking DMV records, police records and a city street directory, police confirmed that defendant lived at the alleged address, that his house fit the description the C-I provided, and that he drove a Mercedes just as the C-I said he did. Probable cause was established for a search warrant.

Note: If the informant appears in person before the magistrate, then the affidavit need not contain extrinsic corroboration of his or her reliability. *Polston v. Commonwealth*, supra.

2. Staleness. If there is an appreciable delay between the occurrence of the circumstances that create probable cause and the time a warrant is issued, the facts supporting the probable cause determination may become "stale", in that, although the alleged facts may have once supported a probable

cause determination, presently, they may not. Courts reason that information demonstrating that evidence of a crime could once be found in a given location, does not mean that evidence of a crime may necessarily be found there now. Stale information creates the mere suspicion crime has been committed, and does not rise to the level of probable cause.

Note that staleness is not judged solely by counting the number of days between the occurrence of the facts relied on in the affidavit and the issuance of the warrant (though that is a factor to consider). The Court must weigh all the facts and circumstances of the case, including the nature and length of the alleged illegal activity and the nature of the property to be seized. *Perez v. Commonwealth*, 486 S.E.2d 578 (Va. Ct. App. 1997).

3. Anticipatory Warrants. When seeking an anticipatory warrant, law enforcement is, in essence, asserting that in the near future a crime will be committed in a certain place, and that evidence of that crime will be found there. Virginia courts may issue such a warrant when the evidence is on a "sure course" (e.g., in the mails, posted to a specific address) to the exact destination to be searched. *McNeill v. Commonwealth*, 395 S.E.2d 460 (Va. Ct. App. 1990).

D. Particularity Requirement

The Fourth Amendment requires that a warrant specifically name both the places to be searched and the items to be seized. The purpose of this particularity requirement is to prevent general searches, i.e., a rummaging for incriminating evidence without cause. The warrant must state the items and the places with distinctiveness, so that the officer executing the warrant will have no question, and no room for guesswork or discretionary choices, as to where he or she is to search, and for what they are looking. A valid warrant authorizes the executing officer to look for a particular item in any place it could logically be found. (e.g., narcotics may be reasonably expected to be found in a dresser drawer; a stolen Harley Davidson motorcycle, on the other hand, would not.) However, the particularity requirement limits any arbitrary decisions as to what items may be seized. The warrant and the supporting affidavit may generally be read together to arrive at a sufficiently particular description.

The particularity requirement has two prongs: (i) a particularly described place, and (ii) particularly described items.

1. Places To Be Searched. The search warrant must describe the location to be searched with sufficient particularity that the executing officer can, with reasonable effort, ascertain and identify the place intended. *Wilson v. Commonwealth*, 429 S.E.2d 229 (Va. Ct. App.), on reh'g, 436 S.E.2d 193 (1993). Generally, a description containing the address as it would appear on a mailing envelope, along with the name of the resident, and a cursory listing of the physical appearance of the building itself, is sufficient for single unit dwellings. A problem arises, however, when the place to be searched is in a multi-unit structure, like an apartment in a complex, or an office in a professional building. The general rule is that the description must describe the specific sub-unit to be searched, not the whole building. If the description merely lists the address of a building, which itself contains many residences or offices, and the law enforcement agents executing the warrant have no means to determine which of the individual units is to be searched, the warrant may be invalid. See *Wilson v. Commonwealth*, supra.

2. Items To Be Seized. The search warrant must also describe the items to be seized with "reasonable specificity;" it must limit the discretion of the executing officers by directing them to seize only evidence of a specific crime. *Morke v. Commonwealth*, 419 S.E.2d 410 (Va. Ct. App. 1992). The degree of particularity with which the items must be described will fluctuate, depending on the nature and individual attributes of the subject items. However, a certain minimum level of specificity will always be required. For example, generic descriptions of contraband, such as "controlled and dangerous substances" or "all controlled substances" or "narcotic drugs", etc., are generally held to be sufficient descriptions, if the affidavit suggests the presence of more than one drug.

E. Execution of the Warrant

1. Time Limit. A search warrant must be executed "forthwith." This has been held to mean "with reasonable dispatch and undue delay." *Turner v. Commonwealth*, 420 S.E.2d 235 (Va. Ct. App. 1992) (eleven-day delay before execution of a warrant valid when the warrant specified both a residence and an individual, and the first six times officers went to the residence, nobody was home; the warrant was immediately served once police learned the subject had returned home). When any delay occurs, officers should make sure before executing the warrant that probable cause still exists. In any event, a search warrant must be executed within fifteen days of its issuance or else be returned to the magistrate who issued it to be voided. (Virginia Code §19.2-56).

2. Knock or No-knock. As a matter of course, when executing a search warrant, law enforcement officers should knock on the door of a residence or business, announce their purpose and authority, and give the occupants a reasonable opportunity to answer before forcing their way inside. *U.S. v. Grogins*, 163 F.3d 795 (4th Cir. 1998); *Spivey v. Commonwealth*, 479 S.E.2d 543 (Va. Ct. App. 1997). See also *Wynne v. Commonwealth*, 427 S.E.2d 228 (Va. Ct. App. 1993) (five seconds was too short a wait to provide defendant with a reasonable opportunity to answer, particularly when officers could see him through a glass door and he made no furtive movements).

However, there is no constitutional mandate that an officer must knock and announce his office and purpose before entering a dwelling in every instance. In situations where exigent circumstances are present, an unannounced entry may be reasonable (e.g., presence of weapons that may put officers at peril, the destruction of evidence, etc.). "A no-knock entry is justified when the police have a reasonable suspicion that knocking and announcing their presence, under the particular circumstances, would be dangerous or futile, or that it would inhibit the effective investigation of the crime." *Richards v. Wisconsin*, 520 U.S.385 (1997). See also *Wilson v. Arkansas*, 514 U.S. 927 (1995); *U.S. v. Ramirez*, 523 U.S. 65 (1998). Police are not required to possess the higher standard of probable cause to believe that exigent circumstances exist, but only the less stringent standard of reasonable suspicion. The failure to knock and announce is not a per se constitutional violation, and there are no rigid rules to determine when an unannounced entry will be excused; rather, the constitutionality of the entry will be judged on the particular facts and circumstances of each case. Nevertheless, the failure to knock and announce may render an entry unreasonable, and therefore unconstitutional, where there is no showing of exigent circumstances which justify the failure to first knock.

In *Spivey v. Commonwealth*, supra, Portsmouth police used information from a reliable informant to obtain a warrant to search defendant's residence for cocaine. The informant told police that defendant was "known to have a .38 [handgun]." In addition, he stated that defendant's son, Duane, was her supplier, and that Duane lived within one city block of defendant's residence and frequently stayed there. Police knew Duane had been arrested just ten days before for discharging a firearm into an unoccupied vehicle.

Because police reasonably feared that they might face two armed dealers, an unannounced entry was justified.

Note: The knock and announce requirement is waived if police gain entry by consent; this is true even if the officers use a ruse or stratagem to get the suspect to open the door and invite them in. *Commonwealth v. Viar*, 425 S.E.2d 86 (Va. Ct. App. 1992).

3. Scope of the Search. When executing a search warrant, officers are entitled to search the entire named premises for the items listed, and any closed containers, drawers, closets, etc., where they have probable cause to believe those items may be found. "A lawful search of fixed premises generally extends to the entire area in which the object of the search may be found and is not limited by the possibility that separate acts of entry or opening may be required to complete the search. Thus, a warrant that authorizes an officer to search a home for illegal weapons also provides authority to open closets, chests, drawers and containers in which the weapon might be found. A warrant to open a footlocker to search for marijuana would also authorize the opening of packages found inside." *U.S. v. Ross*, 456 U.S. 798 (1982).

Compare with *Beavers v. Commonwealth*, 427 S.E.2d 411 (Va.), cert. denied, 510 U.S. 859 (1993). Defendant broke into the victim's home and raped her. Police soon connected defendant to the crime, and obtained both an arrest warrant and a search warrant for his home. One of the items listed in the search warrant was "bloodstained white medical gauze tape," which the victim reported defendant had wrapped around his hand after he cut himself while breaking in. Given the nature of gauze tape – which can easily be compressed to fit almost anywhere – officer was authorized to search a small, multi-colored pouch he found in defendant's chest of drawers. (Although this pouch did not contain the gauze, it did contain jewelry which the officer recognized as having been taken from another rape-murder victim a year earlier; this jewelry was validly seized under the plain view doctrine).

But see *Holloman v. Commonwealth*, 275 S.E.2d 620 (Va. 1981) (when ABC investigators were executing a search warrant for beer and whiskey at defendant's store, which did not have a liquor license, they could not validly search "five small [brown paper] bags" found behind the counter; the size of the bags, as well as their shape and weight when lifted, clearly indicated that they could not hold bottles or cans).

In addition, a valid warrant implicitly carries with it the limited authority to detain the occupants of the premises, or recall and similarly detain those seen leaving, while a proper search is conducted. *Michigan v. Summers*, 452 U.S. 692 (1981). However, the authority to detain those present but not named in the warrant does not include the authority to search those persons, absent an independent justification for the search. *Ybarra v. Illinois*, 444 U.S. 85 (1979). For example, in *Ybarra*, a warrant issued to search a bar for narcotics gave the police authority to search the bartender, named in the warrant, but not a patron who just happened to be there. Compare with *Hayes v. Commonwealth*, 514 S.E.2d 357 (Va. Ct. App. 1999) (police had no right to search defendant, who was seated on the porch outside a Petersburg residence where a search warrant for drugs was being executed, when the warrant did not list any specific persons to be searched or state that all persons at the residence were to be searched).

Note: The search warrant itself can authorize a search of "all persons present" at the time of execution, so long as a showing of probable cause is made in the supporting affidavit. *Morton v. Commonwealth*, 434 S.E.2d 890 (Va. Ct. App. 1993) ("all persons present" warrant valid when the search was of a private residence, the object sought was crack cocaine, which could easily be hidden on the body, and surveillance had seen several known and convicted drug dealers enter the apartment over the past 60 days).

When executing a warrant, officers may seize contraband or other evidence, not listed in the warrant, in plain view, if the requirements of that doctrine are met. (See further discussion under Warrantless Searches, below).

Note: A search warrant for a dwelling also authorizes a search of any of the occupant's automobiles found within the curtilage of the dwelling, even if they were not specifically named in the warrant. *Glenn v. Commonwealth*, 390 S.E.2d 505 (Va. Ct. App. 1990).

4. Inventory An officer who conducts a search pursuant to a warrant should note the date of execution on the warrant. If any property was seized as a result of the search, then the officer should fill out a list of such items. If no items were seized, this should be noted on the warrant. The warrant, the affidavit, and the list of property, if there is one, should then be filed in the court in which the warrant was obtained. (Virginia Code §19.2-57.)

Note: The U.S. Supreme Court has ruled that when law enforcement agents seize property pursuant to a search warrant, Due Process requires that they give notice so that the owner can pursue any remedies available for return under state law; however, agents are not required to give owners notice of state law remedies established by published, generally available statutes and case law. *City of West Covina v. Perkins*, 525 U.S. 234 (1999).

F. Search of Containers

Regardless of whether the subject of a search is a container, like a briefcase, purse, suitcase or footlocker, instead of a house, car, office building or person, the general rule is the same; a warrant must be obtained before the container may be opened. The Fourth Amendment "proscribes – except in certain well defined circumstances – the search of that property unless accomplished pursuant to a judicial warrant issued on probable cause." *U.S. v. Ross*, 456 U.S. 798 (1982). These "well-defined circumstances", e.g., a search incident to arrest or a booking search, are discussed under Warrantless Searches, below. The rationale advanced in this situation is similar to the reasoning behind the rule requiring warrants for the search of a home. When an individual manifests an expectation that certain items remain private, by placing them in a closed container, it is unreasonable for the government to intrude on that expectation of privacy without the protections of a warrant, based on a clear showing of probable cause. When dealing with items of personalty, the procedure prior to a search may be somewhat different, in that it is permissible to briefly detain personal property, based on a reasonable suspicion that it contains contraband.

Note: Once police have the container in their custody, they generally cannot justify a warrantless search based on exigent circumstances. *Arkansas v. Sanders*, 442 U.S. 753 (1979).

A crucial, and often dispositive distinction must be made between closed containers seized and detained from the possession of a person, and those containers taken from an automobile. If the container is found in an automobile, the police may almost always open and search the container without a warrant, if they have probable cause to think the container, or the car transporting it, contains contraband.

G. Exceptions to the Warrant Requirement (Warrantless Searches)

The general rule is that all searches and seizures conducted without a warrant are presumptively unreasonable and therefore unconstitutional. To justify a warrantless search, the state must show that the search falls into one of the narrowly drawn exceptions to warrant requirement. Courts have, however, crafted "a few specifically established and well-delineated" exceptions to the general principle, and they are discussed in detail, below.

1. Exigent Circumstances. The situations that often fall under the exigent circumstances exception can be grouped into three general categories. An exigency exists if: 1) there is a good chance evidence – either contraband, instrumentalities used in the crime, or the fruits of the crime – is being or will be destroyed or concealed; 2) it is likely a suspect will flee; 3) there is a real danger to people. The rationale advanced for permitting warrantless searches under such circumstances is that extreme situations dictate that police act quickly, where there is no time to secure a warrant. The warrant requirement may be dispensed with when officers take actions that are necessary responses to an emergency situation. Courts permit warrantless searches where officers have probable cause and a qualifying set of circumstances.

2. Destruction or Removal of Evidence. Where police have a reasonable belief that evidence is being or about to be destroyed, a warrantless entry may be permitted under this exception. Where the police have an objectively reasonable fear that the evidence is being or about to be destroyed and a reasonable belief that there are people within the home presently capable of destroying or hiding the evidence, and the officer's fear is of an immediate or imminent destruction, the requirements of the exception are met. Some courts say that in order to invoke this exception, the state must demonstrate that the seized evidence is of an "evanescent" nature (i.e., an easily destructible item, like narcotics, which can be easily burned, secreted or flushed).

Note: The fact that the grounds for arrest involve narcotics, standing alone, does not create an exigent circumstance. The arrest of a narcotics suspect on his front doorstep, without any indication drugs are being hidden or destroyed, will not justify the arresting officers conducting a warrantless search of the arrestee's home for narcotics.

3. Flight of the Suspect. If police have evidence demonstrating a suspect is an immediate flight risk, and has the present ability to flee the jurisdiction, a warrantless entry may be permitted to apprehend that suspect before flight.

4. Safety of the Officer or Others. If the officer believes that the suspect is armed and presents a real and immediate danger to the officers or other people, a warrantless entry is permitted. The officers are entitled to conduct such a warrantless search of a residence, if the shooting occurred outside the residence.

5. Hot Pursuit. This doctrine may be analyzed as a specific application of the exigent circumstance doctrine discussed above. A warrantless entry of a private dwelling will be allowed when police are in hot pursuit of a suspect who they have probable cause to believe committed a felony. The pursuing officers must also have probable cause to believe the suspect entered a specific dwelling. After following the suspect into a dwelling, the police may seize contraband, weapons, instrumentalities or fruits of crime that are in plain view.

See, e.g., *Commonwealth v. Talbert*, 478 S.E.2d 331 (Va. Ct. App. 1996). Alexandria police were conducting undercover surveillance at the corner of Alfred and Montgomery Streets. Officer William Bunney watched as defendant, who was in a wheelchair, broke off a piece from a large rock of crack cocaine he had, then gave it to another man. Defendant then wrapped plastic around his remaining crack and placed the rock by his side. After Officer Bunney radioed this information, other officers quickly moved in and apprehended the man who had just acquired the crack, who put up a struggle. When Officer Bunney looked again, he realized that he could no longer see defendant. He then saw a man backing a wheelchair into a house directly adjacent to the alley where the transaction had taken place; the man was lifting the wheelchair up the porch steps and backing into the house. Officer Bunney radioed his observations to his fellow officers, and told them to hurry. When the other officer reached the house, they saw a man walking into the house, with his back to the doorway. The inside door was completely open, while the outside door (which had an upper half made of glass) was still "open about a foot." One of the officers, who knew defendant, could see him in the living room through the glass portion of the exterior door. The Court found that the officers were in "hot pursuit" of defendant, and could therefore enter the house without a warrant.

Note: This exception generally applies only to a "fleeing felon". If the police are pursuing a suspect for a misdemeanor or a non- jailable offense, or other minor infraction, hot pursuit will ordinarily not apply. The burden is upon the state to prove that the hot pursuit exception applies to specific facts.

6. Search Incident to Arrest. Upon the lawful arrest of a person, the arresting officer is entitled to search not only the person of the arrestee, but also the area that was in the immediate control of the suspect prior to the arrest. This exception is premised on the notion that the arrest of a suspect, when based on probable cause, is per se reasonable with respect to the Fourth Amendment. Since this intrusion on an individual's freedom is by definition lawful, a search incident to the arrest requires no additional justification. It is the fact of the arrest which establishes the authority to search. Notice that the arrest must be lawful, i.e., based on probable cause. If the arrest is later deemed improper, all evidence seized incident to that arrest will be suppressed. Under this exception, a search of all effects in the suspect's possession is permissible. However, as mentioned, the scope of the search must be limited to the suspect's person, or what is in, or potentially could be in, the suspect's immediate control. Courts say that a region is within the immediate control of the suspect when he or she might immediately and easily gain possession of a weapon or destructible evidence from that area. *Chimel v. California*, 395 U.S. 752 (1969).

Note: A strip search or search of the arrestee's body cavities is not justifiable as incident to arrest, unless there is a "clear indication" that evidence or a weapon is located within the suspect's body, and exigent circumstances are present. *Moss v. Commonwealth*, 516 S.E.2d 246 (Va. Ct. App. 1999)

The search may precede the arrest, so long as probable cause for the arrest exists independently of what is found during the search, and probable cause to arrest exists before the search is conducted. In other words, an officer may not use the fruits of a search as the basis for the arrest of the suspect, and then seek to justify the search as one incident to the arrest. *Rawlings v. Kentucky*, 448 U.S. 98 (1980); *U.S. v. Han*, 74 F.3d 53 (4th Cir. 1996), cert. denied 517 U.S. 1239 (1996).

A proper search incident to an arrest should be conducted contemporaneously with the arrest, i.e., immediately preceding or succeeding that actual physical act of arrest. However, a search of articles in the possession of the defendant at the time of arrest may not only be conducted at the time of the arrest, but may be conducted later, and at a different location, if a reasonable explanation for the delay is put forth. *U.S. v. Edwards*, 415 U.S. 800 (1974) (delay of ten hours between arrest and station house search permissible). However, such a search will not be allowed of luggage or other personal property "not immediately associated with the person of the arrestee" when it has been reduced to the exclusive control of the police, and there is no longer a danger that the arrestee might gain access to the property and seize a weapon or destroy evidence. *U.S. v. Chadwick*, 433 U.S. 1 (1977) (search of defendants' footlocker over an hour after it was moved to a secure police storage facility inaccessible to defendants was not a valid search incident to arrest).

Similarly, when a law enforcement official arrests the occupant of a car, he or she may search the passenger compartment, and any open, or unopened containers therein, as incident to the arrest. In *New York v. Belton*, 453 U.S. 454 (1981), after a state trooper stopped a car for speeding and ordered all the occupants out of the car, he smelled marijuana and observed an envelope on the car floor which resembled a type frequently used to sell that substance. After inspecting the envelope and finding marijuana, he arrested all the occupants. The U.S. Supreme Court held that the search incident to an arrest can extend to any part of the passenger compartment of the automobile compartment including open or closed containers, glove compartments, consoles and luggage.

Compare with *White v. Commonwealth*, 482 S.E.2d 876 (Va. Ct. App. 1997). Earlier in the day, officer had cited defendant for driving with a suspended license. Later that same day, officer again saw defendant driving, and decided to pull him over and arrest him. As defendant neared his home, officer activated his patrol car's flashing lights; defendant responded by pulling into his driveway, exiting his car, and walking away rapidly. Officer ordered him back to the car, then arrested him. Because defendant was a recent occupant of the car, officer could search it incident to his arrest, and validly seized a bag of crack cocaine he found between the front seats. (This discovery, in turn, established probable cause for a search of the entire car under the "Automobile Exception", discussed below, so that officer's seizure of $2,691 in mixed bills from the trunk was also upheld.)

In *Pack v. Commonwealth*, 368 S.E.2d 921 (Va. Ct. App. 1988), defendant arrived at National Airport with an overnight bag containing a half- pound of cocaine. He met his contact, Robert Williams, and placed the bag on the floorboard behind the front seat in Williams car, then rode off with him. Unfortunately for defendant, Williams had been arrested by Arlington County police three days earlier, and was now fully cooperating with them. Police stopped the car, then arrested, handcuffed and searched both men (Williams was subjected to a sham arrest, to protect his cover). Officers then retrieved the overnight bag, which was partially locked, and searched that as well, finding the cocaine. Even though both men had been removed from the car and handcuffed, and even though the bag was partially locked, the bag was lawfully searched under the *Belton* doctrine.

Note: So long as probable cause existed at the time of arrest to arrest the suspect for *some* offense, then the search incident to arrest will be valid, even if the officer subjectively believed he or she was arresting for another offense and even if the suspect was told that the arrest was for another offense. *Golden v. Commonwealth*, 519 S.E.2d 378 (Va. Ct. App. 1999).

In *Golden*, supra, after Suffolk officers offered to give defendant a ride, she entered their car and offered to perform fellatio for $10. The officers arrested defendant for prostitution, and searched her person incident to the arrest, finding two "crack stems." The Court found that probable cause did not exist to arrest defendant for prostitution, because there had been "no substantial act in furtherance" of the offense. Nevertheless, the officers did have probable cause to arrest defendant for solicitation; therefore the search incident to arrest was still valid.

7. Emergency Aid. Under this doctrine, a police officer can enter a premises without a warrant to protect individuals in distress, to assist victims of crimes that have just occurred or to investigate suspicious signs of impending danger. This exigency, therefore, is based on the officer's obligation to protect life and property.

This right applies for firemen to enter a dwelling to extinguish a fire, and continues for a reasonable time after the fire has been put out so that fire officials can make sure the blaze will not rekindle and can investigate its cause. *Jones v. Commonwealth*, 512 S.E.2d 165 (Va. Ct. App. 1999).

See, e.g., *Commonwealth v. Thornton*, 483 S.E.2d 487 (Va. Ct. App. 1997). The Leesburg Volunteer Fire Department received a call regarding a possible fire at the Cavalier Arms Apartments. When the Captain arrived, he met a person who said he had smelled smoke and heard an alarm. While police, who had arrived on the scene in conjunction with the alarm, began to evacuate the building, the Captain knocked on the door of the apartment where the fire was reported, but received no answer. He did hear "what sounded like a smoke detector" inside. He then directed another firefighter to a rear window; this firefighter saw neither smoke nor flame, but did hear the smoke detector. He removed the screen and entered through the window; inside, on a table, he found an extremely loud pager which had been the source of the alarm-like noise. Next to the pager sat a marijuana cigarette. In addition, the firefighter saw a plastic bag with a green leafy substance in plain view on a coffee table. The firefighters handed this contraband over to the police officers as they left the scene. Because the firefighters reasonably believed that a fire was burning inside the apartment, their entry and seizure of the contraband was valid.

In *People v. Mitchell*, 39 NY2d 173, 383 NYS2d 246 (1976), the Court held that there are three basic requirements for the application of the emergency doctrine: (i) the police must have reasonable cause to believe that there is an emergency at hand and an immediate need for their assistance for the protection of life or property; (ii) the search must not be primarily motivated by an intent to arrest and seize evidence; and (iii) there must be some reasonable basis to associate the emergency with the area or property to be searched. Once the police respond and enter a premises pursuant to this exigency, they have the right to "restore or maintain the status quo during the emergency to control the dangerous or dynamic situation." This right enables the officer to take a number of intrusive actions ranging from a command to halt to a seizure of an individual. During the investigation of an emergency situation, the police may search for weapons to protect themselves and others and may look for injured or missing persons.

See, e.g., *Reynolds v. Commonwealth*, 388 S.E.2d 659 (Va. Ct. App. 1990). A Hanover County deputy stopped a car driven by Mark Fogg, and discovered stolen items in his possession, including a television and two shotguns. When pressed, Fogg admitted that he had stolen the items from the defendants' residence about an hour earlier. Several officers went to the residence to investigate; even though it was late at night, the front door was open, as defendant had left it. An investigator on the scene feared that the residents might be injured or dead, and entered to investigate. He found no persons, injured or otherwise, but did discover 29 marijuana plants in small paper cups in plain view. This was a valid entry – the officer reasonably feared for the safety of the residents of the house, knowing that it had recently been burglarized by an armed man. Until the marijuana plants were discovered, police thought of defendant as a victim, not a suspect, so the search was not a pretext to discover evidence.

8. Consent. A tool often employed by law enforcement officers is to simply ask a suspect for permission to search his or her person, car or residence. If the request is granted,

the individual has in effect waived his or her privacy interest in the area searched. This being so, a lawful, warrantless search may be conducted pursuant to consent given by the suspect. *Deer v. Commonwealth*, 441 S.E.2d 33 (Va. Ct. App. 1994). Valid consent may be rendered verbally (express consent), or inferred from the conduct or actions of the person from whom the police seek consent (implied consent).

Permission to search may also be obtained from a third party who possessed common authority over, or other sufficient relationship to the premises or effects sought to be inspected. Moreover, even where the party granting permission does not in fact have legally sufficient control over the premises, the consent may nonetheless be valid if the officer reasonably believes that the party had common control. *Illinois v. Rodriguez*, 497 U.S. 177 (1990).

See, e.g., *Jones v. Commonwealth*, 432 S.E.2d 517 (Va. Ct. App. 1993). Officer responded to a call at Room 57 of the Richmond Motel, where a maid had found "suspected narcotics.". There were no cars parked in the parking lot near the room, and the doors to Room 57 and several surrounding rooms were open, as if the rooms were being cleaned. When the officer looked through the open doorway into Room 57, he saw no luggage or other personal effects. The maid met him at the doorway, and he followed her into the room, where she showed him the drugs, hidden in an air conditioner. Officer then went to the front office, where he learned that the room was still registered to defendant. Even though the maid did not actually have authority to consent to the officer's entry (as the room was still technically defendant's), the officer reasonably believed that she did based on the surrounding circumstances, so his entry was valid.

Compare with *Caldwell v. Commonwealth*, 425 S.E.2d 534 (Va. Ct. App. 1993). Defendant's sister invited police to enter her mother's home in order to see items that her brother had stolen. The sister told police that although she did not live there, her mother was in Texas and had left her in charge of the house; she did, in fact, have a key. Unbeknownst to police, defendant also lived at his mother's house, and he was present at the time of the search. However, he did not object to the search, and the police reasonably relied on the sister's representation of authority.

To be valid, consent must be given voluntarily. Courts will examine the circumstances under which the consent was given and ascertain if it was rendered intentionally and deliberately. Courts will inquire if the permission was the product of an essentially free and unconstrained choice by its maker. In making this determination, a court will consider the age, maturity, education, intelligence and experience of the individual giving permission, as well as the circumstances under which the consent was given, such as the number of officers present and their actions, and the duration, location and timing of the encounter. The Commonwealth has the burden of proof to show by the preponderance of the evidence that the consent to search was freely and voluntarily given. *Anderson v. Commonwealth*, 507 S.E.2d 339 (Va. 1998).

There is no requirement that officers tell an individual he or she has a right to refuse permission to search. While an individual's knowledge, or lack thereof, concerning his or her right to refuse permission, is a factor to be considered in assessing the voluntariness of any consent given, it is not dispositive. *Commonwealth v. Rice*, 504 S.E.2d 877 (Va. Ct. App. 1998). Similarly, following a valid traffic stop, there is no requirement that an officer tell an individual that he or she is free to leave, before asking for permission to search his or her vehicle. *Ohio v. Robinette*, 519 U.S. 33 (1996).

The search must be limited to those areas to which the defendant actually or impliedly gives permission to search. The scope of the search is generally determined with reference to that which the officer is seeking, i.e., to areas or containers where the stated subject of the search could be located. In *Florida v. Jimeno*, 500 U.S. 248 (1991), the Court approved the search of a paper bag, found on the floor of a car, for narcotics, after the defendant had given consent to a general search of his car. The Court concluded that, based on these facts, it was reasonable for the searching officer to believe the scope of the consent given permitted him to open the bag. The defendant knew the purpose of the search was to look for drugs, and it was objectively reasonable to assume drugs could be found there.

Compare with *Bynum v. Commonwealth*, 477 S.E.2d 750 (Va. Ct. App. 1996). Virginia Beach police were executing a search warrant for drugs on a motel room when defendant and two companions walked in; as soon as they saw the officers, they turned around and left. An officer followed and asked if he could help defendant; in the ensuing conversation, defendant denied possession of any drugs, and consented to a search of his person for narcotics, specifically crack cocaine. Because the officer was searching for a "very small item," he "stuck [his] hands in [defendant's] pockets and removed the contents" without objection from defendant. What he found was a Toyota key, which struck the officer as unusual, as defendant previously claimed he had been dropped off at the motel because he did not have a car. Defendant said he had found the key, and had no objection to the officer keeping it; later, this key was connected to a stolen car, and defendant was arrested for the theft. Defendant's pockets were a legitimate place where crack might have been stored, and defendant did not object to the officer's search of them; therefore, the key was not outside the scope of defendant's consent, and was validly seized.

But see *Camden v. Commonwealth*, 441 S.E.2d 38 (Va. Ct. App. 1994). Officer asked defendant if he could perform a pat-down search for weapons, and defendant agreed. However, the officer exceeded the scope of this consent when he searched defendant's wallet.

Note: If, in an attempt to gain consent to search a residence, officers mislead a person by saying or implying they have a warrant and will search anyway, when in reality they do not, any permission given is invalid. *Crosby v. Commonwealth*, 367 S.E.2d 730 (Va. Ct. App. 1988). However, the threat to obtain a warrant, while bearing on the voluntariness of consent, is not treated the same. Stating that a warrant can and will be obtained, if police in fact have the requisite grounds, will not automatically vitiate an ensuing consent. *Deer v. Commonwealth*, supra.

9. Inventory and Booking. So long as preexisting, standardized procedures are followed, police may conduct a warrantless search of a lawfully impounded automobile and its contents (i.e., Inventory). Similarly, a lawful warrantless search of an arrestee, and containers in his or her possession, may be made prior to incarceration (i.e., Booking). These exceptions are premised on the notion that the police are, in addition to their other duties, fulfilling a caretaking role. They are protecting the property of the arrestee from loss or theft or vandalism, and other fellow detainees from the possibility of assault if a weapon is smuggled in. They are also protecting themselves from possible charges of theft. See *Hogan v. Commonwealth*, 423 S.E.2d 841 (Va. Ct. App. 1992). Courts caution, however, that the extent of the search must be tailored to serve these objectives. An inventory or booking search must not be a ruse for a general rummaging in order to discover incriminating evidence.

With respect to the legitimacy of inventory searches, courts have found that reasonable departmental regulations relating to inventory procedures, when carried out in good faith, satisfy the Constitution. The presence of preexisting and standardized procedures, as well as the absence of bad faith on the part of officers conducting the search, guard against the threat of using an inventory search as a pretext for looking for contraband or other evidence of crime without any individualized suspicion. Objects that are open to view in the vehicle are treated the same as objects that are hidden or otherwise concealed, so that when acting pursuant to the aforementioned criteria, officers conducting the search may open closed containers found in the vehicle, and inventory their contents.

The vehicle searched must lawfully be in police custody (i.e., there are sufficient grounds for impoundment) at the time of the search. Impoundment may be proper for a number of reasons.

Similarly, the search of an arrestee, and his or her personal effects, including closed containers, prior to incarceration, is reasonable under the Fourth Amendment. "A stationhouse search of every item carried on or by the person who has lawfully been taken into custody by the police" is permissible. *Illinois v. Layfayette*, 462 U.S. 640 (1983). In *Layfayette*, police arrested the defendant and transported him to the precinct headquarters. At the time he was carrying a shoulder bag. The bag was opened and emptied, and found to contain contraband. The defendant argued that the search exceeded the scope of a permissible booking search. The Supreme Court disagreed, reasoning that the search served the important government interests of protecting the property of the arrestee, as well as protecting the police department from false claims. A routine booking and search is a reasonable way to promote these interests, and thus reasonable under the Fourth Amendment.

10. Automobile. If police have probable cause to believe a moveable car contains contraband or evidence of a crime, they may lawfully conduct a search of the entire automobile, and any containers which could reasonably be expected to contain contraband, whether open or closed, without first securing a warrant. *Taylor v. Commonwealth*, 284 S.E.2d 833 (Va. 1981).

See, e.g., *Leeth v. Commonwealth*, 288 S.E.2d 475 (Va. 1982). At around 10:25 p.m., a state trooper was stationed along Interstate 81 when he saw defendant driving toward him in excess of the speed limit. When defendant's car was within range, the trooper activated his police radar. The brake lights on defendant's car instantly came on, and the car "braked suddenly, almost to the point of skidding." The trooper proceeded to follow the car, and, with the use of his headlights, he could see"a small cord hanging down from the interior rear view mirror" and "the driver fumbling over the sun visor on the driver's side of the vehicle." Once defendant stopped, the trooper had probable cause to make a warrantless search of the car for a radar detector (which he found under the front seat).

See also *Alvarez v. Commonwealth*, 485 S.E.2d 646 (Va. Ct. App. 1997). Two New Orleans, Louisiana, detectives were investigating a Greyhound bus at the New Orleans Union Passenger Terminal. The dog who accompanied them, "K-9 Robbie," "hit" on a box in one of the bus' cargo areas by biting it, indicating that it contained narcotics. The package was addressed to the defendant's Martinsville, Virginia, residence. K-9 Robbie's "hit" established probable cause to believe that the package contained a controlled substance. Because the package was on a bus – a movable vehicle analogous to an automobile – the detectives could validly search it without first obtaining a warrant.

This exception applies to all containers, whether owned by the driver or a passenger, and irregardless of whether or not there is individualized probable cause to search a specific container. *Wyoming v. Houghton*, 526 U.S. 295 (1999) (after officer saw a syringe in plain view in the driver's pocket, he was entitled to search purse belonging to back seat passenger for narcotics). So long as there is probable cause to search the automobile, officers need not show facts establishing exigency. *Maryland v. Dyson*, 527 U.S. 465 (1999).

Historically, this exception to the warrant requirement was premised on the notion that a car is readily mobile. As such, there is a potential exigency, in that a vehicle containing contraband may be driven from the jurisdiction before officers have an opportunity to secure a warrant. More recently, courts have focused on the pervasive government regulation of automobiles. Because the state has a hand in so many facets of automobile ownership and use (e.g., licensing, registration, emission and safety inspections, et al.), one's expectation of privacy in the solitude of his or her automobile and its contents is diminished. Automobiles, in our society, do not occupy the same sacrosanct position courts attribute to the home. With a lessened privacy interest, a greater intrusion becomes more reasonable, and permissible under the Fourth Amendment.

Note: Stopping a car for a minor traffic violation, without more, will not create probable cause to believe the car contains contraband and justify a search of the vehicle. The officer must have a reasonable belief that a more serious crime has been committed, and probable cause to think that evidence of it can be found in the car. In *Pennsylvania v. Labron*, 518 U.S. 938 (1996), the U.S. Supreme Court discussed the applicability of the automobile exception in two cases. In one case, officers watched the defendant engage in a series of drug transactions on a street corner. The officers proceeded to arrest the defendant and others, and conducted a warrantless search of the trunk, from which the drugs were sold, and in which they found cocaine. In another case, an undercover informant bought drugs from the defendant's accomplice. To obtain the drugs for sale, the accomplice drove to a farmhouse, where she picked up the drugs and met with the defendant. After the sale, the defendant and the accomplice were arrested. Acting with the consent of the owner, police searched the farmhouse. Without a warrant, they also searched the defendant's truck, which was parked on the property, because they had seen the defendant walk to the truck from the house several times. Cocaine was found in the truck. Both defendants argued that the drugs should have been suppressed. In these cases, both trial courts found that the officers had probable cause to search, and no further justification for the search, like exigent circumstances, was needed. The Pennsylvania Supreme Court found that there was probable cause to search each of these vehicles, but suppressed the cocaine anyway, holding that police could not conduct a warrantless search of an automobile, unless exigent circumstances are present, and finding that none existed here. The U.S. Supreme Court reversed, noting that the state was not required to demonstrate exigent circumstances. "If a car is readily mobile, and probable cause exists to believe it contains contraband, the Fourth Amendment permits police to search the vehicle without more." *Pennsylvania v. Labron*, supra.

Stated broadly, police have justification to conduct a warrantless search of a car, or an area or container within the car, in the following circumstances: (i) search of the entire car, where the car is readily mobile, including the trunk and any closed containers, when they possess probable cause to believe the car contains contraband or the fruits and instrumentalities of crime; (ii) the area within an occupant's immediate control, to ensure the officer's safety during a *Terry* stop; (iii) the entire passenger area of the car when they place an occupant of the car under arrest; (iv) the entire car, and generally any closed containers, when the car has been impounded, as part of an inventory procedure; (v) the entire car, when the car has been abandoned or someone attempts to drive it across an international border; (vi) the entire car, when valid consent has been given, or specific areas or containers, when permission to search has been limited to those areas.

The effective officer should keep these principles in mind when making the decision to act without a warrant. Although the rule remains that warrantless searches are per se invalid, warrantless searches are permissible in a variety of situations. However, the justifications permitting warrantless searches differ. The thorough officer should make sure that the circumstances with which he or she is confronted fit within the aforementioned exceptions, before deciding on a course of action.

Note: Watercraft are considered similar to automobiles and searches of watercraft may be conducted under the same circumstances as that of an automobile. *United States v. Villamonte-Marquez*, 462 U.S. 579 (1983).

11. Administrative Searches. Searches and seizures may be undertaken, by a state and its agents, wholly apart from those pursued by law enforcement agencies. The constraints imposed by the Constitution apply to the state and federal governments, and their subdivisions or agents. The U.S. Supreme Court has never limited the Amendment's prohibition on unreasonable searches and seizures to operations conducted by the police. Rather, the Court has long spoken of the Fourth Amendment's strictures as restraints imposed upon "governmental action" – that is, upon "the activities of sovereign authority." *New Jersey v. T.L.O.*, 469 U.S. 325 (1985).

Note: If a search is conducted by a private person, or at the direction of a private sector entity, no constitutional concerns arise. The Constitution places limits on government, not private, action. *Buonocore v. Chesapeake & Potomac Telephone Company of Virginia*, 492 S.E.2d 439 (Va. 1997); *Burke v. Commonwealth*, 515 S.E.2d 777 (Va. Ct. App. 1999).

Detailed below are U.S. Supreme Court cases assessing the constitutionality of searches of an administrative character. In these instances, the Court has upheld searches in several situations where no law enforcement officials were involved, but where those individuals conducting the search could be deemed agents of a state or political subdivision, (i.e., intermediaries acting at the state's behest or in some way advancing the state's agenda), and their actions thus subject to constitutional limitations.

These warrantless intrusions by state actors are justified by the rationale that particular situations may involve special needs of the government. The special needs doctrine concerns governmental objectives that go beyond the normal day to day needs of law enforcement agencies. If special governmental needs are demonstrated, a reviewing court will balance the privacy interests of the individual against the magnitude of the state's need, to determine if a warrant, or at least some level of individualized suspicion (i.e., probable cause or reasonable suspicion) is required to justify a search in each particular context.

The Court approved a warrantless search by school officials of schoolchildren, *New Jersey v. T.L.O.*, 469 U.S. 325 (1985); warrantless drug tests on student athletes, *Veronia School District 47j v. Acton*, 515 U.S. 646 (1995); a warrantless search by an employer of employee's desks, offices or file cabinets, *O'conner v. Ortega*, 480 U.S. 709 (1987); a warrantless search of a probationer's home, *Griffin v. Wisconsin*, 483 U.S. 868 (1987); mandatory warrantless drug testing of both railway employees, *Skinner v. Railway Labor Executives Ass'n.*, 489 U.S. 602 (1989); and of customs officials, *National Treasury Employees Union v. Von Raab*, 489 U.S. 656 (1989). However, in *Chandler v. Miller*, 520 U.S. 305 (1997), the U.S. Supreme Court struck down a Georgia statutory provision requiring that candidates for specified state political offices pass a urinalysis drug test within 30 days prior to qualifying for election. The Court reasoned that Georgia had failed to show a special need important enough to override the individual privacy interests of the candidates. The Court found that the "certification requirement is not well designed to identify candidates who violate anti-drug laws" and that the statute failed to show any concrete danger posed by a state official possibly using drugs.

V. EXPECTATION OF PRIVACY

In *Katz v. United States*, 389 U.S. 347 (1967), the U.S. Supreme Court held that the Fourth Amendment safeguards, against unreasonable searches and seizures, will only extend to those places or objects with respect to which a person has exhibited some expectation of privacy. This expectation is one which society is prepared to recognize as reasonable. There are three varieties of property to which courts have consistently held no reasonable privacy expectation applies, and to which no constitutional protections will attach. These are: objects in open fields, objects placed in plain view, and objects that have been abandoned. These places can be searched, and items in those areas seized, without first securing a warrant.

The Supreme Court has noted that "the touchstone" of any claimed Fourth Amendment violation is always the reasonableness of the governments intrusion upon a citizen's personal security. It is often said that the Fourth Amendment does not prohibit all searches and seizures, only unreasonable ones. The threshold question in determining if government conduct is reasonable, is inquiring whether a legitimate privacy interest has been invaded. In *Katz*, supra, the Court spelled out the analysis that will be used to determine when Fourth Amendment protections are implicated, and when they are not. "The Constitution will protect people from government intrusion only with respect to those areas and items which they subjectively have privacy expectations and that expectation is plainly one that society is prepared to recognize as justifiable." The Fourth Amendment protects "people – and not simply areas – against unreasonable searches and seizures." The Court noted that an expectation of privacy will vary from person to person, and place to place; "objects, activities or statements that one exposes to outsiders may fall outside the protection of the Fourth Amendment because (one) has displayed them freely and has shown an intention of keeping them private. One may also exhibit an expectation of privacy in an item, even though he or she takes it to a public place, if his or her acts manifest an intent to keep the item private." If no privacy violation occurred, the Fourth Amendment is not implicated, and there is no need to further examine government conduct. Likewise, if another person's privacy concerns have been trodden upon, individuals whose interests were not interfered with do not have legal grounds, or standing, to challenge the government's conduct, and that conduct need not be analyzed.

If, however, a privacy violation has occurred, the courts will proceed to examine the conduct in question, and endeavor to determine if it was reasonable under the circumstances. If the actions are deemed reasonable, they are legal; if unreasonable, they are unconstitutional, bringing the specter of suppression and civil liability into the forefront. To aid in this reasonableness determination, courts employ a balancing analysis. On one side of the scale rests a person's privacy concerns regarding his home, body and possessions. On the other side of the scale rests the government's interest in advancing or promoting the law enforcement conduct in question. If the privacy interest is weighty (e.g., the inviolability of one's home), then intrusive government conduct is less likely to be reasonable under the circumstances. If, on the other hand, the government interest is significant (e.g., curtailing the drug epidemic), and the individual's privacy interest is lessened (e.g., items that may be carried about in one's car), then more intrusive government action is more likely to be deemed constitutionally reasonable under the circumstances.

Nonetheless, there remains a judicial preference for warrants, and the general rule remains that warrantless searches are per se unreasonable. The Supreme Court has provided some clear cut guidelines in specific instances, the so called "bright-line rules" (e.g., requirement of a warrant for an in-home arrest, search of a passenger compartment when the occupant is arrested, etc.) Courts routinely state they are hesitant to pronounce far reaching rules of universal applicability. Rather, there is an increasing tendency to evaluate each case on its own facts, and resort to the balancing test to determine the reasonableness, and hence the constitutionality, of any given law enforcement action. There are many circumstances to which no precedent applies. In cases that fall beyond the confines of these "bright line" rules, where government conduct is in the periphery, or gray area of Fourth Amendment law, courts are increasingly likely to employ the balancing test. The outcome, obviously, will vary depending on the unique circumstances of each factual setting. In these cases, rather than employing a rule requiring a warrant for virtually all law enforcement actions, subject to limited exceptions, courts will instead employ the above criteria to answer the question begged by the Fourth Amendment: Was the conduct reasonable?

The following doctrines concern areas, and objects within those areas, or classes of property, with respect to which courts have consistently held individuals do not have a reasonable expectation of privacy. Because there is no privacy expectation, no search, within the meaning of the Constitution, can take place; i.e., the Fourth Amendment is not implicated, there is no need to examine government acts, and no basis for suppression of evidence seized.

A. Plain View Doctrine

Under the plain view doctrine, the warrantless seizure of a piece of evidence which is in plain view is permissible when three criteria are met. First, the evidence must be seen from a lawful vantage point. Second, the seizing officer must have a right of lawful access to the object itself. Finally, it must be immediately apparent to the viewer that the object observed is incriminating evidence. In other words, the observing officer must have probable cause to believe the evidence in question is contraband or incriminating evidence. *U.S. v. Wells*, 98 F.3d 808 (4th Cir. 1996); *Harris v. Commonwealth*, 400 S.E.2d 191 (Va. 1991).

Lawful vantage point means that the officer has a legal justification for his place of observation. Immediately apparent means that the officer needs to conduct no further investigation on the object or item in question to realize its evidentiary value.

See, e.g., *Arnold v. Commonwealth*, 437 S.E.2d 235 (Va. Ct. App. 1993). Defendant was a passenger in car stopped for lack of a rear license plate. The officer noticed a Hecht's bag in the back seat next to defendant. Based on the way the bag was folded and the officer's experience in retail security, he suspected that the bag was lined with foil, a method often used by shoplifters to disable the anti-theft devices commonly placed on clothing. (As the officer later explained, a plastic bag, after being folded down or rolled up, "will tend to open back up on its own[;]" foil-lined bags, however, stay rigid and keep their shape if rolled or folded.) The officer also knew that possession of such a device is a misdemeanor. He validly seized and searched the bag; inside, he found six dresses on hangers with the store security tags still attached.

Compare with *Hogan v. Commonwealth*, 423 S.E.2d 841 (Va. Ct. App. 1992). Officer stopped a car for running a red light. From outside the vehicle, he saw two white plastic bags which contained a powdery substance. These were validly seized under the plain view doctrine, and later determined to be cocaine.

The theory behind the plain view doctrine is that when a police officer is conducting a lawful search and comes across an item or object that is not the object of a search, but is plainly incriminating, then the officer may seize that item. The justification for such a warrantless seizure is not a lack of privacy interest in the item, (probable cause to believe that the object or item is contraband, evidence, or fruits or instrumentality of a crime is necessary), but that there is no intrusion beyond that which is already justified.

The importance of the plain view doctrine is that, technically, when conducting a search, an officer may seize only those objects or items described in a warrant or, in a warrantless search, those objects or items which the officer is lawfully authorized to seize under an exception to the warrant requirement. Thus, without the plain view doctrine, an officer searching an automobile for weapons would be forced to ignore evidence which was not a weapon. However, under the plain view doctrine, a seizure of other evidence is lawful.

Use of a flashlight to view an object does not make a plain view seizure unlawful. *Wells v. Commonwealth*, 371 S.E.2d 19 (1988).

Similar to plain view is the theory of open view. However, in open view an officer needs no justification for his vantage point in that the object or item is in a place in which no person could have a reasonable expectation of privacy. Thus, there is no search being conducted when an officer finds an object or item in open view.

See *U.S. v. Taylor*, 90 F.3d 903 (4th Cir. 1996). Officers arrived at defendant's house to return a handgun seized during an earlier traffic stop. Through a picture window, about eight feet to the left of the front door, they saw a large sum of currency and a bag of white powder on a table in the well-lit dining room. This evidence was visible from the street as well as from the front walkway and porch; officers had the same right to view it as any other member of the public or guest would, and were justified in making a warrantless entry and seizure.

"The seizure of property in plain view involves no invasion of privacy and is presumptively reasonable, assuming that there is probable cause to associate the property with criminal activity." *Payton v. New York*, 445 U.S. 573 (1980). This doctrine is premised on the notion that if an article is already in plain view, the owner of the property has not manifested any expectation of privacy in the object. Often, the critical factor in deciding the applicability of the doctrine to the admission of proffered evidence, involves a determination of whether or not the seizing officers are lawfully in the position from which they view the seized item. So long as law enforcement officials have a proper justification for being where they conduct their observation, and have a right of access to the item seized, they may seize all contraband, fruits and instrumentalities of crime, or those items which they have probable cause to believe are contraband, fruits or instrumentalities of crime. Adequate justifications for being at a given vantage point would include being in a public area (e.g., street, or business open to the public), working under the authority of a warrant, or where the intrusion that brings the police within plain view of the evidence is supported by one of the exceptions to the warrant requirement (e.g., hot pursuit or exigent circumstances). A proper justification for the officers being where they are viewing from, in essence, means that the officer did not violate the defendant's constitutional rights in establishing his vantage point. To fall within the purview of this exception, the discovery of the incriminating items need not be inadvertent, (i.e., the seizing officer can be operating under the assumption that incriminating evidence will be found, or have an idea of what he or she will find), but the incriminating nature of the item must be immediately apparent. *Conway v. Commonwealth*, 407 S.E.2d 310 (Va. Ct. App. 1991).

Courts sometimes draw a distinction between items seized in "plain" view, and items seized in "open" view. Under this analysis, items in plain view are in a constitutionally protected area (i.e., one in which there is a reasonable expectation of privacy). When these items are seized the question a reviewing court will ask is, once the item has been seen, is there a justification, like a warrant or an applicable exception, that will permit access? Or, if the item is seen from a constitutionally protected area, is there a justification for the law enforcement personnel being in that protected area? For example, if contraband is seen in plain view, and the officer is justified in being at his vantage point, it does not always mean the contraband is subject to immediate seizure. If the contraband is in a home, or in the curtilage, and seen from without, a warrant must be procured, absent an applicable exception to the warrant requirement, before the home can be entered and the evidence seized. Items in open view, on the other hand, are items seen in an area that is not constitutionally protected (i.e., where there is no reasonable expectation of privacy). Examples often cited are objects in open fields, on the body of a person, in a public building, or in a car. In this respect, the open view doctrine is essentially identical to the open fields concept, discussed below.

B. Areas and Items Surrounding the Home

The home is clearly a bastion of Fourth Amendment rights. The area around the home, often referred to as the "curtilage", also enjoys protection. This includes areas such as the garage, garden, or the immediate yard. However, courts have held that the area outside the curtilage is not worthy of the same protection.

1. Curtilage. The sanctity of one's home is at the core of Fourth Amendment rights. While objects in open areas do not receive the benefit of Fourth Amendment protections, courts have also ruled that constitutional safeguards will extend to zones immediately outside the home, an area called the curtilage. The extent of the curtilage is determined by factors that bear upon whether an individual reasonably may expect that the area in question should be treated as the home itself. Courts look to see if the area is used for the "intimate activity associated with the sanctity of a man's home and the privacies of life." The analysis employed by courts entails an examination of four factors: the proximity of the area claimed to be curtilage to the home; whether the area is enclosed, for example, by a fence or hedge; the types of activities for which the homeowner uses the area; the measures taken by the resident to guard the area from observation by people passing by. *U.S. v. Dunn*, 480 U.S. 294, reh'g denied, 481 U.S. 1024 (1987); *Jefferson v. Commonwealth*, 497 S.E.2d 474 (Va. Ct. App. 1998).

As a consequence of the interplay between these two doctrines, the home and the curtilage are protected by the Constitution, and a warrant will generally be required to enter and search them. The open areas that surround those private protected zones do not occupy the same position of reverence and are not accorded the same protections.

2. Aerial Search. Courts have found that it is unreasonable to have a privacy expectation in the aerial view of one's property. This is due to the fact that any private citizen may obtain such a view. Since there is no protected privacy interest in the view, police may conduct aerial searches without a warrant. *Dow Chemicals Co. v. United States*, 476 U.S. 227 (1986).

3. Open Fields. Courts have said that people cannot maintain a reasonable expectation of privacy as to items placed in open fields, or concerning activities conducted there. Because there is no intrusion on a constitutionally protected zone of privacy, the Fourth Amendment is not implicated when law enforcement officials survey structures found, or activities conducted, in an open field. Because the Fourth Amendment does not protect open fields, the examination of objects therein does not constitute a search, and neither a warrant, nor any exception to the warrant requirement, need be shown to justify the seizure of articles in an open field.

The type of land a court may deem an open field will depend on the unique circumstances of each parcel. A variety of circumstantial factors will be examined to determine if the area is treated as a non-private area, or if the owner has manifested a privacy interest, or has exhibited an intent to keep outsiders away. The presence or absence of "No Trespassing" signs, and the extent to which such a policy is enforced, is relevant in this determination, as is the presence or absence of a fence or hedge surrounding the field, and the extent to which the owner controls access to the field by use of a gate or chain across an entry lane.

Courts have held that it is generally unreasonable to have an expectation of privacy in open areas of land. Even if the land shows evidence of an expectation of privacy, the courts will still only look at the reasonableness of that expectation. *Oliver v. U.S.*, 466 U.S. 170 (1984).

4. Abandoned Items or Garbage. When property has been abandoned, it no longer falls within the area of protection afforded by the Fourth Amendment, and therefore can be searched or seized without a warrant or any other justification. When determining if property has been abandoned, courts will analyze the actions of the individual alleged to have discarded the article. The focus is not whether the defendant relinquished dominion and control of the property with respect to his possession, as would be the case if the ownership of the item were in dispute, but rather, whether the individual has relinquished his reasonable expectation of privacy in the article. When police conduct is lawful (e.g., they have a lawful right to approach and question a person) and a suspect discards an item in a public place, then he can be said to have abandoned that item. Police may secure the item and, if incriminating, retain it for use later as evidence, without fear of the suspect claiming that the evidence was seized from him unlawfully.

See, e.g., *Wechsler v. Commonwealth*, 455 S.E.2d 744 (Va. Ct. App. 1995). Defendant was stopped at Washington National Airport because he fit the profile of a drug courier (one-way ticket from Tucson, bought with cash minutes before the flight). DEA agents learned from the airline that defendant had checked two bags. However, after making eye contact with the agents in the baggage claim area, defendant left without claiming any bags. During a consensual interview outside the airport, defendant denied that he had checked any bags. Even after a consensual search of defendant's carry-on bag found claim checks for two bags attached to his ticket, defendant continued his denials. By choosing to forego possession of the bags by leaving the airport without them, and then repeatedly denying ownership of them, defendant abandoned the bags, and could no longer object to the agents' warrantless search of them.

Conversely, if officers do not have a justification for their initial actions (e.g., detaining without reasonable suspicion), and the item is discarded in response to this unlawful activity, the evidence may be suppressed as the fruit of illegal law enforcement activity. In this instance, courts say that the unlawful police action forced the abandonment. *Moss v. Commonwealth*, 373 S.E.2d 170 (Va. Ct. App. 1988).

See, e.g., *Motley v. Commonwealth*, 437 S.E.2d 232 (Va. Ct. App. 1993). Officer received a radio dispatch to be on the look-out for a "black male with a yellow hat and black Kings coat." No explanation was offered why this man was being sought by police. Nevertheless, when officer saw defendant, who matched the description, he ordered him to stop. Upon hearing the officer, defendant dropped an object to the ground, later determined to be cocaine. Because the officer had no reasonable suspicion to stop defendant, his abandonment of the cocaine was "forced" by an illegal stop, and the evidence was inadmissible.

When an individual abandons an item of personal property, he relinquishes a reasonable expectation of privacy in the discarded item. This is true whether an individual is putting trash to the curb or dropping evidence while fleeing from police. A showing of actual intent to abandon is not necessary. It is only necessary to show that the individual asserting a privacy interest in the property in question had relinquished sufficient control over the property so that he no longer had any reasonable expectation of privacy in the object or item. See *California v. Greenwood*, 486 U.S. 35 (1988) (renounce any expectation of privacy in garbage set out on the street).

5. Disclaimer of Ownership. If a defendant disclaims ownership of property or any possessory interest, police may use such a denial as sufficient proof of either an intent to abandon the property or a lack of ownership of the property.

C. The Caretaker Function

The "caretaker function" was first developed by the United States Supreme Court in the case of *Cady v. Dombrowski*, 413 U.S. 433 (1973). The concept of the "caretaker function" is that the police are not always involved in the adversarial process of arresting criminals. Sometimes the police may act in other ways to help the public. This may be to render assistance to individuals in need or to provide protection for the rights and property of members of the general public. The "caretaker function" also applies to certain acts performed by police to secure a suspect's rights or property. The Courts will examine the reasonableness of any such act. However, probable cause is not necessary. Evidence that is found during such acts will be admissible.

See, e.g., *Commonwealth v. Waters*, 456 S.E.2d 527 (Va. Ct. App. 1995). A Leesburg officer was patrolling an apartment complex when he observed defendant swaying and walking unsteadily. Defendant appeared either intoxicated or ill. The officer approached him, tapped him on the shoulder, and said he wanted to make sure he could find his way home. The officer was reasonably concerned about defendant's safety; therefore, this was not an illegal stop. When defendant began making threatening gestures and statements, and the officer noticed a bulge on his left side, reasonable suspicion developed, so that a pat-down was then justified.

But see *Barrett v. Commonwealth*, 435 S.E.2d 902 (Va. Ct. App. 1993). Officer was driving along Route 360 in Northumberland County when he saw defendant's truck driving partially on the shoulder of the road and partially on private property. He later testified that he stopped the truck solely to determine whether it was experiencing mechanical problems, not because of any perceived violation of the law. The caretaker function did not justify this stop, as the vehicle was moving without apparent difficulty and was not creating a public safety hazard.

D. Wiretaps

Any police officer who wishes to get authorization to conduct a wiretap must fill out an application. The application must state: (1) the identity of the attorney for the Commonwealth and the identity of the police officer making the application; (2) "[a] full and complete statement of the facts and circumstance relied upon by the applicant to justify his belief that an order should be issued, including (i) details as to the particular offense that has been, is being, or is about to be committed, (ii)...a particular description of the nature and location of the facilities from which or the place where the communication is to be intercepted is to take place, (iii) a particular description of the type of communication sought to be intercepted (iv) the identity of the person, if known, committing the offense and whose communications are to be intercepted" (Virginia Code §19.2-68(2)); (3) the other investigative means that have failed, or why they would fail or be too dangerous; (4) the time period that the intercept will be needed, also any reasons why the intercept should continue after the information described has been obtained; (5) the facts concerning any past attempt to obtain an intercept on any of the suspects in the present application.

All applications must be made through the Attorney General or Deputy Attorney General. The Attorney General or Deputy Attorney General will review the application, verify it, and have it presented to a magistrate in the jurisdiction in which the communications will take place. The magistrate will then make a probable cause determination. (Virginia Code §§19.2-66 and 19.2-68.) See Virginia Code §§19.2-61 through 19.2-70.3 for further details.

Note that Virginia Code §19.2-62 makes unlawful wiretaps a class 6 felony, while §19.2-69 provides for civil damages.

VI. THE EXCLUSIONARY RULE

The frequent result of unconstitutional actions by law enforcement is the imposition of a judicially created remedy – banning the use of evidence gathered under such circumstances – called suppression. The exclusionary rule mandates that all evidence obtained by searches and seizures violative of the rights of an accused are inadmissible against that person in a subsequent trial. The rule is premised on the notion that if private, constitutionally protected areas can be searched, and items taken unlawfully are used to obtain a conviction, the protections of the Fourth Amendment are of little, if any, value. The exclusionary rule is in essence an enforcement mechanism, serving to give teeth to constitutional guarantees. The rule bars the use of all forms of illegally obtained evidence. Physical evidence as well as statements are subject to suppression, if they derive from an unconstitutional act, such as an unlawful arrest, illegal search or coercive interrogation. If law enforcement officials come by evidence through exploitation of their illegal conduct, the evidence is said to be "tainted", and evidence tainted by illegal conduct on the part of law enforcement is inadmissible against an accused.

The exclusionary rule applies not only to the illegally obtained evidence itself, but also bars the use of evidence derived from the initially obtained illegal evidence, because of the initial illegality. This derivative, or secondary evidence, including an officer's testimony based on knowledge garnered as a result of the illegal conduct, is often referred to as the "fruit of the poisonous tree." To invoke the protection of the "poisonous tree" principle, the defendant must first demonstrate there was a primary illegality (i.e., an unconstitutional search or arrest, or a coerced confession), and secondly, a nexus, or connection, between the illegality and the derivative evidence. The nexus between the illegal act and the subject evidence must be so strong that police can be said to have obtained the evidence only by an exploitation of their illegal actions. If another event, or outside factor weakens the connection between the illegality and the evidence, a principle referred to as attenuation, so that the evidence can no longer be said to be a by-product of the unlawful conduct, then suppression is not appropriate. The attenuating factor removes the stigma of the illegal law enforcement action, so that denying the admission of the seized evidence does not serve the deterrent purposes of the exclusionary rule.

See *U.S. v. Sprinkle*, 106 F. 3d 613 (4th Cir. 1997). Officers conducted an unjustified *Terry* stop of the defendant. Because this initial stop was illegal, normally any evidence seized as a result of that stop would be inadmissible at trial. However, an independent act of the defendant constituted a new crime, and gave the arresting officers a separate, and constitutional, basis for arrest. As officers told him they were going to pat him down for weapons, defendant pushed away and began to run. The officers gave chase, and after about 100 feet defendant pulled a handgun from his jacket, and fired a shot in the general direction of one of the officers. Defendant then put the gun to his own head and said if the officer's did not leave, he would shoot himself. After a period of negotiation, defendant was persuaded to drop the weapon. The officers seized the gun, and placed defendant under arrest. On appeal, the Court held that the gun was admissible, even though the initial detention was not justified. Defendant committed a new crime when he fired the gun at the officers. "At this point officer had probable cause to arrest defendant because the new crime purged the taint of the prior illegal stop. And the gun, which was in plain view at the scene of the new crime could be legitimately seized."

The exclusionary rule is not mandated by the language of the Constitution. It is, rather, a judicially created remedy. Exclusion is appropriate where the underlying purposes of the Bill of Rights (i.e., freedom from unbridled government intrusion) are best served. The rule prohibiting the use of illegally obtained evidence has its roots in the notion that we live in a society governed by the rule of law, not rule by law. If a government is not held to the standards found in the document that created it, then how can a government expect citizens to respect and abide by its pronouncements? Moreover, the rule is not designed to penalize officers for their mistakes or oversights, or to hamper their legitimate efforts. "The criminal does not go free because the constable blundered, but because the Constitution prohibits securing the evidence against" the defendant. *People v. Cahan*, 44 Cal.2d 434, 282 P. 2d 905 (Cal. 1955). However, the rule does serve as a deterrent, in that it discourages officers from obtaining evidence in an illegal manner. If the evidence cannot be used to obtain a conviction, then the incentive to obtain it disappears. Put another way, law enforcement is encouraged to respect constitutional guarantees in evidence gathering, for only evidence taken in accordance with those principles will be of any use.

There are three well recognized exceptions to the above rule: (i) the "independent source" and (ii) "inevitable discovery" doctrines, and (iii) the "good faith" exception. The first two are analogous to the attenuation concept, discussed above, where the connection between police misconduct and evidence of crime may be sufficiently protracted to permit the use of that evidence at trial. If an event, or an act is interposed between the initial illegality and the discovery of the evidence offered, then it may be argued that the evidence is not a byproduct or direct result of action tainted by illegal conduct. An attenuation argument may lead to the admission of evidence seized as a result of an illegal arrest or search in certain circumstances. For example, if a suspect's response to illegal police actions is itself a distinct and separate crime, then the suspect may be arrested or searched on the basis of that crime, even if the initial police conduct was illegal. The independent, intervening illegal act may be said to purge the seized evidence of the taint of the initial illegality. The relationship between any illegal conduct and the seizure is adequately attenuated, so that the effect is not the result of an illegality, and the admission of the seized item does not offend constitutional guarantees.

With respect to the independent source and inevitable discovery exceptions, the prosecution is, in effect, arguing that there is no nexus between the illegal conduct and the evidence, but rather the evidence was derived from other, constitutionally permissible sources. Attenuation analysis focuses on whether the proffered evidence has come to the attention of officers by an exploitation of illegal action or instead by means sufficiently distinguishable to be purged of the primary taint.

A. Independent Source

"The Fourth Amendment does not require the suppression of evidence initially discovered during police officer's illegal entry of private premises, if that evidence is also discovered during a later search pursuant to a valid warrant that is wholly independent of the initial illegal entry. The independent source doctrine permits the introduction of evidence initially discovered during, or as a consequence of, an unlawful search, but later obtained independently from lawful activities untainted by the initial illegality." *Murray v. U.S.*, 487 U.S. 573 (1988). The circumstances that justify the second lawful search must have no connection to the initial, unlawful conduct. The facts supporting the second search must arise wholly apart from those which purportedly justified the initial search. (e.g., a judicial finding of probable cause, and a warrant issued based on that finding, where the facts in the supporting affidavit derive completely from a source independent of facts garnered during an initial, illegal search.)

In *Murray v. U.S.*, supra, officers conducting a narcotics investigation had probable cause to believe a large quantity of drugs were being stored in a warehouse. Before securing a warrant, they illegally entered the warehouse, and confirmed their beliefs, finding several bales of marijuana. The officer subsequently applied for and obtained a search warrant, but made no mention of their entry to the issuing judge, basing their application only on facts they had accumulated prior to the unlawful entry. The Supreme Court held that if the earlier information in the affidavit in fact supported the probable cause determination, so that the later seizure of the marijuana was not a result of the illegal entry, but rather the result of a warrant executed pursuant to the independent probable cause finding, the evidence would not be suppressed.

B. Inevitable Discovery

"If the prosecution can establish by a preponderance of the evidence that the information ultimately or inevitably would have been discovered by lawful means then the deterrence rationale has so little basis that the evidence should be received." *Nix v. Williams*, 467 U.S. 431 (1984). Generally, courts will find evidence would have been inevitably discovered if the evidence would have been discovered, in the same condition, through an independent line of investigation, and where the independent investigation was already in progress at the time of the illegal search.

In *Nix*, supra, two officers illegally obtained from a suspect the location of the body of a child he had murdered. The defendant argued that testimony concerning the location and condition of the body should be suppressed as a result of this illegality. The Supreme Court disagreed, holding that if the prosecution could demonstrate that the child's body would have been discovered without the benefit of the defendant's statements, suppression was not appropriate. In this case, there was an extremely good chance that the state could demonstrate the body's location would have been inevitably discovered, as there was a 200 member search party, combing the area, which in fact was scheduled to search the area where the body was found.

C. Good Faith Exception

This exception is a logical extension of the deterrent rationale behind the exclusionary rule. In effect, the exception represents a judicial recognition that an officer will not be encouraged to abide by constitutional rights, or discouraged from infringing upon them, where he or she objectively, reasonably and in good faith performs his or her duties, only to have a mistake, oversight or technical error by a third party hamper his or her efforts. Where an officer, operating in good faith, bases an arrest on a violation of a criminal statute or ordinance, and that statute is later deemed unconstitutional, retroactively rendering the arrest illegal, evidence discovered incident to that arrest will not be suppressed. *U.S. v. Leon*, 468 U.S. 897 (1984). Similarly, suppression is inappropriate where an officer conducting a search or arrest in reasonable, good faith reliance on a warrant issued by a neutral and detached magistrate, and that warrant is later found defective or technically deficient.

Virginia follows the good faith exception. *McCary v. Commonwealth*, 321 S.E.2d 637 (Va. 1984).

The U.S. Supreme Court has held that the exclusionary rule will not apply to evidence seized pursuant to a warrant executed in good faith, where the warrant is subsequently deemed defective because of clerical errors. *Arizona v. Evans*, 514 U.S.1 (1995). In *Evans*, a motorist was pulled over for a routine traffic stop. The officer's in-dash computer indicated the motorist had an outstanding warrant for his arrest. He was placed under arrest, and a search of his car revealed a bag of marijuana. The officer did not know that the warrant under which he arrested the motorist had been quashed, and a clerk forgot to make the appropriate entry. The motorist sought to have the evidence suppressed as the fruit of an unlawful arrest. The Supreme Court denied suppression and held that "the exclusionary rule does not require suppression of evidence seized in violation of the Fourth Amendment where the erroneous information resulted from clerical errors of court employees."

The prosecution is not entitled to the benefit of the good faith exception in four circumstances: (i) when the warrant is based on an affidavit containing knowing or reckless falsity; (ii) when the magistrate simply acted as a rubber stamp for the police; (iii) when the supporting affidavit does not provide the magistrate with a substantial basis for determining the existence of probable cause; (iv) when the warrant is so facially deficient that the officer could not reasonably rely on it. *Janis v. Commonwealth*, 472 S.E.2d 649 (Va. Ct. App.), on reh'g, 479 S.E.2d 534 (1996).

VII. LIABILITY

A. Criminal Liability

Law enforcement officers may be held criminally liable under both 18 U.S.C. 241 and 18 U.S.C. 242. However, neither 18 U.S.C. 241 nor 18 U.S.C. 242 provide individual relief for the party whose rights were violated.

Under 18 U.S.C. 241, a law enforcement office is liable if he or she enters into a conspiracy to deprive any citizen of any right or privilege guaranteed by the Constitution. For this section, the only act that is necessary for a violation is an act in furtherance of the conspiracy. The penalty under this section is up to ten years in prison and/or up to a $10,000 fine. If death results then the prison term may be for life.

18 U.S.C. 242 makes it an offense for a law enforcement officer to act under color of law to willfully deprive any inhabitant of the United States of rights guaranteed by the Constitution or laws of the United States. Under color of law means under the pretense of law. The penalty under this section is up to one year in jail and/or up to a $1,000 fine.

B. Civil Liability

Under Title 42, Chapter 21, Subchapter 1, §1983 of the United States Code, (commonly referred to as a "§1983" action), any person who, under pretense of law, deprives another of any constitutional right, "shall be liable to the party injured in an action at law, suit in equity, or other proper proceeding for redress."

Under this section the U.S. Supreme Court has held that an officer (and the department) may be sued for money damages by the victim of an unlawful arrest. *Malley v. Briggs*, 475 U.S. 335 (1986). Furthermore, the same civil liability for an objectively unreasonable arrest will apply to an objectively unreasonable search. *Anderson v. Creighton*, 483 U.S. 635 (1987).

It is important to note that a police officer's intent in making a false arrest is not material to an action for deprivation of civil rights brought under this statute. *Caballero v. City of Concord*, 956 F.2d 204 (9th Cir. 1992).

Once probable cause to arrest is established, a law enforcement officer cannot be held liable for false arrest under state laws or for deprivation of civil rights under this statute. *Hunter v. Clardy*, 558 F.2d 290 (5th Cir. 1977). Any collateral bad motive or intent on the part of the arresting officer is immaterial.

Qualified immunity is an affirmative defense against §1983 claims. Its purpose is to shield public officials from undue interference with their duties and from potentially disabling threats of liability where the official acts objectively and reasonably in the good faith performance of his or her duties. The defense provides immunity from suit, not merely liability. *Wilson v. Weeks*, 52 F.3d 1547 (10th Cir. 1995).

Some examples of the types of cases which have been brought under this statute are: (i) failure to advise grounds for arrest and detention, *Tilson v. Forrest City Police Dept.*, 28 F.3d 802 (8th Cir. 1994), cert. denied, 514 U.S. 1004 (1995); (ii) detaining the person arrested for too long a period, *Tilson v. Forrest City Police Dept.*, supra; (iii) use of unreasonable or excessive force during arrest or detention, *Elliott v. Leavitt*, 99 F.3d 640 (4th Cir. 1996). But see *City of Sacramento v. Lewis*, 523 U.S. 833 (1998) ("High-speed chases with no intent to harm suspects physiçally or to worsen their legal plight do not give rise to liability under the 14th Amendment redressable by an action under 42 U.S.C. 1983.").

Title 42 U.S.C. 1985(3), is the conspiracy counterpart of §1983. This section makes any person, who conspires with another to deprive a third person of any constitutional right, liable to that third person for damages. The violated individual may sue one or all of the conspirators.

Title 42 U.S.C. §1983 provides that every person who, under color of law, deprives another of any rights, privileges and immunities secured by the Constitution shall be liable to the party injured. Actions by a suspect, an arrestee or defendant may be premised, for example, on a claim of an unlawful arrest, the use of excessive force, a coerced confession, or an illegal search. See *Quinones v. Szorc*, 771 F.2d 289, (7th Cir. 1985); *Munson v. Friske*, 754 F.2d 683, (7th Cir. 1985); *Mass v. McClenahan*, 893 F.Supp. 225 (S.D. N.Y. 1995).

Individual officers, and the municipality, but not the state, in which they work, may be rendered liable under this section. See, e.g., *Board of County Com'rs of Bryan County,*

Okl. v. Brown, 520 U.S. 397 (1997), where the plaintiff sought to sue the county for alleged excessive force used by a deputy. The plaintiff's theory of recovery was that the county, and its agent, in this case the sheriff who hired the deputy, were negligent in hiring the deputy. She maintained that a brief background check would have revealed that there was a strong likelihood, based on the deputy's past behavior, that he would routinely use excessive force. The Supreme Court disagreed, reasoning that a county or municipality cannot be liable under §1983 merely because they employ a tort feasor. The plaintiff must show that there was a policy or custom of employing tort feasors. Moreover, the plaintiff must demonstrate a causal link between the municipality's conduct and the alleged injury. Here, the plaintiff did not prove any culpability on the part of the municipality. The state itself cannot be a defendant in a §1983 action. The Court has ruled that a state, unlike a municipality, a county, or an individual officer, is not a person within the meaning of the statute, and therefore not amenable to suit.

Courts will, and routinely do, provide immunity from liability under this section. Immunity from suit "is the rule, not the exception". The doctrine of qualified immunity protects law enforcement officers to the extent that their discretionary actions do not clearly violate a suspect's federal statutory or constitutional rights. To raise a triable "§1983" claim, the plaintiff must initially demonstrate that the rights allegedly transgressed were clearly established at the time of the alleged violation. In other words, in order for conduct to fall outside the scope of the qualified immunity doctrine and render an officer or his employer liable, the plaintiff must demonstrate it would be clear to a reasonable officer in that position that his or her actions are offending a well-settled constitutional or statutory right. Conversely, if the officer objectively, reasonably, and in good faith performs his duties, he will be shielded from a damage claim. An officer is immune for harm resulting from his actions, for example, if a reasonable officer could have believed a search to be lawful in light of clearly established law and the information the searching officers possessed, or if a reasonable officer would have believed there was probable cause to arrest. See *Anderson v. Creighton*, supra; *Gould v. Davis*, 165 F.3d 265 (4th Cir. 1998).

In addition to suits under §1983, officers may be liable for damages resulting from their unlawful actions, in suits based on state law tort principles. (See, e.g., Virginia Code §19.2-59.)

VIII. FIFTH AMENDMENT RIGHTS AND PRIVILEGES

The Fifth Amendment of the U.S. Constitution contains numerous rights and privileges. However, two of particular importance in the area of police procedure are the privilege against self-incrimination and the right to an attorney during any custodial police interrogation. The privilege against self-incrimination may also be called the right to remain silent. The remedy for police violation of these rights is exclusion of all evidence obtained as a result of the violation. Also, individual officers may be liable in a civil or criminal context, or both, if found in violation of these rights.

The Fifth Amendment's prohibition against compelled self-incrimination requires that any custodial interrogation be preceded by advice to the suspect that he has the right to remain silent and also the right to the presence of an attorney. The Fifth Amendment itself does not mandate that *Miranda* warnings be given. Instead, the warnings, and the suppression of statements given by a custodial suspect in the absence of the warnings, are enforcement mechanisms, employed by the courts to preserve the essence of the right guaranteed by the amendment. The result of the rule is that custodial suspect, not given these warnings prior to an interrogation, may not have any statements he or she may make during that interrogation, used against them in a subsequent prosecution.

Moreover, if the suspect indicates that he wishes to remain silent, the interrogation must cease immediately, although the questioning generally may be resumed later. If he requests counsel, the interrogation must cease until an attorney is present. Furthermore, if a suspect indicates he wants to deal with the police only through counsel, officers may not resume questioning unless the suspect initiates the contact and indicates he wishes to proceed without the benefit of counsel. To this extent, police conduct is determined by which right the defendant invokes. If he invokes the right to counsel, one must be provided, and the police cannot initiate further communications with the suspect without counsel present, unless the suspect approaches the officers and himself reinitiates the interrogation. If however, the suspect invokes his right to remain silent, police may generally reinitiate questioning after a break and after fresh warnings are administered, if the request that questioning cease is initially honored. New warnings at the resumption of questioning may not always be required. If the court finds that the initial warnings are not too remote, and still sufficiently fresh to apprise the suspect of his rights, subsequent warnings may not be necessary.

Apart from these court created rules, the Fifth Amendment, by its terms, prohibits the state from forcing a criminal defendant into self incrimination. Notice that the statements or evidence that a suspect is compelled to give must be testimonial or communicative in nature to fall under the Fifth Amendment's protection. The Fifth Amendment prohibits the state from marshaling evidence against a defendant only by "the cruel expedient of compelling it from his own mouth." Coercing a suspect into confessing, taking a statement prior to reading a custodial suspect *Miranda* warnings, or failing to honor a request for counsel or to remain silent, are methods by which courts have determined law enforcement may offend the guarantees of the Fifth Amendment. However, even if potentially incriminating, the following statements are not considered testimonial: statements used for voice exemplars; answers to general on-the-scene questions during routine investigatory stops; answers to routine booking questions prior to incarceration. Moreover, the privilege does not prohibit the state from compelling a suspect to provide what may ultimately be used as evidence against him in another fashion. Therefore, a suspect does not have a privilege against revealing the color of his eyes, skin, the way his face looks, or the way he is dressed, his fingerprints or measurements, assuming a particular posture or stance, or making a specific gesture. These displays, which certainly may point to the suspect's identity and guilt, and in that regard be incriminating, are nonetheless real or physical evidence as opposed to testimonial, and a suspect may be compelled to show these physical attributes.

Note: Although the Fifth Amendment may not prohibit the use of physical evidence obtained in such fashion, the Fourth Amendment's ban on unreasonable searches may, where evidence is taken from the body of a person, without first obtaining a warrant.

A. *Miranda Rights*

Suspects must be informed of their Fifth Amendment rights once they are in custody. Any statement made by a suspect in custody before they are apprised of their rights will be inadmissible. Suspects must be informed that: they have the right to remain silent; anything they say can be used against them; they have the right to an attorney; if the suspect wants an attorney, but cannot afford one, then one will be provided.

These rights must be presented to the suspect due to the fact that the United States Supreme Court has held that being interrogated while in custody is an inherently coercive situation. *Miranda v. Arizona*, 384 U.S. 436 (1966).

Note: A statement by a suspect who is illegally in custody will not be admissible, even if the suspect has been read his or her rights. *Watson v. Commonwealth*, 454 S.E.2d 358 (Va. Ct. App. 1995).

B. Custody and Interrogation

Note that a suspect is only accorded these protections during a custodial interrogation. Both elements (i.e., custody and interrogation) must be present before the requirement that the warnings be given arises. *Burket v. Commonwealth*, 450 S.E.2d 124 (Va. 1994), cert. denied, 514 U.S. 1053 (1995); *Timbers v. Commonwealth*, 503 S.E.2d 233 (Va. Ct. App. 1998).

Interrogation is referred to as questioning initiated by law enforcement officers – either direct questioning or its functional equivalent. The term interrogation refers not only to express questioning, but also to any words or actions on the part of the police (other than those normally attendant to arrest and custody, e.g., "routine booking questions") that the police should reasonably expect to elicit an incriminating response. *Gates v. Commonwealth*, 516 S.E.2d 731 (Va. Ct. App. 1999).

In *Gates*, supra, defendant, who was already in custody on unrelated charges, was brought to an interview room, where officers served him with an arrest warrant, told him he was being charged with murder, and began to read the warrant to him. Defendant interrupted, saying "look, if y'all want to know the truth, I am going to tell you the truth." He then admitted to having been at the murder scene. The reading of the warrant to defendant was a routine part of the booking process, and should not have been expected to elicit an incriminating response. Therefore, there was no interrogation, and defendant's statement was admissible.

Compare with *Giles v. Commonwealth*, 507 S.E.2d 102 (Va. Ct. App. 1998). Defendant invoked his right to counsel, so the questioning investigator left him alone. Later, another officer approached defendant, and asked "Did you speak with the investigator?" This was not a coercive question intended to elicit an incriminating statement, but merely a routine communication between police and the accused. The officer was merely inquiring about the status of the investigation. Therefore, the question did not constitute interrogation.

Contrast with *Timbers v. Commonwealth*, 503 S.E.2d 233 (Va. Ct. App. 1998). After her arrest, defendant had signed her fingerprint card and Central Criminal Records Exchange form "Gwendolyn Timbers." Later that evening, a woman came into the police station with an item of clothing she said was for "Kelly Timbers." His suspicions raised, officer went to the holding cell and called out, "Kelly Timbers?" Defendant looked over at him. Officer then said that if defendant's name was really "Kelly" then "she needed to come forward with that information." Even though officer did not directly ask defendant if she lied about her name, his statement nevertheless constituted interrogation, because a reasonable observer would find that it was designed to elicit an incriminating response.

Note that spontaneous, volunteered statements are not subject to the *Miranda* requirement. *Blain v. Commonwealth*, 371 S.E.2d 838 (Va. Ct. App. 1988).

The warnings must be read to suspects in custody. If statements are made in a non-custodial setting, no warnings are required. Hence a defendant cannot later attempt to bar the use of his statements at trial on the ground that they were elicited without the benefit of the *Miranda* warnings. Custody is a legal status during which the suspect has been formally arrested or is deprived of his or her freedom of action in any significant way, i.e. to a degree normally associated with formal arrest. *U.S. v. Sullivan*, 138 F.3d 126 (4th Cir. 1998); *Harris v. Commonwealth*, 500 S.E.2d 257 (Va. Ct. App. 1998). Whether or not a suspect is in custody for purposes of *Miranda* warnings is an objective determination, based on all of the components of the setting, and determined on the basis of how a reasonable person in the suspect's situation would understand the circumstances. *Bynum v. Commonwealth*, 506 S.E.2d 30 (Va. Ct. App. 1998). A custodial setting is not determined with reference to a suspect's belief that he is in police custody, or by a subjective belief on the part of the interrogating officers that they have placed the suspect in custody, unless that fact has been communicated to the suspect. *Bynum*, supra.

Factors a court will weigh in deciding whether a suspect was in custody include: (i) the manner in which the suspect was summoned by police; (ii) whether the surroundings were familiar or neutral to the suspect; (iii) the number of officers present; (iv) the degree of physical restraint imposed on the suspect (e.g. handcuffs); (v) the duration and character of the interrogation; (vi) the extent to which the officers' beliefs regarding the suspect's potential culpability were manifested to the suspect. *Harris v. State*, supra.

See, e.g., *Ford v. Commonwealth*, 503 S.E.2d 803 (Va. Ct. App. 1998). A detective saw defendant stash a bag in the woods outside a mall; when the detective checked the bag, he learned it contained clothing with the store tags still attached, but no receipt or sales slip. Later, when the defendant left the mall, officers detained him for questioning. Although four officers approached defendant, he was with two other people, and only one detective actually questioned him; defendant was at no point surrounded by officers. This encounter took place in a public place in the middle of the afternoon, and lasted less than a minute. Defendant was not handcuffed or searched. Defendant was never told that he was suspected of grand larceny; the detective only asked for his identification and whether he had been in the store from which the abandoned merchandise had been taken. Defendant was not in custody, so *Miranda* warnings were not required.

Note: A suspect not under formal arrest may nonetheless be in custody for *Miranda* purposes.

Similar to an arrest situation, in determining whether an individual was in custody for *Miranda* purposes, courts will not try to determine the subjective intent of the officers involved. Whether a person is in custody for *Miranda* purposes depends on whether the person is physically denied his freedom of action in any significant way or is placed in a situation in which he reasonably believes that his freedom of action or movement is restricted. Thus, police need not give *Miranda* warnings to an individual who is not restrained in any way and freely accompanies them to the police station.

See, e.g., *Bottenfield v. Commonwealth*, 487 S.E.2d 883 (Va. Ct. App. 1997). A sergeant with the Augusta County Sheriff's Department asked defendant to come down to the Department building to discuss allegations of sexual abuse which had been made against him. Defendant agreed, and came in the next day for a 35 minute interview. Defendant drove himself to the Sheriff's Department in his own vehicle. Once there, he was never told that he was under arrest or that he was going to be charged. The door to the sergeant's office remained open throughout the interview. The Court concluded that defendant was not in custody, so that his un*Mirandized* statements were admissible.

Compare with *Bynum v. Commonwealth*, supra. Defendant shot his wife while she was sitting in his truck in the driveway of their Portsmouth home; the wound was non-fatal, and the victim left the scene. (Apparently, defendant did not even realize he had hit her). The next morning, police asked defendant to come to the station for questioning, and he agreed. He was given the option of driving himself, but chose to receive a ride from one of the officers. At the station, defendant was continually reassured that he was not under arrest and was free to leave at any time. He was never handcuffed during the interview, and when it ended, he was given a ride home. Even though defendant was the only suspect police had, he was not in custody during this interview, so *Miranda* warnings were not required.

Merely informing an individual of his or her *Miranda* rights does not necessarily create an in-custody situation.

A motorist stopped for an ordinary traffic violation is not in custody for *Miranda* purposes. *Pennsylvania v. Bruder*, 488 U.S. 9 (1988). However, a motorist who is subsequently arrested, or otherwise placed in- custody, must be given *Miranda* warnings prior to any questioning. Otherwise, any statements by the defendant may be inadmissible. *Berkemer v. McCarty*, 468 U.S. 420 (1984).

C. Invocation of Rights

After a suspect has been informed of his or her rights, the police may wish to ask the suspect questions. It is at this point that suspects must invoke their right to remain silent and/or their right to have counsel present. A suspect that does not invoke either right will be subject to further questioning. Note that if the suspect gives a response to questioning that is ambiguous but may be construed as invoking the right to counsel, the officers conducting the questioning are not required to clarify the response, and may continue questioning. Officers must stop all questioning only if there is an unambiguous, unequivocal request for counsel. *Davis v. U.S.*, 512 U.S. 452 (1994) ("Maybe I should talk to a lawyer" was not an unequivocal request for counsel, so continued questioning by police was upheld).

Compare with *Midkiff v. Commonwealth*, 462 S.E.2d 112 (Va. 1995) ("I'm scared to say anything without talking to a lawyer" merely showed a reservation on defendant's part about continuing with the interrogation, and was not an invocation of his right to an attorney); *Mueller v. Commonwealth*, 422 S.E.2d 380 (Va. 1992) ("Do you think I need an attorney here?" too ambiguous a statement to invoke the right to counsel).

However, in *McDaniel v. Commonwealth*, 518 S.E.2d 851 (Va. Ct. App. 1999), defendant's statement "I think I would rather have an attorney speak for me" was a clear, unambiguous invocation of the right to counsel, so that all police questioning should have ceased.

Similarly, any invocation of the right to remain silent must also be clear and unequivocal. *Green v. Commonwealth*, 500 S.E.2d 835 (Va. Ct. App. 1998) (when defendant stated that he "didn't have anything more to say," there was no invocation of the right to remain silent, so continued questioning by police was proper). Compare with *Mitchell v. Commonwealth*, 518 S.E.2d 330 (Va. Ct. App. 1999) (after being *Mirandized*, defendant responded, "I ain't got shit to say to y'all," but then began talking about the crime anyway; his statement was too ambiguous to serve as an invocation, especially when he immediately began to talk anyway).

1. Right To Remain Silent. When a suspect informs the police that he or she wishes not to speak then the police must "scrupulously honor" the suspect's right to remain silent. At this point all questioning must cease and the police are not allowed to say or do anything that is intended to elicit a response from the suspect or that is likely to elicit a response from the suspect. *Giles v. Commonwealth*, 507 S.E.2d 102 (Va. Ct. App. 1998). If they do elicit a response, then such response will be inadmissible.

The police may start questioning again at a later time, so long as the suspect's first invocation of the right to remain silent was "scrupulously honored". Factors a court will consider in making this determination include: (i) whether, before questioning initially began, the suspect was "carefully advised" of the right to remain silent; (ii) whether questioning ceased immediately upon the suspect's invocation of the right, and no attempt was made by police to persuade the suspect to reconsider; (iii) whether a "significant period of time" has passed; (iv) whether fresh *Miranda* warnings have been given; (v) whether the new questioning concerns a different subject matter. *Weeks v. Commonwealth*, 450 S.E.2d 379 (Va. 1994), cert. denied, 516 U.S. 829 (1995). Of course, the suspect may once again refuse to speak.

In *Weeks*, supra, defendant was initially advised of his right to silence, and police immediately ceased questioning when he invoked this right. Ten hours later, officers re-approached defendant, and although they did not re-read him the *Miranda* rights, they asked if he remembered them from "earlier today" and he said that he did. Even though defendant was questioned regarding the same crime as before, the officers had uncovered new facts, so they were not repeating the same questions from earlier in the day. This time around, defendant answered the questions freely and without hesitation. The Court concluded that this reinitiation of questioning was proper, and, therefore, defendant's statements were admissible.

2. Right to Counsel. When a suspect invokes his or her right to counsel all questioning must cease until the suspect meets with an attorney. The only way that the police may then speak to the suspect without an attorney is if the suspect initiates the conversation. *Arizona v. Edwards*, 451 U.S. 477 (1981). However, for any statement to be admissible, the police will still have to show that the suspect waived his or her rights. *Arizona v. Edwards*, supra. Also, once a suspect has asked to speak to an attorney, the police may not initiate any questioning unless an attorney representing the suspect is present. *Minnick v. Mississippi*, 498 U.S. 146 (1990). This is true whether the questioning is for the original offense or a different offense. *Arizona v. Roberson*, 486 U.S. 675 (1988).

3. Waiver. The U.S. Supreme Court in *North Carolina v. Butler*, 441 U.S. 369 (1979), held that courts may find a valid waiver even if the defendant only implicitly waives his or her *Miranda* rights.

A suspect may waive his or her Fifth Amendment rights at any time. However, the prosecution will be asked to show that any such waiver was not only knowing and voluntary, but that the suspect understood the right that he or she was waiving. *Cherrix v. Commonwealth*, 513 S.E.2d 642 (Va. 1999). The Commonwealth bears the burden of proving the voluntariness of a statement by a preponderance of the evidence. *Bottenfield v. Commonwealth*, 487 S.E.2d 883 (Va. Ct. App. 1997). In checking to see that a waiver was legally sufficient, the courts will look to both the suspect's background (e.g. age, intelligence, prior experience with the criminal justice system), as well as the circumstances surrounding the interview. See *Gwaltney v. Commonwealth*, 452 S.E.2d 687 (Va. Ct. App. 1995). The state has the burden of showing by a preponderance of the evidence that the consent was voluntary. Suspects who are in pain, intoxicated or on drugs may be more susceptible to police coercion, and therefore be less able to give a voluntary waiver. *Commonwealth v. Peterson*, 424 S.E.2d 722 (Va. Ct. App. 1992). A suspect may invoke or re-invoke either of these rights at any time and the police must act accordingly. Waivers obtained

 Zv

by improper means, such as suggesting that the suspect may receive some specific benefit by talking, are invalid.

Once a custodial suspect has been given the warnings, he or she can, of course, waive his or her right to be silent or to counsel, and decide to talk to the police. If the suspect voluntarily waives these rights, police may continue to question until the suspect requests an attorney, or effectively renounces his or her waiver, and relates that he or she wishes to remain silent. Waivers of *Miranda* rights must not only be voluntary, but must also constitute a knowing and intelligent relinquishment of a known right. When addressing waiver issues, and the voluntariness of a confession, a court will examine the particular facts and circumstances of each case, including the background, experience, and conduct of the accused. Voluntariness and coercion are different sides of the same coin. If a confession or statement has been coerced, or taken from a custodial suspect in the absence of *Miranda* warnings, there was no waiver. The statement is involuntary, and therefore not the product of a free relinquishment of a known right, hence not be allowed in evidence at a trial. Conversely, if a confession or statement is voluntary, the suspect has either impliedly or expressly waived his rights, and the statement or confession has not been coerced, and it, and any other incriminating evidence deriving from it, is admissible.

One way in which a defendant may attempt to show his statement was involuntary is to show that actual physical or psychological force was used on him to coerce the confession (e.g., actual or threatened bodily harm, or threats of adverse consequences).

But see *U.S. v. Braxton*, 112 F.3d 777 (4th Cir.), cert. denied, 118 S. Ct. 192 (1997) (officer's statement "you're not coming clean...you can do five years because you're not coming clean" did not render defendant's subsequent statement involuntary, because it was a truthful statement regarding the penalty for giving a false statement to law enforcement).

A defendant may also attempt to show that the atmosphere surrounding the interrogation was so inherently coercive that his will was overborne, and the statement or confession was given involuntarily (e.g., suspect was denied sleep, food and drink, use of restroom facilities, handcuffed, or left alone for extended periods).

Another way a defendant may demonstrate involuntariness is to show that a promise of leniency was made, and in return for his cooperation, told that his punishment will be less severe. To prevail, the defendant must show, not just that such a promise was made, but that he relied on it to such an extent that his will was overborne, and his statement was therefore involuntary. The promise must cause the statement. Mere exhortations to tell the truth or promises to tell the prosecution of any cooperation, however, will not render a subsequent statement involuntary.

Note: The use of a ruse or deliberate falsehood by police will not necessarily render a subsequent statement involuntary. *Arthur v. Commonwealth*, 480 S.E.2d 749 (Va. Ct. App. 1997). In *Arthur*, police prepared a "dummy" report indicating that defendant's fingerprints had been found at a murder scene (even though no fingerprints had in fact been recovered), then confronted defendant with it at an interview. The Court found that this false report was not enough to overcome defendant's will or critically impair his capacity for self-determination, and his subsequent confession was therefore held to be voluntary.

D. Actions Not Protected by the Fifth Amendment

The Fifth Amendment only provides protection for suspects from being forced to give testimony that is self-incriminating. Suspects may still be forced to provide evidence that is not testimonial in nature. Thus suspects may be forced to provide answers to booking questions, such as name, address, and telephone number. Suspects may also be forced to allow the taking of physical evidence such as voice exemplars, handwriting samples, blood samples, hair samples, or evidence of physical characteristics. *Schmerber v. California*, 384 U.S. 757 (1966). Courts have also allowed videotaped dexterity tests, as well as other conduct on videotape as long as it is not testimonial evidence.

Note that although the Fifth Amendment allows the taking of such evidence, the Fourth Amendment and its protections (i.e. the warrant requirement) may still be implicated. See *Hassell v. City of Chesapeake*, 64 F. Supp.2d 573 (E.D. Va. 1999) (urinalysis test and blood test are both "searches" within the meaning of the Fourth Amendment); *Tipton v. State*, 444 S.E.2d 1 (Va. Ct. App. 1994) (blood test constitutes a "search" under the Fourth Amendment).

E. Public Safety Exception

The U.S. Supreme Court has held that, in certain instances, statements made by a custodial suspect, in response to questions asked by law enforcement may be admissible even if no *Miranda* warnings were given prior to the statement. *New York v. Quarles*, 467 U.S. 649 (1984). The Court reasoned that "police officers can and will distinguish almost instinctively between questions necessary to secure their own safety or the safety of the public and questions designed solely to elicit testimonial evidence from a suspect." If the question is motivated primarily out of concern for the officer's safety, or that of the public at large, rather than a deliberate attempt to obtain an incriminating statement, there is no reason to bar the statement's subsequent use against its maker. In *Quarles*, the Court held an officer was not required to give warning to a suspect before asking – "Where's the gun?" – when the officer had a reasonable fear for the safety of bystanders. As a result the suspect's reply – "It's over there." – to the question was admissible at trial, even though it was incriminating, and rendered without the benefit of the *Miranda* warnings.

IX. SIXTH AMENDMENT RIGHT TO COUNSEL

The Sixth Amendment right to counsel differs from the Fifth Amendment right to counsel in two principal ways. First, the right attaches when the criminal justice process has reached a critical stage, at the initiation of the prosecution, rather than during a custodial interrogation. A prosecution is initiated, for example, when 1) formal charges are filed, 2) a preliminary hearing is held, 3) an indictment or information is filed, or 4) an arraignment is held. So, for example, there is a right to have counsel present during a post arraignment line-up. But, the stage of the proceeding and the nature of the confrontation must be "trial-like" for the right to be implicated (e.g., there is no Sixth Amendment right to counsel when police bring in a witness to examine a photo spread, because the accused is not being confronted). Secondly, the right is offense specific. Once the right has attached for a given charge, the suspect cannot be questioned about that charge without counsel present. He can, however, be questioned regarding unrelated offenses for which the Sixth Amendment right has not yet attached, without violating that provision. *McNeil v. Wisconsin*, 501 U.S. 171 (1991). On the other hand, the *Miranda* Fifth Amendment right to counsel is not offense specific. If a suspect has invoked his Fifth Amendment right to have counsel present during a custodial interrogation, he cannot be questioned, regarding any offense, without counsel present. Of course, the suspect may waive his Sixth Amendment right to counsel, so long as it is knowing, intelligent and voluntary. This right to counsel is safeguarded by the exclusionary rule as well. If a statement is obtained in violation of the Sixth Amendment, it, and any other evidence that may come to light as a result of the statement, will be suppressed.

X. SUSPECT IDENTIFICATION

Frequently, the state will attempt to elicit at trial, identification testimony from a witness to a crime, who has made an out of court identification of the defendant. Typically, the testimony culminates in the witness pointing to the defendant in court and identifying him or her as the perpetrator. The defendant may challenge the admission of this testimony, claiming that the in-court identification was in fact the result of a suggestive, prior, out of court identification, orchestrated by law enforcement. The Fourteenth Amendment provides that no person shall lose his life, liberty or property without due process of law. The "due process" clause protects a suspect from police identification procedures that are so impermissibly suggestive as to create a very significant likelihood of irreparable misidentification. *Bryant v. Commonwealth*, 393 S.E.2d 216 (Va. Ct. App. 1990).

A suspect can challenge an identification by raising the issue of impermissible suggestiveness. If the requisite showing is made, a hearing will be held, after which the judge will make a ruling regarding the admissibility of testimony concerning the identification. To determine which practices are so unfairly suggestive so as to deprive a suspect of Due Process, a court looks to the totality of the circumstances surrounding the out-of-court identification.

Even if an identification procedure is found to be unnecessarily suggestive, the resulting identification may still be admissible, if the reliability of the witness who made it can be independently established. Factors a court will consider in determining reliability include: (i) the opportunity of the witness to view the defendant during the crime; (ii) the level of attention the witness was paying to the defendant; (iii) the accuracy of descriptions of the defendant made by the witness prior to the suggestive procedure; (iv) the witness' level of certainty in his or her identification; (v) the time between the crime and confrontation. *U.S. v. Johnson*, 113 F.3d 435 (4th Cir. 1997), cert. denied, 118 S. Ct. 257 (1998); *Charity v. Commonwealth*, 482 S.E.2d 59 (Va. Ct. App. 1997).

See, e.g., *Bryant v. State*, supra. The eight-year-old victim fell asleep watching television, then awoke to find herself being carried off out of her apartment by defendant. Once outside the apartment building, she managed to escape and sought help. Later that night, after defendant was arrested, police showed the victim three photographs, all of which depicted defendant, and told her that the photos were of a man who had just been arrested while prowling around her building; the victim then identified defendant as her abductor. The Court found that this "array" was impermissibly suggestive. Nevertheless, the Court concluded that the victim's identification of defendant was still reliable. The lighting in the apartment was adequate to see defendant's face, and, obviously, her attention "was riveted...on the person who was carrying her in his arms." The victim drew a picture of her abductor, and her description was remarkably accurate – she described defendant's "smooth" brown hair, his blue jacket and jeans, and mustache, and noted that he used to work at the Farm Fresh store across the street from her apartment building. In fact, this description was accurate enough that officers relied on it in arresting defendant. The victim immediately identified defendant's photo as both the man who kidnapped her and the man who used to work in the Farm Fresh store; the fact that she was already familiar with defendant before the crime added to the reliability of her identification. Finally, the victim made her identification just two hours after the crime, so the events were fresh in her memory.

XI. DIPLOMATIC IMMUNITY

The following information is provided for the guidance of the law enforcement officer. Failure of the authorities of the United States to fully respect the privileges of foreign diplomatic and consular personnel may complicate diplomatic relations between the United States and the other State concerned. It also may lead to harsher treatment of U.S. personnel abroad, since the principle of reciprocity is integral to diplomatic and consular relations.

Diplomatic immunity does not exempt diplomatic officers from the obligation of conforming with national and local laws and regulations. Diplomatic immunity is not intended to serve as a license for such persons to flout the law and purposely avoid liability for their actions. The purpose of these privileges and immunities is not to benefit individuals but to ensure the efficient and effective performance of their official missions. This is a crucial point for law enforcement officers to understand in their dealings with foreign diplomatic and consular personnel. While police officers are obliged under international customary and treaty law to recognize the immunity of the envoy, they must not ignore or condone the commission of crimes. The proper performance of police procedures in such cases is often essential in order for the United States to formulate appropriate measures through diplomatic channels to deal with such offenders.

A. Categories of Persons Entitled to Privileges and Immunities

1. Staffs of Diplomatic Missions. The categories of diplomatic mission personnel are defined primarily with reference to the functions performed.

"Diplomatic agent" is the term assigned to ambassadors and other diplomatic officers who generally have the function of dealing directly with the host country officials. This category enjoys the highest degree of immunity.

The next category is the "members of the administrative and technical staff" of the mission, which includes those persons who perform sophisticated and often sensitive duties but serve primarily in support of the activities of diplomatic agents. This category includes secretaries, certain clerical personnel, office managers and certain professional security personnel. Members of the administrative and technical staff also enjoy a high level of privileges and immunities but one which in some respects is less than diplomatic agents.

The last category is "members of the service staff" of the diplomatic mission who perform more menial tasks such as driving, cleaning, and building and grounds maintenance. These persons are afforded significantly less in the way of privileges and immunities.

It should be noted that the private servants of diplomatic personnel enjoy no jurisdictional immunity or inviolability in the United States.

Police officers usually do not have to deal with the distinctions given below. The U.S. Department of State will normally have issued identity documents. If no identity documents are available, telephone identification can be made as explained below.

a. Diplomatic Agents. Diplomatic agents enjoy the highest degree of privileges and immunities. They enjoy complete personal inviolability, which means that they may not be arrested or detained; they are owed a special measure of respect and protection; and neither their property nor residences may be entered or searched. Diplomatic agents also enjoy complete immunity from the criminal jurisdiction of the host State and thus cannot be prosecuted no matter how serious the offense. (Although it is not ordinarily of concern to police authorities, they also have immunity from civil suit except (i) in connection with real property transactions not conducted on behalf of the mission; (ii) in connection with any role they may play as executor for or as an heir to an estate being distributed in the host country; (iii) in connection with the performance of professional or commercial activities outside the scope of their official duties; or (iv) in respect of counter- claims in connection with activities outside the scope of their official duties when they have been the initiating party in a law suit.)

Diplomatic agents enjoy complete immunity from the obligation to provide evidence as witnesses and cannot be required to testify. This immunity is absolute and even extends to cases when they themselves have been the victim of a crime.

Family members forming part of the household of diplomatic agents enjoy precisely the same privileges and immunities as do the sponsoring diplomatic agents. The U.S. Department of State has held that family members enjoying this absolute immunity consist of the spouse, children under the age of 21, and children under the age of 23 who are full-time students at an institution of higher learning. Other persons than the above may be considered family members for the purpose of obtaining this absolute immunity if agreed to by the U.S. Department of State in extraordinary circumstances.

b. Members of Administrative and Technical Staff. Members of the administrative and technical staff of a diplomatic mission perform tasks critical to the inner workings of the embassy. Accordingly, they enjoy privileges and immunities identical to those of diplomatic agents regarding personal inviolability, immunity from criminal (and sometimes civil) jurisdiction, and immunity from the obligation to provide evidence as witnesses. Immunity from civil jurisdiction for members of the administrative and technical staff exists only for acts performed in connection with the performance of their official duties. This type of immunity is known as "official acts" or "functional" immunity. Like the family members of diplomatic agents, the recognized family members of administrative and technical staff enjoy the same privileges and immunities from the host country's criminal jurisdiction as their sponsors. Because these family members have no official duties to perform, they enjoy no immunity from civil jurisdiction.

c. Members of Service Staff. Members of the service staff of diplomatic missions perform more menial support tasks for the missions and are therefore accorded much less in the way of privileges and immunities than are those in the other categories. Service staff members have only official acts immunity in connection with all aspects of the host State jurisdiction, and they enjoy no personal inviolability or immunity from the obligation to provide evidence as witnesses. The families of service staff members enjoy no privileges or immunities.

d. Nationals or Permanent Residents of the United States. The general rules regarding immunity, as set forth above, assume that the staff members of a diplomatic mission are nationals of the sending country or some third country. Traditionally, countries are unwilling to surrender any jurisdiction over their own nationals. The United States, as a matter of policy, does not normally accept the accreditation of its own nationals or permanent residents as diplomatic agents. If it did so, such diplomatic agents would enjoy inviolability and jurisdictional immunity only in connection with the performance of official acts. The family members of diplomatic agents enjoy no privileges or immunities if they are "nationals" of the United States. If members of the administrative and technical staff (including their families) and members of the service staff are U.S. nationals or "permanent residents" of the United States, they enjoy no privileges or immunities.

e. Special Bilateral Agreements. There are some foreign countries in respect of which the categories set forth above are not applicable. These are countries with which the United States has concluded bilateral agreements which grant to all members of the staff of their respective embassies (provided that they are nationals of the sending country) the privileges and immunities to which only diplomatic agents are normally entitled. Although identity documents will normally clarify this situation, police officers should be aware of this distinction because they may have to confront situations where a chauffeur or mechanic from the embassy of one of these countries asserts a right to full diplomatic privileges and immunities.

f. Waiver. The privileges and immunities held by staffs of diplomatic missions are extended from one country to another in order to permit their respective representatives to effectively perform their duties. It may be said that the sending countries "own" these privileges and immunities. Although the individual enjoying such immunities may not effectively waive them, the sending State can, and occasionally does so. Police authorities should never address the commission of a serious crime by a person enjoying full criminal immunity with the belief that there is no possibility that a prosecution could result. The seeking of waiver of immunity is handled entirely via diplomatic channels. Effective and informed police work remains the foundation of a successful prosecution should the Department of State succeed in obtaining a waiver of immunity in a particular case.

2. Members of Consular Posts (Normal and Special Bilateral). Consulates and their foreign personnel are often erroneously considered to be identical to foreign embassies and their staffs in the popular view of privileges and immunities. Traditionally, however, the function of consular posts is fundamentally different from that of the diplomatic missions. Consulates do not have the principal role of providing communication between the two countries but rather perform a variety of functions of principal interest to their respective sending countries (e.g., issuance of travel documents, attending to the difficulties of their own countrymen who are present in the host country, and generally promoting the commerce of the sending country). Countries have long recognized the importance of consular functions to their overall relations but have been willing to grant only a significantly lower measure of privileges and immunities to the persons assigned to their countries at consular posts.

a. Consular Officers. Consular officers, generally speaking, are those members of consular posts who are recognized by both the sending and the host country as fully authorized to perform the broad array of formal consular functions. They have only official acts or functional immunity in respect of both criminal and civil matters (no civil immunity under any circumstances for actions arising from personal contracts or accidents caused by vehicles, vessels or aircraft which they are operating), and their personal inviolability is quite limited. Consular officers may be arrested pending trial provided that the underlying offense is a felony and that the arrest is made pursuant to a decision by a competent judicial authority (e.g., a warrant issued by an appropriate court). Consular officers enjoy complete immunity from the obligation to provide evidence as witnesses in connection with matters involving their official duties, to produce official documents or to provide expert witness testimony on the laws of the sending country. Without a special bilateral agreement to the contrary, the family members of consular officers enjoy no personal inviolability and no jurisdictional immunity of any kind.

The concept of "official acts" immunity pertains in numerous different circumstances. It is very important that law enforcement officers understand the nature of this protection. No law enforcement (or State Department) officer is expected or authorized to determine whether a given set of circumstances constitutes an "official act". This is an issue which may only be resolved, as a matter of law, by the host country court with subject matter jurisdiction over the alleged crime. Thus a person enjoying official acts immunity from criminal jurisdiction may always be prosecuted if the responsible host government authorities believe that the criminal act is outside the scope of the individual's official duties, and may in this connection always be required to appear in court (in person or through counsel). At this point, however, such person may assert as an affirmative defense, that the actions complained of, arose in connection with the performance of official acts. If, upon examination of the circumstances complained of, the court agrees, then the court is without jurisdiction to proceed and the case must be dismissed. Although only a court may finally rule in such cases, it is reasonable for law enforcement authorities to make decisions on whether or not to proceed with a case based on their own assessment of the court's likely decision on a particular fact situation.

b. Consular Employees. Consular employees perform the administrative and technical services for the consular post. They have no personal immunity, only official acts immunity. They enjoy immunity from the obligation to provide evidence as witnesses only in respect of official acts. Their family members enjoy no personal inviolability or jurisdictional immunities of any kind.

c. Consular Service Staff. Consular service staff do not enjoy personal inviolability or jurisdictional immunity of any kind. They do have immunity from the obligation to provide evidence as witnesses in respect of official acts. Their family members enjoy no personal immunity or jurisdictional immunity of any kind.

d. Nationals or Permanent Residents of the United States. As is the case with staff of diplomatic missions, members of consular posts have reduced privileges and immunities if they are U.S. nationals or permanent residents. In particular, consular officers who are U.S. nationals or permanent residents have personal inviolability only in respect of the performance of official acts; jurisdictional immunity only in connection with official acts; and immunity from the obligation to provide evidence as witnesses only in respect of official acts. Consular employees and consular service staff who are U.S. nationals or permanent residents enjoy no personal inviolability or jurisdictional immunity in the United States.

e. Honorary Consuls. Consular officers who are accredited as full- time practitioners of consular functions are referred to as "career" consular officers. These officers are normally nationals of the sending country who are sent to the United States to perform these functions for a specific period and then are transferred to a further assignment. Career consular officers are in fact prohibited by international law from engaging in professional or commercial activities outside the scope of their official consular functions.

Another category is that of "honorary" consular officers. These are generally part-time employees of the sending country who provide a degree of consular representation in places not covered by career consular officers. The privileges and immunities of honorary consular officers approximate those of career consular officers with limitations in certain respects. It is U.S. policy to recognize as honorary consular officers only those who are U.S. nationals or permanent residents. Accordingly, honorary consular officers in the United States have personal inviolability only in connection with official acts (arrest of honorary consuls is not limited only to felonies and does not require a warrant, as is the case with career consular officers), and enjoy only the more restricted form of official acts immunity accorded U.S. nationals or permanent residents, and immunity from the obligation to provide evidence as witnesses only in respect of official acts. Their family members enjoy no personal inviolability and no jurisdictional immunity of any kind.

3. International Organization Personnel and National Missions to Such Organizations. International organizations, such as the United Nations, are a relatively modern development. The privileges and immunities of the personnel of such organizations and the personnel of national missions to such organizations have a different basis than that of diplomatic and consular representatives. In the case of international organizations, the nations concerned have agreed that the important purposes of such organizations may only be accomplished if a certain measure of privileges and immunities are afforded to their participants. The nations concerned have concluded treaties embodying such grants of privileges and immunities and have also (e.g., in the case of the United States) enacted domestic legislation granting certain minimal privileges and immunities to certain categories of persons not covered by the treaties. In determining the degree of inviolability or immunity, law enforcement officers will be governed primarily by the identity documents which have been issued to such persons.

a. Personnel of International Organizations. International organizations which have headquarters or other offices in the United States are staffed with the number of administrative and executive employees necessary to carry out their functions.

The vast majority of these employees enjoy only official acts immunity as provided for by U.S. domestic legislation (the International Organizations Immunities Act, 22 U.S.C. 288) and no personal inviolability. In certain cases, however, the most senior executives of such organizations have been accorded privileges and immunities equal to those afforded diplomatic agents. This is the case for the Secretary General and all assistant secretaries- general of the United Nations.

b. Personnel of National Missions to International Organizations. The United Nations and the Organization of American States are headquartered in the United States. Most of their member States maintain permanent missions in the United States. The persons staffing these missions are accredited to the international organization concerned (not to the United States). Their privileges and immunities are nonetheless often defined by reference to the status of diplomatic personnel who are accredited to the United States.

As is the case with diplomatic missions, the assignment of privileges and immunities is differentiated generally on the basis of the functions performed. Pursuant to international law, the most senior representatives in these missions to international organizations have privileges and immunities equivalent to those afforded diplomatic agents. The remainder of the staffs of these missions have only official acts immunity pursuant to the International Organizations Immunities Act and no personal inviolability.

Persons visiting in the United States on short-term official duty with diplomatic missions are ordinarily not recognized as enjoying any privileges and immunities (law enforcement authorities should nonetheless always seek prompt verification from the Department of State in particular cases involving such individuals). In the case of the United Nations, however, a different legal situation exists. Short-term official visitors from other States to the United Nations or to international conferences convened by the United Nations may enjoy full diplomatic immunity equivalent to that afforded diplomatic agents. Owing to the temporary nature of their visit, such officials will normally not have the usual official identity documents recognizable in the United States. Law enforcement officials (particularly in New York) should therefore be sensitive to the existence of this situation and always coordinate with the U.S. authorities indicated below if confronted with an apparent offender appearing to fall into this category.

B. Identification of Persons Entitled to Privileges and Immunities in the United States

1. Foreign Diplomatic Passports and U.S. "Diplomatic" Visas: Not Conclusive. Most foreigners in the United States who enjoy any degree of privileges and immunities possess a diplomatic passport issued by their country with a so-called "diplomatic" ("A" or "G") visa entered by U.S. authorities.* However, foreign diplomatic passports (even those which contain U.S. diplomatic visas) are not authoritative indications that their bearers enjoy any degree of privileges or immunities in the United States. This is the case because both foreign diplomatic passports and U.S. diplomatic-type visas are issued to a broad range of persons, including those who have no association with the categories of persons described and who therefore enjoy no privileges and immunities in the United States.

Law enforcement officials should bear in mind, however, that the possession of these documents is an indication that the bearer might be entitled to privileges and immunities in the United States. For example, temporary duty visitors to the United Nations might have only such documents and might nonetheless be entitled to immunity in the United States. A similar situation could arise in connection with the foreign officer who has just joined a diplomatic mission or consular post and has not yet received the appropriate U.S. identity documents. In cases of doubt, police officers should always coordinate with U.S. authorities. (See Telephonic Information/Verification below.)

**All foreign personnel assigned to official duty at bilateral diplomatic or consular missions in the U.S. would have A-category visas. G-category visas are the equivalent, and are issued to foreigners assigned to duty at an international organization in the U.S. or at a foreign country's mission to such organization.*

2. Tax Exemption Cards: Not Conclusive. Under international law, most members of diplomatic missions and consular posts and certain people associated with international organizations would normally be entitled to exemption from sales taxation in the United States. However, significant numbers of these individuals do not enjoy this privilege owing to considerations based on reciprocity. The Department of State issues tax exemption cards to all those entitled to such exemptions, but this does not cover all persons in the United States who are entitled to privileges and immunities, nor do such tax cards give a definitive indication of the degree of immunity to which the bearer is entitled. Accordingly, tax exemption cards should not be relied upon for immunity purposes and should be considered only as an indication that the bearer may be entitled to some degree of immunity.

3. Automobile Registration, License Plates, Drivers Licenses: Not Conclusive. The Department of State has recently taken over the registration of automobiles of persons entitled to privileges and immunities in the United States; the issuance of distinctive license plates for such vehicles; and the issuance of operator's permits for such persons to drive in the United States. As is the case with tax exemption cards, the purpose of these Federal registration documents and driver's licenses is not definitively to reflect the degree of privileges and immunities of the bearer. They should be relied upon only as an indication that the bearer is very likely entitled to at least some degree of immunity.

Vehicle license plates issued by the Department of State, in particular, must be properly understood by police authorities in order to avoid confusion. These plates are issued to persons entitled to privileges and immunities in the United States. The plates are coded to correspond generally with the degree of immunity to which the owner or principal operator is entitled (e.g., the vehicle(s) of a diplomatic agent would have a "D" prefix; that of a member of the administrative and technical staff of a diplomatic mission would have an "S" prefix; and vehicles of consular personnel have a "C" prefix). These plates may be taken as a preliminary indication that the person operating the vehicle probably enjoys the degree of immunity indicated by the license code. It is ultimately only by determining the personal identity of the operator that his or her immunity may be established. Police officers should bear in mind that a car with "C" plates may in fact on occasion be operated by an ambassador (diplomatic agent) who is visiting a consulate. On the other hand, a diplomatic agent may not always be driving a vehicle with any kind of Federal plates; a rented or borrowed car may be in use at a particular time. The distinctive license plates are designed to provide helpful assistance in identifying vehicles which may be operated by persons enjoying diplomatic or consular immunity. However, they are not a definitive indication that such a person is operating the vehicle at any particular time.

Vehicle registration cards are issued by the Department of State to accompany diplomatic license plates. The card provides the vehicle description, name and address of the registered owner, and the license plate number assigned to the vehicle. Verification of the registered owner, vehicle or license plate can be made through standard access of "NLETS." Neither the registration cards nor the drivers licenses issued by the Department of State should be relied upon as conclusive indications of the status or immunity of the bearer.

4. Formal Identity Documents Issued by the Department of State. All of the forms of identity mentioned above provide an indication of possible immunity of a person possessing them. However, the only authoritative identity document is the identity card issued by the Department of State, Protocol Office.

Beginning in 1987, a new series of identification cards was issued to all diplomatic and consular personnel and to persons associated with international organizations who are entitled to privileges and immunities. Identification cards were issued initially to embassy personnel and at a later date to consular personnel.

There are three types of identification cards: "Diplomatic" (blue border for diplomats), "Official" (green border for employees), and "Consular" (red border for consular personnel). The new identification cards are 3¾ x 2½ and contain a photograph of the bearer. The bearer's name, title, mission, city and state, date of birth, identification number, expiration date, and a U.S. Department of State seal appear on the front of the card. A brief statement of the bearer's immunity is printed on the reverse side. Space also is provided for the bearer's signature.

While this form of identification is generally to be relied upon, law enforcement authorities are nonetheless urged immediately to seek verification as indicated below in connection with any serious incident or in any case where they have reason to doubt the validity of the card.

Police officers should be alert to the fact that newly arrived members of diplomatic and consular staffs may not yet have these official identity documents and should be prepared to contact the U.S. Department of State, Protocol Office, for verification if confronted with such situations.

5. Telephonic Information/Verification. Inquiry must be promptly made to the Department of State in any case where an individual claims immunity and cannot present satisfactory identification or in any case where the officer has reason to believe that invalid identification is being presented, or in any case where arrest or detention is made. The following telephone numbers are provided for use in this connection:

(202) 647-2663 during business hours; and

(202) 647-7277 after hours diplomatic security office.

C. Incidents: Guidance for Police

1. Generally. The vast majority of the persons entitled to privileges and immunities in the United States are judicious in their actions and keenly aware of the significance attached to their actions as representatives of their sending country. On rare occasions, however, a member of this class or of his or her family may be involved in a criminal law violation. The more common violations involve traffic offenses such as illegal parking, speeding, and, less frequently, driving while intoxicated. Whatever the offense or circumstances of contact, police officers should keep in mind that such persons are official representatives of foreign governments who are to be accorded the maximum degree of respect possible under the circumstances. It is not an exaggeration to say that police handling incidents in this country may have a direct effect on the treatment of U.S. diplomatic or consular personnel abroad.

When, in the course of responding to or investigating an apparent violation of criminal law, a police officer is confronted with a person claiming immunity, official Department of State identification should immediately be requested in order to verify the person's status and immunity. Should the individual be unable to produce satisfactory identification, and the situation would normally warrant arrest or detention, the officer should inform the individual that he or she will be detained until proper identity can be confirmed. As described previously, this can be accomplished by contacting the appropriate Department of State office.

When proper identification is available, the individual's immunity should be fully respected to the degree to which the particular individual is entitled. If it is established that the individual is entitled to the full inviolability and immunity of a diplomatic agent, he or she may not be arrested and should not, except in extraordinary circumstances (see Personal Inviolability vs. Public Safety below), be handcuffed or detained in any way. However, in an incident involving any person entitled to immunity, the officer should record all pertinent details from the identity card and fully record the details and circumstances of the incident in accordance with normal police procedures. Proper documentation of incidents is essential to permit the Department of State to take consequential steps, should they be considered appropriate.

2. Personal Inviolability vs. Public Safety. Personal inviolability is enjoyed to some degree by a majority of foreign diplomatic or consular personnel. In its most extreme form, this inviolability precludes arrest or detention in any form and forbids U.S. authorities from intruding into their residences, automobiles, or other property. All such personal inviolability is, however, qualified by the understanding, well established in international law, that the host country does not give up its right to protect the safety and welfare of its populace and retains the right, in extraordinary circumstances, to prevent the commission of a crime. Thus, in circumstances where public safety is in imminent danger or it is apparent that a serious crime may otherwise be committed, police authorities may intervene to the extent necessary to halt such activity. This naturally includes the power of the police to defend themselves from personal harm.

3. Traffic Enforcement. Stopping a diplomatic or consular officer and issuing a traffic citation does not constitute arrest or detention and is permissible, although signature of the citation by such individual may not be required. Accordingly, a police officer should never hesitate to follow normal procedures to intervene in a traffic violation which he or she has observed – even if immunity ultimately bars any further action at the scene. The officer should always stop persons committing moving violations, issue a citation if appropriate, and report the incident in accordance with usual procedures. Sobriety tests may be offered in accordance with local procedures but may not be required or compelled. If the police officer judges the individual to be intoxicated, the officer should not (even in the case of diplomatic agents) permit the individual to continue to drive. The officer's primary concern in this connection should be the safety of the community and of the intoxicated individual. Depending on the circumstances, the following options are available: The officer may, with the individual's permission, take the individual to the police station or other location where he or she may recover sufficiently to drive; the officer may summon, or allow the individual to summon, a friend or relative to drive; or the police officer may call a taxi for the individual. If appropriate, the police may choose to provide the individual with transportation.

In any event, the police officer involved with the incident should fully document the facts of the incident and the identity of the individual, and a written report of the incident should be promptly forwarded to the Department of State. (In serious cases, report by telephone is also urged.) It is Department of State's policy to suspend the operators license of foreign mission personnel not considered to be responsible drivers, and this policy may only be effectively enforced if all driving-related infractions (DUI, reckless driving, etc.) are fully reported to the Department of State.

The property of a person enjoying full immunity, including his or her vehicle, may not be searched or seized. Such vehicles may not be impounded or "booted" but may be towed the distance necessary to remove them from obstructing traffic or endangering public safety. If the vehicle is suspected of being stolen or used in the commission of a crime, occupants of the vehicle may be required to present vehicle documentation to permit police verification of the vehicle's status through standard access to "NLETS." Should the vehicle prove to have been stolen or to have been used by unauthorized persons in the commission of a crime, the inviolability to which the vehicle would normally be entitled must be considered temporarily suspended, and normal search of the vehicle and, if appropriate, its detention, are permissible.

4. Correct Understanding of Immunity. Frequently (and erroneously), immunity is understood to mean pardon, total exoneration or total release from the responsibility to comply with the law. In actuality, immunity is simply a legal barrier which precludes U.S. courts from exercising jurisdiction over cases against persons who enjoy it and in no way releases such persons from the duty, embodied in international law, to respect the laws and regulations of the United States. Even those who properly understand the concept of immunity sometimes believe that it is senseless to waste valuable police time in the investigation and paperwork essential to building a legal case, when there is no possibility that a conviction will result. This too is an incorrect perception. It can never be ascertained with certainty at the investigation stage that the person involved will continue to enjoy immunity when his or her government is confronted with the alleged criminal actions of such person and, in any event, there are

diplomatic remedies available to deal with such persons even when immunity bars prosecution and conviction. As is explained in greater detail below, there are a number of important reasons for police authorities to give careful attention to the documentation of incidents involving persons enjoying privileges and immunities. Such incidents should always be promptly reported to the Department of State.

5. Waiver of Immunity. Even though individuals ultimately enjoy the protections afforded by diplomatic or consular privileges and immunities, it is for the benefit of the sending country that these protections are actually devised. This concept is well established in international law and explains the fact that the individual concerned does not "own" the immunity. Such immunity may always be waived, in whole or in part, by the country which employs such person. While waiver of immunity in the face of criminal charges is not common, it is routinely sought and occasionally granted. The Department's ability to secure such waiver may depend to a large degree on the strength (and documentation) of the case at issue. Similarly, it is of little avail for the Department to secure waiver of immunity in a particular case, if the case has not been developed with sufficient care and completeness to permit a successful subsequent prosecution. Proper documentation and reporting by law enforcement authorities plays a critical role in both of these respects.

6. The Persona Non Grata (PNG) Procedure. The criminal immunity which foreign diplomatic and consular personnel enjoy protects them, to the extent that it is not waived by their government, from the normal jurisdiction of the courts in respect of alleged criminal activity.

One of the oldest concepts of international diplomatic law, however, is that host countries may strip persons who become unacceptable to them of their privileges and immunities, allowing such persons only a reasonable time to remove themselves from the territory of the host country. This is known as the *persona non grata* (PNG) procedure. It may be employed by the host country at any time. There is no requirement, under international law, for such countries to justify their action.

For the United States, however, use of this procedure has inherent constraints. Even though their immunity may deprive such PNG persons of due process in the formal sense, it is felt that in most cases this remedy should be employed only when there is reasonable certainty that a criminal act has actually been committed. The United States' reputation for being a society governed by the rule of law is not served if it may be pointed to as having acted in an arbitrary, capricious or prejudiced manner in invoking the extreme diplomatic tool of declaring a foreign diplomat PNG. Similarly, any PNG action which the U.S. Government is not able to defend in appropriate detail may be understood by the other country involved as a political action and might thus result in the reciprocal PNG of an entirely innocent American diplomat abroad. A high standard of police investigation, records and reporting in diplomatic incident cases is therefore essential to permit the Department responsibly to exercise the diplomatic tools available to remove persons engaged in criminal activity from the United States.

7. Official Acts Immunity. Official acts immunity is not a prima facie bar to the exercise of jurisdiction by U.S. courts. Rather, it is an affirmative defense to be raised before the U.S. court with subject matter jurisdiction over the alleged crime. If such court, in the full light of all the relevant facts, determines that the action complained of was an official act, only at that point does international law preclude the further exercise of jurisdiction by the U.S. court. Because the judicial determination in a case of this type is very much dependent on the facts surrounding the incident, a full and complete police report may be critical in permitting the court to make a just decision.

8. Termination of Immunity. Criminal immunity, to the extent that it is enjoyed by a particular individual and to the extent that it is not waived by the sending State concerned, precludes the exercise by courts of the United States of jurisdiction over alleged criminal activity by such persons, whether such activity occurred during or prior to the period during which such person enjoys criminal immunity in the United States. This jurisdictional bar is, however, not a perpetual benefit for such person. With the exception of immunity for official acts (which subsists indefinitely), criminal immunity expires upon the termination of the diplomatic or consular tour of the individual enjoying such immunity, including a reasonable period of time for such person to depart the U.S. territory. Thereafter, if the law enforcement authorities of the United States can obtain personal jurisdiction over a person alleged to have committed criminal acts in the United States, normal prosecution may go forward. This assumes, of course, that the case against such individual has been adequately developed at the time of the alleged action and that any applicable statute of limitations has not run. Obviously, careful and complete police work is required at the time of the alleged crime in order to lay the basis for such delayed prosecution, and it is important that the charges against such person be pushed as far as possible in the U.S. judicial system in order to lay the basis for such prosecution. Obtaining an indictment, information, or arrest warrant, even though they would be without immediate legal effect, would lay the basis for a prosecution at a later date.

The existence of an outstanding arrest warrant may be entered into the records of the U.S. immigration authorities and thus serve to bar the subsequent issuance of a U.S. visa permitting such person to enter the United States. It also should be kept in mind that persons who once resided in the United States in a status affording criminal immunity may later return for pleasure or otherwise under conditions affording them no criminal immunity. Additionally, in the case of serious crimes and with respect to foreign countries with which the United States enjoys an extradition relationship, it is not precluded under international law that international extradition may be effected.

D. Conclusion

It is important that the law enforcement authorities of the United States always treat foreign diplomatic and consular personnel with respect and with due regard for the privileges and immunities to which they are entitled under international law. Any shortcomings have the potential of casting into doubt the commitment of the United States to carry out its international obligations or of negatively influencing larger foreign policy interests. Appropriate caution on the part of law enforcement authorities should never escalate into a total "hands off" attitude in connection with criminal law enforcement actions involving diplomats. Foreign diplomats who violate traffic laws should be cited. Allegations of serious crimes should be fully investigated, promptly reported to the Department of State, and procedurally developed to the maximum permissible extent. Local law enforcement authorities should never be inhibited in their efforts to protect the public welfare in extreme situations. The U.S. Department of State should be advised promptly of any serious difficulties arising in connection with diplomatic or consular personnel. It has provided offices to assist police authorities in verifying individuals who may enjoy inviolability or immunity. Police departments should feel free to contact the Department of State for general advice in any matter bearing on diplomatic or consular personnel.

CODE OF VIRGINIA

TITLE 18.2
CRIMES AND OFFENSES GENERALLY
(Complete Title)

CHAPTER 1
IN GENERAL

ARTICLE 1
TRANSITION PROVISIONS

§18.2-1. Repealing clause.
All acts and parts of acts, all sections of this Code, and all provisions of municipal charters, inconsistent with the provisions of this title, are, except as herein otherwise provided, repealed to the extent of such inconsistency.

§18.2-2. Effect of repeal of Title 18.1 and enactment of this title.
The repeal of Title 18.1, effective as of October 1, 1975, shall not affect any act or offense done or committed, or any penalty or forfeiture incurred, or any right established, accrued or accruing on or before such date, or any prosecution, suit or action pending on that day. Except as herein otherwise provided, neither the repeal of Title 18.1 nor the enactment of this title shall apply to offenses committed prior to October 1, 1975, and prosecutions for such offenses shall be governed by the prior law, which is continued in effect for that purpose. For the purposes of this section, an offense was committed prior to October 1, 1975, if any of the essential elements of the offense occurred prior thereto.

§18.2-3. Certain notices, recognizances and processes validated.
Any notice given, recognizance taken, or process or writ issued before October 1, 1975, shall be valid although given, taken or to be returned to a day after such date, in like manner as if this title had been effective before the same was given, taken or issued.

§18.2-4. References to former sections, articles and chapters of Title 18.1 and others.
Whenever in this title any of the conditions, requirements, provisions or contents of any section, article or chapter of Title 18.1 or any other title of this Code as such titles existed prior to October 1, 1975, are transferred in the same or in modified form to a new section, article or chapter of this title or any other title of this Code and whenever any such former section, article or chapter is given a new number in this or any other title, all references to any such former section, article or chapter of Title 18.1 or such other title appearing elsewhere in this Code than in this title shall be construed to apply to the new or renumbered section, article or chapter containing such conditions, requirements, provisions or contents or portions thereof.

ARTICLE 2
CONSTRUCTION AND DEFINITIONS

§18.2-5. Rules of construction.
In the construction of this title, and of each section thereof, the rules of construction set forth in Chapter 2 (§1-10 et seq.) of Title 1 of this Code shall be observed, unless such construction would be inconsistent with the manifest intent of the General Assembly.

§18.2-6. Meaning of certain terms.
As used in this title:

The word "court," unless otherwise clearly indicated by the context in which it appears, shall mean and include any court vested with appropriate jurisdiction under the Constitution and laws of this Commonwealth.

The word "judge," unless otherwise clearly indicated by the context in which it appears, shall mean and include any judge, associate judge or substitute judge, or police justice, of any court.

The words "motor vehicle," "semitrailer," "trailer" and "vehicle" shall have the respective meanings assigned to them by §46.2-100.

§18.2-7. Criminal act not to merge civil remedy.
The commission of a crime shall not stay or merge any civil remedy.

ARTICLE 3
CLASSIFICATION OF CRIMINAL OFFENSES AND PUNISHMENT THEREFOR

§18.2-8. Felonies, misdemeanors and traffic infractions defined.
Offenses are either felonies or misdemeanors. Such offenses as are punishable with death or confinement in a state correctional facility are felonies; all other offenses are misdemeanors. Traffic infractions are violations of public order as defined in §46.2-100 and not deemed to be criminal in nature.

§18.2-9. Classification of criminal offenses.
(1) Felonies are classified, for the purposes of punishment and sentencing, into six classes:

(a) Class 1 felony;
(b) Class 2 felony;
(c) Class 3 felony;
(d) Class 4 felony;
(e) Class 5 felony;
(f) Class 6 felony.

(2) Misdemeanors are classified, for the purposes of punishment and sentencing, into four classes:

(a) Class 1 misdemeanor;
(b) Class 2 misdemeanor;
(c) Class 3 misdemeanor;
(d) Class 4 misdemeanor.

§18.2-10. Punishment for conviction of felony.
The authorized punishments for conviction of a felony are:

(a) For Class 1 felonies, death, if the person so convicted was sixteen years of age or older at the time of the offense, or imprisonment for life and, subject to subdivision (g), a fine of not more than $100,000. If the person was under sixteen years of age at the time of the offense, the punishment shall be imprisonment for life and, subject to subdivision (g), a fine of not more than $100,000.

(b) For Class 2 felonies, imprisonment for life or for any term not less than twenty years and, subject to subdivision (g), a fine of not more than $100,000.

(c) For Class 3 felonies, a term of imprisonment of not less than five years nor more than twenty years and, subject to subdivision (g), a fine of not more than $100,000.

(d) For Class 4 felonies, a term of imprisonment of not less than two years nor more than ten years and, subject to subdivision (g), a fine of not more than $100,000.

(e) For Class 5 felonies, a term of imprisonment of not less than one year nor more than ten years, or in the discretion of the jury or the court trying the case without a jury, confinement in jail for not more than twelve months and a fine of not more than $2,500, either or both.

(f) For Class 6 felonies, a term of imprisonment of not less than one year nor more than five years, or in the discretion of the jury or the court trying the case without a jury, confinement in jail for not more than twelve months and a fine of not more than $2,500, either or both.

(g) Except as specifically authorized in subdivision (e) or (f), or in Class 1 felonies for which a sentence of death is imposed, the court shall impose either a sentence of imprisonment together with a fine, or imprisonment only. However, if the defendant is not a natural person, the court shall impose only a fine.

For any felony offense committed (i) on or after January 1, 1995, the court may, and (ii) on or after July 1, 2000, shall, except in cases in which the court orders a suspended term of confinement of at least six months, impose an additional term of not less than six months nor more than three years, which shall be suspended conditioned upon successful completion of a period of postrelease supervision pursuant to §19.2-295.2 and compliance with such other terms as the sentencing court may require. However, such additional term may only be imposed when the sentence includes an active term of incarceration in a correctional facility.

For a felony offense prohibiting proximity to children as described in subsection A of §18.2-370.2, the sentencing court is authorized to impose the punishment set forth in subsection B of that section in addition to any other penalty provided by law.
(Chgd. by L.1995 ch. 427; L.2000 chs. 361, 767, 770, eff. 7/1/2000.)

§18.2-11. Punishment for conviction of misdemeanor.
The authorized punishments for conviction of a misdemeanor are:

(a) For Class 1 misdemeanors, confinement in jail for not more than twelve months and a fine of not more than $2,500, either or both.

(b) For Class 2 misdemeanors, confinement in jail for not more than six months and a fine of not more than $1,000, either or both.

(c) For Class 3 misdemeanors, a fine of not more than $500.

(d) For Class 4 misdemeanors, a fine of not more than $250.

For a misdemeanor offense prohibiting proximity to children as described in subsection A of §18.2-370.2, the sentencing court is authorized to impose the punishment set forth in subsection B of that section in addition to any other penalty provided by law.
(Chgd. by L.2000 ch. 770, eff. 7/1/2000.)

§18.2-12. Same; where no punishment or maximum punishment prescribed.
A misdemeanor for which no punishment or no maximum punishment is prescribed by statute shall be punishable as a Class 1 misdemeanor.

§18.2-13. Same; by reference.
Where a statute in this Code prescribes punishment by stating that the offense is a misdemeanor, or that it is punishable as provided for in §18.2-12, the offense shall be deemed to be a Class 1 misdemeanor.

§18.2-14. How unclassified offenses punished.
Offenses defined in Title 18.2 and in other titles in the Code, for which punishment is prescribed without specification as to the class of the offense, shall be punished according to the punishment prescribed in the section or sections thus defining the offense.

§18.2-15. Place of punishment.
Imprisonment for conviction of a felony shall be by confinement in a state correctional facility, unless in Class 5 and Class 6 felonies the jury or court trying the case without a jury fixes the punishment at confinement in jail. Imprisonment for conviction of a misdemeanor shall be by confinement in jail.

§18.2.16. How common-law offenses punished.
A common-law offense, for which punishment is prescribed by statute, shall be punished only in the mode so prescribed.

§18.2-17. When capital punishment inflicted.
No crime shall be punished with death unless it be authorized by statute.

CHAPTER 2
PRINCIPALS AND ACCESSORIES

§18.2-18. How principals in second degree and accessories before the fact punished.

In the case of every felony, every principal in the second degree and every accessory before the fact may be indicted, tried, convicted and punished in all respects as if a principal in the first degree; provided, however, that except in the case of a killing for hire under the provisions of subdivision 2 of §18.2-31 or a killing pursuant to the direction or order of one who is engaged in a continuing criminal enterprise under the provisions of subdivision 10 of §18.2-31, an accessory before the fact or principal in the second degree to a capital murder shall be indicted, tried, convicted and punished as though the offense were murder in the first degree.
(Chgd. by L.1997 ch. 313, eff. 7/1/97.)

§18.2-19. How accessories after the fact punished; certain exceptions.

In the case of every felony, every accessory after the fact shall be guilty of a Class 1 misdemeanor; provided, however, no person in the relation of husband or wife, parent or grandparent, child or grandchild, brother or sister, by consanguinity or affinity, or servant to the offender, who, after the commission of a felony, shall aid or assist a principal felon or accessory before the fact to avoid or escape from prosecution or punishment, shall be deemed an accessory after the fact.

§18.2-21. When and where accessories tried; how indicted.

An accessory, either before or after the fact, may, whether the principal felon be convicted or not, or be amenable to justice or not, be indicted, tried, convicted and punished in the county or corporation in which he became accessory, or in which the principal felon might be indicted. Any such accessory before the fact may be indicted either with such principal or separately.

CHAPTER 3
INCHOATE OFFENSES

ARTICLE 1
CONSPIRACIES

§18.2-22. Conspiracy to commit felony.

(a) If any person shall conspire, confederate or combine with another, either within or without this Commonwealth, to commit a felony within this Commonwealth, or if he shall so conspire, confederate or combine with another within this Commonwealth to commit a felony either within or without this Commonwealth, he shall be guilty of a felony which shall be punishable as follows:

(1) Every person who so conspires to commit an offense which is punishable by death shall be guilty of a Class 3 felony;

(2) Every person who so conspires to commit an offense which is a noncapital felony shall be guilty of a Class 5 felony; and

(3) Every person who so conspires to commit an offense the maximum punishment for which is confinement in a state correctional facility for a period of less than five years shall be confined in a state correctional facility for a period of one year, or, in the discretion of the jury or the court trying the case without a jury, may be confined in jail not exceeding twelve months and fined not exceeding $500, either or both.

(b) However, in no event shall the punishment for a conspiracy to commit an offense exceed the maximum punishment for the commission of the offense itself.

(c) Jurisdiction for the trial of any person accused of a conspiracy under this section shall be in the county or city wherein any part of such conspiracy is planned or in the county or city wherein any act is done toward the consummation of such plan or conspiracy.

(d) The penalty provisions of this section shall not apply to any person who conspires to commit any offense defined in Chapter 34 of Title 54.1 or of Article 1 (§18.2-247 et seq.), Chapter 7 of this title. The penalty for any such violation shall be as provided in §18.2-256.

§18.2-23. Conspiring to trespass after having been forbidden to do so.

If any person shall conspire, confederate or combine with another or others in this Commonwealth to go upon or remain upon the lands, buildings or premises of another, or any part, portion or area thereof, having knowledge that any of them have been forbidden, either orally or in writing, to do so by the owner, lessee, custodian or other person lawfully in charge thereof, or having knowledge that any of them have been forbidden to do so by a sign or signs posted on such lands, buildings, premises or part, portion or area thereof at a place or places where it or they may reasonably be seen, he shall be deemed guilty of a Class 3 misdemeanor.

Jurisdiction for the trial of any such person shall be in the county or city wherein any part of such conspiracy is planned, or in the county or city wherein any act is done toward the consummation of such plan or conspiracy.

§18.2-23.1. Completed substantive offense bars conviction for conspiracy.

Notwithstanding any other provision of this article or of §18.2-256, in any case where a defendant has been tried and convicted of an act he has also conspired to commit, such defendant shall be subject to conviction only for the completed substantive offense and not thereafter be convicted for the underlying conspiracy.

ARTICLE 2
ATTEMPTS

§18.2-25. Attempts to commit capital offenses; how punished.

If any person attempts to commit an offense which is punishable with death, he shall be guilty of a Class 2 felony.

§18.2-26. Attempts to commit noncapital felonies; how punished.

Every person who attempts to commit an offense which is a noncapital felony shall be punished as follows:

(1) If the felony attempted is punishable by a maximum punishment of life imprisonment or a term of years in excess of twenty years, an attempt thereat shall be punishable as a Class 4 felony.

(2) If the felony attempted is punishable by a maximum punishment of twenty years' imprisonment, an attempt thereat shall be punishable as a Class 5 felony.

(3) If the felony attempted is punishable by a maximum punishment of less than twenty years' imprisonment, an attempt thereat shall be punishable as a Class 6 felony.

§18.2-27. Attempts to commit misdemeanors; how punished.

Every person who attempts to commit an offense which is a misdemeanor shall be punishable by the same punishment prescribed for the offense the commission of which was the object of the attempt.

§18.2-28. Maximum punishment for attempts.

Any provision in this article notwithstanding, in no event shall the punishment for an attempt to commit an offense exceed the maximum punishment had the offense been committed.

§18.2-29. Criminal solicitation; penalty.

Any person who commands, entreats, or otherwise attempts to persuade another person to commit a felony, shall be guilty of a Class 6 felony. Any person age eighteen or older who commands, entreats, or otherwise attempts to persuade another person under age eighteen to commit a felony, shall be guilty of a Class 5 felony.

CHAPTER 4
CRIMES AGAINST THE PERSON

ARTICLE 1
HOMICIDE

§18.2-30. Murder and manslaughter declared felonies.

Any person who commits capital murder, murder of the first degree, murder of the second degree, voluntary manslaughter, or involuntary manslaughter, shall be guilty of a felony.

§18.2-31. Capital murder defined; punishment.

The following offenses shall constitute capital murder, punishable as a Class 1 felony:

1. The willful, deliberate, and premeditated killing of any person in the commission of abduction, as defined in §18.2-48, when such abduction was committed with the intent to extort money or a pecuniary benefit or with the intent to defile the victim of such abduction;

2. The willful, deliberate, and premeditated killing of any person by another for hire;

3. The willful, deliberate, and premeditated killing of any person by a prisoner confined in a state or local correctional facility as defined in §53.1-1, or while in the custody of an employee thereof;

4. The willful, deliberate, and premeditated killing of any person in the commission of robbery or attempted robbery;

5. The willful, deliberate, and premeditated killing of any person in the commission of, or subsequent to, rape or attempted rape, forcible sodomy or attempted forcible sodomy or object sexual penetration;

6. The willful, deliberate, and premeditated killing of a law-enforcement officer as defined in §9-169(9) or any law-enforcement officer of another state or the United States having the power to arrest for a felony under the laws of such state or the United States, when such killing is for the purpose of interfering with the performance of his official duties;

7. The willful, deliberate, and premeditated killing of more than one person as a part of the same act or transaction;

8. The willful, deliberate, and premeditated killing of more than one person within a three-year period;

9. The willful, deliberate, and premeditated killing of any person in the commission of or attempted commission of a violation of §18.2-248, involving a Schedule I or II controlled substance, when such killing is for the purpose of furthering the commission or attempted commission of such violation;

10. The willful, deliberate, and premeditated killing of any person by another pursuant to the direction or order of one who is engaged in a continuing criminal enterprise as defined in subsection I of §18.2-248;

11. The willful, deliberate and premeditated killing of a pregnant woman by one who knows that the woman is pregnant and has the intent to cause the involuntary termination of the woman's pregnancy without a live birth; and

12. The willful, deliberate and premeditated killing of a person under the age of fourteen by a person age twenty-one or older.

If any one or more subsections, sentences, or parts of this section shall be judged unconstitutional or invalid, such adjudication shall not affect, impair, or invalidate the remaining provisions thereof but shall be confined in its operation to the specific provisions so held unconstitutional or invalid.

(Chgd. by L.1995 ch. 340; L.1996 chs. 876, 959; L.1997 chs. 235, 313, 514, 709; L.1998 ch. 887, eff. 7/1/98.)

§18.2-32. First and second degree murder defined; punishment.

Murder, other than capital murder by poison, lying in wait, imprisonment, starving, or by any willful, deliberate, and premeditated killing, or in the commission of, or attempt to commit, arson, rape, forcible sodomy, inanimate or animate object sexual penetration, robbery, burglary or abduction, except as provided in §18.2-31, is murder of the first degree, punishable as a Class 2 felony.

All murder other than capital murder and murder in the first degree is murder of the second degree and is punishable by confinement in a state correctional facility for not less than five nor more than forty years.

(Chgd. by L.1998 ch. 281, eff. 7/1/98.)

§18.2-32.1. Murder of a pregnant woman; penalty.

The willful and deliberate killing of a pregnant woman without premeditation by one who knows that the woman is pregnant and has the intent to cause the involuntary termination of the woman's pregnancy without a live birth shall be punished by a term of imprisonment of not less than ten years nor more than forty years.

(Added by L.1997 ch. 709, eff. 7/1/97.)

§18.2-33. Felony homicide defined; punishment.

The killing of one accidentally, contrary to the intention of the parties, while in the prosecution of some felonious act other than those specified in §§18.2-31 and 18.2-32, is murder of the second degree and is punishable by confinement in a state correctional facility for not less than five years nor more than forty years.

(Chgd. by L.1999 ch. 282, eff. 7/1/99.)

§18.2-35. How voluntary manslaughter punished.

Voluntary manslaughter is punishable as a Class 5 felony.

§18.2-36. How involuntary manslaughter punished.

Involuntary manslaughter is punishable as a Class 5 felony.

§18.2-36.1. Certain conduct punishable as involuntary manslaughter.

A. Any person who, as a result of driving under the influence in violation of clause (ii), (iii), or (iv) of §18.2-266 or any local ordinance substantially similar thereto unintentionally causes the death of another person, shall be guilty of involuntary manslaughter.

B. If, in addition, the conduct of the defendant was so gross, wanton and culpable as to show a reckless disregard for human life, he shall be guilty of aggravated involuntary manslaughter, a felony punishable by a term of imprisonment of not less than one nor more than twenty years, one year of which shall be a mandatory, minimum term of imprisonment.

C. The provisions of this section shall not preclude prosecution under any other homicide statute. This section shall not preclude any other revocation or suspension required by law. The driver's license of any person convicted under this section shall be revoked pursuant to subsection B of §46.2-391.

(Chgd. by L.1999 chs. 945, 987; L.2000 chs. 956, 982, eff. 7/1/2000.)

§18.2-37. How and where homicide prosecuted and punished if death occur without the Commonwealth.

If any person be stricken or poisoned in this Commonwealth, and die by reason thereof out of this Commonwealth, the offender shall be as guilty, and shall be prosecuted and punished, as if the death had occurred in the county or corporation in which the stroke or poison was given or administered.

ARTICLE 2
CRIMES BY MOBS

§18.2-38. "Mob" defined.

Any collection of people, assembled for the purpose and with the intention of committing an assault or a battery upon any person or an act of violence as defined in §19.2-297.1, without authority of law, shall be deemed a "mob."

(Chgd. by L.1999 ch. 623, eff. 7/1/99.)

§18.2-39. "Lynching" defined.

Any act of violence by a mob upon the body of any person, which shall result in the death of such person, shall constitute a "lynching."

§18.2-40. Lynching deemed murder.

Every lynching shall be deemed murder. Any and every person composing a mob and any and every accessory thereto, by which any person is lynched, shall be guilty of murder, and upon conviction, shall be punished as provided in Article 1 (§18.2-30 et seq.) of this chapter.

§18.2-41. Shooting, stabbing, etc., with intent to maim, kill, etc., by mob.

Any and every person composing a mob which shall maliciously or unlawfully shoot, stab, cut or wound any person, or by any means cause him bodily injury with intent to maim, disable, disfigure or kill him, shall be guilty of a Class 3 felony.

§18.2-42. Assault or battery by mob.

Any and every person composing a mob which shall commit a simple assault or battery shall be guilty of a Class 1 misdemeanor.

§18.2-42.1. Acts of violence by mob.

Any and every person composing a mob which commits an act of violence as defined in §19.2-297.1 shall be guilty of that act of violence and, upon conviction, shall be punished as provided in the section of this title which makes that act of violence unlawful.

(Added by L.1999 ch. 623, eff. 7/1/99.)

§18.2-43. Apprehension and prosecution of participants in lynching.

The attorney for the Commonwealth of any county or city in which a lynching may occur shall promptly and diligently endeavor to ascertain the identity of the persons who in any way participated therein, or who composed the mob which perpetrated the same, and have them apprehended, and shall promptly proceed with the prosecution of any and all persons so found; and to the end that such offenders may not escape proper punishment, such attorney for the Commonwealth may be assisted in all such endeavors and prosecutions by the Attorney General, or other prosecutors designated by the Governor for the purpose; and the Governor may have full authority to spend such sums as he may deem necessary for the purpose of seeking out the identity, and apprehending the members of such mob.

§18.2-44. Civil liability for lynching.

No provisions of this article shall be construed to relieve any member of a mob from civil liability to the personal representative of the victim of a lynching.

§18.2-45. Persons suffering death from mob attempting to lynch another person.

Every person suffering death from a mob attempting to lynch another person shall come within the provisions of this article, and his personal representative shall be entitled to relief in the same manner and to the same extent as if he were the originally intended victim of such mob.

§18.2-46. Jurisdiction.

Jurisdiction of all actions and prosecutions under any of the provisions of this article shall be in the circuit court of the county or city wherein a lynching or other violation of any of the provisions of this article may have occurred, or of the county or city from which the person lynched or assaulted may have been taken as aforesaid.

ARTICLE 2.1
CRIMES BY GANGS

(Added by L.2000 ch. 332, eff. 7/1/2000.)

§18.2-46.1. Definitions.

As used in this article unless the context requires otherwise or it is otherwise provided:

"Act of violence" means those felony offenses described in subsection A of §19.2-297.1.

"Criminal street gang" means any ongoing organization, association, or group of three or more persons, whether formal or informal, (i) which has as one of its primary objectives or activities the commission of one or more predicate criminal acts, (ii) which has an identifiable name or identifying sign or symbol, and (iii) whose members individually or collectively engage in or have engaged in a pattern of criminal gang activity.

"Pattern of criminal gang activity" means commission of, attempt to commit, conspiracy to commit, or solicitation of two or more predicate criminal acts, at least one of which is an act of violence, provided such predicate criminal acts (i) were not part of a common act, transaction or scheme or (ii) were committed by two or more persons who are members of, or belong to, the same criminal street gang.

"Predicate criminal act" means an act of violence, any violation of §§18.2-51, 18.2-51.1, 18.2-52, 18.2-53, 18.2-55, 18.2-57, 18.2-57.2, 18.2-121, 18.2-127, 18.2-128, 18.2-137, 18.2-138, 18.2-146, or §18.2-147, or any violation of a local ordinance adopted pursuant to §18.2-138.1.

(Added by L.2000 ch. 332, eff. 7/1/2000.)

§18.2-46.2. Prohibited criminal street gang participation; penalty.

A. Any person who actively participates in or is a member of a criminal street gang and who knowingly and willfully participates in any predicate criminal act committed for the benefit of, at the direction of, or in association with any criminal street gang shall be guilty of a Class 5 felony. However, if such participant in or member of a criminal street gang is age eighteen years or older and knows or has reason to know that such criminal street gang also includes a juvenile member or participant, he shall be guilty of a Class 4 felony.

B. Violation of this section shall constitute a separate and distinct offense. If the acts or activities violating this section also violate another provision of law, a prosecution under this section shall not prohibit or bar any prosecution or proceeding under such other provision or the imposition of any penalties provided for thereby.

(Added by L.2000 ch. 332, eff. 7/1/2000.)

§18.2-46.3. Recruitment of juveniles for criminal street gang; penalty.

Any person age eighteen years or older who solicits, invites, recruits, encourages or otherwise causes or attempts to cause a juvenile to actively participate in or become a member of a criminal street gang shall be guilty of a Class 6 felony.

(Added by L.2000 ch. 332, eff. 7/1/2000.)

ARTICLE 3
KIDNAPPING AND RELATED OFFENSES

§18.2-47. Abduction and kidnapping defined; punishment.

A. Any person, who, by force, intimidation or deception, and without legal justification or excuse, seizes, takes, transports, detains or secretes the person of another, with the intent to deprive such other person of his personal liberty or to withhold or conceal him from any person, authority or institution lawfully entitled to his charge, shall be deemed guilty of "abduction"; but the provisions of this section shall not apply to any law-enforcement officer in the performance of his duty. The terms "abduction" and "kidnapping" shall be synonymous in this Code. Abduction for which no punishment is otherwise prescribed shall be punished as a Class 5 felony.

B. If such offense is committed by the parent of the person abducted and punishable as contempt of court in any proceeding then pending, the offense shall be a Class 1 misdemeanor in addition to being punishable as contempt of court. Provided further, however, that such offense, if committed by the parent of the person abducted and punishable as contempt of court in any proceeding then pending and the person abducted is removed from the Commonwealth by the abducting parent, shall be a Class 6 felony in addition to being punishable as contempt of court.

(Chgd. by L.1997 ch. 747, eff. 7/1/97.)

§18.2-48. Abduction with intent to extort money or for immoral purpose.

Abduction (i) with the intent to extort money or pecuniary benefit, (ii) of any person with intent to defile such person, or (iii) of any child under sixteen years of age for the purpose of concubinage or prostitution, shall be a Class 2 felony.

(Chgd. by L.1997 ch. 747, eff. 7/1/97.)

§18.2-48.1. Abduction by prisoners; penalty.

Any prisoner in a state, local or community correctional facility, or in the custody of an employee thereof, or who has escaped from any such facility or from any person in charge of such prisoner, who abducts or takes any person hostage shall be guilty of a Class 3 felony.

§18.2-49. Threatening, attempting or assisting in such abduction.

Any person who (1) threatens, or attempts, to abduct any other person with intent to extort money, or pecuniary benefit, or (2) assists or aids in the abduction of, or threatens to abduct, any person with the intent to defile such person, or (3) assists or aids in the abduction of, or threatens to abduct, any female under sixteen years of age for the purpose of concubinage or prostitution, shall be guilty of a Class 5 felony.

§18.2-49.1. Violation of court order regarding custody and visitation; penalty.

A. Any person who knowingly, wrongfully and intentionally withholds a child from the child's custodial parent in a clear and significant violation of a court order respecting the custody or visitation of such child, provided such child is withheld outside of the Commonwealth, shall be guilty of a Class 6 felony.

B. Any person who knowingly, wrongfully and intentionally engages in conduct which constitutes a clear and significant violation of a court order respecting the custody or visitation of a child shall be guilty of a Class 4 misdemeanor upon conviction of a first offense. A second conviction for a violation of this section within twelve months of a first conviction shall be a Class 3 misdemeanor, and a third conviction occurring within twenty-four months of the first conviction shall be a Class 2 misdemeanor.

§18.2-50. Disclosure of information and assistance to law-enforcement officers required.

Whenever it is brought to the attention of the members of the immediate family of any person that such person has been abducted, or that threats or attempts have been made to abduct any such person, such members shall make immediate report thereof to the police or other law-enforcement officers of the county, city or town where such person resides, and shall render all such possible assistance to such officers in the capture and conviction of the person or persons guilty of the alleged offense. Any person violating any of the provisions of this section shall be guilty of a Class 2 misdemeanor.

§18.2-50.2. Emergency control of telephone service in hostage or barricaded person situation.

A. The Superintendent of the State Police or the chief law-enforcement officer or sheriff of any county, city or town may designate one or more law-enforcement officers with appropriate technical training or expertise as a hostage and barricade communications specialist.

B. Each telephone company providing service to Virginia residents shall designate a department or one or more individuals to provide liaison with law-enforcement agencies for the purposes of this section and shall designate telephone numbers, not exceeding two, at which such law-enforcement liaison department or individual can be contacted.

C. The supervising law-enforcement officer, who has jurisdiction in any situation in which there is probable cause to believe that the criminal enterprise of hostage holding is occurring or that a person has barricaded himself within a structure and poses an immediate threat to the life, safety or property of himself or others, may order a telephone company, or a hostage and barricade communications specialist to interrupt, reroute, divert, or otherwise control any telephone communications service involved in the hostage or barricade situation for the purpose of preventing telephone communication by a hostage holder or barricaded person with any person other than a law-enforcement officer or a person authorized by the officer.

D. A hostage and barricade communication specialist shall be ordered to act under subsection C only if the telephone company providing service in the area has been contacted and requested to act under subsection C or an attempt to contact has been made, using the telephone company's designated liaison telephone numbers and:

1. The officer's attempt to contact after ten rings for each call is unsuccessful;
2. The telephone company declines to respond to the officer's request because of a threat of personal injury to its employees; or
3. The telephone company indicates when contacted that it will be unable to respond appropriately to the officer's request within a reasonable time from the receipt of the request.

E. The supervising law-enforcement officer may give an order under subsection C only after that supervising law-enforcement officer has given or attempted to give written notification or oral notification of the hostage or barricade situation to the telephone company providing service to the area in which it is occurring. If an order is given on the basis of an oral notice, the oral notice shall be followed by a written confirmation of that notice within forty-eight hours of the order.

F. Good faith reliance on an order by a supervising law-enforcement officer who has the real or apparent authority to issue an order under this section shall constitute a complete defense to any action against a telephone company or a telephone company employee that rises out of attempts by the telephone company or the employees of the telephone company to comply with such an order.

ARTICLE 4
ASSAULTS AND BODILY WOUNDINGS

Section

§18.2-51. Shooting, stabbing, etc., with intent to maim, kill, etc.

If any person maliciously shoot, stab, cut, or wound any person or by any means cause him bodily injury, with the intent to maim, disfigure, disable, or kill, he shall, except where it is otherwise provided, be guilty of a Class 3 felony. If such act be done unlawfully but not maliciously, with the intent aforesaid, the offender shall be guilty of a Class 6 felony.

§18.2-51.1. Malicious bodily injury to law-enforcement officers or firefighters; penalty; lesser included offense.

If any person maliciously causes bodily injury to another by any means including the means set out in §18.2-52, with intent to maim, disfigure, disable or kill, and knowing or having reason to know that such other person is a law-enforcement officer, as defined hereinafter, or firefighter, as defined in §65.2-102, engaged in the performance of his public duties as a law-enforcement officer or firefighter, such person shall be guilty of a felony punishable by imprisonment for a period of not less than five years nor more than thirty years and, subject to subdivision (g) of §18.2-10, a fine of not more than $100,000. Upon conviction, the sentence of such person shall include a mandatory, minimum term of imprisonment of two years.

If any person unlawfully, but not maliciously, with the intent aforesaid, causes bodily injury to another by any means, knowing or having reason to know such other person is a law-enforcement officer as defined hereinafter, or firefighter, as defined in §65.2-102, engaged in the performance of his public duties as a law-enforcement officer or firefighter, he shall be guilty of a Class 6 felony, and upon conviction, the sentence of such person shall include a mandatory, minimum term of imprisonment of one year.

Nothing in this section shall be construed to affect the right of any person charged with a violation of this section from asserting and presenting evidence in support of any defenses to the charge that may be available under common law.

As used in this section the term "mandatory, minimum" means that the sentence it describes shall be served with no suspension of sentence in whole or in part.

As used in this section a law-enforcement officer means any full-time or part-time employee of a police department or sheriff's office which is part of or administered by the Commonwealth or any political subdivision thereof, and who is responsible for the prevention or detection of crime and the enforcement of the penal, traffic or highway laws of this Commonwealth, any conservation officer of the Department of Conservation and Recreation commissioned pursuant to §10.1-115, and includes auxiliary police officers appointed or provided for pursuant to §§15.1-159.2 and 15.1-159.4 and auxiliary deputy sheriffs appointed pursuant to §15.1-48.

The provisions of §18.2-51 shall be deemed to provide a lesser included offense hereof.

(Chgd. by L.1997 chs. 8, 120, eff. 7/1/97.)

§18.2-51.2. Aggravated malicious wounding; penalty.

A. If any person maliciously shoots, stabs, cuts or wounds any other person, or by any means causes bodily injury, with the intent to maim, disfigure, disable or kill, he shall be guilty of a Class 2 felony if the victim is thereby severely injured and is caused to suffer permanent and significant physical impairment.

B. If any person maliciously shoots, stabs, cuts or wounds any other woman who is pregnant, or by any other means causes bodily injury, with the intent to maim, disfigure, disable or kill the pregnant woman or to cause the involuntary termination of her pregnancy, he shall be guilty of a Class 2 felony if the victim is thereby severely injured and is caused to suffer permanent and significant physical impairment.

C. For purposes of this section, the involuntary termination of a woman's pregnancy shall be deemed a severe injury and a permanent and significant physical impairment.

(Chgd. by L.1997 ch. 709, eff. 7/1/97.)

§18.2-51.3. Prohibition against reckless endangerment of others by throwing objects from places higher than one story; penalty.

A. It shall be unlawful for any person, with the intent to cause injury to another, to intentionally throw from a balcony, roof top, or other place more than one story above ground level any object capable of causing any such injury.

B. A violation of this section shall be punishable as a Class 6 felony.

§18.2-51.4. Maiming, etc., of another resulting from driving while intoxicated.

A. Any person who, as a result of driving while intoxicated in violation of §18.2-266 or any local ordinance substantially similar thereto in a manner so gross, wanton and culpable as to show a reckless disregard for human life, unintentionally causes the serious bodily injury of another person resulting in permanent and significant physical impairment shall be guilty of a Class 6 felony. The drivers' license of any person convicted under this section shall be revoked pursuant to subsection B of §46.2-391.

B. The provisions of Article 2 (§18.2-266 et seq.) of Chapter 7 of Title 18.2 shall apply, mutatis mutandis, upon arrest for a violation of this section.

(Added by L.1997 ch. 691; chgd. by L.1999 chs. 945, 987; L.2000 chs. 956, 982, eff. 7/1/2000.)

§18.2-52. Malicious bodily injury by means of any caustic substance or agent or use of any explosive or fire.

If any person maliciously causes any other person bodily injury by means of any acid, lye or other caustic substance or agent or use of any explosive or fire, he shall be guilty of a felony and shall be punished by confinement in a state correctional facility for a period of not less than five years nor more than thirty years. If such act is done unlawfully but not maliciously, the offender shall be guilty of a Class 6 felony.

(Chgd. by L.1995 ch. 439, eff. 7/1/95.)

§18.2-52.1. Possession of infectious biological substances.

A. Any person who possesses, with the intent thereby to injure another, an infectious biological substance capable of causing death, is guilty of a Class 5 felony.

B. Any person who destroys or damages, or attempts to destroy or damage, any facility, equipment or material involved in the sale, manufacturing, storage or distribution of an infectious biological substance capable of causing death, with the intent to injure another by releasing the substance, is guilty of a Class 4 felony.

An "infectious biological substance" includes any bacteria, virus, fungi, protozoa, or rickettsiae capable of causing death.

(Added by L.1996 ch. 769, eff. 7/1/96.)

§18.2-53. Shooting, etc., in committing or attempting a felony.

If any person, in the commission of, or attempt to commit, felony, unlawfully shoot, stab, cut or wound another person he shall be guilty of a Class 6 felony.

§18.2-53.1. Use or display of firearm in committing felony.

It shall be unlawful for any person to use or attempt to use any pistol, shotgun, rifle, or other firearm or display such weapon in a threatening manner while committing or attempting to commit murder, rape, forcible sodomy, inanimate or animate object sexual penetration as defined in §18.2-67.2, robbery, carjacking, burglary, malicious wounding as defined in §18.2-51, malicious bodily injury to a law-enforcement officer as defined in §18.2-51.1, aggravated malicious wounding as defined in §18.2-51.2, malicious wounding by mob as defined in §18.2-41 or abduction. Violation of this section shall constitute a separate and distinct felony and any person found guilty thereof shall be sentenced to a term of imprisonment of three years for a first conviction, and for a term of five years for a second or subsequent conviction under the provisions of this section. Notwithstanding any other provision of law, the sentence prescribed for a violation of the provisions of this section shall not be suspended in whole or in part, nor shall anyone convicted hereunder be placed on probation. Such punishment shall be separate and apart from, and shall be made to run consecutively with, any punishment received for the commission of the primary felony.

§18.2-54. Conviction of lesser offenses under certain indictments.

On any indictment for maliciously shooting, stabbing, cutting or wounding a person or by any means causing him bodily injury, with intent to maim, disfigure, disable or kill him, or of causing bodily injury by means of any acid, lye or other caustic substance or agent, the jury or the court trying the case without a jury may find the accused not guilty of the offense charged but guilty of unlawfully doing such act with the intent aforesaid, or of assault and battery if the evidence warrants.

§18.2-54.1. Attempts to poison.

If any person administers or attempts to administer any poison or destructive substance in food, drink, prescription or over-the-counter medicine, or otherwise, or poisons any spring, well, or reservoir of water with intent to kill or injure another person, he shall be guilty of a Class 3 felony.

§18.2-54.2. Adulteration of food, drink, drugs, cosmetics, etc.; penalty.

Any person who adulterates or causes to be adulterated any food, drink, prescription or over-the-counter medicine, cosmetic or other substance with the intent to kill or injure any individual who ingests, inhales or uses such substance shall be guilty of a Class 3 felony.

§18.2-55. Bodily injuries caused by prisoners, probationers or parolees.

A. It shall be unlawful for a person confined in a state, local or regional correctional facility as defined in §53.1-1; in a secure facility or detention home as defined in §16.1-228 or in any facility designed for the secure detention of juveniles; or while in the custody of an employee thereof to knowingly and willfully inflict bodily injury on:

1. An employee thereof, or
2. Any other person lawfully admitted to such facility, except another prisoner or person held in legal custody, or
3. Any person who is supervising or working with prisoners or persons held in legal custody, or
4. Any such employee or other person while such prisoner or person held in legal custody is committing any act in violation of §53.1-203.

B. It shall be unlawful for a probationer or parolee, under the supervision of a probation or parole officer as defined in §16.1-237 or §53.1-145, to knowingly and willfully inflict bodily injury on such officer while in the performance of such officer's duty.

Any person violating any provision of this section shall be guilty of a Class 5 felony.

(Chgd. by L.1996 ch. 527; L.1999 chs. 618, 658, eff. 7/1/99.)

§18.2-56. Hazing unlawful; civil and criminal liability; duty of school, etc., officials.

It shall be unlawful to haze, or otherwise mistreat so as to cause bodily injury, any student at any school, college, or university.

Any person found guilty thereof shall be guilty of a Class 1 misdemeanor, unless the injury would be such as to constitute a felony, and in that event the punishment shall be inflicted as is otherwise provided by law for the punishment of such felony.

Any person receiving bodily injury by hazing or mistreatment shall have a right to sue, civilly, the person or persons guilty thereof, whether adults or infants.

The president, or other presiding official of any school, college or university, receiving appropriations from the state treasury shall, upon satisfactory proof of the guilt of any student found guilty of hazing or mistreating another student so as to cause bodily injury, expel such student so found guilty, and shall make report thereof to the attorney for the Commonwealth of the county or city in which such school, college or university is, who shall present the same to the grand jury of such city or county convened next after such report is made to him.

§18.2-56.1. Reckless handling of firearms; reckless handling while hunting.

A. It shall be unlawful for any person to handle recklessly any firearm so as to endanger the life, limb or property of any person. Any person violating this section shall be guilty of a Class 1 misdemeanor.

B. If this section is violated while the person is engaged in hunting, trapping or pursuing game, the trial judge may, in addition to the penalty imposed by the jury or the court trying the case without a jury, revoke such person's hunting or trapping license or privilege to hunt or trap while possessing a firearm for a period of one year to life.

C. Upon a revocation pursuant to subsection B hereof, the clerk of the court in which the case is tried pursuant to this section shall forthwith send to the Department of Game and Inland Fisheries (i) such person's revoked hunting or trapping license or notice that such person's privilege to hunt or trap while in possession of a firearm has been revoked and (ii) a notice of the length of revocation imposed. The Department shall keep a list which shall be furnished upon request to any law-enforcement officer, Commonwealth's attorney or court in this Commonwealth, and such list shall contain the names and addresses of all persons whose license or privilege to hunt or trap while in possession of a firearm has been revoked and the court which took such action.

D. If any person whose license to hunt and trap, or whose privilege to hunt and trap while in possession of a firearm, has been revoked pursuant to this section, thereafter hunts or traps while in possession of a firearm, he shall be guilty of a Class 1 misdemeanor, and, in addition to any penalty imposed by the jury or the court trying the case without a jury, the trial judge may revoke such person's hunting or trapping license, or privilege to hunt or trap while in possession of a firearm, for an additional period not to exceed five years. The clerk of the court shall notify the Department of Game and Inland Fisheries as is provided in subsection C herein.

§18.2-56.2. Allowing access to firearms by children; penalty.

A. It shall be unlawful for any person to recklessly leave a loaded, unsecured firearm in such a manner as to endanger the life or limb of any child under the age of fourteen. Any person violating the provisions of this subsection shall be guilty of a Class 3 misdemeanor.

B. It shall be unlawful for any person knowingly to authorize a child under the age of twelve to use a firearm except when the child is under the supervision of an adult. Any person violating this subsection shall be guilty of a Class 1 misdemeanor. For purposes of this subsection, "adult" shall mean a parent, guardian, person standing in loco parentis to the child or a person twenty-one years or over who has the permission of the parent, guardian, or person standing in loco parentis to supervise the child in the use of a firearm.

§18.2-57. Assault and battery.

A. Any person who commits a simple assault or assault and battery shall be guilty of a Class 1 misdemeanor, and if the person intentionally selects the person against whom a simple assault is committed because of his race, religious conviction, color or national origin, the penalty upon conviction shall include a mandatory, minimum term of confinement of at least six months, thirty days of which shall not be suspended, in whole or in part.

B. However, if a person intentionally selects the person against whom an assault and battery resulting in bodily injury is committed because of his race, religious conviction, color or national origin, the person shall be guilty of a Class 6 felony, and the penalty upon conviction shall include a mandatory, minimum term of confinement of at least six months, thirty days of which shall not be suspended, in whole or in part.

C. In addition, if any person commits an assault or an assault and battery against another knowing or having reason to know that such other person is a law-enforcement officer as defined hereinafter, a correctional officer as defined in §53.1-1, a person employed by the Department of Corrections directly involved in the care, treatment or supervision of inmates in the custody of the Department or a firefighter as defined in §65.2-102, engaged in the performance of his public duties as such, such person shall be guilty of a Class 6 felony, and, upon conviction, the sentence of such person shall include a mandatory, minimum term of confinement for six months which mandatory, minimum term shall not be suspended, in whole or in part.

Nothing in this subsection shall be construed to affect the right of any person charged with a violation of this section from asserting and presenting evidence in support of any defenses to the charge that may be available under common law.

D. In addition, if any person commits a battery against another knowing or having reason to know that such other person is a full-time or part-time teacher, principal, assistant principal, or guidance counselor of any public or private elementary or secondary school and is engaged in the performance of his duties as such, he shall be guilty of a Class 1 misdemeanor and the sentence of such person upon conviction shall include a mandatory, minimum sentence of fifteen days in jail, two days of which shall not be suspended in whole or in part. However, if the offense is committed by use of a firearm or other weapon prohibited on school property pursuant to §18.2-308.1, the person shall serve a mandatory, minimum sentence of confinement of six months which shall not be suspended in whole or in part.

E. As used in this section, a "law-enforcement officer" means any full-time or part-time employee of a police department or sheriff's office which is part of or administered by the Commonwealth or any political subdivision thereof, who is responsible for the prevention or detection of crime and the enforcement of the penal, traffic or highway laws of this Commonwealth, and any conservation officer of the Department of Conservation and Recreation commissioned pursuant to §10.1-115, and game wardens appointed pursuant to §29.1-200, and such officer also includes jail officers in local correctional facilities, all deputy sheriffs, whether assigned to law-enforcement duties, court services or local jail responsibilities, auxiliary police officers appointed or provided for pursuant to §§15.2-1731 and 15.2-1733 and auxiliary deputy sheriffs appointed pursuant to §15.2-1603.

F. "Simple assault" or "assault and battery" shall not be construed to include the use of, by any teacher, in the course and scope of his acting official capacity, any of the following: (i) incidental, minor or reasonable physical contact or other actions designed to maintain order and control; (ii) reasonable and necessary force to quell a disturbance or remove a student from the scene of a disturbance that threatens physical injury to persons or damage to property; (iii) reasonable and necessary force to prevent a student from inflicting physical harm on himself; (iv) reasonable and necessary force for self-defense or the defense of others; or (v) reasonable and necessary force to obtain possession of weapons or other dangerous objects or controlled substances or associated paraphernalia that are upon the person of the student or within his control.

In determining whether a person was acting within the exceptions provided in this subsection, due deference shall be given to reasonable judgments at the time of the event that were made by a teacher.

(Chgd. by L.1997 ch. 833; L.1999 chs. 771, 1036; L.2000 chs. 288, 682, eff. 7/1/2000.)

§18.2-57.01. Pointing laser at law-enforcement officer unlawful; penalty.

If any person, knowing or having reason to know another person is a law-enforcement officer as defined in §18.2-57, a probation or parole officer appointed pursuant to §53.1-143, a correctional officer as defined in §53.1-1, or a person employed by the Department of Corrections directly involved in the care, treatment or supervision of inmates in the custody of the Department engaged in the performance of his public duties as such, intentionally projects at such other person a beam or a point of light from a laser, a laser gun sight, or any device that simulates a laser, shall be guilty of a Class 2 misdemeanor.

(Added by L.2000 ch. 350, eff. 7/1/2000.)

§18.2-57.1. *(Repealed by L.1997 ch. 833, eff. 7/1/97.)*

§18.2-57.2. Assault and battery against a family or household member.

A. Any person who commits an assault and battery against a family or household member shall be guilty of a Class 1 misdemeanor.

B. On a third or subsequent conviction for assault and battery against a family or household member, where it is alleged in the warrant, information, or indictment on which a person is convicted, that (i) such person has been previously convicted twice of assault and battery against a family or household member, or of a similar offense under the law of any other jurisdiction, within ten years of the third or subsequent offense and (ii) each such assault and battery occurred on different dates, such person shall be guilty of a Class 6 felony.

C. Whenever a warrant for a violation of this section is issued, the magistrate shall issue an emergency protective order as authorized by §16.1-253.4, except if the defendant is a minor, an emergency protective order shall not be required.

D. The definition of "family or household member" in §16.1-228 applies to this section.

(Chgd. by L.1996 ch. 866; L.1997 ch. 603; L.1999 chs. 697, 721, 807, eff. 7/1/99.)

§18.2-57.3. Persons charged with first offense of assault and battery against a family or household member may be placed on probation; conditions; screening, evaluation, testing, education and treatment programs; costs and fees; violations; discharge.

When a person who is no younger than eighteen years of age or who is considered an adult at the time of conviction has not previously been convicted of any offense under this article or under any statute of the United States or of any state or any ordinance of any local government relating to assault and battery against a family or household member or has not previously had a proceeding against him for violation of such an offense dismissed as provided in this section, pleads guilty to or enters a plea of not guilty to a violation of §18.2-57.2, the court, upon such plea if the facts found by the court would justify a finding of guilt, without entering a judgment of guilt and with the consent of the accused, may defer further proceedings and place him on probation upon terms and conditions.

As a term or condition, the court shall require the accused to be evaluated and, based on the results of screening, assessment, evaluation, and testing, to enter an education or treatment program, if available, such as, in the opinion of the court, may be best suited to the needs of the accused.

The court shall require the person entering such education or treatment program under the provisions of this section to pay all or part of the costs of the program, including the costs of the screening, evaluation, testing, education and treatment, based upon the accused's ability to pay unless the person is determined by the court to be indigent.

As a condition of local probation, the court shall require the accused to successfully complete all treatment and/or education programs required and to be of good behavior for a period of not less than two years following the completion of local probation supervision.

The court shall, unless done at arrest, order the accused to report to the original arresting law-enforcement agency to submit to fingerprinting.

Upon violation of a term or condition, the court may enter an adjudication of guilt and proceed as otherwise provided. Upon fulfillment of the terms and conditions, the court shall discharge the person and dismiss the proceedings against him. Discharge and dismissal under this section shall be without adjudication of guilt and is a conviction only for the purposes of applying this section in subsequent proceedings. As such, no charges dismissed pursuant to this section shall be eligible for expungement under §19.2-392.2.

Notwithstanding any other provision of this section, whenever a court places an individual on probation upon terms and conditions pursuant to this section, such action shall be treated as a conviction for purposes of §18.2-308.

(Added by L.1999 ch. 963; chgd. by L.2000 ch. 1040, eff. 7/1/2000.)

ARTICLE 5
ROBBERY

§18.2-58. How punished.

If any person commit robbery by partial strangulation, or suffocation, or by striking or beating, or by other violence to the person, or by assault or otherwise putting a person in fear of serious bodily harm, or by the threat or presenting of firearms, or other deadly weapon or instrumentality whatsoever, he shall be guilty of a felony and shall be punished by confinement in a state correctional facility for life or any term not less than five years.

§18.2-58.1. Carjacking; penalty.

A. Any person who commits carjacking, as herein defined, shall be guilty of a felony punishable by imprisonment for life or a term not less than fifteen years.

B. As used in this section "carjacking" means the intentional seizure or seizure of control of a motor vehicle of another with intent to permanently or temporarily deprive another in possession or control of the vehicle of that possession or control by means of partial strangulation, or suffocation, or by striking or beating, or by other violence to the person, or by assault or otherwise putting a person in fear of serious bodily harm, or by the threat or presenting of firearms, or other deadly weapon or instrumentality whatsoever. "Motor vehicle" shall have the same meaning as set forth in §46.2-100.

C. The provisions of this section shall not preclude the applicability of any other provision of the criminal law of the Commonwealth which may apply to any course of conduct which violates this section.

ARTICLE 6
EXTORTION AND OTHER THREATS

§18.2-59. Extorting money, etc., by threats.

If any person threaten injury to the character, person, or property of another person or accuse him of any offense and thereby extort money, property, or pecuniary benefit or any note, bond, or other evidence of debt from him or any other person, he shall be guilty of a Class 5 felony.

§18.2-60. Threats of death or bodily injury to a person or member of his family; certain threats communicated to persons; penalty.

A. If any person write or compose and also send or procure the sending of any letter, inscribed communication or electronically transmitted communication producing a visual or electronic message, so written or composed, whether such letter or communication be signed or anonymous, to any person, containing a threat to kill or do bodily injury to the person to whom such letter or communication is sent, or a threat to kill or do bodily injury to any member of his or her family, the person so writing or composing and sending or procuring the sending of such letter or communication shall be guilty of a Class 6 felony and may be prosecuted either in the county, city or town in which the letter or inscribed communication is composed, written, sent or procured to be sent or in the county, city or town in which the letter or inscribed communication is received.

B. If any person orally makes a threat to any employee of any elementary, middle or secondary school, while on a school bus, on school property or at a school-sponsored activity, to kill or to do bodily injury to such person, he shall be guilty of a Class 1 misdemeanor.

(Chgd. by L.1998 chs. 687, 788, eff. 7/1/98.)

§18.2-60.1. Threatening the Governor or his immediate family.

Any person who shall knowingly and willfully send, deliver or convey, or cause to be sent, delivered or conveyed, to the Governor or his immediate family any threat to take the life of or inflict bodily harm upon the Governor or his immediate family, whether such threat be oral or written, shall be guilty of a Class 6 felony.

§18.2-60.2. Members of the Governor's immediate family.

As used in §18.2-60.1, the immediate family of the Governor shall include any parent, sibling, child, grandchild, spouse, parent of a spouse, and spouse of a sibling, child or grandchild who resides in the same household as the Governor.

§18.2-60.3. Stalking; penalty.

A. Any person who on more than one occasion engages in conduct directed at another person with the intent to place, or with the knowledge that the conduct places, that other person in reasonable fear of death, criminal sexual assault, or bodily injury to that other person or to that other person's family or household member shall be guilty of a Class 1 misdemeanor.

B. A third or subsequent conviction occurring within five years of a conviction for an offense under this section or for a similar offense under the law of any other jurisdiction shall be a Class 6 felony.

C. A person may be convicted under this section irrespective of the jurisdiction or jurisdictions within the Commonwealth wherein the conduct described in subsection A occurred, if the person engaged in that conduct on at least one occasion in the jurisdiction where the person is tried. Evidence of any such conduct which occurred outside the Commonwealth may be admissible, if relevant, in any prosecution under this section provided that the prosecution is based upon conduct occurring within the Commonwealth.

D. Upon finding a person guilty under this section, the court shall, in addition to the sentence imposed, issue an order prohibiting contact between the defendant and the victim or the victim's family or household member.

E. The Department of Corrections, sheriff or regional jail director shall give notice prior to the release from a state correctional facility or a local or regional jail of any person incarcerated upon conviction of a violation of this section, to any victim of the offense who, in writing, requests notice, or to any person designated in writing by the victim. The notice shall be given at least fifteen days prior to release of a person sentenced to a term of incarceration of more than thirty days or, if the person was sentenced to a term of incarceration of at least forty-eight hours but no more than thirty days, twenty-four hours prior to release. If the person escapes, notice shall be given as soon as practicable following the escape. The victim shall keep the Department of Corrections, sheriff or regional jail director informed of the current mailing address and telephone number of the person named in the writing submitted to receive notice.

All information relating to any person who receives or may receive notice under this subsection shall remain confidential and shall not be made available to the person convicted of violating this section.

For purposes of this subsection, "release" includes a release of the offender from a state correctional facility or a local or regional jail (i) upon completion of his term of incarceration or (ii) on probation or parole.

No civil liability shall attach to the Department of Corrections nor to any sheriff or regional jail director or their deputies or employees for a failure to comply with the requirements of this subsection.

F. As used in this section the term "family or household member" shall have the same meaning as provided in §16.1-228.

(Chgd. by L.1995 ch. 824; L.1996 chs. 540, 866; L.1998 ch. 570, eff. 7/1/98.)

§18.2-60.4. Violation of stalking protective orders; penalty.

Any person who violates any provision of a protective order issued pursuant to §§19.2-152.8, 19.2-152.9 or §19.2-152.10 is guilty of a Class 1 misdemeanor. Conviction hereunder shall bar a finding of contempt for the same act.

(Added by L.1998 ch. 569, eff. 7/1/98.)

ARTICLE 7
CRIMINAL SEXUAL ASSAULT

§18.2-61. Rape.

A. If any person has sexual intercourse with a complaining witness who is not his or her spouse or causes a complaining witness, whether or not his or her spouse, to engage in sexual intercourse with any other person and such act is accomplished (i) against the complaining witness's will, by force, threat or intimidation of or against the complaining witness or another person, or (ii) through the use of the complaining witness's mental incapacity or physical helplessness, or (iii) with a child under age thirteen as the victim, he or she shall be guilty of rape.

B. If any person has sexual intercourse with his or her spouse and such act is accomplished against the spouse's will by force, threat or intimidation of or against the spouse or another, he or she shall be guilty of rape.

However, no person shall be found guilty under this subsection unless, at the time of the alleged offense, (i) the spouses were living separate and apart, or (ii) the defendant caused bodily injury to the spouse by the use of force or violence.

C. A violation of this section shall be punishable, in the discretion of the court or jury, by confinement in a state correctional facility for life or for any term not less than five years. There shall be a rebuttable presumption that a juvenile over the age of 10 but less than 12, does not possess the physical capacity to commit a violation of this section. In any case deemed appropriate by the court, all or part of any sentence imposed for a violation of subsection B may be suspended upon the defendant's completion of counseling or therapy, if not already provided, in the manner prescribed under §19.2-218.1 if, after consideration of the views of the complaining witness and such other evidence as may be relevant, the court finds such action will promote maintenance of the family unit and will be in the best interest of the complaining witness.

D. Upon a finding of guilt under subsection B in any case tried by the court without a jury, the court, without entering a judgment of guilt, upon motion of the defendant and with the consent of the complaining witness and the attorney for the Commonwealth, may defer further proceedings and place the defendant on probation pending completion of counseling or therapy, if not already provided, in the manner prescribed under §19.2-218.1. If the defendant fails to so complete such counseling or therapy, the court may make final disposition of the case and proceed as otherwise provided. If such counseling is completed as prescribed under §19.2-218.1, the court may discharge the defendant and dismiss the proceedings against him if, after consideration of the views of the complaining witness and such other evidence as may be relevant, the court finds such action will promote maintenance of the family unit and be in the best interest of the complaining witness.

(Chgd. by L.1997 ch. 330; L.1999 ch. 367, eff. 7/1/99.)

§18.2-62. Testing of certain persons for human immunodeficiency virus.

A. As soon as practicable following arrest, the attorney for the Commonwealth may request, after consultation with any victim, that any person charged with any crime involving sexual assault pursuant to this article or any offenses against children as prohibited by §§18.2-361, 18.2-366, 18.2-370, and 18.2-370.1 be requested to submit to testing for infection with human immunodeficiency virus. The person so charged shall be counseled about the meaning of the test, about acquired immunodeficiency syndrome, and about the transmission and prevention of infection with human immunodeficiency virus.

If the person so charged refuses to submit to the test, the court with jurisdiction of the case shall, after a finding of probable cause that the individual has committed the crime with which he is charged, order the accused to undergo testing for infection with human immunodeficiency virus.

B. Upon conviction, or adjudication as delinquent in the case of a juvenile, of any crime involving sexual assault pursuant to this article or any offenses against children as prohibited by §§18.2-361, 18.2-366, 18.2-370, and 18.2-370.1, the attorney for the Commonwealth may, after consultation with any victim and, upon the request of any victim shall, request and the court shall order the defendant to submit to testing for infection with human immunodeficiency virus. Any test conducted following conviction shall be in addition to such tests as may have been conducted following arrest pursuant to subsection A.

C. Confirmatory tests shall be conducted before any test result shall be determined to be positive. The results of the tests for infection with human immunodeficiency virus shall be confidential as provided in §32.1-36.1; however, the Department of Health shall also disclose the results to any victim and offer appropriate counseling as provided by subsection B of §32.1-37.2. The Department shall conduct surveillance and investigation in accordance with §32.1-39.

The results of such tests shall not be admissible as evidence in any criminal proceeding.

The cost of such tests shall be paid by the Commonwealth and taxed as part of the cost of such criminal proceedings.

§18.2-63. Carnal knowledge of child between thirteen and fifteen years of age.

If any person carnally knows, without the use of force, a child thirteen years of age or older but under fifteen years of age, such person shall be guilty of a Class 4 felony.

However, if such child is thirteen years of age or older but under fifteen years of age and consents to sexual intercourse and the accused is a minor and such consenting child is three years or more the accused's junior, the accused shall be guilty of a Class 6 felony. If such consenting child is less than three years the accused's junior, the accused shall be guilty of a Class 4 misdemeanor.

In calculating whether such child is three years or more a junior of the accused minor, the actual dates of birth of the child and the accused, respectively, shall be used.

For the purposes of this section, (i) a child under the age of thirteen years shall not be considered a consenting child and (ii) "carnal knowledge" includes the acts of sexual intercourse, cunnilingus, fellatio, anallingus, anal intercourse, and animate and inanimate object sexual penetration.

§18.2-63.1. Death of victim.

When the death of the victim occurs in connection with an offense under this article, it shall be immaterial in the prosecution thereof whether the alleged offense occurred before or after the death of the victim.

§18.2-64.1. Carnal knowledge of certain minors.

If any person providing services, paid or unpaid, to juveniles under the purview of the Juvenile and Domestic Relations District Court Law, or to juveniles who have been committed to the custody of the State Department of Juvenile

Justice, carnally knows, without the use of force, any minor fifteen years of age or older, when such minor is confined or detained in jail, is detained in any facility mentioned in §16.1-249, or has been committed to the custody of the Department of Juvenile Justice pursuant to §16.1-278.8, knowing or having good reason to believe that (i) such minor is in such confinement or detention status, (ii) such minor is a ward of the Department of Juvenile Justice, or (iii) such minor is on probation, furlough, or leave from or has escaped or absconded from such confinement, detention, or custody, he shall be guilty of a Class 6 felony.

For the purposes of this section, "carnal knowledge" includes the acts of sexual intercourse, cunnilingus, fellatio, anallingus, anal intercourse, and animate and inanimate object sexual penetration.

(Chgd. by L.1996 ch. 616, eff. 7/1/96.)

§18.2-64.2. Carnal knowledge of an inmate, parolee, probationer, or pretrial or posttrial offender; penalty.

An accused shall be guilty of carnal knowledge of an inmate, parolee, probationer, or pretrial or posttrial offender if he or she is an employee or contractual employee of, or a volunteer with, a state or local correctional facility or regional jail, the Department of Corrections, a local community-based probation program or a pretrial services program; is in a position of authority over the inmate, probationer, parolee, or a pretrial or posttrial offender; knows that the inmate, probationer, parolee, or pretrial or posttrial offender is under the jurisdiction of the state or local correctional facility, a regional jail, the Department of Corrections, a local community-based probation program, or a pretrial services program; and carnally knows, without the use of force, threat or intimidation (i) an inmate who has been committed to jail or convicted and sentenced to confinement in a state or local correctional facility or regional jail or (ii) a probationer, parolee, or a pretrial or posttrial offender under the jurisdiction of the Department of Corrections, a local community-based probation program, a pretrial services program, a local or regional jail for the purposes of imprisonment, a work program or any other parole/probationary or pretrial services program. Such offense is a Class 6 felony.

For the purposes of this section, "carnal knowledge" includes the acts of sexual intercourse, cunnilingus, fellatio, anallingus, anal intercourse and animate or inanimate object sexual penetration.

(Added by L.1999 ch. 294; chgd. by L.2000 ch. 1040, eff. 7/1/2000.)

§18.2-66. Effect of subsequent marriage to child over fourteen years of age.

If the carnal knowledge is with the consent of the child and such child is fourteen years of age or older, the subsequent marriage of the parties may be pleaded to any indictment found against the accused. The court, upon proof of such marriage, and that the parties are living together as husband and wife, and that the accused has properly provided for, supported, and maintained and is at the time properly providing, supporting and maintaining the spouse and the issue of such marriage, if any, shall continue the case from time to time and from term to term, until the spouse reaches the age of sixteen years. Thereupon the court shall dismiss the indictment already found against the accused for the aforesaid offense. However, if the accused deserts such spouse before the spouse reaches the age of sixteen without just cause, any indictment found against the accused for such offense shall be tried without regard to the number of times the case has been continued, and whether such continuance is entered upon the order book.

§18.2-67. Depositions of complaining witnesses in cases of criminal sexual assault and attempted criminal sexual assault.

Before or during the trial for an offense or attempted offense under this article, the judge of the court in which the case is pending, with the consent of the accused first obtained in open court, by an order of record, may direct that the deposition of the complaining witness be taken at a time and place designated in the order, and the judge may adjourn the taking thereof to such other time and places as he may deem necessary. Such deposition shall be taken before a judge of a circuit court in the county or city in which the offense was committed or the trial is had, and the judge shall rule upon all questions of evidence, and otherwise control the taking of the same as though it were taken in open court. At the taking of such deposition the attorney for the Commonwealth, as well as the accused and his attorneys, shall be present and they shall have the same rights in regard to the examination of such witness as if he or she were testifying in open court. No other person shall be present unless expressly permitted by the judge. Such deposition shall be read to the jury at the time such witness might have testified if such deposition had not been taken, and shall be considered by them, and shall have the same force and effect as though such testimony had been given orally in court. The judge may, in like manner, direct other depositions of the complaining witness, in rebuttal or otherwise, which shall be taken and read in the manner and under the conditions herein prescribed as to the first deposition. The cost of taking such depositions shall be paid by the Commonwealth.

§18.2-67.1. Forcible sodomy.

A. An accused shall be guilty of forcible sodomy if he or she engages in cunnilingus, fellatio, anallingus, or anal intercourse with a complaining witness who is not his or her spouse, or causes a complaining witness, whether or not his or her spouse, to engage in such acts with any other person, and

1. The complaining witness is less than thirteen years of age, or

2. The act is accomplished against the will of the complaining witness, by force, threat or intimidation of or against the complaining witness or another person, or through the use of the complaining witness's mental incapacity or physical helplessness.

B. An accused shall be guilty of forcible sodomy if (i) he or she engages in cunnilingus, fellatio, anallingus, or anal intercourse with his or her spouse, and (ii) such act is accomplished against the will of the spouse, by force, threat or intimidation of or against the spouse or another person.

However, no person shall be found guilty under this subsection unless, at the time of the alleged offense, (i) the spouses were living separate and apart, or (ii) the defendant caused bodily injury to the spouse by the use of force or violence.

C. Forcible sodomy is a felony punishable by confinement in a state correctional facility for life or for any term not less than five years. In any case deemed appropriate by the court, all or part of any sentence imposed for a violation of subsection B may be suspended upon the defendant's completion of counseling or therapy, if not already provided, in the manner prescribed under §19.2-218.1 if, after consideration of the views of the complaining witness and such other evidence as may be relevant, the court finds such action will promote maintenance of the family unit and will be in the best interest of the complaining witness.

D. Upon a finding of guilt under subsection B in any case tried by the court without a jury, the court, without entering a judgment of guilt, upon motion of the defendant and with the consent of the complaining witness and the attorney

for the Commonwealth, may defer further proceedings and place the defendant on probation pending completion of counseling or therapy, if not already provided, in the manner prescribed under §19.2-218.1. If the defendant fails to so complete such counseling or therapy, the court may make final disposition of the case and proceed as otherwise provided. If such counseling is completed as prescribed under §19.2-218.1, the court may discharge the defendant and dismiss the proceedings against him if, after consideration of the views of the complaining witness and such other evidence as may be relevant, the court finds such action will promote maintenance of the family unit and be in the best interest of the complaining witness.
(Chgd. by L.1999 ch. 367, eff. 7/1/99.)

§18.2-67.2. Object sexual penetration; penalty.

A. An accused shall be guilty of inanimate or animate object sexual penetration if he or she penetrates the labia majora or anus of a complaining witness who is not his or her spouse with any object, other than for a bona fide medical purpose, or causes such complaining witness to so penetrate his or her own body with an object or causes a complaining witness, whether or not his or her spouse, to engage in such acts with any other person or to penetrate, or to be penetrated by, an animal, and

1. The complaining witness is less than thirteen years of age, or

2. The act is accomplished against the will of the complaining witness, by force, threat or intimidation of or against the complaining witness or another person, or through the use of the complaining witness's mental incapacity or physical helplessness.

B. An accused shall be guilty of inanimate or animate object sexual penetration if (i) he or she penetrates the labia majora or anus of his or her spouse with any object other than for a bona fide medical purpose, or causes such spouse to so penetrate his or her own body with an object and (ii) such act is accomplished against the spouse's will by force, threat or intimidation of or against the spouse or another person.

However, no person shall be found guilty under this subsection unless, at the time of the alleged offense, (i) the spouses were living separate and apart or (ii) the defendant caused bodily injury to the spouse by the use of force or violence.

C. Inanimate or animate object sexual penetration is a felony punishable by confinement in the state correctional facility for life or for any term not less than five years. In any case deemed appropriate by the court, all or part of any sentence imposed for a violation of subsection B may be suspended upon the defendant's completion of counseling or therapy, if not already provided, in the manner prescribed under §19.2-218.1 if, after consideration of the views of the complaining witness and such other evidence as may be relevant, the court finds such action will promote maintenance of the family unit and will be in the best interest of the complaining witness.

D. Upon a finding of guilt under subsection B in any case tried by the court without a jury, the court, without entering a judgment of guilt, upon motion of the defendant and with the consent of the complaining witness and the attorney for the Commonwealth, may defer further proceedings and place the defendant on probation pending completion of counseling or therapy, if not already provided, in the manner prescribed under §19.2-218.1. If the defendant fails to so complete such counseling or therapy, the court may make final disposition of the case and proceed as otherwise provided. If such counseling is completed as prescribed under §19.2-218.1, the court may discharge the defendant and dismiss the proceedings against him if, after consideration of the views of the complaining witness and such other evidence as may be relevant, the court finds such action will promote maintenance of the family unit and be in the best interest of the complaining witness.
(Chgd. by L.1999 ch. 367, eff. 7/1/99.)

§18.2-67.2:1. Marital sexual assault.

A. An accused shall be guilty of marital sexual assault if (i) he or she engages in sexual intercourse, cunnilingus, fellatio, anallingus or anal intercourse with his or her spouse, or penetrates the labia majora or anus of his or her spouse with any object other than for a bona fide medical purpose, or causes such spouse to so penetrate his or her own body with an object, and (ii) such act is accomplished against the spouse's will by force or a present threat of force or intimidation of or against the spouse or another person.

B. A violation of this section shall be punishable by confinement in a state correctional facility for a term of not less than one year nor more than twenty years or, in the discretion of the court or jury, by confinement in jail for not more than twelve months and a fine of not more than $1,000, either or both. In any case deemed appropriate by the court, all or part of any sentence may be suspended upon the defendant's completion of counseling or therapy if not already provided, in the manner prescribed under §19.2-218.1 if, after consideration of the views of the complaining witness and such other evidence as may be relevant, the court finds such action will promote maintenance of the family unit and will be in the best interest of the complaining witness.

C. Upon a finding of guilt under this section in any case tried by the court without a jury, the court, without entering a judgment of guilt, upon motion of the defendant and with the consent of the complaining witness and the attorney for the Commonwealth, may defer further proceedings and place the defendant on probation pending completion of counseling or therapy, if not already provided, in the manner prescribed under §19.2-218.1. If the defendant fails to so complete such counseling or therapy, the court may enter an adjudication of guilt and proceed as otherwise provided. If such counseling is completed as prescribed under §19.2-218.1, the court may discharge the defendant and dismiss the proceedings against him if, after consideration of the views of the complaining witness and such other evidence as may be relevant, the court finds such action will promote maintenance of the family unit and be in the best interest of the complaining witness.

D. A violation of this section shall constitute a lesser, included offense of the respective violation set forth in §§18.2-61 B, 18.2-67.1 B or §18.2-67.2 B.
(Chgd. by L.1999 ch. 367, eff. 7/1/99.)

§18.2-67.3. Aggravated sexual battery.

A. An accused shall be guilty of aggravated sexual battery if he or she sexually abuses the complaining witness, and

1. The complaining witness is less than thirteen years of age, or

2. The act is accomplished against the will of the complaining witness, by force, threat or intimidation, or through the use of the complaining witness's mental incapacity or physical helplessness, and

a. The complaining witness is at least thirteen but less than fifteen years of age, or

b. The accused causes serious bodily or mental injury to the complaining witness, or

c. The accused uses or threatens to use a dangerous weapon.

B. Aggravated sexual battery is a felony punishable by confinement in a state correctional facility for a term of not less than one nor more than twenty years and by a fine of not more than $100,000.

§18.2-67.4. Sexual battery.

A. An accused shall be guilty of sexual battery if he or she sexually abuses, as defined in §18.2-67.10, (i) the complaining witness against the will of the complaining witness, by force, threat, intimidation or ruse, or through the use of the complaining witness's mental incapacity or physical helplessness, or (ii) an inmate who has been committed to jail or convicted and sentenced to confinement in a state or local correctional facility or regional jail, and the accused is an employee or contractual employee of, or a volunteer with, the state or local correctional facility or regional jail; is in a position of authority over the inmate; and knows that the inmate is under the jurisdiction of the state or local correctional facility or regional jail, or (iii) a probationer, parolee, or a pretrial or posttrial offender under the jurisdiction of the Department of Corrections, a local community-based probation program, a pretrial services program, a local or regional jail for the purposes of imprisonment, a work program or any other parole/probationary or pretrial services program and the accused is an employee or contractual employee of, or a volunteer with, the Department of Corrections, a local community-based probation program, a pretrial services program or a local or regional jail; is in a position of authority over an offender; and knows that the offender is under the jurisdiction of the Department of Corrections, a local community-based probation program, a pretrial services program or a local or regional jail.

B. Sexual battery is a Class 1 misdemeanor.

(Chgd. by L.1997 ch. 643; L.1999 ch. 294; L.2000 chs. 832, 1040, eff. 7/1/2000.)

§18.2-67.4:1. Infected sexual battery; penalty.

Any person who, knowing he is infected with HIV, syphilis, or hepatitis B, has sexual intercourse, cunnilingus, fellatio, anallingus or anal intercourse with the intent to transmit the infection to another person shall be guilty of a Class 6 felony.

"HIV" means the human immunodeficiency virus or any other related virus that causes acquired immunodeficiency syndrome (AIDS).

Nothing in this section shall prevent the prosecution of any other crime against persons under Chapter 4 (§18.2-30 et seq.) of this title. Any person charged with a violation of this section alleging he is infected with HIV shall be subject to the testing provisions of §18.2-62.

(Added by L.2000 ch. 831, eff. 7/1/2000.)

§18.2-67.5. Attempted rape, forcible sodomy, object sexual penetration, aggravated sexual battery, and sexual battery.

A. An attempt to commit rape, forcible sodomy, or inanimate or animate object sexual penetration shall be punishable as a Class 4 felony.

B. An attempt to commit aggravated sexual battery shall be a felony punishable as a Class 6 felony.

C. An attempt to commit sexual battery is a Class 1 misdemeanor.

§18.2-67.5:1. Punishment upon conviction of third misdemeanor offense.

When a person is convicted of sexual battery in violation of §18.2-67.4, attempted sexual battery in violation of subsection C of §18.2-67.5, a violation of §18.2-371 involving consensual intercourse with a child, or indecent exposure of himself or procuring another to expose himself in violation of §18.2-387 and it is alleged in the warrant, information or indictment on which the person is convicted and found by the court or jury trying the case, that the person has previously been convicted within the ten-year period immediately preceding the offense charged of two or more of the offenses specified in this section, each such offense occurring on a different date, he shall be guilty of a Class 6 felony.

§18.2-67.5:2. Punishment upon conviction of certain subsequent felony sexual assault.

A. Any person convicted of (i) more than one offense specified in subsection B or (ii) one of the offenses specified in subsection B of this section and one of the offenses specified in subsection B of §18.2-67.5:3 when such offenses were not part of a common act, transaction or scheme, and who has been at liberty as defined in §53.1-151 between each conviction shall, upon conviction of the second or subsequent such offense, be sentenced to the maximum term authorized by statute for such offense, and shall not have all or any part of such sentence suspended, provided it is admitted, or found by the jury or judge before whom the person is tried, that he has been previously convicted of at least one of the specified offenses.

B. The provisions of subsection A shall apply to felony convictions for:

1. Carnal knowledge of a child between thirteen and fifteen years of age in violation of §18.2-63 when the offense is committed by a person over the age of eighteen;
2. Carnal knowledge of certain minors in violation of §18.2-64.1;
3. Aggravated sexual battery in violation of §18.2-67.3;
4. Crimes against nature in violation of subsection B of §18.2-361;
5. Adultery or fornication with one's own child or grandchild in violation of §18.2-366;
6. Taking indecent liberties with a child in violation of §18.2-370 or §18.2-370.1; or
7. Conspiracy to commit any offense listed in subdivisions 1 through 6 pursuant to §18.2-22.

C. For purposes of this section, prior convictions shall include (i) adult convictions for felonies under the laws of any state or the United States that are substantially similar to those listed in subsection B and (ii) findings of not innocent, adjudications or convictions in the case of a juvenile if the juvenile offense is substantially similar to those listed in subsection B, the offense would be a felony if committed by an adult in the Commonwealth and the offense was committed less than twenty years before the second offense.

The Commonwealth shall notify the defendant in writing, at least thirty days prior to trial, of its intention to seek punishment pursuant to this section.

(Added by L.1995 ch. 834; chgd. by L.2000 ch. 333, eff. 7/1/2000.)

§18.2-67.5:3. Punishment upon conviction of certain subsequent violent felony sexual assault.

A. Any person convicted of more than one offense specified in subsection B, when such offenses were not part of a common act, transaction or scheme, and who has been at liberty as defined in §53.1-151 between each conviction shall, upon conviction of the second or subsequent such offense, be sentenced to life imprisonment and shall not have all or any portion of the sentence suspended, provided it is admitted, or found by the jury or judge before whom he is tried, that he has been previously convicted of at least one of the specified offenses.

B. The provisions of subsection A shall apply to convictions for:

1. Rape in violation of §18.2-61;
2. Forcible sodomy in violation of §18.2-67.1;
3. Object sexual penetration in violation of §18.2-67.2;
4. Abduction with intent to defile in violation of §18.248; or
5. Conspiracy to commit any offense listed in subdivisions 1 through 4 pursuant to §18.2-22.

C. For purposes of this section, prior convictions shall include (i) adult convictions for felonies under the laws of any state or the United States that are substantially similar to those listed in subsection B and (ii) findings of not innocent, adjudications or convictions in the case of a juvenile if the juvenile offense is substantially similar to those listed in subsection B, the offense would be a felony if committed by an adult in the Commonwealth and the offense was committed less than twenty years before the second offense.

The Commonwealth shall notify the defendant in writing, at least thirty days prior to trial, of its intention to seek punishment pursuant to this section.
(Added by L.1995 ch. 834, eff. 7/1/95.)

§18.2-67.6. Proof of physical resistance not required.
The Commonwealth need not demonstrate that the complaining witness cried out or physically resisted the accused in order to convict the accused of an offense under this article, but the absence of such resistance may be considered when relevant to show that the act alleged was not against the will of the complaining witness.

§18.2-67.7. Admission of evidence.
A. In prosecutions under this article, general reputation or opinion evidence of the complaining witness's unchaste character or prior sexual conduct shall not be admitted. Unless the complaining witness voluntarily agrees otherwise, evidence of specific instances of his or her prior sexual conduct shall be admitted only if it is relevant and is:

1. Evidence offered to provide an alternative explanation for physical evidence of the offense charged which is introduced by the prosecution, limited to evidence designed to explain the presence of semen, pregnancy, disease, or physical injury to the complaining witness's intimate parts; or

2. Evidence of sexual conduct between the complaining witness and the accused offered to support a contention that the alleged offense was not accomplished by force, threat or intimidation or through the use of the complaining witness's mental incapacity or physical helplessness, provided that the sexual conduct occurred within a period of time reasonably proximate to the offense charged under the circumstances of this case; or

3. Evidence offered to rebut evidence of the complaining witness's prior sexual conduct introduced by the prosecution.

B. Nothing contained in this section shall prohibit the accused from presenting evidence relevant to show that the complaining witness had a motive to fabricate the charge against the accused. If such evidence relates to the past sexual conduct of the complaining witness with a person other than the accused, it shall not be admitted and may not be referred to at any preliminary hearing or trial unless the party offering same files a written notice generally describing the evidence prior to the introduction of any evidence, or the opening statement of either counsel, whichever first occurs, at the preliminary hearing or trial at which the admission of the evidence may be sought.

C. Evidence described in subsections A and B of this section shall not be admitted and may not be referred to at any preliminary hearing or trial until the court first determines the admissibility of that evidence at an evidentiary hearing to be held before the evidence is introduced at such preliminary hearing or trial. The court shall exclude from the evidentiary hearing all persons except the accused, the complaining witness, other necessary witnesses, and required court personnel. If the court determines that the evidence meets the requirements of subsections A and B of this section, it shall be admissible before the judge or jury trying the case in the ordinary course of the preliminary hearing or trial. If the court initially determines that the evidence is inadmissible, but new information is discovered during the course of the preliminary hearing or trial which may make such evidence admissible, the court shall determine in an evidentiary hearing whether such evidence is admissible.

§18.2-67.8. Closed preliminary hearings.
In preliminary hearings for offenses charged under this article or under §§18.2-361, 18.2-366, 18.2-370, or §18.2-370.1, the court may, on its own motion or at the request of the Commonwealth, the complaining witness, the accused, or their counsel, exclude from the courtroom all persons except officers of the court and persons whose presence, in the judgment of the court, would be supportive of the complaining witness or the accused and would not impair the conduct of a fair hearing.

§18.2-67.9. Testimony by child victims using two-way closed-circuit television.
A. In any criminal proceeding, including preliminary hearings, involving an alleged offense against a child, relating to a violation of the laws pertaining to kidnapping (§18.2-47 et seq.), criminal sexual assault (§18.2-61 et seq.) or family offenses pursuant to Article 4 (§18.2-362 et seq.) of Chapter 8 of Title 18.2, the Commonwealth's attorney or the defendant may apply for an order from the court that the testimony of the alleged victim or a child witness be taken in a room outside the courtroom and be televised by two-way closed-circuit television. The party seeking such order shall apply for the order at least seven days before the trial date or at least seven days before such other preliminary proceeding to which the order is to apply.

A1. The provisions of this section shall apply to the following:

1. An alleged victim who was fourteen years of age or under at the time of the alleged offense and is sixteen or under at the time of the trial; and

2. Any child witness who is fourteen years of age or under at the time of the trial.

B. The court may order that the testimony of the child be taken by closed-circuit television as provided in subsections A and A1 if it finds that the child is unavailable to testify in open court in the presence of the defendant, the jury, the judge, and the public, for any of the following reasons:

1. The child's persistent refusal to testify despite judicial requests to do so;

2. The child's substantial inability to communicate about the offense; or

3. The substantial likelihood, based upon expert opinion testimony, that the child will suffer severe emotional trauma from so testifying.

Any ruling on the child's unavailability under this subsection shall be supported by the court with findings on the record or with written findings in a court not of record.

C. In any proceeding in which closed-circuit television is used to receive testimony, the Commonwealth's attorney and the defendant's attorney shall be present in the room with the child, and the child shall be subject to direct and cross-examination. The only other persons allowed to be present in the room with the child during his testimony shall be those persons necessary to operate the closed-circuit equipment, and any other person whose presence is determined by the court to be necessary to the welfare and well-being of the child.

D. The child's testimony shall be transmitted by closed-circuit television into the courtroom for the defendant, jury, judge and public to view. The defendant shall be provided with a means of private, contemporaneous communication with his attorney during the testimony.

E. Notwithstanding any other provision of law, none of the cost of the two-way closed-circuit television shall be assessed against the defendant.
(Chgd. by L.1999 ch. 668, eff. 7/1/99.)

§18.2-67.10. General definitions.

As used in this article:

1. "Complaining witness" means the person alleged to have been subjected to rape, forcible sodomy, inanimate or animate object sexual penetration, marital sexual assault, aggravated sexual battery, or sexual battery.

2. "Intimate parts" means the genitalia, anus, groin, breast, or buttocks of any person.

3. "Mental incapacity" means that condition of the complaining witness existing at the time of an offense under this article which prevents the complaining witness from understanding the nature or consequences of the sexual act involved in such offense and about which the accused knew or should have known.

4. "Physical helplessness" means unconsciousness or any other condition existing at the time of an offense under this article which otherwise rendered the complaining witness physically unable to communicate an unwillingness to act and about which the accused knew or should have known.

5. The complaining witness's "prior sexual conduct" means any sexual conduct on the part of the complaining witness which took place before the conclusion of the trial, excluding the conduct involved in the offense alleged under this article.

6. "Sexual abuse" means an act committed with the intent to sexually molest, arouse, or gratify any person, where:

a. The accused intentionally touches the complaining witness's intimate parts or material directly covering such intimate parts;

b. The accused forces the complaining witness to touch the accused's, the witness's own, or another person's intimate parts or material directly covering such intimate parts or;

c. The accused forces another person to touch the complaining witness's intimate parts or material directly covering such intimate parts.

ARTICLE 9
ABORTION

§18.2-71. Producing abortion or miscarriage, etc.; penalty.

Except as provided in other sections of this article, if any person administer to, or cause to be taken by a woman, any drug or other thing, or use means, with intent to destroy her unborn child, or to produce abortion or miscarriage, and thereby destroy such child, or produce such abortion or miscarriage, he shall be guilty of a Class 4 felony.

§18.2-72. When abortion lawful during first trimester of pregnancy.

Notwithstanding any of the provisions of §18.2-71, it shall be lawful for any physician licensed by the Virginia State Board of Medicine to practice medicine and surgery, to terminate or attempt to terminate a human pregnancy or aid or assist in the termination of a human pregnancy by performing an abortion or causing a miscarriage on any woman during the first trimester of pregnancy.

§18.2-73. When abortion lawful during second trimester of pregnancy.

Notwithstanding any of the provisions of §18.2-71 and in addition to the provisions of §18.2-72, it shall be lawful for any physician licensed by the Virginia State Board of Medicine to practice medicine and surgery, to terminate or attempt to terminate a human pregnancy or aid or assist in the termination of a human pregnancy by performing an abortion or causing a miscarriage on any woman during the second trimester of pregnancy and prior to the third trimester of pregnancy provided such procedure is performed in a hospital licensed by the State Department of Health or under the control of the State Board of Mental Health, Mental Retardation and Substance Abuse Services.

§18.2-74. When abortion or termination of pregnancy lawful after second trimester of pregnancy.

Notwithstanding any of the provisions of §18.2-71 and in addition to the provisions of §§18.2-72 and 18.2-73, it shall be lawful for any physician licensed by the Virginia State Board of Medicine to practice medicine and surgery to terminate or attempt to terminate a human pregnancy or aid or assist in the termination of a human pregnancy by performing an abortion or causing a miscarriage on any woman in a stage of pregnancy subsequent to the second trimester provided the following conditions are met:

(a) Said operation is performed in a hospital licensed by the Virginia State Department of Health or under the control of the State Board of Mental Health, Mental Retardation and Substance Abuse Services.

(b) The physician and two consulting physicians certify and so enter in the hospital record of the woman, that in their medical opinion, based upon their best clinical judgment, the continuation of the pregnancy is likely to result in the death of the woman or substantially and irremediably impair the mental or physical health of the woman.

(c) Measures for life support for the product of such abortion or miscarriage must be available and utilized if there is any clearly visible evidence of viability.

§18.2-74.1. Abortion, etc., when necessary to save life of woman.

In the event it is necessary for a licensed physician to terminate a human pregnancy or assist in the termination of a human pregnancy by performing an abortion or causing a miscarriage on any woman in order to save her life, in the opinion of the physician so performing the abortion or causing the miscarriage, §§18.2-71, 18.2-73 and 18.2-74 shall not be applicable.

§18.2-74.2. Partial birth abortion prohibited.

A. Notwithstanding the provisions of §§18.2-72, 18.2-73 and 18.2-74, a physician shall not knowingly perform a partial birth abortion that is not necessary to save the life of a mother. A violation of this section shall be punishable as a Class 1 misdemeanor.

B. A physician charged with an offense under this section may seek a review pursuant to subsection E before a medical necessity advisory committee on whether the partial birth abortion was necessary to save the life of a mother. In any case in which a physician charged with an offense under this section intends to seek a review before a medical necessity advisory committee he, or his counsel, shall give notice in writing to the attorney for the Commonwealth, at least twenty-one days prior to his trial, of his intention to seek such a review. The defendant shall be entitled to a continuance of his criminal trial proceedings for the review to occur. The report and findings of the committee shall be admissible upon motion of either party at the trial of the defendant. In the event that such a notice of intention to seek review before a medical necessity advisory committee is not given to the attorney for the Commonwealth as described above, the review is waived by the defendant. A waiver of review in the general district court shall constitute a waiver of review in any subsequent proceedings, regardless of the court in which such subsequent proceedings may be held. A defendant may have no more than one review; and an appeal, trial de novo or retrial shall not entitle the defendant to request a second review.

C. A woman upon whom a partial birth abortion is performed may not be prosecuted under this section for a conspiracy to violate this section or for any other offense arising out of the performance of a partial birth abortion.

D. As used in this section:

"Partial birth abortion" means an abortion in which the person performing the abortion deliberately and intentionally delivers a living fetus or a substantial portion thereof into the vagina for the purpose of performing a procedure the person knows will kill the fetus, performs the procedure, kills the fetus and completes the delivery.

"Physician" means a doctor of medicine or osteopathy licensed and legally authorized by the Board of Medicine to practice medicine and surgery, or any other individual legally authorized to perform abortions.

E. Upon written request of a physician made pursuant to subsection B for a review by a medical necessity advisory committee, the Clerk of the Supreme Court of Virginia shall promptly appoint a medical necessity advisory committee consisting of three impartial practitioners licensed and actively practicing medicine in the Commonwealth, no more than one of whom has limited his practice to obstetrics and gynecology. No more than one such practitioner shall have his principal office in the city or county in which the alleged violation of this section occurred. Such appointments shall be made from a list of practitioners submitted to the Clerk by the Board of Medicine from nominations made by the deans of the medical schools located in the Commonwealth. The Clerk shall designate one member of the committee as chairman. No person appointed to serve on a medical malpractice review panel which is investigating a complaint involving the defendant shall be eligible to serve on a medical necessity advisory committee investigating a complaint under review by the medical malpractice review panel.

The function of a medical necessity advisory committee appointed pursuant to this section shall be to examine whether the performance of a partial birth abortion was necessary to save the life of a mother. The committee shall conduct a review of the pertinent medical records and provide an opportunity for the attorney for the Commonwealth and the physician and his counsel to meet with the committee and present additional information to the committee.

When a dispute regarding the information to be considered by the committee is not resolved by the committee, the chairman of the committee shall submit the issue to the court in which the criminal case is pending for resolution. Proceedings of the committee shall be in accordance with rules established by the committee. Testimony before the committee need not be recorded.

At the conclusion of its review, but in no event later than forty days after its appointment, the committee shall submit all documentary evidence and records to the court, accompanied by a report containing a summary of the evidence and one of the following findings:

1. The evidence presented to the committee supports a conclusion that the partial birth abortion was necessary to save the life of the mother; or

2. The evidence presented to the committee supports a conclusion that the partial birth abortion was not necessary to save the life of the mother.

An individual member of the committee may include in the report his separate views if he is unable to agree with the committee's report. Upon receipt, the court shall promptly transmit to all counsel of record copies of the report and other materials submitted to the court by the committee.

No member of the medical necessity advisory committee may be called as a witness in the criminal proceeding. A member of the committee shall have immunity from civil liability resulting from any communication, finding, opinion or conclusion made in the course of his duties as a member of the committee unless such person acted in bad faith or with malicious intent.

F. If any one or more subsections, provisions, clauses, phrases or words of this section or the application thereof to any person or circumstance is found to be unconstitutional, the same is hereby declared to be severable and the balance of this section shall remain effective.

(Added by L.1998 chs. 448, 579, eff. 7/1/98.)

§18.2-75. Conscience clause.

Nothing in §§18.2-72, 18.2-73 or 18.2-74 shall require a hospital or other medical facility or physician to admit any patient under the provisions hereof for the purpose of performing an abortion. In addition, any person who shall state in writing an objection to any abortion or all abortions on personal, ethical, moral or religious grounds shall not be required to participate in procedures which will result in such abortion, and the refusal of such person, hospital or other medical facility to participate therein shall not form the basis of any claim for damages on account of such refusal or for any disciplinary or recriminatory action against such person, nor shall any such person be denied employment because of such objection or refusal. The written objection shall remain in effect until such person shall revoke it in writing or terminate his association with the facility with which it is filed.

§18.2-76. Informed consent required.

Before performing any abortion or inducing any miscarriage or terminating a pregnancy as provided for in §§18.2-72, 18.2-73 or §18.2-74, the physician shall obtain the informed written consent of the pregnant woman; provided, however, if such woman has been adjudicated incapacitated by any court of competent jurisdiction or if the physician knows or has good reason to believe that such woman is incapacitated as adjudicated by a court of competent jurisdiction, then only after permission is given in writing by a parent, guardian, committee, or other person standing in loco parentis to the woman, may the physician perform the abortion or otherwise terminate the pregnancy.

The physician shall inform the pregnant woman of the nature of the proposed procedure to be utilized and the risks, if any, in her particular case to her health in terminating or continuing the pregnancy.

(Chgd. by L.1997 ch. 801, eff. 1/1/98.)

§18.2-76.1. Encouraging or promoting abortion.

If any person, by publication, lecture, advertisement, or by the sale or circulation of any publication, or through the use of a referral agency for profit, or in any other manner, encourage or promote the performing of an abortion or the inducing of a miscarriage in this Commonwealth which is prohibited under this article, he shall be guilty of a Class 3 misdemeanor.

§18.2-76.2. *(Omitted due to limited applicability.)*

CHAPTER 5
CRIMES AGAINST PROPERTY

Article

ARTICLE 1
ARSON AND RELATED CRIMES

Section

§18.2-77. Burning or destroying dwelling house, etc.

A. If any person maliciously (i) burns, or by use of any explosive device or substance destroys, in whole or in part, or causes to be burned or destroyed, or (ii) aids, counsels or procures the burning or destruction of any dwelling house or manufactured home whether belonging to himself or another, or any occupied hotel, hospital, mental health facility, or other house in which persons usually dwell or lodge, any occupied railroad car, boat, vessel, or river craft in which persons usually dwell or lodge, or any occupied jail or prison, or any occupied church or occupied building owned or leased by a church that is immediately adjacent to a church, he shall be guilty of a felony, punishable by imprisonment for life or for any period not less than five years and, subject to subdivision g of §18.2-10, a fine of not more than $100,000. Any person who maliciously sets fire to anything, or aids, counsels or procures the setting fire to anything, by the burning whereof such occupied dwelling house, manufactured home, hotel, hospital, mental health facility or other house, or railroad car, boat, vessel, or river craft, jail or prison, church or building owned or leased by a church that is immediately adjacent to a church, is burned shall be guilty of a violation of this subsection.

B. Any such burning or destruction when the building or other place mentioned in subsection A is unoccupied, shall be punishable as a Class 4 felony.

C. For purposes of this section, "church" shall be defined as in §18.2-127.

(Chgd. by L.1997 ch. 832, eff. 7/1/97.)

§18.2-78. What not deemed dwelling house.

No outhouse, not adjoining a dwelling house, nor under the same roof, although within the curtilage thereof, shall be deemed a part of such dwelling house, within the meaning of this chapter, unless some person usually lodge therein at night.

§18.2-79. Burning or destroying meeting house, etc.

If any person maliciously burns, or by the use of any explosive device or substance, maliciously destroys, in whole or in part, or causes to be burned or destroyed, or aids, counsels, or procures the burning or destroying, of any meeting house, courthouse, townhouse, college, academy, schoolhouse, or other building erected for public use except an asylum, hotel, jail, prison or church or building owned or leased by a church that is immediately adjacent to a church, or any banking house, warehouse, storehouse, manufactory, mill, or other house, whether the property of himself or of another person, not usually occupied by persons lodging therein at night, at a time when any person is therein, or if he maliciously sets fire to anything, or causes to be set on fire, or aids, counsels, or procures the setting on fire of anything, by the burning whereof any building mentioned in this section is burned, at a time when any person is therein, he shall be guilty of a Class 3 felony. If such offense is committed when no person is in such building mentioned in this section, the offender shall be guilty of a Class 4 felony.

(Chgd. by L.1997 ch. 832, eff. 7/1/97.)

§18.2-80. Burning or destroying any other building or structure.

If any person maliciously, or with intent to defraud an insurance company or other person, burn, or by the use of any explosive device or substance, maliciously destroy, in whole or in part, or cause to be burned or destroyed, or aid, counsel or procure the burning or destruction of any building, bridge, lock, dam or other structure, whether the property of himself or of another, at a time when any person is therein or thereon, the burning or destruction whereof is not punishable under any other section of this chapter, he shall be guilty of a Class 3 felony. If he commits such offense at a time when no person is in such building, or other structure, and such building, or other structure, with the property therein, be of the value of $200, or more, he shall be guilty of a Class 4 felony, and if it and the property therein be of less value, he shall be guilty of a Class 1 misdemeanor.

§18.2-81. Burning or destroying personal property, standing grain, etc.

If any person maliciously, or with intent to defraud an insurance company or other person, set fire to or burn or destroy by any explosive device or substance, or cause to be burned, or destroyed by any explosive device or substance, or aid, counsel, or procure the burning or destroying by any explosive device or substance, of any personal property, standing grain or other crop, he shall, if the thing burnt or destroyed, be of the value of $200 or more, be guilty of a Class 4 felony, and if the thing burnt or destroyed be of less value, he shall be guilty of a Class 1 misdemeanor.

§18.2-82. Burning building or structure while in such building or structure with intent to commit felony.

If any person while in any building or other structure unlawfully, with intent to commit a felony therein, shall burn or cause to be burned, in whole or in part, such building or other structure, the burning of which is not punishable under any other section of this chapter, he shall be guilty of a Class 4 felony.

§18.2-83. Threats to bomb or damage buildings or means of transportation; false information as to danger to such buildings, etc.; punishment; venue.

A. Any person (a) who makes and communicates to another by any means any threat to bomb, burn, destroy or in any manner damage any place of assembly, building or other structure, or any means of transportation, or (b) who communicates to another, by any means, information, knowing the same to be false, as to the existence of any peril of bombing, burning, destruction or damage to any such place of assembly, building or other structure, or any means of transportation, shall be guilty of a Class 5 felony; provided, however, that if such person be under fifteen years of age, he shall be guilty of a Class 1 misdemeanor.

B. A violation of this section may be prosecuted either in the jurisdiction from which the communication was made or in the jurisdiction where the communication was received.

§18.2-84. Causing, inciting, etc., commission of act proscribed by §18.2-83.

Any person fifteen years of age or over, including the parent of any child, who shall cause, encourage, incite, entice or solicit any person, including a child, to commit any act proscribed by the provisions of §18.2-83, shall be guilty of a Class 5 felony.

§18.2-85. Manufacture, possession, use, etc., of fire bombs or explosive materials or devices; penalties.

For the purpose of this section:

"Fire bomb" means any container of a flammable material such as gasoline, kerosene, fuel oil, or other chemical compound, having a wick or other substance or device which, if set or ignited, is capable of igniting such flammable material or chemical compound but does not include a similar device commercially manufactured and used solely for the purpose of illumination or cooking.

"Explosive material" means any chemical compound, mechanical mixture or device that is commonly used or can be used for the purpose of producing an explosion and which contains any oxidizing and combustive agents or other ingredients in such proportions, quantities or packaging that an ignition by fire, friction, concussion, percussion, detonation or by any part of the compound or mixture may cause a sudden generation of highly heated gases. These materials include, but are not limited to, gunpowder, powders for blasting, high explosives, blasting materials, fuses (other than electric circuit breakers), detonators, and other detonating agents and smokeless powder.

"Device" means any instrument, apparatus or contrivance, including its component parts, that is capable of producing or intended to produce an explosion but shall not include fireworks and defined in §59.1-142.

"Hoax explosive device" means any device which by its design, construction, content or characteristics appears to be or to contain a bomb or other destructive device or explosive but which is, in fact, an imitation of any such device or explosive.

Any person who (i) possesses materials with which fire bombs or explosive materials or devices can be made with the intent to manufacture fire bombs or explosive materials or devices or (ii) manufactures, transports, distributes, possesses or uses a fire bomb or explosive materials or devices shall be guilty of a Class 5 felony. Any person who constructs, uses, places, sends, or causes to be sent any hoax explosive device so as to intentionally cause another person to believe that such device is a bomb or explosive shall be guilty of a Class 6 felony.

Nothing in this section shall prohibit the authorized manufacture, transportation, distribution, use or possession of any material, substance, or device by a member of the armed forces of the United States, fire fighters or law-enforcement officers, nor shall it prohibit the manufacture, transportation, distribution, use or possession of any material, substance or device to be used solely for scientific research, educational purposes or for any lawful purpose, subject to the provisions of §§27-97 and 27-97.2.

(Chgd. by L.2000 ch. 951, eff. 7/1/2000, ch. 1065, eff. 1/1/2001.)

§18.2-86. Setting fire to woods, fences, grass, etc.

If any person maliciously set fire to any wood, fence, grass, straw or other thing capable of spreading fire on land, he shall be guilty of a Class 6 felony.

§18.2-87. Setting woods, etc., on fire intentionally whereby another is damaged or jeopardized.

Any person who intentionally sets or procures another to set fire to any woods, brush, leaves, grass, straw, or any other inflammable substance capable of spreading fire, and who intentionally allows the fire to escape to lands not his own, whereby the property of another is damaged or jeopardized, shall be guilty of a Class 1 misdemeanor, and shall be liable for the full amount of all expenses incurred in fighting the fire.

§18.2-87.1. Setting off chemical bombs capable of producing smoke in certain public buildings.

It shall be unlawful for any person to willfully and intentionally set off or cause to be set off any chemical bomb capable of producing smoke in any building used for public assembly or regularly used by the public including, but not limited to, schools, theaters, stores, office buildings, shopping malls, coliseums and arenas. Any person convicted of a violation of this section shall be guilty of a Class 2 misdemeanor.

§18.2-88. Carelessly damaging property by fire.

If any person carelessly, negligently or intentionally set any woods or marshes on fire, or set fire to any stubble, brush, straw, or any other substance capable of spreading fire on lands, whereby the property of another is damaged or jeopardized, he shall be guilty of a Class 4 misdemeanor, and shall be liable for the full amount of all expenses incurred in fighting the fire.

ARTICLE 2
BURGLARY AND RELATED OFFENSES

§18.2-89. Burglary; how punished.

If any person break and enter the dwelling house of another in the nighttime with intent to commit a felony or any larceny therein, he shall be guilty of burglary, punishable as a Class 3 felony; provided, however, that if such person was armed with a deadly weapon at the time of such entry, he shall be guilty of a Class 2 felony.

§18.2-90. Entering dwelling house, etc., with intent to commit murder, rape, robbery or arson.

If any person in the nighttime enters without breaking or in the daytime breaks and enters or enters and conceals himself in a dwelling house or an adjoining, occupied outhouse or in the nighttime enters without breaking or at any time breaks and enters or enters and conceals himself in any office, shop, manufactured home, storehouse, warehouse, banking house, church as defined in §18.2-127, or other house, or any ship, vessel or river craft or any railroad car, or any automobile, truck or trailer, if such automobile, truck or trailer is used as a dwelling or place of human habitation, with intent to commit murder, rape, robbery or arson in violation of §§18.2-77, 18.2-79 or §18.2-80, he shall be deemed guilty of statutory burglary, which offense shall be a Class 3 felony. However, if such person was armed with a deadly weapon at the time of such entry, he shall be guilty of a Class 2 felony.

(Chgd. by L.1997 ch. 832, eff. 7/1/97.)

§18.2-91. Entering dwelling house, etc., with intent to commit larceny, assault and battery or other felony.

If any person commits any of the acts mentioned in §18.2-90 with intent to commit larceny, or any felony other than murder, rape, robbery or arson in violation of §§18.2-77, 18.2-79 or §18.2-80, or if any person commits any of the acts mentioned in §18.2-89 or §18.2-90 with intent to commit assault and battery, he shall be guilty of statutory burglary, punishable by confinement in a state correctional facility for not less than one or more than twenty years or, in the discretion of the jury or the court trying the case without a jury, be confined in jail for a period not exceeding twelve months or fined not more than $2,500, either or both. However, if the person was armed with a deadly weapon at the time of such entry, he shall be guilty of a Class 2 felony.

(Chgd. by L.1996 ch. 1040; L.1997 ch. 832, eff. 7/1/97.)

§18.2-92. Breaking and entering dwelling house with intent to commit other misdemeanor.

If any person break and enter a dwelling house while said dwelling is occupied, either in the day or nighttime, with the intent to commit any misdemeanor except assault and battery or trespass, he shall be guilty of a Class 6 felony. However, if the person was armed with a deadly weapon at the time of such entry, he shall be guilty of a Class 2 felony.

§18.2-93. Entering bank, armed, with intent to commit larceny.

If any person, armed with a deadly weapon, shall enter any banking house, in the daytime or in the nighttime, with intent to commit larceny of money, bonds, notes, or other evidence of debt therein, he shall be guilty of a Class 2 felony.

§18.2-94. Possession of burglarious tools, etc.

If any person have in his possession any tools, implements or outfit, with intent to commit burglary, robbery or larceny, upon conviction thereof he shall be guilty of a Class 5 felony. The possession of such burglarious tools, implements or outfit by any person other than a licensed dealer, shall be prima facie evidence of an intent to commit burglary, robbery or larceny.

ARTICLE 3
LARCENY AND RECEIVING STOLEN GOODS

§18.2-95. Grand larceny defined; how punished.

Any person who (i) commits larceny from the person of another of money or other thing of value of $5 or more, (ii) commits simple larceny not from the person of another of goods and chattels of the value of $200 or more, or (iii) commits simple larceny not from the person of another of any firearm, regardless of the firearm's value, shall be guilty of grand larceny, punishable by imprisonment in a state correctional facility for not less than one nor more than twenty years or, in the discretion of the jury or court trying the case without a jury, be confined in jail for a period not exceeding twelve months or fined not more than $2,500, either or both. *(Chgd. by L.1998 ch. 821, eff. 7/1/98.)*

§18.2-96. Petit larceny defined; how punished.

Any person who:

1. Commits larceny from the person of another of money or other thing of value of less than $5, or

2. Commits simple larceny not from the person of another of goods and chattels of the value of less than $200, except as provided in subdivision (iii) of §18.2-95, shall be deemed guilty of petit larceny, which shall be punishable as a Class 1 misdemeanor.

§18.2-96.1. Identification of certain personalty.

A. The owner of personal property may permanently mark such property, including any part thereof, for the purpose of identification with the social security number of the owner, preceded by the letters "VA."

B. *(Repealed.)*

C. It shall be unlawful for any person to remove, alter, deface, destroy, conceal, or otherwise obscure the manufacturer's serial number or marks, including personalty marked with a social security number preceded by the letters "VA," from such personal property or any part thereof, without the consent of the owner, with intent to render it or other property unidentifiable.

D. It shall be unlawful for any person to possess such personal property or any part thereof, without the consent of the owner, knowing that the manufacturer's serial number or any other distinguishing identification number or mark, including personalty marked with a social security number preceded by the letters "VA," has been removed, altered, defaced, destroyed, concealed, or otherwise obscured with the intent to violate the provisions of this section.

E. A person in possession of such property which is otherwise in violation of this section may apply in writing to the Bureau of Criminal Investigation, Virginia State Police, for assignment of a number for the personal property providing he can show that he is the lawful owner of the property. If a number is issued in conformity with the provisions of this section, then the person to whom it was issued and any person to whom the property is lawfully disposed of shall not be in violation of this section. This subsection shall apply only when the application has been filed by a person prior to arrest or authorization of a warrant of arrest for that person by a court.

F. Any person convicted of an offense under this section, when the value of the personalty is less than $200, shall be guilty of a Class 1 misdemeanor and, when the value of the personalty is $200 or more, shall be guilty of a Class 5 felony.

§18.2-97. Larceny of certain animals and poultry.

Any person who shall be guilty of the larceny of a dog, horse, pony, mule, cow, steer, bull or calf shall be guilty of a Class 5 felony; and any person who shall be guilty of the larceny of any poultry of the value of $5 or more, but of the value of less than $200, or of a sheep, lamb, swine, or goat, of the value of less than $200, shall be guilty of a Class 6 felony.

§18.2-98. Larceny of bank notes, checks, etc., or any book of accounts.

If any person steal any bank note, check, or other writing or paper of value, whether the same represents money and passes as currency, or otherwise, or any book of accounts, for or concerning money or goods due or to be delivered, he shall be deemed guilty of larceny thereof, and receive the same punishment, according to the value of the thing stolen, prescribed for the punishment of the larceny of goods and chattels. The provisions of this section shall be construed to embrace all bank notes and papers of value representing money and passing as currency, whether the same be the issue of this Commonwealth or any other state, or of the United States, or of any corporation, and shall include all other papers of value, of whatever description. In a prosecution under this section, the money due on or secured by the writing, paper or book, and remaining unsatisfied, or which in any event might be collected thereon, or the value of the property or money affected thereby, shall be deemed to be the value of the article stolen.

§18.2-99. Larceny of things fixed to the freehold.

Things which savor of the realty, and are at the time they are taken part of the freehold, whether they be of the substance or produce thereof, or affixed thereto, shall be deemed goods and chattels of which larceny may be committed, although there be no interval between the severing and taking away.

§18.2-100. Removal of crop by tenant before rents and advances are satisfied.

It shall be unlawful for any person renting the lands of another, either for a share of the crop or for money consideration, to remove therefrom, without the consent of the landlord, any part of such crop until the rents and advances are satisfied. Every such offense shall be punishable as a Class 3 misdemeanor.

§18.2-101. Selling, etc., of goods distrained or levied on.

If any person fraudulently sell, pledge, encumber, remove, destroy, receive or secrete any goods, chattels or other personal property of any kind whatsoever that has been distrained or levied upon, with intent to defeat such distress or levy, he shall be deemed guilty of the larceny thereof.

§18.2-102. Unauthorized use of animal, aircraft, vehicle or boat; consent; accessories or accomplices.

Any person who shall take, drive or use any animal, aircraft, vehicle, boat or vessel, not his own, without the consent of the owner thereof and in the absence of the owner, and with intent temporarily to deprive the owner thereof of his possession thereof, without intent to steal the same, shall be guilty of a Class 6 felony; provided, however, that if the value of such animal, aircraft, vehicle, boat or vessel shall be less than $200, such person shall be guilty of a Class 1 misdemeanor. The consent of the owner of an animal, aircraft, vehicle, boat or vessel to its taking, driving or using shall not in any case be presumed or implied because of such owner's consent on a previous occasion to the taking, driving or using of such animal, aircraft, vehicle, boat or vessel by the same or a different person. Any person who assists in, or is a party or accessory to, or an accomplice in, any such unauthorized taking, driving or using shall be subject to the same punishment as if he were the principal offender.

§18.2-102.1. Removal of shopping cart from store premises.

(1) The term "shopping cart" when used in this section means those push carts of the type or types which are commonly provided by grocery stores, drugstores, or other merchant stores or markets for the use of the public in transporting commodities in stores and markets from the store to a place outside the store.

(2) It shall be unlawful for any person to remove a shopping cart from the premises, of the owner of such shopping cart without the consent, of the owner or of his agent, servant, or employee given at the time of such removal. For the purpose of this section, the premises shall include all the parking area set aside by the owner, or on behalf of the

owner, for the parking of cars for the convenience of the patrons of the owner.

(3) Any person convicted of a violation under subsection (2) shall be guilty of a Class 3 misdemeanor.

§18.2-102.2. Unauthorized use of dairy milk cases or milk crates; penalty.

It shall be unlawful for any person to:

1. Buy, sell, or dispose of any milk case or milk crate bearing the name or label of the owner without the written consent of the owner or his designated agent;

2. Refuse, upon written demand of the owner or his designated agent, to return to the owner or his designated agent any milk case or milk crate bearing the name or label of the owner; or

3. Deface, obliterate, erase, cover up, or otherwise remove or conceal any name, label, registered trademark, insignia, or other business identification of an owner of a milk case or milk crate without the consent of the owner, for the purpose of destroying or removing from the milk case or milk crate evidence of its ownership.

A violation of this section shall be punishable as a Class 4 misdemeanor.

For purposes of this section, milk cases or milk crates shall be deemed to bear a name or label of an owner when there is imprinted or attached on the case or crate a name, insignia, mark, business identification, or label showing ownership or sufficient information to ascertain ownership. The term "milk case" or "milk crate" means a wire or plastic container which holds sixteen quarts or more of beverage and is used by distributors or retailers or their agents as a means to transport, store, or carry dairy products.

§18.2-103. Concealing or taking possession of merchandise; altering price tags; transferring goods from one container to another; counseling, etc., another in performance of such acts.

Whoever, without authority, with the intention of converting goods or merchandise to his own or another's use without having paid the full purchase price thereof, or of defrauding the owner of the value of the goods or merchandise, (i) willfully conceals or takes possession of the goods or merchandise of any store or other mercantile establishment, or (ii) alters the price tag or other price marking on such goods or merchandise, or transfers the goods from one container to another, or (iii) counsels, assists, aids or abets another in the performance of any of the above acts, when the value of the goods or merchandise involved in the offense is less than $200, shall be guilty of petit larceny and, when the value of the goods or merchandise involved in the offense is $200 or more, shall be guilty of grand larceny. The willful concealment of goods or merchandise of any store or other mercantile establishment, while still on the premises thereof, shall be prima facie evidence of an intent to convert and defraud the owner thereof out of the value of the goods or merchandise.

§18.2-104. Punishment for conviction of misdemeanor larceny.

When a person is convicted of an offense of larceny or any offense deemed to be or punished as larceny under any provision of the Code, and it is alleged in the warrant, indictment or information on which he is convicted, and admitted, or found by the jury or judge before whom he is tried, that he has been before convicted in the Commonwealth of Virginia or in another jurisdiction for any offense of larceny or any offense deemed or punishable as larceny, or of any substantially similar offense in any other jurisdiction, regardless of whether the prior convictions were misdemeanors, felonies, or a combination thereof, he shall be confined in jail not less than thirty days nor more than twelve months; and for a third, or any subsequent offense, he shall be guilty of a Class 6 felony.

§18.2-104.1. Liability upon conviction under §18.2-103.

Any person who has been convicted of violating the provisions of §18.2-103 shall be civilly liable to the owner for the retail value of any goods and merchandise illegally converted and not recovered by the owner, and for all costs incurred in prosecuting such person under the provisions of §18.2-103. Such costs shall be limited to actual expenses, including the base wage of one employee acting as a witness for the Commonwealth and suit costs. Provided, however, the total amount of allowable costs granted hereunder shall not exceed $250, excluding the retail value of the goods and merchandise.

§18.2-105. Exemption from civil liability in connection with arrest or detention of suspected person.

A merchant, agent or employee of the merchant, who causes the arrest or detention of any person pursuant to the provisions of §18.2-95 or §18.2-96 or §18.2-103, shall not be held civilly liable for unlawful detention, if such detention does not exceed one hour, slander, malicious prosecution, false imprisonment, false arrest, or assault and battery of the person so arrested or detained, whether such arrest or detention takes place on the premises of the merchant, or after close pursuit from such premises by such merchant, his agent or employee, provided that, in causing the arrest or detention of such person, the merchant, agent or employee of the merchant, had at the time of such arrest or detention probable cause to believe that the person had shoplifted or committed willful concealment of goods or merchandise. The activation of an electronic article surveillance device as a result of a person exiting the premises or an area within the premises of a merchant where an electronic article surveillance device is located shall constitute probable cause for the detention of such person by such merchant, his agent or employee, provided such person is detained only in a reasonable manner and only for such time as is necessary for an inquiry into the circumstances surrounding the activation of the device, and provided that clear and visible notice is posted at each exit and location within the premises where such a device is located indicating the presence of an antishoplifting or inventory control device. For purposes of this section, "electronic article surveillance device" means an electronic device designed and operated for the purpose of detecting the removal from the premises, or a protected area within such premises, of specially marked or tagged merchandise.

§18.2-105.1. Detention of suspected shoplifter.

A merchant, agent or employee of the merchant, who has probable cause to believe that a person has shoplifted in violation of §§18.2-95 or 18.2-96 or 18.2-103, on the premises of the merchant, may detain such person for a period not to exceed one hour pending arrival of a law-enforcement officer.

§18.2-105.2. Manufacture, sale, etc., of devices to shield against electronic detection of shoplifting prohibited; penalty.

It shall be unlawful to manufacture, sell, offer for sale, distribute or possess any specially coated or laminated bag or other device primarily designed and intended to shield shoplifted merchandise from detection by an anti-theft electronic alarm sensor, with the intention that the same be used to aid in the shoplifting of merchandise. A violation of this section shall be punishable as a Class 3 misdemeanor.

§18.2-106. "Agents of the merchant" defined.

As used in this article "agents of the merchant" shall include attendants at any parking lot owned or leased by the merchant, or generally used by customers of the merchant through any contract or agreement between the owner of the parking lot and the merchant.

§18.2-107. Theft or destruction of public records by others than officers.

If any person steal or fraudulently secrete or destroy a public record or part thereof, including a microphotographic copy thereof, he shall, if the offense be not embraced by §18.2-472 be guilty of a Class 6 felony.

§18.2-108. Receiving, etc., stolen goods.

If any person buy or receive from another person, or aid in concealing, any stolen goods or other thing, knowing the same to have been stolen, he shall be deemed guilty of larceny thereof, and may be proceeded against, although the principal offender be not convicted.

§18.2-108.1. Receipt of stolen firearm.

Notwithstanding the provisions of §18.2-108, any person who buys or receives a firearm from another person or aids in concealing a firearm, knowing that the firearm was stolen, shall be guilty of a Class 6 felony and may be proceeded against although the principal offender is not convicted.
(Chgd. by L.1998 ch. 821, eff. 7/1/98.)

§18.2-109. Receipt or transfer of possession of stolen vehicle, aircraft or boat.

Any person who, with intent to procure or pass title to a vehicle, aircraft, boat or vessel, which he knows or has reason to believe has been stolen, shall receive or transfer possession of the same from one to another or who shall with like intent have in his possession any vehicle, aircraft, boat or vessel which he knows or has reason to believe has been stolen, and who is not an officer of the law engaged at the time in the performance of his duty as an officer, shall be guilty of a Class 6 felony.

§18.2-110. Forfeiture of motor vehicles used in commission of certain crimes.

Any vehicle knowingly used by the owner thereof or used by another with his knowledge of and during the commission of, or in an attempt to commit, a second or subsequent offense of §§18.2-346, 18.2-347, 18.2-348, 18.1-349, 18.2-355, 18.2-356 or §18.2-357 or of a similar ordinance of any county, city or town or knowingly used for the transportation of any stolen goods, chattels or other property, when the value of such stolen goods, chattels or other property is $200 or more, or any stolen property obtained as a result of a robbery, without regard to the value of the property, shall be forfeited to the Commonwealth. The vehicle shall be seized by any law-enforcement officer arresting the operator of such vehicle for the criminal offense, and delivered to the sheriff of the county or city in which the offense occurred. The officer shall take a receipt therefor.

Forfeiture of such vehicle shall be enforced as is provided in §§4.1-339 through 4.1-348 as to vehicles used for the transportation of illegally acquired alcoholic beverages, and the provisions of §§4.1-339 through 4.1-348 shall apply, mutatis mutandis, to proceedings for the enforcement of such forfeiture except that venue for the forfeiture proceeding shall be in the county or city in which the offense occurred.

The agency seizing the motor vehicle or other conveyance shall, for such period of time as the court prescribes, be permitted the use and operation of the motor vehicle or other conveyance, after court forfeiture, for the investigation of crimes against the Commonwealth by the agency seizing the motor vehicle or other conveyance. The agency using or operating each motor vehicle shall have insurance on each vehicle used or operated for liability and property damage.

ARTICLE 4
EMBEZZLEMENT AND FRAUDULENT CONVERSIONS

§18.2-111. Embezzlement deemed larceny; indictment; statement from attorney for the Commonwealth.

If any person wrongfully and fraudulently use, dispose of, conceal or embezzle any money, bill, note, check, order, draft, bond, receipt, bill of lading or any other personal property, tangible or intangible, which he shall have received for another or for his employer, principal or bailor, or by virtue of his office, trust, or employment, or which shall have been entrusted or delivered to him by another or by any court, corporation or company, he shall be guilty of embezzlement. Embezzlement shall be deemed larceny and upon conviction thereof, the person shall be punished as provided in §18.2-95 or §18.2-96.

§18.2-111.1. Conversion of military property by person discharged from national guard or naval militia.

If any person comes into the possession of arms or articles of military property belonging to the United States or the Commonwealth, as a member of the Virginia national guard or naval militia, and willfully and intentionally fails and refuses to return the same upon discharge as such member, he shall be deemed guilty of larceny thereof, and receive the same punishment, according to the value of the thing stolen, prescribed for the larceny of goods and chattels.

§18.2-111.2. Failure to pay withheld child support; embezzlement.

If any employer withholds money from the pay of his employee for the purpose of paying administrative or court-ordered child support on behalf of the employee and then wrongfully and fraudulently fails to make payment of the money withheld, the employer shall be guilty of embezzlement.
(Added by L.1999 ch. 56, eff. 7/1/99.)

§18.2-112. Embezzlement by officers, etc., of public or other funds; default in paying over funds evidence of guilt.

If any officer, agent or employee of the Commonwealth or of any city, town, county, or any other political subdivision, or the deputy of any such officer having custody of public funds, or other funds coming into his custody under his official capacity, knowingly misuse or misappropriate the same or knowingly dispose thereof otherwise than in accordance with law, he shall be guilty of a Class 4 felony; and any default of such officer, agent, employee or deputy in paying over any such funds to the proper authorities when required by law to do so shall be deemed prima facie evidence of his guilt.

§18.2-113. Fraudulent entries, etc., in accounts by officers or clerks of banks or joint stock companies.

If any officer or clerk of any bank, savings institution or joint stock company make, alter or omit to make any entry in any account kept in such bank, or by such company, with intent, in so doing, to conceal the true state of such account, or to defraud such bank, institution or company, or to enable or assist any person to obtain money to which he was not entitled, such officer or clerk shall be guilty of a Class 4 felony. *(Chgd. by L.1996 ch. 77, eff. 7/1/96.)*

§18.2-114. Sale, etc., of goods, etc., of another and failure to pay over proceeds.

If any person store or ship goods, wares, merchandise, grain, flour or other produce or commodity, in his own name, being in the possession thereof for or on account of another, and sell, negotiate, pledge or hypothecate the same or any part thereof, or the receipts or bill of lading received therefor, and fraudulently fail to account for or pay over to his principal or the owner of the property the amount so received on such sale, negotiation, pledge or hypothecation, he shall be deemed guilty of larceny thereof.

§18.2-114.1. When collection of money by commissioner, etc., larceny.

If any special commissioner or receiver, appointed by any court to collect money, and required by law, or decree of the court, to give bond before collecting the same, shall collect such money, or any part thereof, without giving such bond, and fail properly to account for the same, he shall be deemed guilty of larceny of the money so collected and not so accounted for.

§18.2-115. Fraudulent conversion or removal of property subject to lien or title to which is in another.

Whenever any person is in possession of any personal property, including motor vehicles or farm products, in any capacity, the title or ownership of which he has agreed in writing shall be or remain in another, or on which he has given a lien, and such person so in possession shall fraudulently sell, pledge, pawn or remove such property from the premises where it has been agreed that it shall remain, and refuse to disclose the location thereof, or otherwise dispose of the property or fraudulently remove the same from the Commonwealth, without the written consent of the owner or lienor or the person in whom the title is, or, if such writing be a deed of trust, without the written consent of the trustee or beneficiary in such deed of trust, he shall be deemed guilty of the larceny thereof.

In any prosecution hereunder, the fact that such person after demand therefor by the lienholder or person in whom the title or ownership of the property is, or his agent, shall fail or refuse to disclose to such claimant or his agent the location of the property, or to surrender the same, shall be prima facie evidence of the violation of the provisions of this section. In the case of farm products, failure to pay the proceeds of the sale of the farm products to the secured party, lienholder or person in whom the title or ownership of the property is, or his agent, within ten days after the sale or other disposition of the farm products unless otherwise agreed by the lender and borrower in the obligation of indebtedness, note or other evidence of the debt shall be prima facie evidence of a violation of the provisions of this section. The venue of prosecutions against persons fraudulently removing any such property, including motor vehicles, from the Commonwealth shall be the county or city in which such property or motor vehicle was purchased or in which the accused last had a legal residence.

This section shall not be construed to interfere with the rights of any innocent third party purchasing such property, unless such writing shall be docketed or recorded as provided by law.

§18.2-115.1. Unlawful sublease of a motor vehicle; penalty.

A. It shall be unlawful for any person, for profit in the course of business, who is not a party to a lease contract, conditional sales contract, or security agreement which transfers any right or interest in a motor vehicle, knowing that the motor vehicle is subject to a lease, security interest or lien, to:

1. Obtain or exercise control over a motor vehicle and sell, transfer, assign, or lease the motor vehicle to another person without the prior written authorization of the secured creditor, lessor, or lienholder if he receives compensation or other consideration for the sale, transfer, assignment, or lease of the motor vehicle; or

2. Assist, cause, or arrange the actual or purported sale, transfer, assignment, or lease the motor vehicle to another person without the prior written authorization of the secured creditor, lessor, or lienholder if he receives compensation or other consideration for assisting, causing, or arranging the sale, transfer, assignment, or lease of the motor vehicle.

B. A violation of this section is punishable as a Class 3 misdemeanor.

C. This section shall not apply to any employee acting upon request of his employer.

D. This section shall not apply if the entire indebtedness owed under or secured by the lease, conditional sales contract, or security agreement through the date of payment is paid in full and received by the lessor or secured party within 30 days after the sale, transfer, assignment, or lease of the motor vehicle.

§18.2-116. Failure to pay for or return goods delivered for selection or approval.

If any person shall solicit and obtain from any merchant any goods, wares or merchandise for examination or approval, and shall thereafter, upon written demand, refuse or fail to return the same to such merchant in unused condition, or to pay for the same, such person so offending shall be deemed guilty of the larceny thereof. But the provisions of this section shall not apply unless such written demand be made within five days after delivery, and unless the goods, wares or merchandise shall have attached to them or to the package in which they are contained a label, card or tag containing the words, "Delivered for selection or approval."

§18.2-117. Failure of bailee to return animal, aircraft, vehicle or boat.

If any person comes into the possession as bailee of any animal, aircraft, vehicle, boat or vessel, and fail to return the same to the bailor, in accordance with the bailment agreement, he shall be deemed guilty of larceny thereof and receive the same punishment, according to the value of the thing stolen, prescribed for the punishment of the larceny of goods and chattels. The failure to return to the bailor such animal, aircraft, vehicle, boat or vessel, within five days from the time the bailee has agreed in writing to return the same shall be prima facie evidence of larceny by such bailee of such animal, aircraft, vehicle, boat or vessel.

§18.2-118. Fraudulent conversion or removal of leased personal property.

(a) Whenever any person is in possession or control of any personal property, by virtue of or subject to a written lease of such property, except property described in §18.2-117, and such person so in possession or control shall, with intent to defraud, sell, secrete, or destroy the property, or dispose of the property for his own use, or fraudulently remove the same from the Commonwealth without the written consent of the lessor thereof, or fail to return such property to the lessor thereof within ten days after expiration of the lease or rental period for such property stated in such written lease, he shall be deemed guilty of the larceny thereof.

(b) The fact that such person signs the lease or rental agreement with a name other than his own, or fails to return such property to the lessor thereof within ten days after the giving of written notice to such person that the lease or rental period for such property has expired, shall be prima facie evidence of intent to defraud. For purposes of this section, notice mailed by certified mail and addressed to such person at the address of the lessee stated in the lease, shall be sufficient giving of written notice under this section.

(c) The venue of prosecution under this section shall be the county or city in which such property was leased or in which such accused person last had a legal residence.

ARTICLE 5
TRESPASS TO REALTY

§18.2-119. Trespass after having been forbidden to do so; penalties.

If any person without authority of law goes upon or remains upon the lands, buildings or premises of another, or any portion or area thereof, after having been forbidden to do so, either orally or in writing, by the owner, lessee, custodian or other person lawfully in charge thereof, or after having been forbidden to do so by a sign or signs posted by such persons or by the holder of any easement or other right-of-way authorized by the instrument creating such interest to post such signs on such lands, structures, premises or portion or area thereof at a place or places where it or they may be reasonably seen, or if any person, whether he is the owner, tenant or otherwise entitled to the use of such land, building or premises, goes upon, or remains upon such land, building or premises after having been prohibited from doing so by a court of competent jurisdiction by an order issued pursuant to §§16.1-253, 16.1-253.1, 16.1-253.4, 16.1-278.2 through 16.1-278.6, 16.1-278.8, 16.1-278.14, 16.1-278.15, 16.1-279.1, 19.2-152.8, 19.2-152.9 or §19.2-152.10 or an ex parte order issued pursuant to §20-103, and after having been served with such order, he shall be guilty of a Class 1 misdemeanor. This section shall not be construed to affect in any way the provisions of §§18.2-132 through 18.2-136.
(Chgd. by L.1998 chs. 569, 684, eff. 7/1/98.)

§18.2-119.1. Validity of signs forbidding trespass; penalty.

If any person knowingly and intentionally posts No Trespassing signs on the land of another without the permission of a person authorized to post such signs on that land, he shall be guilty of a Class 3 misdemeanor.
(Added by L.1999 ch. 274, eff. 7/1/99.)

§18.2-120. Instigating, etc., such trespass by others; preventing service to persons not forbidden to trespass.

If any person shall solicit, urge, encourage, exhort, instigate or procure another or others to go upon or remain upon the lands, buildings, or premises of another, or any part, portion or area thereof, knowing such other person or persons to have been forbidden, either orally or in writing, to do so by the owner, lessee, custodian or other person lawfully in charge thereof, or knowing such other person or persons to have been forbidden to do so by a sign or signs posted on such lands, buildings, premises or part, portion or area thereof at a place or places where it or they may reasonably be seen; or if any person shall, on such lands, buildings, premises or part, portion or area thereof prevent or seek to prevent the owner, lessee, custodian, person in charge or any of his employees from rendering service to any person or persons not so forbidden, he shall be guilty of a Class 1 misdemeanor.

§18.2-121. Entering property of another for purpose of damaging it, etc.

It shall be unlawful for any person to enter the land, dwelling, outhouse or any other building of another for the purpose of damaging such property or any of the contents thereof or in any manner to interfere with the rights of the owner, user or the occupant thereof to use such property free from interference.

Any person violating the provisions of this section shall be guilty of a Class 1 misdemeanor. However, if a person intentionally selects the property entered because of the race, religious conviction, color or national origin of the owner, user or occupant of the property, the person shall be guilty of a Class 6 felony, and the penalty upon conviction shall include a mandatory, minimum term of confinement of at least

six months, thirty days of which shall not be suspended, in whole or in part.
(Chgd. by L.1997 ch. 833, eff. 7/1/97.)

§18.2-121.1. Permitting certain animals to run at large.

The owner or manager of any animal mentioned in §55-316, who shall knowingly permit such animal to run at large in any county or portion thereof, under quarantine, shall be deemed to be guilty of a Class 4 misdemeanor.

§18.2-121.2. Trespass by spotlight on agricultural land.

If any person shall willfully use a spotlight or similar lighting apparatus to cast a light upon private property used for livestock or crops without the written permission of the person in legal possession of such property, he shall be guilty of a Class 3 misdemeanor.

The prohibition of this section shall not apply to light cast by (i) permanently installed outdoor lighting fixtures, (ii) headlamps on vehicles moving in normal travel on public or private roads, (iii) railroad locomotives or rolling stock being operated on the tracks or right-of-way of a railroad company, (iv) aircraft or watercraft, (v) apparatus used by employees of any public utility in maintaining the utility's lines and equipment, (vi) apparatus used by members of rescue squads or fire departments in the performance of their official duties, (vii) apparatus used by any law-enforcement officer in the performance of his official duties, or (viii) farm machinery or motor vehicles being used in normal farming operations.

§18.2-122. *(Repealed by L.1998 ch. 6, eff. 7/1/98.)*

§18.2-123. Dogs not permitted at large in Capitol Square.

It shall be unlawful for any person to bring any dog, or to allow any dog over which for the time being he has control, to follow or come with him into the Capitol Square unless such dog is held in control by leash or otherwise. Any person violating this section shall be deemed guilty of a misdemeanor and shall be fined not less than one dollar nor more than ten dollars. Moreover, any dog found on the Capitol Square without its owner may be driven from the limits of the square or caught and placed in the custody of the dog warden of the City of Richmond.

§18.2-124. Jurisdiction over offenses committed in Capitol Square.

The Circuit Court of the City of Richmond shall have jurisdiction to try cases of offenses committed in Capitol Square except as hereinafter provided. The District Court of the City of Richmond shall have jurisdiction to try cases of misdemeanor arising under §§18.2-122 and 18.2-123, and all other offenses committed in the Capitol Square of which it would have jurisdiction if committed within the corporate limits and jurisdiction of the city; and the Capitol Police, or any member thereof, shall have the same authority to arrest and to swear out warrants for offenses committed on the Capitol Square as policemen of the City of Richmond have to arrest or to swear out warrants for offenses committed within the jurisdiction of the city.

§18.2-125. Trespass at night upon any cemetery.

If any person, without the consent of the owner, proprietor or custodian, go or enter in the nighttime, upon the premises, property, driveways or walks of any cemetery, either public or private, for any purpose other than to visit the burial lot or grave of some member of his family, he shall be guilty of a Class 4 misdemeanor.

§18.2-126. Violation of sepulture; defilement of a dead human body; penalties.

A. If a person unlawfully disinters or displaces a dead human body, or any part of a dead human body which has been deposited in any vault, grave or other burial place, he is guilty of a Class 4 felony.

B. If a person willfully and intentionally physically defiles a dead human body he is guilty of a Class 6 felony. For purposes of this section, the term "defile" shall not include any autopsy or the recovery of organs or tissues for transplantation, or any other lawful purpose.
(Chgd. by L.1995 ch. 306, eff. 7/1/95.)

§18.2-127. Injuries to churches, church property, cemeteries, burial grounds, etc.; penalty.

A. Any person who willfully or maliciously commits any of the following acts is guilty of a Class 1 misdemeanor:

(1) Destroys, removes, cuts, breaks or injures any tree, shrub, or plant on any church property or within any cemetery or lot of any memorial or monumental association;

(2) Destroys, mutilates, injures, or removes and carries away any flowers, wreaths, vases, or other ornaments placed within any church or on church property, or placed upon or around any grave, tomb, monument, or lot in any cemetery, graveyard, or other place of burial; or

(3) Obstructs proper ingress to and egress from any church or any cemetery or lot belonging to any memorial or monumental association.

B. Any person who willfully or maliciously destroys, mutilates, defaces, injures or removes any object or structure permanently attached of affixed within any church or on church property, any tomb, monument, gravestone, or other structure placed within any cemetery, graveyard, or place of burial, or within any lot belonging to any memorial or monumental association, or any fence, railing, or other work for the protection or ornament of any tomb, monument, gravestone, or other structure aforesaid, or of any cemetery lot within any cemetery is guilty of a Class 6 felony.

C. This section shall not apply to any work which is done by the authorities of a church or congregation in the maintenance or improvement of any church property or any burial ground or cemetery belonging to it and under its management or control and which does not injure or result in the removal of a tomb, monument, gravestone, grave marker or vault. For purposes of this section, "church" shall mean any place of worship, and "church property" shall mean any educational building or community center owned or rented by a church.

§18.2-128. Trespass upon church or school property.

A. Any person who, without the consent of some person authorized to give such consent, goes or enters upon, in the nighttime, the premises or property of any church or upon any school property for any purpose other than to attend a meeting or service held or conducted in such church or school property, shall be guilty of a Class 3 misdemeanor.

B. It shall be unlawful for any person, whether or not a church member or student, to enter upon or remain upon any church or school property in violation of (i) any direction to vacate the property by a person authorized to give such direction or (ii) any posted notice which contains such information, posted at a place where it reasonably may be seen. Each time such person enters upon or remains on the posted premises or after such direction that person refuses to vacate such property, it shall constitute a separate offense.

A violation of this subsection shall be punishable as a Class 1 misdemeanor, except that any person, other than a parent, who violates this subsection on school property with the intent to abduct a student shall be guilty of a Class 6 felony.

C. For purposes of this section: (i) "school property" includes a school bus as defined in §46.2-100 and (ii) "church" means any place of worship and includes any educational building or community center owned or leased by a church. *(Chgd. by L.1995 chs. 493, 642; L.1997 ch. 779, eff. 7/1/97.)*

§18.2-130. Peeping or spying into dwelling or enclosure.

A. It shall be unlawful for any person to enter upon the property of another and secretly or furtively peep, spy or attempt to peep or spy into or through a window, door or other aperture of any building, structure, or other enclosure of any nature occupied or intended for occupancy as a dwelling, whether or not such building, structure or enclosure is permanently situated or transportable and whether or not such occupancy is permanent or temporary.

B. It shall be unlawful for any person to use a peephole or other aperture to secretly or furtively peep, spy or attempt to peep or spy into a restroom, dressing room, locker room, hotel room, motel room, tanning bed, tanning booth, bedroom or other location or enclosure for the purpose of viewing any nonconsenting person who is totally nude, clad in undergarments, or in a state of undress exposing the genitals, pubic area, buttocks or female breast and the circumstances are such that the person would otherwise have a reasonable expectation of privacy.

C. The provisions of this section shall not apply to a lawful criminal investigation or a correctional official or local or regional jail official conducting surveillance for security purposes or during an investigation of alleged misconduct involving a person committed to the Department of Corrections or to a local or regional jail.

D. As used in this section, "peephole" means any hole, crack or other similar opening through which a person can see.

E. A violation of this section is a Class 1 misdemeanor. *(Chgd. by L.1999 ch. 351, eff. 7/1/99.)*

§18.2-131. Trespass upon licensed shooting preserve.

It shall be unlawful for any person to trespass on a licensed shooting preserve. Any person convicted of such trespass shall be guilty of a Class 4 misdemeanor and shall be responsible for all damage. Owners or keepers of dogs trespassing on preserves shall be responsible for all damage done by such dogs.

§18.2-132. Trespass by hunters and fishers.

Any person who goes on the lands, waters, ponds, boats or blinds of another to hunt, fish or trap without the consent of the landowner or his agent shall be deemed guilty of a Class 3 misdemeanor.

§18.2-133. Refusal of person on land, etc., of another to identify himself.

Any person who goes on the lands, waters, ponds, boats or blinds of another to hunt, fish, or trap and willfully refuses to identify himself when requested by the landowner or his agent so to do shall be deemed guilty of a Class 4 misdemeanor.

§18.2-134. Trespass on posted property.

Any person who goes on the lands, waters, ponds, boats or blinds of another, which have been posted in accordance with the provisions of §18.2-134.1, to hunt, fish or trap except with the written consent of or in the presence of the owner or his agent shall be guilty of a Class 1 misdemeanor.

§18.2-134.1. Method of posting lands.

A. The owner or lessee of property described in §18.2-134 may post property by (i) placing signs prohibiting hunting, fishing or trapping where they may reasonably be seen; or (ii) placing identifying paint marks on trees or posts at each road entrance and adjacent to public roadways and public waterways adjoining the property. Each paint mark shall be a vertical line of at least two inches in width and at least eight inches in length and the center of the mark shall be no less than three feet nor more than six feet from the ground or normal water surface. Such paint marks shall be readily visible to any person approaching the property.

B. The type and color of the paint to be used for posting shall be prescribed by the Department of Game and Inland Fisheries.

§18.2-135. Destruction of posted signs; posting land of another.

Any person who shall mutilate, destroy or take down any "posted," "no hunting" or similar sign or poster on the lands or waters of another, or who shall post such sign or poster on the lands or waters of another, without the consent of the landowner or his agent, shall be deemed guilty of a Class 3 misdemeanor and his hunting license shall be revoked for a period not exceeding the expiration date of such license.

§18.2-136. Right of certain hunters to go on lands of another; carrying firearms or bows and arrows prohibited.

Fox hunters and coon hunters, when the chase begins on other lands, may follow their dogs on prohibited lands, and hunters of all other game, when the chase begins on other lands, may go upon prohibited lands to retrieve their dogs, but may not carry firearms or bows and arrows on their persons or hunt any game while thereon. The use of vehicles to retrieve dogs on prohibited lands shall be allowed only with the permission of the landowner or his agent.

§18.2-136.1. Enforcement of §§18.2-131 through 18.2-135.

Game wardens, sheriffs and all other law-enforcement officers shall enforce the provisions of §§18.2-131, 18.2-132, 18.2-133, 18.2-134 and 18.2-135.

ARTICLE 6
DAMAGE TO REALTY AND PERSONALTY THEREON

§18.2-137. Injuring, etc., any property, monument, etc.

A. If any person unlawfully destroys, defaces, damages or removes without the intent to steal any property, real or personal, not his own, or breaks down, destroys, defaces, damages or removes without the intent to steal, any monument or memorial for war veterans described in §15.2-1812, any monument erected for the purpose of marking the site of any engagement fought during the War between the States, or for the purpose of designating the boundaries of any city, town, tract of land, or any tree marked for that purpose, he shall be guilty of a Class 3 misdemeanor; provided that the court may, in its discretion, dismiss the charge if the locality or organization responsible for maintaining the injured property, monument, or memorial files a written affidavit with the court stating it has received full payment for the injury.

B. If any person intentionally causes such injury, he shall be guilty of (i) a Class 1 misdemeanor if the value of or damage to the property, memorial or monument is less than $1,000 or (ii) a Class 6 felony if the value of or damage to the property, memorial or monument is $1,000 or more. The amount of loss caused by the destruction, defacing, damage or removal of such property, memorial or monument may be established by proof of the fair market cost of repair or fair market replacement value. Upon conviction, the court may order that the defendant pay restitution.

(Chgd. by L.1999 ch. 625, eff. 7/1/99.)

§18.2-138. Damaging public buildings, etc.; penalty.

Any person who willfully and maliciously (i) breaks any window or door of the Capitol, any courthouse, house of public worship, college, school house, city or town hall, or other public building or library, (ii) damages or defaces the Capitol or any other public building or any statuary in the Capitol, on the Capitol Square, or in or on any other public buildings or public grounds, or (iii) destroys any property in any of such buildings shall be guilty of a Class 6 felony if damage to the property is $1,000 or more or a Class 1 misdemeanor if the damage is less than $1,000.

Any person who willfully and unlawfully damages or defaces any book, newspaper, magazine, pamphlet, map, picture, manuscript, or other property located in any library, reading room, museum, or other educational institution shall be guilty of a Class 6 felony if damage to the property is $1,000 or more or a Class 1 misdemeanor if the damage is less than $1,000.

§18.2-138.1. Willful and malicious damage to or defacement of public or private facilities; penalty.

A. Any county, city or town may by ordinance make unlawful the willful and malicious damage to or defacement of any public buildings, facilities and personal property or of any private buildings, facilities and personal property if the damage to the private property is less than $1,000. The penalty for violation of such ordinance shall be a Class 1 misdemeanor.

B. Upon a finding of guilt under any such ordinance in any case tried before the court without a jury, in the event the violation constitutes a first offense which results in property damage or loss, the court, without entering a judgment of guilt, upon motion of the defendant, may defer further proceedings and place the defendant on probation pending completion of a plan of community service work. If the defendant fails or refuses to complete the community service as ordered by the court, the court may make final disposition of the case and proceed as otherwise provided. If the community service work is completed as the court prescribes, the court may discharge the defendant and dismiss the proceedings against him. Discharge and dismissal under this section shall be without adjudication of guilt and is a conviction only for the purposes of applying the ordinance in subsequent proceedings.

C. The ordinance shall direct that the community service, to the extent feasible, include the repair, restoration or replacement of any damage or defacement to property within the locality, and may include clean-up, beautification, landscaping or other appropriate community service within the locality. Any ordinance adopted pursuant to this section shall make provision for a designee of the locality to supervise the performance of any community service work required and to report thereon to the court imposing such requirement. At or before the time of sentencing under the ordinance, the court shall receive and consider any plan for making restitution or performing community service submitted by the defendant. The court shall also receive and consider the recommendations of the supervisor of community service in the locality concerning the plan.

D. Notwithstanding any other provision of law, no person convicted of a violation of an ordinance adopted pursuant to this section shall be placed on probation or have his sentence suspended unless such person shall make at least partial restitution for such property damage or is compelled to perform community services, or both, as is more particularly set forth in §19.2-305.1.

(Added by L.1995 ch. 251; chgd. by L.1997 chs. 445, 461, eff. 7/1/97.)

§18.2-139. Injuries to trees, fences or herbage on grounds of Capitol, or in any public square.

If any person:

(1) Cut down, pull up, girdle or otherwise injure or destroy any tree growing in the grounds of the Capitol, or in any public square or grounds, without the consent of the Governor, or of the circuit court of the county or city in which such grounds or square is situated; or

(2) Willfully and maliciously injure the fences or herbage of the Capitol grounds, or of any such square or grounds,

he shall be guilty of a Class 3 misdemeanor.

§18.2-140. Destruction of trees, shrubs, etc.

It shall be unlawful for any person to pick, pull, pull up, tear, tear up, dig, dig up, cut, break, injure, burn or destroy, in whole or in part, any tree, shrub, vine, plant, flower or turf found, growing or being upon the land of another, or upon any land reserved, set aside or maintained by the Commonwealth as a public park, or as a refuge or sanctuary for wild animals, birds or fish, or upon any land reserved, set aside or maintained as a public park by a park authority created under the provisions of §15.2-5702, without having previously obtained the permission in writing of such other or his agent or of the superintendent or custodian of such park, refuge or sanctuary so to do, unless the same be done under the personal direction of such owner, his agent, tenant or lessee or superintendent or custodian of such park, refuge or sanctuary.

Any person violating this section shall be guilty of a Class 3 misdemeanor; provided, however, that the approval of the owner, his agent, tenant or lessee, or the superintendent or custodian of such park or sanctuary afterwards given in writing or in open court shall be a bar to further prosecution or suit.

(Chgd. by L.1998 ch. 81, eff. 7/1/98.)

§18.2-141. Cutting or destroying trees; carrying axe, saw, etc., while hunting.

It shall be unlawful for any person while hunting for game or wildlife on the property of another to carry any axe other than a belt axe with a handle less than twenty inches, saw or other tool or instrument customarily used for the purpose of cutting, felling, mutilating or destroying trees without obtaining prior permission of the landowner. Any person violating the provisions of this section shall be guilty of a Class 3 misdemeanor.

Game wardens, sheriffs and all law-enforcement officers shall enforce the provisions of this section.

§18.2-143. Pulling down fences or leaving open gates.

If any person, without permission of the owner, pull down the fence of another and leave the same down, or, without permission, open and leave open the gate of another, or any gate across a public road established by order of court, or if any person other than the owner or owners of the lands through which a line of railroad runs open and leave open a gate at any public or private crossing of the right-of-way of a railroad, he shall be guilty of a Class 4 misdemeanor.

ARTICLE 7
DAMAGE TO AND TAMPERING WITH PROPERTY

§18.2-144. Maiming, killing or poisoning animals, fowl, etc.

Except as otherwise provided for by law, if any person maliciously shoot, stab, wound or otherwise cause bodily injury to, or administer poison to or expose poison with intent that it be taken by, any horse, mule, pony, cattle, swine or other livestock of another, with intent to maim, disfigure, disable or kill the same, or if he do any of the foregoing acts to any animal of his own with intent to defraud any insurer thereof, he shall be guilty of a Class 5 felony. If any person do any of the foregoing acts to any fowl or to any companion animal with any of the aforesaid intents, he shall be guilty of a Class 1 misdemeanor, except that any second or subsequent offense shall be a Class 6 felony if the current offense or any previous offense resulted in the death of an animal or the euthanasia of an animal based on the recommendation of a licensed veterinarian upon determination that such euthanasia was necessary due to the condition of the animal, and such condition was a direct result of a violation of this section.

(Chgd. by L.1999 ch. 620, eff. 7/1/99.)

§18.2-144.1. Prohibition against killing or injuring police animals; penalty.

It shall be unlawful for any person to maliciously shoot, stab, wound or otherwise cause bodily injury to, or administer poison to or expose poison with intent that it be taken by a dog, horse or other animal owned, used or trained by a law-enforcement agency, regional jail or the Department of Corrections while such animal is performing his lawful duties or is being kept in a kennel, pen or stable while off-duty. A violation of this section shall be punishable as a Class 5 felony. The court shall order that the defendant pay restitution for the cost of any animal killed or rendered unable to perform its duties. Such cost shall include training expenses.

(Chgd. by L.1998 ch. 8, eff. 7/1/98.)

§18.2-144.2. Prohibition against making a false representation of ownership of an animal to an animal shelter or pound; penalty.

A. It shall be unlawful for any person to deliver or release any animal not owned by that person to a pound, animal shelter or humane society, as these terms are defined in §3.1-796.66, or to any other similar facility for animals, or any agent thereof, and to falsely represent to such facility or agent that such person is the owner of the animal.

B. A violation of subsection A shall be punished as a Class 1 misdemeanor.

C. No pound, animal shelter, humane society or other similar facility for animals, or the directors or employees of any such business or facility, shall, in the absence of gross negligence, be civilly liable for accepting and disposing of any animal in good faith from a person who falsely claims to be the owner of the animal.

§18.2-145. Protection of homing pigeons.

It shall be unlawful for any person at any time or in any manner to hunt, pursue, take, capture, wound, maim, disfigure, or kill any homing pigeon of another person, or to make use of any pit or pitfall, scaffold, cage, snare, trap, net, baited hook or similar device or drug, poison chemical or explosive, for the purpose of injuring, capturing or killing any such homing pigeon, provided that any officer, employee or agent of a city or county acting pursuant to authority of an ordinance thereof may take, capture and kill pigeons in, on and about any building or structure devoted to business, commercial or industrial purposes when any pigeons are using such premises for roosting, resting or congregating thereon; all pigeons taken upon such premises shall be conclusively deemed not to be homing pigeons or the property of any person.

Any person violating any of the foregoing provisions shall be guilty of a Class 3 misdemeanor.

§18.2-146. Breaking, injuring, defacing, destroying or preventing the operation of vehicle, aircraft or boat.

Any person who shall individually or in association with one or more others willfully break, injure, tamper with or remove any part or parts of any vehicle, aircraft, boat or vessel for the purpose of injuring, defacing or destroying said vehicle, aircraft, boat or vessel, or temporarily or permanently preventing its useful operation, or for any purpose against the will or without the consent of the owner of such vehicle, aircraft, boat or vessel, or who shall in any other manner willfully or maliciously interfere with or prevent the running or operation of such vehicle, aircraft, boat or vessel, shall be guilty of a Class 1 misdemeanor.

§18.2-147. Entering or setting in motion, vehicle, aircraft, boat, locomotive or rolling stock of railroad; exceptions.

Any person who shall, without the consent of the owner or person in charge of a vehicle, aircraft, boat, vessel, locomotive or other rolling stock of a railroad, climb into or upon such vehicle, aircraft, boat, vessel, locomotive or other rolling stock of a railroad, with intent to commit any crime, malicious mischief, or injury thereto, or who, while a vehicle, aircraft, boat, vessel, locomotive or other rolling stock of a railroad is at rest and unattended, shall attempt to manipulate any of the levers and starting crank or other device, brakes or mechanism thereof or to set into motion such vehicle, aircraft, boat, vessel, locomotive or other rolling stock of a railroad, with the intent to commit any crime, malicious mischief, or injury thereto, shall be guilty of a Class 1 misdemeanor, except that the foregoing provision shall not apply when any such act is done in an emergency or in furtherance of public safety or by or under the direction of an officer in the regulation of traffic or performance of any other official duty.

§18.2-147.1. Breaking and entering into railroad cars, motortrucks, aircraft, etc., or pipeline systems.

Any person who breaks the seal or lock of any railroad car, vessel, aircraft, motortruck, wagon or other vehicle or of any pipeline system, containing shipments of freight or express or other property, or breaks and enters any such vehicle or pipeline system with the intent to commit larceny or any felony therein shall be guilty of a Class 4 felony; provided, however, that if such person is armed with a firearm at the time of such breaking and entering, he shall be guilty of a Class 3 felony.

§18.2-147.2. Devices for puncturing motor vehicle tires.

It shall be unlawful for any person to manufacture, distribute, have in his possession or place upon any highway or private property jackrocks which are primarily designed for the purpose of disabling motor vehicles by the puncturing of tires. Any person convicted of unlawful manufacture, distribution, possession or use of such device shall be guilty of a Class 1 misdemeanor.

§18.2-148. Bona fide repossession under lien.

The provisions of §§18.2-102, 18.2-146 and 18.2-147 shall not apply to a bona fide repossession of a vehicle, aircraft, boat or vessel by the holder of a lien on such vehicle, aircraft, boat or vessel, or by the agents or employees of such lienholder.

§18.2-149. Injury to hired animal, aircraft, vehicle or boat.

If any person after having rented or leased from any other person an animal, aircraft, vehicle, boat or vessel shall willfully injure or damage the same, by hard or reckless driving or using, or by using the same in violation of any statute of this Commonwealth, or allow or permit any other person so to do, or hire the same to any other person without the consent of the bailor, such person shall be guilty of a Class 3 misdemeanor.

§18.2-150. Willfully destroying vessel, etc.

If any person willfully scuttle, cast away or otherwise dispose of, or in any manner destroy, except as otherwise provided, a ship, vessel or other watercraft, with intent to injure or defraud any owner thereof or of any property on board the same, or any insurer of such ship, vessel or other watercraft, or any part thereof, or of any such property on board the same, if the same be of the value of $200, he shall be guilty of a Class 4 felony, but if it be of less value than $200, he shall be guilty of a Class 1 misdemeanor.

§18.2-151. Opening or carrying away pumps, etc., used for dispensing gasoline, etc.

If any person, with intent to commit larceny therefrom, break and open, or open, or carry away, any pump, tank, or other similar equipment or container used for dispensing or storing kerosene, gasoline or motor oils, he shall be guilty of a Class 6 felony.

§18.2-152. Stealing from or tampering with parking meter, vending machine, pay telephone, etc.

Any person who enters, forces or attempts to force an entrance into, tampers with, or inserts any part of an instrument into any parking meter, vending machine, pay telephone, money changing machine, or any other device designed to receive money, with intent to steal therefrom, shall for the first conviction thereof be guilty of a Class 1 misdemeanor, and for any subsequent conviction of a violation thereof shall be guilty of a Class 6 felony.

ARTICLE 7.1
COMPUTER CRIMES

§18.2-152.1. Short title.

This article shall be known and may be cited as the "Virginia Computer Crimes Act."

§18.2-152.2. Definitions.

For purposes of this article:

"Computer" means an electronic, magnetic, optical, hydraulic or organic device or group of devices which, pursuant to a computer program, to human instruction, or to permanent instructions contained in the device or group of devices, can automatically perform computer operations with or on computer data and can communicate the results to another computer or to a person. The term "computer" includes any connected or directly related device, equipment, or facility which enables the computer to store, retrieve or communicate computer programs, computer data or the results of computer operations to or from a person, another computer or another device.

"Computer data" means any representation of information, knowledge, facts, concepts, or instructions which is being prepared or has been prepared and is intended to be processed, is being processed, or has been processed in a computer or computer network. "Computer data" may be in any form, whether readable only by a computer or only by a human or by either, including, but not limited to, computer printouts, magnetic storage media, punched cards, or stored internally in the memory of the computer.

"Computer network" means two or more computers connected by a network.

"Computer operation" means arithmetic, logical, monitoring, storage or retrieval functions and any combination thereof, and includes, but is not limited to, communication with, storage of data to, or retrieval of data from any device or human hand manipulation of electronic or magnetic impulses. A "computer operation" for a particular computer may also be any function for which that computer was generally designed.

"Computer program" means an ordered set of data representing coded instructions or statements that, when executed by a computer, causes the computer to perform one or more computer operations.

"Computer services" means computer time or services, including data processing services, Internet services, electronic mail services, electronic message services, or information or data stored in connection therewith.

"Computer software" means a set of computer programs, procedures and associated documentation concerned with computer data or with the operation of a computer, computer program, or computer network.

"Electronic mail service provider" means any person who (i) is an intermediary in sending or receiving electronic mail and (ii) provides to end-users of electronic mail services the ability to send or receive electronic mail.

"Financial instrument" includes, but is not limited to, any check, draft, warrant, money order, note, certificate of deposit, letter of credit, bill of exchange, credit or debit card, transaction authorization mechanism, marketable security, or any computerized representation thereof.

"Network" means any combination of digital transmission facilities and packet switches, routers, and similar equipment interconnected to enable the exchange of computer data.

"Owner" means an owner or lessee of a computer or a computer network or an owner, lessee, or licensee of computer data, computer programs, or computer software.

"Person" shall include any individual, partnership, association, corporation or joint venture.

"Property" shall include:

1. Real property;
2. Computers and computer networks;
3. Financial instruments, computer data, computer programs, computer software and all other personal property regardless of whether they are:
   a. Tangible or intangible;
   b. In a format readable by humans or by a computer;
   c. In transit between computers or within a computer network or between any devices which comprise a computer; or
   d. Located on any paper or in any device on which it is stored by a computer or by a human; and
4. Computer services.

A person "uses" a computer or computer network when he:

1. Attempts to cause or causes a computer or computer network to perform or to stop performing computer operations;
2. Attempts to cause or causes the withholding or denial of the use of a computer, computer network, computer program, computer data or computer software to another user; or
3. Attempts to cause or causes another person to put false information into a computer.

A person is "without authority" when (i) he has no right or permission of the owner to use a computer or he uses a computer in a manner exceeding such right or permission or (ii) he uses a computer, a computer network, or the computer services of an electronic mail service provider to transmit unsolicited bulk electronic mail in contravention of the authority granted by or in violation of the policies set by the electronic mail service provider. Transmission of electronic mail from an organization to its members shall not be deemed to be unsolicited bulk electronic mail.

(Chgd. by L.1999 chs. 886, 904, 905; L.2000 ch. 627, eff. 7/1/2000.)

§18.2-152.3. Computer fraud.

Any person who uses a computer or computer network without authority and with the intent to:

1. Obtain property or services by false pretenses;
2. Embezzle or commit larceny; or
3. Convert the property of another

shall be guilty of the crime of computer fraud. If the value of the property or services obtained is $200 or more, the crime of computer fraud shall be punishable as a Class 5 felony. Where the value of the property or services obtained is less than $200, the crime of computer fraud shall be punishable as a Class 1 misdemeanor.

§18.2-152.4. Computer trespass; penalty.

A. It shall be unlawful for any person to use a computer or computer network without authority and with the intent to:

1. Temporarily or permanently remove, halt, or otherwise disable any computer data, computer programs, or computer software from a computer or computer network;
2. Cause a computer to malfunction, regardless of how long the malfunction persists;
3. Alter or erase any computer data, computer programs, or computer software;
4. Effect the creation or alteration of a financial instrument or of an electronic transfer of funds;
5. Cause physical injury to the property of another;
6. Make or cause to be made an unauthorized copy, in any form, including, but not limited to, any printed or electronic form of computer data, computer programs, or computer software residing in, communicated by, or produced by a computer or computer network; or
7. Falsify or forge electronic mail transmission information or other routing information in any manner in connection with the transmission of unsolicited bulk electronic mail through or into the computer network of an electronic mail service provider or its subscribers.

B. It shall be unlawful for any person knowingly to sell, give or otherwise distribute or possess with the intent to sell, give or distribute software which (i) is primarily designed or produced for the purpose of facilitating or enabling the falsification of electronic mail transmission information or other routing information; (ii) has only limited commercially significant purpose or use other than to facilitate or enable the falsification of electronic mail transmission information or other routing information; or (iii) is marketed by that person or another acting in concert with that person with that person's knowledge for use in facilitating or enabling the falsification of electronic mail transmission information or other routing information.

C. Any person who violates this section shall be guilty of computer trespass, which offense shall be punishable as a Class 3 misdemeanor. If there is damage to the property of another valued at $2,500 or more caused by such person's reckless disregard for the consequences of his act in violation of this section, the offense shall be punished as a Class 1 misdemeanor. If there is damage to the property of another valued at $2,500 or more caused by such person's malicious act in violation of this section, the offense shall be punishable as a Class 6 felony.

D. Nothing in this section shall be construed to interfere with or prohibit terms or conditions in a contract or license related to computers, computer data, computer networks, computer operations, computer programs, computer services, or computer software or to create any liability by reason of terms or conditions adopted by, or technical measures implemented by, a Virginia-based electronic mail service provider to prevent the transmission of unsolicited electronic mail in violation of this article.

(Chgd. by L.1998 ch. 892; L.1999 chs. 886, 904, 905, eff. 7/1/99.)

§18.2-152.5. Computer invasion of privacy.

A. A person is guilty of the crime of computer invasion of privacy when he uses a computer or computer network and intentionally examines without authority any employment, salary, credit or any other financial or personal information relating to any other person. "Examination" under this section requires the offender to review the information relating to any other person after the time at which the offender knows or should know that he is without authority to view the information displayed.

B. The crime of computer invasion of privacy shall be punishable as a Class 3 misdemeanor.

§18.2-152.6. Theft of computer services.

Any person who willfully uses a computer or computer network, with intent to obtain computer services without authority, shall be guilty of the crime of theft of computer services, which shall be punishable as a Class 1 misdemeanor.

§18.2-152.7. Personal trespass by computer.

A. A person is guilty of the crime of personal trespass by computer when he uses a computer or computer network without authority and with the intent to cause physical injury to an individual.

B. If committed maliciously, the crime of personal trespass by computer shall be punishable as a Class 3 felony. If such act be done unlawfully but not maliciously, the crime of personal trespass by computer shall be punishable as a Class 1 misdemeanor.

§18.2-152.7:1. Harassment by computer; penalty.

If any person, with the intent to coerce, intimidate, or harass any person, shall use a computer or computer network to communicate obscene, vulgar, profane, lewd, lascivious, or indecent language, or make any suggestion or proposal of an obscene nature, or threaten any illegal or immoral act, he shall be guilty of a Class 1 misdemeanor.
(Added by L.2000 ch. 849, eff. 7/1/2000.)

§18.2-152.8. Property capable of embezzlement.

For purposes of §18.2-111, personal property subject to embezzlement shall include:

1. Computers and computer networks;

2. Financial instruments, computer data, computer programs, computer software and all other personal property regardless of whether they are:

a. Tangible or intangible;

b. In a format readable by humans or by a computer;

c. In transit between computers or within a computer network or between any devices which comprise a computer; or

d. Located on any paper or in any device on which it is stored by a computer or by a human; and

3. Computer services.

§18.2-152.9. Limitation of prosecution.

Notwithstanding the provisions of §19.2-8, prosecution of a crime which is punishable as a misdemeanor pursuant to this article must be commenced before the earlier of (i) five years after the commission of the last act in the course of conduct constituting a violation of this article or (ii) one year after the existence of the illegal act and the identity of the offender are discovered by the Commonwealth, by the owner, or by anyone else who is damaged by such violation.

§18.2-152.10. Venue for prosecution.

For the purpose of venue under this article, any violation of this article shall be considered to have been committed in any county or city:

1. In which any act was performed in furtherance of any course of conduct which violated this article;

2. In which the owner has his principal place of business in the Commonwealth;

3. In which any offender had control or possession of any proceeds of the violation or of any books, records, documents, property, financial instrument, computer software, computer program, computer data, or other material or objects which were used in furtherance of the violation;

4. From which, to which, or through which any access to a computer or computer network was made whether by wires, electromagnetic waves, microwaves, or any other means of communication;

5. In which the offender resides; or

6. In which any computer which is an object or an instrument of the violation is located at the time of the alleged offense.

§18.2-152.11. Article not exclusive.

The provisions of this article shall not be construed to preclude the applicability of any other provision of the criminal law of this Commonwealth which presently applies or may in the future apply to any transaction or course of conduct which violates this article, unless such provision is clearly inconsistent with the terms of this article.

§18.2-152.12. Civil relief; damages.

A. Any person whose property or person is injured by reason of a violation of any provision of this article may sue therefor and recover for any damages sustained and the costs of suit. Without limiting the generality of the term, "damages" shall include loss of profits.

B. If the injury arises from the transmission of unsolicited bulk electronic mail, the injured person, other than an electronic mail service provider, may also recover attorneys' fees and costs, and may elect, in lieu of actual damages, to recover the lesser of ten dollars for each and every unsolicited bulk electronic mail message transmitted in violation of this article, or $25,000 per day. The injured person shall not have a cause of action against the electronic mail service provider which merely transmits the unsolicited bulk electronic mail over its computer network.

C. If the injury arises from the transmission of unsolicited bulk electronic mail, an injured electronic mail service provider may also recover attorneys' fees and costs, and may elect, in lieu of actual damages, to recover the greater of ten dollars for each and every unsolicited bulk electronic mail message transmitted in violation of this article, or $25,000 per day.

D. At the request of any party to an action brought pursuant to this section, the court may, in its discretion, conduct all legal proceedings in such a way as to protect the secrecy and security of the computer, computer network, computer data, computer program and computer software involved in order to prevent possible recurrence of the same or a similar act by another person and to protect any trade secrets of any party.

E. The provisions of this article shall not be construed to limit any person's right to pursue any additional civil remedy otherwise allowed by law.

F. A civil action under this section must be commenced before expiration of the time period prescribed in §8.01-40.1. In actions alleging injury arising from the transmission of unsolicited bulk electronic mail, personal jurisdiction may be exercised pursuant to §8.01-328.1.
(Chgd. by L.1999 chs. 886, 904, 905, eff. 7/1/99.)

§18.2-152.13. Severability.

If any provision or clause of this article or application thereof to any person or circumstances is held to be invalid, such invalidity shall not affect other provisions or applications of this article which can be given effect without the invalid provision or application, and to this end the provisions of this article are declared to be severable.

§18.2-152.14. Computer as instrument of forgery.

The creation, alteration, or deletion of any computer data contained in any computer or computer network, which if done on a tangible document or instrument would constitute forgery under Article 1 (§18.2-168 et seq.) of Chapter 6 of this Title, will also be deemed to be forgery. The absence of a tangible writing directly created or altered by the offender shall not be a defense to any crime set forth in Article 1 (§18.2-168 et seq.) of Chapter 6 of this Title if a creation, alteration, or deletion of computer data was involved in lieu of a tangible document or instrument.

§18.2-152.15. Encryption used in criminal activity.

Any person who willfully uses encryption to further any criminal activity shall be guilty of an offense which is separate and distinct from the predicate criminal activity and punishable as a Class 1 misdemeanor.

"Encryption" means the enciphering of intelligible data into unintelligible form or the deciphering of unintelligible data into intelligible form.

(Added by L.1999 ch. 455, eff. 7/1/99.)

ARTICLE 8
OFFENSES RELATING TO RAILROADS AND OTHER UTILITIES

Section

§18.2-153. Obstructing or injuring canal, railroad, power line, etc.

If any person maliciously obstruct, remove or injure any part of a canal, railroad or urban, suburban or interurban electric railway, or any lines of any electric power company, or any bridge or fixture thereof, or maliciously obstruct, tamper with, injure or remove any machinery, engine, car, trolley, supply or return wires or any other work thereof, or maliciously open, close, displace, tamper with or injure any switch, switch point, switch lever, signal lever or signal of any such company, whereby the life of any person on such canal, railroad, urban, suburban or interurban electric railway, is put in peril, he shall be guilty of a Class 4 felony; and, in the event of the death of any such person resulting from such malicious act, the person so offending shall be deemed guilty of murder, the degree to be determined by the jury or the court trying the case without a jury.

If any such act be committed unlawfully, but not maliciously, the person so offending shall be guilty of a Class 6 felony; and in the event of the death of any such person resulting from such unlawful act, the person so offending shall be deemed guilty of involuntary manslaughter.

§18.2-154. Shooting at or throwing missiles, etc., at train, car, vessel, etc.; penalty.

Any person who maliciously shoots at, or maliciously throws any missile at or against, any train or cars on any railroad or other transportation company or any vessel or other watercraft, or any motor vehicle or other vehicles when occupied by one or more persons, whereby the life of any person on such train, car, vessel, or other watercraft, or in such motor vehicle or other vehicle, may be put in peril, shall be guilty of a Class 4 felony. In the event of the death of any such person, resulting from such malicious shooting or throwing, the person so offending shall be deemed guilty of murder, the degree to be determined by the jury or the court trying the case without a jury.

If any such act is committed unlawfully, but not maliciously, the person so offending shall be guilty of a Class 6 felony and, in the event of the death of any such person, resulting from such unlawful act, the person so offending shall be deemed guilty of involuntary manslaughter.

If any person commits a violation of this section by maliciously or unlawfully shooting, with a firearm, at a conspicuously marked law-enforcement, fire or rescue squad vehicle, ambulance or any other emergency medical vehicle, the sentence imposed shall include a mandatory, minimum term of imprisonment of one year which shall not be suspended in whole or in part.

§18.2-155. Injuring, etc., signal used by railroad.

If any person maliciously injure, destroy, molest, or remove any switchlamp, flag or other signal used by any railroad, or any line, wire, post. lamp or any other structure or mechanism used in connection with any signal on a railroad, or destroys or in any manner interferes with the proper working of any signal on a railroad, whereby the life of any person is or may be put in peril he shall be guilty of a Class 4 felony; and in the event of the death of such person resulting from such malicious injuring, destroying or removing, the person so offending shall be deemed guilty of murder, the degree to be determined by the jury or the court trying the case without a jury. If such act be done unlawfully but not maliciously the offender shall be guilty of a Class 1 misdemeanor, provided that in the event of the death of any such person resulting from such unlawful injuring, destroying or removing, the person so offending shall be deemed guilty of involuntary manslaughter.

§18.2-156. Taking or removing waste or packing from journal boxes.

If any person shall willfully and maliciously take or remove the waste or packing from any journal box of any locomotive, engine, tender, carriage, coach, car, caboose or truck used or operated upon any railroad, whether the same be operated by steam or electricity, he shall be guilty of a Class 6 felony.

§18.2-157. Injury to fences or cattle stops along line of railroad.

Any person who shall willfully or maliciously cut, break down, injure or destroy any fence erected along the line of any railroad for the purpose of fencing the track or depot grounds of such road, or shall break down, injure or destroy any cattle stop along the line of any railroad, shall be guilty of a Class 3 misdemeanor.

§18.2-158. Driving, etc., animal on track to recover damages.

If any person, with a view to the recovery of damages against a railroad company, willfully ride, drive, or lead any animal, or otherwise contrive for any animal to go, on the railroad track of such company, and such animal is by reason thereof killed or injured, he shall be guilty of a Class 3 misdemeanor.

§18.2-159. Trespassing on railroad track.

Any person who goes upon the track of a railroad other than to pass over such road at a public or private crossing, or who willfully rides, drives or leads any animal or contrives for any animal to go on such track except to cross as aforesaid, without the consent of the railroad company or person operating such road, shall be guilty of a Class 4 misdemeanor. A second violation of the provisions of this section occurring within two years of the first violation shall be punishable as a Class 3 misdemeanor. A third or subsequent violation of the provisions of this section occurring within two years of a second or subsequent violation shall be punishable as a Class 1 misdemeanor. This section shall not apply to any section of track which has been legally abandoned pursuant to an order of a federal or state agency having jurisdiction over the track and is not being used for railroad service.

For purposes of this section, track shall mean the rail, ties, and ballast of the railroad.

§18.2-160. Trespassing on railroad trains.

If any person, not being a passenger or employer, shall be found trespassing upon any railroad car or train of any railroad in this Commonwealth, by riding on any car, or any part thereof, on its arrival, stay or departure at or from any station or depot of such railroad, or on the passage of any such car or train over any part of any such railroad, such person shall be guilty of a Class 4 misdemeanor.

§18.2-160.1. Boarding transportation district train without payment of fare.

It shall be unlawful for any person to board or ride a train operated by or under contract with a transportation district created pursuant to Chapter 32 (§15.1-1342 et seq.) of Title 15.1 when such person has failed or refused to pay the posted fare published by the transportation district. A violation of this section shall be punishable by a fine of not less than $150 nor more than $250. A violation of this section shall be deemed to continue from the point of boarding through termination of the train's scheduled trip.

Any person who has been convicted of violating the provisions of §18.2-160.1 shall be civilly liable to the transportation district for all costs incurred in prosecuting such person under the provisions of §18.2-160.1. The costs shall be limited to actual expenses, including the base wage of one employee acting as a witness for the Commonwealth and suit costs, but the total costs recovered shall not exceed $250.

§18.2-161. Trespassers forbidden to jump on or off railroad cars or trains.

If any person, not being a passenger or employee, but a trespasser, shall jump on or off any railroad car or train on its arrival, stay or departure at or from any station or depot of such railroad, or on the passage of any such car or train over any part of any such railroad, such person shall be guilty of a Class 4 misdemeanor.

§18.2-162. Damage or trespass to public services or utilities.

Any person who shall intentionally destroy or damage any facility which is used to furnish oil, telegraph, telephone, electric, gas, sewer, wastewater or water service to the public, shall be guilty of a Class 4 felony, provided that in the event the destruction or damage may be remedied or repaired for $200 or less such act shall constitute a Class 3 misdemeanor. On electric generating property marked with no trespassing signs, the security personnel of a utility may detain a trespasser for a period not to exceed one hour pending arrival of a law-enforcement officer.

Notwithstanding any other provisions of this title, any person who shall intentionally destroy or damage, or attempt to destroy or damage, any such facility, equipment or material connected therewith, the destruction or damage of which might, in any manner, threaten the release of radioactive materials or ionizing radiation beyond the areas in which they are normally used or contained, shall be guilty of a Class 4 felony, provided that in the event the destruction or damage results in the death of another due to exposure to radioactive materials or ionizing radiation, such person shall be guilty of a Class 2 felony; provided further, that in the event the destruction or damage results in injury to another, such person shall be guilty of a Class 3 felony.

§18.2-162.1. Diverting wastewater line; diverting or wasting public water supply.

Any person who willfully and maliciously (i) diverts any public wastewater or sewer line or (ii) diverts or wastes any public water supply by tampering with any fire hydrant shall be guilty of a Class 2 misdemeanor.

§18.2-163. Tampering with metering device; diverting service; civil liability.

A. Any person who (i) tampers with any metering device incident to the facilities set forth in §18.2-162, or otherwise intentionally prevents such a metering device from properly registering the degree, amount or quantity of service supplied, or (ii) diverts such service, except telephonic or electronic extension service not owned or controlled by any such company without authorization from the owner of the facility furnishing the service to the public, shall be guilty of a Class 1 misdemeanor.

B. The presence of any metering device found to have been altered, tampered with, or bypassed in a manner that would cause the metering device to inaccurately measure and register the degree, amount or quantity of service supplied or which would cause the service to be diverted from the recording apparatus of the meter shall be prima facie evidence of intent to violate and of the violation of this section by the person to whose benefit it is that such service be unmetered, unregistered or diverted.

C. The court may order restitution for the value of the services unlawfully used and for all costs. Such costs shall be limited to actual expenses, including the base wages of employees acting as witnesses for the Commonwealth, and suit costs. However, the total amount of allowable costs granted hereunder shall not exceed $250, excluding the value of the service.

§18.2-164. Unlawful use of, or injury to, telephone and telegraph lines; copying or obstructing messages.

Any person who shall:

(1) Maliciously injure, molest, cut down or destroy any telephone or telegraph line, wire, cable or pole, or the material or property belonging thereto; or

(2) Maliciously cut, break, tap or make any connection with any telephone or telegraph line, wire, cable or instrument of any telegraph or telephone company which has

legally acquired the right-of-way by purchase, condemnation, or otherwise; or

(3) Maliciously copy in any unauthorized manner any message, either social, business, or otherwise, passing over any telephone or telegraph line, wire or cable in this Commonwealth; or

(4) Willfully or maliciously prevent, obstruct or delay by any means or contrivance whatsoever the sending, conveyance or delivery in this Commonwealth of any authorized communication by or through any telephone or telegraph line, wire or cable under the control of any telephone or telegraph company doing business in this Commonwealth; or

(5) Maliciously aid, agree with, employ or conspire with any unauthorized person or persons unlawfully to do or cause to be done any of the acts herein before mentioned,

shall be guilty of a Class 3 misdemeanor.

§18.2-165. Unlawful use of, or injury to, television or radio signals and equipment.

Any person who shall willfully or maliciously break, injure or otherwise destroy or damage any of the posts, wires, towers or other materials or fixtures employed in the construction or use of any line of a television coaxial cable, or a microwave radio system, or willfully or maliciously interfere with such structure so erected, or in any way attempt to lead from its uses or make use of the electrical signal or any portion thereof properly belonging to or in use or in readiness to be made use of for the purpose of using said electrical signal from any television coaxial cable company or microwave system or owner of such property, shall be guilty of a Class 3 misdemeanor.

§18.2-165.1. Tampering with or unlawful use of cable television service.

Any person who (i) shall knowingly obtain or attempt to obtain cable television service from another by means, artifice, trick, deception or device without the payment to the operator of such service of all lawful compensation for each type of service obtained; (ii) shall knowingly, and with intent to profit thereby from any consideration received or expected, assist or instruct any other person in obtaining or attempting to obtain any cable television service without the payment to the operator of said service of all lawful compensation; (iii) shall knowingly tamper or otherwise interfere with or connect to by any means whether mechanical, electrical, acoustical or other, any cables, wires, or other devices used for the distribution of cable television service without authority from the operator of such service; or (iv) shall knowingly sell, rent, lend, promote, offer or advertise for sale, rental or use any device of any description or any plan for making or assembling the same to any person, with knowledge that the person intends to use such device or plan to do any of the acts hereinbefore mentioned or if the device or plan was represented either directly or indirectly by the person distributing it as having the ability to facilitate the doing of any of the acts hereinbefore mentioned, shall be guilty of a Class 6 felony if convicted under clause (ii) or (iv) above and shall be guilty of a Class 1 misdemeanor if convicted under clause (i) or (iii) above.

As used herein, cable television service shall include any and all services provided by or through the facilities of any cable television system or closed circuit coaxial cable communications system or any microwave, satellite or similar transmission service used in connection with any cable television system or other similar closed circuit coaxial cable communications system.

In any prosecution under this section, the existence on property in the actual possession of the accused, of any connection, wire, conductor, or any device whatsoever, which permits the use of cable television service without the same being reported for payment to and specifically authorized by the operator of the cable television service shall be prima facie evidence of intent to violate and of the violation of this section by the accused.

Nothing contained in this section shall be construed so as to abrogate or interfere with any contract right or remedy of any person having a contract with the owner of a television coaxial cable, or a cablevision system, or a microwave radio system.

§18.2-165.2. Unlawful interference with emergency two-way radio communications; penalty.

A. It shall be unlawful for any person to knowingly and willfully (i) interfere with the transmission of a radio communication, the purpose of which is to inform or to inquire about an emergency or (ii) transmit false information about an emergency.

B. For the purposes of this section, "emergency" means a condition or circumstance in which an individual is or is reasonably believed by the person transmitting the communication to be in imminent danger of death or serious bodily harm or in which property is in imminent danger of damage or destruction.

C. Any person who violates the provisions of this section shall be guilty of a Class 1 misdemeanor.

§18.2-166. Disclosing or inducing disclosure of certain information concerning customers of telephone companies.

Any person:

(1) Who is an employee of a telephone company, or an employee of a company which prints or otherwise handles lists of telephone customers for a telephone company and who discloses to another the names, addresses, or telephone numbers of any two or more customers of telephone service, knowing that such disclosure is without the consent of the telephone company furnishing said service; or

(2) Who knowingly induces such an employee to make such disclosure by giving offering, or promising to such employee any gift, gratuity, or thing of value, or by doing or promising to do any act beneficial to such employee; or

(3) Who takes, copies, or compiles any list containing the aforesaid information knowing that such conduct is without the consent of the telephone company furnishing said service; or

(4) Who attempts, aids or abets another, or conspires with another, to commit any of the aforesaid acts,

shall be guilty of a Class 3 misdemeanor.

§18.2-167. Selling or transferring certain telephonic instruments.

(a) It shall be unlawful for any person knowingly to make, sell, offer or advertise for sale, possess, or give or otherwise transfer to another any instrument, apparatus, equipment, or device or plans or instructions for making or assembling any instrument, apparatus, equipment or device which has been designed, adapted, used, or employed with the intent or for the purpose of (1) obtaining long distance toll telephone or telegraph service or the transmission of a long distance toll message, signal, or other communication by telephone or telegraph, or over telephone or telegraph facilities, without the payment of charges for any such long distance message, signal or other communication; or (2) concealing or assisting another to conceal from any supplier of telephone or telegraph service or from any person charged with the responsibility of enforcing this section, the existence or place of origin or of destination of any long distance toll message, signal, or other communication by telephone or telegraph, or over telephone or telegraph facilities. Persons violating any provision of this section shall be guilty of a Class 3 misdemeanor.

(b) Any such instrument, apparatus, equipment or device, or plans or instructions therefor, may be seized by court order or under a warrant; and, upon a final conviction of any person owning the seized materials, or having any ownership interest therein, for a violation of any provision of this section, the instrument, apparatus, equipment, device, or plans or instructions shall be ordered destroyed as contraband by the court in which the person is convicted.

§18.2-167.1. Interception or monitoring of customer telephone calls; penalty.

It shall be unlawful for any person, firm or corporation to intercept or monitor, or attempt to intercept or monitor, the transmission of a message, signal or other communication by telephone between an employee or other agent of such person, firm or corporation and a customer of such person, firm or corporation.

The provisions of this section shall not apply if the person, firm or corporation gives notice to such employee or agent that such monitoring may occur at any time during the course of such employment.

Any person, firm or corporation violating the provisions of this section shall be guilty of a Class 4 misdemeanor. The provisions of this section shall not apply to any wiretap or other interception of any communication authorized pursuant to Chapter 6 of Title 19.2 (§19.2-61 et seq.).

CHAPTER 6
CRIMES INVOLVING FRAUD

Article

ARTICLE 1
FORGERY

Section

§18.2-168. Forging public records, etc.

If any person forge a public record, or certificate, return, or attestation, of any public officer or public employee, in relation to any matter wherein such certificate, return, or attestation may be received as legal proof, or utter, or attempt to employ as true, such forged record, certificate, return, or attestation, knowing the same to be forged, he shall be guilty of a Class 4 felony.

§18.2-169. Forging, or keeping an instrument for forging, a seal.

If any person forge, or keep or conceal any instrument for the purpose of forging the seal of the Commonwealth, the seal of a court, or of any public office, or body politic or corporate in this Commonwealth, he shall be guilty of a Class 4 felony.

§18.2-170. Forging coin or bank notes.

If any person (1) forge any coin, note or bill current by law or usage in this Commonwealth or any note or bill of a banking company, (2) fraudulently make any base coin, or a note or bill purporting to be the note or bill of a banking company, when such company does not exist, or (3) utter, or attempt to employ as true, or sell, exchange, or deliver, or offer to sell, exchange, or deliver, or receive on sale, exchange, or delivery, with intent to utter or employ, or to have the same uttered or employed as true, any such false, forged, or base coin, note or bill, knowing it to be so, he shall be guilty of a Class 4 felony.

§18.2-171. Making or having anything designed for forging any writing, etc.

If any person engrave, stamp, or cast, or otherwise make or mend, any plate, block, press, or other thing, adapted and designed for the forging and false making of any writing or other thing, the forging or false making whereof is punishable by this chapter, or if such person have in possession any such plate, block, press, or other thing, with intent to use, or cause or permit it to be used, in forging or false making any such writing or other thing, he shall be guilty of a Class 4 felony.

§18.2-172. Forging, uttering, etc., other writings.

If any person forge any writing, other than such as is mentioned in §§18.2-168 and 18.2-170, to the prejudice of another's right, or utter, or attempt to employ as true, such forged writing, knowing it to be forged, he shall be guilty of a Class 5 felony. Any person who shall obtain, by any false pretense or token, the signature of another person, to any such writing, with intent to defraud any other person, shall be deemed guilty of the forgery thereof, and shall be subject to like punishment.

§18.2-172.1. Falsifying or altering and fraudulently using transcripts or diplomas; penalty.

Any person who materially falsifies or alters a transcript or diploma from an institution of post-secondary education and fraudulently uses the same for pecuniary gain or in furtherance of such person's education shall be guilty of a Class 3 misdemeanor.

§18.2-173. Having in possession forged coin or bank notes.

If any person have in his possession forged bank notes or forged or base coin, such as are mentioned in §18.2-170, knowing the same to be forged or base, with the intent to utter or employ the same as true, or to sell, exchange, or deliver them, so as to enable any other person to utter or employ them as true, he shall, if the number of such notes or coins in his possession at the same time, be ten or more, be guilty of a Class 6 felony; and if the number be less than ten, he shall be guilty of a Class 3 misdemeanor.

ARTICLE 2
IMPERSONATION

§18.2-174. Impersonating officer.

Any person who shall falsely assume or exercise the functions, powers, duties and privileges incident to the office of sheriff, police officer, marshal, or other peace officer, or who shall falsely assume or pretend to be any such officer, shall be deemed guilty of a Class 1 misdemeanor.

§18.2-174.1. Impersonating certain public safety personnel; penalty.

Any person who willfully impersonates any certified emergency medical services personnel, firefighter, including any special forest warden designated pursuant to §10.1-1135, fire marshal, or fire chief shall be guilty of a Class 3 misdemeanor.
(Chgd. by L.2000 ch. 962, eff. 7/1/2000.)

§18.2-175. Unlawful wearing of officer's uniform or insignia; unlawful use of vehicle with word "police" shown thereon.

No person, not such an officer as is referred to in §19.2-78, shall wear any such uniform as is designated pursuant to the provisions of such section or wear an insignia or markings containing the Seal of the Commonwealth or the insignia of any such officer's uniform, nor shall any person not such an officer, or not authorized by such officer, or not authorized by the military police of the armed forces or of the National Guard, or not authorized by the military police of other governmental agencies, use or cause to be used on the public roads or highways of this Commonwealth, any motor vehicle bearing markings with the word "police" shown thereon. However, the prohibition against wearing an insignia or markings containing the Seal of the Commonwealth shall not apply to any certified firefighter or to any certified or licensed emergency medical personnel. Any violation of this section shall be a Class 1 misdemeanor.

§18.2-176. Unauthorized wearing or displaying on motor vehicles of any button, insignia or emblem of certain associations or societies or of Southern Cross of Honor.

(a) No person shall wear the button or insignia of any order of police, trade union or veterans' organization or display upon a motor vehicle the insignia or emblem of any automobile club, medical society, order of police, trade union or veterans' organization or use such button, insignia or emblem to obtain aid or assistance unless entitled to wear, display or use the same under the constitution, bylaws, rules or regulations of the organization concerned.

(b) No person shall wear any Southern Cross of Honor when not entitled to do so by the regulations under which such Crosses of Honor are given.

(c) A violation of this section shall be a Class 3 misdemeanor.

§18.2-177. Illegal use of insignia.

Any person who shall willfully wear, exhibit, display, print, or use, for any purpose, the badge, motto, button, decoration, charm, emblem, rosette, or other insignia of any such association or organization mentioned in §2.1-74, duly registered under Article 2 (§2.1-74 et seq.), Chapter 8, Title 2.1 of this Code, unless he shall be entitled to use and wear the same under the constitution and bylaws, rules and regulations of such association or organization, shall be guilty of a Class 4 misdemeanor.

ARTICLE 3
FALSE PRETENSES

§18.2-178. Obtaining money or signature, etc., by false pretense.

If any person obtain, by any false pretense or token, from any person, with intent to defraud, money or other property which may be the subject of larceny, he shall be deemed guilty of larceny thereof; or if he obtain, by any false pretense or token, with such intent, the signature of any person to a writing, the false making whereof would be forgery, he shall be guilty of a Class 4 felony.

§18.2-179. Unlawful operation of coin box telephone, parking meter, vending machine, etc.

Any person who shall operate, cause to be operated, or attempt to operate or cause to be operated any coin box telephone, parking meter, vending machine or other machine that operates on the coin-in-the-slot principle, whether of like kind or not, designed only to receive lawful coin of the United States of America, in connection with the use or enjoyment of telephone or telegraph service, parking privileges or any other service, or the sale of merchandise or other property, by means of a slug, or any false, counterfeit, mutilated, sweated or foreign coin, or by any means, method, trick or device whatsoever, not authorized by the owner, lessee or licensee of such coin box telephone, parking meter, vending machine or other machine; or who shall obtain or receive telephone or telegraph service, parking privileges, merchandise, or any other service or property from any such coin box telephone, parking meter, vending machine or other machines, designed only to receive lawful coin of the United States of America, without depositing in or surrendering to such coin box telephone, parking meter, vending machine, or other machine lawful coin of the United States of America to the amount required therefor by the owner, lessee or licensee of such coin box telephone, parking meter, vending machine or other machine, shall be guilty of a Class 3 misdemeanor.

§18.2-180. Manufacture, etc., of slugs, etc., for such unlawful use.

Any person who, with intent to cheat or defraud the owner, lessee, licensee or other person entitled to the contents of any such coin box telephone, parking meter, vending machine or other machine operated on the coin-in-the-slot principle, designed only to receive lawful coin of the United States of America, in connection with the use of any such coin box telephone, parking meter, vending machine or other machine, or who, knowing or having reason to believe that the same is intended for such unlawful use, shall manufacture, sell, offer to sell, advertise for sale or give away any slug, device or substance whatsoever, intended or calculated to be placed or deposited in any such coin box telephone, parking meter, vending machine or other machine, shall be guilty of a Class 3 misdemeanor.

The manufacture, sale, offer for sale, advertisement for sale, giving away or possession of any such slug, device or substance whatsoever, intended or calculated to be placed or deposited in any such coin box telephone, parking meter, vending machine or other machine that operates on the coin-in-the-slot principle, shall be prima facie evidence of intent to cheat or defraud within the meaning of this section and §18.2-179.

ARTICLE 4
BAD CHECK LAW

Section

§18.2-181. Issuing bad checks, etc., larceny.

Any person who, with intent to defraud, shall make or draw or utter or deliver any check, draft, or order for the payment of money, upon any bank, banking institution, trust company, or other depository, knowing, at the time of such making, drawing, uttering or delivering, that the maker or drawer has not sufficient funds in, or credit with, such bank, banking institution, trust company, or other depository, for the payment of such check, draft or order, although no express representation is made in reference thereto, shall be guilty of larceny; and, if this check, draft, or order has a represented value of $200 or more, such person shall be guilty of a Class 6 felony. In cases in which such value is less than $200, the person shall be guilty of a Class 1 misdemeanor.

The word "credit" as used herein, shall be construed to mean any arrangement or understanding with the bank, trust company, or other depository for the payment of such check, draft or order.

Any person making, drawing, uttering or delivering any such check, draft or order in payment as a present consideration for goods or services for the purposes set out in this section shall be guilty as provided herein.

§18.2-181.1. Issuance of bad checks.

It shall be a Class 6 felony for any person, within a period of ninety days, to issue two or more checks, drafts or orders for the payment of money in violation of §18.2-181, which have an aggregate represented value of $200 or more and which (i) are drawn upon the same account of any bank, banking institution, trust company or other depository and (ii) are made payable to the same person, firm or corporation.

§18.2-182. Issuing bad checks on behalf of business firm or corporation in payment of wages.

Any person who shall make, draw, or utter, or deliver any check, draft, or order for the payment of money, upon any bank, banking institution, trust company or other depository on behalf of any business firm or corporation, for the purpose of paying wages to any employee of such firm or corporation, or for the purpose of paying for any labor performed by any person for such firm or corporation, knowing, at the time of such making, drawing, uttering or delivering, that the account upon which such check, draft or order is drawn has not sufficient funds, or credit with, such bank, banking institution, trust company or other depository, for the payment of such check, draft or order, although no express representation is made in reference thereto, shall be guilty of a Class 1 misdemeanor.

The word "credit," as used herein, shall be construed to mean any arrangement or understanding with the bank, banking institution, trust company, or other depository for the payment of such check, draft or order.

In addition to the criminal penalty set forth herein, such person shall be personally liable in any civil action brought upon such check, draft or order.

§18.2-182.1. Issuing bad checks in payment of taxes.

Any person who shall make, draw, utter, or deliver two or more checks, drafts, or orders within a period of ninety days which have an aggregate represented value of $1,000 or more, for the payment of money upon any bank, banking institution, trust company, or other depository on behalf of any taxpayer for the payment of any state tax under §58.1-486 or §58.1-637, knowing, at the time of such making, drawing, uttering, or delivering, that the account upon which such check, draft, or order is drawn has not sufficient funds or credit with such bank, banking institution, trust company, or other depository for the payment of such check, draft, or order, although no express representation is made in reference thereto, shall be guilty of a Class 1 misdemeanor.

The word "credit," as used herein, means any arrangement or understanding with the bank, banking institution, trust company, or other depository for the payment of such check, draft, or order.

§18.2-183. Issuance of bad check prima facie evidence of intent and knowledge; notice by certified or registered mail.

In any prosecution or action under the preceding sections, the making or drawing or uttering or delivery of a check, draft, or order, payment of which is refused by the drawee because of lack of funds or credit shall be prima facie evidence of intent to defraud or of knowledge of insufficient funds in, or credit with, such bank, banking institution, trust company or other depository unless such maker or drawer, or someone for him, shall have paid the holder thereof the amount due thereon, together with interest, and protest fees (if any), within five days after receiving written notice that such check, draft, or order has not been paid to the holder thereof. Notice mailed by certified or registered mail, evidenced by return receipt, to the last known address of the maker or drawer shall be deemed sufficient and equivalent to notice having been received by the maker or drawer.

If such check, draft or order shows on its face a printed or written address, home, office, or otherwise, of the maker or drawer, then the foregoing notice, when sent by certified or registered mail to such address, with or without return receipt requested, shall be deemed sufficient and equivalent to notice having been received by the maker or drawer, whether such notice shall be returned undelivered or not.

When a check is drawn on a bank in which the maker or drawer has no account, it shall be presumed that such check was issued with intent to defraud, and the five-day notice set forth above shall not be required in such case.

§18.2-184. Presumption as to notation attached to check, draft or order.

In any prosecution or action under the preceding sections, any notation attached to or stamped upon a check, draft or order which is refused by the drawee because of lack of funds or credit, bearing the terms "not sufficient funds," "uncollected funds," "account closed," or "no account in this name," or words of similar import, shall be prima facie evidence that such notation is true and correct.

§18.2-185. Evidence and presumptions in malicious prosecution actions after issuance of bad check.

In any civil action growing out of an arrest under §§18.2-181 or 18.2-182, no evidence of statements or representations as to the status of the check, draft, order or deposit involved, or of any collateral agreement with reference to the check, draft, or order, shall be admissible unless such statements, or representations, or collateral agreement, be written upon the instrument at the time it is given by the drawer.

If payment of any check, draft, or order for the payment of money be refused by the bank, banking institution, trust company or other depository upon which such instrument is drawn, and the person who drew or uttered such instrument be arrested or prosecuted under the provisions of §§18.2-181 or 18.2-182, for failure or refusal to pay such instrument, the one who arrested or caused such person to be arrested and prosecuted, or either, shall be conclusively deemed to have acted with reasonable or probable cause in any suit for damages that may be brought by the person who drew or uttered such instrument, if the one who arrested or caused such person to be arrested and prosecuted, or either, shall have, before doing so, presented or caused such instrument to be presented to the depository on which it was drawn where it was refused, and then waited five days after notice, as provided in §18.2-183, without the amount due under the provisions of such instrument being paid.

ARTICLE 5
FALSE REPRESENTATIONS TO OBTAIN PROPERTY OR CREDIT

§18.2-186. False statements to obtain property or credit.

A. A person shall be guilty of a Class 2 misdemeanor if he makes, causes to be made or conspires to make directly, indirectly or through an agency, any materially false statement in writing, knowing it to be false and intending that it be relied upon, concerning the financial condition or means or ability to pay of himself, or of any other person for whom he is acting, or any firm or corporation in which he is interested or for which he is acting, for the purpose of procuring, for his own benefit or for the benefit of such person, firm or corporation, the delivery of personal property, the payment of cash, the making of a loan or credit, the extension of a credit, the discount of an account receivable, or the making, acceptance, discount, sale or endorsement of a bill of exchange or promissory note.

B. Any person who knows that a false statement has been made in writing concerning the financial condition or ability to pay of himself or of any person for whom he is acting, or any firm or corporation in which he is interested or for which he is acting and who, with intent to defraud, procures, upon the faith thereof, for his own benefit, or for the benefit of the person, firm or corporation, any such delivery, payment, loan, credit, extension, discount making, acceptance, sale or endorsement, and fails to pay for such loan, credit or benefit so procured, shall, if the value of the thing or the amount of the loan, credit or benefit obtained is $200 or more, be guilty of grand larceny or, if the value is less than $200, be guilty of a Class 1 misdemeanor.

§18.2-186.2. False statements or failure to disclose material facts in order to obtain aid or benefits under any local, state or federal housing assistance program.

Any person who (i) knowingly makes or causes to be made either directly or indirectly or through any agent or agency, any false statement in writing with the intent that it shall be relied upon, or fails to disclose any material fact concerning the financial means or ability to pay of himself or of any other person for whom he is acting, for the purpose of procuring aid and benefits available under any local, state or federally funded housing assistance program, or (ii) knowingly fails to disclose a change in circumstances in order to obtain or continue to receive under any such program aid or benefits to which he is not entitled or who knowingly aids and abets another person in the commission of any such act is guilty of a Class 1 misdemeanor.

§18.2-186.3. Identity fraud; penalty.

A. It shall be unlawful for any person, without the authorization or permission of the person who is the subject of the identifying information, with the intent to defraud, for his own use or the use of a third person, to:

1. Obtain, record or access identifying information which is not available to the general public that would assist in accessing financial resources, obtaining identification documents, or obtaining benefits of such other person; or

2. Obtain goods or services through the use of identifying information of such other person; or

3. Obtain identification documents in such other person's name.

B. It shall be unlawful for any person to use identification documents or identifying information of another to avoid summons, arrest, prosecution, or to impede a criminal investigation.

C. As used in this section, "identifying information" shall include but not be limited to: (i) name; (ii) date of birth; (iii) social security number; (iv) driver's license number; (v) bank account numbers; (vi) credit or debit card numbers; (vii) personal identification numbers (PIN); (viii) electronic identification codes; (ix) automated or electronic signatures; (x) biometric data; (xi) fingerprints; (xii) passwords; or (xiii) any other numbers or information that can be used to access a person's financial resources, obtain identification, act as identification, or obtain goods or services.

D. Violations of this section shall be punishable as a Class 1 misdemeanor. Any violation resulting in financial loss of greater than $200 shall be punishable as a Class 6 felony. Any second or subsequent conviction shall be punishable as a Class 6 felony. Any violation resulting in the arrest and detention of the person whose identification documents or identifying information were used to avoid summons, arrest, prosecution, or to impede a criminal investigation shall be punishable as a Class 6 felony. In any proceeding brought pursuant to this section, the crime shall be considered to have been committed in any locality where the person whose identifying information was appropriated resides, or in which any part of the offense took place, regardless of whether the defendant was ever actually in such locality.

E. Upon conviction, in addition to any other punishment, a person found guilty of this offense shall be ordered by the court to make restitution as the court deems appropriate to any person whose identifying information was appropriated.

(Added by L.2000 ch. 349, eff. 7/1/2000.)

§18.2-187.1. Obtaining or attempting to obtain oil, electric, gas, water, telephone, telegraph or cable television service without payment; penalty; civil liability.

A. It shall be unlawful for any person knowingly, with the intent to defraud, to obtain or attempt to obtain, for himself or for another, oil, electric, gas, water, telephone, telegraph or cable television service by the use of any false information, or in any case where such service has been disconnected by the supplier and notice of disconnection has been given.

B. It shall be unlawful for any person to obtain or attempt to obtain oil, electric, gas, water, telephone, telegraph, or cable television service by the use of any scheme, device, means or method, or by a false application for service with intent to avoid payment of lawful charges therefor.

B1. It shall be unlawful for any person to obtain, or attempt to obtain, telecommunication service as defined in §18.2-190.1 by the use of an unlawful telecommunication device as defined in §18.2-190.1.

C. The word "notice" as used in subsection A hereof shall be notice given in writing to the person to whom the service was assigned. The sending of a notice in writing by registered or certified mail in the United States mail, duly stamped and addressed to such person at his last known address, requiring delivery to the addressee only with return receipt requested, and the actual signing of the receipt for said mail by the addressee, shall be prima facie evidence that such notice was duly received.

D. Any person who violates any provisions of this section, if the value of service, credit or benefit procured is $200 or more, shall be guilty of a Class 6 felony; or if the value is less than $200, shall be guilty of a Class 1 misdemeanor. In addition, the court may order restitution for the value of the services unlawfully used and for all costs. Such costs shall be limited to actual expenses, including the base wages of employees acting as witnesses for the Commonwealth, and suit costs. However, the total amount of allowable costs granted hereunder shall not exceed $250, excluding the value of the service.

§18.2-188. Defrauding hotels, motels, campgrounds, boardinghouses, etc.

It shall be unlawful for any person, without paying therefor, and with the intent to cheat or defraud the owner or keeper to:

1. Put up at a hotel, motel, campground or boardinghouse;
2. Obtain food from a restaurant or other eating house;
3. Gain entrance to an amusement park; or
4. Without having an express agreement for credit, procure food, entertainment or accommodation from any hotel, motel, campground, boardinghouse, restaurant, eating house or amusement park.

It shall be unlawful for any person with intent to cheat or defraud the owner or keeper out of the pay therefor to obtain credit at a hotel, motel, campground, boardinghouse, restaurant or eating house for food, entertainment or accommodation by means of any false show of baggage or effects brought thereto.

It shall be unlawful for any person, with intent to cheat or defraud, to obtain credit at a hotel, motel, campground, boardinghouse, restaurant, eating house or amusement park for food, entertainment or accommodation through any misrepresentation or false statement.

It shall be unlawful for any person, with intent to cheat or defraud, to remove or cause to be removed any baggage or effects from a hotel, motel, campground, boardinghouse, restaurant or eating house while there is a lien existing thereon for the proper charges due from him for fare and board furnished.

Any person who violates any provision of this section shall, if the value of service, credit or benefit procured or obtained is $200 or more, be guilty of a Class 5 felony; or if the value is less than $200, a Class 1 misdemeanor.

§18.2-188.1. Defrauding person having a lien on an animal; penalty.

It shall be unlawful to remove or cause any horse or other animal to be removed from the possession of the owner or keeper of a livery stable or other person having a lien on the horse or animal for keep, support and care pursuant to §43-32, with intent to defraud or cheat the lienholder. A violation of this section shall be punishable as a Class 2 misdemeanor.

§18.2-189. Defrauding keeper of motor vehicles or watercraft.

A person shall be guilty of a Class 2 misdemeanor if he:

1. Stores a motor vehicle, boat or other watercraft with any person, firm or corporation engaged in the business of conducting a garage, marina, watercraft dealership or other facility for the (i) storage of motor vehicles, boats or other watercraft, (ii) furnishing of supplies to motor vehicles, boats or other watercraft, or (iii) alteration or repair of motor vehicles, boats or other watercraft, and obtains storage, supplies, alterations or repairs for such motor vehicle, boat or other watercraft, without having an express agreement for credit, or procures storage, supplies, alterations or repairs on account of such motor vehicle, boat or other watercraft so stored, without paying therefor, and with the intent to cheat or defraud the owner or keeper of the garage, marina or boat repair facility; or
2. With such intent, obtains credit at the garage, marina, watercraft dealership or boat repair facility for such storage, supplies, alterations or repairs through any misrepresentation or false statement; or
3. With such intent, removes or causes to be removed any such motor vehicle, boat or other watercraft from any such garage, marina, watercraft dealership or boat repair facility while there is a lien existing thereon for the proper charges due from him for storage, supplies, alterations or repairs furnished thereon, in accordance with the provisions of §43-32 or §43-33.

§18.2-190. Fraudulent misrepresentation as to breed of bull or cattle.

Any person who, in the sale, gift or transfer, of any bull or cattle, knowingly shall make any false representation that such bull is registered, or entitled to registration, in some recognized standard and accredited herd of cattle, or three-quarters blood of such breed, or that such cattle are from such a herd or breed of cattle, shall be guilty of a Class 1 misdemeanor.

ARTICLE 5.1
OFFENSES INVOLVING TELECOMMUNICATION DEVICES

§18.2-190.1. Definitions.

As used in this article, unless the context requires a different meaning:

"Equipment or materials used to manufacture an unlawful telecommunication device" means (i) a scanner capable of intercepting the electronic serial number or mobile identification number of a cellular or other wireless telephone; (ii) electronic software or hardware capable of altering or changing the factory-installed electronic serial number of a cellular or other wireless telephone or a computer containing such software; or (iii) a list of cellular or other wireless telephone electronic serial numbers with their associated mobile identification numbers possessed without the consent of the telecommunication service provider.

"Manufacture of an unlawful telecommunication device" means to produce or assemble an unlawful telecommunication device, or to modify, alter, program or reprogram a telecommunication device to be capable of acquiring or facilitating the acquisition of telecommunication service without the consent of the telecommunication service provider.

"Sell" means to sell, exchange, give or dispose of to another or to offer or agree to do the same.

"Telecommunication device" means (i) any type of instrument, device, machine or equipment which is capable of transmitting or receiving telephonic, electronic or radio communications or (ii) any part of such an instrument, device, machine or equipment, or any computer circuit, computer chip, electronic mechanism, or other component, which is capable of facilitating the transmission or reception of telephonic or electronic communications.

"Telecommunication service" includes any service provided for a charge or compensation to facilitate the origination, transmission, emission or reception of signs, signals, writings, images and sounds or intelligence of any nature by telephone, including cellular or other wireless telephones, wire, radio, television optical or other electromagnetic system.

"Telecommunication service provider" means a person or entity providing telecommunication service including, but not limited to, a cellular or other wireless telephone or paging company or other person or entity which, for a fee, supplies the facility, cell site, mobile telephone switching office, or other equipment or telecommunication service.

"Unlawful telecommunication device" means any telecommunication device that is capable, or has been altered, modified, programmed or reprogrammed so as to be capable, of acquiring, or facilitating the acquisition of, a telecommunication service without the consent of the telecommunication service provider. Such unlawful devices include, but are not limited to, tumbler phones, clone phones, tumbler microchips, clone microchips and other instruments capable of disguising their identity or location or of gaining access to a communications system operated by a telecommunication service provider.

(Chgd. by L.1998 ch. 518, eff. 7/1/98.)

§18.2-190.2. Possession of an unlawful telecommunication device or equipment, etc., used to manufacture such device.

A person who knowingly possesses (i) an unlawful telecommunication device or (ii) equipment or materials used to manufacture an unlawful telecommunication device as defined in §18.2-190.1 with the intent to manufacture an unlawful telecommunication device shall be guilty of a Class 6 felony unless such possession is by a telecommunication equipment manufacturer or a facilities-based telecommunication service provider licensed by the Federal Communications Commission or by a law-enforcement agency.

(Chgd. by L.1998 ch. 518, eff. 7/1/98.)

§18.2-190.3. Sale of an unlawful telecommunication device.

A person who sells (i) an unlawful telecommunication device or (ii) material, including hardware, data, computer software or other information or equipment, knowing that the purchaser or a third person intends to use such material in the manufacture of an unlawful telecommunication device, shall be guilty of a Class 6 felony.

(Chgd. by L.1998 ch. 518, eff. 7/1/98.)

§18.2-190.4. Manufacture of an unlawful telecommunication device.

A person who manufactures an unlawful telecommunication device shall be guilty of a Class 6 felony.

(Chgd. by L.1998 ch. 518, eff. 7/1/98.)

ARTICLE 6
OFFENSES RELATING TO CREDIT CARDS

§18.2-191. Definitions.

The following words and phrases as used in this article, unless a different meaning is plainly required by the context, shall have the following meanings:

"Acquirer" means a business organization, financial institution or an agent of a business organization or financial institution that authorizes a merchant to accept payment by credit card or credit card number for money, goods, services or anything else of value.

"Cardholder" means the person or organization named on the face of a credit card to whom or for whose benefit the credit card is issued by an issuer.

"Credit card" means any instrument or device, whether known as a credit card, credit plate, payment device number, or by any other name, issued with or without fee by an issuer for the use of the cardholder in obtaining money, goods, services or anything else of value on credit. For the purpose of this article, "credit card" shall also include a similar device, whether known as a debit card, or any other name, issued with or without fee by an issuer for the use of the cardholder in obtaining money, goods, services or anything else of value by charging the account of the cardholder with a bank or any other person even though no credit is thereby extended.

"Expired credit card" means a credit card which is no longer valid because the term shown on it has elapsed.

"Issuer" means the business organization or financial institution or its duly authorized agent which issues a credit card.

"Payment device number" means any code, account number or other means of account access, other than a check, draft or similar paper instrument, that can be used to obtain money, goods, services or anything else of value, or to initiate a transfer of funds. "Payment device number" does not include an encoded or truncated credit card number or payment device number.

"Receives" or "receiving" means acquiring possession or control of the credit card number or payment device number or accepting the same as security for a loan.

"Revoked credit card" means a credit card which is no longer valid because permission to use it has been suspended or terminated by the issuer.

"Sales draft" means a paper form evidencing a purchase of goods, services or anything else of value from a merchant through the use of a credit card.

"Cash advance/withdrawal draft" means a paper form evidencing a cash advance or withdrawal from a bank or other financial institution through the use of a credit card.

§18.2-192. Credit card theft.

(1) A person is guilty of credit card or credit card number theft when:

(a) He takes, obtains or withholds a credit card or credit card number from the person, possession, custody or control of another without the cardholder's consent or who, with knowledge that it has been so taken, obtained or withheld, receives the credit card or credit card number with intent to use it or sell it, or to transfer it to a person other than the issuer or the cardholder; or

(b) He receives a credit card or credit card number that he knows to have been lost, mislaid, or delivered under a mistake as to the identity or address of the cardholder, and who retains possession with intent to use, to sell or to transfer the credit card or credit card number to a person other than the issuer or the cardholder; or

(c) He, not being the issuer, sells a credit card or credit card number or buys a credit card or credit card number from a person other than the issuer; or

(d) He, not being the issuer, during any twelve-month period, receives credit cards or credit card numbers issued in the names of two or more persons which he has reason to know were taken or retained under circumstances which constitute a violation of §18.2-194 and subdivision (1)(c) of this section.

(2) Credit card or credit card number theft is grand larceny and is punishable as provided in §18.2-95.

§18.2-193. Credit card forgery.

(1) A person is guilty of credit card forgery when:

(a) With intent to defraud a purported issuer, a person or organization providing money, goods, services or anything else of value, or any other person, he falsely makes or falsely embosses a purported credit card or utters such a credit card; or

(b) He, not being the cardholder or a person authorized by him, with intent to defraud the issuer, or a person or organization providing money, goods, services or anything else of value, or any other person, signs a credit card; or

(c) He, not being the cardholder or a person authorized by him, with intent to defraud the issuer, or a person or organization providing money, goods, services or anything else of value, or any other person, forges a sales draft or cash advance/withdrawal draft, or uses a credit card number of a card of which he is not the cardholder, or utters, or attempts to employ as true, such forged draft knowing it to be forged.

(2) A person falsely makes a credit card when he makes or draws, in whole or in part, a device or instrument which purports to be the credit card of a named issuer but which is not such a credit card because the issuer did not authorize the making or drawing, or alters a credit card which was validly issued.

(3) A person falsely embosses a credit card when, without the authorization of the named issuer, he completes a credit card by adding any of the matter, other than the signature of the cardholder, which an issuer requires to appear on the credit card before it can be used by a cardholder. Conviction of credit card forgery shall be punishable as a Class 5 felony.

§18.2-194. Unauthorized possession of two or more signed credit cards or credit card numbers.

When a person, other than the cardholder or a person authorized by him, possesses two or more credit cards which are signed or two or more credit card numbers, such possession shall be prima facie evidence that said cards or credit card numbers were obtained in violation of subdivision (1)(b) of §18.2-193.

§18.2-195. Credit card fraud; conspiracy; penalties.

(1) A person is guilty of credit card fraud when, with intent to defraud any person, he:

(a) Uses for the purpose of obtaining money, goods, services or anything else of value a credit card or credit card number obtained or retained in violation of §18.2-192 or a credit card or credit card number which he knows is expired or revoked;

(b) Obtains money, goods, services or anything else of value by representing (i) without the consent of the cardholder that he is the holder of a specified card or credit card number or (ii) that he is the holder of a card or credit card number and such card or credit card number has not in fact been issued;

(c) Obtains control over a credit card or credit card number as security for debt; or

(d) Obtains money from an issuer by use of an unmanned device of the issuer or through a person other than the issuer when he knows that such advance will exceed his available credit with the issuer and any available balances held by the issuer.

(2) A person who is authorized by an issuer to furnish money, goods, services or anything else of value upon presentation of a credit card or credit card number by the cardholder, or any agent or employee of such person, is guilty of a credit card fraud when, with intent to defraud the issuer or the cardholder, he:

(a) Furnishes money, goods, services or anything else of value upon presentation of a credit card or credit card number obtained or retained in violation of §18.2-192, or a credit card or credit card number which he knows is expired or revoked;

(b) Fails to furnish money, goods, services or anything else of value which he represents or causes to be represented in writing or by any other means to the issuer that he has furnished; or

(c) Remits to an issuer or acquirer a record of a credit card or credit card number transaction which is in excess of the monetary amount authorized by the cardholder.

(3) Conviction of credit card fraud is punishable as a Class 1 misdemeanor if the value of all money, goods, services and other things of value furnished in violation of this

section, or if the difference between the value of all money, goods, services and anything else of value actually furnished and the value represented to the issuer to have been furnished in violation of this section, does not exceed $200 in any six-month period; conviction of credit card fraud is punishable as a Class 6 felony if such value exceeds $200 in any six-month period.

(4) Any person who conspires, confederates or combines with another, (i) either within or without the Commonwealth to commit credit card fraud within the Commonwealth or (ii) within the Commonwealth to commit credit card fraud within or without the Commonwealth, is guilty of a Class 6 felony.

§18.2-195.1. Credit card factoring.

A. Any unauthorized person who presents to the issuer or acquirer for payment a credit card or credit card number transaction record of a sale which was not made by such person or his agent or employee, without the express authorization of the acquirer and with intent to defraud the issuer, acquirer or cardholder, is guilty of a Class 5 felony. If such act is done without authorization of the acquirer but without intent to defraud, he shall be guilty of a Class 1 misdemeanor.

B. Any person who, without the express authorization of the acquirer and with intent to defraud the issuer, acquirer or cardholder, employs or otherwise causes an authorized person to remit to an acquirer or issuer a credit card transaction record of sale that was not made by the authorized person is guilty of a Class 5 felony. If such act is done without the authorization of the acquirer but without intent to defraud, he shall be guilty of a Class 1 misdemeanor.

C. As used in this section, "authorized person" means a person authorized by the acquirer to furnish money, goods, services or anything else of value upon presentation of a credit card or credit card number by a cardholder and includes an agent or employee of a person having such authority.

§18.2-195.2. Fraudulent application for credit card; penalties.

A. A person shall be guilty of a Class 2 misdemeanor if he makes, causes to be made or conspires to make, directly, indirectly or through an agency, any materially false statement in writing concerning the financial condition or means or ability to pay of himself or of any other person for whom he is acting or any firm or corporation in which he is interested or for which he is acting, knowing the statement to be false and intending that it be relied upon for the purpose of procuring a credit card. However, if the statement is made in response to a written solicitation from the issuer or an agent of the issuer to apply for a credit card, he shall be guilty of a Class 4 misdemeanor.

B. A person who knows that a false statement has been made in writing concerning the financial condition or ability to pay of himself or of any person for whom he is acting or any firm or corporation in which he is interested or for which he is acting and who (i) with intent to defraud, procures a credit card, upon the faith thereof, for his own benefit, or for the benefit of the person, firm or corporation, and (ii) fails to pay for money, property, services or any thing of value obtained by use of the credit card, shall be guilty of grand larceny if the value so obtained is $200 or more or a Class 1 misdemeanor if the value is less than $200.

§18.2-196. Criminal possession of credit card forgery devices.

(1) A person is guilty of criminal possession of credit card forgery devices when:

(a) He is a person other than the cardholder and possesses two or more incomplete credit cards, with intent to complete them without the consent of the issuer; or

(b) He possesses, with knowledge of its character, machinery, plates or any other contrivance designed to reproduce instruments purporting to be credit cards of an issuer who has not consented to the preparation of such credit cards.

(2) A credit card is incomplete if part of the matter, other than the signature of the cardholder, which an issuer requires to appear on the credit card before it can be used by a cardholder, has not yet been stamped, embossed, imprinted or written upon.

Conviction of criminal possession of credit card forgery devices is punishable as a Class 6 felony.

§18.2-197. Criminally receiving goods and services fraudulently obtained.

A person is guilty of criminally receiving goods and services fraudulently obtained when he receives money, goods, services or anything else of value obtained in violation of subdivision (1) of §18.2-195 with the knowledge or belief that the same were obtained in violation of subdivision (1) of §18.2-195. Conviction of criminal receipt of goods and services fraudulently obtained is punishable as a Class 1 misdemeanor if the value of all money, goods, services and anything else of value, obtained in violation of this section, does not exceed $200 in any six-month period; conviction of criminal receipt of goods and services fraudulently obtained is punishable as a Class 6 felony if such value exceeds $200 in any six-month period.

§18.2-198. Obtaining airline, railroad, steamship, etc., ticket at discount price.

A person who obtains at a discount price a ticket issued by an airline, railroad, steamship or other transportation company from other than an apparent agent of such company which was acquired in violation of subdivision (1) of §18.2-195 without reasonable inquiry to ascertain that the person from whom it was obtained had a legal right to possess it shall be presumed to know that such ticket was acquired under circumstances constituting a violation of subdivision (1) of §18.2-195.

§18.2-198.1. Venue

Notwithstanding the provisions of §19.2-244, a prosecution for a violation of this article may be had in any county or city in which (i) any act in furtherance of the crime was committed or (ii) an issuer or acquirer, or an agent of either, sustained a financial loss as a result of the offense.

§18.2-199. Penalties for violation of article.

Persons violating any provision of this article for which no other specific punishment is provided for shall be guilty of a Class 6 felony.

ARTICLE 7
MISCELLANEOUS FALSE AND FRAUDULENT ACTS

§18.2-200. Failure to perform promise to deliver crop, etc., in return for advances.

If any person obtain from another an advance of money, merchandise or other thing, upon a promise in writing that he will send or deliver to such other person his crop or other property, and fraudulently fail or refuse to perform such promise, and also fail to make good such advance, he shall be deemed guilty of the larceny of such money, merchandise or other thing.

§18.2-200.1. Failure to perform promise for construction, etc., in return for advances.

If any person obtain from another an advance of money, merchandise or other thing, of value, with fraudulent intent, upon a promise to perform construction, removal, repair or improvement or any building or structure permanently annexed to real property, or any other improvements to such real property, including horticulture, nursery or forest products, and fail or refuse to perform such promise, and also fail to substantially make good such advance, he shall be deemed guilty of the larceny of such money, merchandise or other thing if he fails to return such advance within fifteen days of a request to do so sent by certified mail, return receipt requested, to his last known address or to the address listed in the contract.

§18.2-201. Advances secured by fraudulent promise to perform agricultural labor.

If any person enter into a contract of employment, oral or written, for the performance of personal service to be rendered within one year, in and about the cultivation of the soil, and, at any time during the pendency of such contract, thereby obtain from the landowner, or the person so engaged in the cultivation of the soil, advances of money or other thing of value under such contract, with intent to injure or defraud his employer, and fraudulently refuses or fails to perform such service or to refund such money or other thing of value so obtained, he shall be guilty of a Class 3 misdemeanor. But no prosecution hereunder shall be commenced more than sixty days after the breach of such contract.

§18.2-202. False statements by purchaser of real property as to use for personal residence.

It shall be unlawful for any purchaser falsely to represent in writing in any contract for the purchase of real estate that the property referred to in such contract is intended for use as the personal residence of such purchaser. Any person who violates any provision of this section shall be guilty of a Class 3 misdemeanor.

§18.2-203. False statement or willful overvaluation of property for purpose of influencing lending institution.

Whoever knowingly makes any false statement or report, or willfully overvalues any land, property or security, for the purpose of influencing in any way the action of any lending institution licensed under federal law or authorized to transact business under the laws of this Commonwealth upon any application, advance, discount, purchase, purchase agreement, repurchase agreement, commitment, or loan, or any change or extension of any of the same, by renewal, deferment of action or otherwise, or the acceptance, release, or substitution of security therefor, shall be guilty of a Class 3 misdemeanor.

§18.2-204. False statement for the purpose of defrauding industrial sick benefit company.

Any agent, physician or other person who shall knowingly or willfully make any false or fraudulent statement or representation of any material fact:

(1) In or with reference to any application for insurance in any industrial sick benefit company licensed, or which may be licensed, to do business in this Commonwealth,

(2) As to the death or disability of a policy or certificate holder in any such company,

(3) For the purpose of procuring or attempting to procure the payment of any false or fraudulent claim against any such company, or

(4) For the purpose of obtaining or attempting to obtain any money from or benefit in any such company,

shall be guilty of a Class 3 misdemeanor.

Any such person who shall willfully make a false statement of any material fact or thing in a sworn statement as to the death or disability of a policy or certificate holder in any such company for the purpose of procuring payment of a benefit named in the policy or certificate of such holder, shall be guilty of perjury, and shall be proceeded against and punished as provided by the statutes of this Commonwealth in relation to the crime of perjury.

§18.2-204.1. Fraudulent use of birth certificates, drivers' licenses, etc.

A. It shall be unlawful for any person to obtain or possess the birth certificate of another for the purpose of establishing a false identity for himself or for another person.

B. It shall be unlawful for any person to possess, sell or transfer any document for the purpose of establishing a false status, occupation, membership, license or identity for himself or any other person.

C. Any person who shall violate the provisions of this section is guilty of a Class 1 misdemeanor, except when the birth certificate or document is obtained, possessed, sold, or transferred with the intent to use such certificate or document to purchase a firearm, in which case a violation of this section shall be punishable as a Class 6 felony.

D. The provisions of this section shall not apply to members of state, federal, county, city or town law-enforcement agencies in the performance of their duties.

§18.2-204.2. Manufacture, sale, etc., or possession of fictitious, facsimile or simulated official license or identification.

A. It shall be unlawful for any person to manufacture, advertise for sale, sell or possess any fictitious, facsimile or simulated driver's license issued by any state, territory or possession of the United States, the District of Columbia, the Commonwealth of Puerto Rico or any foreign country or government; United States Armed Forces identification card; United States passport or foreign government visa; Virginia Department of Motor Vehicles special identification card; official identification issued by any other federal, state or foreign government agency; or official university or college student identification card, or in any way reproduce any identification card or facsimile thereof in such a manner that it could be mistaken for a valid license or identification of any type specified in this subsection.

B. Any person manufacturing, advertising for sale, selling or reproducing such card or facsimile thereof shall be guilty of a Class 1 misdemeanor.

C. Any person possessing any such card or facsimile thereof shall be guilty of a Class 2 misdemeanor.

§18.2-205. False pretense in obtaining registration of cattle and other animals and giving false pedigree.

Every person who by any false pretense shall obtain from any club, association, society or company for improving the breed of cattle, horses, sheep, swine or other domestic animals the registration of any animal in the herd register or other register of any such club, association, society or company, or a transfer of any such registration, and every person who shall knowingly give a false pedigree of any animal shall be guilty of a Class 3 misdemeanor.

§18.2-206. Procuring an animal, aircraft, vehicle or boat with intent to defraud.

If any person procure any such animal, aircraft, vehicle, boat or vessel mentioned in §18.2-149 by fraud or by misrepresenting himself as some other person or with the intent to cheat or defraud such other person, he shall be guilty of a Class 1 misdemeanor. The failure to pay the rental for or damage to such animal, aircraft, vehicle, boat or vessel, or absconding without paying such rental or damage, shall be prima facie evidence of the intent to defraud at the time of renting or leasing such animal, aircraft, vehicle, boat or vessel.

§18.2-207. Making false entry, etc., in marriage register, etc.

If any clerk of a court, commissioner of the revenue, physician, surgeon, medical examiner or minister celebrating a marriage, or clerk or keeper of the records of any religious society, shall, in any book, register, record, certificate or copy which such person is by Title 20 (§20-13 et seq.) required to keep, make, or give, knowingly make any false, erroneous, or fraudulent entry, record, registration, or written statement, he shall, for every such offense, be guilty of a Class 3 misdemeanor.

§18.2-208. Making false statement, etc., for marriage record, etc.

If any person, upon whose information or statement any record or registration may lawfully be made under Title 20 (§20-13 et seq.), knowingly give any false information, or make any false statement to be used for the purpose of making any such record or registration, he shall, for every such offense, be guilty of a Class 4 misdemeanor.

§18.2-209. False publications.

Any person who knowingly and willfully states, delivers or transmits by any means whatever to any publisher, or employee of a publisher, of any newspaper, magazine, or other publication or to any owner, or employee of an owner, of any radio station, television station, news service or cable service, any false and untrue statement, knowing the same to be false or untrue, concerning any person or corporation, with intent that the same shall be published, broadcast or otherwise disseminated, shall be guilty of a Class 3 misdemeanor.

§18.2-209.1. Penalties for false certificate or failure to give bond.

A. If any clerk make a certificate as to any bond of a special commissioner appointed under Article 11 (§8.01-96 et seq.) of Chapter 3 of Title 8.01, knowing it to be false, he shall be guilty of a Class 3 misdemeanor, and shall, upon conviction, be removed from his office.

B. If any special commissioner appointed under Article 11 of Chapter 3 of Title 8.01 shall advertise property for sale or rent, and shall sell or rent the same before he shall have given bond as is required by §8.01-99, he shall be guilty of a Class 3 misdemeanor.

§18.2-209.2. Failure of clerk to give notice of appointment of special commissioner to collect purchase money or rent.

If any clerk fail to give notice as required by §8.01-103 of a special commissioner, he shall be guilty of a Class 4 misdemeanor.

§18.2-210. Stamping, etc., on newspapers, any word, etc., to cause belief it was done by publisher; circulating such newspapers.

No person, without first obtaining the consent of the publisher so to do, shall affix to, or place or insert in, or print, stamp or impress upon any newspaper or any part thereof, after the same shall have been issued for circulation by the publisher thereof, any word, figure, design, picture, emblem or advertisement with intent to cause, or which when so affixed, placed, inserted, printed, stamped or impressed may cause, the public to believe that such word, figure, design, picture, emblem or advertisement was affixed, placed, printed, inserted, stamped or impressed in and upon such newspaper by the publisher of the same as a part thereof.

No person shall knowingly circulate, distribute or sell, or cause to be circulated, distributed or sold, any newspaper upon which has been so affixed, placed, inserted, printed, stamped or impressed any word, figure, design, picture, emblem or advertisement in violation of the terms hereof.

Any person violating the provisions hereof shall be guilty of a Class 4 misdemeanor. Each violation shall constitute a separate offense.

§18.2-211. Unlawful use of words "Official Tourist Information" or similar language.

It shall be unlawful for any person, firm or corporation in this Commonwealth to use the words "Official Tourist Information" or "Official Information Service" or other similar language for the purpose of informing tourists, motorists and other persons that the information offered is free of charge, or is sponsored by or offered under the authority of the

Commonwealth of Virginia or any department or agency thereof or by any municipality or any chamber of commerce or any civic agency or group of this or any other state, or the District of Columbia. Any person, firm or corporation disseminating information as contemplated in this section must state on any signboards, billboards, or other similar signs in large, easily read and legible letters, and on any advertising or other publicity media, the names of the persons, firms or corporations represented or from whom any remuneration whatsoever was received. Nothing in this section shall be construed to prohibit or affect the giving or advertising of "official tourist information" or other such service by gasoline service stations or other organizations which offer such information without a charge and without any inducement to purchase any services or products.

Any person, firm or corporation violating any provisions of this section shall be guilty of a Class 3 misdemeanor.

§18.2-212. Calling or summoning ambulance or fire-fighting apparatus without just cause; maliciously activating fire alarms in public buildings; venue.

A. Any person who without just cause therefor, calls or summons, by telephone or otherwise, any ambulance, or fire-fighting apparatus, or any person who maliciously activates a manual or automatic fire alarm in any building used for public assembly or for other public use, including, but not limited to, schools, theaters, stores, office buildings, shopping centers and malls, coliseums and arenas, regardless of whether fire apparatus responds or not, shall be deemed guilty of a Class 1 misdemeanor.

B. A violation of this section may be prosecuted either in the jurisdiction from which the call or summons was made or in the jurisdiction where the call or summons was received.

§18.2-212.1. Unlawful for person not blind or incapacitated to carry white, white tipped with red or metallic cane.

It is unlawful for any person, unless totally or partially blind or otherwise incapacitated, while on any public street or highway to carry in a raised or extended position a cane or walking stick which is metallic or white in color or white tipped with red. Any person violating any provisions of this section shall be guilty of a Class 4 misdemeanor.

§18.2-213. Simulation of warrants, processes, writs and notices.

Any person who, for the purpose of collecting money, shall knowingly deliver, mail, send or otherwise use or cause to be used any paper or writing simulating or intended to simulate any warrant, process, writ, notice of execution lien or notice of motion for judgment shall be guilty of a Class 4 misdemeanor.

§18.2-213.1. Obtaining certification as minority or disadvantaged business enterprise by deception; penalty.

A. Except as otherwise provided by §18.2-498.3, a person shall be guilty of a Class 1 misdemeanor if, in the course of business, he:

1. Fraudulently obtains or retains certification as a minority or disadvantaged business enterprise;

2. Willfully makes a false statement knowing it to be untrue, whether by affidavit, report or other representation, to an official or employee of a public body for the purpose of influencing the certification or denial of certification of any business entity as a minority or disadvantaged business enterprise;

3. Willfully obstructs or impedes any agency official or employee who is investigating the qualifications of a business entity which has requested certification as a minority or disadvantaged business enterprise; or

4. Fraudulently obtains public moneys reserved for or allocated or available to minority or disadvantaged business enterprises.

B. For the purposes of this section, "minority business enterprise" shall have the same meaning as defined in §2.1-64.32 and "disadvantaged business enterprise" means a small business that is both owned and controlled by minorities or by women. This means that minorities or women must own fifty-one percent of the business, and that they must control the management and daily operations of the business. Minorities include Blacks, Hispanics, Asian Americans, American Indians and Alaskan Natives and members of other groups or other individuals who the Small Business Administration (SBA) has determined are economically and socially disadvantaged under Section 8(a) of the Small Business Act.

ARTICLE 8
MISREPRESENTATIONS AND OTHER OFFENSES CONNECTED WITH SALES

(For additional remedies for violations of this Article, see Title 59.1, Chapter 4.1.)

Section

§18.2-214. Changing or removing, etc., trademarks, identification marks, etc.

Any person, firm, association or corporation who or which intentionally removes, defaces, alters, changes, destroys or obliterates in any manner or way or who causes to be removed, defaced, altered, changed, destroyed or obliterated in any manner or way any trademark, distinguishment or identification number, serial number or mark on or from any article or device, in order to secrete its identification with intent to defraud, shall be guilty of a Class 1 misdemeanor.

§18.2-214.1. Penalties for failure to report removal or alteration of identification or serial number on business machines.

It shall be unlawful for any person, firm, association, or corporation regularly engaged in the business of repairing, selling, renting or leasing of business machines to fail to report any business machine which such person, firm, association, or corporation knows has an altered or removed identification or serial number. The report shall be made to the appropriate law-enforcement agency for the county, city, or town where such business machine is located.

For purposes of this section, the term "business machines" includes, but is not limited to, typewriters, adding machines, check-writing machines, cash registers, calculators, addressing machines, copying, and accounting equipment, and recording equipment.

Any person, firm, association, or corporation violating the provisions of this section shall be guilty of a Class 4 misdemeanor.

§18.2-215. Removal or alteration of identification numbers on household electrical appliances; possession of such appliances.

No person, firm, association or corporation, either individually or in association with one or more other persons, firms, associations or corporations shall remove, change or alter the serial number or other identification number stamped upon, cut into or attached as a permanent part of any household or electrical or electronic appliance where such number was stamped upon, cut into or attached to such appliance by the manufacturer thereof.

No person, firm, association or corporation shall knowingly have in his or its possession for the purpose of resale or keep in his possession for a period in excess of forty-eight hours without reporting such possession to the appropriate law-enforcement agency in his county, town or city a household or electrical or electronic appliance, with knowledge that the serial number or other identification number has been removed, changed or altered.

Any person, firm, association or corporation violating the provisions of this section shall be guilty of a Class 1 misdemeanor.

§18.2-216. Untrue, deceptive or misleading advertising, inducements, writing or document.

Any person, firm, corporation or association who, with intent to sell or in anywise dispose of merchandise, securities, service or anything offered by such person, firm, corporation or association, directly or indirectly, to the public for sale or distribution or with intent to increase the consumption thereof, or to induce the public in any manner to enter into any obligation relating thereto, or to acquire title thereto, or any interest therein, makes, publishes, disseminates, circulates or places before the public, or causes, directly or indirectly to be made, published, disseminated, circulated or placed before the public, in a newspaper or other publications, or in the form of a book, notice, handbill, poster, blueprint, map, bill, tag, label, circular, pamphlet or letter or in any other way, an advertisement of any sort regarding merchandise, securities, service, land, lot or anything so offered to the public, which advertisement contains any promise, assertion, representation or statement of fact which is untrue, deceptive or misleading, or uses any other method, device or practice which is fraudulent, deceptive or misleading to induce the public to enter into any obligation, shall be guilty of a Class 1 misdemeanor. The words "untrue, deceptive and misleading," as used in this section, shall be construed as including (i) the advertising in any manner by any person of any goods, wares or merchandise as a bankrupt stock, receiver's stock or trustee's stock, if such stock contains any goods, wares or merchandise put therein subsequent to the date of the purchase by such advertiser of such stock, and if such advertisement of any such stock fail to set forth the fact that such stock contains other goods, wares or merchandise put therein, subsequent to the date of the purchase by such advertiser of such stock in type as large as the type used in any other part of such advertisement, including the caption of the same, it shall be a violation of this section; and (ii) the use of any writing or document which appears to be, but is not in fact a negotiable check, negotiable draft or other negotiable instrument notwithstanding the fact that its nonnegotiability is indicated on the writing or document.

§18.2-216.1. Unauthorized use of name or picture of any person; punishment.

A person, firm, or corporation that knowingly uses for advertising purposes, or for the purpose of trade, the name, portrait or picture of any person resident in the Commonwealth, without having first obtained the written consent of such person, or if dead, of his surviving consort, or if none, his next of kin, or, if a minor, of his or her parent or guardian, as well as that of such minor, shall be deemed guilty of a misdemeanor and be fined not less than $50 nor more than $1,000.

§18.2-217. Advertising merchandise, etc., for sale with intent not to sell at price or terms advertised; prima facie evidence of violation.

(a) Any person, firm, corporation or association who in any manner advertises or offers for sale to the public any merchandise, goods, commodity, service or thing with intent not to sell, or with intent not to sell at the price or upon the terms advertised or offered, shall be guilty of a Class 1 misdemeanor.

(b) In any prosecution or civil action under this section, the refusal by any person, firm, corporation or association or any employee, agent or servant thereof to sell, or the refusal to sell at the price or upon the terms advertised or offered, any merchandise, goods, commodity, service or thing advertised or offered for sale to the public, shall be prima facie evidence of a violation of this section; provided, that this subsection shall not apply when it is clearly stated in the advertisement or offer by which such merchandise, goods, commodity, service or thing is advertised or offered for sale to the public, that the advertiser or offer or has a limited quantity or amount of such merchandise, goods, commodity, service or thing for sale, and the advertiser or offeror at the time of such advertisement or offer did in fact have at least such quantity or amount for sale.

§18.2-218. Failure to indicate goods, etc., are "seconds," "irregulars," "secondhand," etc.

Any person, firm, corporation or association who in any manner knowingly advertises or offers for sale to the public any merchandise, goods, commodity or thing which is defective, blemished, secondhand or used, or which has been designated by the manufacturer thereof as "seconds," "irregulars," "imperfects," "not first class," or words of similar import without clearly and unequivocally indicating in the advertisement or offer of the merchandise, goods, commodity or thing or the articles, units or parts, thereof so advertised or offered for sale to the public is defective, blemished, secondhand or used or consists of "seconds," "irregulars," "imperfects" or "not first class," shall be guilty of a Class 1 misdemeanor.

§18.2-220. Use of word "wholesale" or "wholesaler".

Any person, firm, corporation or association who in any manner in any advertisement or offer for sale to the public of any merchandise, goods, commodity or thing uses the words "wholesale" or "wholesaler" to represent or describe the nature of its business shall be guilty of a Class 1 misdemeanor, unless such person, firm, corporation or association is actually engaged in selling at wholesale the merchandise, goods, commodity or thing advertised or offered for sale.

§18.2-221. Advertising new or used automobiles or trucks.

Any person, firm, corporation or association engaged in selling new or used automobiles or trucks to the public shall be guilty of a Class 2 misdemeanor unless, in any printed advertisement or printed offer in which a price is stated, the following is included: (a) the make, year, and model of such automobile or truck; (b) if reference is made to items of optional equipment which are not included in the advertised price, the additional cost of each such items of optional equipment; and (c) if the manufacturer's suggested retail price is stated, whether such price is an F.O.B. factory or delivered price.

§18.2-222. Misrepresentation as to source of merchandise; penalty.

No person, firm, corporation or association selling or offering for sale any article or merchandise, shall in any manner represent, contrary to fact, that the article was made for, or acquired directly or indirectly from, the United States government or its military or naval forces or any agency of the United States government, or that it has been disposed of by the United States government.

Any person, firm, corporation or association violating any provision of this section shall be guilty of a Class 3 misdemeanor.

§18.2-223. "Going out of business" sales; permit required.

It shall be unlawful for any person to advertise, or conduct, a sale for the purpose of discontinuing a retail business, or to modify the word "sale" in any advertisement with the words "going out of business" or any other words which tend to insinuate that the retail business is to be discontinued and the merchandise liquidated, unless such person obtains a permit to conduct such sale from the city, town or county, or from each city, town or county, wherein such sale is to be conducted.

A violation of the provisions of this section shall be punishable as a Class 1 misdemeanor.

§18.2-224. "Going out of business" sales; counties, cities and towns to issue permits; inspections; application for permit; inventory required; commingling of other goods prohibited; duration; additional permits; inclusion of permit number and dates in advertisements; fee.

Every county, town and city shall issue permits to retail merchants for special sales as required by §18.2-223 upon the application of such merchant and shall inspect the advertisement and conducting of such sale to insure that it is being advertised and conducted in conformity with the required permit.

All applications for special sale permits shall be accompanied by an inventory, including the kind and quantity of all goods which are to be offered for sale during the sale and only the goods specified in the inventory list may be advertised or sold during the sale period. Goods not included on the inventory of special sale goods shall not be commingled with or added to the special sale goods. Each county, city or town shall have the right to revoke a special sale permit upon proof that goods not appearing on the original inventory of special sale goods have been commingled with or added to the special sale goods.

Each special sale permit shall be valid for a period of no longer than sixty days, and any extension of that time shall constitute a new special sale and shall require an additional permit and inventory. A maximum of one permit beyond the initial sixty-day permit may be granted solely for the purpose of liquidating only those goods contained in the initial inventory list which remain unsold.

Any person who advertises such sale shall conspicuously include in the advertisement the permit number assigned for the sale by the city, town or county wherein the sale is to be conducted and the effective dates of the sale as authorized in the permit.

Each county, town and city is authorized to charge a fee for the issuance of special sale permits. Such fee shall not exceed sixty-five dollars for each permit.

§18.2-225. Misrepresentations as to agricultural products.

Misrepresentation by advertising in the press or by radio or by television, or misrepresentation by letter, statement, mark representing grade, quality or condition, label or otherwise in handling, selling, offering or exposing for sale any agricultural commodities is hereby prohibited.

Any person, firm, association or corporation who shall violate any of the provisions of this section shall be guilty of a Class 3 misdemeanor.

The Director of the Division of Markets, with the approval of the Commissioner of Agriculture and Consumer Services, may, in his discretion, cause prosecutions for violations of this section to be instituted through the attorneys for the Commonwealth, or otherwise, in counties or cities of the Commonwealth where in his opinion violations of this section are found.

§18.2-226. Fraud and misrepresentation in sale of liquid fuels, lubricating oils and similar products.

It shall be unlawful for any person, firm, association or corporation, to store, sell, expose for sale or offer for sale any liquid fuels, lubricating oils or other similar products, in any manner whatsoever, so as to deceive or tend to deceive the purchaser as to the nature, quality and identity of the product so sold or offered for sale.

§18.2-227. Same; sale from pump indicating other brand.

It shall be unlawful for any person, firm, association or corporation to store, keep, expose for sale, offer for sale or sell, from any tank or container, or from any pump or other distributing device or equipment, any other liquid fuels, lubricating oils or other similar products than those indicated by the name, trade name, symbol, sign or other distinguishing mark or device of the manufacturer or distributor, appearing upon the tank, container, pump or other distributing equipment from which the same are sold, offered for sale or distributed.

§18.2-228. Same; imitating indicia of other brands.

It shall be unlawful, for any person, firm, association or corporation to disguise or camouflage his or their own equipment by imitating the design, symbol or trade name of the equipment under which recognized brands of liquid fuels, lubricating oils and similar products are generally marketed.

§18.2-229. Same; false trade name or mixing brands.

It shall be unlawful for any person, firm, association or corporation to expose for sale, offer for sale or sell, under any trademark or trade name in general use, any liquid fuels, lubricating oils or other like products, except those manufactured or distributed by the manufacturer or distributor marketing liquid fuels, lubricating oils or other like products under such trademark or trade name, or to substitute, mix or adulterate the liquid fuels, lubricating oils or other similar products sold, offered for sale or distributed under such trademark or trade name.

§18.2-230. Same; assisting in violation of §§18.2-226 through 18.2-229.

It shall be unlawful for any person, firm, association or corporation to aid or assist any other person, firm, association or corporation in the violation of the provisions of §§18.2-226 through 18.2-229 by depositing or delivering into any tank, receptacle or other container any other liquid fuels, lubricating oils or like products than those intended to be stored therein and distributed therefrom, as indicated by the name of the manufacturer or distributor or the trademark or trade name of the product displayed on the container itself, or on the pump or other distributing device used in connection therewith.

§18.2-231. Same; label required.

There shall be firmly attached to or painted at or near the point of outlet from which lubricating oil is drawn or poured out for sale or delivery a sign or label consisting of the word or words in letters not less than one inch in height comprising the brand or trade name of such lubricating oil. But if any lubricating oil shall have no brand or trade name, the above sign or label shall consist of the words "lubricating oil, no brand."

§18.2-232. Same; punishment for violation of §§18.2-226 through 18.2-231.

Any person, firm, association or corporation or any officer, agent or employee thereof who shall violate any provision of §§18.2-226 through 18.2-231, shall be guilty of a Class 3 misdemeanor; and a second or any subsequent offense shall be punishable as a Class 1 misdemeanor.

§18.2-233. Sale of goods marked "sterling" and "sterling silver".

A person who makes or sells or offers to sell or dispose of or has in his possession with intent to sell or dispose of any article of merchandise marked, stamped or branded with the words "sterling" or "sterling silver," or encased or enclosed in any box, package, cover or wrapper, or other thing in or by which such article is packed, enclosed or otherwise prepared for sale or disposition, having thereon any engraving or printed label, stamp, imprint, mark or trademark indicating or denoting by such marking, stamping, branding, engraving or printing that such article is silver, sterling silver or solid silver, unless nine hundred and twenty-five one-thousandths part of the component parts of the metal of which such article is manufactured is pure silver, shall be guilty of a Class 2 misdemeanor.

§18.2-234. Sale of goods marked "coin" and "coin silver".

A person who makes or sells or offers to sell or dispose of, or has in his possession with intent to sell or dispose of, any article of merchandise marked, stamped or branded with words "coin" or "coin silver," or encased or enclosed in any box, package, cover, wrapper or other thing in or by which such article is packed, enclosed, or otherwise prepared for sale or disposition, having thereon any engraving or printed label, stamp, imprint, mark or trademark indicating or denoting by such marking, stamping, branding, engraving or printing that such article is coin or coin silver, unless nine hundred one-thousandths part of the component parts of the metal of which such article is manufactured is pure silver, shall be guilty of a Class 2 misdemeanor.

§18.2-235. Regulating sale of merchandise made of gold.

Any person who marks or sells or offers to sell or dispose of or has in his possession with intent to sell or dispose of any article of merchandise made of gold of a less carat of fineness than is stamped or marked on it or of a less carat of fineness than is engraved, stamped or imprinted on the tag, card, box, label, package, wrapper, cover or other thing in or by which such article is packed, enclosed or otherwise prepared for sale or disposition shall be guilty of a Class 2 misdemeanor.

§18.2-236. Regulating sale of kosher meat and meat preparations.

Any person, who, with intent to defraud, sells or exposes for sale any meat or meat preparation, and falsely represents the same: (1) to be kosher, whether such meat or meat preparation be raw or prepared for human consumption, or (2) as having been prepared under, and of a product or products sanctioned by, the orthodox Hebrew religious requirements; or who, with like intent, falsely represents any food product or the contents of any package or container to be so constituted and prepared, by having or permitting to be inscribed thereon the word "kosher" in any language, shall be guilty of a Class 1 misdemeanor.

§18.2-237. Buying, etc., certain secondhand materials; intent; possession.

If any person buy or receive secondhand grate baskets, keys, bells and bell fixtures, gas fixtures, water fixtures, water pipes, gas pipes, or any part of such fixtures or pipes with intent to defraud, he shall be guilty of a Class 2 misdemeanor. Possession of any such secondhand baskets, keys, bells and bell fixtures, water fixtures, gas fixtures, water pipes, gas pipes, or any part of such fixtures or pipes if bought or received from any other person than the manufacturer thereof or his authorized agent or the owner thereof shall be prima facie evidence of such intent.

§18.2-238. Buying, etc., pig iron, etc., with intent to defraud; possession; evidence of intent.

If any person buy or receive pig iron or railroad, telephone, telegraph, coal mining, industrial, manufacturing or public utility iron, brass, copper, metal or any composition thereof with intent to defraud, he shall be guilty of a Class 6 felony. Possession of any pig iron or railroad, telephone, telegraph, coal mining, industrial, manufacturing or public utility iron, brass, copper, metal or any composition thereof, if bought or received from any other person than the manufacturer thereof or his authorized agent or of a regularly licensed dealer therein, shall be prima facie evidence of such intent.

§18.2-239. Pyramid promotional schemes; misdemeanor; definitions; contracts void.

Every person who contrives, prepares, sets up, operates, advertises or promotes any pyramid promotional scheme shall be guilty of a Class 1 misdemeanor. For the purposes of this section:

(a) "Pyramid promotional scheme" means any program utilizing a pyramid or chain process by which a participant gives a valuable consideration for the opportunity to receive compensation or things of value in return for inducing other persons to become participants in the program;

(b) "Compensation" does not mean payment based on sales of goods or services to persons who are not participants in the scheme and who are not purchasing in order to participate in the scheme; and

(c) "Promotes" shall mean inducing one or more other persons to become a participant.

All contracts and agreements, now existing or hereafter formed, whereof the whole or any part of the consideration is given for the right to participate in pyramid promotional scheme programs, are against public policy, void and unenforceable.

§18.2-240. Same; injunction.

Any Commonwealth's attorney may petition a court of competent jurisdiction to enjoin the further prosecution of any pyramid promotional scheme as defined in §18.2-239, and to appoint receivers to secure and distribute in an equitable manner any assets received by any participant as a result of such scheme, any such distribution to effect reimbursement, to the extent possible, for uncompensated payments made to become a participant in the scheme. The procedure in any such suit shall be similar to the procedure in other suits for equitable relief, except that no bond shall be required upon the granting of either a temporary or permanent injunction therein. Any person who organizes an endless chain scheme and, either directly or through an agent, promotes such scheme within the Commonwealth shall be deemed subject to the personal jurisdiction of such court of competent jurisdiction under §§8.01-328 through 8.01-330, and shall be liable for reasonable costs and attorneys' fees in such suit.

§18.2-241. Acceptance of promissory notes in payment for food sold at retail.

As used in this section, "food" includes food, groceries and beverages, for human consumption. "Retailer" means a person who sells food for consumption and not for resale.

It shall be unlawful for any retailer to accept, in payment for any food sold by him to a customer, a promissory note or notes for an amount in excess of twice the sales price of food delivered by him to the customer. As used in this section the word "delivered" means that actual physical delivery into the exclusive custody and control of the customer is made within seven days of the receipt of the note by the seller.

Any person who violates the provisions of this section shall be guilty of a Class 3 misdemeanor.

§18.2-242. Use of games, lotteries, etc., for promoting sale of certain products.

(a) No retail establishment in this Commonwealth shall use any game, contest, lottery or other scheme or device, whereby a person or persons may receive gifts, prizes or gratuities as determined by chance for the purpose of promoting, furthering or advertising the sale of any product or products having both a federal and state excise tax placed upon it, and the fact that no purchase is required in order to participate in such game, contest, lottery or scheme shall not exclude such game, contest, lottery or scheme from the provisions of this section.

(b) Any person violating the provision of this section shall be guilty of a Class 3 misdemeanor.

§18.2-242.1. Certain referral transactions in connection with consumer sales or leases prohibited; effect of such transactions.

(a) For the purpose of this section, the term "consumer sale or lease of goods or services" means the sale or lease of goods or services which are purchased or leased by a natural person primarily for a personal, family or household purpose, and not for resale.

(b) With respect to a consumer sale or lease of goods or services, no seller or lessor shall give or offer to give a rebate or discount or otherwise pay or offer to pay value to the buyer or lessee as an inducement for the sale or lease in return for the buyer's giving to the seller or lessor the names of prospective buyers or lessees, or otherwise aiding the seller or lessor in entering into a transaction with another buyer or lessee, if the earning of the rebate, discount, or other value is contingent upon the occurrence of any sale, lease, appointment, demonstration, interview, conference, seminar, bailment, testimonial or endorsement subsequent to the time the buyer or lessee enters into the agreement of sale or lease.

(c) Agreements made in whole or in part pursuant to a referral transaction as above described shall be void and unenforceable by the seller or lessor. The buyer or lessee shall be entitled to retain the goods, services or money received pursuant to a referral transaction without obligation to make any further or future payments of any sort on the transaction total, or he shall be entitled to avoid the transaction and to recover from the seller or lessor any sums paid to the seller or lessor pursuant to the transaction.

§18.2-243. When issuer or distributor of advertisements not guilty of violation; inadvertent error.

A person, firm, corporation or association who or which, for compensation, issues or distributes any advertisement or offer, written, printed, oral or otherwise, in reliance upon the copy or information supplied him by the advertiser or offeror, shall not be deemed to have violated the provisions of this article, nor shall an inadvertent error on the part of any such person, firm, corporation or association be deemed a violation of such provisions.

§18.2-244. Right to select clientele or customers not affected.

Nothing in this article shall be deemed to impair the right of any person, firm, corporation or association to select its clientele or customers.

§18.2-245. Enjoining violation of this article.

(a) Any person, firm, corporation or association who violates any one or more of the sections in this article, may be enjoined by any court of competent jurisdiction notwithstanding the existence of an adequate remedy at law. In any action under this section, it shall not be necessary that damages be alleged or proved.

(b) Actions for injunctive relief under this section may be brought by a Commonwealth's attorney in the name of the Commonwealth of Virginia upon their own complaint or upon the complaint of any person, firm, corporation or association. The bringing of an action under this section shall not prevent the institution or continuation of criminal proceedings against the same defendant or defendants.

§18.2-246. Penalty in general for violations.

Unless otherwise provided, any person who shall violate any provision of any section in this article shall be guilty of a Class 1 misdemeanor.

ARTICLE 9
VIRGINIA COMPREHENSIVE MONEY LAUNDERING ACT

(Added by L.1999 ch. 348, eff. 7/1/99.)

§18.2-246.1. Title.

This article shall be known and may be cited as the "Virginia Comprehensive Money Laundering Act."

(Added by L.1999 ch. 348, eff. 7/1/99.)

§18.2-246.2. Definitions.

"Conduct" or "conducts" includes initiating, concluding, participating in, or assisting in a financial transaction.

"Financial transaction" means any purchase, sale, trade, loan, pledge, investment, gift, transfer, transmission, transportation, delivery, deposit, withdrawal, payment, transfer between accounts, exchange of currency, extension of credit, purchase or sale of monetary instruments, use of a safe-deposit box, or any other acquisition or disposition of monetary instruments by any means including the movement of funds by wire or other electronic means, which is knowingly designed in whole or in part to conceal or disguise the nature, location, source, ownership or control of the property involved in the transaction.

"Monetary instruments" means (i) coin or currency of the United States or of any other country, travelers' checks, personal checks, bank checks, cashier's checks, and money orders or (ii) securities or other negotiable instruments, in bearer form or otherwise.

"Proceeds" means property acquired or derived, directly or indirectly, from, produced through, realized through, or caused by an act or omission and includes property, real or personal, of any kind.

"Property" means anything of value, and includes any interest therein, including any benefit, privilege, claim or right with respect to anything of value, whether real or personal, tangible or intangible.

(Added by L.1999 ch. 348, eff. 7/1/99.)

§18.2-246.3. Money laundering; penalties.

A. It shall be unlawful for any person knowingly to conduct a financial transaction where the person knows the property involved in the transaction represents the proceeds of an activity which is punishable as a felony under the laws of the Commonwealth, another state or territory of the United States, the District of Columbia, or the United States. A violation of this section is punishable by imprisonment of not more than forty years or a fine of not more than $500,000 or by both imprisonment and a fine.

B. Any person who, for compensation, converts cash into negotiable instruments or electronic funds for another, knowing the cash is the proceeds of some form of activity which is punishable as a felony under the laws of the Commonwealth, another state or territory of the United States, the District of Columbia, or the United States, shall be guilty of a Class 1 misdemeanor. Any second or subsequent violation of this subsection shall be punishable as a Class 6 felony.

(Added by L.1999 ch. 348, eff. 7/1/99.)

§18.2-246.4. Seizure of property used in connection with money laundering.

The following property shall be subject to lawful seizure by any officer charged with enforcing the provisions of this article: (i) all money, equipment, motor vehicles, and all other personal and real property of any kind or character used in substantial connection with the laundering of proceeds of some form of activity punishable as a felony under the laws of the Commonwealth and (ii) all money or other property, real or personal, traceable to the proceeds of some form of activity punishable as a felony under the laws of the Commonwealth, together with any interest or profits derived from the investment of such proceeds or other property. Real property shall not be subject to seizure unless the minimum prescribed punishment for the violation under this article is a term of imprisonment of not less than five years. All seizures and forfeitures under this section shall be governed by Chapter 22.1 (§19.2-386.1 et seq.) of Title 19.2, and the procedures specified therein shall apply, mutatis mutandis, to all forfeitures under this article.

(Added by L.1999 ch. 348, eff. 7/1/99.)

§18.2-246.5. Forfeiture of business license or registration upon conviction of sale or distribution of imitation controlled substance; money laundering.

Any person, firm or corporation holding a license or registration to operate any business as required by either state or local law shall forfeit such license or registration upon conviction of a violation of (i) §18.2-248 relating to an imitation controlled substance or (ii) §18.2-246.3 relating to money laundering. Upon a conviction under this section the attorney for the Commonwealth shall notify any appropriate agency.

(Added by L.1999 ch. 348, eff. 7/1/99.)

CHAPTER 7
CRIMES INVOLVING HEALTH AND SAFETY

ARTICLE 1
DRUGS

§18.2-247. Use of terms "controlled substances," "marijuana," "Schedules I, II, III, IV, V and VI" and "imitation controlled substance" in Title 18.2.

A. Wherever the terms "controlled substances" and "Schedules I, II, III, IV, V and VI" are used in Title 18.2, such terms refer to those terms as they are used or defined in the Drug Control Act (§54.1-3400 et seq.).

B. The term "imitation controlled substance" when used in this article means a pill, capsule, tablet, or substance in any form whatsoever which is not a controlled substance subject to abuse, and:

1. Which by overall dosage unit appearance, including color, shape, size, marking and packaging or by representations made, would cause the likelihood that such a pill, capsule, tablet, or substance in any other form whatsoever will be mistaken for a controlled substance unless such substance was introduced into commerce prior to the initial introduction into commerce of the controlled substance which it is alleged to imitate; or

2. Which by express or implied representations purports to act like a controlled substance as a stimulant or depressant of the central nervous system and which is not commonly used or recognized for use in that particular formulation for any purpose other than for such stimulant or depressant effect, unless marketed, promoted, or sold as permitted by the United States Food and Drug Administration.

C. In determining whether a pill, capsule, tablet, or substance in any other form whatsoever, is an "imitation controlled substance," there shall be considered, in addition to all other relevant factors, comparisons with accepted methods of marketing for legitimate nonprescription drugs for medicinal purposes rather than for drug abuse or any similar nonmedicinal use, including consideration of the packaging of the drug and its appearance in overall finished dosage form, promotional materials or representations, oral or written, concerning the drug, and the methods of distribution of the drug and where and how it is sold to the public.

D. The term "marijuana" when used in this article means any part of a plant of the genus Cannabis, whether growing or not, its seeds or resin; and every compound, manufacture, salt, derivative, mixture, or preparation of such plant, its seeds, or its resin. Marijuana shall not include any oily extract containing one or more cannabinoids unless such extract contains less then twelve percent of tetrahydrocannabinol by weight, or the mature stalks of such plant, fiber produced from such stalk, oil or cake made from the seed of such plant, unless such stalks, fiber, oil or cake is combined with other parts of plants of the genus Cannabis.
(Chgd. by L.1999 chs. 661, 722, eff. 7/1/99.)

§18.2-248. Manufacturing, selling, giving, distributing or possessing with intent to manufacture, sell, give or distribute a controlled substance or an imitation controlled substance prohibited; penalties.

A. Except as authorized in the Drug Control Act (§54.1-3400 et seq.), it shall be unlawful for any person to manufacture, sell, give, distribute, or possess with intent to manufacture, sell, give or distribute a controlled substance or an imitation controlled substance.

B. In determining whether any person intends to manufacture, sell, give or distribute an imitation controlled substance, the court may consider, in addition to all other relevant evidence, whether any distribution or attempted distribution of such pill, capsule, tablet or substance in any other form whatsoever included an exchange of or a demand for money or other property as consideration, and, if so, whether the amount of such consideration was substantially greater than the reasonable value of such pill, capsule, tablet or substance in any other form whatsoever, considering the actual chemical composition of such pill, capsule, tablet or substance in any other form whatsoever and, where applicable, the price at which over-the-counter substances of like chemical composition sell.

C. Any person who violates this section with respect to a controlled substance classified in Schedule I or II shall upon conviction be imprisoned for not less than five nor more than forty years and fined not more than $500,000. Upon a second or subsequent conviction of such a violation, any such person may, in the discretion of the court or jury imposing the sentence, be sentenced to imprisonment for life or for any period not less than five years and be fined not more than $500,000.

When a person is convicted of a third or subsequent offense under this subsection and it is alleged in the warrant, indictment or information that he has been before convicted of two or more such offenses or of substantially similar offenses in any other jurisdiction which offenses would be felonies if committed in the Commonwealth and such prior convictions occurred before the date of the offense alleged in the warrant, indictment, or information, he shall be sentenced to imprisonment for life or for a period of not less than five years, three years of which shall be a mandatory, minimum term of imprisonment not to be suspended in whole or in part and to be served consecutively with any other sentence and shall be fined not more than $500,000.

D. If such person proves that he gave, distributed or possessed with intent to give or distribute a controlled substance classified in Schedule I or II only as an accommodation to another individual who is not an inmate in a community correctional facility, local correctional facility or state correctional facility as defined in §53.1-1 or in the custody of an employee thereof, and not with intent to profit thereby from any consideration received or expected nor to induce the recipient or intended recipient of the controlled substance to use or become addicted to or dependent upon such controlled substance, he shall be guilty of a Class 5 felony.

E. If the violation of the provisions of this article consists of the filling by a pharmacist of the prescription of a person authorized under this article to issue the same, which prescription has not been received in writing by the pharmacist prior to the filling thereof, and such written prescription is in fact received by the pharmacist within one week of the time of filling the same, or if such violation consists of a request by such authorized person for the filling by a pharmacist of a prescription which has not been received in writing by the pharmacist and such prescription is, in fact, written at the time of such request and delivered to the pharmacist within one week thereof, either such offense shall constitute a Class 4 misdemeanor.

F. Any person who violates this section with respect to a controlled substance classified in Schedule III, IV or V or an imitation controlled substance which imitates a controlled substance classified in Schedule III, IV or V, except for an anabolic steroid classified in Schedule III constituting a violation of §18.2-248.5, shall be guilty of a Class 1 misdemeanor.

G. Any person who violates this section with respect to an imitation controlled substance which imitates a controlled substance classified in Schedule I or II shall be guilty of a Class 6 felony. In any prosecution brought under this subsection, it is not a defense to a violation of this subsection that the defendant believed the imitation controlled substance to actually be a controlled substance.

H. Any person who manufactures, sells, gives, distributes or possesses with the intent to manufacture, sell, give or distribute the following:

1. 1.0 kilograms or more of a mixture or substance containing a detectable amount of heroin;

2. 5.0 kilograms or more of a mixture or substance containing a detectable amount of:

a. Coca leaves, except coca leaves and extracts of coca leaves from which cocaine, ecgonine, and derivatives of ecgonine or their salts have been removed;

b. Cocaine, its salts, optical and geometric isomers, and salts of isomers;

c. Ecgonine, its derivatives, their salts, isomers, and salts of isomers; or

d. Any compound, mixture, or preparation which contains any quantity of any of the substances referred to in subdivisions a through c;

3. 2.5 kilograms or more of a mixture or substance described in subdivision 2 which contains cocaine base;

4. 100 kilograms or more of a mixture or substance containing a detectable amount of marijuana; or

5. 100 grams or more of methamphetamine, its salts, isomers, or salts of its isomers or 200 grams or more of a mixture or substance containing a detectable amount of methamphetamine, its salts, isomers, or salts of its isomers

shall be guilty of a felony punishable by a fine of not more than one million dollars and imprisonment for twenty years to life, twenty years of which shall be a mandatory, minimum sentence which shall be served with no suspension in whole or in part. Such mandatory, minimum sentence shall not be applicable if the court finds that (i) the person does not have a prior conviction for an offense listed in subsection C of §17.1-805, (ii) the person did not use violence or credible threats of violence or possess a firearm or other dangerous weapon in connection with the offense or induce another participant in the offense to do so, (iii) the offense did not result in death or serious bodily injury to any person, (iv) the person was not an organizer, leader, manager, or supervisor of others in the offense, and was not engaged in a continuing criminal enterprise as defined in subsection I of this section, and (v) not later than the time of the sentencing hearing, the person has truthfully provided to the Commonwealth all information and evidence the person has concerning the offense or offenses that were part of the same course of conduct or of a common scheme or plan, but the fact that the person has no relevant or useful other information to provide or that the Commonwealth already is aware of the information shall not preclude a determination by the court that the defendant has complied with this requirement.

H1. Any person who was the principal or one of several principal administrators, organizers or leaders of a continuing criminal enterprise shall be guilty of a felony if (i) the enterprise received at least $100,000 but less than $250,000 in gross receipts during any twelve-month period of its existence from the manufacture, importation, or distribution of heroin or cocaine or ecgonine or methamphetamine or the derivatives, salts, isomers, or salts of isomers thereof or marijuana or (ii) the person engaged in the enterprise to manufacture, sell, give, distribute or possess with the intent to manufacture, sell, give or distribute the following during any twelve-month period of its existence:

1. At least 1.0 kilograms but less than 5.0 kilograms of a mixture or substance containing a detectable amount of heroin;

2. At least 5.0 kilograms but less than 10 kilograms of a mixture or substance containing a detectable amount of:

a. Coca leaves, except coca leaves and extracts of coca leaves from which cocaine, ecgonine, and derivatives of ecgonine or their salts have been removed;

b. Cocaine, its salts, optical and geometric isomers, and salts of isomers;

c. Ecgonine, its derivatives, their salts, isomers, and salts of isomers; or

d. Any compound, mixture, or preparation which contains any quantity of any of the substances referred to in subdivisions a through c;

3. At least 2.5 kilograms but less than 5.0 kilograms of a mixture or substance described in subdivision 2 which contains cocaine base;

4. At least 100 kilograms but less than 250 kilograms of a mixture or substance containing a detectable amount of marijuana; or

5. At least 100 grams but less than 250 grams of methamphetamine, its salts, isomers, or salts of its isomers or at least 200 grams but less than 1.0 kilograms of a mixture or substance containing a detectable amount of methamphetamine, its salts, isomers, or salts of its isomers.

A conviction under this section shall be punishable by a fine of not more than one million dollars and imprisonment for twenty years to life, twenty years of which shall be a mandatory, minimum sentence which shall be served with no suspension in whole or in part.

H2. Any person who was the principal or one of several principal administrators, organizers or leaders of a continuing criminal enterprise if (i) the enterprise received $250,000 or more in gross receipts during any twelve-month period of its existence from the manufacture, importation, or distribution of heroin or cocaine or ecgonine or methamphetamine or the derivatives, salts, isomers, or salts of isomers thereof or marijuana or (ii) the person engaged in the enterprise to manufacture, sell, give, distribute or possess with the intent to manufacture, sell, give or distribute the following during any twelve-month period of its existence:

1. At least 5.0 kilograms of a mixture or substance containing a detectable amount of heroin;

2. At least 10 kilograms of a mixture or substance containing a detectable amount of:

a. Coca leaves, except coca leaves and extracts of coca leaves from which cocaine, ecgonine, and derivatives of ecgonine or their salts have been removed;

b. Cocaine, its salts, optical and geometric isomers, and salts of isomers;

c. Ecgonine, its derivatives, their salts, isomers, and salts of isomers; or

d. Any compound, mixture, or preparation which contains any quantity of any of the substances referred to in subdivisions a through c;

3. At least 5.0 kilograms of a mixture or substance described in subdivision 2 which contains cocaine base;

4. At least 250 kilograms of a mixture or substance containing a detectable amount of marijuana; or

5. At least 250 grams of methamphetamine, its salts, isomers, or salts of its isomers or at least 1.0 kilograms of a mixture or substance containing a detectable amount of methamphetamine, its salts, isomers, or salts of its isomers shall be guilty of a felony punishable by a fine of not more than one million dollars and imprisonment for life, which shall be served with no suspension in whole or in part. Such punishment shall be made to run consecutively with any other sentence. However, the court may impose a mandatory, minimum sentence of forty years if the court finds that the defendant substantially cooperated with law-enforcement authorities.

I. For purposes of this section, a person is engaged in a continuing criminal enterprise if (i) he violates any provision of this section, the punishment for which is a felony and (ii) such violation is a part of a continuing series of violations of this section which are undertaken by such person in concert with five or more other persons with respect to whom such person occupies a position of organizer, a supervisory position, or any other position of management, and from which such person obtains substantial income or resources.

(Chgd. by L.1995 ch. 538; L.1999 ch. 722; L.2000 chs. 1020, 1041, eff. 7/1/2000.)

§18.2-248.01. Transporting controlled substances into the Commonwealth; penalty.

Except as authorized in the Drug Control Act (§54.1-3400 et seq.) it is unlawful for any person to transport into the Commonwealth by any means with intent to sell or distribute one ounce or more of cocaine, coca leaves or any salt, compound, derivative or preparation thereof as described in Schedule II of the Drug Control Act or one ounce or more of any other Schedule I or II controlled substance or five or more pounds of marijuana. A violation of this section shall constitute a separate and distinct felony. Upon conviction, the person shall be sentenced to not less than five years nor more than forty years imprisonment, three years of which shall be a minimum, mandatory term of imprisonment, and a fine not to exceed $1,000,000. A second or subsequent conviction hereunder shall be punishable by a minimum, mandatory term of imprisonment of ten years which shall not be suspended in whole or in part and shall be served consecutively with any other sentence.

(Chgd. by L.2000 chs. 1020, 1041, eff. 7/1/2000.)

§18.2-248.1. Penalties for sale, gift, distribution or possession with intent to sell, give or distribute marijuana.

Except as authorized in the Drug Control Act, Chapter 34 of Title 54.1, it shall be unlawful for any person to sell, give, distribute or possess with intent to sell, give or distribute marijuana.

(a) Any person who violates this section with respect to:

(1) Not more than one-half ounce of marijuana is guilty of a Class 1 misdemeanor;

(2) More than one-half ounce but not more than five pounds of marijuana is guilty of a Class 5 felony;

(3) More than five pounds of marijuana is guilty of a felony punishable by imprisonment of not less than five nor more than thirty years.

If such person proves that he gave, distributed or possessed with intent to give or distribute marijuana only as an accommodation to another individual and not with intent to profit thereby from any consideration received or expected nor to induce the recipient or intended recipient of the marijuana to use or become addicted to or dependent upon such marijuana, he shall be guilty of a Class 1 misdemeanor.

(b) Any person who gives, distributes or possesses marijuana as an accommodation and not with intent to profit thereby, to an inmate of a state or local correctional facility as defined in §53.1-1, or in the custody of an employee thereof shall be guilty of a Class 4 felony.

(c) Any person who manufactures marijuana, or possesses marijuana with the intent to manufacture such substance, not for his own use is guilty of a felony punishable by imprisonment of not less than five nor more than thirty years and a fine not to exceed $10,000.

(d) When a person is convicted of a third or subsequent felony offense under this section and it is alleged in the warrant, indictment or information that he has been before convicted of two or more felony offenses under this section or of substantially similar offenses in any other jurisdiction which offenses would be felonies if committed in the Commonwealth and such prior convictions occurred before the date of the offense alleged in the warrant, indictment or information, he shall be sentenced to imprisonment for life or for any period not less than five years, three years of which shall be a minimum, mandatory term of imprisonment not to be suspended in whole or in part and to be served consecutively with any other sentence and shall be fined not more than $500,000.

(Chgd. by L.2000 chs. 819, 1020, 1041, eff. 7/1/2000.)

§18.2-248.3. Professional use of imitation controlled substances.

No civil or criminal liability shall be imposed by virtue of this article on any person licensed under the Drug Control Act, Chapter 34 of Title 54.1, who manufactures, sells, gives or distributes an imitation controlled substance for use as a placebo by a licensed practitioner in the course of professional practice or research.

§18.2-248.4. Advertisement of imitation controlled substances prohibited; penalty.

It shall be a Class 1 misdemeanor for any person knowingly to sell or display for sale, or to distribute, whether or not any charge is made therefor, any book, pamphlet, handbill or other printed matter which he knows is intended to promote the distribution of an imitation controlled substance.

§18.2-248.5. Illegal stimulants and steroids; penalty.

A. Except as authorized in the Drug Control Act (§54.1-3400 et seq.), Chapter 34 of Title 54.1, it shall be unlawful for any person to knowingly manufacture, sell, give, distribute or possess with intent to manufacture, sell, give or distribute any anabolic steroid.

A violation of subsection A shall be punishable by a term of imprisonment of not less than one year nor more than ten years or, in the discretion of the jury or the court trying the case without a jury, confinement in jail for not more than twelve months or a fine of not more than $20,000, either or both. Any person violating the provisions of this subsection shall, upon conviction, be incarcerated for a minimum, mandatory term of six months which shall not be suspended in whole or in part and shall be served consecutively with any other sentence.

B. It shall be unlawful for any person to knowingly sell or otherwise distribute, without prescription, to a minor any pill, capsule or tablet containing any combination of caffeine and ephedrine sulfate.

A violation of this subsection B shall be punishable as a Class 1 misdemeanor.

(Chgd. by L.2000 chs. 1020, 1041, eff. 7/1/2000.)

§§18.2-248.6, 18.2-248.7. *(Repealed by L.1999 ch. 348, eff. 7/1/99.)*

§18.2-249. Seizure of property used in connection with or derived from illegal drug transactions.

A. The following property shall be subject to lawful seizure by any officer charged with enforcing the provisions of this article: (i) all money, medical equipment, office equipment, laboratory equipment, motor vehicles, and all other personal and real property of any kind or character, used in substantial connection with (a) the illegal manufacture, sale or distribution of controlled substances or possession with intent to sell or distribute controlled substances in violation of §18.2-248, (b) the sale or distribution of marijuana or possession with intent to distribute marijuana in violation of subdivisions (a)(2), (a)(3) and (c) of §18.2-248.1, or (c) a drug-related offense in violation of §18.2-474.1; (ii) everything of value furnished, or intended to be furnished, in exchange for a controlled substance in violation of §18.2-248 or for marijuana in violation of §18.2-248.1 or for a controlled substance or marijuana in violation of §18.2-474.1; and (iii) all moneys or other property, real or personal, traceable to such an exchange, together with any interest or profits derived from the investment of such money or other property. Under the provisions of clause (i), real property shall not be subject to lawful seizure unless the minimum prescribed punishment for the violation is a term of not less than five years.

B. All seizures and forfeitures under this section shall be governed by the procedures contained in Chapter 22.1 (§19.2-386.1 et seq.) of Title 19.2.

(Chgd. by L.1999 ch. 269, eff. 7/1/99.)

§18.2-250. Possession of controlled substances unlawful.

A. It is unlawful for any person knowingly or intentionally to possess a controlled substance unless the substance was obtained directly from, or pursuant to, a valid prescription or order of a practitioner while acting in the course of his professional practice, or except as otherwise authorized by the Drug Control Act (§54.1-3400 et seq.).

Upon the prosecution of a person for a violation of this section, ownership or occupancy of premises or vehicle upon or in which a controlled substance was found shall not create a presumption that such person either knowingly or intentionally possessed such controlled substance.

(a) Any person who violates this section with respect to any controlled substance classified in Schedule I or II of the Drug Control Act shall be guilty of a Class 5 felony.

(b) Any person other than an inmate of a penal institution as defined in §53.1-1 or in the custody of an employee thereof, who violates this section with respect to a controlled substance classified in Schedule III shall be guilty of a Class 1 misdemeanor.

(b1) Violation of this section with respect to a controlled substance classified in Schedule IV shall be punishable as a Class 2 misdemeanor.

(b2) Violation of this section with respect to a controlled substance classified in Schedule V shall be punishable as a Class 3 misdemeanor.

(c) Violation of this section with respect to a controlled substance classified in Schedule VI shall be punishable as a Class 4 misdemeanor.

B. The provisions of this section shall not apply to members of state, federal, county, city or town law-enforcement agencies, jail officers, or correctional officers, as defined in §53.1-1, certified as handlers of dogs trained in the detection of controlled substances when possession of a controlled substance or substances is necessary in the performance of their duties.

(Chgd. by L.1998 ch. 116, eff. 7/1/98.)

§18.2-250.1. Possession of marijuana unlawful.

A. It is unlawful for any person knowingly or intentionally to possess marijuana unless the substance was obtained directly from, or pursuant to, a valid prescription or order of a practitioner while acting in the course of his professional practice, or except as otherwise authorized by the Drug Control Act (§54.1-3400 et seq.).

Upon the prosecution of a person for violation of this section, ownership or occupancy of the premises or vehicle upon or in which marijuana was found shall not create a presumption that such person either knowingly or intentionally possessed such marijuana.

Any person who violates this section shall be guilty of a misdemeanor, and be confined in jail not more than thirty days and a fine of not more than $500, either or both; any person, upon a second or subsequent conviction of a violation of this section, shall be guilty of a Class 1 misdemeanor.

B. The provisions of this section shall not apply to members of state, federal, county, city or town law-enforcement agencies, jail officers, or correctional officers, as defined in §53.1-1, certified as handlers of dogs trained in the detection of controlled substances when possession of marijuana is necessary for the performance of their duties.

(Chgd. by L.1998 ch. 116, eff. 7/1/98.)

§18.2-251. Persons charged with first offense may be placed on probation; conditions; screening, assessment and education programs; drug tests; costs and fees; violations; discharge.

Whenever any person who has not previously been convicted of any offense under this article or under any statute of the United States or of any state relating to narcotic drugs, marijuana, or stimulant, depressant, or hallucinogenic drugs, or has not previously had a proceeding against him for violation of such an offense dismissed as provided in this section, pleads guilty to or enters a plea of not guilty to possession of a controlled substance under §18.2-250 or to possession of marijuana under §18.2-250.1, the court, upon such plea if the facts found by the court would justify a finding of guilt, without entering a judgment of guilt and with the consent of the accused, may defer further proceedings and place him on probation upon terms and conditions.

As a term or condition, the court shall require the accused to undergo a substance abuse assessment pursuant to §18.2-251.01 and enter a treatment and/or education program, if available, such as, in the opinion of the court, may be best suited to the needs of the accused based upon consideration of the substance abuse assessment. This program may be located in the judicial district in which the charge is brought or in any other judicial district as the court may provide. The services shall be provided by a program licensed by the Department of Mental Health, Mental Retardation and Substance Abuse Services, by a similar program which is made available through the Department of Corrections if the court imposes a sentence of one year or more or, if the court imposes a sentence of twelve months or less, by a similar program available through a local or regional jail, a community corrections program established pursuant to §53.1-180, or an ASAP program certified by the Commission on VASAP.

The court shall require the person entering such program under the provisions of this section to pay all or part of the costs of the program, including the costs of the screening, assessment, testing, and treatment, based upon the accused's ability to pay unless the person is determined by the court to be indigent.

As a condition of probation, the court shall require the accused (i) to successfully complete the treatment or education program, (ii) to remain drug and alcohol free during the period of probation and submit to such tests during that period as may be necessary and appropriate to determine if the accused is drug and alcohol free, (iii) to make reasonable efforts to secure and maintain employment, and (iv) to comply with a plan of at least 100 hours of community service. Such testing shall be conducted by personnel of the supervising probation agency or personnel of any program or agency approved by the supervising probation agency.

The court shall, unless done at arrest, order the accused to report to the original arresting law-enforcement agency to submit to fingerprinting.

Upon violation of a term or condition, the court may enter an adjudication of guilt and proceed as otherwise provided. Upon fulfillment of the terms and conditions, the court shall discharge the person and dismiss the proceedings against him. Discharge and dismissal under this section shall be without adjudication of guilt and is a conviction only for the purposes of applying this section in subsequent proceedings.

Notwithstanding any other provision of this section, whenever a court places an individual on probation upon terms and conditions pursuant to this section, such action shall be treated as a conviction for purposes of §§18.2-259.1 and 46.2-390.1, and the driver's license forfeiture provisions of those sections shall be imposed. The provisions of this paragraph shall not be applicable to any offense for which a juvenile has had his license suspended or denied pursuant to §16.1-278.9 for the same offense.

(Chgd. by L.1997 ch. 380; L.1998 chs. 688, 783, 840; L.2000 chs. 1020, 1041, eff. 7/1/2000.)

§18.2-251.01. Substance abuse screening and assessment for felony convictions.

A. When a person is convicted of a felony, not a capital offense, committed on or after January 1, 2000, he shall be required to undergo a substance abuse screening and, if the screening indicates a substance abuse or dependence problem, an assessment by a certified substance abuse counselor as defined in §54.1-3500 employed by the Department of Corrections or by an agency employee under the supervision of such counselor. If the person is determined to have a substance abuse problem, the court shall require him to enter a treatment and/or education program, if available, which, in the opinion of the court, is best suited to the needs of the person. This program may be located in the judicial district in which the conviction was had or in any other judicial district as the court may provide. The treatment and/or education program shall be licensed by the Department of Mental Health, Mental Retardation and Substance Abuse Services or shall be a similar program which is made available through the Department of Corrections if the court imposes a sentence of one year or more or, if the court imposes a sentence of twelve months or less, by a similar program available through a local or regional jail, a community corrections program established pursuant to §53.1-180, or an ASAP program certified by the Commission on VASAP. The program may require the person entering such program under the provisions of this section to pay a fee for the education and treatment component, or both, based upon the defendant's ability to pay.

B. As a condition of any suspended sentence and probation, the court shall order the person to undergo periodic testing and treatment for substance abuse, if available, as the court deems appropriate based upon consideration of the substance abuse assessment.

(Added by L.1998 chs. 783, 840; chgd. by L.1999 chs. 891, 913; L.2000 chs. 1020, 1041, eff. 7/1/2000.)

§18.2-251.02. Drug Offender Assessment Fund.

There is hereby established in the state treasury the Drug Offender Assessment Fund which shall consist of moneys received from fees imposed on certain drug offense convictions pursuant to subdivisions A 10 and A 11 of §17.1-275 and §16.1-69.48:3. All interest derived from the deposit and investment of moneys in the Fund shall be

credited to the Fund. Any moneys not appropriated by the General Assembly shall remain in the Drug Offender Assessment Fund and shall not be transferred or revert to the general fund at the end of any fiscal year. All moneys in the Fund shall be subject to annual appropriation by the General Assembly to the Department of Corrections, the Department of Juvenile Justice and the Commission on VASAP to implement and operate the offender substance abuse screening and assessment program.
(Added by L.1998 chs. 783, 840, eff. 7/1/98.)

§18.2-251.1. Possession or distribution of marijuana for medical purposes permitted.

A. No person shall be prosecuted under §§18.2-250 or 18.2-250.1 for the possession of marijuana or tetrahydrocannabinol when that possession occurs pursuant to a valid prescription issued by a medical doctor in the course of his professional practice for treatment of cancer or glaucoma.

B. No medical doctor shall be prosecuted under §§18.2-248 or 18.2-248.1 for dispensing or distributing marijuana or tetrahydrocannabinol for medical purposes when such action occurs in the course of his professional practice for treatment of cancer or glaucoma.

C. No pharmacist shall be prosecuted under §§18.2-248 to 18.2-248.1 for dispensing or distributing marijuana or tetrahydrocannabinol to any person who holds a valid prescription of a medical doctor for such substance issued in the course of such doctor's professional practice for treatment of cancer or glaucoma.

§18.2-251.2. Possession and distribution of flunitrazepam; enhanced penalty.

Notwithstanding the provisions of §§54.1-3446 and 54.1-3452, the drug flunitrazepam shall be deemed to be listed on Schedule I for the purposes of penalties for violations of the Drug Control Act (§54.1-3400 et seq.). Any person knowingly manufacturing, selling, giving, distributing or possessing the drug flunitrazepam shall be punished under the penalties prescribed for such violations in accordance with §§18.2-248 and 18.2-250.
(Added by L.1997 ch. 595, eff. 7/1/97.)

§18.2-251.3. Possession and distribution of gamma-butyrolactone; 1, 4 - butanediol; enhanced penalty.

Any person who knowingly manufactures, sells, gives, distributes or possesses with the intent to distribute the substances gamma-butyrolactone; or 1, 4 - butanediol, when intended for human consumption shall be guilty of a Class 3 felony.
(Added by L.2000 ch. 348, eff. 7/1/2000.)

§18.2-252. Suspended sentence conditioned upon substance abuse screening, assessment, testing, and treatment or education.

The trial judge or court trying the case of any person found guilty of violating any law concerning the use, in any manner, of drugs, controlled substances, narcotics, marijuana, noxious chemical substances and like substances, shall condition any suspended sentence by first requiring such person to agree to undergo a substance abuse screening pursuant to §18.2-251.01 and to submit to such periodic substance abuse testing, to include alcohol testing, as may be directed by the court. Such testing shall be conducted by the supervising probation agency or by personnel of any program or agency approved by the supervising probation agency. The cost of such testing ordered by the court shall be paid by the Commonwealth and taxed as a part of the costs of such criminal proceedings. The judge or court shall order the person, as a condition of any suspended sentence, to undergo such treatment or education for substance abuse, if available, as the judge or court deems appropriate based upon consideration of the substance abuse assessment. The treatment or education shall be provided by a program licensed by the Department of Mental Health, Mental Retardation and Substance Abuse Services, by a similar program available through the Department of Corrections if the court imposes a sentence of one year or more or, if the court imposes a sentence of twelve months or less, by a similar program available through a local or regional jail, a community corrections program established pursuant to §53.1-180, or an ASAP program certified by the Commission on VASAP.
(Chgd. by L.1998 chs. 783, 840; L.2000 chs. 1020, 1041, eff. 7/1/2000.)

§18.2-253. Disposal of seized substances.

A. All controlled substances, imitation controlled substances, marijuana or paraphernalia the lawful possession of which is not established or the title to which cannot be ascertained, which have come into the custody of a peace officer or have been seized in connection with violations of this chapter, shall be forfeited and disposed of as follows:

1. Upon written application by the Division of Forensic Science the court may order the forfeiture of any such substance or paraphernalia to the Division for research and training purposes and for destruction pursuant to regulations of the United States Department of Justice Drug Enforcement Administration and of the State Board of Pharmacy once these purposes have been fulfilled.

2. In the event no application is made under subdivision 1 of this subsection, the court shall order the destruction of all such substances or paraphernalia which order shall state the existence and nature of the substance or paraphernalia, the quantity thereof, the location where seized, the person or persons from whom the substance or paraphernalia was seized, if known, and the manner whereby such item shall be destroyed. A return under oath, reporting the time, place and manner of destruction shall be made to the court and to the Board of Pharmacy by the officer to whom the order is directed. A copy of the order and affidavit shall be made a part of the record of any criminal prosecution in which the substance or paraphernalia was used as evidence and shall, thereafter, be prima facie evidence of its contents. In the event a law enforcement agency recovers, seizes, finds, is given or otherwise comes into possession of any such substances or paraphernalia which are not evidence in a trial in the Commonwealth, the chief law-enforcement officer of the agency may, with the written consent of the appropriate attorney for the Commonwealth, order destruction of same; provided that, a statement under oath, reporting a description of the substances and paraphernalia destroyed, and the time, place and manner of destruction is made to the chief law-enforcement officer and to the Board of Pharmacy by the officer to whom the order is directed.

B. No such substance or paraphernalia used or to be used in a criminal prosecution under this chapter shall be disposed of as provided by this section until all rights of appeal have been exhausted, except as provided in §18.2-253.1.
(Chgd. by L.1995 ch. 578, eff. 7/1/95.)

§18.2-253.1. Destruction of seized substances prior to trial.

Where seizures of controlled substances or marijuana are made in excess of ten pounds in connection with any prosecution or investigation under this chapter, the appropriate law-enforcement agency may retain ten pounds of the substance randomly selected from the seized substance for representative purposes as evidence and destroy the remainder of the seized substance.

Before any destruction is carried out under this section, the law-enforcement agency shall cause the material seized to be photographed with identification case numbers or other means of identification and shall prepare a report identifying the seized material. It shall also notify the accused or other interested party, if known, or his attorney, at least five days in advance that the photography will take place and that they may be present. Prior to any destruction under this section, the law-enforcement agency shall also notify the accused or other interested party, if known, and his attorney at least seven days prior to the destruction of the time and place the destruction will occur. Any notice required under the provisions of this section shall be by first class mail to the last known address of the person required to be notified. In addition to the substance retained for representative purposes as evidence, all photographs and records made under this section and properly identified shall be admissible in any court proceeding for any purposes for which the seized substance itself would have been admissible.

§18.2-253.2. Judge may order law-enforcement agency to maintain custody of controlled substances.

Upon request of the clerk of any court, a judge of the court may order a law-enforcement agency to take into its custody or to maintain custody of substantial quantities of any controlled substances, imitafion controlled substances, chemicals, marijuana or paraphernalia used or to be used in a criminal prosecution under this chapter. The court in its order may make provision for ensuring integrity of these items until further order of the court.

§18.2-254. Commitment of convicted person for treatment for drug or alcohol abuse.

A. Whenever any person who has not previously been convicted of any offense under this article or under any statute of the United States or of any state relating to narcotic drugs, marijuana, stimulant, depressant, or hallucinogenic drugs, or has not previously had a proceeding against him for violation of such an offense dismissed as provided in §18.2-251, is found guilty of violating any law concerning the use, in any manner, of drugs, controlled substances, narcotics, marijuana, noxious chemical substances and like substances, the judge or court shall require such person to undergo a substance abuse screening pursuant to §18.2-251.01 and to submit to such periodic substance abuse testing, to include alcohol testing, as may be directed by the court. The cost of such testing ordered by the court shall be paid by the Commonwealth and taxed as a part of the costs of the criminal proceedings. The judge or court shall also order the person to undergo such treatment or education for substance abuse, if available, as the judge or court deems appropriate based upon consideration of the substance abuse assessment. The treatment or education shall be provided by a program licensed by the Department of Mental Health, Mental Retardation and Substance Abuse Services or by a similar program available through the Department of Corrections if the court imposes a sentence of one year or more or, if the court imposes a sentence of twelve months or less, by a similar program available through a local or regional jail, a community corrections program established pursuant to §53.1-180, or an ASAP program certified by the Commission on VASAP.

B. The court trying the case of any person alleged to have committed any offense designated by this article or by the Drug Control Act (§54.1-3400 et seq.) or in any other criminal case in which the commission of the offense was motivated by, or closely related to, the use of drugs and determined by the court, pursuant to a substance abuse screening and assessment to be in need of treatment for the use of drugs may commit, based upon a consideration of the substance abuse assessment, such person, upon his conviction, to any facility for the treatment of persons for the intemperate use of narcotic or other controlled substances, licensed by the Department of Mental Health, Mental Retardation and Substance Abuse Services, if space is available in such facility, for a period of time not in excess of the maximum term of imprisonment specified as the penalty for conviction of such offense or, if sentence was determined by a jury, not in excess of the term of imprisonment as set by such jury. Confinement under such commitment shall be, in all regards, treated as confinement in a penal institution and the person so committed may be convicted of escape if he leaves the place of commitment without authority. The court may revoke such commitment, at any time, and transfer the person to an appropriate state or local correctional facility. Upon presentation of a certified statement from the director of the treatment facility to the effect that the confined person has successfully responded to treatment, the court may release such confined person prior to the termination of the period of time for which such person was confined and may suspend the remainder of the term upon such conditions as the court may prescribe.

C. The court trying a case in which commission of the offense was related to the defendant's habitual abuse of alcohol and in which the court determines, pursuant to a substance abuse screening and assessment, that such defendant is an alcoholic as defined in §37.1-1 and in need of treatment, may commit, based upon a consideration of the substance abuse assessment, such person, upon his conviction, to any facility for the treatment of alcoholics licensed by the Department of Mental Health, Mental Retardation and Substance Abuse Services, if space is available in such facility, for a period of time not in excess of the maximum term of imprisonment specified as the penalty for conviction. Confinement under such commitment shall be, in all regards, treated as confinement in a penal institution and the person so committed may be convicted of escape if he leaves the place of commitment without authority. The court may revoke such commitment, at any time, and transfer the person to an appropriate state or local correctional facility. Upon presentation of a certified statement from the director of the treatment facility to the effect that the confined person has successfully responded to treatment, the court may release such confined person prior to the termination of the period of time for which such person was confined and may suspend the remainder of the term upon such conditions as the court may prescribe.

(Chgd. by L.1998 ch. 724; L.2000 chs. 1020, 1041, eff. 7/1/2000.)

§18.2-255. Distribution of certain drugs to persons under eighteen prohibited; penalty.

A. Except as authorized in the Drug Control Act, Chapter 34 (§54.1-3400 et seq.) of Title 54.1, it shall be unlawful for any person who is at least eighteen years of age to knowingly or intentionally (i) distribute any drug classified in Schedule I, II, III or IV or marijuana to any person under eighteen years of age who is at least three years his junior or (ii) cause any person under eighteen years of age to assist in such distribution of any drug classified in Schedule I, II, III or IV or marijuana. Any person violating this provision shall upon conviction be imprisoned in a state correctional facility for a period not less than ten nor more than fifty years, and fined not more than $100,000. Five years of the sentence imposed shall not be suspended, in whole or in part for a conviction under this section involving a Schedule I or II controlled substance or one ounce or more of marijuana. Two years of the sentence imposed shall not be suspended, in whole or in part, for a conviction involving less than one ounce of marijuana.

B. It shall be unlawful for any person who is at least eighteen years of age to knowingly or intentionally (i) distribute any imitation controlled substance to a person under eighteen years of age who is at least three years his junior or (ii) cause any person under eighteen years of age to assist in such distribution of any imitation controlled substance. Any person violating this provision shall be guilty of a Class 6 felony.

(Chgd. by L.2000 chs. 1020, 1041, eff. 7/1/2000.)

§18.2-255.1. Distribution, sale or display of printed material advertising instruments for use in administering marijuana or controlled substances to minors; penalty.

It shall be a Class 1 misdemeanor for any person knowingly to sell, distribute, or display for sale to a minor any book, pamphlet, periodical or other printed matter which he knows advertises for sale any instrument, device, article, or contrivance for advertised use in unlawfully ingesting, smoking, administering, preparing or growing marijuana or a controlled substance.

§18.2-255.2. Prohibiting the sale of drugs on or near certain properties.

A. It shall be unlawful for any person to manufacture, sell or distribute or possess with intent to sell, give or distribute any controlled substance, imitation controlled substance or marijuana while (i) upon the property, including buildings and grounds, of any public or private elementary, secondary, or post secondary school, or any public or private two-year or four-year institution of higher education; (ii) upon public property or any property open to public use within 1,000 feet of such school property; (iii) on any school bus as defined in §46.2-100; (iv) upon a designated school bus stop, or upon either public property or any property open to public use which is within 1,000 feet of such school bus stop, during the time when school children are waiting to be picked up and transported to or are being dropped off from school or a school-sponsored activity; (v) upon the property, including buildings and grounds, of any publicly owned or publicly operated recreation or community center facility or any public library; or (vi) upon the property of any state hospital as defined in §37.1-1 or upon public property or property open to public use within 1,000 feet of such an institution. Nothing in this section shall prohibit the authorized distribution of controlled substances.

B. Violation of this section shall constitute a separate and distinct felony. Any person violating the provisions of this section shall, upon conviction, be imprisoned for a term of not less than one year nor more than five years and fined not more than $100,000. A second or subsequent conviction hereunder for an offense involving a controlled substance classified in Schedule I, II, or III of the Drug Control Act (§54.1-3400 et seq.) or more than one-half ounce of marijuana shall be punished by a minimum, mandatory term of imprisonment of one year which shall not be suspended in whole or in part and shall be served consecutively with any other sentence. However, if such person proves that he sold such controlled substance or marijuana only as an accommodation to another individual and not with intent to profit thereby from any consideration received or expected nor to induce the recipient or intended recipient of the controlled substance or marijuana to use or become addicted to or dependent upon such controlled substance or marijuana, he shall be guilty of a Class 1 misdemeanor.

C. If a person commits an act violating the provisions of this section, and the same act also violates another provision of law that provides for penalties greater than those provided for by this section, then nothing in this section shall prohibit or bar any prosecution or proceeding under that other provision of law or the imposition of any penalties provided for thereby.

(Chgd. by L.1999 ch. 873; L.2000 chs. 1020, 1041, eff. 7/1/2000.)

§18.2-256. Conspiracy.

Any person who conspires to commit any offense defined in this article or in the Drug Control Act (§54.1-3400 et seq.) is punishable by imprisonment or fine or both which may not be less than the minimum punishment nor exceed the maximum punishment prescribed for the offense, the commission of which was the object of the conspiracy.

§18.2-257. Attempts.

(a) Any person who attempts to commit any offense defined in this article or in the Drug Control Act (§54.1-3400 et seq.) which is a felony shall be imprisoned for not less than one nor more than ten years; provided, however, that any person convicted of attempting to commit a felony for which a lesser punishment may be imposed may be punished according to such lesser penalty.

(b) Any person who attempts to commit any offense defined in this article or in the Drug Control Act which is a misdemeanor shall be guilty of a Class 2 misdemeanor; provided, however, that any person convicted of attempting to commit a misdemeanor for which a lesser punishment may be imposed may be punished according to such lesser penalty.

§18.2-258. Certain premises deemed common nuisance; penalty.

A. Any office, store, shop, restaurant, dance hall, theater, poolroom, clubhouse, storehouse, warehouse, dwelling house, apartment, building of any kind, vehicle, vessel, boat, or aircraft, which with the knowledge of the owner, lessor, agent of any such lessor, manager, chief executive officer, operator, or tenant thereof, is frequented by persons under the influence of illegally obtained controlled substances or marijuana, as defined in §54.1-3401, or for the purpose of illegally obtaining possession of, manufacturing or distributing controlled substances or marijuana, or is used for the illegal possession, manufacture or distribution of controlled substances or marijuana, shall be deemed a common nuisance. Any such owner, lessor, agent of any such lessor, manager, chief executive officer, operator or tenant who knowingly permits, establishes, keeps or maintains such a common nuisance is guilty of a Class 1 misdemeanor and, for a second or subsequent offense, a Class 6 felony. In addition, after due notice and opportunity to be heard on the part of any owner, lessor, or a lienholder not involved in the original offense, by a proceeding similar to that in Chapter 22.1 (§19.2-386.1 et seq.) of Title 19.2 and upon proof of guilty knowledge, a court may order that such house, motor vehicle, aircraft, boat, vessel, or other premises, or any room or part thereof, be closed, but the court may, upon the owner or lessor giving bond in the penalty of not less than $500 and with security to be approved by the court, conditioned that the premises shall not be used for unlawful purposes, turn the same over to its owner or lessor; or proceeding may be had in equity as provided in §18.2-258.01.

B. The penalties provided in this section shall be in addition to any other penalty provided by law, including immediate termination of a rental agreement as provided in §55-248.31.

C. In no civil or in rem proceeding under the provisions of this section shall judgment be entered against the owner, lessor, or lienholder of property unless it is proved: (i) that he knew of the unlawful use of the property and (ii) that he had the right, because of such unlawful use, to enter and repossess the property.

§18.2-258.01. Enjoining nuisances involving illegal drug transactions.

The attorney for the Commonwealth, or any citizen of the county, city, or town, where such a nuisance as is described in §18.2-258 exists, may in addition to the remedies given in and punishment imposed by this chapter, maintain a suit in equity in the name of the Commonwealth to enjoin the same; provided, however, the attorney for the Commonwealth shall not be required to prosecute any suit brought by a citizen under this section. In every case where the bill charges, on the knowledge or belief of complainant, and is sworn to by two witnesses, that a nuisance exists as described in §18.2-258, a temporary injunction may be granted as soon as the bill is presented to the court provided reasonable notice has been given. The injunction shall enjoin and restrain any owners, tenants, their agents, employees, and any other person from contributing to or maintaining the nuisance and may impose such other requirements as the court deems appropriate. If, after hearing, the court finds that the material allegations of the bill are true, although the premises complained of may not then be unlawfully used, it shall continue the injunction against such persons or premises for such period of time as it deems appropriate, with the right to dissolve the injunction upon a proper showing by the owner of the premises.

§18.2-258.02. Maintaining a fortified drug house; penalty.

Any office, store, shop, restaurant, dance hall, theater, poolroom, clubhouse, storehouse, warehouse, dwelling house, apartment or building or structure of any kind which is (i) substantially altered from its original status by means of reinforcement with the intent to impede, deter or delay lawful entry by a law-enforcement officer into such structure, (ii) being used for the purpose of manufacturing or distributing controlled substances or marijuana, and (iii) the object of a valid search warrant, shall be considered a fortified drug house. Any person who maintains or operates a fortified drug house is guilty of a Class 5 felony.

(Added by L.1996 ch. 913, eff. 7/1/96.)

§18.2-258.1. Obtaining drugs, procuring administration of controlled substances, etc., by fraud, deceit or forgery.

A. It shall be unlawful for any person to obtain or attempt to obtain any drug or procure or attempt to procure the administration of any controlled substance or marijuana: (i) by fraud, deceit, misrepresentation, embezzlement, or subterfuge; or (ii) by the forgery or alteration of a prescription or of any written order; or (iii) by the concealment of a material fact; or (iv) by the use of a false name or the giving of a false address.

B. It shall be unlawful for any person to furnish false or fraudulent information in or omit any information from, or willfully make a false statement in, any prescription, order, report, record, or other document required by Chapter 34 of Title 54.1.

C. It shall be unlawful for any person to use in the course of the manufacture or distribution of a controlled substance or marijuana a license number which is fictitious, revoked, suspended, or issued to another person.

D. It shall be unlawful for any person, for the purpose of obtaining any controlled substance or marijuana, to falsely assume the title of, or represent himself to be, a manufacturer, wholesaler, pharmacist, physician, dentist, veterinarian or other authorized person.

E. It shall be unlawful for any person to make or utter any false or forged prescription or false or forged written order.

F. It shall be unlawful for any person to affix any false or forged label to a package or receptacle containing any controlled substance.

G. This section shall not apply to officers and employees of the United States, of this Commonwealth or of a political subdivision of this Commonwealth acting in the course of their employment, who obtain such drugs for investigative, research or analytical purposes, or to the agents or duly authorized representatives of any pharmaceutical manufacturer who obtain such drugs for investigative, research or analytical purposes and who are acting in the course of their employment; provided that such manufacturer is licensed under the provisions of the Federal Food, Drug and Cosmetic Act; and provided further, that such pharmaceutical manufacturer, its agents and duly authorized representatives file with the Board such information as the Board may deem appropriate.

H. Except as otherwise provided in this subsection, any person who shall violate any provision herein shall be guilty of a Class 6 felony.

Whenever any person who has not previously been convicted of any offense under this article or under any statute of the United States or of any state relating to narcotic drugs, marijuana, or stimulant, depressant, or hallucinogenic drugs, or has not previously had a proceeding against him for violation of such an offense dismissed, or reduced as provided in this section, pleads guilty to or enters a plea of not guilty to the court for violating §18.2-258.1, upon such plea if the facts found by the court would justify a finding of guilt, the court may place him on probation upon terms and conditions.

As a term or condition, the court shall require the accused to be evaluated and enter a treatment and/or education program, if available, such as, in the opinion of the court, may be best suited to the needs of the accused. This program may be located in the judicial circuit in which the charge is brought or in any other judicial circuit as the court may provide. The services shall be provided by a program certified or licensed by the Department of Mental Health, Mental Retardation and Substance Abuse Services. The court shall require the person entering such program under the provisions of this section to pay all or part of the costs of the program, including the costs of the screening, evaluation, testing and education, based upon the person's ability to pay unless the person is determined by the court to be indigent.

As a condition of supervised probation, the court shall require the accused to remain drug free during the period of probation and submit to such tests during that period as may be necessary and appropriate to determine if the accused is drug free. Such testing may be conducted by the personnel of any screening, evaluation, and education program to which the person is referred or by the supervising agency.

Unless the accused was fingerprinted at the time of arrest, the court shall order the accused to report to the original arresting law-enforcement agency to submit to fingerprinting.

Upon violation of a term or condition, the court may enter an adjudication of guilt upon the felony and proceed as otherwise provided. Upon fulfillment of the terms and conditions of probation, the court shall find the defendant guilty of a Class 1 misdemeanor.

(Chgd. by L.1997 ch. 542, eff. 7/1/97.)

§18.2-259. Penalties to be in addition to civil or administrative sanctions.

Any penalty imposed for violation of this article or of the Drug Control Act (§54.1-3400 et seq.) shall be in addition to, and not in lieu of, any civil or administrative penalty or sanction authorized by law.

§18.2-259.1. Forfeiture of driver's license for violations of article.

A. In addition to any other sanction or penalty imposed for a violation of this article, the (i) judgment of conviction under this article or (ii) placement on probation following deferral of further proceedings under §18.2-251 or subsection H of §18.2-258.1 for any such offense shall of itself operate to deprive the person so convicted or placed on probation after deferral of proceedings under §18.2-251 or subsection H of §18.2-258.1 of the privilege to drive or operate a motor vehicle, engine, or train in the Commonwealth for a period of six months from the date of such judgment or placement on probation. Such license forfeiture shall be in addition to and shall run consecutively with any other license suspension, revocation or forfeiture in effect or imposed upon the person so convicted or placed on probation. However, a juvenile who has had his license suspended or denied pursuant to §16.1-278.9 shall not have his license forfeited pursuant to this section for the same offense.

B. The court trying the case shall order any person so convicted or placed on probation to surrender his driver's license to be disposed of in accordance with the provisions of §46.2-398 and shall notify the Department of Motor Vehicles of any such conviction entered and of the license forfeiture to be imposed.

C. In those cases where the court determines there are compelling circumstances warranting an exception, the court may provide that any individual be issued a restricted license to operate a motor vehicle for any or all of the following purposes: (i) travel to and from his place of employment; (ii) travel to a screening, evaluation and education program entered pursuant to §18.2-251 or subsection H of §18.2-258.1; (iii) travel during the hours of such person's employment if the operation of a motor vehicle is a necessary incident of such employment; (iv) travel to and from school if such person is a student, upon proper written verification to the court that such person is enrolled in a continuing program of education; or (v) such other medically necessary travel as the court deems necessary and proper upon written verification of need by a licensed health professional. No restricted license issued pursuant to this subsection shall permit any person to operate a commercial motor vehicle as defined in the Virginia Commercial Driver's License Act (§46.2-341.1 et seq.). The court shall order the surrender of such person's license in accordance with the provisions of subsection B and shall forward to the Commissioner of the Department of Motor Vehicles a copy of its order entered pursuant to this subsection. This order shall specifically enumerate the restrictions imposed and contain such information regarding the person to whom such a permit is issued as is reasonably necessary to identify such person. The court shall also provide a copy of its order to such person who may operate a motor vehicle on the order until receipt from the Commissioner of the Department of Motor Vehicles of a restricted license, but only if the order provides for a restricted license for that period. A copy of the order and, after receipt thereof, the restricted license shall be carried at all times by such person while operating a motor vehicle. The court may require a person issued a restricted permit under the provisions of this subsection to be monitored by an alcohol safety action program during the period of license suspension. Any violation of the terms of the restricted license or of any condition set forth by the court related thereto, or any failure to remain drug-free during such period shall be reported forthwith to the court by such program. Any person who operates a motor vehicle in violation of any restriction imposed pursuant to this section shall be guilty of a violation of §46.2-301.

(Chgd. by L.1999 ch. 45; L.2000 ch. 325, eff. 7/1/2000.)

§18.2-260. Prescribing, dispensing, etc., drug except as authorized in article and Drug Control Act; violations for which no penalty provided.

It shall be unlawful for any person to prescribe, administer or dispense any drug except as authorized in the Drug Control Act (§54.1-3400 et seq.) or in this article. Any person who violates any provision of the Drug Control Act or of this article, for which no penalty is elsewhere specified in this article or in Article 7 (§54.1-3466 et seq.) of the Drug Control Act, shall be guilty of a Class 1 misdemeanor.

§18.2-260.1. Falsifying patient records.

Any person who fraudulently falsifies any patient record shall be guilty of a Class 3 misdemeanor.

(Added by L.1997 ch. 619, eff. 7/1/97.)

§18.2-261. Monetary penalty.

Any person licensed by the State Board of Pharmacy who violates any of the provisions of the Drug Control Act (§54.1-3400 et seq.) or of this article, and who is not criminally prosecuted, shall be subject to the monetary penalty provided in this section. If, by a majority vote, the Board shall determine that the respondent is guilty of the violation complained of, the Board shall proceed to determine the amount of the monetary penalty for such violation, which shall not exceed the sum of $1,000 for each violation. Such penalty may be sued for and recovered in the name of the Commonwealth.

§18.2-262. Witnesses not excused from testifying or producing evidence because of self-incrimination.

No person shall be excused from testifying or from producing books, papers, correspondence, memoranda or other records for the Commonwealth as to any offense alleged to have been committed by another under this article or under the Drug Control Act (§54.1-3400 et seq.) by reason of his testimony or other evidence tending to incriminate himself, but the testimony given and evidence so produced by such person on behalf of the Commonwealth when called for by the trial judge or court trying the case, or by the attorney for the Commonwealth, or when summoned by the Commonwealth and sworn as a witness by the court or the clerk and sent before the grand jury, shall be in no case used against him nor shall he be prosecuted as to the offense as to which he testifies. Any person who refuses to testify or produce books, papers, correspondence, memoranda or other records, shall be guilty of a Class 2 misdemeanor.

§18.2-263. Unnecessary to negative exception, etc.; burden of proof of exception, etc.

In any complaint, information, or indictment, and in any action or proceeding brought for the enforcement of any provision of this article or of the Drug Control Act (§54.1-3400 et seq.), it shall not be necessary to negative any exception, excuse, proviso, or exemption contained in this article or in the Drug Control Act, and the burden of proof of any such exception, excuse, proviso, or exemption shall be upon the defendant.

§18.2-264. Inhaling drugs or other noxious chemical substances or causing, etc., others to do so.

A. It shall be unlawful, except under the direction of a practitioner as defined in §54-3401, for any person deliberately to smell or inhale any drugs or any other noxious chemical substances including but not limited to fingernail polish or model airplane glue, containing any ketones, aldehydes, organic acetates, ether, chlorinated hydrocarbons or vapors, with the intent to become intoxicated, inebriated, excited, stupefied or to dull the brain or nervous system.

Any person violating the provisions of this subsection shall be guilty of a Class 1 misdemeanor.

B. It shall be unlawful for any person, other than one duly licensed, deliberately to cause, invite or induce any person to smell or inhale any drugs or any other noxious substances or chemicals containing any ketone, aldehydes, organic acetates, ether, chlorinated hydrocarbons or vapors with the intent to intoxicate, inebriate, excite, stupefy or to dull the brain or nervous system of such person.

Any person violating the provisions of this subsection shall be guilty of a Class 2 misdemeanor.

§18.2-264.01. Charges for forensic laboratory analysis.

In all cases where a person is found guilty of a violation of this article (§18.2-247 et seq.), a fee of $100 per case for any forensic laboratory analysis performed for use in prosecution of such violation shall be taxed as costs to the defendant and shall be paid into the general fund of the state treasury. For the purposes of this section, "guilty" includes any case where the defendant pleads guilty, receives a suspended imposition of sentence or is placed on probation without a judgment of guilt under §18.2-251.

(Added by L.1995 ch. 463, eff. 7/1/95.)

ARTICLE 1.1
DRUG PARAPHERNALIA

Section

§18.2-265.1. Definition.

As used in this article, the term "drug paraphernalia" means all equipment, products, and materials of any kind which are either designed for use or which are intended by the person charged with violating §18.2-265.3 for use in planting, propagating, cultivating, growing, harvesting, manufacturing, compounding, converting, producing, processing, preparing, strength testing, analyzing, packaging, repackaging, storing, containing, concealing, injecting, ingesting, inhaling, or otherwise introducing into the human body marijuana or a controlled substance. It includes, but is not limited to:

1. Kits intended for use or designed for use in planting, propagating, cultivating, growing or harvesting of marijuana or any species of plant which is a controlled substance or from which a controlled substance can be derived;

2. Kits intended for use or designed for use in manufacturing, compounding, converting, producing, processing, or preparing marijuana or controlled substances;

3. Isomerization devices intended for use or designed for use in increasing the potency of marijuana or any species of plant which is a controlled substance;

4. Testing equipment intended for use or designed for use in identifying or in analyzing the strength or effectiveness of marijuana or controlled substances;

5. Scales and balances intended for use or designed for use in weighing or measuring marijuana or controlled substances;

6. Diluents and adulterants, such as quinine hydrochloride, mannitol, or mannite, intended for use or designed for use in cutting controlled substances;

7. Separation gins and sifters intended for use or designed for use in removing twigs and seeds from, or in otherwise cleaning or refining, marijuana;

8. Blenders, bowls, containers, spoons, and mixing devices intended for use or designed for use in compounding controlled substances;

9. Capsules, balloons, envelopes, and other containers intended for use or designed for use in packaging small quantities of marijuana or controlled substances;

10. Containers and other objects intended for use or designed for use in storing or concealing marijuana or controlled substances;

11. Hypodermic syringes, needles, and other objects intended for use or designed for use in internally injecting controlled substances into the human body;

12. Objects intended for use or designed for use in ingesting, inhaling, or otherwise introducing marijuana, cocaine, hashish, or hashish oil into the human body, such as:

a. Metal, wooden, acrylic, glass, stone, plastic, or ceramic pipes with or without screens, permanent screens, hashish heads, or punctured metal bowls;

b. Water pipes;

c. Carburetion tubes and devices;

d. Smoking and carburetion masks;

e. Roach clips, meaning objects used to hold burning material, such as a marijuana cigarette, that has become too small or too short to be held in the hand;

f. Miniature cocaine spoons, and cocaine vials;

g. Chamber pipes;

h. Carburetor pipes;

i. Electric pipes;

j. Air-driven pipes;

k. Chillums;

l. Bongs;

m. Ice pipes or chillers.

§18.2-265.2. Evidence to be considered in cases under this article.

In determining whether an object is drug paraphernalia, the court may consider, in addition to all other relevant evidence, the following:

1. Constitutionally admissible statements by the accused concerning the use of the object;

2. The proximity of the object to marijuana or controlled substances, which proximity is actually known to the accused;

3. Instructions, oral or written, provided with the object concerning its use;

4. Descriptive materials accompanying the object which explain or depict its use;

5. National and local advertising within the actual knowledge of the accused concerning its use;

6. The manner in which the object is displayed for sale;

7. Whether the accused is a legitimate supplier of like or related items to the community, such as a licensed distributor or dealer of tobacco products;

8. Evidence of the ratio of sales of the objects defined in §18.2-265.1 to the total sales of the business enterprise;

9. The existence and scope of legitimate uses for the object in the community;

10. Expert testimony concerning its use or the purpose for which it was designed;

11. Relevant evidence of the intent of the accused to deliver it to persons who he knows, or should reasonably know, intend to use the object with an illegal drug. The innocence of an owner, or of anyone in control of the object, as to a direct violation of this article shall not prevent a finding that the object is intended for use or designed for use as drug paraphernalia.

§18.2-265.3. Penalties for sale, etc., of drug paraphernalia.

A. Any person who sells or possesses with intent to sell drug paraphernalia, knowing, or under circumstances where one reasonably should know, that it is either designed for use or intended by such person for use to illegally plant, propagate, cultivate, grow, harvest, manufacture, compound, convert, produce, process, prepare, test, analyze, pack, repack, store, contain, conceal, inject, ingest, inhale, or otherwise introduce into the human body marijuana or a controlled substance, shall be guilty of a Class 1 misdemeanor.

B. Any person eighteen years of age or older who violates subsection A hereof by selling drug paraphernalia to a minor who is at least three years junior to the accused in age shall be guilty of a Class 6 felony.

C. Any person eighteen years of age or older who distributes drug paraphernalia to a minor shall be guilty of a Class 1 misdemeanor.

§18.2-265.4. Seizure and forfeiture of drug paraphernalia.

All drug paraphernalia as defined in this article shall be forfeited to the Commonwealth and may be seized and disposed of in the same manner as provided in §18.2-253 of the Code, subject to the rights of an innocent lienor, to be recognized as under §4.1-343.

§18.2-265.5. Advertisement of drug paraphernalia prohibited; penalty.

It shall be unlawful for any person to place in any newspaper, magazine, handbill or other publication any advertisement, knowing or under circumstances where one reasonably should know, that the purpose of the advertisement, in whole or in part, is to promote the sale of objects designed or intended by such person for use as drug paraphernalia. A violation of this section shall be punishable as a Class 1 misdemeanor.

ARTICLE 2
DRIVING MOTOR VEHICLE, ETC., WHILE INTOXICATED

§18.2-266. Driving motor vehicle, engine, etc., while intoxicated, etc.

It shall be unlawful for any person to drive or operate any motor vehicle, engine or train (i) while such person has a blood alcohol concentration of 0.08 percent or more by weight by volume or 0.08 grams or more per 210 liters of breath as indicated by a chemical test administered as provided in this article, (ii) while such person is under the influence of alcohol, (iii) while such person is under the influence of any narcotic drug or any other self-administered intoxicant or drug of whatsoever nature, or any combination of such drugs, to a degree which impairs his ability to drive or operate any motor vehicle, engine or train safely, or (iv) while such person is under the combined influence of alcohol and any drug or drugs to a degree which impairs his ability to drive or operate any motor vehicle, engine or train safely. A charge alleging a violation of this section shall support a conviction under clauses (i), (ii), (iii) or (iv).

For the purposes of this section, the term "motor vehicle" includes mopeds, while operated on the public highways of this Commonwealth.

(Chgd. by L.1996 ch. 439, eff. 7/1/96.)

§18.2-266.1. Persons under age twenty-one driving after illegally consuming alcohol; penalty.

A. It shall be unlawful for any person under the age of twenty-one to operate any motor vehicle after illegally consuming alcohol. Any such person with a blood alcohol concentration of 0.02 percent or more by weight by volume or 0.02 grams or more per 210 liters of breath but less than 0.08 by weight by volume or less than 0.08 grams per 210 liters of breath as indicated by a chemical test administered as provided in this article shall be in violation of this section.

B. A violation of this section shall be punishable by forfeiture of such person's license to operate a motor vehicle for a period of six months from the date of conviction and by a fine of not more than $500. The penalties and license forfeiture provisions set forth in §§16.1-278.9, 18.2-270 and 18.2-271 shall not apply to a violation of this section. Any person convicted of a violation of this section shall be eligible to attend an Alcohol Safety Action Program under the provisions of §18.2-271.1 and may, in the discretion of the court, be issued a restricted license during the term of license suspension.

C. Notwithstanding §§16.1-278.8 and 16.1-278.9, upon adjudicating a juvenile delinquent based upon a violation of this section, the juvenile and domestic relations district court shall order disposition as provided in subsection B.

(Chgd. by L.1995 ch. 31, eff. 7/1/95.)

§18.2-267. Preliminary analysis of breath to determine alcoholic content of blood.

A. Any person who is suspected of a violation of §18.2-266 or §18.2-266.1 shall be entitled, if such equipment is available, to have his breath analyzed to determine the probable alcoholic content of his blood. The person shall also be entitled, upon request, to observe the process of analysis and to see the blood-alcohol reading on the equipment used to perform the breath test. His breath may be analyzed by any police officer of the Commonwealth, or of any county, city or town, or by any member of a sheriff's department in the normal discharge of his duties.

B. The Department of Criminal Justice Services, Division of Forensic Science, shall determine the proper method and equipment to be used in analyzing breath samples taken pursuant to this section and shall advise the respective police and sheriff's departments of the same.

C. Any person who has been stopped by a police officer of the Commonwealth, or of any county, city or town, or by any member of a sheriff's department and is suspected by such officer to be guilty of a violation of §18.2-266 or §18.2-266.1, shall have the right to refuse to permit his breath to be so analyzed, and his failure to permit such analysis shall not be evidence in any prosecution under §18.2-266 or §18.2-266.1.

D. Whenever the breath sample analysis indicates that alcohol is present in the person's blood, the officer may charge the person with a violation of §18.2-266 or §18.2-266.1, or a similar ordinance of the county, city or town where the arrest is made. The person so charged shall then be subject to the provisions of §§18.2-268.1 through 18.2-268.12, or of a similar ordinance of a county, city or town.

E. The results of the breath analysis shall not be admitted into evidence in any prosecution under §18.2-266 or §18.2-266.1, the purpose of this section being to permit a preliminary analysis of the alcoholic content of the blood of a person suspected of having violated the provisions of §18.2-266 or §18.2-266.1.

F. Police officers or members of any sheriff's department shall, upon stopping any person suspected of having violated the provisions of §18.2-266 or §18.2-266.1, advise the person of his rights under the provisions of this section.

G. Nothing in this section shall be construed as limiting the provisions of §§18.2-268.1 through 18.2-268.12.
(Chgd. by L.1996 chs. 154, 952, eff. 7/1/96.)

§18.2-268.1. Chemical testing to determine alcohol or drug content of blood; definitions.

As used in §§18.2-268.2 through 18.2-268.12, unless the context clearly indicates otherwise:

The phrase "alcohol or drug" means alcohol, a drug or drugs, or any combination of alcohol and a drug or drugs.

The phrase "blood or breath" means either or both.

"Chief police officer" means the sheriff in any county not having a chief of police, the chief of police of any county having a chief of police, the chief of police of the city, or the sergeant or chief of police of the town in which the charge will be heard, or their authorized representatives.

"Director" means the Director of the Division of Forensic Science.

"Division" means the Division of Forensic Science.

"License" means any driver's license, temporary driver's license, or instruction permit authorizing the operation of a motor vehicle upon the highways.

"Ordinance" means a county, city or town ordinance.

§18.2-268.2. Implied consent to post-arrest chemical test to determine drug or alcohol content of blood.

A. Any person, whether licensed by Virginia or not, who operates a motor vehicle upon a highway, as defined in §46.2-100, in this Commonwealth shall be deemed thereby, as a condition of such operation, to have consented to have samples of his blood, breath, or both blood and breath taken for a chemical test to determine the alcohol, drug, or both alcohol and drug content of his blood, if he is arrested for violation of §18.2-266 or §18.2-266.1 or of a similar ordinance within two hours of the alleged offense.

B. Any person so arrested for a violation of §18.2-266 (i) or (ii) or both, or §18.2-266.1 or of a similar ordinance shall submit to a breath test. If the breath test is unavailable or the person is physically unable to submit to the breath test, a blood test shall be given. The accused shall, prior to administration of the test, be advised by the person administering the test that he has the right to observe the process of analysis and to see the blood alcohol reading on the equipment used to perform the breath test. If the equipment automatically produces a written printout of the breath test result, the printout, or a copy, shall be given to the accused.

C. A person, after having been arrested for a violation of §18.2-266 (iii) or (iv) or §18.2-266.1 or of a similar ordinance, may be required to submit to a blood test to determine the drug or both drug and alcohol content of his blood. When a person, after having been arrested for a violation of §18.2-266 (i) or (ii) or both, submits to a breath test in accordance with subsection B of this section or refuses to take or is incapable of taking such a breath test, he may be required to submit to tests to determine the drug or both drug and alcohol content of his blood if the law-enforcement officer has reasonable cause to believe the person was driving under the influence of any drug or combination of drugs, or the combined influence of alcohol and drugs.
(Chgd. by L.1995 ch. 23, eff. 2/23/95.)

§18.2-268.3. Refusal of tests; procedures.

A. If a person, after having been arrested for a violation of §§18.2-51.4, 18.2-266 or §18.2-266.1 or of a similar ordinance and after having been advised by the arresting officer that a person who operates a motor vehicle upon a public highway in this Commonwealth is deemed thereby, as a condition of such operation, to have consented to have samples of his blood and breath taken for chemical tests to determine the alcohol or drug content of his blood, and that the unreasonable refusal to do so constitutes grounds for the revocation of the privilege of operating a motor vehicle upon the highways of this Commonwealth, refuses to permit blood or breath or both blood and breath samples to be taken for such tests, the arresting officer shall take the person before a committing magistrate. If he again so refuses after having been further advised by the magistrate of the law requiring blood or breath samples to be taken and the penalty for refusal, and so declares again his refusal in writing upon a form provided by the Supreme Court, or refuses or fails to so declare in writing and such fact is certified as prescribed below, then no blood or breath samples shall be taken even though he may later request them.

B. The form shall contain a brief statement of the law requiring the taking of blood or breath samples and the penalty for refusal, a declaration of refusal, and lines for the signature of the person from whom the blood or breath sample is sought, the date, and the signature of a witness to the signing. If the person refuses or fails to execute the declaration, the magistrate shall certify such fact and that the magistrate advised the person that a refusal to permit a blood or breath sample to be taken, if found to be unreasonable, constitutes grounds for revocation of the person's privilege to operate a motor vehicle on the highways of this Commonwealth. The

 Zv

magistrate shall promptly issue a warrant or summons charging the person with a violation of §18.2-268.2. The warrant or summons shall be executed in the same manner as criminal warrants.

C. Venue for the trial of the warrant or summons shall lie in the court of the county or city in which the offense of driving under the influence of intoxicants is to be tried. The executed declaration of refusal or the certificate of the magistrate, as the case may be, shall be attached to the warrant and shall be forwarded by the magistrate to the aforementioned court.

D. When the court receives the declaration or certificate and the warrant or summons charging refusal, the court shall fix a date for the trial of the warrant or summons, at such time as the court designates but subsequent to the defendant's criminal trial for driving under the influence of intoxicants.

E. The declaration of refusal or certificate of the magistrate shall be prima facie evidence that the defendant refused to allow a blood or breath sample to be taken to determine the alcohol or drug content of his blood. However, this shall not prohibit the defendant from introducing on his behalf evidence of the basis for his refusal. The court shall determine the reasonableness of such refusal.

(Chgd. by L.1997 ch. 691, eff. 7/1/97.)

§18.2-268.4. Appeal and trial; sanctions for refusal.

The procedure for appeal and trial shall be the same as provided by law for misdemeanors; if requested by either party on appeal to the circuit court, trial by jury shall be as provided in Article 4 (§19.2-260 et seq.) of Chapter 15 of Title 19.2, and the Commonwealth shall be required to prove its case beyond a reasonable doubt.

If the court or jury finds the defendant guilty as charged in the warrant or summons issued pursuant to §18.2-268.3, the court shall suspend the defendant's privilege to drive for a period of one year. This suspension period is in addition to the suspension period provided under §46.2-391.2. However, if the defendant pleads guilty to a violation of §18.2-266 or §18.2-266.1 or of a similar ordinance, the court may dismiss the warrant or summons.

The court shall forward the defendant's license to the Commissioner of the Department of Motor Vehicles of Virginia as in other cases of similar nature for suspension of license. However, if the defendant appeals his conviction, the court shall return the license to him upon his appeal being perfected; however, the defendant's license shall not be returned during any period of suspension imposed under §46.2-391.2.

§18.2-268.5. Qualifications and liability of persons authorized to take blood sample; procedure for taking samples.

For the purposes of this article, only a physician, registered professional nurse, graduate laboratory technician or a technician or nurse designated by order of a circuit court acting upon the recommendation of a licensed physician, using soap and water, polyvinylpyrrolidone iodine or benzalkonium chloride to cleanse the part of the body from which the blood is taken and using instruments sterilized by the accepted steam sterilizer or some other sterilizer which will not affect the accuracy of the test, or using chemically clean sterile disposable syringes, shall withdraw blood for the purpose of determining its alcohol or drug content or both alcohol and drug content. It is a Class 3 misdemeanor to reuse single-use-only needles or syringes. No civil liability shall attach to any person authorized to withdraw blood as a result of the act of withdrawing blood as provided in this section from any person submitting thereto, provided the blood was withdrawn according to recognized medical procedures. However, the person shall not be relieved from liability for negligence in the withdrawing of any blood sample.

No person arrested for a violation of §18.2-266 or §18.2-266.1 or a similar ordinance shall be required to execute in favor of any person or corporation a waiver or release of liability in connection with the withdrawal of blood and as a condition precedent to the withdrawal of blood as provided for in this section.

§18.2-268.6. Transmission of blood samples.

Adequate portions of the blood samples withdrawn pursuant to §18.2-268.5 shall be placed in vials provided by the Division of Forensic Science. The vials shall be sealed by the person taking the sample or at his direction. The person who seals the vial shall complete the prenumbered certificate of blood withdrawal form attached to the vial by the Division. The completed withdrawal certificate for each vial shall show the name of the accused, the name of the person taking the blood sample, the date and time the blood sample was taken and information identifying the arresting or accompanying officer. The officer shall initial the completed certificate. The vials shall be divided between two containers provided by the Division, and the containers shall be sealed to prevent tampering with the vial. The arresting or accompanying officer shall take possession of the two containers as soon as the vials are placed in such containers and sealed, and shall promptly transport or mail one of the containers to the Division. Immediately after taking possession of the second container, the officer shall give to the accused a form provided by the Division which sets forth the procedure to obtain an independent analysis of the blood in the second container, and a list of the names and addresses of laboratories approved by the Division. The form shall contain a space for the accused or his counsel to direct the officer possessing the second container to forward it to an approved laboratory for analysis, if desired. If the accused directs the officer in writing on the form to forward the second container to an approved laboratory of the accused's choice, the officer shall do so.

If the accused does not direct otherwise on the form, the officer having the second container shall deliver it to the chief police officer. The chief police officer, upon receiving the container, shall retain it for a period of seventy-two hours, during which time the accused or his counsel may, in writing, on the form provided hereinabove, direct the chief police officer to mail the second container to the laboratory the accused has chosen from the approved list.

The contents of the second container shall be transmitted, tested and admitted in evidence in the same manner and in accordance with procedures established for the sample sent to the Division; however, an analysis of the second blood sample to determine the presence of a drug or drugs shall not be performed unless an analysis of the first blood sample by the Division has indicated the presence of such drug or drugs.

If the chief police officer having possession of the second container is not directed as herein provided to mail it within seventy-two hours after receiving the container, he shall destroy it.

§18.2-268.7. Transmission of blood test results; use as evidence.

Upon receipt of a blood sample forwarded to the Division for analysis pursuant to §18.2-268.6, the Division shall have it examined for its alcohol or drug or both alcohol and drug content and the Director shall execute a certificate of analysis indicating the name of the accused; the date, time and by whom the blood sample was received and examined; a statement that the seal on the vial had not been broken or otherwise tampered with; a statement that the container and vial were provided by the Division and that the vial was one to which the completed withdrawal certificate was attached; and a statement of the sample's alcohol or drug or alcohol and drug content. The Director shall remove the withdrawal certificate from the vial, attach it to the certificate of analysis and state in the certificate of analysis that it was so removed and attached. The certificate of analysis with the withdrawal certificate shall be returned to the clerk of the court in which the charge will be heard. The vial and blood sample shall be destroyed after completion of the analysis. A similar certificate of analysis, with the withdrawal certificate from the independent laboratory which analyzes the second blood sample on behalf of the accused, shall be returned to the clerk of the court in which the charge will be heard. The blood sample shall be destroyed after completion of the analysis by the independent laboratory.

When a blood sample taken in accordance with the provisions of §§18.2-268.2 through 18.2-268.6 is forwarded for analysis to the Division, a report of the test results shall be filed in that office. Upon proper identification of the certificate of withdrawal, the certificate of analysis, with the withdrawal certificate attached, shall, when attested by the Director, be admissible in any court, in any criminal or civil proceeding, as evidence of the facts therein stated and of the results of such analysis. On motion of the accused, the certificate prepared for the second sample shall be admissible in evidence when attested by the pathologist or by the supervisor of the approved laboratory.

Upon request of the person whose blood was analyzed, the test results shall be made available to him.

The Director may delegate or assign these duties to an employee of the Division of Forensic Science.

§18.2-268.8. Fees.

Payment for withdrawing blood shall not exceed twenty-five dollars, which shall be paid out of the appropriation for criminal charges. If the person whose blood sample was withdrawn is subsequently convicted for a violation of §18.2-266 or §18.2-266.1 or a similar ordinance, or is placed under the purview of a probational, educational, or rehabilitational program as set forth in §18.2-271.1, the amount charged by the person withdrawing the sample shall be taxed as part of the costs of the criminal case and shall be paid into the general fund of the state treasury.

Approved laboratories determining the alcohol content of the second blood sample shall be allowed a fee of no more than twenty-five dollars, which shall be paid out of the appropriation for criminal charges. Payment for determining the presence of a drug or drugs in the second sample may not exceed the amount established on the Division's fee schedule and shall be paid out of the appropriation for criminal charges.

If the person whose blood sample was withdrawn is subsequently convicted for violation of §18.2-266 or §18.2-266.1 or a similar ordinance, (i) the fee paid by the Commonwealth to the laboratory for testing the second blood sample and (ii) a fee of twenty-five dollars for testing the first blood sample by the Division shall be taxed as part of the costs of the criminal case and shall be paid into the general fund of the state treasury.

§18.2-268.9. Assurance of breath-test validity; use of test results as evidence.

To be capable of being considered valid as evidence in a prosecution under §18.2-266, §18.2-266.1, or a similar ordinance, chemical analysis of a person's breath shall be performed by an individual possessing a valid license to conduct such tests, with a type of equipment and in accordance with methods approved by the Department of Criminal Justice Services, Division of Forensic Science. The Division shall test the accuracy of the breath-testing equipment at least once every six months.

The Division shall establish a training program for all individuals who are to administer the breath tests. Upon a person's successful completion of the training program, the Division may license him to conduct breath-test analyses. Such license shall identify the specific types of breath-test equipment upon which the individual has successfully completed training.

Any individual conducting a breath test under the provisions of §18.2-268.2 shall issue a certificate which will indicate that the test was conducted in accordance with the Division's specifications, the equipment on which the breath test was conducted has been tested within the past six months and has been found to be accurate, the name of the accused, that prior to administration of the test the accused was advised of his right to observe the process and see the blood alcohol reading on the equipment used to perform the breath test, the date and time the sample was taken from the accused, the sample's alcohol content, and the name of the person who examined the sample. This certificate, when attested by the individual conducting the breath test, shall be admissible in any court in any criminal or civil proceeding as evidence of the facts therein stated and of the results of such analysis. Any such certificate of analysis purporting to be signed by a person authorized by the Division shall be admissible in evidence without proof of seal or signature of the person whose name is signed to it. A copy of the certificate shall be promptly delivered to the accused.

The officer making the arrest, or anyone with him at the time of the arrest, or anyone participating in the arrest of the accused, if otherwise qualified to conduct such test as provided by this section, may make the breath test or analyze the results.

(Chgd. by L.1996 chs. 154, 952; L.1997 ch. 256; L.1999 ch. 273, eff. 7/1/99.)

§18.2-268.10. Evidence of violation of §18.2-266 or of §18.2-266.1.

In any trial for a violation of §18.2-266 or §18.2-266.1 or a similar ordinance, the admission of the blood or breath test results shall not limit the introduction of any other relevant evidence bearing upon any question at issue before the court, and the court shall, regardless of the result of any blood or breath tests, consider other relevant admissible evidence of the condition of the accused. If the test results indicate the presence of any drug other than alcohol, the test results shall be admissible only if other competent evidence has been presented to relate the presence of the drug or drugs to the impairment of the accused's ability to drive or operate any motor vehicle, engine or train safely.

The failure of an accused to permit a blood or breath sample to be taken to determine the alcohol or drug content of his blood is not evidence and shall not be subject to comment by the Commonwealth at the trial of the case, except in rebuttal; nor shall the fact that a blood or breath test had been offered the accused be evidence or the subject of comment by the Commonwealth, except in rebuttal.

The court or jury trying the case involving a violation of clause (ii), (iii) or (iv) of §18.2-266 or §18.2-266.1 shall determine the innocence or guilt of the defendant from all the evidence concerning his condition at the time of the alleged offense.

§18.2-268.11. Substantial compliance.

The steps set forth in §§18.2-268.2 through 18.2-268.9 relating to taking, handling, identifying, and disposing of blood or breath samples are procedural and not substantive. Substantial compliance shall be sufficient. Failure to comply with any steps or portions thereof, or a variance in the results of the two blood tests shall not of itself be grounds for finding the defendant not guilty, but shall go to the weight of the evidence and shall be considered with all the evidence in the case; however, the defendant shall have the right to introduce evidence on his own behalf to show noncompliance with the aforesaid procedures or any part thereof, and that as a result his rights were prejudiced.

§18.2-268.12. Ordinances.

The governing bodies of counties, cities and towns are authorized to adopt ordinances paralleling the provisions of §§18.2-268.1 through 18.2-268.11.

§18.2-269. Presumptions from alcoholic content of blood.

A. In any prosecution for a violation of §18.2-36.1 or §18.2-266 (ii), or any similar ordinance, the amount of alcohol in the blood of the accused at the time of the alleged offense as indicated by a chemical analysis of a sample of the accused's blood or breath to determine the alcohol content of his blood in accordance with the provisions of §§18.2-268.1 through 18.2-268.12 shall give rise to the following rebuttable presumptions:

(1) If there was at that time 0.05 percent or less by weight by volume of alcohol in the accused's blood or 0.05 grams or less per 210 liters of the accused's breath, it shall be presumed that the accused was not under the influence of alcohol intoxicants at the time of the alleged offense;

(2) If there was at that time in excess of 0.05 percent but less than 0.08 percent by weight by volume of alcohol in the accused's blood or 0.05 grams but less than 0.08 grams per 210 liters of the accused's breath, such facts shall not give rise to any presumption that the accused was or was not under the influence of alcohol intoxicants at the time of the alleged offense, but such facts may be considered with other competent evidence in determining the guilt or innocence of the accused; or

(3) If there was that time 0.08 percent or more by weight by volume of alcohol in the accused's blood or 0.08 grams or more per 210 liters of the accused's breath, it shall be presumed that the accused was under the influence of alcohol intoxicants at the time of the alleged offense.

B. The provisions of this section shall not apply to and shall not affect any prosecution for a violation of §46.2-341.24.

§18.2-270. Penalty for driving while intoxicated; subsequent offense; prior conviction.

A. Except as otherwise provided herein, any person violating any provision of §18.2-266 shall be guilty of a Class 1 misdemeanor. If the person's blood alcohol level as indicated by the chemical test administered as provided in this article was at least 0.20, but not more than 0.25, he shall be confined in jail for an additional minimum, mandatory period of five days or, if the level was more than 0.25, for an additional minimum, mandatory period of ten days. The additional minimum, mandatory period of confinement shall not be suspended by the court.

B. 1. Any person convicted of a second offense committed within less than five years after a first offense under §18.2-266 shall be punishable by a fine of not less than $200 nor more than $2,500 and by confinement in jail for not less than one month nor more than one year. [Forty-eight hours] *Five days* of such confinement shall be a mandatory, minimum sentence not subject to suspension by the court.

2. Any person convicted of a second offense committed within a period of five to ten years of a first offense under §18.2-266 shall be punishable by a fine of not less than $200 nor more than $2,500 and by confinement in jail for not less than one month nor more than one year.

3. Upon conviction of a second offense within ten years of a first offense, if the person's blood alcohol level as indicated by the chemical test administered as provided in this article was at least 0.20, but not more than 0.25, he shall be confined in jail for an additional minimum, mandatory period of ten days or, if the level was more than 0.25, for an additional minimum, mandatory period of twenty days. The additional minimum, mandatory period of confinement shall not be suspended by the court.

C. Any person convicted of three or more offenses of §18.2-266 committed within a ten-year period shall be guilty of a Class 6 felony, *and the sentence shall include a mandatory, minimum sentence of confinement for ten days that shall not be subject to suspension by the court. Any person convicted of a third offense committed within five years of an offense under §18.2-266 shall be guilty of a Class 6 felony, and the sentence shall include a mandatory, minimum sentence of confinement for thirty days that shall not be subject to suspension by the court.* Upon conviction for a fourth or subsequent offense within ten years, the sentence shall include a mandatory, minimum term of imprisonment of one year, none of which may be suspended in whole or in part. Unless otherwise modified by the court, the defendant shall remain on probation and under the terms of any suspended sentence for the same period as his operator's license was suspended, not to exceed three years.

D. In addition to the penalty otherwise authorized by this section or §16.1-278.9, any person convicted of a violation of §18.2-266 committed while transporting a person seventeen years of age or younger shall be (i) fined an additional minimum of $500 and not more that $1,000 and (ii) sentenced to perform forty hours of community service in a program benefiting children or, for a subsequent offense, eighty hours of community service in such a program.

E. For the purpose of this section, an adult conviction of any person, or finding of guilty in the case of a juvenile, under the following shall be considered a prior conviction: (i) the provisions of §18.2-36.1 or the substantially similar laws of any other state or of the United States, (ii) the provisions of §§18.2-51.4, 18.2-266, former §18.1-54 (formerly §18-75), the ordinance of any county, city or town in this Commonwealth or the laws of any other state or of the United States substantially similar to the provisions of §18.2-51.4, and §§18.2-266 through 18.2-269, or (iii) the provisions of subsection A of §46.2-341.24 or the substantially similar laws of any other state or of the United States

(Chgd. by L.1997 ch. 691; L.1999 chs. 743, 945, 949, 987; L.2000 chs. 784, 956, eff. 7/1/2000, chs. 958, 980, eff. 10/1/2000, ch. 982, eff. 7/1/2000. Matter in brackets eff. only until 10/1/2000. Matter in italics eff. 10/1/2000.)

§18.2-270.1. Ignition interlock systems; penalty.

A. For purposes of this section and §18.2-270.2:

"Commission" means the Commission on VASAP.

"Department" means the Department of Motor Vehicles.

"Ignition interlock system" means a device that (i) connects a motor vehicle ignition system to an analyzer that measures a driver's blood alcohol content; (ii) prevents a motor vehicle ignition from starting if a driver's blood alcohol content exceeds 0.025 percent; and (iii) is equipped with the ability to perform a rolling retest and to electronically log the blood alcohol content during ignition, attempted ignition and rolling retest.

"Rolling retest" means a test of the vehicle operator's blood alcohol content required at random intervals during operation of the vehicle, which triggers the sounding of the horn and flashing of lights if (i) the test indicates that the operator has a blood alcohol content which exceeds 0.025 percent or (ii) the operator fails to take the test.

B. In addition to any [other] penalty provided by law for conviction of a first offense under §18.2-51.4 or §18.2-266 or a substantially similar ordinance of any county, city or town, any court of proper jurisdiction may, or, for a second or subsequent offense shall, as a condition of a restricted license *or as a condition of license restoration under subsection C of §18.2-271.1 or §46.2-391*, prohibit an offender from operating a motor vehicle that is not equipped with a functioning, certified ignition interlock system for any period of time not to exceed the period of license suspension and restriction, *not less than six months, and shall require that such a system be installed on each motor vehicle, as defined in §46.2-100, owned by or registered to the offender, in whole or in part, for such period of time*. Such condition shall be in addition to any purposes for which a restricted license may be issued pursuant to §18.2-271.1. The court may order the installation of an ignition interlock system to commence immediately upon conviction. A fee of twenty dollars to cover court and administrative costs related to the ignition interlock system shall be paid by any such offender to the clerk of the court. The court shall require the offender to install an electronic log device with the ignition interlock system on a vehicle designated by the court to measure the blood alcohol content at each attempted ignition and random rolling retest during operation of the vehicle. The offender shall be enrolled in and supervised by an alcohol safety action program pursuant to §18.2-271.1 and to conditions established by regulation under §18.2-270.2 by the Commission during the period for which the court has ordered installation of the ignition interlock system. The offender shall be further required to provide to such program, at least quarterly during the period of [license restriction] *court ordered ignition interlock installation*, a printout from such electronic log indicating the offender's blood alcohol content during such ignitions, attempted ignitions, and rolling retests, and showing attempts to circumvent or tamper with the equipment.

C. In any case in which the court requires the installation of an ignition interlock system, the court shall direct the offender not to operate any motor vehicle which is not equipped with such a system for [a specified] *the* period of time [not to exceed the period of license suspension and restriction] *that installation is ordered*. The clerk of the court shall file with the Department of Motor Vehicles a copy of the order, which shall become a part of the offender's operator's license record maintained by the Department. The Department shall issue to the offender for the installation period required by the court, a restricted license which shall appropriately set forth the restrictions required by the court under this subsection *and any other restrictions imposed upon the offender's driving privilege*, and shall also set forth any exception granted by the court under subsection F.

D. The offender shall be ordered to provide the appropriate ASAP program, within thirty days of the effective date of the order of court, proof of the installation of the ignition interlock system. The Program shall require the offender to have the system monitored and calibrated for proper operation at least every thirty days by an entity approved by the Commission under the provisions of §18.2-270.2 and to demonstrate proof thereof. The offender shall pay the cost of leasing or buying and monitoring and maintaining the ignition interlock system. Absent good cause shown, the court may revoke the offender's [restricted license] *driving privilege* for failing to (i) timely install such system or (ii) have the system properly monitored and calibrated.

E. No person shall start or attempt to start a motor vehicle equipped with an ignition interlock system for the purpose of providing an operable motor vehicle to a person who is prohibited under this section from operating a motor vehicle that is not equipped with an ignition interlock system. No person shall tamper with, or in any way attempt to circumvent the operation of, an ignition interlock system that has been installed in the motor vehicle of a person under this section. Except as authorized in subsection G, no person shall knowingly furnish a motor vehicle not equipped with a functioning ignition interlock system to any person prohibited under subsection B from operating any motor vehicle which is not equipped with such system. A violation of this subsection shall be punishable as a Class 1 misdemeanor.

F. Any person prohibited from operating a motor vehicle under subsection B may, solely in the course of his employment, operate a motor vehicle which is owned or provided by his employer without installation of an ignition interlock system, if the court expressly permits such operation as a condition of a restricted license *at the request of the employer, but such person may not operate a commercial motor vehicle as defined in §46.2-341.4*. This subsection shall not apply if such employer is an entity wholly or partially owned or controlled by the person otherwise prohibited from operating a vehicle without an ignition interlock system.

G. The Commission shall promulgate such regulations and forms as are necessary to implement the procedures outlined in this section.

(Added by L.1995 ch. 486; chgd. by L.1996 ch. 841; L.1997 ch. 691; L.1998 chs. 783, 840; L.1999 ch. 734; L.2000 chs. 958, 980, eff. 10/1/2000. Matter in brackets eff. only until 10/1/2000. Matter in italics eff. 10/1/2000.)

§18.2-270.2. Ignition interlock system; certification by Commission on VASAP; regulations; sale or lease; monitoring use; reports.

A. The Executive Director of the Commission on VASAP or his designee shall, pursuant to approval by the Commission, certify ignition interlock systems for use in this Commonwealth and adopt regulations and forms for the installation, maintenance and certification of such ignition interlock systems.

The regulations adopted shall include requirements that ignition interlock systems:

1. Do not impede the safe operation of the vehicle;
2. Minimize opportunities to be bypassed, circumvented or tampered with, and provide evidence thereof;
3. Correlate accurately with established measures of blood alcohol content and be calibrated according to the manufacturer's specifications;
4. Work accurately and reliably in an unsupervised environment;
5. Have the capability to provide an accurate written measure of blood alcohol content for each ignition, attempted ignition, and rolling retest, and record each attempt to circumvent or tamper with the equipment;
6. Minimize inconvenience to other users;
7. Be manufactured or distributed by an entity responsible for installation, user training, service, and maintenance, and meet the safety and operational requirements promulgated by the National Highway Transportation Safety Administration;
8. Operate reliably over the range of motor vehicle environments or motor vehicle manufacturing standards;
9. Be manufactured by an entity which is adequately insured against liability, in an amount established by the Commission, including product liability and installation and maintenance errors;
10. Provide for an electronic log of the driver's experience with the system with an information management system capable of electronically delivering information to the agency supervising the interlock user within twenty-four

hours of the collection of such information from the datalogger; and

11. Provide for a rolling retest of the operator's blood alcohol content.

Such regulations shall also provide for the establishment of a fund, using a percentage of fees received by the manufacturer or distributor providing ignition interlock services, to afford persons found by the court to be indigent all or part of the costs of an ignition interlock system.

The Commission shall design and adopt a warning label to be affixed to an ignition interlock system upon installation. The warning label shall state that a person tampering with, or attempting to circumvent the ignition interlock system shall be guilty of a Class 1 misdemeanor and, upon conviction, shall be subject to a fine or incarceration or both.

The Commission shall publish a list of certified ignition interlock systems and shall ensure that such systems are available throughout the Commonwealth. The local alcohol safety action program shall make the list available to eligible offenders, who shall have the responsibility and authority to choose which certified ignition interlock company will supply the offender's equipment. A manufacturer or distributor of an ignition interlock system that seeks to sell or lease the ignition interlock system to persons subject to the provisions of §18.2-270.1 shall pay the reasonable costs of obtaining the required certification, as set forth by the Commission.

B. A person may not sell or lease or offer to sell or lease an ignition interlock system to any person subject to the provisions of §18.2-270.1 unless:

1. The system has been certified by the Commission; and

2. The warning label adopted by the Commission is affixed to the system.

C. A manufacturer or distributor of an ignition interlock system shall provide such services as may be required at no cost to the Commonwealth. Such services shall include a toll free, twenty-four-hour telephone number for the users of ignition interlock systems.

(Added by L.1995 ch. 486; chgd. by L.2000 chs. 341, 362, eff. 7/1/2000.)

§18.2-271. Forfeiture of driver's license for driving while intoxicated.

A. Except as provided in §18.2-271.1, the judgment of conviction if for a first offense under §18.2-266 or for a similar offense under any county, city, or town ordinance, or for a first offense under subsection A of §46.2-341.24, shall of itself operate to deprive the person so convicted of the privilege to drive or operate any motor vehicle, engine or train in the Commonwealth for a period of one year from the date of such judgment. This suspension period shall be in addition to the suspension period provided under §46.2-391.2.

B. Any adult convicted, or any juvenile found guilty, of violating §18.2-266 or subsection A of §46.2-341.24, or any substantially similar local ordinance, or law of any other jurisdiction, two or more times in any combination within ten years shall, upon the second conviction, have his driver's license revoked as provided in subsection A of §46.2-391. This suspension period shall be in addition to the suspension period provided under §46.2-391.2. Any period of license suspension or revocation imposed pursuant to this section, in any case, shall run consecutively with any period of suspension for failure to permit a blood or breath sample to be taken as required by §§18.2-268.1 through 18.2-268.12 or §§46.2-341.26:1 through 46.2-341.26:11.

C. Any adult convicted, or any juvenile found guilty, of violating §18.2-266 or subsection A of §46.2-341.24, or any substantially similar local ordinance, or law of any other jurisdiction, three or more times in any combination within ten years shall not be eligible for participation in a program pursuant to §18.2-271.1 and shall, upon the third conviction, have his license revoked as provided in subsection B of §46.2-391. The court trying such case shall order the surrender of the person's driver's license, to be disposed of in accordance with §46.2-398, and shall notify such person that his license has been revoked indefinitely.

D. Notwithstanding any other provision of this section, the period of license revocation or suspension shall not begin to expire until the person convicted has surrendered his license to the court or to the Department of Motor Vehicles.

E. The provisions of this section shall not apply to, and shall have no effect upon, any disqualification from operating a commercial motor vehicle imposed under the provisions of the Commercial Driver's License Act (§46.2-341.1 et seq.).

(Chgd. by L.2000 chs. 956, 982, eff. 7/1/2000.)

§18.2-271.1. Probation, education and rehabilitation of person charged or convicted; person convicted under law of another state.

A. Any person convicted of a first or second offense of §18.2-266 (i), (ii), (iii) or (iv), or any ordinance of a county, city, or town similar to the provisions thereof, or provisions of subsection A of §46.2-341.24, shall be required by court order, as a condition of probation or otherwise, to enter into and successfully complete an alcohol safety action program in the judicial district in which such charge is brought or in any other judicial district upon such terms and conditions as the court may set forth. However, upon motion of a person convicted of any such offense following an assessment of the person conducted by an alcohol safety action program, the court, for good cause, may decline to order participation in such a program *if the assessment by the alcohol safety action program indicates that treatment is not appropriate for such person*. In no event shall such persons be permitted to enter any such program which is not certified as meeting minimum standards and criteria established by the Commission on the Virginia Alcohol Safety Action Program (VASAP) pursuant to subsection H of this section and to §18.2-271.2. However, any person charged with a violation of a first or second offense of §18.2-266 (i), (ii), (iii) or (iv), or any ordinance of a county, city, or town similar to the provisions thereof, or provisions of subsection A of §46.2-341.24, may, at any time prior to trial, enter into an alcohol safety action program in the judicial district in which such charge is brought or in any other judicial district.

B. The court shall require the person entering such program under the provisions of this section to pay a fee of no less than $250 but no more than $300. A reasonable portion of such fee, as may be determined by the Commission on VASAP, but not to exceed ten percent, shall be forwarded monthly to be deposited with the State Treasurer for expenditure by the Commission on VASAP, and the balance shall be held in a separate fund for local administration of driver alcohol rehabilitation programs. Upon a positive finding that the defendant is indigent, the court may reduce or waive the fee. In addition to the costs of the proceeding, fees as may reasonably be required of defendants referred for intervention under any such program may be charged.

C. Upon conviction of a violation of §18.2-266 or any ordinance of a county, city or town similar to the provisions thereof, or subsection A of §46.2-341.24, the court shall impose the sentence authorized by §18.2-270 or §46.2-341.28 and the license revocation as authorized by §18.2-271. *In addition, if the conviction was for a second offense committed within less than five years after a first such offense, the court shall order that restoration of the person's license to drive be conditioned upon the installation of an ignition interlock system on each motor vehicle, as defined in §46.2-100, owned by or registered to the person, in whole or in part, for a period of six months beginning at the end of the three year license revocation, unless such a system has already been installed for six months prior to that time pursuant to a restricted license order under subsection E of this section.* Upon a finding that a person so convicted is required to participate in the program described herein, the court shall enter the conviction on the warrant, and shall note that the person so convicted has been referred to such program. The court may then proceed to issue an order in accordance with subsection E of this section, if the court finds that the person so convicted is eligible for a restricted license. If the court finds good cause for a person not to participate in such program or subsequently that such person has violated, without good cause, any of the conditions set forth by the court in entering the program, the court shall dispose of the case as if no program had been entered, in which event the revocation provisions of §46.2-389 and subsection A of §46.2-391 shall be applicable to the conviction. The court shall, upon final disposition of the case, send a copy of its order to the Commissioner of the Department of Motor Vehicles. If such order provides for the issuance of a restricted license, the Commissioner of the Department of Motor Vehicles, upon receipt thereof, shall issue a restricted license. Appeals from any such disposition shall be allowed as provided by law. The time within which an appeal may be taken shall be calculated from the date of the final disposition of the case or any motion for rehearing, whichever is later.

D. Any person who has been convicted in another state of the violation of a law of such state substantially similar to the provisions of §18.2-266 or subsection A of §46.2-341.24, and whose privilege to operate a motor vehicle in this Commonwealth is subject to revocation under the provisions of §46.2-389 and subsection A of §46.2-391, may petition the general district court of the county or city in which he resides that he be given probation and assigned to a program as provided in subsection A of this section and that, upon entry into such program, he be issued an order in accordance with subsection E of this section. If the court finds that such person would have qualified therefor if he had been convicted in this Commonwealth of a violation of §18.2-266 or subsection A of §46.2-341.24, the court may grant the petition and may issue an order in accordance with subsection E of this section as to the period of license suspension or revocation imposed pursuant to §46.2-389 or subsection A of §46.2-391. Such order shall be conditioned upon the successful completion of a program by the petitioner. If the court subsequently finds that such person has violated any of the conditions set forth by the court, the court shall dispose of the case as if no program had been entered and shall notify the Commissioner, who shall revoke the person's license in accordance with the provisions of §46.2-389 or subsection A of §46.2-391. A copy of the order granting the petition or subsequently revoking or suspending such person's license to operate a motor vehicle shall be forthwith sent to the Commissioner of the Department of Motor Vehicles.

No period of license suspension or revocation shall be imposed pursuant to this subsection which, when considered together with any period of license suspension or revocation previously imposed for the same offense in any state, results in such person's license being suspended for a period in excess of the maximum periods specified in this subsection.

E. Except as otherwise provided herein, whenever a person enters a certified program pursuant to this section, and such person's license to operate a motor vehicle, engine or train in the Commonwealth has been suspended or revoked, the court may, in its discretion and for good cause shown, provide that such person be issued a restricted permit to operate a motor vehicle for any or all of the following purposes: (i) travel to and from his place of employment; (ii) travel to and from an alcohol rehabilitation program entered pursuant to this subsection; (iii) travel during the hours of such person's employment if the operation of a motor vehicle is a necessary incident of such employment; (iv) travel to and from school if such person is a student, upon proper written verification to the court that such person is enrolled in a continuing program of education; (v) such other medically necessary travel as the court deems necessary and proper upon written verification of need by a licensed health professional; or (vi) travel necessary to transport a minor child under the care of such person to and from school, day care, and facilities housing medical service providers. No restricted license issued pursuant to this subsection shall permit any person to operate a commercial motor vehicle as defined in the Virginia Commercial Driver's License Act (§46.2-341.1 et seq.). The court shall order the surrender of such person's license to operate a motor vehicle to be disposed of in accordance with the provisions of §46.2-398 and shall forward to the Commissioner of the Department of Motor Vehicles a copy of its order entered pursuant to this subsection, which shall specifically enumerate the restrictions imposed and contain such information regarding the person to whom such a permit is issued as is reasonably necessary to identify such person. The court shall also provide a copy of its order to the person so convicted who may operate a motor vehicle on the order until receipt from the Commissioner of the Department of Motor Vehicles of a restricted license, if the order provides for a restricted license for that time period. A copy of such order and, after receipt thereof, the restricted license shall be carried at all times while operating a motor vehicle. Any person who operates a motor vehicle in violation of any restrictions imposed pursuant to this section shall be guilty of a violation of §18.2-272. Such restricted license shall be conditioned upon enrollment within fifteen days in, and successful completion of, a program as described in subsection A of this section. No restricted license shall be issued during the first four months of a revocation imposed pursuant to subsection B of §18.2-271 or subsection A of §46.2-391 for a second offense of the type described therein committed within ten years of a first such offense. *No restricted license shall be issued during the first year of a revocation imposed pursuant to subsection B of §18.2-271 or subsection A of §46.2-391 for a second offense of the type described therein committed within five years of a first such offense.* No restricted license shall be issued during any revocation period imposed pursuant to subsection C of §18.2-271 or subsection B of §46.2-391. Notwithstanding the provisions of §46.2-411, the fee charged pursuant to §46.2-411 for reinstatement of the driver's license of any person whose privilege or license has been suspended or revoked as a result of a violation of §18.2-266, subsection A of §46.2-341.24 or of any ordinance of a county, city or town, or of any federal law or the laws of any other state similar to the provisions of §18.2-266 or subsection A of §46.2-341.24 shall be $105. Forty dollars of such reinstatement fee shall be retained by the Department of Motor Vehicles as provided in §46.2-411, forty dollars shall be transferred to the Commission on VASAP, and twenty-five dollars shall be transferred to the Commonwealth Neurotrauma Initiative Trust Fund.

F. The court shall have jurisdiction over any person entering such program under any provision of this section until such time as the case has been disposed of by either successful completion of the program, or revocation due to ineligibility or violation of a condition or conditions imposed by the court, whichever shall first occur. Revocation proceedings shall be commenced by notice to show cause why the court should not revoke the privilege afforded by this section. Such notice shall be made by first-class mail to the last known address of such person, and shall direct such person to appear before the court in response thereto on a date contained in such notice, which shall not be less than ten days from the date of mailing of the notice. Failure to appear in response to such notice shall of itself be grounds for revocation of such privilege. Notice of revocation under this subsection shall be sent forthwith to the Commissioner of the Department of Motor Vehicles.

G. The State Treasurer, the Commission on VASAP or any city or county is authorized to accept any gifts or bequests of money or property, and any grant, loan, service, payment or property from any source, including the federal government, for the purpose of driver alcohol education. Any such gifts, bequests, grants, loans or payments shall be deposited in the separate fund provided in subsection B.

H. The Commission on VASAP, or any county, city, town, or any combination thereof may establish and, if established, shall operate, in accordance with the standards and criteria required by this subsection, alcohol safety action programs in connection with highway safety. Each such program shall operate under the direction of a local independent policy board chosen in accordance with procedures approved and promulgated by the Commission on VASAP. Local sitting or retired district court judges who regularly hear or heard cases involving driving under the influence and are familiar with their local alcohol safety action programs may serve on such boards. The Commission on VASAP shall establish minimum standards and criteria for the implementation and operation of such programs and shall establish procedures to certify all such programs to ensure that they meet the minimum standards and criteria stipulated by the Commission. The Commission shall also establish criteria for the administration of such programs for public information activities, for accounting procedures, for the auditing requirements of such programs and for the allocation of funds. Funds paid to the Commonwealth hereunder shall be utilized in the discretion of the Commission on VASAP to offset the costs of state programs and local programs run in conjunction with any county, city or town and costs incurred by the Commission. The Commission shall submit an annual report as to actions taken at the close of each calendar year to the Governor and the General Assembly.

I. Notwithstanding any other provisions of this section or of §18.2-271, nothing in this section shall permit the court to suspend, reduce, limit, or otherwise modify any disqualification from operating a commercial motor vehicle imposed under the provisions of the Virginia Commercial Driver's License Act (§46.2-341.1 et seq.).

(Chgd. by L.1996 ch. 984; L.1997 chs. 472, 508; L.1998 ch. 703; L.1999 ch. 743; L.2000 ch. 958, eff. 10/1/2000, ch. 970, eff. 7/1/2000, ch. 980, eff. 10/1/2000. Matter in italics eff. 10/1/2000.)

§18.2-271.2. Commission on VASAP.

A. There is hereby established a Commission on the Virginia Alcohol Safety Action Program (VASAP) which shall be composed of three current or former members from the House Committee for Courts of Justice, to be appointed by the Speaker of the House of Delegates and two members from the Senate Committee for Courts of Justice, to be appointed by the Senate Privileges and Elections Committee; three sitting or retired judges, one each from the circuit, general district, and juvenile and domestic relations district courts, who regularly hear or heard cases involving driving under the influence and are familiar with their local alcohol safety action programs, to be appointed by the Chairman of the Committee on District Courts; two directors of local alcohol safety action programs, to be appointed by the legislative members of the Commission; one representative from the law-enforcement profession, to be appointed by the Speaker of the House and one citizen at large, to be appointed by the Senate Committee on Privileges and Elections; one representative from the Virginia Department of Motor Vehicles whose duties are substantially related to matters to be addressed by the Commission to be appointed by the Commissioner of the Department of Motor Vehicles, and one representative from the Department of Mental Health, Mental Retardation and Substance Abuse Services whose duties also substantially involve such matters, to be appointed by the Commissioner of the Department of Mental Health, Mental Retardation. and Substance Abuse Services. All Commission members, other than those members appointed from the House or Senate Committee for Courts of Justice, shall serve two-year terms. However, one-half of such members initially appointed to the Commission shall serve one-year terms and the other one-half shall serve two-year terms. Thereafter, all such appointments shall be for two years.

B. The Commission shall meet quarterly at such places as it may from time to time designate. The Commission shall be empowered to establish and assure the maintenance of minimum standards and criteria for program operations and performance, accounting, auditing, public information and administrative procedures for the various local alcohol safety action programs and shall be responsible for overseeing the administration of the statewide VASAP system. Such programs shall be certified by the Commission in accordance with procedures set forth in the Commission on VASAP Certification Manual. The Commission shall also oversee program plans, operations and performance and a system for allocating funds to cover deficits which may occur in the budgets of local programs.

C. The Commission shall appoint and employ and, at its pleasure, remove an executive director and such other persons as it may deem necessary, and determine their duties and fix their salaries or compensation.

D. The Commission shall appoint a Virginia Alcohol Safety Action Program Advisory Board to make recommendations to the Commission regarding its duties and administrative functions. The membership of such Board shall be appointed in the discretion of the Commission and include personnel from (i) local safety action programs, (ii) state or local boards of mental health and mental retardation and (iii) other community mental health services organizations. An assistant attorney general who provides counsel in matters relating to driving under the influence shall also be appointed to the Board.

E. For the performance of their duties, the Commission members shall be reimbursed for their actual expenses out of that portion of moneys paid in VASAP defendant entry fees which is forwarded to the State Virginia Alcohol Safety Action Program. In addition, per diem compensation shall be allowed for current members of the General Assembly for each day spent in performing their duties.

§18.2-271.3. *(Repealed by L.1999 ch. 734, eff. 7/1/99.)*

§18.2-272. Driving after forfeiture of license.

If any person so convicted shall, during the time for which he is deprived of his right so to do, drive or operate any motor vehicle, engine or train in this Commonwealth, he shall be guilty of a Class 1 misdemeanor. Nothing in this section or §§18.2-266, 18.2-270 or §18.2-271, shall be construed as conflicting with or repealing any ordinance or resolution of any city, town or county which restricts still further the right of such persons to drive or operate any such vehicle or conveyance.

§18.2-273. Report of conviction to Department of Motor Vehicles.

The clerk of every court of record and the judge of every court not of record shall, within thirty days after final conviction of any person in his court under the provisions of this article, report the fact thereof and the name, post-office address and street address of such person, together with the license plate number on the vehicle operated by such person to the Commissioner of the Department of Motor Vehicles who shall preserve a record thereof in his office.

ARTICLE 4
DANGEROUS USE OF FIREARMS OR OTHER WEAPONS

Section

§18.2-279. Discharging firearms or missiles within or at building or dwelling house.

If any person maliciously discharges a firearm within any building when occupied by one or more persons in such a manner as to endanger the life or lives of such person or persons, or maliciously shoots at, or maliciously throws any missile at or against any dwelling house or other building when occupied by one or more persons, whereby the life or lives of any such person or persons may be put in peril, the person so offending shall be guilty of a Class 4 felony. In the event of the death of any person, resulting from such malicious shooting or throwing, the person so offending shall be guilty of murder, the degree to be determined by the jury or the court trying the case without a jury.

If any such act be done unlawfully, but not maliciously, the person so offending shall be guilty of a Class 6 felony; and, in the event of the death of any person resulting from such unlawful shooting or throwing, the person so offending shall be guilty of involuntary manslaughter. If any person willfully discharges a firearm within or shoots at any school building whether occupied or not, he shall be guilty of a Class 4 felony.

§18.2-280. Willfully discharging firearms in public places.

A. If any person willfully discharges or causes to be discharged any firearm in any street in a city or town, or in any place of public business or place of public gathering, and such conduct results in bodily injury to another person, he shall be guilty of a Class 6 felony. If such conduct does not result in bodily injury to another person, he shall be guilty of Class 1 misdemeanor.

B. If any person willfully discharges or causes to be discharged any firearm upon any public, private or parochial elementary, middle or high school, including the buildings and grounds or upon public property within 1,000 feet of such school property, he shall be guilty of a Class 4 felony.

C. This section shall not apply to any law-enforcement officer in the performance of his official duties nor to any other person whose said willful act is otherwise justifiable or excusable at law in the protection of his life or property, or is otherwise specifically authorized by law. In addition, subsection B shall not apply to any otherwise lawful discharge while actually engaged in lawful hunting, a program or curriculum sponsored by or conducted with permission of the school or while in or on an established shooting range.

D. Nothing in this statute shall preclude the Commonwealth from electing to prosecute under any other applicable provision of law instead of this section.
(Chgd. by L.1999 ch. 996, eff. 7/1/99.)

§18.2-281. Setting spring gun or other deadly weapon.

It shall be unlawful for any person to set or fix in any manner any firearm or other deadly weapon so that it may be discharged or activated by a person coming in contact therewith or with any string, wire, spring, or any other contrivance attached thereto or designed to activate such weapon remotely. Any person violating this section shall be guilty of a Class 6 felony.

§18.2-282. Pointing, holding, or brandishing firearm or object similar in appearance; penalty.

A. It shall be unlawful for any person to point, hold or brandish any firearm, as hereinafter described, or any object similar in appearance to a firearm, whether capable of being fired or not, in such manner as to reasonably induce fear in the mind of another or hold a firearm in a public place in such manner as to reasonably induce fear in the mind of another of being shot or injured. However, this section shall not apply to any person engaged in excusable or justifiable self-defense. Persons violating the provisions of this section shall be guilty of a Class 1 misdemeanor or, if the violation occurs upon any public, private or parochial elementary, middle or high school, including buildings and grounds or upon public property within 1,000 feet of such school property, he shall be guilty of a Class 6 felony.

B. Any police officer in the performance of his duty, in making an arrest under the provisions of this section, shall not be civilly liable in damages for injuries or death resulting to the person being arrested if he had reason to believe that the person being arrested was pointing, holding, or brandishing such firearm, or object which was similar in appearance to a firearm, with intent to induce fear in the mind of another.

C. For purposes of this section, the word "firearm" shall mean any weapon in which ammunition may be used or discharged by explosion or pneumatic pressure. The word "ammunition," as used herein, shall mean a cartridge, pellet, ball, missile or projectile adapted for use in a firearm.

§18.2-283. Carrying dangerous weapon to place of religious worship.

If any person carry any gun, pistol, bowie knife, dagger or other dangerous weapon, without good and sufficient reason, to a place of worship while a meeting for religious purposes is being held at such place he shall be guilty of a Class 4 misdemeanor.

§18.2-283.1. Carrying weapon into courthouse.

It shall be unlawful for any person to possess in or transport into any courthouse in this Commonwealth any (i) gun or other weapon designed or intended to propel a missile or projectile of any kind, (ii) frame, receiver, muffler, silencer, missile, projectile or ammunition designed for use with a dangerous weapon and (iii) any other dangerous weapon, including explosives, tasers, stun weapons and those weapons specified in subsection A of §18.2-308. Any such weapon shall be subject to seizure by a law-enforcement officer. A violation of this section is punishable as a Class 1 misdemeanor, and upon the person's conviction, the weapon seized shall be forfeited to the Commonwealth and disposed of as provided in subsection A of §18.2-308.

The provisions of this section shall not apply to any police officer, sheriff, law-enforcement agent or official, game warden, conservator of the peace, magistrate, court officer, or judge while in the conduct of such person's official duties.

§18.2-284. Selling or giving toy firearms.

No person shall sell, barter, exchange, furnish, or dispose of by purchase, gift or in any other manner any toy gun, pistol, rifle or other toy firearm, if the same shall, by means of powder or other explosive, discharge blank or ball charges. Any person violating the provisions of this section shall be guilty of a Class 4 misdemeanor. Each sale of any of the articles hereinbefore specified to any person shall constitute a separate offense.

Nothing in this section shall be construed as preventing the sale of what are commonly known as cap pistols.

§18.2-285. Hunting with firearms while under influence of intoxicant or narcotic drug.

It shall be unlawful for any person to hunt with firearms in the Commonwealth of Virginia while under the influence of alcohol, or while under the influence of any narcotic drug or any other self-administered intoxicant or drug of whatsoever nature. Any person violating the provisions of this section shall be guilty of a Class 2 misdemeanor. Game wardens, sheriffs and all other law-enforcement officers shall enforce the provisions of this section.

(Chgd. by L.1999 ch. 543, eff. 7/1/99.)

§18.2-286. Shooting in or across road or in street.

If any person discharges a firearm, crossbow or bow and arrow in or across any road, or within the right-of-way thereof, or in a street of any city or town, he shall, for each offense, be guilty of a Class 4 misdemeanor.

The provisions of this section shall not apply to firing ranges or shooting matches maintained, and supervised or approved, by law-enforcement officers and military personnel in performance of their lawful duties.

§18.2-286.1. Shooting from vehicles so as to endanger persons; penalty.

Any person who, while in or on a motor vehicle, intentionally discharges a firearm so as to create the risk of injury or death to another person or thereby cause another person to have a reasonable apprehension of injury or death shall be guilty of a Class 5 felony. Nothing in this section shall apply to a law-enforcement officer in the performance of his duties.

§18.2-287. Counties may regulate carrying of loaded firearms on public highways.

The governing body of any county is hereby empowered to adopt ordinances making it unlawful for any person to carry or have in his possession while on any part of a public highway within such county a loaded firearm when such person is not authorized to hunt on the private property on both sides of the highway along which he is standing or walking; and to provide a penalty for violation of such ordinance not to exceed a fine of $100. The provisions of this section shall not apply to persons carrying loaded firearms in moving vehicles, nor to persons acting at the time in defense of persons or property.

§18.2-287.1. Transporting a loaded rifle or shotgun.

The governing body of any county or city is hereby empowered to adopt ordinances making it unlawful for any person to transport, possess or carry a loaded shotgun or loaded rifle in any vehicle on any public street, road, or highway within such locality. Any violation of such ordinance shall be punishable by a fine of not more than $100. Game wardens, sheriffs and all other law-enforcement officers shall enforce the provisions of this section. No ordinance adopted pursuant to this section shall be enforceable unless the governing body adopting such ordinance so notifies the Director of the Department of Game and Inland Fisheries by registered mail prior to May 1 of the year in which such ordinance is to take effect.

The provisions of this section shall not apply to duly authorized law enforcement officers or military personnel in the performance of their lawful duties, nor to any person who reasonably believes that a loaded rifle or shotgun is necessary for his personal safety in the course of his employment or business.

§18.2-287.2. Wearing of body armor while committing a crime; penalty.

Any person who, while committing a crime of violence as defined in §18.2-288 (2) or a felony violation of §18.2-248 or subdivisions (a) 2 or 3 of §18.2-248.1, has in his possession a firearm or knife and is wearing body armor designed to diminish the effect of the impact of a bullet or projectile shall be guilty of a Class 4 felony.

(Chgd. by L.1997 ch. 311, eff. 7/1/97.)

§18.2-287.4. Carrying loaded firearms in public areas prohibited; penalty.

It shall be unlawful for any person to carry a loaded firearm on or about his person on any public street, road, alley, sidewalk, public right-of-way, or in any public park or any other place of whatever nature that is open to the public (i) in any city with a population of 160,000 or more or (ii) in any county having an urban county executive form of government or any county or city surrounded thereby or adjacent thereto or in any county having a county manager form of government. The provisions of this section shall not apply to law-enforcement officers, licensed security guards, military personnel in the performance of their lawful duties, or any person having a valid permit to carry such firearm or to any person actually engaged in lawful hunting or lawful recreational shooting activities at an established shooting range or shooting contest. Any person violating the provisions of this section shall be guilty of a Class 1 misdemeanor.

For purposes of this section, "firearm" means any (i) semi-automatic center-fire rifle or pistol which expels a projectile by action of an explosion and is equipped at the time of the offense with a magazine which will hold more than twenty rounds of ammunition or designed by the manufacturer to accommodate a silencer or equipped with a folding stock or (ii) shotgun with a magazine which will hold more than seven rounds of the longest ammunition for which it is chambered.

Any firearm carried in violation of this section may be forfeited to the Commonwealth pursuant to the provisions of §18.2-310.

The exemptions set out in §18.2-308 shall apply, mutatis mutandis, to the provisions of this section.

ARTICLE 5
UNIFORM MACHINE GUN ACT

§18.2-288. Definitions.

When used in this article:

(1) "Machine gun" applies to any weapon which shoots or is designed to shoot automatically more than one shot, without manual reloading, by a single function of the trigger.

(2) "Crime of violence" applies to and includes any of the following crimes or an attempt to commit any of the same, namely, murder, manslaughter, kidnapping, rape, mayhem, assault with intent to maim, disable, disfigure or kill, robbery, burglary, housebreaking, breaking and entering and larceny.

(3) "Person" applies to and includes firm, partnership, association or corporation.

§18.2-289. Use of machine gun for crime of violence.

Possession or use of a machine gun in the perpetration or attempted perpetration of a crime of violence is hereby declared to be a Class 2 felony.

§18.2-290. Use of machine gun for aggressive purpose.

Unlawful possession or use of a machine gun for an offensive or aggressive purpose is hereby declared to be a Class 4 felony.

§18.2-291. What constitutes aggressive purpose.

Possession or use of a machine gun shall be presumed to be for an offensive or aggressive purpose:

(1) When the machine gun is on premises not owned or rented for bona fide permanent residence or business occupancy by the person in whose possession the machine gun may be found;

(2) When the machine gun is in the possession of, or used by, a person who has been convicted of a crime of violence in any court of record, state or federal, of the United States of America, its territories or insular possessions;

(3) When the machine gun has not been registered as required in §18.2-295; or

(4) When empty or loaded shells which have been or are susceptible of use in the machine gun are found in the immediate vicinity thereof.

§18.2-292. Presence prima facie evidence of use.

The presence of a machine gun in any room, boat or vehicle shall be prima facie evidence of the possession or use of the machine gun by each person occupying the room, boat, or vehicle where the weapon is found.

§18.2-293. What article does not apply to.

The provisions of this article shall not be applicable to:

(1) The manufacture for, and sale of, machine guns to the armed forces or law-enforcement officers of the United States or of any state or of any political subdivision thereof, or the transportation required for that purpose; and

(2) Machine guns and automatic arms issued to the national guard of Virginia by the United States or such arms used by the United States army or navy or in the hands of troops of the national guards of other states or territories of the United States passing through Virginia, or such arms as may be provided for the officers of the State Police or officers of penal institutions.

§18.2-293.1. What article does not prohibit.

Nothing contained in this article shall prohibit or interfere with:

(1) The possession of a machine gun for scientific purposes, or the possession of a machine gun not usable as a weapon and possessed as a curiosity, ornament, or keepsake; and

(2) The possession of a machine gun for a purpose manifestly not aggressive or offensive. Provided, however, that possession of such machine guns shall be subject to the provisions of §18.2-295.

§18.2-294. Manufacturer's and dealer's register; inspection of stock.

Every manufacturer or dealer shall keep a register of all machine guns manufactured or handled by him. This register shall show the model and serial number, date of manufacture, sale, loan, gift, delivery or receipt of every machine gun, the name, address, and occupation of the person to whom the machine gun was sold, loaned, given or delivered, or from whom it was received. Upon demand every manufacturer or dealer shall permit any marshal, sheriff or police officer to inspect his entire stock of machine guns, parts, and supplies therefor, and shall produce the register, herein required, for inspection. A violation of any provisions of this section shall be punishable as a Class 3 misdemeanor.

§18.2-295. Registration of machine guns.

Every machine gun in this Commonwealth shall be registered with the Department of State Police within twenty-four hours after its acquisition or, in the case of semi-automatic weapons which are converted, modified or otherwise altered to become machine guns, within twenty-four hours of the conversion, modification or alteration. Blanks for registration shall be prepared by the Superintendent of State Police, and furnished upon application. To comply with this section the application as filed shall be notarized and shall show the model and serial number of the gun, the name, address and occupation of the person in possession, and from whom and the purpose for which, the gun was acquired or altered. The Superintendent of State Police shall upon registration required in this section forthwith furnish the registrant with a certificate of registration, which shall be valid as long as the registrant remains the same. Certificates of registration shall be retained by the registrant and produced by him upon demand by any peace officer. Failure to keep or produce such certificate for inspection shall be a Class 3 misdemeanor, and any peace officer, may without warrant, seize the machine gun and apply for its confiscation as provided in §18.2-296. Upon transferring a registered machine gun, the transferor shall forthwith notify the Superintendent in writing, setting forth the date of transfer and name and address of the transferee. Failure to give the required notification shall constitute a Class 3 misdemeanor. Registration data shall not be subject to inspection by the public.

§18.2-296. Search warrants for machine guns.

Warrant to search any house or place and seize any machine gun possessed in violation of this article may issue in the same manner and under the same restrictions as provided by law for stolen property, and any court of record, upon application of the attorney for the Commonwealth, a police officer or conservator of the peace, may order any machine gun, thus or otherwise legally seized, to be confiscated and either destroyed or delivered to a peace officer of the Commonwealth or a political subdivision thereof.

§18.2-297. How article construed.

This article shall be so interpreted and construed as to effectuate its general purpose to make uniform the law of those states which enact it.

§18.2-298. Short title of article.

This article may be cited as the "Uniform Machine Gun Act."

ARTICLE 6
"SAWED-OFF" SHOTGUN AND "SAWED-OFF" RIFLE ACT

§18.2-299. Definitions.

When used in this article:

" 'Sawed-off ' shotgun" applies to any weapon, loaded or unloaded, originally designed as a shoulder weapon, utilizing a self-contained cartridge from which a number of ball shot pellets or projectiles may be fired simultaneously from a smooth or rifled bore by a single function of the firing device and which has a barrel length of less than eighteen inches for smooth bore weapons and sixteen inches for rifled weapons. Weapons of less than .225 caliber shall not be included.

" 'Sawed-off ' rifle" means a rifle of any caliber, loaded or unloaded, which expels a projectile by action of an explosion and is designed as a shoulder weapon with a barrel or barrels length of less than sixteen inches or which has been modified to an overall length of less than twenty-six inches.

"Crime of violence" applies to and includes any of the following crimes or an attempt to commit any of the same, namely, murder, manslaughter, kidnapping, rape, mayhem, assault with intent to maim, disable, disfigure or kill, robbery, burglary, housebreaking, breaking and entering and larceny.

"Person" applies to and includes firm, partnership, association or corporation.

§18.2-300. Possession or use of "sawed-off" shotgun or rifle.

A. Possession or use of a "sawed-off" shotgun or "sawed-off" rifle in the perpetration or attempted perpetration of a crime of violence is a Class 2 felony.

B. Possession or use of a "sawed-off" shotgun or "sawed-off" rifle for any other purpose, except as permitted by this article and official use by those persons permitted possession by §18.2-303, is a Class 4 felony.

§18.2-303. What article does not apply to.

The provisions of this article shall not be applicable to:

(1) The manufacture for, and sale of, "sawed-off" shotguns or "sawed-off" rifles to the armed forces or law-enforcement officers of the United States or of any state or of any political subdivision thereof or the transportation required for that purpose; and

(2) "Sawed-off" shotguns, "sawed-off" rifles and automatic arms issued to the national guard of Virginia by the United States or such arms used by the United States army or navy or in the hands of troops of the national guards of other states or territories of the United States passing through Virginia, or such arms as may be provided for the officers of the State Police or officers of penal institutions.

§18.2-303.1. What article does not prohibit.

Nothing contained in this article shall prohibit or interfere with the possession of a "sawed-off" shotgun or "sawed-off" rifle for scientific purposes, the possession of a "sawed-off" shotgun or "sawed-off" rifle possessed in compliance with federal law or the possession of a "sawed-off" shotgun or "sawed-off" rifle not usable as a firing weapon and possessed as a curiosity, ornament, or keepsake.

§18.2-304. Manufacturer's and dealer's register; inspection of stock.

Every manufacturer or dealer shall keep a register of all "sawed-off" shotguns and "sawed-off" rifles manufactured or handled by him. This register shall show the model and serial number, date of manufacture, sale, loan, gift, delivery or receipt of every "sawed-off" shotgun and "sawed-off" rifle, the name, address, and occupation of the person to whom the "sawed-off" shotgun or "sawed-off" rifle was sold, loaned, given or delivered, or from whom it was received. Upon demand every manufacturer or dealer shall permit any marshal, sheriff or police officer to inspect his entire stock of "sawed-off" shotguns and "sawed-off" rifles, and "sawed-off" shotgun or "sawed-off" rifle barrels, and shall produce the register, herein required, for inspection. A violation of any provision of this section shall be punishable as a Class 3 misdemeanor.

§18.2-306. Search warrants for "sawed-off" shotguns and rifles; confiscation and destruction.

Warrant to search any house or place and seize any "sawed-off" shotgun or "sawed-off" rifle possessed in violation of this article may issue in the same manner and under the same restrictions as provided by law for stolen property, and any court of record, upon application of the attorney for the Commonwealth, a police officer or conservator of the peace, may order any "sawed-off" shotgun or "sawed-off" rifle thus or otherwise legally seized, to be confiscated and either destroyed or delivered to a peace officer of the Commonwealth or a political subdivision thereof.

§18.2-307. Short title of article.

This article may be cited as the "Sawed-Off Shotgun and Sawed-Off Rifle Act."

ARTICLE 7
OTHER ILLEGAL WEAPONS

§18.2-308. Personal protection; carrying concealed weapons; when lawful to carry.

A. If any person carries about his person, hidden from common observation, (i) any pistol, revolver, or other weapon designed or intended to propel a missile of any kind; (ii) any dirk, bowie knife, switchblade knife, ballistic knife, razor, slingshot, spring stick, metal knucks, or blackjack; (iii) any flailing instrument consisting of two or more rigid parts connected in such a manner as to allow them to swing freely, which may be known as a nun chahka, nun chuck, nunchaku, shuriken, or fighting chain; (iv) any disc, of whatever configuration, having at least two points or pointed blades which is designed to be thrown or propelled and which may be known as a throwing star or oriental dart; or (v) any weapon of like kind as those enumerated in this subsection, he shall be guilty of a Class 1 misdemeanor. A second violation of this section or a conviction under this section subsequent to any conviction under any substantially similar ordinance of any county, city, or town shall be punishable as a Class 6 felony, and a third or subsequent such violation shall be punishable as a Class 5 felony. Any weapon used in the commission of a violation of this section shall be forfeited to the Commonwealth and may be seized by an officer as forfeited, and such as may be needed for police officers, conservators of the peace, and the Division of Forensic Science shall be devoted to that purpose, subject to any registration requirements of federal law, and the remainder shall be disposed of as provided in §18.2-310. For the purpose of this section, a weapon shall be deemed to be hidden from common observation when it is observable but is of such deceptive appearance as to disguise the weapon's true nature.

B. This section shall not apply to any person while in his own place of abode or the curtilage thereof.

Except as provided in subsection J1, this section shall not apply to:

1. Any person while in his own place of business;

2. Any police officers, including Capitol Police officers, sergeants, sheriffs, deputy sheriffs or regular game wardens appointed pursuant to Chapter 2 (§29.1-200 et seq.) of Title 29.1;

3. Any regularly enrolled member of a target shooting organization who is at, or going to or from, an established shooting range, provided that the weapons are unloaded and securely wrapped while being transported;

4. Any regularly enrolled member of a weapons collecting organization who is at, or going to or from, a bona fide weapons exhibition, provided that the weapons are unloaded and securely wrapped while being transported;

5. Any person carrying such weapons between his place of abode and a place of purchase or repair, provided the weapons are unloaded and securely wrapped while being transported;

6. Campus police officers appointed pursuant to Chapter 17 (§23-232 et seq.) of Title 23;

7. Any person actually engaged in lawful hunting, as authorized by the Board of Game and Inland Fisheries, under inclement weather conditions necessitating temporary protection of his firearm from those conditions; and

8. Any State Police officer retired from the Department of State Police, any local law-enforcement officer retired from a police department or sheriff's office within the Commonwealth and any special agent retired from the Alcoholic Beverage Control Board (i) with a service-related disability or (ii) following at least fifteen years of service with any such law-enforcement agency, board or any combination thereof, other than a person terminated for cause, provided such officer carries with him written proof of consultation with and favorable review of the need to carry a concealed handgun issued by the chief law-enforcement officer of the last such agency from which the officer retired or, in the case of special agents, issued by the Alcoholic Beverage Control Board. A copy of the proof of consultation and favorable review shall be forwarded by the chief or the Board to the Department of State Police for entry into the Virginia Criminal Information Network. The chief law-enforcement officer shall not without cause withhold such written proof if the retired law-enforcement officer otherwise meets the requirements of this section.

For purposes of applying the reciprocity provisions of subsection P, any person granted the privilege to carry a concealed handgun pursuant to this subdivision, while carrying the proof of consultation and favorable review required, shall be deemed to have been issued a concealed handgun permit.

C. This section shall also not apply to any of the following individuals while in the discharge of their official duties, or while in transit to or from such duties:

1. Carriers of the United States mail;

2. Officers or guards of any state correctional institution;

3. *(Repealed.)*

4. Conservators of the peace, except that the following conservators of the peace shall not be permitted to carry a concealed handgun without obtaining a permit as provided in subsection D hereof: (a) notaries public; (b) registrars; (c)

drivers, operators or other persons in charge of any motor vehicle carrier of passengers for hire; or (d) commissioners in chancery;

5. Noncustodial employees of the Department of Corrections designated to carry weapons by the Director of the Department of Corrections pursuant to §53.1-29;

6. Law-enforcement agents of the Armed Forces of the United States and federal agents who are otherwise authorized to carry weapons by federal law while engaged in the performance of their duties;

7. Law-enforcement agents of the United States Naval Criminal Investigative Service; and

8. Harbormaster of the City of Hopewell.

D. Any person twenty-one years of age or older may apply in writing to the clerk of the circuit court of the county or city in which he resides for a five-year permit to carry a concealed handgun. Notwithstanding §15.2-915, a county or city may enact an ordinance which requires any applicant for a concealed handgun permit to submit to fingerprinting for the purpose of obtaining the applicant's state or national criminal history record. The application shall be made under oath before a notary or other person qualified to take oaths and shall be made only on a form prescribed by the Department of State Police, in consultation with the Supreme Court, requiring only that information necessary to determine eligibility for the permit. The court shall consult with the law-enforcement authorities of the county or city and receive a report from the Central Criminal Records Exchange. As a condition for issuance of a concealed handgun permit, the applicant shall submit to fingerprinting if required by local ordinance in the county or city where the applicant resides and provide personal descriptive information to be forwarded with the fingerprints through the Central Criminal Records Exchange to the Federal Bureau of Investigation for the purpose of obtaining criminal history record information regarding the applicant, and obtaining fingerprint identification information from federal records pursuant to criminal investigations by state and local law-enforcement agencies. Upon completion of the criminal history records check, the State Police shall return the fingerprint cards to the submitting local agency. The local agency shall then promptly notify the person that he has twenty-one days from the date of the notice to request return of the fingerprint cards. All fingerprint cards not claimed by the applicant within twenty-one days of notification by the local agency shall be destroyed. Fingerprints taken for the purposes described in this section shall not be copied, held or used for any other purposes. The court shall issue the permit within forty-five days of receipt of the completed application unless it is determined that the applicant is disqualified. An application is deemed complete when all information required to be furnished by the applicant is delivered to the clerk of court. If the applicant is later found by the court to be disqualified, the permit shall be revoked.

E. The following persons shall be deemed disqualified from obtaining a permit:

1. An individual who is ineligible to possess a firearm pursuant to §§18.2-308.1:1, 18.2-308.1:2 or §18.2-308.1:3 or the substantially similar law of any other state or of the United States.

2. An individual who was ineligible to possess a firearm pursuant to §18.2-308.1:1 and who was discharged from the custody of the Commissioner pursuant to §19.2-182.7 less than five years before the date of his application for a concealed handgun permit.

3. An individual who was ineligible to possess a firearm pursuant to §18.2-308.1:2 and whose competency or capacity was restored pursuant to former §37.1-134.1 or §37.1-134.16 less than five years before the date of his application for a concealed handgun permit.

4. An individual who was ineligible to possess a firearm under §18.2-308.1:3 and who was released from commitment less than five years before the date of this application for a concealed handgun permit.

5. An individual who is subject to a restraining order, or to a protective order and prohibited by §18.2-308.1:4 from purchasing or transporting a firearm.

6. An individual who is prohibited by §18.2-308.2 from possessing or transporting a firearm, except that a permit may be obtained in accordance with subsection C of that section.

7. An individual who has been convicted of two or more misdemeanors within the five-year period immediately preceding the application, if one of the misdemeanors was a Class 1 misdemeanor, but the judge shall have the discretion to deny a permit for two or more misdemeanors that are not Class 1. Traffic infractions or reckless driving shall not be considered for purposes of this disqualification.

8. An individual who is addicted to, or is an unlawful user or distributor of, marijuana or any controlled substance.

9. An individual who has been convicted of a violation of §18.2-266 or a substantially similar local ordinance or of public drunkenness within the three-year period immediately preceding the application, or who is a habitual drunkard as determined pursuant to §4.1-333.

10. An alien other than an alien lawfully admitted for permanent residence in the United States.

11. An individual who has been discharged from the Armed Forces of the United States under dishonorable conditions.

12. An individual who is a fugitive from justice.

13. An individual who it is alleged, in a sworn written statement submitted to the court by the sheriff, chief of police or attorney for the Commonwealth in the opinion of such sheriff, chief of police or attorney for the Commonwealth, is likely to use a weapon unlawfully or negligently to endanger others. The statement of the sheriff, chief of police or the attorney for the Commonwealth shall be based upon personal knowledge or upon the sworn written statement of a competent person having personal knowledge.

14. An individual who has been convicted of any assault, assault and battery, sexual battery, discharging of a firearm in violation of §18.2-280 or §18.2-286.1 or brandishing of a firearm in violation of §18.2-282 within the three-year period immediately preceding the application.

15. An individual who has been convicted of stalking.

16. An individual whose previous convictions or adjudications of delinquency were based on an offense which would have been at the time of conviction a felony if committed by an adult under the laws of any state, the District of Columbia, the United States or its territories. For purposes of this disqualifier, only convictions occurring within sixteen years following the later of the date of (i) the conviction or adjudication or (ii) release from any incarceration imposed upon such conviction or adjudication shall be deemed to be "previous convictions."

17. An individual who has a felony charge pending or a charge pending for an offense listed in subdivision 14 or 15.

18. An individual who has received mental health treatment or substance abuse treatment in a residential setting within five years prior to the date of his application for a concealed handgun permit.

19. An individual not otherwise ineligible pursuant to this section, who, within the three-year period immediately preceding the application for the permit, was found guilty of any criminal offense set forth in Article 1 (§18.2-247 et seq.) of Chapter 7 of Title 18.2 or of a criminal offense of illegal

possession or distribution of marijuana or any controlled substance, under the laws of any state, the District of Columbia, or the United States or its territories.

20. An individual, not otherwise ineligible pursuant to this section, with respect to whom, within the three-year period immediately preceding the application, upon a charge of any criminal offense set forth in Article 1 (§18.2-247 et seq.) of Chapter 7 of Title 18.2 or upon a charge of illegal possession or distribution of marijuana or any controlled substance under the laws of any state, the District of Columbia, or the United States or its territories, the trial court found that the facts of the case were sufficient for a finding of guilt and disposed of the case pursuant to §18.2-251 or the substantially similar law of any other state, the District of Columbia, or the United States or its territories.

F. The making of a materially false statement in an application under this section shall constitute perjury, punishable as provided in §18.2-434.

G. The court may further require proof that the applicant has demonstrated competence with a handgun and the applicant may demonstrate such competence by one of the following:

1. Completing any hunter education or hunter safety course approved by the Department of Game and Inland Fisheries or a similar agency of another state;

2. Completing any National Rifle Association firearms safety or training course;

3. Completing any firearms safety or training course or class available to the general public offered by a law-enforcement agency, junior college, college, or private or public institution or organization or firearms training school utilizing instructors certified by the National Rifle Association or the Department of Criminal Justice Services;

4. Completing any law-enforcement firearms safety or training course or class offered for security guards, investigators, special deputies, or any division or subdivision of law enforcement or security enforcement;

5. Presenting evidence of equivalent experience with a firearm through participation in organized shooting competition or current military service or proof of an honorable discharge from any branch of the armed services;

6. Obtaining or previously having held a license to carry a firearm in this Commonwealth or a locality thereof, unless such license has been revoked for cause;

7. Completing any firearms training or safety course or class conducted by a state-certified or National Rifle Association-certified firearms instructor; or

8. Completing any other firearms training which the court deems adequate.

A photocopy of a certificate of completion of any of the courses or classes; an affidavit from the instructor, school, club, organization, or group that conducted or taught such course or class attesting to the completion of the course or class by the applicant; or a copy of any document which shows completion of the course or class or evidences participation in firearms competition shall constitute evidence of qualification under this subsection.

H. The permit to carry a concealed handgun shall specify only the following information: name, address, date of birth, gender, height, weight, color of hair, color of eyes, and signature of the permittee; the signature of the judge issuing the permit, or of the clerk of court who has been authorized to sign such permits by the issuing judge; the date of issuance; and the expiration date. The person issued the permit shall have such permit on his person at all times during which he is carrying a concealed handgun and must display the permit and a photo-identification issued by a government agency of the Commonwealth or by the United States Department of Defense or United States State Department (passport) upon demand by a law-enforcement officer.

I. Persons who previously have held a concealed handgun permit shall be issued, upon application as provided in subsection D, a new five-year permit unless there is good cause shown for refusing to reissue a permit. If the circuit court denies the permit, the specific reasons for the denial shall be stated in the order of the court denying the permit. Upon denial of the application, the clerk shall provide the person with notice, in writing, of his right to an ore tenus hearing. Upon request of the applicant made within twenty-one days, the court shall place the matter on the docket for an ore tenus hearing. The applicant may be represented by counsel, but counsel shall not be appointed, and the rules of evidence shall apply. The final order of the court shall include the court's findings of fact and conclusions of law.

J. Any person convicted of an offense that would disqualify that person from obtaining a permit under subsection E or who violates subsection F shall forfeit his permit for a concealed handgun to the court. Upon receipt by the Central Criminal Records Exchange of a record of the arrest, conviction or occurrence of any other event which would disqualify a person from obtaining a concealed handgun permit under subsection E, the Central Criminal Records Exchange shall notify the court having issued the permit of such disqualifying arrest, conviction or other event.

J1. Any person permitted to carry a concealed handgun, who is under the influence of alcohol or illegal drugs while carrying such handgun in a public place, shall be guilty of a Class 1 misdemeanor. Conviction of any of the following offenses shall be prima facie evidence, subject to rebuttal, that the person is "under the influence" for purposes of this section: manslaughter in violation of §18.2-36.1, maiming in violation of §18.2-51.4, driving while intoxicated in violation of §18.2-266, public intoxication in violation of §18.2-388, or driving while intoxicated in violation of §46.2-341.24. Upon such conviction that court shall revoke the person's permit for a concealed handgun and promptly notify the issuing circuit court. A person convicted of a violation of this subsection shall be ineligible to apply for a concealed handgun permit for a period of five years.

J2. An individual who has a felony charge pending or a charge pending for an offense listed in subdivision E 14 or E 15, holding a permit for a concealed handgun, may have the permit suspended by the court before which such charge is pending or by the court which issued the permit.

J3. No person shall carry a concealed handgun onto the premises of any restaurant or club as defined in §4.1-100 for which a license to sell and serve alcoholic beverages for on-premises consumption has been granted by the Virginia Alcoholic Beverage Control Board under Title 4.1 of the Code of Virginia; however, nothing herein shall prohibit any sworn law-enforcement officer from carrying a concealed handgun on the premises of such restaurant or club or any owner or event sponsor or his employees from carrying a concealed handgun while on duty at such restaurant or club if such person has a concealed handgun permit.

J4. Any individual for whom it would be unlawful to purchase, possess or transport a firearm under §18.2-308.1:2 or §18.2-308.1:3, who holds a concealed handgun permit, may have the permit suspended by the court which issued the permit during the period of incompetency, incapacity or disability.

K. No fee shall be charged for the issuance of such permit to a person who has retired from service (i) as a magistrate in the Commonwealth; (ii) as a law-enforcement officer with the Department of State Police or with a sheriff or police department, bureau or force of any political subdivision of the Commonwealth of Virginia, after completing twenty years' service or after reaching age fifty-five; or (iii) to any person who has retired after completing twenty years' service or after reaching age fifty-five from service as a law-enforcement officer with the United States Federal Bureau of Investigation, Bureau of Alcohol, Tobacco and Firearms, Secret Service Agency, Drug Enforcement Administration, Immigration and Naturalization Service, Customs Service, Department of State Diplomatic Security Service or Naval Criminal Investigative Service. The clerk shall charge a fee of ten dollars for the processing of an application or issuing of a permit, including his costs associated with the consultation with law-enforcement agencies. The local law-enforcement agency conducting the background investigation may charge a fee not to exceed thirty-five dollars to cover the cost of conducting an investigation pursuant to this section. The thirty-five-dollar fee shall include any amount assessed by the Federal Bureau of Investigation for providing criminal history record information, and the local law-enforcement agency shall forward the amount assessed by the Federal Bureau of Investigation to the State Police with the fingerprints taken from the applicant. The State Police may charge a fee not to exceed five dollars to cover their costs associated with processing the application. The total amount assessed for processing an application for a permit shall not exceed fifty dollars, with such fees to be paid in one sum to the person who accepts the application. Payment may be made by any method accepted by that court for payment of other fees or penalties. No payment shall be required until the application is accepted by the court as a complete application. The order issuing such permit shall be provided to the State Police and the law-enforcement agencies of the county or city. The State Police shall enter the permittee's name and description in the Virginia Criminal Information Network so that the permit's existence and current status will be made known to law-enforcement personnel accessing the Network for investigative purposes.

L. Any person denied a permit to carry a concealed handgun under the provisions of this section may present a petition for review to the Court of Appeals. The petition for review shall be filed within sixty days of the expiration of the time for requesting an ore tenus hearing pursuant to subsection I, or if an ore tenus hearing is requested, within sixty days of the entry of the final order of the circuit court following the hearing. The petition shall be accompanied by a copy of the original papers filed in the circuit court, including a copy of the order of the circuit court denying the permit. Subject to the provisions of §17.1-410 B, the decision of the Court of Appeals or judge shall be final. Notwithstanding any other provision of law, if the decision to deny the permit is reversed upon appeal, taxable costs incurred by the person shall be paid by the Commonwealth.

M. For purposes of this section:

"Handgun" means any pistol or revolver or other firearm, except a machine gun, originally designed, made and intended to fire a projectile by means of an explosion from one or more barrels when held in one hand.

"Lawfully admitted for permanent residence" means the status of having been lawfully accorded the privilege of residing permanently in the United States as an immigrant in accordance with the immigration laws, such status not having changed.

N. As used in this article:

"Spring stick" means a spring-loaded metal stick activated by pushing a button which rapidly and forcefully telescopes the weapon to several times its original length.

"Ballistic knife" means any knife with a detachable blade that is propelled by a spring-operated mechanism.

O. The granting of a concealed handgun permit shall not thereby authorize the possession of any handgun or other weapon on property or in places where such possession is otherwise prohibited by law or is prohibited by the owner of private property.

P. A valid concealed handgun permit or license issued by another state shall be valid in the Commonwealth, provided (i) the issuing authority provides the means for instantaneous verification of the validity of all such permits or licenses issued within that state, accessible twenty-four hours a day, (ii) the requirements and qualifications of that state's law are substantially similar to or exceed the provisions of this section, and (iii) a state meeting the requirements and qualifications of this section grants the same privilege to residents of the Commonwealth who have valid concealed handgun permits in their possession while carrying concealed weapons in that state. The Superintendent of State Police shall (a) in consultation with the Office of the Attorney General determine which states meet the requirements and qualifications of this section, (b) maintain a registry of such states on the Virginia Criminal Information Network (VCIN), and (c) make the registry available to law-enforcement officers for investigative purposes.

Q. The provisions of this statute or the application thereof to any person or circumstances which are held invalid shall not affect the validity of other provisions or applications of this statute which can be given effect without the invalid provisions or applications. This subsection is to reiterate §1-17.1 and is not meant to add to or delete from that provision.

(Chgd. by L.1995 ch. 829; L.1997 chs. 916, 921, 922; L.1998 chs. 662, 670, 846, 847; L.1999 chs. 628, 666, 679, eff. 7/1/99.)

§18.2-308.1. Possession of firearm, stun weapon, or other weapon on school property prohibited.

A. If any person possesses any (i) stun weapon or taser as defined in this section, (ii) knife having a metal blade of three inches or longer, or (iii) weapon, other than a firearm, designated in subsection A of §18.2-308 upon (i) the property of any public, private or parochial elementary, middle or high school, including buildings and grounds, (ii) that portion of any property open to the public used for school-sponsored functions or extracurricular activities while such functions or activities are taking place, or (iii) any school bus owned or operated by any such school, he shall be guilty of a Class 1 misdemeanor.

B. If any person possesses any firearm designed or intended to propel a missile of any kind while such person is upon (i) any public, private or parochial elementary, middle or high school, including buildings and grounds, (ii) that portion of any property open to the public used for school-sponsored functions or extracurricular activities while such functions or activities are taking place, or (iii) any school bus owned or operated by any such school, he shall be guilty of a Class 6 felony; however, if the person possesses any firearm within a public, private or parochial elementary, middle or high school building and intends to use, or attempts to use, such firearm, or displays such weapon in a threatening manner, such person shall not be eligible for probation and shall be sentenced to a minimum, mandatory term of imprisonment of five years, which shall not be suspended in whole or in part and which shall be served consecutively with any other sentence.

The exemptions set out in §18.2-308 shall apply, mutatis mutandis, to the provisions of this section. The provisions of this section shall not apply to (i) persons who possess such weapon or weapons as a part of the school's curriculum or activities, (ii) a person possessing a knife customarily used for food preparation or service and using it for such purpose, (iii) persons who possess such weapon or weapons as a part of any program sponsored or facilitated by either the school or any organization authorized by the school to conduct its programs either on or off the school premises, (iv) any law-enforcement officer while engaged in his duties as such, (v) any person who possesses a knife or blade which he uses customarily in his trade, or (vi) a person who possesses an unloaded firearm which is in a closed container, or a knife having a metal blade, in or upon a motor vehicle, or an unloaded shotgun or rifle in a firearms rack in or upon a motor vehicle. For the purposes of this paragraph, "weapon" includes a knife having a metal blade of three inches or longer.

As used in this section:

"Stun weapon" means any mechanism that is (i) designed to emit an electronic, magnetic, or other type of charge that exceeds the equivalency of a five milliamp sixty hertz shock and (ii) used for the purpose of temporarily incapacitating a person; and

"Taser" means any mechanism that is (i) designed to emit an electronic, magnetic, or other type of charge or shock through the use of a projectile and (ii) used for the purpose of temporarily incapacitating a person.

(Chgd. by L.1995 ch. 511; L.1999 chs. 587, 829, 846, eff. 7/1/99.)

§18.2-308.1:1. Possession or transportation of firearms by persons acquitted by reason of insanity; penalty; permit.

A. It shall be unlawful for any person acquitted by reason of insanity and committed to the custody of the Commissioner of Mental Health, Mental Retardation and Substance Abuse Services, pursuant to §19.2-181, on a charge of treason, any felony or any offense punishable as a misdemeanor under Title 54.1 or a Class 1 or Class 2 misdemeanor under Title 18.2, except those misdemeanor violations of (i) Article 2 (§18.2-266 et seq.) Chapter 7 of Title 18.2, (ii) Article 2 (§18.2-415 et seq.) of Chapter 9 of Title 18.2, or (iii) §18.2-119, or (iv) an ordinance of any county, city, or town similar to the offenses specified in (i), (ii), or (iii), to knowingly and intentionally possess or transport any firearm. A violation of this section shall be punishable as a Class 1 misdemeanor.

B. Any person so acquitted may, upon discharge from the custody to the Commissioner, petition the circuit court in which he resides for a permit to possess or carry a firearm. The court may, in its discretion and for good cause shown, grant the petition and issue a permit, in which event the provisions of subsection A do not apply.

§18.2-308.1:2. Purchase, possession or transportation of firearm by persons adjudicated legally incompetent or mentally incapacitated; penalty.

A. It shall be unlawful for any person who has been adjudicated (i) legally incompetent pursuant to former §37.1-128.02 or former §37.1-134, (ii) mentally incapacitated pursuant to former §37.1-128.1 or former §37.1-132 or (iii) incapacitated pursuant to Article 1.1 (§37.1-134.6 et seq.) of Chapter 4 of Title 37.1 and whose competency or capacity has not been restored pursuant to former §37.1-134.1 or §37.1-134.16, to purchase, possess, or transport any firearm. A violation of this subsection shall be punishable as a Class 1 misdemeanor.

B. Any firearm possessed or transported in violation of this section shall be forfeited to the Commonwealth and disposed of as provided in §18.2-310.

(Chgd. by L.1997 ch. 921, eff. 1/1/98.)

§18.2-308.1:3. Purchase, possession or transportation of firearm by persons involuntarily committed; penalty.

A. It shall be unlawful for any person involuntarily committed pursuant to §37.1-67.3 to purchase, possess or transport a firearm during the period of such person's commitment. A violation of this subsection shall be punishable as a Class 1 misdemeanor.

B. Any firearm possessed or transported in violation of this section shall be forfeited to the Commonwealth and disposed of as provided in §18.2-310.

C. Any person prohibited from purchasing, possessing or transporting firearms under this subsection may, at any time following his release from commitment, petition the circuit court in the city or county in which he resides to restore his right to purchase, possess or transport a firearm. The court may, in its discretion and for good cause shown, grant the petition. The clerk shall certify and forward forthwith to the Central Criminal Records Exchange, on a form provided by the Exchange, a copy of any such order.

§18.2-308.1:4. Purchase or transportation of firearm by persons subject to protective orders; penalty.

A. It shall be unlawful for any person who is subject to (i) a protective order entered pursuant to §§16.1-253, 16.1-253.1, 16.1-253.4, 16.1-279.1, 19.2-152.8, 19.2-152.9, or §19.2-152.10; (ii) an order issued pursuant to subsection b of §20-103; or (iii) an order entered pursuant to subsection E of §18.2-60.3 to purchase or transport any firearm while the order is in effect. A violation of this subsection shall be punishable as a Class 1 misdemeanor.

B. Any firearm purchased or transported in violation of this section shall be forfeited to the Commonwealth and disposed of as provided in §18.2-310.

(Chgd. by L.1996 ch. 866; L.1998 ch. 569, eff. 7/1/98.)

§18.2-308.1:5. Purchase or transportation of firearm by persons convicted of certain drug offenses prohibited.

Any person who, within a thirty-six consecutive month period, has been convicted of two misdemeanor offenses under §18.2-250 or §18.2-250.1 shall be ineligible to purchase or transport a handgun. However, upon expiration of a period of five years from the date of the second conviction and provided the person has not been convicted of any such offense within that period, the ineligibility shall be removed.

(Added by L.1995 ch. 577, eff. 7/1/95.)

§18.2-308.2. Possession or transportation of firearms or concealed weapons by convicted felons; penalties; petition for permit; when issued.

A. It shall be unlawful for (i) any person who has been convicted of a felony or (ii) any person under the age of twenty-nine who was found guilty as a juvenile fourteen years of age or older at the time of the offense of a delinquent act which would be a felony if committed by an adult, whether such conviction or adjudication occurred under the laws of this Commonwealth, or any other state, the District of Columbia, the United States or any territory thereof, to knowingly and intentionally possess or transport any firearm or to knowingly and intentionally carry about his person, hidden from common observation, any weapon described in §18.2-308 A. Any person who violates this section shall be guilty of a Class 6 felony. However, any person who violates this section by knowingly and intentionally possessing or transporting any firearm and who was previously convicted of a violent felony as defined in §17.1-805 shall not be eligible for probation, and shall be sentenced to a minimum, mandatory term of imprisonment of five years. Any person who violates this section by knowingly and intentionally possessing or transporting any firearm and who was previously convicted of any other felony shall not be eligible for probation, and shall be sentenced to a minimum, mandatory term of imprisonment of two years. The minimum, mandatory terms of imprisonment prescribed for violations of this section shall not be suspended in whole or in part and shall be served consecutively with any other sentence. Any firearm or any concealed weapon possessed, transported or carried in violation of this section shall be forfeited to the Commonwealth and disposed of as provided in §18.2-310.

B. The prohibitions of subsection A shall not apply to (i) any person who possesses a firearm or other weapon while carrying out his duties as a member of the armed forces of the United States or of the National Guard of Virginia or of any other state, (ii) any law-enforcement officer in the performance of his duties, or (iii) any person who has been pardoned or whose political disabilities have been removed pursuant to Article V, Section 12 of the Constitution of Virginia provided the Governor, in the document granting the pardon or removing the person's political disabilities, may expressly place conditions upon the reinstatement of the person's right to ship, transport, possess or receive firearms.

C. Any person prohibited from possessing, transporting or carrying a firearm under subsection A, may petition the circuit court of the jurisdiction in which he resides for a permit to possess or carry a firearm; however, no person who has been convicted of a felony shall be qualified to petition for such a permit unless his civil rights have been restored by the Governor or other appropriate authority. The court may, in its discretion and for good cause shown, grant such petition and issue a permit. The provisions of this section shall not apply to any person who has been granted a permit pursuant to this subsection.

(Chgd. by L.1998 ch. 810; L.1999 chs. 829, 846, eff. 7/1/99.)

§18.2-308.2:01. Possession or transportation of certain firearms by aliens.

It shall be unlawful for any person who is not a citizen of the United States or who is not a person lawfully admitted for permanent residence to knowingly and intentionally possess or transport any assault firearm or to knowingly and intentionally carry about his person, hidden from common observation, an assault firearm. A violation of this section shall be punishable as a Class 6 felony. Any firearm possessed, transported or carried in violation of this section shall be forfeited to the Commonwealth and disposed of as provided in §18.2-310.

For purposes of this section "assault firearm" means any semi-automatic center-fire rifle or pistol which expels a projectile by action of an explosion and is equipped at the time of the offense with a magazine which will hold more than twenty rounds of ammunition or designed by the manufacturer to accommodate a silencer or equipped with a folding stock.

§18.2-308.2:1. Prohibiting the selling, etc., of firearms to certain felons.

Any person who sells, barters, gives or furnishes, or has in his possession or under his control with the intent of selling, bartering, giving or furnishing, any firearm to any person he knows is prohibited from possessing or transporting a firearm pursuant to §§18.2-308.1:1, 18.2-308.2 or §18.2-308.7 shall be guilty of a Class 6 felony. However, this prohibition shall not be applicable when the person convicted of the felony, adjudicated delinquent or acquitted by reason of insanity has (i) been issued a permit pursuant to §18.2-308.2 C or §18.2-308.1:1 B, (ii) been pardoned or had his political disabilities removed in accordance with §18.2-308.2 B or (iii) obtained a permit to ship, transport, possess or receive firearms pursuant to the laws of the United States. Any firearm sold, bartered, given or furnished or possessed or controlled with intent to do so in violation of this section shall be forfeited to the Commonwealth and disposed of as provided in §18.2-310.

§18.2-308.2:2. Criminal history record information check required for the transfer of certain firearms; firearm safety information to be provided.

A. Any person purchasing from a dealer a firearm as herein defined shall consent in writing, on a form to be provided by the Department of State Police, to have the dealer obtain criminal history record information. Such form shall include only, in addition to the information required by subdivision B 1, the identical information required to be included on the firearms transaction record required by regulations administered by the Bureau of Alcohol, Tobacco and Firearms of the U.S. Department of the Treasury, except that the copies of such forms mailed or delivered to the Department of State Police shall not include any information related to the firearm purchased or transferred.

B. 1. No dealer shall sell, rent, trade or transfer from his inventory any such firearm to any other person who is a resident of Virginia until he has (i) obtained written consent as specified in subsection A, and provided the Department of State Police with the name, birth date, gender, race, and social security and/or any other identification number and the number of firearms by category intended to be sold, rented, traded or transferred and (ii) requested criminal history record information by a telephone call to the State Police and is authorized by subdivision B 2 of this section to complete the sale or other such transfer. To establish personal identification and residence in Virginia for purposes of this section, a dealer must require any prospective purchaser to present one photo-identification form issued by a governmental agency of the Commonwealth or by the United States Department of Defense, and other documentation of residence. Except where the photo-identification was issued by the United States Department of Defense, the other documentation of residence shall show an address identical to that shown on the photo-identification form, such as evidence of currently paid personal property tax or real estate tax, or a current (i) lease, (ii) utility or telephone bill, (iii) voter registration card, (iv) bank check, (v) passport, (vi) automobile registration, or (vii) hunting or fishing license; other current identification allowed as evidence of residency by Part 178.124 of Title 27 of the Code of Federal Regulations and ATF Ruling 79–7; or other documentation of residence determined to be acceptable by the Department of Criminal Justice Services, that corroborates that the prospective purchaser currently resides in Virginia. Where the photo-identification was issued by the Department of Defense, permanent orders may be used as documentation of residence. Additionally, when the photo-identification presented to a dealer by the prospective purchaser is a driver's license or other photo-identification issued by the Department of Motor Vehicles, and such identification form contains a date of issue, the dealer shall not, except for a renewed driver's license or other photo-identification issued by the Department of Motor Vehicles, sell or otherwise transfer a firearm to the prospective purchaser until thirty days after the date of issue of an original or duplicate driver's license unless the prospective purchaser also presents a copy of his Virginia Department of Motor Vehicles driver's record showing that the original date of issue of the driver's license was more than thirty days prior to the attempted purchase.

In addition, no dealer shall sell, rent, trade or transfer from his inventory any assault firearm to any person who is not a citizen of the United States or who is not a person lawfully admitted for permanent residence. To establish citizenship or lawful admission for a permanent residence for purposes of purchasing an assault firearm, a dealer shall require a prospective purchaser to present a certified birth certificate or a certificate of birth abroad issued by the United States State Department, a certificate of citizenship or a certificate of naturalization issued by the Immigration and Naturalization Service, an unexpired U.S. passport, a United States citizen identification card, a current voter registration card, a current selective service registration card, or an immigrant visa or other documentation of status as a person lawfully admitted for permanent residence issued by the Immigration and Naturalization Service.

Upon receipt of the request for a criminal history record information check, the State Police shall (i) review its criminal history record information to determine if the buyer or transferee is prohibited from possessing or transporting a firearm by state or federal law, (ii) inform the dealer if its record indicates that the buyer or transferee is so prohibited, and (iii) provide the dealer with a unique reference number for that inquiry.

2. The State Police shall provide its response to the requesting dealer during the dealer's call, or by return call without delay. If the criminal history record information check indicates the prospective purchaser or transferee has a criminal record or has been acquitted by reason of insanity and committed to the custody of the Commissioner of Mental Health, Mental Retardation and Substance Abuse Services, the State Police shall have until the end of the dealer's next business day to advise the dealer if its records indicate the buyer or transferee is prohibited from possessing or transporting a firearm by state or federal law. If not so advised by the end of the dealer's next business day, a dealer who has fulfilled the requirements of subdivision B 1 of this subsection may immediately complete the sale or transfer and shall not be deemed in violation of this section with respect to such sale or transfer. In case of electronic failure or other circumstances beyond the control of the State Police, the dealer shall be advised immediately of the reason for such delay and be given an estimate of the length of such delay. After such notification, the State Police shall, as soon as possible but in no event later than the end of the dealer's next business day, inform the requesting dealer if its records indicate the buyer or transferee is prohibited from possessing or transporting a firearm by state or federal law. A dealer who fulfills the requirements of subdivision B 1 of this subsection and is told by the State Police that a response will not be available by the end of the dealer's next business day may immediately complete the sale or transfer and shall not be deemed in violation of this section with respect to such sale or transfer.

3. Except as required by subsection D of §9-192, the State Police shall not maintain records longer than thirty days, except for multiple handgun transactions for which records shall be maintained for twelve months, from any dealer's request for a criminal history record information check pertaining to a buyer or transferee who is not found to be prohibited from possessing and transporting a firearm under state or federal law. However, the log on requests made may be maintained for a period of twelve months, and such log shall consist of the name of the purchaser, the dealer identification number, the unique approval number and the transaction date.

4. On the last day of the week following the sale or transfer of any firearm, the dealer shall mail or deliver the written consent form required by subsection A to the Department of State Police. The State Police shall immediately initiate a search of all available criminal history record information to determine if the purchaser is prohibited from possessing or transporting a firearm under state or federal law. If the search discloses information indicating that the buyer or transferee is so prohibited from possessing or transporting a firearm, the State Police shall inform the chief law-enforcement officer in the jurisdiction where the sale or transfer occurred and the dealer without delay.

5. Notwithstanding any other provisions of this section, rifles and shotguns may be purchased by persons who are citizens of the United States or persons lawfully admitted for permanent residence but residents of other states under the terms of subsections A and B upon furnishing the dealer with proof of citizenship or status as a person lawfully admitted for permanent residence and one photo-identification form issued by a governmental agency of the person's state of residence and one other form of identification determined to be acceptable by the Department of Criminal Justice Services.

6. For the purposes of this subsection, the phrase "dealer's next business day" shall not include December 25.

C. No dealer shall sell, rent, trade or transfer from his inventory any firearm, other than a rifle or a shotgun, to any person who is not a resident of Virginia unless he has first obtained from the Department of State Police a report indicating that a search of all available criminal history record information has not disclosed that the person is prohibited from possessing or transporting a firearm under state or federal law. The dealer shall obtain the required report by mailing or delivering the written consent form required under subsection A to the State Police within twenty-four hours of its execution. If the dealer has complied with the provisions of this subsection and has not received the required report from the State Police within ten days from the date the written consent form was mailed to the Department of State Police, he shall not be deemed in violation of this section for thereafter completing the sale or transfer.

D. Nothing herein shall prevent a resident of this Commonwealth, at his option, from buying, renting or receiving a firearm from a dealer by obtaining a criminal history record information check through the dealer as provided in subsection C.

E. If any buyer or transferee is denied the right to purchase a firearm under this section, he may exercise his right of access to and review and correction of criminal history record information under §9-192 or institute a civil action as provided in §9-194, provided any such action is initiated within thirty days of such denial.

F. Any dealer who willfully and intentionally requests, obtains, or seeks to obtain criminal history record information under false pretenses, or who willfully and intentionally disseminates or seeks to disseminate criminal history record information except as authorized in this section shall be guilty of a Class 2 misdemeanor.

G. For purposes of this section:

"Antique firearm" means any firearm, including those with a matchlock, flintlock, percussion cap, or similar type of ignition system, manufactured in or before 1898 and any replica of such a firearm if such replica (i) is not designed or redesigned for using rimfire or conventional center-fire fixed ammunition or (ii) uses rimfire or conventional center-fire fixed ammunition which is no longer manufactured in the United States and which is not readily available in the ordinary channels of commercial trade.

"Assault firearm" means any semi-automatic center-fire rifle or pistol which expels a projectile by action of an explosion and is equipped at the time of the offense with a magazine which will hold more than twenty rounds of ammunition or designed by the manufacturer to accommodate a silencer or equipped with a folding stock.

"Dealer" means any person licensed as a dealer pursuant to 18 U.S.C. §921 et seq.

"Firearm" means any handgun, shotgun, or rifle which expels a projectile by action of an explosion.

"Handgun" means any pistol or revolver or other firearm originally designed, made and intended to fire a projectile by means of an explosion from one or more barrels when held in one hand.

"Lawfully admitted for permanent residence" means the status of having been lawfully accorded the privilege of residing permanently in the United States as an immigrant in accordance with the immigration laws, such status not having changed.

H. The Department of Criminal Justice Services shall promulgate regulations to ensure the identity, confidentiality and security of all records and data provided by the Department of State Police pursuant to this section.

I. The provisions of this section shall not apply to (i) transactions between persons who are licensed as firearms importers or collectors, manufacturers or dealers pursuant to 18 U.S.C. §921 et seq., (ii) purchases by or sales to any law-enforcement officer or agent of the United States, the Commonwealth or any local government, (iii) antique firearms or (iv) transactions in any county, city or town that has a local ordinance adopted prior to January 1, 1987, governing the purchase, possession, transfer, ownership, conveyance or transportation of firearms which is more stringent than this section.

J. All licensed firearms dealers shall collect a fee of two dollars for every transaction for which a criminal history record information check is required pursuant to this section, except that a fee of five dollars shall be collected for every transaction involving an out-of-state resident. Such fee shall be transmitted to the Department of State Police by the last day of the month following the sale for deposit in a special fund for use by the State Police to offset the cost of conducting criminal history record information checks under the provisions of this section.

K. Any person willfully and intentionally making a materially false statement on the consent form required in subsection B or C shall be guilty of a Class 5 felony.

L. Except as provided in §18.2-308.2:1, any dealer who willfully and intentionally sells, rents, trades or transfers a firearm in violation of this section shall be guilty of a Class 6 felony.

M. Any person who purchases a firearm with the intent to (i) resell or otherwise provide such firearm to any person who he knows or has reason to believe is ineligible to purchase or otherwise receive from a dealer a firearm for whatever reason or (ii) transport such firearm out of the Commonwealth to be resold or otherwise provided to another person who the transferor knows is ineligible to purchase or otherwise receive a firearm, shall be guilty of a Class 5 felony. However, if the violation of this subsection involves such a transfer of more than one firearm, the person shall be sentenced to a mandatory minimum term of imprisonment of five years, which shall not be suspended in whole or in part nor shall the person be eligible for parole during that period.

N. Any person who is ineligible to purchase or otherwise receive or possess a firearm in the Commonwealth who solicits, employs or assists any person in violating subsection M shall be guilty of a Class 5 felony and shall be sentenced to a mandatory minimum term of imprisonment of five years, which shall not be suspended in whole or in part nor shall the person be eligible for parole during that period.

O. All driver's licenses issued on or after July 1, 1994, shall carry a letter designation indicating whether the driver's license is an original, duplicate or renewed driver's license.

P. The Department of Education, in conjunction with the Department of Game and Inland Fisheries, shall develop a standard informational form and posted notice to be furnished to each licensed firearms dealer in the Commonwealth at no cost to the dealer. The form and notice shall provide basic information of the laws governing the purchase, possession and use of firearms by juveniles and adults.

Copies of the form shall be made available by the dealer whenever a firearm is purchased.

Every firearms dealer shall conspicuously post the written notice which shall be at least eight and one-half inches by eleven inches in size and printed in boldface type of a minimum size of ten points. A licensed firearms dealer shall not be liable for damages for injuries resulting from the discharge of a firearm purchased from the dealer if, at the time of the purchase, the dealer failed to provide the form or failed to post the written notice.

Q. Except as provided in subdivisions 1, 2 and 3 of this subsection, it shall be unlawful for any person who is not a licensed firearms dealer to purchase more than one handgun within any thirty-day period. A violation of this subsection shall be punishable as a Class 1 misdemeanor.

1. Purchases in excess of one handgun within a thirty-day period may be made upon completion of an enhanced background check, as described herein, by special application to the Department of State Police listing the number and type of handguns to be purchased and transferred for lawful business or personal use, in a collector series, for collections, as a bulk purchase from estate sales and for similar purposes. Such applications shall be signed under oath by the applicant on forms provided by the Department of State Police, shall state the purpose for the purchase above the limit, and shall require satisfactory proof of residency and identity. Such application shall be in addition to the firearms sales report required by the Bureau of Alcohol, Tobacco and Firearms (ATF). The Superintendent of State Police shall promulgate regulations, pursuant to the Administrative Process Act (§9-6.14:1 et seq.), for the implementation of an application process for purchases of handguns above the limit.

Upon being satisfied that these requirements have been met, the Department of State Police shall forthwith issue to the applicant a nontransferable certificate which shall be valid for seven days from the date of issue. The certificate shall be surrendered to the dealer by the prospective purchaser prior to the consummation of such sale and shall be kept on file at the dealer's place of business for inspection as provided in §54.1-4201 for a period of not less than two years. Upon request of any local law-enforcement agency, and pursuant to its regulations, the Department of State Police may certify such local law-enforcement agency to serve as its agent to receive applications and, upon authorization by the Department of State Police, issue certificates forthwith pursuant to this subsection. Applications and certificates issued under this subsection shall be maintained as records as provided in subdivision 3 of subsection B. The Department of State Police shall make available to local law-enforcement agencies all records concerning certificates issued pursuant to this subsection and all records provided for in subdivision 3 of subsection B.

2. The provisions of this subsection shall not apply to:

a. A law-enforcement agency;

b. An agency duly authorized to perform law-enforcement duties;

c. State and local correctional facilities;

d. A private security company licensed to do business within the Commonwealth;

e. The purchase of antique firearms as herein defined; or

f. A person whose handgun is stolen or irretrievably lost who deems it essential that such handgun be replaced immediately. Such person may purchase another handgun, even if the person has previously purchased a handgun within a thirty-day period, provided (i) the person provides the firearms dealer with a copy of the official police report or a summary thereof, on forms provided by the Department of

State Police, from the law-enforcement agency that took the report of the lost or stolen handgun; (ii) the official police report or summary thereof contains the name and address of the handgun owner, the description of the handgun, the location of the loss or theft, the date of the loss or theft, and the date the loss or theft was reported to the law-enforcement agency; and (iii) the date of the loss or theft as reflected on the official police report or summary thereof occurred within thirty days of the person's attempt to replace the handgun. The firearms dealer shall attach a copy of the official police report or summary thereof to the original copy of the Virginia firearms transaction report completed for the transaction and retain it for the period prescribed by the Department of State Police.

3. For the purposes of this subsection, "purchase" shall not include the exchange or replacement of a handgun by a seller for a handgun purchased from such seller by the same person seeking the exchange or replacement within the thirty-day period immediately preceding the date of exchange or replacement.

(Chgd. by L.1997 ch. 341; L.1998 ch. 844, eff. 7/1/98.)

§18.2-308.2:3. Criminal background check required for employees of a gun dealer to transfer firearms.

A. No person, corporation or proprietorship licensed as a firearms dealer pursuant to 18 U.S.C. §921 et seq. shall employ any person to act as a seller, whether full-time or part-time, permanent, temporary, paid or unpaid, for the transfer of firearms under §18.2-308.2:2, if such employee would be prohibited from possessing a firearm under §§18.2-308.1:1 through 18.2-308.1:7, 18.2-308.2, 18.2-308.2:01 or is an illegal alien.

B. Prior to permitting an applicant to begin employment, the dealer shall obtain a written statement or affirmation from the applicant that he is not disqualified from possessing a firearm and shall submit the applicant's fingerprints and personal descriptive information to the Central Criminal Records Exchange to be forwarded to the Federal Bureau of Investigation (FBI) for the purpose of obtaining national criminal history record information regarding the applicant.

C. Prior to August 1, 2000, the dealer shall obtain written statements or affirmations from persons employed before July 1, 2000, to act as a seller under §18.2-308.2:2 that they are not disqualified from possessing a firearm. Within five working days of the employee's next birthday, after August 1, 2000, the dealer shall submit the employee's fingerprints and personal descriptive information to the Central Criminal Records Exchange to be forwarded to the Federal Bureau of Investigation (FBI) for the purpose of obtaining national criminal history record information regarding the request.

D. The Department of State Police, upon receipt of an individual's record or notification that no record exists, shall submit an eligibility report to the requesting dealer within thirty days of the applicant beginning his duties for new employees or within 30 days of the applicant's birthday for a person employed prior to July 1, 2000.

E. If any applicant is denied employment because of information appearing on the criminal history record and the applicant disputes the information upon which the denial was based, the Central Criminal Records Exchange shall, upon written request, furnish to the applicant the procedures for obtaining a copy of the criminal history record from the Federal Bureau of Investigation. The information provided to the dealer shall not be disseminated except as provided in this section.

F. The cost of obtaining the criminal history record shall be borne by the applicant, unless the dealer, at his option, decides to pay such cost.

G. Upon receipt of the request for a criminal history record information check, the State Police shall establish a unique number for that firearm seller. Beginning September 1, 2001, the firearm seller's signature, firearm seller's number and the dealer's identification number shall be on all firearm transaction forms. The State Police shall void the firearm seller's number when a disqualifying record is discovered. The State Police may suspend a firearm seller's identification number upon the arrest of the firearm seller for a potentially disqualifying crime.

H. No transfer of a firearm at any place other than at a dealership or at any event required to be registered as a gun show shall be restricted by this section.

I. Any person who willfully and intentionally requests, obtains, or seeks to obtain criminal history record information under false pretenses, or who willfully and intentionally disseminates or seeks to disseminate criminal history record information except as authorized by this section and §18.2-308.2:2, shall be guilty of a Class 2 misdemeanor.

J. Any person willfully and intentionally making a materially false statement on the personal descriptive information required in this section shall be guilty of a Class 5 felony. Any person who offers for transfer any firearm in violation of this section shall be guilty of a Class 1 misdemeanor. Any dealer who willfully and knowingly employs or permits a person to act as a firearm seller in violation of this section shall be guilty of a Class 1 misdemeanor.

K. There shall be no civil liability for any seller for the actions of any purchaser or subsequent transferee of a firearm lawfully transferred pursuant to this section.

L. The provisions of this section requiring a seller's background check shall not apply to a licensed dealer.

M. For purposes of this section:

"Dealer" means any person, corporation or proprietorship licensed as a dealer pursuant to 18 U.S.C. §921 et seq.

"Firearm" means any handgun, shotgun, or rifle, which expels a projectile by action of an explosion.

"Place of business" means any place or premises where a dealer may lawfully transfer firearms.

"Seller" means for the purpose of any single sale of a firearm any person who is a dealer or an agent of a dealer, who may lawfully transfer firearms and who actually performs the criminal background check in accordance with the provisions of §18.2-308.2:2.

"Transfer" means any act performed with intent to sell, rent, barter, trade or otherwise transfer ownership or permanent possession of a firearm at the place of business of a dealer.

(Added by L.2000 ch. 794, eff. 7/1/2000.)

§18.2-308.3. Use or attempted use of restricted ammunition in commission or attempted commission of crimes prohibited; penalty.

A. When used in this section:

"Restricted firearm ammunition" applies to bullets, projectiles or other types of ammunition that are: (i) coated with or contain, in whole or in part, polytetrafluorethylene* or a similar product, (ii) commonly known as "KTW" bullets or "French Arcanes," or (iii) any cartridges containing bullets coated with a plastic substance with other than lead or lead alloy cores, jacketed bullets with other than lead or lead alloy cores, or cartridges of which the bullet itself is wholly comprised of a metal or metal alloy other than lead. This definition shall not be construed to include shotgun shells or solid plastic bullets.

**Probably should be "polytetrafluoro-ethylene".*

B. It shall be unlawful for any person to knowingly use or attempt to use restricted firearm ammunition while committing or attempting to commit a crime. Violation of this section shall constitute a separate and distinct felony and any person found guilty thereof shall be guilty of a Class 5 felony.

§18.2-308.4. Possession of firearms while in possession of certain controlled substances.

A. It shall be unlawful for any person unlawfully in possession of a controlled substance classified in Schedule I or II of the Drug Control Act (§54.1-3400 et seq.) of Title 54.1 to simultaneously with knowledge and intent possess any firearm.

B. It shall be unlawful for any person to possess, use, or attempt to use any pistol, shotgun, rifle, or other firearm or display such weapon in a threatening manner while committing or attempting to commit the illegal manufacture, sale, distribution, or the possession with the intent to manufacture, sell, or distribute a controlled substance classified in Schedule I or Schedule II of the Drug Control Act (§54.1-3400 et seq.) of Title 54.1 or more than one pound of marijuana.

Violation of this section shall constitute a separate and distinct felony and any person convicted thereof shall be guilty of a Class 6 felony, shall not be eligible for probation, and shall be sentenced to a minimum, mandatory term of imprisonment of five years, which shall not be suspended in whole or in part. Such punishment shall be separate and apart from, and shall be made to run consecutively with, any punishment received for the commission of the primary felony.

C. Any firearm possessed in violation of this section shall be forfeited to the Commonwealth pursuant to the provisions of §18.2-310.

(Chgd. by L.1999 chs. 829, 846, eff. 7/1/99.)

§18.2-308.5. Manufacture, import, sale, transfer or possession of plastic firearm prohibited.

It shall be unlawful for any person to manufacture, import, sell, transfer or possess any plastic firearm. As used in this section "plastic firearm" means any firearm, including machine guns and sawed-off shotguns as defined in this chapter, containing less than 3.7 ounces of electromagnetically detectable metal in the barrel, slide, cylinder, frame or receiver of which, when subjected to inspection by X–ray machines commonly used at airports, does not generate an image that accurately depicts its shape. A violation of this section shall be punishable as a Class 5 felony.

Any firearm manufactured, imported, sold, transferred or possessed in violation of this section shall be forfeited to the Commonwealth and disposed of in accordance with §18.2-310.

§18.2-308.6. Possession of unregistered firearm mufflers or silencers prohibited; penalty.

It shall be unlawful for any person to possess any firearm muffler of firearm silencer which is not registered to him in the National Firearms Registration and Transfer Record. A violation of this section shall be punishable as a Class 6 felony.

§18.2-308.7. Possession or transportation of certain firearms by persons under the age of eighteen; penalty.

It shall be unlawful for any person under eighteen years of age to knowingly and intentionally possess or transport a handgun or assault firearm anywhere in the Commonwealth. For the purposes of this section, "handgun" means any pistol or revolver or other firearm originally designed, made and intended to fire a projectile by means of an explosion from one or more barrels when held in one hand and "assault firearm" means any (i) semi-automatic centerfire rifle or pistol which expels a projectile by action of an explosion and is equipped at the time of the offense with a magazine which will hold more than twenty rounds of ammunition or designed by the manufacturer to accommodate a silencer or equipped with a folding stock or (ii) shotgun with a magazine which will hold more than seven rounds of the longest ammunition for which it is chambered. A violation of this section shall be a Class 1 misdemeanor. Any handgun possessed or transported in violation of this section shall be forfeited to the Commonwealth and disposed of as provided in §18.2-310.

This section shall not apply to:

1. Any person (i) while in his home or on his property, (ii) while in the home or on the property of his parent, grandparent, or legal guardian; or (iii) while on the property of another who has provided prior permission, and with the prior permission of his parent or legal guardian if the person has the landowner's written permission on his person while on such property;

2. Any person who, while accompanied by an adult, is at, or going to and from, a lawful shooting range or firearms educational class, provided that the weapons are unloaded while being transported;

3. Any person actually engaged in lawful hunting or going to and from a hunting area or preserve, provided that the weapons are unloaded while being transported; and

4. Any person while carrying out his duties in the armed forces of the United States or the National Guard of this Commonwealth or any other state.

§18.2-308.8. Importation, sale, possession or transfer of Striker 12's prohibited; penalty.

It sale be unlawful for any person to import, sell, possess or transfer the following firearms: the Striker 12, commonly called a "streetsweeper," or any semi-automatic folding stock shotgun of like kind with a spring tension drum magazine capable of holding twelve shotgun shells. A violation of this section shall be punishable as a Class 6 felony.

§18.2-309. Furnishing certain weapons to minors.

A. If any person sells, barters, gives or furnishes, or causes to be sold, bartered, given or furnished, to any minor a dirk, switchblade knife or bowie knife, having good cause to believe him to be a minor, such person shall be guilty of a Class 1 misdemeanor.

B. If any person sells, barters, gives or furnishes, or causes to be sold, bartered, given or furnished, to any minor a handgun, having good cause to believe him to be a minor, such person shall be guilty of a Class 6 felony. This subsection shall not apply to any transfer made between family members or for the purpose of engaging in a sporting event or activity.

§18.2-310. Forfeiture of certain weapons used in commission of criminal offense.

All pistols, shotguns, rifles, dirks, bowie knives, switchblade knives, ballistic knives, razors, slingshots, brass or metal knucks, blackjacks, stun weapons and tasers, and other weapons used by any person in the commission of a criminal offense, shall, upon conviction of such person, be forfeited to the Commonwealth by order of the court trying the case. The court shall dispose of such weapons as it deems proper by entry of an order of record. Such disposition may include the destruction of the weapons or, subject to any registration requirements of federal law, sale of the firearms to a licensed dealer in such firearms in accordance with the provisions of Chapter 22 (§19.2-369 et seq.) of Title 19.2 regarding sale of property forfeited to the Commonwealth.

The proceeds of any sale of such weapon shall be paid in accordance with the provisions of Article VIII, Section 8 of the Constitution of Virginia. In addition, the court may authorize the seizing law-enforcement agency to use the weapon for a period of time as specified in the order. When the seizing agency ceases to so use the weapon, it shall be disposed of as otherwise provided in this section.

However, upon petition to the court and notice to the attorney for the Commonwealth, the court, upon good cause shown, shall return any such weapon to its lawful owner after conclusion of all relevant proceedings if such owner (i) did not know and had no reason to know of the conduct giving rise to the forfeiture and (ii) is not otherwise prohibited by law from possessing the weapon. The owner shall acknowledge in a sworn affidavit to be filed with the record in the case or cases that he has retaken possession of the weapon involved.

§18.2-311. Prohibiting the selling or having in possession blackjacks, etc.

If any person sells or barters, or exhibits for sale or for barter, or gives or furnishes, or causes to be sold, bartered, given or furnished, or has in his possession, or under his control, with the intent of selling, bartering, giving or furnishing, any blackjack, brass or metal knucks, any disc of whatever configuration having at least two points or pointed blades which is designed to be thrown or propelled and which may be known as a throwing star or oriental dart, switchblade knife, ballistic knife, or like weapons, such person shall be guilty of a Class 4 misdemeanor. The having in one's possession of any such weapon shall be prima facie evidence, except in the case of a conservator of the peace, of his intent to sell, barter, give or furnish the same.

§18.2-311.1. Removing, altering, etc., serial number or other identification on firearm.

Any person, firm, association or corporation who or which intentionally removes, defaces, alters, changes, destroys or obliterates in any manner or way or who or which causes to be removed, defaced, altered, changed, destroyed or obliterated in any manner or way the name of the maker, model, manufacturer's or serial number, or any other mark or identification on any pistol, shotgun, rifle, machine gun or any other firearm shall be guilty of a Class 1 misdemeanor.

§18.2-311.2. Third conviction of firearm offenses; penalty.

On a third or subsequent conviction of any offense contained in Article 4, 5, 6, or 7 of Chapter 7 of Title 18.2, which would ordinarily be punished as a Class 1 misdemeanor, where it is alleged in the information or indictment on which the person is convicted, that (i) such person has been twice previously convicted of a violation of any Class 1 misdemeanor or felony offense contained in either Article 4, 5, 6, or 7 of Chapter 7 of Title 18.2 or §18.2-53.1, or of a substantially similar offense under the law of any other jurisdiction of the United States, and (ii) each such violation occurred on a different date, such person shall be guilty of a Class 6 felony.

ARTICLE 8
MISCELLANEOUS DANGEROUS CONDUCT

§18.2-312. Illegal use of tear gas, phosgene and other gases.

If any person maliciously release or cause or procure to be released in any private home, place of business or place of public gathering any tear gas, mustard gas, phosgene gas or other noxious or nauseating gases or mixtures of chemicals designed to, and capable of, producing vile or injurious or nauseating odors or gases, and bodily injury results to any person from such gas or odor, the offending person shall be guilty of a Class 3 felony.

If such act be done unlawfully, but not maliciously, the offending person shall be guilty of a Class 6 felony.

Nothing herein contained shall prevent the use of tear gas or other gases by police officers or other peace officers in the proper performance of their duties, or by any person or persons in the protection of person, life or property.

§18.2-313. Handling or using snakes so as to endanger human life or health.

It shall be unlawful for any person, or persons, to display, exhibit, handle or use any poisonous or dangerous snake or reptile in such a manner as to endanger the life or health of any person.

Any person violating the provisions of this section shall be guilty of a Class 4 misdemeanor.

§18.2-313.1. Withholding information about possibly rabid animal; penalty.

It shall be unlawful for any person to knowingly withhold information from, or knowingly give false information to any lawfully authorized governmental agent which would reasonably lead to the discovery or location and capture of any animal reasonably identifiable as one which has bitten a human being.

Any person violating the provisions of this section shall be guilty of a Class 2 misdemeanor.

§18.2-314. Failing to secure medical attention for injured child.

Any parent or other person having custody of a minor child which child shows evidence of need for medical attention as the result of physical injury inflicted by an act of any member of the household, whether the injury was intentional or unintentional, who knowingly fails or refuses to secure prompt and adequate medical attention, or who conspires to prevent the securing of such attention, for such minor child, shall be guilty of a Class 1 misdemeanor; provided, however, that any parent or other person having custody of a minor child that is being furnished Christian Science treatment by a duly accredited Christian Science practitioner shall not, for that reason alone, be considered in violation of this section.

§18.2-316. Duty of persons causing well or pit to be dug to fill it before abandonment.

Any person who has caused to be dug on his own land or the land of another any well or pit, shall fill such well or pit with earth so that the same shall not be dangerous to human beings, animals or fowls before such well or such pit is abandoned; and any person owning land whereon any such well or pit is located shall in the same manner fill with earth any such well or pit which has been abandoned, provided such person has knowledge of the existence of such well or pit.

But in the case of mining operations in lieu of filling the shaft or pit the owner or operator thereof on ceasing operations in such shaft or pit shall securely fence the same and keep the same at all times thereafter securely fenced.

Any person violating any provision of this section shall be deemed guilty of a Class 3 misdemeanor.

§18.2-317. Covers to be kept on certain wells.

Every person owning or occupying any land on which there is a well having a diameter greater than six inches and which is more than ten feet deep shall at all times keep the same covered in such a manner as not to be dangerous to human beings, animals or fowls.

Any person violating the provisions of this section shall be guilty of a Class 3 misdemeanor.

§18.2-318. Authority of counties, cities and towns to require and regulate well covers.

Notwithstanding the provisions of §18.2-317, the governing body of any county, city or town may adopt ordinances requiring persons owning or occupying any land within such county, city or town on which there is a well having a diameter greater than six inches and which is more than ten feet deep to keep the same covered in such a manner as not to be dangerous to human beings, animals or fowls.

Any such ordinance may specify and require reasonable minimum standards for the construction, installation and maintenance of such covers, including the manner in which any concrete used in connection therewith shall be reinforced, and may prescribe punishment for violations not inconsistent with general law.

§18.2-319. Discarding or abandoning iceboxes, etc.; precautions required.

It shall be unlawful for any person, firm or corporation to discard, abandon, leave or allow to remain in any place any icebox, refrigerator or other container, device or equipment of any kind with an interior storage area of more than two cubic feet of clear space which is airtight, without first removing the door or doors or hinges from such icebox, refrigerator, container, device or equipment.

This section shall not apply to any icebox, refrigerator, container, device or equipment which is being used for the purpose for which it was originally designed, or is being used for display purposes by any retail or wholesale merchant, or is crated, strapped or locked to such an extent that it is impossible for a child to obtain access to any airtight compartment thereof.

Any violation of the provisions of this section shall be punishable as a Class 3 misdemeanor.

§18.2-320. Sale, etc., of plastic bags; warning required.

(a) No person shall sell, offer for sale, or deliver, or offer for delivery, or give away any plastic bag or partial plastic bag intended to enclose freshly cleaned clothing, the length of which totals twenty-five inches or more and the material of which is less than one mil ($\frac{1}{1,000}$ inch) in thickness; unless such plastic bag bears the following warning statement, or a warning statement which the Commissioner of Health has approved as the equivalent thereof:

"WARNING: To avoid danger of suffocation, keep this plastic bag away from babies and children. Do not use this bag in cribs, beds, carriages or playpens."

(b) Such warning statement shall be imprinted in a prominent place on the plastic bag or shall appear on a label securely attached to the bag in a prominent place, and shall be printed in legible type of at least thirty-six point type.

(c) Violators of this section shall be guilty of a Class 3 misdemeanor.

§18.2-321. Using X ray, fluoroscope, etc., in the fitting of footwear.

It shall be unlawful for any person to use any X ray, fluoroscope, or other equipment or apparatus employing roentgen rays, in the fitting of shoes or other footwear. This section shall not apply to any licensed physician or surgeon in the practice of his profession. Any person violating the provisions of this section shall be guilty of a Class 3 misdemeanor.

§18.2-322. Expectorating in public places.

No person shall spit, expectorate, or deposit any sputum, saliva, mucus, or any form of saliva or sputum upon the floor, stairways, or upon any part of any public building or place where the public assemble, or upon the floor of any part of any public conveyance, or upon any sidewalk abutting on any public street, alley or lane of any town or city.

Any person violating any provision of this section shall be guilty of a Class 4 misdemeanor.

§18.2-322.1. *(Repealed by L.1997 ch. 391, eff. 7/1/97.)*

§18.2-323. Leaving disabled or dead animal in road, or allowing dead animal to remain unburied.

If any person cast any dead animal into a road or knowingly permit any dead animal to remain unburied upon his property when offensive to the public or, having in custody any maimed, diseased, disabled or infirm animal, leave it to lie or be in a street, road or public place, he shall be guilty of a Class 3 misdemeanor.

§18.2-323.01. Prohibition against disposal of dead body.

It shall be unlawful for any person to dispose of a dead body as defined in §32.1-249 (i) on private property without the written permission of the landowner or (ii) on public property.

A violation of this section shall be punishable as a Class 1 misdemeanor.

§18.2-323.1. Drinking while operating a motor vehicle; penalty.

It shall be unlawful for any person to consume an alcoholic beverage while driving a motor vehicle upon a public highway of this Commonwealth. A violation of this section is punishable as a Class 4 misdemeanor.

§18.2-324. Throwing or depositing certain substances upon highway; removal of such substances.

No person shall throw or deposit or cause to be deposited upon any highway any glass bottle, glass, nail, tack, wire, can, or any other substance likely to injure any person or animal, or damage any vehicle upon such highway, nor shall any person throw or deposit or cause to be deposited upon any highway any soil, sand, mud, gravel or other substances so as to create a hazard to the traveling public. Any person who drops, or permits to be dropped or thrown, upon any highway any destructive, hazardous or injurious material shall immediately remove the same or cause it to be removed. Any person removing a wrecked or damaged vehicle from a highway shall remove any glass or other injurious substance dropped upon the highway from such vehicle. Any persons violating the provisions of this section shall be guilty of a Class 1 misdemeanor.

This section shall not apply to the use, by a law-enforcement officer while in the discharge of official duties, of any device designed to deflate tires. The Division of Purchase and Supply shall, pursuant to §2.1-446, set minimum standards for such devices and shall give notice of such standards to law-enforcement offices in the Commonwealth. No such device shall be used which does not meet or exceed the standards.

(Chgd. by L.1997 ch. 136, eff. 7/1/97.)

§18.2-324.1. Punishment for violation of §§55-298.1 through 55-298.5, relating to electric fences.

The violation of any provision of §§55-298.1 through 55.298.5 shall constitute a Class 1 misdemeanor.

CHAPTER 8
CRIMES INVOLVING MORALS AND DECENCY

Article

ARTICLE 1
GAMBLING

Section

§18.2-325. Definitions.

1. "Gambling device" includes:

a. Any device, machine, paraphernalia, equipment, or other thing, including books, records and other papers, which are actually used in an illegal gambling operation or activity, and

b. Any machine, apparatus, implement, instrument, contrivance, board or other thing, including but not limited to those dependent upon the insertion of a coin or other object for their operation, which operates, either completely automatically or with the aid of some physical act by the player or operator, in such a manner that, depending upon elements of chance, it may eject something of value or determine the prize or other thing of value to which the player is entitled; provided, however, that the return to the user of nothing more than additional chances or the right to use such machine is not deemed something of value within the meaning of this subsection; and provided further, that machines that only sell, or entitle the user to, items of merchandise of equivalent value that may differ from each other in composition, size, shape or color, shall not be deemed gambling devices within the meaning of this subsection.

Such devices are no less gambling devices if they indicate beforehand the definite result of one or more operations but not all the operations. Nor are they any less a gambling device because, apart from their use or adaptability as such, they may also sell or deliver something of value on a basis other than chance.

2. "Illegal gambling" means the making, placing or receipt, of any bet or wager in this Commonwealth of money or other thing of value, made in exchange for a chance to win a prize, stake or other consideration or thing of value, dependent upon the result of any game, contest or any other event the outcome of which is uncertain or a matter of chance, whether such game, contest or event, occurs or is to occur inside or outside the limits of this Commonwealth.

3. "Interstate gambling" means the conduct of an enterprise for profit which engages in the purchase or sale within the Commonwealth of any interest in a lottery of another state or country whether or not such interest is an actual lottery ticket, receipt, contingent promise to pay, order to purchase, or other record of such interest.

4. "Operator" includes any person, firm or association of persons, who conducts, finances, manages, supervises, directs or owns all or part of an illegal gambling enterprise, activity or operation.

§18.2-326. Penalty for illegal gambling.

Except as otherwise provided in this article, any person who illegally gambles or engages in interstate gambling as defined in §18.2-325 shall be guilty of a Class 3 misdemeanor. If an association or pool of persons illegally gamble, each person therein shall be guilty of illegal gambling.

§18.2-327. Winning by fraud; penalty.

If any person while gambling cheats or by fraudulent means wins or acquires for himself or another money or any other valuable thing, he shall be fined not less than five nor more than ten times the value of such winnings. This penalty shall be in addition to any other penalty imposed under this article.

§18.2-328. Conducting illegal gambling operation; penalties.

The operator of an illegal gambling enterprise, activity or operation shall be guilty of a Class 6 felony. However, any such operator who engages in an illegal gambling operation which (i) has been or remains in substantially continuous operation for a period in excess of thirty days or (ii) has gross revenue of $2,000 or more in any single day shall be fined not more than $20,000 and imprisoned not less than one year nor more than ten years.

As used in this section, the term "gross revenue" means the total amount of illegal gambling transactions handled, dealt with, received by or placed with such operation, as distinguished from any net figure or amount from which deductions are taken, without regard to whether money or any other thing of value actually changes hands.

§18.2-329. Owners, etc., of gambling place permitting its continuance; penalty.

If the owner, lessee, tenant, occupant or other person in control of any place or conveyance, knows, or reasonably should know, that it is being used for illegal gambling, and permits such gambling to continue without having notified a law-enforcement officer of the presence of such illegal gambling activity, he shall be guilty of a Class 1 misdemeanor.

§18.2-330. Accessories to gambling activity; penalty.

Any person, firm or association of persons, other than those persons specified in other sections of this article, who knowingly aids, abets or assists in the operation of an illegal gambling enterprise, activity or operation, shall be guilty of a Class 1 misdemeanor.

§18.2-331. Illegal possession, etc., of gambling device; penalty.

A person is guilty of illegal possession of a gambling device when he manufactures, sells, transports, rents, gives away, places or possesses, or conducts or negotiates any transaction affecting or designed to affect ownership, custody or use of any gambling device, believing or having reason to believe that the same is to be used in the advancement of unlawful gambling activity. Violation of any provision of this section shall constitute a Class 1 misdemeanor.

§18.2-332. Certain acts not deemed "consideration" in prosecution under this article.

In any prosecution under this article, no consideration shall be deemed to have passed or been given because of any person's attendance upon the premises of another; his execution, mailing or delivery of an entry blank; his answering of questions, verbally or in writing; his witnessing of a demonstration or other proceeding; or any one or more thereof, where no charge is made to, paid by, or any purchase required of him in connection therewith.

§18.2-333. Exceptions to article; certain sporting events.

Nothing in this article shall be construed to prevent any contest of speed or skill between men, animals, fowl or vehicles, where participants may receive prizes or different percentages of a purse, stake or premium dependent upon whether they win or lose or dependent upon their position or score at the end of such contest.

Any participant who, for the purpose of competing for any such purse, stake or premium offered in any such contest, knowingly and fraudulently enters any contestant other than the contestant purported to be entered or knowingly and fraudulently enters a contestant in a class in which it does not belong, shall be guilty of a Class 3 misdemeanor.

§18.2-334. Exception to article; private residences.

Nothing in this article shall be construed to make it illegal to participate in a game of chance conducted in a private residence, provided such private residence is not commonly used for such games of chance and there is no operator as defined in subsection 4 of §18.2-325.

§18.2-334.2. Same; bingo games, raffles, and duck races conducted by certain organizations.

Nothing in this article shall apply to any bingo game, instant bingo, raffle, or duck race conducted solely by organizations as defined in §18.2-340.16 which have received a permit as set forth in §18.2-340.25, or which are exempt from the permit requirement under §18.2-340.23. *(Chgd. by L.1995 ch. 837, eff. 7/1/96.)*

§18.2-334.3. Exemptions to article; state lottery.

Nothing in this article shall apply to any lottery conducted by the Commonwealth of Virginia pursuant to Chapter 40 of Title 58.1.

§18.2-334.4. Exemptions to article; pari-mutuel wagering.

Nothing in this article shall be construed to make it illegal to participate in any race meeting or pari-mutuel wagering conducted in accordance with Chapter 28 (§59.1-353 et seq.) of Title 59.1.

§18.2-336. Forfeiture of money, gambling devices, etc., seized from illegal gambling enterprise; innocent owners or lienors.

All money, gambling devices, office equipment and other personal property used in connection with an illegal gambling enterprise or activity, and all money, stakes and things of value received or proposed to be received by a winner in any illegal gambling transaction, which are lawfully seized by any law-enforcement officer or which shall lawfully come into his custody, shall be forfeited to the Commonwealth by order of the court in which a conviction under this article is obtained. Such court shall order all money so forfeited to be paid over to the Commonwealth, and by order shall make such disposition of other property so forfeited as the court deems proper, including award of such property to any State agency or charitable organization for lawful purposes, or in case of the sale thereof, the proceeds therefrom to be paid over to the Commonwealth. Provided, however, that such forfeiture shall not extinguish the rights of any person without knowledge of the illegal use of such property who is the lawful owner or who has a lien on the same which has been perfected in the manner provided by law.

§18.2-337. Immunity of witnesses from prosecution.

No witness called by the Commonwealth or by the court, giving evidence either before the grand jury or in any prosecution under this article, shall ever be prosecuted for the offense being prosecuted concerning which he testifies. Such witness shall be compelled to testify and for refusing to do so may be punished for contempt.

§18.2-338. Enforcement of §18.2-331 by Governor and Attorney General.

If it shall come to the knowledge of the Governor that §18.2-331 is not being enforced in any county, city or town, the Governor may call upon the Attorney General to direct its enforcement in such county, city or town, and thereupon the Attorney General may instruct the attorney for the Commonwealth, sheriff and chief of police, if any, of such county, or the attorney for the Commonwealth and chief of police of such city, or the attorney for the Commonwealth of the county in which such town is located and the chief of police or sergeant of such town, to take such steps as may be necessary to insure the enforcement of such section in such county, city or town, and if any such officers, after receiving such instructions, shall thereafter fail or refuse to exercise diligence in the enforcement of §18.2-331, the Attorney General shall make report thereof in writing to the Governor and to the judge of the circuit court having jurisdiction over the acts thereby prohibited, and thereupon the Attorney

General upon being directed so to do by the Governor, shall take such steps as he may deem proper in directing the institution and prosecution of criminal proceedings, to secure the enforcement of §18.2-331.

§18.2-339. Enjoining offenses relating to gambling.

Whenever any person shall be engaged in committing, or in permitting to be committed, or shall be about to commit, or permit, any act prohibited by any one or more of the sections in this article, the attorney for the Commonwealth of the county or city in which such act is being, or is about to be, committed or permitted, or the Attorney General of the Commonwealth, may institute and maintain a suit in equity in the appropriate court, in the name of the Commonwealth, upon the relation of such attorney for the Commonwealth, or the Attorney General, to enjoin and restrain such person from committing, or permitting, such prohibited act or acts. The procedure in any such suit shall be similar to the procedure in other suits for injunctions, except that no bond shall be required upon the granting of either a temporary or permanent injunction therein.

§18.2-340. County ordinances prohibiting illegal gambling.

The governing body of any county may adopt ordinances prohibiting illegal gambling and other illegal activity related thereto, including provision for forfeiture proceedings in the name of the county. Such ordinances shall not conflict with the provisions of this article or with other state laws and any penalties provided for violation of such ordinances shall not exceed a fine of $2,500 or confinement in jail for twelve months, either or both.

ARTICLE 1.1
BINGO AND RAFFLES

(Repealed by L.1995 ch. 837, eff. 7/1/96.)

§§18.2-340.1 to 18.2-340.14. *(Repealed by L.1995 ch. 837, eff. 7/1/96.)*

ARTICLE 1.1:1
CHARITABLE GAMING

(Added by L.1995 ch. 837, eff. 7/1/95.)

Section

§18.2-340.15. State control of charitable gaming.

A. Charitable gaming as authorized herein shall be permitted in the Commonwealth as a means of funding qualified organizations. The Charitable Gaming Commission is vested with control of all charitable gaming in the Commonwealth, with plenary power to prescribe regulations and conditions under which such gaming shall be conducted to ensure that it is conducted in a manner consistent with the purpose for which it is permitted.

B. The conduct of any charitable gaming is a privilege which may be granted or denied by the Charitable Gaming Commission or its duly authorized representatives in its discretion in order to effectuate the purposes set forth in this article.

(Added by L.1995 ch. 837, eff. 7/1/96.)

§18.2-340.16. Definitions.

As used in this article unless the context requires a different meaning:

"Bingo" means a specific game of chance played with (i) individual cards having randomly numbered squares ranging from one to seventy-five, (ii) Commission-approved electronic devices which display facsimiles of bingo cards and are used for the purpose of marking and monitoring players' cards as numbers are called, or (iii) Commission-approved cards pursuant to subdivision 13 of §18.2-340.18, in which prizes are awarded on the basis of designated numbers on such cards conforming to a predetermined pattern of numbers selected at random. Such cards shall have five columns headed respectively by the letters B.I.N.G.O.

"Bona fide member" means an individual who participates in activities of a qualified organization other than such organization's charitable gaming activities.

"Charitable gaming" or "charitable games" means those raffles and games of chance explicitly authorized by this article.

"Charitable gaming supplies" includes bingo cards or sheets, devices for selecting bingo numbers, instant bingo cards, pull-tab cards and seal cards, and any other equipment or product manufactured for or intended to be used in the conduct of charitable games. However, for the purposes of this article, charitable gaming supplies shall not include items incidental to the conduct of charitable gaming, such as markers, wands, or tape.

"Commission" means the Charitable Gaming Commission.

"Gaming expenses" means prizes, supplies, costs of publicizing gaming activities, audit and administration or permit fees, and a portion of the rent, utilities, accounting and legal fees and such other reasonable and proper expenses as are directly incurred for the conduct of charitable gaming.

"Gross receipts" means the total amount of money received by an organization from charitable gaming before the deduction of expenses, including prizes.

"Instant bingo" means a specific game of chance played by the random selection of one or more individually prepacked cards, made completely of paper or paper products, with winners being determined by the preprinted appearance of concealed letters, numbers or symbols that must be exposed by the player to determine wins and losses and may include the use of a seal card which conceals one or more numbers or symbols that have been designated in advance as prize winners. Such cards may be dispensed by electronic or mechanical equipment.

"Jackpot" means a bingo game, exclusive of a "winner-take-all" bingo game, in which (i) all numbers on the card are covered, each number being selected at random, and with no more than one free space and (ii) the prize amount is greater than $100.

"Landlord" means any person or his agent, firm, association, organization, partnership, or corporation, or employee thereof, which owns and leases, or leases any premise devoted in whole or in part to the conduct of bingo games, and any person residing in the same household as a landlord.

"Organization" means any one of the following:

1. A volunteer fire department or rescue squad or auxiliary unit thereof which has been recognized in accordance with §15.2-955. by an ordinance or resolution of the political subdivision where the volunteer fire department or rescue squad is located as being a part of the safety program of such political subdivision;

2. An organization operated exclusively for religious, charitable, community or educational purposes;

3. An association of war veterans or auxiliary units thereof organized in the United States;

4. A fraternal association or corporation operating under the lodge system;

5. A local chamber of commerce; or

6. A nonprofit organization that raises funds by conducting raffles which generate annual gross receipts of less than $75,000, provided such gross receipts from the raffle, less expenses and prizes, are used exclusively for charitable, educational, religious or community purposes.

"Qualified organization" means any organization to which a valid permit has been issued by the Commission to conduct charitable gaming or any organization which is exempt pursuant to §18.2-340.23.

"Raffle" means a lottery in which the prize is won by (i) a random drawing of the name or prearranged number of one or more persons purchasing chances or (ii) a random contest in which the winning name or preassigned number of one or more persons purchasing chances is determined by a race involving inanimate objects floating on a body of water, commonly referred to as a "duck race."

For the purpose of this article, "raffle" shall include the use of individually prepackaged cards made completely of paper or paper products, with winners being determined by the appearance of preprinted concealed letters, numbers or symbols that must be exposed by the player to determine wins and losses, such cards being commonly referred to as "pull tabs" or "seal cards" which conceal one or more numbers or symbols that have been designated in advance as prize winners. Such cards may be dispensed by electronic or mechanical equipment.

"Reasonable and proper business expenses" means business expenses actually incurred by a qualified organization and not otherwise allowed under this article or under Commission regulations on real estate and personal property tax payments, travel expenses, payments of utilities and trash collection services, legal and accounting fees, costs of business furniture, fixtures and office equipment and costs of acquisition, maintenance, repair or construction of an organization's real property. For the purpose of this definition, salaries and wages of employees whose primary responsibility is to provide services for the principal benefit of an organization's members shall not qualify as a business expense.

"Supplier" means any person who offers to sell, sells or otherwise provides charitable gaming supplies to any qualified organization.

(Added by L.1995 ch. 837; chgd. by L.1996 ch. 919; L.1997 chs. 777, 838; L.1998 chs. 57, 398; L.1999 ch. 534, eff. 7/1/99.)

§18.2-340.17. Charitable Gaming Commission established.

A. There is hereby established, in the Office of the Secretary of Administration, the Charitable Gaming Commission. The Commission shall consist of seven members appointed by the Governor, subject to confirmation by the General Assembly. Each member of the Commission shall have been a resident of the Commonwealth for a period of at least three years next preceding his appointment, and his continued residency shall be a condition of his tenure in office. To the extent practicable, the Commission shall consist of individuals from different geographic regions of the Commonwealth. Upon initial appointment, three members shall be appointed for four-year terms, two for three-year terms, and two for two-year terms. Thereafter, all members shall be appointed for four-year terms. Vacancies shall be filled by the Governor in the same manner as the original appointment for the unexpired portion of the term. Each Commission member shall be eligible for reappointment for a second consecutive term at the discretion of the Governor. Persons who are first appointed to initial terms of less than four years shall thereafter be eligible for reappointment to two consecutive terms of four years each. The Commission shall elect a chairman from among its members. No member of the General Assembly while serving as a member shall be eligible for appointment to the Commission.

B. The members of the Commission shall serve at the pleasure of the Governor.

C. For each day or part thereof spent in the performance of his duties, each member of the Commission shall receive such compensation and reimbursement for his reasonable expenses as provided in §2.1-20.3.

D. A quorum shall consist of four members. The decision of a majority of those members present and voting shall constitute a decision of the Commission.

E. The Commission shall adopt rules and procedures for the conduct of its business. The Commission shall establish and maintain a business office within the Commonwealth at a place to be determined by the Commission. The Commission shall meet at least six times a year, and other meetings may be held at any time or place determined by the Commission or upon call of the chairman or upon a written request to the chairman by any two members. Except for emergency meetings and meetings governed by §2.1-343.1 requiring a longer notice, all members shall be duly notified of the time and place of any regular or other meeting at least ten days in advance of such meetings.

F. The Commission shall keep a complete and accurate record of its proceedings. A copy of the record and any other public records not exempt from disclosure under the Freedom of Information Act (§2.1-340 et seq.) shall be available for public inspection and copying during regular office hours at its principal office.

(Added by L.1995 ch. 837; chgd. by L.2000 ch. 639, eff. 7/1/2000.)

§18.2-340.18. Powers and duties of the Commission.

The Commission shall have all powers and duties necessary to carry out the provisions of this article and to exercise the control of charitable gaming as set forth in §18.2-340.15. Such powers and duties shall include but not be limited to the following:

1. The Commission is vested with jurisdiction and supervision over all charitable gaming authorized under the provisions of this article and including all persons that conduct or provide goods, services or premises used in the conduct of charitable gaming. It may employ such persons as are necessary to ensure that charitable gaming is conducted in conformity with the provisions of this article and the regulations of the Commission. The Commission may designate such agents and employees as it deems necessary and appropriate to be vested with like power to enforce the provisions of this article and the criminal laws of the Commonwealth as is vested in the chief law-enforcement officer of any county, city or town.

2. The Commission, its agents and employees and any law-enforcement officers charged with the enforcement of charitable gaming laws shall have free access to the offices, facilities or any other place of business of any organization, including any premises devoted in whole or in part to the conduct of charitable gaming. These individuals may enter such places or premises for the purpose of carrying out any duty imposed by this article, securing records required to be maintained by an organization, investigating complaints, or conducting audits.

3. The Commission may compel the production of any books, documents, records, or memoranda of any organizations or supplier for the purpose of satisfying itself that this article and its regulations are strictly complied with. In addition, the Commission may require the production of an annual balance sheet and operating statement of any person granted a permit pursuant to the provisions of this article and may require the production of any contract to which such person is or may be a party.

4. The Commission shall promulgate regulations under which charitable gaming shall be conducted in the Commonwealth and all such other regulations that it deems necessary and appropriate to effect the purposes of this article. Such regulations may include penalties for violations. The regulations shall be subject to the Administrative Process Act (§9-6.14:1 et seq.).

5. The Commission may issue subpoenas for the attendance of witnesses before it, administer oaths, and compel production of records or other documents and testimony of such witnesses whenever, in the judgment of the Commission, it is necessary to do so for the effectual discharge of its duties.

6. The Commission may compel any person holding a permit to file with the Commission such documents, information or data as shall appear to the Commission to be necessary for the performance of its duties.

7. The Commission may enter into arrangements with any governmental agency of this or any other state or any locality in the Commonwealth for the purposes of exchanging information or performing any other act to better ensure the proper conduct of charitable gaming.

8. The Commission may issue interim certification of tax-exempt status and collect a fee therefor in accordance with subsection B of §18.2-340.24.

9. The Commission shall report annually to the Governor and the General Assembly, which report shall include a financial statement of the operation of the Commission and any recommendations for legislation applicable to charitable gaming in the Commonwealth.

10. The Commission, its agents and employees may conduct such audits, in addition to those required by §18.2-340.31, as they deem necessary and desirable.

11. The Commission may limit the number of organizations for which a person may manage, operate or conduct charitable games.

12. The Commission may report any alleged criminal violation of this article to the appropriate attorney for the Commonwealth for appropriate action.

13. The Commission may, by regulation, approve variations to the card formats for bingo games provided such variations result in bingo games which are conducted in a manner consistent with the provisions of this article. Commission-approved variations may include, but are not limited to, bingo games commonly referred to as player selection games and 90-number bingo.

(Added by L.1995 ch. 837; chgd. by L.1997 chs. 777, 838, eff. 7/1/97.)

§18.2-340.19. Regulations of the Commission.

The Commission shall adopt regulations which:

1. Require, as a condition of receiving a permit, that the applicant use a predetermined percentage of its gross receipts for (i) those lawful religious, charitable, community or educational purposes for which the organization is specifically chartered or organized or (ii) those expenses relating to the acquisition, construction, maintenance or repair of any interest in real property involved in the operation of the organization and used for lawful religious, charitable, community or educational purposes. The regulation may provide for a graduated scale of percentages of gross receipts to be used in the foregoing manner based upon factors the Commission finds appropriate to and consistent with the purpose of charitable gaming.

2. Require the organization to have at least fifty percent of its membership consist of residents of the Commonwealth and specify the conditions under which a complete list of the organization's members who participate in the management, operation or conduct of charitable gaming may be required in order for the Commission to ascertain the percentage of Virginia residents; however, if an organization (i) does not consist of bona fide members and (ii) is exempt under §501(c)(3) of the United States Internal Revenue Code, the Commission shall exempt such organizations from the regulations adopted pursuant to this subdivision.

Membership lists furnished to the Commission in accordance with this subdivision shall not be a matter of public record and shall be exempt from disclosure under the provisions of the Freedom of Information Act (§2.1-340 et seq.).

3. Prescribe fees for processing applications for charitable gaming permits. Such fees may reflect the nature and extent of the charitable gaming activity proposed to be conducted.

4. Establish requirements for the audit of all reports required in accordance with §18.2-340.30.

5. Define electronic and mechanical equipment used in the conduct of charitable gaming.

6. Prescribe the conditions under which a qualified organization may (i) provide food and nonalcoholic beverages to its members who participate in the management, operation or conduct of bingo and (ii) permit members who participate in the management, operation or conduct of bingo to play bingo.

7. Prescribe the conditions under which a qualified organization located in the Northern Virginia Planning District may sell raffle tickets for a raffle drawing which will be held outside the Commonwealth pursuant to subsection C of §18.2-340.26.

8. Prescribe the conditions under which persons who are bona fide members of a qualified organization or a child, above the age of eleven years, of a bona fide member of such organization may participate in the conduct or operation of bingo games.

9. Prescribe the conditions under which a person below the age of eighteen years may play bingo, provided such person (i) has the consent of his parent or legal guardian or (ii) is accompanied by his parent or legal guardian.

10. Require all qualified organizations that are subject to Commission regulations to post in a conspicuous place in every place where charitable gaming is conducted a sign which bears a toll-free telephone number for "Gamblers Anonymous" or other organization which provides assistance to compulsive gamblers.

(Added by L.1995 ch. 837; chgd. by L.1996 ch. 919; L.1997 chs. 777, 838; L.1998 ch. 845, eff. 7/1/98.)

§18.2-340.20. Denial, suspension or revocation of permit; hearings and appeals.

A. The Commission may deny, suspend or revoke the permit of any organization found not to be in strict compliance with the provisions of this article and the regulations of the Commission. The action of the Commission in denying, suspending, or revoking any permit shall be subject to the Administrative Process Act (§9-6.14:1 et seq.).

B. Except as provided in §§18.2-340.30 and 18.2-340.36, no permit to conduct charitable gaming shall be denied, suspended or revoked except upon notice stating the proposed basis for such action and the time and place for the hearing. At the discretion of the Commission, hearings may be conducted by hearing officers who shall be selected from the list prepared by the Executive Secretary of the Supreme Court. After a hearing on the issues, the Commission may refuse to issue or may suspend or revoke any such permit if it determines that the organization has not complied with the provisions of this article or the regulations of the Commission.

C. Any person aggrieved by a refusal of the Commission to issue any permit, the suspension or revocation of a permit, or any other action of the Commission, may seek review of such action in accordance with Article 4 (§9-6.14:15 et seq.) of the Administrative Process Act.

D. *(Subsection effective only until 7/1/2001 by the third enactment of L.2000 ch. 1000.)* Until July 1, 2001, the Charitable Gaming Commission shall not deny, suspend, or revoke the permit of any organization solely because of its failure to meet the required minimum percentage of its gross receipts required to be used for charitable purposes, as prescribed by regulations adopted pursuant to subdivision 1 of §18.2-340.19, unless requested by the organization, provided that (i) the organization was conducting gaming in a rented facility prior to January 1, 2000, and (ii) the organization is otherwise in compliance with the laws and regulations governing charitable gaming in the Commonwealth.

(Added by L.1995 ch. 837; chgd. by L.1996 ch. 573; L.1997 chs. 777, 838; L.2000 ch. 1000, eff. 7/1/2000.)

§18.2-340.21. Executive Secretary; staff.

The Commission shall appoint an Executive Secretary and such other employees as it deems essential to perform its duties under this article, who shall possess such authority and perform such duties as the Commission shall prescribe or delegate to them. Such employees shall be compensated as provided by the Commission.

The Executive Secretary, in addition to any other duties prescribed by the Commission, shall keep a true and full record of all proceedings of the Commission and preserve at the Commission's principal office all books, documents and papers of the Commission.

(Added by L.1995 ch. 837, eff. 7/1/95.)

§18.2-340.22. Only raffles, bingo and instant bingo games permitted; prizes not gaming contracts.

A. This article permits qualified organizations to conduct raffles, bingo and instant bingo games. All games not explicitly authorized by this article or Commission regulations adopted in accordance with §18.2-340.18 are prohibited.

B. The award of any prize money for any charitable game shall not be deemed to be part of any gaming contract within the purview of §11-14.

C. Nothing in this article shall prohibit an organization from using the State Lottery Department's Pick-3 number or any number or other designation selected by the State Lottery Department in connection with any lottery, as the basis for determining the winner of a raffle.

(Added by L.1995 ch. 837; chgd. by L.1997 chs. 777, 838, eff. 7/1/97.)

§18.2-340.23. Organizations exempt from certain permit, financial reporting and audit requirements.

A. No organization that reasonably expects, based on prior charitable gaming annual results or any other quantifiable method, to realize gross receipts of $25,000 or less in any twelve-month period shall be required to (i) notify the Commission of its intention to conduct charitable gaming, (ii) file a resolution of its board of directors as required by subsection B, or (iii) comply with Commission regulations. If any organization's actual gross receipts for the twelve-month period exceed $25,000, the Commission may require the organization to file by a specified date the report required by §18.2-340.30.

B. Any volunteer fire department or rescue squad or auxiliary unit thereof which has been recognized in accordance with §15.1-26.01 by an ordinance or resolution of the political subdivision where the volunteer fire department or rescue squad is located as being part of the safety program of such political subdivision shall be exempt from the requirements of §18.2-340.25 if, prior to conducting charitable gaming, it notifies the Commission, on a form prescribed by the Commission, that it will conduct charitable gaming. The organization must receive notification of its exempt status from the Commission prior to conducting charitable gaming. Any such organization also shall be exempt from the financial reporting requirements of this article and the payment of audit fees but shall file with the Commission, at such time as may be required by the Commission, a resolution of its board of directors stating that the organization has complied with the provisions of this article. Nothing in this subsection shall be construed as exempting volunteer fire departments and rescue squads from any other provisions of this article or other Commission regulations.

C. Nothing in this section shall prevent the Commission from conducting any investigation or audit it deems appropriate to ensure an organization's compliance with the provisions of this article and, to the extent applicable, Commission regulations.

(Added by L.1995 ch. 837; chgd. by L.1997 chs. 777, 838, eff. 7/1/97.)

§18.2-340.24. Eligibility for permit; exceptions; where valid.

A. To be eligible for a permit to conduct charitable gaming, an organization shall:

1. Have been in existence and met on a regular basis in the county, city or town or in a county, city or town adjacent to the county, city or town wherein the organization proposes to conduct charitable gaming for a period of at least three years immediately prior to applying for a permit.

The three-year residency requirement shall not apply (i) to any lodge or chapter of a national or international fraternal order or of a national or international civic organization which is exempt under §501(c) of the United States Internal Revenue Code and which has a lodge or chapter holding a charitable gaming permit issued under the provisions of this article anywhere within the Commonwealth; (ii) to booster clubs which have been operating for less than three years and which have been established solely to raise funds for school-sponsored activities in public schools which are less than three years old; (iii) to recently established volunteer fire and rescue companies or departments, after county, city or town approval; or (iv) to an organization which relocates its meeting place on a permanent basis from one jurisdiction to another, complies with the requirements of subdivision 2 of this section, and was the holder of a valid permit at the time of its relocation.

2. Be operating currently and have always been operated as a nonprofit organization.

B. Any organization whose gross receipts from all charitable gaming exceeds or can be expected to exceed $75,000 in any calendar year shall have been granted tax-exempt status pursuant to §501(c) of the United States Internal Revenue Code. At the same time tax-exempt status is sought from the Internal Revenue Service, the same documentation may be filed with the Commission for an interim certification of tax-exempt status. If such documentation is filed, the Commission may, after reviewing such documentation it deems necessary, issue its determination of tax-exempt status within sixty days of receipt of such documentation. The Commission may charge a reasonable fee, not to exceed $500. This interim certification of tax-exempt status shall be valid until the Internal Revenue Service issues its determination of tax-exempt status, or for eighteen months, whichever is earlier.

C. A permit shall be valid only for the locations designated in the permit.

(Added by L.1995 ch. 837, eff. 7/1/96; chgd. by L.1996 ch. 919, eff. 7/1/96.)

§18.2-340.25. Permit required; application fee; form of application.

A. Except as provided for in §18.2-340.23, prior to the commencement of any charitable game, an organization shall obtain a permit from the Commission.

B. All complete applications for a permit shall be acted upon by the Commission within forty-five days from the filing thereof. Upon compliance by the applicant with the provisions of this article, and at the discretion of the Commission, a permit may be issued. All permits when issued shall be valid for the period specified in the permit unless it is sooner suspended or revoked. No permit shall be valid for longer than two years. The application shall be a matter of public record.

All permits shall be subject to regulation by the Commission to ensure the public safety and welfare in the operation of charitable games. The permit shall only be granted after a reasonable investigation has been conducted by the Commission.

C. In no case shall an organization receive more than one permit allowing it to conduct charitable gaming; however, nothing in this section shall be construed to prohibit granting special permits pursuant to §18.2-340.27.

D. Application for a charitable gaming permit shall be made on forms prescribed by the Commission and shall be accompanied by payment of the fee for processing the application.

(Added by L.1995 ch. 837; chgd. by L.1997 chs. 777, 838; L.1999 ch. 361, eff. 7/1/99.)

§18.2-340.26. Sale of raffle tickets; drawings.

A. Except as provided in subsection C, a qualified organization may sell raffle tickets both in and out of the jurisdiction designated in its permit and shall conduct the drawing within the Commonwealth.

B. Pull tabs or seal cards used as part of a raffle as defined in §18.2-340.16 may be sold only upon the premises owned or exclusively leased by the organization and at such times as the portion of the premises in which the pull tabs or seal cards are sold is open only to members and their guests.

C. A qualified organization located in the Northern Virginia Planning District may sell raffle tickets for a raffle drawing which will be held outside the Commonwealth, provided the raffle is conducted in accordance with (i) the regulations of the Commission and (ii) the laws and regulations of the jurisdiction in which the raffle drawing will be held.

(Added by L.1995 ch. 837; chgd. by L.1997 chs. 777, 838, eff. 7/1/97.)

§18.2-340.27. Conduct of bingo games; special permits.

A. A qualified organization shall accept only cash or, at its option, checks in payment of any charges or assessments for players to participate in bingo games. However, no such organization shall accept postdated checks in payment of any charges or assessments for players to participate in bingo games.

B. No qualified organization or any person on the premises shall extend lines of credit or accept any credit or debit card or other electronic fund transfer in payment of any charges or assessments for players to participate in bingo games.

C. Bingo games may be held by qualified organizations no more frequently than two calendar days in any calendar week except in accordance with subsection D.

D. A special permit may be granted a qualified organization which entitles it to conduct more frequent operations of bingo games during carnivals, fairs and other similar events which are located in the jurisdiction designated in the permit.

(Added by L.1995 ch. 837, eff. 7/1/96.)

§18.2-340.28. Conduct of instant bingo.

A. Any organization qualified to conduct bingo games pursuant to the provisions of this article may play instant bingo as a part of such bingo game and only at such location and at such times as designated in the permit for regular bingo games.

B. Any organization conducting instant bingo shall maintain a record of the date, quantity and card value of instant bingo supplies purchased as well as the name and address of the supplier of such instant bingo supplies. The organization shall also maintain a written invoice or receipt from a nonmember of the organization verifying any information required by this subsection. Instant bingo supplies shall be paid for only by check drawn on an account of the organization. During the conduct of instant bingo, the supplier's invoice, or a legible true copy thereof, for the instant bingo supplies being used shall be maintained by the organization on the premises where the instant bingo is being conducted.

C. No qualified organization shall sell any instant bingo card to any individual under eighteen years of age.

(Added by L.1995 ch. 837; chgd. by L.1997 chs. 777, 838, eff. 7/1/97.)

§18.2-340.29. Joint operation of bingo games; written reports; special permit required.

A. Any two qualified organizations may jointly organize and conduct bingo games provided both have fully complied with all other provisions of this article.

B. Any two qualified organizations jointly conducting such games shall be (i) subject to the same restrictions and prohibitions contained in this article that would apply to a single organization conducting bingo games and (ii) required to furnish to the Commission a written report setting forth the location where such games will be held, the division of manpower, costs, and proceeds for each game to be jointly conducted.

Upon a finding that the division of manpower and costs for each game bears a reasonable relationship to the division of proceeds, the Commission shall issue a special permit for the joint conduct of all approved games.

C. No bingo game shall be jointly conducted until the special permit issued pursuant to subsection B is obtained by the organizations.

(Added by L.1995 ch. 837, eff. 7/1/96.)

§18.2-340.30. Reports of gross receipts and disbursements required; form of reports; failure to file.

A. Each qualified organization shall keep a complete record of all receipts from its charitable gaming operation and all disbursements related to such operation. Except as provided in §18.2-340.23, each qualified organization shall file at least annually, on a form prescribed by the Commission, a report of all such receipts and disbursements, the amount of money on hand attributable to charitable gaming as of the end of the period covered by the report and any other information related to its charitable gaming operation that the Commission may require. In addition, the Commission, by regulation, may require any qualified organization whose receipts exceed a specified amount during any three-month period to file a report of its receipts and disbursements for such period. All reports filed per this section shall be a matter of public record.

B. All reports required by this section shall be acknowledged in the presence of a notary public and filed on or before the date prescribed by the Commission.

C. Except as provided in §18.2-340.23, each qualified organization shall designate an individual who shall be responsible for filing an annual, and, if required, quarterly, financial report if the organization goes out of business or otherwise ceases to conduct charitable gaming activities. The Commission shall require such reports as it deems necessary until all proceeds of any charitable gaming have been used for the purposes specified in §18.2-340.19 or have been disbursed in a manner approved by the Commission.

D. Each qualified organization shall maintain (i) for three years a written record of the dates on which bingo games are played, the number of people in attendance on each date and the amount of the gross receipts and prizes paid on each day; (ii) a record of the name and address of each individual to whom a regular or special bingo game prize or jackpot from the playing of bingo is awarded, as well as the amount of the award; and (iii) an itemized record of all receipts and disbursements, including operating costs and use of proceeds incurred in operating bingo games.

E. The failure to file reports within thirty days of the time such reports are due, shall cause the automatic revocation of the permit, and no organization shall conduct any bingo game or raffle thereafter until the report is properly filed and a new permit is obtained. However, the Commission may grant an extension of time for filing such reports for a period not to exceed forty-five days if requested by an organization, provided the organization requests an extension within fifteen days of the time such reports are due. For the term of any such extension, the organization's permit shall not be automatically revoked, such organization may continue to conduct charitable gaming, and no new permit shall be required.

(Added by L.1995 ch. 837; chgd. by L.1997 chs. 777, 838; L.1999 ch. 360, eff. 7/1/99.)

§18.2-340.31. Audit of reports; exemption; audit and administration fee.

A. Except as provided in §18.2-340.23, all reports filed pursuant to §18.2-340.30 shall be subject to audit by the Commission in accordance with Commission regulations. The Commission may engage the services of independent certified public accountants to perform any audits deemed necessary to fulfill the Commission's responsibilities under this article.

B. The Commission shall prescribe a reasonable audit and administration fee to be paid by any organization conducting charitable gaming under a permit issued by the Commission unless the organization is exempt from such fee pursuant to §18.2-340.23. Such fee shall not exceed one and one-half percent of the gross receipts which an organization reports pursuant to §18.2-340.30. Beginning July 1, 1998, the audit and administration fee charged by the Commission shall not exceed one and one-quarter percent of the gross receipts which an organization reports pursuant to §18.2-340.30. The audit and administration fee shall accompany each annual report or each three-month report if such report is required by the Commission pursuant to §18.2-340.30.

C. The audit and administration fee shall be payable to the Commission. All such fees received by the Commission shall be separately accounted for and shall be used only for the purposes of auditing and regulating charitable gaming.

(Added by L.1995 ch. 837; chgd. by L.1997 chs. 777, 838, eff. 7/1/97.)

§18.2-340.32. Authority of local governments; proceeds exempt from local taxation.

A. The governing body of any county, city or town may adopt an ordinance consistent with this article and the regulations of the Commission which (i) prohibits the playing of instant bingo and (ii) establishes reasonable hours during which bingo games may be played within such jurisdiction. If the governing body of any town adopts an ordinance pursuant to the provisions of this section, such town shall not be subject to any ordinance adopted by the county within which such town lies.

B. No governing body of any county, city or town may impose a gross receipts, entertainment, admission or any other tax based on revenues of qualified organizations derived from the conduct of charitable gaming.

(Added by L.1995 ch. 837; chgd. by L.1997 chs. 777, 838; L.1998 ch. 679, eff. 7/1/98.)

§18.2-340.33. Prohibited practices.

In addition to those other practices prohibited by this article, the following acts or practices are prohibited:

1. No part of the gross receipts derived by a qualified organization may be used for any purpose other than (i) reasonable and proper gaming expenses, (ii) reasonable and proper business expenses, (iii) those lawful religious, charitable, community or educational purposes for which the organization is specifically chartered or organized, and (iv) expenses relating to the acquisition, construction, maintenance, or repair of any interest in the real property involved in the operation of the organization and used for lawful religious, charitable, community or educational purposes. For the purposes of clause (iv), such expenses may include the expenses of a corporation formed for the purpose of serving as the real estate holding entity of a qualified organization, provided (a) such holding entity is qualified as a tax exempt organization under §501(c) (3), (7) or (10) of the Internal

Revenue Code and (b) the membership of the qualified organization is identical to such holding entity.

2. No qualified organization shall enter into a contract with or otherwise employ for compensation any person for the purpose of organizing, managing, or conducting any charitable games. However, organizations composed of or for deaf or blind persons may use a part of their gross receipts for costs associated with providing clerical assistance in the conduct of charitable gaming.

The provisions of this subdivision shall not prohibit the joint operation of bingo games held in accordance with §18.2-340.29.

3. No person shall pay or receive for use of any premises devoted, in whole or in part, to the conduct of any charitable games, any consideration in excess of the current fair market rental value of such property. Fair market rental value consideration shall not be based upon or determined by reference to a percentage of the proceeds derived from the operation of any charitable games or to the number of people in attendance at such charitable games.

(Paragraph effective only until 7/1/2001 by the third enactment of L.2000 ch. 1000.) No lease or rental of any premises devoted to the conduct of charitable gaming shall be conditioned upon the use or purchase of any services, products, or readily portable property from any landlord or other person, unless they are included in the rent being paid for the premises. Nothing herein shall prohibit any landlord from requiring in such lease or rental of any such premises that the organization shall provide certain services, products, or readily portable property related to the lease or rental of such premises.

4. No building or other premises shall be utilized in whole or in part for the purpose of conducting bingo games more frequently than two calendar days in any one calendar week. However, no building or other premises owned by (i) a qualified organization which is exempt from taxation pursuant to §501(c) of the Internal Revenue Code or (ii) any county, city or town shall be utilized in whole or in part for the purpose of conducting bingo games more frequently than four calendar days in any one calendar week.

The provisions of this subdivision shall not apply to the playing of bingo games pursuant to a special permit issued in accordance with §18.2-340.27.

5. No person shall participate in the management, operation or conduct of any charitable game unless such person is and, for a period of at least thirty days immediately preceding such participation, has been a bona fide member of the organization.

The provisions of this subdivision shall not apply to (i) persons employed as clerical assistants by qualified organizations composed of or for deaf or blind persons; (ii) employees of a corporate sponsor of a qualified organization, provided such employees' participation is limited to the management, operation or conduct of no more than one raffle per year; or (iii) the spouse or family member of any such bona fide member of a qualified organization provided at least one bona fide member is present.

6. No person shall receive any remuneration for participating in the management, operation or conduct of any charitable game, except that:

a. Persons employed by organizations composed of or for deaf or blind persons may receive remuneration not to exceed thirty dollars per event for providing clerical assistance in the conduct of charitable games only for such organizations;

b. Persons under the age of nineteen who sell raffle tickets for a qualified organization to raise funds for youth activities in which they participate may receive nonmonetary incentive awards or prizes from the organization;

c. Remuneration may be paid to off-duty law-enforcement officers from the jurisdiction in which such bingo games are played for providing uniformed security for such bingo games even if such officer is a member of the sponsoring organization, provided the remuneration paid to such member is in accordance with off-duty law-enforcement personnel work policies approved by the local law-enforcement official and further provided that such member is not otherwise engaged in the management, operation or conduct of the bingo games of that organization; and

d. A member of a qualified organization lawfully participating in the management, operation or conduct of a bingo game may be provided food and nonalcoholic beverages by such organization for on-premises consumption during the bingo game provided the food and beverages are provided in accordance with Commission regulations.

7. No landlord shall, at bingo games conducted on the landlord's premises, (i) participate in the conduct, management, or operation of any bingo games; (ii) sell, lease or otherwise provide for consideration any bingo supplies, including, but not limited to, bingo cards, instant bingo cards, or other game pieces; or (iii) require as a condition of the lease or by contract that a particular manufacturer, distributor or supplier of bingo supplies or equipment be used by the organization. If equipment or services are included by a landlord in any lease or contract, the lease or contract shall itemize the amount attributable to the rent of the premises, equipment, and each service to be provided by the landlord.

The provisions of this subdivision shall not apply to any qualified organization conducting bingo games on its own behalf at premises owned by it.

8. No qualified organization shall enter into any contract with or otherwise employ or compensate any member of the organization on account of the sale of bingo supplies or equipment.

9. No organization shall award any bingo prize money or any merchandise valued in excess of the following amounts:

a. No bingo door prize shall exceed $25;

b. No regular bingo or special bingo game prize shall exceed $100;

c. No instant bingo prize for a single card shall exceed $500; and

d. No bingo jackpot of any nature whatsoever shall exceed $1,000, nor shall the total amount of bingo jackpot prizes awarded in any one calendar day exceed $1,000.

The provisions of this subdivision shall not apply to any bingo game in which all the gross receipts from players for that game, up to $1,000, are paid as prize money back to the players, provided there is no more than one such game per calendar day of play and the prize money from any such game does not exceed $1,000, such games being commonly referred to as "winner-take-all" games.

10. No organization shall award any raffle prize valued at more than $100,000.

The provisions of this subdivision shall not apply to (i) a raffle conducted no more than once per calendar year by a qualified organization qualified as a tax-exempt organization pursuant to §501(c)(3) of the Internal Revenue Code for a prize consisting of a lot improved by a residential dwelling where 100 percent of the moneys received from such a raffle, less deductions for the fair market value for the cost of acquisition of the land and materials, are donated to lawful religious, charitable, community, or educational organizations specifically chartered or organized under the laws of the Commonwealth and qualified as a §501(c)(3) tax-exempt organization or (ii) pull tabs or seal cards when played as permitted in §18.2-340.26, which prize award for a single card shall not exceed $500.

11. No qualified organization composed of or for deaf or blind persons which employs a person not a member to provide clerical assistance in the conduct of any charitable games shall conduct such games unless it has in force fidelity insurance, as defined in §38.2-120, written by an insurer licensed to do business in the Commonwealth.

12. No person shall participate in the management, operation or conduct of any charitable game if, within the preceding five years, he has been convicted of a felony or crime of moral turpitude. In addition, no person shall participate in the management, operation or conduct of any charitable game if that person, within the preceding five years, has participated in the management, operation, or conduct of any charitable game which was found by the Commission or a court of competent jurisdiction to have been operated in violation of state law, local ordinance or Commission regulation.

13. Qualified organizations jointly conducting bingo games pursuant to §18.2-340.29 shall not circumvent any restrictions and prohibitions which would otherwise apply if a single organization were conducting such games. These restrictions and prohibitions shall include, but not be limited to, the frequency with which bingo games may be held, the value of merchandise or money awarded as prizes, or any other practice prohibited under this section.

14. A qualified organization shall not purchase any charitable gaming supplies for use in this Commonwealth from any person who is not currently registered with the Commission as a supplier pursuant to §18.2-340.34.

15. Unless otherwise permitted in this article, no part of an organization's charitable gaming gross receipts shall be used for an organization's social or recreational activities.
(Added by L.1995 ch. 837; chgd. by L.1996 ch. 919; L.1997 chs. 777, 838; L.1998 chs. 57, 398; L.1999 ch. 534; L.2000 ch. 1000, eff. 7/1/2000.)

§18.2-340.34. Suppliers of charitable gaming supplies; registration; qualification; suspension, revocation or refusal to renew certificate; maintenance, production, and release of records.

A. No person shall offer to sell, sell or otherwise provide charitable gaming supplies to any qualified organization unless and until such person has made application for and has been issued a registration certificate by the Commission. An application for registration shall be made on forms prescribed by the Commission and shall be accompanied by a fee in the amount of $500. Each registration certificate shall remain valid for a period of one year from the date of issuance. Application for renewal of a registration certificate shall be accompanied by a fee in the amount of $500 and shall be made on forms prescribed by the Commission.

B. The Commission shall have authority to prescribe by regulation reasonable criteria consistent with the provisions of this article for the registration of suppliers. The Commission may refuse to register any supplier who has, or which has any officer, director, partner, or owner who has (i) been convicted of or pleaded nolo contendere to a felony in any state or federal court or has been convicted of any offense which, if committed in the Commonwealth, would be a felony; (ii) been convicted of or pleaded nolo contendere to a crime involving gambling; (iii) had any license, permit, certificate or other authority related to activities defined as charitable gaming in the Commonwealth suspended or revoked in the Commonwealth or in any other jurisdiction; or (iv) failed to file or has been delinquent in excess of one year in the filing of any tax returns or the payment of any taxes due the Commonwealth.

C. The Commission may suspend, revoke or refuse to renew the registration certificate of any supplier for any conduct described in subsection B or for any violation of this article or regulation of the Commission. Before taking any such action, the Commission shall give the supplier a written statement of the grounds upon which it proposes to take such action and an opportunity to be heard. Every hearing in a contested case shall be conducted in accordance with the Administrative Process Act (§9-6.14:1 et seq.).

D. Each supplier shall document each sale of charitable gaming supplies and other items incidental to the conduct of charitable gaming, such as markers, wands or tape, to a qualified organization on an invoice which clearly shows (i) the name and address of the qualified organization to which such supplies or items were sold; (ii) the date of the sale; (iii) the name or form and serial number of each deal of instant bingo cards and pull-tab raffle cards, the quantity of deals sold and the price per deal paid by the qualified organization; (iv) the serial number of the top sheet in each packet of bingo paper, the serial number for each series of uncollated bingo paper, and the cut, color and quantity of bingo paper sold; and (v) any other information with respect to charitable gaming supplies or other items incidental to the conduct of charitable gaming as the Commission may prescribe by regulation. A legible copy of the invoice shall accompany the charitable gaming supplies when delivered to the qualified organization.

E. Each supplier shall maintain a legible copy of each invoice required by subsection D for a period of three years from the date of sale. Each supplier shall make such documents immediately available for inspection and copying to any agent or employee of the Commission upon request made during normal business hours. This subsection shall not limit the right of the Commission to require the production of any other documents in the possession of the supplier which relate to its transactions with qualified organizations. All documents and other information of a proprietary nature furnished to the Commission in accordance with this subsection shall not be a matter of public record and shall be exempt from disclosure under the provisions of the Freedom of Information Act (§2.1-340 et seq.).
(Added by L.1995 ch. 837; chgd. by L.1996 ch. 919; L.1997 chs. 777, 838; L.1999 ch. 534, eff. 7/1/99.)

§18.2-340.35. Assistance from Department of State Police.

The Department of the State Police, upon request of the Commission, shall assist in the conduct of investigations by the Commission.
(Added by L.1995 ch. 837, eff. 7/1/96.)

§18.2-340.36. Suspension of permit.

A. When any officer charged with the enforcement of the charitable gaming laws of the Commonwealth has reasonable cause to believe that the conduct of charitable gaming is being conducted by an organization in violation of this article or the regulations of the Commission, he may apply to any judge, magistrate, or other person having authority to issue criminal warrants for the immediate suspension of the permit of the organization conducting the bingo game or raffle. If the judge, magistrate, or person to whom such application is presented is satisfied that probable cause exists to suspend the permit, he shall suspend the permit. Immediately upon such suspension, the officer shall notify the organization in writing of such suspension.

B. Written notice specifying the particular basis for the immediate suspension shall be provided by the officer to the organization within one business day of the suspension and a hearing held thereon by the Commission or its designated hearing officer within ten days of the suspension unless the organization consents to a later date. No charitable gaming shall be conducted by the organization until the suspension

has been lifted by the Commission or a court of competent jurisdiction.
(Added by L.1995 ch. 837, eff. 7/1/96.)

§18.2-340.37. Criminal penalties.

A. Any person who violates the provisions of this article or who willfully and knowingly files, or causes to be filed, a false application, report or other document or who willfully and knowingly makes a false statement, or causes a false statement to be made, on any application, report or other document required to be filed with or made to the Commission shall be guilty of a Class 1 misdemeanor.

B. Each day in violation shall constitute a separate offense.
(Added by L.1995 ch. 837; chgd. by L.1996 ch. 919, eff. 7/1/96.)

§18.2-340.38. Transitional provisions.

A. In order to implement the statewide regulation of charitable gaming expeditiously, rules and regulations shall be adopted by the Commission but shall not be subject to the Administrative Process Act (§9-6.14:1 et seq.) during the first twenty-four-month period following the earliest effective date of any portion of this article. Thereafter, all rules and regulations shall fully comply with the provisions of the Administrative Process Act.

B. The Commission may issue temporary licenses upon conditions as it deems necessary, subject however to all limitations set forth in this article, for a term which shall not extend beyond one year after the latest effective date of any portion of this article.
(Added by L.1995 ch. 837; chgd. by L.1996 ch. 919, 7/1/96.)

ARTICLE 2
SUNDAY OFFENSES

Section

§18.2-341. Working or transacting business on Sunday.

A. On the first day of the week, commonly known and designated as Sunday, no person shall engage in work, labor or business or employ others to engage in work, labor or business except in the following industries and businesses:

1. Transportation by whatever means and supporting facilities;
2. Public services and utilities, manufacturing, processing and plant operation of all types;
3. Publishing, including the distribution and sale of the products thereof;
4. Servicing, fueling and repair of motor vehicles, boats and aircraft, and the selling of parts and supplies therefor;
5. Operation of motion picture theatres and the production of radio and television programs;
6. Medical services; and other services on an emergency basis;
7. Sports, athletic events and the operation of historic, entertainment and recreational facilities, and the sale or rental of boats, and swimming, fishing and boating equipment;
8. Agriculture, including the operation of nurseries and florist establishments;
9. Preparation and sale of prescription and nonprescription drugs and the sale of medical and hygienic supplies and baby supplies;
10. Wholesale food warehouses and ship chandleries;
11. Restaurants and delicatessens;
12. Janitorial, custodial and like services;
13. Operation of hotels and motels and funeral homes and cemeteries;
14. Mining and supporting facilities;
15. Sale of food, ice and beverages;
16. Sale of tobacco and related products;
17. A drugstore, a majority of the sales receipts of which consist of prescription and nonprescription drugs, health and beauty aids;
18. Sale of novelties, cameras, photographic supplies (including film and flash bulbs), antiques, pictures, paintings, art supplies, souvenirs, animals as pets, including tropical fish, and pet supplies;
19. Sale or leasing of noncommercial real property, mobile homes, and the sale of residential modular, panelized or other prefabricated houses, notwithstanding that such houses are not then erected or constructed on a site;
20. Providing of any service, product or other thing by means of a mechanical device not requiring the labor of any person;
21. Sale of any item, provided such sale takes place on publicly owned property or property designated by the governing body of any county, city or town, on a case-by-case basis, as the site of a festival, trade show, convention, festival market place or other type of public celebration or gathering. The governing body of a county, city or town may extend such a designation to nonpublicly owned property only when more than fifty percent of the area in which sales are made is used for otherwise exempt activities; and
22. Providing of any service or product by means of a mechanical device requiring only a telephone operator or answerer who may accept, but not process, orders.

This section shall not be applicable to works of charity conducted solely for charitable purposes by any person or organization not organized or engaged in business for a profit.

B. Any person violating the provisions of this section shall be guilty of a misdemeanor.

C. Nothing contained herein shall be construed to permit any fine or penalty against any employee or agent who has been caused, directed or authorized by his employer to violate any provision of this section, in which case the employer shall be subject to the sanctions prescribed by this section.

§18.2-342. Applicability of §18.2-341 within certain counties and cities.

The provisions of §18.2-341 shall have no force or effect within any county or city in the Commonwealth which has by ordinance expressed the sense of its citizens, as provided in §15.1-29.5, that such laws are not necessary.

§18.2-343. Observance of Saturday as Sabbath.

The penalties imposed by §18.2-341 shall not be incurred by any person who conscientiously believes that the seventh day of the week ought to be observed as a Sabbath, and actually refrains from all secular business and labor on that day, provided he does not compel an apprentice or servant, not of his belief to do secular work or business on a Sunday.

ARTICLE 3
SEXUAL OFFENSES, PROSTITUTION, ETC.

Section

§18.2-344. Fornication.

Any person, not being married, who voluntarily shall have sexual intercourse with any other person, shall be guilty of fornication, punishable as a Class 4 misdemeanor.

§18.2-345. Lewd and lascivious cohabitation.

If any persons, not married to each other, lewdly and lasciviously associate and cohabit together, or, whether married or not, be guilty of open and gross lewdness and lasciviousness, each of them shall be guilty of a Class 3 misdemeanor; and upon a repetition of the offense, and conviction thereof, each of them shall be guilty of a Class 1 misdemeanor.

§18.2-346. Being a prostitute or prostitution.

A. Any person who, for money or its equivalent, commits adultery, fornication or any act in violation of §18.2-361, or offers to commit adultery, fornication or any act in violation of §18.2-361 and thereafter does any substantial act in furtherance thereof, shall be guilty of being a prostitute, or prostitution, which shall be punishable as a Class 1 misdemeanor.

B. Any person who offers money or its equivalent to another for the purpose of engaging in sexual acts as enumerated above and thereafter does any substantial act in furtherance thereof shall be guilty of solicitation of prostitution and shall be guilty of a Class 1 misdemeanor.

§18.2-346.1. Testing of convicted prostitutes for infection with human immunodeficiency virus.

As soon as practicable following conviction of any person for violation of §18.2-346 or §18.2-361, such person shall be required to submit to testing for infection with human immunodeficiency virus. The convicted person shall receive counseling from personnel of the Department of Health concerning (i) the meaning of test, (ii) acquired immunodeficiency syndrome and (iii) the transmission and prevention of infection with human immunodeficiency virus.

Tests shall be conducted to confirm any initial positive test results before any test result shall be determined to be positive for infection. The results of such test shall be confidential as provided in §32.1-36.1 and shall be disclosed to the person who is the subject of the test and to the Department of Health as required by §32.1-36. The Department shall conduct surveillance and investigation in accordance with the requirements of §32.1-39.

The results of the test shall not be admissible in any criminal proceeding related to prostitution.

The cost of the test shall be paid by the Commonwealth and taxed as part of the cost of such criminal proceedings.

§18.2-347. Keeping, residing in or frequenting a bawdy place; "bawdy place" defined.

It shall be unlawful for any person to keep any bawdy place, or to reside in or at or visit, for immoral purposes, any such bawdy place. Each and every day such bawdy place shall be kept, resided in or visited, shall constitute a separate offense. In a prosecution under this section the general reputation of the place may be proved.

As used in this Code, "bawdy place" shall mean any place within or without any building or structure which is used or is to be used for lewdness, assignation or prostitution.

§18.2-348. Aiding prostitution or illicit sexual intercourse.

It shall be unlawful for any person or any officer, employee or agent of any firm, association or corporation, with knowledge of, or good reason to believe, the immoral purpose of such visit, to take or transport or assist in taking or transporting, or offer to take or transport on foot or in any way, any person to a place, whether within or without any building or structure, used or to be used for the purpose of lewdness, assignation or prostitution within this Commonwealth; or procure or assist in procuring for the purpose of illicit sexual intercourse, or any act violative of §18.2-361, or to give any information or direction to any person with intent to enable such person to commit an act of prostitution.

§18.2-349. Using vehicles to promote prostitution or unlawful sexual intercourse.

It shall be unlawful for any owner or chauffeur of any vehicle, with knowledge or reason to believe the same is to be used for such purpose, to use the same or to allow the same to be used for the purpose of prostitution or unlawful sexual intercourse, or to aid or promote such prostitution or unlawful sexual intercourse by the use of any such vehicle.

§18.2-350. Confinement of convicted prostitutes and persons violating §§18.2-347 through 18.2-349.

Every person convicted of being a prostitute and every person convicted of violating any of the provisions of §§18.2-347 through 18.2-349 shall be guilty of a Class 1 misdemeanor; provided, however, that in any case in which a city or county farm or hospital is available for the confinement of persons so convicted, confinement may be in such farm or hospital, in the discretion of the court or judge.

§18.2-351. Commitment of persons convicted of certain offenses; investigation and report; reduction of period.

Whenever any circuit court or judge thereof, or any general district court or juvenile and domestic relations district court or judge thereof, in the exercise of sound discretion shall determine that it is necessary for the protection of the public health or safety or for the promotion of the public welfare, through the rehabilitation of any person, such court or judge may, in lieu of imposing any sentence or fine provided by law for such offenses, commit to the control and supervision of the Director of the Department of Corrections, for an indeterminate period of not less than three months not more than twelve months any person who, in such court or before such judge, is convicted in this Commonwealth:

(1) Of being a prostitute, or

(2) Of being a keeper, inmate or frequenter of a bawdy place, or

(3) Of soliciting for immoral purposes, or

(4) Of contributing to the delinquency, neglect, or dependency of a minor.

When a person is tried for any offense enumerated in this section or is adjudged guilty of such offense, the court may, before fixing punishment, imposing sentence, or ordering a commitment, direct any probation officer or agency performing probation services for such court to thoroughly investigate and report upon the history of the accused and any and all relevant facts, to the end that the court may be fully advised as to the appropriate and just sentence to be imposed or commitment to be ordered.

All such institutions, except state institutions, shall receive from the Commonwealth the same fees as are allowed by law to jailers.

During any such period of commitment, the committing court or judge thereof may, upon its own motion or upon application of the Director, reduce such period of commitment.

Notwithstanding the provisions of §53.1-151 or §53.1-153, no person who, upon conviction of an offense enumerated in this section, is committed to the control and supervision of the Director of the Department of Corrections pursuant to this section or is otherwise incarcerated in a penal institution shall be eligible for parole.
(Chgd. by L.1996 ch. 616, eff. 7/1/96.)

§18.2-352. Examination and investigation of such persons; reports to committing court.

The Department of Corrections shall make a careful physical, mental and social examination of every person committed to it under the provisions of §18.2-351, and shall investigate such person's personal and family history in order that it may properly evaluate the convicted person's progress during confinement. The committing court may require the Department to report at any time or times, subsequent to the minimum commitment period prescribed by §18.2-351, upon the Department's observations, findings and recommendations with respect to any such person and terminate such sentence or change it to probation at any time upon recommendation of the Department of Corrections.

§18.2-353. Probation or release of such persons.

If the Director of Corrections finds it not possible or expedient to place such persons as are committed to him under the provisions of §18.2-351 in the institutions referred to in that section, the committing court on application of the Director may place such persons on probation. The Director or his authorized agents may at any time order the release of such persons when satisfied that such release is conducive to the welfare of such persons and will not be detrimental to the public health or the public welfare, and may prescribe reasonable terms or conditions upon which such release is granted. If any person so released violates the terms or conditions of his or her release, the general district court or juvenile and domestic relations district court exercising jurisdiction in the city or county wherein such violation occurs may revoke the order of release and direct his or her apprehension and detention by the proper law-enforcement officers and his or her return to the Director, and such court, on its own motion or on application of the Director, may recommit such person to an institution or make such other disposition as may be provided by law. In no case shall the total period of probation, confinement, supervision and reconfinement exceed three years.
(Chgd. by L.1996 ch. 616, eff. 7/1/96.)

§18.2-355. Taking, detaining, etc., person for prostitution, etc., or consenting thereto.

Any person who:

(1) For purposes of prostitution or unlawful sexual intercourse, takes any person into, or persuades, encourages or causes any person to enter, a bawdy place, or takes or causes such person to be taken to any place against his or her will for such purposes; or,

(2) Takes or detains a person against his or her will with the intent to compel such person, by force, threats, persuasions, menace or duress, to marry him or her or to marry any other person, or to be defiled; or,

(3) Being parent, guardian, legal custodian or one standing in loco parentis of a person, consents to such person being taken or detained by any person for the purpose of prostitution or unlawful sexual intercourse;

is guilty of pandering, and shall be guilty of a Class 4 felony.
(Chgd. by L.1997 ch. 555, eff. 7/1/97.)

§18.2-356. Receiving money for procuring person.

Any person who shall receive any money or other valuable thing for or on account of procuring for or placing in a house of prostitution or elsewhere any person for the purpose of causing such person to engage in unlawful sexual intercourse or any act in violation of §18.2-361 shall be guilty of a Class 4 felony.

§18.2-357. Receiving money from earnings of male or female prostitute.

Any person who shall knowingly receive any money or other valuable thing from the earnings of any male or female engaged in prostitution, except for a consideration deemed good and valuable in law, shall be guilty of pandering, punishable as a Class 4 felony.

§18.2-358. Detaining male or female in bawdy place against his or her will.

Any person who shall detain any male or female in a bawdy place against his or her will, shall be guilty of a Class 4 felony.

§18.2-359. Venue where any person transported for criminal sexual assault, attempted criminal sexual assault, or purposes of unlawful sexual intercourse, crimes against nature, and indecent liberties with children.

A. Any person transporting or attempting to transport through or across this Commonwealth, any person for the purposes of unlawful sexual intercourse or prostitution, or for the purpose of committing any crime specified in §18.2-361 or §18.2-370, may be presented, indicted, tried, and convicted in any county or city in which any part of such transportation occurred.

B. Venue for the trial of any person charged with committing or attempting to commit criminal sexual assault under Article 7 (§18.2-61 et seq.) of Chapter 4 of this title may be had in the county or city in which such crime is alleged to have occurred or in any county or city through which the victim was transported by the defendant prior to the commission of such offense.

§18.2-360. Competency of persons to testify in prosecutions under §§18.2-355 through 18.2-361.

Any male or female referred to in §§18.2-355 through 18.2-361 shall be a competent witness in any prosecution under such sections to testify to any and all matters, including conversations by or with the accused with third persons in his or her presence, notwithstanding he or she may have married the accused either before or after the violation of any of the provisions of this section; but such witness shall not be compelled to testify after such marriage.

§18.2-361. Crimes against nature.

A. If any person carnally knows in any manner any brute animal, or carnally knows any male or female person by the anus or by or with the mouth, or voluntarily submits to such carnal knowledge, he or she shall be guilty of a Class 6 felony, except as provided in subsection B.

B. Any person who carnally knows by the anus or by or with the mouth his daughter or granddaughter, son or grandson, brother or sister, or father or mother shall be guilty of a Class 5 felony. However, if a parent or grandparent commits any such act with his child or grandchild and such child or grandchild is at least thirteen but less than eighteen years of age at the time of the offense, such parent or grandparent shall be guilty of a Class 3 felony.

ARTICLE 4
FAMILY OFFENSES; CRIMES AGAINST CHILDREN, ETC.

§18.2-362. Person marrying when husband or wife is living.

If any person, being married, shall, during the life of the husband or wife, marry another person in this Commonwealth, or if the marriage with such other person take place out of the Commonwealth, shall thereafter cohabit with such other person in this Commonwealth, he or she shall be guilty of a Class 4 felony.

§18.2-363. Leaving Commonwealth to evade law against bigamy.

If any persons, resident in this Commonwealth, one of whom has a husband or wife living, shall, with the intention of returning to reside in this Commonwealth, go into another state or country and there intermarry and return to and reside in this Commonwealth cohabiting as man and wife, such marriage shall be governed by the same law, in all respects, as if it had been solemnized in this Commonwealth.

§18.2-364. Exceptions to preceding sections.

Sections 18.2-362 and 18.2-363 shall not extend to a person whose husband or wife shall have been continuously absent from such person for seven years next before marriage of such person to another, and shall not have been known by such person to be living within that time; nor to a person who can show that the second marriage was contracted in good faith under a reasonable belief that the former consort was dead; nor to a person who shall, at the time of the subsequent marriage, have been divorced from the bond of the former marriage; nor to a person whose former marriage was void.

§18.2-365. Adultery defined; penalty.

Any person, being married, who voluntarily shall have sexual intercourse with any person not his or her spouse shall be guilty of adultery, punishable as a Class 4 misdemeanor.

§18.2-366. Adultery and fornication by persons forbidden to marry; incest.

A. Any person who commits adultery or fornication with any person whom he or she is forbidden by law to marry shall be guilty of a Class 1 misdemeanor except as provided in subsection B.

B. Any person who commits adultery or fornication with his daughter or granddaughter, or with her son or grandson, or her father or his mother, shall be guilty of a Class 5 felony. However, if a parent or grandparent commits adultery or fornication with his or her child or grandchild, and such child or grandchild is at least thirteen years of age but less than eighteen years of age at the time of the offense, such parent or grandparent shall be guilty of a Class 3 felony.

§18.2-367. Conspiring to cause spouse to commit adultery.

If any person, being married, shall conspire with any other person or persons to cause the spouse of such married person to commit adultery and any act in furtherance of such conspiracy is done, such married person shall be guilty of a Class 5 felony; and if any person shall conspire with a married person to cause the spouse of such married person to commit adultery and any act in furtherance of such conspiracy is done, such person shall be guilty of a Class 6 felony.

§18.2-368. Placing or leaving wife for prostitution.

Any person who, by force, fraud, intimidation or threats, places or leaves, or procures any other person to place or leave his wife in a bawdy place for the purpose of prostitution or unlawful sexual intercourse, shall be guilty of pandering, punishable as a Class 4 felony.

§18.2-369. Abuse and neglect of incapacitated adults; penalty.

A. It shall be unlawful for any responsible person to abuse or neglect any incapacitated adult as defined in this section. Any responsible person who abuses or neglects an incapacitated adult in violation of this section shall be guilty of a Class 1 misdemeanor. Any responsible person who is convicted of a second or subsequent offense under this section shall be guilty of a Class 6 felony.

In any event, if a violation results in serious bodily injury or disease to another, conviction of an offense shall be punishable as a Class 6 felony. For purposes of this subsection, "serious bodily injury or disease" shall include but not be limited to (i) disfigurement, (ii) a fracture, (iii) a severe burn or laceration, (iv) mutilation, (v) maiming, or (vi) life threatening internal injuries or conditions, whether or not caused by trauma.

B. For purposes of this section:

"Abuse" means (i) knowing and willful conduct that causes physical injury or pain or (ii) knowing and willful use of physical restraint, including confinement, as punishment, for convenience or as a substitute for treatment, except where such conduct or physical restraint, including confinement, is a part of care or treatment and is in furtherance of the health and safety of the incapacitated person.

"Incapacitated adult" means any person eighteen years or older who is impaired by reason of mental illness, mental retardation, physical illness or disability, advanced age or other causes to the extent the adult lacks sufficient understanding or capacity to make, communicate or carry out reasonable decisions concerning his well-being.

"Neglect" means the knowing and willful failure by a responsible person to provide treatment, care, goods or services which results in injury to the health or endangers the safety of an incapacitated adult.

"Responsible person" means a person who has responsibility for the care, custody or control of an incapacitated person by operation of law or who has assumed such responsibility voluntarily, by contract or in fact.

C. No responsible person shall be in violation of this section whose conduct was (i) in accordance with the informed consent of the incapacitated person or a person authorized to consent on his behalf; (ii) in accordance with a declaration by the incapacitated person under the Natural Death Act of Virginia (§54.1-2981 et seq.) or with the provisions of a valid medical power of attorney; (iii) in accordance with the wishes of the incapacitated person or a person authorized to consent on behalf of the incapacitated person and in accord with the tenets and practices of a church or religious denomination; (iv) incident to necessary movement of, placement of or protection from harm to the incapacitated person; or (v) a bona fide, recognized or approved practice to provide medical care.

(Chgd. by L.2000 ch. 796, eff. 7/1/2000.)

§18.2-370. Taking indecent liberties with children.

A. Any person eighteen years of age or over, who, with lascivious intent, shall knowingly and intentionally:

(1) Expose his or her sexual or genital parts to any child under the age of fourteen years to whom such person is not legally married or propose that any such child expose his or her sexual or genital parts to such person; or

(2) *(Repealed.)*

(3) Propose that any such child feel or fondle the sexual or genital parts of such person or propose that such person feel or fondle the sexual or genital parts of any such child; or

(4) Propose to such child the performance of an act of sexual intercourse or any act constituting an offense under §18.2-361; or

(5) Entice, allure, persuade, or invite any such child to enter any vehicle, room, house, or other place, for any of the purposes set forth in the preceding subdivisions of this section; or

(6) Receive money, property, or any other remuneration for allowing, encouraging, or enticing any person under the age of eighteen years to perform in or be a subject of sexually explicit visual material as defined in §18.2-374.1 or who knowingly encourages such person to perform in or be a subject of sexually explicit material;

shall be guilty of a Class 6 felony.

B. Any person who is convicted of a second or subsequent violation of this section shall be guilty of a Class 5 felony; provided, that (i) the offenses were not part of a common act, transaction or scheme, (ii) the accused was at liberty as defined in §53.1-151 between each conviction, and (iii) it is admitted, or found by the jury or judge before whom the person is tried, that the accused was previously convicted of a violation of this section.

(Chgd. by L.2000 ch. 333, eff. 7/1/2000.)

§18.2-370.01. Indecent liberties by children; penalty.

Any child over the age of thirteen years but under the age of eighteen who, with lascivious intent, knowingly and intentionally exposes his or her sexual or genital parts to any other child under the age of fourteen years who, measured by actual dates of birth, is five or more years the accused's junior, or propose that any such child expose his or her sexual or genital parts to such person, shall be guilty of a Class 1 misdemeanor.

(Added by L.1998 ch. 825, eff. 7/1/98.)

§18.2-370.1. Taking indecent liberties with child by person in custodial or supervisory relationship.

Any person eighteen years of age or older who maintains a custodial or supervisory relationship over a child under the age of eighteen, including but not limited to the parent, step-parent, grandparent, step-grandparent, or who stands in loco parentis with respect to such child and is not legally married to such child, and who, with lascivious intent, knowingly and intentionally (i) proposes that any such child feel or fondle the sexual or genital parts of such person or that such person feel or handle the sexual or genital parts of the child, or (ii) proposes to such child the performance of an act of sexual intercourse or any act constituting an offense under §18.2-361, or (iii) exposes his or her sexual or genital parts to such child, or (iv) proposes that any such child expose his or her sexual or genital parts to such person, or (v) proposes to the child that the child engage in sexual intercourse, sodomy or fondling of sexual or genital parts with another person, or (vi) sexually abuses the child as defined in §18.2-67.10(6), shall be guilty of a Class 6 felony.

§18.2-370.2. Sex offenses prohibiting proximity to children.

A. "Offense prohibiting proximity to children" means a violation or an attempt to commit a violation of (i) subsection A of §18.2-47, clause (ii) or (iii) of §18.2-48, subsection B of §18.2-361, or subsection B of §18.2-366, where the victim of one of the foregoing offenses was a minor, or (ii) subsection A (iii) of §18.2-61, §§18.2-63, 18.2-64.1, subdivision A 1 of §18.2-67.1, subdivision A 1 of §18.2-67.2, or subdivision A 1 or A 2(a) of §18.2-67.3, or §§18.2-370, 18.2-370.1, clause (ii) of §18.2-371, §§18.2-374.1, 18.2-374.1:1 or §18.2-379.

B. Every adult who is convicted of an offense prohibiting proximity to children when the offense occurred on or after July 1, 2000, shall as part of his sentence be forever prohibited from loitering within 100 feet of the premises of any place he knows or has reason to know is a primary, secondary or high school. A violation of this section is punishable as a Class 6 felony.

(Added by L.2000 ch. 770, eff. 7/1/2000.)

§18.2-371. Causing or encouraging acts rendering children delinquent, abused, etc.; penalty.

Any person eighteen years of age or older, including the parent of any child, (i) who willfully contributes to, encourages, or causes any act, omission, or condition which renders a child delinquent, in need of services, in need of supervision, or abused or neglected as defined in §16.1-228, or (ii) engages in consensual sexual intercourse with a child fifteen or older not his spouse, child, or grandchild shall be guilty of a Class 1 misdemeanor. This section shall not be construed as repealing, modifying, or in any way affecting §§18.2-18, 18.2-19, 18.2-61, 18.2-63, 18.2-66, 18.2-68, and 18.2-347.

§18.2-371.1. Abuse and neglect of children; penalty.

A. Any parent, guardian, or other person responsible for the care of a child under the age of eighteen who by willful act or omission or refusal to provide any necessary care for the child's health causes or permits serious injury to the life or health of such child shall be guilty of a Class 4 felony. For purposes of this subsection, "serious injury" shall include but not be limited to (i) disfigurement, (ii) a fracture, (iii) a severe burn or laceration, (iv) mutilation, (v) maiming, (vi) forced ingestion of dangerous substances, or (vii) life-threatening internal injuries.

B. Any parent, guardian, or other person responsible for the care of a child under the age of eighteen whose willful act or omission in the care of such child was so gross, wanton and culpable as to show a reckless disregard for human life shall be guilty of a Class 6 felony.

C. Any parent, guardian or other person having care, custody, or control of a minor child who in good faith is under treatment solely by spiritual means through prayer in accordance with the tenets and practices of a recognized church or religious denomination shall not, for that reason alone, be considered in violation of this section.

§18.2-371.2. Prohibiting purchase or possession of tobacco products by minors or sale of tobacco products to minors.

A. No person shall sell to, distribute to, purchase for or knowingly permit the purchase by any person less than eighteen years of age, knowing or having reason to believe that such person is less than eighteen years of age, any tobacco product, including but not limited to cigarettes, cigars, and bidis. Tobacco products may be sold from a vending machine only if the machine is (i) posted with a notice, in a conspicuous manner and place, indicating that the purchase or possession of tobacco products by minors is unlawful and (ii) located in a place which is not open to the general public and is not generally accessible to minors. An establishment which prohibits the presence of minors unless accompanied by an adult is not open to the general public.

B. No person less than eighteen years of age shall purchase or possess any tobacco product, including but not limited to cigarettes, cigars, and bidis. The provisions of this subsection shall not be applicable to the possession of tobacco products by a person less than eighteen years of age making a delivery of tobacco products in pursuance of his employment.

C. No person shall sell a tobacco product, including but not limited to cigarettes, cigars, and bidis, to any individual who does not demonstrate, by producing a driver's license or similar photo identification issued by a government agency, that the individual is at least eighteen years of age. Such identification is not required from an individual whom the person has reason to believe is at least eighteen years of age or who the person knows is at least eighteen years of age. Proof that the person demanded, was shown, and reasonably relied upon a photo identification stating that the individual was at least eighteen years of age shall be a defense to any action brought under this subsection. In determining whether a person had reason to believe an individual is at least eighteen years of age, the trier of fact may consider, but is not limited to, proof of the general appearance, facial characteristics, behavior and manner of the individual.

This subsection shall not apply to mail order sales.

D. A violation of subsection A or C by an individual or by a separate retail establishment that involves a tobacco product other than a bidi shall be punishable by a civil penalty not to exceed $100 for a first violation, a civil penalty not to exceed $200 for a second violation, and a civil penalty not to exceed $500 for a third or subsequent violation. A violation of subsection A or C by an individual or by a separate retail establishment that involves the sale, distribution or purchase of a bidi shall be punishable by a civil penalty in the amount of $500 for a first violation, a civil penalty in the amount of $1,000 for a second violation, and a civil penalty in the amount of $2,500 for a third or subsequent violation. Where a defendant retail establishment offers proof that it has trained its employees concerning the requirements of this section, the court shall suspend all of the penalties imposed hereunder. However, where the court finds that a retail establishment has failed to so train its employees, the court may impose a civil penalty not to exceed $1,000 in lieu of any penalties imposed hereunder for a violation of subsection A or C involving a tobacco product other than a bidi.

A violation of subsection B shall be punishable by a civil penalty not to exceed $100 for a first violation and a civil penalty not to exceed $250 for a second or subsequent violation. A court may, as an alternative to the civil penalty, and upon motion of the defendant, prescribe the performance of up to 20 hours of community service for a first violation of subsection B and up to 40 hours of community service for a second or subsequent violation. If the defendant fails or refuses to complete the community service as prescribed, the court may impose the civil penalty. Upon a violation of subsection B, the judge may enter an order pursuant to subdivision 9 of §16.1-278.8.

Any attorney for the Commonwealth of the county or city in which an alleged violation occurred may bring an action to recover the civil penalty, which shall be paid into the state treasury. Any law-enforcement officer may issue a summons for a violation of subsection A, B, or C.

E. 1. Cigarettes shall be sold only in sealed packages provided by the manufacturer, with the required health warning. The proprietor of every retail establishment which offers for sale any tobacco product, including but not limited to cigarettes, cigars, and bidis, shall post in a conspicuous manner and place a sign or signs indicating that the sale of tobacco products to any person under eighteen years of age is prohibited by law. Any attorney for the county, city or town in which an alleged violation of this subsection occurred may enforce this subsection by civil action to recover a civil penalty not to exceed fifty dollars. The civil penalty shall be paid into the local treasury. No filing fee or other fee or cost shall be charged to the county, city or town which instituted the action.

2. For the purpose of compliance with regulations of the Substance Abuse and Mental Health Services Administration published at 61 Federal Register 1492, the Department of Agriculture and Consumer Services may promulgate regulations which allow the Department to undertake the activities necessary to comply with such regulations.

3. Any attorney for the county, city or town in which an alleged violation of this subsection occurred may enforce this subsection by civil action to recover a civil penalty not to exceed $100. The civil penalty shall be paid into the local treasury. No filing fee or other fee or cost shall be charged to the county, city or town which instituted the action.

F. Nothing in this section shall be construed to create a private cause of action.

G. Agents of the Virginia Alcoholic Beverage Control Board designated pursuant to §4.1-105 may issue a summons for any violation of this section.

H. As used in this section, "bidi" means a product containing tobacco that is wrapped in temburni leaf (diospyros melanoxylon) or tendu leaf (diospyros exculpra), or any other product that is offered to, or purchased by, consumers as a bidi or beedie.

(Chgd. by L.1995 ch. 675; L.1996 chs. 509, 517; L.1997 chs. 812, 882; L.1998 ch. 363; L.1999 ch. 1020; L.2000 ch. 883, eff. 7/1/2000.)

§18.2-371.3. Tattooing or body piercing of minors.

No person shall tattoo or perform body piercing on a person less than eighteen years of age, knowing or having reason to believe such person is less than eighteen years of age except (i) in the presence of the person's parent or guardian, or (ii) when done by or under the supervision of a medical doctor, registered nurse or other medical services personnel licensed pursuant to Title 54.1 in the performance of their duties. A person who violates this section is guilty of a Class 2 misdemeanor. Any second or subsequent violation of this section shall be punished as a Class 1 misdemeanor.

For the purposes of this section:

"Body-piercing" means the act of penetrating the skin to make a hole, mark, or scar, generally permanent in nature. "Body piercing" does not include the use of a mechanized, presterilized ear-piercing system that penetrates the outer perimeter or lobe of the ear or both.

"Tattoo" means to place any design, letter, scroll, figure, symbol or any other mark upon or under the skin of any person with ink or any other substance resulting in the permanent coloration of the skin by the aid of needles or any other instrument designed to touch or puncture the skin.
(Added by L.1997 ch. 586; chgd. by L.2000 ch. 842, eff. 7/1/2000.)

ARTICLE 5
OBSCENITY AND RELATED OFFENSES

§18.2-372. "Obscene" defined.

The word "obscene" where it appears in this article shall mean that which, considered as a whole, has as its dominant theme or purpose an appeal to the prurient interest in sex, that is, a shameful or morbid interest in nudity, sexual conduct, sexual excitement, excretory functions or products thereof or sadomasochistic abuse, and which goes substantially beyond customary limits of candor in description or representation of such matters and which, taken as a whole, does not have serious literary, artistic, political or scientific value.

§18.2-373. Obscene items enumerated.

Obscene items shall include:

(1) Any obscene book;

(2) Any obscene leaflet, pamphlet, magazine, booklet, picture, painting, bumper sticker, drawing, photograph, film, negative, slide, motion picture, videotape recording;

(3) Any obscene figure, object, article, instrument, novelty device, or recording or transcription used or intended to be used in disseminating any obscene song, ballad, words, or sounds; or

(4) Any obscene writing, picture or similar visual representation, or sound recording, stored in an electronic or other medium retrievable in a perceivable form.
(Chgd. by L.2000 ch. 1009, eff. 7/1/2000.)

§18.2-374. Production, publication, sale, possession, etc., of obscene items.

It shall be unlawful for any person knowingly to:

(1) Prepare any obscene item for the purposes of sale or distribution; or

(2) Print, copy, manufacture, produce, or reproduce any obscene item for purposes of sale or distribution; or

(3) Publish, sell, rent, lend, transport in intrastate commerce, or distribute or exhibit any obscene item, or offer to do any of these things; or

(4) Have in his possession with intent to sell, rent, lend, transport, or distribute any obscene item. Possession in public or in a public place of any obscene item as defined in this article shall be deemed prima facie evidence of a violation of this section.

For the purposes of this section, "distribute" shall mean delivery in person, by mail, messenger or by any other means by which obscene items as defined in this article may pass from one person, firm or corporation to another.

§18.2-374.1. Production, publication, sale, possession with intent to distribute, financing, etc., of sexually explicit items involving children; presumption as to age; severability.

A. For the purposes of this article and Article 4 (§18.2-362 et seq.) of this chapter, the term "sexually explicit visual material" means a picture, photograph, drawing, sculpture, motion picture film, digital image or similar visual representation which depicts sexual bestiality, a lewd exhibition of nudity, as nudity is defined in §18.2-390, or sexual excitement, sexual conduct or sadomasochistic abuse, as also defined in §18.2-390, or a book, magazine or pamphlet which contains such a visual representation. An undeveloped photograph or similar visual material may be sexually explicit material notwithstanding that processing or other acts may be required to make its sexually explicit content apparent.

B. A person shall be guilty of a Class 5 felony who:

1. Accosts, entices or solicits a person less than eighteen years of age with intent to induce or force such person to perform in or be a subject of sexually explicit visual material; or

2. Produces or makes or attempts or prepares to produce or make sexually explicit visual material which utilizes or has as a subject a person less than eighteen years of age; or

3. Who knowingly takes part in or participates in the filming, photographing or other reproduction of sexually explicit visual material by any means, including but not limited to computer-generated reproduction, which utilizes or has as a subject a person less than eighteen years of age; or

4. Sells, gives away, distributes, electronically transmits, displays with lascivious intent, purchases, or possesses with intent to sell, give away, distribute, transmit or display with lascivious intent sexually explicit visual material which utilizes or has as a subject a person less than eighteen years of age.

C. A person shall be guilty of a Class 4 felony who knowingly finances or attempts or prepares to finance sexually explicit visual material which utilizes or has as a subject a person less than eighteen years of age.

D. For the purposes of this section a person who is depicted as or presents the appearance of being less than eighteen years of age in sexually explicit visual material is prima facie presumed to be less than eighteen years of age.

E. The provisions of this section shall be severable and, if any of its provisions shall be held unconstitutional by a court of competent jurisdiction, then the decision of such court shall not affect or impair any of the remaining provisions.

(Chgd. by L.1995 ch. 839, eff. 7/1/95.)

§18.2-374.1:1. Possession of child pornography; penalty.

A. Any person who knowingly possesses any sexually explicit visual material utilizing or having as a subject a person less than eighteen years of age shall be guilty of a Class 1 misdemeanor. However, no prosecution for possession of material prohibited by this section shall lie where the prohibited material comes into the possession of the person charged from a law-enforcement officer or law-enforcement agency.

B. The provisions of this section shall not apply to any such material which is possessed for a bona fide artistic, medical, scientific, educational, religious, governmental, judicial or other proper purpose by a physician, psychologist, sociologist, scientist, teacher, person pursuing bona fide studies or research, librarian, clergyman, attorney, judge, or other person having a proper interest in the material.

C. All sexually explicit visual material which utilizes or has as a subject a person less than eighteen years of age shall be subject to lawful seizure and forfeiture pursuant to §18.2-374.2.

D. Any person convicted of a second or subsequent offense under this section shall be guilty of a Class 6 felony.

(Chgd. by L.1999 ch. 659, eff. 7/1/99.)

§18.2-374.2. Seizure and forfeiture of property used in connection with production of sexually explicit items involving children.

All audio and visual equipment, electronic equipment, devices and other personal property used in connection with the production, distribution, publication, sale, possession with intent to distribute or making of sexually explicit visual material having a person less than eighteen years of age as a subject shall be subject to lawful seizure by a law-enforcement officer and shall be subject to forfeiture to the Commonwealth pursuant to Chapter 22 (§19.2-369 et seq.) of Title 19.2 by order of the court in which a conviction under §18.2-374.1 is obtained. Notwithstanding the provisions of §19.2-381, the court shall dispose of the forfeited property as it deems proper, including awarding the property to a state agency for lawful purposes. If the property is disposed of by sale, the court shall provide that the proceeds be paid into the Literary Fund.

A forfeiture under this section shall not extinguish the rights of any person without knowledge of the illegal use of the property who (i) is the lawful owner or (ii) has a valid and perfected lien on the property.

(Chgd. by L.1999 ch. 659, eff. 7/1/99.)

§18.2-374.3. Use of communications systems to facilitate certain offenses involving children.

A. It shall be unlawful for any person to use a communications system, including but not limited to computers or computer networks or bulletin boards, or any other electronic means for the purposes of procuring or promoting the use of a minor for any activity in violation of §18.2-370 or §18.2-374.1. A violation of this section shall be punishable as a Class 6 felony.

B. It shall be unlawful for any person over the age of eighteen to use a communications system, including but not limited to computers or computer networks or bulletin boards, or any other electronic means, for the purposes of soliciting any person he knows or has reason to believe is a minor for (i) any activity in violation of §§18.2-355, 18.2-358, 18.2-361 or §18.2-370, (ii) any activity in violation of §18.2-374.1, or (iii) a violation of §18.2-374.1:1. As used in this subsection, "use a communications system" means making personal contact or direct contact through any agent or agency, any print medium, the United States mail, any common carrier or communication common carrier, any electronic communications system, or any telecommunications, wire, computer, or radio communications system. A violation of this section shall be punishable as a Class 5 felony.

(Chgd. by L.1999 ch. 659, eff. 7/1/99.)

§18.2-375. Obscene exhibitions and performances.

It shall be unlawful for any person knowingly to:

(1) Produce, promote, prepare, present, manage, direct, carry on or participate in, any obscene exhibitions or performances, including the exhibition or performance of any obscene motion picture, play, drama, show, entertainment, exposition, tableau or scene; provided, that no employee of any person or legal entity operating a theatre, garden, building, structure, room or place which presents such obscene exhibition or performance shall be subject to prosecution under this section if the employee is not the manager of the theatre or an officer of such entity, and has no financial interest in such theatre other than receiving salary and wages; or

(2) Own, lease or manage any theatre, garden, building, structure, room or place and lease, let, lend or permit such theatre, garden, building, structure, room or place to be used for the purpose of presenting such obscene exhibition or performance or to fail to post prominently therein the name and address of a person resident in the locality who is the manager of such theatre, garden, building, structure, room or place.

§18.2-376. Advertising, etc., obscene items, exhibitions or performances.

It shall be unlawful for any person knowingly to prepare, print, publish, or circulate, or cause to be prepared, printed, published or circulated, any notice or advertisement of any obscene item proscribed in §18.2-373, or of any obscene performance or exhibition proscribed in §18.2-375, stating or indicating where such obscene item, exhibition, or performance may be purchased, obtained, seen or heard.

§18.2-377. Placards, posters, bills, etc.

It shall be unlawful for any person knowingly to expose, place, display, post up, exhibit, paint, print, or mark, or cause to be exposed, placed, displayed, posted, exhibited, painted, printed or marked, in or on any building, structure, billboard, wall or fence, or on any street, or in or upon any public place, any placard, poster, banner, bill, writing, or picture which is obscene, or which advertises or promotes any obscene item proscribed in §18.2-373 or any obscene exhibition or performance proscribed in §18.2-375, or knowingly to permit the same to be displayed on property belonging to or controlled by him.

§18.2-378. Coercing acceptance of obscene articles or publications.

It shall be unlawful for any person, firm, association or corporation, as a condition to any sale, allocation, consignment or delivery for resale of any paper, magazine, book, periodical or publication to require that the purchaser or consignee receive for resale any other article, book, or other publication which is obscene; nor shall any person, firm, association or corporation deny or threaten to deny any franchise or impose or threaten to impose any penalty, financial or otherwise, by reason of the failure or refusal of any person to accept such articles, books, or publications, or by reason of the return thereof.

§18.2-379. Employing or permitting minor to assist in offense under article.

It shall be unlawful for any person knowingly to hire, employ, use or permit any minor to do or assist in doing any act or thing constituting an offense under this article.

§18.2-380. Punishment for first offense.

Any person, firm, association or corporation convicted for the first time of an offense under §§18.2-374, 18.2-375, 18.2-376, 18.2-377, 18.2-378 or §18.2-379, shall be guilty of a Class 1 misdemeanor.

§18.2-381. Punishment for subsequent offenses; additional penalty for owner.

Any person, firm, association or corporation convicted of a second or other subsequent offense under §§18.2-374 through 18.2-379 shall be guilty of a Class 6 felony. However, if the person, firm, association or corporation convicted of such subsequent offense is the owner of the business establishment where each of the offenses occurred, a fine of not more than $10,000 shall be imposed in addition to the penalties otherwise prescribed by this section.

§18.2-382. Photographs, slides and motion pictures.

Every person who knowingly:

(1) Photographs himself or any other person, for purposes of preparing an obscene film, photograph, negative, slide or motion picture for purposes of sale or distribution; or

(2) Models, poses, acts, or otherwise assists in the preparation of any obscene film, photograph, negative, slide or motion picture for purposes of sale or distribution;

shall be guilty of a Class 3 misdemeanor.

§18.2-383. Exceptions to application of article.

Nothing contained in this article shall be construed to apply to:

(1) The purchase, distribution, exhibition, or loan of any book, magazine, or other printed or manuscript material by any library, school, or institution of higher learning, supported by public appropriation;

(2) The purchase, distribution, exhibition, or loan of any work of art by any museum of fine arts, school, or institution of higher learning, supported by public appropriation;

(3) The exhibition or performance of any play, drama, tableau, or motion picture by any theatre, museum of fine arts, school or institution of higher learning, supported by public appropriation.

§18.2-384. Proceeding against book alleged to be obscene.

(1) Whenever he has reasonable cause to believe that any person is engaged in the sale or commercial distribution of any obscene book, any citizen or the attorney for the Commonwealth of any county or city, or city attorney, in which the sale or commercial distribution of such book occurs may institute a proceeding in the circuit court in said city or county for adjudication of the obscenity of the book.

(2) The proceeding shall be instituted by filing with the court a petition:

(a) Directed against the book by name or description;

(b) Alleging the obscene nature of the book; and

(c) Listing the names and addresses, if known, of the author, publisher, and all other persons interested in its sale or commercial distribution.

(3) Upon the filing of a petition pursuant to this article, the court in term or in vacation shall forthwith examine the book alleged to be obscene. If the court find no probable cause to believe the book obscene, the judge thereof shall dismiss the petition; but if the court find probable cause to believe the book obscene, the judge thereof shall issue an order to show cause why the book should not be adjudicated obscene.

(4) The order to show cause shall be:

(a) Directed against the book by name or description;

(b) Published once a week for two successive weeks in a newspaper of general circulation within the county or city in which the proceeding is filed;

(c) If their names and addresses are known, served by registered mail upon the author, publisher, and all other persons interested in the sale or commercial distribution of the book; and

(d) Returnable twenty-one days after its service by registered mail or the commencement of its publication, whichever is later.

(5) When an order to show cause is issued pursuant to this article, and upon four days notice to be given to the persons and in the manner prescribed by the court, the court may issue a temporary restraining order against the sale or distribution of the book alleged to be obscene.

(6) On or before the return date specified in the order to show cause, the author, publisher, and any person interested in the sale or commercial distribution of the book may appear and file an answer. The court may by order permit any other person to appear and file an answer amicus curiae.

(7) If no one appears and files an answer on or before the return date specified in the order to show cause, the court, upon being satisfied that the book is obscene, shall order the clerk of court to enter judgment that the book is obscene, but the court in its discretion may except from its judgment a restricted category of persons to whom the book is not obscene.

(8) If an appearance is entered and an answer filed, the court shall order the proceeding set on the calendar for a prompt hearing. The court shall conduct the hearing in accordance with the rules of civil procedure applicable to the trial of cases by the court without a jury. At the hearing, the court shall receive evidence, including the testimony of experts, if such evidence be offered, pertaining to:

(a) The artistic, literary, medical, scientific, cultural and educational values, if any, of the book considered as a whole;

(b) The degree of public acceptance of the book, or books of similar character, within the county or city in which the proceeding is brought;

(c) The intent of the author and publisher of the book;

(d) The reputation of the author and publisher;

(e) The advertising, promotion, and other circumstances relating to the sale of the book;

(f) The nature of classes of persons, including scholars, scientists, and physicians, for whom the book may not have prurient appeal, and who may be subject to exception pursuant to subsection (7).

(9) In making a decision on the obscenity of the book, the court shall consider, among other things, the evidence offered pursuant to subsection (8), if any, and shall make a written determination upon every such consideration relied

upon in the proceeding in his findings of fact and conclusions of law or in a memorandum accompanying them.

(10) If he finds the book not obscene, the court shall order the clerk of court to enter judgment accordingly. If he finds the book obscene, the court shall order the clerk of court to enter judgment that the book is obscene, but the court, in its discretion, may except from its judgment a restricted category of persons to whom the book is not obscene.

(11) While a temporary restraining order made pursuant to subsection (5) is in effect, or after the entry of a judgment pursuant to subsection (7), or after the entry of judgment pursuant to subsection (10), any person who publishes, sells, rents, lends, transports in intrastate commerce, or commercially distributes or exhibits the book, or has the book in his possession with intent to publish, sell, rent, lend, transport in intrastate commerce, or commercially distribute or exhibit the book, is presumed to have knowledge that the book is obscene under §§18.2-372 through 18.2-378 of this article.

(12) Any party to the proceeding, including the petitioner, may appeal from the judgment of the court to the Supreme Court of Virginia, as otherwise provided by law.

(13) It is expressly provided that the petition and proceeding authorized under this article, relating to books alleged to be obscene, shall be intended only to establish scienter in cases where the establishment of such scienter is thought to be useful or desirable by the petitioner; and the provisions of §18.2-384 shall in nowise be construed to be a necessary prerequisite to the filing of criminal charges under this article.

§18.2-385. Section 18.2-384 applicable to motion picture films.

The provisions of §18.2-384 shall apply mutatis mutandis in the case of motion picture film.

§18.2-386. Showing previews of certain motion pictures.

It shall be unlawful for any person to exhibit any trailer or preview of any motion picture which has a motion picture industry rating which would not permit persons in the audience viewing the feature motion picture to see the complete motion picture from which the trailer or preview is taken. Persons violating the provisions of this section shall be guilty of a Class 1 misdemeanor.

§18.2-386.1. Unlawful filming, videotaping or photographing of another; penalty.

A. It shall be unlawful for any person to videotape, photograph, or film any nonconsenting person if (i) that person is totally nude, clad in undergarments, or in a state of undress so as to expose the genitals, pubic area, buttocks or female breast in a restroom, dressing room, locker room, hotel room, motel room, tanning bed, tanning booth, bedroom or other location and (ii) the circumstances are otherwise such that the person being videotaped, photographed or filmed would have a reasonable expectation of privacy.

B. The provisions of this section shall not apply to filming, videotaping or photographing by (i) law-enforcement officers pursuant to a criminal investigation which is otherwise lawful or (ii) correctional officials and local or regional jail officials for security purposes or for investigations of alleged misconduct involving a person committed to the Department of Corrections or to a local or regional jail, or to any sound recording of an oral conversation made as a result of any videotaping or filming pursuant to Chapter 6 (§19.2-61 et seq.) of Title 19.2

C. A violation of subsection A shall be punishable as a Class 1 misdemeanor.

§18.2-387. Indecent exposure.

Every person who intentionally makes an obscene display or exposure of his person, or the private parts thereof, in any public place, or in any place where others are present, or procures another to so expose himself, shall be guilty of a Class 1 misdemeanor. No person shall be deemed to be in violation of this section for breastfeeding a child in any public place or any place where others are present.

§18.2-388. Profane swearing and intoxication in public; penalty; transportation of public inebriates to detoxification center.

If any person profanely curses or swears or is intoxicated in public, whether such intoxication results from alcohol, narcotic drug or other intoxicant or drug of whatever nature, he shall be deemed guilty of a Class 4 misdemeanor. In any area in which there is located a court-approved detoxification center a law-enforcement officer may authorize the transportation, by police or otherwise, of public inebriates to such detoxification center in lieu of arrest; however, no person shall be involuntarily detained in such center.

§18.2-389. Adoption of ordinances prohibiting obscenity.

The governing body of any county, city or town may adopt ordinances to prohibit obscenity or conduct paralleling the provisions of this article and of Article 6 (§18.2-390 et seq.) of this chapter, and ordinances prohibiting the dissemination to juveniles of, and their access to, materials deemed harmful to juveniles as defined in §18.2-390(6) in public at places frequented by juveniles or where juveniles are or may be invited as part of the general public. Exceptions as provided in §18.2-391.1 shall apply thereto. The governing body may not provide a penalty for violating the provisions of such ordinance which is greater than the penalty imposed for a Class 1 misdemeanor.

ARTICLE 6
PROHIBITED SALES AND LOANS TO JUVENILES

Section

§18.2-390. Definitions.

As used in this article:

(1) "Harmful to juveniles" means that quality of any description or representation, in whatever form, of nudity, sexual conduct, sexual excitement, or sadomasochistic abuse, when it (a) predominantly appeals to the prurient, shameful or morbid interest of juveniles, (b) is patently offensive to prevailing standards in the adult community as a whole with respect to what is suitable material for juveniles, and (c) is, when taken as a whole, lacking in serious literary, artistic, political or scientific value for juveniles.

(2) "Juvenile" means a person less than eighteen years of age.

(3) "Knowingly" means having general knowledge of, or reason to know, or a belief or ground for belief which warrants further inspection or inquiry of both (a) the character and content of any material described herein which is reasonably susceptible of examination by the defendant, and (b) the age of the juvenile, provided however, that an honest mistake shall constitute an excuse from liability hereunder if the defendant made a reasonable bona fide attempt to ascertain the true age of such juvenile.

(4) "Nudity" means a state of undress so as to expose the human male or female genitals, pubic area or buttocks with less than a full opaque covering, or the showing of the female

breast with less than a fully opaque covering of any portion thereof below the top of the nipple, or the depiction of covered or uncovered male genitals in a discernibly turgid state.

(5) "Sadomasochistic abuse" means actual or explicitly simulated flagellation or torture by or upon a person who is nude or clad in undergarments, a mask or bizarre costume, or the condition of being fettered, bound or otherwise physically restrained on the part of one so clothed.

(6) "Sexual conduct" means actual or explicitly simulated acts of masturbation, homosexuality, sexual intercourse, or physical contact in an act of apparent sexual stimulation or gratification with a person's clothed or unclothed genitals, pubic area, buttocks or, if such be female, breast.

(7) "Sexual excitement" means the condition of human male or female genitals when in a state of sexual stimulation or arousal.

§18.2-391. Unlawful acts.

A. It shall be unlawful for any person knowingly to sell, rent or loan to a juvenile, or to knowingly display for commercial purpose in a manner whereby juveniles may examine and peruse:

1. Any picture, photography, drawing, sculpture, motion picture film, electronic file or message containing an image, or similar visual representation or image of a person or portion of the human body which depicts sexually explicit nudity, sexual conduct or sadomasochistic abuse and which is harmful to juveniles, or

2. Any book, pamphlet, magazine, printed matter however reproduced, electronic file or message containing words, or sound recording which contains any matter enumerated in subdivision 1 of this subsection, or explicit and detailed verbal descriptions or narrative accounts of sexual excitement, sexual conduct or sadomasochistic abuse and which, taken as a whole, is harmful to juveniles.

However, if a person uses services of an Internet service provider or an electronic mail service provider in committing acts prohibited under this subsection, such Internet service provider or electronic mail service provider shall not be held responsible for violating this subsection.

B. It shall be unlawful for any person knowingly to sell to a juvenile an admission ticket or pass, or knowingly to admit a juvenile to premises whereon there is exhibited a motion picture, show or other presentation which, in whole or in part, depicts sexually explicit nudity, sexual conduct or sadomasochistic abuse and which is harmful to juveniles or to exhibit any such motion picture at any such premises which are not designed to prevent viewing from any public way of such motion picture by juveniles not admitted to any such premises.

C. It shall be unlawful for any juvenile falsely to represent to any person mentioned in subsection A or subsection B hereof, or to his agent, that such juvenile is eighteen years of age or older, with the intent to procure any material set forth in subsection A, or with the intent to procure such juvenile's admission to any motion picture, show or other presentation, as set forth in subsection B.

D. It shall be unlawful for any person knowingly to make a false representation to any person mentioned in subsection A or subsection B hereof or to his agent, that he is the parent or guardian of any juvenile, or that any juvenile is eighteen years of age, with the intent to procure any material set forth in subsection A, or with the intent to procure such juvenile's admission to any motion picture, show or other presentation, as set forth in subsection B.

E. Violation of any provision hereof shall constitute a Class 1 misdemeanor.

(Chgd. by L.1999 ch. 936; L.2000 ch. 1009, eff. 7/1/2000.)

§18.2-391.1. Exceptions to application of article.

Nothing contained in this article shall be construed to apply to:

1. The purchase, distribution, exhibition, or loan of any work of art, book, magazine, or other printed or manuscript material by any accredited museum, library, school, or institution of higher learning.

2. The exhibition or performance of any play, drama, tableau, or motion picture by any theatre, museum, school or institution of higher learning, either supported by public appropriation or which is an accredited institution supported by private funds.

ARTICLE 8
OFFENSES INVOLVING ANIMALS

Section

§18.2-403.1. Offenses involving animals – Class 1 misdemeanors.

The following unlawful acts and offenses against animals shall constitute and be punished as a Class 1 misdemeanor:

1. Violation of subsection A of §3.1-796.122 pertaining to cruelty to animals, except as provided for second or subsequent violations in that section.

2. Violation of §3.1-796.69 pertaining to transporting animals under certain conditions.

3. Making a false claim or receiving money on a false claim under §3.1-796.118 pertaining to compensation for livestock and poultry killed by dogs.

4. Violation of §3.1-796.83:1 pertaining to boarding establishments and groomers as defined in §3.1-796.68.

(Chgd. by L.1996 ch. 249; L.1999 ch. 620, eff. 7/1/99.)

§18.2-403.2. Offenses involving animals – Class 3 misdemeanors.

The following unlawful acts and offenses against animals shall constitute and be punished as a Class 3 misdemeanor:

1. Violation of §3.1-796.71 pertaining to the failure of a shopkeeper or pet dealer to provide adequate care to animals.

2. Violation of §3.1-796.72 pertaining to the misrepresentation of an animal's condition by the shopkeeper or pet dealer.

3. Violation of §3.1-796.73 and subsection C of §3.1-796.122 pertaining to the abandonment of animals.

4. Violation of §3.1-796.70 pertaining to the sale of baby fowl.

5. Violation of §3.1-796.125 pertaining to fighting cocks, dogs and other animals.

6. Violation of §3.1-796.123 pertaining to soring horses.

7. Violation of §3.1-796.83:2 pertaining to notice of consumer remedies required to be supplied by boarding establishments.

(Chgd. by L.1999 ch. 620, eff. 7/1/99.)

§18.2-403.3. Offenses involving animals – Class 4 misdemeanors.

The following unlawful acts and offenses against animals shall constitute and be punished as a Class 4 misdemeanor:

1. Violation of §3.1-796.111 pertaining to interference of agents charged with preventing cruelty to animals.

2. Violation of §3.1-796.126 pertaining to shooting pigeons.

3. Violation of §3.1-796.121 pertaining to disposing of the body of a dead companion animal.

4. Violation of ordinances passed pursuant to §§3.1-796.98 and 3.1-796.100 pertaining to rabid dogs and preventing the spread of rabies and the running at large of vicious dogs.

5. Violation of an ordinance passed pursuant to §3.1-796.95 requiring dogs to be on a leash.

6. Failure by any person to secure and exhibit the permits required by §29.1-422 pertaining to field trials, night trials and foxhounds.

7. Diseased dogs. – For the owner of any dog with a contagious or infectious disease to permit such dog to stray from his premises if such disease is known to the owner.

8. License application. – For any person to make a false statement in order to secure a dog or cat license to which he is not entitled.

9. License tax. – For any dog or cat owner to fail to pay any license tax required by §3.1-796.88 before February 1 for the year in which it is due. In addition, the court may order confiscation and the proper disposition of the dog or cat.

10. Concealing a dog or cat. – For any person to conceal or harbor any dog or cat on which any required license tax has not been paid.

11. Removing collar and tag. – For any person, except the owner or custodian, to remove a legally acquired license tag from a dog or cat without the permission of the owner or custodian.

12. Violation of §3.1-796.68 pertaining to care of animals by owner.

§18.2-403.4. Unauthorized release of animals; penalty.

Any person who intentionally releases an animal, as defined in §3.1-796.66, lawfully confined for scientific, research, commercial, agricultural or educational purposes without the consent of the owner or custodian of the animal and with the intent to impede or obstruct any such lawful purpose shall be guilty of a Class 1 misdemeanor.

CHAPTER 9
CRIMES AGAINST PEACE AND ORDER

Article

ARTICLE 1
RIOT AND UNLAWFUL ASSEMBLY

Section

§18.2-404. Obstructing free passage of others.

Any person or persons who in any public place or on any private property open to the public unreasonably or unnecessarily obstructs the free passage of other persons to and from or within such place or property and who shall fail or refuse to cease such obstruction or move on when requested to do so by the owner or lessee or agent or employee of such owner or lessee or by a duly authorized law-enforcement officer shall be guilty of a Class 1 misdemeanor. Nothing in this section shall be construed to prohibit lawful picketing.

§18.2-405. What constitutes a riot; punishment.

Any unlawful use, by three or more persons acting together, of force or violence which seriously jeopardizes the public safety, peace or order is riot.

Every person convicted of participating in any riot shall be guilty of a Class 1 misdemeanor.

If such person carried, at the time of such riot, any firearm or other deadly or dangerous weapon, he shall be guilty of a Class 5 felony.

§18.2-406. What constitutes an unlawful assembly; punishment.

Whenever three or more persons assembled share the common intent to advance some lawful or unlawful purpose by the commission of an act or acts of unlawful force or violence likely to jeopardize seriously public safety, peace or order, and the assembly actually tends to inspire persons of ordinary courage with well-grounded fear of serious and immediate breaches of public safety, peace or order, then such assembly is an unlawful assembly. Every person who participates in any unlawful assembly shall be guilty of a Class 1 misdemeanor. If any such person carried, at the time of his participation in an unlawful assembly, any firearm or other deadly or dangerous weapon, he shall be guilty of a Class 5 felony.

§18.2-407. Remaining at place of riot or unlawful assembly after warning to disperse.

Every person, except the owner or lessee of the premises, his family and nonrioting guests, and public officers and persons assisting them, who remains at the place of any riot or unlawful assembly after having been lawfully warned to disperse, shall be guilty of a Class 3 misdemeanor.

§18.2-408. Conspiracy; incitement, etc., to riot.

Any person who conspires with others to cause or produce a riot, or directs, incites, or solicits other persons who participate in a riot to acts of force or violence, shall be guilty of a Class 5 felony.

§18.2-409. Resisting or obstructing execution of legal process.

Every person acting jointly or in combination with any other person to resist or obstruct the execution of any legal process shall be guilty of a Class 1 misdemeanor.

§18.2-410. Power of Governor to summon law-enforcement agencies, national guard, etc., to execute process or preserve the peace.

If it appears to the Governor that the power of the locality is not sufficient to enable the sheriff or other officer to execute process delivered to him or to suppress riots and to preserve the peace, he may order law-enforcement agencies, national guard, militia or other agencies of the Commonwealth or localities as may be necessary to execute such process and to preserve the peace. All persons so ordered or summoned by the Governor are required to attend and act. Any person who, without lawful cause, refuses or neglects to obey the command, shall be guilty of a Class 1 misdemeanor.

§18.2-411. Dispersal of unlawful or riotous assemblies; duties of officers.

When any number of persons, whether armed or not, are unlawfully or riotously assembled, the sheriff of the county and his deputies, the police officials of the county, city or town, and any assigned militia, or any of them, shall go among the persons assembled or as near to them as safety will permit and command them in the name of the Commonwealth immediately to disperse. If upon such command the persons unlawfully assembled do not disperse immediately, such sheriff, officer or militia may use such force as is reasonably necessary to disperse them and to arrest those who fail or refuse to disperse. To accomplish this end, the sheriff or other law-enforcement officer may request and use the assistance and services of private citizens. Every endeavor shall be used, both by such sheriff or other officers and by the officer commanding any other force, which can be made consistently with the preservation of life, to induce or force those unlawfully assembled to disperse before an attack is made upon those unlawfully assembled by which their lives may be endangered.

§18.2-412. Immunity of officers and others in quelling a riot or unlawful assembly.

No liability, criminal or civil, shall be imposed upon any person authorized to disperse or assist in dispersing a riot or unlawful assembly for any action of such person which was taken after those rioting or unlawfully assembled had been commanded to disperse, and which action was reasonably necessary under all the circumstances to disperse such riot or unlawful assembly or to arrest those who failed or refused to disperse.

§18.2-413. Commission of certain offenses in county, city or town declared by Governor to be in state of riot or insurrection.

Any person, who after the publication of a proclamation by the Governor, or who after lawful notice to disperse and retire, resists or aids in resisting the execution of process in any county, city or town declared to be in a state of riot or insurrection, or who aids or attempts the rescue or escape of another from lawful custody or confinement, or who resists or aids in resisting a force ordered out by the Governor or any sheriff or other officer to quell or suppress an insurrection or riot, shall be guilty of a Class 5 felony.

§18.2-414. Injury to property or persons by persons unlawfully or riotously assembled.

If any person or persons, unlawfully or riotously assembled, pull down, injure, or destroy, or begin to pull down, injure or destroy any dwelling house or other building, or assist therein, or perpetrate any premeditated injury on the person of another, he shall be guilty of a Class 6 felony.

§18.2-414.1. Obstructing members of rescue squad in performance of mission.

Any person or persons who unreasonably or unnecessarily obstruct a member or members of a rescue squad, whether governmental, private or volunteer, in the performance of their rescue mission or who shall fail or refuse to cease such obstruction or move on when requested to do so by a member of a rescue squad going to or at the site of a rescue mission, shall be guilty of a Class 4 misdemeanor.

§18.2-414.2. Crossing established police lines, perimeters or barricades.

It shall be unlawful for any person to cross or remain within police lines or barricades which have been established pursuant to §15.1-140.1 without proper authorization.

Any person violating the provisions of this section shall be guilty of a Class 3 misdemeanor.

ARTICLE 2
DISORDERLY CONDUCT

§18.2-415. Disorderly conduct in public places.

A person is guilty of disorderly conduct if, with the intent to cause public inconvenience, annoyance or alarm, or recklessly creating a risk thereof, he:

A. In any street, highway, public building, or while in or on a public conveyance, or public place engages in conduct having a direct tendency to cause acts of violence by the person or persons at whom, individually, such conduct is directed; or

B. Willfully or being intoxicated, whether willfully or not, and whether such intoxication results from self-administered alcohol or other drug of whatever nature, disrupts any meeting of the governing body of any political subdivision of this Commonwealth or a division or agency thereof, or of any school, literary society or place of religious worship, if the disruption (i) prevents or interferes with the orderly conduct of the meeting or (ii) has a direct tendency to cause acts of violence by the person or persons at whom, individually, the disruption is directed; or

C. Willfully or while intoxicated, whether willfully or not, and whether such intoxication results from self-administered alcohol or other drug of whatever nature, disrupts the operation of any school or any activity conducted or sponsored by any school, if the disruption (i) prevents or interferes with the orderly conduct of the operation or activity or (ii) has a direct tendency to cause acts of violence by the person or persons at whom, individually, the disruption is directed.

However, the conduct prohibited under subsection A, B or C shall not be deemed to include the utterance or display of any words or to include conduct otherwise made punishable under this title.

The person in charge of any such building, place, conveyance, meeting operation or activity may eject therefrom any person who violates any provision of this section, with the aid, if necessary, of any persons who may be called upon for such purpose.

The governing bodies of counties, cities and towns are authorized to adopt ordinances prohibiting and punishing the acts and conduct prohibited by this section, provided that the punishment fixed therefor shall not exceed that prescribed for a Class 1 misdemeanor. A person violating any provision of this section shall be guilty of a Class 1 misdemeanor.

ARTICLE 3
ABUSIVE AND INSULTING LANGUAGE

§18.2-416. Punishment for using abusive language to another.

If any person shall, in the presence or hearing of another, curse or abuse such other person, or use any violent abusive language to such person concerning himself or any of his relations, or otherwise use such language, under circumstances reasonably calculated to provoke a breach of the peace, he shall be guilty of a Class 3 misdemeanor.

§18.2-417. Slander and libel.

Any person who shall falsely utter and speak, or falsely write and publish, of and concerning any female of chaste character, any words derogatory of such female's character for virtue and chastity, or imputing to such female acts not virtuous and chaste, or who shall falsely utter and speak, or falsely write and publish, of and concerning another person, any words which from their usual construction and common acceptation are construed as insults and tend to violence and breach of the peace or shall use grossly insulting language to any female of good character or reputation, shall be guilty of a Class 3 misdemeanor.

The defendant shall be entitled to prove upon trial in mitigation of the punishment, the provocation which induced the libelous or slanderous words, or any other fact or circumstance tending to disprove malice, or lessen the criminality of the offense.

ARTICLE 4
PICKETING OF DWELLING PLACES

§18.2-418. Declaration of policy.

It is hereby declared that the protection and preservation of the home is the keystone of democratic government; that the public health and welfare and the good order of the community require that members of the community enjoy in their homes a feeling of well-being, tranquility, and privacy, and when absent from their homes carry with them the sense of security inherent in the assurance that they may return to the enjoyment of their homes; that the practice of picketing before or about residences and dwelling places causes emotional disturbance and distress to the occupants; that such practice has as its object the harassing of such occupants; and without resort to such practice, full opportunity exists, and under the terms and provisions of this article will continue to exist, for the exercise of freedom of speech and other constitutional rights; and that the provisions hereinafter enacted are necessary in the public interest, to avoid the detrimental results herein set forth.

§18.2-419. Picketing or disrupting tranquility of home.

Any person who shall engage in picketing before or about the residence or dwelling place of any individual, or who shall assemble with another person or persons in a manner which disrupts or threatens to disrupt any individual's right to tranquility in his home, shall be guilty of a Class 3 misdemeanor. Each day on which a violation of this section occurs shall constitute a separate offense.

Nothing herein shall be deemed to prohibit (1) the picketing in any lawful manner, during a labor dispute, of the place of employment involved in such labor dispute; (2) the picketing in any lawful manner of a construction site; or (3) the holding of a meeting or assembly on any premises commonly used for the discussion of subjects of general public interest.

Notwithstanding the penalties herein provided, any court of general equity jurisdiction may enjoin conduct, or threatened conduct, proscribed by this article, and may in any such proceeding award damages, including punitive damages, against the persons found guilty of actions made unlawful by this section.

ARTICLE 5
ACTIVITIES TENDING TO CAUSE VIOLENCE

§18.2-420. "Clandestine organization" defined.

"Clandestine organization" means: any organization (1) which conceals, or attempts to conceal, its name, activities or membership, or the names, activities or membership of any chapter, branch, unit or affiliate thereof, by the use of covernames, codes, or any deceptive practice or other means, or (2) whose members shall be required, urged, or instructed, or shall adopt any practice, to conceal their membership or affiliation and that of others in or with such organization, or (3) whose members shall take any oath or pledge, or shall administer any such oath or pledge to those associated with them, to maintain in secrecy any matter or knowledge committed to them by the organization or by any member thereof, or (4) which shall transact business or advance any purpose at any secret meeting or meetings which are guarded or secured against intrusion by persons not associated with it, and (5) whose purpose, policy or activity includes the unlawful use of violence, threats, or intimidation in accomplishing any of its objectives.

§18.2-421. Information to be filed by clandestine organization with State Corporation Commission.

Every existing membership corporation and every existing unincorporated association which is a clandestine organization as defined in §18.2-420, shall file with the clerk of the State Corporation Commission a sworn copy of its constitution, bylaws, rules, regulations, and oath of membership, together with a roster of its membership and a list of its officers for the current year. Every such corporation and association shall, in case its constitution, bylaws, rules, regulations or oath of membership or any part thereof be revised, changed or amended, within ten days after such revision or amendment, file with the clerk of the State Corporation Commission a sworn copy of such revised, changed or amended constitution, bylaw, rule, regulation or oath of membership. Every such corporation or association shall, within thirty days after a change has been made in its officers, file with the clerk of the State Corporation Commission a sworn statement showing such change. Every such corporation or association shall, at intervals of six months, file with the clerk of the State Corporation Commission, a sworn statement showing the names and addresses of such additional members as have been received in such corporation or association during such interval.

The violation of any provision of this section shall constitute a Class 3 misdemeanor.

The provisions of §§18.2-420 and 18.2-421 shall not apply to fraternal organizations which are organized for charitable, benevolent, and educational objectives and whose transactions and list of members are open for public inspection.

§18.2-422. Prohibition of wearing of masks in certain places; exceptions.

It shall be unlawful for any person over sixteen years of age while wearing any mask, hood or other device whereby a substantial portion of the face is hidden or covered so as to conceal the identity of the wearer, to be or appear in any public place, or upon any private property in this Commonwealth without first having obtained from the owner or tenant thereof consent to do so in writing. However, the provisions of this section shall not apply to persons (i) wearing traditional holiday costumes; (ii) engaged in professions, trades, employment or other activities and wearing protective masks which are deemed necessary for the physical safety of the wearer or other persons; (iii) engaged in any bona fide theatrical production or masquerade ball; or (iv) wearing a mask, hood or other device for bona fide medical reasons upon the advice of a licensed physician or osteopath and carrying on his person an affidavit from the physician or osteopath specifying the medical necessity for wearing the device and the date on which the wearing of the device will no longer be necessary and providing a brief description of the device. The violation of any provisions of this section shall constitute a Class 6 felony.

§18.2-423. Burning cross on property of another or public place with intent to intimidate; penalty; prima facie evidence of intent.

It shall be unlawful for any person or persons, with the intent of intimidating any person or group of persons, to burn, or cause to be burned, a cross on the property of another, a highway or other public place. Any person who shall violate any provision of this section shall be guilty of a Class 6 felony.

Any such burning of a cross shall be prima facie evidence of an intent to intimidate a person or group of persons.

§18.2-423.1. Placing swastika on certain property with intent to intimidate; penalty; prima facie evidence of intent.

It shall be unlawful for any person or persons, with the intent of intimidating another person or persons, to place or cause to be placed a swastika on any church, synagogue or other building or place used for religious worship, or on any school, educational facility or community center owned or operated by a church or religious body.

A violation of this section shall be punishable as a Class 6 felony.

For the purposes of this section, any such placing of a swastika shall be prima facie evidence of an intent to intimidate another person or group of persons.

ARTICLE 6
UNLAWFUL USE OF TELEPHONES

§18.2-424. Relinquishing telephone party lines in emergency.

Any person who fails to relinquish a telephone party line after he has been requested to do so to permit another to place an emergency call, shall be guilty of a Class 4 misdemeanor; provided, that this section shall not apply to any person who is using the telephone party line for an emergency call.

§18.2-425. Requesting relinquishment on pretext.

Any person who requests another to relinquish a telephone party line on the pretext that he must place an emergency call, knowing such pretext to be false, shall be guilty of a Class 4 misdemeanor.

§18.2-425.1. Certain solicitation calls prohibited; penalties.

A. Any person who uses recorded solicitation calls for initial sales contacts shall be guilty of a Class 4 misdemeanor.

B. Any person who uses recorded solicitation calls which do not disengage or terminate when the party called attempts to terminate the call by any method which is in accordance with normal operating procedures of his receiver shall be guilty of a Class 3 misdemeanor.

C. Nothing contained herein shall be construed to permit any fine or penalty against any employee or agent who has been caused, directed or authorized by his employer to violate the provisions of this section. In such cases, the employer shall be subject to the sanctions prescribed in this section.

§18.2-426. "Emergency call," "emergency personnel" and "telephone party line" defined.

As used in this article:

"Emergency call" means a call to report a fire or summon police, or for medical aid or ambulance service, in a situation where human life or property is in jeopardy and the prompt summoning of aid is essential.

"Emergency personnel" means any persons, paid or volunteer, who receive calls for dispatch of police, fire, or emergency medical service personnel, and includes law-enforcement officers, firefighters, including special forest wardens designated pursuant to §10.1-1135, and emergency medical service personnel.

"Telephone party line" means a subscriber's line circuit consisting of two or more main telephone stations connected therewith, each station with a distinctive ring or telephone number.

(Chgd. by L.1995 ch. 791; L.2000 ch. 962, eff. 7/1/2000.)

 Zv

§18.2-427. Use of profane, threatening or indecent language over public airways.

If any person shall use obscene, vulgar, profane, lewd, lascivious, or indecent language, or make any suggestion or proposal of an obscene nature, or threaten any illegal or immoral act with the intent to coerce, intimidate, or harass any person, over any telephone or citizens band radio, in this Commonwealth, he shall be guilty of a Class 1 misdemeanor.

§18.2-428. Giving certain false information to another by telephone.

If any person maliciously advises or informs another over any telephone in this Commonwealth of the death of, accident to, injury to, illness of, or disappearance of some third party, knowing the same to be false, he shall be guilty of a Class 1 misdemeanor.

§18.2-429. Causing telephone to ring with intent to annoy.

Any person who, with or without intent to communicate but with intent to annoy any other person, causes any telephone or digital pager, not his own, to ring or to otherwise signal, and any person who permits or condones the use of any telephone under his control for such purpose shall be guilty of a Class 3 misdemeanor.

Any person who, with or without intent to converse, but with intent to annoy, harass, hinder or delay emergency personnel in the performance of their duties as such, causes a telephone to ring, which is owned or leased for the purpose of receiving emergency calls by a public or private entity providing fire, police or emergency medical service, and any person who knowingly permits the use of a telephone under his control for such purpose, shall be guilty of a Class 1 misdemeanor.

(Chgd. by L.1995 chs. 410, 478, 791, eff. 7/1/95.)

§18.2-430. Venue for offenses under this article.

Any person violating any of the provisions of this article may be prosecuted either in the county or city from which he called or in the county or city in which the call was received.

§18.2-431. Duty of telephone companies; notices in directories.

(1) It shall be the duty, on pain of contempt of court, of each telephone company in this Commonwealth to furnish immediately in response to a subpoena issued by a circuit court such information as it, its officers and employees may possess which, in the opinion of the court, may aid in the apprehension of persons suspected of violating the provisions of this article or the provisions of §18.2-83 or §18.2-212.

(2) Every telephone directory distributed to the public which lists the calling numbers of telephones or of any telephone exchange located in this Commonwealth shall contain a notice which explains the offenses made punishable under this article, such notice to be printed in type which conforms with and is comparable to other type on the same page, and to be placed in a prominent place in such directory. Any violation of this subsection shall be punishable as a Class 4 misdemeanor.

ARTICLE 7
PLACES OF AMUSEMENT AND DANCE HALLS

Section

§18.2-432. Counties, cities and towns authorized to regulate minors in public places of amusement.

The governing body of any county, city or town may, by ordinance, regulate the frequenting, playing in or loitering in public places of amusement by minors, and may prescribe punishment for violations of such ordinances not to exceed that prescribed for a Class 3 misdemeanor.

§18.2-433. Regulation of dance halls by counties, cities and towns.

A public dance hall, within the meaning of this section, shall be construed to mean any place open to the general public where dancing is permitted; provided, however, that a restaurant located in any city licensed under §4.1-210 to serve food and beverages having a dance floor with an area not exceeding ten per centum of the total floor area of the establishment shall not be considered a public dance hall.

The governing body of any county, city or town may, by ordinance, regulate public dance halls in such county, city or town, and prescribe punishment for violation of such ordinance not to exceed that prescribed for a Class 3 misdemeanor.

Such ordinance shall prescribe for: (1) the issuance of permits to operate public dance halls, grounds for revocation and procedure for revocation of such permits; (2) a license tax not to exceed $600 on every person operating or conducting any such dance hall; and (3) rules and regulations for the operation of such dance halls. Such ordinances may exempt from their operation dances held for benevolent or charitable purposes, or when the same are conducted under the auspices of religious, educational, civic or military organizations.

No county ordinance adopted under the provisions of this section shall be in effect in any town in which an ordinance adopted under the provisions of this section is in effect.

ARTICLE 8
UNLAWFUL PARAMILITARY ACTIVITY

Section

§18.2-433.1. Definitions.

As used in this article:

"Civil disorder" means any public disturbance within the United States or any territorial possessions thereof involving acts of violence by assemblages of three or more persons, which causes an immediate danger of or results in damage or injury to the property or person of any other individual.

"Explosive or incendiary device" means (i) dynamite and all other forms of high explosives, (ii) any explosive bomb, grenade, missile, or similar device, or (iii) any incendiary bomb or grenade, fire bomb, or similar device, including any device which consists of or includes a breakable container including a flammable liquid or compound, and a wick composed of any material which, when ignited, is capable of igniting such flammable liquid or compound, and can be carried or thrown by one individual acting alone.

"Firearm" means any weapon which is designed to or may readily be converted to expel any projectile by the action of an explosive; or the frame or receiver of any such weapon.

"Law-enforcement officer" means any officer as defined in subdivision 9 of §9-169 or any such officer or member of the armed forces of the United States, any state, any political subdivision of a state, or the District of Columbia, and such term shall specifically include, but shall not be limited to, members of the National Guard, as defined in §101(9) of Title 10, United States Code, members of the organized militia of any state or territory of the United States, the Commonwealth of Puerto Rico, or the District of Columbia, not included within the definition of National Guard as defined by such §101(9), and members of the armed forces of the United States.

§18.2-433.2. Paramilitary activity prohibited.

A person shall be guilty of unlawful paramilitary activity, punishable as a Class 5 felony if he:

1. Teaches or demonstrates to any other person the use, application, or making of any firearm, explosive or incendiary device, or technique capable of causing injury or death to persons, knowing or having reason to know or intending that such training will be employed for use in, or in furtherance of, a civil disorder; or

2. Assembles with one or more persons for the purpose of training with, practicing with, or being instructed in the use of any firearm, explosive or incendiary device, or technique capable of causing injury or death to persons, intending to employ such training for use in, or in furtherance of, a civil disorder.

§18.2-433.3. Exceptions.

Nothing contained in this article shall be construed to apply to:

1. Any act of a law-enforcement officer performed in the otherwise lawful performance of the officer's official duties;

2. Any activity, undertaken without knowledge of or intent to cause or further a civil disorder, which is intended to teach or practice self-defense or self-defense techniques such as karate clubs or self-defense clinics, and similar lawful activity;

3. Any facility, program or lawful activity related to firearms instruction and training intended to teach the safe handling and use of firearms; or

4. Any other lawful sports or activities related to the individual recreational use or possession of firearms, including but not limited to hunting activities, target shooting, self-defense and firearms collection.

Notwithstanding any language contained herein, no activity of any individual, group, organization or other entity engaged in the lawful display or use of firearms or other weapons or facsimiles thereof shall be deemed to be in violation of this statute.

CHAPTER 10
CRIMES AGAINST THE ADMINISTRATION OF JUSTICE

ARTICLE 1
PERJURY

§18.2-434. What deemed perjury; punishment and penalty.

If any person to whom an oath is lawfully administered on any occasion willfully swear falsely on such occasion touching any material matter or thing, or if a person falsely make oath that any other person is eighteen years of age in order to obtain a marriage license for such other person, he shall be guilty of perjury, punishable as a Class 5 felony. Upon the conviction of any person for perjury, such person thereby shall be adjudged forever incapable of holding any office of honor, profit or trust under the Constitution of Virginia, or of serving as a juror.

§18.2-435. Giving conflicting testimony on separate occasions as to same matter; indictment; sufficiency of evidence.

It shall likewise constitute perjury for any person, with the intent to testify falsely, to knowingly give testimony under oath as to any material matter or thing and subsequently to give conflicting testimony under oath as to the same matter or thing. In any indictment for such perjury, it shall be sufficient to allege the offense by stating that the person charged therewith did, knowingly and with the intent to testify falsely, on one occasion give testimony upon a certain matter and, on a subsequent occasion, give different testimony upon the same matter. Upon the trial on such indictment, it shall be sufficient to prove that the defendant, knowingly and with the intent to testify falsely, gave such differing testimony and that the differing testimony was given on two separate occasions.

§18.2-436. Inducing another to give false testimony; sufficiency of evidence.

If any person procure or induce another to commit perjury or to give false testimony under oath in violation of any provision of this article, he shall be punished as prescribed in §18.2-434.

In any prosecution under this section, it shall be sufficient to prove that the person alleged to have given false testimony shall have been procured induced, counselled or advised to give such testimony by the party charged.

§18.2-437. Immunity of witnesses.

No witness called by the attorney for the Commonwealth, or by the court, and required to give evidence for the prosecution in a proceeding under this article shall ever be proceeded against for the offense concerning which he testified. Such witness shall be compelled to testify and may be punished for contempt for refusing to do so.

ARTICLE 2
BRIBERY AND RELATED OFFENSES

§18.2-438. Bribes to officers or candidates for office.

If any person corruptly give, offer or promise to any executive, legislative or judicial officer, sheriff or police officer, or to any candidate for such office, either before or after he shall have taken his seat, any gift or gratuity, with intent to influence his act, vote, opinion, decision or judgment on any matter, question, cause or proceeding, which is or may be then pending, or may by law come or be brought before him in his official capacity, he shall be guilty of a Class 4 felony and shall forfeit to the Commonwealth any such gift or gratuity given. This section shall also apply to a resident of this Commonwealth who, while temporarily absent therefrom for that purpose, shall make such gift, offer or promise.

§18.2-439. Acceptance of bribe by officer or candidate.

If any executive, legislative or judicial officer, sheriff or police officer, or any candidate for such office, accept in this Commonwealth, or if, being resident in this Commonwealth, such officer or candidate shall go out of this Commonwealth and accept and afterwards return to and reside in this Commonwealth, any gift or gratuity or any promise to make a gift or do any act beneficial to such officer or candidate under an agreement, or with an understanding, that his vote, opinion or judgment shall be given on any particular side of any question, cause or proceeding which is or may be by law brought before him in his official capacity or that in such capacity he shall make any particular nomination or appointment or take or fail to take any particular action or perform any duty required by law, he shall be guilty of a Class 4 felony and shall forfeit his office and be forever incapable of holding any office of honor, profit or trust under the Constitution of Virginia. The word candidate as used in this section and §18.2-438, shall mean anyone who has filed his candidacy with the appropriate electoral official or who is a candidate as defined in subdivision (2) of §24.1-1.

§18.2-440. Bribes to officers to prevent service of process.

If any officer authorized to serve legal process receive any money or other thing of value for omitting or delaying to perform any duty pertaining to his office, he shall be guilty of a Class 2 misdemeanor.

§18.2-441. Giving bribes to, or receiving bribes by, commissioners, jurors, etc.

If any person give, offer or promise to give any money or other thing of value to a commissioner appointed by a court, auditor, arbitrator, umpire or juror (although not impaneled), with intent to bias his opinion influence his decision in relation to any matter in which he is acting or is to act, or if any such commissioner, auditor, arbitrator, umpire or juror corruptly take or receive such money or other thing, he shall be guilty of a Class 4 felony.

§18.2-441.1. Bribery of witnesses.

If any person give, offer, or promise to give any money or other thing of value to anyone with intent to prevent such person from testifying as a witness in any civil or criminal proceeding or with intent to cause that person to testify falsely, he shall be guilty of a Class 6 felony.

§18.2-442. Bribery of participants in games, contests or sports.

Whoever gives, promises or offers any valuable thing to any professional or amateur participant or prospective participant in any game, contest or sport, with intent to influence him to lose or try to lose or cause to be lost or to limit his or his team's margin of victory in any professional or amateur game, contest or sport in which such participant is taking part or expects to take part, or has any duty or connection therewith, shall be guilty of a Class 5 felony.

§18.2-443. Solicitation or acceptance of bribes by participants or by managers, coaches or trainers.

A professional or amateur participant or prospective participant in any game, contest or sport or a manager, coach or trainer of any team or individual participant or prospective participant in any such game, contest or sport, who solicits or accepts any valuable thing to influence him to lose or try to lose or cause to be lost or to limit his or his team's margin of victory in any game, contest or sport in which he is taking part, or expects to take part, or has any duty or connection therewith, shall be guilty of a Class 5 felony.

§18.2-444. Corruptly influencing, or being influenced as, agents, etc.

(1) Any person who gives, offers or promises to an agent, employee or servant any gift or gratuity whatever, without the knowledge and consent of the principal, employer or master of such agent, employee or servant, with intent to influence his action to the prejudice of his principal's, employer's or master's business; or

(2) An agent, employee or servant who, without the knowledge and consent of his principal, employer or master requests or accepts a gift or gratuity or a promise to make a gift or to do an act beneficial to himself, under an agreement or with an understanding that he shall act in any particular manner as to his principal's, employer's or master's business; or

(3) An agent, employee or servant who, being authorized to procure materials, supplies or other articles either by purchase or contract for his principal, employer or master or to employ service or labor for his principal, employer or master receives directly or indirectly, for himself or for another, a commission, discount or bonus from the person who makes such sale or contract, or furnishes such materials, supplies or other articles, or from a person who renders such service or labor; or

(4) Any person who gives or offers such an agent, employee or servant such commission, discount or bonus; shall be guilty of a Class 3 misdemeanor.

§18.2-444.2. Giving or accepting a fee or gift for purposes of influencing decisions of financial institution.

A. No officer, director, or employee of a financial institution or subsidiary, affiliate or holding company thereof, or stockholder owning ten percent or more of the issued capital stock of any such financial institution or holding company, shall accept, receive or acquire any fee, gift, property interest, or other thing of value with the intent to influence the decision of the financial institution, subsidiary, affiliate or holding company with regard to any extension of credit, investment, or purchase or sale of assets by such financial institution, subsidiary, affiliate or holding company. No person shall give, provide or cause to be transferred to any such officer, director, employee or stockholder, any fee, gift, property interest or other thing of value with the intent to influence the decision of the financial institution, subsidiary, affiliate or holding company with regard to any extension of credit, investment or purchase or sale of assets by the financial institution, subsidiary, affiliate or holding company. The foregoing provisions shall not apply to salary, wages, fees or other compensation or consideration paid by, or expenses paid or reimbursed by, such financial institution, subsidiary, affiliate or holding company. The violation of this section shall be punishable as a Class 6 felony.

B. The provisions of this section shall not apply to any such officer, director, employee or stockholder who is a member of a firm of licensed brokers, in buying for or from or selling to, or for the account of, the financial institution, in the ordinary course of business, real estate or bonds, stocks, or other evidences of debt at the usual rate of commission for such service, if the officer, director, employee or stockholder notifies the board of directors of the financial institution, its cashier or secretary, in writing, that such services will be rendered for compensation prior to the rendition of the services or within five business days following the commencement of the services. If a continuing business relationship exists, an annual disclosure may be made.

C. The provisions of this section shall not apply to fees paid to any such officer, director, employee, or stockholder who renders services to a borrower outside of his relationship with the financial institution in connection with the preparation of a loan application, or in connection with the closing of a loan, in evaluating the security or affecting a lien on the collateral, where the fact of rendition of such services for compensation is disclosed in writing to the board of directors of the financial institution, or its cashier or secretary, prior to the time such services are rendered or within five business days following the commencement of the services. If a continuing business relationship exists, an annual disclosure may be made.

§18.2-445. Immunity of witnesses.

No witness called by the court or attorney for the Commonwealth and giving evidence for the prosecution, either before the grand jury or the court in any prosecution, under this article shall ever be proceeded against for any offense of giving, or offering to give, or accepting a bribe committed by him at the time and place indicated in such prosecution; but such witness shall be compelled to testify, and for refusing to answer questions may, by the court, be punished for contempt.

ARTICLE 3
BRIBERY OF PUBLIC SERVANTS AND PARTY OFFICIALS

Section

§18.2-446. Definitions.

The following words and phrases when used in this article shall have the meanings respectively ascribed to them in this section except where the context clearly requires a different meaning:

(1) "Administrative proceeding" means any proceeding other than a judicial proceeding, the outcome of which is required to be based on a record or documentation prescribed by law including specifically, but not limited to, proceedings before a planning commission and board of zoning appeals.

(2) "Benefits" means a gain or advantage, or anything regarded by the beneficiary as a gain or advantage, including a benefit to any other person or entity in whose welfare he is interested, but shall not mean an advantage promised generally to a group or class of voters as a consequence of public measures which a candidate engages to support or oppose;

(3) "Party official" means a person who holds an elective or appointive post in a political party in the United States by virtue of which he directs or conducts, or participates in directing or conducting party affairs at any level of responsibility;

(4) "Pecuniary benefit" means a benefit in the form of money, property, commercial interest or anything else the primary significance of which is economic gain;

(5) "Public servant" means any officer or employee of this Commonwealth or any political subdivision thereof, including members of the General Assembly and judges, and any person participating as a juror, advisor, consultant or otherwise, in performing any governmental function; but the term does not include witnesses;

§18.2-447. When person guilty of bribery.

A person shall be guilty of bribery under the provisions of this article:

(1) If he offers, confers or agrees to confer upon another (a) any pecuniary benefit as consideration for or to obtain or influence the recipient's decision, opinion, recommendation, vote or other exercise of discretion as a public servant or party official, or (b) any benefit as consideration for or to obtain or influence either the recipient's decision, opinion, recommendation, vote or other exercise of official discretion in a judicial or administrative proceeding or the recipient's violation of a known legal duty as a public servant or party official; or

(2) If he accepts or agrees to accept from another (a) any pecuniary benefit offered, conferred or agreed to be conferred as consideration for or to obtain or influence the recipient's decision, opinion, recommendation, vote or other exercise of discretion as a public servant or party official, or (b) any benefit offered, conferred or agreed to be conferred as consideration for or to obtain or influence either the recipient's decision, opinion, recommendation, vote or other exercise of official discretion in a judicial or administrative proceeding or the recipient's violation of a known legal duty as a public servant or party official; or

(3) If he solicits from another (a) any pecuniary benefit or promise of pecuniary benefit as consideration for or in exchange for his decision, opinion, recommendation, vote or other exercise of discretion as a public servant or party official, or (b) any benefit or promise of benefit as consideration for or in exchange for his decision, opinion, recommendation, vote or other exercise of official discretion in a judicial or administrative proceeding or his violation of a known legal duty as a public servant or party official.

§18.2-448. Certain matters not to constitute defenses.

It shall be no defense to any prosecution under §18.2-447 that a person whom the actor sought to influence was not qualified to act in the desired way, whether because he had not yet assumed office, or lacked jurisdiction, or for any other reason. Also it shall be no defense to a prosecution under §18.2-447 that a resident of this Commonwealth charged with committing an act of bribery was temporarily absent from this Commonwealth at the time such act was committed.

§18.2-449. Punishment.

Any person found guilty of bribery under the provisions of this article shall be guilty of a Class 4 felony, and if such person be a public servant he shall in addition forfeit his public office and shall be forever incapable of holding any public office in this Commonwealth.

§18.2-450. Immunity of witnesses.

No witness called by the court or attorney for the Commonwealth and giving evidence for the prosecution, either before the grand jury or the court in any prosecution under this article shall ever be proceeded against for any offense of giving, or offering to give, or accepting a bribe committed by him at the time and place indicated in such prosecution; but such witness shall be compelled to testify, and for refusing to answer questions, may by the court, be punished for contempt.

ARTICLE 4
BARRATRY

§18.2-451. Definitions; application and construction of article.

(a) "Barratry" is the offense of stirring up litigation.

(b) A "barrator" is an individual, partnership, association or corporation who or which stirs up litigation.

(c) "Stirring up litigation" means instigating or attempting to instigate a person or persons to institute a suit at law or equity.

(d) "Instigating" means bringing it about that all or part of the expenses of the litigation are paid by the barrator or by a person or persons (other than the plaintiffs) acting in concert with the barrator, unless the instigation is justified.

(e) "Justified" means that the instigator is related by blood or marriage to the plaintiff whom he instigates, or that the instigator is entitled by law to share with the plaintiff in money or property that is the subject of the litigation or that the instigator has a direct interest in the subject matter of the litigation or occupies a position of trust in relation to the plaintiff; or that the instigator is acting on behalf of a duly constituted legal aid society approved by the Virginia State Bar which offers advice or assistance in all kinds of legal matters to all members of the public who come to it for advice or assistance and are unable because of poverty to pay legal fees.

(f) "Direct interest" means a personal right or a pecuniary right or liability.

This article shall not be applicable to attorneys who are parties to contingent fee contracts with their clients where the attorney does not protect the client from payment of the costs and expense of litigation, nor shall this article apply to any matter involving annexation, zoning, bond issues, or the holding or results of any election or referendum, nor shall this article apply to suits pertaining to or affecting possession of or title to real or personal property, regardless of ownership, nor shall this article apply to suits involving the legality of assessment or collection of taxes or the rates thereof, nor shall this article apply to suits involving rates or charges or services by common carriers or public utilities, nor shall this article apply to criminal prosecutions nor to the payment of attorneys by legal aid societies approved by the Virginia State Bar, nor to proceedings to abate nuisances. Nothing herein shall be construed to be in derogation of the constitutional rights of real parties in interest to employ counsel or to prosecute any available legal remedy under the laws of this Commonwealth.

§18.2-452. Barratry unlawful.

Any person, if an individual, who shall engage in barratry shall be guilty of a Class 1 misdemeanor; and if a corporation, may be fined not more than $10,000. If the corporation be a foreign corporation, its certificate of authority to transact business in Virginia shall be revoked by the State Corporation Commission.

§18.2-453. Aiders and abettors.

A person who aids and abets a barrator by giving money or rendering services to or for the use or benefit of the barrator for committing barratry shall be guilty of barratry and punished as provided in §18.2-452.

§18.2-454. Enjoining barratry.

Suits to enjoin barratry may be brought by the Attorney General or the attorney for the Commonwealth in the appropriate circuit court.

§18.2-455. Unprofessional conduct; revocation of license.

Conduct that is made illegal by this article on the part of an attorney at law or any person holding license from the Commonwealth to engage in a profession is unprofessional conduct. Upon hearing pursuant to the provisions of §54.1-3935, or other statute applicable to the profession concerned, if the defendant be found guilty of barratry, his license to practice law or any other profession shall be revoked for such period as provided by law.

ARTICLE 5
CONTEMPT OF COURT

§18.2-456. Cases in which courts and judges may punish summarily for contempt.

The courts and judges may issue attachments for contempt, and punish them summarily, only in the cases following:

(1) Misbehavior in the presence of the court, or so near thereto as to obstruct or interrupt the administration of justice;

(2) Violence, or threats of violence, to a judge or officer of the court, or to a juror, witness or party going to, attending or returning from the court, for or in respect of any act or proceeding had or to be had in such court;

(3) Vile, contemptuous or insulting language addressed to or published of a judge for or in respect of any act or proceeding had, or to be had, in such court, or like language used in his presence and intended for his hearing for or in respect of such act or proceeding;

(4) Misbehavior of an officer of the court in his official character;

(5) Disobedience or resistance of an officer of the court, juror, witness or other person to any lawful process, judgment, decree or order of the court.

§18.2-457. Fine and imprisonment by court limited unless jury impaneled.

No court shall, without a jury, for any such contempt as is mentioned in the first class embraced in §18.2-456, impose a fine exceeding $250 or imprison more than ten days; but in any such case the court may, without an indictment, information or any formal pleading, impanel a jury to ascertain the fine or imprisonment proper to be inflicted and may give judgment according to the verdict.
(Chgd. by L.1999 ch. 626, eff. 7/1/99.)

§18.2-458. Power of judge of district court to punish for contempt.

A judge of a district court shall have the same power and jurisdiction as a judge of a circuit court to punish summarily for contempt, but in no case shall the fine exceed $250, or the imprisonment exceed ten days, for the same contempt.
(Chgd. by L.1999 ch. 626, eff. 7/1/99.)

§18.2-459. Appeal from sentence of such judge.

Any person sentenced to pay a fine, or to confinement, under §18.2-458, may appeal therefrom to the circuit court of the county or city in which the sentence was pronounced, upon entering into recognizance before the sentencing judge, with surety and in penalty deemed sufficient, to appear before such circuit court to answer for the offense. If such appeal be taken, a certificate of the conviction and the particular circumstances of the offense, together with the recognizance, shall forthwith be transmitted by the sentencing judge to the clerk of such circuit court, who shall immediately deliver the same to the judge thereof. Such judge may hear the case upon the certificate and any legal testimony adduced on either side, and make such order therein as may seem to him proper.

ARTICLE 6
INTERFERENCE WITH ADMINISTRATION OF JUSTICE

§18.2-460. Obstructing justice.

A. If any person without just cause knowingly obstructs a judge, magistrate, justice, juror, attorney for the Commonwealth, witness or any law-enforcement officer in the performance of his duties as such or fails or refuses without just cause to cease such obstruction when requested to do so by such judge, magistrate, justice, juror, attorney for the Commonwealth, witness, or law-enforcement officer, he shall be guilty of a Class 2 misdemeanor.

B. If any person, by threats or force, knowingly attempts to intimidate or impede a judge, magistrate, justice, juror, attorney for the Commonwealth, witness, or any law-enforcement officer, lawfully engaged in his duties as such, or to obstruct or impede the administration of justice in any court, he shall be deemed to be guilty of a Class 1 misdemeanor.

C. If any person by threats of bodily harm or force knowingly attempts to intimidate or impede a judge, magistrate, justice, juror, witness, or any law-enforcement officer, lawfully engaged in the discharge of his duty, or to obstruct or impede the administration of justice in any court relating to a violation of or conspiracy to violate §18.2-248 or §18.2-248.1 (a)(3), (b) or (c), or relating to the violation of or conspiracy to commit any violent felony offense listed in subsection C of §17.1-805, he shall be guilty of a Class 5 felony.
(Chgd. by L.1996 ch. 718; L.1999 chs. 770, 800, eff. 7/1/99.)

§18.2-460.1. Unlawful disclosure of existence of order authorizing wire or oral interception of communication.

Except as provided in Chapter 6 (§19.2-61 et seq.) of Title 19.2, it shall be unlawful for any person who, by virtue of his position of authority or in the course of his employment by a court, a public utility, a law-enforcement agency, or by any other agency of state or local government, obtains knowledge of the fact that an order authorizing interception of wire or oral communication has been entered or is sought to be entered, intentionally to disclose such information to any person, except In the performance of his duties. Persons violating this section shall be guilty of a Class 1 misdemeanor.

Nothing herein precludes a court authorizing an interception under this chapter from prohibiting any other person from disclosing the existence of an order, interception, or device and imposing contempt sanctions for any willful disclosure.

§18.2-461. Falsely summoning or giving false reports to law-enforcement officials.

It shall be unlawful for any person (i) to knowingly give a false report as to the commission of any crime to any law-enforcement official with intent to mislead, or (ii) without just cause and with intent to interfere with the operations of any law-enforcement official, to call or summon any law-enforcement official by telephone or other means, including engagement or activation of an automatic emergency alarm. Violation of the provisions of this section shall be punishable as a Class 1 misdemeanor.
(Chgd. by L.1996 chs. 753, 815, eff. 7/1/96.)

§18.2-462. Concealing or compounding offenses.

If any person knowing of the commission of an offense take any money or reward, or an engagement therefor, upon an agreement or understanding, expressed or implied, to compound or conceal such offense, or not to prosecute therefor, or not to give evidence thereof, he shall, if such offense be a felony, be guilty of a Class 2 misdemeanor; and if such offense be not a felony, unless it be punishable merely by forfeiture to him, he shall be guilty of a Class 4 misdemeanor.

§18.2-462.1. Use of police radio during commission of crime.

Any person who has in his possession or who uses a device capable of receiving a police radio signal, message, or transmission, while in the commission of a felony, is guilty of a Class 1 misdemeanor. A prosecution for or conviction of the crime of use or possession of a police radio is not a bar to conviction for any other crime committed while possessing or using the police radio.

§18.2-463. Refusal to aid officer in execution of his office.

If any person on being required by any sheriff or other officer refuse or neglect to assist him: (1) in the execution of his office in a criminal case, (2) in the preservation of the peace, (3) in the apprehending or securing of any person for a breach of the peace, or (4) in any case of escape or rescue, he shall be guilty of a Class 2 misdemeanor.

§18.2-464. Failure to obey order of conservator of the peace.

If any person, being required by a conservator of the peace on view of a breach of the peace or other offense to bring before him the offender, refuse or neglect to obey the conservator of the peace, he shall be guilty of a Class 2 misdemeanor; and if the conservator of the peace declare himself or be known to be such to the person so refusing or neglecting, ignorance of his office shall not be pleaded as an excuse.

§18.2-465. Officer summoning juror to act impartially.

If any sheriff or other officer corruptly, or through favor or ill-will, summon a juror, with intent that such juror shall find a verdict for or against either party, he shall be guilty of a Class 3 misdemeanor, and forfeit his office; and he shall be forever incapable of holding any office of honor, profit or trust under the Constitution of Virginia.

§18.2-465.1. Penalizing employee for court appearance or service on jury panel.

Any person who is summoned to serve on jury duty or any person, except a defendant in a criminal case, who is summoned or subpoenaed to appear in any court of law or equity when a case is to be heard shall neither be discharged from employment, nor have any adverse personnel action taken against him, nor shall he be required to use sick leave or vacation time, as a result of his absence from employment due to such jury duty or court appearance, upon giving reasonable notice to his employer of such court appearance or summons. Any employer violating the provisions of this section shall be guilty of a Class 3 misdemeanor.

(Chgd. by L.2000 ch. 295, eff. 7/1/2000.)

§18.2-466. Corruptly procuring juror to be summoned.

If any person procure or attempt to procure a juror to be summoned, with intent that such juror shall find a verdict for or against either party, he shall be guilty of a Class 3 misdemeanor.

§18.2-467. Fraud in drawing jurors, etc.

If any person be guilty of any fraud, either by tampering with the jury box prior to a draft, or in drawing a juror, or in returning into the jury box the name of any person which has lawfully been drawn out and drawing and substituting another in his stead, or in any other way in drawing of jurors, he shall be guilty of a Class 1 misdemeanor.

§18.2-468. Making sound recordings of jury deliberations.

If any person shall install or cause to be installed or use or cause to be used any microphone or device designed for recording or transmitting for recording sound in any jury room in this Commonwealth for the purpose of recording the deliberations of any jury or for the purpose of preparing a summary of such deliberations, he shall be guilty of a Class 6 felony.

§18.2-469. Officer refusing, delaying, etc., to execute process for criminal.

If any officer willfully and corruptly refuse to execute any lawful process requiring him to apprehend or confine a person convicted of, or charged with, an offense, or willfully and corruptly omit or delay to execute such process, whereby such person shall escape and go at large, such officer shall be guilty of a Class 3 misdemeanor.

§18.2-470. Extortion by officer.

If any officer, for performing an official duty for which a fee or compensation is allowed or provided by law knowingly demand and receive a greater fee or compensation than is so allowed or provided, he shall be guilty of a Class 4 misdemeanor.

§18.2-471. Fraudulent issue of fee bills.

If any person authorized by law to charge fees for services performed by him and issue bills therefor fraudulently issue a fee bill for a service not performed by him, or for more than he is entitled to, he shall be guilty of a Class 3 misdemeanor and shall forfeit his office and be forever incapable of holding office of honor, profit or trust under the Constitution of Virginia.

§18.2-472. False entries or destruction of records by officers.

If a clerk of any court or other public officer fraudulently make a false entry, or erase, alter, secrete or destroy any record, including a microphotographic copy, in his keeping and belonging to his office, he shall be guilty of a Class 1 misdemeanor and shall forfeit his office and be forever incapable of holding any office of honor, profit or trust under the Constitution of Virginia.

§18.2-472.1. Providing false information or failing to provide registration information; penalty.

Any person subject to §19.2-298.1, other than a sexually violent offender, who knowingly fails to register or reregister, or who knowingly provides materially false information to the Sex Offender and Crimes Against Minors Registry shall be guilty of a Class 1 misdemeanor. However, any person convicted of a sexually violent offense, as defined in §19.2-298.1, who knowingly fails to register or reregister, or who knowingly provides materially false information to the Registry established pursuant to §19.2-390.1 shall be guilty of a Class 6 felony.

A prosecution pursuant to this section shall be brought in the city or county where the registrant can be found or where the offender last registered or reregistered or, if the offender failed to comply with the duty to register, where the offender was last convicted of an offense for which registration or reregistration is required.

(Added by L.1997 ch. 747; chgd. by L.1999 ch. 845, eff. 7/1/99.)

ARTICLE 7
ESCAPE OF, COMMUNICATIONS WITH AND DELIVERIES TO PRISONERS

Section

§18.2-473. Persons aiding escape of prisoner or child.

When a person is lawfully detained as a prisoner in any jail or prison or held in custody, or when a child is placed in a local juvenile detention home, or committed to the Department of Juvenile Justice in any juvenile correctional center, or Reception and Diagnostic Center for Children or held in custody, if any person: (1) conveys anything into the jail, prison, juvenile detention home, juvenile correctional center or Reception and Diagnostic Center for Children with intent to facilitate a person's escape therefrom, (2) in any way aids such prisoner or child to escape, or in an attempt to escape, from such jail, prison, juvenile detention home, juvenile correctional center, Reception and Diagnostic Center for Children or custody, or (3) forcibly takes, or attempts to take him therefrom, such person, if the taking or escape is effected, shall, if the prisoner or child was detained on conviction, commitment or charge of felony, be confined in a state correctional facility not less than one year nor more than five years. If the same is not effected, or if the prisoner or child was not detained on such conviction, commitment or charge, he shall be guilty of a Class 1 misdemeanor.

(Chgd. by L.1996 chs. 755, 914, eff. 7/1/96.)

§18.2-473.1. Communication with prisoners; penalty.

It shall be unlawful for any person outside of any state or local correctional facility, other than the jailers or custodial officers in charge of the prisoners, to communicate without authority by word or sign with any prisoner confined within a state or local correctional facility. Any person violating this section shall be guilty of a Class 4 misdemeanor.

(Chgd. by L.2000 ch. 286, eff. 7/1/2000.)

§18.2-474. Delivery of articles to prisoners.

No person shall willfully in any manner deliver, or attempt to deliver, to any prisoner confined under authority of the Commonwealth of Virginia, or of any political subdivision thereof, any article of any nature whatsoever, without first securing the permission of the person in whose charge such prisoner is, and who may in his discretion grant or refuse permission. Any person violating this section shall be guilty of a Class 1 misdemeanor.

Nothing herein contained shall be construed to repeal or amend §18.2-473.

§18.2-474.1. Delivery of drugs, firearms, explosives, etc., to prisoners.

Notwithstanding the provisions of §18.2-474, any person who shall willfully in any manner deliver, attempt to deliver, or conspire with another to deliver to any prisoner confined under authority of the Commonwealth of Virginia, or of any political subdivision thereof, any drug which is a controlled substance regulated by the Drug Control Act in Chapter 34 of Title 54.1 or marijuana, shall be guilty of a Class 5 felony. Any person who shall willfully in any manner so deliver or attempt to deliver or conspire to deliver to any such prisoner, firearms, ammunitions, or explosives of any nature shall be guilty of a Class 3 felony.

Nothing herein contained shall be construed to repeal or amend §18.2-473.

§18.2-475. Officers, etc., voluntarily allowing prisoner convicted of or charged with felony to escape; penalty.

If any sheriff, jailer or other officer, or any guard or other person summoned or employed by any such sheriff, jailer or other officer, voluntarily allows a prisoner convicted of or charged with felony to escape from his custody, he shall be guilty of a Class 4 felony.

§18.2-476. Officers, etc., willfully and deliberately permitting prisoner not convicted of or charged with felony to escape or willfully refusing to receive prisoner; penalty.

If any sheriff, jailer or other officer, or any guard or other person summoned or employed by such sheriff, jailer or other officer, willfully and deliberately permits a prisoner convicted of or charged with an offense not a felony, to escape from his custody, or willfully refuses to receive into his custody a person lawfully committed thereto, he shall be guilty of a Class 2 misdemeanor.

§18.2-477. Prisoner escaping from jail; how punished.

If any person confined in jail or in custody after conviction of a criminal offense shall escape by force or violence, other than by setting fire thereto, he shall be guilty of a Class 6 felony. The term of confinement under this section shall commence from the expiration of the former sentence.

§18.2-477.1. Escapes from juvenile facility; penalty.

A. It shall be unlawful for any person to escape or remain away without proper authority from a group home or other residential care facility for children in need of services, delinquent or alleged delinquent youths in which he had been placed by the juvenile and domestic relations court or as a result of his commitment as a juvenile to the Department of Juvenile Justice. Any person violating this subsection shall be taken into custody and brought before the juvenile and domestic relations court. The court may find the person in violation of §16.1-292 or, if the court finds the person amenable to further treatment in a juvenile facility, the court may return him to the custody of the Department.

B. It shall be unlawful for any person to escape or remain away without proper authority from a secure facility operated by or under contract with the Department of Juvenile Justice or from a secure juvenile detention facility in which he had been placed by the juvenile and domestic relations court or as a result of his commitment as a juvenile to the Department of Juvenile Justice. Any person who escapes from a facility specified in this subsection by force or by violence shall be guilty of a Class 6 felony or, if violation of this subsection occurs other than by force or violence, a Class 1 misdemeanor.

(Chgd. by L.1996 ch. 616; L.1997 ch. 749, eff. 7/1/97.)

§18.2-477.2. Punishment for certain offenses committed within a secure juvenile facility or detention home.

It shall be unlawful for a person detained in a secure juvenile facility or detention home to commit any of the offenses enumerated in subdivisions 1 through 9 of §53.1-203. A violation of this section shall be punishable as a Class 1 misdemeanor.

(Added by L.1999 ch. 21, eff. 7/1/99.)

§18.2-478. Escape from jail or custody by force or violence without setting fire to jail.

If any person lawfully imprisoned in jail and not tried or sentenced on a criminal offense escapes from jail by force or violence, other than by setting fire thereto or if any person lawfully in the custody of any police officer on a charge of criminal offense escapes from such custody by force or violence, he shall be guilty of a Class 6 felony.

§18.2-479. Escape without force or violence or setting fire to jail.

A. If any person lawfully confined in jail or lawfully in the custody of any court or officer thereof or of any law-enforcement officer on a charge or conviction of a misdemeanor escapes, otherwise than by force or violence or by setting fire to the jail, he shall be guilty of a Class 1 misdemeanor.

B. If any person lawfully confined in jail or lawfully in the custody of any court or officer thereof or of any law-enforcement officer on a charge or conviction of a felony escapes, otherwise than by force or violence or by setting fire to the jail, he shall be guilty of a Class 6 felony.

§18.2-480. Escape, etc., by setting fire to jail.

If any person lawfully imprisoned in jail escape, or attempt to escape therefrom, by setting fire thereto, he shall be guilty of a Class 4 felony.

§18.2-480.1. Admissibility of records of Department of Corrections in escape cases.

In any prosecution for, or preliminary hearing for, the offense of escape under this article or Title 53.1, the records maintained by the Department of Corrections or the Department of Juvenile Justice, when such records are duly attested by the custodian of such records, shall be admissible in evidence as evidence of the fact, location and dates of confinement, provided that the records shall be filed with the clerk of the court hearing the case at least seven days prior to the trial or preliminary hearing. On motion of the accused, the court may require the custodian to appear as a witness and be subject to cross-examination; provided such motion is made within a reasonable time prior to the day on which the case is set for trial; and provided further, that the custodian so appearing shall be considered the Commonwealth's witness.

CHAPTER 11
OFFENSES AGAINST THE SOVEREIGNTY OF THE COMMONWEALTH

Article

ARTICLE 1
TREASON AND RELATED OFFENSES

Section

§18.2-481. Treason defined; how proved and punished.

Treason shall consist only in:

(1) Levying war against the Commonwealth;

(2) Adhering to its enemies, giving them aid and comfort;

(3) Establishing, without authority of the legislature, any government within its limits separate from the existing government;

(4) Holding or executing, in such usurped government, any office, or professing allegiance or fidelity to it; or

(5) Resisting the execution of the laws under color of its authority.

Such treason, if proved by the testimony of two witnesses to the same overt act, or by confession in court, shall be punishable as a Class 2 felony.

§18.2-482. Misprision of treason.

If any person knowing of such treason shall not, as soon as may be, give information thereof to the Governor, or some conservator of the peace, he shall be guilty of a Class 6 felony.

§18.2-483. Attempting, or instigating others, to establish usurped government.

If any person attempt to establish any such usurped government and commit any overt act therefor or by writing or speaking endeavor to instigate others to establish such government, he shall be guilty of a Class 1 misdemeanor.

§18.2-484. Advocacy of change in government by force, violence or other unlawful means.

It shall be unlawful for any person, group, or organization to advocate any change, by force, violence, or other unlawful means in the government of the Commonwealth of Virginia or any of its subdivisions or in the government of the United States of America.

It shall be unlawful for any person to join, assist or otherwise contribute to any group or organization which, to the knowledge of such person, advocates or has as its purpose, aim or objective, any change by force, violence, or other unlawful means in the government of the Commonwealth of Virginia or any of its subdivisions or in the government of the United States of America.

Violation of this section shall be punishable as a Class 6 felony.

Nothing herein shall be construed to limit or prohibit the advocacy, orally or otherwise, of any change, by peaceful means, in the government of the Commonwealth or any of its subdivisions or in the government of the United States.

§18.2-485. Conspiring to incite one race to insurrection against another race.

If any person conspire with another to incite the population of one race to acts of violence and war against the population of another race, he shall, whether such acts of violence and war be made or not, be guilty of a Class 4 felony.

ARTICLE 2
UNIFORM FLAG ACT

Section

§18.2-486. Definition of flag, standard, etc.

The words flag, standard, color, ensign or shield, as used in this article, shall include any flag, standard, color, ensign or shield, or copy, picture or representation thereof, made of any substance or represented or produced thereon, and of any size, evidently purporting to be such flag, standard, color, ensign or shield of the United States, or of this Commonwealth, or a copy, picture or representation thereof.

§18.2-487. Exhibition or display.

No person shall, in any manner, for exhibition or display:

(1) Place or cause to be placed any word, figure, mark, picture, design, drawing or advertisement of any nature upon any flag, standard, color, ensign or shield of the United States or of this Commonwealth, or authorized by any law of the United States or of this Commonwealth;

(2) Expose to public view any such flag, standard, color, ensign or shield upon which shall have been printed, painted or otherwise produced, or to which shall have been attached, appended, affixed or annexed, any such word, figure, mark, picture, design, drawing or advertisement; or

(3) Expose to public view for sale, manufacture or otherwise, or sell, give or have in possession for sale, for gift or for use for any purpose, any substance, being an article of merchandise, or receptacle, or thing for holding or carrying merchandise, upon or to which shall have been produced or attached any such flag, standard, color, ensign or shield, in order to advertise, call attention to, decorate, mark or distinguish such article or substance.

§18.2-488. Mutilating, defacing, etc.

No person shall publicly burn with contempt, mutilate, deface, defile, trample upon, or wear with intent to defile any such flag, standard, color, ensign or shield.

§18.2-489. To what article applies.

This article shall not apply to any act permitted by the statutes of the United States or by the laws of this Commonwealth, or by the United States armed forces regulations, nor shall it apply to any printed or written document or production, stationery, ornament, picture or jewelry whereon shall be depicted such flag, standard, color, ensign or shield, with no design or words thereon and disconnected with any advertisement.

§18.2-490. Penalty.

Any violation of this article shall be punishable as a Class 1 misdemeanor.

§18.2-491. Construction.

This article shall be so construed as to effectuate its general purpose, and to make uniform the laws of the states which enact it.

§18.2-492. Short title.

This article may be cited as the Uniform Flag Act.

CHAPTER 12
MISCELLANEOUS

Article

ARTICLE 1
LIQUEFIED PETROLEUM GAS CONTAINERS

Section

§18.2-493. Definitions.

As used in this article, unless the text indicates otherwise:

(a) "Person" shall mean any person, firm or corporation.

(b) "Owner" shall mean any person who holds a written bill of sale under which title or ownership to a container was transferred to such person, or any manufacturer of a container who has not sold or transferred ownership thereof by written bill of sale.

(c) "Liquefied petroleum gas" shall mean any material which is composed predominately* of any of the following hydrocarbons or mixtures of the same: propane, propylene, butanes (normal butane and isobutane) and butylenes.

**Probably should be "predominantly".*

§18.2-494. Unlawful use of, filling or refilling or trafficking in containers.

No person except the owner thereof or person authorized in writing by the owner shall fill or refill with liquefied petroleum gas, or any other gas or compound, a liquefied petroleum gas container; or buy, sell, offer for sale, give, take, loan, deliver or permit to be delivered, or otherwise use, dispose of, or traffic in a liquefied petroleum gas container or containers if the container bears upon the surface thereof in plainly legible characters the name, initials, mark or other device of the owner; nor shall any person other than the owner of a liquefied petroleum gas container or a person authorized in writing by the owner deface, erase, obliterate, cover up, or otherwise remove or conceal any name, mark, initial or device thereon.

§18.2-495. Presumptive evidence.

The use of a liquefied petroleum gas container or containers by any person other than the person whose name, mark, initial or device is on the liquefied petroleum gas container or containers, without written consent, or purchase of the marked and distinguished liquefied petroleum gas container for the sale of liquefied petroleum gas or filling or refilling with liquefied petroleum gas, or possession of the liquefied petroleum gas containers by any person other than the person having his name, mark, initial or other device thereon, without the written consent of such owner, is presumptive evidence of the unlawful use, filling or refilling, or trafficking in of such liquefied petroleum gas containers.

§18.2-496. Punishment for violation.

Any person who fails to comply with any of the foregoing provisions of this article is guilty of a Class 3 misdemeanor for each separate offense.

§18.2-497. Fines and costs.

The costs incurred in the enforcement of this article shall be assessed and collected in the same manner as in criminal cases, and all fines collected by virtue of this article shall be turned over in the same manner and for the same purposes as criminal and misdemeanor fines are disposed of by law.

§18.2-498. Exempt containers.

Nothing in this article applies to or shall be construed to affect a liquefied petroleum gas container having a total capacity of five gallons or less.

ARTICLE 1.1
VIRGINIA GOVERNMENTAL FRAUDS ACT

§18.2-498.1. Short title.

This article shall be known and cited as the Virginia Governmental Frauds Act.

§18.2-498.2. Definitions.

When used in this article, the term:

1. "Person" includes any natural person, any trust or association of persons, formal or otherwise, or any corporation, partnership, company or other legal or commercial entity.

2. "Commercial dealing" shall mean any offer, acceptance agreement, or solicitation to sell or offer to sell or distribute goods, services or construction, to the Commonwealth of Virginia, or any local government within the Commonwealth or any department or agency thereof.

§18.2-498.3. Misrepresentations prohibited.

Any person, in any commercial dealing in any matter within the jurisdiction of any department or agency of the Commonwealth of Virginia, or any local government within the Commonwealth or any department or agency thereof who knowingly falsifies, conceals, misleads, or covers up by any trick, scheme, or device a material fact, or makes any false, fictitious or fraudulent statements or representations, or makes or uses any false writing or document knowing the same to contain any false, fictitious or fraudulent statement or entry, shall be guilty of a Class 6 felony.

§18.2-498.4. Duty to provide certified statement.

A. The Commonwealth, or any department or agency thereof, and any local government or any department or agency thereof, may require that any person seeking, offering or agreeing to transact business or commerce with it, or seeking, offering or agreeing to receive any portion of the public funds or moneys, submit a certification that the offer or agreement or any claim resulting therefrom is not the result of, or affected by, any act of collusion with another person engaged in the same line of business or commerce; or any act of fraud punishable under this article.

B. Any person required to submit a certified statement as provided in subsection A above who knowingly makes a false statement shall be guilty of a Class 6 felony.

§18.2-498.5. Actions on behalf of Commonwealth or localities.

The Attorney General on behalf of the Commonwealth, or the Commonwealth's attorney, on behalf of the county or city as the case may be may institute actions and proceedings for any and all violations occurring within their jurisdictions.

ARTICLE 2
CONSPIRACY TO INJURE ANOTHER IN TRADE, BUSINESS OR PROFESSION

§18.2-499. Combinations to injure others in their reputation, trade, business or profession; rights of employees.

A. Any two or more persons who combine, associate, agree, mutually undertake or concert together for the purpose of (i) willfully and maliciously injuring another in his reputation, trade, business or profession by any means whatever or (ii) willfully and maliciously compelling another to do or perform any act against his will, or preventing or hindering another from doing or performing any lawful act, shall be jointly and severally guilty of a Class 1 misdemeanor. Such punishment shall be in addition to any civil relief recoverable under §18.2-500.

B. Any person who attempts to procure the participation, cooperation, agreement or other assistance of any one or more persons to enter into any combination, association, agreement, mutual understanding or concert prohibited in subsection A of this section shall be guilty of a violation of this section and subject to the same penalties set out in subsection A.

C. This section shall not affect the right of employees lawfully to organize and bargain concerning wages and conditions of employment, and take other steps to protect their rights as provided under state and federal laws.

§18.2-500. Same; civil relief; damages and counsel fees; injunctions.

(a) Any person who shall be injured in his reputation, trade, business or profession by reason of a violation of §18.2-499, may sue therefor and recover three-fold the damages by him sustained, and the costs of suit, including a reasonable fee to plaintiff's counsel; and without limiting the generality of the term, "damages" shall include loss of profits. Such counsel shall in no case receive any other, further or additional compensation except that allowed by the court and any contract to the contrary shall be null and void.

(b) Whenever a person shall duly file a bill in chancery in the circuit court of any county or city against any person alleging violations of the provisions of §18.2-499 and praying that such party defendant be restrained and enjoined from continuing the acts complained of, such court shall have jurisdiction to hear and determine the issues involved, to issue injunctions pendente lite and permanent injunctions and to decree damages and costs of suit, including reasonable counsel fees to complainants' and defendants' counsel.

§18.2-501. Same; protection of persons testifying or producing evidence.

(a) No natural person shall be prosecuted or be subjected to any penalty or forfeiture for or on account of any transaction, matter or thing concerning which he may testify or produce evidence, documentary or otherwise, in any action, suit, or prosecution authorized by this article; provided, that no person so testifying shall be exempt from prosecution or punishment for perjury committed in so testifying.

(b) As used in this article a "person" is any person, firm, corporation, partnership or association.

ARTICLE 3
MISCELLANEOUS OFFENSES IN GENERAL

§18.2-502. Medical referral for profit.

(a) No person, firm, partnership, association or corporation, or agent or employee thereof, shall for profit engage in any business which in whole or in part includes the referral or recommendation of persons to a physician, hospital, health related facility, or dispensary for any form of medical care or treatment of any ailment or physical condition unless the person is advised of the criteria of selection of the physicians, hospitals, health-related facilities or dispensaries considered for the referral or recommendation. The acceptance of a fee or charge for any such referral or recommendation shall create a presumption that the business is engaged in such service for profit. A violation of the provisions of this section shall be punishable as a Class 1 misdemeanor.

(b) Whenever there is a violation of this section, in addition to the criminal sanctions, an application may be made by the Attorney General to the circuit court of the city or county in which the offense occurred, to issue an injunction, and upon notice to the defendant of not less than five days, to enjoin and restrain the continuance of such violation. If it appears to the satisfaction of the court or judge that the defendant has, in fact, violated this section, an injunction may be issued by such court or judge enjoining and restraining any further violation, without requiring proof that any person has, in fact, been injured or damaged thereby. Nothing in this section shall be construed to limit, prohibit, forbid or prevent any licensed physician or practitioner of the healing arts in the ordinary course of his professional practice from making referrals or recommendations to other members of such groups, so long as no fee is received for such referral or recommendation.

The criminal and civil provisions of this section shall not apply to any individual association or corporation not organized or incorporated for pecuniary profit or financial gain, or to any organization or association which is exempt from taxation pursuant to §501(c) of Title 26 of the United States Code (Int. Rev. Code of 1954).

(c) Nothing in this section shall be construed to authorize any division of fees prohibited by §54.1-2962 or any remuneration for referral prohibited by federal law or regulation.

§18.2-502.1. Weight loss centers or clinics; disclosure.

No weight loss center or clinic shall, in its name or advertisements, use the words "physicians" or "doctors" or refer to its clients as "patients" or indicate that "medical teams" are available in its facility unless (i) the facility employs at least one registered nurse full-time and employs or contracts with at least one physician licensed by the Board of Medicine for services or consultation in connection with the facility's activities; or (ii) the facility is under the full-time supervision of a physician; or (iii) the clinic or program is operated by or in conjunction with a licensed hospital. Any physician affiliated with a weight loss center or clinic for purposes of consultation or supervision shall have primary responsibility for decisions made within the scope of that affiliation relating to the provision of medical services or care to persons using the services of that facility and shall have primary responsibility for medical decisions relating to the evaluation of the appropriateness of the admission of persons to the weight loss program. Any person who violates the provisions of this section shall be guilty of a Class 1 misdemeanor.

§18.2-502.2. Warning required for certain medical tests; penalty.

No commercial medical testing kit designed for consumer home use shall be sold in this Commonwealth unless a warning is provided to the consumer to the effect that such tests may produce erroneous results and that medical testing is more accurate when performed by professionals within the controlled conditions of a laboratory. The consumer shall be advised to seek professional medical consultation and, if recommended, another test for validation of such test results.

Any person who violates the provisions of this section shall be guilty of a Class 4 misdemeanor.

§18.2-503. Possession or duplication of certain keys.

(a) No person shall knowingly possess any key to the lock of any building or other property owned by the Commonwealth of Virginia, or a department, division, agency or political subdivision thereof, without receiving permission from a person duly authorized to give such permission to possess such key.

(b) No person, without receiving permission from a person duly authorized to give such permission, shall knowingly duplicate, copy or make a facsimile of any key to a lock of a building or other property owned by the Commonwealth of Virginia, or a department, division, agency or political subdivision thereof.

Violation of this section shall constitute a Class 3 misdemeanor.

§18.2-504. Destroying or concealing wills.

If any person fraudulently destroy or conceal any will or codicil, with intent to prevent the probate thereof, he shall be guilty of a Class 6 felony.

§18.2-504.1. Unlawful change of name; punishment.

If any person residing in this Commonwealth changes his name or assumes another name, unlawfully, he shall be guilty of a Class 3 misdemeanor.

§18.2-505. Preparation, etc., of papers to be submitted for academic credit.

(a) No person shall prepare, cause to be prepared or sell any term paper, thesis, dissertation or other written material for another person, for with the knowledge, or under circumstances in which he should reasonably have known, that such term paper, thesis, dissertation or other written material is to be submitted by any other person for academic credit at any public or private college, university or other institution of higher learning in this Commonwealth.

(b) No person shall make or disseminate, with the intent to induce any other person to enter into any obligation relating thereto, any statement, written or oral, that he will prepare or cause to be prepared, any term paper, thesis, dissertation or other written material, to be sold for profit, for or on behalf of any person who has been assigned the written preparation of such term paper, thesis, dissertation or other written material for academic credit at any public or private college, university or other institution of higher learning in this Commonwealth.

§18.2-506. "Person" and "prepare" defined.

(a) As used in this article, "person" means any individual, partnership, corporation or association.

(b) As used in this article, "prepare" means to put into condition for intended use. "Prepare" does not include the mere typing or assembling of papers, nor the mere furnishing of information or research.

§18.2-507. Injunctions against violation of §18.2-505.

Whenever a college, university or other institution of higher learning in this Commonwealth shall duly file a bill in chancery in the circuit court of any county or city against any person alleging violations of the provisions of §18.2-505, and praying that such party defendant be restrained and enjoined from continuing the acts complained of, such court shall have jurisdiction to hear and determine the issues involved, to issue injunctions pendente lite and permanent injunctions and to decree damages and costs of suit, including reasonable counsel fees to complainants' counsel.

§18.2-508. Penalties.

Any person found guilty of violating any provisions of §18.2-505 shall be guilty of a misdemeanor and shall be punished by a fine not to exceed $1,000.

§18.2-509. Employment of lights under certain circumstances.

Any person in any motor vehicle or otherwise who, between a half hour after sunset on any day and a half hour before sunrise the following day, employs a light attached to such vehicle, or employs a spotlight to cast a light beyond the surface of the roadway upon any poultry house or other building inhabited by animals that causes such animals to panic or become injured, except upon his own land or upon private land on which he has permission, shall be guilty of a Class 4 misdemeanor.

§18.2-510. Burial or cremation of animals or fowls which have died.

When the owner of any animal or grown fowl which has died knows of such death, such owner shall forthwith have its body cremated or buried, and, if he fails to do so, any judge of a general district court, after notice to the owner if he can be ascertained, shall cause any such dead animal or fowl to be cremated or buried by an officer or other person designated for the purpose. Such officer or other person shall be entitled to recover of the owner of every such animal so cremated or buried the actual cost of the cremation or burial, not to exceed seventy-five dollars, and of the owner of every such fowl so cremated or buried the actual cost of the cremation or burial, not to exceed five dollars, to be recovered in the same manner as officers fees are recovered, free from all exemptions in favor of such owner. Any person violating the provisions of this section shall be guilty of a Class 4 misdemeanor.

Nothing in this section shall be deemed to require the burial or cremation of the whole or portions of any animal or fowl which is to be used for food or in any commercial manner.

This section shall not apply to any county until the governing body thereof shall adopt the same.

TITLE 19.2
CRIMINAL PROCEDURE
(Complete Title)

Chapter

CHAPTER 1
GENERAL PROVISIONS

Section

§19.2-1. Repealing clause.

All acts and parts of acts, all sections of this Code, and all provisions of municipal charters, inconsistent with the provisions of this title, are, except as herein otherwise provided, repealed to the extent of such inconsistency.

§19.2-2. Effect of repeal of Title 19.1 and enactment of this title.

The repeal of Title 19.1 effective as of October 1, 1975, shall not affect any act or offense done or committed, or any penalty or forfeiture incurred, or any right established, accrued, or accruing on or before such date, or any prosecution, suit or action pending on that day. Except as herein otherwise provided, neither the repeal of Title 19.1 nor the enactment of this title shall apply to offenses committed prior to October 1, 1975, and prosecutions for such offenses shall be governed by the prior law, which is continued in effect for that purpose. For the purposes of this section, an offense was committed prior to October 1, 1975, if any of the essential elements of the offense occurred prior thereto.

§19.2-3. Certain notices, recognizances and processes validated.

Any notice given, recognizance taken, or process or writ issued before October 1, 1975, shall be valid although given, taken or to be returned to a day after such date, in like manner as if this title had been effective before the same was given, taken or issued.

§19.2-3.1. Personal appearance by two-way electronic video and audio communication; standards.

A. Where an appearance is required or permitted before a magistrate, intake officer or, prior to trial, before a judge, the appearance may be by (i) personal appearance before the magistrate, intake officer or judge or (ii) use of two-way electronic video and audio communication. If two-way electronic video and audio communication is used, a magistrate, intake officer or judge may exercise all powers conferred by law and all communications and proceedings shall be conducted in the same manner as if the appearance were in person, and any documents filed may be transmitted by electronically transmitted facsimile process. The facsimile may be served or executed by the officer or person to whom sent, and returned in the same manner, and with the same force, effect, authority, and liability as an original document. All signatures thereon shall be treated as original signatures.

B. Any two-way electronic video and audio communication system used for an appearance shall meet the following standards:

1. The persons communicating must simultaneously see and speak to one another;
2. The signal transmission must be live, real time;

3. The signal transmission must be secure from interception through lawful means by anyone other than the persons communicating; and

4. Any other specifications as may be promulgated by the Chief Justice of the Supreme Court.

(Chgd. by L.1996 chs. 755, 914, eff. 7/1/96.)

§19.2-4. References to former sections, articles or chapters of Titles 18.1 and 19.1.

Whenever in this title any of the conditions, requirements, provisions or contents of any section, article or chapter of Titles 18.1 and 19.1, as such titles existed prior to October 1, 1975, are transferred in the same or in modified form to a new section, article or chapter of this title or of Title 18.2, and whenever any such former section, article or chapter is given a new number in this title or in Title 18.2, all references to any such former section, article or chapter of Title 19.1 or of Title 18.1 appearing elsewhere in this Code than in this title or in Title 18.2, shall be construed to apply to the new or renumbered section, article or chapter containing such conditions, requirements, provisions or contents or portions thereof.

§19.2-5. Rules of construction; meaning of certain terms.

In the construction of this title and of each section thereof, the rules of construction set forth in Chapter 2 (§1-10 et seq.) of Title 1 of this Code shall be observed, unless such construction would be inconsistent with the manifest intent of the General Assembly.

The word "court" as used in this title, unless otherwise clearly indicated by the context in which it appears, shall mean and include any court vested with appropriate jurisdiction under the Constitution and laws of this Commonwealth.

The word "judge" as used in this title, unless otherwise clearly indicated by the context in which it appears, shall mean and include any judge, associate judge or substitute judge, or magistrate, of any court.

The words "courts not of record," and "district court" as used in this title, unless otherwise clearly indicated by the context in which they appear, shall have the respective meanings assigned to them in Chapter 4.1 (§16.1-69.1 et seq.) of Title 16.1 of this Code.

§19.2-6. Appointive power of circuit courts.

Unless otherwise specifically provided, whenever an appointive power is given to the judge of a circuit court, that power shall be exercised by a majority of the judges of the circuit. In case of a tie, such fact shall be communicated to the Chief Justice of the Supreme Court, who shall appoint a circuit judge from another circuit who shall act as a tie breaker. Where the power of appointment is to be exercised by a majority of the judges of the Second Judicial Circuit and such appointment is to a local post, board or commission in Accomack or Northampton County, the resident judge or judges of the County of Accomack or Northampton shall exercise such appointment power as if he or they comprise the majority of the judges of the Circuit.

§19.2-7. Rewards for arrest of persons convicted of or charged with offenses; rewards for conviction of unknown offenders.

The Governor may offer a reward for apprehending and securing any person convicted of an offense or charged therewith, who shall have escaped from lawful custody or confinement, or for apprehending and securing any person charged with an offense, who, there is reason to fear, cannot be arrested in the common course of proceeding. The Governor may also offer a reward for the detection and conviction of the person guilty of an offense when such offense has been committed but the person guilty thereof is unknown.

Any sheriff, deputy sheriff, sergeant, deputy sergeant or any other officer may claim and receive any reward which may be offered for the arrest and detention of any offender against the criminal laws of this or any other state or nation.

§19.2-8. Limitation of prosecutions.

A prosecution for a misdemeanor, or any pecuniary fine, forfeiture, penalty or amercement, shall be commenced within one year next after there was cause therefor, except that a prosecution for petit larceny may be commenced within five years, and for an attempt to produce abortion, within two years after commission of the offense.

A prosecution for violation of laws governing the placement of children for adoption without a license pursuant to §63.1-196 shall be commenced within one year from the date of the filing of the petition for adoption.

A prosecution for making a false statement or representation of a material fact knowing it to be false or knowingly failing to disclose a material fact, to obtain or increase any benefit or other payment under the Virginia Unemployment Compensation Act (§60.2-100 et seq.) shall be commenced within three years next after the commission of the offense.

A prosecution for any violation of §§10.1-1320, 62.1-44.32(b), 62.1-194.1, or Article 11 (§62.1-44.34:14 et seq.) of Chapter 3.1 of Title 62.1 which involves the discharge, dumping or emission of any toxic substance as defined in §32.1-239 shall be commenced within three years next after the commission of the offense.

Prosecution of Building Code violations under §36-106 shall commence within one year of discovery of the offense by the owner or by the building official; provided that such discovery occurs within two years of the date of initial occupancy or use after construction of the building or structure, or the issuance of a certificate of use and occupancy for the building or structure, whichever is later. However, prosecutions under §36-106 relating to the maintenance of existing buildings or structures as contained in the Uniform Statewide Building Code shall commence within one year of the discovery of the offense.

Prosecution of nonfelonious offenses which constitute malfeasance in office shall commence within two years next after the commission of the offense.

Prosecution of any violation of §§55-79.87, 55-79.88, 55-79.89, 55-79.90, 55-79.93, 55-79.94, 55-79.95, 55-79.103, or any rule adopted under or order issued pursuant to §55-79.98, shall commence within three years next after the commission of the offense.

Prosecution of illegal sales or purchases of wild birds, wild animals and freshwater fish under §29.1-553 shall commence within three years after commission of the offense.

Prosecution of violations under Title 58.1 for offenses involving false or fraudulent statements, documents or returns, or for the offense of willfully attempting in any manner to evade or defeat any tax or the payment thereof, or for the offense of willfully failing to pay any tax, or willfully failing to make any return at the time or times required by law or regulations shall commence within three years next after the commission of the offense, unless a longer period is otherwise prescribed.

Prosecution of violations of subsection A or B of §3.1-796.122 shall commence within five years of the commission of the offense, except violations regarding agricultural animals shall commence within one year of the commission of the offense.

A prosecution for a violation of §18.2-386.1 shall be commenced within five years of the commission of the offense.

A prosecution for any violation of the Campaign Finance Disclosure Act (§24.2-900 et seq.) shall commence within one year of the discovery of the offense but in no case more than three years after the date of the commission of the offense.

Nothing in this section shall be construed to apply to any person fleeing from justice or concealing himself within or without this Commonwealth to avoid arrest or be construed to limit the time within which any prosecution may be commenced for desertion of a spouse or child or for neglect or refusal or failure to provide for the support and maintenance of a spouse or child.

(Chgd. by L.1996 ch. 484; L.1998 ch. 566; L.1999 ch. 620, eff. 7/1/99.)

§19.2-9. Prosecution of certain criminal cases removed from state to federal courts; costs.

When any person indicted in the courts of this Commonwealth for a violation of its laws, has his case removed to the district court of the United States under §33 of the Judicial Code of the United States, it shall be the duty of the attorney for the Commonwealth for the county or city in which any such indictment is found to prosecute any such case in the United States district court to which the same shall be so removed, and for his services in this behalf he shall be paid a fee of $100 for each case tried by him in such United States district court, and mileage at the rate now allowed by law to the members of the General Assembly for all necessary travel in going to and returning from such court, to be paid on his account when approved by the Attorney General.

A per diem of one dollar and fifty cents for each day of actual attendance upon such United States district court and mileage at a rate as provided by law for every mile of necessary travel in going to and returning from such court shall be paid out of the state treasury to each witness for the Commonwealth in every such case upon accounts therefor against the Commonwealth, certified by the attorney for the Commonwealth prosecuting such case and approved by the Attorney General.

It shall not be the duty of the Attorney General to appear for the Commonwealth in such cases unless he can do so without interfering with the efficient discharge of the duties imposed upon him by law; but he may appear with the attorney for the Commonwealth prosecuting such case in any case when the interests of the Commonwealth may in his judgment require his presence.

The Comptroller shall from time to time draw his warrants upon the state treasury in favor of the parties entitled to be paid the above compensation and expenses, or their assigns, upon bills certified and approved as above prescribed.

§19.2-9.1. Written notice required for complaining witness who is requested to take polygraph test.

If a complaining witness is requested to submit to a polygraph examination during the course of a criminal investigation, such witness shall be informed in writing prior to the examination that (i) the examination is voluntary, (ii) the results thereof are inadmissible as evidence and (iii) the agreement of the complaining witness to submit thereto shall not be the sole condition for initiating or continuing the criminal investigation.

§19.2-10. Outlawry abolished.

No proceeding of outlawry shall hereafter be instituted or prosecuted.

§19.2-11. Procedure in contempt cases.

No court or judge shall impose a fine upon a juror, witness or other person for disobedience of its process or any contempt, unless he either be present in court at the time, or shall have been served with a rule, returnable to a certain time, requiring him to show cause why the fine should not be imposed and shall have failed to appear and show cause.

CHAPTER 1.1
CRIME VICTIM AND WITNESS RIGHTS ACT

§19.2-11.01. Crime victim and witness rights.

A. In recognition of the Commonwealth's concern for the victims and witnesses of crime, it is the purpose of this chapter to ensure that the full impact of crime is brought to the attention of the courts of the Commonwealth; that crime victims and witnesses are treated with dignity, respect and sensitivity; and that their privacy is protected to the extent permissible under law. It is the further purpose of this chapter to ensure that victims and witnesses are informed of the rights provided to them under the laws of the Commonwealth; that they receive authorized services as appropriate; and that they have the opportunity to be heard by law-enforcement agencies, attorneys for the Commonwealth, corrections agencies and the judiciary at all critical stages of the criminal justice process to the extent permissible under law. Unless otherwise stated and subject to the provisions of §19.2-11.1, it shall be the responsibility of a locality's crime victim and witness assistance program to provide the information and assistance required by this chapter.

Following a crime, law-enforcement personnel shall provide the victim with a standardized form listing the specific rights afforded to crime victims. The form shall include a telephone number by which the victim can receive further information and assistance in securing the rights afforded crime victims.

1. Victim and witness protection.

a. In order that victims and witnesses receive protection from harm and threats of harm arising out of their cooperation with law-enforcement, or prosecution efforts, they shall be provided with information as to the level of protection which may be available pursuant to §52-35 or to any other federal, state or local program providing protection, and shall be assisted in obtaining this protection from the appropriate authorities.

b. Victims and witnesses shall be provided, where available, a separate waiting area during court proceedings that affords them privacy and protection from intimidation.

2. Financial assistance.

a. Victims shall be informed of financial assistance and social services available to them as victims of a crime, including information on their possible right to file a claim for compensation from the Crime Victims' Compensation Fund pursuant to Chapter 21.1 (§19.2-368.1 et seq.) of this title and on other available assistance and services.

b. Victims shall be assisted in having any property held by law-enforcement agencies for evidentiary purposes returned promptly in accordance with §§19.2-270.1 and 19.2-270.2.

c. Victims shall be advised that restitution is available for damages or loss resulting from an offense and shall be assisted in seeking restitution in accordance with §§19.2-305, 19.2-305.1, Chapter 21.1 (§19.2-368.1 et seq.) of this title, Article 21 (§58.1-520 et seq.) of Chapter 3 of Title 58.1, and other applicable laws of the Commonwealth.

3. Notices.

a. Victims and witnesses shall be (i) provided with appropriate employer intercession services to ensure that employers of victims and witnesses will cooperate with the criminal justice process in order to minimize an employee's loss of pay and other benefits resulting from court appearances and (ii) advised that pursuant to §18.2-465.1 it is unlawful for an employer to penalize an employee for appearing in court pursuant to a summons or subpoena.

b. Victims shall receive advance notification when practicable from the attorney for the Commonwealth of judicial proceedings relating to their case and shall be notified when practicable of any change in court dates in accordance with §19.2-265.01 if they have provided their names, current addresses and telephone numbers.

c. Victims shall receive notification, if requested, subject to such reasonable procedures as the Attorney General may require pursuant to §2.1-124, from the Attorney General of the filing and disposition of any appeal or habeas corpus proceeding involving their case.

d. Victims shall be notified by the Department of Corrections or a sheriff or jail superintendent in whose custody an escape, change of name, transfer, release or discharge of a prisoner occurs pursuant to the provisions of §§53.1-133.02 and 53.1-160 if they have provided their names, current addresses and telephone numbers in writing.

e. Victims shall be advised that, in order to protect their right to receive notices and offer input, all agencies and persons having such duties must have current victim addresses and telephone numbers given by the victims.

4. Victim input.

a. Victims shall be given the opportunity, pursuant to §19.2-299.1, to prepare a written victim impact statement prior to sentencing of a defendant and may provide information to any individual or agency charged with investigating the social history of a person or preparing a victim impact statement under the provisions of §§16.1-273 and 53.1-155 or any other applicable law.

b. Victims shall have the right to remain in the courtroom during a criminal trial or proceeding pursuant to the provisions of §19.2-265.01.

c. On motion of the attorney for the Commonwealth, victims shall be given the opportunity, pursuant to §§19.2-264.4 and 19.2-295.3, to testify prior to sentencing of a defendant regarding the impact of the offense.

5. Courtroom assistance.

a. Victims and witnesses shall be informed that their addresses and telephone numbers may not be disclosed, pursuant to the provisions of §§19.2-11.2 and 19.2-269.2, except when necessary for the conduct of the criminal proceeding.

b. Victims and witnesses shall be advised that they have the right to the services of an interpreter in accordance with §§19.2-164 and 19.2-164.1.

c. Victims of certain sexual offenses shall be advised that there may be a closed preliminary hearing in accordance with §18.2-67.8 and, if a victim was fourteen years of age or younger on the date of the offense and is sixteen or under at the time of the trial, two-way closed-circuit television may be used in the taking of testimony in accordance with §18.2-67.9.

B. For purposes of this chapter, "victim" means (i) a person who has suffered physical, psychological or economic harm as a direct result of the commission of a felony or of assault and battery in violation of §§18.2-57, 18.2-57.1 or §18.2-57.2, stalking in violation of §18.2-60.3, sexual battery in violation of §18.2-67.4, attempted sexual battery in violation of §18.2-67.5, maiming or driving while intoxicated in violation of §18.2-51.4 or §18.2-266, (ii) a spouse or child of such a person, (iii) a parent or legal guardian of such a person who is a minor, or (iv) a spouse, parent, sibling or legal guardian of such a person who is physically or mentally incapacitated or was the victim of a homicide; however, "victim" does not mean a parent, child, spouse, sibling or legal guardian who commits a felony or other enumerated criminal offense against a victim as defined in clause (i) of this subsection.

C. Officials and employees of the judiciary, including court services units, law-enforcement agencies, the Department of Corrections, attorneys for the Commonwealth and public defenders, shall be provided with copies of this chapter by the Department of Criminal Justice Services or a crime victim and witness assistance program. Each agency, officer or employee who has a responsibility or responsibilities to victims under this chapter or other applicable law shall make reasonable efforts to become informed about these responsibilities and to ensure that victims and witnesses receive such information and services to which they may be entitled under applicable law, provided that no liability or cause of action shall arise from the failure to make such efforts or from the failure of such victims or witnesses to receive any such information or services.

(Added by L.1995 ch. 687; chgd. by L.1996 ch. 546; L.1997 ch. 691; L.1998 ch. 485; L.1999 chs. 668, 702, 844; L.2000 chs. 272, 827, eff. 7/1/2000.)

§19.2-11.1. Establishment of crime victim-witness assistance programs; funding; minimum standards.

Any local governmental body which establishes, operates and maintains a crime victim and witness assistance program, whose funding is provided in whole or part by grants administered by the Department of Criminal Justice Services pursuant to §9-173.3, shall operate the program in accordance with guidelines which shall be established by the Department to implement the provisions of this chapter and other applicable laws establishing victims' rights.

(Chgd. by 1994, chs. 361, 598; L.1995 ch. 687; L.1996 ch. 545, eff. 7/1/96.)

§19.2-11.2. Crime victim's right to nondisclosure of certain information; exceptions; testimonial privilege.

Upon request of any crime victim, neither a law-enforcement agency, the Commonwealth's attorney, a court nor the Department of Corrections, nor any employee of any of them, may disclose, except among themselves, the residential address, telephone number, or place of employment of the victim or a member of the victim's family, except to the extent that disclosure is (i) of the site of the crime, (ii) required by law or Rules of the Supreme Court, (iii) necessary for law-enforcement purposes, or (iv) permitted by the court for good cause.

Except with the written consent of the victim, a law-enforcement agency may not disclose to the public information which directly or indirectly identifies the victim of a crime involving any sexual assault or abuse, except to the extent that disclosure is (i) of the site of the crime, (ii) required by law, (iii) necessary for law-enforcement purposes, or (iv) permitted by the court for good cause.

Nothing herein shall limit the right to examine witnesses in a court of law or otherwise affect the conduct of any criminal proceeding.

§19.2-11.3. Virginia Crime Victim-Witness Fund.

There is hereby established the Virginia Crime Victim-Witness Fund as a special nonreverting fund to be administered by the Department of Criminal Justice Services to support victim and witness services that meet the minimum standards prescribed for such programs under §19.2-11.1. Three dollars collected pursuant to subdivisions 15 and 16 of

§14.1-112 and to subdivision 1 of §14.1-123 shall be deposited into the state treasury to the credit of this Fund. The Fund shall be distributed according to grant procedures adopted pursuant to §9-173.3 and shall be established on the books of the Comptroller. Any funds remaining in such Fund at the end of the biennium shall not revert to the general fund, but shall remain in the Fund. Interest earned on the Fund shall be credited to the Fund.
(Added by L.1995 ch. 371, eff. 7/1/95.)

§19.2-11.4. Establishment of victim-offender reconciliation program.

A. Any Crime Victim and Witness Assistance Program may establish a victim-offender reconciliation program to provide an opportunity after conviction for a victim, at his request and upon the subsequent agreement of the offender, to:

1. Meet with the offender in a safe, controlled environment;
2. Give to the offender, either orally or in writing, a summary of the financial, emotional, and physical effects of the offense on the victim or the victim's family; and
3. Discuss a proposed restitution agreement which may be submitted for consideration by the sentencing court for damages incurred by the victim as a result of the offense.

B. If the victim chooses to participate in a victim-offender reconciliation program under this section, the victim shall execute a waiver releasing the Crime Victim and Witness Assistance Program, attorney for the offender and the attorney for the Commonwealth from civil and criminal liability for actions taken by the victim or offender as a result of participation by the victim or the offender in a victim-offender reconciliation program.

C. A victim shall not be required to participate in a victim-offender reconciliation program under this section.

D. The failure of any person to participate in a reconciliation program pursuant to this section shall not be used directly or indirectly at sentencing.
(Added by L.1995 ch. 628, eff. 7/1/95.)

CHAPTER 2
CONSERVATORS OF THE PEACE AND SPECIAL POLICEMEN

ARTICLE 1
APPOINTMENT

§19.2-12. Who are conservators of the peace.

Every judge throughout the Commonwealth and every magistrate within the geographical area for which he is appointed or elected, shall be a conservator of the peace. In addition, every commissioner in chancery, while sitting as such commissioner, any special agent or law-enforcement officer of the United States Department of Justice, National Marine Fisheries Service of the United States Department of Commerce, Department of Treasury, Department of Agriculture, Department of State, and Department of Interior, any inspector, law-enforcement official or police personnel of the United States Postal Inspection Service and any United States marshal or deputy United States marshal whose duties involve the enforcement of the criminal laws of the United States, any officer of the Virginia Marine Patrol, any criminal investigator of the United States Department of Labor, and any special agent of the United States Naval Criminal Investigative Service shall be a conservator of the peace, while engaged in the performance of their official duties.
(Chgd. by L.1997 ch. 34, eff. 7/1/97.)

§19.2-13. Special conservators of the peace; authority; jurisdiction; bond; liability of employers.

A. Upon the application of any corporation authorized to do business in the Commonwealth or the owner, proprietor or authorized custodian of any place within the Commonwealth and the showing of a necessity for the security of property or the peace, the circuit court of any county or city, in its discretion, may appoint one or more special conservators of the peace who shall serve as such for such length of time as the court may designate, but not exceeding four years under any one appointment. The order of appointment may provide that a special conservator of the peace shall have all the powers, functions, duties, responsibilities and authority of any other conservator of the peace within such geographical limitations as the court may deem appropriate, whenever such special conservator of the peace is engaged in the performance of his duties as such. The order may also provide that the special conservator of the peace is a "law-enforcement officer" for the purposes of §§37.1-67.01 and 37.1-67.1. Prior to granting an application for appointment, the circuit court shall order the local law-enforcement agency to conduct a background investigation, in accordance with §15.1-131.8(ii), of the prospective appointee and file a report of such investigation with the court unless the prospective appointee is a police officer as defined in §9-169. The local law-enforcement agency may charge the prospective appointee a reasonable fee not to exceed the lesser of the actual cost to the local law-enforcement agency or $300 for the time and costs expended in preparing the investigative report.

When the application is made by a corporation, the circuit court shall specify in the order of appointment the geographic jurisdiction of the special conservator of the peace, and this jurisdiction may include any or all counties and cities of the Commonwealth wherein the corporation does business. The clerk of the appointing circuit court shall certify a copy of the order of appointment to the circuit court of every jurisdiction specified in said order, and each special conservator of the peace so appointed on application of a corporation shall present his credentials to the chief of police or sheriff of all such jurisdictions.

Every person initially appointed on or after July 1, 1996, as a special conservator of the peace pursuant to the provisions of this section, before entering upon the duties of such office, shall be required by the court to enter into a bond with approved security before the clerk of the circuit court of the county or city wherein such duties are to be performed, in the penalty of such sum as may be fixed by the court, conditioned upon the faithful performance of such duties. Such bond shall be conditioned upon the faithful performance of such duties in any locality in which he is authorized to act pursuant to the order of the court. No such bond shall be required, however, if such person so appointed has met the minimum entry-level law-enforcement training requirements established by the Department of Criminal Justice Services under §9-170 within three years of the date of initial appointment or has been employed as a law-enforcement officer as defined by subdivision 9 of §9-169 within the preceding three years.

If any such special conservator of the peace is the employee, agent or servant of another, his appointment as special conservator of the peace shall not relieve his employer, principal or master, from civil liability to another arising out of any wrongful action or conduct committed by such special conservator of the peace while within the scope of his employment.

B. The court may limit or prohibit the carrying of weapons by any special conservator of the peace initially appointed on or after July 1, 1996, while the appointee is within the scope of his employment as such. If the order of appointment does not prohibit the carrying of weapons, the court may require that the appointee meet the minimum entry training requirements established by the Department of Criminal Justice Service under §9-170 for law-enforcement officers within twelve months of his appointment.
(Chgd. by L.1996 chs. 850, 956, eff. 7/1/96.)

§19.2-14. Conservators of the peace for fairgrounds and cemeteries; bond required.

The superintendent or other person in charge of any fairgrounds or any public or private cemetery shall, for the purpose of maintaining order and enforcing the criminal and police laws of the Commonwealth, or the county or city in which such fairgrounds or cemetery is situated, have all the powers, functions, duties, responsibilities and authority of a conservator of the peace within the fairgrounds or cemetery over which he may have charge and within one-half of a mile around the same.

The provisions of §19.2-13 relative to the giving of bond and the liability of an employer, principal or master, shall be applicable to every person exercising any powers of a conservator of the peace under this section.

§19.2-15. When conservator appointed under §19.2-13 need not be a citizen.

Any such conservator appointed under the provisions of §19.2-13 whose jurisdiction is limited to the grounds attached to an airport, need not be a citizen of the Commonwealth if the proprietors of such airport shall, before any such conservator shall enter upon the duties of the office, enter into bond with approved surety before the clerk of the circuit court having jurisdiction over such airport in the penalty of $1,000 for each conservator so appointed, with condition for the faithful discharge of his official duties.

§19.2-17. *(Repealed by L.1996 ch. 850, eff. 7/1/96.)*

ARTICLE 2
POWERS AND DUTIES

§19.2-18. Powers and duties generally.

Every conservator of the peace shall have authority to arrest without a warrant in such instances as are set out in §§19.2-19 and 19.2-81. Upon making an arrest without a warrant, the conservator of the peace shall proceed in accordance with the provisions of §19.2-22 or §19.2-82 as the case may be.

§19.2-19. Recognizance to keep the peace; when required.

If any person threatens to kill or injure another or to commit violence or injury against his person or property, or to unlawfully trespass upon his property, he shall be required to give a recognizance to keep the peace for such period not to exceed one year as the court hearing the complaint may determine.

§19.2-20. Same; complaint and issuance of warrant therefor.

If complaint be made to any magistrate or judge that a person should be required to give a recognizance to keep the peace due to any of the reasons set forth in §19.2-19, such magistrate or judge shall examine on oath the complainant, and any witness who may be produced, reduce the complaint to writing, and cause it to be signed by the complainant; and if probable cause is established, such magistrate or judge shall issue a warrant, reciting the complaint, and requiring the person complained of forthwith to be apprehended and brought before the district court having appropriate jurisdiction.

§19.2-21. Same; procedure when accused appears.

When such person appears, if the judge, on hearing the parties, considers that there is not good cause for the complaint, he shall discharge such person, and may give judgment in his favor against the complainant for his costs. If he considers that there is good cause therefor, he may require a recognizance of the person against whom it is, and give judgment against him for the costs of the prosecution, or any part thereof; and, unless such recognizance be given, he shall commit him to jail by a warrant, stating the sum and time in and for which the recognizance is directed. The person given judgment under this section for costs may issue a writ of fieri facias thereon, if an appeal be not allowed; and proceedings thereupon may be according to §§16.1-99 through 16.1-101.

§19.2-22. Same; arrest without a warrant.

A person arrested without a warrant by any conservator of the peace or other law-enforcement officer for any of the acts set forth in §19.2-19 committed in the presence of such conservator of the peace or law-enforcement officer, shall be brought forthwith before a magistrate or judge, and proceedings shall be had in accordance with §§19.2-20 and 19.2-21.

§19.2-23. Payment of fees or mileage allowances into county or city treasury.

Any conservator or policeman appointed under the provisions of this chapter shall not be entitled to fees or mileage for performance of his duties as such conservator or policeman.

ARTICLE 3
APPEALS

§19.2-24. When appeal may be taken; witnesses recognized; bail.

Any person from whom a recognizance is required under the provisions of this chapter or who has been committed to jail for failure to give security therefor, may appeal to the circuit court of the county or city, and, in such case, the judge from whose judgment the appeal is taken shall recognize such of the witnesses as he thinks proper; provided, however, that the person taking the appeal may be required to give bail, with good security, for his appearance at the circuit court of the county or city.

§19.2-25. Power of court on appeal.

The court may dismiss the complaint or affirm the judgment, and make what order it sees fit as to the costs. If it award costs against the appellant, the recognizance which he may have given shall stand as security therefor. When there is a failure to prosecute the appeal, such recognizance shall remain in force, although there be no order of affirmance. On any appeal the court may require of the appellant a new recognizance if it see fit.

Any person committed to jail under this chapter may be discharged by the circuit court of the county or city on such terms as it may deem reasonable.

CHAPTER 3
MAGISTRATES

ARTICLE 1
TRANSITION PROVISIONS

§19.2-26. Repeal of inconsistent statutes, municipal charters, etc.

All acts and parts of acts, all sections of this Code, and all provisions of municipal charters, inconsistent with the provisions of this title, are, except as herein otherwise provided, repealed to the extent of such inconsistency.

§19.2-27. Effect of repeal of Title 39.1 on prior acts, offenses, etc.

The repeal of Title 39.1 effective as of January 1, 1974, shall not affect any act or offense done or committed or any penalty or forfeiture incurred, or any right established, accrued, or accruing on or before such date, or any prosecution, suit or action pending on that day.

§19.2-28. Certain notices, recognizances and processes validated.

Any notice given, recognizance taken, or process or writ issued, before January 1, 1974, shall be valid although given, taken or to be returned to a day after such date, in like manner as if this title had been effective before the same was given, taken or issued.

§19.2-29. References to former sections, articles and chapters in Title 39.1.

Whenever in Chapters 3 (§19.2-26 et seq.) and 4 (§19.2-49 et seq.) of this title any of the conditions, requirements, provisions or contents of any section, article or chapter of Title 39.1, as such title existed prior to January 1, 1974, are transferred in the same or modified form to a new section, article or chapter, and whenever any such former section, article or chapter is given a new number in Chapters 3 and 4 of this title all references to any such former section, article or chapter of Title 39.1 appearing elsewhere in this Code than in Chapters 3 and 4 of this title shall be construed to apply to the new or renumbered section, article or chapter containing such conditions, requirements, provisions or contents or portions thereof.

ARTICLE 2
ABOLITION OF JUSTICE OF THE PEACE SYSTEM

§19.2-30. Abolition of justice of the peace system.

The office of justice of the peace having been abolished effective as of January 1, 1974, nevertheless, any justice of the peace in office December 31, 1973, may continue in office as a magistrate under the provisions of Chapters 3 (§19.2-26 et seq.) and 4 (§19.2-49 et seq.) of this title for the remainder of the term for which he had been elected or appointed and shall be eligible for future appointment to serve as a magistrate notwithstanding §19.2-37.

§19.2-31. Abolition of office of issuing justice.

Effective January 1, 1974, the office of issuing justice as provided for in Chapter 2 (§39.1-20 et seq.) of Title 39.1 having been abolished, nevertheless, any such special justice of the peace in office December 31, 1973, and elected by the town council for a specific term to expire after that date, may continue in office for the remainder of that term. If he continues in office as provided herein, such justice shall exercise the same powers, perform the same duties, and receive such compensation as he was receiving as of December 31, 1973.

§19.2-32. References to justices of the peace.

References in law to justices of the peace shall be deemed to apply to magistrates unless the provisions of Chapters 3 (§19.2-26 et seq.) and 4 (§19.2-49 et seq.) of this title shall render such reference inapplicable.

ARTICLE 3
THE MAGISTRATE SYSTEM

§19.2-33. Office of magistrate.

The office of magistrate shall be vested with all the authority, duties and obligations previously vested in the office of justice of the peace prior to January 1, 1974.

§19.2-34. Number of magistrates.

There shall be appointed for each judicial district as many magistrates as are necessary for the effective administration of justice, such magistrates and any other personnel in the office of the magistrates shall be authorized by the

Committee on District Courts established pursuant to §16.1-69.33.

§19.2-35. Appointment; supervision generally.

Magistrates and any other personnel in the office of the magistrate shall be appointed by the chief judge of the circuit court having jurisdiction within the district. Each magistrate shall be appointed to serve the entire judicial district for which the appointment is made. The chief circuit judge shall have full supervisory authority over the magistrates so appointed, but may delegate this authority to the chief general district judge. Notwithstanding any other provision of law, the only methods for the selection of magistrates and special magistrates shall be as set out in this section and Chapter 4 (§19.2-49 et seq.) of this title, respectively.

The chief judge may also appoint so many substitute magistrates as may be authorized by the Committee on District Courts. The order of appointment of such substitute magistrate shall specify the period such substitute magistrate shall serve and during this period such substitute magistrate shall exercise all the powers enumerated in §19.2-45 in the judicial district for which the appointment is made.

If a magistrate of any district is absent or unable through sickness or other disability to perform his duties, the chief magistrate of that district may call upon any off-duty magistrate of an adjoining district to serve in a replacement capacity. When so designated, the replacement magistrate shall have all the authority and power of a magistrate of that district.

§19.2-36. Chief magistrates.

The chief circuit judge of a circuit may appoint a chief magistrate, for the purpose of maintaining the proper schedules, assisting in the training of the magistrates within such judicial district and to be responsible to the chief circuit judge for the conduct of the magistrates and to further assist the chief circuit judge in the operation of the magistrate system. The chief magistrate shall exercise direct daily supervision over the magistrates within the district and shall have the power to suspend without pay a magistrate after consultation and with the concurrence of the chief circuit judge.

§19.2-37. Who may be appointed magistrate.

Any person may be appointed to the office of magistrate under this title subject to the limitations of Chapter 4 (§2.1-30 et seq.) of Title 2.1 of the Code and of this section.

A person shall be eligible for appointment to the office of magistrate under the provisions of this title: (a) if such person or his spouse is not a law-enforcement officer; (b) if such person or his spouse is not a clerk, deputy or assistant clerk, or employee charged with the duty of enforcing any of the laws of this Commonwealth or any ordinance of any political subdivision thereof, of any such clerk of a district court or police department or sheriff's office in any county or city with respect to appointment to the office of magistrate of such county or city, provided that the Committee on District Courts may authorize a magistrate to assist in the district court clerk's office on a part-time basis; (c) if the appointment does not create a parent-child, husband-wife, or brother-sister relationship between a district court judge and such person serving within the same judicial district; (c1) if such person is not the chief executive officer, or a member of the board of supervisors, town or city council, or other governing body for any political subdivision of this Commonwealth; (d) if such person is a United States citizen and a resident of the judicial district for which he is appointed to serve as magistrate or an adjoining judicial district. Any magistrate serving in the City of Norfolk on July 1, 1996, shall be eligible for reappointment pursuant to this article regardless of the judicial district of his residence. No magistrate shall issue any warrant or process in complaint of his spouse, child, grandchild, parent, grandparent, parent-in-law, child-in-law, brother, sister, brother-in-law or sister-in-law, nephew, niece, uncle, aunt, first cousin, guardian or ward. The residence provisions contained in this section shall not be a bar to the reappointment of any magistrate in office on July 1, 1973, provided he is otherwise eligible to serve under the provisions of this chapter.
(Chgd. by L.1996 ch. 112; L.1999 ch. 267, eff. 7/1/99.)

§19.2-38. Terms; probationary period; compensation and benefits; vacancies; revocation of appointment.

Persons appointed as magistrates under the provisions of this chapter shall serve for a term of four years. Such term shall commence upon appointment and qualification, provided that any magistrate appointed for the first time to any term commencing after July 1, 1980, shall serve initially for a six-month probationary period during which the magistrate must complete the minimum training program as established by the Committee on District Courts and satisfactorily complete a certification examination. Failure to successfully pass the certification examination shall preclude the magistrate from serving beyond the six-month probationary period. Magistrates shall be entitled to compensation and other benefits only from the time they take office. Vacancies shall be filled for the unexpired term by the chief circuit judge. Appointments made under the provisions of this chapter shall be revocable at the pleasure of the chief circuit judge.

§19.2-38.1. Training standards; training prerequisite to reappointment; waiver.

The Committee on District Courts shall establish minimum training standards for magistrates in accordance with such rules and regulations as may be established by the Committee. Every magistrate appointed to an original term commencing on or after July 1, 1980, shall comply with the minimum training standards established by the Committee on District Courts and such magistrates must complete the minimum training standards as a prerequisite for continuing to serve as magistrate beyond the six-month probationary period as established by §19.2-38. All magistrates shall be required to complete the minimum training standards prior to reappointment for a new term. The Committee on District Courts upon request may waive any portion of the minimum training standards for an individual magistrate.

Every magistrate appointed to an original term commencing on or after July 1, 1985, shall be required to have a high school diploma or General Education Development Certificate.

Every magistrate appointed to an original term commencing on or after July 1, 1995, shall be required to have a bachelor's degree from an accredited institution of higher learning or equivalent experience.
(Chgd. by L.1995 ch. 611, eff. 7/1/95.)

§19.2-39. Bond.

Every magistrate appointed under the provisions of this chapter shall enter into bond in the sum of $5,000, made payable to the Commonwealth, before the clerk of the circuit court which exercises jurisdiction over the political subdivision wherein such magistrate shall serve, for the faithful performance of his duties. The premium for such bond shall be paid by the Commonwealth. Provided, however, that in lieu of specific bonds, the Committee on District Courts may in its discretion procure faithful performance of duty blanket bonds for any or all of the districts enumerated in §16.1-69.6 covering all magistrates included in such districts and for the penalty contained in this section, unless in the discretion of the Committee, bonds with a larger penalty should be obtained. Such blanket bonds shall be made payable to the

Commonwealth and shall cover all funds handled by a magistrate whether such funds belong to the Commonwealth or any political subdivision thereof. Provided further, that in those instances where specific bonds for magistrates are in effect, the Committee on District Courts may, whenever it deems it advisable, terminate such specific bonds upon obtaining a blanket bond covering such magistrates with appropriate refunds or credit being made for the unearned premiums on the specific bonds terminated. A copy of any such blanket bond so procured shall be filed with the State Comptroller and with the clerk of the respective circuit court which exercises jurisdiction over the district wherein such magistrate shall serve. The premiums for such blanket bonds shall be paid by the Commonwealth.

ARTICLE 4
SUPERVISION

§19.2-41. When chief general district judge to exercise general supervisory power; rules and regulations.

When delegated the authority by the chief circuit judge, the chief general district judge shall exercise general supervisory power over the administration of magistrates within the district. When such authority is delegated, it shall be the duty of the chief general district judge to supervise the magistrates within the district and to promulgate such reasonable rules and regulations as may be deemed necessary to supplement or clarify the provisions of this chapter with respect to such magistrates, to include fixing the time and place of the sitting of such magistrates.

§19.2-42. Duty of attorney for the Commonwealth.

It shall be the duty of the attorney for the Commonwealth to render legal advice to the magistrates within his city or county and to advise them, when necessary, of changes in law and procedure.

§19.2-43. Duty of Executive Secretary of Supreme Court.

It shall be the duty of the Executive Secretary of the Supreme Court to assist the chief general district judges and general district courts in the supervision and mandatory training of magistrates for which purpose he shall be authorized to conduct training sessions and meetings for magistrates and provide information and materials for their use. He may appoint one or more magistrates to assist him and, in addition, with the approval of the Chief Justice, require annual reports to be filed by the magistrates on their work as such, fees associated therewith and other information pertinent to their office, on forms to be furnished by him.

ARTICLE 5
JURISDICTION AND POWERS

§19.2-44. Territorial jurisdiction.

A magistrate shall exercise the powers conferred by this title only in the judicial district for which he is appointed. However, a magistrate may exercise these powers in a contiguous political subdivision when so authorized by his appointing authority and the chief circuit court judge of the district to which assistance is to be provided.

(Chgd. by L.1995 ch. 551, eff. 7/1/95.)

§19.2-45. Powers enumerated.

A magistrate shall have the following powers only:

(1) To issue process of arrest in accord with the provisions of §§19.2-71 to 19.2-82 of the Code;

(2) To issue search warrants in accord with the provisions of §§19.2-52 to 19.2-60 of the Code;

(3) To admit to bail or commit to jail all persons charged with offenses subject to the limitations of and in accord with general laws on bail;

(4) The same power to issue warrants and subpoenas within such county or city as is conferred upon district courts. Such attachments, warrants and subpoenas shall be returnable before a district court or any court of limited jurisdiction continued in operation pursuant to §16.1-70.1;

(5) To issue civil warrants directed to the sheriff or constable of the county or city wherein the defendant resides, together with a copy thereof, requiring him to summon the person against whom the claim is, to appear before a district court on a certain day, not exceeding thirty days from the date thereof to answer such claim. If there be two or more defendants and any defendant resides outside the jurisdiction in which the warrant is issued, the summons for such defendant residing outside the jurisdiction may be directed to the sheriff of the county or city of his residence, and such warrant may be served and returned as provided in §16.1-80;

(6) To administer oaths and take acknowledgments;

(7) To act as conservators of the peace;

(8), (9) *(Repealed.)*

(10) To perform such other acts or functions specifically authorized by law.

ARTICLE 6
COMPENSATION AND FEES

§19.2-46. Compensation.

The salaries of all magistrates shall be fixed and paid as provided in Article 5.1 (§14.1-44.1 et seq.) of Chapter 1 of Title 14.1. The salaries referred to herein shall be in lieu of all fees which may accrue to the recipient by virtue of his office.

Each substitute magistrate shall receive for his services a per diem compensation as may be established by the Committee on District Courts.

§19.2-46.1. Salaries to be fixed by Committee on District Courts; limitations; mileage allowance.

Salaries of magistrates and any other personnel in the office of the magistrate shall be fixed by the Committee on District Courts established pursuant to §16.1-69.33. Such salaries shall be fixed by the Committee at least annually at such time as it deems proper and as soon as practicable thereafter certified to the Comptroller and the Executive Secretary of the Supreme Court.

In addition to the salary authorized by this section, a magistrate may be reimbursed by the county or city for reasonable mileage expenses actually incurred in the performance of his duties.

In determining the salary of any magistrate, the Committee shall consider the work load of and territory and population served by the magistrate and such other factors it deems relevant. It may require of any magistrate or district judge information on the operation of the office of the magistrate.

The governing body of any county or city may add to the fixed compensation of magistrates such amount as the governing body may appropriate with the total amount not to exceed fifty percent of the amount paid by the Commonwealth to magistrates. No additional amount paid by a local governing body shall be chargeable to the Executive Secretary of the Supreme Court, nor shall it remove or supersede any authority, control or supervision of the Executive Secretary or Committee on District Courts.
(Added by L.1998 ch. 872, eff. 10/1/98.)

§19.2-46.2. Full-time magistrates; certification for retirement coverage.

The Committee on District Courts shall certify to the director of the Virginia Retirement System the names of those magistrates serving on a regular full-time basis. Certification by the Committee shall qualify a magistrate as a state employee, for purposes of §§51.1-124.3 and 51.1-152 of the Virginia Retirement System (§51.1-124.1 et seq.), effective on the date given in the certificate as the date on which such magistrate first served on a regular full-time basis on or after January 1, 1974.
(Added by L.1998 ch. 872, eff. 10/1/98.)

§19.2-47. Magistrate not to receive claims or evidence of debt for collection.

No magistrate shall receive claims or evidence of debt for collection; and it shall be unlawful for any magistrate to receive claims of any kind for collection, or to accept or receive money or any other things of value by way of commission or compensation for or on account of any collection made by or through him on any such claim, either before or after judgment. Any magistrate violating this section shall be guilty of a Class 1 misdemeanor.

§19.2-47.1. Disposition of funds.

All funds paid to and collected by or on behalf of a magistrate shall be paid promptly to the appropriate district court clerk, circuit court clerk, commissioner in chancery, department of the Commonwealth, federal agency or as otherwise authorized by statute.
(Added by L.1998 ch. 872, eff. 10/1/98.)

§19.2-48. Audits.

The Auditor of Public Accounts shall audit the records of all magistrates who serve in any county or city when auditing the records of the district courts of such county or city or upon request of the chief district judge of the district in which such county or city is located.

§19.2-48.1. Quarters for magistrates.

A. Each county and city having a general district court or juvenile and domestic relations district court and having one or more magistrates appointed pursuant to Article 3 (§19.2-33 et seq.) of this chapter, shall provide suitable quarters for such magistrates. Insofar as possible, such quarters should be located in a public facility and should be appropriate to conduct the affairs of a judicial officer as well as provide convenient access to the public and law-enforcement officers. The county or city shall also provide all furniture and other equipment necessary for the efficient operation of the office.

B. Wherever practical, the office of magistrate shall be located at the county seat. However, offices may be located at other locations in the county, or city adjacent thereto, whenever such additional offices are necessary to effect the efficient administration of justice.
(Chgd. by L.1996 ch. 616, eff. 7/1/96.)

CHAPTER 5
SEARCH WARRANTS

Section

19.2-52.	When search warrant may issue.
19.2-53.	What may be searched and seized.
19.2-54.	Affidavit preliminary to issuance of search warrant; general search warrant prohibited; effect of failure to file affidavit.
19.2-55.	Issuing general search warrant or search warrant without affidavit deemed malfeasance.
19.2-56.	To whom search warrant directed; what it shall command; warrant to show date and time of issuance; copy of affidavit to be part of warrant and served therewith; warrants not executed within fifteen days.
19.2-56.1.	Warrant issued for search of attorney's office.
19.2-57.	Execution and return of warrant; list of property seized.
19.2-58.	Disposition of property seized.
19.2-59.	Search without warrant prohibited; when search without warrant lawful.
19.2-59.1.	Strip searches prohibited; exceptions; how strip searches conducted.
19.2-60.	Motion for return of seized property and to suppress.

§19.2-52. When search warrant may issue.

Except as provided in §19.2-56.1, search warrants, based upon complaint on oath supported by an affidavit as required in §19.2-54, may be issued by any judge, magistrate or other person having authority to issue criminal warrants, if he be satisfied from such complaint and affidavit that there is reasonable and probable cause for the issuance of such search warrant.

§19.2-53. What may be searched and seized.

Search warrants may be issued for the search of or for specified places, things or persons, and seizure therefrom of the following things as specified in the warrant:

(1) Weapons or other objects used in the commission of crime;

(2) Articles or things the sale or possession of which is unlawful;

(3) Stolen property or the fruits of any crime;

(4) Any object, thing, or person, including without limitation, documents, books, papers, records or body fluids, constituting evidence of the commission of crime.

Notwithstanding any other provision in this chapter to the contrary, no search warrant may be issued as a substitute for a witness subpoena.

§19.2-54. Affidavit preliminary to issuance of search warrant; general search warrant prohibited; effect of failure to file affidavit.

No search warrant shall be issued until there is filed with the officer authorized to issue the same an affidavit of some person reasonably describing the place, thing, or person to be searched, the things or persons to be searched for thereunder, alleging briefly material facts, constituting the probable cause for the issuance of such warrant and alleging substantially the offense in relation to which such search is to be made and that the object, thing, or person searched for constitutes evidence of the commission of such offense. Such affidavit shall be certified by the officer who issues such warrant and delivered by such officer or other officer authorized to certify such warrants to the clerk of the circuit court of the county or city wherein the search is made within seven days after the issuance of such warrant and shall by such clerk be preserved as a record and shall at all times be subject to inspection by the public; however such affidavit may be temporarily sealed by the appropriate court upon application of the attorney for the Commonwealth for good cause shown in an ex parte hearing. Any individual arrested and claiming to be aggrieved by such search and seizure or any person who claims to be entitled to lawful possession of such property seized may move the appropriate court for the unsealing of such affidavit, and the burden of proof with respect to continued sealing shall be upon the Commonwealth. Each such clerk shall maintain an index of all such affidavits filed in his office in order to facilitate inspection. No such warrant shall be issued on an affidavit omitting such essentials, and no general warrant for the search of a house, place, compartment, vehicle or baggage shall be issued. The term "affidavit" as used in this section, means statements made under oath or affirmation and preserved verbatim.

Failure of the officer issuing such warrant to file the required affidavit shall not invalidate any search made under the warrant unless such failure shall continue for a period of thirty days. If the affidavit is filed prior to the expiration of the thirty-day period, nevertheless, evidence obtained in any such search shall not be admissible until a reasonable time after the filing of the required affidavit.

§19.2-55. Issuing general search warrant or search warrant without affidavit deemed malfeasance.

Any person having authority to issue criminal warrants who wilfully and knowingly issues a general search warrant or a search warrant without the affidavit required by §19.2-54 shall be deemed guilty of a malfeasance.

§19.2-56. To whom search warrant directed; what it shall command; warrant to show date and time of issuance; copy of affidavit to be part of warrant and served therewith; warrants not executed within fifteen days.

The judge, magistrate or other official authorized to issue criminal warrants, shall issue a search warrant if he finds from the facts or circumstances recited in the affidavit that there is probable cause for the issuance thereof.

Every search warrant shall be directed to (i) the sheriff, sergeant, or any policeman of the county, city or town in which the place to be searched is located, (ii) any law-enforcement officer or agent employed by the Commonwealth and vested with the powers of sheriffs and police, or (iii) jointly to any such sheriff, sergeant, policeman or law-enforcement officer or agent and an agent or officer of the Federal Bureau of Investigation, the Bureau of Alcohol, Tobacco and Firearms of the United States Treasury or the Drug Enforcement Administration. The warrant shall (i) name the affiant, (ii) recite the offense in relation to which the search is to be made, (iii) name or describe the place to be searched, (iv) describe the property or person to be searched for, and (v) recite that the magistrate has found probable cause to believe that the property or person constitutes evidence of a crime (identified in the warrant) or tends to show that a person (named or described therein) has committed or is committing a crime.

The warrant shall command that the place be forthwith searched, either in day or night, and that the objects or persons described in the warrant, if found there, be seized. An inventory shall be produced before a court having jurisdiction of the offense in relation to which the warrant was issued as provided in §19.2-57.

Any such warrant as provided in this section shall be executed by the policeman or other law-enforcement officer or agent into whose hands it shall come or be delivered. If the warrant is directed jointly to a sheriff, sergeant, policeman or law-enforcement officer or agent of the Commonwealth and a federal agent or officer as otherwise provided in this section, the warrant may be executed jointly or by the policeman, law-enforcement officer or agent into whose hands it is delivered. No other person may be permitted to be present during or participate in the execution of a warrant to search a place except (i) the owners and occupants of the place to be searched when permitted to be present by the officer in charge of the conduct of the search and (ii) persons designated by the officer in charge of the conduct of the search to assist or provide expertise in the conduct of the search.

Every search warrant shall contain the date and time it was issued. However, the failure of any such search warrant to contain the date and time it was issued shall not render the warrant void, provided that the date and time of issuing of said warrant is established by competent evidence.

The judge, magistrate, or other official authorized to issue criminal warrants shall attach a copy of the affidavit required by §19.2-54, which shall become a part of the search warrant and served therewith. However, this provision shall not be applicable in any case in which the affidavit is made by means of a voice or videotape recording or where the affidavit has been sealed pursuant to §19.2-54.

Any search warrant not executed within fifteen days after issuance thereof shall be returned to, and voided by, the officer who issued such search warrant.

(Chgd. by L.2000 ch. 738, eff. 7/1/2000.)

§19.2-56.1. Warrant issued for search of attorney's office.

A. Any warrant sought for the search of a premises or the contents thereof belonging to or under the control of any licensed attorney-at-law to search for evidence of any crime solely involving a client of such attorney shall be issued only by a circuit court judge. Any evidence seized pursuant to this section shall be inventoried forthwith by the clerk of the issuing court and sealed by the issuing judge. As soon thereafter as is practicable, the issuing judge shall conduct an in camera inspection of the seized evidence in the presence of the attorney from whom the evidence was seized. Following such inspection the issuing judge shall return any evidence so seized which is determined to be within the scope of the attorney-client privilege and not otherwise subject to seizure.

B. Nothing herein shall bar the standing of the client to challenge the admissibility of any evidence seized pursuant to this section in any trial or proceeding.

§19.2-57. Execution and return of warrant; list of property seized.

The warrant shall be executed by the search of the place described in the warrant and, if property described in the warrant be found there, by the seizure of the property. The officer who seizes any property shall prepare an inventory thereof, under oath. An inventory of any seized property shall be produced before the court designated in the warrant. The officer executing the warrant shall endorse the date of execution thereon and shall file the warrant, with the inventory attached (or a notation that no property was seized) and the accompanying affidavit, unless such affidavit was made by voice or videotape recording, within three days after the execution of such search warrant in the circuit court clerk's office, wherein the search was made, as provided in §19.2-54. Saturdays, Sundays, or any federal or state legal holiday shall not be used in computing the three-day filing period.

§19.2-58. Disposition of property seized.

If any such warrant be executed by the seizure of property, or of any other of the things aforesaid, the same shall be safely kept by the direction of such judge or court, to be used as evidence, and thereafter be disposed of as provided by law; provided, however, that any such property seized under such warrant which is not used in evidence and any property which is stolen or embezzled property shall be restored to its owner, and the things mentioned in §19.2-53 may be burnt or otherwise destroyed, under such direction, as soon as there is no further need for its use as evidence unless it is otherwise expressly provided by law.

§19.2-59. Search without warrant prohibited; when search without warrant lawful.

No officer of the law or any other person shall search any place, thing or person, except by virtue of and under a warrant issued by a proper officer. Any officer or other person searching any place, thing or person otherwise than by virtue of and under a search warrant, shall be guilty of malfeasance in office. Any officer or person violating the provisions of this section shall be liable to any person aggrieved thereby in both compensatory and punitive damages. Any officer found guilty of a second offense under this section shall, upon conviction thereof, immediately forfeit his office, and such finding shall be deemed to create a vacancy in such office to be filled according to law.

Provided, however, that any officer empowered to enforce the game laws or marine fisheries laws as set forth in Title 28.2 may without a search warrant enter for the purpose of enforcing such laws, any freight yard or room, passenger depot, baggage room or warehouse, storage room or warehouse, train, baggage car, passenger car, express car, Pullman car or freight car of any common carrier, or any boat, automobile or other vehicle; but nothing in this proviso contained shall be construed to permit a search of any occupied berth or compartment on any passenger car or boat or any baggage, bag, trunk, box or other closed container without a search warrant.
(Chgd. by L.1997 ch. 147, eff. 7/1/97.)

§19.2-59.1. Strip searches prohibited; exceptions; how strip searches conducted.

A. No person in custodial arrest for a traffic infraction, Class 3 or Class 4 misdemeanor, or a violation of a city, county, or town ordinance, which is punishable by no more than thirty days in jail shall be strip searched unless there is reasonable cause to believe on the part of a law-enforcement officer authorizing the search that the individual is concealing a weapon. All strip searches conducted under this section shall be performed by persons of the same sex as the person arrested and on premises where the search cannot be observed by persons not physically conducting the search.

B. A regional jail superintendent or the chief of police or the sheriff of the county or city shall develop a written policy regarding strip searches.

C. A search of any body cavity must be performed under sanitary conditions and a search of any body cavity, other than the mouth, shall be conducted either by or under the supervision of medically trained personnel.

D. Strip searches authorized pursuant to the exceptions stated in subsection A of this section shall be conducted by a law-enforcement officer as defined in subdivision 9 of §9-169.

E. The provisions of this section shall not apply when the person is taken into custody by or remanded to a law-enforcement officer pursuant to a circuit or district court order.

F. For purposes of this section, "strip search" shall mean having an arrested person remove or arrange some or all of his clothing so as to permit a visual inspection of the genitals, buttocks, anus, female breasts, or undergarments of such person.

G. Nothing in this section shall prohibit a sheriff or a regional jail superintendent from requiring that inmates take hot water and soap showers and be subjected to visual inspection upon assignment to the general population area of the jail or upon determination by the sheriff or regional jail superintendent that the inmate must be held at the jail by reason of his inability to post bond after reasonable opportunity to do so.
(Chgd. by L.1995 ch. 112, eff. 7/1/95.)

§19.2-60. Motion for return of seized property and to suppress.

A person aggrieved by an allegedly unlawful search or seizure may move the court to return any seized property and to suppress it for use as evidence. The court shall receive evidence on any issue of fact necessary to the decision of the motion. If the motion is granted by a court of record, any seized property shall be restored as soon as practicable unless otherwise subject to lawful detention, and such property shall not be admissible in evidence at any hearing or trial. If the motion is granted by a court not of record, such property shall not be admissible in evidence at any hearing or trial before that court, but the ruling shall have no effect on any hearing or trial in a court of record.

CHAPTER 6
INTERCEPTION OF WIRE, ELECTRONIC OR ORAL COMMUNICATIONS

 Zv

§19.2-61. Definitions.

As used in this chapter:

"Wire communication" means any aural transfer made in whole or in part through the use of facilities for the transmission of communications by the aid of wire, cable, or other like connection, including the use of such connection in a switching station, furnished or operated by any person engaged in providing or operating such facilities for the transmission of communications and includes electronic storage of such communication;

"Oral communication" means any oral communication uttered by a person exhibiting an expectation that such communication is not subject to interception under circumstances justifying such expectations but does not include any electronic communication;

"Intercept" means any aural or other means of acquisition of the contents of any wire, electronic or oral communication through the use of any electronic, mechanical or other device;

"Electronic, mechanical or other device" means any device or apparatus which can be used to intercept a wire, electronic or oral communication other than:

(a) Any telephone or telegraph instrument, equipment or facility, or any component thereof, (i) furnished to the subscriber or user by a provider of wire or electronic communication service in the ordinary course of its business and being used by the subscriber or user in the ordinary course of its business or furnished by the subscriber or user for connection to the facilities of such service and used in the ordinary course of the subscriber's or user's business; or (ii) being used by a communications common carrier in the ordinary course of its business, or by an investigative or law-enforcement officer in the ordinary course of his duties;

(b) A hearing aid or similar device being used to correct subnormal hearing to not better than normal;

"Person" means any employee or agent of the Commonwealth or a political subdivision thereof, and any individual, partnership, association, joint stock company, trust or corporation;

"Investigative or law-enforcement officer" means any officer of the United States or of a state or political subdivision thereof, who is empowered by law to conduct investigations of or to make arrests for offenses enumerated in this chapter, and any attorney authorized by law to prosecute or participate in the prosecution of such offenses;

"Contents" when used with respect to any wire, electronic or oral communication, includes any information concerning the substance, purport or meaning of that communication;

"Judge of competent jurisdiction" means a judge of any circuit court of the Commonwealth with general criminal jurisdiction;

"Communications common carrier" means any person engaged as a common carrier for hire in communication by wire or radio or in radio transmission of energy;

"Aggrieved person" means a person who was a party to any intercepted wire, electronic or oral communication or a person against whom the interception was directed;

"Electronic communication" means any transfer of signs, signals, writing, images, sounds, data, or intelligence of any nature transmitted in whole or in part by a wire, radio, electromagnetic, photoelectronic or photooptical system. The term does not include:

1. Any wire communication or oral communication as defined herein;

2. Any communication made through a tone-only paging device; or

3. Any communication from an electronic or mechanical device which permits the tracking of the movement of a person or object;

"User" means any person or entity who uses an electronic communication service and is duly authorized by the provider of such service to engage in such use;

"Electronic communication system" means any wire, radio, electromagnetic, photooptical or photoelectronic facilities for the transmission of electronic communications, and any computer facilities or related electronic equipment for the electronic storage of such communications;

"Electronic communication service" means any service which provides to users thereof the ability to send or receive wire or electronic communications;

"Readily accessible to the general public" means, with respect to a radio communication, that such communication is not (i) scrambled or encrypted, (ii) transmitted using modulation techniques whose essential parameters have been withheld from the public with the intention of preserving the privacy of such communication; (iii) carried on a subcarrier or other signal subsidiary to a radio transmission, (iv) transmitted over a communication system provided by a communications common carrier, unless the communication is a tone-only paging system communication; or (v) transmitted on frequencies allocated under Part 25, subpart D, E, or F of Part 74, or Part 94 of the Rules of the Federal Communications Commission, unless, in the case of a communication transmitted on a frequency allocated under Part 74 that is not exclusively allocated to broadcast auxiliary services, the communication is a two-way voice communication by radio;

"Electronic storage" means any temporary, intermediate storage of a wire or electronic communication incidental to the electronic transmission thereof and any storage of such communication by an electronic communication service for purposes of backup protection of such communication;

"Aural transfer" means a transfer containing the human voice at any point between and including the point of origin and the point of reception;

"Pen register" means a device which records or decodes electronic or other impulses which identify the numbers dialed or otherwise transmitted on the telephone line to which such device is attached. The term does not include any device used by a provider or customer of a wire or electronic communication service for billing, or recording as an incident to billing, for communications services provided by such provider or any device used by a provider or customer of a wire communication service for cost accounting or other like purposes in the ordinary course of the provider's or customer's business;

"Trap and trace device" means a device which captures the incoming electronic or other impulses identifying the originating number of an instrument or device from which a wire or electronic communication was transmitted; and

"Remote computing service" means the provision to the public of computer storage or processing services by means of an electronic communications system.

§19.2-62. Interception, disclosure, etc., of wire, electronic or oral communications unlawful; penalties; exceptions.

A. Except as otherwise specifically provided in this chapter any person who:

1. Intentionally intercepts, endeavors to intercept or procures any other person to intercept or endeavor to intercept, any wire, electronic or oral communication;

2. Intentionally uses, endeavors to use, or procures any other person to use or endeavor to use any electronic, mechanical or other device to intercept any oral communication;

3. Intentionally discloses, or endeavors to disclose, to any other person the contents of any wire, electronic or oral communication knowing or having reason to know that the information was obtained through the interception of a wire, electronic or oral communication; or

4. Intentionally uses, or endeavors to use, the contents of any wire, electronic or oral communication, knowing or having reason to know that the information was obtained through the interception of a wire or oral communication; shall be guilty of a Class 6 felony.

B. 1. It shall not be unlawful under this chapter for an operator of a switchboard, or an officer, employee or agent of a provider of wire or electronic communications service, whose facilities are used in the transmission of a wire communication, to intercept, disclose or use that communication in the normal course of his employment while engaged in any activity which is a necessary incident to the rendition of his service or to the protection of the rights or property of the provider of that service. However, a provider of wire communication service to the public shall not utilize service observing or random monitoring except for mechanical or service quality control checks. It shall not be a criminal offense under this chapter for providers of wire or electronic communications service, their officers, employees and agents, landlords, custodians, or other persons pursuant to a court order under this chapter, to provide information facilities or technical assistance to an investigative or law-enforcement officer, who, pursuant to this chapter, is authorized to intercept a wire, electronic or oral communication.

2. It shall not be a criminal offense under this chapter for a person to intercept a wire, electronic or oral communication, where such person is a party to the communication or one of the parties to the communication has given prior consent to such interception.

3. It shall not be a criminal offense under this chapter for any person:

(a) To intercept or access an electronic communication made through an electronic communication system that is configured so that such electronic communication is readily accessible to the general public;

(b) To intercept any radio communication which is transmitted (i) by any station for the use of the general public, or that relates to ships, aircraft, vehicles, or persons in distress, (ii) by any governmental, law-enforcement, civil defense, private land mobile, or public safety communications system, including police and fire, readily accessible to the general public, (iii) by a station operating on an authorized frequency within the bands allocated to the amateur, citizens band, or general mobile radio services; or (iv) by any marine or aeronautical communications system;

(c) To intercept any wire or electronic communication the transmission of which is causing harmful interference to any lawfully operating station or consumer electronic equipment, to the extent necessary to identify the source of such interference;

(d) Using the same frequency to intercept any radio communication made through a system that utilizes frequencies monitored by individuals engaged in the provision or the use of such system, if such communication is not scrambled or encrypted;

(e) To use a pen register or a trap and trace device pursuant to §§19.2-70.1 and 19.2-70.2; or

(f) Who is a provider of electronic communication service to record the fact that a wire or electronic communication was initiated or completed in order to protect such provider, another provider furnishing service toward the completion of the wire or electronic communication, or a user of that service, from fraudulent, unlawful or abusive use of such service.

C. A person or entity providing an electronic communication service to the public shall not intentionally divulge the contents of any communication, other than one to such person or entity or an agent thereof, while in transmission on that service to any person or entity other than an addressee or intended recipient of such communication or an agent of the addressee or intended recipient. However, a person or entity providing electronic communication service to the public may divulge the contents of any such communication:

1. As authorized in subdivision B 1 of this section or §19.2-67;

2. With the lawful consent of the originator or any addressee or intended recipient of such communication;

3. To a person employed or authorized, or whose facilities are used, to forward such communication to its destination; or

4. Which were inadvertently obtained by the service provider and which appear to pertain to the commission of a crime, to a law-enforcement agency.

Conduct otherwise an offense under this subsection that consists of or relates to the interception of a satellite transmission that is not encrypted or scrambled and that is transmitted (i) to a broadcasting station for purposes of retransmission to the general public, or (ii) as an audio subcarrier intended for redistribution to facilities open to the public, but not including data transmissions or telephone calls, is not an offense under this section unless the conduct is for the purposes of direct or indirect commercial advantage or private financial gain. Further, private viewing of a satellite video communication that is not scrambled or encrypted and interception of a radio communication that is transmitted on frequencies allocated under subpart D of Part 74 of the Rules of the Federal Communications Commission that is not scrambled or encrypted when the viewing or interception is not done for a tortious or illegal purpose or for purposes of direct or indirect commercial advantage or private commercial gain, shall not be offenses under this chapter.

Violation of this subsection shall be punishable as a Class 1 misdemeanor.

§19.2-63. Manufacture, possession, sale or advertising of certain devices unlawful; penalties; exceptions.

A. Except as otherwise specifically provided in this chapter, any person who intentionally:

1. Manufactures, assembles, possesses, or sells any electronic, mechanical, or other device, knowing or having reason to know that the design of such device renders it primarily useful for the purpose of the surreptitious interception of wire, electronic or oral communications; or

2. Places in any newspaper, magazine, handbill, or other publication any advertisement of:

(a) Any electronic, mechanical, or other device knowing or having reason to know that the design of such device renders it primarily useful for the purpose of the surreptitious interception of wire, electronic or oral communications, or

(b) Any other electronic, mechanical, or other device where such advertisement promotes the use of such device for the purpose of the surreptitious interception of wire, electronic or oral communications; shall be guilty of a Class 6 felony.

B. It shall not be unlawful under this section for:

1. A provider of wire or electronic communication service or an officer, agent, or employee of, or a person under contract with, such provider in the normal course of the provider's business, or

2. An officer, agent, or employee of, or a person under contract with the United States, the Commonwealth or a

political subdivision thereof, in the normal course of the activities of the United States, the Commonwealth, or a political subdivision thereof, to manufacture, assemble, possess, or sell any electronic, mechanical, or other device, knowing or having reason to know that the design of such device renders it primarily useful for the purpose of the surreptitious interception of wire, electronic or oral communications.

§19.2-63.1. Supervision and control of devices; unauthorized possession.

Any electronic, mechanical or other device as defined in this chapter which is in the possession of any sheriff's office or police department of a county, city or town, or in the possession of any employee of such office, shall be under the direct control and supervision of the sheriff or chief of police of the office or department. Unauthorized possession of any such device under the provisions of this section by any such employee is unlawful, notwithstanding the provisions of subdivision B 2 of §19.2-63, and a Class 1 misdemeanor.

§19.2-64. Forfeiture of unlawful devices.

Any electronic, mechanical or other device used, manufactured, assembled, possessed, sold, or advertised in violation of §19.2-62 or §19.2-63 may be seized and forfeited to the Commonwealth, and turned over to the court of record in the city or county in which it was seized and such property shall be disposed of in such manner as the court may direct.

§19.2-65. When intercepted communications and evidence derived therefrom not to be received in evidence.

Whenever any wire or oral communication has been intercepted, no part of the contents of such communication and no evidence derived therefrom may be received in evidence in any trial, hearing or other proceeding in or before any court, grand jury, department, officer, commission, regulatory body, legislative committee or other agency of this State or a political subdivision thereof if the disclosure of that information would be in violation of this chapter.

§19.2-66. When Attorney General or Chief Deputy Attorney General may apply for order authorizing interception of communications.

The Attorney General or Chief Deputy Attorney General, if the Attorney General so designates in writing, in any case where the Attorney General is authorized by law to prosecute or pursuant to a request in his official capacity of an attorney for the Commonwealth in any city or county, may apply to a judge of competent jurisdiction for the jurisdiction where the proposed intercept is to be made for an order authorizing the interception of wire, electronic or oral communications by the Department of State Police, when such interception may reasonably be expected to provide evidence of the commission of a felonious offense of extortion, bribery, kidnapping, murder, any felony violation of §18.2-248 or §18.2-248.1, any felony violation of Chapter 29 (§59.1-364 et seq.) of Title 59.1, or any conspiracy to commit any of the foregoing offenses. The Attorney General or Chief Deputy Attorney General may apply for authorization for the observation or monitoring of the interception by a police department of a county or city or by law-enforcement officers of the United States. Such application shall be made, and such order may be granted, in conformity with the provisions of §19.2-68. Application for installation of a mobile interception device may be made to and granted by any court of competent jurisdiction in the Commonwealth.

§19.2-67. Disclosure of information obtained by authorized means.

A. Any investigative or law-enforcement officer, or police officer of a county or city, who, by any means authorized by this chapter, has obtained knowledge of the contents of any wire, electronic or oral communication, or evidence derived therefrom, may disclose such contents to another investigative or law-enforcement officer, or police officer of a county or city, to the extent that such disclosure is appropriate to the proper performance of the official duties of the officer making or receiving the disclosure.

B. Any investigative or law-enforcement officer or police officer of a county or city, who, by any means authorized by this chapter, has obtained knowledge of the contents of any wire, electronic or oral communication or evidence derived therefrom may use such contents to the extent such use is appropriate to the proper performance of his official duties.

C. Any person who has received, by any means authorized by this chapter, any information concerning a wire, electronic or oral communication, or evidence derived therefrom intercepted in accordance with the provisions of this chapter may disclose the contents of that communication or such derivative evidence while giving testimony under oath or affirmation in any criminal proceeding for an offense specified in §19.2-66, or any conspiracy or attempt to commit the same, in any court of the United States or of any state or in any federal or state grand jury proceeding.

D. No wire, electronic or oral communication which is a privileged communication between the parties to the conversation which is intercepted in accordance with, or in violation of, the provisions of this chapter shall lose its privileged character, nor shall it be disclosed or used in any way.

E. When an investigative or law-enforcement officer, or police officer of a county or city, while engaged in intercepting wire, electronic or oral communications in the manner authorized herein, or observing or monitoring such interception intercepts, observes or monitors wire, electronic or oral communications relating to offenses other than those specified in the order of authorization, the contents thereof, and evidence derived therefrom, shall not be disclosed or used as provided in subsections A, B and C of this section, unless such communications or derivative evidence relates to a felony, in which case use or disclosure may be made as provided in subsections A, B and C of this section. Such use and disclosure pursuant to subsection C of this section shall be permitted only when approved by a judge of competent jurisdiction where such judge finds, on subsequent application, that such communications were otherwise intercepted in accordance with the provisions of this chapter. Violations of this subsection E shall be punishable as provided in §19.2-62.

§19.2-68. Application for and issuance of order authorizing interception; contents of order; recording and retention of intercepted communications, applications and orders; notice to parties; introduction in evidence of information obtained.

A. Each application for an order authorizing the interception of a wire, electronic or oral communication shall be made in writing upon oath or affirmation to the appropriate judge of competent jurisdiction and shall state the applicant's authority to make such application. Each application shall be verified by the Attorney General to the best of his knowledge and belief and shall include the following information:

1. The identity of the attorney for the Commonwealth and law-enforcement officer who requested the Attorney General to apply for such order;

2. A full and complete statement of the facts and circumstances relied upon by the applicant to justify his belief that an order should be issued, including (i) details as to the particular offense that has been, is being or is about to be committed, (ii) except as provided in subsection I, a particular description of the nature and location of the facilities from which or the place where the communication is to be intercepted, (iii) a particular description of the type of communications sought to be intercepted, (iv) the identity of the person, if known, committing the offense and whose communications are to be intercepted;

3. A full and complete statement as to whether or not other investigative procedures have been tried and failed or why they reasonably appear to be unlikely to succeed if tried or to be too dangerous;

4. A statement of the period of time for which the interception is required to be maintained. If the nature of the investigation is such that the authorization for interception should not automatically terminate when the described type of communication has been first obtained, a particular description of facts establishing probable cause to believe that additional communications of the same type will occur thereafter;

5. A full and complete statement of the facts concerning all previous applications known to the individual authorizing and making the application, made to any judge for authorization to intercept wire, electronic or oral communications involving any of the same persons, facilities or places specified in the application, and the action taken by the judge on each such application;

6. Where the application is for the extension of an order, a statement setting forth the results thus far obtained from the interception, or a reasonable explanation of the failure to obtain such results; and

7. If authorization is requested for observation or monitoring by a police department of a county or city or by law-enforcement officers of the United States, a statement containing the name of the police department or United States agency, and an explanation of the reasons such observation or monitoring is necessary.

The judge may require the applicant to furnish additional testimony or documentary evidence in support of the application.

B. Upon such application the judge may enter an ex parte order, as requested or as modified, authorizing interception of wire, electronic or oral communications within the territorial jurisdiction of the court in which the judge is sitting, and outside that jurisdiction but within the Commonwealth in the case of a mobile interception device authorized by a court of competent jurisdiction within such jurisdiction, if the judge determines on the basis of the facts submitted by the applicant that:

1. There is probable cause for belief that an individual is committing, has committed or is about to commit an offense enumerated in §19.2-66 of this chapter;

2. There is probable cause for belief that particular communications concerning that offense will be obtained through such interception;

3. Normal investigative procedures have been tried and have failed, or reasonably appear to be unlikely to succeed if tried, or to be too dangerous; and interception under this chapter is the only alternative investigative procedure available;

4. Except as provided in subsection I, there is probable cause for belief that the facilities from which, or the place where, the wire, electronic or oral communications are to be intercepted are being used, or are about to be used, in connection with the commission of such offense, or are leased to, listed in the name of, or commonly used by such person;

5. A wire, electronic or oral communication shall be deemed to be intercepted pursuant to subsection B of this section in the jurisdiction where the communication is actually intercepted and the monitoring of such intercepted communication may be at any location within the Commonwealth of Virginia. For the purposes of this section, the definition of "intercept" means the acquisition of the contents of any wire, electronic or oral communication through the use of any electronic, mechanical or other device.

C. Each order authorizing the interception of any wire, electronic or oral communication shall specify:

1. The identity of the person, if known, whose communications are to be intercepted;

2. The nature and location of the communications facilities as to which, or the place where, authority to intercept is granted;

3. A particular description of the type of communication sought to be intercepted, and a statement of the particular offense enumerated in §19.2-66 to which it relates;

4. That such interception is to be conducted only by the Department of State Police;

5. If observation or monitoring by the police department of a county or city or by law-enforcement officers of the United States is authorized, only that police department or agency shall observe or monitor the interception; and

6. The period of time during which such interception is authorized, including a statement as to whether or not the interception shall automatically terminate when the described communication has been first obtained.

An order authorizing the interception of a wire, electronic or oral communication shall, upon request of the applicant, direct that a provider of wire or electronic communications service, landlord, custodian or other person shall furnish the Department of State Police forthwith all information, facilities and technical assistance necessary to accomplish the interception unobtrusively and with a minimum of interference with the services that such service provider, landlord, custodian or person is providing the person whose communications are to be intercepted. Any provider of wire or electronic communications service, landlord, custodian or other person furnishing such facilities or technical assistance shall be compensated therefor by the Commonwealth for reasonable and actual expenses incurred in providing such facilities or assistance, to be paid out of the criminal fund.

D. No order entered under this section may authorize the interception of any wire, electronic or oral communication for any period longer than is necessary to achieve the objective of the authorization, nor in any event longer than thirty days which period begins to run on the earlier of the day on which the investigative or law-enforcement officer begins to conduct an interception under the order or ten days after the date of entry of the order. Extensions of an order may be granted, but only upon application for an extension made in accordance with subsection A of this section and the court's making the findings required by subsection B of this section. The period of extension shall be no longer than the authorizing judge deems necessary to achieve the purposes for which it was granted and in no event for longer than thirty days. Every order and extension thereof shall contain a provision that the authorization to intercept shall be executed as soon as practicable, shall be conducted in such a way as to minimize the interception of communications not otherwise subject to interception under this chapter, and must terminate upon attainment of the authorized objective, or in any event in thirty days. In the event the intercepted communication is in a code or foreign language, and an expert in that foreign language or code is not reasonably available during the interception period, minimization may be accomplished as soon as practicable after such interception.

E. Whenever an order authorizing interception is entered pursuant to this chapter, the order shall require reports to be made to the judge who issued the order showing what progress has been made toward achievement of the authorized objective and the need for continued interception. Such reports shall be made at such intervals as the judge shall require.

F. 1. The contents of any wire, electronic or oral communication intercepted by any means authorized by this chapter shall, if possible, be recorded on tape or wire or other comparable device. Should it not be possible to record the intercepted communication, a detailed resume of such communication shall forthwith be reduced to writing and filed with the court. The recording of the contents of any wire, electronic or oral communication under this subsection shall be done in such way as will protect the recording from editing or other alterations and shall not be duplicated except upon order of the court as hereafter provided. Immediately upon the expiration of the period of the order, or extensions thereof, such recording or detailed resume shall be made available to the judge issuing such order and sealed under his directions. Custody of any recordings or detailed resumes shall be vested with the court and shall not be destroyed for a period of ten years from the date of the order and then only by direction of the court; provided, however, should any interception fail to reveal any information related to the offense or offenses for which it was authorized, such recording or resume shall be destroyed after the expiration of sixty days after the notice required by subdivision 4 of this subsection is served. Duplicate recordings may be made for use or disclosure pursuant to the provisions of subsections A and B of §19.2-67 for investigations. The presence of the seal provided for by this subsection, or a satisfactory explanation for the absence thereof, shall be a prerequisite for the use or disclosure of the contents of any wire, electronic or oral communication or evidence derived therefrom under subsection C of §19.2-67.

2. Applications made and orders granted or denied under this chapter shall be sealed by the judge. Custody of the applications and orders shall be wherever the judge directs. Such applications and orders shall be disclosed only upon a showing of good cause before a judge of competent jurisdiction and shall not be destroyed except on order of the issuing or denying judge, and in any event shall be kept for ten years.

3. Any violation of the provisions of this subsection may be punished as contempt of the issuing or denying court.

4. Within a reasonable time but not later than ninety days after the filing of an application for an order of authorization which is denied or the termination of the period of an order or extensions thereof, the issuing or denying judge shall cause to be served, on the persons named in the order or the application, and such other parties to intercepted communications as the judge may determine in his discretion that is in the interest of justice, an inventory which shall include notice of:

(a) The fact of the entry of the order or the application;

(b) The date of the entry and the period of authorized interception, or the denial of the application;

(c) The fact that during the period wire, electronic or oral communications were or were not intercepted; and

(d) The fact that unless he files a motion with the court within sixty days after the service of notice upon him, the recordation or resume may be destroyed in accordance with subdivision 1 of this subsection.

The judge, upon the filing of a motion, shall make available to such person or his counsel for inspection the intercepted communications, applications and orders. The serving of the inventory required by this subsection may be postponed for additional periods, not to exceed thirty days each, upon the ex parte showing of good cause to a judge of competent jurisdiction.

G. The contents of any intercepted wire, electronic or oral communication or evidence derived therefrom shall not be received in evidence or otherwise disclosed in any trial, hearing or other proceeding in a state court unless each party to the communication and to such proceeding, not less than ten days before the trial, hearing or proceeding, has been furnished with a copy of the court order, accompanying application under which the interception was authorized and the contents of any intercepted wire, electronic or oral communication that is to be used in any trial, hearing or other proceeding in a state court. This ten-day period may be waived by the judge if he finds that it was not possible to furnish the party with the above information ten days before the trial, hearing or proceeding and that the party will not be prejudiced by the delay in receiving such information; provided that such information in any event shall be given prior to the day of the trial, and the inability to comply with such ten-day period shall be grounds for the granting of a continuance to either party.

The judge who considers an application for an interception under this chapter, whether issuing or denying the order, shall be disqualified from presiding at any trial resulting from or in any manner connected with such interception, regardless of whether the evidence acquired thereby is used in such trial.

H. Any aggrieved person in any trial, hearing or proceeding in or before any court, department, officer, agency, regulatory body or other authority of the Commonwealth, or a political subdivision thereof, may move to suppress the contents of any intercepted wire, electronic or oral communication, or evidence derived therefrom, on the grounds that:

1. The communication was unlawfully intercepted, or was not intercepted in compliance with this chapter; or

2. The order of the authorization or approval under which it was intercepted is insufficient on its face; or

3. The interception was not made in conformity with the order of authorization or approval; or

4. The interception is not admissible into evidence in any trial, proceeding or hearing in a state court under the applicable rules of evidence.

Such motion shall be made before the trial, hearing or proceeding unless there was no opportunity to make such motion or the person was not aware of the grounds of the motion. If the motion is granted pursuant to subdivision 1, 2 or 3 of this subsection, the contents of the intercepted wire, electronic or oral communication or evidence derived therefrom shall be treated as having been obtained in violation of this chapter. The judge, upon the filing of such motion by the aggrieved person, shall make available to the aggrieved person, or his counsel, for inspection the intercepted communication.

I. The requirements of subdivision 2 of subsection A and subdivision 4 of subsection B of this section relating to the specification of the facilities from which, or the place where, the communication is to be intercepted do not apply if:

1. In the case of an application with respect to the interception of an oral communication:

(a) The application contains a full and complete statement as to why such specification is not practical and identifies the person committing the offense and whose communications are to be intercepted; and

(b) The judge finds that such specification is not practical; or

2. In the case of an application with respect to a wire or electronic communication:

(a) the application identifies the person believed to be committing the offense and whose communications are to be intercepted and the applicant makes a showing of a purpose, on the part of that person, to thwart interception by changing facilities; and

(b) the judge finds that such purpose has been adequately shown.

The interception of a communication under an order issued pursuant to this subsection shall not begin until the facilities from which, or the place where, the communication is to be intercepted is ascertained by the person implementing the interception order. A provider of wire or electronic communications service that has received an order issued pursuant to this subdivision 2 may move the court to modify or quash the order on the ground that its assistance with respect to the interception cannot be performed in a timely or reasonable fashion. The court, upon notice to the Attorney General, shall decide the motion expeditiously.

§19.2-69. Civil action for unlawful interception, disclosure or use.

Any person whose wire, electronic or oral communication is intercepted, disclosed or used in violation of this chapter shall (i) have a civil cause of action against any person who intercepts, discloses or uses, or procures any other person to intercept, disclose or use such communications, and (ii) be entitled to recover from any such person:

1. Actual damages but not less than liquidated damages computed at the rate of $100 a day for each day of violation or $1,000, whichever is higher;
2. Punitive damages; and
3. A reasonable attorney's fee and other litigation costs reasonably incurred.

A good faith reliance on a court order or legislative authorization shall constitute a complete defense to any civil or criminal action brought under this chapter or under any other law.

§19.2-70. Reports to be filed by courts and Attorney General.

All courts of the Commonwealth and the Attorney General shall file all reports required by 18 U.S.C. §2519. The Attorney General shall file a written report with the Clerks of the Senate and House of Delegates on or before December 31 of each year setting forth the number of applications made pursuant to this chapter, the number of interceptions authorized, the number of arrests resulting from each application, the number of convictions including a breakdown by offense, the cost of each application granted and the number of requests denied. Such information shall be made available by such Clerks to any member of the General Assembly upon request.

§19.2-70.1. General prohibition on pen register and trap and trace device use; exceptions.

Except as provided in this section, no person may install or use a pen register or a trap and trace device without first obtaining a court order under §19.2-70.2.

However, a court order shall not be required for use of a pen register or trap and trace device by a provider of electronic or wire communication service (i) relating to the operation, maintenance, and testing of a wire or electronic communication service or to the protection of the rights or property of the provider, or to the protection of users of that service from abuse of service or unlawful use of service; (ii) to record the fact that a wire or electronic communication was initiated or completed in order to protect such provider, another provider furnishing service toward the completion of the wire communication, or a user of that service, from fraudulent, unlawful or abusive use of service; or (iii) where the consent of the user of that service has been obtained.

Any person who knowingly violates this section shall be guilty of a Class 1 misdemeanor.

§19.2-70.2. Application for and issuance of order for a pen register or trap and trace device; assistance in installation and use.

A. An investigative or law-enforcement officer may make application for an order or an extension of an order authorizing or approving the installation and use of a pen register or a trap and trace device, in writing under oath or equivalent affirmation, to a court of competent jurisdiction. The application shall include:

1. The identity of the officer making the application and the identity of the law-enforcement agency conducting the investigation; and
2. A certification by the applicant that the information likely to be obtained is relevant to an ongoing criminal investigation being conducted by that agency.

The application may include a request that the order require information, facilities and technical assistance necessary to accomplish the installation be furnished.

B. Upon application, the court shall enter an ex parte order authorizing the installation and use of a pen register or a trap and trace device within the jurisdiction of the court if the court finds that the investigative or law-enforcement officer has certified to the court that the information likely to be obtained by such installation and use is relevant to an ongoing criminal investigation.

The order shall specify:

1. The identity, if known, of the person in whose name the telephone line to which the pen register or trap and trace device is to be attached is listed or to whom the line is leased;
2. The identity, if known, of the person who is the subject of the criminal investigation;
3. The number and, if known, the physical location of the telephone line to which the pen register or trap and trace device is to be attached and, in the case of a trap and trace device, the geographic limits of the trap and trace order; and
4. A statement of the offense to which the information likely to be obtained by the pen register or trap and trace device relates.

C. Installation and use of a pen register or a trap and trace device shall be authorized for a period not to exceed sixty days. Extensions of the order may be granted, but only upon application made and order issued in accordance with this section. The period of an extension shall not exceed sixty days.

D. An order authorizing or approving the installation and use of a pen register or a trap and trace device shall direct that:

1. The order and application be sealed until otherwise ordered by the court;
2. Information, facilities and technical assistance necessary to accomplish the installation be furnished if requested in the application; and
3. The person owning or leasing the line to which the pen register or trap and trace device is attached, or who has been ordered by the court to provide assistance to the applicant, not disclose the existence of the pen register or trap and trace device or the existence of the investigation to the listed subscriber, or to any other person, unless or until otherwise ordered by the court.

E. Upon request of an investigative or a law-enforcement officer authorized by the court to install and use a pen register, a provider of wire or electronic communication service, a landlord, custodian or any other person so ordered by the court shall, as soon as practicable, furnish the officer with all information, facilities, and technical assistance necessary to accomplish the installation of the pen register unobtrusively and with a minimum of interference with the services that the person so ordered by the court accords the party with respect to whom the installation and use is to take place.

F. Upon request of an investigative or law-enforcement officer authorized by the court to receive the results of a trap and trace device under this section, a provider of wire or electronic communication service, a landlord, custodian or any other person so ordered by the court shall, as soon as practicable, install the device on the appropriate line and furnish the officer with all additional information, facilities and technical assistance, including installation and operation of the device, unobtrusively and with a minimum of interference with the services that the person so ordered by the court accords the party with respect to whom the installation and use is to take place. Unless otherwise ordered by the court, the results of the trap and trace device shall be furnished to the investigative or law-enforcement officer designated by the court at reasonable intervals during regular business hours for the duration of the order.

G. A provider of a wire or electronic communication service, a landlord, custodian or other person who furnishes facilities or technical assistance pursuant to this section shall be reasonably compensated for reasonable and actual expenses incurred in providing such facilities and assistance. The expenses shall be paid out of the criminal fund.

H. No cause of action shall lie in any court against a provider of a wire or electronic communication service, its officers, employees, agents or other specified persons for providing information, facilities, or assistance in accordance with the terms of a court order issued pursuant to this section. Good faith reliance on a court order, a legislative authorization or a statutory authorization is a complete defense against any civil or criminal action based upon a violation of this chapter.

§19.2-70.3. Obtaining records concerning electronic communication service or remote computing service.

A. A provider of electronic communication service or remote computing service shall disclose a record or other information pertaining to a subscriber to or customer of such service, excluding the contents of electronic communications, to an investigative or law-enforcement officer only pursuant to:

1. A subpoena issued by a grand jury of a court of this Commonwealth;

2. A search warrant issued by a magistrate, general district court or a circuit court;

3. A court order for such disclosure issued as provided in this section; or

4. The consent of the subscriber or customer to such disclosure.

B. A court shall issue an order for disclosure under this section only if the investigative or law-enforcement officer shows that there is reason to believe the records or other information sought are relevant to a legitimate law-enforcement inquiry. A court issuing an order pursuant to this section, on a motion made promptly by the service provider, may quash or modify the order, if the information or records requested are unusually voluminous in nature or compliance with such order would otherwise cause an undue burden on such provider.

C. No cause of action shall lie in any court against a provider of a wire or electronic communication service, its officers, employees, agents, or other specified persons for providing information, facilities, or assistance in accordance with the terms of a court order, warrant or subpoena under this section.

CHAPTER 7
ARREST

§19.2-71. Who may issue process of arrest.

A. Process for the arrest of a person charged with a criminal offense may be issued by the judge, or clerk of any circuit court, any general district court, any juvenile and domestic relations district court, or any magistrate as provided for in Chapters 3 (§19.2-26 et seq.) and 4 (§19.2-49 et seq.) of this title.

B. No law-enforcement officer shall seek issuance of process by any judicial officer, for the arrest of a person for the offense of capital murder as defined in §18.2-31, without prior authorization by the attorney for the Commonwealth. Failure to comply with the provisions of this subsection shall not be (i) a basis upon which a warrant may be quashed or deemed invalid, (ii) deemed error upon which a conviction or

sentence may be reversed or vacated, or (iii) a basis upon which a court may prevent or delay execution of sentence.
(Chgd. by L.1996 ch. 616; L.1999 ch. 266, eff. 7/1/99.)

§19.2-72. When it may issue; what to recite and require.

On complaint of a criminal offense to any officer authorized to issue criminal warrants he shall examine on oath the complainant and any other witnesses, or when such officer shall suspect that an offense punishable otherwise than by a fine has been committed he may, without formal complaint, issue a summons for witnesses and shall examine such witnesses. If upon such examination such officer finds that there is probable cause to believe the accused has committed an offense, such officer shall issue a warrant for his arrest. The warrant shall (i) be directed to an appropriate officer or officers, (ii) name the accused or, if his name is unknown, set forth a description by which he can be identified with reasonable certainty, (iii) describe the offense charged with reasonable certainty, (iv) command that the accused be arrested and brought before a court of appropriate jurisdiction in the county, city or town in which the offense was allegedly committed, and (v) be signed by the issuing officer. The warrant shall require the officer to whom it is directed to summon such witnesses as shall be therein named to appear and give evidence on the examination. But in a city or town having a police force, the warrant shall be directed "To any policeman, sheriff or his deputy sheriff of such city (or town)," and shall be executed by the policeman, sheriff or his deputy sheriff into whose hands it shall come or be delivered. A sheriff or his deputy may execute an arrest warrant throughout the county in which he serves and in any city surrounded thereby.
(Chgd. by L.2000 ch. 170, eff. 7/1/2000.)

§19.2-73. Issuance of summons instead of warrant in certain cases.

In any misdemeanor case or in any class of misdemeanor cases, or in any case involving complaints made by any state or local governmental official or employee having responsibility for the enforcement of any statute, ordinance or administrative regulation, the magistrate or other issuing authority having jurisdiction may issue a summons instead of a warrant when there is reason to believe that the person charged will appear in the courts having jurisdiction over the trial of the offense charged. Any person on whom such summons is served shall appear on the date set forth in same, and if such person fails to appear in such court at such time and on such date then he shall be treated in accordance with the provisions of §19.2-128, regardless of the disposition of, and in addition to, the charge upon which he was originally arrested.

§19.2-73.1. Notice of issuance of warrant or summons; appearance; failure to appear.

In any misdemeanor case or in any class of misdemeanor cases and in a Class 5 or Class 6 felony case, the chief-of-police of the city or county or his designee, or the sheriff or deputy sheriff of the county, if the county has no police department, in which the case is pending may notify the accused of the issuance of the warrant or summons and direct the accused to appear at the time and place directed for the purpose of the execution of the summons or warrant. However, the issuing judicial officer may direct the execution of such process prior to any such notification. If the accused does not appear, then the warrant or summons shall be executed and returned as provided by §19.2-76.

§19.2-73.2. Law-enforcement officers to issue subpoenas; penalty.

Law-enforcement officers as defined in §9-169 and state police officers, in the course of their duties, in the investigation of any Class 3 or Class 4 misdemeanor or any traffic infraction, may, within seventy-two hours of the time of the offense, issue a subpoena to any witness to appear in court and testify with respect to any such criminal charge or traffic infraction brought against any person as a result of such investigation. The return of service thereof shall be made within seventy-two hours after service to the appropriate court clerk. A subpoena so issued shall have the same force and effect as if issued by the court.

Any person failing to appear in response to a subpoena issued as provided in this section shall be punished as provided by law.
(Added by L.1995 ch. 335, eff. 7/1/95.)

§19.2-74. Issuance and service of summons in place of warrant in misdemeanor case; issuance of summons by special policemen and conservators of the peace.

A. 1. Whenever any person is detained by or is in the custody of an arresting officer for any violation committed in such officer's presence which offense is a violation of any county, city or town ordinance or of any provision of this Code punishable as a Class 1 or Class 2 misdemeanor or any other misdemeanor for which he may receive a jail sentence, except as otherwise provided in Title 46.2, or §18.2-266, or an arrest on a warrant charging an offense for which a summons may be issued, and when specifically authorized by the judicial officer issuing the warrant, the arresting officer shall take the name and address of such person and issue a summons or otherwise notify him in writing to appear at a time and place to be specified in such summons or notice. Upon the giving by such person of his written promise to appear at such time and place, the officer shall forthwith release him from custody. However, if any such person shall fail or refuse to discontinue the unlawful act, the officer may proceed according to the provisions of §19.2-82.

Anything in this section to the contrary notwithstanding, if any person is believed by the arresting officer to be likely to disregard a summons issued under the provisions of this subsection, or if any person is reasonably believed by the arresting officer to be likely to cause harm to himself or to any other person, a magistrate or other issuing authority having jurisdiction shall proceed according to the provisions of §19.2-82.

2. Whenever any person is detained by or is in the custody of an arresting officer for a violation of any county, city, or town ordinance or of any provision of this Code, punishable as a Class 3 or Class 4 misdemeanor or any other misdemeanor for which he cannot receive a jail sentence, except as otherwise provided in Title 46.2, or to the offense of public drunkenness as defined in §18.2-388, the arresting officer shall take the name and address of such person and issue a summons or otherwise notify him in writing to appear at a time and place to be specified in such summons or notice. Upon the giving of such person of his written promise to appear at such time and place, the officer shall forthwith release him from custody. However, if any such person shall fail or refuse to discontinue the unlawful act, the officer may proceed according to the provisions of §19.2-82.

3. Any person so summoned shall not be held in custody after the issuance of such summons for the purpose of complying with the requirements of Chapter 23 (§19.2-387 et seq.) of this title. Reports to the Central Criminal Records Exchange concerning such persons shall be made after a disposition of guilt is entered as provided for in §19.2-390.

Any person refusing to give such written promise to appear under the provisions of this section shall be taken immediately by the arresting or other police officer before a magistrate or other issuing authority having jurisdiction, who shall proceed according to provisions of §19.2-82.

Any person who willfully violates his written promise to appear, given in accordance with this section, shall be treated in accordance with the provisions of §19.2-128, regardless of the disposition of, and in addition to, the charge upon which he was originally arrested.

Any person charged with committing any violation of §18.2-407 may be arrested and immediately brought before a magistrate who shall proceed as provided in §19.2-82.

B. Special policemen of the counties as provided in §15.1-144, special policemen or conservators of the peace appointed under Chapter 2 (§19.2-12 et seq.) of this title and special policemen appointed by authority of a city's charter may issue summonses pursuant to this section, if such officers are in uniform, or displaying a badge of office. On application, the chief law-enforcement officer of the county or city shall supply each officer with a supply of summons forms, for which such officer shall account pursuant to regulation of such chief law-enforcement officer.

C. The summons used by a law-enforcement officer pursuant to this section shall be in form the same as the uniform summons for motor vehicle law violations as prescribed pursuant to §46.2-388.

(Chgd. by L.1995 ch. 471, eff. 7/1/95.)

§19.2-75. Copy of process to be left with accused; exception.

Except as provided in §46.2-936, any process issued against a person charged with a criminal offense shall be in duplicate and the officer serving such process shall leave a copy with the person charged.

§19.2-76. Execution and return of warrant, capias or summons; arrest outside county or city where charge is to be tried.

A law-enforcement officer may execute within his jurisdiction a warrant, capias or summons issued anywhere in the Commonwealth. A warrant or capias shall be executed by the arrest of the accused, and a summons shall be executed by delivering a copy to the accused personally.

If the accused is a corporation, partnership, unincorporated association or legal entity other than an individual, a summons may be executed by service on the entity in the same manner as provided in Title 8.01 for service of process on that entity in a civil proceeding. However, if the summons is served on the entity by delivery to a registered agent or to any other agent who is not an officer, director, managing agent or employee of the entity, such agent shall not be personally subject to penalty for failure to appear as provided in §19.2-128, nor shall the agent be subject to punishment for contempt for failure to appear under his summons as provided in §19.2-129.

The law-enforcement officer executing a warrant or capias shall endorse the date of execution thereon and make return thereof to a judicial officer. The law-enforcement officer executing a summons shall endorse the date of execution thereon and make return thereof to the court to which the summons is returnable.

Whenever a person is arrested upon a warrant or capias in a county or city other than that in which the charge is to be tried, the law-enforcement officer making the arrest shall either (i) bring the accused forthwith before a judicial officer in the locality where the arrest was made or where the charge is to be tried or (ii) commit the accused to the custody of an officer from the county or city where the charge is to be tried who shall bring the accused forthwith before a judicial officer in the county or city in which the charge is to be tried. The judicial officer before whom the accused is brought shall immediately conduct a bail hearing and either admit the accused to bail or commit him to jail for transfer forthwith to the county or city where the charge is to be tried.

(Chgd. by L.1997 ch. 10; L.1998 ch. 615, eff. 7/1/98.)

§19.2-76.1. Submission of quarterly reports concerning unexecuted felony and misdemeanor warrants and other criminal process; destruction.

It shall be the duty of the chief law-enforcement officer of the police department or sheriff's office, whichever is responsible for such service, in each county, town or city of the Commonwealth to submit quarterly reports to the attorney for the Commonwealth for the county, town or city concerning unexecuted felony and misdemeanor arrest warrants, summonses, capiases or other unexecuted criminal processes as hereinafter provided. The reports shall list those existing felony arrest warrants in his possession which have not been executed within seven years of the date of issuance and those misdemeanor arrest warrants, summonses and capiases and other criminal processes in his possession which have not been executed within three years from the date of issuance. The reports shall be submitted in writing no later than the tenth day of April, July, October, and January of each year, together with the unexecuted felony and misdemeanor warrants, or other unexecuted criminal processes listed therein. Upon receipt of the report and the warrants listed therein, the attorney for the Commonwealth shall petition the circuit court of the county or city for the destruction of such unexecuted felony and misdemeanor warrants, summonses, capiases or other unexecuted criminal processes. The attorney for the Commonwealth may petition that certain of the unexecuted warrants, summonses, capiases and other unexecuted criminal processes not be destroyed based upon justifiable continuing active investigation of the cases. The circuit court shall order the destruction of each such unexecuted felony warrant and each unexecuted misdemeanor warrant, summons, capias and other criminal process except (i) any warrant which charges capital murder and (ii) any unexecuted criminal process whose preservation is deemed justifiable by the court. No arrest shall be made under the authority of any warrant or other process which has been ordered destroyed pursuant to this section. Nothing in this section shall be construed to relate to or affect the time within which a prosecution for a felony or a misdemeanor shall be commenced.

As used herein, the term "chief law-enforcement officer" refers to the chiefs of police of cities, counties and towns and sheriffs of cities and counties, unless a political subdivision has otherwise designated its chief law-enforcement officer by appropriate resolution or ordinance, in which case the local designation shall be controlling.

§19.2-76.2. Mailing of summons in certain cases.

Notwithstanding the provisions of §19.2-76, whenever a summons for a violation of a county, city or town parking ordinance is served in any county, city or town it may be executed by mailing by first-class mail a copy thereof to the address of the owner of the vehicle as shown on the records of the Department of Motor Vehicles. In addition, whenever a summons for a violation of a county, city or town trash ordinance punishable as a misdemeanor under §15.1-11 is served in any county, city or town, it may be executed by mailing a copy by first-class mail to the person who occupies the subject premises. If the person fail to appear on the date of return set out in the summons mailed pursuant to this section, the summons shall be executed in the manner set out in §19.2-76.3 of this Code.

No proceedings for contempt or arrest of a person summoned by mailing shall be instituted for his failure to appear on the return date of the summons.

§19.2-76.3. Failure to appear on return date for summons issued under §19.2-76.2.

A. If any person fails to appear on the date of the return contained in the summons issued in accordance with §19.2-76.2, then a summons shall be delivered to the sheriff of the county, city or town for service on that person as set out in §8.01-296.

B. If such person then fails to appear on the date of return as contained in the summons so issued, a summons shall be executed in the manner set out in §19.2-76.

C. No proceedings for contempt or arrest of any person summoned under the provisions of this section shall be instituted unless such person has been personally served with a summons and has failed to appear on the return date contained therein.

§19.2-77. Escape, flight and pursuit; arrest anywhere in Commonwealth.

Whenever a person in the custody of an officer shall escape or whenever a person shall flee from an officer attempting to arrest him, such officer, with or without a warrant, may pursue such person anywhere in the Commonwealth and, when actually in close pursuit, may arrest him wherever he is found. If the arrest is made in a county or city adjoining that from which the accused fled, or in any area of the Commonwealth within one mile of the boundary of the county or city from which he fled, the officer may forthwith return the accused before the proper official of the county or city from which he fled. If the arrest is made beyond the foregoing limits, the officer shall proceed according to the provisions of §19.2-76, and if such arrest is made without a warrant, the officer shall procure a warrant from the magistrate of the county or city wherein the arrest was made, charging the accused with the offense committed in the county or city from which he fled.

§19.2-78. Uniform of officer making arrest.

All officers whose duties are to make arrests acting under the authority of any law of this Commonwealth or any subdivision thereof, who shall make any arrest, search or seizure on any public road or highway of this Commonwealth shall be dressed at the time of making any such arrest, search or seizure in such uniform as he may customarily wear in the performance of his duties which will clearly show him to casual observation to be an officer.

Nothing in this section shall render unlawful any arrest, search or seizure by an officer who is not in such customary uniform.

§19.2-79. Arrest by officers of other states of United States.

Any member of a duly organized state, county or municipal peace unit of another state of the United States who enters this Commonwealth in close pursuit, and continues within this Commonwealth in such close pursuit, of a person in order to arrest him on the ground that he has committed a felony in such other state shall have the same authority to arrest and hold in custody such person as members of a duly organized state, county or municipal peace unit of this Commonwealth have to arrest and hold in custody a person on the ground that he has committed a felony in this State, if the state from which such person has fled extends similar privileges to any member of a duly organized state, county or municipal peace unit of this Commonwealth.

If an arrest is made in this Commonwealth by an officer of another state in accordance with the provisions of the first paragraph of this section, he shall without unnecessary delay take the person arrested before a judge of a general district court, or of the circuit court, of the county or city in which the arrest was made, who shall conduct a hearing for the purpose of determining the lawfulness of the arrest. If the judge determines that the arrest was lawful he shall commit the person arrested to await for a reasonable time the issuance of an extradition warrant by the Governor. If the judge determines that the arrest was unlawful he shall discharge the person arrested.

The first paragraph of this section shall not be construed so as to make unlawful any arrest in this Commonwealth which would otherwise be lawful.

For the purpose of this section the word "State" shall include the District of Columbia.

§19.2-80. Duty of arresting officer; bail.

In any case in which an officer does not issue a summons pursuant to §19.2-74 or §46.2-936, a law-enforcement officer making an arrest under a warrant or capias shall bring the arrested person without unnecessary delay before a judicial officer. The judicial officer shall immediately conduct a bail hearing and either admit the accused to bail or commit him to jail. However, if (i) the accused is charged with a misdemeanor and is brought before a judge of the court having jurisdiction to try the case and (ii) both the accused and the Commonwealth consent, the judge may proceed to trial instead of conducting a bail hearing.
(Chgd. by L.1997 ch. 10, eff. 7/1/97.)

§19.2-80.1. When arrested person operating motor vehicle; how vehicle removed from scene of arrest.

In any case in which a police officer arrests the operator of a motor vehicle and there is no legal cause for the retention of the motor vehicle by the officer, the officer shall allow the person arrested to designate another person who is present at the scene of the arrest and a licensed driver to drive the motor vehicle from the scene to a place designated by the person arrested. If such a designation is not made, the officer may cause the vehicle to be taken to the nearest appropriate place for safekeeping.

§19.2-80.2. Duty of arresting officer; providing magistrate or court with criminal history information.

In any case in which an officer proceeds under §§19.2-76, 19.2-80 and 19.2-82, such officer shall, to the extent possible, obtain and provide the magistrate or court with the arrested person's criminal history information prior to any proceeding under Article 1 (§19.2-119 et seq.) of Chapter 9 of this title. A pretrial services program established pursuant to §19.2-152.4 may, in lieu of the arresting officer, provide the criminal history to the magistrate or court.
(Added by L.1999 chs. 829, 846, eff. 7/1/99.)

§19.2-81. Arrest without warrant authorized in certain cases.

The following officers shall have the powers of arrest as provided in this section:

1. Members of the State Police force of the Commonwealth,

2. Sheriffs of the various counties and cities, and their deputies,

3. Members of any county police force or any duly constituted police force of any city or town of the Commonwealth,

4. The Commissioner, members and employees of the Marine Resources Commission granted the power of arrest pursuant to §28.2-900,

5. Regular game wardens appointed pursuant to §29.1-200,

6. United States Coast Guard and United States Coast Guard Reserve commissioned, warrant, and petty officers authorized under §29.1-205 to make arrests, and

7. The special policemen of the counties as provided by §15.2-1737, provided such officers are in uniform, or displaying a badge of office.

Such officers may arrest, without a warrant, any person who commits any crime in the presence of the officer and any person whom he has reasonable grounds or probable cause to suspect of having committed a felony not in his presence.

Any such officer may arrest without a warrant any person whom the officer has probable cause to suspect of operating a watercraft or motor boat (i) while intoxicated in violation of subsection B of §29.1-738 or (ii) in violation of an order issued pursuant to §29.1-738.4, in his presence, and may thereafter transfer custody of the person suspected of the violation to another officer, who may obtain a warrant based upon statements made to him by the arresting officer.

Any such officer may, at the scene of any accident involving a motor vehicle, watercraft as defined in §29.1-712 or motorboat, or at any hospital or medical facility to which any person involved in such accident has been transported, or in the apprehension of any person charged with the theft of any motor vehicle, on any of the highways or waters of the Commonwealth, upon reasonable grounds to believe, based upon personal investigation, including information obtained from eyewitnesses, that a crime has been committed by any person then and there present, apprehend such person without a warrant of arrest.

Such officers may arrest, without a warrant, persons duly charged with a crime in another jurisdiction upon receipt of a photocopy of a warrant, telegram, computer printout, facsimile printout, a radio, telephone or teletype message, in which photocopy of a warrant, telegram, computer printout, facsimile printout, radio, telephone or teletype message shall be given the name or a reasonably accurate description of such person wanted and the crime alleged.

Such officers may arrest, without a warrant, for an alleged misdemeanor not committed in his presence when the officer receives a radio message from his department or other law-enforcement agency within the Commonwealth that a warrant for such offense is on file.

Such officers may also arrest without a warrant for an alleged misdemeanor not committed in their presence involving (i) shoplifting in violation of §18.2-96 or §18.2-103 or a similar local ordinance, (ii) carrying a weapon on school property in violation of §18.2-308.1, (iii) assault and battery, (iv) brandishing a firearm in violation of §18.2-282, or (v) destruction of property in violation of §18.2-137, when such property is located on premises used for business or commercial purposes, or a similar local ordinance, when any such arrest is based on probable cause upon reasonable complaint of the person who observed the alleged offense. The arresting officer may issue a summons to any person arrested under this section for a misdemeanor violation involving shoplifting.

(Chgd. by L.1995 ch. 465; L.1996 chs. 866, 929, 1015; L.1998 ch. 684, eff. 7/1/98.)

§19.2-81.1. Arrest without warrant by correctional officers in certain cases.

Any correctional officer, as defined in §53.1-1, may arrest, in the same manner as provided in §19.2-81, persons for crimes involving:

(a) The escape of an inmate from a correctional institution, as defined in §53.1-1 of this Code;

(b) Assisting an inmate to escape from a correctional institution, as defined in §53.1-1 of this Code;

(c) The delivery of contraband to an inmate in violation of §18.2-474 or §18.2-474.1; and

(d) Any other criminal offense which may contribute to the disruption of the safety, welfare, or security of the population of a correctional institution.

§19.2-81.2. Power of correctional officers and designated noncustodial employees to detain.

A. A correctional officer, as defined in §53.1-1, who has completed the minimum training standards established by the Department of Criminal Justice Services, or other noncustodial employee of the Department of Corrections who has been designated to carry a weapon by the Director of the Department of Corrections pursuant to §53.1-29 of the Code and who has completed the basic course in detention training as approved by the Department of Criminal Justice Services, may, while on duty in or on the grounds of a correctional institution, or with custody of prisoners without the confines of a correctional institution, detain any person whom he has reasonable suspicion to believe has committed a violation of §§18.2-473 through 18.2-475, or of aiding or abetting a prisoner in violating the provisions of §53.1-203. Such detention shall be for the purpose of summoning a law-enforcement officer in order that the law-enforcement officer can arrest the person who is alleged to have violated any of the above sections.

B. Any employee of the Department of Corrections having the authority to detain any person pursuant to subsection A hereof shall not be held civilly liable for unlawful detention, slander, malicious prosecution, false imprisonment, false arrest, or assault and battery of the person so detained, whether such detention takes place within or without the grounds of a correctional institution, provided that, in causing the detention of such person, the employee had at the time of the detention reasonable suspicion to believe that the person committed a violation for which the detention was undertaken.

C. It is the purpose and intent of this section to ensure that the safety, stability, welfare and security of correctional institutions be preserved insofar as possible.

§19.2-81.3. Arrest without a warrant authorized in cases of assault and battery against a family or household member and stalking and for violations of protective orders; procedure, etc.

A. Any law-enforcement officer, as defined in §19.2-81, may arrest without a warrant for an alleged violation of §§18.2-57.2, 18.2-60.4 or §16.1-253.2 regardless of whether such violation was committed in his presence, if such arrest is based on probable cause or upon personal observations or the reasonable complaint of a person who observed the alleged offense or upon personal investigation.

B. A law-enforcement officer having probable cause to believe that a violation of §18.2-57.2 or §16.1-253.2 has occurred shall arrest and take into custody the person he has probable cause to believe, based on the totality of the circumstances, was the primary physical aggressor unless there are special circumstances which would dictate a course of action other than an arrest.

C. Regardless of whether an arrest is made, the officer shall file a written report with his department of any incident in which he has probable cause to believe family abuse has occurred, including, where required, a statement in writing that there are special circumstances which would dictate a course of action other than an arrest. Upon request of the allegedly abused person, the department shall make a summary of the report available to the allegedly abused person. The officer shall also provide the allegedly abused person, both orally and in writing, information regarding the legal and community resources available to the allegedly abused person.

D. In every case in which a law-enforcement officer makes an arrest under this section, he shall petition for an emergency protective order as authorized in §16.1-253.4 when the person arrested and taken into custody is brought before the magistrate, except if the person arrested is a minor, a petition for an emergency protective order shall not be required. Regardless of whether an arrest is made, if the officer has probable cause to believe that a danger of acts of family abuse exists, the law-enforcement officer shall seek an emergency protective order under §16.1-253.4, except if the suspected abuser is a minor, a petition for an emergency protective order shall not be required.

E. A law-enforcement officer investigating any complaint of family abuse, including but not limited to assault and battery against a family or household member may, upon request, transport, or arrange for the transportation of an abused person to a hospital, safe shelter, or magistrate. Any local law-enforcement agency may adopt a policy requiring an officer to transport or arrange for transportation of an abused person as provided in this subsection.

F. The definition of "family or household member" in §16.1-228 applies to this section.

G. As used in this section, a "law-enforcement officer" means (i) any full-time or part-time employee of a police department or sheriff's office which is part of or administered by the Commonwealth or any political subdivision thereof and who is responsible for the prevention and detection of crime and the enforcement of the penal, traffic or highway laws of this Commonwealth and (ii) any member of an auxiliary police force established pursuant to subsection B of §15.2-1731. Part-time employees are compensated officers who are not full-time employees as defined by the employing police department or sheriff's office.

(Chgd. by L.1995 chs. 413, 433; L.1996 ch. 866; L.1997 ch. 603; L.1998 ch. 569; L.1999 chs. 697, 721, 807, eff. 7/1/99.)

§19.2-81.4. Policies and procedures for the Virginia State Police and local law-enforcement officials.

The Virginia State Police and each local police and sheriff's department shall establish an arrest policy and procedures to implement this section. Any local police or sheriff's department is authorized to adopt an arrest policy that prescribes additional requirements under this section. Any policies and procedures established under this section shall at a minimum provide guidance to law-enforcement officers on the following:

1. The department's arrest policy;
2. The standards for determining who is the primary physical aggressor including (i) the intent of the law to protect the health and safety of family and household members, (ii) prior complaints of family abuse by the allegedly abusing person involving the family or household members and (iii) the relative severity of the injuries inflicted on persons involved in the incident and whether any injuries were inflicted in self-defense;
3. The standards for completion of a required incident report to be filed with the department including the existence of any special circumstances which would dictate a course of action other than arrest;
4. The department's policy on providing transportation to an allegedly abused person; and
5. The legal and community resources available to allegedly abused persons in the department's jurisdiction.

(Added by L.1996 ch. 866, eff. 7/1/97.)

§19.2-81.5. Cooperation with a law-enforcement officer.

Upon receipt of a request and documentation of an indictment or issuance of a warrant from a law-enforcement agency, any public agency within the Commonwealth may disclose to the requesting law-enforcement agency from agency records, to the extent permitted by federal law, the address of an individual who has been indicted or for whom a warrant for arrest for a crime punishable by incarceration has been issued.

(Added by L.1998 ch. 436, eff. 7/1/98.)

§19.2-82. Procedure upon arrest without warrant.

A person arrested without a warrant shall be brought forthwith before a magistrate or other issuing authority having jurisdiction who shall proceed to examine the officer making the arrest under oath. If the magistrate or other issuing authority having jurisdiction has lawful probable cause upon which to believe that a criminal offense has been committed, and that the person arrested has committed such offense, he shall issue either a warrant under the provisions of §19.2-72 or a summons under the provisions of §19.2-73.

As used in this section the term "brought before a magistrate or other issuing authority having jurisdiction" shall include a personal appearance before such authority or any two-way electronic video and audio communication meeting the requirements of §19.2-3.1, in order that the accused and the arresting officer may simultaneously see and speak to such magistrate or authority. If electronic means are used, any documents filed may be transmitted in accordance with §19.2-3.1.

If a warrant is issued the case shall thereafter be disposed of under the provisions of §§19.2-183 through 19.2-190, if the issuing officer is a judge; under the provisions of §§19.2-119 through 19.2-134, if the issuing officer is a magistrate or other issuing officer having jurisdiction. If such warrant or summons is not issued, the person so arrested shall be released; however, this section shall not bar a judge of a district court from proceeding in accord with the provisions of §16.1-129.1.

§19.2-83.1. Report of arrest of school employees for certain offenses.

Every state official or agency and every sheriff, police officer, or other local law-enforcement officer or conservator of the peace having the power to arrest for a felony, upon arresting a person who is known or discovered by the arresting official to be a full-time, part-time, permanent, or temporary teacher or other employee in any public school division in this Commonwealth for a felony; a misdemeanor involving (i) sexual assault as established in Article 7 (§18.2-61 et seq.) of Chapter 4 of Title 18.2, (ii) obscenity and related offenses as established in Article 5 (§18.2-372 et seq.) of Chapter 8 of Title 18.2, (iii) drugs as established in Article 1 (§18.2-247 et seq.) of Chapter 7 of Title 18.2, (iv) moral turpitude, or (v) the physical or sexual abuse or neglect of a child; or an equivalent offense in another state shall file a report of such arrest with the division superintendent of the employing division as soon as reasonably practical. The contents of the report required pursuant to this section shall be utilized by the local school division solely to implement the provisions of §§22.1-296.2 B and 22.1-315.

(Chgd. by L.1996 chs. 958, 960; L.1997 ch. 721, eff. 7/1/97.)

CHAPTER 8
EXTRADITION OF CRIMINALS

ARTICLE 1
FUGITIVES FROM FOREIGN NATIONS

§19.2-84. Governor to surrender on requisition of President.

The Governor shall whenever required by the executive authority of the United States, pursuant to the Constitution and laws thereof, deliver over to justice any person found within the Commonwealth, who is charged with having committed any crime without the jurisdiction of the United States.

ARTICLE 2
UNIFORM CRIMINAL EXTRADITION ACT

§19.2-85. Definitions.

When appearing in this chapter:

(1) The term "Governor" includes any person performing the functions of Governor by authority of the law of this Commonwealth;

(2) The term "executive authority" includes the Governor, and any person performing the functions of Governor in a state other than this Commonwealth;

(3) The term "State," referring to a state other than this Commonwealth, includes any other state or territory, organized or unorganized, of the United States of America, and the District of Columbia; and

(4) The term "judge" means a judge of a court of record having criminal jurisdiction.

§19.2-86. Fugitives from justice; duty of Governor.

Subject to the provisions of this chapter, the provisions of the Constitution of the United States controlling, and any and all acts of Congress enacted in pursuance thereof, the Governor shall have arrested and delivered up to the executive authority of any other of the United States any person charged in that state with treason, felony, or other crime, who has fled from justice and is found in this Commonwealth.

§19.2-87. Form of demand.

No demand for the extradition of a person charged with, or convicted of, crime in another state shall be recognized by the Governor unless in writing alleging, except in cases arising under §19.2-91, that the accused was present in the demanding state at the time of the commission of the alleged crime and that thereafter he fled from such state, and accompanied: (1) by a copy of an indictment found, (2) by a copy or an information supported by an affidavit filed in the state having jurisdiction of the crime, (3) by a copy of an affidavit made before a magistrate in such state together with a copy of any warrant which was issued thereupon, or (4) by a copy of a judgment of conviction or of a sentence imposed in execution thereof together with a statement by the executive authority of the demanding state that the person claimed has escaped from confinement or has broken the terms of his bail, probation or parole. The indictment, information or affidavit made before the magistrate must substantially charge the person demanded with having committed a crime under the law of that state; and the copy of the indictment, information, affidavit, judgment of conviction or sentence must be authenticated by the executive authority making the demand.

§19.2-88. Governor may investigate case.

When a demand shall be made upon the Governor by the executive authority of another state for the surrender of a person so charged with, or convicted of, crime, the Governor may call upon the Attorney General or any other officer of this Commonwealth to investigate or assist in investigating the demand and to report to him the situation and circumstances of the person so demanded and whether he ought to be surrendered.

§19.2-89. Extradition of persons imprisoned or awaiting trial in another state.

When it is desired to have returned to this Commonwealth a person charged in this State with a crime and such person is imprisoned or is held under criminal proceedings then pending against him in another state, the Governor may agree with the executive authority of such other state for the extradition of such person before the conclusion of such proceedings or his term of sentence in such other state, upon condition that such person be returned to such other state at the expense of this Commonwealth as soon as the prosecution in this Commonwealth is terminated.

§19.2-90. Extradition of persons who have left demanding state involuntarily.

The Governor may also surrender on demand of the executive authority of any other state any person in this Commonwealth who is charged in the manner provided in §§19.2-109 to 19.2-111, with having violated the laws of the state whose executive authority is making the demand, even though such person left the demanding state involuntarily.

§19.2-91. Extradition of persons not in demanding state at time of commission of crime.

The Governor may also surrender, on demand of the executive authority of any other state, any person in this Commonwealth charged in such other state in the manner provided in §19.2-87 with committing an act in this Commonwealth, or in a third state, intentionally resulting in a crime in the state whose executive authority is making the demand. The provisions of this chapter not otherwise inconsistent shall apply to such cases, even though the accused was not in that state at the time of the commission of the crime, and has not fled therefrom.

§19.2-92. Issuance of Governor's warrant of arrest; its recitals.

If the Governor decides that a demand for the extradition of a person, charged with, or convicted of, crime in another state should be complied with, he shall sign a warrant of arrest, which shall be sealed with the state seal, and be directed to the sheriff or sergeant of any county or city or to any peace officer or other person whom he may think fit to entrust with the execution thereof. The warrant must substantially recite the facts necessary to the validity of its issuance.

§19.2-93. Manner and place of execution of warrant.

Such warrant shall authorize the officer or other person to whom it is directed to arrest the accused at any time and at any place where he may be found within the Commonwealth and to command the aid of all peace officers or other persons in the execution of the warrant and to deliver the accused, subject to the provisions of this chapter, to the duly authorized agent of the demanding state.

§19.2-94. Assistance to arresting officer.

Every officer or other person empowered to make the arrest, as provided in the preceding section, shall have the same authority, in arresting the accused, to command assistance therein as the sheriffs and sergeants of the several counties and cities of this Commonwealth have by law in the execution of any criminal process directed to them, with like penalties against those who refuse to render their assistance.

§19.2-95. Rights of accused persons; application for writ of habeas corpus.

No person arrested upon such warrant shall be delivered over to the agent whom the executive authority demanding him shall have appointed to receive him unless he shall first be taken forthwith before a judge of a circuit or general district court in this Commonwealth, who shall inform him of the demand made for his surrender and of the crime with which he is charged, and that he has the right to demand and procure legal counsel; and if the prisoner or his counsel shall state that he or they desire to test the legality of his arrest, the judge or trial justice shall fix a reasonable time to be allowed him within which to apply for a writ of habeas corpus. When such writ is applied for, notice thereof and of the time and place of hearing thereon shall be given to the attorney for the Commonwealth of the county or city in which the arrest is made and in which the accused is in custody, and to the agent of the demanding state.

§19.2-96. Penalty for noncompliance with preceding section.

Any officer who shall deliver to the agent for extradition of the demanding state a person in his custody under the Governor's warrant in willful disobedience to the last preceding section shall be guilty of a Class 1 misdemeanor.

§19.2-97. Confinement in jail when necessary.

The officer or persons executing the Governor's warrant of arrest, or the agent of the demanding state to whom the prisoner may have been delivered, may, when necessary, confine the prisoner in the jail of any county or city through which he may pass; and the keeper of such jail shall receive and safely keep the prisoner until the officer or person having charge of him is ready to proceed on his route, such officer or person being chargeable with the expense of keeping.

§19.2-98. Same; for prisoners being taken through Commonwealth.

The officer or agent of a demanding state to whom a prisoner may have been delivered following extradition proceedings in another state or to whom a prisoner may have been delivered after waiving extradition in such other state, and who is passing through this Commonwealth with such prisoner for the purpose of returning immediately such prisoner to the demanding state may, when necessary, confine the prisoner in the jail of any county or city through which he may pass; and the keeper of such jail shall receive and safely keep the prisoner until the officer or agent having charge of him is ready to proceed on his route, such officer or agent, however, being chargeable with the expense of keeping, provided, however, that such officer or agent shall deliver to the jailer the warrant or legal order authorizing custody of the prisoner. Such prisoner shall not be entitled to demand a new requisition while in this Commonwealth.

§19.2-99. Arrest prior to requisition.

Whenever: (1) any person within this Commonwealth shall be charged on the oath of any credible person before any judge, magistrate or other officer authorized to issue criminal warrants in this Commonwealth with the commission of any crime in any other state and, except in cases arising under §19.2-91, (a) with having fled from justice, (b) with having been convicted of a crime in that state and of having escaped from confinement, or (c) of having broken the terms of his bail, probation, or parole, or (2) complaint shall have been made before any such judge, magistrate or other officer in this Commonwealth setting forth on the affidavit of any credible person in another state that a crime has been committed in such other state and that the accused has been charged in such state with the commission of the crime, and, except in cases arising under §19.2-91, (a) has fled from justice, (b) having been convicted of a crime in that state has escaped from confinement, or (c) broken the terms of his bail, probation or parole, and that the accused is believed to be in this Commonwealth, such judge, magistrate or other officer shall issue a warrant directed to any sheriff or to any peace officer commanding him to apprehend the person named therein, wherever he may be found in this Commonwealth, and to bring him before any judge who may be available in or convenient of access to the place where the arrest may be made, to answer the charge of complaint and affidavit. A certified copy of the sworn charge or complaint and affidavit upon which the warrant is issued shall be attached to the warrant.

§19.2-100. Arrest without warrant.

The arrest of a person may be lawfully made also by any peace officer or private person without a warrant upon reasonable information that the accused stands charged in the courts of a state with a crime punishable by death or imprisonment for a term exceeding one year. But when so arrested the accused shall be taken before a judge, magistrate or other officer authorized to issue criminal warrants in this Commonwealth with all practicable speed and complaint made against him under oath setting forth the ground for the arrest as in the preceding section; and thereafter his answer shall be heard as if he had been arrested on a warrant.

§19.2-101. Confinement to await requisition; bail.
If from the examination before the judge it appears that the person held pursuant to either of the two preceding sections is the person charged with having committed the crime alleged and, except in cases arising under §19.2-91, that he has fled from justice, the judge shall, by a warrant reciting the accusation, commit him to jail for such a time, not exceeding thirty days, specified in the warrant as will enable the arrest of the accused to be made under a warrant of the Governor on a requisition of the executive authority of the state having jurisdiction of the offense, unless the accused give bail as provided in the next section, or until he shall be legally discharged.

§19.2-102. In what cases bail allowed; conditions of bond.
Unless the offense with which the prisoner is charged is shown to be an offense punishable by death or life imprisonment under the laws of the state in which it was committed, any judge, magistrate or other person authorized by law to admit persons to bail in this Commonwealth may admit the person arrested to bail by bond, with sufficient sureties, and in such sum as he deems proper, conditioned upon his appearance before a judge at a time specified in such bond and upon his surrender for arrest upon the warrant of the Governor of this Commonwealth.

§19.2-103. Discharge, recommitment or renewal of bail.
If the accused is not arrested under warrant of the Governor by the expiration of the time specified in the warrant or bond, any judge in this Commonwealth may discharge him or may recommit him for a further period not to exceed sixty days, or such judge may again take bail for his appearance and surrender, as provided in the preceding section, but within a period not to exceed sixty days after the date of such new bond.

§19.2-104. Forfeiture of bail.
If the prisoner is admitted to bail and fails to appear and surrender himself according to the conditions of his bond, any judge of a circuit or general district court by proper order, shall declare the bond forfeited and order his immediate arrest without warrant if he be within this Commonwealth. Recovery may be had on such bond in the name of the Commonwealth as in the case of other bonds given by the accused in criminal proceedings within this Commonwealth.

§19.2-105. Persons under criminal prosecution in this Commonwealth at time of requisition.
If a criminal prosecution has been instituted against such person under the laws of this Commonwealth and is still pending, the Governor, in his discretion, either may surrender him on demand of the executive authority of another state or hold him until he has been tried and discharged or convicted and punished in this Commonwealth.

§19.2-106. When guilt or innocence of accused inquired into.
The guilt or innocence of the accused as to the crime of which he is charged may not be inquired into by the Governor or in any proceeding after the demand for extradition accompanied by a charge of crime in legal form as above provided shall have been presented to the Governor, except as it may be involved in identifying the person held as the person charged with the crime.

§19.2-107. Governor may recall warrant or issue alias.
The Governor may recall his warrant of arrest or may issue another warrant whenever he deems it proper.

§19.2-108. Fugitives from this Commonwealth; duty of Governor.
Whenever the Governor shall demand a person charged with crime or with escaping from confinement or breaking the terms of his bail, probation or parole in this Commonwealth, from the executive authority of any other state, or from the chief justice or an associate justice of the Supreme Court of the District of Columbia authorized to receive such demand under the laws of the United States, he shall issue a warrant under the seal of this Commonwealth to some agent commanding him to receive the person so charged if delivered to him and convey him to the proper officer of the county or city in this Commonwealth in which the offense was committed.

§19.2-109. Application for requisition for return of person charged with crime.
When the return to this Commonwealth of a person charged with crime in this Commonwealth is required, the attorney for the Commonwealth shall present to the Governor his written application for a requisition for the return of the person charged, in which application shall be stated the name of the person so charged, the crime charged against him, the approximate time, place and circumstances of its commission, the state in which he is believed to be, including the location of the accused therein at the time the application is made, and certifying that, in the opinion of the attorney for the Commonwealth, the ends of justice require the arrest and return of the accused to this Commonwealth for trial and that the proceeding is not instituted to enforce a private claim.

§19.2-110. Application for requisition for return of escaped convict, etc.
When the return to this Commonwealth is required of a person who has been convicted of a crime in this Commonwealth and has escaped from confinement or broken the terms of his bail, probation or parole, the attorney for the Commonwealth, of the county or city in which the offense was committed, or the warden of the institution or sheriff of the county or city from which the escape was made, shall present to the Governor a written application for a requisition for the return of such person, in which application shall be stated the name of the person, the crime of which he was convicted, the circumstances of his escape from confinement or of the breach of the terms of his bail, probation or parole and the state in which he is believed to be, including the location of the person therein at the time application is made.

§19.2-111. Form of such applications; copies, etc.
The application shall be verified by affidavit, shall be executed in duplicate and shall be accompanied by two certified copies of the indictment returned, or information and affidavit filed, or of the complaint made to the judge of a circuit or general district court or other officer issuing the warrant stating the offense with which the accused is charged, or of the judgment of conviction or of the sentence. The attorney for the Commonwealth, warden or sheriff may also attach such further affidavits and other documents in duplicate as he shall deem proper to be submitted with such application. One copy of the application, with the action of the Governor indicated by endorsement thereon, and one of the certified copies of the indictment, complaint, information, and affidavits, or of the judgment of conviction or of the

sentence shall be filed in the office of the Secretary of the Commonwealth, to remain of record in that office. The other copies of all papers shall be forwarded with the Governor's requisition.

§19.2-112. Costs and expenses of extradition.

A. The expenses incident to the extradition of any person under the four preceding sections may be paid out of the state treasury, on warrants of the Comptroller issued upon vouchers signed by the Governor, or such other person as may be designated by him for such purpose.

B. If the person was extradited after illegally leaving the Commonwealth while on parole or on probation, the person extradited, and not the Commonwealth, shall be responsible for the costs and expenses of extradition. The state treasury shall continue to reimburse local jurisdictions for the costs and expenses of extradition. The fugitive shall pay the costs and expenses of his extradition into the state treasury.
(Chgd. by L.1999 ch. 322, eff. 7/1/99.)

§19.2-113. Immunity from service of process in certain civil actions.

A person brought into this Commonwealth by, or after waiver of, extradition based on a criminal charge shall not be subject to service of personal process in civil actions arising out of the same facts as the criminal proceeding to answer which he is being or has been returned, until he has been convicted in the criminal proceeding, or, if acquitted, until he has had reasonable opportunity to return to the state from which he was extradited.

§19.2-114. Written waiver of extradition proceedings.

Any person arrested in this Commonwealth charged with having committed any crime in another state or alleged to have escaped from confinement, or broken the terms of his bail, probation or parole may waive the issuance and service of the warrant provided for in §§19.2-92 and 19.2-93 and all other procedures incidental to extradition proceedings by executing or subscribing in the presence of a judge of a circuit or district court within this Commonwealth a writing which states that he consents to return to the demanding state. However, before the waiver is executed or subscribed by the person, it shall be the duty of the judge to inform the person of his rights to the issuance and service of a warrant of extradition and to obtain a writ of habeas corpus as provided for in §19.2-95.

If and when such consent has been duly executed, it shall forthwith be forwarded to the office of the Governor and filed therein. The judge shall direct the officer having the person in custody to promptly deliver him to the duly accredited agent of the demanding state, and shall deliver or cause to be delivered to such agent a copy of the consent.

This section shall not be deemed to limit the rights of the accused person to return voluntarily and without formality to the demanding state, nor shall this waiver procedure be deemed to be an executive procedure or to limit the powers, rights or duties of the officers of the demanding state or of this Commonwealth.

§19.2-115. Nonwaiver by this Commonwealth.

Nothing in this chapter contained shall be deemed to constitute a waiver by this Commonwealth of its right, power or privilege to try such demanded person for crime committed within this Commonwealth, or of its right, power or privilege to regain custody of such person by extradition proceedings or otherwise for the purpose of trial, sentence or punishment for any crime committed within this Commonwealth, nor shall any proceedings had under this chapter which result in, or fail to result in, extradition be deemed a waiver by this Commonwealth of any of its rights, privileges or jurisdiction in any way whatsoever.

§19.2-116. No right of asylum; no immunity from other criminal prosecutions while in this Commonwealth.

After a person has been brought back to this Commonwealth by, or after waiver of, extradition proceedings he may be tried in this Commonwealth for other crimes which he may be charged with having committed here as well as that specified in the requisition for his extradition.

§19.2-117. Interpretation of article.

The provisions of this article shall be so interpreted and construed as to effectuate its general purposes to make uniform the law of those states which enact statutes similar thereto.

§19.2-118. Short title.

This article may be cited as the Uniform Criminal Extradition Act.

CHAPTER 9
BAIL AND RECOGNIZANCES

ARTICLE 1
BAIL

§19.2-119. Definitions.

As used in this chapter:

"Bail" means the pretrial release of a person from custody upon those terms and conditions specified by order of an appropriate judicial officer.

"Bond" means the posting by a person or his surety of a written promise to pay a specific sum, secured or unsecured, ordered by an appropriate judicial officer as a condition of bail to assure performance of the terms and conditions contained in the recognizance.

"Criminal history" means records and data collected by criminal justice agencies or persons consisting of identifiable descriptions and notations of arrests, detentions, indictments, informations or other formal charges, and any deposition arising therefrom.

"Judicial officer" means, unless otherwise indicated, any magistrate within his jurisdiction, any judge of a district court and the clerk or deputy clerk of any district court or circuit court within their respective cities and counties, any judge of a circuit court, any judge of the Court of Appeals and any justice of the Supreme Court of Virginia.

"Person" means any accused, or any juvenile taken into custody pursuant to §16.1-246.

"Recognizance" means a signed commitment by a person to appear in court as directed and to adhere to any other terms ordered by an appropriate judicial officer as a condition of bail.

(Chgd. by L.1999 chs. 829, 846, eff. 7/1/99.)

§19.2-120. Admission to bail.

Prior to conducting any hearing on the issue of bail, release or detention, the judicial officer shall, to the extent feasible, obtain the person's criminal history.

A. A person who is held in custody pending trial or hearing for an offense, civil or criminal contempt, or otherwise shall be admitted to bail by a judicial officer, unless there is probable cause to believe that:

1. He will not appear for trial or hearing or at such other time and place as may be directed, or

2. His liberty will constitute an unreasonable danger to himself or the public.

B. The judicial officer shall presume, subject to rebuttal, that no condition or combination of conditions will reasonably assure the appearance of the person or the safety of the public if the person is currently charged with:

1. An act of violence as defined in §19.2-297.1;

2. An offense for which the maximum sentence is life imprisonment or death;

3. A violation of §§18.2-248, 18.2-248.01, 18.2-255 or §18.2-255.2 involving a Schedule I or II controlled substance if (i) the maximum term of imprisonment is ten years or more and the person was previously convicted of a like offense or (ii) the person was previously convicted as a "drug kingpin" as defined in §18.2-248;

4. A violation of §§18.2-308.1, 18.2-308.2, or §18.2-308.4 and which relates to a firearm and provides for a minimum, mandatory sentence;

5. Any felony, if the person has been convicted of two or more offenses described in subdivision 1 or 2, whether under the laws of this Commonwealth or substantially similar laws of the United States;

6. Any felony committed while the person is on release pending trial for a prior felony under federal or state law or on release pending imposition or execution of sentence or appeal of sentence or conviction; or

7. An offense listed in subsection B of §18.2-67.5:2 and the person had previously been convicted of an offense listed in §18.2-67.5:2 and the judicial officer finds probable cause to believe that the person who is currently charged with one of these offenses committed the offense charged.

C. The court shall consider the following factors and such others as it deems appropriate in determining, for the purpose of rebuttal of the presumption against bail described in subsection B, whether there are conditions of release that will reasonably assure the appearance of the person as required and the safety of the public:

1. The nature and circumstances of the offense charged;

2. The history and characteristics of the person, including his character, physical and mental condition, family ties, employment, financial resources, length of residence in the community, community ties, past conduct, history relating to drug or alcohol abuse, criminal history, and record concerning appearance at court proceedings; and

3. The nature and seriousness of the danger to any person or the community that would be posed by the person's release.

D. The judicial officer shall inform the person of his right to appeal from the order denying bail or fixing terms of bond or recognizance consistent with §19.2-124.

(Chgd. by L.1996 ch. 973; L.1997 chs. 6, 476; L.1999 chs. 829, 846; L.2000 ch. 797, eff. 7/1/2000.)

§19.2-121. Fixing terms of bail.

If the person is admitted to bail, the terms thereof shall be such as, in the judgment of any official granting or reconsidering the same, will be reasonably fixed to assure the appearance of the accused and to assure his good behavior pending trial. The judicial officer shall take into account (i) the nature and circumstances of the offense; (ii) whether a firearm is alleged to have been used in the offense; (iii) the weight of the evidence; (iv) the financial resources of the accused or juvenile and his ability to pay bond; (v) the character of the accused or juvenile including his family ties, employment or involvement in education; (vi) his length of residence in the community; (vii) his record of convictions; (viii) his appearance at court proceedings or flight to avoid prosecution or failure to appear at court proceedings; (ix) whether the person is likely to obstruct or attempt to obstruct justice, or threaten, injure, or intimidate, or attempt to threaten, injure, or intimidate a prospective witness, juror, or victim; and (x) any other information available which the court considers relevant to the determination of whether the accused or juvenile is unlikely to appear for court proceedings.

In any case where the accused has appeared and otherwise met the conditions of bail, no bond therefor shall be used to satisfy fines and costs unless agreed to by the person who posted such bond.

(Chgd. by L.1999 chs. 829, 846, eff. 7/1/99.)

§19.2-123. Release of accused on unsecured bond or promise to appear; conditions of release.

A. Any person arrested for a felony who has previously been convicted of a felony, or who is presently on bond for an unrelated arrest in any jurisdiction, or who is on probation or parole, may be released only upon a secure bond. This provision may be waived with the approval of the judicial officer and with the concurrence of the attorney for the Commonwealth or the attorney for the county, city or town. Subject to the foregoing, any judicial officer may impose any one or any combination of the following conditions of release:

1. Place the person in the custody and supervision of a designated person, organization or pretrial services agency which, for the purposes of this section, shall not include a court services unit established pursuant to §16.1-233;

2. Place restrictions on the travel, association or place of abode of the person during the period of release and restrict contacts with household members for a period not to exceed seventy-two hours;

2a. Require the execution of an unsecured bond;

3. Require the execution of a secure bond which at the option of the accused shall be satisfied with sufficient solvent sureties, or the deposit of cash in lieu thereof. Only the actual value of any interest in real estate or personal property owned by the proposed surety shall be considered in determining solvency and solvency shall be found if the value of the proposed surety's equity in the real estate or personal property equals or exceeds the amount of the bond;

3a. Require that the person do any or all of the following: (i) maintain employment or, if unemployed, actively seek employment; (ii) maintain or commence an educational program; (iii) avoid all contact with an alleged victim of the crime and with any potential witness who may testify concerning the offense; (iv) comply with a specified curfew; (v) refrain from possessing a firearm, destructive device, or other dangerous weapon; (vi) refrain from excessive use of alcohol, or use of any illegal drug or any controlled substance not prescribed by a health care provider; and (vii) submit to testing for drugs and alcohol until the final disposition of his case; or

4. Impose any other condition deemed reasonably necessary to assure appearance as required, and to assure his good behavior pending trial, including a condition requiring that the person return to custody after specified hours or be placed on home electronic incarceration pursuant to §53.1-131.2.

Upon satisfaction of the terms of recognizance, the accused shall be released forthwith.

In addition, where the accused is a resident of a state training center for the mentally retarded, the judicial officer may place the person in the custody of the director of the state facility, if the director agrees to accept custody. Such director is hereby authorized to take custody of such person and to maintain him at the training center prior to a trial or hearing under such circumstances as will reasonably assure the appearance of the accused for the trial or hearing.

B. In any jurisdiction served by a pretrial services agency which offers a drug or alcohol screening or testing program approved for the purposes of this subsection by the chief general district court judge, any such person charged with a crime may be requested by such agency to give voluntarily a urine sample, submit to a drug or alcohol screening, or take a breath test for presence of alcohol. A sample may be analyzed for the presence of phencyclidine (PCP), barbiturates, cocaine, opiates or such other drugs as the agency may deem appropriate prior to any hearing to establish bail. The judicial officer and agency shall inform the accused or juvenile being screened or tested that test results shall be used by a judicial officer only at a bail hearing and only to determine appropriate conditions of release or to reconsider the conditions of bail at a subsequent hearing. All screening or test results, and any pretrial investigation report containing the screening or test results, shall be confidential with access thereto limited to judicial officers, the attorney for the Commonwealth, defense counsel, other pretrial service agencies, any criminal justice agency as defined in §9-169 and, in cases where a juvenile is screened or tested, the parents or legal guardian or custodian of such juvenile. However, in no event shall the judicial officer have access to any screening or test result prior to making a bail release determination or to determining the amount of bond, if any. Following this determination, the judicial officer shall consider the screening or test results and the screening or testing agency's report and accompanying recommendations, if any, in setting appropriate conditions of release. In no event shall a decision regarding a release determination be subject to reversal on the sole basis of such screening or test results. Any accused or juvenile whose urine sample has tested positive for such drugs and who is admitted to bail may, as a condition of release, be ordered to refrain from use of alcohol or illegal drugs and may be required to be tested on a periodic basis until final disposition of his case to ensure his compliance with the order. Sanctions for a violation of any condition of release, which violations shall include subsequent positive drug or alcohol test results or failure to report as ordered for testing, may be imposed in the discretion of the judicial officer and may include imposition of more stringent conditions of release, contempt of court proceedings or revocation of release. Any test given under the provisions of this subsection which yields a positive drug or alcohol test result shall be reconfirmed by a second test if the person tested denies or contests the initial drug or alcohol test positive result. The results of any drug or alcohol test conducted pursuant to this subsection shall not be admissible in any judicial proceeding other than for the imposition of sanctions for a violation of a condition of release.

C. *(Repealed.)*

D. Nothing in this section shall be construed to prevent an officer taking a juvenile into custody from releasing that juvenile pursuant to §16.1-247. If any condition of release imposed under the provisions of this section is violated, a judicial officer may issue a capias or order to show cause why the recognizance should not be revoked.

(Chgd. by L.1999 chs. 829, 846; L.2000 chs. 885, 1020, 1041, eff. 7/1/2000.)

§19.2-124. Appeal from order denying bail or fixing terms of bond or recognizance.

A. If a judicial officer denies bail to a person, requires excessive bond, or fixes unreasonable terms of a recognizance under this article, the person may appeal therefrom successively to the next higher court or judge thereof, up to and including the Supreme Court of Virginia or any justice thereof where permitted by law.

B. If a court grants bail to a person or fixes a term of recognizance under this article over the objection of the attorney for the Commonwealth, the attorney for the Commonwealth may appeal therefrom successively to the next higher court or judge thereof, up to and including the Supreme Court of Virginia or any justice thereof.

(Chgd. by L.1999 chs. 829, 846, eff. 7/1/99.)

§19.2-125. Release pending appeal from conviction in court not of record.

A person who has been convicted of an offense in a district court and who has noted an appeal shall be given credit for any bond that he may have posted in the court from which he appeals and shall be treated in accordance with the provisions of this article.

(Chgd. by L.1999 chs. 829, 846, eff. 7/1/99.)

§19.2-126. *(Repealed by L.1999 chs. 829, 846, eff. 7/1/99.)*

§19.2-127. Conditions of release of material witness.

If it appears by affidavit that the testimony of a person is material in any criminal proceeding, and it reasonably appears that it will be impossible to secure his presence by a subpoena, a judge shall inquire into the conditions of his release pursuant to this article.

(Chgd. by L.1999 chs. 829, 846, eff. 7/1/99.)

§19.2-128. Penalties for failure to appear.

A. Whoever, having been released pursuant to this chapter or §19.2-319 or on a summons pursuant to §19.2-73 or §19.2-74, willfully fails to appear before any court or judicial officer as required, shall, after notice to all interested parties, incur a forfeiture of any security which may have been given or pledged for his release, unless one of the parties can show good cause for excusing the absence, or unless the court, in its sound discretion, shall determine that neither the interests of justice nor the power of the court to conduct orderly proceedings will be served by such forfeiture.

B. Any person (i) charged with a felony offense or (ii) convicted of a felony offense and execution of sentence is suspended pursuant to §19.2-319 who willfully fails to appear before any court as required shall be guilty of a Class 6 felony.

C. Any person (i) charged with a misdemeanor offense or (ii) convicted of a misdemeanor offense and execution of sentence is suspended pursuant to §19.2-319 who willfully

fails to appear before any court as required shall be guilty of a Class 1 misdemeanor.
(Chgd. by L.1999 ch. 821, eff. 7/1/99.)

§19.2-129. Power of court to punish for contempt.
Nothing in this chapter shall interfere with or prevent the exercise by any court of the Commonwealth of its power to punish for contempt, except that a person shall not be sentenced for contempt and under the provisions of §19.2-128 for the same absence.

§19.2-130. Bail in subsequent proceeding arising out of initial arrest.
Any person admitted to bail by a judge or clerk of a district court or by a magistrate shall not be required to be admitted to bail in any subsequent proceeding arising out of the initial arrest unless the court having jurisdiction of such subsequent proceeding deems the initial amount of bond or security taken inadequate. When the court having jurisdiction of the proceeding believes the amount of bond or security inadequate, it may increase the amount of such bond or security or require new and additional sureties.

§19.2-131. Bail for person held in jurisdiction other than that of trial.
In any case in which a person charged with a misdemeanor or felony, or a juvenile taken into custody pursuant to §16.1-246 is held in some county, city or town other than that in which he is to be tried upon such charge, he may be admitted to bail by any judicial officer of the county, city or town in which he is so held in accordance with the provisions of law concerning the granting of bail in cases in which persons are so admitted to bail, when held in the county, city or town in which they are to be tried.

In such case, such judicial officer before whom he is brought may, without trial or examination, let him to bail, upon taking a recognizance for his appearance before the court having cognizance of the case. The fact of taking such recognizance shall be certified by the court or officer taking it upon the warrant under which such person was arrested or taken into custody and the warrant and recognizance shall be returned forthwith to the clerk of the court before whom the accused or juvenile taken into custody pursuant to §16.1-246 is to appear. And to such court, the judicial officer who issued such warrant shall recognize or cause to be summoned such witnesses as he may think proper.

§19.2-132. Motion to increase amount of bond fixed by magistrate or clerk; when bond may be increased.
A. Although a person has been admitted to bail, if the amount of any bond is subsequently deemed insufficient, or the security taken inadequate, or if it appears that bail should have been denied, the attorney for the Commonwealth of the county or city in which the person is held for trial may, on reasonable notice to the person and to any surety on the bond of such person, move the court, or the appropriate judicial officer to increase the amount of such bond or to revoke bail. The court may, in accordance with subsection B, grant such motion and may require new or additional sureties therefor, or both or revoke bail. Any surety in a bond for the appearance of such person may take from his principal collateral or other security to indemnify such surety against liability. The failure to notify the surety will not prohibit the court from proceeding with the bond hearing.

B. Subsequent to an initial appearance before any judicial officer where the conditions of bail have been determined, no person, after having been released on a bond, shall be subject to a motion to increase such bond or revoke bail unless (i) the person has violated a term or condition of his release, or is convicted of or arrested for a felony or misdemeanor, or (ii) the attorney for the Commonwealth presents evidence that incorrect or incomplete information regarding the person's family ties; employment; financial resources; length of residence in the community; record of convictions; record of appearance at court proceedings or flight to avoid prosecution or failure to appear at court proceedings; whether the person is likely to obstruct or attempt to obstruct justice, or threaten, injure, or intimidate, or attempt to threaten, injure, or intimidate, a prospective witness, juror, or victim; or other information relevant to the bond determination was relied upon by the court or magistrate establishing initial bond.
(Chgd. by L.1999 chs. 829, 846, eff. 7/1/99.)

§19.2-134. When bail piece to be delivered to accused; form of bail piece.
In all cases in which recognizances, at the suit of the Commonwealth, may have been, or shall hereafter be entered into, it shall be the duty of the clerk of the court in which, or in the clerk's office of which, any recognizance is filed, to deliver to the accused and his sureties upon request, a bail piece, in substance, as follows: "A. B. of the county or city of..........., is delivered to bail, unto C. D. of the county or city of..........., at the suit of the Commonwealth. Given under my hand, this day of.........., in the year....."

ARTICLE 2
RECOGNIZANCES

Section

§19.2-135. Commitment for trial; recognizance; notice to attorney for Commonwealth; remand on violation of condition.
When a judicial officer considers that there is sufficient cause for charging the accused or juvenile taken into custody pursuant to §16.1-246 with a felony, unless it be a case wherein it is otherwise specially provided, the commitment shall be for trial or hearing. Any recognizance taken of the accused or juvenile shall be upon the following conditions: (1) that he appear to answer for the offense with which he is charged before the court or judge before whom the case will be tried at such time as may be stated in the recognizance and at any time or times to which the proceedings may be continued and before any court or judge thereafter in which

proceedings on the charge are held; (2) that he shall not depart from the Commonwealth unless the judicial officer taking recognizance or a court in a subsequent proceeding specifically waives such requirement; and (3) that he shall keep the peace and be of good behavior until the case is finally disposed of. Every such recognizance shall also include a waiver such as is required by §49-12 in relation to the bonds therein mentioned and though such waiver be not expressed in the recognizance it shall be deemed to be included therein in like manner and with the same effect as if it was so expressed. The judge shall return to the clerk of the court wherein the accused or juvenile is to be tried, or the case be heard as soon as may be, a certificate of the nature of the offense, showing whether the accused or juvenile was committed to jail or recognized for his appearance; and the clerk, as soon as may be, shall inform the attorney for the Commonwealth of such certificate.

The court may, in its discretion, in the event of a violation of any condition of a recognizance taken pursuant to this section, remand the principal to jail until the case is finally disposed of, and if the principal is remanded to jail, the surety is discharged from liability.

When a recognizance is taken of a witness in a case against an accused or juvenile, the condition thereof shall be that he appear to give evidence in such case and that he shall not depart from the Commonwealth without the leave of such court or judge.

§19.2-136. How bonds in recognizances payable; penalty.

Bonds in recognizances in criminal or juvenile cases, where the violation is committed against the Commonwealth or where the Commonwealth is a party, shall be payable to the Commonwealth of Virginia. Bonds in recognizances in criminal cases where the violation is a violation of a county, city or town ordinance, shall be payable to such county, city or town. Every bond under this title shall be in such sum as the court or officer requiring it may direct.

§19.2-137. Order of court on recognizance.

When such recognizance is taken by a court of a person to answer a charge or of a witness to give evidence it shall be sufficient for the order of the court taking the recognizance to state that the party or parties recognized were duly recognized upon a bond in such sum as the court may have directed with such surety as the court may have accepted for his or their appearance before such court at such time as may have been prescribed by the court to answer for the offense with which such person is charged or to give evidence, as the case may be.

§19.2-141. How recognizance taken for incapacitated or insane person or one under disability.

A recognizance which would be taken of a person but for his being a minor, insane or otherwise mentally incapacitated, may be taken of another person and without further surety, if such other person is deemed sufficient, for the performance by such minor, insane or otherwise incapacitated person, of the conditions of the recognizance.

(Chgd. by L.1997 ch. 801, eff. 1/1/98.)

§19.2-142. Where recognizance taken out of court to be sent.

A person taking a recognizance out of court shall forthwith transmit it to the clerk of the court for appearance before which it is taken; or, if it be not for appearance before a court, to the clerk of the circuit court of the county or city in which it is taken; and it shall remain filed in the clerk's office.

§19.2-143. Where default recorded; process on recognizance; forfeiture on recognizance; when copy may be used; cash bond.

When a person, under recognizance in a case, either as party or witness, fails to perform the condition of appearance thereof, if it is to appear before a court of record, or a district court, a hearing shall be held upon reasonable notice to all parties affording them opportunity to show cause why the recognizance or any part thereof should not be forfeited. The show cause notice shall be issued within forty-five days of the breach of the condition of appearance.

If the court finds the recognizance or any part thereof should be forfeited, the default shall be recorded therein, unless, the defendant or juvenile is brought before the court within sixty days of the findings of default. After sixty days of the finding of default, his default shall be recorded therein, and if it is to appear before a district court, his default shall be entered by the judge of such court, on the page of his docket whereon the case is docketed unless the defendant or juvenile has been delivered or appeared before the court. The process on any such forfeited recognizance shall be issued from the court before which the appearance was to be, and wherein such forfeiture was recorded or entered. Any such process issued by a judge when the penalty of the recognizance so forfeited is in excess of the maximum jurisdictional amount specified in §16.1-77(1) shall be made returnable to the circuit court of his county or city, and when not in excess of such amount it shall be made returnable before, and tried by, such judge, who shall promptly transmit to the clerk of the circuit court of his county or city wherein deeds are recorded an abstract of such judgment as he may render thereon, which shall be forthwith docketed by the clerk of such court.

If the defendant or juvenile appears before or is delivered to the court within twelve months of the findings of default, the court shall remit any bond previously ordered forfeited by the courts, less such costs as the court may direct.

If it is brought to the attention of the court that the defendant or juvenile is incarcerated in another state or country within twelve months of the finding of default, thereby preventing his delivery or appearance within that period, the court shall remit any bond previously ordered forfeited. If the defendant or juvenile left the Commonwealth with the permission of the court, the bond shall be remitted without deduction of costs; otherwise, the cost of returning him to the Commonwealth shall be deducted from the bond.

Evidence that the defendant or juvenile is incarcerated or subject to court process in another jurisdiction on the day his appearance is required or a medical certificate from a duly licensed physician that the defendant was physically unable to so appear shall be considered evidence of good cause why the recognizance should not be forfeited.

If such recognizance so forfeited is not for such appearance, process thereon shall be issued from the court in which it was taken, or the court to which it was made returnable, and in a proceeding in one court on a recognizance entered in another a copy thereof shall be evidence in like manner as the original would be if it had been entered in the court wherein the proceeding is being had thereon.

However, when any defendant or juvenile who posted a cash bond and failed to appear is tried in his absence and is convicted, the court or judge trying the case shall first apply the cash bond, or so much thereof as may be necessary, to the payment of any fines or costs, or both, adjudged against the defendant or juvenile or imposed by law. Any remaining funds shall be forfeited without further notice. However, if a rehearing is granted, the court may remit part or all of such cash bond not applied ultimately to fines or costs, and order a refund of the same by the State Treasurer, but only if good cause is shown.

If the defendant or juvenile posted a cash bond and failed to appear, but is not tried in his absence, the bond shall be forfeited promptly without further notice. However, if the defendant or juvenile appears in court within sixty days after the bond is forfeited, the judge may remit part or all of any bond previously forfeited and order a refund of the same by the State Treasurer.
(Chgd. by L.2000 ch. 885, eff. 7/1/2000.)

§19.2-144. Forfeiture of recognizance while in military or naval service.

If in any motion, action, suit or other proceeding made or taken in any court of this Commonwealth on a forfeited bail bond or forfeited recognizance, or to enforce the payment of the bond in any manner or any judgment thereon, or to forfeit any bail bond or recognizance, it appears that the person for whose alleged default such bail bond or recognizance was forfeited or judgment rendered, or such motion is made or proceeding taken, was prevented from complying with the condition of such bail bond or recognizance by reason of his having enlisted or been drafted in the army or navy of the United States, then judgment or decree on such motion, action, suit or other proceeding shall be given for the defendant.

§19.2-145. How penalty remitted.

When in an action or on a motion to extend the period for enforcement of a judgment on a recognizance the penalty is adjudged to be forfeited the court may on an application of a defendant or juvenile remit the penalty or any part of it and render judgment on such terms and conditions as it deems reasonable.

§19.2-146. Defects in form of recognizance not to defeat action or judgment.

No action or judgment on a recognizance shall be defeated or arrested by reason of any defect in the form of the recognizance, if it appear to have been taken by a court or officer authorized to take it and be substantially sufficient.

§19.2-147. Docketing judgment on forfeited recognizance or bond.

Whenever a judgment is entered in any court of record in favor of the Commonwealth of Virginia upon a forfeited recognizance or bond, the clerk of the court in which the judgment is rendered shall certify an abstract of the same to the clerk of the circuit court of the county or city wherein the judgment debtor resides or of any city or county in which he may own real property, who shall thereupon enter the abstract of judgment upon his judgment docket.

§19.2-148. Surety discharged on payment of amount, etc., into court.

A surety on a bond in a recognizance may, after default, pay into the court from which the process has issued, or may issue thereon, the amount for which he is bound, with such costs as the court may direct, and be thereupon discharged.

§19.2-149. How surety on a bond in recognizance may surrender principal and be discharged from liability.

A surety on a bond in a recognizance may at any time arrest his principal and surrender him to the court before which the recognizance was taken or before which such principal's appearance is required, or to the sheriff, sergeant or jailer of the county or city wherein the court before which such principal's appearance is required is located; in addition to the above authority, upon the application of the surety, the court, or the clerk thereof, before which the recognizance was taken, or before which such principal's appearance is required, shall issue a capias for the arrest of such principal, and such capias may be executed by such surety, or his authorized agent, or by any sheriff, sergeant or police officer, and the person executing such capias shall deliver such principal and such capias to the sheriff or jailer of the county or the sheriff, sergeant or jailer of the city in which the appearance of such principal is required, and thereupon the said surety shall be discharged from liability for any act of the principal subsequent thereto. Such sheriff, sergeant or jailer shall thereafter deliver such capias to the clerk of such court, with his endorsement thereon acknowledging delivery of such principal to his custody.

§19.2-150. Proceeding when surety surrenders principal.

If the surrender is to the court, the court shall make such order as it deems proper; if the surrender is to a sheriff or jailer, the officer to whom the accused has been surrendered shall give the surety a certificate of the fact. After such surrender the person shall be treated in accordance with the provisions of Article 1 (§19.2-119 et seq.) of Chapter 9 of this title unless the court or judge thereof has reason to believe that no one or more conditions of release will reasonably assure that the person will not flee or pose a danger to any other person or to the community.
(Chgd. by L.1999 chs. 829, 846, eff. 7/1/99.)

ARTICLE 3
SATISFACTION AND DISCHARGE

Section

§19.2-151. Satisfaction and discharge of assault and similar charges.

When a person is in jail or under a recognizance to answer a charge of assault and battery or other misdemeanor, or has been indicted for an assault and battery or other misdemeanor for which there is a remedy by civil action, unless the offense was committed (i) by or upon any law-enforcement officer, (ii) riotously in violation of §§18.2-404 to 18.2-407, (iii) against a family or household member in violation of §18.2-57.2, or (iv) with intent to commit a felony, if the person injured appears before the court which made the commitment or took the recognizance, or before the court in which the indictment is pending, and acknowledges in writing that he has received satisfaction for the injury, the court may, in its discretion, by an order, supersede the commitment, discharge the recognizance, or dismiss the prosecution, upon payment by the defendant of costs accrued to the Commonwealth or any of its officers.
(Chgd. by L.1997 ch. 532; L.1999 ch. 963, eff. 7/1/99.)

§19.2-152. Order discharging recognizance or superseding commitment; judgment for costs.

Every order discharging a recognizance shall be filed with the clerk before the session of the court at which the party was to appear. Where a person is held under a commitment, any order superseding a commitment shall be delivered to the jailer, who shall forthwith discharge the witnesses, if any, and the accused or juvenile, and judgment against the accused or juvenile shall be entered in the court for the costs of the prosecution.

ARTICLE 4
BAIL BONDSMEN

§19.2-152.1. Bondsmen's certificate; limitations on bail business.

The revenue license authorized in §58.1-3724 shall not be issued by any county, city or town unless and until the applicant shall have first obtained a certificate from the judge of the circuit court of the county or city, in which he desires to carry on the business of professional bondsman, approving the issuance of the license and certifying that the applicant is of good moral character, that his past conduct before the courts of said county or city has not been unsatisfactory and is suitable to be so licensed. Before the issuance of such certificate the judge of the circuit court may review the record of the applicant as furnished by the Federal Bureau of Investigation. Prior to the issuance of such certificate, the judge of the circuit court may confer with the judge or judges of those courts in which such bondsman seeks to act. A license granted to a professional bondsman in any such county or city pursuant to §58.1-3724 shall authorize such person to enter into such bonds in any other county or city, provided that upon entering into any bond conditioned upon real estate, cash or certificates of deposit issued by a federally insured institution, or any combination thereof as collateral in any other county or city such bondsman makes affidavit that the aggregate of the penalty of such bond together with all other bonds in the Commonwealth on which he has not been released from liability is not in excess of the true market value of the equity in his real estate, cash or certificates of deposit issued by a federally insured institution, or any combination thereof.

No professional bondsman shall enter into any such bond if the aggregate of the penalty of such bond and all other bonds, on which he has not been released from liability, is in excess of the true market value of his real estate, cash or certificates of deposit issued by a federally insured institution, or any combination thereof. Each professional bondsman, if so directed by the judge of the circuit court of the county or of the city in which he is licensed, shall place a deed of trust on the real estate that he is using for the limit of his expected bonded indebtedness to secure the Commonwealth of Virginia and shall name the attorney for the Commonwealth of the affected locality as trustee under the deed of trust or shall place the requisite cash or certificates of deposit issued by a federally insured institution, or any combination thereof with the court. In addition thereto, he shall furnish the clerk of the appropriate court an acceptable appraisal and title certificate of the real estate subject to any such deed of trust. Each professional bondsman licensed hereunder shall file with the clerk of the circuit court of the county or city in which he is licensed not later than the fifth day of each month a list of all outstanding bonds on which he was obligated as of the last day of the preceding month, together with the amount of the penalty of each such bond.

No court shall certify and no revenue license shall be issued as provided in this section to a person who had not obtained a certification and license prior to July 1, 1989, unless such person provides to the issuing court collateral of $200,000 on his bonds and $200,000 on the bonds of each of his agents.

Any professional bondsman or agent for any professional bondsman, qualified under this section, shall be subject to and governed by any reasonable rules of conduct or procedure set up by the judge of the court in which he is acting as a bondsman. Such rules shall include the requirement that such bondsman give written notice to the clerk of the circuit court of each change in the number of agents in his employ within seven days of such change and provide $200,000 collateral for each additional agent and may include a requirement that such bondsman or agent place a reasonable amount of cash or negotiable instruments in escrow with the clerk of said court to be held during the time such bondsman or agent is acting as a bondsman in said court, provided that said clerk is acting under a bond of sufficient amount and coverage to insure protection against loss, theft, or misappropriation. Upon his violation of such rules, he may, after hearing upon a charge of such violation, be suspended from entering into further bonds in said court by the judge thereof. If such bondsman or agent fails to have in escrow with the clerk of said court a sum sufficient to cover any forfeiture of bond against him and fails or refuses to pay such forfeiture after notice and demand by the judge of the court he may be suspended by such judge from entering into further bonds in said court until the forfeiture is paid or it is adjudicated that he is not liable thereon.

No person after July 1, 1981, who has previously not been licensed shall be licensed hereunder either as a professional bondsman or agent for any professional bondsman, when such person, his or her spouse, or a member of his or her immediate family holds any office as magistrate, clerk or deputy clerk of any court.

Nothing in this section shall be construed to apply to guaranty, indemnity, fidelity and security companies doing business in Virginia or their agents and attorneys-in-fact, under the provisions of Chapter 24 (§38.2-2400 et seq.) of Title 38.2, except that agents and attorneys-in-fact of guaranty, indemnity, fidelity and security companies entering into bonds for bail, appearances, costs or appeal in criminal cases, shall be required to obtain a certificate from the judge of the circuit court in which he desires to carry on the business of professional bondsman, certifying that the applicant is of good moral character, that his past conduct before the courts of said county or city has not been unsatisfactory and he is suitable to be a licensed bondsman. Such certificate shall authorize such persons to enter into such bonds in any other county or city. Such agents and attorneys-in-fact shall be subject to any reasonable rules of conduct or procedure and discipline for the violation of same as may be ordered by the judge of the court in which they act for such companies. No person may act as such an agent or attorney-in-fact when such person, his or her spouse, or a member of his or her immediate family holds any office as magistrate, clerk or deputy clerk of any court.

(Chgd. by L.1997 ch. 455, eff. 7/1/97.)

ARTICLE 5
PRETRIAL SERVICES ACT

§19.2-152.2. Purpose; establishment of program.

It is the purpose of this article to provide more effective protection of society by establishing programs which will assist judicial officers in discharging their duties pursuant to Article 1 (§19.2-119 et seq.) of Chapter 9 of this title. Such

programs are intended to provide better information and services for use by judicial officers in determining the risk to public safety and the assurance of appearance of persons held in custody and charged with an offense, other than an offense punishable by death, who are pending trial or hearing. Any city, county or combination thereof may establish a pretrial services program and any city, county or combination thereof required to submit a community-based corrections plan pursuant to §53.1-82.1 shall establish a pretrial services program.
(Chgd. by L.1999 chs. 829, 846, eff. 7/1/99.)

§19.2-152.3. Department of Criminal Justice Services to prescribe standards; biennial plan.

The Department of Criminal Justice Services shall prescribe standards for the development, implementation, operation and evaluation of programs authorized by this article. The Department of Criminal Justice Services shall develop risk assessment and other instruments to be used by pretrial services programs in assisting judicial officers in discharging their duties pursuant to Article 1 (§19.2-119 et seq.) of Chapter 9 of this title. Any city, county or combination thereof which establishes a pretrial services program pursuant to this article shall submit a biennial plan to the Department of Criminal Justice Services for review and approval.
(Chgd. by L.1999 chs. 829, 846, eff. 7/1/99.)

§19.2-152.4. Mandated services.

Any city, county or combination thereof which elects or is required to establish a pretrial services program shall provide all information and services for use by judicial officers as set forth in Article 1 (§19.2-119 et seq.) of Chapter 9 of this title.
(Chgd. by L.1999 chs. 829, 846, eff. 7/1/99.)

§19.2-152.4:1. Form of oath of office for local pretrial services officer; authorization to seek capias or warrant.

Every pretrial services officer who is an employee of a local pretrial services agency established by any city, county or combination thereof or operated pursuant to this article shall take an oath of office as prescribed in §49-1 and to provide services pursuant to the requirements of this article before entering the duties of his office. The oath of office shall be taken before any general district or circuit court judge in any county or city which has established services for use by judicial officers pursuant to this article.

In addition, any officer of a pretrial services agency established or operated pursuant to this article may seek a warrant or capias from any judicial officer for the arrest of any person under the agency's custody and supervision for failure to comply with any conditions of release imposed by a judicial officer, for failure to comply with the conditions of pretrial supervision as established by a pretrial services agency, or when there is reason to believe that the person will fail to appear, will leave, or has left the jurisdiction to avoid prosecution.
(Added by L.2000 ch. 1040, eff. 7/1/2000.)

§19.2-152.5. Community criminal justice boards.

Each city, county or combination thereof establishing a pretrial services program shall also establish a community criminal justice board pursuant to §53.1-183.

§19.2-152.6. Withdrawal from program.

Any participating city or county may, at the beginning of any calendar quarter, by ordinance or resolution of its governing authority, notify the Department of Criminal Justice Services of its intention to withdraw from the pretrial services program. Such withdrawal shall be effective as of the last day of the quarter in which such notice is given.

§19.2-152.7. Funding; failure to comply.

Counties and cities shall be required to establish a pretrial services program only to the extent funded by the Commonwealth through the general appropriation act. The Department of Criminal Justice Services shall periodically review each program established under this article to determine compliance with the submitted plan and operating standards. If the Department determines that a program is not in substantial compliance with the submitted plan or standards, the Department may suspend all or any portion of financial aid made available to the locality for purposes of this article until there is compliance.

CHAPTER 9.1
PROTECTIVE ORDERS FOR STALKING
(Added by L.1997 ch. 831, eff. 7/1/97.)

Section

§19.2-152.8. Emergency protective orders authorized in cases of stalking.

A. Any judge of a circuit court, general district court, juvenile and domestic relations district court or magistrate may issue a written or oral ex parte emergency protective order pursuant to this section in order to protect the health or safety of any person.

B. When a law-enforcement officer or an allegedly stalked person asserts under oath to a judge or magistrate that such person is being or has been subjected to stalking and on that assertion or other evidence the judge or magistrate finds that (i) there is probable danger of a further such offense being committed by the respondent against the allegedly stalked person, and (ii) a warrant for the arrest of the respondent has been issued, the judge or magistrate shall issue an ex parte emergency protective order imposing one or more of the following conditions on the respondent:

1. Prohibiting acts of stalking in violation of §18.2-60.3;
2. Prohibiting such contacts by the respondent with the allegedly stalked person or such person's family or household members as the judge or magistrate deems necessary to protect the safety of such persons; and
3. Such other conditions as the judge or magistrate deems necessary to prevent further acts of stalking, communication or other contact of any kind by the respondent.

C. An emergency protective order issued pursuant to this section shall expire seventy-two hours after issuance. If the expiration of the seventy-two-hour period occurs at a time that the court is not in session, the emergency protective order shall be extended until 5 p.m. of the next business day that the court which issued the order is in session. The respondent may at any time file a motion with the court requesting a hearing to dissolve or modify the order. The hearing on the motion shall be given precedence on the docket of the court.

D. A law-enforcement officer may request an emergency protective order pursuant to this section orally, in person or by electronic means, and the judge of a circuit court, general district court, or juvenile and domestic relations district court or a magistrate may issue an oral emergency protective order. An oral emergency protective order issued pursuant to this section shall be reduced to writing, by the law-enforcement officer requesting the order or the magistrate, on a preprinted form approved and provided by the Supreme Court of Virginia. The completed form shall include a statement of the grounds for the order asserted by the officer or the allegedly stalked person.

E. As soon as practicable after receipt of the order by a local law-enforcement agency for service, the agency shall enter the name of the person subject to the order and other appropriate information required by the Department of State Police into the Virginia criminal information network system established and maintained by the Department pursuant to Chapter 2 (§52-12 et seq.) of Title 52. A copy of an emergency protective order issued pursuant to this section shall be served upon the respondent as soon as possible, and upon service, the agency making service shall enter the date and time of service into the Virginia criminal information network system. One copy of the order shall be given to the allegedly stalked person. The original copy shall be verified by the judge or magistrate who issued the order and then filed with the clerk of the appropriate district court within five business days of the issuance of the order. If the order is later dissolved or modified, a copy of the dissolution or modification order shall also be attested, forwarded and entered in the system as described above. Upon request, the clerk shall provide the allegedly stalked person with information regarding the date and time of service.

F. The issuance of an emergency protective order shall not be considered evidence of any wrongdoing by the respondent.

G. As used in this section, a "law-enforcement officer" means any (i) person who is a full-time or part-time employee of a police department or sheriff's office which is part of or administered by the Commonwealth or any political subdivision thereof and who is responsible for the prevention and detection of crime and the enforcement of the penal, traffic or highway laws of the Commonwealth and (ii) member of an auxiliary police force established pursuant to subsection B of §15.2-1731. Part-time employees are compensated officers who are not full-time employees as defined by the employing police department or sheriff's office.

H. As used in this section, "copy" includes a facsimile copy.

I. No fee shall be charged for filing or serving any petition pursuant to this section.

(Added by L.1997 ch. 831; chgd. by L.1998 chs. 569, 684; L.1999 ch. 371, eff. 7/1/99.)

§19.2-152.9. Preliminary protective orders in cases of stalking.

A. Upon the filing of a petition alleging that (i) the petitioner is or has been, within a reasonable period of time, subjected to stalking and (ii) a warrant has been issued for the arrest of the alleged stalker, the court may issue a preliminary protective order against the alleged stalker in order to protect the health and safety of the petitioner or any family or household member of the petitioner. The order may be issued in an ex parte proceeding upon good cause shown when the petition is supported by an affidavit or sworn testimony before the judge or intake officer. Immediate and present danger of stalking or evidence sufficient to establish probable cause that stalking has recently occurred shall constitute good cause.

A preliminary protective order may include any one or more of the following conditions to be imposed on the respondent:

1. Prohibiting acts of stalking in violation of §18.2-60.3;
2. Prohibiting such other contacts by the respondent with the petitioner or the petitioner's family or household members as the court deems necessary for the health and safety of such persons; and
3. Such other conditions as the court deems necessary to prevent further acts of stalking, communication or other contact of any kind by the respondent.

B. As soon as practicable after receipt of the order by a local law-enforcement agency for service, the agency shall enter the name of the person subject to the order and other appropriate information required by the Department of State Police into the Virginia criminal information network system established and maintained by the Department pursuant to Chapter 2 (§52-12 et seq.) of Title 52. Where feasible and practical, the court may transfer information electronically to the Virginia criminal information network system. A copy of a preliminary protective order shall be served as soon as possible on the alleged stalker in person as provided in §16.1-264, and upon service, the agency making service shall enter the date and time of service into the Virginia criminal information network system. The preliminary order shall specify a date for the full hearing. The hearing shall be held within fifteen days of the issuance of the preliminary order. Upon request after the order is issued, the clerk shall provide the petitioner with a copy of the order and information regarding the date and time of service. The order shall further specify that either party may at any time file a motion with the court requesting a hearing to dissolve or modify the order. The hearing on the motion shall be given precedence on the docket of the court.

Upon receipt of the return of service or other proof of service pursuant to subsection C of §16.1-264, the clerk shall forward forthwith an attested copy of the preliminary protective order to the local police department or sheriff's office which shall, on the date of receipt, enter into the Virginia criminal information network system any other information required by the State Police which was not previously entered. If the order is later dissolved or modified, a copy of the dissolution or modification order shall also be attested, forwarded and entered into the Virginia criminal information network system as described above.

C. The preliminary order is effective upon personal service on the alleged stalker. Except as otherwise provided in §16.1-253.2, a violation of the order shall constitute contempt of court.

D. At a full hearing on the petition, the court may issue a protective order pursuant to §19.2-152.10 if the court finds that the petitioner has proven the allegation of stalking by a preponderance of the evidence.

E. No fees shall be charged for filing or serving petitions pursuant to this section.

F. As used in this section, "copy" includes a facsimile copy.

(Added by L.1997 ch. 831; chgd. by L.1998 chs. 569, 684; L.1999 ch. 371, eff. 7/1/99.)

§19.2-152.10. Protective order in cases of stalking.

A. The court may issue a protective order pursuant to this chapter to protect the health and safety of the petitioner and family or household members of a petitioner upon (i) the issuance of a warrant for a violation of §18.2-60.3, (ii) a hearing held pursuant to subsection D of §19.2-152.9, or (iii) a conviction for a violation of §18.2-60.3. A protective order issued under this section may include any one or more of the following conditions to be imposed on the respondent:

1. Prohibiting further acts of stalking in violation of §18.2-60.3;
2. Prohibiting such contacts by the respondent with the petitioner or family or household members of the petitioner as the court deems necessary for the health or safety of such persons;
3. Any other relief necessary to prevent further acts of stalking, communication or other contact of any kind by the respondent.

B. The protective order may be issued for a specified period; however, unless otherwise authorized by law, a protective order may not be issued under this section for a period longer than two years. A copy of the protective order shall be served on the respondent and provided to the petitioner as soon as possible. The clerk shall forward forthwith an attested copy of the order to the local police department or sheriff's office which shall, on the date of receipt, enter the name of the person subject to the order and other appropriate information required by the Department of State Police into the Virginia criminal information network system established and maintained by the Department pursuant to Chapter 2 (§52-12 et seq.) of Title 52. Where feasible and practical, the court may transfer information electronically to the Virginia criminal information network system. If the order is later dissolved or modified, a copy of the dissolution or modification order shall also be attested, forwarded and entered into the system as described above.

C. Except as otherwise provided, a violation of a protective order issued under this section shall constitute contempt of court.

D. The court may assess costs and attorneys' fees against either party regardless of whether an order of protection has been issued as a result of a full hearing.

E. Any judgment, order or decree, whether permanent or temporary, issued by a court of appropriate jurisdiction in another state, the United States or any of its territories, possessions or Commonwealths, the District of Columbia or by any tribal court of appropriate jurisdiction for the purpose of preventing violent or threatening acts or harassment against or contact or communication with or physical proximity to another person, including any of the conditions specified in subsection A, shall be accorded full faith and credit and enforced in the Commonwealth as if it were an order of the Commonwealth, provided reasonable notice and opportunity to be heard were given by the issuing jurisdiction to the person against whom the order is sought to be enforced sufficient to protect such person's due process rights and consistent with federal law. A person entitled to protection under such a foreign order may file the order in any appropriate district court by filing with the court, an attested or exemplified copy of the order. Upon such a filing, the clerk shall forward forthwith an attested copy of the order to the local police department or sheriff's office which shall, on the date of receipt, enter the name of the person subject to the order and other appropriate information required by the Department of State Police into the Virginia criminal information network system established and maintained by the Department pursuant to Chapter 2 (§52-12 et seq.) of Title 52.

Upon inquiry by any law-enforcement agency of the Commonwealth, the clerk shall make a copy available of any foreign order filed with that court. A law-enforcement officer may, in the performance of his duties, rely upon a copy of a foreign protective order or other suitable evidence which has been provided to him by any source and may also rely upon the statement of any person protected by the order that the order remains in effect.

F. Either party may at any time file a written motion with the court requesting a hearing to dissolve or modify the order. Proceedings to modify or dissolve a protective order shall be given precedence on the docket of the court.

G. No fees shall be charged for filing or serving petitions pursuant to this section.

H. As used in this section, "copy" includes a facsimile copy.

(Added by L.1997 ch. 831; chgd. by L.1998 chs. 569, 684; L.1999 ch. 371, eff. 7/1/99.)

CHAPTER 10
DISABILITY OF JUDGE OR ATTORNEY FOR COMMONWEALTH; COURT-APPOINTED COUNSEL; INTERPRETERS; TRANSCRIPTS

ARTICLE 1
DISABILITY OF JUDGE

§19.2-153. When judge cannot sit on trial; how another judge procured to try the case.

When the judge of a circuit court in which a prosecution is pending is connected with the accused or party injured, or is so situated in respect to the case as in his opinion to render it improper that he should preside at the trial, or if he has rejected a plea bargain agreement submitted by both parties and the parties do not agree that he may hear the case, he shall enter the fact of record and the clerk of the court shall at once certify this fact to the Chief Justice of the Supreme Court and thereupon another judge shall be appointed, in the manner prescribed by §17-7, to preside at the trial.

§19.2-154. Death or disability of judge during trial; how another judge procured to continue with trial.

If by reason of death, sickness or other disability the judge who presided at a criminal jury trial is unable to proceed with and finish the trial, another judge of that court or a judge designated by the Chief Justice of the Supreme Court or by a justice designated by him for that purpose, may proceed with and finish the trial or, in his discretion, may grant and preside at a new trial. If by reason of such disability, the judge who presided at any trial is unable to perform the duties to be performed by the court after a finding of guilty by the jury or the court, another judge of that court, or a judge designated as provided in the preceding sentence, may perform those duties or, in his discretion, may grant and preside at a new trial. Before proceeding with the trial or performing such duties, such judge shall certify that he has familiarized himself with the record of the trial.

ARTICLE 2
DISABILITY OF ATTORNEY FOR COMMONWEALTH

§19.2-155. Disqualification or temporary disability of attorney for Commonwealth; appointment of substitute; powers, duties and compensation of such appointee.

If the attorney for the Commonwealth of any county or city is connected by blood or marriage with the accused, or is so situated with respect to such accused as to render it improper, in his opinion, concurred in by the judge, for him to act, or if such attorney for the Commonwealth of any county or city is unable to act, or to attend to his official duties as attorney for the Commonwealth, due to sickness, disability or other reason of a temporary nature, then upon notification by such attorney for the Commonwealth, or upon the certificate of his attending physician, or the clerk of the court, which fact shall be entered of record, the judge of the circuit court shall appoint from another jurisdiction an attorney for the Commonwealth or an assistant attorney for the Commonwealth, with the consent of such attorney for the Commonwealth or assistant, who is not authorized by law to engage in private practice for such case or cases, term or terms of court, or period or periods of time, as may be necessary or desirable, and the same to be forthwith entered of record. However, if the circuit court determines that the appointment of such attorney for the Commonwealth or such assistant attorney for the Commonwealth is not appropriate or that such an attorney or assistant is unavailable, or for other good cause, then the circuit court may appoint an attorney-at-law who shall be compensated pursuant to §19.2-332. Such appointee shall act in place of, and otherwise perform the duties and exercise the powers of, such disqualified or disabled attorney for the Commonwealth, in regard to such case or cases, for the term or terms of the court, or the period or periods of time, for which the appointment and designation is made, or until the disqualified or disabled attorney for the Commonwealth shall again be able to attend to his duties as such. Nothing herein shall prevent a court from appointing as a special assistant attorney for the Commonwealth, without additional compensation, an attorney employed by a state agency when such appointment is requested by the attorney for the Commonwealth and the court determines such appointment will aid in the prosecution of a particular case or cases.

An attorney for the Commonwealth or assistant attorney for the Commonwealth who is required by law to devote full time to his duties as such shall not receive additional compensation for services rendered on appointment pursuant to this section. However, such attorney for the Commonwealth or assistant may receive reimbursement for actual expenses incurred, as approved by the Compensation Board to be paid by the Compensation Board, provided such expenses are not otherwise reimbursed by the county or city which he is elected or appointed to serve or by the Compensation Board.
(Chgd. by L.1996 ch. 968, eff. 7/1/96.)

§19.2-156. Prolonged absence of attorney for Commonwealth.

If it shall be necessary for the attorney for the Commonwealth of any county or city to absent himself for a prolonged period of time from the performance of the duties of his office, then, upon notification by such attorney for the Commonwealth, or by the court on its own motion, and the facts being entered of record, the judge of the circuit court shall appoint an attorney-at-law as acting attorney for the Commonwealth to serve for such length of time as may be necessary. Such acting attorney for the Commonwealth shall act in place of and otherwise perform the duties and exercise the powers of such regular attorney for the Commonwealth, and while so acting shall receive the salary and allowance for expenses fixed by the State Compensation Board for such regular attorney for the Commonwealth, who during such length of time shall not receive any such salary or allowance.

ARTICLE 3
APPOINTMENT OF ATTORNEY FOR ACCUSED

§19.2-157. Duty of court when accused appears without counsel.

Except as may otherwise be provided in §§16.1-266 through 16.1-268, whenever a person charged with a criminal offense the penalty for which may be death or confinement in the state correctional facility or jail, including charges for revocation of suspension of imposition or execution of sentence or probation, appears before any court without being represented by counsel, the court shall inform him of his right to counsel. The accused shall be allowed a reasonable opportunity to employ counsel or, if appropriate, the statement of indigence provided for in §19.2-159 may be executed.

§19.2-158. When person not free on bail shall be informed of right to counsel and amount of bail.

Every person charged with an offense described in §19.2-157, who is not free on bail or otherwise, shall be brought before the judge of a court not of record, unless the circuit court issues process commanding the presence of the person, in which case the person shall be brought before the circuit court, on the first day on which such court sits after the person is charged, at which time the judge shall inform the accused of the amount of his bail and his right to counsel. The court shall also hear and consider motions by the person or Commonwealth relating to bail or conditions of release pursuant to Article 1 (§19.2-119 et seq.) of Chapter 9 of this title. If the court not of record sits on a day prior to the scheduled sitting of the court which issued process, the person shall be brought before the court not of record.

No hearing on the charges against the accused shall be had until the foregoing conditions have been complied with, and the accused shall be allowed a reasonable opportunity to employ counsel of his own choice, or, if appropriate, the statement of indigence provided for in §19.2-159 may be executed.
(Chgd. by L.1998 ch. 773; L.1999 chs. 829, 846, eff. 7/1/99.)

§19.2-159. Determination of indigency; guidelines; statement of indigence; appointment of counsel.

If the accused shall claim that he is indigent, and the charge against him is a criminal offense which may be punishable by death or confinement in the state correctional facility or jail, subject to the provisions of §19.2-160, the court shall determine from oral examination of the accused or other competent evidence whether or not the accused is

 Zv

indigent within the contemplation of law pursuant to the guidelines set forth in this section.

In making its finding, the court shall determine whether or not the accused is a current recipient of a state or federally funded public assistance program for the indigent. If the accused is a current recipient of such a program and does not waive his right to counsel or retain counsel on his own behalf, he shall be presumed eligible for the appointment of counsel. This presumption shall be rebuttable where the court finds that a more thorough examination of the financial resources of the defendant is necessary. If the accused shall claim to be indigent and is not presumptively eligible under the provisions of this section, then a thorough examination of the financial resources of the accused shall be made with consideration given to the following:

1. The net income of the accused, which shall include his total salary and wages minus deductions required by law. The court also shall take into account income and amenities from other sources including but not limited to social security funds, union funds, veteran's benefits, other regular support from an absent family member, public or private employee pensions, dividends, interests, rents, estates, trusts, or gifts.

2. All assets of the accused which are convertible into cash within a reasonable period of time without causing substantial hardship or jeopardizing the ability of the accused to maintain home and employment. Assets shall include all cash on hand as well as in checking and savings accounts, stocks, bonds, certificates of deposit, and tax refunds. All personal property owned by the accused which is readily convertible into cash shall be considered, except property exempt from attachment. Any real estate owned by the accused shall be considered in terms of the amounts which could be raised by a loan on the property. For purposes of eligibility determination, the income, assets, and expenses of the spouse, if any, who is a member of the accused's household, shall be considered, unless the spouse was the victim of the offense or offenses allegedly committed by the accused.

3. Any exceptional expenses of the accused and his family which would, in all probability, prohibit him from being able to secure private counsel. Such items shall include but not be limited to costs for medical care, family support obligations, and child care payments.

The available funds of the accused shall be calculated as the sum of his total income and assets less the exceptional expenses as provided in paragraph 3 above. If the accused does not waive his right to counsel or retain counsel on his own behalf, counsel shall be appointed for the accused if his available funds are equal to or below 125% of the federal poverty income guidelines prescribed for the size of the household of the accused by the federal Department of Health and Human Services. The Supreme Court of Virginia shall be responsible for distributing to all courts the annual updates of the federal poverty income guidelines made by the Department.

If the available funds of the accused exceed 125% of the federal poverty income guidelines and the accused fails to employ counsel and does not waive his right to counsel, the court may, in exceptional circumstances, and where the ends of justice so require, appoint an attorney to represent the accused. However, in making such appointments, the court shall state in writing its reasons for so doing. The written statement by the court shall be included in the permanent record of the case.

If the court determines that the accused is indigent as contemplated by law pursuant to the guidelines set forth in this section, the court shall provide the accused with a statement which shall contain the following:

"I have been advised this.... day of........, 19.., by the (name of court) court of my right to representation by counsel in the trial of the charge pending against me; I certify that I am without means to employ counsel and I hereby request the court to appoint counsel for me."

....
(signature of accused)

The court shall also require the accused to complete a written financial statement to support the claim of indigency and to permit the court to determine whether or not the accused is indigent within the contemplation of law. The accused shall execute the said statements under oath, and the said court shall appoint competent counsel to represent the accused in the proceeding against him, including an appeal, if any, until relieved or replaced by other counsel.

The executed statements by the accused and the order of appointment of counsel shall be filed with and become a part of the record of such proceeding.

All other instances in which the appointment of counsel is required for an indigent shall be made in accordance with the guidelines prescribed in this section.

Except in jurisdictions having a public defender pursuant to Article 4 (§19.2-163.1 et seq.) of Chapter 10 of Title 19.2, counsel appointed by the court for representation of the accused shall be selected by a fair system of rotation among members of the bar practicing before the court whose practice regularly includes representation of persons accused of crimes and who have indicated their willingness to accept such appointments.

§19.2-159.1. Interrogation by court; filing; change in circumstances; investigation by attorney for Commonwealth.

A. The court shall thoroughly interrogate any person making the statement of indigency required in §19.2-159 and shall further advise such person of the penalty which might result from false swearing, as provided in §19.2-161.

B. The statement and oath of the defendant shall be filed with the papers in the case, and shall follow and be in effect at all stages of the proceedings against him without further oath. In the event the defendant undergoes a change of circumstances so that he is no longer indigent, the defendant shall thereupon obtain private counsel and shall forthwith advise the court of the change of circumstances. The court shall grant reasonable continuance to allow counsel to be obtained and to prepare for trial. When private counsel has been retained, appointed counsel shall forthwith be relieved of further responsibility and compensated for his services, pro rata, pursuant to §19.2-163.

C. Upon the request of the court, it shall be the duty of the attorney for the Commonwealth of the county or city in which such statement and oath was made to make an investigation as to the indigency of the defendant, or of any other person making such statement. The attorney for the Commonwealth is authorized to delegate the responsibility for such investigation to any subordinate in his office, or to any agency, state or local, which possesses the facilities to quickly make such investigation. Such investigation shall be reduced to writing and forwarded to the court in which the statement and oath was made within fourteen days after such request by the court is made. Such report shall be placed with the papers in the case.

§19.2-160. Appointment of counsel or waiver of right.

If the charge against the accused is a crime the penalty for which may be incarceration, and the accused is not represented by counsel, the court shall ascertain by oral examination of the accused whether or not the accused desires to waive his right to counsel.

In the event the accused desires to waive his right to counsel, and the court ascertains that such waiver is voluntary and intelligently made, then the court shall provide the accused with a statement to be executed by the accused to document his waiver. The statement shall be in a form designed and provided by the Supreme Court. Any executed statement herein provided for shall be filed with and become a part of the record of such proceeding.

In the absence of a waiver of counsel by the accused, and if he shall claim that he is indigent, the court shall proceed in the same manner as is provided in §19.2-159.

Should the defendant refuse or otherwise fail to sign either of the statements described in this section and §19.2-159, the court shall note such refusal on the record. Such refusal shall be deemed to be a waiver of the right to counsel, and the court, after so advising the accused and offering him the opportunity to rescind his refusal shall, if such refusal is not rescinded and the accused's signature given, proceed to hear and decide the case. However, if, prior to the commencement of the trial, the court states in writing, either upon the request of the attorney for the Commonwealth or, in the absence of the attorney for the Commonwealth, upon the court's own motion, that a sentence of incarceration will not be imposed if the defendant is convicted, the court may try the case without appointing counsel, and in such event no sentence of incarceration shall be imposed.

§19.2-161. Penalty for false swearing with regard to statement of indigence.

Any person charged with a felony who shall falsely swear or who shall execute the statement provided for in §19.2-159 knowing such statement to be false, shall be guilty of perjury, punishable as a Class 5 felony.

Any person charged with a misdemeanor punishable by confinement in jail who shall falsely swear or who shall execute the statement provided for in §19.2-159 knowing such statement to be false shall be guilty of a Class 1 misdemeanor.

§19.2-162. Continuances to be granted if necessary.

Courts before which criminal proceedings are pending shall afford such continuances and take such other action as is necessary to comply with the provisions of this chapter.

§19.2-163. Compensation of court-appointed counsel.

Counsel appointed to represent an indigent accused in a criminal case shall be compensated for his services in an amount fixed by each of the courts in which he appears according to the time and effort expended by him in the particular case, not to exceed the amounts specified in the following schedule:

1. In a district court, a sum not to exceed [$100] *$120* or such other amount as may be provided by law; such amount shall be allowed in any case wherein counsel conducts the defense of a single charge against the indigent through to its conclusion or a charge of violation of probation at any hearing conducted under §19.2-306, without a requirement for accounting of time devoted thereto; thereafter, compensation for additional charges against the same accused also conducted by the same counsel shall be allowed on the basis of additional time expended as to such additional charges;

2. In a circuit court (i) to defend a felony charge that may be punishable by death an amount deemed reasonable by the court; (ii) to defend a felony charge that may be punishable by confinement in the state correctional facility for a period of more than twenty years, or a charge of violation of probation for such offense, a sum not to exceed [$845 beginning July 1, 1998, and $882 beginning July 1, 1999, and thereafter] *$1,235*; (iii) to defend any other felony charge, or a charge of violation of probation for such offense, a sum not to exceed [$305 beginning July 1, 1998, and $318 beginning July 1, 1999, and thereafter] *$445*; and (iv) to defend any misdemeanor charge punishable by confinement in jail or a charge of violation of probation for such offense, a sum not to exceed [$132] *$158*. In the event any case is required to be retried due to a mistrial for any cause or reversed on appeal, the court may allow an additional fee for each case in an amount not to exceed the amounts allowable in the initial trial. In the event counsel is appointed to defend an indigent charged with a felony that may be punishable by death, such counsel shall continue to receive compensation as provided in this paragraph for defending such a felony, regardless of whether the charge is reduced or amended to a felony that may not be punishable by death, prior to final disposition of the case.

The circuit or district court shall direct the payment of such reasonable expenses incurred by such court-appointed attorney as it deems appropriate under the circumstances of the case. Counsel appointed by the court to represent an indigent charged with repeated violations of the same section of the Code of Virginia, with each of such violations arising out of the same incident, occurrence, or transaction, shall be compensated in an amount not to exceed the fee prescribed for the defense of a single charge, if such offenses are tried as part of the same judicial proceeding. The trial judge shall consider any guidelines established by the Supreme Court but shall have the sole discretion to fix the amount of compensation to be paid counsel appointed by the court to defend a felony charge that may be punishable by death.

The circuit or district court shall direct that the foregoing payments shall be paid out by the Commonwealth, if the defendant is charged with a violation of a statute, or by the county, city or town, if the defendant is charged with a violation of a county, city or town ordinance, to the attorney so appointed to defend such person as compensation for such defense.

Counsel representing a defendant charged with a Class 1 felony may submit to the court, on a monthly basis, a statement of all costs incurred and fees charged by him in the case during that month. Whenever the total charges as are deemed reasonable by the court for which payment has not previously been made or requested exceed $1,000, the court may direct that payment be made as otherwise provided in this section.

When such directive is entered upon the order book of the court, the Commonwealth, county, city or town, as the case may be, shall provide for the payment out of its treasury of the sum of money so specified. If the defendant is convicted, the amount allowed by the court to the attorney appointed to defend him shall be taxed against the defendant as a part of the costs of prosecution and, if collected, the same shall be paid to the Commonwealth, or the county, city or town, as the case may be. An abstract of such costs shall be docketed in the judgment docket and execution lien book maintained by such court.

Any statement submitted by an attorney for payments due him for indigent representation or for representation of a child pursuant to §16.1-266 shall, after the submission of the statement, be forwarded forthwith by the clerk to the Commonwealth, county, city or town, as the case may be, responsible for payment.

For the purposes of this section, the defense of a case may be considered conducted through to its conclusion and an appointed counsel entitled to compensation for his services in the event an indigent accused fails to appear in court subject to a capias for his arrest or a show cause summons for his failure to appear and remains a fugitive from justice for one year following the issuance of the capias or the summons to show cause, and appointed counsel has appeared at a hearing on behalf of the accused.

(Chgd. by L.1995 chs. 571, 713; L.1997 ch. 492; L.1998 chs. 440, 451; L.2000 chs. 436, 448, eff. pending funding by the 2000 Session of the General Assembly. Matter in italics eff. only if funded; otherwise matter in brackets continues in effect.)

ARTICLE 4
PUBLIC DEFENDERS

§19.2-163.1. Public Defender Commission to be appointed; membership; expenses.

There is hereby created a Public Defender Commission, which shall be composed of nine citizens and residents of this Commonwealth. Members of the Commission shall be appointed by the Speaker of the House of Delegates in consultation with the chairmen of the Courts of Justice Committees of the House of Delegates and the Senate. Members shall be appointed for staggered terms of three years, with the term of one judicial appointment, one lawyer appointment, and one public appointment expiring each year, except that the terms of the nine members initially appointed shall be in equal numbers of one-year, two-year, and three-year terms. The Commission shall annually elect one of its members chairman. The Commission shall consist of two members who are judges of courts of record, one of whom may be retired or inactive, one member who is an active general district court judge, three members who are active members of the Virginia State Bar and have practiced law in the Commonwealth for ten or more years immediately preceding their appointment and three public members who shall not be active or retired judges and shall never have been licensed lawyers. Members of this Commission shall receive compensation for their services pursuant to §2.1-20.3 and shall be paid their reasonable and necessary expenses incurred in the performance of their duties.

§19.2-163.2. Commission to appoint public defenders in selected locations; compensation, assistants, offices, etc., of public defenders.

The duties of the Public Defender Commission, hereinafter referred to as "the Commission," are:

1. To recommend to the General Assembly the areas in which a public defender office is to be established, and to establish such an office in:

a. the City of Virginia Beach;

b. the City of Petersburg;

c. the Cities of Buena Vista, Lexington, Staunton and Waynesboro and the Counties of Augusta and Rockbridge;

d. the City of Roanoke;

e. the City of Portsmouth;

f. the City of Richmond;

g. the Counties of Clarke, Frederick, Page, Shenandoah and Warren, and the City of Winchester;

h. the City and County of Fairfax;

i. the City of Alexandria;

j. the City of Radford and the Counties of Bland, Pulaski and Wythe;

k. the Counties of Fauquier, Loudoun and Rappahannock;

l. the City of Suffolk;

m. the City of Franklin and the Counties of Isle of Wight and Southampton;

n. the City of Bedford and the County of Bedford;

o. the City of Danville;

p. the Counties of Halifax, Lunenburg and Mecklenburg;

q. the city of Fredericksburg and the Counties of King George, Stafford and Spotsylvania;

r. the City of Lynchburg;

s. the City of Martinsville and the Counties of Henry and Patrick; and

t. the City of Charlottesville and the County of Albemarle.

2. To appoint a public defender for each of the above offices to serve at the pleasure of the Commission, who shall devote his full time to his duties and not engage in the private practice of law. The Commission shall fix the compensation of each public defender and all other personnel in each public defender office.

3. To authorize the public defender to employ such assistants as authorized by the Commission. Such assistants shall devote such time to the performance of their duties as may be required by the public defender or the Commission and may engage in the private practice of law.

4. To authorize the public defender to employ such staff, including secretarial and investigative personnel, as may be necessary to carry out the duties imposed upon the public defender office.

5. To authorize the public defender to secure such office space as needed, to purchase or rent office equipment, to purchase supplies and to incur such expenses as are necessary to carry out the duties imposed upon him.

6. To receive and expend moneys appropriated by the General Assembly of Virginia and to receive other moneys as they become available to it and expend the same in order to carry out the duties imposed upon it.

7. In any case in which a public defender or his assistant represents an indigent person charged with an offense and such person is convicted, such sum as would have been allowed a court-appointed attorney as compensation and as reasonable expenses shall be taxed against the person defended as a part of the costs of the prosecution, and, if collected, shall be paid to the Commonwealth or to the appropriate county, city or town if payment was made to the Commonwealth by a locality for defense of a local ordinance violation. An abstract of such costs shall be docketed in the judgment lien docket and execution book of the court.

(Chgd. by L.1998 chs. 519, 526, 530, eff. 7/1/98.)

§19.2-163.3. Duties of public defenders and assistants.

Public defenders and their assistants shall carry out the following duties:

(a) To secure office space, to employ a staff, to fix salaries and to do such other things necessary to carry out the duties imposed upon them with the approval of the Commission.

(b) To represent within their respective jurisdictions as set out in §19.2-163.2 indigent persons charged with a crime or offense when such persons are entitled to be represented by law by court-appointed counsel in a court of record or a court not of record.

(c) To represent indigent persons who are entitled to be represented by court-appointed counsel in an appeal of their conviction to the Court of Appeals or the Supreme Court of Virginia.

(d) To represent indigent prisoners when a habeas corpus proceeding is brought by such prisoners.

(e) To submit such reports as required by the Commission.

§19.2-163.4. Inapplicability of §§14.1-183 and 19.2-163 where public defender offices established; exception.

In counties and cities in which public defender offices are established pursuant to §19.2-163.2, defense services for indigents charged with jailable offenses shall be provided by the public defenders unless (i) the public defender is unable to represent the defendant or petitioner by reason of conflict of interest or (ii) the court finds that appointment of other counsel is necessary to attain the ends of justice. Except for the provisions of §19.2-163 relating to reasonable expenses, §§14.1-183 and 19.2-163 shall not apply when defense services are provided by the public defenders.

§19.2-163.5. Legal services to public defenders and/or assistant public defenders.

At the request of a public defender, the Attorney General shall provide legal services to such attorney, his assistants, or members of his staff in any proceeding brought against him, his assistants, or staff for money damages, when the cause of action allegedly arises out of the duties of his office.

Any costs chargeable against the defendant or defendants in any such case shall be paid by the Commonwealth from the appropriation for the payment of criminal charges.

§19.2-163.6. Executive director, consultants and other personnel.

The Commission shall be authorized to appoint and employ and, at pleasure, remove, an executive director, counsel, and such other persons as it may deem necessary; and to determine their duties and fix their salaries or compensation within the amounts appropriated therefor.

ARTICLE 4.1
COUNSEL IN CAPITAL CASES

§19.2-163.7. Counsel in capital cases.

In any case in which an indigent defendant is charged with a capital offense, the judge of the circuit court, upon request for the appointment of counsel, shall appoint one or more attorneys from the list or lists established by the Public Defender Commission pursuant to §19.2-163.8 to represent the defendant at trial and, if the defendant is sentenced to death, on appeal. If the sentence of death is affirmed on appeal, the court shall, within thirty days after the decision of the Supreme Court of Virginia, appoint counsel from the same list, or such other list as the Commissioner may establish, to represent an indigent prisoner under sentence of death in a state habeas corpus proceeding. The Attorney General shall have no standing to object to the appointment of counsel for the petition.
(Chgd. by L.1995 ch. 503, eff. 7/1/95.)

§19.2-163.8. List of qualified attorneys.

A. The Public Defender Commission, in conjunction with the Virginia State Bar, shall adopt standards for the appointment of counsel in capital cases, which take into consideration, to the extent practicable, the following criteria: (i) license or permission to practice law in Virginia; (ii) general background in criminal litigation; (iii) demonstrated experience in felony practice at trial and appeal; (iv) experience in death penalty litigation; (v) familiarity with the requisite court system; (vi) current training in death penalty litigation; and (vii) demonstrated proficiency and commitment to quality representation.

B. The Public Defender Commission shall maintain a list or lists of attorneys admitted to practice law in Virginia who are qualified to represent indigent defendants charged with capital murder or sentenced to death. In establishing such a list or lists, the Commission shall consider all relevant factors, including but not limited to, the attorney's background, experience, and training and the Commission's assessment of whether the attorney is competent to provide quality legal representation.

C. Notwithstanding the requirements of §19.2-163.7, the judge of the circuit court may appoint counsel who is not included on the list or lists, but who otherwise qualifies under the standards established and maintained by the Commission.

D. Noncompliance with the requirements of this article shall not form the basis of a claim of error at trial, on appeal, or in any habeas corpus proceeding. The performance of habeas corpus counsel appointed pursuant to this article shall not form a basis for relief in any subsequent habeas corpus proceeding.

E. By July 1, 1992, the Public Defender Commission shall, in conjunction with the Virginia State Bar, promulgate and thereafter maintain standards for the qualifications of counsel who shall be considered eligible to be placed on a list for appointment.

F. The provisions of this article, with the exception of subsection (E), shall not become effective until July 1, 1992.

ARTICLE 5
INTERPRETERS

§19.2-164. Interpreters for non-English-speaking persons.

In any criminal case in which a non-English-speaking person is the accused, an interpreter for the non-English-speaking person shall be appointed. In any criminal case in which a non-English-speaking person is a victim or witness, an interpreter shall be appointed by the judge of the court in which the case is to be heard unless the court finds that the person does not require the services of a court-appointed interpreter. An English-speaking person fluent in the language of the country of the accused, a victim or a witness shall be appointed by the judge of the court in which the case is to be heard, unless such person obtains an interpreter of his own choosing who is approved by the court as being competent. The compensation of an interpreter appointed by the court pursuant to this section shall be fixed by the court and shall be paid from the general fund of the state treasury as part of the expense of trial. Such fee shall not be assessed as part of the costs. Whenever a person communicates through an interpreter to any person under such circumstances that the communication would be privileged, and such person could not be compelled to testify as to the communications, this privilege shall also apply to the interpreter. The provisions of this section shall apply in both circuit courts and district courts.
(Chgd. by L.1995 ch. 546; L.1996 ch. 402, eff. 7/1/96.)

§19.2-164.1. Interpreters for the deaf.

In any criminal case in which a deaf person is the accused, an interpreter for the deaf person shall be appointed. In any criminal case in which a deaf person is the victim or a witness, an interpreter for the deaf person shall be appointed by the court in which the case is to be heard unless the court finds that the deaf person does not require the services of a court-appointed interpreter and the deaf person waives his rights. Such interpreter shall be procured by the judge of the court in which the case is to be heard through the Department for the Deaf and Hard-of-Hearing.

The compensation of an interpreter appointed by the court pursuant to this section shall be fixed by the court and paid from the general fund of the state treasury as part of the expense of trial. Such fee shall not be assessed as part of the costs.

Any person entitled to the services of an interpreter under this section may waive these services for all or a portion of the proceedings. Such a waiver shall be made by the person upon the record after an opportunity to consult with legal counsel. A judicial officer, utilizing an interpreter obtained in accordance with this section, shall explain to the deaf person the nature and effect of any waiver. Any waiver shall be approved in writing by the deaf person's legal counsel. If the person does not have legal counsel, approval shall be made in writing by a judicial officer. A person who waives his right to an interpreter may provide his own interpreter at his own expense without regard to whether the interpreter is qualified under this section.

The provisions of this section shall apply in both circuit courts and district courts.

Whenever a person communicates through an interpreter to any person under such circumstances that the communication would be privileged, and such person could not be compelled to testify as to the communications, this privilege shall also apply to the interpreter.

In any judicial proceeding, the judge on his own motion or on the motion of a party to the proceeding may order all of the testimony of a deaf person and the interpretation thereof to be visually electronically recorded for use in verification of the official transcript of the proceedings.

(Chgd. by L.1995 ch. 546; L.1996 ch. 402, eff. 7/1/96.)

ARTICLE 6
RECORDING EVIDENCE AND INCIDENTS OF TRIAL

§19.2-165. Recording evidence and incidents of trial in felony cases; cost of recording; cost of transcripts; certified transcript deemed prima facie correct; request for copy of transcript.

In all felony cases, the court or judge trying the case shall by order entered of record provide for the recording verbatim of the evidence and incidents of trial either by a court reporter or by mechanical or electronic devices approved by the court. The expense of reporting or recording the trial of criminal cases shall be paid by the Commonwealth out of the appropriation for criminal charges, upon approval of the trial judge. However, if the defendant is convicted, the Commonwealth shall be entitled to receive the amount allocated to the court reporter fund under the fixed felony fee. Localities that maintain mechanical or electronic devices for this purpose shall be entitled to retain their reasonable expenses attributable to the cost of operating and maintaining such equipment.

In all felony cases where it appears to the court from the affidavit of the defendant and other evidence that the defendant intends to seek an appeal and is financially unable to pay such costs or to bear the expense of a copy of the transcript of the evidence for an appeal, the trial court shall, upon the motion of counsel for the defendant, order the evidence transcribed for such appeal and all costs therefor paid by the Commonwealth out of the appropriation for criminal charges. If the conviction is not reversed, all costs paid by the Commonwealth, under the provisions hereof, shall be assessed against the defendant.

The reporter or other individual designated to report and record the trial shall file the original shorthand notes or other original records with the clerk of the circuit court who shall preserve them in the public records of the court for not less than five years if an appeal was taken and a transcript was prepared, or ten years if no appeal was taken. The transcript in any case certified by the reporter or other individual designated to report and record the trial shall be deemed prima facie a correct statement of the evidence and incidents of trial.

Upon the request of any counsel of record, or of any party not represented by counsel, and upon payment of the reasonable cost thereof, the court reporter covering any proceeding shall provide the requesting party with a copy of the transcript of such proceeding or any requested portion thereof.

The court shall not direct the court reporter to cease recording any portion of the proceeding without the consent of all parties or of their counsel of record.

The administration of this section shall be under the direction of the Supreme Court of Virginia.

(Chgd. by L.1999 ch. 9, eff. 7/1/99.)

§19.2-165.1. Payment of medical fees in certain criminal cases.

All medical fees involved in the gathering of evidence for all criminal cases where medical evidence is necessary to establish a crime has occurred and for cases involving abuse of children under the age of eighteen shall be paid by the Commonwealth out of the appropriation for criminal charges, provided that any medical evaluation, examination, or service rendered be performed by a physician or facility specifically designated by the attorney for the Commonwealth in the city or county having jurisdiction of such case for such a purpose. If no such physician or facility is reasonably available in such city or county, then the attorney for the Commonwealth may designate a physician or facility located outside and adjacent to such city or county.

Where there has been no prior designation of such a physician or facility, medical fees shall be paid out of the appropriation for criminal charges upon authorization by the attorney for the Commonwealth of the city or county having jurisdiction over the case. Such authorization may be granted prior to or within forty-eight hours after the medical evaluation, examination, or service rendered.

(Chgd. by L.1997 ch. 322; L.1999 ch. 853; L.2000 ch. 292, eff. 7/1/2000.)

§19.2-166. Court reporters.

Each judge of a court of record having jurisdiction over criminal proceedings shall be authorized, in all felony cases, to appoint a court reporter to report proceedings or to operate mechanical or electrical devices for recording proceedings, to transcribe the report or record of such proceedings, to perform any stenographic work related to such report, record or transcript, and to perform stenographic work relating to habeas corpus proceedings within such court's jurisdiction, including work pertinent to the court's findings of fact and conclusions of law pertinent thereto. Such reporter shall be paid by the Commonwealth on a per diem or work basis as appropriate out of the appropriation for criminal charges.

CHAPTER 11 PROCEEDINGS ON QUESTION OF INSANITY

Section

§19.2-167. Accused not to be tried while insane or feebleminded.

No person shall, while he is insane or feebleminded, be tried for a criminal offense.

§19.2-168. Notice to Commonwealth of intention to present evidence of insanity; continuance if notice not given.

In any case in which a person charged with a crime intends (i) to put in issue his sanity at the time of the crime charged and (ii) to present testimony of an expert to support his claim on this issue at his trial, he, or his counsel, shall give notice in writing to the attorney for the Commonwealth, at least twenty-one days prior to his trial, of his intention to present such evidence. In the event that such notice is not given, and the person proffers such evidence at his trial as a defense, then the court may in its discretion, either allow the Commonwealth a continuance or, under appropriate circumstances, bar the defendant from presenting such evidence. The period of any such continuance shall not be counted for speedy trial purposes under §19.2-243.

§19.2-168.1. Evaluation on motion of the Commonwealth after notice.

A. If the attorney for the defendant gives notice pursuant to §19.2-168, and the Commonwealth thereafter seeks an evaluation of the defendant's sanity at the time of the offense, the court shall appoint one or more qualified mental health experts to perform such an evaluation. The court shall order the defendant to submit to such an evaluation and advise the defendant on the record in court that a refusal to cooperate with the Commonwealth's expert could result in exclusion of the defendant's expert evidence. The qualification of the experts shall be governed by §19.2-169.5 A. The location of the evaluation shall be governed by §19.2-169.5 B. The attorney for the Commonwealth shall be responsible for providing the experts the information specified in §19.2-169.5 C. After performing their evaluation, the experts shall report their findings and opinions, and provide copies of psychiatric, psychological, medical or other records obtained during the course of the evaluation to the attorneys for the Commonwealth and the defense.

B. If the court finds, after hearing evidence presented by the parties, that the defendant has refused to cooperate with an evaluation requested by the Commonwealth, it may admit evidence of such refusal or, in the discretion of the court, bar the defendant from presenting expert psychiatric or psychological evidence at trial on the issue of his sanity at the time of the offense.

§19.2-169.1. Raising question of competency to stand trial or plead; evaluation and determination of competency.

A. Raising competency issue; appointment of evaluators. If, at any time after the attorney for the defendant has been retained or appointed and before the end of trial, the court finds, upon hearing evidence or representations of counsel for the defendant or the attorney for the Commonwealth, that there is probable cause to believe that the defendant lacks substantial capacity to understand the proceedings against him or to assist his attorney in his own defense, the court shall order that a competency evaluation be performed by at least one psychiatrist, clinical psychologist or master's level psychologist who is qualified by training and experience in forensic evaluation.

B. Location of evaluation. The evaluation shall be performed on an outpatient basis at a mental health facility or in jail unless the court specifically finds that outpatient evaluation services are unavailable or unless the results of outpatient evaluation indicate that hospitalization of the defendant for evaluation on competency is necessary. If either finding is made, the court, under authority of this subsection, may order the defendant sent to a hospital designated by the Commissioner of Mental Health, Mental Retardation and Substance Abuse Services as appropriate for evaluations of persons under criminal charge. The defendant shall be hospitalized for such time as the director of the hospital deems necessary to perform an adequate evaluation of the defendant's competency, but not to exceed thirty days from the date of admission to the hospital.

C. Provision of information to evaluators. The court shall require the attorney for the Commonwealth to provide to the evaluators appointed under subsection A any information relevant to the evaluation, including, but not limited to (i) a copy of the warrant or indictment; (ii) the names and addresses of the attorney for the Commonwealth, the attorney for the defendant, and the judge ordering the evaluation; (iii) information about the alleged crime; and (iv) a summary of the reasons for the evaluation request. The court shall require the attorney for the defendant to provide any available psychiatric records and other information that is deemed relevant.

D. The competency report. Upon completion of the evaluation, the evaluators shall promptly submit a report in writing to the court and the attorneys of record concerning (i) the defendant's capacity to understand the proceedings against him; (ii) his ability to assist his attorney; and (iii) his need for treatment in the event he is found incompetent. No statements of the defendant relating to the time period of the alleged offense shall be included in the report.

E. The competency determination. After receiving the report described in subsection D, the court shall promptly determine whether the defendant is competent to stand trial. A hearing on the defendant's competency is not required unless one is requested by the attorney for the Commonwealth or the attorney for the defendant, or unless the court has reasonable cause to believe the defendant will be hospitalized under §19.2-169.2. If a hearing is held, the party alleging that the defendant is incompetent shall bear the burden of proving by a preponderance of the evidence the defendant's incompetency. The defendant shall have the right to notice of the hearing, the right to counsel at the hearing and the right to personally participate in and introduce evidence at the hearing.

The fact that the defendant claims to be unable to remember the time period surrounding the alleged offense shall not, by itself, bar a finding of competency if the defendant otherwise understands the charges against him and can assist in his defense. Nor shall the fact that the defendant is under the influence of medication bar a finding of competency if the defendant is able to understand the charges against him and assist in his defense while medicated.

§19.2-169.2. Disposition when defendant found incompetent.

A. Upon finding pursuant to §19.2-169.1 E that the defendant is incompetent the court shall order that the defendant receive treatment to restore his competency on an outpatient basis or, if the court specifically finds that the defendant requires inpatient hospital treatment, at a hospital designated by the Commissioner of Mental Health, Mental Retardation and Substance Abuse Services as appropriate for treatment of persons under criminal charge. Any reports submitted pursuant to §19.2-169.1 D shall be made available to the director of the treating facility.

B. If, at any time after the defendant is ordered to undergo treatment under paragraph A of this section, the director of the treatment facility believes the defendant's competency is restored, the director shall immediately send a report to the court as prescribed in §19.2-169.1 D. The court shall make a ruling on the defendant's competency according to the procedures specified in §19.2-169.1 E.

§19.2-169.3. Disposition of the unrestorably incompetent defendant.

A. If, at any time after the defendant is ordered to undergo treatment pursuant to subsection A of §19.2-169.2, the director of the treating facility concludes that the defendant is likely to remain incompetent for the foreseeable future, he shall send a report to the court so stating. The report shall also indicate whether, in the director's opinion, the defendant should be released, *committed pursuant to §37.1-67.3,* committed pursuant to §37.1-70.9, or certified pursuant to §37.1-65.1 in the event he is found to be unrestorably incompetent. Upon receipt of the report, the court shall make a competency determination according to the procedures specified in subsection E of §19.2-169.1. If the court finds that the defendant is incompetent and is likely to remain so for the foreseeable future, it shall order that he be (i) released, (ii) committed pursuant to §37.1-67.3, *(iii) reviewed for commitment pursuant to §37.1-70.6,* or [(iii)] *(iv)* certified pursuant to §37.1-65.1. If the court finds the defendant incompetent but restorable to competency in the foreseeable future, it may order treatment continued until six months have elapsed from the date of the defendant's initial admission under subsection A of §19.2-169.2.

B. At the end of six months from the date of the defendant's initial admission under subsection A of §19.2-169.2 if the defendant remains incompetent in the opinion of the director, the director shall so notify the court and make recommendations concerning disposition of the defendant as described above. The court shall hold a hearing according to the procedures specified in subsection E of §19.2-169.1 and, if it finds the defendant unrestorably incompetent, shall order one of the dispositions described above. If the court finds the defendant incompetent but restorable to competency, it may order continued treatment under subsection A of §19.2-169.2 for additional six-month periods, provided a hearing pursuant to subsection E of §19.2-169.1 is held at the completion of each such period and the defendant continues to be incompetent but restorable to competency in the foreseeable future.

C. If not dismissed without prejudice at an earlier time, charges against an [unrestorable] *unrestorably* incompetent defendant shall be dismissed on the date upon which his sentence would have expired had he been convicted and received the maximum sentence for the crime charged, or on the date five years from the date of his arrest for such charges, whichever is sooner.

D. If the court orders an unrestorably incompetent defendant to be reviewed for commitment pursuant to §37.1-70.6, it shall order the attorney for the Commonwealth in the jurisdiction wherein the defendant was charged and the Commissioner of the Department of Mental Health, Mental Retardation and Substance Abuse Services to provide the Attorney General with any information relevant to the review, including, but not limited to: (i) a copy of the warrant or indictment, (ii) a copy of the defendant's criminal record, (iii) information about the alleged crime, (iv) a copy of the competency report completed pursuant to §19.2-169.1, and (v) a copy of the report prepared by the director of the defendant's treating facility pursuant to this section. The court shall further order that the defendant be held in the custody of the Department of Mental Health, Mental Retardation and Substance Abuse Services for secure confinement and treatment until the Attorney General's review and any subsequent hearing or trial are completed. If the court receives notice that the Attorney General has declined to file a petition for the commitment of an unrestorably incompetent defendant as a sexually violent predator after conducting a review pursuant to §37.1-70.6, the court shall order that the defendant be released, committed pursuant to §37.1-67.3, or certified pursuant to §37.1-65.1.

(Chgd. by L.1999 chs. 946, 985, eff. 7/1/2001 as chgd. by L.2000 ch. 1024, eff. 7/1/2000. Matter in brackets eff. only until 7/1/2001. Matter in italics eff. 7/1/2001.)

§19.2-169.4. Litigating certain issues when the defendant is incompetent.

A finding of incompetency does not preclude the adjudication, at any time before trial, of a motion objecting to the sufficiency of the indictment, nor does it preclude the adjudication of similar legal objections which, in the court's opinion, may be undertaken without the personal participation of the defendant.

§19.2-169.5. Evaluation of sanity at the time of the offense; disclosure of evaluation results.

A. Raising issue of sanity at the time of offense; appointment of evaluators. If, at any time before trial, the court finds, upon hearing evidence or representations of counsel for the defendant, that there is probable cause to believe that the defendant's sanity will be a significant factor in his defense and that the defendant is financially unable to pay for expert assistance, the court shall appoint one or more qualified mental health experts to evaluate the defendant's sanity at the time of the offense and, where appropriate, to assist in the development of an insanity defense. Such mental health expert shall be (i) a psychiatrist, a clinical psychologist, or an individual with a doctorate degree in clinical psychology who has successfully completed forensic evaluation training as approved by the Commissioner of Mental Health, Mental Retardation and Substance Abuse Services and (ii) qualified by specialized training and experience to perform forensic evaluations. The defendant shall not be entitled to a mental health expert of his own choosing or to funds to employ such expert.

B. Location of evaluation. The evaluation shall be performed on an outpatient basis, at a mental health facility or in jail, unless the court specifically finds that outpatient services are unavailable, or unless the results of the outpatient evaluation indicate that hospitalization of the defendant for further evaluation of his sanity at the time of the offense is necessary. If either finding is made, the court, under authority of this subsection, may order that the defendant be sent to a hospital designated by the Commissioner of Mental Health, Mental Retardation and Substance Abuse Services as appropriate for evaluation of the defendant under criminal charge. The defendant shall be hospitalized for such time as the director of the hospital deems necessary to perform an adequate evaluation of the defendant's sanity at the time of the offense, but not to exceed thirty days from the date of admission to the hospital.

C. Provision of information to evaluators. The court shall require the party making the motion for the evaluation, and such other parties as the court deems appropriate, to provide to the evaluators appointed under subsection A any information relevant to the evaluation, including, but not limited to (i) copy of the warrant or indictment; (ii) the names and addresses of the attorney for the Commonwealth, the attorney for the defendant and the judge who appointed the expert; (iii) information pertaining to the alleged crime, including statements by the defendant made to the police and transcripts of preliminary hearings, if any; (iv) a summary of the reasons for the evaluation request; (v) any available psychiatric, psychological, medical or social records that are deemed relevant; and (vi) a copy of the defendant's criminal record, to the extent reasonably available.

D. The report. The evaluators shall prepare a full report concerning the defendant's sanity at the time of the offense, including whether he may have had a significant mental disease or defect which rendered him insane at the time of the offense. The report shall be prepared within the time period designated by the court, said period to include the time necessary to obtain and evaluate the information specified in subsection C.

E. Disclosure of evaluation results. The report described in subsection D shall be sent solely to the attorney for the defendant and shall be deemed to be protected by the lawyer-client privilege. However, the Commonwealth shall be given the report, the results of any other evaluation of the defendant's sanity at the time of the offense, and copies of psychiatric, psychological, medical, or other records obtained during the course of any such evaluation, after the attorney for the defendant gives notice of an intent to present psychiatric or psychological evidence pursuant to §19.2-168.

(Chgd. by L.1996 chs. 937, 980, eff. 7/1/96.)

§19.2-169.6. Emergency treatment prior to trial.

A. Any defendant who is not subject to the provisions of §19.2-169.2 may be hospitalized for psychiatric treatment prior to trial if:

1. The court with jurisdiction over the defendant's case finds clear and convincing evidence that the defendant (i) is being properly detained in jail prior to trial; (ii) is mentally ill and imminently dangerous to self or others in the opinion of a qualified mental health professional; and (iii) requires treatment in a hospital rather than the jail in the opinion of a qualified mental health professional; or

2. The person having custody over a defendant who is awaiting trial has reasonable cause to believe that (i) the defendant is mentally ill and imminently dangerous to himself or others and (ii) requires treatment in a hospital rather than jail and the person having such custody arranges for an evaluation of the defendant by a person skilled in the diagnosis and treatment of mental illness provided a judge, as defined in §37.1-1 or, if a judge is not available, a magistrate, upon the advice of a person skilled in the diagnosis and treatment of mental illness, subsequently issues a temporary order of detention for treatment in accordance with the procedures specified in §37.1-67.1. In no event shall the defendant have the right to make application for voluntary admission and treatment as may be otherwise provided in §37.1-65 or §37.1-67.3.

If the defendant is committed pursuant to subdivision 1 of this subsection, the attorney for the defendant shall be notified that the court is considering hospitalizing the defendant for psychiatric treatment and shall have the opportunity to challenge the findings of the qualified mental health professional. If the defendant is detained pursuant to subdivision 2 of this subsection, the court having jurisdiction over the defendant's case and the attorney for the defendant shall be given notice prior to the detention pursuant to a temporary order of detention or as soon thereafter as is reasonable. Upon detention pursuant to subdivision 2 of this subsection, a hearing shall be held, upon notice to the attorney for the defendant, either (i) before the court having jurisdiction over the defendant's case or (ii) before a judge as defined in §37.1-1, in accordance with the provisions of §37.1-67.4, in which case the defendant shall be represented by counsel as specified in §37.1-67.3; the hearing shall be held within forty-eight hours of execution of the temporary order to allow the court which hears the case to make the findings, based upon clear and convincing evidence, which are specified in subdivision 1 of this subsection. If the forty-eight-hour period herein specified terminates on a Saturday, Sunday or legal holiday, such person may be detained for the same period allowed for detention pursuant to an order for temporary detention issued pursuant to §37.1-67.1.

In any case in which the defendant is hospitalized pursuant to this section, the court having jurisdiction over the defendant's case may provide by order that the admitting hospital evaluate the defendant's competency to stand trial and his mental state at the time of the offense pursuant to §§19.2-169.1 and 19.2-169.5.

B. A defendant subject to this section shall be treated at a hospital designated by the Commissioner as appropriate for treatment and evaluation of persons under criminal charge. The director of the hospital shall, within thirty days of the defendant's admission, send a report to the court with jurisdiction over the defendant addressing the defendant's continued need for treatment as mentally ill and imminently dangerous to self or others and, if so ordered by the court, the defendant's competency to stand trial, pursuant to §19.2-169.1 D, and his mental state at the time of the offense, pursuant to §19.2-169.5 D. Based on this report, the court shall either (i) find the defendant incompetent to stand trial pursuant to §19.2-169.1 E and proceed accordingly, (ii) order that the defendant be discharged from custody pending trial, (iii) order that the defendant be returned to jail pending trial, or (iv) make other appropriate disposition, including dismissal of charges and release of the defendant.

C. A defendant may not be hospitalized longer than thirty days under this section unless the court which has criminal jurisdiction over him or a judge as defined in §37.1-1 holds a hearing at which the defendant shall be represented by an attorney and finds clear and convincing evidence that the defendant continues to be (i) mentally ill, (ii) imminently dangerous to self or others, and (iii) in need of psychiatric treatment in a hospital. Hospitalization may be extended in this manner for periods of sixty days, but in no event may such hospitalization be continued beyond trial, nor shall such hospitalization act to delay trial, so long as the defendant remains competent to stand trial.
(Chgd. by L.1995 ch. 844, eff. 7/1/95.)

§19.2-169.7. Disclosure by defendant during evaluation or treatment; use at guilt phase of trial.

No statement or disclosure by the defendant concerning the alleged offense made during a competency evaluation ordered pursuant to §19.2-169.1, a mental state at the time of the offense evaluation ordered pursuant to §19.2-169.5, or treatment ordered pursuant to §19.2-169.2 or §19.2-169.6 may be used against the defendant at trial as evidence or as a basis for such evidence, except on the issue of his mental condition at the time of the offense after he raises the issue pursuant to §19.2-168.

§19.2-174.1. Information required prior to admission to a mental health facility.

Prior to any person being placed into the custody of the Commissioner for evaluation or treatment pursuant to §§19.2-169.2, *19.2-169.3,* 19.2-169.6, 19.2-176, 19.2-177.1, 19.2-182.2, and 19.2-182.3, *and Article 1.1 (37.1-70.1 et seq.) of Chapter 2 of Title 37.1,* the court or special justice shall provide the Commissioner with the following, if available: (i) the commitment order, (ii) the names and addresses for the attorney for the Commonwealth, the attorney for the person and the judge holding jurisdiction over the person, (iii) a copy of the warrant or indictment, and (iv) a copy of the criminal incident information as defined in §2.1-341 or a copy of the arrest report or a summary of the facts relating to the crime. The party requesting the placement into the Commissioner's custody or, in the case of admissions pursuant to §§*19.2-169.3,* 19.2-169.6, 19.2-176, and 19.2-177.1, *and Article 1.1 (37.1-70.1 et seq.) of Chapter 2 of Title 37.1,* the person having custody over the defendant shall gather the above information for submission to the court at the hearing. If the information is not available at the hearing, it shall be provided by the party requesting placement or the person having custody directly to the Commissioner within ninety-six hours of the person being placed into the Commissioner's custody.
(Added by L.1995 ch. 645; chgd. by L.1999 chs. 946, 985, eff. 7/1/2001 as chgd. by L.2000 ch. 1024, eff. 7/1/2000. Matter in italics eff. 7/1/2001.)

§19.2-175. Compensation of experts.

Each psychiatrist, clinical psychologist or other expert appointed by the court to render professional service pursuant to §§19.2-168.1, 19.2-169.1, 19.2-169.5, subsection A of §§19.2-176, 19.2-182.8, 19.2-182.9, 19.2-264.3:1, or §19.2-301, who is not regularly employed by the Commonwealth of Virginia except by the University of Virginia School of Medicine and the Medical College of Virginia, shall receive a reasonable fee for such service. The fee shall be determined in each instance by the court that appointed the expert, in accordance with guidelines established by the Supreme Court after consultation with the Department of Mental Health, Mental Retardation and Substance Abuse Services. Except in capital murder cases the fee shall not exceed $400, but in addition if any such expert is required to appear as a witness in any hearing held pursuant to such sections, he shall receive mileage and a fee of $100 for each day during which he is required so to serve. Itemized account of expense, duly sworn to, must be presented to the court, and when allowed shall be certified to the Supreme Court for payment out of the state treasury, and be charged against the appropriations made to pay criminal charges. Allowance for the fee and for the per diem authorized shall also be made by order of the court, duly certified to the Supreme Court for payment out of the appropriation to pay criminal charges.
(Chgd. by L.1995 ch. 645, eff. 7/1/95.)

§19.2-176. Determination of insanity after conviction but before sentence; hearing.

A. If, after conviction and before sentence of any person, the judge presiding at the trial shall find reasonable ground to question such person's mental state, he may order an evaluation of such person's mental state by at least one psychiatrist or clinical psychologist who is qualified by training and experience to perform such evaluations. If the judge, based on the evaluation, and after hearing representations of the defendant's counsel, finds clear and convincing evidence that the defendant (i) is mentally ill, and (ii) requires treatment in a mental hospital rather than the jail, he may order the defendant hospitalized in a facility designated by the Commissioner as appropriate for treatment of persons convicted of crime. The time such person is confined to such hospital shall be deducted from any term for which he may be sentenced to any penal institution, reformatory or elsewhere.

B. If it appears from all evidence readily available that the defendant is mentally ill and poses an imminent danger to himself or others if not immediately hospitalized, a temporary order of detention may be issued in accordance with §19.2-169.6 A 2 and a hearing shall be conducted in accordance with subsections A and C hereof within forty-eight hours of execution of the temporary order of detention, or if the forty-eight hour period herein specified terminates on a Saturday, Sunday or legal holiday, such person may be detained for the same period allowed for detention pursuant to an order for temporary detention issued pursuant to §37.1-67.1.

C. A defendant may not be hospitalized longer than thirty days under this section unless the court which has criminal jurisdiction over him, or a court designated by such court, holds a hearing, at which the defendant shall be represented by an attorney, and finds clear and convincing evidence that the defendant continues to be (i) mentally ill, (ii) imminently dangerous to self or others, and (iii) in need of psychiatric treatment in a hospital. Hospitalization may be extended in this manner for periods of 180 days, but in no event may such hospitalization be continued beyond the date upon which his sentence would have expired had he received the maximum sentence for the crime charged.

§19.2-177.1. Determination of mental illness after sentencing; hearing.

A person convicted of a crime who is in the custody of a local correctional facility after sentencing may be the subject of a mental commitment proceeding in accordance with the procedures provided in Chapter 2 (§37.1-63 et seq.) of Title 37.1. Such proceeding shall be commenced upon petition of the person having custody over the prisoner. If the person having custody over the prisoner has reasonable cause to believe that (i) the prisoner is mentally ill and imminently dangerous to himself or others and (ii) requires treatment in a hospital rather than a local correctional facility and the person having such custody arranges for an evaluation of the prisoner by a person skilled in the diagnosis and treatment of mental illness, then a judge, as defined in §37.1-1 or, if a judge is not available, a magistrate, upon the advice of a person skilled in the diagnosis and treatment of mental illness, may issue a temporary order of detention for treatment in accordance with the procedures specified in subdivision A 2 of §19.2-169.6.

In all other respects, the involuntary civil detention and commitment procedures specified in Chapter 2 of Title 37.1 shall be applicable, except:

1. Any detention or commitment shall be only to a facility designated for this purpose by the Commissioner;

2. In no event shall the prisoner have the right to make application for voluntary admission and treatment as may be otherwise provided in §37.1-65 or §37.1-67.3;

3. The time that such prisoner is confined to a hospital shall be deducted from any term for which he may be sentenced, but in no event may such hospitalization be continued beyond the date upon which his sentence would have expired;

4. Any prisoner hospitalized pursuant to this section who has not completed service of his sentence upon discharge from the hospital shall serve the remainder of his sentence.

(Chgd. by L.1995 ch. 844, eff. 7/1/95.)

§19.2-178. Where prisoner kept when no vacancy in facility or hospital.

When a court shall have entered any of the orders provided for in §§19.2-168.1, 19.2-169.1, 19.2-169.5, 19.2-169.6, 19.2-177.1, or §19.2-176, the sheriff of the county or city or the proper officer of the penal institution shall immediately proceed to ascertain whether a vacancy exists at the proper facility or hospital and until it is ascertained that there is a vacancy such person shall be kept in the jail of such county or city or in such custody as the court may order, or in the penal institution in which he is confined, until there is room in such facility or hospital. Any person whose care and custody is herein provided for shall be taken to and from the facility or hospital to which he was committed by an officer of the penal institution having custody of him, or by the sheriff of the county or city whose court issued the order of commitment, and the expenses incurred in such removals shall be paid by such penal institution, county or city.

(Chgd. by L.1995 ch. 645, eff. 7/1/95.)

§19.2-180. Sentence or trial of prisoner when restored to sanity.

When a prisoner whose trial or sentence was suspended by reason of his being found to be insane or feebleminded, has been found to be mentally competent and is brought from a hospital and committed to jail, if already convicted, he shall be sentenced, and if not, the court shall proceed to try him as if no delay had occurred on account of his insanity or feeblemindedness.

§19.2-182. Representation by counsel in proceeding for commitment.

A. In any proceeding for commitment under this title, the judge before whom or upon whose order the proceeding is being held, shall ascertain if the person whose commitment is sought is represented by counsel. If the person is not represented by counsel, the judge shall appoint an attorney at law to represent him in the proceeding. The attorney shall receive a fee of twenty-five dollars for his services, to be paid by the Commonwealth.

B. Any attorney representing any person in any proceeding for commitment under this title shall, prior to such proceeding, personally consult with such person.

CHAPTER 11.1
DISPOSITION OF PERSONS ACQUITTED BY REASON OF INSANITY

Section

§19.2-182.2. Verdict of acquittal by reason of insanity to state the fact; temporary custody and evaluation.

When the defense is insanity of the defendant at the time the offense was committed, the jurors shall be instructed, if they acquit him on that ground, to state the fact with their verdict. The court shall place the person so acquitted ("the acquittee") in temporary custody of the Commissioner of Mental Health, Mental Retardation and Substance Abuse Services (hereinafter referred to in this chapter as the "Commissioner") for evaluation as to whether the acquittee may be released with or without conditions or requires commitment. The evaluation shall be conducted by (i) one psychiatrist and (ii) one clinical psychologist. The psychiatrist or clinical psychologist shall be skilled in the diagnosis of mental illness and mental retardation and qualified by training and experience to perform such evaluations. The Commissioner shall appoint both evaluators, at least one of whom shall not be employed by the hospital in which the acquittee is primarily confined. The evaluators shall determine whether the acquittee is currently mentally ill or mentally retarded and shall assess the acquittee and report on his condition and need for hospitalization with respect to the factors set forth in §19.2-182.3. The evaluators shall conduct their examinations and report their findings separately within forty-five days of the Commissioner's assumption of custody. Copies of the report shall be sent to the acquittee's attorney, the attorney for the Commonwealth for the jurisdiction where the person was acquitted and the community services board serving the locality where the acquittee was acquitted. If either evaluator recommends conditional release or release

without conditions of the acquittee, the court shall extend the evaluation period to permit the hospital in which the acquittee is confined and the appropriate community services board to jointly prepare a conditional release or discharge plan, as applicable, prior to the hearing.
(Chgd. by L.1996 chs. 937, 980, eff. 7/1/96.)

§19.2-182.3. Commitment; civil proceedings.

Upon receipt of the evaluation report and, if applicable, a conditional release or discharge plan, the court shall schedule the matter for hearing on an expedited basis, giving the matter priority over other civil matters before the court, to determine the appropriate disposition of the acquittee. Except as otherwise ordered by the court, the attorney who represented the defendant at the criminal proceedings shall represent the acquittee through the proceedings pursuant to this section. The matter may be continued on motion of either party for good cause shown. The acquittee shall be provided with adequate notice of the hearing, of the right to be present at the hearing, the right to the assistance of counsel in preparation for and during the hearing, and the right to introduce evidence and cross-examine witnesses at the hearing. The hearing is a civil proceeding.

At the conclusion of the hearing, the court shall commit the acquittee if it finds that he is mentally ill or mentally retarded and in need of inpatient hospitalization. For the purposes of this chapter, mental illness includes any mental illness, as this term is defined in §37.1-1, in a state of remission when the illness may, with reasonable probability, become active. The decision of the court shall be based upon consideration of the following factors:

1. To what extent the acquittee is mentally ill or mentally retarded, as those terms are defined in §37.1-1;
2. The likelihood that the acquittee will engage in conduct presenting a substantial risk of bodily harm to other persons or to himself in the foreseeable future;
3. The likelihood that the acquittee can be adequately controlled with supervision and treatment on an outpatient basis; and
4. Such other factors as the court deems relevant.

If the court determines that an acquittee does not need inpatient hospitalization solely because of treatment or habilitation he is currently receiving, but the court is not persuaded that the acquittee will continue to receive such treatment or habilitation, it may commit him for inpatient hospitalization. The court shall order the acquittee released with conditions pursuant to §§19.2-182.7 through 19.2-182.9 if it finds that he is not in need of inpatient hospitalization but that he meets the criteria for conditional release set forth in §19.2-182.7. If the court finds that the acquittee does not need inpatient hospitalization nor does he meet the criteria for conditional release, it shall release him without conditions, provided the court has approved a discharge plan prepared jointly by the hospital staff and the appropriate community services board.

§19.2-182.4. Confinement and treatment; interfacility transfers; out-of-hospital visits; notice of change in treatment.

Upon commitment of an acquittee for inpatient hospitalization, the Commissioner shall determine the appropriate placement for him, based on his clinical needs and security requirements. The Commissioner may make interfacility transfers and treatment and management decisions regarding acquittees in his custody without obtaining prior approval of or review by the committing court. If the Commissioner is of the opinion that a temporary visit from the hospital would be therapeutic for the acquittee and that such a visit would pose no substantial danger to others, the Commissioner may grant such visit not to exceed forty-eight hours. The Commissioner shall notify the attorney for the Commonwealth for the committing jurisdiction in writing of changes in an acquittee's course of treatment which will involve authorization for the acquittee to leave the grounds of the hospital in which he is confined.

§19.2-182.5. Review of continuation of confinement hearing; procedure and reports; disposition.

A. The committing court shall conduct a hearing twelve months after the date of commitment to assess each confined acquittee's need for inpatient hospitalization. A hearing for assessment shall be conducted at yearly intervals for five years and at biennial intervals thereafter. The court shall schedule the matter for hearing as soon as possible after it becomes due, giving the matter priority over all pending matters before the court.

B. Prior to the hearing, the Commissioner shall provide to the court a report evaluating the acquittee's condition and recommending treatment, to be prepared by a psychiatrist or a psychologist. The psychologist who prepares the report shall be a clinical psychologist and any evaluating psychiatrist or clinical psychologist shall be skilled in the diagnosis of mental illness and qualified by training and experience to perform forensic evaluations. If the examiner recommends release or the acquittee requests release, the acquittee's condition and need for inpatient hospitalization shall be evaluated by a second person with such credentials who is not currently treating the acquittee. A copy of any report submitted pursuant to this subsection shall be sent to the attorney for the Commonwealth for the jurisdiction from which the acquittee was committed.

C. The acquittee shall be provided with adequate notice of the hearing, of the right to be present at the hearing, the right to the assistance of counsel in preparation for and during the hearing, and the right to introduce evidence and cross-examine witnesses at the hearing. Written notice of the hearing shall be provided to the attorney for the Commonwealth for the committing jurisdiction. The hearing is a civil proceeding.

According to the determination of the court following the hearing, and based upon the report and other evidence provided at the hearing, the court shall (i) release the acquittee from confinement if he does not need inpatient hospitalization and does not meet the criteria for conditional release set forth in §19.2-182.7, provided the court has approved a discharge plan prepared jointly by the hospital staff and the appropriate community services board; (ii) place the acquittee on conditional release if he meets the criteria for conditional release, and the court has approved a conditional release plan prepared jointly by the hospital staff and the appropriate community services board; or (iii) order that he remain in the custody of the Commissioner if he continues to require inpatient hospitalization based on consideration of the factors set forth in §19.2-182.3.
(Chgd. by L.1996 chs. 937, 980, eff. 7/1/96.)

§19.2-182.6. Petition for release; conditional release hearing; notice; disposition.

A. The Commissioner may petition the committing court for conditional or unconditional release of the acquittee at any time he believes the acquittee no longer needs hospitalization. The petition shall be accompanied by a report of clinical findings supporting the petition and by a conditional release or discharge plan, as applicable, prepared jointly by the hospital and the appropriate community services board. The acquittee may petition the committing court for release only once in each year in which no annual judicial review is required pursuant to §19.2-182.5. The party petitioning for release shall transmit a copy of the petition to the attorney for the Commonwealth for the committing jurisdiction.

B. Upon receipt of a petition for release, the court shall order the Commissioner to appoint two persons in the same manner as set forth in §19.2-182.2 to assess and report on the acquittee's need for inpatient hospitalization by reviewing his condition with respect to the factors set forth in §19.2-182.3. The evaluators shall conduct their evaluations and report their finding in accordance with the provisions of §19.2-182.2, except that the evaluations shall be completed and findings reported within forty-five days of issuance of the court's order for evaluation.

The Commissioner shall give notice of the hearing to any victim of the act resulting in the charges on which the acquittee was acquitted or the next of kin of the victim at the last known address, provided the person submits a written request for such notification to the Commissioner.

C. Upon receipt of the reports of evaluation, the court shall conduct a hearing on the petition. The hearing shall be scheduled on an expedited basis and given priority over other civil matters before the court. The acquittee shall be provided with adequate notice of the hearing, of the right to be present at the hearing, the right to the assistance of counsel in preparation for and during the hearing, and the right to introduce evidence and cross-examine witnesses. Written notice of the hearing shall be provided to the attorney for the Commonwealth for the committing jurisdiction. The hearing is a civil proceeding.

At the conclusion of the hearing, based upon the report and other evidence provided at the hearing, the court shall order the acquittee (i) released from confinement if he does not need inpatient hospitalization and does not meet the criteria for conditional release set forth in §19.2-182.3, provided the court has approved a discharge plan prepared jointly by the hospital and the appropriate community services board; (ii) placed on conditional release if he meets the criteria for such release as set forth in §19.2-182.7, and the court has approved a conditional release plan prepared jointly by the hospital and the appropriate community services board; or (iii) retained in the custody of the Commissioner if he continues to require inpatient hospitalization based on consideration of the factors set forth in §19.2-182.3.

D. Persons committed pursuant to this chapter shall be released only in accordance with the procedures set forth governing release and conditional release.

§19.2-182.7. Conditional release; criteria; conditions; reports.

At any time the court considers the acquittee's need for inpatient hospitalization pursuant to this chapter, it shall place the acquittee on conditional release if it finds that (i) based on consideration of the factors which the court must consider in its commitment decision, he does not need inpatient hospitalization but needs outpatient treatment or monitoring to prevent his condition from deteriorating to a degree that he would need inpatient hospitalization; (ii) appropriate outpatient supervision and treatment are reasonably available; (iii) there is significant reason to believe that the acquittee, if conditionally released, would comply with the conditions specified; and (iv) conditional release will not present an undue risk to public safety. The court shall subject a conditionally released acquittee to such orders and conditions it deems will best meet the acquittee's need for treatment and supervision and best serve the interests of justice and society.

The community services board serving the locality in which the acquittee will reside upon release shall implement the court's conditional release orders and shall submit written reports to the court on the acquittee's progress and adjustment in the community no less frequently than every six months.

After a finding by the court that the acquittee has violated the conditions of his release but does not require inpatient hospitalization pursuant to §19.2-182.8, the court may hold the acquittee in contempt of court for violation of the conditional release order.

(Chgd. by L.1999 chs. 700, 746, eff. 7/1/99.)

§19.2-182.8. Revocation of conditional release.

If at any time the court which released an acquittee pursuant to §19.2-182.7 finds reasonable ground to believe that an acquittee on conditional release (i) has violated the conditions of his release or is no longer a proper subject for conditional release based on application of the criteria for conditional release and (ii) requires inpatient hospitalization, it may order an evaluation of the acquittee by a psychiatrist or clinical psychologist, provided the psychiatrist or clinical psychologist is qualified by training and experience to perform forensic evaluations. If the court, based on the evaluation and after hearing evidence on the issue, finds by a preponderance of the evidence that an acquittee on conditional release (i) has violated the conditions of his release or is no longer a proper subject for conditional release based on application of the criteria for conditional release and (ii) is mentally ill or mentally retarded and requires inpatient hospitalization, the court may revoke the acquittee's conditional release and order him returned to the custody of the Commissioner.

At any hearing pursuant to this section, the acquittee shall be provided with adequate notice of the hearing, of the right to be present at the hearing, the right to the assistance of counsel in preparation for and during the hearing, and the right to introduce evidence and cross-examine witnesses at the hearing. Written notice of the hearing shall be provided to the attorney for the Commonwealth for the committing jurisdiction. The hearing is a civil proceeding.

(Chgd. by L.1996 chs. 937, 980, eff. 7/1/96.)

§19.2-182.9. Emergency custody of conditionally released acquittee.

When exigent circumstances do not permit compliance with revocation procedures set forth in §19.2-182.8, any judge as defined in §37.1-1 or a magistrate may issue an emergency custody order, upon the sworn petition of any responsible person or upon his own motion based upon probable cause to believe that an acquittee on conditional release (i) has violated the conditions of his release or is no longer a proper subject for conditional release and (ii) requires inpatient hospitalization. The emergency custody order shall require the acquittee within his judicial district to be taken into custody and transported to a convenient location where a person designated by the community services board who is skilled in the diagnosis and treatment of mental illness shall evaluate such acquittee and assess his need for inpatient hospitalization. A law-enforcement officer who, based on his observation or the reliable reports of others, has probable cause to believe that any acquittee on conditional release has violated the conditions of his release and is no longer a proper subject for conditional release and requires emergency evaluation to assess the need for inpatient hospitalization, may take the acquittee into custody and transport him to an appropriate location to assess the need for hospitalization without prior judicial authorization. The evaluation shall be conducted immediately. The acquittee shall remain in custody until a temporary detention order is issued or until he is released, but in no event shall the period of custody exceed four hours. If it appears from all evidence readily available (i) that the acquittee has violated the conditions of his release or is no longer a proper subject for conditional release and (ii) that he requires emergency evaluation to assess the need for inpatient hospitalization, the judge as defined in

§37.1-1, or magistrate upon the advice of such person skilled in the diagnosis and treatment of mental illness may issue an order of temporary detention authorizing the executing officer to place the acquittee in an appropriate institution for a period not to exceed forty-eight hours prior to a hearing. If the forty-eight-hour period terminates on a Saturday, Sunday or legal holiday, the acquittee may be detained until the next day which is not a Saturday, Sunday or legal holiday, but in no event may he be detained for longer than seventy-two hours or ninety-six hours when the legal holiday occurs on a Monday or Friday. For purposes of this section, a Saturday, Sunday or legal holiday shall be deemed to include the time period up to 8 a.m. of the next day which is not a Saturday, Sunday or legal holiday.

The committing court or any judge as defined in §37.1-1 shall have jurisdiction to hear the matter. Prior to the hearing, the acquittee shall be examined by a psychiatrist or licensed clinical psychologist, provided the psychiatrist or clinical psychologist is skilled in the diagnosis of mental illness, who shall certify whether the person is in need of hospitalization. At the hearing the acquittee shall be provided with adequate notice of the hearing, of the right to be present at the hearing, the right to the assistance of counsel in preparation for and during the hearing, and the right to introduce evidence and cross-examine witnesses at the hearing. Following the hearing, if the court determines, based on a preponderance of the evidence presented at the hearing, that the acquittee (i) has violated the conditions of his release or is no longer a proper subject for conditional release and (ii) is mentally ill or mentally retarded and is in need of inpatient hospitalization, the court shall revoke the acquittee's conditional release and place him in the custody of the Commissioner. When an acquittee on conditional release pursuant to this chapter is taken into emergency custody, detained or hospitalized, such action shall be considered to have been taken pursuant to this section, notwithstanding the fact that his status as an insanity acquittee was not known at the time of custody, detention or hospitalization. Detention or hospitalization of an acquittee pursuant to provisions of law other than those applicable to insanity acquittees pursuant to this chapter shall not render the detention or hospitalization invalid. If a person's status as an insanity acquittee on conditional release is not recognized at the time of emergency custody or detention, at the time his status as such is verified, the provisions applicable to such persons shall be applied and the court hearing the matter shall notify the committing court of the proceedings.
(Chgd. by L.1996 chs. 937, 980, eff. 7/1/96.)

§19.2-182.10. Release of person whose conditional release was revoked.

If an acquittee is returned to the custody of the Commissioner for inpatient treatment pursuant to revocation proceedings, and his condition improves to the degree that, within thirty days of resumption of custody following the hearing, the acquittee, in the opinion of hospital staff treating the acquittee and the supervising community services board, is an appropriate candidate for conditional release, he may be, with the approval of the court, conditionally released as if revocation had not taken place. If treatment is required for longer than thirty days, the acquittee shall be returned to the custody of the Commissioner for a period of hospitalization and treatment which is governed by the provisions of this chapter applicable to committed acquittees.

§19.2-182.11. Modification or removal of conditions; notice; objections; review.

A. The committing court may modify conditions of release or remove conditions placed on release pursuant to §19.2-182.7, upon petition of the supervising community services board, the attorney for the Commonwealth, or the acquittee or upon its own motion based on reports of the supervising community services board. However, the acquittee may petition only annually commencing six months after the conditional release order is issued. Upon petition, the court shall require the supervising community services board to provide a report on the acquittee's progress while on conditional release.

B. As it deems appropriate based on the community services board's report and any other evidence provided to it, the court may issue a proposed order for modification or removal of conditions. The court shall provide notice of the order, and their right to object to it within ten days of its issuance, to the acquittee, the supervising community services board and the attorney for the Commonwealth for the committing jurisdiction and for the jurisdiction where the acquittee is residing on conditional release. The proposed order shall become final if no objection is filed within ten days of its issuance. If an objection is so filed, the court shall conduct a hearing at which the acquittee, the attorney for the Commonwealth, and the supervising community services board have an opportunity to present evidence challenging the proposed order. At the conclusion of the hearing, the court shall issue an order specifying conditions of release or removing existing conditions of release.

§19.2-182.12. Representation of Commonwealth and acquittee.

The attorney for the Commonwealth shall represent the Commonwealth in all proceedings held pursuant to this chapter. The court shall appoint counsel for the acquittee unless the acquittee waives his right to counsel. The court shall consider appointment of the person who represented the acquittee at the last proceeding.

§19.2-182.13. Authority of Commissioner; delegation to board; liability.

The Commissioner may delegate any of the duties and powers imposed on or granted to him by this chapter to an administrative board composed of persons with demonstrated expertise in such matters. The Department of Mental Health, Mental Retardation and Substance Abuse Services shall assist the board in its administrative and technical duties. Members of the board shall exercise their powers and duties without compensation and shall be immune from personal liability while acting within the scope of their duties except for intentional misconduct.

§19.2-182.14. Escape of persons placed or committed; penalty.

Any person placed in the temporary custody of the Commissioner pursuant to §19.2-182.2 or committed to the custody of the Commissioner pursuant to §19.2-182.3 who escapes from such custody shall be guilty of a Class 6 felony.

§19.2-182.15. Escape of persons placed on conditional release; penalty.

Any person placed on conditional release pursuant to §19.2-182.7 who leaves the Commonwealth without permission from the court which conditionally released the person shall be guilty of a Class 6 felony.

§19.2-182.16. Copies of orders to Commissioner.

Copies of all orders and notices issued pursuant to this chapter shall be sent to the Commissioner of the Department of Mental Health, Mental Retardation and Substance Abuse Services.

CHAPTER 12
PRELIMINARY HEARING

§19.2-183. Examination of witnesses; assistance of counsel; evidentiary matters and remedies; power to adjourn case.

A. The judge before whom any person is brought for an offense shall, as soon as may be practical, in the presence of such person, examine on oath the witnesses for and against him. Before conducting the hearing or accepting a waiver of the hearing, the judge shall advise the accused of his right to counsel and, if the accused is indigent and the offense charged be punishable by confinement in jail or the state correctional facility, the judge shall appoint counsel as provided by law.

B. At the hearing the judge shall, in the presence of the accused, hear testimony presented for and against the accused in accordance with the rules of evidence applicable to criminal trials in this Commonwealth. In felony cases, the accused shall not be called upon to plead, but he may cross-examine witnesses, introduce witnesses in his own behalf, and testify in his own behalf.

C. A judge may adjourn a trial, pending before him, not exceeding ten days at one time, without the consent of the accused.

§19.2-183.1. Joint preliminary hearings.

Upon motion of the Commonwealth's attorney, preliminary hearings for persons alleged to have participated in contemporaneous and related acts or occurrences or in a series of such acts or occurrences constituting an offense or offenses may be heard jointly if jurisdiction over each person and offense lies in the same court, unless the court finds that such joint preliminary hearing would constitute prejudice to a defendant. Upon such a finding, the court shall order that the preliminary hearing for that defendant be held separately.

§19.2-184. Witnesses may be separated.

While a witness is under such examination all other witnesses may by order of the judge be excluded from the place of examination and kept separate from each other.

§19.2-185. Testimony may be reduced to writing and subscribed.

When the judge deems it proper the testimony of the witnesses may be reduced to writing, and, if required by him, shall be signed by them respectively.

The judge of the court of record to which the case may be or has been certified may order the testimony of the witnesses at the preliminary hearing to be reduced to writing.

§19.2-186. When accused to be discharged, tried, committed or bailed by judge.

The judge shall discharge the accused if he considers that there is not sufficient cause for charging him with the offense.

If a judge considers that there is sufficient cause only to charge the accused with an offense which the judge has jurisdiction to try, then he shall try the accused for such offense and convict him if he deems him guilty and pass judgment upon him in accordance with law just as if the accused had first been brought before him on a warrant charging him with such offense.

If a judge considers that there is sufficient cause to charge the accused with an offense that he does not have jurisdiction to try then he shall certify the case to the appropriate court having jurisdiction and shall commit the accused to jail or let him to bail pursuant to the provisions of Article 1 (§19.2-119 et seq.) of Chapter 9 of this title.
(Chgd. by L.1999 chs. 829, 846, eff. 7/1/99.)

§19.2-187. Admission into evidence of certain certificates of analysis.

In any hearing or trial of any criminal offense or in any proceeding brought pursuant to Chapter 22.1 (§19.2-386.1 et seq.) of this title, a certificate of analysis of a person performing an analysis or examination, performed in any laboratory operated by the Division of Consolidated Laboratory Services or the Division of Forensic Science or authorized by such Division to conduct such analysis or examination, or performed by the Federal Bureau of Investigation, the federal Postal Inspection Service, the federal Bureau of Alcohol, Tobacco and Firearms, the Naval Criminal Investigative Service, the National Fish and Wildlife Forensics Laboratory, the federal Drug Enforcement Administration, or the United States Secret Service Laboratory when such certificate is duly attested by such person, shall be admissible in evidence as evidence of the facts therein stated and the results of the analysis or examination referred to therein, provided (i) the certificate of analysis is filed with the clerk of the court hearing the case at least seven days prior to the hearing or trial and (ii) a copy of such certificate is mailed or delivered by the clerk or attorney for the Commonwealth to counsel of record for the accused at least seven days prior to the hearing or trial upon request made by such counsel to the clerk with notice of the request to the attorney for the Commonwealth. The request to the clerk shall be in writing at least ten days prior to trial and shall clearly state in its heading "Request for Copy of Certificate of Analysis."

The certificate of analysis of any examination conducted by the Division of Forensic Science relating to a controlled substance or marijuana shall be mailed or forwarded by personnel of the Division of Forensic Science to the attorney for the Commonwealth of the jurisdiction where such offense may be heard. The attorney for the Commonwealth shall acknowledge receipt of the certificate on forms provided by the laboratory.

Any such certificate of analysis purporting to be signed by any such person shall be admissible as evidence in such hearing or trial without any proof of the seal or signature or

of the official character of the person whose name is signed to it.
(Chgd. by L.1995 ch. 437; L.1999 ch. 296; L.2000 ch. 336, eff. 7/1/2000.)

§19.2-187.01. Certificate of analysis as evidence of chain of custody of material described therein.
A report of analysis duly attested by the person performing such analysis or examination in any laboratory operated by (i) the Division of Consolidated Laboratory Services, the Division of Forensic Science or any of its regional laboratories, or by any laboratory authorized by either Division to conduct such analysis or examination, (ii) the Federal Bureau of Investigation, (iii) the federal Bureau of Alcohol, Tobacco, and Firearms, (iv) the Naval Criminal Investigative Service, (v) the federal Drug Enforcement Administration, (vi) the Postal Inspection Service, or (vii) the United States Secret Service shall be prima facie evidence in a criminal or civil proceeding as to the custody of the material described therein from the time such material is received by an authorized agent of such laboratory until such material is released subsequent to such analysis or examination. Any such certificate of analysis purporting to be signed by any such person shall be admissible as evidence in such hearing or trial without any proof of the seal or signature or of the official character of the person whose name is signed to it. The signature of the person who received the material for the laboratory on the request for laboratory examination form shall he deemed prima facie evidence that the person receiving the material was an authorized agent and that such receipt constitutes proper receipt by the laboratory for purposes of this section.
(Chgd. by L.1995 ch. 437, eff. 7/1/95.)

§19.2-187.1. Right to examine person performing analysis or involved in chain of custody.
The accused in any hearing or trial in which a certificate of analysis is admitted into evidence pursuant to §19.2-187 or §19.2-187.01 shall have the right to call the person performing such analysis or examination or involved in the chain of custody as a witness therein, and examine him in the same manner as if he had been called as an adverse witness. Such witness shall be summoned and appear at the cost of the Commonwealth.

§19.2-187.2. Procedure for subpoena duces tecum of analysis evidence.
No subpoena duces tecum shall issue for the production of writings or documents used to reach the conclusion contained in a certificate of analysis prepared pursuant to §19.2-187 except upon affidavit that the requested writings or documents are material. Upon a showing by the Commonwealth that the production of such writings and documents would place an undue burden on the Division of Forensic Science, the Court may order that the subpoena duces tecum be satisfied by making the writings and documents available for inspection by the requesting party at the laboratory site where the analysis was performed or at the laboratory operated by the Division of Forensic Science which is closest to the court in which the case is pending.

§19.2-188. Reports and records received as evidence.
Reports of investigations made by the Chief Medical Examiner or his assistants or by medical examiners, and the records and reports of autopsies made under the authority of Title 32.1 of this Code, shall be received as evidence in any court or other proceeding, and copies of records, photographs, laboratory findings and records in the office of the Chief Medical Examiner or any medical examiner, when duly attested by the Chief Medical Examiner or one of his Assistant Chief Medical Examiners, or the medical examiner in whose office the same are, shall be received as evidence in any court or other proceeding for any purpose for which the original could be received without proof of the official character or the person whose name is signed thereto.

§19.2-188.1. Testimony regarding identification of controlled substances.
In any preliminary hearing on a violation of Article 1 (§18.2-247 et seq.) of Chapter 7 of Title 18.2, any law-enforcement officer shall be permitted to testify as to the results of field tests which have been approved by the Division Forensic Science pursuant to regulations adopted in accordance with the Administrative Process Act (§9-6.14:1 et seq.), regarding whether or not any substance the identity of which is at issue in such hearing is a controlled substance, imitation controlled substance, or marijuana, as defined in §18.2-247.

§19.2-188.2. Certificate of surgeon as evidence.
A. In any criminal proceeding, the certificate of a duly qualified surgeon stating that he has removed organs or other body parts from a decedent for transplant in accordance with Chapter 8 (§32.1-277 et seq.) of Title 32.1, shall be admissible in evidence as evidence of the facts stated therein. The certificate shall be competent evidence to show that such organs or body parts were functional at the time of recovery and not affected by any injury or illness that caused the decedent's death.
B. A copy of the certificate shall be filed with the attorney for the Commonwealth in the jurisdiction in which the decedent's fatal injury occurred. The certificate shall not be admitted into evidence unless the attorney for the Commonwealth has provided a copy of the certificate to counsel for the defendant at least fourteen days prior to the proceeding in which it is to be offered into evidence.
C. Any such certificate, when properly notarized, purporting to be signed by the surgeon who removed the organs or other body parts shall be admissible in evidence without proof of seal or signature of the person whose name is signed to it. In any hearing or trial the accused shall have the right to call the person signing the certificate and the provisions of §19.2-187.1 shall apply, mutatis mutandis.
(Added by L.1997 ch. 557, eff. 7/1/97.)

§19.2-189. Commitment of accused for further examination.
If the accused be committed, it shall be by an order of the judge stating that he is committed for further examination on a day specified in the order. And on that day he may be brought before such judge by his verbal order to the officer by whom he was committed, or by a written order to a different person.

§19.2-190. To whom, and when, examination and recognizance to be certified.
Every examination and recognizance for a felony taken under this chapter, shall, by the person taking it, be certified to the clerk of the circuit court of the county or city in which the party charged is to be tried, or the witness is to appear, on or before the first day of its next term. If he fail he may be compelled to do so by attachment as for a contempt.

CHAPTER 13
GRAND JURIES

Article

ARTICLE 1
IN GENERAL

§19.2-191. Functions of a grand jury.

The functions of a grand jury are two-fold:

(1) To consider bills of indictment prepared by the attorney for the Commonwealth and to determine whether as to each such bill there is sufficient probable cause to return such indictment "a true bill." This function shall be performed solely by a regular grand jury.

(2) To investigate and make report thereon concerning any condition which involves or tends to promote criminal activity, either in the community or by any governmental authority, agency or official thereof. This function may be exercised by either a special grand jury or a regular grand jury as hereinafter provided.

§19.2-192. Secrecy in grand jury proceedings.

Except as otherwise provided in this chapter, every member of a regular or special grand jury shall keep secret all proceedings which occurred during sessions of the grand jury; provided, however, in a prosecution for perjury of a witness examined before a regular grand jury, a regular grand juror may be required by the court to testify as to the testimony given by such witness before the regular grand jury.

ARTICLE 2
REGULAR GRAND JURIES

§19.2-193. Number of regular grand juries.

There shall be a regular grand jury at each term of the circuit court of each county and city, unless the court, on the motion of the attorney for the Commonwealth or with his concurrence, finds that it is unnecessary or impractical to impanel a grand jury for the particular term and enters an order to that effect.

Whenever the number of cases to be considered by the grand jury at a given term is so great as to hamper the intelligent consideration thereof by a single grand jury, the court may order two or more regular grand juries to be impanelled to sit separately at the same or a different time during the term.

Whenever a regular grand jury has been discharged, the court, during the term, may impanel another regular grand jury.

§19.2-194. When and how grand jurors to be selected and summoned; lists to be delivered to clerk.

The judges of such courts shall annually, in the month of June, July, or August, select from citizens of each city and county of their respective circuits at least 60 persons and not more than 120 persons 18 years of age or over, of honesty, intelligence and good demeanor and suitable in all respects to serve as grand jurors, who, except as hereinafter provided, shall be the grand jurors for the county or city from which they are selected for the next twelve months. The judge making the selection shall at once furnish to the clerk of his court in each county and city of his circuit a list of those selected for that county or city. The clerk, not more than twenty days before the commencement of each term of his court at which a regular grand jury is required, shall issue a venire facias to the sheriff of his county or city, commanding him to summon not less than five nor more than seven of the persons selected as aforesaid (the number to be designated by the judge of the court by an order entered of record) to be named in the writ to appear on the first day of the court to serve as grand jurors. No such person shall be required to appear more than once until all the others have been summoned once, nor more than twice until the others have been twice summoned, and so on. The Circuit Court of James City County, or the judge thereof in vacation, shall select the grand jurors for each court from such county and the City of Williamsburg in such proportion from each as he may think proper.

Any person who has legal custody of and is responsible for a child sixteen years of age or younger or a person having a mental or physical impairment requiring continuous care during normal court hours shall be excused from jury service upon his request.

§19.2-195. Number and qualifications of grand jurors.

A regular grand jury shall consist of not less than five nor more than seven persons. Each grand juror shall be a citizen of this Commonwealth, eighteen years of age or over, and shall have been a resident of this Commonwealth one year and of the county or corporation in which the court is to be held six months, and in other respects a qualified juror, and, when the grand juror is for a circuit court of a county, not an inhabitant of a city, except in those cases in which the circuit court of the county has jurisdiction in the city.

§19.2-196. How deficiency of jurors supplied.

If a sufficient number of grand jurors do not appear, the court may order the deficiency to be supplied from the bystanders or from a list furnished by the judge to the sheriff or sergeant.

§19.2-197. Foreman of grand jury; oaths of jurors and witnesses.

From among the persons summoned who attend the court shall select a foreman who shall be sworn as follows: "You shall diligently inquire, and true presentment make, of all such matters as may be given you in charge, or come to your knowledge, touching the present service. You shall present no person through prejudice or ill-will, nor leave any unpresented through fear or favor, but in all your presentments you shall present the truth, the whole truth, and nothing but the truth. So help you God." The other grand jurors shall afterwards be sworn as follows: "The same oath that your foreman has taken on his part, you and each of you shall observe and keep on your part. So help you God." Any witness testifying before the grand jury may be sworn by the foreman.

§19.2-198. When new foreman or juror may be sworn in.

If the foreman or any grand juror, at any time after being sworn, fail or be unable to attend another may be sworn in his stead.

§19.2-199. Judge to charge grand jury.

The grand jury, after being sworn, shall be charged by the judge of the court and shall then be sent to their room. In the charge given by the court to a regular grand jury, the court shall instruct it to advise the court after their considerations of the bills of indictment whether it desires to be impanelled as a special grand jury to consider any matters provided for in paragraph (2) of §19.2-191.

§19.2-200. Duties of grand jury.

The grand jury shall inquire of and present all felonies, misdemeanors and violations of penal laws committed within the jurisdiction of the respective courts wherein it is sworn; except that no presentment shall be made of a matter for which there is no corporal punishment, but only a fine, where the fine is limited to an amount not exceeding five dollars. After a regular grand jury has concluded its deliberation on bills of indictment and made its return thereon, the court shall inquire of it whether it recommends that a special grand jury be impanelled to perform any of the functions provided for in paragraph (2) of §19.2-191. If a majority of the grand jurors responds in the affirmative, the court shall impanel so many of that jury as answer in the affirmative and are also willing to serve thereon, plus any additional members as may be necessary to complete the panel, as a special grand jury and if a minority of the grand jurors responds in the affirmative, the court may impanel a special grand jury in the same manner.

§19.2-201. Officers to give information of violation of penal laws to attorney for Commonwealth.

Every commissioner of the revenue, sheriff, constable or other officer shall promptly give information of the violation of any penal law to the attorney for the Commonwealth, who shall forthwith institute and prosecute all necessary and proper proceedings in such case, whether in the name of the Commonwealth or of a county or corporation, and may in such case issue or cause to be issued a summons for any witnesses he may deem material to give evidence before the court or grand jury. Except as otherwise provided in this chapter, no attorney for the Commonwealth shall go before any grand jury except when duly sworn to testify as a witness, but he may advise the foreman of a regular grand jury or any member or members thereof in relation to the discharge of their duties.

§19.2-202. How indictments found and presentment made.

At least four of a regular grand jury must concur in finding or making an indictment or presentment. It may make a presentment or find an indictment upon the information of two or more of its own body, or on the testimony of witnesses called on by the grand jury, or sent to it by the court. If only one of their number can testify as to an offense, he shall be sworn as any other witness. When a presentment or indictment is so made or found, the names of the grand jurors giving the information, or of the witnesses, shall be written at the foot of the presentment or indictment.

§19.2-203. Indictments ignored may be sent to another grand jury; what irregularities not to vitiate indictment, etc.

Although a bill of indictment be returned not a true bill the same or another bill of indictment against the same person for the same offense may be sent to, and acted on, by the same or another grand jury. No irregularity in the time or manner of selecting the jurors, or in the writ of venire facias, or in the manner of executing the same, shall vitiate any presentment, indictment or finding of a grand jury.

§19.2-204. Penalties on officers and jurors for failure of duty.

A court whose officer fails without good cause, when it is his duty, to summon a grand jury and return a list of its names shall fine him twenty dollars. A person summoned and failing to attend a court as a grand juror shall be fined by the court not less than five dollars nor more than twenty dollars, unless, after being summoned to show cause against the fine, he gives a reasonable excuse for his failure.

§19.2-205. Pay and mileage of grand jurors.

Every person who serves upon a grand jury, regular or special, shall receive the same compensation and mileage allowed jurors in civil cases by §14.1-195.1 and the same shall be paid out of the county or corporation levy.

ARTICLE 3
SPECIAL GRAND JURIES

§19.2-206. When impanelled.

A. Special grand juries may be impanelled by a circuit court (i) at any time upon its own motion, or (ii) upon recommendation of a minority of the members of a regular grand jury that a special grand jury be impanelled, to perform the functions provided for in subdivision (2) of §19.2-191.

B. A special grand jury shall be impanelled by a circuit court upon the recommendation of a majority of the members of a regular grand jury if the court finds probable cause to believe that a crime has been committed which should be investigated by a special grand jury impanelled to perform the functions provided for in subdivision (2) of §19.2-191.

§19.2-207. Composition of a special grand jury.

Special grand juries shall consist of not less than seven and not more than eleven members, and shall be summoned from a list prepared by the court. Members of a special grand jury shall possess the same qualifications as those prescribed for members of a regular grand jury. The court shall appoint one of the members as foreman.

§19.2-208. Subpoena power of special grand jury.

The special grand jury may subpoena persons to appear before it to testify and to produce specified records, papers and documents, but before any witness testifies, he shall be warned by the foreman that he need not answer any questions or produce any evidence that would tend to incriminate him, and that the witness may have counsel of his own procurement present when he appears to testify, and at the same time the foreman also shall warn each witness that he may later be called upon to testify in any case that might grow out of the investigation and report of the special grand jury. Notwithstanding the provisions of this section, all provisions of this

Code relative to immunity granted to witnesses who testify before a grand jury shall remain applicable.

The foreman shall administer the oath prescribed by law for witnesses, and any member of the special grand jury may examine a witness.

§19.2-209. Presence of counsel for a witness.

Any witness appearing before a special grand jury shall have the right to have counsel of his own procurement present when he testifies. Such counsel shall have the right to consult with and advise the witness during his examination, but shall not have the right to conduct an examination of his own of the witness.

§19.2-210. Presence of attorney for Commonwealth.

The attorney for the Commonwealth shall not be present at any time while the special grand jury is in session except that during the investigatory stage of its proceedings he may be present when his presence is requested by the special grand jury or when the special grand jury was empanelled upon his motion. When present before the special grand jury he may interrogate witnesses provided the special grand jury requests or consents to such interrogation.

The attorney for the Commonwealth shall not be present during or after the investigative stage of the proceedings at any time while the special grand jury is discussing, evaluating or considering the testimony of a witness or is deliberating in order to reach decisions or prepare its report, except that he may be present when his legal advice is requested by the special grand jury.

§19.2-211. Provision for special counsel and other personnel.

At the request of the special grand jury, the court may designate special counsel to assist it in its work, and may also provide it with appropriate specialized personnel for investigative purposes.

§19.2-212. Provision for court reporter; use and disposition of notes, tapes and transcriptions.

A court reporter shall be provided for a special grand jury to record, manually or electronically, and transcribe all oral testimony taken before a special grand jury, but such reporter shall not be present during any stage of its deliberations. The notes, tapes and transcriptions of the reporter are for the sole use of the special grand jury, and the contents thereof shall not be divulged by anyone except as hereinafter provided. After the special grand jury has completed its use of the said notes, tapes and transcriptions, the foreman shall cause them to be sealed, the container dated, and delivered to the court.

The court shall cause the sealed container to be kept safely. If any witness testifying before the special grand jury is prosecuted subsequently for perjury, the court, on motion of either the attorney for the Commonwealth or the defendant, shall permit them both to have access to the testimony given by the defendant when a witness before the special grand jury, and the said testimony shall be admissible in the perjury case.

If no prosecution for perjury is instituted within three years from the date of the report of the special grand jury, the court shall cause the sealed container to be destroyed.

§19.2-213. Report by special grand jury.

At the conclusion of its investigation and deliberation, the special grand jury shall file a report of its findings with the court, including therein any recommendations that it may deem appropriate, after which it shall be discharged. Such report shall be sealed and not open to public inspection, other than by order of the court.

§19.2-213.1. Discharge of special grand jury.

If a special grand jury has not filed a report pursuant to §19.2-213 within six months of its impaneling, the circuit court appointing it shall discharge it; provided, however, if such court, in its discretion, determines that the special grand jury is making progress in its investigation, the court may direct that special grand jury to continue its investigation pursuant to this article.

§19.2-214. Prosecutions resulting from report.

Any bill of indictment for alleged criminal offenses, which may follow as a result of the report of the special grand jury, shall be prepared by the attorney for the Commonwealth for presentation to a regular grand jury.

§19.2-215. Costs of special grand jury.

All costs incurred for services provided by the court for a special grand jury shall be paid by the Commonwealth.

ARTICLE 4
MULTI-JURISDICTION GRAND JURIES

Section

§19.2-215.1. Functions of a multijurisdiction grand jury.

The functions of a multijurisdiction grand jury are:

1. To investigate any condition which involves or tends to promote criminal violations of:

a. Title 10.1 for which punishment as a felony is authorized;

b. §13.1-520;

c. §§18.2-47 and 18.2-48;

d. §§18.2-111 and 18.2-112;

e. Article 6 (§18.2-59 et seq.) of Chapter 4 of Title 18.2;

f. Article 7.1 (§18.2-152.1 et seq.) of Chapter 5 of Title 18.2;

g. Article 1 (§18.2-247 et seq.) and Article 1.1 (§18.2-265.1 et seq.) of Chapter 7 of Title 18.2;

h. Article 1 (§18.2-325 et seq.) and Article 1.1 (§18.2-340.1 et seq.) of Chapter 8 of Title 18.2, Chapter 29 (§59.1-364 et seq.) of Title 59.1 or any other provision prohibiting, limiting, regulating, or otherwise affecting gaming or gambling activity;

i. §18.2-434, when violations occur before a multijurisdiction grand jury;

j. Article 2 (§18.2-438 et seq.) and Article 3 (§18.2-446 et seq.) of Chapter 10 of Title 18.2;

k. §18.2-460 for which punishment as a felony is authorized;

l. Article 1.1 (§18.2-498.1 et seq.) of Chapter 12 of Title 18.2;

m. Article 1 (§32.1-310 et seq.) of Chapter 9 of Title 32.1;

n. Chapter 4.2 (§59.1-68.6 et seq.) of Title 59.1;

o. Article 6 (§3.1-796.122 et seq.) of Chapter 27.4 of Title 3.1;

p. Article 1 (§18.2-30 et. seq.) of Chapter 4 of Title 18.2; and

q. Any other provision of law when such condition is discovered in the course of an investigation which a multijurisdiction grand jury is otherwise authorized to undertake and to investigate any condition which involves or tends to promote any attempt, solicitation or conspiracy to violate the laws enumerated in this section.

2. To report evidence of any criminal offense enumerated in subdivision 1 to the attorney for the Commonwealth or United States attorney of any jurisdiction where such offense could be prosecuted or investigated and, when appropriate, to the Attorney General.

3. To consider bills of indictment prepared by a special counsel to determine whether there is sufficient probable cause to return each such indictment as a "true bill." Only bills of indictment which allege an offense enumerated in subdivision 1 may be submitted to a multijurisdiction grand jury.

4. The provisions of this section shall not abrogate the authority of an attorney for the Commonwealth in a particular jurisdiction to determine the course of a prosecution in that jurisdiction.

(Chgd. by L.1995 ch. 552; L.2000 ch. 359, eff. 7/1/2000.)

§19.2-215.2. Application for such grand jury.

Provided the Attorney General has approved the application in writing prior to submission, application for a multi-jurisdiction grand jury may be made to the Supreme Court of Virginia by two or more attorneys for the Commonwealth from jurisdictions which would be within the original scope of the investigation. The application shall be in writing and shall state (i) which jurisdictions will be involved in the original scope of the investigation, (ii) in which jurisdiction it is requested that the multi-jurisdiction grand jury be convened, (iii) the name or names of the attorneys for the Commonwealth or their assistants who will serve as special counsel to the grand jury, (iv) the name of the attorney who shall direct the grand jury proceedings. The presiding judge may extend or limit the jurisdictional territory of the investigation, for good cause shown, upon the motion of a grand jury already convened. Notice of every such application shall be given to the attorneys for the Commonwealth in the jurisdictions named in the application and, if the original scope of the investigation is extended into other jurisdictions, notice of such extension shall be given to the attorneys for the Commonwealth in the jurisdictions into which the investigation is extended.

§19.2-215.3. When impaneled; impaneling order.

Upon application by two or more attorneys for the Commonwealth, the Chief Justice of the Supreme Court, or any justice designated by the Chief Justice, may within twenty days thereafter order the impaneling of a multi-jurisdiction grand jury for a term of twelve months. The term of such a grand jury may be extended for successive periods of not more than six months by the Chief Justice, or by any justice designated by the Chief Justice, upon the petition of a majority of the members of the grand jury.

The impaneling order shall appoint a judge of a circuit court from one of the jurisdictions named on the application as the presiding judge and shall designate where the multi-jurisdiction grand jury shall be convened. The impaneling order shall also designate special counsel and each special counsel who will assist the multi-jurisdiction grand jury as listed in the application. The presiding judge shall substitute or appoint additional special counsel upon motion of special counsel.

§19.2-215.4. Number and qualifications of jurors; grand jury list; when convened; compensation of jurors.

A. A multi-jurisdiction grand jury shall consist of not less than seven nor more than eleven members. Each member of a multi-jurisdiction grand jury shall be a citizen of this Commonwealth, eighteen years of age or older, and a resident of this Commonwealth for one year and of one of the jurisdictions named in the application for six months.

B. The presiding judge shall determine the number of grand jurors to be drawn and shall draw them so that, to the extent practicable, each of the jurisdictions named in the application is represented by at least one juror residing in that jurisdiction, but in no event shall said panel have more than eleven members. The grand jurors shall be summoned from a list prepared by the presiding judge. In the preparation of this list, the presiding judge shall select only persons who have been selected as regular grand jurors pursuant to the provisions of §19.2-194 in the jurisdiction named in the application.

C. The provisions of §19.2-192 dealing with secrecy in grand jury proceedings are incorporated herein by reference.

D. The presiding judge shall determine the time, date and place within the designated jurisdiction where the multi-jurisdiction grand jury is to be convened. The presiding judge shall also appoint one of the grand jurors to serve as foreman. Members of the multi-jurisdiction grand jury shall be compensated according to the provisions of §19.2-205. The expense of a multi-jurisdiction grand jury shall be borne by the Commonwealth.

§19.2-215.5. Subpoena power; counsel for witness; oath.

A multi-jurisdiction grand jury has statewide subpoena power and may subpoena persons to appear before it to testify or to produce evidence in the form of specified records, papers, documents or other tangible things. Mileage and such other reasonable expenses as are approved by the presiding judge shall be paid such persons from funds appropriated for such purpose.

A witness before a multi-jurisdiction grand jury shall be entitled to the presence of counsel in the grand jury room, but he may not participate in the proceedings.

The foreman shall administer the oath required by law for witnesses.

§19.2-215.6. Role and presence of special counsel; examination of witnesses.

Special counsel may be present during the investigatory stage of a multi-jurisdiction grand jury proceeding and may examine any witness who is called to testify or produce evidence. The examination of a witness by special counsel shall in no way affect the right of any grand juror to examine the witness.

Special counsel, however, may not be present at any time during the deliberations of a multi-jurisdiction grand jury except when the grand jury requests the legal advice of special counsel as to specific questions of law.

§19.2-215.7. Warnings given to witnesses; when witness in contempt; use of testimony compelled after witness invokes right against self-incrimination.

A. Every witness testifying before a multi-jurisdiction grand jury shall be warned by special counsel or by the foreman of the grand jury that he need not answer any question that would tend to incriminate him, and that he may later be called upon to testify in any case that may result from the grand jury proceedings.

B. A witness who has been called to testify or produce evidence before a multi-jurisdiction grand jury, and who refuses to testify or produce evidence by expressly invoking his right not to incriminate himself, may be compelled to testify or produce evidence by the presiding judge. A witness who refuses to testify or produce evidence after being ordered to do so by the presiding judge may be held in contempt and may be incarcerated until the contempt is purged by compliance with the order.

C. When a witness is compelled to testify or produce evidence after expressly invoking his right not to incriminate himself, and the presiding judge has determined that the assertion of the right is bona fide, the compelled testimony, or any information directly or indirectly derived from such testimony or other information, shall not be used against the witness in any criminal proceeding except a prosecution for perjury.

§19.2-215.8. Returning a "true bill" of indictment; jurisdiction to be set out.

In order to return a "true bill" of indictment, a majority, but in no instance less than five, of the multi-jurisdiction grand jurors must concur in that finding. A multi-jurisdiction grand jury may return a "true bill" of indictment upon the testimony of, or evidence produced by, any witness who was called by the grand jury, upon evidence presented to it by special counsel, or upon evidence sent to it by the presiding judge.

Every "true bill" of indictment returned by a multi-jurisdiction grand jury shall state in which jurisdiction or jurisdictions the offense is alleged to have occurred. Thereafter, when venue is proper in more than one jurisdiction, the presiding judge who directed the grand jury proceeding shall elect in which one of the jurisdictions named in the indictment the indictment is to be prosecuted.

§19.2-215.9. Court reporter provided; safekeeping of transcripts, notes, etc.; when disclosure permitted; access to record of testimony and evidence.

A. A court reporter shall be provided for a multi-jurisdiction grand jury to record, manually or electronically, and transcribe all oral testimony taken before a multi-jurisdiction grand jury, but such a reporter shall not be present during any stage of its deliberations. Such transcription shall include the original or copies of all documents, reports or other evidence presented to the multi-jurisdiction grand jury. The notes, tapes and transcriptions of the reporter are for the use of the multi-jurisdiction grand jury, and the contents thereof shall not be used or divulged by anyone except as provided in this article. After the multi-jurisdiction grand jury has completed its use of the notes, tapes and transcriptions, the foreman shall cause them to be delivered to the presiding judge.

B. The presiding judge shall cause the notes, tapes and transcriptions or other evidence to be kept safely. Upon motion to the presiding judge, special counsel shall be permitted to review any of the evidence which was presented to the multi-jurisdiction grand jury, and shall be permitted to make notes and to duplicate portions of the evidence as he deems necessary for use in a criminal investigation or proceeding. Special counsel shall maintain the secrecy of all information obtained from a review or duplication of the evidence presented to the multi-jurisdiction grand jury, except that this information may be disclosed pursuant to the provisions of subdivision 2 of §19.2-215.1. Upon motion to the presiding judge by a person indicted by a multi-jurisdiction grand jury, similar permission to review, note or duplicate evidence shall be extended if it appears that the permission is consistent with the ends of justice and is necessary to reasonably inform such person of the nature of the evidence to be presented against him, or to adequately prepare his defense.

C. If any witness who voluntarily testified or produced evidence before the multi-jurisdiction grand jury is prosecuted on the basis of his testimony or the evidence he produced, or if any witness who was compelled to testify or to produce evidence is prosecuted for perjury on the basis of his testimony or the evidence he produced before the multi-jurisdiction grand jury, the presiding judge, on motion of either the Commonwealth or the defendant, shall permit both the Commonwealth and the defendant access to the testimony of or evidence produced by the defendant before the multi-jurisdiction grand jury. The testimony and the evidence produced by the defendant voluntarily before the multi-jurisdiction grand jury shall then be admissible in the trial of the criminal offense with which the defendant is charged, for the purpose of impeaching the defendant.

§19.2-215.10. Participation by office of Attorney General; assistance of special counsel permitted in certain prosecutions.

Upon request by the applicants or upon motion to the presiding judge by special counsel, the office of Attorney General may participate as special counsel in the multi-jurisdiction grand jury proceedings and any prosecutions arising therefrom. In any prosecution arising out of the multi-jurisdiction grand jury, the attorney for the Commonwealth may also obtain the assistance of the special counsel to the grand jury as a special assistant attorney for the Commonwealth.

§19.2-215.11. Discharge of grand jury.

At any time during the original or extended term of a multi-jurisdiction grand jury, the presiding judge may discharge the grand jury if, in the opinion of the presiding judge, the existence of the multi-jurisdiction grand jury is no longer necessary.

CHAPTER 14
PRESENTMENTS, INDICTMENTS AND INFORMATIONS

ARTICLE 1
NECESSITY FOR INDICTMENT, ETC.

§19.2-216. Definition of indictment, presentment and information.

An indictment is a written accusation of crime, prepared by the attorney for the Commonwealth and returned "a true bill" upon the oath or affirmation of a legally impanelled grand jury.

A presentment is a written accusation of crime prepared and returned by a grand jury from their own knowledge or observation, without any bill of indictment laid before them.

An information is a written accusation of crime or a complaint for forfeiture of property or money or for imposition of a penalty, prepared and presented by a competent public official upon his oath of office.

§19.2-217. When information filed; prosecution for felony to be by indictment or presentment; waiver; process to compel appearance of accused.

An information may be filed by the attorney for the Commonwealth based upon a complaint in writing verified by the oath of a competent witness; but no person shall be put upon trial for any felony, unless an indictment or presentment shall have first been found or made by a grand jury in a court of competent jurisdiction or unless such person, by writing signed by such person before the court having jurisdiction to try such felony or before the judge of such court shall have waived such indictment or presentment, in which event he may be tried on a warrant or information. If the accused be in custody, or has been recognized or summoned to answer such information, presentment or indictment, no other process shall be necessary; but the court may, in its discretion, issue process to compel the appearance of the accused.

§19.2-217.1. Central file of capital murder indictments.

Upon the return by a grand jury of an indictment for capital murder and the arrest of the defendant, the clerk of the circuit court in which the indictment is returned shall forthwith file a certified copy of the indictment with the clerk of the Supreme Court of Virginia. All such indictments shall be maintained in a single place by the clerk of the Supreme Court, and shall be available to members of the public upon request. Failure to comply with the provisions of this section shall not be (i) a basis upon which an indictment may be quashed or deemed invalid; (ii) deemed error upon which a conviction may be reversed or a sentence vacated; or (iii) a basis upon which a court may prevent or delay execution of a sentence.

§19.2-218. Preliminary hearing required for person arrested on charge of felony; waiver.

No person who is arrested on a charge of felony shall be denied a preliminary hearing upon the question of whether there is reasonable ground to believe that he committed the offense and no indictment shall be returned in a court of record against any such person prior to such hearing unless such hearing is waived in writing by the accused.

§19.2-218.1. Preliminary hearings involving marital sexual assault and certain other sexual crimes against spouses.

A. In any preliminary hearing of a charge against a person for a violation under §§18.2-61 B, 18.2-67.1 B, 18.2-67.2 B or §18.2-67.2:1, upon a finding of probable cause the court may request that its court services unit, in consultation with any appropriate social services organization, local board of mental health and mental retardation, or other community mental health services organization, prepare a report analyzing the feasibility of providing counseling or other forms of therapy for the accused and the probability such treatment will be successful. Based upon this report and any other relevant evidence, the court may, (i) with the consent of the accused, the complaining witness and the attorney for the Commonwealth in any case involving a violation of §§18.2-61 B, 18.2-67.1 B or §18.2-67.2 B or (ii) with the consent of the accused and after consideration of the views of the complaining witness in any case involving a violation of §18.2-67.2:1, authorize the accused to submit to and complete a designated course of counseling or therapy. In such case, the hearing shall be adjourned until such time as counseling or therapy is completed or terminated. Upon the completion of counseling or therapy by the accused and after consideration of a final evaluation to be furnished to the court by the person responsible for conducting such counseling or therapy and such further report of the court services unit as the court may require, and after consideration of the views of the complaining witness, the court, in its discretion, may discharge the accused if the court finds such action will promote maintenance of the family unit and be in the best interest of the complaining witness.

B. No statement or disclosure by the accused concerning the alleged offense made during counseling or any other form of therapy ordered pursuant to this section or §§18.2-61, 18.2-67.1, 18.2-67.2, 18.2-67.2:1 or §19.2-218.2 may be used against the accused in any trial as evidence, nor shall any evidence against the accused be admitted which was discovered through such statement or disclosure.

§19.2-218.2. Hearing before juvenile and domestic relations district court required for persons accused of certain violations against their spouses.

A. In any case involving a violation of subsection B of §18.2-61, subsection B of §18.2-67.1, subsection B of §18.2-67.2 or subsection B of §18.2-67.2:1 where a preliminary hearing pursuant to §19.2-218.1 has not been held prior to indictment or trial, the court shall refer the case to the appropriate juvenile and domestic relations district court for a hearing to determine whether counseling or therapy is appropriate prior to further disposition unless the hearing is waived in writing by the accused. The court conducting this hearing may order counseling or therapy for the accused in compliance with the guidelines set forth in §19.2-218.1.

B. After such hearing pursuant to which the accused has completed counseling or therapy and upon the recommendation of the juvenile and domestic relations district court judge conducting the hearing, the judge of the circuit court may dismiss the charge with the consent of the attorney for the Commonwealth and if the court finds such action will promote maintenance of the family unit and be in the best interest of the complaining witness.

(Chgd. by L.1996 ch. 616, eff. 7/1/96.)

§19.2-219. When capias need not be issued; summons; judgment.

No capias need be issued on a presentment or indictment of an offense for which there is no punishment but a fine or forfeiture, limited to an amount not exceeding twenty dollars; but a summons to answer such presentment or indictment may be issued against the accused; and if it be served ten days before the return day thereof, and he does not appear, judgment may be rendered against him for the penalty. If he appear, the court may, unless he demand a jury, hear and determine the matter and give judgment thereon.

ARTICLE 2
FORM AND REQUISITES

§19.2-220. Contents of indictment in general.

The indictment or information shall be a plain, concise and definite written statement, (1) naming the accused, (2) describing the offense charged, (3) identifying the county, city or town in which the accused committed the offense, and (4) reciting that the accused committed the offense on or about a certain date. In describing the offense, the indictment or information may use the name given to the offense by the common law, or the indictment or information may state so much of the common law or statutory definition of the offense as is sufficient to advise what offense is charged.

§19.2-221. Form of prosecutions generally; murder and manslaughter.

The prosecutions for offenses against the Commonwealth, unless otherwise provided, shall be by presentment, indictment or information. While any form of presentment, indictment or information which informs the accused of the nature and cause of the accusation against him shall be good the following shall be deemed sufficient for murder and manslaughter:

State of Virginia............ county (or city) to-wit: The grand jurors of the State of Virginia, in and for the body of the county (or city) of............, upon their oaths present that A................ B................, on the.... day of........, 19.., in the county (or city) of............ feloniously did kill and murder one C................ D................ against the peace and dignity of the Commonwealth.

A grand jury may, in case of homicide, which in their opinion amounts to manslaughter only, and not to murder, find an indictment against the accused for manslaughter and in such case the indictment shall be sufficient if it be in form or effect as follows:

State of Virginia............ county (or city) to-wit: The grand jurors of the State of Virginia, in and for the body of the county (or city) of............, upon their oaths present that A................ B................, on the.... day of........, 19.. in the county (or city) of............ feloniously and unlawfully did kill and slay one C...................... D................, against the peace and dignity of the Commonwealth.

§19.2-222. *(Repealed by L.1996 ch. 676, eff. 7/1/96.)*

§19.2-223. Charging several acts of embezzlement; description of money.

In a prosecution against a person accused of embezzling or fraudulently converting to his own use bullion, money, bank notes or other security for money or items of personal property subject to larceny it shall be lawful in the same indictment or accusation to charge and thereon to proceed against the accused for any number of distinct acts of such embezzlements or fraudulent conversions which may have been committed by him within six months from the first to the last of the acts charged in the indictment; and it shall be sufficient to allege the embezzlement or fraudulent conversion to be of money without specifying any particular money, gold, silver, note or security. Such allegation, so far as it regards the description of the property, shall be sustained if the accused be proved to have embezzled any bullion, money, bank note or other security for money or items of personal property subject to larceny although the particular species be not proved.

And in a prosecution for the larceny of United States currency or for obtaining United States currency by a false pretense or token, or for receiving United States currency knowing the same to have been stolen, it shall be sufficient if the accused be proved guilty of the larceny of national bank notes or United States treasury notes, certificates for either gold or silver coin, fractional coin, currency, or any other form of money issued by the United States government, or of obtaining the same by false pretense or token, or of receiving the same knowing it to have been stolen although the particular species be not proved.

§19.2-224. In prosecution for forgery, unnecessary to set forth copy of forged instrument.

In a prosecution for forging or altering any instrument or other thing, or attempting to employ as true any forged instrument or other thing, or for any of the offenses mentioned in Article 1 (§18.2-168 et seq.) of Chapter 6 of Title 18.2, it shall not be necessary to set forth any copy or facsimile of such instrument or other thing; but it shall be sufficient to describe the same in such manner as would sustain an indictment for stealing such instrument or other thing, supposing it to be the subject of larceny.

§19.2-225. Allegation of intent.

Where an intent to injure, defraud or cheat is required to constitute an offense, it shall be sufficient, in an indictment or accusation therefor, to allege generally an intent to injure, defraud or cheat without naming the person intended to be injured, defrauded or cheated; and it shall be sufficient, and not be deemed a variance, if there appear to be an intent to injure, defraud or cheat the United States, or any state, or any county, corporation, officer or person.

§19.2-226. What defects in indictments not to vitiate them.

No indictment or other accusation shall be quashed or deemed invalid:

(1) For omitting to set forth that it is upon the oaths of the jurors or upon their oaths and affirmations;

(2) For the insertion of the words "upon their oath," instead of "upon their oaths";

(3) For not in terms alleging that the offense was committed "within the jurisdiction of the court" when the averments show that the case is one of which the court has jurisdiction;

(4) For the omission or misstatement of the title, occupation, estate, or degree of the accused or of the name or place of his residence;

(5) For omitting the words "with force and arms" or the statement of any particular kind of force and arms;

(6) For omitting to state, or stating imperfectly, the time at which the offense was committed when time is not the essence of the offense;

(7) For failing to allege the kind or value of an instrument which caused death or to allege that it was of no value;

(8) For omitting to charge the offense to be "against the form of the statute or statutes"; or

(9) For the omission or insertion of any other words of mere form or surplusage.

Nor shall it be abated for any misnomer of the accused; but the court may, in case of a misnomer appearing before or in the course of a trial, forthwith cause the indictment or accusation to be amended according to the fact.

§19.2-227. When judgment not to be arrested or reversed.

Judgment in any criminal case shall not be arrested or reversed upon any exception or objection made after a verdict to the indictment or other accusation, unless it be so defective as to be in violation of the Constitution.

§19.2-228. Name and address of complaining witness to be written on indictment, etc., for misdemeanor.

In a prosecution for a misdemeanor the name and address of the complaining witness, if there be one, shall be written at the foot of the presentment, indictment or information when it is made, found or filed. In case the grand jury that brings in such presentment or indictment or the attorney for the Commonwealth who files such information fail to write the name of a complaining witness at the foot of the presentment, indictment or information, then the name of a complaining witness may be entered of record as such by the court on the motion of the defendant or the attorney for the Commonwealth at any time before the judgment.

§19.2-229. When complaining witness required to give security for costs.

For good cause the court may require a complaining witness to give security for the costs and if he fails to do so dismiss the prosecution at his costs.

§19.2-230. Bill of particulars.

A court of record may direct the filing of a bill of particulars at any time before trial. A motion for a bill of particulars shall be made before a plea is entered and at least seven days before the day fixed for trial and the bill of particulars shall be filed within such time as is fixed by the court.

ARTICLE 3
AMENDMENTS

Section

§19.2-231. Amendment of indictment, presentment or information.

If there be any defect in form in any indictment, presentment or information, or if there shall appear to be any variance between the allegations therein and the evidence offered in proof thereof, the court may permit amendment of such indictment, presentment or information, at any time before the jury returns a verdict or the court finds the accused guilty or not guilty, provided the amendment does not change the nature or character of the offense charged. After any such amendment the accused shall be arraigned on the indictment, presentment or information as amended, and shall be allowed to plead anew thereto, if he so desires, and the trial shall proceed as if no amendment had been made; but if the court finds that such amendment operates as a surprise to the accused, he shall be entitled, upon request, to a continuance of the case for a reasonable time.

ARTICLE 4
PROCESS

Section

§19.2-232. What process to be awarded against accused on indictment, etc.

When an indictment or presentment is found or made, or information filed, the court, or the judge thereof, shall award process against the accused to answer the same, if he be not in custody. Such process, if the prosecution be for a felony, shall be a capias; if it be for a misdemeanor, for which imprisonment may be imposed, it may be a capias or summons, in the discretion of the court or judge; in all other cases, it shall be, in the first instance a summons, but if a summons be returned executed and the defendant does not appear, or be returned not found, the court or judge may award a capias. The officer serving the summons or capias shall also serve a copy of the indictment, presentment or information therewith.

§19.2-233. How awarded, directed, returnable and executed.

Sections 8.01-292 and 8.01-295 shall apply to process in criminal, as well as in civil cases; and the court may, in the same case against the same person, award at the same time, or different times, several writs of summons or capias directed to officers of different counties or cities. An officer having a capias under which the accused is let to bail shall give a certificate of the fact, which shall protect him against any other capias which may have been issued for the same offense. A summons shall be served by delivering a copy thereof to the party in person and the clerk issuing such summons shall deliver or transmit therewith as many copies thereof as there are persons named therein on whom it is to be served.

§19.2-234. Procedure when person arrested under capias.

An officer who, under a capias from any court, arrests a person accused of an offense shall proceed in accordance with §19.2-80 and Article 1 (§19.2-119 et seq.) of Chapter 9 of Title 19.2 regarding bail.

§19.2-235. Clerks to mail process to officers in other counties, etc.

The clerk of every court shall forward, by mail, all process issued for the Commonwealth, directed to the officer of any county or city other than his own.

§19.2-236. Where process of arrest may be executed.

When process of arrest in a criminal prosecution is issued from a court, either against a party accused or a witness, the officer to whom it is directed or delivered may execute it in any part of the Commonwealth.

§19.2-237. Process on indictment or presentment for misdemeanor.

On any indictment or presentment for a misdemeanor process shall be issued immediately. If the accused appear and plead to the charge, the trial shall proceed without delay, unless good cause for continuance be shown. If, in any misdemeanor case the accused fails to appear and plead, when required the court may either award a capias or proceed to trial in the same manner as if the accused had appeared, plead not guilty and waived trial by jury, provided, that the court shall not in any such case enforce a jail sentence.

§19.2-238. Summons against corporation; proceedings; expense of publication.

A summons against a corporation to answer an indictment, presentment or information may be served as provided in §§8.01-299 through 8.01-301; and if the defendant after being so served fail to appear, the court may proceed to trial and judgment, without further process, as if the defendant had appeared, plead not guilty and waived trial by jury. And when, in any such case, publication of a copy of the process is required according to such sections, the expense of such publication may be certified by the court to the Comptroller, and shall be paid out of the state treasury; but the same shall be taxed with other costs and collected from the defendant, if judgment be for the Commonwealth, and be paid into the state treasury by the officer collecting the same.

CHAPTER 15
TRIAL AND ITS INCIDENTS

ARTICLE 1
JURISDICTION

§19.2-239. Jurisdiction in criminal cases.

The circuit courts, except where otherwise provided, shall have exclusive original jurisdiction for the trial of all presentments, indictments and informations for offenses committed within their respective circuits.

§19.2-240. Clerks shall make out criminal docket.

Before every term of any court in which criminal cases are to be tried the clerk of the court shall make out a separate docket of criminal cases then pending, in the following order, numbering the same:

1. Felony cases;
2. Misdemeanor cases.

He shall docket all felony cases in the order in which the indictments are found and all misdemeanor cases in the order in which the presentments or indictments are found or informations are filed or appeals are allowed by magistrates and as soon as any presentments or indictments are made at a term of court he shall forthwith docket the same in the order required above.

Traffic infractions shall be docketed with misdemeanor cases. Cases appealed from the juvenile and domestic relations district court shall not be placed on the criminal docket except for cases involving criminal offenses committed by adults as provided in §16.1-302. Cases transferred to a circuit court from a juvenile and domestic relations district court pursuant to Article 7 (§16.1-269.1 et seq.) of Chapter 11 of Title 16.1 shall be docketed as provided in this section upon return of a true bill of indictment by the grand jury.
(Chgd. by L.1996 ch. 616, eff. 7/1/96.)

§19.2-241. Time within which court to set criminal cases for trial.

The judge of each circuit court shall fix a day of his court when the trial of criminal cases will commence, and may make such general or special order in reference thereto, and to the summoning of witnesses, as may seem proper, but all criminal cases shall be disposed of before civil cases, unless the court shall direct otherwise.

When an indictment is found against a person for felony or when an appeal has been perfected from the conviction of a misdemeanor or traffic infraction, the accused, if in custody, or if he appear according to his recognizance, may be tried at the same term and shall be tried within the time limits fixed in §19.2-243; provided that no trial shall be held on the first day of the term unless it be with consent of the attorney for the Commonwealth and the accused and his attorney.

§19.2-242. Accused discharged from jail if not indicted in time.

A person in jail on a criminal charge shall be discharged from imprisonment if a presentment, indictment or information be not found or filed against him before the end of the second term of the court at which he is held to answer, unless it appear to the court that material witnesses for the Commonwealth have been enticed or kept away or are prevented from attendance by sickness or inevitable accident, and except, also, in the case provided in §19.2-169. A discharge under the provisions of this section shall not, however, prevent a reincarceration after a presentment or indictment has been found.

§19.2-243. Limitation on prosecution of felony due to lapse of time after finding of probable cause; misdemeanors; exceptions.

Where a general district court has found that there is probable cause to believe that the accused has committed a felony, the accused, if he is held continuously in custody thereafter, shall be forever discharged from prosecution for such offense if no trial is commenced in the circuit court within five months from the date such probable cause was found by the district court; and if the accused is not held in custody but has been recognized for his appearance in the circuit court to answer for such offense, he shall be forever discharged from prosecution therefor if no trial is commenced in the circuit court within nine months from the date such probable cause was found.

If there was no preliminary hearing in the district court, or if such preliminary hearing was waived by the accused, the commencement of the running of the five and nine months periods, respectively, set forth in this section, shall be from the date an indictment or presentment is found against the accused.

If an indictment or presentment is found against the accused but he has not been arrested for the offense charged

 Zv

therein, the five and nine months periods, respectively, shall commence to run from the date of his arrest thereon.

Where a case is before a circuit court on appeal from a conviction of a misdemeanor or traffic infraction in a district court, the accused shall be forever discharged from prosecution for such offense if the trial de novo in the circuit court is not commenced (i) within five months from the date of the conviction if the accused has been held continuously in custody or (ii) within nine months of the date of the conviction if the accused has been recognized for his appearance in the circuit court.

The provisions of this section shall not apply to such period of time as the failure to try the accused was caused:

1. By his insanity or by reason of his confinement in a hospital for care and observation;
2. By the witnesses for the Commonwealth being enticed or kept away, or prevented from attending by sickness or accident;
3. By the granting of a separate trial at the request of a person indicted jointly with others for a felony;
4. By continuance granted on the motion of the accused or his counsel, or by concurrence of the accused or his counsel in such a motion by the attorney for the Commonwealth, or by the failure of the accused or his counsel to make a timely objection to such a motion by the attorney for the Commonwealth, or by reason of his escaping from jail or failing to appear according to his recognizance; or
5. By the inability of the jury to agree in their verdict.

But the time during the pendency of any appeal in any appellate court shall not be included as applying to the provisions of this section.
(Chgd. by L.1995 chs. 37, 352, eff. 7/1/95.)

ARTICLE 2
VENUE

§19.2-244. Venue in general.

Except as otherwise provided by law, the prosecution of a criminal case shall be had in the county or city in which the offense was committed. Except as to motions for a change of venue, all other questions of venue must be raised before verdict in cases tried by a jury and before the finding of guilty in cases tried by the court without a jury.

§19.2-245. Offenses committed without and made punishable within Commonwealth; embezzlement or larceny committed within Commonwealth; where prosecuted.

Prosecution for offenses committed wholly or in part without and made punishable within this Commonwealth may be in any county or city in which the offender is found or to which he is sent by any judge or court; and if any person shall commit larceny or embezzlement beyond the jurisdiction of this Commonwealth and bring the stolen property into the same he shall be liable to prosecution and punishment for larceny or embezzlement in any county or city into which he shall have taken the property as if the same had been wholly committed therein; and if any person shall commit larceny or embezzlement within this Commonwealth and take the stolen property into any county or city other than the county or city within which the same was committed he shall be liable to prosecution and punishment for such larceny or embezzlement in any such county or city into which he shall have taken the property as if the same had been wholly committed therein; provided, that if any person shall commit embezzlement within this Commonwealth he shall be liable as aforesaid or to prosecution and punishment for his offense in the county or city in which he was legally obligated to deliver the embezzled funds or property.

§19.2-245.1. Forgery; where prosecuted.

If any person commits forgery, that forgery may be prosecuted in any county or city (i) where the writing was forged, or where the same was used or passed, or attempted to be used or passed, or deposited or placed with another person, firm, association, or corporation either for collection or credit for the account of any person, firm, association, or corporation or (ii) where the writing is found in the possession of the defendant.
(Chgd. by L.2000 ch. 327, eff. 7/1/2000.)

§19.2-245.2. Tax offenses; where prosecuted.

If an offense involving tax, as defined in Title 58.1, is committed, that offense may be prosecuted in either any county or city where a false or fraudulent tax return, document, or statement was filed, or the county or city where the offender resides. However, venue shall not be in the City of Richmond solely because a false or fraudulent tax return, document or statement was filed directly with the Department of Taxation.

§19.2-246. Injury inflicted by person within Commonwealth upon one outside Commonwealth.

If a mortal wound or other violence or injury be inflicted by a person within this Commonwealth upon one outside of the same, or upon one in this State who afterwards dies from the effect thereof out of the Commonwealth, the offender shall be amenable to prosecution and punishment for the offense in the courts of the county or city in which he was at the time of the commission thereof as if the same had been committed in such county or city.

§19.2-247. Venue in certain homicide cases.

Where evidence exists that a homicide has been committed either within or without this Commonwealth, under circumstances which make it unknown where such crime was committed, the offense shall be amenable to prosecution in the courts of the county or city where the body of the victim may be found, as if the offense has been committed in such county or city. In a prosecution for capital murder pursuant to subdivision 8 of §18.2-31, the offense may be prosecuted in any jurisdiction in the Commonwealth in which any one of the killings may be prosecuted.
(Chgd. by L.1996 ch. 959, eff. 7/1/96.)

§19.2-248. Venue when mortal wound, etc., inflicted in one county and death ensues in another.

If a mortal wound, or other violence or injury, be inflicted, or poison administered in one county or city, and death ensues therefrom in another county or city, the offense may be prosecuted in either.

§19.2-249. Offenses committed on boundary of two counties, or county and city, etc.; where prosecuted.

An offense committed on the boundary of 2 counties, or on the boundary of a county and city, or within 300 yards thereof, may be alleged to have been committed, and may be prosecuted and punished, in either county, or the county or city, and any sheriff, deputy sheriff, or other police officer shall have jurisdiction to make arrests and preserve the peace for a like distance on either side of the boundary line between such counties, or such county and city.

§19.2-249.1. Offenses committed within towns situated in two or more counties; where prosecuted.

An offense or traffic infraction committed within a town situated in two or more counties within the Commonwealth may be alleged to have been committed, and may be prosecuted and punished, in any one of such counties.

§19.2-250. How far jurisdiction of corporate authorities extends.

A. Notwithstanding any other provision of this article and except as provided in subsection B hereof, the jurisdiction of the corporate authorities of each town or city, in criminal cases involving offenses against the Commonwealth, shall extend within the Commonwealth one mile beyond the corporate limits of such town or city; except that such jurisdiction of the corporate authorities of towns situated in counties having a density of population in excess of 300 inhabitants per square mile, or in counties adjacent to cities having a population of 170,000 or more, shall extend for 300 yards beyond the corporate limits of such town or, in the case of the criminal jurisdiction of an adjacent county, for 300 yards within such town.

B. Notwithstanding any other provision of this article, the jurisdiction of the authorities of a county adjoining the City of Richmond and having a population between 209,200 and 209,500 or a county adjoining the City of Richmond and having a population between 217,800 and 217,900, according to the 1990 census, in criminal cases involving offenses against the Commonwealth, shall extend one mile beyond the limits of such county into the City of Richmond.

(Chgd. by L.1998 ch. 428, eff. 7/1/98.)

§19.2-251. When and how venue may be changed.

A circuit court may, on motion of the accused or of the Commonwealth, for good cause, order the venue for the trial of a criminal case in such court to be changed to some other circuit court. Such motion when made by the accused may be made in his absence upon a petition signed and sworn to by him.

Whenever the mayor of any city, or the sheriff of any county, shall call on the Governor for military force to protect the accused from violence, the judge of the circuit court of the city or county having jurisdiction of the offense shall, upon a petition signed and sworn to by the accused, whether he be present or not, at once order the venue to be changed to the circuit court of a city or county sufficiently remote from the place where the offense was committed to insure the safe and impartial trial of the accused.

§19.2-252. Court ordering change of venue may admit accused to bail and recognize witnesses; remand of accused not admitted to bail.

When the venue is so changed, the court making the order may admit the accused to bail and shall recognize the witnesses and the accused if admitted to bail and the bail be given, to appear on some certain day before the court to which the case is removed; if the accused be not admitted to bail or the bail required be not given, the court shall remand him to its own jail and order its officer to remove him thence to the jail of the court to which the case is removed, so that he shall be there before the day for the appearance of the witnesses.

§19.2-253. Procedure upon and after change of venue.

The clerk of the court which orders a change of venue shall certify copies of the recognizances aforesaid and of the record of the case to the clerk of the court to which the case is removed, who shall thereupon issue a venire facias, directed to the officer of such court; and such court shall proceed with the case as if the prosecution had been originally therein; and for that purpose the certified copies aforesaid shall be sufficient.

ARTICLE 3
ARRAIGNMENT; PLEAS; TRIAL WITHOUT JURY

§19.2-254. Arraignment; pleas; when court may refuse to accept plea.

Arraignment shall be conducted in open court. It shall consist of reading to the accused the charge on which he will be tried and calling on him to plead thereto. In a felony case, arraignment is not necessary when waived by the accused. In a misdemeanor case, arraignment is not necessary when waived by the accused or his counsel, or when the accused fails to appear.

An accused may plead not guilty, guilty or nolo contendere. The court may refuse to accept a plea of guilty to any lesser offense included in the charge upon which the accused is arraigned; but, in misdemeanor and felony cases the court shall not refuse to accept a plea of nolo contendere.

With the approval of the court and the consent of the Commonwealth, a defendant may enter a conditional plea of guilty in a felony case, reserving the right, on appeal from the judgment, to a review of the adverse determination of any specified pretrial motion. If the defendant prevails on appeal, he shall be allowed to withdraw his plea.

§19.2-254.1. Procedure in traffic infraction cases.

In a traffic infraction case, as defined in §46.2-100, involving an offense included in the uniform fine schedule established pursuant to §16.1-69.40:1, a defendant may elect to enter a written appearance and waive court hearing, except in instances in which property damage or personal injury resulted. Arraignment is not necessary when waived by the accused or his counsel, when the accused fails to appear, or when such written appearance has been elected.

 Zv

An accused may plead not guilty, guilty, or nolo contendere; and the court shall not refuse to accept a plea of nolo contendere. A plea of guilty may be entered in writing without court appearance.

When an accused tenders payment without executing a written waiver of court hearing and entry of guilty plea, such tender of payment shall itself be deemed a waiver of court hearing and entry of guilty plea.

In districts with traffic violations bureaus on July 1, 1977, the chief judge of the district may designate the traffic violations bureau for the receipt of a written appearance, waiver of court hearing and guilty plea.

§19.2-254.2. Procedure in nontraffic offenses for which prepayment is authorized.

In any prepayable nontraffic offense case as defined in §16.1-69.40:2 a defendant may elect to enter a written appearance and waive court hearing. Arraignment is not necessary when waived by the accused or his counsel, when the accused fails to appear, or when such written appearance has been elected.

An accused may plead not guilty, guilty, or nolo contendere; and the court shall not refuse to accept a plea of nolo contendere. A plea of guilty may be entered in writing without court appearance.

When an accused tenders payment without executing a written waiver of court hearing and entry of guilty plea, such tender of payment shall itself be deemed a waiver of court hearing and entry of guilty plea. Likewise when a person charged with a prepayable nontraffic offense fails to enter a written or court appearance, he shall be deemed to have waived court hearing and the case may be heard in his absence. In all other respects prepayable traffic offenses shall be treated as all other misdemeanors.

§19.2-255. Defendant allowed to plead several matters of law or fact.

The defendant in any criminal prosecution may plead as many several matters, whether of law or fact, as he shall think necessary, and he may file pleas in bar at the same time with pleas in abatement, or within a reasonable time thereafter; but the issues on the pleas in abatement shall be first tried.

§19.2-256. Approvers.

Approvers shall not be admitted in any case.

§19.2-257. Trial without jury in felony cases.

Upon a plea of guilty in a felony case, tendered in person by the accused after being advised by counsel, the court shall hear and determine the case without the intervention of a jury; or if the accused plead not guilty, with his consent after being advised by counsel and the concurrence of the attorney for the Commonwealth and of the court entered of record, the court shall hear and determine the case without the intervention of a jury. In such cases the court shall have and exercise all the powers, privileges and duties given to juries by any statute relating to crimes and punishments.

§19.2-258. Trial of misdemeanors by court without jury; failure to appear deemed waiver of jury.

In all cases of a misdemeanor upon a plea of guilty, tendered in person by the accused or his counsel, the court shall hear and determine the case without the intervention of a jury. If the accused plead not guilty, in person or by his counsel, the court, in its discretion, with the concurrence of the accused and the attorney for the Commonwealth, may hear and determine the case without the intervention of a jury. In each instance the court shall have and exercise all the powers and duties vested in juries by any statute relating to crimes and punishments.

When a person charged with a misdemeanor has been admitted to bail or released upon his own recognizance for his appearance before a court of record having jurisdiction of the case, for a hearing thereon and fails to appear in accordance with the condition of his bail or recognizance, he shall be deemed to have waived trial by a jury and the case may be heard in his absence as upon a plea of not guilty.

§19.2-258.1. Trial of traffic infractions; measure of proof; failure to appear.

For any traffic infraction cases tried in a district court, the court shall hear and determine the case without the intervention of a jury. For any traffic infraction case appealed to a circuit court, the defendant shall have the right to trial by jury. The defendant shall be presumed innocent until proven guilty beyond a reasonable doubt.

When a person charged with a traffic infraction fails to enter a written or court appearance, he shall be deemed to have waived court hearing and the case may be heard in his absence, after which he shall be notified of the court's finding. He shall be advised that if he fails to comply within ten days of the date of the notice with any order of the court therein, the court may order suspension of his driver's license as provided in §46.2-395 but the court shall not issue a warrant for his failure to appear pursuant to §46.2-938.

§19.2-259. On trial for felony, accused to be present; when court may enter plea for him, and trial go on.

A person tried for felony shall be personally present during the trial. If when arraigned he will not plead or answer and does not confess his guilt the court shall have the plea of not guilty entered and the trial shall proceed as if the accused had put in that plea. But for the purposes of this section a motion for a continuance, whether made before or after arraignment, shall not be deemed to be part of the trial.

ARTICLE 4
TRIAL BY JURY

§19.2-260. Provisions of Title 8.01 apply except as provided in this article.

Except as otherwise provided in this article, trial by jury in criminal cases shall be regulated as provided for in Chapter 11 (§8.01-336 et seq.) of Title 8.01.

§19.2-261. Charging grand jury in presence of person selected as juror.

The court shall not charge the grand jury in the presence of any person selected as a juror to try any person indicted by the said grand jury. A violation of this provision shall constitute reversible error in any criminal case tried by a jury composed of one or more such veniremen.

§19.2-262. Waiver of jury trial; numbers of jurors in criminal cases; how jurors selected from panel.

A. In any criminal case in which trial by jury is dispensed with as provided by law, the whole matter of law and fact shall be heard and judgment given by the court. In appeals from juvenile and domestic relations district courts the infant, through his guardian ad litem or counsel, may waive a jury.

B. Twelve persons from a panel of twenty shall constitute a jury in a felony case. Seven persons from a panel of thirteen shall constitute a jury in a misdemeanor case.

C. The parties or their counsel, beginning with the attorney for the Commonwealth, shall alternately strike off one name from the panel until the number remaining shall be reduced to the number required for a jury.

D. In any case in which persons indicted for felony are tried jointly, if counsel or the accused are unable to agree on the full number to be stricken, or, if for any other reason counsel or the accused fail or refuse to strike off the full number of jurors allowed such party, the clerk shall place in a box ballots bearing the names of the jurors whose names have not been stricken and shall cause to be drawn from the box such number of ballots as may be necessary to complete the number of strikes allowed the party or parties failing or refusing to strike. Thereafter, if the opposing side is entitled to further strikes, they shall be made in the usual manner.
(Chgd. by L.1996 ch. 616; L.1997 chs. 516, 518, eff. 7/1/97.)

§19.2-262.1. Joinder of defendants.

On motion of the Commonwealth, for good cause shown, the court shall order persons charged with participating in contemporaneous and related acts or occurrences or in a series of acts or occurrences constituting an offense or offenses, to be tried jointly unless such joint trial would constitute prejudice to a defendant. If the court finds that a joint trial would constitute prejudice to a defendant, the court shall order severance as to that defendant or provide such other relief justice requires.
(Chgd. by L.1997 ch. 518, eff. 7/1/97.)

§19.2-263.1. Contact between judge and juror prohibited.

No judge shall communicate in any way with a juror in a criminal proceeding concerning the juror's conduct or any aspect of the case during the course of the trial outside the presence of the parties or their counsel.

§19.2-263.2. Jury instructions.

A proposed jury instruction submitted by a party, which constitutes an accurate statement of the law applicable to the case, shall not be withheld from the jury solely for its nonconformance with model jury instructions.

§19.2-264. When jury need not be kept together in felony case; sufficient compliance with requirement that jury be kept together.

In any case of a felony the jury shall not be kept together unless the court otherwise directs. Whenever a jury is required to be kept together, it shall be deemed sufficient compliance although the court for good cause permits one or more of such jurors to be separated from the others; provided all such jurors, whether separated or not, be kept in charge of officers provided therefor.

§19.2-264.1. Views by juries.

The jury in any criminal case may, at the request of either the attorney for the Commonwealth or any defendant, be taken to view the premises or place in question, or any property, matter or thing relating to the case, when it shall appear to the court that such view is necessary to a just decision.

ARTICLE 4.1
TRIAL OF CAPITAL CASES

§19.2-264.2. Conditions for imposition of death sentence.

In assessing the penalty of any person convicted of an offense for which the death penalty may be imposed, a sentence of death shall not be imposed unless the court or jury shall (1) after consideration of the past criminal record of convictions of the defendant, find that there is a probability that the defendant would commit criminal acts of violence that would constitute a continuing serious threat to society or that his conduct in committing the offense for which he stands charged was outrageously or wantonly vile, horrible or inhuman in that it involved torture, depravity of mind or an aggravated battery to the victim; and (2) recommend that the penalty of death be imposed.

§19.2-264.3. Procedure for trial by jury.

A. In any case in which the offense may be punishable by death which is tried before a jury the court shall first submit to the jury the issue of guilt or innocence of the defendant of the offense charged in the indictment, or any other offense supported by the evidence for which a lesser punishment is provided by law and the penalties therefor.

B. If the jury finds the defendant guilty of an offense for which the death penalty may not be imposed, it shall fix the punishment as provided in §19.2-295.1.

C. If the jury finds the defendant guilty of an offense which may be punishable by death, then a separate proceeding before the same jury shall be held as soon as is practicable on the issue of the penalty, which shall be fixed as is provided in §19.2-264.4.

If the sentence of death is subsequently set aside or found invalid, and the defendant or the Commonwealth requests a jury for purposes of resentencing, the court shall impanel a different jury on the issue of penalty.

§19.2-264.3:1. Expert assistance when defendant's mental condition relevant to capital sentencing.

A. Upon (i) motion of the attorney for a defendant charged with or convicted of capital murder and (ii) a finding by the court that the defendant is financially unable to pay for expert assistance, the court shall appoint one or more qualified mental health experts to evaluate the defendant and to assist the defense in the preparation and presentation of information concerning the defendant's history, character, or mental condition, including (i) whether the defendant acted under extreme mental or emotional disturbance at the time of the offense; (ii) whether the capacity of the defendant to appreciate the criminality of his conduct or to conform his conduct to the requirements of the law was significantly impaired at the time of the offense; and (iii) whether there are any other factors in mitigation relating to the history or character of the defendant or the defendant's mental condition at the time of the offense. The mental health expert appointed pursuant to this section shall be (i) a psychiatrist, a clinical psychologist, or an individual with a doctorate degree in clinical psychology who has successfully completed forensic evaluation training as approved by the Commissioner of Mental Health, Mental Retardation and Substance Abuse Services and (ii) qualified by specialized training and experience to perform forensic evaluations. The defendant shall not be entitled to a mental health expert of the defendant's own choosing or to funds to employ such expert.

B. Evaluations performed pursuant to subsection A may be combined with evaluations performed pursuant to §19.2-169.5 and shall be governed by subsections B and C of §19.2-169.5.

C. The expert appointed pursuant to subsection A shall submit to the attorney for the defendant a report concerning the history and character of the defendant and the defendant's mental condition at the time of the offense. The report shall include the expert's opinion as to (i) whether the defendant acted under extreme mental or emotional disturbance at the time of the offense, (ii) whether the capacity of the defendant to appreciate the criminality of his conduct or to conform his conduct to the requirements of the law was significantly impaired, and (iii) whether there are any other factors in mitigation relating to the history or character of the defendant or the defendant's mental condition at the time of the offense.

D. The report described in subsection C shall be sent solely to the attorney for the defendant and shall be protected by the attorney-client privilege. However, the Commonwealth shall be given the report and the results of any other evaluation of the defendant's mental condition conducted relative to the sentencing proceeding and copies of psychiatric, psychological, medical or other records obtained during the course of such evaluation, after the attorney for the defendant gives notice of an intent to present psychiatric or psychological evidence in mitigation pursuant to subsection E.

E. In any case in which a defendant charged with capital murder intends, in the event of conviction, to present testimony of an expert witness to support a claim in mitigation relating to the defendant's history, character or mental condition, he or his attorney shall give notice in writing to the attorney for the Commonwealth, at least twenty-one days before trial, of his intention to present such testimony. In the event that such notice is not given and the defendant tenders testimony by an expert witness at the sentencing phase of the trial, then the court may, in its discretion, upon objection of the Commonwealth, either allow the Commonwealth a continuance or, under appropriate circumstances, bar the defendant from presenting such evidence.

F. 1. If the attorney for the defendant gives notice pursuant to subsection E and the Commonwealth thereafter seeks an evaluation concerning the existence or absence of mitigating circumstances relating to the defendant's mental condition at the time of the offense, the court shall appoint one or more qualified experts to perform such an evaluation. The court shall order the defendant to submit to such an evaluation, and advise the defendant on the record in court that a refusal to cooperate with the Commonwealth's expert could result in exclusion of the defendant's expert evidence. The qualification of the experts shall be governed by subsection A. The location of the evaluation shall be governed by subsection B of §19.2-169.5. The attorney for the Commonwealth shall be responsible for providing the experts the information specified in subsection C of §19.2-169.5. After performing their evaluation, the experts shall report their findings and opinions and provide copies of psychiatric, psychological, medical or other records obtained during the course of the evaluation to the attorneys for the Commonwealth and the defense.

2. If the court finds, after hearing evidence presented by the parties, out of the presence of the jury, that the defendant has refused to cooperate with an evaluation requested by the Commonwealth, the court may admit evidence of such refusal or, in the discretion of the court, bar the defendant from presenting his expert evidence.

G. No statement or disclosure by the defendant made during a competency evaluation performed pursuant to §19.2-169.1, an evaluation performed pursuant to §19.2-169.5 to determine sanity at the time of the offense, treatment provided pursuant to §19.2-169.2 or §19.2-169.6 or a capital sentencing evaluation performed pursuant to this section, and no evidence derived from any such statements or disclosures may be introduced against the defendant at the sentencing phase of a capital murder trial for the purpose of proving the aggravating circumstances specified in §19.2-264.4. Such statements or disclosures shall be admissible in rebuttal only when relevant to issues in mitigation raised by the defense.

(Chgd. by L.1996 chs. 937, 980, eff. 7/1/96.)

§19.2-264.3:2. Notice to the defendant of intention to present evidence of unadjudicated criminal conduct.

Upon motion of the defendant, in any case in which the offense for which the defendant is to be tried may be punishable by death, if the attorney for the Commonwealth intends to introduce during a sentencing proceeding held pursuant to §19.2-264.4 evidence of defendant's unadjudicated criminal conduct, the attorney for the Commonwealth shall give notice in writing to the attorney for the defendant of such intention. The notice shall include a description of the alleged unadjudicated criminal conduct and, to the extent such information is available, the time and place such conduct will be alleged to have occurred.

The court shall specify the time by which such notice shall be given.

§19.2-264.4. Sentence proceeding.

A. Upon a finding that the defendant is guilty of an offense which may be punishable by death, a proceeding shall be held which shall be limited to a determination as to whether the defendant shall be sentenced to death or life imprisonment. Upon request of the defendant, a jury shall be instructed that for all Class 1 felony offenses committed after January 1, 1995, a defendant shall not be eligible for parole if sentenced to imprisonment for life. In case of trial by jury, where a sentence of death is not recommended, the defendant shall be sentenced to imprisonment for life.

A1. In any proceeding conducted pursuant to this section, the court shall permit the victim, as defined in §19.2-11.01, upon the motion of the attorney for the Commonwealth, and with the consent of the victim, to testify in the presence of the accused regarding the impact of the offense upon the victim. The court shall limit the victim's testimony to the factors set forth in clauses (i) through (vi) of subsection A of §19.2-299.1.

B. In cases of trial by jury, evidence may be presented as to any matter which the court deems relevant to sentence, except that reports under the provisions of §19.2-299, or under any rule of court, shall not be admitted into evidence.

Evidence which may be admissible, subject to the rules of evidence governing admissibility, may include the circumstances surrounding the offense, the history and background of the defendant, and any other facts in mitigation of the offense. Facts in mitigation may include, but shall not be limited to, the following: (i) the defendant has no significant history of prior criminal activity, (ii) the capital felony was committed while the defendant was under the influence of extreme mental or emotional disturbance, (iii) the victim was a participant in the defendant's conduct or consented to the act, (iv) at the time of the commission of the capital felony, the capacity of the defendant to appreciate the criminality of his conduct or to conform his conduct to the requirements of law was significantly impaired, (v) the age of the defendant at the time of the commission of the capital offense, or (vi) mental retardation of the defendant.

C. The penalty of death shall not be imposed unless the Commonwealth shall prove beyond a reasonable doubt that there is a probability based upon evidence of the prior history of the defendant or of the circumstances surrounding the commission of the offense of which he is accused that he would commit criminal acts of violence that would constitute a continuing serious threat to society, or that his conduct in committing the offense was outrageously or wantonly vile, horrible or inhuman, in that it involved torture, depravity of mind or aggravated battery to the victim.

D. The verdict of the jury shall be in writing, and in one of the following forms:

(1) "We, the jury, on the issue joined, having found the defendant guilty of (here set out statutory language of the offense charged) and that (after consideration of his prior history that there is a probability that he would commit criminal acts of violence that would constitute a continuing serious threat to society) or his conduct in committing the offense is outrageously or wantonly vile, horrible or inhuman in that it involved (torture) (depravity of mind) (aggravated battery to the victim), and having considered the evidence in mitigation of the offense, unanimously fix his punishment at death.

Signed...................., foreman"

or

(2) "We, the jury, on the issue joined, having found the defendant guilty of (here set out statutory language of the offense charged) and having considered all of the evidence in aggravation and mitigation of such offense, fix his punishment at imprisonment for life.

Signed...................., foreman"

E. In the event the jury cannot agree as to the penalty, the court shall dismiss the jury, and impose a sentence of imprisonment for life.

(Chgd. by L.1998 ch. 485; L.2000 ch. 838, eff. 7/1/2000.)

§19.2-264.5. Post-sentence reports.

When the punishment of any person has been fixed at death, the court shall, before imposing sentence, direct a probation officer of the court to thoroughly investigate the history of the defendant and any and all other relevant facts, to the end that the court may be fully advised as to whether the sentence of death is appropriate and just. Reports shall be made, presented and filed as provided in §19.2-299 except that, notwithstanding any other provision of law, such reports shall in all cases contain a Victim Impact Statement. Such statement shall contain the same information and be prepared in the same manner as Victim Impact Statements prepared pursuant to §19.2-299.1. After consideration of the report, and upon good cause shown, the court may set aside the sentence of death and impose a sentence of imprisonment for life.

ARTICLE 5
MISCELLANEOUS PROVISIONS

Section

§19.2-265. Opening statement of counsel.

On the trial of any case of felony or misdemeanor and before any evidence is submitted on either side, the attorney for the Commonwealth and counsel for the accused, respectively, shall have the right to make an opening statement of their case.

§19.2-265.01. Victims, certain members of the family and support persons not to be excluded.

During the trial of every criminal case and in all court proceedings attendant to trial, whether before, during or after trial, including any proceedings occurring after an appeal by the defendant or the Commonwealth, at which attendance by the defendant is permitted, whether in a circuit or district court, any victim as defined in §19.2-11.01 may remain in the courtroom and shall not be excluded unless the court determines, in its discretion, the presence of the victim would impair the conduct of a fair trial. In any case involving a minor victim, the court may permit an adult chosen by the minor to be present in the courtroom during any proceedings in addition to or in lieu of the minor's parent or guardian.

The attorney for the Commonwealth shall give prior notice when practicable of such trial and attendant proceedings and changes in the scheduling thereof to any known victim and to any known adult chosen in accordance with this section by a minor victim, at the address or telephone number, or both, provided in writing by such person.

(Chgd. by L.1995 ch. 687; L.1996 ch. 546; L.1999 ch. 844; L.2000 ch. 339, eff. 7/1/2000.)

§19.2-265.1. Exclusion of witnesses.

In the trial of every criminal case, the court, whether a court of record or a court not of record, may upon its own motion and shall upon the motion of either the attorney for the Commonwealth or any defendant, require the exclusion of every witness to be called, including, by not limited to, police officers or other investigators; however, each defendant who is an individual and one officer or agent of each defendant which is a corporation or association shall be exempt from the rule of this section as a matter of right.

§19.2-265.2. Judicial notice of laws.

A. Whenever, in any criminal case it becomes necessary to ascertain what the law, statutory or otherwise, of this Commonwealth, of another state, of the United States, of another country, or of any political subdivision or agency of the same is, or was, at any time, the court shall take judicial notice thereof whether specially pleaded or not.

B. The court, in taking such notice, shall consult any book, record, register, journal, or other official document or publication purporting to contain, state, or explain such law, and may consider any evidence or other information or argument that is offered on the subject.

§19.2-265.3. Nolle prosequi; discretion of court upon good cause shown.

Nolle prosequi shall be entered only in the discretion of the court, upon motion of the Commonwealth with good cause therefor shown.

§19.2-265.4. Failure to provide discovery.

A. In any criminal prosecution for a felony in a circuit court or for a misdemeanor brought on direct indictment, the attorney for the Commonwealth shall have a duty to adequately and fully provide discovery as provided under Rule 3A:11 of the Rules of the Supreme Court. Rule 3A:11 shall be construed to apply to such felony and misdemeanor prosecutions. This duty to disclose shall be continuing and shall apply to any additional evidence or material discovered by the Commonwealth prior to or during trial which is subject to discovery or inspection and has been previously requested by the accused.

B. If at any time during the course of the proceedings it is brought to the attention of the court that the attorney for the Commonwealth has failed to comply with this section, the court may order the Commonwealth to permit the discovery or inspection, grant a continuance, or prohibit the Commonwealth from introducing evidence not disclosed, or the court may enter such other order as it deems just under the circumstances.

(Chgd. by L.1995 ch. 504, eff. 7/1/95.)

§19.2-265.5. Prosecuting misdemeanor cases without attorney.

Notwithstanding any of the provisions of §19.2-265.1, whenever in a misdemeanor case neither an attorney for the Commonwealth nor any other attorney for the prosecution is present, the complaining witness may be allowed to remain in court throughout the entire trial if necessary for the orderly presentation of witnesses for the prosecution.

§19.2-266. Exclusion of persons from trial; photographs and broadcasting permitted under designated guidelines; exceptions.

In the trial of all criminal cases, whether the same be felony or misdemeanor cases, the court may, in its discretion, exclude from the trial any persons whose presence would impair the conduct of a fair trial, provided that the right of the accused to a public trial shall not be violated.

A court may solely in its discretion permit the taking of photographs in the courtroom during the progress of judicial proceedings and the broadcasting of judicial proceedings by radio or television and the use of electronic or photographic means for the perpetuation of the record or parts thereof in criminal and in civil cases, but only in accordance with the rules set forth hereunder. In addition to such rules, the Supreme Court and the Court of Appeals shall have the authority to promulgate any other rules they deem necessary to govern electronic media and still photography coverage in their respective courts. The following rules shall serve as guidelines, and a violation of these rules may be punishable as contempt:

COVERAGE ALLOWED

1. The presiding judge shall at all times have authority to prohibit, interrupt or terminate electronic media and still photography coverage of public judicial proceedings. The presiding judge shall advise the parties of such coverage in advance of the proceedings and shall allow the parties to object thereto. For good cause shown, the presiding judge may prohibit coverage in any case and may restrict coverage as he deems appropriate to meet the ends of justice.

2. Coverage of the following types of judicial proceedings shall be prohibited: adoption proceedings, juvenile proceedings, child custody proceedings, divorce proceedings, temporary and permanent spousal support proceedings, proceedings concerning sexual offenses, proceedings for the hearing of motions to suppress evidence, proceedings involving trade secrets, and in camera proceedings.

3. Coverage of the following categories of witnesses shall be prohibited: police informants, minors, undercover agents and victims and families of victims of sexual offenses.

4. Coverage of jurors shall be prohibited expressly at any stage of a judicial proceeding, including that portion of a proceeding during which a jury is selected. The judge shall inform all potential jurors at the beginning of the jury selection process of this prohibition.

5. To protect the attorney-client privilege and the right to counsel, there shall be no recording or broadcast of sound from such conferences which occur in a court facility between attorneys and their clients, between co-counsel of a client, between adverse counsel, or between counsel and the presiding judge held at the bench or in chambers.

LOCATION OF EQUIPMENT AND PERSONNEL

1. The location of recording and camera equipment shall be strictly regulated so as not to be intrusive.

2. Media personnel shall not enter or leave the courtroom once the proceedings are in session except during a court recess or adjournment.

3. Electronic media equipment and still photography equipment shall not be taken into the courtroom or removed from the designated media area except at the following times:

a. Prior to the convening of proceedings;

b. During any luncheon recess;

c. During any court recess with the permission of the trial judge; and

d. After adjournment for the day of the proceedings.

OFFICIAL REPRESENTATIVES OF THE MEDIA

The Virginia Association of Broadcasters and the Virginia Press Association may designate one person to represent the television media, one person to represent the radio broadcasters, and one person to represent still photographers in each jurisdiction in which electronic media and still photographic coverage is desired. The names of the persons so designated shall be forwarded to the chief judge of the court in the county or city in which coverage is desired so that arrangements can be made for the "pooling" of equipment and personnel. Such persons shall also be the only persons authorized to speak for the media to the presiding judge concerning the coverage of any judicial proceedings.

EQUIPMENT AND PERSONNEL

1. No distracting lights or sounds shall be permitted.

2. Not more than two television cameras shall be permitted in any proceeding.

3. Not more than one still photographer, utilizing not more than two still cameras with not more than two lenses for each camera and related equipment for print purposes, shall be permitted in any proceeding.

4. Not more than one audio system for broadcast purposes shall be permitted in any proceeding.

Audio pickup for all media purposes shall be accomplished with existing audio systems present in the court facility. If no technically suitable audio system exists in the court facility, microphones and related wiring essential for media purposes may be installed and maintained at media expense. The microphones and wiring must be unobtrusive and shall be located in places designated in advance of any proceeding by the chief judge of the court in which coverage is desired.

5. Any "pooling" arrangements among the media required by these limitations on equipment and personnel shall be the sole responsibility of the media without calling upon the presiding judge to mediate any dispute as to the

appropriate media representative or equipment authorized to cover a particular proceeding. In the absence of advance media agreement on disputed equipment or personnel issues, the presiding judge may exclude all contesting media personnel from a proceeding.

6. In no event shall the number of personnel in the designated area exceed the number necessary to operate the designated equipment.

7. Only television photographic and audio equipment which does not produce distracting sound or light shall be employed to cover judicial proceedings. No artificial lighting device of any kind shall he employed in connection with the television camera.

8. Only still camera equipment which does not produce distracting sound or light shall be employed to cover judicial proceedings. No artificial lighting device of any kind shall be employed in connection with a still camera.

9. With the concurrence of the chief judge of the court in which coverage is desired, modifications and additions may be made in light sources existing in the facility, provided such modifications or additions are installed and maintained without public expense.

IMPERMISSIBLE USE OF MEDIA MATERIAL

None of the film, video tape, still photographs or audio reproductions developed during or by virtue of coverage of a judicial proceeding shall be admissible as evidence (i) in the proceeding out of which it arose, (ii) in any proceeding subsequent and collateral thereto, or (iii) upon any retrial or appeal of such proceedings.

All electronic media and still photography coverage of public judicial proceedings authorized by this section, with the exception of electronic or photographic means authorized for the perpetuation of the record or parts thereof shall be conducted at no cost to the Commonwealth.

§19.2-266.1. Conviction of lesser offense on indictment for homicide.

In any trial upon an indictment charging homicide, the jury or the court may find the accused not guilty of the specific offense charged in the indictment, but guilty of any degree of homicide supported by the evidence for which a lesser punishment is provided by law.

§19.2-266.2. Defense objections to be raised before trial; hearing; bill of particulars.

Defense motions or objections seeking (i) suppression of evidence on the grounds such evidence was obtained in violation of the provisions of the Fourth, Fifth or Sixth Amendments to the Constitution of the United States or Article I, Section 8, 10 or 11 of the Constitution of Virginia proscribing illegal searches and seizures and protecting rights against self-incrimination, or (ii) dismissal of a warrant, information, or indictment or any count or charge thereof on the ground that a statute upon which it was based is unconstitutional shall be raised by motion or objection, in writing, before trial. The motions or objections shall be filed and notice given to opposing counsel not later than seven days before trial. A hearing on all such motions or objections shall be held not later than three days prior to trial, unless such period is waived by the accused, as set by the trial judge. The court may, however, for good cause shown and in the interest of justice, permit the motions or objections to be raised at a later time.

To assist the defense in filing such motions or objections in a timely manner, the trial court shall, upon motion of the defendant, direct the Commonwealth to file a bill of particulars pursuant to §19.2-230. The trial court shall fix the time within which such bill of particulars is to be filed. Upon further motion of the defendant, the trial court may, upon a showing of good cause, direct the Commonwealth to supplement its bill of particulars. The attorney for the Commonwealth shall certify that the matters stated in the bill of particulars are true and accurate to the best of his knowledge and belief.

CHAPTER 16
EVIDENCE AND WITNESSES

Article

ARTICLE 1
IN GENERAL

Section

§19.2-267. Provisions applicable to witnesses in criminal as well as civil cases; obligation to attend; summons.

Sections 8.01-396.1, 8.01-402, 8.01-405 and 8.01-407 to 8.01-410, inclusive, shall apply to a criminal as well as a civil case in all respects, except that a witness in a criminal case shall be obliged to attend, and may be proceeded against for failing to do so, although there may not previously have been any payment, or tender to him of anything for attendance, mileage, or tolls. In a criminal case a summons for a witness may be issued by the attorney for the Commonwealth or other attorney charged with the responsibility for the prosecution of a violation of any ordinance; however, any attorney who issues such a summons shall, at the time of the issuance, file with the clerk of the court the names and addresses of such witnesses.

§19.2-267.1. Authority of law-enforcement officer to issue summons to witness; failure to appear.

A summons may be issued by a law-enforcement officer during the course of his immediate investigation of an alleged misdemeanor for which an arrest warrant is not required pursuant to §19.2-81 to any person he reasonably believes was a witness to the offense. The summons shall command the person to appear and testify at the trial of any criminal charge brought against any person as the result of the offense.

A summons issued pursuant to this section shall have the same force as if issued by the court. The failure of any person so summoned to appear after receiving written notice of the date, time and place of the trial at least five days prior to the trial shall be punishable as contempt of the court in accordance with §18.2-456(5).

§19.2-268. Right of accused to testify.

In any case of felony or misdemeanor, the accused may be sworn and examined in his own behalf, and if so sworn and examined, he shall be deemed to have waived his privilege of not giving evidence against himself, and shall be subject to cross-examination as any other witness; but his failure to testify shall create no presumption against him, nor be the subject of any comment before the court or jury by the prosecuting attorney.

§19.2-268.1. Contradiction by prior inconsistent writing.

A witness in a criminal case may be cross-examined as to previous statements made by him in writing or reduced into writing, relative to the subject matter of the proceeding, without such writing being shown to him; but if it is intended to contradict such witness by the writing, his attention must, before such contradictory proof can be given, be called to the particular occasion on which the writing is supposed to have been made, and he may be asked if he did not make a writing of the purport of the one to be offered to contradict him, and if he denies making it, or does not admit its execution, it shall then be shown to him, and if he admits its genuineness, he shall be allowed to make his own explanation of it; but it shall be competent for the court at any time during the trial to require the production of the writing for its inspection, and the court may thereupon make such use of it for the purpose of the trial as it may think best.

§19.2-268.2. Recent complaint hearsay exception.

Notwithstanding any other provision of law, in any prosecution for criminal sexual assault under Article 7 (§18.2-61 et seq.) of Chapter 4 of Title 18.2, a violation of §§18.2-361, 18.2-366, 18.2-370 or §18.2-370.1, the fact that the person injured made complaint of the offense recently after commission of the offense is admissible, not as independent evidence of the offense, but for the purpose of corroborating the testimony of the complaining witness.

§19.2-269. Convicts as witnesses.

A person convicted of a felony or perjury shall not be incompetent to testify, but the fact of conviction may be shown in evidence to affect his credit.

§19.2-269.1. Convicts, etc., as witnesses.

Whenever the Commonwealth or a defendant in a criminal prosecution in any circuit court in this Commonwealth shall require as a witness in his behalf, a convict or prisoner in a correctional or penal institution as defined in §53.1-1, the court, on the application of such defendant or his attorney, or the attorney for the Commonwealth, shall issue an order to the Director of the Department of Corrections to deliver such witness to the sheriff of the county, or sergeant of the city, as the case may be, who shall go where such witness may then be and carry him to the court to testify as such witness, and after he shall have so testified and been released as such witness, carry him back to the place whence he came, for all of which service such officers shall be paid out of the criminal expense funds in the state treasury such compensation as the court in which the case is pending may certify to be reasonable.

§19.2-269.2. Nondisclosure of addresses or telephone numbers of crime victims and witnesses.

During any criminal proceeding, upon motion of the defendant or the attorney for the Commonwealth, a judge may prohibit testimony as to the current residential or business address or telephone number of a victim or witness if the judge determines that this information is not material under the circumstances of the case.

§19.2-270. When statement by accused as witness not received as evidence.

In a criminal prosecution, other than for perjury, or in an action on a penal statute, evidence shall not be given against the accused of any statement made by him as a witness upon a legal examination, in a criminal or civil action, unless such statement was made when examined as a witness in his own behalf.

§19.2-270.1. Use of photographs as evidence in certain larceny and burglary prosecutions.

In any prosecution for larceny under the provisions of §§18.2-95, 18.2-96 or §18.2-98, or for shoplifting under the provisions of §18.2-103, or for burglary under the provisions of §§18.2-89, 18.2-90, 18.2-91 or §18.2-92, photographs of the goods, merchandise, money or securities alleged to have been taken or converted shall be deemed competent evidence of such goods, merchandise, money or securities and shall be admissible in any proceeding, hearing or trial of the case to the same extent as if such goods, merchandise, money or securities had been introduced as evidence. Such photographs shall bear a written description of the goods, merchandise, money or securities alleged to have been taken or converted, the name of the owner of such goods, merchandise, money or securities and the manner of the identification of same by such owner, or the name of the place wherein the alleged offense occurred, the name of the accused, the name of the arresting or investigating police officer or conservator of the peace, the date of the photograph and the name of the photographer. Such writing shall be made under oath by the arresting or investigating police officer or conservator of the peace, and the photographs identified by the signature of the photographer. Upon the filing of such photograph and writing with the police authority or court holding such goods and merchandise as evidence, such goods or merchandise shall be returned to their owner, or the proprietor or manager of the store or establishment wherein the alleged offense occurred.

(Chgd. by L.1995 ch. 447, eff. 7/1/95.)

§19.2-270.2. Disposition of money, securities or documents seized upon arrest, etc., and pertinent as evidence.

A. When in the course of investigation or arrest, the investigating or arresting officer shall seize or come into the possession of moneys, cash, or negotiable or nonnegotiable instruments or securities, hereinafter called "moneys or securities," taken or retained unlawfully from a financial institution or other person, and such moneys or securities, or a portion thereof, shall be pertinent evidence in a pending prosecution or appeal therefrom, the officer or agency having possession thereof, may retain, pending such prosecution or appeal thereof, sufficient of such moneys or securities as shall be necessary to prove the crime of grand larceny or other crimes requiring a specific amount in value. The court upon motion of the attorney for the Commonwealth and for good cause shown may order the release of all moneys or securities, subject to the provisions of this section. The remaining excess moneys or securities, if any, may be released to the owner thereof, upon proper receipt therefor, which release shall be with the consent of the attorney for the Commonwealth. The officer or agency authorizing such release shall make an appropriate record of such moneys or securities released, including designation or copying of serial numbers, and such record or receipt shall be admissible into evidence in any proceeding, hearing or trial of the case to the same extent as if such moneys or securities had been introduced. Such record or receipt shall contain the name of the financial institution or person from whom such moneys or securities were taken, the place from which taken, the name of the accused, and the name of the arresting officer or officers coming into initial possession of such moneys or securities. Pictures shall be taken of any instruments or securities and such pictures shall be attached to the receipt or record above and shall contain further, in the case of such copying, the date of the photograph and the name of the photographer.

B. When in the course of investigation or arrest, the investigating or arresting officer seizes or comes into the possession of moneys or securities under the provisions of this section, and such moneys or securities, or a portion thereof, are introduced as an exhibit in a prosecution or appeal therefrom, the court may, with the consent of the attorney for the Commonwealth, authorize the clerk of the circuit court, upon all appeal rights being exhausted to deposit such moneys or cash in an interest-bearing account.
(Chgd. by L.1995 ch. 447, eff. 7/1/95.)

§19.2-270.3. Admissible evidence as to identity of party presenting bad check, draft or order.

In any prosecution under §18.2-181 or §18.2-182 for the presentation of a bad check, draft or order, the following shall be admissible in any proceeding, hearing or trial of the case:

1. The unpaid or dishonored check, draft or order, bearing a notation thereon of the full name, residence address, home telephone number, and either the driver's license, social security or other governmentally issued identification number of the person who delivered such check, draft or order to the payee, the cashing party or its representative, and bearing the initials of the representative of the payee or cashing party to whom the check, draft or order was delivered, as evidence that such information was transcribed on such check, draft or order at the time of such delivery; or

2. A composite photograph of the check, draft or order, and of the person delivering such check, draft or order, and of other documentation identifying such person, such as a driver's license, social security card, or other governmentally issued identification card, taken together at the time the check, draft or order was delivered by such person to the payee, the cashing party or its representative.

If such evidence is introduced, it may invoke an inference sufficient for the trier of fact to find that the person whose identifying information appears on the check, draft or order was the person who delivered the check, draft, or order in question to the payee, cashing party or its representative.

§19.2-270.4. When donation, destruction or return of exhibits received in evidence authorized.

A. Unless objection with sufficient cause is made, the trial court in any criminal case may order the donation or destruction of any or all exhibits received in evidence during the course of the trial (i) at any time after the expiration of the time for filing an appeal from the final judgment of the court if no appeal is taken or (ii) if an appeal is taken, at any time after exhaustion of all appellate remedies. The order of donation or destruction may require that photographs be made of all exhibits ordered to be donated or destroyed and that such photographs be appropriately labeled for future identification. In addition, the order shall state the nature of the exhibit subject to donation or destruction, identify the case in which such exhibit was received and from whom such exhibit was received, if known, and the manner by which the exhibit is to be destroyed or to whom donated.

B. A circuit court for good cause shown, on notice to the attorney for the Commonwealth and any attorney for a defendant in the case, may order the return of any or all exhibits to the owners thereof, notwithstanding the pendency of any appeal. The order may be upon such conditions as the court deems appropriate for future identification and inclusion in the record of a case subject to retrial. In addition, the owner shall acknowledge in a sworn affidavit to be filed with the record of the case, that he has retaken possession of such exhibit or exhibits.

C. Any photographs taken pursuant to an order of donation or destruction or an order returning exhibits to the owners shall be retained with the record in the case and, if necessary, shall be admissible in any subsequent trial of the same cause, subject to all other rules of evidence.

D. Upon petition of any organization which is exempt from taxation under §501(c)(3) of the Internal Revenue Code, the court in its sound discretion may order the donation of an exhibit to such charitable organization.

§19.2-270.5. DNA profile admissible in criminal proceeding.

In any criminal proceeding, DNA (deoxyribonucleic acid) testing shall be deemed to be a reliable scientific technique and the evidence of a DNA profile comparison may be admitted to prove or disprove the identity of any person. This section shall not otherwise limit the introduction of any relevant evidence bearing upon any question at issue before the court, including the accuracy and reliability of the procedures employed in the collection and analysis of a particular DNA sample. The court shall, regardless of the results of the DNA analysis, if any, consider such other relevant evidence of the identity of the accused as shall be admissible in evidence.

At least twenty-one days prior to commencement of the proceeding in which the results of a DNA analysis will be offered as evidence, the party intending to offer the evidence shall notify the opposing party, in writing, of the intent to offer the analysis and shall provide or make available copies of the profiles and the report or statement to be introduced. In the event that such notice is not given, and the person proffers such evidence, then the court may in its discretion either allow the opposing party a continuance or, under appropriate circumstances, bar the person from presenting such evidence. The period of any such continuance shall not be counted for speedy trial purposes under §19.2-243. If the opposing party intends to object to the admissibility of such evidence he shall give written notice of that fact and the basis for his objections at least ten days prior to commencement of the proceedings.

No blood sample submitted to the Division of Forensic Science for analysis and use as provided in this section and no results of the analysis performed shall be included in the DNA data bank established by the Division pursuant to §19.2-310.5 or otherwise used in any way with identifying information on the person whose sample was submitted.
(Chgd. by L.1997 ch. 315, eff. 7/1/97.)

§19.2-270.6. Evidence of abuse admissible in certain criminal trials.

In any criminal prosecution alleging personal injury or death, or the attempt to cause personal injury or death, relevant evidence of repeated physical and psychological abuse of the accused by the victim shall be admissible, subject to the general rules of evidence.

§19.2-271. Certain judicial officers incompetent to testify under certain circumstances.

No judge shall be competent to testify in any criminal or civil proceeding as to any matter which came before him in the course of his official duties.

No clerk of any court, magistrate, or other person having the power to issue warrants, shall be competent to testify in any criminal or civil proceeding, except proceedings wherein the defendant is charged with perjury, as to any matter which came before him in the course of his official duties. Such person shall be competent to testify in any criminal proceeding wherein the defendant is charged pursuant to the provisions of §18.2-460 or in any proceeding authorized pursuant to §19.2-353.3. Notwithstanding any other provision of this section, any judge, clerk of any court, magistrate, or other person having the power to issue warrants, who is the victim of a crime, shall not be incompetent solely because of his office to testify in any criminal or civil proceeding arising out of the crime.

§19.2-271.1. Competency of husband and wife to testify.

Husband and wife shall be competent witnesses to testify for or against each other in criminal cases, except as otherwise provided.

§19.2-271.2. Testimony of husband and wife in criminal cases.

In criminal cases husband and wife shall be allowed, and, subject to the rules of evidence governing other witnesses and subject to the exception stated in §8.01-398, may be compelled to testify in behalf of each other, but neither shall be compelled to be called as a witness against the other, except (i) in the case of a prosecution for an offense committed by one against the other or against a minor child of either, (ii) in any case where either is charged with forgery of the name of the other or uttering or attempting to utter a writing bearing the allegedly forged signature of the other or (iii) in any proceeding relating to a violation of the laws pertaining to criminal sexual assault (§§18.2-61 through 18.2-67.10), crimes against nature (§18.2-361) involving a minor as a victim and provided the defendant and the victim are not married to each other, incest (§18.2-366), or abuse of children (§§18.2-370 through 18.2-371). The failure of either husband or wife to testify, however, shall create no presumption against the accused, nor be the subject of any comment before the court or jury by any attorney.

In the prosecution for a criminal offense as set forth in (i), (ii) or (iii) above, each shall be a competent witness except as to privileged communications.

(Chgd. by L.1996 ch. 423, eff. 7/1/96.)

§19.2-271.3. Communications between ministers of religion and persons they counsel or advise.

No regular minister, priest, rabbi or accredited practitioner over the age of eighteen years, of any religious organization or denomination usually referred to as a church, shall be required in giving testimony as a witness in any criminal action to disclose any information communicated to him by the accused in a confidential manner, properly entrusted to him in his professional capacity and necessary to enable him to discharge the functions of his office according to the usual course of his practice or discipline, where such person so communicating such information about himself or another is seeking spiritual counsel and advice relative to and growing out of the information so imparted.

ARTICLE 2
WITNESSES FROM OR FOR ANOTHER STATE

§19.2-272. Definitions.

"Witness" as used in this article shall include a person whose testimony is desired in any proceeding or investigation by a grand jury or in a criminal action, prosecution or proceeding.

The word "state" shall include any territory of the United States and the District of Columbia.

The word "summons" shall include a subpoena (both subpoena ad testificandum and subpoena duces tecum), order or other notice requiring the appearance of a witness or production of documents.

§19.2-273. Certificate that witness is needed in another state; hearing.

If a judge of a court of record in any state which by its laws has made provisions for commanding persons within that state to attend and testify in this Commonwealth certifies under the seal of such court (1) that there is a criminal prosecution pending in such court or that a grand jury investigation has commenced or is about to commence, (2) that a person being within this Commonwealth is a material witness in such prosecution or grand jury investigation and (3) that his presence will be required for a specified number of days, upon presentation of such certificate to any judge of a court of record in the county or city in which such person is, such judge shall fix a time and place for hearing and shall make an order directing the witness to appear at a time and place certain for the hearing.

§19.2-274. When court to order witness to attend.

If at such hearing the judge determines that the witness is material and necessary, that it will not cause undue hardship to the witness to be compelled to attend and testify in the prosecution or grand jury investigation in the other state and that the laws of the state in which the prosecution is pending, or grand jury investigation has commenced or is about to commence (and of any other state through which the witness may be required to pass by ordinary course of travel) will give to him protection from arrest and the service of civil and criminal process, the judge shall issue a summons, with a copy of the certificate attached, directing the witness to attend and testify in the court where the prosecution is pending, or where a grand jury investigation has commenced or is about to commence at a time and place specified in the summons. In any such hearing the certificate shall be prima facie evidence of all the facts stated therein.

§19.2-275. Arrest of witness.

If the certificate recommends that the witness be taken into immediate custody and delivered to an officer of the requesting state to assure his attendance in the requesting state, such judge may, in lieu of notification of the hearing, direct that such witness be forthwith brought before him for the hearing; and the judge at the hearing being satisfied of the desirability of such custody and delivery, for which determination the certificate shall be prima facie proof of such desirability, may, in lieu of issuing subpoena or summons, order that the witness be forthwith taken into custody and delivered to an officer of the requesting state.

§19.2-276. Penalty for failure to attend and testify.

If the witness who is summoned as above provided, after being paid or tendered by some properly authorized person reimbursement for reasonable travel and lodging expenses as provided in §14.1-5 for each day he is required to travel and attend as a witness, fails without good cause to attend and testify as directed in the summons, he shall be punished in the manner provided for the punishment of any witness who disobeys a Virginia circuit court summons.

§19.2-277. Summoning witnesses in another state to testify in this Commonwealth.

If a person in any state which by its laws has made provision for commanding persons within its borders to attend and testify in criminal prosecutions or grand jury investigations commenced or about to commence in this Commonwealth is a material witness in a prosecution pending in a court of record in this Commonwealth, or in a grand jury investigation which has commenced or is about to commerce, a judge of such court may issue a certificate under the seal of the court stating these facts and specifying the number of days the witness will be required. The certificate may include a recommendation that the witness be taken into immediate custody and delivered to an officer of this Commonwealth to assure his attendance in this Commonwealth. This certificate shall be presented to a judge of a court of record in the county in which the witness is found.

§19.2-278. Reimbursement for daily mileage to such witnesses; issuance of warrant necessary to make tender.

If the witness is summoned to attend and testify in this Commonwealth he shall receive such reimbursement for his daily mileage as prescribed in §14.1-5 for each day that he is required to travel and attend as a witness. A witness who has appeared in accordance with the provisions of the summons shall not be required to remain within this Commonwealth a longer period of time than the period mentioned in the certificate, unless otherwise ordered by the court.

The judge issuing the certificate prescribed in §19.2-277 may, by order, direct the clerk of the court involved to issue such warrant or warrants payable out of the state treasury, as may be necessary to make the tender hereinabove prescribed; and after the entry of such order, such clerk, upon application of the attorney for the Commonwealth of the county or city involved, or of the accused, if certificate for the attendance of witness has been issued by such judge on his behalf as authorized by §19.2-330, shall issue such warrant or warrants and deliver them to the said attorney for the Commonwealth, who shall, forthwith, cause such tender to be made. Upon issuance of any such warrant or warrants said clerk shall deliver a certified copy of the court's order to the Supreme Court, and the said warrant or warrants shall be paid out of the state treasury upon presentation.

Unless and until appropriate forms shall be obtained, such warrants may be issued on the regular forms provided for the payment of witness fees and allowances, but in such event the clerk issuing the same shall make a notation thereon that they were issued pursuant to the provisions of this section.

§19.2-279. Penalty for failure of such witnesses to testify.

If such witness, after coming into this Commonwealth, fails without good cause to attend and testify as directed in the summons, he shall be punished in the manner provided for the punishment of any witness who disobeys a summons issued from a court of record in this Commonwealth.

§19.2-280. Exemption of such witnesses from arrest or service of process.

If a person comes into this Commonwealth in obedience to a summons directing him to attend and testify in this Commonwealth he shall not while in this Commonwealth pursuant to such summons be subject to arrest or the service of process, civil or criminal, in connection with matters which arose before his entrance into this Commonwealth under the summons.

If a person passes through this Commonwealth while going to another state in obedience to a summons to attend and testify in that state or while returning therefrom, he shall not while so passing through this Commonwealth be subject to arrest or the service of process, civil or criminal, in connection with matters which arose before his entrance into this Commonwealth under the summons.

§19.2-281. Construction of article.

This article shall be so interpreted and construed as to effectuate its general purpose to make uniform the law of the states which enact it.

§19.2-282. How article cited.

This article may be cited as the "Uniform Act to Secure the Attendance of Witnesses from without a State in Criminal Proceedings."

CHAPTER 17
CONVICTIONS; EFFECT THEREOF

Article

ARTICLE 1
PROOF AND VERDICTS

Section

§19.2-283. How accused may be convicted of felony.

No person shall be convicted of felony, unless by his confession of guilt in court, or by his plea, or by the verdict of a jury, accepted and recorded by the court, or by judgment of the court trying the case without a jury according to law.

§19.2-284. Proof of ownership in offense relating to property.

In a prosecution for an offense committed upon, relating to or affecting real estate, or for stealing, embezzling, destroying, injuring or fraudulently receiving or concealing any personal estate it shall be sufficient to prove that when the offense was committed the actual or constructive possession, or a general or special property, in the whole or any part of such estate was in the person or entity alleged in the indictment or other accusation to be the owner thereof.

§19.2-285. Accused guilty of part of offense charged; sentence; on new trial what tried.

If a person indicted of a felony be by the jury acquitted of part of the offense charged, he shall be sentenced for such part as he is so convicted of, if the same be substantially charged in the indictment, whether it be felony or misdemeanor. If the verdict be set aside and a new trial granted the accused, he shall not be tried for any higher offense than that of which he was convicted on the last trial.

§19.2-286. Conviction of attempt or as accessory on indictment for felony; effect of general verdict of not guilty.

On an indictment for felony the jury may find the accused not guilty of the felony but guilty of an attempt to commit such felony, or of being an accessory thereto; and a general verdict of not guilty, upon such indictment, shall be a bar to a subsequent prosecution for an attempt to commit such felony, or of being an accessory thereto.

§19.2-287. Verdict and judgment, when jury agree as to some and disagree as to others.

When two or more persons are charged and tried jointly, the jury may render a verdict as to any of them as to whom they agree. Thereupon judgment shall be entered according to the verdict; and as to the others the case shall be tried by another jury.

§19.2-288. Verdict when accused found guilty of punishable homicide.

If a person indicted for murder be found by the jury guilty of any punishable homicide, they shall in their verdict fix the degree thereof and ascertain the extent of the punishment to be inflicted within the bounds prescribed by §§18.2-30 to 18.2-36.

§19.2-289. Conviction of petit larceny.

In a prosecution for grand larceny, if it be found that the thing stolen is of less value than $200, the jury may find the accused guilty of petit larceny.

§19.2-290. Conviction of petit larceny though thing stolen worth more than $200.

In a prosecution for petit larceny, though the thing stolen be of the value of $200 or more, the jury may find the accused guilty; and upon a conviction under this section or §19.2-289 the accused shall be sentenced for petit larceny.

§19.2-291. Faulty counts; motion to strike; general verdict of guilty.

When there are several counts in the indictment one or more or which are faulty, the accused may move to strike the faulty count or counts or move the court to instruct the jury to disregard them. If he does neither and a general verdict of guilty is found, judgment shall be entered against the accused, if any count be good, though others be faulty, unless the court can plainly see that the verdict could not have been found on the good count. If the accused demurs to the faulty count or moves the court to instruct the jury to disregard it and his demurrer or motion is overruled and there is a general verdict of guilty and it cannot be seen on which count the verdict was founded, if the jury has been discharged, it shall be set aside; but if it is manifest that it could not have been found on the bad count, the verdict shall be allowed to stand.

ARTICLE 2
FORMER JEOPARDY

§19.2-292. Acquittal by jury on merits bar to further prosecution for same offense.

A person acquitted upon the facts and merits on a former trial, may plead such acquittal in bar of a second prosecution for the same offense, notwithstanding any defect in the form or substance of the indictment or accusation on which he was acquitted, unless the case be for a violation of the law relating to the state revenue and the acquittal be reversed on a writ of error on behalf of the Commonwealth.

§19.2-293. When acquittal not a bar to further prosecution for same offense.

A person acquitted of an offense on the ground of a variance between the allegations and the proof of the indictment or other accusation, or upon an exception to the form or substance thereof, may be arraigned again on a new indictment or other proper accusation, and tried and convicted for the same offense, notwithstanding such former acquittal.

§19.2-294. Offense against two or more statutes or ordinances.

If the same act be a violation of two or more statutes, or of two or more ordinances, or of one or more statutes and also one or more ordinances, conviction under one of such statutes or ordinances shall be a bar to a prosecution or proceeding under the other or others. Furthermore, if the same act be a violation of both a state and a federal statute a prosecution under the federal statute shall be a bar to a prosecution under the state statute.

For purposes of this section, a prosecution under a federal statute shall be deemed to be commenced with the return of an indictment by a grand jury or the filing of an information by a United States Attorney.

§19.2-294.1. Dismissal of one of dual charges for driving while intoxicated and reckless driving upon conviction of other charge.

Whenever any person is charged with a violation of §18.2-51.4 or §18.2-266 or any similar ordinances of any county, city, or town and reckless driving growing out of the same act or acts and is convicted of one of these charges, the court shall dismiss the remaining charge.

(Chgd. by L.1997 ch. 691, eff. 7/1/97.)

ARTICLE 3
CONVICTION OF ALIENS

§19.2-294.2. Procedure when aliens convicted of certain felonies; duties of probation and parole officer.

A. Whenever a person is (i) convicted in a circuit court of any felony and (ii) referred to a probation or parole officer for a report pursuant to §19.2-299, or for probation supervision, the probation or parole officer shall inquire as to the citizenship of such person. If upon inquiry it is determined that the person may be an alien based upon his failure to produce evidence of United States citizenship, the probation or parole officer shall report this determination to the Central Criminal Records Exchange of the Department of State Police on forms provided by the Exchange.

B. The inquiry required by this section need not be made if it is apparent that a report on alien status has previously been made to the Central Criminal Records Exchange pursuant to this section.

C. It shall be the responsibility of the Central Criminal Records Exchange of the Department of State Police to review arrest reports submitted by law-enforcement agencies and reports of suspected alien-status inquiries made by probation or parole officers, and to report within sixty days of final disposition to the Immigration and Naturalization Service the identity of all convicted offenders suspected of being an alien.

CHAPTER 18
SENTENCE; JUDGMENT; EXECUTION OF SENTENCE

ARTICLE 1
GENERAL PROVISIONS

§19.2-295. Ascertainment of punishment.

Within the limits prescribed by law, the term of confinement in the state correctional facility or in jail and the amount of fine, if any, of a person convicted of a criminal offense, shall be ascertained by the jury, or by the court in cases tried without a jury.

§19.2-295.1. Sentencing proceeding by the jury after conviction for a felony.

In cases of trial by jury, upon a finding that the defendant is guilty of a felony, a separate proceeding limited to the ascertainment of punishment shall be held as soon as practicable before the same jury. At such proceeding, the Commonwealth shall present the defendant's prior criminal convictions by certified, attested or exemplified copies of the record of conviction, including adult convictions and juvenile convictions and adjudications of delinquency. Prior convictions shall include convictions and adjudications of delinquency under the laws of any state, the District of Columbia, the United States or its territories. The Commonwealth shall provide to the defendant fourteen days prior to trial notice of its intention to introduce evidence of the defendant's prior criminal convictions. Such notice shall include (i) the date of each prior conviction, (ii) the name and jurisdiction of the court where each prior conviction was had and (iii) each offense of which he was convicted. Prior to commencement of the trial, the Commonwealth shall provide the defendant photocopies of certified copies of the defendant's prior criminal convictions which it intends to introduce at sentencing. After the Commonwealth has introduced such evidence of prior convictions, or if no such evidence is introduced, the defendant may introduce relevant, admissible evidence related to punishment. Nothing in this section shall prevent the Commonwealth or the defendant from introducing relevant, admissible evidence in rebuttal. If the defendant is found guilty of an offense other than a felony, punishment shall be fixed as otherwise provided by law.

If the jury cannot agree on a punishment and if the defendant, the attorney for the Commonwealth, and the court agree, in the manner provided in §19.2-257, then the court shall fix punishment.

If the sentence on appeal is subsequently set aside or found invalid solely due to an error in the sentencing proceeding, the court shall impanel a different jury to ascertain punishment, unless the defendant, the attorney for the Commonwealth and the court agree, in the manner provided in §19.2-257, that the court shall fix punishment.

(Chgd. by L.1995 ch. 567; L.1996 ch. 664, eff. 7/1/96.)

§19.2-295.2. Postrelease supervision of felons sentenced for offenses committed on and after January 1, 1995, and on and after July 1, 2000.

A. At the time the court imposes sentence upon a conviction for any felony offense committed (i) on or after January 1, 1995, the court may, and (ii) on or after July 1, 2000, shall, in addition to any other punishment imposed if such other punishment includes an active term of incarceration in a state or local correctional facility, except in cases in which the court orders a suspended term of confinement of at least six months, impose a term of postrelease supervision of not less than six months nor more than three years, as the court may determine. Such additional term shall be suspended and the defendant placed under postrelease supervision upon release from the active term of incarceration. The period of supervision shall be established by the court; however, such period shall not be less than six months nor more than three years. Periods of postrelease supervision imposed pursuant to this section upon more than one felony conviction may be ordered to run concurrently. Periods of postrelease supervision imposed pursuant to this section may be ordered to run concurrently with any period of probation the defendant may also be subject to serve.

B. The period of postrelease supervision shall be under the supervision and review of the Virginia Parole Board. The Board shall review each felon prior to release and establish conditions of postrelease supervision. Failure to successfully abide by such terms and conditions shall be grounds to terminate the period of postrelease supervision and recommit the defendant to the Department of Corrections or to the local correctional facility from which he was previously released. Procedures for any such termination and recommitment shall be conducted in the same manner as procedures for the revocation of parole.

C. Postrelease supervision programs shall be operated through the probation and parole districts established pursuant to §53.1-141.

D. Nothing in this section shall be construed to prohibit the court from exercising any authority otherwise granted by law.

(Chgd. by L.1995 chs. 502, 574; L.2000 ch. 767, eff. 7/1/2000.)

§19.2-295.3. Admission of victim impact testimony.

In cases of trial by jury or by the court, upon a finding that the defendant is guilty of a felony, the court shall permit the victim, as defined in §19.2-11.01, upon motion of the attorney for the Commonwealth, to testify in the presence of the accused regarding the impact of the offense upon the victim. The court shall limit the victim's testimony to the factors set forth in clauses (i) through (vi) of subsection A of §19.2-299.1. In the case of trial by jury, the court shall permit the victim to testify at the sentencing hearing conducted pursuant to §19.2-295.1 or in the case of trial by the court, the court shall permit the victim to testify before the court prior to the imposition of a sentence. Victim impact testimony in all capital murder cases shall be admitted in accordance with §19.2-264.4.

(Added by L.1998 ch. 485, eff. 7/1/98.)

§19.2-296. Withdrawal of plea of guilty.

A motion to withdraw a plea of guilty or nolo contendere may be made only before sentence is imposed or imposition of a sentence is suspended; but to correct manifest injustice, the court within twenty-one days after entry of a final order may set aside the judgment of conviction and permit the defendant to withdraw his plea.

§19.2-297.1. Sentence of person twice previously convicted of certain violent felonies.

A. Any person convicted of two or more separate acts of violence when such offenses were not part of a common act, transaction or scheme, and who has been at liberty as defined in §53.1-151 between each conviction, shall, upon conviction of a third or subsequent act of violence, be sentenced to life imprisonment and shall not have all or any portion of the sentence suspended, provided it is admitted, or found by the jury or judge before whom he is tried, that he has been previously convicted of two or more such acts of violence. For the purposes of this section, "act of violence" means (i) any one of the following violations of Chapter 4 (§18.2-30 et seq.) of Title 18.2:

a. First and second degree murder and voluntary manslaughter under Article 1 (§18.2-30 et seq.);

b. Mob-related felonies under Article 2 (§18.2-38 et seq.);

c. Any kidnapping or abduction felony under Article 3 (§18.2-47 et seq.);

d. Any malicious felonious assault or malicious bodily wounding under Article 4 (§18.2-51 et seq.);

e. Robbery under §18.2-58 and carjacking under §18.2-58.1;

f. Except as otherwise provided in §18.2-67.5:2 or §18.2-67.5:3, criminal sexual assault punishable as a felony under Article 7 (§18.2-61 et seq.); or

g. Arson in violation of §18.2-77 when the structure burned was occupied or a Class 3 felony violation of §18.2-79.

(ii) conspiracy to commit any of the violations enumerated in clause (i) of this section; and (iii) violations as a principal in the second degree or accessory before the fact of the provisions enumerated in clause (i) of this section.

B. Prior convictions shall include convictions under the laws of any state or of the United States for any offense substantially similar to those listed under "act of violence" if such offense would be a felony if committed in the Commonwealth.

The Commonwealth shall notify the defendant in writing, at least thirty days prior to trial, of its intention to seek punishment pursuant to this section.

C. Any person sentenced to life imprisonment pursuant to this section shall not be eligible for parole and shall not be eligible for any good conduct allowance or any earned sentence credits under Chapter 6 (§53.1-186 et seq.) of Title 53.1. However, any person subject to the provisions of this section, other than a person who was sentenced under subsection A of §18.2-67.5:3 for criminal sexual assault convictions specified in subdivision f, (i) who has reached the age of sixty-five or older and who has served at least five years of the sentence imposed or (ii) who has reached the age of sixty or older and who has served at least ten years of the sentence imposed may petition the Parole Board for conditional release. The Parole Board shall promulgate regulations to implement the provisions of this subsection. *(Chgd. by L.1995 ch. 834; L.1996 ch. 539, eff. 7/1/96.)*

§19.2-298. Pronouncement of sentence.

After a finding of guilty, sentence shall be pronounced, or decision to suspend the imposition of sentence shall be announced, without unreasonable delay. Pending pronouncement, the court may commit the accused to jail or may continue or alter the bail except that in those cases where the accused is convicted of a murder in the first degree, the court shall commit him to jail and he shall not be allowed bail pending the pronouncement of sentence. Before pronouncing the sentence, the court shall inquire of the accused if he desires to make a statement and if he desires to advance any reason why judgment should not be pronounced against him.

§19.2-298.01. Use of discretionary sentencing guidelines.

A. In all felony cases, other than Class 1 felonies, the court shall (i) have presented to it the appropriate discretionary sentencing guidelines worksheets and (ii) review and consider the suitability of the applicable discretionary sentencing guidelines established pursuant to Chapter 8 (§17.1-800 et seq.) of Title 17.1. Before imposing sentence, the court shall state for the record that such review and consideration have been accomplished and shall make the completed worksheets a part of the record of the case and open for inspection. In cases tried by a jury, the jury shall not be presented any information regarding sentencing guidelines.

B. In any felony case, other than Class 1 felonies, in which the court imposes a sentence which is either greater or less than that indicated by the discretionary sentencing guidelines, the court shall file with the record of the case a written explanation of such departure.

C. In felony cases, other than Class 1 felonies, tried by a jury and in felony cases tried by the court without a jury upon a plea of not guilty, the court shall direct a probation officer of such court to prepare the discretionary sentencing guidelines worksheets. In felony cases tried upon a plea of guilty, including cases which are the subject of a plea agreement, the court shall direct a probation officer of such court to prepare the discretionary sentencing guidelines worksheets, or, with the concurrence of the accused, the court and the attorney for the Commonwealth, the worksheets shall be prepared by the attorney for the Commonwealth.

D. Except as provided in subsection E, discretionary sentencing guidelines worksheets prepared pursuant to this section shall be subject to the same distribution as presentence investigation reports prepared pursuant to subsection A of §19.2-299.

E. Following the entry of a final order of conviction and sentence in a felony case, the clerk of the circuit court in which the case was tried shall cause a copy of such order or orders, the original of the discretionary sentencing guidelines worksheets prepared in the case, and a copy of any departure explanation prepared pursuant to subsection B to be forwarded to the Virginia Criminal Sentencing Commission within five days.

F. The failure to follow any or all of the provisions of this section or the failure to follow any or all of the provisions of this section in the prescribed manner shall not be reviewable on appeal or the basis of any other post-conviction relief.

G. The provisions of this section shall apply only to felony cases in which the offense is committed on or after January 1, 1995, and for which there are discretionary sentencing guidelines. For purposes of the discretionary sentencing guidelines only, a person sentenced to a boot camp incarceration program pursuant to §19.2-316.1, a detention center incarceration program pursuant to §19.2-316.2 or a diversion center incarceration program pursuant §19.2-316.3 shall be deemed to be sentenced to a term of incarceration. *(Chgd. by L.1996 ch. 552; L.1997 ch. 345; L.1998 chs. 200, 353; L.1999 ch. 286, eff. 7/1/99.)*

§19.2-298.1. Registration required of persons convicted of certain offenses.

A. For purposes of this section:

"Offense for which registration is required" means a violation or attempted violation of:

1. §§18.2-63, 18.2-64.1, 18.2-67.2:1, subsection B of §18.2-67.5, §18.2-90 with the intent to commit rape, §§18.2-370, 18.2-370.1, 18.2-374.1 or subsection D of 18.2-374.1:1, or a third or subsequent conviction of §18.2-67.4 or of subsection C of §18.2-67.5;

2. A "sexually violent offense"; or

3. Where the victim is a minor or is physically helpless or mentally incapacitated as defined in §18.2-67.10, a violation or attempted violation of subsection A of §18.2-47, clause (iii) of §18.2-48, subsection B of §18.2-361 or subsection B of §18.2-366, or subdivision B 1 of §18.2-374.1.

"Sexually violent offense" means a violation or attempted violation of:

1. Clause (ii) of §18.2-48, §§18.2-61, 18.2-67.1, 18.2-67.2, 18.2-67.3 or subsection A of §18.2-67.5; or

2. §§18.2-63, 18.2-64.1, 18.2-67.2:1, subsection B of §18.2-67.5, §18.2-90 with the intent to commit rape, §§18.2-370, 18.2-370.1 or, where the victim is a minor or is physically helpless or mentally incapacitated as defined in §18.2-67.10, a violation or attempted violation of subsection A of §18.2-47, clause (iii) of §18.2-48, subsection B of §18.2-361, subsection B of §18.2-366, or subdivision B 1 of §18.2-374.1. Conviction of an offense listed under this subdivision shall be deemed a sexually violent offense only if the person has been convicted of any two or more such offenses occurring within a ten-year period, provided that person had been at liberty between such convictions.

B. Every person convicted on or after July 1, 1997, including juveniles tried and convicted in the circuit courts pursuant to §16.1-269, whether sentenced as adults or juveniles, of an offense for which registration is required shall be required as a part of the sentence imposed upon conviction to register and reregister with the Department of State Police as provided in this section. The court shall remand the person to the custody of the local law-enforcement agency of the county or city for the purpose of obtaining the person's fingerprints and photographs of a type and kind specified by the Department of State Police for inclusion in the Sex Offender and Crimes Against Minors Registry established pursuant to §19.2-390.1. The court shall order the person to provide to the local law-enforcement agency all information required by the State Police for inclusion in the Registry.

It shall be the duty of the local law-enforcement agency to forward to the State Police all the necessary registration information within seven days of the date of sentencing and to promptly provide to the State Police such information as is necessary for any reregistration.

C. Every person serving a sentence of confinement or under community supervision as defined in §53.1-1 on July 1, 1997, for an offense for which registration is required shall be required to register with the Department of State Police and shall be given notice of the duty to register pursuant to §53.1-116.1 or §53.1-160.1 as appropriate. In addition, any person who was convicted under Chapter 17* (18 U.S.C. 2421 et seq.) of Title 18 of the United States Code, and who resides in or was convicted in Virginia, shall be required to register with the Department of State Police.

**Probably should be "Chapter 117".*

D. Every person required to register shall register within ten days of his release from confinement in a state, local or juvenile correctional facility or, if a sentence of confinement is not imposed, within ten days of suspension of the sentence or in the case of a juvenile, of disposition. In addition, all persons convicted of violations under the laws of the United States or any other state substantially similar to an offense for which registration is required shall provide to the local agency all necessary information for inclusion in the Registry within ten days of establishing a residence within the Commonwealth. The local law-enforcement agency shall obtain from the person who presents himself for registration or reregistration, two sets of fingerprints and two photographs of a type and kind specified by the State Police for inclusion in the Registry and advise the person of his duties regarding reregistration. Any person required to register shall also be required to reregister within ten days following any change of residence, whether within or without the Commonwealth. If a probation or parole officer becomes aware of a change of residence for any of his probationers or parolees required to register, the probation or parole officer shall notify the State Police within ten days. Whenever a person subject to registration changes residence to another state, the State Police shall notify the designated law-enforcement agency of that state.

The local law-enforcement agency shall promptly submit to the State Police all necessary information for registrations and reregistrations pursuant to this subsection.

E. The registration shall be maintained in the Registry established pursuant to §19.2-390.1 and shall include the person's name, all aliases which he has used or under which he may have been known, the date and locality of the conviction for which registration is required, his fingerprints and a photograph of a type and kind specified by the State Police, his date of birth, social security number, current address and a description of the offense or offenses for which he was convicted and shall, if applicable, provide the same information on convictions prior to July 1, 1997, for any of the specified offenses or under a substantially similar law of the United States or any other state.

F. Every person required to register under this section, other than a person convicted of a sexually violent offense but including persons required to register between July 1, 1994, and July 1, 1997, shall reregister with the State Police on an annual basis from the date of the initial registration. Every person convicted of a sexually violent offense, including persons convicted of a sexually violent offense who were required to register between July 1, 1994, and July 1, 1997, shall reregister with the State Police every ninety days from the date of initial registration. For purposes of this section, reregistration means that the person has notified the State Police, confirmed his then current address and provided such other information, including identifying information, which the State Police may, pursuant to this section and by regulation, require. Upon registration and as may be necessary thereafter, the State Police shall provide the person with an address verification form to be used for reregistration. The form shall contain in bold print a statement indicating that failure to comply with the registration required is punishable as a Class 1 misdemeanor or a Class 6 felony as provided in §18.2-472.1.

G. Nonresident offenders entering the Commonwealth for employment, to carry on a vocation, or as a student attending school who are required to register in their state of residence or who would be required to register under this section if a resident of the Commonwealth shall, within ten days of accepting employment or enrolling in school in the Commonwealth, be required to register and reregister pursuant to this section. For purposes of this section, "employment" and "carry on a vocation" include employment that is full-time or part-time for a period of time exceeding fourteen days or for an aggregate period of time exceeding thirty days during any calendar year, whether financially compensated, volunteered, or for the purpose of government or educational benefit. For purposes of this section "student" means a person who is enrolled on a full-time or part-time basis, in any public or private educational institution, including any secondary school, trade or professional institution, or institution of higher education.

H. Whenever it appears from the records of the State Police that a person has failed to comply with the duty to register or reregister, the State Police shall promptly cause a warrant for the arrest of the person to be issued charging a violation of §18.2-472.1 by the jurisdiction in which the offender last registered or reregistered or, if the offender failed to comply with the duty to register, in the jurisdiction in which the offender was last convicted of an offense for which registration or reregistration is required. The State Police shall also promptly notify the local law-enforcement agency of the jurisdiction of the offender's last known residence as shown in the records of the State Police.

(Chgd. by L.1997 chs. 670, 672, 747; L.1998 chs. 785, 834; L.1999 chs. 659, 662, 801, 845, eff. 7/1/99.)

§19.2-298.2. Duration of registration requirement.

Any person required by §19.2-298.1 to register or reregister shall be required to register for a period of ten years from the date of initial registration. However, any person who has been convicted of any sexually violent offense shall have a continuing duty to reregister, for life.

Any period of confinement in a state or local correctional facility, hospital or any other institution or facility during the otherwise applicable ten-year period shall toll the registration period and the duty to reregister shall be extended.

(Chgd. by L.1997 ch. 747; L.1998 chs. 785, 834, eff. 7/1/98.)

§19.2-298.3. Expungement from Registry.

A. Any person required by §19.2-298.1 to register, other than a person who has been convicted of any sexually violent offense as defined in §19.2-298.1, may petition the circuit court in which he was convicted or the circuit court in the jurisdiction where he then resides for removal of his name and all identifying information from the Registry. A petition may not be filed earlier than ten years after the date of the initial registration pursuant to subsection D of §19.2-298.1. The court shall hold a hearing on the petition at which the applicant and any interested persons may present witnesses and other evidence. If, after such hearing, the court is satisfied that such person no longer poses a risk to public safety, the court shall grant the petition. In the event the petition is not granted, the person shall wait at least twenty-four months from the date of the denial to file a new petition for removal from the Registry. A petition for expungement shall not be granted to any person convicted of two or more offenses for which registration is required or convicted of any sexually violent offense.

B. The name of any person required to register under §19.2-298.1 and all identifying information shall be removed from the Registry by the Department of State Police upon receipt of an order granting a petition pursuant to subsection A or at the end of the period for which the person is required to register under §19.2-298.2.

(Chgd. by L.1997 ch. 747; L.1998 chs. 785, 834, eff. 7/1/98.)

§19.2-298.4. Relief from registration or reregistration.

A. Upon expiration of three years from the date upon which the duty to register as a sexually violent offender is imposed, any person convicted of a sexually violent offense as defined in §19.2-298.1 may petition the court in which he was convicted for relief from the requirement to reregister every ninety days. The court shall hold a hearing on the petition, on notice to the attorney for the Commonwealth, to determine whether the person suffers from a mental abnormality or a personality disorder that makes the person a menace to the health and safety of others or significantly impairs his ability to control his sexual behavior. Prior to the hearing the court shall order a comprehensive assessment of the applicant by a panel of three certified sex offender treatment providers as defined in §54.1-3600. A report of the assessment shall be filed with the court prior to the hearing. The costs of the assessment shall be taxed as costs of the proceeding.

If, after consideration of the report and such other evidence as may be presented at the hearing, the court finds by clear and convincing evidence that the person does not suffer from a mental abnormality or a personality disorder that makes the person a menace to the health and safety of others or significantly impairs his ability to control his sexual behavior, the petition shall be granted and the duty to reregister every ninety days shall be terminated. The State Police shall be notified promptly upon entry of an order granting the petition and Registry information on the offender shall be removed from the Internet system developed and maintained by the State Police pursuant to subsection D of §19.2-390.1.

The person shall, however, be under a continuing duty to register annually in accordance with subsection F of §19.2-298.1.

If the petition is denied, the duty to reregister every ninety days shall continue. An appeal from the denial of a petition shall lie to the Supreme Court.

A petition for relief pursuant to this subsection may not be filed within three years from the date on which any previous petition for such relief was denied.

B. The duly appointed guardian of a person convicted of an offense requiring registration or reregistration as either a sex offender or sexually violent offender under §19.2-298.1, who due to a physical condition is incapable of (i) reoffending and (ii) reregistering, may petition the court in which the person was convicted for relief from the requirement to reregister. The court shall hold a hearing on the petition, on notice to the attorney for the Commonwealth, to determine whether the person suffers from a physical condition that makes the person (i) no longer a menace to the health and safety of others and (ii) incapable of reregistering. Prior to the hearing the court shall order a comprehensive assessment of the applicant by at least two licensed physicians other than the person's primary care physician. A report of the assessment shall be filed with the court prior to the hearing. The costs of the assessment shall be taxed as costs of the proceeding.

If, after consideration of the report and such other evidence as may be presented at the hearing, the court finds by clear and convincing evidence that due to his physical condition the person (i) no longer poses a menace to the health and safety of others and (ii) is incapable of reregistering, the petition shall be granted and the duty to reregister shall be terminated. The State Police shall be notified promptly upon entry of an order granting the petition and Registry information on the offender shall be removed from the Internet system developed and maintained by the State Police pursuant to subsection D of §19.2-390.1.

If the petition is denied, the duty to reregister shall continue. An appeal from the denial of a petition shall be to the Virginia Supreme Court.

A petition for relief pursuant to this subsection may not be filed within three years from the date on which any previous petition for such relief was denied.

The Department of State Police shall annually verify and report to the attorney for the Commonwealth in the jurisdiction in which the person resides that a person whose obligation to reregister was terminated under this section continues to suffer from the physical condition that resulted in such termination.

If, at any time, the person's physical condition changes so that he is capable of reoffending or reregistering, the attorney for the Commonwealth shall file a petition with the circuit court in the jurisdiction where the person resides and the court shall hold a hearing on the petition, with notice to the person and his guardian, to determine whether the person still suffers from a physical condition that makes the person (i) no longer a menace to the health and safety of others and (ii) incapable of reregistering. Prior to the hearing the court shall order a comprehensive assessment of the applicant by at least two licensed physicians other than the person's primary care physician. A report of the assessment shall be filed with the court prior to the hearing. The costs of the assessment shall be taxed as costs of the proceeding.

(Added by L.1997 ch. 747; chgd. by L.1998 chs. 785, 834; L.1999 ch. 845, eff. 7/1/99.)

§19.2-299. Investigations and reports by probation officers in certain cases.

A. When a person is tried in a circuit court (i) upon a charge of assault and battery in violation of §§18.2-57, 18.2-57.1 or §18.2-57.2, stalking in violation of §18.2-60.3, sexual battery in violation of §18.2-67.4, attempted sexual battery in violation of §18.2-67.5, or maiming or driving while intoxicated in violation of §18.2-51.4 or §18.2-266, and is adjudged guilty of such charge, the court may, or on motion of the defendant shall, or (ii) upon a felony charge, the court may when there is a plea agreement between the defendant and the Commonwealth and shall when the defendant pleads guilty without a plea agreement or is found guilty by the court after a plea of not guilty, direct a probation officer of such court to thoroughly investigate and report upon the history of the accused, including a report of the accused's criminal record as an adult and available juvenile court records, and all other relevant facts, to fully advise the court so the court may determine the appropriate sentence to be imposed. The probation officer, after having furnished a copy of this report at least five days prior to sentencing to counsel for the accused and the attorney for the Commonwealth for their permanent use, shall submit his report in advance of the sentencing hearing to the judge in chambers, who shall keep such report confidential. The probation officer shall be available to testify from this report in open court in the presence of the accused, who shall have been advised of its contents and be given the right to cross-examine the investigating officer as to any matter contained therein and to present any additional facts bearing upon the matter. The report of the investigating officer shall at all times be kept confidential by each recipient, and shall be filed as a part of the record in the case. Any report so filed shall be sealed upon the entry of the sentencing order by the court and made available only by court order, except that such reports or copies thereof shall be available at any time to any criminal justice agency, as defined in §9-169, of this or any other state or of the United States; to any agency where the accused is referred for treatment by the court or by probation and parole services; and to counsel for any person who has been indicted jointly for the same felony as the person subject to the report. Any report prepared pursuant to the provisions hereof shall without court order be made available to counsel for the person who is the subject of the report if that person is charged with a felony subsequent to the time of the preparation of the report. The presentence report shall be in a form prescribed by the Department of Corrections. In all cases where such report is not ordered, a simplified report shall be prepared on a form prescribed by the Department of Corrections.

B. As a part of any presentence investigation conducted pursuant to subsection A when the offense for which the defendant was convicted was a felony, the court probation officer shall advise any victim of such offense in writing that he may submit to the Virginia Parole Board a written request (i) to be given the opportunity to submit to the Board a written statement in advance of any parole hearing describing the impact of the offense upon him and his opinion regarding the defendant's release and (ii) to receive copies of such other notifications pertaining to the defendant as the Board may provide pursuant to subsection B of §53.1-155.

C. As part of any presentence investigation conducted pursuant to subsection A when the offense for which the defendant was convicted was a felony drug offense set forth in Article 1 (§18.2-247 et seq.) of Chapter 7 of Title 18.2, the presentence report shall include any known association of the defendant with illicit drug operations or markets.

D. As a part of any presentence investigation conducted pursuant to subsection A, when the offense for which the defendant was convicted was a felony, not a capital offense, committed on or after January 1, 2000, the defendant shall be required to undergo a substance abuse screening pursuant to §18.2-251.01.

(Chgd. by L.1995 chs. 687, 778; L.1997 ch. 691; L.1998 chs. 783, 840; L.1999 chs. 891, 903, 913, eff. 7/1/99.)

§19.2-299.1. When Victim Impact Statement required; contents; uses.

The presentence report prepared pursuant to §19.2-299 shall, with the consent of the victim, as defined in §19.2-11.01, in all cases involving offenses other than capital murder, include a Victim Impact Statement. Victim Impact Statements in all cases involving capital murder shall be prepared and submitted in accordance with the provisions of §19.2-264.5.

A Victim Impact Statement shall be kept confidential and shall be sealed upon entry of the sentencing order. If prepared by someone other than the victim, it shall (i) identify the victim, (ii) itemize any economic loss suffered by the victim as a result of the offense, (iii) identify the nature and extent of any physical or psychological injury suffered by the victim as a result of the offense, (iv) detail any change in the victim's personal welfare, lifestyle or familial relationships as a result of the offense, (v) identify any request for psychological or medical services initiated by the victim or the victim's family as a result of the offense, and (vi) provide such other information as the court may require related to the impact of the offense upon the victim.

If the court does not order a presentence investigation and report, the attorney for the Commonwealth shall, at the request of the victim, submit a Victim Impact Statement. In any event, a victim shall be advised by the local crime victim and witness assistance program that he may submit in his own words a written Victim Impact Statement prepared by the victim or someone the victim designates in writing.

The Victim Impact Statement may be considered by the court in determining the appropriate sentence. A copy of the statement prepared pursuant to this section shall be made available to the defendant or counsel for the defendant without court order at least five days prior to the sentencing hearing. The statement shall not be admissible in any civil proceeding for damages arising out of the acts upon which the conviction was based. The statement, however, may be utilized by the Virginia Worker's Compensation Commission in its determinations on claims by victims of crimes pursuant to Chapter 21.1 (§19.2-368.1 et seq.) of this title.

(Chgd. by L.1995 chs. 687, 720; L.1996 ch. 398, eff. 7/1/96.)

§19.2-299.2. Alcohol and substance abuse screening and assessment for designated Class 1 misdemeanor convictions.

A. When a person is convicted of any offense committed on or after January 1, 2000, under Article 1 (§18.2-247 et seq.) or Article 1.1 (§18.2-265.1 et seq.) of Chapter 7 of Title 18.2, and such offense is punishable as a Class 1 misdemeanor, the court shall order the person to undergo a substance abuse screening as part of the sentence if the defendant's sentence includes probation supervision by a local community-based probation program established pursuant to Article 2 (§53.1-180 et seq.) of Chapter 5 of Title 53.1 or participation in a local alcohol safety action program. *Whenever a court requires a person to enter into and successfully complete an alcohol safety action program pursuant to §18.2-271.1 for a second offense of the type described therein, or orders an evaluation of a person to be conducted by an alcohol safety action program pursuant to any provision of §46.2-391, the alcohol safety action program shall assess such person's degree of alcohol abuse before determining the appropriate level of treatment to be provided or to be recommended for such person being evaluated pursuant to §46.2-391.*

The court may order such screening upon conviction as part of the sentence of any other Class 1 misdemeanor if the defendant's sentence includes probation supervision by a local community-based probation program established pursuant to Article 2 (§53.1-180 et seq.) of Chapter 5 of Title 53.1, participation in a local alcohol safety action program or any other sanction and the court has reason to believe the defendant has a substance abuse or dependence problem.

B. A substance abuse screening ordered pursuant to this section shall be conducted by the local alcohol safety action program. When an offender is ordered to enter programming under the local community-based probation program established pursuant to Article 2 (§53.1-180 et seq.) of Chapter 5 of Title 53.1, rather than the local alcohol safety action program, the local community-based probation program shall be responsible for the screening. However, if a local community-based probation program has not been established for the locality, the local alcohol safety action program shall conduct the screening as part of the sentence.

C. If the screening indicates that the person has a substance abuse or dependence problem, an assessment shall be completed and if the assessment confirms that the person has a substance abuse or dependence problem, as a condition of a suspended sentence and probation, the court shall order the person to complete the substance abuse education and intervention component, or both as appropriate, of the local alcohol safety action program or such other treatment program, if available, such as in the opinion of the court would be best suited to the needs of the person. If the referral is to the local alcohol safety action program, the program may

charge a fee for the education and intervention component, or both, not to exceed $300, based upon the defendant's ability to pay.
(Added by L.1998 chs. 783, 840; chgd. by L.1999 chs. 891, 913; L.2000 chs. 958, 980, eff. 10/1/2000, ch. 1040, eff. 7/1/2000. Matter in italics eff. 10/1/2000.)

§19.2-300. Deferring for mental examination sentence of person convicted of offense indicating sexual abnormality.
In the case of the conviction in any circuit court of any person for any criminal offense which indicates sexual abnormality, the trial judge may on his own initiative, or shall upon application of the attorney for the Commonwealth, the defendant, or counsel for defendant or other person acting for the defendant, defer sentence until the report of a mental examination conducted as provided in §19.2-301 of the defendant can be secured to guide the judge in determining what disposition shall be made of the defendant.

§19.2-301. Judge shall require examination under §19.2-300; by whom made; report; expenses of psychiatrist.
The judge shall order the defendant examined by at least one psychiatrist or clinical psychologist who is qualified by specialized training and experience to perform such evaluations. The examination shall be performed on an outpatient basis at a mental health facility or in jail. However, if the court specifically finds that outpatient examination services are unavailable or if the results of outpatient examination indicate that hospitalization of the defendant for further examination is necessary, the court may order the defendant sent to a hospital designated by the Commissioner of Mental Health, Mental Retardation, and Substance Abuse Services as appropriate for examination of persons convicted of crimes. The defendant shall then be hospitalized for such time as the director of the hospital deems necessary to perform an adequate examination, but not to exceed thirty days from the date of admission to the hospital. Upon completion of the examination, the examiners shall prepare a written report of their findings and conclusions and shall furnish copies of such report to the judge, the defendant, counsel for the defendant, and the attorney for the Commonwealth.

§19.2-302. Construction and administration of §§19.2-300 and 19.2-301.
Nothing contained in §19.2-300 or §19.2-301 shall be construed to conflict with or repeal any statute in regard to the Department of Mental Health, Mental Retardation and Substance Abuse Services, and such sections shall be administered with due regard to the authority of, and in cooperation with, the Commissioner of Mental Health, Mental Retardation and Substance Abuse Services.

§19.2-303. Suspension or modification of sentence; probation; taking of fingerprints as condition of probation.
After conviction, whether with or without jury, the court may suspend imposition of sentence or suspend the sentence in whole or part and in addition may place the accused on probation under such conditions as the court shall determine or may, as a condition of a suspended sentence, require the accused to make at least partial restitution to the aggrieved party or parties for damages or loss caused by the offense for which convicted, or to perform community service, or both, under terms and conditions which shall be entered in writing by the court. The judge, after convicting the accused of a felony, shall determine whether a copy of the accused's fingerprints are on file at the Central Criminal Records Exchange. In any case where fingerprints are not on file, the judge shall require that fingerprints be taken as a condition of probation. Such fingerprints shall be submitted to the Central Criminal Records Exchange under the provisions of subsection D of §19.2-390 of the Code.

If a person is sentenced to jail upon conviction of a misdemeanor or a felony, the court may, at any time before the sentence has been completely served, suspend the unserved portion of any such sentence, place the person on probation for such time as the court shall determine, or otherwise modify the sentence imposed.

If a person has been sentenced for a felony to the Department of Corrections but has not actually been transferred to a receiving unit of the Department, the court which heard the case, if it appears compatible with the public interest and there are circumstances in mitigation of the offense, may, at any time before the person is transferred to the Department, suspend or otherwise modify the unserved portion of such a sentence. The court may place the person on probation for such time as the court shall determine.

§19.2-303.1. Fixing period of suspension of sentence.
In any case where a court suspends the imposition or execution of a sentence, it may fix the period of suspension for a reasonable time, having due regard to the gravity of the offense, without regard to the maximum period for which the defendant might have been sentenced.

§19.2-303.2. Persons charged with first offense may be placed on probation.
Whenever any person who has not previously been convicted of any felony pleads guilty to or enters a plea of not guilty to any crime against property constituting a misdemeanor, under Articles 5, 6, 7 and 8 of Chapter 5 (§18.2-119 et seq.) of Title 18.2, the court, upon such plea if the facts found by the court would justify a finding of guilt, without entering a judgment of guilt and with the consent of the accused, may defer further proceedings and place him on probation subject to terms and conditions, which may include restitution for losses caused, set by the court. Upon violation of a term or condition, the court may enter an adjudication of guilt and proceed as otherwise provided. Upon fulfillment of the terms and conditions, the court shall discharge the person and dismiss the proceedings against him. Discharge and dismissal under this section shall be without adjudication of guilt and is a conviction only for the purpose of applying this section in subsequent proceedings.

§19.2-303.3. Sentence to local community-based probation program; eligibility for participation; evaluation; sentencing; withdrawal or removal from program; payment for costs.
A. Any defendant who is (i) convicted on or after July 1, 1995, of a misdemeanor or a felony that is not a felony act of violence as defined in §19.2-297.1, and for which the court imposes a sentence of twelve months of less, (ii) no younger than eighteen years of age or is considered an adult at the time of conviction; and (iii) who meets other eligibility criteria pursuant to this section and §53.1-180 may be sentenced to a local community-based probation program established pursuant to §53.1-181 by the local governing bodies within that judicial district or circuit.

B. Prior to or at the time of sentencing, the court may order the defendant placed in a local community-based probation program pursuant to §53.1-181 upon a determination by the court that the defendant may benefit from the program and is capable of returning to society as a productive citizen with a reasonable amount of supervision and intervention including programs and services set forth in §53.1-182.1. All or part of any sentence imposed that has been suspended, shall be conditioned upon the defendant's successful completion of any program established pursuant to §53.1-181.

The court may impose terms and conditions of supervision as it deems appropriate, including that the defendant abide by any additional requirements of supervision imposed or established by the program during the period of probation supervision.

C. Any officer of a local probation program established or operated pursuant to the Comprehensive Community Corrections Act for Local-Responsible Offenders (§53.1-180 et seq.) may seek a warrant or capias from any judicial officer for the arrest of any person on probation and under its supervision for removal from the program for (i) intractable behavior; (ii) refusal to comply with the terms and conditions imposed by the court; (iii) refusal to comply with the requirements of local probation supervision established by the program; or (iv) the commission of a new offense while on local probation and under program supervision. Upon arrest, the defendant shall be brought before the court for a hearing. Upon finding that the defendant exhibited intractable behavior as defined herein, or refused to comply with terms and conditions imposed, the court may revoke all or part of the suspended sentence and supervision, and commit the defendant to serve whatever sentence was originally imposed or impose such other terms and conditions of supervision as it deems appropriate. "Intractable behavior" is that behavior which, in the determination of the court, indicates a defendant's unwillingness or inability to conform his behavior to that which is necessary for successful completion of the program or that the defendant's behavior is so disruptive as to threaten the successful completion of the program by other participants.

D. The court may order a defendant sentenced pursuant to this section to pay an amount to defray the cost of the services received in accordance with subsection D of §53.1-185.2.

(Chgd. by L.1995 chs. 502, 574; L.1999 ch. 372; L.2000 ch. 1040, eff. 7/1/2000.)

§19.2-303.4. Payment of costs when proceedings deferred and defendant placed on probation.

A circuit or district court, which had deferred further proceedings, without entering a judgment of guilt, and placed a defendant on probation subject to terms and conditions pursuant to §§16.1-278.8, 16.1-278.9, 18.2-57.3, 18.2-61, 18.2-67.1, 18.2-67.2, 18.1-67.2:1, 18.2-251 or §19.2-303.2, may impose upon the defendant costs.

(Added by L.1995 ch. 485; chgd. by L.2000 ch. 186, eff. 7/1/2000.)

§19.2-304. Increasing or decreasing probation period and modification of conditions.

The court may subsequently increase or decrease the probation period and may revoke or modify any condition of probation, but only upon a hearing after reasonable notice to both the defendant and the attorney for the Commonwealth.

§19.2-305. Requiring fines, costs, restitution for damages, support or community services from probationer.

A. While on probation the defendant may be required to pay in one or several sums a fine or costs, or both such fine and costs, imposed at the time of being placed on probation as a condition of such probation, and the failure of the defendant to pay such fine or costs, or both such fine and costs, at the prescribed time or times may be deemed a breach of such probation. The provisions of this subsection shall also apply to any person ordered to pay costs pursuant to §19.2-303.3.

B. A defendant placed on probation following conviction may be required to make at least partial restitution or reparation to the aggrieved party or parties for damages or loss caused by the offense for which conviction was had, or may be required to provide for the support of his wife or others for whose support he may be legally responsible, or may be required to perform community services. The defendant may submit a proposal to the court for making restitution, for providing for support or for performing community services.

(Chgd. by L.1995 ch. 485, eff. 7/1/95.)

§19.2-305.1. Restitution for property damage or loss; community services.

A. Notwithstanding any other provision of law, no person convicted of a crime in violation of any provision in Title 18.2, except the provisions of Article 2 (§18.2-266 et seq.) of Chapter 7 of Title 18.2, on or after July 1, 1977, which resulted in property damage or loss, shall be placed on probation or have his sentence suspended unless such person shall make at least partial restitution for such property damage or loss, or shall be compelled to perform community services, or both, or shall submit a plan for doing that which appears to the court to be feasible under the circumstances.

A1. Notwithstanding any other provision of law, any person who, on or after July 1, 1995, commits, and is convicted of, a crime in violation of any provision in Title 18.2 except the provisions of Article 2 (§18.2-266 et seq.) of Chapter 7 of Title 18.2 shall make at least partial restitution for any property damage or loss caused by the crime or for actual medical expenses incurred by the victim as a result of the crime, may be compelled to perform community services and, if the court so orders, shall submit a plan for doing that which appears to be feasible to the court under the circumstances.

B. At or before the time of sentencing, the court shall receive and consider any plan for making restitution submitted by the defendant. The plan shall include the defendant's home address, place of employment and address, social security number and bank information. If the court finds such plan to be reasonable and practical under the circumstances, it may consider probation or suspension of whatever portion of the sentence that it deems appropriate. By order of the court incorporating the defendant's plan or a reasonable and practical plan devised by the court, the defendant shall make restitution while he is free on probation or work release or following his release from confinement. Additionally, the court may order that the defendant make restitution during his confinement, if feasible, based upon both his earning capacity and net worth as determined by the court at sentencing.

C. At the time of sentencing, the court, in its discretion, shall determine the amount to be repaid by the defendant and the terms and conditions thereof. If community service work is ordered, the court shall determine the terms and conditions upon which such work shall be performed. The court shall include such findings in the judgment order. The order may specify that sums paid under such order shall be paid to the clerk, who shall disburse such sums as the court may, by order, direct. Any court desiring to participate in the Setoff Debt Collection Act (§§58.1-520 through 58.1-535) for the purpose of collecting fines or costs or providing restitution shall, at the time of sentencing, obtain the social security number of each defendant.

D. Unreasonable failure to execute the plan by the defendant shall result in revocation of the probation or imposition of the suspended sentence. A hearing shall be held in accordance with the provisions of this Code relating to revocation of probation or imposition of a suspended sentence before either such action is taken.

E. If restitution is ordered to be paid by the defendant to the victim of a crime and the victim can no longer be located or identified, the clerk shall deposit any such restitution collected to the Criminal Injuries Compensation Fund for the

benefit of crime victims. The administrator shall reserve a sum sufficient in the Fund from which he shall make prompt payment to the victim for any proper claims. Before making the deposit he shall record the name, last known address and amount of restitution due each victim appearing from the clerk's report to be entitled to restitution.
(Chgd. by L.1995 chs. 434, 687; L.2000 ch. 775, eff. 7/1/2000.)

§19.2-305.2. Amount of restitution; enforcement.
A. The court, when ordering restitution pursuant to §19.2-305.1, may require that such defendant, in the case of an offense resulting in damage to or loss or destruction of property of a victim of the offense (i) return the property to the owner or (ii) if return of the property is impractical or impossible, pay an amount equal to the greater of the value of the property at the time of the offense or the value of the property at the time of sentencing.
B. An order of restitution may be docketed as provided in §8.01-446 when so ordered by the court or upon written request of the victim and may be enforced by a victim named in the order to receive the restitution in the same manner as a judgment in a civil action.

§19.2-305.3. *(Repealed by L.1997 ch. 140, eff. 7/1/97.)*

§19.2-305.4. When interest to be paid on award of restitution.
The court, when ordering restitution pursuant to §19.2-305 or §19.2-305.1, may provide in the order for interest on the amount so ordered from the date of the loss or damage at the rate specified in §6.1-330.54.
(Added by L.1996 ch. 544, eff. 7/1/96.)

§19.2-306. Revocation of suspension of sentence and probation.
The court may, for any cause deemed by it sufficient which occurred at any time within the probation period, or if none, within the period of suspension fixed by the court, or if neither, within the maximum period for which the defendant might originally have been sentenced to be imprisoned, revoke the suspension of sentence and any probation, if the defendant be on probation, and cause the defendant to be arrested and brought before the court at any time within one year after the probation period, or if no probation period has been prescribed then within one year after the period of suspension fixed by the court, or if neither a probation period nor a period of suspension has been prescribed then within one year after the maximum period for which the defendant might originally have been sentenced to be imprisoned, whereupon, in case the imposition of sentence has been suspended, the court may pronounce whatever sentence might have been originally imposed. In case the execution of the sentence has been suspended, the original sentence shall be in full force and effect, and neither the time of probation or of suspension shall be taken into account to diminish the original sentence. In the event that any person placed on probation shall leave the jurisdiction of the court without the consent of the judge, or having obtained leave to remove to another locality violates any of the terms of his probation, he may be apprehended and returned to the court and dealt with as provided above. Provided, however, that nothing contained herein shall be construed to deprive any person of his right to appeal in the manner provided by law to the circuit court having criminal jurisdiction from a judgment or order revoking any suspended sentence. Provided, further, that if any court has, after hearing, found no cause to impose a sentence which might have been originally imposed, or to revoke a suspended sentence or probation, any further hearing to impose a sentence, or revoke a suspended sentence or probation, based solely on the alleged violation for which the hearing was held shall be barred.

§19.2-307. Contents of judgment order.
The judgment order shall set forth the plea, the verdict or findings and the adjudication and sentence, whether or not the case was tried by jury, and if not, whether the consent of the accused was concurred in by the court and the attorney for the Commonwealth. If the accused is found not guilty, or for any other reason is entitled to be discharged, judgment shall be entered accordingly. If an accused is tried at one time for two or more offenses, the court may enter one judgment order respecting all such offenses. The final judgment order shall be entered on a form promulgated by the Supreme Court.
(Chgd. by L.1996 ch. 60, eff. 1/1/97.)

§19.2-308. When two or more sentences run concurrently.
When any person is convicted of two or more offenses, and sentence to confinement, such sentences shall not run concurrently, unless expressly ordered by the court.

§19.2-308.1. When sentence may run concurrently with sentence in another jurisdiction.
Notwithstanding any other provision of law, in the event that a person is convicted of a criminal offense in any court of this Commonwealth and such person has also been sentenced to imprisonment for a term of one year or more by a court of the United States, or any other state or territory, and, at the time of sentencing in this Commonwealth, is incarcerated in a federal or state penal institution, the court may order the sentence to run concurrently with the sentence imposed by such other court.

§19.2-309. Sentence of confinement for conviction of a combination of felony and misdemeanor offenses.
When any person is convicted of a combination of felony and misdemeanor offenses and sentenced to confinement therefor, in determining the sequence of confinement, the felony sentence and commitment shall take precedence and such person shall first be committed to serve the felony sentence.

§19.2-309.1. *(Omitted due to limited applicability.)*

§19.2-310. Transfer of prisoners to custody of Director of Department of Corrections.
Every person sentenced by a court to the Department of Corrections upon conviction of a felony shall be conveyed to an appropriate receiving unit operated by the Department in the manner hereinafter provided. The clerk of the court in which the person is sentenced shall forthwith transmit to the Central Criminal Records Exchange the report of dispositions required by §19.2-390. The clerk of the court within thirty days from the date of the judgment shall forthwith transmit to the Director of the Department a certified copy or copies of the order of trial and a certified copy of the complete final order, and if he fails to do so he shall forfeit $100. Such copy or copies shall contain, as nearly as ascertainable, the birth date of the person sentenced. The sheriff shall certify to the Director of the Department any jail credits to which the person to be confined is entitled at such time as that person is transferred to the custody of the Director of the Department.
Following receipt of the order of trial and a certified copy of the complete final order, the Director or his designee shall dispatch a correctional officer to the county or city with a warrant directed to the sheriff authorizing him to deliver the prisoner to the correctional officer whose duty it shall be to take charge of the person and convey him to an appropriate receiving unit designated by the Director or his designee.

The Director or his designee shall allocate space available in the receiving unit or units by giving first priority to the transportation, as the transportation facilities of the Department may permit, of those persons held in jails who in the opinion of the Director or his designee except as required by §53.1-20 require immediate transportation to a receiving unit. In making such a determination of priority, the Director shall give due regard to the capacity of local as well as state correctional facilities and, to the extent feasible, shall seek to balance between local and state correctional facilities the excess of prisoners requiring detention.

§19.2-310.01. Transmission of sentencing documents.
Within thirty days of the receipt of a request from the Department of Corrections for certified copies of sentencing documents for any misdemeanor conviction, the clerk of the court receiving such request shall transmit the requested documents to the Director of the Department. In accordance with the provisions of §14.1-90, the requested documents shall be provided to the Director without the payment of any fee.

ARTICLE 1.1
DNA ANALYSIS AND DATA BANK

Section

§19.2-310.2. Blood, saliva or tissue sample required for DNA analysis upon conviction of a felony.
Every person convicted of a felony on or after July 1, 1990, and every person convicted of a felony offense under Article 7 (§18.2-61 et seq.) of Chapter 4 of Title 18.2 who was incarcerated on July 1, 1989, shall have a sample of his blood, saliva or tissue taken for DNA (deoxyribonucleic acid) analysis to determine identification characteristics specific to the person. The analysis shall be performed by the Division of Forensic Science, Department of Criminal Justice Services. The identification characteristics of the profile resulting from the DNA analysis shall be stored and maintained by the Division in a DNA data bank and shall be made available only as provided in §19.2-310.5.

After July 1, 1990, the blood, saliva or tissue sample shall be taken prior to release from custody.

Notwithstanding the provisions of §53.1-159, any person convicted of a felony who is in custody after July 1, 1990, shall provide a blood, saliva or tissue sample prior to his release. Every person so convicted after July 1, 1990, who is not sentenced to a term of confinement shall provide a blood, saliva or tissue sample as a condition of such sentence.
(Chgd. by L.1996 chs. 154, 952; L.1998 ch. 280, eff. 7/1/98.)

§19.2-310.3. Procedures for withdrawal of blood, saliva or tissue sample for DNA analysis.
Each sample required pursuant to §19.2-310.2 from persons who are to be incarcerated shall be withdrawn at the receiving unit or at such other place as is designated by the Department of Corrections or, in the case of a juvenile, the Department of Juvenile Justice. The required samples from persons who are not sentenced to a term of confinement shall be withdrawn at a time and place specified by the sentencing court. Only a correctional health nurse technician or a physician, registered professional nurse, licensed practical nurse, graduate laboratory technician, or phlebotomist shall withdraw any sample to be submitted for analysis. No civil liability shall attach to any person authorized to withdraw blood, saliva or tissue as provided herein as a result of the act of withdrawing blood, saliva or tissue from any person submitting thereto, provided the blood, saliva or tissue was withdrawn according to recognized medical procedures. However, no person shall be relieved from liability for negligence in the withdrawing of any blood, saliva or tissue sample.

Chemically clean sterile disposable needles and vacuum draw tubes or swabs shall be used for all samples. The tube containing the sample shall be sealed and labelled with the subject's name, social security number, date of birth, race and gender, the name of the person collecting the sample, the date and place of collection. The tubes containing the samples shall be secured to prevent tampering with the contents. The steps herein set forth relating to the taking, handling, identification, and disposition of blood, saliva or tissue samples are procedural and not substantive. Substantial compliance therewith shall be deemed to be sufficient. The samples shall be transported to the Division of Forensic Science not more than fifteen days following withdrawal and shall be analyzed and stored in the DNA data bank in accordance with §§19.2-310.4 and 19.2-310.5.
(Chgd. by L.1997 ch. 862; L.1998 ch. 280, eff. 7/1/98.)

§19.2-310.4. Procedures for conducting DNA analysis of blood, saliva or tissue sample.
Whether or not the results of an analysis are to be included in the data bank, the Division shall conduct the DNA analysis in accordance with procedures adopted by the Division to determine identification characteristics specific to the individual whose sample is being analyzed. The Director or his designated representative shall complete and maintain on file a form indicating the name of the person whose sample is to be analyzed, the date and by whom the blood, saliva or tissue sample was received and examined, and a statement that the seal on the tube containing the sample had not been broken or otherwise tampered with. The remainder of a blood, saliva or tissue sample submitted for analysis and inclusion in the data bank pursuant to §19.2-310.2 may be divided, labeled as provided for the original sample, and securely stored by the Division in accordance with specific procedures adopted by regulation of the Division to ensure the integrity and confidentiality of the samples. All or part of the remainder of that sample may be used only (i) to create a statistical data base provided no identifying information on the individual whose sample is being analyzed is included or (ii) for retesting by the Division to validate or update the original analysis.

A report of the results of a DNA analysis conducted by the Division as authorized, including the profile and identifying information, shall be made and maintained at the Division. A certificate and the results of the analysis shall be admissible in any court as evidence of the facts therein stated. Except as specifically provided in this section and §19.2-310.5, the results of the analysis shall be securely stored and shall remain confidential.
(Chgd. by L.1998 ch. 280, eff. 7/1/98.)

§19.2-310.5. DNA data bank exchange.
It shall be the duty of the Division to receive blood, saliva or tissue samples and to analyze, classify, and file the results of DNA identification characteristics profiles of blood, saliva or tissue samples submitted pursuant to §19.2-310.2 and to make such information available as provided in this section. The results of an analysis and comparison of the identification characteristics from two or more blood, saliva or tissue samples shall be made available directly to federal,

state and local law-enforcement officers upon request made in furtherance of an official investigation of any criminal offense. The Division shall confirm whether or not there is a DNA profile on file for a specific individual if a federal, state or local law-enforcement officer requests that information in furtherance of an official investigation of any criminal offense. A request may be made by personal contact, mail, or electronic means. The name of the requestor and the purpose for which the information is requested shall be maintained on file with the Division.

Upon his request, a copy of the request for search shall be furnished to any person identified and charged with an offense as the result of a search of information in the data bank.

The Division shall adopt regulations governing (i) the methods of obtaining information from the data bank in accordance with this section and (ii) procedures for verification of the identity and authority of the requestor. The Division shall specify the positions in that agency which require regular access to the data bank and samples submitted as a necessary function of the job.

The Division shall create a separate statistical data base comprised of DNA profiles of blood, saliva or tissue samples of persons whose identity is unknown. Nothing in this section or §19.2-310.6 shall prohibit the Division from sharing or otherwise disseminating the information in the statistical data base with law-enforcement or criminal justice agencies within or without the Commonwealth.

The Division may charge a reasonable fee to search and provide a comparative analysis of DNA profiles in the data bank to any authorized law-enforcement agency outside of the Commonwealth.

(Chgd. by L.1998 ch. 280; L.2000 ch. 284, eff. 7/1/2000.)

§19.2-310.6. Unauthorized uses of DNA data bank; forensic samples; penalties.

Any person who, without authority, disseminates information contained in the data bank shall be guilty of a Class 3 misdemeanor. Any person who disseminates, receives, or otherwise uses or attempts to so use information in the data bank, knowing that such dissemination, receipt, or use is for a purpose other than as authorized by law, shall be guilty of a Class 1 misdemeanor.

Except as authorized by law, any person who, for purposes of having DNA analysis performed, obtains or attempts to obtain any sample submitted to the Division of Forensic Science for analysis shall be guilty of a Class 5 felony.

§19.2-310.7. Expungement.

A person whose DNA profile has been included in the data bank pursuant to this chapter may request expungement on the grounds that the felony conviction on which the authority for including his DNA profile was based has been reversed and the case dismissed. The Division shall purge all records and identifiable information in the data bank pertaining to the person and destroy all samples from the person upon receipt of (i) a written request for expungement pursuant to this section and (ii) a certified copy of the court order reversing and dismissing the conviction.

ARTICLE 2
INDETERMINATE COMMITMENT

Section

§19.2-311. Indeterminate commitment to Department of Corrections in certain cases; duration and character of commitment; concurrence by Department.

A. The judge, after a finding of guilt, when fixing punishment in those cases specifically enumerated in subsection B of this section, may, in his discretion, in lieu of imposing any other penalty provided by law and, with consent of the person convicted, commit such person for a period of four years, which commitment shall be indeterminate in character. In addition, the court shall impose a period of confinement which shall be suspended. Subject to the provisions of subsection C hereof, such persons shall be committed to the Department of Corrections for a confinement in a state facility for youthful offenders established pursuant to §53.1-63. Such confinement shall be followed by at least one and one-half years of supervisory parole, conditioned on good behavior. The sentence of indeterminate commitment and eligibility for continuous evaluation and parole under §19.2-313 shall remain in effect but eligibility for use of programs and facilities established pursuant to §53.1-63 shall lapse if such person (i) exhibits intractable behavior as defined in §53.1-66 or (ii) is convicted of a second criminal offense which is a felony. A sentence imposed for any second criminal offense shall run consecutively with the indeterminate sentence.

B. The provisions of subsection A of this section shall be applicable to first convictions in which the person convicted:

1. Committed the offense of which convicted before becoming twenty-one years of age;

2. Was convicted of a felony offense other than any of the following: capital murder, murder in the first degree or murder in the second degree or a violation of §§18.2-61, 18.2-67.1, 18.2-67.2 or subdivision A 1 of §18.2-67.3; and

3. Is considered by the judge to be capable of returning to society as a productive citizen following a reasonable amount of rehabilitation.

C. Subsequent to a finding of guilt and prior to fixing punishment, the Department of Corrections shall, concurrently with the evaluation required by §19.2-316, review all aspects of the case to determine whether (i) such defendant is physically and emotionally suitable for the program, (ii) such indeterminate sentence of commitment is in the best interest of the Commonwealth and of the person convicted, and (iii) facilities are available for the confinement of such person. After the review such person shall be again brought before the court, which shall review the findings of the Department. The court may impose a sentence as authorized in subsection A, or any other penalty provided by law.

D. Upon the defendant's failure to complete the program established pursuant to §53.1-63 or to comply with the terms and conditions through no fault of his own, the defendant shall be brought before the court for hearing. Notwithstanding the provisions for pronouncement of sentence as set forth in §19.2-306, the court, after hearing, may pronounce whatever sentence was originally imposed, pronounce a reduced sentence, or impose such other terms and conditions of probation as it deems appropriate.

(Chgd. by L.1996 chs. 755, 914; L.1997 ch. 387; L.2000 chs. 668, 690, eff. 7/1/2000.)

§19.2-313. Eligibility for release.

Any person committed under the provisions of §19.2-311 shall be eligible for release at the discretion of the Parole Board upon certification by the Director of the Department of Corrections that the person has successfully completed the program established pursuant to §53.1-63 and a determination that he has demonstrated that such release is compatible with the interests of society and of such person and his successful rehabilitation to that extent. The Department and Parole Board shall make continuous evaluation of his progress to determine his readiness for release. All such persons, in any event, shall be released after four years' confinement. Any person committed under §19.2-311 who was convicted of a misdemeanor and is determined to be unsuitable for the program established pursuant to §53.1-63 shall be released after one year of confinement or the maximum confinement for the misdemeanor whichever is less.

(Chgd. by L.2000 chs. 668, 690, eff. 7/1/2000.)

§19.2-314. Supervision of persons released.

Every person released under §19.2-313 shall receive intensive parole supervision for a period of at least one and one-half years and may have parole supervision continued for a longer period, if the Parole Board deems it advisable.

(Chgd. by L.2000 chs. 668, 690, eff. 7/1/2000.)

§19.2-315. Compliance with terms and conditions of parole; time on parole not counted as part of commitment period.

Every person on parole under §19.2-314 shall comply with such terms and conditions as may be prescribed by the Board according to §53.1-157 and shall be subject to the penalties imposed by law for a violation of such terms and conditions. Notwithstanding any other provision of the Code, if parole is revoked as a result of any such violation, such person may be returned to the institution established pursuant to §53.1-63 upon the direction of the Parole Board with the concurrence of the Department of Corrections, provided such person has not been convicted since his release on parole of an offense constituting a felony under the laws of the Commonwealth. Time on parole shall not be counted as part of the four-year period of commitment under this section. In addition, such person may be brought before the sentencing court for imposition of all or part of the suspended sentence.

(Chgd. by L.2000 chs. 668, 690, eff. 7/1/2000.)

§19.2-316. Evaluation and report prior to determining punishment.

Following conviction and prior to sentencing the court shall order such defendant committed to the Department of Corrections for a period not to exceed sixty days from the date of referral for evaluation and diagnosis by the Department to determine the person's potential for rehabilitation through confinement and treatment in the facilities and programs established pursuant to §53.1-63. The evaluation and diagnosis shall include a complete physical and mental examination of the defendant and may be conducted by the Department of Corrections at any state or local facility, probation and parole office, or other location deemed appropriate by the Department. The Department of Corrections shall conduct the evaluation and diagnosis and shall review all aspects of the case within sixty days from the date of conviction or revocation of ordinary probation and shall recommend that the defendant be committed to the facility established pursuant to §53.1-63 upon finding that (i) such defendant is physically and emotionally suitable for the program, (ii) such commitment is in the best interest of the Commonwealth and the defendant, and (iii) facilities are available for confinement of the defendant.

If the Director of the Department of Corrections determines such person should be confined in a facility other than one established pursuant to §53.1-63, a written report giving the reasons for such decision shall be submitted to the sentencing court. The court shall not be bound by such written report in the matter of determining punishment. Additionally, the person may be committed or transferred to a mental hospital or like institution, as provided by law, during such sixty-day period.

(Chgd. by L.2000 chs. 668, 690, eff. 7/1/2000.)

ARTICLE 3
BOOT CAMP INCARCERATION PROGRAM

Section

§19.2-316.1. Eligibility for participation; evaluation; sentencing; withdrawal or removal from program.

An individual may be eligible to be sentenced as provided herein if he (i) is convicted on or after January 1, 1991, of a nonviolent felony, or is deemed by the court to be nonviolent in character, (ii) is no older than twenty-four at the time of conviction for the offense, (iii) has never before been incarcerated upon a felony conviction in a correctional facility of any state, the District of Columbia, the United States or its territories, and (iv) has not been confined for more than twelve months nor for more than one term of confinement in a local correctional facility of any such jurisdiction; however, confinement for misdemeanor traffic convictions shall not be considered in determining eligibility.

Following conviction and prior to sentencing, upon motion of the defendant, the court may order such defendant committed to the Department of Corrections for a period not to exceed sixty days from the date of referral or the date of revocation of ordinary probation, as the case may be, for evaluation and diagnosis by the Department to determine suitability for participation in the Boot Camp Incarceration Program established pursuant to §53.1-67.1. The evaluation and diagnosis shall include a complete physical and mental examination of the defendant and may be conducted by the Department of Corrections at any state or local facility, probation and parole office, or other location deemed appropriate by the Department.

The Department of Corrections shall conduct the evaluation and diagnosis and shall review all aspects of the case within sixty days from the date of conviction or revocation of ordinary probation and shall recommend that the defendant be committed to the Boot Camp Incarceration Program upon finding that (i) such defendant is physically and emotionally suitable for the program, (ii) such commitment is in the best interest of the Commonwealth and the defendant, and (iii) facilities are available for confinement of the defendant.

Upon receipt of such a recommendation and written consent of the defendant to participate in the program, and a determination by the court that the defendant will benefit from the program and is capable of returning to society as a productive citizen following a reasonable amount of intensive supervision and rehabilitation including program components set forth in §53.1-67.1, and the defendant would otherwise be committed to the Department of Corrections for a period of confinement, the court shall impose such sentence of confinement as authorized by law and suspend the sentence and place the defendant on probation. Such probation shall be conditioned upon the defendant's entry into and successful completion of a Boot Camp Incarceration Program established by the Department of Corrections pursuant to §53.1-67.1. The court may impose such other terms and conditions of probation as it deems appropriate.

Upon the defendant's (i) voluntary withdrawal from the program, (ii) removal from the program by the Department of Corrections for intractable behavior, or (iii) refusal to comply with the terms and conditions of probation imposed by the court, the defendant shall be brought before the court for hearing. Upon a finding that the defendant voluntarily chooses to withdraw from the program, exhibited intractable behavior as defined herein, or refused to comply with terms and conditions of probation, the court may revoke all or part of the suspended sentence and probation. Upon revocation of the suspension and probation, the provisions of §§53.1-191, 53.1-196 and 53.1-198 through 53.1-201 shall apply retroactively to the date of sentencing.

Upon the defendant's failure to complete the program or to comply with the terms and conditions of probation imposed by the court through no fault of his own, the defendant shall be brought before the court for hearing. Notwithstanding the provisions for pronouncement of sentence as set forth in §19.2-306, the court, after hearing, may pronounce whatever sentence was originally imposed, pronounce a reduced sentence, or impose such other terms and conditions of probation as it deems appropriate.

"Intractable behavior" means that behavior which, in the determination of the Department of Corrections, (i) indicates an inmate's unwillingness or inability to conform his behavior to that necessary to his successful completion of the program or (ii) is so disruptive as to threaten the successful completion of the program by other participants.

"Nonviolent felony" means any felony except those considered an "act of violence" pursuant to §19.2-297.1 or any attempt to commit any of those crimes.

(Chgd. by L.1995 ch. 117; L.1996 chs. 809, 938; L.2000 ch. 769, eff. 7/1/2000.)

ARTICLE 4
DETENTION CENTER INCARCERATION PROGRAM

Section

§19.2-316.2. Eligibility for participation in detention center incarceration program; evaluation; sentencing; withdrawal or removal from program.

A. A defendant who otherwise would have been sentenced to incarceration for a nonviolent felony as defined in §19.2-316.1 or who has been previously incarcerated for a nonviolent felony as defined in §19.2-316.1 but otherwise meets the following criteria and (i) who is determined by the court to need more security or supervision than provided by the diversion center incarceration program under §53.1-67.7, (ii) whose age or physical condition disqualifies him from the Boot Camp Incarceration Program under §53.1-67.1, and (iii) who can benefit from a regimented environment and structured program, may be considered for commitment to a detention center as established under §53.1-67.8 as follows:

1. Following conviction and prior to imposition of sentence or following a finding that the defendant's probation should be revoked, upon motion of the defendant, the court may order such defendant committed to the Department of Corrections for a period not to exceed sixty days from the date of commitment for evaluation and diagnosis by the Department to determine suitability for participation in the Detention Center Incarceration Program. The evaluation and diagnosis shall include a complete physical and mental examination of the defendant and may be conducted by the Department at any state or local correctional facility, probation and parole office, or other location deemed appropriate by the Department.

2. Upon determination that (i) such defendant is physically and emotionally suited for the program, (ii) such commitment is in the best interest of the Commonwealth and the defendant, and (iii) facilities are available for the confinement of the defendant, the Department shall recommend to the court in writing that the defendant be committed to the Detention Center Incarceration Program.

3. Upon receipt of such a recommendation and a determination by the court that the defendant will benefit from the program and is capable of returning to society as a productive citizen following successful completion of the program, and if the defendant would otherwise be committed to the Department, the court (i) shall impose sentence, suspend the sentence, and place the defendant on probation or (ii) following a finding that the defendant has violated the terms and conditions of his probation previously ordered, shall place the defendant on probation pursuant to this section. Such probation shall be conditioned upon the defendant's entry into and successful completion of the Detention Center Incarceration Program. The court shall order that, upon successful completion of the program, the defendant shall be released from confinement and be under intensive probation supervision for a period to be specified by the court followed by an additional period of regular probation of not less than one year. The court shall further order that the defendant, following release from confinement, shall (i) make reasonable efforts to secure and maintain employment, (ii) comply with a plan of restitution or community service, (iii) comply with a plan for payment of fines, if any, and costs of court, and (iv) undergo appropriate substance abuse treatment, if necessary. The court may impose such other terms and conditions of probation as it deems appropriate.

4. Upon the defendant's (i) voluntary withdrawal from the program, (ii) removal from the program by the Department for intractable behavior as defined in §19.2-316.1, or (iii) failure to comply with the terms and conditions of probation, the court shall cause the defendant to show cause why his probation and suspension of sentence should not be revoked. Upon a finding that the defendant voluntarily withdrew from the program, was removed from the program by the Department for intractable behavior, or failed to comply with the terms and conditions of probation, the court may revoke all or part of the probation and suspended sentence and commit the defendant as otherwise provided in this chapter.

B. Any offender as described in §19.2-316.1 paroled under §53.1-155 or mandatorily released under §53.1-159 and for whom probable cause that a violation of parole or mandatory release, other than for the occurrence of a new felony or Class 1 or Class 2 misdemeanor, has been determined under §53.1-165, may be considered by the Parole Board for commitment to a detention center as established under §53.1-67.8 as follows:

1. The Parole Board or its authorized hearing officer, with the violator's consent, may order the violator to be evaluated and diagnosed by the Department of Corrections to determine suitability for participation in the Detention Center Incarceration Program. The evaluation and diagnosis may be conducted by the Department at any state or local correctional facility, probation or parole office, or other location deemed appropriate by the Department.

2. Upon determination that (i) such commitment is in the best interest of the Commonwealth and the violator and (ii) facilities are available for the confinement of the violator, the Department shall recommend to the Parole Board in writing

that the violator be committed to the Detention Center Incarceration Program. The Department shall have the final authority to determine an individual's suitablity for the program.

3. Upon receipt of such a recommendation and a determination by the Parole Board that the violator will benefit from the program and is capable of returning to society as a productive citizen following successful completion of the program, the violator shall be placed under parole supervision for a period of not less than one year. The Parole Board may impose such other terms and conditions of parole or mandatory release as it deems appropriate. The time spent in the program shall not be counted as service of any part of a term of imprisonment for which he was sentenced upon his conviction.

4. Upon the violator's (i) voluntary withdrawal from the program, (ii) removal from the program for intractable behavior as defined in §19.2-316.1, or (iii) failure to comply with the terms and conditions of parole or mandatory release, the Department shall conduct a preliminary parole violation hearing to determine if probable cause exists to revoke his parole or mandatory release. Upon a finding that the violator voluntarily withdrew from the program, was removed from the program by the Department for intractable behavior, or failed to comply with the terms and conditions of parole or mandatory release, the Parole Board shall revoke parole or mandatory release and recommit the violator as provided in §53.1-165.

(Chgd. by L.1995 chs. 502, 574; L.2000 ch. 338, eff. 7/1/2000.)

ARTICLE 5
DIVERSION CENTER INCARCERATION PROGRAM

Section

§19.2-316.3. Eligibility for participation in diversion center incarceration program; evaluation; sentencing; withdrawal or removal from program; payment for costs.

A. A defendant (i) who otherwise would have been sentenced to incarceration for a nonviolent felony as defined in §19.2-316.1 and who the court determines requires more security or supervision than provided by intensive probation supervision or (ii) whose suspension of sentence would otherwise be revoked after a finding that the defendant has violated the terms and conditions of probation for a nonviolent felony as defined in §19.2-316.1, may be considered for commitment to a diversion center as established under §53.1-67.7 as follows:

1. Following conviction and prior to imposition of sentence or following a finding that the defendant's probation should be revoked, upon motion of the defendant, the court may order such defendant committed to the Department of Corrections for a period not to exceed forty-five days from the date of commitment for evaluation and diagnosis by the Department to determine suitability for participation in the Diversion Center Incarceration Program. The evaluation and diagnosis may be conducted by the Department at any state or local correctional facility, probation and parole office, or other location deemed appropriate by the Department.

2. Upon determination that (i) such commitment is in the best interest of the Commonwealth and the defendant and (ii) facilities are available for the confinement of the defendant, the Department shall recommend to the court in writing that the defendant be committed to the Diversion Center Incarceration Program.

3. Upon receipt of such a recommendation and a determination by the court that the defendant will benefit from the program and is capable of returning to society as a productive citizen following successful completion of the program, and if the defendant would otherwise be committed to the Department, the court (i) shall impose sentence, suspend the sentence, and place the defendant on probation pursuant to this section or (ii) following a finding that the defendant has violated the terms and conditions of his probation previously ordered, shall place the defendant on probation pursuant to this section. Such probation shall be conditioned upon the defendant's entry into and successful completion of the Diversion Center Incarceration Program. The court shall order that, upon successful completion of the program, the defendant shall be released from confinement and be under intensive probation supervision for a period to be specified by the court followed by an additional period of regular probation of not less than one year. The court shall further order that the defendant, prior to release from confinement, shall (i) make reasonable efforts to secure and maintain employment, (ii) comply with a plan of restitution or community service, (iii) comply with a plan for payment of fines, if any, and costs of court, and (iv) undergo substance abuse treatment, if necessary. The court may impose such other terms and conditions of probation as it deems appropriate.

4. Upon the defendant's (i) voluntary withdrawal from the program, (ii) removal from the program by the Department for intractable behavior as defined in §19.2-316.1, or (iii) failure to comply with the terms and conditions of probation, the court shall cause the defendant to show cause why his probation and suspension of sentence should not be revoked. Upon a finding that the defendant voluntarily withdrew from the program, was removed from the program by the Department for intractable behavior, or failed to comply with the terms and conditions of probation, the court may revoke all or part of the probation and suspended sentence, and commit the defendant as otherwise provided in this chapter.

B. Any offender as described in §19.2-316.1 paroled under §53.1-155 or mandatorily released under §53.1-159 and for whom probable cause that a violation of parole or mandatory release, other than the occurrence of a new felony or Class 1 or Class 2 misdemeanor, has been determined under §53.1-165, may be considered by the Parole Board for commitment to a diversion center as established under §53.1-67.7 as follows:

1. The Parole Board or its authorized hearing officer, with the violator's consent, may order the violator to be evaluated and diagnosed by the Department of Corrections to determine suitability for participation in the Diversion Center Incarceration Program. The evaluation and diagnosis may be conducted by the Department at any state or local correctional facility, probation or parole office, or other location deemed appropriate by the Department.

2. Upon determination that (i) such commitment is in the best interest of the Commonwealth and the violator and (ii) facilities are available for the confinement of the violator, the Department shall recommend to the Parole Board in writing that the violator be committed to the Diversion Center Incarceration Program. The Department shall have the final authority to determine an individual's suitability for the program.

3. Upon receipt of such a recommendation and a determination by the Parole Board that the violator will benefit from the program and is capable of returning to society as a productive citizen following successful completion of the program and if the violator would otherwise be committed to

the Department, the Parole Board shall restore the violator to parole supervision conditioned upon entry into and successful completion of the Diversion Center Incarceration Program. The Parole Board shall order that, upon successful completion of the program, the violator shall be placed under parole supervision for a period of not less than one year. The Parole Board may impose such other terms and conditions of parole or mandatory release as it deems appropriate. The time spent in the program shall not be counted as service of any part of a term of imprisonment for which he was sentenced upon his conviction.

4. Upon the violator's (i) voluntary withdrawal from the program, (ii) removal from the program by the Department for intractable behavior as defined in §19.2-316.1, or (iii) failure to comply with the terms and conditions of parole or mandatory release, the Parole Board may revoke parole or mandatory release and recommit the violator as provided in §53.1-165.

C. A person sentenced pursuant to this article shall be required to pay an amount to be determined by the Board of Corrections pursuant to regulation to defray the cost of his keep.

(Chgd. by L.1995 502, 574; L.2000 ch. 338, eff. 7/1/2000.)

CHAPTER 19
EXCEPTIONS AND WRITS OF ERROR

Section

§19.2-317. When writ of error lies in criminal case for accused; when for Commonwealth; when for county, city or town.

A. A writ of error shall lie in a criminal case to the judgment of a circuit court or the judge thereof, from the Court of Appeals as provided in §17.1-406. It shall lie in any such case for the accused and if the case is for the violation of any law relating to the state revenue, it shall lie also for the Commonwealth.

B. A writ of error shall also lie for any county, city or town from the Supreme Court to the judgment of any circuit court declaring an ordinance of such county, city or town to be unconstitutional or otherwise invalid, except when the violation of any such ordinance is made a misdemeanor by state statute.

C. A writ of error shall also lie for the Commonwealth from the Supreme Court to a judgment of the Court of Appeals in a criminal case, except where the decision of the Court of Appeals is made final under §17.1-410 or §19.2-408.

(Chgd. by L.1997 ch. 358, eff. 7/1/97.)

§19.2-318. Appeal on writ of error to judgment for contempt.

From a judgment for any civil contempt of court an appeal may be taken to the Court of Appeals. A writ of error shall lie from the Court of Appeals to a judgment for criminal contempt of court. This section shall also be construed to authorize an appeal from or writ of error to a judgment of a circuit court rendered on appeal from a judgment of a district court for civil or criminal contempt.

§19.2-319. When execution of sentence to be suspended; bail; appeal from denial.

If a person sentenced by a circuit court to death or confinement in the state correctional facility indicates an intention to apply for a writ of error, the circuit court shall postpone the execution of such sentence for such time as it may deem proper.

In any other criminal case wherein judgment is given by any court to which a writ of error lies, and in any case of judgment for any civil or criminal contempt, from which an appeal may be taken or to which a writ of error lies, the court giving such judgment may postpone the execution thereof for such time and on such terms as it deems proper.

In any case after conviction if the sentence, or the execution thereof, is suspended in accordance with this section, or for any other cause, the court, or the judge thereof, may, and in any case of a misdemeanor shall, set bail in such penalty and for appearance at such time as the nature of the case may require; provided that, if the conviction was for a violent felony as defined in §19.2-297.1 and the defendant was sentenced to serve a period of incarceration not subject to suspension, then the court shall presume, subject to rebuttal, that no condition or combination of conditions of bail will reasonably assure the appearance of the convicted person or the safety of the public.

In any case in which the court denies bail, the reason for such denial shall be stated on the record of the case. A writ of error from the Court of Appeals shall lie to any such judgment refusing bail or requiring excessive bail, except that in any case where a person has been sentenced to death, a writ of error shall lie from the Supreme Court. Upon review by the Court of Appeals or the Supreme Court, if the decision by the trial court to deny bail is overruled, the appellate court shall set bail.

(Chgd. by L.1999 ch. 821, eff. 7/1/99.)

§19.2-320. Petitioner for writ of error to comply with Rules of Court.

Any party for whom a writ of error lies may apply therefor by complying with the provisions of the Rules of the Supreme Court of Virginia relative to the appeal of criminal cases to the Court of Appeals, or where an appeal is taken to the Supreme Court, with the Rules of the Supreme Court relative to appeal of criminal cases to the Supreme Court.

§19.2-321. With whom petition for writ of error filed.

A. The petition to the Court of Appeals shall be filed with the clerk of the Court in the manner and within the time provided by law.

B. The petition in a case wherein a writ of error lies from the Supreme Court shall be filed with the clerk of that Court in the manner and within the time provided by law.

§19.2-322.1. Suspension of execution of judgment on appeal.

Execution of a judgment from which an appeal to the Court of Appeals or the Supreme Court is sought may be suspended during an appeal provided the appeal is timely prosecuted and an appeal bond is filed as provided in §8.01-676.1.

§19.2-323. Denial by judge or justice no bar to allowance by Court.

The denial of a writ of error by a judge or justice of an appellate court, in the vacation of that court, shall not prevent the allowance of the writ by the Court, if by it deemed proper, on presentation of the petition to that Court at its next term.

§19.2-324. Decision of appellate court.

The court from which a writ of error lies shall affirm the judgment, if there be no error therein, and reverse the same in whole or in part, if erroneous, and enter such judgment as the court whose error is sought to be corrected ought to have entered; or remand the cause and direct a new trial; affirming in those cases where the voices on both sides are equal.

§19.2-325. Provisions which apply to criminal as well as civil cases; when plaintiff in error unable to pay printing costs.

Sections 8.01-675.1, 8.01-675.2, 8.01-675.3, 8.01-684 and 14.1-120 shall apply as well to criminal cases as to civil cases. In a felony case in the Court of Appeals or the Supreme Court, if the plaintiff in error files with the clerk of the Court an affidavit that he is unable to pay or secure to be paid the costs of printing the record in the case, together with a certificate of the judge of the trial court to the effect that he has investigated the matter and is of opinion that the plaintiff in error is unable to pay, or secure to be paid, such costs, the printing shall be done as if the costs had been paid and the clerk shall not be required to account for and pay the same into the state treasury. However, if the costs are not paid or secured to be paid and upon the hearing of the case the judgment of the court below is wholly affirmed by the Court of Appeals and no appeal granted by the Supreme Court, or wholly affirmed by the Supreme Court where appeal is granted, the Court in affirming the judgment shall also give judgment in behalf of the Commonwealth against the plaintiff in error for the amount of the costs to be taxed by its clerk.

§19.2-326. Payment of expenses of appeals of indigent defendants.

In any felony or misdemeanor case wherein the judge of the circuit court, from the affidavit of the defendant or any other evidence certifies that the defendant is financially unable to pay his attorneys' fees, costs and expenses incident to an appeal, the court to which an appeal is taken shall order the payment of such attorneys' fees in an amount not less than $300, costs or necessary expenses of such attorneys in an amount deemed reasonable by the court, by the Commonwealth out of the appropriation for criminal charges. If the conviction is upheld on appeal, the attorney's fees, costs and necessary expenses of such attorney paid by the Commonwealth under the provisions hereof shall be assessed against the defendant.

§19.2-327. How judgment of appellate court certified and entered.

The judgment of the Court of Appeals or of the Supreme Court shall be certified to the court to whose judgment the writ of error was allowed. The court or the clerk thereof shall cause the same to be entered on its order book as its own judgment.

CHAPTER 20
TAXATION AND ALLOWANCE OF COSTS

§19.2-328. When jailers and sheriffs to summon or employ guards and other persons; allowances therefor.

Whenever in the discretion of the court it is necessary for the safekeeping of a prisoner under charge of, or sentence for, crime, whether the prisoner be in jail, hospital, court or elsewhere, the court may order the jailer to summon a sufficient guard, and whenever ordered by the court to do so, the sheriff of any county or city shall summon or employ temporarily such person or persons as may be needed to preserve proper order or otherwise to aid the court in its proper operation and functioning, and for such guard or other service the court may allow therefor so much as it deems proper, not exceeding the hourly equivalent of the minimum annual salary paid a full-time deputy sheriff who performs like services in the same county or city; in addition, mileage and other expenses for rendering the services shall be paid for each person, the same to be paid out of the budget allotted to the sheriff as approved by the Compensation Board, except when payment for such guard is otherwise provided under the provisions of §53.1-94 of the Code of Virginia.

§19.2-329. Allowance to witnesses.

Sections 14.1-190 to 14.1-194, inclusive, shall apply to a person attending as a witness, under a recognizance or summons in a criminal case, as well as to a person attending under a summons in a civil case, except that a person residing out of this Commonwealth, who attends a court therein as a witness, shall be allowed by the court a proper compensation for attendance and travel to and from the place of his abode, the amount of the same to be fixed by the court.

§19.2-330. Compensation to witnesses from out of Commonwealth.

Any witness from without the Commonwealth whose attendance is compelled under the provisions of Chapter 16, Article 2 (§19.2-272 et seq.) of this title shall be deemed to render a service within the meaning of §19.2-332 and the compensation and expenses of such witness, whether on behalf of the Commonwealth or the accused, may be paid out of the state treasury in accordance with the provisions of such section. But the compensation and expenses of any witness summoned on behalf of an accused shall not be certified to the state treasury as a compensation under such section except in cases when the court or judge thereof is satisfied that the defendant is without means to pay same and is unable to provide the costs incident thereto.

§19.2-331. When Commonwealth pays witnesses in case of misdemeanor.

Payment shall not be made out of the state treasury to a witness attending for the Commonwealth in any prosecution for a misdemeanor unless it appears that the sum to which the witness is entitled cannot be obtained:

(1) If it be a case wherein there is a prosecutor and the defendant is convicted, by reason of the insolvency of the defendant, or

(2) If it be a case in which there is no prosecutor, by reason of the acquittal or insolvency of the defendant or other cause.

§19.2-332. Compensation to officer or other person for services not otherwise compensable.

Whenever in a criminal case an officer or other person renders any service required by law for which no specific compensation is provided, or whenever any other service has been rendered pursuant to the request or prior approval of the court, the court shall allow therefor such sum as it deems reasonable, including mileage at a rate provided by law, and such allowance shall be paid out of the state treasury from the appropriation for criminal charges on the certificate of the court stating the nature of the service. This section shall not prevent any payment under §2.1-223.6, which could have been made if this section had not been enacted.

This section shall not be construed to authorize the payment of any additional compensation to an officer or other employee of the Commonwealth who is compensated for his services exclusively by salary unless it be otherwise expressly provided by law.

§19.2-333. No state fees to attorney for the Commonwealth.

No fee to an attorney for the Commonwealth shall be payable out of the state treasury, unless it be expressly so provided.

§19.2-334. By whom certificate of allowance to be made; vouchers to accompany it; proof of correctness; what entry to state.

Any other expense incident to a proceeding in a criminal case which is payable out of the state treasury otherwise than under §§2.1-223.6, 19.2-330 or §19.2-332 shall be certified by the court. If it be a judge of a district court exercising jurisdiction, it shall be certified by such judge to the Supreme Court. With the certificate of allowance there shall be transmitted to the Supreme Court the vouchers on which it is made. The court, in passing upon any account for fees or expenses required to be certified by it under this section, before certifying the account, may, in its discretion, require proof of the correctness of any item thereof.

The entry of such certificate of allowance shall state how much thereof is on account of each person prosecuted.

§19.2-335. Judge of district court to certify to clerk of circuit court costs of proceedings in criminal cases before him.

A judge of a district court before whom there is any proceeding in a criminal case, including any proceeding which has been deferred upon probation of the defendant pursuant to §§16.1-278.8, 16.1-278.9, 18.2-61, 18.2-67.1, 18.2-67.2, 18.2-67.2:1, 18.2-251 or §19.2-303.2, shall certify to the clerk of the circuit court of his county or city, and a judge or court before whom there is, in a criminal case, any proceeding preliminary to conviction in another court, upon receiving information of the conviction from the clerk of the court wherein it is, shall certify to such clerk all the expenses incident to such proceedings which are payable out of the state treasury.

(Chgd. by L.1995 ch. 485, eff. 7/1/95.)

§19.2-336. Clerk to make up statement of whole cost, and issue execution therefor.

In every criminal case the clerk of the circuit court in which the accused is found guilty or is placed on probation during deferral of the proceedings pursuant to §§16.1-278.8, 16.1-278.9, 18.2-61, 18.2-67.1, 18.2-67.2, 18.2-67.2:1, 18.2-251 or §19.2-303.2, or, if the conviction is in a district court, the clerk to which the judge thereof certifies as aforesaid, shall, as soon as may be, make up a statement of all the expenses incident to the prosecution, including such as are certified under §19.2-335, and execution for the amount of such expenses shall be issued and proceeded with. Chapter 21 (§19.2-339 et seq.) of this title shall apply thereto in like manner as if, on the day of completing the statement, there was a judgment in such court in favor of the Commonwealth against the accused for such amount as a fine. However, in any case in which an accused waives trial by jury, at least ten days before trial, but the Commonwealth or the court trying the case refuses to so waive, then the cost of the jury shall not be included in such statement or judgment.

(Chgd. by L.1995 ch. 485, eff. 7/1/95.)

§19.2-337. Claims not presented in time to be disallowed.

If by reason of the failure of a person to present his claim in due time a sum be not included in such execution which would have been included if so presented, such claim, unless there be good cause for the failure, shall be disallowed.

§19.2-338. Collection by town of cost of transporting prisoners.

(1) Notwithstanding any provision of any charter or any law to the contrary, any town may provide that any person convicted of violating any ordinance of the town may be charged, in addition to all other costs, fines, fees and charges, the costs of transporting such person so convicted to and from a jail or other penal institution outside the corporate limits of such town designated by the town as a place of confinement for persons arrested for violating the ordinances of the town and required to be held in jail pending trial upon such charge. The cost of such transportation shall be taxed as a part of the costs payable by persons convicted of violating such ordinances.

(2) No officer transporting any person convicted of violating any ordinance of the town, as provided in subsection (1) hereof, shall charge or be paid, nor shall such town receive directly or indirectly, more than the cost of transporting such person when more than one person is transported.

(Chgd. by L.1995 ch. 51, eff. 7/1/95.)

CHAPTER 21
RECOVERY OF FINES AND PENALTIES

Article

ARTICLE 1
PROCEEDINGS TO RECOVER

§19.2-339. Word "fine" construed.

Whenever the word "fine" is used in this chapter, it shall be construed to refer solely to the pecuniary penalty imposed by a court or jury upon a defendant who has been found guilty of a crime. The word "fine" shall not include other forfeitures, penalties, costs, amercements or the like, even though they follow as a consequence of conviction of crime.

§19.2-340. Fines; how recovered; in what name.

When any statute or ordinance prescribes a fine, unless it is otherwise expressly provided or would be inconsistent with the manifest intention of the General Assembly, it shall be paid to the Commonwealth if prescribed by a statute and recoverable by presentment, indictment, information or warrant and paid to the locality if prescribed by an ordinance and recoverable by warrant. Fines imposed and costs taxed in a criminal or traffic prosecution, including a prosecution for a violation of an ordinance adopted pursuant to §46.2-1220, for committing an offense shall constitute a judgment and, if not paid at the time they are imposed, execution may issue thereon in the same manner as upon any other monetary judgment, subject to the period of limitations provided by §19.2-341.

(Chgd. by L.1995 ch. 438, eff. 7/1/95.)

§19.2-341. Penalties other than fines; how recovered; in what name; limitation of actions.

When any statute or ordinance prescribes a monetary penalty other than a fine, unless it is otherwise expressly provided or would be inconsistent with the manifest intention of the General Assembly, it shall be paid to the Commonwealth if prescribed by statute and paid to the locality if prescribed by an ordinance and recoverable by warrant, presentment, indictment, or information. Penalties imposed and costs taxed in any such proceeding shall constitute a judgment and, if not paid at the time they are imposed, execution may issue thereon in the same manner as upon any other monetary judgment. No such proceeding of any nature, however, shall be brought or had for the recovery of such a penalty or costs due the Commonwealth or any political subdivision thereof, unless within twenty years from the date of the offense or delinquency giving rise to imposition of such penalty if imposed by a circuit court, or within ten years if imposed by a general district court.

(Chgd. by L.1995 ch. 438, eff. 7/1/95.)

§19.2-342. Where and in what court proceeding to be.

In a proceeding under §19.2-341, such warrant, presentment, indictment or information shall be in the county or city wherein the offense was committed or the delinquency occurred.

ARTICLE 3
COLLECTION AND DISPOSITION
OF FINES

§19.2-348. Attorneys for Commonwealth or clerks to superintend issue of executions, etc.

The attorney for the Commonwealth or the clerk of the circuit court shall superintend the issuing of all executions or judgments for fines and penalties going wholly or in part to the Commonwealth or a county, city or town, in the circuit court or appropriate district court of his county or city.

§19.2-349. Responsibility for collections; clerks to report unsatisfied fines, etc.; duty of attorneys for Commonwealth; assistance by the office of the Attorney General.

A. The clerk of the circuit court and district court of every county and city shall submit to the judge of his court, the Department of Taxation, the State Compensation Board and the attorney for the Commonwealth of his county or city a monthly report of all fines, costs, forfeitures and penalties which are delinquent more than thirty days, including court-ordered restitution of a sum certain, imposed in his court for a violation of state law or a local ordinance which remain unsatisfied, including those which are delinquent in installment payments. The monthly report shall include the social security number or driver's license number of the defendant, if known, and such other information as the Department of Taxation and the Compensation Board deem appropriate. The Executive Secretary shall make the report required by this subsection on behalf of those clerks who participate in the Supreme Court's automated information system.

B. It shall be the duty of the attorney for the Commonwealth to cause proper proceedings to be instituted for the collection and satisfaction of all fines, costs, forfeitures, penalties and restitution. The attorney for the Commonwealth shall determine whether it would be impractical or uneconomical for such service to be rendered by the office of the attorney for the Commonwealth. If the defendant does not enter into an installment payment agreement under §19.2-354, the attorney for the Commonwealth and the clerk may agree to a process by which collection activity may be commenced ten days after judgment.

If the attorney for the Commonwealth does not undertake collection, he shall contract with (i) private attorneys or private collection agencies, (ii) enter into an agreement with a local governing body, or (iii) use the services of the Department of Taxation, upon such terms and conditions as may be established by guidelines promulgated by the Office of the Attorney General, the Executive Secretary of the Supreme Court with the Department of Taxation and the Compensation Board. If the attorney for the Commonwealth undertakes collection, he shall follow the procedures established by the Department of Taxation and the Compensation Board. Such guidelines shall not supersede contracts between attorneys for the Commonwealth and private attorneys and collection agencies when active collection efforts are being undertaken.

The fees of any private attorneys or collection agencies shall be paid on a contingency fee basis out of the proceeds of the amounts collected. However, in no event shall such attorney or collection agency receive a fee for amounts collected by the Department of Taxation under the Setoff Debt Collection Act (§58.1-520 et seq.).

C. The Department of Taxation and the State Compensation Board shall be responsible for the collection of any judgment which remains unsatisfied or does not meet the conditions of §19.2-354. Persons owing such unsatisfied judgments or failing to comply with installment payment agreements under §19.2-354 shall be subject to the delinquent tax collection provisions of Title 58.1. The Department of Taxation and the State Compensation Board shall establish procedures to be followed by clerks of courts, attorneys for the Commonwealth, other state agencies and any private attorneys or collection agents and may employ private attorneys or collection agencies, or engage other state agencies to collect the judgment. The Department of Taxation and the Commonwealth shall be entitled to deduct a fee for services from amounts collected for violations of local ordinances.

The Department of Taxation and the State Compensation Board shall annually report to the Governor and the General Assembly the total of fines, costs, forfeitures and penalties assessed, collected and unpaid and those which remain unsatisfied or do not meet the conditions of §19.2-354 by each circuit and district court. The report shall include the procedures established by the Department of Taxation and the State Compensation Board pursuant to this section and a plan for increasing the collection of unpaid fines, costs, forfeitures and penalties. The Auditor of Public Accounts shall annually report to the Governor, the Executive Secretary of the Supreme Court and the General Assembly as to the adherence of clerks of courts, attorneys for the Commonwealth and other state agencies to the procedures established by the Department of Taxation and the State Compensation Board.

§19.2-350. When sheriff not to receive fines.

No sheriff or other law-enforcement officer shall receive any fine, penalty or costs imposed by a court not of record, except under process duly issued.

§19.2-351. How fines disposed of; informer.

Although a law may allow an informer or person prosecuting to have part of a fine or penalty, the whole thereof shall go to the Commonwealth, unless the name of such informer or prosecutor be endorsed on, or written at the foot of, the presentment at the time it is made, or of the indictment before it is presented to the grand jury, or of the information before it is filed, or of the writ issued in the action, or the process on the warrant, or the notice of the motion before service of such writ, process, or notice.

§19.2-352. Officers to pay fines to clerks; default; forfeiture, etc.

Every sheriff or other officer receiving money under a writ of fieri facias or capias pro fine shall pay the same to the clerk of the court from which such process issued, on or before the return day of such process; and if such sheriff or other officer fail to pay the money, or fail to return such writ of fieri facias or capias pro fine, he shall, for every such failure, unless good cause be shown therefor, forfeit twenty dollars; and the clerk shall, within ten days from the return day of such process, report the failure to pay such money, or to return such process, to the attorney for the Commonwealth, who shall proceed at once against such officer in default to recover such money and the forfeiture aforesaid.

§19.2-353. Certain fines paid into Literary Fund.

The proceeds of all fines and penalties collected for offenses committed against the Commonwealth, and directed by Article VIII, §8 of the Constitution of Virginia to be set apart as a part of a perpetual and permanent literary fund, shall be paid and collected only in lawful money of the United States, and shall be paid into the state treasury to the credit of the Literary Fund, and shall be used for no other purpose whatsoever.

§19.2-353.1. Fieri facias and proceedings thereon.

Any writ of fieri facias issued under this chapter and the proceedings on the same shall conform to the writ of fieri facias and proceedings thereon under Article 19 (§8.01-196 et seq.) of Chapter 3 of Title 8.01.

§19.2-353.3. Acceptance of checks and credit cards in lieu of money; additional fee.

Notwithstanding the provisions of §19.2-353, personal checks and credit cards shall be accepted in lieu of money to collect and secure all fees, fines, restitution, forfeiture, penalties and costs collected for offenses tried in a district court, including motor vehicle violations, committed against the Commonwealth or against any county, city or town. Notwithstanding the provisions of §19.2-353, personal checks shall be accepted in lieu of money to collect and secure all fees, fines, restitution, forfeiture, penalties and costs collected for offenses tried in a circuit court, including motor vehicle violations, committed against the Commonwealth or against any county, city or town. The clerk of any circuit court shall not be required to but may, in his discretion, accept credit card payment in lieu of money to collect and secure all fees, fines, restitution, forfeitures, penalties, and costs collected for such offenses. The Committee on District Courts shall devise a procedure for approving and accepting checks and credit cards that shall be accepted by the district courts. Court personnel shall not be held to be guarantors of the payment made in such manner and shall not be personally liable for any sums uncollected. The clerk of the court, in addition to any fees, fines, restitution, forfeiture, penalties or costs, may add to such payment a sum not to exceed four percent of the amount paid as a service charge for the acceptance of a credit card.

If a check is returned unpaid by the financial institution on which it is drawn or notice is received from the credit card issuer that payment will not be made, for any reason, the fine, restitution, forfeiture, penalty or costs shall be treated as unpaid and the court may pursue all available remedies to obtain payment. The clerk of the court to whom the dishonored check or credit card was tendered may impose a fee of twenty dollars or ten percent of the value of the payment, whichever is greater, in addition to the fine and costs already imposed.

The clerk of court may refuse acceptance of checks or credit cards of an individual if (i) he has been convicted of a violation of Chapter 6 (§18.2-168 et seq.) of Title 18.2 in which a check, credit card, or credit card information was used to commit the offense, (ii) he has previously tendered to the court a check which was not ultimately honored or a credit card or credit card information which did not ultimately result in payment by the credit card issuer, (iii) authorization of payment is not given by the bank or credit card issuer, (iv) the validity of the check or credit card cannot be verified, or (v) the payee of the check is other than the court.

(Chgd. by L.1996 ch. 616; L.1997 ch. 819; L.1998 chs. 720, 731, eff. 7/1/98.)

§19.2-353.5. Interest on fines and costs.

No interest shall accrue on any fine or costs imposed in a criminal case or in a case involving a traffic infraction for a period of forty days from the date of the final judgment imposing such fine or costs or during any period the defendant is incarcerated as a result of that case. In no event shall interest accrue in such cases during any period in which a fine, costs, or both a fine and costs are being paid in deferred or installment payments pursuant to an order of the court.

Whenever interest on any unpaid fine or costs accrues, it shall accrue at the judgment rate of interest set forth in §6.1-330.54.
(Chgd. by L.1995 chs. 375, 566; L.1996 ch. 226, eff. 7/1/96.)

ARTICLE 4
PAYMENT OF FINES AND COSTS ON INSTALLMENT BASIS, ETC.

§19.2-354. Authority of court to order payment of fine, costs, forfeitures, penalties or restitution in installments or upon other terms and conditions; community work in lieu of payment.

A. Whenever (i) a defendant, convicted of a traffic infraction or a violation of any criminal law of the Commonwealth or of any political subdivision thereof, or found not innocent in the case of a juvenile, is sentenced to pay a fine, restitution, forfeiture or penalty and (ii) the defendant is unable to make payment of the fine, restitution, forfeiture, or penalty and costs within ten days of sentencing, the court shall order the defendant to pay such fine, restitution, forfeiture or penalty and any costs which the defendant may be required to pay in deferred payments or installments. The court may authorize the clerk to establish and approve the conditions of all deferred or installment payment agreements, pursuant to guidelines established by the court. As a condition of every such agreement, a defendant who enters into an installment or deferred payment agreement shall promptly inform the court of any change of mailing address during the term of the agreement. If the defendant is unable to make payment within ten days of sentencing, the court may assess a one-time fee not to exceed ten dollars to cover the costs of management of the defendant's account until such account is paid in full. This one-time fee shall not apply to cases in which costs are assessed pursuant to §§17.1-275.1, 17.1-275.2, 17.1-275.3, or §17.1-275.4. Installment or deferred payment agreements shall include terms for payment if the defendant participates in a program as provided in subsection B or C. The court, if such sum or sums are not paid in full by the date ordered, shall proceed in accordance with §19.2-358.

B. When a person sentenced to the Department of Corrections or a local correctional facility owes any fines, costs, forfeitures, restitution or penalties, he shall be required as a condition of participating in any work release, home/electronic incarceration or nonconsecutive days program as set forth in §§53.1-60, 53.1-131, 53.1-131.1, or §53.1-131.2 to either make full payment or make payments in accordance with his installment or deferred payment agreement while participating in such program. If, after the person has an installment or deferred payment agreement, the person fails to pay as ordered, his participation in the program may be terminated until all fines, costs, forfeitures, restitution and penalties are satisfied. The Director of the Department of Corrections and any sheriff or other administrative head of any local correctional facility shall withhold such ordered payments from any amounts due to such person. Distribution of the money collected shall be made in the following order of priority to:

1. Meet the obligation of any judicial or administrative order to provide support and such funds shall be disbursed according to the terms of such order;
2. Pay any fines, restitution or costs as ordered by the court;
3. Pay travel and other such expenses made necessary by his work release employment or participation in an education or rehabilitative program, including the sums specified in §53.1-150; and
4. Defray the offender's keep.

The balance shall be credited to the offender's account or sent to his family in an amount the offender so chooses.

The Board of Corrections shall promulgate regulations governing the receipt of wages paid to persons participating in such programs, the withholding of payments and the disbursement of appropriate funds.

C. The court shall establish a program to provide an option to any person upon whom a fine and costs have been imposed to discharge all or part of the fine or costs by earning credits for the performance of community service work before or after imprisonment. The program shall specify the rate at which credits are earned and provide for the manner of applying earned credits against the fine or costs. The court shall have such other authority as is reasonably necessary for or incidental to carrying out this program.

D. When the court has authorized deferred payment or installment payments, the clerk shall give notice to the defendant that upon his failure to pay as ordered he may be fined or imprisoned pursuant to §19.2-358 and his privilege to operate a motor vehicle will be suspended pursuant to §46.2-395.

E. The failure of the defendant to enter into a deferred payment or installment payment agreement with the court or the failure of the defendant to make payments as ordered by the agreement shall allow the Tax Commissioner to act in accordance with §19.2-349 to collect all fines, costs, forfeitures and penalties.
(Chgd. by L.1995 chs. 380, 441; L.1996 ch. 273; L.1998 ch. 831; L.1999 ch. 9, eff. 7/1/99.)

§19.2-355. Petition of defendant.

(a) In determining whether the defendant is unable to pay such fine forthwith, the court may require such defendant to file a petition, under oath, with the court, upon a form provided by the court, setting forth the financial condition of the defendant.

(b) Such form shall be a questionnaire, and shall include, but shall not be limited to: the name and residence of the defendant; his occupation, if any; his family status and the number of persons dependent upon him; his monthly income; whether or not his dependents are employed and, if so, their approximate monthly income; his banking accounts, if any; real estate owned by the defendant, or any interest he may have in real estate; income produced therefrom; any independent income accruing to the defendant; tangible and intangible personal property owned by the defendant, or in which he may have an interest; and a statement listing the approximate indebtedness of the defendant to other persons. Such form shall also include a payment plan of the defendant, if the court should exercise its discretion in permitting the payment of such fine and costs in installments or other conditions to be fixed by the court. At the end of such form there shall be printed in bold face type, in a distinctive color the following: THIS STATEMENT IS MADE UNDER OATH, ANY FALSE STATEMENT OF A MATERIAL FACT TO ANY QUESTION CONTAINED HEREIN

SHALL CONSTITUTE PERJURY UNDER THE PROVISIONS OF §18.2-434 OF THE CODE OF VIRGINIA. THE MAXIMUM PENALTY FOR PERJURY IS CONFINEMENT IN THE PENITENTIARY FOR A PERIOD OF TEN YEARS. A copy of the petition shall be retained by the defendant.

(c) If the defendant is unable to read or write, the court, or the clerk, may assist the defendant in completing the petition and require him to affix his mark thereto. The consequences of the making of a false statement shall be explained to such defendant.

§19.2-356. Payment of fine or costs as condition of probation or suspension of sentence.

If a defendant is placed on probation, or imposition or execution of sentence is suspended, or both, the court may make payment of any fine, or costs, or fine and costs, either on a certain date or on an installment basis, a condition of probation or suspension of sentence.

§19.2-357. Requiring that defendant be of peace and good behavior until fine and costs are paid.

If a defendant is permitted to pay a fine or fine and costs on an installment basis, or under such other conditions as the court shall fix under the provisions of §19.2-354, the court may require as a condition that the defendant be of peace and good behavior until the fine and costs are paid.

§19.2-358. Procedure on default in deferred payment or installment payment of fine, costs, forfeiture, restitution or penalty.

A. When an individual obligated to pay a fine, costs, forfeiture, restitution or penalty defaults in the payment or any installment payment, the court upon the motion of the Commonwealth in the case of a conviction of a violation of a state law, or attorney for a locality or for the Commonwealth in the event of a conviction of a violation of a local law or ordinance, or upon its own motion, may require him to show cause why he should not be confined in jail or fined for nonpayment. A show cause proceeding shall not be required prior to issuance of a capias if an order to appear on date certain in the event of nonpayment was issued pursuant to subsection A of §19.2-354 and the defendant failed to appear.

B. Following the order to show cause or following a capias issued for a defendant's failure to comply with a court order to appear issued pursuant to subsection A of §19.2-354, unless the defendant shows that his default was not attributable to an intentional refusal to obey the sentence of the court, or not attributable to a failure on his part to make a good faith effort to obtain the necessary funds for payment, or unless the defendant shows that any failure to appear was not attributable to an intentional refusal to obey the order of the court, the court may order the defendant confined as for a contempt for a term not to exceed sixty days or impose a fine not to exceed $500. The court may provide in its order that payment or satisfaction of the amounts in default at any time will entitle the defendant to his release from such confinement or, after entering the order, may at any time reduce the sentence for good cause shown, including payment or satisfaction of such amounts.

C. If it appears that the default is excusable under the standards set forth in subsection B hereof, the court may enter an order allowing the defendant additional time for payment, reducing the amount due or of each installment, or remitting the unpaid portion in whole or in part.

D. Nothing in this section shall be deemed to alter or interfere with the collection of fines by any means authorized for the enforcement of money judgments rendered in favor of the Commonwealth or any locality within the Commonwealth.

ARTICLE 5
RECEIPTS FOR FINES

Section

§19.2-359. Official receipts to be given for fines.

Every officer collecting a fine, fine and costs or costs when no fine is imposed shall give an official receipt therefor to the person making the payment, and the clerk of the court shall use the official receipt in receipting to a court not of record for payments made to the clerk; and when the fine, fine and costs or costs are collected by execution, the clerk shall receipt to the officer making payment to him upon the official receipts.

§19.2-360. Forms of receipts; distribution; record of disposition.

The Executive Secretary of the Supreme Court shall prescribe and prepare forms of official receipts for fines and distribute them to the clerks of the circuit courts and to the clerks of the district courts for their use. A record of the disposition of each receipt form shall be maintained as prescribed by the Executive Secretary.

§19.2-361. Misuse, misappropriation or willful failure to account for fines is embezzlement.

If any officer misuse, misappropriate, or willfully fail to return or account for, a fine collected by him he shall be deemed guilty of embezzlement and shall be punished as for the embezzlement of public funds and the failure, without good cause, to produce or account for any receipt form received by him shall be prima facie evidence of his embezzlement of the amount represented thereby.

ARTICLE 6
RELIEF FROM FINES AND PENALTIES

Section

§19.2-362. Court not to remit fine or penalty, other than fine for contempt, except as provided in §19.2-358.

No court shall remit any fine or penalty, except for a contempt, which the court during the same term may remit either wholly or in part, and except as provided in §19.2-358. This section shall not impair the judicial power of the court to set aside a verdict or judgment, or to grant a new trial.

§19.2-363. Authority of Governor to grant relief from fines and penalties.

The Governor shall have power, in his discretion, to remit, in whole or in part, fines and penalties, in all cases of felony or misdemeanor, after conviction, whether paid into the state treasury or not, except when judgment shall have been rendered against any person for contempt of court, for nonperformance of or disobedience to some order, decree or judgment of such court, or when the fine or penalty has been imposed by the State Corporation Commission, or when the prosecution has been carried on by the House of Delegates. The Governor may, in his discretion, remit, refund or release, in whole or in part, any forfeited recognizance or any judgment rendered thereon, provided, in the opinion of the Governor, the evidence accompanying such application warrants the granting of the relief asked for. But the provisions of the three following sections and §19.2-368 shall be complied with as a condition precedent to such action by the Governor; provided, that when the party against whom the fine or penalty has been imposed and judgment rendered therefor has departed this life leaving a spouse or children surviving, the Governor may remit such fine or penalty upon the certificate of the judge of the circuit court of the county or city wherein such fine or penalty was imposed and judgment rendered, that to enforce the same against the estate, real or personal, of the decedent, would impose hardship upon the spouse or children. In any case when the Governor remits, in whole or in part, a fine or penalty, if the same has been paid into the state treasury, on the order of the Governor such fine or penalty or so much thereof as is remitted shall be paid by the State Treasurer, on the warrant of the Comptroller, out of the fund into which the fine or penalty was paid.

§19.2-364. Petition for relief; in what court filed; notice to attorney for Commonwealth.

Such person or his personal representative, as the case may be, shall file a petition in the clerk's office of the circuit court of the county or city wherein such fine or penalty was imposed, or such liability established, at least fifteen days before the term of the court at which the same is to be heard, and shall set forth the grounds upon which relief is asked. Ten days' notice thereof in writing shall be given to the attorney for the Commonwealth of the county or city.

§19.2-365. Duties of attorney for Commonwealth upon filing of such petition.

The attorney for the Commonwealth, at or before the hearing of such petition, shall file an answer to the same. He shall cause to be summoned such witnesses and shall introduce all such testimony as may be necessary and proper to protect the interest of the Commonwealth; and the petitioner may cause to be summoned such witnesses and shall introduce all such testimony as may be necessary and proper to protect his interest.

§19.2-366. Duty of court in which petition filed; certificate and opinion.

The court wherein such petition is filed shall hear all such testimony as may be offered, either by the petitioner or attorney for the Commonwealth, and after the evidence has been heard shall cause to be made out by the clerk of the court a certificate of the facts proved, and file with the same an opinion, in writing, as to the propriety of granting the relief prayed for.

§19.2-367. Proceedings to be according to common law.

All proceedings had before the court under the provisions of the three preceding sections shall be according to the course of the common-law practice, except that no formal pleadings shall be necessary.

§19.2-368. Course of proceeding when relief asked of the Governor.

Whenever application shall be made to the Governor by or on behalf of any person desiring to be relieved, in whole or in part, of any such fine or penalty, the petition, answer, certificate of facts, and opinion of the court provided for in §§19.2-364, 19.2-365 and 19.2-366, duly authenticated by the clerk of the court, shall accompany the application, which shall be in writing. In all cases in which the Governor shall remit a fine or penalty he shall issue his order to the clerk of the court by which such fine or penalty was imposed; or if such fine or penalty was imposed by a court not of record, to the clerk of the circuit court of the county or city in which the judge of such court not of record holds office, and such court shall, at its next term, or immediately, if then in session, cause such order to be spread upon the law order book of its court; and the clerk of such court shall immediately, upon the receipt of such order, mark the judgment for such fine or penalty, and costs, or so much thereof as the person may have been relieved of, "remitted by the Governor," upon the Judgment Lien Docket of the court of the county or city in which it may have been recorded. The Governor shall communicate to the General Assembly at each session the particulars of every case of fine or penalty remitted, with his reason for remitting the same.

CHAPTER 21.1
COMPENSATING VICTIMS OF CRIME

§19.2-368.1. Findings; legislative intent.

The General Assembly finds that many innocent persons suffer personal physical injury or death as a result of criminal acts or in their efforts to prevent crime or apprehend persons committing or attempting to commit crimes. Such persons or their dependents may thereby suffer disability, incur financial hardships or become dependent upon public assistance. The General Assembly finds and determines that there is a need for governmental financial assistance for such victims of crime. Therefore, it is the intent of the General Assembly that aid, care and support be provided by the Commonwealth as a matter of moral responsibility for such victims of crime.

§19.2-368.2. Definitions.

For the purpose of this chapter:

"Claimant" means the person filing a claim pursuant to this chapter.

"Commission" means the Virginia Workers' Compensation Commission.

"Crime" means an act committed by any person in the Commonwealth of Virginia which would constitute a crime as defined by the Code of Virginia or at common law. However, no act involving the operation of a motor vehicle which results in injury shall constitute a crime for the purpose of this chapter unless the injuries (i) were intentionally inflicted through the use of such vehicle or (ii) resulted from a violation of §18.2-51.4 or §18.2-266.

"Family," when used with reference to a person, means (i) any person related to such person within the third degree of consanguinity or affinity, (ii) any person residing in the same household with such person, or (iii) a spouse.

"Victim" means a person who suffers personal physical injury or death as a direct result of a crime, including a person who is injured or killed as a result of foreign terrorism, or who suffers personal emotional injury as a direct result of being the subject of a violent felony offense, as defined in subsection C of §17.1-805, or attempted robbery or abduction.

(Chgd. by L.1997 chs. 528, 691; L.1998 ch. 484; L.1999 ch. 286, eff. 7/1/99.)

§19.2-368.3. Powers and duties of Commission.

The Commission shall have the following powers and duties in the administration of the provisions of this chapter:

1. To adopt, promulgate, amend and rescind suitable rules and regulations to carry out the provisions and purposes of this chapter.

2. Notwithstanding the provisions of §2.1-342.2, to acquire from the attorneys for the Commonwealth, State Police, local police departments, sheriffs' departments, and the Chief Medical Examiner such investigative results, information and data as will enable the Commission to determine if, in fact, a crime was committed or attempted, and the extent, if any, to which the victim or claimant was responsible for his own injury. These data shall include prior adult arrest records and juvenile court disposition records of the offender. For such purposes and in accordance with §16.1-305, the Commission may also acquire from the juvenile and domestic relations district courts a copy of the order of disposition relating to the crime. The use of any information received by the Commission pursuant to this subdivision shall be limited to carrying out the purposes set forth in this section, and this information shall be confidential and shall not be disseminated further. The agency from which the information is requested may submit original reports, portions thereof, summaries, or such other configurations of information as will comply with the requirements of this section.

3. To hear and determine all claims for awards filed with the Commission pursuant to this chapter, and to reinvestigate or reopen cases as the Commission deems necessary.

4. To require and direct medical examination of victims.

5. To hold hearings, administer oaths or affirmations, examine any person under oath or affirmation and to issue summonses requiring the attendance and giving of testimony of witnesses and require the production of any books, papers, documentary or other evidence. The powers provided in this subsection may be delegated by the Commission to any member or employee thereof.

6. To take or cause to be taken affidavits or depositions within or without the Commonwealth.

7. To render each year to the Governor and to the General Assembly a written report of its activities.

8. To accept from the government of the United States grants of federal moneys for disbursement under the provisions of this chapter.

(Chgd. by L.1996 ch. 616; L.1998 ch. 484; L.1999 chs. 703, 726, eff. 7/1/99.)

§19.2-368.3:1. Crime victims' ombudsman.

A. The Commission shall employ a crime victims' ombudsman and adequate staff to facilitate the prompt review and resolution of crime victim compensation claims and to assure that crime victims' rights are safeguarded and protected during the claims process. The ombudsman shall report directly to the Commission.

B. The ombudsman shall ensure that all parties, including service providers and Criminal Injuries Compensation Fund personnel, are acting in the best interests of the crime victim. The ombudsman shall also provide assistance to crime victims in filling out the necessary forms for compensation and obtaining necessary documentation.

(Added by L.1998 ch. 484, eff. 7/1/98.)

§19.2-368.4. Persons eligible for awards.

A. The following persons shall be eligible for awards pursuant to this chapter unless the award would directly and unjustly benefit the person who is criminally responsible:

1. A victim of a crime.

2. A surviving spouse, parent, grandparent, sibling or child, including posthumous children, of a victim of a crime who died as a direct result of such crime.

3. Any person, except a law-enforcement officer engaged in the performance of his duties, who is injured or killed while trying to prevent a crime or an attempted crime from occurring in his presence, or trying to apprehend a person who had committed a crime in his presence or had, in fact, committed a felony.

4. A surviving spouse, parent, grandparent, sibling or child, including posthumous children, of any person who dies as a direct result of trying to prevent a crime or attempted crime from occurring in his presence, or trying to apprehend a person who had committed a crime in his presence or had, in fact, committed a felony.

5. Any other person legally dependent for his principal support upon a victim of crime who dies as a result of such crime, or legally dependent for his principal support upon any person who dies as a direct result of trying to prevent a crime or an attempted crime from occurring in his presence or trying to apprehend a person who had committed a crime in his presence or had, in fact, committed a felony.

B. A person who is criminally responsible for the crime upon which a claim is based, or an accomplice or accessory of such person, shall not be eligible to receive an award with respect to such claim.

C. A resident of Virginia who is the victim of a crime occurring outside Virginia and any other person as defined in subsection A who is injured as a result of a crime occurring outside Virginia shall be eligible for an award pursuant to this chapter if (i) the person would be eligible for benefits had the crime occurred in Virginia and (ii) the state in which the crime occurred does not have a crime victims' compensation program deemed eligible pursuant to the provisions of the federal Victims of Crime Act and does not compensate nonresidents.

(Chgd. by L.1996 ch. 86, eff. 7/1/96.)

§19.2-368.5. Filing of claims; deferral of proceedings.

A. A claim may be filed by a person eligible to receive an award, as provided in §19.2-368.4, or if such person is a minor, by his parent or guardian. In any case in which the person entitled to make a claim is incapacitated, the claim may be filed on his behalf by his guardian, conservator or such other individual authorized to administer his estate.

B. A claim shall be filed by the claimant not later than one year after the occurrence of the crime upon which such claim is based, or not later than one year after the death of the victim. However, (i) in cases involving claims made on behalf of a minor or a person who is incapacitated, the provisions of subsection A of §8.01-229 shall apply to toll the one-year period and (ii) in cases involving claims made by a victim against profits of crime forfeited and held in escrow pursuant to Chapter 21.2 (§19.2-368.19 et seq.) of this title, the claim shall be filed within five years of the date of the order of forfeiture. In all other cases, upon good cause shown, the Commission may extend the time for filing for a period not exceeding, under any circumstances, two years after such occurrence.

C. Claims shall be filed in the office of the Commission in person or by mail. The Commission shall accept for filing all claims submitted by persons eligible under subsection A of this section and alleging the jurisdictional requirements set forth in this chapter and meeting the requirements as to form in the rules and regulations of the Commission.

D. Upon filing of a claim pursuant to this chapter, the Commission shall promptly notify the attorney for the Commonwealth of the jurisdiction wherein the crime is alleged to have occurred. If, within ten days after such notification, the attorney for the Commonwealth so notified advises the Commission that a criminal prosecution is pending upon the same alleged crime, the Commission shall defer all proceedings under this chapter until such time as such criminal prosecution has been concluded in the circuit court unless notification is received from the attorney for the Commonwealth that no objection is made to a continuation of the investigation and determination of the claim. When such criminal prosecution has been concluded in the circuit court the attorney for the Commonwealth shall promptly so notify the Commission. Nothing in this section shall be construed to mean that the Commission is to defer proceedings upon the filing of an appeal, nor shall this section be construed to limit the authority of the Commission to grant emergency awards as hereinafter provided.

(Chgd. by L.1997 ch. 801; L.1998 ch. 484, eff. 7/1/98.)

§19.2-368.5:1. Failure to perfect claim; denial.

Notwithstanding the provisions of §19.2-368.5, if, following the initial filing of a claim, a claimant fails to take such further steps to support or perfect the claim as may be required by the Commission within 180 days after written notice of such requirement is sent by the Commission to the claimant, the claimant shall be deemed in default. If the claimant is in default, the Commission shall notify the claimant that the claim is denied and the claimant shall be forever barred from reasserting it; however, the Commission may reopen the proceeding upon a showing by claimant that the failure to do the acts required by the Commission was beyond the control of the claimant.

(Chgd. by L.1998 ch. 484, eff. 7/1/98.)

§19.2-368.6. Assignment of claims; investigation; hearing; confidentiality of records; decisions.

A. A claim, when accepted for filing, shall be properly investigated, and, if necessary, assigned by the chairman to a commissioner, deputy commissioner or other proper party for disposition. All claims arising from the death of an individual shall be considered together by the same person.

B. The person to whom such claim is assigned shall examine the papers filed in support of the claim and shall thereupon cause an investigation to be conducted into the validity of the claim. The investigation shall include, but not be limited to, an examination of police, court and official records and reports concerning the crime, and an examination of medical and hospital reports relating to the injury upon which the claim is based. Health care providers, as defined in §8.01-581.1, shall provide medical and hospital reports relating to the diagnosis and treatment of the injury upon which the claim is based to the Commission, upon request.

C. Claims shall be investigated and determined, regardless of whether the alleged criminal has been apprehended or prosecuted for, or convicted of, any crime based upon the same incident, or has been acquitted, or found not guilty of the crime in question owing to a lack of criminal responsibility or other legal exemption.

D. There shall be a rebuttable presumption that the claimant did not contribute to and was not responsible for the infliction of his injury.

E. The person to whom a claim is assigned may decide the claim in favor of a claimant on the basis of the papers filed in support thereof and the report of the investigation of the claim. If he is unable to decide the claim, upon the basis of the said papers and report, he shall order a hearing. At the hearing any relevant evidence, not legally privileged, shall be admissible. The hearing of any claim involving a claimant or victim who is a juvenile shall be closed. All records, papers, and reports involving such claim shall be confidential except as to the amount of the award and nonidentifying information concerning the claimant or victim.

F. For purposes of this chapter, confidentiality provided for by law applicable to a claimant's or victim's juvenile court records shall not be applicable to the extent that the Commission shall have access to those records only for the purposes set forth in this chapter.

G. After examining the papers filed in support of the claim, and the report of investigation, and after a hearing, if any, a decision shall be made either granting an award pursuant to §19.2-368.11:1 of this chapter or denying the claim.

H. The person making a decision shall issue a written report setting forth such decision and his reasons therefor, and shall notify the claimant and furnish him a copy of such report.

(Chgd. by L.1996 ch. 616; L.1997 ch. 528; L.1998 ch. 484, eff. 7/1/98.)

§19.2-368.7. Review by Commission.

A. The claimant may, within forty-five days from the date of the report, apply in writing to the Commission for review of the decision by the full Commission. The Commission may extend the time for filing under this section, upon good cause shown, for a period not to exceed two years from the date of the occurrence.

B. Upon receipt of an application pursuant to subsection A of this section, or upon its own motion, the Commission shall review the record and affirm or modify the decision of the person to whom the claim was assigned. The action of the Commission in affirming or modifying such decision shall be final. If the Commission receives no application pursuant to subsection A of this section, or takes no action upon its own motion, the decision of the person to whom the claim was assigned shall become the final decision of the Commission.

C. The Commission shall promptly notify the claimant and the Comptroller of the final decision of the Commission and furnish each with a copy of the report setting forth the decision.

(Chgd. by L.2000 ch. 455, eff. 7/1/2000.)

§19.2-368.8. Reinvestigation of decision; reconsideration of award; judicial review.

A. The Commission, on its own motion, or upon request of the claimant, may reinvestigate or reopen a decision making or denying an award. Under no circumstances shall the Commission reopen or reinvestigate a case after the expiration of two years from the date of occurrence of the crime upon which the claim is based.

B. The Commission shall reconsider, at least annually, every award upon which periodic payments are being made. An order or reconsideration of an award shall not require refund of amounts previously paid unless the award was obtained by fraud. The right of reconsideration does not affect the finality of a Commission decision for the purposes of judicial review.

C. Within thirty days of the date of the report containing the final decision of the Commission, the claimant may, if in his judgment the award is improper, appeal such decision to the Court of Appeals, as provided in §65.2-706. The Attorney General may appear in such proceedings as counsel for the Commission.

§19.2-368.9. Emergency awards.

Notwithstanding any other provisions of this chapter, if it appears to the Commission, that (1) such claim is one with respect to which an award probably will be made, and (2) undue hardship will result to the claimant if immediate payment is not made, the Commission may make an emergency award to the claimant, pending a final decision in the case, provided that (i) the amount of such emergency award shall not exceed $2,000, (ii) the amount of such emergency award shall be deducted from any final award made to the claimant, and (iii) the excess of the amount of such emergency award over the final award, or the full amount of the emergency award if no final award is made, shall be repaid by the claimant to the Commission.

§19.2-368.10. When awards to be made.

No award shall be made unless the Commission finds that (1) a crime was committed, (2) such crime directly resulted in personal physical injury to, or death of the victim, and (3) police records show that such crime was promptly reported to the proper authorities, and in no case may an award be made where the police records show that such report was made more than 120 hours after the occurrence of such crime, unless the Commission, for good cause shown, finds the delay to have been justified. The Commission, upon finding that any claimant or award recipient has not fully cooperated with all law-enforcement agencies, may deny, reduce or withdraw any award, as the case may be.

§19.2-368.11:1. Amount of award.

A. Compensation for Total Loss of Earnings: An award made pursuant to this chapter for total loss of earnings which results directly from incapacity incurred by a crime victim shall be payable during total incapacity to the victim or to such other eligible person, at a weekly compensation rate equal to sixty-six and two-thirds percent of the victim's average weekly wages. The total amount of weekly compensation shall not exceed $200. The victim's average weekly wages shall be determined as provided in §65.2-101.

B. Compensation for Partial Loss of Earnings: An award made pursuant to this chapter for partial loss of earnings which results directly from incapacity incurred by a crime victim shall be payable during incapacity at a weekly rate equal to sixty-six and two-thirds percent of the difference between the victim's average weekly wages before the injury and the weekly wages which the victim is able to earn thereafter. The combined total of actual weekly earnings and compensation for partial loss of earnings shall not exceed $200 per week.

C. Compensation for Dependents of a Victim Who Is Killed: If death results to a victim of crime entitled to benefits, dependents of the victim shall be entitled to compensation in accordance with the provisions of §§65.2-512 and 65.2-515 in an amount not to exceed the maximum aggregate payment or the maximum weekly compensation which would have been payable to the deceased victim under this section.

D. Compensation for Unreimbursed Medical Costs, Funeral Expenses, Services, etc.: Awards may also be made on claims or portions of claims based upon the claimant's actual expenses incurred as are determined by the Commission to be appropriate, for (i) unreimbursed medical expenses or indebtedness reasonably incurred for medical expenses; (ii) expenses reasonably incurred in obtaining ordinary and necessary services in lieu of those the victim would have performed, for the benefit of himself and his family, if he had not been a victim of crime; (iii) expenses in any way related to funeral or burial, not to exceed $3,500; (iv) expenses attributable to pregnancy resulting from forcible rape; (v) mental health counseling for survivors as defined under subdivisions A 2 and A 4 of §19.2-368.4, not to exceed $2,500 per claim; (vi) reasonable and necessary moving expenses, not to exceed $500, incurred by a victim or survivors as defined under subdivisions A 2 and A 4 of §19.2-368.4; and (vii) any other reasonable and necessary expenses and indebtedness incurred as a direct result of the injury or death upon which such claim is based, not otherwise specifically provided for.

E. Any claim made pursuant to this chapter shall be reduced by the amount of any payments received or to be received as a result of the injury from or on behalf of the person who committed the crime or from any other public or private source, including an emergency award by the Commission pursuant to §19.2-368.9.

F. To qualify for an award under this chapter, a claim must have a minimum value of $100, and payments for injury or death to a victim of crime, to the victim's dependents or to others entitled to payment for covered expenses, after being reduced as provided in subsection E, shall not exceed $15,000 in the aggregate.

(Chgd. by L.1996 ch. 86; L.1998 ch. 484; L.2000 ch. 847, eff. 7/1/2000.)

§19.2-368.12. Awards not subject to execution or attachment; apportionment; reductions.

A. No award made pursuant to this chapter shall be subject to execution or attachment other than for expenses resulting from the injury which is the basis for the claim.

B. If there are two or more persons entitled to an award as a result of the death of a person which is the direct result of a crime, the award shall be apportioned among the claimants.

C. In determining the amount of an award, the Commission shall determine whether, because of his conduct, the victim of such crime contributed to the infliction of his injury, and the Commission shall reduce the amount of the award or reject the claim altogether, in accordance with such determination; provided, however, that the Commission may disregard for this purpose the responsibility of the victim for his own injury where the record shows that such responsibility was attributable to efforts by the victim to prevent a crime or an attempted crime from occurring in his presence, or to apprehend a person who had committed a crime in his presence or had, in fact, committed a felony.

§19.2-368.14. Public record; exception.

Except as provided in §19.2-368.6 concerning juvenile claimants or victims, the record of any proceedings under this chapter shall be a public record; provided, however, that any record or report obtained by the Commission, the confidentiality of which is protected by any other law or regulation, shall remain confidential, subject to such law or regulation.

§19.2-368.15. Subrogation of Commonwealth to claimant's right of action; disposition of funds collected.

Acceptance of an award made pursuant to this chapter shall subrogate the Commonwealth, to the extent of such award, to any right or right of action accruing to the claimant or the victim to recover payments on account of losses resulting from the crime with respect to which the award is made.

However, the Commonwealth shall not institute any proceedings in connection with its right of subrogation under this section within one year from the date of commission of the crime, unless any claimant or victim's right or action shall have been previously terminated. All funds collected by the Commonwealth in a proceeding instituted pursuant to this section shall be paid over to the Comptroller for deposit into the Criminal Injuries Compensation Fund.

§19.2-368.16. Claims to be made under oath.

All claims shall be made under oath. Any person who asserts a false claim under the provisions of this chapter shall be guilty of perjury and, in addition, shall be subject to prosecution under the provisions of Article 3 (§18.2-95 et seq.) of Chapter 5 of Title 18.2 of the Code of Virginia, and shall further forfeit any benefit received and shall reimburse and repay the Commonwealth for payments received or paid on his behalf pursuant to any of the provisions hereunder.

§19.2-368.17. Public information program.

The Commission shall establish and conduct a public information program to assure extensive and continuing publicity and public awareness of the provisions of this chapter. The public information program shall include brochures, posters and public service advertisements for television, radio and print media for dissemination to the public of information regarding the right to compensation for innocent victims of crime, including information on the right to file a claim, the scope of coverage, and the procedures to be utilized incident thereto.

Whenever a crime which directly resulted in personal physical injury to, or death of, an individual is reported within the time required by §19.2-368.10, the law-enforcement agency to which the report is made shall make reasonable efforts, where practicable, to notify the victim or other potential claimant in writing on forms prepared by the Commission of his or her possible right to file a claim under this chapter. In any event, no liability or cause of action shall arise from the failure to so notify a victim of crime or other potential claimant.

§19.2-368.18. Criminal Injuries Compensation Fund.

A. There is hereby created a special fund to be administered by the Comptroller, known as the Criminal Injuries Compensation Fund.

B. Where any person is convicted, after July 1, 1996, by a court with criminal jurisdiction of (i) treason or any other felony or (ii) any offense punishable as a misdemeanor under Title 18.2 or pursuant to local ordinance substantially similar to a misdemeanor under Title 18.2, with the exception of a public drunkenness violation, a cost shall be imposed in addition to any other costs required to be imposed by law. This additional cost shall be thirty dollars in any case under clause (i) and twenty dollars in any case under clause (ii) of this subsection. Such additional sum shall be paid over to the Comptroller to be deposited into the Criminal Injuries Compensation Fund. Under no condition shall a political subdivision be held liable for the payment of this sum.

C. No claim shall be accepted under the provisions of this chapter when the crime which gave rise to such claim occurred prior to July 1, 1977.

D. Sums available in the Criminal Injuries Compensation Fund shall be used for the purpose of payment of the costs and expenses necessary for the administration of this chapter and for the payment of claims pursuant to this chapter.

E. All revenues deposited into the Criminal Injuries Compensation Fund, and appropriated for the purposes of this chapter, shall be immediately available for the payment of claims.

(Chgd. by L.1996 chs. 760, 976, eff. 7/1/96.)

CHAPTER 21.2
PROFITS FROM CRIME

§19.2-368.19. Definitions.

For purposes of this chapter, the following terms shall have the following meanings unless the context requires otherwise:

"Defendant" means any person who pleads guilty to, is convicted of, or is found not guilty by reason of insanity with respect to a felony resulting in physical injury to or death of another person.

"Division" means the Division of Crime Victims' Compensation.

"Interested party" means the victim, the defendant, and any transferee of proceeds due the defendant under a contract, the person with whom the defendant has contracted, the prosecuting attorney for the Commonwealth, and the Division of Crime Victims' Compensation.

"Victim" means a person who suffers personal, physical, mental, emotional, or pecuniary loss as a direct result of a crime and includes the spouse, parent, child, or sibling of the victim.

§19.2-368.20. Order of special forfeiture.

Any proceeds or profits received or to be received directly or indirectly by a defendant or a transferee of that defendant from any source, as a direct or indirect result of his crime or sentence, or the notoriety which such crime or sentence has conferred upon him, shall be subject to forfeiture pursuant to Chapter 22 (§19.2-369 et seq.) of Title 19.2.

Income from the defendant's employment in a position unrelated to his crime or the notoriety which such crime has conferred upon him but obtained through the assistance of or rehabilitative training by correctional or mental health programs or personnel shall not be subject to forfeiture under this section, and nothing in this section shall be construed to prohibit or hinder the return of property belonging to victims of crime to its rightful owners. Any proceeds from a contract relating to a depiction or discussion of the defendant's crime in a movie, book, newspaper, magazine, radio or television production, or live entertainment or publication of any kind shall not be subject to forfeiture unless an integral part of the work is a depiction or discussion of the defendant's crime or an impression of the defendant's thoughts, opinions, or emotions regarding such crime.

Upon petition of the attorney for the Commonwealth filed at any time after conviction of such defendant or his acquittal by reason of insanity and after notice to the interested parties, a hearing upon the motion and a finding for the Commonwealth, for good cause shown, any circuit court in which the petition is filed shall order that such proceeds be forfeited.

An order issued under this section shall require that the defendant and the person with whom the defendant contracts pay to the Division any proceeds due the defendant under the contract.

§19.2-368.21. Distribution.

A. Proceeds paid to the Division under §19.2-368.20 shall be retained in escrow in the Criminal Injuries Compensation Fund for five years after the date of the order, but during that five-year period may be levied upon to satisfy:

1. A money judgment rendered by a court or award of the Workers' Compensation Commission in favor of a victim of an offense for which the defendant has been convicted or

acquitted by reason of insanity, or a legal representative of the victim; and

2. Any fines or costs assessed against the defendant by a court of this Commonwealth.

B. If ordered by a circuit court in the interest of justice, after motion, notice to all interested parties, and opportunity for hearing, such escrow fund shall be used to:

1. Satisfy a money judgment rendered in the court hearing the matter, in favor of a victim of any offense for which the defendant has been convicted; and

2. Pay for legal representation of the defendant in criminal proceedings, including the appeals process. No more than twenty-five percent of the total proceeds in escrow may be used for legal representation.

C. At the end of the five-year period, the remaining proceeds shall be paid into the Criminal Injuries Compensation Fund. However, (i) if a civil action under this section is pending against the defendant, the proceeds shall be held in escrow until completion of the action or (ii) if the defendant has appealed his conviction and the appeals process is not final, the proceeds shall be held in escrow until the appeals process is final, and upon disposition of the charges favorable to the defendant, the Division shall immediately pay any money in the escrow account to the defendant.

§19.2-368.22. Actions to defeat chapter void.

Any action taken by any person convicted of a felony, whether by way of execution of a power of attorney, creation of corporate entities, or otherwise, to defeat the purpose of this chapter shall be void.

CHAPTER 22
ENFORCEMENT OF FORFEITURES

Section

§19.2-369. Information to be filed by attorney for Commonwealth.

If any statute provides for the forfeiture of any property or money, or if any property or money be seized as forfeited for a violation of any of the provisions of this Code, and a different mode of enforcing the forfeiture is not prescribed, in order to enforce the same the attorney for the Commonwealth for the county or city wherein the forfeiture was incurred shall file in the clerk's office of the circuit court of his county or city an information in the name of the Commonwealth against such property or money by name or general designation.

§19.2-370. Contents of information.

The information shall allege the seizure, and set forth in general terms the causes or grounds of forfeiture. It shall also pray that the property be condemned as forfeited to the Commonwealth and be sold and the proceeds of sale disposed of according to law, and that all persons concerned in interest be cited to appear and show cause why the property should not be condemned and sold to enforce the forfeiture.

§19.2-371. Signing and swearing to information.

If the proceeding be instituted by an informer, he shall sign and swear to the information. The attorney for the Commonwealth also shall sign it, but if the law on which the proceeding is based contains no provisions as to informers, the signature of the attorney for the Commonwealth alone shall be sufficient.

§19.2-372. Issuance of warrant.

Upon the filing of the information, the clerk shall forthwith issue a warrant directed to the sheriff or other law-enforcement officer of the county or city, commanding him to take the property into his possession and hold the same subject to further proceedings in the cause. If from any cause the warrant be not executed, other like warrants may be successively issued until one be executed.

§19.2-373. Execution and return of warrant.

The officer serving the warrant shall take the property into his possession and forthwith return the warrant and report to the clerk in writing thereon his action thereunder.

§19.2-374. Notice issued by clerk.

As soon as the warrant has been executed and returned, the clerk shall issue a notice reciting briefly the filing of the information, the object thereof, the issuing of the warrant and the seizure of the property thereunder, and citing all persons concerned in interest to appear on a day fixed on said notice which date shall not be less than ten days from the date of such notice, and show cause why the prayer of the information for condemnation and sale should not be granted. He shall, at least ten days before the day fixed by the notice for appearance, post a copy of the notice at the front door of the courthouse of his county or city. Such posting shall be sufficient service of the notice on all persons concerned in interest, except as provided in §§19.2-375 and 19.2-376.

§19.2-375. Notice to Commissioner of Department of Motor Vehicles; duties of Commissioner.

If the property so seized be a motor vehicle required by the motor vehicle laws of Virginia to be registered, the attorney for the Commonwealth shall forthwith notify the Commissioner of the Department of Motor Vehicles, by certified mail, of such seizure and the motor number of the vehicle so seized, and the Commissioner shall promptly certify to such attorney for the Commonwealth the name and address of the person in whose name such vehicle is registered, together with the name and address of any person holding a lien thereon, and the amount thereof. The Commissioner shall also forthwith notify such registered owner and lienor, in writing, of the reported seizure and the county or city wherein such seizure was made.

The certificate of the Commissioner, concerning such registration and lien shall be received in evidence in any proceeding, either civil or criminal, under any provision of this chapter, in which such facts may be material to the issue involved.

§19.2-376. Owners, purchasers and lienors of vehicles to be made parties defendant; notice of hearing.

The owner of and all persons in any manner then indebted or liable for the purchase price of the property, if such property be a conveyance or vehicle of any kind, and any person having a lien thereon, if they be known to the attorney who files the information, shall be made parties defendant thereto, and shall be served with notice in the manner provided by law for serving a notice, at least ten days before the date therein specified for the hearing on the information, if they be residents of this Commonwealth; and if they be unknown or nonresidents, or cannot with reasonable diligence be found in this Commonwealth, they shall be deemed sufficiently served by publication of the notice once a week for two successive weeks in some newspaper published in such county or city, or if none be published therein, then in some newspaper having general circulation therein, and a notice shall be sent by registered mail of such seizure to the last known address of the owner of such conveyance or vehicle.

§19.2-377. Bond by owner or lienor to secure possession.

If the owner or lienor of the seized property shall desire to obtain possession thereof before the hearing on the information filed against the same, such property shall be appraised by the sheriff of the county or city in which the court where such information is filed is located, who shall promptly inspect and appraise the property, under oath, at its fair cash value, and forthwith make return thereof in writing, to the clerk's office of the court in which the proceedings are pending. Upon the return, the owner or lienor may give a bond payable to the Commonwealth, in a penalty of the amount equal to the appraised value of the property plus the court costs which may accrue, with security to be approved by the clerk, and conditioned for the performance of the final judgment of the court, on the trial of the information, and with a further condition to the effect that, if upon the hearing on the information, the judgment of the court be that such property, or any part thereof, or such interest and equity as the owner or lienor may have therein, be forfeited, judgment may thereupon be entered against the obligors on such bond for the penalty thereof, without further or other proceedings against them thereon, to be discharged by the payment of the appraised value of the property so seized and forfeited and costs, upon which judgment, execution may issue, on which the clerk shall endorse, "no security to be taken." Upon giving of the bond, the property shall be delivered to the owner or lienor.

§19.2-378. Sale of property liable to deterioration, etc.

If the property seized under the warrant be perishable or liable to deterioration, decay, or injury by being detained in custody pending the proceedings the court or the judge thereof may order the same to be sold upon such notice as he in his discretion may deem proper and hold the proceeds of sale to abide the event of such proceedings, or if such property may be stored without deterioration, decay or injury, the court in its discretion may order the same to be stored pending final outcome of the proceedings.

§19.2-379. Defense to information; rights of owners or lienors without knowledge of illegal use.

Any person concerned in interest may appear and make defense to the information, which may be done by answer on oath. The fact that the person by whom the property was used in violating the law has not been convicted of such violation shall be no defense. The information shall be independent of any proceeding against such person or any other for violation of law. Unless otherwise specifically provided by law, no forfeiture shall extinguish the rights of any person without knowledge of the illegal use of such property who is the lawful owner or who has a lien on the same which has been perfected in the manner provided by law.

§19.2-380. Trial of issues of fact.

When the case is ready for trial, such issues of fact as are made by the pleadings, or as the court may direct, shall be tried by a jury, unless a trial by jury be dispensed with by consent of parties, in which case, the court shall determine the whole matter of law and fact.

§19.2-381. Judgment of condemnation and sale of property; when judgment given on bond of owner or lienor; destruction of contraband.

If the forfeiture be established, the judgment shall be that the property be condemned as forfeited to the Commonwealth and further that the same be sold, unless a sale thereof has been already made under §19.2-378 or unless the court shall determine that the property forfeited is of such minimal value that the sale thereof would not be in the best interest of the Commonwealth. If such sale has been made, the further judgment shall be against the proceeds. If the property condemned has been delivered to the claimant under §19.2-377, such further judgment shall be against the obligors in the bond for the penalty thereof to be discharged by the payment of the appraised value of the property, upon which judgment, process of execution shall be awarded and the clerk shall endorse thereon, "No security is to be taken."

Money that is forfeited shall be disposed of pursuant to the provisions of §19.2-383.

Contraband, the sale or possession of which is unlawful, and property not sold because of the minimal value thereof, shall be ordered destroyed by the court.

§19.2-382. Sale to be for cash; title of purchaser.

Any sale ordered in the cause shall be made for cash, after due advertisement, and shall vest in the purchaser a clear and absolute title to the property sold.

§19.2-383. Disposition of proceeds of sale.

The proceeds of sale, and whatever may be realized on any bond given under §19.2-377, and any money forfeited, shall be disposed of by the court according to the rights of the parties.

§19.2-384. Payment of expenses and costs.

Expenses and costs incurred in the proceedings shall be paid as the court, in its discretion, shall determine; except that no costs shall be adjudged against the Commonwealth.

§19.2-385. Writ of error and supersedeas.

For the purpose of review on a writ of error or supersedeas, a final judgment or order in the cause shall be deemed a final judgment or order in a civil case (not in chancery) within the meaning of §8.01-670.

§19.2-386. How forfeitures of property not otherwise provided for are enforced.

Except as otherwise specifically provided by law, whenever any property is forfeited to the Commonwealth by reason of the violation of any law, the court before which the offender is convicted shall order sale or other disposition of the property and proceeds of any such sale as provided for in §§19.2-381 through 19.2-384.

CHAPTER 22.1
FORFEITURES IN DRUG CASES

§19.2-386.1. Commencing an action of forfeiture.

An action against any property subject to seizure under the provisions of §18.2-249 shall be commenced by the filing of an information in the clerk's office of the circuit court. Any information shall be filed in the name of the Commonwealth by the attorney for the Commonwealth or may be filed by the Attorney General if so requested by the attorney for the Commonwealth. Venue for an action of forfeiture shall lie in the county or city where (i) the property is located, (ii) the property is seized, or (iii) an owner of the property could be prosecuted for the illegal conduct alleged to give rise to the forfeiture. Such information shall (i) name as parties defendant all owners and lienholders then known or of record and the trustees named in any deed of trust securing such lienholder, (ii) specifically describe the property, (iii) set forth in general terms the grounds for forfeiture of the named property, (iv) pray that the same be condemned and sold or otherwise be disposed of according to law, and (v) ask that all persons concerned or interested be notified to appear and show cause why such property should not be forfeited. In all cases, an information shall be filed within three years of the date of actual discovery by the Commonwealth of the last act giving rise to the forfeiture or the action for forfeiture will be barred.

§19.2-386.2. Seizure of named property.

A. When any property subject to seizure under §18.2-249 has not been seized at the time an information naming that property is filed, the clerk of the circuit court, upon motion of the attorney for the Commonwealth wherein the information is filed, shall issue a warrant to the sheriff or other state or local law-enforcement officer authorized to serve criminal process in the jurisdiction where the property is located, describing the property named in the complaint and authorizing its immediate seizure.

B. In all cases of seizure of real property, a notice of lis pendens shall be filed with the clerk of the circuit court of the county or city wherein the property is located and shall be indexed in the land records in the name or names of those persons whose interests appear to be affected thereby.

§19.2-386.3. Notice of seizure for forfeiture and notice of motion for judgment.

A. If an information has not been filed, then upon seizure of any property under §18.2-249, the agency seizing the property shall forthwith notify in writing the attorney for the Commonwealth in the county or city in which the seizure occurred, who shall, within twenty-one days of receipt of such notice, file a notice of seizure for forfeiture with the clerk of the circuit court. Such notice of seizure for forfeiture shall specifically describe the property seized, set forth in general terms the grounds for seizure, identify the date on which the seizure occurred, and identify all owners and lien holders then known or of record. The clerk shall forthwith mail by first-class mail notice of seizure for forfeiture to the last known address of all identified owners and lien holders. When property has been seized under §18.2-249 prior to filing an information, then an information against that property shall be filed within ninety days of the date of seizure or the property shall be released to the owner or lien holder.

B. Except as to corporations, all parties defendant shall be served, in accordance with §8.01-296, with a copy of the information and a notice to appear prior to any motion for default judgment on the information. The notice shall contain a statement warning the party defendant that his interest in the property shall be subject to forfeiture to the Commonwealth unless within thirty days after service on him of the notice, or before the date set forth in the order of publication with respect to the notice, an answer under oath is filed in the proceeding setting forth (i) the nature of the defendant's claim, (ii) the exact right, title or character of the ownership or interest in the property and the evidence thereof, and (iii) the reason, cause, exemption or defense he may have against the forfeiture of his interest in the property, including but not limited to the exemptions set forth in §19.2-386.8. Service upon corporations shall be made in accordance with §8.01-299 or subdivision 1 or 2 of §8.01-301; however, if such service cannot be thus made, it shall be made by publication in accordance with §8.01-317.

(Chgd. by L.1996 ch. 673, eff. 7/1/96.)

§19.2-386.4. Records and handling of seized property.

Any agency seizing property under §18.2-249 or under §19.2-386.2, pending forfeiture and final disposition, may do any of the following:

1. Place the property under constructive seizure by posting notice of seizure for forfeiture on the property or by filing notice of seizure for forfeiture in any appropriate public record relating to property;
2. Remove the property to a storage area for safekeeping or, if the property is a negotiable instrument or money, deposit it in an interest-bearing account;
3. Remove the property to a place designated by the circuit court in the county or city wherein the property was seized; or
4. Provide for another custodian or agency to take custody of the property and remove it to an appropriate location within or without the jurisdiction of the circuit court in the county or city wherein the property was seized or in which the complaint was filed.

A report regarding the type of property subject to forfeiture and its handling pursuant to this section and §19.2-386.5, and the final disposition of the property shall be filed by the seizing agency with the Department of Criminal Justice Services in accordance with regulations promulgated by the Board.

§19.2-386.5. Release of seized property.

At any time prior to the filing of an information, the attorney for the Commonwealth in the county or city in which the property has been seized pursuant to §18.2-249 may, in his discretion, upon the payment of costs incident to the custody of the seized property, return the seized property to an owner or lien holder, without requiring that the owner or lien holder post bond as provided in §19.2-386.6, if he believes the property is properly exempt from forfeiture pursuant to §19.2-386.8.

§19.2-386.6. Bond to secure possession.

If the owner or lien holder of the named property desires to obtain possession thereof before the hearing on the information filed against the same, such property shall be appraised by the clerk of the court where such information is filed. The clerk shall promptly cause the property to be appraised at its fair cash value, and forthwith make return thereof in writing to the court. Any appraisal fee shall be taxed as costs as provided in §19.2-386.12. Upon the return of the appraisal, the owner or lien holder may give a bond payable to the Commonwealth, in a penalty of the amount equal to the appraised value of the property plus the court costs which may accrue, with security to be approved by the clerk and conditioned for the performance of the final judgment of the court, on the trial of the information. A further condition shall be that, if upon the hearing on the information, the judgment of the court is that such property, or any part thereof, or such interest and equity as the owner or lien holder may have therein, is forfeited, judgment may thereupon be entered against the obligors on such bond for the penalty thereof, without further or other proceedings against them thereon, to be discharged by the payment of the appraised value of the property so seized and forfeited, and costs. Upon such judgment, execution may issue, on which the clerk shall endorse, "No security to be taken." Upon giving of the bond, the property shall be delivered to the owner or lien holder.

§19.2-386.7. Sale of property liable to deterioration.

If the property seized is perishable or liable to deterioration, decay, or injury by being detained in custody pending the proceedings, the circuit court for the county or city in which the information is filed or in which the property is located, may order the same to be sold upon such notice as the court, in its discretion, may deem proper and hold the proceeds of sale pending the final disposition of such proceedings.

§19.2-386.8. Exemptions.

The following exemptions shall apply to property otherwise subject to forfeiture:

1. No conveyance used by any person as a lawfully certified common carrier in the transaction of business as a common carrier may be forfeited under the provisions of this section unless the owner of the conveyance was a consenting party or privy to the conduct giving rise to forfeiture or knew or had reason to know of it.

2. No conveyance may be forfeited under the provisions of this section for any conduct committed by a person other than the owner while the conveyance was unlawfully in the possession of a person other than the owner in violation of the criminal laws of this Commonwealth, or any other state, the District of Columbia, the United States or any territory thereof.

3. No owner's interest may be forfeited under this chapter if the court finds that:

a. He did not know and had no reason to know of the conduct giving rise to forfeiture;

b. He was a bona fide purchaser for value without notice; and

c. The conduct giving rise to forfeiture occurred without his connivance or consent, express or implied.

4. No lien holder's interest may be forfeited under this chapter if the court finds that:

a. The lien holder did not know of the conduct giving rise to forfeiture at the time the lien was granted;

b. The lien holder held a bona fide lien on the property subject to forfeiture and had perfected the same in the manner prescribed by law prior to seizure of the property; and

c. The conduct giving rise to forfeiture occurred without his connivance or consent, express or implied.

In the event the interest has been sold to a bona fide purchaser for value in order to avoid the provisions of this chapter, the Commonwealth shall have a right of action against the seller of the property for the proceeds of the sale.

§19.2-386.9. Appearance by owner or lien holder.

Any person claiming to be an owner or lien holder of the named property may appear at any time within thirty days after service on him of notice to appear or on or before the date certain set forth in any order of publication under §8.01-317 or such longer time as the court in its discretion may allow to prevent a miscarriage of justice. Any person without actual or constructive notice of the forfeiture proceedings claiming to be an owner or lienholder may appear at any time before final judgment of the trial court and be made a party to the action. Such appearance shall be by answer, under oath, which shall clearly set forth (i) the nature of the defendant's claim; (ii) the exact right, title or character of the ownership or interest in the property and the evidence thereof; and (iii) the reason, cause, exemption or defense he may have against the forfeiture of the property.

§19.2-386.10. Trial.

A. A party defendant who fails to appear as provided in §19.2-386.9 shall be in default. The forfeiture shall be deemed established as to the interest of any party in default upon entry of judgment as provided in §19.2-386.11. Within twenty-one days after entry of judgment, any party defendant against whom judgment has been so entered may petition the Department of Criminal Justice Services for remission of his interest in the forfeited property. For good cause shown and upon proof that the party defendant's interest in the property is exempt under subdivision 2, 3 or 4 of §19.2-386.8, the Department of Criminal Justice Services shall grant the petition and direct the state treasury to either (i) remit the party defendant an amount not exceeding the party defendant's interest in the proceeds of sale of the forfeited property after deducting expenses incurred and payable pursuant to subsection B of §19.2-386.12 or (ii) convey clear and absolute title to the forfeited property in extinguishment in such interest.

If any party defendant appears in accordance with §19.2-386.9, the court shall proceed to trial of the case, unless trial by jury is demanded by the Commonwealth or any party defendant. At trial, the Commonwealth has the burden of proving that the property is subject to forfeiture under this chapter. Upon such a showing by the Commonwealth, the claimant has the burden of proving that the claimant's interest in the property is exempt under subdivision 2, 3 or 4 of §19.2-386.8. The proof of all issues shall be by a preponderance of the evidence.

B. The information and trial thereon shall be independent of any criminal proceeding against any party or other person for violation of law. However, upon motion and for good cause shown, the court may stay a forfeiture proceeding that is related to any indictment or information.

§19.2-386.11. Judgment of condemnation; destruction.

A. If the forfeiture is established, the judgment shall be that the property be condemned as forfeited to the Commonwealth subject to any remission granted under subsection A of §19.2-386.10 and further that the same be sold, unless (i) a sale thereof has been already made under §19.2-386.7, (ii) the court determines that the property forfeited is of such minimal value that the sale would not be in the best interest of the Commonwealth or (iii) the court finds that the property may be subject to return to a participating agency. If the court finds that the property may be subject to return to an agency participating in the seizure in accordance with subsection C of §19.2-386.14, the order shall provide for storage of the property until the determination to return it is made or, if return is not made, for sale of the property as provided in this section and §19.2-386.12. If sale has been made, the judgment shall be against the proceeds of sale, subject to the rights of any lien holder whose interest is not forfeited. If the property condemned has been delivered to the claimant under §19.2-386.6, further judgment shall be against the obligors in the bond for the penalty thereof to be discharged by the payment of the appraised value of the property, upon which judgment, process of execution shall be awarded and the clerk shall endorse thereon, "No security is to be taken."

B. Forfeited cash and negotiable instruments shall be disposed of pursuant to the provisions of §19.2-386.12.

C. Contraband, the sale or possession of which is unlawful, weapons and property not sold because of the minimal value thereof, may be ordered destroyed by the court.

§19.2-386.12. Sale of forfeited property.

A. Any sale of forfeited property shall be made for cash, after due advertisement. The sale shall be by public sale or other commercially feasible means authorized by the court in the order of forfeiture and shall vest in the purchaser a clear and absolute title to the property sold subject to the rights of any lien holder whose interest is not forfeited. The proceeds of sale, and whatever may be realized on any bond given under §19.2-386.6, and any money forfeited shall be paid over to the state treasury into a special fund of the Department of Criminal Justice Services in Accordance with §19.2-386.14.

B. In all cases of forfeiture under this section, the actual expenses incident to the custody, preservation, and management of the seized property prior to forfeiture, the actual expenses incident to normal legal proceedings to perfect the Commonwealth's interest in the seized property through forfeiture, and the actual expenses incident to the sale thereof, including commissions, shall be costs and shall be paid to the person or persons who incurred these costs out of the net proceeds from the sale of such property. If there are no proceeds, the actual expenses shall be paid by the Commonwealth from the Criminal Fund. Actual expenses in excess of the available net proceeds, shall be paid by the Commonwealth from the Criminal Fund. The party or parties in interest to any forfeiture proceeding commenced under this section shall be entitled to reasonable attorney's fees and costs if the forfeiture proceeding is terminated in favor of such party or parties. Such fees and costs shall be paid by the Commonwealth from the Criminal Fund.

The residue, if any, shall be paid and disbursed as provided in subsection A of §19.2-386.10 and §19.2-386.14 and regulations promulgated by the Criminal Justice Services Board.

§19.2-386.13. Writ of error and supersedeas.

For the purpose of review on a writ of error or supersedeas, a final judgment or order in the cause shall be deemed a final judgment or order in a civil case (not in chancery) within the meaning of §8.01-670.

§19.2-386.14. Sharing of forfeited drug assets.

A. All cash, negotiable instruments and proceeds from a sale conducted pursuant to §19.2-386.7 or §19.2-386.12, after deduction of expenses, fees and costs as provided in §19.2-386.12, shall, as soon after entry of the forfeiture as is practicable, be paid over to the state treasury into a special fund of the Department of Criminal Justice Services for distribution in accordance with this section. The forfeited property and proceeds, less ten percent, shall be made available to federal, state and local agencies to promote law enforcement in accordance with this section and regulations adopted by the Criminal Justice Services Board to implement the asset-sharing program.

The ten percent retained by the Department shall be held in a nonreverting fund, known as the Asset Sharing Administrative Fund. Administrative costs incurred by the Department to manage and operate the asset-sharing program shall be paid from the Fund. Any amounts remaining in the Fund after payment of these costs shall be used to promote state or local law-enforcement activities. Distributions from the Fund for these activities shall be based upon need and shall be made from time to time in accordance with regulations promulgated by the Board.

B. Any federal, state or local agency or office that directly participated in the investigation or other law-enforcement activity which led, directly or indirectly, to the seizure and forfeiture shall be eligible for, and may petition the Department for, return of the forfeited asset or an equitable share of the net proceeds, based upon the degree of participation in the law-enforcement effort resulting in the forfeiture, taking into account the total value of all property forfeited and the total law-enforcement effort with respect to the violation of law on which the forfeiture is based. Upon finding that the petitioning agency is eligible for distribution and that all participating agencies agree on the equitable share of each, the Department shall distribute each share directly to the appropriate treasury of the participating agency.

If all eligible participating agencies cannot agree on the equitable shares of the net proceeds, the shares shall be determined by the Criminal Justice Services Board in accordance with regulations which shall specify the criteria to be used by the Board in assessing the degree of participation in the law-enforcement effort resulting in the forfeiture.

C. After the order of forfeiture is entered, any seizing agency may petition the Department for return of any forfeited motor vehicle, boat or aircraft or other tangible personal property which is not subject to a grant or pending petition for remission. Where all the participating agencies agree upon the equitable distribution of the tangible personal property, the Department shall return the property to those agencies upon finding that (i) the agency meets the criteria for distribution as set forth in subsection B and (ii) the agency has a clear and reasonable law-enforcement need for the forfeited property.

If all eligible participating agencies cannot agree on the distribution of the property, distribution shall be determined by the Criminal Justice Services Board as in subsection B, taking into consideration the clear and reasonable law-enforcement needs for the property which the agencies may have. In order to equitably distribute tangible personal property, the Criminal Justice Services Board may require the agency receiving the property to reimburse the Department in cash for the difference between the fair market value of the forfeited property and the agency's equitable share as determined by the Criminal Justice Services Board.

D. All forfeited property, including its proceeds or cash equivalent, received by a participating state or local agency pursuant to this section shall be used to promote law enforcement but shall not be used to supplant existing programs or funds. The Board shall promulgate regulations establishing an audit procedure to ensure compliance with this section.

CHAPTER 23
CENTRAL CRIMINAL RECORDS EXCHANGE

Section

§19.2-387. Exchange to operate as a division of Department of State Police; authority of Superintendent of State Police.

A. The Central Criminal Records Exchange shall operate as a separate division within the Department of State Police and shall be the sole criminal record-keeping agency of the Commonwealth, except for (i) the Department of Corrections pursuant to Chapter 10 of Title 16.1 (§16.1-222 et seq.), (ii) the Department of Motor Vehicles, (iii) for purposes of the DNA data bank, the Bureau of Forensic Science within the Division of Consolidated Laboratory Services* and (iv) for the purpose of making parole determinations pursuant to subdivisions 1, 2, 3 and 5 of §53.1-136, the Virginia Parole Board.

**See now the Division of Forensic Science within the Department of Criminal Justice Services.*

B. The Superintendent of State Police is hereby authorized to employ such personnel, establish such offices and acquire such equipment as shall be necessary to carry out the purposes of this chapter and is also authorized to enter into agreements with other state agencies for services to be performed for it by employees of such other agencies.

§19.2-388. Duties and authority of Exchange.

A. It shall be the duty of the Central Criminal Records Exchange to receive, classify and file criminal history record information as defined in §9-169 and other records required to be reported to it by §§16.2-299 and 19.2-390. The Exchange is authorized to prepare and furnish to all state and local law-enforcement officials and agencies; to clerks of circuit courts, general district courts, and juvenile and domestic relations district courts; and to corrections and penal officials, forms which shall be used for the making of such reports.

B. Juvenile records received pursuant to §16.1-299 shall be maintained separately from adult records.
(Chgd. by L.1996 chs. 755, 914, eff. 7/1/96.)

§19.2-389. Dissemination of criminal history record information.

A. Criminal history record information shall be disseminated, whether directly or through an intermediary, only to:

1. Authorized officers or employees of criminal justice agencies, as defined by §9-169, for purposes of the administration of criminal justice and the screening of an employment application or review of employment by a criminal justice agency with respect to its own employees or applicants, and dissemination to the Virginia Parole Board, pursuant to this subdivision, of such information on all state-responsible inmates for the purpose of making parole determinations pursuant to subdivisions 1, 2, 3, and 5 of §53.1-136 shall include collective dissemination by electronic means every thirty days;

2. Such other individuals and agencies which require criminal history record information to implement a state or federal statute or executive order of the President of the United States or Governor that expressly refers to criminal conduct and contains requirements and/or exclusions expressly based upon such conduct, except that information concerning the arrest of an individual may not be disseminated to a noncriminal justice agency or individual if an interval of one year has elapsed from the date of the arrest and no disposition of the charge has been recorded and no active prosecution of the charge is pending;

3. Individuals and agencies pursuant to a specific agreement with a criminal justice agency to provide services required for the administration of criminal justice pursuant to that agreement which shall specifically authorize access to data, limit the use of data to purposes for which given, and ensure the security and confidentiality of the data;

4. Individuals and agencies for the express purpose of research, evaluative, or statistical activities pursuant to an agreement with a criminal justice agency which shall specifically authorize access to data, limit the use of data to research, evaluative, or statistical purposes, and ensure the confidentiality and security of the data;

5. Agencies of state or federal government which are authorized by state or federal statute or executive order of the President of the United States or Governor to conduct investigations determining employment suitability or eligibility for security clearances allowing access to classified information;

6. Individuals and agencies where authorized by court order or court rule;

7. Agencies of any political subdivision of the Commonwealth for the conduct of investigations of applicants for public employment, permit, or license whenever, in the interest of public welfare or safety, it is necessary to determine under a duly enacted ordinance if the past criminal conduct of a person with a conviction record would be compatible with the nature of the employment, permit, or license under consideration;

8. Public or private agencies when and as required by federal or state law or interstate compact to investigate applicants for foster or adoptive parenthood subject to the restriction that the data shall not be further disseminated by the agency to any party other than a federal or state authority or court as may be required to comply with an express requirement of law for such further dissemination;

9. To the extent permitted by federal law or regulation, public service companies as defined in §56-1, for the conduct of investigations of applicants for employment when such employment involves personal contact with the public or when past criminal conduct of an applicant would be

incompatible with the nature of the employment under consideration;

10. The appropriate authority for purposes of granting citizenship and for purposes of international travel, including but not limited to, issuing visas and passports;

11. A person requesting a copy of his own criminal history record information as defined in §9-169 at his cost, except that criminal history record information shall be supplied at no charge to a person who has applied to be a volunteer (i) with a Virginia affiliate of Big Brothers/Big Sisters of America, (ii) with a volunteer fire company or volunteer rescue squad, (iii) with the Volunteer Emergency Families for Children, or (iv) with any affiliate of Prevent Child Abuse, Virginia;

12. Administrators and board presidents of and applicants for licensure or registration as a child welfare agency as defined in §63.1-195 for dissemination to the Commissioner of Social Services' representative pursuant to §63.1-198 for the conduct of investigations with respect to employees of and volunteers at such facilities, caretakers, and other adults living in family day-care homes or homes approved by family day-care systems, and foster and adoptive parent applicants of private child-placing agencies, pursuant to §63.1-198.1, subject to the restriction that the data shall not be further disseminated by the facility or agency to any party other than the data subject, the Commissioner of Social Services' representative or a federal or state authority or court as may be required to comply with an express requirement of law for such further dissemination;

13. The school boards of the Commonwealth for the purpose of screening individuals who are offered or who accept public school employment and those current school board employees for whom a report of arrest has been made pursuant to §19.2-83.1;

14. The State Lottery Department for the conduct of investigations as set forth in the State Lottery Law (§58.1-4000 et seq.);

15. Licensed nursing homes, hospitals and home care organizations for the conduct of investigations of applicants for compensated employment in licensed nursing homes pursuant to §32.1-126.01, hospital pharmacies pursuant to §32.1-126.02, and home care organizations pursuant to §32.1-162.9:1, subject to the limitations set out in subsection E;

16. Licensed homes for adults, licensed district homes for adults, and licensed adult day-care centers for the conduct of investigations of applicants for compensated employment in licensed homes for adults pursuant to §63.1-173.2, in licensed district homes for adults pursuant to §63.1-189.1, and in licensed adult day-care centers pursuant to §63.1-194.13, subject to the limitations set out in subsection F;

17. The Alcoholic Beverage Control Board for the conduct of investigations as set forth in §4.1-103.1;

18. The State Board of Elections and authorized officers and employees thereof in the course of conducting necessary investigations with respect to registered voters, limited to any record of felony convictions;

19. The Commissioner of the Department of Mental Health, Mental Retardation and Substance Abuse Services for those individuals who are committed to the custody of the Commissioner pursuant to §§19.2-169.2, 19.2-169.6, 19.2-176, 19.2-177.1, 19.2-182.2, 19.2-182.3, 19.2-182.8 and 19.2-182.9 for the purpose of placement, evaluation, and treatment planning;

20. Any alcohol safety action program certified by the Commission on the Virginia Alcohol Safety Action Program for (i) assessments of habitual offenders under §46.2-360, (ii) interventions with first offenders under §18.2-251, or (iii) services to offenders under §§18.2-51.4, 18.2-266 or §18.2-266.1;

21. Residential facilities for juveniles regulated or operated by the Department of Social Services, the Department of Education, or the Department of Mental Health, Mental Retardation and Substance Abuse Services for the purpose of determining applicants' fitness for employment or for providing volunteer or contractual services;

22. The Department of Mental Health, Mental Retardation and Substance Abuse Services and facilities operated by the Department for the purpose of determining an individual's fitness for employment pursuant to departmental instructions;

23. Pursuant to §22.1-296.3, the governing boards or administrators of private or parochial elementary or secondary schools which are accredited by a statewide accrediting organization recognized, prior to January 1, 1996, by the State Board of Education or a private organization coordinating such records information on behalf of such governing boards or administrators pursuant to a written agreement with the Department of State Police;

24. Public and nonprofit private colleges and universities for the purpose of screening individuals who are offered or accept employment;

25. Executive directors of community services boards or the personnel director serving the community services board for the purpose of determining an individual's fitness for employment pursuant to §37.1-197.2;

26. Executive directors of behavioral health authorities as defined in §37.1-243 for the purpose of determining an individual's fitness for employment pursuant to §37.1-197.2;

27. The Commissioner of the Department of Social Services for the purpose of locating persons who owe child support or who are alleged in a pending paternity proceeding to be a putative father, provided that only the name, address, demographics and social security number of the data subject shall be released;

28. Authorized officers or directors of agencies licensed pursuant to Chapter 8 (§37.1-179 et seq.) of Title 37.1 by the Department of Mental Health, Mental Retardation and Substance Abuse Services for the purpose of determining if any applicant who accepts employment in any direct consumer care position has been convicted of a crime that affects their fitness to have responsibility for the safety and well-being of persons with mental illness, mental retardation and substance abuse pursuant to §§37.1-183.3 and 37.1-197.2; and

29. Other entities as otherwise provided by law.

Upon an ex parte motion of a defendant in a felony case and upon the showing that the records requested may be relevant to such case, the court shall enter an order requiring the Central Criminal Records Exchange to furnish the defendant, as soon as practicable, copies of any records of persons designated in the order on whom a report has been made under the provisions of this chapter.

Notwithstanding any other provision of this chapter to the contrary, upon a written request sworn to before an officer authorized to take acknowledgments, the Central Criminal Records Exchange, or the criminal justice agency in cases of offenses not required to be reported to the Exchange, shall furnish a copy of conviction data covering the person named in the request to the person making the request; however, such person on whom the data is being obtained shall consent in writing, under oath, to the making of such request. A person receiving a copy of his own conviction data may utilize or further disseminate that data as he deems appropriate. In the event no conviction data is maintained on the data subject, the person making the request shall be furnished at his cost a certification to that effect.

B. Use of criminal history record information disseminated to noncriminal justice agencies under this section shall be limited to the purposes for which it was given and may not be disseminated further.

C. No criminal justice agency or person shall confirm the existence or nonexistence of criminal history record information for employment or licensing inquiries except as provided by law.

D. Criminal justice agencies shall establish procedures to query the Central Criminal Records Exchange prior to dissemination of any criminal history record information on offenses required to be reported to the Central Criminal Records Exchange to ensure that the most up-to-date disposition data is being used. Inquiries of the Exchange shall be made prior to any dissemination except in those cases where time is of the essence and the normal response time of the Exchange would exceed the necessary time period. A criminal justice agency to whom a request has been made for the dissemination of criminal history record information that is required to be reported to the Central Criminal Records Exchange may direct the inquirer to the Central Criminal Records Exchange for such dissemination. Dissemination of information regarding offenses not required to be reported to the Exchange shall be made by the criminal justice agency maintaining the record as required by §15.2-1722.

E. Criminal history information provided to licensed nursing homes, hospitals and to home care organizations pursuant to subdivision A 15 shall be limited to the convictions on file with the Exchange for any offense specified in §§32.1-126.01, 32.1-126.02 and 32.1-162.9:1.

F. Criminal history information provided to licensed adult care residences, licensed district homes for adults, and licensed adult day-care centers pursuant to subdivision A 16 shall be limited to the convictions on file with the Exchange for any offense specified in §§63.1-173.2, 63.1-189.1 or §63.1-194.13.

(Chgd. by L.1995 chs. 409, 645, 731, 781, 809; L.1996 chs. 428, 432, 747, 881, 927, 944; L.1997 chs. 169, 177, 606, 691, 721, 743, 796, 895; L.1998 chs. 113, 405, 445, 882; L.1999 chs. 383, 685, eff. 7/1/99.)

§19.2-389.1. Dissemination of juvenile record information.

Record information maintained in the Central Criminal Records Exchange pursuant to the provisions of §16.1-299 shall be disseminated only (i) to make the determination as provided in §§18.2-308.2 and 18.2-308.2:2 of eligibility to possess or purchase a firearm, (ii) to aid in the preparation of a pre-sentence or post-sentence investigation report pursuant to §19.2-264.5 or §19.2-299 or in the preparation of the discretionary sentencing guidelines worksheets pursuant to subsection C of §19.2-298.01, (iii) to aid all court service units serving juvenile delinquent offenders, (iv) for fingerprint comparison utilizing the fingerprints maintained in the Automated Fingerprint Information System (AFIS) computer, and (v) to attorneys for the Commonwealth to secure information incidental to sentencing and to attorneys for the Commonwealth and probation officers to prepare the discretionary sentencing guidelines worksheets pursuant to subsection C of §19.2-298.01.

(Chgd. by L.1996 chs. 755, 870, 914, eff. 7/1/96.)

§19.2-390. Reports to be made by local law-enforcement officers, conservators of the peace, clerks of court, Secretary of the Commonwealth and Corrections officials to State Police; material submitted by other agencies.

A. 1. Every state official or agency having the power to arrest, the sheriffs of counties, the police officials of cities and towns, and any other local law-enforcement officer or conservator of the peace having the power to arrest for a felony shall make a report to the Central Criminal Records Exchange, on forms provided by it, of any arrest, including those arrests involving the taking into custody of, or service of process upon, any person on charges resulting from an indictment, presentment or information, the arrest on capias or warrant for failure to appear, and the service of a warrant for another jurisdiction, on any of the following charges:

a. Treason;

b. Any felony;

c. Any offense punishable as a misdemeanor under Title 54.1; or

d. Any misdemeanor punishable by confinement in jail under Title 18.2 or 19.2, except an arrest for a violation of §18.2-119, Article 2 (§18.2-266 et seq.) of Chapter 7 of Title 18.2, Article 2 (§18.2-415 et seq.) of Chapter 9 of Title 18.2, or any similar ordinance of any county, city or town.

The reports shall contain such information as is required by the Exchange and shall be accompanied by fingerprints of the individual arrested. Fingerprint cards prepared by a law-enforcement agency for inclusion in a national criminal justice file shall be forwarded to the Exchange for transmittal to the appropriate bureau.

2. For persons arrested and released on summonses in accordance with §19.2-74, such report shall not be required until (i) a conviction is entered and no appeal is noted or if an appeal is noted, the conviction is upheld upon appeal or the person convicted withdraws his appeal; (ii) the court dismisses the proceeding pursuant to §18.2-251; or (iii) an acquittal by reason of insanity pursuant to §19.2-182.2 is entered. Upon such conviction or acquittal, the court shall remand the individual to the custody of the office of the chief law-enforcement officer of the county or city. It shall be the duty of the chief law-enforcement officer, or his designee who may be the arresting officer, to ensure that such report is completed after a determination of guilt or acquittal by reason of insanity. The court shall require the officer to complete the report immediately following the person's conviction or acquittal, and the individual shall be discharged from custody forthwith, unless the court has imposed a jail sentence to be served by him or ordered him committed to the custody of the Commissioner of the Department of Mental Health, Mental Retardation and Substance Abuse Services.

B. Within seventy-two hours following the receipt of (i) a warrant or capias for the arrest of any person on a charge of a felony or (ii) a Governor's warrant of arrest of a person issued pursuant to §19.2-92, the law-enforcement agency which received the warrant shall enter the person's name and other appropriate information required by the Department of State Police into the "information system", known as the Virginia Criminal Information Network (VCIN), established and maintained by the Department pursuant to Chapter 2 (§52-12 et seq.) of Title 52. The report shall include the person's name, date of birth, social security number and such other known information which the State Police may require. Any unexecuted criminal process which has been entered into the VCIN system shall be removed forthwith by the entering law-enforcement agency when the criminal process has been ordered destroyed pursuant to §19.2-76.1.

C. The clerk of each circuit court and district court shall make a report to the Central Criminal Records Exchange of (i) any dismissal, indefinite postponement or continuance, charge still pending due to mental incompetency or incapacity, nolle prosequi, acquittal, or conviction of, including any sentence imposed, or failure of a grand jury to return a true bill as to, any person charged with an offense listed in subsection A of this section, including any action which may have resulted from an indictment, presentment or information, and (ii) any adjudication of delinquency based upon an act which, if committed by an adult, would require fingerprints to be filed pursuant to subsection A. In the case of offenses not required to be reported to the Exchange by subsection A of this section, the reports of any of the foregoing dispositions shall be filed by the law-enforcement agency making the arrest with the arrest record required to be maintained by §15.1-135.1. Upon conviction of any person, including juveniles tried and convicted in the circuit courts pursuant to §16.1-269.1, whether sentenced as adults or juveniles, for an offense for which registration is required as defined in §19.2-298.1, the clerk shall within seven days of sentencing submit a report to the Sex Offender and Crimes Against Minors Registry. The report to the Registry shall include the name of the person convicted and all aliases which he is known to have used, the date and locality of the conviction for which registration is required, his date of birth, social security number, last known address, and specific reference to the offense for which he was convicted. No report of conviction or adjudication in a district court shall be filed unless the period allowed for an appeal has elapsed and no appeal has been perfected. In the event that the records in the office of any clerk show that any conviction or adjudication has been nullified in any manner, he shall also make a report of that fact to the Exchange and, if appropriate, to the Registry. In addition, each clerk of a circuit court, upon receipt of certification thereof from the Supreme Court, shall report to the Exchange or the Registry, or to the law-enforcement agency making the arrest in the case of offenses not required to be reported to the Exchange, on forms provided by the Exchange or Registry, as the case may be, any reversal or other amendment to a prior sentence or disposition previously reported. When criminal process is ordered destroyed pursuant to §19.2-76.1, the clerk shall report such action to the law-enforcement agency that entered the warrant or capias into the VCIN system.

D. In addition to those offenses enumerated in subsection A of this section, the Central Criminal Records Exchange may receive, classify and file any other fingerprints and records of arrest or confinement submitted to it by any law-enforcement agency or any correctional institution.

E. Corrections officials, sheriffs, and jail superintendents of regional jails, responsible for maintaining correctional status information, as required by the regulations of the Department of Criminal Justice Services, with respect to individuals about whom reports have been made under the provisions of this chapter shall make reports of changes in correctional status information to the Central Criminal Records Exchange. The reports to the Exchange shall include any commitment to or release or escape from a state or local correctional facility, including commitment to or release from a parole or probation agency.

F. Any pardon, reprieve or executive commutation of sentence by the Governor shall be reported to the Exchange by the office of the Secretary of the Commonwealth.

G. Officials responsible for reporting disposition of charges, and correctional changes of status of individuals under this section, including those reports made to the Registry, shall adopt procedures reasonably designed at a minimum (i) to ensure that such reports are accurately made as soon as feasible by the most expeditious means and in no instance later than thirty days after occurrence of the disposition or correctional change of status and (ii) to report promptly any correction, deletion, or revision of the information.

H. Upon receiving a correction, deletion, or revision of information, the Central Criminal Records Exchange shall notify all criminal justice agencies known to have previously received the information.

As used in this section, the term "chief law-enforcement officer" means the chief of police of cities and towns and sheriffs of counties, unless a political subdivision has otherwise designated its chief law-enforcement officer by appropriate resolution or ordinance, in which case the local designation shall be controlling.

(Chgd. by L.1996 chs. 429, 755, 806, 914; L.1997 chs. 27, 509, 747, eff. 7/1/97, ch. 801, eff. 1/1/98.)

§19.2-390.1. Sex Offender and Crimes Against Minors Registry; maintenance; access.

A. The Department of State Police shall keep and maintain a Sex Offender and Crimes Against Minors Registry, separate and apart from all other records maintained by it. The purpose of the Registry shall be to assist the efforts of law-enforcement agencies to protect their communities from repeat sex offenders and to protect children from becoming victims of criminal offenders by helping to prevent such individuals from being hired or allowed to volunteer to work directly with children.

The Registry shall include conviction data received from the courts, including the disposition records for juveniles tried and convicted in the circuit courts pursuant to §16.1-269.1, on convictions for offenses for which registration is required as defined in §19.2-298.1 and registrations and reregistrations received from persons required to do so by §19.2-298.1, whether such requirement arose before, on, or after July 1, 1997.

The Registry shall also include a separate indication that a person has been convicted of a sexually violent offense.

Upon receipt of a registration or reregistration pursuant to §19.2-298.1 the State Police shall forthwith notify the chief law-enforcement officer of the county, city or town of the locality listed as the person's address on the registration or reregistration and any person who has requested automatic notification pursuant to §19.2-390.2. The State Police shall forthwith transmit the appropriate information as required by the Federal Bureau of Investigation for inclusion in the National Sex Offender Registry. The State Police shall promulgate regulations governing the giving of notice to the chief local law-enforcement officer, the operation and maintenance of the Registry and the expungement of records on persons who are deceased, whose convictions have been reversed or who have been pardoned, and those for whom an order of expungement or relief from frequent registration has been entered pursuant to §§19.2-298.3, 19.2-298.4 or §19.2-392.1.

B. Except as provided in subsection A, C or D, Registry information shall be disseminated upon request made directly to the Department of State Police or to the State Police through a local law-enforcement agency. Such information may be disclosed to any person requesting information on a specific individual in accordance with subsection C. The Department of State Police shall make Registry information available, upon request, to criminal justice agencies including local law-enforcement agencies through the Virginia Criminal Information Network (VCIN). Registry information provided under this section shall be used for the purposes of the administration of criminal justice, for the screening of current or prospective employees or volunteers or otherwise for the protection of the public in general and children in particular. Use of the information for purposes not authorized by this section is prohibited and a willful violation of this section with the intent to harass or intimidate another shall be punished as a Class 1 misdemeanor.

The VCIN and any form or document used by the Department of State Police to disseminate information from the Registry shall provide notice that any unauthorized use of the information with the intent to harass or intimidate another is a crime punishable as a Class 1 misdemeanor. The

Department of State Police may by regulation establish a fee not to exceed fifteen dollars for responding to requests for information from the Registry pursuant to this subsection. Any fees collected shall be deposited in a special account to be used to offset the costs of administering the Registry.

C. Information regarding a specific person requested pursuant to subsection B shall be disseminated upon receipt of an official request form which may be submitted directly to the Department of State Police or to the State Police through a local law-enforcement agency. The official request form shall include a statement of the reason for the request; the name and address of the person requesting the information; the name, address and, if known, the social security number of the person about whom information is sought; and such other information as the State Police may require to ensure reliable identification. Unlawful use of the information for purposes of intimidating or harassing another is prohibited and a willful violation of this section shall be punished as a Class 1 misdemeanor.

D. On or before January 1, 1999, the State Police shall develop and maintain a system for making certain Registry information on violent sex offenders publicly available by means of the Internet. The information to be made available shall include the offender's name; all aliases which he has used or under which he may have been known; the date and locality of the conviction and a brief description of the offense; his date of birth, current address and photograph; and such other information as the State Police may from time to time determine is necessary to preserve public safety. The system shall be secure and not capable of being altered except by the State Police. The system shall be updated each business day with newly received registrations and reregistrations. The State Police shall remove all information which it knows to be inaccurate from the Internet system.

E. No liability shall be imposed upon any law-enforcement official who disseminates information or fails to disseminate information in good faith compliance with the requirements of this section, but this provision shall not be construed to grant immunity for gross negligence or willful misconduct.

(Chgd. by L.1996 chs. 418, 542, 880; L.1997 chs. 670, 672, 747; L.1998 chs. 785, 834; L.2000 ch. 250, eff. 7/1/2000.)

§19.2-390.2. Automatic notification of registration to certain entities.

On and after January 1, 1999, any public, parochial, denominational or private elementary or secondary school, day-care service and child-minding service, and any state-regulated or state-licensed child caring institution, child day center, child day program, family day home, foster home or group home as defined in §63.1-195 may request from the State Police pursuant to this section and, upon compliance with the requirements therefor established by the State Police, shall be eligible to receive from the State Police electronic notice of the registration or reregistration of any sex offender registered pursuant to §19.2-298.1. Agencies that request and are entitled to this notification, and which do not have the capability of receiving such electronic notice, may register with the Department of State Police to receive written notification of sex offender registration or reregistration.

Within three business days of receipt by the State Police of registration or reregistration pursuant to §19.2-298.1, the State Police shall electronically or in writing notify an entity which has requested such notification, has complied with the requirements therefor established by the State Police and is located in the same zip code area as the address of the offender as shown on the registration or any contiguous zip code area.

The State Police shall establish reasonable guidelines governing the automatic dissemination of Registry information pursuant to this section, which may include the payment of a fee, whether a one-time fee or a regular assessment, to maintain the electronic access. The fee, if any, shall defray the costs of establishing and maintaining the electronic notification system and notice by mail.

For the purposes of this section, the term "day-care service" means provision of supplementary care and protection during a part of the day for the minor child of another, and "child-minding service" means provision of temporary custodial care or supervisory services for the minor child of another.

(Added by L.1998 chs. 785, 834; chgd. by L.1999 ch. 845, eff. 7/1/99.)

§19.2-391. Records to be made available to Exchange by state officials and agencies; duplication of records.

Each state official and agency shall make available to the Central Criminal Records Exchange such of their records as are pertinent to its functions and shall cooperate with the Exchange in the development and use of equipment and facilities on a joint basis, where feasible. No state official or agency shall maintain records which are a duplication of the records on deposit in the Central Criminal Records Exchange, except to the extent necessary for efficient internal administration of such agency. Furthermore, the Virginia Parole Board may receive and use electronically disseminated criminal history record information from the Central Criminal Records Exchange as required to make parole determinations pursuant to subdivisions (1), (2), (3), and (5) of §53.1-136, provided the data is (i) temporarily stored with the Board solely for operational purposes, (ii) purged within thirty days of receipt of updated data by the Board, and (iii) accessed and viewed solely by Parole Board members and authorized staff pursuant to subdivision (6) of §9-169 and §9-191.

§19.2-392. Fingerprints and photographs by police authorities.

A. All duly constituted police authorities having the power of arrest may take the fingerprints and photographs of: (i) any person arrested by them and charged with a felony or a misdemeanor an arrest for which is to be reported by them to the Central Criminal Records Exchange, or (ii) any person who pleads guilty or is found guilty after being summoned in accordance with §19.2-74. Such authorities shall make such records available to the Central Criminal Records Exchange. Such authorities are authorized to provide, on the request of duly appointed law-enforcement officers, copies of any fingerprint records they may have, and to furnish services and technical advice in connection with the taking, classifying and preserving of fingerprints and fingerprint records.

B. Such police authorities may establish and collect a reasonable fee not to exceed five dollars for the taking of fingerprints when voluntarily requested by any person for purposes other than criminal violations.

§19.2-392.01. Judges may require taking of fingerprints and photographs in certain misdemeanor cases.

The judge of a district court may, in his discretion, on motion of the attorney for the Commonwealth, require the duly constituted police officers of the county, city or town within the territorial jurisdiction of the court to take the fingerprints and photograph of any person who has been arrested and charged with a misdemeanor other than a misdemeanor which is a violation of any provision of Title 46.2.

(Added by L.1995 ch. 407; chgd. by L.1996 chs. 755, 914, eff. 7/1/96.)

§19.2-392.02. National criminal background checks by businesses and organizations regarding employees or volunteers providing care to children, the elderly and disabled.

(Section effective 1/1/2001.)

A. For purposes of this section:

"Barrier crime" means any offense set forth in §63.1-198.1 or §63.1-248.7:2.

"Barrier crime information" means the following facts concerning a person who has been arrested for, or has been convicted of, a barrier crime, regardless of whether the person was a juvenile or adult at the time of the arrest or conviction: full name, race, sex, date of birth, height, weight, fingerprints, a brief description of the barrier crime or offenses for which the person has been arrested or has been convicted, the disposition of the charge, and any other information that may be useful in identifying persons arrested for or convicted of a barrier crime.

"Care" means the provision of care, treatment, education, training, instruction, supervision, or recreation to children, the elderly or disabled.

"Department" means the Department of State Police.

"Employed by" means any person who is employed by, volunteers for, seeks to be employed by, or seeks to volunteer for a qualified entity.

"Identification document" means a document made or issued by or under the authority of the United States government, a state, a political subdivision of a state, a foreign government, political subdivision of a foreign government, an international governmental or an international quasi-governmental organization that, when completed with information concerning a particular individual, is of a type intended or commonly accepted for the purpose of identification of individuals.

"Provider" means a person who (i) is employed by a qualified entity, and has, seeks to have, or may have unsupervised access to a child or to an elderly or disabled person to whom the qualified entity provides care or (ii) owns, operates or seeks to own or operate a qualified entity.

"Qualified entity" means a business or organization that provides care to children, the elderly or disabled, whether governmental, private, for profit, nonprofit or voluntary, except organizations exempt pursuant to subdivision A 10 of §63.1-196.001.

B. Notwithstanding §§63.1-198.1 and 63.1-198.2, a qualified entity may request the Department of State Police to conduct a national criminal background check on any provider who is employed by such entity. No qualified entity may request a national criminal background check on a provider until such provider has:

1. Been fingerprinted at any local or state law-enforcement agency and provided two sets of the fingerprints to the qualified entity; and

2. Completed and signed a statement, furnished by the entity, that includes (i) his name, address, and date of birth as it appears on a valid identification document, (ii) a disclosure of whether or not the provider has ever been convicted of or is the subject of pending charges for a criminal offense within or outside the Commonwealth, and if the provider has been convicted of a crime, a description of the crime and the particulars of the conviction, (iii) a notice to the provider that the entity may request a background check, (iv) a notice to the provider that he is entitled to obtain a copy of any background check report, to challenge the accuracy and completeness of any information contained in any such report, and to obtain a prompt determination as to the validity of such challenge before a final determination is made by the Department, and (v) a notice to the provider that prior to the completion of the background check the qualified entity may choose to deny the provider unsupervised access to children, the elderly or disabled for whom the qualified entity provides care.

C. Upon receipt of (i) a qualified entity's written request to conduct a background check on a provider, (ii) the provider's fingerprints, and (iii) a completed, signed statement as described in subsection B, the Department shall make a determination whether the provider has been convicted of or is the subject of charges of a barrier crime. To conduct its determination regarding the provider's barrier crime information, the Department shall access the national criminal history background check system, which is maintained by the Federal Bureau of Investigation and is based on fingerprints and other methods of identification, and shall access the Central Criminal Records Exchange maintained by the Department. If the Department receives a background report lacking disposition data, the Department shall conduct research in whatever state and local record-keeping systems are available in order to obtain complete data. The Department shall make reasonable efforts to respond to a qualified entity's inquiry within fifteen business days.

D. Any background check conducted pursuant to this section for a provider employed by a private entity shall be screened by the Department of State Police. If the provider has been convicted of or is under indictment for a barrier crime, the qualified entity shall be notified that the provider is not qualified to work or volunteer in a position that involves unsupervised access to children, the elderly or disabled.

E. Any background check conducted pursuant to this section for a provider employed by a governmental entity shall be provided to that entity.

F. In the case of a provider who desires to volunteer at a qualified entity and who is subject to a national criminal background check, the Department and the Federal Bureau of Investigation may each charge the provider the lesser of eighteen dollars or the actual cost to the entity of the background check conducted with the fingerprints.

G. The failure to request a criminal background check pursuant to subsection B shall not be considered negligence per se in any civil action.

(Added by L.2000 ch. 860, eff. 1/1/2001.)

CHAPTER 23.1
EXPUNGEMENT OF CRIMINAL RECORDS

Section

§19.2-392.1. Statement of policy.

The General Assembly finds that arrest records can be a hindrance to an innocent citizen's ability to obtain employment, an education and to obtain credit. It further finds that the police and court records of those of its citizens who have been absolutely pardoned for crimes for which they have been unjustly convicted can also be a hindrance. This chapter is intended to protect such persons from the unwarranted damage which may occur as a result of being arrested and convicted.

§19.2-392.2. Expungement of police and court records.

A. If a person is charged with the commission of a crime and

1. Is acquitted, or

2. A nolle prosequi is taken or the charge is otherwise dismissed, including dismissal by accord and satisfaction pursuant to §19.2-151, or

3. Is granted an absolute pardon for the commission of a crime for which he has been unjustly convicted,

he may file a petition setting forth the relevant facts and requesting expungement of the police records and the court records relating to the charge.

B. If any person whose name or other identification has been used without his consent or authorization by another person who has been charged or arrested using such name or identification, he may petition the court disposing of the charge for relief pursuant to this section.

C. The petition with a copy of the warrant or indictment if reasonably available shall be filed in the circuit court of the county or city in which the case was disposed of by acquittal or being otherwise dismissed and shall contain, except where not reasonably available, the date of arrest and the name of the arresting agency. Where this information is not reasonably available, the petition shall state the reason for such unavailability. The petition shall further state the specific criminal charge to be expunged, the date of final disposition of the charge as set forth in the petition, the petitioner's date of birth, and the full name used by the petitioner at the time of arrest.

D. A copy of the petition shall be served on the attorney for the Commonwealth of the city or county in which the petition is filed. The attorney for the Commonwealth may file an objection or answer to the petition within twenty-one days after it is served on him.

E. Hearing by court; granting or denial of expungement. The court shall conduct a hearing on the petition. If the court finds that the continued existence and possible dissemination of information relating to the arrest of the petitioner causes or may cause circumstances which constitute a manifest injustice to the petitioner, it shall enter an order requiring the expungement of the police and court records relating to the charge. Otherwise, it shall deny the petition. However, if the petitioner has no prior criminal record and the arrest was for a misdemeanor violation, the petitioner shall be entitled, in the absence of good cause shown to the contrary by the Commonwealth, to expungement of the police and court records relating to the charge, and the court shall enter an order of expungement.

F. The Commonwealth shall be made party defendant to the proceeding. Any party aggrieved by the decision of the court may appeal, as provided by law in civil cases.

G. Notwithstanding any other provision of this section, when the charge is dismissed because the court finds that the person arrested or charged is not the person named in the summons, warrant, indictment or presentment, the court dismissing the charge shall, upon motion of the person improperly arrested or charged, enter an order requiring expungement of the police and court records relating to the charge. Such order shall contain a statement that the dismissal and expungement are ordered pursuant to this subsection. Upon the entry of such order, it shall be treated as provided in subsection H hereof.

H. Upon the entry of an order of expungement, the clerk of the court shall cause a copy of such order to be forwarded to the Department of Criminal Justice Services, which Department shall, pursuant to rules and regulations adopted pursuant to §9-190 of this Code, direct the manner by which the appropriate expungement or removal of such records shall be effected.

I. Costs shall be as provided by §14.1-113, but shall not be recoverable against the Commonwealth.

§19.2-392.3. Disclosure of expunged records.

A. It shall be unlawful for any person having or acquiring access to an expunged court or police record to open or review it or to disclose to another person any information from it without an order from the court which ordered the record expunged.

B. Upon a verified petition filed by the attorney for the Commonwealth alleging that the record is needed by a law-enforcement agency for purposes of employment application as an employee of a law-enforcement agency or for a pending criminal investigation and that the investigation will be jeopardized or that life or property will be endangered without immediate access to the record, the court may enter an ex parte order, without notice to the person, permitting such access. An ex parte order may permit a review of the record, but may not permit a copy to be made of it.

C. Any person who willfully violates this section is guilty of a Class 1 misdemeanor.

§19.2-392.4. Prohibited practices by employers, educational institutions, agencies, etc., of state and local governments.

A. An employer or educational institution shall not, in any application, interview, or otherwise, require an applicant for employment or admission to disclose information concerning any arrest or criminal charge against him that has been expunged. An applicant need not, in answer to any question concerning any arrest or criminal charge that has not resulted in a conviction, include a reference to or information concerning arrests or charges that have been expunged.

B. Agencies, officials, and employees of the state and local governments shall not, in any application, interview, or otherwise, require an applicant for a license, permit, registration, or governmental service to disclose information concerning any arrest or criminal charge against him that has been expunged. An applicant need not, in answer to any question concerning any arrest or criminal charge that has not resulted in a conviction, include a reference to or information concerning charges that have been expunged. Such an application may not be denied solely because of the applicant's refusal to disclose information concerning any arrest or criminal charge against him that has been expunged.

C. A person who willfully violates this section is guilty of a Class 1 misdemeanor for each violation.

CHAPTER 24
INSPECTION WARRANTS

Section

§19.2-393. Definitions.

An "inspection warrant" is an order in writing, made in the name of the Commonwealth, signed by any judge of the circuit court whose territorial jurisdiction encompasses the property or premises to be inspected or entered, and directed to a state or local official, commanding him to enter and to conduct any inspection, testing or collection of samples for testing required or authorized by state or local law or regulation in connection with the manufacturing, emitting or presence of a toxic substance, and which describes, either directly or by reference to any accompanying or attached supporting affidavit, the property or premises where the inspection, testing or collection of samples for testing is to occur. Such warrant shall be sufficiently accurate in description so that the official executing the warrant and the owner or custodian of the property or premises can reasonably determine from the warrant the activity, condition, circumstance, object or property of which inspection, testing or collection of samples for testing is authorized.

For the purposes of this chapter, "manufacturing" means producing, formulating, packaging, or diluting any substance for commercial sale or resale; "emitting" means the release of any substance, whether or not intentional or avoidable, into the work environment, into the air, into the water, or otherwise into the human environment; and "toxic substance" means any substance, including (i) any raw material, intermediate product, catalyst, final product and by-product of any operation conducted in a commercial establishment and (ii) any biological organism, that has the capacity, through its physical, chemical, or biological properties, to pose a substantial risk to humans, aquatic organisms or any other animal of illness, death or impairment of normal functions, either immediately or over a period of time.

§19.2-394. Issuance of warrant.

An inspection warrant may be issued for any inspection, testing or collection of samples for testing or for any administrative search authorized by state or local law or regulation in connection with the presence, manufacturing or emitting of toxic substances, whether or not such warrant be constitutionally required. Nothing in this chapter shall be construed to require issuance of an inspection warrant where a warrant is not constitutionally required or to exclude any other lawful means of search, inspection, testing or collection of samples for testing, whether without warrant or pursuant to a search warrant issued under any other provision of the Code of Virginia. No inspection warrant shall be issued pursuant to this chapter except upon probable cause, supported by affidavit, particularly describing the place, things or persons to be inspected or tested and the purpose for which the inspection, testing or collection of samples for testing is to be made. Probable cause shall be deemed to exist if either reasonable legislative or administrative standards for conducting such inspection, testing or collection of samples for testing are satisfied with respect to the particular place, things or persons or there exists probable cause to believe that there is a condition, object, activity or circumstance which legally justifies such inspection, testing or collection of samples for testing. The supporting affidavit shall contain either a statement that consent to inspect, test or collect samples for testing has been sought and refused or facts or circumstances reasonably justifying the failure to seek such consent in order to enforce effectively the state or local law or regulation which authorizes such inspection, testing or collection of samples for testing. The issuing judge may examine the affiant under oath or affirmation to verify the accuracy of any matter indicated by the statement in the affidavit.

§19.2-395. Duration of warrant.

An inspection warrant shall be effective for the time specified therein, for a period of not more than ten days, unless extended or renewed by the judicial officer who signed and issued the original warrant, upon satisfying himself that such extension or renewal is in the public interest. Such warrant shall be executed and returned to the judicial officer by whom it was issued within the time specified in the warrant or within the extended or renewed time. After the expiration of such time, the warrant, unless executed shall be void.

§19.2-396. Conduct of inspection, testing or collection of samples for testing; special procedure for dwelling.

An inspection, testing or collection of samples for testing pursuant to such warrant may not be made in the absence of the owner, custodian or possessor of the particular place, things or persons unless specifically authorized by the issuing judge upon a showing that such authority is reasonably necessary to effectuate the purpose of the law or regulation being enforced. An entry pursuant to this warrant shall not be made forcibly, except that the issuing judge may expressly authorize a forcible entry where facts are shown sufficient to create a reasonable suspicion of an immediate threat to public health or safety, or where facts are shown establishing that reasonable attempts to serve a previous warrant have been unsuccessful. In the case of entry into a dwelling, prior consent must be sought and refused and notice that a warrant has been issued must be given at least twenty-four hours before the warrant is executed, unless the issuing judge finds that failure to seek consent is justified and that there is a reasonable suspicion of an immediate threat to public health or safety.

§19.2-397. Refusal to permit authorized inspection; penalty.

Any person who willfully refuses to permit an inspection, testing or collection of samples for testing lawfully authorized by warrant issued pursuant to this chapter shall be guilty of a Class 3 misdemeanor.

CHAPTER 25
APPEALS BY THE COMMONWEALTH

§19.2-398. When appeal by the Commonwealth in felony actions allowed.

A. A petition for appeal from a circuit court may be taken by the Commonwealth only in felony cases, before a jury is impaneled and sworn in a jury trial, or before the court begins to hear or receive evidence or the first witness is sworn, whichever occurs first, in a nonjury trial. The appeal may be taken from:

1. An order of a circuit court dismissing a warrant, information or indictment, or any count or charge thereof on the ground that a statute upon which it was based is unconstitutional; or

2. An order of a circuit court prohibiting the use of certain evidence at trial on the grounds such evidence was obtained in violation of the provisions of the Fourth, Fifth or Sixth Amendments to the Constitution of the United States or Article I, Section 8, 10 or 11 of the Constitution of Virginia prohibiting illegal searches and seizures and protecting

rights against self-incrimination, provided the Commonwealth certifies the evidence is essential to the prosecution.

B. A petition for appeal may be taken by the Commonwealth in a felony case from any order of release on conditions pursuant to Article 1 (§19.2-119 et seq.) of Chapter 9 of this title.

C. Nothing in this chapter shall affect the Commonwealth's right to appeal in civil matters or cases involving a violation of law relating to the state revenue or appeals pursuant to §17.1-411 or subsection C of §19.2-317.

(Chgd. by L.1998 ch. 251; L.1999 chs. 829, 846, eff. 7/1/99.)

§19.2-400. Appeal lies to the Court of Appeals; time for filing notice.

An appeal taken pursuant to §19.2-398, including such an appeal in a capital murder case, will lie to the Court of Appeals of Virginia.

No appeal shall be allowed the Commonwealth pursuant to this chapter unless within seven days after entry of the order of the circuit court from which the appeal is taken, and before a jury is impaneled and sworn if there is to be trial by jury or, in cases to be tried without a jury, before the court begins to hear or receive evidence or the first witness is sworn, whichever occurs first, the Commonwealth files a notice of appeal with the clerk of the trial court. If the appeal relates to suppressed evidence, the attorney for the Commonwealth shall certify in the notice of appeal that such evidence is essential to the prosecution. All other requirements related to the notice of appeal shall be governed by Part Five A of the Rules of the Supreme Court. Upon the filing of a timely notice of appeal, the order from which the appeal is taken and further trial proceedings in the circuit court, except for a bail hearing pursuant to §19.2-403, shall thereby be suspended pending disposition of the appeal.

§19.2-401. Cross appeal; when allowed; time for filing.

The defendant shall have no independent right of appeal pursuant to §19.2-398. If the Commonwealth appeals, the defendant may cross appeal from any orders from which the Commonwealth may appeal, pursuant to §19.2-398. The defendant shall be under no obligation to defend an appeal filed by the Commonwealth. However, when an appeal is taken by the Commonwealth, and the defendant wishes to defend or cross appeal, the circuit court shall, where the defendant is indigent, appoint counsel to represent the defendant on appeal. The remuneration to be awarded appointed counsel shall be governed by §19.2-326. The defendant shall file a notice of cross appeal with the clerk of the circuit court within seven days following the notice of appeal filed by the Commonwealth. Any brief on cross appeal shall be consolidated with the defendant's brief as appellee, if any.

§19.2-402. Petition for appeal; brief in opposition; time for filing.

When a notice of appeal has been filed pursuant to §19.2-400, the Commonwealth may petition the Court of Appeals for an appeal pursuant to §19.2-398. The Commonwealth shall be represented by the attorney for the Commonwealth prosecuting the case. The petition for appeal shall be filed with the clerk of the Court of Appeals not more than fourteen days after the date that the transcript or written statement of facts is filed, or if there are objections thereto, within fourteen days after the judge signs the transcript or written statement. The accused may file a brief in opposition with the clerk of the Court of Appeals within fourteen days after the filing of the petition for appeal. If the accused has filed a notice of cross appeal, he shall file a petition for cross appeal to be consolidated with, and filed within the same time period as, his brief in opposition. The Commonwealth may file a brief in opposition to any petition for cross appeal within ten days after the petition for cross appeal is filed. Except as specifically provided in this section, all other requirements for the petition for appeal and brief in opposition shall conform as nearly as practicable to Part Five A of the Rules of the Supreme Court of Virginia.

§19.2-403. Procedures on petition for appeal.

The procedures on an appeal to the Court of Appeals by the Commonwealth pursuant to §19.2-398, and on a cross appeal by the accused pursuant to §19.2-401, shall be governed by the provisions of subsections C and D of §17-116.05:2. The Court of Appeals, however, shall grant or deny the petition for appeal, and the petition for cross appeal, if any, not later than thirty days after the brief in opposition is timely filed or the time for such filing has expired. No petition for rehearing may be filed. If the petition for appeal is denied, the Court's mandate shall immediately issue and the clerk of the Court of Appeals shall return the record forthwith to the clerk of the trial court.

§19.2-404. Procedures on awarded appeal.

If the Court of Appeals grants the Commonwealth's petition for appeal, the Attorney General shall thereafter represent the Commonwealth during that appeal. The Commonwealth shall file its opening brief in the office of the clerk of the Court of Appeals within twenty-five days after the date of the certificate awarding the appeal. The brief of the appellee shall be filed in the office of the clerk of the Court of Appeals within twenty-five days after the filing of the Commonwealth's opening brief. The Commonwealth may then file a reply brief, including its response to any cross appeal, in the office of the clerk of the Court of Appeals within fifteen days after the filing of the brief of the accused. With the permission of a judge of the Court of Appeals, the time for filing any brief may be extended for good cause shown.

Four copies of each brief shall be filed and three copies shall be mailed or delivered to opposing counsel on or before the date of filing. Except as specifically provided in this section, all other requirements of the brief shall conform as nearly as practicable to Part Five A of the Rules of the Supreme Court of Virginia.

The Court of Appeals shall accelerate the appeal on its docket and render its decision not later than sixty days after the filing of the appellee's brief or after the time for filing such brief has expired. When the opinion is rendered by the Court of Appeals, the mandate shall immediately issue and the clerk of the Court of Appeals shall return the record forthwith to the clerk of the trial court. No petition for rehearing may be filed.

§19.2-405. Record on appeal; transcript; written statement; time for filing.

The record on appeal shall conform, as nearly as practicable, to the requirements of Part Five A of the Rules of the Supreme Court for the record on appeal, except as hereinafter provided. The transcript or written statement of facts shall be filed by the Commonwealth with the clerk of the circuit court from which the appeal is being taken, within twenty-five days following entry of the order of the circuit court. Upon motion of the Commonwealth, the Court of Appeals may grant an extension of up to forty-five days for filing the transcript or written statement for good cause shown. If the Commonwealth files a transcript or written statement, it must also file with the clerk of the circuit court a notice, signed by the attorney for the Commonwealth, who is counsel for the appellant, identifying the transcript or written statement and reciting its delivery to the clerk. There shall be appended to the notice a certificate by the attorney for the

Commonwealth that a copy of the notice has been mailed or delivered to opposing counsel.

Any party may object to the transcript or written statement on the ground that it is erroneous or incomplete. Notice of the objection specifying the errors alleged or deficiencies asserted shall be tendered to the trial judge within ten days after the transcript or written statement is filed in the office of the clerk. The trial judge shall, within three days after the filing of such objection, either overrule the objection, or take steps deemed necessary to make the record complete or certify the respect in which the record is incomplete, and sign the transcript or written statement to verify its accuracy. The clerk of the trial court shall forthwith transmit the record to the clerk of the Court of Appeals.

§19.2-406. Bail pending appeal pursuant to §19.2-398.

Upon appeal being taken by the Commonwealth pursuant to §19.2-398, if the defendant moves the trial court for release on bail, that court shall promptly, but in no event later than three days after the Commonwealth's notice of appeal is filed, hold a hearing to determine the issue of bail. The burden shall be upon the Commonwealth to show good cause why the bail should not be reduced or the accused released on his own recognizance. If it is determined that the accused shall be released on bail, bail shall be set and determined in accordance with Article 1 (§19.2-119 et seq.) of Chapter 9 of this title.

(Chgd. by L.1999 chs. 829, 846, eff. 7/1/99.)

§19.2-407. Review by the Supreme Court.

Pursuant to §17-116.06, the Supreme Court in its discretion may certify an appeal taken pursuant to §19.2-398, or a cross appeal taken pursuant to §19.2-401, for expedited review by the Supreme Court before it has been determined by the Court of Appeals. Such certification may be made only when the Supreme Court determines that at least one of the conditions set forth in §17-116.06 B exists.

§19.2-408. Finality of decision of the Court of Appeals.

The decision of the Court of Appeals shall be final for purposes of an appeal pursuant to §19.2-398, or a cross appeal taken pursuant to §19.2-401, and no further pretrial appeal shall lie to the Supreme Court.

§19.2-409. Exclusion of appeal period from time within which accused must be tried; reconsideration of issues after conviction.

The provisions of §19.2-243 shall not apply to the period of time commencing when the Commonwealth's notice of appeal is filed pursuant to this chapter and ending when the Court of Appeals or Supreme Court issues its mandate disposing of the appeal. Such finality of the Court of Appeals decision shall not preclude a defendant, if he is convicted, from requesting the Court of Appeals or Supreme Court on direct appeal to reconsider an issue which was the subject of the pretrial appeal.

TITLE 46.2
MOTOR VEHICLES
(Complete Title)

SUBTITLE I
GENERAL PROVISIONS; DEPARTMENT OF MOTOR VEHICLES

CHAPTER 1
GENERAL PROVISIONS

§46.2-100. Definitions.

The following words and phrases when used in this title shall, for the purpose of this title, have the meanings respectively ascribed to them in this section except in those instances where the context clearly indicates a different meaning:

"Antique motor vehicle" means every motor vehicle, as defined in this section, which was actually manufactured or designated by the manufacturer as a model manufactured in a calendar year not less than twenty-five years prior to January 1 of each calendar year and is owned solely as a collector's item.

"Automobile or watercraft transporters" means any tractor truck, lowboy, vehicle, or combination, including vehicles or combinations which transport motor vehicles or watercraft on their power unit, designed and used exclusively for the transportation of motor vehicles or watercraft.

"Bicycle" means a device propelled solely by human power, having pedals, two or more wheels, and a seat height of more than twenty-five inches from the ground when adjusted to its maximum height. For purposes of Chapter 8 (§46.2-800 et seq.) of this title, a bicycle shall be a vehicle while operated on the highway.

"Business district" means the territory contiguous to a highway where seventy-five percent or more of the property contiguous to a highway, on either side of the highway, for a distance of 300 feet or more along the highway, is occupied by land and buildings actually in use for business purposes.

"Camping trailer" means every vehicle which has collapsible sides and contains sleeping quarters but may or may not contain bathing and cooking facilities and is designed to be drawn by a motor vehicle.

"Cancel" or "cancellation" means that the document or privilege cancelled has been annulled or terminated because of some error, defect, or ineligibility, but the cancellation is without prejudice and reapplication may be made at any time after cancellation.

"Chauffeur" means every person employed for the principal purpose of driving a motor vehicle and every person who drives a motor vehicle while in use as a public or common carrier of persons or property.

"Commission" means the State Corporation Commission.

"Commissioner" means the Commissioner of the Department of Motor Vehicles of the Commonwealth.

"Crosswalk" means that part of a roadway at an intersection included within the connections of the lateral lines of the sidewalks on opposite sides of the highway measured from the curbs or, in the absence of curbs, from the edges of the traversable roadway; or any portion of a roadway at an intersection or elsewhere distinctly indicated for pedestrian crossing by lines or other markings on the surface.

"Decal" means a device to be attached to a license plate that validates the license plate for a predetermined registration period.

"Department" means the Department of Motor Vehicles of the Commonwealth.

"Disabled parking license plate" means a license plate that displays the international symbol of access in the same size as the numbers and letters on the plate and in a color that contrasts with the background.

"Disabled veteran" means a veteran who (i) has either lost, or lost the use of, a leg, arm, or hand; (ii) is blind; or (iii) is permanently and totally disabled as certified by the U.S. Veterans Administration. A veteran shall be considered blind if he has a permanent impairment of both eyes to the following extent: (i) central visual acuity of 20/200 or less in the better eye, with corrective lenses, or central visual acuity of more than 20/200, if there is a field defect in which the peripheral field has contracted to such an extent that the widest diameter of visual field subtends an angular distance no greater than twenty degrees in the better eye.

"Driver's license" means any license, including a commercial driver's license as defined in the Virginia Commercial Driver's License Act (§46.2-341.1 et seq.), issued under the laws of the Commonwealth authorizing the operation of a motor vehicle.

"Essential parts" means all integral parts and body parts, the removal, alteration, or substitution of which will tend to conceal the identity of a vehicle.

"Farm tractor" means every motor vehicle designed and used as a farm, agricultural, or horticultural implement for drawing plows, mowing machines, and other farm, agricultural, or horticultural machinery and implements including self-propelled mowers designed and used for mowing lawns.

"Federal safety requirements" means applicable provisions of the National Traffic and Motor Vehicle Safety Act of 1966 as amended (15 U.S.C. §1381 et seq.) and all administrative regulations and policies adopted pursuant thereto.

"Financial responsibility" means the ability to respond in damages for liability thereafter incurred arising out of the ownership, maintenance, use, or operation of a motor vehicle, in the amounts provided for in §46.2-472.

"Foreign market vehicle" means any motor vehicle originally manufactured outside the United States, which was not manufactured in accordance with the National Traffic and Motor Vehicle Safety Act as amended (15 U.S.C. §1381 et seq.) and the policies and regulations adopted pursuant to that Act, and for which a Virginia title or registration is sought.

"Foreign vehicle" means every motor vehicle, trailer, or semitrailer which is brought into the Commonwealth otherwise than in the ordinary course of business by or through a manufacturer or dealer and which has not been registered in the Commonwealth.

"Golf cart" means a self-propelled vehicle which is designed to transport persons playing golf and their equipment on a golf course.

"Gross weight" means the aggregate weight of a vehicle or combination of vehicles and the load thereon.

"Highway" means the entire width between the boundary lines of every way or place open to the use of the public for purposes of vehicular travel in the Commonwealth, including the streets and alleys, and, for law-enforcement purposes, the entire width between the boundary lines of all private roads or private streets which have been specifically designated "highways" by an ordinance adopted by the governing body of the county, city, or town in which such private roads or streets are located.

"Intersection" means (i) the area embraced within the prolongation or connection of the lateral curblines or, if none, then the lateral boundary lines of the roadways of two highways which join one another at, or approximately at, right angles, or the area within which vehicles traveling on different highways joining at any other angle may come in conflict; (ii) where a highway includes two roadways thirty feet or more apart, then every crossing of each roadway of such divided highway by an intersecting highway shall be regarded as a separate intersection, in the event such intersecting highway also includes two roadways thirty feet or more apart, then every crossing of two roadways of such highways shall be regarded as a separate intersection; or (iii) for purposes only of authorizing installation of traffic-control devices, every crossing of a highway or street at grade by a pedestrian crosswalk.

"Law-enforcement officer" means any officer authorized to direct or regulate traffic or to make arrests for violations of this title or local ordinances authorized by law. For the purposes of access to law-enforcement databases regarding motor vehicle registration and ownership only, this term shall also include city and county commissioners of the revenue and treasurers, together with their duly designated deputies and employees, when such officials are actually engaged in the enforcement of §§46.2-752, 46.2-753 and 46.2-754 and local ordinances enacted thereunder.

"License plate" means a device containing letters, numerals, or a combination of both, attached to a motor vehicle, trailer, or semitrailer to indicate that the vehicle is properly registered with the Department.

"Light" means a device for producing illumination or the illumination produced by the device.

"Manufactured home" means a structure subject to federal regulation, transportable in one or more sections, which in the traveling mode is eight body feet or more in width or forty body feet or more in length, or, when erected on site, is 320 or more square feet, and which is built on a permanent chassis and designed to be used as a dwelling with or without a permanent foundation when connected to the required utilities, and includes the plumbing, heating, air conditioning, and electrical systems contained therein.

"Moped" means a conveyance that is either (i) a bicycle-like device with pedals and a helper motor which is rated at no more than two brake horsepower and which produces speeds up to a maximum of thirty miles per hour or (ii) a motorcycle with an engine displacement of 50 cubic centimeters or less and a maximum speed of less than thirty miles per hour. For purposes of Chapter 8 of this title, a moped shall be a vehicle while operated on a highway.

"Motor home" means every private motor vehicle with a normal seating capacity of not more than ten persons, including the driver, designed primarily for use as living quarters for human beings.

"Motor vehicle" means every vehicle as defined in this section which is self-propelled or designed for self-propulsion except as otherwise provided in this title. Any structure designed, used, or maintained primarily to be loaded on or affixed to a motor vehicle to provide a mobile dwelling, sleeping place, office, or commercial space shall be considered a part of a motor vehicle. For the purposes of this title, any device herein defined as a bicycle or a moped shall be deemed not to be a motor vehicle.

"Motorcycle" means every motor vehicle designed to travel on not more than three wheels in contact with the ground, except any vehicle included within the term "farm tractor" or "moped" as defined in this section.

"Nonresident" means every person who is not domiciled in the Commonwealth, except: (i) any foreign corporation which is authorized to do business in the Commonwealth by the State Corporation Commission shall be a resident of the Commonwealth for the purpose of this title; in the case of corporations incorporated in the Commonwealth but doing business outside the Commonwealth, only such principal place of business or branches located within the Commonwealth shall be dealt with as residents of the Commonwealth; (ii) a person who becomes engaged in a gainful occupation in the Commonwealth for a period exceeding sixty days shall be a resident for the purposes of this title except for the purposes of Chapter 3 (§46.2-300 et seq.) of this title; (iii) a person, other than a nonresident student as defined in this section, who has actually resided in the Commonwealth for a period of six months, whether employed or not, or who has registered a motor vehicle, listing an address in the Commonwealth in the application for registration shall be deemed a resident for the purposes of this title, except for the purposes of the Virginia Commercial Driver's License Act (§46.2-341.1 et seq.).

"Nonresident student" means every nonresident person who is enrolled as a full-time student in an accredited institution of learning in the Commonwealth and who is not gainfully employed.

"Operation or use for rent or for hire, for the transportation of passengers, or as a property carrier for compensation," and "business of transporting persons or property" mean any owner or operator of any motor vehicle, trailer, or semitrailer operating over the highways in the Commonwealth who accepts or receives compensation for the service, directly or indirectly; but these terms do not mean a "truck lessor" as defined in this section and do not include persons or businesses that receive compensation for delivering a product that they themselves sell or produce, where a separate charge is made for delivery of the product or the cost of delivery is included in the sale price of the product, but where the person or business does not derive all or a substantial portion of its income from the transportation of persons or property except as part of a sales transaction.

"Operator" or "driver" means every person who either (i) drives or is in actual physical control of a motor vehicle on a highway or (ii) is exercising control over or steering a vehicle being towed by a motor vehicle.

"Owner" means a person who holds the legal title to a vehicle; however, if a vehicle is the subject of an agreement for its conditional sale or lease with the right of purchase on performance of the conditions stated in the agreement and with an immediate right of possession vested in the conditional vendee or lessee or if a mortgagor of a vehicle is entitled to possession, then the conditional vendee or lessee or mortgagor shall be the owner for the purpose of this title. In all such instances when the rent paid by the lessee includes charges for services of any nature or when the lease does not provide that title shall pass to the lessee on payment of the rent stipulated, the lessor shall be regarded as the owner of the vehicle, and the vehicle shall be subject to such requirements of this title as are applicable to vehicles operated for compensation. A "truck lessor" as defined in this section shall be regarded as the owner, and his vehicles shall be subject to such requirements of this title as are applicable to vehicles of private carriers.

"Passenger car" means every motor vehicle other than a motorcycle designed and used primarily for the transportation of no more than ten persons including the driver.

"Payment device" means any credit card as defined in 15 U.S.C. §1602(k) or any "accepted card or other means of access" set forth in 15 U.S.C. §1693(a)(1). For the purposes of this title, this definition shall also include a card that enables a person to pay for transactions through the use of value stored on the card itself.

"Pickup or panel truck" means every motor vehicle designed for the transportation of property and having a registered gross weight of 7,500 pounds or less.

"Private road or driveway" means every way in private ownership and used for vehicular travel by the owner and those having express or implied permission from the owner, but not by other persons.

"Reconstructed vehicle" means every vehicle of a type required to be registered under this title materially altered from its original construction by the removal, addition, or substitution of new or used essential parts.

"Residence district" means the territory contiguous to a highway, not comprising a business district, where seventy-five percent or more of the property abutting such highway, on either side of the highway, for a distance of 300 feet or more along the highway consists of land improved for dwelling purposes, or is occupied by dwellings, or consists of land or buildings in use for business purposes.

"Revoke" or "revocation" means that the document or privilege revoked is not subject to renewal or restoration except through reapplication after the expiration of the period of revocation.

"Roadway" means that portion of a highway improved, designed, or ordinarily used for vehicular travel, exclusive of the shoulder. A highway may include two or more roadways if divided by a physical barrier or barriers or an unpaved area.

"Safety zone" means the area officially set apart within a roadway for the exclusive use of pedestrians and which is protected or is so marked or indicated by plainly visible signs.

"School bus" means any motor vehicle, other than a station wagon, automobile, truck, or commercial bus, which is: (i) designed and used primarily for the transportation of pupils to and from public, private or parochial schools, or used for the transportation of the mentally or physically handicapped to and from a sheltered workshop; (ii) painted yellow and bears the words "School Bus" in black letters of a specified size on front and rear; and (iii) is equipped with warning devices prescribed in §46.2-1090. A yellow school bus may have a white roof provided such vehicle is painted in accordance with regulations promulgated by the Department of Education.

"Semitrailer" means every vehicle of the trailer type so designed and used in conjunction with a motor vehicle that some part of its own weight and that of its own load rests on or is carried by another vehicle.

"Shoulder" means that part of a highway between the portion regularly traveled by vehicular traffic and the lateral curbline or ditch.

"Snowmobile" means a self-propelled vehicle designed to travel on snow or ice, steered by skis or runners, and supported in whole or in part by one or more skis, belts, or cleats.

"Specially constructed vehicle" means any vehicle which was not originally constructed under a distinctive name, make, model, or type by a generally recognized manufacturer of vehicles and not a reconstructed vehicle as herein defined.

"Stinger-steered automobile or watercraft transporter" means an automobile or watercraft transporter configured as a semitrailer combination wherein the fifth wheel is located on a drop frame behind and below the rearmost axle of the power unit.

"Superintendent" means the Superintendent of the Department of State Police of the Commonwealth.

"Suspend" or "suspension" means that the document or privilege suspended has been temporarily withdrawn, but may be reinstated following the period of suspension unless it has expired prior to the end of the period of suspension.

"Towing and recovery operator" means a person engaged in the business of (i) removing disabled vehicles, parts of vehicles, their cargoes, and other objects to facilities for repair or safekeeping and (ii) restoring to the highway or other location where they either can be operated or removed to other locations for repair or safekeeping vehicles which have come to rest in places where they cannot be operated.

"Tractor truck" means every motor vehicle designed and used primarily for drawing other vehicles and not so constructed as to carry a load other than a part of the load and weight of the vehicle attached thereto.

"Traffic infraction" means a violation of law punishable as provided in §46.2-113, which is neither a felony nor a misdemeanor.

"Traffic lane" or "lane" means that portion of a roadway designed or designated to accommodate the forward movement of a single line of vehicles.

"Trailer" means every vehicle without motive power designed for carrying property or passengers wholly on its own structure and for being drawn by a motor vehicle, including manufactured homes.

"Truck" means every motor vehicle designed to transport property on its own structure independent of any other vehicle and having a registered gross weight in excess of 7,500 pounds.

"Truck lessor" means a person who holds the legal title to any motor vehicle, trailer, or semitrailer which is the subject of a bona fide written lease for a term of one year or more to another person, provided that: (i) neither the lessor nor the lessee is a common carrier by motor vehicle or restricted common carrier by motor vehicle or contract carrier by motor vehicle as defined in §46.2-2000; (ii) the leased motor vehicle, trailer, or semitrailer is used exclusively for the transportation of property of the lessee; (iii) the lessor is not employed in any capacity by the lessee; (iv) the operator of the leased motor vehicle is a bona fide employee of the lessee and is not employed in any capacity by the lessor; and (v) a true copy of the lease, verified by affidavit of the lessor, is filed with the Commissioner.

"Vehicle" means every device in, on or by which any person or property is or may be transported or drawn on a highway, except devices moved by human power or used exclusively on stationary rails or tracks. For the purposes of Chapter 8 of this title, bicycles and mopeds shall be vehicles while operated on a highway.

"Wheel chair or wheel chair conveyance" means a chair or seat equipped with wheels, typically used to provide mobility for persons who, by reason of physical disability, are otherwise unable to move about as pedestrians. The term includes both three-wheeled and four-wheeled devices. So long as it is operated only as provided in §46.2-677, a self-propelled wheel chair or self-propelled wheel chair conveyance shall not be considered a motor vehicle.

(Chgd. by L.1996 chs. 943, 994; L.1997 chs. 9, 186, 486, 783, 904; L.1998 ch. 888; L.1999 chs. 67, 77, eff. 7/1/99.)

§46.2-101. Applicability of title to vehicles on certain toll roads and parking facilities.

This title shall apply to any vehicle and any person operating or owning a vehicle operated on any toll facility controlled by the Department of Transportation or any political subdivision of the Commonwealth.

This title shall also apply to any vehicle and any person operating or owning a vehicle operated on or in parking lots, parking garages, or other parking facilities owned, controlled, or leased by the Commonwealth or any of its agencies, instrumentalities, or political subdivisions.

§46.2-102. Enforcement by law-enforcement officers; officers to be uniformed; officers to be paid fixed salaries.

State police officers and law-enforcement officers of every county, city, town, or other political subdivision of the Commonwealth shall enforce the provisions of this title punishable as felonies, misdemeanors, or traffic infractions. Additionally, notwithstanding §52-22, state police officers may enforce local ordinances, adopted under subsection G of §46.2-752, requiring the obtaining and displaying of local motor vehicle licenses. Fifty percent of the revenue collected from such enforcement shall be remitted by the locality to the Department of State Police and disposed of by the Department to cover its costs of operation. Every law-enforcement officer shall be uniformed at the time of the enforcement or shall display his badge or other sign of authority. All officers making arrests incident to the enforcement of this title shall be paid fixed salaries for their services and shall have no interest in, nor be permitted by law to accept the benefit of, any fine or fee resulting from the arrest or conviction of an offender against any provision of this title.

With the consent of the landowner, any such officer or other uniformed employee of the local law-enforcement agency may patrol the landowner's property to enforce state, county, city, or town motor vehicle registration and licensing requirements.

Any law-enforcement officer may patrol the streets and roads within subdivisions of real property or within land submitted to a horizontal property regime pursuant to Chapter 4.1 (§55-79.1 et seq.) or 4.2 (§55-79.39 et seq.) of Title 55, which streets and roads are maintained by the owners of the lots or parcels of land within the subdivision or the owners of condominium units within any horizontal property regime or any association of owners, on the request or with the consent of the owners or association of owners, to enforce the provisions of this title punishable as felonies, misdemeanors, or traffic infractions.

(Chgd. by L.1995 ch. 132, eff. 7/1/95.)

§46.2-103. Stopping vehicles for inspection or to secure information.

Except as prohibited by §19.2-59, on his request or signal, any law-enforcement officer who is in uniform or displays his badge or other sign of authority may:

1. Stop any motor vehicle, trailer, or semitrailer to inspect its equipment, operation, manufacturer's serial or engine number; or
2. Stop any property-carrying motor vehicle, trailer, or semitrailer to inspect its contents or load or to obtain other necessary information.

§46.2-104. Possession of registration cards; exhibiting registration card and licenses; failure to carry license or registration card.

The operator of any motor vehicle, trailer, or semitrailer being operated on the highways in the Commonwealth, shall have in his possession: (i) the registration card issued by the Department or the registration card issued by the state or country in which the motor vehicle, trailer, or semitrailer is registered, and (ii) his driver's license, learner's permit, or temporary driver's permit.

The owner or operator of any motor vehicle, trailer, or semitrailer shall stop on the signal of any law-enforcement officer who is in uniform or shows his badge or other sign of authority and shall, on the officer's request, exhibit his registration card, driver's license, learner's permit, or temporary driver's permit and write his name in the presence of the officer, if so required, for the purpose of establishing his identity.

Every person licensed by the Department as a driver or issued a learner's or temporary driver's permit who fails to carry his license or permit, and the registration card for the vehicle which he operates, shall be guilty of a traffic infraction and upon conviction punished by a fine of ten dollars. However, if any person summoned to appear before a court for failure to display his license, permit, or registration card presents to the officer issuing the summons or a magistrate of the county or city in which the summons was issued, before the return date of the summons, a license or permit issued to him prior to the time the summons was issued or a registration card, as the case may be, or appears pursuant to the summons and produces before the court a license or permit issued to him prior to the time the summons was issued or a registration card, as the case may be, he shall have complied with the provisions of this section.

§46.2-105. Making false affidavit or swearing falsely, perjury.

Any person who knowingly makes any false affidavit or knowingly swears or affirms falsely to any matter or thing required by this title or the Commissioner incidental to his administration of this title to be sworn to or affirmed shall be guilty of perjury.

§46.2-105.1. Unlawful procurement of certificate, license or permit; unauthorized possession of examination or answers; penalty.

A. It shall be unlawful:

1. For any person to procure, or assist another to procure, through theft, fraud or other illegal means, a certificate, license or permit, from the Department of Motor Vehicles;
2. For any person, other than an authorized agent of the Department of Motor Vehicles, to procure or have in his possession or furnish to another person, prior to the beginning of an examination, any question intended to be used by the Department of Motor Vehicles in conducting an examination;

 Zv

3. For any person to receive or furnish to any person taking an examination, prior to or during an examination, any written or printed material purporting to be answers to questions intended to be used by the Department of Motor Vehicles in conducting an examination;

4. For any person to attempt to procure, through theft, fraud or other illegal means, any questions intended to be used by the Department of Motor Vehicles in conducting an examination, or the answers to the questions; or

5. To promise or offer any valuable or other consideration to a person having access to the questions or answers as an inducement to procure for delivery to the promisor, or any other person, a copy or copies of any questions or answers.

B. If an examination is divided into separate parts, each of the parts shall be deemed an examination for the purposes of this section.

C. Any violation of any provision of subsection A of this section shall be punishable as a Class 2 misdemeanor.

§46.2-105.2. Obtaining documents from the Department when not entitled thereto; penalty.

A. It shall be unlawful for any person to obtain a Virginia driver's license, special identification card, vehicle registration, certificate of title, or other document issued by the Department if such person has not satisfied all legal and procedural requirements for the issuance thereof, or is otherwise not legally entitled thereto.

B. It shall be unlawful to aid any person to obtain any driver's license, special identification card, vehicle registration, certificate of title, or other document in violation of the provisions of subsection A.

C. It shall be unlawful to knowingly possess or use for any purpose any driver's license, special identification card, vehicle registration, certificate of title, or other document obtained in violation of the provisions of subsection A.

D. A violation of any provision of this section shall constitute a Class 2 misdemeanor; however, if a person is charged and convicted of a violation of subsection B which involved aid to five or more persons, such offense shall constitute a Class 4 felony.

E. Whenever it appears to the satisfaction of the Commissioner that any driver's license, special identification card, vehicle registration, certificate of title, or other document issued by the Department has been obtained in violation of this section, it may be cancelled by the Commissioner, who shall mail notice of the cancellation to the address of record maintained by the Department.

§46.2-106. Reciprocity Board; reciprocal agreements entered into by Governor.

The Reciprocity Board, hereinafter called the Board, is hereby created. The Board shall consist of three ex officio members: the Commissioner of the Department of Motor Vehicles, the Commonwealth Transportation Commissioner, and one of the members of the State Corporation Commission. A majority of the members of the Board shall constitute a quorum and the action of the majority of the members in attendance at any meeting shall be the action of the Board. Whenever a member of the Board is absent from a meeting of the Board, he may designate one of his assistants or employees to attend on his behalf. The assistant or employee shall be entitled to participate in the discussion and proceedings of the Board, but he shall not vote.

The Governor may, with the advice of the Board, enter into reciprocal agreements on behalf of the Commonwealth with the appropriate authorities of any state of the United States with respect to all taxes imposed by the Commonwealth and by any other state of the United States on motor vehicles, the operation of motor vehicles, or any transaction incident to the operation of motor vehicles.

Except as provided in this section, all agreements entered into by the Governor with respect to any subject of reciprocity as to which provision is expressly made by statute shall conform to the provisions of that statute. As to any other subject of reciprocity appropriate to the powers vested in the Governor by this section, the Governor may, with the advice of the Board, agree to whatever terms and conditions as in his judgment are best calculated to promote the interests of the Commonwealth. Except as provided in this section, it is the policy of the Commonwealth to grant reciprocity to the residents of another state when that state grants reciprocity to the residents of the Commonwealth.

All agreements entered into by the Governor pursuant to this section shall be reduced to writing, and a copy shall be furnished to the Secretary of the Commonwealth, each member of the Reciprocity Board, and the Superintendent of State Police.

(Chgd. by L.1995 chs. 744, 803, eff. 7/1/95.)

§46.2-107. Lists of vehicles used for rent or hire, or by contract carriers.

Every person engaged in hiring or renting motor vehicles for the transportation of passengers or property and every contract carrier by motor vehicle of passengers or property who operates, or who should operate, under a permit issued by the State Corporation Commission or by the Interstate Commerce Commission, as provided by law, shall furnish to the Commissioner, whenever required to do so, a list and description of motor vehicles used in his business.

§46.2-108. Records required of persons renting motor vehicles without drivers; inspections; insurance.

A. Every person engaged in the business of renting motor vehicles without drivers who rents any vehicle without a driver, otherwise than as a part of a bona fide transaction involving the sale of the motor vehicle, shall maintain a record of the identity of the person to whom the vehicle is rented and the exact time the vehicle is the subject of the rental or in possession of the person renting and having the use of the vehicle. These records shall be public records and open to inspection by any person damaged as to his person or property by the operation of the vehicle or by law-enforcement personnel in the discharge of their duties. Any person who has been damaged as to his person or property may require a production of the written record in person or by his authorized agent or attorney.

B. It shall be unlawful for any person who rents a motor vehicle as provided in this section to fail to make or have in possession or to refuse an inspection of the record required in this section.

C. The Commissioner shall prescribe and the owner shall use the form for the keeping of the record provided in this section.

D. No person engaged in the business of renting automobiles and trucks without drivers shall rent any vehicle without a driver unless the vehicle is an insured motor vehicle as defined in §46.2-705. A violation of this subsection shall constitute a Class 1 misdemeanor.

§46.2-109. Reports by persons in charge of garages and repair shops; vehicles equipped with bullet-proof glass or smoke projectors or struck by bullets.

The person in charge of any garage or repair shop to which is brought any motor vehicle equipped with bullet-proof glass or any smoke screen device or that shows evidence of having been struck by a bullet shall report in writing, on forms furnished by the Superintendent of State Police, to the nearest police station or to the State Police, within twenty-four hours after the motor vehicle is received, the engine number, registration number, serial number or identification number, and the name and address of the owner or operator of the vehicle if known.

§46.2-110. Right to inspect vehicles in garages.

Any law-enforcement officer or Department officer or employee who is in uniform or exhibits a badge or other sign of authority shall have the right to inspect any motor vehicle, trailer, or semitrailer in any public garage or repair shop for the purpose of locating stolen motor vehicles, trailers, and semitrailers and for investigating the title and registration of motor vehicles, trailers, and semitrailers. For this purpose the owner of any garage or repair shop shall permit any law-enforcement officer or Department officer or employee freely to make investigation as authorized in this section.

§46.2-111. Flares and other signals relating to disabled vehicles.

A. Whenever any bus, truck, trailer, house trailer, or manufactured home is disabled and stops on any roadway in the Commonwealth, except within the corporate limits of cities or on highways which are artificially lighted at night, at any time during which lights are required on motor vehicles by §46.2-1030, the operator of such vehicle shall place or cause to be placed on the roadway three red flares or torches of a type approved by the Superintendent. One of the flares or torches shall be placed in the center of the lane of traffic occupied by the disabled vehicle and not less than 100 feet therefrom in the direction of traffic approaching in that lane, a second not less than 100 feet from such vehicle in the opposite direction and a third at the traffic side of such vehicle not closer than ten feet from its front or rear. However, if such vehicle is disabled within 500 feet of a curve or crest of a hill, or other obstruction to view, the flares or torches in that direction shall be so placed as to afford ample warning to other users of the highway, but in no case less than 500 feet from the disabled vehicle. Red reflectorized triangular warning devices of a type approved by the Superintendent may be used in lieu of flares or torches.

The exception provided in this subsection with respect to highways within the corporate limits of cities or on streets or highways which are artificially lighted at night shall not apply to any portion of any interstate highway within the corporate limits of any city.

B. If any such vehicle is used for the transportation of flammable liquids in bulk, whether loaded or empty, or for transporting inflammable gases, red flares or red electric lanterns of a type approved by the Superintendent of State Police shall be used. Such reflectors or lanterns shall be lighted and placed on the roadway in the manner provided in subsection A of this section.

C. During such time as lights on motor vehicles are not required, red flags not less than twelve inches both in length and width shall be used in the place of flares, torches, or lanterns. The flags shall be placed on the roadway in the manner prescribed in subsections A and B of this section for flares, torches, and lanterns, except that no flag shall be required to be placed at the side of such vehicle. If the disablement of such vehicle continues into the period when lights on motor vehicles are required, flares, torches, reflectors, or lanterns shall be placed as required by subsections A and B of this section. Red reflectorized triangular warning devices of a type approved by the Superintendent may be used in lieu of flags.

(Chgd. by L.1999 ch. 77, eff. 7/1/99.)

§46.2-112. Tampering with odometer; penalty; civil liability.

A. It shall be unlawful to knowingly cause, either personally or through an agent, the changing, tampering with, disconnection, or nonconnection of any odometer or similar device designed to show by numbers or words the distance which a motor vehicle has traveled or the use it has sustained.

B. It shall be unlawful for any person to sell a motor vehicle if he knows or should reasonably know that the odometer or similar device of the motor vehicle has been changed, tampered with, or disconnected to reflect a lesser mileage or use, unless he gives clear and unequivocal notice of such tampering, etc., or of his reasonable belief thereof, to the purchaser in writing prior to the sale. In a prosecution under this subsection, evidence that a person or his agent has changed, tampered with, disconnected, or failed to connect an odometer or similar device of a motor vehicle shall constitute prima facie evidence of knowledge thereof.

C. It shall be unlawful for any person to advertise for sale, sell, or use any device designed primarily for the purpose of resetting the odometer or similar device of a motor vehicle in any manner.

D. The provisions of this section shall not apply to the following:

1. The changing of odometer or similar device readings registered in the course of predelivery testing of any motor vehicle by its manufacturer prior to its delivery to a dealer.
2. Any necessary repair or replacement of an odometer or similar device, provided that the repaired or replaced odometer or similar device is forthwith set at a reading determined by the reading on the device immediately prior to repair or replacement plus a bona fide estimate of the use of the vehicle sustained between the period when the device ceased to accurately record that use and the time of repair or replacement.
3. Passenger vehicles having a capacity in excess of fifteen persons.
4. Trucks having a net weight in excess of 10,000 pounds.

E. Any person convicted of a violation of the provisions of subsections A through D of this section shall, for a first offense, be fined not more than $10,000 and sentenced to a term of confinement in jail for not more than twelve months, either or both. Any person convicted of a subsequent offense under this section shall be fined not more than $50,000 and sentenced to a term of confinement in a state correctional facility for not less than one year nor more than five years, either or both, for each offense if the offense is committed with the intent thereby to defraud another. Each violation of this section shall constitute a separate offense.

F. Any person who with intent to defraud violates subsection A or B of this section shall be liable in a civil action in an amount equal to three times the amount of actual damages sustained or $1,500, whichever is greater. In the case of a successful action to enforce the foregoing liability, the costs of the action, together with reasonable attorney fees as determined by the court, shall be assessed against the person committing the violation. An action under this subsection shall be brought within two years from the date on which liability arises. For the purpose of this subsection, liability arises when the injured party discovers, or with due diligence should have discovered, the violation.

§46.2-113. Violations of this title; penalties.

It shall be unlawful for any person to violate any of the provisions of this title, or any regulation adopted pursuant to this title, or local ordinances adopted pursuant to the authority granted in §46.2-1300. Unless otherwise stated, these violations shall constitute traffic infractions punishable by a fine of not more than $200.

If it is found by the judge of a court of proper jurisdiction that the violation of any provision of this title (i) was a serious traffic violation as defined in §46.2-341.20 and (ii) that such violation was committed while operating a vehicle or combination of vehicles used to transport property that

either: (a) has a gross vehicle weight rating of 26,001 or more pounds or (b) has a gross combination weight rating of 26,001 or more pounds inclusive of a towed vehicle with a gross vehicle weight rating of more than 10,000 pounds, the judge may assess, in addition to any other penalty assessed, a further monetary penalty not exceeding $500.
(Chgd. by L.1997 ch. 637, eff. 7/1/97.)

§46.2-114. Disposition of fines and forfeitures.

All fines or forfeitures collected on conviction or on a forfeiture of bail of any person charged with a violation of any of the provisions of this title punishable as felonies, misdemeanors, or traffic infractions shall be paid into the state treasury to be credited to the Literary Fund unless a different form of payment is required specifically by this title.

§46.2-115. Inapplicability of title on Tangier Island; adoption of local ordinances; penalties.

Except for this section, no provisions of this title shall apply in the Town of Tangier.

The council of the Town of Tangier may adopt such ordinances paralleling any provision of this title and adapt their provisions to suit the Town's unique situation. No penalty for any violation of such ordinance, however, shall exceed the penalty imposed for a violation of the parallel provision of this title.
(Added by L.1995 ch. 670, eff. 7/1/95.)

CHAPTER 2
DEPARTMENT OF MOTOR VEHICLES

Article

ARTICLE 1
POWERS AND DUTIES OF DEPARTMENT, GENERALLY

Section

§46.2-200. Department of Motor Vehicles.

There shall be a Department of Motor Vehicles in the executive department, responsible to the Secretary of Transportation. The Department shall be under the supervision and management of the Commissioner of the Department of Motor Vehicles.

The Department shall be responsible for the administration of the motor vehicle license, registration and title laws; the issuance, suspension, and revocation of driver's licenses; the examination of applicants for and holders of driver's licenses; the administration, training, disciplining, and assignment of examiners of applicants for driver's licenses; the administration of the safety responsibility laws, fuel tax laws, the provisions of this title relating to transportation safety, and dealer licensing laws; the registration of carriers of passengers or property and vehicles that may be required to be registered under the International Registration Plan or pay road tax as described under Chapter 27 (§58.1-2700 et seq.) of Title 58.1 under the International Fuel Tax Agreement; the audit of carriers of passengers or property for compliance with registration and road tax requirements; proof of financial responsibility; and any other services that may be required to create a single point of contact for motor carriers operating within and without the Commonwealth.
(Chgd. by L.1995 chs. 744, 803; L.1997 ch. 283, eff. 7/1/97.)

§46.2-201. Appointment of Commissioner; term; vacancies.

The Commissioner shall be appointed by the Governor, subject to confirmation by the General Assembly, if in session when such appointment is made and if not in session, then at its next succeeding session. He shall hold his office at the pleasure of the Governor for a term coincident with that of each Governor making the appointment or until his successor shall be appointed and qualified. Vacancies shall be filled for the unexpired term in the same manner as original appointments are made.

§46.2-202. Oath and bond; salary.

The Commissioner, before entering on the discharge of his duties, shall take an oath that he will faithfully and impartially discharge all the duties of his office and he shall give bond in such penalty as may be fixed by the Governor, conditioned on the faithful discharge of his duties. The premium on the bond shall be paid out of the funds available for the maintenance and operation of his office. The Commissioner shall receive the salary appropriated for the purpose.

§46.2-203. Regulations; violation; forms for applications, certificates, licenses, etc.

Subject to the provisions of Chapter 1.1:1 (§9-6.14:1 et seq.) of Title 9, the Commissioner may adopt reasonable administrative regulations necessary to carry out the laws administered by the Department and may enforce these regulations and laws through the agencies of the Commonwealth he may designate. A violation of any such regulation shall constitute a Class 4 misdemeanor. He shall also provide suitable forms for applications, certificates of title, registration cards, license plates, and driver's licenses. Unless otherwise required in this title, he shall provide all other forms requisite for the purpose of this title.

§46.2-203.1. Provision of updated addresses by persons completing forms; acknowledgment of future receipt of official notices.

Whenever any person completes a form for an application, certificate of title, registration card, license plate, driver's license, and any other form requisite for the purpose of this title, or whenever any person is issued a summons for a violation of the motor vehicle laws of the Commonwealth, he shall provide his current address on the form or summons. By signing the form or summons, the person acknowledges that (i) the address is correct, (ii) any official notice, including an order of suspension, will be sent by prepaid first class mail to the address on the signed form with the most current date, and (iii) the notice shall be deemed to have been accepted by the person at that address. In addition, upon signing a summons for a violation of the motor vehicle laws, the person shall acknowledge that his failure to appear in court and pay fines and costs could result in suspension of his operator's license.

§46.2-204. Medical Advisory Board.

For the purpose of enabling the Department of Motor Vehicles to comply with its responsibilities under this title, there is hereby created a Medical Advisory Board for the Department. The Board shall consist of seven licensed physicians currently practicing medicine in Virginia appointed by the Governor. Appointments to the Board shall be for four-year terms and vacancies shall be filled by appointment for the unexpired portion of a term. The Governor shall designate the chairman of the Board.

The Commissioner may refer to the Board for an advisory opinion the case of any person applying for a driver's license or renewal thereof, or of any person whose license has been suspended or revoked, or of any person being examined under the provisions of §46.2-322, when he has cause to believe that such person suffers from a physical or mental disability or disease which will prevent his exercising reasonable and ordinary control over a motor vehicle while driving it on the highways. In addition, the Board shall assist the Commissioner through the development of medical and health standards for use in the issuance of driver's licenses by the Department to avoid the issuance of licenses to persons suffering from any physical or mental disability or disease that will prevent their exercising reasonable and ordinary control over a motor vehicle while driving it on the highways.

The Board shall meet at the pleasure of the Commissioner. Each member shall serve without compensation but shall be reimbursed for his necessary expenses from funds appropriated to the Department of Motor Vehicles.

§46.2-205. Department offices and agencies.

The Commissioner shall maintain his office in the Commonwealth at a location which he determines to be appropriate. He may appoint agents and maintain branch offices in the Commonwealth in whatever locations he determines to be necessary to carry out this title.

The personnel of each branch office and each agency shall be appointed by the Commissioner and shall be bonded in an amount fixed by the Commissioner. The person in charge of the branch office and each agency shall deposit daily in the local bank, or at such other intervals as may be designated by the Commissioner, to the account of the State Treasurer, all moneys collected, and shall submit daily to the Commissioner, or at such other intervals as may be designated by the Commissioner, a complete record of what each deposit is intended to cover. The Commissioner shall not be held liable in the event of the loss of any moneys collected by such agents resulting from their failure to deposit such money to the account of the State Treasurer.

The compensation of the personnel of each branch office and each agency is to be fixed by the Commissioner. The compensation fixed for each nonautomated agency for the purpose of maintaining adequate annual service to the public shall be three and one-half percent of the first $500,000 of gross collections made by the agency, two percent of the next $500,000 of gross collections made by the agency, and one percent of all gross collections in excess of $1,000,000 made by the agency during each fiscal year.

The compensation fixed for each automated agency for the purpose of maintaining adequate annual service to the public shall be three and one-half percent of the first $1,000,000 of gross collections made by the agency and one percent of all gross collections in excess of $1,000,000 made by the agency during each fiscal year.

The compensation awarded shall belong to the agents for their services under this section, and the Commissioner shall cause to be paid all freight, cartage, premium on bond and postage, but not any extra clerk hire or other expenses occasioned by their duties.

(Chgd. by L.1999 ch. 308, eff. 7/1/99.)

§46.2-206. Disposition of fees.

Except as otherwise provided in this title, all fees and moneys collected pursuant to the provisions of Chapters 1, 2, 3, 6, 8, 10, 12, and 16 through 26 of this title shall be paid into the state treasury, and warrants for the expenditure of funds necessary for the proper enforcement of this title shall be issued by the Comptroller on certificates of the Commissioner or his representatives, designated by him and bonded, that the parties are entitled thereto, and shall be paid by the State Treasurer out of such funds, not exceeding the amount appropriated in the general appropriation bill.

These funds, except as is otherwise provided in this section, shall constitute special funds within the Commonwealth Transportation Fund to be expended (i) under the direction of the Commonwealth Transportation Commissioner for the construction, reconstruction, and maintenance of roads and bridges in the state highway system, interstate system, and secondary system of state highways and (ii) as authorized by the Commissioner for the expenses incident to the maintenance of the Department, including its customer service centers, and for other expenses incurred in the enforcement of this title. Any funds available for construction or reconstruction under the provisions of this section shall be, as nearly as possible, equitably apportioned by the Commonwealth Transportation Commission among the several construction districts. Beginning July 1, 1998, any balances remaining in these funds at the end of the fiscal year shall be available for use in subsequent years for the purposes set forth in this section, and any interest income on such funds shall accrue to the respective individual special funds.

There may be paid out of these funds such sums as may be provided by law for (i) contributions toward the construction, reconstruction, and maintenance of streets in cities or towns and (ii) the operation and maintenance of the Department of Transportation, the Department of Rail and Public Transportation, the Department of Aviation, the Virginia Port Authority, the Department of State Police, and the Department of Motor Vehicles.

(Chgd. by L.1997 ch. 423, eff. 7/1/97.)

§46.2-207. Uncollected checks tendered for license fees or taxes.

If any bank on which an uncertified check tendered to the Department or to any agent acting on behalf of the Department refuses payment on the check due to insufficient funds in the account of the drawer, no account in the name of the drawer, or account of the drawer closed, and the check shall be returned to the Department or agent unpaid, there shall be a penalty of twenty-five dollars or ten percent of the amount of the check, whichever is greater, imposed on the person from whom the payment is due the Department. This penalty shall apply to checks tendered for any fee or tax required or authorized to be collected by the Department and shall be in addition to any other penalties imposed by the Motor Vehicle Laws of Virginia, except in a case where there is a specific penalty set forth by statute for the nonpayment or late payment of fees or taxes, in which case this section shall apply only in the amount it exceeds the specific penalty. All moneys collected by the Commissioner from the penalties imposed under this section shall be paid into the state treasury and set aside as a special fund to be used to meet the expenses of the Department of Motor Vehicles.

§46.2-208. Records of Department; when open for inspection; release of privileged information.

A. All records in the office of the Department containing the specific classes of information outlined below shall be considered privileged records:

1. Personal information, including all data defined as "personal information" in §2.1-379;

2. Driver information, including all data that relates to driver's license status and driver activity; and

3. Vehicle information, including all descriptive vehicle data and title, registration, and vehicle activity data.

B. The Commissioner shall release such information only under the following conditions:

1. Notwithstanding other provisions of this section, medical data included in personal data shall be released only to a physician as provided in §46.2-322.

2. Insurance data may be released as specified in §§46.2-372, 46.2-380, and 46.2-706.

3. Notwithstanding other provisions of this section, information disclosed or furnished shall be assessed a fee as specified in §46.2-214.

4. When the person requesting the information is (i) the subject of the information, (ii) the parent or guardian of the subject of the information, (iii) the authorized representative of the subject of the information, or (iv) the owner of the vehicle that is the subject of the information, the Commissioner shall provide him with the requested information and a complete explanation of it. Requests for such information need not be made in writing or in person and may be made orally or by telephone, provided that the Department is satisfied that there is adequate verification of the requester's identity. When so requested in writing by (i) the subject of the information, (ii) the parent or guardian of the subject of the information, (iii) the authorized representative of the subject of the information, or (iv) the owner of the vehicle that is the subject of the information, the Commissioner shall verify and, if necessary, correct the personal information provided and furnish driver and vehicle information in the form of an abstract of the record.

5. On the written request of any insurance carrier, surety, or representative of an insurance carrier or surety, the Commissioner shall furnish such insurance carrier, surety, or representative an abstract of the record of any person subject to the provisions of this title. The abstract shall include any record of any conviction of a violation of any provision of any statute or ordinance relating to the operation or ownership of a motor vehicle or of any injury or damage in which he was involved and a report of which is required by §46.2-372. No such report of any conviction or accident shall be made after sixty months from the date of the conviction or accident unless the Commissioner or court used the conviction or accident as a reason for the suspension or revocation of a driver's license or driving privilege, in which case the revocation or suspension and any conviction or accident pertaining thereto shall not be reported after sixty months from the date that the driver's license or driving privilege has been reinstated. This abstract shall not be admissible in evidence in any court proceedings.

6. On the written request of any business organization or its agent, in the conduct of its business, the Commissioner shall compare personal information supplied by the business organization or agent with that contained in the Department's records and, when the information supplied by the business organization or agent is different from that contained in the Department's records, provide the business organization or agent with correct information as contained in the Department's records. Personal information provided under this subdivision shall be used solely for the purpose of pursuing remedies which require locating an individual.

7. The Commissioner shall provide vehicle information to any business organization or agent on such business' or agent's written request. Disclosures made under this subdivision shall not include any personal information and shall not be subject to the limitations contained in subdivision 6 of this subsection.

8. On the written request of any motor vehicle rental or leasing company or its designated agent, the Commissioner shall (i) compare personal information supplied by the company or agent with that contained in the Department's records and, when the information supplied by the company or agent is different from that contained in the Department's records, provide the company or agent with correct information as contained in the Department's records and (ii) provide the company or agent with driver information in the form of an abstract of any person subject to the provisions of this title. Such abstract shall include any record of any conviction of a violation of any provision of any statute or ordinance relating to the operation or ownership of a motor vehicle or of any injury or damage in which the subject of the abstract was involved and a report of which is required by §46.2-372. No such abstract shall include any record of any conviction or accident more than sixty months after the date of such conviction or accident unless the Commissioner or court used the conviction or accident as a reason for the suspension or revocation of a driver's license or driving privilege, in which case the revocation or suspension and any conviction or accident pertaining thereto shall cease to be included in such abstract after sixty months from the date on which the driver's license or driving privilege was reinstated. No abstract released under this subdivision shall be admissible in evidence in any court proceedings.

9. On the request of any federal, state, or local governmental entity, law-enforcement officer, attorney for the Commonwealth, court, or the authorized agent of any of the

foregoing, the Commissioner shall (i) compare personal information supplied by the governmental entity, officer, attorney for the Commonwealth, court, or the authorized agent of any of the foregoing, with that contained in the Department's records and, when the information supplied by the governmental entity, officer, attorney for the Commonwealth, court, or the authorized agent of any of the foregoing, is different from that contained in the Department's records, provide the governmental entity, officer, attorney for the Commonwealth, court, or the authorized agent of any of the foregoing, with correct information as contained in the Department's records and (ii) provide driver and vehicle information in the form of an abstract of the record showing all convictions, accidents, driver's license suspensions or revocations, and other appropriate information as the governmental entity, officer, attorney for the Commonwealth, court, or the authorized agent of any of the foregoing, may require in order to carry out its official functions.

10. On request of the driver licensing authority in any other state or foreign country, the Commissioner shall provide whatever classes of information the requesting authority shall require in order to carry out its official functions.

11. On the written request of any employer, prospective employer, or authorized agent of either, and with the written consent of the individual concerned, the Commissioner shall (i) compare personal information supplied by the employer, prospective employer, or agent with that contained in the Department's records and, when the information supplied by the employer, prospective employer, or agent is different from that contained in the Department's records, provide the employer, prospective employer, or agent with correct information as contained in the Department's records and (ii) provide the employer, prospective employer, or agent with driver information in the form of an abstract of an individual's record showing all convictions, accidents, driver's license suspensions or revocations, and any type of driver's license that the individual currently possesses, provided that the individual's position or the position that the individual is being considered for involves the operation of a motor vehicle.

12. On the written request of any member of or applicant for membership in a volunteer fire company or volunteer rescue squad, the Commissioner shall (i) compare personal information supplied by the volunteer fire company or volunteer rescue squad with that contained in the Department's records and, when the information supplied by the volunteer fire company or volunteer rescue squad is different from that contained in the Department's records, provide the volunteer fire company or volunteer rescue squad with correct information as contained in the Department's records and (ii) provide driver information in the form of an abstract of the member's or applicant's record showing all convictions, accidents, license suspensions or revocations, and any type of driver's license that the individual currently possesses. Such abstract shall be provided free of charge if the request is accompanied by appropriate written evidence that the person is a member of or applicant for membership in a volunteer fire company or volunteer rescue squad and the abstract is needed by a volunteer fire company or volunteer rescue squad to establish the qualifications of the member or applicant to operate equipment owned by the volunteer fire company or volunteer rescue squad.

13. On the written request of any person who has applied to be a volunteer with a Virginia affiliate of Big Brothers/Big Sisters of America, the Commissioner shall (i) compare personal information supplied by a Virginia affiliate of Big Brothers/Big Sisters of America with that contained in the Department's records and, when the information supplied by a Virginia affiliate of Big Brothers/Big Sisters of America is different from that contained in the Department's records, provide the Virginia affiliate of Big Brothers/Big Sisters of America with correct information as contained in the Department's records and (ii) provide driver information in the form of an abstract of the applicant's record showing all convictions, accidents, license suspensions or revocations, and any type of driver's license that the individual currently possesses. Such abstract shall be provided free of charge if the request is accompanied by appropriate written evidence that the person has applied to be a volunteer with a Virginia affiliate of Big Brothers/Big Sisters of America.

14. On the written request of any person who has applied to be a volunteer with a court-appointed special advocate program pursuant to §9-173.8, the Commissioner shall provide an abstract of the applicant's record showing all convictions, accidents, license suspensions or revocations, and any type of driver's license that the individual currently possesses. Such abstract shall be provided free of charge if the request is accompanied by appropriate written evidence that the person has applied to be a volunteer with a court-appointed special advocate program pursuant to §9-173.8.

15. Upon the request of any employer, prospective employer, or authorized representative of either, the Commissioner shall (i) compare personal information supplied by the employer, prospective employer, or agent with that contained in the Department's records and, when the information supplied by the employer, prospective employer, or agent is different from that contained in the Department's records, provide the employer, prospective employer, or agent with correct information as contained in the Department's records and (ii) provide driver information in the form of an abstract of the driving record of any individual who has been issued a commercial driver's license, provided that the individual's position or the position that the individual is being considered for involves the operation of a commercial motor vehicle. Such abstract shall show all convictions, accidents, license suspensions, revocations, or disqualifications, and any type of driver's license that the individual currently possesses.

16. Upon the receipt of a completed application and payment of applicable processing fees, the Commissioner may enter into an agreement with any governmental authority or business to exchange information specified in this section by electronic or other means.

17. Upon the request of an attorney representing a person in a motor vehicle accident, the Commissioner shall provide vehicle information, including the owner's name and address, to the attorney.

18. Upon the request, in the course of business, of any authorized representative of an insurance company or of any not-for-profit entity organized to prevent and detect insurance fraud, the Commissioner shall provide all vehicle information, including the owner's name and address, descriptive data and title, registration, and vehicle activity data to such person.

19. Upon the request of an officer authorized to issue criminal warrants, for the purpose of issuing a warrant for arrest for unlawful disposal of trash or refuse in violation of §33.1-346, the Commissioner shall provide vehicle information, including the owner's name and address.

20. Upon written request of the compliance agent of a private security services business, as defined in §9-183.1, which is licensed by the Department of Criminal Justice Services, the Commissioner shall provide the name and address of the registered owner of the vehicle under procedures determined by the Commissioner.

21. Upon the request of the operator of a toll facility, or an authorized agent or employee of a toll facility operator,

for the purpose of obtaining vehicle owner data under subsection H of §46.2-819.1.

C. Whenever the Commissioner issues an order to suspend or revoke the driver's license or driving privilege of any individual, he may notify the National Driver Register Service operated by the United States Department of Transportation and any similar national driver information system and provide whatever classes of information the authority may require.

D. Accident reports may be inspected under the provisions of §§46.2-379 and 46.2-380.

E. Whenever the Commissioner takes any licensing action pursuant to the provisions of the Virginia Commercial Driver's License Act (§46.2-341.1 et seq.), he may provide information to the Commercial Driver License Information System, or any similar national commercial driver information system, regarding such action.

F. In addition to the foregoing provisions of this section, vehicle information may also be inspected under the provisions of §§43-33, 43-34, 46.2-633 and 46.2-1200.1 through 46.2-1237.

G. The Department may promulgate regulations to govern the means by which personal, vehicle, and driver information is requested and disseminated.

H. Driving records of any person accused of an offense involving the operation of a motor vehicle shall be provided by the Commissioner upon request to any person acting as counsel for the accused. If such counsel is from the public defender's office or has been appointed by the court, such records shall be provided free of charge.

I. The Department shall maintain the records of persons convicted of violations of subsection B of §29.1-738 and §§29.1-738.02, 29.1-738.2, and 29.1-738.4, which shall be forwarded by every general district court or circuit court or the clerk thereof, pursuant to §46.2-383. Such records shall be electronically available to any law-enforcement officer as provided for under clause of subdivision B 9 of this section.
(Chgd. by L.1995 chs. 118, 657, 676, 686; L.1998 chs. 147, 802, eff. 7/1/98, special session I ch. 2, eff. 5/20/98.)

§46.2-208.1. Electronic transfer of information in Department records for voter registration purposes.

Notwithstanding the provisions of §46.2-208, the Commissioner shall provide for the electronic transfer of information from the Department's records to the State Board of Elections and the general registrars for the purpose of voter registration as required by Chapter 4 of Title 24.2. Except as provided in §24.2-444, the State Board of Elections and the general registrars shall not make information provided by the Department available to the public and shall not provide such information to any third party.
(Added by L.1999 ch. 118, eff. 7/1/99.)

§46.2-209. Release of information in Department records for motor vehicle research purposes.

Notwithstanding the provisions of §46.2-208, the Commissioner may furnish information for motor vehicle research purposes when the information is furnished in such a manner that individuals cannot be identified by social security or license number or in other cases wherein, in his opinion, highway safety or the general welfare of the public will be promoted by furnishing the information and the recipient of the information has agreed in writing with the Commissioner or his designee that the information furnished will be used for no purpose other than the purpose for which it was furnished. No such information shall be used for solicitation of sales.
(Chgd. by L.1995 ch. 118, eff. 3/8/95.)

§46.2-209.1. Release of vehicle information by Department to prospective vehicle purchasers.

Notwithstanding the provisions of §46.2-208, the Commissioner may furnish vehicle information to a prospective purchaser of that vehicle, if the prospective purchaser completes an application therefor, including the vehicle's make, model, year, and vehicle identification number, and pays the fee prescribed by the Commissioner. Such information furnished by the Commissioner may be provided from the Department's own records, or may be obtained by the Commissioner through the National Motor Vehicle Title Information System or any other nationally recognized system providing similar information.

Nothing in this section shall be construed to authorize the release of any personal information as defined in §2.1-379.
(Added by L.2000 chs. 87, 92, 235, 257, eff. 7/1/2000.)

§46.2-210. List of registrations and titles.

The Commissioner shall have prepared a list of registrations and titles and furnish it to the commissioner of the revenue of each county and city without cost. The Commissioner shall not make such list available to the public, nor shall any commissioner of the revenue make such list available to any third party.

§46.2-211. Commissioner to advise local commissioners of revenue of situs of certain vehicles.

Before issuing any registration or certificate of title for any tractor truck, or any three-axle truck, trailer, or semitrailer with a registered gross weight in excess of 26,000 pounds, the Commissioner shall determine the county, city, or town in which the vehicle is or will be normally garaged or parked, and shall advise each commissioner of the revenue of the situs of such vehicles as may be in his jurisdiction. The provisions of this section shall not apply to motor vehicles and rolling stock of certificated intrastate common carriers, or electric power, gas, pipeline transmission, railroad, telegraph, telephone, and water companies.

§46.2-212. Notice given for records supplied.

Whenever any records held by the Department are supplied to third persons, the third persons shall notify the subject of the records that the records have been supplied and shall send to the subject a copy of the records.

As used in this section "records supplied to third persons" means all abstracts of operating records held by the Department in which the person who is the subject of the records is identified or identifiable, where the records are made available, in any way, to a person who is not the subject of the records.

This section shall not apply to records supplied to any officials, including court and police officials of the Commonwealth and of any of the counties, cities, and towns of the Commonwealth, and court and law-enforcement officials of other states and of the federal government, provided the records or information supplied is for official use; nor shall this section apply to any records supplied to any insurer or its agents unless insurance is denied or the premium charged therefor is increased either wholly or in part because of information contained in such records.

§46.2-212.1. Payments by payment devices.

The Commissioner may authorize the acceptance of payment devices in lieu of money for payment of any fees, fines, penalties, and taxes collected by the Department of Motor Vehicles or agents acting on behalf of the Department. The Department may add to such payment an amount of no more than four percent of the payment as a service charge for the acceptance of a payment device.

The Commissioner may authorize a Department transaction receipt to be used with existing Department documents

as evidence that the holder has complied with Department payment requirements, provided the transaction is completed before the document's expiration date. Any such transaction receipt shall include detailed information as to length of time by which the document's period of validity will be extended and how the transaction receipt is to be verified.
(Chgd. by L.1996 chs. 943, 994; L.2000 ch. 122, eff. 7/1/2000.)

§46.2-213. Certificate of license plate number; prima facie evidence of ownership.

The Commissioner, on request of any person, shall furnish a certificate, under seal of the Department, setting forth a distinguishing number or license plate of a motor vehicle, trailer, or semitrailer, together with the name and address of its owner. The certificate shall be prima facie evidence in any court in the Commonwealth of the ownership of the vehicle to which the distinguishing number or license plate has been assigned by the Department. Certificates furnished under this section shall be provided free of charge to law-enforcement officers of the Commonwealth, any other state, or the federal government, but the Commissioner may charge a reasonable fee for certificates furnished under this section to other persons.

§46.2-214. Charges for information supplied by Department.

The Commissioner may make a reasonable charge for furnishing information under this title, but no fee shall be charged to any officials, including court and police officials, of the Commonwealth and of any of the counties, towns, and cities of the Commonwealth and court, police, and licensing officials of other states and of the federal government, provided that the information requested is for official use. The fees received by the Commissioner under this section shall be paid into the state treasury and shall be set aside as a special fund to be used to meet the expenses of the Department.

§46.2-215. Certification of certain records and admissibility in evidence.

Whenever any record, including records maintained by electronic media, by photographic processes, or paper, in the office of the Department is admissible in evidence, a copy, a machine-produced transcript, or a photograph of the record or paper attested by the Commissioner or his designee may be admitted as evidence in lieu of the original. In any case in which the records are transmitted by electronic means a machine imprint of the Commissioner's name purporting to authenticate the record shall be the equivalent of attestation or certification by the Commissioner.

Any copy, transcript, photograph, or any certification purporting to be sealed or sealed and signed by the Commissioner or his designee or imprinted with the Commissioner's name may be admitted as evidence without any proof of the seal or signature or of the official character of the person whose name is signed thereto. If an issue as to the authenticity of any information transmitted by electronic means is raised, the court shall require that a record attested by the Commissioner or his designee be submitted for admission into evidence.

§46.2-216. Destruction of records.

In accordance with the provisions of Chapter 7 (§42.1-76 et seq.) of Title 42.1, the Commissioner may establish standards for the disposal of any paper or record which need not be preserved as a permanent record.

§46.2-216.1. Acceptance of electronic filing in lieu of written documents.

Whenever this title provides that a written certificate or other document is to be filed with the Department, the Commissioner may establish procedures for and accept in lieu of such paper document a filing made by electronic means. Such filing by electronic means shall be accepted only if the content of the filing satisfies all of the requirements of the statute which provides for the written document and the Commissioner has made a written, affirmative finding that the lack of a paper document will not compromise or reduce the effectiveness of the record-keeping system established by the statute. The Commissioner shall develop a method to ensure that the electronic filing is received and stored accurately and that it is readily available to satisfy the requirements of the statutes which call for a written document.

§46.2-216.2. Agreements to provide electronic documents in lieu of written documents.

Whenever this title provides that a written certificate or other document is to be delivered to an owner, registrant, licensee, lien holder or other party by the Department or the Commissioner, the Commissioner may enter into an agreement with the owner, registrant, licensee, lien holder or other party to provide the written certificate or other document by electronic means. The electronic document may consist of all of the information included in the paper certificate or document or it may be an abstract or listing of the information held in electronic form by the Department. The Department may not require any owner, registrant, licensee, lien holder or other party to accept electronic certificates and documents. When an agreement is made to accept electronic certificates and documents, the Department will not be required to produce a written certificate or document until requested to do so by the owner, registrant, licensee, lien holder or other party.
(Added by L.1996 chs. 943, 994, eff. 7/1/96.)

§46.2-216.3. Discounts and other incentives.

In addition to those authorized in §46.2-697.1, the Commissioner may authorize discounts and other incentives to encourage customers to conduct transactions with the Department through the mail or by means of electronic technologies.
(Added by L.1999 ch. 593, eff. 7/1/99.)

§46.2-217. Enforcement of laws by Commissioner; authority of officers.

The Commissioner, his several assistants, including those who are full-time sworn members of the enforcement division of the Department of Motor Vehicles, and police officers appointed by him are vested with the powers of sheriffs for the purpose of enforcing the laws of the Commonwealth which the Commissioner is required to enforce. Such full-time sworn members of the enforcement division of the Department of Motor Vehicles are hereby authorized to enforce the criminal laws of the Commonwealth, when violations of same are committed in their presence or occur in their plain view, while they are otherwise engaged in enforcing the laws of the Commonwealth which the Commissioner is required to enforce. Any such violations, which do not relate to laws the Commissioner is required to enforce and which may require follow-up investigatory or other work, shall be promptly referred to the appropriate law-enforcement or criminal justice agency or department.

Nothing in this title shall relieve any law-enforcement officer, commissioner of the revenue, or any other official invested with police powers and duties, state or local, of the duty of assisting in the enforcement of such laws within the scope of his respective authority and duty.

All law-enforcement officers appointed by the Commissioner may administer oaths and take acknowledgments and affidavits incidental to the administration and enforcement of this title and all other laws relating to the operation of motor vehicles, applications for driver's licenses, and the collection and refunding of taxes levied on gasoline. They shall receive no compensation for administering oaths or taking acknowledgments.

§46.2-218. Fees not allowed law-enforcement officers.

No court in the Commonwealth shall, in any case in which a fine is assessed for the violation of any law of the Commonwealth or any subdivision thereof, assess as a part of the cost of the case any fee for arrest, or as a witness, for the benefit of any law-enforcement officer of the Department; nor shall any Department law-enforcement officer receive any such fee. Any Department law-enforcement officer who accepts or receives any such fee shall be guilty of a Class 4 misdemeanor and, in addition, the Commissioner may remove him therefor. Department law-enforcement officers are not prohibited, however, from accepting or receiving rewards.

§46.2-219. Bonds of Commissioner, Deputy Commissioners, assistants, administrators, and law-enforcement officers; liability insurance policies.

The Commissioner, the Deputy Commissioners, the assistant commissioners, the administrators, and law-enforcement officers appointed by the Commissioner and engaged in the enforcement of criminal laws and the laws relating to the operation of motor vehicles on the highways in the Commonwealth shall, before entering on or continuing in their duties, enter into bond with some solvent guaranty, indemnity, fidelity, or casualty company authorized to do business in the Commonwealth as surety, in the penalty of $100,000 and with condition for the faithful and lawful performance of their duties. These bonds shall be filed in the office of the Department and the premiums thereon shall be paid out of the fund appropriated for the enforcement of the laws concerning motor vehicles. All persons injured or damaged in any manner by the unlawful, negligent, or improper conduct of any such officer while on duty may maintain an action on the bond.

In lieu of posting bond as provided in this section, any assistant or law-enforcement officer may furnish an adequate liability insurance policy as proof of his ability to respond in damages which may be adjudged against him in favor of any person or persons injured or damaged in any manner resulting from his unlawful, negligent, or improper conduct while on official duty, to the amount of $100,000. The premiums on any such insurance policy or policies shall be paid out of the funds appropriated for the enforcement of the laws concerning motor vehicles.

All such bonds and insurance policies shall be approved by the Commissioner.

§46.2-220. Special counsel for defense of law-enforcement officers.

If any law-enforcement officer appointed by the Commissioner is arrested, indicted, or prosecuted on any charge arising out of any act committed in the discharge of his official duties, the Commissioner may employ special counsel approved by the Attorney General to defend him. The compensation for special counsel employed pursuant to this section shall, subject to approval of the Attorney General, be paid out of the funds appropriated for the administration of the Department.

§46.2-221. Certain state agencies to report to Department concerning the blind and nearly blind; use of such information by Department; Department to report names of persons refused licenses for defective vision.

Every state agency having knowledge of the blind or visually handicapped, maintaining any register of the blind, or administering either tax deductions or exemptions for or aid to the blind or visually handicapped shall report in January of each year to the Department the names of all persons so known, registered or benefitting from such deductions or exemptions, for aid to the blind or visually handicapped. This information shall be used by the Department only for the purpose of determining qualifications of these persons for licensure under Chapter 3 of this title.

The Department shall report to the Virginia Department for the Visually Handicapped* and the Department of Rehabilitative Services at least annually the name and address of every person who has been refused a driver's license solely or partly because of failure to pass the Department's visual examination.

If any employee of the State Department for the Visually Handicapped* makes a report to the Department of Motor Vehicles as required by this section concerning any client of the agency, it shall not be deemed to have been made in violation of the client-agency relationship.

**Redesignated the Department for the Blind and Vision Impaired by L.2000 ch. 498, eff. 1/1/2001.*

ARTICLE 2
POWERS AND DUTIES OF DEPARTMENT RELATED TO TRANSPORTATION SAFETY

Section

§46.2-222. General powers of Commissioner with respect to transportation safety.

The Commissioner shall have the following general powers to carry out the purposes of this article:

1. To employ required personnel.
2. To enter into all contracts and agreements necessary or incidental to the performance of the Department's duties and the execution of its powers under this article, including, but not limited to, contracts with the United States, other states, and agencies and governmental subdivisions of the Commonwealth.
3. To accept grants from the United States government and its agencies and instrumentalities and any other source. To these ends, the Department shall have the power to comply with conditions and execute agreements necessary, convenient or desirable.
4. To do all acts necessary or convenient to carry out the purposes of this article.

§46.2-223. Additional powers and duties of Commissioner.

The Commissioner shall have the following powers and duties related to transportation safety:

1. To evaluate safety measures currently in use by all transport operators in all modes which operate in or through the Commonwealth, with particular attention to the safety of equipment and appliances and methods and procedures of operation;
2. To engage in training and educational activities aimed at enhancing the safe transport of passengers and property in and through the Commonwealth;
3. To cooperate with all relevant entities of the federal government, including, but not limited to, the Department of Transportation, the Federal Railway Administration, the Federal Aviation Administration, the Coast Guard, and the Independent Transportation Safety Board in matters concerning transportation safety;

4. To initiate, conduct, and issue special studies on matters pertaining to transportation safety;

5. To evaluate transportation safety efforts, practices, and procedures of the agencies or other entities of the government of the Commonwealth and make recommendations to the Secretary of Transportation, the Governor, and the General Assembly on ways to increase transportation safety consciousness or improve safety practices;

6. To assist entities of state government and political subdivisions of the Commonwealth in enhancing their efforts to ensure safe transportation, including the dissemination of relevant materials and the rendering of technical or other advice;

7. To collect, tabulate, correlate, analyze, evaluate, and review the data gathered by various entities of the state government in regard to transportation operations, management, and accidents, especially the information gathered by the Department of Motor Vehicles, the Department of State Police, and the State Corporation Commission;

8. To develop, implement, and review, in conjunction with relevant state and federal entities, a comprehensive highway safety program for the Commonwealth, and to inform the public about it;

9. To assist towns, counties and other political subdivisions of the Commonwealth in the development, implementation, and review of local highway safety programs as part of the state program;

10. To review the activities, role, and contribution of various state entities to the Commonwealth's highway safety program and to report annually and in writing to the Governor and General Assembly on the status, progress, and prospects of highway safety in the Commonwealth;

11. To recommend to the Secretary of Transportation, the Governor, and the General Assembly any corrective measures, policies, procedures, plans, and programs which are needed to make the movement of passengers and property on the highways of the Commonwealth as safe as practicable;

12. To design, implement, administer, and review special programs or projects needed to promote highway safety in the Commonwealth;

13. To integrate highway safety activities into the framework of transportation safety in general; and

14. To administer the Traffic Safety Fund established pursuant to §46.2-749.2:10 and to accept grants, gifts, bequests, and other moneys contributed to, deposited in, or designated for deposit in the Fund.

(Chgd. by L.1998 ch. 743, eff. 7/1/98.)

§46.2-224. Board of Transportation Safety.

There is hereby established within the Department of Motor Vehicles a Board of Transportation Safety, hereinafter referred to in this section as "the Board," to advise the Commissioner of Motor Vehicles, the Secretary of Transportation, and the Governor on transportation safety matters. The Board shall elect a chairman and meet at his call, and shall seek to identify the elements of a comprehensive safety program for all transport modes operating in Virginia. In addition, the Board may consider, study, and report on the following issues: (i) the identification of the unique safety needs of each particular mode of transportation; (ii) the identification of the common elements of safe transportation operation, regardless of mode of transportation; (iii) the adoption of proven safety practices and technology in use in one mode to other modes of transportation; (iv) the identification of the common elements of accident situations; and (v) the allocation of grant funds made available to the Department.

The Board shall consist of twelve members appointed by the Governor, subject to confirmation of the General Assembly. One member shall be appointed from each of the geographic operating districts used by the Department and shall reside in the district from which he is appointed. The remaining members shall be at-large members representing transportation safety interests in the areas of air, rail, water, motor carriers, pupil transportation, and public transit and, insofar as practical, should reflect fair and equitable statewide representation. Members shall serve for terms of four years, and no member shall serve for more than two full consecutive terms. Appointment and confirmation of Board members under this section shall occur only as the terms of the current members of the Board expire under prior law.

Board members shall be reimbursed for their necessary and actual expenses incurred in the performance of their duties.

(Chgd. by L.2000 ch. 141, eff. 7/1/2000.)

SUBTITLE II
TITLING, REGISTRATION AND LICENSURE

CHAPTER 3
LICENSURE OF DRIVERS

ARTICLE 1
UNLICENSED DRIVING PROHIBITED

§46.2-300. Driving without license prohibited; penalties.

No person, except those expressly exempted in §§46.2-303 through 46.2-309, shall drive any motor vehicle on any highway in the Commonwealth until such person has applied for a driver's license, as provided in this article, satisfactorily passed the examination required by §46.2-325, and obtained a driver's license, nor unless the license is valid.

A conviction of a violation of this section shall constitute a Class 2 misdemeanor.

§46.2-301. Driving while license, permit, or privilege to drive suspended or revoked.

A. In addition to any other penalty provided by this section, any motor vehicle administratively impounded or immobilized under the provisions of §46.2-301.1 may, in the discretion of the court, be impounded or immobilized for an additional period of up to ninety days upon conviction of an offender for driving while his driver's license, learner's permit, or privilege to drive a motor vehicle has been suspended or revoked for (i) a violation of §§18.2-36.1, 18.2-51.4, 18.2-266 or §46.2-341.24 or a substantially similar ordinance or law in any other jurisdiction or (ii) driving after adjudication as an habitual offender, where such adjudication was based in whole or in part on an alcohol-related offense, or where such person's license has been administratively suspended under the provisions of §46.2-391.2. However, if, at the time of the violation, the offender was driving a motor vehicle owned by another person, the court shall have no jurisdiction over such motor vehicle but may order the impoundment or immobilization of a motor vehicle owned solely by the offender at the time of arrest. All costs of impoundment or immobilization, including removal or storage expenses, shall be paid by the offender prior to the release of his motor vehicle.

B. Except as provided in §§46.2-304 and 46.2-357, no resident or nonresident (i) whose driver's license, learner's permit, or privilege to drive a motor vehicle has been suspended or revoked or (ii) who has been directed not to drive by any court, by the Commissioner, or by operation of law pursuant to this title or (iii) who has been forbidden, as prescribed by law, by the Commissioner, the State Corporation Commission, the Commonwealth Transportation Commissioner, any court, or the Superintendent of State Police, to operate a motor vehicle in the Commonwealth shall thereafter drive any motor vehicle or any self-propelled machinery or equipment on any highway in the Commonwealth until the period of such suspension or revocation has terminated. A clerk's notice of suspension of license for failure to pay fines or costs given in accordance with §46.2-395 shall be sufficient notice for the purpose of maintaining a conviction under this section. For the purposes of this section, the phrase "motor vehicle or any self-propelled machinery or equipment" shall not include mopeds.

C. A first or second offense of violating this section shall constitute a Class 1 misdemeanor. A third or subsequent offense shall constitute a Class 1 misdemeanor punishable by a minimum, mandatory term of confinement in jail of ten days which shall not be suspended in whole or in part. However, the court shall not be required to impose a minimum, mandatory term of confinement in any case where a motor vehicle is operated in violation of this section in a situation of apparent extreme emergency which requires such operation to save life or limb.

In addition, the court shall suspend the person's driver's license for the same period for which it had been previously suspended or revoked when the person violated this section.

D. In the event the person has violated this section by driving during a period of suspension or revocation which was not for a definite period of time, the court shall suspend the person's license, permit or privilege to drive for an additional period not to exceed ninety days. Any additional suspension ordered under the provisions of this section shall commence upon the expiration of the previous suspension or revocation unless the previous suspension or revocation has expired prior to the ordering of an additional suspension or revocation.

(Chgd. by L.1997 ch. 691; L.2000 chs. 956, 982, eff. 7/1/2000.)

§46.2-301.1. Administrative impoundment of motor vehicle for certain driving while license suspended or revoked offenses; judicial impoundment upon conviction; penalty for permitting violation with one's vehicle.

A. The motor vehicle being driven by any person (i) whose driver's license, learner's permit or privilege to drive a motor vehicle has been suspended or revoked for a violation of §18.2-51.4 or driving while under the influence in violation of §§18.2-266, 46.2-341.24 or a substantially similar ordinance or law in any other jurisdiction, (ii) driving after adjudication as an habitual offender, where such adjudication was based in whole or in part on an alcohol-related offense, or where such person's license has been administratively suspended under the provisions of §46.2-391.2, or (iii) driving after such person's driver's license, learner's permit or privilege to drive a motor vehicle has been suspended or revoked for unreasonable refusal of tests in violation of §§18.2-268.3, 46.2-341.26:3 or a substantially similar ordinance or law in any other jurisdiction, shall be impounded or immobilized by the arresting law-enforcement officer at the time the person is arrested for driving after his driver's license, learner's permit or privilege to drive has been so revoked or suspended. The impoundment or immobilization shall be for a period of thirty days.

The arresting officer, acting on behalf of the Commonwealth, shall serve notice of the impoundment upon the arrested person. The notice shall include information on the person's right to petition for review of the impoundment pursuant to subsection B. A copy of the notice of impoundment shall be delivered to the magistrate and thereafter promptly forwarded to the clerk of the general district court of the jurisdiction where the arrest was made and to the Commissioner. Transmission of the notice may be by electronic means.

At least five days prior to the expiration of the period of impoundment imposed pursuant to this section or §46.2-301, the clerk shall provide the offender with information on the location of the motor vehicle and how and when the vehicle will be released.

All reasonable costs of impoundment or immobilization, including removal and storage expenses, shall be paid by the offender prior to the release of his motor vehicle. Notwithstanding the above, where the arresting law-enforcement officer discovers that the vehicle was being rented or leased from a vehicle renting or leasing company, the officer shall not impound the vehicle or continue the impoundment but shall notify the rental or leasing company that the vehicle is available for pickup and shall notify the clerk and the Commissioner if they have previously been notified of the impoundment.

B. Any driver who is the owner of the motor vehicle that is impounded or immobilized under subsection A may, during the period of the impoundment, petition the general district court of the jurisdiction in which the arrest was made to review that impoundment. The court shall review the impoundment within the same time period as the court hears an appeal from an order denying bail or fixing terms of bail or terms of recognizance, giving this matter precedence over all other matters on its docket. If the person proves to the court by a preponderance of the evidence that the arresting law-enforcement officer did not have probable cause for the arrest, or that the magistrate did not have probable cause to issue the warrant, the court shall rescind the impoundment. Upon rescission, the motor vehicle shall be released and the Commonwealth shall pay or reimburse the person for all reasonable costs of impoundment or immobilization, including removal or storage costs paid or incurred by him. Otherwise, the court shall affirm the impoundment. If the person requesting the review fails to appear without just cause, his right to review shall be waived.

The court's findings are without prejudice to the person contesting the impoundment or to any other potential party as to any proceedings, civil or criminal, and shall not be evidence in any proceedings, civil or criminal.

C. The owner or co-owner of any motor vehicle impounded or immobilized under subsection A who was not the driver at the time of the violation, may petition the general district court in the jurisdiction where the violation occurred for the release of his motor vehicle. The motor vehicle shall be released if the owner or co-owner proves by a preponderance of the evidence that he (i) did not know that the offender's driver's license was suspended or revoked when he authorized the offender to drive such motor vehicle or (ii) did not consent to the operation of the motor vehicle by the offender. If the owner proves by a preponderance of the evidence that his immediate family has only one motor vehicle and will suffer a substantial hardship if that motor vehicle is impounded or immobilized for thirty days, the court, in its discretion, may release the vehicle after some period of less than thirty days.

D. Notwithstanding any provision of this section, a subsequent dismissal or acquittal of the charge of driving on a suspended or revoked license shall result in an immediate rescission of the impoundment or immobilization provided in subsection A. Upon rescission, the motor vehicle shall be released and the Commonwealth shall pay or reimburse the person for all reasonable costs of impoundment or immobilization, including removal or storage costs, incurred or paid by him.

E. Any person who knowingly authorizes the operation of a motor vehicle by a person he knows has had his driver's license, learner's permit or privilege to drive a motor vehicle suspended or revoked for any of the reasons set forth in subsection A, shall be guilty of a Class 1 misdemeanor.

F. Notwithstanding the provisions of this section or §46.2-301, nothing in this section shall impede or infringe upon a valid lienholder's rights to cure a default under an existing security agreement. Furthermore, such lienholder shall not be liable for any cost of impoundment or immobilization, including removal or storage expenses which may accrue pursuant to the provisions of this section or §46.2-301. In the event a lienholder repossesses or removes a vehicle from storage pursuant to an existing security agreement, the Commonwealth shall pay all reasonable costs of impoundment or immobilization, including removal and storage expenses, to any person or entity providing such services to the Commonwealth, except to the extent such costs or expenses have already been paid by the offender to such person or entity. Such payment shall be made within seven calendar days after a request is made by such person or entity to the Commonwealth for payment. Nothing herein, however, shall relieve the offender from liability to the Commonwealth for reimbursement or payment of all such reasonable costs and expenses.

(Chgd. by L.1995 chs. 426, 435; L.1997 chs. 378, 478, 691, eff. 7/1/97.)

§46.2-302. Driving while restoration of license is contingent on furnishing proof of financial responsibility.

No resident or nonresident (i) whose driver's license or learner's permit has been suspended or revoked by any court or by the Commissioner or by operation of law, pursuant to the provisions of this title or of §18.2-271, or who has been disqualified pursuant to the provisions of the Virginia Commercial Driver's License Act (§46.2-341.1 et seq.), or (ii) who has been forbidden as prescribed by law by the Commissioner, the State Corporation Commission, the Commonwealth Transportation Commissioner, or the Superintendent of State Police, to drive a motor vehicle in the Commonwealth shall drive any motor vehicle in the Commonwealth during any period wherein the restoration of license or privilege is contingent upon the furnishing of proof of financial responsibility, unless he has given proof of financial responsibility in the manner provided in Article 15 (§46.2-435 et seq.) of Chapter 3 of this title. Any person who drives a motor vehicle on the roads of the Commonwealth and has furnished proof of financial responsibility but who has failed to pay a reinstatement fee, shall be tried under §46.2-300.

A first offense violation of this section shall constitute a Class 2 misdemeanor. A second or subsequent violation of this section shall constitute a Class 1 misdemeanor.

ARTICLE 2
WHEN LICENSE NOT REQUIRED

§46.2-303. Licenses not required for operating road roller or farm tractor.

No person shall be required to obtain a driver's license to operate a road roller or road machinery used under the supervision and control of the Department of Transportation for construction or maintenance purposes. No person shall be required to obtain a driver's license for the purpose of operating any farm tractor, farm machinery, or vehicle defined in §§46.2-663 through 46.2-674, temporarily drawn, moved, or propelled on the highways. The term "road machinery" shall not include motor vehicles required to be licensed by the Department of Motor Vehicles.

§46.2-304. Limited operation of farm tractor by persons convicted of driving under influence of intoxicants or drugs.

The conviction of a person for driving under the influence of intoxicants or some other self-administered drug in violation of any state law or local ordinance shall not prohibit the person from operating a farm tractor on the highways when it is necessary to move the tractor from one tract of land used for agricultural purposes to another tract of land used for the same purposes, provided that the distance between the said tracts of land does not exceed five miles.

§46.2-305. Exemption of persons in armed services.

Every person in the armed services of the United States, when furnished with a driver's license, and when operating an official motor vehicle in such service, shall be exempt from licensure under this chapter.

§46.2-306. Exemption of armed services personnel and spouses and dependent children of armed services personnel.

Notwithstanding §46.2-100, a person on active duty with the armed services of the United States or a spouse or a dependent child not less than sixteen years of age of a person on active duty with the armed services of the United States who has been licensed as a driver under a law requiring the licensing of drivers in his home state or country and who has in his immediate possession a valid driver's license issued to him in his home state or country shall be permitted without examination or license under this chapter to drive a motor vehicle on the highways in the Commonwealth. The provisions of this section shall not be affected by the person's, spouse's, or dependent child's ownership of a motor vehicle registered in Virginia.

§46.2-307. Nonresidents licensed under laws of home state or country; extension of reciprocal privileges.

A. A nonresident over the age of sixteen years who has been duly licensed as a driver under a law requiring the licensing of drivers in his home state or country and who has in his immediate possession a driver's license issued to him in his home state or country shall be permitted, without a Virginia license, to drive a motor vehicle on the highways of the Commonwealth.

B. Notwithstanding any other provisions of this chapter, the Commissioner, with the consent of the Governor, may extend to nonresidents from foreign countries the same driver's licensing privileges which are granted by the foreign country, or political subdivision wherein such nonresidents are residents, to residents of this Commonwealth residing in such foreign country or political subdivision.

C. Driver's license privileges may be extended to nonresidents from foreign countries or political subdivisions who are over the age of sixteen years, have been duly licensed as drivers under a law requiring the licensing of drivers in their home country or political subdivision, and have in their immediate possession a driver's license issued to them in their home country or political subdivision.
(Chgd. by L.1997 ch. 486, eff. 7/1/97.)

§46.2-308. Temporary exemption for new resident licensed under laws of another state; privately owned vehicle driver's licenses.

A resident over the age of sixteen years who has been duly licensed as a driver under a law of another state or country requiring the licensing of drivers shall, for the first thirty days of his residency in the Commonwealth, be permitted, without a Virginia license, to drive a motor vehicle on the highways of the Commonwealth.

Persons to whom military privately-owned vehicle driver's licenses have been issued by the Department of Defense shall, for the first thirty days of their residency in the Commonwealth, be permitted, without a Virginia license, to drive motor vehicles on the highways of the Commonwealth.

§46.2-309. Nonresidents not licensed in home state.

It shall be unlawful for any nonresident whose home state or country does not require the licensing of drivers and who has not been licensed either as a driver in his home state or country to operate any motor vehicle on any highway in the Commonwealth. But any such unlicensed nonresident who is over the age of sixteen years may operate any motor vehicle which is not a commercial motor vehicle as defined in the Virginia Commercial Driver's License Act (§46.2-341.1 et seq.) and which has been duly registered for the current calendar year in the state or country of which the owner is a resident on the highways of the Commonwealth for a period of not more than thirty days in any one year without a Virginia driver's license, on the condition that he may be required at any time or place to prove lawful possession of or the right to drive the motor vehicle and establish his proper identity.

§46.2-310. Localities may not require license except for taxicabs; prosecutions for operation of vehicle without license or while suspended.

Counties, cities, and towns shall not require any local permit to drive, except as provided in this section. Counties, cities, and towns may adopt regulations for the licensing of drivers of taxicabs and similar for-hire passenger vehicles and for the control of the operation of such for-hire vehicles. This section shall not preclude any county, city, or town from prosecuting, under a warrant issued by such county, city, or town, a person charged with violation of a local ordinance prohibiting operation of a motor vehicle without a driver's license or while his driver's license or privilege to drive is suspended or revoked.

ARTICLE 3
PERSONS NOT TO BE LICENSED

Section

§46.2-311. Persons having defective vision; minimum standards of visual acuity and field of vision; tests of vision.

A. The Department shall not issue a driver's license or learner's permit (i) to any person unless he demonstrates a visual acuity of at least 20/40 in one or both eyes with or without corrective lenses or (ii) to any such person unless he demonstrates at least a field of 100 degrees of horizontal vision in one or both eyes. However, a license permitting the driving of motor vehicles during a period beginning one-half hour after sunrise and ending one-half hour before sunset, may be issued to a person who demonstrates a visual acuity of at least 20/70 in one or both eyes without or with corrective lenses provided he demonstrates at least a field of seventy degrees of horizontal vision, and further provided that if such person has vision in one eye only, he demonstrates at least a field of forty degrees temporal and thirty degrees nasal horizontal vision.

B. The Department shall not issue a driver's license or learner's permit to any person authorizing the driving of a commercial motor vehicle as defined in the Virginia Commercial Driver's License Act (§46.2-341.1 et seq.) unless he demonstrates a visual acuity of at least 20/40 in each eye and at least a field of 140 degrees of horizontal vision.

C. Every person applying to renew a driver's license and required to be reexamined as a prerequisite to the renewal of the license, shall:

1. Appear before a license examiner of the Department to demonstrate his visual acuity and horizontal field of vision, or

2. Accompany his application with a report of such examination made within ninety days prior thereto by an ophthalmologist or optometrist.

D. The test of horizontal visual fields made by license examiners of the Department shall be performed at thirty-three and one-third centimeters with a ten millimeter round white test object or may, at the discretion of the Commissioner, be performed with electronic or other devices designed for the purpose of testing visual acuity and horizontal field of vision. The report of examination of visual acuity and horizontal field of vision made by an ophthalmologist or optometrist shall have precedence over an examination made by a license examiner of the Department in administrative determination as to the issuance of a license to drive. Any such report may, in the discretion of the Commissioner, be referred to a medical advisory board or to the State Health Commissioner for evaluation.

E. Notwithstanding the provisions of subsection B of this section, any person who is licensed to drive any motor vehicle may, on special application to the Department, be licensed to drive any vehicle, provided the operation of the vehicle would not unduly endanger the public safety, as determined by the Commissioner pursuant to regulations established by the Department.

§46.2-312. Persons using bioptic telescopic lenses.

A. Persons using bioptic telescopic lenses shall be eligible for driver's licenses if they:

1. Demonstrate a visual acuity of at least 20/200 in one or both eyes and a field of seventy degrees horizontal vision without or with corrective carrier lenses, or if these persons have vision in one eye only, they demonstrate a field of at least forty degrees temporal and thirty degrees nasal horizontal vision;

2. Demonstrate a visual acuity of at least 20/70 in one or both eyes with the bioptic telescopic lenses and without the use of field expanders;

3. Meet all other criteria for licensure;

4. Accompany the license application with a report of examination by an ophthalmologist or optometrist on a form prescribed by the Department for evaluation by the Medical Advisory Board.

B. Persons using bioptic telescopic lenses shall be eligible for learner's permits issued under §46.2-335 provided they first meet the requirements of subsection A of this section, except for that part of the examination requiring the applicant to drive a motor vehicle.

C. Persons using bioptic telescopic lenses shall be subject to the following restrictions:

1. They shall not be eligible for any of the driver's license endorsements provided for in §46.2-328;

2. Their driver's licenses shall permit the operation of motor vehicles only during the period beginning one-half hour after sunrise and ending one-half hour before sunset.

D. Notwithstanding the provisions of subsection C 2 of this section, persons using bioptic telescopic lenses may be licensed to drive motor vehicles between one-half hour before sunset and one-half hour after sunrise if they:

1. Demonstrate a visual acuity of at least 20/40 in one or both eyes with the bioptic telescopic lenses and without the use of field expanders;

2. Have been licensed under subdivision C of this section for at least one year; and

3. Pass a skills test taken at night.

§46.2-313. Persons with suspended or revoked licenses.

The Department shall not issue a driver's license to any person whose license has been suspended, during the period of the suspension; nor to any person whose license has been revoked, or should have been revoked, under the provisions of this title, until the expiration of one year after the license was revoked, unless otherwise permitted by the provisions of this title.

§46.2-314. Mental incapacity.

No driver's license shall be issued to any applicant who has previously been adjudged incapacitated and who has not, at the time of such application, been (i) adjudged restored to capacity by judicial decree or (ii) released from a hospital for the mentally ill on a certificate of the superintendent of the hospital that the person is capable. In either case, no driver's license shall be issued to him unless the Department is satisfied that he is competent to drive a motor vehicle with safety to persons and property.

(Chgd. by L.1997 ch. 801, eff. 1/1/98.)

§46.2-315. Disabled persons.

The Department shall not issue a driver's license to any person when, in the opinion of the Department, the person is suffering from a physical or mental disability or disease which will prevent his exercising reasonable and ordinary control over a motor vehicle while driving it on the highways, nor shall a license be issued to any person who is unable to understand highway warning or direction signs.

The words "disability or disease" shall not mean inability of a person to hear or to speak, or both, when he has good vision and can satisfactorily demonstrate his ability to drive a motor vehicle and has sufficient knowledge of traffic rules and regulations.

§46.2-316. Persons convicted or found not innocent of certain offenses; requirement of proof of financial responsibility for certain offenses.

A. The Department shall not issue a driver's license or learner's permit to any resident or nonresident person while his license or other privilege to drive is suspended or revoked because of his conviction, or finding of not innocent in the case of a juvenile, or forfeiture of bail upon the following charges of offenses committed in violation of either a law of the Commonwealth or a valid local ordinance or of any federal law or law of any other state or any valid local ordinance of any other state:

1. Voluntary or involuntary manslaughter resulting from the operation of a motor vehicle.

2. Perjury, the making of a false affidavit to the Department under any law requiring the registration of motor vehicles or regulating their operation on the highways, or the making of a false statement in any application for a driver's license.

3. Any crime punishable as a felony under the motor vehicle laws or any felony in the commission of which a motor vehicle is used.

4. Violation of the provisions of §18.2-51.4, pertaining to maiming while under the influence, §18.2-266, pertaining to driving while under the influence of intoxicants or drugs, or of §18.2-272, pertaining to driving while the driver's license has been forfeited for a conviction, or finding of not innocent in the case of a juvenile, under §§18.2-51.4, 18.2-266 or §18.2-272, or for violation of the provisions of any federal law or law of any other state or any valid local ordinance similar to §§18.2-51.4, 18.2-266 or §18.2-272.

5. Failure of a driver of a motor vehicle, involved in an accident resulting in death or injury to another person, to stop and disclose his identity at the scene of the accident.

6. On a charge of operating or permitting the operation, for the second time, of a passenger automobile for the transportation of passengers for rent or for hire, without having first obtained a license for the privilege as provided in §46.2-694.

B. The Department shall not issue a driver's license or learner's permit to any person convicted of a crime mentioned in subsection A of this section for a further period of three years after he otherwise becomes entitled to a license or permit until he proves to the Commissioner his ability to respond in damages as provided in Article 15 (§46.2-435 et seq.) of Chapter 3 of this title or any other law of the Commonwealth requiring proof of financial responsibility.
(Chgd. by L.1997 ch. 691, eff. 7/1/97.)

§46.2-317. Persons making false statement in application.

The Department shall not issue, for a period of one year, a driver's license or learner's permit when the records of the Department clearly show to the satisfaction of the Commissioner that the person has made a willful material false statement on any application for a driver's license.

§46.2-318. Cancellation or revocation of license where application is false in material particular.

The Commissioner may cancel or revoke any license or permit issued pursuant to this title when it appears that the information set forth in the application for the license or permit is false in any material particular.

§46.2-319. Refusal or revocation of license for certain fraudulent acts in obtaining a driver's license.

The Department shall not issue any permit or license under this title to any person who has been convicted, or found not innocent in the case of a juvenile, of violating §46.2-348, when the violation was based on the taking of any examination under §§46.2-311, 46.2-322, §46.2-325 or the provisions of the Virginia Commercial Driver's License Act (§46.2-341.1 et seq.) for another person, or the appearance for another for renewal of a license under this chapter, for a period of ten years from the date of conviction, or finding of not innocent in the case of a juvenile. If the person has a license or permit issued pursuant to this title, the Commissioner shall revoke the license or permit for a period of ten years from the date of the conviction, or finding of not innocent in the case of a juvenile.

§46.2-320. Other grounds for refusal or suspension.

A. The Department may refuse to grant an application for a driver's license in any of the circumstances set forth in §46.2-608 as circumstances justifying the refusal of an application for the registration of a motor vehicle. The Department may refuse to issue or reissue a driver's license for the willful failure or refusal to pay any taxes or fees required to be collected or authorized to be collected by the Department.

B. The Commissioner may enter into an agreement with the Department of Social Services whereby the Department may suspend or refuse to renew the driver's license of any person upon receipt of notice from the Department of Social Services that the person (i) is delinquent in the payment of child support by ninety days or more or in an amount of $5,000 or more or (ii) has failed to comply with a subpoena, summons or warrant relating to paternity or child support proceedings. A suspension or refusal to renew authorized pursuant to this section shall not be effective until thirty days after service on the delinquent obligor of notice of intent to suspend or refuse to renew. The notice of intent shall be served on the obligor by the Department of Social Services (i) by certified mail, return receipt requested, sent to the obligor's last known addresses as shown in the records of the Department or the Department of Social Services, or (ii) pursuant to §8.01-296, or (iii) service may be waived by the obligor in accordance with procedures established by the Department of Social Services. The obligor shall be entitled to a judicial hearing if a request for a hearing is made, in writing, to the Department of Social Services within ten days from service of the notice of intent. Upon receipt of the request for a hearing, the Department of Social Services shall petition the court that entered or is enforcing the order, requesting a hearing on the proposed suspension or refusal to renew. The court shall authorize the suspension or refusal to renew only if it finds that the obligor's noncompliance with the child support order was willful. Upon a showing by the Department of Social Services that the obligor is delinquent in the payment of child support by ninety days or more or in an amount of $5,000 or more, the burden of proving that the delinquency was not willful shall rest upon the obligor. The Department shall not suspend or refuse to renew the driver's license until a final determination is made by the court.

C. At any time after service of a notice of intent, the person may petition the juvenile and domestic relations district court in the jurisdiction where he resides for the issuance of a restricted license to be used if the suspension or refusal to renew becomes effective. Upon such petition and a finding of good cause, the court may provide that such person be issued a restricted permit to operate a motor vehicle for any or all of the following purposes: (i) travel to and from his place of employment and for travel during the hours of such person's employment if the operation of a motor vehicle is a necessary incident of such employment; (ii) travel to and from school if such person is a student, upon proper written verification to the court that such person is enrolled in a continuing program of education; (iii) travel to and from visitation with a child of such person; or (iv) such other medically necessary travel as the court deems necessary and proper upon written verification of need by a licensed health professional. A restricted license issued pursuant to this subsection shall not permit any person to operate a commercial motor vehicle as defined in §46.2-341.4. The court shall order the surrender of the person's license to operate a motor vehicle, to be disposed of in accordance with the provisions of §46.2-398, and shall forward to the Commissioner a copy of its order entered pursuant to this subsection. The order shall specifically enumerate the restrictions imposed and contain such information regarding the person to whom such a permit is issued as is reasonably necessary to identify him.

D. The Department shall not renew a driver's license or terminate a license suspension imposed pursuant to this section until it has received from the Department of Social Services a certification that the person has (i) paid the delinquency in full, (ii) reached an agreement with the Department of Social Services to satisfy the delinquency within a period not to exceed ten years and at least one payment, representing at least five percent of the total delinquency or $500, whichever is greater, has been made pursuant to the agreement, or (iii) complied with a subpoena, summons or warrant relating to a paternity or child support proceeding. Certification by the Department of Social Services shall be made by electronic or telephonic communication and shall be made on the same work day that payment required by clause (i) or (ii) is made.

(Chgd. by L.1995 ch. 595; L.1996 chs. 785, 1013; L.1997 chs. 473, 794, 857, 898; L.1999 ch. 615, eff. 3/28/99.)

§46.2-321. Appeal from denial, suspension, or revocation of license; operation of vehicle pending appeal.

Any person denied a license or whose license has been revoked, suspended, or cancelled under this article may appeal in accordance with the provisions of the Administrative Process Act (§9-6.14:1 et seq.). From the final judgment of the court, either the petitioner or the Commonwealth shall have an appeal as a matter of right to the Court of Appeals.

While an appeal is pending from the action of the Department denying a license or from the court affirming the action of the Department, the person aggrieved shall not drive a motor vehicle on the highways of the Commonwealth.

§46.2-322. Examination of licensee believed incapacitated; suspension, or restriction of license; license application to include questions as to physical or mental conditions of applicant; false answers; examination of applicant; physician's statement.

A. If the Department has good cause to believe that a driver is incapacitated and therefore unable to drive a motor vehicle safely, after written notice of at least fifteen days to the person, it may require him to submit to an examination to determine his fitness to drive a motor vehicle. If the driver so requests in writing, the Department shall give the Department's reasons for the examination, including the identity of all persons who have supplied information to the Department regarding the driver's fitness to drive a motor vehicle. However, the Department shall not supply the reasons or information if its source is a relative of the driver or a physician treating the driver.

B. As a part of its examination, the Department may require a physical examination by a licensed physician and a report on the results thereof. When it has completed its examination, the Department shall take whatever action may be appropriate and may suspend the license or privilege to drive a motor vehicle in the Commonwealth of the person or permit him to retain his license or privilege to drive a motor vehicle in the Commonwealth, or may issue a license subject to the restrictions authorized by §46.2-329. Refusal or neglect of the person to submit to the examination or comply with restrictions imposed by the Department shall be grounds for suspension of his license or privilege to drive a motor vehicle in the Commonwealth.

C. The Commissioner shall include, as a part of the application for an original driver's license, or renewal thereof, questions as to the existence of physical or mental conditions which impair the ability of the applicant to drive a motor vehicle safely. Any person knowingly giving a false answer to any such question shall be guilty of a Class 2 misdemeanor. If the answer to any such question indicates the existence of such condition, the Commissioner shall require an examination of the applicant by a licensed physician as a prerequisite to the issuance of the driver's license. The report of the examination shall contain a statement that, in the opinion of the physician, the applicant's physical or mental condition at the time of the examination does or does not preclude his safe driving of motor vehicles.

(Chgd. by L.1997 ch. 801, eff. 1/1/98.)

ARTICLE 4
OBTAINING LICENSES, GENERALLY

§46.2-323. Application for driver's license; proof of completion of driver education program; penalty.

A. Every application for a driver's license, temporary driver's permit, learner's permit, or motorcycle learner's permit shall be made on a form prescribed by the Department and the applicant shall write his usual signature in ink in the space provided on the form. The form shall include notice to the applicant of the duty to register with the Department of State Police as provided in §19.2-298.1, if the applicant has been convicted of a felony in violation of §§18.2-61, 18.2-63, 18.2-64.1, 18.2-67.1, 18.2-67.2, 18.2-67.3, 18.2-67.5, 18.2-370 or §18.2-370.1 or, where the victim is a minor or is physically helpless or mentally incapacitated as defined in §18.2-67.10, subsection B of §18.2-361 or subsection B of §18.2-366, including juveniles tried and convicted in the circuit courts pursuant to §16.1-269 whether sentenced as adults or juveniles, or a felony under a substantially similar law of the United States or any other state.

B. Every application shall state the name, year, month and date of birth, social security number, sex, and residence address of the applicant; whether or not the applicant has previously been licensed as a driver and, if so, when and by what state, and whether or not his license has ever been suspended or revoked and, if so, the date of and reason for such suspension or revocation. The Department, as a condition for the issuance of any driver's license, temporary driver's permit, learner's permit, or motorcycle learner's permit may require the surrender of any driver's license or, in the case of a motorcycle learner's permit, a motorcycle license issued by another state and held by the applicant. The applicant shall also answer any questions on the application form or otherwise propounded by the Department incidental to the examination. The applicant may also be required to present to the person conducting the examination a birth certificate or other evidence, reasonably acceptable to the Department, of his name and date of birth.

The applicant shall also certify that he is a resident of the Commonwealth by signing a certification statement, on a form prescribed by the Commissioner, and by providing satisfactory proof that he is a resident of the Commonwealth. The Commissioner may adopt regulations to determine the process by which applicants prove that they are residents of the Commonwealth.

If the applicant either (i) fails or refuses to sign the certification statement or (ii) fails to follow the process determined by the Commissioner for proving residency, the Department shall not issue the applicant a driver's license, temporary driver's permit, learner's permit or motorcycle learner's permit.

Any applicant who knowingly makes a false certification of Virginia residency or supplies false or fictitious evidence of Virginia residency shall be punished as provided in §46.2-348.

The Commissioner may, on a case-by-case basis, waive any provision of such regulations for good cause shown.

C. Every application for a driver's license shall include a color photograph of the applicant supplied under arrangements made by the Department. The photograph shall be processed by the Department so that the photograph can be made part of the issued license.

D. Notwithstanding the provisions of §46.2-334, every unlicensed applicant for a driver's license who is under nineteen years of age shall furnish the Department with satisfactory proof of his successful completion of a driver education program approved by the State Department of Education.

(Chgd. by L.1998 ch. 322, eff. 7/1/98.)

§46.2-323.1. Certification of Virginia residency; nonresidents not to be issued driver's licenses, commercial driver's licenses, or learner's permits; penalty.

No driver's license, commercial driver's license, or learner's permit shall be issued to any person who is not a Virginia resident. Every person applying for a driver's license, commercial driver's license, or learner's permit shall execute and furnish to the Commissioner his certificate that he is a resident of Virginia. The Commissioner or his duly authorized agent may require any such applicant to supply, along with his application, such evidence of his Virginia residency as the Commissioner may deem appropriate and adequate. It shall be unlawful for any applicant knowingly to make a false certification of Virginia residency or supply false or fictitious evidence of Virginia residency. Any violation of this section shall be punished as provided in §46.2-348.

§46.2-324. Applicants and license holders to notify Department of change of address.

Whenever any person, after applying for or obtaining a driver's license shall move from the address shown in the application or on the license, he shall, within thirty days, notify the Department of his change of address.

There may be imposed upon anyone failing to comply with this section a fee of five dollars, which fee shall be used to defray the expenses incurred by the Department.

(Chgd. by L.1996 chs. 943, 994, eff. 1/1/97.)

§46.2-324.1. Requirements for initial licensure of certain applicants.

No driver's license shall be issued to any applicant unless he either (i) provides written evidence of having satisfactorily completed a course of driver instruction at a commercial driver training school licensed under Chapter 17 (§46.2-1700 et seq.) of this title or a comparable course approved by the Department or Department of Education or (ii) has held a learner's permit issued by the Department for at least thirty days prior to his first behind-the-wheel examination by the Department.

The provisions of this section shall only apply to persons who are at least 19 years old and who either (i) have never held a driver's license issued by Virginia or any other state or territory of the United States or foreign country with which the Commissioner has established reciprocal driver's licensing privileges or (ii) have never been licensed or held the license endorsement or classification required to operate the type of vehicle which they now propose to operate. The provisions of this section shall apply to applicants for commercial driver's licenses who have never before held a commercial driver's license.

(Added by L.2000 ch. 685, eff. 7/1/2000.)

§46.2-325. Examination of applicants; waiver of Department's examination under certain circumstances.

The Department shall examine every applicant for a driver's license before issuing any license to determine (i) his physical and mental qualifications and his ability to drive a motor vehicle without jeopardizing the safety of persons or property and (ii) if any facts exist which would bar the issuance of a license under §§46.2-311 through 46.2-316, 46.2-334 or §46.2-335. The examination, however, shall not include investigation of any facts other than those directly pertaining to the ability of the applicant to drive a motor vehicle with safety, or other than those facts declared to be prerequisite to the issuance of a license under this chapter. No applicant otherwise competent shall be required to demonstrate ability to park any motor vehicle except in an adequate parking space between horizontal markers, and not between flags or sticks simulating parked vehicles. Applicants for licensure to drive motor vehicles of the classifications referred to in §46.2-328 shall submit to examinations which relate to the operation of those vehicles.

Except for applicants subject to §46.2-312, if the Commissioner is satisfied that an applicant has demonstrated the same proficiency as required by the Department's examination through successful completion of either (i) the driver education course approved by the Department of Education or (ii) a driver training course offered by a commercial driver training school licensed under Chapter 17 (§46.2-1700 et seq.) of this title, he may waive those parts of the Department's examination provided for in this section that require the applicant to drive and park a motor vehicle.

(Chgd. by L.1995 ch. 847; L.1997 ch. 841, eff. 7/1/97.)

§46.2-326. Designation of examiners; conduct of examination; reports.

The Commissioner shall designate persons within the Commonwealth to act for the Department in examining driver's license applicants. Any person so designated shall conduct examinations of driver's license applicants under this title and report his findings and recommendations to the Department.

§46.2-327. Copies of applications; record of licenses and learner's permits issued, suspended, or revoked.

The Department shall retain a copy of every application for a driver's license or learner's permit. The Department shall index and maintain a record of all licenses and learner's permits issued, suspended, or revoked.

§46.2-328. Department to issue licenses; endorsements, classifications, and restrictions authorizing operation of certain vehicles.

A. The Department shall issue to every person licensed as a driver, a driver's license. Every driver's license shall contain all appropriate endorsements, classifications, and restrictions, where applicable, if the licensee has been licensed:

1. To operate a motorcycle as defined in §46.2-100, or
2. To operate a school bus as defined in §46.2-100, or
3. To operate a commercial motor vehicle pursuant to the provisions of the Virginia Commercial Driver's License Act (§46.2-341.1 et seq.).

B. Every applicant intending to operate one or more of the motor vehicles described in subsection A of this section, when applying for a driver's license, shall state in his application the classification of the vehicle or vehicles that he intends to operate and for which he seeks to be licensed and submit to and pass the examination provided for in §46.2-325 and, if applicable, §§46.2-337 and 46.2-341.14, using the type of vehicle or vehicles for which he seeks to be licensed.

C. Every applicant intending to drive a motorcycle, when applying for a license endorsed to authorize the driving of a motorcycle, shall submit to and pass the examination provided for in §46.2-337. A classification on any license to drive a motorcycle shall indicate that the license is classified for the purpose of authorizing the licensee to drive only motorcycles. However, if the applicant has a valid license at the time of application for a classification to drive a motorcycle, or if the applicant, at the time of such application, applies for a regular driver's license and submits to and passes the examination provided for in §46.2-325, he shall be granted a classification on his license to drive motorcycles in addition to any other vehicles his driver's license or commercial driver's license may authorize him to operate.

D. The Department may make any changes in the classifications and endorsements during the validity of the license as may be appropriate.

E. The provisions of this section shall be applicable to persons applying for learner's permits as otherwise provided for in this title.

F. Every person issued a driver's license or commercial driver's license who drives any motor vehicle of the classifications in this section, and whose driver's license does not carry an endorsement or indication that the licensee is licensed as provided in this section shall be guilty of a Class 1 misdemeanor.

(Chgd. by L.2000 ch. 269, eff. 7/1/2000.)

§46.2-329. Special restrictions on particular licensees.

The Department, on issuing a driver's license may, whenever good cause appears, impose restrictions suitable to the licensee's driving ability with respect to the type of, or special mechanical control devices required on, a motor vehicle which the licensee may drive, or any other restrictions applicable to the licensee as the Department may determine. When it appears from the records of the Department that the licensee has failed or refused to comply with the restrictions imposed on the licensee's driving of a motor vehicle, the Department may, after ten days' written notice to the address indicated in the records of the Department, suspend the person's driver's license and the suspension shall remain in effect until this section has been complied with.

Any person issued a driver's license on which there are printed or stamped restrictions as provided by this section, and who drives a motor vehicle in violation of these restrictions shall be guilty of a Class 2 misdemeanor.

§46.2-330. Expiration and renewal of licenses; examinations required.

A. Every driver's license shall expire on the last day of the month of birth of the applicant in years in which the applicant attains an age equally divisible by five. At no time shall any driver's license be issued for less than three nor more than seven years. Thereafter the driver's license shall be renewed in the birthday month of the licensee and shall be valid for five years, expiring in the next year in which the licensee's age is equally divisible by five.

B. Within one year prior to the date shown on the driver's license as the date of expiration, the Department shall mail notice, to the holder thereof, at the address shown on the records of the Department in its driver's license file, that his license will expire on a date specified therein, whether he must be reexamined, and when he may be reexamined. Nonreceipt of the notice shall not extend the period of validity of the driver's license beyond its expiration date.

Any driver's license may be renewed by application, which shall include the applicant's certification of Virginia residency, after the applicant has taken and successfully completed those parts of the examination provided for in §§46.2-311, 46.2-325 and the Virginia Commercial Driver's License Act (§46.2-341.1 et seq.), including visual and written tests, other than the parts of the examination requiring the applicant to drive a motor vehicle. All drivers applying in person for renewal of a license shall take and successfully complete the examination each renewal year.

C. Notwithstanding any other provision of this section, the Commissioner, in his discretion, may require any applicant for renewal to be fully examined as provided in §§46.2-311, 46.2-325 and the Virginia Commercial Driver's License Act (§46.2-341.1 et seq.). Furthermore, the Commissioner may waive the visual examination for any applicant for renewal of a driver's license which is not a commercial driver's license, and the requirement or the taking of the written test as provided in subsection B of this section, §46.2-325 and the Virginia Commercial Driver's License Act (§46.2-341.1 et seq.), for any applicant for renewal if the applicant's driver's license record on file at the Department contains, for the five years prior to the expiration date of the license being renewed, a record of no more than one conviction for any offense reportable under §§46.2-382, 46.2-382.1, and 46.2-383. However, in no case shall there be any waiver of the visual examination for applicants for renewal of a commercial driver's license or of the knowledge test required by the Virginia Commercial Driver's License Act for the hazardous materials endorsement on a commercial driver's license.

D. Every applicant for renewal of a driver's license, whether renewal shall or shall not be dependent on any examination of the applicant, shall appear in person before the Department to apply for renewal, unless specifically notified by the Department that renewal may be accomplished in another manner as provided in the notice.

E. This section shall not modify the provisions of §46.2-331.

(Chgd. by L.1997 ch. 486, eff. 7/1/97.)

§46.2-331. Extension of licenses for persons in armed services or foreign service.

Any driver's license issued under this chapter shall be held not to have expired during the period of the licensee's service, if any, outside the Commonwealth of Virginia, in the armed services of the United States or as a member of the diplomatic service of the United States of America, appointed under the Foreign Service Act of 1946, serving outside the United States and six months thereafter. However, no extension granted under this section shall exceed five years from the date of expiration shown on the individual's driver's license. Any person whose license is extended under this section shall have documentary or other proof, when operating any motor vehicle, that he is entitled to the benefits of this section.

§46.2-332. Fees.

On and after January 1, 1990, the fee for each driver's license other than a commercial driver's license shall be two dollars and forty cents per year. If the license is a commercial driver's license or seasonal restricted commercial driver's license, the fee shall be six dollars per year. Persons twenty-one years old or older may be issued a scenic driver's license, learner's permit, or commercial driver's license for an additional fee of five dollars. For any one or more driver's license endorsements, except a motorcycle endorsement, there shall be an additional fee of one dollar per year; for a motorcycle endorsement, there shall be an additional fee of two dollars per year. For any and all driver's license classifications, there shall be an additional fee of one dollar per year. For any revalidation of a seasonal restricted commercial driver's license, the fee shall be five dollars.

A reexamination fee of two dollars shall be charged for each administration of the knowledge portion of the driver's license examination taken by an applicant who is eighteen years of age or older if taken more than once within a fifteen-day period. The reexamination fee shall be charged each time the examination is administered until the applicant successfully completes the examination, if taken prior to the fifteenth day.

An applicant who is less than eighteen years of age who does not successfully complete the knowledge portion of the driver's license examination shall not be permitted to take the knowledge portion more than once in fifteen days.

If the applicant for a driver's license is an employee of the Commonwealth, or of any county, city, or town who drives a motorcycle or a commercial motor vehicle solely in the line of his duty, he shall be exempt from the additional fee otherwise assessable for a motorcycle classification or a commercial motor vehicle endorsement. The Commissioner may prescribe the forms as may be requisite for completion by persons claiming exemption from additional fees imposed by this section.

No additional fee above two dollars and forty cents per year shall be assessed for the driver's license or commercial driver's license required for the operation of a school bus.

Excluding the two-dollar reexamination fee, one dollar and fifty cents of all fees collected for each original or renewal driver's license shall be paid into the driver education fund of the state treasury and expended as provided by law. Unexpended funds from the driver education fund shall be retained in the fund and be available for expenditure in ensuing years as provided therein.

All fees for motorcycle endorsements shall be distributed as provided in §46.2-1191.

This section shall supersede conflicting provisions of this chapter.

(Chgd. by L.1996 chs. 943, 994; L.1997 chs. 104, 493; L.1999 ch. 593, eff. 7/1/99.)

§46.2-333. Disposition of fees; expenses.

Except as otherwise provided in this chapter, all fees accruing under the provisions of this chapter shall be paid to, and received by the Commissioner, and by him forthwith paid into the state treasury and set aside as a special fund to be used to meet the necessary expenses incurred by the Department.

ARTICLE 5
LICENSURE OF MINORS, STUDENT DRIVERS, SCHOOL BUS DRIVERS, AND MOTORCYCLISTS

Section

§46.2-334. Conditions and requirements for licensure of persons under eighteen; requests for cancellation of minor's driver's license; temporary driver's licenses; Board of Education approved programs; fee.

A. Minors at least sixteen years old may be issued driver's licenses under the following conditions:

1. The minor shall submit a proper application and satisfactory evidence that he (i) is a resident of the Commonwealth; (ii) has successfully completed a driver education course approved by either the State Department of Education or, in the case of a course offered by a commercial driver training school licensed under Chapter 17 (§46.2-1700 et seq.) of this title, by the Department of Motor Vehicles; and (iii) is mentally, physically, and otherwise qualified to drive a motor vehicle safely.

2. The minor's application for a driver's license must be signed by a parent of the applicant, otherwise by the guardian having custody of him. However, in the event a minor has no parent or guardian, then a driver's license shall not be issued to him unless his application is signed by the judge of the juvenile and domestic relations district court of the city or county in which he resides. If the minor making the application is married or otherwise emancipated, in lieu of any parent's, guardian's or judge's signature, the minor may present proper evidence of the solemnization of the marriage or the order of emancipation.

3. The minor shall be required to state in his application whether or not he has been convicted of an offense triable by, or tried in, a juvenile and domestic relations district court or found by such court to be a child in need of supervision, as defined in §16.1-228. If it appears that the minor has been adjudged not innocent of the offense alleged or has been found to be a child in need of supervision, the Department shall not issue a license without the written approval of the judge of the juvenile and domestic relations district court making an adjudication as to the minor or the like approval of a similar court of the county or city in which the parent or guardian, respectively, of the minor resides.

4. The application for a permanent driver's license by a minor of the age of persons required to attend school pursuant to §22.1-254 shall be accompanied by evidence of compliance with the compulsory school attendance law set forth in Article 1 (§22.1-254 et seq.) of Chapter 14 of Title 22.1. This evidence shall be provided in writing by the minor's parent. If the minor is unable to provide such evidence, he shall not be granted a driver's license until he reaches the age of eighteen, presents proper evidence of solemnization of his marriage or an order of emancipation or the parent, as defined in §22.1-1, or other person standing in loco parentis, has provided written authorization for the minor to obtain a driver's license.

A minor may, however, present a high school diploma or its equivalent or a certificate indicating completion of a prescribed course of study as defined by the local school board pursuant to §22.1-253.13:4 as evidence of compulsory school attendance compliance.

5. The minor applicant shall certify in writing, on a form prescribed by the Commissioner, that he is a resident of the Commonwealth. The applicant's parent or guardian shall also certify that the applicant is a resident by signing the certification. Any minor providing proper evidence of the solemnization of his marriage or a certified copy of a court order of emancipation shall not be required to provide the parent's certification of residence.

B. Any custodial parent or guardian of an unmarried or unemancipated minor may, after the issuance of a permanent driver's license to such minor, file with the Department a written request that the license of the minor be canceled. When such request is filed, the Department shall cancel the license of the minor and the license shall not thereafter be reissued by the Department until a period of six months has elapsed from the date of cancellation or the minor reaches his eighteenth birthday, whichever shall occur sooner.

C. The provisions of subsection A of this section requiring that an application for a driver's license be signed by the parent or guardian shall be waived by the Commissioner if the application is accompanied by proper evidence of the solemnization of the minor's marriage or a certified copy of a court order, issued under the provisions of Article 15 (§16.1-331 et seq.) of Chapter 11 of Title 16.1, declaring the applicant to be an emancipated minor.

D. A learner's permit accompanied by documentation verifying the minor's successful completion of an approved driver's education course, signed by the minor's parent, guardian, legal custodian or other person standing in loco parentis, shall constitute a temporary driver's license for purposes of driving unaccompanied by a licensed driver as required in §46.2-335, if all other requirements of this chapter have been met. The temporary license shall only be valid until the permanent license is presented as provided in §46.2-336.

E. Notwithstanding the provisions of subsection A of this section requiring the successful completion of a driver education course approved by the State Department of Education, the Commissioner, on application therefor by a person at least sixteen years of age but less than eighteen years of age, shall issue to the applicant a temporary driver's license valid for six months if he (i) certifies by signing, together with his parent or guardian, on a form prescribed by the Commissioner that he is a resident of the Commonwealth; (ii) is the holder of a valid driver's license from another state; and (iii) has not been found guilty of or otherwise responsible for an offense involving the operation of a motor vehicle. No temporary license issued under this subsection shall be renewed, nor shall any second or subsequent temporary license under this subsection be issued to the same applicant. Any such minor providing proper evidence of the solemnization of his marriage or a certified copy of a court order of emancipation shall not be required to obtain the signature of his parent or guardian for the temporary driver's license.

F. For persons qualifying for a driver's license through driver education courses approved by the Department of Education or courses offered by commercial driver training schools licensed by the Department, the application for the learner's permit shall be used as the application for the driver's license pursuant to §46.2-335.

G. Driver's licenses shall be issued by the Department to minors successfully completing driver education courses approved by the Department of Education (i) when the Department receives from the school proper certification that the student (a) has successfully completed such course, including a road skills examination and (b) is regularly attending school and is in good academic standing or, if not in such standing or submitting evidence thereof, whose parent or guardian, having custody of such minor, provides written authorization for the minor to obtain a driver's license, which written authorization shall be obtained on forms provided by the Department and indicating the Commonwealth's interest in the good academic standing and regular school attendance of such minors; and (ii) upon payment of a fee of $2.40 per year, based on the period of the license's validity. For applicants attending public schools, good academic standing may be certified by the public school principal or any of his designees. For applicants attending nonpublic schools, such certification shall be made by the private school principal or any of his designees; for minors receiving home schooling, such certification shall be made by the home schooling parent or tutor. Any minor providing proper evidence of the solemnization of his marriage or a certified copy of a court order of emancipation shall not be required to provide the certification of good academic standing or any written authorization from his parent or guardian to obtain a driver's license.

(Chgd. by L.1995 ch. 535; L.1996 chs. 616, 943, 994, 1011, 1022; L.1997 ch. 841; L.1999 chs. 459, 462, 887, eff. 7/1/99.)

§46.2-334.01. Licenses issued to persons less than eighteen years old subject to certain restrictions.

Any learner's permit or driver's license issued on or after July 1, 1998, to any person less than eighteen years old shall be subject to the following:

1. Notwithstanding the provisions of §46.2-498, whenever the driving record of a person less than eighteen years old shows that he has been convicted of (i) an offense for which demerit points have been assessed or are assessable under Article 19 (§46.2-489 et seq.) of this chapter or (ii) a violation of any provision of Article 12 (§46.2-1091 et seq.) or Article 13 (§46.2-1095 et seq.) of Chapter 10 of this title:

a. The Commissioner shall direct such person to attend a driver improvement clinic. No safe driving points shall be awarded for such clinic attendance, nor shall any safe driving points be awarded for voluntary or court-assigned clinic attendance.

b. No motor vehicle, while being operated by any person holding a learner's permit or driver's license subject to the restrictions contained in this section, shall transport more than three passengers, in addition to the driver, who are less than eighteen years old. This limitation, however, shall not apply to (i) members of the driver's family or household or (ii) a driver less than eighteen years old who is driving to or from either school or his place of employment. No citation for a violation of this subdivision shall be issued unless the officer issuing such citation has cause to stop or arrest the driver of such motor vehicle for the violation of some other provision of this Code or local ordinance relating to the operation, ownership, or maintenance of a motor vehicle or any criminal statute. For the purpose of this subdivision, "members of the driver's family or household" means (i) the driver's spouse, whether or not he or she resides in the same home with the driver; (ii) the driver's former spouse, whether or not he or she resides in the same home with the driver; (iii) the driver's children, stepchildren, brothers, sisters, half brothers, and half sisters, whether or not they reside in the same home with the driver; (iv) the driver's brothers-in-law and sisters-in-law who reside in the same home with the driver; (v) any individual who has a child in common with the driver, whether or not the driver and that individual have been married or have resided together at any time; or (vi) any individual who cohabits or who, within the previous twelve months, cohabited with the driver, and any children of either of them residing in the same home with the driver.

2. If any person less than eighteen years old is convicted a second time of (i) an offense for which demerit points have been assessed or are assessable under Article 19 (§46.2-489 et seq.) of this chapter or (ii) a violation of any provision of Article 12 (§46.2-1091 et seq.) or Article 13 (§46.2-1095 et seq.) of Chapter 10 of this title, the Commissioner shall suspend such person's driver's license or privilege to operate a motor vehicle for ninety days. Such suspension shall be consecutive to, and not concurrent with, any other period of license suspension, revocation or denial.

3. If any such person is convicted a third time of (i) an offense for which demerit points have been assessed or are assessable under Article 19 (§46.2-489 et seq.) of this chapter or (ii) a violation of any provision of Article 12 (§46.2-1091 et seq.) or Article 13 (§46.2-1095 et seq.) of Chapter 10 of this title, the Commissioner shall revoke such person's driver's license or privilege to operate a motor vehicle for one year or until such person reaches the age of eighteen years, whichever is longer. Such revocation shall be consecutive to, and not concurrent with, any other period of license suspension, revocation or denial.

4. In no event shall a driver who is under the age of eighteen and subject to the provisions of this section, be subject to the suspension or revocation provisions of subdivision 2 or 3 of this section for multiple convictions arising out of the same transaction or occurrence.

(Added by L.1998 chs. 124, 792, eff. 7/1/98.)

§46.2-334.1. Knowledge test; waiting period prior to reexamination.

Any person under the age of eighteen who applies for a driver's license under §46.2-334 and fails the motor vehicle knowledge test administered pursuant to that section shall not be eligible for retesting for at least fifteen days.

(Added by L.1996 ch. 1035, eff. 7/1/96.)

§46.2-335. Learner's permits; fees.

A. The Department, on receiving from any Virginia resident over the age of fifteen years an application for a learner's permit or motorcycle learner's permit, may, subject to the applicant's satisfactory documentation of meeting the requirements of this chapter and successful completion of the written or automated knowledge and vision examinations and, in the case of a motorcycle learner's permit applicant, the automated motorcycle test, issue a permit entitling the applicant, while having the permit in his immediate possession, to drive a motor vehicle or, if the application is made for a motorcycle learner's permit, a motorcycle, on the highways, when accompanied by any licensed driver twenty-one years of age or older or by his parent or legal guardian, or by a brother, sister, half-brother, half-sister, step-brother, or step-sister eighteen years of age or older. The accompanying person shall be (i) actually occupying a seat beside the driver or, for motorcycle instruction, providing immediate supervision from a separate accompanying motorcycle and (ii) lawfully permitted to operate the motor vehicle or accompanying motorcycle at that time.

The Department shall not, however, issue a learner's permit or motorcycle learner's permit to any minor applicant required to provide evidence of compliance with the compulsory school attendance law set forth in Article 1 (§22.1-254 et seq.) of Chapter 14 of Title 22.1, unless such applicant is in good academic standing or, if not in such standing or submitting evidence thereof, whose parent or guardian, having custody of such minor, provides written authorization for the minor to obtain a learner's permit or motorcycle learner's permit, which written authorization shall be obtained on forms provided by the Department and indicating the Commonwealth's interest in the good academic standing and regular school attendance of such minors. Any minor providing proper evidence of the solemnization of his marriage or a certified copy of a court order of emancipation shall not be required to provide the certification of good academic standing or any written authorization from his parent or guardian to obtain a learner's permit or motorcycle learner's permit.

Such permit, except a motorcycle learner's permit, shall be valid until the holder thereof either is issued a driver's license as provided for in this chapter or no longer meets the qualifications for issuance of a learner's permit as provided in this section. Motorcycle learner's permits shall be valid for twelve months. When a motorcycle learner's permit expires, the permittee may, upon submission of an application, payment of the application fee, and successful completion of the examinations, be issued another motorcycle learner's permit valid for twelve months.

B. The provisions of §§46.2-323 and 46.2-334 relating to evidence and certification of Virginia residence and, in the case of persons of school age, compliance with the compulsory school attendance law shall apply, mutatis mutandis, to applications for learner's permits and motorcycle learner's permits issued under this section.

C. For persons qualifying for a driver's license through driver education courses approved by the Department of Education or courses offered by commercial driver training schools licensed by the Department, the application for the learner's permit shall be used as the application for the driver's license.

D. The Department shall charge a fee of three dollars for each learner's permit and motorcycle learner's permit issued under this section. Fees for issuance of learner's permits shall be paid into the driver education fund of the state treasury; fees for issuance of motorcycle learner's permits shall be paid into the state treasury and credited to the Motorcycle Rider Safety Training Program Fund created pursuant to §46.2-1191. It shall be unlawful for any person, after having received a learner's permit, to drive a motor vehicle without being accompanied by a licensed driver as provided in the foregoing provisions of this section; however, a learner's permit other than a motorcycle learner's permit, accompanied by documentation verifying that the driver is at least sixteen years of age and has successfully completed an approved driver's education course, signed by the minor's parent, guardian, legal custodian or other person standing in loco parentis, shall constitute a temporary driver's license for the purpose of driving unaccompanied by a licensed driver eighteen years of age or older, if all other requirements of this chapter have been met. Such temporary driver's license shall only be valid until the driver has received his permanent license pursuant to §46.2-336.

E. Nothing in this section shall be construed to permit the issuance of a learner's permit entitling a person to drive a commercial motor vehicle, except as provided by the Virginia Commercial Driver's License Act (§46.2-341.1 et seq.).

F. The following limitations shall apply to operation of motorcycles by persons holding motorcycle learner's permits:

1. Operation shall be limited to the period between one-half hour after sunrise and one-half hour before sunset.
2. Operation on limited access highways is prohibited.
3. The operator shall wear an approved safety helmet as provided in §46.2-910.
4. Operation shall be under the immediate supervision of a person licensed to operate a motorcycle who is twenty-one years of age or older or by his parent or legal guardian, or by a brother, sister, half-brother, half-sister, step-brother, or step-sister eighteen years of age or older.
5. No person other than the operator shall occupy the motorcycle.

G. No holder of a learner's permit or motorcycle learner's permit shall be allowed to take the behind-the-wheel examination administered by the Department more than three times in any three-month period.

H. Any violation of this section shall be punishable as a Class 2 misdemeanor.

(Chgd. by L.1995 chs. 254, 337, 535, 847; L.1996 chs. 892, 894, 918, 943, 994, 1011, 1022, 1035; L.1997 ch. 841; L.1998 ch. 322; L.1999 chs. 459, 462; L.2000 ch. 686, eff. 7/1/2000.)

§46.2-335.1. Knowledge test; waiting period prior to reexamination.

Any person under the age of eighteen who applies for a learner's permit under §46.2-335 and fails the motor vehicle knowledge test administered pursuant to that section shall not be eligible for retesting for at least fifteen days.

(Added by L.1996 ch. 1035, eff. 7/1/96.)

§46.2-335.2. Learner's permits; required before driver's license; minimum holding period.

A. Effective July 1, 1996, no person under the age of eighteen years shall be eligible to receive a driver's license pursuant to §46.2-334 unless the Department has previously issued such person a learner's permit pursuant to §46.2-335 and such person has satisfied the minimum holding period requirements set forth in subsection B, or unless such person is the holder of a valid driver's license from another state and qualifies for a temporary license under subdivision 3 of §46.2-334. However, persons under the age of eighteen years to whom the Department has issued a learner's permit prior to July 1, 1996, shall not be subject to the minimum holding period requirements set forth in subsection B before obtaining a driver's license pursuant to §46.2-334.

B. Effective July 1, 1996, any person under the age of eighteen years issued a learner's permit pursuant to §46.2-335 shall hold such permit for a minimum period of six months or until he reaches the age of eighteen years, whichever occurs first.

(Added by L.1996 ch. 1035, eff. 7/1/96.)

§46.2-336. Manner of issuing original driver's licenses to minors.

The Department shall forward all original driver's licenses issued to applicants under the age of eighteen years to the judge of the juvenile and domestic relations court in the city or county in which the licensee resides. The judge or a substitute judge shall issue to each person to be licensed the license so forwarded, and shall, at the time of issuance, conduct a formal, appropriate ceremony, in which he shall illustrate to the licensee the responsibility attendant on the privilege of driving a motor vehicle. If the licensee was under the age of eighteen years at the time his application was made, he shall be accompanied at the ceremony by a parent, his guardian, spouse, or other person in loco parentis. However, the judge, for good cause shown, may mail or otherwise deliver the driver's license to any person who is a student at any educational institution outside of the Commonwealth of Virginia at the time such license is received by the judge as prescribed in this section.

The provisions of this section shall not apply to the issuance of Virginia driver's licenses to persons who hold valid driver's licenses issued by other states.

(Chgd. by L.1996 ch. 616; L.1998 ch. 472, eff. 7/1/98.)

§46.2-337. Examination and road test required for license to operate motorcycle; regulations.

No person shall drive any motorcycle on a highway in the Commonwealth unless he has passed a special examination, including written material and a road test, pertaining to his ability to drive a motorcycle with reasonable competence and with safety to other persons using the highways. The Department shall adopt regulations as may be necessary to provide for the special examination under §46.2-325 of persons desiring to qualify to drive motorcycles in the Commonwealth and for the granting of licenses or permits suitably endorsed for qualified applicants.

§46.2-339. Qualifications of school bus driver; examination.

No person shall drive any school bus on a highway in the Commonwealth unless he has had a reasonable amount of experience in driving motor vehicles, and has passed a special examination pertaining to his ability to drive a school bus with safety to its passengers and to other persons using the highways. Such person shall obtain a commercial driver's license with the applicable classifications and endorsements, issued pursuant to the Virginia Commercial Driver's License Act (§46.2-341.1 et seq.), if the school bus he drives is a commercial motor vehicle as defined in the Virginia Commercial Driver's License Act. For the purpose of preparing for the examination required by this section, any person holding a valid driver's license issued under Article 4 of this chapter, may drive, under the direct supervision of a person holding a valid school bus license endorsement, a school bus which contains no other passengers, provided that, on and after April 1, 1992, only persons holding a valid commercial driver's license or instruction permit issued under the provisions of the Virginia Commercial Driver's License Act, may operate, under the direct supervision of a person holding a valid commercial driver's license with a school bus endorsement, a school bus which is a commercial motor vehicle as defined in the Virginia Commercial Driver's License Act and which contains no pupil passengers. The Department may adopt regulations necessary to provide for the examination of persons desiring to qualify to drive school buses in the Commonwealth and for the granting of permits to qualified applicants.

§46.2-340. Information concerning school bus drivers and driver education instructors.

A. At the beginning of each school year, and whenever changes need to be made, each local school division shall furnish to the Department of Motor Vehicles the name, driver's license number, and commercial driver's license number of all persons driving school buses for that school division. Whenever any commercial driver's license with a school bus driver's endorsement is suspended or revoked, or the holder of a driver's license with a school bus driver's endorsement or commercial driver's license with a school bus driver's endorsement is convicted in any court of reckless driving or driving while intoxicated, the Department shall notify the affected local school division of the name and driver's license number or commercial driver's license number of the driver involved.

B. At the beginning of each school year, and whenever changes need to be made, each local school division and private school providing a driver education program approved by the Department of Education shall furnish to the Department of Motor Vehicles the name and driver's license number of all persons providing instruction in driver education for that school division or private school. Whenever a driver's license of a person providing such instruction is suspended or revoked, or such person is convicted in any court of reckless driving or driving while intoxicated, the Department shall notify the affected local school division or private school of the name and driver's license number of the driver involved.

If the driving record of such driver education instructor accumulates more than six demerit points based on convictions occurring in any calendar year, the Department shall notify the relevant local school division or private school of the name and driver's license number of the driver. Safe driving points shall not be used to reduce the six demerit points. No driver education program in a public school division or a private school shall retain its approval by the Department of Education unless such a person who has accumulated such six demerit points is removed from providing behind-the-wheel driver education instruction in the private school or public school division for a period of twenty-four months.

C. The provisions of the Privacy Protection Act of 1976 (Chapter 26 of Title 2.1, §2.1-377 et seq.) shall not apply to the exchange of information under this section.
(Chgd. by L.1999 ch. 463, eff. 7/1/99.)

ARTICLE 6.1
COMMERCIAL DRIVER'S LICENSES

Section

§46.2-341.1. Title.

This Act may be cited as the "Virginia Commercial Driver's License Act."

§46.2-341.2. Statement of intent and purpose.

The purpose of this Act is to improve the safety of commercial motor vehicle operations in the Commonwealth and to implement in Virginia the applicable provisions of the federal Commercial Motor Vehicle Safety Act of 1986 (Title XII of Pub. Law 99–570), as amended. It is intended that the adoption of this Act, in conjunction with the

 Zv

adoption of similar legislation in all other states, will improve the safety of commercial motor vehicle operations in Virginia and in the United States by (i) permitting commercial drivers to hold only one driver's license and to have only one driving record; (ii) disqualifying drivers from the operation of commercial motor vehicles for certain offenses and violations; and (iii) strengthening licensing and testing standards for commercial drivers.

§46.2-341.3. Conflicts; supplement to driver licensing statutes.

This article is intended to supplement, not supplant, the laws of the Commonwealth relating to drivers, driver licensing, vehicles and vehicle operations, which laws shall continue to apply to persons required to be licensed pursuant to this article, unless the context clearly indicates otherwise. To the extent that any provisions of this article conflict with such other laws of the Commonwealth, the provisions of this article shall prevail. Where this article is silent, such other laws shall apply.

Notwithstanding the provisions of §46.2-1300, the governing bodies of counties, cities or towns shall not be authorized to adopt ordinances that are substantially similar to the provisions of this article.

§46.2-341.4. Definitions.

The following definitions shall apply to this article, unless a different meaning is clearly required by the context:

"Commercial driver's license" means any driver's license issued to a person in accordance with the provisions of this article, or if the license is issued by another state, any license issued to a person in accordance with the federal Commercial Motor Vehicle Safety Act, which authorizes such person to drive a commercial motor vehicle of the class and type and with the restrictions indicated on the license.

"Commercial motor vehicle" means: Except for those vehicles specifically excluded in this subsection, every motor vehicle, vehicle or combination of vehicles used to transport passengers or property which either: (i) has a gross vehicle weight rating of 26,001 or more pounds; or (ii) has a gross combination weight rating of 26,001 or more pounds inclusive of a towed vehicle with a gross vehicle weight rating of more than 10,000 pounds; or (iii) is designed to transport sixteen or more passengers including the driver; or (iv) is of any size and is used in the transportation of hazardous materials as defined in this section. Every such motor vehicle or combination of vehicles shall be considered a commercial motor vehicle whether or not it is used in a commercial or profit-making activity.

The following shall be excluded from the definition of commercial motor vehicle: any vehicle when used by an individual solely for his own personal purposes, such as personal recreational activities; or any vehicle which (i) is controlled and operated by a farmer, whether or not it is owned by the farmer, and which is used exclusively for farm use, as defined in §46.2-698, (ii) is used to transport either agricultural products, farm machinery or farm supplies to or from a farm, (iii) is not used in the operation of a common or contract motor carrier and (iv) is used within 150 miles of the farmer's farm; or any military vehicle when operated by active duty military personnel, or members of the military reserves or national guard when on active duty, in the pursuit of military purposes; or emergency equipment operated by a member of a firefighting, rescue, or emergency entity in the performance of his official duties.

"Commercial Motor Vehicle Safety Act" means the federal Commercial Motor Vehicle Safety Act of 1986, Title XII of Public Law 99–570, as amended.

"Conviction" means an unvacated adjudication of guilt, or a determination that a person has violated or failed to comply with the law in a court of original jurisdiction, an unvacated forfeiture of bond, bail or collateral deposited to secure the person's appearance in court, a plea of guilty or nolo contendere accepted by the court, the payment of a fine or court costs in lieu of trial, a violation of a condition of release without bail, regardless of whether the penalty is rebated, suspended or probated, or, for the purposes of alcohol or drug-related offenses involving the operation of a motor vehicle, a civil or an administrative determination of a violation. For the purposes of this definition, an administrative determination shall include an unvacated certification or finding by an administrative or authorized law-enforcement official that a person has violated a provision of law.

"Disqualification" means a prohibition against driving, operating or being in physical control of a commercial motor vehicle for a specified period of time, imposed by a court or a magistrate, or by an authorized administrative or law-enforcement official or body.

"Domicile" means a person's true, fixed and permanent home and principal residence, to which he intends to return whenever he is absent.

"Gross combination weight rating" means the value specified by the manufacturers of an articulated vehicle or combination of vehicles as the maximum loaded weight of such vehicles. In the absence of such a value specified by the manufacturer, the gross combination weight rating shall be the greater of (i) the gross vehicle weight rating of the power units of the combination vehicle plus the total weight of the towed units, including any loads thereon, or (ii) the gross weight at which the articulated vehicle or combination of vehicles is registered in its state of registration.

"Gross vehicle weight rating" means the value specified by the manufacturer of the vehicle as the maximum loaded weight of a single vehicle. In the absence of such a value specified by the manufacturer, the gross vehicle weight rating shall be the gross weight at which the vehicle is registered in its state of registration.

"Hazardous materials" means materials determined to be hazardous in accordance with §103 of the federal Hazardous Materials Transportation Act (49 U.S.C. §1801 et seq.), as amended, and which require placarding when transported by motor vehicle as provided in the federal Hazardous Materials Regulations (49 C.F.R. Part 172, Subpart F).

"Seasonal restricted commercial driver's license" means a commercial driver's license issued, under the authority of the waiver promulgated by the federal Department of Transportation (57 Federal Register 13650) by Virginia or any other jurisdiction to an individual who has not passed the knowledge or skills tests required of other commercial driver's license holders. This license authorizes operation of a commercial motor vehicle only on a seasonal basis, stated on the license, by a seasonal employee of a farm service business, within 150 miles of the place of business or the farm currently being served.

"State" means one of the fifty states of the United States or the District of Columbia.

(Chgd. by L.1998 ch. 883, eff. 7/1/98.)

§46.2-341.5. Regulations consistent with Commercial Motor Vehicle Safety Act.

The Department is authorized to promulgate regulations and establish procedures to enable it to issue commercial driver's licenses, maintain and exchange driver records, and impose licensing sanctions consistent with the provisions of this article and with the minimum standards of the federal Commercial Motor Vehicle Safety Act and the federal regulations promulgated thereunder.

§46.2-341.6. Limitation on number of driver's licenses.

No person who drives a commercial motor vehicle shall have more than one driver's license.

§46.2-341.7. Commercial driver's license required; penalty.

A. No person shall drive a commercial motor vehicle in the Commonwealth unless he has been issued a commercial driver's license and unless such license authorizes the operation of the type and class of vehicle so driven, and unless such license is valid.

B. Every driver of a commercial motor vehicle, while driving such vehicle in the Commonwealth, shall have in his immediate possession the commercial driver's license authorizing the operation of such vehicle and shall make it available to any law-enforcement officer upon request. Failure to comply with this subsection shall be punishable as provided in §46.2-104.

C. No person shall drive a commercial vehicle in Virginia in violation of any of the restrictions or limitations stated on his commercial driver's license. A violation of the subsection shall constitute a Class 2 misdemeanor.

§46.2-341.8. Nonresidents and new residents.

Any person who is not domiciled in the Commonwealth, who has been duly issued a commercial driver's license by his state of domicile, who has such license in his immediate possession, whose privilege or license to drive any motor vehicle is not suspended, revoked, or cancelled, and who has not been disqualified from driving a commercial motor vehicle, shall be permitted without further examination or licensure by the Commonwealth, to drive a commercial motor vehicle in the Commonwealth.

Within thirty days after becoming domiciled in this Commonwealth, any person who has been issued a commercial driver's license by another state and who intends to drive a commercial motor vehicle shall apply to the Department for a Virginia commercial driver's license. The Commissioner may establish, by regulation, the criteria by which the test requirements for a commercial driver's license may be waived for any such applicant.

§46.2-341.9. Eligibility for commercial driver's license.

A Virginia commercial driver's license shall be issued only to a person who drives or intends to drive a commercial motor vehicle and who is domiciled in the Commonwealth, provided that any person who is domiciled in a jurisdiction outside the United States, but has resided in the Commonwealth for a period of six weeks, shall be eligible for a commercial driver's license under such terms and conditions as the Department may require.

No person shall be eligible for a Virginia commercial driver's license until he has applied for such license and has passed the applicable vision, knowledge and skills tests required by this article, and has satisfied all other applicable licensing requirements imposed by the laws of the Commonwealth.

No person shall be eligible for a Virginia commercial driver's license during any period in which he is disqualified from driving a commercial motor vehicle, or his driver's license or privilege to drive is suspended, revoked or cancelled in any state, or during any period wherein the restoration of his license or privilege is contingent upon the furnishing of proof of financial responsibility.

No person shall be eligible for a Virginia commercial driver's license until he surrenders all other driver's licenses issued to him by any state.

No person under the age of twenty-one years shall be eligible for a commercial driver's license, except that a person who is at least eighteen years of age may be issued a commercial driver's license, provided that such person is exempt from or is not subject to the age requirements of the federal Motor Carrier Safety Regulations contained in 49 C.F.R. Part 391, and is not prohibited from operating a commercial motor vehicle by the Virginia Motor Carrier Safety Regulations, and has so certified. No person under the age of twenty-one years shall be issued a hazardous materials endorsement.

§46.2-341.9:1. Commissioner to grant variances for commercial drivers transporting hazardous wastes.

The Commissioner may, to the extent allowed by federal law, grant variances from the regulations with respect to the physical qualifications for drivers of commercial motor vehicles transporting hazardous materials if:

1. The driver is regularly employed in a job requiring the operation of a commercial motor vehicle transporting hazardous materials;
2. The driver is at least twenty-one years of age;
3. A physician licensed in Virginia certifies that, in his professional opinion, the driver is capable of safely operating a commercial motor vehicle transporting hazardous materials; and
4. In the opinion of the Commissioner, the driver is able to perform the normal tasks associated with operating a commercial motor vehicle and comply with the applicable regulations authorized by §10.1-1450.

The Commissioner may promulgate regulations addressing such variances.

(Added by L.1997 ch. 260, eff. 7/1/97.)

§46.2-341.10. Special provisions relating to commercial driver's instruction permit.

The Department, upon receiving an application on forms prescribed by the Commissioner and upon the applicant's satisfactory completion of the vision and knowledge tests required for the class and type of commercial motor vehicle to be driven by the applicant may, in its discretion, issue to such applicant a commercial driver's instruction permit. Such permit shall expire one year after issuance and shall entitle the applicant to drive a commercial motor vehicle of the class and type designated on the permit, but only when accompanied by a person licensed to drive the class and type of commercial motor vehicle driven by the applicant. The person accompanying the permit holder shall occupy the seat closest to the driver's seat for the purpose of giving instruction to the permit holder in driving the commercial motor vehicle.

No person shall be issued a commercial driver's instruction permit unless he possesses a valid Virginia driver's license or has satisfied all the requirements necessary to obtain such a license.

It shall be unlawful for any instruction permit holder to operate a commercial motor vehicle without being accompanied by a licensed driver as provided in this section. Persons who violate this section shall be guilty of a Class 2 misdemeanor.

The Department shall charge a fee of three dollars for each instruction permit issued under the provisions of this section.

§46.2-341.10:1. Seasonal restricted commercial drivers' licenses.

A. The Commissioner may, in his discretion, issue seasonal restricted commercial drivers' licenses in accordance with this section.

B. A Virginia seasonal restricted commercial driver's license shall be issued only to a person who (i) is a seasonal employee of a farm retail outlet or supplier, a custom harvester, a livestock feeder, or an agri-chemical business, (ii) is a Virginia-licensed driver with at least one year of driving experience as a licensed driver, and (iii) has satisfied every requirement for issuance of a commercial driver's license except successful completion of the knowledge and skills test.

C. The Department shall not issue or renew a seasonal restricted commercial driver's license and shall not revalidate the seasonal period for which such license authorizes operation of a commercial motor vehicle, unless:

1. The applicant has not, and certifies that he has not, at any time during the two years immediately preceding the date of application:

a. Had more than one driver's license;

b. Had any driver's license or driving privilege suspended, revoked, or canceled;

c. Had any convictions involving any kind of motor vehicle for any of the offenses listed in §§46.2-341.18, 46.2-341.19, or §46.2-341.20;

d. Been convicted of a violation of state or local laws relating to motor vehicle traffic control, other than a parking violation, which violation arose in connection with any reportable traffic accident;

e. Been convicted of any serious traffic violation, as defined in §46.2-341.20, whether or not committed in a commercial motor vehicle; and

2. The applicant certifies and provides evidence satisfactory to the Commissioner that he is employed on a seasonal basis by a farm retail outlet or supplier, custom harvester, livestock feeder, or agri-chemical business in a job requiring the operation of a commercial motor vehicle.

D. Such seasonal restricted license shall entitle the licensee to drive a commercial motor vehicle of the class and type designated on the license, but shall not authorize operation of a Class A vehicle.

E. Each seasonal restricted license shall authorize operation of a commercial motor vehicle only during the seasonal period or periods prescribed by the Commissioner and stated on the license, provided the total number of calendar days in any twelve-month period for which seasonal restricted license authorizes operation of a commercial motor vehicle shall not exceed 180. The license is valid for operation of a commercial motor vehicle during the seasonal period or periods for which it has been validated and must be revalidated annually by the Department for each successive seasonal period or periods for which commercial vehicle operation is sought; such license shall authorize operation of noncommercial motor vehicles at any time, unless it has been suspended, revoked, or canceled, or has expired.

F. Such seasonal restricted license shall not authorize operation of a commercial motor vehicle during any period during which the licensee is not employed by an entity described in subdivision B hereof, nor if such operation is not directly related to such employment.

G. Such seasonal restricted license shall not authorize the licensee to operate any vehicle transporting hazardous materials as defined in this article, except that a seasonal licensee may drive a vehicle transporting:

1. Diesel fuel in quantities of 1,000 gallons or less;

2. Liquid fertilizers to be used as plant nutrients, in a vehicle or implement of husbandry with a total capacity of 3,000 gallons or less; or

3. Solid plant nutrients that are not transported with any organic substance.

H. Such seasonal restricted license shall authorize operation of a commercial motor vehicle only within 150 miles of the place of business of the licensee's employer or the farm being served.

§46.2-341.11. Commercial drivers required to notify the Department of change of address.

A. If any person who is licensed by the Department to drive a commercial motor vehicle changes the mailing or residential address he most recently submitted to the Department, such person shall notify the Department in writing within thirty days after his change of address.

B. Any violation of this subsection shall constitute a traffic infraction.

§46.2-341.12. Application for commercial driver's license.

A. Every application to the Department for a commercial driver's license shall be made upon a form approved and furnished by the Department, and the applicant shall write his usual signature in ink in the space provided. The applicant shall provide the following information:

1. Full legal name;

2. Current mailing and residential addresses;

3. Physical description including sex, height, weight and eye and hair color;

4. Year, month and date of birth;

5. Social Security number; and

6. Any other information required on the application form.

B. Every applicant for a commercial driver's license shall also submit to the Department the following:

1. A consent to release driving record information;

2. Certifications that:

a. He either meets the federal qualification requirements of 49 C.F.R. Part 391, or he is exempt from or is not subject to such federal requirements;

b. He either meets the state qualification requirements established pursuant to §52-8.4, or he is exempt from or is not subject to such requirements;

c. The motor vehicle in which the applicant takes the skills test is representative of the class and, if applicable, the type of motor vehicle for which the applicant seeks to be licensed;

d. He is not subject to any disqualification, suspension, revocation or cancellation of his driving privileges;

e. He does not have more than one driver's license;

3. Other certifications required by the Department;

4. Any evidence required by the Department to establish proof of identity, including but not limited to a birth certificate; and

5. A statement indicating whether the applicant has ever been licensed as a driver and, if so, when and by what state and whether or not he has ever been disqualified, or his license suspended, revoked or cancelled and, if so, the date of and reason therefor.

C. Every application for a commercial driver's license shall include a color photograph of the applicant supplied under arrangements made therefor by the Department in accordance with §46.2-323.

D. The Department shall disqualify any commercial driver for a period of one year when the records of the Department clearly show to the satisfaction of the Commissioner that such person has made a material false statement on any application or certification made for a commercial driver's license. The Department shall take such action within thirty days after discovering such falsification.

E. The Department shall review the driving record of any person who applies for a Virginia commercial driver's license, for the renewal or reinstatement of such license or for an additional commercial classification or endorsement. The Department's review shall include research through the Commercial Driver License Information System established pursuant to the Commercial Motor Vehicle Safety Act, the

National Driver Register, and the driver record maintained by the applicant's state of licensure.

§46.2-341.13. Disposition of fees.

Except as otherwise provided, all fees accruing under the provisions of this chapter shall be paid to and received by the Commissioner, and by him forthwith paid into the state treasury and shall be set aside as a special fund in the state treasury to be used to meet the necessary additional expenses incurred by the Department of Motor Vehicles and the Commissioner in the performance of the duties required by this article.

§46.2-341.14. Testing requirements for commercial driver's license.

A. The Department shall conduct an examination of every applicant for a commercial driver's license, which examination shall comply with the minimum federal standards established pursuant to the federal Commercial Motor Vehicle Safety Act. The examination shall be designed to test the vision, knowledge, and skills required for the safe operation of the class and type of commercial motor vehicle for which the applicant seeks a license.

B. An applicant's skills test shall be conducted in a vehicle that is representative of or meets the description of the class of vehicle for which the applicant seeks to be licensed. In addition, applicants who seek to be licensed to drive vehicles with air brakes, passenger-carrying vehicles, or school buses must take the skills test in a vehicle that is representative of such vehicle type. Such vehicle shall be furnished by the applicant and shall be properly licensed, inspected and insured.

C. Prior to April 1, 1992, the Commissioner may waive the skills test for applicants licensed at the time they apply for a commercial driver's license if:

1. The applicant has not, and certifies that he has not, at any time during the two years immediately preceeding* the date of application:

**Probably should be "preceding".*

a. Had more than one driver's license, except during the ten-day period beginning on the date such person is issued a driver's license, or unless, prior to December 31, 1989, such applicant was required to have more than one license by a state law enacted before June 1, 1986;

b. Had any driver's license or driving privilege suspended, revoked or canceled;

c. Had any convictions involving any kind of motor vehicle for the offenses listed in §§46.2-341.18, 46.2-341.19, or §46.2-341.20; and

d. Been convicted of a violation of state or local laws relating to motor vehicle traffic control, other than a parking violation, which violation arose in connection with any reportable traffic accident; and

2. The applicant certifies and provides evidence satisfactory to the Commissioner that he is regularly employed in a job requiring the operation of a commercial motor vehicle, and either:

a. Has previously taken and successfully completed a skills test which was administered by a state with a classified licensing and testing system and that test was behind the wheel in a vehicle representative of the class and, if applicable, the type of commercial motor vehicle for which the applicant seeks to be licensed; or

b. Has operated, for at least two years immediately preceding the application date, a vehicle representative of the class and, if applicable, the type of commercial motor vehicle for which the applicant seeks to be licensed.

D. The Commissioner may, in his discretion, designate such persons as he deems fit, including private or governmental entities, to administer the skills tests required of applicants for a commercial driver's license. Any person so designated shall comply with all regulations promulgated by the Commissioner with respect to the administration of such skills tests.

E. Every applicant for a commercial driver's license who is required by the Commissioner to take a vision test shall either (i) appear before a license examiner of the Department of Motor Vehicles to demonstrate his visual acuity and horizontal field of vision; or (ii) submit with his application a report of such examination made within ninety days of the application date by an ophthalmologist or optometrist. The Commissioner may, by regulation, determine whether any other visual tests will satisfy the requirements of this title for commercial drivers.

§46.2-341.15. Commercial driver's license document.

A. The commercial driver's license issued by the Department shall be identified as a Virginia commercial driver's license and shall include at least the following:

1. Full name, address, and signature of the licensee;
2. A color photograph of the licensee;
3. A physical description of the licensee, including sex and height;
4. The licensee's date of birth and Social Security number;
5. A designation of the class and type of commercial motor vehicle or vehicles which the licensee is authorized to drive, together with any restrictions; and
6. The date of license issuance and expiration.

B. The commercial driver's instruction permit shall be identified as such but shall in all other respects conform to subsection A of this section.

§46.2-341.16. Vehicle classifications and endorsements.

A. A commercial driver's license shall authorize the licensee to operate only the classes and types of commercial motor vehicles designated thereon. The classes of commercial motor vehicles for which such license may be issued are:

1. Class A – Combination heavy vehicle. – Any combination of vehicles with a gross combination weight rating of 26,001 or more pounds, provided the gross vehicle weight rating of the vehicles being towed is in excess of 10,000 pounds;
2. Class B – Heavy straight vehicle or other combination. – Any single motor vehicle with a gross vehicle weight rating of 26,001 or more pounds, or any such vehicle towing a vehicle with a gross vehicle weight rating that is not in excess of 10,000 pounds; and
3. Class C – Small vehicle. – Any vehicle that does not fit the definition of a Class A or Class B vehicle and is either (i) designed to transport sixteen or more passengers including the driver or (ii) is used in the transportation of hazardous materials.

B. Commercial driver's licenses shall be issued with endorsements and restrictions authorizing the driver to operate or restricting the driver to the types of vehicles identified as follows:

1. Type T – Vehicles with double or triple trailers;
2. Type P – Vehicles carrying passengers;
3. Type N – Vehicles with cargo tanks;
4. Type H – Vehicles required to be placarded for hazardous materials; and
5. Type K – Vehicles not equipped with air brakes.

C. Persons authorized to drive Class A vehicles are also authorized to drive Classes B and C vehicles, provided such persons possess the requisite endorsements for the type of vehicle driven.

D. Persons authorized to drive Class B vehicles are also authorized to drive Class C vehicles, provided such persons possess the requisite endorsements for the type of vehicle driven.

E. Any licensee who seeks to add a classification or endorsement to his commercial driver's license must submit the application forms, certifications and other updated information required by the Department and shall take and successfully complete the tests required for such classification or endorsement.

§46.2-341.17. Penalty for violation of this article.

Unless otherwise provided in this article or by the laws of the Commonwealth, any person who violates any provision of this article shall be guilty of a Class 2 misdemeanor.

§46.2-341.18. Disqualification for certain offenses.

A. Except as otherwise provided in this section, the Commissioner shall disqualify for a period of one year any person whose record, as maintained by the Department of Motor Vehicles, shows that he has been convicted of any of the following offenses, if such offense was committed while operating a commercial motor vehicle:

1. A violation of any provision of §46.2-341.24 or a violation of any federal law or the law of another state substantially similar to §46.2-341.24;
2. A violation of any provision of §18.2-51.4 or §18.2-266 or a violation of a local ordinance paralleling or substantially similar to §18.2-51.4 or §18.2-266, or a violation of any federal, state or local law or ordinance substantially similar to §18.2-51.4 or §18.2-266;
3. Refusal to submit to a chemical test to determine the alcohol or drug content of the person's blood or breath in accordance with §§18.2-268.1 through 18.2-268.12 or this article, or the comparable laws of any other state or jurisdiction;
4. Failure of the driver whose vehicle is involved in an accident which results in the death of or injury to another person, to stop and disclose his identity at the scene of the accident; or
5. Commission of any crime punishable as a felony in the commission of which a motor vehicle is used, other than a felony described in §46.2-341.19.

B. The Commissioner shall disqualify any such person for a period of three years if the offense listed in subsection A of this section was committed while driving a commercial motor vehicle used in the transportation of hazardous materials required to be placarded under federal Hazardous Materials Regulations (49 C.F.R. Part 172, Subpart F).

C. The Commissioner shall disqualify for life any person whose record, as maintained by the Department, shows that he has been convicted of two or more violations of any of the offenses listed in subsection A of this section, if each offense arose from a separate incident. If two or more such disqualification offenses arise from the same incident, the disqualification periods imposed pursuant to subsection A or B of this section shall run consecutively and not concurrently.

D. The Department may issue, if permitted by federal law, regulations establishing guidelines, including conditions, under which a disqualification for life under subsection C may be reduced to a period of not less than ten years.

E. Only offenses committed on or after January 1, 1990, shall be subject to provisions of this section.

(Chgd. by L.1997 ch. 691, eff. 7/1/97.)

§46.2-341.19. Controlled substance felony; disqualification.

No person shall use a commercial motor vehicle in the commission of any felony involving manufacturing, distributing or dispensing a controlled substance or possession with intent to manufacture, distribute or dispense such controlled substance. For the purpose of this section, a controlled substance shall be defined as provided in §102(6) of the federal Controlled Substances Act (21 U.S.C. §802(6)) and includes all substances listed on Schedules I through V of 21 C.F.R. Part 1308 as they may be revised from time to time.

Violation of this section shall constitute a separate and distinct offense and any person violating this section shall be guilty of a Class 1 misdemeanor. Punishment for a violation of this section shall be separate and apart from any punishment received from the commission of the primary felony.

The Commissioner shall, upon receiving a record of a conviction of a violation of this section, disqualify for life any person who is convicted of such violation.

§46.2-341.20. Disqualification for multiple serious traffic violations.

A. For the purposes of this section, the following offenses, if committed in a commercial motor vehicle, are serious traffic violations:

1. Driving at a speed fifteen or more miles per hour in excess of the posted speed limits;
2. Reckless driving;
3. A violation of a state law or local ordinance relating to motor vehicle traffic control arising in connection with a fatal traffic accident;
4. Improper or erratic traffic lane change; and
5. Following the vehicle ahead too closely.

For the purposes of this section, parking vehicle weight, and vehicle defect violations shall not be considered traffic violations.

B. The Department shall disqualify for the following periods of time, any person whose record as maintained by the Department shows that he has committed, within any three-year period, the requisite number of serious traffic violations:

1. A sixty-day disqualification period for any person convicted of two serious traffic violations; or
2. A 120-day disqualification period for any person convicted of three serious traffic violations.

C. Any disqualification period imposed pursuant to this section shall run consecutively, and not concurrently, with any other disqualification period imposed hereunder.

D. Only offenses committed on or after January 1, 1990, shall be subject to the provisions of this section.

§46.2-341.21. Driving while disqualified; penalties.

No person whose privilege to drive a commercial motor vehicle has been suspended or revoked or who has been disqualified from operating a commercial motor vehicle or who has been ordered out of service, and who has been given notice of, or reasonably should know of the suspension, revocation, disqualification, or out-of-service order shall operate a commercial motor vehicle anywhere in the Commonwealth until the period of such suspension, revocation, disqualification, or out-of-service order has terminated.

Any person who violates this section shall, for the first offense, be guilty of a Class 2 misdemeanor, and for the second or any subsequent offense, be guilty of a Class 1 misdemeanor; however, if the offense is the violation of an out-of-service order, the minimum fine shall be $1,000 for any driver so convicted and $2,500 for any motor carrier so convicted, and the maximum fine shall be $2,500 for any driver so convicted and $10,000 for any motor carrier so convicted. Upon receipt of a record of a violation of this section, the Commissioner shall impose an additional suspension, revocation, or disqualification period equal to the period for which the driver's privilege to operate a motor vehicle was suspended or revoked or for which the driver was disqualified when he violated this section; however, if the offense was the violation of an out-of-service order, the Commissioner shall impose a disqualification period of 180 days, unless the records of the Department show that the driver has been previously convicted of violating an out-of-service order for an offense committed within ten years of the current offense, in which case the Commissioner shall impose a disqualification period of three years.

Notice of disqualification or of revocation or suspension of the license or privilege to operate a commercial motor vehicle is sufficient if served in accordance with the provisions of §46.2-416.

(Chgd. by L.1995 chs. 145, 151, eff. 7/1/95.)

§46.2-341.22. Requirements upon disqualification.

Any person who has been disqualified pursuant to any provision of this Act shall be subject to the provisions of §§46.2-370 and 46.2-414, and shall be required to comply with the provisions of §§46.2-370 and 46.2-411 as conditions to the reinstatement of his privilege to drive a commercial motor vehicle.

Any person who has been disqualified pursuant to the provisions of §46.2-341.18 or §46.2-341.19 shall be required as further conditions to reinstatement of his privilege to operate a commercial motor vehicle, to (i) apply for such license; (ii) pass the knowledge and skills tests required for the class and type of commercial motor vehicle for which he seeks to be licensed; and (iii) satisfy all other applicable licensing requirements, including the payment of licensing fees, imposed by the laws of the Commonwealth.

The provisions of this section shall not apply to out-of-service orders issued pursuant to §§46.2-341.26:2 and 46.2-341.26:3.

§46.2-341.23. Offenses under substantially similar laws.

Except as otherwise provided, whenever in this Act reference is made to an offense which is a violation of a provision of this Code, such reference shall be deemed to include offenses under any local ordinance, any federal law, any law of another state or any local ordinance of another state, substantially similar to such provision of this Code.

§46.2-341.24. Driving a commercial motor vehicle while intoxicated, etc.

A. It shall be unlawful for any person to drive or operate any commercial motor vehicle (i) while such person has a blood alcohol concentration of 0.08 percent or more by weight by volume or 0.08 grams per 210 liters of breath as indicated by a chemical test administered as provided in this article; (ii) while such person is under the influence of alcohol; (iii) while such person is under the influence of any narcotic drug or any other self-administered intoxicant or drug of whatsoever nature, or any combination of such drugs, to a degree which impairs his ability to drive or operate any commercial motor vehicle safely; or (iv) while such person is under the combined influence of alcohol and any drug or drugs to a degree which impairs his ability to drive or operate any commercial motor vehicle safely.

B. It shall be unlawful and a lesser included offense of an offense under provision (i), (ii), or (iv) of subsection A of this section for a person to drive or operate a commercial motor vehicle while such person has a blood alcohol concentration of 0.04 percent or more by weight by volume or 0.04 grams or more per 210 liters of breath as indicated by a chemical test administered in accordance with the provisions of this article.

§46.2-341.25. Preliminary analysis of breath of commercial drivers to determine alcohol content of blood.

A. Any person who is reasonably suspected of a violation of §46.2-341.24 or of having any alcohol in his blood while driving or operating a commercial motor vehicle may be required by any law-enforcement officer to provide a sample of such person's breath for a preliminary screening to determine the probable alcohol content of his blood. Such person shall be entitled, upon request, to observe the process of analysis and to see the blood-alcohol reading on the equipment used to perform the breath test. Such breath may be analyzed by any police officer of the Commonwealth, or of any county, city, or town, or by any member of a sheriff's department in the normal discharge of his duties.

B. The Department of Criminal Justice Services, Division of Forensic Science, shall determine the proper method and equipment to be used in analyzing breath samples taken pursuant to this section and shall advise the respective police and sheriff's departments of the same.

C. If the breath sample analysis indicates that there is alcohol present in the person's blood, or if the person refuses to provide a sample of his breath for a preliminary screening, such person shall then be subject to the provisions of §§46.2-341.26:1 through 46.2-341.26:11.

D. The results of a breath analysis conducted pursuant to this section shall not be admitted into evidence in any prosecution under §46.2-341.24 or §46.2-341.31, but may be used as a basis for charging a person for a violation of the provisions of §46.2-341.24 or §46.2-341.31.

E. The law-enforcement officer requiring the preliminary screening test shall advise the person of his obligations under this section and of the provisions of subsection C of this section.

(Chgd. by L.1996 chs. 154, 952, eff. 7/1/96.)

§46.2-341.26:1. Use of chemical tests to determine alcohol or drug content of blood of commercial driver; definitions.

As used in §§46.2-341.26:2 through 46.2-341.26:11, unless the context clearly indicates otherwise:

The phrase "alcohol or drug" means alcohol, drug or drugs, or any combination of alcohol and a drug or drugs.

The phrase "blood or breath" means either or both.

"Chief police officer" means the sheriff in any county not having a chief of police, the chief of police of any county having a chief of police, the chief of police of the city, or the sergeant or chief of police of the town in which the charge will be heard, or their authorized representatives.

"Director" means the Director of the Division of Forensic Science.

"Division" means the Division of Forensic Science.

§46.2-341.26:2. Implied consent to post-arrest chemical test to determine alcohol or drug content of blood of commercial driver.

A. Any person, whether licensed by Virginia or not, who operates a commercial motor vehicle upon a highway as defined in §46.2-100 in the Commonwealth shall be deemed thereby, as a condition of such operation, to have consented to have samples of his blood, breath, or both blood and breath taken for a chemical test to determine the alcohol, drug or both alcohol and drug content of his blood, if he is arrested for violation of §46.2-341.24 or §46.2-341.31 within two hours of the alleged offense.

B. Such person shall be required to have a breath sample taken and shall be entitled, upon request, to observe the process of analysis and to see the blood-alcohol reading on the equipment used to perform the breath test. If the equipment automatically produces a written printout of the breath test result, the printout or a copy shall be given to the suspect. If a breath test is not available, then a blood test shall be required.

C. The person may be required to submit to blood tests to determine the drug content of his blood if he has been arrested pursuant to provision (iii) or (iv) of subsection A of

§46.2-341.24, or if he has taken the breath test required pursuant to subsection B and the law-enforcement officer has reasonable cause to believe the person was driving under the influence of any drug or combination of drugs, or the combined influence of alcohol and drugs.

D. If the certificate of analysis referred to in §46.2-346.26:9 indicates the presence of alcohol in the suspect's blood, the suspect shall be taken before a magistrate to determine whether the magistrate should issue an out-of-service order prohibiting the suspect from driving any commercial motor vehicle for a twenty-four-hour period. If the magistrate finds that there is probable cause to believe that the suspect was driving a commercial motor vehicle with any measurable amount of alcohol in his blood, the magistrate shall issue an out-of-service order prohibiting the suspect from driving any commercial motor vehicle for a period of twenty-four hours. The magistrate shall forward a copy of the out-of-service order to the Department within seven days after issuing the order. The order shall be in addition to any other action or sanction permitted or required by law to be taken against or imposed upon the suspect.

§46.2-341.26:3. Refusal of tests; issuance of out-of-service orders; disqualification.

A. If a person arrested for a violation of §46.2-341.24 or §46.2-341.31 after having been advised by a law-enforcement officer that a person who operates a commercial motor vehicle on a public highway in the Commonwealth is deemed thereby, as a condition of such operation, to have consented to have samples of his blood or breath taken for chemical tests to determine the alcohol or drug content of his blood and that the unreasonable refusal to do so constitutes grounds for the issuance of an out-of-service order and for the disqualification of such person from operating a commercial motor vehicle, then refuses to permit blood or breath samples to be taken for such tests, the law-enforcement officer shall take the person before a magistrate. If he again refuses after having been further advised by the magistrate of the law requiring blood or breath samples to be taken and the sanctions for refusal, and declares again his refusal in writing on a form provided by the Supreme Court, or refuses or fails to so declare in writing and such fact is certified as prescribed below, then no blood or breath samples shall be taken even though he may later request them.

B. The form shall contain a brief statement of the law requiring the taking of blood or breath samples and the sanctions for refusal; a declaration of refusal; and lines for the signature of the person from whom the blood or breath sample is sought, the date, and the signature of a witness to the signing. If the person refuses or fails to execute the declaration, the magistrate shall certify such fact and that the magistrate advised the person that a refusal to permit a blood or breath sample to be taken, if found to be unreasonable, constitutes grounds for immediate issuance of an out-of-service order prohibiting him from driving a commercial vehicle for a period of twenty-four hours, and for the disqualification of such person from operating a commercial motor vehicle.

C. If the magistrate finds that there was probable cause to believe the refusal was unreasonable, he shall immediately issue an out-of-service order prohibiting the person from operating a commercial motor vehicle for a period of twenty-four hours and shall issue a warrant or summons charging such person with a violation of §46.2-341.26:2. The warrant or summons shall be executed in the same manner as criminal warrants. Venue for the trial of the warrant or summons shall lie in the court of the county or city in which the criminal offense is to be tried.

D. The executed declaration of refusal or the certificate of the magistrate, as the case may be, shall be attached to the warrant and shall be forwarded by the magistrate to the court.

E. When the court receives the declaration or certificate together with the warrant or summons charging refusal, the court shall fix a date for the trial of the warrant or summons, at such time as the court designates but subsequent to the defendant's trial for a violation of §46.2-341.24 or §46.2-341.31.

F. The declaration of refusal or certificate under §46.2-341.26:3 shall be prima facie evidence that the defendant refused to allow a blood or breath sample to be taken to determine the alcohol or drug content of his blood. However, this shall not prohibit the defendant from introducing on his behalf evidence of the basis for his refusal. The court shall determine the reasonableness of such refusal.

§46.2-341.26:4. Appeal and trial; sanctions for refusal; procedures.

The procedure for appeal and trial shall be the same as provided by law for misdemeanors. If requested by either party on appeal to the circuit court, trial by jury shall be as provided in Article 4 (§19.2-260 et seq.) of Chapter 15 of Title 19.2, and the Commonwealth shall be required to prove its case beyond a reasonable doubt.

If the court or jury finds the defendant guilty as charged in the warrant or summons referred to in §46.2-341.26:3, the defendant shall be disqualified as provided in §46.2-341.18. However, if the defendant pleads guilty to a violation of §46.2-341.24, the court may dismiss the warrant or summons.

The court shall notify the Commissioner of any such finding of guilt and shall forward the defendant's license to the Commissioner as in other cases of similar nature for suspension of license unless the defendant appeals his conviction. In such case the court shall return the license to the defendant upon his appeal being perfected.

§46.2-341.26:5. Qualifications and liability of persons authorized to take blood samples; procedure for taking samples.

For purposes of this article, only a physician, registered professional nurse, graduate laboratory technician or a technician or nurse designated by order of a circuit court acting on the recommendation of a licensed physician, using soap and water, polyvinylpyrrolidone iodine or benzalkonium chloride to cleanse the part of the body from which the blood is taken and using instruments sterilized by the accepted steam sterilizer or some other sterilizer which will not affect the accuracy of the test, or using chemically clean sterile disposable syringes, shall withdraw blood for the purpose of determining its alcohol or drug content. It is a Class 3 misdemeanor to reuse single-use-only needles or syringes. No civil liability shall attach to any person authorized by this section to withdraw blood as a result of the act of withdrawing blood from any person submitting thereto, provided the blood was withdrawn according to recognized medical procedures. However, the person shall not be relieved from liability for negligence in the withdrawing of any blood sample.

No person arrested for a violation of §46.2-341.24 or §46.2-341.31 shall be required to execute in favor of any person or corporation a waiver or release of liability in connection with the withdrawal of blood or as a condition precedent to the withdrawal of blood as provided for in this section.

§46.2-341.26:6. Transmission of blood samples.

A. Adequate portions of the blood samples withdrawn pursuant to §46.2-341.26:5 shall be place in vials provided by the Division of Forensic Science. The vials shall be sealed by the person taking the sample or at his direction. The person who seals the vial shall complete the prenumbered certificate of blood withdrawal form attached to the vial by the Division. The completed withdrawal certificate for each vial shall show the name of the suspect, the name of the person taking the blood sample, and the date and time the blood sample was taken and information identifying the arresting or accompanying officer. The officer shall initial the completed certificate. The vials shall be divided between two containers provided by the Division, and the containers shall be sealed to prevent tampering with the vial. A law-enforcement officer shall take possession of the two containers as soon as the vials are placed in such containers and sealed, and shall promptly transport or mail one of the containers to the Division. Immediately after taking possession of the second container, the officer shall give to the suspect a form provided by the Division which sets forth the procedure to obtain an independent analysis of the blood in the second container, and a list of the names and addresses of laboratories approved by the Division. The form shall contain a space for the suspect or his counsel to direct the officer possessing the second container to forward that container to an approved laboratory for analysis, if desired. If the accused directs the officer in writing on the form to forward the second container to an approved laboratory of the accused's choice, the officer shall do so.

If the accused does not direct otherwise on the form, the officer having the second container shall deliver it to the chief police officer of the locality in which the case will be heard. The chief police officer, on receiving the second container, shall retain it for a period of seventy-two hours, during which time the suspect or his counsel may, in writing, on the form provided hereinabove, direct the chief police officer to mail it to the laboratory the suspect has chosen from the approved list.

B. The contents of the second container shall be transmitted, tested and admitted in evidence in the same manner and in accordance with the procedures established for the sample sent to the Division; however, an analysis of the second blood sample to determine the presence of a drug or drugs shall not be performed unless an analysis of the first blood sample by the Division has indicated the presence of such drug or drugs.

C. If the chief police officer having possession of the second container is not directed to mail it within seventy-two hours after receiving the container, he shall destroy such container.

§46.2-341.26:7. Transmission of results.

A. Upon receipt of a blood sample forwarded to the Division for analysis pursuant to §46.2-341.26:6, the Division shall have it examined for its alcohol or drug content, and the Director shall execute a certificate of analysis indicating the name of the suspect; the date, time, and by whom the blood sample was received and examined; a statement that the seal on the vial had not been broken or otherwise tampered with; a statement that the container and vial were provided by the Division and that the vial was one to which the completed withdrawal certificate was attached; and a statement of the sample's alcohol or drug content. The Director or his representative shall remove the withdrawal certificate from the vial, attach it to the certificate of analysis and state in the certificate of analysis that it was so removed and attached. The certificate of analysis with the withdrawal certificate shall be returned to the clerk of the court in which the charge will be heard. The vial and blood sample shall be destroyed after completion of the analysis. A similar certificate of analysis, with the withdrawal certificate from the independent laboratory which analyzes the second blood sample on behalf of the suspect, shall be returned to the clerk of the court in which the case will be heard. The blood sample shall be destroyed after completion of the analysis by the independent laboratory.

B. When a blood sample taken in accordance with the provisions of §§46.2-341.26:2 through 46.2-341.26:6 is forwarded for analysis to the Division, a report of the test results shall be filed in that office. On proper identification of the certificate of withdrawal, the certificate of analysis, with the withdrawal certificate attached, shall, when attested by the Director, be admissible in any court, in any criminal or civil proceeding, as evidence of the facts therein stated and of the results of such analysis. On motion of the accused, the certificate prepared for the second sample shall be admissible in evidence when attested by the pathologist or by the supervisor of the approved laboratory.

Upon request of the person whose blood or breath was analyzed, the test results shall be made available to him.

§46.2-341.26:8. Fees.

Payment for withdrawing blood shall not exceed twenty-five dollars, which shall be paid out of the appropriation for criminal charges. Laboratories determining the alcohol content of the second blood sample shall be allowed no more than twenty-five dollars, which shall be paid out of the appropriation for criminal charges. Payment for determining the presence of a drug or drugs in the second sample may not exceed the amount established on the Division's fee schedule and shall be paid out of the appropriation for criminal charges.

If the person whose blood sample was withdrawn is subsequently convicted for violation of §46.2-341.24 or §46.2-341.31, any fees paid by the Commonwealth to the person withdrawing the sample and to the laboratory for testing the blood sample shall be taxed as part of the costs of the criminal case and shall be paid into the general fund of the state treasury.

§46.2-341.26:9. Assurance of breath test validity; use as evidence.

To be capable of being considered valid in a prosecution under §46.2-341.24 or §46.2-341.31, chemical analysis of a person's breath shall be performed by an individual possessing a valid license to conduct such tests, with the type of equipment and in accordance with methods approved by the Division under the provisions of §18.2-268.9.

Any individual conducting a breath test under the provisions of §46.2-341.26:2 shall issue a certificate which includes the name of the suspect, the date and time the sample was taken from the suspect, the alcohol content of the sample, and the identity of the person who examined the sample. The certificate will also indicate that the test was conducted in accordance with the Division's specifications and that the equipment on which the breath test was conducted in accordance with the Division's specifications and that the equipment on which the breath test was conducted has been tested within the past six months and has been found to be accurate. The certificate, when attested by the authorized individual conducting the breath test, shall be admissible in any court in any criminal or civil proceeding as evidence of the facts therein stated and of the results of such analysis. Any such certificate of analysis purporting to be signed by a person authorized by the Division shall be admissible in evidence without proof of seal or signature of the person whose name is signed to it.

A copy of such certificate shall be promptly delivered to the suspect. The law-enforcement officer requiring the test or anyone with such officer at the time if otherwise qualified to conduct such test as provided by this section, may administer the breath test or analyze the results thereof.

§46.2-341.26:10. Evidence.

A. In any trial for a violation of §46.2-341.24, admission of the blood or breath test results shall not limit the introduction of any other relevant evidence bearing upon any question at issue before the court, and the court shall, regardless of the results of the blood or breath tests, consider other relevant admissible evidence of the condition of the accused. If the test results indicate the presence of any drugs other than alcohol, the test results shall be admissible only if other competent evidence has been presented to relate the presence of the drug or drugs to the impairment of the accused's ability to drive or operate any commercial motor vehicle safely.

The failure of an accused to permit a blood or breath sample to be taken to determine the alcohol or drug content of his blood is not evidence and shall not be subject to any comment by the Commonwealth at the trial of the case, except in rebuttal; nor shall the fact that a blood or breath test had been offered the accused be evidence or the subject of comment by the Commonwealth, except in rebuttal.

B. The court or jury trying the case involving a violation of clause (ii), (iii) or (iv) of §46.2-341.24 shall determine the innocence or guilt of the defendant from all the evidence concerning his condition at the time of the alleged offense.

§46.2-341.26:11. Substantial compliance.

The steps set forth in §§46.2-341.26:2 through 46.2-341.26:9 relating to taking, handling, identifying, and disposing of blood or breath samples are procedural and not substantive. Substantial compliance shall be sufficient. Failure to comply with any steps or portions thereof, or a variance in the results of the two blood tests shall not of itself be grounds for finding the defendant not guilty, but shall go to the weight of the evidence and shall be considered with all the evidence in the case; however, the defendant shall have the right to introduce evidence on his own behalf to show noncompliance with the aforesaid procedures or any part thereof, and that as a result his rights were prejudiced.

§46.2-341.27. Presumptions from alcoholic content of blood.

In any prosecution for a violation of provision (ii) of subsection A of §46.2-341.24, the amount of alcohol in the blood of the accused at the time of the alleged offense as indicated by a chemical analysis of a sample of the suspect's blood or breath to determine the alcoholic content of his blood in accordance with the provisions of §§46.2-341.26:1 through 46.2-341.26:11 shall give rise to the following rebuttable presumption: if there was at that time 0.08 percent or more by weight by volume of alcohol in the accused's blood or 0.08 grams or more per 210 liters of the accused's breath, it shall be presumed that the accused was under the influence of alcoholic intoxicants.

If there was at that time less than 0.08 percent by weight by volume of alcohol in the accused's blood or 0.08 grams or more per 210 liters of the accused's breath, such fact shall not give rise to any presumption that the accused was or was not under the influence of alcoholic intoxicants, but such fact may be considered with other competent evidence in determining the guilt or innocence of the accused.

§46.2-341.28. Penalty for driving commercial motor vehicle while intoxicated; subsequent offense; prior conviction.

Any person violating any provision of subsection A of §46.2-341.24 shall be guilty of a Class 1 misdemeanor.

Any person convicted of a second offense committed within less than five years after a first offense under subsection A of §46.2-341.24 shall be punishable by a fine of not less than $200 nor more than $2,500 and by confinement in jail for not less than one month nor more than one year. [Forty-eight hours] *Five days* of such confinement shall be a mandatory, minimum sentence not subject to suspension by the court. Any person convicted of a second offense committed within a period of five to ten years of a first offense under subsection A of §46.2-341.24 shall be punishable by a fine of not less than $200 nor more than $2,500 and by confinement in jail for not less than one month nor more than one year. Any person convicted of a third offense or subsequent offense committed within ten years of an offense under subsection A of §46.2-341.24 shall be punishable by a fine of not less than $500 nor more than $2,500 and by confinement in jail for not less than two months nor more than one year. Thirty days of such confinement shall be a mandatory, minimum sentence not subject to suspension by the court if the third or subsequent offense occurs within less than five years. Ten days of such confinement shall be a mandatory, minimum sentence not subject to suspension by the court if the third or subsequent offense occurs within a period of five to ten years of a first offense.

For the purposes of this section a conviction or finding of not innocent in the case of a juvenile under (i) §18.2-51.4 or §18.2-266, (ii) the ordinance of any county, city or town in this Commonwealth substantially similar to the provisions of §18.2-51.4 or §18.2-266, (iii) subsection A of §46.2-341.24, or (iv) the laws of any other state substantially similar to the provisions of §§18.2-51.4, 18.2-266 or subsection A of §46.2-341.24, shall be considered a prior conviction.

(Chgd. by L.1997 ch. 691; L.2000 chs. 958, 980, eff. 10/1/2000. Matter in brackets eff. only until 10/1/2000. Matter in italics eff. 10/1/2000.)

§46.2-341.29. Penalty for driving commercial motor vehicle with blood alcohol content equal to or greater than 0.04.

Any person violating the provisions of subsection B of §46.2-341.24 shall be guilty of a Class 3 misdemeanor.

§46.2-341.30. Disqualification for driving commercial motor vehicle while intoxicated, etc.

A. The judgment of conviction under any provision of §46.2-341.24 shall of itself operate to disqualify the person so convicted from the privilege to drive or operate any commercial motor vehicle as provided in §46.2-341.18. Notwithstanding any other provision of law, such disqualification shall not be subject to any suspension, reduction, limitation or other modification by the court or the Commissioner.

B. A judgment of conviction under any provision of subsection A of §46.2-341.24, in addition to causing the disqualification under subsection A of this section, shall also operate to deprive the person so convicted of his privilege to drive or operate any motor vehicle as provided in §18.2-271.

§46.2-341.31. Driving commercial motor vehicle with any alcohol in blood.

No person shall drive a commercial motor vehicle while having any amount of alcohol in his blood, as measured by a test administered pursuant to the provisions of §§46.2-341.26:1 through 46.2-341.26:11. Any person found to have so driven a commercial motor vehicle shall be guilty of a traffic infraction.

§46.2-341.32. Authority to enter into agreements.

The Department may procure and enter into agreements or arrangements for the purpose of participating in the Commercial Driver License System or any other similar information system established to implement the requirements of the Commercial Motor Vehicle Safety Act, and may procure and enter into other agreements or arrangements to carry out the provisions of this article.

§46.2-341.33. Severability and savings clause.

The provisions of this article shall be severable and if any phrase, clause, sentence or provision of this article is declared to be contrary to the laws or Constitution of Virginia or the United States, the validity of the remainder of this article shall not be affected thereby.

§46.2-341.34. Appeals.

Any person denied a commercial driver's license or who has been disqualified from operating a commercial motor vehicle under the provisions of this article is entitled to judicial review in accordance with the provisions of the Administrative Process Act (§9-6.14:1 et seq.). No appeal shall lie in any case in which such denial or disqualification was mandatory except to determine the identity of the person concerned when the question of identity is in dispute.

From the final decision of the circuit court, either party shall have an appeal as of right to the Court of Appeals.

While an appeal is pending from the action of the Department disqualifying the person or denying him a license, or from the court affirming the action of the Department, the person aggrieved shall not drive a commercial motor vehicle.

ARTICLE 7
FORM OF LICENSES; IDENTITY DOCUMENTS ISSUED BY DEPARTMENT

§46.2-342. What license to contain; organ donor information; Uniform Donor Document.

A. Every license issued under this chapter shall bear:

1. For new, renewal, or replacement licenses issued on or after September 1, 1995, either (i) a license number which shall be the same as the licensee's social security number or (ii) a control number which shall be assigned by the Department to the licensee if he either (i) has no social security number or (ii) requests in writing on a form prescribed by the Commissioner that his social security number not be shown on the license;
2. A color photograph of the licensee;
3. The licensee's name, year, month, and date of birth;
4. The licensee's address;
5. A brief description of the licensee for the purpose of identification;
6. A space for the signature of the licensee; and
7. Any other information deemed necessary by the Commissioner for the administration of this title.

No abbreviated names or nicknames shall be shown on any license.

A1. At the option of the licensee, the address shown on the license may be either the post office box, business, or residence address of the licensee. However, regardless of which address is shown on the license, the licensee shall supply the Department with his residence address. This residence address shall be maintained in the Department's records. Whenever the licensee's address shown either on his license or in the Department's records changes, he shall notify the Department of such change as required by §46.2-324.

B. The license shall be made of a material and in a form to be determined by the Commissioner.

C. Licenses issued to persons less than twenty-one years old shall be immediately and readily distinguishable from those issued to persons twenty-one years old or older. Distinguishing characteristics shall include unique design elements of the document and descriptors within the photograph area to identify persons who are at least fifteen years old but less than twenty-one years old. These descriptors shall include the month, day, and year when the person will become twenty-one years old.

D. The Department shall establish a method by which an applicant for a driver's license or an identification card may designate his willingness to be an organ donor as provided in Article 2 (§32.1-289 et seq.) of Chapter 8 of Title 32.1 and shall cooperate with the Virginia Transplant Council to ensure that such method is designed to encourage organ donation with a minimum of effort on the part of the donor and the Department.

E. If an applicant designates his willingness to be a donor pursuant to subsection D, the Department may make a notation of this designation on his license or card and shall make a notation of this designation in his driver record.

F. The donor designation authorized in subsection E shall be sufficient legal authority for the removal, following death, of the subject's organs or tissues without additional authority from the donor, or his family or estate. No family member, guardian, agent named pursuant to an advance directive or person responsible for the decedent's estate shall refuse to honor the donor designation or, in any way, seek to avoid honoring the donor designation.

G. The donor designation provided pursuant to subsection D may only be rescinded by appearing in person at a Department branch office. The Department shall notify the prospective donor of this requirement at the time he authorizes donor designation.

H. With the written consent of his parent or legal guardian, a minor may make a donor designation.

I. When requested by the applicant, and upon presentation of a signed statement by a licensed physician confirming the applicant's condition, the Department shall indicate on the applicant's driver's license that the applicant is an insulin-dependent diabetic.

J. In the absence of gross negligence or willful misconduct, the Department and its employees shall be immune from any civil or criminal liability in connection with the making of or failure to make a notation of donor designation on any license or card or in any person's driver record.

K. Notwithstanding the foregoing provisions of this section, the Department shall continue to use the uniform donor document, as formerly set forth in subsection D above, for organ donation designation until such time as a new method is fully implemented, which shall be no later than July 1, 1994. Any such uniform donor document, shall, when properly executed, remain valid and shall continue to be subject to all conditions for execution, delivery, amendment, and revocation as set out in Article 2 (§32.1-289 et seq.) of Chapter 8 of Title 32.1.

L. The Department shall, in coordination with the Virginia Transplant Council, prepare an organ donor information brochure describing the organ donor program and providing instructions for completion of the uniform donor document and include a copy of such brochure with every driver's license renewal notice or application mailed to licensed drivers in Virginia.

(Chgd. by L.1995 chs. 350, 372; L.1997 ch. 486; L.1998 ch. 322; L.1999 ch. 330; L.2000 ch. 810, eff. 7/1/2000.)

§46.2-343. Duplicate driver's license, reissued driver's licenses, learner's permit; fees.

If a driver's license or learner's permit issued under the provisions of this chapter is lost, stolen, or destroyed, the person to whom it was issued may obtain a duplicate or substitute thereof on furnishing proof satisfactory to the

Department that his license or permit has been lost, stolen, or destroyed, or that there are good reasons why a duplicate should be issued.

There shall be a fee of five dollars for each duplicate license and two dollars for each duplicate learner's permit. An additional fee of five dollars shall be charged to add or change the scene on a duplicate license or duplicate learner's permit.

There shall be a fee of five dollars for reissuance of any driver's license upon the termination of driving restrictions imposed upon the licensee by the Department or a court. An additional fee of five dollars shall be charged to add or change the scene on a license upon reissuance.

(Chgd. by L.1995 ch. 468; L.1997 ch. 486; L.1999 ch. 593, eff. 7/1/99.)

§46.2-344. Temporary driver's permit.

The Department, upon determining, after an examination, that an applicant is mentally, physically, and otherwise qualified to receive a license, may issue to him a temporary driver's permit entitling him, while having the permit in his immediate possession, to drive a motor vehicle on the highways for a period of ninety days, pending the issuance to such person of a driver's license.

§46.2-345. Issuance of special identification cards; fee; confidentiality; penalties.

A. On the application of any person who is a resident of the Commonwealth or the parent or legal guardian of any such person who is under the age of fifteen, the Department shall issue a special identification card to the person provided:

1. Application is made on a form prescribed by the Department;

2. The applicant presents a birth certificate or other evidence acceptable to the Department of his name and date of birth; and

3. The Department is satisfied that the applicant needs an identification card or the applicant shows he has a bona fide need for such a card.

B. The fee for the issuance of a special identification card is five dollars. Persons twenty-one years old or older may be issued a scenic special identification card for an additional fee of five dollars.

C. A special identification card shall expire five years from its date of issuance except that those cards issued to children under the age of fifteen shall expire on the child's fifteenth birthday or five years from the date of issuance, whichever occurs first.

D. A special identification card issued under this section may be similar in size, shape, and design to a driver's license, and include a color photograph of its holder, but the card shall be readily distinguishable from a driver's license and shall clearly state that it does not authorize the person to whom it is issued to drive a motor vehicle.

E. Special identification cards, for persons at least fifteen years old but less than twenty-one years old, shall be immediately and readily distinguishable from those issued to persons twenty-one years old or older. Distinguishing characteristics shall include unique design elements of the document and descriptors within the photograph area to identify persons who are at least fifteen years old but less than twenty-one years old. These descriptors shall include the month, day, and year when the person will become twenty-one years old.

F. Special identification cards for persons under age fifteen shall bear a full face photograph. The special identification card issued to persons under age fifteen shall be readily distinguishable from a driver's license and from other special identification cards issued by the Department. Such cards shall clearly indicate that it does not authorize the person to whom it is issued to drive a motor vehicle.

G. Any personal information, as identified in §2.1-379, which is retained by the Department from an application for the issuance of a special identification card is confidential and shall not be divulged to any person, association, corporation, or organization, public or private, except to the legal guardian or the attorney of the applicant or to a person, association, corporation, or organization nominated in writing by the applicant, his legal guardian, or his attorney. This subsection shall not prevent the Department from furnishing the application or any information thereon to any law-enforcement agency.

H. Any person who uses a false or fictitious name or gives a false or fictitious address in any application for an identification card or knowingly makes a false statement or conceals a material fact or otherwise commits a fraud in any such application shall be guilty of a Class 2 misdemeanor. However, where the name or address is given, or false statement is made, or fact is concealed, or fraud committed, with the intent to purchase a firearm or where the identification card is obtained for the purpose of committing any offense punishable as a felony, a violation of this section shall constitute a Class 4 felony.

I. The Department may promulgate regulations necessary for the effective implementation of the provisions of this section.

J. The Department shall utilize the various communications media throughout the Commonwealth to inform Virginia residents of the provisions of this section and to promote and encourage the public to take advantage of its provisions.

(Chgd. by L.1997 ch. 486; L.1998 ch. 322; L.1999 ch. 593, eff. 7/1/99.)

ARTICLE 8
PROHIBITED USES OF DRIVER'S LICENSES

Section

§46.2-346. Unlawful acts enumerated.

A. No person shall:

1. Display, cause or permit to be displayed, or have in his possession any driver's license which he knows to be fictitious or to have been cancelled, revoked, suspended, or altered, or photographed for the purpose of evading the intent of this chapter;

2. Lend to, or knowingly permit the use of by one not entitled thereto, any driver's license issued to the person so lending or permitting the use thereof;

3. Display or represent as his own any driver's license not issued to him;

4. Reproduce by photograph or otherwise, any driver's license, temporary driver's permit, or learner's permit issued by the Department without obtaining prior written consent of the Department;

5. Fail or refuse to surrender to the Department, on demand, any driver's license issued in the Commonwealth or any other state when the license has been suspended, cancelled, or revoked by proper authority in the Commonwealth, or

any other state as provided by law, or to fail or refuse to surrender the suspended, cancelled, or revoked license to any court in which a driver has been tried and convicted for the violation of any law or ordinance of the Commonwealth or any county, city, or town thereof, regulating or affecting the operation of a motor vehicle.

B. Any law-enforcement officer empowered to enforce the provisions of this title may retain any driver's license held in violation of this section and shall submit the license to the appropriate court for evidentiary purposes.

§46.2-347. Fraudulent use of driver's license or Department of Motor Vehicles identification card to obtain alcoholic beverages; penalties.

Any underage person as specified in §4.1-304 who knowingly uses or attempts to use a forged, deceptive, or otherwise nongenuine driver's license issued by any state, territory or possession of the United States, the District of Columbia, the Commonwealth of Puerto Rico or any foreign country or government; United States Armed Forces identification card; United States passport or foreign government visa; Virginia Department of Motor Vehicles special identification card; official identification issued by any other federal, state or foreign government agency; or official university or college student identification card to obtain alcoholic beverages shall be guilty of a Class 3 misdemeanor, and upon conviction of a violation of this section, the court shall revoke such convicted person's driver's license or privilege to drive a motor vehicle for a period of not less than thirty days nor more than one year.

§46.2-348. Fraud or false statements in applications for license; penalties.

Any person who uses a false or fictitious name or gives a false or fictitious address in any application for a driver's license, or any renewal or duplicate thereof, or knowingly makes a false statement or conceals a material fact or otherwise commits a fraud in his application shall be guilty of a Class 2 misdemeanor. However, where the license is used, or the fact concealed, or fraud is done, with the intent to purchase a firearm, a violation of this section shall be punishable as a Class 4 felony.

§46.2-349. Unlawful to permit violations of chapter.

No person shall authorize or knowingly permit a motor vehicle owned by him or under his control to be driven by any person who has no legal right to do so or in violation of any of the provisions of this chapter.

§46.2-350. Penalty for violation.

Notwithstanding §46.2-113, except as otherwise provided any violation of any provision of this chapter not declared to be a felony shall constitute a Class 2 misdemeanor.

ARTICLE 9
HABITUAL OFFENDERS

Section

§46.2-351. *(Repealed by L.1999 chs. 945, 987, eff. 7/1/99.)*

§§46.2-351.1, 46.2-351.2. *(Repealed by L.1999 chs. 945, 987, eff. 7/1/99.)*

§§46.2-352 to 46.2-355. *(Repealed by L.1999 chs. 945, 987, eff. 7/1/99.)*

§46.2-355.1. Intervention required for certain offenders; fee; penalty; notice.

A. Upon receiving notification of a second conviction entered on or after July 1, 1999, for driving while the offender's license, permit or privilege to drive is suspended or revoked in violation of §46.2-301, the Commissioner shall notify such person that he shall report to a Virginia Alcohol Safety Action Program within sixty days of the date of such notice for intervention. Intervention shall be in accordance with §18.2-271.1. The program shall provide the Commissioner with information of the offender's compliance.

B. An interview shall be conducted by a representative of a Virginia Alcohol Safety Action Program. The representative shall review all applicable laws with the person attending the interview, provide guidance with respect to budgeting for payment of court fines and costs, if applicable, and explain the laws and the consequences of future offenses and may refer the person to any driver improvement clinic. A fee of thirty dollars shall be paid to the Virginia Alcohol Safety Action Program for attendance at a driver intervention interview. All fees collected by a Virginia Alcohol Safety Action Program shall be used to meet its expenses.

C. The Commissioner shall suspend the driving privilege of any person who fails to complete and pay the required fee for an intervention interview within the sixty-day period. The suspension shall continue until such time as the person has completed and paid for the intervention interview.

D. Notice to report for intervention shall be sent by the Department by certified mail, return receipt requested, to the driver at the last known address supplied by the driver and on file with the Department.

E. Failure of the offender to attend as required or failure of the Department to notify the offender upon the second offense shall not prevent conviction for any subsequent offense committed in violation of §46.2-301.

(Added by L.1999 chs. 945, 987, eff. 7/1/99.)

§46.2-356. Period during which habitual offender not to be licensed to drive motor vehicle.

No license to drive motor vehicles in Virginia shall be issued to any person determined or adjudicated an habitual offender (i) for a period of ten years from the date of any final order of a court entered under this article or if no such order was entered then the notice of the determination by the Commissioner finding the person to be an habitual offender and (ii) until the privilege of the person to drive a motor vehicle

in the Commonwealth has been restored by an order of a court entered in a proceeding as provided in this article.
(Chgd. by L.1995 ch. 799; L.1999 chs. 945, 987, eff. 7/1/99.)

§46.2-357. Operation of motor vehicle or self-propelled machinery or equipment by habitual offender prohibited; penalty; enforcement of section.

A. It shall be unlawful for any person determined or adjudicated an habitual offender to drive any motor vehicle or self-propelled machinery or equipment on the highways of the Commonwealth while the revocation of the person's driving privilege remains in effect. However, the revocation determination shall not prohibit the person from operating any farm tractor on the highways when it is necessary to move the tractor from one tract of land used for agricultural purposes to another tract of land used for agricultural purposes, provided that the distance between the said tracts of land is no more than five miles.

B. Except as provided in subsection D, any person found to be an habitual offender under this article, who is thereafter convicted of driving a motor vehicle or self-propelled machinery or equipment in the Commonwealth while the revocation determination is in effect, shall be punished as follows:

1. If such driving does not of itself endanger the life, limb, or property of another, such person shall be guilty of a Class 1 misdemeanor punishable by a minimum, mandatory term of confinement in jail for no less than ten days, which shall not be suspended except in cases designated in subdivision 2(ii) of this subsection.

2. If such driving of itself endangers the life, limb, or property of another or takes place while such person is in violation of §§18.2-36.1, 18.2-51.4, 18.2-266 or §46.2-341.24, irrespective of whether the driving of itself endangers the life, limb or property of another and the person has been previously convicted of a violation of §§18.2-36.1, 18.2-51.4, 18.2-266 or §46.2-341.24, such person shall be guilty of a felony punishable by confinement in a state correctional facility for not less than one year nor more than five years or, in the discretion of the jury or the court trying the case without a jury, by confinement in jail for twelve months and no portion of such sentence shall be suspended. However, (i) if the sentence is more than one year in a state correctional facility, any portion of such sentence in excess of one year may be suspended or (ii) in cases wherein such operation is necessitated in situations of apparent extreme emergency which require such operation to save life or limb, said sentence, or any part thereof may be suspended. For the purposes of this section, an offense in violation of a valid local ordinance, or law of any other jurisdiction, which ordinance or law is substantially similar to any provision of law herein shall be considered an offense in violation of such provision of law.

3. If the offense of driving while a determination as an habitual offender is in effect is a second or subsequent such offense, such person shall be punished as provided in subdivision 2 of this subsection, irrespective of whether the offense, of itself, endangers the life, limb, or property of another.

C. For the purpose of enforcing this section, in any case in which the accused is charged with driving a motor vehicle or self-propelled machinery or equipment while his license, permit, or privilege to drive is suspended or revoked or is charged with driving without a license, the court before hearing the charge shall determine whether the person has been determined an habitual offender and, by reason of this determination, is barred from driving a motor vehicle or self-propelled machinery or equipment on the highways in the Commonwealth. If the court determines the accused has been determined to be an habitual offender and finds there is probable cause that the alleged offense under this section is a felony, it shall certify the case to the circuit court of its jurisdiction for trial.

D. Notwithstanding the provisions of subdivisions 2 and 3 of subsection B, following conviction and prior to imposition of sentence with the consent of the defendant, the court may order the defendant to be evaluated for and to participate in the Boot Camp Incarceration Program pursuant to §19.2-316.1, or the Detention Center Incarceration Program pursuant to §19.2-316.2, or the Diversion Center Incarceration Program pursuant to §19.2-316.3.
(Chgd. by L.1995 ch. 799; L.1997 chs. 5, 344; L.1998 ch. 298; L.1999 chs. 945, 987; L.2000 chs. 956, 982, eff. 7/1/2000.)

§46.2-358. Restoration of privilege of driving motor vehicle; when petition may be brought; terms and conditions.

In any case where the provisions of §46.2-360 or §46.2-361 do not apply, five years from the date of any final order of a court entered under this article, or if no such order was entered then the notice of the determination by the Commissioner finding a person to be an habitual offender and revoking his privilege to drive a motor vehicle in the Commonwealth, the person may petition the court in which he was found to be an habitual offender, or any court of record in Virginia having criminal jurisdiction in the political subdivision in which he then resides, for restoration of his privilege to drive a motor vehicle in the Commonwealth. On such petition, and for good cause shown, the court may, upon a finding that such person does not constitute a threat to the safety and welfare of himself or others with regard to the driving of a motor vehicle, (i) restore to the person the privilege to drive a motor vehicle in the Commonwealth on whatever conditions the court may prescribe or (ii) order that the person be issued a restricted license to drive a motor vehicle in the Commonwealth for any of the purposes set forth in and in accordance with the procedures of subsection E of §18.2-271.1, subject to other provisions of law relating to the issuance of driver's licenses.
(Chgd. by L.1995 ch. 799, eff. 1/1/96.)

§46.2-359. Restoration of driving privilege to certain persons.

Any person eighteen years of age or older who has been adjudged an habitual offender based in whole or in part on findings of not innocent as a juvenile may petition the court in which he was found to be an habitual offender, or any circuit court in Virginia having criminal jurisdiction in the political subdivision in which the person now resides, for restoration of his privilege to operate a motor vehicle in the Commonwealth. On such petition, and for good cause shown, the court may, in its discretion, restore to him the privilege to drive a motor vehicle in the Commonwealth on whatever conditions the court may prescribe, subject to other provisions of law relating to the issuance of driver's licenses.

§46.2-360. Restoration of privilege of operating motor vehicle; restoration of privilege to persons convicted under certain other provisions of Habitual Offender Act.

Any person who has been found to be an habitual offender where the determination or adjudication was based in part and dependent on a conviction as set out in subdivision 1 b of former §46.2-351, may petition the court in which he was found to be an habitual offender, or the circuit court in the political subdivision in which he then resides to:

1. Restore his privilege to drive a motor vehicle in the Commonwealth, provided that five years have elapsed from the date of the final order of a court entered under this article, or if no such order was entered then the notice of the

determination by the Commissioner. On such petition, and for good cause shown, the court may, in its discretion, restore to the person the privilege to drive a motor vehicle in the Commonwealth on whatever conditions the court may prescribe, subject to other provisions of law relating to the issuance of driver's licenses, if the court is satisfied from the evidence presented that: (i) at the time of the previous convictions, the petitioner was addicted to or psychologically dependent on the use of alcohol or other drugs; (ii) at the time of the hearing on the petition, he is no longer addicted to or psychologically dependent on the use of alcohol or such other drug; and (iii) the person does not constitute a threat to the safety and welfare of himself or others with regard to the driving of a motor vehicle. However, prior to acting on the petition, the court shall order that an evaluation of the person be conducted by a Virginia Alcohol Safety Action Program and recommendations therefrom be submitted to the court. The court may, in lieu of restoring the person's privilege to drive, authorize the issuance of a restricted license for a period not to exceed five years in accordance with the provisions of subsection E of §18.2-271.1. The local Virginia Alcohol Safety Action Program shall during the term of the restricted license monitor the person's compliance with the terms of the restrictions imposed by the court. Any violation of the restrictions shall be reported to the court, and the court may then modify the restrictions or revoke the license.

2. Issue a restricted permit to authorize such person to drive a motor vehicle in the Commonwealth in the course of his employment, to and from his home to the place of his employment or such other medically necessary travel as the court deems necessary and proper upon written verification of need by a licensed physician, provided that three years have elapsed from the date of the final order, or if no such order was entered then the notice of the determination by the Commissioner. The court may order that a restricted license for such purposes be issued in accordance with the procedures of subsection E of §18.2-271.1, if the court is satisfied from the evidence presented that (i) at the time of the previous convictions, the petitioner was addicted to or psychologically dependent on the use of alcohol or other drugs, (ii) at the time of the hearing on the petition, he is no longer addicted to or psychologically dependent on the use of alcohol or such other drugs, and (iii) the defendant does not constitute a threat to the safety and welfare of himself and others with regard to the driving of a motor vehicle. The court may prohibit the person to whom a restricted license is issued from operating a motor vehicle that is not equipped with a functioning, certified ignition interlock system during all or any part of the term for which the restricted license is issued, in accordance with the provisions set forth in §18.2-270.1. However, prior to acting on the petition, the court shall order that an evaluation of the person be conducted by a Virginia Alcohol Safety Action Program and recommendations therefrom be submitted to the court. The local Virginia Alcohol Safety Action Program shall during the term of the restricted license monitor the person's compliance with the terms of the restrictions imposed by the court. Any violation of the restrictions shall be reported to the court, and the court may then modify the restrictions or revoke the license.

In the computation of the five-year and three-year periods under subdivisions 1 and 2 of this section, such person shall be given credit for any period his driver's license was administratively revoked under subsection B of §46.2-391 prior to the final order or notification by the Commissioner of the habitual offender determination.

A copy of any petition filed hereunder shall be served on the attorney for the Commonwealth for the jurisdiction wherein the petition was filed, and shall also be served on the Commissioner of the Department of Motor Vehicles, who shall provide to the attorney for the Commonwealth a certified copy of the petitioner's driving record. The Commissioner shall also advise the attorney for the Commonwealth whether there is anything in the records maintained by the Department that might make the petitioner ineligible for restoration, and may also provide notice of any potential ineligibility to the Attorney General's Office, which may join in representing the interests of the Commonwealth where it appears that the petitioner is not eligible for restoration. The hearing on a petition filed pursuant to this article shall not be set for a date sooner than thirty days after the petition is filed and served as provided herein.

(Chgd. by L.1995 chs. 486, 799; L.1996 ch. 374; L.1998 ch. 749; L.1999 ch. 742, eff. 3/28/99, chs. 945, 987, eff. 7/1/99.)

§46.2-361. Restoration of privilege after driving while license revoked or suspended for failure to pay fines or costs, furnish proof of financial responsibility or pay uninsured motorist fee.

A. Any person who has been found to be an habitual offender, where the determination or adjudication was based in part and dependent on a conviction as set out in subdivision 1 c of former §46.2-351, may, after three years from the date of the final order of a court entered under this article, or if no such order was entered then the notice of the determination or adjudication by the Commissioner, petition the court in which he was found to be an habitual offender, or the circuit court in the political subdivision in which he then resides, for restoration of his privilege to drive a motor vehicle in the Commonwealth. In no event, however, shall the provisions of this subsection apply when such person's determination or adjudication was also based in part and dependent on a conviction as set out in subdivision 1 b of former §46.2-351. In such case license restoration shall be in compliance with the provisions of §46.2-360.

B. Any person who has been found to be an habitual offender, where the determination or adjudication was based entirely upon a combination of convictions of §46.2-707 and convictions as set out in subdivision 1 c of former §46.2-351, may, after payment in full of all outstanding fines, costs and judgments relating to his determination, and furnishing proof of (i) financial responsibility and (ii) compliance with the provisions of Article 8 (§46.2-705 et seq.) of Chapter 6 of this title or both, if applicable, petition the court in which he was found to be an habitual offender, or the circuit court in the political subdivision in which he then resides, for restoration of his privilege to drive a motor vehicle in the Commonwealth.

C. This section shall apply only where the conviction or convictions as set out in subdivision 1 c of former §46.2-351 resulted from a suspension or revocation ordered pursuant to (i) §46.2-395 for failure to pay fines and costs, (ii) §46.2-459 for failure to furnish proof of financial responsibility, or (iii) §46.2-417 for failure to satisfy a judgment, provided the judgment has been paid in full prior to the time of filing the petition or was a conviction under §46.2-302 or former §46.1-351.

D. On any such petition, the court, in its discretion, may restore to the person his privilege to drive a motor vehicle, on whatever conditions the court may prescribe, if the court is satisfied from the evidence presented that the petitioner does not constitute a threat to the safety and welfare of himself or others with respect to the operation of a motor vehicle, and that he has satisfied in full all outstanding court costs, court fines and judgments relating to determination as an habitual offender and furnished proof of financial responsibility, if applicable.

E. A copy of any petition filed hereunder shall be served on the attorney for the Commonwealth for the jurisdiction wherein the petition was filed, and shall also be served on the

Commissioner of the Department of Motor Vehicles, who shall provide to the attorney for the Commonwealth a certified copy of the petitioner's driving record. The Commissioner shall also advise the attorney for the Commonwealth whether there is anything in the records maintained by the Department that might make the petitioner ineligible for restoration, and may also provide notice of any potential ineligibility to the Attorney General's Office, which may join in representing the interests of the Commonwealth where it appears that the petitioner is not eligible for restoration. The hearing on a petition filed pursuant to this article shall not be set for a date sooner than thirty days after the petition is filed and served as provided herein.
(Chgd. by L.1995 ch. 799; L.1998 ch. 749; L.1999 chs. 945, 987; L.2000 ch. 792, eff. 7/1/2000.)

§46.2-362. Appeals.

An appeal to the circuit court may be taken from any final action or order of the general district court under former §46.2-355 in the same manner and form as provided in §§16.1-106 and 16.1-107. An appeal to the Court of Appeals may be taken from any final action or order of a circuit court entered under this article in the same manner and form as such an appeal would be taken in any criminal case.
(Chgd. by L.1996 ch. 414; L.1999 chs. 945, 987, eff. 7/1/99.)

§46.2-363. Construction of article.

Nothing in this article shall be construed as amending, modifying, or repealing any existing law of Virginia or any existing ordinance of any political subdivision relating to the driving or licensing of motor vehicles, the licensing of persons to drive motor vehicles, or providing penalties for violations. Nor shall this article preclude the exercise of the regulatory powers of any division, agency, department, or political subdivision of the Commonwealth having the statutory power to regulate driving and licensing.

ARTICLE 10
DRIVER RESPONSIBILITIES, GENERALLY

Section

§46.2-364. Definitions.

For the purposes of this chapter, unless a different meaning is clearly required by the context:

"Conviction" means conviction on a plea of guilty or the determination of guilt by a jury or by a court though no sentence has been imposed or, if imposed, has been suspended and includes a forfeiture of bail or collateral deposited to secure appearance in court of the defendant unless the forfeiture has been vacated, in any case of a charge, the conviction of which requires or authorizes the Commissioner to suspend or revoke the license of the defendant;

"Insured" means the person in whose name a motor vehicle liability policy has been issued, as defined in this section, and any other person insured under its terms;

"Judgment" means any judgment for $200 dollars or more arising out of a motor vehicle accident because of injury to or destruction of property, including loss of its use, or any judgment for damages, including damages for care and loss of services, because of bodily injury to or death of any person arising out of the ownership, use or operation of any motor vehicle, including any judgment for contribution between joint tort-feasors arising out of any motor vehicle accident which occurred within the Commonwealth, except a judgment rendered against the Commonwealth, which has become final by expiration without appeal in the time within which an appeal might be perfected or by final affirmance on appeal rendered by a court of competent jurisdiction of the Commonwealth or any other state or court of the United States or Canada or its provinces;

"Motor vehicle" means every vehicle which is self-propelled or designed for self-propulsion and every vehicle drawn by or designed to be drawn by a motor vehicle and includes every device in, on or by which any person or property is or can be transported or drawn on a highway, except devices moved by human or animal power and devices used exclusively on rails or tracks, and vehicles used in the Commonwealth but not required to be licensed by the Commonwealth;

"Motor vehicle liability policy" means an owner's or a driver's policy of liability insurance certified, as provided in this chapter, by an insurance carrier licensed to do business in the Commonwealth or by an insurance carrier not licensed to do business in the Commonwealth on compliance with the provisions of this chapter, as proof of financial responsibility.
(Chgd. by L.1996 chs. 474, 489, eff. 1/1/97.)

§46.2-365. Plaintiff not prevented from relying upon other legal process.

This article shall not prevent the plaintiff in any action at law from relying upon any other process provided by law.

§46.2-366. Partial application to certain motor vehicles.

This chapter, except its provisions as to the requirements of making reports of motor vehicle accidents and as to the filing of proof of financial responsibility by a common carrier for its drivers, shall not apply to any motor vehicle:

1. Operated under a certificate of convenience and necessity issued by the State Corporation Commission, if public liability and property damage insurance for the protection of the public is required to be carried on it, or
2. Owned by the Commonwealth.

§46.2-367. Persons included within scope of chapter.

Persons who have, by any law of the Commonwealth, been required to file proof of financial responsibility are included within the scope of this chapter. Persons who have been convicted of violations of any law of the Commonwealth or law of any other state or county, city, or town ordinance of either or a federal law pertaining to the driver or driving of motor vehicles or of violations of any provisions of this title are also included.

§46.2-368. Certificate of self-insurance exempts from chapter.

A. This chapter, except §§46.2-371 through 46.2-373, shall not apply to any person who has registered in his name in the Commonwealth more than twenty motor vehicles, nor to any person operating more than twenty vehicles whether as owner or as lessee, if the person seeking exemption under this section obtains from the Commissioner a certificate of self-insurance as provided in subsection B of this section.

B. The Commissioner may, in his discretion and on the application of such a person, issue a certificate of self-insurance when he is reasonably satisfied (i) that the person has and will continue to have financial ability to respond to a judgment as provided in this chapter, obtained against the person, arising out of the ownership, maintenance, use, or operation of his motor vehicles and (ii) that the certificate provides for protection against the uninsured or underinsured motorist to the extent required by §38.2-2206. However, protection against the uninsured or underinsured motorist required under this section shall not exceed the financial requirements of §46.2-472 and shall be secondary coverage to any other valid and collectible insurance providing the same protection which is available to any person otherwise entitled to assert a claim to such protection by virtue of this section.

C. No holder of a certificate of self-insurance shall be liable to pay any judgment arising out of the use or operation of any motor vehicle covered by such certificate by a person who used or operated the vehicle without the permission of the owner of such vehicle; nor shall any holder of a certificate of self-insurance be liable to pay any judgment arising out of the use or operation of any motor vehicle covered by such certificate by a permissive user of such vehicle, where the permissive user has prejudicially failed to cooperate in the defense of the claim which resulted in the judgment. This subsection shall only apply to a holder of a certificate of self-insurance who has provided notice of its intention to rely on the provisions of this subsection as set forth in §38.2-2226.

D. On due notice and hearing, the Commissioner may, in his discretion and on reasonable grounds, cancel a certificate of self-insurance.

(Chgd. by L.1995 ch. 85; L.1997 ch. 553, eff. 7/1/97.)

§46.2-369. Commissioner to administer and enforce chapter; regulations; summoning witnesses and taking testimony.

The Commissioner shall administer and enforce the provisions of this chapter and he may adopt regulations for its administration. He may issue subpoenas for witnesses to attend, administer oaths, and take testimony in, the hearings provided in this chapter for the purpose of finding whether driver's licenses, license plates, or registrations should be suspended or revoked. If any person fails or refuses to obey the subpoena, or to give testimony, the Commissioner shall notify the circuit or district court of the county or city in which the hearing is or was to have been held. On receipt of the notice, the court shall, by appropriate process, compel his attendance or testimony or both, to the same extent that it could be required in a proceeding in the court.

§46.2-370. Revoked driver's licenses, special identification cards, certificates of title, license plates, registration cards to be returned; Commissioner may take possession of them.

A. Any person whose driver's license, special identification card, certificate of title, registration card, or license plates have been suspended, cancelled, or revoked as provided in this title or in Title 18.2 and have not been reinstated, shall immediately return every such license, unless it has been surrendered to the court as required by law, special identification card, certificate of title, registration card, and set of license plates or decals held by him to the Commissioner.

B. The Commissioner may take possession of any driver's license, special identification card, certificate of title, registration card, or set of license plates or decals on their suspension, cancellation, or revocation under the provisions of this title or in Title 18.2 or may direct any law-enforcement officer to take possession of and return them to the office of the Commissioner. Whenever any person fails or refuses to surrender a driver's license, special identification card, certificate of title, registration card, license plates, or decals requiring a representative of the Department designated by the Commissioner to serve the order of suspension, cancellation, or revocation, or whenever the Department directs a sheriff to effect service of a decision, order, or notice pursuant to §46.2-416, the person sought to be served shall, in addition to any other required statutory fees, pay a fee of ten dollars to partially defray the cost of administration incurred by the Department and the Commissioner. No such revoked, cancelled, or suspended license, special identification card, certificate of title, or registration items shall be reinstated before the ten-dollar fee is paid. All fees collected under the provisions of this section shall be paid by the Commissioner into the state treasury and shall be set aside as a special fund to be used to meet the expenses of the Department.

ARTICLE 11
ACCIDENT REPORTS

§46.2-371. Driver to give immediate notice of certain accidents.

The driver of any vehicle involved in any accident resulting in injury to or death of any person, or some person acting for him, shall immediately give notice of the accident to a law-enforcement officer. A willful failure to make the report required in this section shall constitute a Class 4 misdemeanor.

§46.2-372. Driver to report certain accidents in writing; certification of financial responsibility to Department; supplemental reports; reports by witnesses.

A. Any person involved in an accident (i) resulting in injury to or death of any person or property damage, or (ii) when there is reason to believe a motor vehicle involved in the accident was uninsured at the time of the accident, may make a written report of it to the Commissioner, on a form prescribed by the Department.

B. If any accident report filed pursuant to the provisions of this article is alleged to be false or inaccurate, the Commissioner shall withhold any action under this section or imposition of any penalty and shall investigate and determine the true circumstances of the accident, including a determination of the identity of the parties involved.

C. For the purposes of this article the definitions provided in subsection B of §38.2-2206 shall apply.

D. The Commissioner shall require the owner of a motor vehicle involved in any accident of which report is made pursuant to this section to provide information relating to certification of insurance or bond if there was in effect at the time of the accident with respect to the motor vehicle involved:

1. A standard provisions automobile liability policy in form approved by the State Corporation Commission and issued by an insurance carrier authorized to do business in the Commonwealth or, if the motor vehicle was not registered in the Commonwealth or was a motor vehicle which was registered elsewhere than in the Commonwealth at the effective date of the policy, or at its most recent renewal, an automobile liability policy acceptable to that Commission as substantially the equivalent of a standard provisions automobile liability policy; in either event, every automobile liability policy is subject to the limits provided in §46.2-472.

2. Any other form of liability insurance policy issued by an insurance carrier authorized to do business in the Commonwealth or by a bond; provided that every such policy or bond mentioned herein is subject to limits set out in §46.2-472.

E. The Commissioner shall forward the certification of insurance or bond to the insurance company or surety company, whichever is applicable, for verification as to whether or not the policy or bond certified was applicable to any liability that may arise out of the accident as to the named insured. A copy of the certification of insurance or bond shall be retained by the Commissioner and shall be disclosed pursuant to §46.2-380.

§46.2-373. Report by law-enforcement officer investigating accident.

A. Every law-enforcement officer who in the course of duty investigates a motor vehicle accident resulting in injury to or death of any person or total property damage to an apparent extent of $1,000 or more, either at the time of and at the scene of the accident or thereafter and elsewhere, by interviewing participants or witnesses shall, within twenty-four hours after completing the investigation, forward a written report of the accident to the Department. The report shall include the name or names of the insurance carrier or of the insurance agent of the automobile liability policy on each vehicle involved in the accident.

B. Any report filed pursuant to subsection A of this section shall include information as to (i) the speed of each vehicle involved in the accident and (ii) the type of vehicles involved in all accidents between passenger vehicles and vehicles or combinations of vehicles used to transport property, and (iii) whether any trucks involved in such accidents were covered or uncovered.

C. The Department shall supply copies of accident reports received under this section to the Commonwealth Transportation Commissioner who shall exercise the authority granted to him under §§46.2-870 through 46.2-878 to reduce speed limits where accident frequency or severity or other factors may indicate the course of action to be warranted.

§46.2-374. Department to prepare and supply forms for reports.

The Department shall prepare and, on request, supply to police departments, medical examiners or other officials exercising like functions, sheriffs, and other suitable agencies forms for accident reports and other reports required to be made to the Department, appropriate with respect to the persons required to make the reports and the purpose to be served. The forms for accident reports shall include suitable spaces for the name or names of the insurance carrier of the automobile liability policy of each vehicle involved in the accidents as required to be reported by §46.2-373.

§46.2-375. Reports by medical examiners of deaths resulting from accidents.

Every person holding the office of medical examiner shall report to the Commissioner: (i) the death of a person in his jurisdiction as a result of a motor vehicle accident, immediately after learning of the death; (ii) on or before the tenth day of each month, all deaths resulting from motor vehicle accidents during the preceding calendar month. These reports shall be made in the form prescribed by the Commissioner.

§46.2-376. Report required of person in charge of garage or repair shop.

The person in charge of any garage or repair shop to which is brought any motor vehicle (i) that shows evidence of having been involved in a serious motor vehicle accident or (ii) with evidence of bloodstains shall report to the nearest police station or to the State Police, within twenty-four hours after the motor vehicle is received, giving the engine number, registration number and the name and address of the owner or operator of the vehicle if known. Reports required by this section shall be made upon forms furnished by the Superintendent of State Police.

§46.2-377. Reports made by garages to be without prejudice and confidential; exceptions.

All accident reports made by garages pursuant to this article shall be without prejudice to the individual so reporting and shall be for the confidential use of the State Police, local law-enforcement agencies, or by agencies having use for the records for accident prevention purposes.

§46.2-378. Extent to which reports may be used as evidence.

No report submitted pursuant to this article shall be used as evidence in any trial, civil or criminal, arising out of an accident, except that the Department shall furnish, on demand of any person who has or claims to have made such a report, or upon demand of any court, a certificate showing that a specified accident report has or has not been made to the Department, solely to prove compliance or noncompliance with the requirement that the report be made to the Department.

§46.2-379. Use of accident reports made by investigating officers.

All accident reports made by investigating officers shall be for the confidential use of the Department and of other state agencies for accident prevention purposes and shall not be used as evidence in any trial, civil or criminal, arising out of any accident. The Department shall disclose from the reports, on request of any person, the date, time, and location of the accident, and the names and addresses of the drivers, the owners of the vehicles involved, the injured persons, the witnesses, and one investigating officer.

§46.2-380. Reports made under certain sections open to inspection by certain persons; copies; maintenance of reports and photographs for three-year period.

A. Any report of an accident made pursuant to §§46.2-372, 46.2-373, 46.2-375, or §46.2-377 shall be maintained by the Department for a period of at least thirty-six months from the date of the accident and shall be open to the inspection of any person involved or injured in the accident or as a result thereof, or his attorney or any authorized representative of any insurance carrier reasonably anticipating exposure to civil liability as a consequence of the accident or to which the person has applied for issuance or renewal of a policy of automobile insurance. The Commissioner or Superintendent, or the area or division offices of the Department of State Police having a copy of the report, shall on written request of the person or attorney or any authorized representative of any insurance carrier reasonably anticipating exposure to civil liability as a consequence of the accident or to which the person has applied for issuance or renewal of a policy of automobile insurance, furnish a copy of the report at the expense of the person, attorney, or representative. Any such report shall also be open to inspection by the personal representative of any person injured or killed in the accident, including his guardian, conservator, executor, committee, or administrator, or, if the person injured or killed is under eighteen years old, his parent or guardian. The Commissioner or Superintendent shall only be required to furnish under this section copies of reports required by the provisions of this article to be made directly to the Commissioner or Superintendent, or to the area or division offices of the Department of State Police having a copy of any such report, as the case may be. The Commissioner and the Superintendent, acting jointly, may set a reasonable fee for furnishing a copy of any report, provide to whom payment shall be made, and establish a procedure for payment. Nothing contained in this section shall require any division office of the Department of State Police to furnish any copy when duplicating equipment is not available.

B. The Commissioner or Superintendent of State Police having a copy of any photograph taken by a law-enforcement officer relating to a nonfatal accident, shall maintain the negatives for such photographs in their records for at least thirty-six months from the date of the accident.
(Chgd. by L.1997 ch. 801; L.1998 ch. 522, eff. 7/1/98.)

§46.2-381. Accident reports required by county or municipal ordinance; copies.

Any county, city, or town may, by ordinance, require that the driver of a vehicle involved in an accident file with a designated department a report of the accident. These reports shall be for the confidential use of the department and subject to the provisions of this article. The county, city, or town may, by ordinance, require the designated department to make the reports, including the report of the law-enforcement officer, and including any photographs taken by law-enforcement officers, available for inspection by any person involved or injured in the accident or his attorney or any authorized representative of any insurance carrier reasonably anticipating exposure to civil liability as a consequence of the accident. The county, city, or town may, by ordinance, prescribe fees to be charged for copies of the reports and photographs and require the designated department to furnish copies of the reports and photographs, after payment of the prescribed fees, to any such person, attorney, or authorized representative.

§46.2-382. Courts to keep full records of certain cases.

Every general district court or circuit court or the clerk thereof shall keep a full record of every case in which:

1. A person is charged with (i) a violation of any law of the Commonwealth pertaining to the operator or operation of a motor vehicle; (ii) a violation of any ordinance of any county, city, or town pertaining to the operator or operation of any motor vehicles, except parking regulations; (iii) any theft of a motor vehicle or unauthorized use thereof or theft of any part attached to it; or (iv) a violation of subsection B of §29.1-738 or §§29.1-738.02, 29.1-738.2, or §29.1-738.4;

2. A person is charged with manslaughter or any other felony in the commission of which a motor vehicle was used; or

3. There is rendered a judgment for damages, the rendering and nonpayment of which under the terms of this title require the Commissioner to suspend the driver's license and registration in the name of the judgment debtor.
(Chgd. by L.1998 ch. 147, eff. 7/1/98.)

§46.2-382.1. Courts to make findings relating to commercial motor vehicles.

For the purpose of enforcing the Virginia Commercial Driver's License Act (§46.2-341.1 et seq.), in any case in which a person is charged with a violation of any law of the Commonwealth or of any ordinance of any county, city or town pertaining to the operator or operation of a motor vehicle, except parking violations, and the warrant or summons indicates that the motor vehicle so operated was a commercial motor vehicle as defined in the Virginia Commercial Driver's License Act, or that it was a commercial motor vehicle carrying hazardous materials as defined by the Virginia Commercial Driver's License Act, the court hearing such case shall make a finding, which shall be noted on the record, as to whether such vehicle was in fact a commercial motor vehicle and, if applicable, whether such vehicle was carrying hazardous materials.

If the offense charged is one in which operation of a commercial motor vehicle is an element of the offense, the conviction of the offense shall constitute the court's finding that the vehicle was a commercial motor vehicle, but a separate finding shall be made as to whether such vehicle was carrying hazardous materials, if applicable. If the offense charged is one in which operation of a commercial motor vehicle is not an element of the offense, then the court, after convicting the person charged, shall make a separate finding as to whether the vehicle was a commercial motor vehicle and, if applicable, whether it was carrying hazardous materials. The separate findings required by this section shall be noted on the conviction record, and the following procedures shall apply to such separate findings:

1. If the person charged prepays fines and costs pursuant to §19.2-254.1, he shall be deemed to have admitted that such motor vehicle was a commercial motor vehicle and, if applicable, that it carried hazardous materials at the time of the violation, as indicated on the warrant or summons, and such admission or admissions shall be noted on the conviction record as the court's finding.

2. In all other cases, the Commonwealth shall have the burden of proving by a preponderance of the evidence that

the vehicle was a commercial motor vehicle and, if applicable, that it carried hazardous materials.

§46.2-383. Courts to forward abstracts of records or furnish abstract data of conviction by electronic means in certain cases; records in office of Department; inspection; clerk's fee for reports.

A. In the event (i) a person is convicted of a charge described in subdivision 1 or 2 of §46.2-382 or §46.2-382.1 or (ii) a person fails or refuses to pay any fine, costs, forfeiture, restitution or penalty, or any installment thereof, imposed in any traffic case, or (iii) a person forfeits bail or collateral or other deposit to secure the defendant's appearance on the charges, unless the conviction has been set aside or the forfeiture vacated, or (iv) a court assigns a defendant to a driver education program or alcohol treatment or rehabilitation program, or both such programs, as authorized by §18.2-271.1, or (v) compliance with the court's probation order is accepted by the court in lieu of a conviction under §18.2-266 or the requirements specified in §18.2-271 as provided in §18.2-271.1, or (vi) there is rendered a judgment for damages against a person as described in §46.2-382, every district court or clerk of a circuit court shall forward an abstract of the record to the Commissioner within fifteen days, or in the case of civil judgments, on the request of the judgment creditor or his attorney, thirty days after the conviction, forfeiture, assignment, acceptance, or judgment has become final without appeal or has become final by affirmance on appeal.

B. Abstract data of conviction may be furnished to the Commissioner by electronic means provided that the content of the abstract and the certification complies with the requirements of §46.2-386. In cases where the abstract data is furnished by electronic means, the paper abstract shall not be required to be forwarded to the Commissioner. The Commissioner shall develop a method to ensure that all data is received accurately. The Commissioner, with the approval of the Governor, may destroy the record of any conviction, forfeiture, assignment, acceptance, or judgment, when three years has elapsed from the date thereof, except records of conviction or forfeiture on charges of reckless driving and speeding, which records may be destroyed when five years has elapsed from the date thereof, and further excepting those records that alone, or in connection with other records, will require suspension or revocation or disqualification of a license or registration under any applicable provisions of this title.

C. The records required to be kept may, in the discretion of the Commissioner, be kept by electronic media or by photographic processes and when so done the abstract of the record may be destroyed.

§46.2-384. Law-enforcement officers arresting drivers for certain offenses to request abstracts or transcripts of drivers' conviction records.

Every law-enforcement officer who has arrested any person for (i) driving while under the influence of intoxicants or drugs in violation of §18.2-51.4 or §18.2-266 or a parallel local ordinance, or §46.2-341.24, (ii) reckless driving in violation of §§46.2-852 through 46.2-865 or a parallel local ordinance, (iii) failure to stop at the scene of an accident in violation of §§46.2-894 through 46.2-899 or a parallel local ordinance or (iv) driving without a license or while his license has been suspended or revoked in violation of §18.2-51.4 or §18.2-272 or §§46.2-300 through 46.2-302 or a parallel local ordinance or while he is disqualified in violation of §46.2-341.21 of the Commercial Vehicle Driver's License Act (§46.2-341.1 et seq.), shall request from the Department an abstract or transcript of the person's driver's conviction record on file at the Department. The Department shall furnish the abstract or transcript to the attorney for the Commonwealth of the jurisdiction in which the case will be heard, to be held available for the court in which the person is to be tried for the violation or charge. However, the failure of the attorney for the Commonwealth to receive the abstract or transcript in any case shall not constitute grounds for the granting of a continuance of such case. In any such prosecution wherein a necessary element of the offense charged is that the defendant was previously convicted of the same or similar offense, a copy, certified as provided in §46.2-215, of (1) the abstract of the relevant prior conviction, certified as provided in §46.2-386, or (2) that portion of the transcript relating to the relevant prior conviction, shall be prima facie evidence of the facts stated therein with respect to the prior offense.

(Chgd. by L.1997 ch. 691, eff. 7/1/97.)

§46.2-385. Prosecuting attorneys to appear in certain cases.

If requested by the judge trying the case, attorneys for the Commonwealth and all city and town attorneys whose general duties include the prosecution of offenses which are reportable by the courts to the Department under §46.2-383, shall appear on behalf of the Commonwealth or the locality in any contested criminal case wherein a resulting conviction is required to be reported to the Department under §46.2-383.

The failure of the attorney to appear shall, in no case, affect the validity of any conviction.

§46.2-386. Forms for and information to be contained in abstracts; certification.

Abstracts required by §46.2-383 shall be made on forms prepared by or approved by the Department and the Department of State Police. They shall include all information as to the parties to the case. In the event the abstract relates to a person convicted or found not innocent of a charge described in subdivision 1 or 2 of §46.2-382, it shall include the nature and date of the offense, the date of conviction or finding of not innocent, the plea, the judgment, the penalty or forfeiture as the case may be, and the driver's license number if any, the month, day and year of birth, the sex and the residence address or whereabouts of the defendant and shall indicate whether the defendant appeared and was represented by or waived counsel. Every such abstract shall be certified by the general district court or juvenile and domestic relations district court judge or clerk of the general district court or juvenile and domestic relations district court or clerk of a circuit court as a true abstract of the records of the court as it relates to the charge, judgment and penalty.

Abstracts transmitted to the Department by electronic means may be certified by machine imprint of the name of the general district court or juvenile and domestic relations district court judge or the clerk's name of the general district court or juvenile and domestic relations district court or the name of the clerk of the circuit court that furnished the record as a true abstract of the records of the court as it relates to the charge, judgment, and penalty.

(Chgd. by L.1996 ch. 616, eff. 7/1/96.)

§46.2-387. Penalty for failure to forward record of conviction or of judgment for damages.

Any person required to forward to the Commissioner a record of a conviction or of a judgment for damages as provided in this chapter who fails, refuses, or neglects so to do without reasonable cause shall be guilty of a Class 4 misdemeanor and may be suspended or removed from office or otherwise disciplined for dereliction of duty.

The Commissioner shall call every such failure to the attention of the person guilty of the dereliction and to the judge of the court of which he is an officer in cases of dereliction on the part of officers of courts and also to the appropriate attorney for the Commonwealth.

Discipline for dereliction of the duties provided by this chapter is cumulative to the other penalties prescribed and may be imposed by the court having jurisdiction over the official whose negligence is complained of.

§46.2-388. Uniform summons to be used for reportable motor vehicle law violations; citations.

A. The Attorney General, after consultation with the Committee on District Courts, the Superintendent of State Police and the Commissioner, shall approve a form for the summons and all revisions to the form to be used by all law-enforcement officers throughout the Commonwealth in cases of motor vehicle law violations reportable to the Department under the provisions of §§46.2-382 and 46.2-383 and for other offenses charged on a summons pursuant to §19.2-74. The commencement and termination date for the use of the form and each revised version of the form shall be made by the Attorney General after consultation with the Committee on District Courts, the Superintendent of State Police and the Commissioner.

The form of the summons shall include multiple copies with the original to be used for court records and other copies in sufficient number to permit the use of one copy by the courts for purposes of filing abstracts of records with the Department as required by §46.2-383 and shall be a form prepared by the Department within the meaning of §46.2-386. The form of the summons shall also include appropriate space for use in cases of violation of either state laws or local ordinances.

B. A separate citation which has been approved in the manner prescribed in subsection A of this section shall be used for violations of §§46.2-1122 through 46.2-1127 and 46.2-1130. The citation shall be directed to the owner, operator or other person responsible for the overweight violation, and shall advise him of:

1. The nature of the violation charged against him;
2. The amount of monetary fees, penalties, and damages that may be assessed for violations;
3. The requirement that he either pay the fees, penalties, and damages in full or deliver a notice of his intent to contest the charge to the Department;
4. The procedures and time limits for making the payments or contesting such charge, which shall include the trial date, which shall in no event be earlier than sixty days after the violation; and
5. The consequences of a failure to timely pay or contest the charge.

ARTICLE 12
SUSPENSION AND REVOCATION OF LICENSES, GENERALLY; ADDITIONAL PENALTIES

Section

§46.2-389. Required revocation for one year upon conviction or finding of guilty of certain offenses; exceptions.

A. The Commissioner shall forthwith revoke, and not thereafter reissue for a period of time specified in subsection B, except as provided in §18.2-271 or §18.2-271.1, the driver's license of any resident or nonresident on receiving a record of his conviction or a record of his having been found guilty in the case of a juvenile of any of the following crimes, committed in violation of a state law or a valid county, city, or town ordinance or law of the United States, or a law of any other state, substantially paralleling and substantially conforming to a like state law and to all changes and amendments of it:

1. Voluntary or involuntary manslaughter resulting from the driving of a motor vehicle;
2. Violation of §18.2-266 or §18.2-272, or subsection A of §46.2-341.24 or violation of a substantially similar local ordinance;
3. Perjury or the making of a false affidavit to the Department under this chapter or any other law of the Commonwealth requiring the registration of motor vehicles or regulating their operation on the highways;
4. The making of a false statement to the Department on any application for a driver's license;
5. Any crime punishable as a felony under the motor vehicle laws of the Commonwealth or any other felony in the commission of which a motor vehicle is used;
6. Failure to stop and disclose his identity at the scene of the accident, on the part of a driver of a motor vehicle involved in an accident resulting in the death of or injury to another person; or
7. Violation of §18.2-36.1 or §18.2-51.4.

B. Upon conviction of an offense set forth in subsection A, the person's driver's license shall be revoked for one year; however, for a violation of subdivision A 1 or A 7, the driver's license shall be revoked as provided in subsection B of §46.2-391. However, in no such event shall the Commissioner reinstate the driver's license of any person convicted of a violation of §18.2-266, or of a substantially similar valid local ordinance or law of another jurisdiction, until receipt of notification that such person has successfully completed an alcohol safety action program if such person was required by a court to do so unless the requirement for completion of the program has been waived by the court for good cause shown.
(Chgd. by L.1997 chs. 486, 691; L.1999 chs. 945, 987; L.2000 chs. 956, 959, 982, 985, eff. 7/1/2000.)

§46.2-390. Required suspension for conviction of theft or unauthorized use of a motor vehicle.

When any person is convicted, or found guilty in the case of a juvenile, of any theft of a motor vehicle or its unauthorized use, or the theft of any of its parts, whether the motor vehicle is used in the commission of a theft or not, then in addition to any penalties provided by law, the driver's license of the person shall be suspended by the court for a period of not less than sixty days nor more than six months. In case of conviction the court shall order the surrender of the license to the court where it shall be disposed of in accordance with §46.2-398. If the conviction is a second or subsequent offense, the license shall be suspended at least sixty days and not more than one year, and the court shall transmit the license to the Department as provided by law. If the person has not obtained a license as required by this chapter, or is a nonresident, the court shall direct in the judgment of conviction that the person shall not drive any motor vehicle in the Commonwealth for a period to coincide with the judgment of the court. This section shall not apply in the event that the theft is one in which the revocation of the license of any person is required under the provisions of subdivision 5 of §46.2-389. Sections 46.2-391.1 and 46.2-411 shall not apply to any person whose license is suspended under this section.

§46.2-390.1. Required revocation for conviction of drug offenses or deferral of proceedings.

A. Except as otherwise ordered pursuant to §18.2-259.1, the Commissioner shall forthwith revoke, and not thereafter reissue for six months from the later of (i) the date of conviction or deferral of proceedings under §18.2-251 or (ii) the next date of eligibility to be licensed, the driver's license, registration card, and license plates of any resident or nonresident on receiving notification of (i) his conviction, (ii) his having been found guilty in the case of a juvenile or (iii) the deferral of further proceedings against him under §18.2-251 for any violation of any provisions of Article 1 (§18.2-247 et seq.) of Chapter 7 of Title 18.2, or of any state or federal law or valid county, city or town ordinance, or a law of any other state substantially similar to provisions of such Virginia laws. Such license revocation shall be in addition to and shall run consecutively with any other license suspension, revocation or forfeiture in effect against such person.

B. Any person whose license has been revoked pursuant to this section and §18.2-259.1 shall be subject to the provisions of §§46.2-370 and 46.2-414 and shall be required to show proof of financial responsibility and pay a reinstatement fee as provided in §§46.2-411 and 46.2-412 in order to have his license restored.
(Chgd. by L.1997 ch. 486, eff. 7/1/97.)

§46.2-391. Revocation of license for multiple convictions of driving while intoxicated; exception; petition for restoration of privilege.

A. The Commissioner shall forthwith revoke and not thereafter reissue for three years the driver's license of any person on receiving a record of the conviction of any person who is convicted of (i) any combination of two or more offenses, if the second or subsequent violation occurred within ten years of the prior adjudication, in violation of the provisions of subsection A of §46.2-341.24 (driving a commercial motor vehicle under the influence of drugs or intoxicants), or §18.2-266 (driving under the influence of drugs or intoxicants), or (ii) any two or more offenses of §18.2-272 (driving while the driver's license has been forfeited for a conviction under §18.2-266) if the second or subsequent violation occurred within ten years of the prior adjudication. However, if the Commissioner has received a copy of a court order as provided in subsection E of §18.2-271.1, he shall proceed as provided in the order of the court. For the purposes of this subsection, an offense in violation of a valid local ordinance, or law of any other jurisdiction, which ordinance or law is substantially similar to any provision of Virginia law herein shall be considered an offense in violation of such provision of Virginia law. Additionally, in no event shall the Commissioner reinstate the driver's license of any person convicted of a violation of §18.2-266, or of a substantially similar valid local ordinance or law of another jurisdiction, until receipt of notification that such person has successfully completed an alcohol safety action program if such person was required by court order to do so unless the requirement for completion of the program has been waived by the court for good cause shown.

B. The Commissioner shall forthwith revoke and not thereafter reissue the driver's license of any person after receiving a record of the conviction of any person convicted of (i) a violation of §18.2-36.1 or §18.2-51.4 or (ii) any combination of three convictions within a period of ten years of a violation of the provisions of subsection A of §46.2-341.24 or §§18.2-266, 18.2-272 or a substantially similar ordinance or law of any other jurisdiction. [At the expiration of ten years from the date of the revocation hereunder, the person may petition the circuit court in the county or city in which he resides, and for good cause shown, his license may in the discretion of the court be restored on such conditions as the court may prescribe.]

C. Any person who has had his driver's license revoked in accordance with subsection B of this section may petition the circuit court of his residence, or, if a nonresident of Virginia, any circuit court:

1. For restoration of his privilege to drive a motor vehicle in the Commonwealth after the expiration of five years from the date of his last conviction. On such petition, and for good cause shown, the court may, in its discretion, restore to the person the privilege to drive a motor vehicle in the Commonwealth on *condition that such person install an ignition interlock system in accordance with §18.2-270.1 on all motor vehicles, as defined in §46.2-100, owned by or registered to him, in whole or in part, for a period of at least six months, and upon* whatever *other* conditions the court may prescribe, subject to the provisions of law relating to issuance of driver's licenses, if the court is satisfied from the evidence presented that: (i) at the time of his previous convictions, the petitioner was addicted to or psychologically dependent on the use of alcohol or other drugs; (ii) at the time of the hearing on the petition, he is no longer addicted to or psychologically dependent on the use of alcohol or other drugs; and (iii) the defendant does not constitute a threat to the safety and welfare of himself or others with regard to the driving of a motor vehicle. However, prior to acting on the petition, the court shall order that an evaluation of the person, *to include an assessment of his degree of alcohol abuse and the appropriate treatment therefor, if any,* be conducted by a Virginia Alcohol Safety Action Program and recommendations therefrom be submitted to the court. The court may, in lieu of restoring the person's privilege to drive, authorize the issuance of a restricted license for a period not to exceed five years in accordance with the provisions of *§18.2-270.1 and* subsection E of §18.2-271.1. The court shall notify the Virginia Alcohol Safety Action Program which shall during the term of the restricted license monitor the person's compliance with the terms of the restrictions imposed by the court. Any violation of the restrictions shall be reported to the court, and the court may then modify the restrictions or revoke the license.

2. For a restricted license to authorize such person to drive a motor vehicle in the Commonwealth in the course of his employment and to drive a motor vehicle to and from his home to the place of his employment after the expiration of three years from the date of his last conviction. The court may order that a restricted license for such purposes be issued in accordance with the procedures of subsection E of §18.2-271.1, if the court is satisfied from the evidence presented that (i) at the time of the previous convictions, the petitioner was addicted to or psychologically dependent on the use of alcohol or other drugs; (ii) at the time of the hearing on the petition, he is no longer addicted to or psychologically dependent on the use of alcohol or such other drugs; and (iii) the defendant does not constitute a threat to the safety and welfare of himself and others with regard to the driving of a motor vehicle. The court [may] *shall* prohibit the person to whom a restricted license is issued from operating a motor vehicle that is not equipped with a functioning, certified ignition interlock system during all or any part of the term for which the restricted license is issued, in accordance with the provisions set forth in §18.2-270.1. However, prior to acting on the petition, the court shall order that an evaluation of the person, *to include an assessment of his degree of alcohol abuse and the appropriate treatment therefor, if any,* be conducted by a Virginia Alcohol Safety Action Program and recommendations therefrom be submitted to the court. The Virginia Alcohol Safety Action Program shall during the term of the restricted license monitor the person's compliance with the terms of the restrictions imposed by the court. Any violation of the restrictions shall be reported to the court, and the court may then modify the restrictions or revoke the license.

[In the computation of the five-year and three-year periods under subdivisions 1 and 2 of this subsection, such person shall be given credit for any period his driver's license was revoked under §46.2-360 after adjudication as a habitual offender.] *The ignition interlock system installation requirement under subdivisions 1 and 2 of this subsection need only be satisfied once as to any since revocation under subsection B of this section for any person seeking restoration under subdivision 1 following the granting of a restricted license under subdivision 1 or 2.*

D. Any person convicted of driving a motor vehicle or any self-propelled machinery or equipment (i) while his license is revoked pursuant to subsection A or B or (ii) in violation of the terms of a restricted license issued pursuant to subsection C shall, *provided such revocation was based on at least one conviction for an offense committed after July 1, 1999,* be punished as follows:

1. If such driving does not of itself endanger the life, limb, or property of another, such person shall be guilty of a Class 1 misdemeanor punishable by a minimum, mandatory term of confinement in jail for no less than ten days, which shall not be suspended except in cases designated in subdivision 2 b(ii) of this subsection.

2. a. If such driving (i) of itself endangers the life, limb, or property of another or (ii) takes place while such person is in violation of §§18.2-36.1, 18.2-51.4, 18.2-266, subsection A of §46.2-341.24, or a substantially similar law or ordinance of another jurisdiction, irrespective of whether the driving of itself endangers the life, limb or property of another and the person has been previously convicted of a violation of §§18.2-36.1, 18.2-51.4, 18.2-266, subsection A of §46.2-341.24, or a substantially similar local ordinance, or law of another jurisdiction, such person shall be guilty of a felony punishable by confinement in a state correctional facility for not less than one year nor more than five years or, in the discretion of the jury or the court trying the case without a jury, by confinement in jail for twelve months and no portion of such sentence shall be suspended.

b. However, (i) if the sentence is more than one year in a state correctional facility, any portion of such sentence in excess of one year may be suspended or (ii) in cases wherein such operation is necessitated in situations of apparent extreme emergency which require such operation to save life or limb, said sentence, or any part thereof may be suspended.

3. If any such offense of driving is a second or subsequent violation, such person shall be punished as provided in subdivision 2 of this subsection, irrespective of whether the offense, of itself, endangers the life, limb, or property of another.

E. Notwithstanding the provisions of subdivisions 2 and 3 of subsection D, following conviction and prior to imposition of sentence with the consent of the defendant, the court may order the defendant to be evaluated for and to participate in the Boot Camp Incarceration Program pursuant to §19.2-316.1, or the Detention Center Incarceration Program pursuant to §19.2-316.2, or the Diversion Center Incarceration Program pursuant to §19.2-316.3.

F. *(As added by L.2000 chs. 956, 982, See other subsection F below.)* Any period of driver's license revocation imposed pursuant to this section shall commence with the surrender of the license to the court or to the Department of Motor Vehicles.

F. *(As added by L.2000 chs. 958, 980. See other subsection F above.)* Any person who operates a motor vehicle or any self-propelled machinery or equipment (i) while his license is revoked pursuant to subsection A or B, or (ii) in violation of the terms of a restricted license issued pursuant to subsection C, where the provisions of subsection D do not apply, shall be guilty of a violation of §18.2-272.

G. Nothing in this section shall prohibit a person from operating any farm tractor on the highways when it is necessary to move the tractor from one tract of land used for agricultural purposes to another such tract of land when the distance between the tracts is no more than five miles.

(Chgd. by L.1995 ch. 486; L.1997 chs. 691, 706; L.1999 chs. 945, 987; L.2000 chs. 243, 956, eff. 7/1/2000, ch. 958, eff. 10/1/2000, ch. 959, eff. 7/1/2000, ch. 980, eff. 10/1/2000, chs. 982, 985, eff. 7/1/2000. Matter in brackets eff. only until 10/1/2000. Matter in italics eff. 10/1/2000.)

§46.2-391.1. Suspension of registration certificates and plates upon suspension or revocation of driver's license.

Whenever the Commissioner, under the authority of law of the Commonwealth, suspends or revokes the driver's license of any person upon receiving record of that person's conviction, or whenever the Commissioner is notified that a court has suspended a person's driving privilege pursuant to §46.2-395, the Commissioner shall also suspend all of the registration certificates and license plates issued for any motor vehicles registered solely in the name of such person and shall not issue any registration certificate or license plate for any other vehicle that such person seeks to register solely in his name. Except for persons whose privileges have been suspended by a court pursuant to §46.2-395, the Commissioner shall not suspend such registration certificates or license plates in the event such person has previously given or gives and thereafter maintains proof of his financial responsibility in the future, in the manner specified in this chapter, with respect to each and every motor vehicle owned and registered by such person. In this event it shall be lawful for said vehicle or vehicles to be operated during this period of suspension by any duly licensed driver when so authorized by the owner.

§46.2-391.2. Administrative suspension of license or privilege to operate a motor vehicle.

A. If a breath test is taken pursuant to §18.2-268.2 or any similar ordinance of any county, city or town and the results show a blood alcohol content of 0.08 percent or more by weight by volume or 0.08 grams or more per 210 liters of breath, or the person refuses to submit to the breath test in violation of §18.2-268.3 or any similar local ordinance, and upon issuance of a petition or summons, or upon issuance of a warrant by the magistrate, for a violation of §§18.2-51.4, 18.2-266 or §18.2-268.3, or any similar local ordinance, the person's license shall be suspended immediately for seven days or in the case of (i) an unlicensed person, (ii) a person whose license is otherwise suspended or revoked, or (iii) a person whose driver's license is from a jurisdiction other than the Commonwealth, such person's privilege to operate a motor vehicle in the Commonwealth shall be suspended immediately for seven days.

A law-enforcement officer, acting on behalf of the Commonwealth, shall serve a notice of suspension personally on the arrested person. When notice is served, the arresting officer shall promptly take possession of any driver's license held by the person and issued by the Commonwealth and shall promptly deliver it to the magistrate. Any driver's license taken into possession under this section shall be forwarded promptly by the magistrate to the clerk of the general district court or, as appropriate, the court with jurisdiction over juveniles of the jurisdiction in which the arrest was made together with any petition, summons or warrant, the results of the breath test, if any, and the report required by subsection B. A copy of the notice of suspension shall be forwarded forthwith to both (i) the general district court or, as appropriate, the court with jurisdiction over juveniles of the jurisdiction in which the arrest was made and (ii) the Commissioner. Transmission of this information may be made by electronic means.

The clerk shall promptly return the suspended license to the person at the expiration of the seven-day suspension. Whenever a suspended license is to be returned under this section or §46.2-391.4, the person may elect to have the license returned in person at the clerk's office or by mail to the address on the person's license or to such other address as he may request.

B. Promptly after arrest and service of the notice of suspension, the arresting officer shall forward to the magistrate a sworn report of the arrest that shall include (i) information which adequately identifies the person arrested and (ii) a statement setting forth the arresting officer's grounds for belief that the person violated §18.2-51.4 or §18.2-266 or a similar local ordinance or refused to submit to a breath test in violation of §18.2-268.3 or a similar local ordinance. The report required by this subsection shall be submitted on forms supplied by the Supreme Court.

C. Any person whose license or privilege to operate a motor vehicle has been suspended under subsection A may, during the period of the suspension, request the general district court or, as appropriate, the court with jurisdiction over juveniles of the jurisdiction in which the arrest was made to review that suspension. The court shall review the suspension within the same time period as the court hears an appeal from an order denying bail or fixing terms of bail or terms of recognizance, giving this matter precedence over all other matters on its docket. If the person proves to the court by a preponderance of the evidence that the arresting officer did not have probable cause for the arrest, that the magistrate did not have probable cause to issue the warrant, or that there was not probable cause for issuance of the petition, the court shall rescind the suspension, and the clerk of the court shall forthwith (i) return the suspended license, if any, to the person unless the license has been otherwise suspended or revoked, (ii) deliver to the person a notice that the suspension under §46.2-391.2 has been rescinded, and (iii) forward to the Commissioner a copy of the notice that the suspension under §46.2-391.2 has been rescinded. Otherwise, the court shall affirm the suspension. If the person requesting the review fails to appear without just cause, his right to review shall be waived.

The court's findings are without prejudice to the person contesting the suspension or to any other potential party as to any proceedings, civil or criminal, and shall not be evidence in any proceedings, civil or criminal.

D. If a person whose license or privilege to operate a motor vehicle is suspended under subsection A is convicted under §18.2-51.4 or §18.2-266 or any similar local ordinance during the seven-day suspension imposed by subsection A, and if the court decides to issue the person a restricted permit under subsection E of §18.2-271.1, such restricted permit shall not be issued to the person before the expiration of the seven-day suspension imposed under subsection A.

(Chgd. by L.1996 chs. 865, 1007; L.1997 ch. 691, eff. 7/1/97.)

§46.2-391.3. Content of notice of suspension.

A notice of suspension issued pursuant to §46.2-391.2 shall clearly specify (i) the reason and statutory grounds for the suspension, (ii) the effective date and duration of the suspension, (iii) the right of the offender to request a review of that suspension by the appropriate district court of the jurisdiction in which the arrest was made, and (iv) the procedures for requesting such a review.

§46.2-391.4. When suspension to be rescinded.

Notwithstanding any other provision of §46.2-391.2, a subsequent dismissal or acquittal of all the charges under §§18.2-51.4, 18.2-266 and 18.2-268.3 or any similar local ordinances, for the same offense for which a person's driver's license or privilege to operate a motor vehicle was suspended under §46.2-391.2 shall result in the immediate rescission of the suspension. In any such case, the clerk of the court shall forthwith (i) return the suspended license, if any, to the person unless the license has been otherwise suspended or revoked, (ii) deliver to the person a notice that the suspension under §46.2-391.2 has been rescinded and (iii) forward to the Commissioner a copy of the notice that the suspension under §46.2-391.2 has been rescinded.

(Chgd. by L.1997 ch. 691, eff. 7/1/97.)

§46.2-391.5. Preparation and distribution of forms.

The Supreme Court shall develop policies and regulations pertaining to the notice of suspension under subsection A of §46.2-391.2 and the notice that the suspension has been rescinded under subsection C of §46.2-391.2 and §46.2-391.4, and shall furnish appropriate forms to all law-enforcement officers and district courts, respectively.

§46.2-392. Suspension of license or issuance of a restricted license on conviction of reckless driving; probationary conditions required; generally.

In addition to the penalties for reckless driving prescribed in §46.2-868 any court may suspend any license issued to a convicted person under Articles 1 through 9 (§46.2-300 et seq.) of this chapter for a period of not less than ten days nor more than six months and the court shall require the convicted person to surrender his license so suspended to the court where it will be disposed of in accordance with §46.2-398. Additionally, any person convicted of a reckless driving offense which the court has reason to believe is alcohol-related or drug-related may be required as a condition of probation or otherwise to enter into and successfully complete an alcohol safety action program.

If a person so convicted has not obtained the license required by this chapter, or is a nonresident, the court may direct in the judgment of conviction that he shall not, for a period of not less than ten days or more than six months as may be prescribed in the judgment, drive any motor vehicle in the Commonwealth. The court or the clerk of court shall transmit the license to the Commissioner along with the report of the conviction required to be sent to the Department.

The court may, in its discretion and for good cause shown, provide that such person be issued a restricted permit to operate a motor vehicle during the period of suspension for any or all of the following purposes: (i) travel to and from his place of employment; (ii) travel during the hours of such person's employment if the operation of a motor vehicle is a necessary incident of such employment; (iii) travel to and from school if such person is a student, upon proper written verification to the court that such person is enrolled in a continuing program of education; or (iv) such other medically necessary travel as the court deems necessary and proper upon written verification of need by a licensed health professional. The court shall order the surrender of such person's license to operate a motor vehicle to be disposed of in accordance with the provisions of §46.2-398 and shall forward to the Commissioner a copy of its order entered pursuant to this subsection, which shall specifically enumerate the restrictions imposed and contain such information regarding the person to whom such a permit is issued as is reasonably necessary to identify such person. The court shall also provide a copy of its order to the person who may operate a motor vehicle on the order until receipt from the Commissioner of a restricted license. A copy of such order and, after receipt thereof, the restricted license shall be carried at all times while operating a motor vehicle. Any person who operates a motor vehicle in violation of any restrictions imposed pursuant to this section shall be punished as provided in subsection C of §46.2-301. No restricted license issued pursuant to this section shall permit any person to operate a commercial motor vehicle as defined in the Virginia Commercial Driver's License Act (§46.2-341.1 et seq.).

(Chgd. by L.1996 ch. 615; L.2000 ch. 342, eff. 7/1/2000.)

§46.2-393. Suspension of license on conviction of reckless driving involving driving twenty or more miles per hour faster than speed limit.

When any person is convicted of reckless driving as provided in §§46.2-853 through 46.2-864, in addition to any penalties provided by law, the driver's license of the person may be suspended by the court for a period of not less than sixty days nor more than six months. In case of conviction the court shall order the surrender of the license to the court where it shall be disposed of in accordance with the provisions of §46.2-398. Where the conviction is a second conviction which would require revocation under the provisions of §46.2-389, the court shall suspend the driver's license of the person and transmit it to the Department as provided by law. If the person so convicted has not obtained a license required by this chapter or is a nonresident, the court shall direct in the judgment of conviction that the person shall not drive any motor vehicle in the Commonwealth for a period of not less than sixty days nor more than six months.

§46.2-394. Revocation of license for fourth conviction of certain offenses.

If any person is convicted four times of a violation of §§46.2-865, 46.2-894, or §46.2-895, or any substantially similar ordinance or law of any other jurisdiction, the court shall revoke his driver's license for five years.

(Chgd. by L.1997 ch. 691; L.2000 chs. 956, 982, eff. 7/1/2000.)

§46.2-395. Suspension of license for failure or refusal to pay fines or costs.

A. Any person, whether licensed by Virginia or not, who drives a motor vehicle on the highways in the Commonwealth shall thereby, as a condition of such driving, consent to pay all lawful fines, court costs, forfeitures, restitution, and penalties assessed against him for violations of the laws of the Commonwealth; of any county, city, or town; or of the United States. For the purpose of this section, such fines and costs shall be deemed to include any fee assessed by the court under the provisions of §18.2-271.1 for entry by a person convicted of a violation of §18.2-51.4 or §18.2-266 into an alcohol safety action program.

B. In addition to any penalty provided by law, when any person is convicted of any violation of the law of the Commonwealth or of the United States or of any valid local ordinance and fails or refuses to provide for immediate payment in full of any fine, costs, forfeitures, restitution, or penalty lawfully assessed against him, or fails to make deferred payments or installment payments as ordered by the court, the court shall forthwith suspend the person's privilege to drive a motor vehicle on the highways in the Commonwealth. The driver's license of the person shall continue suspended until the fine, costs, forfeiture, restitution, or penalty has been paid in full. However, if the defendant, after having his license suspended, pays the reinstatement fee to the Department of Motor Vehicles and enters into an agreement under §19.2-354 that is acceptable to the court to make deferred payments or installment payments of unpaid fines, costs, forfeitures, restitution, or penalties as ordered by the court, the court shall restore the defendant's driver's license. If the person has not obtained a license as provided in this chapter, or is a nonresident, the court may direct in the judgment of conviction that the person shall not drive any motor vehicle in Virginia for a period to coincide with the nonpayment of the amounts due.

C. Before transmitting to the Commissioner a record of the person's failure or refusal to pay all or part of any fine, costs, forfeiture, restitution, or penalty or a failure to comply with an order issued pursuant to §19.2-354, the clerk of the court that convicted the person shall send or provide the person written notice of the suspension of his license or privilege to drive a motor vehicle in Virginia, effective ten days from the date of conviction, if the fine, costs, forfeiture, restitution, or penalty is not paid prior to the effective date of the suspension as stated on the notice. Notice shall be provided to the person at the time of trial or shall be mailed by first-class mail to the address certified on the summons or bail recognizance document as the person's current mailing address, or to such mailing address as the person has subsequently provided to the court as a change of address. If so mailed on the date of conviction or within two business days thereof, or if delivered to the person at the time of trial, such notice shall be adequate notice of the license suspension and of the person's ability to avoid suspension by paying the fine, costs, forfeiture, restitution, or penalty prior to the effective date. No other notice shall be required to make the suspension effective. A record of the person's failure or refusal and of the license suspension shall be sent to the Commissioner if the fine, costs, forfeiture, restitution, or penalty remains unpaid on the effective date of the suspension specified in the notice or on the failure to make a scheduled payment.

C1. Whenever a person provides for payment of a fine, costs, forfeiture, restitution or penalty other than by cash and such provision for payment fails, the clerk of the court that convicted the person shall send to the person written notice of the failure and of the suspension of his license or privilege to drive in Virginia. The license suspension shall be effective ten days from the date of the notice. The notice shall be the effective notice of the suspension and of the person's ability to avoid the suspension by paying the full amount owed by cash, cashier's check or certified check prior to the effective date of the suspension if the notice is mailed by first class mail to the address provided by the person to the court pursuant to subsection C or §19.2-354. Upon such a failure of payment and notice, the fine, costs, forfeiture, restitution or penalty due shall be paid only by cash, cashier's check or certified check, unless otherwise ordered by the court, for good cause shown.

D. If the person pays the amounts assessed against him subsequent to the time the suspended license has been transmitted to the Department, and his license is not under suspension or revocation for any other lawful reason, except pursuant to this section, then the Commissioner shall return the license to the person on presentation of the official report of the court evidencing the payment of the fine, costs, forfeiture, restitution, or penalty.

E. If the court has suspended or revoked the driver's license for any lawful reason other than this section, or the conviction is one for which revocation or suspension is required under any provision of this title, except for this section, then the suspension permitted under this section shall be in addition to, and run consecutively with, the revocation or suspension. The period of suspension shall be calculated from the date of the assessment of the fine, costs, forfeiture, restitution, or penalty until the date it has been paid.

(Chgd. by L.1997 ch. 691; L.1998 ch. 831; L.2000 chs. 956, 982, eff. 7/1/2000.)

§46.2-396. Suspension of license for reckless driving resulting in death of any person.

When any person is convicted of reckless driving as provided for in §§46.2-853 through 46.2-864 and the reckless driving was the cause of the death of any person, then in addition to any other penalties provided by law, the driver's license of the person may be suspended by the court for no more than twelve months. In case of conviction the court may order the surrender of the license to the court where it shall be disposed of in accordance with the provisions of §46.2-398. If the person so convicted has not obtained a license required by this chapter or is a nonresident, the court may direct in the judgment of conviction that the person shall not drive any motor vehicle in the Commonwealth for a period not to exceed twelve months. The fact of the suspension shall not be admissible as evidence in any related civil proceeding.

§46.2-397. Suspension of license for certain violations while transporting explosives, inflammable gas or liquid.

When the driver of any motor vehicle is convicted of any violation of §§46.2-816, 46.2-820 through 46.2-823, 46.2-825, 46.2-826 or §§46.2-852 through 46.2-864, or of any of the applicable speed limits prescribed in §§46.2-870 through 46.2-878 and the violation was committed while driving a motor vehicle, tractor truck, trailer, or semitrailer, transporting explosives or any inflammable gas or liquid, in addition to any penalty imposed, the court may suspend the driver's license of the convicted person for a period of ninety days from the date of conviction.

§46.2-398. Disposition of surrendered licenses on revocation or suspension.

In any case in which the accused is convicted of an offense, on the conviction of which the law requires or permits revocation or suspension of the driver's license of the person so convicted, the court shall order the surrender of such license, which shall remain in the custody of the court during the period of revocation or suspension if the period does not exceed thirty days, or (i) if the period exceeds thirty days, until the time allowed by law for appeal has elapsed, when it shall be forwarded to the Commissioner, or (ii) until an appeal is effected and proper bond posted, at which time it shall be returned to the accused.

However, when the time of suspension or revocation coincides or approximately coincides with the appeal time, the court may retain the license and return it to the accused on the expiration of the suspension or revocation.

§46.2-399. Revocation of license for improper use or failure to pay certain taxes.

The Department shall revoke a driver's license whenever the person to whom the license has been issued makes or permits to be made an unlawful use of it or permits the use of it by a person not entitled to it or fails or refuses to pay within the time prescribed by law, any lawful taxes due the Commonwealth imposed under Chapter 27 (§58.1-2700 et seq.) of Title 58.1.

§46.2-400. Suspension of license of incapacitated person or person incompetent because of inebriety or drug addiction; return of license; duty of clerk of court.

The Commissioner, on receipt of notice that any person has been legally adjudged to be incapacitated in accordance with Article 1.1 (§37.1-134.6 et seq.) of Chapter 4 of Title 37.1 or that a person discharged from an institution operated or licensed by the Department of Mental Health, Mental Retardation and Substance Abuse Services is, in the opinion of the authorities of the institution, not competent because of mental illness, mental retardation, inebriety, or drug addiction to drive a motor vehicle with safety to persons or property, shall forthwith suspend his license; but he shall not suspend the license if the person has been adjudged competent by judicial order or decree.

In any case in which the person's license has been suspended prior to his discharge it shall not be returned to him unless the Commissioner is satisfied, after an examination such as is required of applicants by §46.2-325, that the person is competent to drive a motor vehicle with safety to persons and property.

The clerk of the court in which the adjudication is made shall forthwith send a certified copy or abstract of such adjudication to the Commissioner.

(Chgd. by L.1997 ch. 921, eff. 1/1/98.)

§46.2-401. Reports to Commissioner of discharge of patients from state institutions.

Whenever practicable, at least ten days prior to the time when any patient is to be discharged from any institution operated or licensed by the Department of Mental Health, Mental Retardation and Substance Abuse Services, if the mental condition of the patient is, because of mental illness, mental retardation, inebriety, or drug addiction, in the judgment of the director or chief medical officer of the institution such as to prevent him from being competent to drive a motor vehicle with safety to persons and property, the director or chief medical officer shall forthwith report to the Commissioner, in sufficient detail for accurate identification, the date of discharge of the patient, together with a statement concerning his ability to drive a motor vehicle.

§46.2-402. When Commissioner may suspend or revoke license for not more than one year after hearing.

A. The Commissioner may, after due hearing, after giving not less than five days' written notice by registered letter to the most recent address of the driver on file at the Department, suspend or revoke for not more than one year and not thereafter reissue during the period of suspension or revocation the Virginia driver's license issued to any person whenever it is satisfactorily proved at the hearing conducted by the Commissioner or other personnel of the Department designated by him, that the licensee under charges:

1. Has, by reckless or unlawful operation of a motor vehicle, caused or contributed to an accident resulting in death or injury to any other person or in serious property damage,
2. Is incompetent to drive a motor vehicle,
3. Suffers from mental or physical infirmities or disabilities rendering it unsafe for him to drive a motor vehicle on the highways,
4. Is habitually a reckless or negligent driver of a motor vehicle, or
5. Has committed a serious violation of the motor vehicle laws of this Commonwealth.

B. The Commissioner, in determining the propriety of suspending or revoking a license as provided in this section, may take into consideration facts and conditions antedating the issuance of the current license.

(Chgd. by L.1996 chs. 943, 994, eff. 1/1/97.)

§46.2-403. Contents of notice of hearing.

A. The notice of a hearing when mailed to any person, as provided in §46.2-402 shall contain:

1. A specific statement of the alleged offense or offenses or other grounds for suspension or revocation of the license, including the date, time and place thereof when applicable;
2. The date, time and place of the hearing;
3. The names and addresses of all known witnesses whose testimony is proposed to be taken at the hearing;
4. As to any record of conviction of any offense which is to be offered as evidence, the date of the conviction and the court in which the same was had.

B. If these requirements are complied with it shall be sufficient regardless of whether the licensee appeared and regardless of whether the notice was ever received.

§46.2-404. Where and before whom hearing held.

The hearing shall be in the county or city where the licensee resides or in the county or city in which the licensee works or, with the consent of the licensee, in any other county or city to which the county or city of his residence is contiguous. The hearing shall be before the Commissioner or any of the personnel of the Department designated by him.

§46.2-405. How hearings to be conducted.

A. In any such hearing all relevant and material evidence shall be received, except that: (i) the rules relating to privileged communications and privileged topics shall be observed; (ii) hearsay evidence shall be received only according to the rules of evidence prevailing in courts of record; and (iii) secondary evidence of the contents of a document shall be received only if the original is not readily available.

B. All reports of inspectors and subordinates of the Department and other records and documents in the possession of the Department bearing on the case subject to the provisions of subsection A of this section shall be introduced at the hearing. Any certified copy of any conviction forwarded to the Commissioner under the provisions of §46.2-383, shall be prima facie evidence of the conviction, and may be introduced in evidence.

C. Subject to the provisions of subsection A of this section, every party shall have the right to cross-examine adverse witnesses and any inspector or subordinate of the Department whose report is in evidence, and to submit rebuttal evidence.

D. The decision shall be based only on evidence received at the hearing and matters of which a court of record could take judicial notice.

§46.2-406. Appointment and authority of hearing officers.

The Commissioner may appoint one or more persons to conduct the hearings provided for in this title. The hearing officers are hereby authorized to administer oaths, take acknowledgements and affidavits, take testimony and depositions, and perform other duties which are incidental to conducting the hearings.

§46.2-407. Form and contents of decision; copies.

Any decision or order of the Commissioner to be valid must be reduced to writing and contain the explicit findings of fact and conclusions of law upon which the decision or order of the Commissioner is based. Certified copies of the decision or order shall be delivered to any party affected by it.

§46.2-408. When Commissioner may suspend or revoke license for no more than five years.

On any reasonable ground appearing in the records of the Department, the Commissioner may, when he deems it necessary for the safety of the public on the highways in the Commonwealth and after notice as provided in §46.2-403 and hearing as provided in §§46.2-404, 46.2-405, 46.2-406 and 46.2-407 suspend or revoke for no more than five years, and not reissue during the period of suspension or revocation, the driver's license of any person who is a violator of any of the provisions of this title punishable as felonies, misdemeanors, or traffic infractions and he may suspend or revoke for a like period, and not reissue during the period of suspension or revocation, any or all of his registration cards and license plates for any motor vehicle.

§46.2-409. Certain abstracts of conviction to be prima facie evidence of conviction.

In any administrative hearing conducted by the Commissioner or his designee pursuant to this article, an abstract showing a conviction of the violation of any of the provisions of this title, submitted as provided by §46.2-383 by the court in which the conviction was had, shall be prima facie evidence that the person named in the abstract was duly convicted of the violation, and the burden shall be on any person challenging the propriety of the conviction to show that the conviction was improper.

§46.2-410. Appeals from order suspending or revoking license or registration.

Any person aggrieved by an order or act of the Commissioner requiring suspension or revocation of a license or registration under the provisions of this chapter is entitled to judicial review in accordance with the provisions of the Administrative Process Act (§9-6.14:1 et seq.). No appeal shall lie in any case in which the suspension or revocation of the license or registration was mandatory except to determine the identity of the person concerned when the question of identity is in dispute.

From the final decision of the circuit court, either the person who petitioned the court for an appeal or the Commissioner shall have an appeal as of right to the Court of Appeals.

§46.2-411. Reinstatement of suspended or revoked license or other privilege to operate or register a motor vehicle; proof of financial responsibility; reinstatement fee.

The Commissioner may refuse, after a hearing if demanded, to issue to any person whose license has been suspended or revoked any new or renewal license, or to register any motor vehicle in the name of the person, whenever he deems or in case of a hearing finds it necessary for the safety of the public on the highways in the Commonwealth.

Before granting or restoring a license or registration to any person whose driver's license or other privilege to drive motor vehicles or privilege to register a motor vehicle has been revoked or suspended pursuant to §§46.2-389, 46.2-391, 46.2-391.1 or §46.2-417, the Commissioner shall require proof of financial responsibility in the future as provided in Article 15 (§46.2-435 et seq.) of this chapter, but no person shall be licensed who may not be licensed under the provisions of §§46.2-389 through 46.2-431.

Whenever the driver's license or registration cards, license plates and decals, or other privilege to drive or to register motor vehicles of any resident or nonresident person is suspended or revoked by the Commissioner or by a district court or circuit court pursuant to the provisions of Title 18.2 or this title, or any valid local ordinance, the order of suspension or revocation shall remain in effect and the driver's license, registration cards, license plates and decals, or other privilege to drive or register motor vehicles shall not be reinstated and no new driver's license, registration cards, license plates and decals, or other privilege to drive or register motor vehicles shall be issued or granted unless such person, in addition to complying with all other provisions of law, pays to the Commissioner a reinstatement fee of thirty dollars. The reinstatement fee shall be increased by thirty dollars whenever such suspension or revocation results from conviction of involuntary manslaughter in violation of §18.2-36.1; conviction of maiming resulting from driving while intoxicated in violation of §18.2-51.4; conviction of driving while intoxicated in violation of §18.2-266 or §46.2-341.24; conviction of driving after illegally consuming alcohol in violation of §18.2-266.1 or failure to comply with court imposed conditions pursuant to subsection D of §18.2-271.1; unreasonable refusal to submit to drug or alcohol testing in violation of §18.2-268.2; conviction of driving while a license, permit or privilege to drive was suspended or revoked in violation of §46.2-301 or §46.2-341.21; disqualification pursuant to §46.2-341.20; violation of driver's license probation pursuant to §46.2-499; failure to attend a driver improvement clinic pursuant to §46.2-503 or habitual offender interventions pursuant to former §46.2-351.1; conviction of eluding police in violation of §46.2-817; conviction of hit and run in violation of §46.2-894; conviction of reckless driving in violation of Article 7 (§46.2-852 et seq.) of Chapter 8 of Title 46.2 or a conviction, finding or adjudication under any similar local ordinance, federal law or law of any other state. Five dollars of the additional amount shall be retained by the Department as provided in this section and twenty-five dollars shall be transferred to the Commonwealth Neurotrauma Initiative Trust Fund established pursuant to Article 12 (§32.1-73.1 et seq.) of Chapter 2 of Title 32.1. When three years have elapsed from the termination date of the order of suspension or revocation and the person has complied with all other provisions of law, the Commissioner may relieve him of paying the reinstatement fee.

No reinstatement fee shall be required when the suspension or revocation of license results from the person's suffering from mental or physical infirmities or disabilities from natural causes not related to the use of self-administered intoxicants or drugs. No reinstatement fee shall be collected from any person whose license is suspended by a court of competent jurisdiction for any reason, other than a cause for mandatory suspension as provided in this title, provided the court ordering the suspension is not required by §46.2-398 to forward the license to the Department during the suspended period.

Except as otherwise provided in this section and §18.2-271.1, reinstatement fees collected under the provisions of this section shall be paid by the Commissioner into the state treasury and shall be set aside as a special fund to be used to meet the expenses of the Department.

(Chgd. by L.1998 ch. 703; L.1999 chs. 945, 987, eff. 7/1/99.)

§46.2-411.1. Reinstatement of driver's license suspended or revoked for a conviction of driving while intoxicated.

A. Before restoring a driver's license to any person (i) whose license to drive a motor vehicle has been suspended or revoked as a result of a conviction for driving while intoxicated in violation of §18.2-266, or of any substantially similar valid local ordinance or law of another jurisdiction, or of subsection A of §46.2-341.24 and (ii) who has been required by a court order to successfully complete an alcohol safety action program pursuant to §18.2-271.1 because of that conviction, the Commissioner shall require written confirmation that the person has successfully completed such program.

B. Any person who drives a motor vehicle in the Commonwealth after the period of license suspension has expired and after all requirements for reinstatement have been satisfied except for successful completion of such program shall be guilty of a violation of §46.2-300.

(Added by L.2000 chs. 959, 985, eff. 7/1/2000.)

§46.2-412. Time suspension or revocation.

Every suspension or revocation shall remain in effect and the Commissioner shall not issue any new or renewal license or register in his name any motor vehicle, until permitted under the provisions of this chapter. When three years shall have elapsed from the date of the termination of the revocation provided by §46.2-389 or §46.2-391, or in the case of a suspension pursuant to the provisions of §46.2-417, when three years has elapsed from the date of satisfaction of the judgment or judgments, the person may be relieved of giving proof of his financial responsibility in the future, provided he is not required to furnish or maintain proof of financial responsibility under any other provision of this chapter. The requirement of this section for giving and maintaining proof of financial responsibility shall not, however, apply in the case of a person whose license has been suspended under §46.2-400.

§46.2-413. Effect of reversal of conviction.

Reversal on appeal of any conviction because of which conviction any license or registration has been suspended or revoked pursuant to the provisions of this chapter shall entitle the holder to the restoration of his license or registration forthwith without proof of financial responsibility.

§46.2-414. Commencement of periods for suspension or revocation of licenses, registration cards, or license plates.

Wherever it is provided in this title that the driver's license, registration cards, or license plates of any person be suspended or revoked for a period of time on conviction of certain offenses, or after a hearing before the Commissioner as provided by law, the period shall be counted from 180 days after the conviction becomes final or after the order of the Commissioner, as a result of the hearing, becomes final, or shall be counted from the date on which the license, cards, or plates are surrendered to the Commissioner or his agent, or to the court or clerk thereof, regardless of whether the record of conviction has been received by the Commissioner or his agent, whichever period shall first commence. However, the provisions of this section shall not apply in any case where the person whose license is subject to suspension or revocation gives a false name or otherwise conceals his identity.

§46.2-415. United States magistrates and judges of district courts authorized to revoke or suspend driver's license under certain conditions.

When any person is found guilty of a violation of any traffic regulation by a United States magistrate or a judge of a district court of the United States, which violation occurred on a federal reservation, and, for which, if the violation had occurred on the highways in the Commonwealth, revocation or suspension of the person's driver's license would be mandatory or discretionary with a court of the Commonwealth, the magistrate or judge is authorized to revoke or suspend the person's driver's license, provided it is forwarded to the Commissioner as is provided by law as to courts of the Commonwealth.

§46.2-416. Notice of suspension or revocation of license.

Whenever it is provided in this title that a driver's license may or shall be suspended or revoked either by the Commissioner or by a court, notice of the suspension or revocation or any certified copy of the decision or order of the Commissioner may be sent by the Department by certified mail to the driver at the most recent address of the driver on file at the Department. If the driver has previously been notified by mail or in person of the suspension or revocation or of an impending suspension for failure to pay fines and costs pursuant to §46.2-395, whether notice is given by the court or law-enforcement officials as provided by law, and the Department has been notified by the court that notice was so given and the fines and costs were not paid within ten days, no notice of suspension shall be sent by the Department to the driver. If the certificate of the Commissioner or someone designated by him for that purpose shows that the notice or copy has been so sent or provided, it shall be deemed prima facie evidence that the notice or copy has been sent and delivered or otherwise provided to the driver for all purposes involving the application of the provisions of this title. In the discretion of the Commissioner, service may be made as provided in §8.01-296, which service on the driver shall be made by delivery in writing to the driver in person in accordance with subdivision 1 of §8.01-296 by a sheriff or deputy sheriff in the county or city in which the address is located, who shall, as directed by the Commissioner, take possession of any suspended or revoked license, registration card, or set of license plates or decals and return them to the office of the Commissioner. No such service shall be made if, prior to service, the driver has complied with the requirement which caused the issuance of the decision or order. In any such case, return shall be made to the Commissioner.

In lieu of making a direct payment to sheriffs as a fee for delivery of the Department's processes, the Commissioner shall effect a transfer of funds, on a monthly basis, to the Compensation Board to be used to provide additional support to sheriffs' departments. The amount of funds so transferred shall be as provided in the general appropriation act.

(Chgd. by L.1996 chs. 943, 994, eff. 1/1/97.)

§46.2-416.1. Suspension for failure to comply with traffic citation issued under federal law.

On receipt of a notice from a United States District Court in Virginia that a person licensed to drive in Virginia has failed to comply with a traffic citation issued under the laws of the United States for a violation occurring in Virginia, the Commissioner may suspend the driving privileges of such person, if the person has been provided written notice mailed to his last known address that his license or privilege to drive a motor vehicle in Virginia will be suspended if he has not complied with the terms of the citation within ten days, and if the person has not so complied.

ARTICLE 13
SUSPENSION OF LICENSES FOR UNSATISFIED JUDGMENTS AND AFTER CERTAIN ACCIDENTS

Section

§46.2-417. Suspension for failure to satisfy motor vehicle accident judgment; exceptions; insurance in liquidated company; insurer obligated to pay judgment.

A. Upon the application of any judgment creditor, the Commissioner shall suspend the driver's license and all of the registration certificates and license plates of any person who has failed for thirty days to satisfy any judgment in an amount and on a cause of action as hereinafter stated in this subsection, immediately upon receiving an authenticated judgment order or abstract thereof in an action for damages in a motor vehicle accident, if (i) the order or abstract is received by the Commissioner within ten years of the date of judgment or (ii) the judgment has been revived. However, if judgment is marked satisfied on the court records on or before the Commissioner's issuance of suspension, the order of suspension shall be invalid.

B. The Commissioner shall not, however, suspend the license of an owner or driver if the insurance carried by him was in a company which was authorized to transact business in this Commonwealth and which subsequent to an accident involving the owner or driver and prior to settlement of the claim therefor went into liquidation, so that the owner or driver is thereby unable to satisfy the judgment arising out of the accident.

C. The Commissioner shall not suspend the driver's license or driving privilege or any registration certificate, license plates, or decals under this section or §46.2-418, if the Commissioner finds that an insurer authorized to do business in the Commonwealth was obligated to pay the judgment upon which suspension is based, or that a policy of the insurer covers the person subject to the suspension, if the insurer's obligation or the limits of the policy are in an amount sufficient to meet the minimum amounts required by §46.2-472, even though the insurer has not paid the judgment for any reason. A finding by the Commissioner that an insurer is obligated to pay a judgment, or that a policy of an insurer covers the person, shall not be binding upon the insurer and shall have no legal effect whatever except for the purpose of administering this article. Whenever in any judicial proceeding it is determined by any final judgment, decree, or order that an insurer is not obligated to pay the judgment, the Commissioner, notwithstanding any contrary finding made by him, forthwith shall suspend the driver's license or driving privilege, or any registration card, license plates or decals of any person against whom the judgment was rendered, as provided in subsection A of this section.

§46.2-418. Nonpayment of judgments of Virginia and other states.

The Commissioner shall take action as required in §46.2-417 on receiving proper evidence that the person has failed for a period of thirty days to satisfy any judgment, in amount and on a cause of action as stated in §§46.2-364 and 46.2-417, rendered by a court of competent jurisdiction of the Commonwealth, any other state of the United States, the United States, Canada or its provinces.

§46.2-419. When judgment satisfied.

A. Every judgment for damages in any motor vehicle accident referred to in this chapter shall, for the purpose of this chapter, be satisfied:

1. When paid in full or when $25,000 has been credited upon any judgment or judgments rendered in excess of that amount because of bodily injury to or death of one person as the result of any one accident;

2. When, subject to the limit of $25,000 because of bodily injury to or death of one person, the judgment has been paid in full or when the sum of $50,000 has been credited upon any judgment or judgments rendered in excess of that amount because of bodily injury to or death of two or more persons as the result of any one accident;

3. When the judgment has been paid in full or when $20,000 has been credited upon any judgment or judgments rendered in excess of that amount because of injury to or destruction of property of others as a result of any one accident; or

4. When the judgment has been discharged in bankruptcy.

B. Payments made in settlement of any claims because of bodily injury, death or property damage arising from a motor vehicle accident shall be credited in reduction of the amount provided in this section.

§46.2-420. Order for payment of judgment in installments.

A judgment debtor, on five days' notice to the judgment creditor, may apply to the court in which the judgment was obtained for the privilege of paying it in installments. The court, without prejudice to other legal remedies which the judgment creditor may have, may so order, fixing the amounts and times of payment of the installments.

§46.2-421. Effect of order for such payment and proof of financial responsibility.

The Commissioner shall not suspend a license or registration of a motor vehicle and shall restore any license or registration suspended following nonpayment of a judgment, if the judgment debtor obtains an order from the court in which the judgment was rendered permitting payment of the judgment in installments and if the judgment debtor gives proof of his financial responsibility in the future as provided in this chapter.

§46.2-422. Suspension on failure to pay installments.

If the judgment debtor fails to pay any installment as permitted by the order of the court, then on notice of default, the Commissioner shall forthwith suspend the driver's license, registration cards, and license plates of the judgment debtor until the judgment is satisfied as provided in this chapter. The judgment debtor may apply, after due notice to the judgment creditor, to the court which allowed installment payment of the judgment, within thirty days after the default, for resumption of the privilege of paying the judgment in installments, if past-due installments are first paid.

§46.2-423. Creditor's consent to license notwithstanding default in payment.

If the judgment creditor consents in writing, in whatever form the Commissioner prescribes, that the judgment debtor be allowed a driver's license and motor vehicle registration, the Commissioner may allow the same, notwithstanding default in the payment of the judgment or any installment thereof, for six months from the date of consent and thereafter until it is revoked in writing, if the judgment debtor furnishes proof of his financial responsibility in the future as provided in this chapter.

§46.2-424. Duty of insurance carrier after notice of accident; report of omissions by insurers to State Corporation Commission; investigation and assessment for omissions.

On receipt of the certificate of insurance, the insurance carrier or surety company named in the certificate of f insurance shall determine whether the policy or bond was applicable to liability, if any, as to the named insured. Thereupon and not later than thirty days following receipt of the certificate of insurance, the insurance company or surety company shall cause to be filed with the Commissioner a written notice if the policy or bond was not applicable to liability, if any, as to the named insured resulting from the accident. The Commissioner shall prescribe the manner in which the written notice shall be made.

When the insurance company or surety company notifies the Commissioner that the policy or bond named in the certificate of insurance was not applicable to liability resulting from the accident, the Department shall determine, under §46.2-708, whether suspension of the driver's license, registration cards, and license plates issued to the owner of the motor vehicle involved in the accident is required.

If the records of the Department reasonably indicate that any insurance carrier or surety company does not cause to be filed the notice herein required, the Commissioner shall report every such omission to the State Corporation Commission.

The State Corporation Commission shall investigate every such report of omission. If the Commission finds that any insurance carrier or surety company licensed to transact business in the Commonwealth, has failed, without good reason, to cause to be filed the notice required hereunder, the State Corporation Commission may assess the carrier or company fifty dollars for each omission.

§46.2-425. Driver or owner having no license issued by Department.

In case a driver or owner has no driver's license issued by the Department or no motor vehicle registered in his name in the Commonwealth, he shall not be allowed a driver's license or motor vehicle registration until he has complied with this chapter to the same extent as would be necessary if he had held a driver's license or a motor vehicle registration at the time of the accident in which he was involved or at the time of the commission of the offense resulting in a conviction as is mentioned in §§46.2-389 and 46.2-391.

§46.2-426. Custody and application of cash or securities deposited; limitation of actions; assignment.

Cash or securities furnished in compliance with the requirements of this chapter shall be placed by the Commissioner in the custody of the State Treasurer and shall be applicable only to the payment of any judgment against the depositor for damages arising out of the accident in question in an action at law in a court in the Commonwealth begun not later than one year after the date of the accident. The cash or securities may be assigned by the depositor for the benefit of the person or persons damaged or injured in the accident as the result of which the cash or securities were filed or deposited without the damaged or injured person being required to institute legal proceedings. The Commissioner shall accept the assignment if, in his opinion, the rights of any other person or persons shall not be prejudiced thereby.

§46.2-427. When suspensions to remain effective; relief from furnishing proof of financial responsibility; prohibition against registration in name of another person.

The suspension required by the provisions of §46.2-417 shall continue except as otherwise provided by §§46.2-421 and 46.2-423 until the person satisfies the judgment or judgments as prescribed in §46.2-419 and gives proof of his financial responsibility in the future.

The motor vehicle involved in the accident on which the suspension under §46.2-417 is based shall not be registered in the name of any other person when the Commissioner has reasonable grounds to believe that the registration of the vehicle will have the effect of defeating the purpose of the chapter and no other motor vehicle shall be registered, and no driver's license or learner's permit shall be issued in the name of the person suspended, except as prescribed in §46.2-437 until the suspension is terminated.

This section shall not relieve any person from giving or maintaining proof of his financial responsibility when he is required so to do for some reason rather than having been involved in a motor vehicle accident.

§46.2-428. Commonwealth responsible for deposits.

The Commonwealth shall be responsible for the safekeeping of all bonds, cash, and securities deposited with the State Treasurer under the provisions of this chapter, and if the deposit or any part of the deposit is lost, destroyed, or misappropriated the Commonwealth shall make good the loss to any person entitled thereto.

§46.2-429. Release of deposits only upon consent of Commissioner.

Bonds, cash, or securities deposited with the State Treasurer pursuant to this chapter shall only be released by the State Treasurer upon consent of the Commissioner given in conformity with this chapter.

ARTICLE 14
SUSPENSION OF LICENSES OF NONRESIDENTS OR FOR ACCIDENTS IN OTHER STATES

§46.2-430. Power over nonresidents.

Whenever by the laws of the Commonwealth the Commissioner may suspend or revoke: (i) the license of a resident driver, or (ii) the registration cards and license plates of a resident owner, he may:

1. Suspend or revoke the privilege of operating a motor vehicle in the Commonwealth by a nonresident driver, and
2. Suspend the privilege of driving a vehicle owned by a nonresident regardless of whether the vehicle is registered in the Commonwealth.

§46.2-431. Chapter applies to nonresidents.

Every provision of this chapter applies to any person who is not a resident of the Commonwealth under the same circumstances as it would apply to a resident. No nonresident may drive any motor vehicle in the Commonwealth and no motor vehicle owned by him may be driven in the Commonwealth, unless the nonresident has complied with the requirements of this chapter with respect to giving proof of financial responsibility in the future.

§46.2-432. Failure of nonresident to report accident.

The failure of a nonresident to report an accident as required in this title shall constitute sufficient ground for suspension or revocation of his privileges of driving a motor vehicle in the Commonwealth and of driving within the Commonwealth of any motor vehicle owned by him.

§46.2-433. Notification of officers in nonresident's home state.

On conviction of a nonresident or in case any unsatisfied judgment results in suspension of a nonresident's driving privileges in the Commonwealth and the prohibition of driving within the Commonwealth of any motor vehicle, or on suspension of a nonresident's driving privileges in the Commonwealth pursuant to any other provision of this chapter, the Commissioner shall transmit a certified copy of the record of the conviction or the unsatisfied judgment, or any other action pursuant to this chapter resulting in suspension of a nonresident's driving privileges of any motor vehicle owned by such nonresident, to the motor vehicle commissioner or officer performing the functions of a commissioner in the state of the United States, or possession under the exclusive control of the United States, or Canada or its provinces in which the nonresident resides.

§46.2-434. Conviction of or judgment against resident in another jurisdiction.

The Commissioner shall suspend or revoke the license and registration certificate and plates of any resident of the Commonwealth upon receiving notice of his conviction, in a court of competent jurisdiction of the Commonwealth, any other state of the United States, the United States, Canada or its provinces or any territorial subdivision of such state or country, of an offense therein which, if committed in the Commonwealth, would be grounds for the suspension or revocation of the license granted to him or registration of any motor vehicle registered in his name. No suspension or revocation under this subsection shall continue for a longer period than it would have, had the offense been committed in the Commonwealth, provided the person gives proof of his financial responsibility in the future for the period provided in §46.2-412.

The Commissioner shall take like action upon receipt of notice that a resident of the Commonwealth has failed, for a period of thirty days, to satisfy any final judgment in amount and upon a cause of action as stated herein, rendered against him in a court of competent jurisdiction of any other state of the United States, the United States, Canada or its provinces, or any territorial subdivision of such state or country.
(Chgd. by L.1997 ch. 486, eff. 7/1/97.)

ARTICLE 15
PROOF OF FINANCIAL RESPONSIBILITY

Section

§46.2-435. Proof of financial responsibility to be furnished for each vehicle.

Proof of financial responsibility in the amounts required by this chapter shall be furnished for each motor vehicle registered by the person required to furnish such proof.

§46.2-436. Methods of proving financial responsibility.

Proof of financial responsibility when required under this chapter may be given by proof that:

1. A policy or policies of motor vehicle liability insurance have been obtained and are in full force;
2. A bond has been duly executed;
3. A deposit has been made of money or securities; or
4. A self-insurance certificate has been filed, all as provided in this chapter.

§46.2-437. Proof of financial responsibility by owner in lieu of driver.

When the Commissioner finds that any person required to give proof of financial responsibility under this title is or later becomes a driver, however designated, or a member of the immediate family or household, in the employ or home of an owner of a motor vehicle, the Commissioner shall accept proof of financial responsibility given by the owner in lieu of proof of financial responsibility by such person to permit him to operate a motor vehicle for which the owner has given proof of financial responsibility as provided in this chapter. The Commissioner shall designate the restrictions imposed by this section on the face of the person's driver's license.

§46.2-438. Proof by owner of vehicles operated under permit or certificate of State Corporation Commission or Department of Motor Vehicles.

If the owner of a motor vehicle is one whose vehicles are operated under a permit or a certificate of convenience and necessity issued by the State Corporation Commission or the Department, proof by the owner on behalf of another as provided by this chapter may be made if there is filed with the Commissioner satisfactory evidence that the owner has

complied with the law with respect to his liability for damage caused by the operation of his vehicles by providing the required insurance or other security or has qualified as a self-insurer as described in §46.2-368.
(Chgd. by L.1997 ch. 283, eff. 7/1/97.)

§46.2-439. Certificate of insurance carrier.

Proof of financial responsibility, when requested, shall be made by filing with the Commissioner the written certificate of any insurance carrier authorized to do business in the Commonwealth, certifying that there is in effect a motor vehicle liability policy for the benefit of the person required to furnish proof of financial responsibility. This certificate shall give its effective date and the effective date of the policy.

§46.2-440. Certificate for nonresident may be by carrier not qualified in Commonwealth.

A nonresident owner of a vehicle not registered in Virginia may give proof of financial responsibility by filing with the Commissioner a written certificate or certificates of an insurance carrier not authorized to transact business in the Commonwealth but authorized to transact business in any other state, any territory or possession of the United States and under its exclusive control, Canada or its provinces, or the territorial subdivisions of such states or countries, in which any motor vehicle described in the certificate and all replacement vehicles of similar classification are registered or, if the nonresident does not own a motor vehicle, then in the like jurisdiction in which the insured resides and otherwise conforming to the provisions of this chapter. The Commissioner shall accept the same if the insurance carrier, in addition to having complied with all other provisions of this chapter as requisite, shall:

1. Execute a power of attorney authorizing the Commissioner to accept service on its behalf of notice or process in any action arising out of a motor vehicle accident in the Commonwealth;
2. Duly adopt a resolution, which shall be binding upon it, declaring that its policies are to be deemed to be modified to comply with the law of the Commonwealth and the terms of this chapter relating to the terms of motor vehicle liability policies issued herein;
3. Agree to accept as final and binding the judgment of any court of competent jurisdiction in the Commonwealth from which judgment no appeal is or can be taken, duly rendered in any action arising out of a motor vehicle accident;
4. Deposit with the State Treasurer cash or securities as are mentioned in §46.2-453 or the surety bond of a company authorized to do business in Virginia equal in value to $60,000 for each insurance policy filed as proof of financial responsibility.

(Chgd. by L.1995 ch. 121, eff. 7/1/95.)

§46.2-441. Nonresident may file proof of future financial responsibility of insurance company or other state-authorized entity providing insurance.

Notwithstanding the requirement of §§46.2-439 and 46.2-440, a nonresident required to file proof of future financial responsibility under this chapter may file proof of future financial responsibility of an insurance company or other state-authorized entity providing insurance and authorized or licensed to do business in the nonresident's state of residence as long as such proof of future financial responsibility is in the amounts equal to those required by §46.2-472.
(Chgd. by L.1995 ch. 121, eff. 7/1/95.)

§46.2-442. Default of foreign insurance carrier.

If any insurance carrier not authorized to do business in the Commonwealth which is qualified to furnish proof of financial responsibility defaults in any of its undertakings or agreements, the Commissioner shall not thereafter accept any certificate of that carrier so long as the default continues and shall revoke licenses previously granted on the basis of its policies unless the default is immediately repaired.

§46.2-443. Chapter not applicable to certain policies of insurance.

This chapter does not apply to:

1. Policies of automobile insurance against liability which may now or hereafter be required by any other law of the Commonwealth and such policies if endorsed to the requirements of this chapter shall be accepted as proof of financial responsibility when required under this chapter; or
2. Policies insuring solely the insured named in the policy against liability resulting from the maintenance, use, or operation by persons in the insured's employ or in his behalf of motor vehicles not owned by the insured.

§46.2-444. Surety requirements of bond.

The bond mentioned in subdivision 2 of §46.2-436 shall be duly executed by the person giving proof and by a surety company duly authorized to transact business in the Commonwealth or by the person giving proof and by one or more individual sureties owning real estate within the Commonwealth and having an equity therein in at least the amount of the bond and the real estate shall be scheduled in the bond. But the Commissioner may not accept any real estate bond unless it is first approved by the circuit court of the jurisdiction wherein the real estate is located.

§46.2-445. How bond to be conditioned.

The Commissioner shall not accept any bond unless it is conditioned for payments in amounts and under the same circumstances as would be required in a motor vehicle liability policy furnished by the person giving proof.

§46.2-446. Notice to Commissioner prerequisite to cancellation of bond; cancellation not to affect rights arising prior thereto.

No bond shall be cancelled unless twenty days' prior written notice of cancellation is given the Commissioner, but cancellation of the bond shall not prevent recovery thereon with respect to any right or cause of action arising prior to the date of cancellation.

§46.2-447. Bond to constitute lien on real estate of surety.

A bond with individual sureties shall constitute a lien in favor of the Commonwealth on the real estate of any individual surety. The lien shall exist in favor of any holder of any final judgment against the principal on account of damage to property or injury to or death of any person or persons resulting from the ownership, maintenance, use, or operation of his, or any other, motor vehicle, upon the recording of the bond in the office of the clerk of the court where deeds are admitted to record of the city or county where the real estate is located.

§46.2-448. Notice of cancellation; record; fees.

Notice of cancellation is to be signed by the Commissioner or by someone designated by him and the seal of the Department placed thereon. Notwithstanding any other provision of law the clerk shall record the notice in the books kept for the recording of deeds and shall index the same in the indices thereto for grantors and grantees, under the respective names of the individual sureties in the column for grantors, and the Commonwealth of Virginia in the column for grantees, for which he shall receive two dollars and fifty cents to be paid by the principal in full payment of all services in connection with the recordation and release of the bond. The clerk shall place on the notice a statement showing the time of recording and the book and page of recording and return the notice to the Commissioner.

§46.2-449. Cancellation of bond with individual sureties; certificates of cancellation.

When a bond with individual sureties filed with the Commissioner is no longer required under this chapter, the Commissioner shall, on request, cancel it as to liability for damage to property or injury to or death of any person or persons thereafter caused and when a bond has been cancelled by the Commissioner or otherwise he shall, on request, furnish a certificate of the cancellation signed by him or by someone designated by him and bearing the seal of the Department. The certificate, notwithstanding any other provision of law, may be recorded in the office of the clerk of the court in which the bond was admitted to record.

§46.2-450. Order discharging lien of bond.

On satisfactory proof that the bond filed with the Commissioner as provided for in this chapter has been cancelled and that there are no claims or judgments against the principal in the bond on account of damage to property or injury to or death of any person or persons resulting from the ownership, maintenance, use, or operation of a motor vehicle of the principal caused while the bond was in effect, the court in which the bond was admitted to record may enter an order discharging the lien of the bond on the real estate of the sureties thereon, upon their petition and at their proper cost.

§46.2-451. Action or suit on bond.

If a final judgment rendered against the principal on the bond filed with the Commissioner as provided in this chapter is not satisfied within fifteen days after its rendition, the judgment creditor may, for his own use and benefit and at his sole expense, bring an action on the bond in the name of the Commonwealth against the company or persons executing the bond.

§46.2-452. Parties to suit on bond with individual sureties.

When the sureties on the bond filed with the Commissioner as provided in this chapter are individuals the judgment creditor may proceed against any or all parties to the bond at law for a judgment or in equity for a decree and foreclosure of the lien on the real estate of the sureties. The proceeding whether at law or in equity may be against one, all, or any intermediate number of the parties to the bond and when less than all are joined other or others may be impleaded in the same proceeding and after final judgment or decree other proceedings may be instituted until full satisfaction is obtained.

§46.2-453. Proof of financial responsibility by delivering cash or securities.

A person may give proof of financial responsibility by delivering to the Commissioner cash or securities equal to the sum of the liability coverage required for bodily injury or death of two or more persons in any one accident and injury to or destruction of property of others in any one accident as prescribed by §46.2-472. Securities so deposited shall be such as public bodies may invest in according to §2.1-327.

§46.2-454. Moneys or securities to be deposited with State Treasurer subject to execution.

All moneys or securities delivered to the Commissioner pursuant to this chapter shall be placed by him in the custody of the State Treasurer and shall be subject to execution to satisfy any judgment within the limits on amounts required by this chapter for motor vehicle liability insurance policies. The State Treasurer shall certify the value of such moneys or securities to the Commissioner as soon as practicable after their delivery to him.

§46.2-455. Assessment for expense of holding deposits.

For the purpose of defraying the expense of the safekeeping and handling of the cash or securities deposited with him under the provisions of this title, in December of each year the State Treasurer shall levy against each person having cash or securities deposited with him an assessment of not more than one-tenth of one percent of the cash or of the par value of the securities deposited to his account, and shall collect the assessment in January of each year. These funds shall be deposited to the general fund of the state treasury. If any assessment is not paid by January 31 of each year, the State Treasurer shall so notify the Commissioner in writing, attaching thereto a dated copy of the original assessment.

§46.2-456. Additional security if fund impaired by any legal process, or otherwise.

Whenever the moneys or securities are subjected to attachment, garnishment, execution, or other legal process or are otherwise depleted or threatened with depletion or impairment in amount or value the depositor must immediately furnish additional moneys or securities, free from lien, claim, or threat of impairment, in sufficient amount or value fully to comply with the requirements of this chapter.

The Treasurer shall notify the Commissioner promptly of any depletion, impairment, or decrease or of any legal threat of depletion, impairment, or decrease in the value of the securities or in the moneys on deposit with him under the provisions of this chapter.

§46.2-457. Substitution of new proof; cancellation or return of old.

The Commissioner may cancel any bond or return any certificate of insurance and on the substitution and acceptance by him of other adequate proof of financial responsibility pursuant to this chapter, and on his direction to such effect the State Treasurer shall return any money or securities on deposit with him to the person entitled to it.

§46.2-458. Interpleader to determine rights in deposits; other proceedings.

The Commissioner and the State Treasurer, or either, may proceed in equity by bill of interpleader for the determination of any dispute as to ownership of or rights in any deposit held by the State Treasurer pursuant to this chapter and may have recourse to any other appropriate proceeding for determination of any question that arises as to their rights or liabilities or as to the rights or liabilities of the Commonwealth under this chapter.

§46.2-459. When other proof of financial responsibility required; suspension of license pending furnishing of proof required.

Whenever any proof of financial responsibility filed by any person under this chapter no longer fulfills the purpose for which required, the Commissioner shall require other proof of financial responsibility as required by this chapter and shall suspend the person's driver's license, registration cards and license plates pending the furnishing of proof as required.

Nonpayment of the assessment provided for in §46.2-455 shall also be reason for suspension of the driver's license, registration cards and license plates of a person offering cash or securities as proof of financial responsibility under this chapter. The suspension shall be promptly initiated by the Commissioner on receipt of written notice of nonpayment of the assessment from the State Treasurer and shall take effect ten days from the date of a written notice sent by the Commissioner to the person by first-class mail, the notice to notify the person of the forthcoming suspension if payment is not received within the ten-day period.

§46.2-460. When Commissioner to consent to cancellation of bond or policy, or return of money or securities.

The Commissioner, on request and subject to the provisions of §46.2-461, shall consent to the cancellation of any bond or insurance policy or to the return to the person entitled thereto of any money or securities deposited pursuant to this chapter as proof of financial responsibility or he shall not require proof of financial responsibility in the event:

1. Of the death of the person on whose behalf the proof was filed;
2. Of his permanent incapacity to operate a motor vehicle; or
3. That the person who has given proof of financial responsibility surrenders his driver's license, and all of his registration cards, and license plates to the Commissioner.

§46.2-461. When Commissioner not to release proof of financial responsibility; affidavit of nonexistence of facts.

A. Notwithstanding the provisions of §46.2-460 the Commissioner shall not release the proof in the event:

1. Any action for damages upon a liability included in this chapter is then pending;
2. Any judgment on any liability is then outstanding and unsatisfied; or
3. The Commissioner has received notice that the person involved has within the period of twelve months immediately preceding been involved as a driver in any motor vehicle accident.

B. An affidavit of the applicant of the nonexistence of these facts shall be sufficient evidence thereof in the absence of evidence in the records of the Department tending to indicate the contrary.

§46.2-462. New license or registration to person to whom proof surrendered.

Whenever any person to whom proof has been surrendered as provided in §46.2-460 applies for a driver's license or the registration of a motor vehicle, the application shall be refused unless the applicant re-establishes proof as required by this chapter.

§46.2-463. Penalty for forging evidence of financial responsibility.

Any person who forges or without authority signs any evidence of ability to respond in damages or knowingly attempts to employ or use any evidence of ability to respond in damages, as required by the Commissioner in the administration of this chapter shall be guilty of a Class 1 misdemeanor.

ARTICLE 16
ASSIGNMENT OF INSURANCE RISKS

Section

§46.2-464. Application for assignment of risk to insurance carrier.

Every person who has been unable to obtain a motor vehicle liability policy shall have the right to apply to the State Corporation Commission to have his risk assigned to an insurance carrier licensed to write and writing motor vehicle liability insurance in the Commonwealth and the insurance carrier, whether a stock or mutual company, reciprocal, or interinsurance exchange, or other type or form of insurance organization, as provided in this article shall issue a motor vehicle liability policy which will meet at least the minimum requirements for establishing financial responsibility as provided in this chapter, and in addition shall provide, at the option of the insured, reasonable motor vehicle physical damage and medical payments coverages, (both as defined in §38.2-124) in the same policy.

Every person who has otherwise obtained a motor vehicle liability insurance policy, or who has been afforded motor vehicle liability insurance under the provisions of §38.2-2015, but who was not afforded motor vehicle medical payments insurance or motor vehicle physical damage insurance in the same policy, or who was not afforded such coverages under the provisions of that section, shall have the right to apply to the Commission to have his risk assigned to an insurance carrier, as provided above, licensed to write and writing either or both coverages, and the insurance carrier shall issue a policy providing the coverage or coverages applied for.

§46.2-465. Optional coverage for persons occupying insured motor vehicle and for named insured and his family.

Once an assigned risk policy has been issued to an insured, every insurer licensed in the Commonwealth issuing or delivering any policy or contract of bodily injury liability insurance, or of property damage liability insurance, covering liability arising from the ownership, maintenance, or use of any motor vehicle shall provide on request of the insured, on payment of premium established by law for the coverage (i) to the named insured and, while resident of the named insured's household, the spouse and relatives of the named insured while occupying a motor vehicle or if struck by a motor vehicle while not occupying a motor vehicle; and (ii) to persons occupying the insured motor vehicle, the following health care and disability benefit for each accident:

1. Medical and chiropractic payments (accident insurance as defined in Article 2, §38.2-101 et seq. of Chapter 1 of Title 38.2) coverages incurred within two years after the date of the accident, up to $2,000 per person;
2. If the person is usually engaged in a remunerative occupation, an amount equal to the loss of income incurred within one year after the date of the accident resulting from injuries received in the accident up to $100 per week during the period from the first work day lost as a result of the accident up to the date on which the person is able to return to his usual occupation and for a period not to exceed fifty-two weeks or any part thereof; and
3. The insured has the option of purchasing either or both of the coverages set forth in subdivisions 1 and 2 of this section.

§46.2-466. Regulations for assignment, rate classifications, and schedules.

The Commission may make reasonable regulations for the assignment of risks to insurance carriers.

It shall establish rate classifications, rating schedules, rates, and regulations to be used by insurance carriers issuing assigned risk, policies of motor vehicle liability, physical damage, and medical payments insurance in accordance with this chapter as appear to it to be proper.

In the establishment of rate classifications, rating schedules, rates, and regulations, it shall be guided by the principles and practices which have been established under its statutory authority to regulate motor vehicle liability, physical damage, and medical payments insurance rates and it may act in conformity with its statutory discretionary authority in such matters.

§46.2-467. Action within power of Commission.

The Commission may, in its discretion, after reviewing all information pertaining to the applicant or policyholder available from its records, the records of the Department or from other sources:

1. Refuse to assign an application;
2. Approve the rejection of an application by an insurance carrier;
3. Approve the cancellation of a policy of motor vehicle liability, physical damage, and medical payments insurance by an insurance carrier; or
4. Refuse to approve the renewal or the reassignment of an expiring policy.

§46.2-468. Information filed with Commission by insurance carrier confidential.

Any information filed with the Commission by an insurance carrier in connection with an assigned risk shall be confidential and solely for the information of the Commission and its staff and shall not be disclosed to any person, including an applicant, policyholder, and any other insurance carrier.

§46.2-469. Commission not required to disclose reasons for action; liability of Commission for act or omission.

A. The Commission shall not be required to disclose to any person, including the applicant or policyholder, its reasons for:

1. Refusing to assign an application;
2. Approving the rejection of an application by an insurance carrier;
3. Approving the cancellation of a policy of motor vehicle liability, physical damage, and medical payments insurance by an insurance carrier; or
4. Refusing to approve the renewal or the reassignment of an expiring policy.

B. The Commission or anyone acting for it shall not be held liable for any act or omission in connection with the administration of the duties imposed upon it by the provisions of this chapter, except upon proof of actual malfeasance.

§46.2-470. Assignment of risks for nonresidents.

The provisions of this chapter relevant to assignment of risks shall be available to nonresidents who are unable to obtain a policy of motor vehicle liability, physical damage, and medical payments insurance with respect only to motor vehicles registered and used in the Commonwealth.

§46.2-471. Assignment of risks for certain carriers.

Notwithstanding the provisions of §46.2-366, the provisions of this chapter relating to assignment of risks shall be available to carriers by motor vehicle who are required by law to carry public liability and property damage insurance for the protection of the public.

ARTICLE 17
MOTOR VEHICLE LIABILITY INSURANCE POLICIES

Section

§46.2-472. Coverage of owner's policy.

Every motor vehicle owner's policy shall:

1. Designate by explicit description or by appropriate reference, all motor vehicles with respect to which coverage is intended to be granted.
2. Insure as insured the person named and any other person using or responsible for the use of the motor vehicle or motor vehicles with the permission of the named insured.
3. Insure the insured or other person against loss from any liability imposed by law for damages, including damages for care and loss of services, because of bodily injury to or death of any person, and injury to or destruction of property caused by accident and arising out of the ownership, use, or operation of such motor vehicle or motor vehicles within the Commonwealth, any other state in the United States, or Canada, subject to a limit exclusive of interest and costs, with respect to each motor vehicle, of $25,000 because of bodily injury to or death of one person in any one accident and, subject to the limit for one person, to a limit of $50,000 because of bodily injury to or death of two or more persons in any one accident, and to a limit of $20,000 because of injury to or destruction of property of others in any one accident.

§46.2-473. Coverage of driver's policy.

Every driver's policy shall insure the person named therein as insured against loss from the liability imposed upon him by law for damages, including damages for care and loss of services, because of bodily injury to or death of any person, and injury to or destruction of property arising out of the use by him of any motor vehicle not owned by him, within the territorial limits and subject to the limits of liability set forth with respect to a motor vehicle owner's policy.

§46.2-474. Policy must contain certain agreement; additional coverage.

Every policy of insurance subject to the provisions of this chapter:

1. Shall contain an agreement that the insurance is provided in accordance with the coverage defined in this chapter as respects bodily injury, death, property damage, and destruction and that it is subject to all the provisions of this chapter and of the laws of the Commonwealth relating to this kind of insurance; and

2. May grant any lawful coverage in excess of or in addition to the coverage herein specified and this excess or additional coverage shall not be subject to the provisions of this chapter but shall be subject to other applicable laws of the Commonwealth.

§46.2-475. Policy must comply with law.
No policy required under this chapter shall be issued or delivered in the Commonwealth unless it complies with §§38.2-2218 through 38.2-2225, with all other applicable and not inconsistent laws of the Commonwealth, and with the terms and conditions of this chapter.

§46.2-476. Liability covered by workers' compensation law.
Policies issued under this chapter shall not insure any liability of the employer on account of bodily injury to, or death of, an employee of the insured for which benefits are payable under any workers' compensation law.

§46.2-477. When chapter applicable to policy.
This chapter shall not apply to any policy of insurance except as to liability thereunder incurred after certification thereof as proof of financial responsibility.

§46.2-478. Several policies together meeting requirements of chapter.
Several policies of one or more insurance carriers which together meet the requirements of this chapter shall be deemed a motor vehicle liability policy within the meaning of this chapter.

§46.2-479. Provisions to which every policy shall be subject but need not contain.
Every policy shall be subject to the following provisions which need not be contained therein:

1. The liability of any insurance carrier to the insured under a policy becomes absolute when loss or damage covered by the policy occurs and the satisfaction by the insured of a judgment for the loss or damage shall not be a condition precedent to the right or duty of the carrier to make payment on account of the loss or damage;

2. No policy shall be cancelled or annulled, as respects any loss or damage, by any agreement between the carrier and the insured after the insured has become responsible for the loss or damage and any attempted cancellation or annulment shall be void;

3. If the death of the insured occurs after the insured has become liable, during the policy period, for loss or damage covered by the policy, the policy shall not be terminated by the death with respect to the liability and the insurance carrier shall be liable hereunder as though death had not occurred;

4. On the recovery of a judgment against any person for loss or damage, if the person or the decedent he represents was at the accrual of the cause of action insured against the liability under the policy, the judgment creditor shall be entitled to have the insurance money applied to the satisfaction of the judgment;

5. If the death, insolvency, or bankruptcy of the insured occurs within the policy period, the policy during the unexpired portion of the period shall cover the legal representatives of the insured; and

6. No statement made by the insured or on his behalf and no violation of the terms of the policy shall operate to defeat or avoid the policy so as to bar recovery within the limits provided in this chapter.

§46.2-480. Reimbursement of carrier and proration of insurance.
Any policy may provide:

1. That the insured, or any other person covered by the policy, shall reimburse the insurance carrier for payments made on account of any accident, claim, or suit involving a breach of the terms, provisions, or conditions of the policy; or

2. For proration of the insurance with other applicable valid and collectible insurance.

§46.2.481. Binder or endorsement in lieu of policy.
Insurance carriers authorized to issue policies as provided in this chapter may, pending the issuance of the policy, execute an agreement to be known as a binder, which shall not be valid beyond sixty days from the date it becomes effective, or may, in lieu of a policy, issue an endorsement to an existing policy, each of which shall be construed to provide indemnity or protection in like manner and to the same extent as a formal policy. The provisions of this chapter apply to these binders and endorsements.

§46.2-482. Notification of cancellation or termination of certified policy.
When any insurance policy certified under this chapter is cancelled or terminated, the insurer shall report the fact to the Commissioner within fifteen days after the cancellation on a form prescribed by the Commissioner.

ARTICLE 18
DRIVER LICENSE COMPACT

Section

§46.2-483. Compact enacted into law; terms.
The Driver License Compact is hereby enacted into law and entered into with all other jurisdictions legally joining therein in the form substantially as follows:

THE DRIVER LICENSE COMPACT

Article I
Findings and Declaration of Policy

(a) The party states find that:

(1) The safety of their streets and highways is materially affected by the degree of compliance with state and local ordinances relating to the operation of motor vehicles.

(2) Violation of such a law or ordinance is evidence that the violator engages in conduct which is likely to endanger the safety of persons and property.

(3) The continuance in force of a license to drive is predicated upon compliance with laws and ordinances relating to the operation of motor vehicles, in whichever jurisdiction the vehicle is operated.

(b) It is the policy of each of the party states to:

(1) Promote compliance with the laws, ordinances, and administrative rules and regulations relating to the operation of motor vehicles by their operators in each of the jurisdictions where such operators drive motor vehicles.

(2) Make the reciprocal recognition of licenses to drive and eligibility therefor more just and equitable by considering the overall compliance with motor vehicle laws, ordinances and administrative rules and regulations as a condition precedent to the continuance or issuance of any license by reason of which the licensee is authorized or permitted to operate a motor vehicle in any of the party states.

Article II
Definitions

As used in this compact:

(a) "State" means a state, territory or possession of the United States, the District of Columbia, or the Commonwealth of Puerto Rico.

(b) "Home state" means the state which has issued and has the power to suspend or revoke the use of the license or permit to operate a motor vehicle.

(c) "Conviction" means a conviction of any offense related to the use or operation of a motor vehicle which is prohibited by state law, municipal ordinance or administrative rule or regulation, or a forfeiture of bail, bond, or other security deposited to secure appearance by a person charged with having committed any such offense, and which conviction or forfeiture is required to be reported to the licensing authority.

Article III
Reports of Conviction

The licensing authority of a party state shall report each conviction of a person from another party state occurring within its jurisdiction to the licensing authority of the home state of the licensee. Such report shall clearly identify the person convicted; describe the violation specifying the section of the statute, code or ordinance violated; identify the court in which action was taken; indicate whether a plea of guilty or not guilty was entered, or the conviction was a result of the forfeiture of bail, bond or other security; and shall include any special findings made in connection therewith.

Article IV
Effect of Conviction

(a) The licensing authority in the home state, for the purposes of suspension, revocation or limitation of the license to operate a motor vehicle, shall give the same effect to the conduct reported, pursuant to Article III of this compact, as it would if such conduct had occurred in the home state, in the case of convictions for:

(1) Manslaughter or negligent homicide resulting from the operation of a motor vehicle;

(2) Driving a motor vehicle while under the influence of intoxicating liquor or a narcotic drug, or under the influence of any other drug to a degree which renders the driver incapable of safely driving a motor vehicle;

(3) Any felony in the commission of which a motor vehicle is used;

(4) Failure to stop and render aid in the event of a motor vehicle accident resulting in the death or personal injury of another.

(b) As to other convictions, reported pursuant to Article III, the licensing authority in the home state shall give such effect to the conduct as is provided by the laws of the home state.

(c) If the laws of a party state do not provide for offenses or violations denominated or described in precisely the words employed in subdivision (a) of this article, such party state shall construe the denominations and descriptions appearing in subdivision (a) hereof as being applicable to and identifying those offenses or violations of a substantially similar nature and the laws of such party state shall contain such provisions as may be necessary to ensure that full force and effect is given to this article.

Article V
Applications for New Licenses

Upon application for a license to drive, the licensing authority in a party state shall ascertain whether the applicant has ever held, or is the holder of a license to drive issued by any other party state. The licensing authority in the state where application is made shall not issue a license to drive to the applicant if:

(1) The applicant has held such a license, but the same has been suspended by reason, in whole or in part, of a violation and if such suspension period has not terminated.

(2) The applicant has held such a license, but the same has been revoked by reason, in whole or in part, of a violation and if such revocation has not terminated, except that after the expiration of one year from the date the license was revoked, such person may make application for a new license if permitted by law. The licensing authority may refuse to issue a license to any such applicant if, after investigation, the licensing authority determines that it will not be safe to grant to such person the privilege of driving a motor vehicle on the public highways.

(3) The applicant is the holder of a license to drive issued by another party state and currently in force unless the applicant surrenders such license.

Article VI
Applicability of Other Laws

Except as expressly required by provisions of this compact, nothing contained herein shall be construed to affect the right of any party state to apply any of its other laws relating to licenses to drive to any person or circumstance, nor to invalidate or prevent any driver license agreement or other cooperative arrangement between a party state and a nonparty state.

Article VII
Compact Administrator and Interchange of Information

(a) The head of the licensing authority of each party state shall be the administrator of this compact for his state. The administrators, acting jointly, shall have the power to formulate all necessary and proper procedures for the exchange of information under this compact.

(b) The administrator of each party state shall furnish to the administrator of each other party state any information or documents reasonably necessary to facilitate the administration of this compact.

Article VIII
Entry Into Force and Withdrawal

(a) This compact shall enter into force and become effective as to any state when it has enacted the same into law.

(b) Any party state may withdraw from this compact by enacting a statute repealing the same, but no such withdrawal shall take effect until six months after the executive head of the withdrawing state has given notice of the withdrawal to the executive heads of all other party states. No withdrawal shall affect the validity or applicability by the licensing authorities of states remaining party to the compact of any report of conviction occurring prior to the withdrawal.

Article IX
Construction and Severability

This compact shall be liberally construed so as to effectuate the purposes thereof. The provisions of this compact shall be severable and if any phrase, clause, sentence or provision of this compact is declared to be contrary to the constitution of any party state or of the United States or the applicability thereof to any government, agency, person or circumstance is held invalid, the validity of the remainder of this compact and the applicability thereof to any government, agency, person or circumstance shall not be affected thereby. If this compact shall be held contrary to the constitution of any state party thereto, the compact shall remain in full force and effect as to the remaining states and in full force and effect as to the state affected as to all severable matters.

§46.2-484. Department of Motor Vehicles to be "licensing authority" within meaning of compact; duties of Department.

As used in the compact, the term "licensing authority" with reference to this Commonwealth shall mean the Department of Motor Vehicles. The Department shall furnish to the appropriate authorities of any other party state any information or documents reasonably necessary to facilitate the administration of Articles III, IV, and V of the compact.

§46.2-485. Compensation and expenses of compact administrator.

The compact administrator provided for in Article VII of the compact shall not be entitled to any additional compensation on account of his service as such administrator, but shall be entitled to expenses incurred in connection with his duties and responsibilities as such administrator, in the same manner as for expenses incurred in connection with any other duties or responsibilities of his office or employment.

§46.2-486. Governor to be "executive head" within meaning of compact.

As used in the compact, with reference to the Commonwealth, the term "executive head" shall mean the Governor.

§46.2-487. Statutes and ordinances deemed to cover offenses specified in subdivision (a) of Article IV of compact.

For the purposes of complying with subdivisions (a) and (c) of Article IV of the compact, the following sections of the Code of Virginia and county, city, or town ordinances substantially paralleling such sections shall be deemed to cover the offenses of subdivision (a) of Article IV: With respect to subdivision (2), §§18.2-266 and 46.2-341.24 A; with respect to subdivision (4), §§46.2-894 through 46.2-899 subject to the limitation that the accident resulted in the death or personal injury of another; with respect to subdivisions (1) and (3), the Department shall determine which offenses are covered in the same manner as under §46.2-389.

§46.2-488. Question to be included in application for driver's license; surrender of license issued by another party state.

For the purpose of enforcing subdivision (3) of Article V of this compact, the Department shall include as part of the form for application for a driver's license under §46.2-323 a question whether the applicant is currently licensed in another state and shall, if the applicant is so licensed, require the surrender of such license prior to the granting of such application in accordance with the provisions of Chapter 3 of Title 46.2 of the Code of Virginia.

ARTICLE 19
DRIVER IMPROVEMENT PROGRAM

§46.2-489. Regulations; appeals.

The Commissioner may, subject to the provisions of §46.2-203, promulgate regulations which he deems necessary to carry out the provisions of this article.

Any person receiving an order of the Commissioner to suspend or revoke his driver's license or licensing privilege or to require attendance at a driver improvement clinic or placing him on probation may, within thirty days from the date of the order, file a petition of appeal in accordance with §46.2-410.

(Chgd. by L.1995 ch. 672, eff. 7/1/95.)

§46.2-490. Establishment of driver improvement clinic program; application fees.

A. The Commissioner shall, in his discretion, contract with such entities as the Commissioner deems fit, including private or governmental entities, to develop curricula for a statewide driver improvement clinic program. The driver improvement clinic program shall be established for the purpose of instructing persons identified by the Department and the court system as problem drivers in need of driver improvement education and training and for those drivers interested in improved driving safety. The clinics shall be composed of uniform education and training programs designed for the rehabilitation of problem drivers, and for the purpose of creating a lasting and corrective influence on their driving performance. The clinics shall operate in localities based on their geographical location so as to be reasonably accessible to persons attending these clinics.

B. All businesses, organizations, governmental entities or individuals that want to provide driver improvement clinic instruction in the Commonwealth using approved curricula shall apply to the Department to be certified to do so, based on criteria established by the Department. A nonrefundable annual application fee of $100 shall be paid to the Department by all such businesses, organizations, governmental entities or individuals. All such application fees collected by the Department shall be paid by the Commissioner into the

state treasury and shall be set aside as a special fund to be used to meet the expenses of the Department.
(Chgd. by L.1995 ch. 672, eff. 7/1/95.)

§46.2-490.1. Section 46.2-391.1 not applicable.
The provisions of §46.2-391.1 shall not apply to any person whose license or other privilege to operate a motor vehicle is suspended or revoked in accordance with the provisions of this article.

§46.2-490.2. Time frame for program transition.
A. The Department shall continue to provide group interviews and personal interviews through September 30, 1995, in order to accommodate persons notified by the Department prior to July 1, 1995, to attend such interviews.

The group interview order shall be terminated on October 1, 1995, for those persons who fail to complete a required group interview by September 30, 1995. Any associated group interview and reinstatement fees shall be waived. The Department shall mail notices to these persons informing them of the termination.

The personal interview order shall be terminated on October 1, 1995, for those persons who fail to complete a required personal interview by September 30, 1995. Any associated personal interview and reinstatement fees shall be waived. The Department shall mail notices to these persons informing them of the termination, requiring them to complete a driver improvement clinic and placing them on a six-month probation period in accordance with §§46.2-498 and 46.2-499 of this article.

No group or personal interview notices shall be issued on or after July 1, 1995. Persons required to complete a driver improvement clinic as a result of a notice issued prior to July 1, 1995, shall continue to be required to satisfy such notice.

B. As necessary, the Department shall provide clinic instruction until such time as curricula for use in driver improvement clinics have been approved and are in use by those businesses, organizations, governmental entities or individuals certified by the Department to provide driver improvement clinic instruction. No materials, instructors, instructor fees or any other form of subsidy shall be provided by the Department to any business, organization, governmental entity or individual providing driver improvement clinic instruction on or after July 1, 1995.
(Added by L.1995 ch. 672, eff. 7/1/95.)

§46.2-491. Persons included within scope of chapter.
This article shall apply to (i) every resident of the Commonwealth, regardless of whether he possesses a driver's license issued by the Department and (ii) every nonresident to whom the Department has issued a driver's license.
(Chgd. by L.1995 ch. 672, eff. 7/1/95.)

§46.2-492. Uniform Demerit Point System.
A. The Commissioner shall assign point values to those convictions, or findings of not innocent in the case of a juvenile, which are required to be reported to the Department in accordance with §46.2-383 for traffic offenses committed in violation of the laws of the Commonwealth or any county, city, or town ordinance paralleling and substantially conforming to state law, provided that no conviction, or finding of not innocent in the case of a juvenile for any offense, relating to registration, insurance, or equipment shall be included except as otherwise provided by this title.

B. The Commissioner shall assign point values to those convictions received from any other state of the United States, the United States, Canada or its provinces, or any territorial subdivision of any of them, of an offense therein, which if committed in this Commonwealth, would be required to be reported to the Department by §46.2-383.

C. No point assignment shall be made for any conviction which results from a vehicle's having been parked or stopped, in order for the driver to sleep or rest, on the shoulder or other portion of a highway not ordinarily used for vehicular traffic. The court shall make a separate finding on this issue and note such finding on the conviction record.

D. The Uniform Demerit Point System standard for rating convictions of traffic offenses shall be based on the severity of the offense and the potential hazardous exposure to other users of the highways and streets. The Commissioner shall designate the point values assigned to convictions, or findings of not innocent in the case of a juvenile, on a graduated scale not to exceed six demerit points for any single conviction. The Commissioner shall develop point system assignments as follows:

1. Serious traffic offenses such as driving while intoxicated in violation of §18.2-266, persons under age twenty-one driving after illegally consuming alcohol in violation of §18.2-266.1, reckless driving in violation of §46.2-852, speeding twenty or more miles per hour above the posted speed limit, racing in violation of §46.2-865, and other serious traffic offenses as the Commissioner may designate, shall be assigned six demerit points.

2. Relatively serious traffic offenses such as failure to yield the right-of-way in violation of §§46.2-820 through 46.2-823, speeding between ten and nineteen miles per hour above the posted speed limit, following too closely in violation of §46.2-816, failure to stop when entering a highway in violation of §46.2-863, and other relatively serious traffic offenses as the Commissioner may designate, shall be assigned four demerit points.

3. Traffic offenses of a less serious nature such as improper driving in violation of §46.2-869, speeding between one and nine miles per hour above the posted speed limit, improper passing in violation of §46.2-836, failure to obey a highway sign in violation of §46.2-830 and other offenses of a less serious nature as the Commissioner may designate, shall be assigned three demerit points.

E. When a person is convicted of two or more traffic offenses committed on a single occasion, he shall be assessed points for one offense only and if the offenses involved have different point values, he shall be assessed points for the offense having the greater point value.
(Chgd. by L.1998 ch. 430, eff. 7/1/98.)

§46.2-493. Demerit points valid for two years.
Demerit points, assigned to any conviction, or finding of not innocent in the case of a juvenile, shall be valid for a period of two years from the date the offense was committed. Demerit points used prior to the termination of the two-year period as the basis for suspension, revocation, probation, or other action which extends beyond the two-year period shall remain valid until the suspension, revocation, probationary period, or other action has terminated.

§46.2-494. Safe driving point credit.
Every resident or nonresident person holding a valid Virginia driver's license whose driving record does not contain any suspension, revocation, conviction, or finding of not innocent in the case of a juvenile, of a traffic violation, during any calendar year shall be awarded one safe driving point. One safe driving point shall be awarded for each calendar year of safe driving, but no person shall be permitted to accumulate more than five safe driving points. The Commissioner shall apply these points to offset an equivalent number of demerit points, if any, to the chronologically earliest offense conviction, or finding of not innocent in the case of a juvenile, for which demerit points have been assigned and are valid. If subsequent to awarding a safe driving point to any person, the Department receives a conviction, or finding

of not innocent in the case of a juvenile, for an offense which occurred during the period for which a safe driving point was awarded for and which requires the Department to assess demerit points, the safe driving point shall be invalidated.

§46.2-495. Advisory letters.

Whenever the driving record of any person who is eighteen years old or older shows an accumulation of at least eight demerit points based on convictions for traffic offenses committed within a period of twelve consecutive months, or at least twelve demerit points based on convictions for traffic offenses committed within a period of twenty-four consecutive months, respectively, the Commissioner may mail, by first-class mail, to the last known address of the person an advisory letter listing his convictions and the demerit points assigned thereto, including his safe driving points, if any, and furnish any other information deemed appropriate and applicable to the rehabilitation of the person, for the purpose of preventing subsequent traffic offenses.

The Department's failure to mail, or the citizen's nonreceipt of the advisory letter shall not be grounds for waiving any other provision of this article.

(Chgd. by L.1995 ch. 672; L.1998 chs. 124, 792, eff. 7/1/98.)

§§46.2-496, 46.2-497. *(Repealed by L.1995 ch. 672, eff. 7/1/95.)*

§46.2-498. Driver improvement clinics; voluntary attendance.

A. Whenever the driving record of any person who is eighteen years old or older shows an accumulation of at least twelve demerit points based on convictions for traffic offenses committed within a period of twelve consecutive months, or at least eighteen demerit points based on convictions for traffic offenses committed within a period of twenty-four consecutive months, respectively, the Commissioner shall direct the person to attend a driver improvement clinic.

B. Except for those persons whose licenses are subject to the restrictions of §46.2-334.01, whenever the driving record of a person under the age of eighteen years shows an accumulation of (i) at least nine points based on convictions for traffic offenses committed within a period of twelve consecutive months or (ii) at least twelve points based on convictions for traffic offenses committed within a period of twenty-four consecutive months, the Commissioner shall direct the person to attend a driver improvement clinic and such person shall be subject to probation pursuant to §46.2-499.

C. Except as provided in subsection D of this section and in §§46.2-334.01 and 46.2-505, every person who attends a driver improvement clinic conducted by the Department or those businesses, organizations, governmental entities or individuals certified by the Department to provide driver improvement clinic instruction and who satisfactorily completes the clinic shall have five demerit points subtracted from his total accumulation of demerit points, except in those instances where a person has not accumulated five demerit points, in which case a reduction in demerit points and/or the award of safe driving points will be made. No person shall be allowed to accumulate more than five safe driving points.

Safe driving points shall be awarded or reductions in premium charges, as set forth in §38.2-2217, shall be received for the completion of a driver improvement clinic only once within a period of two years from the date a person satisfactorily completes the clinic. Persons shall be eligible to voluntarily attend a driver improvement clinic again for either safe driving points or a reduction in premium charges, whichever was not awarded or received previously, one year from the date of satisfactory completion of a driver improvement clinic in which safe driving points or a reduction in premium charges was received or awarded.

D. Any resident or nonresident person holding a valid license to drive a motor vehicle in Virginia, whether or not he has accumulated demerit points, may apply to any business, organization, governmental entity or individual certified by the Department to provide driver improvement clinic instruction for permission to attend a driver improvement clinic on a voluntary basis. Such businesses, organizations, governmental entities or individuals may, when seating space is available, schedule the person to attend a driver improvement clinic.

Persons who voluntarily attend and satisfactorily complete a driver improvement clinic shall be eligible (i) to have five demerit points subtracted from their total accumulation of demerit points, except in those instances where a person has not accumulated five demerit points, in which case a reduction in demerit points and/or the award of safe driving points will be made, or (ii) to receive a reduction in premium charges as set forth under §38.2-2217, either of which, but not both, shall be awarded or received no more than once in a two-year period, as set forth in subsection C of this section. Such persons shall inform the business, organization or individual providing instruction if they are attending to be awarded safe driving points or to receive a reduction in premium charges as set forth under §38.2-2217.

(Chgd. by L.1995 chs. 226, 672; L.1996 chs. 307, 1035; L.1998 chs. 124, 792, eff. 7/1/98.)

§46.2-499. Driver's license probation.

A. The Commissioner shall place on probation for a period of six months any person who has been directed to attend a driver improvement clinic pursuant to the provisions of §46.2-498. In addition, the Commissioner shall place any person on probation for a period of six months on receiving a record of a conviction of such person of any offense for which demerit points are assessed and the offense was committed within any driver control period imposed pursuant to §46.2-500. Whenever a person who has been placed on probation is convicted, or found not innocent in the case of a juvenile, of any offense for which demerit points are assessed, and the offense was committed during the probation period, the Commissioner shall suspend the person's license for a period of ninety days when six demerit points are assigned, for a period of sixty days when four demerit points are assigned, and for a period of forty-five days when three demerit points are assigned. In addition, the Commissioner shall again place the person on probation for a period of six months, effective on termination of the suspension imposed pursuant to this section.

B. Upon request, the Commissioner shall grant a restricted license during the first period of suspension imposed pursuant to subsection A of this section provided the person is otherwise eligible to be licensed. Any person whose driver's license is suspended for a second or subsequent time under subsection A of this section shall be eligible to receive a restricted driver's license only if the violation occurred within a probation period that was immediately preceded by a control period. A restricted license may be issued for any or all of the following purposes: (i) travel to and from his place of employment; (ii) travel during the hours of such person's employment if the operation of a motor vehicle is a necessary incident of such employment; (iii) travel to and from school if such person is a student; or (iv) such other medically necessary travel. Written verifications of the person's employment, continuing education or medically necessary travel shall also be required and made available to the Commissioner. Whenever a person who has been granted a restricted license pursuant to this subsection is convicted, or found not innocent in the case of a juvenile, of any offense for which demerit points are assessed, and the offense was committed during the restricted license period, the Commissioner shall suspend the person's license using the same demerit point criteria and suspension periods set forth in subsection A of this section. No restricted license issued pursuant to this subsection shall permit any person to operate a commercial motor vehicle as defined in the Virginia Commercial Driver's License Act (§46.2-341.1 et seq.).

C. Whenever the Department receives notice from the court that restricted license privileges have been granted to a person who has an existing restricted license issued pursuant to subsection B of this section, the existing restricted license shall be cancelled, and the Commissioner shall suspend the person's license for the period of time remaining on the original order of suspension. No court-granted restricted license shall be issued until the end of the suspension period imposed by the Commissioner.

(Chgd. by L.1995 ch. 672; L.1996 chs. 943, 994, eff. 7/1/96.)

§46.2-500. Driver control period.

Whenever an individual is placed on probation pursuant to §§46.2-498, 46.2-499 or §46.2-506, the Commissioner shall also place the person on driver control status for a period of eighteen months following the termination of the probationary period. If the individual commits any violation during the driver control period for which points are assessed, the Commissioner shall again place the individual on probation for a period of six months and on driver control status for an additional period of eighteen months following the probationary period.

(Chgd. by L.1995 ch. 672, eff. 7/1/95.)

§46.2-501. Notice to attend driver improvement clinic.

A. Any notice to attend a driver improvement clinic must contain:

1. Information on how to schedule a driver improvement clinic.

2. The purpose of the driver improvement clinic, including the consequences of not attending the clinic program.

3. An explanation of the terms of the probationary licensing period.

4. A requirement stating that the clinic must be satisfactorily completed within ninety days from the date of notice.

B. The notice directing any person to attend a driver improvement clinic shall be forwarded by certified mail to the last known address of the person, as shown on the records of the Department.

(Chgd. by L.1995 ch. 672, eff. 7/1/95.)

§46.2-502. Clinic fees.

A. The Department and all businesses, organizations, governmental entities or individuals certified by the Department to provide driver improvement clinic instruction may charge a fee not to exceed seventy-five dollars, which shall include the processing fee set forth in subsection B of this section, to persons notified by the Department, to attend a driver improvement clinic. No person shall be permitted to attend a driver improvement clinic unless the person first pays the required attendance fee to the business, organization, governmental entity or individual providing the driver improvement clinic instruction.

B. All businesses, organizations, governmental entities or individuals certified by the Department to provide driver improvement clinic instruction shall collect for the Department a processing fee of ten dollars from each person attending a driver improvement clinic taught by such businesses, organizations, governmental entities or individuals. Such processing fee payments shall accompany the clinic rosters submitted to the Department by such businesses, organizations, governmental entities or individuals. No such processing fee, however, shall be required or collected from members of volunteer rescue squads and volunteer fire departments who attend such clinics in order to successfully complete training for emergency vehicle operation. All fees collected by the Department under this subsection shall be paid by the Commissioner into the state treasury and shall be set aside as a special fund to be used to meet the expenses of the Department.

(Chgd. by L.1995 ch. 672; L.1996 ch. 171; L.1998 ch. 437, eff. 7/1/98.)

§46.2-503. Suspension of privilege to operate a motor vehicle for failure to attend clinics.

The Commissioner shall suspend the privilege to operate a motor vehicle of any person who fails to satisfactorily complete a driver improvement clinic. This suspension shall remain in effect until such person satisfactorily completes the driver improvement clinic. This section shall not be applicable to persons attending clinics on a voluntary basis.

(Chgd. by L.1995 ch. 672, eff. 7/1/95.)

§46.2-504. Form and contents of order of probation, suspension or revocation; service.

Whenever the Commissioner issues a probation, suspension or revocation order in accordance with any provision of this chapter, the order shall provide the addressee with a minimum of ten days' notice and shall be served as provided in §46.2-416.

§46.2-505. Court may direct defendant to attend driver improvement clinic.

Any circuit or general district court or juvenile court of the Commonwealth, or any federal court, charged with the duty of hearing traffic cases for offenses committed in violation of any law of the Commonwealth, or any valid local ordinance, or any federal law regulating the movement or operation of a motor vehicle, may require any person found guilty, or in the case of a juvenile found not innocent, of a violation of any state law, local ordinance, or federal law, to attend a driver improvement clinic. The attendance requirement may be in lieu of or in addition to the penalties prescribed by §46.2-113, the ordinance, or federal law. The court shall determine if a person is to receive safe driving points upon satisfactory completion of a driver improvement clinic conducted by the Department or by any business, organization, governmental entity or individual certified by the Department to provide driver improvement clinic instruction. In the absence of such notification, no safe driving points shall be awarded by the Department.

Persons required by the court to attend a driver improvement clinic shall notify the court if the driver improvement clinic has or has not been attended and satisfactorily completed, in compliance with the court order. Failure of the person to attend and satisfactorily complete a driver improvement clinic, in compliance with the court order, may be punished as contempt of such court.

(Chgd. by L.1995 ch. 672, eff. 7/1/95.)

§46.2-506. Formal hearings; suspension for excessive point accumulation.

A. Whenever the operating record of any person shows a continued disregard of the motor vehicle laws subsequent to being placed on probation, he may be charged as a reckless or negligent driver of a motor vehicle, and cited for a formal hearing in accordance with the provisions of §§46.2-402 through 46.2-408. If the hearing results in the suspension of a person's driving privilege, the person shall be placed on probation at the end of the suspension period in accordance with the provisions of §46.2-499.

B. Whenever the operating record of any person shows an accumulation of at least eighteen demerit points based on

convictions, or findings of not innocent in the case of a juvenile, for traffic violations committed within any twelve consecutive months, or at least twenty-four demerit points based on convictions, or findings of not innocent in the case of a juvenile, for traffic violations committed within any twenty-four consecutive months, respectively, the Commissioner shall suspend the person's license or licenses for a period of ninety days and thereafter until he attends and satisfactorily completes a driver improvement clinic. At the end of this suspension period, the person shall be placed on probation in accordance with the provisions of §46.2-499.
(Chgd. by L.1995 ch. 672, eff. 7/1/95.)

CHAPTER 6
TITLING AND REGISTRATION OF MOTOR VEHICLES

Article

ARTICLE 1
TITLING AND REGISTRATION, GENERALLY

Section

§46.2-600. Owner to secure registration and certificate of title or certificate of ownership.

Except as otherwise provided in this chapter every person who owns a motor vehicle, trailer or semitrailer, or his authorized attorney-in-fact, shall, before it is operated on any highway in the Commonwealth, register with the Department and obtain from the Department the registration card and certificate of title for the vehicle. Persons applying for registration shall provide the Department with either the home or business street address of the owner of the motor vehicle being registered.

Unless he has previously applied for registration and a certificate of title or he is exempted under §§46.2-619, 46.2-631, and 46.2-1206, every person residing in the Commonwealth who owns a motor vehicle, trailer, or semitrailer, or his duly authorized attorney-in-fact, shall, within thirty days of the purchase or transfer, apply to the Department for a certificate of ownership.

§46.2-601. Appointment of Commissioner agent for service of process.

Each nonresident owner of a motor vehicle, trailer, or semitrailer applying for the registration thereof in the Commonwealth shall file with the application a duly executed instrument, constituting the Commissioner and his successors in office his attorney on whom all lawful process against and notice to the owner may be served in any action or legal proceeding brought as the result of the operation or use of any motor vehicle, trailer, or semitrailer registered by or for him, in the Commonwealth; and therein shall agree that any process against or notice to the owner shall have the same effect as if served on the owner within the Commonwealth. The service of the process or notice shall be made by leaving a copy of it in the office of the Commissioner with a service fee of three dollars to be taxed as a part of the costs of the suit. The Commissioner shall forthwith notify the owner of the service by letter.

§46.2-602. Titling and registration of foreign market vehicles.

A. The Department shall not issue a permanent certificate of title or registration for a foreign market vehicle until the applicant submits proof that the vehicle complies with federal safety requirements.

B. The Department shall accept as proof that a foreign market vehicle complies with federal safety requirements documents from either the United States Department of Transportation or the United States Customs Service stating that the vehicle conforms or has been brought into conformity with federal safety requirements.

C. The certificate of title of any foreign market vehicle titled under this section shall contain an appropriate notation that the owner has submitted proof that it complies with federal safety requirements.

D. Any foreign market vehicle previously titled in the Commonwealth shall be titled and registered without further proof of compliance with federal safety requirements. If, however, proof of compliance is not submitted to the Department, the certificate of title shall contain an appropriate notation that the owner of the foreign market vehicle has not submitted proof that the vehicle complies with federal safety requirements.

E. No foreign market vehicle manufactured prior to 1968 shall be subject to this section.

F. Notwithstanding the provisions of subsection A of this section, the Department shall issue a nonnegotiable title for a foreign market vehicle on submission of a complete application for a title including all necessary documents of ownership. A negotiable title will be issued on proof of compliance as provided in subsection A of this section. The Department shall show on the face of any title issued under this section any negotiable security interests in the motor vehicle as provided in §§46.2-636 through 46.2-643.

G. The Department shall not transfer the title to a foreign market vehicle if ownership of the vehicle is evidenced by a nonnegotiable title, unless the nonnegotiable title owner is deceased. If the nonnegotiable title owner is deceased, a new, nonnegotiable title may be issued to the legatee or distributee in accordance with §§46.2-633 and 46.2-634.

H. A nonnegotiable title may be issued for the purpose of recording a lien. A negotiable certificate of title shall be issued on proof of compliance with all regulations prescribed in this section.

I. Notwithstanding other provisions of this section, the Department shall issue, on application, a temporary, nonrenewable 180-day registration to a foreign market vehicle upon:

1. Proof that the vehicle has been brought into compliance with all federal safety requirements and that the applicant is merely waiting for documentary releases from the Federal Department of Transportation;

2. Proof of satisfactory passage of a Virginia safety inspection; and

3. Submission of a complete application for a title, including all necessary documents of ownership.

J. The Department shall withhold delivery of the certificate of title during the 180-day period of conditional registration and shall not issue the permanent title until the requirements of subsection A of this section have been met.

K. Upon application, the Department shall issue a temporary one-trip permit for the purpose of transporting a foreign market vehicle from the port of entry to the applicant's home or to a conversion facility. The one-trip permit shall be issued in accordance with §46.2-651.

§46.2-603. Issuance of certificate of title and registration card.

The Department, on receiving an application for a certificate of title for a motor vehicle, trailer, or semitrailer, shall issue to the owner a certificate of title and a registration card as separate documents.

§46.2-604. Contents of registration card and certificate; vehicle color data; notation of certain disabled owners.

The registration card and the certificate of title shall each contain the date issued, the registration number assigned to the motor vehicle, trailer, or semitrailer, the name and address of the owner, a description of the registered motor vehicle, trailer, or semitrailer, and other statement of facts as may be determined by the Department. Every applicant for registration or renewal of registration shall indicate on his application the color that best describes the predominant color of the vehicle. In so doing, the applicant shall select a color from a list of standard, primary colors, developed by the Commissioner. Such color information shall be maintained in the Department's records and made available to law-enforcement agencies for their official use and may, in the discretion of the Commissioner, be indicated on the registration card and the certificate of title.

Whenever (i) disabled parking license plates are issued under §46.2-731 or DV disabled parking license plates are issued under subsection B of §46.2-739 and (ii) the vehicle for which such license plates are issued is registered in the name of more than one owner, the registration card for such vehicle shall include a notation indicating which owner or owners of the vehicle is a "person with a disability that limits or impairs his ability to walk" as defined in §46.2-1240. However, no vehicle owned and used by an organization for the transportation of disabled persons shall be subject to the notation requirement imposed by this paragraph.

The registration card shall contain forms for providing notice to the Department of a transfer of the ownership of the motor vehicle, trailer, or semitrailer. Whenever a Virginia-registered motor vehicle is sold or its ownership otherwise transferred, the seller or transferor shall notify the Department of the sale or transfer by completing the appropriate portion of the registration card. Section 46.2-113 shall not apply to failures to provide such notification.

The certificate of title shall contain a statement of the owner's title and of all liens or encumbrances on the motor vehicle, trailer, or semitrailer described in the certificate and whether possession is held by the owner under a lease, contract, or conditional sale or other like agreement. The certificate of title shall also contain forms of assignment of title or interest and warranty of title with space for notation of liens and encumbrances on the motor vehicle, trailer, or semitrailer at the time of a transfer.

(Chgd. by L.1998 chs. 285, 302; L.2000 ch. 667, eff. 7/1/2000.)

§46.2-605. Altering or forging certificate of title, salvage/nonrepairable certificate, or registration card; penalty.

Any person who (i) with fraudulent intent alters any certificate of title, salvage/nonrepairable certificate, or registration card issued by the Department or by any other state, (ii) with fraudulent intent, makes a false statement on any application for a certificate of title, salvage/nonrepairable certificate, or registration card issued by the Department or any other state, (iii) forges or counterfeits any certificate of title, salvage/nonrepairable certificate, or registration card purporting to have been issued by the Department under the provisions of this title or by any other state under a similar law or laws or, with fraudulent intent, alters or falsifies, or forges any assignment of title, or salvage/nonrepairable certificate, (iv) holds or uses any certificate, registration card, or assignment, knowing the same to have been altered, forged, or falsified, shall be guilty of a Class 6 felony.

It shall be unlawful for any person to conspire with any other person to violate the provisions of this section.

(Chgd. by L.1996 chs. 591, 917, eff. 7/1/96.)

§46.2-606. Notice of change of address.

Whenever any person who has applied for or obtained the registration or title to a vehicle moves from the address shown in his application, registration card or certificate of title, he shall notify the Department of his change of address within thirty days.

Anyone failing to comply with this section may be charged a fee of five dollars, to be used to cover the Department's expenses.

(Chgd. by L.1996 chs. 943, 994, eff. 1/1/97.)

§46.2-607. Duplicates for lost or mutilated indicia of titling and registration.

If any license plate, decal, registration card, or certificate of title is lost, mutilated, or has become illegible, the person who is entitled to the certificate shall immediately apply for and obtain a replacement after furnishing information of the fact satisfactory to the Department and after payment of the required fees.

A person who has twice obtained a replacement set of license plates or decals shall not be entitled to obtain another set of license plates or decals during the license period for which the original set of plates was issued unless the Commissioner finds that the replacement license plates or decals have been lost or mutilated without the fault of the person entitled to them.

§46.2-608. When application for registration or certificate of title rejected.

The Department may reject an application for the registration of a motor vehicle, trailer, or semitrailer or certificate of title when:

1. The applicant for registration is not entitled to it under the provisions of this title or Title 43;

2. The applicant has neglected or refused to furnish the Department with the information required on the appropriate official form or other information required by the Department;

3. The required fees have not been paid;

4. The vehicle is not equipped with equipment required by this title or the vehicle is equipped with equipment prohibited by this title;

5. The applicant, if not a resident of the Commonwealth, has not filed with the Commissioner a power of attorney appointing him the applicant's authorized agent or attorney-in-fact upon whom process or notice may be served as required in §46.2-601; or

6. There is reason to believe that the application or accompanying documents have been altered or contain any false statement.

§46.2-609. When registration may be revoked.

The Department may revoke the registration of a motor vehicle, trailer, or semitrailer and may revoke the registration card, license plates, or decals whenever the person to whom the registration card, license plates, or decals have been issued makes or permits to be made an unlawful use of any of them or permits their use by a person not entitled to them, or fails or refuses to pay, within the time prescribed by law, any fuel taxes or other taxes or fees required to be collected or authorized to be collected by the Department regardless of whether the fee applies to that particular vehicle.

§46.2-610. Suspension of registration on theft or embezzlement of vehicle; notices.

Whenever the owner of any motor vehicle, trailer, or semitrailer which is stolen or embezzled notifies the Department directly or through law-enforcement authorities of the theft or embezzlement, the Department shall immediately suspend the registration of that motor vehicle, trailer, or semitrailer until such time as it shall be notified that the owner has recovered his motor vehicle, trailer, or semitrailer. In the event of an embezzlement the owner shall obtain a warrant for the arrest of the person charged with the embezzlement before the Department shall suspend the registration. Any such suspension shall be effective only for the current registration period in which the notice was given. If during that period the motor vehicle, trailer, or semitrailer is not recovered, a new notice may be given with like effect during the ensuing period. Every owner who has given a notice of theft or embezzlement shall immediately notify the Department of the recovery of his motor vehicle, trailer, or semitrailer.

§46.2-611. Appeal.

From any action by the Department under this title suspending or revoking, rescinding or cancelling the registration of any motor vehicle, trailer, or semitrailer or suspending, revoking, cancelling, or repossessing any registration card, license plates, or decals or denying an application for transfer of title, an appeal shall lie in accordance with the Administrative Process Act (§9-6.14:1 et seq.).

§46.2-612. Failure to surrender revoked certificate of title, registration card, license plates or decals.

It shall be unlawful for the owner of any motor vehicle, trailer, or semitrailer, for which license plates, decals, or registration cards have been revoked pursuant to this article, to fail or refuse to surrender to the Department, on demand, a certificate of title if it is incorrect in any material particular, or a revoked registration card, license plates, and decals. Violation of this section shall constitute a Class 2 misdemeanor.

§46.2-613. Offenses relating to registration, licensing, and certificates of title; penalty.

No person shall:

1. Operate or permit the operation of a motor vehicle, trailer, or semitrailer owned, leased, or otherwise controlled by him to be operated on a highway unless (i) it is registered, (ii) a certificate of title therefor has been issued, and (iii) it has displayed on it the license plate or plates and decal or decals, if any, assigned to it by the Department for the current registration period, subject to the exemptions mentioned in §46.2-626, Article 5 (§46.2-655 et seq.), and Article 6 (§46.2-662 et seq.) of this chapter.

2. Display, cause or permit to be displayed, or have in possession any registration card, certificate of title, or license plate or decal which he knows is fictitious or which he knows has been cancelled, revoked, suspended, or altered; or display or cause or permit to be displayed on any motor vehicle, trailer, or semitrailer any license plate or decal that he knows is currently issued for another vehicle.

3. Lend or knowingly permit the use of any registration card, license plate, or decal by anyone not entitled to it.

4. Fail or refuse to surrender to the Department or the Department of State Police, on demand, any certificate of title, registration card, or license plate or decal which has been suspended, cancelled, or revoked.

5. Use a false name or address in any application for the registration of any motor vehicle, trailer, or semitrailer or for a certificate of title or for any renewal or duplicate certificate, or knowingly to make a false statement of a material fact or to conceal a material fact or otherwise commit a fraud in any registration application.

(Chgd. by L.1997 ch. 283; L.1999 ch. 212, eff. 7/1/99.)

§46.2-614. Right to recover damages not affected.

Nothing contained in this chapter shall affect the right of any person injured in his person or property by the negligent operation of any motor vehicle, trailer, semitrailer, or locomotive to sue and recover damages.

§46.2-615. Registration effective after death of owner.

Upon the death of an owner of a registered motor vehicle, trailer, or semitrailer, its registration shall continue in force as a valid registration until (i) the end of the registration period for which the license plates or decals are issued or (ii) the ownership of the motor vehicle, trailer, or semitrailer is transferred before the end of the registration period by the executor or administrator of the estate of the deceased owner or by a legatee or distributee of the estate, as provided in §46.2-632 or §46.2-633, or (iii) its ownership is transferred to a new owner before the end of the registration period by the survivor of its two joint owners.

ARTICLE 2
TITLING VEHICLES

§46.2-616. Acquiring vehicle from vendor who does not have certificate of title.

Except as otherwise provided in this title, no person shall purchase, trade, exchange, or barter for a motor vehicle, trailer, or semitrailer in the Commonwealth, knowing or having reason to believe that its seller has not secured a certificate of title, or knowing or having reason to believe that its seller does not legally have in his possession a certificate of title to the vehicle issued to its owner.

§46.2-617. Sale of vehicle without certificate of title.

Except as provided in §43-34, any person who sells, trades, exchanges, or barters a motor vehicle, trailer, or semitrailer in the Commonwealth without first having secured a certificate of title for it or without legally having in his possession a certificate of title for the vehicle issued to its owner, except as otherwise provided in this title, shall be guilty of a Class 3 misdemeanor.

§46.2-618. When unlawful to have in possession certificate of title issued to another.

It shall constitute a Class 1 misdemeanor for any person in the Commonwealth to possess a certificate of title issued by the Commissioner to a person other than the holder thereof, unless the certificate of title has been assigned to the holder as provided in this title. This section, however, shall apply neither to secured parties who legally hold certificates of title as provided in this title nor to the spouse of the person to whom the certificate of title was issued.

§46.2-619. New indicia of title; procedure as to leased vehicles.

When the Department receives a certificate of title properly assigned and acknowledged, accompanied by an application for registration, it shall register the motor vehicle, trailer, or semitrailer described in the application and shall issue to the person entitled to it by reason of the transfer a new registration card, license plate, or plates and certificate of title in the manner and form and for the fees provided in this chapter for original registration. For leased vehicles, such application shall include, when available, the name and address of the lessee and the name of the locality in which the leased vehicle will be principally garaged or parked. The Department shall also make this information available to the commissioner of the revenue or other assessing officer of the locality in which the leased vehicle is to be principally garaged or parked.
(Chgd. by L.1996 ch. 761, eff. 7/1/96.)

§46.2-620. Period of validity of certificate of title.

Every certificate of title issued under this chapter shall be valid for the life of the motor vehicle, trailer, or semitrailer so long as the owner to whom it is issued shall retain legal title or right of possession of or to the vehicle. Such certificates need not be renewed except on a transfer of title or interest of the owner and except as provided in §46.2-626.

§46.2-621. Application for certificate of title.

The owner of a vehicle, or his duly authorized attorney-in-fact, shall apply for a certificate of title in the name of the owner on appropriate forms prescribed and furnished by the Commissioner. Officers and employees of the Department are vested with the authority to administer oaths and take acknowledgments and affidavits incidental to the administration and enforcement of this section and all other laws relating to the operation of motor vehicles, the collection and refunding of taxes levied on motor fuels and sales and use tax, for which services they shall receive no compensation.

§46.2-622. Issuance of certificate of title in names of joint owners.

When the Department receives an application for a certificate of title for a motor vehicle, trailer, or semitrailer, to be issued in the names of two natural persons, jointly with right of survivorship, the Department shall issue to its owners a certificate of title accordingly. Any certificate issued in the name of two persons may contain an expression such as "or the survivor of them," which shall be deemed sufficient to create joint ownership during the lives of the two owners, and individual ownership in the survivor. A certificate issued in the names of two persons, with their names separated only by "or," shall create joint ownership during the lives of the owners, and individual ownership in the survivor of them.

Nothing herein shall (i) prohibit the issuance of a certificate of title in the names of two or more persons as owners in common which shall be sufficient evidence of ownership of undivided interests in the vehicle or (ii) grant immunity from enforcement of any liability of any person owning the vehicle, as one of two joint owners, to the extent of his interest in the vehicle, during the lives of its owners or (iii) permit the issuance of a certificate of title in the names of two persons as tenants by the entireties.

§46.2-623. Statements in application.

A. Every application for a certificate of title shall contain (i) a statement of the applicant's title and of all liens or encumbrances on the vehicle and the names and addresses of all persons having any interest in the vehicle and the nature of every interest in the vehicle; (ii) the Social Security number, if any, of the owner and, if the application is in the name of an employer for a business vehicle, the employer's identification number assigned by the United States Internal Revenue Service; and (iii) a brief description of the vehicle to be registered, including the name of the maker, the vehicle identification or serial number and, when registering a new vehicle, the date of sale by the manufacturer or dealer to the person first operating the vehicle.

B. Not later than July 15, 1998, the lessor of a qualifying vehicle, as defined in §58.1-3523, shall send a report to the Department for each such qualifying vehicle it was leasing as of July 1, 1998, and has leased between January 1, 1998, and June 30, 1998, containing (i) the name and address of the lessee as it appears in the lease contract; (ii) the social security number of the lessee; and (iii) the registration number of the vehicle as described under Article 1 (§46.2-600 et seq.) of Chapter 6 of Title 46.2.

C. Beginning with August, 1998, such lessor shall send a monthly report to the Department, by the fifteenth day of the month or such later day as may be prescribed in the guidelines promulgated under §58.1-3532, listing any changes, additions or deletions to the information provided under subsection B as of the last day of the preceding month.

D. The application shall contain such additional information as may be required by the Department.

(Chgd. by L.1998 special session I ch. 2, eff. 5/20/98.)

§46.2-624. Information required on transfer of titles of taxicabs or vehicles damaged by water.

A. Unless there is attached to the certificate of title of the vehicle a statement signed by the owner to the effect that the vehicle has been used as a taxicab or has been damaged by water, it shall be unlawful for any person knowingly to sell, transfer, or otherwise dispose of any motor vehicle that:

1. Has been used as a taxicab, or
2. Has been damaged by water to such an extent that the insurance company insuring it has paid a claim of $1,000 or more because of this water damage or has determined the motor vehicle to be a total loss.

B. Violation of subsection A of this section shall constitute a Class 1 misdemeanor.

C. On receipt of a certificate of title to which the information required in subsection A of this section is attached, the Commissioner shall, on issuing a new certificate of title, place an appropriate indicator upon such certificate in order to convey that information to the new owner of the motor vehicle.

§46.2-625. Specially constructed or foreign vehicles.

If a vehicle for which the registration or a certificate of title is applied is a specially constructed, reconstructed, or foreign vehicle, the fact shall be stated in the application and, in the case of any foreign vehicle registered outside the Commonwealth, the owner shall present to the Department the certificate of title and registration card or other evidence of registration as he may have. The Commissioner may require such other evidence of ownership as he may deem advisable and promulgate regulations establishing what additional evidence of ownership, if any, shall be required for titling and registration of specially constructed, reconstructed, or foreign vehicles.

§46.2-626. *(Repealed by L.1996 chs. 591, 917, eff. 7/1/96.)*

§46.2-627. Fee for certificate of title; use in special fund.

The fee to be paid to the Department for the issuance of each original certificate of title shall be ten dollars. The fee to record a supplemental lien and issue a new title shall be six dollars. All fees collected under the provisions of this section shall be paid into the state treasury and set aside as a special fund to be used to meet the expenses of the Department.

§46.2-628. How certificate of title transferred.

The owner of a motor vehicle, trailer, or semitrailer registered under this chapter, when transferring or assigning his title or interest thereto, shall fully and correctly endorse the assignment and warranty of title on the certificate of title of the motor vehicle, trailer, or semitrailer to its purchaser, with a statement of all security interests on it, and shall deliver the certificate to the purchaser or transferee at the time of delivering the motor vehicle, trailer, or semitrailer. Any owner who willfully fails fully and correctly to endorse the assignment and warranty of title shall be guilty of a Class 3 misdemeanor.

§46.2-629. Odometer reading to be reported on certificate of title, application, or power of attorney.

A. Every owner or transferor of any motor vehicle, including a dealer, shall, at the time of transfer of ownership of any motor vehicle by him, record on the certificate of title, if one is currently issued on the vehicle in the Commonwealth, and on any application for certificate of title the reading on the odometer or similar device plus any known additional distance traveled not shown by the odometer or similar device of the motor vehicle at the time of transfer. If, however, a transferor gives his power of attorney to a dealer or other person for the purpose of assigning the transferor's interest in a motor vehicle, the transferor shall conspicuously record on the power of attorney the reading on the odometer or similar device at the time of the assignment.

B. The Department shall not issue to any transferee any new certificate of title to a motor vehicle unless subsection A of this section has been complied with.

C. It shall be unlawful for any person knowingly to record an incorrect odometer or similar device reading plus any known additional distance not shown by the odometer or similar device on any certificate of title or application for a title, or on any power of attorney as described in subsection A of this section.

D. Violation of this section shall constitute a Class 1 misdemeanor.

E. The provisions of subsections A and B of this section shall not apply to transfers under §46.2-633.

§46.2-630. Transfer and application for certificate of title forwarded to Department.

The transferee shall write his name and address in ink on the certificate of title and, except as provided in §§46.2-619 and 46.2-631, shall within thirty days forward the certificate to the Department with an application for the registration of the motor vehicle, trailer, or semitrailer and for a certificate of title.

§46.2-631. When transferred certificate of title need not be forwarded.

When the transferee of a motor vehicle, trailer, or semitrailer is a dealer who holds it for resale and operates it only for sales purposes under a dealer's license plate, the transferee shall not be required to register it nor forward the certificate of title to the Department, as provided in §46.2-630, but the transferee, on transferring his title or interest to another person, shall notify the Department of the transfer and shall endorse and acknowledge an assignment and warranty of title on the certificate and deliver it to the person to whom the transfer is made.

§46.2-632. Transfer when certificate of title lost.

Whenever the applicant for the registration of a motor vehicle, trailer, or semitrailer or a new certificate of title is unable to present a certificate of title because the certificate has been lost or unlawfully detained by one in possession of it or whenever the certificate of title is otherwise not available, the Department may receive the application and investigate the circumstances of the case and may require the filing of affidavits or other information. When the Department is satisfied that the applicant is entitled to the title, it may register the motor vehicle, trailer, or semitrailer and issue a new registration card, license plate, or plates and certificate of title to the person entitled to it.

§46.2-633. Transfer of title by operation of law.

Except as otherwise provided in §46.2-615 in the event of the transfer by operation of law of the title or interest of an owner in and to a motor vehicle, trailer, or semitrailer registered under the provisions of this chapter to anyone as legatee or distributee or as surviving joint owner or by an order in bankruptcy or insolvency, execution sale, sales as provided for in §43-34, repossession on default in the performing of the terms of a lease or executory sales contract or of any written agreement ratified or incorporated in a decree or order of a court of record, or otherwise than by the voluntary act of the person whose title or interest is so transferred, the transferee or his legal representative shall apply to the Department for a certificate of title, giving the name and address of the person entitled to it, and accompany his application with the registration card and certificate of title previously issued for the motor vehicle, trailer, or semitrailer, if available, together with whatever instruments or documents of authority, or certified copies of them, are required by law to evidence or effect a transfer of title or interest in or to chattels in the case. The Department shall cancel the registration of the motor vehicle, trailer, or semitrailer and issue a new certificate of title to the person entitled to it.

§46.2-634. Transfer of title when no qualification on estate.

If the holder of a certificate of title is dead and there has been no qualification on his estate, a transfer may be made by a legatee or distributee if there is presented to the Department a statement made by a legatee or distributee to the effect that there has not been and there is not expected to be a qualification on the estate and that the decedent's debts have been paid or that the proceeds from the sale of the motor vehicle will be applied against his debts. The statement shall contain the name, residence at the time of death, date of death, and the names of any other persons having an interest in the motor vehicle which is sought to be transferred and, if these persons are of legal age, they shall signify in writing their consent to the transfer of the title.

§46.2-635. Surrender of certificates for vehicles to be demolished; securing new title certificates.

Every person disposing of a motor vehicle, trailer, or semitrailer which is to be demolished shall make an assignment of title to the transferee as provided in §46.2-628. The assigned certificate of title, when available, however, shall be delivered to the Department, accompanied by a form provided by the Commissioner, stating that the vehicle is to be demolished. On receipt of this form and the assigned title, the Commissioner shall forward to the transferee a receipt for them.

If the person, in lieu of demolishing the vehicle, sells, transfers, or operates the motor vehicle, trailer, or semitrailer, he shall first secure a certificate of title from the Department. Before issuing the new certificate of title, the Department shall inspect, or have inspected, the reconstructed vehicle.

If a motor vehicle, trailer, or semitrailer obtained for use or resale, is subsequently demolished, the owner shall immediately surrender its certificate of title to the Department.

§46.2-636. Certificate to show security interests.

When the Department receives an application for a certificate of title to a motor vehicle, trailer, or semitrailer showing security interests on the motor vehicle, trailer, or semitrailer, the certificate of title issued by the Department to the owner of the vehicle shall show all security interests disclosed by the application. All security interests shown on the certificate of title shall be shown in the order of their priority according to the information contained in the application.

§46.2-637. Security interests subsequently created.

Security interests, other than those in inventory held for sale, in motor vehicles, trailers, or semitrailers created by the voluntary act of the owner after the original issue of a certificate of title to the owner must be shown on the certificate of title. In such cases, the owner shall file an application with the Department on a form furnished for that purpose, setting forth the security interests and whatever additional information the Department may deem necessary. If satisfied that it is proper for the security interest to be recorded, when the certificate of title covering the motor vehicle, trailer, or semitrailer, is surrendered, the Department shall issue a new certificate of title, showing security interests in the order of their priority according to the date of the filing of the application. For the purpose of recording a subsequent security interest, the Commissioner may require any secured party to deliver to him the certificate of title. The new certificate shall be sent or delivered to the secured party from whom the prior certificate was obtained. Notwithstanding any other provision of law, a security interest in a motor vehicle, trailer, or semitrailer which is inventory held for sale shall be perfected only as provided in §§8.9-301 through 8.9-408.

§46.2-638. Certificate as notice of security interest.

A certificate of title, when issued by the Department showing a security interest, shall be adequate notice to the Commonwealth, creditors, and purchasers that a security interest in the motor vehicle exists and the recording or filing of such creation or reservation of a security interest in the county or city wherein the purchaser or debtor resides or elsewhere is not necessary and shall not be required. Motor vehicles, trailers or semitrailers, other than those which are inventory held for sale, registered or for which a certificate of title shall have been issued under this title shall not be subjected to, but shall be exempt from the provisions of §§8.9-301 through 8.9-408 and §55-96 whether or not inventory held for sale shall be exempt from the provisions of §55-152, nor shall recordation or filing of such security interest, except a security interest in inventory held for sale in any other place for any other purpose, be required or have any effect.

§46.2-639. Security interest may be filed within thirty days after purchase.

If application for the registration or recordation of a security interest to be placed on a motor vehicle, trailer, or semitrailer is filed with the Department, it shall be deemed perfected as of the date of filing, and, if the date of filing is within thirty days from the date of an applicant's purchase of the motor vehicle, trailer, or semitrailer, it shall be as valid as

to all persons, including the Commonwealth, as if that registration had been accomplished on the day the security interest was acquired.
(Chgd. by L.2000 ch. 71, eff. 7/1/2000.)

§46.2-640. Priority of security interests shown on certificates of title.

The security interests, except security interests in motor vehicles, trailers and semitrailers which are inventory held for sale and are perfected under §§8.9-301 through 8.9-408, shown upon such certificates of title issued by the Department pursuant to applications for same shall have priority over any other liens or security interests against such motor vehicle, trailer, or semitrailer, however created and recorded. The foregoing provisions of this section shall not apply to liens for taxes as provided in §58.1-3942, liens of keepers of garages to the extent given by §43-32 and liens of mechanics for repairs to the extent given by §43-33 if the requirements therefor exist, provided the garage keeper or mechanic furnishes the holder of any recorded lien who may request it with an itemized sworn statement of the storage charges, work done, and materials supplied for which the lien is claimed.
(Chgd. by L.1999 ch. 299, eff. 7/1/99.)

§46.2-640.1. Vehicle leases that are not sales or security interests.

Notwithstanding any other provision of law, in the case of motor vehicles, trailers or semi-trailers, a transaction does not create a sale or security interest merely because it provides that the rental price is permitted or required to be adjusted under the agreement either upward or downward by reference to the amount realized upon sale or other disposition of the motor vehicle or trailer.

§46.2-641. Who to hold certificate of title subject to security interest.

The certificate of title of a motor vehicle, trailer, or semitrailer shall be delivered to the person holding the security interest having first priority on the motor vehicle, trailer, or semitrailer and retained by him until the entire amount of his security interest is fully paid by the owner. When the security interest is fully paid, the certificate of title shall be delivered to the secured party next in order of priority or, if none, then to the owner.

§46.2-642. Release of security interest shown on certificate of title.

When an owner secures the release of any security interest on a motor vehicle, trailer, or semitrailer shown on its certificate of title, he may exhibit the documents evidencing the release, signed by the person or persons making the release, and the certificate of title to the Department. However, when it is impossible to secure the release from the secured party, the owner may exhibit to the Department whatever evidence may be available showing that the debt secured has been satisfied, together with a statement by the owner under oath that the debt has been paid. The Department, when satisfied as to the genuineness and regularity of the release, shall issue to the owner either a new certificate of title or an endorsement or rider showing the release of the security interest, which the Department shall attach to the outstanding certificate of title.

§46.2-643. Surrender of certificate of title required when security interest paid.

It shall constitute a Class 3 misdemeanor for a secured party who holds a certificate of title as provided in this title to refuse or fail to mark satisfied and surrender it to the person legally entitled thereto within ten days after his security interest is satisfied.

§46.2-644. Levy of execution.

A levy made by virtue of an execution, fieri facias, or other court order, on a motor vehicle, trailer, or semitrailer for which a certificate of title has been issued by the Department, shall constitute a lien, subsequent to security interests previously recorded by the Department and subsequent to security interests in inventory held for sale and perfected as otherwise permitted by law, when the officer making the levy reports to the Department on forms provided by the Department, that the levy has been made and that the motor vehicle, trailer, or semitrailer levied on has been seized by him. If the lien is thereafter satisfied or should the motor vehicle, trailer, or semitrailer thus levied on and seized thereafter be released by the officer, he shall immediately report that fact to the Department. Any owner who, after the levy and seizure by an officer and before the officer reports the levy and seizure to the Department, shall fraudulently assign or transfer his title to or interest in a motor vehicle, trailer, or semitrailer or cause its certificate of title to be assigned or transferred or cause a security interest to be shown on its certificate of title shall be guilty of a Class 1 misdemeanor.

ARTICLE 3
REGISTRATION OF VEHICLES

§46.2-645. Registration of vehicles.

The Department shall file each motor vehicle registration application received and, when satisfied that the applicant is entitled to register the vehicle, shall register the vehicle.

§46.2-646. Expiration and renewal of registration.

A. Every registration under this title, unless otherwise provided, shall expire on the last day of the twelfth month next succeeding the date of registration. Every registration, unless otherwise provided, shall be renewed annually on application by the owner and by payment of the fees required by law, the renewal to take effect on the first day of the month succeeding the date of expiration.

B. All motor vehicles, trailers, and semitrailers registered in the Commonwealth shall, at the discretion of the Commissioner, be placed in a system of registration on a monthly basis to distribute the work of registering motor vehicles as uniformly as practicable throughout the twelve months of the year. All such motor vehicles, trailers, and semitrailers, unless otherwise provided, shall be registered for a period of twelve months. The registration shall be extended, at the discretion of the Commissioner, on receipt of appropriate prorated fees, as required by law, for a period of not less than one month nor more than eleven months as is necessary to distribute the registrations as equally as practicable on a monthly basis. The Commissioner shall, on request, assign to any owner or owners of two or more motor vehicles, trailers, or semitrailers the same registration period. The expiration date shall be the last day of the twelfth month or the last day of the designated month. Except for motor vehicles, trailers, and semitrailers registered for more than one year under subsection C of this section, every registration shall be renewed annually on application by the owner and by payment of fees required by law, the renewal to take effect on the first day of the succeeding month.

C. The Commissioner may offer, at his discretion, an optional multi-year registration for all motor vehicles, trailers, and semitrailers except for (i) those registered under the International Registration Plan and (ii) those registered as uninsured motor vehicles. When this option is offered and chosen by the registrant, all annual and twelve-month fees due at the time of registration shall be multiplied by the number of years or fraction thereof that the vehicle will be registered.

§46.2-647. Grace period for replacement of license plates or decals and renewal of registrations.

The Commissioner may, on finding either that the Department is unable to efficiently handle the replacement of license plates or decals or the renewal of registrations scheduled to expire during a specific month, or that persons seeking to secure license plates, decals, or registration renewals are, as a group, unable to do so without being substantially inconvenienced, declare a grace period for the replacement of license plates or decals and the renewal of registrations. The declaration of a grace period shall have the effect of postponing the expiration of those license plates, decals, and registrations scheduled to expire on the last day of that month to the fifteenth day of the succeeding month.

§46.2-648. Registration of logging vehicles.

On receipt of an application on a form prescribed by him, the Commissioner shall register in a separate category trucks, tractor trucks, trailers, and semitrailers used exclusively in connection with logging operations. For the purposes of this section, the term "logging" shall mean the harvesting of timber and transportation from forested sites to places of sale.

Fees for the registration of vehicles under this section shall be the same as those ordinarily charged for the type of vehicle being registered.

§46.2-648.1. Optional registration of tow dolly and converter gear.

The Department may, upon request, register any tow dolly or converter gear as defined in §46.2-1119. For the purpose of determining the applicable fee for any such registration, the tow dolly or converter gear shall be considered a trailer and the registration fee determined in accordance with §46.2-694.1. The fee for reserved numbers or letters on license plates for any tow dolly or converter gear shall be determined in accordance with §46.2-726.

(Added by L.1999 ch. 593, eff. 7/1/99.)

§46.2-649. Certain vehicles required to show evidence of payment of taxes and of registration or exemption from registration with Department of Motor Vehicles.

A. Before the Commissioner registers or reregisters any motor vehicle, trailer, or semitrailer under §§46.2-697, 46.2-698, 46.2-700 or §46.2-703, the applicant shall furnish evidence satisfactory to the Commissioner that all state, local, and federal taxes levied on that motor vehicle, trailer, or semitrailer have been paid and that the motor vehicle, trailer, or semitrailer either (i) is registered with the Department as required by law or (ii) is not required so to register.

B. The Commissioner, in consultation with local commissioners of the revenue and directors of finance, and with appropriate federal officials, by regulation shall provide for the kinds of evidence required to satisfy the provisions of subsection A of this section.

C. The provisions of this section shall not apply to (i) pickup trucks, (ii) panel trucks, or (iii) trucks having a registered gross weight less than 33,000 pounds.

(Chgd. by L.1997 ch. 283, eff. 7/1/97.)

§46.2-649.1. Registration of tow trucks; fees.

A. For the purposes of this section, "tow truck" means a motor vehicle for hire (i) designed to lift, pull, or carry another vehicle by means of a hoist or other mechanical apparatus and (ii) having a manufacturer's gross vehicle weight rating of at least 10,000 pounds. The term "tow truck" also includes vehicles designed with a ramp on wheels and a hydraulic lift with a capacity to haul or tow another vehicle, commonly referred to as "rollbacks." The term "tow truck" does not include any "automobile or watercraft transporter," "stinger-steered automobile or watercraft transporter," or "tractor truck" as those terms are defined in §46.2-100.

B. No tow truck registered under this section shall be subject to registration under the international registration plan or subject to any other state registration requirements under this chapter. Registration under this section shall not prohibit the use of "rollbacks" to transport storage sheds, similar structures, or other cargoes.

C. Vehicles registered under this section shall be subject to the following annual fees, based upon their manufacturer's gross vehicle weight ratings:

less than 15,000 pounds	$ 100
15,000 to 22,999 pounds	$ 200
23,000 to 29,499 pounds	$ 300
more than 29,499 pounds	$ 400

D. Motor vehicles having manufacturer's gross vehicle weight ratings of at least 7,000 but less than 10,000 pounds that otherwise would meet the definition of "tow truck" under subsection A of this section may, until January 1, 2000, be registered under this section as long as (i) the vehicle is continuously registered under this section and (ii) the title to the vehicle is not transferred to another owner prior to that time.

E. No vehicle shall be registered under this section unless there is in force as to such vehicle at the time of its registration commercial liability insurance coverage for those classes of insurance defined in §§38.2-117 and 38.2-118 in the amount of at least $750,000.

§46.2-649.1:1. Registration of vehicles owned and used by volunteer rescue squads or volunteer fire departments.

Upon application therefor, the Commissioner shall register and issue permanent license plates without year or month decals for display on any (i) firefighting truck, trailer, and semitrailer on which firefighting apparatus is permanently attached when any such vehicle is owned or under exclusive control of a volunteer fire department or (ii) ambulance or other vehicle owned or used exclusively by a volunteer fire department or volunteer lifesaving or first aid crew or rescue squad if any such vehicle is used exclusively as an ambulance or lifesaving and first aid vehicle and is not rented, leased, or lent to any private individual, firm, or corporation, and no charge is made by the organization for the use of the vehicle. The equipment shall be painted a distinguishing color and conspicuously display in letters and figures not less than three inches in height the identity of the volunteer fire department, lifesaving or first aid crew or rescue squad having control of its operation.

No fee shall be charged for any vehicle registration or license plate issuance under this section.
(Added by L.1999 ch. 329, eff. 7/1/99.)

§46.2-649.2. Certain vehicles to comply with clean alternative fuel fleet standards prior to registration; penalty.

The Commissioner shall not register a motor vehicle subject to §46.2-1179.1 which does not comply with the requirements of that section. Upon a determination that a motor vehicle is exempt from the requirements of §46.2-1179.1, it shall forever be exempt, and the exemption shall be noted on its title. Whoever, through fraud or misrepresentation, procures or attempts to procure the registration of a motor vehicle in violation of the provisions of this section shall be guilty of a Class 1 misdemeanor.

ARTICLE 4
TEMPORARY REGISTRATION

§46.2-650. Temporary permits or duplicate applications.

The Department may promulgate regulations providing that on application for a certificate of title and registration of a vehicle, either new or after a transfer, the vehicle may be operated on the highway under (i) a temporary permit issued by the Department or (ii) a duplicate application carried in the vehicle.

§46.2-651. One-trip permits; regulations; fees.

A. The Department may, on application on forms provided by the Department, issue a one-trip permit to any owner of a motor vehicle, trailer, or semitrailer which would otherwise be subject to registration plates but is not currently registered. If the vehicle operating under the permit is a vehicle designed as a property-carrying vehicle, it shall be unladen at the time of operation under the permit. The permit shall be valid for three days and shall show the registration or permit number, the date of issue, the date of expiration, the make of vehicle, the vehicle identification number, the beginning point and the point of destination. Any vehicle so operated shall only operate between the beginning and destination points. The fee for the permit shall be five dollars.

B. For vehicles to be purchased in another state by a Virginia resident and registered in Virginia, the Department shall issue to the prospective purchaser upon his application therefor one-trip permits as provided in subsection A of this section, except that permits issued under this subsection shall not be valid unless and until the prospective purchaser receives an original bill of sale pertaining to the vehicle purchased. Permits issued under this subsection shall be valid for three days, beginning on the date of the original bill of sale, and shall be kept with the original bill of sale in the purchased vehicle at all times during the trip until the vehicle is properly registered with the Department. Any vehicle so operated shall only operate between the beginning and destination points. The Commissioner may charge a reasonable fee, adequate to recover the Department's costs, for the issuance of permits under this subsection, and may promulgate such regulations as he deems necessary or convenient in carrying out the provisions of this subsection.
(Chgd. by L.2000 ch. 144, eff. 7/1/2000.)

§46.2-652. Temporary registration for vehicles.

The Commonwealth Transportation Commissioner, in cooperation with the Commissioner may grant a temporary registration or permit for the operation of (i) a vehicle or equipment that cannot be licensed because the vehicle, excluding any load thereon, is overweight, oversize, or both or (ii) a licensed vehicle that exceeds statutory weight limits on the highways in the Commonwealth from one point to another within the Commonwealth, or from the Commonwealth to a point or points outside the Commonwealth, or from outside the Commonwealth to a point or points within the Commonwealth. Any temporary registration or permit issued under this section shall show the registration or permit number, the date of issue, the date of expiration, and the route to be traveled or other restrictions and shall be displayed in a prominent place on the vehicle.

For a single-trip temporary registration or permit issued under this section, the applicant shall pay a fee of ten cents per mile for every mile to be traveled, in addition to any administrative fee required by the Department of Transportation. In lieu of a single-trip permit, an annual multi-trip permit may be issued for a fee of forty dollars, in addition to any administrative fee required by the Department of Transportation.
(Chgd. by L.1997 ch. 283, eff. 7/1/97.)

§46.2-653. Temporary registration or permit for transportation of manufactured homes or house trailers exceeding the size permitted by law.

The Commonwealth Transportation Commissioner, in cooperation with the Commissioner may grant a temporary registration or permit for the transportation of manufactured homes or house trailers, which exceed the size permitted by law, on the highways in the Commonwealth from one point to another within the Commonwealth, or from the Commonwealth to a point or points outside the Commonwealth, or from outside the Commonwealth to a point or points within the Commonwealth. Such temporary registration or permit shall show the registration or permit number, the date of issue, the date of expiration, and the route to be traveled or other restrictions and shall be displayed in a prominent place on the vehicle. The owner of every manufactured home or house trailer of this sort purchased in the Commonwealth for use within the Commonwealth or brought into the Commonwealth for use within the Commonwealth shall apply within thirty days to the Department for title in the name of the owner. This requirement shall not apply to inventory held by licensed Virginia dealers for the purpose of resale. After a manufactured home has been titled in the Commonwealth and at such time as the wheels and other equipment previously used for mobility have been removed and the unit has been attached to the realty, then the Virginia title issued for the unit may be returned to the Department for cancellation and the unit shall thereafter be transferred only as real estate is transferred. The validity of any security interest perfected pursuant to §§46.2-636 through 46.2-641 shall continue, notwithstanding the provisions of this section.

The authorities in cities and towns regulating the movement of traffic may prescribe the route or routes over which these manufactured homes or house trailers may be transported, and no manufactured home or house trailer of this sort shall be transported through any city or town except along a prescribed route or routes.

For each temporary single-trip registration or permit issued hereunder, the applicant shall pay a fee of one dollar, in addition to any administrative fee required by the Department of Transportation. In lieu of a single-trip permit, an annual multi-trip permit may be issued for a fee of forty dollars, in addition to any administrative fee required by the Department of Transportation.

No permit, as provided in this section, shall be issued covering any manufactured home or house trailer that is subject to a license plate.

(Chgd. by L.1997 ch. 283; L.1999 ch. 77, eff. 7/1/99.)

§46.2-654. Issuance of temporary registration certificates by motor vehicle auctions.

In addition to the provisions of §46.2-1542, businesses licensed by the Department to conduct sales of motor vehicles by auction may issue to persons who purchase motor vehicles through auctions conducted by these businesses temporary certificates of registration.

Issuance of certificates under this section shall be subject to regulations promulgated by the Commissioner.

ARTICLE 5
RECIPROCITY FOR NONRESIDENTS

Section

§46.2-655. Reciprocity required.

The privileges extended under this article to nonresident owners of foreign motor vehicles, trailers, and semitrailers operated in the Commonwealth are extended only on condition that the same privileges are granted by the state of the United States or foreign country wherein such nonresident owners are residents to residents of the Commonwealth operating motor vehicles, trailers, or semitrailers in such state of the United States or foreign country.

§46.2-656. Nonresident may operate temporarily without registration.

Except as otherwise provided in this article, a nonresident owner of a passenger car which has been registered for the current calendar year in the state or country of which the owner is a resident and which at all times when operated in the Commonwealth displays the license plate or plates issued for such vehicle in the place of residence of such owner, may operate or permit the operation of such passenger car within or partly within this Commonwealth for a period of six months without registering the passenger car or paying any fees to the Commonwealth. If, however, at the expiration of such six months the passenger car is still in the Commonwealth, its owner shall apply for registration of the vehicle and shall pay a fee for such registration based on the time operation of the vehicle in the Commonwealth commenced.

§46.2-657. When registration by nonresident not required.

Notwithstanding other provisions of this article, any nonresident from a state that does not require the registration of a vehicle like that owned by such nonresident when such vehicle is owned and operated by a resident of Virginia in the state in which the foreign vehicle owned or operated by such nonresident is registered, shall not be required to register such vehicle in the Commonwealth. This section, however, shall not permit the operation of any truck, trailer, or semitrailer the weight, length, width, or height of which vehicle or combination of vehicles is in violation of the provisions of this title or at a speed in violation of this title; nor shall the privileges provided in this section apply to common carriers or passenger cars.

§46.2-658. Regular operation other than for pleasure.

Except as provided in §46.2-657, a nonresident owner of a foreign motor vehicle, trailer, or semitrailer which is regularly operated in the Commonwealth, or from a point or points outside the Commonwealth to a point or points within the Commonwealth, or from a point or points within the Commonwealth to a point or points outside the Commonwealth, or through the Commonwealth, for purposes other than purposes of pleasure, shall, unless otherwise provided in this chapter, register such vehicle and pay the same fees therefor as are required with reference to like vehicles owned by residents of the Commonwealth. Any owner who operates or permits to be operated one or more of these vehicles either simultaneously or alternately as often as four times in any one month shall be considered to be regularly operating them in the Commonwealth.

§46.2-659. *(Repealed by L.1997 ch. 283, eff. 7/1/97.)*

§46.2-660. Operating vehicles in business in Commonwealth.

Every nonresident, including any foreign corporation, conducting business in the Commonwealth and owning and regularly operating in such business any motor vehicle, trailer, or semitrailer in the Commonwealth shall be required to register the vehicle and pay the same fees required for registration of similar vehicles owned by residents of the Commonwealth.

§46.2-661. Extension of reciprocal privileges.

Notwithstanding the other provisions of this chapter, the Commissioner, with the consent of the Governor, may extend to the owners of foreign vehicles operated in the Commonwealth the same privileges which are granted by the state of the United States or foreign country wherein the owners of the foreign vehicles are residents to residents of this Commonwealth operating vehicles in such state of the United States or foreign country.

ARTICLE 6
EXEMPTIONS FROM REGISTRATION

Section

§46.2-662. Temporary exemption for new resident operating vehicle registered in another state or country.

A resident owner of any passenger car, pickup or panel truck, or motorcycle, other than those provided for in §46.2-652, which has been duly registered for the current calendar year in another state or country and which at all times when operated in the Commonwealth displays the license plate or plates issued for the vehicle in the other state or country, may operate or permit the operation of the passenger car, pickup or panel truck, or motorcycle within or partly within the Commonwealth for the first thirty days of his residency in the Commonwealth without registering the passenger car, pickup or panel truck, or motorcycle or paying any fees to the Commonwealth.

§46.2-663. Backhoes.

No person shall be required to obtain the registration certificate, license plates, and decals or to pay a registration fee for any backhoe operated on any highway for a distance of no more than twenty miles from its operating base.

§46.2-664. Vehicles used for spraying fruit trees and other plants.

No person shall be required to obtain the registration certificate, license plates and decals, or pay a registration fee for any vehicle on which is securely attached a machine for spraying fruit trees and other plants of the owner or lessee of the truck.

§46.2-665. Vehicles used for agricultural or horticultural purposes.

A. No person shall be required to obtain the registration certificate, license plates and decals, or pay a registration fee for any motor vehicle, trailer, or semitrailer used exclusively for agricultural or horticultural purposes on lands owned or leased by the vehicle's owner.

B. This exemption shall only apply to vehicles which are not operated on or over any public highway in this Commonwealth for any purpose other than:

1. Crossing a highway;

2. Operating along a highway for a distance of no more than thirty miles from one part of the owner's land to another, irrespective of whether the tracts adjoin;

3. Taking the vehicle or attached fixtures to and from a repair shop for repairs;

4. Taking another vehicle exempt from registration under any provision of §§46.2-664 through 46.2-668 or §46.2-672, or any part or subcomponent of such a vehicle, to or from a repair shop for repairs, including return trips;

5. Operating along a highway to and from a refuse disposal facility for the purpose of disposing of trash and garbage generated on a farm; or

6. Operating along a highway for a distance of no more than thirty miles for the purpose of obtaining seeds, fertilizers, chemicals, or animal feed and returning.

(Chgd. by L.2000 ch. 318, eff. 7/1/2000.)

§46.2-666. Vehicles used for seasonal transportation of farm produce and livestock.

No person shall be required to obtain the registration certificate, license plates and decals, or pay a registration fee prescribed for any motor vehicle, trailer, or semitrailer owned by the owner or lessee of a farm and used by him on a seasonal basis in transporting farm produce and livestock along public highways for a distance of no more than thirty miles or the distance to the nearest storage house, packing plant, or market, but in no event more than fifty miles.

(Chgd. by L.1995 ch. 126; L.1998 ch. 323, eff. 7/1/98.)

§46.2-667. Farm machinery and tractors.

No person shall be required to obtain the registration certificate, license plates and decals, or pay the prescribed fee for any farm machinery or tractor when operated on a highway (i) between one tract of land and another regardless of whether the land is owned by the same person or (ii) to and from a repair shop for repairs.

(Chgd. by L.1996 ch. 55; L.2000 ch. 318, eff. 7/1/2000.)

§46.2-668. Vehicles validly registered in other states and used in conjunction with harvesting operations.

A. No person shall be required to obtain the registration certificate, license plates and decals, or pay a registration fee for any motor vehicle, trailer, or semitrailer which is validly registered in another state and bears valid license plates issued by that state when the use of the vehicle has been contracted for by the owner or lessee of a farm as an incidental part of the harvesting of a crop from his farm. This exemption shall only be valid while the vehicle is engaged in transporting farm produce from the farm:

1. As an incidental part of harvesting operations;

2. Along a public highway for a distance of not more than twenty miles to a storage house, packing plant, market, or transportation terminal;

3. When the use is a seasonal operation; and

4. When the owner of the vehicle has secured from the Commissioner an exemption permit for each vehicle.

B. The Commissioner, upon receipt of certification by the Superintendent of State Police that a vehicle is entitled to the exemption set forth in this subsection, shall issue an exemption permit on a form prescribed by him. The exemption permit shall be carried at all times by the operator of the vehicle for which it is issued or displayed in a conspicuous place on the vehicle. The exemption permit shall be valid for a period of ninety days from date of issue and shall be renewable by the procedure set forth in the foregoing provisions of this section.

§46.2-669. Tractors and similar vehicles owned by sawmill operators.

No person shall be required to obtain the registration certificate, license plates and decals, or pay a registration fee for any tractor, trailer, log cart, or similar vehicle owned by a sawmill operator when the vehicle is operated or moved:

1. Along a highway from one sawmill or sawmill site to another;

2. To or from a repair shop for repairs; or

3. Across a highway from one contiguous tract of land to another.

§46.2-670. Vehicles owned by farmers and used to transport certain wood products.

No person shall be required to obtain the registration certificate, license plates and decals, or pay a registration fee for any motor vehicle, trailer, or semitrailer owned by a farm owner when the vehicle is operated or moved along a highway for no more than twenty miles between a sawmill or sawmill site and his farm to transport sawdust, wood shavings, slab wood, and other wood wastes.

§46.2-671. Vehicles used at mines.

No person shall be required to obtain the registration certificate, license plates and decals, or pay a registration fee for any motor vehicle, trailer, or semitrailer used at mines when operated on the highway for no more than twenty miles between mines or to or from a repair shop for repairs.

§46.2-672. Certain vehicles transporting fertilizer, cotton, or peanuts.

No person shall be required to obtain the registration certificate, license plates and decals, or pay a registration fee for any motor vehicle or trailer, semitrailer, or fertilizer spreader drawn by a farm tractor used by a farmer, his tenant, agent or employee or a cotton ginner, peanut buyer, or fertilizer distributor to transport unginned cotton, peanuts, or fertilizer owned by the farmer, cotton ginner, peanut buyer, or fertilizer distributor from one farm to another, from farm to gin, from farm to dryer, from farm to market, or from fertilizer distributor to farm and on return to the distributor.

The provisions of this section shall not apply to vehicles operated on a for-hire basis.

§46.2-673. Return trips of exempted farm vehicles.

No person shall be required to obtain the registration certificate, license plates and decals, or pay a registration fee for any farm vehicle exempted from registration under the provisions of this article when that vehicle is:

1. Making a return trip from any marketplace;
2. Transporting back to a farm ordinary and essential food and other products for home and farm use; or
3. Transporting supplies to the farm.

§46.2-674. Vehicles used by commercial fishermen.

No person shall be required to obtain the registration certificate, license plates and decals, or pay a registration fee for any motor vehicle, trailer, or semitrailer used by commercial fishermen, their agents, or employees for the purpose of:

1. Transporting boats or other equipment used in commercial fishing no more than thirty miles between his place of residence or business and the waters within the territorial limits of the Commonwealth or the adjacent marginal seas;
2. Any return trip to his place of residence or business; or
3. Transporting harvested seafood no more than thirty miles between the place where the seafood is first brought ashore and the transporter's place of business or the location of the seafood's first point of sale.

(Chgd. by L.1997 ch. 500, eff. 7/1/97.)

§46.2-675. Certain vehicles engaged in mining or quarrying operations; permit when such vehicle required to cross public highways.

No person shall be required to obtain the registration certificate, license plates and decals or to pay a registration fee prescribed for any motor vehicle engaged in coal mining operations or other types of mining and quarrying operations, if the sole function of the motor vehicle is to haul coal from mine to tipple or to haul other mined or quarried products from mine or quarry to a processing plant. The owner of the vehicle, however, shall first obtain, without charge, a permit from the Commonwealth Transportation Commissioner in any case in which the motor vehicle is required to cross the public highways. The Commonwealth Transportation Commissioner shall not issue the permit unless he is satisfied that the owner of the motor vehicle has, at his own expense, strengthened the highway crossing so that it will adequately bear the load and has provided adequate signs, lights, or flagmen as may be required for the protection of the public. Any damage done to the highways as a result of this operation shall be repaired in a manner satisfactory to the Commonwealth Transportation Commissioner at the expense of the vehicle's owner.

§46.2-676. Golf carts.

A. No person shall be required to obtain the registration certificates, license plates or decals, or to pay any registration fee, for any golf cart which is not operated on or over any public highway in the Commonwealth for any other purpose other than operating it across a highway from one portion of a golf course to another portion thereof or to another adjacent golf course. Nor shall any person be required to obtain registration certificates, license plates or decals, or to pay any fees to operate a golf cart across any highway if the person driving the golf cart has with him in the vehicle a valid special parking placard issued to him under §46.2-1241.

B. No person shall be required to obtain registration certificates, license plates or decals, or to pay any registration fee to operate a golf cart along a road between his home and golf course if: (i) the trip would not be longer than one-half mile in either direction, (ii) the speed limit on the road is no more than thirty-five miles per hour, (iii) the driver of the vehicle is at least sixteen years old, and (iv) while operating along a highway, the vehicle displays a slow-moving vehicle emblem in conformity with §46.2-1081.

C. No person shall be required to obtain registration certificates, license plates or decals, or to pay any registration fee to operate a golf cart owned by the County of Halifax on the public highways if such golf cart displays a slow-moving vehicle emblem in conformity with §46.2-1081 and is being operated on highways with speed limits of thirty-five miles per hour or less within the Town of Halifax on official business of the maintenance department of the County of Halifax by an employee of that department who is a licensed driver.

D. No person shall be required to obtain registration certificates, license plates or decals, or to pay any registration fee to operate a golf cart owned by the County of Goochland on the public highways if such golf cart displays a slow-moving vehicle emblem in conformity with §46.2-1081 and is being operated on highways with speed limits of thirty-five miles per hour or less at Goochland Courthouse on official business of the maintenance department of the County of Goochland by an employee of that department who is a licensed driver.

E. No person shall be required to obtain registration certificates, license plates or decals, or to pay any registration fee, to operate a golf cart, utility vehicle, or similar vehicle intended for off-road use having no more than twenty-five horsepower, on any highway within the property limits of any public or private two-year or four-year institution of higher education, provided such vehicle: (i) displays a slow-moving vehicle emblem in conformity with §46.2-1081, (ii) is being operated on highways with speed limits of thirty-five miles per hour or less, and (iii) is operated by an employee of the institution of higher education who is a licensed driver, on official business of such institution.

F. Every vehicle operated upon a highway pursuant to this section shall be operated only between sunrise and sunset unless equipped with such lights as are required in

Article 3 (§46.2-1010 et seq.) of Chapter 10 of this title, for different classes of vehicles.
(Chgd. by L.1995 ch. 670; L.1996 ch. 920; L.1997 chs. 485, 783, 904; L.1999 ch. 211, eff. 7/1/99.)

§46.2-677. Self-propelled wheel chairs.

No person shall be required to obtain the registration certificate, license plates and decals, or pay any registration fee for any self-propelled wheelchair or self-propelled wheelchair conveyance provided it is:

1. Operated by a person who is capable of operating it properly and safely but who, by reason of physical disability, is otherwise unable to move about as a pedestrian; and
2. Not operated on a public highway in this Commonwealth except to the extent necessary to cross the highway.

§46.2-678. Forklift trucks.

A. No person shall be required to obtain the registration certificate, license plates and decals, or pay a registration fee for any forklift truck provided it is:

1. Operated by a person holding a valid Virginia driver's license;
2. Operated along or across highways only in traveling from one plant, factory, or job site to another by the most direct route;
3. Not carrying or transporting any object or person, other than the driver;
4. Displaying a slow-moving vehicle emblem in conformity with §46.2-1081;
5. In compliance with requirements of the federal Occupational Safety and Health Administration;
6. Not operated on or along any limited access highway; and
7. Not operated for a distance of more than ten miles.

B. For the purposes of this section, "forklift truck" means a self-propelled machine used for hoisting and transporting heavy objects by means of steel fingers inserted under the load.

§46.2-679. Snowmobiles.

No person shall be required to obtain the registration certificate, license plates and decals, or pay a registration fee for any snowmobile.

§46.2-680. Vehicles transporting oyster shells.

No person shall be required to obtain the registration certificates, license plates and decals, or to pay any registration fee for any motor vehicle properly registered in Maryland and used for the purpose of hauling oyster shells for a distance of less than three miles on a public highway of this Commonwealth to navigable waters to be further transported by water to Maryland.

§46.2-681. *(Repealed by L.1999 ch. 329, eff. 7/1/99.)*

§46.2-682. Tractors, rollers, and other machinery used for highway purposes.

Tractors, rollers, and other machinery used for highway purposes need not be registered under this chapter.

§46.2-683. Traction engines; vehicles operating on rails.

Nothing in this chapter shall apply to machines known as traction engines or to any locomotives or electric cars operating on rails.

§46.2-684. Nocturnal use of highways by exempted vehicles.

It shall be unlawful for any vehicle exempted under this article from registration under this chapter to use the highways between sunset and sunrise unless it is equipped with lights as required by law.

ARTICLE 7
FEES FOR REGISTRATION

§46.2-685. Payment of fees into special fund.

All fees collected by the Commissioner under §§46.2-651, 46.2-652, and 46.2-653 shall be paid into the state treasury and set aside as a special fund to be used to meet the expenses of the Department.

§46.2-686. Portion of certain fees to be paid into special fund.

Except as provided in subdivision 13 of subsection A of §46.2-694 and §46.2-703, an amount equal to twenty percent of the fees collected, after refunds, from the registration of motor vehicles, trailers, and semitrailers pursuant to this chapter, calculated at the rates in effect on December 31, 1986, shall be transferred from the special fund established by the provisions of §46.2-206 to a special fund in the state treasury to be used to meet the expenses of the Department.

§46.2-687. Failure to pay certain fees; penalty.

Any person who operates or permits the operation over any highway in the Commonwealth of any motor vehicle, trailer, or semitrailer for the transportation of passengers without first having paid to the Commissioner the fee prescribed by §46.2-694 shall be guilty of a Class 2 misdemeanor.

§46.2-688. Refund of fees paid.

Any person holding a registration card and license plate or license plates with decal who disposes of, elects not to use the vehicle for which it was issued on the highways in the Commonwealth, or transfers another valid license plate to the vehicle, may surrender, prior to the beginning of the registration period, the license plates or license plates with decals and registration card or provide other evidence of registration of the vehicle to the Commissioner with a statement that the vehicle for which the license plate or license plate with decal was issued has been disposed of, election has been made not to use the vehicle on the highways in the Commonwealth, or another valid license plate has been transferred to the vehicle and request a refund of the fee paid. The Commissioner shall retain five dollars of the fee to cover the costs incurred in issuing the plates and processing the refund.

The Commissioner shall refund to the applicant a proration, in six-month increments, of the total cost of the registration and license plates or license plates with decals if application for the refund is made when there are six or more months remaining in the registration period. No charge or deduction shall be assessed for any refund made under this subsection.

§46.2-689. Refund of certain registration fees.

Upon application on a form prescribed by the Commissioner, any person registering any vehicle whose fees are set under §46.2-697 shall be refunded that portion of the registration fee for a gross weight in excess of that set forth §46.2-1126.

§46.2-690. Refund for certain for-hire vehicles.

Notwithstanding any other provision of law, the owner of any motor vehicle which is required to be licensed under §46.2-697 as a for-hire vehicle, may apply for a refund of that portion of the license fee paid in excess of the fee required if it were licensed not for-hire, subject to the conditions and limitations set forth in this section.

If the motor vehicle, while licensed as a for-hire vehicle, is used exclusively in seasonal operation for the transportation of agricultural, horticultural, or forest products and seed and fertilizer therefor to and from the land of the producer, for compensation, the owner may surrender the for-hire license plates issued at any times prior to the expiration of an accumulated total of not more than ninety days. A refund may be obtained for seventy-five percent of that portion of the fee paid in excess of the license fee required for private carrier license plates. The Commissioner shall refund this surcharge on application on forms prescribed by him and submitted to the Department within thirty days of the registration expiration date of the license plates.

§46.2-691. Credit to truck owner inducted into armed forces.

The owner of any truck who secured and paid for a license therefor but was prevented from operating the truck for the full license year by induction into the armed forces of the United States and who, after his discharge from the service, resumes his trucking operations, shall be entitled to a pro rata credit on any new license purchased by him, in the proportion that the part of the year for which he had paid the license and during which part the truck was not in operation bears to the full license year.

The application for a credit shall be made during the license year for which credit is sought and each application shall be accompanied by the registration card and license plate issued the owner for the year for which credit is sought and an affidavit that the owner has been or will be inducted into the armed forces.

All such affidavits shall set forth that the vehicle cannot be operated due to the owner's service in the armed forces.

The Commissioner, when the owner is entitled to a refund, shall issue to him a credit to be applied on the purchase of a new license, in the proportion that the part of the year for which the license fee was paid and during which the truck will not be operated bears to the full license year.

§46.2-692. Fee for replacement of lost, mutilated, or illegible indicia of titling and registration.

The fee for the replacement of license plates, decals, registration cards, or certificates of title which are lost, mutilated or illegible shall be as follows:

1. For any type of replacement or duplication of vehicle registration cards, International Registration Plan cab cards, registration cards for overload permits, or dealer registration cards, two dollars;
2. For a certificate of title, five dollars;
3. For license plates or license plates with decals, ten dollars;
4. For a license plate with decals issued for trailers, five dollars; and
5. For one or two decals, one dollar.

(Chgd. by L.1997 ch. 486; L.2000 ch. 579, eff. 7/1/2000.)

§46.2-692.1. Sample license plates; fee; use.

Upon application therefor, the Commissioner may issue samples of authorized license plates currently issued by the Department. Sample license plates may display, as requested by the applicant and approved by the Commissioner, a combination of up to seven numbers or letters, when feasible. Notwithstanding the provisions of this section, every such license plate shall display the word "SAMPLE" on its face, in a manner prescribed by the Commissioner.

The fee for sample license plates not displaying numbers or letters requested by the applicant shall be ten dollars for each license plate. The fee for sample license plates displaying numbers or letters requested by the applicant shall be twenty dollars for each license plate. Sample license plates shall not be valid for registration purposes and shall not be mounted or displayed on any motor vehicle.

(Added by L.1996 ch. 1026; chgd. by L.1997 chs. 774, 816, eff. 7/1/97.)

§46.2-693. Use of old plates and registration number on another vehicle.

Upon receipt of a proper application, an owner who sells or transfers a registered vehicle may have the license plates and registration number assigned to another vehicle titled in the name of the owner. If the vehicle requires identical registration fees, the transfer fee shall be two dollars. If the license fee required for the second vehicle requires a greater registration fee, the fee shall be two dollars plus the difference in registration fees between the two vehicles. All fees collected under the provisions of this section shall be paid by the Commissioner into the state treasury and shall be set aside as a special fund to meet the expenses of the Department.

§46.2-694. Fees for vehicles designed and used for transportation of passengers; weights used for computing fees; burden of proof.

A. The annual registration fees for motor vehicles, trailers, and semitrailers designed and used for the transportation of passengers on the highways in the Commonwealth are:

1. Twenty-three dollars for each private passenger car or motor home if the passenger car or motor home weighs 4,000 pounds or less, provided that it is not used for the transportation of passengers for compensation and is not kept or used for rent or for hire, or is not operated under a lease without a chauffeur.

2. Twenty-eight dollars for each passenger car or motor home which weighs more than 4,000 pounds, provided that it is not used for the transportation of passengers for compensation and is not kept or used for rent or for hire, or is not operated under a lease without a chauffeur.

3. Thirty cents per 100 pounds or major fraction thereof for a private motor vehicle other than a motorcycle with a normal seating capacity of more than ten adults including the driver if the private motor vehicle is not used for the transportation of passengers for compensation and is not kept or used for rent or for hire or is not operated under a lease without chauffeur. In no case shall the fee be less than twenty-three dollars if the vehicle weighs 4,000 pounds or less or twenty-eight dollars if the vehicle weighs more than 4,000 pounds.

4. Thirty cents per 100 pounds or major fraction thereof for a school bus. In no case shall the fee be less than twenty-three dollars if the vehicle weighs 4,000 pounds or less or twenty-eight dollars if the vehicle weighs more than 4,000 pounds.

5. Twenty-three dollars for each trailer or semitrailer designed for use as living quarters for human beings.

6. Thirteen dollars plus thirty cents per 100 pounds or major fraction thereof for each motor vehicle, trailer, or semitrailer used as a common carrier of passengers, operating either intrastate or interstate. Interstate common carriers of interstate passengers may elect to be licensed and pay the fees prescribed in subdivision 7 of this subsection on submission to the Commissioner of a declaration of operations and equipment as he may prescribe. An additional five dollars shall be charged if the motor vehicle weighs more than 4,000 pounds.

7. Thirteen dollars plus seventy cents per 100 pounds or major fraction thereof for each motor vehicle, trailer, or semitrailer used as a common carrier of interstate passengers if election is made to be licensed under this subsection. An additional five dollars shall be charged if the motor vehicle weighs more than 4,000 pounds. In lieu of the foregoing fee of seventy cents per 100 pounds, a motor carrier of passengers, operating two or more vehicles both within and outside the Commonwealth and registered for insurance purposes with the Surface Transportation Board of the United States Department of Transportation, Federal Highway Administration, may apply to the Commissioner for prorated registration. Upon the filing of such application, in such form as the Commissioner may prescribe, the Commissioner shall apportion the registration fees provided in this subsection so that the total registration fees to be paid for such vehicles of such carrier shall be that proportion of the total fees, if there were no apportionment, that the total number of miles traveled by such vehicles of such carrier within the Commonwealth bears to the total number of miles traveled by such vehicles within and outside the Commonwealth. Such total mileage in each instance is the estimated total mileage to be traveled by such vehicles during the license year for which such fees are paid, subject to the adjustment in accordance with an audit to be made by representatives of the Commissioner at the end of such license year, the expense of such audit to be borne by the carrier being audited. Each vehicle passing into or through Virginia shall be registered and licensed in Virginia and the annual registration fee to be paid for each such vehicle shall not be less than thirty-three dollars. For the purpose of determining such apportioned registration fees, only those motor vehicles, trailers, or semitrailers operated both within and outside the Commonwealth shall be subject to inclusion in determining the apportionment provided for herein.

8. Thirteen dollars plus eighty cents per 100 pounds or major fraction thereof for each motor vehicle, trailer or semitrailer kept or used for rent or for hire or operated under a lease without chauffeur for the transportation of passengers. An additional fee of five dollars shall be charged if the vehicle weighs more than 4,000 pounds. This subsection does not apply to vehicles used as common carriers.

9. Twenty-three dollars for a taxicab or other vehicle which is kept for rent or hire operated with a chauffeur for the transportation of passengers, and which operates or should operate under permits issued by the Department as required by law. An additional fee of five dollars shall be charged if the vehicle weighs more than 4,000 pounds. This subsection does not apply to vehicles used as common carriers.

10. Eighteen dollars for a motorcycle, with or without a sidecar. To this fee shall be added a surcharge of three dollars which shall be distributed as provided in §46.2-1191.

11. Twenty-three dollars for a bus used exclusively for transportation to and from Sunday school or church, for the purpose of divine worship. If the empty weight of the vehicle exceeds 4,000 pounds, the fee shall be twenty-eight dollars.

12. Thirteen dollars plus seventy cents per 100 pounds or major fraction thereof for other passenger-carrying vehicles.

13. An additional fee of two dollars per year shall be charged and collected at the time of registration of each pickup or panel truck and each motor vehicle under subdivisions 1 through 12 of this subsection. All funds collected pursuant to this subdivision shall be paid into the state treasury and shall be set aside as a special fund to be used only for emergency medical service purposes. The moneys in the special fund shall be distributed as follows:

a. Two and one-half percent shall be distributed to the Virginia Association of Volunteer Rescue Squads;

b. Thirteen and one-half percent shall be distributed to the State Department of Health to support (i) emergency medical services training programs (excluding advanced life support classes), (ii) advanced life support training, and (iii) recruitment and retention programs (all funds for such support shall be used to recruit and retain volunteer emergency medical services personnel only, including public awareness campaigns, technical assistance programs, and similar activities). Any funds set aside for distribution under this provision and remaining undistributed at the end of any fiscal year shall revert to the Rescue Squad Assistance Fund;

c. Thirty-one and three-quarters percent shall be distributed to the Rescue Squad Assistance Fund;

d. Twenty-seven and one-quarter percent shall be available to the State Department of Health for use in emergency medical services; and

e. Twenty-five percent shall be returned by the Comptroller to the locality wherein such vehicle is registered, to provide funding for training of volunteer or salaried emergency medical service personnel of licensed, nonprofit emergency medical services agencies and for the purchase of necessary equipment and supplies for use in such locality for licensed, nonprofit emergency medical and rescue services.

The Comptroller shall clearly designate on the warrant, check, or other means of transmitting these funds that such moneys are only to be used for purposes set forth in this subdivision. Such funds shall be in addition to any local appropriations and local governing bodies shall not use these funds to supplant local funds. Each local governing body shall report annually to the Board of Health on the use of the twenty-five percent of the funds which were returned to it. In any case in which the local governing body grants the funds to a regional emergency medical services council to be distributed to the licensed, nonprofit emergency medical and rescue services, the local governing body shall remain responsible for the proper use of the funds. If, at the end of any fiscal year, a report on the use of the twenty-five percent of the funds for that year has not been received from a local governing body, any funds due to that local governing body for the next fiscal year shall be retained until such time as the report has been submitted to the Board.

B. All motor vehicles, trailers, and semitrailers registered as provided in subsection B of §46.2-646 shall pay a registration fee equal to one-twelfth of all fees required by subsection A of this section or §46.2-697 for such motor vehicle, trailer, or semitrailer, computed to the nearest cent, multiplied by the number of months in the registration period for such motor vehicles, trailers, and semitrailers.

C. The manufacturer's shipping weight or scale weight shall be used for computing all fees required by this section to be based upon the weight of the vehicle.

D. The applicant for registration bears the burden of proof that the vehicle for which registration is sought is entitled by weight, design, and use to be registered at the fee tendered by the applicant to the Commissioner or to his authorized agent.

(Chgd. by L.1997 ch. 283, eff. 7/1/97.)

§46.2-694.1. Fees for trailers and semitrailers not designed and used for transportation of passengers.

Unless otherwise specified in this title, the registration fees for trailers and semitrailers not designed and used for the transportation of passengers on the highways in the Commonwealth shall be as follows:

Registered Gross Weight	1-Year Fee	2-Year Fee	Permanent Fee
0–1,500 lbs	$ 8.00	$16.00	$50.00
1,501–4,000 lbs	$18.50	$37.00	$50.00
4,001 lbs & above	$23.50	$47.00	$50.00

From the foregoing registration fees, the following amounts, regardless of weight category, shall be paid by the Department into the state treasury and set aside for the payment of the administrative costs of the safety inspection program provided for in Article 21 (§46.2-1157 et seq.) of Chapter 10 of this title: (i) from each one-year registration fee, one dollar and fifty cents; (ii) from each two-year registration fee, three dollars; and (iii) from each permanent registration fee, four dollars.

(Added by L.1997 ch. 283, eff. 7/1/97.)

§46.2-695. Small rented vehicles jointly operated.

The fees required by subdivisions 8 and 9 of §46.2-694 to be paid for registration of motor vehicles used for rent or hire shall not be required for the operation of any motor vehicle with a normal seating capacity of not more than twelve adults including the driver while used (i) not for profit in transporting persons who, as a common undertaking, bear or agree to bear all or a part of the actual costs of such operation, or (ii) by a lessee renting or hiring such vehicle for a period of twelve months or longer under a written lease or agreement. For the purposes of §46.2-694, every such motor vehicle shall be treated as a private motor vehicle for which the fee for the annual registration card and license plates shall be fifteen dollars. If, however, the vehicles weigh more than 4,000 pounds, the fee shall be twenty dollars.

§46.2-696. Exemption of buses operated in special or chartered service.

The provisions of §§46.2-107, 46.2-687, 46.2-694, and 46.2-695 shall not apply to any carrier operating under a certificate of public convenience and necessity issued by the State Corporation Commission or the Department for buses operated in special or chartered party service, nor shall the provisions of subdivisions 8 and 9 of subsection A of §46.2-694 apply to any carrier that is: (i) operating under a certificate of public convenience and necessity issued by the State Corporation Commission or the Department, (ii) registered for insurance purposes with the Surface Transportation Board of the United States Department of Transportation, Federal Highway Administration, or (iii) operating under a local franchise granted by any city or town.

(Chgd. by L.1997 ch. 283, eff. 7/1/97.)

§46.2-697. Fees for vehicles not designed or used for transportation of passengers.

A. Except as otherwise provided in this section, the fee for registration of all motor vehicles not designed and used for the transportation of passengers shall be thirteen dollars plus an amount determined by the gross weight of the vehicle or combination of vehicles of which it is a part, when loaded to the maximum capacity for which it is registered and licensed, according to the schedule of fees set forth in this section. For each 1,000 pounds of gross weight, or major fraction thereof, for which any such vehicle is registered, there shall be paid to the Commissioner the fee indicated in the following schedule immediately opposite the weight group and under the classification established by the provisions of subsection B of §46.2-711 into which such vehicle, or any combination of vehicles of which it is a part, falls when loaded to the maximum capacity for which it is registered and licensed. The fee for a pickup or panel truck shall be twenty-three dollars if its gross weight is 4,000 pounds or less, and twenty-eight dollars if its gross weight is 4,001 pounds through 6,500 pounds. The fee shall be twenty-nine dollars for any motor vehicle with a gross weight of 6,501 pounds through 10,000 pounds.

Fee Per Thousand Pounds of Gross Weight

Gross Weight Groups (pounds)	Private Carriers	For Rent or For Hire Carriers
10,001 — 11,000	$ 2.60	$ 4.75
11,001 — 12,000	2.80	4.90
12,001 — 13,000	3.00	5.15
13,001 — 14,000	3.20	5.40
14,001 — 15,000	3.40	5.65
15,001 — 16,000	3.60	5.90
16,001 — 17,000	4.00	6.15
17,001 — 18,000	4.40	6.40
18,001 — 19,000	4.80	7.50
19,001 — 20,000	5.20	7.70
20,001 — 21,000	5.60	7.90
21,001 — 22,000	6.00	8.10
22,001 — 23,000	6.40	8.30
23,001 — 24,000	6.80	8.50
24,001 — 25,000	6.90	8.70
25,001 — 26,000	6.95	8.90
26,001 — 27,000	8.25	10.35
27,001 — 28,000	8.30	10.55
28,001 — 29,000	8.35	10.75
29,001 — 40,000	8.45	10.95
40,001 — 45,000	8.55	11.15
45,001 — 50,000	8.75	11.25
50,001 — 55,000	9.25	13.25
55,001 — 76,000	11.25	15.25
76,001 — 80,000	13.25	16.25

For all such motor vehicles exceeding a gross weight of 6,500 pounds, an additional fee of five dollars shall be imposed.

B. In lieu of registering any motor vehicle referred to in this section for an entire licensing year, the owner may elect to register the vehicle only for one or more quarters of a licensing year, and in such case, the fee shall be twenty-five percent of the annual fee plus five dollars for each quarter that the vehicle is registered.

C. When an owner elects to register and license a motor vehicle under subsection B of this section, the provisions of §§46.2-646 and 46.2-688 shall not apply.

D. Notwithstanding any other provision of law, no vehicle designed, equipped, and used to tow disabled or inoperable motor vehicles shall be required to register in accordance with any gross weight other than the gross weight of the towing vehicle itself, exclusive of any vehicle being towed.

E. All registrations and licenses issued for less than a full year shall expire on the date shown on the license and registration.

(Chgd. by L.1997 ch. 283, eff. 7/1/97.)

§46.2-697.1. Reduction in vehicle registration fees.

To encourage owners (i) to register their vehicles for multi-year periods or (ii) to use the mail or electronic technologies when registering their vehicles, the Commissioner may authorize a discount or other incentives for multi-year, basic mail-in or electronic registrations of motor vehicles, trailers, or semitrailers required to be registered under this chapter.

(Chgd. by L.1997 ch. 486, eff. 7/1/97.)

§46.2-698. Fees for farm vehicles.

A. The fees for registration of farm motor vehicles having gross weights of 7,500 pounds or more, when such vehicles are used exclusively for farm use as defined in this section, shall be one-half of the fee per 1,000 pounds of gross weight for private carriers as calculated under the provisions of §46.2-697 and one-half of the fee for overload permits under §46.2-1128, but the annual registration fee to be paid for each farm vehicle shall not be less than fifteen dollars.

B. A farm motor vehicle is used exclusively for farm use:

1. When owned by a person who is engaged either as an owner, renter, or operator of a farm of a size reasonably requiring the use of such vehicle or vehicles and when such vehicle is:

a. Used in the transportation of agricultural commodities, poultry, dairy products, or livestock of the farm he is working to market, or to other points for sale or processing, or when used to transport materials, tools, equipment, or supplies which are to be used or consumed on the farm he is working, or when used for any other transportation incidental to the regular operation of such farm;

b. Used in transporting forest products, including forest materials originating on a farm or incident to the regular operation of a farm, to the farm he is working or transporting for any purpose forest products which originate on the farm he is working; or

c. Used in the transportation of farm produce, supplies, equipment, or materials to a farm not worked by him, pursuant to a mutual cooperative agreement.

2. When the nonfarm use of such motor vehicle is limited to the personal use of the owner and his immediate family in attending church or school, securing medical treatment or supplies, or securing other household or family necessities.

C. As used in this section, the term "farm" shall include one or more farms, orchards, or ranches, but does not include a tree farm unless it is part of what otherwise is a farm.

D. The first application for registration of a vehicle under this section shall be made on forms provided by the Department and shall include:

1. The location and acreage of each farm on which the vehicle to be registered is to be used;

2. The type of agricultural commodities, poultry, dairy products or livestock produced on such farms and the approximate amounts produced annually;

3. A statement, signed by the vehicle's owner, that the vehicle to be registered will only be used for one or more of the purposes specified in subsection B of this section;

4. Other information required by the Department; and

5. The above information is not required for the renewal of a vehicle's registration under this section.

E. The Department shall issue appropriately designated license plates for those motor vehicles registered under this section. The manner in which such license plates are designated shall be at the discretion of the Commissioner.

F. The owner of a farm vehicle shall inform the Commissioner within 30 days or at the time of his next registration renewal, whichever comes first, when such vehicle is no longer used exclusively for farm use as defined in this section, and shall pay the appropriate registration fee for the vehicle based on its type of operation. It shall constitute a Class 2 misdemeanor to: (i) operate or to permit the operation of any farm motor vehicle for which the fee for registration and license plates is herein prescribed on any highway in the Commonwealth without first having paid the prescribed registration fee; or (ii) operate or permit the operation of any motor vehicle, registered under this section, for purposes other than as provided under subsection B of this section; or (iii) operate as a for-hire vehicle.

G. Nothing in this section shall affect the exemptions of agricultural and horticultural vehicles under §§46.2-664 through 46.2-670.

H. Notwithstanding other provisions of this section, vehicles licensed under this section may be used by volunteer rescue squad members and volunteer firefighters in responding to emergency calls, in reporting for regular duty, and in attending squad meetings and drills.

(Chgd. by L.1996 chs. 943, 994; L.1997 chs. 774, 816, eff. 7/1/97.)

§46.2-699. *(Repealed by L.1997 ch. 283, eff. 7/1/97.)*

§46.2-700. Fees for vehicles for transporting well-drilling machinery and specialized mobile equipment.

A. The fee for registration of any motor vehicle, trailer, or semitrailer on which well-drilling machinery is attached and which is permanently used solely for transporting the machinery shall be fifteen dollars.

B. The fee for the registration of specialized mobile equipment shall be fifteen dollars. "Specialized mobile equipment" shall mean any self-propelled motor vehicle manufactured for a specific purpose, other than for the transportation of passengers or property, which is used on a job site and whose movement on any highway is incidental to the purpose for which it was designed and manufactured. The vehicle must be constructed to fall within all size and weight requirements as contained in §§46.2-1105, 46.2-1110, 46.2-1113 and Article 17 of Chapter 10 (§46.2-1122 et seq.) of this title and must be capable of maintaining sustained highway speeds of forty miles per hour or more. Vehicles registered under this section shall be exempt from the requirements of §46.2-1157.

C. Specialized mobile equipment which cannot maintain a sustained highway speed in excess of forty miles per hour, and trailers or semitrailers which are designed and manufactured for a specific purpose and whose movement on the highway is incidental to the purpose for which it was manufactured and which are not designed or used to transport persons or property, shall not be required to be registered under this chapter.

§46.2-701. Combinations of tractor trucks and semitrailers; five-year registration of certain trailer fleets.

A. Each vehicle of a combination of a truck or tractor truck and a trailer or semitrailer shall be registered as a separate vehicle, and separate vehicle license plates shall be issued for each vehicle, but, for the purpose of determining the gross weight group into which any vehicle falls pursuant to §46.2-697, the combination of vehicles of which such vehicle constitutes a part shall be considered a unit, and the aggregate gross weight of the entire combination shall determine the gross weight group. The fee for the registration card and license plates for a trailer or semitrailer constituting a part of the combination shall be as provided in §46.2-694.1.

B. In determining the fee to be paid for the registration of a truck or tractor truck constituting a part of such combination the fee shall be assessed on the total gross weight and the fee per 1,000 pounds applicable to the gross weight of the combination when loaded to the maximum capacity for which it is registered and licensed.

C. Existing five-year registrations for fleets of fifty or more trailers previously issued under this section shall remain valid through the five-year period, but shall not be renewable.

(Chgd. by L.1997 ch. 283, eff. 7/1/97.)

§46.2-702. Fees for service or wrecking vehicles.

For the purpose of determining the registration and license fees paid by the owners of motor vehicles used as service or wrecking cranes, these motor vehicles, when used in connection with the business of any person engaged in selling motor vehicles or repairing the same, shall be treated as private motor vehicles and not as motor vehicles operated for compensation or for hire.

§46.2-703. Reciprocal agreement with other states; assessment and collection of fees on an apportionment or allocation basis; registration of vehicles and reporting of road tax.

Notwithstanding any other provision of this title, the Governor may on the advice of the Department, enter into reciprocal agreements on behalf of the Commonwealth with the appropriate authorities of any state of the United States or a state or province of a country providing for the assessing and collecting of license fees for motor vehicles, tractor trucks, trucks, trailers, and semitrailers on an apportionment or allocation basis, as outlined in the International Registration Plan developed by the International Registration Plan, Inc.

The Commissioner is authorized to audit the records of any owner, lessor, or lessee to verify the accuracy of any information required by any jurisdiction to determine the registration fees due. Based on this audit, the Commissioner may assess any owner, lessor, or lessee for any license fees due this Commonwealth, including interest and penalties as provided in this section. In addition to any other penalties prescribed by law, the Commissioner or the Reciprocity Board may deny the owner, lessor, or lessee the right to operate any motor vehicle on the highways in the Commonwealth until the assessment has been paid.

Trip permit registration may be issued for any vehicle or combination of vehicles which could be lawfully operated in the jurisdiction if full registration or proportional registration were obtained. The fee for this permit shall be fifteen dollars and the permit shall be valid for ten days.

Any person who operates or permits the operation of any motor vehicle, trailer, or semitrailer over any highway in the Commonwealth without first having paid to the Commissioner the fees prescribed and payable under this section shall be guilty of a Class 2 misdemeanor.

If the Commissioner ascertains that any fees which he is authorized to assess any owner, lessor, or lessee for any license year have not been assessed or have been assessed for less than the law required for the year because of failure or refusal of any owner, lessor, or lessee to make his records available for audit as provided herein, or if any owner, lessor, or lessee misrepresents, falsifies, or conceals any of these records, the Commissioner shall determine from any information obtainable the lawful fees at the rate prescribed for that year, plus a penalty of five percent and interest at the rate of six percent per year, which shall be computed on the fees and penalty from the date the fees became due to the date of assessment, and is authorized to make an assessment therefor against the owner, lessor, or lessee. If the assessment is not paid within thirty days after its date, interest at the rate of six percent per year shall accrue thereon from the date of such assessment until the fees and penalty are paid. The notice of the assessment shall be forthwith sent to the owner, lessor, or lessee by registered or certified mail to the address of the owner, lessor, or lessee as it appears on the records in the office of the Department. The notice, when sent in accordance with these requirements, shall be sufficient regardless of whether it was received.

If any owner, lessor, or lessee fails to pay the fees, penalty, and interest, or any portion thereof, assessed pursuant to this section, in addition to any other provision of law, the Attorney General or the Commissioner shall bring an appropriate action before the Circuit Court of the City of Richmond for the recovery of the fees, penalty, and interest, and judgment shall be rendered for the amount found to be due together with costs. If it is found that the failure to pay was willful on the part of the owner, lessor or lessee, judgment shall be rendered for double the amount of the fees found to be due, plus costs.

Notwithstanding any other provision of this title or Chapter 27 (§58.1-2700 et seq.) of Title 58.1, the Governor, on the advice of the Department, may enter into reciprocal agreements on behalf of the Commonwealth with the duly authorized representatives of other jurisdictions providing for the road tax registration of vehicles, establishing periodic road tax reporting and road tax payment requirements from owners of such vehicles, and disbursement of funds collected due to other jurisdictions based on mileage traveled and fuel used in those jurisdictions.

Notwithstanding any statute contrary to the provisions of any reciprocal agreement entered into by the Governor or his duly authorized representative as authorized by this title, the provisions of the reciprocal agreement shall govern and apply to all matters relating to administration and enforcement of the road tax. In the event the language of any reciprocal agreement entered into by the Governor as authorized by this title is later amended so that it conflicts with or is contrary to any statute, the Department shall consider the amended language of the reciprocal agreement controlling and shall administer and enforce the road tax in accordance with the amended language of the reciprocal agreement.

An agreement may provide for determining the base state for motor carriers, records requirements, audit procedures, exchange of information, persons eligible for tax licensing, defining qualified motor vehicles, determining if bonding is required, specifying reporting requirements and periods, including defining uniform penalties and interest rates for late reporting, determining methods for collecting and forwarding of motor fuel taxes and penalties to another jurisdiction, and other provisions as will facilitate the administration of the agreement.

The Governor may, as required by the terms of the agreement, forward to officers of another member jurisdiction any information in the Department's possession relative to the use of motor fuels by any motor carrier. The Department may disclose to officers of another state the location of offices, motor vehicles, and other real and personal property of motor carriers.

An agreement may provide for each state to audit the records of motor carriers based in the state to determine if the road taxes due each member jurisdiction are properly reported and paid. Each member jurisdiction shall forward the findings of the audits performed on motor carriers based in the member jurisdiction to each jurisdiction in which the carrier has taxable use of motor fuels. For motor carriers not based in the Commonwealth and which have taxable use of motor fuel in the Commonwealth, the Department may serve the audit findings received from another jurisdiction, in the form of an assessment, on the carrier as though an audit had been conducted by the Department.

Any agreement entered into pursuant to this chapter does not preclude the Department from auditing the records of any motor carrier covered by the provisions of this chapter.

The Department shall not enter into any agreement which would affect the motor fuel road tax rate.

The Department may adopt and promulgate such rules, regulations, and procedures as may be necessary to effectuate and administer this title. Nothing in this title shall be construed to affect the tax rate provisions found in Chapter 27 (§58.1-2700 et seq.) of Title 58.1.

Notwithstanding any other provision in this title or Title 56, the Governor, on the advice of the Department, may participate in the reciprocal standards for registration with states as authorized under 49 U.S.C. §11506 and 49 C.F.R. Part 1023.

(Chgd. by L.1995 chs. 744, 803, eff. 7/1/95.)

§46.2-703.1. Additional fee for fleets of vehicles registered under §46.2-703.

In addition to any other fees required to be paid for vehicles registered under the provisions of §46.2-703, the Department shall charge an administrative fee of one dollar per year per fleet for each application processed. All fees collected under this section shall be used exclusively for the administration and support of reciprocity activities described in §46.2-703.

§46.2-704. Prohibited operations; checking on weights; penalties.

A. No person shall operate or permit the operation of any motor vehicle, trailer, or semitrailer for which the fee for registration is prescribed by §46.2-697 on any highway in the Commonwealth, under any of the following circumstances:

1. Without first having paid the registration fee hereinabove prescribed.

2. If, at the time of the operation, the gross weight of the vehicle or of the combination of vehicles of which it is a part, is in excess of the gross weight on the basis of which it is registered. In any case where a pickup truck is used in combination with another vehicle, operation shall be unlawful only if the combined gross weight exceeds the combined gross weight on the basis of which each vehicle is registered.

B. Any officer authorized to enforce the motor vehicle laws, having reason to believe that the gross weight of any motor vehicle, trailer, or semitrailer being operated on any highway in the Commonwealth exceeds that on the basis of which the vehicle is registered, may weigh the vehicle by whatever means the Superintendent may prescribe and the operator, or other person in possession of the vehicle, shall permit this weighing whenever requested by the officer.

C. Any person who violates any provision of this section or who operates or permits the operation of a trailer or semitrailer designed for the use of human beings as living quarters, on the highways in the Commonwealth without having first paid to the Commissioner the fee prescribed in subdivision 5 of subsection A of §46.2-694 is guilty of a Class 2 misdemeanor.

ARTICLE 8
REGISTRATION OF UNINSURED MOTOR VEHICLES

§46.2-705. Definitions.

For the purposes of this article, the following terms shall have the meanings respectively ascribed to them in this section:

"Motor vehicle" means a vehicle capable of self-propulsion which is either (i) required to be titled and licensed and for which a license fee is required to be paid by its owner, or (ii) owned by or assigned to a motor vehicle manufacturer, distributor, or dealer licensed in the Commonwealth.

"Insured motor vehicle" means a motor vehicle as to which there is bodily injury liability insurance and property damage liability insurance, both in the amounts specified in §46.2-472, issued by an insurance carrier authorized to do business in the Commonwealth, or as to which a bond has been given or cash or securities delivered in lieu of the insurance; or as to which the owner has qualified as a self-insurer in accordance with the provisions of §46.2-368.

"Uninsured motor vehicle" means a motor vehicle as to which there is no such bodily injury liability insurance and property damage liability insurance, or no such bond has been given or cash or securities delivered in lieu thereof, or the owner of which has not so qualified as a self-insurer.

§46.2-706. Additional fee; proof of insurance required of applicants for registration of insured motor vehicles; verification of insurance; suspension of driver's license, registration certificates, and license plates for certain violations.

In addition to any other fees prescribed by law, every person registering an uninsured motor vehicle, as defined in §46.2-705, at the time of registering or reregistering the uninsured vehicle, shall pay a fee of $500; however, if the uninsured motor vehicle is being registered or reregistered for a period of less than a full year, the uninsured motor vehicle fee shall be prorated for the unexpired portion of the registration period. If the vehicle is a motor vehicle being registered or reregistered as provided in subsection B of §46.2-697, the fee shall be one-fourth of the annual uninsured motor vehicle fee for each quarter for which the vehicle is registered.

If the owner of a motor vehicle registered under this article as an uninsured motor vehicle, during the period for which such vehicle is registered, obtains insurance coverage

 Zv

adequate to permit such vehicle's registration as an insured motor vehicle and presents evidence satisfactory to the Commissioner of the existence of such insurance coverage, the Commissioner shall amend the Department's records to show such vehicle to be registered as an insured motor vehicle and shall refund to the owner a prorated portion of the additional fee required by this section for registration of an uninsured motor vehicle. Such proration shall be on a monthly basis, except that no such refund shall be made (i) as to any registration during the last three months of its validity or (ii) on any portion of any such fee required to be paid resulting from a determination by the Department or any court that a vehicle was uninsured and no fee had been paid.

Every person applying for registration of a motor vehicle and declaring it to be an insured motor vehicle shall, under the penalties set forth in §46.2-707, execute and furnish to the Commissioner his certificate that the motor vehicle is an insured motor vehicle as defined in §46.2-705, or that the Commissioner has issued to its owner, in accordance with §46.2-368, a certificate of self-insurance applicable to the vehicle sought to be registered. The Commissioner, or his duly authorized agent, may verify that the motor vehicle is properly insured by comparing owner and vehicle identification information on file at the Department of Motor Vehicles with liability information on the owner and vehicle transmitted to the Department by any insurance company licensed to do business in the Commonwealth as provided in §46.2-706.1. If no record of liability insurance is found, the Department may require the motor vehicle owner to verify insurance in a method prescribed by the Commissioner.

The refusal or neglect of any owner within thirty days to submit the liability insurance information when required by the Commissioner or his duly authorized agent, or the electronic notification by the insurance company or surety company that the policy or bond named in the certificate of insurance is not in effect, shall require the Commissioner to suspend any driver's license and all registration certificates and license plates issued to the owner of the motor vehicle until the person (i) has paid to the Commissioner a fee of $500 to be disposed of as provided for in §46.2-710 with respect to the motor vehicle determined to be uninsured and (ii) furnishes proof of financial responsibility for the future in the manner prescribed in Article 15 (§46.2-435 et seq.) of Chapter 3 of this title. No order of suspension required by this section shall become effective until the Commissioner has offered the person an opportunity for an administrative hearing to show cause why the order should not be enforced. Notice of the opportunity for an administrative hearing may be included in the order of suspension. When three years have elapsed from the effective date of the suspension required in this section, the Commissioner may relieve the person of the requirement of furnishing proof of future financial responsibility.

The Commissioner shall suspend the driver's license and all registration certificates and license plates of any person on receiving a record of his conviction of a violation of any provisions of §46.2-707, but the Commissioner shall dispense with the suspension when the person is convicted for a violation of §46.2-707 and the Department's records show conclusively that the motor vehicle was insured or that the fee applicable to the registration of an uninsured motor vehicle has been paid by the owner prior to the date and time of the alleged offense.

(Chgd. by L.1996 chs. 474, 489; L.1998 ch. 404, eff. 7/1/98.)

§46.2-706.1. Insurance and surety companies to furnish certain insurance information.

Any liability insurance information relating to individually identified vehicles or persons, received from such companies under this section, shall be considered privileged information and not subject to the Virginia Freedom of Information Act (§2.1-340 et seq.).

Such information shall be used in conjunction with information supplied under §46.2-706 to verify insurance for motor vehicles certified by their owners to be insured.

Insurance companies licensed to do business in Virginia shall provide to the Department monthly electronic updates of insured information and vehicle descriptions required by the Commissioner when they (i) cancel liability insurance for vehicles registered in Virginia, (ii) add liability insurance for vehicles registered in Virginia, or (iii) provide liability insurance for vehicles registered in Virginia newly satisfying financial responsibility requirements. Insurance companies having less than 1,000 policies may report the information manually or electronically.

(Chgd. by L.1996 chs. 474, 489, eff. 1/1/97.)

§46.2-707. Operating uninsured motor vehicle without payment of fee; verification of insurance; false evidence of insurance.

Any person who owns an uninsured motor vehicle (i) licensed in the Commonwealth, (ii) subject to registration in the Commonwealth, or (iii) displaying temporary license plates provided for in §46.2-1558 who operates or permits the operation of that motor vehicle without first having paid to the Commissioner the uninsured motor vehicle fee required by §46.2-706, to be disposed of as provided by §46.2-710, shall be guilty of a Class 3 misdemeanor.

Any person who is the operator of such an uninsured motor vehicle and not the titled owner, who knows that the required fee has not been paid to the Commissioner, shall be guilty of a Class 3 misdemeanor.

The Commissioner or his duly authorized agent, having reason to believe that a motor vehicle is being operated or has been operated on any specified date, may require the owner of such motor vehicle to verify insurance in a method prescribed by the Commissioner as provided for by §46.2-706. The refusal or neglect of the owner who has not, prior to the date of operation, paid the uninsured motor vehicle fee required by §46.2-706 as to such motor vehicle, to provide such verification shall be prima facie evidence that the motor vehicle was an uninsured motor vehicle at the time of such operation.

Any person who falsely verifies insurance to the Commissioner or gives false evidence that a motor vehicle sought to be registered is an insured motor vehicle, shall be guilty of a Class 3 misdemeanor.

However, the foregoing portions of this section shall not be applicable if it is established that the owner had good cause to believe and did believe that such motor vehicle was an insured motor vehicle, in which event the provisions of §46.2-609 shall be applicable.

Any person who owns an uninsured motor vehicle (i) licensed in the Commonwealth, (ii) subject to registration in the Commonwealth, or (iii) displaying temporary license plates provided for in §46.2-1558, and who has not paid the uninsured motor vehicle fee required by §46.2-706, shall immediately surrender the vehicle's license plates to the Department. Any person who fails to immediately surrender his vehicle's license plates shall be guilty of a Class 3 misdemeanor.

Abstracts of records of conviction, as defined in this title, of any violation of any of the provisions of this section shall be forwarded to the Commissioner as prescribed by §46.2-383.

The Commissioner shall suspend the driver's license and all registration certificates and license plates of any titled owner of an uninsured motor vehicle upon receiving a record of his conviction of a violation of any provisions of this section, and he shall not thereafter reissue the driver's license and the registration certificates and license plates issued in the name of such person until such person pays the fee applicable to the registration of an uninsured motor vehicle as prescribed in §46.2-706 and furnishes proof of future financial responsibility as prescribed by Article 15 (§46.2-435 et seq.) of Chapter 3 of this title. However, when three years have elapsed from the date of the suspension herein required, the Commissioner may relieve such person of the requirement of furnishing proof of future financial responsibility. When such suspension results from a conviction for presenting or causing to be presented to the Commissioner false verification as to whether a motor vehicle is an insured motor vehicle or false evidence that any motor vehicle sought to be registered is insured, then the Commissioner shall not thereafter reissue the driver's license and the registration certificates and license plates issued in the name of such person so convicted for a period of 180 days from the date of such order of suspension, and only then when all other provisions of law have been complied with by such person.

The Commissioner shall suspend the driver's license of any person who is the operator but not the titled owner of a motor vehicle upon receiving a record of his conviction of a violation of any provisions of this section and he shall not thereafter reissue the driver's license until thirty days from the date of such order of suspension.
(Chgd. by L.1996 chs. 474, 489, eff. 1/1/97.)

§46.2-708. Suspension of driver's license and registration when uninsured motor vehicle is involved in reportable accident; hearing prior to suspension.

When it appears to the Commissioner from the records of his office that an uninsured motor vehicle as defined in §46.2-705, subject to registration in the Commonwealth, is involved in a reportable accident in the Commonwealth resulting in death, injury or property damage with respect to which motor vehicle the owner thereof has not paid the uninsured motor vehicle fee as prescribed in §46.2-706, the Commissioner shall, in addition to enforcing the applicable provisions of Article 13 (§46.2-417 et seq.) of Chapter 3 of this title, suspend such owner's driver's license and all of his license plates and registration certificates until such person has complied with Article 13 of Chapter 3 of this title and has paid to the Commissioner a fee of $500, to be disposed of as provided by §46.2-710, with respect to the motor vehicle involved in the accident and furnishes proof of future financial responsibility in the manner prescribed in Article 15 (§46.2-435 et seq.) of Chapter 3 of this title. However, no order of suspension required by this section shall become effective until the Commissioner has offered the person an opportunity for an administrative hearing to show cause why the order should not be enforced. Notice of the opportunity for an administrative hearing may be included in the order of suspension.

However, when three years have elapsed from the effective date of the suspension herein required, the Commissioner may relieve such person of the requirement of furnishing proof of future financial responsibility. The presentation by a person subject to the provisions of this section of a certificate of insurance, executed by an agent or representative of an insurance company qualified to do business in this Commonwealth, showing that on the date and at the time of the accident the vehicle was an insured motor vehicle as herein defined, or, presentation by such person of evidence that the additional fee applicable to the registration of an uninsured motor vehicle had been paid to the Department prior to the date and time of the accident, shall be sufficient bar to the suspension provided for in this section.
(Chgd. by L.1998 ch. 404, eff. 7/1/98.)

§46.2-709. Requiring other proof of financial responsibility; suspended driver's license, registration certificate and license plates to be returned to Commissioner; Commissioner may take possession thereof.

Whenever any proof of financial responsibility filed by any person as required by this article no longer fulfills the purpose for which required, the Commissioner shall require other proof of financial responsibility as required by this article and shall suspend such person's driver's license, registration certificates, and license plates and decals pending the furnishing of proof as required.

Any person whose driver's license or registration certificates, or license plates and decals have been suspended as provided in this article and have not been reinstated shall immediately return every such license, registration certificate, and set of license plates and decals held by him to the Commissioner. Any person failing to comply with this requirement shall be guilty of a traffic infraction and upon conviction thereof shall be punished as provided in §46.2-113.

The Commissioner is authorized to take possession of any license, registration certificate, or set of license plates and decals on their suspension under the provisions of this chapter or to direct any police officer to take possession of and return them to the office of the Commissioner.

§46.2-710. Disposition of funds collected.

All funds collected by the Commissioner under the provisions of this article shall be paid into the state treasury and held in a special fund to be known as the Uninsured Motorists Fund to be disbursed as provided by law. The Commissioner may expend monies from such funds, for the administration of this article, in accordance with the General Appropriations Act.

ARTICLE 9
LICENSE PLATES, GENERALLY

Section

§46.2-711. Furnishing number and design of plates; displaying on vehicles required.

A. The Department shall furnish one license plate for every registered motorcycle, tractor truck, semitrailer, or trailer, and two license plates for every other registered motor vehicle, except to licensed motor vehicle dealers and persons delivering unladen vehicles who shall be furnished one license plate. The license plates for trailers, semitrailers, commercial vehicles, and trucks, other than license plates for dealers, may be of such design as to prevent removal without mutilating some part of the indicia forming a part of the license plate, when secured to the bracket.

B. The Department shall issue appropriately designated license plates for:

1. Passenger-carrying vehicles for rent or hire for the transportation of passengers for private trips;
2. Taxicabs;
3. Executive sedans as defined in §46.2-2500;
4. Limousines as defined in §46.2-2500;
5. Passenger-carrying vehicles operated by common carriers or restricted common carriers;
6. Property-carrying motor vehicles to applicants who operate as private carriers only;
7. Applicants who operate motor vehicles as carriers for rent or hire; and
8. Trailers and semitrailers.

C. The Department shall issue appropriately designated license plates for motor vehicles held for rental as defined in §58.1-2401.

D. No vehicles shall be operated on the highways in the Commonwealth without displaying the license plates required by this chapter.

E. Pickup or panel trucks are exempt from the provisions of subsection B of this section with reference to displaying for-hire license plates when operated as a carrier for rent or hire.

(Chgd. by L.1995 ch. 46; L.1997 chs. 774, 816, eff. 7/1/97.)

§46.2-712. Requirements of license plates and decals.

A. Every license plate shall display the registration number assigned to the motor vehicle, trailer, or semitrailer and to the owner thereof, the name of the Commonwealth, which may be abbreviated, and the year or the month and year, which may be abbreviated and in the form of decals, for which it is issued. Subject to the need for legibility, the size of the plate, the letters, numerals, and decals thereon, and the color of the plate, letters, numerals, and decals shall be in the discretion of the Commissioner. Decals shall be placed on the license plates in the manner prescribed by the Commissioner, and shall indicate the month and year of expiration. On the issuance of the decals, a new registration card shall be issued with the same date of expiration as the decals.

B. Notwithstanding any other provision of this title, the Department may issue permanent license plates without decals and without a month and year of expiration for all trailers and semitrailers, regardless of weight, trucks and tractor trucks with a gross vehicle weight rating or gross combination weight rating of more than 26,000 pounds, and taxicabs or other motor vehicles performing a taxicab service as defined in §46.2-2000 that are in compliance with the requirements of §§46.2-757 through 46.2-768 and Chapter 20 (§46.2-2000, et seq.) of this title. In addition, the Department may issue permanent license plates without decals and without a month and year of expiration for trucks and tractor trucks with gross vehicle weight ratings or gross combination weight ratings of at least 7,501 pounds but not more than 26,000 pounds, provided that such vehicles are for business use only, and for farm vehicles registered with the Department pursuant to §46.2-698.

C. Notwithstanding any contrary provision of this section, any person who, pursuant to former §56-304.3, repealed by Chapters 744 and 803 of the Acts of Assembly of 1995, obtained from the State Corporation Commission an exemption from the marker or decal requirements of former §§56-304, 56-304.1 or §56-304.2, and who has painted or, in the case of newly acquired vehicles, who paints an identifying number on the sides of any vehicle with respect to which such exemption applies and, in all other respects, continues to comply with the requirements of former §56-304.3, shall be deemed to be in compliance with subsections C and D of §46.2-761.

(Chgd. by L.1997 ch. 283; L.1999 ch. 593; L.2000 ch. 133, eff. 7/1/2000.)

§46.2-713. License plates and decals remain property of Department.

Every license plate and decal issued by the Department shall remain the property of the Department and shall be subject to be revoked, cancelled, and repossessed by the Department at any time as provided in this title.

§46.2-714. Permanent license plates.

Notwithstanding the provisions of §§46.2-711 and 46.2-712 the Department may, in its discretion, issue a type of license plate suitable for permanent use on motor vehicles, trailers, semitrailers, and motorcycles, together with decals, unless decals are not required under §46.2-712, to be attached to the license plates to indicate the registration period for which such vehicles have been properly licensed. The design of the license plates and decals, when required, shall be determined by the Commissioner.

Every permanent license plate and decal, when required, shall be returned to the Department whenever the owner of a vehicle disposes of it by sale or otherwise and when not actually in use on a motor vehicle, except dealer's plates temporarily not in use. The person in whose name the license plate is registered may apply, during the registration period for which it is issued, for the return thereof if the license plate is intended to be used on a subsequently acquired motor vehicle.

Every permanent license plate and decal, when issued, shall be returned to the Department whenever the owner of a vehicle elects to garage the vehicle and discontinue the use of it on the highway. The person in whose name the license plate is registered may apply, during the registration period for which it is issued, for the return thereof if the vehicle is to be returned to use on the highway.

(Chgd. by L.1997 ch. 283, eff. 7/1/97.)

§46.2-715. Display of license plates.

License plates assigned to a motor vehicle, other than a motorcycle, tractor truck, trailer, or semitrailer, or to persons licensed as motor vehicle dealers or transporters of unladen vehicles, shall be attached to the front and the rear of the vehicle. The license plate assigned to a motorcycle, trailer, or semitrailer shall be attached to the rear of the vehicle. The license plate assigned to a tractor truck shall be attached to the front of the vehicle. The license plates issued to licensed motor vehicle dealers and to persons licensed as transporters of unladen vehicles shall consist of one plate for each set issued and shall be attached to the rear of the vehicle to which it is assigned.

§46.2-716. How license plates fastened to vehicle; altering appearance of license plates.

A. Every license plate shall be securely fastened to the motor vehicle, trailer, or semitrailer to which it is assigned:

1. So as to prevent the plate from swinging,
2. In a position to be clearly visible, and
3. In a condition to be clearly legible.

B. No colored glass, colored plastic, or any other type of covering shall be placed, mounted, or installed on or over any license plate if such glass, plastic, or other type of covering in any way alters or obscures the alpha-numeric information or color of the license plate. No insignia, emblems, or trailer hitches or couplings shall be mounted in such a way as to hide or obscure any portion of the license plate or render any portion of the license plate illegible.

C. The Superintendent may make such regulations as he may deem advisable to enforce the proper mounting and securing of the license plate on the vehicle.
(Chgd. by L.2000 ch. 258, eff. 7/1/2000.)

§46.2-717. *(Repealed by L.1997 ch. 486, eff. 7/1/97.)*

§46.2-718. Use of old license plates or decals after application for new.

An owner who has applied for renewal of registration of a motor vehicle, trailer, or semitrailer fifteen days prior to the day the registration period begins, but who has not received the license plates, decals, or registration card for the ensuing registration period shall be entitled to operate or permit the operation of the vehicle on the highways on displaying on the vehicle the license plates or decals issued for the preceding registration period for such time to be prescribed by the Department as it may find necessary to issue new license plates or decals.

§46.2-719. Permit for emergency use of license plates.

A. The Commissioner may, in his discretion, grant a special permit for the use of license plates on a vehicle other than the vehicle for which the license plates were issued, when the vehicle for which the license plates were issued is undergoing repairs in a licensed motor vehicle dealer's repair shop and when the license plates are being used on a vehicle owned by the dealer in whose repair shop the vehicle is being repaired.

B. Application for the permit shall be made jointly by the dealer and the person whose vehicle is being repaired, on forms provided by the Department and shall show, in addition to whatever other information may be required by the Commissioner, that an emergency exists which would warrant the issuance of the permit.

C. The permit shall be evidenced by a certificate, issued by the Commissioner, which shall show the date of issuance, the person to whom issued, the motor number, serial number or identification number of the vehicle on which the license plates are to be used, and shall be in the immediate possession of the person operating the vehicle at all times while operating it. The certificate shall be valid for a period of five days from its issuance. On its expiration, application may be made for a renewal permit in the manner provided for the original permit, but only one renewal permit shall be issued to cover any one emergency.

D. The Commissioner may, subject to the limitations and conditions set forth in this section, authorize a motor vehicle dealer licensed in the Commonwealth to issue such permit on behalf of the Commissioner in accordance with the provisions of subsections A, B, and C of this section provided such permits are issued only with regard to the transfer in an emergency situation of license plates from a vehicle undergoing repairs in that dealer's repair shop. Any dealer to whom the authority is delegated by the Commissioner shall use the forms provided by the Commissioner and shall maintain in permanent form a record of all permits issued by him and any other relevant information that may be required by the Commissioner. Each record shall be kept by the dealer for not less than three years from the date of entry. The dealer shall allow full access to these records, during regular business hours, to duly authorized representatives of the Department and to law-enforcement officers. One copy of any permit of this kind issued by a dealer and the application form submitted for the permit shall be filed promptly by the dealer with the Department. The Commissioner, on determining that the provisions of this section or the directions of the Department are not being complied with by a dealer, may suspend the right of such dealer to issue license plate transfer permits.

§46.2-720. Use of license plates from another vehicle in certain circumstances.

The owner of a motor vehicle to which license plates have been assigned by the Department may remove the license plates from the motor vehicle and use them on another motor vehicle owned by a person operating a garage or owned by a motor vehicle dealer provided such use does not extend for more than five days and provided the use is limited to the time during which the first motor vehicle is being repaired or while the second motor vehicle is loaned to him for demonstration, as provided by §46.2-719.

§46.2-721. Application of liability insurance policy to vehicle carrying plates from insured vehicle.

The policy of liability insurance issued to the owner of a motor vehicle and covering the operation thereof shall extend to and be the primary insurance applicable to his operation of a motor vehicle on which he has placed license tags from another motor vehicle as provided in §46.2-720.

§46.2-722. Altered or forged license plates or decals; use as evidence of knowledge.

Any person who, with fraudulent intent, alters any license plate or decal issued by the Department or by any other state, forges or counterfeits any license plate or decal purporting to have been issued by the Department under the provisions of this title or by any other state under a similar law or who, with fraudulent intent, alters, falsifies, or forges any assignment thereof, or who holds or uses any license plate or decal knowing it to have been altered, forged, or falsified, shall be guilty of a Class 1 misdemeanor.

The owner of a vehicle who operates it while it displays altered or forged license plates or decals shall be presumed to have knowledge of the alteration or forgery.

§46.2-723. License plates for transporting manufactured homes used as temporary offices at construction sites.

The Department shall issue to persons engaged in the business of transporting from one construction site to another manufactured homes or house trailers used on those sites as temporary offices, license plates to be affixed to such manufactured homes or house trailers while being transported. The plates shall not be issued or used to transport manufactured homes or house trailers which exceed normally permissible load dimensions. The fee for each plate issued under this section shall be twenty-two dollars per year.

§46.2-724. Operation for hire of certain vehicles registered as not-for-hire; penalty.

If a motor vehicle of over 10,000 pounds registered gross weight that is registered to be operated exclusively not-for-hire is operated for-hire, the licensee shall be guilty of a traffic infraction. This penalty shall be in addition to the penalty prescribed by §46.2-704.
(Chgd. by L.1995 ch. 46; L.1997 chs. 774, 816, eff. 7/1/97.)

ARTICLE 10
SPECIAL LICENSE PLATES

**Multiple Sections 46.2-746.4:2, 46.2-749.32 enacted.*

§46.2-725. Special license plates, generally.

A. No series of special license plates shall be created or issued by the Commissioner or the Department except as authorized in this article. No special license plates in any series not provided for in this article and no registration decal for any such license plate shall be issued, reissued, or renewed on or after July 1, 1995. However, subject to the limitations contained in subdivisions 1 and 2 of subsection B of this section, the Commissioner may issue special license plates that are combinations of no more than two series of special license plates authorized in this article and currently issued by the Department; the fee for any such combination shall be equal to the sum of the fees for the two series plus the fee for reserved numbers and letters, if applicable. The provisions of subdivisions 1 and 2 of subsection B of this section shall not apply to special license plates that are combinations of two series of special license plates authorized in this article and currently issued by the Department if one of the two combined designs, when feasible, incorporates or includes the international symbol of access.

B. Except as otherwise provided in this article:

1. No license plates provided for in this article shall be issued until the Commissioner receives at least 350 prepaid applications therefor. In the event that 350 or more prepaid applications have not been received on or before the last day of the third year from the date the license plates were last authorized, no such license plates shall be issued unless the license plates are reauthorized by the General Assembly. Such reauthorized license plates shall remain subject to the provisions of this article;

2. No additional license plates shall be issued or reissued in any series that, after five or more years of issuance, has fewer than 100 active sets of plates, unless applications therefor again meet the criterion of subdivision 1 of this subsection; and

3. The annual fee for the issuance of any license plates issued pursuant to this article shall be ten dollars plus the prescribed fee for state license plates. Applications for all special license plates issued pursuant to this article shall be on forms prescribed by the Commissioner. All special license plates issued pursuant to this article shall be of designs prescribed by the Commissioner and shall bear unique letters and numerals, clearly distinguishable from any other license plate designs, and be readily identifiable by law-enforcement personnel.

No other state license plates shall be required on any vehicles bearing special license plates issued under the provisions of this article.

All fees collected by the Department under this article shall be paid by the Commissioner into the state treasury and shall be set aside as a special fund to be used to meet the expenses of the Department.

C. The provisions of this article relating to registration fees shall apply only to those vehicles registered as passenger cars, motor homes, and pick-up or panel trucks, as defined in §46.2-100. All other vehicle types registered with special license plates shall be subject to the appropriate special license plate fees, registration fees and other fees prescribed by law for such vehicle types.

(Chgd. by L.1995 ch. 747; L.1996 chs. 922, 1026; L.1997 chs. 774, 816, eff. 7/1/97.)

§46.2-725.1. *(Repealed by L.1995 ch. 747, eff. 7/1/95.)*

§46.2-726. License plates with reserved numbers or letters; fees.

The Commissioner may, in his discretion, reserve license plates with certain registration numbers or letters or combinations thereof for issuance to persons requesting license plates so numbered and lettered.

License plates with reserved numbers or letters may be issued for and displayed on vehicles operated as ambulances by private ambulance services.

The annual fee or, in the case of permanent license plates for trailers and semitrailers, the one-time fee, for the issuance of any license plates with reserved numbers or letters shall be ten dollars plus the prescribed fee for state license plates. If those license plates with reserved numbers or letters are subject to an additional fee beyond the prescribed fee for state license plates, the fee for such special license plates with reserved numbers or letters shall be ten dollars plus the additional fee for the special license plates plus the prescribed fee for state license plates.

The annual fee for reissuing licenses plates with the same combination of letters and numbers as license plates that were previously issued but not renewed shall be ten dollars plus the prescribed fee for state license plates. If those license plates are special license plates subject to an additional fee beyond the prescribed fee for state license plates, the fee shall be ten dollars plus the additional fee for the special license plates plus the prescribed fee for state license plates.

License plates with reserved numbers or letters or combinations thereof shall have at least one number or letter and may have as many as eight numbers, letters, or numbers and letters, but no more.

(Chgd. by L.1995 ch. 747; L.1997 chs. 94, 283; L.2000 ch. 126, eff. 7/1/2000.)

§46.2-727. Bicentennial license plates and decals; fees.

Bicentennial license plates and decals issued to any properly registered passenger motor vehicle from January 1, 1976, through December 31, 1981, may continue in use for a period determined by the Commissioner if the proper fee is paid as required in §46.2-694.

§46.2-728. Special license plates incorporating the Great Seal of Virginia; fees.

On receipt of an application, the Commissioner shall issue license plates incorporating the Great Seal of Virginia. These license plates shall be valid for whatever period the Commissioner determines.

For each set of license plates issued under this section the Commissioner shall charge, in addition to the prescribed cost of state license plates, a one-time fee of twenty-five dollars.

§46.2-728.1. Special license plates incorporating the official bird and the floral emblem of the Commonwealth; fee.

On receipt of an application, the Commissioner shall issue license plates incorporating the official bird and the floral emblem of the Commonwealth. These license plates shall be valid for whatever period the Commissioner determines.

For each set of license plates issued under this section the Commissioner shall charge, in addition to the prescribed cost of state license plates, a one-time fee of ten dollars at the time the plates are issued.

§46.2-728.2. Special license plates displaying a scenic design of Virginia; fees.

On receipt of an application, the Commissioner shall issue license plates displaying a scenic design of Virginia. These license plates shall be valid for whatever period the Commissioner determines.

For each set of license plates issued under this section, the Commissioner shall charge, in addition to the prescribed cost of state license plates, a one-time fee of ten dollars at the time the plates are issued.

§46.2-728.3. Special license plates displaying the official insect of the Commonwealth; fees.

On receipt of an application, the Commissioner shall issue license plates displaying the official insect of the Commonwealth as designated by §7.1-40.5.
(Chgd. by L.1995 ch. 747, eff. 7/1/95.)

§46.2-729. *(Repealed by L.1995 ch. 747, eff. 7/1/95.)*

§46.2-729.1. Presidential inauguration license plates.

Notwithstanding any other provisions of law, presidential inauguration license plates duly issued by the District of Columbia may be displayed on any motor vehicle duly registered and licensed in Virginia in lieu of license plates assigned to that motor vehicle. Such presidential license plates shall not be displayed except for the period beginning January 1 through the last day of March in the year of such inauguration.
(Added by L.1997 chs. 774, 816, eff. 7/1/97.)

§46.2-730. License plates for antique motor vehicles; fee.

A. On receipt of an application, the Commissioner shall issue appropriately designed license plates to owners of antique motor vehicles. These license plates shall be valid so long as title to the vehicle is vested in the applicant. The fee for the registration card and license plates of any of these vehicles shall be ten dollars.

B. On receipt of an application, the Commissioner may authorize for use on antique motor vehicles Virginia license plates manufactured prior to 1976 and designed for use without decals, if such license plates are embossed with or are of the same year of issue as the model year of the antique motor vehicle on which they are to be displayed. Original metal year tabs issued in place of license plates for years 1943 and 1953 and used with license plates issued in 1942 and 1952, respectively, also may be authorized by the Commissioner for use on antique motor vehicles that are of the same model year as the year the metal tab was originally issued. These license plates and metal tabs shall remain valid so long as title to the vehicle is vested in the applicant. The fee for the registration card and permission to use the license plates and metal tabs on any of these vehicles shall be ten dollars.

C. Notwithstanding the provisions of §§46.2-711 and 46.2-715, antique motor vehicles may display single license plates if the original manufacturer's design of the antique motor vehicles allows for the use of only single license plates or if the license plate was originally issued in one of the following years and is displayed in accordance with the provisions of subsection B of this section: 1906, 1907, 1908, 1909, 1945, or 1946.

D. Except as provided in subsection E of this section, motor vehicles registered with license plates issued under this section shall not be used for general transportation purposes, including, but not limited to, daily travel to and from the owner's place of employment, but shall only be used:

1. For participation in club activities, exhibits, tours, parades, and similar events; and

2. On the highways of the Commonwealth for the purpose of testing their operation, obtaining repairs or maintenance, transportation to and from events as described in subdivision 1 of this subsection, and for occasional pleasure driving not exceeding 250 miles from the residence of the owner.

E. Notwithstanding the foregoing provision of this section, antique motor vehicles displaying license plates issued pursuant to subsection B and C of this section may be used for general transportation purposes if the following conditions are met:

1. The physical condition of the vehicle's license plate or plates has been inspected and approved by the Department;

2. The license plate or plates are registered to the specific vehicle by the Department;

3. The owner of the vehicle periodically registers the vehicle with the Department and pays a registration fee for the vehicle equal to that which would be charged to obtain regular state license plates for that vehicle;

4. The vehicle passes a periodic safety inspection as provided in Article 21 (§46.2-1157 et seq.) of Chapter 10 of this title;

5. The vehicle displays current decals attached to the license plate, issued by the Department, indicating the valid registration period for the vehicle; and

6. When applicable, the vehicle meets the requirement of Article 22 (§46.2-1176 et seq.) of Chapter 10 of this title.

If more than one request is made for use, as provided in this subsection, of license plates having the same number, the Department shall accept only the first such application. Only vehicles titled to the person seeking to use license plates as provided in this subsection shall be eligible to use license plates as provided in this subsection.
(Chgd. by L.1999 ch. 292; L.2000 ch. 259, eff. 7/1/2000.)

§46.2-731. Disabled parking license plates; owners of vehicles specially equipped and used to transport persons with disabilities; fees.

On receipt of an application, the Commissioner shall issue appropriately designed disabled parking license plates to persons with physical disabilities that limit or impair their ability to walk. The Commissioner shall request that the application be accompanied by a certification of a licensed physician that the applicant meets the definition of "person with a disability that limits or impairs his ability to walk" contained in §46.2-1240. The issuance of a disabled parking license plate shall not preclude the issuance of a permanent removable windshield placard.

On application of an organization, the Commissioner shall issue disabled parking license plates for vehicles registered in the applicant's name if the vehicles are primarily used to transport persons with disabilities. The application shall include a certification by the applicant, under criteria determined by the Commissioner, that the vehicle is primarily used to transport persons with disabilities that limit or impair their ability to walk, as defined in §46.2-1240.

The fee for the issuance of a disabled parking license plate under this section may not exceed the fee charged for a similar license plate for the same class vehicle.
(Chgd. by L.1995 ch. 776; L.1997 chs. 783, 904, eff. 7/1/97.)

§46.2-732. Special license plates and decals for the deaf; fees.

On receipt of an application, the Commissioner shall issue appropriately designed license plates to deaf persons. For purposes of this section, a deaf person shall be defined as a person who cannot hear and understand normal speech. The fee for these license plates shall be as provided in §46.2-694.

The Commissioner shall also issue to any deaf person a removable decal, to be used on any passenger car, pickup or panel truck operated by such person. The decals shall be of a design determined by the Commissioner and shall be displayed in a manner determined by the Superintendent of State Police. A reasonable fee to be determined by the Commissioner shall be charged each person issued a decal under this section, but no fee shall be charged any person exempted from fees by §46.2-739.

It shall be unlawful for any person who is not a person described in this section to willfully and falsely represent himself as having the qualifications to obtain the special plates or decal.

The provisions of subdivisions 1 and 2 of subsection B of §46.2-725 shall not apply to license plates issued under this section.

(Chgd. by L.1995 ch. 747, eff. 7/1/95.)

§46.2-733. License plates for persons delivering unladen vehicles; fees.

A. On receipt of an application, the Commissioner shall issue appropriately designed license plates to persons engaged in the business of delivering unladen motor vehicles under their own power from points of assembly or distribution.

B. Every applicant for license plates to be issued under this section shall, before he begins delivery of any of these vehicles, apply to the Commissioner for a registration card and license plates. On the payment of a fee of seventy-five dollars a registration card and license plates shall be issued to the applicant in a form prescribed by the Commissioner. The Commissioner shall issue to the applicant two license plates. For each additional license plate a fee of twenty dollars per plate shall be paid by the applicant.

C. It shall be unlawful for any person to use these license plates other than on unladen motor vehicles, trailers, and semitrailers which are being delivered from points of assembly or distribution in the usual course of his delivery business or which are used as provided in subsection D of this section. The operators of such vehicles being delivered, bearing license plates issued under this section, shall at all times during their operation have in their possession a proper bill of lading showing the point of origin and destination of the vehicle being delivered and describing it.

D. License plates issued under this section may be used by any financial institutions specifically excluded from the definition of "motor vehicle dealer" in provision 5 of §46.2-1500 for the purpose of using them in the normal course of business in taking, repossessing, or otherwise transporting vehicles for the purpose of preservation, sale, allowing a prospective buyer to test-drive the vehicle if the prospective buyer is accompanied by an employee of the financial institution or has the written permission of the financial institution on a form provided by the Department, or otherwise in connection with repossession or foreclosure of the vehicle on which there is a security interest securing a loan to a financial institution.

E. License plates issued under this section may be issued to any business engaged in the mounting, installing, servicing, or repairing of equipment on or in a vehicle. The use of license plates issued under this section shall be limited to the pick-up and delivery of a vehicle and shall not be used on vehicles employed for general transportation.

(Chgd. by L.1998 ch. 370, eff. 7/1/98.)

§46.2-734. Reconstructed and specially constructed vehicles; registration and licensing; inspection requirements; storage of unlicensed vehicles.

For the purposes of this section, "hobbyist" means the owner of one or more reconstructed or specially constructed vehicles who collects, purchases, acquires, trades, or disposes of reconstructed or specially constructed vehicles or parts thereof for his own use in order to build, reconstruct, restore, preserve, and maintain a reconstructed or specially constructed vehicle for historic or hobby interest.

Any owner of a reconstructed vehicle assembled from a vehicle manufactured twenty years or more prior to the time of applying for registration or transfer of title of the vehicle or any owner of a specially constructed vehicle, may register it as a reconstructed or specially constructed vehicle on payment of the registration fee as set out in §46.2-694 or §46.2-697 and be furnished, upon request, reserved hobbyist series license plates issued by the Commissioner under §46.2-726.

These vehicles shall be registered and titled according to their chassis numbers or, if no chassis number exists, then by their motor serial numbers. The vehicles shall meet inspection requirements applicable to the model year shown on the registration certificate.

A hobbyist may store unlicensed, operable or inoperable, vehicles on his property provided the vehicles and the outdoor storage area are maintained in such a manner that they do not constitute a health hazard and are screened from ordinary public view by a fence, rapidly growing trees, shrubbery, billboards or other appropriate means. The hobbyist shall, however, not be exempt from local zoning ordinances governing the storage of these vehicles.

§46.2-734.1. Special license plates for certain law-enforcement officers.

On receipt of an application and written confirmation that the applicant is a law-enforcement officer, the Commissioner shall issue to the applicant special license plates.

(Added by L.1997 chs. 774, 816, eff. 7/1/97.)

§46.2-735. Special license plates for members of volunteer rescue squads and volunteer rescue squad auxiliaries; fees.

The Commissioner, on application, shall supply members of volunteer rescue squads and members of volunteer rescue squad auxiliaries special license plates bearing the letters "R S" followed by numbers or letters or any combination thereof.

Only one application shall be required from each volunteer rescue squad or volunteer rescue squad auxiliary. The application shall contain the names and residence addresses of all members who request license plates. The Commissioner shall charge the prescribed cost of state license plates for each set of license plates issued under this section.

(Chgd. by L.1996 ch. 1026, eff. 7/1/96.)

§46.2-736. Special license plates for professional or volunteer fire fighters and members of volunteer fire department auxiliaries; fees.

The Commissioner, on application, shall supply professional fire fighters, members of volunteer fire departments, members of volunteer fire department auxiliaries, and volunteer members of any fire department license plates bearing the letters "F D" followed by numbers or letters or any combination thereof.

An application shall be required from each professional fire fighter, volunteer fire fighter, or member of a volunteer

fire department auxiliary. The application shall be approved by the chief or head of the fire department and shall contain the name and residence address of the applicant. The Commissioner shall charge each professional fire fighter a fee of one dollar in addition to the prescribed cost of state license plates, for each set of license plates issued under this section. No additional fee shall be charged to members of volunteer fire departments, members of volunteer fire department auxiliaries, or volunteer members of any fire department.
(Chgd. by L.1996 ch. 1026, eff. 7/1/96.)

§46.2-736.1. Special license plates for certain officials.

On request, the Commissioner shall issue special license plates to the following officials: the Speaker of the House of Delegates, members of the House of Delegates, members of the Virginia Senate, the Clerk of the House of Delegates, the Clerk of the Virginia Senate, the Governor of Virginia, the Lieutenant Governor of Virginia, the Attorney General of Virginia, United States Congressmen, and United States Senators.

The provisions of subdivisions 1 and 2 of subsection B of §46.2-725 shall not apply to license plates issued under this section.
(Added by L.1995 ch. 747, eff. 7/1/95.)

§46.2-736.2. Special license plates for certain elected or appointed officials.

The Commissioner, on application, shall issue to honorary consuls, upon receipt of written evidence from the United States Department of State that the applicant is an honorary consul on active status, and members of county boards of supervisors, state commissions and boards and to other state officials appointed by the Governor special license plates bearing decals or stickers bearing the legend "HONORARY CONSUL" or identifying the commission, board, or office to which the applicant has been elected or appointed.
(Added by L.1995 ch. 747; chgd. by L.1996 ch. 1026, eff. 7/1/96.)

§46.2-737. Special license plates for certain constitutional officers.

The Commissioner, on application, shall issue to sheriffs, county and city treasurers and commissioners of revenue, attorneys for the Commonwealth, and circuit court clerks special license plates identifying the office held by the applicant.

The provisions of subdivisions 1 and 2 of subsection B of §46.2-725 shall not apply to license plates issued under this section.
(Chgd. by L.1995 ch. 747, eff. 7/1/95.)

§46.2-738. Special license plates for amateur radio operators.

The Commissioner, on request, may supply any amateur radio operator licensed by the federal government or an agency thereof, and having radio transmitting and receiving equipment permanently installed in his motor vehicle, license plates bearing his official call letters.

If more than one request is made for use, as provided in this section, of license plates having the same alpha-numeric, the Department shall accept the first such application. Persons receiving amateur radio operator special license plates shall affix such plates only to vehicles to which they are the titled owner.

The Commissioner shall charge a fee of one dollar in addition to the prescribed cost of state license plates, for each set of license plates issued under the provisions of this section.
(Chgd. by L.1996 chs. 943, 994, eff. 7/1/96.)

§46.2-738.1. Special license plates; members of the American Radio Relay League.

On receipt of an application therefor and written evidence that the applicant is a member, the Commissioner shall issue special license plates to members of the American Radio Relay League. When so requested and feasible, the license plates issued by the Commissioner under this section to any applicant who (i) is licensed by the federal government or an agency thereof as an amateur radio operator and (ii) has radio transmitting and receiving equipment permanently installed in the motor vehicle on which license plates issued under this section are to be displayed shall bear the applicant's official call letters and/or numbers. If more than one application is made under this section for license plates bearing the same combination of letters and/or numbers, the Department shall accept only the first such application.

License plates issued under this section shall be issued only to persons who are the titled owners of the vehicles on which the license plates are to be displayed and shall be displayed only on those vehicles.
(Added by L.1998 ch. 508, eff. 7/1/98.)

§46.2-739. Special license plates for certain disabled veterans; fees.

A. On receipt of an application, the Commissioner shall issue special license plates to applicants who are disabled veterans as defined in §46.2-100 or unremarried surviving spouses of such disabled veterans. These license plates shall be special permanent red, white, and blue license plates bearing the letters "DV." The application shall be accompanied by a certification from the U.S. Veterans Administration that the veteran has been so designated and that his disability is service-connected. License plates issued under this subsection shall not permit the vehicles upon which they are displayed to use parking spaces reserved for persons with disabilities that limit or impair their ability to walk.

B. On receipt of an application, the Commissioner shall issue special DV disabled parking license plates displaying the international symbol of access in the same size as the numbers and letters on the plate and in a color that contrasts to the background to veterans who are also persons with disabilities that limit or impair their ability to walk as defined in §46.2-100. The Commissioner shall require that such application be accompanied by a certification from a licensed physician to that effect. Special DV disabled parking license plates issued under this subsection shall authorize the vehicles upon which they are displayed to use parking spaces reserved for persons with disabilities that limit or impair their ability to walk.

No annual registration fee, as prescribed in §46.2-694, and no annual fee, as set forth in subdivision 3 of subsection B of §46.2-725, shall be required for any one motor vehicle owned and used personally by any veteran, provided such vehicle displays license plates issued under this section.

The provisions of subdivisions 1 and 2 of subsection B of §46.2-725 shall not apply to license plates issued under this section.
(Chgd. by L.1995 ch. 747; L.1997 chs. 774, 816, eff. 7/1/97.)

§46.2-740. Special license plates for survivors of Battle of Chosin Reservoir.

On receipt of an application and written evidence that the applicant is a survivor of the Battle of Chosin Reservoir, the Commissioner shall issue special license plates to the applicant.

The provisions of subdivisions 1 and 2 of subsection B of §46.2-725 shall not apply to license plates under this section.
(Chgd. by L.1995 ch. 747, eff. 7/1/95.)

§46.2-741. Special license plates for survivors of attack on Pearl Harbor; fees.

On receipt of an application and written evidence that the applicant is an honorably discharged former member of one of the armed forces of the United States and, while serving in the armed forces of the United States, was present during the attack on the island of Oahu, Territory of Hawaii, on December 7, 1941, between the hours of 7:55 a.m. and 9:45 a.m., Hawaii time, the Commissioner shall issue to the applicant special license plates identifying the vehicle as registered to a Pearl Harbor survivor.

For each set of license plates issued under this section, the Commissioner shall charge, in addition to the prescribed cost of state license plates, a one-time fee of ten dollars at the time the plates are issued.

The provisions of subdivisions 1 and 2 of subsection B of §46.2-725 shall not apply to license plates issued under this section.

(Chgd. by L.1995 ch. 747; L.1997 chs. 774, 816, eff. 7/1/97.)

§46.2-742. Special license plates for persons awarded Purple Heart; fee.

On receipt of an application and written evidence that the applicant has been awarded the Purple Heart, the Commissioner shall issue to the applicant special license plates.

For each set of license plates issued under this section, the Commissioner shall charge, in addition to the prescribed cost of state license plates, a one-time fee of ten dollars at the time the plates are issued.

Unremarried surviving spouses of persons eligible to receive special license plates under this section may also be issued special license plates under this section.

The provisions of subdivisions 1 and 2 of subsection B of §46.2-725 shall not apply to license plates under this section.

(Chgd. by L.1995 ch. 747; L.1996 chs. 922, 1026, eff. 7/1/96.)

§46.2-742.1. Special license plates for persons awarded the Bronze Star, Bronze Star with a "V" for valor, or the Silver Star; fee.

On receipt of an application and written evidence that the applicant has been awarded a Bronze Star, Bronze Star with a "V" for valor, or Silver Star Medal, the Commissioner shall issue to the applicant special license plates.

For each set of license plates issued under this section, the Commissioner shall charge, in addition to the prescribed cost of state license plates, a one-time fee of ten dollars at the time the plates are issued.

The provisions of subdivisions 1 and 2 of subsection B of §46.2-725 shall not apply to license plates issued under this section.

(Chgd. by L.1995 ch. 747; L.1996 ch. 1026; L.1999 ch. 907, eff. 7/1/99.)

§46.2-742.2. Special license plates for persons awarded the Navy Cross, the Distinguished Service Cross, the Air Force Cross, or the Distinguished Flying Cross.

On receipt of an application and written evidence that the applicant has been awarded the Navy Cross, the Distinguished Service Cross, the Air Force Cross, or the Distinguished Flying Cross, the Commissioner shall issue to the applicant special license plates.

The provisions of subdivisions 1 and 2 of subsection B of §46.2-725 shall not apply to license plates issued under this section.

Unremarried surviving spouses of persons eligible to receive special license plates under this section may also be issued special license plates under this section.

(Chgd. by L.1995 ch. 747; L.1996 ch. 1026; L.1997 chs. 774, 816, eff. 7/1/97.)

§46.2-743. Special license plates for certain veterans.

A. On receipt of an application and written evidence that the applicant is an honorably discharged former member of one of the armed forces of the United States, the Commissioner shall issue to the applicant special license plates.

B. On receipt of an application and written evidence that the applicant is on active duty with, has been honorably discharged after at least six months of active duty service in, or has retired from the United States Marine Corps, the Commissioner shall issue to the applicant special license plates whose design incorporates an emblem of the United States Marine Corps.

C. On receipt of an application and written evidence that the applicant is a veteran of World War II, the Commissioner shall issue special license plates to veterans of World War II.

D. On receipt of an application and written evidence that the applicant is a veteran of the Korean War, the Commissioner shall issue special license plates to veterans of the Korean War.

E. On receipt of an application and written evidence that the applicant is a veteran of the Vietnam War, the Commissioner shall issue special license plates to veterans of the Vietnam War.

F. On receipt of an application and written evidence that the applicant is a veteran of Operation Desert Shield or Operation Desert Storm, the Commissioner shall issue special license plates to veterans of those military operations.

G. On receipt of an application and written evidence that the applicant is a veteran of the Asiatic-Pacific Campaign, the Commissioner shall issue special license plates to veterans of that campaign.

H. The provisions of subdivisions 1 and 2 of subsection B of §46.2-725 shall not apply to license plates issued under subsection A, C, D, or E of this section.

(Chgd. by L.1995 ch. 747; L.1996 ch. 1026; L.1997 chs. 774, 816; L.1999 chs. 883, 907; L.2000 chs. 75, 190, eff. 7/1/2000.)

§46.2-744. Special license plates for members of Virginia National Guard; fees.

On receipt of an application and written confirmation that the applicant is a member of the National Guard, the Commissioner shall issue to the applicant special license plates.

The fee for license plates issued under this section to members of Virginia National Guard units shall be one-half the fee prescribed in §46.2-694, unless the plates bear reserved numbers or letters as provided for in §46.2-726. In this latter case, the fee for the issuance of license plates shall be the same as for those issued under §46.2-726.

The fee for members of non-Virginia National Guard units shall be ten dollars per year plus the prescribed cost for state license plates, unless the plates bear reserved numbers or letters as provided for in §46.2-726. In this latter case, such license plates shall be subject to an additional charge of ten dollars per year for the reserved numbers or letters.

The provisions of subdivisions 1 and 2 of subsection B of §46.2-725 shall not apply to license plates issued under this section.

(Chgd. by L.1995 chs. 252, 747, eff. 7/1/95.)

§46.2-745. Special license plates for persons awarded the Medal of Honor; fees.

On receipt of an application and written confirmation from one of the armed services that the applicant has been awarded the Medal of Honor, the Commissioner shall issue special license plates to such persons and to unremarried surviving spouses of such persons. No fee shall be charged for the issuance of these license plates.

It shall be unlawful for any person who is not a person described in this section to willfully and falsely represent himself as having the qualifications to obtain the special license plates herein provided for.

The provisions of subdivisions 1 and 2 of subsection B of §46.2-725 shall not apply to license plates issued under this section.

(Chgd. by L.1995 ch. 747, eff. 7/1/95.)

§46.2-746. Special license plates for former prisoners of war; fees.

On receipt of an application and written evidence from one of the armed forces that the applicant was a prisoner of war and was honorably discharged, if not currently a member of the armed forces, the Commissioner shall issue special license plates to persons who have been prisoners of the enemy in any war. No fee shall be charged for license plates issued under the provisions of this section.

It shall be unlawful for any person to willfully and falsely represent himself as having the qualifications to obtain the special plates provided for in this section.

No individual shall be issued special license plates under this section for more than one vehicle.

On presentation of appropriate written evidence from the Foreign Claims Settlement Commission of the United States, special license plates provided for in this section shall also be issued by the Commissioner to persons who were not members of the armed forces.

Unremarried surviving spouses of persons eligible to receive special license plates under this section may also be issued special license plates under this section.

The provisions of subdivisions 1 and 2 of subsection B of §46.2-725 shall not apply to license plates issued under this section.

(Chgd. by L.1995 ch. 747, eff. 7/1/95.)

§46.2-746.01. Special license plates for persons once declared missing in action.

On receipt of an application therefor and written evidence from one of the armed forces that the applicant was once declared missing in action, the Commissioner shall issue special license plates to the person once declared missing in action.

(Added by L.1998 ch. 511, eff. 7/1/98.)

§46.2-746.1. Special license plates for members of military assault forces.

On receipt of an application and written evidence that the applicant is or has been, while serving in the armed forces of the United States, a member of a military assault force, the Commissioner shall issue to the applicant special license plates. For the purposes of this section, a military assault force is a unit or element of the armed forces of the United States engaged in or charged with the invasion or capture of territory under the control of enemy forces.

The provisions of subdivisions 1 and 2 of subsection B of §46.2-725 shall not apply to license plates issued under this section.

(Chgd. by L.1995 ch. 747, eff. 7/1/95.)

§46.2-746.2. *(Repealed by L.1999 ch. 907, eff. 7/1/99.)*

§46.2-746.2:1. Special license plates; members of the 82nd Airborne Division Association.

On receipt of an application therefor and presentation of written evidence that the applicant is a member of the 82nd Airborne Division Association, the Commissioner shall issue to the applicant special license plates.

(Added by L.1999 ch. 907, eff. 7/1/99.)

§46.2-746.2:2. Special license plates; members of the Society of the 173rd Airborne Brigade.

On receipt of an application therefor and presentation of written evidence that the applicant is a member of the Society of the 173rd Airborne Brigade, the Commissioner shall issue to the applicant special license plates.

(Added by L.1999 ch. 907, eff. 7/1/99.)

§46.2-746.3. Special license plates for members of certain military reserve organizations.

The Commissioner, on application therefor, shall issue special license plates to members of the Air Force Reserve, the Army Reserve, the Coast Guard Reserve, the Marine Reserve, and the Naval Reserve. Such special license plates may, when feasible, bear decals or stickers identifying the reserve organization of which the applicant is a member.

(Added by L.1995 ch. 747; chgd. by L.1996 ch. 1026, eff. 7/1/96.)

§46.2-746.4. Special license plates for members of certain military veterans' organizations.

On receipt of an application and written evidence that the applicant is a member of any of the following military veterans' organizations, the Commissioner shall issue special license plates to the members of the following organizations: the American Legion, the Disabled American Veterans, the Legion of Valor of the USA, the Marine Corps League, the Retired Officers Association, the Special Forces Association, the Veterans of the Battle of Iwo Jima, and the Vietnam Veterans of America.

The provisions of subdivisions 1 and 2 of subsection B of §46.2-725 shall not apply to license plates issued to members of the Legion of Valor of the USA under this section.

(Added by L.1995 ch. 747; chgd. by L.1996 ch. 1026; L.1997 chs. 774, 816; L.2000 chs. 75, 111, eff. 7/1/2000.)

§46.2-746.4:1. *(Repealed by L.2000 ch. 766, eff. 7/1/2000.)*

§46.2-746.4:2. Special license plates; U.S. Submarine Force centennial.

(As added by L.2000 ch. 145. Section effective only until 7/1/2005. See other Section 46.2-746.4:2 below.)

On receipt of an application therefor, the Commissioner shall issue special license plates celebrating the U.S. Submarine Force centennial.

The provisions of this section shall expire on July 1, 2005.

(Added by L.2000 ch. 145, eff. 7/1/2000. Repealed by its own terms, eff. 7/1/2005.)

§46.2-746.4:2. Special license plates for submarine service veterans.

(As added by L.2000 ch. 766. See other Section 46.2-746.4:2 above.)

On receipt of an application and written evidence that the applicant is a submarine service veteran, the Commissioner shall issue special license plates to submarine service veterans.

(Added by L.2000 ch. 766, eff. 7/1/2000.)

§46.2-746.5. Special license plates for National Guard retirees; fees.

On receipt of an application and written evidence that the applicant is a retired member of the National Guard, the Commissioner shall issue special license plates to National Guard retirees.

The fee for license plates issued under this section to retired members of the Virginia National Guard shall be the fee prescribed in §46.2-694, unless the plates bear reserved numbers or letters as provided for in §46.2-726. In this latter case, the fee for the issuance of license plates shall be the same as for those issued under §46.2-726.

The fee for non-Virginia National Guard retirees shall be ten dollars per year plus the prescribed cost for state license plates, unless the plates bear reserved numbers or letters as provided for in §46.2-726. In this latter case, such license plates shall be subject to an additional charge of ten dollars per year for the reserved numbers or letters.
(Added by L.1995 ch. 747; chgd. by L.1997 chs. 774, 816, eff. 7/1/97.)

§46.2-746.6. Special license plates for members of certain volunteer search and rescue organizations.

On receipt of an application and written evidence that the applicant is a member, the Commissioner shall issue special license plates to members of the following organizations: the Civil Air Patrol, the Coast Guard Auxiliary, and any other volunteer search and rescue organization.
(Added by L.1995 ch. 747, eff. 7/1/95.)

§46.2-746.6:1. *(Repealed by L.2000 chs. 75, 766, eff. 7/1/2000.)*

§46.2-746.6:2. Special license plates for supporters of the American Red Cross.

On receipt of an application, the Commissioner shall issue special license plates to supporters of the American Red Cross.
(Added by L.2000 ch. 766, eff. 7/1/2000.)

§46.2-746.7. Special license plates for members of certain civic and fraternal organizations.

On receipt of an application and written evidence that the applicant is a member of such organization, the Commissioner shall issue special license plates to members of the following organizations: the Exchange Club, the Jaycees, the Kiwanis, the Lions of Virginia, the Loyal Order of Moose, Ruritan National, the Freemasons, the Shriners, the Most Worshipful Prince Hall Grand Lodge of Virginia, the Order of the Eastern Star, the Knights of Columbus, and college and university fraternities and sororities.
(Added by L.1995 ch. 747; chgd. by L.1996 ch. 1026; L.1998 ch. 175; L.1999 ch. 907; L.2000 ch. 75, eff. 7/1/2000.)

§46.2-746.8. Special license plates for members of certain occupational associations.

On receipt of an application and written evidence that the applicant is a member of such organization, the Commissioner shall issue special license plates to members of the following organizations: the National Society of Black Engineers, the Fraternal Order of Police, the International Association of Firefighters, the Virginia State Firefighters Association, the State Fire Chiefs Association of Virginia, the Association of Realtors, and the Society of Certified Public Accountants.
(Added by L.1995 ch. 747; chgd. by L.1997 chs. 774, 816; L.1999 ch. 907; L.2000 ch. 75, eff. 7/1/2000.)

§46.2-746.8:1. Special license plates for members of the Fraternal Order of Police Associates or the Fraternal Order of Police Auxiliary.

On receipt of an application and written evidence that the applicant is a member of either the Fraternal Order of Police Associates or the Fraternal Order of Police Auxiliary, the Commissioner shall issue to the applicant special license plates. All license plates issued under this section shall be of the same design.
(Added by L.1998 ch. 654; chgd. by L.2000 ch. 267, eff. 7/1/2000.)

§46.2-746.9. Special license plates for certain occupations.

On receipt of an application and written evidence that the applicant is a magistrate, pharmacist, registered nurse, general registrar, or postmaster, the Commissioner shall issue special license plates to the applicant.
(Added by L.1995 ch. 747; chgd. by L.2000 ch. 148, eff. 7/1/2000.)

§46.2-746.10. Special license plates for supporters of the AFL–CIO.

On receipt of an application therefor, the Commissioner shall issue special license plates to supporters of the AFL–CIO.
(Added by L.1997 chs. 774, 816, eff. 7/1/97.)

§46.2-746.11. Special license plates for supporters of certain aviation education facilities; fees.

A. On receipt of an application and payment of the fee prescribed by this section, the Commissioner shall issue special license plates bearing the following legend: NATIONAL AIR AND SPACE MUSEUM.

B. The annual fee for plates issued pursuant to this section shall be twenty-five dollars in addition to the prescribed fee for state license plates. For each such twenty-five-dollar fee collected in excess of 1,000 registrations pursuant to this section, fifteen dollars shall be paid into the state treasury and credited to the special nonreverting fund known as the Aviation Education Facilities Fund, established within the Department of Accounts, for use by the Department of Aviation to support aviation education facilities located in the Commonwealth that are annexes of or affiliated with similar national facilities located in the nation's capital.
(Added by L.1998 chs. 286, 295, eff. 7/1/98.)

§46.2-746.12. Special license plates for supporters of credit unions.

On receipt of an application therefor, the Commissioner shall issue special license plates to supporters of credit unions.
(Added by L.1998 ch. 288, eff. 7/1/98.)

§46.2-746.13. Special license plates; National Speleological Society.

On receipt of an application therefor, the Commissioner shall issue special license plates bearing the legend: NATIONAL SPELEOLOGICAL SOCIETY.
(Added by L.1998 ch. 293, eff. 7/1/98.)

§46.2-746.14. Special license plates; aviation enthusiasts.

On receipt of an application therefor, the Commissioner shall issue special license plates to aviation enthusiasts.
(Added by L.1998 ch. 294, eff. 7/1/98.)

§46.2-746.15. Special license plates; supporters of Great Meadow.

On receipt of an application therefor, the Commissioner shall issue special license plates to supporters of Great Meadow.
(Added by L.1998 ch. 297, eff. 7/1/98.)

§46.2-746.16. Special license plates; returned Peace Corps volunteers.

On receipt of an application therefor and written evidence that the applicant is a returned Peace Corps volunteer, the Commissioner shall issue special license plates to returned Peace Corps volunteers.
(Added by L.1998 ch. 297, eff. 7/1/98.)

§46.2-746.17. Special license plates; Wildlife Foundation of Virginia.

On receipt of an application therefor, the Commissioner shall issue special license plates bearing the legend: WILDLIFE FOUNDATION OF VIRGINIA.
(Added by L.1998 ch. 429, eff. 7/1/98.)

§46.2-746.18. Special license plates; Virginia Wildlife Federation.

On receipt of an application therefor, the Commissioner shall issue special license plates bearing the legend: VIRGINIA WILDLIFE FEDERATION.
(Added by L.1998 ch. 429, eff. 7/1/98.)

§46.2-746.19. Special license plates; employees of the Virginia Department of Transportation.

On receipt of an application therefor and written evidence that the applicant is an employee of the Virginia Department of Transportation, the Commissioner shall issue special license plates to employees of the Virginia Department of Transportation.
(Added by L.1998 ch. 710, eff. 7/1/98.)

§46.2-746.20. Special license plates; supporters of the American Automobile Association.

On receipt of an application therefor, the Commissioner shall issue special license plates to supporters of the American Automobile Association.
(Added by L.1998 ch. 849, eff. 7/1/98.)

§46.2-746.21. Special license plates; Tercentenary of the City of Williamsburg.

(Repealed by its own terms, eff. 7/1/2003.)

On receipt of an application therefor, the Commissioner shall issue special license plates commemorating the Tercentenary of the City of Williamsburg.

The provisions of this section shall expire on July 1, 2003.
(Added by L.1998 ch. 849, eff. 7/1/98.)

§46.2-746.22. Special license plates; members of the Sons of Confederate Veterans.

On receipt of an application therefor and written evidence that the applicant is a member of the Sons of Confederate Veterans, the Commissioner shall issue special license plates to members of the Sons of Confederate Veterans. No logo or emblem of any description shall be displayed or incorporated into the design of license plates issued under this section.
(Added by L.1999 ch. 902, eff. 7/1/99.)

§46.2-747. Special license plates for street rods.

On receipt of an application, the Commissioner shall issue special license plates to owners of street rods. For the purposes of this section, "street rods" shall mean modernized private passenger motor vehicles either manufactured prior to 1949 or designed or manufactured to resemble vehicles manufactured prior to 1949.

§46.2-747.1. Special license plates for members of the Gold Wing Road Riders Association.

On receipt of an application and written evidence that the applicant is a member of the Gold Wing Road Riders Association, the Commissioner shall issue special license plates to members of the Gold Wing Road Riders Association.
(Added by L.1997 chs. 774, 816, eff. 7/1/97.)

§46.2-748. Special license plates for members of "REACT."

On receipt of an application, the Commissioner shall issue special license plates to members of Radio Emergency Associated Communications Teams (REACT).

The provisions of subdivisions 1 and 2 of subsection B of §46.2-725 shall not apply to license plates issued under this section prior to July 1, 1997.
(Chgd. by L.1996 ch. 1026, eff. 7/1/96.)

§46.2-748.1. *(Repealed by L.2000 ch. 75, eff. 7/1/2000.)*

§46.2-748.2. Special license plates; Virginia Scuba Diver.

On receipt of an application therefor, the Commissioner shall issue to the applicant special license plates bearing the legend: VIRGINIA SCUBA DIVER.
(Added by L.1997 chs. 774, 816, eff. 7/1/97.)

§46.2-749. Issuance of license plates bearing seal, symbol, emblem, or logotype of certain institutions of higher education; fees.

A. On receipt of an application, the Commissioner may issue for any accredited college or university, in accordance with policies and procedures established by the Commissioner and in accordance with an agreement between the institution and the Department, special license plates bearing the seal, symbol, emblem, or logotype of that institution of higher education.

For each set of license plates issued hereunder, the Commissioner shall charge, in addition to the prescribed cost of state license plates, an annual fee of twenty-five dollars.

B. Any institution of higher education that enters into an agreement with the Department pursuant to this section thereby waives any royalty fees to which it might otherwise be entitled for use of its seal, symbol, emblem, or logotype as provided in this section. However, any such institution located in Virginia shall annually receive an allocation of fifteen dollars for each set of license plates in excess of 1,000 registrations pursuant to the institution's agreement with the Department during the term of the agreement. The allocated funds shall be deposited by the Department into the state treasury and credited to the relevant institution to be used to support scholarships for eligible undergraduate students enrolled in the institution. Only students who (i) are bona fide domiciliaries of Virginia as defined in §23-7.4 and (ii) are enrolled in educational programs whose primary purpose is not to provide religious training or theological education shall be eligible to receive such scholarships.

The State Council of Higher Education for Virginia shall review and approve plans for each participating institution for the implementation of these scholarship programs. These plans shall include, but need not be limited to, criteria for the awarding of the scholarships and procedures for determining the recipients.

The provisions of subdivisions 1 and 2 of subsection B of §46.2-725 shall not apply to license plates issued under this section for any institution of higher education located in Virginia.
(Chgd. by L.1995 ch. 747; L.1996 ch. 1026, eff. 7/1/96.)

§46.2-749.1. Special wildlife conservation plates.

A. On receipt of an application and payment of the fee prescribed by this section, the Commissioner shall issue special license plates bearing the following legend: WILDLIFE CONSERVATIONIST.

B. The annual fee for plates issued pursuant to this section shall be twenty-five dollars plus the prescribed fee for state license plates. For each such twenty-five dollar fee collected in excess of 1,000 registrations pursuant to this section, fifteen dollars shall be paid into the state treasury and credited to the special fund known as the game protection fund.
(Chgd. by L.1995 ch. 747, eff. 7/1/95.)

§46.2-749.2. Special Chesapeake Bay preservation plates.

A. On receipt of an application and payment of the fee prescribed by this section, the Commissioner shall issue special license plates bearing the following legend: FRIEND OF THE CHESAPEAKE.

B. The annual fee for plates issued pursuant to this section shall be twenty-five dollars in addition to the prescribed fee for state license plates. For each such twenty-five dollar fee collected in excess of 1,000 registrations pursuant to this section, fifteen dollars shall be paid into the state treasury and credited to the special nonreverting fund known as the Chesapeake Bay Restoration Fund, established within the Department of Accounts, for use by the Commonwealth of Virginia for environmental education and restoration projects relating to the Chesapeake Bay and its tributaries. Interest earned on the Fund will accrue to the Fund.
(Chgd. by L.1995 chs. 747, 749, 823, eff. 7/1/95.)

§46.2-749.2:1. Special license plates for supporters of certain children's programs; fees.

On receipt of an application and payment of the fee prescribed by this section, the Commissioner shall issue special license plates bearing, at the applicant's option, either (i) a heart, (ii) a five-pointed star, (iii) a child's handprint, or (iv) another design or device approved by the Commissioner.

The annual fee for plates issued pursuant to this section shall be twenty-five dollars plus the prescribed fee for state license plates. For each such twenty-five-dollar fee collected in excess of 1,000 registrations pursuant to this section, fifteen dollars shall be paid into the state treasury and credited to the special fund known as the Children's Programs Support Fund for use as follows: one-half shall be paid into the Family and Children's Trust Fund and one-half shall be paid to the Department of Health for use by the Safe Kids Coalition.
(Chgd. by L.1995 ch. 747; L.1996 ch. 922, eff. 7/1/96.)

§46.2-749.2:2. Special license plates for Virginians for the Arts; fees.

A. On receipt of an application and payment of the fee prescribed by this section, the Commissioner shall issue special license plates bearing the following legend: VIRGINIANS FOR THE ARTS.

B. The annual fee for plates issued pursuant to this section shall be twenty-five dollars in addition to the prescribed fee for state license plates. For each such twenty-five-dollar fee collected in excess of 1,000 registrations pursuant to this section, fifteen dollars shall be paid into the state treasury and credited to the special nonreverting fund known as the Virginia Arts Foundation Fund established within the Department of Accounts, for use by the Virginia Arts Foundation.
(Added by L.1996 ch. 1026; chgd. by L.1997 ch. 878, eff. 7/1/97.)

§§46.2-749.2:3, 46.2-749.2:4. *(Repealed by L.2000 ch. 75, eff. 7/1/2000.)*

§46.2-749.2:5. *(Repealed by its own terms and by L.2000 ch. 75, eff. 7/1/2000.)*

§46.2-749.2:6. *(Repealed by L.2000 ch. 75, eff. 7/1/2000.)*

§46.2-749.2:7. Special license plates for supporters of dog and cat sterilization programs; fees.

A. On receipt of an application and payment of the fee prescribed by this section, the Commissioner shall issue special license plates to supporters of dog and cat sterilization programs.

B. The annual fee for plates issued pursuant to this section shall be twenty-five dollars in addition to the prescribed fee for state license plates. For each such twenty-five-dollar fee collected in excess of 1,000 registrations pursuant to this section, fifteen dollars shall be paid into the state treasury and credited to a special nonreverting fund known as the Dog and Cat Sterilization Fund, established within the Department of Accounts. These funds shall be paid annually to the locality in which the vehicle is registered and shall be used by the localities to which they are paid to support sterilization programs for dogs and cats.

Each affected locality shall annually certify in a manner prescribed by the Commissioner that these funds have been or are being used to support sterilization programs for dogs and cats. If an affected locality does not have such a sterilization program, it shall (i) make the funds available to any private, nonprofit sterilization program for dogs and cats in that locality; (ii) return the funds to the Commissioner; or (iii) refuse the funds. Any funds refused, returned to the Commissioner, or otherwise not paid to an affected locality shall be distributed to other affected localities on a pro rata basis.
(Added by L.1996 ch. 922, eff. 7/1/96.)

§46.2-749.2:8. Special license plates for supporters of the Virginia's Western Highlands Travel Council.

On receipt of an application therefor, the Commissioner shall issue special license plates to supporters of the Virginia's Western Highlands Travel Council.
(Added by L.1997 chs. 774, 816, eff. 7/1/97.)

§46.2-749.2:9. Special license plates for supporters of the Virginia Drug Abuse Resistance Education Association (D.A.R.E.), Inc.

On receipt of an application therefor, the Commissioner shall issue special license plates to supporters of the Virginia Drug Abuse Resistance Education Association (D.A.R.E.), Inc.
(Added by L.1997 chs. 774, 816, eff. 7/1/97.)

§46.2-749.2:10. Special license plates for supporters of community traffic safety programs in the Commonwealth; fees.

A. On receipt of an application and payment of the fee prescribed by this section, the Commissioner shall issue special license plates bearing the following legend: DRIVE SMART.

B. The annual fee for plates issued pursuant to this section shall be twenty-five dollars in addition to the prescribed fee for state license plates. For each such twenty-five-dollar fee collected in excess of 1,000 registrations pursuant to this section, fifteen dollars shall be paid into the state treasury and credited to the special nonreverting fund known as the Traffic Safety Fund, established within the Department of Accounts, for use by the Department of Motor Vehicles to support community traffic safety programs in the Commonwealth.
(Added by L.1997 chs. 774, 816, eff. 7/1/97.)

§46.2-749.2:11. Special license plates for supporters of the Virginia Education Foundation.

On receipt of an application therefor, the Commissioner shall issue special license plates to supporters of the Virginia Education Foundation.
(Added by L.1997 chs. 774, 816, eff. 7/1/97.)

§46.2-749.2:12. Special license plates for supporters of Operation Smile.

On receipt of an application therefor, the Commissioner shall issue special license plates to supporters of Operation Smile.
(Added by L.1997 chs. 774, 816, eff. 7/1/97.)

§46.2-749.2:13. Special license plates commemorating the 400th anniversary of the establishment of the Jamestown settlement; fees.

(Section effective only until 1/1/2013.)

A. On receipt of an application therefor on or after November 1, 1997, and payment of the fee prescribed by this section, the Commissioner shall issue special license plates commemorating the 400th anniversary of the establishment of the Jamestown settlement.

B. For each set of license plates issued under this section, the Commissioner shall charge, in addition to the prescribed cost of state license plates, a one-time fee of fifteen dollars at the time the plates are issued. For each such fifteen-dollar fee collected, five dollars shall be paid into the state treasury and credited to a special nonreverting fund known as the Jamestown-Yorktown Foundation Fund, established within the Department of Accounts, to be paid annually to the Jamestown-Yorktown Foundation.

C. On receipt of an application therefor from a member of the Senate or House of Delegates, the Commissioner shall issue to the applicant special license plates combining the designs of special license plates issued under subsection A of this section and special license plates issued to members of the Senate or House of Delegates, as the case may be, under §46.2-736.1. The fee for issuance of special license plates under this subsection shall be the same as provided in subsection B of this section.

D. The provisions of subdivisions 1 and 2 of subsection B of §46.2-725 shall not apply to license plates issued under this section.

E. The provisions of this section shall expire on January 1, 2013.

(Added by L.1997 ch. 90; chgd. by L.1998 ch. 763, eff. 7/1/98. Repealed by its own terms, eff. 1/1/2013.)

§46.2-749.2:14. Special license plates commemorating the 1999 Bicentennial of George Washington.

(Section effective only until 7/1/2003.)

On receipt of an application therefor, the Commissioner shall issue to the applicant special license plates commemorating the 1999 Bicentennial of George Washington.

(Added by L.1998 chs. 174, 181, eff. 7/1/98. Repealed by L.1998 chs. 174, 181, eff. 7/1/2003.)

§46.2-749.2:15. Special license plates commemorating the 250th anniversary of the City of Alexandria.

(Section effective only until 7/1/2003.)

On receipt of an application therefor, the Commissioner shall issue special license plates commemorating the 250th anniversary of the City of Alexandria.

(Added by L.1998 ch. 284, eff. 7/1/98. Repealed by L.1998 ch. 284, eff. 7/1/2003.)

§46.2-749.2:16. Special license plates commemorating the 250th anniversary of the County of Chesterfield.

(Section effective only until 7/1/2003.)

On receipt of an application therefor, the Commissioner shall issue special license plates commemorating the 250th anniversary of the County of Chesterfield.

(Added by L.1998 ch. 284, eff. 7/1/98. Repealed by L.1998 ch. 284, eff. 7/1/2003.)

§46.2-749.2:17. Special license plates commemorating the 250th anniversary of the County of Culpeper.

(Section effective only until 7/1/2003.)

On receipt of an application therefor, the Commissioner shall issue special license plates commemorating the 250th anniversary of the County of Culpeper.

(Added by L.1998 ch. 284, eff. 7/1/98. Repealed by L.1998 ch. 284, eff. 7/1/2003.)

§46.2-749.3. Special license plates for clean special fuel vehicles.

The owner of any motor vehicle, except a motorcycle, that may utilize clean special fuel may purchase special license plates indicating the motor vehicle utilizes clean special fuels. Upon receipt of an application, the Commissioner shall issue special license plates to the owners of such vehicles. [Notwithstanding §46.2-725, for license plates issued under this section prior to July 1, 1998, the Commissioner shall charge only the prescribed cost of state license plates, and no additional fee shall be charged.]

For those motor vehicles required by law to display official government-use license plates, the Commissioner shall provide by regulation for the issuance, display, and fee for issuance of an alternative device indicating that the vehicle displaying the device is a clean special fuel vehicle. For the purposes of §33.1-46.2, vehicles displaying such a device as provided in such regulation shall be treated as vehicles displaying special license plates issued under this section.

As used in this section, "clean special fuel" means any product or energy source used to propel a highway vehicle, the use of which, compared to conventional gasoline or reformulated gasoline, results in lower emissions of oxides of nitrogen, volatile organic compounds, carbon monoxide or particulates or any combination thereof. The term includes compressed natural gas, liquefied natural gas, liquefied petroleum gas, hydrogen, hythane (a combination of compressed natural gas and hydrogen), and electricity.

(Chgd. by L.1995 ch. 134; L.1999 ch. 883; L.2000 chs. 729, 758, eff. 1/1/2001. Matter in brackets eff. only until 1/1/2001. Matter in italics eff. 1/1/2001.)

§46.2-749.4. Special license plates bearing the seal, symbol, emblem, or logotype of certain localities.

On receipt of a minimum of 350 paid applications therefor, the Commissioner may design and issue special license plates whose design incorporates the seal, symbol, emblem, or logotype of any county, city or town.

The annual fee for plates issued pursuant to this section shall be twenty-five dollars plus the prescribed fee for state license plates. For each such twenty-five-dollar fee collected in excess of 1,000 registrations pursuant to this section, fifteen dollars shall be paid to the locality whose seal, symbol, emblem, or logotype appears on the plate. These funds shall be paid to the affected localities annually and may be used as provided by the local governing body.

(Chgd. by L.1995 ch. 747; L.1996 ch. 1026; L.1999 chs. 883, 907, eff. 7/1/99.)

§46.2-749.4:1. Special license plates for Historic Yorktown.

A. On receipt of an application and payment of the fee prescribed by this section, the Commissioner shall issue special license plates bearing the following legend: HISTORIC YORKTOWN.

B. The annual fee for plates issued pursuant to this section shall be twenty-five dollars in addition to the prescribed fee for state license plates. For each such twenty-five-dollar fee collected in excess of 1,000 registrations pursuant to this section, fifteen dollars shall be paid into the state treasury and credited to the special nonreverting fund known as the Historic Yorktown Fund, established within the Department of Accounts. These funds shall be paid annually to the Town of Yorktown and may be used as provided by the governing body.

(Added by L.1997 chs. 774, 816, eff. 7/1/97.)

§46.2-749.4:2. Special license plates for Gloucester County; fees.

A. On receipt of an application and payment of the fee prescribed by this section, the Commissioner shall issue special license plates bearing the following legend: GLOUCESTER COUNTY.

B. The annual fee for plates issued pursuant to this section shall be twenty-five dollars in addition to the prescribed fee for state license plates. For each such twenty-five-dollar fee collected in excess of 1,000 registrations pursuant to this section, fifteen dollars shall be paid into the state treasury and credited to the special nonreverting fund known as the Gloucester County Fund, established within the Department of Accounts. These funds shall be paid annually to the County of Gloucester and may be used as provided by the governing body.

(Added by L.1997 chs. 774, 816, eff. 7/1/97.)

§46.2-749.4:3. Special license plates for supporters of parental involvement in local public school programs.

On receipt of an application therefor, the Commissioner shall issue special license plates to supporters of parental involvement in local public school programs.

(Added by L.1997 chs. 774, 816, eff. 7/1/97.)

§46.2-749.5. Special license plates celebrating Virginia's tobacco heritage.

On receipt of an application, the Commissioner shall issue special license plates celebrating Virginia's tobacco heritage. For each set of license plates issued under this section, the Commissioner shall charge, in addition to the prescribed cost of state license plates, an annual fee of ten dollars.

§46.2-749.6. Special license plates for supporters of the National Rifle Association.

On receipt of an application therefor, the Commissioner shall issue special license plates to supporters of the National Rifle Association.

(Added by L.1995 ch. 747, eff. 7/1/95.)

§46.2-749.6:1. Special license plates for supporters of the Washington D.C. United soccer team.

On receipt of an application therefor, the Commissioner shall issue special license plates to supporters of the Washington D.C. United soccer team.

(Added by L.1997 chs. 774, 816, eff. 7/1/97.)

§46.2-749.6:1.1. Special license plates for supporters of the Richmond Braves, the Salem Avalanche, the Norfolk Tides, the Prince William Cannons, the Pulaski Rangers, the Lynchburg Hillcats, the Martinsville Phillies, the Danville Braves, and the Bristol Tigers baseball teams.

On receipt of an application therefor, the Commissioner shall issue special license plates to supporters of the Richmond Braves, the Salem Avalanche, the Norfolk Tides, the Prince William Cannons, the Pulaski Rangers, the Lynchburg Hillcats, the Martinsville Phillies, the Danville Braves, and the Bristol Tigers baseball teams.

(Added by L.1998 ch. 501, eff. 7/1/98.)

§46.2-749.7. Special license plates for supporters of Ducks Unlimited.

On receipt of an application therefor, the Commissioner shall issue special license plates to supporters of Ducks Unlimited.

(Added by L.1995 ch. 747, eff. 7/1/95.)

§46.2-749.7:1. *(Repealed by L.2000 ch. 75, eff. 7/1/2000.)*

§46.2-749.7:2. Special license plates; Old Dominion Boat Club.

On receipt of an application therefor, the Commissioner shall issue to the applicant special license plates bearing the following legend: OLD DOMINION BOAT CLUB.

(Added by L.1997 chs. 774, 816, eff. 7/1/97.)

§46.2-749.7:3. Special license plates promoting tourism on Virginia's Eastern Shore.

On receipt of an application therefor, the Commissioner shall issue special license plates promoting tourism on Virginia's Eastern Shore.

(Added by L.1998 ch. 381, eff. 7/1/98.)

§46.2-749.8. Special license plates for Harley-Davidson motor vehicle owners.

On receipt of an application therefor, the Commissioner shall issue special license plates to owners of Harley-Davidson motor vehicles.

(Added by L.1995 ch. 747, eff. 7/1/95.)

§46.2-749.9. Special license plates; Virginia Bowler.

On receipt of an application therefor, the Commissioner shall issue to the applicant special license plates bearing the legend: Virginia Bowler.

(Added by L.1995 ch. 747, eff. 7/1/95.)

§46.2-749.10. Special license plates for ride-sharing vehicles.

On receipt of an application therefor, the Commissioner shall issue special license plates for display on ride-sharing vehicles. License plates shall be issued under this section only for privately owned motor vehicles (i) with seating for fewer than sixteen persons and (ii) participating in ride-sharing arrangements.

(Added by L.1995 ch. 747, eff. 7/1/95.)

§46.2-749.11. *(Repealed by L.2000 ch. 75, eff. 7/1/2000.)*

§46.2-749.12. Special license plates; supporters of the Chincoteague Pony Association.

On receipt of an application therefor, the Commissioner shall issue special license plates to supporters of the Chincoteague Pony Association.

(Added by L.1999 ch. 907, eff. 7/1/99.)

§46.2-749.13. Special license plates; Internet commerce industry.

On receipt of an application therefor, the Commissioner shall issue to the applicant special license plates designed to represent the Internet commerce industry.

(Added by L.1999 ch. 907, eff. 7/1/99.)

§46.2-749.14. Special license plates; supporters of greyhound adoption programs.

On receipt of an application therefor, the Commissioner shall issue special license plates to supporters of greyhound adoption programs.

(Added by L.1999 ch. 907, eff. 7/1/99.)

§46.2-749.15. Special license plates; Eagle Scouts.

On receipt of an application therefor and presentation of written evidence that the applicant is an Eagle Scout, the Commissioner shall issue to the applicant special license plates bearing the legend: EAGLE SCOUT.

(Added by L.1999 ch. 907, eff. 7/1/99.)

§46.2-749.16. Special license plates; members of the Navy League of the United States.

On receipt of an application therefor and presentation of appropriate written evidence that the applicant is a member of the Navy League of the United States, the Commissioner shall issue special license plates to the applicant.

(Added by L.1999 ch. 907, eff. 7/1/99.)

§46.2-749.17. Special license plates; members of the Order of AHEPA.

On receipt of an application therefor and receipt of appropriate written evidence that the applicant is a member of the Order of AHEPA, the Commissioner shall issue special license plates to the applicant.

(Added by L.1999 ch. 907, eff. 7/1/99.)

§46.2-749.18. Special license plates; horse enthusiasts.

On receipt of an application therefor, the Commissioner shall issue special license plates to horse enthusiasts.

(Added by L.1999 ch. 907, eff. 7/1/99.)

§46.2-749.19. Special license plates; supporters of public schools; fees.

A. On receipt of an application and payment of the fee prescribed by this section, the Commissioner shall issue to the applicant special license plates for supporters of public schools.

B. The annual fee for plates issued pursuant to this section shall be twenty-five dollars in addition to the prescribed fee for state license plates. For each such twenty-five-dollar fee collected in excess of 1,000 registrations pursuant to this section, fifteen dollars shall be paid into the state treasury and credited to a special nonreverting fund known as the Helping Schools Fund, established within the Department of Accounts. These funds shall be paid annually to the school division of the locality in which the vehicle is registered and used for the purchase of classroom supplies, textbooks, or equipment in grades K through 12.

(Added by L.1999 ch. 907; chgd. by L.2000 ch. 107, eff. 7/1/2000.)

§46.2-749.20. Special license plates; members of the Virginia State Police Alumni, Inc.

On receipt of an application and presentation of written evidence that the applicant is a member of the Virginia State Police Alumni, Inc., the Commissioner shall issue special license plates to members of the Virginia State Police Alumni, Inc.

(Added by L.1999 chs. 883, 907, eff. 7/1/99.)

§46.2-749.21. Special license plates; Hampton Roads.

On receipt of an application therefor, the Commissioner shall issue to the applicant special license plates bearing the legend: HAMPTON ROADS.

(Added by L.1999 ch. 907, eff. 7/1/99.)

§46.2-749.22. Special license plates; public safety communications professionals.

On receipt of an application and appropriate written evidence signed by a chief law-enforcement officer, fire chief, or public safety administrator, that the applicant is a public safety communications professional, the Commissioner shall issue special license plates to the applicant.

(Added by L.1999 ch. 907, eff. 7/1/99.)

§46.2-749.23. Special license plates; Virginia is for lovers.

On receipt of an application therefor, the Commissioner shall issue to the applicant special license plates bearing the legend: VIRGINIA IS FOR LOVERS.

(Added by L.1999 ch. 907, eff. 7/1/99.)

§46.2-749.24. Special license plates celebrating the history of Fairfax County.

A. On receipt of an application and payment of the fee prescribed by this section, the Commissioner shall issue to the applicant special license plates celebrating the history of Fairfax County.

B. The annual fee for plates issued pursuant to this section shall be twenty-five dollars in addition to the prescribed fee for state license plates. For each such twenty-five-dollar fee collected in excess of 1,000 registrations pursuant to this section, fifteen dollars shall be paid into the state treasury and credited to a special nonreverting fund known as the Fairfax County Historical Preservation Fund, established within the Department of Accounts. These funds shall be paid annually to Fairfax County to assist in historic preservation activities and programs within the County.

(Added by L.1999 ch. 907, eff. 7/1/99.)

§46.2-749.25. Special license plates commemorating the 300th anniversary of the City of Falls Church.

(Section effective only until 7/1/2004.)

On receipt of an application therefor, the Commissioner shall issue to the applicant special license plates commemorating the 300th anniversary of the City of Falls Church.

The provisions of this section shall expire on July 1, 2004.

(Added by L.1999 ch. 907, eff. 7/1/99. Repealed by its own terms, eff. 7/1/2004.)

§46.2-749.26. Special license plates; Natural Bridge of Virginia.

On receipt of an application therefor, the Commissioner shall issue to the applicant special license plates celebrating the Natural Bridge of Virginia.

(Added by L.1999 ch. 907, eff. 7/1/99.)

§46.2-749.27. Special license plates; members of the Amateur Radio Emergency Service (ARES).

On receipt of an application therefor and presentation of written evidence that the applicant is a member of the Amateur Radio Emergency Service (ARES), the Commissioner shall issue to the applicant special license plates.

(Added by L.1999 ch. 883, eff. 7/1/99; renumbered in 1999 from Section 46.2-749.12.)

§46.2-749.28. Special license plates; Oceana Naval Air Station.

On receipt of an application therefor, the Commissioner shall issue to the applicant special license plates bearing the legend: OCEANA NAVAL AIR STATION.

(Added by L.1999 ch. 883, eff. 7/1/99; renumbered in 1999 from Section 46.2-749.14.)

§46.2-749.29. Special license plates; supporters of Operation Wildflower; fees.

A. On receipt of an application and payment of the fee prescribed by this section, the Commissioner shall issue special license plates to supporters of Operation Wildflower.

B. The annual fee for plates issued pursuant to this section shall be twenty-five dollars in addition to the prescribed fee for state license plates. For each such twenty-five-dollar fee collected in excess of 1,000 registrations pursuant to this section, fifteen dollars shall be paid into the state treasury and credited to a special nonreverting fund known as the Operation Wildflower Fund, established within the Department of Accounts. These funds shall be paid annually to the Virginia Department of Transportation and used to support its Operation Wildflower program.

(Added by L.1999 ch. 883, eff. 7/1/99; renumbered in 1999 from Section 46.2-749.15.)

§46.2-749.30. Special license plates; supporters of the Boy Scouts of America.

On receipt of an application therefor, the Commissioner shall issue special license plates to supporters of the Boy Scouts of America.

(Added by L.1999 ch. 883, eff. 7/1/99; renumbered in 1999 from Section 46.2-749.16.)

§46.2-749.31. Special license plates; Virginia lighthouses.

On receipt of an application therefor, the Commissioner shall issue to the applicant special license plates celebrating Virginia lighthouses.

(Added by L.1999 ch. 883, eff. 7/1/99; renumbered in 1999 from Section 46.2-749.17.)

§46.2-749.32. Special license plates; Corvette motor vehicle enthusiasts.

(As added by L.2000 ch. 44. See other Sections 46.2-749.32 below.)

On receipt of an application therefor, the Commissioner shall issue special license plates to Corvette motor vehicle enthusiasts.

(Added by L.2000 ch. 44, eff. 7/1/2000.)

§46.2-749.32. Special license plates; members of the National Association of Retired Federal Employees.

(As added by L.2000 ch. 76. See other Sections 46.2-749.32 above and below.)

On receipt of an application therefor and written evidence that the applicant is a member of the National Association of Retired Federal Employees, the Commissioner shall issue special license plates to members of the National Association of Retired Federal Employees.

(Added by L.2000 ch. 76, eff. 7/1/2000.)

§46.2-749.32. Special license plates; seal of the Virginia Federation of Women's Clubs.

(As added by L.2000 ch. 78. See other Sections 46.2-749.32 above and below.)

On receipt of an application therefor, the Commissioner shall issue to the applicant special license plates bearing the seal of the Virginia Federation of Women's Clubs.

(Added by L.2000 ch. 78, eff. 7/1/2000.)

§46.2-749.32. Special license plates; local government attorneys.

(As added by L.2000 ch. 80. See other Sections 46.2-749.32 above and below.)

On receipt of an application and written evidence that the applicant is a local government attorney, the Commissioner shall issue to the applicant special license plates.

(Added by L.2000 ch. 80, eff. 7/1/2000.)

§46.2-749.32. Special license plates; supporters of the Motorcycle Rider Safety Training Program.

(As added by L.2000 ch. 81. See other Sections 46.2-749.32 above and below.)

A. On receipt of an application and payment of the fee prescribed by this section, the Commissioner shall issue to the applicant special license plates bearing the legend: SHARE THE ROAD.

B. The annual fee for plates issued pursuant to this section shall be twenty-five dollars in addition to the prescribed fee for state license plates. For each such twenty-five-dollar fee collected in excess of 1,000 registrations pursuant to this section, fifteen dollars shall be paid into the state treasury and credited to the Motorcycle Rider Safety Training Program Fund created pursuant to §46.2-1191.

(Added by L.2000 ch. 81, eff. 7/1/2000.)

§46.2-749.32. Special license plates; twenty-fifth anniversary of the City of Poquoson.

(As added by L.2000 ch. 85. Section effective only until 7/1/2005. See other Sections 46.2-749.32 above and below.)

On receipt of an application therefor, the Commissioner shall issue to the applicant special license plates commemorating the twenty-fifth anniversary of the City of Poquoson.

The provisions of this section shall expire on July 1, 2005.

(Added by L.2000 ch. 85, eff. 7/1/2000. Repealed by its own terms, eff. 7/1/2005.)

§46.2-749.32. Special license plates; 250th anniversary of the Town of Dumfries.

(As added by L.2000 ch. 124. Section effective only until 7/1/2005. See other Sections 46.2-749.32 above and below.)

On receipt of an application therefor, the Commissioner shall issue to the applicant special license plates commemorating the 250th anniversary of the Town of Dumfries.

The provisions of this section shall expire on July 1, 2005.

(Added by L.2000 ch. 124, eff. 7/1/2000. Repealed by its own terms, eff. 7/1/2005.)

§46.2-749.32. Special license plates; Virginia Statute for Religious Freedom.

(As added by L.2000 ch. 127. See other Sections 46.2-749.32 above and below.)

On receipt of an application therefor, the Commissioner shall issue to the applicant special license plates celebrating the Virginia Statute for Religious Freedom.

(Added by L.2000 ch. 127, eff. 7/1/2000.)

§46.2-749.32. Special license plates; Class–J No. 611 steam locomotive.

(As added by L.2000 ch. 143. See other Sections 46.2-749.32 above and below.)

On receipt of an application therefor, the Commissioner shall issue to the applicant special license plates commemorating the Class–J No. 611 steam locomotive.

(Added by L.2000 ch. 143, eff. 7/1/2000.)

§46.2-749.32. Special license plates; Marriage Encounter Movement.

(As added by L.2000 ch. 146. See other Sections 46.2-749.32 above and below.)

On receipt of an application therefor, the Commissioner shall issue to the applicant special license plates for supporters of the Marriage Encounter Movement.

(Added by L.2000 ch. 146, eff. 7/1/2000.)

§46.2-749.32. Special license plates; retired state employees.

(As added by L.2000 ch. 150. See other Sections 46.2-749.32 above and below.)

On receipt of an application therefor and presentation of written evidence that the applicant is a retired state employee, the Commissioner shall issue special license plates to retired state employees.

(Added by L.2000 ch. 150, eff. 7/1/2000.)

§46.2-749.32. Special license plates; POW/MIA logo.

(As added by L.2000 ch. 189. See other Sections 46.2-749.32 above and below.)

On receipt of an application therefor, the Commissioner shall issue to the applicant special license plates bearing the POW/MIA logo.

(Added by L.2000 ch. 189, eff. 7/1/2000.)

§46.2-749.32. Special license plates; supporters of the Monitor-Merrimac Memorial Foundation.

(As added by L.2000 ch. 226. See other Sections 46.2-749.32 above and below.)

A. On receipt of an application and payment of the fee prescribed by this section, the Commissioner shall issue special license plates to supporters of the Monitor-Merrimac Memorial Foundation.

B. The annual fee for plates issued pursuant to this section shall be twenty-five dollars in addition to the prescribed

fee for state license plates. For each such twenty-five-dollar fee collected in excess of 1,000 registrations pursuant to this section, fifteen dollars shall be paid into the state treasury and credited to a special nonreverting fund known as the Monitor-Merrimac Memorial Foundation Fund, established within the Department of Accounts. These funds shall be paid annually to the Mariner's Museum and used exclusively to further the construction of the USS Monitor Center.
(Added by L.2000 ch. 226, eff. 7/1/2000.)

§46.2-749.32. Special license plates; supporters of the Virginia Breast Cancer Foundation.
(As added by L.2000 ch. 319. See other Sections 46.2-749.32 above and below.)

A. On receipt of an application and payment of the fee prescribed by this section, the Commissioner shall issue to the applicant special license plates bearing the legend: Virginia Breast Cancer Foundation.

B. The annual fee for plates issued pursuant to this section shall be twenty-five dollars in addition to the prescribed fee for state license plates. For each such twenty-five-dollar fee collected in excess of 1,000 registrations pursuant to this section, fifteen dollars shall be paid into the state treasury and credited to a special nonreverting fund known as the Virginia Breast Cancer Foundation Fund, established within the Department of Accounts. These funds shall be paid annually to the Virginia Breast Cancer Foundation and used to support statewide breast cancer educational programs.
(Added by L.2000 ch. 319, eff. 7/1/2000.)

§46.2-749.32. Special license plates; naval aviators.
(As added by L.2000 ch. 766. See other Sections 46.2-749.32 above.)

On receipt of an application and written evidence that the applicant is or has been a naval aviator, the Commissioner shall issue to the applicant special license plates.
(Added by L.2000 ch. 766, eff. 7/1/2000.)

§46.2-749.33. Special license plates; insurance agents.

On receipt of an application therefor, the Commissioner shall issue to the applicant special license plates bearing the legend: INSURANCE AGENT.
(Added by L.2000 ch. 766, eff. 7/1/2000.)

§46.2-749.34. Special license plates for supporters of Family and Children's Trust Fund; fees.

On receipt of an application and payment of the fee prescribed by this section, the Commissioner shall issue special license plates for supporters of the Family and Children's Trust Fund.

The annual fee for plates issued pursuant to this section shall be twenty-five dollars plus the prescribed fee for state license plates. For each such twenty-five-dollar fee collected in excess of 1,000 registrations pursuant to this section, fifteen dollars shall be paid into the state treasury and credited to the Family and Children's Trust Fund.
(Added by L.2000 ch. 766, eff. 7/1/2000.)

ARTICLE 11
STATE AND LOCAL MOTOR VEHICLE REGISTRATION

Section

§46.2-750. Vehicles of Commonwealth and subdivisions.

A. Motor vehicles, trailers, and semitrailers owned by the Commonwealth and political subdivisions thereof and used solely for governmental purposes shall be registered and shall display license plates as provided in this section. The fee for such license plates shall be equal to the cost incurred by the Department in the purchase or manufacture of such license plates. The fees received by the Commissioner under this section shall be paid into the state treasury and shall be set aside as a special fund to be used to meet the expenses of the Department of Motor Vehicles.

License plates issued for vehicles owned by the Commonwealth, except plates issued to be used (i) on vehicles devoted solely to police work, (ii) by the Virginia Economic Development Partnership to the extent approved by the Governor, or (iii) by the Governor and the Attorney General, shall have conspicuously and legibly inscribed, stamped, or printed thereon words stating that the vehicle is for official state use only. The Commissioner shall reserve a unique series of numbers for use on such license plates and shall provide for a design and combination of colors which distinguish such license plates from those issued for vehicles owned by the political subdivisions of the Commonwealth.

License plates issued for vehicles owned by political subdivisions of the Commonwealth, except such plates issued to be used (i) on vehicles used by any local or regional economic development authority, agency, instrumentality, or organization, upon the request of the chief administrative officer of the affected locality (or, in the case of regional organizations, the chief administrative officer of any of the affected localities) or (ii) on vehicles devoted solely to police work, shall have conspicuously and legibly inscribed, stamped, or printed thereon words stating that the vehicle is for official local government use only. The Commissioner shall reserve a unique series of numbers for use on such license plates and shall provide for a design and combination of colors which distinguish such license plates from those issued for vehicles owned by the Commonwealth.

License plates issued for vehicles owned by the Commonwealth and the political subdivisions thereof which have inscribed, stamped, or printed thereon the words "Public Use" may be used only on the vehicle for which they were issued prior to January 1, 1990, but in no case shall such license plates be used for any vehicle after December 31, 1992.

No other license plates shall be used on vehicles for which official use plates have been issued, except for vehicles used solely for police work and as provided in subsection B of this section.

B. In addition to any other license plate authorized by this section, the Commissioner may issue permanent or temporary license plates for use on vehicles owned by the Commonwealth or any of its departments, institutions, boards, or agencies and used for security or transportation purposes in conjunction with conferences, meetings, or other events involving the Governor or members of the General Assembly. No state agency shall use government funds to cover the costs of any license plates issued under this subsection. The design of these license plates shall be at the discretion of the Commissioner. These license plates shall be issued under the following conditions:

1. For each set of permanent plates issued, the Commissioner shall charge a fee of $100. The Commissioner shall limit the validity of any set of license plates issued under this subdivision to no more than thirty consecutive days. The Commissioner's written authorization for use of any set of license plates issued under this subdivision shall be kept in the vehicle on which the license plates are displayed until expiration of the authorization.

2. The Commissioner shall limit the validity of each set of temporary license plates to no more than fourteen consecutive days. For each set of temporary license plates, the Commissioner shall charge a fee of twenty-five dollars for the first set and two dollars for each additional set. The Commissioner's written authorization for use of any set of license plates issued under this subdivision shall be kept in the vehicle on which the license plates are displayed until expiration of the authorization.

(Chgd. by L.1995 chs. 432, 747; L.1996 chs. 590, 598, 1026, eff. 7/1/96.)

§46.2-750.1. Vehicles used for police work.

Motor vehicles, trailers, and semitrailers owned by the Commonwealth and the counties, cities, and towns thereof and used solely for police work may be issued the same license plates as those issued in registration of vehicles owned by private citizens. The head of a state agency, the chief of police of a city, county, or town having a police department, or the sheriff of a city or county, shall certify under oath and the law-enforcement agencies of the federal government shall certify to the Commissioner of Motor Vehicles the vehicles to be used solely for police work.

§46.2-751. State-owned passenger vehicles.

Except at provided in subsection B of §46.2-750, the Commissioner shall not issue any license plates for use on vehicles owned by the Commonwealth or any of its departments, institutions, boards, or agencies and used for passenger transportation unless written application has been filed with the Governor showing the necessity for the use and unless the Governor has directed the Commissioner to issue the license plates.

§46.2-752. Taxes and license fees imposed by counties, cities, and towns; limitations on amounts; disposition of revenues; requiring evidence of payment of personal property taxes; prohibiting display of licenses after expiration; failure to display valid local license required by other localities.

A. Except as provided in §46.2-755, counties, cities, and towns may levy and assess taxes and charge license fees on motor vehicles, trailers, and semitrailers. However, none of these taxes and license fees shall be assessed or charged by any county on vehicles owned by residents of any town located in the county when such town constitutes a separate school district if the vehicles are already subject to town license fees and taxes. The amount of the license fee or tax imposed by any county, city, or town on any motor vehicle, trailer, or semitrailer shall not be greater than the amount of the license tax imposed by the Commonwealth on the motor vehicle, trailer, or semitrailer. The license fees and taxes shall be imposed in such manner, on such basis, for such periods, and subject to proration for fractional periods of years, as the proper local authorities may determine. Local licenses may be issued free of charge for any or all of the following:

1. Vehicles powered by clean special fuels as defined in §58.1-2101, including dual-fuel and bi-fuel vehicles,
2. Vehicles owned by volunteer rescue squads,
3. Vehicles owned by volunteer fire departments,
4. Vehicles owned or leased by active members of volunteer rescue squads,
5. Vehicles owned or leased by active members of volunteer fire departments,
6. Vehicles owned or leased by auxiliary police officers,
7. Vehicles owned or leased by volunteer police chaplains,
8. Vehicles owned by surviving spouses of persons qualified to receive special license plates under §46.2-739,
9. Vehicles owned or leased by auxiliary deputy sheriffs or volunteer deputy sheriffs,
10. Vehicles owned by persons qualified to receive special license plates under §46.2-739,
11. Vehicles owned by any of the following who served at least ten years in the locality: former members of volunteer rescue squads, former members of volunteer fire departments, former auxiliary police officers, former volunteer police chaplains, and former volunteer special police officers appointed under §15.2-1737. In the case of active members of volunteer rescue squads and volunteer fire departments, applications for such licenses shall be accompanied by written evidence, in a form acceptable to the locality, of their active membership, and no member shall be issued more than one such license free of charge, or
12. All vehicles having a situs for the imposition of licensing fees under this section in the locality.

The governing body of any county, city, or town issuing licenses under this section may by ordinance provide for a fifty percent reduction in the fee charged for the issuance of any such license issued for any vehicle owned or leased by any person who is sixty-five years old or older. No such discount, however, shall be available for more than one vehicle owned or leased by the same person.

The governing body of any county, city, or town issuing licenses free of charge under this subsection may by ordinance provide for (i) the limitation, restriction, or denial of such free issuance to an otherwise qualified applicant, including without limitation the denial of free issuance to a taxpayer who has failed to timely pay personal property taxes due with respect to the vehicle and (ii) the grounds for such limitation, restriction, or denial.

The situs for the imposition of licensing fees under this section shall in all cases, except as hereinafter provided, be the county, city, or town in which the motor vehicle, trailer, or semitrailer is normally garaged, stored, or parked. If it cannot be determined where the personal property is normally garaged, stored, or parked, the situs shall be the domicile of its owner. In the event the owner of the motor vehicle is a full-time student attending an institution of higher education, the situs shall be the domicile of such student, provided the student has presented sufficient evidence that he has paid a personal property tax on the motor vehicle in his domicile.

B. The revenue derived from all county, city, or town taxes and license fees imposed on motor vehicles, trailers, or semitrailers shall be applied to general county, city, or town purposes.

C. A county, city, or town may require that no motor vehicle, trailer, or semitrailer shall be locally licensed until the applicant has produced satisfactory evidence that all personal property taxes on the motor vehicle, trailer, or semitrailer to be licensed have been paid and satisfactory evidence that any delinquent motor vehicle, trailer, or semitrailer personal property taxes owing have been paid which have been properly assessed or are assessable against the applicant by the county, city, or town. A county, city, or town may also provide that no motor vehicle license shall be issued unless the tangible personal property taxes properly assessed or assessable by that locality on any tangible personal property used or usable as a dwelling titled by the Department of Motor Vehicles and owned by the taxpayer have been paid. Any county and any town within any such county may by agreement require that all personal property taxes assessed by either the county or the town on any vehicle be paid before licensure of such vehicle by either the county or the town.

C1. Any county having a population of at least 24,000, but no more than 24,600, may, by ordinance or resolution adopted after public notice and hearing and, with the consent of the treasurer, require that no license may be issued under this section unless the applicant has produced satisfactory evidence that all fees, including delinquent fees, payable to such county or local solid waste authority, for the disposal of solid waste pursuant to the Virginia Water and Waste Authorities Act (§15.2-5100 et seq.), have been paid in full. For purposes of this subsection, all fees, including delinquent fees, payable to a county for waste disposal services described herein, shall be paid to the treasurer of such county.

D. The Counties of Arlington, Fairfax, Loudoun, and Prince William and towns within them and any city may require that no motor vehicle, trailer, or semitrailer shall be licensed by that jurisdiction unless all fines owed to the jurisdiction by the owner of the vehicle, trailer, or semitrailer for violation of the jurisdiction's ordinances governing parking of vehicles have been paid. The provisions of this subsection shall not apply to vehicles owned by firms or companies in the business of renting motor vehicles.

E. If in any county imposing license fees and taxes under this section, a town therein imposes like fees and taxes on vehicles of owners resident in the town, the owner of any vehicle subject to the fees or taxes shall be entitled, on the owner's displaying evidence that he has paid the fees or taxes, to receive a credit on the fees or taxes imposed by the county to the extent of the fees or taxes he has paid to the town. Nothing in this section shall deprive any town now imposing these licenses and taxes from increasing them or deprive any town not now imposing them from hereafter doing so, but subject to the limitations provided in subsection D of this section. The governing body of any county and the governing body of any town in that county wherein each imposes the license tax herein provided may provide mutual agreements so that not more than one license plate or decal in addition to the state plate shall be required.

F. Notwithstanding the provisions of subsection E of this section, in a consolidated county wherein a tier-city exists, the tier-city may, in accordance with the provisions of the agreement or plan of consolidation, impose license fees and taxes under this section in addition to those fees and taxes imposed by the county, provided that the combined county and tier-city rates do not exceed the maximum provided in subsection A of this section. No credit shall be allowed on the fees or taxes imposed by the county for fees or taxes paid to the tier-city, except as may be provided by the consolidation agreement or plan. The governing body of any county and the governing body of any tier-city in said county wherein each imposes the license tax herein may provide by mutual agreement that no more than one license plate or decal in addition to the state license plate shall be required.

G. Any county, city, or town may by ordinance provide that it shall be unlawful for any owner or operator of a motor vehicle, trailer, or semitrailer to fail to obtain and display the local license required by any ordinance of the county, city or town in which the vehicle is registered or to display upon a motor vehicle, trailer, or semitrailer any such local license after its expiration date. The ordinance may provide that a violation shall constitute a misdemeanor the penalty for which shall not exceed that of a Class 4 misdemeanor and may, in the case of a motor vehicle registered to a resident of the locality where such vehicle is registered, authorize the issuance by local law-enforcement officers of citations, summonses, parking tickets, or uniform traffic summonses for violations. Any such ordinance may also provide that a violation of the ordinance by the registered owner of the vehicle may not be discharged by payment of a fine except upon presentation of satisfactory evidence that the required license has been obtained.

H. Except as provided by subsections E and F, no vehicle shall be subject to taxation under the provisions of this section in more than one jurisdiction.

I. Purchasers of new or used motor vehicles shall be allowed at least a ten-day grace period, beginning with the date of purchase, during which to pay license fees charged by local governments under authority of this section.

J. Beginning October 1, 1992, the treasurer or director of finance of any county, city, or town may enter into an agreement with the Commissioner whereby the Commissioner will refuse to issue or renew any vehicle registration of any applicant therefor who owes to such county, city or town any delinquent tangible personal property tax levied with respect to such vehicle in excess of $50. Before being issued any vehicle registration or renewal of such license or registration by the Commissioner, the applicant must first satisfy all such delinquent taxes and present evidence satisfactory to the Commissioner that all such delinquent taxes have been paid in full. The Commissioner shall charge a reasonable fee to cover the costs of such enforcement action, and the treasurer or director of finance may add the cost of this fee to the delinquent tax bill. The treasurer or director of finance of any county, city, or town seeking to collect delinquent taxes through the withholding of registration or renewal thereof by the Commissioner as provided for in this subsection shall notify the Commissioner in the manner provided for in his agreement with the Commissioner and supply to the Commissioner information necessary to identify the debtor whose registration or renewal is to be denied. Any agreement entered into pursuant to the provisions of this subsection shall provide the debtor notice of the intent to deny renewal of registration at least thirty days prior to the expiration date of a current vehicle registration. For the purposes of this subsection, notice by first-class mail to the registrant's address as maintained in the records of the Department of Motor Vehicles shall be deemed sufficient.

K. The governing bodies of any two or more counties, cities, or towns may enter into compacts for the regional enforcement of local motor vehicle license requirements. The governing body of each participating jurisdiction may by ordinance require the owner or operator of any motor vehicle, trailer, or semitrailer to display on his vehicle a valid local license issued by another county, city, or town that is a party to the regional compact, provided that the owner or operator is required by the jurisdiction of situs, as provided in §58.1-3511, to obtain and display such license. The ordinance may provide that a violation shall constitute a misdemeanor the penalty for which shall not exceed that of a Class 4 misdemeanor. Any such ordinance may also provide that a violation of the ordinance by the owner of the vehicle may not be discharged by payment of a fine except upon presentation of satisfactory evidence that the required license has been obtained.

(Chgd. by L.1995 chs. 91, 412, 449, 460, 479, 659; L.1996 chs. 89, 562; L.1997 chs. 246, 499, 905, 911; L.1998 ch. 649; L.1999 ch. 236; L.2000 ch. 303, eff. 7/1/2000.)

§46.2-753. Additional license fees in certain localities.

Notwithstanding any other provision of law, the governing bodies of Alexandria, Arlington, Fairfax County, Fairfax City, and Falls Church are authorized to charge annual license fees, in addition to those specified in §46.2-752, on passenger cars not used for the transportation of passengers for compensation. The additional fee shall be no more than five dollars. The total local license fee shall be no more than twenty-five dollars on any vehicle and this license fee shall not be imposed on any motor vehicle exempted under §46.2-739.

The governing bodies are also authorized to charge additional annual license fees on the motor vehicles, trailers, and semitrailers as specified in §46.2-697 in an amount of no more than five dollars for each such vehicle. This authorization shall not increase the maximum chargeable by more than five dollars or affect any existing exemption.

Any funds acquired in excess of those allowed by §46.2-752, shall be allocated to the Northern Virginia Transportation Commission to be a credit to that jurisdiction making the payment for its share of any operating deficit assigned to it by the Washington Metropolitan Area Transit Authority.

§46.2-754. Local motor vehicle licenses in Arlington County.

Arlington County may by ordinance require the owner of any motor vehicle, trailer, or semitrailer to obtain and display a license from the county licensing authority designated by the ordinance. The ordinance may also require that the license be obtained only after showing satisfactory evidence that all personal property taxes on the motor vehicle, trailer, or semitrailer have been paid, and that any delinquent personal property taxes assessed or assessable against the vehicle have been paid. The ordinance may also prohibit the display of the license after its expiration date and may prescribe the form of the license. This license requirement shall be imposed in such manner, on such basis, for such period, and subject to proration for fractional periods of years as the governing body requires.

The situs for the imposition of the license requirement under the ordinance shall be the locality in which the vehicle is normally garaged, stored, or parked. If it cannot be determined where it is normally garaged, stored, or parked, the situs shall be the domicile of its owner.

The ordinance may provide that no motor vehicle, trailer, or semitrailer may be licensed by the county unless all fines owed by the owner of the vehicle for violation of the county's parking ordinances have been paid.

The ordinance may provide that a violation of such ordinance constitutes a misdemeanor the penalty for which shall not exceed that of a Class 4 misdemeanor.

§46.2-755. Limitations on imposition of motor vehicle license taxes and fees.

A. No county, city, or town shall impose any motor vehicle license tax or fee on any motor vehicle, trailer, or semitrailer when:

1. A similar tax or fee is imposed by the county, city, or town wherein the vehicle is normally garaged, stored or parked;

2. The vehicle is owned by a nonresident of such locality and is used exclusively for pleasure or personal transportation and not for hire or for the conduct of any business or occupation other than that set forth in subdivision 3 of this subsection;

3. The vehicle is (i) owned by a nonresident and (ii) used for transporting into and within the locality, for sale in person or by his employees, wood, meats, poultry, fruits, flowers, vegetables, milk, butter, cream, or eggs produced or grown by him, and not purchased by him for sale;

4. The motor vehicle, trailer, or semitrailer is owned by an officer or employee of the Commonwealth who is a nonresident of such county, city, or town and who uses the vehicle in the performance of his duties for the Commonwealth under an agreement for such use;

5. The motor vehicle, trailer, or semitrailer is kept by a dealer or manufacturer for sale or for sales demonstration;

6. The motor vehicle, trailer, or semitrailer is operated by a common carrier of persons or property operating between cities and towns in the Commonwealth and not in intracity transportation or between cities and towns on the one hand and points and places outside cities and towns on the other and not in intracity transportation.

B. No county, city, or town shall impose a license fee for any one motor vehicle owned and used personally by any veteran who holds a current state motor vehicle registration card establishing that he has received a disabled veteran's exemption from the Department and has been issued a disabled veteran's motor vehicle license plate as prescribed in §46.2-739.

C. No county, city, or town shall impose any license tax or license fee or the requirement of a license tag, sticker or decal upon any daily rental vehicle as defined in §58.1-2401, the rental of which is subject to the tax imposed by §58.1-2402 A 4.

D. As used in this section, common carrier of persons or property includes any person who undertakes, whether directly or by lease or any other arrangement, to transport passengers or household goods for the general public by motor vehicle for compensation over the highways of the Commonwealth, whether over regular or irregular routes, that has obtained the required certificate of public convenience and necessity from the Department of Motor Vehicles pursuant to §46.2-2004.

(Chgd. by L.1997 chs. 283, 496, 853, eff. 7/1/97.)

§46.2-756. Collection by Department of certain license fees.

The Department may, upon the written request of the governing body of any county, city, or town, collect motor vehicle, trailer, and semitrailer license fees, or portions thereof, provided the portions are for the identical period as the state license plate, levied by such county, city, or town. The Department may make any contractual arrangements in connection with these collections which do not conflict with this chapter. The Department may make such charge as may be proper to defray the cost of handling such fees, and such moneys as may be received shall be used by the Commissioner to defray the expenses of the Department incurred hereunder. The receipts from the fees collected shall be disposed of as provided in the contract between the Department and the counties, cities, and towns involved. However, before a registration or certificate of title is issued under the requirements of §46.2-600 the owner of the motor vehicle, trailer, or semitrailer shall advise the Department of the situs, as provided in subsection A of §46.2-752, of the motor vehicle, trailer, or semitrailer. The Department of Motor Vehicles shall not collect the motor vehicle, trailer, or semitrailer license fee of a county, city, or town on motor vehicles or vehicles falling within the provisions of §46.2-755.

ARTICLE 12
INSURANCE REQUIREMENTS FOR MOTOR CARRIERS

§46.2-757. Definitions and application of article.

A. The following words and phrases when used in this article shall have the following meanings, except where the context clearly indicates a different meaning:

"Authorized insurer" means, in the case of an interstate motor carrier whose operations may or may not include intrastate activity, an insurer authorized to transact business in any one state, or, in the case of a solely intrastate motor carrier, an insurer authorized to transact business in the Commonwealth.

"Identification marker" means a decal or other visible identification issued by the Department to show (i) that the operator of the vehicle has registered with the Department for the payment of the road tax imposed under Chapter 27 (§58.1-2700 et seq.) of Title 58.1, and/or (ii) proof of the possession of a certificate or permit issued pursuant to Chapters 19, 20, 21, 22, 23, 24, and 25 of this title.

"Motor carrier" means a common carrier by motor vehicle, a contract carrier by motor vehicle, or a private carrier of property or passengers by motor vehicle.

"Operation" means the movement on a public highway of the Commonwealth of a loaded or empty motor vehicle that is owned by, leased to, or rented to a motor carrier.

"Operator" means the employer or person actually driving a motor vehicle or combination of vehicles.

"Single State Insurance Receipt" means any receipt issued pursuant to 49 C.F.R. 1023 evidencing that the carrier has the required insurance and paid the requisite fees to the Commonwealth and other qualified jurisdictions.

B. Unless otherwise stated, this article shall apply to all motor carriers that have registered with the Department for the payment of registration fees as required under this title.
(Added by L.1995 chs. 744, 803, eff. 7/1/95.)

§46.2-758. Surety bonds, insurance, letter of credit or securities required prior to issuance of registration.

A. No certificate, permit, identification marker, registration card or license plate shall be issued by the Department to any vehicle operated by a motor carrier until the motor carrier certifies to the Department that the vehicle is covered by:

1. An insurance policy or bond;

2. A certificate of insurance in lieu of the insurance policy or bond, certifying that such policy or bond covers the liability of such motor carrier in accordance with the provisions of this article, is issued by an authorized insurer, or in the case of bonds, is in an amount approved by the Department. The bonds may be issued by the Commonwealth of Virginia, the United States of America, or any municipality in the Commonwealth. Such bonds shall be deposited with the State Treasurer and the surety shall not be reduced except in accordance with an order of the Department;

3. An unconditional letter of credit, issued by a bank doing business in Virginia, for an amount approved by the Department. The letter of credit shall be in effect so long as the motor carrier operates motor vehicles in the Commonwealth; or

4. In the case of a lessor who acts as a registrant for purposes of consolidating lessees' vehicle registration applications, a statement that the registrant has, before leasing a vehicle, obtained from the lessee an insurance policy, bond, or certificate of insurance in lieu of the insurance policy or bond and can make available said proof of insurance coverage upon demand.

Vehicles belonging to carriers who have filed proof of financial responsibility in accordance with the provisions of §11506 of Title 49 of the United States Code are deemed to have fulfilled the requirements of this title for insurance purposes, provided there is on board the vehicle a copy of a single state insurance receipt issued pursuant to 49 C.F.R. 1023. The Department is further authorized to issue single state registration receipts to any qualified carrier as well as to collect and disperse the fees for and to qualified jurisdictions.

B. All motor carriers shall keep in force at all times insurance, a bond or bonds, in an amount required by the Department for motor carriers operating in intrastate commerce under this section; however, for any motor vehicle used in the transportation of property alone, the required amount shall in no case exceed the following: $100,000 for death or injury to any one person; $500,000 total public liability for any one accident; property damage, $50,000; and cargo liability, $10,000. Motor carriers engaged exclusively in the transportation of commodities in bulk shall not be required to file any cargo insurance, bond or bonds for cargo liability.

C. The minimum insurance for motor carriers operating in interstate commerce shall not be less than the minimum required by federal law, rule, or regulation.
(Added by L.1995 chs. 744, 803, eff. 7/1/95.)

§46.2-759. Policies or surety bonds to be filed with the Department and securities with State Treasurer.

Each motor carrier which is the holder of a registration card, license plate, certificate, permit or identification marker issued by the Department shall keep on file with the Department proof of an insurance policy or bond in accordance with this article. Such prior filings as have been made on behalf of interstate motor carriers to the State Corporation Commission shall be kept in full force at all times at the Department. The policy or bond shall remain in the files of the Department six months after the certificate, registration card, license plate, identification marker or permit is canceled for any cause. If federal, state, or municipal bonds are deposited with the State Treasurer in lieu of an insurance policy, the bonds shall remain deposited until six months after the registration card, license plate, certificate, permit or identification marker is canceled for any cause unless otherwise ordered by the Department.
(Added by L.1995 chs. 744, 803; chgd. by L.1997 ch. 283, eff. 7/1/97.)

§46.2-760. Condition or obligation of security.

The insurance, bond or other security provided for in §46.2-759 shall obligate the insurer or surety to pay any final judgment for (i) damages sustained by the shippers or consignees for injury to any passenger or passengers or for loss or damage to property entrusted to such motor carrier when a cargo policy is required and (ii) any and all injuries to persons and loss of or damage to property resulting from the negligent operation of any motor vehicle.
(Added by L.1995 chs. 744, 803, eff. 7/1/95.)

§46.2-761. Effect of failure to give security; penalty.

A. Failure of any motor carrier which is the holder of a registration card, license plate, certificate, permit or identification marker issued by and under the authority of the Department to comply with any of the requirements of this article shall be cause for either (i) the revocation or suspension of all registration cards, license plates, certificates, permits, and identification markers issued to that holder or (ii) a civil penalty not exceeding $1,000.

B. When informed that the right to operate a vehicle has been denied, the driver shall drive the vehicle to a nearby location off the public highways and not move it or allow it to be moved until the judgment or penalty has been satisfied. Failure by the driver to comply with this provision shall constitute a Class 4 misdemeanor.

C. Each carrier who is required to file insurance under this article or is engaged in operations governed by Chapter 19, 20, 21, 22, 23, 24, or 25 of Title 46.2 shall be issued, at the discretion of the Department, an identification marker. The expiration dates and costs will be in accordance with the provisions of §58.1-2700.1.

D. All carriers holding permits and certificates issued by the Department, or required to show proof of insurance under this article, shall place the identification markers issued by the Department on each vehicle operated in the Commonwealth in the place prescribed by the Department, unless the operation is interstate in nature and the carrier has been issued a single state registration receipt by the Department or other qualified jurisdiction. Failure to comply with this provision will constitute a Class 4 misdemeanor.

(Added by L.1995 chs. 744, 803, eff. 7/1/95.)

§46.2-762. Temporary emergency operation.

In an emergency, the Department or its agents may, by letter, telegram, or other means, authorize a vehicle to be operated in the Commonwealth without a proper registration card or identification marker for not more than ten days.

(Added by L.1995 chs. 744, 803; chgd. by L.1997 ch. 283, eff. 7/1/97.)

§46.2-763. Title to plates and markers.

All registration cards and identification markers issued by the Department shall remain the property of the Department.

(Added by L.1995 chs. 744, 803, eff. 7/1/95.)

§46.2-764. Application blanks.

The Department shall prepare forms to be used in making applications in accordance with this article, and the applicant shall furnish all material information called for by such forms.

(Added by L.1995 chs. 744, 803, eff. 7/1/95.)

§46.2-765. Violations declared to be misdemeanors; penalties.

A. The following violations of laws shall be punished as follows:

1. Any person who does not obtain a proper registration card, identification marker, or other evidence of registration as required by this article shall be guilty of a Class 4 misdemeanor.

2. Any person who operates or causes to be operated on any highway in the Commonwealth any motor vehicle that does not carry the proper registration and identification that this article requires or any motor vehicle that does not display (i) an identification marker in such manner as is prescribed by the Department or (ii) other identifying information that this article requires it to display shall be guilty of a Class 4 misdemeanor.

3. Any person who knowingly displays or uses on any vehicle operated by him any identification marker or other identification which has not been issued to the owner or operator thereof for such vehicle and any person who knowingly assists him to do so shall be guilty of a Class 3 misdemeanor.

4. Any person who operates or causes to be operated on any highway in the Commonwealth any motor vehicle requiring registration from the Department under this article after such registration cards or identification markers have been revoked, canceled or suspended shall be guilty of a Class 3 misdemeanor.

B. The officer charging the violation under this article shall serve a citation on the operator of the vehicle in violation. Such citation shall be directed to the owner, operator or other person responsible for the violation as determined by the officer. Service of the citation on the vehicle operator shall constitute service of process upon the owner, operator, or other person charged with the violation under this article, and shall have the same legal force as if served within the Commonwealth personally upon the owner, operator, or other person charged with the violation, whether such owner, operator, or other person charged is a resident or nonresident.

(Added by L.1995 chs. 744, 803, eff. 7/1/95.)

§46.2-766. Other offenses; penalties.

The Department may impose a civil penalty not exceeding $1,000 if it is proved that the defendant has:

1. Made any misrepresentation of a material fact to obtain proper operating credentials as required by this article or other requirements in this Code regulating the operation of motor vehicles;

2. Failed to make any report required in this article;

3. Failed to pay any fee or tax properly assessed against him; or

4. Failed to comply with any lawful order, rule or regulation of the Department.

Any such penalty shall be imposed by order entered after a hearing. Notice of such hearing shall be served on the defendant not less than ten days before the date of the hearing. Instead of or in addition to imposing such penalty, the Department may suspend, revoke, or cancel any registration card or identification marker issued pursuant to this article. If, in any such case, it appears that the defendant owes any fee or tax to the Commonwealth, the Department shall enter order therefor.

(Added by L.1995 chs. 744, 803, eff. 7/1/95.)

§46.2-767. Participation in federal programs; regulations.

The Department may promulgate regulations implementing the requirements of any program established under federal law intended to accomplish objectives similar to those provided in this article.

(Added by L.1995 chs. 744, 803, eff. 7/1/95.)

§46.2-768. Vehicle seizure; penalty.

A. Any police officer of the Commonwealth authorized to serve process may hold a motor vehicle owned by a person against whom an order or penalty has been entered, but only for such time as is reasonably necessary to promptly petition for a writ of fieri facias. The Commonwealth shall not be required to post bond in order to hold and levy upon any vehicle held pursuant to this section.

B. Upon notification of the judgment or penalty entered against the owner of the vehicle and notice to such person of the failure to satisfy the judgment or penalty, any investigator, special agent, or officer of the Commonwealth shall thereafter deny the offending person the right to operate the motor vehicle on the highways of the Commonwealth.

(Added by L.1995 chs. 744, 803, eff. 7/1/95.)

§46.2-769. *(Repealed by L.1997 ch. 283, eff. 7/1/97.)*

SUBTITLE III
OPERATION

CHAPTER 8
REGULATION OF TRAFFIC

ARTICLE 1
GENERAL AND MISCELLANEOUS

§46.2-800. Riding bicycles or mopeds; riding or driving animals.

Every person riding a bicycle, moped or an animal or driving an animal on a highway shall be subject to the provisions of this chapter and shall have all of the rights and duties applicable to the driver of a vehicle, unless the context of the provision clearly indicates otherwise.

The provisions of subsections A and C of §46.2-920 applicable to operation of emergency vehicles under emergency conditions shall also apply, mutatis mutandis, to bicycles and mopeds operated under similar emergency conditions by law-enforcement officers.

§46.2-800.1. Riding animals on highways after sunset.

A. No person riding upon any animal on a highway between sunset and sunrise shall ride the animal on the roadway unless the rider:

1. Wears a hat made of or coated with reflectorized material; or

2. Wears upper body clothing made of or coated with reflectorized material visible from 360 degrees; or

3. Displays at least 100 square inches of solid reflectorized material at shoulder level visible from 360 degrees; or

4. Carries a light visible in clear weather from a distance of 500 feet.

B. The requirements of subsection A of this section shall only apply to the riders of the first and last animals in a group riding one behind the other.

C. A violation of this section shall not be construed as negligence per se in any civil action.

§46.2-801. Chapter applicable to drivers of all vehicles regardless of ownership.

The provisions of this chapter applicable to the drivers of vehicles on the highways shall apply to the drivers of all vehicles regardless of their ownership, subject to such exceptions as are set forth in this chapter.

§46.2-802. Drive on right side of highways.

Except as otherwise provided by law, on all highways of sufficient width, the driver of a vehicle shall drive on the right half of the highway, unless it is impracticable to travel on such side of the highway and except when overtaking and passing another vehicle, subject to the provisions applicable to overtaking and passing set forth in Article 4 (§46.2-837 et seq.) of this chapter.

§46.2-803. Keep to the right in crossing intersections or railroads.

Except as otherwise provided by law, when crossing an intersection of highways or the intersection of a highway by a railroad right-of-way, the driver of a vehicle shall drive on the right half of the roadway unless it is obstructed or impassable. When crossing an intersection of highways, however, the driver of a vehicle may overtake or pass another vehicle in the intersection if such intersection is designated and marked as a passing zone.

§46.2-803.1. Commercial vehicles limited to use of certain lanes of certain interstate highways.

Except where the posted speed limit is less than sixty-five miles per hour, no person shall drive any commercial motor vehicle, as defined in §46.2-341.4, on the left-most of any interstate highway having more than two lanes in each direction.

Furthermore, within the Eighth Planning District, no person shall drive any commercial motor vehicle, as defined in §46.2-341.4, on the left-most lane of any interstate highway having more than two lanes in each direction, regardless of the posted speed limit.

The provisions of this section shall not apply to (i) buses or school buses or (ii) other commercial vehicles when (a) preparing to exit a highway via a left exit or (b) being used to perform maintenance or construction work on an interstate highway.

(Paragraph effective only until 7/1/2002 by the second enactment of L.2000 chs. 60, 306.) The provisions of this section shall not apply to Interstate Route 295.

(Added by L.1997 ch. 733; chgd. by L.1998 ch. 555; L.2000 chs. 60, 306, 407, eff. 7/1/2000.)

§46.2-804. Special regulations applicable on highways laned for traffic.

Whenever any roadway has been divided into clearly marked lanes for traffic, drivers of vehicles shall obey the following:

1. Any vehicle proceeding at less than the normal speed of traffic at the time and place and under the conditions existing, shall be driven in the lane nearest the right edge or right curb of the highway when such lane is available for travel except when overtaking and passing another vehicle or in preparation for a left turn or where right lanes are reserved for slow-moving traffic as permitted in this section;

2. A vehicle shall be driven as nearly as is practicable entirely within a single lane and shall not be moved from that lane until the driver has ascertained that such movement can be made safely;

3. Except as otherwise provided in subdivision 5 of this section, on a highway which is divided into three lanes, no vehicle shall be driven in the center lane except when overtaking and passing another vehicle or in preparation for a left turn or unless such center lane is at the time allocated exclusively to traffic moving in the direction the vehicle is proceeding and is signed or marked to give notice of such allocation. Traffic-control devices may be erected directing specified traffic to use a designated lane or designating those lanes to be used by traffic moving in a particular direction regardless of the center of the roadway and drivers of vehicles shall obey the directions of every such device;

4. The Commonwealth Transportation Board, or local authorities in their respective jurisdictions, may designate right lanes for slow-moving vehicles;

5. Wherever a highway is marked with double traffic lines consisting of a solid line immediately adjacent to a broken line, no vehicle shall be driven to the left of such line if the solid line is on the right of the broken line, but it shall be lawful to make a left turn for the purpose of entering or leaving a public, private, or commercial road or entrance. Where the middle lane of a highway is marked on both sides with a solid line immediately adjacent to a broken line, such middle lane shall be considered a left-turn or holding lane and it shall be lawful to drive to the left of such line if the solid line is on the right of the broken line for the purpose of turning left into any road or entrance, provided that the vehicle may not travel in such lane further than 150 feet;

6. Wherever a highway is marked with double traffic lines consisting of two immediately adjacent solid lines, no vehicle shall be driven to the left of such lines, except when turning left.

§46.2-805. Lane direction control signals.

When lane direction control signals are placed over the individual lanes of a highway, vehicular traffic may travel in any lane over which a green signal is shown, but shall not enter or travel in any lane over which a red signal is shown and shall vacate as soon as possible any lane over which an amber signal is shown.

§46.2-806. One-way roadways and highways.

The Commonwealth Transportation Board may designate any highway or any separate roadway under its jurisdiction for one-way traffic and shall erect appropriate signs. Traffic thereon shall move only in the direction designated.

§46.2-807. Rotary traffic islands.

A vehicle passing around a rotary traffic island shall be driven only to the right of such island.

§46.2-808. Commonwealth Transportation Board may prohibit certain uses of controlled access highways; penalty.

A. The Commonwealth Transportation Board may, when necessary to promote safety, prohibit the use of controlled access highways or any part thereof by any or all of the following:

1. Pedestrians,
2. Persons riding bicycles or mopeds,
3. Horse-drawn vehicles,
4. Self-propelled machinery or equipment, and
5. Animals led, ridden or driven on the hoof.

B. The termini of any section of controlled access highways, use of which is restricted under the provisions of this section, shall be clearly indicated by a conspicuous marker.

C. This section shall not apply to any vehicle or equipment owned or controlled by the Virginia Department of Transportation, while actually engaged in the construction, reconstruction, or maintenance of highways or to any vehicle or equipment for which a permit has been obtained for operation on such highway.

Any person violating a restriction or prohibition imposed pursuant to this section shall be guilty of a traffic infraction.

§46.2-808.1. Use of crossovers on controlled access highways; penalty.

It shall be unlawful for the driver of any vehicle other than an authorized vehicle to use or attempt to use any crossover posted for authorized vehicles only on any controlled access highway.

For the purposes of this section, "authorized vehicle" means (i) Department of Transportation vehicles, (ii) law-enforcement vehicles, (iii) emergency vehicles as defined in §46.2-920, (iv) towing and recovery vehicles operating under the direction of law-enforcement officers, (v) vehicles for which permits authorizing use of such crossovers have been issued by the Department of Transportation, and (vi) other vehicles operating in medical emergency situations.

Violation of any provision of this section shall constitute a traffic infraction punishable by a fine of no more than $250.
(Added by L.1997 ch. 881, eff. 7/1/97.)

§46.2-809. Regulation of truck traffic on secondary highways.

The Commonwealth Transportation Board in response to a formal request by a local governing body, after such body has held public hearings, may, after due notice and a proper hearing, prohibit or restrict the use by through traffic of any part of a secondary highway if a reasonable alternate route is provided. Such restriction may apply to any truck or truck and trailer or semitrailer combination, except a pickup or panel truck, as may be necessary to promote the health, safety, and welfare of the citizens of the Commonwealth. Nothing in this section shall affect the validity of any city charter provision or city ordinance heretofore adopted.

The provisions of this section shall not apply in (i) cities, (ii) any town which maintains its own system of streets, and (iii) in any county which owns, operates, and maintains its own system of roads and streets.

§46.2-809.1. Regulation of residential cut-through traffic by Board.

The Commonwealth Transportation Board may develop a residential cut-through traffic policy and procedure for the control of residential cut-through traffic on designated secondary highways.

For the purposes of this section, "residential cut-through traffic" means vehicular traffic passing through a residential area without stopping or without at least an origin or destination within the area.

The provisions of this section shall not apply in (i) cities, (ii) any town that maintains its own system of streets, and (iii) any county that owns, operates and maintains its own system of highways.
(Added by L.1995 ch. 556, eff. 7/1/95.)

§46.2-810. Age limits for drivers of public passenger-carrying vehicles.

No person, whether licensed or not, under the age of eighteen years shall drive a motor vehicle while in use as a public passenger-carrying vehicle.

§46.2-811. Coasting prohibited.

The driver of any motor vehicle traveling on a downgrade on any highway shall not coast with the gears of the vehicle in neutral.

§46.2-812. Driving more than thirteen hours in twenty-four prohibited.

No person shall drive any motor vehicle on the highways of the Commonwealth for more than thirteen hours in any period of twenty-four hours or for a period which, when added to the time such person may have driven in any other state, would make an aggregate of more than thirteen hours in any twenty-four-hour period. The provisions of this section, however, shall not apply to the operation of motor vehicles used in snow or ice control or removal operations or similar emergency situations.

No owner of any vehicle shall cause or permit it to be driven in violation of this section.

§46.2-813. Occupation of trailer being towed on highways.

No person shall occupy a house trailer or camping trailer while it is being towed on a public highway in this Commonwealth. No operator of a towing vehicle shall knowingly permit another person to occupy a house trailer or camping trailer as defined in §46.2-100 while it is being towed.

In any civil proceeding, the violation of this section shall not constitute negligence per se.

§46.2-814. Driving through safety zone prohibited.

No driver of a vehicle shall drive through or over a safety zone.

§46.2-815. Hauling certain cargoes through tunnels in violation of posted signs; penalty.

The hauling of any explosive, flammable, or other hazardous cargo, as prohibited by the Department of Transportation under the authority of §§33.1-12 and 33.1-49, through any tunnel on any highway in the Commonwealth in violation of any lawfully posted sign shall constitute a Class 1 misdemeanor.

§46.2-816. Following too closely.

The driver of a motor vehicle shall not follow another motor vehicle, trailer, or semitrailer more closely than is reasonable and prudent, having due regard to the speed of both vehicles and the traffic on, and conditions of, the highway at the time.

§46.2-817. Disregarding signal by law-enforcement officer to stop; eluding police; penalties.

A. Any person who, having received a visible or audible signal from any law-enforcement officer to bring his motor vehicle to a stop, drives such motor vehicle in a willful and wanton disregard of such signal or who attempts to escape or elude such law-enforcement officer, shall be guilty of a Class 3 misdemeanor. It shall be an affirmative defense to a charge of a violation of this subsection if the defendant shows he reasonably believed he was being pursued by a person other than a law-enforcement officer.

B. Any person who, having received a visible or audible signal from any law-enforcement officer to bring his motor vehicle to a stop, drives such motor vehicle in a willful and wanton disregard of such signal so as to interfere with or endanger the operation of the law-enforcement vehicle or endanger a person shall be guilty of a Class 6 felony. It shall be an affirmative defense to a charge of a violation of this subsection if the defendant shows he reasonably believed he was being pursued by a person other than a law-enforcement officer.

C. When any person is convicted of a misdemeanor under this section, in addition to the other penalties provided in this section, the driver's license of such person may be suspended by the court for a period of not less than thirty days nor more than one year. However, in any case where the speed of such person is determined to have exceeded the maximum allowed by twenty miles per hour, his driver's license shall be suspended by the court trying the case for a period of not less than ninety days. In case of conviction and suspension, the court or judge shall order the surrender of the license to the court, which shall dispose of it in accordance with the provisions of §46.2-398.
(Chgd. by L.1996 chs. 577, 817; L.1999 ch. 720; L.2000 ch. 315, eff. 7/1/2000.)

§46.2-818. Stopping vehicle of another; blocking access to premises; damaging or threatening commercial vehicle or operator thereof; penalties.

No person shall intentionally and willfully:

1. Stop the vehicle of another for the sole purpose of impeding its progress on the highways, except in the case of an emergency or mechanical breakdown;

2. Block the access to or egress from any premises of any service facility operated for the purposes of (i) selling fuel for motor vehicles, (ii) performing repair services on motor vehicles, or (iii) furnishing food, rest, or any other convenience for the use of persons operating motor vehicles engaged in intrastate and interstate commerce on the highways of this Commonwealth;

3. Damage any vehicle engaged in commerce on the highways of this Commonwealth, or threaten, assault, or otherwise harm the person of any operator of a motor vehicle being used for the transportation of property for hire.

Any person violating any provision of this section shall be guilty of a Class 1 misdemeanor, and in addition, his driver's license may be suspended by the court for a period of not more than one year. The court shall forward such license to the Department as provided by §46.2-398.

The provisions of this section shall not apply to any law-enforcement officer, school guard, fire fighter, or member of a rescue squad engaged in the performance of his duties nor to any vehicle owned or controlled by the Virginia Department of Transportation while engaged in the construction, reconstruction, or maintenance of highways.

§46.2-819. Use of toll facility without payment of toll; circumstances to be considered in assessing penalty.

Except for those permitted free use of toll facilities under §33.1-252, it shall be unlawful for the driver of a motor vehicle to use a toll facility without payment of the specified toll.

However, in considering the case of anyone accused of violating this section, the court shall take into consideration (i) except for lanes equipped for payment of tolls through an automatic vehicle identification system, whether the toll booth or collection facility at which the defendant failed to pay the toll was manned at the time, (ii) whether the defendant was required to pay the toll with the exact amount in change, (iii) whether the defendant had change to make the payment, and (iv) whether the defendant had been afforded appropriate advance notice, by signs or other means, that he would be required to pay a toll and pay it with the exact change. Where any photo-monitoring system provided for in §46.2-819.1 is in operation, no person shall be subject to both prosecution under this section and to the provisions of §46.2-819.1 for actions arising out of the same transaction or occurrence.

(Chgd. by L.1998 ch. 802, eff. 7/1/98.)

§46.2-819.1. Installation and use of photo-monitoring system in conjunction with certain toll facilities; penalty.

A. The operator of any toll facility or the locality within which such toll facility is located may install and operate or cause to be installed and operated a photo-monitoring system at locations where tolls are collected for the use of such toll facility.

B. The operator of a vehicle shall be liable for a civil penalty of no more than twenty-five dollars for a first offense or no more than fifty dollars for any subsequent offense if the vehicle is found, as evidenced by information obtained from a photo-monitoring system as provided in this section, to have used such a toll facility without payment of the required toll.

C. Proof of a violation of this section shall be evidenced by information obtained from a photo-monitoring system as provided in this section. A certificate, sworn to or affirmed by a technician employed or authorized by the operator of a toll facility or by the locality wherein the toll facility is located, or a facsimile of such a certificate, based on inspection of photographs, microphotographs, videotapes, or other recorded images produced by a photo-monitoring system, shall be prima facie evidence of the facts contained therein. Any photographs, microphotographs, videotape, or other recorded images evidencing such a violation shall be available for inspection in any proceeding to adjudicate the liability for such violation under this section.

D. It shall be prima facie evidence that the vehicle described in the summons issued pursuant to subsection G of this section was operated in violation of this section.

Upon a finding by a court of competent jurisdiction that the vehicle described in the summons issued pursuant to subsection G of this section was in violation of this section, the court shall impose a civil penalty upon the registered owner of such vehicle in accordance with the amounts specified in subsection B of this section. Such civil penalty shall constitute a lien on such vehicle, subordinate to any other liens on the vehicle, unless such civil penalty is paid to the court within thirty days of imposition of such civil penalty.

The registered owner of such vehicle shall be given reasonable notice by way of a summons as provided in subsection G of this section that his vehicle had been used in violation of this section and such owner shall be given notice of the time and place of the hearing as well as the civil penalty and costs for such offense.

Such summons shall be dismissed upon the filing of an affidavit by the registered owner of the vehicle stating that he was not the driver of the vehicle on the date of the violation.

In addition thereto, if the registered owner of the vehicle produces a certified copy of a police report showing that the vehicle had been reported to the police as stolen prior to the time of the alleged offense, then the court shall dismiss the summons.

E. For purposes of this section, "owner" means the registered owner of such vehicle on record with the Department of Motor Vehicles. For purposes of this section, "owner" does not mean a vehicle rental or vehicle leasing company. For purposes of this section, "photo-monitoring system" means a vehicle sensor installed to work in conjunction with a toll collection device that automatically produces one or more photographs, one or more microphotographs, a videotape, or other recorded images of each vehicle at the time it is used or operated in violation of this section.

F. Imposition of a civil penalty pursuant to this section shall not be deemed a conviction as an operator and shall not be made part of the operating record of the person upon whom such civil penalty is imposed nor shall it be used for insurance purposes in the provision of motor vehicle insurance coverage.

G. A summons for a violation of this section may be executed pursuant to §19.2-76.2. Notwithstanding the provisions of §19.2-76, a summons for a violation of this section may be executed by mailing by first-class mail a copy thereof to the address of the owner of the vehicle as shown on the records of the Department of Motor Vehicles. If the summoned person fails to appear on the date of return set out in the summons mailed pursuant to this section, the summons shall be executed in the manner set out in §19.2-76.3. No proceedings for contempt or arrest of a person summoned by mailing shall be instituted for failure to appear on the return date of the summons.

H. The operator of a toll facility may enter into an agreement with the Department of Motor Vehicles, in accordance with the provisions of subdivision 21 of subsection B of §46.2-208, to obtain vehicle owner information regarding the registered owners of vehicles that fail to pay tolls required for the use of toll facilities.

I. Where any photo-monitoring system provided for in this section is in operation, no person shall be subject to both the provisions of this section and to prosecution under §46.2-819 for actions arising out of the same transaction or occurrence.

(Added by L.1998 ch. 802, eff. 7/1/98.)

§46.2-819.2. Driving a motor vehicle from establishment where motor fuel offered for sale; suspension of license; penalty.

(Section effective 1/1/2001.)

A. No person shall drive a motor vehicle off the premises of an establishment at which motor fuel offered for retail sale was dispensed into the fuel tank of such motor vehicle unless payment for such fuel has been made.

B. Any person who violates this section shall be liable for a civil penalty not to exceed $100.

C. The driver's license of any person found to have violated this section (i) may be suspended, for the first offense, for a period of up to 30 days and (ii) shall be suspended for a period of 30 days for the second and subsequent offenses.

(Added by L.2000 chs. 729, 758, eff. 1/1/2001.)

ARTICLE 2
RIGHT-OF-WAY

§46.2-820. Right-of-way at uncontrolled intersections, generally.

Except as otherwise provided in this article, when two vehicles approach or enter an uncontrolled intersection at approximately the same time, the driver of the vehicle on the left shall yield the right-of-way to the vehicle on the right.

§46.2-821. Vehicles before entering certain highways shall stop or yield right-of-way.

The driver of a vehicle approaching an intersection on a highway controlled by a stop sign shall, immediately before entering such intersection, stop at a clearly marked stop line, or, in the absence of a stop line, stop before entering the crosswalk on the near side of the intersection, or, in the absence of a marked crosswalk, stop at the point nearest the intersecting roadway where the driver has a view of approaching traffic on the intersecting roadway. Before proceeding, he shall yield the right-of-way to the driver of any vehicle approaching on such other highway from either direction.

Where a "Yield Right-of-Way" sign is posted, the driver of a vehicle approaching or entering such intersection shall slow down to a speed reasonable for the existing conditions, yield the right-of-way to the driver of another vehicle approaching or entering such intersection from another direction, and, if required for safety, shall stop at a clearly marked stop line, or, in the absence of a stop line, stop before entering the crosswalk on the near side of the intersecting roadway where the driver has a view of approaching traffic on the intersecting roadway, and shall yield the right-of-way to the driver of any vehicle approaching on such other highway from either direction.

§46.2-822. Right-of-way at traffic circles.

At traffic circles vehicles already in the circle shall have the right-of-way over vehicles approaching and entering the circle.

§46.2-823. Unlawful speed forfeits right-of-way.

The driver of any vehicle traveling at an unlawful speed shall forfeit any right-of-way which he might otherwise have under this article.

§46.2-824. Right-of-way at uncontrolled "T" intersections.

When vehicles arrive at approximately the same time at an uncontrolled "T" intersection, the driver of the vehicle on the highway that intersects but does not cross the other highway shall yield the right-of-way to any vehicle traveling on the other highway.

§46.2-825. Left turn traffic to yield right-of-way.

The driver of a vehicle, intending to turn left within an intersection or into an alley, private road, or driveway shall yield the right-of-way to any vehicle approaching from the opposite direction if it is so close as to constitute a hazard. At intersections controlled by traffic lights with separate left-turn signals, any vehicle making a left turn when so indicated by the signal shall have the right-of-way over all other vehicles approaching the intersection.

§46.2-826. Stop before entering public highway or sidewalk from private road, etc.; yielding right-of-way.

The driver of a vehicle entering a public highway or sidewalk from a private road, driveway, alley, or building shall stop immediately before entering such highway or sidewalk and yield the right-of-way to vehicles approaching on such public highway and to pedestrians or vehicles approaching on such public sidewalk.

The provisions of this section shall not apply at an intersection of public and private roads controlled by a traffic signal. At any such intersection, all movement of traffic into and through the intersection shall be controlled by the traffic signal.

§46.2-827. Right-of-way of United States forces, troops, national guard, etc.

United States forces or troops, or any portion of the Virginia national guard or naval militia, parading or performing any duty according to law, or any civil defense personnel performing any duty according to law, shall have the right-of-way in any highway through which they may pass. Such passage, however, shall not interfere with the carrying of the United States mails and the legitimate functions of police and fire fighters or with the passage of emergency vehicles as defined in §46.2-920.

§46.2-828. Right-of-way for funeral processions under police or sheriff's escort; improper joining of, passing through, or interfering with processions prohibited.

Funeral processions traveling under police or sheriff's escort shall have the right-of-way in any highway through which they may pass. Localities may, by ordinance, provide for such escort service and provide for the imposition of reasonable fees to defray the cost of such service.

The sheriff in any locality not having a separate police department may provide traffic control for funeral processions when equipment and personnel are not otherwise engaged in law-enforcement activities.

No vehicle that is not properly part of a funeral procession shall join, pass through, or interfere with the passage of any funeral procession under escort as provided in this section.

§46.2-828.1. Impeding or disrupting certain funeral processions; penalty.

A. It shall be unlawful for the operator of any motor vehicle intentionally to impede or disrupt a funeral procession. Any person convicted of violating this subsection shall be guilty of a traffic infraction and shall, in addition to a penalty assessed pursuant to §46.2-113, be assessed four driver demerit points.

B. This section shall apply only to funeral processions that are either (i) travelling under police or sheriff's escort as provided in §46.2-828 or (ii) escorted or led by vehicles displaying warning lights as provided in §46.2-1025.
(Added by L.2000 ch. 274, eff. 7/1/2000.)

§46.2-829. Approach of law-enforcement or firefighting vehicles, rescue vehicles, or ambulances; violation as failure to yield right-of-way.

Upon the approach of any emergency vehicle as defined in §46.2-920 giving audible signal by siren, exhaust whistle, or air horn designed to give automatically intermittent signals, and displaying a flashing, blinking, or alternating emergency light or lights as provided in §§46.2-1022 through 46.2-1024, the driver of every other vehicle shall, as quickly as traffic and other highway conditions permit, drive to the nearest edge of the roadway, clear of any intersection of highways, and stop and remain there, unless otherwise directed by a law-enforcement officer, until the emergency vehicle has passed. This provision shall not relieve the driver of any such vehicle to which the right-of-way is to be yielded of the duty to drive with due regard for the safety of all persons using the highway, nor shall it protect the driver of any such vehicle from the consequences of an arbitrary exercise of such right-of-way.

Violation of this section shall constitute failure to yield the right-of-way; however, any violation of this section that involves overtaking or passing a moving emergency vehicle giving an audible signal and displaying activated warning lights as provided for in this section shall constitute reckless driving, punishable as provided in §46.2-868.

ARTICLE 3
TRAFFIC SIGNS, LIGHTS, AND MARKINGS

§46.2-830. Uniform marking and signing of highways; drivers to obey signs; enforcement of section.

The Commonwealth Transportation Board may classify, designate, and mark state highways and provide a uniform system of marking and signing such highways under the jurisdiction of the Commonwealth. Such system of marking and signing shall correlate with and, so far as possible, conform to the system adopted in other states.

All drivers of vehicles shall obey lawfully erected signs.

No provision of this section relating to the prohibition of disobeying signs or violating local traffic signals, markings, and lights shall be enforced against an alleged violator if, at the time and place of the alleged violation, any such sign, signal, marking, or light is not in proper position and sufficiently legible to be seen by an ordinarily observant person.
(Chgd. by L.1997 ch. 881, eff. 7/1/97.)

§46.2-830.1. Failure to obey highway sign where driver sleeping or resting.

Upon the trial of a person charged with failure to obey a highway sign in violation of §46.2-830 where the court finds that the violation resulted from the vehicle's having been parked or stopped by the driver on the shoulder or other portion of the highway nor ordinarily used for vehicular traffic in order for the driver to sleep or rest, the court may, in lieu of convicting under §46.2-830, find the driver guilty of violating this section, which shall be a lesser-included offense of §46.2-830. No demerit points shall be assigned pursuant to the Uniform Demerit Point System for convictions pursuant to this section.

§46.2-831. Unofficial signs prohibited; penalties.

No unauthorized person shall erect or maintain on any highway any warning or direction sign, signal, or light in imitation of any official sign, signal, or light erected as provided by law. No person shall erect or maintain on any highway any traffic or highway sign or signal bearing any commercial advertising.

Nothing in this section shall prohibit the erection or maintenance of signs or signals bearing the name of an organization authorized to erect it by the Commonwealth Transportation Board or by the local authorities of counties, cities, and towns as provided by law. Nor shall this section be construed to prohibit the erection by contractors or public utility companies of temporary signs approved by the Virginia Department of Transportation warning motorists that work is in progress on or adjacent to the highway.

Any violation of this section shall constitute a Class 4 misdemeanor.

§46.2-832. Injuring signs.

Any person who defaces, injures, knocks down, or removes any legally posted sign shall be guilty of a Class 2 misdemeanor.

§46.2-833. Traffic lights.

A. Signals by traffic lights shall be as follows:

Steady red indicates that moving traffic shall stop and remain stopped as long as the red signal is shown, except in the direction indicated by a lighted green arrow.

Green indicates the traffic shall move in the direction of the signal and remain in motion as long as the green signal is given, except that such traffic shall yield to other vehicles and pedestrians lawfully within the intersection.

Steady amber indicates that a change is about to be made in the direction of the moving of traffic. When the amber signal is shown, traffic which has not already entered the intersection, including the crosswalks, shall stop if it is not reasonably safe to continue, but traffic which has already entered the intersection shall continue to move until the intersection has been cleared. The amber signal is a warning that the steady red signal is imminent.

Flashing red indicates that traffic shall stop before entering an intersection.

Flashing amber indicates that traffic may proceed through the intersection or past such signal with reasonable care under the circumstances.

B. The driver of any motor vehicle may be detained for a violation of this section if the detaining law-enforcement officer is in uniform, displays his badge of authority, and (i) has observed the violation or (ii) has received a radio message from another law-enforcement officer who observed the violation. In the case of a person being detained based on a radio message, the message shall be sent immediately after the violation is observed, and the observing officer shall furnish the license number or other positive identification of the vehicle to the detaining officer.

(Chgd. by L.2000 ch. 834, eff. 7/1/2000.)

§46.2-833.01. Use of photo-monitoring systems to enforce traffic light signals; penalty.

(Section effective only until 7/1/2005.)

A. The governing body of any city having a population of more than 390,000, any city having a population of at least 200,000 but less than 225,000, any county having the urban county executive form of government, any county adjacent to such county, and any city or town adjacent to or surrounded by such county except any county having the county executive form of government and the cities surrounded by such county may provide by ordinance for the establishment of a demonstration program imposing monetary liability on the operator of a motor vehicle for failure to comply with traffic light signals in such locality in accordance with the provisions of this section. Each such locality may install and operate traffic light signal photo-monitoring systems at no more than twenty-five intersections within each locality at any one time.

B. The operator of a vehicle shall be liable for a monetary penalty imposed pursuant to this section if such vehicle is found, as evidenced by information obtained from a traffic light signal violation monitoring system, to have failed to comply with a traffic light signal within such locality.

C. Proof of a violation of this section shall be evidenced by information obtained from a traffic light signal violation monitoring system authorized pursuant to this section. A certificate, sworn to or affirmed by a technician employed by a locality authorized to impose penalties pursuant to this section, or a facsimile thereof, based upon inspection of photographs, microphotographs, videotape, or other recorded images produced by a traffic light signal violation monitoring system, shall be prima facie evidence of the facts contained therein. Any photographs, microphotographs, videotape, or other recorded images evidencing such a violation shall be available for inspection in any proceeding to adjudicate the liability for such violation pursuant to an ordinance adopted pursuant to this section.

D. In the prosecution of an offense established under this section, prima facie evidence that the vehicle described in the summons issued pursuant to this section was operated in violation of this section, together with proof that the defendant was at the time of such violation the owner, lessee, or renter of the vehicle, shall constitute in evidence a rebuttable presumption that such owner, lessee, or renter of the vehicle was the person who committed the violation. Such presumption shall be rebutted if the owner, lessee, or renter of the vehicle (i) files an affidavit by regular mail with the clerk of the general district court that he or she was not the operator of the vehicle at the time of the alleged violation or (ii) testifies in open court under oath that he or she was not the operator of the vehicle at the time of the alleged violation. Such presumption shall also be rebutted if a certified copy of a police report, showing that the vehicle had been reported to the police as stolen prior to the time of the alleged violation of this section, is presented, prior to the return date established on the summons issued pursuant to this section, to the court adjudicating the alleged violation.

E. For purposes of this section "owner" means the registered owner of such vehicle on record with the Department of Motor Vehicles. For purposes of this section, "traffic light signal violation-monitoring system" means a vehicle sensor installed to work in conjunction with a traffic light that automatically produces two or more photographs, two or more microphotographs, a videotape, or other recorded images of each vehicle at the time it is used or operated in violation of §§46.2-833, 46.2-835, or §46.2-836. For each such vehicle, at least one recorded image shall be of the vehicle before it has illegally entered the intersection, and at least one recorded image shall be of the same vehicle after it has illegally entered that intersection.

F. Imposition of a penalty pursuant to this section shall not be deemed a conviction as an operator and shall not be made part of the operating record of the person upon whom such liability is imposed nor shall it be used for insurance purposes in the provision of motor vehicle insurance coverage. No monetary penalty imposed under this section shall exceed fifty dollars nor shall it include court costs.

G. A summons for a violation of this section may be executed pursuant to §19.2-76.2. Notwithstanding the provisions of §19.2-76, a summons for a violation of this section may be executed by mailing by first-class mail a copy thereof to the address of the owner, lessee, or renter of the vehicle as shown, in the case of vehicle owners, in the records of the Department of Motor Vehicles or, in the case of vehicle lessees or renters, in the records of the lessor or rentor. Every such mailing shall include, in addition to the summons, a notice of (i) the summoned person's ability to rebut the presumption that he was the operator of the vehicle at the time of the alleged violation through the filing of an affidavit as provided in subsection D of this section and (ii) instructions for filing such affidavit, including the address to which the affidavit is to be sent. If the summoned person fails to appear on the date of return set out in the summons mailed pursuant to this section, the summons shall be executed in the manner set out in §19.2-76.3. No proceedings for contempt or arrest of a person summoned by mailing shall be instituted for failure to appear on the return date of the summons.

H. In any action at law brought by any person or entity as the result of personal injury or death or damage to property, such evidence derived from a photo-monitoring system shall be admissible in the same method prescribed as required in the prosecution of an offense established under this section without the requirements of authentication as otherwise required by law.

I. On behalf of a locality, a private entity may not obtain records regarding the registered owners of vehicles which fail to comply with traffic light signals. A private entity may enter into an agreement with a locality to be compensated for providing the traffic light signal violation-monitoring system or equipment, and all related support services, to include consulting, operations and administration. However, only an employee of the locality may swear to or affirm the certificate required by subsection C.

J. The provisions of this section shall expire on July 1, 2005.

(Added by L.1995 ch. 492; chgd. by L.1996 ch. 392; L.1998 chs. 663, 685; L.1999 ch. 884; L.2000 ch. 575, eff. 7/1/2000. Repealed by its own terms, eff. 7/1/2005.)

§46.2-833.1. Evasion of traffic control devices.

It shall be unlawful for the driver of any motor vehicle to drive off the roadway and onto or across any public or private property in order to evade any stop sign, yield sign, traffic light, or other traffic control device.

§46.2-834. Signals by law-enforcement officers and crossing guards.

A. Law-enforcement officers may assume control of traffic at any intersection, regardless of whether such intersection is controlled by lights, controlled by other traffic control devices, or uncontrolled. Whenever any law-enforcement officer so assumes control of traffic, all drivers of vehicles shall obey his signals.

B. Law-enforcement officers and uniformed school crossing guards may assume control of traffic otherwise controlled by lights and in such event, signals by such officers and uniformed crossing guards shall take precedence over such traffic control devices.

§46.2-835. Right turn on steady red light after stopping.

Notwithstanding the provisions of §46.2-833, except where signs are placed prohibiting turns on steady red, vehicular traffic facing a steady red signal, after coming to a full stop, may cautiously enter the intersection and make a right turn.

Such turning traffic shall yield the right-of-way to pedestrians lawfully within an adjacent crosswalk and to other traffic using the intersection.

§46.2-836. Left turn on steady red after stopping.

Notwithstanding the provisions of §46.2-833, except where signs are placed prohibiting turns on steady red, vehicular traffic facing a steady red signal on a one-way highway, after coming to a full stop, may cautiously enter the intersection and make a left turn onto another one-way highway.

Such turning traffic shall yield the right-of-way to pedestrians lawfully within an adjacent crosswalk and to other traffic using the intersection.

ARTICLE 4
PASSING

§46.2-837. Passing vehicles proceeding in opposite directions.

Drivers of vehicles proceeding in opposite directions on highways not marked to indicate traffic lanes shall pass each other to the right, each giving to the other, as nearly as possible, one-half of the main traveled portion of the roadway.

§46.2-838. Passing when overtaking a motor vehicle.

The driver of any vehicle overtaking another motor vehicle proceeding in the same direction shall pass at least two feet to the left of the overtaken vehicle and shall not again drive to the right side of the highway until safely clear of such overtaken vehicle, except as otherwise provided in this article.

(Chgd. by L.1999 ch. 999, eff. 7/1/99.)

§46.2-839. Passing bicycle, moped, animal or animal-drawn vehicle.

In approaching or passing a person riding a bicycle, moped, animal or animal-drawn vehicle, the driver of a motor vehicle shall pass at a safe distance and at a reasonable speed.

(Chgd. by L.1999 ch. 999, eff. 7/1/99.)

§46.2-840. *(Repealed by L.1996 ch. 147, eff. 7/1/96.)*

§46.2-841. When overtaking vehicle may pass on right.

A. The driver of a vehicle may overtake and pass to the right of another vehicle only:

1. When the overtaken vehicle is making or about to make a left turn, and its driver has given the required signal;
2. On a highway with unobstructed pavement, not occupied by parked vehicles, of sufficient width for two or more lines of moving vehicles in each direction;
3. On a one-way street or on any one-way roadway when the roadway is free from obstructions and of sufficient width for two or more lines of moving vehicles.

B. The driver of a vehicle may overtake and pass another vehicle on the right only under conditions permitting such movement in safety. Except where driving on paved shoulders is permitted by lawfully placed signs, no such movement shall be made by driving on the shoulder of the highway or off the pavement or main traveled portion of the roadway.

§46.2-842. Driver to give way to overtaking vehicle.

Except when overtaking and passing on the right is permitted, the driver of an overtaken vehicle shall give way to the right in favor of the overtaking vehicle on audible signal and shall not increase the speed of his vehicle until completely passed by the overtaking vehicle. Any over-width, or slow-moving vehicle as defined by §46.2-1081 shall be removed from the roadway at the nearest suitable location when necessary to allow traffic to pass.

§46.2-842.1. Drivers to give way to certain overtaking vehicles on divided highways.

It shall be unlawful to fail to give way to overtaking traffic when driving a motor vehicle to the left and abreast of another motor vehicle on a divided highway. On audible or light signal, the driver of the overtaken vehicle shall move to the right to allow the overtaking vehicle to pass as soon as the overtaken vehicle can safely do so. A violation of this section shall not be construed as negligence per se in any civil action.

§46.2-843. Limitations on overtaking and passing.

The driver of a vehicle shall not drive to the left side of the center line of a highway in overtaking and passing another vehicle proceeding in the same direction unless such left side is clearly visible and is free of oncoming traffic for a sufficient distance ahead to permit such overtaking and passing to be made safely.

No person operating a truck or combination of vehicles shall pass or attempt to pass any truck or combination of vehicles going in the same direction on an upgrade if such passing will impede the passage of following traffic.

§46.2-844. Passing stopped school buses; penalty.

The driver of a motor vehicle approaching from any direction a clearly marked school bus which is stopped on any highway or school driveway for the purpose of taking on or discharging children, the elderly, or mentally or physically handicapped persons, who, in violation of §46.2-859, fails to stop and remain stopped until all such persons are clear of the highway or school driveway, shall be subject to a civil penalty of $250 and any such prosecution shall be instituted and conducted in the same manner as prosecutions for traffic infractions.

A prosecution or proceeding under §46.2-859 shall be a bar to a prosecution or proceeding under this section for the same act and a prosecution or proceeding under this section shall be a bar to a prosecution or proceeding under §46.2-859 for the same act.

In any prosecution for which a summons charging a violation of this section was issued within ten days of the alleged violation, proof that the motor vehicle described in the summons was operated in violation of this section, together with proof that the defendant was at the time of such violation the registered owner of the vehicle, as required by Chapter 6 (§46.2-600 et seq.) of this title shall give rise to a rebuttable presumption that such registered owner of the vehicle was the person who operated the vehicle at the place where, and for the time during which, such violation occurred.

(Chgd. by L.1997 chs. 622, 800, 908, eff. 7/1/97.)

ARTICLE 5
TURNING

Section

§46.2-845. Limitation on U–turns.

The driver of a vehicle within cities, towns or business districts of counties shall not turn his vehicle so as to proceed in the opposite direction except at an intersection.

No vehicle shall be turned so as to proceed in the opposite direction on any curve, or on the approach to or near the crest of a grade, where the vehicle cannot be seen by the driver of any other vehicle approaching from any direction within 500 feet.

§46.2-846. Required position and method of turning at intersections; local regulations.

A. Except where turning is prohibited, a driver intending to turn at an intersection or other location on any highway shall execute the turn as provided in this section.

1. Right turns: Both the approach for a right turn and a right turn shall be made as close as practicable to the right curb or edge of the roadway.

2. Left turns on two-way roadways: At any intersection where traffic is permitted to move in both directions on each roadway entering the intersection, an approach for a left turn shall be made from the right half of the roadway and as close as possible to the roadway's center line, passing to the right of the center line where it enters the intersection. After entering the intersection, the left turn shall be made so as to leave the intersection to the right of the center line of the roadway being entered. Whenever practicable, the left turn shall be made to the left of the center of the intersection.

3. Left turns on other than two-way roadways: At any intersection where traffic is restricted to one direction on one or more of the roadways, and at any crossover from one roadway of a divided highway to another roadway thereof on which traffic moves in the opposite direction, the driver intending to turn left at any such intersection or crossover shall approach the intersection or crossover in the extreme left lane lawfully available to traffic moving in the direction of travel of such vehicle and after entering the intersection or crossover the left turn shall be made so as to leave the intersection or crossover, as nearly as practicable, in the left lane lawfully available to traffic moving in such direction upon the roadway being entered.

B. Local authorities having the power to regulate traffic in their respective jurisdictions may cause markers or signs to be placed within or adjacent to intersections and thereby direct that a different course from that specified in this section be traveled by vehicles turning at any intersection. When markers or signs are so placed, no driver shall turn a vehicle at an intersection other than as directed by such markers or signs.

§46.2-847. Left turns by bicycles and mopeds.

A person riding a bicycle or moped and intending to turn left shall either follow a course described in §46.2-846 or make the turn as provided in this section.

A person riding a bicycle or moped and intending to turn left shall approach the turn as close as practicable to the right curb or edge of the roadway. After proceeding across the intersecting roadway, the rider shall comply with traffic signs or signals and continue his turn as close as practicable to the right curb or edge of the roadway being entered.

Notwithstanding the foregoing provisions of this section, the Commonwealth Transportation Board and local authorities, in their respective jurisdictions, may cause official traffic control devices to be placed at intersections to direct that a specific course be traveled by turning bicycles and mopeds. When such devices are so placed, no person shall turn a bicycle or moped other than as directed by such devices.

ARTICLE 6
SIGNALS BY DRIVERS

Section

§46.2-848. Signals required on backing, stopping, or turning.

Every driver who intends to back, stop, turn, or partly turn from a direct line shall first see that such movement can be made safely and, whenever the operation of any other vehicle may be affected by such movement, shall give the signals required in this article, plainly visible to the driver of such other vehicle, of his intention to make such movement.

§46.2-849. How signals given.

A. Signals required by §46.2-848 shall be given by means of the hand and arm or by some mechanical or electrical device approved by the Superintendent, in the manner specified in this section. Whenever the signal is given by means of the hand and arm, the driver shall indicate his intention to start, stop, turn, or partly turn by extending the hand and arm beyond the left side of the vehicle in the manner following:

1. For left turn or to pull to the left, the arm shall be extended in a horizontal position straight from and level with the shoulder;

2. For right turn or to pull to the right, the arm shall be extended upward;

3. For slowing down or stopping, the arm shall be extended downward.

B. Wherever the lawful speed is more than 35 miles per hour, such signals shall be given continuously for a distance of at least 100 feet, and in all other cases at least fifty feet, before slowing down, stopping, turning, or partly turning.

C. A person riding a bicycle or moped shall signal his intention to stop, or turn. Such signals, however, need not be given continuously if both hands are needed in the control or operation of the bicycle or moped.

§46.2-850. Change of course after giving signal.

Drivers having once given a hand or light signal shall continue the course thus indicated, unless they alter the original signal.

§46.2-851. Signals prior to moving standing vehicles into traffic.

Drivers of vehicles stopped at the curb or edge of a highway, before moving such vehicles, shall signal their intentions to move into traffic, as provided in this article, before turning in the direction the vehicle will proceed from the curb.

ARTICLE 7
RECKLESS DRIVING AND IMPROPER DRIVING

Section

§46.2-852. Reckless driving; general rule.

Irrespective of the maximum speeds permitted by law, any person who drives a vehicle on any highway recklessly or at a speed or in a manner so as to endanger the life, limb, or property of any person shall be guilty of reckless driving.

§46.2-853. Driving vehicle which is not under control; faulty brakes.

A person shall be guilty of reckless driving who drives a vehicle which is not under proper control or which has inadequate or improperly adjusted brakes on any highway in the Commonwealth.

§46.2-854. Passing on or at the crest of a grade or on a curve.

A person shall be guilty of reckless driving who, while driving a vehicle, overtakes and passes another vehicle proceeding in the same direction, on or approaching the crest of a grade or on or approaching a curve in the highway, where the driver's view along the highway is obstructed, except where the overtaking vehicle is being operated on a highway having two or more designated lanes of roadway for each direction of travel or on a designated one-way roadway or highway.

§46.2-855. Driving with driver's view obstructed or control impaired.

A person shall be guilty of reckless driving who drives a vehicle when it is so loaded, or when there are in the front seat such number of persons, as to obstruct the view of the driver to the front or sides of the vehicle or to interfere with the driver's control over the driving mechanism of the vehicle.

§46.2-856. Passing two vehicles abreast.

A person shall be guilty of reckless driving who passes or attempts to pass two other vehicles abreast, moving in the same direction, except on highways having separate roadways of three or more lanes for each direction of travel, or on designated one-way streets or highways. This section shall not apply, however, to a motor vehicle passing two other vehicles when one or both of such other vehicles is a bicycle or moped; nor shall this section apply to a bicycle or moped passing two other vehicles.

§46.2-857. Driving two abreast in a single lane.

A person shall be guilty of reckless driving who drives any motor vehicle, including any motorcycle, so as to be abreast of another vehicle in a lane designed for one vehicle, or drives any motor vehicle, including any motorcycle, so as to travel abreast of any other vehicle traveling in a lane designed for one vehicle. However, this section shall not apply to any validly authorized parade, motorcade, or motorcycle escort, nor shall it apply to a motor vehicle traveling in the same lane of traffic as a bicycle or moped.

§46.2-858. Passing at a railroad grade crossing.

A person shall be guilty of reckless driving who overtakes or passes any other vehicle proceeding in the same direction at any railroad grade crossing or at any intersection of highways unless such vehicles are being operated on a highway having two or more designated lanes of roadway for each direction of travel or unless such intersection is designated and marked as a passing zone or on a designated one-way street or highway, or while pedestrians are passing or about to pass in front of either of such vehicles, unless permitted so to do by a traffic light or law-enforcement officer.

§46.2-859. Passing a stopped school bus.

A person shall be guilty of reckless driving who fails to stop, when approaching from any direction, any school bus which is stopped on any highway or school driveway for the purpose of taking on or discharging children, the elderly, or mentally or physically handicapped persons, and to remain stopped until all such persons are clear of the highway or school driveway and the bus is put in motion. The driver of a vehicle, however, need not stop when approaching a school bus if such school bus is stopped on the other roadway of a divided highway, on an access road, or on a driveway when such other roadway, access road, or driveway is separated from the roadway on which he is driving by a physical barrier or an unpaved area. The driver of a vehicle also need not stop when approaching a school bus which is loading or discharging passengers from or onto property immediately adjacent to a school if such driver is directed by a law-enforcement officer or other duly authorized uniformed school crossing guard to pass such school bus. This section shall apply to school buses which are equipped with warning devices prescribed in §46.2-1090 and are painted yellow with the words "School Bus" in black letters at least eight inches high on the front and rear thereof. Only school buses which are painted yellow and equipped with the required lettering and warning devices shall be identified as school buses.

§46.2-860. Failing to give proper signals.

A person shall be guilty of reckless driving who fails to give adequate and timely signals of intention to turn, partly turn, slow down, or stop, as required by Article 6 (§46.2-848 et seq.) of this chapter.

§46.2-861. Driving too fast for highway and traffic conditions.

A person shall be guilty of reckless driving who exceeds a reasonable speed under the circumstances and traffic conditions existing at the time, regardless of any posted speed limit.

§46.2-862. Exceeding speed limit.

A person shall be guilty of reckless driving who drives a motor vehicle on the highways in the Commonwealth (i) at a speed of twenty miles per hour or more in excess of the applicable maximum speed limit where the applicable speed limit is thirty miles per hour or less, (ii) at a speed of sixty miles per hour or more where the applicable maximum speed limit is thirty-five miles per hour, (iii) at a speed of twenty miles per hour or more in excess of the applicable maximum speed limits where the applicable maximum speed limit is forty miles per hour or more, or (iv) in excess of eighty miles per hour regardless of the applicable maximum speed limit.

§46.2-863. Failure to yield right-of-way.

A person shall be guilty of reckless driving who fails to bring his vehicle to a stop immediately before entering a highway from a side road when there is traffic approaching on such highway within 500 feet of such point of entrance, unless (i) a "Yield Right-of-Way" sign is posted or (ii) where such sign is posted, fails, upon entering such highway, to yield the right-of-way to the driver of a vehicle approaching on such highway from either direction.

§46.2-864. Reckless driving on parking lots, etc.

A person shall be guilty of reckless driving who operates any motor vehicle at a speed or in a manner so as to endanger the life, limb, or property of any person:

1. On any driveway or premises of a church, school, recreational facility, or business property open to the public; or
2. On the premises of any industrial establishment providing parking space for customers, patrons, or employees; or
3. On any highway under construction or not yet open to the public.

§46.2-865. Racing; penalty.

Any person who engages in a race between two or more motor vehicles on the highways in the Commonwealth or on any driveway or premises of a church, school, recreational facility, or business property open to the public in the Commonwealth shall be guilty of reckless driving, unless authorized by the owner of the property or his agent. When any person is convicted of reckless driving under this section, in addition to any other penalties provided by law the driver's license of such person shall be suspended by the court for a period of not less than six months nor more than two years. In case of conviction the court shall order the surrender of the license to the court where it shall be disposed of in accordance with the provisions of §46.2-398.

§46.2-866. Racing; aiders or abettors.

Any person, although not engaged in a race as defined in §46.2-865, who aids or abets any such race, shall be guilty of a Class 1 misdemeanor.

§46.2-867. Racing; seizure of motor vehicle.

If the owner of a motor vehicle is convicted of racing such vehicle in a prearranged, organized, and planned speed competition in violation of §46.2-865, or is present in the vehicle which is being operated by another in violation of §46.2-865, and knowingly consents to the racing, the vehicle shall be seized and disposed of in the manner provided in §§4.1-339 through 4.1-348 for seizure and forfeiture of conveyances or vehicles used in the illegal transportation of alcoholic beverages. Such sections shall apply mutatis mutandis.

The penalties imposed by these sections are in addition to any other penalty imposed by law.

§46.2-868. Reckless driving; penalties.

Every person convicted of reckless driving under the provisions of this article shall be guilty of a Class 1 misdemeanor.

§46.2-869. Improper driving; penalty.

Notwithstanding the foregoing provisions of this article, upon the trial of any person charged with reckless driving where the degree of culpability is slight, the court in its discretion may find the accused not guilty of reckless driving but guilty of improper driving. However, an attorney for the Commonwealth may reduce a charge of reckless driving to improper driving at any time prior to the court's decision and shall notify the court of such change. Improper driving shall be punishable as a traffic infraction punishable by a fine of not more than $500.
(Chgd. by L.2000 ch. 340, eff. 7/1/2000.)

ARTICLE 8
SPEED

Section

§46.2-870. Maximum speed limits generally.

Except as otherwise provided in this article, the maximum speed limit shall be fifty-five miles per hour on interstate highways or other limited access highways with divided roadways, nonlimited access highways having four or more lanes, and all state primary highways.

The maximum speed limit on all other highways shall be fifty-five miles per hour if the vehicle is a passenger motor vehicle, bus, pickup or panel truck, or a motorcycle, but forty-five miles per hour on such highways if the vehicle is a truck, tractor truck, or combination of vehicles designed to transport property, or is a motor vehicle being used to tow a vehicle designed for self-propulsion, or a house trailer.

Notwithstanding the foregoing provisions of this section, the maximum speed limits on (i) highways constructed pursuant to the Virginia Highway Corporation Act of 1988 (§56-535 et seq.) (ii) those rural interstate highways where both (a) permitted by federal laws and (b) indicated by lawfully placed signs, (iii) Virginia Route 288, and (iv) other limited access highways in any county having a population of at least 45,700 but no more than 45,800, where indicated by lawfully placed signs, shall be sixty-five miles per hour.
(Chgd. by L.1996 ch. 1; L.1998 chs. 546, 560; L.1999 ch. 142, eff. 7/1/99.)

§46.2-871. Maximum speed limit for school buses.

The maximum speed limit for school buses shall be forty-five miles per hour or the minimum speed allowable, whichever is greater, on any highway where the maximum speed limit is fifty-five miles* or less, and fifty-five miles per hour on all interstate highways and on other highways where the maximum speed limit is more than fifty-five miles per hour. However, for any such vehicle which takes on or discharges children, the maximum speed limit shall be thirty-five miles per hour between the first stop and the last stop, not including the school. The school and the designated school bus parking area shall not be considered the first or last stop.
(Chgd. by L.1999 ch. 166, eff. 7/1/99.)
**Probably should be "miles per hour".*

§46.2-872. Maximum speed limits for vehicles operating under special permits.

The maximum speed limit shall be fifty-five miles per hour on any highway having a posted speed limit of fifty-five miles or more per hour if the vehicle or combination of vehicles is operating under a special permit issued by the Commonwealth Transportation Commissioner in accordance with §46.2-1139 or §46.2-1149.2. The Commissioner may, however, further reduce the speed limit on any permit issued in accordance with §46.2-1139.
(Chgd. by L.1995 ch. 113; L.1996 chs. 36, 87; L.1998 ch. 439, eff. 7/1/98.)

§46.2-873. Maximum speed limits at school crossings; penalty.

A. The maximum speed limit shall be twenty-five miles per hour between portable signs, tilt-over signs, or fixed blinking signs placed in or along any highway and bearing the word "school" or "school crossing." Any signs erected under this section shall be placed not more than 600 feet from the limits of the school property or crossing in the vicinity of the school. However, "school crossing" signs may be placed in any location if the Department of Transportation or the council of the city or town or the board of supervisors of a county maintaining its own system of secondary roads approves the crossing for such signs. If the portion of the highway to be posted is within the limits of a city or town, such portable signs shall be furnished and delivered by such city or town. If the portion of highway to be posted is outside the limits of a city or town, such portable signs shall be furnished and delivered by the Department of Transportation. The principal or chief administrative officer of each school or a school board designee, preferably not a classroom teacher, shall place such portable signs in the highway at a point not more than 600 feet from the limits of the school property and remove such signs when their presence is no longer required by this section. Such portable signs, tilt-over signs, or fixed blinking signs shall be placed in a position plainly visible to vehicular traffic approaching from either direction, but shall not be placed so as to obstruct the roadway.

B. Such portable signs, tilt-over signs, or blinking signs shall be in a position, or be turned on, for thirty minutes preceding regular school hours, for thirty minutes thereafter, and during such other times as the presence of children on such school property or going to and from school reasonably requires a special warning to motorists. The governing body of any county, city, or town may, however, decrease the period of time preceding and following regular school hours during which such portable signs, tilt-over signs, or blinking signs shall be in position or lit if it determines that no children will be going to or from school during the period of time that it subtracts from the thirty-minute period.

C. The governing body of any city or town may, if the portion of the highway to be posted is within the limits of such city or town, increase or decrease the speed limit provided in this section only after justification for such increase or decrease has been shown by an engineering and traffic investigation, and no such increase or decrease in speed limit shall be effective unless such increased or decreased speed limit is conspicuously posted on the portable signs, tilt-over signs, or fixed blinking signs required by this section.

D. Any city having a population of 390,000 or more may establish school zones as provided in this section and mark such zones with flashing warning lights as provided in this section on and along all highways adjacent to Route 58.

E. Any person operating any motor vehicle in excess of a maximum speed limit established specifically for a school crossing zone, when such school crossing zone is (i) indicated by appropriately placed signs displaying the maximum speed limit and (ii) in operation pursuant to subsection B of this section shall be guilty of a traffic infraction punishable by a fine of not more than $250, in addition to other penalties provided by law.

For the purposes of this section, "school crossing zone" means an area located within the vicinity of a school at or near a highway where the presence of children on such school property or going to and from school reasonably requires a special warning to motorists. Such zones are marked and operated in accordance with the requirements of this section with appropriate warning signs or other traffic control devices indicating that a school crossing is in progress.

F. Notwithstanding the foregoing provisions of this section, the maximum speed limit in school zones in residential areas may be decreased to fifteen miles per hour if (i) the school board having jurisdiction over the school nearest to the affected school zone passes a resolution requesting the reduction of the maximum speed limit for such school zone from twenty-five miles per hour to fifteen miles per hour and (ii) the local governing body of the jurisdiction in which such school is located enacts an ordinance establishing the speed-limit reduction requested by the school board.
(Chgd. by L.1997 chs. 629, 781, eff. 7/1/97.)

§46.2-873.1. Maximum speed limit on nonsurface treated highways.

The maximum speed limit on nonsurface treated highways shall be thirty-five miles per hour. The maximum speed limit upon such highways may be increased or decreased by the Commonwealth Transportation Commissioner or other authority having jurisdiction over highways. However, such increased or decreased maximum speed limit shall be effective only when indicated by sign on the highway. For such highways upon which maximum speed limit is not indicated by sign, the maximum speed limit shall be thirty-five miles per hour.

The provisions of this section shall apply only in counties having populations of at least 86,000 but less than 170,000.
(Added by L.2000 ch. 262, eff. 7/1/2000.)

§46.2-874. Maximum speed limit in city and town business and residence districts.

The maximum speed shall be twenty-five miles per hour on highways in business or residential districts, except on interstate or other limited access highways with divided roadways.

§46.2-875. Maximum speed limit on other highways in cities and towns.

The maximum speed limit shall be thirty-five miles per hour on highways in any city or town, except on interstate or other limited access highways with divided roadways and in business or residence districts.

§46.2-876. Maximum speed limit for passenger vehicles towing certain trailers.

The maximum speed limit for passenger motor vehicles while towing utility, camping, or boat trailers not exceeding an actual gross weight of 2,500 pounds shall be the same as that for passenger motor vehicles.

§46.2-877. Minimum speed limits.

No person shall drive a motor vehicle at such a slow speed as to impede the normal and reasonable movement of traffic except when reduced speed is necessary for safe operation or in compliance with law.

Whenever the Commonwealth Transportation Commissioner or local authorities within their respective jurisdictions determine on the basis of a traffic engineering and traffic investigation that slow speeds on any part of a highway consistently impede the normal and reasonable movement of traffic, the Commissioner or such local authority may determine and declare a minimum speed limit to be set forth on signs posted on such highway below which no person shall drive a vehicle except when necessary for safe operation or in compliance with law.

§46.2-878. Authority to change speed limits.

Notwithstanding the other provisions of this article, the Commonwealth Transportation Commissioner or other authority having jurisdiction over highways may decrease the speed limits set forth in §46.2-870 and may increase or decrease the speed limits set forth in §§46.2-873 through 46.2-875 on any highway under its jurisdiction; and may establish differentiated speed limits for daytime and nighttime by decreasing for nighttime driving the speed limits set forth in §46.2-870 and by increasing for daytime or decreasing for nighttime the speed limits set forth in §§46.2-873 through 46.2-875 on any highway under his jurisdiction. Such increased or decreased speed limits and such differentiated speed limits for daytime and nighttime driving shall be effective only when prescribed after a traffic engineering investigation and when indicated on the highway by signs. It shall be unlawful to operate any motor vehicle in excess of speed limits established and posted as provided in this section. The increased or decreased speed limits over highways under the control of the Commonwealth Transportation Commissioner shall be effective only when prescribed in writing by the Transportation Commissioner and kept on file in the Central Office of the Department of Transportation. Whenever the speed limit on any highway has been increased or decreased or a differential speed limit has been established and such speed limit is properly posted, there shall be a rebuttable presumption that the change in speed was properly established in accordance with the provisions of this section.

§46.2-878.1. Maximum speed limits in highway work zones; penalty.

Operation of any motor vehicle in excess of a maximum speed limit established specifically for a highway work zone, when workers are present and when such highway work zone is indicated by appropriately placed signs displaying the maximum speed limit and the penalty for violations, shall be unlawful and constitute a traffic infraction punishable by a fine of not more than $250.

For the purposes of this section, "highway work zone" means a construction or maintenance area that is located on or beside a highway and marked by appropriate warning signs or other traffic control devices indicating that work is in progress.

Nothing in this section shall preclude the prosecution or conviction for reckless driving of any motor vehicle operator whose operation of any motor vehicle in a highway work zone, apart from speed, demonstrates a reckless disregard for life, limb, or property.
(Chgd. by L.1995 ch. 54, eff. 7/1/95.)

§46.2-878.2. Maximum speed limits in certain residence districts; penalty.

Operation of any motor vehicle in excess of a maximum speed limit established for a highway in a residence district, when indicated by appropriately placed signs displaying the maximum speed limit and the penalty for violations, shall be unlawful and constitute a traffic infraction punishable by a fine of not more than $200, in addition to other penalties provided by law. The Commonwealth Transportation Board shall develop criteria for the overall applicability for the installation of signs. Such criteria shall not exclude highways, functionally classified as minor arterials, serving areas that either (i) were built as residential developments or (ii) have grown to resemble residential developments, provided, in either case, (i) such highways are experiencing documented speeding problems and (ii) the local governing body requests the application of this section to such highway.
(Added by L.1996 ch. 172; chgd. by L.1999 ch. 87, eff. 7/1/99.)

§46.2-879. No conviction for speeding in certain areas unless markers installed.

No person shall be convicted of a violation of a statute or an ordinance enacted by local authorities pursuant to the provisions of §46.2-1300 decreasing the speed limit established in this article when such person has exceeded the speed limit in an area where the speed limit has been decreased unless such area is clearly indicated by a conspicuous marker at the termini of such area.

§46.2-880. Tables of speed and stopping distances.

All courts shall take notice of the following tables of speed and stopping distances of motor vehicles, which shall not raise a presumption, in actions in which inquiry thereon is pertinent to the issues:

SPEED IN		AVERAGE STOPPING DISTANCES			TOTAL STOPPING DISTANCES: DRIVER AND	
Miles Per Hour	Feet Per Second	Automobile Brakes (In Feet)	Truck Brakes (Brakes on All Wheels) (In Feet)	Average Driver Reaction Time (¾ Second) (In Feet)	Automobiles (In Feet)	Trucks (In Feet)
10	14.67	5	7	11	16	18
15	22.0	12	17	16	28	33
20	29.34	21	30	22	43	52
25	36.62	32	47	27	59	74
30	44.0	47	67	33	80	100
35	51.3	63	92	38	101	130
40	58.7	82	120	44	126	164
45	66.0	104	152	50	154	202
50	73.3	128	187	55	183	242
55	80.7	155	227	61	216	288
60	88.0	185	270	66	251	336
65	95.3	217	316	71	288	387
70	102.6	252	367	77	329	444
75	109.9	289	422	82	371	504
80	117.2	328	480	88	416	568
90	132.0	425	607	99	524	706
100	146.6	514	750	109	623	859

The courts shall further take notice that such tables are the result of experiments made with motor vehicles, unloaded except for the driver, equipped with four-wheel brakes, in good condition, on dry, hard, approximately level stretches of highway free from loose material.

§46.2-881. Special speed limitation on bridges and tunnels.

It shall be unlawful to drive any motor vehicle, trailer, or semitrailer on any public bridge, causeway, viaduct, or in any tunnel at a speed exceeding that indicated as a maximum by signs posted thereon or at its approach by or on the authority of the Commonwealth Transportation Commissioner.

The Commonwealth Transportation Commissioner, on request or on his own initiative, may conduct an investigation of any public bridge, causeway, viaduct, or tunnel and, on the basis of his findings, may set the maximum speed of vehicles which such structure can withstand or which is necessitated in consideration of the benefit and safety of the traveling public and the safety of the structure. The Commonwealth Transportation Commissioner is expressly authorized to establish and indicate variable speed limits on such structures to be effective under such conditions as would in his judgment, warrant such variable limits, including but not limited to darkness, traffic conditions, atmospheric conditions, weather, emergencies, and like conditions which may affect driving safety. Any speed limits, whether fixed or variable, shall be prominently posted in such proximity to such structure as deemed appropriate by the Commonwealth Transportation Commissioner. The findings of the Commissioner shall be conclusive evidence of the maximum safe speed which can be maintained on such structure.

§46.2-882. Determining speed with various devices; certificate as to accuracy of device; arrest without warrant.

The speed of any motor vehicle may be determined by the use of (i) a laser speed determination device, (ii) radar, (iii) a microcomputer device that is physically connected to an odometer cable and both measures and records distance traveled and elapsed time to determine the average speed of a motor vehicle, or (iv) a microcomputer device that is located aboard an airplane or helicopter and measures and records distance traveled and elapsed time to determine the average speed of a motor vehicle being operated on highways within the Interstate System of highways as defined in §33.1-48. The results of such determinations shall be accepted as prima facie evidence of the speed of such motor vehicle in any court or legal proceeding where the speed of the motor vehicle is at issue.

In any court or legal proceeding in which any question arises about the calibration or accuracy of any laser speed determination device, radar, or microcomputer device as described in this section used to determine the speed of any motor vehicle, a certificate, or a true copy thereof, showing the calibration or accuracy of the speedometer of any vehicle or of any tuning fork employed in calibrating or testing the device, and when and by whom the calibration was made, shall be admissible as evidence of the facts therein stated. No calibration or testing of such device shall be valid for longer than six months.

The driver of any such motor vehicle may be arrested without a warrant under this section if the arresting officer is in uniform and displays his badge of authority and if the officer has observed the registration of the speed of such motor vehicle by the laser speed determination device, radar, or microcomputer device as described in this section, or has received a radio message from the officer who observed the speed of the motor vehicle registered by the laser speed determination device, radar, or microcomputer device as described in this section. However, in case of an arrest based on such a message, such radio message shall have been dispatched immediately after the speed of the motor vehicle was registered and furnished the license number or other positive identification of the vehicle and the registered speed to the arresting officer.

Law-enforcement officers shall not have the authority to use laser speed determination devices or radar, as described herein in airplanes or helicopters for the purpose of determining the speed of motor vehicles.

State Police officers may use laser speed determination devices, radar, and/or microcomputer devices as described in this section. All localities may use radar; (i) counties having populations of at least 85,000 but less than 150,000 and towns within such counties; (ii) counties having populations of at least 79,000 but less than 86,000, (iii) counties having populations of at least 68,000 but less than 73,000; (iv) towns having populations of at least 14,000 but less than 15,000 and located within a county operating under the urban county executive form of government; (v) counties having the county manager form of government; (vi) counties having populations of at least 61,000 but less than 63,000; and (vii) cities having populations of at least 40,000 but less than 50,000 may use laser speed determination devices to measure speed. Any county, city or town located within the boundaries of Planning District No. 8 may use laser speed determination devices, radar, or both to measure speed. The Cities of Alexandria, Fairfax, Falls Church, Manassas, and Manassas Park and the Counties of Arlington, Fairfax, Loudoun, and Prince William and towns within such counties may use microcomputer devices as described in this section.

The Division of Purchases and Supply, pursuant to §2.1-446, shall determine the proper equipment used to determine the speed of motor vehicles and shall advise the respective law-enforcement officials of the same. Police chiefs and sheriffs shall ensure that all such equipment and devices purchased on or after July 1, 1986, meet or exceed the standards established by the Division.

Law-enforcement officers using motor vehicle-based microcomputer devices or laser speed determination devices as provided for in this section shall, on request of any affected motorist, permit such motorist to observe the reading on the device. Nothing in this section, however, shall require any law-enforcement officer to allow affected motorists to observe any reading on any microcomputer device on any airplane or helicopter.

(Chgd. by L.1997 ch. 33; L.1998 ch. 423; L.1999 chs. 693, 694, 698, 724, 729, 733; L.2000 chs. 354, 357, 365, eff. 7/1/2000.)

§46.2-883. Signs indicating legal rate of speed and measurement of speed by radar.

Signs to indicate the legal rate of speed and that the speed of motor vehicles may be measured by radar or other electrical devices shall be placed at or near the State boundary on those interstate and primary highways which connect the Commonwealth to other jurisdictions at such locations as the Commonwealth Transportation Commissioner, in his discretion, may select. There shall be a prima facie presumption that such signs were placed at the time of the commission of the offense of exceeding the legal rate of speed, and a certificate by the Commonwealth Transportation Commissioner as to the placing of such signs shall be admissible in evidence to support or rebut the presumption. Such legal rate of speed and notice of measurement of speed by radar or other electrical devices may be posted on different signs and need not be posted on the same sign.

ARTICLE 9
RAILROAD CROSSINGS

§46.2-884. Railroad warning signals must be obeyed.

No person driving a vehicle shall disobey a clearly visible or audible crossing signal which gives warning of the immediate approach of a train at a railroad grade crossing.

§46.2-885. When vehicles to stop at railroad grade crossings.

A. Except in cities or towns, whenever any person driving a vehicle approaches a railroad grade crossing under any of the circumstances stated in this section, the driver of the vehicle shall stop within fifty feet but not less than fifteen feet from the nearest rail of such railroad, and shall not proceed until he can do so safely. The foregoing requirements shall apply when:

1. A clearly visible electric or mechanical signal device gives warning of the immediate approach of a train;
2. A crossing gate is lowered or a flagman gives or continues to give a signal of the approach or passage of a train;
3. A train approaching such crossing gives the signals required by §56-414;
4. An approaching train is plainly visible and is in hazardous proximity to such crossing.

B. No person shall drive any vehicle through, around, or under any crossing gate or barrier at a railroad crossing while such gate or barrier is closed or is being opened or closed.

§46.2-886. When drivers of certain vehicles to stop, look, and listen at railroad crossings; crossing tracks without shifting gears.

Except in cities or towns, the driver of any motor vehicle carrying passengers for hire, or of any vehicle carrying explosive substances or flammable liquids as a cargo or part of a cargo, before crossing at grade any railroad track, shall stop such vehicle within fifty feet but not less than fifteen feet from the nearest rail of such railroad and while stopped shall listen and look in both directions along the track for any approaching train, and for signals indicating the approach of a train, except as hereinafter provided in this section, and shall not proceed until he can do so safely. After stopping and upon proceeding when it is safe to do so, the driver of any vehicle shall cross only in such gear of the vehicle that there will be no necessity for changing gears while traversing the crossing.

Before crossing any railroad tracks at grade, the driver of any school bus shall stop the school bus within fifty feet but not less than fifteen feet from the nearest rail of such railroad and while stopped shall listen and look in both directions along the track for any approaching train, except as hereinafter provided in this section, and shall not proceed until he can do so safely. After stopping and upon proceeding when it is safe to do so, the driver of any school bus shall cross only in such gear of the vehicle that there will be no necessity for changing gears while traversing the crossing.

Notwithstanding the foregoing provisions of this section, no stop need be made at any such crossing where a law-enforcement officer or a traffic-control signal directs traffic to proceed.

§46.2.887. Moving crawler-type tractors, steam shovels, derricks, rollers, etc., over railroad grade crossings.

Except in cities or towns, no person shall move any crawler-type tractor, steam shovel, derrick, roller, or any equipment or structure having a normal operating speed of ten or less miles per hour or a vertical body or load clearance of less than one-half inch per foot of the distance between any two adjacent axles or in any event of less than nine inches, measured above the level surface of a roadway, on or across any tracks at a railroad grade crossing without first complying with this section.

Notice of any intended crossing shall be given to a station agent of the railroad and a reasonable time shall be given to the railroad to provide proper protection at the crossing.

Before making any such crossing, the person moving any such vehicle or equipment shall first stop it not less than fifteen feet nor more than fifty feet from the nearest rail of the railroad and while so stopped shall listen and look in both directions along such track for any approaching train and for signals indicating the approach of a train, and shall not proceed until the crossing can be made safely.

No such crossing shall be made when warning is given by automatic signal, crossing gates, a flagman, or otherwise of the immediate approach of a train. If a flagman is provided by the railroad, movement over the crossing shall be under his direction.

ARTICLE 10
STOPPING ON HIGHWAYS

§46.2-888. Stopping on highways; general rule.

No person shall stop a vehicle in such manner as to impede or render dangerous the use of the highway by others, except in the case of an emergency, an accident, or a mechanical breakdown. In the event of such an emergency, accident, or breakdown, the emergency flashing lights of such vehicle shall be turned on if the vehicle is equipped with such lights and such lights are in working order. If the driver is capable of doing so and the vehicle is movable, the driver may move the vehicle only so far as is necessary to prevent obstructing the regular flow of traffic; provided, however, that the movement of the vehicle to prevent the obstruction of traffic shall not relieve the law-enforcement officer of his duty pursuant to §46.2-373. A report of the vehicle's location shall be made to the nearest law-enforcement officer as soon as practicable, and the vehicle shall be moved from the roadway to the shoulder as soon as possible and removed from the shoulder without unnecessary delay. If the vehicle is not promptly removed, such removal may be ordered by a law-enforcement officer at the expense of the owner if the disabled vehicle creates a traffic hazard.
(Chgd. by L.1997 ch. 431, eff. 7/1/97.)

§46.2-889. Location of parked vehicles.

No vehicle shall be stopped except close to and parallel to the right edge of the curb or roadway, except that a vehicle may be stopped close to and parallel to the left curb or edge of the roadway on one-way streets or may be parked at an angle where permitted by the Commonwealth Transportation Board or local authorities with respect to highways under their jurisdiction.

§46.2-890. Stopping in vicinity of fire or emergency.

No vehicle shall be stopped at or in the vicinity of a fire, vehicle or airplane accident, or other area of emergency, in such a manner as to create a traffic hazard or interfere with law-enforcement officers, fire fighters, rescue workers, or others whose duty it is to deal with such emergencies. Any vehicle found unlawfully parked in the vicinity of a fire, accident, or area of emergency may be removed by order of a law-enforcement officer or, in the absence of a law-enforcement officer, by order of the uniformed fire or rescue officer in charge, at the risk and expense of the owner if such vehicle creates a traffic hazard or interferes with the necessary procedures of law-enforcement officers, fire fighters, rescue workers, or others whose assigned duty it is to deal with such emergencies. The charge for such removal shall not exceed the actual and necessary cost. Vehicles being used by accredited information services, such as press, radio, and television, when being used for the gathering of news, shall be exempt from the provisions of this section, except when actually obstructing the law-enforcement officers, firefighters, and rescue workers dealing with such emergencies.

§46.2-891. Exemption for highway construction and maintenance vehicles.

The provisions of this article shall not apply to any vehicle owned or controlled by the Virginia Department of Transportation or counties, cities or towns, while actually engaged in the construction, reconstruction, or maintenance of highways.

§46.2-892. Rural mail carriers stopping on highways.

The provisions of §46.2-888 shall not apply to any rural mail carrier stopping on the highway while collecting or delivering the United States mail at a mailbox, provided there is lettered on the back of the vehicle operated by such rural mail carrier, or lettered on a sign securely attached to and displayed at the rear of such vehicle, in letters at least four inches in height:

CAUTION
FREQUENT STOPS
U.S. MAIL

Additionally, the provisions of §46.2-888 shall not apply to such rural mail carrier so stopping if, in lieu of such sign, the vehicle has, and is using supplemental turn signals mounted at each side of the roof of the vehicle. Between the lights on the assembly shall be mounted a sign with the words "U.S. Mail." The sign shall be yellow with black letters at least four inches in height, and the lights shall be of the type approved by the Superintendent of State Police. The lettered sign shall be displayed only when the vehicle is engaged in the collection or delivery of the United States mail.

Nothing in this section shall be construed to relieve any such mail carrier from civil liability for such stopping on any highway if he is negligent in so doing, and if the negligence proximately contributes to any personal injury or property damage resulting therefrom.
(Chgd. by L.1998 ch. 411, eff. 7/1/98.)

§46.2-893. Stopping on highways to discharge cargo or passengers; school buses.

No truck or bus, except a school bus, shall be stopped wholly or partially on the traveled portion of any highway outside of cities and towns for the purpose of taking on or discharging cargo or passengers unless the operator cannot leave the traveled portion of the highway with safety. A school bus may be stopped on the traveled portion of the highway when taking on or discharging school children, but these stops shall be made only at points where the bus can be clearly seen for a safe distance from both directions.

ARTICLE 11
ACCIDENTS

§46.2-894. Duty of driver to stop, etc., in event of accident involving injury or death or damage to attended property.

The driver of any vehicle involved in an accident in which a person is killed or injured or in which an attended vehicle or other attended property is damaged shall immediately stop as close to the scene of the accident as possible without obstructing traffic, as provided in §46.2-888, and report his name, address, driver's license number, and vehicle registration number forthwith to the State Police or local law-enforcement agency, to the person struck and injured if such person appears to be capable of understanding and retaining the information, or to the driver or some other occupant of the vehicle collided with or to the custodian of other damaged property. The driver shall also render reasonable assistance to any person injured in such accident, including taking such injured person to a physician, surgeon, or hospital if it is apparent that medical treatment is necessary or is requested by the injured person.

Where, because of injuries sustained in the accident, the driver is prevented from complying with the foregoing provisions of this section, the driver shall, as soon as reasonably possible, make the required report to the State Police or local law-enforcement agency and make a reasonable effort to locate the person struck, or the driver or some other occupant of the vehicle collided with, or the custodian of the damaged property, and report to such person or persons his name, address, driver's license number, and vehicle registration number.

(Chgd. by L.1997 ch. 431, eff. 7/1/97.)

§46.2-895. Duty of certain persons accompanying driver to report accidents involving injury, death, or damage to attended property.

If the driver fails to stop and make the report required by §46.2-894, every person sixteen years of age or older in the vehicle with the driver at the time of the accident, who has knowledge of the accident, shall have a duty to ensure that a report is made within twenty-four hours from the time of the accident to the State Police or, if the accident occurs in a city or town, to the local law-enforcement agency. The report shall include his name, address, and such other information within his knowledge as the driver is required to report pursuant to §46.2-894.

§46.2-896. Duties of driver in event of accident involving damage only to unattended property.

The driver of any vehicle involved in an accident in which no person is killed or injured, but in which an unattended vehicle or other unattended property is damaged, shall make a reasonable effort to find the owner or custodian of such property and shall report to the owner or custodian the information which the driver is required to report pursuant to §46.2-894 if such owner or custodian is found. If the owner or custodian of such damaged vehicle or property cannot be found, the driver shall leave a note in a conspicuous place at the scene of the accident and shall report the accident in writing within twenty-four hours to the State Police or the local law-enforcement agency. Such note and written report shall contain the information which the driver is required to report pursuant to §46.2-894. The written report shall, in addition, state the date, time, and place of the accident and the driver's estimate of the property damage.

Where, because of injuries sustained in the accident, the driver is prevented from complying with the foregoing provisions of this section, the driver shall, as soon as reasonably possible, make the required report to the State Police or local law-enforcement agency and make a reasonable effort to locate the owner or custodian of the unattended vehicle or property and report to him the information required by §46.2-894.

(Chgd. by L.1997 ch. 431, eff. 7/1/97.)

§46.2-897. Duty of certain persons accompanying driver to report accidents involving damage only to unattended property.

If the driver fails to stop and make a reasonable search for the owner or custodian of an unattended vehicle or property or to leave a note for such owner or custodian as required by §46.2-896, every person sixteen years of age or older in the vehicle with the driver at the time of the accident who has knowledge of the accident shall have a duty to ensure that a report is made within twenty-four hours from the time of the accident to the State Police or, if the accident occurs in a city or town, to the local law-enforcement agency. The report shall include his name, address, and such other facts within his knowledge as are required by §46.2-896 to be reported by the driver.

§46.2-898. Reports are in addition to others.

The reports required by §§46.2-894 through 46.2-897 are in addition to other accident reports required by this title and shall be made irrespective of the amount of property damage involved.

§46.2-899. Article applies to accidents on private or public property.

The provisions of this article shall apply irrespective of whether such accident occurs on the public streets or highways or on private property.

§46.2-900. Penalty for violation of §§46.2-894 through 46.2-897.

Any person convicted of violating the provisions of §§46.2-894 through 46.2-897 shall, if such accident results in injury to or the death of, any person, be guilty of a Class 6 felony. If such accident results only in damage to property, the person so convicted shall be guilty of a Class 1 misdemeanor; however, if the vehicle or other property struck is unattended and such damage is less than $ 250, such person shall be guilty of a Class 4 misdemeanor. A motor vehicle operator convicted of a Class 4 misdemeanor under this section shall be assigned three demerit points by the Commissioner of the Department of Motor Vehicles.

§46.2-901. Suspension of driver's license for failure to report certain accidents.

Any person convicted of violating the provisions of §§46.2-894 through 46.2-897 may be punished, in addition to the penalties provided in §46.2-900, if such accident resulted only in damage to property and such damage exceeded $ 500, by suspension of his license or privilege to operate a motor vehicle on the highways of the Commonwealth for a period not to exceed six months by the court. This section shall in no case be construed to limit the authority or duty of the Commissioner with respect to revocation of licenses for violation of §§46.2-894 through 46.2-897 as provided in Article 10 of Chapter 3 (§46.2-364 et seq.) of this title. Any license revoked under the provisions of this section shall be surrendered to the court to be disposed of in accordance with the provisions of §46.2-398.

§46.2-902. Leaving scene of accident when directed to do so by officer.

A person shall leave the scene of a traffic accident when directed to do so by a law-enforcement officer.

ARTICLE 12
BICYCLES

§46.2-903. Riding or driving vehicles other than bicycles on sidewalks.

No person shall ride or drive any vehicle other than (i) an emergency vehicle, as defined in §46.2-920, (ii) a vehicle engaged in snow or ice removal and control operations, (iii) a wheel chair or wheel chair conveyance, whether self-propelled or otherwise, or (iv) a bicycle on the sidewalks of any county, city, or town of the Commonwealth.

§46.2-904. Use of roller skates and skateboards on sidewalks; operation of bicycles on sidewalks and crosswalks; local ordinances.

The governing body of any county, city, or town may by ordinance prohibit the use of roller skates and skateboards and/or the riding of bicycles on designated sidewalks or crosswalks, including those of any church, school, recreational facility, or any business property open to the public where such activity is prohibited. Signs indicating such prohibition shall be conspicuously posted in general areas where use of roller skates and skateboards and/or bicycle riding is prohibited.

A person riding a bicycle on a sidewalk, or across a roadway on a crosswalk, shall yield the right-of-way to any pedestrian and shall give an audible signal before overtaking and passing any pedestrian.

No person shall ride a bicycle on a sidewalk, or across a roadway on a crosswalk, where such use of bicycles is prohibited by official traffic control devices.

A person riding a bicycle on a sidewalk, or across a roadway on a crosswalk, shall have all the rights and duties of a pedestrian under the same circumstances.

A violation of any ordinance adopted pursuant to this section shall be punishable by a civil penalty of not more than $50.
(Chgd. by L.1999 ch. 943, eff. 7/1/99.)

§46.2-905. Riding bicycles and mopeds on roadways and bicycle paths.

Any person operating a bicycle or moped on a roadway shall ride as close as practicable to the right curb or edge of the roadway, except under any of the following circumstances:

1. When overtaking and passing another vehicle proceeding in the same direction;
2. When preparing for a left turn at an intersection or into a private road or driveway; and
3. When reasonably necessary to avoid conditions including, but not limited to, fixed or moving objects, parked or moving vehicles, pedestrians, animals, surface hazards, or substandard width lanes that make it unsafe to continue along the right curb or edge.

For purposes of this section, a "substandard width lane" is a lane too narrow for a bicycle or moped and another vehicle to pass safely side by side within the lane.

Persons riding bicycles on a highway shall not ride two or more abreast except on paths or parts of highways set aside for the exclusive use of bicycles.

The governing body of any locality may by ordinance provide that wherever a usable path for bicycles has been provided adjacent to a roadway, bicycle riders shall use such path and shall not use the roadway.

§46.2-906. Carrying articles on bicycles and mopeds.

No person operating a bicycle or moped on a highway shall carry any package, bundle, or article which prevents the driver from keeping at least one hand on the handlebars.

§46.2-906.1. Local ordinances may require bicyclists to wear helmets.

The governing body of any county, city or town may, by ordinance, provide that every person fourteen years of age or younger shall wear a protective helmet that meets the standards promulgated by the American National Standards Institute or the Snell Memorial Foundation whenever riding or being carried on a bicycle on any highway as defined in §46.2-100, sidewalk, or public bicycle path.

Violation of any such ordinance shall be punishable by a fine of twenty-five dollars. However, such fine shall be suspended (i) for first-time violators and (ii) for violators who, subsequent to the violation but prior to imposition of the fine, purchase helmets of the type required by the ordinance.

Violation of any such ordinance shall not constitute negligence, assumption of risk, be considered in mitigation of damages of whatever nature, be admissible in evidence, or be the subject of comment by counsel in any action for the recovery of damages arising out of the operation of any bicycle, nor shall anything in this section change any existing law, rule, or procedure pertaining to any civil action.
(Chgd. by L.1995 chs. 42, 671, eff. 7/1/95.)

§46.2-907. Overtaking and passing vehicles.

A person riding a bicycle or moped may overtake and pass another vehicle on either the left or right side, staying in the same lane as the overtaken vehicle, or changing to a different lane, or riding off the roadway as necessary to pass with safety.

A person riding a bicycle or moped may overtake and pass another vehicle only under conditions which permit the movement to be made with safety.

A person riding a bicycle or moped shall not travel between two lanes of traffic moving in the same direction, except where one lane is a separate turn lane or a mandatory turn lane.

Except as otherwise provided in this section, a person riding a bicycle or moped shall comply with all rules applicable to the driver of a motor vehicle when overtaking and passing.

§46.2-908. Registration of bicycle serial numbers.

Any person who owns a bicycle may register its serial number with the local law-enforcement agency of the political subdivision in which such person resides.

ARTICLE 13
MOTORCYCLES AND MOPEDS AND ALL-TERRAIN VEHICLES

§46.2-909. Riding on motorcycles, generally.

Every person operating a motorcycle, as defined in §46.2-100 excluding three-wheeled vehicles, shall ride only upon the permanent seat attached to the motorcycle, and such operator shall not carry any other person. No other person shall ride on a motorcycle unless the motorcycle is designed to carry more than one person, in which event a passenger may ride on the permanent seat if designed for two persons, or on another seat firmly attached to the rear or side of the seat for the operator. If the motorcycle is designed to carry more than one person, it shall also be equipped with a footrest for the use of such passenger.

§46.2-910. Motorcyclist to wear helmets, etc.; certain sales prohibited; penalty.

A. Every person operating a motorcycle shall wear a face shield, safety glasses or goggles, or have his motorcycle equipped with safety glass or a windshield at all times while operating the vehicle, and operators and any passengers thereon shall wear protective helmets. Operators and passengers riding on motorcycles with wheels of eight inches or less in diameter or in three-wheeled motorcycles which have nonremovable roofs, windshields and enclosed bodies shall not be required to wear protective helmets. The windshields, face shields, glasses or goggles, and protective helmets required by this section shall meet or exceed the standards and specifications of the Snell Memorial Foundation, the American National Standards Institute, Inc., or the federal Department of Transportation. Failure to wear a face shield, safety glasses or goggles, or protective helmets shall not constitute negligence per se in any civil proceeding. The provisions of this section requiring the wearing of protective helmets shall not apply to operators of or passengers on motorcycles being operated (i) as part of an organized parade authorized by the Department of Transportation or the locality in which the parade is being conducted and escorted, accompanied, or participated in by law-enforcement officers of the jurisdiction wherein the parade is held and (ii) at speeds of no more than fifteen miles per hour.

No motorcycle operator shall use any face shield, safety glasses or goggles, or have his motorcycle equipped with safety glass or a windshield unless of a type either (i) approved by the Superintendent prior to July 1, 1996, or (ii) that meets or exceeds the standards and specifications of the Snell Memorial Foundation, the American National Standards Institute, Inc., or the federal Department of Transportation and is marked in accordance with such standards.

B. It shall be unlawful to sell or offer for sale, for highway use in Virginia, any protective helmet that fails to meet or exceed any standard as provided in the foregoing provisions of this section. Any violation of this subsection shall constitute a Class 4 misdemeanor.
(Chgd. by L.1996 ch. 690; L.1998 ch. 789, eff. 7/1/98.)

§46.2-912. Operating motorcycle without headlight, horn or rearview mirror.

A. Notwithstanding any other provision of law, motorcycles may be operated without headlights, horns, or rearview mirrors on public highways if all the following conditions are met:

1. The motorcycles are designed for use in trail riding and endurance runs;
2. The motorcycles are being driven by duly licensed persons;
3. The motorcycles are being operated between sunrise and sunset; and
4. The motorcycles are being operated during endurance runs sanctioned by the American Motorcycle Association.

B. No person shall operate motorcycles without such equipment on the public highways of the Commonwealth other than at the times and under the circumstances set forth in this section.

§46.2-913. Vendors of certain motorcycles to furnish statements of registration and licensing requirements.

Every retailer of motorcycles having a rating of seven horsepower or less, shall provide written statements to every vendee regarding registration and licensing of such vehicles and the requirement of a motor vehicle driver's license.

§46.2-914. Limitations on operation of mopeds.

No moped shall be driven on any highway or public vehicular area (i) faster than thirty miles per hour or (ii) by any person under the age of sixteen.

§46.2-915. Stickers required on mopeds.

Any dealer who sells any moped at retail shall affix to any such moped, or verify that there is affixed thereto a permanent decal or sticker which states (i) that the operation of mopeds on highways and public vehicular areas by persons under the age of sixteen is prohibited by Virginia law, (ii) the maximum horsepower of the moped, and (iii) the maximum speed at which the moped may be ridden.

Any dealer who sells any such moped which does not have affixed thereto such a permanent decal or sticker or who sells a motorcycle with such a sticker or decal attached thereto indicating that its motor is rated at no more than two brake horsepower producing only ordinary speeds up to a maximum of thirty miles per hour shall be guilty of a Class 1 misdemeanor.

§46.2-915.1. All-terrain vehicles; penalty.

A. No all-terrain vehicle shall be operated:

1. On any public highway, or other public property, except as authorized by proper authorities or to the extent necessary to cross a public highway by the most direct route;
2. By any person under the age of sixteen, except that children between the ages of twelve and sixteen may operate all-terrain vehicles powered by engines of no less than seventy nor more than ninety cubic centimeters displacement;
3. By any person unless he is wearing a protective helmet of a type approved by the Superintendent of State Police for use by motorcycle operators;
4. On another person's property without the written consent of the owner of the property or as explicitly authorized by law; or
5. With a passenger at any time.

B. Any retailer selling any all-terrain vehicle shall affix thereto, or verify that there is affixed thereto, a decal or sticker, approved by the Superintendent of State Police, which clearly and completely states the prohibition contained in subsection A of this section.

C. A violation of this section shall not constitute negligence, be considered in mitigation of damages of whatever nature, be admissible in evidence or be the subject of comment by counsel in any action for the recovery of damages arising out of the operation, ownership, or maintenance of an all-terrain vehicle, nor shall anything in this section change any existing law, rule, or procedure pertaining to any such civil action, nor shall this section bar any claim which otherwise exists.

D. Violation of any provision of this section shall be punishable by a civil penalty of not more than $500.

E. The provisions of this section shall not apply:

1. To any all-terrain vehicle being used in conjunction with farming activities; or

2. To members of the household or employees of the owner or lessee of private property on which the all-terrain vehicle is operated.

F. For the purposes of this section, "all-terrain vehicle" shall mean a three-wheeled or four-wheeled motor vehicle, generally characterized by large, low-pressure tires, a seat designed to be straddled by the operator, and handlebars for steering, which is intended for off-road use by an individual rider on various types of non-paved terrain. The term does not include four-wheeled vehicles which have low centers of gravity and are typically used in racing and on relatively level surfaces, commonly known as "go-carts."
(Chgd. by L.1995 ch. 670, eff. 7/1/95.)

§46.2-915.2. Ordinances providing for certain safety equipment for mopeds; effect of violation; penalty.

The governing body of any county, city, or town may, by ordinance, provide that every person operating a moped, as defined in §46.2-100, on a public street or highway shall wear a face shield, safety glasses, or goggles of a type approved by the Superintendent or have his moped equipped with safety glass or a windshield at all times while operating such vehicle, and operators and passengers thereon, if any, shall wear protective helmets of a type approved by the Superintendent. A violation of any such ordinance shall not constitute negligence, be considered in mitigation of damages of whatever nature, be admissible in evidence or be the subject of comment by counsel in any action for the recovery of damages arising out of the operation, ownership, or maintenance of a moped or motor vehicle, nor shall anything in this section change any existing law, rule, or procedure pertaining to any such civil action. Any person who knowingly violates any such ordinance shall be guilty of a traffic infraction and be subject to a fine of not more than fifty dollars.

§46.2-916. Ordinances providing for the disposition of unregistered or unlicensed motorcycles.

The governing bodies of counties, cities, and towns may by ordinance provide for the lawful seizure, impounding and disposition of unlicensed or unregistered motorcycles operated either on the highways or on private property without the consent of the private property owner.

ARTICLE 14
SCHOOL BUSES

§46.2-917. Operation of yellow motor vehicles of certain seating capacity on state highways prohibited; exceptions; penalty.

It shall be unlawful for any motor vehicle licensed in Virginia having a seating capacity of more than fifteen persons to be operated on the highways of the Commonwealth if it is yellow, unless it is used in transporting students who attend public, private, or parochial schools or used in transporting the elderly or mentally or physically handicapped persons.

Any violation of this section shall constitute a Class 1 misdemeanor.

§46.2-917.1. School buses hired to transport children.

Notwithstanding §46.2-917, any person may contract to hire school buses for the purpose of transporting students to or from school, camp, or any other place during any part of the year. All provisions of this title applicable to school buses shall also apply to any school bus hired under the provisions of this section.

§46.2-917.2. School buses operating under State Corporation Commission or Department certificate.

Notwithstanding §46.2-917, any person holding a special or charter party certificate issued by the State Corporation Commission or the Department pursuant to Chapter 23 (§46.2-2300 et seq.) of this title may transport special or charter parties in school buses provided all lettering required by §46.2-1089 and warning devices required by §46.2-1090 are covered with some opaque detachable material.
(Chgd. by L.1997 ch. 283, eff. 7/1/97.)

§46.2-918. School buses to be routed so as to avoid necessity of pupils' crossing divided highways.

All school buses transporting pupils to and from all public, private, or parochial schools or in connection with such schools, operating on any highway in the Commonwealth which has two or more roadways separated by a physical barrier or barriers or an unpaved area, or which have five or more lanes the center lane of which is a flush median marked for use by turning traffic only, shall be routed so that no pupil shall be picked up or discharged at any point which will require any pupil to cross such highway as described in this section, in order for such pupil to reach such bus or to return to his residence. Any violation of this section shall constitute a Class 1 misdemeanor.

§46.2-919. Age limit for drivers of school buses.

It shall be unlawful for any person, whether licensed or not, who is under the age of eighteen years to drive a motor vehicle while in use as a school bus for the transportation of pupils.

ARTICLE 15
EMERGENCY VEHICLES

§46.2-920. Emergency vehicles exempt from regulations in certain situations; exceptions and additional requirements.

A. The driver of any emergency vehicle, when such vehicle is being used in the performance of public services, and when such vehicle is operated under emergency conditions, may, without subjecting himself to criminal prosecution:

1. Disregard speed limits, while having due regard for safety of persons and property;

2. Proceed past any steady or flashing red signal, traffic light, stop sign, or device indicating moving traffic shall stop if the speed of the vehicle is sufficiently reduced to enable it to pass a signal, traffic light, or device with due regard to the safety of persons and property;

3. Park or stop notwithstanding the other provisions of this chapter;

4. Disregard regulations governing a direction of movement of vehicles turning in specified directions so long as the operator does not endanger life or property;

5. Pass or overtake, with due regard to the safety of persons and property, another vehicle at any intersection;

6. Pass or overtake with due regard to the safety of persons and property, while en route to an emergency, stopped or slow-moving vehicles, by going to the left of the stopped or slow-moving vehicle either in a no-passing zone or by crossing the highway centerline;

7. Pass or overtake with due regard to the safety of persons and property, while en route to an emergency, stopped or slow-moving vehicles, by going off the paved or main traveled portion of the roadway on the right. Notwithstanding other provisions of this section, vehicles exempted in this instance will not be required to sound a siren or any device to give automatically intermittent signals.

B. The exemptions granted to emergency vehicles by subsection A of this section shall apply only when the operator of such vehicle displays a flashing, blinking, or alternating emergency light or lights as provided in §§46.2-1022 and 46.2-1023 and sounds a siren, exhaust whistle, or air horn designed to give automatically intermittent signals, as may be reasonably necessary, and, only when there is in force and effect for such vehicle either (i) standard motor vehicle liability insurance covering injury or death to any person in the sum of at least $100,000 because of bodily injury to or death of one person in any one accident and, subject to the limit for one person, to a limit of $300,000 because of bodily injury to or death of two or more persons in any one accident, and to a limit of $20,000 because of injury to or destruction of property of others in any one accident or (ii) a certificate of self-insurance issued pursuant to §46.2-368. Such exemptions shall not, however, protect the operator of any such vehicle from criminal prosecution for conduct constituting reckless disregard of the safety of persons and property. Nothing in this section shall release the operator of any such vehicle from civil liability for failure to use reasonable care in such operation.

C. For the purposes of this section, the term "emergency vehicle" shall mean:

1. Any law-enforcement vehicle operated by or under the direction of a federal, state, or local law-enforcement officer (i) in the chase or apprehension of violators of the law or persons charged with or suspected of any such violation or (ii) in response to an emergency call;

2. Any regional detention center vehicle operated by or under the direction of a correctional officer responding to an emergency call or operating in an emergency situation;

3. Any vehicle used to fight fire, including publicly owned state forest warden vehicles, when traveling in response to a fire alarm or emergency call;

4. Any ambulance, rescue, or life-saving vehicle designed or used for the principal purpose of supplying resuscitation or emergency relief where human life is endangered;

5. Any Department of Emergency Services vehicle or Office of Emergency Medical Services vehicle, when responding to an emergency call or operating in an emergency situation; and

6. Any Department of Corrections vehicle designated by the Director of the Department of Corrections, when (i) responding to an emergency call at a correctional facility, (ii) participating in a drug-related investigation, (iii) pursuing escapees from a correctional facility, or (iv) responding to a request for assistance from a law-enforcement officer.

D. Any law-enforcement vehicle operated by or under the direction of a federal, state, or local law-enforcement officer may disregard speed limits, while having due regard for safety of persons and property, (i) in testing the accuracy of speedometers of such vehicles or (ii) in testing the accuracy of speed measuring devices specified in §46.2-882.

(Chgd. by L.1995 ch. 92; L.2000 ch. 120, eff. 7/1/2000.)

§46.2-920.1. Operation of tow trucks under certain circumstances.

When operating at or en route to or from the scene of a traffic accident or similar emergency and when specifically directed by a law-enforcement officer present at the scene of a motor vehicle crash or similar incident, tow truck operators may:

1. Operate on a highway in a direction opposite that otherwise permitted for traffic;

2. Cross medians of divided highways;

3. Use cross-overs and turn-arounds otherwise reserved for use only by authorized vehicles;

4. Drive on a portion of the highway other than the roadway;

5. Stop or stand on any portion of the highway; and

6. Operate in any other manner as directed by a law-enforcement officer at the scene.

Nothing in this section, however, shall (i) immunize the driver of any tow truck from criminal prosecution for conduct constituting reckless disregard of the safety of persons and property or (ii) release the driver of any tow truck from any civil liability for failure to use reasonable care in operations permitted in this section.

§46.2-921. Following or parking near fire apparatus or rescue squad vehicle.

It shall be unlawful, in any county, city, or town for the driver of any vehicle, other than one on official business, to follow any fire apparatus or rescue squad vehicle traveling in response to a fire alarm or emergency call at any distance closer than 500 feet to such apparatus or rescue squad vehicle or to park such vehicle within 500 feet of where fire apparatus has stopped in answer to a fire alarm.

§46.2-922. Driving over fire hose.

It shall be unlawful, without the consent of the fire department official in command, for the driver of any vehicle to drive over any unprotected hose of a fire department laid down for use at any fire or alarm of fire.

ARTICLE 16
PEDESTRIANS

§46.2-923. How and where pedestrians to cross highways.

When crossing highways, pedestrians shall not carelessly or maliciously interfere with the orderly passage of vehicles. They shall cross, wherever possible, only at intersections or marked crosswalks. Where intersections contain no marked crosswalks, pedestrians shall not be guilty of negligence as a matter of law for crossing at any such intersection or between intersections when crossing by the most direct route.

The governing body of any town or city or the governing body of a county authorized by law to regulate traffic may by ordinance permit pedestrians to cross an intersection diagonally when all traffic entering the intersection has been halted by lights, other traffic control devices, or by a law-enforcement officer.

§46.2-924. Right-of-way of pedestrians; installation of certain signs; penalty.

A. The driver of any vehicle on a highway shall yield the right-of-way to any pedestrian crossing such highway:

1. At any clearly marked crosswalk, whether at mid-block or at the end of any block;

2. At any regular pedestrian crossing included in the prolongation of the lateral boundary lines of the adjacent sidewalk at the end of a block;

3. At any intersection when the driver is approaching on a highway or street where the legal maximum speed does not exceed thirty-five miles per hour.

B. Notwithstanding the provisions of subsection A of this section, at intersections or crosswalks where the movement of traffic is being regulated by law-enforcement officers or traffic control devices, the driver shall yield according to the direction of the law-enforcement officer or device.

No pedestrian shall enter or cross an intersection in disregard of approaching traffic.

The drivers of vehicles entering, crossing, or turning at intersections shall change their course, slow down, or stop if necessary to permit pedestrians to cross such intersections safely and expeditiously.

Pedestrians crossing highways at intersections shall at all times have the right-of-way over vehicles making turns into the highways being crossed by the pedestrians.

C. The governing body of any county having the county manager plan of government, or any city with a population between 110,000 and 115,000, may by ordinance provide for the installation and maintenance of highway signs at marked crosswalks specifically requiring operators of motor vehicles, at the locations where such signs are installed, to yield the right-of-way to pedestrians crossing or attempting to cross the highway. Any operator of a motor vehicle who fails at such locations to yield the right-of-way to pedestrians as required by such signs shall be guilty of a traffic infraction punishable by a fine of no less than $100 or more than $500. The Commonwealth Transportation Board shall develop criteria for the design, location, and installation of such signs. The provisions of this section shall not apply to any limited access highway.

(Chgd. by L.2000 ch. 323, eff. 7/1/2000.)

§46.2-925. Pedestrian control signals.

Whenever special pedestrian control signals exhibiting the words "Walk" or "Don't Walk" are in place such signals shall indicate as follows:

Walk. Pedestrians facing such signal may proceed across the highway in the direction of the signal and shall be given the right-of-way by the drivers of all vehicles.

Don't Walk. No pedestrian shall start to cross the highway in the direction of such signal, but any pedestrian who has partially completed his crossing on the Walk signal shall proceed to a sidewalk or safety island and remain there while the Don't Walk signal is showing.

§46.2-926. Pedestrians stepping into highway where they cannot be seen.

No pedestrian shall step into a highway open to moving vehicular traffic at any point between intersections where his presence would be obscured from the vision of drivers of approaching vehicles by a vehicle or other obstruction at the curb or side. The foregoing prohibition shall not apply to a pedestrian stepping into a highway to board a bus or to enter a safety zone, in which event he shall cross the highway only at right angles.

§46.2-927. Boarding or alighting from buses.

When actually boarding or alighting from buses, pedestrians shall have the right-of-way over vehicles, but shall not, in order to board or alight from buses, step into the highway sooner or remain there longer than is absolutely necessary.

§46.2-928. Pedestrians not to use roadway except when necessary; keeping to left.

Pedestrians shall not use the roadways for travel, except when necessary to do so because of the absence of sidewalks which are reasonably suitable and passable for their use. If they walk on the hard surface, or the main travelled portion of the roadway, they shall keep to the extreme left side or edge thereof, or where the shoulders of the highway are of sufficient width to permit, they may walk on either shoulder thereof.

§46.2-929. Pedestrians soliciting rides.

Pedestrians shall not stand or stop in any roadway for the purpose of soliciting rides.

§46.2-930. Loitering on bridges.

Pedestrians shall not loiter on any bridge on which the Commonwealth Transportation Commissioner has posted signs prohibiting such action. Any person violating the provisions of this section shall be guilty of a traffic infraction.

§46.2-931. Certain counties may prohibit distribution of handbills, etc., solicitation of contributions and sale of merchandise on highways.

Arlington and Henrico Counties are hereby authorized to adopt ordinances prohibiting:

1. The distribution of handbills, leaflets, bulletins, literature, advertisements, or similar material to the drivers of motor vehicles or passengers therein on secondary highways located within such counties;
2. The solicitation of contributions of any nature from the drivers of motor vehicles or passengers therein on secondary highways located within such counties;
3. The sale of merchandise or the attempted sale of merchandise to the drivers of motor vehicles or passengers therein on secondary highways located within such counties.

Ordinances adopted pursuant to this section may provide that any person violating the provisions of such ordinances shall be guilty of a traffic infraction.

§46.2-932. Playing on highways; roller skates, skateboards, toys, or other devices on wheels or runners; persons riding bicycles, mopeds, etc., not to attach to vehicles.

No person shall play on a highway, other than on the sidewalks thereof, within a city or town or on any part of a highway outside the limits of a city or town designated by the Commonwealth Transportation Commissioner exclusively for vehicular travel. No person shall use roller skates, skateboards, toys, or other devices on wheels or runners, except bicycles, mopeds, and motorcycles, on highways where play is prohibited. The governing bodies of counties, cities, and towns may designate areas on highways under their control where play is permitted and may impose reasonable restrictions on play on such highways. If the highways have only two traffic lanes, persons using such devices, except bicycles, mopeds, and motorcycles, shall keep as near as reasonably possible to the extreme left side or edge of the left traffic lane so that they will be facing oncoming traffic at all times.

No person riding on any bicycle, moped, roller skates, skateboards, toys, or other devices on wheels or runners, shall attach the same or himself to any vehicle on a roadway.

§46.2-933. When vehicles to stop for pedestrian guided by dog or carrying white, red-tipped white, or metallic cane.

Whenever a totally or partially blind pedestrian crossing or attempting to cross a highway in accordance with the provisions of §46.2-923 is guided by a dog guide or carrying a cane which is predominantly metallic or white in color, with or without a red tip, the driver of every vehicle approaching the intersection or place of crossing shall bring his vehicle to a full stop before arriving at such intersection or place of crossing, unless such intersection or place of crossing is controlled by a law-enforcement officer or traffic light. Any person violating any provision of this section shall be guilty of a Class 3 misdemeanor.

§46.2-934. Failure to use cane or guide dog not contributory negligence.

Nothing contained in §46.2-933 shall be construed to deprive any totally or partially blind or otherwise incapacitated person not carrying such a cane or walking stick or not being guided by a dog, of the rights and privileges conferred by law upon pedestrians crossing highways. Nor shall the failure of such totally or partially blind or otherwise incapacitated person to carry a cane or walking stick, or to be guided by a guide dog on the highways or sidewalks of the Commonwealth, be held to constitute nor be evidence of contributory negligence.

§46.2-935. Regulation by ordinance in counties, cities, and towns.

The governing bodies of counties, cities, and towns may enact ordinances requiring pedestrians to obey signs and signals erected on highways therein for the direction and control of traffic, to obey the orders of law-enforcement officers engaged in directing traffic on such highways, and may provide penalties not exceeding those of a traffic infraction.

ARTICLE 17
LEGAL PROCEDURES AND REQUIREMENTS

§46.2-936. Arrest for misdemeanor; release on summons and promise to appear; right to demand hearing immediately or within twenty-four hours; issuance of warrant on request of officer for violations of §§46.2-301 and 46.2-302; refusal to promise to appear; violations.

Whenever any person is detained by or in the custody of an arresting officer, including an arrest on a warrant, for a violation of any provision of this title punishable as a misdemeanor, the arresting officer shall, except as otherwise provided in §46.2-940, take the name and address of such person and the license number of his motor vehicle and issue a summons or otherwise notify him in writing to appear at a time and place to be specified in such summons or notice. Such time shall be at least five days after such arrest unless the person arrested demands an earlier hearing. Such person shall, if he so desires, have a right to an immediate hearing, or a hearing within twenty-four hours at a convenient hour, before a court having jurisdiction under this title within the county, city, or town wherein such offense was committed. Upon the giving by such person of his written promise to appear at such time and place, the officer shall forthwith release him from custody.

Notwithstanding the foregoing provisions of this section, if prior general approval has been granted by order of the general district court for the use of this section in cases involving violations of §§46.2-301 and 46.2-302, the arresting officer may take the person before the appropriate judicial officer of the county or city in which the violation occurred and make oath as to the offense and request issuance of a warrant. If a warrant is issued, the judicial officer shall proceed in accordance with the provisions of Article 1 (§19.2-119 et seq.) of Chapter 9 of Title 19.2.

Notwithstanding any other provision of this section, in cases involving a violation of §46.2-341.24 or §46.2-341.31, the arresting officer shall take the person before a magistrate as provided in §§46.2-341.26:2 and 46.2-341.26:3. The magistrate may issue either a summons or a warrant as he shall deem proper.

Any person refusing to give such written promise to appear under the provisions of this section shall be taken immediately by the arresting officer before a magistrate or other issuing officer having jurisdiction who shall proceed according to the provisions of §46.2-940.

Any person who willfully violates his written promise to appear, given in accordance with this section, shall be treated in accordance with the provisions of §46.2-938.

Any officer violating any of the provisions of this section shall be guilty of misconduct in office and subject to removal therefrom upon complaint filed by any person in a court of competent jurisdiction. This section shall not be construed to limit the removal of a law-enforcement officer for other misconduct in office.

(Chgd. by L.1999 chs. 829, 846, eff. 7/1/99.)

§46.2-937. Traffic infractions treated as misdemeanors for arrest purposes.

For purposes of arrest, traffic infractions shall be treated as misdemeanors. Except as otherwise provided by this title, the authority and duties of arresting officers shall be the same for traffic infractions as for misdemeanors.

§46.2-938. Issuance of warrant upon failure to comply with summons; penalties; suspension of licenses for failure to appear.

Upon the failure of any person to comply with the terms of a summons or notice as provided in §46.2-936, such person shall be guilty of a Class 1 misdemeanor and the court may order a warrant for his arrest. The warrant shall be returnable to the court having jurisdiction of the offense and shall be accompanied by a report by the arresting officer which shall clearly identify the person arrested, specifying the section of the Code of Virginia or ordinance violated, the location of the offense, a description of the motor vehicle and its registration or license number.

If the warrant is returned to the court with the notation "not found" or the person named in the warrant does not appear on the return date thereof, the court shall forward a certificate of the fact of nonservice or nonappearance, with a copy of the report specified in the foregoing provisions of this section, to the Commissioner of the Department of Motor Vehicles, who shall forthwith suspend the driver's license of such person. The order of suspension shall specify the reason for the suspension. Such suspension shall continue until such time as the court has notified the Commissioner that the defendant has appeared before the court under the terms of the summons or notice and the warrant.

§46.2-939. Authority of law-enforcement officers to issue subpoenas.

Local law-enforcement officers and state police officers, in the course of their duties in the investigation of any accident involving a motor vehicle or vehicles, may, at the scene of any such accident, issue a subpoena to any witness to appear in court and testify with respect to any criminal charge brought against any person as a result of such accident. State police officers, additionally, may issue such subpoenas at any other location within seventy-two hours of the time of such accident, with the return of service thereof made to the appropriate court clerk within forty-eight hours after such service. A subpoena so issued shall have the same force and effect as if issued by the court.

Any person failing to appear in response to a subpoena issued as provided in this section shall be punished as provided by law.

§46.2-940. When arresting officer shall take person before issuing authority.

If any person is: (i) believed by the arresting officer to have committed a felony; (ii) believed by the arresting officer to be likely to disregard a summons issued under §46.2-936; or (iii) refuses to give a written promise to appear under the provisions of §46.2-936 or §46.2-945; the arresting officer shall promptly take him before a magistrate or other issuing authority having jurisdiction to determine whether probable cause exists that such person is likely to disregard a summons. The magistrate or other authority may issue either a summons or warrant as he shall determine proper.

§46.2-941. Conditions precedent to issuance of summons for violation of parking ordinance; notice.

Before any summons shall be issued for the prosecution of a violation of an ordinance of any county, city, or town regulating parking, the violator shall have been first notified by mail at his last known address or at the address shown for such violator on the records of the Department of Motor Vehicles, that he may pay the fine provided by law for such violation, within five days of receipt of such notice, and the authorized person issuing such summons shall be notified that the violator has failed to pay such fine within such time. The notice to the violator, required by the provisions of this section, shall be contained in an envelope bearing the words "Law-Enforcement Notice" stamped or printed on the face thereof in fourteen point or larger type.

(Chgd. by L.1999 ch. 291, 323, eff. 7/1/99.)

§46.2-942. Admissibility of results of speedometer test in prosecution for exceeding speed limit.

In the trial of any person charged with exceeding any maximum speed limit in the Commonwealth, the court shall receive as evidence a sworn report of the results of a calibration test of the accuracy of the speedometer in the motor vehicle operated by the defendant or the arresting officer at the time of the alleged offense. The report shall be considered by the court or jury in both determining guilt or innocence and in fixing punishment.

§46.2-943. Court or jury may consider defendant's prior traffic record before sentencing.

The term "traffic offense" when used in this section shall mean any moving traffic violation described or enumerated in subdivisions 1 and 2 of §46.2-382, whether such violation was committed within or outside the Commonwealth according to the records of the Department of Motor Vehicles.

The term "prior traffic record" when used in this section shall mean the record of prior suspensions and revocations of a driver's license, and the record of prior convictions of traffic offenses described in the foregoing provisions of this section.

When any person is found guilty of a traffic offense, the court or jury trying the case may consider the prior traffic record of the defendant before imposing sentence as provided by law. After the prior traffic record of the defendant has been introduced, the defendant shall be afforded an opportunity to present evidence limited to showing the nature of his prior convictions, suspensions, and revocations.

ARTICLE 18
ARREST OF NONRESIDENTS

§46.2-944. Definitions.

As used in this article:

"Citation" means any summons, ticket, or other official document issued by a police officer for a traffic violation containing an order which requires the motorist to respond.

"Collateral" or "bond" means any cash or other security deposited to secure an appearance for trial, following the issuance by a police officer of a citation for a traffic violation.

"Compliance" means the motorist must appear for a hearing and/or pay court fines and costs.

"Court" means a court of law or traffic tribunal.

"Driver's license" means any license or privilege to operate a motor vehicle issued under the laws of the home jurisdiction.

"Home jurisdiction" means the jurisdiction that issued the driver's license of the traffic violator.

"Issuing jurisdiction" means the jurisdiction in which the traffic citation was issued to the motorist.

"Jurisdiction" means a state, territory, or possession of the United States, the District of Columbia, or the Commonwealth of Puerto Rico.

"Motorist" means a driver of a motor vehicle operating in a party jurisdiction other than the home jurisdiction.

"Party jurisdiction" means any jurisdiction which by its laws or by written agreement with the Commonwealth extends to residents of Virginia substantially the rights and privileges provided by this article.

"Personal recognizance" means a signed agreement by a motorist made at the time of issuance of the traffic citation that he will comply with the terms of that traffic citation.

"Police officer" means any individual authorized by the party jurisdiction to issue a citation for a traffic violation.

"Terms of the citation" means those options expressly stated upon the citation.

§46.2-945. Issuance of citation to motorist; party jurisdiction; police officer to report noncompliance with citation.

A. When issuing a citation for a traffic violation, a police officer shall issue the citation to a motorist who is a resident of or holds a driver's license issued by a party jurisdiction and shall not, subject to the exceptions noted in subsection C of this section, require such motorist to post collateral or bond to secure appearance for trial, but shall accept such motorist's written promise that he will comply with the terms of such citation; provided, however, the motorist shall have the right upon his request to post collateral or bond in a manner provided by law and, in such case, the provisions of this article shall not apply.

B. In the absence of the motorist's written promise, the officer shall proceed according to the provisions of §46.2-940.

C. No motorist shall be entitled to receive a citation under the terms of subsection A of this section nor shall any police officer issue such citation under the same in the event the offense for which the citation is issued shall be one of the following: (i) an offense for which the issuance of a citation in lieu of a hearing or the posting of collateral or bond is prohibited by the laws of this Commonwealth; or (ii) an offense, the conviction of or the forfeiture of collateral for which requires the revocation of the motorist's license.

D. Upon the failure of any motorist to comply with the terms of a traffic citation, the police officer or the appropriate official shall report this fact to the Department of Motor Vehicles. Such report shall clearly identify the motorist; describe the violation, specifying the section of the statute, code or ordinance violated; shall indicate the location of the offense, give description of vehicle involved, and show the registration or license number of the vehicle. Such report shall be signed by the police officer or appropriate official.

§46.2-946. Department to transmit officer's report to party jurisdiction; suspension of resident's license for noncompliance with citation issued by party jurisdiction.

Upon receipt of the report as described in §46.2-945, the Department of Motor Vehicles shall transmit a certified copy of such report to the official in charge of the issuance of driver's licenses in the home jurisdiction in which the motorist resides or by which he is licensed.

Upon receipt from the issuing jurisdiction of a certification of noncompliance with a citation by a motorist holding a driver's license issued by this Commonwealth, the Commissioner of the Department of Motor Vehicles forthwith shall suspend such motorist's driver's license. The order of suspension shall indicate the reason for the order, and shall notify the motorist that his license shall remain suspended until he has furnished evidence satisfactory to the Commissioner that he has fully complied with the terms of the citation which was the basis for the suspension order.

The licensing authority of the issuing jurisdiction may suspend the privilege of a motorist for whom a report has been transmitted.

It shall be the duty of the Commissioner of Motor Vehicles to ascertain and remain informed as to which jurisdictions are party jurisdictions hereunder and, accordingly, to maintain a current listing of such jurisdictions, which listing he shall from time to time cause to be disseminated among the appropriate departments, divisions, bureaus and agencies of this Commonwealth, the principal executive officers of the several counties, cities and towns of this Commonwealth and the licensing authorities in all other jurisdictions which are, have been, or claim to be a party jurisdiction pursuant hereto.

Consistent with the terms of the applicable Nonresident Violator Compact, the home jurisdiction shall take no action regarding any report transmitted by the issuing jurisdiction, which is transmitted more than six months after the date on which the traffic citation was issued.

Consistent with the terms of the applicable Nonresident Violator Compact, the home jurisdiction shall take no action regarding any report on any violation where the date of issuance of the citation predates the entry into the compact for the two party jurisdictions affected.

CHAPTER 10
MOTOR VEHICLE AND EQUIPMENT SAFETY

ARTICLE 1
VEHICLE AND EQUIPMENT SAFETY, GENERALLY

Section

§46.2-1000. Department to suspend registration of vehicles lacking certain equipment; officer to take possession of registration card, license plates and decals when observing defect in motor vehicle; when to be returned.

The Department shall suspend the registration of any motor vehicle, trailer, or semitrailer which the Department or the Department of State Police determines is not equipped with proper (i) brakes, (ii) lights, (iii) horn or warning device, (iv) turn signals, (v) safety glass when required by law, (vi) mirror, (vii) muffler, (viii) windshield wiper, (ix) steering gear adequate to ensure the safe movement of the vehicle as required by this title or when such vehicle is equipped with a smoke screen device or cutout or when such motor vehicle, trailer, or semitrailer is otherwise unsafe to be operated.

Any law-enforcement officer shall, when he observes any defect in a motor vehicle as described above, take possession of the registration card, license plates, and decals of any such vehicle and retain the same in his possession for a period of fifteen days unless the owner of the vehicle corrects the defects or obtains a new safety inspection sticker from an authorized safety inspection station. When the defect or defects are corrected as indicated above the registration card, license plates, and decals shall be returned to the owner.

§46.2-1001. Removal of unsafe vehicles; penalty.

Any motor vehicle, trailer, or semitrailer examined by a law-enforcement officer certified to perform vehicle safety inspections and found to be operating with defective brakes, tires, wheels, steering mechanism, or any other condition which is likely to cause an accident or a breakdown of the motor vehicle, trailer, or semitrailer may be removed from the highway and not permitted to operate again on the highway until the defects have been corrected and the law-enforcement officer has found the corrections to be satisfactory. Such law-enforcement officer may allow any motor vehicle, trailer, or semitrailer discovered to be in such an unsafe condition while being operated on the highway to continue in operation only to the nearest place where repairs can be safely effected and only if such operation is less hazardous to the public than to permit the motor vehicle, trailer, or semitrailer to remain on the highway.

No person shall operate a motor vehicle, trailer, or semitrailer which has been removed from service as provided in the foregoing provisions of this section prior to correction and proper authorization by a law-enforcement officer certified to perform vehicle safety inspection procedures.

For the purpose of this section, the term "law-enforcement officer certified to perform vehicle safety inspections" shall include (i) State Police officers and (ii) those law-enforcement officers of the Cities of Alexandria, Chesapeake, Fairfax, Falls Church, Harrisonburg, Lynchburg, Manassas, Norfolk, Suffolk, and Virginia Beach; the Town of Herndon; and the Counties of Arlington, Bedford, Chesterfield, Fairfax, Henrico, Loudoun, Prince William, Roanoke, Rockingham, and Wythe who have satisfactorily completed a course of instruction as prescribed by the U.S. Department of Transportation, Federal Highway Administration, Bureau of Motor Carrier Safety, in federal motor carrier safety regulations, safety inspection procedures, and out-of-service criteria. Those law-enforcement officers certified to place vehicles out of service must receive annual in-service training in current federal motor carrier safety regulations, safety inspection procedures, and out-of-service criteria. The Superintendent of State Police shall be responsible for coordinating the annual in-service training. The agency administrator of the law-enforcement agencies authorized to perform vehicle safety inspections shall submit to the Department of State Police the names of each law-enforcement officer certified to perform vehicle safety inspections who has satisfactorily completed a course of instruction as prescribed by the U.S. Department of Transportation, Federal Highway Administration, Bureau of Motor Carrier Safety.

Every vehicle inspected by a local law-enforcement officer pursuant to this section and found to be free of defects which would constitute grounds for removal of the vehicle from service shall be issued a sticker as evidence of such inspection and freedom from defects. Such stickers shall be valid for ninety days. Any vehicle displaying a valid sticker shall be exempt from local or State Police inspections under this section. However, the fact that a vehicle displays a valid sticker shall not prevent any local or State Police officer from stopping and inspecting the vehicle if he observes an obvious safety defect. The Superintendent of State Police shall work cooperatively with local law-enforcement agencies of localities whose officers are authorized to perform

 Zv

inspections pursuant to this section to develop a standard sticker as provided for in this section and uniform policies and procedures for issuance and display of such stickers.

However, notwithstanding the foregoing provisions of this section, before placing any vehicle out of service, the vehicle operator shall be allowed two hours to effect repairs to his vehicle. Such repairs may be performed at the site where the vehicle was inspected and found to be unsafe, provided the vehicle requiring repair is off the highway, where the repairs can be effected safely. If such repairs remedy the condition or conditions that would have caused it to be taken out of service, it shall not be taken out of service, but allowed to resume its operations. No such repairs, however, shall be allowed if the vehicle's load consists of hazardous material as defined in §10.1-1400.

(Chgd. by L.1995 chs. 39, 458; L.1996 chs. 24, 91, 144, 525; L.1997 ch. 35; L.1999 chs. 68, 279; L.2000 chs. 59, 112, eff. 7/1/2000.)

§46.2-1002. Illegal possession or sale of certain unapproved equipment.

It shall be unlawful for any person to possess with intent to sell or offer for sale, either separately or as a part of the equipment of a motor vehicle, or to use or have as equipment on a motor vehicle operated on a highway any lighting device, warning device, signal device, safety glass, or other equipment for which approval is required by any provision of this chapter or any part or parts tending to change or alter the operation of such device, glass, or other equipment unless of a type that has been submitted to and approved by the Superintendent or meets or exceeds the standards and specifications of the Society of Automotive Engineers, the American National Standards Institute, Incorporated or the federal Department of Transportation.

§46.2-1003. Illegal use of defective or unsafe equipment.

It shall be unlawful for any person to use or have as equipment on a motor vehicle operated on a highway any device or equipment mentioned in §46.2-1002 which is defective or in unsafe condition.

§46.2-1004. Trademark or name and instructions required.

Each device or other equipment mentioned in §46.2-1002 and offered for sale in the Commonwealth shall bear a trademark or name or be identified in keeping with the Superintendent's regulations and shall be accompanied by printed instructions as to the proper mounting, use, and candlepower of any bulbs to be used therewith and any particular methods of mounting or adjustments necessary to meet the requirements of this title and any regulation of the Superintendent.

ARTICLE 2
TESTING, EVALUATION, AND APPROVAL OF EQUIPMENT

Section

§46.2-1005. Procedure for approval of equipment.

The Superintendent may establish a procedure for the approval of equipment required to be approved by him. Such procedure shall include the submission of a sample of the device for test and record purposes, submission of evidence that the device complies with this title and with recognized testing standards which the Superintendent is hereby authorized to adopt, and payment of the fee as provided by §46.2-1008. The Superintendent shall then, within a reasonable time, either disapprove the device or issue a certificate of approval therefor.

The Superintendent may waive such approval and the issuance of a certificate of approval when the device or equipment required to be approved by this title is identified as complying with the standards and specifications of the Society of Automotive Engineers, the American National Standards Institute, Incorporated, or the regulations of the federal Department of Transportation.

§46.2-1006. Approval of brake and head light testing methods and equipment.

The Superintendent shall approve methods of brake testing and head light testing. Approval of the use of mechanical brake and light testing equipment may be given by the Superintendent. When necessary, the Superintendent may call upon the United States Bureau of Standards or some other recognized testing agency to assist him in determining whether such mechanical testing equipment shall be approved for the purpose set forth in this chapter.

§46.2-1007. Retesting of devices and revocation of approval certificates.

The Superintendent, when having reason to believe that an approved device or equipment for which a certificate of approval has been issued and which is being sold commercially does not, under ordinary conditions of use, comply with the requirements of this chapter, may, after notice to the manufacturer thereof, suspend or revoke the certificate of approval issued therefor, until or unless the device is resubmitted to and retested by an authorized testing agency and is found to meet the requirements of this chapter. If the certificate of approval for such device or equipment has been waived by the Superintendent as provided in §46.2-1005, the notice to the manufacturer as provided in this section shall have the effect of making further sales of such device or equipment unlawful in the Commonwealth until such device or equipment has been submitted to the Superintendent and a certificate of approval has been issued in accordance with the procedure established pursuant to §46.2-1005. The Superintendent may, at the time of retest, purchase in the open market and submit to the testing agency one or more sets of the approved device, and if the device fails to meet the requirements of this title, the Superintendent may permanently revoke the certificate of approval of the device. In the discretion of the Superintendent, an approval for the sale and use of any such device may be amended to permit the continued use of such devices already sold but to prohibit further sales of the device.

§46.2-1008. Fees for approval certificates.

Any person who applies to the Superintendent for a certificate of approval required by this article shall pay a fee not to exceed the following amounts:

1. For approval and recordation of head lights, warning devices, safety glass, signal devices, and other devices required by this title to be approved by the Superintendent and not provided for elsewhere in this section, $150.

2. For approval and recordation of tail lights, spot lights or any other lighting devices, seventy-five dollars.

3. For approval and recordation of brake-testing and light-testing machines, $100 for each type approved.

4. For approval and recordation of safety lap belts and shoulder straps or harnesses or any combination lap belt and shoulder strap or harness, fifty dollars.

5. For approval and recordation of safety glasses, face shields, or goggles for motorcycle operators, fifty dollars.

Fees collected under this section shall be used by the Superintendent in examining and testing devices to be approved and for maintaining and publishing necessary records.

§46.2-1009. Exemptions for certain electrically powered vehicles; standards and permits for such vehicles.

The provisions of §§46.2-1002 through 46.2-1008 shall not apply to vehicles which are powered solely by electricity, capable of speeds of no more than fifteen miles per hour. The Superintendent may establish standards for safety equipment to be used on such vehicles. Upon the establishment of such standards, permits to use such vehicles may be issued to persons owning vehicles meeting such standards by the officer in charge of the division of the Department of State Police having jurisdiction in the county, city, or town in which such person resides.

ARTICLE 3
LIGHTS AND TURN SIGNALS

Section

§46.2-1010. Equipment required.

Every vehicle driven or moved on a highway within the Commonwealth shall at all times be equipped with such lights as are required in this chapter for different classes of vehicles. The lights shall at all times be capable of being lighted, except as otherwise provided. This section shall not apply, however, to any vehicle for transporting well-drilling machinery licensed under §46.2-700 when operated only between the hours of sunrise and sunset.

§46.2-1011. Head lights on motor vehicles.

Every motor vehicle other than a motorcycle, road roller, road machinery, or tractor used on a highway shall be equipped with at least two head lights as approved by the Superintendent, at the front of and on opposite sides of the motor vehicle.

§46.2-1012. Head lights on motorcycles; auxiliary head lights.

Every motorcycle shall be equipped with at least one and not more than two head lights which shall be of a type that has been approved by the Superintendent and shall be capable of projecting sufficient light to the front of such motorcycle to render discernible a person or object at a distance of 200 feet. However, the lights shall not project a glaring or dazzling light to persons approaching such motorcycles. In addition, each motorcycle may be equipped with not more than two auxiliary head lights of a type approved by the Superintendent.

Motorcycles may be equipped with means of modulating the high beam of their head lights between high and low beam at a rate of 200 to 280 flashes per minute. Such head lights shall not be so modulated during periods when head lights would ordinarily be required to be lighted under §46.2-1030.

§46.2-1013. Tail lights.

Every motor vehicle, trailer, or semitrailer which is being drawn at the end of one or more other vehicles, or motorcycles shall carry at the rear a red light plainly visible in clear weather from a distance of 500 feet to the rear of such vehicle. Such tail lights shall be constructed and so mounted in their relation to the rear license plate as to illuminate the license plate with a white light so that the same may be read from a distance of 50 feet to the rear of such vehicle. Alternatively, a separate white light shall be so mounted as to illuminate the rear license plate from a distance of 50 feet to the rear of such vehicle. Any such tail light or special white light shall be of a type approved by the Superintendent.

In any instance where the tail light is to be installed on a boat trailer and the boat extends beyond the end of the trailer or to the end of the trailer, an approved portable light assembly or assemblies may be attached to the exposed rear of the boat, provided such installation complies with the visibility requirements of this section.

§46.2-1014. Brake lights.

Every motor vehicle, trailer, or semitrailer, except an antique vehicle not originally equipped with a brake light, registered in the Commonwealth and operated on the highways in the Commonwealth shall be equipped with at least one brake light of a type approved by the Superintendent. Such brake lights shall automatically exhibit a red or amber light plainly visible in clear weather from a distance of 500 feet to the rear of such vehicle when the brake is applied.

Motorcycles may be equipped with one or more auxiliary brake lights of a type approved by the Superintendent. The Superintendent may by regulation prescribe or limit the size, number, location, and configuration of such auxiliary brake lights.
(Chgd. by L.2000 chs. 54, 63, eff. 7/1/2000.)

§46.2-1014.1. Supplemental high mount stop light.
Whenever operated on the highways, every Virginia-registered passenger car manufactured for the 1986 or subsequent model year shall be equipped with a supplemental center high mount stop light of a type approved by the Superintendent or which meets the standards adopted by the United States Department of Transportation. The light shall be mounted as near the vertical center line of the vehicle as possible. The light shall be actuated only in conjunction with the vehicle's brake lights and hazard lights. Any supplemental high mount stop light installed on any other vehicle shall comply with those requirements.

§46.2-1015. Lights on bicycles and mopeds.
Every bicycle and moped when in use between sunset and sunrise shall be equipped with a white light on the front which shall be visible in clear weather from a distance of at least 500 feet to the front and with a red reflector on the rear. Such reflector shall be of a type approved by the Superintendent and shall be visible in clear weather from fifty feet to 300 feet to the rear when directly in front of lawful high beams of head lights on a motor vehicle. A red light visible in clear weather for 500 feet to the rear may be used in lieu of or in addition to the red reflector. Such lights and reflector shall be of types approved by the Superintendent.

§46.2-1016. Lights on other vehicles; reflectors.
All vehicles or other mobile equipment not otherwise in this article required to be equipped with specified lights shall carry at least one or more white lights to the front and a red light to the rear visible in clear weather from a distance of not less than 500 feet to the front and rear of such vehicles.

In lieu of or in addition to the lights, a reflector of a type, size, and color approved by the Superintendent may be permanently affixed to the rear and front of such vehicle.

§46.2-1017. Dimension or marker lights and reflectors, generally.
All motor vehicles, trailers, or semitrailers exceeding seven feet in width or the widest portion of which extends four inches beyond the front fender extremes shall be equipped with amber lights mounted at the extreme right and left front top corners of such vehicle. Each such light shall be visible in clear weather for a distance of at least 500 feet to the front of such vehicle. Such vehicles shall also be equipped with red lights mounted at the extreme right and left rear top corners of such vehicle. Each such light shall be visible in clear weather for at least 500 feet to the rear of such vehicle. Any tractor truck, however, need not be equipped with rear red dimension or marker lights. If the front or the rear of such vehicle is not the widest portion of the vehicle, the dimension or marker lights required in this section shall be mounted on the widest portions of the vehicle with the amber lights herein required visible from the front as herein required and the red lights herein required visible from the rear as herein required. The lights herein required shall be of a type approved by the Superintendent.

In addition to the lights required in this section, each such vehicle shall be equipped with amber reflectors located on each side thereof, at or near the front. Red reflectors shall be used on the rear of each such vehicle. Such reflectors shall be securely fastened to the vehicle not less than fifteen inches and not more than sixty inches from the ground. For a vehicle that is less than fifteen inches tall, however, such reflectors shall be securely fastened thereto at the highest point the structure of a vehicle will permit. The reflectors shall be of a type approved by the Superintendent.

If any vehicle is so constructed as to make compliance with the requirements of this section impractical, the lights and reflectors shall be placed on the vehicle in accordance with the Superintendent's regulations.

If any vehicle required by this section to be equipped with dimension or marker lights has installed on its rear, as close as practicable to the top of the vehicle and as close as practicable to the vertical centerline of the vehicle, three red identification lights of a type approved by the Superintendent, with the light centers spaced not less than six inches or more than twelve inches apart, the rear dimension or marker lights may be mounted at any height but must indicate as nearly as practicable the extreme width of the vehicle.
(Chgd. by L.1997 ch. 23, eff. 7/1/97.)

§46.2-1018. Marker lights on vehicles or loads exceeding thirty-five feet.
Whenever any motor vehicle or combination of vehicles whose actual length, including its load, exceeds thirty-five feet and is not subject to the provisions of §46.2-1017, such vehicle shall be equipped with reflectors of a type approved by the Superintendent when operated between sunset and sunrise. Such reflectors shall be mounted on the widest part of the vehicle or its load so as to be visible from the front and sides of the vehicle.

§46.2-1019. Spotlights.
Any motor vehicle or motorcycle may be equipped with one or two spotlights which, when lighted, shall be aimed and used so that no portion of the beam will be directed to the left of the center of the highway at any time or more than 100 feet ahead of the vehicle. Any such lights shall be of a type approved by the Superintendent. No such spotlights shall be used in conjunction with or as a substitute for required head lights, except in case of emergency.

§46.2-1020. Other permissible lights.
Any motor vehicle may be equipped with one or two fog lights, one or two auxiliary driving lights if so equipped by the manufacturer, two daytime running lights, two side lights of not more than six candlepower, an interior light or lights of not more than fifteen candlepower each, and signal lights.

The provision of this section limiting interior lights to no more than fifteen candlepower shall not apply to (i) alternating, blinking, or flashing colored emergency lights mounted inside law-enforcement motor vehicles which may otherwise legally be equipped with such colored emergency lights, or (ii) flashing shielded red or red and white lights, authorized under §46.2-1024, mounted inside vehicles owned by members of volunteer fire companies or volunteer rescue squads or owned or used by professional fire fighters.

Unless such lighting device is both covered and unlit, no motor vehicle which is equipped with any lighting device other than lights required or permitted in this article, required or approved by the Superintendent, or required by the federal Department of Transportation shall be operated on any highway in the Commonwealth. Nothing in this section shall permit any vehicle, not otherwise authorized, to be equipped with colored emergency lights, whether blinking or steady-burning.
(Chgd. by L.1995 ch. 122, eff. 7/1/95.)

§46.2-1021. Additional lights permitted on certain commercial vehicles.
In addition to other lights permitted in this article, buses operated as public carriers, taxicabs as defined in §46.2-2000, and commercial motor vehicles as defined in §52-8.4 may be equipped with (i) illuminated vacant or destination

signs and (ii) single steady-burning white lights, emitting a diffused light of such intensity as not to project a glaring or dazzling light, for the nighttime illumination of exterior advertising.

In addition to other lights authorized by this article, buses operated as public carriers may be equipped with flashing white warning lights of types authorized by the Superintendent of State Police. These warning lights shall be installed in a manner authorized by the Superintendent and shall be lighted while the bus is transporting passengers during periods of reduced visibility caused by atmospheric conditions other than darkness. These warning lights may also be lighted at other times while the bus is transporting passengers.

(Chgd. by L.1998 ch. 419, eff. 7/1/98.)

§46.2-1021.1. Additional lights permitted on certain privately owned cars.

Privately owned passenger cars used for home delivery of commercially prepared food may be equipped with one steady-burning white light for the nighttime illumination of a sign identifying the business delivering the food. Such sign shall not utilize primarily green, red or blue colors. Such sign shall not exceed eighteen inches in height nor have more than four sides, no side of which shall exceed fifteen by twenty-four inches. Such light shall emit diffused illumination of such an intensity as not to project a glaring or dazzling light. Such light may only be illuminated during delivery.

§46.2-1022. Flashing blue, red and blue, blue and white, or red, white and blue warning lights.

Department of Corrections vehicles designated by the Director of the Department of Corrections and law-enforcement vehicles may be equipped with flashing, blinking, or alternating blue, blue and red, blue and white, or red, white, and blue combination warning lights of types approved by the Superintendent.

(Chgd. by L.1996 chs. 141, 347, eff. 7/1/96.)

§46.2-1023. Flashing red or red and white warning lights.

Fire apparatus, forest warden vehicles, ambulances, rescue and life-saving vehicles, vehicles of the Department of Emergency Services, vehicles of the Office of Emergency Medical Services, animal warden vehicles, and vehicles used by security personnel of the Newport News Shipbuilding and Drydock Company, Bassett-Walker, Inc., Tultex Corporation, and, within those areas specified in their orders of appointment, by special conservators of the peace and policemen for certain places appointed pursuant to §§19.2-13 and 19.2-17 may be equipped with flashing, blinking, or alternating red or red and white combination warning lights of types approved by the Superintendent.

(Chgd. by L.1995 ch. 92, eff. 7/1/95.)

§46.2-1024. Flashing or steady-burning red or red and white warning lights.

Any member of a fire department, volunteer fire company, or volunteer rescue squad and any ambulance driver employed by a privately owned ambulance service may equip one vehicle owned by him with no more than two flashing or steady-burning red or red and white combination warning lights of types approved by the Superintendent. Warning lights permitted by this section shall be lit only when answering emergency calls.

§46.2-1025. Flashing amber or purple warning lights.

A. The following vehicles may be equipped with flashing, blinking, or alternating amber warning lights of types approved by the Superintendent:

1. Vehicles used for the principal purpose of towing or servicing disabled vehicles;
2. Vehicles used in constructing, maintaining, and repairing highways or utilities on or along public highways;
3. Vehicles used for the principal purpose of removing hazardous or polluting substances from state waters and drainage areas on or along public highways;
4. Vehicles used for servicing automatic teller machines, provided the amber lights are not lit while the vehicle is in motion;
5. Vehicles used in refuse collection, provided the amber lights are lit only when the vehicles are engaged in refuse collection operations;
6. Vehicles used by individuals for emergency snow-removal purposes;
7. Hi-rail vehicle, provided the amber lights are lit only when the vehicles are operated on railroad rails;
8. Fire apparatus, ambulances, and rescue and life-saving vehicles, provided the amber lights are used in addition to lights permitted under §46.2-1023 and are so mounted or installed as to be visible from behind the vehicle;
9. Vehicles owned and used by businesses providing security services, provided the amber lights are not lit while the vehicle is being operated on a public highway;
10. Vehicles used to collect and deliver the United States mail, provided the amber lights are lit only when the vehicle is actually engaged in such collection or delivery;
11. Vehicles used to transport petroleum products, provided the amber light is mounted on the rear of the vehicle and is lit only when the vehicle's back-up lights are lit and its device producing an audible signal when the vehicle is operated in reverse gear, as provided for in §46.2-1175.1, is in operation;
12. Vehicles used by law-enforcement agency personnel in the enforcement of laws governing motor vehicle parking;
13. Government-owned law-enforcement vehicles, provided the lights are used for the purpose of giving directional warning to vehicular traffic to move one direction or another and are not lit while the vehicle is being operated on a public highway;
14. Chase vehicles when used to unload a hot air balloon or used to load a hot air balloon after landing, provided the amber lights are not lit while the vehicle is in motion;
15. Vehicles used for farm, agricultural, or horticultural purposes, or any farm tractor;
16. Vehicles owned and used by construction companies operating under Virginia contractors licenses;
17. Vehicles used to lead or provide escorts for bicycle races authorized by the Department of Transportation or the locality in which the race is being conducted;
18. Vehicles used by radio or television stations for remote broadcasts, provided that the amber lights are not lit while the vehicle is in motion;
19. Vehicles used as pace cars, security vehicles, or fire-fighting vehicles by any speedway or motor vehicle race track, provided that the amber lights are not lit while the vehicle is being operated on a public highway; and
20. Vehicles used by municipal safety officers in the performance of their official duties. For the purpose of this subdivision, "municipal safety officers" means municipal employees responsible for managing municipal safety programs and ensuring municipal compliance with safety and environmental regulatory mandates.

B. Except as otherwise provided in this section, such amber lights shall be lit only when performing the functions which qualify them to be equipped with such lights.

C. Vehicles used to lead or provide escorts for funeral processions may use either amber warning lights or purple warning lights, but amber warning lights and purple warning lights shall not simultaneously be used on the same vehicle. The Superintendent of State Police shall develop standards and specifications for purple lights authorized in this subsection.

(Chgd. by L.1995 ch. 727; L.1997 ch. 149; L.1998 chs. 134, 417; L.1999 chs. 18, 72, 232; L.2000 chs. 84, 121, 278, eff. 7/1/2000.)

§46.2-1026. Flashing high-intensity amber warning lights.

High-intensity flashing, blinking, or alternating amber warning lights visible for at least 500 feet, of types approved by the Superintendent, shall be used on any vehicle engaged in either escorting or towing over-dimensional materials, equipment, boats, or manufactured housing units by authority of a highway hauling permit issued pursuant to §46.2-1139. Such lights shall be mounted on the top of the escort and tow vehicles and on the upper rear end of the over-dimensional vehicles or loads for maximum visibility, front and rear. However, any vehicles operating under a permit issued pursuant to §46.2-1139 shall be deemed to be in compliance with the requirements of this section if accompanied by escort vehicles.

The provisions of this section shall apply only to vehicles or loads which are either (i) more than twelve feet wide or (ii) more than seventy-five feet long.

§46.2-1027. Warning lights on certain demonstrator vehicles.

Dealers or businesses engaged in the sale of fire, rescue, or law-enforcement vehicles or ambulances may, for demonstration purposes, equip such vehicles with colored warning lights.

§46.2-1028. Auxiliary lights on fire-fighting, Virginia Department of Transportation and other emergency vehicles.

Any fire-fighting vehicle, ambulance, rescue or life-saving vehicle, Virginia Department of Transportation vehicle or wrecker may be equipped with clear auxiliary lights which shall be used exclusively for lighting emergency scenes. Such lights shall be of a type approved by the Superintendent, and shall not be used in a manner which may blind or interfere with the vision of the drivers of approaching vehicles. In no event shall such lights be lighted while the vehicle is in motion.

(Chgd. by L.1996 ch. 403, eff. 7/1/96.)

§46.2-1029. Auxiliary lights on law-enforcement vehicles.

Notwithstanding any other provision of this article, any government-owned law-enforcement vehicle may be equipped with clear auxiliary lights of a type approved by the Superintendent. Such lights may be used to light emergency scenes and other areas for the purpose of detecting offenders, apprehending violators of law, and in performing other reasonably necessary law-enforcement functions. Such lights may be used when the vehicle on which they are mounted is standing or proceeding at a speed of no more than fifteen miles per hour. Such lights shall not be used in a manner which may blind or interfere with the vision of the operators of approaching vehicles.

Any law-enforcement officer may also use spotlights, as authorized in §46.2-1019, for the purpose and in the manner described herein.

§46.2-1029.1. Flashing of head lights on certain vehicles.

Emergency vehicles as defined in subsection C of §46.2-920 may be equipped with the means to flash their head lights when their warning lights are activated if (i) the head lights are wired to allow either the high beam or low beam to flash, but not both, and (ii) the head light system includes a switch or device which prevents flashing of head lights when head lights are required to be lighted under §46.2-1030.

§46.2-1030. When lights to be lighted; number of lights to be lighted at any time; use of warning lights.

A. Every vehicle in operation on a highway in the Commonwealth shall display lighted headlights and illuminating devices as required by this article (i) from sunset to sunrise, (ii) during any other time when, because of rain, smoke, fog, snow, sleet, insufficient light, or other unfavorable atmospheric conditions, visibility is reduced to a degree whereby persons or vehicles on the highway are not clearly discernible at a distance of 500 feet, and (iii) whenever windshield wipers are in use as a result of fog, rain, sleet, or snow. The provisions of this subsection, however, shall not apply to instances when windshield wipers are used intermittently in misting rain, sleet, or snow.

B. Not more than four lights used to provide general illumination ahead of the vehicle, including at least two headlights and any other combination of fog lights or other auxiliary lights approved by the Superintendent, shall be lighted at any time. However, this limitation shall not preclude the display of warning lights authorized in §§46.2-1020 through 46.2-1027, or other lights as may be authorized by the Superintendent.

C. Vehicles equipped with warning lights authorized in §§46.2-1020 through 46.2-1027 shall display lighted warning lights as authorized in such sections at all times when responding to emergency calls, towing disabled vehicles, or constructing, repairing, and maintaining public highways or utilities on or along public highways, except that amber lights on vehicles designed with a ramp on wheels and a hydraulic lift with a capacity to haul or tow another vehicle, commonly referred to as "rollbacks," need not be lit while the vehicle is in motion unless it is actually towing a vehicle.

D. The failure to display lighted headlights and illuminating devices under the conditions set forth in clause (iii) of subsection A of this section shall not constitute negligence per se, nor shall violation of clause (iii) of subsection A of this section constitute a defense to any claim for personal injury or recovery of medical expenses for injuries sustained in a motor vehicle accident.

E. No demerit points shall be assessed for failure to display lighted headlights and illuminating devices during periods of fog, rain, sleet, or snow in violation of clause (iii) of subsection A of this section.

F. No citation for a violation of clause (iii) of subsection A of this section shall be issued unless the officer issuing such citation has cause to stop or arrest the driver of such motor vehicle for the violation of some other provision of this Code or local ordinance relating to the operation, ownership, or maintenance of a motor vehicle or any criminal statute.

(Chgd. by L.1997 chs. 25, 589, eff. 7/1/97.)

§46.2-1031. Requirements as to single-beam head lights.

Approved single-beam head lights shall be aimed in accordance with regulations promulgated by the Superintendent so as not to project a glaring or dazzling light to persons approaching such head lights and shall be of sufficient intensity to reveal persons and objects at a distance of at least 200 feet.

§46.2-1032. Requirements as to multiple-beam head lights.

Approved multiple-beam head lights shall be aimed in accordance with regulations promulgated by the Superintendent, based on recommendations of the Society of Automotive Engineers. The high beam of any such lights shall be of sufficient intensity to reveal persons and objects at least 350 feet ahead. At least one nonglaring low beam shall be provided and shall be of such intensity as to reveal persons and objects at least 100 feet ahead.

§46.2-1033. Indicator light required.

Every motor vehicle operated on a highway shall be equipped with a working indicator light that indicates to the driver when the high beam of the head lights is being used.

§46.2-1034. When dimming head lights required.

Whenever a vehicle is being driven on a highway or a portion thereof which is sufficiently lighted to reveal any person or object upon such highway at a distance of 350 feet ahead, the operator of such vehicle shall use the low beam of his vehicle's head lights or shall dim the head lights if the vehicle has single-beam lights. Whenever a vehicle approaches an oncoming vehicle within 500 feet, the driver of such vehicle shall use the low beam of his vehicle's head lights so aimed that glaring rays are not projected into the eyes of the oncoming driver or dim the head lights, if the vehicle has single-beam lights. Whenever the driver of any motor vehicle approaches from the rear or follows within 200 feet of another vehicle proceeding in the same direction, the driver shall use the low beam of his vehicle's head lights or shall dim the head lights if the vehicle has single-beam lights.

§46.2-1035, Dimming head lights on parked vehicles.

Whenever a vehicle is parked so that the beam from its head lights will glare into the eyes of the driver of a vehicle approaching on a highway, the operator of the parked vehicle shall dim or use the low beam of such lights so that glaring rays are not projected into the eyes of an approaching driver.

§46.2-1036. Acetylene lights on antique motor vehicles.

Antique motor vehicles as defined in §46.2-100 may be equipped with acetylene head lights, tail lights, and lights to illuminate their rear license plates as provided in regulations promulgated by the Superintendent.

§46.2-1037. Lights on parked vehicles.

Any vehicle parked or stopped on a highway, whether attended or unattended, between sunset and sunrise shall display at least one light projecting a white or amber light visible in clear weather from a distance of 500 feet to the front of such vehicle and projecting a red light visible under like conditions from a distance of 500 feet to the rear. No lights, however, need be displayed upon any such vehicle when legally parked.

§46.2-1038. When turn signals required; exceptions.

A. Any motor vehicle, trailer, or semitrailer which is so constructed or carries a load in such a manner as to prevent a hand and arm signal required in §46.2-849 from being visible both to the front and rear of such motor vehicle, trailer, or semitrailer or any vehicle the driver of which is incapable of giving the required hand and arm signals, shall be equipped with electrical turn signals which meet the requirements of this title and are of a type that has been approved by the Superintendent. A tractor truck, however, need not be equipped with electrical turn signals on the rear if it is equipped with double faced signal lights mounted on the front fenders or on the sides near the front of the vehicle clearly visible to the rear.

B. It shall be unlawful for any person to drive on any highway a motor vehicle registered in the Commonwealth and manufactured or assembled after January 1, 1955, unless such vehicle is equipped with such turn signals on both front and rear.

C. Any such turn signal may be used in lieu of the hand and arm signal required by §46.2-849.

D. Subsections A and B of this section shall not apply to any motorcycle. The provisions of this section shall not apply to motor vehicles, trailers, or semitrailers used for agricultural or horticultural purposes and exempted from registration under Article 6 (§46.2-662 et seq.) of Chapter 6 of this title.

§46.2-1039. Requirements of turn signals; regulations.

Every turn signal used to give a signal of intention to turn a vehicle shall be so constructed and so installed as to give a signal plainly visible in clear weather and under normal traffic conditions from a distance of at least 100 feet to the rear and 100 feet to the front of the vehicle. No front turn signal, however, shall be required on vehicles manufactured before January 1, 1943.

The Superintendent may promulgate regulations not inconsistent with this section and §46.2-1038 governing the construction, location, and operation of turn signals and the color of lights which may be used in any such signal device. Nothing contained herein, however, shall prohibit the requiring of turn signals on any vehicle whose driver is prevented by any reason from giving the hand and arm signal required in §46.2-849.

§46.2-1040. Hazard lights.

Motor vehicles, trailers, and semitrailers, when temporarily stopped on the traveled or paved portion of the highway so as to create a traffic hazard, shall flash all four turn signals simultaneously to signal approaching motorists of the existing hazard whenever such vehicle is equipped with a device which will cause the four turn signals to flash simultaneously. All four turn signals may be flashed simultaneously on a vehicle slowed or stopped at the scene of a traffic hazard or when traveling at a speed of thirty miles per hour or less, but in no other event shall all four signals be flashed simultaneously while the vehicle is traveling faster than thirty miles per hour.

School buses shall flash all four turn signals when approaching and stopping at railroad grade crossings.

ARTICLE 4
TIRES

§46.2-1041. Restrictions as to solid rubber tires.

Every tire, other than a pneumatic tire, made of rubber on a vehicle moved on any highway shall have rubber on its entire traction surface at least one inch thick above the edge of the flange of the entire periphery. No vehicle equipped with such tires shall be operated on any highway in the Commonwealth unless a permit therefor is first secured from the Commonwealth Transportation Board.

§46.2-1042. Sale, etc., of regrooved or recut tires prohibited.

No person shall sell or offer for sale, or have in his possession with intent to sell any motor vehicle tire unless that tire (i) meets or exceeds standards established by the Society of Automotive Engineers, the American National Standards Institute, Inc., or the federal Department of Transportation and (ii) is marked in accordance with those standards.

No person shall knowingly operate on any highway in the Commonwealth a Virginia registered motor vehicle equipped with any regrooved or recut tire unless that tire (i) meets or exceeds standards established by the Society of Automotive Engineers, the American National Standards Institute, Inc., or the federal Department of Transportation and (ii) is marked in accordance with those standards.

Any person violating the provisions of this section shall be guilty of a Class 1 misdemeanor.

(Chgd. by L.1996 ch. 92, eff. 7/1/96.)

§46.2-1043. Tire tread depth.

A. No person shall operate a motor vehicle, trailer, or semitrailer on any highway in the Commonwealth if it is equipped with one or more tires which:

1. When measured in any two adjacent major tread grooves where the tread is thinnest, at three equally spaced intervals around the circumference of the tire and exclusive of "tiebars" by a tread depth gauge calibrated in thirty-seconds of an inch, are found to have tread depth of less than two thirty-seconds of an inch at such locations; or

2. When equipped with tread wear indicators, are found to have such indicators in contact with pavement at any two adjacent grooves at three equally spaced intervals around the circumference of the tire.

B. No motor vehicle, trailer, or semitrailer shall be issued a safety inspection approval sticker if equipped with any tire whose use is prohibited under the provisions of this section.

C. This section shall not apply to tires mounted on dual wheels installed on motor vehicles which have seats for more than seven passengers and are (i) operated wholly within a municipality, or (ii) operated by urban and suburban bus lines. For purposes of this section, "urban and suburban bus lines" are defined as bus lines operating over regular scheduled routes the majority of whose passengers use the buses for traveling one-way distances not exceeding forty miles on the same day between their residence and their place of work, shopping areas, or schools.

D. The foregoing exemptions shall not apply to buses owned or operated by any public school district, private school, or contract operator of school buses.

E. The provisions of this section shall not apply to any vehicle not required to be registered or licensed.

§46.2-1044. Cleats, etc., on tires; chains; tires with studs.

No tire on a vehicle moved on a highway shall have on its periphery any block, stud, flange, cleat, spike, or any other protuberance of any material other than rubber which projects beyond the tread of the traction surface of the tire. It shall be permissible, however, to use on the highways farm machinery having protuberances which will not injure the highway and to use tire chains of reasonable proportions when required for safety because of snow, ice, or other conditions tending to cause a vehicle to slide or skid. It shall also be permissible to use on any vehicle whose gross weight does not exceed 10,000 pounds tires with studs which project no more than one-sixteenth of an inch beyond the tread of the traction surface of the tire when compressed if the studs cover no more than three percent of the traction surface of the tire.

The use of studded tires shall be permissible only from October 15 to April 15.

§46.2-1045. Sale of tires having cleats, etc., prohibited; studded tires excepted.

No person shall sell to any resident of the Commonwealth a tire which shall have on its periphery any block, stud, flange, cleat, spike, or any other protuberance of any material other than rubber which projects beyond the tread of the traction surface of the tire. Farm machinery having protuberances which will not injure the highway and tire chains of reasonable proportions may, however, be sold. It shall also be permissible to sell studded tires whose use is permitted under the provisions of this article. Violation of this section shall constitute a Class 1 misdemeanor.

§46.2-1046. Traction engines and tractors.

The Commonwealth Transportation Board and local authorities in their respective jurisdictions may, in their discretion, issue special permits authorizing the operation on a highway of traction engines or tractors having movable tracks with transverse corrugations upon the periphery of such movable tracks.

ARTICLE 5
EXHAUST SYSTEM

Section

§46.2-1047. Muffler cutout, etc., illegal.

It shall be unlawful to sell or offer for sale any (i) muffler without interior baffle plates or other effective muffling device or (ii) gutted muffler, muffler cutout, or straight exhaust. It shall be unlawful for any person to operate on the highways in the Commonwealth a motor vehicle equipped with a gutted muffler, muffler cutout, or straight exhaust.

§46.2-1048. Pollution control systems or devices.

No motor vehicle registered in the Commonwealth and manufactured for the model year 1973 or for subsequent model years shall be operated on the highways in the Commonwealth unless it is equipped with an air pollution control system, device, or combination of such systems or devices installed in accordance with federal laws and regulations.

It shall be unlawful for any person to operate a motor vehicle, as herein described, on the highways in the Commonwealth with its pollution control system or device removed or otherwise rendered inoperable.

It shall be unlawful for any person to operate on the highways in the Commonwealth a motor vehicle, as described in this section, equipped with any emission control system or device unless it is of a type installed as standard factory equipment, or comparable to that designed for use upon the particular vehicle as standard factory equipment.

No motor vehicle, as described in this section, shall be issued a safety inspection approval sticker unless it is equipped as provided under the foregoing provisions of this section or if it violates this section.

The provisions of this section shall not prohibit or prevent shop adjustments or replacements of equipment for maintenance or repair or the conversion of engines to low polluting fuels, such as, but not limited to, natural gas or propane, so long as such action does not degrade the antipollution capabilities of the vehicle power system.

§46.2-1049. Exhaust system in good working order.

No person shall drive and no owner of a motor vehicle shall permit or allow the operation of any vehicle on a highway unless it is equipped with an exhaust system of a type installed as standard factory equipment, or comparable to that designed for use on the particular vehicle as standard factory equipment, in good working order and in constant operation to prevent excessive or unusual noise. An exhaust system shall not be deemed to prevent excessive or unusual noise if it permits the escape of noise in excess of that permitted by the standard factory equipment exhaust system of private passenger motor vehicles or trucks of standard make.

The term "exhaust system," as used in this section, means all the parts of a motor vehicle through which the exhaust passes after leaving the engine block.

Chambered pipes are not an effective muffling device to prevent excessive or unusual noise.

§46.2-1050. Mufflers on motorcycles.

It shall be unlawful for any person to operate or cause to be operated any motorcycle not equipped with a muffler or other sound dissipative device in good working order and in constant operation.

No person shall remove or render inoperative, or cause to be removed or rendered inoperative, other than for purposes of maintenance, repair or replacement, any muffler or sound dissipative device on a motorcycle.

§46.2-1051. Certain local governments may impose restrictions on operations of certain mopeds, mini-bikes, trail-bikes, and go-carts.

The governing body of any county, city, or town which is located within the Northern Virginia Planning District may provide by ordinance that no person shall operate and no owner shall permit the operation of, either on a highway or on public or private property within 500 feet of any residential district, any motorcycle, moped, motorized bicycle, motorcycle-like device commonly known as a trail-bike or mini-bike, or motorized cart commonly known as a go-cart unless it is equipped with an exhaust system of a type installed as standard equipment, or comparable to that designed for use on that particular vehicle or device as standard factory equipment, in good working order and in constant operation to prevent excessive noise.

ARTICLE 6
WINDSHIELDS AND WINDOWS

§46.2-1052. Tinting films, signs, decals, and stickers on windshields, etc.; penalties.

A. Except as otherwise provided in this article or permitted by federal law, it shall be unlawful for any person to operate any motor vehicle on a highway with any sign, poster, colored or tinted film, sun-shading material, or other colored material on the windshield, front or rear side windows, or rear windows of such motor vehicle. This provision, however, shall not apply to any certificate or other paper required by law or permitted by the Superintendent to be placed on a motor vehicle's windshield or window.

The size of stickers or decals used by counties, cities, and towns in lieu of license plates shall be in compliance with regulations promulgated by the Superintendent. Such stickers shall be affixed on the windshield at a location designated by the Superintendent.

B. Notwithstanding the foregoing provisions of this section, whenever a motor vehicle is equipped with a mirror on each side of such vehicle, so located as to reflect to the driver of such vehicle a view of the highway for at least 200 feet to the rear of such vehicle, any or all of the following shall be lawful:

1. To drive a motor vehicle equipped with one optically grooved clear plastic right-angle rear view lens attached to one rear window of such motor vehicle, not exceeding eighteen inches in diameter in the case of a circular lens or not exceeding eleven inches by fourteen inches in the case of a rectangular lens, which enables the driver of the motor vehicle to view below the line of sight as viewed through the rear window;

2. To have affixed to the rear side windows, rear window or windows of a motor vehicle any sticker or stickers, regardless of size; or

3. To drive a motor vehicle when the driver's clear view of the highway through the rear window or windows is otherwise obstructed.

C. Except as provided in §46.2-1053, but notwithstanding the foregoing provisions of this section, no sun-shading or tinting film may be applied or affixed to any window of a motor vehicle unless such motor vehicle is equipped with a mirror on each side of such motor vehicle, so located as to reflect to the driver of the vehicle a view of the highway for at least 200 feet to the rear of such vehicle, and the sun-shading or tinting film is applied or affixed in accordance with the following:

1. No sun-shading or tinting films may be applied or affixed to the rear side windows or rear window or windows of any motor vehicle operated on the highways of this Commonwealth that reduce the total light transmittance of such window to less than thirty-five percent;

2. No sun-shading or tinting films may be applied or affixed to the front side windows of any motor vehicle operated on the highways of this Commonwealth that reduce total light transmittance of such window to less than fifty percent;

3. No sun-shading or tinting films shall be applied or affixed to any window of a motor vehicle that (i) have a reflectance of light exceeding twenty percent or (ii) produce a holographic or prism effect.

Any person who operates a motor vehicle on the highways of this Commonwealth with sun-shading or tinting films that (i) have a total light transmittance less than that required by subdivisions 1 and 2 of this subsection, (ii) have a reflectance of light exceeding twenty percent, or (iii) produce holographic or prism effects shall be guilty of a traffic infraction but shall not be awarded any demerit points by the Commissioner for the violation.

Any person or firm who applies or affixes to the windows of any motor vehicle in Virginia sun-shading or tinting films that (i) reduce the light transmittance to levels less than that allowed in subdivisions 1 and 2 of this subsection, (ii) have a reflectance of light exceeding twenty percent, or (iii) produce holographic or prism effects shall be guilty of a Class 3 misdemeanor for the first offense and of a Class 2 misdemeanor for any subsequent offense.

D. The Division of Purchases and Supply, pursuant to §2.1-446, shall determine the proper standards for equipment or devices used to measure light transmittance through windows of motor vehicles. Law-enforcement officers shall use only such equipment or devices to measure light transmittance through windows that meet the standards established by the Division. Such measurements made by law-enforcement officers shall be given a tolerance of minus seven percentage points.

E. No film or darkening material may be applied on the windshield except to replace the sunshield in the uppermost area as installed by the manufacturer of the vehicle.

F. Nothing in this section shall prohibit the affixing to the rear window of a motor vehicle of a single sticker no larger than twenty square inches if such sticker is totally contained within the lower five inches of the glass of the rear window, nor shall subsection B of this section apply to a motor vehicle to which but one such sticker is so affixed.

G. Nothing in this section shall prohibit applying to the rear side windows or rear window of any multi-purpose passenger vehicle or pickup truck sun-shading or tinting films that reduce the total light transmittance of such window or windows below thirty-five percent.

H. As used in this article:

"Front side windows" means those windows located adjacent to and forward of the driver's seat;

"Holographic effect" means a picture or image that may remain constant or change as the viewing angle is changed;

"Multipurpose passenger vehicle" means any motor vehicle that is (i) designed to carry no more than ten persons and (ii) constructed either on a truck chassis or with special features for occasional off-road use;

"Prism effect" means a visual, iridescent, or rainbow-like effect that separates light into various colored components that may change depending on viewing angle;

"Rear side windows" means those windows located to the rear of the driver's seat;

"Rear window" or "rear windows" means those windows which are located to the rear of the passenger compartment of a motor vehicle and which are approximately parallel to the windshield.

I. Notwithstanding the foregoing provisions of this section, sun-shading material which was applied or installed prior to July 1, 1987, in a manner and on which windows not then in violation of Virginia law, shall continue to be lawful, provided that it can be shown by appropriate receipts that such material was installed prior to July 1, 1987.

J. Where a person is convicted within one year of a second or subsequent violation of this section involving the operation of the same vehicle having a tinted or smoked windshield, the court, in addition to any other penalty, may order the person so convicted to remove such tinted or smoked windshield from the vehicle.

K. The provisions of this section shall not apply to law-enforcement vehicles.

L. The provisions of subdivision C 1 of this section shall not apply to sight-seeing carriers as defined in §46.2-2200 and limousine and executive sedan carriers as defined in §46.2-2500.

(Chgd. by L.1997 chs. 744, 880; L.1998 ch. 133; L.1999 ch. 75, eff. 7/1/99.)

§46.2-1053. Equipping certain motor vehicles with sun-shading or tinting films or applications.

Notwithstanding the provisions of §46.2-1052, a motor vehicle operated by or regularly used to transport any person with a medical condition which renders him susceptible to harm or injury from exposure to sunlight or bright artificial light may be equipped, on its windshield and any or all of its windows, with sun-shading or tinting films or applications which reduce the transmission of light into the vehicle to levels not less than thirty-five percent. Such sun-shading or tinting film when applied to the windshield of a motor vehicle shall not cause the total light transmittance to be reduced to any level less than seventy percent except for the upper five inches of such windshield or the AS–1 line, whichever is closer to the top of the windshield. Vehicles equipped with such sun-shading or tinting films shall not be operated on any highway unless, while being so operated, the driver or an occupant of the vehicle has in his possession a written authorization issued by the Commissioner of the Department of Motor Vehicles authorizing such operation. The Commissioner shall issue such written authorization only upon receipt of a signed statement from a licensed physician or licensed optometrist (i) identifying with reasonable specificity the person seeking the written authorization and (ii) stating that, in the physician's or optometrist's professional opinion, the equipping of a vehicle with sun-shading or tinting films or applications is necessary to safeguard the health of the person seeking the written authorization. Written authorizations issued by the Commissioner under this section shall be valid so long as the condition requiring the use of sun-shading or tinting films or applications persists or until the vehicle is sold, whichever first occurs. Such written authorizations shall permit the approval of any such vehicle upon its safety inspection as required by this chapter if such vehicle otherwise qualifies for inspection approval. In the discretion of the Commissioner, one or more written authorizations may be issued to an individual or a family. The Division of Purchases and Supply, pursuant to §2.1-446, shall determine the proper standards for equipment or devices used to measure light transmittance through windows of motor vehicles. Law-enforcement officers shall use only such equipment or devices to measure light transmittance through windows that meet the standards established by the Division. Such measurements made by law-enforcement officers shall be given a tolerance of minus seven percentage points.

(Chgd. by L.1996 chs. 943, 994, eff. 7/1/96.)

§46.2-1054. Suspension of objects or alteration of vehicle so as to obstruct view of driver.

It shall be unlawful for any person to drive a motor vehicle on a highway in the Commonwealth with any object or objects, other than a rear view mirror, sun visor, or other equipment of the motor vehicle approved by the Superintendent, suspended from any part of the motor vehicle in such a manner as to obstruct the driver's clear view of the highway through the windshield, the front side windows, or the rear window, or to alter a passenger-carrying vehicle in such a manner as to obstruct the driver's view through the windshield. However, this section shall not apply (i) when the driver's clear view of the highway through the rear window is obstructed if such motor vehicle is equipped with a mirror on each side, so located as to reflect to the driver a view of the highway for at least 200 feet to the rear of such vehicle or (ii) to safety devices installed on the windshields of vehicles owned by private waste haulers or local governments and used to transport solid waste.

§46.2-1055. Windshield wipers.

Every permanent windshield on a motor vehicle shall be equipped with a device for cleaning snow, rain, moisture, or other matter from the windshield directly in front of the driver. The device shall be so constructed as to be controlled or operated by the driver of the vehicle. Every such device on a school bus or a vehicle designed or used to carry passengers for compensation or hire or as a public conveyance shall be of a mechanically or electrically operated type. The device or devices on any motor vehicle manufactured or assembled after January 1, 1943, shall clean both the right and left sides of the windshield and shall be of a mechanically or electrically operated type.

§46.2-1055.1. Windshield defroster or defogger.

Every Virginia-registered motor vehicle manufactured for the 1969 or subsequent model years and required to be equipped with a windshield shall be equipped with a windshield defroster or defogger. The defroster or defogger shall be in good working order at all times when the vehicle is operated on the highways.

§46.2-1056. When safety glass required.

It shall be unlawful for any person to drive on any highway a motor vehicle registered in the Commonwealth and manufactured or assembled after January 1, 1935, and designed or used for the purpose of carrying persons for compensation or hire or as a public conveyance to transport school children and others, unless such vehicle is equipped with safety glass wherever glass is used in doors, windows, and windshields.

It shall be unlawful to drive on any highway any motor vehicle registered in the Commonwealth, manufactured or assembled after January 1, 1936, unless the vehicle is equipped with safety glass approved by the Superintendent, or meets the standards and specifications of the American National Standards Institute, Incorporated, or the regulations of the federal Department of Transportation whenever glass is used in doors, windows, and windshields.

The term "safety glass" as used in this section shall mean any product composed of glass so manufactured, fabricated or treated as substantially to prevent shattering and flying of the glass when struck or broken. The Commissioner shall maintain a list of types of glass approved by the Superintendent as conforming to the specifications and requirements for safety glass as set forth in this section and shall not issue a license for or relicense any motor vehicle subject to the provisions herein stated unless such motor vehicle is equipped as herein provided with the approved type of glass.

No glazing material other than safety glass shall be used in any motor vehicle registered in the Commonwealth, except that the Superintendent may permit safety glazing materials other than glass to be used in lieu of safety glass in portions of motor vehicles, trailers, and semitrailers designated by him, provided any such material bears a trade name or identifying mark, and has been submitted to and approved by the Superintendent.

If any person drives any vehicle in violation of this section while under a certificate issued by the State Corporation Commission, in addition to the penalty provided in §46.2-113, the certificate of such person may, in the discretion of the State Corporation Commission, be suspended until this section is satisfactorily complied with.

Replacement safety glass installed in any part of a vehicle other than the windshield need not bear a trademark or name, provided (i) the glass consists of two or more sheets of glass separated by a glazing material, (ii) the glass is cut from a piece of approved safety glass, and (iii) the edge of the glass can be observed.

§46.2-1057. Windshields.

It shall be unlawful for any person to drive on a highway in the Commonwealth any motor vehicle or reconstructed motor vehicle, other than a motorcycle, registered in the Commonwealth, which was manufactured, assembled or reconstructed after July 1, 1970, unless the motor vehicle is equipped with a windshield.

§46.2-1058. Replacement of glass in vehicle.

It shall be unlawful for any person to replace any glass in any vehicle with any material other than an approved type of safety glass. Safety glazing materials other than glass approved by the Superintendent as provided in §46.2-1056 may, however, be used to replace safety glass in any portion of a motor vehicle which has been designated for such use by the Superintendent.

ARTICLE 7
HORNS, SIRENS, AND WHISTLES

§46.2-1059. Horns.

Every motor vehicle driven on a highway shall be equipped with a working horn capable of emitting sound audible under normal conditions for at least 200 feet.

§46.2-1060. Illegal sirens, whistles, etc.; unlawful use of warning devices; exceptions.

It shall be unlawful for any vehicle to be equipped with or for any person to use on any vehicle any siren or exhaust, compression or spark plug whistle, or horn except as may be authorized in this title. It shall be unlawful for any vehicle operated on a public highway to be equipped with any warning device that is not of a type that has been approved by the Superintendent. It shall further be unlawful for any person at any time to use a horn otherwise than as a reasonable warning or to make any unnecessary or unreasonably loud or harsh sound by means of a horn or other warning device. However, vehicles of common carriers or extraordinarily large and heavy vehicles may be equipped with such type of warning device as the Superintendent may require or permit.

Notwithstanding the provisions of this article, a siren, bell, or supplemental horn may be used on a vehicle as a noisemaker for an alarm system if the device is installed so as to prohibit actuation of the system by the driver while the vehicle is in motion.

§46.2-1061. Sirens or exhaust whistles on emergency vehicles.

Every law-enforcement vehicle, every vehicle authorized to be equipped with warning lights pursuant to §§46.2-1022 and 46.2-1023 shall be equipped with a siren, exhaust whistle, or air horn designed to give automatically intermittent signals. Such devices shall be of types not prohibited by the Superintendent.

§46.2-1062. Approval of warning devices.

The Superintendent may promulgate regulations relating to the construction, mounting, use, and number of warning devices for which there shall be an approval fee as prescribed in §46.2-1008.

ARTICLE 8
STEERING AND SUSPENSION SYSTEMS

§46.2-1063. Alteration of suspension system; bumper height limits; raising body above frame rail.

No person shall drive on a public highway any motor vehicle registered as a passenger motor vehicle if it has been modified by alteration of its altitude from the ground to the extent that its bumpers, measured to any point on the lower edge of the main horizontal bumper bar, exclusive of any bumper guards, are not within the range of fourteen inches to twenty-two inches above the ground. Notwithstanding the foregoing provisions of this section, the range of bumper heights for motor vehicles bearing street rod license plates issued pursuant to §46.2-747 shall be nine to twenty-two inches.

No vehicle shall be modified to cause the vehicle body or chassis to come in contact with the ground, expose the fuel tank to damage from collision, or cause the wheels to come in contact with the body under normal operation. No part of the original suspension system of a motor vehicle shall be disconnected to defeat the safe operation of its suspension system. However, nothing contained in this section shall prevent the installation of heavy duty equipment, including shock absorbers and overload springs. Nothing contained in this section shall prohibit the driving on a public highway of a motor vehicle with normal wear to the suspension system if such normal wear does not adversely affect the control of the vehicle.

No person shall drive on a public highway any motor vehicle registered as a truck if it has been modified by alteration of its altitude from the ground to the extent that its bumpers, measured to any point on the lower edge of the main horizontal bumper bar, exclusive of any bumper guards, do not fall within the limits specified herein for its gross vehicle weight rating category. The front bumper height of trucks whose gross vehicle weight ratings are 4,500 pounds or less shall be no less than 14 inches and no more than 28 inches and their rear bumper height shall be no less than 14 inches and no more than 28 inches. The front bumper height of trucks whose gross vehicle weight ratings are 4,501 pounds to 7,500 pounds shall be no less than 14 inches and no more than 29 inches, and their rear bumper height shall be no less than 14 inches and no more than 30 inches. The front bumper height of trucks whose gross vehicle weight ratings are 7,501 pounds to 15,000 pounds shall be no less than 14 inches and no more than 30 inches and their rear bumper height shall be no less than 14 inches and no more than 31 inches. Bumper height limitations contained in this section shall not apply to trucks with gross vehicle weight ratings in excess of 15,000 pounds. For the purpose of this section, the term "truck" includes pickup and panel trucks, and "gross vehicle weight ratings" means manufacturer's gross vehicle weight ratings established for that vehicle as indicated by a number, plate, sticker, decal, or other device affixed to the vehicle by its manufacturer.

In the absence of bumpers, and in cases where bumper heights have been lowered, height measurements under the foregoing provisions of this section shall be made to the bottom of the frame rail. However, if bumper heights have been raised, height measurements under the foregoing provisions of this section shall be made to the bottom of the main horizontal bumper bar.

No vehicle shall be operated on a public highway if it has been modified by any means so as to raise its body more than three inches, in addition to any manufacturer's spacers and bushings, above the vehicle's frame rail or manufacturer's attachment points on the frame rail.

This section shall not apply to specially designed or modified motor vehicles when driven off the public highways in races and similar events. Such motor vehicles may be lawfully towed on the highways of the Commonwealth.

§46.2-1064. Modification of front-end suspension by use of lift blocks.

No motor vehicle whose front-end suspension has been modified by the use of lift blocks shall be driven on any highway in the Commonwealth.

§46.2-1065. Steering gear; installation, sale, etc., of repair kit or preventive maintenance kit for use on part of steering gear prohibited.

Every motor vehicle driven on a highway shall be equipped with steering gear adequate to ensure the safe control of the vehicle. Such steering gear shall not show signs of weakness or breaking under ordinary conditions. The Superintendent may promulgate regulations establishing standards of adequacy of steering gear, which shall be the current standard specifications of steering gear adopted by the United States Bureau of Standards or the Society of Automotive Engineers, or the regulations of the federal Department of Transportation, for determining whether or not any motor vehicle operated on any highway conforms to the requirements of the Department of State Police.

No Virginia-registered motor vehicle shall be issued a safety inspection approval sticker or be operated on a highway in the Commonwealth if equipped with a repair kit or preventive maintenance kit installed on a tie rod end, idler arm, ball joint or any other part of the vehicle's steering gear.

It shall be unlawful for any person to sell or offer for sale any repair kit or preventive maintenance kit for use on a tie rod end, idler arm, ball joint, or any other part of a vehicle's steering gear to prevent wear or to repair or remove play or looseness in the steering gear components.

Nothing contained in this section shall prohibit or prevent shop adjustments or the replacement of parts or complete components of a motor vehicle's steering gear that meet Society of Automotive Engineers standards of excellence, in order to correct deficiencies in the steering gear.

ARTICLE 9
BRAKES

Section

46.2-1066. Brakes.
46.2-1067. Within what distances brakes should stop vehicle.
46.2-1068. Emergency or parking brakes.
46.2-1069. Brakes on motorcycles.
46.2-1070. Brakes on trailers.
46.2-1071. Requirements for parking.

§46.2-1066. Brakes.

Every motor vehicle when driven on a highway shall be equipped with brakes adequate to control the movements of and to stop and hold such vehicle. The brakes shall be maintained in good working order and shall conform to the provisions of this article.

Every bicycle and moped when operated on a highway shall be equipped with a brake which will enable the operator to make the braked wheels skid on dry, level, clean pavement.

§46.2-1067. Within what distances brakes should stop vehicle.

On a dry, hard, approximately level stretch of highway free from loose material, the service braking system shall be capable of stopping a motor vehicle or combination of vehicles at all times and under all conditions of loading at a speed of twenty miles per hour within the following distances:

1. Passenger motor vehicles, except buses and antique vehicles, twenty-five feet.
2. Buses, trucks, and tractor trucks, forty feet.
3. Motor vehicles registered or qualified to be registered as antique vehicles, when equipped with two-wheel brakes, forty-five feet; four-wheel brakes, twenty-five feet.
4. All combinations of vehicles, forty feet.
5. Motorcycles, thirty feet.

§46.2-1068. Emergency or parking brakes.

Every motor vehicle and combination of vehicles, except motorcycles, shall be equipped with emergency or parking brakes adequate to hold the vehicle or vehicles on any grade on which it is operated, under all conditions of loading on a surface free from snow, ice, or loose material.

§46.2-1069. Brakes on motorcycles.

Every motorcycle manufactured after July 1, 1974, and driven on a highway in the Commonwealth shall be equipped with either a split-service brake system or two independently actuated brake systems which shall act on the front as well as the rear wheel or wheels.

It shall be unlawful for any person to drive on a highway in the Commonwealth a motorcycle which was originally equipped with a brake system on both the front or rear wheel or wheels if the brake system has been altered by removing or disconnecting any of the brake-system components from any of the wheels.

§46.2-1070. Brakes on trailers.

Every semitrailer, trailer, or separate vehicle attached by a drawbar, chain, or coupling to a towing vehicle other than a farm tractor or a vehicle not required to obtain a registration certificate and having an actual gross weight of 3,000 pounds or more, shall be equipped with brakes controlled or operated by the driver of the towing vehicle, which shall conform to the specifications set forth in §46.2-1067 and shall be of a type approved by the Superintendent. Farm trailers used exclusively for hauling raw agricultural produce from farm to farm or farm to packing shed or processing plant within the normal growing area of the packing shed or processing plant and trailers or semitrailers drawn by a properly licensed motor vehicle but exempt from registration, shall be exempt from the requirements of this section.

"Gross weight" for the purpose of this section includes weight of the vehicle and the load upon such semitrailer, trailer, or separate vehicle.

This section shall not apply to any vehicle being towed for repairs, repossession, in an emergency, or being moved by a wrecker when two wheels of the towed vehicle are off the ground.

§46.2-1071. Requirements for parking.

No person having control of a motor vehicle shall allow such vehicle to stand on any highway unattended without first effectively setting the emergency or parking brake thereon, stopping the motor, and turning the front wheels into the curb or side of the roadway.

ARTICLE 10
MISCELLANEOUS EQUIPMENT

Section

§46.2-1072. Operation of vehicle without serial or identification number; requirements for stamping, cutting, or embossing numbers; regulations.

It shall be unlawful to sell or to drive on any highway in the Commonwealth any motor vehicle which does not have stamped on or cut into its motor its motor number or which does not bear a permanent serial or other identification number assigned by the manufacturer or by the Commissioner, or any trailer or semitrailer which does not bear a permanent serial or other identification number assigned by its manufacturer or the Commissioner. The number shall be stamped, cut, embossed, or attached in such a manner that it cannot be changed, altered, or removed without plainly showing evidence which would be readily detectable or which would destroy the attached plate. The number shall be die stamped, cut, or embossed into or attached to a permanent part of the vehicle which is easily accessible for verification. However, nonresident owners who are permitted to operate motor vehicles, trailers, or semitrailers without registration, under the registration provision relating to nonresidents contained in §§46.2-655 through 46.2-661 shall not be required to comply with this section before operating a motor vehicle, trailer, or semitrailer on the highways in the Commonwealth.

The Commissioner may adopt regulations to carry out the provisions of this section.

(Chgd. by L.1997 ch. 96, eff. 7/1/97.)

§46.2-1072.1. Fees.

The Commissioner may charge an appropriate fee, not to exceed twenty-five dollars per vehicle, for the examination, verification, or identification of the serial or identification number of any vehicle, motor vehicle, trailer, or semitrailer. The Commissioner may also receive applications for the issuance of an identification number and investigate the circumstances of the application. When the Commissioner is satisfied that the applicant is entitled to the identification number, the fee for the issuance of such identification number shall be five dollars. If any inspection under this provision is done at the same time as an inspection under §46.2-1605, then only one twenty-five-dollar fee shall be charged for both inspections.

(Added by L.1997 ch. 96, eff. 7/1/97.)

§46.2-1073. Engine or serial number illegible, removed, or obliterated.

The owner of a motor vehicle, trailer, or semitrailer on which the engine, serial, or other identification number has become illegible or has been removed or obliterated shall immediately apply to the Department for a new identification number for such motor vehicle, trailer, or semitrailer. The Department, when satisfied that the applicant is the lawful owner or possessor of the motor vehicle, trailer, or semitrailer may assign a new identification number and shall require that such number, together with the name of the Commonwealth or a symbol indicating the Commonwealth and the date of such assignment, be stamped, inscribed, or affixed upon such portion of the motor vehicle, trailer, or semitrailer as shall be designated by the Department. Whenever a new identification number has been assigned to and stamped, inscribed, or affixed on a motor vehicle, trailer, or semitrailer as provided in this section, the Department shall insert the number on the registration card and certificate of title or salvage/nonrepairable certificate issued the motor vehicle, trailer, or semitrailer.

(Chgd. by L.1996 chs. 591, 917, eff. 7/1/96.)

§46.2-1074. Removing or altering serial or identification numbers, decals and devices without consent of Department.

Any person who, individually or in association with one or more others, knowingly removes, changes, alters, or conceals any motor number, serial, or other identification number, decal or device affixed to a motor vehicle, trailer, semitrailer or motor vehicle part as required by federal law without the consent of the Department, shall be guilty of a Class 6 felony.

(Chgd. by L.1996 chs. 591, 917, eff. 7/1/96.)

§46.2-1075. Possession of vehicles with serial numbers removed or altered.

Any person who shall knowingly have in his possession a motor vehicle, motor vehicle part, trailer, or semitrailer whose motor number, serial number, identification number, decal or device as required by federal law has been removed, changed, or altered without the consent of the Department shall be guilty of a Class 6 felony.

(Chgd. by L.1996 chs. 591, 917, eff. 7/1/96.)

§46.2-1075.1. Tampering with gross vehicle weight ratings; penalty.

It shall be unlawful for any person willfully to remove, alter, deface, or tamper with any number, plate, bracket, sticker, decal, indication, or other device indicating the manufacturer's gross vehicle weight rating of any vehicle which (i) has a manufacturer's gross vehicle weight rating of 15,000 pounds or less and (ii) has been modified by alteration of its height from the ground. Violation of this section shall constitute a Class 3 misdemeanor.

§46.2-1076. Lettering on certain vehicles used to transport property.

A. No person shall drive, cause to be driven, or permit the driving of a "for hire" motor vehicle on the highways in the Commonwealth unless the name and address of the owner of the vehicle is plainly displayed on both sides of the vehicle. The letters and numerals in the display shall be of such size, shape, and color as to be readily legible during daylight hours from a distance of fifty feet while the vehicle is not in motion. The display shall be kept legible and may take the form of a removable device which meets the identification and legibility requirements of this section.

B. This section shall not apply to any motor vehicle:

1. Having a registered gross weight of less than 10,000 pounds;

2. Which is used exclusively for wedding, ambulance, or funeral services; or

3. Which is rented without chauffeur and operated under a valid lease which gives the lessee exclusive control of the vehicle.

C. Notwithstanding the exemptions contained in subsection B of this section, the requirements of subsection A of this section shall also apply to all motor vehicles leased to common or contract carriers of persons or property which are required to operate under certificates or permits issued by the State Corporation Commission or the Interstate Commerce Commission.

D. Subsection A of this section shall also apply to tow trucks used in providing service to the public for hire. For the purposes of this section, "tow truck" means any motor vehicle which is constructed and used primarily for towing, lifting, or otherwise moving disabled vehicles.

E. No person shall drive on the highways in the Commonwealth a pickup or panel truck, tractor truck, trailer, or semitrailer bearing any name other than that of the vehicle's owner or lessee. However, the provisions of this subsection shall not apply to advertising material for another, displayed pursuant to a valid contract.

§46.2-1077. Motor vehicles not to be equipped with television within view of driver.

No motor vehicle registered in the Commonwealth of Virginia shall be equipped with, nor shall there be used therein, a television receiver forward of the driver's seat or the screen of which would otherwise be visible to the driver while driving the vehicle. The operator of a motor vehicle which is not required to be registered in Virginia shall not operate a television receiver which violates the provisions of this section while driving in the Commonwealth.

The prohibitions contained in the foregoing provisions of this section shall not, however, include:

1. Electronic displays used in conjunction with vehicle navigation systems;

2. Closed circuit video monitors designed to operate only in conjunction with dedicated video cameras and used in rear-view systems on trucks and motor homes; and

3. Television receivers or monitors used in government-owned vehicles by law-enforcement officers and employees of the Virginia Department of Transportation in the course of their official duties.

§46.2-1078. Unlawful to operate motor vehicle, moped, or bicycle while using earphones.

It shall be unlawful for any person to operate a motor vehicle, moped, or bicycle on the highways in the Commonwealth while using earphones on or in both ears.

For the purpose of this section, "earphones" shall mean any device worn on or in both ears which converts electrical energy to sound waves or which impairs or hinders the person's ability to hear, but shall not include (i) any prosthetic device which aids the hard of hearing, (ii) earphones installed in helmets worn by motorcycle operators and riders and used as part of a communications system, or (iii) nonprosthetic, closed-ear, open-back, electronic noise-cancellation devices designed and used to enhance the hearing ability of persons who operate vehicles in high-noise environments, provided any such device is being worn by the operator of a vehicle with a gross vehicle weight rating of 26,000 pounds or more. The provisions of this section shall not apply to the driver of any emergency vehicle as defined in §46.2-920.

(Chgd. by L.1997 ch. 36, eff. 7/1/97.)

§46.2-1079. Radar detectors; demerit points not to be awarded.

A. It shall be unlawful for any person to operate a motor vehicle on the highways of the Commonwealth when such vehicle is equipped with any device or mechanism, passive or active, to detect or purposefully interfere with or diminish the measurement capabilities of any radar, laser, or other device or mechanism employed by law-enforcement personnel to measure the speed of motor vehicles on the highways of the Commonwealth for law-enforcement purposes. It shall be unlawful to use any such device or mechanism on any such motor vehicle on the highways. It shall be unlawful to sell any such device or mechanism in the Commonwealth. However, provisions of this section shall not apply to any receiver of radio waves utilized for lawful purposes to receive any signal from a frequency lawfully licensed by any state or federal agency.

This section shall not be construed to authorize the forfeiture to the Commonwealth of any such device or mechanism. Any such device or mechanism may be taken by the arresting officer if needed as evidence, and, when no longer needed, shall be returned to the person charged with a violation of this section, or at that person's request, and his expense, mailed to an address specified by him. Any unclaimed devices may be destroyed on court order after six months have elapsed from the final date for filing an appeal.

Except as provided in subsection B of this section, the presence of any such prohibited device or mechanism in or on a motor vehicle on the highways of the Commonwealth shall constitute prima facie evidence of the violation of this section. The Commonwealth need not prove that the device or mechanism in question was in an operative condition or being operated.

B. A person shall not be guilty of a violation of this section when the device or mechanism in question, at the time of the alleged offense, had no power source and was not readily accessible for use by the driver or any passenger in the vehicle.

C. This section shall not apply to motor vehicles owned by the Commonwealth or any political subdivision thereof and used by law-enforcement officers in their official duties, nor to the sale of any such device or mechanism to law-enforcement agencies for use in their official duties.

D. No demerit points shall be awarded by the Commissioner for violations of this section. Any demerit points awarded by the Commissioner prior to July 1, 1992, for any violation of this section shall be rescinded and the driving record of any person awarded demerit points for a violation of this section shall be amended to reflect such rescission.
(Chgd. by L.1998 ch. 300, eff. 7/1/98.)

§46.2-1080. Speedometer in good working order.

It shall be unlawful for any person to possess with intent to sell or offer for sale, either separately or as a part of the equipment of a motor vehicle, or to use or have as a part of the equipment of a motor vehicle, or to use or have as equipment on a motor vehicle operated on a highway any speedometer which is not in good working order.

§46.2-1081. Slow-moving vehicle emblems.

A. Every farm tractor, self-propelled unit of farm equipment or implement of husbandry, and any other vehicle designed for operation at speeds not in excess of twenty-five miles per hour or normally operated at speeds not in excess of twenty-five miles per hour, shall display a triangular slow-moving vehicle emblem on the rear of the vehicle when traveling on a public highway at any time of the day or night.

B. Should a slow-moving vehicle tow a unit on a public highway, then the towing vehicle or the towed unit shall be equipped with the slow-moving vehicle emblem as follows:

1. If the towed unit or any load thereon obscures the slow-moving vehicle emblem on the towing vehicle, the towed unit shall be equipped with a slow-moving vehicle emblem, in which case the towing vehicle need not display such emblem.

2. If the slow-moving vehicle emblem on the towing vehicle is not obscured by the towed unit or any load thereon, then either or both such vehicles may be equipped with such emblem.

C. The standards and specifications for the slow-moving vehicle emblem and the position of mounting of the emblem shall conform to standards and specifications adopted by the American Society of Agricultural Engineers, the Society of Automotive Engineers, the American National Standards Institute, Inc., or the federal Department of Transportation.

D. The use of the slow-moving vehicle emblem shall be restricted to the uses specified in this title.
(Chgd. by L.1996 ch. 82, eff. 7/1/96.)

§46.2-1082. Mirrors.

No person shall drive a motor vehicle on a highway in the Commonwealth if the vehicle is not equipped with a mirror which reflects to the driver a view of the highway for a distance of not less than 200 feet to the rear of such vehicle.

No motor vehicle registered in the Commonwealth, designed and licensed primarily for passenger vehicular transportation on the public highways and manufactured after 1968 shall be driven on the highways in the Commonwealth unless equipped with at least one outside and at least one inside rear view mirror meeting the requirements of this section.

Notwithstanding the other provisions of this section, no motor vehicle which either has no rear window, or which has a rear window so obstructed as to prevent rearward vision by means of an inside rear view mirror, shall be required to be equipped with an inside rear view mirror if such motor vehicle has horizontally and vertically adjustable outside rear view mirrors installed on both sides of such motor vehicle in such a manner as to provide the driver of such motor vehicle a rearward view along both sides of such motor vehicle for at least 200 feet.

§46.2-1083. Rear fenders, flaps, or guards required for certain motor vehicles.

No person shall operate on a highway any motor vehicle or combination of vehicles having a licensed gross weight in excess of 40,000 pounds unless the motor vehicle or combination of vehicles is equipped with rear fenders, flaps, or guards of sufficient size to substantially prevent the projection of rocks, dirt, water, or other substances to the rear. Vehicles used exclusively for hauling logs and tractor trucks shall be exempt from the provisions of this section.

§46.2-1084. Vehicle to have securely affixed seat for driver; location of such seat.

It shall be unlawful for any person to drive any motor vehicle on a highway in the Commonwealth unless it is equipped with a securely affixed seat for the driver. The seat shall be so located as to permit the driver to adequately control the steering and braking mechanisms and other instruments necessary for the safe operation of the motor vehicle.

§46.2-1085. Handlebars of motorcycles.

It shall be unlawful for any person to register or to drive any motorcycle on a highway in the Commonwealth if the motorcycle is equipped with handlebars or other type of steering mechanisms that are more than fifteen inches above the level of the motorcycle's seat.

§46.2-1086. Devices for emission of smoke screens, gas projectors or flame throwers; prohibited.

It shall be a Class 6 felony to install or to aid or abet in installing, in any manner, in or on any motor vehicle any device, appliance, equipment, or instrument of any kind, character, or description, or any part of such device, appliance, equipment, or instrument, designed for generating or emitting smoke, thereby creating what is commonly known as a "smoke screen," or of emitting any gas or flame which may be a hindrance or obstruction to traffic. It shall also be a Class 6 felony to knowingly possess or drive on the highways any motor vehicle so equipped.

Additionally, the driver's license of any person convicted of a violation of this section shall be suspended for six months from the date of conviction.

The provisions of this section shall not apply to vehicles used in applying herbicides, insecticides, or pesticides.

§46.2-1087. Forfeiture of vehicles equipped with smoke projectors, etc.

Any motor vehicle found to be equipped with any device, appliance, equipment, or instrument, as mentioned in §46.2-1086, or equipped for the installation or attachment of any "smoke screen" or gas or flame emitting device, appliance, equipment, or instrument, as so mentioned, shall be forfeited to the Commonwealth, subject to the rights of an innocent owner and lien holders. No such forfeiture, however, shall take place unless the owner or operator knows that such vehicle is so equipped.

§46.2-1088. Air conditioning units.

No motor vehicle operated on any highway shall be equipped with any air conditioning unit unless such device is of a type approved as to safety by the Superintendent. The Superintendent is authorized to promulgate regulations setting specifications relating to the design, construction, installation, maintenance, and use of such air conditioning units. No refrigerant used in such unit shall be explosive, flammable, or toxic.

§46.2-1088.1. Hood scoops.

No motor vehicle shall be operated on a public highway in the Commonwealth if any hood scoop installed thereon exceeds any of the following dimensions:

1. For any hood scoop installed on any motor vehicle manufactured for the 1990 or earlier model year: thirty-eight inches wide at its widest point, two and one-quarter inches high at its highest point measured from the junction of the dashboard and the windshield, and fifty-two and one-quarter inches long at its longest point.

2. For any hood scoop installed on any motor vehicle manufactured for the 1991 or subsequent model year: thirty-eight inches wide at its widest point, one and one-eighth inches high at its highest point measured from the junction of the dashboard and the windshield, and fifty and one-half inches long at its longest point.

ARTICLE 11
PAINT, LETTERING, AND SPECIAL EQUIPMENT FOR SCHOOL BUSES

Section

§46.2-1089. Paint and lettering on school bus.

School buses shall be painted yellow with the words "School Bus" on the front and rear in letters at least eight inches high. All school buses shall be equipped with warning devices prescribed in §46.2-1090. Only school buses as defined in §46.2-100 may be painted yellow, identified by lettering as provided in this section, and equipped with the specified warning devices. A vehicle which merely transports pupils or residents at a school from one point to another without intermittent stops for the purpose of picking up or discharging pupils need not comply with the requirements of this section.

§46.2-1089.1. Signs and markings on school buses using alternative fuels.

The State Board of Education may provide by regulation for the display of appropriate signs or other markings on school buses using alternative fuels. Such signs or markings shall conspicuously identify the vehicle as an alternatively fueled vehicle and indicate the type of alternative fuel used. No such sign or marking shall be more than 4¾ inches long or more than 3¼ inches high.

For the purposes of this section: (i) "alternative fuel" means a motor fuel used as an alternative to gasoline or diesel fuel; (ii) alcohol/gasoline blended fuels which contain less than eighty-five percent ethanol or methanol shall not be considered alternative fuels; and (iii) dual-fuel and bi-fuel vehicles equipped to operate on both a conventional fuel and an alternative fuel shall be considered alternatively fueled vehicles.

Signs and markings provided for under this section shall be in addition to other markings permitted or required by this title.

§46.2-1090. Warning devices on school buses; other buses; use thereof; penalties.

Every bus used for the principal purpose of transporting school children shall be equipped with a warning device of such type as may be prescribed by the State Board of Education after consultation with the Superintendent of State Police. Such a warning device shall indicate when such bus is either (i) stopped or about to stop to take on or discharge children, the elderly, or mentally or physically handicapped persons or (ii) stopped or about to stop for another such bus, when approaching from any direction, that is stopped or about to stop to take on or discharge any such persons. Such warning device shall be used and in operation for at least 100 feet before any proposed stop of such bus if the lawful speed limit is less than thirty-five miles per hour, and for at least 200 feet before any proposed stop of such bus if the lawful speed limit is thirty-five miles per hour or more.

Failure of a warning device to function on any school bus shall not relieve any person operating a motor vehicle from his duty to stop as provided in §§46.2-844 and 46.2-859.

Any person operating such bus who fails or refuses to equip such vehicle being driven by him with such equipment, or who fails to use such warning devices in the operation of such vehicle shall be guilty of a Class 3 misdemeanor.

Transit buses used to transport school children in the City of Hampton may be equipped with an advisory sign that extends from the left side of the bus and displays the words: "CAUTION – STUDENTS." Such sign may be equipped with not more than two warning lights of a type approved for use by the Superintendent of State Police.

(Chgd. by L.1995 ch. 106; L.1996 ch. 512, eff. 7/1/96.)

§46.2-1090.1. Warning lights on school buses.

In addition to other lights authorized by law, school buses may be equipped with flashing white or amber warning lights of types authorized by the Board of Education after consultation with the Superintendent of State Police. These warning lights shall be installed in a manner authorized by the Board after consultation with the Superintendent and shall be lighted while the bus is transporting school children during periods of reduced visibility caused by atmospheric conditions other than darkness. These warning lights may also be lighted at other times while the bus is transporting school children. Drivers of motor vehicles approaching school buses displaying lighted warning lights authorized in

this section shall not be required to stop except as required in §§46.2-844 and 46.2-859.
(Chgd. by L.1997 ch. 65, eff. 7/1/97.)

ARTICLE 12
SAFETY BELTS

§46.2-1091. Safety belts to be worn by certain bus drivers.

Any person operating a school bus shall wear the appropriate safety belt system when the bus is in motion.

Violation of this section shall constitute a Class 3 misdemeanor.

§46.2-1092. Safety lap belts or a combination of lap belts and shoulder harnesses to be installed in certain motor vehicles.

No passenger car registered in the Commonwealth and manufactured for the year 1963 or for subsequent years shall be operated on the highways in the Commonwealth unless the front seats thereof are equipped with adult safety lap belts or a combination of lap belts and shoulder harnesses of types approved by the Superintendent.

Failure to use the safety lap belts or a combination of lap belts and shoulder harnesses after installation shall not be deemed to be negligence. Nor shall evidence of such nonuse of such devices be considered in mitigation of damages of whatever nature.

No motor vehicle registered in the Commonwealth and manufactured after January 1, 1968, shall be issued a safety inspection approval sticker if any lap belt, combination of lap belt and shoulder harness, or passive belt systems required to be installed at the time of manufacture by the federal Department of Transportation have been either removed from the motor vehicle or rendered inoperable.

No passenger car, except convertibles, registered in the Commonwealth and manufactured on or after September 1, 1990, shall be operated on the highways in the Commonwealth unless the forward-facing rear outboard seats thereof are equipped with rear seat lap/shoulder belts of types required to be installed at the time of manufacture by the federal Department of Transportation.

No passenger car, including convertibles, registered in the Commonwealth and manufactured on or after September 1, 1991, shall be operated on the highways in the Commonwealth unless the forward-facing rear outboard seats thereof are equipped with rear seat lap/shoulder belts of types required to be installed at the time of manufacture by the federal Department of Transportation.

No truck, multi-purpose vehicle, or bus, except school buses and motor homes, with a gross vehicle weight rating of 10,000 pounds or less, registered in the Commonwealth and manufactured on or after September 1, 1991, shall be operated on the highways in the Commonwealth unless the forward-facing rear outboard seats thereof are equipped with rear seat lap/shoulder belts of types required to be installed at the time of manufacture by the federal Department of Transportation.

Passenger cars, trucks, multipurpose vehicles, and buses, except school buses and motor homes, registered in the Commonwealth and manufactured on or after September 1, 1992, shall not be operated on the highways in the Commonwealth unless equipped with rear seat lap/shoulder belts of types required to be installed at the time of manufacture by the federal Department of Transportation for each forward-facing rear outboard seating position on a readily removable seat.

For the purposes of this section, forward-facing rear outboard seats are defined as those designated seating positions for passengers in outside front facing seats behind the driver and front passenger seats, except any designated seating position adjacent to a walkway that is located between the seat and the near side of the vehicle and is designed to allow access to a more rearward seating position.

The Superintendent of State Police shall include in the Official Motor Vehicle Inspection Regulations a section which identifies each classification of motor vehicle required to be equipped with any of the devices described in the foregoing provisions of this section.

Such regulations shall also include a listing of the exact devices which are required to be installed in each motor vehicle classification and the model year of each motor vehicle classification on which the standards of the federal Department of Transportation first became applicable.

§46.2-1093. Requirements for safety lap belts, shoulder harnesses and combinations thereof.

Any safety lap belt or shoulder harness or any combination of lap belt and shoulder harness installed in a vehicle shall be designed and installed in such manner as to prevent or materially reduce movement of any person using the same in the event of collision or upset of the vehicle.

The Superintendent shall establish specifications or requirements for approved type safety lap belts and shoulder harnesses or any combination of lap belt and shoulder harness, attachments, and installation, in accordance with the provisions of this section. Such specifications or requirements may be the same as those specifications or requirements for safety lap belts or shoulder harnesses or any combination of lap belt and shoulder harness established by the Civil Aeronautics Administration Technical Standard Orders or regulations established by the Society of Automotive Engineers or the standards of the federal Department of Transportation, for safety lap belts and shoulder harnesses or combination of lap belts and shoulder harnesses.

No person shall sell or offer for sale any safety lap belt, shoulder harness, or any combination of lap belt and shoulder harness or attachments thereto for use in a vehicle, unless of a type which has been approved by the Superintendent.

§46.2-1094. Occupants of front seats of motor vehicles required to use safety lap belts and shoulder harnesses; penalty.

A. Each person at least sixteen years of age and occupying the front seat of a motor vehicle equipped or required by the provisions of this title to be equipped with a safety belt system, consisting of lap belts, shoulder harnesses, combinations thereof or similar devices, shall wear the appropriate safety belt system at all times while the motor vehicle is in motion on any public highway. A child under the age of sixteen years, however, shall be protected as required by the provisions of this chapter.

B. This section shall not apply to:

1. Any person for whom a licensed physician determines that the use of such safety belt system would be impractical by reason of such person's physical condition or other medical reason, provided the person so exempted carries on his person or in the vehicle a signed written statement

of the physician identifying the exempted person and stating the grounds for the exemption; or

2. Any law-enforcement officer transporting persons in custody or traveling in circumstances which render the wearing of such safety belt system impractical; or

3. Any person while driving a motor vehicle and performing the duties of a rural mail carrier for the United States Postal Service; or

4. Any person driving a motor vehicle and performing the duties of a rural newspaper route carrier, newspaper bundle hauler or newspaper rack carrier; or

5. Drivers of taxicabs; or

6. Personnel of commercial or municipal vehicles while actually engaged in the collection or delivery of goods or services, including but not limited to solid waste, where such collection or delivery requires the personnel to exit and enter the cab of the vehicle with such frequency and regularity so as to render the use of safety belt systems impractical and the safety benefits derived therefrom insignificant. Such personnel shall resume the use of safety belt systems when actual collection or delivery has ceased or when the vehicle is in transit to or from a point of final disposition or disposal, including but not limited to solid waste facilities, terminals, or other location where the vehicle may be principally garaged; or

7. Any person driving a motor vehicle and performing the duties of a utility meter reader; or

8. Law-enforcement agency personnel driving motor vehicles to enforce laws governing motor vehicle parking.

C. Any person who violates this section shall be subject to a civil penalty of twenty-five dollars to be paid into the state treasury and credited to the Literary Fund. No assignment of demerit points shall be made under Article 19 of Chapter 3 (§46.2-489 et seq.) of this title and no court costs shall be assessed for violations of this section.

D. A violation of this section shall not constitute negligence, be considered in mitigation of damages of whatever nature, be admissible in evidence or be the subject of comment by counsel in any action for the recovery of damages arising out of the operation, ownership, or maintenance of a motor vehicle, nor shall anything in this section change any existing law, rule, or procedure pertaining to any such civil action.

E. A violation of this section may be charged on the uniform traffic summons form.

F. No citation for a violation of this section shall be issued unless the officer issuing such citation has cause to stop or arrest the driver of such motor vehicle for the violation of some other provision of this Code or local ordinance relating to the operation, ownership, or maintenance of a motor vehicle or any criminal statute.

G. The governing body of any city having a population of at least 66,000 but no more than 67,000 may adopt an ordinance not inconsistent with the provisions of this section, requiring the use of safety belt systems. The penalty for violating any such ordinance shall not exceed a fine or civil penalty of twenty-five dollars.

(Chgd. by L.1997 ch. 793, eff. 7/1/97.)

ARTICLE 13
CHILD RESTRAINTS

§46.2-1095. Child restraint devices required; safety belts for children four to sixteen required; penalty.

A. Any person who drives on the highways of Virginia any motor vehicle manufactured after January 1, 1968, shall ensure that any child under the age of four whom he transports therein is provided with and properly secured in a child restraint device of a type which meets the standards adopted by the United States Department of Transportation.

B. Any person transporting any child at least four years of age, but less than sixteen years of age, shall ensure that such child is provided with and properly secured by an appropriate safety belt system when driving on the highways of Virginia in any motor vehicle manufactured after January 1, 1968, equipped or required by the provisions of this title to be equipped with a safety belt system, consisting of lap belts, shoulder harnesses, combinations thereof or similar devices.

C. A violation of this section shall not constitute negligence, be considered in mitigation of damages of whatever nature, be admissible in evidence or be the subject of comment by counsel in any action for the recovery of damages in a civil action.

D. Any person who violates subsection B of this section shall be subject to a civil penalty of twenty-five dollars to be paid into the state treasury and credited to the Child Restraint Device Special Fund pursuant to §46.2-1097. No assignment of demerit points shall be made under Article 19 (§46.2-489 et seq.) of Chapter 3 of this title and no court costs shall be assessed for violations of this section.

E. A violation of this section may be charged on the uniform traffic summons form.

F. Nothing in this section shall apply to taxicabs, school buses, executive sedans, limousines, or the rear cargo area of vehicles other than pickup trucks.

(Chgd. by L.1997 ch. 793; L.2000 ch. 736, eff. 7/1/2000.)

§46.2-1096. Exceptions for certain children.

Whenever any physician licensed to practice medicine in the Commonwealth or any other state determines, through accepted medical procedures, that use of a child restraint system by a particular child would be impractical by reason of the child's weight, physical unfitness, or other medical reason, the child shall be exempt from the provisions of this article. Any person transporting a child so exempted shall carry on his or her person or in the vehicle a signed written statement of the physician identifying the child so exempted and stating the grounds therefor.

§46.2-1097. Child restraint devices; special fund created.

The Department of Health shall operate a program to promote, purchase, and distribute child restraint devices to applicants who need a child restraint device but are unable to acquire one because of financial inability. A special fund, known as the Child Restraint Device Special Fund, shall fund the program. The Department of Health shall determine the number of child restraint devices that can be purchased by the program, based upon the amount of funds in the Child Restraint Device Special Fund, provided, however, that the requirements of the Virginia Public Procurement Act (§11-35 et seq.) shall not apply to child restraint device purchases by the Department of Health pursuant to this section. The Child Restraint Device Special Fund shall consist of all civil penalties that are collected pursuant to §46.2-1098 and other funds that may be appropriated for that purpose.

(Chgd. by L.1996 ch. 145, eff. 10/1/96.)

§46.2-1098. Penalties; violations not negligence per se.

Any person, including those subject to jurisdiction of a juvenile and domestic relations district court, found guilty of violating this article shall be subject to a civil penalty of fifty dollars for a violation of §46.2-1095, or, if applicable, a civil penalty of twenty dollars for failure to carry a statement as required by §46.2-1096. The court may waive or suspend the imposition of the penalty for a violation of §46.2-1095 if it finds that the failure of the defendant to comply with the section was due to his financial inability to acquire a child restraint system. All civil penalties collected pursuant to this section shall be paid into the Child Restraint Device Special Fund as provided for in §46.2-1097.

Violations of this article shall not constitute negligence per se; nor shall violation of this article constitute a defense to any claim for personal injuries to a child or recovery of medical expenses for injuries sustained in any motor vehicle accident.

(Chgd. by L.1996 ch. 616, eff. 7/1/96.)

§46.2-1099. Further exemptions.

This article shall not apply to:

The transporting of any child in a vehicle having an interior design which makes the use of such device impractical; or

The transporting of children by public transportation, bus, school bus, or farm vehicle.

For the purposes of this section, "farm vehicle" means a vehicle which is either (i) exempt from registration pursuant to §46.2-664, §46.2-665, §46.2-666, §46.2-667, §46.2-670, or §46.2-672, (ii) registered as a farm vehicle pursuant to §46.2-698, or (iii) owned by a resident of another state as a farm vehicle or exempt from registration by virtue of its use as a farm vehicle.

§46.2-1100. Use of standard seat belts permitted.

The use of a seat belt of the type which is standard equipment in new automobiles sold in the Commonwealth shall not violate this article if (i) the affected child is between three and four years old and (ii) the weight and size of the child is such as to make the use of such seat belt practical and the use of an approved child restraint impractical.

ARTICLE 14
MAXIMUM VEHICLE SIZE, GENERALLY

§46.2-1101. Limitations applicable throughout Commonwealth; alteration by local authorities.

The maximum size and weight of vehicles specified in Articles 14 through 17 (§46.2-1101 et seq.) of this chapter shall apply throughout the Commonwealth. Local authorities shall not alter such limitations except as expressly authorized in this title.

§46.2-1102. Size limitations inapplicable to farm machinery, agricultural multipurpose drying units, and fire-fighting equipment; amber warning lights.

A. The vehicle size limitations contained in Articles 14 through 17 (§46.2-1101 et seq.) of this chapter shall not apply to any farm machinery or agricultural multipurpose drying unit when such farm machinery or agricultural multipurpose drying unit is temporarily propelled, hauled, transported, or moved on the highway by a farm machinery distributor or dealer, fertilizer distributor, or farmer in the ordinary course of business. Nor shall those limitations apply to fire-fighting equipment of any county, city, town, or fire-fighting company or association. Any farm tractor or agricultural multipurpose drying unit wider than 108 inches, however, which is so propelled, hauled, transported, or moved on the highway shall be equipped with a safety light of a type approved by the Superintendent of State Police. The light shall be plainly visible from the rear of the tractor or agricultural multipurpose drying unit.

B. Notwithstanding subsection A of this section, any farm tractor or other farm, agricultural, or horticultural vehicle wider than 108 inches may be equipped with an amber flashing, blinking, or alternating warning light as provided in §46.2-1025. Any such light may be installed in lieu of or in addition to the safety light described in subsection A of this section. The absence of amber flashing, blinking, or alternating warning lights on any farm tractor or other farm, agricultural, or horticultural vehicle, as authorized under this subsection, shall not constitute negligence, be considered in mitigation of damages of whatever nature, be admissible in evidence or be the subject of comment by counsel in any action for the recovery of damages arising out of the operation, ownership, or maintenance of any motor vehicle or farm tractor, nor shall anything in this section change any existing law, rule, or procedure pertaining to any such civil action.

(Chgd. by L.1997 ch. 149, eff. 7/1/97.)

§46.2-1103. Greater size, weight, and load limits permitted by interstate commerce regulations.

If a federal regulation of interstate commerce permits the use in interstate commerce over the highways of Virginia or any of them, of a greater size, weight, or load limit than prescribed in this title, the Board shall prescribe a similar size, weight, and load limit for vehicles in intrastate commerce operated over the same highways.

§46.2-1104. Reduction of limits by Commonwealth Transportation Commissioner and local authorities; penalties.

The Commonwealth Transportation Commissioner, acting through district or resident engineers, may prescribe the weight, width, height, length, or speed of any vehicle or combination of vehicles passing over any highway or section of highway or bridge constituting a part of the interstate, primary, or secondary system of highways. Any limitations thus prescribed may be less than those prescribed in this title whenever an engineering study discloses that it would promote the safety of travel or is necessary for the protection of any such highway.

If the reduction of limits as provided in this section is to be effective for more than ninety days, the Commonwealth Transportation Commissioner shall prescribe such reduction in writing which shall be kept on file at the central office of the Department of Transportation. In instances where the limits, including speed limits, are to be temporarily reduced, the resident engineer for the Department of Transportation in the county wherein such highway is located shall immediately notify the Chief Engineer for the Department of Transportation of such reduction. The Chief Engineer shall either affirm or rescind the action of reducing such limits within five days from the date the limits have been posted as hereinafter provided. A list of all highways on which there has been a reduction of limits as herein provided shall be kept on file at the central office of the Department of Transportation. Anyone aggrieved by such reduction of limits may appeal directly to the Commonwealth Transportation

Commissioner for redress, and if he affirms the action of reducing such limits, the Commonwealth Transportation Board shall afford any such aggrieved person the opportunity of being heard at its next regular meeting.

The local authorities of counties, cities, and towns, where the highways are under their jurisdiction, may adopt regulations or pass ordinances decreasing the weight limits prescribed in this title for a total period of no more than ninety days in any calendar year, when an engineering study discloses that operation over such highways or streets by reason of deterioration, rain, snow, or other climatic conditions will seriously damage such highways unless such weights are reduced.

In all instances where the limits for weight, size, or speed have been reduced by the Commonwealth Transportation Commissioner or the weights have been reduced by local authorities pursuant to this section, signs stating the weight, height, width, length, or speed permitted on such highway shall be erected at each end of the section of highway affected and no such reduced limits shall be effective until such signs have been posted.

It shall be unlawful to operate a vehicle or combination of vehicles on any public highway or section thereof when the weight, size, or speed thereof exceeds the maximum posted by authority of the Commonwealth Transportation Commissioner or local authorities pursuant to this section.

Any violation of any provision of this section shall constitute a Class 2 misdemeanor. Furthermore, the vehicle or combination of vehicles involved in such violation may be held upon an order of the court until all fines and costs have been satisfied.

ARTICLE 15
MAXIMUM VEHICLE WIDTHS AND HEIGHTS

§46.2-1105. Width of vehicles generally; exceptions.

No vehicle, including any load thereon, but excluding the mirror required by §46.2-1082 and any warning device installed on a school bus pursuant to §46.2-1090, shall exceed a total outside width as follows:

1. Passenger bus operated in an incorporated city or town when authorized under §46.2-1300 – 102 inches;
2. School buses – 100 inches;
3. Vehicles hauling boats or other watercraft – 102 inches.
4. Other vehicles – 102 inches.

(Chgd. by L.1996 chs. 446, 506, eff. 7/1/96.)

§46.2-1106. *(Omitted due to limited applicability.)*

§46.2-1107. Bus widths in certain counties.

Upon application by the governing body of any county, the Commonwealth Transportation Board may permit within that county the operation of passenger buses wider than 96 inches but no wider than 102 inches.

§46.2-1108. Bus widths to comply with federal law.

If federal law permits the operation of passenger buses wider than 96 inches on the interstate highway system, the Commonwealth Transportation Board may permit the operation of passenger buses of a total outside width, excluding the mirror required by §46.2-1082, of more than 96 inches, but not exceeding more than 102 inches, on interstate and defense highways or any other four lane divided highways under the jurisdiction of the Commonwealth Transportation Board. The use of any other state highways between the aforesaid highways and the passenger bus terminals may be permitted upon application to the Board by the governing body of any county, city, or town in which such other highways are located. Any such increase in width of passenger buses or designation of highways to be used by them shall not exceed the federal law which may hereafter be adopted, or jeopardize the Commonwealth's allotment of or qualification for federal aid highway funds.

§46.2-1109. Widths of commercial vehicles.

No commercial vehicle shall exceed 102 inches in width when operating on any interstate highway or on any highway designated by the Commonwealth Transportation Board. The width limitation in this section shall not include rear view mirrors, turn signal lights, handholds for cab entry and egress, splash suppressant devices, and load-induced tire bulge. Safety devices, with the exception of rear view mirrors, shall not extend more than three inches on each side of a vehicle. The Commonwealth Transportation Board shall designate reasonable access to terminals, facilities for food, fuel, repairs, and rest. Household goods carriers and any tractor truck semitrailer combination in which the semitrailer has a length of no more than twenty-eight and one-half feet shall not be denied reasonable access to points of loading and unloading, except as designated, based on safety considerations, by the Commonwealth Transportation Board. No reasonable access designation shall be made, however, until notice of any proposed designation has been provided by the Commonwealth Transportation Commissioner to the governing body of every locality wherein any highway affected by the proposed designation is located.

For the purposes of this section, a commercial vehicle is defined as a loaded or empty motor vehicle, trailer, or semitrailer designed or regularly used for carrying freight, merchandise, or more than ten passengers, including buses, but not including vehicles used for vanpools.

(Chgd. by L.1997 ch. 773, eff. 7/1/97.)

§46.2-1110. Height of vehicles; damage to overhead obstruction; penalty.

No loaded or unloaded vehicle shall exceed a height of thirteen feet, six inches.

Nothing contained in this section shall require either the public authorities or railroad companies to provide vertical clearances of overhead bridges or structures in excess of twelve feet, six inches, or to make any changes in the vertical clearances of existing overhead bridges or structures crossing highways. The driver or owner of vehicles on highways shall be held financially responsible for any damage to overhead bridges or structures that results from collisions therewith.

The driver or owner of any vehicle colliding with an overhead bridge or structure shall immediately notify, either in person or by telephone, a law-enforcement officer or the public authority or railroad company, owning or maintaining such overhead bridge or structure of the fact of such collision, and his name, address, driver's license number, and the registration number of his vehicle. Failure to give such notice immediately, either in person or by telephone, shall constitute a Class 1 misdemeanor.

On any highway over which there is a bridge or structure having a vertical clearance of less than thirteen feet, six inches, the Commonwealth Transportation Commissioner shall have at least two signs erected setting forth the height of the bridge or structure. Such signs shall be located at least 1,500 feet ahead of the bridge or structure.

§46.2-1111. Extension of loads beyond line of fender or body.

No vehicle shall carry any load extending more than six inches beyond the line of the fender or body. Nor shall such load exceed a total outside width as prescribed by §§46.2-1105 through 46.2-1109.

Notwithstanding the foregoing provisions of this section, watercraft carried on vehicles may extend more than six inches beyond the line of the fender or body of such vehicle if the total width of watercraft and the carrier upon which it is carried does not exceed seventy-six inches.

ARTICLE 16
MAXIMUM VEHICLE LENGTHS

§46.2-1112. Length of vehicles, generally; special permits; tractor truck semitrailer combinations, etc., operating on certain highways.

Except for buses, no motor vehicle longer than forty feet shall be operated on any highway in the Commonwealth. The actual length of any combination of vehicles coupled together including any load thereon shall not exceed a total of sixty-five feet. No bus longer than forty-five feet shall be operated on any highway in the Commonwealth. No tolerance shall be allowed that exceeds twelve inches.

The Commonwealth Transportation Board, however, when good cause is shown, may issue a special permit for combinations either in excess of sixty-five feet, including any load thereon, or where the object or objects to be carried cannot be moved otherwise. Such permits may also be issued by the Board when the total number of otherwise overdimensional loads of modular housing of no more than two units may be reduced by permitting the use of an overlength trailer not exceeding fifty-four feet.

No overall length restrictions, however, shall be imposed on any tractor truck semitrailer combinations drawing one trailer or any tractor truck semitrailer combinations when operated on any interstate highway or on any highway as designated by the Commonwealth Transportation Board. No such designation shall be made, however, until notice of any proposed designation has been provided by the Commonwealth Transportation Commissioner to the governing body of every locality wherein any highway affected by the proposed designation is located.

No individual semitrailer or trailer being drawn in a tractor truck semitrailer trailer combination, however, shall exceed twenty-eight and one-half feet in length, and no semitrailer being operated in a tractor truck semitrailer combination shall exceed forty-eight feet in length, except when semitrailers have a distance of not more than forty-one feet between the kingpin of the semitrailer and the rearmost axle or a point midway between the rear tandem axles, such semitrailer shall be allowed not more than fifty-three feet in length.

The length limitations on semitrailers and trailers in the foregoing provisions of this section shall be exclusive of safety and energy conservation devices, steps and handholds for entry and egress, rubber dock guards, flexible fender extensions, mudflaps, refrigeration units, and air compressors. The Commonwealth Transportation Board shall designate reasonable access to terminals, facilities for food, fuel, repairs and rest. Household goods carriers and any tractor truck semitrailer combination in which the semitrailer has a length of no more than twenty-eight and one-half feet shall not be denied reasonable access to points of loading and unloading, except as designated, based on safety considerations, by the Commonwealth Transportation Board.

(Chgd. by L.1995 ch. 71; L.1997 ch. 773, eff. 7/1/97.)

§46.2-1113. Length exceptions for certain passenger buses.

Passenger buses longer than thirty-five feet, but not longer than forty-five feet, may be operated on the streets of cities and towns when authorized pursuant to §46.2-1300. Passenger buses may exceed the forty-five-foot limitation when such excess length is caused by the projection of a front or rear safety bumper or both. Such safety bumper shall not cause the length of the bus to exceed the maximum legal limit by more than one foot in the front and one foot in the rear. "Safety bumper" means any device which may be fitted on an existing bumper or which replaces the bumper and is so constructed, treated, or manufactured to absorb energy upon impact.

§46.2-1114. Length of automobile or watercraft transporters; operation on certain highways.

Automobile or watercraft transporters shall not exceed a length of sixty-five feet when operated on any interstate highway or on any highway as designated by the Commonwealth Transportation Board. Stinger-steered automobile or watercraft transporters shall not exceed a length of seventy-five feet when operated on any interstate highway or on any highway designated by the Commonwealth Transportation Board. In addition, watercraft may be transported on a truck/trailer combination no more than sixty-five feet long when operated on any interstate highway or on any highway designated by the Commonwealth Transportation Board. Any such vehicle shall display a sign of a size and type approved by the Commonwealth Transportation Board warning that the vehicle is an over-length vehicle. However, an additional three-foot overhang shall be allowed beyond the front and a four-foot overhang shall be allowed beyond the rear of the vehicle. Such combinations shall have reasonable access to terminals, facilities for food, fuel, repairs, and rest as designated by the Commonwealth Transportation Board.

§46.2-1115. Lengths of manufactured homes or house trailers.

The actual length of any combination of a towing vehicle and any manufactured home or house trailer, coupled together, shall not exceed a total length of sixty-five feet, including coupling.

(Chgd. by L.1996 chs. 39, 146; L.1999 ch. 77, eff. 7/1/99.)

§46.2-1116. Vehicles having more than one trailer, etc., attached thereto; exceptions.

Except as provided in this section and §46.2-1117, no motor vehicle shall be driven on a highway while drawing or having attached thereto more than one motor vehicle, trailer, or semitrailer unless such vehicle is being operated under a special permit from the Commonwealth Transportation Board. This limitation, however, shall not apply between sunrise and sunset to farm trailers or semitrailers being moved from one farm to another farm owned or operated by the same person within a radius of ten miles. This limitation also shall not apply to a combination of vehicles coupled together by a saddle mount device used to transport motor vehicles in a drive-away service when not more than two saddle mounts are used. Vehicles coupled together by not more than three saddle mounts shall not exceed seventy-five feet when operated on any interstate highway or any primary highway as designated by the Commonwealth Transportation Board. Use of saddle mounts as provided in this section shall be in conformity with safety regulations adopted by the federal Department of Transportation.

The Commonwealth Transportation Board shall designate reasonable access to terminals and facilities for food, fuel, repairs, and rest.

The governing body of any city may by ordinance permit motor vehicles to be driven on the highways of their respective cities while drawing or having attached thereto more than one other vehicle, trailer, or semitrailer.

(Chgd. by L.1996 ch. 340, eff. 7/1/96.)

§46.2-1117. Tractor truck semitrailer combinations operating on certain highways; access to certain facilities.

A tractor truck semitrailer combination may draw one trailer when operating on any interstate highway and any highway as designated by the Commonwealth Transportation Board. The Commonwealth Transportation Board shall designate reasonable access to terminals, facilities for food, fuel, repairs, and rest, and points of loading and unloading for carriers of household goods.

§46.2-1118. Connection between vehicles.

The connection between any two vehicles, one of which is towing or drawing the other on a highway, shall consist of a fifth wheel, drawbar, or other similar device not to exceed fifteen feet in length from one vehicle to the other. Any such two vehicles shall, in addition to such drawbar or other similar device, be equipped at all times when so operated on the highway with an emergency chain.

The foregoing provisions of this section shall not apply to any farm tractor, as defined in §46.2-100, when such farm tractor is towing any farm implement or farm machinery by means of a drawbar coupled with a safety hitch pin or manufacturer's coupling device.

§46.2-1119. Tow dolly and converter gear.

No axle-like device, commonly called a "tow dolly," used to support the front or rear wheels of a passenger vehicle or pick-up or panel truck for towing purposes, and no axle-like device, commonly called "converter gear," on which is mounted a fifth wheel used to convert a semitrailer to a full trailer, shall be considered vehicles. Either such device, when used on the public highways, shall be equipped with a safety chain or chains of a strength to restrain the device and vehicle being towed, should the connection fail. In addition, either device, when moved on the public highway, shall be equipped with rear marker lights or reflectors when towed without a load. When a tow dolly or converter gear is used to tow a vehicle, the towed vehicle must comply with all requirements of law pertaining to towed vehicles.

§46.2-1120. Extension of loads beyond front of vehicles.

No vehicle shall carry any load extending more than three feet beyond the front thereof.

§46.2-1121. Flag or light at end of load.

Whenever the load on any vehicle extends more than four feet beyond the rear of the bed or body thereof, there shall be displayed at the end of the load, in such a position as to be clearly visible at all times from the rear of the load, a red flag, not less than twelve inches, both in length and width. Between sunset and sunrise, however, there shall be displayed at the end of the load a red light plainly visible in clear weather at least 500 feet to the sides and rear of the vehicle.

ARTICLE 17
MAXIMUM VEHICLE WEIGHTS

Section

§46.2-1122. Definitions.

For the purposes of this article the following terms shall have the following meanings, unless the context clearly indicates otherwise:

"Single axle" means an assembly of two or more wheels whose centers are in one transverse vertical plane or may be included between two parallel transverse vertical planes forty inches apart, extending across the full width of the vehicle.

"Tandem axle" means any two or more consecutive axles whose centers are more than forty inches but not more than ninety-six inches apart, and are individually attached to and/or articulated from a common attachment to the vehicle including a connecting mechanism designed to equalize the load between axles.

"Single axle weight" means the total weight transmitted to the highway by all wheels whose centers may be included between two parallel transverse vertical planes forty inches apart, extending across the full width of the vehicle.

"Tandem axle weight" means the total weight transmitted to the highway by two or more consecutive axles whose centers may be included between parallel transverse vertical planes spaced more than forty inches and not more than ninety-six inches apart, extending across the full width of the vehicle.

"Group of axles" means any two or more consecutive axles located under a vehicle or combination.

§46.2-1123. Weight of vehicles and loads.

The maximum gross weight and axle weight to be permitted on the road surface of any highway shall be in accordance with the provisions of this article. Any notice by the Department of Transportation to truckers as to the provisions of this article shall include all limits as provided in this article.

§46.2-1124. Maximum single axle weight, generally; maximum weight per inch of tire width.

The single axle weight of any vehicle or combination shall not exceed 20,000 pounds, nor shall it exceed 650 pounds per inch, width of tire, measured in contact with the surface of the highway.

§46.2-1125. Maximum tandem axle weight, generally.

The tandem axle weight of any vehicle or combination shall not exceed 34,000 pounds, and no one axle of such tandem unit shall exceed the weight permitted for a single axle. Furthermore, the weight imposed on the highway by two or more consecutive axles, individually attached to the vehicle and spaced not less than forty inches nor more than ninety-six inches apart, shall not exceed 34,000 pounds and no one axle of such unit shall exceed the weight permitted for a single axle.

§46.2-1126. Maximum gross weight, generally.

Except as provided in §46.2-1128, the gross weight imposed on the highway by a vehicle or combination shall not exceed the maximum weight given for the respective distance between the first and last axle of the vehicle or combination, nor shall any two or more consecutive axles exceed the maximum weight given, when measured longitudinally with any fraction of a foot rounded to the next highest as set forth in the following table:

Distance in feet between the extremes of any group of two or more consecutive axles	or Maximum weight in pounds on any group of axles					
	2 axles	3 axles	4 axles	5 axles	6 axles	7 axles
4	34,000	...	...	...	...	...
5	34,000	...	...	...	...	...
6	34,000	...	...	...	...	...
7	34,000	...	...	...	...	...
8	34,000	34,000	...	...	...	...
9	39,000	42,500	...	...	...	...
10	40,000	43,500	...	...	...	...
11	...	44,000	...	...	...	...
12	...	45,000	50,000	...	...	...
13	...	45,000	50,500	...	...	...
14	...	46,500	51,500	...	...	...
15	...	47,000	52,000	...	...	...
16	...	48,000	52,500	58,000	...	...
17	...	48,500	53,500	58,500	...	...
18	...	49,500	54,000	59,000	...	...
19	...	50,000	54,500	60,000	...	...
20	...	51,000	55,500	60,500	66,000	...
21	...	51,500	56,000	61,000	66,500	...
22	...	52,500	56,500	61,500	67,000	...
23	...	53,000	57,500	62,500	68,000	...
24	...	54,000	58,000	63,000	68,500	74,000
25	...	54,500	58,500	63,500	69,000	74,500
26	...	55,500	59,500	64,000	69,500	75,000
27	...	56,000	60,000	65,000	70,000	75,500
28	...	57,000	60,500	65,500	71,000	76,500
29	...	57,500	61,500	66,000	71,500	77,000
30	...	58,500	62,000	66,500	72,000	77,500
31	...	59,000	62,500	67,500	72,500	78,000
32	...	60,000	63,500	68,000	73,000	78,500
33	...	...	64,000	68,500	74,000	79,000
34	...	...	64,500	69,000	74,500	80,000
35	...	...	65,500	70,000	75,000	...
36	...	...	66,000	70,500	75,500	...
37	...	...	66,500	71,000	76,000	...
38	...	...	67,500	72,000	77,000	...
39	...	...	68,000	72,500	77,500	...
40	...	...	68,500	73,000	78,000	...
41	...	...	69,500	73,500	78,500	...
42	...	...	70,000	74,000	79,000	...
43	...	...	70,500	75,000	80,000	...
44	...	...	71,500	75,500	...	...
45	...	...	72,000	76,000	...	...
46	...	...	72,500	76,500	...	...
47	...	...	73,500	77,500	...	...
48	...	...	74,000	78,000	...	...
49	...	...	74,500	78,500	...	...
50	...	...	75,500	79,000	...	...
51	...	...	76,000	80,000	...	...

§46.2-1127. Weight limits for vehicles using interstate highways.

No motor vehicle or combination of vehicles shall travel on an interstate highway in the Commonwealth with (i) a single axle weight in excess of 20,000 pounds, or (ii) a tandem axle weight in excess of 34,000 pounds, or (iii) a gross weight, based on axle spacing, greater than that permitted in §46.2-1126, or (iv) a gross weight, regardless of axle spacing, in excess of 80,000 pounds, unless otherwise permitted by the proper authority. If such weights on interstate highways are increased, the Governor, upon recommendation of the Department of Transportation, may authorize the axle and gross weights set forth in this section to be used on interstate highways in the Commonwealth.

§46.2-1128. Extensions of weight limits; fees.

The owner of any motor vehicle may obtain an extension of single axle, tandem axle, and gross weight set forth in this article by purchasing an overload permit for such vehicle. The permit shall extend the single axle weight limit of 20,000 pounds, tandem axle weight limit of 34,000 pounds, and gross weight limit based on axle spacing and number of axles on such vehicle. However, no such permit shall authorize the operation of a motor vehicle whose gross weight exceeds 80,000 pounds, nor shall any such permit authorize any extension of the limitations provided in §46.2-1127 for interstate highways.

Permits under this section shall be valid for one year and shall be issued according to the following fee schedule:

Percentage	Fee for Permit
1%	$ 35
2%	75
3%	115
4%	160
5%	200

The Commissioner shall make the permit available to vehicles registered outside the Commonwealth under the same conditions and restrictions which are applicable to vehicles

registered within the Commonwealth. The Commissioner shall promulgate regulations governing such permits. Except as provided in this section and §46.2-1129, no weights in excess of those authorized by law shall be tolerated.
(Chgd. by L.1997 ch. 283, eff. 7/1/97.)

§46.2-1129. Further extensions of weight limits for certain vehicles hauling Virginia-grown farm or forest products.

The owner of any motor vehicle used for hauling Virginia-grown forest or farm products, as defined in §3.1-692, from the place where they are first produced, cut, harvested, or felled to the location where they are first processed may obtain from the Commissioner an extension for such vehicle of the single axle, tandem axle, and gross weight limits set forth in this title. The permit shall extend the single axle weight limit, tandem axle, and gross weight limits set forth in this title. The permit shall extend the single axle weight limit, tandem axle weight limit, and gross weight limit based on axle spacing and number of axles on such vehicle by five percent, respectively.

No permit issued under this section shall permit the operation on an interstate highway of any vehicle with (i) a single axle weight in excess of 20,000 pounds, or (ii) a tandem axle weight in excess of 34,000 pounds, or (iii) a gross weight, based on axle spacing, greater than that permitted in §46.2-1126, or (iv) a gross weight, regardless of axle spacing, in excess of 80,000 pounds. The Commissioner shall promulgate regulations governing such permits.

Weight extensions provided in this section shall be in addition to those provided in §46.2-1128, but no weights beyond those permitted by the combination of the extensions provided in this section and §46.2-1128 shall be tolerated.
(Chgd. by L.1997 ch. 283, eff. 7/1/97.)

§46.2-1130. Crossing bridge or culvert by vehicle heavier than allowed; where weight signs to be erected.

No vehicle shall cross any bridge or culvert in the Commonwealth if the gross weight of such vehicle is greater than the amount posted for the bridge or culvert as its carrying capacity.

Signs stating the carrying capacity shall be erected and maintained near each end of the bridge or culvert on the approaches to such bridge or culvert. Whenever the weight capacity of any structure on the interstate or primary system is reduced below the weight limit permitted on the road of which it is a part, a sign indicating that there is a restricted structure shall be placed in advance of the last alternate route on the road upon which there is a restricted structure. Whenever the weight capacity of any structure is reduced below the weight limit permitted on the road of which it is a part, a sign indicating that there is a restricted structure, shall be placed in advance of the last alternate route on the road upon which there is a restricted structure.

§46.2-1131. Penalty for violation of weight limits; record of conviction, etc., forwarded to Department.

Any person violating any weight limit as provided in this chapter or any permit issued by either the Department of Transportation or by local authorities pursuant to this article shall be subject to a civil penalty of twenty-five dollars and a processing fee of twenty dollars in addition to any liquidated damages and weighing fees imposed by this article. Upon collection by the Department, except as provided in §46.2-1138, civil penalties shall be paid to the Literary Fund, but processing fees shall be paid to the state treasury and, beginning July 1, 1990, shall be set aside as a special fund to be used to meet the expenses of the Department of Motor Vehicles. In addition, liquidated damages and weighing fees shall be distributed as provided in §§46.2-1135 and 46.2-1137, respectively, except as provided in §46.2-1138.

The penalties, damages, and fees specified in this section shall be in addition to any other liability which may be legally fixed against the owner, operator, or other person charged with the weight violation for damage to a highway or bridge attributable to such weight violation.

§46.2-1132. Service of process in weight violation cases.

Any person, whether resident or nonresident, who permits the operation of a motor vehicle in the Commonwealth by his agent or employee shall be deemed to have appointed the operator of such motor vehicle his statutory agent for the purpose of service of process in any proceeding against such person growing out of any weight violation involving such motor vehicle. Acceptance by a nonresident of the rights and privileges conferred by §§46.2-655 through 46.2-661 shall have the same effect under this section as operation of such motor vehicle by such nonresident, his agent, or his employee.

§46.2-1133. Special processing provisions for overweight violations.

Notwithstanding any other provision of law, all violations of any weight limit as provided in this article or any permit issued by either the Department of Transportation or by local authorities pursuant to this chapter shall be processed in the following manner:

1. The officer charging the violation shall serve a citation on the operator of the overweight vehicle. The citation shall be directed to the owner, operator, or other person responsible for the overweight violation as determined by the officer. Service of the citation on the vehicle operator shall constitute service of process upon the owner, operator, or other person charged with the weight violation as provided in §46.2-1136.

2. The officer charging the violation shall cause the citation to be delivered or mailed by first-class mail to the Department within twenty-four hours after it is served.

3. The owner, operator, or other person charged with the weight violation shall, within twenty-one days after the citation is served upon the vehicle operator, either make full payment to the Department of the civil penalty, liquidated damages, weighing fee, and processing fee as stated on the citation, or deliver to the Department a written notice of his election to contest the overweight charge in court.

4. Failure of the owner, operator, or other person charged with the weight violation to timely deliver to the Department either payment in full of the uncontested civil penalty, liquidated damages, weighing fee, and processing fee or a notice of contest of the weight violation shall cause the Department to issue an administrative order of assessment against such person. A copy of the order shall be sent by first-class mail to the person charged with the weight violation. Any such administrative order shall have the same effect as a judgment for liquidated damages entered by a general district court.

5. Upon timely receipt of a notice of contest of an overweight charge, the Department shall:

a. Forward the citation to the general district court named in the citation and

b. Send by first-class mail to the person charged with the weight violation, and to the officer who issued the citation, confirmation that the citation has been forwarded to the court for trial.

6. Notices and pleadings may be served by first-class mail sent to the address shown on the citation as the address of the person charged with the weight violation or, if none is

shown, to the address of record for the person to whom the vehicle is registered.

7. An alleged weight violation which is contested shall be tried as a civil case. The attorney for the Commonwealth shall represent the interests of the Commonwealth. The disposition of the case shall be recorded in an appropriate order, a copy of which shall be sent to the Department in lieu of any record which may be otherwise required by §46.2-383. If judgment is for the Commonwealth, payment shall be made to the Department.

§46.2-1134. Special overweight seizure provisions; penalty.

Any officer authorized to serve process or weigh vehicles under the provisions of this chapter may hold an overweight vehicle without an attachment summons or court order, but only for such time as is reasonably necessary to promptly petition for an attachment summons to attach the vehicle.

After finding reasonable cause for the issuance of an attachment summons, the judicial officer conducting the hearing shall inform the operator of the vehicle of his option to either pay the liquidated damages, civil penalty, weighing fee, and processing fee, or contest the charge through the attachment proceeding. If the operator chooses to make payment, he shall do so to the judicial officer who shall transmit the citation, liquidated damages, civil penalty, weighing fee, and processing fee to the Department for distribution in accordance with §46.2-1131.

The Commonwealth shall not be required to post bond in order to attach a vehicle pursuant to this section. The officer authorized to hold the overweight vehicle pending a hearing on the attachment petition shall also be empowered to execute the attachment summons if issued. Any bond for the retention of the vehicle or for release of the attachment shall be given in accordance with §8.01-553 except that the bond shall be taken by a judicial officer. The judicial officer shall return the bond to the clerk of the appropriate court in place of the officer serving the attachment as otherwise provided in §8.01-554.

In the event the civil penalty, liquidated damages, weighing fee, and processing fee are not paid in full, or no bond is given by or for the person charged with the weight violation, the vehicle involved in the weight violation shall be stored in a secure place, as may be designated by the owner or operator of the vehicle. If no place is designated, the officer executing the attachment summons shall designate the place of storage. The owner or operator shall be afforded the right of unloading and removing the cargo from the vehicle. The risk and cost of the storage shall be borne by the owner or operator of the vehicle.

Whenever an attachment summons is issued for a weight violation, the court shall forward to the Department both a copy of the order disposing of the case and the weight violation citation prepared by the officer but not served.

Upon notification of the judgment or administrative order entered for such weight violation and notification of the failure of such person to satisfy the judgment or order, the Department or the Department of State Police or any law-enforcement officer shall thereafter deny the offending person the right to operate a motor vehicle or vehicles upon the highways of the Commonwealth until the judgment or order has been satisfied.

When informed that the right to operate the motor vehicle has been denied, the driver shall drive the motor vehicle to a nearby location off the public highways and not move it or permit it to be moved until such judgment or order has been satisfied. Failure by the driver to comply with this provision shall constitute a Class 4 misdemeanor.

All costs incurred by the Commonwealth and all judgments, if any, against the Commonwealth due to action taken pursuant to this section shall be paid from the fund into which liquidated damages are paid.

Police officers of the Department of State Police and all other law-enforcement officers are vested with the same powers with respect to the enforcement of this chapter as they have with respect to the enforcement of the criminal laws of the Commonwealth.

§46.2-1135. Liquidated damages for violation of weight limits; powers of enforcement officers; forfeiture of vehicle and cargo.

A. Any person violating any weight limit as provided in this chapter or in any permit issued either by the Virginia Department of Transportation or by local authorities pursuant to this chapter shall be assessed liquidated damages. The amount of those damages shall be two cents per pound for each pound of excess weight over the prescribed limit in this article for an excess which does not exceed 5,000 pounds, five cents per pound for each pound of excess weight over the prescribed limit in this article when such excess is more than 5,000 pounds, two cents per pound for each pound of excess axle weight over the prescribed limit in any permit issued pursuant to Article 18 (§46.2-1139 et seq.) of this chapter when the excess is 5,000 pounds or less, five cents per pound for each pound of excess axle weight over the prescribed limit in any permit issued pursuant to Article 18 (§46.2-1139 et seq.) of this chapter when such excess is more than 5,000 pounds and ten cents per pound for each pound of excess gross weight over the prescribed limit in any permit issued pursuant to Article 18 (§46.2-1139 et seq.) of this chapter. However, whenever any vehicle does not exceed the gross weight permitted according to the table provided in §46.2-1139 and exceeds the axle weight in this article by 2,000 pounds or less, the liquidated damages shall be assessed in the amount of one cent per pound for each pound of excess weight over the prescribed axle limit in this article. If a person has no prior violations under the motor vehicle weight laws, and the excess weight does not exceed 2,500 pounds, the general district court may waive the liquidated damages against such person. Except as provided by §46.2-1138, such assessment shall be entered by the court or by the Department as a judgment for the Commonwealth, the entry of which shall constitute a lien upon the overweight vehicle. Except as provided by §46.2-1138, such sums shall be paid to the Department or collected by the attorney for the Commonwealth and forwarded to the State Treasurer and allocated to the fund appropriated for the construction and maintenance of state highways.

B. If the gross weight of the vehicle exceeds lawful limits by at least twenty-five percent but no more than fifty percent, the amount of the liquidated damages shall be two times the amount provided for in the foregoing provisions of this section; if the gross weight of the vehicle exceeds lawful limits by more than fifty percent, the amount of the liquidated damages shall be three times the amount provided for in the foregoing provisions of this section. The provisions of this subsection shall not apply to pickup or panel trucks.
(Chgd. by L.1997 ch. 479, eff. 7/1/97.)

§46.2-1136. Procedures for issuing and serving process in overweight vehicle cases.

Any officer authorized to enforce overweight vehicle laws may issue a citation for a violation of such laws. Such officer may also serve an attachment summons issued by a judge or magistrate in connection with a weight violation.

Service of any such citation shall be made upon the driver of the motor vehicle involved in the violation. Such service on the driver shall have the same legal force and validity as if served within the Commonwealth personally upon the owner, operator, or other person charged with the weight violation, whether such owner, operator, or other person charged is a resident or nonresident.

§46.2-1137. Weighing vehicles; procedure; shifting loads; unloading excess load; weighing fee; certificate as to accuracy of scales admissible in evidence; penalties.

Any officer authorized to enforce the law under this title, having reason to believe that the weight of a vehicle and load is unlawful, is authorized to weigh the load and the vehicle. If the place where the vehicle is stopped is ten road miles or less from a permanent weighing station, the officer may, and upon demand of the driver shall, require the vehicle to proceed to such station. If the distance to the nearest permanent weighing station is more than ten road miles such vehicle may be weighed by wheel load weighers. Any driver who fails or unreasonably refuses to drive his vehicle to such permanent weighing station or such scales or wheel load weighers upon the request and direction of the officer to do so shall be guilty of a Class 4 misdemeanor. The penalty for such violation shall be in addition to any other penalties prescribed for exceeding the maximum weight permitted or for any other violation.

In the event of such failure or unreasonable refusal, where the officer has reason to believe the vehicle is overweight, the officer may use whatever reasonable means are available to have the vehicle weighed, including the employment of a tow truck to move the vehicle to the weighing area. He may also use whatever means are necessary to reload the vehicle if the load is intentionally dumped. In such a case, any expenses incurred in having the vehicle weighed may be taxed as costs to be imposed upon the operator who failed or unreasonably refused to drive his vehicle to such weighing area, when he has been convicted of such failure or refusal and an overweight violation. In all cases where such failure or refusal or overweight charges are dismissed, payment shall be made from highway funds.

Should the officer find that the weight of any vehicle and its load is greater than that permitted by this title or that the weight of the load carried in or on such vehicle is greater than that which the vehicle is licensed to carry under the provisions of this title, he may require the driver to unload, at the nearest place where the property unloaded may be stored or transferred to another vehicle, such portion of the load as may be necessary to decrease the gross weight of the vehicle to the maximum therefor permitted by this title.

However, notwithstanding the provisions of §§46.2-1122 through 46.2-1127, should the officer find that the gross weight of the vehicle and its load is within limits permitted under this title and does not exceed the limit for which the vehicle is registered, but that the axle weight of any axle or axles of the vehicle exceeds that permitted under this title, the driver shall be allowed two hours to shift his load within or on that same vehicle in order to bring the axle weight or axle weights within proper limits. Such load shifting shall be performed at the site where the vehicle was weighed and found to exceed allowable axle weight limits. No such load shifting shall be allowed if such load is required to be placarded as defined in §10.1-1450 and consists of hazardous material as defined in §10.1-1400. Any property so unloaded shall be stored or cared for by the owner or operator of the overweight vehicle at the risk of such owner or operator.

If the driver of an overloaded vehicle is convicted, forfeits bail, or purchases an increased license as a result of such weighing, the court in addition to all other penalties shall assess and collect a weighing fee of two dollars from the owner or operator of the vehicle and shall forward such fee to the State Treasurer. Upon receipt of the fee, the State Treasurer shall allocate the same to the fund appropriated for the administration and maintenance of the Department of State Police.

In any court or legal proceedings in which any question arises as to the calibration or accuracy of any such scales at permanent weighing stations or wheel load weighers, a certificate, executed and signed under oath by the inspector calibrating or testing such device as to its accuracy as well as to the accuracy of the test weights used in such test, and stating the date of such test, type of test and results of testing, shall be admissible when attested by one such inspector who executed and signed it as evidence of the facts therein stated and the results of such testing.

(Chgd. by L.1996 ch. 422, eff. 7/1/96.)

§46.2-1138. *(Omitted due to limited applicability.)*

§46.2-1138.1. City ordinances fixing weight limits on certain roads.

The governing body of any city may adopt ordinances providing weight limits in accordance with the weight limits established by §§46.2-1123 through 46.2-1127 for any vehicle or combination of vehicles passing over any such roads under the jurisdiction of such city, and providing further for the assessment of liquidated damages as to overweight vehicles at rates and amounts not exceeding those applicable to the liquidated damages under §46.2-1135. Such ordinances may provide:

Upon a finding of a violation of any weight limit prescribed therein, the court shall assess the owner, operator or other person causing the operation of such overweight vehicle at such rate and amount as may be provided in such ordinance;

The assessment shall be entered by the court as a judgment for such city;

The entry of such judgment shall constitute a lien upon the overweight vehicles;

Such sums shall be paid into the treasury of such city, and allocated to the fund appropriated by such city for the construction and maintenance of such roads under its jurisdiction.

Such ordinances may include additional provisions relating to payment of such assessment and enforcement powers applicable to such city and corresponding to the provisions of §§46.2-1131, 46.2-1133, 46.2-1134 and 46.2-1135, except that civil penalties, liquidated damages and weighing fees collected pursuant to such ordinances shall be paid to the city, and the city attorney or his designee shall represent the city in any court proceeding.

§46.2-1138.2. Town ordinances concerning weight limits on certain roads.

A. The governing body of any town that provided, on January 1, 1993, town-owned and -maintained weight scales for the purpose of enforcing the weight limits established by §§46.2-1123 through 46.2-1127 for any vehicle or combination of vehicles passing over any roads in the town may adopt ordinances for the assessment of liquidated damages as to overweight vehicles in accordance with the liquidated damages under §46.2-1135. Such ordinances may provide that:

1. Upon a finding of a violation of any weight limit prescribed therein, the court shall assess the owner, operator or other person causing the operation of such overweight vehicle at such rate and amount as may be provided in such ordinance;

2. The assessment shall be entered by the court as a judgment for such town;

3. The entry of such judgment shall constitute a lien upon the overweight vehicle; and

4. Such sum shall be paid into the treasury of the town and allocated to the fund appropriated by the town for the construction and maintenance of roads under its jurisdiction.

B. Such ordinances may include additional provisions relating to the payment of such assessment and the enforcement powers applicable to such town and corresponding to the provisions of §§46.2-1131, 46.2-1133, 46.2-1134, and 46.2-1135, except that civil penalties, liquidated damages and weighing fees collected pursuant to such ordinances shall be paid to the town, and the town attorney or his designee shall represent the town in any court proceeding.

ARTICLE 18
PERMITS FOR EXCESSIVE SIZE AND WEIGHT

§46.2-1139. Permits for excessive size and weight generally; penalty.

A. The Commonwealth Transportation Commissioner and local authorities of cities and towns, in their respective jurisdictions, may, upon written application and good cause being shown, issue a permit authorizing the applicant to operate on a highway a vehicle of a size or weight exceeding the maximum specified in this title. Any such permit may designate the route to be traversed and contain any other restrictions or conditions deemed necessary by the body granting the permit.

B. Except for permits issued under §46.2-1141 for overweight vehicles transporting containerized freight and permits issued for overweight vehicles transporting irreducible loads, no overweight permit issued by the Commissioner or any local authority under any provision of this article shall be valid for the operation of any vehicle on an interstate highway if the vehicle has:

1. A single axle weight in excess of 20,000 pounds; or
2. A tandem axle weight in excess of 34,000 pounds; or
3. A gross weight, based on axle spacing, greater than that permitted in §46.2-1127; or
4. A gross weight, regardless of axle spacing, in excess of 80,000 pounds.

C. Every permit issued under this article for the operation of oversize or overweight vehicles shall be carried in the vehicle to which it refers and may be inspected by any officer. Violation of any term of any permit issued under this article shall constitute a Class 1 misdemeanor.

D. Any permit issued by the Commonwealth Transportation Commissioner or local authorities of cities and towns pursuant to state law may be restricted so as to prevent travel on any federal-aid highway if the continuation of travel on such highway would result in a loss of federal-aid funds. Before any such permit is restricted by the Commissioner, or local authority, written notice shall be given to the permittee.

E. When application is made for permits issued by the Commonwealth Transportation Commissioner as well as local authorities of one or more cities and towns, any fees imposed therefor by the Commonwealth Transportation Commissioner as well as all affected local authorities may be paid by the applicant, at the applicant's option, to the Commonwealth Transportation Commissioner, who shall promptly transmit the local portion of the total fee to the appropriate locality or localities.

(Chgd. by L.1996 chs. 36, 87; L.1997 ch. 70, eff. 7/1/97.)

§46.2-1140. Authority to use certain streets and highways in cities and towns.

When the Commonwealth Transportation Commissioner issues a permit to a person to move a vehicle of excessive size and weight along specified highways in Virginia, the Commissioner may also include within such permit, after coordinating with the authorities of a city or town, the authority to use specified highways at specified times within any such city or town which highways constitute extensions of any part of the primary highway system. No city or town otherwise having jurisdiction over its highways, shall have authority to prohibit the use of its highways to a person holding a permit issued by the Commissioner so long as such person travels upon the highways specified in the permit.

(Chgd. by L.1996 chs. 36, 87, eff. 7/1/96.)

§46.2-1141. Overweight permits for containerized freight.

Permits to operate on the highways a vehicle exceeding the maximum weight specified in this title shall be granted without costs if the vehicle is hauling containerized cargo in a sealed, seagoing container bound to or from a seaport and has been or will be transported by marine shipment. In order to qualify for such a permit the contents of such seagoing container shall not be changed from the time it is loaded by the consignor or his agents to the time it is delivered to the consignee or his agents. Cargo moving in vehicles conforming to specifications shown in this section shall be considered irreducible and eligible for permits under regulations of the Commonwealth Transportation Commissioner.

(Chgd. by L.1995 ch. 146; L.1996 chs. 36, 87, eff. 7/1/96.)

§46.2-1142. Overweight permits for concrete haulers.

The Commonwealth Transportation Commissioner and local authorities of cities and towns, in their respective jurisdictions, upon written application made by the owner or operator, shall issue overweight permits for operation of certain vehicles used to haul concrete. Permits under this section shall be issued only for vehicles that are used exclusively for the mixing of concrete in transit or at a project site or for transporting necessary components in a compartmentalized vehicle to produce concrete immediately upon arrival at a project site and either have (i) four axles with more than twenty-two feet between the first and last axle of the vehicle or (ii) three axles. Any vehicle operating under a permit issued pursuant to this section shall have a gross weight of no more than 60,000 pounds for three-axle vehicles and 70,000 pounds for four-axle vehicles, a single axle weight of no more than 20,000 pounds, a tandem axle weight of no more than 40,000 pounds, and a tri-axle grouping weight of no more than 50,000 pounds, with no single axle of such tri-axle grouping exceeding the weight permitted for a single axle. Such permits shall be issued without cost. Such permit shall not designate the route to be traversed nor contain restrictions or conditions not applicable to other vehicles in their general use of the highways.

Each vehicle, when loaded according to the provisions of a permit issued under this section, shall be operated at a reduced speed. The reduced speed limit is to be ten miles per hour slower than the legal speed limit in fifty-five, forty-five and thirty-five miles per hour speed limit zones.

(Chgd. by L.1996 chs. 36, 87; L.2000 ch. 265, eff. 7/1/2000.)

§46.2-1142.1. Extensions of overweight limits authorized under §46.2-1142 for vehicles used to haul concrete; fees.

Owners or operators of vehicles used exclusively to haul concrete may apply for permits to extend the single axle weight limit of 20,000 pounds, the tandem axle weight limit of 40,000, the four axle weight of 70,000 pounds, the tri-axle grouping weight of 50,000 pounds, and the three-axle weight of 60,000 pounds provided for in §46.2-1142, by the percentages and upon payment of the fees set forth in this section:

Percentage	Fee for Permit
1%	$ 35
2%	75
3%	115
4%	160
5%	200

Permits issued under this section shall be valid for one year from the date of issuance. No permit issued under this section shall authorize any extension of the limitation provided for in §46.2-1127 for interstate highways, nor authorize violations of any weight limitation for bridges or culverts promulgated and posted in accordance with §46.2-1130.

The Commissioner shall make the permit available to vehicles registered outside the Commonwealth under the same conditions and restrictions which are applicable to vehicles registered within the Commonwealth. The Commissioner may promulgate regulations governing such permits. Except as provided in this section and §46.2-1142, no weights in excess of those authorized by law shall be tolerated.

(Chgd. by L.1997 ch. 283; L.2000 ch. 265, eff. 7/1/2000.)

§46.2-1143. Overweight permits for coal haulers; trucks hauling gravel, sand, or crushed stone in certain counties; penalties.

A. The Commonwealth Transportation Commissioner and local authorities of cities and towns in their respective jurisdictions, upon written application by the owner or operator of vehicles used exclusively for hauling coal from a mine or other place of production to a preparation plant, loading dock, or railroad shall issue, without cost, a permit authorizing those vehicles to operate with gross weights in excess of those established in §46.2-1126 on the conditions set forth in this section.

B. Vehicles with three axles may have a maximum gross weight, when loaded, of no more than 60,000 pounds, a single axle weight of not more than 24,000 pounds and a tandem axle weight of no more than 45,000 pounds. Vehicles with four axles may have a maximum gross weight, when loaded, of no more than 70,000 pounds, a single axle weight of no more than 24,000 pounds, and a tri-axle weight of no more than 50,000 pounds. Vehicles with five axles having no less than thirty-five feet of axle space between extreme axles may have a maximum gross weight, when loaded, of no more than 90,000 pounds, a single axle weight of no more than 20,000 pounds, and a tandem axle weight of no more than 40,000 pounds.

C. No load of any vehicle operating under a permit issued according to this section shall rise above the top of the bed of such vehicle, not including extensions of the bed. Three-axle vehicles shall not carry loads in excess of the maximum bed size in cubic feet for such vehicle which shall be computed by a formula of 60,000 pounds minus the weight of the empty truck divided by the average weight of coal. For the purposes of this section, the average weight of coal shall be fifty-two pounds per cubic foot. Four-axle vehicles shall not carry loads in excess of the maximum bed size for such vehicle which shall be computed by a formula of 70,000 pounds minus the weight of the truck empty divided by the average weight of coal.

D. For the purposes of this section, the term bed shall mean that part of the vehicle used to haul coal. Bed size shall be measured by its interior dimensions with volume expressed in cubic feet. In order to ensure compliance with this section by visual inspection, if the actual bed size of the vehicle exceeds the maximum as provided above, the owner or operator shall be required to paint a horizontal line two inches wide on the sides of the outside of the bed of the vehicle, clearly visible to indicate the uppermost limit of the maximum bed size applicable to the vehicle as provided in this section. In addition, one hole two inches high and six inches long on each side of the bed shall be cut in the center of the bed and at the top of the painted line. Any vehicle in violation of this section shall subject the vehicle's owner or operator or both to a penalty of $250 for a first offense, $500 for a second offense within a twelve-month period, and $1,000 and revocation of the permit for a third offense within a twelve-month period from the first offense.

E. If the bed of any vehicle is enlarged beyond the maximum bed size for which its permit was granted, or if the line or holes required are altered so that the vehicle exceeds the bed size for which its permit was granted, the owner, operator, or both shall be subject to a penalty of $1,000 for each offense and revocation of the permit. Upon revocation, a permit shall not be reissued for six months. The penalties provided in this section shall be in lieu of those imposed under §46.2-1135.

F. For any vehicle with a valid permit issued pursuant to the conditions required by this section, when carrying loads which do not rise above the top of the bed or the line indicating the bed's maximum size, if applicable, it shall be, in the absence of proof to the contrary, prima facie evidence that the load is within the applicable weight limits. If any vehicle is stopped by enforcement officials for carrying a load rising above the top of the bed or the line indicating the bed's maximum size, the operator of the vehicle shall be permitted to shift his load within the bed to determine whether the load can be contained in the bed without rising above its top or above the line.

G. No such permit shall be valid for the operation of any such vehicle for a distance of more than thirty-five miles from the preparation plant, loading dock, or railroad.

H. Until July 1, 2001, in counties that impose a severance tax on coal and gases as authorized by §58.1-3712, the weight limits prescribed in subsection B of this section shall also apply to trucks hauling gravel, sand, or crushed stone no more than fifty miles from origin to destination. Nothing contained in this subsection shall authorize any extension of weight limits provided in §46.2-1127 for operation on interstate highways. Any weight violation hauling sand, gravel, or crushed stone under this subsection shall be subject to the penalties authorized by §46.2-1135. The Virginia Department of Transportation shall monitor the operation of vehicles under this subsection and the effects of such operation on the condition of the affected highways and report to the Governor and the 2001 Regular Session of the General Assembly its findings and recommendations as to whether the provisions of this subsection should be allowed to expire on July 1, 2001, or continued, either in its present or some modified form, for some specific or indefinite period. During such monitoring, should the Virginia Department of Transportation determine that the additional weight limits authorized by this subsection are negatively impacting the condition of such highways, the Department is authorized to prohibit the additional weight limits authorized by this subsection.

(Chgd. by L.1996 chs. 36, 87; L.1999 ch. 915, eff. 7/1/99.)

§46.2-1144. Overweight permits for solid waste haulers.

The Commonwealth Transportation Commissioner, upon written application by the owner or operator of vehicles used exclusively for hauling solid waste other than hazardous waste, shall issue without cost a permit authorizing the operation on the highway of such vehicles at gross weights in excess of those set forth in §46.2-1126.

No permit issued under this section shall authorize a single axle weight of more than 20,000 pounds or a tandem axle weight of more than 40,000 pounds. No such permit shall be issued for a total gross weight in excess of 40,000 pounds for a two-axle vehicle, or of more than 60,000 pounds for a three-axle vehicle. Such permit shall be obtained annually at the time the vehicle is registered. The Commissioner shall promulgate regulations governing such permits.

No such permit shall authorize the operation of any vehicle enumerated in this section beyond the boundary of the county or city where it is principally garaged or for a distance of more than twenty-five miles from the place where it is principally garaged, whichever is greater. However, the permit shall not designate the route to be traversed nor contain restrictions or conditions not applicable to other vehicles in their general use of the highways. Each vehicle, when loaded according to the provisions of a permit issued under this section, shall be operated at a reduced speed of ten miles per hour slower than the legal speed limit in fifty-five, forty-five and thirty-five miles per hour speed limit zones.

For the purposes of this section, the terms "solid waste" and "hazardous waste" shall have the meanings provided in §10.1-1400.

(Chgd. by L.1996 chs. 36, 87, eff. 7/1/96.)

§46.2-1145. Overweight permits for certain trucks operated by Arlington County.

The Commonwealth Transportation Commissioner, upon written application by Arlington County, shall issue without cost to such county a permit authorizing the county's operation of vehicles used for hauling household waste and vehicles used for highway or utility construction, operation, or maintenance upon the highways of such county at gross weights exceeding those set forth in §46.2-1126. Permits issued hereunder shall specify that vehicles with two axles may have a maximum gross weight of no more than 48,000 pounds and a single axle weight of not more than 24,000 pounds and that vehicles with three axles may have a maximum gross weight of not more than 60,000 pounds and a single axle weight of not more than 24,000 pounds and a tandem axle weight of not more than 40,000 pounds.

The permit shall not designate the route to be traversed nor contain restrictions or conditions not applicable to other vehicles in their general use of the highways. Each vehicle, when loaded according to the provisions of a permit issued under this section shall be operated at a reduced speed of ten miles per hour slower than the legal speed limit in fifty-five, forty-five, and thirty-five miles per hour speed limit zones.

(Chgd. by L.1996 chs. 36, 87, eff. 7/1/96.)

§46.2-1146. Excess height and length permits for haulers of certain imported goods.

The Commonwealth Transportation Commissioner and local authorities of cities and towns in their respective jurisdictions, upon written application by the owners or operators of motor vehicles used to transport items arriving at a Virginia port by ship from overseas points of origin and consigned to an assembly plant in this Commonwealth, shall issue without cost permits for the operation of such motor vehicles on the highways if those vehicles do not exceed the height limitation set forth in §46.2-1110 by more than one and one-half feet and not exceeding the length limitation as set forth in §§46.2-1112 and 46.2-1113 by more than three feet. The Commissioner and local authorities may designate the routes such permittees shall use from the port to the assembly plant.

(Chgd. by L.1996 chs. 36, 87, eff. 7/1/96.)

§46.2-1147. Permits for excessive size and weight for articulated buses.

The Commonwealth Transportation Commissioner and local authorities of cities and towns in their respective jurisdictions, upon written application by the owner or operator of passenger buses having three or more axles consisting of two sections joined together by an articulated joint with the trailer being equipped with a mechanically steered rear axle, and having a gross weight of no more than 60,000 pounds, a single axle weight of no more than 25,000 pounds and a width of no more than 102 inches shall issue to such owner or operator, without cost, a written permit authorizing the operation of such vehicles on the highways.

(Chgd. by L.1996 chs. 36, 87, eff. 7/1/96.)

§46.2-1148. Overweight permit for hauling Virginia-grown farm produce.

In addition to other permits provided for in this article, the Commonwealth Transportation Commissioner and local authorities of cities and towns, in their respective jurisdictions, upon written application by the owner or operator of any three-axle vehicle used for hauling farm produce grown in Virginia shall issue permits for overweight operation of such vehicles as provided in this section. Such permits shall allow the vehicles to have a gross weight of no more than 50,000 pounds, a single axle weight of no more than 20,000 pounds, and a tandem axle weight of no more than 36,000 pounds. Additionally, any five-axle combination used for hauling Virginia-grown farm products may have a gross weight of no more than 80,000 pounds and any four-axle combination hauling Virginia-grown produce, may have a tandem axle weight of 36,000 pounds.

Except as otherwise provided in this section, no such permit shall designate the route to be traversed nor contain restrictions or conditions not applicable to other vehicles in their general use of the highways.

No permit issued under this section shall authorize any vehicle whose axle weights or axle spacing would not be permissible under §§46.2-1122 through 46.2-1127 to cross any bridge constituting a part of any public road.

Permits issued under this section shall be valid only in Accomack and Northampton Counties.

(Chgd. by L.1996 chs. 36, 87, eff. 7/1/96.)

§46.2-1149. Unladen, oversize and overweight, rubber-tired, self-propelled haulers and loaders; permits; engineering analysis; costs.

The Commonwealth Transportation Commissioner and local authorities of cities and towns in their respective jurisdictions, upon written application by the owner or operator of any empty, oversize and overweight, rubber-tired, self-propelled hauler or loader used in the construction and coal mining industries, may issue to such owner or operator a permit authorizing operation upon the highways of such equipment with gross empty weights in excess of those established in §§46.2-1122 through 46.2-1127 and sizes in excess of those established in §§46.2-1105 through 46.2-1108. The permits shall be issued only after an engineering analysis of a proposed routing has been conducted by the affected jurisdictions to assess the ability of the roadway and bridges to be traversed to sustain the vehicles' size and weight. Costs shall be assessed against the applicant to cover engineering analysis.

No permit issued under this section shall be valid for the operation of the equipment for a distance of more than thirty-five miles.

(Chgd. by L.1996 chs. 36, 87; L.2000 ch. 129, eff. 7/1/2000.)

§46.2-1149.1. Excess tandem axle weight permits for cotton module haulers.

The Commonwealth Transportation Commissioner, upon application made by the owner or operator of vehicles used exclusively to transport seed cotton modules, shall issue without cost a permit authorizing the operation on the highway of such vehicles, from September 1 through December 31 of each year, at tandem axle weights in excess of that authorized in §46.2-1125. The Commissioner shall promulgate regulations governing such permits. Such permits shall allow the vehicles to have tandem axle weights of no more than 44,000 pounds. No permit issued under this section shall authorize a single axle weight in excess of that authorized in §46.2-1124 or a gross weight in excess of 56,000 pounds.

(Added by L.1995 ch. 419; chgd. by L.1996 chs. 29, 36, 87, eff. 7/1/96.)

§46.2-1149.2. Permit authorizing transportation of tree-length logs.

The Commonwealth Transportation Commissioner, upon application made by the owner or operator of vehicles used to transport tree-length logs, shall issue a permit authorizing the operation on the highways of such vehicles in excess of lengths authorized in Article 16 (§46.2-1112 et seq.) of this chapter. Such permit shall be issued in accordance with regulations promulgated as provided in Chapter 1.1:1 (§9-6.14:1 et seq.) of Title 9, subdivision (3) of §33.1-12, and §33.1-49.

(Added by L.1997 ch. 283, eff. 7/1/97.)

ARTICLE 19
TOWING AND TOWED VEHICLES

§46.2-1150. Towing certain unlicensed or uninspected vehicles.

Nothing in this title shall prohibit towing an unlicensed motor vehicle or motor vehicle which has not been inspected pursuant to Article 21 (§46.2-1157 et seq.) or 22 (§46.2-1176 et seq.) of Chapter 10 of this title.

Nothing in this title shall prohibit the towing of an unlicensed trailer or semitrailer used on a construction site as an office or for storage or a trailer or semitrailer which has been used on a construction site as an office or for storage, but which has not been inspected pursuant to Article 21 of Chapter 10 of this title, provided that any such unlicensed or uninspected trailer or semitrailer (i) is towed by a tow truck, wrecker, or other vehicle designed and equipped for the towing of inoperable or disabled vehicles; (ii) is operated only in intrastate commerce; (iii) has an actual gross weight, including contents, of no more than 15,000 pounds; (iv) is secured to the towing vehicle by means of safety chains; and (v) is equipped with rear-mounted bar lights which function as tail lights, brake lights, and turn signals as provided in Article 3 (§46.2-1010 et seq.) of Chapter 10 of this title. However, nothing in this section shall authorize the towing or drawing of an unlicensed or uninspected trailer or semitrailer by means of a tractor truck except for the purpose of having such trailer or semitrailer inspected as provided in §46.2-1157.

§46.2-1151. Weight limit exception as to vehicles designed for towing disabled vehicles.

The provisions of §§46.2-1122 through 46.2-1127 shall not apply to a vehicle designed for towing disabled vehicles, when towing such vehicle in an emergency in such manner that a part of the combined weight of the two vehicles rests upon an axle or axles of the towing vehicle, provided the towed and towing vehicles each are within the weight limits prescribed in §§46.2-1122 through 46.2-1127. This section shall not permit the violation of any lawfully established load limit on any bridge. For the purpose of this section, "emergency" includes towing disabled inoperative vehicles to places designated by owners.

§46.2-1152. Certain tow trucks need not be weighed.

Notwithstanding any other provision of law, no truck designed and equipped for the towing of inoperative or disabled motor vehicles shall be required to be weighed at state-operated permanent weighing stations when not actually engaged in towing another vehicle.

§46.2-1153. Permissible lengths of combination vehicles being towed in emergencies.

In an emergency as provided in §46.2-1149*, the towing of disabled vehicles which cannot be separated for safety, physical, or mechanical reasons and which exceed length limits established in Article 16 (§46.2-1112 et seq.) of this chapter, shall be permissible for the purpose of towing any such vehicle to the nearest facility which can make the necessary repairs but not more than fifty miles from the point such vehicle was disabled.

**Probably should be "§46.2-1151".*

§46.2-1154. Length of vehicles; exceptions in case of breakdown.

The provisions of §46.2-1118 shall not apply to vehicles which, because of a mechanical breakdown or an accident, are towed to the nearest repair facility which can furnish the required service. In any such case such connection may consist solely of a chain, rope, or cable of no more than fifteen feet long. A licensed driver shall be at the controls of the towed vehicle to brake, steer and control its lights.

ARTICLE 20
LOADS AND CARGOES

§46.2-1155. Fastening load of logs, barrels, etc.

No vehicle which is designed or used for the purpose of hauling logs, poles, lumber, barrels, hogsheads, or other materials or containers which by their nature may shift or roll, shall be operated or moved on any highway unless its load is securely fastened by adequate log chains, metal cables, nylon webbing, steel straps or other restraining devices so as to prevent the load from shifting or falling from the vehicle. Tobacco hogsheads may, however, be secured by manila or hemp rope, at least five-eighths inch in diameter, of sufficient strength securely to fasten the hogshead against shifting, falling, or rolling.

Nothing in this section shall release the owner or operator from liability for failure to use reasonable care to prevent the load from shifting or falling.

§46.2-1156. Construction, maintenance and loading must prevent escape of contents; load covers; exemptions.

A. No vehicle shall be operated or moved on any highway unless it is so constructed, maintained, and loaded as to prevent its contents from dropping, sifting, leaking, or otherwise escaping. No provision of this section, however, shall apply to any (i) motor vehicle that is used exclusively for agricultural purposes as provided in §46.2-698 and is not licensed in any other state; (ii) agricultural vehicle, tractor, or other vehicle exempted from registration and licensing requirements pursuant to Article 6 (§46.2-662 et seq.) of Chapter 6 of this title; or (iii) motor vehicle transporting forest products, poultry, or livestock.

B. The loads of all trucks, trailers and semitrailers carrying gravel, sand, coal or other nonagricultural and nonforestry products on interstate, primary, or secondary highways or roads maintained by cities, counties or incorporated towns shall be either (i) secured to the vehicle in which they are being transported or (ii) covered. Public service company vehicles, pickup trucks, and emergency snow removal equipment while engaged in snow removal operations shall be excluded from the provisions of this subsection.

(Chgd. by L.1997 ch. 283, eff. 7/1/97.)

§46.2-1156.1. Transportation of persons less than sixteen years old in pickup truck beds prohibited; exception.

No person under sixteen years of age shall be transported in the rear cargo area of any pickup truck on the highways of Virginia. The provisions of this section shall not apply to transportation of persons in the bed of any pickup truck being operated (i) as part of an organized parade authorized by the Department of Transportation or the locality in which the parade is being conducted or (ii) on or across a highway from one field or parcel of land to another field or parcel of land in connection with farming operations.

(Added by L.2000 ch. 736, eff. 7/1/2000.)

ARTICLE 21
SAFETY INSPECTIONS

§46.2-1157. Requirement of inspection; well-drilling machinery, antique motor vehicle excepted.

The Superintendent may compel, by proclamation of the Governor or otherwise, the owner or operator of any motor vehicle, trailer, or semitrailer registered in Virginia and operated on a highway within this Commonwealth to submit his vehicle to an inspection of its mechanism and equipment by an official inspection station, designated for that purpose, in accordance with §46.2-1158. No owner or operator shall fail to submit a motor vehicle, trailer, or semitrailer operated on the highways in this Commonwealth to such inspection or fail or refuse to correct or have corrected in accordance with the requirements of this title any mechanical defects found by such inspection to exist.

The provisions of this section requiring safety inspections of motor vehicles shall also apply to vehicles used for fire fighting; inspections of fire-fighting vehicles shall be conducted pursuant to regulations promulgated by the Superintendent of State Police, taking into consideration the special purpose of such vehicles and the conditions under which they operate.

Each day during which such motor vehicle, trailer, or semitrailer is operated on any highway in this Commonwealth after failure to comply with this law shall constitute a separate offense. However, no penalty shall be imposed on any owner or operator for operation of a motor vehicle, trailer, or semitrailer after the expiration of a period fixed for the inspection thereof, over the most direct route between the place where such vehicle is kept or garaged and an official inspection station, for the purpose of having it inspected pursuant to a prior appointment with such station.

Further, no penalty shall be imposed on any owner or operator of a truck, tractor truck, trailer, or semitrailer for which the period fixed for inspection has expired while the vehicle was outside the Commonwealth and that penalty is for operation of such vehicle (i) from a point outside the Commonwealth to the place where such vehicle is kept or garaged within the Commonwealth or (ii) to a destination within the Commonwealth where such vehicle will be (a) unloaded within twenty-four hours of entering the Commonwealth, (b) inspected within such twenty-four hour period, and (c) after being unloaded, will be operated only to an inspection station or to the place where it is kept or garaged within the Commonwealth.

The provisions of this section shall not apply to any vehicle for transporting well-drilling machinery licensed under §46.2-700 or to any antique motor vehicle as defined in §46.2-100 and licensed pursuant to §46.2-730.

Notwithstanding the penalty provisions of §46.2-1171, a violation of this section constitutes a traffic infraction.
(Chgd. by L.1995 ch. 670; L.1997 ch. 283, eff. 7/1/97.)

§46.2-1158. Frequency of inspection; scope of inspection.

Motor vehicles, trailers, and semitrailers required to be inspected pursuant to the provisions of §46.2-1157 shall be reinspected within twelve months of the month of the first inspection and at least once every twelve months thereafter.

Each inspection shall be a complete inspection. A reinspection of a rejected vehicle by the same station during the period of validity of the rejection sticker on such vehicle, however, need only include an inspection of the item or items previously found defective unless there is found an obvious defect that would warrant further rejection of the vehicle.

A rejection sticker shall be valid for fifteen calendar days beyond the day of issuance. A complete inspection shall be performed on any vehicle bearing an expired rejection sticker.

§46.2-1159. Logtrailers defined; exempt from inspection under certain conditions.

For the purpose of this section, a "logtrailer" shall be any vehicle designed and used solely as an implement for hauling logs, lumber, or other forest products from the forest to the mill or loading platform. Log trailers shall be exempt from the requirements of §46.2-1157 if operation on the highways in the Commonwealth does not exceed two miles and is made during daylight hours.

§46.2-1160. Towed vehicle defined; exempt from inspection requirement.

For the purpose of this section a towed vehicle shall be any motor vehicle designed or altered and used exclusively for racing or other exhibition purposes at places other than the highways in the Commonwealth where such vehicle does not operate under its own power on the highways in the Commonwealth in going to or from such places. A towed vehicle as defined in this section shall be exempt from the requirements of §46.2-1157.

§46.2-1161. Exemption of certain trailers not equipped with brakes.

No boat, utility, or travel trailer which is not equipped with brakes shall be required to be inspected.

§46.2-1161.1. Inspections of trailers and semitrailers equipped with heating or cooking appliances.

If any trailer or semitrailer subject to the periodic safety inspections required by this article is equipped with a heating or cooking appliance, the safety inspection of such trailer or semitrailer shall include a visual inspection of the venting of such cooking or heating appliance to the outside of the trailer or semitrailer. No safety inspection approval sticker shall be issued to any such trailer or semitrailer unless any such heating or cooking appliance is adequately vented to prevent the asphyxiation of occupants of any such trailer or semitrailer by the operation of the heating or cooking appliance.

§46.2-1162. Inspection of certain trailers.

Any trailer required to be inspected under the provisions of this article may, only if the size or configuration of the trailer and the size and configuration of the facilities of the inspection station prevent the trailer from being inspected inside the inspection station, be inspected outside the inspection station. The provisions of this section shall apply only to trailers as defined in §46.2-100 and shall not apply to recreational vehicles commonly known as "motor homes" or to any vehicle required to be equipped with head lights.

§46.2-1163. Official inspection stations; safety inspection approval stickers; actions of Superintendent subject to the Administrative Process Act.

The Superintendent may designate, furnish instructions to, and supervise official inspection stations for the inspection of motor vehicles, trailers, and semitrailers and for adjusting and correcting equipment enumerated in this chapter in such a manner as to conform to specifications hereinbefore set forth. The Superintendent shall adopt and furnish to such official inspection stations regulations governing the making of inspections required by this chapter. The Superintendent may at any time, after five days' notice, revoke the designation of any official inspection station designated by him.

If no defects are discovered or when the equipment has been corrected in accordance with this title, the official inspection station shall issue to the operator or owner of the vehicle, on forms furnished by the Department of State Police, a duplicate of which is retained by such station, a certificate showing the date of correction, registration number of the vehicle, and the official designation of such station. There also shall be placed on the windshield of the vehicle at a place to be designated by the Superintendent an approval sticker furnished by the Department of State Police. If any vehicle is not equipped with a windshield, the approval sticker shall be placed on the vehicle in a location designated by the Superintendent. This sticker shall be displayed on the windshield of such vehicle or at such other designated place upon the vehicle at all times when it is operated on the highways in the Commonwealth and until such time as a new inspection period shall be designated and a new inspection sticker issued. Common carriers, operating under certificate from the State Corporation Commission or the Department of Motor Vehicles, who desire to do so may use with the approval of the Superintendent private inspection stations for the inspection and correction of their equipment.

Actions of the Superintendent relating to official inspection stations shall be governed by the provisions of the Administrative Process Act (§9-6.14:1 et seq.).
(Chgd. by L.1996 ch. 573, eff. 7/1/96.)

§46.2-1164. Reinspection not required when windshield replaced; transfer of inspection sticker to new windshield; replacement of lost or damaged stickers.

When any vehicle requires the replacement of a windshield pursuant to §46.2-1058, it shall not be necessary to inspect such vehicle at the time of replacement if a valid state inspection sticker is displayed on the windshield being replaced.

The sticker found on the broken windshield may be removed and placed on the new windshield.

The Superintendent may designate certain State Police officers to issue safety inspection approval stickers to vehicles from which the original valid safety inspection approval sticker has been lost, stolen or damaged without causing the vehicle to be reinspected, provided the vehicle owner or operator produces the original safety inspection approval sticker receipt issued to the vehicle within the past eleven months. Such replacement safety inspection approval stickers shall be issued in accordance with regulations promulgated by the Superintendent.

§46.2-1165. Regulations for inspection of vehicles; posting.

The Superintendent shall promulgate regulations for the inspection of motor vehicles under this title and shall furnish each official inspection station with a printed set of such regulations suitable for posting. Such station shall post the regulations in a conspicuous place in the portion of its premises where inspections are made and shall cause its employees making official inspections to be conversant with such regulations.

§46.2-1166. Minimum standards required for inspection stations.

The Superintendent shall not designate any person, firm, or corporation as an official inspection station unless and until such person, firm or corporation satisfies the Superintendent, under such regulations as the Superintendent shall prescribe, that such person, firm, or corporation has met and will continue to meet the following standards:

1. The station has sufficient mechanical equipment and skilled and competent mechanics to make a complete inspection in accordance with the provisions of this article;

2. Adequate means are provided by the station to test the brakes, headlights, and steering mechanism of motor vehicles and to ascertain that motor vehicles inspected by the station meet the safety standards prescribed by the Superintendent under the terms of this title;

3. The person making the actual inspection or under whose immediate supervision such inspection is made shall have at least one year's practical experience as an automotive mechanic, or has satisfactorily completed a training program in automotive mechanics approved by the Superintendent of State Police;

4. No person shall be designated by such station to make such inspections unless the person has been approved for that purpose by the Department of State Police;

5. The Superintendent of State Police may, at his discretion, waive the experience and training requirements of this section for inspections of motorcycles and trailers when, in the Superintendent's opinion, the person performing such inspections is otherwise qualified to perform such inspections.

§46.2-1167. Charges for inspection and reinspection; exemption.

Each official safety inspection station may charge ten dollars for each inspection, but the charge shall not be mandatory. No such charge shall be made unless the station has previously contracted therefor.

Each official safety inspection station may charge one dollar for each reinspection of a vehicle rejected by the station, as provided in §46.2-1158, if the vehicle is submitted for reinspection within the validity period of the rejection sticker. If a rejected vehicle is not submitted to the same station within the validity period of the rejection sticker or is submitted to another official safety inspection station, ten dollars may be charged for the inspection.

Notwithstanding the foregoing provisions of this section, the maximum fee for the inspection of motorcycles shall be one-half the fee permitted for the inspection of other vehicles.

§46.2-1168. Additional registration fee.

In addition to any other fees imposed, at the time of registration the owner of every motor vehicle, trailer, or semitrailer required to be registered in this Commonwealth shall pay to the Department of Motor Vehicles one dollar and fifty cents per year of registration or, in the case of trailers and semitrailers, such other fee as is provided in §46.2-694.1, to be paid into the state treasury and set aside for the payment of the administrative costs of the official motor vehicle safety inspection program as appropriated by the General Assembly.

(Chgd. by L.1997 ch. 283, eff. 7/1/97.)

§46.2-1169. Inspection defined; making of repairs or adjustments.

The term "inspection" as herein used shall not include repairs or adjustments. Repairs or adjustments necessary to bring the vehicle into conformity with this title may be made by agreement between the owner and such station or whatever repair station the owner may select. If such adjustments or repairs are made by anyone other than an official inspection station, such vehicle shall again be inspected by an official inspection station.

§46.2-1170. Advertising, etc., of official inspection station when not authorized.

No person, firm, or corporation, unless designated as such in accordance with the provisions of this article, shall, either directly or indirectly, display, advertise, or represent that such person, firm or corporation is an official inspection station.

§46.2-1171. Penalties for violation of article.

Any person violating this article shall be guilty of a Class 3 misdemeanor for the first offense and guilty of a Class 1 misdemeanor for each subsequent offense except as otherwise provided in this article. If the violation of this article or regulations of the Superintendent made pursuant thereto is by an official inspection station in addition to or in lieu of such fine imposed by a court the Superintendent may, whether or not the violation is a first offense against this article or regulation of the Superintendent, suspend the appointment of the inspection station or, if in his opinion after a hearing, the facts warrant such action, the Superintendent may revoke the designation of such inspection station.

§46.2-1172. Unauthorized taking, possession, or use of inspection stickers, etc.; penalty.

No person shall remove any inspection sticker or any paper issued by the Superintendent in connection with vehicle safety inspections from the custody of any person to whom the same has been issued by or under the authority of the Superintendent of State Police. Nor shall any person have any such sticker or paper in his possession or use otherwise than as authorized by the Superintendent. In any case where the Superintendent has suspended or revoked the designation of any official inspection station designated by him, such station shall surrender possession to the Superintendent or his

duly authorized representative all inspection stickers and other forms and papers used in connection with safety inspection of vehicles on or before the effective date of such suspension or revocation. Any person violating the provisions of this section shall be guilty of a Class 1 misdemeanor.
(Chgd. by L.1998 ch. 299, eff. 7/1/98.)

§46.2-1173. Imitation or counterfeit inspection stickers.
No person shall make, issue, or knowingly use any imitation or counterfeit of an official safety inspection sticker.

No person shall display or cause or permit to be displayed upon any vehicle any safety inspection sticker knowing it to be fictitious or issued for another vehicle.

§46.2-1174. Superintendent authorized to enter into Uniform Vehicle Inspection Reciprocity Agreement.
The Superintendent is authorized to enter into the Uniform Vehicle Inspection Reciprocity Agreement, adopted by the American Association of Motor Vehicles Administrators on January 1, 1967.

§46.2-1175. Operators of certain commuter buses to maintain certain records; inspection of records and buses by employees of Department of State Police; penalty.
Persons, firms, corporations, and other business entities operating commuter buses for compensation in intrastate commerce shall maintain records of all maintenance performed on such buses. Such records shall include the dates of service, the odometer reading of the bus on that date, the maintenance performed, and the name of the person or persons performing the maintenance. Such records shall be open to inspection during the operator's normal business hours by employees of the Department of State Police specifically designated by the Superintendent. Employees of the Department of State Police designated for that purpose by the Superintendent shall also be authorized with the consent of the owner, operator, or agent in charge or with an appropriate warrant obtained under the procedure prescribed in Chapter 24 (§19.2-393 et seq.) of Title 19.2 to go onto the property of business entities operating commuter buses for compensation in intrastate commerce to inspect buses directly on such property or on the property where such buses are principally garaged at any time during normal business hours. Such inspections may be either for the purpose of determining the safe condition of the buses or to verify the accuracy of the maintenance logs or for both purposes.

A violation of any provision of this section shall constitute a Class 3 misdemeanor.

The provisions of this section shall not apply to local or regional governments, to authorities created to provide local or regional mass transit service, or to buses which those governments or authorities own or operate.

For the purpose of this section, "commuter bus" means a motor vehicle which has a seating capacity of more than seventeen passengers, is used primarily to transport workers directly to and from factories, plants, offices, or other places where they work, and is registered with the Department for such operation.
(Chgd. by L.1997 ch. 283, eff. 7/1/97.)

§46.2-1175.1. Inspection of certain refuse collection and highway maintenance vehicles.
No safety inspection approval sticker shall be issued under this article to any publicly or privately owned vehicle (i) used for garbage and refuse collection and disposal or (ii) having a manufacturer's gross vehicle weight rating of 10,001 pounds or more and used primarily for highway repair or maintenance unless any such vehicle is equipped with a device, in good working order, which automatically emits an audible alarm signal when the vehicle is operated in reverse gear. Any such device shall be of a type approved by the Superintendent of State Police.

ARTICLE 22
EMISSIONS INSPECTIONS

§46.2-1176. Definitions.
The following words and phrases when used in this article shall have the following meanings except where the context clearly indicates a different meaning:

"Basic, test and repair program" means a motor vehicle emissions inspection system established by regulations of the Board which shall designate the use of a BAR–90, designed so it may be upgraded in the future to an ASM 50–15 (acceleration simulation mode or method), as the only authorized testing equipment. Only those computer software programs and emissions testing procedures necessary to comply with the applicable provisions of Title I of the Clean Air Act shall be included. Such testing equipment shall be approvable for motor vehicle manufacturers' warranty repairs.

"Board" means the State Air Pollution Control Board.

"Certificate of emissions inspection" means a document, device, or symbol, prescribed by the Director and issued pursuant to this article, which indicates that (i) a motor vehicle has satisfactorily complied with the emissions standards and passed the emissions inspection provided for in this article; (ii) the requirement of compliance with such emissions standards has been waived; or (iii) the motor vehicle has failed such emissions inspection.

"Director" means the Director of the Department of Environmental Quality.

"Emissions inspection station" means any facility or portion of a facility which has obtained an emissions inspection station permit from the Director authorizing the facility to perform emissions inspections in accordance with this article.

"Enhanced emissions inspection program" means a motor vehicle emissions inspection system established by regulations of the Board which shall designate the use of the ASM 50–15 (acceleration simulation mode or method) as the only authorized testing equipment. Only those computer software programs and emissions testing procedures necessary to comply with applicable provisions of Title I of the Clean Air Act shall be included. Such testing equipment shall be approvable for motor vehicle manufacturers' warranty repairs.

"Fleet emissions inspection station" means any inspection facility operated under a permit issued to a qualified fleet owner or lessee as determined by the Director.

"Motor vehicle" means any vehicle which:

1. Was actually manufactured or designated by the manufacturer as a model manufactured in a calendar year less than twenty-five calendar years prior to January 1 of the present calendar year;

2. Is designed for the transportation of persons or property; and

3. Is powered by an internal combustion engine.

"On-road testing" means tests of motor vehicle emissions or emissions control devices by means of roadside pullovers or remote sensing devices.

"Referee station" means an inspection facility operated or used by the Department of Environmental Quality (i) to determine program effectiveness, (ii) to resolve emissions inspection conflicts between motor vehicle owners and emissions inspection stations, and (iii) to provide such other technical support and information, as appropriate, to emissions inspection stations and vehicle owners.

"Remote sensing" means the measurement of motor vehicle emissions through electronic or light-sensing equipment from a remote location such as the roadside. Remote sensing equipment may include devices to detect and record the vehicle's registration or other identification numbers.

"Test and repair" means motor vehicle emissions inspection facilities that perform official motor vehicle emissions inspections and may also perform vehicle repairs. No regulation of the Board pertaining to test and repair shall bar inspection facilities from also performing vehicle repairs.

(Chgd. by L.1995 chs. 836, 851; L.2000 ch. 311, eff. 7/1/2000.)

§46.2-1177. Emissions inspection program.

The Director shall administer an emissions inspection program. Such program shall require biennial inspections of motor vehicles at official emissions inspection stations in accordance with this article and may require additional inspections of motor vehicles that have been shown by on-road testing to exceed emissions standards established by the Board.

The emissions inspections required in §46.2-1178 shall not apply to any:

1. Vehicle powered by a clean special fuel as defined in §58.1-2101, provided provisions of the Federal Clean Air Act permit such exemption for vehicles powered by a clean special fuel;

2. Motorcycle;

3. Vehicle which, at the time of its manufacture was not designed to meet emissions standards set or approved by the federal government;

4. Antique motor vehicle as defined in §46.2-100 and licensed pursuant to §46.2-730; or

5. Vehicle for which no testing standards have been adopted by the Board.

(Chgd. by L.1995 chs. 836, 851, eff. 7/1/95.)

§46.2-1178. Administration and scope of emissions inspection program.

A. Except as otherwise provided in this section, the emissions inspection program provided for in this article shall apply to motor vehicles having actual gross weights of 8,500 pounds or less that are registered in the Counties of Arlington, Fairfax, and Prince William, and the Cities of Alexandria, Fairfax, Falls Church, Manassas, and Manassas Park. The provisions of this subsection shall expire when the provisions of subsection C of this section become effective.

B. An emissions inspection program as required by regulations adopted by the Board under this article shall apply to motor vehicles that have actual gross weights of 8,500 pounds or less and are registered or operated primarily, as defined by the Board in accordance with the provisions of the Administrative Process Act (§9-6.14:1 et seq.), in the Counties of Chesterfield, Hanover, and Henrico and the Cities of Colonial Heights, Hopewell, and Richmond. Such emissions inspection program shall be a basic, test and repair program with the greatest number of inspection facilities consistent with the consumer protection and fee provisions herein as consistent with the Clean Air Act.

The provisions of this subsection shall apply but not necessarily be limited to (i) motor vehicles owned by governmental entities, (ii) motor vehicles owned by military personnel residing in those localities, (iii) motor vehicles owned by leasing or rental companies, and (iv) motor vehicles owned or leased by employees of the federal government and operated on a federal installation. The provisions of this subsection shall become effective July 1, 1995. The Board may promulgate regulations to implement the provisions of this article, but such regulations shall not require inspections in the localities mentioned in this subsection prior to the later of: (i) July 1, 1996; or (ii) the date on which the Federal Environmental Protection Agency, pursuant to the Clean Air Act, formally and in writing approves this program for such localities or on such later date as may be provided by regulations of the Board.

C. The emissions inspection program provided for in this subsection shall be a test and repair enhanced emissions inspection program with the greatest number of inspection facilities consistent with the consumer protection and fee provisions herein and may include on-road testing and remote sensing devices. Any enhanced emissions inspection program provided for in this article shall apply to motor vehicles that have actual gross weights of 10,000 pounds or less and are registered or operated primarily, as defined by the Board in accordance with the provisions of the Administrative Process Act (§9-6.14:1 et seq.) in the Counties of Arlington, Fairfax, Loudoun, Prince William, and Stafford and the Cities of Alexandria, Fairfax, Falls Church, Manassas, and Manassas Park.

The provisions of this subsection shall apply but not necessarily be limited to (i) motor vehicles owned by governmental entities, (ii) motor vehicles owned by military personnel residing in those localities, (iii) vehicles owned by leasing or rental companies, and (iv) motor vehicles owned or leased by employees of the federal government and operated on a federal installation.

The provisions of this subsection shall be effective January 1, 1996, or on such later date as may be provided by regulations of the Board. However, the provisions of this subsection may become effective immediately provided that (i) the federal Environmental Protection Agency, pursuant to the Clean Air Act, formally and in writing approves the program for such localities, (ii) the Governor determines in writing that expedited promulgation of such regulations is in the best interest of the Commonwealth, determining that such shall constitute an "emergency situation" pursuant to

§9-6.14:4.1, and (iii) the Governor authorizes the Board to promulgate the regulations as emergency regulations in accordance with this section.

D. Any emissions inspection program regulations in effect at the time the 1995 amendments to this section become effective shall remain in effect until the Board promulgates new regulations or amends or repeals existing regulations in accordance with this section.

(Chgd. by L.1995 chs. 836, 851; L.1997 ch. 507, eff. 7/1/97.)

§46.2-1178.1. On-road testing of motor vehicle emissions; authority to adopt regulations; civil charges.

A. The emissions inspection program authorized by §46.2-1177 and provided for in §46.2-1178 shall include on-road testing of motor vehicle emissions. The Board may promulgate regulations establishing on-road testing requirements including, but not limited to, collecting of data and information necessary to comply with the federal Clean Air Act Amendments of 1990, random testing of motor vehicle emissions, procedures to notify owners of test results, and assessment of civil charges for noncompliance with emissions standards adopted by the Board.

B. If an emissions test performed pursuant to this section indicates that a motor vehicle does not meet emissions standards established by the Board, the Board may collect from the owner of the vehicle a civil charge based on actual emissions. The Board shall establish a schedule of civil charges to be collected pursuant to this section. Such civil penalties shall not exceed $450 using 1990 as the base year and adjusted annually by the Consumer Price Index. The schedule of charges and their assessment shall be established by regulations promulgated to be in accordance with the provisions of the Administrative Process Act (§9-6.14:1 et seq.).

C. Civil charges assessed pursuant to this section shall be waived by the Board if, within ninety days of notice of the violation, the vehicle's owner provides proof that the vehicle (i) since the date of the violation, has passed a vehicle emissions test as provided in §46.2-1178, (ii) qualifies for an emissions inspection waiver as provided in §46.2-1181, or (iii) has qualified for an emissions inspection waiver as provided in §46.2-1181 within the twelve months prior to the violation.

D. Civil charges collected pursuant to this section shall be paid into the state treasury and deposited by the State Treasurer into the Vehicle Emissions Inspection Program Fund pursuant to §46.2-1182.2.

E. If on-road testing indicates that a motor vehicle does not exceed emissions standards adopted by the Board for on-road testing pursuant to §46.2-1179, such testing may be considered proof of compliance for the purposes of §46.2-1183 and may be considered to satisfy the requirements of §46.2-1177 for a biennial inspection. The Board shall establish criteria under which such testing shall satisfy the requirements of §46.2-1183.

(Added by L.1995 chs. 836, 851; chgd. by L.1996 chs. 35, 100, eff. 7/1/96.)

§46.2-1179. Board to adopt emissions standards.

The Board shall adopt emissions standards necessary to implement the emissions inspection program provided for in this article.

(Chgd. by L.1995 chs. 836, 851, eff. 7/1/95.)

§46.2-1179.1. Board to adopt clean alternative fuel fleet standards for motor vehicles; penalty.

A. For the purposes of this section:

"Clean alternative fuel" means any fuel including methanol, ethanol, other alcohols, reformulated gasoline, diesel, natural gases, liquified petroleum gas, hydrogen, and electricity or other power source used in a clean fuel vehicle that complies with the standards applicable to such vehicle under the federal Clean Air Act when using such fuel or other power source. In the case of a flexible fuel vehicle or dual fuel vehicle, "clean alternative fuel" means only a fuel for which the vehicle was certified when operating on clean alternative fuel.

"Fleet" means any centrally fueled fleet of ten or more motor vehicles owned or operated by a single entity. "Fleet" does not include motor vehicles held for lease or rental to the general public, motor vehicles held for sale by motor vehicle dealers, motor vehicles used for manufacturer product tests, law-enforcement and other emergency vehicles, or nonroad vehicles, including farm and construction vehicles.

B. The Board may adopt by regulation motor vehicle clean alternative fuel fleet standards consistent with the provisions of Part C of Title II of the federal Clean Air Act for model years beginning with the model year 1998 or the first succeeding model year for which adoption of such standards is practicable. If adoption and implementation by the Board of an equivalent air pollution reduction program is approved by the federal Environmental Protection Agency, the regulation and program authorized by this section shall not become effective. Such regulations shall contain the minimum phase-in schedule contained in Section 246(b) of Part C of Title II of the Clean Air Act. However, nothing in this section shall preclude affected fleet owners from exceeding the minimum requirements of the federal Clean Air Act. Beginning in 1995 and upon adoption of the standards by the Board, the Board shall require the fleet owned by the federal government to meet the clean alternative fuel fleet standard and phase-in schedule established by the Board. If necessary to meet the Board's standards and phase-in schedule, the Board shall require fleets owned by the federal government to convert a portion of existing fleet vehicles to the use of clean alternative fuels as defined by the federal Clean Air Act. The standards specified in this subsection shall apply only to (i) motor vehicles registered in localities designated by the federal Environmental Protection Agency, pursuant to the federal Clean Air Act, as serious, severe, or extreme air quality nonattainment areas, or as maintenance areas formerly designated serious, severe, or extreme and (ii) motor vehicles not registered in the above-mentioned localities, but having either (a) a base of operations or (b) a majority of their annual travel in one or more of those localities.

C. An owner of a covered fleet shall not use any motor vehicle or motor vehicle engine which is manufactured during or after the first model year to which the standards specified in subsection A of this section are applicable, if such vehicle or engine is registered or has its base of operations in the localities specified in subsection B of this section and has not been certified in accordance with regulations promulgated by the Board. The Board may promulgate regulations providing for reasonable exceptions consistent with the provisions of Part C of Title II of the federal Clean Air Act. Motor vehicles exempted from the provisions of this section shall forever be exempt.

D. Any person that violates the requirements of this section or any regulation adopted hereunder shall be subject to the penalties in §§46.2-1187 and 46.2-1187.2. Each day of violation shall be a separate offense, and each motor vehicle shall be treated separately in assessing violations.

E. In order to limit adverse economic and administrative impacts on covered fleets operating both in Virginia and in neighboring states, the Department of Environmental Quality shall, to the maximum extent practicable, coordinate the provisions of its regulations promulgated under this section with neighboring states' statutes and regulations relating to the use of clean alternative fuels by motor vehicle fleets.

F. The State Corporation Commission, as to matters within its jurisdiction, and the Department of Environmental Quality, as to other matters, may, should they deem such action necessary, promulgate regulations necessary or convenient to ensure the availability of clean alternative fuels to operators of fleets covered by the provisions of this section. The State Air Pollution Control Board may delegate to the Commissioner of Agriculture its authority under the Air Pollution Control Law of Virginia, Chapter 13 (§10.1-1300 et seq.) of Title 10.1, to implement and enforce any provisions of its regulations covering the availability of clean alternative fuels. Upon receiving such delegation, the authority to implement and enforce the regulations under the Air Pollution Control Law of Virginia shall be invested in the Commissioner, notwithstanding any provision of law contained in Title 10.1, except as provided in this section. The State Air Pollution Control Board, in delegating its authority under this section, may make the delegation subject to any conditions it deems appropriate to ensure effective implementation of the regulations according to the policies of the State Air Pollution Control Board.

(Chgd. by L.1995 ch. 141; L.1998 chs. 401, 421, eff. 7/1/98.)

§46.2-1180. Board to adopt regulations; exemption of certain motor vehicles.

A. The Board is authorized to adopt such regulations for purposes of implementation, administration, and regulation as may be necessary to carry out the provisions of this article. Such regulations shall include but not necessarily be limited to requirements for the following:

1. The collection of data and maintenance of records of emissions inspection test results and vehicle repairs under this article and the inspection results of the air pollution control systems or devices in accordance with §46.2-1048 and regulations of the Board.
2. The calibration of emissions testing equipment by emissions inspection stations to ensure conformance with the standards adopted by the Board.
3. The establishment of appropriate referee stations.
4. The permitting of emissions inspection stations and fleet emissions inspection stations and the licensing of emissions inspectors, including the suspension or revocation of such permit or license.
5. The protection of consumer interests in accordance with regulations of the Board concerning, but not limited to: (i) the number of inspection facilities and inspection lanes relative to population density, (ii) the proximity of inspection facilities to motor vehicle owners, (iii) the time spent waiting for inspections, and (iv) the days and hours of operation of inspection facilities.
6. The prohibition of any manufacturer or distributor of emissions testing equipment from directly or indirectly owning or operating any emissions testing facility or having any direct or indirect financial interest in any such facility other than the leasing of or providing financing for equipment related to emissions testing.
7. The certification of motor vehicle emissions repair technicians and emissions repair facilities, including the suspension or revocation of such certification. The regulations shall apply to emissions repair technicians and emissions repair facilities that conduct emissions-related repairs for vehicles that have failed a motor vehicle emissions test according to regulations adopted by the Board.

The Director shall administer these regulations and seek compliance with conditions of any contractual arrangements which the Commonwealth may make for inspection services related to air pollution control.

B. Motor vehicles being titled for the first time may be registered for up to two years without being subject to an emissions inspection, and the four immediately preceding model years being held in a motor vehicle dealer's inventory for resale may be registered in the localities mentioned in subsection C of §46.2-1178 for up to one year without being subject to an emissions inspection, provided that the dealer states in writing that the emissions equipment on the motor vehicle was operating in accordance with the manufacturer's or distributor's warranty at the time of resale.

C. No motor vehicle for which the Board has not adopted emissions inspection standards shall be subject to an emissions inspection.

D. The Director may enter into bilateral agreements with other states providing for assistance in enforcing each state's statutes and regulations relating to motor vehicle emissions and motor vehicle emissions programs as to vehicles registered in one state and operated in another. Subject to such bilateral agreement, owners of motor vehicles registered in other states and operated in Virginia shall be subject to the on-road testing provisions of §46.2-1178.1, and shall be notified of test results and assessment of civil charges for noncompliance with emissions standards adopted by the Board. Such notification shall also be provided to the appropriate motor vehicle agency in the state of registration.

(Chgd. by L.1995 chs. 836, 851; L.1997 ch. 559, eff. 7/1/97.)

§46.2-1181. Emissions inspection; cost of repairs; waivers.

A. A motor vehicle shall qualify for an emissions inspection waiver in the event that such vehicle has failed an initial inspection and subsequently failed a reinspection if the owner provides written proof that (i) at least the amount specified in this section has been spent by the owner on the maintenance and repair of the vehicle's engine and emission control system and related equipment and (ii) any emission control system or part thereof which has been removed, damaged, or rendered inoperable by any act enumerated in §46.2-1048 has been replaced and restored to operating condition.

B. The Executive Director shall establish and revise, as necessary, specifications and procedures for motor vehicle maintenance and repair of pollution control devices and systems.

C. For the purposes of subsection A of this section:

For motor vehicles subject to emissions inspections under subsection A of §46.2-1178, cost limitations on repairs under the emissions inspection program, including parts and labor, but excluding costs of repairs covered by warranties shall be $175 for pre-1980 model vehicles and $200 for 1980 and newer vehicles.

For motor vehicles subject to emissions inspections under subsection C of §46.2-1178, the cost limitations shall be a base amount of $450 per vehicle using 1990, or a later date if allowed by federal regulations and approved by the Board, as the base year and annually adjusted by the Consumer Price Index. The Board may phase in waiver amounts.

Repairs credited toward this waiver must be done by a repair technician certified in accordance with §46.2-1180. Repairs shall include parts and labor.

D. For the purposes of subsection A of this section, for motor vehicles subject to emissions inspections under subsection B of §46.2-1178, the cost limitations on repairs under the emissions inspection program, including parts and labor but excluding costs of repairs covered by warranties, shall be:

1. $75 for pre-1981 vehicles; and
2. $200 for 1981 and newer vehicles.

(Chgd. by L.1995 chs. 836, 851, eff. 7/1/95.)

§46.2-1182. Emissions inspection fees; exemption.

Emissions inspection stations performing emissions inspections under subsection A of §46.2-1178 may charge

$11.40 for each emissions inspection, but such charge shall not be mandatory. Any such fee shall be paid to the emissions inspection station.

Each emissions inspection station performing emissions inspections under subsection B of §46.2-1178 may charge for each emissions inspection an amount not to exceed $17.00. Any such fee shall be paid to and retained by the emissions inspection station.

Beginning at such date upon which the program becomes an enhanced emissions program, each emissions inspection station performing emissions inspections under subsection C of §46.2-1178 may charge an amount not to exceed $20.00 for each emissions inspection. Any such fee shall be paid to and retained by the emissions inspection station.

Within fourteen days of an initial failure of an emissions inspection, the vehicle's owner shall be entitled to one free reinspection at the station that conducted the original inspection.

(Chgd. by L.1995 chs. 836, 851, eff. 7/1/95.)

§46.2-1182.1. Additional registration fee; exemption.

Beginning July 1, 1994, in addition to any other fees imposed, at the time of registration by the Department of Motor Vehicles, the owner of any motor vehicle subject to registration in Virginia and subject to the program by virtue of the locality in which it is registered shall pay two dollars per year.

Beginning July 1, 1995, or later if required by regulation of the Board, owners of motor vehicles which are subject to the program by virtue of the location of their base of operation or the location where they are primarily operated shall remit a fee of two dollars per vehicle per year to the Department of Environmental Quality. Payment shall be made according to procedures and on a schedule prescribed by the Department of Environmental Quality. State and local governmental units and agencies shall be exempt from the payment of fees under this subsection.

(Chgd. by L.1995 chs. 836, 851, eff. 7/1/95.)

§46.2-1182.2. Vehicle Emissions Inspection Program Fund established; use of moneys.

A special nonreverting fund known as the Vehicle Emissions Inspection Program Fund is hereby established in the state treasury.

Notwithstanding the provisions of §2.1-180, all moneys collected pursuant to §46.2-1182.1 shall be paid into the treasury and credited to the Vehicle Emissions Inspection Program Fund.

No moneys remaining in the Fund at the end of each fiscal year shall revert to the general fund, but shall remain in the Fund. Interest earned on such moneys shall remain in the Fund and be credited to it.

The Department of Environmental Quality may release moneys from the Fund, on warrants issued by the State Comptroller, for covering the costs of the emissions inspection program. The moneys in this Fund may also be released for the purpose of long-term maintenance of air quality and the correction and prevention of nonattainment status for National Ambient Air Quality Standards through air quality programs under the direction of the Director.

§46.2-1183. Emissions inspection required prior to registration of certain vehicles; records.

No vehicle subject to the provisions of this article shall be registered or reregistered until it has passed an emissions inspection or has been issued an emissions inspection waiver. Any (i) proof of compliance with emissions standards and emissions inspection requirements and (ii) emissions inspection waiver issued for any motor vehicle shall be valid for two years from the end of the month in which it is issued, regardless of any sale or trade of the motor vehicle for which either document was issued during that time, unless such motor vehicle has failed on-road testing pursuant to §46.2-1178.1 and has not subsequently passed an emissions inspection or received a waiver. Motor vehicles being titled for the first time shall be considered to have valid emissions inspection certificates for a period of two years from the month of first titling. The Commissioner of Motor Vehicles may enter into an agreement with the Director whereby the Department of Motor Vehicles may refuse to register or reregister those motor vehicles subject to emissions inspection programs set forth in this article if the registration period for such vehicles exceeds the valid emissions inspection period by a period of time to be determined by the Director in consultation with the Department of Motor Vehicles and the Commissioner.

Owners of motor vehicles that are not registered with the Department of Motor Vehicles shall maintain such records pertaining to all vehicles located or operated in the areas specified in §46.2-1178 as the Board may by regulation require. Such records shall contain proof of compliance with this article and be made available to the Department of Environmental Quality upon the Department's request.

(Chgd. by L.1995 chs. 836, 851; L.1996 chs. 35, 100, eff. 7/1/96.)

§46.2-1184. Fleet emissions inspection stations; certificates of inspection; dealer's inventory; investigations; revocation of permit.

Any registered owner or lessee of a fleet of at least twenty vehicles may apply to the Director for a permit to establish a fleet emissions inspection station consistent with federal requirements. The Director shall not issue any fleet emissions inspection station permit until it has found that the applicant:

1. Maintains an established place of business for the applicant's fleet of vehicles;
2. Has obtained approved machinery, tools and equipment to adequately conduct the required emissions inspection in the manner prescribed by regulations of the Board;
3. Employs properly trained and licensed personnel to perform the necessary labor; and
4. Agrees to provide test records and data as may be prescribed by the Director.

Upon issuance of a permit by the Director, the owner or lessee of the motor vehicle fleet may conduct emissions inspections of the vehicles in his fleet. No emissions inspection approval shall be issued to any fleet vehicle until it has been inspected and found to comply with applicable regulations.

No holder of a fleet emissions inspection station permit shall inspect any vehicle for which such permittee is not the registered owner or lessee.

§46.2-1185. Investigation of inspection stations; revocation or suspension of permits for emissions inspection stations.

The Director shall investigate the operation of each emissions inspection station and fleet emissions inspection station as the conditions and circumstances of such operation indicate. He may require the holder of any permit to submit such documentation required concerning the operation of such inspection station. The Director may suspend or revoke and require the forfeiture of any emissions inspection station permit if he finds that such station is not operated in accordance with the provisions of this article and the regulations adopted by the Board or the holder of such permit has failed or refused to submit records or documentation required.

If the Director finds that any permit holder has violated any provision of this article or any order or regulation of the

Board, after notice or a reasonable attempt to give notice to the permit holder, the Director may, without a hearing, suspend the permit of the emissions inspection station and require the permit holder immediately to cease performing emissions inspections. Within ten days of such action, the Director shall, after reasonable notice to the permit holder as to the time and place thereof, hold a hearing to affirm, modify, amend, or cancel the suspension and the requirement to cease performing emissions inspections. With the consent of the permit holder, the Director may forego such hearing and allow the suspension and requirement to cease performing emissions inspections to stand. If the Director finds that a permit holder is not complying with any such suspension or requirement to cease performing emissions inspections, the Director may proceed in accordance with §46.2-1187 or §46.2-1187.2.

Nothing in this section shall limit the Director's authority to proceed against the permit holder directly under §46.2-1187 or §46.2-1187.2.

§46.2-1186. False certificate.

No person shall make, issue, or knowingly use any imitation or otherwise counterfeit official certificate of emissions inspection.

No person shall issue or cause or permit to be issued any certificate of inspection knowing it to be fictitious or knowing it to have been issued for a vehicle other than the vehicle identified on the certificate.

§46.2-1187. Penalties.

Any person violating this article shall be guilty of a Class 3 misdemeanor for the first offense and fined not less than $100 nor more than $1,000 for each subsequent offense except as otherwise provided in this article. If any official emissions inspection station violates this article or regulations of the Director made pursuant hereto, the Director, in addition to or in lieu of such fine imposed by a court, may suspend the permit of the emissions inspection station or if, in the opinion of the Director, the facts warrant such action, the Director may revoke the authority and cancel the permit of such inspection station, whether or not the violation is a first offense against this article.

§46.2-1187.1. Right of entry.

Whenever it is necessary for the purposes of this article, the Executive Director or his duly authorized agent or employee at reasonable times may enter any establishment or upon any public or private property to obtain information or conduct surveys, audits, or investigations.

§46.2-1187.2. Compelling compliance with regulations and order of Board; penalty.

Any emissions inspection station owner violating or failing, neglecting, or refusing to obey any regulation or order of the Board may be compelled to comply by injunction, mandamus, or other appropriate remedy.

Without limiting the remedies which may be obtained under the foregoing provisions of this section, any emissions inspection station owner violating or failing, neglecting, or refusing to obey any regulation or order of the Board or any provision of this article, shall, in the discretion of the court, be subject to a civil penalty of no more than $25,000 for each violation. Each day of violation shall constitute a separate offense. In determining the amount of any civil penalty to be assessed, the court shall consider, in addition to such other factors as it may deem appropriate, the size of the emissions inspection station owner's business, the severity of the economic impact of the penalty on that business, and the seriousness of the violation. Such civil penalties may, in the discretion of the court, be directed to be paid into the treasury of the county, city, or town in which the violation occurred to be used to abate environmental pollution in whatever manner the court, by order, may direct. However, where the emissions inspection station owner is the county, city, or town or an agent thereof, the court shall direct the penalty to be paid into the state treasury.

With the consent of the emissions inspection station owner who has violated or failed, neglected, or refused to obey any regulation or order of the Board or any provision of this article, the Board may, in any order issued by the Board against such owner, provide for the payment of civil charges in specific sums, not to exceed the limit in the foregoing provisions of this section. Such civil charges shall be in lieu of any civil penalty which could be imposed under the foregoing provisions of this section.

Any penalty provided for in this section to which an emissions inspection station owner is subject shall apply to any emissions inspector or certified emissions repair mechanic employed by or at that station.

As to emissions inspection station owners, emissions inspectors, and certified emissions repair mechanics, minor violations as set forth in Board regulations may be punishable by letters of reprimand from the Department. Major violations as set forth in Board regulations may be punishable by probation, suspension and/or license or certificate revocation, depending on the nature and type of violation. Civil penalties may be imposed only for major types of violations.

The Board shall provide by regulation a process whereby emissions inspection station owners, emissions inspectors and certified emissions repair mechanics may appeal penalties for violations. Such regulations regarding the process to appeal penalties for violations shall provide that the appeal process shall be handled by a person other than the Program Manager for the applicable emissions program or one of his regional employees.

(Chgd. by L.1995 chs. 836, 851, eff. 7/1/95.)

§46.2-1187.3. Vehicles used for investigations.

Motor vehicles owned by the Commonwealth and used solely for investigations pursuant to this article may be issued the same license plates as those issued for vehicles owned by private citizens. The Executive Director shall certify under oath to the Commissioner of the Department of Motor Vehicles the vehicles to be used solely for such investigations.

ARTICLE 23
MOTORCYCLE RIDER SAFETY

§46.2-1188. Motorcycle rider safety training courses.

"Motorcycle rider safety training courses" shall mean courses of instruction in the operation of motorcycles, including instruction in the safe on-road operation of motorcycles, the rules of the road, and the laws of the Commonwealth relating to motor vehicles. Courses shall meet the requirements of this article and regulations issued pursuant to this article by the Department of Motor Vehicles and shall be required to be approved by the Department of Motor Vehicles.

§46.2-1189. Authority of the Department of Motor Vehicles.

The Department of Motor Vehicles may do all things necessary to carry out the purposes of this article, including the promulgation of regulations not inconsistent with law. Where such course is authorized at a high school, the Department shall work with the Department of Education's section of driver education to implement such course.

§46.2-1190. Regional motorcycle rider safety training centers.

Any high school, institution of higher education, or safety training expert authorized by the Department may organize a regional motorcycle rider safety training center and offer motorcycle rider safety training courses. The curriculum, accreditation, and geographic areas in which each training center may offer courses shall be provided for by regulations of the Department. Instructors shall meet the requirements of the Department and the requirements of the institution, or safety training expert offering the program. Instructors may be employed on a calendar year basis.

§46.2-1191. Motorcycle Rider Safety Training Program Fund.

To finance the cost of the Motorcycle Rider Safety Training Program, the Department of Motor Vehicles shall deposit the fee collected for the issuance of each motorcycle learner's permit and three dollars of the fee collected for the issuance of each motorcycle registration and all motorcycle driver's license endorsement fees into a special fund to be known as the Motorcycle Rider Safety Training Program Fund. The Department shall use the Fund as necessary for: (i) the costs of the Department of Motor Vehicles incurred in the administration of this article, (ii) the funding or contracts with approved regional cycle rider safety training centers for the conducting of courses, and (iii) for any other purposes related to the administration of this article.

(Chgd. by L.1997 chs. 104, 493; L.1998 ch. 322, eff. 7/1/98.)

§46.2-1192. Awarding of contracts by Department; payments to regional training centers.

The Department of Motor Vehicles is authorized to enter into contracts with regional motorcycle rider safety training centers for the conducting of motorcycle rider safety training courses, and to make payments in fulfillment of those contracts from funds appropriated from the Motorcycle Rider Safety Training Program Fund.

CHAPTER 12
ABANDONED, IMMOBILIZED, UNATTENDED AND TRESPASSING VEHICLES; PARKING

Article

1. Abandoned Vehicles. (Secs. 46.2-1200 to 46.2-1208)
2. Immobilized and Unattended Vehicles. (Secs. 46.2-1209 to 46.2-1215)
3. Trespassing Vehicles, Parking, and Towing. (Secs. 46.2-1216 to 46.2-1239)

ARTICLE 1
ABANDONED VEHICLES

Section

46.2-1200. Definitions.
46.2-1200.1. Abandoning motor vehicles prohibited; penalty.
46.2-1201. Ordinances.
46.2-1202. Notice to owner of vehicle taken into custody.
46.2-1203. Sale of vehicle at public auction; disposition of proceeds.
46.2-1204. Vehicles abandoned in garages.
46.2-1205. Disposition of inoperable abandoned vehicles.
46.2-1206. Surrender of certificate of title, etc., where motor vehicle acquired for demolition; records to be kept by demolisher.
46.2-1207. Certification of disposal; reimbursement of locality by Commissioner.
46.2-1208. Vehicles abandoned on private property other than garages.

§46.2-1200. Definitions.

As used in this article:

"Abandoned motor vehicle" means a motor vehicle, trailer, or semitrailer or part of a motor vehicle, trailer, or semitrailer that:

1. Is inoperable and is left unattended on public property, other than an interstate highway or primary highway, for more than forty-eight hours, or
2. Has remained illegally on public property for more than forty-eight hours, or
3. Has remained for more than forty-eight hours on private property without the consent of the property's owner, regardless of whether it was brought onto the private property with the consent of the owner or person in control of the private property, or
4. Is inoperable, left unattended, or both, on an interstate highway, or
5. Is inoperable, left unattended, or both, on the shoulder of a primary highway.

"Inoperable abandoned motor vehicle" means an abandoned motor vehicle which is inoperable and whose fair market value, as determined by the locality's official responsible for assessing motor vehicles under §58.1-3503, is less than the cost of its restoration to an operable condition.

(Chgd. by L.1997 ch. 431, eff. 7/1/97.)

§46.2-1200.1. Abandoning motor vehicles prohibited; penalty.

No person shall cause any motor vehicle to become an abandoned motor vehicle as defined in §46.2-1200. In any prosecution for a violation of this section, proof that the defendant was, at the time that the vehicle was found abandoned, the owner of the vehicle shall constitute in evidence a rebuttable presumption that the owner was the person who committed the violation. Such presumption, however, shall not arise if the owner of the vehicle provided notice to the Department, as provided in §46.2-604, that he had sold or otherwise transferred the ownership of the vehicle.

A summons for a violation of this section shall be executed by mailing a copy of the summons by first-class mail to the address of the owner of the vehicle as shown on the records of the Department of Motor Vehicles. If the person fails to appear on the date of return set out in the summons, a new summons shall be issued and delivered to the sheriff of the county, city, or town for service on the accused personally. If the person so served then fails to appear on the date of return set out in the summons, proceedings for contempt shall be instituted.

Any person convicted of a violation of this section shall be subject to a civil penalty of no more than $500. If any person fails to pay any such penalty, his privilege to drive a motor vehicle on the highways of the Commonwealth shall be suspended as provided in §46.2-395.

All penalties collected under this section shall be paid into the state treasury to be credited to the Literary Fund as provided in §46.2-114.

§46.2-1201. Ordinances.

The governing body of any county, city, or town may provide by ordinance for taking abandoned vehicles into custody and disposing of them in accordance with this article.

Any county, city, or town may take any abandoned motor vehicle into custody. The locality may employ its own personnel, equipment, and facilities or hire persons, equipment, and facilities, or firms or corporations that may be independent contractors for removing, preserving, storing, and selling at public auction abandoned motor vehicles.

(Chgd. by L.1997 ch. 150, eff. 7/1/97.)

§46.2-1202. Notice to owner of vehicle taken into custody.

Any locality or its authorized agent that takes an abandoned motor vehicle into custody shall, within fifteen days, by registered or certified mail, return receipt requested, notify the owner of record of the motor vehicle and all persons having security interests in the vehicle of record, that it has been taken into custody. The notice shall (i) state the year, make, model, and serial number of the abandoned motor vehicle; (ii) set forth the location of the facility where it is being held; and (iii) inform the owner and any persons having security interests of their right to reclaim it within fifteen days after the date of the notice after payment of all towing, preservation, and storage charges resulting from placing the vehicle in custody. The notice shall state that the failure of the owner or persons having security interests to reclaim the vehicle within the time provided shall constitute (i) a waiver by the owner and all persons having any security interests of all right, title, and interest in the vehicle and (ii) consent to the sale of the abandoned motor vehicle at a public auction.

If records of the Department contain no address for the owner or no address of any person shown by the Department's records to have a security interest, or if the identity and addresses of the owner and all persons having security interests cannot be determined with reasonable certainty, notice by publication once in a newspaper of general circulation in the area where the motor vehicle was abandoned shall be sufficient to meet all requirements of notice pursuant to this article as to any person who cannot be notified pursuant to the foregoing provisions of this section. Notice by publication may contain multiple listings of abandoned motor vehicles. Any notice of this kind shall be within the time requirements prescribed by this section for notice by mail and shall have the same contents required for a notice by mail.

The consequences of failure to reclaim an abandoned motor vehicle shall be as set forth in a notice given in accordance with and pursuant to this section.

(Chgd. by L.1997 ch. 150, eff. 7/1/97.)

§46.2-1203. Sale of vehicle at public auction; disposition of proceeds.

If an abandoned motor vehicle is not reclaimed as provided for in §46.2-1202, the locality or its authorized agent shall, notwithstanding the provisions of §46.2-617, sell it at public auction. The purchaser of the motor vehicle shall take title to the motor vehicle free of all liens and claims of ownership of others, shall receive a sales receipt at the auction, and shall be entitled to apply to and receive from the Department a certificate of title and registration card for the vehicle. The sales receipt from the sale shall be sufficient title only for purposes of transferring the vehicle to a demolisher for demolition, wrecking, or dismantling, and in that case no further titling of the vehicle shall be necessary. From the proceeds of the sale of an abandoned motor vehicle the locality or its authorized agent shall reimburse itself for the expenses of the auction, the cost of towing, preserving, and storing the vehicle which resulted from placing the abandoned motor vehicle in custody, and all notice and publication costs incurred pursuant to §46.2-1202. Any remainder from the proceeds of a sale shall be held for the owner of the abandoned motor vehicle or any person having security interests in the vehicle, as their interests may appear, for ninety days, and then be deposited into the treasury of the locality in which the abandoned motor vehicle was abandoned.

§46.2-1204. Vehicles abandoned in garages.

Notwithstanding §46.2-1200, any motor vehicle, trailer, semitrailer, or part thereof shall be considered abandoned and may be reported by the garagekeeper to the political subdivision if it has been left in a garage for more than ten days or for more than ten days beyond the period the vehicle was to remain on the premises pursuant to a contract, after notice by registered or certified mail, return receipt requested, to the owner of record and all persons having security interests of record therein, to reclaim the vehicle within fifteen days of the notice. Any abandoned motor vehicle left in a garage may be taken into custody by the locality in accordance with §46.2-1201 and shall be subject to the notice and sale provisions contained in §§46.2-1202 and 46.2-1203. If, however, the vehicle is reclaimed in accordance with §46.2-1202, the person reclaiming it, in addition to the other charges required to be paid, shall pay the reasonable charges of the garagekeeper, unless otherwise provided by contract or ordinance. If the vehicle is sold pursuant to §46.2-1203, any garagekeeper's charges shall be paid from, and to the extent of, the excess of the proceeds of sale after paying the expenses of the auction, the costs of towing, preserving, and storing the vehicle which resulted from placing the vehicle in custody and all notice and publication costs incurred pursuant to §46.2-1202. Except as otherwise provided in this article, nothing in this section shall restrict any rights conferred on any person under §§43-32 through 43-36.

For the purposes of this section, "garage" means any commercial parking place, motor vehicle storage facility, or establishment for the servicing, repair, maintenance, or sale of motor vehicles whether or not the vehicle had been brought to that location with the consent of the owner or person in control of the premises and "garagekeeper" means the operator of a garage.

§46.2-1205. Disposition of inoperable abandoned vehicles.

Notwithstanding any other provisions of this article, any inoperable motor vehicle, trailer, semitrailer, or part of a motor vehicle, trailer, or semitrailer which has been taken into custody pursuant to other provisions of this article may be disposed of to a demolisher, without the title and without the notification procedures, by the person or locality on whose property or in whose possession the motor vehicle, trailer, or semitrailer is found. The demolisher, on taking custody of the inoperable abandoned motor vehicle shall notify the Department on forms and in the manner prescribed by the Commissioner. Notwithstanding any other provision of law, no other report or notice shall be required in this instance.

§46.2-1206. Surrender of certificate of title, etc., where motor vehicle acquired for demolition; records to be kept by demolisher.

No demolisher who purchases or otherwise acquires a motor vehicle for wrecking, dismantling, or demolition shall be required to obtain a certificate of title for the motor vehicle in his own name. After the motor vehicle has been demolished, processed, or changed so that it physically is no longer a motor vehicle, the demolisher shall surrender to the Department for cancellation the certificate of title or sales receipt for the vehicle. The Department shall issue the appropriate forms and regulations governing the surrender of sales receipts and certificates of title.

Demolishers shall keep accurate and complete records of all motor vehicles purchased or received by them in the course of their business. These records shall contain the name and address of the person from whom each motor vehicle was purchased or received and the date on which purchases or receipts occurred. These records shall be open for inspection by the Department at any time during normal business hours.

§46.2-1207. Certification of disposal; reimbursement of locality by Commissioner.

On certification by a locality on forms provided by the Department that an inoperable abandoned motor vehicle left on property within the locality has been disposed of as provided in §46.2-1205, the Commissioner shall reimburse the locality fifty dollars for each inoperable abandoned motor vehicle disposed of at the expense of the locality. These reimbursements shall be made from appropriations made in the general appropriations act. In the event the appropriation is insufficient to satisfy requests for reimbursement, payments shall be made in chronological order on the basis of the date on which the requests were received. No payments, however, shall be made for requests received on any date until adequate funds are available to pay all requests received on that date. The Commissioner may promulgate regulations necessary to carry out the provisions of this section. These regulations shall include the requirement of the identification number or motor number of the vehicle for which reimbursement is applied, or an acceptable reason why that number is not furnished.

No reimbursement shall be made to any locality for vehicles which it acquires from sources outside its jurisdiction nor for vehicles it receives from dealers engaged in the business of dismantling used automobiles.

§46.2-1208. Vehicles abandoned on private property other than garages.

Notwithstanding any other provisions of this article, if an abandoned motor vehicle is left on private property, other than an establishment covered by the provisions of §46.2-1204, regardless of whether the vehicle had been brought to that location with the consent of the owner or person in control of the private property, the owner or person in control of the private property may send a notice, by registered or certified mail, return receipt requested, to the owner of record of the motor vehicle and all persons having security interests in the vehicle of record in the office of the Department, describing the motor vehicle by year, make, model, and serial number, and advising that unless the vehicle is reclaimed and removed within thirty days from the date of the notice, its owner and all persons having security interests in the vehicle shall have waived all right, title, and interest in the vehicle. If the motor vehicle is not reclaimed by its owner or a person having a security interest in the vehicle of record within thirty days from the date of the notice, the owner or person in control of the private property on which the motor vehicle was abandoned may apply to the Department for a title to such vehicle. On verification that the notice provisions of this section have been complied with and payment of the certificate of title fee prescribed by §46.2-627, the Department shall issue a certificate of title to the vehicle in the name of the person submitting the application. The Commissioner shall issue appropriate forms and promulgate appropriate regulations governing applications for title to abandoned motor vehicles pursuant to this section.

The provisions of this section shall be applicable in the case of any motor vehicle, trailer, semitrailer, or part of a motor vehicle, trailer, or semitrailer abandoned on private property, whether or not the locality in which the private property is located has provided by ordinance for the removal and disposition of abandoned vehicles in accordance with this article.

The provisions of this section shall apply only to motor vehicles registered in Virginia. In cases of motor vehicles registered in other states, the Commissioner shall issue certificates of title to their owners on proof satisfactory to the Commissioner that the persons required to be notified by registered or certified mail have received actual notice fully containing the information required by this section.

ARTICLE 2
IMMOBILIZED AND UNATTENDED VEHICLES

Section

§46.2-1209. Unattended or immobile vehicles, generally.

No person shall leave any motor vehicle, trailer, semitrailer, or part or combination thereof unattended on or adjacent to any roadway if it constitutes a hazard in the use of the highway. No person shall leave any unattended motor vehicle, trailer, semitrailer, or part or combination thereof longer than twenty-four hours on or adjacent to any roadway outside the corporate limits of any city or town, or on an interstate highway or limited access highway, expressway, or parkway inside the corporate limits of any city or town. Any law-enforcement officer may remove it or have it removed to a storage area for safekeeping and shall report the removal to the Department and to the owner of the motor vehicle, trailer, semitrailer, or combination as promptly as possible. Before obtaining possession of the motor vehicle, trailer, semitrailer, or combination, its owner shall pay to the parties entitled thereto all costs incidental to its removal or storage. In any violation of this section the owner of such motor vehicle, trailer, semitrailer or part or combination of a motor vehicle, trailer, or semitrailer, shall be presumed to be the person committing the violation; however, this presumption shall be rebuttable by competent evidence. Where it is shown to the satisfaction of the court that the motor vehicle, trailer, semitrailer, or part or combination of a motor vehicle, trailer, or semitrailer was stolen or illegally used by a person other than the owner without his authorization, express or implied, it shall be forthwith returned to its owner who shall be relieved of the payment of any costs. In any case in which the identity of the violator cannot be determined, or where it is found by a court that this section was not violated, the costs of the removal and storage of the vehicle shall be paid out of the state treasury from the appropriation for criminal charges. If any person convicted of violating this section fails or refuses to pay these costs or if the identity or whereabouts of the owner is unknown and unascertainable after a diligent search has been made or after notice to the owner at his address as indicated by the records of the Department and to the holder of any lien of record with the Department, against the motor vehicle, trailer, semitrailer, or combination, the Commissioner may, after thirty days and after having the value of such motor vehicle, trailer, semitrailer, or combination determined by three disinterested dealers dispose of it by public or private sale. The proceeds from the sale shall be forthwith paid by him into the state treasury and shall be set aside as a special fund to be used to meet the expenses of the Department in carrying out the duties required by this section and to reimburse the owner of such motor vehicle, trailer, semitrailer, or combination as hereafter provided in this section.

If after the sale or other disposition of the motor vehicle, trailer, semitrailer, or combination the ownership of a motor vehicle, trailer, or semitrailer at the time of its removal is established satisfactorily to the Commissioner by the person claiming its ownership, the Commissioner shall pay him so much of the proceeds from the sale or other disposition of the motor vehicle, trailer, semitrailer, or combination as remains after paying the costs of removal, storage, investigation of ownership, appraisal, and sale.

§46.2-1210. Motor vehicles immobilized by weather conditions or emergencies.

Whenever any motor vehicle, trailer, semitrailer, or combination or part of a motor vehicle, trailer, or semitrailer is immobilized on any roadway by weather conditions or other emergency situations, the Department of Transportation may move or have the vehicle removed to some reasonably accessible portion of the adjacent right-of-way. Disposition thereafter shall be effected as provided by §46.2-1209.

§46.2-1211. Removal of motor vehicles obstructing movement; storage; payment of costs.

Whenever any motor vehicle, trailer, semitrailer, or part of a motor vehicle, trailer, or semitrailer interferes with the free ingress, egress, or movement on any premises, driveway, or parking area, without the permission of the owner of that property, any law-enforcement officer may remove it or have it removed to a storage area for safekeeping and shall report the removal to the Department and to the owner of the motor vehicle, trailer, semitrailer, or other vehicle as promptly as possible. Before obtaining the possession of his property, the owner shall pay to the parties entitled thereto all costs incidental to its removal or storage.

§46.2-1212. Authority to provide for temporary removal and disposition of vehicles involved in accidents.

The governing body of any county, city, or town may provide by ordinance that whenever a motor vehicle, trailer, or semitrailer involved in an accident is so located as to impede the orderly flow of traffic, the police may (i) at no cost to the owner or operator remove the motor vehicle, trailer, or semitrailer to some point in the vicinity where it will not impede the flow of traffic or (ii) have the vehicle removed to a storage area for safekeeping and shall report the removal to the Department and to the owner of the vehicle as promptly as possible. If the vehicle is removed to a storage area under clause (ii), the owner shall pay to the parties entitled thereto all costs incidental to its removal and storage.

§46.2-1212.1. Authority to provide for removal and disposition of vehicles and cargoes of vehicles involved in accidents.

A. As a result of a motor vehicle accident or incident, the Department of State Police and/or local law-enforcement agency in conjunction with other public safety agencies may, without the consent of the owner or carrier, remove:

1. A vehicle, cargo, or other personal property that has been (i) damaged or spilled within the right-of-way or any portion of a roadway in the state highway system and (ii) is blocking the roadway or may otherwise be endangering public safety; or

2. Cargo or personal property that the Department of Transportation, Department of Emergency Services, or the fire officer in charge has reason to believe is a hazardous material, hazardous waste or regulated substance as defined by the Virginia Waste Management Act (§10.1-1400 et seq.), a hazardous waste or regulated substance as defined by the Hazardous Materials Transportation Act (49 U.S.C. §1808 et seq.) or the State Water Control Law (§62.1-44 et seq.), if the Department of Transportation or applicable person complies with the applicable procedures and instructions defined either by the Department of Emergency Services or the fire officer in charge.

B. The Department of Transportation, Department of State Police, Department of Emergency Services, local law-enforcement agency and other local public safety agencies and their officers, employees and agents, shall not be held responsible for any damages or claims that may result from the failure to exercise any authority granted under this section provided they are acting in good faith.

C. The owner and carrier, if any, of the vehicle, cargo or personal property removed or disposed of under the authority of this section shall reimburse the Department of Transportation, Department of State Police, Department of Emergency Services, local law-enforcement agency, and local public safety agencies for all costs incurred in the removal and subsequent disposition of such property.

(Added by L.1997 ch. 431, eff. 7/1/97.)

§46.2-1213. Removal and disposition of unattended, or immobile vehicles; ordinances in counties, cities, and towns.

A. The governing body of any county, city, or town may by ordinance provide for the removal for safekeeping of motor vehicles, trailers, semitrailers, or parts thereof to a storage area if:

1. It is left unattended on a public highway or other public property and constitutes a traffic hazard;

2. It is illegally parked;

3. It is left unattended for more than ten days either on public property or on private property without the permission of the property owner, lessee, or occupant;

4. It is immobilized on a public roadway by weather conditions or other emergency situation.

B. Removal shall be carried out by or under the direction of a law-enforcement officer. The ordinance, however, shall not authorize removal of motor vehicles, trailers, semitrailers, and parts thereof from private property without the written request of the owner, lessee, or occupant of the premises. The ordinance may also provide that the person at whose request the motor vehicle, trailer, semitrailer, or part of a motor vehicle, trailer, or semitrailer is removed from private property shall indemnify the county, city, or town against any loss or expense incurred by reason of removal, storage, or sale thereof. Any such ordinance may also provide that it shall be presumed that such motor vehicle, trailer, semitrailer, or part thereof is abandoned if it (i) lacks either a current license plate; or a current county, city or town license plate or sticker; or a valid state safety inspection certificate or sticker; and (ii) it has been in a specific location for four days without being moved. As promptly as possible, each removal shall be reported to a local governmental office to be designated in the ordinance and to the owner of the motor vehicle, trailer, or semitrailer. Before obtaining possession of the motor vehicle, trailer, semitrailer, or part thereof, the owner shall pay to the parties entitled thereto all costs incidental to its removal and storage and locating the owner. If the owner fails or refuses to pay the cost or if his identity or whereabouts is unknown and unascertainable after a diligent search has been made, and after notice to him at his last known address and to the holder of any lien of record with the office of the Department against the motor vehicle, trailer, semitrailer, or part of a motor vehicle, trailer, or semitrailer, the vehicle shall be treated as an abandoned vehicle under the provisions of Article 1 (§46.2-1200 et seq.) of this chapter.

§46.2-1214. Sale of personal property found in unattended or abandoned vehicles.

Any personal property found in any unattended or abandoned motor vehicle, trailer, or semitrailer may be sold incident to the sale of the vehicle as authorized in this article.

§46.2-1215. Leaving vehicles on private property prohibited; authority of counties, cities, and towns to provide for removal and disposition; notice of disposition.

No person shall leave any motor vehicle, trailer, semitrailer, or part of a motor vehicle, trailer, or semitrailer on the private property of any other person without his consent. The governing body of any county, city, or town may by ordinance provide, that on complaint of the owner of the property on which such motor vehicle, trailer, semitrailer, or part thereof has been left for more than seventy-two hours, that such motor vehicle, trailer, semitrailer, or part thereof, may be removed by or under the direction of a law-enforcement officer to a storage area. The ordinance shall require the owners of private property which is normally open to the public for parking to post or cause to be posted signs warning that vehicles left on the property for more than seventy-two hours will be towed or removed at their owners' expense. The ordinance may also provide that the person at whose request the vehicle, trailer, semitrailer, or part thereof is so removed shall indemnify the county, city, or town against any loss or expense incurred by reason of removal, storage, or sale thereof.

In the case of the removal of a motor vehicle, trailer, semitrailer, or part of a motor vehicle, trailer, or semitrailer from private property, when it cannot be readily sold, the motor vehicle, trailer, semitrailer, or part may be disposed of in whatever manner the governing body of the county, city, or town may provide.

In all other respects, the provisions of §§46.2-1213 and 46.2-1217 shall apply to these removals. Disposal of a motor vehicle, trailer, or semitrailer may at the option of the governing body of the county, city, or town be carried out under either the provisions of §46.2-1213, or under the provisions of this section after a diligent search for the owner, after notice to him at his last known address and to the holder of any lien of record in the office of the Department against the motor vehicle, trailer, or semitrailer, and after the motor vehicle, trailer, or semitrailer has been held at least sixty days.

The Department shall be notified of the disposition of any motor vehicle, trailer, or semitrailer under §46.2-1213 or the provisions of this section.

ARTICLE 3
TRESPASSING VEHICLES, PARKING, AND TOWING

§46.2-1216. Removal or immobilization of motor vehicles against which there are outstanding parking violations; ordinances.

The governing body of any county, city, or town may provide by ordinance that any motor vehicle parked on the public highways or public grounds against which there are three or more unpaid or otherwise unsettled parking violation notices may be removed to a place within such county, city, or town or in an adjacent locality designated by the chief law-enforcement officer for the temporary storage of the vehicle, or the vehicle may be immobilized in a manner which will prevent its removal or operation except by authorized law-enforcement personnel. The governing body of any county having the urban county executive form of government and any county, city, or town adjacent to such county except any county having the county manager plan of government and any city having a 1980 census population of more than 262,000 but less than 265,000 may also provide by ordinance that whenever any motor vehicle against which there are three or more outstanding unpaid or otherwise unsettled parking violation notices is found parked upon private property, including privately owned streets and roads, the vehicle may, by towing or otherwise, be removed or immobilized in the manner provided above; provided that no motor vehicle may be removed or immobilized from property which is owned or occupied as a single family residence. Any such ordinance shall further provide that no such vehicle parked on private property may be removed or immobilized unless written authorization to enforce this section has been given by the owner of the property or an association of owners formed pursuant to Chapter 4.1 (§55-79.1 et seq.) or Chapter 4.2 (§55-79.39 et seq.) of Title 55 and that the local governing body has provided written assurance to the owner of the property that he will be held harmless from all loss, damage, or expense, including costs and attorney's fees, that may be incurred as a result of the towing or otherwise of any motor vehicle pursuant to this section. The ordinance shall provide that the removal or immobilization of the vehicle shall be by or under the direction of, an officer or employee of the police department or sheriff's office.

Any ordinance shall provide that it shall be the duty of the law-enforcement personnel removing or immobilizing the motor vehicle or under whose direction such vehicle is removed or immobilized, to inform as soon as practicable the owner of the removed or immobilized vehicle of the nature and circumstances of the prior unsettled parking violation notices for which the vehicle was removed or immobilized. In any case involving immobilization of a vehicle pursuant to this section, there shall be placed on the vehicle, in a conspicuous manner, a notice warning that the vehicle has been immobilized and that any attempt to move the vehicle might damage it.

Any ordinance shall provide that the owner of an immobilized vehicle, or other person acting on his behalf, shall be allowed at least twenty-four hours from the time of immobilization to repossess or secure the release of the vehicle. Failure to repossess or secure the release of the vehicle within that time period may result in the removal of the vehicle to a storage area for safekeeping under the direction of law-enforcement personnel.

Any ordinance shall provide that the owner of the removed or immobilized motor vehicle, or other person acting on his behalf, shall be permitted to repossess or to secure the release of the vehicle by payment of the outstanding parking violation notices for which the vehicle was removed or immobilized and by payment of all costs incidental to the immobilization, removal, and storage of the vehicle, and the efforts to locate the owner of the vehicle. Should the owner fail or refuse to pay such fines and costs, or should the identity or whereabouts of the owner be unknown and unascertainable, the ordinance may provide for the sale of the motor vehicle in accordance with the procedures set forth in §46.2-1213.

§46.2-1217. Local governing body may regulate certain towing.

The governing body of any county, city, or town by ordinance may regulate services rendered pursuant to police towing requests by any business engaged in the towing or storage of unattended, abandoned, or immobile vehicles. The ordinance may include delineation of service areas for towing services, the limitation of the number of persons engaged in towing services in any area, including the creation of one or more exclusive service areas, and the specification of equipment to be used for providing towing service. The governing body of any county, city, or town may contract for services rendered pursuant to a police towing request with one or more businesses engaged in the towing or storage of unattended, abandoned, or immobile vehicles. The contract may specify the fees or charges to be paid by the owner or operator of a towed vehicle to the person undertaking its towing or storage and may prescribe the geographical area to be served by each person providing towing services. The county, city, or town may establish criteria for eligibility of persons to enter into towing services contracts and, in its discretion, may itself provide exclusive towing and storage service for police-requested towing of unattended, abandoned, or immobile vehicles.

Prior to adopting an ordinance or entering into a contract pursuant to this section, the local governing body shall appoint an advisory board to advise the governing body with regard to the appropriate provisions of the ordinance or terms of the contract. The advisory board shall include representatives of local law-enforcement agencies, towing and recovery operators, and the general public.

"Police-requested towing" or "police towing request," as used in this section, includes all requests made by a law-enforcement officer of the county, city, or town or by a State Police officer within the county, city, or town pursuant to this article or Article 2 (§46.2-1209 et seq.) of this chapter and towing requests made by a law-enforcement officer at the request of the owner or operator of an unattended, abandoned, or immobile vehicle, when no specific service provider is requested by such owner or operator.

If an unattended, abandoned, or immobile vehicle is located so as to impede the free flow of traffic on a highway declared by resolution of the Commonwealth Transportation Board to be a portion of the interstate highway system and a law-enforcement officer determines, in his discretion, that the business or businesses authorized to undertake the towing or storage of the vehicle pursuant to an ordinance or contract adopted pursuant to this section cannot respond in a timely manner, the law-enforcement officer may request towing and storage service from a towing and storage business other than those authorized by such ordinance or contract.

(Chgd. by L.1999 ch. 78, eff. 7/1/99.)

§46.2-1218. Reports by persons in charge of garages, parking places, etc.; unclaimed vehicles.

The person in charge of any garage, repair shop, or automotive service, storage, or parking place shall report on forms furnished by the Superintendent of State Police, to the nearest police station or to the State Police any motor vehicle left unclaimed in his place of business for more than two weeks when he does not know the name of the owner and the reason for the storage.

§46.2-1219. Regulation of vehicular and pedestrian traffic on certain parking lots.

The governing body of any county, city, or town may by ordinance regulate the flow of vehicular and pedestrian traffic, the parking of vehicles, and speed limits on parking lots which are open to the public and designed to accommodate fifty or more vehicles, but no such ordinance shall conflict with state law.

§46.2-1219.1. Regulation or prohibition of vehicular traffic on certain privately owned public parking areas and driveways.

The governing body of any county, city, or town may adopt an ordinance not in conflict with state law regulating or prohibiting the stopping, standing, parking, or flow of vehicles in parking areas or driveways of shopping centers and commercial office and apartment complexes. The ordinance shall be applied to and enforced in a specific center or commercial area upon application in writing by the owner or person in general charge of the operation of such area to the chief law-enforcement officer or other official designated by the ordinance for that purpose.

The provisions of any such ordinance shall be substantially as follows:

CRUISING ORDINANCE.

No person shall drive or permit a motor vehicle under his care, custody, or control to be driven past a traffic control point three or more times within a two-hour period from 6:00 p.m. to 4:00 a.m. Monday through Sunday, in or around a posted no cruising area so as to contribute to traffic congestion; obstruction of streets, sidewalks, parking lots, or public vehicular areas; impediment of access to shopping centers or other buildings open to the public; or interference with the use of property or conduct of business in the area adjacent thereto.

At every point where a public street or alley becomes or provides ingress to a no-cruising area, there shall be posted a sign which designates "No-Cruising" areas and times.

"Traffic control point," as used in this section, means any point or points within the no-cruising area established by the local law-enforcement agency for the purpose of monitoring cruising.

No violations shall occur except upon the third passage past the same traffic control point within a two-hour period.

No area shall be designated or posted as a no-cruising area except upon the passage of a resolution by the local governing body specifically requiring such designation and posting for a particular area.

This ordinance shall not apply to in-service emergency vehicles, taxicabs for hire, buses, and other vehicles being used for business purposes.

Where there is a violation of any provision of this ordinance, a law-enforcement officer charge such violation on the uniform traffic summons form. The ordinance may further provide that any person violating the ordinance shall, upon conviction, be subject to a fine of twenty-five dollars.

Any person convicted of a second or subsequent violation of the ordinance may be punished by a fine of not less than fifty dollars nor more than $100 for each succeeding violation. No assignment of demerit points shall be made under Article 19 (§46.2-489 et seq.) of this title for any violation of the ordinance.

§46.2-1220. Parking, stopping, and standing regulations in cities, towns, and certain counties; parking meters; presumption as to violation of ordinances.

The governing bodies of Albemarle, Arlington, Campbell, Chesterfield, Dinwiddie, Fairfax, Hanover, Henrico, Henry, Isle of Wight, James City, King George, Loudoun, Prince George, Prince William, Roanoke, Rockbridge, Spotsylvania, Stafford, and Tazewell Counties and the governing body of any city or town may by ordinance provide for the regulation of parking, stopping, and standing of vehicles within its limits, including the installation and maintenance of parking meters. The ordinance may require the deposit of a coin of a prescribed denomination, determine the length of time a vehicle may be parked, and designate a department, official, or employee of the local government to administer the provisions of the ordinance. The ordinance may delegate to that department, official, or employee the authority to make and enforce any additional regulations concerning parking that may be required, including, but not limited to, penalties for violations, deadlines for the payment of fines, and late payment penalties for fines not paid when due. In a city having a population of at least 100,000, the ordinance may also provide that a summons or parking ticket for the violation of the ordinance or regulations may be issued by law-enforcement officers, other uniformed city employees, or by uniformed personnel serving under contract with the city. The governing bodies of Augusta, Bath, and Rockingham Counties may by ordinance provide for the regulation of parking, stopping, and standing of vehicles within their limits, but no such ordinance shall authorize or provide for the installation and maintenance of parking meters.

If any ordinance regulates parking on an interstate highway or any arterial highway or any extension of an arterial highway, it shall be subject to the approval of the Transportation Commissioner.

In any prosecution charging a violation of the ordinance or regulation, proof that the vehicle described in the complaint, summons, parking ticket citation, or warrant was parked in violation of the ordinance or regulation, together with proof that the defendant was at the time the registered owner of the vehicle, as required by Chapter 6 (§46.2-600 et seq.) of this title, shall constitute in evidence a prima facie presumption that the registered owner of the vehicle was the person who committed the violation.

(Chgd. by L.1995 ch. 144; L.1996 ch. 348; L.1997 chs. 506, 780, 912; L.1998 ch. 545; L.1999 ch. 71, eff. 7/1/99.)

§46.2-1221. Authority of county to regulate parking on county-owned or leased property or on county highways; parking meters; presumption as to violation of ordinances.

The governing body of any county may, by ordinance, provide for the regulation of parking on county-owned or leased property and may prohibit parking within fifteen feet of any fire hydrant or in any way obstructing a fire hydrant.

In any prosecution charging a violation of the ordinance or regulation, proof that the vehicle described in the complaint, summons, parking ticket citation, or warrant was parked in violation of the ordinance or regulation, together with proof that the defendant was at the time the registered owner of the vehicle, as required by Chapter 6 of this title, shall constitute in evidence a prima facie presumption that the registered owner of the vehicle was the person who committed the violation.

(Chgd. by L.1995 ch. 66, eff. 7/1/95.)

§46.2-1222. *(Omitted due to limited applicability.)*

§46.2-1222.1. Regulation or prohibition of parking of certain vehicles in certain counties.

Any county operating under the urban county executive form of government may by ordinance regulate or prohibit the parking on any public highway in the county of any or all of the following: (i) watercraft; (ii) boat trailers; (iii) motor

homes, as defined in §46.2-100; and (iv) camping trailers, as defined in §46.2-100.
(Added by L.2000 chs. 72, 270, eff. 7/1/2000.)

§46.2-1223. Authority of Commissioner to regulate parking on certain parts of State Highway System.
Except as otherwise provided in this article, the Commonwealth Transportation Commissioner may, by regulation, regulate parking on any part of the primary and secondary systems of state highways.

§46.2-1224. County and town ordinances prohibiting certain parking in streets and highways.
A. The governing body of any county may, by ordinance, prohibit any person from parking any motor vehicle, trailer, or semitrailer on or adjacent to the highways in the county when such person parks any such motor vehicle, trailer, or semitrailer for commercial purposes. The provisions of any such ordinance shall not apply to motor vehicle carriers when picking up or discharging passengers.

B. The governing bodies of (i) counties with populations greater than 500,000 and of towns located therein and (ii) counties with populations of at least 210,000 but less than 217,000 may, by ordinance, prohibit any person from parking any commercial vehicle, as defined in this section, on the highways within their respective jurisdiction in areas zoned for residential use. For the purposes of this section, the term "commercial vehicle" may include: (i) any solid waste collection vehicle, tractor truck or tractor truck/semitrailer or tractor truck/trailer combination, dump truck, concrete mixer truck, towing and recovery vehicle with a registered gross weight of 12,000 pounds or more, and any heavy construction equipment, whether located on the highway or on a truck, trailer, or semitrailer; (ii) any trailer, semitrailer, or other vehicle in which food or beverages are stored or sold; (iii) any trailer or semitrailer used for transporting landscaping or lawn-care equipment whether or not such trailer or semitrailer is attached to another vehicle; and (iv) any vehicle licensed by the Commonwealth for use as a common or contract carrier or as a limousine. Such ordinance shall permit, however, one resident of each single-family dwelling unit zoned for residential use to park one vehicle licensed as a taxicab or limousine on such highways, provided other vehicles are permitted to park thereon. The provisions of any such ordinance shall not apply to a commercial vehicle when picking up or discharging passengers or when temporarily parked pursuant to the performance of work or service at a particular location.

C. Any violation of the provisions of any such ordinance shall be a traffic infraction.
(Chgd. by L.1996 ch. 770; L.1997 ch. 19; L.1998 chs. 391, 403, 424, eff. 7/1/98.)

§46.2-1224.1. Local ordinances regulating certain parking; penalty.
The governing body of any county having the county manager plan of government may by ordinance prohibit idling the engine of a bus for more than ten minutes when the bus is parked, left unattended, or is stopped for other than traffic or maintenance reasons.

Violators of such ordinance shall be subject to a civil penalty not to exceed fifty dollars, the proceeds from which shall be paid into the county's general fund.

The provisions of this section shall not apply to school buses or public transit buses.
(Added by L.1996 ch. 389, eff. 7/1/96.)

§46.2-1225. Enforcement provisions in city or county parking ordinances.
Any city or county ordinance regulating parking under this article shall require:

1. That uncontested payment of parking citation penalties be collected and accounted for by a local administrative official or officials who shall be compensated by the locality;
2. That contest by any person of any parking citation shall be certified on an appropriate form, to the appropriate district court, by such official or officials; and
3. That the local administrative official or officials shall cause complaints, summons, or warrants to be issued for delinquent parking citations.

Every action to collect unpaid parking citation penalties imposed for violation of a city or county ordinance regulating parking under this article shall be commenced within three years of the date upon which such penalty became delinquent.
(Chgd. by L.1995 ch. 459, eff. 7/1/95.)

§46.2-1226. Enforcement of regulations governing parking in Capitol Square.
Any regulation adopted pursuant to §2.1-531 and relating to parking in Capitol Square shall provide:

That uncontested citations issued under those regulations shall be paid to the administrative official or officials appointed under the provisions of this section in the City of Richmond, who shall promptly pay these sums into the general fund of the state treasury; and

That contested or delinquent citations shall be certified or complaint, summons, or warrant shall be issued as provided in §46.2-1225 to the general district court of the City of Richmond. Any sums collected by the court, minus court costs, shall be promptly paid by the clerk to the general fund of the state treasury.

§46.2-1227. Enforcement of state regulations governing parking on primary and secondary highways.
Any regulation of the Commissioner under the provisions of §46.2-1223 relating to parking on any primary or secondary highway shall provide:

1. That uncontested citations issued under the regulation shall be paid to the administrative official or officials appointed under the provisions of this section in the locality in which the part of the highway lies, or in the locality where there is no appointed administrative official the citations shall be paid to the local treasurer, who shall promptly pay them into the general fund of the state treasury; and
2. That contested or delinquent citations shall be certified or complaint, summons, or warrant shall be issued as provided in §46.2-1225 to the general district court in whose jurisdiction the part of the highway lies. Any sums collected by such court, minus court costs, shall be promptly paid by the clerk into the general fund of the state treasury.

§46.2-1228. Enforcement of parking regulations of boards of visitors of educational institutions.
Any regulation of any board of visitors or other governing body of an educational institution pursuant to the provisions of §23-9.2:3 relating to parking on property owned by the institution shall provide:

1. That uncontested citations issued thereunder shall be paid to the administrative official or officials appointed under the provisions of this section in the city or county in which the property of the institution lies, who shall promptly deposit such sums into the state treasury as a special revenue of the institution; and
2. That contested or delinquent citations shall be certified or complaint, summons, or warrant shall be issued as provided in §46.2-1225 to the general district court in whose jurisdiction the institution lies. Any sum collected by the court, minus court costs, shall be promptly deposited by the clerk into the state treasury as a special revenue of the institution. However, nothing in this section shall prevent any

educational institution which adopts, or has adopted, regulations pursuant to §23-9.2:3 providing for administrative disposition of contested, uncontested, or delinquent citations from disposing of those citations in accordance with those regulations, and all moneys collected under those regulations shall be deposited promptly into the state treasury as a special revenue of the institution.

§46.2-1229. Enforcement of parking regulations of State Mental Health, Mental Retardation and Substance Abuse Services Board.

Any regulations of the State Mental Health, Mental Retardation and Substance Abuse Services Board pursuant to the provisions of §37.1-10 relating to parking on property owned or controlled by the Board shall provide:

1. That uncontested citations issued thereunder shall be paid to the administrative official or officials appointed under the provisions of this section in the locality in which the part of the hospital lies, who shall promptly deposit the sums into the state treasury as a special revenue of the Board; and

2. That contested or delinquent citations shall be certified or complaint, summons, or warrant shall be issued as provided in §46.2-1225 to the general district court in whose jurisdiction the hospital lies. Any sum collected by the court, minus court costs, shall be promptly deposited by the clerk into the state treasury as a special revenue of the Board.

§46.2-1230. Authority of counties, cities, and towns to issue parking permits.

The governing body of any county, city, or town may by ordinance provide for the issuance of permits for motor vehicles parking on public streets, to set the rates for the permits, and to set the term of validity of the permits. In setting the rates, the governing body may differentiate between motor vehicles registered in the political subdivision issuing the permit and other motor vehicles.

§46.2-1231. Ticketing, removal, or immobilization of trespassing vehicles by owner or operator of parking or other lot or building; charges.

The owner, operator, or lessee of any parking lot, parking area, or parking space in a parking lot or area or any part of a parking lot or area, or of any other lot or building, including any county, city, or town, or authorized agent of the person having control of such premises may have any vehicle occupying the lot, area, space, or building without the permission of its owner, operator, lessee, or authorized agent of the one having the control of the premises, removed by towing or otherwise to a licensed garage for storage until called for by the owner or his agent if there are posted at all entrances to the parking lot or area signs clearly and conspicuously disclosing that such vehicle, if parked without permission, will be removed, towed or immobilized. The requirements of this section relating to the posting of signs by the owner, operator, or lessee of any parking lot, parking area or space shall not apply to localities in which the local governing body has adopted an ordinance pursuant to §46.2-1232.

Whenever a trespassing vehicle is removed or towed as permitted by this section, notice of this action shall forthwith be given by the tow truck operator to the State Police or the local law-enforcement agency of the jurisdiction from which the vehicle was towed. It shall be unlawful to fail to report such tow as required by this section and violation of the reporting requirement of this section shall constitute a traffic infraction punishable by a fine of not more than $100. Such failure to report may limit the amount which may be charged for the storage and safekeeping of the towed vehicle to an amount no greater than that charged for one day of storage and safekeeping. If the vehicle is removed and stored, the vehicle owner may be charged and the vehicle may be held for a reasonable fee for the removal and storage.

All businesses engaged in towing vehicles without the consent of their owners shall prominently display at their main place of business a comprehensive list of all their fees for towing, recovery, and storage services, or the basis of such charges. Charges in excess of those posted shall not be collectable from any motor vehicle owner whose vehicle is towed, recovered, or stored without his consent.

Notwithstanding the foregoing provisions of this section, if the owner or representative or agent of the owner of the trespassing vehicle is present and removes the trespassing vehicle from the premises before it is actually towed, the trespassing vehicle shall not be towed, but the owner or representative or agent or the owner of the trespassing vehicle shall be liable for a reasonable fee, not to exceed twenty-five dollars or such other limit as the governing body of the county, city, or town may set by ordinance, in lieu of towing.

In lieu of having a trespassing vehicle removed by towing or otherwise, the owner, operator, lessee or authorized agent of the premises on which the trespassing vehicle is parked may cause the vehicle to be immobilized by a boot or other device that prevents a vehicle from being moved by preventing a wheel from turning, provided that the boot or other device does not damage the vehicle or wheel. The charge for the removal of any boot or device shall not exceed twenty-five dollars or such other limit as the governing body of the county, city, or town may set by ordinance. In lieu of having the vehicle removed by towing or otherwise, or in lieu of causing the vehicle to be immobilized, the owner, operator, lessee or authorized agent of the premises on which the trespassing vehicle is parked may cause to have an authorized local government official or law-enforcement officer issue, on the premises, a notice of the violation of a parking ordinance or regulation created pursuant to §46.2-1220 or §46.2-1221 to the registered owner of the vehicle.

This section shall not apply to police, fire, or public health vehicles or where a vehicle, because of a wreck or other emergency, is parked or left temporarily on the property of another. The governing body of every county, city, and town may by ordinance set limits on fees and charges provided for in this section.

§46.2-1231.1. Immunity from liability for certain towing.

No towing and recovery operator shall be liable for damages in any civil action for responding in good faith to the lawful direction of a law-enforcement agency to tow, recover, or store any vehicle, combination of vehicles, their contents, or any other object. The immunity provided by this section shall not extend to the liability for negligence in the towing, recovery, or storage carried out by the towing and recovery operator. For the purposes of this section, any towing, recovery, or storage carried out in compliance with a contract between a towing business and a local law-enforcement agency or local government shall be deemed to have been performed at the lawful direction of a law-enforcement agency.

§46.2-1232. Localities may regulate removal or immobilization of trespassing vehicles.

The governing body of any county, city, or town may by ordinance regulate the removal of trespassing vehicles from property by or at the direction of the owner, operator, lessee, or authorized agent in charge of the property.

§46.2-1233. Localities may regulate towing fees.

The governing body of any county, city, or town may by ordinance set reasonable limits on fees charged for the removal of motor vehicles, trailers, and parts thereof left on private property in violation of §46.2-1231, and for the removal of trespassing vehicles under §46.2-1215, taking into consideration the fair market value of such removal.

§46.2-1233.1. Limitation on charges for towing and storage of motor vehicles.

Unless different limits are established by ordinance of the local governing body pursuant to §46.2-1233, as to vehicles towed or removed from private property, no charges imposed for the towing, storage and safekeeping of any passenger car removed, towed, or stored without consent of its owner shall be in excess of the maximum charges provided for in this section. No hookup and initial towing fee shall exceed eighty-five dollars. For towing a vehicle between seven o'clock p.m. and eight o'clock a.m. or on any Saturday, Sunday, or holiday, an additional fee of ten dollars may be charged. No charge shall be made for storage and safekeeping for a period of twenty-four hours or less. Except for fees or charges imposed by this section or a local ordinance adopted pursuant to §46.2-1233, no other fees or charges shall be imposed during the first twenty-four hour period.

§46.2-1233.2. Advisory Board.

Prior to adopting any ordinance pursuant to §46.2-1232 or §46.2-1233, the local governing body shall appoint an advisory board to advise the governing body with regard to the appropriate provisions of the ordinance. The advisory board shall include representatives of local law-enforcement agencies, towing and recovery operators, and the general public.

§46.2-1234. Liability of persons furnishing free parking accommodations as to motor vehicles and property left therein.

No action shall lie or proceeding be brought against any person conducting any business and maintaining a parking lot at which free parking accommodations are provided for customers or employees of such business, when a motor vehicle is parked in such parking lot, for the total or partial loss of any motor vehicle because of theft or damage by any person other than an employee or for the total or partial loss of property left in the motor vehicle because of theft or damage by any person other than an employee.

As used in this section, "free parking accommodations" means parking accommodations for which no specific charge is made and the patronage of the business by customers and the performance of the regular services for the business by employees shall not constitute the payment of any consideration for the use of the parking accommodations.

Nothing in this section shall relieve any person of liability resulting from his own wrongdoing.

§46.2-1235. *(Omitted due to limited applicability.)*

§46.2-1237. *(Repealed by L.1997 chs. 783, 904, eff. 7/1/97.)*

§46.2-1239. Parking in certain locations; penalty.

No person shall park a vehicle or permit it to stand, whether attended or unattended, on a highway in front of a private driveway, within fifteen feet of a fire hydrant or the entrance to a fire station, within fifteen feet of the entrance to a plainly designated building housing rescue squad equipment or ambulances, or within twenty feet from the intersection of curb lines or, if none, then within fifteen feet of the intersection of property lines at any highway intersection.

CHAPTER 12.1 PARKING FOR PERSONS WITH DISABILITIES

(Added by L.1997 chs. 783, 904, eff. 7/1/97.)

§46.2-1240. Definitions.

"Disabled parking sign" means any sign used to identify parking spaces for use by vehicles bearing valid organizational, permanent, or temporary removable windshield placards, disabled parking license plates, or disabled parking license plates issued under §46.2-739. All disabled parking signs shall be erected and maintained in accordance with signage requirements specified in §36-99.11.

"Organizational removable windshield placard" means a two-sided, hooked placard which includes on each side: (i) the international symbol of access at least three inches in height, centered on the placard, and shown in white on a green background; (ii) the name of the institution or organization; (iii) an identification number; (iv) an expiration date imprinted on the placard and indicated by a month and year hole-punch system or an alternative system designed by the Department; (v) a misuse hotline number designated by the Department; (vi) a warning of the penalties for placard misuse; and (vii) the seal or identifying symbol of the issuing authority.

"Permanent removable windshield placard" means a two-sided, hooked placard which includes on each side: (i) the international symbol of access at least three inches in height, centered on the placard, and shown in white on a blue background; (ii) the name, age, and sex of the person to whom issued; (iii) an identification number; (iv) an expiration date imprinted on the placard and indicated by a month and year hole-punch system or an alternative system designed by the Department; (v) a misuse hotline number designated by the Department; (vi) a warning of the penalties for placard misuse; and (vii) the seal or other identifying symbol of the issuing authority. However, the person to whom the placard is issued may cover his name, as shown on the placard, with opaque, removable tape, provided that no other data on the placard is covered or obscured by such tape.

"Person with a disability that limits or impairs his ability to walk" means a person who, as determined by a licensed physician: (i) cannot walk 200 feet without stopping to rest; (ii) cannot walk without the use of or assistance from a brace, cane, crutch, another person, prosthetic device, wheelchair, or other assistive device; (iii) is restricted by lung disease to such an extent that his forced (respiratory) expiratory volume for one second, when measured by spirometry, is less than one liter, or when at rest, his arterial oxygen tension is less than sixty millimeters of mercury on room air; (iv) uses portable oxygen; (v) has a cardiac condition to the extent that his functional limitations are classified in severity as Class III or Class IV according to standards set by the American Heart Association; (vi) is severely limited in his ability to walk due to an arthritic, neurological, or orthopedic condition; or (vii) has some other debilitating condition that, in the view of a licensed physician, limits or impairs his ability to walk.

Any physician certifying an applicant's disability under clause (vii) of this definition shall specify, in a space provided on the certification form, the medical condition which limits or impairs his patient's ability to walk.

"Temporary removable windshield placard" means a two-sided, hooked placard which includes on each side: (i) the international symbol of access at least three inches in height, centered on the placard, and shown in white on a red background; (ii) the name, age, and sex of the person to whom issued; (iii) an identification number; (iv) an expiration date imprinted on the placard and indicated by a month and year hole-punch system or an alternative system designed by the Department; (v) a misuse hotline number; (vi) a warning of the penalties for placard misuse; and (vii) the seal or other identifying symbol of the issuing authority. However, the person to whom the placard is issued may cover his name, as shown on the placard, with opaque, removable tape, provided that no other data on the placard is covered or obscured by such tape.

(Added by L.1997 chs. 783, 904; chgd. by L.1999 ch. 188, eff. 7/1/99.)

§46.2-1241. Issuance of disabled parking placards.

A. Upon application of a person with a disability that limits or impairs his ability to walk, the Commissioner shall issue a permanent removable windshield placard for use on a passenger car or pickup or panel truck. The Commissioner shall require that the application be accompanied by a certification from a licensed physician on forms prescribed by the Commissioner that the applicant meets the definition of "person with a disability that limits or impairs his ability to walk" contained in §46.2-1240.

1. The Commissioner shall provide for the renewal of such placards every five years as well as a reasonable fee to be charged for each placard, but no fee shall be charged any person exempted from fees in §46.2-739.

2. The placards shall be of a design approved by the Commissioner pursuant to the specifications and definitions contained in §46.2-1240.

B. Upon the application of a person with a disability that limits or impairs his ability to walk and whose disability is temporary, the Commissioner shall issue a temporary removable windshield placard. The application for a temporary removable windshield placard shall be accompanied by a certification from a licensed physician on forms prescribed by the Commissioner that the applicant meets the definition of "person with a condition that limits or impairs his ability to walk" contained in §46.2-1240 and shall also include the period of time that the physician determines the applicant will have the disability, not to exceed six months.

1. The temporary removable windshield placard shall be valid for the period of time for which the physician has determined that the applicant will have the disability, not to exceed six months from the date of issuance.

2. The Commissioner shall provide for a reasonable fee to be charged for the placard. The placards shall be of a design approved by the Commissioner pursuant to the specifications and definitions contained in §46.2-1240.

C. On application, the Commissioner shall issue to hospitals, hospices, nursing homes, and other institutions and organizations meeting criteria determined by the Commissioner organizational removable windshield placards, as provided for in the foregoing provisions of this section, for use by volunteers when transporting disabled persons in passenger vehicles and pickup or panel trucks owned by such volunteers. The provisions of this section relating to other windshield placards issued under this section shall also apply, mutatis mutandis, to windshield placards issued to these institutions and organizations, except that windshield placards issued to institutions and agencies, in addition to their expiration date, shall bear the name of the institution or organization whose volunteers will be using the windshield placards rather than the name, age, and sex of the person to whom issued organizational removable windshield placards.

1. The Commissioner shall provide for the renewal of such placards every five years.

2. The placards shall be of a design approved by the Commissioner pursuant to the specifications and definitions contained in §46.2-1240.

D. No person shall use or display an organizational removable windshield placard, permanent removable windshield placard or temporary removable windshield placard beyond its expiration date.

E. Organizational removable windshield placards, permanent removable windshield placards and temporary removable windshield placards shall be displayed in such a manner that they may be viewed from the front and rear of the vehicle and be hanging from the rearview mirror of a vehicle utilizing a parking space reserved for persons with disabilities that limit or impair their ability to walk. When there is no rearview mirror, the placard shall be displayed on the vehicle's dashboard. No placard shall be displayed from the rearview mirror while a vehicle is in motion.

(Added by L.1997 chs. 783, 904, eff. 7/1/97.)

§46.2-1242. Parking in spaces reserved for persons with disabilities; local ordinances; penalty.

A. No vehicles other than those displaying disabled parking license plates, organizational removable windshield placards, permanent removable windshield placards, or temporary removable windshield placards issued under §46.2-1241, or DV disabled parking license plates issued under subsection B of §46.2-739, shall park in any parking spaces reserved for persons with disabilities.

1. No person without a disability that limits or impairs his ability to walk shall park a vehicle with disabled parking license plates, organizational removable windshield placards, permanent removable windshield placards, temporary removable windshield placards, or DV disabled parking license plates issued under subsection B of §46.2-739 in a parking space reserved for persons with disabilities that limit or impair their ability to walk except when transporting a disabled person in the vehicle.

2. A summons or parking ticket for the offense may be issued by law-enforcement officers, uniformed law-enforcement department employees, or volunteers acting pursuant to

§46.2-1244 without the necessity of a warrant's being obtained by the owner of any private parking area.

3. Parking a vehicle in a space reserved for persons with disabilities in violation of this section shall be punishable by a fine of not less than $100 nor more than $500.

B. The governing body of any county, city, or town may, by ordinance, provide that it shall be unlawful for a vehicle not displaying disabled parking license plates, an organizational removable windshield placard, a permanent removable windshield placard, or a temporary removable windshield placard issued under §46.2-1241, or DV disabled parking license plates issued under subsection B of §46.2-739, to be parked in a parking space reserved for persons with disabilities that limit or impair their ability to walk or for a person who is not limited or impaired in his ability to walk to park a vehicle in a parking space so designated except when transporting a person with such a disability in the vehicle.

1. Any local governing body, by such ordinance, may assess and retain a fine of not less than $100 nor more than $500 for its violation.

2. The ordinance may further provide that a summons or parking ticket for the offense may be issued by law-enforcement officers, volunteers serving in units established pursuant to §46.2-1244, and other uniformed personnel employed by the locality to enforce parking regulations without the necessity of a warrant's being obtained by the owner of the private parking area.

C. In any prosecution charging a violation of this section or an ordinance adopted pursuant to this section, proof that the vehicle described in the complaint, summons, parking ticket, citation, or warrant was parked in violation of this section or the ordinance, together with proof that the defendant was at the time the registered owner of the vehicle, as required by Chapter 6 (§46.2-600 et seq.) of this title, shall constitute prima facie evidence that the registered owner of the vehicle was the person who committed the violation.

D. No violation of this section or an ordinance adopted pursuant to this section shall be dismissed for a property owner's failure to comply strictly with the requirements for disabled parking signs set forth in §36-99.11, provided the space is clearly distinguishable as a parking space reserved for persons with disabilities that limit or impair their ability to walk.

(Added by L.1997 chs. 783, 904, eff. 7/1/97.)

§46.2-1243. Enforcement by private security guards in certain localities.

The local governing bodies of Franklin County and the Cities of Danville and Martinsville may by ordinance provide that, in privately owned parking areas open to the public, a summons for violation of an ordinance promulgated under §46.2-1242 may be issued by private security guards licensed under the provisions of Article 2.1 (§9-183.1 et seq.) of Chapter 27 of Title 9 and deputized to issue a summons for the offense by the chief law-enforcement officer of the county or city in which the private parking area is located.

(Added by L.1997 chs. 783, 904, eff. 7/1/97.)

§46.2-1244. Volunteer disabled parking enforcement units.

A. The governing body of any county, city, or town may by ordinance provide that its law-enforcement agency establish and supervise volunteers to enforce violations of §46.2-1242.

B. Excluding §46.2-1242, volunteers acting pursuant to this section shall not have the power or duty to enforce any other traffic or criminal laws of the state or any county, city, or town.

C. No volunteer acting pursuant to this section shall carry a firearm or other weapon during the course of his volunteer enforcement duties.

(Added by L.1997 chs. 783, 904, eff. 7/1/97.)

§46.2-1245. Four hours' free parking in time-restricted or metered spaces; local option.

A. The disabled person, vehicle owner, or volunteer for an institution or organization to which disabled parking license plates, organizational removable windshield placards, permanent windshield placards, or temporary removable windshield placards are issued or any person to whom disabled parking license plates have been issued under subsection B of §46.2-739 shall be allowed to park the vehicle on which such license plates or placards are displayed for up to four hours in metered or unmetered parking zones restricted as to length of parking time permitted and shall be exempted from paying parking meter fees of any county, city, or town.

B. This section shall not apply to any local ordinance which creates zones where stopping, standing, or parking is prohibited, or which creates parking zones for special types of vehicles, nor shall it apply to any local ordinance which prohibits parking during heavy traffic periods, during specified rush hours, or where parking would clearly present a traffic hazard.

C. The governing body of any county, city, or town may by ordinance provide that this section shall not apply within the boundaries of such county, city, or town. Any county, city, or town adopting an ordinance pursuant to this subsection shall indicate by signs or other reasonable notice that the provisions of this section do not apply in such county, city, or town.

(Added by L.1997 chs. 783, 904, eff. 7/1/97.)

§46.2-1246. Towing of unauthorized vehicles.

A. The owner or duly authorized agent of the owner of a parking space properly designated and clearly marked as reserved for use by persons with disabilities that limit or impair their ability to walk may have any vehicle not displaying disabled parking license plates, organizational removable windshield placards, permanent removable windshield placards, temporary removable windshield placards, or DV disabled parking license plates removed from the parking space and stored.

B. The owner of a vehicle which has been removed and stored may regain possession of his vehicle on payment to the person or persons who removed and stored the vehicle all reasonable costs incidental to the removal and storage. The owner of the vehicle, on notice to the owner or duly authorized agent of the owner of the parking space, may also petition the general district court having jurisdiction over the location where the parking occurred for an immediate determination as to whether the removal of the vehicle was lawful. If the court finds that the removal was unlawful, the court shall direct the owner of the parking space to pay the costs incidental to the removal and storage of the vehicle and return the vehicle to its owner.

(Added by L.1997 chs. 783, 904, eff. 7/1/97.)

§46.2-1247. Counterfeiting disabled parking license plates or placards; penalty.

A. Any person who creates a counterfeit or unauthorized replica of a disabled parking license plate, DV disabled parking license plate which has been issued under subsection B of §46.2-739, organizational removable windshield placard, permanent removable windshield placard, or temporary removable windshield placard, shall be guilty of a Class 2 misdemeanor.

B. The local governing body of any county, city, or town may by ordinance incorporate this provision by reference.
(Added by L.1997 chs. 783, 904, eff. 7/1/97.)

§46.2-1248. Use of counterfeit disabled parking license plates or placards; penalty.

A. Any person who displays a counterfeit or unauthorized replica of a disabled parking license plate, DV disabled parking license plate which has been issued under subsection B of §46.2-739, organizational removable windshield placard, permanent removable windshield placard, or temporary removable windshield placard and parks in a disabled parking space or attempts to use the parking privileges afforded by §46.2-1245, shall be guilty of a Class 2 misdemeanor.

B. The local governing body of any county, city, or town may by ordinance incorporate this provision by reference.
(Added by L.1997 chs. 783, 904, eff. 7/1/97.)

§46.2-1249. Alteration of disabled parking license plates or placards; penalty.

A. Any person who alters a disabled parking license plate, DV disabled parking license plate which has been issued under subsection B of §46.2-739, organizational removable windshield placard, permanent removable windshield placard, or temporary removable windshield placard shall be guilty of a Class 2 misdemeanor.

B. The local governing body of any county, city, or town may by ordinance incorporate this provision by reference.
(Added by L.1997 chs. 783, 904, eff. 7/1/97.)

§46.2-1250. Unauthorized use of disabled parking license plates or placards; penalty.

A. Any person who parks in a space reserved for persons with disabilities that limit or impair their ability to walk or attempts to use the parking privileges afforded by §46.2-1245 and displays a disabled parking license plate, DV disabled parking license plate which has been issued under subsection B of §46.2-739, organizational removable windshield placard, permanent removable windshield placard, or temporary removable windshield placard which has been issued to another person, and is not transporting a person with a disability which limits or impairs his ability to walk, shall be guilty of a Class 2 misdemeanor.

B. The local governing body of any county, city, or town may by ordinance incorporate this provision by reference.
(Added by L.1997 chs. 783, 904, eff. 7/1/97.)

§46.2-1251. Fraudulently obtaining a disabled parking license plate or placard; penalty.

A. Any person who makes a false statement of material fact to obtain or assist an individual in obtaining a disabled parking license plate, DV disabled parking license plate which has been issued under subsection B of §46.2-739, organizational removable windshield placard, permanent removable windshield placard, or temporary removable windshield placard shall be guilty of a Class 2 misdemeanor.

B. The local governing body of any county, city, or town may by ordinance incorporate this provision by reference.
(Added by L.1997 chs. 783, 904, eff. 7/1/97.)

§46.2-1252. Selling or exchanging a disabled parking license plate or placard; penalty.

A. Any person who sells or exchanges for consideration any valid, altered, or counterfeit disabled parking license plate, DV disabled parking license plate which has been issued under subsection B of §46.2-739, organizational removable windshield placard, permanent removable windshield placard, or temporary removable windshield placard shall be guilty of a Class 2 misdemeanor.

B. The local governing body of any county, city, or town may by ordinance incorporate this provision by reference.
(Added by L.1997 chs. 783, 904, eff. 7/1/97.)

§46.2-1253. Providing a disabled parking license plate or placard; penalty.

A. Any person who knowingly provides to another person, without sale or exchange of consideration, any valid, altered, or counterfeit disabled parking license plate, DV disabled parking license plate which has been issued under subsection B of §46.2-739, permanent removable windshield placard, temporary removable windshield placard, or organizational removable windshield placard, shall be guilty of a Class 3 misdemeanor.

B. The local governing body of any county, city, or town may by ordinance incorporate this provision by reference.
(Added by L.1997 chs. 783, 904, eff. 7/1/97.)

§46.2-1254. Photo identification.

Any law-enforcement officer or private security guard acting pursuant to §46.2-1243 may request to examine the driver's license, state identification card, or other form of photo identification of any person using disabled parking privileges afforded by this chapter.
(Added by L.1997 chs. 783, 904, eff. 7/1/97.)

§46.2-1255. Confiscation of disabled parking placards.

A. Any law-enforcement officer or private security guard acting pursuant to §46.2-1243 who issues a summons to or arrests an individual for any violation of §§46.2-1247 through 46.2-1249 and §§46.2-1251 through 46.2-1253 may confiscate the defendant's permanent, temporary, or organizational removable windshield placard and shall notify, by mail or facsimile, the Department of Motor Vehicles of such confiscation and the number of the placard involved.

B. After receiving notice specified in subsection A of this section, the Department may prohibit the issuance of any form of disabled parking license plate or placard to the defendant until the defendant's charge under §§46.2-1247 through 46.2-1249 and §§46.2-1251 through 46.2-1253 reaches final disposition, including appeals.

C. Upon the defendant's acquittal for any violation of §§46.2-1247 through 46.2-1249 and §§46.2-1251 through 46.2-1253, the law-enforcement officer or private security guard shall return the confiscated placard to the defendant and the court shall notify the Department of such acquittal by electronic or other means. Upon the defendant's conviction for any violation of §§46.2-1247 through 46.2-1249 and §§46.2-1251 through 46.2-1253, the law-enforcement officer or private security guard shall send the confiscated placard to the Department and the court shall notify the Department pursuant to §46.2-1256.
(Added by L.1997 chs. 783, 904, eff. 7/1/97.)

§46.2-1256. Notice of convictions; revocation of disabled parking placards and license plates.

A. Upon the entry of a conviction under §§46.2-1247 through 46.2-1253, or under any ordinance which incorporates any of those sections by reference, the court shall send notice of the conviction and the number of the license plate or placard involved to the Commissioner. Such notice may be transmitted by electronic means.

B. Upon receiving notice pursuant to subsection A of this section, the Commissioner may revoke any disabled parking license plate, DV disabled parking license plate, organizational, permanent, or temporary placard of an individual or organization found guilty under §§46.2-1247 through 46.2-1253 if he finds, after a hearing if requested by the person to whom the license plate or placard is issued, that such person (i) is not a person with a disability that limits or impairs his ability to walk and is not otherwise eligible to be

issued a license plate or a placard pursuant to §§46.2-731, 46.2-739, or 46.2-1241, or (ii) is authorized to have such license plate or placard but has allowed the abuse or misuse of the privilege granted thereby so that revocation appears appropriate to remedy the abuse or misuse.
(Added by L.1997 chs. 783, 904, eff. 7/1/97.)

§46.2-1257. Invalidation and re-issuance of organizational and permanent removable windshield placards.

A. Effective October 1, 1998, the Department shall mail a placard meeting the specifications set forth in §§46.2-1240 and 46.2-1259 to each organizational and permanent removable windshield placard holder. The Department shall instruct each organizational and permanent removable windshield placard holder to return by mail their existing placard to the Department by January 1, 1999. The Department shall conduct the exchange during a three-month period commencing October 1, 1998, and ceasing January 1, 1999.

B. The Department shall not require valid placard holders to obtain certification that they have a disability that limits or impairs their ability to walk in order to receive a placard meeting the specifications set forth in §§46.2-1240 and 46.2-1259.

C. All placards issued by the Department pursuant to this section shall bear the valid expiration date of the placard which is replaced by the Department.

D. Effective January 1, 1999, any organizational removable windshield placard or permanent removable windshield placard not meeting the specifications set forth under §46.2-1240 shall be invalid. Any person attempting to use the disabled parking privileges provided by this chapter and displaying an invalid organizational or permanent removable windshield placard may be charged with a violation of §46.2-1242, and any invalid placard shall be subject to confiscation pursuant to §46.2-1255.
(Added by L.1997 chs. 783, 904, eff. 7/1/97.)

§46.2-1258. Reciprocity.

Disabled parking license plates, permanent removable windshield placards, temporary removable windshield placards, and DV disabled parking license plates issued by other states and countries for the purpose of identifying vehicles permitted to use parking spaces reserved for persons with disabilities that limit or impair their ability to walk shall be accorded all rights and privileges accorded vehicles displaying such devices issued in Virginia.
(Added by L.1997 chs. 783, 904, eff. 7/1/97.)

§46.2-1259. Placard issuance; additional requirements.

In developing and issuing organizational, permanent, and temporary removable windshield placards pursuant to the requirements of §46.2-1240, the Commissioner shall, in consultation with representatives of law-enforcement and Disability Services Boards, develop and issue placards that are (i) resistant to tampering, alteration, and counterfeiting, (ii) clear and legible, and (iii) protective of the privacy rights of the placard user to the extent the requirements of §46.2-1240 allow. The Commissioner shall begin issuing placards meeting the requirements of this section and §46.2-1240, on July 1, 1997.
(Added by L.1997 chs. 783, 904, eff. 7/1/97.)

CHAPTER 13
POWERS OF LOCAL GOVERNMENTS

§46.2-1300. Powers of local authorities generally; erection of signs and markers; maximum penalties.

A. The governing bodies of counties, cities, and towns may adopt ordinances not in conflict with the provisions of this title to regulate the operation of vehicles on the highways in such counties, cities, and towns. They may also repeal, amend, or modify such ordinances and may erect appropriate signs or markers on the highway showing the general regulations applicable to the operation of vehicles on such highways. The governing body of any county, city, or town may by ordinance, or may by ordinance authorize its chief administrative officer to:

1. Increase or decrease the speed limit within its boundaries, provided such increase or decrease in speed shall be based upon an engineering and traffic investigation by such county, city or town and provided such speed area or zone is clearly indicated by markers or signs;

2. Authorize the city or town manager or such officer thereof as it may designate, to reduce for a temporary period not to exceed sixty days, without such engineering and traffic investigation, the speed limit on any portion of any highway of the city or town on which work is being done or where the highway is under construction or repair;

3. Require vehicles to come to a full stop or yield the right-of-way at a street intersection if one or more of the intersecting streets has been designated as a part of the state highway system in a town which has a population of less than 3,500.

 Zv

B. No such ordinance shall be violated if at the time of the alleged violation the sign or marker placed in conformity with this section is missing, substantially defaced, or obscured so that an ordinarily observant person under the same circumstances would not be aware of the existence of the ordinance.

C. No governing body of a county, city, or town may provide penalties for violating a provision of an ordinance adopted pursuant to this section which is greater than the penalty imposed for a similar offense under the provisions of this title.

D. No county whose roads are under the jurisdiction of the Department of Transportation shall designate, in terms of distance from a school, the placement of flashing warning lights unless the authority to do so has been expressly delegated to such county by the Department of Transportation, in its discretion.

§46.2-1301. Designation of stop and yield right-of-way intersections.

The governing body of any county, city, or town operating its own system of roads may by ordinance authorize the city or town manager or some other local officer to designate intersections, other than intersections at which one or more of the intersecting streets have been designated as a part of the state highway system in a town which has a population of less than 3,500, at which vehicles shall come to a full stop or yield the right-of-way. No such ordinance shall be violated if, at the time of the alleged violation the sign or marker placed in conformity with this section is missing or is defaced so that an ordinarily observant person under the same circumstances would not be aware of the existence of the regulation.

§46.2-1302. Regulation of operation of vehicles in snow, sleet, etc.; designation of play areas; penalties.

The governing body of any county, city, or town may by ordinance regulate the operation of vehicles on the highways in such county, city, or town in the event of snow, sleet, hail, freezing rain, ice, water, flood, high wind, storm or the threat thereof. In addition to the general powers granted by this section, and any other provisions of this title notwithstanding, any such ordinance may:

1. Prohibit vehicles from parking or operating on designated highways;

2. Authorize the designation and posting of highways as snow routes and prohibit any person to obstruct or impede traffic on a highway designated and posted as a snow route through his failure to have the vehicle operated by him equipped with snow tires or chains;

3. Prohibit the abandoning of vehicles on designated highways;

4. Authorize the removal of vehicles that are stalled, stuck, parked, or abandoned on designated highways;

5. Authorize the storing of removed vehicles and the imposition of reasonable charges for removal and storage;

6. Authorize the designation of certain highways, or portions thereof, as play areas for sledding and similar recreational activities. No city or town shall be liable in any civil action or proceeding for damages resulting from any injury to the person or property of any person caused by an act or omission constituting simple or ordinary negligence on the part of any officer or agent of any such city or town in the designation or operation of any such play area. Every such city or town may be liable in damages for the gross or wanton negligence of any of its officers or agents in the operation of any such play area;

7. Authorize and regulate the operation of snowmobiles on or across streets and highways during periods of snow or ice or at the direction of any law-enforcement officer during an emergency;

8. Set fines for violations. Such fines may be in place of or in addition to the removal and storage of the vehicle and charges therefor, but no such fine shall exceed fifty dollars for each such offense.

(Chgd. by L.1997 ch. 47, eff. 7/1/97.)

§46.2-1303. Issuance of permits to perform construction or repair work within right-of-way lines of public roadways.

The governing body of any county, city, or town having jurisdiction over and responsibility for the construction and maintenance of public roadways within its boundaries may by ordinance authorize an officer or agency of such political subdivision to issue a permit prior to the performance by any person, firm, partnership or corporation of construction and repair work within the right-of-way lines of any public highways under the jurisdiction of the political subdivision. Such authority, however, shall not extend to any railroad crossings or to any highways under the jurisdiction of the Virginia Department of Transportation. Such ordinance may provide that:

1. No person, firm, partnership or corporation shall enter into any repair, alteration, construction, or reconstruction of any type whatever, other than emergency repairs to or maintenance of public utility facilities within the right-of-way lines of any public highway without first having obtained a permit for such work from the agency or officer designated by such ordinance.

2. Such permit may require the notification of all emergency services likely to be affected by such repair, alteration, construction or reconstruction; the types of traffic control devices necessary to properly warn the motoring public and provide for reinspection by the appropriate authority from time to time and at the conclusion of such repair, alteration, construction, or reconstruction.

3. The owner or owners of any such firm, partnership or corporation shall be subject to arrest for a violation of this section or his representative on the site, if the owner is not present.

4. The person, firm, partnership, or corporation requesting such permit shall be responsible for furnishing and maintaining the required traffic control devices in accord with the Virginia Manual of Uniform Traffic Control Devices for Streets and Highways.

5. The penalty for violation of such ordinance shall be a fine of not less than $25 nor more than $100 for the first offense and not less than $100 nor more than $500 for the second and subsequent offenses.

§46.2-1304. Local regulation of trucks and buses.

The governing bodies of counties, cities, and towns may by ordinance, whenever in their judgment conditions so require:

1. Prohibit the use of trucks, except for the purpose of receiving loads or making deliveries on certain designated streets under their jurisdiction;

2. Restrict the use of trucks passing through the city or town to such street or streets under their jurisdiction as may be designated in such ordinance.

Any city having a population of at least 11,200 but no more than 15,000 may restrict the operation of nonscheduled buses, other than school buses, over designated streets under its jurisdiction.

(Chgd. by L.1998 chs. 547, 574, eff. 7/1/98.)

§46.2-1305. Regulation of vehicular and pedestrian traffic on roadways and parking areas in residential subdivisions.

The governing body of any county, city, or town which has adopted ordinances under the provisions of Chapter 22 (§15.2-2200 et seq.) of Title 15.2, may require as a part of such land use regulations for residential subdivisions employing roadways and parking areas open to the public but not in public ownership, the posting and maintenance of signs or other appropriate markings regulating the operation and parking of motor vehicles and pedestrian traffic, and may adopt ordinances applying the regulations to existing and future residential subdivisions.

§46.2-1306. Prohibiting parking near certain fire hydrants.

The governing body of any county may by ordinance prohibit the parking of motor vehicles within a reasonable distance of either side of fire hydrants located on private property.

§46.2-1306.1. Prohibiting parking so as to prevent the use of curb ramps.

The governing body of any county, city, or town may by ordinance prohibit the parking of a vehicle, whether attended or unattended, so as to prevent the use of a curb ramp located on public property or on privately owned property which is open to the public. A summons for the offense may be issued by law-enforcement department employees without the necessity of a warrant being obtained by the owner of any private property.

§46.2-1307. Designation of private roads as highways for law-enforcement purposes.

The governing body of any county, city, or town may adopt ordinances designating the private roads, within any residential development containing 100 or more lots, as highways for law-enforcement purposes.

§46.2-1308. Disposition of fines in traffic cases; failure or neglect to comply with section.

In counties, cities, and towns whose governing bodies adopt the ordinances authorized by §§46.2-1300 and 46.2-1304, all fines imposed for violations of such ordinances shall be paid into the county, city or town treasury. Fees shall be disposed of according to law.

In all cases, however, in which the arrest is made or the summons is issued by an officer of the Department of State Police or of any other division of the state government, for violation of the motor vehicle laws of the Commonwealth, the person arrested or summoned shall be charged with and tried for a violation of some provision of this title and all fines and forfeitures collected upon convictions or upon forfeitures of bail of any person so arrested or summoned shall be credited to the Literary Fund.

Willful failure, refusal or neglect to comply with this provision shall constitute a Class 4 misdemeanor and may be grounds for removal of the guilty person from office. Charges for dereliction of the duties here imposed shall be tried by the circuit court of the jurisdiction served by the officer charged with the violation.

§46.2-1309. Officers may direct traffic; signals.

Law-enforcement officers and uniformed school crossing guards may direct traffic by signals. Such signals other than by voice shall be as follows:

1. To stop traffic by hand. Stand with shoulders parallel to moving traffic. Raise arms forty-five degrees above shoulder with hand extended, palm towards moving traffic to be stopped.

2. To move traffic by hand. Stand with shoulders parallel to traffic to be moved. Extend right arm and hand full length at height of shoulders towards such traffic, fingers extended and joined, palm down. Bring hand sharply in direction traffic is to move. Repeat movement with left arm and hand to start traffic from opposite direction.

3. To stop and start traffic by whistle. One blast, moving traffic to stop; two blasts, traffic in opposite direction to move.

4. Emergency stop of traffic by whistle. Three or more short blasts, all traffic shall immediately clear the intersection and stop.

Such law-enforcement officers and uniformed school crossing guards may also use supplemental traffic direction devices, including but not limited to hand-held stop or go signs, in directing traffic as provided in this section.
(Chgd. by L.1995 ch. 473, eff. 7/1/95.)

§46.2-1310. Authority to deputize persons to direct traffic in certain circumstances.

The chief of police of any county, city, or town, or the sheriff of any county which does not have a chief of police, may deputize persons over the age of eighteen years for the limited purpose of directing traffic in accordance with §46.2-1309 during periods of heavy traffic or congestion. Such persons shall first receive training as the chief of police or sheriff determines necessary to fully acquaint such persons with the techniques of traffic control. They shall not have arrest powers.

Any person who is deputized as provided in the foregoing provisions of this section, shall at all times while engaged in traffic control wear a distinctive uniform, safety vest, or a white reflectorized belt which crosses both the chest and back above the waist.

§46.2-1311. Applicability of county ordinances within towns.

Any traffic ordinance adopted by the governing body of a county shall not apply within the limits of any town in which the traffic is regulated by town ordinances.

§46.2-1312. Size, design, and color of signs, signals, and markings erected by local authorities.

Traffic signs and traffic signals and markings placed or erected by local authorities pursuant to this title shall conform in size, design, and color to those erected for the same purpose by the Department of Transportation.

§46.2-1313. Incorporation of provisions of this title, Article 9 (§16.1-278 et seq.) of Chapter 11 of Title 16.1 and Article 2 (§18.2-266 et seq.) of Chapter 7 of Title 18.2 in ordinances.

Ordinances enacted by local authorities pursuant to this chapter may incorporate appropriate provisions of this title, of Article 9 (§16.1-278 et seq.) of Chapter 11 of Title 16.1, and of Article 2 (§18.2-266 et seq.) of Chapter 7 of Title 18.2 into such ordinances by reference. Nothing contained in this title shall require the readoption of ordinances heretofore validly adopted. Local authorities may adopt ordinances incorporating by reference the appropriate provisions of state law before the effective date of such state law; provided that such local ordinances do not become effective before the effective date of the state law. The provisions of this section are declaratory of existing law.
(Chgd. by L.2000 ch. 48, eff. 7/1/2000.)

§46.2-1314. Traffic schools; requiring attendance by persons convicted of certain violations.

The governing body of any county or city may by ordinance provide for the establishment of a traffic school in the locality, at which instruction concerning laws and ordinances for the regulation of vehicular traffic, safe operation of vehicles, and such other subjects as may be prescribed shall be given. The ordinance shall provide for the supervision of the school, the days and hours of its operation, and its personnel. In the discretion of the governing body, the ordinance establishing a traffic school may vest the direction and conduct of the school in the general district court charged with hearing traffic cases.

The governing body of any county or city may, alternatively, by ordinance provide for the designation of an existing traffic school or course operated as part of a county or city adult education program as a traffic school for the purposes of this section.

Any court in a county or city which provides for a traffic school under this section may require any person found guilty of a violation of any provision of Chapter 8 of this title or local ordinance governing the operation of motor vehicles to attend a traffic school in the county or city where the person is a resident or any traffic school that has been established in any jurisdiction contiguous to the county or city of residence of the convicted violator for a period specified in the order requiring the attendance if the governing body of that contiguous jurisdiction consents thereto. The requirement for attendance may be in lieu of or in addition to the penalties prescribed by §46.2-113 or any such ordinance. Failure to comply with the order of the court shall be punishable as contempt.

CHAPTER 14
RIDESHARING

Section

§46.2-1400. "Ridesharing arrangement" defined.

"Ridesharing arrangement" means the transportation of persons in a motor vehicle when such transportation is incidental to the principal purpose of the driver, which is to reach a destination and not to transport persons for profit. The term includes ridesharing arrangements known as car pools, van pools, and bus pools.

§46.2-1401. Motor carrier laws do not apply.

The following laws and regulations of the Commonwealth shall not apply to any ridesharing arrangement using a motor vehicle with a seating capacity for not more than sixteen persons, including the driver:

1. Laws and regulations containing insurance requirements that are specifically applicable to motor carriers or commercial vehicles;

2. Laws imposing a greater standard of care on motor carriers or commercial vehicles than that imposed on other drivers or owners of motor vehicles;

3. Laws and regulations with equipment requirements and special accident reporting requirements that are specifically applicable to motor carriers or commercial vehicles; and

4. Laws imposing a tax on fuel purchased in another state by a motor carrier or road user taxes on commercial buses.

§46.2-1402. Workers' compensation law does not apply.

Title 65.2 of the Code of Virginia, providing compensation for workers injured during the course of their employment, shall not apply to a person injured while participating in a ridesharing arrangement between his place of residence and place of employment or termini near such places; however, if the employer owns, leases, or contracts for the motor vehicle used in such arrangement, Title 65.2 of the Code of Virginia shall apply.

§46.2-1403. Liability of employer.

An employer shall not be liable for injuries to passengers and other persons resulting from the operation or use of a motor vehicle, not owned, leased or contracted for by the employer, in a ridesharing arrangement.

An employer shall not be liable for injuries to passengers and other persons because he provides information or incentives or otherwise encourages his employees to participate in ridesharing arrangements.

§46.2-1404. Ridesharing payments or transit reduced fares are not income.

Money and other benefits, other than salary, received by a driver in a ridesharing arrangement using a motor vehicle with a seating capacity for not more than sixteen persons, including the driver, shall not constitute income for the purpose of Chapter 3 (§58.1-300 et seq.) of Title 58.1 of the Code of Virginia imposing taxes on income. Neither shall the difference in the amount between discount and full transit fares constitute income for the purpose of Chapter 3 (§58.1-300 et seq.) of Title 58.1 of the Code of Virginia imposing taxes on income.

§46.2-1405. Municipal licenses and taxes.

No county, city, or town may impose a tax on or require a license, including business licenses or gross receipts taxes, for a ridesharing arrangement using a motor vehicle with a seating capacity for not more than sixteen persons, including the driver.

§46.2-1406. Overtime compensation and minimum wage laws.

The participation of an employee in any kind of ridesharing arrangement shall not result in the application of Title 40.1 of the Code of Virginia.

§46.2-1407. Certain ridesharing vehicles are not commercial vehicles or buses.

A motor vehicle used in a ridesharing arrangement that has a seating capacity for not more than sixteen persons, including the driver, shall not be a "bus" under those portions of this title relating to equipment requirements or rules of the road.

A motor vehicle used in a ridesharing arrangement that has a seating capacity for not more than sixteen persons, including the driver, shall not be a "bus" or "commercial vehicle" under the portions of this title relating to registration.

SUBTITLE IV
DEALERS, COMMERCIAL DRIVER TRAINING SCHOOLS, AND SCRAPPAGE PROGRAM

CHAPTER 15
MOTOR VEHICLE DEALERS

ARTICLE 1
MOTOR VEHICLE DEALERS, GENERALLY

§46.2-1500. Definitions.

Unless the context otherwise requires, the following words and terms for the purpose of this chapter shall have the following meanings:

"Board" means the Motor Vehicle Dealer Board.

"Certificate of origin" means the document provided by the manufacturer of a new motor vehicle, or its distributor, which is the only valid indication of ownership between the manufacturer, its distributor, its franchised motor vehicle dealers, and the original purchaser not for resale.

"Dealer-operator" means the individual who works at the established place of business of a dealer and who is responsible for and in charge of day-to-day operations of that place of business.

"Distributor" means a person who is licensed by the Department of Motor Vehicles under Chapter 19 (§46.2-1900 et seq.) of this title and who sells or distributes new motor vehicles pursuant to a written agreement with the manufacturer, to franchised motor vehicle dealers in the Commonwealth.

"Distributor branch" means a branch office licensed by the Department of Motor Vehicles under Chapter 19 (§46.2-1900 et seq.) of this title and maintained by a distributor for the sale of motor vehicles to motor vehicle dealers or for directing or supervising, in whole or in part, its representatives in the Commonwealth.

"Distributor representative" means a person who is licensed by the Department of Motor Vehicles under Chapter 19 (§46.2-1900 et seq.) of this title and employed by a distributor or by a distributor branch, for the purpose of making or promoting the sale of motor vehicles or for supervising or contacting its dealers, prospective dealers, or representatives in the Commonwealth.

"Factory branch" means a branch office maintained by a person for the sale of motor vehicles to distributors or for the sale of motor vehicles to motor vehicle dealers, or for directing or supervising, in whole or in part, its representatives in the Commonwealth.

"Factory representative" means a person who is licensed by the Department of Motor Vehicles under Chapter 19 (§46.2-1900 et seq.) of this title and employed by a person who manufactures or assembles motor vehicles or by a factory branch for the purpose of making or promoting the sale of its motor vehicles or for supervising or contacting its dealers, prospective dealers, or representatives in the Commonwealth.

"Factory repurchase motor vehicle" means a motor vehicle sold, leased, rented, consigned, or otherwise transferred to a person under an agreement that the motor vehicle will be resold or otherwise retransferred only to the manufacturer or distributor of the motor vehicle, and which is reacquired by the manufacturer or distributor, or its agents.

"Family member" means a person who either (i) is the spouse, child, grandchild, spouse of a child, spouse of a grandchild, brother, sister, or parent of the dealer or owner or (ii) has been employed continuously by the dealer for at least five years.

"Franchise" means a written contract or agreement between two or more persons whereby one person, the franchisee, is granted the right to engage in the business of offering and selling, servicing, or offering, selling, and servicing new motor vehicles of a particular line-make or late model or factory repurchase motor vehicles of a particular line-make manufactured or distributed by the grantor of the right, the franchisor, and where the operation of the franchisee's business is substantially associated with the franchisor's trademark, trade name, advertising, or other commercial symbol designating the franchisor, the motor vehicle or its manufacturer or distributor. The term shall include any severable part or parts of a franchise agreement which separately provides for selling and servicing different line-makes of the franchisor.

"Franchised late model or factory repurchase motor vehicle dealer" means a dealer in late model or factory repurchase motor vehicles, including a franchised new motor vehicle dealer, that has a franchise agreement with a manufacturer or distributor of the line-make of the late model or factory repurchase motor vehicles.

"Franchised motor vehicle dealer" means a dealer in new motor vehicles that has a franchise agreement with a manufacturer or distributor of new motor vehicles, trailers, or semitrailers.

"Fund" means the Motor Vehicle Dealer Board Fund.

"Independent motor vehicle dealer" means a dealer in used motor vehicles.

"Late model motor vehicle" means a motor vehicle of the current model year and the immediately preceding model year.

"Line-make" means the name of the motor vehicle manufacturer or distributor and a brand or name plate marketed by the manufacturer or distributor.

"Manufacturer" means a person who is licensed by the Department of Motor Vehicles under Chapter 19 (§46.2-1900 et seq.) of this title and engaged in the business of constructing or assembling new motor vehicles and, in the case of trucks, also means a person engaged in the business of manufacturing engines, power trains, or rear axles, when such engines, power trains, or rear axles are not warranted by the final manufacturer or assembler of the truck.

"Motor vehicle" means the same as provided in §46.2-100, except, for the purposes of this chapter, it shall not include (i) trailers and semitrailers; (ii) manufactured homes, sales of which are regulated under Chapter 4.2 (§36-85.16 et seq.) of Title 36; (iii) motor homes; (iv) motorcycles; (v) nonrepairable vehicles, as defined in §46.2-1600; and (vi) salvage vehicles, as defined in §46.2-1600.

"Motor vehicle dealer" or "dealer" means any person who:

1. For commission, money, or other thing of value, buys, sells, exchanges, either outright or on conditional sale, bailment lease, chattel mortgage, or otherwise or arranges or offers or attempts to solicit or negotiate on behalf of others a sale, purchase, or exchange of an interest in new motor vehicles, new and used motor vehicles, or used motor vehicles alone, whether or not the motor vehicles are owned by him; or

2. Is wholly or partly engaged in the business of selling new motor vehicles, new and used motor vehicles, or used motor vehicles only, whether or not the motor vehicles are owned by him; or

3. Offers to sell, sells, displays, or permits the display for sale, of five or more motor vehicles within any twelve consecutive months.

The term "motor vehicle dealer" does not include:

1. Receivers, trustees, administrators, executors, guardians, conservators or other persons appointed by or acting under judgment or order of any court or their employees when engaged in the specific performance of their duties as employees.

2. Public officers, their deputies, assistants, or employees, while performing their official duties.

3. Persons other than business entities primarily engaged in the leasing or renting of motor vehicles to others when selling or offering such vehicles for sale at retail, disposing of motor vehicles acquired for their own use and actually so used, when the vehicles have been so acquired and used in good faith and not for the purpose of avoiding the provisions of this chapter.

4. Persons dealing solely in the sale and distribution of fire-fighting equipment, ambulances, and funeral vehicles, including motor vehicles adapted therefor; however, this exemption shall not exempt any person from the provisions of §§46.2-1519, 46.2-1520 and 46.2-1548.

5. Any financial institution chartered or authorized to do business under the laws of the Commonwealth or the United States which may have received title to a motor vehicle in the normal course of its business by reason of a foreclosure, other taking, repossession, or voluntary reconveyance to that institution occurring as a result of any loan secured by a lien on the vehicle.

6. An employee of an organization arranging for the purchase or lease by the organization of vehicles for use in the organization's business.

7. Any person licensed to sell real estate who sells a manufactured home or similar vehicle in conjunction with the sale of the parcel of land on which the manufactured home or similar vehicle is located.

8. Any person who permits the operation of a motor vehicle show or permits the display of motor vehicles for sale by any motor vehicle dealer licensed under this chapter.

9. An insurance company authorized to do business in the Commonwealth that sells or disposes of vehicles under a contract with its insured in the regular course of business.

10. Any publication, broadcast, or other communications media when engaged in the business of advertising, but not otherwise arranging for the sale of vehicles owned by others.

11. Any person dealing solely in the sale or lease of vehicles designed exclusively for off-road use.

12. Any credit union authorized to do business in Virginia, provided the credit union does not receive a commission, money, or other thing of value directly from a motor vehicle dealer.

13. Any person licensed as a manufactured home dealer, broker, manufacturer, or salesperson under Chapter 4.2 (§36-85.16 et seq.) of Title 36.

14. The State Department of Social Services or local departments of social services.

"Motor vehicle salesperson" or "salesperson" means any person who is licensed as and employed as a salesperson by a motor vehicle dealer to sell or exchange motor vehicles. It also means any person who is licensed as a motor vehicle dealer and who sells or exchanges motor vehicles.

"Motor vehicle show" means a display of motor vehicles to the general public at a location other than a dealer's location licensed under this chapter where the vehicles are not being offered for sale or exchange during or as part of the display.

"New motor vehicle" means any vehicle which (i) has not been previously sold except in good faith for the purpose of resale, (ii) has not been used as a rental, driver education, or demonstration motor vehicle, or for the personal and business transportation of the manufacturer, distributor, dealer, or any of his employees, (iii) has not been used except for limited use necessary in moving or road testing the vehicle prior to delivery to a customer, (iv) is transferred by a certificate of origin, and (v) has the manufacturer's certification that it conforms to all applicable federal motor vehicle safety and emission standards. Notwithstanding provisions (i) and (iii), a motor vehicle that has been previously sold but not titled shall be deemed a new motor vehicle if it meets the requirements of provisions (ii), (iv), and (v).

"Original license" means a motor vehicle dealer license issued to an applicant who has never been licensed as a motor vehicle dealer in Virginia or whose Virginia motor vehicle dealer license has been expired for more than thirty days.

"Relevant market area" means as follows:

1. In metropolitan localities, the relevant market area shall be a circular area around an existing franchised dealer with a population of 250,000, not to exceed a radius of ten miles but in no case less than seven miles.

2. If the population in an area within a radius of ten miles around an existing franchised dealer is less than 250,000, but the population in an area within a radius of fifteen miles around an existing franchised dealer is 150,000 or more, the relevant market area shall be that area within the fifteen-mile radius.

3. In all other cases the relevant market area shall be an area within a radius of twenty miles around an existing franchised dealer or the area of responsibility defined in the franchise, whichever is greater. In any case where the franchise agreement is silent as to area responsibility, the relevant market area shall be the greater of an area within a radius of twenty miles around an existing franchised dealer or that area in which the franchisor otherwise requires the franchisee to make significant retail sales or sales efforts.

In determining population for this definition, the most recent census by the U.S. Bureau of the Census or the most recent population update, either from the National Planning Data Corporation or other similar recognized source, shall be accumulated for all census tracts either wholly or partially within the relevant market area.

"Retail installment sale" means every sale of one or more motor vehicles to a buyer for his use and not for resale, in which the price of the vehicle is payable in one or more installments and in which the seller has either retained title to the goods or has taken or retained a security interest in the goods under form of contract designated either as a security agreement, conditional sale, bailment lease, chattel mortgage, or otherwise.

"Sale at retail" or "retail sale" means the act or attempted act of selling, bartering, exchanging, or otherwise disposing of a motor vehicle to a buyer for his personal use and not for resale.

"Sale at wholesale" or "wholesale" means a sale to motor vehicle dealers or wholesalers other than to consumers; a sale to one who intends to resell.

"Used motor vehicle" means any vehicle other than a new motor vehicle as defined in this section.

"Wholesale auction" means an auction of motor vehicles restricted to sales at wholesale.

(Chgd. by L.1995 chs. 767, 816; L.1996 ch. 1053; L.1997 chs. 801, 848; L.1999 chs. 77, 910, eff. 7/1/99.)

§46.2-1501. General powers of Commissioner.

The Commissioner shall promote the interest of the retail buyers of motor vehicles and endeavor to prevent unfair methods of competition and unfair or deceptive acts or practices.

§46.2-1502. *(Repealed by L.1995 chs. 767, 816, eff. 7/1/95.)*

§46.2-1503. Motor Vehicle Dealer Board.

A. The Motor Vehicle Dealer Board is hereby created. The Board shall consist of nineteen members appointed by the Governor, subject to confirmation by the General Assembly. Every member appointed by the Governor must be a citizen of the United States and must be a resident of Virginia. The Governor may remove any member as provided in subsection B of §2.1-43. The initial terms of eight of the members appointed in July of 1995 shall commence when appointed and shall be for terms ending on June 30, 1997. Nine members shall be appointed for four-year terms. The members shall be at-large members and, insofar as practical, should reflect fair and equitable statewide representation.

B. Nine members shall be licensed franchised motor vehicle dealers who have been licensed as such for at least two years prior to being appointed by the Governor and seven members shall be licensed independent motor vehicle dealers who (i) have been licensed as such for at least two years prior to being appointed by the Governor and (ii) are not also franchised motor vehicle dealers. One of the independent dealers appointed to the Board shall be a licensed motor vehicle dealer primarily engaged in the business of renting vehicles, and one shall be a licensed independent dealer primarily engaged in the motor vehicle salvage business. One member shall be an individual who has no direct or indirect interest, other than as a consumer, in or relating to the motor vehicle industry.

C. Appointments shall be for terms of four years, and no person other than the Commissioner of the Department of Motor Vehicles and the Commissioner of Agriculture and Consumer Services shall be eligible to serve more than two successive four-year terms. The Commissioner of the Department of Motor Vehicles shall serve as chairman of the Board. Vacancies shall be filled by appointment by the Governor for the unexpired term and shall be effective until thirty days after the next meeting of the ensuing General Assembly and, if confirmed, thereafter for the remainder of the term. Any person appointed to fill a vacancy may serve two additional successive terms.

D. The Commissioner of the Department of Motor Vehicles and the Commissioner of the Department of Agriculture and Consumer Services shall be ex officio voting members of the Board.

E. Members of the Board shall be reimbursed their actual and necessary expenses incurred in carrying out their duties, such reimbursement to be paid from the special fund referred to in §46.2-1520.

(Chgd. by L.1995 chs. 767, 816, eff. 7/1/95.)

§46.2-1503.1. Board to employ Executive Director.

The Board shall employ an executive director who shall serve at the pleasure of the Board. He shall direct the affairs of the Board and keep records of all proceedings, transactions, communications, and official acts of the Board. He shall be custodian of all records of the Board and perform such duties as the Board may require. The Executive Director shall call a meeting of the Board at the direction of the chairman or upon written request of three or more Board members. The Executive Director, with approval of the Board, may employ such additional staff as needed. The annual salary of the Executive Director shall be at Level II of the Executive Compensation Plan contained in the Appropriation Act.

(Added by L.1995 chs. 767, 816, eff. 7/1/95.)

§46.2-1503.2. State Personnel and Public Procurement Acts not applicable.

A. The Executive Director and all staff employed by the Board shall be exempt from the Virginia Personnel Act (§2.1-110 et seq.) of Title 2.1. Personnel actions under this exemption shall be taken without regard to race, sex, color, national origin, religion, age, handicap or political affiliation.

B. The Board and the Executive Director shall be exempt from the Virginia Public Procurement Act (§11-35 et seq.) of Title 11.

(Added by L.1995 chs. 767, 816, eff. 7/1/95.)

§46.2-1503.3. Motor Vehicle Dealer Board Fund; receipts; disbursements.

The Motor Vehicle Dealer Board Fund is established as a special fund in the state treasury. Except as otherwise provided in this chapter, all fees collected as provided in this

chapter and by regulations promulgated by the Board, shall be paid into the state treasury immediately upon collection and credited to the Motor Vehicle Dealer Board Fund. Any interest income shall accrue to the Motor Vehicle Dealer Board Fund. All disbursements from the Fund shall be made by the State Treasurer upon warrants of the Comptroller issued upon vouchers signed by an authorized officer of the Board or the Executive Director as authorized by the Board.
(Added by L.1995 chs. 767, 816; chgd. by L.1998 ch. 325, eff. 10/1/98.)

§46.2-1503.4. General powers and duties of Board.

The powers and duties of the Board shall include, but not be limited to the following:

1. To establish the qualifications of applicants for certification or licensure, provided that all qualifications shall be necessary to ensure competence and integrity.
2. To examine, or cause to be examined, the qualifications of each applicant for certification or licensure, including the preparation, administration and grading of examinations.
3. To certify or license qualified applicants as motor vehicle dealers and motor vehicle salespersons.
4. To levy and collect fees for certification or licensure and renewal that are sufficient to cover all expenses for the administration and operation of the Board.
5. To levy on licensees special assessments necessary to cover expenses of the Board.
6. To revoke, suspend, or fail to renew a certificate or license for just cause as set out in Articles 2, 3.1, 4, 8 and 9 of this chapter or enumerated in regulations promulgated by the Board.
7. To ensure that inspections are conducted relating to the motor vehicle sales industry and to ensure that all licensed dealers and salespersons are conducting business in a professional manner, not in violation of any provision of Articles 2, 3.1, 4, 7, 8 and 9 of this chapter and within the lawful regulations promulgated by the Board.
8. To receive complaints concerning the conduct of persons and businesses licensed by the Board and to take appropriate disciplinary action if warranted.
9. To enter into contracts necessary or convenient for carrying out the provisions of this chapter or the functions of the Board.
10. To establish committees of the Board, appoint persons to such committees, and to promulgate regulations establishing the responsibilities of these committees. Each of these committees shall include at least one Board member and the Advertising, Dealer Practices and Transaction Recovery Fund committees shall include at least one citizen member who is not licensed or certified by the Board. The Board may establish one of each committee in each DMV District. Committees to be established shall include, but not be limited to the following:
    a. Advertising;
    b. Licensing;
    c. Dealer Practices;
    d. Franchise Review and Advisory Committee; and
    e. Transaction Recovery Fund.
11. To do all things necessary and convenient for carrying into effect Articles 2, 3.1, 4, 8 and 9 of this chapter or as enumerated in regulations promulgated by the Board.

(Added by L.1995 chs. 767, 816, eff. 7/1/95.)

§46.2-1503.5. Biennial report.

The Board shall submit a biennial report to the Governor and General Assembly on or before November 1 of each even-numbered year. The biennial report shall contain, at a minimum, the following information: (i) a summary of the Board's fiscal affairs, (ii) a description of the Board's activities, (iii) statistical information regarding the administrative hearings and decisions of the Board, and (iv) a general summary of all complaints received against licensees and the procedures used to resolve the complaints. The biennial report shall be distributed in accordance with the provisions of §2.1-467.
(Added by L.1995 chs. 767, 816, eff. 7/1/95.)

§46.2-1504. Board's powers with respect to hearings under this chapter.

The Board may, in hearings arising under this chapter, except as provided for in Article 7 (§46.2-1566 et seq.), determine the place in the Commonwealth where they shall be held; subpoena witnesses; take depositions of witnesses residing outside the Commonwealth in the manner provided for in civil actions in courts of record; pay these witnesses the fees and mileage for their attendance as is provided for witnesses in civil actions in courts of record; and administer oaths.
(Chgd. by L.1995 chs. 767, 816, eff. 7/1/95.)

§46.2-1505. Suit to enjoin violations.

The Board, whenever it believes from evidence submitted to the Board that any person has been violating, is violating or is about to violate any provision of this chapter, in addition to any other remedy, may bring an action in the name of the Commonwealth to enjoin any violation of this chapter.
(Chgd. by L.1995 chs. 767, 816, eff. 7/1/95.)

§46.2-1506. Regulations.

The Board may promulgate regulations requiring persons licensed under this chapter to keep and maintain records reasonably required for the enforcement of §§46.2-112 and 46.2-629, and any other regulations, not inconsistent with the provisions of this chapter, as it shall consider necessary for the effective administration and enforcement of this chapter. A copy of any regulation promulgated under this section shall be mailed to each motor vehicle dealer licensee thirty days prior to its effective date.
(Chgd. by L.1995 chs. 767, 816, eff. 7/1/95.)

§46.2-1506.1. Additional training.

The Board may promulgate regulations specifying additional training or conditions for individuals seeking certification, licensure, or renewal of certificates or licenses.
(Added. by L.1995 chs. 767, 816, eff. 7/1/95.)

§46.2-1507. Penalties.

Except as otherwise provided in this chapter, any person violating any of the provisions of this chapter may be assessed a civil penalty by the Board. No such civil penalty shall exceed $1,000 for any single violation. Civil penalties collected under this chapter shall be deposited in the Transportation Trust Fund.
(Chgd. by L.1995 chs. 767, 816, eff. 7/1/95.)

ARTICLE 2
MOTOR VEHICLE DEALER LICENSES

Section

§46.2-1508. Licenses required.

It shall be unlawful for any person to engage in business in the Commonwealth as a motor vehicle dealer or salesperson without first obtaining a license as provided in this chapter. It shall be unlawful for any person to engage in business in the Commonwealth as a manufacturer, factory branch, distributor, distributor branch, or factory or distributor representative without first obtaining a license as provided in Chapter 19 (§46.2-1900 et seq.) of this title. Any nonprofit organization exempt from taxation under §501(c)(3) of the Internal Revenue Code, after having obtained a nonprofit organization certificate as provided in this chapter, may consign donated motor vehicles to licensed Virginia motor vehicle dealers. Any person licensed in another state as a motor vehicle dealer may sell motor vehicles at wholesale auctions in the Commonwealth after having obtained a certificate of dealer registration as provided in Chapter 19 of this title. The offering or granting of a motor vehicle dealer franchise in the Commonwealth shall constitute engaging in business in the Commonwealth for purposes of this section, and no new motor vehicle may be sold or offered for sale in the Commonwealth unless the franchisor of motor vehicle dealer franchises for that line-make in the Commonwealth, whether such franchisor is a manufacturer, factory branch, distributor, distributor branch, or otherwise, is licensed under Chapter 19 of this title. In the event a license issued under Chapter 19 to a franchisor of motor vehicle dealer franchises is suspended, revoked, or not renewed, nothing in this section shall prevent the sale of any new motor vehicle of such franchisor's line-make manufactured in or brought into the Commonwealth for sale prior to the suspension, revocation or expiration of the license.

Violation of any provision of this section shall constitute a Class 1 misdemeanor.

(Chgd. by L.1995 chs. 767, 816; L.1997 ch. 848; L.2000 ch. 180, eff. 7/1/2000.)

§46.2-1508.1. Licensure of certain nonprofit organizations.

A. Any nonprofit organization exempt from taxation under §501(c)(3) of the Internal Revenue Code that (i) receives title to motor vehicles as qualified charitable gifts to the organization, (ii) provides no more than twelve of these donated vehicles in any twelve-month period to low-income persons, as defined in §2.1-588, in need of transportation, and (iii) receives from the recipients of the vehicles only reimbursement for the costs of repairs, towing, titles, taxes, license fees and inspection fees shall be required to obtain a dealer's license. However, such nonprofit organization shall be exempt from the requirements of §46.2-1510, Article 3.1 (§46.2-1527.1 et seq.) of Chapter 15 of this title, §§46.2-1533, and 46.2-1534. Transactions of such nonprofit organization shall not be subject to recovery from the Motor Vehicle Transaction Recovery Fund.

B. Upon application to and approval by the Board, any nonprofit organization exempt from taxation under §501(c)(3) of the Internal Revenue Code may be issued a nonprofit organization certificate authorizing it to consign donated motor vehicles to licensed Virginia motor vehicle dealers when the nonprofit organization receives title to such motor vehicles as qualified charitable gifts and titles the vehicles in the name of the nonprofit organization.

(Added by L.1998 ch. 393; chgd. by L.2000 ch. 180, eff. 7/1/2000.)

§46.2-1509. Application for license or certificate of dealer registration.

Application for license or certificate of dealer registration under this chapter shall be made to the Board and contain such information as the Board shall require. The application shall be accompanied by the fee as required by the Board.

The Board shall require, in the application or otherwise, information relating to the matters set forth in §46.2-1575 as grounds for refusing licenses, certificates of dealer registration, and to other pertinent matters requisite for the safeguarding of the public interest, including, if the applicant is a dealer in new motor vehicles with factory warranties, a copy of a current service agreement with the manufacturer or with the distributor, requiring the applicant to perform within a reasonable distance of his established place of business, the service, repair, and replacement work required of the manufacturer or distributor by such vehicle warranty. All of these matters shall be considered by the Board in determining the fitness of the applicant to engage in the business for which he seeks a license or certificate of dealer registration.

(Chgd. by L.1995 chs. 767, 816, eff. 7/1/95.)

§46.2-1510. Dealers required to have established place of business.

No license shall be issued to any motor vehicle dealer unless he has an established place of business, owned or leased by him, where a substantial portion of the sales activity of the business is routinely conducted and which:

1. Satisfies all local zoning regulations;
2. Has sales, service, and office space devoted exclusively to the dealership of at least 250 square feet in a permanent, enclosed building not used as a residence;
3. Houses all records the dealer is required to maintain by §46.2-1529;
4. Is equipped with a desk, chairs, filing space, a working telephone listed in the name of the dealership, and working utilities including electricity and provisions for space heating;
5. Displays a sign and business hours as required by this chapter; and
6. Has contiguous space designated for the exclusive use of the dealer adequate to permit the display of at least ten vehicles.

Any dealer licensed on or before July 1, 1995, shall be considered in compliance with provisions 2 and 6 of the first paragraph of this section for that licensee.

(Chgd. by L.1995 chs. 767, 816; L.1998 ch. 418, eff. 7/1/98.)

§46.2-1511. Dealer-operator to have certificate of qualification.

No license shall be issued to any motor vehicle dealer unless the dealer-operator holds a valid certificate of qualification issued by the Board. Such certificate shall be issued only on application to the Board, payment of an application fee of no more than fifty dollars as determined by the Board, the successful completion of an examination prepared and administered by the Board, and other prerequisites as set forth in this section. However, any individual who is the dealer-operator of a licensed dealer on July 1, 1995, shall be entitled to such a certificate without examination on application to the Board made on or before January 1, 1996.

The Board may establish minimum qualifications for applicants and require applicants to satisfactorily complete courses of study or other prerequisites prior to taking the examination.

(Chgd. by L.1995 chs. 767, 816, eff. 7/1/95.)

§46.2-1512. Salesperson to have certificate of qualification.

No license shall be issued to any motor vehicle salesperson unless he holds a valid certificate of qualification issued by the Board. A certificate shall be issued only on application to the Board, payment of the required application fee of no more than fifty dollars as determined by the Board, the successful completion of an examination prepared and administered by the Board, and other prerequisites as set forth in this section. Any individual who is licensed as a salesperson on July 1, 1995, shall be entitled to such a certificate without examination on application to the Board made on or before January 1, 1996.

The Board may establish minimum qualifications for applicants and require applicants to satisfactorily complete courses of study or other prerequisites prior to taking the examination.

(Chgd. by L.1995 chs. 767, 816, eff. 7/1/95.)

§46.2-1513. Continued operation on loss of a dealer-operator holding certificate of qualification.

Each dealer shall notify the Board in writing immediately when a dealer-operator who holds a certificate of qualification dies, becomes disabled, retires, is removed, or for any other cause ceases to act as dealer-operator. The dealer may continue to operate for 120 days thereafter without a dealer-operator and may be granted approval by the Board to operate for an additional 60 days on application and good cause shown for such delay.

(Chgd. by L.1995 chs. 767, 816, eff. 7/1/95.)

§46.2-1514. Action on applications; hearing on denial; denial for failure to have established place of business.

The Board shall act on all applications for a license or certificate of dealer registration under this chapter within sixty days after receipt by either granting or refusing the application. Any applicant denied a license or certificate shall, on his written request filed within thirty days, be given a hearing at a time and place determined by the Board or a person designated by the Board. All hearings under this section shall be public and shall be held promptly. The applicant may be represented by counsel.

Any applicant denied a license for failure to have an established place of business as provided in §46.2-1510 may not, nor shall anyone, apply for a license for premises for which a license was denied for thirty days from the date of the rejection of the application.

(Chgd. by L.1995 chs. 767, 816, eff. 7/1/95.)

§46.2-1515. Location to be specified; display of license; change of location.

The licenses of motor vehicle dealers shall specify the location of each place of business, branch or other location occupied or to be occupied by the licensee in conducting his business and the license issued therefor shall be conspicuously displayed at each of the premises. In the event any licensee intends to change a licensed location, he shall provide the Board thirty-days' advance written notice and a successful inspection of the new location shall be required prior to approval of a change of location. The Board shall endorse the change of location on the license, without charge, if the new location is within the same county or city. A change in location to another county or city shall require a new license and fee.

(Chgd. by L.1995 chs. 767, 816, eff. 7/1/95.)

§46.2-1516. Supplemental sales locations.

The Board may issue a license for a licensed motor vehicle dealer to display for sale or sell vehicles at locations other than his established place of business, subject to compliance with local ordinances and requirements.

A permanent supplemental license may be issued for premises less than 500 yards from the dealer's established place of business, provided a sign is displayed as required for the established place of business. A supplemental license shall not be required for premises otherwise contiguous to the established place of business except for a public thoroughfare.

A temporary supplemental license may be issued for a period not to exceed seven days, provided that the application is made fifteen days prior to the sale. A temporary supplemental license for the sale of new motor vehicles may be issued only for locations within the dealer's area of responsibility, as defined in his franchise or sales agreement, unless proof is provided that all dealers in the same line-make in whose areas of responsibility, as defined in their franchise or sales agreements, where the temporary supplemental license is sought do not oppose the issuance of the temporary license.

A temporary supplemental license for sale of used motor vehicles may be issued only for the county, city, or town in which the dealer is licensed pursuant to §46.2-1510, or for a contiguous county, city, or town. Temporary licenses may be issued without regard to the foregoing geographic restrictions where the dealer operating under a temporary license provides notice, at least thirty days before any proposed sale under a temporary license, to all other dealers licensed in the jurisdiction in which the sale will occur of the intent to conduct a sale and permits any locally licensed dealer who wishes to do so to participate in the sale on the same terms as the dealer operating under the temporary license. Any locally licensed dealer who chooses to participate in the sale must obtain a temporary supplemental license for the sale pursuant to this section.

A temporary supplemental license may be issued for the sale of boat trailers at a boat show. Any such license shall be valid for no more than fourteen days. Application for such a license shall be made and such license obtained prior to the opening of the show. Temporary supplemental licenses for sale of boat trailers at boat shows may be issued for any boat show located anywhere in the Commonwealth without notification of or approval by other boat trailer dealers.

(Chgd. by L.1995 chs. 767, 816, eff. 7/1/95.)

§46.2-1517. Changes in form of ownership, make, name.

Any change in the form of ownership or the addition or deletion of a partner shall require a new application, license, and fee.

Any addition or deletion of a franchise or change in the name of a dealer shall require immediate notification to the Department and the Board, and the Board shall endorse the change on the license without a fee. The change of an officer or director of a corporation shall be made at the time of license renewal.

(Chgd. by L.1995 chs. 767, 816, eff. 7/1/95.)

§46.2-1518. Display of salesperson's license; notice on termination.

No salesperson shall be employed by more than one dealer, unless the dealers are owned by the same person.

Each dealer shall post and maintain in a place conspicuous to the public a list of salespersons employed.

Each salesperson shall carry his license when engaged in his business and shall display it on request.

Each dealer shall notify the Board in writing not later than the tenth day following the month of the termination of any licensed salesperson's employment. In lieu of written notification, the license of the terminated salesperson may be returned to the Board annotated "terminated" on the face of the license and signed and dated by the dealer-operator, owner, or officer.

(Chgd. by L.1995 chs. 767, 816, eff. 7/1/95.)

§46.2-1519. License and registration fees; additional to other licenses and fees required by law.

A. The fee for each license and registration year or part thereof shall be determined by the Board, subject to the following:

1. For motor vehicle dealers, not more than $300 for each principal place of business, plus not more than $40 for each supplemental license.

2. For motor vehicle salespersons, not more than $50.

B. The licenses, registrations, and fees required by this chapter are in addition to licenses, taxes, and fees imposed by other provisions of law and nothing contained in this chapter shall exempt any person from any license, tax, or fee imposed by any other provision of law.

C. The fee for issuance to a nonprofit organization of a certificate pursuant to subsection B of §46.2-1508.1 shall be $25 per year or any part thereof.

D. No nonprofit organization granted a certificate pursuant to subsection B of §46.2-1508.1 shall, either orally or in writing, assign a value to any donated vehicle for the purpose of establishing tax deduction amounts on any federal or state income tax return.

(Chgd. by L.1995 chs. 767, 816; L.2000 ch. 180, eff. 7/1/2000.)

§46.2-1520. Collection of license and registration fees; payments from fund.

All licensing and registration fees provided for in this chapter, except as identified in Article 3.1 (§46.2-1527.1 et seq.) of this chapter shall be collected by the Board and paid into the state treasury and set aside as a special fund to meet the expenses of the Board.

(Chgd. by L.1995 chs. 767, 816, eff. 7/1/95.)

§46.2-1521. Issuance, expiration, and renewal of licenses and certificates of registration.

A. All licenses and certificates of registration issued under this chapter shall be issued for a period of twelve consecutive months except, at the discretion of the Board, the periods may be adjusted as is necessary to distribute the licenses and certificates as equally as practicable on a monthly basis. The expiration date shall be the last day of the twelfth month of validity or the last day of the designated month. Every license and certificate of registration shall be renewed annually on application by the licensee or registrant and by payment of fees required by law, the renewal to take effect on the first day of the succeeding month.

B. Licenses and certificates of registration issued under this chapter shall be deemed not to have expired if the renewal application and required fees as set forth in this subsection are received by the Board or postmarked not more than thirty days after the expiration date of such license or certificate of registration. Whenever the renewal application is received by the Board or postmarked no more than thirty days after the expiration date of such license or certificate of registration, the license fees shall be 150 percent of the fees provided for in §46.2-1519.

C. The Board may offer an optional multi-year license. When such option is offered and chosen by the licensee, all annual and twelve-month fees due at the time of licensing shall be multiplied by the number of years or fraction thereof for which the license will be issued.

(Chgd. by L.1995 chs. 767, 816; L.1997 ch. 848; L.1998 ch. 325, eff. 1/1/99.)

ARTICLE 3.1
MOTOR VEHICLE TRANSACTION RECOVERY FUND

§46.2-1527.1. Motor Vehicle Transaction Recovery Fund established.

All fees in this article shall be deposited in the Motor Vehicle Transaction Recovery Fund, hereinafter referred to in this article as "the Fund." The Fund shall be a special fund in the state treasury to pay claims against the Fund and for no other purpose, except the Board may expend moneys from the interest earned on the Fund for the administration of this article, in accordance with the general appropriation act. The Fund shall be used to satisfy unpaid judgments, as provided for in §46.2-1527.3. Any interest income shall accrue to the Fund. The Board shall maintain an accurate record of all transactions involving the Fund. The minimum balance of the Fund shall be $250,000.

Every applicant renewing a motor vehicle dealer's license shall pay, in addition to other license fees, an annual Fund fee of $100, and every applicant for a motor vehicle salesperson's license shall pay, in addition to other license fees, an annual Fund fee of ten dollars, prior to license issue. However, annual Fund renewal fees from salespersons shall not exceed $100 per year from an individual dealer. These fees shall be deposited in the Motor Vehicle Transaction Recovery Fund.

Applicants for an original motor vehicle dealer's license shall pay an annual Fund fee of $250 each year for three consecutive years. During this period, the $250 Fund fee will take the place of the annual $100 Fund fee.

In addition to the $250 annual fee, applicants for an original dealer's license shall have a $25,000 bond pursuant to §46.2-1527.2 for three consecutive years. Only those renewing licensees who have not been the subject of a claim against their bond or against the Fund for three consecutive years shall pay the annual $100 fee and will no longer be required to pay the $250 annual fee or hold the $25,000 bond.

In addition to other license fees, applicants for an original Certificate of Dealer Registration or its renewal shall pay a Fund fee of $60.

The Board may suspend or reinstate collection of Fund fees.

The provisions of this section shall not apply to manufactured home dealers as defined in §36-85.16, T&M vehicle dealers as defined in §46.2-1900, trailer dealers as defined in §46.2-1992, motorcycle dealers as defined in §46.2-1993, and nonprofit organizations issued certificates pursuant to subsection B of §46.2-1508.1.
(Chgd. by L.1995 chs. 767, 816; L.1998 ch. 325; L.2000 ch. 180, eff. 7/1/2000.)

§46.2-1527.2. Bonding requirements for applicants for an original license.

Before the Board shall issue to an applicant an original license, the applicant shall obtain and file with the Board a bond in the amount of $25,000. The bond shall come from a corporate surety licensed to do business in the Commonwealth and approved by the Attorney General. The bond shall be conditioned on a statement by the applicant that the applicant will not practice fraud, make any fraudulent representation, or violate any provision of this chapter in the conduct of the applicant's business. The Board may, without holding a hearing, suspend the dealer's license during the period that the dealer does not have a sufficient bond on file.

If a person suffers any of the following: (i) loss or damage in connection with purchase or lease of a motor vehicle by reason of fraud practiced on him or fraudulent representation made to him by a licensed motor vehicle dealer or one of the dealer's salespersons acting within his scope of employment, (ii) loss or damage by reason of the violation by a dealer or salesperson of any provision of this chapter in connection with the purchase or lease of a motor vehicle, or (iii) loss or damage resulting from a breach of an extended service contract entered into on or after the effective date of this act, as defined by §59.1-435, that person shall have a claim against the dealer and the dealer's bond, and may recover such damages as may be awarded to such person by final judgment of a court of competent jurisdiction against the dealer as a proximate result of such loss or damage up to but not exceeding the amount of the bond, from such surety, who shall be subrogated to the rights of such person against the dealer or salesperson. The liability of such surety shall be limited to actual damages, and shall not include any punitive damages or attorneys' fees assessed against the dealer or salesperson.

In those cases in which a dealer's surety shall be liable pursuant to this section, the surety shall be liable only for the first $25,000 in claims against the dealer. Thereafter, the Fund shall be liable for the next $50,000 in those cases in which the Fund itself may be liable. The aggregate liability of the dealer's surety to any and all persons, regardless of the number of claims made against the bond or the number of years the bond remains in force, shall in no event exceed $25,000.

The dealer's surety shall notify the Board when a claim is made against a dealer's bond, when a claim is paid and when the bond is cancelled. Such notification shall include the amount of a claim and the circumstances surrounding the claim. Notification of cancellation shall include the effective date and reason for cancellation. The bond may be cancelled as to future liability by the dealer's surety upon thirty days' notice to the Board.
(Chgd. by L.1995 chs. 767, 816; L.1998 ch. 325, eff. 10/1/98.)

§46.2-1527.3. Recovery from Fund, generally.

Whenever any person is awarded a final judgment in a court of competent jurisdiction in the Commonwealth for (i) any loss or damage in connection with the purchase or lease of a motor vehicle by reason of any fraud practiced on him or fraudulent representation made to him by a licensed or registered motor vehicle dealer or one of a dealer's salespersons acting for the dealer or within the scope of his employment or (ii) any loss or damage by reason of the violation by a dealer or salesperson of any of the provisions of this chapter in connection with the purchase of a motor vehicle, on or after January 1, 1989, or the lease of a motor vehicle on or after October 1, 1998, the judgment creditor may file a verified claim with the Board, requesting payment from the Fund of the amount unpaid on the judgment. The claim shall be filed with the Board no sooner than thirty days and no later than twelve months after the judgment becomes final.

On or after the effective date of this act, the Board shall consider for payment, claims submitted by retail purchasers of motor vehicles, and for purchases of motor vehicles by licensed or registered motor vehicle dealers who contribute to the Fund. The Board shall also consider for payment claims submitted by lessees of motor vehicles leased on or after October 1, 1998, from licensed or registered motor vehicle dealers who contribute to the Fund.
(Chgd. by L.1995 chs. 767, 816; L.1998 ch. 325, eff. 10/1/98.)

§46.2-1527.4. Opportunity to intervene.

Any action instituted by a person against a licensed or registered dealer or a salesperson, which may become a claim against the Fund, shall be served to the Board in the manner prescribed by law. All subsequent pleadings and documents shall also be served to the Board. Included in such service shall be an affidavit stating all acts constituting fraud or violations of this chapter. Upon service of process, the Board, or duly authorized representative, shall have the right to request leave of the court to intervene. The person shall submit such pleadings or documents to the Board by certified mail or the equivalent.
(Chgd. by L.1995 chs. 767, 816, eff. 7/1/95.)

§46.2-1527.5. Limitations on recovery from Fund.

The maximum claim of one judgment creditor against the Fund based on an unpaid final judgment arising out of any loss or damage by reason of a claim submitted under §46.2-1527.2 or §46.2-1527.3 involving a single transaction, shall be limited to $15,000, regardless of the amount of the unpaid final judgment of one judgment creditor.

The aggregate of claims against the Fund based on unpaid final judgments arising out of any loss or damage by reason of a claim submitted under §46.2-1527.3 involving more than one transaction shall be limited to $75,000, regardless of the total amounts of the unpaid final judgments of judgment creditors.

However, aggregate claims against the Fund under §46.2-1527.2 shall be limited to $50,000 and then only after the dealer's $25,000 bond has been exhausted.

If a claim has been made against the Fund, and the Board has reason to believe that there may be additional claims against the Fund from other transactions involving the same licensee or registrant, the Board may withhold any payment from the Fund involving the licensee or registrant for a period not to exceed the end of the relevant license or registration period. After this period, if the aggregate of claims against the licensee or registrant exceeds $75,000, a total of $75,000 shall be prorated among the claimants and paid from the Fund in proportion to the amounts of their unpaid final judgments against the licensee or registrant.

However, claims against motor vehicle dealers and salespersons under §46.2-1527.2 shall be prorated when the aggregate exceeds $50,000. Claims shall be prorated only after the dealer's $25,000 bond has been exhausted.

On receipt of a verified claim filed against the Fund, the Board shall forthwith notify the licensee or registrant who is the subject of the unpaid judgment that a verified claim has been filed and that the licensee or registrant should satisfy the judgment debt. If the judgment debt is not fully satisfied thirty days following the date of the notification by the Board, the Board shall make payment from the Fund subject to the other limitations contained in this article.

Excluded from the amount of any unpaid final judgment on which a claim against the Fund is based shall be any sums representing interest, or punitive or exemplary damages.

If at any time the Fund is insufficient to fully satisfy any claims or claim filed with the Board and authorized by this article, the Board shall pay such claims, claim, or portion thereof to the claimants in the order that the claims were filed with the Board. However, claims by retail purchasers shall take precedence over other claims.

(Chgd. by L.1995 chs. 767, 816; L.1998 ch. 325, eff. 10/1/98.)

§46.2-1527.6. Assignment of claimant's rights to the Board; payment of claims.

Subject to the provisions of this article and on the claimant's execution and delivery to the Board of an assignment to the Board of his rights against the licensee or registrant, to the extent he received satisfaction from the Fund, the Board shall pay the claimant from the Fund the amount of the unpaid final judgment.

(Chgd. by L.1995 chs. 767, 816, eff. 7/1/95.)

§46.2-1527.7. Revocation of license or certificate of registration on payment from the Fund.

On payment by the Board to a claimant from the Fund as provided in this article, the Board shall immediately notify the licensee or registrant in writing of the Board's payment to the claimant and request full reimbursement be made to the Board within thirty days of the notification. Failure to reimburse the Board in full within the specified period shall cause the Board to immediately revoke the license or certificate of the dealer or the license of a salesperson whose fraud, fraudulent representation, or violation of this chapter resulted in this payment. Any person whose license or certificate is revoked shall not be eligible to apply for a license or certificate as a motor vehicle dealer or a license as a salesperson until the person has repaid in full the amount paid from the Fund on his account, plus interest at the rate of eight percent per year from the date of payment.

(Chgd. by L.1995 chs. 767, 816, eff. 7/1/95.)

§46.2-1527.8. No waiver by the Board of disciplinary action against licensee or registrant.

Nothing contained in this article shall limit the authority of the Board to take disciplinary action against any licensee or registrant for any violation of this chapter or any regulation promulgated thereunder, nor shall full repayment of the amount paid from the Fund on a licensee's or registrant's account nullify or modify the effect of any disciplinary action against that licensee or registrant for any violation.

(Chgd. by L.1995 chs. 767, 816, eff. 7/1/95.)

ARTICLE 4
CONDUCT OF BUSINESS

Section

§46.2-1528. Examination or audit of licensee; costs.

The Board or authorized representatives of the Board may examine, during the posted business hours, the records required to be maintained by this chapter. If a licensee is found to have violated this chapter or any order of the Board, the actual cost of the examination shall be paid by the licensee so examined within thirty days after demand therefor by the Board. The Board may maintain an action for the recovery of these costs in any court of competent jurisdiction.

(Chgd. by L.1995 chs. 767, 816, eff. 7/1/95.)

§46.2-1529. Dealer records.

All dealer records regarding employees; lists of vehicles in inventory for sale, resale, or on consignment; vehicle purchases, sales, trades, and transfers of ownership; collections of taxes; titling, uninsured motor vehicle, and registration fees; odometer disclosure statements; records of permanent dealer registration plates assigned to the dealer and temporary transport plates and temporary certificates of ownership; and other records required by the Department or the Board shall be maintained on the premises of the licensed location. The Board may, on written request by a dealer, permit his records to be maintained at a location other than the premises of the licensed location for good cause shown. All dealer records shall be preserved in original form or in film, magnetic, or optical media (including but not limited to microfilm, microfiche, or other electronic media) for a period of five years in a manner that permits systematic retrieval. Certain records may be maintained on a computerized record-keeping system with the prior approval of the Board.

(Chgd. by L.1995 chs. 767, 816; L.2000 ch. 128, eff. 7/1/2000.)

§46.2-1529.1. Sales of used motor vehicles by dealers; disclosures; penalty.

A. If, in any retail sale by a dealer of a used motor vehicle of under 6,000 pounds gross vehicle weight for use on the public highways, and normally used for personal, family or household use, the dealer offers an express warranty, the dealer shall provide the buyer a written disclosure of this warranty. The written disclosure shall be the Buyer's Guide required by federal law, shall be completely filled out and, in addition, signed and dated by the buyer and incorporated as part of the buyer's order.

B. A dealer may sell a used motor vehicle at retail "AS IS" and exclude all warranties only if the dealer provides the buyer, prior to sale, a separate written disclosure as to the effect of an "AS IS" sale. The written disclosure shall be conspicuous and contained on the front of the buyer's order and printed in not less than bold, ten-point type and signed by the buyer: "I understand that this vehicle is being sold "AS IS" with all faults and is not covered by any dealer warranty. I understand that the dealer is not required to make any repairs after I buy this vehicle. I will have to pay for any repairs this vehicle will need." A fully completed Buyer's Guide, as required by federal law, shall be signed and dated by the buyer and incorporated as part of the buyer's order.

C. Failure to provide the applicable disclosure required by subsection A or B of this section shall be punishable by a civil penalty of no more than $1,000. Any such civil penalty shall be paid into the general fund of the state treasury. Furthermore, if the applicable disclosure required by subsection A or B of this section is not provided as required in this section, the buyer may cancel the sale within thirty days. In this case, the buyer shall have the right to return the vehicle to the dealer and obtain a full refund of all payments made toward the purchase of the vehicle, less any damage to the vehicle incurred while ownership was vested in the purchaser, and less a reasonable amount for the use not to exceed one-half the amount allowed per mile by the Internal Revenue Service, as provided by regulation, revenue procedure, or revenue ruling promulgated pursuant to §162 of the Internal Revenue Code, for use of a personal vehicle for business purposes. Notice of the provisions of this subsection shall be included as part of every disclosure made under subsection A or B of this section.

(Added by L.1995 ch. 849, eff. 7/1/95.)

§46.2-1530. Buyer's order.

A. Every motor vehicle dealer shall complete, in duplicate, a buyer's order for each sale or exchange of a motor vehicle. A copy of the buyer's order form shall be made available to a prospective buyer during the negotiating phase of a sale and prior to any sales agreement. The completed original shall be retained for a period of four years in accordance with §46.2-1529, and a duplicate copy shall be delivered to the purchaser at the time of sale or exchange. A buyer's order shall include:

1. The name and address of the person to whom the vehicle was sold or traded.
2. The date of the sale or trade.
3. The name and address of the motor vehicle dealer selling or trading the vehicle.
4. The make, model year, vehicle identification number and body style of the vehicle.
5. The sale price of the vehicle.
6. The amount of any cash deposit made by the buyer.
7. A description of any vehicle used as a trade-in and the amount credited the buyer for the trade-in. The description of the trade-in shall be the same as outlined in subdivision 4 of this subsection.
8. The amount of any sales and use tax, title fee, uninsured motor vehicle fee, registration fee, or other fee required by law for which the buyer is responsible and the dealer has collected. Each tax and fee shall be individually listed and identified.
9. The net balance due at settlement.
10. Any item designated as "processing fee," and the amount charged by the dealer, if any, for processing the transaction. As used in this section processing includes obtaining title and license plates for the purchaser.
11. Any item designated as "dealer's business license tax," and the amount charged by the dealer, if any.
12. For sales involving dealer-arranged financing, the following notice, printed in bold type no less than ten-point:

"THIS SALE IS CONDITIONED UPON APPROVAL OF YOUR PROPOSED RETAIL INSTALLMENT SALE CONTRACT AS SUBMITTED TO OR THROUGH THE DEALER. IF THAT PROPOSED RETAIL INSTALLMENT SALE CONTRACT IS NOT APPROVED UNDER THE TERMS AGREED TO WITH THE DEALER, YOU MAY CANCEL THIS SALE AND ANY DOWNPAYMENT AND/OR TRADE-IN YOU SUBMITTED WILL BE RETURNED TO YOU, PROVIDED THAT ANY VEHICLE DELIVERED TO YOU BY THE DEALER PURSUANT TO THIS AGREEMENT IS RETURNED TO THE DEALER IN THE SAME CONDITION AS DELIVERED TO YOU, NORMAL WEAR AND TEAR EXCEPTED, WITHIN TWENTY-FOUR HOURS OF WRITTEN OR ORAL NOTICE TO YOU OF THE CREDIT DENIAL."

13. For sales of used motor vehicles, the disclosure required by §46.2-1529.1.

If the transaction does not include a policy of motor vehicle liability insurance, the seller shall stamp or mark on the face of the bill of sale in boldface letters no smaller than eighteen point type the following words: "No Liability Insurance Included."

A completed buyer's order when signed by both buyer and seller may constitute a bill of sale.

B. The Board shall approve a buyer's order form and each dealer shall file with each original license application its buyer's order form, on which the processing fee amount is stated.

C. If a processing fee is charged, that fact and the amount of the processing fee shall be disclosed by the dealer. Disclosure shall be by placing a clear and conspicuous sign in the public sales area of the dealership. The sign shall be no smaller than eight and one-half inches by eleven inches and the print shall be no smaller than one-half inch, and in a form as approved by the Board.

(Chgd. by L.1995 chs. 767, 816, 849; L.2000 ch. 116, eff. 7/1/2000.)

§46.2-1531. Consignment vehicles; contract.

Any motor vehicle dealer offering a vehicle for sale on consignment shall have in his possession a consignment contract for the vehicle, executed and signed by the dealer and the consignor. The consignment contract shall include:

1. The complete name, address, and the telephone number of the owners.
2. The name, address, and dealer certificate number of the selling dealer.
3. A complete description of the vehicle on consignment, including the make, model year, vehicle identification number, and body style.
4. The beginning and termination dates of the contract.
5. The percentage of commission, the amount of the commission, or the net amount the owner is to receive, if the vehicle is sold.
6. Any fees for which the owner is responsible.
7. A disclosure of all unsatisfied liens on the vehicle and the location of the certificate of title to the vehicle.
8. A requirement that the motor vehicle pass a safety inspection prior to sale.

If any motor vehicle on consignment from a certified nonprofit organization is found not to be in compliance with any safety inspection requirement, the dealer shall furnish any buyer intending to use that vehicle on the public highways a written disclosure, prior to sale, that the vehicle did not pass a safety inspection.

Any dealer offering a vehicle for sale on consignment shall inform any prospective customer that the vehicle is on consignment.

Dealer license plates shall not be used to demonstrate a vehicle on consignment except on (i) motor vehicles with gross vehicle weight of 15,000 pounds or more, (ii) vehicles on consignment from another licensed motor vehicle dealer, and (iii) vehicles on consignment from a nonprofit organization certified pursuant to subsection B of §46.2-1508.1. The owner's license plates may be used if liability insurance coverage is in effect in the amounts prescribed by §46.2-472.

(Chgd. by L.2000 ch. 180, eff. 7/1/2000.)

§46.2-1532. Odometer disclosure; penalty.

Every motor vehicle dealer shall comply with all requirements of the Federal Odometer Act and §46.2-629 by completing the appropriate odometer mileage statement form for each vehicle purchased, sold or transferred, or in any other way acquired or disposed of. Odometer disclosure statements shall be maintained by the dealer in a manner that permits systematic retrieval. Any person found guilty of violating any of the provisions of this section shall be guilty of a Class 1 misdemeanor.

(Chgd. by L.1995 chs. 767, 816, eff. 7/1/95.)

§46.2-1532.1. Certain disclosures required by manufacturers and distributors.

Motor vehicle manufacturers and distributors shall affix or cause to be affixed in a conspicuous place to every motor vehicle offered for sale as a new vehicle a statement disclosing the place of assembly or manufacture of the vehicle. For disclosures of place of assembly, the assembly plant shall be the same as that designated by the vehicle identification number.

The provisions of this section shall apply only to motor vehicles manufactured for the 1991 or subsequent model years.

§46.2-1533. Business hours.

Each motor vehicle dealer shall be open for business a minimum of twenty hours per week, at least ten of which shall be between the hours of 9:00 a.m. and 5:00 p.m. Monday through Friday, except that the Board, on written request by a dealer, may modify these requirements for good cause. Each licensee engaged in business exclusively as a dealer in used manufactured homes without inventory shall be open for business a minimum of two consecutive hours per week between the hours of 9:00 a.m. and 5:00 p.m. Monday through Friday. The dealer's hours shall be posted and maintained conspicuously on or near the main entrance of each place of business.

Each dealer shall include his business hours on the original and every renewal application for a license, and changes to these hours shall be immediately filed with the Department.

(Chgd. by L.1995 chs. 767, 816, eff. 7/1/95.)

§46.2-1534. Signs.

Each retail motor vehicle dealer's place of business shall be identified by a permanent sign visible from the front of the business office so that the public may quickly and easily identify the dealership. The sign shall contain the dealer's trade name in letters no less than six inches in height unless otherwise restricted by law or contract.

Each licensee engaged in business exclusively as a dealer in used manufactured homes without inventory shall be identified by a permanent sign visible from the front of the business office so that the public may quickly and easily identify the dealership. The sign shall contain the dealer's trade name in letters no less than two inches in height unless otherwise restricted by law or contract.

§46.2-1535. Advertisements.

Unless the dealer is clearly identified by name, whenever any licensee places an advertisement in any newspaper or publication, the abbreviations "VA DLR," denoting a Virginia licensed dealer, shall appear therein.

§46.2-1536. Coercing purchaser to provide insurance coverage on motor vehicle; penalty.

It shall be unlawful for any dealer or salesperson or any employee of a dealer or representative of either to coerce or offer anything of value to any purchaser of a motor vehicle to provide any type of insurance coverage on the motor vehicle.

Nothing in this section shall prohibit a dealer from requiring that a retail customer obtain automobile physical damage insurance to protect collateral secured by an installment sales contract. Any person found guilty of violating any of the provisions of this section shall be guilty of a Class 1 misdemeanor.

(Chgd. by L.1995 chs. 767, 816, eff. 7/1/95.)

§46.2-1537. Prohibited solicitation and compensation.

It shall be unlawful for any motor vehicle dealer or salesperson licensed under this chapter, directly or indirectly, to solicit the sale of a motor vehicle through a pecuniarily interested person, or to pay, or cause to be paid, any commission or compensation in any form whatsoever to any person in connection with the sale of a motor vehicle, unless the person is duly licensed as a salesperson employed by the dealer.

§46.2-1538. Salesman selling for other than his employer prohibited.

It shall be unlawful for any motor vehicle salesman licensed under this chapter to sell or exchange or offer or attempt to sell or exchange any motor vehicle except for the licensed motor vehicle dealer by whom he is employed, or to offer, transfer, or assign any sale or exchange that he may have negotiated to any other dealer or salesman.

§46.2-1539. Inspection of vehicles required; penalty.

No person required to be licensed as a dealer under this chapter shall sell at retail any motor vehicle which is intended by the buyer for use on the public highways, and which is required to comply with the safety inspection requirements provided in Article 21 (§46.2-1157 et seq.) of Chapter 10 of this title unless between the time the vehicle comes into the possession of the dealer and the time it is sold at retail it is inspected by an official safety inspection station. In the event the vehicle is found not to be in compliance with all safety inspection requirements, the dealer shall either take steps to bring it into compliance or shall furnish any buyer intending it for use on the public highway a written disclosure, prior to sale, that the vehicle did not pass a safety inspection. Any person found guilty of violating any of the provisions of this section shall be guilty of a Class 1 misdemeanor.

(Chgd. by L.1995 chs. 767, 816, eff. 7/1/95.)

§46.2-1540. Inspections prior to sale not required of certain sellers.

The provisions of §§46.2-1158 and 46.2-1539 requiring inspection of any motor vehicle prior to sale at retail shall not apply to any person conducting a public auction for the sale of motor vehicles at retail, provided that the individual, firm, or business conducting the auction shall not have taken title to the vehicle, but is acting as an agent for the sale of the vehicle. Nor shall the provisions of §§46.2-1158 and 46.2-1539 requiring inspection of any motor vehicle prior to sale at retail apply to any new motor vehicle or vehicles sold on the basis of a special order placed by a dealer with a manufacturer outside Virginia on behalf of a customer who is a nonresident of Virginia and takes delivery outside Virginia.

§46.2-1541. *(Repealed by L.1995 chs. 767, 816, eff. 7/1/95.)*

§46.2-1542. Temporary certificates of ownership.

A. Notwithstanding §§46.2-617 and 46.2-628, whenever a dealer licensed by the Board sells and delivers to a purchaser a motor vehicle and is unable at the time of the sale to deliver to the purchaser the certificate of title or certificate of origin for the vehicle because the certificate of title or certificate of origin is lost or is being detained by another in possession or for any other reason beyond the dealer's control, the dealer shall execute, on forms provided by the Commissioner, a temporary certificate of ownership. The certificate shall bear its date of issuance, the name and address of the purchaser, the identification number of the vehicle, the registration number to be used temporarily on the vehicle, the name of the state in which the vehicle is to be registered, the name and address of the person from whom the dealer acquired the vehicle, and whatever other information may be required by the Commissioner. A copy of the temporary certificate and a bona fide bill of sale shall be delivered to the purchaser and shall be in the possession of the purchaser at all times when operating the vehicle. One copy of the certificate shall be retained by the dealer and shall be subject to inspection at any time by the Department's agents. The original of the certificate shall be forwarded by the dealer to the Department directly on issuance to the purchaser if the vehicle is to be titled outside the Commonwealth, along with application for title. The issuance of a temporary certificate of ownership to a purchaser pursuant to this section shall have the effect of vesting ownership to the vehicle in the purchaser for the period that the certificate remains effective.

B. A temporary certificate of ownership issued by a dealer to a purchaser pursuant to this section shall expire on receipt by the purchaser of a certificate of title to the vehicle issued by the Department in the name of the purchaser, but in no event shall any temporary certificate of ownership issued under this section be effective for more than thirty days from the date of its issuance. In the event that the dealer fails to produce the old certificate of title or certificate of origin to the vehicle or fails to apply for a replacement certificate of title pursuant to §46.2-632, thereby preventing delivery to the Department or purchaser before the expiration of the temporary certificate of ownership, the purchaser's ownership of the vehicle may terminate and the purchaser shall have the right to return the vehicle to the dealer and obtain a full refund of all payments made toward the purchase of the vehicle, less any damage to the vehicle incurred while ownership was vested in the purchaser, and less a reasonable amount for use not to exceed one-half the amount allowed per mile by the Internal Revenue Service, as provided by regulation, revenue procedure, or revenue ruling promulgated pursuant to §162 of the Internal Revenue Code, for use of a personal vehicle for business purposes.

C. Notwithstanding subsection B of this section, if the dealer fails to deliver the certificate of title or certificate of origin to the purchaser within thirty days, a second temporary certificate of ownership may be issued. However, the dealer shall, not later than the expiration of the first temporary certificate, deliver to the Department an application for title, copy of the bill of sale, all required fees and a written statement of facts describing the dealer's efforts to secure the certificate of title or certificate of origin to the vehicle. On receipt of the title application with attachments as described herein, the Department shall record the purchaser's ownership of the vehicle and may authorize the dealer to issue a second thirty-day temporary certificate of ownership. If the dealer does not produce the certificate of title or certificate of origin to the vehicle before the expiration of the second temporary certificate, the purchaser's ownership of the vehicle may terminate and he shall have the right to return the vehicle as provided in subsection B of this section.

D. If the dealer is unable to produce the certificate of title or certificate of origin to the vehicle within the sixty-day period from the date of issuance of the first temporary certificate, the Department may extend temporary ownership for an additional period of up to ninety days, provided the dealer makes application in the format required by the Department. If the dealer does not produce the certificate of title or certificate of origin to the vehicle before the expiration of the additional ninety-day period, the purchaser's ownership of the vehicle may terminate and he shall have the right to return the vehicle as provided in subsection B of this section.

E. The Commissioner, on determining that the provisions of this section or the directions of the Department are not being complied with by a dealer, may suspend, after a hearing, the right of the dealer to issue temporary certificates of ownership.

(Chgd. by L.1995 chs. 767, 816, eff. 7/1/95.)

§46.2-1543. Use of old license plates and registration number on another vehicle.

An owner who sells or transfers a registered motor vehicle may have the license plates and the registration number transferred to another vehicle titled in the owner's name according to the provisions of Chapter 6 of this title, which is in a like vehicle category as specified in §46.2-694 and which requires an identical registration fee, on application to the Board accompanied by a fee of two dollars or, if the other vehicle requires a greater registration fee than that for which the license plates were assigned, on the payment of a fee of two dollars and the amount of the difference in registration fees between the two vehicles, all such transfers to be in accordance with the regulations of the Department. All fees collected under this section shall be paid by the Commissioner into the state treasury and shall be set aside as a special fund to be used to meet the expenses of the Department. For purposes of this section, a motor vehicle dealer licensed by the Board may be authorized to act as an agent of the Department for the purpose of receiving, processing, and approving applications from its customers for assignment of license plates and registration numbers pursuant to this section, using the forms and following the procedures prescribed by the Department. The Commissioner, on determining that the provisions of this section or the directions of the Department are not being complied with by a dealer, may suspend, after a hearing, the authority of the dealer to receive, process, and approve the assignment of license plates and registration numbers pursuant to this section.

(Chgd. by L.1995 chs. 767, 816, eff. 7/1/95.)

§46.2-1544. Certificate of title for dealers; penalty.

Except as otherwise provided in this chapter, every dealer shall obtain, on the purchase of each vehicle, a certificate of title issued to the dealer or shall obtain an assignment or reassignment of a certificate of title for each vehicle purchased, except that a certificate of title shall not be required for any new vehicle to be sold as such. Any person found guilty of violating any of the provisions of this section shall be guilty of a Class 1 misdemeanor.

(Chgd. by L.1995 chs. 767, 816, eff. 7/1/95.)

§46.2-1545. Termination of business.

No dealer, unless his license has been suspended, revoked, or canceled, shall cease business without a thirty-day prior notification to the Department and the Board. On cessation of the business, the dealer shall immediately surrender to the Board the dealer's certificate of license, all salespersons' licenses and any other materials furnished by the Board. The dealer shall also immediately surrender to the Department all dealer and temporary license plates, all fees and taxes collected, and any other materials furnished by the Department. After cessation of business, the former licensee shall continue to maintain and make available to the Department and the Board dealer records as set forth in this chapter.

(Chgd. by L.1995 chs. 767, 816, eff. 7/1/95.)

ARTICLE 5
DEALER'S LICENSE PLATES

§46.2-1546. Registration of dealers; fees.

Every manufacturer, distributor, or dealer, before he commences to operate vehicles in his inventory for sale or resale, shall apply to the Commissioner for a dealer's certificate of vehicle registration and license plates. For the purposes of this article, a vehicle is in inventory when it is owned by or assigned to a dealer and is offered and available for sale or resale. All dealer's certificates of vehicle registration and license plates issued under this section may, at the discretion of the Commissioner, be placed in a system of staggered issue to distribute the work of issuing vehicle registration certificates and license plates as uniformly as practicable throughout the year. Dealerships which sold fewer than twenty-five vehicles during the last twelve months of the preceding license year shall be eligible to receive no more than two dealer's license plates; dealerships which sold at least twenty-five but fewer than fifty vehicles during the last twelve months of the preceding license year shall be eligible to receive no more than four dealer's license plates. However, dealerships which sold fifty or more vehicles during their current license year may apply for additional license plates not to exceed four times the number of licensed salespersons employed by that dealership. Dealerships which sold fifty or more vehicles during the last twelve months of the preceding license year shall be eligible to receive a number of dealer's license plates not to exceed four times the number of licensed salespersons employed by that dealership. A new applicant for a dealership shall be eligible to receive a number of dealer's license plates not to exceed four times the number of licensed salespersons employed by that dealership. For the purposes of this article, a salesperson or employee shall be considered to be employed only if he (i) works for the dealership at least twenty-five hours each week on a regular basis and (ii) is compensated for this work. All salespersons' or employees' employment records shall be retained in accordance with the provisions of §46.2-1529. A salesperson shall not be considered employed, within the meaning of this section, if he is an independent contractor as defined by the United States Internal Revenue Code. The fee for the issuance of dealer's license plates shall be determined by the Board, but not more than $30 per license plate; however, the fee for the first two dealer's plates shall not be less than twenty-four dollars and the fee for additional dealer's license plates shall not be less than ten dollars and forty cents each. For the first two dealer's license plates issued by the Department to a dealer, twenty-four dollars shall be deposited into the Transportation Trust Fund and the remainder shall be deposited into the Motor Vehicle Dealer Fund. For each additional dealer's license plate issued to a dealer, ten dollars and forty cents shall be deposited into the Transportation Trust Fund and the remainder shall be deposited into the Motor Vehicle Dealer Fund.

(Chgd. by L.1995 chs. 767, 816, eff. 7/1/95.)

§46.2-1547. License under this chapter prerequisite to receiving dealer's license plates; insurance required; Commissioner may revoke plates.

No motor vehicle dealer, unless licensed under this chapter, nor any manufacturer or distributor, unless licensed under Chapter 19 (§46.2-1900 et seq.) of this title, shall be entitled to receive or maintain any dealer's license plates. It shall be unlawful to use or permit the use of any dealer's license plates for which there is no automobile liability insurance coverage or a certificate of self-insurance as defined in §46.2-368 on any motor vehicle. No dealer's license plates shall be issued unless the dealer certifies to the Department that there is automobile liability insurance coverage or a certificate of self-insurance with respect to each dealer's license plate to be issued. Such automobile liability insurance or a certificate of self-insurance shall be maintained as to each dealer's license plate for so long as the registration for the dealer's license plate remains valid without regard to whether the plate is actually being used on a vehicle. If insurance or a certificate of self-insurance is not so maintained, the dealer's license plate shall be surrendered to the Department. The Commissioner shall revoke any dealer's license plate as to which there is no insurance or a certificate of self-insurance. The Commissioner may also revoke any dealer's license plate that has been used in any way not authorized by the provisions of this title.

(Chgd. by L.1995 chs. 767, 816, eff. 7/1/95.)

§46.2-1548. Transferable dealer's license plates.

In lieu of registering each vehicle of a type described in this section, a manufacturer, distributor, or dealer owning and operating any motor vehicle on any highway may obtain a dealer's license plate from the Department, on application therefor on the prescribed form and on payment of the fees required by law. These license plates shall be attached to each vehicle as required by subsection A of §46.2-711. Each plate shall bear a distinctive number, and the name of the Commonwealth, which may be abbreviated, together with the word "dealer" or a distinguishing symbol indicating that the plate is issued to a manufacturer, distributor, or dealer. Month and year decals indicating the date of expiration shall be affixed to each license plate. Any license plates so issued may, during the calendar year or years for which they have been issued, be transferred from one motor vehicle to another, used or operated by the manufacturer, distributor, or dealer, who shall keep a written record of the motor vehicle on which the dealer's license plates are used. This record shall be in a format approved by the Commissioner and shall be open to inspection by any law-enforcement officer or any officer or employee of the Department.

Display of a transferable manufacturer's, distributor's, or dealer's license plate or plates on a motor vehicle shall subject the vehicle to the requirements of §§46.2-1038 and 46.2-1056.

All manufacturer's, distributor's, and dealer's license plates shall be issued for a period of twelve consecutive months except, at the discretion of the Commissioner, the periods may be adjusted as may be necessary to distribute the registrations as equally as practicable on a monthly basis. The expiration date shall be the last day of the twelfth month of validity or the last day of the designated month. Every license plate shall be renewed annually on application by the owner and by payment of fees required by law, such renewal to take effect on the first day of the succeeding month.

The Commissioner may offer an optional multi-year license plate registration to manufacturers, distributors, and dealers licensed pursuant to this chapter provided that he has chosen to offer optional multi-year licensing to such persons pursuant to §46.2-1521. When such option is offered and chosen by the licensee, all annual and twelve-month fees due at the time of registration shall be multiplied by the number of years or fraction thereof the licensee will be licensed pursuant to §46.2-1521.
(Chgd. by L.1995 chs. 767, 816, eff. 7/1/95.)

§46.2-1549. Dealer's license plates to distinguish between various types of dealers.

The Commissioner shall provide for the issuance of appropriate franchised or independent dealer's license plates.
(Chgd. by L.1995 chs. 767, 816, eff. 7/1/95.)

§46.2-1549.1. Dealer's promotional license plates.

In addition to any other license plate authorized by this article, the Commissioner may issue permanent or temporary dealer's promotional license plates to a dealer for use on vehicles held for sale or resale in the dealer's inventory. The design of these license plates shall be at the discretion of the Commissioner. These license plates shall be for use as authorized by the Commissioner. These plates shall be issued under the following conditions:

1. For each permanent promotional license plate issued or renewed, the Commissioner shall charge an annual fee of $100. Issuance of license plates pursuant to this subdivision shall be subject to the insurance requirement contained in §46.2-1547. The Commissioner shall limit the validity of any license plate issued under this subdivision to no more than thirty consecutive days. Upon written request from the dealership, the Commissioner may consider an extended use of a license plate issued under this subdivision. The Commissioner's authorization for use of any license plate issued under this subdivision shall be kept in the vehicle on which the license plate is displayed until expiration of the authorization. These license plates shall be included in the number of dealer's license plates authorized under §46.2-1546 and not in addition thereto.

2. The Commission shall limit the validity of each temporary promotional license plate to no more than fourteen consecutive days. For each request, the Commissioner shall charge a fee of twenty-five dollars for the first plate and two dollars for each additional plate. Issuance of license plates pursuant to this subdivision shall be subject to the insurance requirement contained in §46.2-1547. The Commissioner's authorization for use of any license plate issued under this subdivision shall be kept in the vehicle on which the license plate is displayed until expiration of the authorization. License plates issued under this subdivision shall not be included in the number of dealer's license plates authorized under §46.2-1546.

§46.2-1550. Use of dealer's license plates, generally.

A. Dealer's license plates may be used on vehicles in the inventory of licensed motor vehicle manufacturers, distributors, and dealers in the Commonwealth when operated on the highways of Virginia by dealers or dealer-operators, their spouses, or employees of manufacturers, distributors, and dealers as permitted in this article. Except as otherwise explicitly permitted in this article, it shall be unlawful for any dealer to cause or permit: (i) use of dealer's license plates on vehicles other than those held in inventory for sale or resale; (ii) dealer's license plates to be lent, leased, rented, or placed at the disposal of any persons other than those permitted by this article to use dealer's license plates; and (iii) use of dealer's license plates on any vehicle of a type for which their use is not authorized by this article. It shall be unlawful for any dealer to cause or permit dealer's license plates to be used on:

1. Motor vehicles such as tow trucks, wrecking cranes, or other service motor vehicles;

2. Vehicles used to deliver or transport (i) other vehicles; (ii) portions of vehicles; (iii) vehicle components, parts, or accessories; or (iv) fuel;

3. Courtesy vehicles; or

4. Vehicles used in conjunction with any other business.

B. A dealer may permit his license plates to be used in the operation of a motor vehicle:

1. By any person whom the dealer reasonably believes to be a bona fide prospective purchaser who is either accompanied by a licensed salesperson or has the written permission of the dealer;

2. When the plates are being used by a customer on a vehicle owned by the dealer in whose repair shop the customer's vehicle is being repaired; or

3. By a person authorized by the dealer on a vehicle that is being driven to or from (i) a point of sale, (ii) an auction, (iii) a repair facility for the purpose of mechanical repairs, painting, or installation of parts or accessories, or (iv) a dealer exchange.

The dealer shall issue to the prospective purchaser, customer whose vehicle is being repaired, or other person authorized under subdivision 3 of this subsection, a certificate on forms provided by the Department, a copy of which shall be retained by the dealer and open at all times to the inspection of the Commissioner or any of the officers or agents of the Department. The certificate shall be in the immediate possession of the person operating or authorized to operate the vehicle. The certificate shall entitle a person to operate with dealer's license plates under (i) subdivision 1 or 2 of this subsection for a specific period of no more than five days or (ii) subdivision 3 of this subsection for no more than twenty-four hours. No more than two certificates may be issued by a dealer to the same person under subdivision 1 or 2 of this subsection for successive periods.
(Chgd. by L.1995 chs. 767, 816; L.1998 ch. 827, eff. 7/1/98.)

§46.2-1550.1. Use of dealer's license plates and temporary transport plates on certain vehicles.

Notwithstanding the provisions of §46.2-1550, dealer's license plates or dealer's temporary transport plates may be used on vehicles being transported (i) from a motor vehicle auction or other point of purchase or sale, (ii) between properties owned or controlled by the same dealership, or (iii) for repairs, painting, or installation of parts or accessories. This section shall also apply to return trips by such vehicles.

§46.2-1550.2. Issuance and use of temporary transport plates, generally.

The Department, subject to the limitations and conditions set forth in this section and the insurance requirements contained in §46.2-1547, may provide for the issuance of temporary transport plates designed by the Department to any dealer licensed under this chapter who applies for at least ten plates and who encloses with his application a fee of one dollar for each plate. The application shall be made on a form prescribed and furnished by the Department. Temporary transport plates may be used for those purposes outlined in §46.2-1550.1. Every dealer who has applied for temporary transport plates shall maintain a permanent record of (i) all temporary transport plates delivered to him, (ii) all temporary transport plates issued by him, and (iii) any other information pertaining to the receipt or the issuance of temporary transport plates which may be required by the Department.

Every dealer who issues temporary transport plates shall insert clearly and indelibly on the face of the temporary transport plates the name of the issuing dealer, the date of issuance and expiration, and the make and identification number of the vehicle for which issued.

The dealer shall issue to the operator of the specified vehicle a certificate on forms provided by the Department, a copy which shall be retained by the dealer and open at all times to the inspection of the Commissioner or any of the officers or agents of the Department. The certificate shall be in the immediate possession of the person operating or authorized to operate the vehicle. The certificate shall entitle the person to operate with the dealer's temporary transport plate for a period of no more than five days. Temporary transport plates may also be used by the dealer to demonstrate types of vehicles taken in trade but for which he has not been issued dealer's license plates.

§46.2-1551. Use of dealer's license plates or temporary transport plates on certain vehicles traveling from one establishment to another for purpose of having special equipment installed.

Notwithstanding the provisions of §46.2-1550, dealer's license plates or temporary transport plates may be used on tractor trucks or trucks for the purpose of delivering these vehicles to another establishment for the purpose of having a fifth wheel, body, or any special permanently mounted equipment installed on the vehicles, and for the purpose of returning the vehicle to the dealer whose plates are attached to the tractor truck or truck, whether or not the title to the vehicle has been retained by the dealer, and no other license, permit, warrant, exemption card, or classification plate from any other agency of the Commonwealth shall be required under these circumstances. No other statute or regulation in conflict with the provisions of this section shall be applicable to the extent of the conflict. This section shall also apply to trips into the Commonwealth by a vehicle owned and operated outside the Commonwealth to an establishment within the Commonwealth and to the return trip of that vehicle from the Commonwealth to another state, provided the operator of the vehicle carries on his person when so operating a bill of sale for the fifth wheel, body, or special equipment.

(Chgd. by L.1995 chs. 767, 816, eff. 7/1/95.)

§46.2-1552. Use of dealer's license plates on newly purchased vehicles.

Notwithstanding the provisions of §46.2-1550, any dealer who sells and delivers to a purchaser a motor vehicle at a time when the main offices of the Department, its branch offices, or offices of its local agents, are not open for business and the purchaser is therefore unable to register the vehicle, may permit the purchaser to use, for a period not exceeding five days, on the newly purchased vehicle, license plates which have been issued to the dealer, provided that, at the time of the purchase, the dealer executes in duplicate, on forms provided by the Commissioner, a certificate bearing the date of issuance, the name and address of the purchaser, the identification number of the vehicle, the registration number to be used temporarily on the vehicle, the name of the state in which the vehicle is to be registered, and whatever other information may be required by the Commissioner. The original of the certificate and a bona fide bill of sale shall be delivered to the purchaser and shall be in the possession of the purchaser at all times when operating the vehicle under dealer plates. One copy of the certificate shall be retained by the dealer, filed by him, and shall be subject to inspection at any time by the Department's agents. If the vehicle is to be titled and registered in the Commonwealth, application for title and registration shall be made by the purchaser on the first business day following issuance of the certificate and a copy of the certificate shall accompany the applications.

License plates temporarily used by the purchaser shall be returned to the dealer by the purchaser not later than five days after the issuance of the certificate.

§46.2-1552.1. Use of dealer's license plates or temporary transport plates for demonstrating trucks or tractor trucks.

Notwithstanding any other provision of this chapter, dealer's license plates issued under §46.2-1548 and temporary transport plates issued under §46.2-1550.2 may be used on trucks or tractor trucks in the inventory of licensed motor vehicle dealers for the purpose of demonstrating trucks or tractor trucks in the inventory of a licensed dealer by a bona fide prospective purchaser. Any such demonstration vehicle may be loaded in a manner consistent with the prospective purchaser's usual commercial activities. Such use of dealer's license plates on demonstration trucks or tractor trucks in a prospective purchaser's commercial activities shall be for not more than three days or 750 miles, whichever comes first, and shall not thereafter be used on the same truck or tractor truck by the same prospective purchaser for a period of sixty days. The dealer shall issue to the prospective purchaser, or to his authorized agent, a certificate on forms provided by the Department, a copy of which shall be retained by the dealer and open at all times to the inspection of the Commissioner or any of the officers or agents of the Department. The certificate shall be in the immediate possession of the person operating or authorized to operate the truck or tractor truck. The certificate shall entitle the person to operate with the dealer's license plate or temporary transport plate for a specific period of no more than three days. This certificate shall be in lieu of any other registration, permit, and motor fuel road tax identification otherwise required by law.

(Chgd. by L.1997 ch. 283, eff. 7/1/97.)

§46.2-1553. Operation without license plate prohibited.

No manufacturer or distributor of or dealer in motor vehicles shall cause or permit any motor vehicle owned by him to be operated or moved on a public highway without there being displayed on the motor vehicle a license plate or plates issued to him, either under §46.2-711 or under §46.2-1548, except as otherwise authorized in §§46.2-733, 46.2-1554 and 46.2-1555.

(Chgd. by L.1995 chs. 767, 816, eff. 7/1/95.)

§46.2-1554. Movement by manufacturer to place of shipment or delivery.

Any manufacturer of motor vehicles may operate or move or cause to be moved or operated on the highways for a distance of no more than twenty-five miles motor vehicles from the factory where manufactured or assembled to a railway depot, vessel, or place of shipment or delivery, without registering them and without license plates attached thereto, under a written permit first obtained from the local law-enforcement authorities having jurisdiction over the highways and on displaying in plain sight on each motor vehicle a placard bearing the name and address of the manufacturer authorizing or directing the movement.

(Chgd. by L.1995 chs. 767, 816, eff. 7/1/95.)

§46.2-1555. Movement by dealers to salesrooms.

Any dealer in motor vehicles may operate or move, or cause to be operated or moved, any motor vehicle on the highways for a distance of no more than twenty-five miles from a vessel, railway depot, warehouse, or any place of shipment or from a factory where manufactured or assembled to a salesroom, warehouse, or place of shipment or transshipment without registering them and without license plates attached thereto, under a written permit first obtained from the local law-enforcement authorities having jurisdiction over the highways and on displaying in plain sight on each motor vehicle a placard bearing the name and address of the dealer authorizing or directing the movement.

(Chgd. by L.1995 chs. 767, 816, eff. 7/1/95.)

§46.2-1556. Operation under foreign dealer's license.

It shall be unlawful, except as provided for by reciprocal agreement, for any person to operate a motor vehicle or for the owner thereof to permit a motor vehicle to be operated in the Commonwealth on a foreign dealer's license, unless the operation of the motor vehicle on the license is specifically authorized by the Commissioner.

(Chgd. by L.1995 chs. 767, 816, eff. 7/1/95.)

§46.2-1557. Use of certain foreign-registered motor vehicles in driver education programs.

Dealer's license plates may be displayed on motor vehicles used by Virginia school systems in connection with driver education programs approved by the State Board of Education. In the event of such use of a motor vehicle or vehicles by a school system, any dealer, his employees and agents furnishing the motor vehicle or vehicles shall be immune from liability in any suit, claim, action, or cause of action, including but not limited to, actions or claims for injury to persons or property arising out of such use. Nothing in this section shall authorize the sale of any motor vehicle or vehicles so used in such driver education program as a demonstrator vehicle.

Notwithstanding the provisions of §§46.2-1500 and 46.2-1556, school divisions either (i) bordering on Kentucky, Maryland, North Carolina, Tennessee, or West Virginia, or (ii) located in Accomack or Northampton County may use motor vehicles bearing foreign motor vehicle dealer's license plates in connection with their driver education programs.

§46.2-1557.1. Removal of plates by Department of Motor Vehicles investigators; cancellation; reissuance.

If any Department of Motor Vehicles investigator finds that a vehicle bearing license plates or temporary transport plates issued under this article is being operated in a manner inconsistent with (i) the requirements of this article or (ii) the Commissioner's authorization provided for in this article, the Department of Motor Vehicles investigator may remove the license plate for cancellation. Once a license plate has been cancelled, the dealership may reapply for the license plate. Reissuance of the license plate shall be subject to the approval of the Commissioner and the payment of the fee prescribed for issuance of license plates under this article.

§46.2-1557.2. Penalties for violations of article; service of summons.

Notwithstanding §46.2-1507, any person violating any of the provisions of this article shall be guilty of a Class 3 misdemeanor. Any summons issued for any violation of any provision of this article relating to use or misuse of dealer's license plates shall be served upon the dealership to whom the plates were issued or to the person expressly permitting the unlawful use, or upon the operator of the motor vehicle if the plates are used contrary to the use authorized by the certificate issued pursuant to §45.2-1550.

ARTICLE 6
ISSUANCE OF TEMPORARY LICENSE PLATES BY DEALERS

§46.2-1558. Issuance of temporary license plates to dealers and vehicle owners.

The Department may, subject to the limitations and conditions set forth in this article, deliver temporary license plates designed by the Department to any dealer licensed under this chapter who applies for at least ten sets of plates and who encloses with his application a fee of two dollars for each set applied for. The application shall be made on a form prescribed and furnished by the Department. Dealers, subject to the limitations and conditions set forth in this article, may issue temporary license plates to owners of vehicles. The owners shall comply with the provisions of this article and §§46.2-705, 46.2-706 and 46.2-707. Dealers issuing temporary license plates may do so free of charge, but if they charge a fee for issuing temporary plates, the fee shall be no more than the fee charged the dealer by the Department under this section.

Display of a temporary license plate or plates on a motor vehicle, trailer, or semitrailer shall subject the vehicle to the requirements of §§46.2-1038 and 46.2-1056.

§46.2-1559. Records to be kept by dealers; inspection.

Every dealer who has applied for temporary license plates shall maintain a permanent record of (i) all temporary license plates delivered to him, (ii) all temporary license plates issued by him, and (iii) any other information pertaining to the receipt or the issuance of temporary license plates which may be required by the Department. Each record shall be kept for at least one year from the date of entry. Every dealer shall allow full access to these records during regular business hours to authorized representatives of the Department and to law-enforcement officers.

§46.2-1560. Application for temporary license plate.

No dealer shall issue a temporary license plate except on written application by the person entitled to receive the license plate, which application shall be forwarded by the dealer to the Department as provided in §46.2-1542.

§46.2-1561. To whom temporary plates shall not be issued; dealer to forward application for current titling and registration; misstatements and false information.

No dealer shall issue, assign, transfer, or deliver temporary license plates to other than the bona fide purchaser or owner of a vehicle, whether or not the vehicle is to be registered in Virginia. If the vehicle is to be registered in Virginia, the dealer shall submit to the Department a written application for the current titling and registration of the purchased vehicle, accompanied by the prescribed fees. Any dealer who issues temporary license plates to a purchaser who fails or declines to request that his application be forwarded promptly to the Department forthwith shall notify the Department of the issuance in the manner provided in this article. No dealer shall issue temporary license plates to any person who possesses current license plates for a vehicle that has been sold or exchanged, nor shall any dealer lend temporary license plates to any person for use on any vehicle. If the dealer does not have in his possession the certificate of title or certificate of origin he shall issue temporary license plates even though the purchaser has current license plates to be transferred. The dealer shall present the title or certificate of origin to the customer within thirty days of purchase and after this transaction is completed the customer shall transfer his current license plates to the vehicle. If the title or certificate of origin cannot be produced for a vehicle within thirty days, a second set of temporary license plates may be issued provided that a temporary certificate of ownership is issued as provided in §46.2-1542. It shall be unlawful for any person to issue any temporary license plates containing any misstatement of fact, or for any person issuing or using temporary license plates knowingly to insert any false information on their face.

§46.2-1562. Dealer to insert his name, date of issuance and expiration, make and identification number of vehicle.

Every dealer who issues temporary license plates shall insert clearly and indelibly on the face of each temporary license plate the name of the issuing dealer, the date of issuance and expiration, and the make and identification number of the vehicle for which issued.

§46.2-1563. Suspension of right of dealer to issue.

The Commissioner, on determining that the provisions of this chapter or the directions of the Department are not being complied with by any dealer, may suspend, after a hearing, the right of a dealer to issue temporary license plates.

§46.2-1564. Plates to be destroyed on expiration.

Every person to whom temporary license plates have been issued shall destroy them on the thirtieth day after issue or immediately on receipt of the permanent license plates from the Department, whichever occurs first.

§46.2-1565. When plates to expire; refunds or credit.

Temporary license plates shall expire on the receipt of the permanent license plates from the Department, or on the rescission of a contract to purchase a motor vehicle, or on the expiration of thirty days from the date of issuance, whichever occurs first. No refund or credit of fees paid by dealers to the Department for temporary license plates shall be allowed, except that when the Department discontinues the right of a dealer to issue temporary license plates, the dealer, on returning temporary license plates to the Department, may receive a refund or a credit for them.

§46.2-1565.1. Penalties.

Any person violating any of the provisions of this article shall be guilty of a Class 3 misdemeanor. Any summons issued for any violation of any provision of this article relating to use or misuse of temporary license plates shall be served upon the dealership to whom the plates were issued or to the person expressly permitting the unlawful use, or upon the operator of the motor vehicle if the plates are used contrary to the use authorized pursuant to §46.2-1561.
(Added by L.1995 chs. 767, 816, eff. 7/1/95.)

ARTICLE 7
FRANCHISES

Section

§46.2-1566. Filing of franchises.

A. It shall be the responsibility of each motor vehicle manufacturer, factory branch, distributor, distributor branch, or subsidiary thereof to file with the Commissioner by certified mail a true copy of each new, amended, modified, or different form or addendum offered to more than one dealer which affects the rights, responsibilities, or obligations of the parties of a franchise or sales, service, or sales and service agreement to be offered to a motor vehicle dealer or prospective motor vehicle dealer in the Commonwealth no later than sixty days prior to the date the franchise or sales agreement is offered. In no event shall a new, amended, modified, or different form of franchise or sales, service, or sales and service agreement be offered a motor vehicle dealer in the Commonwealth until the form has been determined by the Commissioner as not containing terms inconsistent with the provisions of this chapter. At the time a filing is made with the Commissioner pursuant to this section, the manufacturer, factory branch, distributor, distributor branch, or subsidiary shall also give written notice together with a copy of the papers so filed to the affected dealer or dealers.

B. The Department shall inform the manufacturer, factory branch, distributor, distributor branch, or subsidiary and the dealer or dealers or other parties named in the agreement of a preliminary recommendation as to the consistency of the agreement with the provisions of this chapter. If any of the parties involved have comments on the preliminary recommendation, they must be submitted to the Commissioner within thirty days of receiving the preliminary recommendation. The Commissioner shall render his decision within fifteen days of receiving comments from the parties involved. If the Commissioner does not receive comments

within the thirty-day time period, he shall make the final determination as to the consistency of the agreement with the provisions of this chapter.
(Chgd. by L.1995 chs. 767, 816, eff. 7/1/95.)

§46.2-1567. Exemption of franchises from Retail Franchising Act.

Franchises subject to the provisions of this chapter shall not be subject to any requirement contained in Chapter 8 (§13.1-557 et seq.) of Title 13.1.

§46.2-1568. Coercion of retail dealer by manufacturer or distributor with respect to retail installment sales contracts prohibited; penalty.

A. It shall be unlawful for any manufacturer or distributor, or any officer, agent, or representative of either, to coerce or attempt to coerce any retail motor vehicle dealer or prospective retail motor vehicle dealer in the Commonwealth to sell, assign, or transfer any retail installment sales contract obtained by the dealer in connection with the sale by him in the Commonwealth of motor vehicles manufactured or sold by the manufacturer or distributor, to a specified finance company or class of finance companies or to any other specified persons by any of the following:

1. By any statement, suggestion, promise, or threat that the manufacturer or distributor will in any manner benefit or injure the dealer, whether the statement, suggestion, threat, or promise is express or implied or made directly or indirectly.

2. By any act that will benefit or injure the dealer.

3. By any contract, or any express or implied offer of contract, made directly or indirectly to the dealer, for handling the motor vehicle on the condition that the dealer sell, assign, or transfer his retail installment sales contract on the vehicle, in the Commonwealth, to a specified finance company or class of finance companies or to any other specified person.

4. By any express or implied statement or representation made directly or indirectly that the dealer is under any obligation whatsoever to sell, assign, or transfer any of his retail sales contracts in the Commonwealth on motor vehicles manufactured or sold by the manufacturer or distributor to a finance company, or class of finance companies, or other specified person, because of any relationship or affiliation between the manufacturer or distributor and the finance company or companies or the specified person or persons.

B. Any such statements, threats, promises, acts, contracts, or offers of contracts, when their effect may be to lessen or eliminate competition or tend to create a monopoly, are declared unfair trade practices and unfair methods of competition and are prohibited.

C. Any person found guilty of violating any of the provisions of this section shall be guilty of a Class 1 misdemeanor.
(Chgd. by L.1995 chs. 767, 816, eff. 7/1/95.)

§46.2-1569. Other coercion of dealers; transfer, grant, succession to and cancellation of dealer franchises; delivery of vehicles, parts, and accessories.

Notwithstanding the terms of any franchise agreement, it shall be unlawful for any manufacturer, factory branch, distributor, or distributor branch, or any field representative, officer, agent, or their representatives:

1. To coerce or attempt to coerce any dealer to accept delivery of any motor vehicle or vehicles, parts or accessories therefor, or any other commodities, which have not been ordered by the dealer.

2. To coerce or attempt to coerce any dealer to enter into an agreement with the manufacturer, factory branch, distributor, or distributor branch, or representative thereof, or do any other act unfair to the dealer, by threatening to cancel any franchise existing between the manufacturer, factory branch, distributor, distributor branch, or representative thereof and the dealer.

2a. To coerce or attempt to coerce any dealer to join, contribute to, or affiliate with any advertising association.

3. To prevent or refuse to approve the sale or transfer of the ownership of a dealership by the sale of the business, stock transfer, or otherwise, or the transfer, sale, or assignment of a dealer franchise, or a change in the executive management or principal operator of the dealership, unless the franchisor provides written notice to the dealer of its objection and the reasons therefor at least thirty days prior to the proposed effective date of the transfer, sale, assignment, or change. No such objection shall be effective to prevent the sale, transfer, assignment, or change if the Commissioner has determined, if requested in writing by the dealer within thirty days after receipt of an objection to the proposed sale, transfer, or change, and after a hearing on the matter, that the failure to permit or honor the sale, transfer, assignment, or change is unreasonable under the circumstances. No franchise may be sold, assigned, or transferred unless (i) the franchisor has been given at least ninety days' prior written notice by the dealer as to the identity, financial ability, and qualifications of the proposed transferee, and (ii) the sale or transfer of the franchise and business will not involve, without the franchisor's consent, a relocation of the business.

4. To grant an additional franchise for a particular line-make of motor vehicle in a relevant market area in which a dealer or dealers in that line-make are already located unless the franchisor has first advised in writing all other dealers in the line-make in the relevant market area. No such additional franchise may be established at the proposed site unless the Commissioner has determined, if requested by a dealer of the same line-make in the relevant market area within thirty days after receipt of the franchisor's notice of intention to establish the additional franchise, and after a hearing on the matter, that there is reasonable evidence that after the grant of the new franchise, the market will support all of the dealers in that line-make in the relevant market area. Establishing a franchised dealer in a relevant market area to replace a franchised dealer that has not been in operation for more than two years shall constitute the establishment of a new franchise subject to the terms of this subdivision. The two-year period for replacing a franchised dealer shall begin on the day the franchise was terminated, or, if a termination hearing was held, on the day the franchisor was legally permitted finally to terminate the franchise. This subdivision shall not apply to (i) the relocation of an existing dealer within that dealer's relevant market area if the relocation site is to be more than ten miles distant from any other dealer for the same line-make; (ii) the relocation of an existing dealer within that dealer's relevant market area if the relocation site is to be more distant than the existing site from all other dealers of the same line-make in that relevant market area; or (iii) the relocation of an existing new motor vehicle dealer within two miles of the existing site of the relocating dealer.

5. Except as otherwise provided in this subdivision and notwithstanding the terms of any franchise, to terminate, cancel, or refuse to renew the franchise of any dealer without good cause and unless (i) the dealer and the Commissioner have received written notice of the franchisor's intentions at least sixty days prior to the effective date of such termination, cancellation, or the expiration date of the franchise, setting forth the specific grounds for the action, and (ii) the Commissioner has determined, if requested in writing by the dealer within the sixty-day period and, after a hearing on the matter, that there is good cause for the termination, cancellation, or nonrenewal of the franchise. In any case where a petition is made to the Commissioner for a determination as

to good cause for the termination, cancellation, or nonrenewal of a franchise, the franchise in question shall continue in effect pending the Commissioner's decision or, if that decision is appealed to the circuit court, pending the decision of the circuit court. In any case in which a franchisor neither advises a dealer that it does not intend to renew a franchise nor takes any action to renew a franchise beyond its expiration date, the franchise in question shall continue in effect on the terms last agreed to by the parties. Notwithstanding the other provisions of this subdivision notice of termination, cancellation, or nonrenewal may be provided to a dealer by a franchisor not less than fifteen days prior to the effective date of such termination, cancellation, or nonrenewal when the grounds for such action are any of the following:

a. Insolvency of the franchised motor vehicle dealer or filing of any petition by or against the franchised motor vehicle dealer, under any bankruptcy or receivership law, leading to liquidation or which is intended to lead to liquidation of the franchisee's business.

b. Failure of the franchised motor vehicle dealer to conduct its customary sales and service operations during its posted business hours for seven consecutive business days, except where the failure results from acts of God or circumstances beyond the direct control of the franchised motor vehicle dealer.

c. Revocation of any license which the franchised motor vehicle dealer is required to have to operate a dealership.

d. Conviction of the dealer or any principal of the dealer of a felony.

The change or discontinuance of a marketing or distribution system of a particular line-make product by a manufacturer or distributor, while the name identification of the product is continued in substantial form by the same or different manufacturer or distributor, may be considered to be a franchise termination, cancellation, or nonrenewal. The provisions of this paragraph shall apply to changes and discontinuances made after January 1, 1989, but they shall not be considered by any court in any case in which such a change or discontinuance occurring prior to that date has been challenged as constituting a termination, cancellation or nonrenewal.

5a. To fail to provide continued parts and service support to a dealer which holds a franchise in a discontinued line-make for at least five years from the date of such discontinuance. This requirement shall not apply to a line-make which was discontinued prior to January 1, 1989.

6. To fail to allow a dealer the right at any time to designate a member of his family as a successor to the dealership in the event of the death or incapacity of the dealer. It shall be unlawful to prevent or refuse to honor the succession to a dealership by a member of the family of a deceased or incapacitated dealer if the franchisor has not provided to the member of the family previously designated by the dealer as his successor written notice of its objections to the succession and of such person's right to seek a hearing on the matter before the Commissioner pursuant to this article, and the Commissioner determines, if requested in writing by such member of the family within thirty days of receipt of such notice from the franchisor, and after a hearing on the matter before the Commissioner pursuant to this article, that the failure to permit or honor the succession is unreasonable under the circumstances. No member of the family may succeed to a franchise unless (i) the franchisor has been given written notice as to the identity, financial ability, and qualifications of the member of the family in question, and (ii) the succession to the franchise will not involve, without the franchisor's consent, a relocation of the business.

7. To fail to ship monthly to any dealer, if ordered by the dealer, the number of new vehicles of each make, series, and model needed by the dealer to receive a percentage of total new vehicle sales of each make, series, and model equitably related to the total new vehicle production or importation currently being achieved nationally by each make, series, and model covered under the franchise. Upon the written request of any dealer holding its sales or sales and service franchise, the manufacturer or distributor shall disclose to the dealer in writing the basis upon which new motor vehicles are allocated, scheduled, and delivered to the dealers of the same line-make. In the event that allocation is at issue in a request for a hearing, the dealer may demand the Commissioner to direct that the manufacturer or distributor provide to the dealer, within thirty days of such demand, all records of sales and all records of distribution of all motor vehicles to the same line-make dealers who compete with the dealer requesting the hearing.

7a. To fail or refuse to offer to its same line-make franchised dealers all models manufactured for the line-make, or require a dealer to pay an extra fee, or remodel, renovate, or recondition the dealer's existing facilities, or purchase unreasonable advertising displays or other materials as a prerequisite to receiving a model or a series of vehicles.

7b. To require or otherwise coerce a dealer to underutilize the dealer's facilities.

8. To include in any franchise with a motor vehicle dealer terms that are contrary to, prohibited by, or otherwise inconsistent with the requirements of this chapter.

8a. For any franchise agreement to require a motor vehicle dealer to pay the attorney's fees of the manufacturer or distributor related to hearings and appeals brought under this article.

9. To fail to include in any franchise with a motor vehicle dealer the following language: "If any provision herein contravenes the laws or regulations of any state or other jurisdiction wherein this agreement is to be performed, or denies access to the procedures, forums, or remedies provided for by such laws or regulations, such provision shall be deemed to be modified to conform to such laws or regulations, and all other terms and provisions shall remain in full force," or words to that effect.

(Chgd. by L.1995 chs. 767, 816; L.1998 ch. 682, eff. 7/1/98.)

§46.2-1569.1. Manufacturer or distributor right of first refusal.

Notwithstanding the terms of any franchise agreement, in the event of a proposed sale or transfer of dealership, the manufacturer or distributor shall be permitted to exercise a right of first refusal to acquire the new vehicle dealer's assets or ownership, if such sale or transfer is conditioned upon the manufacturer's or dealer's* entering into a dealer agreement with the proposed new owner or transferee, only if all the following requirements are met:

**Probably should be "manufacturer or dealer".*

1. To exercise its right of first refusal, the manufacturer or distributor must notify the dealer in writing within forty-five days of its receipt of the completed proposal for the proposed sale transfer;

2. The exercise of the right of first refusal will result in the dealer's and dealer's owner's* receiving the same or greater consideration as they have contracted to receive in connection with the proposed change of ownership or transfer;

**Probably should be "dealer and dealer owner".*

3. The proposed sale or transfer of the dealership's assets does not involve the transfer or sale to a member or members of the family of one or more dealer owners, or to a qualified manager or a partnership or corporation controlled by such persons; and

4. The manufacturer or distributor agrees to pay the reasonable expenses, including attorney's fees which do not exceed the usual, customary, and reasonable fees charged for similar work done for other clients, incurred by the proposed new owner and transferee prior to the manufacturer's or distributor's exercise of its right of first refusal in negotiating and implementing the contract for the proposed sale or transfer of the dealership or dealership assets. Notwithstanding the foregoing, no payment of such expenses and attorney's fees shall be required if the dealer has not submitted or caused to be submitted an accounting of those expenses within thirty days of the dealer's receipt of the manufacturer's or distributor's written request for such an accounting. Such accounting may be requested by a manufacturer or distributor before exercising its right of first refusal.

§46.2-1570. Discontinuation of distributors.

If the contract between a distributor and a manufacturer or importer is terminated or otherwise discontinued, all franchises granted to motor vehicle dealers in Virginia by that distributor shall continue in full force and shall not be affected by the discontinuance, except that the manufacturer, factory branch, distributor, representative, or other person who undertakes to distribute motor vehicles of the same line-make or the same motor vehicles of a re-named line-make shall be substituted for the discontinued distributor under the existing motor vehicle dealer franchises and those franchises shall be modified accordingly.

§46.2-1571. Warranty obligations.

A. Each motor vehicle manufacturer, factory branch, distributor, or distributor branch shall (i) specify in writing to each of its motor vehicle dealers licensed in the Commonwealth the dealer's obligations for preparation, delivery, and warranty service on its products and (ii) compensate the dealer for warranty parts, service and diagnostic work required of the dealer by the manufacturer or distributor as follows:

1. Compensation of a dealer for warranty parts, service and diagnostic work shall not be less than the amounts charged by the dealer for the manufacturer's or distributor's original parts, service and diagnostic work to retail customers for nonwarranty service, parts and diagnostic work installed or performed in the dealer's service department unless the amounts are not reasonable. Warranty parts compensation shall be stated as a percentage of markup, which shall be an agreed reasonable approximation of retail markup and which shall be uniformly applied to all of the manufacturer's or distributor's parts unless otherwise provided for in this section. If the dealer and manufacturer or distributor cannot agree on the warranty parts compensation markup to be paid to the dealer, the markup shall be determined by an average of the dealer's retail markup on all of the manufacturer's or distributor's parts as described in subdivisions 2 and 3 of this subsection.

2. For purposes of determining warranty parts and service compensation paid to a dealer by the manufacturer or distributor, menu-priced parts or services, group discounts, special event discounts, and special event promotions shall not be considered in determining amounts charged by the dealer to retail customers. For purposes of determining labor compensation for warranty body shop repairs paid to a dealer by the manufacturer or distributor, internal and insurance-paid repairs shall not be considered in determining amounts charged by the dealer to retail customers.

3. Increases in dealer warranty parts and service compensation and diagnostic work compensation, pursuant to this section, shall be requested by the dealer in writing, shall be based on 100 consecutive repair orders or all repair orders over a ninety-day period, whichever occurs first and, in the case of parts, shall be stated as a percentage of markup which shall be uniformly applied to all the manufacturer's or distributor's parts.

4. In the case of warranty parts compensation, the provisions of this subsection shall be effective only for model year 1992 and succeeding model years.

5. If a manufacturer or distributor furnishes a part to a dealer at no cost for use by the dealer in performing work for which the manufacturer or distributor is required to compensate the dealer under this section, the manufacturer or distributor shall compensate the dealer for the part in the same manner as warranty parts compensation, less the wholesale costs, for such part as listed in the manufacturer's current price schedules. A manufacturer or distributor may pay the dealer a reasonable handling fee instead of the compensation otherwise required by this subsection for special high-performance complete engine assemblies in limited production motor vehicles which constitute less than five percent of model production furnished to the dealer at no cost, if the manufacturer or distributor excludes such special high-performance complete engine assemblies in determining whether the amounts requested by the dealer for warranty compensation are consistent with the amounts that the dealer charges its other retail service customers for parts used by the dealer to perform similar work.

6. In the case of service work, manufacturer original parts or parts otherwise specified by the manufacturer or distributor, and parts provided by a dealer either pursuant to an adjustment program as defined in §59.1-207.34 or as otherwise requested by the manufacturer or distributor, the dealer shall be compensated in the same manner as for warranty service or parts.

This section does not apply to compensation for parts such as components, systems, fixtures, appliances, furnishings, accessories, and features that are designed, used, and maintained primarily for nonvehicular, residential purposes. Warranty and sales incentive audits of dealer records may be conducted by the manufacturer, factory branch, distributor, or distributor branch on a reasonable basis, and dealer claims for warranty or sales incentive compensation shall not be denied except for good cause, such as performance of nonwarranty repairs, lack of material documentation, fraud, or misrepresentation. A dealer's failure to comply with the specific requirements of the manufacturer or distributor for processing the claim shall not constitute grounds for the denial of the claim or reduction of the amount of compensation to the dealer as long as reasonable documentation or other evidence has been presented to substantiate the claim. Claims for dealer compensation shall be paid within thirty days of dealer submission or within thirty days of the end of an incentive program or rejected in writing for stated reasons. The manufacturer, factory branch, distributor, or distributor branch shall reserve the right to reasonable periodic audits to determine the validity of all such paid claims for dealer compensation. Any chargebacks for warranty parts or service compensation and service incentives shall only be for the twelve-month period immediately following the date of the claim and, in the case of chargebacks for sales compensation only, for the eighteen-month period immediately following the date of claim. However, such limitations shall not be effective in the case of intentionally false or fraudulent claims. A dealer shall not be charged back or otherwise liable for sales incentives or charges related to a motor vehicle sold by the dealer and subsequently exported, provided the dealer can demonstrate that he exercised due diligence and that the sale was made in good faith and without knowledge of the purchaser's intention to export the motor vehicle.

B. It shall be unlawful for any motor vehicle manufacturer, factory branch, distributor, or distributor branch to:

1. Fail to perform any of its warranty obligations, including tires, with respect to a motor vehicle;

2. Fail to assume all responsibility for any liability resulting from structural or production defects;

3. Fail to include in written notices of factory recalls to vehicle owners and dealers the expected date by which necessary parts and equipment will be available to dealers for the correction of defects;

4. Fail to compensate any of the motor vehicle dealers licensed in the Commonwealth for repairs effected by the dealer of merchandise damaged in manufacture or transit to the dealer where the carrier is designated by the manufacturer, factory branch, distributor, or distributor branch;

5. Fail to compensate its motor vehicle dealers licensed in the Commonwealth for warranty parts, work, and service pursuant to subsection A of this section, or for legal costs and expenses incurred by such dealers in connection with warranty obligations for which the manufacturer, factory branch, distributor, or distributor branch is legally responsible or which the manufacturer, factory branch, distributor, or distributor branch imposes upon the dealer;

6. Misrepresent in any way to purchasers of motor vehicles that warranties with respect to the manufacture, performance, or design of the vehicle are made by the dealer, either as warrantor or co-warrantor;

7. Require the dealer to make warranties to customers in any manner related to the manufacture, performance, or design of the vehicle; or

8. Shift or attempt to shift to the motor vehicle dealer, directly or indirectly, any liabilities of the manufacturer, factory branch, distributor or distributor branch under the Virginia Motor Vehicle Warranty Enforcement Act (§59.1-207.9 et seq.), unless such liability results from the act or omission by the dealer.

C. Notwithstanding the terms of any franchise, it shall be unlawful for any motor vehicle manufacturer, factory branch, distributor, or distributor branch to fail to indemnify and hold harmless its motor vehicle dealers against any losses or damages arising out of complaints, claims, or suits relating to the manufacture, assembly, or design of motor vehicles, parts, or accessories, or other functions by the manufacturer, factory branch, distributor, or distributor branch beyond the control of the dealer, including, without limitation, the selection by the manufacturer, factory branch, distributor, or distributor branch of parts or components for the vehicle or any damages to merchandise occurring in transit to the dealer where the carrier is designated by the manufacturer, factory branch, distributor, or distributor branch. The dealer shall notify the manufacturer of pending suits in which allegations are made which come within this subsection whenever reasonably practicable to do so. Every motor vehicle dealer franchise issued to, amended, or renewed for motor vehicle dealers in Virginia shall be construed to incorporate provisions consistent with the requirements of this subsection.

D. On any new motor vehicle, any uncorrected damage or any corrected damage exceeding three percent of the manufacturer's or distributor's suggested retail price as defined in 15 U.S.C. §§1231–1233, as measured by retail repair costs, must be disclosed to the dealer in writing prior to delivery. Factory mechanical repair and damage to glass, tires, and bumpers are excluded from the three percent rule when properly replaced by identical manufacturer's or distributor's original equipment or parts. Whenever a new motor vehicle is damaged in transit, when the carrier or means of transportation is determined by the manufacturer or distributor, or whenever a motor vehicle is otherwise damaged prior to delivery to the new motor vehicle dealer, the new motor vehicle dealer shall:

1. Notify the manufacturer or distributor of the damage within three business days from the date of delivery of the new motor vehicle to the new motor vehicle dealership or within the additional time specified in the franchise; and

2. Request from the manufacturer or distributor authorization to replace the components, parts, and accessories damaged or otherwise correct the damage, unless the damage to the vehicle exceeds the three percent rule, in which case the dealer may reject the vehicle within three business days.

E. If the manufacturer or distributor refuses or fails to authorize correction of such damage within ten days after receipt of notification, or if the dealer rejects the vehicle because damage exceeds the three percent rule, ownership of the new motor vehicle shall revert to the manufacturer or distributor, and the new motor vehicle dealer shall have no obligation, financial or otherwise, with respect to such motor vehicle. Should either the manufacturer, distributor, or the dealer elect to correct the damage or any other damage exceeding the three percent rule, full disclosure shall be made by the dealer in writing to the buyer and an acknowledgment by the buyer is required. If there is less than three percent damage, no disclosure is required, provided the damage has been corrected. Predelivery mechanical work shall not require a disclosure. Failure to disclose any corrected damage within the knowledge of the selling dealer to a new motor vehicle in excess of the three percent rule shall constitute grounds for revocation of the buyer order, provided that, within thirty days of purchase, the motor vehicle is returned to the dealer with an accompanying written notice of the grounds for revocation. In case of revocation pursuant to this section, the dealer shall accept the vehicle and refund any payments made to the dealer in connection with the transaction, less a reasonable allowance for the consumer's use of the vehicle as defined in §59.1-207.11.

F. If there is a dispute between the manufacturer, factory branch, distributor, or distributor branch and the dealer with respect to any matter referred to in subsection A, B, or C of this section, either party may petition the Commissioner in writing, within thirty days after either party has given written notice of the dispute to the other, for a hearing. The decision of the Commissioner shall be binding on the parties, subject to rights of judicial review and appeal as provided in Chapter 1.1:1 (§9-6.14:1 et seq.) of Title 9. However, nothing contained in this section shall give the Commissioner any authority as to the content or interpretation of any manufacturer's or distributor's warranty.

(Chgd. by L.1995 chs. 421, 477; L.1997 ch. 484; L.1998 ch. 681, eff. 7/1/98.)

§46.2-1572. Operation of dealership by manufacturer.

It shall be unlawful for any motor vehicle manufacturer, factory branch, distributor, distributor branch, or subsidiary thereof, to own, operate, or control any motor vehicle dealership in the Commonwealth. However, this section shall not prohibit:

1. The operation by a manufacturer, factory branch, distributor, distributor branch, or subsidiary thereof, of a dealership for a temporary period, not to exceed one year, during the transition from one owner or operator to another;

2. The ownership or control of a dealership by a manufacturer, factory branch, distributor, distributor branch, or subsidiary thereof, while the dealership is being sold under a bona fide contract or purchase option to the operator of the dealership;

3. The ownership, operation, or control of a dealership by a manufacturer, factory branch, distributor, distributor branch, or subsidiary thereof, if the manufacturer, factory branch, distributor, distributor branch, or subsidiary has

 Zv

been engaged in the retail sale of motor vehicles through the dealership for a continuous period of three years prior to July 1, 1972, and if the Commissioner determines, after a hearing on the matter at the request of any party, that there is no dealer independent of the manufacturer or distributor, factory branch or distributor branch, or subsidiary thereof available in the community to own and operate the franchise in a manner consistent with the public interest;

4. The ownership, operation, or control of a dealership by a manufacturer, factory branch, distributor, distributor branch, or subsidiary thereof if the Commissioner determines, after a hearing at the request of any party, that there is no dealer independent of the manufacturer or distributor, factory branch or distributor branch, or subsidiary thereof available in the community or trade area to own and operate the franchise in a manner consistent with the public interest;

5. The ownership, operation, or control of a dealership dealing exclusively with school buses by a school bus manufacturer or school bus parts manufacturer or a person who assembles school buses; or

6. The ownership, operation, or control of a dealership dealing exclusively with refined fuels truck tanks by a manufacturer of refined fuels truck tanks or by a person who assembles refined fuels truck tanks.

§46.2-1572.1. Ownership of service facilities.

It shall be unlawful for any motor vehicle manufacturer, factory branch, distributor, distributor branch, or subsidiary thereof, to own, operate, or control, either directly or indirectly, any motor vehicle warranty or service facility located in the Commonwealth. Nothing in this section shall prohibit any motor vehicle manufacturer, factory branch, distributor, distributor branch, or subsidiary thereof, from owning, operating, or controlling any warranty or service facility for warranty or service of motor vehicles owned or operated by the manufacturer, factory branch, distributor, distributor branch, or subsidiary thereof. Nothing contained in this section shall prohibit a motor vehicle manufacturer, factory branch, distributor, or distributor branch from performing service for reasons of compliance with an order of a court of competent jurisdiction or of warranty under Chapter 17.3 (§59.1-207.9 et seq.) of Title 59.1.

The preceding provisions of this section shall not apply to manufacturers of refined fuels truck tanks or to persons who assemble refined fuels truck tanks or to persons who exclusively manufacture or assemble school buses or school bus parts.

§46.2-1572.2. Mediation of disputes.

At any time before a hearing under this article is commenced before the Commissioner, either party to a franchise agreement for the sale or service of passenger cars, pickup trucks or trucks may demand that a dispute be submitted to nonbinding mediation as a condition precedent to the right to a hearing before the Commissioner.

A demand for mediation may be served on the other party and shall be filed with the Commissioner at any time before a hearing is commenced by the Commissioner. The service of the demand for mediation shall, of itself, toll the time required to file requests for hearings and for the time for commencing and completing hearings under this article until mediation is concluded.

A demand for mediation shall be in writing and shall be served upon the other party by certified mail at an address designated in the franchise agreement or in the records of the Department. The demand for mediation shall contain a brief statement of the dispute and the relief sought by the party filing the demand.

Within ten days after the date on which the demand for mediation is served, the Commissioner shall select one mediator from his approved list of mediators or from the lists of hearing officers as set forth in §9-6.14:14.1. Within twenty-five days of the date of demand, the parties shall meet with the mediator for the purpose of attempting to resolve the dispute. The meeting place shall be within the Commonwealth at a location selected by the mediator. The mediator may extend the date of the meeting for good cause shown by either party or upon the stipulation of both parties.

§46.2-1573. Hearings and other remedies; civil penalties.

A. In every case of a hearing before the Commissioner authorized under this article, the Commissioner shall give reasonable notice of each hearing to all interested parties, and the Commissioner's decision shall be binding on the parties, subject to the rights of judicial review and appeal as provided in Chapter 1.1:1 (§9-6.14:1 et seq.) of Title 9.

B. Hearings before the Commissioner under this article shall commence within ninety days of the request for a hearing and the Commissioner's decision shall be rendered within sixty days from the receipt of the hearing officer's recommendation. Hearings authorized under this article shall be presided over by a hearing officer selected from a list prepared by the Executive Secretary of the Supreme Court of Virginia. On request of the Commissioner, the Executive Secretary will name a hearing officer from the list, selected on a rotation system administered by the Executive Secretary. The hearing officer shall provide recommendations to the Commissioner within ninety days of the conclusion of the hearing.

C. Notwithstanding any contrary provision of this article, the Commissioner shall initiate investigations, conduct hearings, and determine the rights of parties under this article whenever he is provided information by the Motor Vehicle Dealer Board or any other person indicating a possible violation of any provision of this article.

D. For purposes of any matter brought to the Commissioner under subdivisions 3, 4, 5, 6 and 7b of §46.2-1569 with respect to which the Commissioner is to determine whether there is good cause for a proposed action or whether it would be unreasonable under the circumstances, the Commissioner shall consider:

1. The volume of the affected dealer's business in the relevant market area;

2. The nature and extent of the dealer's investment in its business;

3. The adequacy of the dealer's service facilities, equipment, parts, supplies, and personnel;

4. The effect of the proposed action on the community;

5. The extent and quality of the dealer's service under motor vehicle warranties;

6. The dealer's performance under the terms of its franchise;

7. Other economic and geographical factors reasonably associated with the proposed action; and

8. The recommendations, if any, from a three-member panel composed of members of the Board who are franchised dealers not of the same line-make involved in the hearing and who are appointed to the panel by the Commissioner.

With respect to subdivision 6 of this subsection, any performance standard or program for measuring dealership performance that may have a material effect on a dealer, and the application of any such standard or program by a manufacturer or distributor, shall be fair, reasonable, and equitable and, if based upon a survey, shall be based upon a statistically valid sample. Upon the request of any dealer, a manufacturer or distributor shall disclose in writing to the dealer a description of how a performance standard or program is designed and all relevant information used in the application of the performance standard or program to that dealer.

E. An interested party in a hearing held pursuant to subsection A of this section shall comply with the effective date of compliance established by the Commissioner in his decision in such hearing, unless a stay or extension of such date is granted by the Commissioner or the Commissioner's decision is under judicial review and appeal as provided in subsection A of this section. If, after notice to such interested party and an opportunity to comment, the Commissioner finds an interested party has not complied with his decision by the designated date of compliance, unless a stay or extension of such date has been granted by the Commissioner or the Commissioner's decision is under judicial review and appeal, the Commissioner may assess such interested party a civil penalty not to exceed $1,000 per day of noncompliance. Civil penalties collected under this subsection shall be deposited into the Transportation Trust Fund.

(Chgd. by L.1995 chs. 767, 816; L.2000 ch. 106, eff. 7/1/2000.)

ARTICLE 7.1
LATE MODEL AND FACTORY REPURCHASE FRANCHISES

§46.2-1573.1. Late model and factory repurchase franchises.

Franchised late model or factory repurchase motor vehicle dealers shall have the same rights and obligations as provided for franchised new motor vehicle dealers in Article 7 (§46.2-1566 et seq.) of this chapter, mutatis mutandis.

ARTICLE 8
DENIAL, SUSPENSION, AND REVOCATION OF DEALER LICENSES

§46.2-1574. Acts of officers, directors, partners, and salespersons.

If a licensee or registrant is a partnership or corporation, it shall be sufficient cause for the denial, suspension, or revocation of a license or certificate of dealer registration that any officer, director, or trustee of the partnership or corporation, or any member in the case of a partnership or the dealer-operator, has committed any act or omitted any duty which would be cause for refusing, suspending, or revoking a license or certificate of dealer registration issued to him as an individual under this chapter. Each licensee or registrant shall be responsible for the acts of any of his salespersons while acting as his agent, if the licensee approved of those acts or had knowledge of those acts or other similar acts and after such knowledge retained the benefit, proceeds, profits, or advantages accruing from those acts or otherwise ratified those acts.

§46.2-1575. Grounds for denying, suspending, or revoking licenses or certificates of dealer registration or qualification.

A license or certificate of dealer registration or qualification issued under this subtitle may be denied, suspended, or revoked on any one or more of the following grounds:

1. Material misstatement or omission in application for license, dealer's license plates, certificate of dealer registration, certificate of qualification, or certificate of title;
2. Failure to comply subsequent to receipt of a written warning from the Department or the Board or any willful failure to comply with any provision of this chapter or any regulation promulgated by the Commissioner or the Board under this chapter;
3. Failure to have an established place of business as defined in §46.2-1510 or failure to have as the dealer-operator an individual who holds a valid certificate of qualification;
4. Defrauding any retail buyer, to the buyer's damage, or any other person in the conduct of the licensee's or registrant's business;
5. Employment of fraudulent devices, methods or practices in connection with compliance with the requirements under the statutes of the Commonwealth with respect to the retaking of vehicles under retail installment contracts and the redemption and resale of those vehicles;
6. Having used deceptive acts or practices;
7. Knowingly advertising by any means any assertion, representation, or statement of fact which is untrue, misleading, or deceptive in any particular relating to the conduct of the business licensed or registered or for which a license or registration is sought;
8. Having been convicted of any fraudulent act in connection with the business of selling vehicles or any consumer-related fraud;
9. Having been convicted of any criminal act involving the business of selling vehicles;
10. Willfully retaining in his possession title to a motor vehicle that has not been completely and legally assigned to him;
11. Failure to comply with any provision of Chapter 4.1 (§36-85.2 et seq.) of Title 36 or any regulation promulgated pursuant to that chapter;
12. Leasing, renting, lending, or otherwise allowing the use of a dealer's license plate by persons not specifically authorized under this title;
13. Having been convicted of a felony;
14. Failure to submit to the Department, within thirty days from the date of sale, any application, tax, or fee collected for the Department on behalf of a buyer;
15. Having been convicted of larceny of a vehicle or receipt or sale of a stolen vehicle;
16. Having been convicted of odometer tampering or any related violation;
17. If a salvage dealer, salvage pool, or rebuilder, failing to comply with any provision of Chapter 16 (§46.2-1600 et seq.) of this title or any regulation promulgated by the Commissioner under that chapter;
18. Failing to maintain automobile liability insurance, issued by a company licensed to do business in the Commonwealth, or a certificate of self-insurance as defined in §46.2-368, with respect to each dealer's license plate issued to the dealer by the Department; or
19. Failing or refusing to pay civil penalties imposed by the Board pursuant to §46.2-1507.

(Chgd. by L.1995 chs. 767, 816; L.1999 ch. 217, eff. 7/1/99.)

 Zv

§46.2-1576. Suspension, revocation, and refusal to renew licenses or certificates of dealer registration or qualification; notice and hearing.

A. Except as provided in §46.2-1527.7 and subsections B and C of this section, no license or certificate of dealer registration or qualification issued under this subtitle shall be suspended or revoked, or renewal thereof refused, until a written copy of the complaint made has been furnished to the licensee, registrant, or qualifier against whom the same is directed and a public hearing thereon has been had before a hearing officer designated by the Board. At least ten days' written notice of the time and place of the hearing shall be given to the licensee, registrant, or qualifier by registered mail addressed to his last known post office address or as shown on his license or certificate or other record of information in possession of the Board. At the hearing the licensee, registrant, or qualifier shall have the right to be heard personally or by counsel. The hearing officer shall provide recommendations to the Board within ninety days of the conclusion of the hearing. After receiving the recommendations from the hearing officer, the Board may suspend, revoke, or refuse to renew the license or certificate in question. A Board member shall disqualify himself and withdraw from any case in which he cannot accord fair and impartial consideration. Any party may request the disqualification of any Board member by stating with particularity the grounds upon which it is claimed that fair and impartial consideration cannot be accorded. The remaining members of the Board shall determine whether the individual should be disqualified. Immediate notice of any suspension, revocation, or refusal shall be given to the licensee, registrant, or qualifier in the manner provided in this section in the case of notices of hearing.

B. Should a dealer fail to maintain an established place of business, the Board may cancel the license of the dealer without a hearing after notification of the intent to cancel has been sent, by return receipt mail, to the dealer at the dealer's residence and business addresses, and the notices are returned undelivered or the dealer does not respond within twenty days from the date the notices were sent. Any subsequent application for a dealer's license shall be treated as an original application.

C. Should a dealer fail or refuse to pay civil penalties imposed by the Board pursuant to §46.2-1507, the Board may deny, revoke, or suspend the dealer's license without a hearing after notice of imposition of civil penalties has been sent, by certified mail, return receipt requested, to the dealer at the dealer's business address and such civil penalty is not paid in full within thirty days after receipt of the notice.

(Chgd. by L.1995 chs. 767, 816; L.1996 chs. 639, 658; L.1999 ch. 217, eff. 7/1/99.)

§46.2-1577. Appeals from actions of the Commissioner.

Any person aggrieved by the action of the Board in refusing to grant or renew a license or certificate of dealer registration or qualification issued under this chapter, or by any other action of the Board which is alleged to be improper, unreasonable, or unlawful under the provisions of this chapter is entitled to judicial review in accordance with the provisions of the Administrative Process Act (§9-6.14:1 et seq.).

(Chgd. by L.1995 chs. 767, 816, eff. 7/1/95.)

§46.2-1578. Appeals to Court of Appeals.

Either party may appeal from the decision of the court under §46.2-1577 to the Court of Appeals. These appeals shall be taken and prosecuted in the same manner and with like effect as is provided by law in other cases appealed as a matter of right to the Court of Appeals.

(Chgd. by L.1996 ch. 573, eff. 7/1/96.)

§46.2-1579. Equitable remedies not impaired.

The remedy at law provided by §§46.2-1577 and 46.2-1578 shall not in any manner impair the right to applicable equitable relief. That right to equitable relief is hereby preserved, notwithstanding the provisions of §§46.2-1577 and 46.2-1578.

ARTICLE 9
MOTOR VEHICLE DEALER ADVERTISING

Section

§46.2-1580. *(Omitted due to limited applicability.)*

§46.2-1581. Regulated advertising practices.

For purposes of this chapter, a violation of the following regulated advertising practices shall be an unfair, deceptive, or misleading act or practice.

1. A vehicle shall not be advertised as new, either by word or implication, unless it is one which conforms to the requirements of §46.2-1500.

2. When advertising any vehicle which does not conform to the definition of "new" as provided in §46.2-1500, the fact that it is used shall be clearly and unequivocally expressed by the term "used" or by such other term as is commonly understood to mean that the vehicle is used. By way of example but not by limitation, "special purchase" by itself is not a satisfactory disclosure; however, such terms as "demonstrator" or "former leased vehicles" used alone clearly express that the vehicles are used for advertising purposes.

3. Advertisement of finance charges or other interest rates shall not be used when there is a cost to buy-down said charge or rate which is passed on, in whole or in part, to the purchaser.

4. Terms, conditions, and disclaimers shall be stated clearly and conspicuously. An asterisk or other reference symbol may be used to point to a disclaimer or other information, but shall not be used as a means of contradicting or changing the meaning of an advertised statement.

5. The expiration date of an advertised sale shall be clearly and conspicuously disclosed.

6. The term "list price," "sticker price," or "suggested retail price" and similar terms, shall be used only in reference to the manufacturer's suggested retail price for new vehicles or the dealer's own usual and customary price for used vehicles.

7. Terms such as "at cost," "below cost," "$ off cost" shall not be used in advertisements because of the difficulty in determining a dealer's actual net cost at the time of the sale. Terms such as "invoice price," "$ over invoice," may be used, provided that the invoice referred to is the manufacturer's factory invoice or a bona fide bill of sale and the invoice or bill of sale is available for customer inspection.

"Manufacturer's factory invoice" means that document supplied by the manufacturer to the dealer listing the manufacturer's charge to the dealer before any deduction for holdback, group advertising, factory incentives or rebates, or any governmental charges.

8. When the price or credit terms of a vehicle are advertised, the vehicle shall be fully identified as to year, make, and model. In addition, in advertisements placed by individual dealers and not line-make marketing groups, the advertised price or credit terms shall include all charges which the buyer must pay to the seller, except buyer-selected options, state and local fees and taxes, and manufacturer's or distributor's freight or destination charges, and a processing

fee, if any. If a processing fee or freight or destination charges are not included in the advertised price, the amount of any such processing fee and freight or destination charge must be (i) clearly and conspicuously disclosed in not less than eight-point boldface type or (ii) not smaller than the largest typeface within the advertisement. If the processing fee is not included in the advertised price, the amount of the processing fee may be omitted from any advertisement in which the largest type size is less than eight-point typeface, so long as the dealer participates in a media-provided listing of processing fees and the dealer's advertisement includes an asterisk or other such notation to refer the reader to the listing of the fees.

9. Advertisements which set out a policy of matching or bettering competitors' prices shall not be used unless the terms of the offer are specific, verifiable and reasonable.

10. Advertisements of "dealer rebates" shall not be used. This does not affect advertisement of manufacturer rebates.

11. "Free," "at no cost," or other words to that effect shall not be used unless the "free" item, merchandise, or service is available without a purchase. This provision shall not apply to advertising placed by manufacturers, distributors, or line-make marketing groups.

12. "Bait" advertising, in which an advertiser may have no intention to sell at the price or terms advertised, shall not be used. By way of example, but not by limitation:

a. If a specific vehicle is advertised, the seller shall be in possession of a reasonable supply of said vehicles, and they shall be available at the advertised price. If the advertised vehicle is available only in limited numbers or only by order, that shall be stated in the advertisement. For purposes of this subdivision, the listing of a vehicle by stock number or vehicle identification number in the advertisement for a used vehicle is one means of satisfactorily disclosing a limitation of availability. Stock numbers or vehicle identification numbers shall not be used in advertising a new vehicle unless the advertisement clearly and conspicuously discloses that it relates to only one vehicle.

b. Advertising a vehicle at a certain price, including "as low as" statements, but having available for sale only vehicles equipped with dealer added cost "options" which increase the selling price, above the advertised price, shall also be considered "bait" advertising.

c. If a lease payment is advertised, the fact that it is a lease arrangement shall be disclosed.

13. The term "repossessed" shall be used only to describe vehicles that have been sold, registered, titled and then taken back from a purchaser and not yet resold to an ultimate user. Advertisers offering repossessed vehicles for sale shall provide proof of repossession upon request.

14. Words such as "finance" or "loan" shall not be used in a motor vehicle advertiser's firm name or trade name, unless that person is actually engaged in the financing of motor vehicles.

15. Any advertisement which gives the impression a dealer has a special arrangement or relationship with the distributor or manufacturer, as compared to similarly situated dealers, shall not be used.

(Chgd. by L.1996 ch. 1027; L.1998 ch. 325, eff. 10/1/98.)

§46.2-1582. Enforcement; regulations.

The Board may promulgate regulations reasonably necessary for enforcement of this article.

In addition to any other sanctions or remedies available to the Board under this chapter, the Board may assess a civil penalty not to exceed $1,000 for any single violation of this article. Each day that a violation continues shall constitute a separate violation.

(Chgd. by L.1995 chs. 767, 816, eff. 7/1/95.)

CHAPTER 16
SALVAGE, NONREPAIRABLE, AND REBUILT VEHICLES

Section

§46.2-1600. Definitions.

The following words, terms, and phrases when used in this chapter shall have the meaning ascribed to them in this section, except where the context indicates otherwise:

"Actual cash value," as applied to a vehicle, means the retail cash value of the vehicle prior to damage as determined, using recognized evaluation sources, either (i) by an insurance company responsible for paying a claim or (ii) if no insurance company is responsible therefor, by the Department.

"Current salvage value," as applied to a vehicle, means (i) the salvage value of the vehicle, as determined by the insurer responsible for paying the claim or (ii) if no insurance company is responsible therefor, twenty-five percent of the actual cash value.

"Demolisher" means any person whose business is to crush, flatten, or otherwise reduce a vehicle to a state where it can no longer be considered a vehicle.

"Diminished value compensation" means the amount of compensation that an insurance company pays to a third party vehicle owner, in addition to the cost of repairs, for the reduced value of a vehicle due to damage.

"Independent appraisal firm" means any business providing cost estimates for the repair of damaged motor vehicles for insurance purposes and having all required business licenses and zoning approvals. This term shall not include insurance companies that provide the same service, nor shall any such entity be a rebuilder or affiliated with a rebuilder.

"Late model vehicle" means the current-year model of a vehicle and the six preceding model years, or any vehicle whose actual cash value is determined to have been at least $7,500 prior to being damaged.

"Licensee" means any person who is licensed or is required to be licensed under this chapter.

"Major component" means any one of the following subassemblies of a motor vehicle: (i) front clip assembly, consisting of the fenders, grille, hood, bumper, and related parts; (ii) engine; (iii) transmission; (iv) rear clip assembly, consisting of the quarter panels, floor panels, trunk lid, bumper, and related parts; (v) frame; (vi) air bags; and (vii) any door that displays a vehicle identification number.

"Nonrepairable certificate" means a document of ownership issued by the Department for any nonrepairable vehicle, upon surrender or cancellation of the vehicle's title and registration or salvage certificate.

"Nonrepairable vehicle" means (i) any late model vehicle that has been damaged and whose estimated cost of repair exceeds ninety percent of its actual cash value prior to damage, or (ii) any vehicle which has been determined to be nonrepairable by its insurer or owner, and for which a nonrepairable certificate has been issued or applied for, or (iii) any other vehicle which has been damaged, is inoperable, and has no value except for use as parts and scrap metal.

"Rebuilder" means any person who acquires and repairs, for use on the public highways, two or more salvage vehicles within a twelve-month period.

"Rebuilt vehicle" means (i) any salvage vehicle that has been damaged as a result of collision, fire, flood, accident, trespass, or any other occurrence and has been repaired and the estimated cost of repair exceeded seventy-five percent of its actual cash value, for use on the public highways or (ii) any late model vehicle which has been repaired and the estimated cost of repair exceeded seventy-five percent of its actual cash value, excluding the cost to repair damage to the engine, transmission, or drive axle assembly.

"Salvage certificate" means a document of ownership issued by the Department for any salvage vehicle upon surrender or cancellation of the vehicle's title and registration.

"Salvage dealer" means any person who acquires any vehicle for the purpose of reselling any parts thereof.

"Salvage pool" means any person providing a storage service for salvage vehicles or nonrepairable vehicles who either displays the vehicles for resale or solicits bids for the sale of salvage vehicles or nonrepairable vehicles, but this definition shall not apply to an insurance company which stores and displays fewer than 100 salvage vehicles and nonrepairable vehicles in one location; however, any two or more insurance companies who display salvage and nonrepairable vehicles for resale, using the same facilities, shall be considered a salvage pool.

"Salvage vehicle" means (i) any late model vehicle which has been (a) acquired by an insurance company as a part of the claims process other than a stolen vehicle or (b) damaged as a result of collision, fire, flood, accident, trespass, or any other occurrence to such an extent that its estimated cost of repair, excluding charges for towing, storage, and temporary replacement/rental vehicle or payment for diminished value compensation, would exceed its actual cash value less its current salvage value; (ii) any recovered stolen vehicle acquired by an insurance company as a part of the claims process, whose estimated cost of repair exceeds seventy-five percent of its actual cash value; or (iii) any other vehicle which is determined to be a salvage vehicle by its owner or an insurance company by applying for a salvage certificate for the vehicle, provided that such vehicle is not a nonrepairable vehicle.

"Scrap metal processor" means any person who is engaged in the business of processing vehicles into scrap for remelting purposes who, from a fixed location, utilizes machinery and equipment for processing and manufacturing ferrous and nonferrous metallic scrap into prepared grades, and whose principal product is metallic scrap.

"Vehicle removal operator" means any person who acquires a vehicle for the purpose of reselling it to a demolisher, scrap metal processor, or salvage dealer.

(Chgd. by L.2000 chs. 123, 235, 257, eff. 7/1/2000.)

§46.2-1601. Licensing of dealers of salvage vehicles; fees.

It shall be unlawful for any person to engage in business in the Commonwealth as a demolisher, rebuilder, salvage dealer, salvage pool, or vehicle removal operator without first acquiring a license issued by the Commissioner for each such business at each location. The fee for the first such license issued or renewed under this chapter shall be $100 per license year or part thereof. The fee for each additional license issued or renewed under this chapter for the same location shall be $25 per license year or part thereof. However, no fee shall be charged for supplemental locations of a business located within 500 yards of the licensed location. No license shall be issued or renewed for any person unless the licensed business contains at least 600 square feet of enclosed space and is shown to be in compliance with all applicable zoning ordinances. Nothing in this section shall authorize any person to act as a motor vehicle dealer or salesperson without being licensed under Chapter 15 of this title and meeting all requirements imposed by such chapter.

The Commissioner may offer an optional multiyear license for any license set forth in this section. When such option is offered and chosen by the licensee, all fees due at the time of licensing shall be multiplied by the number of years for which the license will be issued.

On due notice and hearing, the Commissioner may suspend or revoke any license issued under this chapter for any violation of any provision of this chapter or a violation of §46.2-1074 or §46.2-1075. Suspension or revocation shall only be imposed on the specific business found to be in violation.

(Chgd. by L.1999 ch. 53, eff. 7/1/99.)

§46.2-1602. Certain sales prohibited; exceptions.

A. It shall be unlawful:

1. For any scrap metal processor to sell a vehicle or vehicle components or parts;

2. For any salvage pool to sell a salvage vehicle to any person who is not a scrap metal processor or licensed as a salvage dealer, rebuilder, demolisher, motor vehicle dealer, or vehicle removal operator;

3. For any person to sell a nonrepairable vehicle to any person who is not a scrap metal processor or licensed as a salvage dealer, demolisher, or vehicle removal operator; or

4. For any person to sell a rebuilt vehicle without first having disclosed the fact that the vehicle is a rebuilt vehicle to the buyer in writing on a form prescribed by the Commissioner.

B. Notwithstanding the provisions of subsection A of this section, it shall not be unlawful:

1. For a salvage dealer to sell vehicle components or parts to unlicensed persons; or

2. For an individual to dispose of a salvage vehicle acquired or retained for his own use when it has been acquired and retained and used in good faith and not for the purpose of avoiding the provisions of this chapter.

§46.2-1602.1. Duties of insurance companies upon acquiring certain vehicles.

Every insurance company which acquires, as a result of the claims process, any late model vehicle titled in the Commonwealth or any recovered stolen vehicle whose estimated cost of repair exceeds seventy-five percent of its actual cash value shall apply to and obtain from the Department either (i) a salvage certificate or certificate of title as provided in §46.2-1603 or (ii) a nonrepairable certificate as provided in §46.2-1603.2 for each such vehicle. An insurance company may apply to and obtain from the Department either a salvage certificate as provided in §46.2-1603 or a nonrepairable certificate as provided in §46.2-1603.2 for any other vehicle

which is determined to be either a salvage vehicle or a nonrepairable vehicle.
(Chgd. by L.2000 chs. 235, 257, eff. 7/1/2000.)

§46.2-1603. Obtaining salvage certificate or certificate of title for an unrecovered stolen vehicle.

A. The owner of any vehicle titled in the Commonwealth may declare such vehicle to be a salvage vehicle and apply to the Department and obtain a salvage certificate for that vehicle.

B. Every insurance company or its authorized agent shall apply to the Department and obtain a salvage certificate for each late model vehicle acquired by the insurance company as the result of the claims process if such vehicle is titled in the Commonwealth and is a salvage vehicle.

C. Every insurance company or its authorized agent shall apply to the Department and obtain a certificate of title for each stolen vehicle acquired by the insurance company as the result of the claims process if such vehicle is titled in the Commonwealth and has not been recovered at the time of application to the Department. For each recovered stolen vehicle, acquired as a result of the claims process, whose estimated cost of repair exceeds seventy-five percent of its actual cash value, the insurance company or its authorized agent shall apply to the Department and obtain a salvage certificate. The application shall be accompanied by the vehicle's title certificate and shall contain a description of the damage to the salvage vehicle and an itemized estimate of the cost of repairs up to the point where a nonrepairable certificate would be issued. Application for the certificate of title shall be made within fifteen days after payment has been made to the owner, lienholder, or both. Application for the salvage certificate shall be made within fifteen days after the stolen vehicle is recovered.

D. Every insurance company or its authorized agent shall notify the Department of each late model vehicle titled in the Commonwealth on which a claim for damage to the vehicle has been paid by the insurance company if (i) the estimated cost of repair exceeds seventy-five percent of actual cash value of the vehicle and (ii) the vehicle is to be retained by its owner. No such notification shall be required for a vehicle when a supplemental claim has been paid for the cost of repairs to the engine, transmission, or drive axle assembly if such components are replaced by components of like kind and quality.

E. Every owner of an uninsured or self-insured late model vehicle which sustains damage to such an extent that the estimated cost of repairs exceeds seventy-five percent of the actual cash value of the vehicle prior to being damaged shall similarly apply for and obtain a salvage certificate. If no estimated cost of repairs is available from an insurance company, the owner of the vehicle may provide an estimate from an independent appraisal firm. Any such estimate from an independent appraisal firm shall be verified by the Department in such a manner as may be provided for by Department regulations.

F. The fee for issuance of the salvage certificate shall be ten dollars. If a salvage vehicle is sold after a salvage certificate has been issued, the owner of the salvage vehicle shall make proper assignment to the purchaser.

G. The Department, upon receipt of an application for a salvage certificate for a vehicle titled in the Commonwealth, or upon receipt of notification from an insurance company or its authorized agent as provided in subsection D of this section, shall cause the title of such vehicle to be cancelled and the appropriate certificate issued to the vehicle's owner.

H. All provisions of this Code applicable to a motor vehicle certificate of title shall apply, mutatis mutandis, to a salvage certificate, except that no registration or license plates shall be issued for the vehicle described in the salvage certificate. A vehicle for which a salvage certificate has been issued may be retitled for use on the highways in accordance with the provisions of §46.2-1605.
(Chgd. by L.2000 chs. 235, 257, eff. 7/1/2000.)

§46.2-1603.1. Duties of licensees.

A. If a salvage vehicle is purchased by a salvage dealer and the vehicle is sold as a unit to anyone other than a demolisher, rebuilder, vehicle removal operator or scrap metal processor, the purchaser shall obtain from the Department a salvage certificate. If the sale is to a demolisher or vehicle removal operator, the salvage vehicle shall be assigned in the space provided for such assignments on the existing salvage certificate. If a vehicle is purchased by a salvage dealer and disassembled for parts only or demolished by a demolisher, the salvage dealer shall immediately and conspicuously indicate on the salvage certificate or title that the vehicle was disassembled for parts only or demolished and immediately forward the salvage certificate or title to the Department for cancellation. The Department shall cancel the title or salvage certificate and issue a nonrepairable certificate for the vehicle to the salvage dealer.

1. If a vehicle for which a title or salvage certificate or other ownership document has been issued by a foreign jurisdiction and is purchased by a salvage dealer or demolisher and disassembled for parts only or demolished by a demolisher, the salvage dealer or demolisher shall immediately and conspicuously indicate on the salvage certificate, title, or other ownership document that the vehicle was disassembled for parts only or demolished and immediately forward the salvage certificate, title or other ownership document to the Department for cancellation. The Department shall cancel the title, salvage certificate, or other ownership document and issue a nonrepairable certificate for the vehicle to the salvage dealer.

2. There shall be no fee for the issuance of a nonrepairable certificate.

B. If a licensee acquires any late model vehicle, he shall immediately compare the vehicle identification number assigned by the manufacturer or the Department or the identification number issued or assigned by another state with the title or salvage certificate of the vehicle and shall notify the Department as provided in subsection C of this section. Such comparison and notification shall not be required of a demolisher if the vehicle was acquired from a licensed salvage dealer, rebuilder, salvage pool, or vehicle removal operator and such licensee delivers to the demolisher a title or salvage certificate for the vehicle.

C. If the vehicle identification number has been altered, is missing, or appears to have been otherwise tampered with, the licensee shall take no further action with regard to the vehicle except to safeguard it in its then-existing condition and shall promptly notify the Department. The Department shall, after an investigation has been made, notify the licensee whether the vehicle can be freed from this limitation. In no event shall the vehicle be disassembled, demolished, processed, or otherwise modified or removed prior to authorization by the Department. If the vehicle is a motorcycle, the licenses shall cause to be noted on the title or salvage certificate, certifying on the face of the document, in addition to the above requirements, the frame number of the motorcycle and motor number, if available.

D. After a vehicle has been demolished, the demolisher shall, within five working days, deliver to the Department the salvage certificate or title, certifying on the face of the document that the vehicle has been destroyed.

E. It shall be unlawful for any licensee to purchase, receive, take into inventory, or otherwise accept from any person any late model vehicle unless, as a part of any such transaction, the licensee also receives a title, salvage

certificate, nonrepairable certificate, or other ownership documents, issued by an appropriate regulatory agency within or without the Commonwealth, relating to such vehicle. Every licensee shall maintain as a part of his business records a title, salvage certificate, nonrepairable certificate, or other ownership documents, issued by an appropriate regulatory agency within or without the Commonwealth, pertaining to every late model vehicle in his inventory or possession.
(Chgd. by L.1995 chs. 390, 394, eff. 7/1/95.)

§46.2-1603.2. Owner may declare vehicle nonrepairable; insurance company required to obtain a nonrepairable certificate; applicability of certain other laws to nonrepairable certificates; titling and registration of nonrepairable vehicle prohibited.

A. The owner of any vehicle titled in the Commonwealth may declare such vehicle to be a nonrepairable vehicle by applying to the Department for a nonrepairable certificate.

B. Every insurance company or its authorized agent shall apply to the Department and obtain a nonrepairable certificate for each vehicle acquired by the insurance company as a result of the claims process if such vehicle is titled in the Commonwealth and is (i) a late model nonrepairable vehicle or (ii) a stolen vehicle that has been recovered and determined to be a nonrepairable vehicle. The application shall be accompanied by the vehicle's title certificate or salvage certificate and shall contain a description of the damage to the nonrepairable vehicle. Application for the nonrepairable certificate shall be made within fifteen days after payment has been made to the owner, lienholder, or both.

C. Every insurance company or its authorized agent shall notify the Department of each late model vehicle titled in the Commonwealth upon which a claim has been paid if such vehicle is a nonrepairable vehicle that is retained by its owner.

D. The Department, upon receipt of an application for a nonrepairable certificate for a vehicle titled in the Commonwealth, or upon receipt of notification from an insurance company or its authorized agent as provided in subsection C of this section that a vehicle registered in the Commonwealth has become a nonrepairable vehicle, shall cause the title of such vehicle to be cancelled and a nonrepairable certificate issued to the vehicle's owner.

There shall be no fee for the issuance of a nonrepairable certificate. All provisions of this Code applicable to a motor vehicle certificate of title shall apply, mutatis mutandis, to a nonrepairable certificate, except that no registration or license plates shall be issued for the vehicle described in a nonrepairable certificate. No vehicle for which a nonrepairable certificate has been issued shall ever be titled or registered for use on the highways in the Commonwealth.

E. The Department, upon receipt of a title, salvage certificate, or other ownership document from a licensed salvage dealer or demolisher pursuant to §46.2-1603.1 A 1, shall cause the title, salvage certificate, or other ownership document to such vehicle to be cancelled and a nonrepairable certificate issued to the vehicle's owner.
(Chgd. by L.1995 ch. 390, eff. 7/1/95.)

§46.2-1604. Rebuilders required to possess certificate of title.

Each rebuilder shall have in his possession a certificate of title assigned to him for each vehicle in his inventory for resale. If a rebuilder purchases a salvage vehicle to be used or sold for parts only, he shall conspicuously indicate on the salvage certificate that the vehicle will be sold or used as parts only and immediately forward the salvage certificate to the Department for cancellation. The Department shall issue a nonrepairable certificate for that vehicle.

§46.2-1605. Vehicles repaired or rebuilt for highway use; examinations; branding of titles.

Each salvage vehicle that has been repaired or rebuilt for use on the highways shall be examined by the Department prior to the issuance of a title for the vehicle. The examination shall include a review of all documentation for the parts and labor used for the repair of the salvage vehicle and a verification of the vehicle's identification number, confidential number, and odometer reading. The Commissioner shall ensure that, in scheduling and performing examinations of salvage vehicles under this section, single vehicles owned by private owner-operators are afforded no lower priority than examinations of vehicles owned by motor vehicle dealers, salvage dealers, demolishers, rebuilders, salvage pools, or vehicle removal operators. The Commissioner may charge an appropriate fee, not to exceed twenty-five dollars per vehicle, for the examination of repaired and rebuilt vehicles.

Any salvage vehicle whose vehicle identification number or confidential number has been altered, is missing, or appears to have been tampered with may be impounded by the Department until completion of an investigation by the Department. The vehicle may not be moved, sold, or tampered with until the completion of this investigation. Upon completion of an investigation by the Department, if the vehicle identification number is found to be missing or altered, a new vehicle identification number may be issued by the Department. If the vehicle is found to be a stolen vehicle and its owner can be determined, the vehicle shall be returned to him. If the owner cannot be determined or located and the person seeking to title the vehicle has been convicted of a violation of §46.2-1074 or §46.2-1075, the vehicle shall be deemed forfeited to the Commonwealth. Each such vehicle shall be sold at public auction and the proceeds thereof, after satisfaction of any liens, returned to the state treasury for use by the Department. If the Department's examination of a repaired or rebuilt salvage vehicle indicates no irregularities, a title and registration may be issued for the vehicle upon application therefor to the Department by the owner of the salvage vehicle. If the vehicle is a rebuilt vehicle, the title issued by the Department and any subsequent title thereafter issued for the vehicle shall be permanently branded to indicate that it is a rebuilt vehicle. If the repaired vehicle is not a rebuilt vehicle, the Department shall issue a certificate of title without branding. All rebuilt vehicles shall be subject to all safety equipment requirements provided by law. No title or registration shall be issued by the Department for any vehicle for which a nonrepairable certificate has ever been issued.
(Chgd. by L.1996 chs. 21, 843, eff. 7/1/96.)

§46.2-1606. Certificates of title issued by other states.

The Commissioner may accept certificates of titles for salvage vehicles or other documents deemed appropriate by the Department issued by other states indicating a vehicle has been declared salvage, and shall carry forward all appropriate brands or indicators. If the vehicle has not been rebuilt and the requirements of §46.2-1605 have not been met, the Department shall issue a salvage certificate for the vehicle.

§46.2-1607. Inspection of records and examination of inventory.

The Commissioner or any person authorized by the Commissioner or any law-enforcement officer, during the usual business hours, may examine any records, books, papers, or other documents required to be maintained by this chapter, and may examine any vehicle or component part of any vehicle located in the yard, garage, or storage area of any salvage dealer, rebuilder, demolisher, salvage pool, scrap metal processor, or vehicle removal operator to ensure compliance with this chapter.

§46.2-1608. Maintenance and contents of records.

Each licensee shall maintain a record of the receipt of any vehicle. The record shall contain the date of receipt of the vehicle, its make, year, model, identification number, name and address of the person from whom it was acquired, the vehicle's title number, and state of issuance. If any major component, as defined in §46.2-1600, is sold, the salvage dealer shall provide, upon request of any law-enforcement official, the information required by this section as to the vehicle from which the part was taken.

(Chgd. by L.2000 ch. 123, eff. 7/1/2000.)

§46.2-1609. Penalties.

Violation of any provision of this chapter shall constitute a Class 1 misdemeanor.

§46.2-1610. Disposition of fees.

All fees collected under this chapter shall be paid by the Commissioner into the state treasury and set aside as a special fund to be used to meet the expenses of the Department.

CHAPTER 17
COMMERCIAL DRIVER TRAINING SCHOOLS

§46.2-1700. Definitions.

As used in this chapter, unless the context requires a different meaning:

"Class A licensee" means a school which provides occupational training in the operation of tractor-trailers or motor vehicles in excess of 20,000 pounds, exclusive of any load.

"Class B licensee" means a school which provides training in the operation of any type of motor vehicle other than those included in Class A licensure.

"Commercial driver training school" or "school" means a business enterprise conducted by an individual, association, partnership, or corporation, for the education and training of persons, either practically or theoretically or both, to operate or drive motor vehicles, and charging a consideration or tuition for such services. "Commercial driver training school" or "school" does not mean any college, university, school established pursuant to §46.2-1314, school maintained or classes conducted by employers for their own employees where no fee or tuition is charged, schools or classes owned and operated by or under the authority of bona fide religious institutions, or by the Commonwealth or any political subdivision thereof, or schools accredited by accrediting associations approved by the Department of Education.

"Instructor" means any person, whether acting for himself as operator of a commercial driver training school or for such school for compensation, who teaches, conducts classes, gives demonstrations, or supervises persons learning to operate or drive a motor vehicle.

§46.2-1701. Licenses required for school and instructor; fees.

No commercial driver training school shall be established or continue operation unless the school obtains from the Commissioner a license authorizing the school to operate within this Commonwealth.

No instructor shall perform the actions enumerated in the definition of "instructor" in §46.2-1700 unless he obtains from the Commissioner a license authorizing him to act as driving instructor.

The Commissioner shall have authority to set and collect school and instructor licensing fees. All licensing fees collected by the Commissioner under this chapter shall be paid into the state treasury and set aside as a special fund to meet the expenses of the Department of Motor Vehicles.

§46.2-1701.1. Bond of applicants.

The applicant shall file a surety bond in the amount of $100,000 for a Class A licensee and $5,000 for a Class B licensee. The bond shall be payable to the Commonwealth of Virginia and conditioned to protect the contractual rights of students. The bonding requirement for a Class A license may be reduced, at the discretion of the Department, on a showing by the school that no course of study for which tuition is collected lasts longer than thirty days or that the school collects no advance tuition other than equal monthly installments based on the length of the course of study. The minimum bond for any school shall be $5,000.

§46.2-1702. Certification of driver education courses by Commissioner.

The Commissioner shall have the authority to approve as a driver education course satisfying the requirements of §46.2-334 any course which is offered by any commercial driver training school licensed under the provisions of this chapter if he finds that the course is of comparable content and quality to that offered in the Commonwealth's public schools. In making such finding, the Commissioner shall not require that the instructors of any commercial driver training school meet the certification requirements of teachers in the Commonwealth's public schools. The Commissioner may accept twenty years' service with the Virginia Department of State Police by a person who retired or resigned while in good standing from such Department in lieu of requirements established by the Department of Education for instructor qualification.

§46.2-1703. Authority to promulgate regulations.

The Commissioner may promulgate regulations necessary to enforce the provisions of this chapter, to provide adequate training for students, and to carry out the other provisions of this chapter. These regulations shall include but need not be limited to curriculum requirements, contractual arrangements with students, obligations to students, facilities and equipment, qualifications of instructors, and financial stability of schools.

§46.2-1704. Action on applications; hearing on denial.

The Commissioner shall act on any application for a license under this chapter within thirty days after receipt by either granting or denying the application. Any applicant denied a license shall, on his written request made within thirty days, be given a hearing at a time and place determined by the Commissioner or his designee. All hearings under this section shall be public and shall be held promptly. The applicant may be represented by counsel. Any applicant denied a license may not apply again for a license for thirty days from the date of denial of the application.

§46.2-1705. Suspension, revocation, cancellation or refusal to renew license; limitations on operations; imposition of monetary penalties.

A. Except as otherwise provided in this section, no license issued under this chapter shall be suspended, revoked, or cancelled or renewal thereof denied, no limitation on operations shall be imposed pursuant to subsection F of this section, and no monetary penalty shall be imposed pursuant to §46.2-1706, unless the licensee has been furnished a written copy of the complaint against him and the grounds upon which the action is taken and has been offered an opportunity for an administrative hearing to show cause why such action should not be taken.

B. The order suspending, revoking, cancelling, or denying renewal of a license, imposing a limitation on operation, or imposing a monetary penalty, except as otherwise provided in subsection E of this section, shall not become effective until the licensee has had thirty days after notice of the opportunity for a hearing to make a written request for such a hearing. If no hearing has been requested within such thirty-day period, the order shall become effective and no hearing shall thereafter be held. A timely request for a hearing shall automatically stay operation of the order until after the hearing.

C. Notice of an order suspending, revoking, cancelling or denying renewal of a license, imposing a limitation on operation, or imposing a monetary penalty and advising the licensee of the opportunity for a hearing shall be mailed to the licensee by registered mail to the school address and the licensee's residence address as shown on the licensee's application for license and shall be considered served when mailed.

D. No licensee whose license has been revoked or cancelled or who has been denied renewal shall apply for a new license within 180 days of such action.

E. Notwithstanding the provisions of subsection B of this section, an order suspending, revoking, or denying renewal of an instructor license shall be effective immediately if the order is based upon a finding by the Commissioner that the instructor's driving record is such that he is not presently qualified to act as an instructor. Such finding by the Commissioner shall be based on records of driver's license suspension or revocation, upon records of conviction of serious motor vehicle related offenses punishable as a misdemeanor or felony including driving under the influence or reckless driving, and upon such other criteria as the Commissioner may establish by regulation.

F. If the Commissioner makes a finding that the conduct of a licensee is in violation of this chapter or regulations adopted pursuant to this chapter, he may order the licensee, in accordance with subsections A, B and C of this section, to limit the types of driver education training provided, restrict the use of the licensee's training vehicles, or both. Whenever the Commissioner takes action under this subsection, the Commissioner shall require the licensee to post conspicuous notice of the Commissioner's action under this subsection at the same location as the licensee's license was issued under this chapter, as soon as the Commissioner's order becomes effective. Orders of the Commissioner limiting operations and requiring posting of notices shall remain in effect until the Commissioner makes a finding that the violations causing the imposition of such limitations have been remedied by the licensee or the Commissioner's order is lifted as the result of an appeal under §46.2-1704 or by a court of competent jurisdiction.

G. If the Commissioner makes a finding, after conducting a preliminary investigation, that the conduct of a licensee (i) is in violation of this chapter or regulations adopted pursuant to this chapter and (ii) such violation constitutes a danger to public safety, the Commissioner may issue an order suspending the licensee's license to operate a commercial driver training school. Notice of the suspension shall be in writing and mailed in accordance with subsection C of this section. Upon receipt of a request for a hearing appealing the suspension, the licensee shall be afforded the opportunity for a hearing within 30 days. The suspension shall remain in effect pending the outcome of the hearing.
(Chgd. by L.2000 ch. 179, eff. 7/1/2000.)

§46.2-1706. Civil penalties.

In addition to any other sanctions or remedies available to the Commissioner under this chapter, the Commissioner may assess a civil penalty not to exceed $1,000 for any violation or any provision of this chapter or any regulation promulgated thereunder. The penalty may be sued for and recovered in the name of the Commonwealth.

§46.2-1707. Unlawful acts; prosecution; proceedings in equity.

A. It shall be unlawful for any person to engage in any of the following acts:

1. Practicing as a commercial driving training school or as an instructor without holding a valid license as required by statute or regulation;
2. Making use of any designation provided by statute or regulation to denote a standard of professional or occupational competence without being duly certified or licensed;
3. Performing any act or function which is restricted by statute or regulation to persons holding a commercial driver training school or instructor license or certification, without being duly certified or licensed;
4. Materially misrepresenting facts in an application for licensure, certification or registration;
5. Willfully refusing to furnish the Department information or records required or requested pursuant to statute or regulation; or
6. Violating any statute or regulation governing the practice of any commercial driver training school or instructor regulated pursuant to this chapter.

Any person who willfully engages in any unlawful act enumerated in this section shall be guilty of a Class 1 misdemeanor. However, the third or any subsequent conviction for violating this section during a thirty-six-month period shall constitute a Class 6 felony.

B. In addition to the provisions of subsection A of this section, the Department may institute proceedings in equity to enjoin any person from engaging in any unlawful act enumerated in this section. Such proceedings shall be brought in the name of the Commonwealth in the circuit court of the city or county in which the unlawful act occurred or in which the defendant resides.

CHAPTER 18
VIRGINIA MOTOR VEHICLE SCRAPPAGE PROGRAM

(Repealed by L.1996 chs. 165, 926, eff. 7/1/96.)

§§46.2-1801 to 46.2-1805. *(Repealed by L.1996 chs. 165, 926, eff. 7/1/96.)*

CHAPTER 19
T&M VEHICLE DEALERS

(Added by L.1995 chs. 767, 816, eff. 7/1/95.)

ARTICLE 1
T&M VEHICLE DEALERS GENERALLY

§46.2-1900. Definitions.

Unless the context otherwise requires, the following words and terms for the purpose of this chapter shall have the following meanings:

"Certificate of origin" means the document provided by the manufacturer of a new T&M vehicle, or its distributor, which is the only valid indication of ownership between the manufacturer, its distributor, its franchised T&M vehicle dealers, and the original purchaser not for resale.

"Dealer-operator" means the individual who works at the established place of business of a dealer and who is responsible for and in charge of day-to-day operations of that place of business.

"Distributor" means a person who sells or distributes new T&M vehicles pursuant to a written agreement with the manufacturer, to franchised T&M vehicle dealers in the Commonwealth.

"Distributor branch" means a branch office maintained by a distributor for the sale of T&M vehicles to T&M vehicle dealers or for directing or supervising, in whole or in part, its representatives in the Commonwealth.

"Distributor representative" means a person employed by a distributor or by a distributor branch, for the purpose of making or promoting the sale of T&M vehicles or for supervising or contacting its dealers, prospective dealers, or representatives in the Commonwealth.

"Factory branch" means a branch office maintained by a person for the sale of T&M vehicles to distributors or for the sale of T&M vehicles to T&M vehicle dealers, or for directing or supervising, in whole or in part, its representatives in the Commonwealth.

"Factory representative" means a person employed by a person who manufactures or assembles T&M vehicles, or by a factory branch for the purpose of making or promoting the sale of its T&M vehicles, or for supervising or contacting its dealers, prospective dealers, or representatives in the Commonwealth.

"Factory repurchase T&M vehicle" means a T&M vehicle sold, leased, rented, consigned, or otherwise transferred to a person under an agreement that the T&M vehicle will be resold or otherwise retransferred only to the manufacturer or distributor of the T&M vehicle, and which is reacquired by the manufacturer or distributor, or its agents.

"Family member" means a person who either (i) is the spouse, child, grandchild, spouse of a child, spouse of a grandchild, brother, sister, or parent of the dealer or owner, or (ii) has been employed continuously by the dealer for at least five years.

"Franchise" means a written contract or agreement between two or more persons whereby one person, the franchisee, is granted the right to engage in the business of offering and selling, servicing, or offering, selling, and servicing new T&M vehicles of a particular line-make or late model or factory repurchase T&M vehicles of a particular line-make manufactured or distributed by the grantor of the right, the franchisor, and where the operation of the franchisee's business is substantially associated with the franchisor's trademark, trade name, advertising, or other commercial symbol designating the franchisor, the T&M vehicle or its manufacturer or distributor. The term shall include any severable part or parts of a franchise agreement which separately provides for selling and servicing different line-makes of the franchisor.

"Franchised late model or factory repurchase T&M vehicle dealer" means a dealer in late model or factory repurchase T&M vehicles, including a franchised new T&M vehicle dealer, that has a franchise agreement with a manufacturer or distributor of the line-make of the late model or factory repurchase T&M vehicles.

"Franchised T&M vehicle dealer" or "franchised dealer" means a dealer in new T&M vehicles that has a franchise agreement with a manufacturer or distributor of new T&M vehicles.

"Independent T&M vehicle dealer" means a dealer in used T&M vehicles.

"Late model T&M vehicle" means a T&M vehicle of the current model year and the immediately preceding model year.

"Manufacturer" means a person engaged in the business of constructing or assembling new T&M vehicles or a person engaged in the business of manufacturing engines, power trains, or rear axles, when such engines, power trains, or rear axles are not warranted by the final manufacturer or assembler of the motor home.

"Motor home" means a motor vehicle with a normal seating capacity of not more than ten persons, including the driver, designed primarily for use as living quarters for human beings.

"Motor vehicle dealer," "motor vehicle manufacturer," "motor vehicle factory branch," "motor vehicle distributor," "motor vehicle distributor branch," "motor vehicle factory representative," and "motor vehicle distributor representative" mean the same as provided in §46.2-1500.

"New T&M vehicle" means any T&M vehicle which (i) has not been previously sold except in good faith for the purpose of resale, (ii) has not been used as a rental, driver education, or demonstration T&M vehicle, or for the personal and business transportation of the manufacturer, distributor, dealer, or any of his employees, (iii) has not been used except for limited use necessary in moving or road testing the T&M vehicle prior to delivery to a customer, (iv) is transferred by a certificate of origin, and (v) has the manufacturer's certification that it conforms to all applicable federal T&M vehicle safety and emission standards. Notwithstanding provisions (i) and (iii), a T&M vehicle that has been previously sold but not titled shall be deemed a new T&M vehicle if it meets the requirements of provisions (ii), (iv), and (v) of this definition.

"Original license" means a T&M vehicle dealer license issued to an applicant who has never been licensed as a T&M vehicle dealer in Virginia or whose Virginia T&M vehicle dealer license has been expired for more than thirty days.

"Relevant market area" means as follows:

1. In metropolitan localities with a population of 250,000, the relevant market area shall be a circular area around an existing franchised dealer not to exceed a radius of ten miles, but in no case less than seven miles.

2. If the population in an area within a radius of ten miles around an existing franchised dealer is less than 250,000, but the population in an area within a radius of fifteen miles around an existing franchised dealer is 150,000 or more, the relevant market area shall be that area within the fifteen-mile radius.

3. In all other cases the relevant market area shall be an area within a radius of twenty miles around an existing franchised dealer or the area of responsibility defined in the franchise, whichever is greater. In any case where the franchise agreement is silent as to area responsibility, the relevant market area shall be the greater of an area within a radius of twenty miles around an existing franchised dealer or that area in which the franchisor otherwise requires the franchisee to make significant retail sales or sales efforts.

In determining population for this definition, the most recent census by the U.S. Bureau of the Census or the most recent population update, either from the National Planning Data Corporation or other similar recognized source, shall be accumulated for all census tracts either wholly or partially within the relevant market area.

"Retail installment sale" means every sale of one or more T&M vehicles to a buyer for his use and not for resale, in which the price of the T&M vehicle is payable in one or more installments and in which the seller has either retained title to the goods or has taken or retained a security interest in the goods under form of contract designated either as a security agreement, conditional sale, bailment lease, chattel mortgage, or otherwise.

"Sale at retail" or "retail sale" means the act or attempted act of selling, bartering, exchanging, or otherwise disposing of a T&M vehicle to a buyer for his personal use and not for resale.

"Sale at wholesale" or "wholesale" means a sale to T&M vehicle dealers or wholesalers other than to consumers, or a sale to one who intends to resell.

"T&M vehicle" means motor homes and travel trailers as defined in this section.

"T&M vehicle dealer" or "dealer" means any person who:

1. For commission, money, or other thing of value, buys, sells, exchanges, either outright or on conditional sale, bailment lease, chattel mortgage, or otherwise or arranges or offers or attempts to solicit or negotiate on behalf of others a sale, purchase, or exchange of an interest in new T&M vehicles, new and used T&M vehicles, or used T&M vehicles alone, whether or not the T&M vehicles are owned by him;

2. Is wholly or partly engaged in the business of selling new T&M vehicles, new and used T&M vehicles, or used T&M vehicles only, whether or not the T&M vehicles are owned by him; or

3. Offers to sell, sells, displays, or permits the display for sale, of five or more T&M vehicles within any twelve consecutive months.

The term "T&M vehicle dealer" does not include:

1. Receivers, trustees, administrators, executors, guardians, conservators or other persons appointed by or acting under judgment or order of any court or their employees when engaged in the specific performance of their duties as employees.

2. Public officers, their deputies, assistants, or employees, while performing their official duties.

3. Persons other than business entities primarily engaged in the leasing or renting of T&M vehicles to others when selling or offering such vehicles for sale at retail, disposing of T&M vehicles acquired for their own use and actually so used, when the T&M vehicles have been so acquired and used in good faith and not for the purpose of avoiding the provisions of this chapter.

4. Persons dealing solely in the sale and distribution of fire-fighting equipment, ambulances, and funeral vehicles, including T&M vehicles adapted therefor; however, this exemption shall not exempt any person from the provisions of §§46.2-1919, 46.2-1920 and 46.2-1949.

5. Any financial institution chartered or authorized to do business under the laws of the Commonwealth or the United States which may have received title to a T&M vehicle in the normal course of its business by reason of a foreclosure, other taking, repossession, or voluntary reconveyance to that institution occurring as a result of any loan secured by a lien on the T&M vehicle.

6. An employee of an organization arranging for the purchase or lease by the organization of T&M vehicles for use in the organization's business.

7. Any person licensed to sell real estate who sells a manufactured home or similar vehicle in conjunction with the sale of the parcel of land on which the manufactured home or similar vehicle is located.

8. Any person who permits the operation of a T&M vehicle show or permits the display of T&M vehicles for sale by any T&M vehicle dealer licensed under this chapter.

9. An insurance company authorized to do business in the Commonwealth that sells or disposes of T&M vehicles under a contract with its insured in the regular course of business.

10. Any publication, broadcast, or other communications media when engaged in the business of advertising, but not otherwise arranging for the sale of T&M vehicles owned by others.

11. Any person dealing solely in the sale or lease of T&M vehicles designed exclusively for off-road use.

12. Any credit union authorized to do business in Virginia, provided the credit union does not receive a commission, money, or other thing of value directly from a T&M vehicle dealer.

13. Any person licensed as a manufactured home dealer, broker, manufacturer, or salesperson under Chapter 4.2 (§36-85.16 et seq.) of Title 36.

"T&M vehicle salesperson" or "salesperson" means any person who is licensed as and employed as a salesperson by a T&M vehicle dealer to sell or exchange T&M vehicles.

"T&M vehicle show" means a display of T&M vehicles to the general public at a location other than a dealer's location licensed under this chapter where the T&M vehicles are not being offered for sale or exchange during or as part of the display.

"Travel trailer" means a vehicle designed to provide temporary living quarters of such size or weight as not to require special highway movement permits when towed by a motor vehicle and having a gross trailer area less than 320 square feet.

"Used T&M vehicle" means any T&M vehicle other than a new T&M vehicle as defined in this section.

"Wholesale auction" means an auction of T&M vehicles restricted to sales at wholesale.
(Added by L.1995 chs. 767, 816; chgd. by L.1996 chs. 1043, 1052; L.1997 chs. 801, 848; L.1999 ch. 77, eff. 7/1/99.)

§46.2-1901. General powers of Commissioner.

The Commissioner shall promote the interest of the retail buyers of T&M vehicles and endeavor to prevent unfair methods of competition and unfair or deceptive acts or practices.
(Added by L.1995 chs. 767, 816, eff. 7/1/95.)

§§46.2-1902, 46.2-1903. *(Repealed by L.1996 chs. 1043, 1052, eff. 7/1/96.)*

§46.2-1904. Commissioner's powers with respect to hearings under this chapter.

The Commissioner may, in hearings arising under this chapter, determine the place in the Commonwealth where they shall be held; subpoena witnesses; take depositions of witnesses residing outside the Commonwealth in the manner provided for in civil actions in courts of record; pay these witnesses the fees and mileage for their attendance as is provided for witnesses in civil actions in courts of record; and administer oaths.
(Added by L.1995 chs. 767, 816, eff. 7/1/95.)

§46.2-1905. Suit to enjoin violations.

The Commissioner, whenever he believes from evidence submitted to him that any person has been violating, is violating or is about to violate any provision of this chapter, in addition to any other remedy, may bring an action in the name of the Commonwealth to enjoin any violation of this chapter.
(Added by L.1995 chs. 767, 816, eff. 7/1/95.)

§46.2-1906. Regulations.

The Commissioner may promulgate regulations requiring persons licensed under this chapter to keep and maintain records reasonably required for the enforcement of §§46.2-112 and 46.2-629, and any other regulations, not inconsistent with the provisions of this chapter, as he shall consider necessary for the effective administration and enforcement of this chapter. A copy of any regulation promulgated under this section shall be mailed to each T&M vehicle dealer licensee thirty days prior to its effective date.
(Added by L.1995 chs. 767, 816, eff. 7/1/95.)

§46.2-1907. Penalties.

Except as otherwise provided in this chapter, any person violating any of the provisions of this chapter may be assessed a civil penalty not to exceed $1,000 for any single violation. Civil penalties collected under this chapter shall be deposited into the Transportation Trust Fund.
(Added by L.1995 chs. 767, 816; chgd. by L.1996 chs. 1043, 1052, eff. 7/1/96.)

ARTICLE 2
T&M VEHICLE DEALER LICENSES

Section

§46.2-1908. Licenses required.

It shall be unlawful for any person to engage in business in the Commonwealth as a T&M vehicle dealer, salesperson, manufacturer, factory branch, distributor, distributor branch, or factory or distributor representative or as a motor vehicle manufacturer, factory branch, distributor, distributor branch, or factory or distributor representative as defined in §46.2-1500, without first obtaining a license as provided in this chapter. Every person licensed as a manufactured home dealer under Chapter 4.2 (§36-85.16 et seq.) of Title 36 shall obtain a certificate of dealer registration as provided in this chapter. Any person licensed in another state as a motor vehicle dealer or T&M vehicle dealer may sell motor vehicles or T&M vehicles at wholesale auctions in the Commonwealth after having obtained a certificate of dealer registration as provided in this chapter. Any nonprofit organization exempt from taxation under §501(c)(3) of the Internal Revenue Code, after having obtained a nonprofit organization certificate as provided in this chapter, may consign donated T&M vehicles to licensed Virginia T&M vehicle dealers. The offering or granting of a T&M vehicle dealer franchise in the Commonwealth shall constitute engaging in business in the Commonwealth for purposes of this section, and no new T&M vehicle may be sold or offered for sale in the Commonwealth unless the franchisor of T&M vehicle dealer franchises for that line-make in the Commonwealth, whether such franchisor is a manufacturer, factory branch, distributor, distributor branch, or otherwise, is licensed under this chapter. In the event a license issued under this chapter to a franchisor of T&M vehicle dealer franchises is suspended, revoked, or not renewed, nothing in this section shall prevent the sale of any new T&M vehicle of such franchisor's line-make manufactured in or brought into the Commonwealth for sale prior to the suspension, revocation or expiration of the license.

Violation of any provision of this section shall constitute a Class 1 misdemeanor.
(Added by L.1995 chs. 767, 816; chgd. by L.1997 ch. 848; L.2000 ch. 180, eff. 7/1/2000.)

§46.2-1908.1. Certification of certain nonprofit organizations.

Upon application to and approval by the Department, any nonprofit organization exempt from taxation under §501(c)(3) of the Internal Revenue Code may be issued a nonprofit organization certificate authorizing it to consign donated T&M vehicles to licensed Virginia T&M vehicle dealers when the nonprofit organization receives title to such T&M vehicles as qualified charitable gifts and titles the T&M vehicles in the name of the nonprofit organization.
(Added by L.2000 ch. 180, eff. 7/1/2000.)

§46.2-1909. Application for license or certificate of dealer registration.

Application for license or certificate of dealer registration under this chapter shall be made to the Commissioner and contain such information as the Commissioner shall require. The application shall be accompanied by the required fee.

The Commissioner shall require, in the application or otherwise, information relating to the matters set forth in §46.2-1985 as grounds for refusing licenses, certificates of dealer registration, and to other pertinent matters requisite for the safeguarding of the public interest, including, if the applicant is a dealer in new T&M vehicles with factory warranties, a copy of a current service agreement with the manufacturer or with the distributor, requiring the applicant to perform within a reasonable distance of his established place of business, the service, repair, and replacement work required of the manufacturer or distributor by such T&M vehicle warranty. All of these matters shall be considered by the Commissioner in determining the fitness of the applicant to engage in the business for which he seeks a license or certificate of dealer registration.

(Added by L.1995 chs. 767, 816; chgd. by L.1996 chs. 1043, 1052, eff. 7/1/96.)

§46.2-1910. Dealers required to have established place of business.

No license shall be issued to any T&M vehicle dealer unless he has an established place of business, owned or leased by him, where a substantial portion of the sales activity of the business is routinely conducted and which:

1. Satisfies all local zoning regulations;
2. Has sales, service, and office space devoted exclusively to the dealership of at least 250 square feet in a permanent, enclosed building not used as a residence;
3. Houses all records the dealer is required to maintain by §46.2-1929;
4. Is equipped with a desk, chairs, filing space, a working telephone listed in the name of the dealership, and working utilities including electricity and provisions for space heating;
5. Displays a sign and business hours as required by this chapter; and
6. Has contiguous space designated for the exclusive use of the dealer adequate to permit the display of at least ten T&M vehicles.

However, any licensee engaging in business exclusively as a dealer in used manufactured homes without inventory need not have contiguous display space and need have only 120 square feet of sales and office space devoted exclusively to its business.

Any person licensed by the Department as a dealer under any provision of this subtitle on June 30, 1996, shall be considered in compliance with subdivisions 2 and 6 of this section for that licensee.

(Added by L.1995 chs. 767, 816; chgd. by L.1996 chs. 1043, 1052, eff. 7/1/96.)

§46.2-1911. Dealer-operator to have certificate of qualification.

No license shall be issued to any T&M vehicle dealer unless the dealer-operator holds a valid certificate of qualification issued by the Department. Such certificate shall be issued only on application to the Department, payment of a twenty-five dollar application fee, the successful completion of an examination prepared and administered by the Department, and other prerequisites as set forth in this section. However, any individual who is the dealer-operator of a dealer licensed by the Department under any provision of this subtitle on June 30, 1996, shall be entitled to such a certificate without examination on application to the Department made on or before January 1, 1997.

The Commissioner may establish minimum qualifications for applicants and require applicants to satisfactorily complete courses of study or other prerequisites prior to taking the examination.

(Added by L.1995 chs. 767, 816; chgd. by L.1996 chs. 1043, 1052, eff. 7/1/96.)

§46.2-1912. Salesperson to have certificate of qualification.

No license shall be issued to any T&M vehicle salesperson unless he holds a valid certificate of qualification issued by the Department. A certificate shall be issued only on application to the Department, payment of a twenty-five dollar application fee, the successful completion of an examination prepared and administered by the Department, and other prerequisites as set forth in this section. However, any individual who is licensed as a salesperson by the Department under any provision of this subtitle on June 30, 1996, shall be entitled to such a certificate without examination on application to the Department made on or before January 1, 1997.

The Commissioner may establish minimum qualifications for applicants and require applicants to satisfactorily complete courses of study or other prerequisites prior to taking the examination.

(Added by L.1995 chs. 767, 816; chgd. by L.1996 chs. 1043, 1052, eff. 7/1/96.)

§46.2-1913. Continued operation on loss of a dealer-operator holding certificate of qualification.

Each dealer shall notify the Department in writing immediately when a dealer-operator who holds a certificate of qualification dies, becomes disabled, retires, is removed, or for any other cause ceases to act as dealer-operator. The dealer may continue to operate for 120 days thereafter without a dealer-operator and may be granted approval by the Department to operate for an additional sixty days on application and with good cause shown for such delay.

(Added by L.1995 chs. 767, 816, eff. 7/1/95.)

§46.2-1914. Action on applications; hearing on denial; denial for failure to have established place of business.

The Commissioner shall act on all applications for a license or certificate of dealer registration under this chapter within sixty days after receipt by either granting or refusing the application. Any applicant denied a license or certificate shall, on his written request filed within thirty days, be given a hearing at a time and place determined by the Commissioner or a person designated by him. All hearings under this section shall be public and shall be held promptly. The applicant may be represented by counsel.

Any applicant denied a license for failure to have an established place of business as provided in §46.2-1910 may not, nor shall anyone, apply for a license for premises for which a license was denied for thirty days from the date of the rejection of the application.

(Added by L.1995 chs. 767, 816, eff. 7/1/95.)

§46.2-1915. Location to be specified; display of license; change of location.

The licenses of T&M vehicle dealers, manufacturers, factory branches, distributors, and distributor branches and the licenses of motor vehicle manufacturers, factory branches, distributors and distributor branches, shall specify the location of each place of business, branch or other location occupied or to be occupied by the licensee in conducting his business and the license issued therefor shall be conspicuously displayed at each of the premises. If any licensee intends to change a licensed location, he shall provide the Commissioner thirty days' advance written notice, and a successful inspection of the new location shall be required prior to approval of a change of location. The Commissioner shall endorse the change of location on the license, without charge, if the new location is within the same county or city. A change in location to another county or city shall require a new license and fee. Nothing contained in this section shall prevent a licensee engaged in business exclusively as a dealer in used manufactured homes without inventory from conducting business in any county or city other than the county or city in which his established place of business is maintained.

(Added by L.1995 chs. 767, 816, eff. 7/1/95.)

§46.2-1916. Supplemental sales locations.

The Commissioner may issue a license for a licensed T&M vehicle dealer to display for sale or sell T&M vehicles at locations other than his established place of business, subject to compliance with local ordinances and requirements.

A permanent supplemental license may be issued for premises less than 500 yards from the dealer's established place of business, provided a sign is displayed as required for the established place of business. A supplemental license shall not be required for premises otherwise contiguous to the established place of business except for a public thoroughfare.

A temporary supplemental license may be issued for a period not to exceed seven days, provided that the application is made fifteen days prior to the sale. A temporary supplemental license for the sale of new T&M vehicles may be issued only for locations within the dealer's area of responsibility, as defined in his franchise or sales agreement, unless proof is provided that all dealers in the same line-make in whose areas of responsibility, as defined in their franchise or sales agreements, where the temporary supplemental license is sought do not oppose the issuance of the temporary license.

However, the application for a temporary supplemental license may be made five business days prior to the sale if the applicant submits evidence that the location is in compliance with all applicable local ordinances and that all other requirements of this section have been met. The application shall include affirmative proof of no opposition, in the form of letters signed by all dealers in the same line-make in whose areas of responsibility, as defined in their franchise or sales agreements, where the temporary supplemental license is sought, approving the Department's granting the temporary supplemental license.

A temporary supplemental license for sale of used T&M vehicles may be issued only for the county, city, or town in which the dealer is licensed pursuant to §46.2-1910, or for a contiguous county, city, or town. Temporary licenses may be issued without regard to the foregoing geographic restrictions where the dealer operating under a temporary license provides notice, at least thirty days before any proposed sale under a temporary license, to all other dealers licensed in the jurisdiction in which the sale will occur of the intent to conduct a sale and permits any locally licensed dealer who wishes to do so to participate in the sale on the same terms as the dealer operating under the temporary license. Any locally licensed dealer who chooses to participate in the sale must obtain a temporary supplemental license for the sale pursuant to this section.

(Added by L.1995 chs. 767, 816; chgd. by L.1996 chs. 1043, 1052, eff. 7/1/96.)

§46.2-1917. Changes in form of ownership, line-make, name.

Any change in the form of ownership or the addition or deletion of a partner shall require a new application, license, and fee.

Any addition or deletion of a franchise or change in the name of a dealer shall require immediate notification to the Department, and the Commissioner shall endorse the change on the license without a fee. The change of an officer or director of a corporation shall be made at the time of license renewal.

(Added by L.1995 chs. 767, 816, eff. 7/1/95.)

§46.2-1918. Display of salesperson's license; notice on termination.

No salesperson shall be employed by more than one dealer, unless the dealers are owned by the same person.

Each dealer shall maintain a list of salespersons employed.

Each salesperson and each T&M vehicle and motor vehicle factory representative and distributor representative shall carry his license when engaged in his business and shall display it on request.

Each dealer and each motor vehicle and T&M vehicle manufacturer and distributor shall notify the Department in writing not later than the tenth day of the month following the termination of any licensed salesperson's or representative's employment. In lieu of written notification, the license of the terminated salesperson or representative may be returned to the Department annotated "terminated" on the face of the license and signed and dated by the dealer-operator, owner, or officer.

(Added by L.1995 chs. 767, 816; chgd. by L.1996 chs. 1043, 1052, eff. 7/1/96.)

§46.2-1919. License and registration fees; additional to other licenses and fees required by law.

A. The fee for each license and registration year or part thereof shall be as follows:

1. For T&M vehicle dealers, $100 for each principal place of business, plus $20 for each supplemental license.

2. For T&M and motor vehicle manufacturers, distributors, and each factory branch and distributor branch, $100.

3. For T&M and motor vehicle rebuilder salespersons, factory representatives, and distributor representatives, $10.

4. For motor vehicle dealers and T&M vehicle dealers licensed in other states, but not in Virginia, a registration fee of $50.

5. For manufactured home dealers, a registration fee of $50.

B. The licenses, registrations, and fees required by this chapter are in addition to licenses, taxes, and fees imposed by other provisions of law and nothing contained in this chapter shall exempt any person from any license, tax, or fee imposed by any other provision of law. However, the Commissioner may waive fees for those licensed under Chapter 15, 19.1, or 19.2 of this title; the Commissioner shall waive the fee for nonprofit organizations certified under Chapter 15, 19.1, or 19.2 of this title.

C. The fee for any nonprofit organization issued a certificate pursuant to §46.2-1908.1 shall be $25 per year or any part thereof.

D. No nonprofit organization granted a certificate pursuant to §46.2-1908.1 shall, either orally or in writing, assign a value to any donated vehicle for the purpose of establishing tax deduction amounts on any federal or state income tax return.

(Added by L.1995 chs. 767, 816; chgd. by L.1996 chs. 1043, 1052; L.2000 ch. 180, eff. 7/1/2000.)

§46.2-1920. Collection of license and registration fees; payments from fund.

All licensing and registration fees provided for in this chapter, except as identified in Article 3 (§46.2-1927) of this chapter, shall be collected by the Commissioner and paid

into the state treasury and set aside as a special fund to meet the expenses of the Department.
(Added by L.1995 chs. 767, 816, eff. 7/1/95.)

§46.2-1921. Issuance, expiration, and renewal of licenses and certificates of registration.

A. All licenses and certificates of registration issued under this chapter shall be issued for a period of twelve consecutive months except, at the discretion of the Commissioner, the periods may be adjusted as is necessary to distribute the licenses and certificates as equally as practicable on a monthly basis. The expiration date shall be the last day of the twelfth month of validity or the last day of the designated month. Every license and certificate of registration shall be renewed annually on application by the licensee or registrant and by payment of fees required by law, the renewal to take effect on the first day of the succeeding month.

B. Licenses and certificates of registration issued under this chapter shall be deemed not to have expired if the renewal application and required fees as set forth in this subsection are received by the Commissioner or postmarked not more than thirty days after the expiration date of such license or certificate of registration. Whenever the renewal application is received by the Commissioner or postmarked no more than thirty days after the expiration date of such license or certificate of registration, the license fees shall be 150 percent of the fees provided for in §46.2-1919.

C. The Commissioner may offer an optional multi-year license. When such option is offered and chosen by the licensee, all annual and twelve-month fees due at the time of licensing shall be multiplied by the number of years or fraction thereof for which the license will be issued.
(Added by L.1995 chs. 767, 816; chgd. by L.1997 ch. 848; L.1998 ch. 325, eff. 1/1/99.)

ARTICLE 3
BONDING REQUIREMENTS

§46.2-1927. Bonding requirements for applicants for license.

Every applicant for an original, second year renewal, and third year renewal dealer's license shall obtain and file with the Commissioner a bond in the amount of $25,000. However, no dealer shall be required to obtain more than one $25,000 bond for all licenses held under this subtitle. Any dealer who is licensed under Chapter 15 of this title and who obtains a T&M vehicle dealer license under this chapter, shall be exempt from the bond requirements set out in this section. In addition, any person who purchases a T&M vehicle from a dealer who is licensed under Chapter 15 of this title, shall have access to the Motor Vehicle Transaction Recovery Fund as prescribed in Article 3 (§46.2-1527 et seq.) of Chapter 15 of this title. The bond shall come from a corporate surety licensed to do business in the Commonwealth and approved by the Attorney General. The bond shall be conditioned on a statement by the applicant that the applicant will not practice fraud, make any fraudulent representation, or violate any provision of this chapter in the conduct of the applicant's business. The Commissioner may, without holding a hearing, suspend the dealer's license during the period that the dealer does not have a sufficient bond on file.

If a person suffers any of the following: (i) loss or damage in connection with the purchase of a T&M vehicle by reason of fraud practiced on him or fraudulent representation made to him by a licensed T&M vehicle dealer or one of the dealer's salespersons acting within his scope of employment; (ii) loss or damage by reason of the violation by a dealer or salesperson of any provision of this chapter in connection with the purchase of a T&M vehicle; or (iii) loss or damage resulting from a breach of an extended service contract entered into on or after the effective date of this act, as defined by §59.1-435, that person shall have a claim against the dealer and the dealer's bond, and may recover such damages as may be awarded to such person by final judgment of a court of competent jurisdiction against the dealer as a proximate result of such loss or damage up to, but not exceeding, the amount of the bond, from such surety, who shall be subrogated to the rights of such person against the dealer or salesperson. The liability of such surety shall be limited to actual damages, and shall not include any punitive damages or attorneys' fees assessed against the dealer or salesperson.

The dealer's surety shall notify the Department when a claim is made against a dealer's bond, when a claim is paid and when the bond is cancelled. Such notification shall include the amount of a claim and the circumstances surrounding the claim. Notification of cancellation shall include the effective date and reason for cancellation. The bond may be cancelled as to future liability by the dealer's surety upon thirty days' notice to the Department.
(Added by L.1995 chs. 767, 816; chgd. by L.1996 chs. 1043, 1052, eff. 7/1/96.)

ARTICLE 4
CONDUCT OF BUSINESS

§46.2-1928. Examination or audit of licensee; costs.

The Commissioner or authorized representatives of the Department may examine, during the posted business hours, the records required to be maintained by this chapter. If a licensee is found to have violated this chapter or any order of the Commissioner, the actual cost of the examination shall be paid by the licensee so examined within thirty days after demand therefor by the Commissioner. The Commissioner may maintain an action for the recovery of these costs in any court of competent jurisdiction.
(Added by L.1995 chs. 767, 816, eff. 7/1/95.)

§46.2-1929. Dealer records.

All dealer records regarding employees; lists of vehicles in inventory for sale, resale, or on consignment; vehicle purchases, sales, trades, and transfers of ownership; collections of taxes; titling, uninsured T&M vehicle and registration fees; odometer disclosure statements; records of permanent dealer registration plates assigned to the dealer and temporary transport plates and temporary certificates of ownership; and other records required by the Department shall be maintained on the premises of the licensed location. The Commissioner may, on written request by a dealer, permit his records to be maintained at a location other than the premises of the licensed location for good cause shown. All dealer records shall be preserved in original form or in film, magnetic, or optical media (including but not limited to microfilm, microfiche, or other electronic media) for a period of five years in a manner that permits systematic retrieval. Certain records may be maintained on a computerized record-keeping system with the prior approval of the Commissioner.

(Added by L.1995 chs. 767, 816; chgd. by L.2000 ch. 128, eff. 7/1/2000.)

§46.2-1930. Buyer's order.

A. Every T&M vehicle dealer shall complete, in duplicate, a buyer's order for each sale or exchange of a vehicle. A copy of the buyer's order form shall be made available to a prospective buyer during the negotiating phase of a sale and prior to any sales agreement. The completed original shall be retained for a period of four years in accordance with §46.2-1929, and a duplicate copy shall be delivered to the purchaser at the time of sale or exchange. A buyer's order shall include:

1. The name and address of the person to whom the vehicle was sold or traded.
2. The date of the sale or trade.
3. The name and address of the T&M vehicle dealer selling or trading the vehicle.
4. The make, model year, vehicle identification number and body style of the vehicle.
5. The sale price of the vehicle.
6. The amount of any cash deposit made by the buyer.
7. A description of any vehicle used as a trade-in and the amount credited the buyer for the trade-in. The description of the trade-in shall be the same as outlined in subdivision 4 of this subsection.
8. The amount of any sales and use tax, title fee, uninsured vehicle fee, registration fee, or other fee required by law for which the buyer is responsible and the dealer has collected. Each tax and fee shall be individually listed and identified.
9. The net balance due at settlement.
10. Any item designated as "processing fee," and the amount charged by the dealer, if any, for processing the transaction. As used in this section processing includes obtaining title and license plates for the purchaser.
11. Any item designated as "dealer's business license tax," and the amount charged by the dealer, if any.
12. For sales involving dealer-arranged financing, the following notice, printed in bold type no less than ten-point:

"THIS SALE IS CONDITIONED UPON APPROVAL OF YOUR PROPOSED RETAIL INSTALLMENT SALE CONTRACT AS SUBMITTED TO OR THROUGH THE DEALER. IF THAT PROPOSED RETAIL INSTALLMENT SALE CONTRACT IS NOT APPROVED UNDER THE TERMS AGREED TO WITH THE DEALER, YOU MAY CANCEL THIS SALE AND ANY DOWN PAYMENT AND/OR TRADE-IN YOU SUBMITTED WILL BE RETURNED TO YOU, PROVIDED THAT ANY VEHICLE DELIVERED TO YOU BY THE DEALER PURSUANT TO THIS AGREEMENT IS RETURNED TO THE DEALER IN THE SAME CONDITION AS DELIVERED TO YOU, NORMAL WEAR AND TEAR EXCEPTED, WITHIN TWENTY-FOUR HOURS OF WRITTEN OR ORAL NOTICE TO YOU OF THE CREDIT DENIAL."

If the transaction does not include a policy of liability insurance, the seller shall stamp or mark on the face of the bill of sale in boldface letters no smaller than eighteen point type the following words: "No Liability Insurance Included."

A completed buyer's order when signed by both buyer and seller may constitute a bill of sale.

B. The Commissioner shall approve a buyer's order form and each dealer shall file with each original license application its buyer's order form, on which the processing fee amount is stated.

C. If a processing fee is charged, that fact and the amount of the processing fee shall be disclosed by the dealer. Disclosure shall be by placing a clear and conspicuous sign in the public sales area of the dealership. The sign shall be no smaller than eight and one-half inches by eleven inches and the print shall be no smaller than one-half inch, and in a form as approved by the Commissioner.

(Added by L.1995 chs. 767, 816; chgd. by L.1996 chs. 1043, 1052; L.2000 ch. 116, eff. 7/1/2000.)

§46.2-1931. Consignment vehicles; contract.

Any T&M vehicle dealer offering a T&M vehicle for sale on consignment shall have in his possession a consignment contract for the T&M vehicle, executed and signed by the dealer and the consignor. The consignment contract shall include:

1. The complete name, address, and the telephone number of the owners.
2. The name, address, and dealer certificate number of the selling dealer.
3. A complete description of the T&M vehicle on consignment, including the make, model year, vehicle identification number, and body style.
4. The beginning and termination dates of the contract.
5. The percentage of commission, the amount of the commission, or the net amount the owner is to receive, if the T&M vehicle is sold.
6. Any fees for which the owner is responsible.
7. A disclosure of all unsatisfied liens on the T&M vehicle and the location of the certificate of title to the T&M vehicle.
8. A requirement that the T&M vehicle pass a safety inspection prior to sale.

If any T&M vehicle on consignment from a certified nonprofit organization is found not to be in compliance with any safety inspection requirement, the T&M dealer shall furnish any buyer intending to use that T&M vehicle on the public highways a written disclosure, prior to sale, that the T&M vehicle did not pass a safety inspection.

Any dealer offering a T&M vehicle for sale on consignment shall inform any prospective customer that the T&M vehicle is on consignment.

Dealer license plates shall not be used to demonstrate a T&M vehicle on consignment except on (i) T&M vehicles with gross vehicle weight of 15,000 pounds or more, (ii) T&M vehicles on consignment from another licensed T&M vehicle dealer, and (iii) T&M vehicles on consignment from a nonprofit organization certified pursuant to §46.2-1908.1. The owner's license plates may be used if liability insurance coverage is in effect in the amounts prescribed by §46.2-472.

No vehicles other than T&M vehicles shall be sold on consignment by T&M vehicle dealers.
(Added by L.1995 chs. 767, 816; chgd. by L.1996 chs. 1043, 1052; L.2000 ch. 180, eff. 7/1/2000.)

§46.2-1932. Odometer disclosure.

Every T&M vehicle dealer shall comply with all requirements of the Federal Odometer Act and §46.2-629 by completing the appropriate odometer mileage statement form for each vehicle purchased, sold or transferred, or in any other way acquired or disposed of. Odometer disclosure statements shall be maintained by the dealer in a manner that permits systematic retrieval. Any person found violating any of the provisions of this section shall be guilty of a Class 1 misdemeanor.
(Added by L.1995 chs. 767, 816, eff. 7/1/95.)

§46.2-1933. Certain disclosures required by manufacturers and distributors.

T&M vehicle manufacturers and distributors shall affix or cause to be affixed in a conspicuous place to every T&M vehicle offered for sale as a new T&M vehicle a statement disclosing the place of assembly or manufacture of the T&M vehicle. For disclosures of place of assembly, the assembly plant shall be the same as that designated by the T&M vehicle identification number.

The provisions of this section shall apply only to T&M vehicles manufactured for the 1991 or subsequent model years.
(Added by L.1995 chs. 767, 816; chgd. by L.1996 chs. 1043, 1052, eff. 7/1/96.)

§46.2-1934. Business hours.

Each T&M vehicle dealer shall be open for business a minimum of twenty hours per week, at least ten of which shall be between the hours of 9:00 a.m. and 5:00 p.m. Monday through Friday, except that the Commissioner, on written request by a dealer, may modify these requirements for good cause. Each licensee engaged in business exclusively as a dealer in used manufactured homes without inventory shall be open for business a minimum of two consecutive hours per week between the hours of 9:00 a.m. and 5:00 p.m. Monday through Friday. The dealer's hours shall be posted and maintained conspicuously on or near the main entrance of each place of business.

Each dealer shall include his business hours on the original and every renewal application for a license, and changes to these hours shall be immediately filed with the Department.
(Added by L.1995 chs. 767, 816, eff. 7/1/95.)

§46.2-1935. Signs.

Each retail T&M vehicle dealer's place of business shall be identified by a permanent sign visible from the front of the business office so that the public may quickly and easily identify the dealership. The sign shall contain the dealer's trade name in letters no less than six inches in height unless otherwise restricted by law or contract.

Each licensee engaged in business exclusively as a dealer in used manufactured homes without inventory shall be identified by a permanent sign visible from the front of the business office so that the public may quickly and easily identify the dealership. The sign shall contain the dealer's trade name in letters no less than two inches in height unless otherwise restricted by law or contract.
(Added by L.1995 chs. 767, 816, eff. 7/1/95.)

§46.2-1936. Advertisements.

Unless the dealer is clearly identified by name, whenever any licensee places an advertisement in any newspaper or publication, the abbreviations "VA DLR," denoting a Virginia licensed dealer, shall appear therein.
(Added by L.1995 chs. 767, 816, eff. 7/1/95.)

§46.2-1937. Coercing purchaser to provide insurance coverage on T&M vehicle.

It shall be unlawful for any dealer or salesperson or any employee of a dealer or representative of either to coerce or offer anything of value to any purchaser of a T&M vehicle to provide any type of insurance coverage on the T&M vehicle.

Nothing in this section shall prohibit a dealer from requiring that a retail customer obtain automobile physical damage insurance to protect collateral secured by an installment sales contract. Any person found guilty of violating any provisions of this section shall be guilty of a Class 1 misdemeanor.
(Added by L.1995 chs. 767, 816, eff. 7/1/95.)

§46.2-1938. Prohibited solicitation and compensation.

It shall be unlawful for any T&M vehicle dealer or salesperson licensed under this chapter, directly or indirectly, to solicit the sale of a T&M vehicle through a person with a pecuniary interest, or to pay, or cause to be paid, any commission or compensation in any form whatsoever to any person in connection with the sale of a T&M vehicle, unless the person is duly licensed as a salesperson employed by the dealer.
(Added by L.1995 chs. 767, 816, eff. 7/1/95.)

§46.2-1939. Salesperson selling for other than his employer prohibited.

It shall be unlawful for any T&M vehicle salesperson licensed under this chapter to sell or exchange or offer or attempt to sell or exchange any T&M vehicle except for the licensed T&M vehicle dealer by whom he is employed, or to offer, transfer, or assign any sale or exchange that he may have negotiated to any other dealer or salesperson.
(Added by L.1995 chs. 767, 816, eff. 7/1/95.)

§46.2-1940. Inspection of vehicles required.

No person required to be licensed as a dealer under this chapter shall sell at retail any T&M vehicle which is intended by the buyer for use on the public highways, and which is required to comply with the safety inspection requirements provided in Article 21 (§46.2-1157 et seq.) of Chapter 10 of this title unless between the time the vehicle comes into the possession of the dealer and the time it is sold at retail it is inspected by an official safety inspection station. If the vehicle is found not to be in compliance with all safety inspection requirements, the dealer shall either take steps to bring it into compliance or shall furnish any buyer intending it for use on the public highway a written disclosure, prior to sale, that the vehicle did not pass a safety inspection. Any person found guilty of violating any provisions of this section shall be guilty of a Class 1 misdemeanor.
(Added by L.1995 chs. 767, 816, eff. 7/1/95.)

§46.2-1941. Inspections prior to sale not required of certain sellers.

The provisions of §§46.2-1158 and 46.2-1940 requiring inspection of any T&M vehicle prior to sale at retail shall not apply to any person conducting a public auction for the sale of T&M vehicles at retail, provided that the individual, firm, or business conducting the auction has not taken title to the vehicle, but is acting as an agent for the sale of the vehicle. Nor shall the provisions of §§46.2-1158 and 46.2-1940 requiring inspection of any T&M vehicle prior to sale at retail apply to any new T&M vehicle or vehicles sold on the basis of a special order placed by a dealer with a manufacturer outside Virginia on behalf of a customer who is a nonresident of Virginia and takes delivery outside Virginia.
(Added by L.1995 chs. 767, 816, eff. 7/1/95.)

§46.2-1942. *(Repealed by L.1996 chs. 1043, 1052, eff. 7/1/96.)*

§46.2-1943. Temporary certificates of ownership.

A. Notwithstanding §§46.2-617 and 46.2-628, whenever a dealer licensed by the Department sells and delivers to a purchaser a vehicle and is unable at the time of the sale to deliver to the purchaser the certificate of title or certificate of origin for the vehicle because the certificate of title or certificate of origin is lost or is being detained by another in possession or for any other reason beyond the dealer's control, the dealer shall execute, on forms provided by the Commissioner, a temporary certificate of ownership. The certificate shall bear its date of issuance, the name and address of the purchaser, the identification number of the vehicle, the registration number to be used temporarily on the vehicle, the name of the state in which the vehicle is to be registered, the name and address of the person from whom the dealer acquired the vehicle, and whatever other information may be required by the Commissioner. A copy of the temporary certificate and a bona fide bill of sale shall be delivered to the purchaser and shall be in the possession of the purchaser at all times when operating the vehicle. One copy of the certificate shall be retained by the dealer and shall be subject to inspection at any time by the Department's agents. The original of the certificate shall be forwarded by the dealer to the Department directly on issuance to the purchaser if the vehicle is to be titled outside the Commonwealth, along with application for title. The issuance of a temporary certificate of ownership to a purchaser pursuant to this section shall have the effect of vesting ownership of the vehicle in the purchaser for the period that the certificate remains effective.

B. A temporary certificate of ownership issued by a dealer to a purchaser pursuant to this section shall expire on receipt by the purchaser of a certificate of title to the vehicle issued by the Department in the name of the purchaser, but in no event shall any temporary certificate of ownership issued under this section be effective for more than thirty days from the date of its issuance. In the event that the dealer fails to produce the old certificate of title or certificate of origin to the vehicle or fails to apply for a replacement certificate of title pursuant to §46.2-632, thereby preventing delivery to the Department or purchaser before the expiration of the temporary certificate of ownership, the purchaser's ownership of the vehicle may terminate and the purchaser shall have the right to return the vehicle to the dealer and obtain a full refund of all payments made toward the purchase of the vehicle, less any damage to the vehicle incurred while ownership was vested in the purchaser, and less a reasonable amount for use not to exceed one-half the amount allowed per mile by the Internal Revenue Service, as provided by regulation, revenue procedure, or revenue ruling promulgated pursuant to §162 of the Internal Revenue Code, for use of a personal vehicle for business purposes.

C. Notwithstanding subsection B of this section, if the dealer fails to deliver the certificate of title or certificate of origin to the purchaser within thirty days, a second temporary certificate of ownership may be issued. However, the dealer shall, not later than the expiration of the first temporary certificate, deliver to the Department an application for title, copy of the bill of sale, all required fees and a written statement of facts describing the dealer's efforts to secure the certificate of title or certificate of origin to the vehicle. On receipt of the title application with attachments as described herein, the Department shall record the purchaser's ownership of the vehicle and may authorize the dealer to issue a second thirty-day temporary certificate of ownership. If the dealer does not produce the certificate of title or certificate of origin to the vehicle before the expiration of the second temporary certificate, the purchaser's ownership of the vehicle may terminate and he shall have the right to return the vehicle as provided in subsection B of this section.

D. If the dealer is unable to produce the certificate of title or certificate of origin to the vehicle within the sixty-day period from the date of issuance of the first temporary certificate, the Department may extend temporary ownership for an additional period of up to ninety days, provided the dealer makes application in the format required by the Department. If the dealer does not produce the certificate of title or certificate of origin to the vehicle before the expiration of the additional ninety-day period, the purchaser's ownership of the vehicle may terminate and he shall have the right to return the vehicle as provided in subsection B of this section.

E. The Commissioner, on determining that the provisions of this section or the directions of the Department are not being complied with by a dealer, may, after a hearing, suspend the right of the dealer to issue temporary certificates of ownership.

(Added by L.1995 chs. 767, 816; chgd. by L.1996 chs. 1043, 1052, eff. 7/1/96.)

§46.2-1944. Use of old license plates and registration number on a motor home.

An owner who sells or transfers a registered T&M vehicle may have the license plates and the registration number transferred to a T&M vehicle titled in the owner's name according to the provisions of Chapter 6 (§46.2-600 et seq.), which is in a like vehicle category as specified in §46.2-694 and which requires an identical registration fee, on application to the Department accompanied by a fee of two dollars or, if the T&M vehicle requires a greater registration fee than that for which the license plates were assigned, on the payment of a fee of two dollars and the amount of the difference in registration fees between the two vehicles, all such transfers shall be in accordance with the regulations of the Department. All fees collected under this section shall be paid by the Commissioner into the state treasury and shall be set aside as a special fund to be used to meet the expenses of the Department. For purposes of this section, a T&M vehicle dealer licensed by the Department may be authorized to act as an agent of the Department for the purpose of receiving, processing, and approving applications from its customers for assignment of license plates and registration numbers pursuant to this section, using the forms and following the procedures prescribed by the Department. The Commissioner, on determining that the provisions of this section or the directions of the Department are not being complied with by a dealer, may suspend, after a hearing, the authority of the dealer to receive, process, and approve the assignment of license plates and registration numbers pursuant to this section.

(Added by L.1995 chs. 767, 816; chgd. by L.1996 chs. 1043, 1052, eff. 7/1/96.)

§46.2-1945. Certificate of title for dealers.

Except as otherwise provided in this chapter, every dealer shall obtain, on the purchase of each vehicle, a certificate of title issued to the dealer or shall obtain an assignment or reassignment of a certificate of title for each vehicle purchased, except that a certificate of title shall not be required for any new vehicle to be sold as such.

(Added by L.1995 chs. 767, 816, eff. 7/1/95.)

§46.2-1946. Termination of business.

No dealer, unless his license has been suspended, revoked, or canceled, shall cease business without a thirty-day prior notification to the Department. On cessation of the business, the dealer shall immediately surrender to the Department the dealer's certificate of license, all salespersons'

licenses, all dealer and temporary license plates, all fees and taxes collected, and any other materials furnished by the Department. After cessation of business, the former licensee shall continue to maintain and make available to the Department dealer records as set forth in this chapter.
(Added by L.1995 chs. 767, 816, eff. 7/1/95.)

ARTICLE 5
T&M DEALER LICENSE PLATES

§46.2-1947. Registration of dealers; fees.

Every manufacturer, distributor, or dealer, before he commences to operate T&M vehicles in his inventory for sale or resale, shall apply to the Commissioner for a dealer's certificate of vehicle registration and license plates. For the purposes of this article, a vehicle is in inventory when it is owned by, or assigned to, a dealer and is offered and available for sale or resale. All dealer's certificates of vehicle registration and license plates issued under this section may, at the discretion of the Commissioner, be placed in a system of staggered issue to distribute the work of issuing vehicle registration certificates and license plates as uniformly as practicable throughout the year. Dealerships which sold fewer than twenty-five vehicles during the last twelve months of the preceding license year shall be eligible to receive no more than two dealer's license plates; dealerships which sold at least twenty-five but fewer than fifty vehicles during the last twelve months of the preceding license year shall be eligible to receive no more than four dealer's license plates. However, dealerships which sold fifty or more T&M vehicles during their current license year may apply for additional license plates not to exceed four times the number of licensed salespersons employed by that dealership. Dealerships which sold fifty or more T&M vehicles during the last twelve months of the preceding license year shall be eligible to receive a number of dealer's license plates not to exceed four times the number of licensed salespersons employed by that dealership. A new applicant for a dealership shall be eligible to receive a number of dealer's license plates not to exceed four times the number of licensed salespersons employed by that dealership. For the purposes of this article, a salesperson or employee shall be considered to be employed only if he (i) works for the dealership at least twenty-five hours each week on a regular basis and (ii) is compensated for this work. All salespersons' or employees' employment records shall be retained in accordance with the provisions of §46.2-1929. A salesperson shall not be considered employed, within the meaning of this section, if he is an independent contractor as defined by the United States Internal Revenue Code. The fee for the issuance of dealer's license plates shall be thirty dollars per year for the first two dealer's license plates and thirteen dollars per year for each additional dealer's license plate.
(Added by L.1995 chs. 767, 816; chgd. by L.1996 chs. 1043, 1052, eff. 7/1/96.)

§46.2-1948. License under this chapter prerequisite to receiving dealer's license plates; insurance required; Commissioner may revoke plates.

No T&M vehicle manufacturer, distributor, or dealer, unless licensed under this chapter, shall be entitled to receive or maintain any dealer's license plates. It shall be unlawful to use or permit the use of any dealer's license plates for which there is no liability insurance coverage or a certificate of self-insurance as defined in §46.2-368 on any T&M vehicle. No dealer's license plates shall be issued unless the dealer certifies to the Department that there is liability insurance coverage or a certificate of self-insurance with respect to each dealer's license plate to be issued. Such liability insurance or a certificate of self-insurance shall be maintained for each dealer's license plate for so long as the registration for the dealer's license plate remains valid without regard to whether the plate is actually being used on a T&M vehicle. If insurance or a certificate of self-insurance is not so maintained, the dealer's license plate shall be surrendered to the Department. The Commissioner shall revoke any dealer's license plate for which there is no insurance or a certificate of self-insurance. The Commissioner may also revoke any dealer's license plate that has been used in any way not authorized by the provisions of this title.
(Added by L.1995 chs. 767, 816; chgd. by L.1996 chs. 1043, 1052, eff. 7/1/96.)

§46.2-1949. Transferable dealer's license plates.

In lieu of registering each T&M vehicle, a manufacturer, distributor, or dealer owning and operating any T&M vehicle on any highway may obtain a dealer's license plate from the Department, on application therefor on the prescribed form and on payment of the fees required by law. These license plates shall be attached to each T&M vehicle as required by subsection A of §46.2-711. Each plate shall bear a distinctive number, and the name of the Commonwealth, which may be abbreviated, together with the word "dealer" or a distinguishing symbol indicating that the plate is issued to a manufacturer, distributor, or dealer. Month and year decals indicating the date of expiration shall be affixed to each license plate. Any license plates so issued may, during the calendar year or years for which they have been issued, be transferred from one T&M vehicle to another, used or operated by the manufacturer, distributor, or dealer, who shall keep a written record of the T&M vehicle on which the dealer's license plates are used. This record shall be in a format approved by the Commissioner and shall be open to inspection by any law-enforcement officer or any officer or employee of the Department.

Display of a transferable manufacturer's, distributor's, or dealer's license plate or plates on a T&M vehicle shall subject the vehicle to the requirements of §§46.2-1038 and 46.2-1056.

All manufacturer's, distributor's, and dealer's license plates shall be issued for a period of twelve consecutive months except, at the discretion of the Commissioner, the periods may be adjusted as may be necessary to distribute the registrations as equally as practicable on a monthly basis. The expiration date shall be the last day of the twelfth month of validity or the last day of the designated month. Every license plate shall be renewed annually on application by the owner and by payment of fees required by law, such renewal to take effect on the first day of the succeeding month.

The Commissioner may offer an optional multi-year license plate registration to manufacturers, distributors, and dealers licensed pursuant to this chapter provided that he has chosen to offer optional multi-year licensing to such persons pursuant to §46.2-1921. When such option is offered and chosen by the licensee, all annual and twelve-month fees due at the time of registration shall be multiplied by the number of years or fraction thereof the licensee will be licensed pursuant to §46.2-1921.

(Added by L.1995 chs. 767, 816; chgd. by L.1996 chs. 1043, 1052, eff. 7/1/96.)

§46.2-1950. Dealer's license plates to distinguish between various types of dealers.

The Commissioner shall provide for the issuance of appropriate franchised or independent dealer's license plates so as to distinguish between factory dealers and T&M dealers.

(Added by L.1995 chs. 767, 816; chgd. by L.1996 chs. 1043, 1052, eff. 7/1/96.)

§46.2-1951. Dealer's promotional license plates.

In addition to any other license plate authorized by this article, the Commissioner may issue dealer's promotional license plates to a dealership for use on T&M vehicles held for sale or resale in the dealership's inventory. The design of these license plates shall be at the discretion of the Commissioner. These license plates shall be for use as authorized by the Commissioner. For each such license plate issued or renewed, the Commissioner shall charge an annual fee of $100. Issuance of license plates pursuant to this section shall be subject to the insurance requirement contained in §46.2-1948. The Commissioner shall limit the validity of any license plate issued under this section to no more than thirty consecutive days. Upon written request from the dealership, the Commissioner may consider an extended use of a license plate issued under this section. The Commissioner's authorization for use of any license plate issued under this section shall be kept in the T&M vehicle on which the license plate is displayed until expiration of the authorization. These license plates shall be included in the number of dealer's license plates authorized under §46.2-1547 and not in addition thereto.

(Added by L.1995 chs. 767, 816; chgd. by L.1996 chs. 1043, 1052, eff. 7/1/96.)

§46.2-1952. Use of dealer's license plates, generally.

A. Dealer's license plates may be used on T&M vehicles in the inventory of licensed T&M vehicle manufacturers, distributors, and dealers in the Commonwealth when operated on the highways of Virginia by dealers or dealer-operators, their spouses, or employees of manufacturers, distributors, and dealers as permitted in this article. Except as otherwise explicitly permitted in this article, it shall be unlawful for any dealer to cause or permit: (i) use of T&M dealer license plates on any T&M vehicle other than one held in inventory for sale or resale; (ii) dealer's license plates to be lent, leased, rented, or placed at the disposal of any persons other than those permitted by this article to use dealer's license plates; and (iii) use of dealer's license plates on any vehicle other than a T&M vehicle. It shall be unlawful for any dealer to cause or permit dealer's license plates to be used on:

1. Vehicles such as tow trucks, wrecking cranes, or other service vehicles;
2. Vehicles used to deliver or transport (i) T&M vehicles; (ii) portions of vehicles; (iii) vehicle components, parts, or accessories; or (iv) fuel;
3. Courtesy vehicles; or
4. Vehicles used in conjunction with any other business.

B. A dealer may permit his license plates to be used in the operation of a T&M vehicle:

1. By any person whom the dealer reasonably believes to be a bona fide prospective purchaser who is either accompanied by a licensed salesperson or has the written permission of the dealer;
2. When the plates are being used by a customer on a T&M vehicle owned by the dealer in whose repair shop the customer's T&M vehicle is being repaired; or
3. By a person authorized by the dealer on a vehicle that is being driven to or from (i) a point of sale, (ii) an auction, (iii) a repair facility for the purpose of mechanical repairs, painting, or installation of parts or accessories, or (iv) a dealer exchange.

The dealer shall issue to the prospective purchaser, customer whose T&M vehicle is being repaired, or other person authorized under subdivision 3 of this subsection, a certificate on forms provided by the Department, a copy of which shall be retained by the dealer and open at all times to the inspection of the Commissioner or any of the officers or agents of the Department. The certificate shall be in the immediate possession of the person operating or authorized to operate the T&M vehicle. The certificate shall entitle a person to operate with dealer's license plates under (i) subdivision 1 or 2 of this subsection for a specific period of no more than five days or (ii) subdivision 3 of this subsection for no more than twenty-four hours. No more than two certificates may be issued by a dealer to the same person under subdivision 1 or 2 of this subsection for successive periods.

(Added by L.1995 chs. 767, 816; chgd. by L.1996 chs. 1043, 1052; L.1998 ch. 827, eff. 7/1/98.)

§46.2-1953. Use of dealer's license plates and temporary transport plates on certain vehicles.

Notwithstanding the provisions of §46.2-1952, dealer's license plates or dealer's temporary transport plates may be used on vehicles being transported (i) to or from a vehicle auction or other point of purchase or sale, (ii) between properties owned or controlled by the same dealership, or (iii) for repairs, painting, or installation of parts or accessories. This section shall also apply to return trips by such vehicles.

(Added by L.1995 chs. 767, 816; chgd. by L.1996 chs. 1043, 1052, eff. 7/1/96.)

§46.2-1954. Issuance and use of temporary transport plates, generally.

The Department, subject to the limitations and conditions set forth in this section and the insurance requirements contained in §46.2-1948, may provide for the issuance of temporary transport plates designed by the Department to any dealer licensed under this chapter who applies for at least ten plates and who encloses with his application a fee of one dollar for each plate. The application shall be made on a form prescribed and furnished by the Department. Temporary transport plates may be used for those purposes outlined in §46.2-1953. Every dealer who has applied for temporary transport plates shall maintain a permanent record of (i) all temporary transport plates delivered to him, (ii) all temporary transport plates issued by him, and (iii) any other information pertaining to the receipt or the issuance of temporary transport plates which may be required by the Department.

Every dealer who issues temporary transport plates shall insert clearly and indelibly on the face of the temporary transport plates the name of the issuing dealer, the date of issuance and expiration, and the make and identification number of the vehicle for which issued.

The dealer shall issue to the operator of the specified vehicle a certificate on forms provided by the Department, a copy of which shall be retained by the dealer and open at all times to the inspection of the Commissioner or any of the officers or agents of the Department. The certificate shall be in the immediate possession of the person operating or authorized to operate the vehicle. The certificate shall entitle the person to operate with the dealer's temporary transport plate for a period of no more than five days. Temporary transport plates may also be used by the dealer to demonstrate types of vehicles taken in trade but for which he has not been issued dealer's license plates.

(Added by L.1995 chs. 767, 816, eff. 7/1/95.)

§46.2-1955. Use of dealer's license plates and temporary transport plates on certain vehicles traveling from one establishment to another for purpose of having special equipment installed.

Notwithstanding the provisions of §46.2-1952, dealer's license plates or temporary transport plates may be used on T&M vehicles for the purpose of delivering these T&M vehicles to another establishment for the purpose of having body work or any special permanently mounted equipment installed on the T&M vehicles, and for the purpose of returning the T&M vehicle to the dealer whose plates are attached to the T&M vehicle, whether or not the title to the T&M vehicle has been retained by the dealer, and no other license, permit, warrant, exemption card, or classification plate from any other agency of the Commonwealth shall be required under these circumstances. No other statute or regulation in conflict with the provisions of this section shall be applicable to the extent of the conflict. This section shall also apply to trips into the Commonwealth by a T&M vehicle owned and operated outside the Commonwealth to an establishment within the Commonwealth and to the return trip of that T&M vehicle from the Commonwealth to another state, provided the operator of the T&M vehicle carries on his person when so operating a bill of sale for the body work or special equipment.

(Added by L.1995 chs. 767, 816; chgd. by L.1996 chs. 1043, 1052, eff. 7/1/96.)

§46.2-1956. Use of dealer's license plates on newly purchased vehicles.

Notwithstanding the provisions of §46.2-1952, any dealer who sells and delivers to a purchaser a T&M vehicle at a time when the main offices of the Department, its branch offices, or offices of its local agents, are not open for business and the purchaser is therefore unable to register the T&M vehicle, may permit the purchaser to use, for a period not exceeding five days, on the newly purchased T&M vehicle, license plates which have been issued to the dealer, provided that, at the time of the purchase, the dealer executes in duplicate, on forms provided by the Commissioner, a certificate bearing the date of issuance, the name and address of the purchaser, the identification number of the T&M vehicle, the registration number to be used temporarily on the T&M vehicle, the name of the state in which the T&M vehicle is to be registered, and whatever other information may be required by the Commissioner. The original of the certificate and a bona fide bill of sale shall be delivered to the purchaser and shall be in the possession of the purchaser at all times when operating the T&M vehicle under dealer plates. One copy of the certificate shall be retained by the dealer, filed by him, and shall be subject to inspection at any time by the Department's agents. If the T&M vehicle is to be titled and registered in the Commonwealth, application for title and registration shall be made by the purchaser on the first business day following issuance of the certificate and a copy of the certificate shall accompany the applications.

License plates temporarily used by the purchaser shall be returned to the dealer by the purchaser not later than five days after the issuance of the certificate.

(Added by L.1995 chs. 767, 816; chgd. by L.1996 chs. 1043, 1052, eff. 7/1/96.)

§46.2-1957. Operation without license plate prohibited.

No manufacturer or distributor of or dealer in T&M vehicles shall cause or permit any T&M vehicle, owned by him to be operated or moved on a public highway without there being displayed on the T&M vehicle, a license plate or plates issued to him, either under §46.2-711 or under §46.2-1949, except as otherwise authorized in §§46.2-733, 46.2-1948 and 46.2-1959.

(Added by L.1995 chs. 767, 816, eff. 7/1/95.)

§46.2-1958. Movement by manufacturer to place of shipment or delivery.

Any manufacturer of T&M vehicles may operate or move or cause to be moved or operated on the highways for a distance of no more than twenty-five miles T&M vehicles from the factory where manufactured or assembled to a railway depot, vessel, or place of shipment or delivery, without registering them and without license plates attached thereto, under a written permit first obtained from the local law-enforcement authorities having jurisdiction over the highways and on displaying in plain sight on each T&M vehicle a placard bearing the name and address of the manufacturer authorizing or directing the movement.

(Added by L.1995 chs. 767, 816, eff. 7/1/95.)

§46.2-1959. Movement by dealers to salesrooms.

Any dealer in T&M vehicles may operate or move, or cause to be operated or moved, any T&M vehicle on the highways for a distance of no more than twenty-five miles from a vessel, railway depot, warehouse, or any place of shipment or from a factory where manufactured or assembled to a salesroom, warehouse, or place of shipment or transshipment without registering them and without license plates attached thereto, under a written permit first obtained from the local law-enforcement authorities having jurisdiction over the highways, and on displaying in plain sight on each T&M vehicle, a placard bearing the name and address of the dealer authorizing or directing the movement.

(Added by L.1995 chs. 767, 816, eff. 7/1/95.)

§46.2-1960. Operation under foreign dealer's license.

It shall be unlawful, except as provided for by reciprocal agreement, for any person to operate a T&M vehicle or for the owner thereof to permit a T&M vehicle to be operated in the Commonwealth on a foreign dealer's license, unless the operation of the T&M vehicle on the license is specifically authorized by the Commissioner.

(Added by L.1995 chs. 767, 816, eff. 7/1/95.)

§46.2-1961. *(Repealed by L.1996 chs. 1043, 1052, eff. 7/1/96.)*

§46.2-1962. Removal of plates by Department investigators; cancellation; reissuance.

If any Department investigator finds that a vehicle bearing license plates or temporary transport plates issued under this article is being operated in a manner inconsistent with (i) the requirements of this article or (ii) the Commissioner's

authorization provided for in this article, the Department of Motor Vehicles investigator may remove the license plate for cancellation. Once a license plate has been cancelled, the dealership may reapply for the license plate. Reissuance of the license plate shall be subject to the approval of the Commissioner and the payment of the fee prescribed for issuance of license plates under this article.
(Added by L.1995 chs. 767, 816, eff. 7/1/95.)

§46.2-1963. Penalties for violations of article; service of summons.

Notwithstanding §46.2-1907, any person violating any of the provisions of this article shall be guilty of a Class 3 misdemeanor. Any summons issued for any violation of any provision of this article relating to use or misuse of dealer's license plates shall be served upon the dealership to whom the plates were issued or to the person expressly permitting the unlawful use, or upon the operator of the T&M vehicle if the plates are used contrary to the use authorized by the certificate issued pursuant to §46.2-1952.
(Added by L.1995 chs. 767, 816, eff. 7/1/95.)

ARTICLE 6
ISSUANCE OF TEMPORARY LICENSE PLATES BY DEALERS

Section

§46.2-1964. Issuance of temporary license plates to dealers and vehicle owners.

The Department may, subject to the limitations and conditions set forth in this article, deliver temporary license plates designed by the Department to any dealer licensed under this chapter who applies for at least ten sets of plates and who encloses with his application a fee of two dollars for each set applied for. The application shall be made on a form prescribed and furnished by the Department. Dealers, subject to the limitations and conditions set forth in this article, may issue temporary license plates to owners of vehicles. The owners shall comply with the provisions of this article and §§46.2-705, 46.2-706 and 46.2-707. Dealers issuing temporary license plates may do so free of charge, but if they charge a fee for issuing temporary plates, the fee shall be no more than the fee charged the dealer by the Department under this section.

Display of a temporary license plate or plates on a T&M vehicle shall subject the vehicle to the requirements of §§46.2-1038 and 46.2-1056.
(Added by L.1995 chs. 767, 816, eff. 7/1/95.)

§46.2-1965. Records to be kept by dealers; inspection.

Every dealer who has applied for temporary license plates shall maintain a permanent record of (i) all temporary license plates delivered to him, (ii) all temporary license plates issued by him, and (iii) any other information pertaining to the receipt or the issuance of temporary license plates which may be required by the Department. Each record shall be kept for at least one year from the date of entry. Every dealer shall allow full access to these records during regular business hours to authorized representatives of the Department and to law-enforcement officers.
(Added by L.1995 chs. 767, 816, eff. 7/1/95.)

§46.2-1966. Application for temporary license plate.

No dealer shall issue a temporary license plate except on written application by the person entitled to receive the license plate, which application shall be forwarded by the dealer to the Department as provided in §46.2-1943.
(Added by L.1995 chs. 767, 816, eff. 7/1/95.)

§46.2-1967. To whom temporary plates shall not be issued; dealer to forward application for current titling and registration; misstatements and false information.

No dealer shall issue, assign, transfer, or deliver temporary license plates to other than the bona fide purchaser or owner of a vehicle, whether or not the vehicle is to be registered in Virginia. If the vehicle is to be registered in Virginia, the dealer shall submit to the Department a written application for the current titling and registration of the purchased vehicle, accompanied by the prescribed fees. Any dealer who issues temporary license plates to a purchaser who fails or declines to request that his application be forwarded promptly to the Department forthwith shall notify the Department of the issuance in the manner provided in this article. No dealer shall issue temporary license plates to any person who possesses current license plates for a vehicle that has been sold or exchanged, nor shall any dealer lend temporary license plates to any person for use on any vehicle. If the dealer does not have in his possession the certificate of title or certificate of origin, he shall issue temporary license plates even though the purchaser has current license plates to be transferred. The dealer shall present the title or certificate of origin to the customer within thirty days of purchase and after this transaction is completed, the customer shall transfer his current license plates to the vehicle. If the title or certificate of origin cannot be produced for a vehicle within thirty days, a second set of temporary license plates may be issued provided that a temporary certificate of ownership is issued as provided in §46.2-1943. It shall be unlawful for any person to issue any temporary license plates containing any misstatement of fact, or for any person issuing or using temporary license plates knowingly to insert any false information on their face.
(Added by L.1995 chs. 767, 816, eff. 7/1/95.)

§46.2-1968. Dealer to insert his name, date of issuance and expiration, make and identification number of vehicle.

Every dealer who issues temporary license plates shall insert clearly and indelibly on the face of each temporary license plate the name of the issuing dealer, the date of issuance and expiration, and the make and identification number of the vehicle for which issued.
(Added by L.1995 chs. 767, 816, eff. 7/1/95.)

§46.2-1969. Suspension of right of dealer to issue.

The Commissioner, on determining that the provisions of this chapter or the directions of the Department are not being complied with by any dealer, may, after a hearing, suspend the right of a dealer to issue temporary license plates.
(Added by L.1995 chs. 767, 816, eff. 7/1/95.)

§46.2-1970. Plates to be destroyed on expiration.

Every person to whom temporary license plates have been issued shall destroy them on the thirtieth day after issue

 Zv

or immediately on receipt of the permanent license plates from the Department, whichever occurs first.
(Added by L.1995 chs. 767, 816, eff. 7/1/95.)

§46.2-1971. When plates to expire; refunds or credit.

Temporary license plates shall expire on the receipt of the permanent license plates from the Department, or on the rescission of a contract to purchase a T&M vehicle, or on the expiration of, or thirty days from the date of issuance, whichever occurs first. No refund or credit of fees paid by dealers to the Department for temporary license plates shall be allowed, except that when the Department discontinues the right of a dealer to issue temporary license plates, the dealer, on returning temporary license plates to the Department, may receive a refund or a credit for them.
(Added by L.1995 chs. 767, 816, eff. 7/1/95.)

§46.2-1972. Penalties.

Any person violating any of the provisions of this article shall be guilty of a Class 1 misdemeanor.
(Added by L.1995 chs. 767, 816, eff. 7/1/95.)

ARTICLE 7
FRANCHISES

Section

§46.2-1973. Filing of franchises.

Each T&M vehicle manufacturer, factory branch, distributor, distributor branch, or subsidiary thereof shall file with the Commissioner a true copy of each new, amended, modified, or different form or addendum offered to more than one dealer which affects the rights, responsibilities, or obligations of the parties of a franchise or sales, service, or sales and service agreement to be offered to a T&M vehicle dealer or prospective T&M vehicle dealer in the Commonwealth no later than sixty days prior to the date the franchise or sales agreement is offered. In no event shall a new, amended, modified, or different form of franchise or sales, service, or sales and service agreement be offered a T&M vehicle dealer in the Commonwealth until the form has been determined by the Commissioner as not containing terms inconsistent with the provisions of this chapter. At the time a filing is made with the Commissioner pursuant to this section, the manufacturer, factory branch, distributor, distributor branch, or subsidiary shall also give written notice together with a copy of the papers so filed to the affected dealer or dealers.
(Added by L.1995 chs. 767, 816, eff. 7/1/95.)

§46.2-1974. Exemption of franchises from Retail Franchising Act.

Franchises subject to the provisions of this chapter shall not be subject to any requirement contained in Chapter 8 (§13.1-557 et seq.) of Title 13.1.
(Added by L.1995 chs. 767, 816, eff. 7/1/95.)

§46.2-1975. Coercion of retail dealer by manufacturer or distributor with respect to retail installment sales contracts prohibited.

A. It shall be unlawful for any manufacturer or distributor, or any officer, agent, or representative of either, to coerce or attempt to coerce any retail T&M vehicle dealer or prospective retail T&M vehicle dealer in the Commonwealth to sell, assign, or transfer any retail installment sales contract obtained by the dealer in connection with the sale by him in the Commonwealth of T&M vehicles manufactured or sold by the manufacturer or distributor, to a specified finance company or class of finance companies or to any other specified persons by any of the following:

1. Any statement, suggestion, promise, or threat that the manufacturer or distributor will in any manner benefit or injure the dealer, whether the statement, suggestion, threat, or promise is expressed or implied or made directly or indirectly.

2. Any act that will benefit or injure the dealer.

3. Any contract, or any expressed or implied offer of contract, made directly or indirectly to the dealer, for handling the T&M vehicle on the condition that the dealer sell, assign, or transfer his retail installment sales contract on the T&M vehicle, in the Commonwealth, to a specified finance company or class of finance companies or to any other specified person.

4. Any expressed or implied statement or representation made directly or indirectly that the dealer is under any obligation whatsoever to sell, assign, or transfer any of his retail sales contracts in the Commonwealth on T&M vehicles manufactured or sold by the manufacturer or distributor to a finance company, or class of finance companies, or other specified person, because of any relationship or affiliation between the manufacturer or distributor and the finance company or companies or the specified person or persons.

B. Any such statements, threats, promises, acts, contracts, or offers of contracts, when their effect may be to lessen or eliminate competition or tend to create a monopoly, are declared unfair trade practices and unfair methods of competition and are prohibited.

C. Any person violating any of the provisions of this article shall be guilty of a Class 1 misdemeanor.
(Added by L.1995 chs. 767, 816; chgd. by L.1996 chs. 1043, 1052, eff. 7/1/96.)

§46.2-1976. Other coercion of dealers; transfer, grant, succession to and cancellation of dealer franchises; delivery of T&M vehicles, parts, and accessories.

It shall be unlawful for any manufacturer, factory branch, distributor, or distributor branch, or any field representative, officer, agent, or their representatives:

1. To coerce or attempt to coerce any dealer to accept delivery of any T&M vehicle or T&M vehicles, parts or accessories therefor, or any other commodities, which have not been ordered by the dealer.

2. To coerce or attempt to coerce any dealer to enter into an agreement with the manufacturer, factory branch, distributor, or distributor branch, or representative thereof, or do any other act unfair to the dealer, by threatening to cancel any franchise existing between the manufacturer, factory branch, distributor, distributor branch, or representative thereof and the dealer.

3. To coerce or attempt to coerce any dealer to join, contribute to, or affiliate with any advertising association.

4. To prevent or refuse to approve the sale or transfer of the ownership of a dealership by the sale of the business, stock transfer, or otherwise, or the transfer, sale, or assignment of a dealer franchise, or a change in the executive management or principal operator of the dealership, unless the franchisor provides written notice to the dealer of its objection and the reasons therefor at least thirty days prior to the proposed effective date of the transfer, sale, assignment, or change. No such objection shall be effective to prevent the sale, transfer, assignment, or change if the Commissioner has determined, if requested in writing by the dealer within thirty days after receipt of an objection to the proposed sale, transfer, or change, and after a hearing on the matter, that the failure to permit or honor the sale, transfer, assignment, or change is unreasonable under the circumstances. No franchise may be sold, assigned, or transferred unless (i) the franchisor has been given at least ninety days' prior written notice by the dealer as to the identity, financial ability, and qualifications of the proposed transferee, and (ii) the sale or transfer of the franchise and business will not involve, without the franchisor's consent, a relocation of the business.

5. To grant an additional franchise for a particular line-make of T&M vehicle in a relevant market area in which a dealer or dealers in that line-make are already located unless the franchisor has first advised in writing all other dealers in the line-make in the relevant market area. No such additional franchise may be established at the proposed site unless the Commissioner has determined, if requested by a dealer of the same line-make in the relevant market area within thirty days after receipt of the franchisor's notice of intention to establish the additional franchise, and after a hearing on the matter, that there is reasonable evidence that after the grant of the new franchise, the market will support all of the dealers in that line-make in the relevant market area. Establishing a franchised dealer in a relevant market area to replace a franchised dealer that has not been in operation for more than two years shall constitute the establishment of a new franchise subject to the terms of this subdivision. The two-year period for replacing a franchised dealer shall begin on the day the franchise was terminated, or, if a termination hearing was held, on the day the franchisor was legally permitted finally to terminate the franchise. This subdivision shall not apply to (i) the relocation of an existing dealer within that dealer's relevant market area if the relocation site is to be more than ten miles distant from any other dealer for the same line-make; (ii) the relocation of an existing dealer within that dealer's relevant market area if the relocation site is to be more distant than the existing site from all other dealers of the same line-make in that relevant market area; or (iii) the relocation of an existing new T&M vehicle dealer within two miles of the existing site of the relocating dealer.

6. Except as otherwise provided in this subdivision and notwithstanding the terms of any franchise, to terminate, cancel, or refuse to renew the franchise of any dealer without good cause and unless (i) the dealer and the Commissioner have received written notice of the franchisor's intentions at least sixty days prior to the effective date of such termination, cancellation, or the expiration date of the franchise, setting forth the specific grounds for the action, and (ii) the Commissioner has determined, if requested in writing by the dealer within the sixty-day period and, after a hearing on the matter, that there is good cause for the termination, cancellation, or nonrenewal of the franchise. In any case where a petition is made to the Commissioner for a determination as to good cause for the termination, cancellation, or nonrenewal of a franchise, the franchise in question shall continue in effect pending the Commissioner's decision or, if that decision is appealed to the circuit court, pending the decision of the circuit court. In any case in which a franchisor neither advises a dealer that it does not intend to renew a franchise nor takes any action to renew a franchise beyond its expiration date, the franchise in question shall continue in effect on the terms last agreed to by the parties. Notwithstanding the other provisions of this subdivision, notice of termination, cancellation, or nonrenewal may be provided to a dealer by a franchisor not less than fifteen days prior to the effective date of such termination, cancellation, or nonrenewal when the grounds for such action are any of the following:

a. Insolvency of the franchised T&M vehicle dealer or filing of any petition by or against the franchised T&M vehicle dealer, under any bankruptcy or receivership law, leading to liquidation or which is intended to lead to liquidation of the franchisee's business;

b. Failure of the franchised T&M vehicle dealer to conduct its customary sales and service operations during its posted business hours for seven consecutive business days, except where the failure results from acts of God or circumstances beyond the direct control of the franchised T&M vehicle dealer;

c. Revocation of any license which the franchised T&M vehicle dealer is required to have to operate a dealership;

d. Conviction of the dealer or any principal of the dealer of a felony.

The change or discontinuance of a marketing or distribution system of a particular line-make product by a manufacturer or distributor, while the name identification of the product is continued in substantial form by the same or different manufacturer or distributor, may be considered to be a franchise termination, cancellation, or nonrenewal. The provisions of this paragraph shall apply to changes and discontinuances made after January 1, 1989, but they shall not be considered by any court in any case in which such a change or discontinuance occurring prior to that date has been challenged as constituting a termination, cancellation or nonrenewal.

7. To fail to provide continued parts and service support to a dealer which holds a franchise in a discontinued line-make for at least five years from the date of such discontinuance. This requirement shall not apply to a line-make which was discontinued prior to January 1, 1989.

8. To fail to allow a dealer the right at any time to designate a member of his family as a successor to the dealership in the event of the death or incapacity of the dealer. It shall be unlawful to prevent or refuse to honor the succession to a dealership by a member of the family of a deceased or incapacitated dealer if the franchisor has not provided to the member of the family previously designated by the dealer as his successor written notice of its objections to the succession and of such person's right to seek a hearing on the matter before the Commissioner pursuant to this article, and the Commissioner determines, if requested in writing by such member of the family within thirty days of receipt of such notice from the franchisor, and after a hearing on the matter before the Commissioner pursuant to this article, that the failure to permit or honor the succession is unreasonable under the circumstances. No member of the family may succeed to a franchise unless (i) the franchisor has been given written notice as to the identity, financial ability, and qualifications of the member of the family in question and (ii) the succession to the franchise will not involve, without the franchisor's consent, a relocation of the business.

9. To fail to ship monthly to any dealer, if ordered by the dealer, the number of new T&M vehicles of each make, series, and model needed by the dealer to receive a percentage of total new T&M vehicle sales of each make, series, and

model equitably related to the total new T&M vehicle production or importation currently being achieved nationally by each make, series, and model covered under the franchise. Upon the written request of any dealer holding its sales or sales and service franchise, the manufacturer or distributor shall disclose to the dealer in writing the basis upon which new T&M vehicles are allocated, scheduled, and delivered to the dealers of the same line-make. If allocation is at issue in a request for a hearing, the dealer may demand the Commissioner to direct that the manufacturer or distributor provide to the dealer, within thirty days of such demand, all records of sales and all records of distribution of all T&M vehicles to the same line-make dealers who compete with the dealer requesting the hearing.

10. To require or otherwise coerce a dealer to underutilize the dealer's facilities.

11. To include in any franchise with a T&M vehicle dealer terms that are contrary to, prohibited by, or otherwise inconsistent with the requirements of this chapter.

12. For any franchise agreement to require a T&M vehicle dealer to pay the attorney's fees of the manufacturer or distributor related to hearings and appeals brought under this article.

13. To fail to include in any franchise with a T&M vehicle dealer the following language: "If any provision herein contravenes the laws or regulations of any state or other jurisdiction wherein this agreement is to be performed, or denies access to the procedures, forums, or remedies provided for by such laws or regulations, such provision shall be deemed to be modified to conform to such laws or regulations, and all other terms and provisions shall remain in full force," or words to that effect.

(Added by L.1995 chs. 767, 816; chgd. by L.1996 chs. 1043, 1052, eff. 7/1/96.)

§46.2-1977. Manufacturer or distributor right of first refusal.

Notwithstanding the terms of any franchise agreement, in the event of a proposed sale or transfer of a dealership, the manufacturer or distributor shall be permitted to exercise a right of first refusal to acquire the new T&M vehicle dealer's assets or ownership, if such sale or transfer is conditioned upon the manufacturer's or dealer's entering into a dealer agreement with the proposed new owner or transferee, only if all the following requirements are met:

1. To exercise its right of first refusal, the manufacturer or distributor must notify the dealer in writing within forty-five days of its receipt of the completed proposal for the proposed sale or transfer;

2. The exercise of the right of first refusal will result in the dealer's and dealer's owner's receiving the same or greater consideration as they have contracted to receive in connection with the proposed change of ownership or transfer;

3. The proposed sale or transfer of the dealership's assets does not involve the transfer or sale to a member or members of the family of one or more dealer owners, or to a qualified manager or a partnership or corporation controlled by such persons; and

4. The manufacturer or distributor agrees to pay the reasonable expenses, including attorney's fees which do not exceed the usual, customary, and reasonable fees charged for similar work done for other clients, incurred by the proposed new owner and transferee prior to the manufacturer's or distributor's exercise of its right of first refusal in negotiating and implementing the contract for the proposed sale or transfer of the dealership or dealership assets. Notwithstanding the foregoing, no payment of such expenses and attorney's fees shall be required if the dealer has not submitted or caused to be submitted an accounting of those expenses within thirty days of the dealer's receipt of the manufacturer's or distributor's written request for such an accounting. Such accounting may be requested by a manufacturer or distributor before exercising its right of first refusal.

(Added by L.1995 chs. 767, 816; chgd. by L.1996 chs. 1043, 1052, eff. 7/1/96.)

§46.2-1978. Discontinuation of distributors.

If the contract between a distributor and a manufacturer or importer is terminated or otherwise discontinued, all franchises granted to T&M vehicle dealers in Virginia by that distributor shall continue in full force and shall not be affected by the discontinuance, except that the manufacturer, factory branch, distributor, representative, or other person who undertakes to distribute T&M vehicles of the same line-make or the same T&M vehicles of a re-named line-make shall be substituted for the discontinued distributor under the existing T&M vehicle dealer franchises and those franchises shall be modified accordingly.

(Added by L.1995 chs. 767, 816, eff. 7/1/95.)

§46.2-1979. Warranty obligations.

A. Each T&M vehicle manufacturer, factory branch, distributor, or distributor branch shall (i) specify in writing to each of its T&M vehicle dealers licensed in the Commonwealth the dealer's obligations for preparation, delivery, and warranty service on its products and (ii) compensate the dealer for warranty parts, service and diagnostic work required of the dealer by the manufacturer or distributor as follows:

1. Compensation of a dealer for warranty parts, service and diagnostic work shall not be less than the amounts charged by the dealer for the manufacturer's or distributor's original parts, service and diagnostic work to retail customers for nonwarranty service, parts and diagnostic work installed or performed in the dealer's service department unless the amounts are not reasonable;

2. For purposes of determining warranty parts and service compensation, menu-priced parts or services, group discounts, special event discounts, and special event promotions shall not be considered in determining amounts charged by the dealer to retail customers;

3. Increases in dealer warranty parts and service compensation and diagnostic work compensation, pursuant to this section, shall be requested by the dealer in writing, shall be based on 100 consecutive repair orders or all repair orders over a ninety-day period, whichever occurs first and, in the case of parts, shall be stated as a percentage of markup which shall be uniformly applied to all the manufacturer's or distributor's parts;

4. In the case of warranty parts compensation, the provisions of this subsection shall be effective only for model year 1992 and succeeding model years;

5. If a manufacturer or distributor furnishes a part to a dealer at no cost for use by the dealer in performing work for which the manufacturer or distributor is required to compensate the dealer under this section, the manufacturer or distributor shall compensate the dealer for the part in the same manner as warranty parts compensation, less the wholesale costs, for such part as listed in the manufacturer's current price schedules. A manufacturer or distributor may pay the dealer a reasonable handling fee instead of the compensation otherwise required by this subsection for special high-performance complete engine assemblies in limited production T&M vehicles which constitute less than five percent of model production furnished to the dealer at no cost, if the manufacturer or distributor excludes such special high-performance complete engine assemblies in determining whether the amounts requested by the dealer for warranty

compensation are consistent with the amounts that the dealer charges its other retail service customers for parts used by the dealer to perform similar work; or

6. In the case of service work, manufacturer original parts or parts otherwise specified by the manufacturer or distributor, and parts provided by a dealer either pursuant to an adjustment program as defined in §59.1-207.34 or as otherwise requested by the manufacturer or distributor, the dealer shall be compensated in the same manner as for warranty service or parts.

This section does not apply to compensation for parts such as components, systems, fixtures, appliances, furnishings, accessories, and features that are designed, used, and maintained primarily for nonvehicular, residential purposes. Warranty audits of dealer records may be conducted by the manufacturer, factory branch, distributor, or distributor branch on a reasonable basis, and dealer claims for warranty compensation shall not be denied except for good cause, such as performance of nonwarranty repairs, lack of material documentation, fraud, or misrepresentation. Claims for dealer compensation shall be paid within thirty days of dealer submission or within thirty days of the end of an incentive program or rejected in writing for stated reasons. The manufacturer, factory branch, distributor, or distributor branch shall reserve the right to reasonable periodic audits to determine the validity of all such paid claims for dealer compensation. Any chargebacks for warranty parts or service compensation and service incentives shall only be for the twelve-month period immediately following the date of the claim and, in the case of chargebacks for sales compensation only, for the eighteen-month period immediately following the date of claim. However, such limitations shall not be effective in the case of intentionally false or fraudulent claims.

B. It shall be unlawful for any T&M vehicle manufacturer, factory branch, distributor, or distributor branch to:

1. Fail to perform any of its warranty obligations, including tires, with respect to a T&M vehicle;

2. Fail to assume all responsibility for any liability resulting from structural or production defects;

3. Fail to include in written notices of factory recalls to T&M vehicle owners and dealers the expected date by which necessary parts and equipment will be available to dealers for the correction of defects;

4. Fail to compensate any of the T&M vehicle dealers licensed in the Commonwealth for repairs effected by the dealer of merchandise damaged in manufacture or transit to the dealer where the carrier is designated by the manufacturer, factory branch, distributor, or distributor branch;

5. Fail to compensate its T&M vehicle dealers licensed in the Commonwealth for warranty parts, work, and service pursuant to subsection A of this section, or for legal costs and expenses incurred by such dealers in connection with warranty obligations for which the manufacturer, factory branch, distributor, or distributor branch is legally responsible or which the manufacturer, factory branch, distributor, or distributor branch imposes upon the dealer;

6. Misrepresent in any way to purchasers of T&M vehicles that warranties with respect to the manufacture, performance, or design of the T&M vehicle are made by the dealer, either as warrantor or co-warrantor;

7. Require the dealer to make warranties to customers in any manner related to the manufacture, performance, or design of the T&M vehicle; or

8. Shift or attempt to shift to the T&M vehicle dealer, directly or indirectly, any liabilities of the manufacturer, factory branch, distributor or distributor branch under the Virginia Motor Vehicle Warranty Enforcement Act (§59.1-207.9 et seq.), unless such liability results from the act or omission by the dealer.

C. Notwithstanding the terms of any franchise, it shall be unlawful for any T&M vehicle manufacturer, factory branch, distributor, or distributor branch to fail to indemnify and hold harmless its T&M vehicle dealers against any losses or damages arising out of complaints, claims, or suits relating to the manufacture, assembly, or design of T&M vehicles, parts, or accessories, or other functions by the manufacturer, factory branch, distributor, or distributor branch beyond the control of the dealer, including, without limitation, the selection by the manufacturer, factory branch, distributor, or distributor branch of parts or components for the T&M vehicle or any damages to merchandise occurring in transit to the dealer where the carrier is designated by the manufacturer, factory branch, distributor, or distributor branch. The dealer shall notify the manufacturer of pending suits in which allegations are made which come within this subsection whenever reasonably practicable to do so. Every T&M vehicle dealer franchise issued to, amended, or renewed for T&M vehicle dealers in Virginia shall be construed to incorporate provisions consistent with the requirements of this subsection.

D. On any new T&M vehicle, any uncorrected damage or any corrected damage exceeding three percent of the manufacturer's or distributor's suggested retail price as defined in 15 U.S.C. §§1231–1233, as measured by retail repair costs, must be disclosed to the dealer in writing prior to delivery. Factory mechanical repair and damage to glass, tires, and bumpers are excluded from the three percent rule when properly replaced by identical manufacturer's or distributor's original equipment or parts. Whenever a new T&M vehicle is damaged in transit, when the carrier or means of transportation is determined by the manufacturer or distributor, or whenever a T&M vehicle is otherwise damaged prior to delivery to the new T&M vehicle dealer, the new T&M vehicle dealer shall:

1. Notify the manufacturer or distributor of the damage within three business days from the date of delivery of the new T&M vehicle to the new T&M vehicle dealership or within the additional time specified in the franchise; and

2. Request from the manufacturer or distributor authorization to replace the components, parts, and accessories damaged or otherwise correct the damage, unless the damage to the T&M vehicle exceeds the three percent rule, in which case the dealer may reject the vehicle within three business days.

E. If the manufacturer or distributor refuses or fails to authorize correction of such damage within ten days after receipt of notification, or if the dealer rejects the T&M vehicle because damage exceeds the three percent rule, ownership of the new T&M vehicle shall revert to the manufacturer or distributor, and the new T&M vehicle dealer shall have no obligation, financial or otherwise, with respect to such T&M vehicle. Should either the manufacturer, distributor, or the dealer elect to correct the damage or any other damage exceeding the three percent rule, full disclosure shall be made by the dealer in writing to the buyer and an acknowledgment by the buyer is required. If there is less than three percent damage, no disclosure is required, provided the damage has been corrected. Predelivery mechanical work shall not require a disclosure. Failure to disclose any corrected damage within the knowledge of the selling dealer to a new T&M vehicle in excess of the three percent rule shall constitute grounds for revocation of the buyer order, provided that, within thirty days of purchase, the T&M vehicle is returned to the dealer with an accompanying written notice of the grounds for revocation. In case of revocation pursuant to this section, the dealer shall accept the T&M vehicle and refund any payments made to the dealer in connection with the transaction, less a reasonable allowance for the consumer's use of the vehicle as defined in §59.1-207.11.

F. If there is a dispute between the manufacturer, factory branch, distributor, or distributor branch and the dealer with respect to any matter referred to in subsection A, B, or C of this section, either party may petition the Commissioner in writing, within thirty days after either party has given written notice of the dispute to the other, for a hearing. The decision of the Commissioner shall be binding on the parties, subject to rights of judicial review and appeal as provided in Chapter 1.1:1 (§9-6.14:1 et seq.) of Title 9. However, nothing contained in this section shall give the Commissioner any authority as to the content or interpretation of any manufacturer's or distributor's warranty.

(Added by L.1995 chs. 767, 816; chgd. by L.1996 chs. 453, 1043, 1052, eff. 7/1/96.)

§46.2-1980. Operation of dealership by manufacturer.

It shall be unlawful for any T&M vehicle manufacturer, factory branch, distributor, distributor branch, or subsidiary thereof, to own, operate, or control any T&M vehicle dealership in the Commonwealth. However, this section shall not prohibit:

1. The operation by a manufacturer, factory branch, distributor, distributor branch, or subsidiary thereof of a dealership for a temporary period, not to exceed one year, during the transition from one owner or operator to another;

2. The ownership or control of a dealership by a manufacturer, factory branch, distributor, distributor branch, or subsidiary thereof, while the dealership is being sold under a bona fide contract or purchase option to the operator of the dealership;

3. The ownership, operation, or control of a dealership by a manufacturer, factory branch, distributor, distributor branch, or subsidiary thereof, if the manufacturer, factory branch, distributor, distributor branch, or subsidiary has been engaged in the retail sale of T&M vehicles through the dealership for a continuous period of three years prior to July 1, 1972, and if the Commissioner determines, after a hearing on the matter at the request of any party, that there is no dealer independent of the manufacturer or distributor, factory branch or distributor branch, or subsidiary thereof available in the community to own and operate the franchise in a manner consistent with the public interest;

4. The ownership, operation, or control of a dealership by a manufacturer, factory branch, distributor, distributor branch, or subsidiary thereof if the Commissioner determines, after a hearing at the request of any party, that there is no dealer independent of the manufacturer or distributor, factory branch or distributor branch, or subsidiary thereof available in the community or trade area to own and operate the franchise in a manner consistent with the public interest;

5. The ownership, operation, or control of a dealership dealing exclusively with school buses by a school bus manufacturer or school bus parts manufacturer or a person who assembles school buses; or

6. The ownership, operation, or control of a dealership dealing exclusively with refined fuels truck tanks by a manufacturer of refined fuels truck tanks or by a person who assembles refined fuels truck tanks.

(Added by L.1995 chs. 767, 816, eff. 7/1/95.)

§46.2-1981. Ownership of service facilities.

It shall be unlawful for any T&M vehicle manufacturer, factory branch, distributor, distributor branch, or subsidiary thereof, to own, operate, or control, either directly or indirectly, any T&M vehicle warranty or service facility located in the Commonwealth. Nothing in this section shall prohibit any T&M vehicle manufacturer, factory branch, distributor, distributor branch, or subsidiary thereof, from owning, operating, or controlling any warranty or service facility for warranty or service of T&M vehicles owned or operated by the manufacturer, factory branch, distributor, distributor branch, or subsidiary thereof. Nothing contained in this section shall prohibit a T&M vehicle manufacturer, factory branch, distributor, or distributor branch from performing service for reasons of compliance with an order of a court of competent jurisdiction or of warranty under Chapter 17.3 (§59.1-207.9 et seq.) of Title 59.1.

The preceding provisions of this section shall not apply to manufacturers of refined fuels truck tanks or to persons who assemble refined fuels truck tanks or to persons who exclusively manufacture or assemble school buses or school bus parts.

(Added by L.1995 chs. 767, 816, eff. 7/1/95.)

§46.2-1982. Hearings and other remedies; civil penalties.

A. In every case of a hearing before the Commissioner authorized under this article, the Commissioner shall give reasonable notice of each hearing to all interested parties, and the Commissioner's decision shall be binding on the parties, subject to the rights of judicial review and appeal as provided in Chapter 1.1:1 (§9-6.14:1 et seq.) of Title 9.

B. Hearings before the Commissioner under this article shall commence within ninety days of the request for a hearing and the Commissioner's decision shall be rendered within sixty days from the receipt of the hearing officer's recommendation. Hearings authorized under this article shall be presided over by a hearing officer selected from a list prepared by the Executive Secretary of the Supreme Court of Virginia. On request of the Commissioner, the Executive Secretary will name a hearing officer from the list, selected on a rotation system administered by the Executive Secretary. The hearing officer shall provide recommendations to the Commissioner within ninety days of the conclusion of the hearing.

C. Notwithstanding any contrary provision of this article, the Commissioner shall initiate investigations, conduct hearings, and determine the rights of parties under this article whenever he is provided information indicating a possible violation of any provision of this article.

D. For purposes of any matter brought to the Commissioner under subdivisions 3, 4, 5, 6 and 9 of §46.2-1976 with respect to which the Commissioner is to determine whether there is good cause for a proposed action or whether it would be unreasonable under the circumstances, the Commissioner shall consider:

1. The volume of the affected dealer's business in the relevant market area;

2. The nature and extent of the dealer's investment in its business;

3. The adequacy of the dealer's service facilities, equipment, parts, supplies, and personnel;

4. The effect of the proposed action on the community;

5. The extent and quality of the dealer's service under T&M vehicle warranties;

6. The dealer's performance under the terms of its franchise; and

7. Other economic and geographical factors reasonably associated with the proposed action.

With respect to subdivision 6 of this subsection, any performance standard or program for measuring dealership performance that may have a material effect on a dealer, and the application of any such standard or program by a manufacturer or distributor, shall be fair, reasonable, and equitable and, if based upon a survey, shall be based upon a statistically valid sample. Upon the request of any dealer, a manufacturer or distributor shall disclose in writing to the dealer a description of how a performance standard or program is designed and all relevant information used in the application of the performance standard or program to that dealer.

E. An interested party in a hearing held pursuant to subsection A of this section shall comply with the effective date of compliance established by the Commissioner in his decision in such hearing, unless a stay or extension of such date is granted by the Commissioner or the Commissioner's decision is under judicial review and appeal as provided in subsection A of this section. If, after notice to such interested party and an opportunity to comment, the Commissioner finds an interested party has not complied with his decision by the designated date of compliance, unless a stay or extension of such date has been granted by the Commissioner or the Commissioner's decision is under judicial review and appeal, the Commissioner may assess such interested party a civil penalty not to exceed $1,000 per day of noncompliance. Civil penalties collected under this subsection shall be deposited into the Transportation Trust Fund.

(Added by L.1995 chs. 767, 816; chgd. by L.2000 ch. 106, eff. 7/1/2000.)

§46.2-1983. Late model and factory repurchase franchises.

Franchised late model or factory repurchase T&M vehicle dealers shall have the same rights and obligations as provided for franchised new T&M vehicle dealers in Article 7 (§46.2-1973 et seq.) of this chapter, mutatis mutandis.

(Added by L.1995 chs. 767, 816, eff. 7/1/95.)

ARTICLE 8
DENIAL, SUSPENSION, AND REVOCATION OF DEALER LICENSES

Section

§46.2-1984. Acts of officers, directors, partners, and salespersons.

If a licensee or registrant is a partnership or corporation, it shall be sufficient cause for the denial, suspension, or revocation of a license or certificate of dealer registration that any officer, director, or trustee of the partnership or corporation, or any member in the case of a partnership or the dealer-operator, has committed any act or omitted any duty which would be cause for refusing, suspending, or revoking a license or certificate of dealer registration issued to him as an individual under this chapter. Each licensee or registrant shall be responsible for the acts of any of his salespersons while acting as his agent, if the licensee approved of those acts or had knowledge of those acts or other similar acts and, after such knowledge, retained the benefit, proceeds, profits, or advantages accruing from those acts or otherwise ratified those acts.

(Added by L.1995 chs. 767, 816, eff. 7/1/95.)

§46.2-1985. Grounds for denying, suspending, or revoking licenses or certificates of dealer registration or qualification.

A license or certificate of dealer registration or qualification issued under this subtitle may be denied, suspended, or revoked on any one or more of the following grounds:

1. Material misstatement or omission in application for license, dealer's license plates, certificate of dealer registration, certificate of qualification, or certificate of title;
2. Failure to comply subsequent to receipt of a written warning from the Department or any willful failure to comply with any provision of this chapter or any applicable provision of this subtitle or any applicable regulation promulgated under this subtitle;
3. Failure to have an established place of business as defined in §46.2-1910 or failure to have as the dealer-operator an individual who holds a valid certificate of qualification;
4. Defrauding any retail buyer, to the buyer's damage, or any other person in the conduct of the licensee's or registrant's business;
5. Employment of fraudulent devices, methods or practices in connection with compliance with the requirements under the statutes of the Commonwealth with respect to the retaking of vehicles under retail installment contracts and the redemption and resale of those vehicles;
6. Having used deceptive acts or practices;
7. Knowingly advertising by any means any assertion, representation, or statement of fact which is untrue, misleading, or deceptive in any particular relating to the conduct of the business licensed or registered under this subtitle or for which a license or registration is sought;
8. Having been convicted of any fraudulent act in connection with the business of selling vehicles or any consumer-related fraud;
9. Having been convicted of any criminal act involving the business of selling vehicles;
10. Willfully retaining in his possession title to a vehicle that has not been completely and legally assigned to him;
11. Failure to comply with any provision of Chapter 4.1 (§36-85.2 et seq.) of Title 36 or any regulation promulgated pursuant to that chapter;
12. Leasing, renting, lending, or otherwise allowing the use of a dealer's license plate by persons not specifically authorized under this title;
13. Having been convicted of a felony;
14. Failure to submit to the Department, within thirty days from the date of sale, any application, tax, or fee collected for the Department on behalf of a buyer;
15. Having been convicted of larceny of a vehicle or receipt or sale of a stolen vehicle;
16. Having been convicted of odometer tampering or any related violation;
17. If a salvage dealer, salvage pool, or rebuilder, failing to comply with any provision of Chapter 16 of this title or any regulation promulgated by the Commissioner under that chapter;
18. Failing to maintain liability insurance, issued by a company licensed to do business in the Commonwealth, or a certificate of self-insurance as defined in §46.2-368, with respect to each dealer's license plate issued to the dealer by the Department; or
19. Failing or refusing to pay civil penalties imposed by the Commissioner pursuant to §46.2-1907.

(Added by L.1995 chs. 767, 816; chgd. by L.1996 chs. 1043, 1052; L.1999 ch. 217, eff. 7/1/99.)

 Zv

§46.2-1986. Suspension, revocation, and refusal to renew licenses or certificates of dealer registration or qualification; notice and hearing.

A. Except as provided in subsections B and C of this section, no license or certificate of dealer registration or qualification issued under this subtitle shall be suspended or revoked, or renewal thereof refused, until a written copy of the complaint made has been furnished to the licensee, registrant, or qualifier against whom the same is directed and a public hearing thereon has been had before the Commissioner. At least ten days' written notice of the time and place of the hearing shall be given to the licensee, registrant, or qualifier by registered mail addressed to his last known post office address or as shown on his license or certificate or other record of information in possession of the Commissioner. At the hearing the licensee, registrant, or qualifier shall have the right to be heard personally or by counsel. After hearing, the Commissioner may suspend, revoke, or refuse to renew the license or certificate in question. Immediate notice of any suspension, revocation, or refusal shall be given to the licensee, registrant, or qualifier in the same manner provided in this section for giving notices of hearing.

B. Should a dealer fail to maintain an established place of business, the Commissioner may cancel the license of the dealer without a hearing after notification of the intent to cancel has been sent, by return receipt mail, to the dealer at the dealer's residence and business addresses, and the notices are returned undelivered or the dealer does not respond within twenty days from the date the notices were sent. Any subsequent application for a dealer's license shall be treated as an original application.

C. Should a dealer fail or refuse to pay civil penalties imposed by the Commissioner pursuant to §46.2-1907, the Commissioner may deny, revoke, or suspend the dealer's license without a hearing after notice of imposition of civil penalties has been sent, by certified mail, return receipt requested, to the dealer at the dealer's business address and such civil penalty is not paid in full within thirty days after receipt of the notice.

(Added by L.1995 chs. 767, 816; chgd. by L.1999 ch. 217, eff. 7/1/99.)

§46.2-1987. Appeals from actions of the Commissioner.

Any person aggrieved by the action of the Commissioner in refusing to grant or renew a license or certificate of dealer registration or qualification issued under this chapter, or by any other action of the Commissioner which is alleged to be improper, unreasonable, or unlawful under the provisions of this chapter is entitled to judicial review in accordance with the provisions of the Administrative Process Act (§9-6.14:1 et seq.).

(Added by L.1995 chs. 767, 816, eff. 7/1/95.)

§46.2-1988. Appeals to Court of Appeals.

Either party may appeal from the decision of the court under §46.2-1987 to the Court of Appeals. These appeals shall be taken and prosecuted in the same manner and with like effect as is provided by law in other cases appealed as a matter of right to the Court of Appeals.

(Added by L.1995 chs. 767, 816; chgd. by L.1996 chs. 1043, 1052; L.1997 ch. 88, eff. 7/1/97.)

§46.2-1989. Equitable remedies not impaired.

The remedy at law provided by §§46.2-1987 and 46.2-1988 shall not in any manner impair the right to applicable equitable relief. That right to equitable relief is hereby preserved, notwithstanding the provisions of §§46.2-1987 and 46.2-1988.

(Added by L.1995 chs. 767, 816, eff. 7/1/95.)

ARTICLE 9
T&M VEHICLE DEALER ADVERTISING

§46.2-1990. Regulated advertising practices.

For purposes of this chapter, a violation of the following regulated advertising practices shall be an unfair, deceptive, or misleading act or practice.

1. A vehicle shall not be advertised as new, either by word or implication, unless it is one which conforms to the requirements of §46.2-1900.

2. When advertising any vehicle which does not conform to the definition of "new" as provided in §46.2-1900, the fact that it is used shall be clearly and unequivocally expressed by the term "used" or by such other term as is commonly understood to mean that the vehicle is used. By way of example but not by limitation, "special purchase" by itself is not a satisfactory disclosure; however, such terms as "demonstrator" or "former leased vehicles" used alone clearly express that the vehicles are used for advertising purposes.

3. Advertisement of finance charges or other interest rates shall not be used when there is a cost to buy-down said charge or rate which is passed on, in whole or in part, to the purchaser.

4. Terms, conditions, and disclaimers shall be stated clearly and conspicuously. An asterisk or other reference symbol may be used to point to a disclaimer or other information, but shall not be used as a means of contradicting or changing the meaning of an advertised statement.

5. The expiration date of an advertised sale shall be clearly and conspicuously disclosed.

6. The term "list price," "sticker price," or "suggested retail price" and similar terms, shall be used only in reference to the manufacturer's suggested retail price for new vehicles or the dealer's own usual and customary price for used vehicles.

7. Terms such as "at cost," "below cost," "$ off cost" shall not be used in advertisements because of the difficulty in determining a dealer's actual net cost at the time of the sale. Terms such as "invoice price," "$ over invoice," may be used, provided that the invoice referred to is the manufacturer's factory invoice or a bona fide bill of sale and the invoice or bill of sale is available for customer inspection.

"Manufacturer's factory invoice" means that document supplied by the manufacturer to the dealer listing the manufacturer's charge to the dealer before any deduction for holdback, group advertising, factory incentives or rebates, or any governmental charges.

8. When the price or credit terms of a vehicle are advertised, the vehicle shall be fully identified as to year, make, and model. In addition, in advertisements placed by individual dealers and not line-make marketing groups, the stated price or credit terms shall include all charges which the buyer must pay to the seller, except buyer-selected options, state and local fees and taxes, and manufacturer's or distributor's freight or destination charges. If freight or destination charges are not included in the advertised price, the amount of any such freight or destination charge must be clearly and conspicuously disclosed.

9. Advertisements which set out a policy of matching or bettering competitors' prices shall not be used unless the terms of the offer are specific, verifiable and reasonable.

10. Advertisements of "dealer rebates" shall not be used. This does not affect advertisement of manufacturer rebates.

11. "Free," "at no cost," or other words to that effect shall not be used unless the "free" item, merchandise, or service is available without a purchase. This provision shall not apply to advertising placed by manufacturers, distributors, or line-make marketing groups.

12. "Bait" advertising, in which an advertiser may have no intention to sell at the price or terms advertised, shall not be used. By way of example, but not by limitation:

a. If a specific vehicle is advertised, the seller shall be in possession of a reasonable supply of said vehicles, and they shall be available at the advertised price. If the advertised vehicle is available only in limited numbers or only by order, that shall be stated in the advertisement. For purposes of this subdivision, the listing of a vehicle by stock number or vehicle identification number in the advertisement for a used vehicle is one means of satisfactorily disclosing a limitation of availability. Stock numbers or vehicle identification numbers shall not be used in advertising a new vehicle unless the advertisement clearly and conspicuously discloses that it relates to only one vehicle;

b. Advertising a vehicle at a certain price, including "as low as" statements, but having available for sale only vehicles equipped with dealer added cost "options" which increase the selling price, above the advertised price, shall also be considered "bait" advertising;

c. If a lease payment is advertised, the fact that it is a lease arrangement shall be disclosed.

13. The term "repossessed" shall be used only to describe vehicles that have been sold, registered, titled and then taken back from a purchaser and not yet resold to an ultimate user. Advertisers offering repossessed vehicles for sale shall provide proof of repossession upon request.

14. Words such as "finance" or "loan" shall not be used in a T&M vehicle advertiser's firm name or trade name, unless that person is actually engaged in the financing of T&M vehicles.

15. Any advertisement which gives the impression a dealer has a special arrangement or relationship with the distributor or manufacturer, as compared to similarly situated dealers, shall not be used.

(Added by L.1995 chs. 767, 816, eff. 7/1/95.)

§46.2-1991. Enforcement; regulations.

The Commissioner may promulgate regulations reasonably necessary for enforcement of this article.

In addition to any other sanctions or remedies available to the Commissioner under this chapter, the Commissioner may assess a civil penalty not to exceed $1,000 for any single violation of this article. Each day that a violation continues shall constitute a separate violation.

(Added by L.1995 chs. 767, 816, eff. 7/1/95.)

CHAPTER 19.1
TRAILER DEALERS

(Added by L.1996 chs. 1043, 1052, eff. 7/1/96.)

Article

ARTICLE 1
TRAILER DEALERS GENERALLY

Section

§46.2-1992. Definitions.

Unless the context otherwise requires, the following words and terms, for the purpose of this chapter, shall have the following meanings:

"Certificate of origin" means the document, provided by the manufacturer or distributor of a new trailer, that is the only valid indication of ownership between the manufacturer, its distributor, its franchised trailer dealers, and the original purchaser not for resale.

"Dealer-operator" means the individual who works at the established place of business of a dealer and who is responsible for and in charge of day-to-day operations of that place of business.

"Distributor" means a person who sells or distributes new trailers, pursuant to a written agreement with the manufacturer, to franchised trailer dealers in the Commonwealth.

"Distributor branch" means a branch office maintained by a distributor for the sale of trailers to trailer dealers or for directing or supervising, in whole or in part, its representatives in the Commonwealth.

"Distributor representative" means a person employed, by a distributor or by a distributor branch, for the purpose of making or promoting the sale of trailers or for supervising or contacting its dealers, prospective dealers, or representatives in the Commonwealth.

"Factory branch" means a branch office maintained by a person for the sale of trailers to distributors, for the sale of trailers to trailer dealers, or for directing or supervising, in whole or in part, its representatives in the Commonwealth.

"Factory representative" means a person employed either by a person who manufactures or assembles trailers or by a factory branch for the purpose of (i) making or promoting the sale of its trailers or (ii) for supervising or contacting its dealers, prospective dealers, or representatives in the Commonwealth.

"Factory repurchase trailer" means a trailer that is (i) sold, leased, rented, consigned, or otherwise transferred to a person under an agreement that the trailer will be resold or otherwise retransferred only to the manufacturer or distributor of the trailer, and (ii) reacquired by the manufacturer or distributor, or its agents.

"Family member" means a person who either (i) is the spouse, child, grandchild, spouse of a child, spouse of a grandchild, brother, sister, or parent of the dealer or owner, or (ii) has been employed continuously by the dealer for at least five years.

"Franchise" means a written contract or agreement between two or more persons whereby one person, the franchisee, is granted the right to engage in the business of offering and selling, servicing, or offering, selling, and servicing new trailers of a particular line-make or late model or factory repurchase trailers of a particular line-make manufactured or distributed by the grantor of the right, the franchisor, and where the operation of the franchisee's business is substantially associated with the franchisor's trademark, trade name, advertising, or other commercial symbol designating the franchisor, the trailer or its manufacturer or distributor. The term shall include any severable part or parts of a franchise agreement which separately provides for selling and servicing different line-makes of the franchisor.

"Franchised late model or factory repurchase trailer dealer" means a dealer in late model or factory repurchase trailers, including a franchised new trailer dealer, that has a franchise agreement with a manufacturer or distributor of the line-make of the late model or factory repurchase trailers.

"Franchised trailer dealer" or "franchised dealer" means a dealer in new trailers that has a franchise agreement with a manufacturer or distributor of new trailers.

"Independent trailer dealer" means a dealer in used trailers.

"Late model trailer" means a trailer of the current model year and the immediately preceding model year.

"Manufacturer" means a person engaged in the business of constructing or assembling new trailers.

"New trailer" means any trailer which (i) has not been previously sold except in good faith for the purpose of resale, (ii) has not been used as a rental, driver education, or demonstration trailer, or for the personal and business transportation of the manufacturer, distributor, dealer, or any of his employees, (iii) has not been used except for limited use necessary in moving or road testing the trailer prior to delivery to a customer, (iv) is transferred by a certificate of origin, and (v) has the manufacturer's certification that it conforms to all applicable federal trailer safety and emission standards. Notwithstanding provisions (i) and (iii), a trailer that has been previously sold but not titled shall be deemed a new trailer if it meets the requirements of provisions (ii), (iv), and (v).

"Original license" means a trailer dealer license issued to an applicant who has never been licensed as a trailer dealer in Virginia or whose Virginia trailer dealer license has been expired for more than thirty days.

"Relevant market area" means as follows:

1. In metropolitan localities with a population of 250,000, the relevant market area shall be a circular area around an existing franchised dealer not to exceed a radius of ten miles, but in no case less than seven miles.

2. If the population in an area within a radius of ten miles around an existing franchised dealer is less than 250,000, but the population in an area within a radius of fifteen miles around an existing franchised dealer is 150,000 or more, the relevant market area shall be that area within the fifteen-mile radius.

3. In all other cases the relevant market area shall be an area within a radius of twenty miles around an existing franchised dealer or the area of responsibility defined in the franchise, whichever is greater. In any case where the franchise agreement is silent as to area responsibility, the relevant market area shall be the greater of an area within a radius of twenty miles around an existing franchised dealer or that area in which the franchisor otherwise requires the franchisee to make significant retail sales or sales efforts.

In determining population for this definition, the most recent census by the U.S. Bureau of the Census or the most recent population update, either from the National Planning Data Corporation or other similar recognized source, shall be accumulated for all census tracts either wholly or partially within the relevant market area.

"Retail installment sale" means every sale of one or more trailers to a buyer for his use and not for resale, in which the price of the trailer is payable in one or more installments and in which the seller has either retained title to the goods or has taken or retained a security interest in the goods under form of contract designated either as a security agreement, conditional sale, bailment lease, chattel mortgage, or otherwise.

"Sale at retail" or "retail sale" means the act or attempted act of selling, bartering, exchanging, or otherwise disposing of a trailer to a buyer for his personal use and not for resale.

"Sale at wholesale" or "wholesale" means a sale to trailer dealers or wholesalers other than to consumers, or a sale to one who intends to resell.

"Trailer" means every vehicle without motive power designed for carrying property or passengers wholly on its own structure and for being drawn by a motor vehicle, including semitrailers but not manufactured homes, sales of which are regulated under Chapter 4.2 (§36-85.16 et seq.) of Title 36, and not (i) watercraft trailers as defined in this section or (ii) travel trailers as defined in §46.2-1900.

"Trailer dealer" or "dealer" means any person who:

1. For commission, money, or other thing of value, buys, sells, exchanges, either outright or on conditional sale, bailment lease, chattel mortgage, or otherwise, arranges, offers or attempts to solicit or negotiate on behalf of others a sale, purchase, or exchange of an interest in new trailers, new and used trailers, or used trailers alone, whether or not the trailers are owned by him;

2. Is wholly or partly engaged in the business of selling new trailers, new and used trailers, or used trailers only, whether or not the trailers are owned by him; or

3. Offers to sell, sells, displays, or permits the display for sale, of five or more trailers within any twelve consecutive months.

The term "trailer dealer" does not include:

1. Receivers, trustees, administrators, executors, guardians, conservators or other persons appointed by or acting under judgment or order of any court or their employees when engaged in the specific performance of their duties as employees.

2. Public officers, their deputies, assistants, or employees, while performing their official duties.

3. Persons other than business entities primarily engaged in the leasing or renting of trailers to others when selling or offering such trailers for sale at retail, disposing of trailers acquired for their own use and actually so used, when the trailers have been so acquired and used in good faith and not for the purpose of avoiding the provisions of this chapter.

4. Persons dealing solely in the sale and distribution of fire-fighting equipment, ambulances, and funeral trailers, including trailers adapted therefor; however, this exemption shall not exempt any person from the provisions of §§46.2-1992.17, 46.2-1992.18 and 46.2-1992.41.

5. Any financial institution chartered or authorized to do business under the laws of the Commonwealth or the United States which may have received title to a trailer in the normal course of its business by reason of a foreclosure, other taking, repossession, or voluntary reconveyance to that institution occurring as a result of any loan secured by a lien on the trailer.

6. An employee of an organization arranging for the purchase or lease by the organization of trailers for use in the organization's business.

7. Any person who permits the operation of a trailer show or permits the display of trailers for sale by any trailer dealer licensed under this chapter.

8. An insurance company authorized to do business in the Commonwealth that sells or disposes of trailers under a contract with its insured in the regular course of business.

9. Any publication, broadcast, or other communications media when engaged in the business of advertising, but not otherwise arranging for the sale of trailers owned by others.

10. Any person dealing solely in the sale or lease of trailers designed exclusively for off-road use.

11. Any credit union authorized to do business in Virginia, provided the credit union does not receive a commission, money, or other thing of value directly from a trailer dealer.

"Trailer salesperson" or "salesperson" means any person who is licensed as and employed as a salesperson by a trailer dealer to sell or exchange trailers.

"Trailer show" means a display of trailers to the general public at a location other than a dealer's location licensed under this chapter where the trailers are not being offered for sale or exchange during or as part of the display.

"Used trailer" means any trailer other than a new trailer as defined in this section.

"Watercraft trailer" means any new or used trailer specifically designed to carry a watercraft or a motorboat and purchased, sold, or offered for sale by a watercraft dealer licensed under Chapter 8 (§29.1-800 et seq.) of Title 29.1.

"Watercraft trailer dealer" means any watercraft dealer licensed under Chapter 8 (§29.1-800 et seq.) of Title 29.1 who obtains a certificate of dealer registration under this chapter.

"Wholesale auction" means an auction of trailers restricted to sales at wholesale.

(Added by L.1996 chs. 1043, 1052; chgd. by L.1997 ch. 801, eff. 1/1/98, ch. 848, eff. 7/1/97.)

§46.2-1992.1. General powers of Commissioner.

The Commissioner shall promote the interest of the retail buyers of trailers and endeavor to prevent unfair methods of competition and unfair or deceptive acts or practices.

(Added by L.1996 chs. 1043, 1052, eff. 7/1/96.)

§46.2-1992.2. Commissioner's powers with respect to hearings under this chapter.

The Commissioner may, in hearings arising under this chapter, determine the place in the Commonwealth where they shall be held; subpoena witnesses; take depositions of witnesses residing outside the Commonwealth in the manner provided for in civil actions in courts of record; pay these witnesses the fees and mileage for their attendance as is provided for witnesses in civil actions in courts of record; and administer oaths.

(Added by L.1996 chs. 1043, 1052, eff. 7/1/96.)

§46.2-1992.3. Suit to enjoin violations.

The Commissioner, whenever he believes from evidence submitted to him that any person has been violating, is violating, or is about to violate any provision of this chapter, in addition to any other remedy, may bring an action in the name of the Commonwealth to enjoin any violation of this chapter.

(Added by L.1996 chs. 1043, 1052, eff. 7/1/96.)

§46.2-1992.4. Regulations.

The Commissioner may promulgate regulations requiring persons licensed under this chapter to keep and maintain records reasonably required for the enforcement of §§46.2-112 and 46.2-629, and any other regulations, not inconsistent with the provisions of this chapter, as he shall consider necessary for the effective administration and enforcement of this chapter. A copy of any regulation promulgated under this section shall be mailed to each trailer dealer licensee thirty days prior to its effective date.

(Added by L.1996 chs. 1043, 1052, eff. 7/1/96.)

§46.2-1992.5. Penalties.

Except as otherwise provided in this chapter, any person violating any of the provisions of this chapter may be assessed a civil penalty not to exceed $1,000 for any single violation. Civil penalties collected under this chapter shall be deposited into the Transportation Trust Fund.

(Added by L.1996 chs. 1043, 1052, eff. 7/1/96.)

ARTICLE 2
TRAILER DEALER LICENSES

Section

§46.2-1992.6. Licenses required.

It shall be unlawful for any person to engage in business in the Commonwealth as a trailer dealer, salesperson, manufacturer, factory branch, distributor, distributor branch, or factory or distributor representative, without first obtaining a license as provided in this chapter. Every person licensed as a watercraft dealer under Chapter 8 (§29.1-800 et seq.) of Title 29.1 and who offers for sale watercraft trailers, shall obtain a certificate of dealer registration as provided in this chapter, but shall not be required to obtain a dealer license unless he also sells other types of trailers. Any person licensed in another state as a trailer dealer may sell trailers at wholesale auctions in the Commonwealth after having obtained a certificate of dealer registration as provided in this chapter. Any nonprofit organization exempt from taxation under §501(c)(3) of the Internal Revenue Code, after having obtained a nonprofit organization certificate as provided in this chapter, may consign donated trailers to licensed Virginia trailer dealers. The offering or granting of a trailer dealer franchise in the Commonwealth shall constitute engaging in business in the Commonwealth for purposes of this section, and no new trailer may be sold or offered for sale in the Commonwealth unless the franchisor of trailer dealer franchises for that line-make in the Commonwealth, whether such franchisor is a manufacturer, factory branch, distributor, distributor branch, or otherwise, is licensed under this chapter. In the event a license issued under this chapter to a franchisor of trailer dealer franchises is suspended, revoked, or not renewed, nothing in this section shall prevent the sale of any new trailer of such franchisor's line-make manufactured in or brought into the Commonwealth for sale prior to the suspension, revocation or expiration of the license.

Violation of any provision of this section shall constitute a Class 1 misdemeanor.

(Added by L.1996 chs. 1043, 1052; chgd. by L.1997 ch. 848; L.2000 ch. 180, eff. 7/1/2000.)

§46.2-1992.6:1. Certification of certain nonprofit organizations.

Upon application to and approval by the Department, any nonprofit organization exempt from taxation under §501(c)(3) of the Internal Revenue Code may be issued a nonprofit organization certificate authorizing it to consign donated trailers to licensed Virginia trailer dealers when the nonprofit organization receives title to such trailers as qualified charitable gifts and titles the trailers in the name of the nonprofit organization.

(Added by L.2000 ch. 180, eff. 7/1/2000.)

§46.2-1992.7. Application for license or certificate of dealer registration.

Application for license or certificate of dealer registration under this chapter shall be made to the Commissioner and contain such information as the Commissioner shall require. The application shall be accompanied by the required fee.

The Commissioner shall require, in the application or otherwise, information relating to the matters set forth in §46.2-1992.79 as grounds for refusing licenses, certificates of dealer registration, and to other pertinent matters requisite for the safeguarding of the public interest, including, if the applicant is a dealer in new trailers with factory warranties, a copy of a current service agreement with the manufacturer or with the distributor, requiring the applicant to perform within a reasonable distance of his established place of business, the service, repair, and replacement work required of the manufacturer or distributor by such trailer warranty. All of these matters shall be considered by the Commissioner in determining the fitness of the applicant to engage in the business for which he seeks a license or certificate of dealer registration.

(Added by L.1996 chs. 1043, 1052, eff. 7/1/96.)

§46.2-1992.8. Dealers required to have established place of business.

No license shall be issued to any trailer dealer unless he has an established place of business, owned or leased by him, where a substantial portion of the sales activity of the business is routinely conducted and which:

1. Satisfies all local zoning regulations;

2. Has sales, service, and office space devoted exclusively to the dealership of at least 250 square feet in a permanent, enclosed building not used as a residence;

3. Houses all records the dealer is required to maintain by §46.2-1992.22;

4. Is equipped with a desk, chairs, filing space, a working telephone listed in the name of the dealership, and working utilities including electricity and provisions for space heating;

5. Displays a sign and business hours as required by this chapter; and

6. Has contiguous space designated for the exclusive use of the dealer adequate to permit the display of at least ten trailers.

Any person licensed as a dealer by the Department under any provision of this subtitle on June 1, 1996, shall be considered in compliance with subdivisions 2 and 6 of this section for that licensee.

(Added by L.1996 chs. 1043, 1052, eff. 7/1/96.)

§46.2-1992.9. Dealer-operator to have certificate of qualification.

No license shall be issued to any trailer dealer unless the dealer-operator holds a valid certificate of qualification issued by the Department. Such certificate shall be issued only on application to the Department, payment of a twenty-five dollar application fee, the successful completion of an examination prepared and administered by the Department, and other prerequisites as set forth in this section. However, any individual who is the dealer-operator of a dealer licensed by the Department under any provision of this subtitle on June 30, 1996, shall be entitled to such a certificate without examination on application to the Department made on or before January 1, 1997.

The Commissioner may establish minimum qualifications for applicants and require applicants to satisfactorily complete courses of study or other prerequisites prior to taking the examination.

(Added by L.1996 chs. 1043, 1052, eff. 7/1/96.)

§46.2-1992.10. Salesperson to have certificate of qualification.

No license shall be issued to any trailer salesperson unless he holds a valid certificate of qualification issued by the Department. A certificate shall be issued only on application to the Department, payment of a twenty-five dollar application fee, the successful completion of an examination prepared and administered by the Department, and other prerequisites as set forth in this section. However, any individual who is licensed as a salesperson by the Department under any provision of this subtitle on June 30, 1996, shall be entitled to such a certificate without examination on application to the Department made on or before January 1, 1997.

The Commissioner may establish minimum qualifications for applicants and require applicants to satisfactorily complete courses of study or other prerequisites prior to taking the examination.

(Added by L.1996 chs. 1043, 1052, eff. 7/1/96.)

§46.2-1992.11. Continued operation on loss of a dealer-operator holding certificate of qualification.

Each dealer shall notify the Department in writing immediately when a dealer-operator who holds a certificate of qualification dies, becomes disabled, retires, is removed, or for any other cause ceases to act as dealer-operator. The dealer may continue to operate for 120 days thereafter without a dealer-operator and may be granted approval by the Department to operate for an additional sixty days on application and with good cause shown for such delay.

(Added by L.1996 chs. 1043, 1052, eff. 7/1/96.)

§46.2-1992.12. Action on applications; hearing on denial; denial for failure to have established place of business.

The Commissioner shall act on all applications for a license or certificate of dealer registration under this chapter within sixty days after receipt by either granting or refusing the application. Any applicant denied a license or certificate shall, on his written request filed within thirty days, be given a hearing at a time and place determined by the Commissioner or a person designated by him. All hearings under this section shall be public and shall be held promptly. The applicant may be represented by counsel.

Any applicant denied a license for failure to have an established place of business as provided in §46.2-1992.8 may not, nor shall anyone, apply for a license for premises for

which a license was denied for thirty days from the date of the rejection of the application.
(Added by L.1996 chs. 1043, 1052, eff. 7/1/96.)

§46.2-1992.13. Location to be specified; display of license; change of location.

The licenses of trailer dealers, manufacturers, factory branches, distributors, and distributor branches shall specify the location of each place of business, branch or other location occupied or to be occupied by the licensee in conducting his business and the license issued therefor shall be conspicuously displayed at each of the premises. If any licensee intends to change a licensed location, he shall provide the Commissioner thirty days' advance written notice, and a successful inspection of the new location shall be required prior to approval of a change of location. The Commissioner shall endorse the change of location on the license, without charge, if the new location is within the same county or city. A change in location to another county or city shall require a new license and fee.
(Added by L.1996 chs. 1043, 1052, eff. 7/1/96.)

§46.2-1992.14. Supplemental sales locations.

The Commissioner may issue a license for a licensed trailer dealer to display for sale or sell trailers at locations other than his established place of business, subject to compliance with local ordinances and requirements.

A permanent supplemental license may be issued for premises less than 500 yards from the dealer's established place of business, provided a sign is displayed as required for the established place of business. A supplemental license shall not be required for premises otherwise contiguous to the established place of business except for a public thoroughfare.

A temporary supplemental license may be issued for a period not to exceed fourteen days, provided that the application is made fifteen days prior to the sale. A temporary supplemental license for the sale of new trailers may be issued only for locations within the dealer's area of responsibility, as defined in his franchise or sales agreement, unless certification is provided that all dealers in the same line-make in whose areas of responsibility, as defined in their franchise or sales agreements, where the temporary supplemental license is sought do not oppose the issuance of the temporary license.

However, the application for a temporary supplemental license may be made five business days prior to the sale, provided the applicant submit evidence that the location is in compliance with all local ordinances and that all other requirements of this section have been met. The application shall include affirmative proof of nonopposition in the form of letters signed by all dealers in the same line-make in whose areas of responsibility, as defined in their franchise or sales agreements, where the temporary supplemental license is sought, approving the Department's granting of the temporary supplemental license.

A temporary supplemental license for sale of used trailers may be issued only for the county, city, or town in which the dealer is licensed pursuant to §46.2-1992.8, or for a contiguous county, city, or town. Temporary licenses may be issued without regard to the foregoing geographic restrictions where the dealer operating under a temporary license provides notice, at least thirty days before any proposed sale under a temporary license, to all other dealers licensed in the jurisdiction in which the sale will occur of the intent to conduct a sale and permits any locally licensed dealer who wishes to do so to participate in the sale on the same terms as the dealer operating under the temporary license. Any locally licensed dealer who chooses to participate in the sale must obtain a temporary supplemental license for the sale pursuant to this section.
(Added by L.1996 chs. 1043, 1052, eff. 7/1/96.)

§46.2-1992.15. Changes in form of ownership, line-make, name.

Any change in the form of ownership or the addition or deletion of a partner shall require a new application, license, and fee.

Any addition or deletion of a franchise or change in the name of a dealer shall require immediate notification to the Department, and the Commissioner shall endorse the change on the license without a fee. The change of an officer or director of a corporation shall be made at the time of license renewal.
(Added by L.1996 chs. 1043, 1052, eff. 7/1/96.)

§46.2-1992.16. Display of salesperson's license; notice on termination.

No salesperson shall be employed by more than one dealer, unless the dealers are owned by the same person.

Each dealer shall maintain a list of salespersons employed.

Each salesperson, factory representative, and distributor representative shall carry his license when engaged in his business and shall display it on request.

Each dealer and each manufacturer and distributor shall notify the Department in writing not later than the tenth day of the month following the termination of any licensed salesperson's or representative's employment. In lieu of written notification, the license of the terminated salesperson or representative may be returned to the Department annotated "terminated" on the face of the license and signed and dated by the dealer-operator, owner, or officer.
(Added by L.1996 chs. 1043, 1052, eff. 7/1/96.)

§46.2-1992.17. License and registration fees; additional to other licenses and fees required by law.

A. The fee for each license and registration year or part thereof shall be as follows:

1. For trailer dealers, $100 for each principal place of business, plus $20 for each supplemental license.
2. For each trailer manufacturer, distributor, factory branch and distributor branch, $100.
3. For trailer rebuilder salespersons, factory representatives, and distributor representatives, $10.
4. For trailer dealers licensed in other states, but not in Virginia, and for watercraft trailer dealers, a registration fee of $50.

B. The licenses, registrations, and fees required by this chapter are in addition to licenses, taxes, and fees imposed by other provisions of law and nothing contained in this chapter shall exempt any person from any license, tax, or fee imposed by any other provision of law. However, the Commissioner may waive fees for those licensed under Chapter 15, 19, or 19.2 of this title; the Commissioner shall waive the fee for nonprofit organizations certified under Chapter 15, 19, or 19.2 of this title.

C. The fee for any nonprofit organization issued a certificate pursuant to §46.2-1992.6:1 shall be $25 per year or any part thereof.

D. No nonprofit organization granted a certificate pursuant to §46.2-1992.6:1 shall, either orally or in writing, assign a value to any donated vehicle for the purpose of establishing tax deduction amounts on any federal or state income tax return.
(Added by L.1996 chs. 1043, 1052; chgd. by L.2000 ch. 180, eff. 7/1/2000.)

§46.2-1992.18. Collection of license and registration fees; payments from fund.

All licensing and registration fees provided for in this chapter, except as identified in Article 3 (§46.2-1992.20 et seq.) of this chapter, shall be collected by the Commissioner

and paid into the state treasury and set aside as a special fund to meet the expenses of the Department.
(Added by L.1996 chs. 1043, 1052, eff. 7/1/96.)

§46.2-1992.19. Issuance, expiration, and renewal of licenses and certificates of registration.

A. All licenses and certificates of registration issued under this chapter shall be issued for a period of twelve consecutive months except, at the discretion of the Commissioner, the periods may be adjusted as is necessary to distribute the licenses and certificates as equally as practicable on a monthly basis. The expiration date shall be the last day of the twelfth month of validity or the last day of the designated month. Every license and certificate of registration shall be renewed annually on application by the licensee or registrant and by payment of fees required by law, the renewal to take effect on the first day of the succeeding month.

B. Licenses and certificates of registration issued under this chapter shall be deemed not to have expired if the renewal application and required fees as set forth in this subsection are received by the Commissioner or postmarked not more than thirty days after the expiration date of such license or certificate of registration. Whenever the renewal application is received by the Commissioner or postmarked no more than thirty days after the expiration date of such license or certificate of registration, the license fees shall be 150 percent of the fees provided for in §46.2-1992.17.

C. The Commissioner may offer an optional multi-year license. When such option is offered and chosen by the licensee, all annual and twelve-month fees due at the time of licensing shall be multiplied by the number of years or fraction thereof for which the license will be issued.
(Added by L.1996 chs. 1043, 1052; chgd. by L.1997 ch. 848; L.1998 ch. 325, eff. 1/1/99.)

ARTICLE 3
BONDING REQUIREMENTS

§46.2-1992.20. Bonding requirements for applicants for license.

Every applicant for an original, second year renewal, and third year renewal trailer dealer's license shall obtain and file with the Commissioner a bond in the amount of $25,000. However, no dealer shall be required to obtain more than one $25,000 bond for all licenses held under this subtitle. Any dealer who is licensed under Chapter 15 of this title and who obtains a trailer dealer license under this chapter, shall be exempt from the bond requirements set out in this section. In addition, any person who purchases a trailer from a dealer who is licensed under Chapter 15 of this title, shall have access to the Motor Vehicle Transaction Recovery Fund as prescribed in Article 3 (§46.2-1527 et seq.) of Chapter 15 of this title. The bond shall come from a corporate surety licensed to do business in the Commonwealth and approved by the Attorney General. The bond shall be conditioned on a statement by the applicant that the applicant will not practice fraud, make any fraudulent representation, or violate any provision of this chapter in the conduct of the applicant's business. The Commissioner may, without holding a hearing, suspend the dealer's license during the period that the dealer does not have a sufficient bond on file.

If a person suffers any of the following: (i) loss or damage in connection with the purchase of a trailer by reason of fraud practiced on him or fraudulent representation made to him by a licensed trailer dealer or one of the dealer's salespersons acting within his scope of employment; (ii) loss or damage by reason of the violation by a dealer or salesperson of any provision of this chapter in connection with the purchase of a trailer; or (iii) loss or damage resulting from a breach of an extended service contract as defined by §59.1-435, and entered into on or after the effective date of this act, that person shall have a claim against the dealer and the dealer's bond, and may recover such damages as may be awarded to such person by final judgment of a court of competent jurisdiction against the dealer as a proximate result of such loss or damage up to, but not exceeding, the amount of the bond, from such surety, who shall be subrogated to the rights of such person against the dealer or salesperson. The liability of such surety shall be limited to actual damages, and shall not include any punitive damages or attorneys' fees assessed against the dealer or salesperson.

The dealer's surety shall notify the Department when a claim is made against a dealer's bond, when a claim is paid and when the bond is canceled. Such notification shall include the amount of a claim and the circumstances surrounding the claim. Notification of cancellation shall include the effective date and reason for cancellation. The bond may be canceled as to future liability by the dealer's surety upon thirty days' notice to the Department.
(Added by L.1996 chs. 1043, 1052, eff. 7/1/96.)

ARTICLE 4
CONDUCT OF BUSINESS

§46.2-1992.21. Examination or audit of licensee; costs.

The Commissioner or authorized representatives of the Department may examine, during the posted business hours, the records required to be maintained by this chapter. If a licensee is found to have violated this chapter or any order of the Commissioner, the actual cost of the examination shall be paid by the licensee so examined within thirty days after demand therefor by the Commissioner. The Commissioner may maintain an action for the recovery of these costs in any court of competent jurisdiction.
(Added by L.1996 chs. 1043, 1052, eff. 7/1/96.)

§46.2-1992.22. Dealer records.

All dealer records regarding employees; lists of vehicles in inventory for sale, resale, or on consignment; vehicle

purchases, sales, trades, and transfers of ownership; collections of taxes; titling, uninsured motor vehicle and registration fees; odometer disclosure statements, records of permanent dealer registration plates assigned to the dealer and temporary transport plates and temporary certificates of ownership; and other records required by the Department shall be maintained on the premises of the licensed location. The Commissioner may, on written request by a dealer, permit his records to be maintained at a location other than the premises of the licensed location for good cause shown. All dealer records shall be preserved in original form or in film, magnetic, or optical media (including but not limited to microfilm, microfiche, or other electronic media) for a period of five years in a manner that permits systematic retrieval. Certain records may be maintained on a computerized record-keeping system with the prior approval of the Commissioner.
(Added by L.1996 chs. 1043, 1052; chgd. by L.2000 ch. 128, eff. 7/1/2000.)

§46.2-1992.23. Buyer's order.
A. Every trailer dealer shall complete, in duplicate, a buyer's order for each sale or exchange of a vehicle. A copy of the buyer's order form shall be made available to a prospective buyer during the negotiating phase of a sale and prior to any sales agreement. The completed original shall be retained for a period of four years in accordance with §46.2-1992.22, and a duplicate copy shall be delivered to the purchaser at the time of sale or exchange. A buyer's order shall include:

1. The name and address of the person to whom the vehicle was sold or traded.
2. The date of the sale or trade.
3. The name and address of the trailer dealer selling or trading the vehicle.
4. The make, model year, vehicle identification number and body style of the vehicle.
5. The sale price of the vehicle.
6. The amount of any cash deposit made by the buyer.
7. A description of any vehicle used as a trade-in and the amount credited the buyer for the trade-in. The description of the trade-in shall be the same as outlined in subdivision 4 of this subsection.
8. The amount of any sales and use tax, title fee, uninsured motor vehicle fee, registration fee, or other fee required by law for which the buyer is responsible and the dealer has collected. Each tax and fee shall be individually listed and identified.
9. The net balance due at settlement.
10. Any item designated as "processing fee," and the amount charged by the dealer, if any, for processing the transaction. As used in this section processing includes obtaining title and license plates for the purchaser.
11. Any item designated as "dealer's business license tax," and the amount charged by the dealer, if any.
12. For sales involving dealer-arranged financing, the following notice, printed in bold type no less than ten-point:

"THIS SALE IS CONDITIONED UPON APPROVAL OF YOUR PROPOSED RETAIL INSTALLMENT SALE CONTRACT AS SUBMITTED TO OR THROUGH THE DEALER. IF THAT PROPOSED RETAIL INSTALLMENT SALE CONTRACT IS NOT APPROVED UNDER THE TERMS AGREED TO WITH THE DEALER, YOU MAY CANCEL THIS SALE AND ANY DOWN PAYMENT AND/OR TRADE-IN YOU SUBMITTED WILL BE RETURNED TO YOU, PROVIDED THAT ANY VEHICLE DELIVERED TO YOU BY THE DEALER PURSUANT TO THIS AGREEMENT IS RETURNED TO THE DEALER IN THE SAME CONDITION AS DELIVERED TO YOU, NORMAL WEAR AND TEAR EXCEPTED, WITHIN TWENTY-FOUR HOURS OF WRITTEN OR ORAL NOTICE TO YOU OF THE CREDIT DENIAL."

A completed buyer's order when signed by both buyer and seller may constitute a bill of sale.

B. The Commissioner shall approve a buyer's order form and each dealer shall file with each original license application its buyer's order form, on which the processing fee amount is stated.

C. If a processing fee is charged, that fact and the amount of the processing fee shall be disclosed by the dealer. Disclosure shall be by placing a clear and conspicuous sign in the public sales area of the dealership. The sign shall be no smaller than eight and one-half inches by eleven inches and the print shall be no smaller than one-half inch, and in a form as approved by the Commissioner.
(Added by L.1996 chs. 1043, 1052; chgd. by L.2000 ch. 116, eff. 7/1/2000.)

§46.2-1992.24. Consignment trailers; contract.
Any trailer dealer offering a trailer for sale on consignment shall have in his possession a consignment contract for the trailer, executed and signed by the dealer and the consignor. The consignment contract shall include:

1. The complete name, address, and the telephone number of the owners.
2. The name, address, and dealer certificate number of the selling dealer.
3. A complete description of the trailer on consignment, including the make and model year.
4. The beginning and termination dates of the contract.
5. The percentage of commission, the amount of the commission, or the net amount the owner is to receive, if the trailer is sold.
6. Any fees for which the owner is responsible.
7. A disclosure of all unsatisfied liens on the trailer and the location of the certificate of title to the trailer.
8. A requirement that the trailer pass a safety inspection prior to sale, if periodic safety inspections of the trailer are required under Article 21 (§46.2-1157) of Chapter 10 of this title.

If any trailer on consignment from a certified nonprofit organization is found not to be in compliance with any safety inspection requirement, the trailer dealer shall furnish any buyer intending to use that trailer on the public highways a written disclosure, prior to sale, that the trailer did not pass a safety inspection.

Any dealer offering a trailer for sale on consignment shall inform any prospective customer that the trailer is on consignment.

Dealer license plates shall not be used to demonstrate a trailer on consignment except on (i) trailers with gross vehicle weight of 15,000 pounds or more, (ii) trailers on consignment from another licensed trailer dealer, and (iii) trailers on consignment from nonprofit organizations certified pursuant to §46.2-1992.6:1. No vehicles other than trailers shall be sold on consignment by trailer dealers.

The provisions of this section shall also apply to watercraft trailers and watercraft trailer dealers.
(Added by L.1996 chs. 1043, 1052; chgd. by L.2000 ch. 180, eff. 7/1/2000.)

§46.2-1992.25. Certain disclosures required by manufacturers and distributors.
Trailer and watercraft trailer manufacturers and distributors shall affix or cause to be affixed in a conspicuous place to every trailer and watercraft trailer offered for sale as

new, a statement disclosing the place of its assembly or manufacture.

The provisions of this section shall apply only to trailers manufactured for the 1991 or subsequent model years.
(Added by L.1996 chs. 1043, 1052, eff. 7/1/96.)

§46.2-1992.26. Business hours.

Each trailer dealer shall be open for business a minimum of twenty hours per week, at least ten of which shall be between the hours of 9:00 a.m. and 5:00 p.m. Monday through Friday, except that the Commissioner, on written request by a dealer, may modify these requirements for good cause. The dealer's hours shall be posted and maintained conspicuously on or near the main entrance of each place of business.

Each dealer shall include his business hours on the original and every renewal application for a license, and changes to these hours shall be immediately filed with the Department.
(Added by L.1996 chs. 1043, 1052, eff. 7/1/96.)

§46.2-1992.27. Signs.

Each retail trailer dealer's place of business shall be identified by a permanent sign visible from the front of the business office so that the public may quickly and easily identify the dealership. The sign shall contain the dealer's trade name in letters no less than six inches in height unless otherwise restricted by law or contract.
(Added by L.1996 chs. 1043, 1052, eff. 7/1/96.)

§46.2-1992.28. Advertisements.

Unless the dealer is clearly identified by name, whenever any licensee places an advertisement in any newspaper or publication, the abbreviations "VA DLR," denoting a Virginia licensed dealer, shall appear therein.
(Added by L.1996 chs. 1043, 1052, eff. 7/1/96.)

§46.2-1992.29. Coercing purchaser to provide insurance coverage on trailer.

It shall be unlawful for any dealer or salesperson or any employee of a dealer or representative of either to coerce or offer anything of value to any purchaser of a trailer to provide any type of insurance coverage on the trailer.

Nothing in this section shall prohibit a dealer from requiring that a retail customer obtain vehicle physical damage insurance to protect collateral secured by an installment sales contract. Any person found guilty of violating any provisions of this section shall be guilty of a Class 1 misdemeanor.
(Added by L.1996 chs. 1043, 1052, eff. 7/1/96.)

§46.2-1992.30. Prohibited solicitation and compensation.

It shall be unlawful for any trailer dealer or salesperson licensed under this chapter, directly or indirectly, to solicit the sale of a trailer through a person with a pecuniary interest, or to pay, or cause to be paid, any commission or compensation in any form whatsoever to any person in connection with the sale of a trailer, unless the person is duly licensed as a salesperson employed by the dealer.
(Added by L.1996 chs. 1043, 1052, eff. 7/1/96.)

§46.2-1992.31. Salesperson selling for other than his employer prohibited.

It shall be unlawful for any trailer salesperson licensed under this chapter to sell or exchange or offer or attempt to sell or exchange any trailer except for the licensed trailer dealer by whom he is employed, or to offer, transfer, or assign any sale or exchange that he may have negotiated to any other dealer or salesperson.
(Added by L.1996 chs. 1043, 1052, eff. 7/1/96.)

§46.2-1992.32. Inspection of vehicles required.

No person required to be licensed as a dealer under this chapter shall sell at retail any vehicle which is intended by the buyer for use on the public highways, and which is required to comply with the safety inspection requirements provided in Article 21 (§46.2-1157 et seq.) of Chapter 10 of this title unless between the time the vehicle comes into the possession of the dealer and the time it is sold at retail it is inspected by an official safety inspection station. If the vehicle is found not to be in compliance with all safety inspection requirements, the dealer shall either take steps to bring it into compliance or shall furnish any buyer intending it for use on the public highway a written disclosure, prior to sale, that the trailer did not pass a safety inspection. Any person found guilty of violating any provisions of this section shall be guilty of a Class 1 misdemeanor.

The provisions of this section shall also apply to watercraft trailers and watercraft trailer dealers.
(Added by L.1996 chs. 1043, 1052, eff. 7/1/96.)

§46.2-1992.33. Inspections prior to sale not required of certain sellers.

The provisions of §§46.2-1158 and 46.2-1992.32 requiring inspection of any vehicle prior to sale at retail shall not apply to any person conducting a public auction for the sale of vehicles at retail, provided that the individual, firm, or business conducting the auction has not taken title to the trailer, but is acting as an agent for the sale of the trailer. Nor shall the provisions of §§46.2-1158 and 46.2-1992.32 requiring inspection of any vehicle prior to sale at retail apply to any new trailer or trailers sold on the basis of a special order placed by a dealer with a manufacturer outside Virginia on behalf of a customer who is a nonresident of Virginia and takes delivery outside Virginia. Nor shall the provisions of §§46.2-1158 and 46.2-1992.32 requiring inspection of any trailer prior to sale at retail apply to the sale of five or more used trailers, to the same buyer, provided the trailers have a valid safety inspection, of trailers with a gross weight of more than 10,000 pounds.

The provisions of this section shall also apply to watercraft trailers.
(Added by L.1996 chs. 1043, 1052, eff. 7/1/96.)

§46.2-1992.34. Inspections or disclosure required before sale of certain trailers.

Any trailer required by any provision of this title to undergo periodic safety inspections shall be inspected by an official inspection station between the time it comes into the possession of a retail dealer and the time the trailer is sold by the dealer or, in lieu of an inspection, the dealer shall present to the purchaser, prior to purchase of the trailer, a written itemization of all the trailer's deficiencies relative to applicable Virginia safety inspection requirements. The provisions of this section shall not apply to sales of trailers or watercraft trailers by individuals not ordinarily engaged in the business of selling trailers or watercraft trailers nor shall this section apply to the retail sale of five or more trailers to the same buyer. Any person found guilty of violating any provisions of this section shall be guilty of a Class 1 misdemeanor.
(Added by L.1996 chs. 1043, 1052, eff. 7/1/96.)

§46.2-1992.35. Temporary certificates of ownership.

A. Notwithstanding §§46.2-617 and 46.2-628, whenever a dealer licensed by the Department sells and delivers to a purchaser a vehicle, and is unable at the time of the sale to deliver to the purchaser the certificate of title or certificate of origin for the vehicle because the certificate of title or certificate of origin is lost or is being detained by another in possession or for any other reason beyond the dealer's control, the dealer shall execute, on forms provided by the

Commissioner, a temporary certificate of ownership. The certificate shall bear its date of issuance, the name and address of the purchaser, the identification number of the vehicle, the registration number to be used temporarily on the vehicle, the name of the state in which the vehicle is to be registered, the name and address of the person from whom the dealer acquired the vehicle, and whatever other information may be required by the Commissioner. A copy of the temporary certificate and a bona fide bill of sale shall be delivered to the purchaser and shall be in the possession of the purchaser at all times when operating the vehicle. One copy of the certificate shall be retained by the dealer and shall be subject to inspection at any time by the Department's agents. The original of the certificate shall be forwarded by the dealer to the Department directly on issuance to the purchaser if the vehicle is to be titled outside the Commonwealth, along with application for title. The issuance of a temporary certificate of ownership to a purchaser pursuant to this section shall have the effect of vesting ownership of the vehicle in the purchaser for the period that the certificate remains effective.

B. A temporary certificate of ownership issued by a dealer to a purchaser pursuant to this section shall expire on receipt by the purchaser of a certificate of title to the vehicle issued by the Department in the name of the purchaser, but in no event shall any temporary certificate of ownership issued under this section be effective for more than thirty days from the date of its issuance. In the event that the dealer fails to produce the old certificate of title or certificate of origin to the vehicle or fails to apply for a replacement certificate of title pursuant to §46.2-632, thereby preventing delivery to the Department or purchaser before the expiration of the temporary certificate of ownership, the purchaser's ownership of the vehicle may terminate and the purchaser shall have the right to return the vehicle to the dealer and obtain a full refund of all payments made toward the purchase of the vehicle, less any damage to the vehicle incurred while ownership was vested in the purchaser.

C. Notwithstanding subsection B of this section, if the dealer fails to deliver the certificate of title or certificate of origin to the purchaser within thirty days, a second temporary certificate of ownership may be issued. However, the dealer shall, not later than the expiration of the first temporary certificate, deliver to the Department an application for title, copy of the bill of sale, all required fees and a written statement of facts describing the dealer's efforts to secure the certificate of title or certificate of origin to the vehicle. On receipt of the title application with attachments as described herein, the Department shall record the purchaser's ownership of the vehicle and may authorize the dealer to issue a second thirty-day temporary certificate of ownership. If the dealer does not produce the certificate of title or certificate of origin to the vehicle before the expiration of the second temporary certificate, the purchaser's ownership of the vehicle may terminate and he shall have the right to return the trailer as provided in subsection B of this section.

D. If the dealer is unable to produce the certificate of title or certificate of origin to the vehicle within the sixty-day period from the date of issuance of the first temporary certificate, the Department may extend temporary ownership for an additional period of up to ninety days, provided the dealer makes application in the format required by the Department. If the dealer does not produce the certificate of title or certificate of origin to the vehicle before the expiration of the additional ninety-day period, the purchaser's ownership of the vehicle may terminate and he shall have the right to return the vehicle as provided in subsection B of this section.

E. The Commissioner, on determining that the provisions of this section or the directions of the Department are not being complied with by a dealer, may, after a hearing, suspend the right of the dealer to issue temporary certificates of ownership.

The provisions of this section shall also apply to watercraft trailers and watercraft trailer dealers.
(Added by L.1996 chs. 1043, 1052, eff. 7/1/96.)

§46.2-1992.36. Use of old license plates and registration number on a trailer.

An owner who sells or transfers a registered trailer may have the license plates and the registration number transferred to a trailer titled in the owner's name according to the provisions of Chapter 6 (§46.2-600 et seq.), which is in a like trailer category as specified in §46.2-694 and which requires an identical registration fee, on application to the Department accompanied by a fee of two dollars or, if the trailer requires a greater registration fee than that for which the license plates were assigned, on the payment of a fee of two dollars and the amount of the difference in registration fees between the two trailers, all such transfers shall be in accordance with the regulations of the Department. All fees collected under this section shall be paid by the Commissioner into the state treasury and shall be set aside as a special fund to be used to meet the expenses of the Department. For purposes of this section, a trailer dealer licensed by the Department may be authorized to act as an agent of the Department for the purpose of receiving, processing, and approving applications from its customers for assignment of license plates and registration numbers pursuant to this section, using the forms and following the procedures prescribed by the Department. The Commissioner, on determining that the provisions of this section or the directions of the Department are not being complied with by a dealer, may suspend, after a hearing, the authority of the dealer to receive, process, and approve the assignment of license plates and registration numbers pursuant to this section.

The provisions of this section shall also apply to watercraft trailers and watercraft trailer dealers.
(Added by L.1996 chs. 1043, 1052, eff. 7/1/96.)

§46.2-1992.37. Certificate of title for dealers.

Except as otherwise provided in this chapter, every dealer shall obtain, on the purchase of each trailer, a certificate of title issued to the dealer or shall obtain an assignment or reassignment of a certificate of title for each trailer purchased, except that a certificate of title shall not be required for any new trailer to be sold as such.

The provisions of this section shall also apply to watercraft trailers and watercraft trailer dealers.
(Added by L.1996 chs. 1043, 1052, eff. 7/1/96.)

§46.2-1992.38. Termination of business.

No dealer, unless his license has been suspended, revoked, or canceled, shall cease business without a thirty-day prior notification to the Department. On cessation of the business, the dealer shall immediately surrender to the Department the dealer's certificate of license, all salespersons' licenses, all dealer and temporary license plates, all fees and taxes collected, and any other materials furnished by the Department. After cessation of business, the former licensee shall continue to maintain and make available to the Department dealer records as set forth in this chapter.

The provisions of this section shall also apply to watercraft trailers and watercraft trailer dealers.
(Added by L.1996 chs. 1043, 1052, eff. 7/1/96.)

ARTICLE 5
TRAILER DEALER LICENSE PLATES

§46.2-1992.39. Registration of dealers; fees.

Every manufacturer, distributor, or dealer, before he commences to operate trailers in his inventory for sale or resale, shall apply to the Commissioner for a dealer's certificate of vehicle registration and license plates. For the purposes of this article, a trailer is in inventory when it is owned by, or assigned to, a dealer and is offered and available for sale or resale. All dealer's certificates of vehicle registration and license plates issued under this section may, at the discretion of the Commissioner, be placed in a system of staggered issue to distribute the work of issuing vehicle registration certificates and license plates as uniformly as practicable throughout the year. Dealerships which sold fewer than twenty-five trailers during the last twelve months of the preceding license year shall be eligible to receive no more than two dealer's license plates; dealerships which sold at least twenty-five but fewer than fifty trailers during the last twelve months of the preceding license year shall be eligible to receive no more than four dealer's license plates. However, dealerships which sold fifty or more trailers during their current license year may apply for additional license plates not to exceed four times the number of licensed salespersons employed by that dealership. Dealerships which sold fifty or more trailers during the last twelve months of the preceding license year shall be eligible to receive a number of dealer's license plates not to exceed four times the number of licensed salespersons employed by that dealership. A new applicant for a dealership shall be eligible to receive a number of dealer's license plates not to exceed four times the number of licensed salespersons employed by that dealership. For the purposes of this article, a salesperson or employee shall be considered to be employed only if he (i) works for the dealership at least twenty-five hours each week on a regular basis and (ii) is compensated for this work. All salespersons' or employees' employment records shall be retained in accordance with the provisions of §46.2-1992.22. A salesperson shall not be considered employed, within the meaning of this section, if he is an independent contractor as defined by the United States Internal Revenue Code. The fee for the issuance of dealer's license plates shall be thirty dollars per year for the first two dealer's license plates and thirteen dollars per year for each additional dealer's license plate.

(Added by L.1996 chs. 1043, 1052, eff. 7/1/96.)

§46.2-1992.40. License under this chapter prerequisite to receiving dealer's license plates; Commissioner may revoke plates.

No trailer manufacturer, distributor, or dealer, unless licensed under this chapter, shall be entitled to receive or maintain any dealer's license plates. The Commissioner may revoke any dealer's license plate that has been used in any way not authorized by the provisions of this title.

(Added by L.1996 chs. 1043, 1052, eff. 7/1/96.)

§46.2-1992.41. Transferable dealer's license plates.

In lieu of registering each trailer of a type described in this section, a manufacturer, distributor, or dealer owning and operating any trailer on any highway may obtain a dealer's license plate from the Department, on application therefor on the prescribed form and on payment of the fees required by law. These license plates shall be attached to each trailer as required by subsection A of §46.2-711. Each plate shall bear a distinctive number, and the name of the Commonwealth, which may be abbreviated, together with the word "dealer" or a distinguishing symbol indicating that the plate is issued to a manufacturer, distributor, or dealer. Month and year decals indicating the date of expiration shall be affixed to each license plate. Any license plates so issued may, during the calendar year or years for which they have been issued, be transferred from one trailer to another, used or operated by the manufacturer, distributor, or dealer, who shall keep a written record of the trailer on which the dealer's license plates are used. This record shall be in a format approved by the Commissioner and shall be open to inspection by any law-enforcement officer or any officer or employee of the Department.

Display of a transferable manufacturer's, distributor's, or dealer's license plate or plates on a trailer shall subject the trailer to the requirements of §§46.2-1038 and 46.2-1056.

All manufacturer's, distributor's, and dealer's license plates shall be issued for a period of twelve consecutive months except, at the discretion of the Commissioner, the periods may be adjusted as may be necessary to distribute the registrations as equally as practicable on a monthly basis. The expiration date shall be the last day of the twelfth month of validity or the last day of the designated month. Every license plate shall be renewed annually on application by the owner and by payment of fees required by law, such renewal to take effect on the first day of the succeeding month.

The Commissioner may offer an optional multi-year license plate registration to manufacturers, distributors, and dealers licensed pursuant to this chapter provided that he has chosen to offer optional multi-year licensing to such persons pursuant to §46.2-1992.19. When such option is offered and chosen by the licensee, all annual and twelve-month fees due at the time of registration shall be multiplied by the number of years or fraction thereof the licensee will be licensed pursuant to §46.2-1992.19.

(Added by L.1996 chs. 1043, 1052, eff. 7/1/96.)

§46.2-1992.42. Dealer's license plates to distinguish between various types of dealers.

The Commissioner shall provide for the issuance of appropriate franchised or independent dealer's license plates so as to distinguish between factory trailer dealers and trailer dealers.

(Added by L.1996 chs. 1043, 1052, eff. 7/1/96.)

§46.2-1992.43. Dealer's promotional license plates.

In addition to any other license plate authorized by this article, the Commissioner may issue dealer's promotional license plates to a dealership for use on trailers held for sale or resale in the dealership's inventory. The design of these license plates shall be at the discretion of the Commissioner. These license plates shall be for use as authorized by the Commissioner. For each such license plate issued or renewed, the Commissioner shall charge an annual fee of $100. The Commissioner shall limit the validity of any license plate issued under this section to no more than thirty consecutive days. Upon written request from the dealership, the Commissioner may consider an extended use of a license plate issued under this section. The Commissioner's authorization for use of any license plate issued under this section shall be kept in the trailer on which the license plate is displayed until expiration of the authorization. These license plates shall be included in the number of dealer's license plates authorized under §46.2-1992.39 and not in addition thereto.

(Added by L.1996 chs. 1043, 1052, eff. 7/1/96.)

§46.2-1992.44. Use of dealer's license plates, generally.

A. Dealer's license plates may be used on trailers in the inventory of licensed trailer manufacturers, distributors, and dealers in the Commonwealth when operated on the highways of Virginia by dealers or dealer-operators, their spouses, or employees of manufacturers, distributors, and dealers as permitted in this article. Except as otherwise explicitly permitted in this article, it shall be unlawful for any dealer to cause or permit: (i) use of dealer's license plates on trailers other than those held in inventory for sale or resale; (ii) dealer's license plates to be lent, leased, rented, or placed at the disposal of any persons other than those permitted by this article to use dealer's license plates; and (iii) use of dealer's license plates on any vehicle other than a trailer or watercraft trailer. It shall be unlawful for any dealer to cause or permit dealer's license plates to be used on:

1. Vehicles such as tow trucks, wrecking cranes, or other service vehicles;
2. Vehicles used to deliver or transport (i) trailers; (ii) portions of vehicles; (iii) vehicle components, parts, or accessories; or (iv) fuel;
3. Courtesy vehicles; or
4. Vehicles used in conjunction with any other business.

B. A dealer may permit his license plates to be used in the operation of a trailer:

1. By any person whom the dealer reasonably believes to be a bona fide prospective purchaser who is either accompanied by a licensed salesperson or has the written permission of the dealer;
2. When the plates are being used by a customer on a trailer owned by the dealer in whose repair shop the customer's trailer is being repaired; or
3. By a person authorized by the dealer on a vehicle that is being operated to or from (i) a point of sale, (ii) an auction, (iii) a repair facility for the purpose of mechanical repairs, painting, or installation of parts or accessories, or (iv) a dealer exchange.

The dealer shall issue to the prospective purchaser, customer whose trailer is being repaired, or other person authorized under subdivision 3 of this subsection, a certificate on forms provided by the Department, a copy of which shall be retained by the dealer and open at all times to the inspection of the Commissioner or any of the officers or agents of the Department. The certificate shall be in the immediate possession of the person operating or authorized to operate the trailer. The certificate shall entitle a person to operate with dealer's license plates under (i) subdivision 1 or 2 of this subsection for a specific period of no more than five days or (ii) subdivision 3 of this subsection for no more than twenty-four hours. No more than two certificates may be issued by a dealer to the same person under subdivision 1 or 2 of this subsection for successive periods.

(Added by L.1996 chs. 1043, 1052; chgd. by L.1998 ch. 827, eff. 7/1/98.)

§46.2-1992.45. Use of dealer's license plates and temporary transport plates on certain trailers.

Notwithstanding the provisions of §46.2-1992.44, dealer's license plates or dealer's temporary transport plates may be used on vehicles being transported (i) to or from a vehicle auction or other point of purchase or sale, (ii) between properties owned or controlled by the same dealership, or (iii) for repairs, painting, or installation of parts or accessories. This section shall also apply to return trips by such vehicles.

(Added by L.1996 chs. 1043, 1052, eff. 7/1/96.)

§46.2-1992.46. Issuance and use of temporary transport plates, generally.

The Department, subject to the limitations and conditions set forth in this section and the insurance requirements contained in §46.2-1992.40, may provide for the issuance of temporary transport plates designed by the Department to any dealer licensed under this chapter who applies for at least ten plates and who encloses with his application a fee of one dollar for each plate. The application shall be made on a form prescribed and furnished by the Department. Temporary transport plates may be used for those purposes outlined in §46.2-1992.45. Every dealer who has applied for temporary transport plates shall maintain a permanent record of (i) all temporary transport plates delivered to him, (ii) all temporary transport plates issued by him, and (iii) any other information pertaining to the receipt or the issuance of temporary transport plates which may be required by the Department.

Every dealer who issues temporary transport plates shall insert clearly and indelibly on the face of the temporary transport plates the name of the issuing dealer, the date of issuance and expiration, and the make and identification number of the trailer for which issued.

The dealer shall issue to the operator of the specified trailer a certificate on forms provided by the Department, a copy of which shall be retained by the dealer and open at all times to the inspection of the Commissioner or any of the officers or agents of the Department. The certificate shall be in the immediate possession of the person operating or authorized to operate the trailer. The certificate shall entitle the person to operate with the dealer's temporary transport plate for a period of no more than five days. Temporary transport plates may also be used by the dealer to demonstrate types of vehicles taken in trade but for which he has not been issued dealer's license plates.

(Added by L.1996 chs. 1043, 1052, eff. 7/1/96.)

§46.2-1992.47. Use of dealer's license plates or temporary transport plates on certain vehicles traveling from one establishment to another for purpose of having special equipment installed.

Notwithstanding the provisions of §46.2-1992.44, dealer's license plates or temporary transport plates may be used on trailers or semitrailers for the purpose of delivering these

vehicles to another establishment for the purpose of having a body or any special permanently mounted equipment installed on the trailers, and for the purpose of returning the vehicle to the dealer whose plates are attached to the trailer or semitrailer, whether or not the title to the trailer has been retained by the dealer, and no other license, permit, warrant, exemption card, or classification plate from any other agency of the Commonwealth shall be required under these circumstances. No other statute or regulation in conflict with the provisions of this section shall be applicable to the extent of the conflict. This section shall also apply to trips into the Commonwealth by a trailer owned and operated outside the Commonwealth to an establishment within the Commonwealth and to the return trip of that trailer from the Commonwealth to another state, provided the operator of the trailer carries on his person when so operating a bill of sale for the body or special equipment.
(Added by L.1996 chs. 1043, 1052, eff. 7/1/96.)

§46.2-1992.48. Use of dealer's license plates on newly purchased trailers.

Notwithstanding the provisions of §46.2-1992.44, any dealer who sells and delivers to a purchaser a trailer at a time when the main offices of the Department, its branch offices, or offices of its local agents, are not open for business and the purchaser is therefore unable to register the trailer, may permit the purchaser to use, for a period not exceeding five days, on the newly purchased trailer, license plates which have been issued to the dealer, provided that, at the time of the purchase, the dealer executes in duplicate, on forms provided by the Commissioner, a certificate bearing the date of issuance, the name and address of the purchaser, the identification number of the vehicle, the registration number to be used temporarily on the trailer, the name of the state in which the trailer is to be registered, and whatever other information may be required by the Commissioner. The original of the certificate and a bona fide bill of sale shall be delivered to the purchaser and shall be in the possession of the purchaser at all times when operating the trailer under dealer plates. One copy of the certificate shall be retained by the dealer, filed by him, and shall be subject to inspection at any time by the Department's agents. If the trailer is to be titled and registered in the Commonwealth, application for title and registration shall be made by the purchaser on the first business day following issuance of the certificate and a copy of the certificate shall accompany the applications.

License plates temporarily used by the purchaser shall be returned to the dealer by the purchaser not later than five days after the issuance of the certificate.
(Added by L.1996 chs. 1043, 1052, eff. 7/1/96.)

§46.2-1992.49. Operation without license plate prohibited.

No manufacturer or distributor of or dealer in trailers shall cause or permit any trailer owned by him to be operated or moved on a public highway without there being displayed on the trailer a license plate or plates issued to him, either under §46.2-711 or under §46.2-1992.41, except as otherwise authorized in §§46.2-733, 46.2-1992.40, and 46.2-1992.51.
(Added by L.1996 chs. 1043, 1052, eff. 7/1/96.)

§46.2-1992.50. Movement by manufacturer to place of shipment or delivery.

Any manufacturer of trailers may operate or move or cause to be moved or operated on the highways for a distance of no more than twenty-five miles trailers from the factory where manufactured or assembled to a railway depot, vessel, or place of shipment or delivery, without registering them and without license plates attached thereto, under a written permit first obtained from the local law-enforcement authorities having jurisdiction over the highways and on displaying in plain sight on each trailer a placard bearing the name and address of the manufacturer authorizing or directing the movement.
(Added by L.1996 chs. 1043, 1052, eff. 7/1/96.)

§46.2-1992.51. Movement by dealers to salesrooms.

Any dealer in trailers may operate or move, or cause to be operated or moved, any trailer on the highways for a distance of no more than twenty-five miles from a vessel, railway depot, warehouse, or any place of shipment or from a factory where manufactured or assembled to a salesroom, warehouse, or place of shipment or transshipment without registering them and without license plates attached thereto, under a written permit first obtained from the local law-enforcement authorities having jurisdiction over the highways, and on displaying in plain sight on each trailer, a placard bearing the name and address of the dealer authorizing or directing the movement.
(Added by L.1996 chs. 1043, 1052, eff. 7/1/96.)

§46.2-1992.52. Operation under foreign dealer's license.

It shall be unlawful, except as provided for by reciprocal agreement, for any person to operate a trailer or for the owner thereof to permit a trailer to be operated in the Commonwealth on a foreign dealer's license, unless the operation of the trailer on the license is specifically authorized by the Commissioner.
(Added by L.1996 chs. 1043, 1052, eff. 7/1/96.)

§46.2-1992.53. Removal of plates by Department of Motor Vehicles investigators; cancellation; reissuance.

If any Department of Motor Vehicles investigator finds that a trailer bearing license plates or temporary transport plates issued under this article is being operated in a manner inconsistent with (i) the requirements of this article or (ii) the Commissioner's authorization provided for in this article, the Department of Motor Vehicles investigator may remove the license plate for cancellation. Once a license plate has been canceled, the dealership may reapply for the license plate. Reissuance of the license plate shall be subject to the approval of the Commissioner and the payment of the fee prescribed for issuance of license plates under this article.
(Added by L.1996 chs. 1043, 1052, eff. 7/1/96.)

§46.2-1992.54. Penalties for violations of article; service of summons.

Notwithstanding §46.2-1992.5, any person violating any of the provisions of this article shall be guilty of a Class 3 misdemeanor. Any summons issued for any violation of any provision of this article relating to use or misuse of dealer's license plates shall be served upon the dealership to whom the plates were issued or to the person expressly permitting the unlawful use, or upon the operator of the trailer if the plates are used contrary to the use authorized by the certificate issued pursuant to §46.2-1992.44.
(Added by L.1996 chs. 1043, 1052, eff. 7/1/96.)

§46.2-1992.55. Watercraft trailers and watercraft trailer dealers.

For the purposes of this article, the term "trailer" shall include watercraft trailers and the terms "dealer" and "trailer dealer" shall include watercraft trailer dealers.
(Added by L.1996 chs. 1043, 1052, eff. 7/1/96.)

ARTICLE 6
ISSUANCE OF TEMPORARY LICENSE PLATES BY DEALERS

§46.2-1992.56. Issuance of temporary license plates to dealers and vehicle owners.

The Department may, subject to the limitations and conditions set forth in this article, deliver temporary license plates designed by the Department to any dealer licensed under this chapter who applies for at least ten sets of plates and who encloses with his application a fee of two dollars for each set applied for. The application shall be made on a form prescribed and furnished by the Department. Dealers, subject to the limitations and conditions set forth in this article, may issue temporary license plates to owners of trailers. The owners shall comply with the provisions of this article and §§46.2-705, 46.2-706 and 46.2-707. Dealers issuing temporary license plates may do so free of charge, but if they charge a fee for issuing temporary plates, the fee shall be no more than the fee charged the dealer by the Department under this section.

Display of a temporary license plate or plates on a vehicle shall subject the vehicle to the requirements of §§46.2-1038 and 46.2-1056.

(Added by L.1996 chs. 1043, 1052, eff. 7/1/96.)

§46.2-1992.57. Records to be kept by dealers; inspection.

Every dealer who has applied for temporary license plates shall maintain a permanent record of (i) all temporary license plates delivered to him, (ii) all temporary license plates issued by him, and (iii) any other information pertaining to the receipt or the issuance of temporary license plates which may be required by the Department. Each record shall be kept for at least one year from the date of entry. Every dealer shall allow full access to these records during regular business hours to authorized representatives of the Department and to law-enforcement officers.

(Added by L.1996 chs. 1043, 1052, eff. 7/1/96.)

§46.2-1992.58. Application for temporary license plate.

No dealer shall issue a temporary license plate except on written application by the person entitled to receive the license plate, which application shall be forwarded by the dealer to the Department as provided in §46.2-1992.35.

(Added by L.1996 chs. 1043, 1052, eff. 7/1/96.)

§46.2-1992.59. To whom temporary plates shall not be issued; dealer to forward application for current titling and registration; misstatements and false information.

No dealer shall issue, assign, transfer, or deliver temporary license plates to other than the bona fide purchaser or owner of a trailer, whether or not the trailer is to be registered in Virginia. If the trailer is to be registered in Virginia, the dealer shall submit to the Department a written application for the current titling and registration of the purchased trailer, accompanied by the prescribed fees. Any dealer who issues temporary license plates to a purchaser who fails or declines to request that his application be forwarded promptly to the Department forthwith shall notify the Department of the issuance in the manner provided in this article. No dealer shall issue temporary license plates to any person who possesses current license plates for a trailer that has been sold or exchanged, nor shall any dealer lend temporary license plates to any person for use on any trailer. If the dealer does not have in his possession the certificate of title or certificate of origin, he shall issue temporary license plates even though the purchaser has current license plates to be transferred. The dealer shall present the title or certificate of origin to the customer within thirty days of purchase and after this transaction is completed, the customer shall transfer his current license plates to the trailer. If the title or certificate of origin cannot be produced for a trailer within thirty days, a second set of temporary license plates may be issued provided that a temporary certificate of ownership is issued as provided in §46.2-1992.35. It shall be unlawful for any person to issue any temporary license plates containing any misstatement of fact, or for any person issuing or using temporary license plates knowingly to insert any false information on their face.

(Added by L.1996 chs. 1043, 1052, eff. 7/1/96.)

§46.2-1992.60. Dealer to insert his name, date of issuance and expiration, make and identification number of trailer.

Every dealer who issues temporary license plates shall insert clearly and indelibly on the face of each temporary license plate the name of the issuing dealer, the date of issuance and expiration, and the make and identification number of the trailer for which issued.

(Added by L.1996 chs. 1043, 1052, eff. 7/1/96.)

§46.2-1992.61. Suspension of right of dealer to issue.

The Commissioner, on determining that the provisions of this chapter or the directions of the Department are not being complied with by any dealer, may, after a hearing, suspend the right of a dealer to issue temporary license plates.

(Added by L.1996 chs. 1043, 1052, eff. 7/1/96.)

§46.2-1992.62. Plates to be destroyed on expiration.

Every person to whom temporary license plates have been issued shall destroy them on the thirtieth day after issue or immediately on receipt of the permanent license plates from the Department, whichever occurs first.

(Added by L.1996 chs. 1043, 1052, eff. 7/1/96.)

§46.2-1992.63. When plates to expire; refunds or credit.

Temporary license plates shall expire on the receipt of the permanent license plates from the Department, or on the rescission of a contract to purchase a trailer, or on the expiration of, or thirty days from the date of issuance, whichever occurs first. No refund or credit of fees paid by dealers to the Department for temporary license plates shall be allowed, except that when the Department discontinues the right of a dealer to issue temporary license plates, the dealer, on

returning temporary license plates to the Department, may receive a refund or a credit for them.
(Added by L.1996 chs. 1043, 1052, eff. 7/1/96.)

§46.2-1992.64. Penalties.
Any person violating any of the provisions of this article shall be guilty of a Class 1 misdemeanor.
(Added by L.1996 chs. 1043, 1052, eff. 7/1/96.)

§46.2-1992.65. Watercraft trailers and watercraft trailer dealers.
For the purposes of this article, the term "trailer" shall include watercraft trailers and the terms "dealer" and "trailer dealer" shall include watercraft trailer dealers.
(Added by L.1996 chs. 1043, 1052, eff. 7/1/96.)

ARTICLE 7
FRANCHISES

Section

§46.2-1992.66. Filing of franchises.
Each trailer manufacturer, factory branch, distributor, distributor branch, or subsidiary thereof shall file with the Commissioner a true copy of each new, amended, modified, or different form or addendum offered to more than one dealer which affects the rights, responsibilities, or obligations of the parties of a franchise or sales, service, or sales and service agreement to be offered to a trailer dealer or prospective trailer dealer in the Commonwealth no later than sixty days prior to the date the franchise or sales agreement is offered. In no event shall a new, amended, modified, or different form of franchise or sales, service, or sales and service agreement be offered a trailer dealer in the Commonwealth until the form has been determined by the Commissioner as not containing terms inconsistent with the provisions of this chapter. At the time a filing is made with the Commissioner pursuant to this section, the manufacturer, factory branch, distributor, distributor branch, or subsidiary shall also give written notice together with a copy of the papers so filed to the affected dealer or dealers.
(Added by L.1996 chs. 1043, 1052, eff. 7/1/96.)

§46.2-1992.67. Exemption of franchises from Retail Franchising Act.
Franchises subject to the provisions of this chapter shall not be subject to any requirement contained in Chapter 8 (§13.1-557 et seq.) of Title 13.1.
(Added by L.1996 chs. 1043, 1052, eff. 7/1/96.)

§46.2-1992.68. Coercion of retail dealer by manufacturer or distributor with respect to retail installment sales contracts prohibited.
A. It shall be unlawful for any manufacturer or distributor, or any officer, agent, or representative of either, to coerce or attempt to coerce any retail trailer dealer or prospective retail trailer dealer in the Commonwealth to sell, assign, or transfer any retail installment sales contract obtained by the dealer in connection with the sale by him in the Commonwealth of trailers manufactured or sold by the manufacturer or distributor, to a specified finance company or class of finance companies or to any other specified persons by any of the following:

1. Any statement, suggestion, promise, or threat that the manufacturer or distributor will in any manner benefit or injure the dealer, whether the statement, suggestion, threat, or promise is expressed or implied or made directly or indirectly.
2. Any act that will benefit or injure the dealer.
3. Any contract, or any expressed or implied offer of contract, made directly or indirectly to the dealer, for handling the trailer on the condition that the dealer sell, assign, or transfer his retail installment sales contract on the trailer, in the Commonwealth, to a specified finance company or class of finance companies or to any other specified person.
4. Any expressed or implied statement or representation made directly or indirectly that the dealer is under any obligation whatsoever to sell, assign, or transfer any of his retail sales contracts in the Commonwealth on trailers manufactured or sold by the manufacturer or distributor to a finance company, or class of finance companies, or other specified person, because of any relationship or affiliation between the manufacturer or distributor and the finance company or companies or the specified person or persons.

B. Any such statements, threats, promises, acts, contracts, or offers of contracts, when their effect may be to lessen or eliminate competition or tend to create a monopoly, are declared unfair trade practices and unfair methods of competition and are prohibited.

C. Any person violating any of the provisions of this article shall be guilty of a Class 1 misdemeanor.
(Added by L.1996 chs. 1043, 1052, eff. 7/1/96.)

§46.2-1992.69. Other coercion of dealers; transfer, grant, succession to and cancellation of dealer franchises; delivery of trailers, parts, and accessories.
It shall be unlawful for any manufacturer, factory branch, distributor, or distributor branch, or any field representative, officer, agent, or their representatives:

1. To coerce or attempt to coerce any dealer to accept delivery of any trailer or trailers, parts or accessories therefor, or any other commodities, which have not been ordered by the dealer.
2. To coerce or attempt to coerce any dealer to enter into an agreement with the manufacturer, factory branch, distributor, or distributor branch, or representative thereof, or do any other act unfair to the dealer, by threatening to cancel any franchise existing between the manufacturer, factory branch, distributor, distributor branch, or representative thereof and the dealer.
3. To coerce or attempt to coerce any dealer to join, contribute to, or affiliate with any advertising association.
4. To prevent or refuse to approve the sale or transfer of the ownership of a dealership by the sale of the business, stock transfer, or otherwise, or the transfer, sale, or assignment of a dealer franchise, or a change in the executive management or principal operator of the dealership, unless the franchisor provides written notice to the dealer of its objection and the reasons therefor at least thirty days prior to

the proposed effective date of the transfer, sale, assignment, or change. No such objection shall be effective to prevent the sale, transfer, assignment, or change if the Commissioner has determined, if requested in writing by the dealer within thirty days after receipt of an objection to the proposed sale, transfer, or change, and after a hearing on the matter, that the failure to permit or honor the sale, transfer, assignment, or change is unreasonable under the circumstances. No franchise may be sold, assigned, or transferred unless (i) the franchisor has been given at least ninety days' prior written notice by the dealer as to the identity, financial ability, and qualifications of the proposed transferee, and (ii) the sale or transfer of the franchise and business will not involve, without the franchisor's consent, a relocation of the business.

5. To grant an additional franchise for a particular line-make of trailer in a relevant market area in which a dealer or dealers in that line-make are already located unless the franchisor has first advised in writing all other dealers in the line-make in the relevant market area. No such additional franchise may be established at the proposed site unless the Commissioner has determined, if requested by a dealer of the same line-make in the relevant market area within thirty days after receipt of the franchisor's notice of intention to establish the additional franchise, and after a hearing on the matter, that there is reasonable evidence that after the grant of the new franchise, the market will support all of the dealers in that line-make in the relevant market area. Establishing a franchised dealer in a relevant market area to replace a franchised dealer that has not been in operation for more than two years shall constitute the establishment of a new franchise subject to the terms of this subdivision. The two-year period for replacing a franchised dealer shall begin on the day the franchise was terminated, or, if a termination hearing was held, on the day the franchisor was legally permitted finally to terminate the franchise. This subdivision shall not apply to (i) the relocation of an existing dealer within that dealer's relevant market area if the relocation site is to be more than ten miles distant from any other dealer for the same line-make; (ii) the relocation of an existing dealer within that dealer's relevant market area if the relocation site is to be more distant than the existing site from all other dealers of the same line-make in that relevant market area; or (iii) the relocation of an existing new trailer dealer within two miles of the existing site of the relocating dealer.

6. Except as otherwise provided in this subdivision and notwithstanding the terms of any franchise, to terminate, cancel, or refuse to renew the franchise of any dealer without good cause and unless (i) the dealer and the Commissioner have received written notice of the franchisor's intentions at least sixty days prior to the effective date of such termination, cancellation, or the expiration date of the franchise, setting forth the specific grounds for the action, and (ii) the Commissioner has determined, if requested in writing by the dealer within the sixty-day period, and after a hearing on the matter, that there is good cause for the termination, cancellation, or nonrenewal of the franchise. In any case where a petition is made to the Commissioner for a determination as to good cause for the termination, cancellation, or nonrenewal of a franchise, the franchise in question shall continue in effect pending the Commissioner's decision or, if that decision is appealed to the circuit court, pending the decision of the circuit court. In any case in which a franchisor neither advises a dealer that it does not intend to renew a franchise nor takes any action to renew a franchise beyond its expiration date, the franchise in question shall continue in effect on the terms last agreed to by the parties. Notwithstanding the other provisions of this subdivision, notice of termination, cancellation, or nonrenewal may be provided to a dealer by a franchisor not less than fifteen days prior to the effective date of such termination, cancellation, or nonrenewal when the grounds for such action are any of the following:

a. Insolvency of the franchised trailer dealer or filing of any petition by or against the franchised trailer dealer, under any bankruptcy or receivership law, leading to liquidation or which is intended to lead to liquidation of the franchisee's business;

b. Failure of the franchised trailer dealer to conduct its customary sales and service operations during its posted business hours for seven consecutive business days, except where the failure results from acts of God or circumstances beyond the direct control of the franchised trailer dealer;

c. Revocation of any license which the franchised trailer dealer is required to have to operate a dealership; or

d. Conviction of the dealer or any principal of the dealer of a felony.

The change or discontinuance of a marketing or distribution system of a particular line-make product by a manufacturer or distributor, while the name identification of the product is continued in substantial form by the same or different manufacturer or distributor, may be considered to be a franchise termination, cancellation, or nonrenewal. The provisions of this paragraph shall apply to changes and discontinuances made after January 1, 1989, but they shall not be considered by any court in any case in which such a change or discontinuance occurring prior to that date has been challenged as constituting a termination, cancellation or nonrenewal.

7. To fail to provide continued parts and service support to a dealer which holds a franchise in a discontinued line-make for at least five years from the date of such discontinuance. This requirement shall not apply to a line-make which was discontinued prior to January 1, 1989.

8. To fail to allow a dealer the right at any time to designate a member of his family as a successor to the dealership in the event of the death or incapacity of the dealer. It shall be unlawful to prevent or refuse to honor the succession to a dealership by a member of the family of a deceased or incapacitated dealer if the franchisor has not provided to the member of the family previously designated by the dealer as his successor written notice of its objections to the succession and of such person's right to seek a hearing on the matter before the Commissioner pursuant to this article, and the Commissioner determines, if requested in writing by such member of the family within thirty days of receipt of such notice from the franchisor, and after a hearing on the matter before the Commissioner pursuant to this article, that the failure to permit or honor the succession is unreasonable under the circumstances. No member of the family may succeed to a franchise unless (i) the franchisor has been given written notice as to the identity, financial ability, and qualifications of the member of the family in question and (ii) the succession to the franchise will not involve, without the franchisor's consent, a relocation of the business.

9. To fail to ship monthly to any dealer, if ordered by the dealer, the number of new trailers of each make, series, and model needed by the dealer to receive a percentage of total new trailer sales of each make, series, and model equitably related to the total new trailer production or importation currently being achieved nationally by each make, series, and model covered under the franchise. Upon the written request of any dealer holding its sales or sales and service franchise, the manufacturer or distributor shall disclose to the dealer in writing the basis upon which new trailers are allocated, scheduled, and delivered to the dealers of the same line-make. If allocation is at issue in a request for a hearing, the dealer may demand the Commissioner to direct that the manufacturer or distributor provide to the dealer, within thirty

days of such demand, all records of sales and all records of distribution of all trailers to the same line-make dealers who compete with the dealer requesting the hearing.

10. To require or otherwise coerce a dealer to under-utilize the dealer's facilities.

11. To include in any franchise with a trailer dealer terms that are contrary to, prohibited by, or otherwise inconsistent with the requirements of this chapter.

12. For any franchise agreement to require a trailer dealer to pay the attorney's fees of the manufacturer or distributor related to hearings and appeals brought under this article.

13. To fail to include in any franchise with a trailer dealer the following language: "If any provision herein contravenes the laws or regulations of any state or other jurisdiction wherein this agreement is to be performed, or denies access to the procedures, forums, or remedies provided for by such laws or regulations, such provision shall be deemed to be modified to conform to such laws or regulations, and all other terms and provisions shall remain in full force," or words to that effect.

(Added by L.1996 chs. 1043, 1052, eff. 7/1/96.)

§46.2-1992.70. Manufacturer or distributor right of first refusal.

Notwithstanding the terms of any franchise agreement, in the event of a proposed sale or transfer of a dealership, the manufacturer or distributor shall be permitted to exercise a right of first refusal to acquire the new trailer dealer's assets or ownership, if such sale or transfer is conditioned upon the manufacturer's or dealer's entering into a dealer agreement with the proposed new owner or transferee, only if all the following requirements are met:

1. To exercise its right of first refusal, the manufacturer or distributor must notify the dealer in writing within forty-five days of its receipt of the completed proposal for the proposed sale or transfer;

2. The exercise of the right of first refusal will result in the dealer's and dealer's owner's receiving the same or greater consideration as they have contracted to receive in connection with the proposed change of ownership or transfer;

3. The proposed sale or transfer of the dealership's assets does not involve the transfer or sale to a member or members of the family of one or more dealer owners, or to a qualified manager or a partnership or corporation controlled by such persons; and

4. The manufacturer or distributor agrees to pay the reasonable expenses, including attorney's fees which do not exceed the usual, customary, and reasonable fees charged for similar work done for other clients, incurred by the proposed new owner and transferee prior to the manufacturer's or distributor's exercise of its right of first refusal in negotiating and implementing the contract for the proposed sale or transfer of the dealership or dealership assets. Notwithstanding the foregoing, no payment of such expenses and attorney's fees shall be required if the dealer has not submitted or caused to be submitted an accounting of those expenses within thirty days of the dealer's receipt of the manufacturer's or distributor's written request for such an accounting. Such accounting may be requested by a manufacturer or distributor before exercising its right of first refusal.

(Added by L.1996 chs. 1043, 1052, eff. 7/1/96.)

§46.2-1992.71. Discontinuation of distributors.

If the contract between a distributor and a manufacturer or importer is terminated or otherwise discontinued, all franchises granted to trailer dealers in Virginia by that distributor shall continue in full force and shall not be affected by the discontinuance, except that the manufacturer, factory branch, distributor, representative, or other person who undertakes to distribute trailers of the same line-make or the same trailers of a renamed line-make shall be substituted for the discontinued distributor under the existing trailer dealer franchises and those franchises shall be modified accordingly.

(Added by L.1996 chs. 1043, 1052, eff. 7/1/96.)

§46.2-1992.72. Warranty obligations.

A. Each trailer manufacturer, factory branch, distributor, or distributor branch shall (i) specify in writing to each of its trailer dealers licensed in the Commonwealth the dealer's obligations for preparation, delivery, and warranty service on its products and (ii) compensate the dealer for warranty parts, service and diagnostic work required of the dealer by the manufacturer or distributor as follows:

1. Compensation of a dealer for warranty parts, service and diagnostic work shall not be less than the amounts charged by the dealer for the manufacturer's or distributor's original parts, service and diagnostic work to retail customers for nonwarranty service, parts and diagnostic work installed or performed in the dealer's service department unless the amounts are not reasonable;

2. For purposes of determining warranty parts and service compensation, menu-priced parts or services, group discounts, special event discounts, and special event promotions shall not be considered in determining amounts charged by the dealer to retail customers;

3. Increases in dealer warranty parts and service compensation and diagnostic work compensation, pursuant to this section, shall be requested by the dealer in writing, shall be based on 100 consecutive repair orders or all repair orders over a ninety-day period, whichever occurs first and, in the case of parts, shall be stated as a percentage of markup which shall be uniformly applied to all the manufacturer's or distributor's parts;

4. In the case of warranty parts compensation, the provisions of this subsection shall be effective only for model year 1992 and succeeding model years;

5. If a manufacturer or distributor furnishes a part to a dealer at no cost for use by the dealer in performing work for which the manufacturer or distributor is required to compensate the dealer under this section, the manufacturer or distributor shall compensate the dealer for the part in the same manner as warranty parts compensation, less the wholesale costs, for such part as listed in the manufacturer's current price schedules; or

6. In the case of service work, manufacturer original parts or parts otherwise specified by the manufacturer or distributor, and parts provided by a dealer either pursuant to an adjustment program as defined in §59.1-207.34 or as otherwise requested by the manufacturer or distributor, the dealer shall be compensated in the same manner as for warranty service or parts.

This section does not apply to compensation for parts such as components, systems, fixtures, appliances, furnishings, accessories, and features that are designed, used, and maintained primarily for nonvehicular, residential purposes. Warranty audits of dealer records may be conducted by the manufacturer, factory branch, distributor, or distributor branch on a reasonable basis, and dealer claims for warranty compensation shall not be denied except for good cause, such as performance of nonwarranty repairs, lack of material documentation, fraud, or misrepresentation. Claims for dealer compensation shall be paid within thirty days of dealer submission or within thirty days of the end of an incentive program or rejected in writing for stated reasons. The manufacturer, factory branch, distributor, or distributor branch shall reserve the right to reasonable periodic audits to determine the validity of all such paid claims for dealer compensation. Any chargebacks for warranty parts or service compensation and service incentives shall only be for the twelve-month period immediately following the date of the claim and, in the case of chargebacks for sales compensation only, for the eighteen-month period immediately following the date of claim. However, such limitations shall not be effective in the case of intentionally false or fraudulent claims.

B. It shall be unlawful for any trailer manufacturer, factory branch, distributor, or distributor branch to:

1. Fail to perform any of its warranty obligations, including tires, with respect to a trailer;

2. Fail to assume all responsibility for any liability resulting from structural or production defects;

3. Fail to include in written notices of factory recalls to trailer owners and dealers the expected date by which necessary parts and equipment will be available to dealers for the correction of defects;

4. Fail to compensate any of the trailer dealers licensed in the Commonwealth for repairs effected by the dealer of merchandise damaged in manufacture or transit to the dealer where the carrier is designated by the manufacturer, factory branch, distributor, or distributor branch;

5. Fail to compensate its trailer dealers licensed in the Commonwealth for warranty parts, work, and service pursuant to subsection A of this section, or for legal costs and expenses incurred by such dealers in connection with warranty obligations for which the manufacturer, factory branch, distributor, or distributor branch is legally responsible or which the manufacturer, factory branch, distributor, or distributor branch imposes upon the dealer;

6. Misrepresent in any way to purchasers of trailers that warranties with respect to the manufacture, performance, or design of the trailer are made by the dealer, either as warrantor or co-warrantor;

7. Require the dealer to make warranties to customers in any manner related to the manufacture, performance, or design of the trailer; or

8. Shift or attempt to shift to the trailer dealer, directly or indirectly, any liabilities of the manufacturer, factory branch, distributor or distributor branch under the Virginia Motor Vehicle Warranty Enforcement Act (§59.1-207.9 et seq.), unless such liability results from the act or omission by the dealer.

C. Notwithstanding the terms of any franchise, it shall be unlawful for any trailer manufacturer, factory branch, distributor, or distributor branch to fail to indemnify and hold harmless its trailer dealers against any losses or damages arising out of complaints, claims, or suits relating to the manufacture, assembly, or design of trailers, parts, or accessories, or other functions by the manufacturer, factory branch, distributor, or distributor branch beyond the control of the dealer, including, without limitation, the selection by the manufacturer, factory branch, distributor, or distributor branch of parts or components for the trailer or any damages to merchandise occurring in transit to the dealer where the carrier is designated by the manufacturer, factory branch, distributor, or distributor branch. The dealer shall notify the manufacturer of pending suits in which allegations are made which come within this subsection whenever reasonably practicable to do so. Every trailer dealer franchise issued to, amended, or renewed for trailer dealers in Virginia shall be construed to incorporate provisions consistent with the requirements of this subsection.

D. On any new trailer, any uncorrected damage or any corrected damage exceeding three percent of the manufacturer's or distributor's suggested retail price as defined in 15 U.S.C. §§1231–1233, as measured by retail repair costs, must be disclosed to the dealer in writing prior to delivery. Factory mechanical repair and damage to glass, tires, and bumpers are excluded from the three percent rule when properly replaced by identical manufacturer's or distributor's original equipment or parts. Whenever a new trailer is damaged in transit, when the carrier or means of transportation is determined by the manufacturer or distributor, or whenever a trailer is otherwise damaged prior to delivery to the new trailer dealer, the new trailer dealer shall:

1. Notify the manufacturer or distributor of the damage within three business days from the date of delivery of the new trailer to the new trailer dealership or within the additional time specified in the franchise; and

2. Request from the manufacturer or distributor authorization to replace the components, parts, and accessories damaged or otherwise correct the damage, unless the damage to the trailer exceeds the three percent rule, in which case the dealer may reject the trailer within three business days.

E. If the manufacturer or distributor refuses or fails to authorize correction of such damage within ten days after receipt of notification, or if the dealer rejects the trailer because damage exceeds the three percent rule, ownership of the new trailer shall revert to the manufacturer or distributor, and the new trailer dealer shall have no obligation, financial or otherwise, with respect to such trailer. Should either the manufacturer, distributor, or the dealer elect to correct the damage or any other damage exceeding the three percent rule, full disclosure shall be made by the dealer in writing to the buyer and an acknowledgment by the buyer is required. If there is less than three percent damage, no disclosure is required, provided the damage has been corrected. Predelivery mechanical work shall not require a disclosure. Failure to disclose any corrected damage within the knowledge of the selling dealer to a new trailer in excess of the three percent rule shall constitute grounds for revocation of the buyer order, provided that, within thirty days of purchase, the trailer is returned to the dealer with an accompanying written notice of the grounds for revocation. In case of revocation pursuant to this section, the dealer shall accept the trailer and refund any payments made to the dealer in connection with the transaction, less a reasonable allowance for the consumer's use of the trailer as defined in §59.1-207.11.

F. If there is a dispute between the manufacturer, factory branch, distributor, or distributor branch and the dealer with respect to any matter referred to in subsection A, B, or C of this section, either party may petition the Commissioner in writing, within thirty days after either party has given written notice of the dispute to the other, for a hearing. The decision of the Commissioner shall be binding on the parties, subject to rights of judicial review and appeal as provided in Chapter 1.1:1 (§9-6.14:1 et seq.) of Title 9. However, nothing contained in this section shall give the Commissioner any authority as to the content or interpretation of any manufacturer's or distributor's warranty.

(Added by L.1996 chs. 1043, 1052, eff. 7/1/96.)

§46.2-1992.73. Operation of dealership by manufacturer.

It shall be unlawful for any trailer manufacturer, factory branch, distributor, distributor branch, or subsidiary thereof, to own, operate, or control any trailer dealership in the Commonwealth. However, this section shall not prohibit:

1. The operation by a manufacturer, factory branch, distributor, distributor branch, or subsidiary thereof, of a dealership for a temporary period, not to exceed one year, during the transition from one owner or operator to another;

2. The ownership or control of a dealership by a manufacturer, factory branch, distributor, distributor branch, or subsidiary thereof, while the dealership is being sold under a bona fide contract or purchase option to the operator of the dealership;

3. The ownership, operation, or control of a dealership by a manufacturer, factory branch, distributor, distributor branch, or subsidiary thereof, if the manufacturer, factory branch, distributor, distributor branch, or subsidiary has been engaged in the retail sale of trailers through the dealership for a continuous period of three years prior to July 1, 1972, and if the Commissioner determines, after a hearing on the matter at the request of any party, that there is no dealer independent of the manufacturer or distributor, factory branch or distributor branch, or subsidiary thereof available in the community to own and operate the franchise in a manner consistent with the public interest; or

4. The ownership, operation, or control of a dealership by a manufacturer, factory branch, distributor, distributor branch, or subsidiary thereof if the Commissioner determines, after a hearing at the request of any party, that there is no dealer independent of the manufacturer or distributor, factory branch or distributor branch, or subsidiary thereof available in the community or trade area to own and operate the franchise in a manner consistent with the public interest.
(Added by L.1996 chs. 1043, 1052, eff. 7/1/96.)

§46.2-1992.74. Ownership of service facilities.

It shall be unlawful for any trailer manufacturer, factory branch, distributor, distributor branch, or subsidiary thereof, to own, operate, or control, either directly or indirectly, any trailer warranty or service facility located in the Commonwealth. Nothing in this section shall prohibit any trailer manufacturer, factory branch, distributor, distributor branch, or subsidiary thereof, from owning, operating, or controlling any warranty or service facility for warranty or service of trailers owned or operated by the manufacturer, factory branch, distributor, distributor branch, or subsidiary thereof. Nothing contained in this section shall prohibit a trailer manufacturer, factory branch, distributor, or distributor branch from performing service for reasons of compliance with an order of a court of competent jurisdiction or of warranty under Chapter 17.3 (§59.1-207.9 et seq.) of Title 59.1.
(Added by L.1996 chs. 1043, 1052, eff. 7/1/96.)

§46.2-1992.75. Hearings and other remedies; civil penalties.

A. In every case of a hearing before the Commissioner authorized under this article, the Commissioner shall give reasonable notice of each hearing to all interested parties, and the Commissioner's decision shall be binding on the parties, subject to the rights of judicial review and appeal as provided in Chapter 1.1:1 (§9-6.14:1 et seq.) of Title 9.

B. Hearings before the Commissioner under this article shall commence within ninety days of the request for a hearing and the Commissioner's decision shall be rendered within sixty days from the receipt of the hearing officer's recommendation. Hearings authorized under this article shall be presided over by a hearing officer selected from a list prepared by the Executive Secretary of the Supreme Court of Virginia. On request of the Commissioner, the Executive Secretary will name a hearing officer from the list, selected on a rotation system administered by the Executive Secretary. The hearing officer shall provide recommendations to the Commissioner within ninety days of the conclusion of the hearing.

C. Notwithstanding any contrary provision of this article, the Commissioner shall initiate investigations, conduct hearings, and determine the rights of parties under this article whenever he is provided information indicating a possible violation of any provision of this article.

D. For purposes of any matter brought to the Commissioner under subdivisions 3, 4, 5, 6 and 9 of §46.2-1992.69 with respect to which the Commissioner is to determine whether there is good cause for a proposed action or whether it would be unreasonable under the circumstances, the Commissioner shall consider:

1. The volume of the affected dealer's business in the relevant market area;
2. The nature and extent of the dealer's investment in its business;
3. The adequacy of the dealer's service facilities, equipment, parts, supplies, and personnel;
4. The effect of the proposed action on the community;
5. The extent and quality of the dealer's service under trailer warranties;
6. The dealer's performance under the terms of its franchise; and
7. Other economic and geographical factors reasonably associated with the proposed action.

With respect to subdivision 6 of this subsection, any performance standard or program for measuring dealership performance that may have a material effect on a dealer, and the application of any such standard or program by a manufacturer or distributor, shall be fair, reasonable, and equitable and, if based upon a survey, shall be based upon a statistically valid sample. Upon the request of any dealer, a manufacturer or distributor shall disclose in writing to the dealer a description of how a performance standard or program is designed and all relevant information used in the application of the performance standard or program to that dealer.

E. An interested party in a hearing held pursuant to subsection A of this section shall comply with the effective date of compliance established by the Commissioner in his decision in such hearing, unless a stay or extension of such date is granted by the Commissioner or the Commissioner's decision is under judicial review and appeal as provided in subsection A of this section. If, after notice to such interested party and an opportunity to comment, the Commissioner finds an interested party has not complied with his decision by the designated date of compliance, unless a stay or extension of such date has been granted by the Commissioner or the Commissioner's decision is under judicial review and appeal, the Commissioner may assess such interested party a civil penalty not to exceed $1,000 per day of noncompliance. Civil penalties collected under this subsection shall be deposited into the Transportation Trust Fund.
(Added by L.1996 chs. 1043, 1052; chgd. by L.2000 ch. 106, eff. 7/1/2000.)

§46.2-1992.76. Late model and factory repurchase franchises.

Franchised late model or factory repurchase trailer dealers shall have the same rights and obligations as provided for franchised new trailer dealers in this article, mutatis mutandis.
(Added by L.1996 chs. 1043, 1052, eff. 7/1/96.)

§46.2-1992.77. Watercraft trailers and watercraft trailer dealers.

For the purposes of this article, the term "trailer" shall include watercraft trailers and the terms "dealer" and "trailer dealer" shall include watercraft trailer dealers.
(Added by L.1996 chs. 1043, 1052, eff. 7/1/96.)

ARTICLE 8
DENIAL, SUSPENSION, AND REVOCATION OF DEALER LICENSES

§46.2-1992.78. Acts of officers, directors, partners, and salespersons.

If a licensee or registrant is a partnership or corporation, it shall be sufficient cause for the denial, suspension, or revocation of a license or certificate of dealer registration that any officer, director, or trustee of the partnership or corporation, or any member in the case of a partnership or the dealer-operator, has committed any act or omitted any duty which would be cause for refusing, suspending, or revoking a license or certificate of dealer registration issued to him as an individual under this chapter. Each licensee or registrant shall be responsible for the acts of any of his salespersons while acting as his agent, if the licensee approved of those acts or had knowledge of those acts or other similar acts and, after such knowledge, retained the benefit, proceeds, profits, or advantages accruing from those acts or otherwise ratified those acts.

(Added by L.1996 chs. 1043, 1052, eff. 7/1/96.)

§46.2-1992.79. Grounds for denying, suspending, or revoking licenses or certificates of dealer registration or qualification.

A license or certificate of dealer registration or qualification issued under this subtitle may be denied, suspended, or revoked on any one or more of the following grounds:

1. Material misstatement or omission in application for license, dealer's license plates, certificate of dealer registration, certificate of qualification, or certificate of title;
2. Failure to comply subsequent to receipt of a written warning from the Department or any willful failure to comply with any provision of this chapter or any applicable provision of this subtitle or any applicable regulation promulgated under this subtitle;
3. Failure to have an established place of business as defined in §46.2-1992.8 or failure to have as the dealer-operator an individual who holds a valid certificate of qualification;
4. Defrauding any retail buyer, to the buyer's damage, or any other person in the conduct of the licensee's or registrant's business;
5. Employment of fraudulent devices, methods or practices in connection with compliance with the requirements under the statutes of the Commonwealth with respect to the retaking of vehicles under retail installment contracts and the redemption and resale of those vehicles;
6. Having used deceptive acts or practices;
7. Knowingly advertising by any means any assertion, representation, or statement of fact which is untrue, misleading, or deceptive in any particular relating to the conduct of the business licensed or registered under this subtitle or for which a license or registration is sought;
8. Having been convicted of any fraudulent act in connection with the business of selling vehicles or any consumer-related fraud;
9. Having been convicted of any criminal act involving the business of selling vehicles;
10. Willfully retaining in his possession title to a vehicle that has not been completely and legally assigned to him;
11. Failure to comply with any provision of Chapter 4.1 (§36-85.2 et seq.) of Title 36 or any regulation promulgated pursuant to that chapter;
12. Leasing, renting, lending, or otherwise allowing the use of a dealer's license plate by persons not specifically authorized under this title;
13. Having been convicted of a felony;
14. Failure to submit to the Department, within thirty days from the date of sale, any application, tax, or fee collected for the Department on behalf of a buyer;
15. Having been convicted of larceny of a vehicle or receipt or sale of a stolen vehicle;
16. Having been convicted of odometer tampering or any related violation;
17. If a salvage dealer, salvage pool, or rebuilder, failing to comply with any provision of Chapter 16 of this title or any regulation promulgated by the Commissioner under that chapter;
18. Failing to maintain liability insurance, issued by a company licensed to do business in the Commonwealth, or a certificate of self-insurance as defined in §46.2-368, with respect to each dealer's license plate issued to the dealer by the Department; or
19. Failing or refusing to pay civil penalties imposed by the Commissioner pursuant to §46.2-1992.5.

(Added by L.1996 chs. 1043, 1052; chgd. by L.1999 ch. 217, eff. 7/1/99.)

§46.2-1992.80. Suspension, revocation, and refusal to renew licenses or certificates of dealer registration or qualification; notice and hearing.

A. Except as provided in subsections B and C of this section, no license or certificate of dealer registration or qualification issued under this subtitle shall be suspended or revoked, or renewal thereof refused, until a written copy of the complaint made has been furnished to the licensee, registrant, or qualifier against whom the same is directed and a public hearing thereon has been had before the Commissioner. At least ten days' written notice of the time and place of the hearing shall be given to the licensee, registrant, or qualifier by registered mail addressed to his last known post office address or as shown on his license or certificate or other record of information in possession of the Commissioner. At the hearing the licensee, registrant, or qualifier shall have the right to be heard personally or by counsel. After hearing, the Commissioner may suspend, revoke, or refuse to renew the license or certificate in question. Immediate notice of any suspension, revocation, or refusal shall be given to the licensee, registrant, or qualifier in the same manner provided in this section for giving notices of hearing.

B. Should a dealer fail to maintain an established place of business, the Commissioner may cancel the license of the dealer without a hearing after notification of the intent to cancel has been sent, by return receipt mail, to the dealer at the dealer's residence and business addresses, and the notices are returned undelivered or the dealer does not respond within twenty days from the date the notices were sent. Any subsequent application for a dealer's license shall be treated as an original application.

C. Should a dealer fail or refuse to pay civil penalties imposed by the Commissioner pursuant to §46.2-1992.5, the Commissioner may deny, revoke, or suspend the dealer's license without a hearing after notice of imposition of civil

penalties has been sent, by certified mail, return receipt requested, to the dealer at the dealer's business address and such civil penalty is not paid in full within thirty days after receipt of the notice.
(Added by L.1996 chs. 1043, 1052; chgd. by L.1999 ch. 217, eff. 7/1/99.)

§46.2-1992.81. Appeals from actions of the Commissioner.

Any person aggrieved by the action of the Commissioner in refusing to grant or renew a license or certificate of dealer registration or qualification issued under this chapter, or by any other action of the Commissioner which is alleged to be improper, unreasonable, or unlawful under the provisions of this chapter is entitled to judicial review in accordance with the provisions of the Administrative Process Act (§9-6.14:1 et seq.).
(Added by L.1996 chs. 1043, 1052, eff. 7/1/96.)

§46.2-1992.82. Appeals to Court of Appeals.

Either party may appeal from the decision of the court under §46.2-1992.81 to the Court of Appeals. These appeals shall be taken and prosecuted in the same manner and with like effect as is provided by law in other cases appealed as a matter of right to the Court of Appeals.
(Added by L.1996 chs. 1043, 1052; chgd. by L.1997 ch. 88, eff. 7/1/97.)

§46.2-1992.83. Equitable remedies not impaired.

The remedy at law provided by §§46.2-1992.81 and 46.2-1992.82 shall not in any manner impair the right to applicable equitable relief. That right to equitable relief is hereby preserved, notwithstanding the provisions of §§46.2-1992.81 and 46.2-1992.82.
(Added by L.1996 chs. 1043, 1052, eff. 7/1/96.)

ARTICLE 9
TRAILER DEALER ADVERTISING

§46.2-1992.84. Regulated advertising practices.

For purposes of this chapter, a violation of the following regulated advertising practices shall be an unfair, deceptive, or misleading act or practice.

1. A trailer shall not be advertised as new, either by word or implication, unless it is one which conforms to the requirements of §46.2-1992.

2. When advertising any trailer which does not conform to the definition of "new" as provided in §46.2-1992, the fact that it is used shall be clearly and unequivocally expressed by the term "used" or by such other term as is commonly understood to mean that the trailer is used. By way of example but not by limitation, "special purchase" by itself is not a satisfactory disclosure; however, such terms as "demonstrator" or "former leased trailers" used alone clearly express that the trailers are used for advertising purposes.

3. Advertisement of finance charges or other interest rates shall not be used when there is a cost to buy-down said charge or rate which is passed on, in whole or in part, to the purchaser.

4. Terms, conditions, and disclaimers shall be stated clearly and conspicuously. An asterisk or other reference symbol may be used to point to a disclaimer or other information, but shall not be used as a means of contradicting or changing the meaning of an advertised statement.

5. The expiration date of an advertised sale shall be clearly and conspicuously disclosed.

6. The term "list price," "sticker price," or "suggested retail price" and similar terms, shall be used only in reference to the manufacturer's suggested retail price for new trailers or the dealer's own usual and customary price for used trailers.

7. Terms such as "at cost," "below cost," "$ off cost" shall not be used in advertisements because of the difficulty in determining a dealer's actual net cost at the time of the sale. Terms such as "invoice price," "$ over invoice," may be used, provided that the invoice referred to is the manufacturer's factory invoice or a bona fide bill of sale and the invoice or bill of sale is available for customer inspection.

"Manufacturer's factory invoice" means that document supplied by the manufacturer to the dealer listing the manufacturer's charge to the dealer before any deduction for holdback, group advertising, factory incentives or rebates, or any governmental charges.

8. When the price or credit terms of a trailer are advertised, the trailer shall be fully identified as to year, make, and model. In addition, in advertisements placed by individual dealers and not line-make marketing groups, the stated price or credit terms shall include all charges which the buyer must pay to the seller, except buyer-selected options, state and local fees and taxes, and manufacturer's or distributor's freight or destination charges. If freight or destination charges are not included in the advertised price, the amount of any such freight or destination charge must be clearly and conspicuously disclosed.

9. Advertisements which set out a policy of matching or bettering competitors' prices shall not be used unless the terms of the offer are specific, verifiable and reasonable.

10. Advertisements of "dealer rebates" shall not be used. This does not affect advertisement of manufacturer rebates.

11. "Free," "at no cost," or other words to that effect shall not be used unless the "free" item, merchandise, or service is available without a purchase. This provision shall not apply to advertising placed by manufacturers, distributors, or line-make marketing groups.

12. "Bait" advertising, in which an advertiser may have no intention to sell at the price or terms advertised, shall not be used. By way of example, but not by limitation:

a. If a specific trailer is advertised, the seller shall be in possession of a reasonable supply of said trailers, and they shall be available at the advertised price. If the advertised trailer is available only in limited numbers or only by order, that shall be stated in the advertisement. For purposes of this subdivision, the listing of a trailer by stock number or vehicle identification number in the advertisement for a used trailer is one means of satisfactorily disclosing a limitation of availability. Stock numbers or vehicle identification numbers shall not be used in advertising a new trailer unless the advertisement clearly and conspicuously discloses that it relates to only one trailer;

b. Advertising a trailer at a certain price, including "as low as" statements, but having available for sale only trailers equipped with dealer added cost "options" which increase the selling price, above the advertised price, shall also be considered "bait" advertising;

c. If a lease payment is advertised, the fact that it is a lease arrangement shall be disclosed.

13. The term "repossessed" shall be used only to describe trailers that have been sold, registered, titled and then taken back from a purchaser and not yet resold to an ultimate user. Advertisers offering repossessed trailers for sale shall provide proof of repossession upon request.

14. Words such as "finance" or "loan" shall not be used in a trailer advertiser's firm name or trade name, unless that person is actually engaged in the financing of trailers.

15. Any advertisement which gives the impression a dealer has a special arrangement or relationship with the distributor or manufacturer, as compared to similarly situated dealers, shall not be used.
(Added by L.1996 chs. 1043, 1052, eff. 7/1/96.)

§46.2-1992.85. Enforcement; regulations.

The Commissioner may promulgate regulations reasonably necessary for enforcement of this article.

In addition to any other sanctions or remedies available to the Commissioner under this chapter, the Commissioner may assess a civil penalty not to exceed $1,000 for any single violation of this article. Each day that a violation continues shall constitute a separate violation.
(Added by L.1996 chs. 1043, 1052, eff. 7/1/96.)

CHAPTER 19.2
MOTORCYCLE DEALERS

(Added by L.1996 chs. 1043, 1052, eff. 7/1/96.)

Article

ARTICLE 1
MOTORCYCLE DEALERS GENERALLY

Section

§46.2-1993. Definitions.

Unless the context otherwise requires, the following words and terms for the purpose of this chapter shall have the following meanings:

"Certificate of origin" means the document provided by the manufacturer of a new motorcycle, or its distributor, which is the only valid indication of ownership between the manufacturer, its distributor, its franchised motorcycle dealers, and the original purchaser not for resale.

"Dealer-operator" means the individual who works at the established place of business of a dealer and who is responsible for and in charge of day-to-day operations of that place of business.

"Distributor" means a person who sells or distributes new motorcycles pursuant to a written agreement with the manufacturer, to franchised motorcycle dealers in the Commonwealth.

"Distributor branch" means a branch office maintained by a distributor for the sale of motorcycles to motorcycle dealers or for directing or supervising, in whole or in part, its representatives in the Commonwealth.

"Distributor representative" means a person employed by a distributor or by a distributor branch, for the purpose of making or promoting the sale of motorcycles or for supervising or contacting its dealers, prospective dealers, or representatives in the Commonwealth.

"Factory branch" means a branch office maintained by a person for the sale of motorcycles to distributors or for the sale of motorcycles to motorcycle dealers, or for directing or supervising, in whole or in part, its representatives in the Commonwealth.

"Factory representative" means a person employed by a person who manufactures or assembles motorcycles, or by a factory branch for the purpose of making or promoting the sale of its motorcycles, or for supervising or contacting its dealers, prospective dealers, or representatives in the Commonwealth.

"Factory repurchase motorcycle" means a motorcycle sold, leased, rented, consigned, or otherwise transferred to a person under an agreement that the motorcycle will be resold or otherwise retransferred only to the manufacturer or distributor of the motorcycle, and which is reacquired by the manufacturer or distributor, or its agents.

"Family member" means a person who either (i) is the spouse, child, grandchild, spouse of a child, spouse of a grandchild, brother, sister, or parent of the dealer or owner, or (ii) has been employed continuously by the dealer for at least five years.

"Franchise" means a written contract or agreement between two or more persons whereby one person, the franchisee, is granted the right to engage in the business of offering and selling, servicing, or offering, selling, and servicing new motorcycles of a particular line-make or late model or factory repurchase motorcycles of a particular line-make manufactured or distributed by the grantor of the right, the franchisor, and where the operation of the franchisee's business is substantially associated with the franchisor's trademark, trade name, advertising, or other commercial symbol designating the franchisor, the motorcycle or its manufacturer or distributor. The term shall include any severable part or parts of a franchise agreement which separately provides for selling and servicing different line-makes of the franchisor.

"Franchised late model or factory repurchase motorcycle dealer" means a dealer in late model or factory repurchase motorcycles, including a franchised new motorcycle dealer, that has a franchise agreement with a manufacturer or distributor of the line-make of the late model or factory repurchase motorcycles.

"Franchised motorcycle dealer" or "franchised dealer" means a dealer in new motorcycles that has a franchise agreement with a manufacturer or distributor of new motorcycles.

"Independent motorcycle dealer" means a dealer in used motorcycles.

"Late model motorcycle" means a motorcycle of the current model year and the immediately preceding model year.

"Manufacturer" means a person engaged in the business of constructing or assembling new motorcycles.

"Motorcycle" means every motor vehicle designed to travel on not more than three wheels in contact with the ground, except any vehicle included within the term "farm vehicle" or "moped" as defined in §46.2-100.

"Motorcycle dealer" or "dealer" means any person who:

1. For commission, money, or other thing of value, buys, sells, exchanges, either outright or on conditional sale, bailment lease, chattel mortgage, or otherwise or arranges or offers or attempts to solicit or negotiate on behalf of others a sale, purchase, or exchange of an interest in new motorcycles, new and used motorcycles, or used motorcycles alone, whether or not the motorcycles are owned by him;

2. Is wholly or partly engaged in the business of selling new motorcycles, new and used motorcycles, or used motorcycles only, whether or not the motorcycles are owned by him; or

3. Offers to sell, sells, displays, or permits the display for sale, of five or more motorcycles within any twelve consecutive months.

The term "motorcycle dealer" does not include:

1. Receivers, trustees, administrators, executors, guardians, conservators or other persons appointed by or acting under judgment or order of any court or their employees when engaged in the specific performance of their duties as employees.

2. Public officers, their deputies, assistants, or employees, while performing their official duties.

3. Persons other than business entities primarily engaged in the leasing or renting of motorcycles to others when selling or offering such motorcycles for sale at retail, disposing of motorcycles acquired for their own use and actually so used, when the motorcycles have been so acquired and used in good faith and not for the purpose of avoiding the provisions of this chapter.

4. Any financial institution chartered or authorized to do business under the laws of the Commonwealth or the United States which may have received title to a motorcycle in the normal course of its business by reason of a foreclosure, other taking, repossession, or voluntary reconveyance to that institution occurring as a result of any loan secured by a lien on the motorcycle.

5. An employee of an organization arranging for the purchase or lease by the organization of motorcycles for use in the organization's business.

6. Any person who permits the operation of a motorcycle show or permits the display of motorcycles for sale by any motorcycle dealer licensed under this chapter.

7. An insurance company authorized to do business in the Commonwealth that sells or disposes of motorcycles under a contract with its insured in the regular course of business.

8. Any publication, broadcast, or other communications media when engaged in the business of advertising, but not otherwise arranging for the sale of motorcycles owned by others.

9. Any person dealing solely in the sale or lease of motorcycles designed exclusively for off-road use.

10. Any credit union authorized to do business in Virginia, provided the credit union does not receive a commission, money, or other thing of value directly from a motorcycle dealer.

"Motorcycle salesperson" or "salesperson" means any person who is licensed as and employed as a salesperson by a motorcycle dealer to sell or exchange motorcycles.

"Motorcycle show" means a display of motorcycles to the general public at a location other than a dealer's location licensed under this chapter where the motorcycles are not being offered for sale or exchange during or as part of the display.

"New motorcycle" means any motorcycle which (i) has not been previously sold except in good faith for the purpose of resale, (ii) has not been used as a rental, driver education, or demonstration motorcycle, or for the personal and business transportation of the manufacturer, distributor, dealer, or any of his employees, (iii) has not been used except for limited use necessary in moving or road testing the motorcycle prior to delivery to a customer, (iv) is transferred by a certificate of origin, and (v) has the manufacturer's certification that it conforms to all applicable federal motorcycle safety and emission standards. Notwithstanding provisions (i) and (iii), a motorcycle that has been previously sold but not titled shall be deemed a new motorcycle if it meets the requirements of provisions (ii), (iv), and (v).

"Original license" means a motorcycle dealer license issued to an applicant who has never been licensed as a motorcycle dealer in Virginia or whose Virginia motorcycle dealer license has been expired for more than thirty days.

"Relevant market area" means as follows:

1. In metropolitan localities with a population of 250,000, the relevant market area shall be a circular area around an existing franchised dealer not to exceed a radius of ten miles, but in no case less than seven miles.

2. If the population in an area within a radius of ten miles around an existing franchised dealer is less than 250,000, but the population in an area within a radius of fifteen miles around an existing franchised dealer is 150,000 or more, the relevant market area shall be that area within the fifteen-mile radius.

3. In all other cases the relevant market area shall be an area within a radius of twenty miles around an existing franchised dealer or the area of responsibility defined in the franchise, whichever is greater. In any case where the franchise agreement is silent as to area responsibility, the relevant market area shall be the greater of an area within a radius of twenty miles around an existing franchised dealer or that area in which the franchisor otherwise requires the franchisee to make significant retail sales or sales efforts.

In determining population for this definition, the most recent census by the U.S. Bureau of the Census or the most recent population update, either from the National Planning Data Corporation or other similar recognized source, shall be accumulated for all census tracts either wholly or partially within the relevant market area.

"Retail installment sale" means every sale of one or more motorcycles to a buyer for his use and not for resale, in which the price of the motorcycle is payable in one or more installments and in which the seller has either retained title to the goods or has taken or retained a security interest in the goods under form of contract designated either as a security agreement, conditional sale, bailment lease, chattel mortgage, or otherwise.

"Sale at retail" or "retail sale" means the act or attempted act of selling, bartering, exchanging, or otherwise disposing of a motorcycle to a buyer for his personal use and not for resale.

"Sale at wholesale" or "wholesale" means a sale to motorcycle dealers or wholesalers other than to consumers, or a sale to one who intends to resell.

"Used motorcycle" means any motorcycle other than a new motorcycle as defined in this section.

"Wholesale auction" means an auction of motorcycles restricted to sales at wholesale.

(Added by L.1996 chs. 1043, 1052; chgd. by L.1997 ch. 801, eff. 1/1/98, ch. 848, eff. 7/1/97.)

§46.2-1993.1. General powers of Commissioner.

The Commissioner shall promote the interest of the retail buyers of motorcycles and endeavor to prevent unfair methods of competition and unfair or deceptive acts or practices.

(Added by L.1996 chs. 1043, 1052, eff. 7/1/96.)

§46.2-1993.2. Commissioner's powers with respect to hearings under this chapter.

The Commissioner may, in hearings arising under this chapter, determine the place in the Commonwealth where they shall be held; subpoena witnesses; take depositions of witnesses residing outside the Commonwealth in the manner provided for in civil actions in courts of record; pay these witnesses the fees and mileage for their attendance as is provided for witnesses in civil actions in courts of record; and administer oaths.

(Added by L.1996 chs. 1043, 1052, eff. 7/1/96.)

§46.2-1993.3. Suit to enjoin violations; manufacturer, factory branch, distributor, distributor branch, factory or distributor representative subject to jurisdiction of courts of the Commonwealth.

A. The Commissioner, whenever he believes from evidence submitted to him that any person has been violating, is violating or is about to violate any provision of this chapter, in addition to any other remedy, may bring an action in the name of the Commonwealth to enjoin any violation of this chapter. In addition, a motorcycle dealer may bring an action to enjoin a violation of §§46.2-1993.31, 46.2-1993.67 or §46.2-1993.67:1.

B. Any manufacturer, factory branch, distributor, distributor branch, or factory or distributor representative who obtains a license under this chapter, is engaged in business in the Commonwealth and is subject to the jurisdiction of the courts of the Commonwealth. Any manufacturer, factory branch, distributor, distributor branch, or factory or distributor representative of motorcycles of a recognized line-make that are sold or leased in the Commonwealth pursuant to a plan, system, or channel of distribution established, approved, authorized, or known to the manufacturer, shall be subject to the jurisdiction of the courts of the Commonwealth in any action seeking relief under or to enforce any of the remedies or penalties provided for in this chapter.

(Added by L.1996 chs. 1043, 1052; chgd. by L.1997 ch. 802, eff. 7/1/97.)

§46.2-1993.4. Regulations.

The Commissioner may promulgate regulations requiring persons licensed under this chapter to keep and maintain records reasonably required for the enforcement of §§46.2-112 and 46.2-629, and any other regulations, not inconsistent with the provisions of this chapter, as he shall consider necessary for the effective administration and enforcement of this chapter. A copy of any regulation promulgated under this section shall be mailed to each motorcycle dealer licensee thirty days prior to its effective date.

(Added by L.1996 chs. 1043, 1052, eff. 7/1/96.)

§46.2-1993.5. Penalties.

Except as otherwise provided in this chapter, any person violating any of the provisions of this chapter may be assessed a civil penalty not to exceed $1,000 for any single violation. Civil penalties collected under this chapter shall be deposited into the Transportation Trust Fund.

(Added by L.1996 chs. 1043, 1052, eff. 7/1/96.)

ARTICLE 2
MOTORCYCLE DEALER LICENSES

Section

§46.2-1993.6. Licenses required.

It shall be unlawful for any person to engage in business in the Commonwealth as a motorcycle dealer, salesperson, manufacturer, factory branch, distributor, distributor branch, or factory or distributor representative, without first obtaining a license as provided in this chapter. Any person licensed in another state as a motorcycle dealer may sell motorcycles at wholesale auctions in the Commonwealth after having obtained a certificate of dealer registration as provided in Chapter 19 (§46.2-1900 et seq.) of this title. Any nonprofit organization exempt from taxation under §501(c)(3) of the Internal Revenue Code, after having obtained a nonprofit organization certificate as provided in this chapter, may consign donated motorcycles to licensed Virginia motorcycle dealers. The offering or granting of a motorcycle dealer franchise in the Commonwealth shall constitute engaging in business in the Commonwealth for purposes of this section, and no new motorcycle may be sold or offered for sale in the Commonwealth unless the franchisor of motorcycle dealer franchises for that line-make in the Commonwealth, whether such franchisor is a manufacturer, factory branch, distributor, distributor branch, or otherwise, is licensed under this chapter. In the event a license issued under this chapter to a franchisor of motorcycle dealer franchises is suspended, revoked, or not renewed, nothing in this section shall prevent the sale of any new motorcycle of such franchisor's line-make manufactured in or brought into the Commonwealth for sale prior to the suspension, revocation or expiration of the license.

Violation of any provision of this section shall constitute a Class 1 misdemeanor.

(Added by L.1996 chs. 1043, 1052; chgd. by L.1997 ch. 848; L.2000 ch. 180, eff. 7/1/2000.)

§46.2-1993.6:1. Certification of certain nonprofit organizations.

Upon application to and approval by the Board, any nonprofit organization exempt from taxation under §501(c)(3) of the Internal Revenue Code may be issued a nonprofit organization certificate authorizing it to consign donated motorcycles to licensed Virginia motorcycle dealers when the nonprofit organization receives title to such motorcycles as qualified charitable gifts and titles the motorcycles in the name of the nonprofit organization.

(Added by L.2000 ch. 180, eff. 7/1/2000.)

§46.2-1993.7. Application for license or certificate of dealer registration.

Application for license or certificate of dealer registration under this chapter shall be made to the Commissioner and contain such information as the Commissioner shall require. The application shall be accompanied by the required fee.

The Commissioner shall require, in the application or otherwise, information relating to the matters set forth in §46.2-1993.76 as grounds for refusing licenses, certificates of dealer registration, and to other pertinent matters requisite for the safeguarding of the public interest, including, if the applicant is a dealer in new motorcycles with factory warranties, a copy of a current service agreement with the manufacturer or with the distributor, requiring the applicant to perform within a reasonable distance of his established place of business, the service, repair, and replacement work required of the manufacturer or distributor by such motorcycle warranty. All of these matters shall be considered by the Commissioner in determining the fitness of the applicant to engage in the business for which he seeks a license or certificate of dealer registration.

(Added by L.1996 chs. 1043, 1052, eff. 7/1/96.)

§46.2-1993.8. Dealers required to have established place of business.

No license shall be issued to any motorcycle dealer unless he has an established place of business, owned or leased by him, where a substantial portion of the sales activity of the business is routinely conducted and which:

1. Satisfies all local zoning regulations;

2. Has sales, service, and office space devoted exclusively to the dealership of at least 250 square feet in a permanent, enclosed building not used as a residence;

3. Houses all records the dealer is required to maintain by §46.2-1993.22;

4. Is equipped with a desk, chairs, filing space, a working telephone listed in the name of the dealership, and working utilities including electricity and provisions for space heating;

5. Displays a sign and business hours as required by this chapter; and

6. Has contiguous space designated for the exclusive use of the dealer adequate to permit the display of at least ten motorcycles.

Any person licensed as a dealer by the Department under any provision of this subtitle on June 30, 1996, shall be considered in compliance with subdivisions 2 and 6 of this section for that licensee.

(Added by L.1996 chs. 1043, 1052, eff. 7/1/96.)

§46.2-1993.9. Dealer-operator to have certificate of qualification.

No license shall be issued to any motorcycle dealer unless the dealer-operator holds a valid certificate of qualification issued by the Department. Such certificate shall be issued only on application to the Department, payment of a twenty-five dollar application fee, the successful completion of an examination prepared and administered by the Department, and other prerequisites as set forth in this section. However, any individual who is the dealer-operator of a dealer licensed by the Department under any provision of this subtitle on June 30, 1996, shall be entitled to such a certificate without examination on application to the Department made on or before January 1, 1997.

The Commissioner may establish minimum qualifications for applicants and require applicants to satisfactorily complete courses of study or other prerequisites prior to taking the examination.

(Added by L.1996 chs. 1043, 1052, eff. 7/1/96.)

§46.2-1993.10. Salesperson to have certificate of qualification.

No license shall be issued to any motorcycle salesperson unless he holds a valid certificate of qualification issued by the Department. A certificate shall be issued only on application to the Department, payment of a twenty-five-dollar application fee, the successful completion of an examination prepared and administered by the Department, and other prerequisites as set forth in this section. However, any individual who is licensed as a salesperson by the Department under any provision of this subtitle on June 30, 1996, shall be entitled to such a certificate without examination on application to the Department made on or before January 1, 1997.

The Commissioner may establish minimum qualifications for applicants and require applicants to satisfactorily complete courses of study or other prerequisites prior to taking the examination.

(Added by L.1996 chs. 1043, 1052, eff. 7/1/96.)

§46.2-1993.11. Continued operation on loss of a dealer-operator holding certificate of qualification.

Each dealer shall notify the Department in writing immediately when a dealer-operator who holds a certificate of qualification dies, becomes disabled, retires, is removed, or for any other cause ceases to act as dealer-operator. The dealer may continue to operate for 120 days thereafter without a dealer-operator and may be granted approval by the Department to operate for an additional sixty days on application and with good cause shown for such delay.

(Added by L.1996 chs. 1043, 1052, eff. 7/1/96.)

§46.2-1993.12. Action on applications; hearing on denial; denial for failure to have established place of business.

The Commissioner shall act on all applications for a license or certificate of dealer registration under this chapter within sixty days after receipt by either granting or refusing the application. Any applicant denied a license or certificate shall, on his written request filed within thirty days, be given a hearing at a time and place determined by the Commissioner or a person designated by him. All hearings under this section shall be public and shall be held promptly. The applicant may be represented by counsel.

Any applicant denied a license for failure to have an established place of business as provided in §46.2-1993.8 may not, nor shall anyone, apply for a license for premises for which a license was denied for thirty days from the date of the rejection of the application.

(Added by L.1996 chs. 1043, 1052, eff. 7/1/96.)

§46.2-1993.13. Location to be specified; display of license; change of location.

The licenses of motorcycle dealers, manufacturers, factory branches, distributors, and distributor branches shall specify the location of each place of business, branch or other location occupied or to be occupied by the licensee in conducting his business and the license issued therefor shall be conspicuously displayed at each of the premises. If any licensee intends to change a licensed location, he shall provide the Commissioner thirty days' advance written notice, and a successful inspection of the new location shall be required prior to approval of a change of location. The Commissioner shall endorse the change of location on the license, without charge, if the new location is within the same county or city. A change in location to another county or city shall require a new license and fee.

(Added by L.1996 chs. 1043, 1052, eff. 7/1/96.)

§46.2-1993.14. Supplemental sales locations.

The Commissioner may issue a license for a licensed motorcycle dealer to display for sale or sell motorcycles at locations other than his established place of business, subject to compliance with local ordinances and requirements.

A permanent supplemental license may be issued for premises less than 500 yards from the dealer's established place of business, provided a sign is displayed as required for the established place of business. A supplemental license shall not be required for premises otherwise contiguous to the established place of business except for a public thoroughfare.

A temporary supplemental license may be issued for a period not to exceed fourteen days, provided that the application is made fifteen days prior to the sale. A temporary supplemental license for the sale of new motorcycles may be issued only for locations within the dealer's area of responsibility, as defined in his franchise or sales agreement, unless certification is provided that all dealers in the same line-make in whose areas of responsibility, as defined in their franchise or sales agreements, where the temporary supplemental license is sought do not oppose the issuance of the temporary license.

However, the application for a temporary supplemental license may be made five business days prior to the sale, provided the applicant submit evidence that the location is in compliance with all local ordinances and that all other requirements of this section have been met. The application shall include affirmative proof of nonopposition in the form of letters signed by all dealers in the same line-make in whose areas of responsibility, as defined in their franchise or sales agreements, where the temporary supplemental license is sought, approving the Department's granting the temporary supplemental license.

A temporary supplemental license for sale of used motorcycles may be issued only for the county, city, or town in which the dealer is licensed pursuant to §46.2-1993.8, or for a contiguous county, city, or town. Temporary licenses may be issued without regard to the foregoing geographic restrictions where the dealer operating under a temporary license provides notice, at least thirty days before any proposed sale under a temporary license, to all other dealers licensed in the jurisdiction in which the sale will occur of the intent to conduct a sale and permits any locally licensed dealer who wishes to do so to participate in the sale on the same terms as the dealer operating under the temporary license. Any locally licensed dealer who chooses to participate in the sale must obtain a temporary supplemental license for the sale pursuant to this section.

(Added by L.1996 chs. 1043, 1052, eff. 7/1/96.)

§46.2-1993.15. Changes in form of ownership, line-make, name.

Any change in the form of ownership or the addition or deletion of a partner shall require a new application, license, and fee.

Any addition or deletion of a franchise or change in the name of a dealer shall require immediate notification to the Department, and the Commissioner shall endorse the change on the license without a fee. The change of an officer or director of a corporation shall be made at the time of license renewal.

(Added by L.1996 chs. 1043, 1052, eff. 7/1/96.)

§46.2-1993.16. Display of salesperson's license; notice on termination.

No salesperson shall be employed by more than one dealer, unless the dealers are owned by the same person.

Each dealer shall maintain a list of salespersons employed.

Each salesperson, factory representative, and distributor representative shall carry his license when engaged in his business and shall display it on request.

Each dealer and each motorcycle manufacturer and distributor shall notify the Department in writing not later than the tenth day of the month following the termination of any licensed salesperson's or representative's employment. In lieu of written notification, the license of the terminated salesperson or representative may be returned to the Department annotated "terminated" on the face of the license and signed and dated by the dealer-operator, owner, or officer.

(Added by L.1996 chs. 1043, 1052, eff. 7/1/96.)

§46.2-1993.17. License and registration fees; additional to other licenses and fees required by law.

A. The fee for each license and registration year or part thereof shall be as follows:

1. For motorcycle dealers, $100 for each principal place of business, plus $20 for each supplemental license.
2. For each motorcycle manufacturer, distributor, factory branch, and distributor branch, $100.
3. For motorcycle rebuilder salespersons, factory representatives, and distributor representatives, $10.
4. For motorcycle dealers licensed in other states, but not in Virginia, a registration fee of $50.

B. The licenses, registrations, and fees required by this chapter are in addition to licenses, taxes, and fees imposed by other provisions of law and nothing contained in this chapter shall exempt any person from any license, tax, or fee imposed by any other provision of law. However, the Commissioner may waive fees for those licensed under Chapter 15, 19, or 19.1 of this title; the Commissioner shall waive the fee for nonprofit organizations certified under Chapter 15, 19, or 19.2 of this title.

C. The fee for any nonprofit organization issued a certificate pursuant to §46.2-1992.6:1 shall be $25 per year or any part thereof.

D. No nonprofit organization granted a certificate pursuant to subsection B of §46.2-1993.6:1 shall, either orally or in writing, assign a value to any donated vehicle for the purpose of establishing tax deduction amounts on any federal or state income tax return.

(Added by L.1996 chs. 1043, 1052; chgd. by L.2000 ch. 180, eff. 7/1/2000.)

§46.2-1993.18. Collection of license and registration fees; payments from fund.

All licensing and registration fees provided for in this chapter, except as identified in Article 3 (§46.2-1993.20) of this chapter, shall be collected by the Commissioner and paid into the state treasury and set aside as a special fund to meet the expenses of the Department.

(Added by L.1996 chs. 1043, 1052, eff. 7/1/96.)

§46.2-1993.19. Issuance, expiration, and renewal of licenses and certificates of registration.

A. All licenses and certificates of registration issued under this chapter shall be issued for a period of twelve consecutive months except, at the discretion of the Commissioner, the periods may be adjusted as is necessary to distribute the licenses and certificates as equally as practicable on a monthly basis. The expiration date shall be the last day of the twelfth month of validity or the last day of the designated month. Every license and certificate of registration shall be renewed annually on application by the licensee or registrant and by payment of fees required by law, the renewal to take effect on the first day of the succeeding month.

B. Licenses and certificates of registration issued under this chapter shall be deemed not to have expired if the renewal application and required fees as set forth in this subsection are received by the Commissioner or postmarked not more than thirty days after the expiration date of such license or certificate of registration. Whenever the renewal application is received by the Commissioner or postmarked no more than thirty days after the expiration date of such license or certificate of registration, the license fees shall be 150 percent of the fees provided for in §46.2-1993.17.

C. The Commissioner may offer an optional multi-year license. When such option is offered and chosen by the licensee, all annual and twelve-month fees due at the time of licensing shall be multiplied by the number of years or fraction thereof for which the license will be issued.
(Added by L.1996 chs. 1043, 1052; chgd. by L.1997 ch. 848; L.1998 ch. 325, eff. 1/1/99.)

ARTICLE 3 BONDING REQUIREMENTS

§46.2-1993.20. Bonding requirements for applicants for license.

Every applicant for an original, second year renewal and third year renewal motorcycle dealer's license shall obtain and file with the Commissioner a bond in the amount of $25,000. However, no dealer shall be required to obtain more than one $25,000 bond for all licenses held under this subtitle. Any dealer who is licensed under Chapter 15 of this title and who obtains a motorcycle dealer license under this chapter, shall be exempt from the bond requirements set out in this section. In addition, any person who purchases a motorcycle from a dealer who is licensed under Chapter 15 of this title, shall have access to the Motor Vehicle Transaction Recovery Fund as prescribed in Article 3 (§46.2-1527 et seq.) of Chapter 15 of this title. The bond shall come from a corporate surety licensed to do business in the Commonwealth and approved by the Attorney General. The bond shall be conditioned on a statement by the applicant that the applicant will not practice fraud, make any fraudulent representation, or violate any provision of this chapter in the conduct of the applicant's business. The Commissioner may, without holding a hearing, suspend the dealer's license during the period that the dealer does not have a sufficient bond on file.

If a person suffers any of the following: (i) loss or damage in connection with the purchase of a motorcycle by reason of fraud practiced on him or fraudulent representation made to him by a licensed motorcycle dealer or one of the dealer's salespersons acting within his scope of employment; (ii) loss or damage by reason of the violation by a dealer or salesperson of any provision of this chapter in connection with the purchase of a motorcycle; or (iii) loss or damage resulting from a breach of an extended service contract entered into on or after the effective date of this act, as defined by §59.1-435, that person shall have a claim against the dealer and the dealer's bond, and may recover such damages as may be awarded to such person by final judgment of a court of competent jurisdiction against the dealer as a proximate result of such loss or damage up to, but not exceeding, the amount of the bond, from such surety, who shall be subrogated to the rights of such person against the dealer or salesperson. The liability of such surety shall be limited to actual damages, and shall not include any punitive damages or attorneys' fees assessed against the dealer or salesperson.

The dealer's surety shall notify the Department when a claim is made against a dealer's bond, when a claim is paid and when the bond is canceled. Such notification shall include the amount of a claim and the circumstances surrounding the claim. Notification of cancellation shall include the effective date and reason for cancellation. The bond may be canceled as to future liability by the dealer's surety upon thirty days' notice to the Department.
(Added by L.1996 chs. 1043, 1052, eff. 7/1/96.)

ARTICLE 4 CONDUCT OF BUSINESS

§46.2-1993.21. Examination or audit of licensee; costs.

The Commissioner or authorized representatives of the Department may examine, during the posted business hours, the records required to be maintained by this chapter. If a licensee is found to have violated this chapter or any order of the Commissioner, the actual cost of the examination shall be paid by the licensee so examined within thirty days after demand therefor by the Commissioner. The Commissioner may maintain an action for the recovery of these costs in any court of competent jurisdiction.
(Added by L.1996 chs. 1043, 1052, eff. 7/1/96.)

§46.2-1993.22. Dealer records.

All dealer records regarding employees; lists of vehicles in inventory for sale, resale, or on consignment; vehicle purchases, sales, trades, and transfers of ownership; collections of taxes; titling, uninsured motor vehicle and registration fees; odometer disclosure statements; records of permanent dealer registration plates assigned to the dealer and temporary transport plates and temporary certificates of ownership; and other records required by the Department shall be maintained on the premises of the licensed location. The Commissioner may, on written request by a dealer, permit his records to be maintained at a location other than the premises of the licensed location for good cause shown. All dealer records shall be preserved in original form or in film, magnetic, or optical media (including but not limited to microfilm, microfiche, or other electronic media) for a period of five years in a manner that permits systematic retrieval. Certain records may be maintained on a computerized record-keeping system with the prior approval of the Commissioner.
(Added by L.1996 chs. 1043, 1052; chgd. by L.2000 ch. 128, eff. 7/1/2000.)

§46.2-1993.23. Buyer's order.

A. Every motorcycle dealer shall complete, in duplicate, a buyer's order for each sale or exchange of a vehicle. A copy of the buyer's order form shall be made available to a prospective buyer during the negotiating phase of a sale and prior to any sales agreement. The completed original shall be retained for a period of four years in accordance with

§46.2-1993.22, and a duplicate copy shall be delivered to the purchaser at the time of sale or exchange. A buyer's order shall include:

1. The name and address of the person to whom the vehicle was sold or traded.

2. The date of the sale or trade.

3. The name and address of the motorcycle dealer selling or trading the vehicle.

4. The make, model year, and vehicle identification number.

5. The sale price of the vehicle.

6. The amount of any cash deposit made by the buyer.

7. A description of any vehicle used as a trade-in and the amount credited the buyer for the trade-in. The description of the trade-in shall be the same as outlined in subdivision 4 of this subsection.

8. The amount of any sales and use tax, title fee, uninsured motor vehicle fee, registration fee, or other fee required by law for which the buyer is responsible and the dealer has collected. Each tax and fee shall be individually listed and identified.

9. The net balance due at settlement.

10. Any item designated as "processing fee," and the amount charged by the dealer, if any, for processing the transaction. As used in this section processing includes obtaining title and license plates for the purchaser.

11. Any item designated as "dealer's business license tax," and the amount charged by the dealer, if any.

12. For sales involving dealer-arranged financing, the following notice, printed in bold type no less than ten-point:

"THIS SALE IS CONDITIONED UPON APPROVAL OF YOUR PROPOSED RETAIL INSTALLMENT SALE CONTRACT AS SUBMITTED TO OR THROUGH THE DEALER. IF THAT PROPOSED RETAIL INSTALLMENT SALE CONTRACT IS NOT APPROVED UNDER THE TERMS AGREED TO WITH THE DEALER, YOU MAY CANCEL THIS SALE AND ANY DOWN PAYMENT AND/OR TRADE-IN YOU SUBMITTED WILL BE RETURNED TO YOU, PROVIDED THAT ANY VEHICLE DELIVERED TO YOU BY THE DEALER PURSUANT TO THIS AGREEMENT IS RETURNED TO THE DEALER IN THE SAME CONDITION AS DELIVERED TO YOU, NORMAL WEAR AND TEAR EXCEPTED, WITHIN TWENTY-FOUR HOURS OF WRITTEN OR ORAL NOTICE TO YOU OF THE CREDIT DENIAL."

If the transaction does not include a policy of liability insurance, the seller shall stamp or mark on the face of the bill of sale in boldface letters no smaller than eighteen point type the following words: "No Liability Insurance Included."

A completed buyer's order when signed by both buyer and seller may constitute a bill of sale.

B. The Commissioner shall approve a buyer's order form and each dealer shall file with each original license application its buyer's order form, on which the processing fee amount is stated.

C. If a processing fee is charged, that fact and the amount of the processing fee shall be disclosed by the dealer. Disclosure shall be by placing a clear and conspicuous sign in the public sales area of the dealership. The sign shall be no smaller than eight and one-half inches by eleven inches and the print shall be no smaller than one-half inch, and in a form as approved by the Commissioner.

(Added by L.1996 chs. 1043, 1052; chgd. by L.2000 ch. 116, eff. 7/1/2000.)

§46.2-1993.24. Consignment motorcycles; contract.

Any motorcycle dealer offering a motorcycle for sale on consignment shall have in his possession a consignment contract for the motorcycle, executed and signed by the dealer and the consignor. The consignment contract shall include:

1. The complete name, address, and the telephone number of the owners.

2. The name, address, and dealer certificate number of the selling dealer.

3. A complete description of the motorcycle on consignment, including the make, model year, vehicle identification number, and body style.

4. The beginning and termination dates of the contract.

5. The percentage of commission, the amount of the commission, or the net amount the owner is to receive, if the motorcycle is sold.

6. Any fees for which the owner is responsible.

7. A disclosure of all unsatisfied liens on the motorcycle and the location of the certificate of title to the motorcycle.

8. A requirement that the motorcycle pass a safety inspection prior to sale.

If any motorcycle on consignment from a certified nonprofit organization is found not to be in compliance with any safety inspection requirement, the motorcycle dealer shall furnish any buyer intending to use that motorcycle on the public highways a written disclosure, prior to sale, that the motorcycle did not pass a safety inspection.

Any dealer offering a motorcycle for sale on consignment shall inform any prospective customer that the motorcycle is on consignment.

Dealer license plates shall not be used to demonstrate a motorcycle on consignment except (i) motorcycles on consignment from another licensed motorcycle dealer and (ii) motorcycles on consignment from nonprofit organizations certified pursuant to §46.2-1993.6:1. The owner's license plates may be used if liability insurance coverage is in effect in the amounts prescribed by §46.2-472. No vehicles other than motorcycles shall be sold on consignment by motorcycle dealers.

(Added by L.1996 chs. 1043, 1052; chgd. by L.2000 ch. 180, eff. 7/1/2000.)

§46.2-1993.25. Odometer disclosure.

Every motorcycle dealer shall comply with all requirements of the Federal Odometer Act and §46.2-629 by completing the appropriate odometer mileage statement form for each vehicle purchased, sold or transferred, or in any other way acquired or disposed of. Odometer disclosure statements shall be maintained by the dealer in a manner that permits systematic retrieval. Any person found violating any of the provisions of this section shall be guilty of a Class 1 misdemeanor.

(Added by L.1996 chs. 1043, 1052, eff. 7/1/96.)

§46.2-1993.26. Certain disclosures required by manufacturers and distributors.

Motorcycle manufacturers and distributors shall affix or cause to be affixed in a conspicuous place to every motorcycle offered for sale as a new motorcycle a statement disclosing the place of assembly or manufacture of the motorcycle. For disclosures of place of assembly, the assembly plant shall be the same as that designated by the vehicle identification number.

The provisions of this section shall apply only to motorcycles manufactured for the 1991 or subsequent model years.

(Added by L.1996 chs. 1043, 1052, eff. 7/1/96.)

§46.2-1993.27. Business hours.

Each motorcycle dealer shall be open for business a minimum of twenty hours per week, at least ten of which shall be between the hours of 9:00 a.m. and 5:00 p.m. Monday through Friday, except that the Commissioner, on written request by a dealer, may modify these requirements for good cause. The dealer's hours shall be posted and maintained conspicuously on or near the main entrance of each place of business.

Each dealer shall include his business hours on the original and every renewal application for a license, and changes to these hours shall be immediately filed with the Department.

(Added by L.1996 chs. 1043, 1052, eff. 7/1/96.)

§46.2-1993.28. Signs.

Each retail motorcycle dealer's place of business shall be identified by a permanent sign visible from the front of the business office so that the public may quickly and easily identify the dealership. The sign shall contain the dealer's trade name in letters no less than six inches in height unless otherwise restricted by law or contract.

(Added by L.1996 chs. 1043, 1052, eff. 7/1/96.)

§46.2-1993.29. Advertisements.

Unless the dealer is clearly identified by name, whenever any licensee places an advertisement in any newspaper or publication, the abbreviations "VA DLR," denoting a Virginia licensed dealer, shall appear therein.

(Added by L.1996 chs. 1043, 1052, eff. 7/1/96.)

§46.2-1993.30. Coercing purchaser to provide insurance coverage on motorcycle.

It shall be unlawful for any dealer or salesperson or any employee of a dealer or representative of either to coerce or offer anything of value to any purchaser of a motorcycle to provide any type of insurance coverage on the motorcycle.

Nothing in this section shall prohibit a dealer from requiring that a retail customer obtain vehicle physical damage insurance to protect collateral secured by an installment sales contract. Any person found guilty of violating any provisions of this section shall be guilty of a Class 1 misdemeanor.

Nothing in this section shall prohibit a dealer from informing the retail customer of Virginia's insurance requirements.

(Added by L.1996 chs. 1043, 1052, eff. 7/1/96.)

§46.2-1993.31. Prohibited solicitation and compensation.

It shall be unlawful for any motorcycle dealer or salesperson licensed under this chapter, directly or indirectly, to solicit the sale of a motorcycle through a person with a pecuniary interest, or to pay, or cause to be paid, any commission or compensation in any form whatsoever to any person in connection with the sale of a motorcycle, unless the person is duly licensed as a salesperson employed by the dealer.

(Added by L.1996 chs. 1043, 1052, eff. 7/1/96.)

§46.2-1993.32. Salesperson selling for other than his employer prohibited.

It shall be unlawful for any motorcycle salesperson licensed under this chapter to sell or exchange or offer or attempt to sell or exchange any motorcycle except for the licensed motorcycle dealer by whom he is employed, or to offer, transfer, or assign any sale or exchange that he may have negotiated to any other dealer or salesperson.

(Added by L.1996 chs. 1043, 1052, eff. 7/1/96.)

§46.2-1993.33. Inspection of vehicles required.

No person required to be licensed as a dealer under this chapter shall sell at retail any vehicle which is intended by the buyer for use on the public highways, and which is required to comply with the safety inspection requirements provided in Article 21 (§46.2-1157 et seq.) of Chapter 10 of this title unless between the time the vehicle comes into the possession of the dealer and the time it is sold at retail it is inspected by an official safety inspection station. If the vehicle is found not to be in compliance with all safety inspection requirements, the dealer shall either take steps to bring it into compliance or shall furnish any buyer intending it for use on the public highway a written disclosure, prior to sale, that the vehicle did not pass a safety inspection. Any person found guilty of violating any provisions of this section shall be guilty of a Class 1 misdemeanor.

(Added by L.1996 chs. 1043, 1052, eff. 7/1/96.)

§46.2-1993.34. Inspections prior to sale not required of certain sellers.

The provisions of §§46.2-1158 and 46.2-1993.33 requiring inspection of any vehicle prior to sale at retail shall not apply to any person conducting a public auction for the sale of vehicles at retail, provided that the individual, firm, or business conducting the auction has not taken title to the vehicle, but is acting as an agent for the sale of the vehicle. Nor shall the provisions of §§46.2-1158 and 46.2-1993.33 requiring inspection of any motorcycle prior to sale at retail apply to any new motorcycle sold on the basis of a special order placed by a dealer with a manufacturer outside Virginia on behalf of a customer who is a nonresident of Virginia and takes delivery outside Virginia.

(Added by L.1996 chs. 1043, 1052, eff. 7/1/96.)

§46.2-1993.35. Temporary certificates of ownership.

A. Notwithstanding §§46.2-617 and 46.2-628, whenever a dealer licensed by the Department sells and delivers to a purchaser a vehicle and is unable at the time of the sale to deliver to the purchaser the certificate of title or certificate of origin for the vehicle because the certificate of title or certificate of origin is lost or is being detained by another in possession or for any other reason beyond the dealer's control, the dealer shall execute, on forms provided by the Commissioner, a temporary certificate of ownership. The certificate shall bear its date of issuance, the name and address of the purchaser, the identification number of the vehicle, the registration number to be used temporarily on the vehicle, the name of the state in which the vehicle is to be registered, the name and address of the person from whom the dealer acquired the vehicle, and whatever other information may be required by the Commissioner. A copy of the temporary certificate and a bona fide bill of sale shall be delivered to the purchaser and shall be in the possession of the purchaser at all times when operating the vehicle. One copy of the certificate shall be retained by the dealer and shall be subject to inspection at any time by the Department's agents. The original of the certificate shall be forwarded by the dealer to the Department directly on issuance to the purchaser if the vehicle is to be titled outside the Commonwealth, along with application for title. The issuance of a temporary certificate of ownership to a purchaser pursuant to this section shall have the effect of vesting ownership of the motorcycle in the purchaser for the period that the certificate remains effective.

B. A temporary certificate of ownership issued by a dealer to a purchaser pursuant to this section shall expire on receipt by the purchaser of a certificate of title to the vehicle issued by the Department in the name of the purchaser, but in no event shall any temporary certificate of ownership issued under this section be effective for more than thirty days from the date of its issuance. In the event that the dealer fails to produce the old certificate of title or certificate of origin to the vehicle or fails to apply for a replacement certificate of title pursuant to §46.2-632, thereby preventing delivery to the Department or purchaser before the expiration of the temporary certificate of ownership, the purchaser's ownership of the vehicle may terminate and the purchaser shall have the right to return the vehicle to the dealer and obtain a full refund of all payments made toward the purchase of the vehicle, less any damage to the vehicle incurred while ownership was vested in the purchaser, and less a reasonable amount for use not to exceed one-half the amount allowed per mile by the Internal Revenue Service, as provided by regulation, revenue procedure, or revenue ruling promulgated pursuant to §162 of the Internal Revenue Code, for use of a personal vehicle for business purposes.

C. Notwithstanding subsection B of this section, if the dealer fails to deliver the certificate of title or certificate of origin to the purchaser within thirty days, a second temporary certificate of ownership may be issued. However, the dealer shall, not later than the expiration of the first temporary certificate, deliver to the Department an application for title, copy of the bill of sale, all required fees and a written statement of facts describing the dealer's efforts to secure the certificate of title or certificate of origin to the vehicle. On receipt of the title application with attachments as described herein, the Department shall record the purchaser's ownership of the vehicle and may authorize the dealer to issue a second thirty-day temporary certificate of ownership. If the dealer does not produce the certificate of title or certificate of origin to the vehicle before the expiration of the second temporary certificate, the purchaser's ownership of the vehicle may terminate and he shall have the right to return the vehicle as provided in subsection B of this section.

D. If the dealer is unable to produce the certificate of title or certificate of origin to the vehicle within the sixty-day period from the date of issuance of the first temporary certificate, the Department may extend temporary ownership for an additional period of up to ninety days, provided the dealer makes application in the format required by the Department. If the dealer does not produce the certificate of title or certificate of origin to the vehicle before the expiration of the additional ninety-day period, the purchaser's ownership of the vehicle may terminate and he shall have the right to return the motorcycle as provided in subsection B of this section.

E. The Commissioner, on determining that the provisions of this section or the directions of the Department are not being complied with by a dealer, may, after a hearing, suspend the right of the dealer to issue temporary certificates of ownership.

(Added by L.1996 chs. 1043, 1052, eff. 7/1/96.)

§46.2-1993.36. Use of old license plates and registration number on a motorcycle.

An owner who sells or transfers a registered motorcycle may have the license plates and the registration number transferred to a motorcycle titled in the owner's name according to the provisions of Chapter 6 (§46.2-600 et seq.), on application to the Department and accompanied by a fee of two dollars. All such transfers shall be in accordance with the regulations of the Department. All fees collected under this section shall be paid by the Commissioner into the state treasury and shall be set aside as a special fund to be used to meet the expenses of the Department. For purposes of this section, a motorcycle dealer licensed by the Department may be authorized to act as an agent of the Department. As an agent for the Department, the dealer is authorized to receive, process, and approve applications from its customers for assignment of license plates and registration numbers pursuant to this section, using the forms and following the procedures prescribed by the Department. The Commissioner, on determining that the provisions of this section or the directions of the Department are not being complied with by a dealer, may suspend, after a hearing, the authority of the dealer to receive, process, and approve the assignment of license plates and registration numbers pursuant to this section.

(Added by L.1996 chs. 1043, 1052, eff. 7/1/96.)

§46.2-1993.37. Certificate of title for dealers.

Except as otherwise provided in this chapter, every dealer shall obtain, on the purchase of each motorcycle, a certificate of title issued to the dealer or shall obtain an assignment or reassignment of a certificate of title for each motorcycle purchased, except that a certificate of title shall not be required for any new motorcycle to be sold as such.

(Added by L.1996 chs. 1043, 1052, eff. 7/1/96.)

§46.2-1993.38. Termination of business.

No dealer, unless his license has been suspended, revoked, or canceled, shall cease business without a thirty-day prior notification to the Department. On cessation of the business, the dealer shall immediately surrender to the Department the dealer's certificate of license, all salespersons' licenses, all dealer and temporary license plates, all fees and taxes collected, and any other materials furnished by the Department. After cessation of business, the former licensee shall continue to maintain and make available to the Department dealer records as set forth in this chapter.

(Added by L.1996 chs. 1043, 1052, eff. 7/1/96.)

ARTICLE 5
MOTORCYCLE DEALER LICENSE PLATES

Section

§46.2-1993.39. Registration of dealers; fees.

Every manufacturer, distributor, or dealer, before he commences to operate motorcycles in his inventory for sale or resale, shall apply to the Commissioner for a dealer's certificate of vehicle registration and license plates. For the purposes of this article, a motorcycle is in inventory when it is owned by, or assigned to, a dealer and is offered and available for sale or resale. All dealer's certificates of vehicle registration and license plates issued under this section may, at the discretion of the Commissioner, be placed in a system of staggered issue to distribute the work of issuing vehicle registration certificates and license plates as uniformly as practicable throughout the year. Dealerships which sold fewer than twenty-five motorcycles during the last twelve months of the preceding license year shall be eligible to receive no more than two dealer's license plates; dealerships which sold at least twenty-five but fewer than fifty motorcycles during the last twelve months of the preceding license year shall be eligible to receive no more than four dealer's license plates. However, dealerships which sold fifty or more motorcycles during their current license year may apply for additional license plates not to exceed four times the number of licensed salespersons employed by that dealership. Dealerships which sold fifty or more motorcycles during the last twelve months of the preceding license year shall be eligible to receive a number of dealer's license plates not to exceed four times the number of licensed salespersons employed by that dealership. A new applicant for a dealership shall be eligible to receive a number of dealer's license plates not to exceed four times the number of licensed salespersons employed by that dealership. For the purposes of this article, a salesperson or employee shall be considered to be employed only if he (i) works for the dealership at least twenty-five hours each week on a regular basis and (ii) is compensated for this work. All salespersons' or employees' employment records shall be retained in accordance with the provisions of §46.2-1993.22. A salesperson shall not be considered employed, within the meaning of this section, if he is an independent contractor as defined by the United States Internal Revenue Code. The fee for the issuance of motorcycle dealer's license plates shall be nine dollars per year for each dealer's license plate.

(Added by L.1996 chs. 1043, 1052, eff. 7/1/96.)

§46.2-1993.40. License under this chapter prerequisite to receiving dealer's license plates; insurance required; Commissioner may revoke plates.

No motorcycle manufacturer, distributor, or dealer, unless licensed under this chapter, shall be entitled to receive or maintain any dealer's license plates. It shall be unlawful to use or permit the use of any dealer's license plates for which there is no liability insurance coverage or a certificate of self-insurance as defined in §46.2-368 on any motorcycle. No dealer's license plates shall be issued unless the dealer certifies to the Department that there is liability insurance coverage or a certificate of self-insurance with respect to each dealer's license plate to be issued. Such liability insurance or a certificate of self-insurance shall be maintained for each dealer's license plate for so long as the registration for the dealer's license plate remains valid without regard to whether the plate is actually being used on a motorcycle. If insurance or a certificate of self-insurance is not so maintained, the dealer's license plate shall be surrendered to the Department. The Commissioner shall revoke any dealer's license plate for which there is no insurance or a certificate of self-insurance. The Commissioner may also revoke any dealer's license plate that has been used in any way not authorized by the provisions of this title.

(Added by L.1996 chs. 1043, 1052, eff. 7/1/96.)

§46.2-1993.41. Transferable dealer's license plates.

In lieu of registering each motorcycle, a manufacturer, distributor, or dealer owning and operating any motorcycle on any highway may obtain a dealer's license plate from the Department, on application therefor on the prescribed form and on payment of the fees required by law. These license plates shall be attached to each motorcycle as required by subsection A of §46.2-711. Each plate shall bear a distinctive number, and the name of the Commonwealth, which may be abbreviated, together with the word "dealer" or a distinguishing symbol indicating that the plate is issued to a manufacturer, distributor, or dealer. Month and year decals indicating the date of expiration shall be affixed to each license plate. Any license plates so issued may, during the calendar year or years for which they have been issued, be transferred from one motorcycle to another, used or operated by the manufacturer, distributor, or dealer, who shall keep a written record of the motorcycle on which the dealer's license plates are used. This record shall be in a format approved by the Commissioner and shall be open to inspection by any law-enforcement officer or any officer or employee of the Department.

Display of a transferable manufacturer's, distributor's, or dealer's license plate or plates on a motorcycle shall subject the motorcycle to the requirements of §§46.2-1038 and 46.2-1056.

All manufacturer's, distributor's, and dealer's license plates shall be issued for a period of twelve consecutive months except, at the discretion of the Commissioner, the periods may be adjusted as may be necessary to distribute the registrations as equally as practicable on a monthly basis. The expiration date shall be the last day of the twelfth month of validity or the last day of the designated month. Every license plate shall be renewed annually on application by the owner and by payment of fees required by law, such renewal to take effect on the first day of the succeeding month.

The Commissioner may offer an optional multi-year license plate registration to manufacturers, distributors, and dealers licensed pursuant to this chapter provided that he has chosen to offer optional multi-year licensing to such persons pursuant to §46.2-1993.19. When such option is offered and chosen by the licensee, all annual and twelve-month fees due at the time of registration shall be multiplied by the number of years or fraction thereof the licensee will be licensed pursuant to §46.2-1993.19.

(Added by L.1996 chs. 1043, 1052, eff. 7/1/96.)

§46.2-1993.42. Dealer's license plates to distinguish between various types of dealers.

The Commissioner shall provide for the issuance of appropriate franchised or independent dealer's license plates so as to distinguish between factory motorcycle dealers and motorcycle dealers.

(Added by L.1996 chs. 1043, 1052, eff. 7/1/96.)

§46.2-1993.43. Dealer's promotional license plates.

In addition to any other license plate authorized by this article, the Commissioner may issue dealer's promotional license plates to a dealership for use on motorcycles held for sale or resale in the dealership's inventory. The design of these license plates shall be at the discretion of the Commissioner. These license plates shall be for use as authorized by the Commissioner. For each such license plate issued or renewed, the Commissioner shall charge an annual fee of $100. Issuance of license plates pursuant to this section shall be subject to the insurance requirement contained in §46.2-1993.40. The Commissioner shall limit the validity of any license plate issued under this section to no more than thirty consecutive days. Upon written request from the dealership, the Commissioner may consider an extended use of a license plate issued under this section. The Commissioner's authorization for use of any license plate issued under this section shall be kept in the motorcycle on which the license plate is displayed until expiration of the authorization. These license plates shall be included in the number of dealer's license plates authorized under §46.2-1993.39 and not in addition thereto.

(Added by L.1996 chs. 1043, 1052, eff. 7/1/96.)

§46.2-1993.44. Use of motorcycle dealer's license plates, generally.

A. Motorcycle dealer's license plates may be used on motorcycles in the inventory of licensed motorcycle manufacturers, distributors, and dealers in the Commonwealth when operated on the highways of Virginia by dealers or dealer-operators, their spouses, or employees of manufacturers, distributors, and dealers as permitted in this article. Except as otherwise explicitly permitted in this article, it shall be unlawful for any dealer to cause or permit: (i) use of dealer's license plates on motorcycles other than those held in inventory for sale or resale; (ii) dealer's license plates to be lent, leased, rented, or placed at the disposal of any persons other than those permitted by this article to use dealer's license plates; and (iii) use of dealer's license plates on any vehicle other than a motorcycle. It shall be unlawful for any dealer to cause or permit dealer's license plates to be used on:

1. Vehicles such as tow trucks, wrecking cranes, or other service vehicles;
2. Vehicles used to deliver or transport (i) motorcycles; (ii) portions of motorcycles; (iii) motorcycle components, parts, or accessories; or (iv) fuel;
3. Courtesy vehicles; or
4. Vehicles used in conjunction with any other business.

B. A dealer may permit his license plates to be used in the operation of a motorcycle:

1. By any person whom the dealer reasonably believes to be a bona fide prospective purchaser who is either accompanied by a licensed salesperson or has the written permission of the dealer;
2. When the plates are being used by a customer on a motorcycle owned by the dealer in whose repair shop the customer's motorcycle is being repaired; or
3. By a person authorized by the dealer on a motorcycle that is being driven to or from (i) a point of sale, (ii) an auction, (iii) a repair facility for the purpose of mechanical repairs, painting, or installation of parts or accessories, or (iv) a dealer exchange.

The dealer shall issue to the prospective purchaser, customer whose motorcycle is being repaired, or other person authorized under subdivision 3 of this subsection, a certificate on forms provided by the Department, a copy of which shall be retained by the dealer and open at all times to the inspection of the Commissioner or any of the officers or agents of the Department. The certificate shall be in the immediate possession of the person operating or authorized to operate the vehicle. The certificate shall entitle a person to operate with dealer's license plates under (i) subdivision 1 or 2 of this subsection for a specific period of no more than five days or (ii) subdivision 3 of this subsection for no more than twenty-four hours. No more than two certificates may be issued by a dealer to the same person under subdivision 1 or 2 of this subsection for successive periods.

(Added by L.1996 chs. 1043, 1052; chgd. by L.1998 ch. 827, eff. 7/1/98.)

§46.2-1993.45. Use of dealer's license plates and temporary transport plates on certain vehicles.

Notwithstanding the provisions of §46.2-1993.44, dealer's license plates or dealer's temporary transport plates may be used on vehicles being transported (i) to and from a vehicle auction or other point of purchase or sale, (ii) between properties owned or controlled by the same dealership, or (iii) for repairs, painting, or installation of parts or accessories. This section shall also apply to return trips by such vehicles.

(Added by L.1996 chs. 1043, 1052, eff. 7/1/96.)

§46.2-1993.46. Issuance and use of temporary transport plates, generally.

The Department, subject to the limitations and conditions set forth in this section and the insurance requirements contained in §46.2-1993.40, may provide for the issuance of temporary transport plates designed by the Department to any dealer licensed under this chapter who applies for at least ten plates and who encloses with his application a fee of one dollar for each plate. The application shall be made on a form prescribed and furnished by the Department. Temporary transport plates may be used for those purposes outlined in §46.2-1993.45. Every dealer who has applied for temporary transport plates shall maintain a permanent record of (i) all temporary transport plates delivered to him, (ii) all temporary transport plates issued by him, and (iii) any other information pertaining to the receipt or the issuance of temporary transport plates which may be required by the Department.

Every dealer who issues temporary transport plates shall insert clearly and indelibly on the face of the temporary transport plates the name of the issuing dealer, the date of issuance and expiration, and the make and identification number of the vehicle for which issued.

The dealer shall issue to the operator of the specified vehicle a certificate on forms provided by the Department, a copy of which shall be retained by the dealer and open at all times to the inspection of the Commissioner or any of the officers or agents of the Department. The certificate shall be in the immediate possession of the person operating or authorized to operate the vehicle. The certificate shall entitle the person to operate with the dealer's temporary transport plate for a period of no more than five days. Temporary transport plates may also be used by the dealer to demonstrate types of vehicles taken in trade but for which he has not been issued dealer's license plates.

(Added by L.1996 chs. 1043, 1052, eff. 7/1/96.)

§46.2-1993.47. Use of motorcycle dealer's license plates on newly purchased motorcycles.

Notwithstanding the provisions of §46.2-1993.44, any dealer who sells and delivers to a purchaser a motorcycle at a time when the main offices of the Department, its branch offices, or offices of its local agents, are not open for business and the purchaser is therefore unable to register the motorcycle, may permit the purchaser to use, for a period not exceeding five days, on the newly purchased motorcycle, license plates which have been issued to the dealer, provided that, at the time of the purchase, the dealer executes in duplicate, on forms provided by the Commissioner, a certificate bearing the date of issuance, the name and address of the purchaser, the identification number of the motorcycle, the registration number to be used temporarily on the motorcycle, the name of the state in which the motorcycle is to be registered, and whatever other information may be required by the Commissioner. The original of the certificate and a bona fide bill of sale shall be delivered to the purchaser and shall be in the possession of the purchaser at all times when operating the motorcycle under dealer plates. One copy of the certificate shall be retained by the dealer, filed by him, and shall be subject to inspection at any time by the Department's agents. If the motorcycle is to be titled and registered in the Commonwealth, application for title and registration shall be made by the purchaser on the first business day following issuance of the certificate and a copy of the certificate shall accompany the applications.

License plates temporarily used by the purchaser shall be returned to the dealer by the purchaser not later than five days after the issuance of the certificate.

(Added by L.1996 chs. 1043, 1052, eff. 7/1/96.)

§46.2-1993.48. Operation without license plate prohibited.

No manufacturer or distributor of or dealer in motorcycles shall cause or permit any motorcycle, owned by him to be operated or moved on a public highway without there being displayed on the motorcycle, a license plate or plates issued to him, either under §46.2-711 or under

§46.2-1993.41, except as otherwise authorized in §§46.2-733, 46.2-1993.40 and 46.2-1993.50.
(Added by L.1996 chs. 1043, 1052, eff. 7/1/96.)

§46.2-1993.49. Movement by manufacturer to place of shipment or delivery.

Any manufacturer of motorcycles may operate or move or cause to be moved or operated on the highways for a distance of no more than twenty-five miles motorcycles from the factory where manufactured or assembled to a railway depot, vessel, or place of shipment or delivery, without registering them and without license plates attached thereto, under a written permit first obtained from the local law-enforcement authorities having jurisdiction over the highways and on displaying in plain sight on each motorcycle a placard bearing the name and address of the manufacturer authorizing or directing the movement.
(Added by L.1996 chs. 1043, 1052, eff. 7/1/96.)

§46.2-1993.50. Movement by dealers to salesrooms.

Any dealer in motorcycles may operate or move, or cause to be operated or moved, any motorcycle on the highways for a distance of no more than twenty-five miles from a vessel, railway depot, warehouse, or any place of shipment or from a factory where manufactured or assembled to a salesroom, warehouse, or place of shipment or transshipment without registering them and without license plates attached thereto, under a written permit first obtained from the local law-enforcement authorities having jurisdiction over the highways, and on displaying in plain sight on each motorcycle, a placard bearing the name and address of the dealer authorizing or directing the movement.
(Added by L.1996 chs. 1043, 1052, eff. 7/1/96.)

§46.2-1993.51. Operation under foreign dealer's license.

It shall be unlawful, except as provided for by reciprocal agreement, for any person to operate a motorcycle or for the owner thereof to permit a motorcycle to be operated in the Commonwealth on a foreign dealer's license, unless the operation of the motorcycle on the license is specifically authorized by the Commissioner.
(Added by L.1996 chs. 1043, 1052, eff. 7/1/96.)

§46.2-1993.52. Use of certain foreign-registered motorcycles in driver education programs.

Dealer's license plates may be displayed on motorcycles used by Virginia school systems in connection with driver education programs approved by the State Board of Education. In the event of such use of a motorcycle by a school system, any dealer, his employees and agents furnishing the motorcycle shall be immune from liability in any suit, claim, action, or cause of action, including but not limited to, actions or claims for injury to persons or property arising out of such use. Nothing in this section shall authorize the sale of any motorcycle so used in such driver education program as a demonstrator motorcycle. Notwithstanding the provisions of §§46.2-1993 and 46.2-1993.51, school divisions either (i) bordering on Kentucky, Maryland, North Carolina, Tennessee, or West Virginia, or (ii) located in Accomack or Northampton County may use motorcycles bearing foreign motorcycle dealer's license plates in connection with their driver education programs.
(Added by L.1996 chs. 1043, 1052, eff. 7/1/96.)

§46.2-1993.53. Removal of plates by Department of Motor Vehicles investigators; cancellation; reissuance.

If any Department of Motor Vehicles investigator finds that a vehicle bearing license plates or temporary transport plates issued under this article is being operated in a manner inconsistent with (i) the requirements of this article or (ii) the Commissioner's authorization provided for in this article, the Department of Motor Vehicles investigator may remove the license plate for cancellation. Once a license plate has been canceled, the dealership may reapply for the license plate. Reissuance of the license plate shall be subject to the approval of the Commissioner and the payment of the fee prescribed for issuance of license plates under this article.
(Added by L.1996 chs. 1043, 1052, eff. 7/1/96.)

§46.2-1993.54. Penalties for violations of article; service of summons.

Notwithstanding §46.2-1993.5, any person violating any of the provisions of this article shall be guilty of a Class 3 misdemeanor. Any summons issued for any violation of any provision of this article relating to use or misuse of dealer's license plates shall be served upon the dealership to whom the plates were issued or to the person expressly permitting the unlawful use, or upon the operator of the motorcycle if the plates are used contrary to the use authorized by the certificate issued pursuant to §46.2-1993.44.
(Added by L.1996 chs. 1043, 1052, eff. 7/1/96.)

ARTICLE 6
ISSUANCE OF TEMPORARY LICENSE PLATES BY DEALERS

§46.2-1993.55. Issuance of temporary license plates to dealers and vehicle owners.

The Department may, subject to the limitations and conditions set forth in this article, deliver temporary license plates designed by the Department to any dealer licensed under this chapter who applies for at least ten sets of plates and who encloses with his application a fee of two dollars for each set applied for. The application shall be made on a form prescribed and furnished by the Department. Dealers, subject to the limitations and conditions set forth in this article, may issue temporary license plates to owners of vehicles. The owners shall comply with the provisions of this article and §§46.2-705, 46.2-706 and 46.2-707. Dealers issuing temporary license plates may do so free of charge, but if they charge a fee for issuing temporary plates, the fee shall be no more than the fee charged the dealer by the Department under this section.

Display of a temporary license plate or plates on a vehicle shall subject the vehicle to the requirements of §§46.2-1038 and 46.2-1056.
(Added by L.1996 chs. 1043, 1052, eff. 7/1/96.)

§46.2-1993.56. Records to be kept by dealers; inspection.

Every dealer who has applied for temporary license plates shall maintain a permanent record of (i) all temporary license plates delivered to him, (ii) all temporary license plates issued by him, and (iii) any other information

pertaining to the receipt or the issuance of temporary license plates which may be required by the Department. Each record shall be kept for at least one year from the date of entry. Every dealer shall allow full access to these records during regular business hours to authorized representatives of the Department and to law-enforcement officers.
(Added by L.1996 chs. 1043, 1052, eff. 7/1/96.)

§46.2-1993.57. Application for temporary license plate.
No dealer shall issue a temporary license plate except on written application by the person entitled to receive the license plate, which application shall be forwarded by the dealer to the Department as provided in §46.2-1993.35.
(Added by L.1996 chs. 1043, 1052, eff. 7/1/96.)

§46.2-1993.58. To whom temporary plates shall not be issued; dealer to forward application for current titling and registration; misstatements and false information.
No dealer shall issue, assign, transfer, or deliver temporary license plates to other than the bona fide purchaser or owner of a motorcycle, whether or not the motorcycle is to be registered in Virginia. If the motorcycle is to be registered in Virginia, the dealer shall submit to the Department a written application for the current titling and registration of the purchased motorcycle, accompanied by the prescribed fees. Any dealer who issues temporary license plates to a purchaser who fails or declines to request that his application be forwarded promptly to the Department forthwith shall notify the Department of the issuance in the manner provided in this article. No dealer shall issue temporary license plates to any person who possesses current license plates for a motorcycle that has been sold or exchanged, nor shall any dealer lend temporary license plates to any person for use on any vehicle. If the dealer does not have in his possession the certificate of title or certificate of origin, he shall issue temporary license plates even though the purchaser has current license plates to be transferred. The dealer shall present the title or certificate of origin to the customer within thirty days of purchase and after this transaction is completed, the customer shall transfer his current license plates to the motorcycle. If the title or certificate of origin cannot be produced for a vehicle within thirty days, a second set of temporary license plates may be issued provided that a temporary certificate of ownership is issued as provided in §46.2-1993.35. It shall be unlawful for any person to issue any temporary license plates containing any misstatement of fact, or for any person issuing or using temporary license plates knowingly to insert any false information on their face.
(Added by L.1996 chs. 1043, 1052, eff. 7/1/96.)

§46.2-1993.59. Dealer to insert his name, date of issuance and expiration, make and identification number of vehicle.
Every dealer who issues temporary license plates shall insert clearly and indelibly on the face of each temporary license plate the name of the issuing dealer, the date of issuance and expiration, and the make and identification number of the motorcycle for which issued.
(Added by L.1996 chs. 1043, 1052, eff. 7/1/96.)

§46.2-1993.60. Suspension of right of dealer to issue.
The Commissioner, on determining that the provisions of this chapter or the directions of the Department are not being complied with by any dealer, may, after a hearing, suspend the right of a dealer to issue temporary license plates.
(Added by L.1996 chs. 1043, 1052, eff. 7/1/96.)

§46.2-1993.61. Plates to be destroyed on expiration.
Every person to whom temporary license plates have been issued shall destroy them on the thirtieth day after issue or immediately on receipt of the permanent license plates from the Department, whichever occurs first.
(Added by L.1996 chs. 1043, 1052, eff. 7/1/96.)

§46.2-1993.62. When plates to expire; refunds or credit.
Temporary license plates shall expire on the receipt of the permanent license plates from the Department, or on the rescission of a contract to purchase a motorcycle, or on the expiration of, or thirty days from the date of issuance, whichever occurs first. No refund or credit of fees paid by dealers to the Department for temporary license plates shall be allowed, except that when the Department discontinues the right of a dealer to issue temporary license plates, the dealer, on returning temporary license plates to the Department, may receive a refund or a credit for them.
(Added by L.1996 chs. 1043, 1052, eff. 7/1/96.)

§46.2-1993.63. Penalties.
Any person violating any of the provisions of this article shall be guilty of a Class 1 misdemeanor.
(Added by L.1996 chs. 1043, 1052, eff. 7/1/96.)

ARTICLE 7
FRANCHISES

Section

§46.2-1993.64. Filing of franchises.
Each motorcycle manufacturer, factory branch, distributor, distributor branch, or subsidiary thereof shall file with the Commissioner a true copy of each new, amended, modified, or different form or addendum offered to more than one dealer which affects the rights, responsibilities, or obligations of the parties of a franchise or sales, service, or sales and service agreement to be offered to a motorcycle dealer or prospective motorcycle dealer in the Commonwealth no later than sixty days prior to the date the franchise or sales agreement is offered. In no event shall a new, amended, modified, or different form of franchise or sales, service, or sales and service agreement be offered a motorcycle dealer in the Commonwealth until the form has been determined by the Commissioner as not containing terms inconsistent with the provisions of this chapter. At the time a filing is made with the Commissioner pursuant to this section, the manufacturer,

 Zv

factory branch, distributor, distributor branch, or subsidiary shall also give written notice together with a copy of the papers so filed to the affected dealer or dealers.
(Added by L.1996 chs. 1043, 1052, eff. 7/1/96.)

§46.2-1993.65. Exemption of franchises from Retail Franchising Act.

Franchises subject to the provisions of this chapter shall not be subject to any requirement contained in Chapter 8 (§13.1-557 et seq.) of Title 13.1.
(Added by L.1996 chs. 1043, 1052, eff. 7/1/96.)

§46.2-1993.66. Coercion of retail dealer by manufacturer or distributor with respect to retail installment sales contracts and extended warranties prohibited.

A. It shall be unlawful for any manufacturer or distributor, or any officer, agent, or representative of either, to coerce or attempt to coerce any retail motorcycle dealer or prospective retail motorcycle dealer in the Commonwealth to sell or offer to sell extended warranties or to sell, assign, or transfer any retail installment sales contract obtained by the dealer in connection with the sale by him in the Commonwealth of motorcycles manufactured or sold by the manufacturer or distributor, to a specified finance company or class of finance companies or to any other specified persons by any of the following:

1. Any statement, suggestion, promise, or threat that the manufacturer or distributor will in any manner benefit or injure the dealer, whether the statement, suggestion, threat, or promise is expressed or implied or made directly or indirectly.

2. Any act that will benefit or injure the dealer.

3. Any contract, or any expressed or implied offer of contract, made directly or indirectly to the dealer, for handling the motorcycle on the condition that the dealer sell, assign, or transfer his retail installment sales contract on the motorcycle, in the Commonwealth, to a specified finance company or class of finance companies or to any other specified person.

4. Any expressed or implied statement or representation made directly or indirectly that the dealer is under any obligation whatsoever to sell, assign, or transfer any of his retail sales contracts in the Commonwealth on motorcycles manufactured or sold by the manufacturer or distributor to a finance company, or class of finance companies, or other specified person, because of any relationship or affiliation between the manufacturer or distributor and the finance company or companies or the specified person or persons.

B. Any such statements, threats, promises, acts, contracts, or offers of contracts, when their effect may be to lessen or eliminate competition or tend to create a monopoly, are declared unfair trade practices and unfair methods of competition and are prohibited.

C. Any person violating any of the provisions of this article shall be guilty of a Class 1 misdemeanor.
(Added by L.1996 chs. 1043, 1052, eff. 7/1/96.)

§46.2-1993.67. Other coercion of dealers; transfer, grant, succession to and cancellation of dealer franchises; delivery of motorcycles, parts, and accessories.

It shall be unlawful for any manufacturer, factory branch, distributor, or distributor branch, or any field representative, officer, agent, or their representatives:

1. To coerce or attempt to coerce any dealer to accept delivery of any motorcycle or motorcycles, parts or accessories therefor, or any other commodities, which have not been ordered by the dealer.

2. To coerce or attempt to coerce any dealer to enter into an agreement with the manufacturer, factory branch, distributor, or distributor branch, or representative thereof, or do any other act unfair to the dealer, by threatening to cancel any franchise existing between the manufacturer, factory branch, distributor, distributor branch, or representative thereof and the dealer.

3. To coerce or attempt to coerce any dealer to join, contribute to, or affiliate with any advertising association.

4. To prevent or refuse to approve the sale or transfer of the ownership of a dealership by the sale of the business, stock transfer, or otherwise, or the transfer, sale, or assignment of a dealer franchise, or a change in the executive management or principal operator of the dealership, unless the franchisor provides written notice to the dealer of its objection and the reasons therefor at least thirty days prior to the proposed effective date of the transfer, sale, assignment, or change. No such objection shall be effective to prevent the sale, transfer, assignment, or change if the Commissioner has determined, if requested in writing by the dealer within thirty days after receipt of an objection to the proposed sale, transfer, or change, and after a hearing on the matter, that the failure to permit or honor the sale, transfer, assignment, or change is unreasonable under the circumstances. No franchise may be sold, assigned, or transferred unless (i) the franchisor has been given at least ninety days' prior written notice by the dealer as to the identity, financial ability, and qualifications of the proposed transferee and (ii) the sale or transfer of the franchise and business will not involve, without the franchisor's consent, a relocation of the business.

5. To grant an additional franchise for a particular line-make of motorcycle in a relevant market area in which a dealer or dealers in that line-make are already located unless the franchisor has first advised in writing all other dealers in the line-make in the relevant market area. No such additional franchise may be established at the proposed site unless the Commissioner has determined, if requested by a dealer of the same line-make in the relevant market area within thirty days after receipt of the franchisor's notice of intention to establish the additional franchise, and after a hearing on the matter, that there is reasonable evidence that after the grant of the new franchise, the market will support all of the dealers in that line-make in the relevant market area. Establishing a franchised dealer in a relevant market area to replace a franchised dealer that has not been in operation for more than two years shall constitute the establishment of a new franchise subject to the terms of this subdivision. The two-year period for replacing a franchised dealer shall begin on the day the franchise was terminated, or, if a termination hearing was held, on the day the franchisor was legally permitted finally to terminate the franchise. This subdivision shall not apply to (i) the relocation of an existing dealer within that dealer's relevant market area if the relocation site is to be more than ten miles distant from any other dealer for the same line-make; (ii) the relocation of an existing dealer within that dealer's relevant market area if the relocation site is to be more distant than the existing site from all other dealers of the same line-make in that relevant market area; or (iii) the relocation of an existing new motorcycle dealer within two miles of the existing site of the relocating dealer.

No new or additional motorcycle dealer franchise shall be established in any county, city or town unless the manufacturer, factory branch, distributor, distributor branch, or factory or distributor representative gives advance notice to any existing franchised dealers of the same line-make. The notice shall be in writing and sent by certified mail, return receipt requested, at least forty-five days prior to the establishment of the new or additional franchise. Any existing franchise dealer may file a protest within thirty days of the date the notice is received. The burden of proof in establishing inadequate representation of such line-make motorcycles shall be on the manufacturer, factory branch, distributor, distributor branch, or factory or distributor representative.

6. Except as otherwise provided in this subdivision and notwithstanding the terms of any franchise, to terminate, cancel, or refuse to renew the franchise of any dealer without good cause and unless (i) the dealer and the Commissioner have received written notice of the franchisor's intentions at least sixty days prior to the effective date of such termination, cancellation, or the expiration date of the franchise, setting forth the specific grounds for the action, and (ii) the Commissioner has determined, if requested in writing by the dealer within the sixty-day period, and after a hearing on the matter, that there is good cause for the termination, cancellation, or nonrenewal of the franchise. In any case where a petition is made to the Commissioner for a determination as to good cause for the termination, cancellation, or nonrenewal of a franchise, the franchise in question shall continue in effect pending the Commissioner's decision or, if that decision is appealed to the circuit court, pending the decision of the circuit court. In any case in which a franchisor neither advises a dealer that it does not intend to renew a franchise nor takes any action to renew a franchise beyond its expiration date, the franchise in question shall continue in effect on the terms last agreed to by the parties. Notwithstanding the other provisions of this subdivision, notice of termination, cancellation, or nonrenewal may be provided to a dealer by a franchisor not less than fifteen days prior to the effective date of such termination, cancellation, or nonrenewal when the grounds for such action are any of the following:

a. Insolvency of the franchised motorcycle dealer or filing of any petition by or against the franchised motorcycle dealer, under any bankruptcy or receivership law, leading to liquidation or which is intended to lead to liquidation of the franchisee's business;

b. Failure of the franchised motorcycle dealer to conduct its customary sales and service operations during its posted business hours for seven consecutive business days, except where the failure results from acts of God or circumstances beyond the direct control of the franchised motorcycle dealer;

c. Revocation of any license which the franchised motorcycle dealer is required to have to operate a dealership;

d. Conviction of the dealer or any principal of the dealer of a felony.

The change or discontinuance of a marketing or distribution system of a particular line-make product by a manufacturer or distributor, while the name identification of the product is continued in substantial form by the same or different manufacturer or distributor, may be considered to be a franchise termination, cancellation, or nonrenewal. The provisions of this paragraph shall apply to changes and discontinuances made after January 1, 1989, but they shall not be considered by any court in any case in which such a change or discontinuance occurring prior to that date has been challenged as constituting a termination, cancellation or nonrenewal.

7. To fail to provide continued parts and service support to a dealer which holds a franchise in a discontinued line-make for at least five years from the date of such discontinuance. This requirement shall not apply to a line-make which was discontinued prior to January 1, 1989.

8. To fail to allow a dealer the right at any time to designate a member of his family as a successor to the dealership in the event of the death or incapacity of the dealer. It shall be unlawful to prevent or refuse to honor the succession to a dealership by a member of the family of a deceased or incapacitated dealer if the franchisor has not provided to the member of the family previously designated by the dealer as his successor written notice of its objections to the succession and of such person's right to seek a hearing on the matter before the Commissioner pursuant to this article, and the Commissioner determines, if requested in writing by such member of the family within thirty days of receipt of such notice from the franchisor, and after a hearing on the matter before the Commissioner pursuant to this article, that the failure to permit or honor the succession is unreasonable under the circumstances. No member of the family may succeed to a franchise unless (i) the franchisor has been given written notice as to the identity, financial ability, and qualifications of the member of the family in question and (ii) the succession to the franchise will not involve, without the franchisor's consent, a relocation of the business.

9. To fail to ship monthly to any dealer, if ordered by the dealer, the number of new motorcycles of each make, series, and model needed by the dealer to receive a percentage of total new motorcycle sales of each make, series, and model equitably related to the total new motorcycle production or importation currently being achieved nationally by each make, series, and model covered under the franchise. Upon the written request of any dealer holding its sales or sales and service franchise, the manufacturer or distributor shall disclose to the dealer in writing the basis upon which new motorcycles are allocated, scheduled, and delivered to the dealers of the same line-make. If allocation is at issue in a request for a hearing, the dealer may demand the Commissioner to direct that the manufacturer or distributor provide to the dealer, within thirty days of such demand, all records of sales and all records of distribution of all motorcycles to the same line-make dealers who compete with the dealer requesting the hearing.

10. To require or otherwise coerce a dealer to underutilize the dealer's facilities.

11. To include in any franchise with a motorcycle dealer terms that are contrary to, prohibited by, or otherwise inconsistent with the requirements of this chapter.

12. For any franchise agreement to require a motorcycle dealer to pay the attorney's fees of the manufacturer or distributor related to hearings and appeals brought under this article.

13. To fail to include in any franchise with a motorcycle dealer the following language: "If any provision herein contravenes the laws or regulations of any state or other jurisdiction wherein this agreement is to be performed, or denies access to the procedures, forums, or remedies provided for by such laws or regulations, such provision shall be deemed to be modified to conform to such laws or regulations, and all other terms and provisions shall remain in full force," or words to that effect.

14. To include in any franchise agreement with a motorcycle dealer terms that prohibit a motorcycle dealer from exercising his right to a trial by jury in any action where such right otherwise exists.

(Added by L.1996 chs. 1043, 1052; chgd. by L.1997 ch. 802, eff. 7/1/97.)

§46.2-1993.67:1. When discontinuation, cancellation, or nonrenewal of franchise unfair.

A discontinuation, cancellation, or nonrenewal of a franchise agreement is unfair if it is not clearly permitted by the franchise agreement, is not undertaken in good faith, is not undertaken for good cause, or is based on an alleged breach of the franchise agreement that is not in fact a material and substantial breach.

(Added by L.1997 ch. 802, eff. 7/1/97.)

§46.2-1993.68. Manufacturer or distributor right of first refusal.

Notwithstanding the terms of any franchise agreement, in the event of a proposed sale or transfer of a dealership, the

 Zv

manufacturer or distributor shall be permitted to exercise a right of first refusal to acquire the new motorcycle dealer's assets or ownership, if such sale or transfer is conditioned upon the manufacturer's or dealer's entering into a dealer agreement with the proposed new owner or transferee, only if all the following requirements are met:

1. To exercise its right of first refusal, the manufacturer or distributor must notify the dealer in writing within forty-five days of its receipt of the completed proposal for the proposed sale or transfer;

2. The exercise of the right of first refusal will result in the dealer's and dealer's owner's receiving the same or greater consideration as they have contracted to receive in connection with the proposed change of ownership or transfer;

3. The proposed sale or transfer of the dealership's assets does not involve the transfer or sale to a member or members of the family of one or more dealer owners, or to a qualified manager or a partnership or corporation controlled by such persons; and

4. The manufacturer or distributor agrees to pay the reasonable expenses, including attorney's fees which do not exceed the usual, customary, and reasonable fees charged for similar work done for other clients, incurred by the proposed new owner and transferee prior to the manufacturer's or distributor's exercise of its right of first refusal in negotiating and implementing the contract for the proposed sale or transfer of the dealership or dealership assets. Notwithstanding the foregoing, no payment of such expenses and attorney's fees shall be required if the dealer has not submitted or caused to be submitted an accounting of those expenses within thirty days of the dealer's receipt of the manufacturer's or distributor's written request for such an accounting. Such accounting may be requested by a manufacturer or distributor before exercising its right of first refusal.

(Added by L.1996 chs. 1043, 1052, eff. 7/1/96.)

§46.2-1993.69. Discontinuation of distributors.

If the contract between a distributor and a manufacturer or importer is terminated or otherwise discontinued, all franchises granted to motorcycle dealers in Virginia by that distributor shall continue in full force and shall not be affected by the discontinuance, except that the manufacturer, factory branch, distributor, representative, or other person who undertakes to distribute motorcycles of the same line-make or the same motorcycles of a re-named line-make shall be substituted for the discontinued distributor under the existing motorcycle dealer franchises and those franchises shall be modified accordingly.

(Added by L.1996 chs. 1043, 1052, eff. 7/1/96.)

§46.2-1993.70. Warranty obligations.

A. Each motorcycle manufacturer, factory branch, distributor, or distributor branch shall (i) specify in writing to each of its motorcycle dealers licensed in the Commonwealth the dealer's obligations for preparation, delivery, and warranty service on its products and (ii) compensate the dealer for warranty parts, service and diagnostic work required of the dealer by the manufacturer or distributor as follows:

1. Compensation of a dealer for warranty parts, service and diagnostic work shall not be less than the amounts charged by the dealer for the manufacturer's or distributor's original parts, service and diagnostic work to retail customers for nonwarranty service, parts and diagnostic work installed or performed in the dealer's service department unless the amounts are not reasonable;

2. For purposes of determining warranty parts and service compensation, menu-priced parts or services, group discounts, special event discounts, and special event promotions shall not be considered in determining amounts charged by the dealer to retail customers;

3. Increases in dealer warranty parts and service compensation and diagnostic work compensation, pursuant to this section, shall be requested by the dealer in writing, shall be based on 100 consecutive repair orders or all repair orders over a ninety-day period, whichever occurs first and, in the case of parts, shall be stated as a percentage of markup which shall be uniformly applied to all the manufacturer's or distributor's parts;

4. In the case of warranty parts compensation, the provisions of this subsection shall be effective only for model year 1992 and succeeding model years;

5. If a manufacturer or distributor furnishes a part to a dealer at no cost for use by the dealer in performing work for which the manufacturer or distributor is required to compensate the dealer under this section, the manufacturer or distributor shall compensate the dealer for the part in the same manner as warranty parts compensation, less the wholesale costs, for such part as listed in the manufacturer's current price schedules. A manufacturer or distributor may pay the dealer a reasonable handling fee instead of the compensation otherwise required by this subsection for special high-performance complete engine assemblies in limited production motorcycles which constitute less than five percent of model production furnished to the dealer at no cost, if the manufacturer or distributor excludes such special high-performance complete engine assemblies in determining whether the amounts requested by the dealer for warranty compensation are consistent with the amounts that the dealer charges its other retail service customers for parts used by the dealer to perform similar work; or

6. In the case of service work, manufacturer original parts or parts otherwise specified by the manufacturer or distributor, and parts provided by a dealer either pursuant to an adjustment program as defined in §59.1-207.34 or as otherwise requested by the manufacturer or distributor, the dealer shall be compensated in the same manner as for warranty service or parts.

Warranty audits of dealer records may be conducted by the manufacturer, factory branch, distributor, or distributor branch on a reasonable basis, and dealer claims for warranty compensation shall not be denied except for good cause, such as performance of nonwarranty repairs, lack of material documentation, fraud, or misrepresentation. Claims for dealer compensation shall be paid within thirty days of dealer submission or within thirty days of the end of an incentive program or rejected in writing for stated reasons. The manufacturer, factory branch, distributor, or distributor branch shall reserve the right to reasonable periodic audits to determine the validity of all such paid claims for dealer compensation. Any chargebacks for warranty parts or service compensation and service incentives shall only be for the twelve-month period immediately following the date of the claim and, in the case of chargebacks for sales compensation only, for the eighteen-month period immediately following the date of claim. However, such limitations shall not be effective in the case of intentionally false or fraudulent claims.

B. It shall be unlawful for any motorcycle manufacturer, factory branch, distributor, or distributor branch to:

1. Fail to perform any of its warranty obligations, including tires, with respect to a motorcycle;

2. Fail to assume all responsibility for any liability resulting from structural or production defects;

3. Fail to include in written notices of factory recalls to motorcycle owners and dealers the expected date by which necessary parts and equipment will be available to dealers for the correction of defects;

4. Fail to compensate any of the motorcycle dealers licensed in the Commonwealth for repairs effected by the dealer of merchandise damaged in manufacture or transit to the dealer where the carrier is designated by the manufacturer, factory branch, distributor, or distributor branch;

5. Fail to compensate its motorcycle dealers licensed in the Commonwealth for warranty parts, work, and service pursuant to subsection A of this section, or for legal costs and expenses incurred by such dealers in connection with warranty obligations for which the manufacturer, factory branch, distributor, or distributor branch is legally responsible or which the manufacturer, factory branch, distributor, or distributor branch imposes upon the dealer;

6. Misrepresent in any way to purchasers of motorcycles that warranties with respect to the manufacture, performance, or design of the motorcycle are made by the dealer, either as warrantor or co-warrantor;

7. Require the dealer to make warranties to customers in any manner related to the manufacture, performance, or design of the motorcycle; or

8. Shift or attempt to shift to the motorcycle dealer, directly or indirectly, any liabilities of the manufacturer, factory branch, distributor or distributor branch under the Virginia Motor Vehicle Warranty Enforcement Act (§59.1-207.9 et seq.), unless such liability results from the act or omission by the dealer.

C. Notwithstanding the terms of any franchise, it shall be unlawful for any motorcycle manufacturer, factory branch, distributor, or distributor branch to fail to indemnify and hold harmless its motorcycle dealers against any losses or damages arising out of complaints, claims, or suits relating to the manufacture, assembly, or design of motorcycles, parts, or accessories, or other functions by the manufacturer, factory branch, distributor, or distributor branch beyond the control of the dealer, including, without limitation, the selection by the manufacturer, factory branch, distributor, or distributor branch of parts or components for the motorcycle or any damages to merchandise occurring in transit to the dealer where the carrier is designated by the manufacturer, factory branch, distributor, or distributor branch. The dealer shall notify the manufacturer of pending suits in which allegations are made which come within this subsection whenever reasonably practicable to do so. Every motorcycle dealer franchise issued to, amended, or renewed for motorcycle dealers in Virginia shall be construed to incorporate provisions consistent with the requirements of this subsection.

D. On any new motorcycle, any uncorrected damage or any corrected damage exceeding three percent of the manufacturer's or distributor's suggested retail price as defined in 15 U.S.C. §§1231–1233, as measured by retail repair costs, must be disclosed to the dealer in writing prior to delivery. Factory mechanical repair and damage to tires are excluded from the three percent rule when properly replaced by identical manufacturer's or distributor's original equipment or parts. Whenever a new motorcycle is damaged in transit, when the carrier or means of transportation is determined by the manufacturer or distributor, or whenever a motorcycle is otherwise damaged prior to delivery to the new motorcycle dealer, the new motorcycle dealer shall:

1. Notify the manufacturer or distributor of the damage within three business days from the date of delivery of the new motorcycle to the new motorcycle dealership or within the additional time specified in the franchise; and

2. Request from the manufacturer or distributor authorization to replace the components, parts, and accessories damaged or otherwise correct the damage, unless the damage to the motorcycle exceeds the three percent rule, in which case the dealer may reject the motorcycle within three business days.

E. If the manufacturer or distributor refuses or fails to authorize correction of such damage within ten days after receipt of notification, or if the dealer rejects the motorcycle because damage exceeds the three percent rule, ownership of the new motorcycle shall revert to the manufacturer or distributor, and the new motorcycle dealer shall have no obligation, financial or otherwise, with respect to such motorcycle. Should either the manufacturer, distributor, or the dealer elect to correct the damage or any other damage exceeding the three percent rule, full disclosure shall be made by the dealer in writing to the buyer and an acknowledgment by the buyer is required. If there is less than three percent damage, no disclosure is required, provided the damage has been corrected. Predelivery mechanical work shall not require a disclosure. Failure to disclose any corrected damage within the knowledge of the selling dealer to a new motorcycle in excess of the three percent rule shall constitute grounds for revocation of the buyer order, provided that, within thirty days of purchase, the motorcycle is returned to the dealer with an accompanying written notice of the grounds for revocation. In case of revocation pursuant to this section, the dealer shall accept the motorcycle and refund any payments made to the dealer in connection with the transaction, less a reasonable allowance for the consumer's use of the motorcycle as defined in §59.1-207.11.

F. If there is a dispute between the manufacturer, factory branch, distributor, or distributor branch and the dealer with respect to any matter referred to in subsection A, B, or C of this section, either party may petition the Commissioner in writing, within thirty days after either party has given written notice of the dispute to the other, for a hearing. The decision of the Commissioner shall be binding on the parties, subject to rights of judicial review and appeal as provided in Chapter 1.1:1 (§9-6.14:1 et seq.) of Title 9. However, nothing contained in this section shall give the Commissioner any authority as to the content or interpretation of any manufacturer's or distributor's warranty.

(Added by L.1996 chs. 1043, 1052, eff. 7/1/96.)

§46.2-1993.71. Operation of dealership by manufacturer.

It shall be unlawful for any motorcycle manufacturer, factory branch, distributor, distributor branch, or subsidiary thereof, to own, operate, or control any motorcycle dealership in the Commonwealth. However, this section shall not prohibit:

1. The operation by a manufacturer, factory branch, distributor, distributor branch, or subsidiary thereof, of a dealership for a temporary period, not to exceed one year, during the transition from one owner or operator to another;

2. The ownership or control of a dealership by a manufacturer, factory branch, distributor, distributor branch, or subsidiary thereof, while the dealership is being sold under a bona fide contract or purchase option to the operator of the dealership;

3. The ownership, operation, or control of a dealership by a manufacturer, factory branch, distributor, distributor branch, or subsidiary thereof, if the manufacturer, factory branch, distributor, distributor branch, or subsidiary has been engaged in the retail sale of motorcycles through the dealership for a continuous period of three years prior to July 1, 1972, and if the Commissioner determines, after a hearing on the matter at the request of any party, that there is no dealer independent of the manufacturer or distributor, factory branch or distributor branch, or subsidiary thereof available in the community to own and operate the franchise in a manner consistent with the public interest;

4. The ownership, operation, or control of a dealership by a manufacturer, factory branch, distributor, distributor branch, or subsidiary thereof if the Commissioner determines, after a hearing at the request of any party, that there is no dealer independent of the manufacturer or distributor, factory branch or distributor branch, or subsidiary thereof available in the community or trade area to own and operate the franchise in a manner consistent with the public interest.
(Added by L.1996 chs. 1043, 1052, eff. 7/1/96.)

§46.2-1993.72. Ownership of service facilities.
It shall be unlawful for any motorcycle manufacturer, factory branch, distributor, distributor branch, or subsidiary thereof, to own, operate, or control, either directly or indirectly, any motorcycle warranty or service facility located in the Commonwealth. Nothing in this section shall prohibit any motorcycle manufacturer, factory branch, distributor, distributor branch, or subsidiary thereof, from owning, operating, or controlling any warranty or service facility for warranty or service of motorcycles owned or operated by the manufacturer, factory branch, distributor, distributor branch, or subsidiary thereof. Nothing contained in this section shall prohibit a motorcycle manufacturer, factory branch, distributor, or distributor branch from performing service for reasons of compliance with an order of a court of competent jurisdiction or of warranty under Chapter 17.3 (§59.1-207.9 et seq.) of Title 59.1.
(Added by L.1996 chs. 1043, 1052, eff. 7/1/96.)

§46.2-1993.73. Hearings and other remedies; civil penalties.
A. In every case of a hearing before the Commissioner authorized under this article, the Commissioner shall give reasonable notice of each hearing to all interested parties, and the Commissioner's decision shall be binding on the parties, subject to the rights of judicial review and appeal as provided in Chapter 1.1:1 (§9-6.14:1 et seq.) of Title 9.

B. Hearings before the Commissioner under this article shall commence within ninety days of the request for a hearing and the Commissioner's decision shall be rendered within sixty days from the receipt of the hearing officer's recommendation. Hearings authorized under this article shall be presided over by a hearing officer selected from a list prepared by the Executive Secretary of the Supreme Court of Virginia. On request of the Commissioner, the Executive Secretary will name a hearing officer from the list, selected on a rotation system administered by the Executive Secretary. The hearing officer shall provide recommendations to the Commissioner within ninety days of the conclusion of the hearing.

C. Notwithstanding any contrary provision of this article, the Commissioner shall initiate investigations, conduct hearings, and determine the rights of parties under this article whenever he is provided information indicating a possible violation of any provision of this article.

D. For purposes of any matter brought to the Commissioner under subdivisions 3, 4, 5, 6 and 9 of §46.2-1993.67 with respect to which the Commissioner is to determine whether there is good cause for a proposed action or whether it would be unreasonable under the circumstances, the Commissioner shall consider:

1. The volume of the affected dealer's business in the relevant market area;
2. The nature and extent of the dealer's investment in its business;
3. The adequacy of the dealer's service facilities, equipment, parts, supplies, and personnel;
4. The effect of the proposed action on the community;
5. The extent and quality of the dealer's service under motorcycle warranties;
6. The dealer's performance under the terms of its franchise; and
7. Other economic and geographical factors reasonably associated with the proposed action.

With respect to subdivision 6 of this subsection, any performance standard or program for measuring dealership performance that may have a material effect on a dealer, and the application of any such standard or program by a manufacturer or distributor, shall be fair, reasonable, and equitable and, if based upon a survey, shall be based upon a statistically valid sample. Upon the request of any dealer, a manufacturer or distributor shall disclose in writing to the dealer a description of how a performance standard or program is designed and all relevant information used in the application of the performance standard or program to that dealer.

E. An interested party in a hearing held pursuant to subsection A of this section shall comply with the effective date of compliance established by the Commissioner in his decision in such hearing, unless a stay or extension of such date is granted by the Commissioner or the Commissioner's decision is under judicial review and appeal as provided in subsection A of this section. If, after notice to such interested party and an opportunity to comment, the Commissioner finds an interested party has not complied with his decision by the designated date of compliance, unless a stay or extension of such date has been granted by the Commissioner or the Commissioner's decision is under judicial review and appeal, the Commissioner may assess such interested party a civil penalty not to exceed $1,000 per day of noncompliance. Civil penalties collected under this subsection shall be deposited into the Transportation Trust Fund.
(Added by L.1996 chs. 1043, 1052; chgd. by L.2000 ch. 106, eff. 7/1/2000.)

§46.2-1993.74. Late model and factory repurchase franchises.
Franchised late model or factory repurchase motorcycle dealers shall have the same rights and obligations as provided for franchised new motorcycle dealers in this article, mutatis mutandis.
(Added by L.1996 chs. 1043, 1052, eff. 7/1/96.)

ARTICLE 8
DENIAL, SUSPENSION, AND REVOCATION OF DEALER LICENSES

§46.2-1993.75. Acts of officers, directors, partners, and salespersons.
If a licensee or registrant is a partnership or corporation, it shall be sufficient cause for the denial, suspension, or revocation of a license or certificate of dealer registration that any officer, director, or trustee of the partnership or corporation, or any member in the case of a partnership or the dealer-operator, has committed any act or omitted any duty which would be cause for refusing, suspending, or revoking a license or

certificate of dealer registration issued to him as an individual under this chapter. Each licensee or registrant shall be responsible for the acts of any of his salespersons while acting as his agent, if the licensee approved of those acts or had knowledge of those acts or other similar acts and, after such knowledge, retained the benefit, proceeds, profits, or advantages accruing from those acts or otherwise ratified those acts.
(Added by L.1996 chs. 1043, 1052, eff. 7/1/96.)

§46.2-1993.76. Grounds for denying, suspending, or revoking licenses or certificates of dealer registration or qualification.

A license or certificate of dealer registration or qualification issued under this subtitle may be denied, suspended, or revoked on any one or more of the following grounds:

1. Material misstatement or omission in application for license, dealer's license plates, certificate of dealer registration, certificate of qualification, or certificate of title;
2. Failure to comply subsequent to receipt of a written warning from the Department or any willful failure to comply with any provision of this chapter or any applicable provision of this subtitle or any applicable regulation promulgated under this subtitle;
3. Failure to have an established place of business as defined in §46.2-1993.8 or failure to have as the dealer-operator an individual who holds a valid certificate of qualification;
4. Defrauding any retail buyer, to the buyer's damage, or any other person in the conduct of the licensee's or registrant's business;
5. Employment of fraudulent devices, methods or practices in connection with compliance with the requirements under the statutes of the Commonwealth with respect to the retaking of vehicles under retail installment contracts and the redemption and resale of those vehicles;
6. Having used deceptive acts or practices;
7. Knowingly advertising by any means any assertion, representation, or statement of fact which is untrue, misleading, or deceptive in any particular relating to the conduct of the business licensed or registered under this subtitle or for which a license or registration is sought;
8. Having been convicted of any fraudulent act in connection with the business of selling vehicles or any consumer-related fraud;
9. Having been convicted of any criminal act involving the business of selling vehicles;
10. Willfully retaining in his possession title to a vehicle that has not been completely and legally assigned to him;
11. Failure to comply with any provision of Chapter 4.1 (§36-85.2 et seq.) of Title 36 or any regulation promulgated pursuant to that chapter;
12. Leasing, renting, lending, or otherwise allowing the use of a dealer's license plate by persons not specifically authorized under this title;
13. Having been convicted of a felony;
14. Failure to submit to the Department, within thirty days from the date of sale, any application, tax, or fee collected for the Department on behalf of a buyer;
15. Having been convicted of larceny of a vehicle or receipt or sale of a stolen vehicle;
16. Having been convicted of odometer tampering or any related violation;
17. If a salvage dealer, salvage pool, or rebuilder, failing to comply with any provision of Chapter 16 of this title or any regulation promulgated by the Commissioner under that chapter;
18. Failing to maintain liability insurance, issued by a company licensed to do business in the Commonwealth, or a certificate of self-insurance as defined in §46.2-368, with respect to each dealer's license plate issued to the dealer by the Department; or
19. Failing or refusing to pay civil penalties imposed by the Commissioner pursuant to §46.2-1993.5.

(Added by L.1996 chs. 1043, 1052; chgd. by L.1999 ch. 217, eff. 7/1/99.)

§46.2-1993.77. Suspension, revocation, and refusal to renew licenses or certificates of dealer registration or qualification; notice and hearing.

A. Except as provided in subsections B and C of this section, no license or certificate of dealer registration or qualification issued under this subtitle shall be suspended or revoked, or renewal thereof refused, until a written copy of the complaint made has been furnished to the licensee, registrant, or qualifier against whom the same is directed and a public hearing thereon has been had before the Commissioner. At least ten days' written notice of the time and place of the hearing shall be given to the licensee, registrant, or qualifier by registered mail addressed to his last known post office address or as shown on his license or certificate or other record of information in possession of the Commissioner. At the hearing the licensee, registrant, or qualifier shall have the right to be heard personally or by counsel. After hearing, the Commissioner may suspend, revoke, or refuse to renew the license or certificate in question. Immediate notice of any suspension, revocation, or refusal shall be given to the licensee, registrant, or qualifier in the same manner provided in this section for giving notices of hearing.

B. Should a dealer fail to maintain an established place of business, the Commissioner may cancel the license of the dealer without a hearing after notification of the intent to cancel has been sent, by return receipt mail, to the dealer at the dealer's residence and business addresses, and the notices are returned undelivered or the dealer does not respond within twenty days from the date the notices were sent. Any subsequent application for a dealer's license shall be treated as an original application.

C. Should a dealer fail or refuse to pay civil penalties imposed by the Commissioner pursuant to §46.2-1993.5, the Commissioner may deny, revoke, or suspend the dealer's license without a hearing after notice of imposition of civil penalties has been sent, by certified mail, return receipt requested, to the dealer at the dealer's business address and such civil penalty is not paid in full within thirty days after receipt of the notice.
(Added by L.1996 chs. 1043, 1052; chgd. by L.1999 ch. 217, eff. 7/1/99.)

§46.2-1993.78. Appeals from actions of the Commissioner.

Any person aggrieved by the action of the Commissioner in refusing to grant or renew a license or certificate of dealer registration or qualification issued under this chapter, or by any other action of the Commissioner which is alleged to be improper, unreasonable, or unlawful under the provisions of this chapter is entitled to judicial review in accordance with the provisions of the Administrative Process Act (§9-6.14:1 et seq.).
(Added by L.1996 chs. 1043, 1052, eff. 7/1/96.)

§46.2-1993.79. Appeals to Court of Appeals.

Either party may appeal from the decision of the court under §46.2-1993.78 to the Court of Appeals. These appeals shall be taken and prosecuted in the same manner and with like effect as is provided by law in other cases appealed as a matter of right to the Court of Appeals.
(Added by L.1996 chs. 1043, 1052; chgd. by L.1997 ch. 88, eff. 7/1/97.)

§46.2-1993.80. Equitable remedies not impaired.

The remedy at law provided by §§46.2-1993.78 and 46.2-1993.79 shall not in any manner impair the right to applicable equitable relief. That right to equitable relief is hereby preserved, notwithstanding the provisions of §§46.2-1993.78 and 46.2-1993.79.

(Added by L.1996 chs. 1043, 1052, eff. 7/1/96.)

ARTICLE 9
MOTORCYCLE DEALER ADVERTISING

§46.2-1993.81. Regulated advertising practices.

For purposes of this chapter, a violation of the following regulated advertising practices shall be an unfair, deceptive, or misleading act or practice.

1. A motorcycle shall not be advertised as new, either by word or implication, unless it is one which conforms to the requirements of §46.2-1993.

2. When advertising any motor vehicle which does not conform to the definition of "new" as provided in §46.2-1993, the fact that it is used shall be clearly and unequivocally expressed by the term "used" or by such other term as is commonly understood to mean that the motor vehicle is used. By way of example but not by limitation, "special purchase" by itself is not a satisfactory disclosure; however, such terms as "demonstrator" or "former leased vehicles" used alone clearly express that the vehicles are used for advertising purposes.

3. Advertisement of finance charges or other interest rates shall not be used when there is a cost to buy-down said charge or rate which is passed on, in whole or in part, to the purchaser.

4. Terms, conditions, and disclaimers shall be stated clearly and conspicuously. An asterisk or other reference symbol may be used to point to a disclaimer or other information, but shall not be used as a means of contradicting or changing the meaning of an advertised statement.

5. The expiration date of an advertised sale shall be clearly and conspicuously disclosed.

6. The term "list price," "sticker price," or "suggested retail price" and similar terms, shall be used only in reference to the manufacturer's suggested retail price for new motorcycles or the dealer's own usual and customary price for used motorcycles.

7. Terms such as "at cost," "below cost," "$ off cost" shall not be used in advertisements because of the difficulty in determining a dealer's actual net cost at the time of the sale. Terms such as "invoice price," "$ over invoice," may be used, provided that the invoice referred to is the manufacturer's factory invoice or a bona fide bill of sale and the invoice or bill of sale is available for customer inspection.

"Manufacturer's factory invoice" means that document supplied by the manufacturer to the dealer listing the manufacturer's charge to the dealer before any deduction for holdback, group advertising, factory incentives or rebates, or any governmental charges.

8. When the price or credit terms of a motorcycle are advertised, the motorcycle shall be fully identified as to year, make, and model. In addition, in advertisements placed by individual dealers and not line-make marketing groups, the stated price or credit terms shall include all charges which the buyer must pay to the seller, except buyer-selected options, state and local fees and taxes, and manufacturer's or distributor's freight or destination charges. If freight or destination charges are not included in the advertised price, the amount of any such freight or destination charge must be clearly and conspicuously disclosed.

9. Advertisements which set out a policy of matching or bettering competitors' prices shall not be used unless the terms of the offer are specific, verifiable and reasonable.

10. Advertisements of "dealer rebates" shall not be used. This does not affect advertisement of manufacturer rebates.

11. "Free," "at no cost," or other words to that effect shall not be used unless the "free" item, merchandise, or service is available without a purchase. This provision shall not apply to advertising placed by manufacturers, distributors, or line-make marketing groups.

12. "Bait" advertising, in which an advertiser may have no intention to sell at the price or terms advertised, shall not be used. By way of example, but not by limitation:

a. If a specific motorcycle is advertised, the seller shall be in possession of a reasonable supply of said motorcycles, and they shall be available at the advertised price. If the advertised motorcycle is available only in limited numbers or only by order, that shall be stated in the advertisement. For purposes of this subdivision, the listing of a motorcycle by stock number or vehicle identification number in the advertisement for a used motorcycle is one means of satisfactorily disclosing a limitation of availability. Stock numbers or vehicle identification numbers shall not be used in advertising a new motorcycle unless the advertisement clearly and conspicuously discloses that it relates to only one motorcycle;

b. Advertising a motorcycle at a certain price, including "as low as" statements, but having available for sale only motorcycles equipped with dealer added cost "options" which increase the selling price, above the advertised price, shall also be considered "bait" advertising;

c. If a lease payment is advertised, the fact that it is a lease arrangement shall be disclosed.

13. The term "repossessed" shall be used only to describe motorcycles that have been sold, registered, titled and then taken back from a purchaser and not yet resold to an ultimate user. Advertisers offering repossessed motorcycles for sale shall provide proof of repossession upon request.

14. Words such as "finance" or "loan" shall not be used in a motorcycle advertiser's firm name or trade name, unless that person is actually engaged in the financing of motorcycles.

15. Any advertisement which gives the impression a dealer has a special arrangement or relationship with the distributor or manufacturer, as compared to similarly situated dealers, shall not be used.

(Added by L.1996 chs. 1043, 1052, eff. 7/1/96.)

§46.2-1993.82. Enforcement; regulations.

The Commissioner may promulgate regulations reasonably necessary for enforcement of this article.

In addition to any other sanctions or remedies available to the Commissioner under this chapter, the Commissioner may assess a civil penalty not to exceed $1,000 for any single violation of this article. Each day that a violation continues shall constitute a separate violation.

(Added by L.1996 chs. 1043, 1052, eff. 7/1/96.)

SUBTITLE V
MOTOR CARRIERS

CHAPTER 20
REGULATION OF MOTOR VEHICLE CARRIERS GENERALLY

(Added by L.1995 chs. 744, 803, eff. 7/1/95.)

§46.2-2000. Definitions.

Whenever used in this chapter unless expressly stated otherwise:

"Broker" means any person not included in the term "motor carrier" and not a bona fide employee or agent of any such carrier, who, as principal or agent, sells or offers for sale any transportation subject to this chapter, or negotiates for, or holds himself out by solicitation, advertisement, or otherwise as one who sells, provides, furnishes, contracts, or arranges for such transportation.

"Certificate" means a certificate of public convenience and necessity issued by the Department of Motor Vehicles to common carriers by motor vehicle and restricted common carriers by motor vehicle under this chapter authorizing the transportation of passengers over the public highways of the Commonwealth; but nothing contained in this chapter shall be construed to mean that the Department can issue any such certificate authorizing intracity transportation.

"Common carrier by motor vehicle" means any person who undertakes, whether directly or by a lease or any other arrangement, to transport passengers for the general public by motor vehicle for compensation over the highways of the Commonwealth, whether over regular or irregular routes,

 Zv

including such motor vehicle operations of carriers by rail or water under this chapter.

"Highway" means every public highway or place of whatever nature open to the use of the public for purposes of vehicular travel in the Commonwealth, including the streets and alleys in towns and cities.

"Minibus" means any motor vehicle having a seating capacity of not less than seven nor more than sixteen passengers and used in the transportation of passengers.

"Motor carrier" includes a common carrier by motor vehicle and a restricted common carrier by motor vehicle.

"Operation" or "operations" includes the operation of all motor vehicles as defined in this section, whether loaded or empty, whether for compensation or not, and whether owned by or leased to the motor carrier who operates them or causes them to be operated

"Permit" means a permit issued by the Department to contract carriers by motor vehicle, or to operators of taxicabs or other vehicles performing taxicab service under this chapter.

"Person" means any individual, firm, copartnership, corporation, company, association or joint-stock association, and includes any trustee, receiver, assignee, or personal representative thereof.

"Restricted common carrier by motor vehicle" means any person who undertakes, whether directly or by a lease or other arrangement, to transport passengers or household goods of any restricted class or classes by motor vehicle for compensation, whether over regular or irregular routes.

"Route", when used in connection with or with respect to a certificate of public convenience and necessity, means the road or highway, or segment thereof, operated over by the holder of a certificate of public convenience and necessity or proposed to be operated over by an applicant therefore, whether such road or highway is designated by one or more highway numbers.

"Services" and "transportation", include the service of, and all transportation by, all vehicles operated by, for, or in the interest of any motor carrier irrespective of ownership or contract, expressed or implied, together with all facilities and property operated or controlled by any such carrier or carriers and used in the transportation of passengers or property or the performance of any service in connection therewith.

"Taxicab or other motor vehicle performing a taxicab service" means any motor vehicle having a seating capacity of not more than six passengers, not operating on a regular route or between fixed terminals used in the transportation of passengers for hire or for compensation, and not a common carrier or restricted common carrier as defined in this chapter.

(Added by L.1995 chs. 744, 803, eff. 7/1/95.)

§46.2-2000.1. Vehicles excluded from operation of chapter.

This chapter shall not be construed to include:

1. Motor vehicles employed solely in transporting school children and teachers;

2. Taxicabs, or other motor vehicles performing bona fide taxicab service, having a seating capacity of not more than six passengers, while operating in a county, city, or town which has or adopts an ordinance regulating and controlling taxicabs and other vehicles performing a bona fide taxicab service, and not operating on a regular route or between fixed termini. Each operator of a motor vehicle performing a bona fide taxicab service shall file insurance as required under §46.2-2028 unless evidence can be shown the Department that the operator is a self-insurer under an ordinance of the city or county where the home office of the operator is located; and failure to keep insurance in force shall subject the operator to cancellation of any authority under this chapter;

3. Motor vehicles owned or operated by or on behalf of hotels while used exclusively for the transportation of hotel patronage between hotels and local railroad or other common carrier stations;

4. Motor vehicles owned and operated by the United States, the District of Columbia, or any state, or any municipality or any other political subdivision of this Commonwealth, including vehicles used exclusively for handling United States mail, and passenger-carrying motor vehicles while being operated under an exclusive contract with the United States;

5. Motor vehicles while used exclusively in transporting only bona fide employees directly to and from the factories, plants, offices or other places of like nature where they are employed and accustomed to work. The operator of such vehicle shall first secure from the Department a permit, and the necessary identification marker for each vehicle so operated, neither of which shall be issued by the Department unless the applicant furnishes to the Department at the time the application is made, a statement in writing signed by the applicant (i) setting forth the names and locations of the factories, plants, offices or other places of like nature to and from which the applicant proposes to operate and (ii) stating that such applicant will transport only bona fide employees of such factories, plants, offices or like places to and from work; the permit shall be subject to revocation or suspension, and the holder thereof subject to the imposition of penalties by the Department for any of the causes and in the manner and to the extent provided for by the Department. Any permit issued by the Department under the provisions of this section prior to July 1, 1950, shall, unless suspended or revoked as herein provided, continue to be valid; but any such permit or permit holder shall in all other respects be subject to the provisions of this section;

6. Any motor vehicle while transporting not more than fifteen passengers in addition to the driver, if the driver and the passengers are engaged in a share-the-ride undertaking and if they share not more than the expenses of operation of the vehicle. Regular payments, toward a capital recovery fund or used to pay for leasing the vehicle are to be considered eligible expenses of operation;

7. Motor vehicles while used exclusively in the transportation of passengers within the corporate limits of incorporated cities or towns, and motor vehicles used exclusively in the regular transportation of passengers within the boundaries of such cities or towns and adjacent counties where such vehicles are being operated by such county or pursuant to a contract with the board of supervisors of such county;

8. Minibuses controlled and operated by a bona fide nonprofit corporation organized or existing under Chapter 10 (§13.1-801 et seq.) of Title 13.1 of the Code of Virginia, or by a tax-exempt organization as defined in §§501(c)(3) and 501(c)(4) of the United States Internal Revenue Code, as from time to time amended, while used exclusively in the transportation, for hire, for compensation, or otherwise, of members of such organization if it is a membership corporation, or of elderly, handicapped or economically disadvantaged members of the community served by such organization if it is not a membership corporation. Such minibuses shall not be operated over the same or an adjacent route and on a similar schedule as a holder of a certificate of public convenience and necessity or as a public transportation authority. Each operator of a minibus hereby excluded shall be issued an identification marker under subsection C of §46.2-761 and shall file insurance as required under §46.2-2028 unless evidence can be shown the Department

that the operator is a self-insurer under an ordinance of the city or an ordinance of the county where the registered office of the operator is located. Failure to keep insurance in force shall subject the operator to cancellation of its exemption card and withdrawal of its classification plate;

9. Motor vehicles while operated under the exclusive regulatory control of a transportation district commission acting pursuant to Chapter 45 (§15.2-4500 et seq.) of Title 15.2;

10. One insured vehicle which is owned by a person as defined in §46.2-2000 and which is more than fifty years old, when operated during the daytime on trips returning to the point of origin;

11. Motor vehicles used for the transportation of passengers by nonprofit, nonstock corporations funded solely by federal, state or local subsidies, the use of which motor vehicles are restricted as to regular and irregular routes to contracts with four or more counties and, at the commencement of the operation, no certificated carrier provides the same or similar services within such counties.

(Added by L.1995 chs. 744, 803, eff. 7/1/95.)

§46.2-2000.2. Section 46.2-2000.1 not to exempt from requirements of Article 12 of Chapter 6.

The provisions of §46.2-2000.1, except subsection 10, shall not be construed to exempt any person or any vehicle from the requirements of Article 12 (§46.2-757 et seq.) of Chapter 6 relating to identification markers.

(Added by L.1995 chs. 744, 803, eff. 7/1/95.)

§46.2-2001. Regulation by Department; reports; prevention of discrimination; regulation of leasing of motor vehicles.

The Department shall supervise, regulate and control all common carriers by motor vehicle and restricted common carriers by motor vehicle, doing business in the Commonwealth, and all matters relating to the performance of their public duties and their charges therefor, and shall correct abuses therein by such carriers; and to that end the Department shall, from time to time, prescribe reasonable rules, regulations, forms and reports for such carriers in furtherance of the administration and operation of this chapter; and the Department shall have the right at all times to require from such motor carriers special reports and statements, under oath, concerning their business.

The Department shall, from time to time, make and enforce such requirements, rules and regulations as may be necessary to prevent unjust or unreasonable discriminations by any carrier in favor of, or against, any person, locality, community or connecting carrier in the matter of service, schedule, efficiency of transportation or otherwise, in connection with the public duties of such carrier. The Department shall administer and enforce all provisions of this chapter, and prescribe reasonable rules, regulations and procedure looking to that end.

The Department may, from time to time, prescribe and enforce such reasonable requirements, rules and regulations in the matter of leasing of motor vehicles as are necessary to prevent evasion of the Department's regulatory powers. This power of the Department to regulate leasing shall not be limited to those motor carriers of property doing business in this Commonwealth but shall include all persons not otherwise exempted who are operating motor vehicles on any highway in Virginia.

(Added by L.1995 chs. 744, 803, eff. 7/1/95.)

§46.2-2002. Regulation of brokers.

The Department shall also regulate brokers and make and enforce reasonable requirements respecting their licenses, financial responsibility, accounts, records, reports, operations and practices.

(Added by L.1995 chs. 744, 803, eff. 7/1/95.)

§46.2-2003. Appointment of police agents.

The president or any other executive officer of a motor carrier company, incorporated in the Commonwealth may, with the approval of the judge of any court of record wherein the motor carrier company has terminal facilities, appoint one or more police agents, who shall have authority in all cases in which the rights of such motor carrier company are involved to exercise, within the Commonwealth, all the powers which can lawfully be exercised by any conservator of the peace for the preservation of the peace, the arrest of offenders and disorderly persons, and for the enforcement of the laws against crime; such president or other executive officer may, with the approval of the judge of any court of record as aforesaid, revoke such appointment. Any judge aforesaid giving such consent may at any time revoke it.

(Added by L.1995 chs. 744, 803, eff. 7/1/95.)

§46.2-2004. Required certificates of public convenience and necessity.

No common carrier by motor vehicle or restricted carrier by motor vehicle not herein exempted shall engage in intrastate operation on any highway within the Commonwealth without first having obtained from the Department a certificate of public convenience and necessity authorizing such operation.

(Added by L.1995 chs. 744, 803, eff. 7/1/95.)

§46.2-2005. Application for certificate; notice, etc.

The Department shall prescribe the form of the application for a certificate of convenience and necessity, and such reasonable requirements as to notices, publication, proof of service and information as may in its judgment be necessary.

(Added by L.1995 chs. 744, 803, eff. 7/1/95.)

§46.2-2006. Filing fees and annual fee.

Every applicant for a certificate and transfer of a certificate under the provisions of the chapter shall, upon the filing of an application, deposit with the Department, as a filing fee, a sum in the amount of fifty dollars.

(Added by L.1995 chs. 744, 803, eff. 7/1/95.)

§46.2-2007. Hearing on application; action of Department.

Upon the filing of an application for a certificate of public convenience and necessity, the Department shall, within a reasonable time, fix a time and place of hearing on such application. If the Department finds the proposed operation justified, it shall issue a certificate to the applicant, subject to such terms, limitations and restrictions as the Department may deem proper. If the Department finds the proposed operation not justified, the application shall be denied.

(Added by L.1995 chs. 744, 803, eff. 7/1/95.)

§46.2-2008. No certificate to issue when service already adequate.

No certificate shall be granted to an applicant proposing to operate over the route of any holder of a certificate unless it is proved to the satisfaction of the Department that the service rendered by such certificate holder, over such route, is inadequate to the requirements of the public necessity and convenience; and if the Department is of the opinion that the service rendered by such certificate holder over such route is in any respect inadequate to the requirements of the public necessity and convenience, such certificate holder shall be given reasonable time and opportunity to remedy such inadequacy before any certificate shall be granted to an applicant proposing to operate over such route.

For the purpose of this section, the transportation of passengers by an urban-suburban bus line, hereby defined as a bus line the majority of whose passengers use the buses for traveling a distance of not exceeding forty miles, measured, one way, on the same day, between their places of abode and their places of work, shopping areas, or schools, shall not be deemed an operation over the route of any common carrier of passengers holding a certificate of public convenience and necessity.
(Added by L.1995 chs. 744, 803, eff. 7/1/95.)

§46.2-2009. Certificates for passenger carriers operating over Interstate Highway System.
Notwithstanding the provisions of §46.2-2008, upon a showing of public convenience and necessity, the Department of Motor Vehicles may, if it finds from the evidence, after a public hearing, that the public interest will be promoted thereby, issue to any carrier of passengers by motor vehicle a certificate or certificates authorizing operations in the Commonwealth upon highways which are part of the Interstate Highway System. The foregoing shall be applicable only to issuance of certificates for operations over such System. Except as indicated in this section, all other applicable provisions of this chapter shall apply to such carriers and to such certificates.
(Added by L.1995 chs. 744, 803, eff. 7/1/95.)

§46.2-2010. Irregular route passenger certificates.
Notwithstanding any of the provisions of §46.2-2008, the Department may grant common carrier of passengers certificates to applicants to serve irregular routes on an irregular schedule within a specified geographic area. The Department shall issue no more certificates than the public convenience and necessity require, and shall place such restrictions upon such certificates as may be reasonably necessary to protect any existing regular or irregular route common carrier of passengers certificate holders operating within the proposed service area, but shall not deny a certificate solely on the ground that the applicant will operate in the same service area that an existing regular or irregular route common carrier of passengers certificate holder is operating. Certificates issued hereunder shall be restricted to operation of vehicles with a passenger-carrying capacity not to exceed fifteen persons and shall be restricted to prohibit pickup or delivery of passengers at their personal residence in any city having a population between 260,000 and 265,000 as determined by the 1990 census. Such restriction shall not apply to specially equipped vehicles for the transportation of disabled persons.
(Added by L.1995 chs. 744, 803, eff. 7/1/95.)

§46.2-2011. Considerations for determination of issuance of certificate.
In determining whether the certificate required by this chapter shall be granted, the Department may, among other things, consider the present transportation facilities over the proposed route of the applicant or, in the case of irregular route applications within the applicant's proposed service area, the volume of traffic over such route or, in the case of irregular route applications within the proposed service area, the financial condition of the applicant, and the condition of the highway over the proposed route or routes or, in the case of passenger applications, within the proposed service area.
(Added by L.1995 chs. 744, 803, eff. 7/1/95.)

§46.2-2011.1. Issuance of temporary authority.
To enable the provision of service for which there is an immediate and urgent need to a point or between points in Virginia where certificated carriers are unable to perform the service, or within a territory having no certificated carrier, the Department may, in its discretion and without hearings or other proceedings, grant temporary authority for such service by a carrier that would otherwise be required to obtain a certificate of public convenience and necessity under this title. Such temporary authority, unless suspended or revoked for good cause, shall be valid for such time as the Department shall specify, but for not more than an aggregate of 180 days, and shall create no presumption of public convenience and necessity or that corresponding permanent authority will be granted thereafter.
(Added by L.1996 ch. 170, eff. 3/9/96.)

§46.2-2012. Schedule changes require Department approval.
A common carrier by motor vehicle or a restricted common carrier by motor vehicle operating under a certificate issued by the Department shall not make any change in schedules or service without having first received the approval of the Department for such change in schedules or service.
(Added by L.1995 chs. 744, 803, eff. 7/1/95.)

§46.2-2013. Permit required for taxicab service.
It shall be unlawful for any taxicab or other motor vehicle performing a taxicab service to operate on any public highway in the Commonwealth outside the corporate limits of incorporated cities or towns without first obtaining from the Department a permit in accordance with the provisions of this chapter.
(Added by L.1995 chs. 744, 803, eff. 7/1/95.)

§46.2-2013.1. Limitations on advertising.
Within the jurisdictions of Planning District Number Eight, no person shall use the term "taxi" or "taxicab" in any advertisement, sign, or trade name, or hold himself out by means of advertising, signs, trade names, or otherwise as an operator of a taxicab or other motor vehicle performing a taxicab service as defined by §46.2-2000, unless he complies with the requirements of §46.2-2013 and any county, city, or town ordinance adopted pursuant to §46.2-2016. This statute, however, shall not preempt, supersede, or affect in any way the authority of the governing body of any county, city, or town to issue local ordinances under §§46.2-2016 through 46.2-2020.1.
(Added by L.1997 ch. 549, eff. 7/1/97.)

§46.2-2014. Notice of abandonment of taxicab service.
Every taxicab operator or operator of a motor vehicle performing a taxicab service who ceases operation or abandons his rights under a permit issued shall notify the Department within thirty days of such cessation or abandonment.
(Added by L.1995 chs. 744, 803, eff. 7/1/95.)

§46.2-2015. Chapter does not make taxicab operators common carriers.
Nothing in this chapter shall be construed to make or constitute operators of taxicabs or other motor vehicles performing a taxicab service common carriers.
(Added by L.1995 chs. 744, 803, eff. 7/1/95.)

§46.2-2016. Regulation of taxicab service by localities; rates and charges.
A. The governing body of any county, city or town in the Commonwealth may by ordinance regulate the rates or charges of any motor vehicles used for the transportation of passengers for a consideration on any highway, street, road, lane or alley in such county, city or town, and may prescribe such reasonable regulations as to filing of schedules of rates, charges and the general operation of such vehicles; provided that, notwithstanding anything contained in this chapter to the contrary, such ordinances and regulations shall not prescribe the wages or compensation to be paid to any driver or

lessor of any such motor vehicle by the owner or lessee thereof.

B. In considering rates or charges, the governing body may require any owner or operator to submit such supporting financial data as may be necessary, including federal or state income tax returns for the two years preceding; provided that such income tax returns submitted shall be used only for consideration of such rates or charges and shall be kept confidential by the governing body concerned; and provided further that the governing body shall not require any owner or operator to submit any audit more extensive than that conducted by such owner or operator in the normal course of business.

(Added by L.1995 chs. 744, 803, eff. 7/1/95.)

§46.2-2017. Same; license and payment of license tax may be required.

The governing body of any county, city or town may require a license for and impose upon and collect a license tax from every person, firm, association or corporation who or which operates or intends to operate in such county, city or town any taxicab or other motor vehicle for the transportation of passengers for a consideration. The tax may be upon each such motor vehicle so operated. The governing body of the county, city or town may by ordinance provide for levying and collecting the tax and may impose penalties for violations of the ordinance and for operating any such vehicle without obtaining the required license. Any person accepting a license issued under authority of this section and operating a taxicab business based in a county, city or town shall be subject to the provision that any complaint relating to taxicab service in the Commonwealth shall be resolved under the license regulations of the county, city or town from which that person obtained a taxicab license.

(Added by L.1995 chs. 744, 803, eff. 7/1/95.)

§46.2-2018. Same; when license may not be required.

No such county, city or town shall require a license or impose a license tax for the operation of any such motor vehicle for which a similar license is imposed or tax levied by the county, city or town of which the owner or operator of the motor vehicle is a resident, except that such license may be required and such license tax imposed by any such county, city or town for the operation of any such motor vehicle if the owner, lessee or operator thereof maintains a taxicab stand or otherwise solicits business within such county, city or town; nor, except as herein expressly authorized, shall more than one county, city or town impose any such license fee or tax on the same vehicle. This chapter shall not be construed to apply to common carriers of persons operating as public carriers by authority of the Department of Motor Vehicles or under a franchise granted by any county, city or town.

(Added by L.1995 chs. 744, 803, eff. 7/1/95.)

§46.2-2019. Same; qualifications of operators; stands.

The governing body of any county, city or town may prescribe such reasonable regulations as to the character and qualifications of operators of any such vehicle as they deem proper and may provide for the designation and allocation, by the sheriff or chief of police, of stands for such vehicles and the persons who may use the same.

(Added by L.1995 chs. 744, 803, eff. 7/1/95.)

§46.2-2020. Same; penalty for violation of provisions of chapter or regulations.

Every owner or operator of a motor vehicle used as a vehicle for the transportation of persons for a consideration on any highway, street, road, lane or alley in any county, city or town who violates any of the provisions of this chapter or regulations of a governing body made pursuant to this chapter shall be guilty of a misdemeanor and upon conviction thereof be fined not more than $100 for the first offense and not more than $500 for each subsequent offense.

(Added by L.1995 chs. 744, 803, eff. 7/1/95.)

§46.2-2020.1. Regulation of number of taxicabs.

A. It is the policy of this Commonwealth, based on the public health, safety and welfare, to assure safe and reliable privately operated taxicab service for the riding public in this Commonwealth; and in furtherance of this policy, it is recognized that it is essential that counties, cities and towns be granted the authority to reasonably regulate such taxicab service as to the number of operators and the number of vehicles which shall provide such service and regulations as to the rates or charges for such taxicab service, even though such regulations may have an anti-competitive effect on such service by limiting the number of operators and vehicles within a particular jurisdiction.

B. The governing body of any county, city or town in the Commonwealth may regulate by ordinance and limit the number of taxicab operators and the number of taxicabs within its jurisdiction in order to provide safe and reliable privately operated taxicab service on any highway, street, road, lane or alley in such county, city or town. The governing body may promulgate such reasonable regulations to further the provisions of this section including, but not limited to, minimum liability insurance requirements. However, such ordinances and regulations shall not prescribe the wages or compensation to be paid to any driver or lessor of any such motor vehicle by the owner or lessee thereof. Further, such ordinances and regulations shall not impose (i) regulatory requirements concerning claims settlement practices beyond those imposed by §46.2-2032 or (ii) financial requirements to qualify as a self-insurer beyond those imposed by §46.2-2028 on any taxicab operator who, in lieu of filing an insurance policy or surety bond, has qualified as a self-insurer pursuant to §46.2-2028 by depositing with the State Treasurer state, federal or municipal bonds or has filed an unconditional letter of credit issued by a bank. Nothing herein shall be construed to affect or control the authority of counties, cities or towns to set the amount, if any, of locally established liability insurance requirements which may be met by a program of self-insurance.

(Added by L.1995 chs. 744, 803, eff. 7/1/95.)

§46.2-2021. When broker's license required.

No person shall for compensation sell or offer for sale transportation subject to this chapter or shall make any contract, agreement, or arrangement to provide, procure, furnish, or arrange for such transportation or shall hold himself out by advertisement, solicitation, or otherwise as one who sells, provides, procures, contracts, or arranges for such transportation, unless such person holds a broker's license issued by the Department to engage in such transactions; however, the provisions of this section shall not apply to any carrier holding a certificate or permit under the provisions of this chapter or to any bona fide employee or agent of such motor carrier, so far as concerns transportation to be furnished wholly by such carrier or jointly with other motor carriers holding like certificates or permits.

(Added by L.1995 chs. 744, 803, eff. 7/1/95.)

§46.2-2022. Application for broker's license.

The Department shall prescribe the form of application for a broker's license and such reasonable requirements and information as may in its judgment be necessary.

(Added by L.1995 chs. 744, 803, eff. 7/1/95.)

§46.2-2023. Fees for issuance or transfer of licenses.

Every applicant for a license or a transfer of a license shall, upon the filing of an application, deposit with the Department as a filing fee the sum of fifty dollars.

(Added by L.1995 chs. 744, 803, eff. 7/1/95.)

§46.2-2024. Hearing on such application and action thereon.

Upon the filing of an application for a broker's license, the Department may fix such requirements as it deems necessary to inquire into the application. If the Department finds the application proper and in the public interest, it shall issue a license, subject to such terms, limitations and restrictions as the Department may deem proper.
(Added by L.1995 chs. 744, 803, eff. 7/1/95.)

§46.2-2025. Authority over brokers; bond.

The Department shall have the same authority over persons operating under and holding a brokerage license as it has over motor carriers under this chapter, and shall require a broker to furnish bond or other security approved by the Department and sufficient for the protection of travelers or shippers by motor vehicle.
(Added by L.1995 chs. 744, 803, eff. 7/1/95.)

§46.2-2026. Broker's license not substitute for other certificates or permits required.

No person who holds a broker's license under this chapter shall engage in transportation subject to this chapter unless he holds a certificate or permit as provided in this chapter. In the execution of any contract, agreement, or arrangement to sell, provide, procure, furnish, or arrange for such transportation, it shall be unlawful for such person to employ any carrier by motor vehicle who is not the lawful holder of an effective certificate or permit issued as provided in this chapter.
(Added by L.1995 chs. 744, 803, eff. 7/1/95.)

§46.2-2027. Transfer or lease of certificate or license.

Any certificate or license issued under this chapter, other than under §§46.2-2016 through 46.2-2020, may be transferred or leased, subject to the approval of the Department, and under such reasonable rules and regulations as may be prescribed by the Department. An application for such approval shall be made jointly by the transferor and transferee, or lessor or lessee.
(Added by L.1995 chs. 744, 803, eff. 7/1/95.)

§46.2-2028. Surety bonds, insurance, letter of credit or securities required prior to issuance of certificate or permit.

No certificate or permit shall be issued by the Department to any motor carrier unless such motor carrier has filed with, and the same has been approved by, the Department:

1. An insurance policy or bond;

2. A certificate of insurance in lieu of the insurance policy or bond, certifying that such policy or bond covers the liability of such motor carrier in accordance with the provisions of this chapter, is issued by an insurer authorized to transact business in the Commonwealth, or in the case of bonds, is an amount approved by the Department, and are bonds of the Commonwealth of Virginia, the United States of America, or of any municipality in the Commonwealth. Such state, federal or municipal bonds shall be deposited with the State Treasurer, and such surety shall not be reduced during the life of such certificate or permit, except in accordance with an order of the Department; or

3. An unconditional letter of credit issued by a bank doing business in Virginia for an amount approved by the Department and the term of which runs concurrently with the certificate or permit.
(Added by L.1995 chs. 744, 803, eff. 7/1/95.)

§46.2-2029. When taxicab operator a self-insurer.

If the operator of any taxicab or other motor vehicle performing a taxicab service is a self-insurer under an ordinance of the city where the home office of the operator is located, such operator shall not be required to obtain and keep on file with the Department insurance as required by law.
(Added by L.1995 chs. 744, 803, eff. 7/1/95.)

§46.2-2030. Bonds or insurance to be kept in force; amounts.

Each holder of a certificate, permit, or license issued by the Department shall keep in force at all times insurance, a bond or bonds, in an amount required by the Department; however, the amount of the insurance policy or bond required by the Department under this section of any motor vehicle used in the transportation of property and/or passengers shall in no case exceed those limits required by the United States Department of Transportation and the Interstate Commerce Commission.
(Added by L.1995 chs. 744, 803, eff. 7/1/95.)

§46.2-2031. Duties of carriers of passengers as to through routes, equipment, rates, regulations, etc.

Every common carrier or restricted common carrier of passengers by motor vehicle shall establish reasonable through routes with other such common carriers and shall provide safe and adequate service, equipment, and facilities for the transportation of passengers; shall establish, observe, and enforce just and reasonable individual and joint rates, fares and charges and just and reasonable regulations and practices relating thereto, and to the issuance, form, and substance of tickets, the carrying of personal, sample, and excess baggage, the facilities for transportation, and all other matters relating to or connected with the transportation of passengers; and in case of such joint rates, fares, and charges, shall establish just, reasonable and equitable divisions thereof as between the carriers participating therein which shall not unduly prefer or prejudice any of such participating carriers.
(Added by L.1995 chs. 744, 803, eff. 7/1/95.)

§46.2-2032. Effect of unfair claims settlement practices on self-insured taxicab owners.

The provisions of subdivisions 4, 6, 11 and 12 of subsection A of §38.2-510 shall apply to each holder of a certificate or permit issued by and under the authority of the Department who, in lieu of filing an insurance policy, has deposited with the State Treasurer state, federal or municipal bonds or has filed an unconditional letter of credit issued by a bank. The failure of any such holder of a certificate or permit to comply with the provisions of §38.2-510 shall be the cause for revocation or suspension of the certificate or permit.
(Added by L.1995 chs. 744, 803, eff. 7/1/95.)

§46.2-2033. Undue preference not permitted.

Except as provided in §46.2-2036, it shall be unlawful for any common carrier or restricted common carrier by motor vehicle to make, give, or cause any undue or unreasonable preference or advantage to any particular person, port, gateway, locality, or description of traffic in any respect whatsoever, or to subject any particular person, port, gateway, locality, or description of traffic to any unjust discrimination or any undue or unreasonable prejudice or disadvantage in any respect whatsoever; however, this section shall not be construed to apply to discriminations, prejudice or disadvantage to the traffic of any other carrier of whatever description.
(Added by L.1995 chs. 744, 803; chgd. by L.1995 ch. 124, eff. 7/1/95.)

§46.2-2034. Complaints; action of Department thereon or on own initiative.

Any person, state board, organization, or body politic may make complaint in writing to the Department that any rate, fare, charge, classification, rule, regulation, or practice

of any common carrier or restricted common carrier by motor vehicle, in effect or proposed to be put into effect, is or will be in violation of §§46.2-2031 and 46.2-2033 or §§46.2-2035 through 46.2-2039. Whenever, after hearing, upon complaint or in an investigation on its own initiative, the Department shall be of the opinion that any individual or joint rate, fare, or charge, demanded, charged, or collected by any common or restricted common carrier by motor vehicle or by any common or restricted common carrier by motor vehicle in conjunction with any common carrier by railroad, or water, or any classification, rule, regulation, or practice whatsoever of such carrier affecting such rate, fare, or charge or the value of the service thereunder, is or will be unjust or unreasonable, or unjustly discriminatory or unduly preferential or unduly prejudicial, it shall determine and prescribe the lawful rate, fare, or charge or the maximum or minimum, or maximum and minimum rate, fare, or charge thereafter to be observed, or the lawful classification, rule, regulation, or practice thereafter to be made effective.
(Added by L.1995 chs. 744, 803, eff. 7/1/95.)

§46.2-2035. Tariffs showing rates, fares and charges, etc.

Every common carrier and restricted common carrier by motor vehicle shall file with the Department, and print, and keep open to the public inspection, tariffs showing all the rates, fares and charges for transportation, and all services in connection therewith, of passengers between points on its own route and between points on its own route and points on the route of any other such carrier, or on the route of any common carrier by railroad, air, or water, when a through route and joint rate shall have been established. Such rates, fares, and charges shall be stated in terms of lawful money of the United States. The tariffs required by this section shall be published, filed, and posted in such form and manner, and shall contain such information, as the Department by regulations shall prescribe. The Department is authorized to reject any tariff filed with it which is not in consonance with this section and with such regulations. Any tariff so rejected by the Department shall be void, and its use shall be unlawful.
(Added by L.1995 chs. 744, 803, eff. 7/1/95.)

§46.2-2036. Unlawful to charge other than published tariff.

A. No common carrier or restricted common carrier by motor vehicle shall charge or demand or collect or receive a greater or less or different compensation for transportation or for any service in connection therewith between the points enumerated in such tariff than the rates, fares, and charges specified in the tariffs in effect at the time; and no such carrier shall refund or remit in any manner or by any device, directly or indirectly, or through any agent or broker or otherwise, any portion of the rates, fares, or charges so specified, or extend to any person any privileges or facilities for transportation except such as are specified in its tariffs.

B. Notwithstanding the provisions of subsection A, common carriers of passengers by motor vehicle and restricted common carriers of passengers by motor vehicle may elect to charge, demand, collect or receive less compensation for transportation or for any service in connection therewith between the points enumerated in such tariff than the rates, fares, and charges specified in the tariffs in effect at the time.
(Added by L.1995 chs. 744, 803; chgd. by L.1995 ch. 124, eff. 7/1/95.)

§46.2-2037. Changes in tariffs.

Except as provided in §46.2-2036, no change shall be made in any rate, fare, charge, or classification, or any rule, regulation, or practice affecting such rate, fare, charge, or classification, or the value of the service thereunder, specified in any effective tariff of a common carrier or restricted common carrier by motor vehicle, except after reasonable notice of the proposed change. Such notice shall plainly state the change proposed to be made and the time when such change will take effect. The Department may, in its discretion and for good cause shown, allow such change upon notice less than that herein specified or modify the requirements of this section with respect to posting and filing of tariffs either in particular instances or by general order applicable to special or peculiar circumstances or conditions.
(Added by L.1995 chs. 744, 803; chgd. by L.1995 ch. 124, eff. 7/1/95.)

§46.2-2038. No transportation except when rates have been filed, etc.

No common carrier or restricted common carrier by motor vehicle, unless otherwise provided by this chapter, shall engage in the transportation of passengers unless the rates, fares, and charges upon which the same are transported by such carrier have been filed and published in accordance with the provisions of this chapter.
(Added by L.1995 chs. 744, 803, eff. 7/1/95.)

§46.2-2039. Free passes or reduced rates; differential rates.

No motor carrier subject to the provisions of this chapter shall, directly or indirectly, issue or give any free ticket, free pass or free transportation for passengers. Nothing in this section shall apply (i) to the free carriage of homeless and destitute persons and the necessary agents employed in such transportation or (ii) to mileage, excursion or commutation passenger tickets.

Nor shall anything in this section be construed to prohibit any motor carrier (i) from giving reduced rates or free passage to ministers of religion, or regular traveling secretaries of the Young Men's Christian Association or Young Women's Christian Association, whose duties require regular travel in supervising and directing Young Men's Christian or Young Women's Christian Association work, or to secretaries of duly organized religious work, or to indigent persons, or to inmates of the Confederate homes or state homes for disabled soldiers and sailors, or to disabled soldiers and sailors, and those returning home after discharge; nor (ii) from giving free carriage to its own officers, employees, and members of their families, representatives of the press and members of the Department of State Police or to any other person or persons to whom the giving of such free carriage is not otherwise prohibited by law.

Nor shall this section be construed to prevent the principal officers of any motor carrier from exchanging passes or tickets with other motor carriers or any rail, air, steamship, or electric railway companies for their officers, employees and members of their families.

The Department shall have authority to establish differential rates according to the time of day and for groupings of passenger classes.
(Added by L.1995 chs. 744, 803, eff. 7/1/95.)

§46.2-2040. Department may seek judgment for refunds due public and collect and distribute same.

If any motor carrier or broker, upon the final decision of an appeal from the action of the Department prescribing rates, charges, or classification of traffic, confirming or modifying the action of the Department, fails to refund in the manner and within the time prescribed in the notice of the Department all amounts which the appealing motor carrier or broker may have collected, pending the appeal, in excess of that authorized by such final decision, upon notice to such motor carrier or broker by the Department of such final

decision, then the Department, after thirty days' notice to any such motor carrier or broker, may, unless the amount required by such final decision is paid to the Department, seek judgment in the name of the Commonwealth, for the use of, the persons, firms and corporations entitled to the same, against any such motor carrier or broker for the aggregate amount of such collections and for costs, and may enforce the amount of such judgment and costs by process of execution, as provided by law. The Department shall, upon the collection of such judgment, forthwith distribute the amount thereof among the parties entitled thereto, respectively, in such manner as it may by its rules or regulations prescribe, and shall, upon the payment or collection of any such judgment, mark the same satisfied upon its records, and have the same entered satisfied on the judgment lien docket of the court where the same may have been docketed; the satisfaction of any such judgment shall be a bar to any further action or recovery against any such motor carrier or broker to the extent of such recovery.
(Added by L.1995 chs. 744, 803, eff. 7/1/95.)

§46.2-2041. Motor bus operators, etc., to be conservators of the peace.
The operators of motor buses operated as common carriers of passengers, and station and depot agents, shall be conservators of the peace, and shall have the same power to make arrests that other conservators of the peace have, except that the agents shall have such power only at their respective places of business. Operators of motor buses and agents may cause any person so arrested by them to be detained, and delivered to the proper authorities for trial as soon as practicable.
(Added by L.1995 chs. 744, 803, eff. 7/1/95.)

§46.2-2042. Waiting rooms and other public facilities.
Motor carriers of passengers shall keep all waiting rooms, rest rooms and other public facilities in good and sanitary condition, and the Department may inspect all waiting rooms, rest rooms or other public facilities at any time, and after inspection may require such changes as the Department may deem proper.
(Added by L.1995 chs. 744, 803, eff. 7/1/95.)

§46.2-2043. Violation by passengers; misdemeanor; ejection.
All persons who fail, while on any motor vehicle of a motor carrier of passengers, to act in an orderly manner so as to permit the safe operation of such vehicle by the driver, or who fail to obey the directions of any such driver, operator or other person in charge to act in such orderly manner, shall be deemed guilty of a Class 4 misdemeanor. Furthermore, such persons may be ejected from any such vehicle by any driver, operator or person in charge of such vehicle, or by any police officer or other conservator of the peace; and in case such persons ejected have paid their fares upon such vehicle, they shall not be entitled to the return of any part of the same. For the refusal of any such passenger to abide by the direction of the person in charge of such vehicle as aforesaid, and his consequent ejection from such vehicle, neither the driver, operator, person in charge, owner, manager nor bus company operating such vehicle shall be liable for damages in any court.
(Added by L.1995 chs. 744, 803, eff. 7/1/95.)

§46.2-2044. Operators are special policemen to enforce §46.2-2043; other powers.
Each driver, operator or person in charge of any motor vehicle of any motor carrier of passengers in the employment of any such motor carrier, while actively engaged in the operation of such vehicle, shall be a special policeman and have all of the powers of conservators of the peace in the enforcement of the provisions of §46.2-2043, and in the discharge of his duty as special policeman, in the enforcement of order upon such vehicle; and such driver, operator or person in charge of any such vehicle shall likewise have the powers of conservators of the peace and of special policemen while in pursuit of persons for disorder upon such vehicle or for violating the provisions of §46.2-2043, and until such persons as may be arrested by him have been placed in confinement or delivered over to the custody of some other conservator of the peace or police officer.
(Added by L.1995 chs. 744, 803, eff. 7/1/95.)

§46.2-2045. Reports, records, etc.
A. The Department is hereby authorized to require annual, periodical, or special reports from all motor carriers, except such as are exempted from the operation of the provisions of this chapter; to prescribe the manner and form in which such reports shall be made; and to require from such carriers specific answers to all questions upon which the Department may deem information to be necessary. Such reports shall be under oath whenever the Department so requires. The Department may also require any motor carrier to file with it a true copy of each or any contract, agreement, or arrangement between such carrier and any other carrier or person in relation to any traffic affected by the provisions of this chapter.

B. The Department may, in its discretion, prescribe (i) the forms of any and all accounts, records, and memoranda to be kept by common carriers and restricted common carriers by motor vehicle and (ii) the length of time such accounts, records, and memoranda shall be preserved, including the accounts, records, and memoranda of the movement of traffic, as well as of the receipts and expenditures of money. The Department or its employees shall at all times have access to all lands, buildings, or equipment of motor carriers used in connection with their operations and also all accounts, records, and memoranda, including all documents, papers, and correspondence now or hereafter existing, and kept, or required to be kept, by motor carriers. The Department and its employees shall have authority to inspect and examine any and all such lands, buildings, equipment, accounts, records, and memoranda, including all documents, papers, and correspondence now or hereafter existing and kept or required to be kept by such carriers. These provisions shall apply to receivers of carriers and to operating trustees and, to the extent deemed necessary by the Department, to persons having control, direct or indirect, over or affiliated with any motor carrier.

C. As used in this section the term "motor carriers" includes brokers.
(Added by L.1995 chs. 744, 803, eff. 7/1/95.)

§46.2-2046. Certificate or permit holder not relieved of liability for negligence.
Nothing in this chapter shall relieve any holder of a certificate or permit by and under the authority of the Department from any liability resulting from his negligence, whether or not he has complied with the requirements of this chapter.
(Added by L.1995 chs. 744, 803, eff. 7/1/95.)

§46.2-2047. Violation; penalties.
A. Any person knowingly and willfully violating any provision of this chapter, or any rule or regulation thereunder, or any term or condition of any certificate, permit, or license, for which a penalty is not otherwise herein provided, shall, upon conviction thereof, be fined not more than $2,500 for the first offense and not more than $5,000 for any subsequent offense. Each day of such violation shall constitute a separate offense.

B. Any person, whether carrier, shipper, consignee, or broker, or any officer, employee, agent, or representative thereof, who shall knowingly offer, grant, or give, or solicit, accept, or receive any rebate, concession, or discrimination in violation of any provision of this chapter, or who, by means of any false statement or representation, or by the use of any false or fictitious bill, bill of lading, receipt, voucher, roll, account, claim, certificate, affidavit, deposition, lease, or bill of sale, or by any other means or device, shall knowingly and willfully assist, suffer or permit any person, natural or artificial, to obtain transportation of passengers subject to this chapter for less than the applicable rate, fare, or charge, or who shall knowingly and willfully by any such means or otherwise fraudulently seek to evade or defeat regulation as in this chapter provided for motor carriers or brokers, shall be deemed guilty of a misdemeanor and, upon conviction thereof, be fined not more than $500 for the first offense and not more than $2,000 for any subsequent offense.

C. Any motor carrier, or broker, or any officer, agent, employee, or representative thereof who willfully fails or refuses to make a report to the Department as required by this chapter or to keep accounts, records, and memoranda in the form and manner approved or prescribed by the Department, or knowingly and willfully falsifies, destroys, mutilates, or alters any such report, account, record or memorandum, or knowingly and willfully files any false report, account, record or memorandum, shall be deemed guilty of a misdemeanor and upon conviction thereof be subject for each offense to a fine of not less than $100 and not more than $5,000.

(Added by L.1995 chs. 744, 803, eff. 7/1/95.)

§46.2-2048. No property rights in highways conferred by chapter.

Nothing in this chapter shall confer any proprietary or property rights in the use of the public highways.

(Added by L.1995 chs. 744, 803, eff. 7/1/95.)

§46.2-2049. Bus terminals; local license taxes on operation.

Counties, cities and towns may impose license taxes for the privilege of operating or conducting terminals for use by common carriers of passengers by motor vehicle. Operation of terminals by such carriers in connection with and incidental to their business as such common carriers, and not for profit, or for such carriers where the local agent receives as his compensation a commission on tickets sold shall not be subject to the imposition of any such taxes. Lots used by such carriers for parking, storage and servicing of motor vehicles used in the business of such carriers and for taking on and discharging passengers shall not be deemed terminals. Nothing herein contained shall be construed to exempt the payment of license taxes on any other business that may be conducted on, at or in any such terminal or lot.

(Added by L.1995 chs. 744, 803, eff. 7/1/95.)

§46.2-2050. Licenses, taxes, etc., not affected.

Nothing in this chapter shall be construed to relieve any person from the payment of any licenses, fees, taxes or levies now or hereafter imposed by law.

(Added by L.1995 chs. 744, 803, eff. 7/1/95.)

CHAPTER 21
REGULATION OF HOUSEHOLD GOODS CARRIERS

(Added by L.1995 chs. 744, 803, eff. 7/1/95.)

§46.2-2100. Definitions.

Whenever used in this chapter, unless expressly stated otherwise:

"Certificate" means a certificate of public convenience and necessity issued by the Department to "household goods carriers" under this chapter.

"Department" means the Department of Motor Vehicles.

"Highway" means every public highway or place of whatever nature open to the use of the public for purposes of vehicle travel in this Commonwealth, excluding the streets and alleys in towns and cities.

"Household goods" means personal effects and property used or to be used in a dwelling, when a part of the equipment or supplies of such dwelling, and similar property if the transportation of such effects or property is (i) arranged and paid for by the householder, including transportation of the property from a factory or store when the property is purchased by the householder with intent to use it in his dwelling or (ii) arranged and paid for by another party.

"Household goods carrier" means any person who undertakes, whether directly or by a lease or other arrangement, to transport "household goods," as herein defined, by motor vehicle for compensation, on any highway in this Commonwealth, between two or more points in this Commonwealth, whether over regular or irregular routes.

"Motor vehicle" means any vehicle, machine, tractor, trailer, or semitrailer propelled or drawn by mechanical power and used upon the highways in the transportation of property, but does not include any vehicle, locomotive or car operated exclusively on a rail or rails.

"Person" means any individual, firm, copartnership, corporation, company, association or joint-stock association, and includes any trustee, receiver, assignee, or personal representative thereof.

"Services" and "transportation" includes all vehicles operated by, for, or in the interest of any "household goods carrier," irrespective of ownership or contract, express or implied, together with all facilities and property operated or controlled by any such carrier or carriers and used in the transportation of "household goods" or in the performance of any service in connection therewith.

(Added by L.1995 chs. 744, 803; chgd. by L.1997 ch. 283, eff. 7/1/97.)

§46.2-2101. Exemptions from chapter.

The following are exempt from this chapter:

1. Motor vehicles owned and operated by the United States, District of Columbia, any state, municipality, or any other political subdivision of the Commonwealth.

2. Transportation of household goods between any point in this Commonwealth and any point outside this Commonwealth, or between any points wholly within the limits of any city or town in this Commonwealth, or for any lesser distance than thirty road miles.

3. Infrequent (not more than twelve trips a year) transportation of "household goods" for a greater distance than thirty road miles, when the point of origin of goods is not within the limits of a city and is not within thirty road miles from the limits of a city.

(Added by L.1995 chs. 744, 803, eff. 7/1/95.)

§46.2-2102. Compliance with chapter required.

No household goods carrier shall operate any motor vehicle for the transportation of property for compensation on any highway in this Commonwealth except in accordance with the provisions of this chapter.

(Added by L.1995 chs. 744, 803, eff. 7/1/95.)

§46.2-2103. Control by Department.

Every such carrier is hereby declared to be subject to control, supervision and regulation by the Department.

(Added by L.1995 chs. 744, 803, eff. 7/1/95.)

§46.2-2104. No property rights in use of highways.

Nothing in this chapter shall confer any proprietary or property rights in the use of the public highways.

(Added by L.1995 chs. 744, 803, eff. 7/1/95.)

§46.2-2105. Provisions of chapter controlling.

As to household goods carriers, the provisions of this chapter shall be controlling, and no laws in conflict herewith, or inconsistent herewith, shall have any application to such carriers.

(Added by L.1995 chs. 744, 803, eff. 7/1/95.)

§46.2-2106. Other applicable laws.

The provisions of §§46.2-2028, 46.2-2030, 46.2-2032, 46.2-2040, 46.2-2045, 46.2-2046, 46.2-2047 and 46.2-2050, with reference to the filing of insurance with the Department by motor carriers, registration for vehicles used by motor carriers, reports, forms and accounts of motor carriers, enforcement of laws applicable to motor carriers, prohibition of rebates and discriminations, shall be applicable to household goods carriers and to the regulation thereof.

(Added by L.1995 chs. 744, 803, eff. 7/1/95.)

§46.2-2107. Necessity of certificate.

No person shall engage in motor vehicle transportation of household goods for compensation on any highway within the Commonwealth unless he has obtained from the Department a certificate of public convenience and necessity as a household goods carrier.

(Added by L.1995 chs. 744, 803, eff. 7/1/95.)

§46.2-2108. Application, notice, etc.

The Department shall prescribe the form of the application for a certificate of convenience and necessity, and such reasonable requirements as to notice, publication, proof of service and information as may in its judgment be necessary.

(Added by L.1995 chs. 744, 803, eff. 7/1/95.)

§46.2-2109. Hearing and determination.

Upon the filing of an application for a certificate of public convenience and necessity as a household goods carrier, the Department shall, within a reasonable time, fix a time and place of hearing on such application. If the Department finds the proposed operation justified by public convenience and necessity, it shall issue a certificate to the applicant, subject to such terms, limitations and restrictions as the Department may deem proper. If the Department finds the proposed operation not justified, the application shall be denied.

(Added by L.1995 chs. 744, 803, eff. 7/1/95.)

§46.2-2110. Suspension, revocation, etc., of certificate; imposition of penalty.

The Department may at any time, after hearing had upon notice to the holder of any such certificate and an opportunity to such holder to be heard, at which it shall be proved that such holder has made any misrepresentation of a material fact in obtaining such certificate, or has violated or refused to observe any of the laws of this Commonwealth touching such certificate, or any of the terms, limitations and restrictions of his certificate, or any of the Department's rules or regulations, impose a penalty not exceeding $2,500; or the Department may suspend, revoke, alter or amend any such certificate, whenever the Department finds after a hearing upon notice as above, that such certificate holder knowingly misrepresented any material fact in obtaining his certificate, or willfully violated or refused to observe any of the laws of this Commonwealth touching his certificate, or willfully violated or failed to observe any of the rules or regulations of the Department, or any term, condition or limitation of such certificate. Proceedings looking to the imposition of any penalty provided for herein may be commenced upon the complaint of any person or upon the Department's own initiative.

(Added by L.1995 chs. 744, 803, eff. 7/1/95.)

§46.2-2111. Transfer or lease of certificate.

Any such certificate may be transferred or leased if the Department after a public hearing finds the proposed transfer or lease justified by public convenience and necessity, and under such terms, limitations and restrictions as may be prescribed by the Department. The application shall be made jointly by the transferor and transferee, seller and purchaser, or assignor and assignee, or lessor and lessee.

(Added by L.1995 chs. 744, 803, eff. 7/1/95.)

§46.2-2112. Fees for issuance or transfer of certificates.

Every household goods carrier, upon filing with the Department an application for a certificate, or application for transfer shall deposit with the Department as a filing fee a sum to be set by the Department. An annual fee shall be imposed for all certificates required by this chapter. The amount of the annual fee as well as the date of payment shall be set by the Department.

(Added by L.1995 chs. 744, 803, eff. 7/1/95.)

§46.2-2113. Power and duty of Department.

The Department shall regulate and control all household goods carriers not herein exempted, doing business in the Commonwealth, in all matters relating to the performance of their duties as such carriers and their rates and charges therefor, which rates and charges shall be filed with and subject to approval by the Department by individual household goods carriers or by groups of such carriers, and correct abuses by such carriers. To that end the Department shall prescribe reasonable rules, regulations, bills of lading, forms and reports for such carriers to administer and enforce the provisions of this chapter. The Department shall have the right at all times to require from such carriers special reports and statements, under oath, concerning their business. It shall make and enforce such requirements, rules, and regulations as may be necessary to prevent unjust or unreasonable discriminations by any such carrier in favor of, or against, any person, locality, community or connecting carrier in the matter of service,

schedule, efficiency of transportation or otherwise, in connection with the duties of such carriers.
(Added by L.1995 chs. 744, 803, eff. 7/1/95.)

§46.2-2114. Notice to carriers; opportunity for hearing, etc.

Before the Department prescribes or fixes any rate, charge, or classification of traffic, and before it makes any rule or regulation directed against any household goods carrier, the carrier affected by such rate, charge, classification, rule, regulation or requirement shall first be given, by the Department, reasonable notice of the time and place when and where the contemplated action will be considered and disposed of, and shall be afforded a reasonable opportunity to introduce evidence and be heard thereon to the end that justice may be done, and shall have process to enforce the attendance of witnesses.
(Added by L.1995 chs. 744, 803, eff. 7/1/95.)

CHAPTER 22
REGULATION OF SIGHT-SEEING CARRIERS
(Added by L.1995 chs. 744, 803, eff. 7/1/95.)

§46.2-2200. Definitions.

When used in this chapter, unless expressly stated otherwise:

"Certificate" means a certificate of public convenience and necessity issued by the Department to a sight-seeing carrier.

"Department" means the Department of Motor Vehicles.

"Person" means any person, firm or corporation.

"Sight-seeing carrier" means a restricted common carrier authorized to transport sightseers under the provisions of this chapter. Except as otherwise provided in this chapter, all provisions of law applicable to common carriers of passengers shall apply to sight-seeing carriers. The provisions of this chapter do not apply to special or chartered parties as defined in §46.2-2300.
(Added by L.1995 chs. 744, 803, eff. 7/1/95.)

§46.2-2201. Certificates.

A certificate issued under this chapter shall authorize the holder named in the certificate to transport sightseers from the point or points of origin named in the certificate over regular routes to the points of interest named in the certificate and back to the point or points of origin. Each passenger shall be issued a ticket on which shall be printed the points of interest and the fare charged for the round trip. Passengers shall be transported only on round trips without stopover privileges, and no part of a fare shall be refunded because of a passenger's refusal to complete the round trip.
(Added by L.1995 chs. 744, 803, eff. 7/1/95.)

§46.2-2202. Filing fee.

Every applicant for a certificate or for the transfer of a certificate, upon the filing of an application, shall deposit with the Department as a filing fee the sum of fifty dollars.
(Added by L.1995 chs. 744, 803, eff. 7/1/95.)

§46.2-2203. When certificate granted.

The public convenience and necessity to be served by this chapter is to encourage sightseers to visit points of interest in Virginia by providing economical, comfortable and convenient transportation, and, in the issuance of certificates, the Department shall consider all facts bearing on that purpose, including existing means of transportation, the character of the applicant, and the kind of equipment he proposes to use. The Department shall issue no more certificates than the public convenience and necessity require, and shall place such restrictions upon such certificates as may be reasonably necessary to protect any existing common carrier operating over the same route or routes under a certificate issued by the Department, but it shall not deny a certificate solely on the ground that the applicant will operate over the route or part of the route of an existing common carrier; however, in granting certificates, preference shall be given to applicants who were intrastate common carriers in Virginia on June 26, 1956.
(Added by L.1995 chs. 744, 803, eff. 7/1/95.)

§46.2-2204. When certificate revoked.

In addition to the grounds on which a certificate issued to a common carrier other than a sight-seeing carrier may be revoked, a certificate may be revoked, after notice and hearing, for failure to furnish economical, comfortable and convenient transportation. A certificate shall be revoked whenever the holder requests in writing that it be revoked.
(Added by L.1995 chs. 744, 803, eff. 7/1/95.)

§46.2-2205. Transfers and leases.

No certificate shall be leased, but a certificate issued to an individual shall be construed to authorize the individual to operate with one or more partners, and a certificate issued to a partnership shall be construed to authorize the firm to operate with more or fewer partners so long as at least one of the partners named in the certificate continues to be active in the business, provided that the names and addresses of all partners engaged in the business are filed with the Department whenever there is a change in the partnership.

Any such certificate may be transferred if the Department finds, after such notice and hearing as required by law, that the proposed transfer is justified by the public convenience and necessity, subject to such terms, limitations and restrictions as may be prescribed by the Department. Any such application shall be made jointly by the transferor and transferee.
(Added by L.1995 chs. 744, 803, eff. 7/1/95.)

§46.2-2206. Corporations.

No certificate shall be issued or transferred to a foreign corporation nor to any domestic corporation that is not organized as a common carrier of passengers.
(Added by L.1995 chs. 744, 803, eff. 7/1/95.)

§46.2-2207. Fares.

The fares charged by sight-seeing carriers shall be fixed by the Department at such rates as will promote the purposes mentioned in §46.2-2207.
(Added by L.1995 chs. 744, 803, eff. 7/1/95.)

§46.2-2208. Schedules.

The schedules operated by sight-seeing carriers shall be filed with and subject to the approval or disapproval of the Department, which may consider the seasonal nature of the business and may authorize the discontinuance of schedules during times when the demand for service does not justify service.
(Added by L.1995 chs. 744, 803, eff. 7/1/95.)

§46.2-2209. Cities and towns.

The provisions of this chapter shall not apply to operations conducted wholly within the corporate limits of a city or a town.

(Added by L.1995 chs. 744, 803, eff. 7/1/95.)

CHAPTER 23
REGULATION OF SPECIAL OR CHARTER PARTY CARRIERS

(Added by L.1995 chs. 744, 803, eff. 7/1/95.)

Section

§46.2-2300. Definitions.

When used in this chapter, unless expressly stated otherwise:

"Certificate" means a certificate of public convenience and necessity issued by the Department to a special or charter party carrier under this chapter.

"Department" means the Department of Motor Vehicles.

"Person" means any person, firm or corporation.

"Special or charter party" means a group movement of passengers transported under a single contract made with one person for an agreed charge for such movement regardless of the number of passengers transported, and for which transportation, no individual or separate fares are solicited, charged, collected or received by the carrier.

"Special or charter party carrier" means a restricted common carrier authorized to transport passengers in special or charter parties under the provisions of this chapter.

(Added by L.1995 chs. 744, 803, eff. 7/1/95.)

§46.2-2301. Exemptions from chapter.

This chapter shall not be construed to apply to:

1. Motor vehicles employed solely in transporting school children and teachers except when such vehicles are used for special or charter party service;

2. Transportation of a special or charter party between any point in this Commonwealth and any point outside this Commonwealth, or between two points within the limits of a city or town in this Commonwealth;

3. Motor vehicles owned and operated by the United States, District of Columbia, any state, or by any municipality or other political subdivision of the Commonwealth, except when such motor vehicles, other than public transit motor vehicles normally used in regular route service, owned and operated by any municipality or other political subdivision of this Commonwealth are operated from point of origin outside the boundaries of such municipality or other political subdivision; and motor vehicles while being operated under an exclusive contract with the United States; or

4. Motor vehicles owned and operated by funeral service establishments when such vehicles are employed in the usual course of business of such establishments.

(Added by L.1995 chs. 744, 803, eff. 7/1/95.)

§46.2-2302. Certificates required unless exempted.

Except as otherwise provided in §46.2-2303, no person shall engage in the business of a special or charter party carrier of passengers by motor vehicle on any highway within the Commonwealth unless such person has secured from the Department a certificate authorizing such business.

(Added by L.1995 chs. 744, 803, eff. 7/1/95.)

§46.2-2303. Authority conferred by "A," "B," and "C" certificates; applications; hearings.

A. An "A" certificate shall authorize the holder named therein to transport passengers in special or charter parties from any point or points within the Commonwealth to other points in the Commonwealth. Upon the filing of an application for an "A" certificate, the Department shall fix a time and place of hearing upon such application, and if the Department finds the proposed operation justified the Department shall issue an "A" certificate to the applicant, subject to such terms, limitations and restrictions as the Department may deem proper. If the Department finds that the proposed operation is not justified, the application shall be denied.

B. A "B" certificate shall authorize the holder named therein to transport passengers in special or charter parties from any point or points within the territory of origin specified in the certificate to other points in the Commonwealth. Upon the filing of an application for a "B" certificate, the Department shall fix a time and place of hearing upon such application, and if the Department finds the proposed operation justified, it shall issue a "B" certificate to the applicant, subject to such terms, limitations and restrictions as the Department may deem proper. If the Department finds that the proposed operation is not justified, the application shall be denied.

C. A "C" certificate shall authorize the holder named therein to transport passengers in special or charter parties from a specified town or city having a population of 10,000 inhabitants or less as the point of origin to other points in the Commonwealth which are not more than thirty miles from the point of origin; however, one trip for a distance exceeding thirty miles may be made by the holder of a "C" certificate during any calendar month. Upon the filing of an application for a "C" certificate, the Department shall require the applicant to give at least ten days' notice to the chairman of the board of supervisors and the attorney for the Commonwealth of the counties adjoining such town or city and also by publication in a newspaper of general circulation in such town or city, or as otherwise directed by the Department, that such an application has been made and that at a certain time and date the Department will grant such application if the Department is then of the opinion that it meets the requirements of §46.2-2304. If a proper objection is filed with the Department before said date, the Department shall fix a time and place for a hearing upon such application and the objection thereto, and if the Department finds the proposed operation justified it shall issue a "C" certificate to the applicant. The Department may issue a "C" certificate subject to such terms, limitations and restrictions as the Department may deem proper. If the Department finds the proposed operation is not justified, the application shall be denied.

(Added by L.1995 chs. 744, 803, eff. 7/1/95.)

§46.2-2304. When certificates granted.

The public convenience and necessity to be served by special or charter party carriers is to provide economical, comfortable and convenient transportation for special or charter parties and, in the issuance of all types of certificates authorized by this chapter, the Department shall consider all facts bearing on that purpose, including existing means of transportation, the character of the applicant, and the kind

and location of the equipment he proposes to use. The Department shall issue no more certificates than the public convenience and necessity require, and shall place such restrictions upon such certificates as may be reasonably necessary to protect any existing motor carrier, whether such carrier is operating under certificates issued by the Department under this chapter or under Chapter 20 (§46.2-2000 et seq.) or Chapter 23 (§46.2-2300 et seq.) or otherwise, but the Department shall not deny a certificate solely on the ground that the applicant may render special or charter party service originating at the same point or points as such other motor carriers. The Department shall protect the private intercity charter industry to the extent reasonably practicable from carriers receiving grants from federal and state agencies where private operators are willing and able to provide such service.
(Added by L.1995 chs. 744, 803, eff. 7/1/95.)

§46.2-2305. When certificates revoked.
In addition to the grounds upon which a certificate issued to a common carrier other than a special or charter party carrier may be revoked, a certificate issued under this chapter may also be revoked, after notice and hearing, for failure to furnish economical, comfortable and convenient transportation or for failure to observe the requirements of this chapter or the rules and regulations hereunder as are prescribed by the Department. A certificate shall be revoked whenever the holder requests in writing that it be revoked.
(Added by L.1995 chs. 744, 803, eff. 7/1/95.)

§46.2-2306. Leases prohibited; transfer.
No certificate may be leased. Any certificate may be transferred if the Department finds, after such notice and hearing as it deems reasonable, that the proposed transfer is justified by the public convenience and necessity, subject to such terms, limitations, and restrictions as may be prescribed by the Department. Any such application shall be made jointly by the transferor and transferee.
(Added by L.1995 chs. 744, 803, eff. 7/1/95.)

§46.2-2307. Foreign corporations and nonresidents.
No certificate shall be issued or transferred to a foreign corporation or to a person who has not been a resident of Virginia for at least sixty days preceding the filing of an application therefor.
(Added by L.1995 chs. 744, 803, eff. 7/1/95.)

§46.2-2308. Rates and tariffs.
No special or charter party carrier shall charge more or less than the fixed rate and/or charge for the type of vehicle involved set out in said carrier's published tariff which shall be on file with the Department.
(Added by L.1995 chs. 744, 803, eff. 7/1/95.)

§46.2-2309. Brokers.
No holder of a certificate under this chapter shall engage in special or charter party service through any broker, except in compliance with the provisions of this chapter and the Department's rules and regulations hereunder.
(Added by L.1995 chs. 744, 803, eff. 7/1/95.)

§46.2-2310. Department may prescribe rules and require reports.
The Department shall have the power to prescribe from time to time reasonable rules and regulations for the control and operation of charter party carriers, including their rates and charges, and may require reports from such carriers in respect thereto.
(Added by L.1995 chs. 744, 803, eff. 7/1/95.)

§46.2-2311. Fees
Every person, upon filing with the Department an application for a certificate or for the transfer of a certificate, shall deposit with the Department as a filing fee, the sum of fifty dollars.
(Added by L.1995 chs. 744, 803, eff. 7/1/95.)

§46.2-2312. Other laws applicable.
Except as otherwise provided in this chapter, all provisions of law applicable to common carriers of passengers shall apply to special or charter party carriers.
(Added by L.1995 chs. 744, 803, eff. 7/1/95.)

CHAPTER 23.1
EXCURSION TRAINS
(Added by L.1997 ch. 393, eff. 7/1/97.)

Section

§46.2-2313. Definitions.
When used in this chapter, unless expressly stated otherwise:

"Certificate" means a certificate of operation issued by the Department to an operator of an excursion train.

"Department" means the Department of Motor Vehicles.

"Excursion train" means any steam-powered train that carries passengers for which the primary purpose of the operation of such train is the passengers' experience and enjoyment of this means of transportation, and does not, in the course of operation, carry (i) freight other than the personal luggage of the passengers or crew or supplies and equipment necessary to serve the needs of the passengers and crew, (ii) passengers who are commuting to work, or (iii) passengers who are traveling to their final destination solely for business or commercial purposes.
(Added by L.1997 ch. 393, eff. 7/1/97.)

§46.2-2314. Certification requirements.
A. A person may apply to the Department for certification as an operator of an excursion train. The Department shall certify an applicant if the Department determines that the applicant will operate a passenger train that:

1. Is primarily used for tourism or public service;

2. Leads to the promotion of the tourist industry in the Commonwealth; and

3. Is primarily operated within a county having a population between 50,000 and 55,000 people.

B. An application for certification shall include:

1. The name and address of each person who owns an interest of at least ten percent of the excursion train operation;

2. An address in this Commonwealth where the excursion train is based;

3. An operations plan including the route to be used and a schedule of operations and stops along the route; and

4. Evidence of insurance that meets the requirements of subsection C.

C. The Department shall not certify a person under subsection A unless the person files with the Department evidence of insurance providing coverage of liability resulting from injury to persons or damages to property in the amount of at least ten million dollars for the operation of the train.

D. The Department shall not certify an applicant under subsection A if the applicant or any other person owning interest in the excursion train also owns or operates a regularly scheduled passenger train service with interstate connection.
(Added by L.1997 ch. 393, eff. 7/1/97.)

§46.2-2315. Assignment of liability.

A. The operator of an excursion train shall be liable for personal injury or wrongful death arising from the operation of such excursion train, including operations, maintenance and signalization of the tracks and facilities upon which the excursion train operates.

B. Any county, city, or town may by resolution determine that the provision of excursion train services within the locality promotes tourism and furthers other public purposes. Upon request of such locality, by resolution, any railroad company which authorizes the operator of an excursion train to use its tracks and facilities for the purposes of this chapter shall not be liable for personal injury or wrongful death arising from the operation of such excursion train, including operations, maintenance, and signalization of the tracks and facilities upon which the excursion train operates.

C. The limitation of liability under subsection B does not apply if:

1. The injury or damages result from intentional misconduct, malice, or gross negligence of the railroad company; or

2. The operator of the excursion train was not operating in accordance with the definition of an excursion train under this chapter and the railroad company had otherwise authorized the operations which were inconsistent with this chapter.

D. Each passenger on the excursion train shall be deemed to have accepted and consented to the limitation of liability under this section. This agreement shall be governed by the laws of the Commonwealth as the place of performance notwithstanding any choice of law rules to the contrary.

E. The railroad company may charge reasonable amounts to the operator of the excursion train for the use of its tracks and facilities as determined by agreement between the railroad company and the operator.

(Added by L.1997 ch. 393, eff. 7/1/97.)

§46.2-2316. Notice to passengers.

The operator of an excursion train shall:

1. Issue each passenger a ticket with the following statement in twelve point boldface type:

"THE RAILROAD COMPANY WHICH OWNS THE TRACKS AND FACILITIES UPON WHICH THIS EXCURSION TRAIN OPERATES SHALL NOT BE LIABLE FOR PERSONAL INJURY OR WRONGFUL DEATH ARISING FROM THE OPERATION OF THE EXCURSION TRAIN, INCLUDING OPERATIONS, MAINTENANCE, AND SIGNALIZATION OF THE TRACKS AND FACILITIES."

2. Post notice near any passenger boarding area containing the same statement contained in subdivision 1, in letters that are at least two inches high.

(Added by L.1997 ch. 393, eff. 7/1/97.)

CHAPTER 24
REGULATION OF CARRIERS BY MOTOR LAUNCH

(Added by L.1995 chs. 744, 803, eff. 7/1/95.)

Section

§46.2-2400. Definitions.

When used in this chapter, unless expressly stated otherwise:

"Carrier by motor launch" means a common carrier or contract carrier authorized to transport passengers under the provisions of this chapter, which carrier uses one or more motor launches operating on the waters within the Commonwealth.

"Certificate" means a certificate of public convenience and necessity issued by the Department to a carrier by motor launch.

"Department" means the Department of Motor Vehicles.

"Motor launch" means a motor vessel which meets the requirements of the U.S. Coast Guard for the carriage of passengers for hire, with a capacity of six or more passengers, but not in excess of fifty passengers. Motor launch, as defined herein, shall not include sightseeing vessels, special or charter party vessels within the provisions of Chapter 26 (§46.2-2600 et seq.) of Title 46.2. A carrier by motor launch shall not be regarded as a steamship company.

"Person" means any person, partnership or corporation.

(Added by L.1995 chs. 744, 803, eff. 7/1/95.)

§46.2-2401. Contents of certificate.

A certificate issued under this chapter shall authorize the holder named in the certificate to transport passengers and property from the point or points of origin named in the certificate over irregular routes to (i) ships anchored or located on the waters within the Commonwealth and (ii) points of land located within the Commonwealth, and to return.

(Added by L.1995 chs. 744, 803; chgd. by L.1997 ch. 91, eff. 7/1/97.)

§46.2-2402. Purpose of chapter; when certificate granted.

The public convenience and necessity to be served by this chapter is to encourage economical, safe and convenient transportation by motor launch on waters within the Commonwealth, and in the issuance of certificates the Department shall consider all facts bearing on that purpose including existing means of transportation and the character of the applicant and the kind of equipment he proposes to use. The Department shall issue no more certificates than the public convenience and necessity require, but the Department shall not deny a certificate solely on the ground that the applicant may render motor launch service originating at the same point or points as other carriers by motor launch.

(Added by L.1995 chs. 744, 803, eff. 7/1/95.)

§46.2-2403. Revocation of certificate.

A certificate may be revoked, after notice and hearing by the Department, for failure of the carrier to comply with the requirements of this chapter or failure of the carrier to furnish economical, safe and convenient transportation. A certificate shall be revoked whenever the holder requests in writing that it be revoked.

(Added by L.1995 chs. 744, 803, eff. 7/1/95.)

§46.2-2404. Leases prohibited; transfer.

No certificate may be leased. Any certificate may be transferred if the Department finds, after such notice and hearing as it deems reasonable, that the proposed transfer is justified by the public convenience and necessity, subject to such terms, limitations and restrictions as may be prescribed by the Department. Any such application shall be made jointly by the transferor and transferee.

(Added by L.1995 chs. 744, 803, eff. 7/1/95.)

§46.2-2405. Fares.

The fares charged by carriers by motor launch shall be fixed by the Department at such rates as will promote the purposes as set forth in §46.2-2402.

(Added by L.1995 chs. 744, 803, eff. 7/1/95.)

§46.2-2406. Schedules.

A carrier by motor launch shall not be required to file a schedule or schedules with the Department, and is authorized to operate on a scheduled or unscheduled basis as required to meet the demands for service.
(Added by L.1995 chs. 744, 803, eff. 7/1/95.)

§46.2-2407. Certificate required as condition to operation.

No person shall engage in business as a carrier by motor launch as defined in §46.2-2400, unless such person has first obtained a certificate of public convenience and necessity issued by the Department pursuant to the provisions of this chapter.
(Added by L.1995 chs. 744, 803, eff. 7/1/95.)

§46.2-2408. Filing fee; issuance of certificate.

Every applicant for a certificate, upon the filing of an application, shall deposit with the Department a filing fee of $200.

The Department shall issue a certificate if it finds, after such notice and hearing as it deems reasonable, that the proposed operation is justified by the public convenience and necessity, subject to such terms, limitations and restrictions as may be prescribed by the Department.
(Added by L.1995 chs. 744, 803, eff. 7/1/95.)

§46.2-2409. Minimum insurance to be kept in force.

Each holder of a certificate issued by the Department shall keep in force at all times marine protection and indemnity insurance in an amount not less than $500,000 for bodily injury and property damage. The Department shall have the authority to require higher minimum insurance limits, not in excess of one million dollars, related to the passenger carrying capacity of vessels covered by this section.
(Added by L.1995 chs. 744, 803, eff. 7/1/95.)

CHAPTER 25
REGULATION OF LIMOUSINES AND EXECUTIVE SEDANS

(Added by L.1995 chs. 744, 803, eff. 7/1/95.)

Section

§46.2-2500. Definitions.

When used in this chapter, unless the context clearly indicates otherwise:

"Certificate" means a certificate issued by the Department to a limousine carrier or an executive sedan carrier under this chapter.

"Department" means the Department of Motor Vehicles.

"Executive sedan" means a chauffeur-driven, unmarked, unmetered sedan automobile having a seating capacity of not more than five passengers transporting a person or his party under a single-contract agreement for a minimum time period of one hour. A person and his party shall be limited to the contracting person, group, family, or employees of a company or corporation. "Executive sedan" shall not include limousines, vehicles used by funeral directors, taxicabs, trucks, vans, minivans, buses, or minibuses.

"Executive sedan carrier" means any person who undertakes, whether directly or by lease, to transport passengers in an executive sedan for compensation over the highways of the Commonwealth.

"Highway" means every public highway or place of whatever nature open to the use of the public for purposes of vehicle travel in the Commonwealth, including the streets and alleys in towns and cities.

"Limousine" means a chauffeur-driven, luxurious automobile with a seating capacity of not more than ten passengers transporting a person or persons under a single contract for a minimum time period of one hour. The automobile shall be equipped with amenities not normally provided in passenger cars. These amenities should be in the nature of, but not limited to or inclusive of, a television, musical sound system, ice storage area, telephone, additional interior lighting, and driver-passenger communication, such as intercom or power-operated divider partitions. "Limousine" shall not include taxicabs, vehicles used by funeral directors, executive sedans, trucks, vans, minivans, buses, or minibuses.

"Limousine carrier" means any person who undertakes, whether directly or by lease, to transport passengers in limousines for compensation over the highways of the Commonwealth.

"Person" means any individual, firm, partnership, corporation, company, association or joint-stock association, and includes any trustee, receiver, assignee, or personal representative thereof.
(Added by L.1995 chs. 744, 803, eff. 7/1/95.)

§46.2-2501. Exemptions from chapter.

This chapter shall not be construed to apply to any of the following:

1. Motor vehicles owned and operated by the United States, District of Columbia, any state or municipality or any other political subdivision of the Commonwealth.
2. Transportation between any point in the Commonwealth and any point outside the Commonwealth.
3. Motor vehicles while used exclusively in transportation within the corporate limits of incorporated cities or towns, provided the incorporated city or town by local ordinance regulates such motor vehicles pursuant to existing regulations.
4. Motor vehicles used exclusively by a funeral service establishment for services related thereto.

(Added by L.1995 chs. 744, 803, eff. 7/1/95.)

§46.2-2502. Operation except in accordance with chapter prohibited.

No limousine carrier or executive sedan carrier shall operate any limousine or executive sedan for the transportation of passengers for compensation on any highway in the Commonwealth except in accordance with the provisions of this chapter. There shall be no subleasing of individual contracts or commingling of unrelated passengers by use of a contract between a limousine carrier or executive sedan carrier and a licensed broker for the transportation of passengers by motor vehicles.

(Added by L.1995 chs. 744, 803, eff. 7/1/95.)

§46.2-2503. Control, supervision and regulation by Department.

Except as provided in subdivision 3 of §46.2-2501, every limousine carrier or executive sedan carrier shall be subject to the exclusive control, supervision, and regulation by the Department, except that enforcement of statutes and Department regulations shall be not only by the Department, but also by the Department of State Police and local law-enforcement agencies. Nothing in this section shall be construed as authorizing the adoption of local ordinances providing for local regulation of executive sedan carriers or limousine carriers.

(Added by L.1995 chs. 744, 803; chgd. by L.1999 ch. 199, eff. 7/1/99.)

§46.2-2504. No proprietary or property rights conferred.

Nothing in this chapter shall confer any proprietary or property rights in the use of the public highways.

(Added by L.1995 chs. 744, 803, eff. 7/1/95.)

§46.2-2505. Provisions of chapter controlling.

As to limousine carriers or executive sedan carriers, the provisions of this chapter shall be controlling. No laws in conflict or inconsistent herewith shall have any application to such carriers. Operation by a limousine carrier or executive sedan carrier, whether over regular or irregular routes, shall not be deemed an operation over the route of a holder of a certificate authorizing operation as a common carrier of passengers for the general public for compensation, issued pursuant to Chapter 20 (§46.2-2000 et seq.) of this title, so long as the operation is conducted within the restrictions and conditions contained in this chapter. It shall be the policy of the Commonwealth to preserve generally the procedures set forth in Chapter 19 for the transportation of passengers in all cases in which such restrictions and conditions are not strictly met.

(Added by L.1995 chs. 744, 803, eff. 7/1/95.)

§46.2-2506. Application of other provisions of law.

All provisions of law applicable to common carriers of passengers, as provided in Chapter 20 (§46.2-2000 et seq.), to the extent not inconsistent with this chapter, shall be applicable to limousine carriers or executive sedan carriers; however, the Department may grant an exemption from or promulgate different or additional regulations pursuant to the laws herein as the Department may, in its discretion, deem appropriate or necessary to accomplish the purposes of this chapter.

(Added by L.1995 chs. 744, 803, eff. 7/1/95.)

§46.2-2507. Certificate for limousine carrier required.

No person, except as exempted by this chapter, shall operate as a limousine carrier for compensation on any highway within the Commonwealth, until the person has obtained from the Department a certificate as a limousine carrier.

(Added by L.1995 chs. 744, 803, eff. 7/1/95.)

§46.2-2508. Certificate for executive sedan carrier required.

No person, except as exempted by this chapter, shall operate as an executive sedan carrier for compensation on any highway within the Commonwealth, until the person has obtained from the Department a certificate as an executive sedan carrier.

(Added by L.1995 chs. 744, 803, eff. 7/1/95.)

§46.2-2509. Statement of approval of size and type of vehicles required.

No limousine carrier or executive sedan carrier shall conduct operations on any highway of the Commonwealth until the carrier has obtained from the Department approval of the size and type of vehicles to be operated under the certificate.

(Added by L.1995 chs. 744, 803, eff. 7/1/95.)

§46.2-2510. Form of application for certificate; notice, etc.

The Department shall prescribe the form of the application for the certificate, and prescribe such reasonable requirements as to notice, publication, proof of service and information as may, in its judgment, be necessary.

(Added by L.1995 chs. 744, 803, eff. 7/1/95.)

§46.2-2510.1. Executive sedan carrier or limousine carrier to have established place of business.

No certificate shall be issued to any executive sedan carrier or limousine carrier unless the carrier has an established place of business, owned or leased by the carrier, where a substantial portion of the activity of his business is routinely conducted and that:

1. Satisfies all applicable local zoning regulations;
2. Houses all records that the carrier is required to maintain by this chapter or by regulations promulgated pursuant to this chapter; and
3. Is equipped with a working telephone listed in the name of the carrier.

(Added by L.1999 ch. 199, eff. 7/1/99.)

§46.2-2511. Hearing upon application; issuance or denial of certificate.

Upon the filing of an application for a certificate, the Department may, within a reasonable time, schedule a hearing on the application. If the Department finds the applicant is fit, willing, and able to supply the service, it shall issue a certificate to the applicant, subject to such terms, limitations and restrictions as the Department may deem proper.

(Added by L.1995 chs. 744, 803, eff. 7/1/95.)

§46.2-2511.1. Operational requirements.

Limousine carriers and executive sedan carriers shall provide service on a prearranged basis only. Limousine carriers and executive sedan carriers shall, prior to and at all times when providing compensated service, carry in each motor vehicle a trip sheet or contract order identifying the name and pickup address of the passengers who have arranged for use of the motor vehicle and the approximate time of pickup. Such trip sheet or contract order shall be made available immediately upon request to authorized representatives of the Department, law-enforcement agencies, and airport authorities and shall be retained and available for inspection at the carrier's place of business for a period of at least three years. Trip sheets or contract orders may be retained (i) in the form of paper records; (ii) by microfilm, microfiche, similar microphotographic process; or (iii) by electronic means. The fact that a limousine carrier or executive sedan carrier stations a motor vehicle at an airport, in front of or across the street from a hotel or motel, or within one hundred feet of a recognized taxicab stand shall constitute prima facie evidence that the limousine carrier or

executive sedan carrier is operating in violation of this section, unless the carrier has (i) a completed trip sheet or contract order in the vehicle or (ii) a written agreement with an airport authority or hotel or motel owner providing office space devoted to the carrier's business in the airport, hotel, or motel. Any violation of this section shall be punishable as a Class 3 misdemeanor.
(Added by L.1999 ch. 199, eff. 7/1/99.)

§46.2-2512. Consideration for determination of issuance of certificate.
When determining whether a certificate should be granted, the Department shall consider, among other things, the experience, fitness and ability of the applicant to render the proposed service. The Department shall not deny a certificate solely on the ground that an applicant will render limousine service or executive sedan service in any area currently served by one or more existing limousine carriers or executive sedan carriers.
(Added by L.1995 chs. 744, 803, eff. 7/1/95.)

§46.2-2513. Imposition of penalties; suspension, revocation, etc., of certificate.
A. The Department may, after notice and hearing, impose a penalty not to exceed $2,500 and suspend, revoke, alter or amend any such certificate, if it finds that such certificate holder (i) knowingly misrepresented any material fact in obtaining the certificate, (ii) has violated any law affecting such certificate, or (iii) has violated any proper order or regulation of the Department or any term, condition or limitation of such certificate.

B. Proceedings for the imposition of any penalty provided for in this section may be commenced upon the complaint of any person or upon the Department's own initiative.
(Added by L.1995 chs. 744, 803, eff. 7/1/95.)

§46.2-2514. Transfer or lease of certificate.
A limousine certificate or executive sedan certificate may be transferred or leased if the Department finds the proposed transfer or lease is in the public interest, subject to such terms, limitations and restrictions as may be prescribed by the Department. The application shall be made by the parties to the transfer or lease.
(Added by L.1995 chs. 744, 803, eff. 7/1/95.)

§46.2-2515. Transfer of baggage.
A certificate authorizing the transportation of passengers as a limousine carrier or executive sedan carrier shall also be deemed to include authority to transport in the same vehicle with passengers the baggage of passengers.
(Added by L.1995 chs. 744, 803, eff. 7/1/95.)

§46.2-2516. Fees.
Pursuant to this chapter, the Department shall collect the following fees:

1. For filing an application for a certificate, a filing fee of fifty dollars.
2. For the transfer of a certificate, a fee of fifty dollars.
3. For the issuance of a duplicate certificate, a fee of three dollars.
4. For the filing of a lease, a fee of five dollars.

(Added by L.1995 chs. 744, 803, eff. 7/1/95.)

§46.2-2517. Chapter not to invalidate certificates previously issued.
Nothing in this chapter shall adversely affect the rights of any person holding a certificate issued by the Department as provided for in Chapter 20 (§46.2-2000 et seq.) or Chapter 21 (§46.2-2100 et seq.) of this title prior to July 1, 1989, and in force on such date. Every certificate issued by the Department prior to such date shall be and continue in full force and effect until suspended, altered, canceled or revoked in the manner provided for herein.
(Added by L.1995 chs. 744, 803, eff. 7/1/95.)

§46.2-2518. Powers of Department; regulations.
The Department shall have the following powers and duties:

1. To supervise, regulate and control all limousine carriers and executive sedan carriers, except as exempted, who are doing business in the Commonwealth, in all matters relating to the performance of their public duties;
2. To correct any abuses by such carriers;
3. To promulgate regulations, forms and reports for such carriers in the administration and operation of this chapter;
4. To require from such carriers special reports and statements, under oath, concerning their business;
5. To make and enforce requirements and regulations as may be necessary to prevent unjust or unreasonable discriminations by any carrier in favor of, or against, any person, locality or community in connection with the duties of such carriers; and
6. To administer and enforce all provisions of this chapter.

(Added by L.1995 chs. 744, 803, eff. 7/1/95.)

§46.2-2519. Tariffs and schedules of service not required.
A limousine carrier or executive sedan carrier operating under a certificate issued by the Department shall not be required to file with the Department a tariff of rates and charges or time schedules showing arrivals and departures of limousines or executive sedans at any locations served.
(Added by L.1995 chs. 744, 803, eff. 7/1/95.)

CHAPTER 26
REGULATION OF SIGHT-SEEING CARRIERS BY BOAT
(Added by L.1995 chs. 744, 803, eff. 7/1/95.)

Section

§46.2-2600. Definitions.
When used in this chapter, unless expressly stated otherwise:

"Certificate" means a certificate of public convenience and necessity issued by the Department to a sight-seeing carrier by boat.

"Department" means the Department of Motor Vehicles.

"Person" means any person, firm or corporation.

"Sight-seeing carrier by boat" means a restricted common carrier authorized to transport sightseers under the provisions of this chapter, which restricted common carrier uses a boat or boats operating on waters within the Commonwealth. The provisions of this chapter shall apply to special or charter parties by boat as hereinafter defined. Sight-seeing carriers by boat and special or charter parties by boat as defined in this chapter shall not be regarded as steamship companies.

"Special or charter party by boat" for purposes of this chapter shall mean a group movement of persons transported under a single contract made with one person for an agreed charge for such movement regardless of the number of persons transported and in connection with which the fare or tariff is set or determined with regard to the number of such persons to be transported and not on an individual basis. Persons engaged in operating boats for fishing or having an approved passenger capacity of twenty-five or less persons shall not be regarded as special or charter parties under this chapter. Such persons may otherwise be subject to the provisions of this chapter if within the definition of sight-seeing carrier by boat.
(Added by L.1995 chs. 744, 803, eff. 7/1/95.)

§46.2-2601. Contents of certificate.

A certificate issued under this chapter shall authorize the holder named in the certificate to transport sightseers and special or charter parties from the point of origin named in the certificate over regular routes to the point or points of interest named in the certificate and back to the point of origin. Only one point of origin shall be named in a certificate.
(Added by L.1995 chs. 744, 803, eff. 7/1/95.)

§46.2-2602. Purpose of chapter; when certificate granted.

The public convenience and necessity to be served by this chapter is to encourage sightseers to visit and view points of interest in Virginia by providing economical, comfortable and convenient transportation, and in the issuance of certificates the Department shall consider all facts bearing on that purpose, including existing means of transportation and the character of the applicant and the kind of equipment he proposes to use. The Department shall issue no more certificates than the public convenience and necessity require, and shall place such restrictions upon such certificates as may be reasonably necessary to protect any existing sight-seeing carrier by boat or special or charter parties by boat operating over the same or substantially the same route or routes under a certificate issued by the Department, but shall not deny a certificate solely on the ground that the applicant will operate over the same route or substantially the same route or part of the route of an existing sight-seeing carrier by boat or special or charter parties by boat.
(Added by L.1995 chs. 744, 803, eff. 7/1/95.)

§46.2-2603. Revocation of certificate.

In addition to the grounds on which a certificate issued to a common carrier other than a sight-seeing carrier by boat and special and charter parties by boat may be revoked, a certificate may be revoked, after notice and hearing, for failure to furnish economical, comfortable and convenient transportation. A certificate shall be revoked whenever the holder requests in writing that it be revoked.
(Added by L.1995 chs. 744, 803, eff. 7/1/95.)

§46.2-2604. Transfer or lease of certificate; operation by individual or partnership.

No certificates shall be transferred or leased, but a certificate issued to an individual shall be construed to authorize the individual to operate with one or more partners and a certificate issued to a partnership shall be construed to authorize the firm to operate with more or fewer partners so long as at least one of the partners named in the certificate continues to be active in the business. The names and addresses of all partners engaged in the business shall be filed with the Department whenever there is a change in the partnership.
(Added by L.1995 chs. 744, 803, eff. 7/1/95.)

§46.2-2605. Fares.

The fares charged by sight-seeing carriers by boat but not special or charter parties by boat shall be fixed by the Department at such rates as will promote the purposes mentioned in §46.2-2600*.
(Added by L.1995 chs. 744, 803, eff. 7/1/95.)
**So in original. Probably should be "§46.2-2602".*

§46.2-2606. Schedules.

The schedules operated by sight-seeing carriers by boat shall be filed with and subject to the approval or disapproval of the Department, which may consider the seasonal nature of the business and may authorize the discontinuance of schedules during times when the demand for service does not justify service. The area of operation of special or charter parties by boat shall also be subject to the approval or disapproval of the Department.
(Added by L.1995 chs. 744, 803, eff. 7/1/95.)

§46.2-2607. Certificate required as condition to operation; penalty.

No person shall engage in business as a sight-seeing carrier by boat or as a special or charter party by boat as defined in this chapter unless such person first has obtained a certificate from the Department pursuant to the provisions of this chapter. The Department may issue a certificate upon verification that the person has proper insurance coverage, in an amount determined by the Department, and has a valid permit issued by the United States Coast Guard. Operation as a sight-seeing carrier by boat or as a special or charter party by boat as defined in this chapter, without having been issued a certificate shall be a Class 1 misdemeanor.
(Added by L.1995 chs. 744, 803, eff. 7/1/95.)

§46.2-2608. Filing fee.

Every applicant for a certificate under §46.2-2607 shall upon filing of an application, deposit with the Department as a filing fee the sum of fifty dollars for the purpose of defraying the expense of administering the provisions of law with respect to the issuance of such certificate.
(Added by L.1995 chs. 744, 803, eff. 7/1/95.)

§46.2-2609. Insurance to be kept in force.

Each holder of a certificate issued by the Department or person operating by virtue of §46.2-2607 shall also keep in force at all times marine protection and indemnity insurance in an amount not less than $100,000 for bodily injury and property damage. The Department shall have the authority to require higher minimum insurance limits, not in excess of $500,000, related to the passenger carrying capacity of vessels covered by this section.
(Added by L.1995 chs. 744, 803, eff. 7/1/95.)

§46.2-2610. Exceptions to application of chapter.

The provisions of this chapter shall not be applicable to any municipal corporation acting as a sight-seeing carrier by boat or special or charter party by boat, if said municipal corporation has a population greater than 89,000 but less than 91,000.
(Added by L.1995 chs. 744, 803, eff. 7/1/95.)

CHAPTER 27
VIRGINIA MOTOR VEHICLE EMISSIONS REDUCTION PROGRAM

(Repealed by L.1997 ch. 117, eff. 7/1/97.)

§§46.2-2700 to 46.2-2703. *(Repealed by L.1997 ch. 117, eff. 7/1/97.)*

TITLE 52
POLICE (STATE)
(Complete Title)

CHAPTER 1
DEPARTMENT OF STATE POLICE

§52-1. Establishment of Department headed by Superintendent; Bureau of Criminal Investigation and division of drug law enforcement and investigation within Department.

There is hereby established as a separate department, a Department of State Police headed by the Superintendent of State Police. There shall be established within the Department of State Police, in addition to any other divisions or bureaus that may be established by statute or otherwise, a Bureau of Criminal Investigation and a division for drug law enforcement and investigation.

(Chgd. by L.2000 chs. 560, 600, eff. 7/1/2000.)

§52-2. Appointment of Superintendent and term of office.

The Superintendent of State Police shall be appointed by the Governor, subject to confirmation by the General Assembly if in session when such appointment is made, and if not in session, then at its next succeeding session. Such officer shall hold his office at the pleasure of the Governor for a term coincident with that of each Governor making the appointment, or until his successor shall be appointed and qualified. Vacancies shall be filled for the unexpired term in the same manner as original appointments are made.

§52-3. Oath, bond and salary of Superintendent.

The Superintendent of State Police, before entering upon the discharge of his duties, shall take an oath that he will faithfully and impartially discharge and perform all the duties of his office, and shall give bond in such penalty as may be fixed by the Governor, conditioned upon the faithful discharge of his duties, the premium on such bond to be paid out of the funds available for the maintenance and operation of his office. The Superintendent shall receive such salary as may be appropriated for the purpose.

§52-4. Functions of Department.

The highway patrol, or state police patrol as it is sometimes called, the police school, the state police radio or communication system, the supervision of inspection stations and of inspectors of motor vehicles, the promotion of highway safety, the establishment and direction of a vehicle accident prevention and safety program for state agencies, the adoption of standards for motor vehicle appliances, accessories and safety devices and the registration of machine guns shall be in the Department of State Police.

§52-4.2. Department of Motor Vehicles to publish statistical information, and conduct research and experiments; copies to be furnished by Department to Commonwealth's attorneys.

(a) The Department of Motor Vehicles shall tabulate and analyze all accident reports and shall publish annually, or more frequently, statistical information based thereon as to the number and circumstances of traffic accidents.

(b) Based upon its findings, after analysis, the Department may conduct further necessary detailed research to determine more fully the cause, control and prevention of highway accidents. It may further conduct experimental field tests within areas of the Commonwealth from time to time to prove the practicability of various ideas advanced in traffic control and accident prevention.

(c) The Department of Motor Vehicles shall promptly furnish a copy of any particular accident report or a proof of financial responsibility to any Commonwealth's attorney upon the request of that person, without charge to be used only in the performance of his official duties.

§52-4.3. Drug Investigation Special Trust Account.

A. There is hereby created in the Department of the Treasury a special nonreverting fund to be known as the Drug Investigation Special Trust Account, consisting of such funds as may be appropriated by the General Assembly from time to time and all interest, dividends and appreciation, including payments to the fund from the federal government by virtue of a grant, gift, forfeiture or other disposition, which may accrue to such fund, for the purpose of providing a timely supplemental source of money to the Department of State Police for use in the detection, investigation and apprehension of persons for the violation of the laws pertaining to the manufacture, sale or distribution of illegal drugs.

B. Funds from the Drug Investigation Special Trust Account shall be used to supplement general appropriations for the Department of State Police Bureau of Criminal Investigations and a division for drug law enforcement and investigation for nonpersonal service expenditures related to illegal drug investigations. They shall be used only for the purposes stated in subsection A and in strict conformity with the rules and regulations promulgated by the Superintendent of State Police to carry out the intent and purposes of this section.

C. No expenditures shall be made from the Drug Investigation Trust Account except in strict compliance with procedures established by the Superintendent of State Police and approved by the State Comptroller. The accounting for all such expenditures shall also be in strict compliance with such procedures.

D. The Drug Investigation Special Trust Account shall be established on the books of the Comptroller so as to segregate the amounts appropriated to the account and the amounts earned or accumulated by such special trust account. No portion of such special trust account shall be used for a purpose other than for drug investigations. Funds remaining in the Drug Investigation Special Trust Account at the end of a biennium shall not revert to the general fund but shall remain in the special trust account, to be used for the purposes set forth in subsections A through C and shall accumulate interest and dividends throughout the existence of the special trust account. Any funds, however, remaining in the special trust account at the end of a biennium in excess of $1,500,000 shall revert to the general fund.
(Chgd. by L.2000 chs. 560, 600, eff. 7/1/2000.)

§52-4.4. Duties relating to criminal history record information checks required by licensed firearms dealers.

The Superintendent of the Department of State Police shall establish a toll-free telephone number which shall be operational seven days a week between the hours of 8:00 a.m. and 10:00 p.m., except December 25, for purposes of responding to inquiries from licensed firearms dealers, as such term is defined in 18 U.S.C. §921 et seq., pursuant to the provisions of §18.2-308.2:2. The Department shall hire and train such personnel as are necessary to administer the provisions of this section.
(Chgd. by L.1997 ch. 341, eff. 7/1/97.)

§52-6. Appointment of additional police officers.

The Superintendent of State Police, with the approval of the Governor, shall have authority to appoint additional police officers, who may or may not be residents of this Commonwealth, to serve for specified periods of time. The police officers so appointed shall receive such compensation as the Superintendent shall approve. Such police officers shall have the same powers and perform the same duties as the regular police officers appointed by the Superintendent.

§52-6.1. Appointment of supervisory officers.

All appointments to sworn police positions above the rank of trooper within the Department of State Police shall be made by the Superintendent of State Police from among the sworn police officers of the Department, except for those positions designated in subdivision A 16 of §2.1-116, or whenever the Superintendent determines, in writing, that a position requires knowledge, skills, or abilities such that a sufficient pool of qualified candidates does not exist within the Department of State Police. It was and is the intent of the General Assembly that the primary factor in the career progression program is satisfactory years of service.

§52-7. Bonds of police officers; liability insurance policies.

All police officers appointed by the Superintendent of State Police, and engaged in the enforcement of criminal laws and the laws relating to the operation of motor vehicles upon the roads and highways of this Commonwealth, shall, before entering upon or continuing in their duties, enter into bond, with some solvent guaranty company authorized to do business in this Commonwealth, as surety, in the penalty of $75,000 and with condition for the faithful and lawful performance of their duties. Such bonds shall be filed in the office of the Department of State Police, and the premiums thereon shall be paid out of the funds appropriated for the maintenance and operation of the Department of State Police. All persons injured or damaged in any manner by the unlawful, negligent or improper conduct of any such officer while on duty may maintain an action upon such bond.

In lieu of posting bond as provided herein, any such police officer may furnish an adequate liability insurance policy as proof of his ability to respond in damages, which may be adjudged against him in favor of any person or persons injured or damaged in any manner resulting from his unlawful, negligent or improper conduct while on official duty, to the amount set forth above. The premiums on any such insurance policy or policies shall be paid out of the funds appropriated for the maintenance and operation of the Department of State Police.

All such bonds and insurance policies shall be approved by the Superintendent of State Police.

§52-8. Powers and duties to enforce criminal laws and investigate aircraft accidents.

The Superintendent of State Police, his several assistants and police officers appointed by him are vested with the powers of a sheriff for the purpose of enforcing all the criminal laws of this Commonwealth and for investigating any aircraft accident which occurs in the Commonwealth, and it shall be the duty of the Superintendent, his several assistants and police officers appointed by him to use their best efforts to enforce the same.

Nothing in this section shall be construed as relieving any sheriff or sergeant, commissioner of the revenue, police officer, or any other official now or hereafter invested with police powers and duties, state or local, from the duty of aiding and assisting in the enforcement of such laws within the scope of his authority and duty.

§52-8.1. Powers and duties of Bureau of Criminal Investigation.

In addition to any other powers and duties which may be provided by statute or otherwise, the Bureau of Criminal Investigation shall conduct an investigation into any matter referred to it by the Governor. The Bureau of Criminal Investigation shall, when requested by the Attorney General, any sheriff, chief of police, Commonwealth's attorney or grand jury, conduct an investigation into the subject matter so directed or requested, if the person or grand jury making the request has reasonable cause to believe the acts committed or about to be committed would constitute a Class 1, 2 or 3 felony, to determine whether any such criminal violations have occurred, are occurring or are about to occur. The Bureau may, in all other requests for investigations made by the Attorney General, any sheriff, chief of police, Commonwealth's attorney or grand jury, conduct an investigation into the subject matter so requested, to determine whether any criminal violations have occurred, are occurring or are about to occur.

§52-8.1:1. Powers and duties of a drug law enforcement and investigation division.

A. In addition to any other powers and duties which may be provided by statute or otherwise, it shall be the duty of a division for drug law enforcement and investigation to enforce the laws of the Commonwealth and conduct investigations related to violations of Articles 1 (§18.2-247 et seq.) and 1.1 (§18.2-265.1 et seq.) of Chapter 7 of Title 18.2 or when requested pursuant to the provisions of §52-8.1.

B. The Superintendent may request and receive, from any federal, state or local agency, cooperation and assistance to aid such division in the performance of its duties, including temporary assignment of personnel which may be necessary to carry out the performance of its functions; provided that the agency consents to the assignment. Consent may not be unreasonably withheld. Any assistance or appropriation given to such division shall be used for the primary purpose of enforcing laws and conducting investigations related to violations of Articles 1 (§18.2-247 et seq.) and 1.1 (§18.2-265.1 et seq.) of Chapter 7 of Title 18.2. Such division shall be a party to any anti-crime partnership agreement established pursuant to §2.1-51.6:3 and may assist any locality declared an Intensified Drug Enforcement Jurisdiction pursuant to §15.2-1715.

C. Such division may enter into agreements with other states pertaining to the enforcement of Articles 1 (§18.2-247 et seq.) and 1.1 (§18.2-265.1 et seq.) of Chapter 7 of Title 18.2 across state boundaries. Such division may share information with law enforcement agencies in other states as is necessary to carry out its work.

(Added by L.2000 chs. 560, 600, eff. 7/1/2000.)

§52-8.2. Certain investigations of elected officials; immunity for witnesses.

A. No investigation of an elected official of the Commonwealth or any political subdivision to determine whether a criminal violation has occurred, is occurring or is about to occur under the provisions of §52-8.1 shall be initiated, undertaken or continued except upon the request of the Governor, Attorney General or a grand jury.

B. In any grand jury proceeding or criminal prosecution involving a person who was at the time of the offense an elected official of the Commonwealth or a political subdivision thereof resulting from an investigation under subsection A, any witness called by the court or attorney for the Commonwealth and required to give evidence for the prosecution who refuses to testify or produce evidence by expressly invoking his right not to incriminate himself may be compelled to testify or produce evidence by the presiding judge. A witness who refuses to testify or produce evidence after being ordered to do so by the presiding judge may be held in contempt and may be incarcerated until the contempt is purged by compliance with the order. When a witness is compelled to testify or produce evidence after expressly invoking his right not to incriminate himself, and the presiding judge has determined that the assertion of the right is bona fide, the compelled testimony, or any information directly or indirectly derived from such testimony or other information, shall not be used against the witness in any criminal proceeding except a prosecution for perjury.

§52-8.3. Disclosure of criminal investigative records and reports; penalty.

Any person employed by a law-enforcement agency or other governmental agency within the Commonwealth who has or has had access in an official capacity to an official written record or report submitted in confidence to the Department of State Police relating to an ongoing criminal investigation, and who uses or knowingly permits another to use such record or report for any purpose not consistent with the exclusions permitted in §§2.1-342.01 and 2.1-342.2, or other provision of state law, shall be guilty of a Class 2 misdemeanor.

The provisions of this section shall not be construed to impede or prohibit full access to information concerning the existence of any criminal investigation or to other verbal disclosures permitted by state police operating procedures.

(Chgd. by L.1999 chs. 703, 726, eff. 7/1/99.)

§52-8.4. Powers and duties to promulgate regulations; inspection of certain records.

A. The Superintendent of State Police, with the cooperation of such other agencies of the Commonwealth as may be necessary, shall promulgate regulations pertaining to commercial motor vehicle safety pursuant to the United States Motor Carrier Act of 1984. These regulations shall set forth criteria relating to driver, vehicle, and cargo safety inspections with which motor carriers and transport vehicles shall comply, and shall be no more restrictive than the applicable provisions of the Federal Motor Carrier Safety Regulations of the United States Department of Transportation. These regulations shall not apply to hours worked by any carrier when transporting passengers or property to or from any portion of the Commonwealth for the purpose of providing relief or assistance in case of earthquake, flood, fire, famine, drought, epidemic, pestilence, major loss of utility services, or other calamity or disaster. The suspension of the regulation provided for in this subsection shall expire if the Secretary of the United States Department of Transportation determines that it is in conflict with the intent of Federal Motor Carrier Safety Regulations.

B. For the purposes of this section:

"Commercial motor vehicle" means any self-propelled or towed vehicle used on the highways in commerce to transport passengers or property if such vehicle (i) has a gross vehicle weight rating or gross combination weight rating of more than 10,000 pounds when operated interstate or more than 26,000 pounds when operated intrastate, (ii) is designed to transport more than fifteen passengers, including the driver, regardless of weight, or (iii) is used to transport hazardous materials in a quantity requiring placards by regulations issued under authority of Article 7 (§10.1-1450 et seq.) of Chapter 14 of Title 10.1.

"Motor carrier" means a common carrier by motor vehicle, a contract carrier by motor vehicle, or a private carrier of property or passengers by motor vehicle. This term also encompasses any agent, officer, representative, or employee who is responsible for the hiring, supervision, training, assignment, or dispatching of drivers.

"Transport vehicle" means any vehicle owned or leased by a motor carrier used in the transportation of goods or persons.

"Safety inspection" means the detailed examination of a vehicle for compliance with safety regulations promulgated under this section and includes a determination of the qualifications of the driver and his hours of service.

C. Except for those offenses listed in §52-8.4:2, any violation of the provisions of the regulations adopted pursuant to this section shall constitute a traffic infraction punishable by a fine of not more than $1,000 for the first offense or by a fine of not more than $5,000 for a subsequent offense. Each day of violation shall constitute a separate offense; however, any violation of any out-of-service order issued under authority of such regulations or under authority of the Federal Motor Carrier Safety regulations shall be punished as provided in §46.2-341.21 and the disqualification provisions of §46.2-341.21 also shall apply to any driver so convicted.

D. The Department of State Police, together with all other law-enforcement officers certified to perform vehicle safety inspections as defined by §46.2-1001 who have satisfactorily completed forty hours of on-the-job training and a course of instruction as prescribed by the U.S. Department of Transportation, Federal Highway Administration, Office of Motor Carriers, in federal motor carrier safety regulations, safety inspection procedures, and out-of-service criteria, shall enforce the regulations and other requirements promulgated pursuant to this section. Those law-enforcement officers certified to enforce the regulations and other requirements promulgated pursuant to this section shall annually receive in-service training in current federal motor carrier safety regulations, safety inspection procedures, and out-of-service criteria.

E. Any records required to be maintained by motor carriers pursuant to regulations promulgated by the Superintendent under the authority of subsection A of this section shall be open to inspection during a carrier's normal business hours by specially trained members of the Department of State Police specifically designated by the Superintendent. Members of the Department of State Police designated for that purpose by the Superintendent shall also be authorized, with the consent of the owner, operator, or agent in charge or with an appropriate warrant obtained under the procedure prescribed in Chapter 24 (§19.2-393 et seq.) of Title 19.2, to go upon the property of motor carriers to verify the accuracy of maintenance records by an inspection of the vehicles to which those records relate.

(Chgd. by L.1995 chs. 145, 151, 744, 803; L.1996 ch. 302; L.1997 ch. 283, eff. 7/1/97.)

§52-8.4:1. Regulations for firearms shows.

The Superintendent of State Police shall provide a form for use by promoters of firearms shows for the purpose of notifying the State Police and the chief of police, or the sheriff in localities without police departments, of their intent to conduct a firearms show pursuant to §54.1-4201.1.

§52-8.4:2. Certain offenses to be considered traffic infractions.

Notwithstanding subsection C of §52-8.4, any violation of any of the following provisions of the regulations adopted pursuant to §52-8.4 shall constitute traffic infractions as defined in §46.2-100 and shall be eligible for designation as traffic infractions for which a pretrial waiver of appearance, plea of guilty, and fine payment may be accepted pursuant to §16.1-69.40:1.

DESCRIPTION OF OFFENSE	CORRESPONDING SECTION OF THE CODE OF FEDERAL REGULATIONS
(a) General Violations	
Marking of motor vehicle	49 C.F.R. §390.21
Railroad crossing/stopping	49 C.F.R. §392.10
(b) Driver Violations	
No medical examiner's certificate	49 C.F.R. §391.41
Improper medical examiner's certificate	49 C.F.R. §391.43
Medical certificate invalid	49 C.F.R. §391.43
No medical waiver	49 C.F.R. §391.49
Ill/fatigued driver	49 C.F.R. §392.3
Possess alcoholic beverage	49 C.F.R. §392.5
Hearing aid to be worn	49 C.F.R. §392.9
Violate 10-hour rule, 15-hour rule	49 C.F.R. §395.3
Violate 60/70-hour rule	49 C.F.R. §395.3
Logbook violation (general)	49 C.F.R. §395.8
No logbook	49 C.F.R. §395.8
Logbook not current	49 C.F.R. §395.8
Fail to retain previous 7 days on logbook	49 C.F.R. §395.8
(c) Equipment Violations	
Equipment–inspection/use	49 C.F.R. §392.7
Emergency equipment–inspection/use	49 C.F.R. §392.8
Safe loading (secured)	49 C.F.R. §392.9
Brakes–inoperative or missing	49 C.F.R. §393.40–§393.52
Fuel tank securement	49 C.F.R. §393.65
Fuel leak/cap	49 C.F.R. §393.67
Coupling/towing devices	49 C.F.R. §393.70; §393.71
Tire exceeds weight limit	49 C.F.R. §393.75
Bus violations	49 C.F.R. §393.89–§393.92
Front end structure	49 C.F.R. §393.106
Frame–cracked, loose, sagging, broken	49 C.F.R. §393.201
Cab/body components–defective	49 C.F.R. §393.203
Wheels/rims defective	49 C.F.R. §393.205
Suspension–defective	49 C.F.R. §393.207
Steering system–defective	49 C.F.R. §393.209
Vehicle maintenance (general)	49 C.F.R. §396.3
No driver vehicle inspection report	49 C.F.R. §396.11
No periodic inspection	49 C.F.R. §396.17–§396.25
(d) Hazardous Materials Driving and Parking	
Fail to attend Division 1.1, 1.2, or 1.3 material	49 C.F.R. §397.5
Fail to attend other hazardous materials class	49 C.F.R. §397.5
Improper parking Division 1.1, 1.2, or 1.3 material	49 C.F.R. §397.7; §397.11
Improper parking other hazardous materials	49 C.F.R. §397.7; §397.11
Fail to have route plan	49 C.F.R. §397.67
Smoking violations	49 C.F.R. §397.13
Instructions and document violations	49 C.F.R. §397.19

(Added by L.1997 ch. 283, eff. 7/1/97.)

 Zv

§52-8.5. Reporting terroristic acts.

A. The Superintendent shall establish and maintain within the Department of State Police a central repository for the collection and analysis of information regarding terroristic acts and groups and individuals carrying out such acts.

B. State, county and municipal law-enforcement agencies shall report to the Department all terroristic acts occurring in their jurisdictions in a form, time and manner prescribed by the Superintendent. Such reports shall not be open to public inspection except insofar as the Superintendent shall permit.

C. For purposes of this section, "terroristic act" means (i) a criminal act committed against a person or his property with the specific intent of instilling fear or intimidation in the individual against whom the act is perpetrated because of race, religion or ethnic origin or which is committed for the purpose of restraining that person from exercising his rights under the Constitution or laws of this Commonwealth or of the United States, (ii) any illegal act directed against any persons or their property because of those persons' race, religion or national origin, and (iii) all other incidents, as determined by law-enforcement authorities, intended to intimidate or harass any individual or group because of race, religion or national origin.

§52-9. Administration of oaths; acknowledgments and affidavits; summoning witnesses in certain cases.

A. All police officers appointed by the Superintendent are vested with the authority and power to administer oaths and take acknowledgments and affidavits incidental to the administration and enforcement of all laws relating to the operation of motor vehicles, applications for driver's licenses and the collection and refunding of taxes levied on gasoline, for which services they shall receive no compensation.

B. Any member of the Bureau of Criminal Investigation conducting an investigation may petition an appropriate judicial officer for the issuance of a summons directed to a sheriff of any county or city, police chief of any town, or to any member of the Bureau of Criminal Investigation, commanding the officer to summon witnesses at such time and place as he may direct. Any such officer to whom the summons is delivered shall forthwith execute it, and make return thereof at the time and place named therein.

C. Any member of the Bureau of Criminal Investigation who is conducting an investigation requested under the provisions of §52-8.2 or investigating frauds or attempts to defraud the Commonwealth or any of its political subdivisions or investigating criminal misconduct related to official duties of any officer, agent, or employee of the Commonwealth or any of its political subdivisions, upon authorization by the Attorney General or an attorney for the Commonwealth, may administer an oath to any complaining witness who is giving a statement or evidence concerning such investigation. If oath is administered pursuant to this statute it shall be administered prior to the taking of any statement, and any statement taken after such oath shall be reduced to writing and subscribed by the witness.

§52-9.1. Distinctive uniform to be adopted for State police officers.

The Superintendent of State Police shall cause to be designed and, with the approval of the Governor, adopt a distinctive uniform with appropriate insignia for the use of the police officers appointed by him. Such uniform, when adopted, shall be worn by all such police officers when on patrol duty, and at such other times as the Superintendent may by regulation prescribe.

§52-9.1:1. Retention of officer's badge upon retirement.

Notwithstanding any provision of law to the contrary, on and after July 1, 1978, every State police officer shall upon retirement be awarded his badge or other insignia of his office for permanent keeping; provided, however, the Superintendent of State Police, prior to tendering such badge or insignia, shall have the same mounted in such a manner that it will be impossible for anyone to display such badge or insignia upon his person.

§52-9.2. Wearing of same or similar uniforms by other persons.

When such official uniform has been adopted by the Superintendent, no police officer of any county, city or town, special policeman, guard or other person shall wear any uniform identical with such official uniform or so similar in appearance as to be likely to deceive the casual observer.

Violations of this or the preceding section (§52-9.1) shall constitute a misdemeanor and be punished as provided by law.

§52-10. Fees and rewards.

No trial justice or court, in this Commonwealth, shall in any case, in which a fine is assessed for the violation of any law of this Commonwealth, or any subdivision thereof, assess, as a part of the cost of the case any fee for arrest, or as a witness, for the benefit of any police officer of the Department of State Police; nor shall any such police officer receive any such fee. Any such police officer who accepts or receives any such fee shall be guilty of a misdemeanor and shall be punished by a fine of not more than $100, and in addition the Superintendent may remove him therefor. But such officers are not prohibited from accepting or receiving rewards.

§52-11. Defense of police officers.

If any police officer appointed by the Superintendent of State Police shall be brought before any regulatory body, summoned before any grand jury, investigated by any other law-enforcement agency, or arrested or indicted or otherwise prosecuted on any charge arising out of any act committed in the discharge of his official duties, the Superintendent may employ special counsel approved by the Attorney General to defend such officer. Upon a finding that (i) the officer did not violate a law or regulation resulting from the act which was the subject of the investigation and (ii) the officer will not be terminated from employment as the result of such act, the Superintendent shall pay for the special counsel employed. The compensation for special counsel employed, pursuant to this section, shall, subject to the approval of the Attorney General, be paid out of the funds appropriated for the administration of the Department of State Police.

§52-11.1. State Health Commissioner to cooperate.

The State Health Commissioner shall cause to be furnished to the Department of State Police all such assistance requested by the Superintendent of State Police or the authorized officers and agents of the Department of State Police as may be afforded by the technical staff of the Department of Health and the Chief Medical Examiner.

The State Health Commissioner may, in his discretion, furnish to any other law-enforcement officer or agency, such assistance as is afforded by the technical staff of the Department of Health and the Chief Medical Examiner.

§52-11.2. Services of State Police in areas of counties that have merged, consolidated or been annexed into cities.

When a county or city merges or consolidates into a city, or when a combination of counties and cities merge into a city, or when any county and all of the incorporated towns

 Zv

located entirely therein merge, consolidate or be annexed or when any county or part thereof be annexed into a city or cities, the governing body of any such city may thereafter request of the Superintendent of State Police, and upon such request he shall grant, the services of the Department of State Police in those areas of the counties which were merged, or consolidated or annexed into such city or cities for a period of ten years after the effective date of such merger, consolidation or annexation which were not previously incorporated.

§52-11.3. Acquisition of military property.

The Superintendent of State Police is authorized to apply for and accept grants or loans of personal property from the United States Department of Defense for use in the law-enforcement activities of the Department of State Police or any other law-enforcement agency of the Commonwealth or its political subdivisions. In connection with the receipt of such property, the Department of State Police and any other law-enforcement agency to which the property is transferred, may agree to hold the United States government harmless against claims for damages arising out of the use of the property received. Such other law-enforcement agencies may also agree to hold the Commonwealth harmless against such claims.

(Added by L.1995 ch. 149, eff. 7/1/95.)

CHAPTER 2
BASIC STATE POLICE COMMUNICATION SYSTEM

§52-12. Establishment of communication system.

There shall be established in the Department of State Police, a basic coordinating police communication system of private line typewriter communication, operating through sending and receiving stations or receiving stations only, and such associated equipment as may be necessary, at the headquarters of the Superintendent of State Police and at such substations or detached posts as shall be designated by the Superintendent, for the purpose of prompt collection and distribution of information throughout the Commonwealth as the police problems of the Commonwealth may require. Authority is hereby granted to connect such basic system directly or indirectly with similar systems in this or adjoining states.

§52-13. Installation, operation and maintenance of system; personnel.

The Superintendent of State Police is authorized to install, operate and maintain the basic system and to employ the necessary personnel for its installation, operation and maintenance. The persons so employed may be members of the State Police, or other State employees, particularly qualified for the duty they are to perform.

§52-14. Availability of system.

The basic system herein provided for may be made available for use by any department or division of the State government and by any county, city, town, railroad or other special police department lawfully maintained by any corporation in this Commonwealth as well as agencies of the federal government, subject to the following terms and conditions:

1. Application for permission to connect with the basic system shall be made to the Superintendent of State Police on forms to be provided by him;
2. Such application may be approved by the Superintendent if, as and when in his discretion such connection is requisite and necessary for the best interests of the entire system;
3. Upon approval of such application and before the applicant shall be connected with the basic system, such applicant must agree to assume and pay all rentals for sending and receiving stations, or receiving stations only, as may be authorized by the Superintendent for installation within the jurisdiction of the applicant, and any and all costs of installation and operation of such stations;
4. a. The Commonwealth shall pay all rental for necessary wire or circuit mileage required to connect such stations operated by criminal justice agencies of the Commonwealth and its political subdivisions, or the Federal Bureau of Investigation, with the basic system.

b. All other agencies shall agree, as a condition of connection or continued service, to assume and pay all rental for necessary wire or circuit mileage required to connect such stations with the basic system.

(Chgd. by L.1999 ch. 150, eff. 7/1/99.)

§52-15. Control of system; orders, rules or regulations.

Such basic system shall remain at all times under the control of the Superintendent of State Police, and such control may be exercised by him through such member of his department as he shall designate for such purpose. The Superintendent may make and issue such orders, rules or regulations for the use of the system as in his discretion are necessary for efficient operation.

CHAPTER 3
JOINT STATE AND LOCAL POLICE COMMUNICATION SYSTEM

§52-16. Governor may establish and maintain radio and teletype system to aid police.

The Governor may in his discretion establish, purchase, lease or otherwise acquire all necessary property, real and personal, for such purpose, and cause to be constructed, equipped, maintained and operated, at such place or places as he may determine, a radio or teletype system or any combination of the two for transmitting and receiving messages, in connection with the work of the police departments of, and officers exercising police powers in, the cities, towns and counties of Virginia and the work of the police officers of the Department of State Police, relating to the detection of crime and the apprehension of criminals and other necessary police activities.

§52-17. Contracts with counties, cities and towns.

In order to make the system effective and of greatest benefit to the people of the Commonwealth, the Governor may in his discretion enter into negotiations with and make contracts and agreements with the cities, counties and towns of the Commonwealth whereby portions of the cost of establishing, purchasing, constructing, maintaining and operating such system will be borne by such localities.

In making agreements with the several localities due consideration shall be given to the population thereof and to any expense incurred, or which may be incurred, by such localities in purchasing, constructing, maintaining and operating local systems for similar purposes.

§52-18. Districts.
The Governor may in his discretion divide the Commonwealth into two or more radio or teletype districts or combination of the two, and in the event of the proper proportionate monetary cooperation upon the part of localities within any one or more of such districts, may arrange for the establishment, purchase, installation, maintenance and operation of such radio or teletype equipment or both within such district or districts.

§52-19. Rules and regulations.
The Governor may cause to be made and issued such reasonable rules and regulations as he may deem necessary for the proper use of such system.

CHAPTER 4
ARRESTS BY STATE POLICE

Section

§52-20. Arrests without warrants in certain cases.
Members of the State Police force of the Commonwealth, provided such officers are in uniform, or displaying a badge of office, may, at the scene of any motor vehicle accident, or in the apprehension of any person charged with the theft of any motor vehicle, on any of the highways of the Commonwealth, upon reasonable grounds to believe, based upon personal investigation, including information obtained from eyewitnesses, that a crime has been committed by any person then and there present, apprehend such person without a warrant of arrest; and such officers may arrest, without a warrant, persons duly charged with crime in another jurisdiction upon receipt of a telegram, a radio or teletype message, in which telegram, radio or teletype message shall be given the name or a reasonably accurate description of such person wanted, the crime alleged and an allegation that such person is likely to flee the jurisdiction of the Commonwealth.

§52-21. Procedure after arrest without warrant.
Except in the case of a violation of a provision of Title 46.2, in which case the officer making the arrest shall proceed as provided in §46.2-936, the officer making the arrest shall forthwith bring the person so arrested before an officer authorized to issue criminal warrants in the county or city where the arrest is made. The officer before whom such person is brought shall proceed to examine the officer making the arrest. If the officer before whom such person is brought has reasonable grounds upon which to believe that a criminal offense has been committed, and that the person arrested has committed such offense, he shall issue such a warrant as might have been issued prior to the arrest of such person under the provisions of §19.2-72. If such a warrant is issued the case shall thereafter be disposed of in like manner as though the warrant had been issued prior to the arrest. If such a warrant be not issued the person so arrested shall be released.

§52-22. Arrests for violations of ordinances.
The Superintendent of State Police, his assistants, and the State troopers, patrolmen and police officers appointed by him, shall have authority to execute warrants of arrest for violations of ordinances of counties, cities and towns when requested so to do by the county, city or town authorities. Such arrests may be made upon information transmitted as provided in §52-20, as well as in cases where the officer is in possession of the warrant.

The execution of any such warrant shall rest entirely in the discretion of the Superintendent and other officers who may be requested to execute the same, and no such officer shall execute the same in any case where it will in any way interfere with, delay or hinder him in the discharge of his official duties.

CHAPTER 5
INVESTIGATORS AND SPECIAL STATE POLICE OFFICERS

Section

§52-23. Appointment by Governor; power and jurisdiction.
The Governor may appoint whenever he deems the same necessary, and may remove at will, investigators and temporary special police officers, who shall be directly responsible to the Governor, be conservators of the peace and have jurisdiction throughout the Commonwealth in the enforcement of the laws of the Commonwealth. Such investigators and special police officers shall have in all the counties, cities and towns of the Commonwealth all the power and authority, in connection with the enforcement of the laws of the Commonwealth, vested by law in sheriffs of the counties and police officers of cities and towns.

§52-24. Compensation.
Such investigators and temporary special police officers shall be paid such compensation as may be allowed by the Governor, such compensation to be paid from such moneys as shall be appropriated to the Governor for the executive control of the Commonwealth, and not otherwise specifically appropriated.

CHAPTER 6
UNIFORM CRIME REPORTING PROGRAM

Section

§52-25. Uniform crime reporting system established.
The Superintendent shall establish, organize, equip, staff and maintain within the Department of State Police, at such departmental locations as the Superintendent may direct, a uniform crime reporting system for the purpose of receiving, compiling, classifying, analyzing and publishing crime statistics of offenses known, persons arrested, and persons charged and other information pertaining to the investigation of crime and the apprehension of criminals, as hereinafter provided. The Superintendent shall appoint or designate necessary personnel to carry out the duties and assignments in accordance with rules and regulations pertaining thereto promulgated by the Superintendent.

§52-25.1. Reporting of confiscated firearms.

The Superintendent shall establish and maintain within the Department of State Police a Criminal Firearms Clearinghouse as a central repository of information regarding all firearms seized, forfeited, found or otherwise coming into the possession of any state or local law-enforcement agency of the Commonwealth which are believed to have been used in the commission of a crime. The Superintendent shall adopt and promulgate regulations prescribing the form for reporting this information and the time and manner of submission of the form.

In addition to any other information which the Superintendent may require, the form shall require (i) the serial number or other identifying information on the firearm, if available, (ii) a brief description of the circumstances under which the firearm came into the possession of the law-enforcement agency, including the crime which was or may have been committed with the firearm, (iii) the name of or other identifying information on the person from whom the firearm was taken, (iv) the original place of sale and, if known, the chain of possession of the firearm, and (v) the disposition of the firearm.

§52-26. Cooperation with other law-enforcement agencies.

The Superintendent is authorized to maintain liaison and to cooperate with law-enforcement and criminal justice agencies of all counties, cities and towns and all other agencies, departments, and institutions of the Commonwealth, other states and of the United States in order to develop and carry on a comprehensive uniform crime reporting program for the Commonwealth. Uniform crime reports for the Commonwealth shall be published by the Superintendent and distributed to all law-enforcement agencies, Commonwealth's attorneys, courts, and to the General Assembly and the office of the Governor, annually.

§52-27. Aid to reporting agencies.

The Department shall render all necessary aid and assistance to all reporting agencies in order to fulfill the requirements of the uniform crime reporting program for the Commonwealth.

§52-28. Duty of Commonwealth and local agencies to make reports.

All Commonwealth, county and municipal law-enforcement agencies shall submit to the Department all periodic uniform crime reports setting forth their activities in connection with law enforcement. The provisions of this chapter shall not apply to any police agency not paid entirely from public funds.

§52-29. Rules and regulations for form, etc.

The Superintendent shall adopt and promulgate rules and regulations prescribing the form, general content, time and manner of submission of such uniform crime reports of all offenses designated by him, including, but not limited to, part I and part II offenses as set out by the Federal Bureau of Investigation.

§52-30. Reports to Federal Bureau of Investigation.

The Department shall correlate reports submitted to it and shall compile and submit reports to the Federal Bureau of Investigation on behalf of all agencies of the Commonwealth, as may be required by the federal standards for the uniform crime reporting program.

CHAPTER 7
MISSING CHILDREN INFORMATION CLEARINGHOUSE

Section

§52-31. Missing Children Information Clearinghouse established.

The Superintendent shall establish, organize, equip, staff and maintain within the Department of State Police a Missing Children Information Clearinghouse as a central repository of information regarding missing children. Such information shall be collected, processed, maintained and disseminated by the Clearinghouse as accurately and completely as possible to assist in the location of missing children.

§52-31.1. Superintendent to establish network.

The Superintendent of State Police shall establish a network to implement reports of the disappearance of children by local law-enforcement agencies to local school division superintendents and the State Registrar of Vital Records. The network shall be designed to establish cooperative arrangements between local law-enforcement agencies and local school divisions concerning reports of missing children and notices to law-enforcement agencies of requests for copies of the cumulative records and birth certificates of missing children. The network shall also establish a mechanism for reporting the identities of all missing children to the State Registrar of Vital Records.

§52-32. Definitions.

As used in this chapter, unless the context requires otherwise or it is otherwise specifically provided:

"Missing child" means any person who is under the age of eighteen years, whose temporary or permanent residence is in Virginia, or is believed to be in Virginia, whose whereabouts are unknown to any parent, guardian, legal custodian or other person standing in loco parentis of the child, and who has been reported as missing to a law-enforcement agency within the Commonwealth.

"Missing child report" means a report prepared in a format prescribed by the Superintendent for use by law-enforcement agencies to report missing child information to the Missing Children Information Clearinghouse.

§52-33. Powers and duties of Clearinghouse.

The Clearinghouse shall have the following powers and duties:

1. To maintain a centralized file for the exchange of information on missing children within the Commonwealth. The Clearinghouse shall accept a missing child report from any law-enforcement officer as defined in §9-169. Any parent, guardian, legal custodian or other person standing in loco parentis of a missing child may contact the Clearinghouse to verify the entry of a missing child report on such child. If the Clearinghouse is requested to verify a missing child report which has not been received, the Clearinghouse shall immediately contact the appropriate law-enforcement agency and take such measures as may be necessary to determine whether a report should be entered in the centralized file.

2. To maintain a system of intrastate communication to receive information relating to the disappearance or sighting of missing children. Such system shall be available twenty-four hours per day, seven days per week.

3. To maintain close liaison with the National Crime Information Center and the National Center for Missing and Exploited Children for the exchange of information on children suspected of interstate travel and for assistance in the operation of the Clearinghouse.

4. To circulate a monthly bulletin on missing children to the news media, all law-enforcement agencies, and every school in the Commonwealth.

5. To provide emergency flyers containing physical and situational descriptions of missing children when requested by law-enforcement agencies.

6. To provide for training of public and private organizations regarding the operation of the Clearinghouse.

7. To provide assistance to law-enforcement agencies in planning and implementing programs to fingerprint children.

§52-34. Notification required when missing child located.

Any law-enforcement officer who has reported a missing child to the Clearinghouse shall notify the Clearinghouse immediately upon determining the location of the child.

CHAPTER 8
WITNESS PROTECTION PROGRAM

§52-35. Witness protection program established.

The Superintendent of State Police may establish and maintain within the Department of State Police a witness protection program to temporarily relocate or otherwise protect witnesses and their families who may be in danger because of their cooperation with the investigation and prosecution of serious violent crimes or felony violations of §18.2-248. The Superintendent may make the services of the program available to law-enforcement and criminal justice agencies of all counties, cities, and towns, and of the Commonwealth, pursuant to regulations promulgated by the Superintendent under the Administrative Process Act. (§9-6.14:1 et seq.).

CHAPTER 9
INSURANCE FRAUD

(Added by L.1998 ch. 590, eff. 1/1/99. Repealed by L.1998 ch. 590, eff. 1/1/2003.)

§52-36. Definitions.

(Section effective only until 1/1/2003.)

As used in this chapter, the following words shall have the following meanings:

"Commission" means the State Corporation Commission.

"Insurance fraud" means any commission or attempted commission of the criminal acts and practices defined in §18.2-178 which involve any type of insurance as defined in §§38.2-110 through 38.2-122.2 and 38.2-124 through 38.2-132.

"Insurance policy" means a contract or other written instrument between an insured and insurer setting forth the obligations and responsibilities of each party.

"Insurance premium finance company" has the same meaning as specified in §38.2-4700.

"Insurance professional" means adjusters, agents, managing general agents, surplus lines brokers, reinsurance intermediaries, insurance consultants, brokers, and attorneys-in-fact.

"Insurance transaction," "insurance business," and "business of insurance" include solicitation, negotiations preliminary to execution of an insurance contract, execution of an insurance contract and the transaction of matters subsequent to execution of a contract and arising out of it, and matters arising out of any relationship among or between an insured, an insurer and a third party for which an insurance policy provides coverage.

"Insured" means any person covered by an insurance policy.

"Insurer" means any person subject to regulation pursuant to Title 38.2, 46.2, or 65.2 engaged in the business of making, or purporting to make contracts of insurance; however, this term shall not include (i) any person licensed by or subject to regulation pursuant to Chapter 18 (§38.2-1800 et seq.) of Title 38.2, (ii) title insurers subject to regulation pursuant to Chapter 46 (§38.2-4600 et seq.) of Title 38.2, (iii) continuing care providers subject to registration pursuant to Chapter 49 (§38.2-4900 et seq.) of Title 38.2, and (iv) purchasing groups authorized by Chapter 51 (§38.2-5100 et seq.) of Title 38.2.

(Added by L.1998 ch. 590; chgd. by L.2000 ch. 526, eff. 7/1/2000. Repealed by L.1998 ch. 590, eff. 1/1/2003.)

§52-37. Insurance Fraud Investigation Unit established; powers and duties of Department of State Police.

(Section effective only until 1/1/2003.)

A. There shall be established within the Department of State Police, Bureau of Criminal Investigation, the Insurance Fraud Investigation Unit. The purposes of this unit shall be to:

1. Initiate independent inquiries and conduct independent investigations when the Department has reason to believe that insurance fraud may have been or is currently being committed, and to undertake studies to determine the extent of such insurance fraud.

2. Respond to notification or complaints alleging insurance fraud generated by federal, state and local police, other law-enforcement authorities, governmental agencies or units, and any other person.

3. Review notices and reports of insurance fraud; select the incidents of suspected fraud that, in its judgment, require further detailed investigation; and conduct the investigations.

B. The Superintendent may appoint such agents as he may deem necessary to assist the Department in carrying out its powers and duties under this chapter.

(Added by L.1998 ch. 590, eff. 1/1/99. Repealed by L.1998 ch. 590, eff. 1/1/2003.)

§52-38. Access to evidence, documentation, and related materials.

(Section effective only until 1/1/2003.)

If the Department seeks evidence, documentation, and related materials located within this Commonwealth pertinent to an investigation or examination and in the possession or control of an insurer or an insurance professional, the Department may request access to the material. The person so requested shall either make the material available to the Department, or shall make the material available for inspection or examination by a designated representative of the Department.

(Added by L.1998 ch. 590, eff. 1/1/99. Repealed by L.1998 ch. 590, eff. 1/1/2003.)

§52-39. Confidentiality and immunity from service of process.

(Section effective only until 1/1/2003.)

A. Papers, records, documents, reports, materials or other evidence relative to the subject of an insurance fraud investigation or examination in the possession of the Department shall remain confidential and shall not be subject to public inspection.

B. Agents employed by the Department shall not be subject to subpoena in civil actions by any court in this Commonwealth to testify concerning any matter of which they have knowledge pursuant to a pending or continuing insurance fraud investigation or examination being conducted by the Department.

(Added by L.1998 ch. 590, eff. 1/1/99. Repealed by L.1998 ch. 590, eff. 1/1/2003.)

§52-40. Duties of insurers, their employees and insurance professionals.

(Section effective only until 1/1/2003.)

A. If any insurer, any employee thereof, or any insurance professional has knowledge of, or has reason to believe that a violation of §18.2-178 will be, is being, or has been committed, that person shall furnish and disclose any information in his possession concerning the fraudulent act to the Department, subject to any legal privilege protecting such information.

B. All applications for insurance and all claim forms provided and required by an insurer or required by law as a condition of payment of a claim shall contain a statement, permanently affixed to, or included as a part of the application or claim form, that clearly states in substance the following:

"It is a crime to knowingly provide false, incomplete or misleading information to an insurance company for the purpose of defrauding the company. Penalties include imprisonment, fines and denial of insurance benefits."

The lack of a statement required in this subsection does not constitute a defense in any criminal prosecution. The statement required by this subsection shall not be required on applications and forms relating to reinsurance.

(Added by L.1998 ch. 590, eff. 1/1/99. Repealed by L.1998 ch. 590, eff. 1/1/2003.)

§52-41. Receipt of information; immunity from liability.

(Section effective only until 1/1/2003.)

A. Any insurer providing information to an authorized representative of the Department pursuant to §52-38 or pursuant to subdivision A 6 of §38.2-613 shall have the right to request relevant information and receive, within thirty days, the information requested.

B. No cause of action in the nature of defamation, invasion of privacy, or negligence shall arise against any person furnishing information concerning any suspected, anticipated or completed criminal violation when the information is provided to or received from the Department, the National Association of Insurance Commissioners, another insurer, any federal or state governmental entity established for the purposes of detecting and preventing insurance fraud, or the National Insurance Crime Bureau.

C. No insurer, its officers or employees, insurance professional or any other person shall be subject to such cause of action for cooperating with, or furnishing evidence or information regarding any suspected criminal violation to the Department.

D. This section shall not provide immunity for those disclosing or furnishing false information with malice or willful intent to injure any person.

E. This section does not abrogate or modify in any way common law or statutory privilege or immunity heretofore enjoyed by any person or entity, nor does it authorize the Department to make public insurance company records which are proprietary in nature.

(Added by L.1998 ch. 590, eff. 1/1/99. Repealed by L.1998 ch. 590, eff. 1/1/2003.)

§52-42. Reward fund.

(Section effective only until 1/1/2003.)

The Department, in cooperation with authorized insurers and insurance professionals, may establish and operate a fund to offer monetary rewards for information sufficient to procure conviction in a court of appropriate jurisdiction of a person or persons responsible for insurance fraud. No law-enforcement officer, employee of the Commission, employee of an insurance company or any insurance professional shall be eligible to receive such reward.

(Added by L.1998 ch. 590, eff. 1/1/99. Repealed by L.1998 ch. 590, eff. 1/1/2003.)

§52-43. Reports.

(Section effective only until 1/1/2003.)

The Department shall submit an annual report to the Governor and General Assembly no later than February 15 of each year on the progress made in deterring insurance fraud. Such report shall detail (i) all expenditures and receipts of the Insurance Fraud Investigation Unit, (ii) the uses to which these funds were put, including payment of salaries and expenses, purchases of equipment and supplies, and other expenditures by type, and (iii) the results achieved as a consequence of such expenditures, including the number of notifications or inquiries received, the number of inquiries and investigations undertaken, the number of inquiries to which an investigation was not initiated, the number of arrests, the number of files presented to prosecutors, the number of prosecutions, the number of convictions and the total dollar amount of restitution resulting from the operation of the Insurance Fraud Investigation Unit.

(Added by L.1998 ch. 590, eff. 1/1/99. Repealed by L.1998 ch. 590, eff. 1/1/2003.)

§52-44. Other law-enforcement authority.

(Section effective only until 1/1/2003.)

This chapter shall not:

1. Preempt the authority or relieve the duty of any law-enforcement agencies to investigate, examine, and prosecute suspected violations of law.

2. Limit any of the powers granted elsewhere by the laws of this Commonwealth to the Commission to investigate and examine possible violations of law and to take appropriate action.

(Added by L.1998 ch. 590, eff. 1/1/99. Repealed by L.1998 ch. 590, eff. 1/1/2003.)

TITLE 54.1
PROFESSIONS AND OCCUPATIONS
(Selected Subtitle)

(See additional sections from Title 54.1 following Title 53.1 in the Related Statutes.)

SUBTITLE III
PROFESSIONS AND OCCUPATIONS REGULATED BY BOARDS WITHIN THE DEPARTMENT OF HEALTH PROFESSIONS
(Selected Chapter)

CHAPTER 34
DRUG CONTROL ACT
(Complete Chapter)

ARTICLE 1
GENERAL PROVISIONS

**Multiple Sections 54.1-3408.01 enacted.*

§54.1-3400. Citation.

This chapter may be cited as "The Drug Control Act."

§54.1-3401. Definitions.

As used in this chapter, unless the context requires a different meaning:

"Administer" means the direct application of a controlled substance, whether by injection, inhalation, ingestion or any other means, to the body of a patient or research subject by (i) a practitioner or by his authorized agent and under his direction or (ii) the patient or research subject at the direction and in the presence of the practitioner.

"Advertisement" means all representations disseminated in any manner or by any means, other than by labeling, for the purpose of inducing, or which are likely to induce, directly or indirectly, the purchase of drugs or devices.

"Agent" means an authorized person who acts on behalf of or at the direction of a manufacturer, distributor, or dispenser. It does not include a common or contract carrier, public warehouseman, or employee of the carrier or warehouseman.

"Anabolic steroid" means any drug or hormonal substance, chemically and pharmacologically related to testosterone, other than estrogens, progestins, and corticosteroids, that promotes muscle growth.

"Animal" means any nonhuman animate being endowed with the power of voluntary action.

"Automated drug dispensing system" means a mechanical or electronic system that performs operations or activities, other than compounding or administration, relating to pharmacy services, including the storage, dispensing, or distribution of drugs and the collection, control, and maintenance of all transaction information, to provide security and accountability for such drugs.

"Board" means the Board of Pharmacy.

"Change of ownership" of an existing entity permitted, registered or licensed by the Board means (i) the sale or transfer of all or substantially all of the assets of the entity or of any corporation that owns or controls the entity; (ii) the creation of a partnership by a sole proprietor, the dissolution of a partnership, or change in partnership composition; (iii) the acquisition or disposal of fifty percent or more of the outstanding shares of voting stock of a corporation owning the entity or of the parent corporation of a wholly owned subsidiary owning the entity, except that this shall not apply to any corporation the voting stock of which is actively traded on any securities exchange or in any over-the-counter market; (iv) the merger of a corporation owning the entity or of the parent corporation of a wholly-owned subsidiary owning the entity with another business or corporation; or (v) the expiration or forfeiture of a corporation's charter.

"Compound" means the taking of two or more ingredients and fabricating them into a single preparation, usually referred to as a dosage form.

"Controlled substance" means a drug, substance or immediate precursor in Schedules I through VI of this chapter. The term shall not include distilled spirits, wine, malt beverages, or tobacco as those terms are defined or used in Title 3.1 or Title 4.1.

"DEA" means the Drug Enforcement Administration, United States Department of Justice, or its successor agency.

"Deliver" or "delivery" means the actual, constructive, or attempted transfer of any item regulated by this chapter, whether or not there exists an agency relationship.

"Device" means instruments, apparatus, and contrivances, including their components, parts and accessories, intended for use in the diagnosis, cure, mitigation, treatment, or prevention of disease in man or animals or to affect the structure or any function of the body of man or animals.

"Dialysis care technician" means an unlicensed individual who, under the supervision of a licensed practitioner of medicine or a registered nurse, assists in the care of patients undergoing renal dialysis treatments in a Medicare-certified renal dialysis facility.

"Dialysis solution" means either the commercially available, unopened, sterile solutions whose purpose is to be instilled into the peritoneal cavity during the medical procedure known as peritoneal dialysis, or commercially available solutions whose purpose is to be used in the performance of hemodialysis not to include any solutions administered to the patient intravenously.

"Dispense" means to deliver a drug to an ultimate user or research subject by or pursuant to the lawful order of a practitioner, including the prescribing and administering, packaging, labeling or compounding necessary to prepare the substance for that delivery.

"Dispenser" means a practitioner who dispenses.

"Distribute" means to deliver other than by administering or dispensing a controlled substance.

"Distributor" means a person who distributes.

"Drug" means (i) articles or substances recognized in the official United States Pharmacopoeia National Formulary or official Homeopathic Pharmacopoeia of the United States, or any supplement to any of them; (ii) articles or substances intended for use in the diagnosis, cure, mitigation, treatment or prevention of disease in man or animals; (iii) articles or substances, other than food, intended to affect the structure or any function of the body of man or animals; or (iv) articles or substances intended for use as a component of any article specified in clause (i), (ii) or (iii). "Drug" does not include devices or their components, parts or accessories.

"Electronic transmission prescription" means any prescription, other than an oral or written prescription or a prescription transmitted by facsimile machine, that is electronically transmitted directly to a pharmacy without interception or intervention from a third party from a practitioner authorized to prescribe or from one pharmacy to another pharmacy.

"Facsimile (FAX) prescription" means a written prescription or order, which is transmitted by an electronic device over telephone lines that sends the exact image to the receiving pharmacy in hard copy form.

"Hashish oil" means any oily extract containing one or more cannabinoids, but shall not include any such extract with a tetrahydrocannabinol content of less than twelve percent by weight.

"Immediate precursor" means a substance which the Board of Pharmacy has found to be and by regulation designates as being the principal compound commonly used or produced primarily for use, and which is an immediate chemical intermediary used or likely to be used in the manufacture of a controlled substance, the control of which is necessary to prevent, curtail, or limit manufacture.

"Label" means a display of written, printed or graphic matter upon the immediate container of any article. A requirement made by or under authority of this chapter that any word, statement or other information appear on the label shall not be considered to be complied with unless such word, statement or other information also appears on the outside container or wrapper, if any, of the retail package of such article, or is easily legible through the outside container or wrapper.

"Labeling" means all labels and other written, printed or graphic matter on an article or any of its containers or wrappers, or accompanying such article.

"Manufacture" means the production, preparation, propagation, compounding, conversion or processing of any item regulated by this chapter, either directly or indirectly by extraction from substances of natural origin, or independently by means of chemical synthesis, or by a combination of extraction and chemical synthesis, and includes any packaging or repackaging of the substance or labeling or relabeling of its container. This term does not include the preparing, compounding, packaging or labeling of a controlled substance by a practitioner as an incident to his administering or dispensing of a controlled substance or marijuana in the course of his professional practice, or by a practitioner, or by his authorized agent under his supervision, for the purpose of, or as an incident to, research, teaching, or chemical analysis and not for sale.

"Manufacturer" means every person who manufactures.

"Marijuana" means any part of a plant of the genus Cannabis whether growing or not, its seeds or resin; and every compound, manufacture, salt, derivative, mixture, or preparation of such plant, its seeds, or its resin. Marijuana shall not include any oily extract containing one or more cannabinoids unless such extract contains less than twelve percent of tetrahydrocannabinol by weight, nor shall marijuana include the mature stalks of such plant, fiber produced from such stalk, oil or cake made from the seeds of such plant, unless such stalks, fiber, oil or cake is combined with other parts of plants of the genus Cannabis.

"Medical equipment supplier" means any person, as defined in §1-13.19, engaged in the delivery to the ultimate consumer, pursuant to the lawful order of a practitioner, of hypodermic syringes and needles, medicinal oxygen, Schedule VI controlled devices, those Schedule VI controlled substances with no medicinal properties which are used for the operation and cleaning of medical equipment and solutions for peritoneal dialysis.

"Narcotic drug" means any of the following, whether produced directly or indirectly by extraction from substances of vegetable origin, or independently by means of chemical synthesis, or by a combination of extraction and chemical synthesis: (i) opium, opiates, and any salt, compound, derivative, or preparation of opium or opiates; (ii) any salt, compound, isomer, derivative, or preparation thereof which is chemically equivalent or identical with any of the substances referred to in clause (i), but not including the isoquinoline alkaloids of opium; (iii) opium poppy and poppy straw; (iv) coca leaves and any salt, compound, derivative, or preparation of coca leaves, and any salt, compound, isomer, derivative, or preparation thereof which is chemically equivalent or identical with any of these substances, but not including decocainized coca leaves or extraction of coca leaves which do not contain cocaine or ecgonine.

"New drug" means: (i) any drug, except a new animal drug or an animal feed bearing or containing a new animal drug, the composition of which is such that such drug is not generally recognized, among experts qualified by scientific training and experience to evaluate the safety and effectiveness of drugs, as safe and effective for use under the conditions prescribed, recommended, or suggested in the labeling, except that such a drug not so recognized shall not be deemed to be a "new drug" if at any time prior to the enactment of this chapter it was subject to the Food and Drugs Act of June 30, 1906, as amended, and if at such time its labeling contained the same representations concerning the conditions of its use; or (ii) any drug, except a new animal drug or an animal feed bearing or containing a new animal drug, the composition of which is such that such drug, as a result of investigations to determine its safety and effectiveness for use under such conditions, has become so recognized, but which has not, otherwise than in such investigations, been used to a material extent or for a material time under such conditions.

"Nuclear medicine technologist" means an individual who holds a current certification with the American Registry of Radiological Technologists or the Nuclear Medicine Technology Certification Board.

"Official compendium" means the official United States Pharmacopoeia National Formulary, official Homeopathic Pharmacopoeia of the United States, or any supplement to any of them.

"Official written order" means an order written on a form provided for that purpose by the United States Drug Enforcement Administration, under any laws of the United States making provision therefor, if such order forms are authorized and required by federal law, and if no such order form is provided then on an official form provided for that purpose by the Board of Pharmacy.

"Opiate" means any substance having an addiction-forming or addiction-sustaining liability similar to morphine or being capable of conversion into a drug having such addiction-forming or addiction-sustaining liability. It does not include, unless specifically designated as controlled under Article 4 (§54.1-3437 et seq.) of this chapter, the dextrorotatory isomer of 3-methoxy-n-methylmorphinan and its salts (dextromethorphan). It does include its racemic and levorotatory forms.

"Opium poppy" means the plant of the species Papaver somniferum L., except the seeds thereof.

"Original package" means the unbroken container or wrapping in which any drug or medicine is enclosed together with label and labeling, put up by or for the manufacturer, wholesaler, or distributor for use in the delivery or display of such article.

"Person" means both the plural and singular, as the case demands, and includes an individual, partnership, corporation, association, governmental agency, trust, or other institution or entity.

"Pharmacist-in-charge" means the person who, being licensed as a pharmacist, signs the application for a pharmacy permit and assumes full legal responsibility for the operation of the relevant pharmacy in a manner complying with the laws and regulations for the practice of pharmacy and the sale and dispensing of controlled substances; the "pharmacist-in-charge" shall personally supervise the pharmacy and the pharmacy's personnel as required by §54.1-3432.

"Poppy straw" means all parts, except the seeds, of the opium poppy, after mowing.

"Practitioner" means a physician, dentist, licensed nurse practitioner pursuant to §54.1-2957.01, licensed physician assistant pursuant to §54.1-2952.1, pharmacist pursuant to §54.1-3300, TPA-certified optometrist pursuant to Article 5 (§54.1-3222 et seq.) of Chapter 32 of this title, veterinarian, scientific investigator, or other person licensed, registered or otherwise permitted to distribute, dispense, prescribe and administer, or conduct research with respect to, a controlled substance in the course of professional practice or research in this Commonwealth.

"Prescriber" means a practitioner who is authorized pursuant to §§54.1-3303 and 54.1-3408 to issue a prescription.

"Prescription" means an order for drugs or medical supplies, written or signed or transmitted by word of mouth, telephone, telegraph or other means of communication to a pharmacist by a duly licensed physician, dentist, veterinarian or other practitioner, authorized by law to prescribe and administer such drugs or medical supplies.

"Prescription drug" means any drug required by federal law or regulation to be dispensed only pursuant to a prescription, including finished dosage forms and active ingredients subject to §503(b) of the federal Food, Drug, and Cosmetic Act.

"Production" or "produce" includes the manufacture, planting, cultivation, growing or harvesting of a controlled substance or marijuana.

"Proprietary medicine" means a completely compounded nonprescription drug in its unbroken, original package which does not contain any controlled substance or marijuana as defined in this chapter and is not in itself poisonous, and which is sold, offered, promoted or advertised directly to the general public by or under the authority of the manufacturer or primary distributor, under a trademark, trade name or other trade symbol privately owned, and the labeling of which conforms to the requirements of this chapter and applicable federal law. However, this definition shall not include a drug which is only advertised or promoted professionally to licensed practitioners, a narcotic or drug containing a narcotic, a drug which may be dispensed only upon prescription or the label of which bears substantially the statement "Warning – may be habit-forming," or a drug intended for injection.

"Radiopharmaceutical" means any drug that exhibits spontaneous disintegration of unstable nuclei with the emission of nuclear particles or photons and includes any non-radioactive reagent kit or radionuclide generator that is intended to be used in the preparation of any such substance, but does not include drugs such as carbon-containing compounds or potassium-containing salts that include trace quantities of naturally occurring radionuclides. The term also includes any biological product that is labeled with a radionuclide or intended solely to be labeled with a radionuclide.

"Sale" includes barter, exchange, or gift, or offer therefor, and each such transaction made by any person, whether as an individual, proprietor, agent, servant or employee.

"Warehouser" means any person, other than a wholesale distributor, engaged in the business of selling or otherwise distributing prescription drugs or devices to any person who is not the ultimate user or consumer. No person shall be subject to any state or local tax by reason of this definition.

"Wholesale distribution" means distribution of prescription drugs to persons other than consumers or patients, subject to the exceptions set forth in §54.1-3401.1.

"Wholesale distributor" means any person engaged in wholesale distribution of prescription drugs including, but not limited to, manufacturers; repackers; own-label distributors; private-label distributors; jobbers; brokers; warehouses, including manufacturers' and distributors' warehouses, chain drug warehouses conducting wholesale distributions, and wholesale drug warehouses; independent wholesale drug traders; and retail pharmacies conducting wholesale distributions. No person shall be subject to any state or local tax as a wholesale merchant by reason of this definition.

The words "drugs" and "devices" as used in Chapter 33 (§54.1-3300 et seq.) of this title and in this chapter shall not include surgical or dental instruments, physical therapy equipment, X–ray apparatus or glasses or lenses for the eyes.

The terms "pharmacist," "pharmacy" and "practice of pharmacy" as used in this chapter shall be defined as provided in Chapter 33 of this title unless the context requires a different meaning.

(Chgd. by L.1996 chs. 37, 152, 158, 407, 408; L.1997 chs. 20, 677, 806; L.1998 ch. 470; L.1999 chs. 661, 750; L.2000 chs. 861, 878, eff. 7/1/2000, ch. 935, eff. 4/9/2000.)

§54.1-3401.1. Practices not considered wholesale distribution.

A. Wholesale distribution, as defined in §54.1-3401, shall not include:

1. Intracompany sales, including any transaction or transfer between any division, subsidiary, parent, and/or affiliated or related company under the common ownership and control of a corporate entity;

2. The purchase or other acquisition by a hospital or other health care entity that is a member of a group purchasing organization of a drug for its own use from the group purchasing organization or from other hospitals or health care entities that are members of such organization;

3. The sale, purchase, or trade of a drug or an offer to sell, purchase, or trade a drug by a charitable organization, described in §501(c)(3) of the Internal Revenue Code of 1986, to a nonprofit affiliate of such organization to the extent otherwise permitted by law;

4. The sale, purchase, or trade of a drug or an offer to sell, purchase, or trade a drug among hospitals or other health care entities that are under common control;

5. The sale, purchase, or trade of a drug or an offer to sell, purchase, or trade a drug for emergency medical reasons;

6. The sale, purchase, or trade of a drug or an offer to sell, purchase, or trade a drug or the dispensing a drug pursuant to a prescription;

7. The distribution of drug samples by manufacturers' representatives or distributors' representatives; or

8. The sale, purchase, or trade of or the offer to sell, purchase, or trade blood and blood components intended for transfusion.

B. For the purposes of this section:

"Blood" means whole blood collected from a single donor and processed either for transfusion or further manufacturing.

"Blood component" means that part of blood separated by physical or mechanical means.

"Common control" means the power to direct or cause the direction of the management and policies of a person or an organization, whether by ownership of stock, voting rights, by contract, or otherwise.

"Drug sample" means a unit of a prescription drug that is not intended to be sold and is intended to promote the sale of the drug.

"Emergency medical reasons" includes transfers of prescription drugs by a retail pharmacy to another retail pharmacy to alleviate a temporary shortage arising from delays in or interruptions of regular distribution schedules.

§54.1-3402. Proprietor of pharmacy exempted.

This article shall not be construed to require the proprietor of a pharmacy to register as a manufacturer or distributor if the products manufactured or purchased are labeled under the name of the pharmacy and dispensed within the premises and not sold for distribution and resale outside the premises.

§54.1-3403. Chapter not applicable to economic poisons.

This chapter shall not be construed to apply (i) to poisons used for the control of insects, animal pests, weeds, fungus diseases or other substances sold for use in agricultural, horticultural or related arts and sciences when such substances which are poisons within the meaning of this chapter are sold in original unbroken packages bearing a label having plainly printed upon it the name of the contents and the word POISON and an effective antidote or (ii) to any person, persons, corporations or associations engaged in the business of selling, making, compounding or manufacturing industrial chemicals for distribution or sale at wholesale or for making, compounding or manufacturing other products.

§54.1-3404. Persons required to keep record of drugs; contents and form of record.

A. Every person manufacturing, compounding, processing, selling, dispensing or otherwise disposing of drugs in Schedules I, II, III, IV or V shall take a complete and accurate inventory of all stocks of Schedules I through V drugs on the date he first engages in business. If there are no controlled substances on hand at that time, he shall record this fact as part of the inventory. An inventory taken by use of an oral recording device shall be promptly reduced to writing and maintained in a written, typewritten or printed form. Such inventory shall be made either as of the opening of business or as of the close of business on the inventory date.

B. After the initial inventory is taken, every person described herein shall take a new inventory at least every two years of all stocks on hand of Schedules I through V drugs. The biennial inventory shall be taken on any date which is within two years of the previous biennial inventory.

C. The record of such drugs received shall in every case show the date of receipt, the name and address of the person from whom received and the kind and quantity of drugs received, the kind and quantity of drugs produced or removed from process of manufacture, and the date of such production or removal from process of manufacture. The record shall in every case show the proportion of morphine, cocaine, or ecgonine contained in or producible from crude opium or coca leaves received or produced.

D. The record of all drugs sold, administered, dispensed, or otherwise disposed of, shall show the date of selling, administering, or dispensing, the name and address of the person to whom or for whose use, or the owner and species of animal for which the drugs were sold, administered or dispensed, and the kind and quantity of drugs. Any person selling, administering, dispensing or otherwise disposing of such drugs shall make and sign such record at the time of each transaction. The keeping of a record required by or under the federal laws, containing substantially the same information as is specified above, shall constitute compliance with this section, except that every such record shall contain a detailed list of any drugs lost, destroyed or stolen, the kind and quantity of such drugs, and the date of the discovery of such loss, destruction or theft. The form of records shall be prescribed by the Board.

E. Whenever any registrant or licensee discovers a theft or any other unusual loss of any controlled substance, he shall immediately report such theft or loss to the Board. If the registrant or licensee is unable to determine the exact kind and quantity of the drug loss, he shall immediately make a complete inventory of all Schedule I through V drugs.

Within thirty days after the discovery of a loss of drugs, the registrant or licensee shall furnish the Board with a listing of the kind, quantity and strength of such drugs lost.

F. All records required pursuant to this section shall be maintained completely and accurately for two years from the date of the transaction recorded.

(Chgd. by L.1998 ch. 105, eff. 7/1/98.)

§54.1-3405. Access to and copies of records; inspections.

Every person required to prepare or obtain, and keep, records, and any carrier maintaining records with respect to any shipment containing any drug, and every person in charge or having custody of such records shall, upon request of an agent designated by the Board, permit such agent at reasonable times to have access to and copy such records.

Any agent designated by the Superintendent of the Department of State Police to conduct drug diversion investigations shall, for the purpose of such investigations, also be permitted access at reasonable times to all such records relevant to a specific investigation and be allowed to inspect and copy such records. However, agents designated by the Superintendent of the Department of State Police to conduct drug diversion investigations shall not copy and remove patient records unless such patient records are relevant to a specific investigation. Any agent designated by the Superintendent of the Department of State Police shall allow the person or carrier maintaining such records, or agent thereof, to examine any copies of records before their removal from the premises. If the agent designated by the Superintendent of State Police copies records on magnetic storage media, he will deliver a duplicate of the magnetic storage media on which the copies are stored to the person or carrier maintaining such records or an agent thereof, prior to removing the copies from the premises. If the original of any record is removed by any agent designated by the Superintendent of State Police, a receipt therefor shall be left with the person or carrier maintaining such records or an agent thereof, and a copy of the removed record shall be provided the person or carrier maintaining such records within a reasonable time thereafter.

For the purposes of verification of such records and of enforcement of this chapter, agents designated by the Board or by the Superintendent are authorized, upon presenting appropriate credentials to the owner, operator, or agent in charge, to enter, at reasonable times, any factory, warehouse, establishment, or vehicle in which any drug is held, manufactured, compounded, processed, sold, delivered, or otherwise disposed of; and to inspect, within reasonable limits and in a reasonable manner, such factory, warehouse, establishment, or vehicle, and all pertinent equipment, finished and unfinished material, containers and labeling, including records, files, papers, processes, controls, and facilities, bearing on violation of this chapter; and to inventory and obtain samples of any stock of any drugs.

If a sample of any drug is obtained, the agent making the inspection shall, upon completion of the inspection and before leaving the premises, give to the owner, operator, or agent in charge a receipt describing the sample. No inspection shall extend to financial data, sales data other than shipment data, pricing data, personnel data or research data.

Any information obtained by a designated State Police agent during an inspection under this section which constitutes evidence of a violation of any provision of this chapter shall be reported to the Department of Health Professions upon its discovery.

Any information obtained by an agent designated by the Board during an inspection under this section which constitutes evidence of a violation of Article 1 (§18.2-247 et seq.) of Chapter 7 of Title 18.2 shall be reported to the Department of State Police upon its discovery.

§54.1-3406. Records confidential.

No agent of the Board or agent designated by the Superintendent of the Department of State Police having knowledge by virtue of his office of any prescriptions, papers, records, or stocks of drugs shall divulge such knowledge, except in connection with a criminal investigation authorized by the Attorney General or attorney for the Commonwealth or with a prosecution or proceeding in court or before a regulatory board or officer, to which investigation, prosecution or proceeding the person to whom such prescriptions, papers or records relate is a subject or party. This section shall not be construed to prohibit the Board president or his designee and the Director of the Department of Health Professions from discharging their duties as provided in this title.

§54.1-3407. Analysis of controlled substances.

A licensed physician or pharmacist may receive controlled substances from or on behalf of a patient for qualitative or quantitative analysis purposes only, without an official order form, if within twenty-four hours of its receipt the physician or pharmacist mails or delivers the entire sample to a laboratory operated by the Commonwealth and designated by the Board to receive such substances. If the sample is mailed, it shall be sent by registered or certified mail, postage prepaid, with return receipt requested. If personally delivered, a receipt shall be obtained from such laboratory. All receipts or returns shall be kept on file for three years and shall be available for inspection by the Board at any reasonable time.

§54.1-3408. Professional use by practitioners.

A practitioner of medicine, osteopathy, podiatry, dentistry, or veterinary medicine or a licensed nurse practitioner pursuant to §54.1-2957.01, a licensed physician assistant pursuant to §54.1-2952.1, or a TPA-certified optometrist pursuant to Article 5 (§54.1-3222 et seq.) of Chapter 32 of this title shall only prescribe, dispense, or administer controlled substances in good faith for medicinal or therapeutic purposes within the course of his professional practice.

The prescribing practitioner's order may be on a written prescription or pursuant to an oral prescription as authorized by this chapter. The prescriber may administer drugs and devices, or he may cause them to be administered by a nurse, physician assistant or intern under his direction and supervision, or he may prescribe and cause drugs and devices to be administered to patients in state-owned or state-operated hospitals or facilities licensed as hospitals by the Board of Health or psychiatric hospitals licensed by the State Mental Health, Mental Retardation and Substance Abuse Services Board by other persons who have been trained properly to administer drugs and who administer drugs only under the control and supervision of the prescriber or a pharmacist or a prescriber may cause drugs and devices to be administered to patients by emergency medical services personnel who have been certified and authorized to administer such drugs and devices pursuant to Board of Health regulations governing emergency medical services and who are acting within the scope of such certification. A prescriber may authorize a certified respiratory therapy practitioner as defined in §54.1-2954 to administer by inhalation controlled substances used in inhalation or respiratory therapy.

Pursuant to an oral or written order or standing protocol, the prescriber, who is authorized by state or federal law to possess and administer radiopharmaceuticals in the scope of his practice, may authorize a nuclear medicine technologist to administer, under his supervision, radiopharmaceuticals used in the diagnosis or treatment of disease.

Pursuant to an oral or written order or standing protocol issued by the prescriber within the course of his professional practice, such prescriber may authorize registered nurses and licensed practical nurses to possess (i) epinephrine for administration in treatment of emergency medical conditions and (ii) heparin and sterile normal saline to use for the maintenance of intravenous access lines.

Pursuant to a written order or standing protocol issued by the prescriber within the course of his professional practice, such prescriber may authorize, with the consent of the parents as defined in §22.1-1, an employee of a school board who is trained in the administration of insulin and glucagon to assist with the administration of insulin or administer glucagon to a student diagnosed as having diabetes and who requires insulin injections during the school day or for whom glucagon has been prescribed for the emergency treatment of hypoglycemia. Such authorization shall only be effective when a licensed nurse, nurse practitioner, physician or physician assistant is not present to perform the administration of the medication.

A prescriber may authorize, pursuant to a protocol approved by the Board of Nursing, the administration of vaccines to adults for immunization, when a practitioner with prescriptive authority is not physically present, (i) by licensed pharmacists, (ii) by registered nurses, or (iii) licensed practical nurses under the immediate and direct supervision of a registered nurse. A prescriber acting on behalf of and in accordance with established protocols of the Department of Health may authorize the administration of vaccines to any person by a pharmacist or nurse when the prescriber is not physically present.

A dentist may cause Schedule VI topical drugs to be administered under his direction and supervision by either a dental hygienist or by an authorized agent of the dentist.

This section shall not prevent the administration of drugs by a person who has satisfactorily completed a training program for this purpose approved by the Board of Nursing and who administers such drugs in accordance with a physician's instructions pertaining to dosage, frequency, and manner of administration, and in accordance with regulations promulgated by the Board of Pharmacy relating to security and record keeping, when the drugs administered would be normally self-administered by (i) a resident of a facility licensed or certified by the State Mental Health, Mental Retardation and Substance Abuse Services Board; (ii) a resident of any adult care residence which is licensed by the Department of Social Services; (iii) a resident of the Virginia Rehabilitation Center for the Blind and [Visually] *Vision* Impaired; (iv) a resident of a facility approved by the Board or Department of Juvenile Justice for the placement of children in need of services or delinquent or alleged delinquent youth; (v) a program participant of an adult day-care center licensed by the Department of Social Services; or (vi) a resident of any facility authorized or operated by a state or local government whose primary purpose is not to provide health care services.

In addition, this section shall not prevent the administration of drugs by a person who administers such drugs in accordance with a physician's instructions pertaining to dosage, frequency, and manner of administration and with written authorization of a parent, and in accordance with school board regulations relating to training, security and record keeping, when the drugs administered would be normally self-administered by a student of a Virginia public school. Training for such persons shall be accomplished through a program approved by the local school boards, in consultation with the local departments of health.

Nothing in this title shall prohibit the administration of normally self-administered oral or topical drugs by unlicensed individuals to a person in his private residence.

This section shall not interfere with any prescriber issuing prescriptions in compliance with his authority and scope of practice and the provisions of this section to a Board agent for use pursuant to subsection G of §18.2-258.1. Such prescriptions issued by such prescriber shall be deemed to be valid prescriptions.

Nothing in this title shall prevent dialysis care technicians, in the ordinary course of their duties in a Medicare-certified renal dialysis facility, from administering heparin, topical needle site anesthetics, dialysis solutions and sterile normal saline solution for the purpose of facilitating renal dialysis treatment, provided such administration of medications occurs under the orders of a licensed physician and under the immediate and direct supervision of a licensed registered nurse. The dialysis care technician administering the medications must have been trained in renal dialysis practices and procedures by a licensed nurse, and must have demonstrated competency as evidenced by satisfactory completion of a training program in accordance with the Core Curriculum for the Dialysis Technician, also known as the Amgen Core Curriculum, or a comparable education and training curriculum.

(Chgd. by L.1995 chs. 88, 529; L.1996 chs. 152, 158, 183, 406, 408, 490; L.1997 chs. 272, 566, 806, 906; L.1998 ch. 112; L.1999 ch. 570; L.2000 ch. 135, eff. 7/1/2000, ch. 498, eff. 1/1/2001, chs. 861, 881, eff. 7/1/2000, ch. 935, eff. 4/9/2000. Matter in brackets eff. only until 1/1/2001. Matter in italics eff. 1/1/2001.)

§54.1-3408.01. Requirements for prescriptions.

(As added by L.2000 ch. 135. See other Section 54.1-3408.01 below.)

A. The written prescription referred to in §54.1-3408 shall be written with ink or individually typed or printed. The prescription shall contain the name, address, and telephone number of the prescriber. A prescription for a controlled substance other than one controlled in Schedule VI shall also contain the federal controlled substances registration number assigned to the prescriber. The prescriber's information shall be either preprinted upon the prescription blank, electronically printed, typewritten, rubber stamped, or printed by hand.

The written prescription shall contain the first and last name of the patient for whom the drug is prescribed. The address of the patient shall either be placed upon the written prescription by the prescriber or his agent, or by the dispenser of the prescription. If not otherwise prohibited by law, the dispenser may record the address of the patient in an electronic prescription dispensing record for that patient in lieu of recording it on the prescription. Each written prescription shall be dated as of, and signed by the prescriber on, the day when issued. The prescription may be prepared by an agent for the prescriber's signature.

This section shall not prohibit a prescriber from using preprinted prescriptions for drugs classified in Schedule VI if all requirements concerning dates, signatures, and other information specified above are otherwise fulfilled.

No written prescription order form shall include more than one prescription. However, this provision does not apply to the entry of any order on a patient's chart in any hospital or any long-term care facility, as defined in Board regulations, in Virginia or to a prescription ordered through a pharmacy operated by or for the Department of Corrections or the Department of Juvenile Justice, the central pharmacy of the Department of Health, or the central outpatient pharmacy operated by the Department of Mental Health, Mental Retardation and Substance Abuse Services.

B. Pursuant to §32.1-87, any prescription form shall include two boxes, one labeled "Voluntary Formulary Permitted" and the other labeled "Dispense As Written." A prescriber may indicate his permission for the dispensing of a drug product included in the Formulary upon signing a prescription form and marking the box labeled "Voluntary Formulary Permitted." A Voluntary Formulary product shall be dispensed if the prescriber fails to indicate his preference. If no Voluntary Formulary product is immediately available or if the patient objects to the dispensing of a generic drug, the pharmacist may dispense a brand name drug. Printed prescription forms shall provide:

"☐ Dispense As Written
☐ Voluntary Formulary Permitted

....
Signature of prescriber

If neither box is marked, a Voluntary Formulary product must be dispensed."

C. Prescribers' orders, whether written as chart orders or prescriptions, for Schedules II, III, IV and V controlled drugs to be administered to (i) patients or residents of long-term care facilities served by a Virginia pharmacy from a remote location or (ii) patients receiving parenteral, intravenous, intramuscular, subcutaneous or intraspinal infusion therapy and served by a home infusion pharmacy from a remote location, may be transmitted to that remote pharmacy by an electronic communications device over telephone lines which send the exact image to the receiver in hard copy form, and such facsimile copy shall be treated as a valid original prescription order. If the order is for a radiopharmaceutical, a physician authorized by state or federal law to possess and administer medical radioactive materials may authorize a nuclear medicine technologist to transmit a prescriber's verbal or written orders for radiopharmaceuticals.

D. The oral prescription referred to in subsection A of this section shall be transmitted to the pharmacy of the patient's choice by the prescriber or his authorized agent. For the purposes of this section, an authorized agent of the prescriber shall be an employee of the prescriber who is under his immediate and personal supervision, or if not an employee, an individual who holds a valid license allowing the administration or dispensing of drugs and who is specifically directed by the prescriber.

(Added by L.2000 ch. 135, eff. 7/1/2000, incorporating changes to Section 54.1-3408 by L.2000 ch. 861, eff. 7/1/2000.)

§54.1-3408.01. Transmission of prescriptions.

(As added by L.2000 ch. 878. See other Section 54.1-3408.01 above.)

Consistent with federal law and in accordance with regulations promulgated by the Board, prescriptions may be transmitted to a pharmacy by electronic transmission or by facsimile machine and shall be treated as valid original prescriptions.

(Added by L.2000 ch. 878, eff. 7/1/2000.)

§54.1-3408.1. Prescription in excess of recommended dosage in certain cases.

In the case of a patient with intractable pain, a physician may prescribe a dosage in excess of the recommended dosage of a pain relieving agent if he certifies the medical necessity for such excess dosage in the patient's medical record. Any person who prescribes, dispenses or administers an excess dosage in accordance with this section shall not be in violation of the provisions of this title because of such excess dosage, if such excess dosage is prescribed, dispensed or administered in good faith for accepted medicinal or therapeutic purposes.

Nothing in this section shall be construed to grant any person immunity from investigation or disciplinary action based on the prescription, dispensing or administration of an excess dosage in violation of this title.

(Chgd. by L.1995 ch. 277, eff. 7/1/95.)

§54.1-3409. Professional use by veterinarians.

A veterinarian may not prescribe controlled substances for human use and shall only prescribe, dispense or administer a controlled substance in good faith for use by animals within the course of his professional practice. He may prescribe, on a written prescription or on oral prescription as authorized by §54.1-3410. He may administer drugs, and he may cause them to be administered by an assistant or orderly under his direction and supervision. Such a prescription shall be dated and signed by the person prescribing on the day when issued, and shall bear the full name and address of the owner of the animal, and the species of the animal for which the drug is prescribed and the full name, address and registry number, under the federal laws of the person prescribing, if he is required by those laws to be so registered.

§54.1-3410. When pharmacist may sell and dispense drugs.

A. A pharmacist, acting in good faith, may sell and dispense drugs and devices to any person pursuant to a prescription of a prescriber as follows:

1. A drug listed in Schedule II shall be dispensed only upon receipt of a written prescription that is properly executed, dated and signed by the person prescribing on the day when issued and bearing the full name and address of the patient for whom, or of the owner of the animal for which, the drug is dispensed, and the full name, address, and registry number under the federal laws of the person prescribing, if he is required by those laws to be so registered. If the prescription is for an animal, it shall state the species of animal for which the drug is prescribed;

2. In emergency situations, Schedule II drugs may be dispensed pursuant to an oral prescription in accordance with the Board's regulations;

3. Whenever a pharmacist dispenses any drug listed within Schedule II on a prescription issued by a prescriber, he shall affix to the container in which such drug is dispensed, a label showing the prescription serial number or name of the drug; the date of initial filling; his name and address, or the name and address of the pharmacy; the name of the patient or, if the patient is an animal, the name of the owner of the animal and the species of the animal; the name of the prescriber by whom the prescription was written; and such directions as may be stated on the prescription.

B. A drug controlled by Schedules III through VI or a device controlled by Schedule VI shall be dispensed upon receipt of a written or oral prescription as follows:

1. If the prescription is written, it shall be properly executed, dated and signed by the person prescribing on the day when issued and bear the full name and address of the patient for whom, or of the owner of the animal for which, the drug is dispensed, and the full name and address of the person

prescribing. If the prescription is for an animal, it shall state the species of animal for which the drug is prescribed.

2. If the prescription is oral, the prescriber shall furnish the pharmacist with the same information as is required by law in the case of a written prescription for drugs and devices, except for the signature of the prescriber.

A pharmacist who dispenses a Schedule III through VI drug or device shall label the drug or device as required in subdivision A 3 of this section.

C. A drug controlled by Schedule VI may be refilled without authorization from the prescriber if, after reasonable effort has been made to contact him, the pharmacist ascertains that he is not available and the patient's health would be in imminent danger without the benefits of the drug. The refill shall be made in compliance with the provisions of §54.1-3411.

If the written or oral prescription is for a Schedule VI drug or device and does not contain the address or registry number of the prescriber, or the address of the patient, the pharmacist need not reduce such information to writing if such information is readily retrievable within the pharmacy.

D. Pursuant to authorization of the prescriber, an agent of the prescriber on his behalf may orally transmit a prescription for a drug classified in Schedules III through VI if, in such cases, the written record of the prescription required by this subsection specifies the full name of the agent of the prescriber transmitting the prescription.

(Chgd. by L.1996 ch. 408, eff. 7/1/96.)

§54.1-3410.1. Requirements for radiopharmaceuticals.

A. A pharmacist who is authorized by the Board and acting in good faith, may sell and dispense radiopharmaceuticals pursuant to the order of a physician who is authorized by state or federal law to possess and administer radiopharmaceuticals for the treatment or diagnosis of disease.

B. When an authorized nuclear pharmacist dispenses a radioactive medical material, he shall assure that the outer container (shield) of the radiopharmaceutical shall bear the following information:

1. The name and address of the nuclear pharmacy;
2. The name of the prescriber (authorized user);
3. The date of dispensing;
4. The serial number assigned to the radiopharmaceutical order;
5. The standard radiation symbol;
6. The name of the diagnostic procedure;
7. The words "Caution: Radioactive Material";
8. The name of the radionuclide;
9. The amount of radioactivity and the calibration date and time;
10. The expiration date and time;
11. In the case of a diagnostic radiopharmaceutical, the patient's name or the words "Per Physician's Order"; and
12. In the case of a therapeutic radiopharmaceutical, the patient's name.

C. Orders for radiopharmaceuticals, whether written or verbal, shall include at least the following information:

1. The name of the institution or facility and the name of the person transmitting the order;
2. The date that the radiopharmaceutical will be needed and the calibration time;
3. The name or generally recognized and accepted abbreviation of the radiopharmaceutical;
4. The dose or activity of the radiopharmaceutical at the time of calibration; and
5. In the case of a therapeutic radiopharmaceutical or a radiopharmaceutical blood product, the name of the patient shall be obtained prior to dispensing.

(Added by L.2000 ch. 861, eff. 7/1/2000.)

§54.1-3411. When prescriptions may be refilled.

Prescriptions may be refilled as follows:

1. A prescription for a drug in Schedule II may not be refilled.

2. A prescription for a drug in Schedules III or IV may not be filled or refilled more than six months after the date on which such prescription was issued and no such prescription may be authorized to be refilled, nor be refilled, more than five times, except that any prescription for such a drug after six months from the date of issue, or after being refilled five times, may be renewed by the prescriber issuing it either in writing, or orally, if promptly reduced to writing and filed by the pharmacist filling it.

3. A prescription in Schedule VI may not be refilled, unless authorized by the prescriber either on the face of the original prescription or orally by the prescriber except as provided in subdivision 4 of this section. Oral instructions shall be reduced promptly to writing by the pharmacist and filed on or with the original prescription.

4. A prescription for a drug controlled by Schedule VI may be refilled without authorization from the prescriber if reasonable effort has been made to communicate with the prescriber, and the pharmacist has determined that he is not available and the patient's health would be in imminent danger without the benefits of the drug. The pharmacist shall inform the patient of the prescriber's unavailability and that the refill is being made without his authorization. The pharmacist shall promptly inform the prescriber of such refill. The date and quantity of the refill, the prescriber's unavailability and the rationale for the refill shall be noted on the reverse side of the prescription.

(Chgd. by L.1996 ch. 408, eff. 7/1/96.)

§54.1-3412. Date of dispensing; initials of pharmacist; automated data processing system.

The pharmacist dispensing any prescription shall record the date of dispensing and his initials on the prescription or in an automated data processing system used for the storage and retrieval of dispensing information for prescriptions pursuant to regulations promulgated by the Board.

§54.1-3413. Manufacturing and administering Schedule I drugs.

It shall be lawful for a person to manufacture, and for a practitioner to administer, Schedule I drugs if:

1. The manufacturer and practitioner are expressly authorized to engage in such activities by the Attorney General of the United States, or pursuant to the federal Food, Drug and Cosmetic Act;
2. The manufacturer or dispenser is registered under all appropriate provisions of this chapter;
3. Any Schedule I drug so manufactured is sold or furnished on an official written order to a practitioner or other authorized person only; and
4. The manufacturer and practitioner comply with all other requirements of this chapter.

§54.1-3414. Official orders for Schedule II drugs.

An official written order for any Schedule II drug shall be signed by the purchasing licensee or by his agent. The original shall be presented to the person who supplies the drug or drugs. If such person accepts the order, each party to the transaction shall preserve his copy of the order for two years in such a way as to be readily accessible for inspection by any public officer or employee engaged in the enforcement of this chapter. It shall be deemed a compliance with this section if the parties to the transaction have complied with the federal laws respecting the requirements governing the use of order forms.

§54.1-3415. Distribution of drugs in Schedules II through VI by manufacturers and wholesalers.

A. A permitted manufacturer or wholesaler may distribute Schedule II drugs to any of the following persons, but only on official written orders:

1. To a manufacturer or wholesaler who has been issued permits pursuant to this chapter;
2. To a licensed pharmacist, permitted pharmacy or a licensed practitioner of medicine, osteopathy, podiatry, dentistry or veterinary medicine;
3. To a person who has been issued a controlled substance registration certificate pursuant to §54.1-3422, if the certificate of such person authorizes such purchase;
4. On a special written order accompanied by a certificate of exemption, as required by the federal laws, to a person in the employ of the United States government or of any state, territorial, district, county, municipal, or insular government, purchasing, receiving or possessing drugs by reason of his official duties;
5. To a master of a ship or a person in charge of any aircraft upon which no physician is regularly employed, for the actual medical needs of persons on board such ship or aircraft when not in port. However, such drugs shall be sold to a master of such ship or person in charge of such aircraft pursuant to a special order form approved by a commissioned medical officer or acting assistant surgeon of the United States Public Health Service; and
6. To a person in a foreign country in compliance with the provisions of the relevant federal laws.

B. A permitted manufacturer or wholesaler may distribute drugs classified in Schedule III through Schedule VI and devices to all persons listed in subsection A of this section without an official written order. However, this section shall not be construed to prohibit the distribution of a Schedule VI drug or device to any person who is otherwise authorized by law to administer, prescribe or dispense such drug or device.
(Chgd. by L.1998 ch. 490, eff. 7/1/98.)

§54.1-3416. No prescription for preparations listed pursuant to Schedule V.

A preparation listed pursuant to Schedule V may be dispensed without a prescription if:

1. The preparation is dispensed only by a pharmacist directly to the person requesting the preparation;
2. The preparation is dispensed only to a person who is at least eighteen years of age;
3. The pharmacist requires the person requesting the preparation to furnish suitable identification including proof of age when appropriate;
4. The pharmacist does not dispense to any one person, or for the use of any one person or animal, any narcotic drug preparation or preparations, when he knows, or can by reasonable diligence ascertain, that such dispensing will provide the person to whom or for whose use, or the owner of the animal for the use of which, such preparation is dispensed, within 48 consecutive hours, with more than 200 milligrams of opium, or more than 270 milligrams of codeine, or more than 130 milligrams of dihydrocodeinone, or more than 65 milligrams of ethylmorphine, or more than $32\frac{5}{10}$ milligrams of diphenoxylate. In dispensing such a narcotic drug preparation, the pharmacist shall exercise professional discretion to ensure that the preparation is being dispensed for medical purposes only.

Any pharmacist shall, at the time of dispensing, make and keep a record showing the date of dispensing, the name and quantity of the preparation, the name and address of the person to whom the preparation is dispensed, and enter his initials thereon. Such records shall be maintained as set forth in §54.1-3404 and the regulations of the Board.

§54.1-3417. Disposing of stocks of Schedules II through V drugs.

The owner of any stocks of drugs included in Schedules II through V obtained in compliance with this chapter, upon discontinuance of dealing in such drugs, may dispose of such stocks only on an official written order as follows:

1. A pharmacy or practitioner or an agent or agents of a pharmacy or practitioner under specific written authorization from the owner of such pharmacy or such practitioner, may dispose of such stocks to a manufacturer or wholesaler holding a valid license to deal in such drugs, or to another pharmacy or practitioner.
2. A manufacturer or wholesaler may dispose of such stocks only to a manufacturer or wholesaler holding a valid permit to deal in such drugs.

§54.1-3418. Sale of aqueous or oleaginous solutions.

A pharmacist, only upon an official written order, may sell to a physician, dentist, or veterinarian, in quantities not exceeding one ounce at any one time, aqueous or oleaginous solutions compounded by the pharmacist, of which the content of narcotic drugs does not exceed a proportion greater than twenty percent of the complete solution, to be used for medical purposes.

§54.1-3419. Dispensing of insulin preparations.

Any insulin preparation shall be dispensed only by or under the supervision of a licensed pharmacist.

§54.1-3420. Distribution of certain drugs; written request or confirmation of receipt.

No manufacturer or distributor of controlled substances shall distribute or dispense any substance listed on Schedules II through V to any person, whether a practitioner of the healing arts or some other profession, except with the written request or confirmation of receipt of the practitioner. Such request or confirmation shall be maintained as required by this chapter.

Subject to the foregoing provisions, no person shall be prohibited from distributing controlled substances listed on Schedules II through V for charitable uses or for use in research or investigations.

§54.1-3420.1. Identification required for filling prescriptions.

Before dispensing any drug listed on Schedules II through V, a pharmacist may require proof of identity from any patient presenting a prescription or requesting a refill of a prescription.

§54.1-3420.2. Delivery of prescription drug order.

Whenever any pharmacy permitted to operate in this Commonwealth or nonresident pharmacy registered to conduct business in the Commonwealth delivers a prescription drug order by mail, common carrier, or delivery service, when the drug order is not personally hand delivered directly, to the patient or his agent at the person's residence or other designated location, the following conditions shall be required:

1. Written notice shall be placed in each shipment alerting the consumer that under certain circumstances chemical degradation of drugs may occur; and
2. Written notice shall be placed in each shipment providing a toll-free or local consumer access telephone number which is designed to respond to consumer questions pertaining to chemical degradation of drugs.

(Added by L.1998 ch. 597, eff. 7/1/98.)

§54.1-3421. New drugs.

A. No person shall sell, deliver, offer for sale, hold for sale or give away any new drug unless an application with respect to the drug has been approved and the approval has not been withdrawn under §505 of the federal Food, Drug, and Cosmetic Act (21 U.S.C. §355).

B. This section shall not apply to a drug subject to the federal act intended solely for investigational use and for which a notice of claimed investigational exemption for a new drug has been filed with the U.S. Food and Drug Administration in accordance with 21 C.F.R. Part 312.

(Chgd. by L.2000 ch. 135, eff. 7/1/2000.)

§54.1-3422. Controlled substances registration certificate required in addition to other requirements; exemptions.

A. Every person who manufactures, distributes or dispenses any substance which is controlled in Schedules I through V or who proposes to engage in the manufacture, distribution or dispensing of any such controlled substance except permitted pharmacies, those persons who are licensed pharmacists, and those persons who are licensed practitioners of medicine, osteopathy, podiatry, dentistry, or veterinary medicine shall obtain annually a controlled substances registration certificate issued by the Board. This registration shall be in addition to other licensing or permitting requirements enumerated in this chapter or otherwise required by law.

B. Registration under this section and under all other applicable registration requirements shall entitle the registrant to possess, manufacture, distribute, dispense, or conduct research with those substances to the extent authorized by this registration and in conformity with the other provisions of this chapter.

C. The following persons need not register and may possess controlled substances listed on Schedules I through VI:

1. An agent or employee of any holder of a controlled substance registration certificate or of any practitioner listed in subsection A of this section as exempt from the requirement for registration, if such agent or employee is acting in the usual course of his business or employment;

2. A common or contract carrier or warehouseman, or his employee, whose possession is in the usual course of business or employment; or

3. An ultimate user or a person in possession of any controlled substance pursuant to a lawful order of a prescriber or in lawful possession of a Schedule V substance.

D. A separate registration is required at each principal place of business or professional practice where the applicant manufactures, distributes, or dispenses controlled substances.

(Chgd. by L.1996 chs. 408, 468, 496; L.1998 ch. 490, eff. 7/1/98.)

§54.1-3423. Board to issue registration unless inconsistent with public interest; authorization to conduct research; application and fees.

A. The Board shall register an applicant to manufacture or distribute controlled substances included in Schedules I through V unless it determines that the issuance of that registration would be inconsistent with the public interest. In determining the public interest, the Board shall consider the following factors:

1. Maintenance of effective controls against diversion of controlled substances into other than legitimate medical, scientific, or industrial channels;

2. Compliance with applicable state and local law;

3. Any convictions of the applicant under any federal and state laws relating to any controlled substance;

4. Past experience in the manufacture or distribution of controlled substances, and the existence in the applicant's establishment of effective controls against diversion;

5. Furnishing by the applicant of false or fraudulent material in any application filed under this chapter;

6. Suspension or revocation of the applicant's federal registration to manufacture, distribute, or dispense controlled substances as authorized by federal law; and

7. Any other factors relevant to and consistent with the public health and safety.

B. Registration under subsection A does not entitle a registrant to manufacture and distribute controlled substances in Schedule I or II other than those specified in the registration.

C. Practitioners must be registered to conduct research with controlled substances in Schedules II through VI. Practitioners registered under federal law to conduct research with Schedule I substances may conduct research with Schedule I substances within this Commonwealth upon furnishing the evidence of that federal registration.

D. The Board may register other persons or entities to possess controlled substances listed on Schedules II through VI upon a determination that (i) there is a documented need, (ii) the issuance of the registration is consistent with the public interest, (iii) the possession and subsequent use of the controlled substances complies with applicable state and federal laws and regulations, and (iv) the subsequent storage, use, and recordkeeping of the controlled substances will be under the general supervision of a licensed pharmacist, practitioner of medicine, osteopathy, podiatry, dentistry or veterinary medicine as specified in the Board's regulations. The Board shall consider, at a minimum, the factors listed in subsection A of this section in determining whether the registration shall be issued. Notwithstanding the exceptions listed in §54.1-3422 A, the Board may mandate a controlled substances registration for sites maintaining certain types and quantities of Schedules II through VI controlled substances as it may specify in its regulations. The Board shall promulgate regulations related to requirements or criteria for the issuance of such controlled substances registration, storage, security, supervision, and recordkeeping. The first such regulations shall be promulgated within 280 days of the enactment of this provision.

E. Applications for controlled substances registration certificates and renewals thereof shall be made on a form prescribed by the Board and such applications shall be accompanied by a fee in an amount to be determined by the Board.

F. Upon (i) any change in ownership or control of a business, (ii) any change of location of the controlled substances stock, (iii) the termination of authority by or of the person named as the responsible party on a controlled substances registration, or (iv) a change in the supervising practitioner, if applicable, the registrant or responsible party shall immediately surrender the registration. The registrant shall, within fourteen days following surrender of a registration, file a new application and, if applicable, name the new responsible party or supervising practitioner.

(Chgd. by L.1996 chs. 468, 496; L.1998 ch. 490, eff. 7/1/98.)

§54.1-3424. Suspension or revocation of registration, license or permit; limitation to particular controlled substance; controlled substances placed under seal; sale of perishables and forfeiture; notification to DEA.

A. A registration to manufacture, distribute, or dispense a controlled substance may be suspended or revoked by the Board upon a finding that the registrant:

1. Has furnished false or fraudulent material information in an application filed under this chapter;

2. Has been convicted of a felony under any state or federal law relating to any controlled substance;

3. Has had his federal registration to manufacture, distribute or dispense controlled substances suspended or revoked;

4. Has violated or cooperated with others in violating any provision of this chapter or regulations of the Board relating to the manufacture, distribution or dispensing of controlled substances.

B. The Board may limit revocation or suspension of a registration to the particular controlled substance with respect to which grounds for revocation or suspension exist.

C. If the Board suspends or revokes a registration, or if the license or permit of a person possessing controlled substances under an exemption in §54.1-3422 A is suspended or revoked by the issuing board, all controlled substances owned or possessed by the registrant, licensee or permittee at the time of suspension or the effective date of the revocation order may be placed under seal. No disposition may be made of substances under seal until the time for taking an appeal has elapsed or until all appeals have been concluded unless a court orders the sale of perishable substances and the deposit of the proceeds of the sale with the court. Upon a revocation order becoming final, all controlled substances shall be forfeited to the Commonwealth.

D. The Board shall promptly notify the DEA of all orders suspending or revoking registration and all forfeitures of controlled substances.

(Chgd. by L.1996 chs. 468, 496; L.1998 ch. 490, eff. 7/1/98.)

§54.1-3425. Issuance of limited permits to humane societies.

The Board may issue, upon such terms and conditions as it finds proper, to any humane society making application, a limited permit only for the purpose of buying, possessing, and using any drug approved by the State Veterinarian for the purpose of euthanizing injured, sick, homeless, and unwanted domestic pets and animals. The application and renewal thereof for such a special permit shall be accompanied by a fee as determined by the Board.

§54.1-3426. Regulations for special packaging.

A. The Board shall adopt standards for special packaging consistent with those promulgated pursuant to the federal Poison Prevention Packaging Act of 1970. The Board may exempt any drug from the requirements of special packaging and shall exempt any drug exempted pursuant to the Poison Prevention Packaging Act of 1970.

B. A prescriber or a purchaser may direct that a drug, which is subject to being dispensed in special packaging, be dispensed in other than special packaging.

(Chgd. by L.1996 ch. 408, eff. 7/1/96.)

§54.1-3427. Dispensing drugs without safety closure container.

When a pharmacist receives the request of any person that a drug or drugs for such person to be dispensed by the pharmacist not be placed in a safety closure container, the pharmacist may dispense such drug or drugs in such nonsafety closure container. The delivering pharmacist shall not be civilly liable simply by reason of dispensing a drug or drugs in such a container if the recipient signs a release covering a period of time or a single delivery, which release provides that the recipient releases the pharmacist from civil liability for not using the safety closure container, unless the pharmacist acted with willful and wanton disregard of safety.

§54.1-3428. Dissemination of information.

The Board may disseminate such information regarding drugs, devices, and cosmetics as the Board deems necessary in the interest of public health and the protection of the consumer against fraud. This section shall not be construed to prohibit the Board from collecting, reporting, and illustrating the results of its investigations.

§54.1-3429. Revocation of permit issued to manufacturer, wholesaler or distributor.

The Board may revoke a permit issued to a manufacturer, wholesaler or distributor for failure to comply with regulations promulgated pursuant to the provisions of this chapter.

§54.1-3430. Display of permit; permits nontransferable; renewal.

Permits issued under the provisions of this chapter shall be displayed in a conspicuous place in the factory or other place of business for which issued.

Permits shall not be transferable and shall be renewed annually.

§54.1-3431. Admission into evidence of certain certificates of analysis.

In any administrative hearing, a certificate of analysis of a chemist, performed in any laboratory operated by the Division of Forensic Science or authorized by such Division to conduct such analysis, when such certificate is attested by such chemist, shall be admissible as evidence. A copy of such certificate shall be delivered to the parties in interest at least seven days prior to the date fixed for the hearing.

Any certificate of analysis purporting to be signed by any chemist shall be admissible as evidence in such hearing without any proof of the seal or signature or of the official character of the chemist whose name is signed to it.

ARTICLE 2
PERMITTING OF PHARMACIES

Section

§54.1-3432. Supervision by pharmacist.

Every pharmacy shall be under the personal supervision of a pharmacist on the premises of the pharmacy.

§54.1-3433. Certain advertising and signs unlawful.

It shall be unlawful for any place of business which is not a pharmacy as defined in this chapter to advertise or to have upon it or in it as a sign the words, "pharmacy," "pharmacist," "apothecary," "drugstore," "druggist," "drugs," "medicine store,", "drug sundries," "prescriptions filled" or any like words indicating that drugs are compounded or sold or prescriptions filled. Each day during which such advertisement appears or such sign is allowed to remain upon or in such place of business shall constitute a separate offense under this section.

§54.1-3434. Permit to conduct pharmacy.

No person shall conduct a pharmacy without first obtaining a permit from the Board.

The application for such permit shall be made on a form provided by the Board and signed by a pharmacist who will be in full and actual charge of the pharmacy and who will be fully engaged in the practice of pharmacy at the location designated on the application.

The application shall (i) show the corporate name and trade name, (ii) list any pharmacist in addition to the pharmacist-in-charge practicing at the location indicated on the application, and (iii) list the hours during which the pharmacy will be open to provide pharmacy services. Any change in the hours of operation, which is expected to last more than one week, shall be reported to the Board in writing and posted, at least fourteen days prior to the anticipated change, in a conspicuous place to provide notice to the public. The Board shall promulgate regulations to provide exceptions to this prior notification.

If the owner is other than the pharmacist making the application, the type of ownership shall be indicated and shall list any partner or partners, and, if a corporation, then the corporate officers and directors. Further, if the owner is not a pharmacist, he shall not abridge the authority of the pharmacist-in-charge to exercise professional judgment relating to the dispensing of drugs in accordance with this act and Board regulations.

The permit shall be issued only to the pharmacist who signs the application as the pharmacist-in-charge and as such assumes the full responsibilities for the legal operation of the pharmacy. This permit and responsibilities shall not be construed to negate any responsibility of any pharmacist or other person.

Upon termination of practice by the pharmacist-in-charge, or upon any change in partnership composition, or upon the acquisition, as defined in Board regulations, of the existing corporation by another person or the closing of a pharmacy, the permit previously issued shall be immediately surrendered to the Board by the pharmacist-in-charge to whom it was issued, or by his legal representative, and an application for a new permit may be made in accordance with the requirements of this chapter.

The Board shall promulgate regulations (i) defining acquisition of an existing permitted, registered or licensed facility or of any corporation under which the facility is directly or indirectly organized; (ii) providing for the transfer, confidentiality, integrity, and security of the pharmacy's prescription dispensing records and other patient records, regardless of where located; and (iii) establishing a reasonable time period for designation of a new pharmacist-in-charge. At the conclusion of the time period for designation of a new pharmacist-in-charge, a pharmacy which has failed to designate a new pharmacist-in-charge shall not operate as a pharmacy nor maintain a stock of prescription drugs on the premises. The Director shall immediately notify the owner of record that the pharmacy no longer holds a valid permit and that the owner shall make provision for the proper disposition of all Schedule II through VI drugs and devices on the premises within fifteen days of receipt of this notice. At the conclusion of the fifteen-day period, the Director or his authorized agent shall seize and indefinitely secure all Schedule II through VI drugs and devices still on the premises, and notify the owner of such seizure. The Director may properly dispose of the seized drugs and devices after six months from the date of the notice of seizure if the owner has not claimed and provided for the proper disposition of the property. The Board shall assess a fee of not less than the cost of storage of said drugs upon the owner for reclaiming seized property.

The succeeding pharmacist-in-charge shall cause an inventory to be made of all Schedule I, II, III, IV and V drugs on hand. Such inventory shall be completed as of the date he becomes pharmacist-in-charge and prior to opening for business on that date.

The pharmacist to whom such permit is issued shall provide safeguards against diversion of all controlled substances.

An application for a pharmacy permit shall be accompanied by a fee determined by the Board. All permits shall expire on December 31 of each year.

Every pharmacy must be equipped so that prescriptions can be properly filled. The Board of Pharmacy shall prescribe the minimum of such professional and technical equipment and reference material which a pharmacy shall at all times possess. No permit shall be issued or continued for the conduct of a pharmacy until or unless there is compliance with the provisions of this chapter and regulations promulgated by the Board.

Each day during which a person is in violation of this section shall constitute a separate offense.

(Chgd. by L.1998 ch. 470; L.2000 ch. 135, eff. 7/1/2000.)

§54.1-3434.01. Notice of pharmacy closing; change of ownership; penalty.

A. Prior to the closing of a pharmacy for more than one week, the owner shall either (i) post a conspicuous notice at least thirty days prior to the anticipated closing or (ii) mail a notice, at least fourteen days prior to the anticipated closing, to every current pharmacy customer having refill authority. Each notice posted or mailed pursuant to this section shall indicate the date of such closing, if available, and the name of the pharmacy to which prescriptions and other required prescription dispensing records and individual patient records will be transferred unless patients indicate their preference to the contrary. The Board of Pharmacy shall promulgate regulations providing for a definition of "closing of a pharmacy" and exceptions to the requirements of this section.

B. Upon any change of ownership of a pharmacy, regardless of how such change may be effectuated, the prescription dispensing records and other patient records for at least two years immediately prior to the change of ownership, shall be transferred, in accordance with Board regulations, to the new owner in a manner to ensure the confidentiality, integrity, and security of the pharmacy's prescription dispensing records and other patient records and the continuity of pharmacy services at substantially the same level as that offered by the previous owner.

Refusing to process a request for the prescription dispensing records and other patient records tendered in accordance with law or regulation shall constitute a closing and the requirements of this section shall apply. Such refusal may constitute a violation of §54.1-111 A 9, depending on the circumstance.

(Chgd. by L.1998 ch. 470, eff. 4/14/98.)

§54.1-3434.02. Automated drug dispensing systems.

A. Hospitals licensed pursuant to Title 32.1 or Title 37.1 may use automated drug dispensing systems, as defined in §54.1-3401, upon meeting the following conditions:

1. Drugs are placed in the automated drug dispensing system in a hospital and are under the control of a pharmacy providing services to the hospital;

2. The pharmacist-in-charge of the pharmacy providing services to the hospital has established procedures for assuring the accurate stocking and proper storage of drugs in the automated drug dispensing system and for ensuring accountability for and security of all drugs utilized in the automated drug dispensing system until the time such drugs are removed from the automated drug dispensing system for administration to the patients;

3. Removal of drugs from any automated drug dispensing system for administration to patients can only be made pursuant to a valid prescription or lawful order of a prescriber;

4. Adequate security for automated drug dispensing systems is provided, as evidenced by written policies and procedures, for (i) preventing unauthorized access, (ii) complying with federal and state regulations on prescribing and dispensing controlled substances, (iii) maintaining patient confidentiality, and (iv) assuring compliance with the requirements of this section;

5. Accountability for drugs dispensed from automated drug dispensing systems is vested in the pharmacist-in-charge of a pharmacy located within the hospital or the pharmacist-in-charge of any outside pharmacy providing pharmacy services to the hospital;

6. Filling and stocking of all drugs in automated drug dispensing systems shall be performed under the direction of the pharmacist-in-charge. The task of filling and stocking of drugs into an automated drug dispensing system shall be performed by a pharmacist or the designee of the pharmacist-in-charge, who shall be an employee of the provider pharmacy and shall be properly trained in accordance with established standards set forth in a policy and procedure manual maintained by the provider pharmacy. Delegation of filling and stocking tasks to a nonpharmacist shall not be conditioned on the use of the automated drug dispensing system as a floor stock system or a patient-specific drug dispensing system; however, the filling and stocking shall be performed by a person who holds current certification by the National Pharmacy Technician Certification Board as a pharmacy technician. The pharmacist stocking and filling the automated drug dispensing system or, if a nonpharmacist is delegated this task, the pharmacist-in-charge shall be responsible for the proper and accurate stocking and filling of the automated drug dispensing system.

B. Drugs placed into and removed from automated drug dispensing systems for administration to patients shall be in the manufacturer's or distributor's sealed original packaging or in unit-dose containers packaged by the pharmacy.

C. The pharmacist-in-charge in a pharmacy located within a hospital or the pharmacist-in-charge of any outside pharmacy providing pharmacy services to a hospital shall be responsible for establishing procedures for (i) periodically inspecting and auditing automated drug dispensing systems to assure the proper storage, security, and accountability for all drugs placed in and removed from automated drug dispensing systems, and (ii) reviewing the operation and maintenance of automated drug dispensing systems. This monitoring shall be reviewed by a pharmacist while on the premises of the hospital and in accordance with the pharmacist-in-charge's procedures and the Board of Pharmacy's regulations.

D. The Board of Pharmacy shall promulgate regulations establishing minimum requirements for random periodic inspections and monthly audits of automated drug dispensing systems to assure the proper storage, security, and accountability of all drugs placed in and removed from automated drug dispensing systems and for reviewing the operation and maintenance of automated drug dispensing systems.
(Added by L.1999 ch. 750, eff. 7/1/99.)

ARTICLE 2.1
REGISTRATION OF NONRESIDENT PHARMACIES

Section

§54.1-3434.1. Nonresident pharmacies to register with Board.

A. Any pharmacy located outside this Commonwealth which ships, mails, or delivers, in any manner, Schedule II through VI drugs or devices pursuant to a prescription into this Commonwealth shall be considered a nonresident pharmacy, shall be registered with the Board, and shall disclose to the Board all of the following:

1. The location, names, and titles of all principal corporate officers and all pharmacists who are dispensing prescription drugs or devices to residents of this Commonwealth. A report containing this information shall be made on an annual basis and within thirty days after any change of office, corporate officer, or principal pharmacist.

2. That it complies with all lawful directions and requests for information from the regulatory or licensing agency of the Commonwealth in which it is licensed as well as with all requests for information made by the Board pursuant to this section. The nonresident pharmacy shall maintain, at all times, a valid unexpired license, permit, or registration to conduct the pharmacy in compliance with the laws of the state in which it is a resident. As a prerequisite to registering with the Board, the nonresident pharmacy shall submit a copy of the most recent inspection report resulting from an inspection conducted by the regulatory or licensing agency of the state in which it is located.

3. That it maintains its records of prescription drugs or dangerous drugs or devices dispensed to patients in this Commonwealth so that the records are readily retrievable from the records of other drugs dispensed and provides a copy or report of such dispensing records to the Board, its authorized agents, or any agent designated by the Superintendent of the Department of State Police upon request within seven days of receipt of a request.

4. That its pharmacists do not knowingly fill or dispense a prescription for a patient in Virginia in violation of §54.1-3303.

B. Any pharmacy subject to this section shall, during its regular hours of operation, but not less than six days per week, and for a minimum of forty hours per week, provide a toll-free telephone service to facilitate communication between patients in this Commonwealth and a pharmacist at the pharmacy who has access to the patient's records. This toll-free number shall be disclosed on a label affixed to each container of drugs dispensed to patients in this Commonwealth.

C. The registration fee shall be the fee specified for pharmacies within Virginia.
(Chgd. by L.2000 ch. 882, eff. 7/1/2000.)

§54.1-3434.2. Permit to be issued.

No out-of-state pharmacy doing business in this Commonwealth which has not obtained a permit shall conduct the business of selling or distributing drugs in Virginia without registering as a nonresident pharmacy.

Applications for a nonresident pharmacy registration, under this section, shall be made on a form furnished by the Board. The Board may require such information as it deems is necessary to carry out the purpose of the section.

The permit or nonresident pharmacy registration shall be renewed annually on or before January 1 of each year.

§54.1-3434.3. Denial, revocation, and suspension of registration.

The Board may deny, revoke, or suspend a nonresident pharmacy registration for conduct which causes serious bodily or serious psychological injury to a resident of the Commonwealth if the Board has referred the matter to the regulatory or licensing agency in the state in which the pharmacy is located and the regulatory or licensing agency fails to initiate an investigation within forty-five days of the referral.

§54.1-3434.4. Prohibited acts.

It is unlawful for any nonresident pharmacy which is not registered under this article to advertise its services in Virginia or for any person who is a resident of Virginia to advertise the pharmacy services of a nonresident pharmacy which has not registered with the Board, with the knowledge that the advertisement will or is likely to induce members of the public in the Commonwealth to use the pharmacy to dispense prescriptions.

ARTICLE 3
WHOLESALE DISTRIBUTORS AND MEDICAL EQUIPMENT SUPPLIERS

Section

§54.1-3435. License to act as wholesale distributor; renewal; fee.

It shall be unlawful for any person to engage in the wholesale distribution of prescription drugs in this Commonwealth without a valid unrevoked license issued by the Board. The applicant for licensure as a wholesale distributor, as defined in §54.1-3401, in this Commonwealth shall apply to the Board for a license, using such forms as the Board may furnish; renew such license using such forms as the Board may furnish, if granted, annually on or before January 1 of each year notify the Board within thirty days of any substantive change in the information reported on the application form previously submitted to the Board; and remit a fee as determined by the Board.

The Board may promulgate such regulations relating to the storage, handling, and distribution of prescription drugs by wholesale distributors as it deems necessary to implement this section, to prevent diversion of prescription drugs, and to protect the public.

§54.1-3435.01. Registration of nonresident wholesale distributors; renewal; fee.

A. Any person located outside this Commonwealth who engages in the wholesale distribution of prescription drugs into this Commonwealth shall be registered with the Board. The applicant for registration as a nonresident wholesale distributor shall apply to the Board using such forms as the Board may furnish; renew such registration, if granted, using such forms as the Board may furnish, annually on or before January 1 of each year; notify the Board within thirty days of any substantive change in the information previously submitted to the Board; and remit a fee, which shall be the fee specified for wholesale distributors located within the Commonwealth.

B. The nonresident wholesale distributor shall at all times maintain a valid, unexpired license, permit, or registration in the state in which it is located and shall furnish proof of such upon application and at each renewal.

C. Records of prescription drugs distributed into this Commonwealth shall be maintained in such a manner that they are readily retrievable from records of distributions into other jurisdictions and shall be provided to the Board, its authorized agent, or any agent designated by the Superintendent of the Department of State Police upon request within seven days of receipt of such request.

D. This section shall not apply to persons who distribute prescription drugs directly to a licensed wholesale distributor located within this Commonwealth.

§54.1-3435.1. Denial, revocation, and suspension of license as wholesale distributor or of registration as a nonresident wholesale distributor.

A. The license as a wholesale distributor or registration as a nonresident wholesale distributor of prescription drugs may be denied, suspended, or revoked by the Board for any of the following:

1. Any conviction of the applicant or licensee under federal or state laws relating to controlled substances, including, but not limited to, drug samples and wholesale or retail prescription drug distribution;
2. Any felony conviction of the applicant or licensee;
3. Any misdemeanor conviction of the applicant or licensee for a crime involving moral turpitude;
4. Conduct in the manufacture or distribution of prescription drugs contrary to the protection of the health, safety, and welfare of the public;
5. Fraud or deceit in any application for licensure or permit under this chapter;
6. Denial, suspension, revocation, or restriction of any federal or state license previously or currently held by the applicant or licensee for the manufacture or distribution of any drug;
7. Violations of licensing requirements under previously held licenses;
8. Failure to maintain and make available to the Board or to federal regulatory officials those records required to be maintained by wholesale distributors of prescription drugs;
9. Violations of the minimum requirements for qualifications, personnel, storage, and handling of prescription drugs and maintenance of prescription drug records as set forth in the federal Prescription Drug Marketing Act of 1987 and Part 205 of Chapter 21 of the Code of Federal Regulations; or
10. Violations of any provision of this chapter or regulations of the Board governing wholesale distributors.

B. Wholesale drug distributors shall allow the Board or its authorized agents to enter and inspect, at reasonable times and in a reasonable manner, their premises and delivery vehicles, and to audit their records and written operating procedures. Such agents shall be required to show appropriate identification prior to being permitted access to wholesale drug distributors' premises and delivery vehicles.

§54.1-3435.2. Permit to act as medical equipment supplier; storage; limitation; regulations.

A. Unless otherwise authorized by this chapter or Chapter 33 (§54.1-3300 et seq.) of this title, it shall be unlawful for any person to act as a medical equipment supplier, as defined in §54.1-3401, in this Commonwealth without a valid unrevoked permit issued by the Board. The applicant for a permit to act as a medical equipment supplier in this Commonwealth shall apply to the Board for a permit, using such form as the Board may furnish; renew such permit, if granted, annually on or before January 1 of each year; and remit a fee as determined by the Board.

B. Prescription drugs received, stored, and distributed by authority of this section shall be limited to those Schedule VI controlled substances with no medicinal properties which are used for the operation and cleaning of medical equipment and solutions for peritoneal dialysis.

C. Distribution of any Schedule VI drug or device or of any hypodermic needle or syringe, or medicinal oxygen by authority of this section is limited to delivery to the ultimate user upon lawful order by a prescriber authorized to prescribe such drugs and devices.

D. The Board may promulgate such regulations relating to the storage, handling, and distribution of prescription drugs, devices and controlled paraphernalia by medical equipment suppliers as it deems necessary to implement this section, to prevent diversion of prescription drugs and devices and controlled paraphernalia, and to protect the public.
(Chgd. by L.1996 ch. 408; L.1997 ch. 677, eff. 7/1/97.)

§54.1-3435.3. Denial, revocation, and suspension of permit as medical equipment supplier.

A. The permit as a medical equipment supplier may be denied, suspended, or revoked by the Board for any of the following:

1. Any conviction of the applicant or permit holder under federal or state laws relating to wholesale or retail distribution or delivery of prescription drugs or devices or controlled substances;
2. Any felony conviction of the applicant or permit holder;
3. Any misdemeanor conviction of the applicant or permit holder for a crime involving moral turpitude;
4. Violations of any provision of this chapter or regulations of the Board governing medical equipment suppliers;
5. Fraud or deceit in any application for licensure or permit under this chapter; or
6. Engaging in or attempting any fraud upon the consumer.

B. Medical equipment suppliers shall allow the Board or its authorized agents to enter and inspect, at reasonable times and in a reasonable manner, their premises and delivery vehicles, and to audit their records and written operating procedures.

§54.1-3435.4. Permit to act as warehouser; regulations.

A. Unless otherwise authorized by this chapter or Chapter 33 (§54.1-3300 et seq.) of this title, it shall be unlawful for any person to act as a warehouser, as defined in §54.1-3401, in this Commonwealth without a valid unrevoked permit issued by the Board. The applicant for a permit to act as a warehouser in this Commonwealth shall apply to the Board for a permit, using such form as the Board may furnish; renew such permit, if granted, annually on or before January 1 of each year; and remit a fee as determined by the Board.

B. The Board may promulgate such regulations relating to the storage, handling, and distribution of prescription drugs and devices by warehousers as it deems necessary to implement this section, to prevent diversion of prescription drugs and devices, and to protect the public.

C. Warehousers shall allow the Board or its authorized agents to enter and inspect, at reasonable times and in a reasonable manner, their premises and delivery vehicles, and to audit their records and written operating procedures. Such agents shall be required to show appropriate identification prior to being permitted access to warehousers' premises and delivery vehicles.

§54.1-3435.5. Denial, revocation, and suspension of permit as warehouser.

The permit as a warehouser may be denied, suspended, or revoked by the Board for any of the following:

1. Conduct in the distribution of prescription drugs or devices contrary to the protection of the health, safety, and welfare of the citizens of this Commonwealth; or
2. Violations of any provisions of this chapter or regulations of the Board governing warehousers.

ARTICLE 4
PERMITTING OF MANUFACTURERS

Section

§54.1-3437. Permit to manufacture drugs.

It shall be lawful to manufacture, make, produce, pack, package, repackage, relabel or prepare any drug not controlled by Schedule I after first obtaining the appropriate permit from the Board. Such permits shall be subject to the Board's regulations on sanitation, equipment, and safeguards against diversion. This provision shall not apply to manufacturers or packers of medicated feeds who manufacture or package no other drugs.
(Chgd. by L.1996 chs. 37, 407, eff. 7/1/96.)

§54.1-3437.1. Limited permit for repackaging drugs.

The Board may issue a limited manufacturing permit for the purpose of repackaging drugs, upon such terms and conditions approved by the Board, to the pharmacy directly operated by the Department of Mental Health, Mental Retardation and Substance Abuse Services and which serves clients of the community services boards.
(Added by L.1997 ch. 218, eff. 7/1/97.)

§54.1-3438. Manufacturing, etc., of drugs or proprietary medicines, to be supervised by pharmacist.

No drugs or proprietary medicines shall be manufactured, made, produced, packed, packaged, repackaged, relabeled or prepared within this Commonwealth, except under the personal and immediate supervision of a pharmacist or such other person as may be approved by the Board of Pharmacy after an investigation and a determination by the Board that they are qualified by scientific or technical training to perform such duties or supervision as may be necessary to protect the public health and safety. This provision shall not apply to manufacturers or packers of medicated feeds who manufacture or pack no other drugs. Medicated feeds are hereby defined as products obtained by mixing a commercial feed and a drug.
(Chgd. by L.1996 chs. 37, 407, eff. 7/1/96.)

§54.1-3439. Application for nonrestricted manufacturing permit; fee.

Every person desiring to manufacture any drug or proprietary medicines shall annually apply to the Board for a nonrestricted manufacturing permit. The application shall be accompanied by the required fee. Separate applications shall be made and separate permits issued for each specific place of manufacturing. Each such permit shall expire on December 31.
(Chgd. by L.1996 chs. 37, 407, eff. 7/1/96.)

§54.1-3440. Persons to whom nonrestricted permit is granted.

No person shall be granted a nonrestricted permit as a manufacturer unless he is of good moral character and properly equipped as to land, buildings, equipment and safeguards against diversion to carry out the functions of a manufacturer with due regard to the protection of the public safety.

§54.1-3441. Restricted manufacturing permit; application; fee; separate application and permit for each place of manufacturing.

Every person desiring to manufacture a proprietary medicine or to repackage medical gases shall apply to the Board for a restricted manufacturing permit. The application shall be accompanied by the required fee. Separate applications shall be made and separate permits issued for each separate place of manufacturing.

(Chgd. by L.1996 chs. 37, 407, eff. 7/1/96.)

§54.1-3442. When permit not to be granted; regulations.

No person shall be granted a restricted manufacturing permit as a manufacturer unless such person is properly equipped as to buildings and equipment to carry out the functions of a manufacturer with due regard to the protection of the public health. The Board shall promulgate regulations in order to carry out the provisions of this section.

ARTICLE 5
STANDARDS AND SCHEDULES

Section

§54.1-3443. Board to administer article.

A. The Board shall administer this article and may add substances to or deschedule or reschedule all substances enumerated in the schedules in this article pursuant to the procedures of the Administrative Process Act (§9-6.14:1 et seq.). In making a determination regarding a substance, the Board shall consider the following:

1. The actual or relative potential for abuse;
2. The scientific evidence of its pharmacological effect, if known;
3. The state of current scientific knowledge regarding the substance;
4. The history and current pattern of abuse;
5. The scope, duration, and significance of abuse;
6. The risk to the public health;
7. The potential of the substance to produce psychic or physical dependence; and
8. Whether the substance is an immediate precursor of a substance already controlled under this article.

B. After considering the factors enumerated in subsection A, the Board shall make findings and issue a regulation controlling the substance if it finds the substance has a potential for abuse.

C. If the Board designates a substance as an immediate precursor, substances which are precursors of the controlled precursor shall not be subject to control solely because they are precursors of the controlled precursor.

D. If any substance is designated, rescheduled, or descheduled as a controlled substance under federal law and notice of such action is given to the Board, the Board may similarly control the substance under this chapter after the expiration of 120 days from publication in the Federal Register of the final order designating a substance as a controlled substance or rescheduling or deleting a substance without following the provisions specified in subsections A and B of this section.

E. Authority to control under this section does not extend to distilled spirits, wine, malt beverages, or tobacco as those terms are defined or used in Title 4.1.

F. The Board shall exempt any nonnarcotic substance from a schedule if such substance may, under the provisions of the federal Food, Drug and Cosmetic Act (21 U.S.C. §301 et seq.) or state law, be lawfully sold over the counter without a prescription.

(Chgd. by L.1996 ch. 408, eff. 7/1/96.)

§54.1-3444. Controlled substances included by whatever name designated.

The controlled substances listed or to be listed in the schedules in this chapter are included by whatever official, common, usual, chemical, or trade name designated.

§54.1-3445. Placement of substance in Schedule I.

The Board shall place a substance in Schedule I if it finds that the substance:

1. Has high potential for abuse; and
2. Has no accepted medical use in treatment in the United States or lacks accepted safety for use in treatment under medical supervision.

§54.1-3446. Schedule I.

The controlled substances listed in this section are included in Schedule I:

1. Any of the following opiates, including their isomers, esters, ethers, salts, and salts of isomers, esters, and ethers, unless specifically excepted, whenever the existence of these isomers, esters, ethers and salts is possible within the specific chemical designation:

Acetylmethadol;
Allylprodine;
Alphamethylfentanyl;
Alphacetylmethadol (except levo-alphacetylmethadol, also known as levo-alpha-acetylmethadol, levomethadyl acetate, or LAAM);
Alphameprodine;
Alphamethadol;
Benzethidine;
Betacetylmethadol;
Betameprodine;
Betamethadol;
Betaprodine;
Clonitazene;
Dextromoramide;
Diampromide;
Diethylthiambutene;
Difenoxin;
Dimenoxadol;
Dimepheptanol;
Dimethylthiambutene;
Dioxaphetylbutyrate;
Dipipanone;
Ethylmethylthiambutene;
Etonitazene;
Etoxeridine;
Furethidine;
Hydroxypethidine;
Ketobemidone;

Levomoramide;
Levophenacylmorphan;
Morpheridine;
Noracymethadol;
Norlevorphanol;
Normethadone;
Norpipanone;
Phenadoxone;
Phenampromide;
Phenomorphan;
Phenoperidine;
Piritramide;
Proheptazine;
Properidine;
Propiram;
Racemoramide;
Trimeperidine.

2. Any of the following opium derivatives, their salts, isomers and salts of isomers, unless specifically excepted, whenever the existence of these salts, isomers and salts of isomers is possible within the specific chemical designation:

Acetorphine;
Acetyldihydrocodeine;
Benzylmorphine;
Codeine methylbromide;
Codeine-N-Oxide;
Cyprenorphine;
Desomorphine;
Dihydromorphine;
Drotebanol;
Etorphine;
Heroin;
Hydromorphinol;
Methyldesorphine;
Methyldihydromorphine;
Morphine methylbromide;
Morphine methylsulfonate;
Morphine-N-Oxide;
Myrophine;
Nicocodeine;
Nicomorphine;
Normorphine;
Phoclodine;
Thebacon.

3. Unless specifically excepted or unless listed in another schedule, any material, compound, mixture, or preparation, which contains any quantity of the following hallucinogenic substances, or which contains any of its salts, isomers, and salts of isomers, whenever the existence of such salts, isomers, and salts of isomers is possible within the specific chemical designation (for purposes of this subdivision only, the term "isomer" includes the optical, position, and geometric isomers):

Alpha-ethyltryptamine (some trade or other names: Monase;a-ethyl-1H-indole-3-ethanamine; 3-[2-aminobutyl] indole; a-ET; AET);

4-Bromo-2,5-dimethoxyphenethylamine (some trade or other names: 2-[4-bromo-2,5-dimethoxyphenyl]-1-aminoethane;alpha-desmethyl DOB;2C-B; Nexus);

3,4-methylenedioxy amphetamine;
5-methoxy-3,4-methylenedioxy amphetamine;
3,4,5-trimethoxy amphetamine;
Bufotenine;
Diethyltryptamine;
Dimethyltryptamine;
4-methyl-2,5-dimethoxyamphetamine;
2,5-dimethoxy-4-ethylamphetamine (DOET);
Ibogaine;
Lysergic acid diethylamide;
Mescaline;

Parahexyl (some trade or other names: 3-Hexyl-1-hydroxy-7, 8, 9, 10-tetrahydro-6, 6, 9-trimethyl-6H-dibenzo [b,d] pyran; Synhexyl);

Peyote;
N-ethyl-3-piperidyl benzilate;
N-methyl-3-piperidyl benzilate;
Psilocybin;
Psilocyn;

Tetrahydrocannabinols, except as present in marijuana and dronabinol in sesame oil and encapsulated in a soft gelatin capsule in a drug product approved by the U.S. Food and Drug Administration;

Hashish oil (some trade or other names: hash oil; liquid marijuana; liquid hashish);

2,5-dimethoxyamphetamine (some trade or other names: 2,5-dimethoxy-a-methylphenethylamine; 2,5-DMA);

3,4-methylenedioxymethamphetamine (MDMA), its optical, positional and geometric isomers, salts and salts of isomers;

3,4-methylenedioxy-N-ethylamphetamine (also known as N-ethyl-alpha-methyl-3,4 (methylenedioxy)phenethylamine, N-ethyl MDA, MDE, MDEA);

4-bromo-2,5-dimethoxyamphetamine (some trade or other names: 4-bromo-2,5-dimethoxy-a-methylphenethylamine; 4-bromo-2,5-DMA);

4-methoxyamphetamine (some trade or other names: 4-methoxy-a-methylphenethylamine; paramethoxyamphetamine; PMA);

N-ethyl analog of phencyclidine;
Pyrrolidine analog of phencyclidine;
Thiophene analog of phencyclidine.

4. Unless specifically excepted or unless listed in another schedule, any material, compound, mixture or preparation which contains any quantity of the following substances having a depressant effect on the central nervous system, including its salts, isomers and salts of isomers whenever the existence of such salts, isomers and salts of isomers is possible within the specific chemical designation:

Gamma hydroxybutyric acid (some other names include GHB; gamma hydroxybutyrate; 4-hydroxybutyrate; 4-hydroxybutanoic acid; sodium oxybate; sodium oxybutyrate);

Mecloqualone;
Methaqualone.

5. Unless specifically excepted or unless listed in another schedule, any material, compound, mixture or preparation which contains any quantity of the following substances having a stimulant effect on the central nervous system, including its salts, isomers and salts of isomers:

Aminorex (some trade or other names: aminoxaphen; 2-amino-5-phenyl-2-oxazoline; 4, 5-dihydro-5-phenyl-2-oxazolamine);

Fenethylline;
Ethylamphetamine;

Cathinone (some trade or other names: 2-amino-1-phenyl-1-propanone, alpha-aminopropiophenone, 2-aminopropiophenone, norephedrone), and any plant material from which Cathinone may be derived;

Methcathinone (some other names: 2-(methylamino)-propiophenone; alpha-(methylamino) propiophenone; 2-(methylamino)-1-phenylpropan-1-one; alpha-N-methylaminopropiophenone; monomethylpropion; ephedrone; N-methylcathinone; methylcathinone; AL-464; AL-422; AL-463 and UR 1432).

6. Any material, compound, mixture or preparation containing any quantity of the following substances:

3-methylfentany-(N-[3-methyl-1-(2-phenyethyl)-4-pipe ridyl] N-phenylpropanamide), its optical and geometric isomers, salts, and salts of isomers;

1-methyl-4-phenyl-4-propionoxypiperidine (MPPP), its optical isomers, salts and salts of isomers;

1-(2-phenylethyl)-4-phenyl-4-acetyloxypiperidine (PEPAP), its optical isomers, salts and salts of isomers;

N-[1-(1-methyl-2-phenyl)ethyl-4-piperidyl]-N-phenylacetamide (acetyl-alpha-methylfentanyl), its optical isomers, salts and salts of isomers;

N-[1-(1-methyl-2-2-thienyl)ethyl-4 piperidyl]-N-phenylpropanamide (alpha-methylthiofentanyl), its optical isomers, salts and salts of isomers;

N-[1-benzyl-4-piperidyl]-N-phenylpropanamide (benzylfentanyl), its optical isomers, salts and salts of isomers;

N-[1-(2-hydroxy-2-phenyl) ethyl-4-piperidyl]-N-phenylpropanamide (beta-hydroxyfentanyl), its optical isomers, salts and salts of isomers;

N-[3-methyl-1-(2-hydroxy-2-phenyl)ethyl-4-piperidyl]-N-phenylpropanamide (beta-hydroxy-3-methylfentanyl), its optical and geometric isomers, salts and salts of isomers;

N-[3-methyl-1-(2-2-thienyl)ethyl-4-piperidyl]-N-phenylpropanamide (3-methylthiofentanyl), its optical and geometric isomers, salts and salts of isomers;

N-[1-(2-thienyl)methyl-4-piperidyl]-N-phenylpropanamide(thenylfentanyl), its optical isomers, salts and salts of isomers;

N-[1-(2-2-thienyl)ethyl-4-piperidyl]-N-phenylpropanimide(thiofentanyl), its optical isomers, salts and salts of isomers.

(Chgd. by L.1996 ch. 408; L.1997 ch. 594; L.1999 ch. 722; L.2000 ch. 348, eff. 7/1/2000.)

§54.1-3447. Placement of substance in Schedule II.

The Board shall place a substance in Schedule II if it finds that:

1. The substance has high potential for abuse;
2. The substance has currently accepted medical use in treatment in the United States, or currently accepted medical use with severe restrictions; and
3. The abuse of the substance may lead to severe psychic or physical dependence.

§54.1-3448. Schedule II.

The controlled substances listed in this section are included in Schedule II:

1. Any of the following substances, except those narcotic drugs listed in other schedules, whether produced directly or indirectly by extraction from substances of vegetable origin, or independently by means of chemical synthesis, or by combination of extraction and chemical synthesis:

Opium and opiate, and any salt, compound, derivative, or preparation of opium or opiate, excluding apomorphine, thebaine-derived butorphanol, dextrorphan, nalbuphine, nalmefene, naloxone naltrexone and their respective salts, but including the following:

Raw opium;
Opium extracts;
Opium fluid extracts;
Powdered opium;
Granulated opium;
Tincture of opium;
Codeine;
Ethylmorphine;
Etorphine hydrochloride;
Hydrocodone;
Hydromorphone;
Metopon;
Morphine;
Oxycodone;
Oxymorphone;
Thebaine.

Any salt, compound, isomer, derivative, or preparation thereof which is chemically equivalent or identical with any of the substances referred to in this subdivision, but not including the isoquinoline alkaloids of opium.

Opium poppy and poppy straw.

Coca leaves and any salt, compound, derivative, or preparation of coca leaves, and any salt, compound, derivative, or preparation thereof which is chemically equivalent or identical with any of these substances, but not including decocainized coca leaves or extractions which do not contain cocaine or ecgonine; cocaine or any salt or isomer thereof.

Concentrate of poppy straw, the crude extract of poppy straw in either liquid, solid or powder form, which contains the phenanthrene alkaloids of the opium poppy.

2. Any of the following opiates, including their isomers, esters, ethers, salts, and salts of isomers, whenever the existence of these isomers, esters, ethers and salts is possible within the specific chemical designation:

Alfentanil;
Alphaprodine;
Anileridine;
Bezitramide;
Bulk dextropropoxyphene (nondosage forms);
Dihydrocodeine;
Diphenoxylate;
Fentanyl;
Isomethadone;
Levo-alphacetylmethadol (levo-alpha-acetylmethadol) (levomethadyl acetate) (LAAM);
Levomethorphan;
Levorphanol;
Metazocine;
Methadone;
Methadone - Intermediate, 4-cyano-2-dimethylamino-4, 4-diphenyl butane;
Moramide - Intermediate, 2-methyl-3-morpholino-1, 1-diphenyl-propane-carboxylicacid;
Pethidine;
Pethidine - Intermediate - A, 4-cyano-1-methyl-4-phenylpiperidine;
Pethidine - Intermediate - B, ethyl-4-phenylpiperidine-4-carboxylate;
Pethidine - Intermediate - C, 1-methyl-4-phenylpiperidine-4-carboxylic acid;
Phenazocine;
Piminodine;
Racemethorphan;
Racemorphan;
Remifentanil.

3. Any material, compound, mixture or preparation which contains any quantity of the following substances having a potential for abuse associated with a stimulant effect on the central nervous system:

Amphetamine, its salts, optical isomers, and salts of its optical isomers;
Phenmetrazine and its salts;
Any substance which contains any quantity of methamphetamine, including its salts, isomers, and salts of isomers;
Methylphenidate.

4. Unless specifically excepted or unless listed in another schedule, any material, compound, mixture, or preparation which contains any quantity of the following substances having a depressant effect on the central nervous

system, including its salts, isomers, and salts of isomers whenever the existence of such salts, isomers, and salts of isomers is possible within the specific chemical designation:

Amobarbital;
Glutethimide;
Secobarbital;
Pentobarbital;
Phencyclidine.

5. The following hallucinogenic substance:
Nabilone.

6. Unless specifically excepted or unless listed in another schedule, any material, compound, mixture, or preparation which contains any quantity of the following substances which are immediate precursors to amphetamine and methamphetamine or phencyclidine:

Phenylacetone;
1-phenylcyclohexylamine;
1-piperidinocyclohexanecarbonitrile.

(Chgd. by L.1998 ch. 105; L.2000 ch. 135, eff. 7/1/2000.)

§54.1-3449. Placement of substance in Schedule III.

The Board shall place a substance in Schedule III if it finds that:

1. The substance has a potential for abuse less than the substances listed in Schedules I and II;
2. The substance has currently accepted medical use in treatment in the United States; and
3. Abuse of the substance may lead to moderate or low physical dependence or high psychological dependence.

§54.1-3450. Schedule III.

The controlled substances listed in this section are included in Schedule III:

1. Unless specifically exempted or listed in another schedule, any material, compound, mixture, or preparation which contains any quantity of the following substances having a depressant effect on the central nervous system:

Any substance which contains any quantity of a derivative of barbituric acid, or any salt of a derivative of barbituric acid, except those substances which are specifically listed in other schedules;

Any compound, mixture or preparation containing amobarbital, secobarbital, or pentobarbital or any salt of amobarbital, secobarbital, or pentobarbital and one or more other active medicinal ingredients which are not listed in Schedules II through V;

Any suppository dosage form containing amobarbital, secobarbital, or pentobarbital or any salt of amobarbital, secobarbital, or pentobarbital and approved by the Food and Drug Administration for marketing only as a suppository;

Chlorhexadol;

Any drug product containing gamma hydroxybutyric acid, including its salts, isomers, and salts of isomers, for which an application is approved under section 505 of the Federal Food, Drug, and Cosmetic Act;

Ketamine, its salts, isomers, and salts of isomers (some other names for ketamine: [±]-2-[2-chlorophenyl]-2-[methylamino]-cyclohexanone);

Lysergic acid;
Lysergic acid amide;
Methyprylon;
Sulfondiethylmethane;
Sulfonethylmethane;
Sulfonmethane;
Tiletamine - zolazepam or any salt thereof;
Nalorphine.

2. Any material, compound, mixture, or preparation containing limited quantities of any of the following narcotic drugs, or any salts thereof:

Not more than 1.8 grams of codeine, or any of its salts, per 100 milliliters or not more than 90 milligrams per dosage unit, with an equal or greater quantity of an isoquinoline alkaloid of opium;

Not more than 1.8 grams of codeine, or any of its salts, per 100 milliliters or not more than 90 milligrams per dosage unit, with one or more active, nonnarcotic ingredients in recognized therapeutic amounts;

Not more than 300 milligrams of dihydrocodeinone, or any of its salts, per 100 milliliters or not more than 15 milligrams per dosage unit, with a fourfold or greater quantity of an isoquinoline alkaloid of opium;

Not more than 300 milligrams of dihydrocodeinone, or any of its salts, per 100 milliliters or not more than 15 milligrams per dosage unit, with one or more active, nonnarcotic ingredients in recognized therapeutic amounts;

Not more than 1.8 grams of dihydrocodeine, or any of its salts, per 100 milliliters or not more than 90 milligrams per dosage unit, with one or more active, nonnarcotic ingredients in recognized therapeutic amounts;

Not more than 300 milligrams of ethylmorphine, or any of its salts, per 100 milliliters or not more than 15 milligrams per dosage unit, with one or more ingredients in recognized therapeutic amounts;

Not more than 500 milligrams of opium per 100 milliliters or per 100 grams, or not more than 25 milligrams per dosage unit, with one or more active, nonnarcotic ingredients in recognized therapeutic amounts;

Not more than 50 milligrams of morphine, or any of its salts, per 100 milliliters or per 100 grams with one or more active, nonnarcotic ingredients in recognized therapeutic amounts.

3. Unless specifically excepted or unless listed in another schedule, any material, compound, mixture, or preparation which contains any quantity of the following substances having a stimulant effect on the central nervous system, including its salts, isomers (whether optical, position, or geometric), and salts of such isomers whenever the existence of such salts, isomers, and salts of isomers is possible within the specific chemical designation:

Benzphetamine;
Chlorphentermine;
Clortermine;
Phendimetrazine.

4. The Board may except by regulation any compound, mixture, or preparation containing any stimulation or depressant substance listed in subdivision 1 from the application of all or any part of this chapter if the compound, mixture, or preparation contains one or more active medicinal ingredients not having a stimulant or depressant effect on the central nervous system, and if the admixtures are included therein in combinations, quantity, proportion, or concentration that vitiate the potential for abuse of the substances which have a stimulant or depressant effect on the central nervous system.

5. Unless specifically excepted or unless listed in another schedule, any material, compound, mixture, or preparation containing any quantity of the following substances, including its salts, isomers, and salts of isomers whenever the existence of such salts of isomers is possible within the specific chemical designation:

Anabolic steroids, including, but not limited to:
Boldenone (Dehydrotestosterone);
Clostebol (4-Chlorotestosterone) (Chlorotestosterone);
Dromostanolone (Drostanolone);
Ethylestrenol;

Fluoxymesterone;
Formyldienolone (Formebolone);
Mesterolone;
Methandriol (methylandrostenediol);
Methandrostenolone (Methandienone) (Dehydromethyltestosterone);
Methenolone;
17-Methyltestosterone (Methyltestosterone);
Mibolerone;
Nandrolone (19-Nortestosterone);
Norethandrolone;
Oxandrolone;
Oxymesterone (Oxymestrone);
Oxymetholone (Anasterone);
Stanolone (4-Dihydrotestosterone) (Dihydrotestosterone);
Stanozolol (Androstanazole);
Testolactone (1-Dehydrotestololactone);
Testosterone;
Trenbolone (Trienbolone) (Trienolone); and

Any salt, ester, or isomer of a drug or substance described or listed in this paragraph, if that salt, ester, or isomer promotes muscle growth. However, such term does not include an anabolic steroid which is expressly intended for administration through implants to cattle or other nonhuman species and which has been approved by the United States Secretary of Health and Human Services for such administration. If any person prescribes, dispenses, or distributes any such steroid for human use, such person shall be considered to have prescribed, dispensed, or distributed an anabolic steroid within the meaning of this subdivision.

6. Dronabinol (synthetic) in sesame oil and encapsulated in a soft gelatin capsule in a drug product approved by the U.S. Food and Drug Administration.
(Chgd. by L.2000 chs. 135, 348, eff. 7/1/2000.)

§54.1-3451. Placement of substance in Schedule IV.

The Board shall place a substance in Schedule IV if it finds that:

1. The substance has a low potential for abuse relative to substances in Schedule III;
2. The substance has currently accepted medical use in treatment in the United States; and
3. Abuse of the substance may lead to limited physical dependence or psychological dependence relative to the substances in Schedule III.

§54.1-3452. Schedule IV.

The controlled substances listed in this section are included in Schedule IV unless specifically excepted or listed in another schedule:

1. Any material, compound, mixture, or preparation which contains any quantity of the following substances having a potential for abuse associated with a depressant effect on the central nervous system:

Alprazolam;
Barbital;
Bromazepam;
Camazepam;
Chloral betaine;
Chloral hydrate;
Chlordiazepoxide;
Clobazam;
Clonazepam;
Clorazepate;
Clotiazepam;
Cloxazolam;
Delorazepam;
Diazepam;
Estazolam;
Ethchlorvynol;
Ethinamate;
Ethyl loflazepate;
Fludiazepam;
Flunitrazepam;
Flurazepam;
Halazepam;
Haloxazolam;
Ketazolam;
Loprazolam;
Lorazepam;
Lormetazepam;
Mebutamate;
Medazepam;
Methohexital;
Meprobamate;
Methylphenobarbital;
Midazolam;
Nimetazapam;
Nitrazepam;
Nordiazepam;
Oxazepam;
Oxazolam;
Paraldehyde;
Petrichloral;
Phenobarbital;
Pinazepam;
Prazepam;
Quazepam;
Temazepam;
Tetrazepam;
Triazolam;
Zaleplon;
Zolpidem.

2. Any compound, mixture or preparation which contains any quantity of the following substances including any salts or isomers thereof:

Fenfluramine.

3. Unless specifically excepted or unless listed in another schedule, any material, compound, mixture, or preparation which contains any quantity of the following substances having a stimulant effect on the central nervous system, including its salts, isomers (whether optical, position, or geometric), and salts of such isomers whenever the existence of such salts, isomers, and salts of isomers is possible within the specific chemical designation:

Cathine (+)-norpseudoephedrine;
Diethylpropion;
Fencamfamin;
Fenproprex;
Mazindol;
Mefenorex;
Modafinil;
Phentermine;
Pemoline (including organometallic complexes and chelates thereof);
Pipradrol;
Sibutramine;
SPA (-)-1-dimethylamino-1,2-diphenylethane.

4. Unless specifically excepted or unless listed in another schedule, any material, compound, mixture, or preparation containing any of the following narcotic drugs, or their salts calculated as the free anhydrous base or alkaloid, in limited quantities as set forth below:

Dextropropoxyphene (alpha-(+)-4-dimethylamino-1,2-diphenyl-3-methyl-2-propionoxy butane);

Not more than 1 milligram of difenoxin and not less than 25 micrograms of atropine sulfate per dosage unit.

5. Unless specifically excepted or unless listed in another schedule, any material, compound, mixture, or preparation which contains any quantity of the following substances, including their salts:

Butorphanol (including its optical isomers);

Pentazocine.

6. The Board may except by regulation any compound, mixture, or preparation containing any depressant substance listed in subdivision 1 from the application of all or any part of this chapter if the compound, mixture, or preparation contains one or more active medicinal ingredients not having a depressant effect on the central nervous system, and if the admixtures are included therein in combinations, quantity, proportion, or concentration that vitiate the potential for abuse of the substances which have a depressant effect on the central nervous system.

(Chgd. by L.1998 ch. 105; L.1999 ch. 605; L.2000 ch. 135, eff. 7/1/2000.)

§54.1-3453. Placement of substance in Schedule V.

The Board shall place a substance in Schedule V if it finds that:

1. The substance has low potential for abuse relative to the controlled substances listed in Schedule IV;
2. The substance has currently accepted medical use in treatment in the United States; and
3. The substance has limited physical dependence or psychological dependence liability relative to the controlled substances listed in Schedule IV.

§54.1-3454. Schedule V.

The controlled substances listed in this section are included in Schedule V:

1. Unless specifically excepted or unless listed in another schedule, any material, compound, mixture, or preparation containing any of the following narcotic drugs and their salts, as set forth below:

Buprenorphine.

2. Any compound, mixture, or preparation containing limited quantities of any of the following narcotic drugs, which also contains one or more nonnarcotic active medicinal ingredients in sufficient proportion to confer upon the compound, mixture, or preparation, valuable medicinal qualities other than those possessed by the narcotic drug alone:

Not more than 200 milligrams of codeine, or any of its salts, per 100 milliliters or per 100 grams;

Not more than 100 milligrams of dihydrocodeine, or any of its salts, per 100 milliliters or per 100 grams;

Not more than 100 milligrams of ethylmorphine, or any of its salts, per 100 milliliters or per 100 grams;

Not more than 2.5 milligrams of diphenoxylate and not less than 25 micrograms of atropine sulfate per dosage unit;

Not more than 100 milligrams of opium per 100 milliliters or per 100 grams;

Not more than 0.5 milligrams of difenoxin and not less than 25 micrograms of atropine sulfate per dosage unit.

The Board may except by regulation any compound, mixture or preparation containing any depressant substance listed in subdivision 2 from the application of all or any part of this chapter and such substances so excepted may be dispensed pursuant to §54.1-3416.

3. Unless specifically excepted or listed in another schedule, any material, compound, mixture, or preparation which contains any quantity of the following substances having a stimulant effect on the central nervous system, including its salts, isomers, and salts of isomers:

Pyrovalerone.

§54.1-3455. Schedule VI.

The following classes of drugs and devices shall be controlled by Schedule VI:

1. Any compound, mixture, or preparation containing any stimulant or depressant drug exempted from Schedules III, IV or V and designated by the Board as subject to this section.
2. Every drug, not included in Schedules I, II, III, IV or V, or device, which because of its toxicity or other potentiality for harmful effect, or the method of its use, or the collateral measures necessary to its use, is not generally recognized among experts qualified by scientific training and experience to evaluate its safety and efficacy as safe for use except by or under the supervision of a practitioner licensed to prescribe or administer such drug or device.
3. Any drug, not included in Schedules I, II, III, IV or V, required by federal law to bear on its label prior to dispensing, at a minimum, the symbol "Rx only," or which bears the legend "Caution: Federal Law Prohibits Dispensing Without Prescription" or "Caution: Federal Law Restricts This Drug To Use By Or On The Order Of A Veterinarian" or any device which bears the legend "Caution: Federal Law Restricts This Device To Sales By Or On The Order Of A ______." (The blank should be completed with the word "Physician," "Dentist," "Veterinarian," or with the professional designation of any other practitioner licensed to use or order such device.)

(Chgd. by L.1999 ch. 605, eff. 7/1/99.)

§54.1-3456. Designer drugs.

Any drug not listed on Schedule I or II in this chapter, which is privately compounded, with the specific intent to circumvent the provisions of this chapter, to emulate or simulate the effects of another drug or class of drugs listed on Schedule I or II in this chapter through chemical changes such as the addition, subtraction or rearranging of a radical or the addition, subtraction or rearranging of a substituent, shall be considered to be listed on the same schedule as the drug or class of drugs which it imitates in the same manner as any isomer, ester, ether, salts of isomers, esters and ethers of such drug or class of drugs.

ARTICLE 6
MISBRANDED AND ADULTERATED DRUGS AND COSMETICS

Section

§54.1-3457. Prohibited acts.

The following acts shall be prohibited:

1. The manufacture, sale, or delivery, holding or offering for sale of any drug, device, or cosmetic that is adulterated or misbranded.
2. The adulteration or misbranding of any drug, device, or cosmetic.

3. The receipt in commerce of any drug, device, or cosmetic that is adulterated or misbranded, and the delivery or proffered delivery thereof for pay or otherwise.

4. The sale, delivery for sale, holding for sale, or offering for sale of any article in violation of §54.1-3421.

5. The dissemination of any false advertisement.

6. The refusal to permit entry or inspection, or to permit the taking of a sample, or to permit access to or copying of any record.

7. The giving of a false guaranty or undertaking.

8. The removal or disposal of a detained article in violation of §54.1-3459.

9. The alteration, mutilation, destruction, obliteration, or removal of the whole or any part of the labeling of, or the doing of any other act with respect to a drug, device, or cosmetic, if such act is done while such article is held for sale and results in such article being adulterated or misbranded.

10. The forging, counterfeiting, simulating, or falsely representing, or without proper authority using any mark, stamp, tag, label, or other identification device authorized or required by regulations promulgated under the provisions of this chapter or of the federal act.

11. The using by any person to his own advantage, or revealing, other than to the Board or its authorized representative or to the courts when relevant in any judicial proceeding under this chapter of any information acquired under authority of this chapter concerning any method or process which as a trade secret is entitled to protection.

12. The using, on the labeling of any drug or in any advertisement relating to such drug, of any representation or suggestion that an application with respect to such drug is effective under §54.1-3421, or that such drug complies with the provisions of such section.

13. In the case of a drug distributed or offered for sale in this Commonwealth, the failure of the manufacturer, packer, or distributor thereof to maintain for transmittal, or to transmit, to any practitioner licensed by applicable law to administer such drug who makes written request for information as to such drug, true and correct copies of all printed matter which is required to be included in any package in which that drug is distributed or sold, or such other printed matter as is approved under the federal act. This subdivision shall not be construed to exempt any person from any labeling requirement imposed by or under other provisions of this chapter.

14. Placing or causing to be placed upon any drug or device or container, with intent to defraud, the trade name or other identifying mark, or imprint of another or any likeness of any of the foregoing; or selling, dispensing, disposing of or causing to be sold, dispensed or disposed of, or concealing or keeping in possession, control or custody, with intent to sell, dispense or dispose of, any drug, device or any container thereof, with knowledge that the trade name or other identifying mark or imprint of another or any likeness of any of the foregoing has been placed thereon in a manner prohibited by this section or making, selling, disposing of, or causing to be made, sold or disposed of, or keeping in possession, control or custody, or concealing any punch, die, plate, stone, or other thing designed to print, imprint, or reproduce the trademark, trade name, or other identifying mark, imprint, or device of another or any likeness of any of the foregoing upon any drug or container or labeling thereof so as to render such drug a counterfeit drug.

15. The doing of any act which causes a drug to be a counterfeit drug, or the sale or dispensing, or the holding for sale or dispensing, of a counterfeit drug.

16. Dispensing or causing to be dispensed, except as provided in §32.1-87 relating to the Virginia Voluntary Formulary, a different drug or brand of drug in place of the drug or brand of drug ordered or prescribed without the permission of the person ordering or prescribing.

§54.1-3458. Violations.

A. Any person who violates any of the provisions of §54.1-3457 shall be guilty of a Class 2 misdemeanor.

B. No person shall be subject to the penalties of this section for having violated subdivisions 1 and 3 of §54.1-3457 if he establishes a guaranty or undertaking signed by, and containing the name and address of, the person residing in this Commonwealth from whom he received in good faith the article, to the effect that such article is not adulterated or misbranded within the meaning of this chapter.

C. No publisher, radio-broadcast licensee, or agency or medium for the dissemination of an advertisement, except the manufacturer, packer, distributor, or seller of the article to which a false advertisement relates, shall be liable under this section for the dissemination of such false advertisement, unless he has refused, on the request of the Board, to furnish the Board the name and post-office address of the manufacturer, packer, distributor, seller, or advertising agency, residing in this Commonwealth who caused him to disseminate such advertisement.

§54.1-3459. Tagging of adulterated or misbranded drugs, devices, or cosmetics; condemnation; destruction; expenses.

A. Whenever a duly authorized agent of the Board finds, or has probable cause to believe, that any drug, device, or cosmetic is adulterated, or so misbranded as to be dangerous or fraudulent, within the meaning of this chapter or is in violation of §54.1-3457, he shall affix to such article a tag or other appropriate marking, giving notice that such article is, or is suspected of being, adulterated or misbranded or in violation of §54.1-3457 and has been detained. The tag shall also warn all persons not to remove or dispose of such article by sale or otherwise until permission for removal or disposal is given by an authorized agent or the court. It shall be unlawful for any person to remove or dispose of such detained article by sale or otherwise without permission.

B. When an article is adulterated or misbranded or is in violation of §54.1-3421, the Board may petition the circuit court in whose jurisdiction the article is detained for condemnation of such article. When an authorized agent finds that an article which has been detained is not adulterated or misbranded, or in violation of §54.1-3421, he shall remove the tag or other marking.

C. If the court finds that a detained article is adulterated or misbranded, or in violation of §54.1-3421, such article shall, after entry of the decree, be destroyed at the expense of the claimant, under the supervision of an authorized agent, and all court costs and fees, and storage and other proper expenses, shall be levied against the claimant or his agent. When the adulteration or misbranding can be corrected by proper labeling or processing of the article, the court shall order the article to be properly labeled or processed. The expense of the supervision shall be paid by the claimant. The article shall be returned to the claimant and the bond shall be discharged on the representation to the court by the Board that the article is no longer in violation of this chapter, and that the expenses of such supervision have been paid.

§54.1-3460. Poisonous or deleterious substance, or color additive.

Any added poisonous or deleterious substance, or any color additive, shall with respect to any particular use or intended use be deemed unsafe with respect to any drug, device, or cosmetic, unless there is a regulation allowing limited use of a quantity of such substance, and the use or intended use of such substance conforms to the terms prescribed by regulation. While such regulations relating to such substance are in effect, a drug or cosmetic shall not, by reason of bearing or containing such substance in accordance with the regulations, be considered adulterated.

§54.1-3461. Adulterated drug or device.

A. A drug or device shall be deemed to be adulterated:

1. If it consists in whole or in part of any filth, putrid or decomposed substance;

2. If it has been produced, prepared, packed, or held under insanitary conditions whereby it has been contaminated with filth, or whereby it has been rendered injurious to health;

3. If it is a drug and the methods used in, or the facilities or controls used for, its manufacture, processing, packing, or holding do not conform to or are not operated or administered in conformity with current good manufacturing practice to assure that such drug meets the requirements of this chapter;

4. If it is a drug and its container is composed, in whole or in part, of any poisonous or deleterious substance which may render the contents injurious to health;

5. If it is a drug and it bears or contains, for purposes of coloring only, a color additive which is unsafe within the meaning of the federal act or §54.1-3460; or

6. It is a color additive, the intended use of which in or on drugs is for purposes of coloring only, and is unsafe within the meaning of the federal act or §54.1-3460.

B. A drug or device shall be deemed to be adulterated if it purports to be or is represented as a drug the name of which is recognized in an official compendium, and its strength differs from, or its quality or purity falls below, the standard set forth in such compendium. Such determination of strength, quality, or purity shall be made in accordance with the tests or methods of assay set forth in such compendium, or in the absence of or inadequacy of such tests or methods of assay, those prescribed under authority of the federal act. No drug defined in an official compendium shall be deemed to be adulterated under this subsection because it differs from the standard of strength, quality, or purity set forth in such compendium, if the difference in strength, quality, or purity from such standard is plainly stated on its label.

Whenever a drug is recognized in both the United States Pharmacopoeia National Formulary and the Homeopathic Pharmacopoeia of the United States it shall be subject to the requirements of the United States Pharmacopoeia National Formulary unless it is labeled and offered for sale as a homeopathic drug, in which case it shall be subject to the provisions of the Homeopathic Pharmacopoeia of the United States and not to those of the United States Pharmacopoeia National Formulary.

C. A drug or device shall be deemed to be adulterated if it is not subject to the provisions of subsection B of this section and its strength differs from, or its purity or quality falls below, that which it purports or is represented to possess.

D. A drug or device shall be deemed to be adulterated if it is a drug and any substance has been (i) mixed or packed with it so as to reduce its quality or strength or (ii) substituted wholly or in part for it.

§54.1-3462. Misbranded drug or device.

A drug or device shall be deemed to be misbranded:

1. If its labeling is false or misleading in any particular.

2. If its package does not bear a label containing the name and place of business of the manufacturer, packer, or distributor. However, all prescription drugs intended for human use and devices shall bear a label containing the name and place of business of the manufacturer of the final dosage form of the drug and, if different, the name and place of business of the packer or distributor and an accurate statement of the quantity of the contents in terms of weight, measure, or numerical count. Reasonable variations shall be permitted, and exemptions for small packages shall be allowed in accordance with regulations of the Board.

3. If any word, statement, or other information required by or under authority of this chapter to appear on the label or labeling is not prominently placed with such conspicuousness, as compared with other words, statements, designs or devices, in the labeling, and in such terms as to render it likely to be read and understood by the ordinary individual under customary conditions of purchase and use.

4. If it is for use by man and contains any quantity of the narcotic or hypnotic substances alpha-eucaine, barbituric acid, beta-eucaine, bromal, carbromal, chloral, coca, cocaine, codeine, morphine, opium, paraldehyde, or sulfonmethane, or any chemical derivative of such substances, which derivative, after investigation has been found to be and designated as, habit forming, by regulations issued by the Board under this chapter, unless its label bears the name and quantity or proportion of such substance or derivative and in juxtaposition therewith the statement "Warning – May Be Habit Forming."

5. If it is a drug, unless its label bears, to the exclusion of any other nonproprietary name, except the applicable systematic chemical name or the chemical formula, the established name of the drug, and in case it is fabricated from two or more ingredients, the established name and quantity of each active ingredient, including the kind and quantity or proportion of any alcohol, and the established name and quantity or proportion of any bromides, ether, chloroform, acetanilid, acetphenetidin, amidopyrine, antipyrine, atropine, hyoscine, hyoscyamine, arsenic, digitalis, digitalis glucosides, mercury, ouabain, strophanthin, strychnine, thyroid, or any derivative or preparation of any such substances. However, the requirement for stating the quantity of the active ingredients, other than the quantity of those specifically named in this subdivision, shall apply only to prescription drugs. Any prescription drug shall have the established name of the drug or ingredient printed on its label prominently and in type at least half as large as that used for any proprietary name or designation for such drug or ingredient. Exemptions may be allowed under regulations of the Board.

As used in this subdivision, the term "established name," with respect to a drug or ingredient, means the applicable official name designated pursuant to §508* of the federal act, or if there is no such name and such drug, or such ingredient, is an article recognized in an official compendium, then the official title in such compendium or if neither exists, then the common or usual name, if any, of such drug or of such ingredient. Whenever, an article is recognized in the United States Pharmacopoeia National Formulary and in the Homeopathic Pharmacopoeia under different official titles, the official title used in the United States Pharmacopoeia National Formulary shall apply unless it is labeled and offered for sale as a homeopathic drug, in which case the official title used in the Homeopathic Pharmacopoeia shall apply.

**See 21 U.S.C. 358.*

6. Unless its labeling bears adequate directions for use and such adequate warnings against use in those pathological conditions or by children where its use may be dangerous to health, or against unsafe dosage or methods or duration of administration or application, in such manner and form, as are necessary for the protection of users. The Board shall promulgate regulations exempting such drug or device from such requirements when these requirements are not necessary to protect the public health and the articles are also exempted under regulations issued under §502(f)* of the federal act.

**See 21 U.S.C. 352(f).*

7. If it purports to be a drug the name of which is recognized in an official compendium, unless it is packaged and labeled as prescribed. The method of packing may be modified with the consent of the Board, or if consent is obtained under the federal act. Whenever a drug is recognized in both the United States Pharmacopoeia National Formulary and the Homeopathic Pharmacopoeia of the United States, it shall be subject to the requirements of the United States Pharmacopoeia National Formulary with respect to packaging and labeling unless it is labeled and offered for sale as a homeopathic drug, in which case it shall be subject to the provisions of the Homeopathic Pharmacopoeia of the United States and not to those of the United States Pharmacopoeia National Formulary. However, in the event of inconsistency between the requirements of this subdivision and those of subdivision 5 as to the name by which the drug or its ingredients shall be designated, the requirements of subdivision 5 shall prevail.

8. If it is dangerous to health when used in the dosage, or with the frequency or duration prescribed, recommended, or suggested in the labeling or advertising.

9. If it is, or purports to be, or is represented as a drug composed wholly or partly of insulin, unless it is from a batch for which a certificate or release has been issued pursuant to §506* of the federal act, and such certificate or release is in effect with respect to such drug.

**See 21 U.S.C. 356.*

10. If it is, or purports to be, or is represented as a drug composed wholly or partly of any kind of penicillin, streptomycin, chlortetracycline, chloramphenicol, bacitracin, or any other antibiotic drug, or any derivative, unless it is from a batch, for which a certificate or release has been issued pursuant to §507* of the federal act, and such certificate or release is in effect for such drug. This subdivision shall not apply to any drug or class of drugs exempted by regulations promulgated under §507(c) or (d) of the federal law.

**See 21 U.S.C. 357.*

For the purpose of this subdivision the term "antibiotic drug" means any drug intended for use by man containing any quantity of any chemical substance which is produced by microorganisms and which has the capacity to inhibit or destroy microorganisms in dilute solution, including, the chemically synthesized equivalent of any such substance.

11. If it is a color additive, the intended use of which in or on drugs is for coloring only, unless its packaging and labeling are in conformity with such packaging and labeling requirements applicable to such color additive, prescribed under the provisions of the federal act.

12. In the case of any prescription drug distributed or offered for sale in this Commonwealth, unless the manufacturer, packer, or distributor includes in all advertisements and other descriptive printed matter a true statement of (i) the established name, as defined in this section, printed prominently and in type at least half as large as that used for any trade or brand name, (ii) the formula showing quantitatively each ingredient of such drug to the extent required for labels under this section, and (iii) such other information in brief summary relating to side effects, contraindications, and effectiveness as are required in regulations issued under the federal act.

13. If a trademark, trade name or other identifying mark, imprint or device of another or any likeness of the foregoing has been placed thereon or upon its container with intent to defraud.

Drugs and devices which are, in accordance with the practice of the trade, to be processed, labeled or repacked in substantial quantities at establishments other than those where originally processed or packed shall be exempt from any labeling or packaging requirements of this chapter if such drugs and devices are being delivered, manufactured, processed, labeled, repacked or otherwise held in compliance with regulations issued by the Board.

§54.1-3463. Exemption of drugs dispensed by filling or refilling prescription.

A. Any drug dispensed by filling or refilling a written or oral prescription of a prescriber shall be exempt from the requirements of §54.1-3462 except subdivisions 1, 9, and 10, and the packaging requirements of subdivision 7, if the drug bears a label containing the name and address of the dispenser, the serial number and date of the prescription or of its filling, the name of the prescriber and the name of the patient, and the directions for use and cautionary statements, if any, contained in such prescription.

B. This section shall not be construed to relieve any person from any requirement prescribed by or under authority of law with respect to drugs now included or which may hereafter be included within the classifications of narcotic drugs or marijuana as defined in the applicable federal and state laws relating to narcotic drugs and marijuana.

(Chgd. by L.1996 ch. 408, eff. 7/1/96.)

§54.1-3464. Adulterated cosmetics.

A cosmetic shall be deemed to be adulterated:

1. If it bears or contains any poisonous or deleterious substance which may render it injurious to users under the conditions of use prescribed in the labeling or advertisement, or under such conditions of use as are customary or usual. This provision shall not apply to coal-tar hair dye, the label of which bears the following legend conspicuously displayed thereon: "Caution – This product contains ingredients which may cause skin irritation on certain individuals and a preliminary test according to accompanying directions should first be made. This product must not be used for dyeing the eyelashes or eyebrows; to do so may cause blindness," and the labeling of which bears adequate directions for such preliminary testing. For the purpose of this subdivision and subdivision 5, the term "hair dye" shall not include eyelash or eyebrow dyes;

2. If it consists in whole or in part of any filthy, putrid, or decomposed substance;

3. If it has been produced, prepared, packed, or held under insanitary conditions whereby it may have become contaminated with filth, or whereby it may have been rendered injurious to health;

4. If its container is composed, in whole or in part, of any poisonous or deleterious substance which may render the contents injurious to health;

5. If it is not a hair dye, and it is or it bears or contains a color additive which is unsafe within the meaning of the federal act or §54.1-3460.

§54.1-3465. Misbranded cosmetics.

A cosmetic shall be deemed to be misbranded:

1. If its labeling is false or misleading in any particular;

2. If in package form unless it bears a label containing the name and place of business of the manufacturer, packer, or distributor and an accurate statement of the quantity of the contents in terms of weight, measure, or numerical count. However, reasonable variations shall be permitted, and exemptions for small packages shall be established by the Board;

3. If any word, statement, or other information required by or under authority of this chapter to appear on the label or labeling is not prominently placed thereon with such conspicuousness, as compared with other words, statements, designs, or devices, in the labeling, and in such terms as to render it likely to be read and understood by the ordinary individual under customary conditions of purchase and use;

4. If its container is so made, formed or filled as to be misleading;

5. If it is a color additive, unless its packaging and labeling are in conformity with packaging and labeling requirements applicable to such color additive under the provisions of the federal act. This subdivision shall not apply to packages of color additives which, with respect to their use for cosmetics, are marketed and intended for use only in or on hair dyes.

A cosmetic which is, in accordance with the practice of the trade, to be processed, labeled or repacked in substantial quantities at an establishment other than the establishment where it was originally processed or packed, is exempted from the affirmative labeling requirements of this chapter while it is in transit in commerce from the one establishment to the other, if such transit is made in good faith for such completion purposes only; but it is otherwise subject to all applicable provisions of this chapter.

ARTICLE 7
CONTROLLED PARAPHERNALIA

Section

§54.1-3466. Possession or distribution of controlled paraphernalia; meaning of controlled paraphernalia; evidence; exceptions.

Except as authorized in this chapter, it shall be a misdemeanor for any person to possess or distribute controlled paraphernalia which shall mean a hypodermic syringe, needle or other instrument or implement or combination thereof adapted for the administration of controlled dangerous substances by hypodermic injections under circumstances which reasonably indicate an intention to use such controlled paraphernalia for purposes of illegally administering any controlled drug, or gelatin capsules, glassine envelopes or any other container suitable for the packaging of individual quantities of controlled drugs in sufficient quantity to and under circumstances which reasonably indicate an intention to use any such item for the illegal manufacture, distribution, or dispensing of any such controlled drug. Evidence of such circumstances shall include, but not be limited to, close proximity of any such controlled paraphernalia to any adulterants or equipment commonly used in the illegal manufacture and distribution of controlled drugs including, but not limited to, scales, sieves, strainers, measuring spoons, staples and staplers, or procaine hydrochloride, mannitol, lactose, quinine, or any controlled drug or any machine, equipment, instrument, implement, device or combination thereof which is adapted for the production of controlled drugs under circumstances which reasonably indicate an intention to use such item or combination thereof to produce, sell, or dispense any controlled drug in violation of the provisions of this chapter.

The provisions of this section shall not apply to persons who have acquired possession and control of controlled paraphernalia in accordance with the provisions of this article or to any person who owns or is engaged in breeding or raising livestock, poultry or other animals to which hypodermic injections are customarily given in the interest of health, safety, or good husbandry; or to hospitals, physicians, pharmacists, dentists, podiatrists, veterinarians, funeral directors and embalmers, persons to whom a permit has been issued, manufacturers, wholesalers or their authorized agents or employees when in the usual course of their business, if the controlled paraphernalia lawfully obtained continues to be used for the legitimate purposes for which they were obtained.

§54.1-3467. Distribution of hypodermic needles or syringes, gelatin capsules, quinine or any of its salts.

Distribution by any method, of any hypodermic needles or syringes, gelatin capsules, quinine or any of its salts, in excess of one-fourth ounce shall be restricted to licensed pharmacists or to others who have received a license or a permit from the Board.

§54.1-3468. Conditions to dispensing device, item, or substance; records.

In dispensing any device, item or substance, the pharmacist or other licensed or permitted person referred to in §54.1-3467 shall:

1. Require the person requesting such device, item or substance to furnish suitable identification, including proof of age when appropriate;

2. Require the person requesting such item, device or substance to furnish written legitimate purposes for which such item, device or substance is being purchased, except in cases of telephone orders for such item, device or substance from customers of known good standing;

3. At the time of dispensing, make and keep a record showing the date of dispensing, the name and quantity of the device, item or substance, the price at which it was sold, the name and address of the person to whom the device, item or substance was dispensed, the reason for its purchase and enter his initials thereon.

No such devices, substances or items shall be sold or distributed to persons under the age of sixteen years except by a physician for legitimate purposes or upon his prescription. Records shall be maintained pursuant to this chapter and the Board's regulations and shall be made available for inspection to any law-enforcement officer or agent of the Board. Persons violating the provisions of this section shall be guilty of a Class 1 misdemeanor.

§54.1-3469. Storage, usage, and disposition of controlled paraphernalia.

Each person, association or corporation which has lawfully obtained possession of any of the controlled paraphernalia mentioned in §54.1-3467 shall exercise reasonable care in the storage, usage and disposition of such devices or substances to ensure that they are not diverted for reuse for any purposes other than those for which they were lawfully obtained. Any person who permits or causes, directly or indirectly, such controlled paraphernalia to be used for any other purpose than that for which it was lawfully obtained shall be guilty of a Class 1 misdemeanor.

§54.1-3470. Obtaining controlled paraphernalia by fraud, etc.

A. No person shall obtain or attempt to obtain any item, device or substance referred to in §54.1-3467 by fraud, deceit, misrepresentation, or subterfuge or by giving a false name or a false address.

B. No person shall furnish false or fraudulent information in or omit any information from, or willfully make a false statement in obtaining or attempting to obtain any of the instruments or substances referred to in §54.1-3467.

C. No person shall, for the purpose of obtaining any such instrument or substance, falsely claim to be a manufacturer, wholesaler, pharmacist, practitioner of the healing arts, funeral director, embalmer or veterinarian.

Persons violating the provisions of this section shall be guilty of a Class 1 misdemeanor.

§54.1-3471. Issuance of permits to certain persons other than registered pharmacists.

The Board shall, upon written application, on a form furnished by the Board, issue a permit to any person other than a licensed pharmacist who in the usual course of business sells any item referred to in §54.1-3467 as a wholesale distributor or distributes at retail to any persons who own or breed or raise livestock, poultry, or other animals to which such items, devices or substances are customarily given to or used upon in the interest of health, safety, or good husbandry. This permit shall not authorize the sale or distribution of these items, devices or substances for human use and the permitted person shall exercise reasonable diligence to assure that the items distributed are not for the purpose of human consumption.

§54.1-3472. Article inapplicable to certain persons.

The provisions of this article shall not apply to legitimate distribution by or possession of controlled paraphernalia by physicians, dentists, podiatrists, veterinarians, funeral directors and embalmers.

TITLE 2.1
ADMINISTRATION OF THE GOVERNMENT GENERALLY
(Selected Chapters)

CHAPTER 5.3
SECRETARY OF PUBLIC SAFETY
(Selected Sections)

§2.1-51.16. Position continued; appointment; term; oath.

The position of Secretary of Transportation and Public Safety is continued as the Secretary of Public Safety. The Secretary shall be appointed by the Governor, subject to confirmation by the General Assembly if in session when the appointment is made, and if not in session, then at its next succeeding session. The Secretary shall hold office at the pleasure of the Governor for a term coincident with that of the Governor making the appointment or until a successor is appointed and qualified. Before entering upon the discharge of duties, the Secretary shall take an oath to faithfully execute the duties of the office.

§2.1-51.17. Subject to supervision by Governor; powers and duties.

A. The Secretary of Public Safety shall be subject to direction and supervision by the Governor. The agencies assigned to the Secretary shall:

1. Exercise their respective powers and duties in accordance with the general policy established by the Governor or by the Secretary acting on behalf of the Governor;
2. Provide such assistance to the Governor or the Secretary as may be required; and
3. Forward all reports to the Governor through the Secretary.

B. Unless the Governor expressly reserves such power to himself, the Secretary is empowered to:

1. Resolve administrative, jurisdictional, operational, program, or policy conflicts between agencies or officials assigned;
2. Direct the formulation of a comprehensive program budget for the functional area identified in §2.1-398 encompassing the services of agencies assigned for consideration by the Governor;
3. Hold agency heads accountable for their administrative, fiscal and program actions in the conduct of the respective powers and duties of the agencies;
4. Direct the development of goals, objectives, policies and plans that are necessary to the effective and efficient operation of government;
5. Sign documents on behalf of the Governor which originate with agencies assigned to the Secretary; and
6. Employ such personnel and contract for such consulting services as may be required to perform the powers and duties conferred upon the Secretary by statute or executive order.

C. The Secretary shall provide annual reports to the Governor and the General Assembly on juvenile offender demographics by offense, age, committing court, previous court contacts of offenders, and, beginning in July, 1998, recidivism rates of juveniles committed to agencies within the Secretariat. The annual report shall also include summaries of any juvenile program evaluations completed in the previous year on programs operated by the Departments of Juvenile Justice, Corrections or Criminal Justice Services and whose evaluation was directed by the General Assembly or the Secretary.

(Chgd. by L.1996 ch. 617, eff. 7/1/96.)

§2.1-51.17:01. Secretary of Public Safety to publish certain list.

The Secretary of Public Safety is hereby directed to publish annually a list of those localities which have acquired any aircraft through forfeiture procedures. Such list shall include a description of each aircraft so acquired. The Secretary shall develop a program to encourage the use of such aircraft for travel associated with law-enforcement purposes, including but not limited to, extradition of prisoners and arrestees within and without the Commonwealth.

(Added by L.1995 ch. 464, eff. 7/1/95.)

§2.1-51.18. Agencies for which responsible.

The Secretary of Public Safety shall be responsible to the Governor for the following agencies: Department of Alcoholic Beverage Control, Department of Corrections, Department of Juvenile Justice, Department of Correctional Education, Department of Criminal Justice Services, Virginia Parole Board, Department of Emergency Services, Department of Military Affairs, Department of State Police, Department of Fire Programs and the Commonwealth's Attorneys' Services Council. The Governor may, by executive order, assign any other state executive agency to the Secretary of Public Safety, or reassign any agency listed above to another secretary.

(Chgd. by L.1996 ch. 503, eff. 7/1/96.)

CHAPTER 10
PERSONNEL ADMINISTRATION
(Selected Section)

§2.1-114.5:01. Certain information not to be made public.

Notwithstanding the provisions of Chapter 21 (§§2.1-340 through 2.1-346.1) of Title 2.1 the Department shall not disclose lists of home addresses of state employees except in accordance with regulations adopted by the Department pursuant to Chapter 1.1:1 (§§9-6.14:1 through 9-6.14:25) of Title 9.

CHAPTER 10.01
THE DEPARTMENT OF EMPLOYMENT DISPUTE RESOLUTION

(Added by L.1995 chs. 770, 818; heading chgd. to conform with L.2000 chs. 947, 1006, eff. 7/1/2000.)

(Selected Sections)

§2.1-116.05. Grievance procedure generally.

A. It shall be the policy of the Commonwealth, as an employer, to encourage the resolution of employee problems and complaints. To that end, employees must be able to freely, and without retaliation, discuss their concerns with their immediate supervisors and management. To the extent that such concerns cannot be resolved informally, the grievance procedure shall afford an immediate and fair method for the resolution of employment disputes which may arise between state agencies and those employees who have access to the procedure under §2.1-116.09.

B. As part of the Commonwealth's program of employee relations management, the Department shall develop a grievance procedure that includes not more than three successively higher grievance resolution steps and a formal hearing as provided in this chapter.

C. Prior to initiating a written grievance, the employee shall be encouraged to pursue an informal complaint with his immediate supervisor. The supervisor shall have authority to resolve the complaint if it involves actions within his control.

D. An employee may pursue a formal written grievance through the grievance resolution steps if the complaint has been presented to management within thirty calendar days of the employee's knowledge of the event that gave rise to the complaint. Employees' rights to pursue grievances shall not be used to harass or otherwise impede the efficient operations of government.

E. Upon receipt of a timely written complaint, management shall review the grievance and respond to the merits thereof. Each level of management review shall have the authority to provide the employee with a remedy. At least one face-to-face meeting between the employee and management shall be required. The persons who may be present at this meeting are the employee, the appropriate manager, an individual selected by the employee, and an individual selected by the manager. Witnesses may be called by either party.

F. Absent just cause, all documents, as defined in the Rules of the Supreme Court of Virginia, relating to the actions grieved shall be made available, upon request from a party to the grievance, by the opposing party. Documents pertaining to nonparties that are relevant to the grievance shall be produced in such a manner as to preserve the privacy of the individuals not personally involved in the grievance. A party shall not be required to create a document if the document does not exist.

G. All time limitations prescribed in the grievance procedure, including, but not limited to, submission of an initial complaint and employee appeal of management decisions, shall be reasonable, specific, and equally applicable to the agency and the employee. Expedited grievance procedures shall be established for terminations, demotions, suspensions, and lost wages or salaries.

H. Within five workdays of the receipt of a written notice of noncompliance, failure of the employee or the agency to comply with a substantial procedural requirement of the grievance procedure without just cause may result in a decision against the noncomplying party on any qualified issue. Written notice of noncompliance by the agency must be made to the agency head. The Director shall render all decisions related to procedural compliance, and such decisions shall contain the reasons for such decision and shall be final.

I. Grievances qualified pursuant to §2.1-116.06 that have not been resolved through the grievance resolution steps shall advance to a hearing which shall be the final step in the grievance procedure.

(Added by L.1995 chs. 770, 818; chgd. by L.1996 chs. 164, 869; L.1999 chs. 703, 726; L.2000 chs. 947, 1006, eff. 7/1/2000.)

§2.1-116.06. Grievances qualifying for a grievance hearing; grievance hearing generally.

A. A grievance qualifying for a hearing shall involve a complaint or dispute by an employee relating to the following adverse employment actions in which the employee is personally involved, including but not limited to: (i) formal disciplinary actions, including suspensions, demotions, transfers and assignments, and dismissals resulting from formal discipline or unsatisfactory job performance; (ii) the application of all written personnel policies, procedures, rules and regulations where it can be shown that policy was misapplied or unfairly applied; (iii) discrimination on the basis of race, color, religion, political affiliation, age, disability, national origin or sex; (iv) arbitrary or capricious performance evaluations; (v) acts of retaliation as the result of the use of or participation in the grievance procedure or because the employee has complied with any law of the United States or of the Commonwealth, has reported any violation of such law to a governmental authority, has sought any change in law before the Congress of the United States or the General Assembly, or has reported an incidence of fraud, abuse, or gross mismanagement; and (vi) retaliation for exercising any right otherwise protected by law.

B. Management reserves the exclusive right to manage the affairs and operations of state government. Management shall exercise its powers with the highest degree of trust. In any employment matter that management precludes from proceeding to a grievance hearing, management's response, including any appropriate remedial actions, shall be prompt, complete, and fair.

C. Complaints relating solely to the following issues shall not proceed to a hearing: (i) establishment and revision of wages, salaries, position classifications, or general benefits; (ii) work activity accepted by the employee as a condition of employment or which may reasonably be expected to be a part of the job content; (iii) contents of ordinances, statutes or established personnel policies, procedures, and rules and regulations; (iv) methods, means, and personnel by which work activities are to be carried on; (v) termination, layoff, demotion, or suspension from duties because of lack of work, reduction in work force, or job abolition; (vi) hiring, promotion, transfer, assignment, and retention of employees within the agency; and (vii) relief of employees from duties of the agency in emergencies.

D. Decisions regarding whether a grievance qualifies for a hearing shall be made in writing by the agency head or his designee within five workdays of the employee's request for a hearing. A copy of the decision shall be sent to the employee. The employee may appeal the denial of a hearing by the agency head to the Director. Upon receipt of an appeal, the agency shall transmit the entire grievance record to the Department within five workdays. The Director shall render a decision on whether the employee is entitled to a hearing upon the grievance record and other probative evidence.

E. Proceedings for review of the decision of the Director may be made by an employee filing a notice of appeal within five workdays of receipt of the decision. Within five workdays thereafter, the agency shall transmit to the clerk of the circuit court in the jurisdiction in which the grievance arose a copy of the grievance record. The court, on motion of the grievant, may issue a writ of certiorari requiring the Director to transmit the record on or before a certain date. Within thirty days of receipt of such records, the court, sitting without a jury, shall hear the appeal on the record and such additional evidence as may be necessary to resolve any controversy as to the correctness of the record. The court, in its discretion, may receive such other evidence as the ends of justice require. The court may affirm the decision of the Director or may reverse or modify the decision. The decision of the court shall be rendered no later than the fifteenth day from the date of the conclusion of the hearing. The decision of the court is final and is not appealable. The circuit court hearing shall be at no cost to the Commonwealth or the grievant.

F. The hearing pursuant to §2.1-116.07 shall be held in the locality in which the employee is employed or in any other locality agreed to by the employee, employer, and hearing officer. The employee and the agency may be represented by legal counsel or a lay advocate, the provisions of §54.1-3904 notwithstanding. The employee and the agency may call witnesses to present testimony and be cross-examined.

(Added by L.1995 chs. 770, 818; chgd. by L.1996 chs. 164, 869, eff. 7/1/96.)

§2.1-116.08. Certain employees of the Departments of Corrections and Juvenile Justice.

A. Employees of the Departments of Corrections and Juvenile Justice who work in institutions or juvenile correctional centers or have client, inmate, or resident contact and who are terminated on the grounds of client, inmate, or resident abuse, criminal conviction, or as a result of being placed on probation under the provisions of §18.2-251, may appeal their termination only through the grievance resolution steps.

B. If no resolution is reached by the conclusion of the last grievance step, the employee may advance the grievance to the circuit court of the jurisdiction in which the grievance occurred for a de novo hearing on the merits. In its discretion, the court may refer the matter to a commissioner in chancery to take such evidence as may be proper and to make a report to the court. Both the grievant and the respondent may call upon appropriate witnesses and be represented by legal counsel or other representatives before the court or the commissioner in chancery. Such representatives may examine, cross-examine, question and present evidence on behalf of the grievant or respondent before the court or commissioner in chancery without being in violation of the provisions of §54.1-3904.

C. A termination shall be upheld unless shown to have been unwarranted by the facts or contrary to law or policy. The decision of the court shall be final and binding.

(Added by L.1995 chs. 770, 818; chgd. by L.1996 chs. 755, 914, eff. 7/1/96.)

§2.1-116.013. Exemptions from chapter.

The provisions of this chapter shall not apply to:

1. Appointees of elected groups or individuals except as provided in subsection B of §2.1-116.09;

2. Agency heads or chief executive officers of government agencies and institutions of higher education appointed by boards and commissions;

3. Law-enforcement officers as defined in §2.1-116.1 whose grievances are subject to Chapter 10.1 (§2.1-116.1 et seq.) and who have elected to resolve such grievances under those provisions; and

4. Employees in positions designated in §2.1-116 as exempt from the Virginia Personnel Act (§2.1-110 et seq.).

(Added by L.1995 chs. 770, 818, eff. 7/1/95.)

CHAPTER 10.1
LAW-ENFORCEMENT OFFICERS' PROCEDURAL GUARANTEES

(Complete Chapter)

§2.1-116.1. Definitions.

As used in this chapter, the following terms have the following meanings:

1. "Law-enforcement officer" means any person, other than a Chief of Police or the Superintendent of the Department of State Police, who, in his official capacity, is (i) authorized by law to make arrests and (ii) a nonprobationary officer of one of the following agencies:

(a) The Department of State Police, The Division of Capitol Police, the Virginia Marine Resources Commission, the Virginia Port Authority, the Department of Alcoholic Beverage Control, or the Department of Motor Vehicles; or

(b) The police department, bureau or force of any political subdivision or the campus police department of any public institution of higher education of the Commonwealth of Virginia where such department, bureau or force has ten or more law-enforcement officers; however, this shall not include the sheriff's department of any city or county.

This term also means any game warden as defined in §9-169(9).

2. "Agency" means:

(a) The Department of State Police, The Division of Capitol Police, the Virginia Marine Resources Commission, the Virginia Port Authority, the Department of Alcoholic Beverage Control, or the Department of Motor Vehicles; or

(b) The political subdivision or the campus police department of any public institution of higher education of the Commonwealth of Virginia employing the law-enforcement officer.

(Chgd. by L.1995 ch. 730, eff. 7/1/95.)

§2.1-116.2. Conduct of investigation.

Whenever an investigation by an agency focuses on matters which could lead to the dismissal, demotion, suspension or transfer for punitive reasons of a law-enforcement officer, the following conditions shall be complied with:

1. Any questioning of the officer shall take place at a reasonable time and place as designated by the investigating officer, preferably when the officer under investigation is on duty and at the office of the command of the investigating officer or at the office of the local precinct or police unit of the officer being investigated, unless circumstances dictate otherwise.

2. Prior to the officer being questioned, he shall be informed of (i) the name and rank of the investigating officer and of any individual to be present during the questioning and (ii) the nature of the investigation.

3. When a blood or urine specimen is taken from a law-enforcement officer for the purpose of determining whether the officer has used drugs or alcohol, the specimen shall be divided and placed into two separate containers. One specimen shall be tested while the other is held in a proper manner to preserve the specimen by the facility collecting or testing the specimen. Should the first specimen test positive, the law-enforcement officer shall have the right to require the second specimen be sent to a laboratory of his choice for independent testing in accordance generally with the procedures set forth in §18.2-268.1 through §18.2-268.12. The officer shall notify the chief of his agency in writing of his request within ten days of being notified of positive specimen results. The laboratory chosen by the officer shall be on the approved list of the Division of Forensic Science.

§2.1-116.3. Personal assets of officers.

No law-enforcement officer shall be required or requested to disclose any item of his property, income, assets, source of income, debts, or personal or domestic expenditures, including those of any member of his family or household, unless such information is necessary in investigating a possible conflict of interest with respect to the performance of his official duties, or unless such disclosure is required by law, or unless such information is related to an investigation. Nothing in this section shall preclude an agency from requiring such law-enforcement officer to disclose any place of off-duty employment and where he may be contacted.

§2.1-116.4. Notice of charges; response; election to proceed under grievance procedure of local governing body.

A. Before any dismissal, demotion, suspension without pay or transfer for punitive reasons may be imposed, the following must be complied with:

1. The law-enforcement officer shall be notified in writing of all charges, the basis therefor, and the action which may be taken;

2. The law-enforcement officer must be given an opportunity, within a reasonable time limit after the date of the written notice provided for above, to respond orally and in writing to the charges. The time limit shall be determined by the agency, but in no event shall it be less than five calendar days unless agreed to by the law-enforcement officer;

3. In making his response, the law-enforcement office may be assisted by counsel at his own expense; and

4. The law-enforcement officer shall be given written notification of his right to initiate a grievance under the grievance procedure established by the local governing body pursuant to §§15.1-7.1 and 15.1-7.2. A copy of the local governing body's grievance procedure shall be provided to the law-enforcement officer upon his request.

B. A law-enforcement officer may proceed under either the local governing body's grievance procedure or the law-enforcement officer's procedural guarantees, but not both.

§2.1-116.5. Hearing.

1. Whenever a law-enforcement officer is dismissed, demoted, suspended or transferred for punitive reasons, he may, within a reasonable amount of time following such action, as set by the agency, request a hearing. If such request is timely made, a hearing shall be held within a reasonable amount of time set by the agency; provided, however, that the hearing shall be set no later than fourteen calendar days following the date of request unless a later date is agreed to by the law-enforcement officer. At the hearing, the law-enforcement officer and his agency shall be afforded the opportunity to present evidence, examine and cross-examine witnesses. The panel shall have the power to, and on the request of either the law-enforcement officer or his agency shall, issue subpoenas requiring the testimony of witnesses who have refused or failed to appear at the hearing. The law-enforcement officer shall also be given the opportunity to be represented by counsel at the hearing unless such officer and agency are afforded, by regulation, the right to counsel in a subsequent de novo hearing. The panel conducting the hearing shall rule on the admissibility of the evidence. A record shall be made of the hearing.

2. The hearing shall be conducted by a panel, such panel to consist of one member from within the agency selected by the grievant, one member from within the agency of equal rank of the grievant but no more than two ranks above appointed by the agency head, and a third member from within the agency to be selected by the other two members. In the event that such two members cannot agree upon their selection, the chief judge of the judicial circuit wherein the duty station of the grievant lies shall choose such third member.

3. At the option of the agency, it may, in lieu of complying with the provisions of §2.1-116.4, give the law-enforcement officer a statement, in writing, of the charges, the basis therefor, the action which may be taken, and provide a hearing as provided for in this section prior to dismissing, demoting, suspending or transferring for punitive reasons the law-enforcement officer.

§2.1-116.6. Immediate suspension.

Nothing in this chapter shall prevent the immediate suspension without pay of any law-enforcement officer whose continued presence on the job is deemed to be a substantial and immediate threat to the welfare of his agency or the public, nor shall anything in this chapter prevent the suspension of a law-enforcement officer for refusing to obey a direct order issued in conformance with the agency's written and disseminated rules and regulations. In such a case, the law-enforcement officer shall, upon request, be afforded the rights provided for under this chapter within a reasonable amount of time set by the agency.

§2.1-116.7. Outcome of hearing.

The recommendations of the panel, and the reasons therefor, shall be in writing, shall be transmitted promptly to the law-enforcement officer or his attorney and to the chief executive officer of the law-enforcement agency. Such recommendations shall be advisory only, but shall be accorded significant weight.

§2.1-116.8. Informal counseling not prohibited.

Nothing in this chapter shall be construed to prohibit the informal counseling of a law-enforcement officer by a supervisor in reference to a minor infraction of policy or procedure which does not result in disciplinary action being taken against the law-enforcement officer.

§2.1-116.9. Chapter accords minimum rights.

The rights accorded law-enforcement officers in this chapter are minimum rights and all agencies shall promulgate grievance procedures not inconsistent herewith; provided that any agency may provide for the rights of law-enforcement officers in addition hereto.

CHAPTER 10.1:2
CIVILIAN PROTECTION IN CASES OF POLICE MISCONDUCT ACT
(Complete Chapter)

§2.1-116.9:6. Civilian protection in cases of police misconduct; minimum standards.

A. State, local, and public law-enforcement agencies, which have ten or more law-enforcement officers, shall have procedures as established in subsection B, allowing citizen submission of complaints regarding the conduct of the law-enforcement agency, law-enforcement officers in the agency, or employees of the agency. The provisions of this chapter shall not apply to constitutional officers.

B. Law-enforcement agencies shall ensure, at a minimum, that in the case of all written complaints:

1. The general public has access to the required forms and information concerning the submission of complaints;
2. The law-enforcement agency assists individuals in filing complaints; and
3. Adequate records are maintained of the nature and disposition of such cases.

CHAPTER 11
ATTORNEY GENERAL AND DEPARTMENT OF LAW
(Selected Sections)

§2.1-121. Legal service in civil matters.

All legal service in civil matters for the Commonwealth, the Governor, and every state department, institution, division, commission, board, bureau, agency, entity, official, court, or judge, including the conduct of all civil litigation in which any of them are interested, shall be rendered and performed by the Attorney General, except as hereinafter provided in this chapter and except for any litigation concerning a justice or judge initiated by the Judicial Inquiry and Review Commission. No regular counsel shall be employed for or by the Governor or any state department, institution, division, commission, board, bureau, agency, entity, or official. The Attorney General, in his discretion, may represent personally or through one or more of his assistants any number of state departments, institutions, divisions, commissions, boards, bureaus, agencies, entities, officials, courts, or judges which are parties to the same transaction or which are parties in the same civil or administrative proceeding and may represent multiple interests within the same department, institution, division, commission, board, bureau, agency, or entity. The Attorney General, in his discretion, may represent personally or through one of his assistants any of the following persons who are made defendant in any civil action for damages arising out of any matter connected with their official duties: any member, agent, or employee of the Alcoholic Beverage Control Board; agent, inspector, or investigator appointed by the State Corporation Commission; agent, investigator, or auditor employed by the Department of Taxation; member, agent, or employee of the State Mental Health, Mental Retardation and Substance Abuse Services Board, the Department of Mental Health, Mental Retardation and Substance Abuse Services, the State Board of Health, the State Department of Health, the Department of General Services, the State Board of Social Services, the Department of Social Services, the State Board of Corrections, the Department of Corrections, the State Board of Juvenile Justice, the Department of Juvenile Justice, the Virginia Parole Board, or the Department of Agriculture and Consumer Services; any person employed by the Commonwealth Transportation Board; any person employed by the Commissioner of Motor Vehicles; any person appointed by the Commissioner of Marine Resources; any police officer appointed by the Superintendent of State Police; any game warden appointed by the Department of Game and Inland Fisheries; or any third impartial panel member appointed to hear a teacher's grievance pursuant to §22.1-312; or any staff member or volunteer participating in a court-appointed special advocate program pursuant to Article 1.4 (§9-173.6 et seq.) of Chapter 27 of Title 9. If, in the opinion of the Attorney General, it is impracticable or uneconomical for such legal service to be rendered by him or one of his assistants, he may employ special counsel for this purpose, whose compensation shall be fixed by the Attorney General.

The Attorney General, in his discretion, may represent personally or through one of his assistants any emergency medical service agency that is a licensee of the Department of Health in any civil matter and any guardian ad litem appointed by a court in a civil matter brought against him for alleged errors or omissions in the discharge of his court-appointed duties.

Upon request of the affected individual, the Attorney General may represent personally or through one of his assistants any basic or advanced emergency medical care attendant or technician possessing a valid certificate issued by authority of the State Board of Health in any civil matter in which a defense of immunity from liability is raised pursuant to §8.01-255.

The compensation for such special counsel shall be paid out of the funds appropriated for the administration of the board, commission, division or department whose members, officers, inspectors, investigators, or other employees are defended pursuant to this section. Notwithstanding any provision of this section to the contrary, the Supreme Court, in its discretion, may employ its own counsel in any matter arising out of its official duties in which it, or any justice, is a party.

§2.1-124. Criminal cases.

A. Unless specifically requested by the Governor to do so, the Attorney General shall have no authority to institute or conduct criminal prosecutions in the circuit courts of the Commonwealth except in cases involving (i) violations of the Alcoholic Beverage Control Act (§4.1-100 et seq.), (ii) violation of laws relating to elections and the electoral process as provided in §24.2-104, (iii) violation of laws relating to motor vehicles and their operation, (iv) the handling of funds by a state bureau, institution, commission or department, (v) the theft of state property, (vi) violation of the criminal laws involving child pornography and sexually explicit visual material involving children, (vii) the practice of law without being duly authorized or licensed or the illegal practice of law, (viii) with the concurrence of the local attorney for the Commonwealth, violations of the Virginia Computer Crimes Act (§18.2-152.1 et seq.), (ix) with the concurrence of the local attorney for the Commonwealth, violations of the Air Pollution Control Law (§10.1-1300 et seq.), the Virginia Waste Management Act (§10.1-1400 et seq.), and the State Water Control Law (§62.1-44.2 et seq.), (x) with the concurrence of the local attorney for the Commonwealth, violations of Chapters 2 (§18.2-18 et seq.), 3 (§18.2-22 et seq.), and 10 (§18.2-434 et seq.) of Title 18.2, if such crimes relate to violations of law listed in clause (ix) of this subsection, and (xi) with the concurrence of the local attorney for the Commonwealth, criminal violations by

Medicaid providers or their employees in the course of doing business, in which cases the Attorney General may leave the prosecution to the local attorney for the Commonwealth, or he may, in his discretion, institute proceedings by information, presentment or indictment, as the one or the other may be appropriate, and conduct the same.

In all other criminal cases in the circuit courts, except where the law provides otherwise, the authority of the Attorney General to appear or participate in the proceedings shall not attach unless and until a petition for appeal has been granted by the Court of Appeals or a writ of error has been granted by the Supreme Court. In all criminal cases before the Court of Appeals or the Supreme Court in which the Commonwealth is a party or is directly interested, the Attorney General shall appear and represent the Commonwealth. In any criminal case in which a petition for appeal has been granted by the Court of Appeals, the Attorney General shall continue to represent the Commonwealth in any further appeal of a case from the Court of Appeals to the Supreme Court.

B. The Attorney General shall, upon request of a person who was the victim of a crime and subject to such reasonable procedures as the Attorney General may require, ensure that such person is given notice of the filing and disposition of any appeal or habeas corpus proceeding involving the case or cases in which such person was a victim. For the purposes of this section, a victim is an individual who has suffered physical, psychological or economic harm as a direct result of the commission of a crime; a spouse, child, parent or legal guardian of a minor or incapacitated victim; or a spouse, child, parent or legal guardian of a victim of a homicide. Nothing in this subsection shall confer upon any person a right to appeal or modify any decision in a criminal, appellate or habeas corpus proceeding; abridge any right guaranteed by law; or create any cause of action for damages against the Commonwealth or any of its political subdivisions, the Attorney General or any of his employees or agents, any other officer, employee or agent of the Commonwealth or any of its political subdivisions, or any officer of the court.

(Chgd. by L.1995 chs. 565, 839; L.1997 ch. 801; L.1998 ch. 507, 510; L.2000 ch. 239, eff. 7/1/2000.)

CHAPTER 11.1
LINE OF DUTY ACT

(Added by L.1995 ch. 156, eff. 7/1/95.)

(Complete Chapter)

Section

§2.1-133.5. Title of chapter.

This chapter shall be known and designated as the Line of Duty Act.

(Added by L.1995 ch. 156, eff. 7/1/95.)

§2.1-133.6. Definitions.

For the purposes of this chapter the following words shall have the following meanings:

"Beneficiary" means the spouse of the deceased and such person or persons as are entitled to take under the will of the deceased if testate, or as his heir at law if intestate.

"Deceased" means any person whose death occurs on or after April 8, 1972, as the direct or proximate result of the performance of his duty, including the presumptions under §§27-40.1, 27-40.2, 51.1-813, and 65.2-402, as a law-enforcement officer of this Commonwealth or any of its political subdivisions; a correctional officer as defined in §53.1-1; a jail officer; a regional jail or jail farm superintendent; a sheriff, deputy sheriff, or city sergeant or deputy city sergeant of the City of Richmond; a member of any fire company or department or rescue squad which has been recognized by an ordinance or a resolution of the governing body of any county, city or town of this Commonwealth as an integral part of the official safety program of such county, city or town; a member of the Virginia National Guard or the Virginia State Defense Force while such member is serving in the Virginia National Guard or the Virginia State Defense Force on official state duty or federal duty under Title 32 of the United States Code; any special agent of the Virginia Alcoholic Beverage Control Board; any agent, investigator, or inspector vested with the power to arrest pursuant to §56-334; any regular or special game warden who receives compensation from a county, city or town or from the Commonwealth appointed pursuant to the provisions of §29.1-200; any commissioned forest warden appointed under the provisions of §10.1-1135; any member or employee of the Virginia Marine Resources Commission granted the power of arrest pursuant to §28.2-900; any Department of Emergency Services hazardous materials officer; any nonfirefighter regional hazardous materials emergency response team member; or any conservation officer of the Department of Conservation and Recreation commissioned pursuant to §10.1-115.

"Disabled employee" means any person who, as the direct or proximate result of the performance of his duty in any position listed in the definition of deceased in this section, has become mentally or physically incapacitated so as to prevent the further performance of duty where such incapacity is likely to be permanent.

"Line of duty" means any action the deceased or disabled employee was obligated or authorized to perform by rule, regulation, condition of employment or service, or law.

(Added by L.1995 chs. 112, 156, 597; chgd. by L.1996 chs. 66, 174; L.1998 ch. 712, eff. 7/1/2000.)

§2.1-133.7. Payments to beneficiaries of certain deceased law-enforcement officers, firefighters, etc., and retirees.

A. If the deceased's death occurred while in the line of duty as the direct or proximate result of the performance of his duty, his beneficiary shall be entitled to receive the sum of $75,000, which shall be payable out of the general fund of the state treasury, in gratitude for and in recognition of his sacrifice on behalf of the people of this Commonwealth.

B. Subject to the provisions of §§27-40.1, 27-40.2, 51.1-813, or 65.2-402, if the deceased's death (a) arose out of and in the course of his employment or (b) was within five years from his date of retirement, his beneficiary shall be entitled to receive the sum of $25,000, which shall be payable out of the general fund of the state treasury.

(Added by L.1995 chs. 156, 597; chgd. by L.2000 ch. 314, eff. 7/1/2000.)

§2.1-133.7:1. Continued health insurance coverage for disabled employees, their spouses and dependents, and for the surviving spouse and dependents of certain deceased law-enforcement officers, firefighters, etc.

A. If the deceased's death: (i) occurred while in the line of duty as the direct or proximate result of the performance of his duty or (ii) was subject to the provisions of §§27-40.1, 27-40.2, 51.1-813 or §65.2-402, and arose out of and in the course of his employment, his surviving spouse and any dependents shall be afforded continued health insurance coverage. The cost of such health insurance coverage shall be paid in full out of the general fund of the state treasury.

B. If the disabled employee's disability: (i) occurred while in the line of duty as the direct or proximate result of the performance of his duty or (ii) was subject to the provisions of §§27-40.1, 27-40.2, 51.1-813 or §65.2-402, and arose out of and in the course of his employment, the disabled employee, his surviving spouse and any dependents shall be afforded continued health insurance coverage. The cost of such health insurance coverage shall be paid in full out of the general fund of the state treasury.

C. The continued health insurance coverage provided by this section shall be the same plan of benefits which the deceased or disabled employee was entitled to on the last day of his active duty or comparable benefits established as a result of a replacement plan.

D. For any spouse, continued health insurance provided by this section shall terminate upon such spouse's death or coverage by alternate health insurance.

E. For dependents, continued health insurance provided by this section shall terminate upon such dependent's death, marriage, coverage by alternate health insurance or twenty-first birthday. Continued health care insurance shall be provided beyond the dependent's twenty-first birthday if the dependent is a full-time college student and shall continue until such time as the dependent ceases to be a full-time student or reaches his twenty-fifth birthday, whichever occurs first. Continued health care insurance shall also be provided beyond the dependent's twenty-first birthday if the dependent is mentally or physically disabled, and such coverage shall continue until three months following the cessation of the disability.

F. For any disabled employee, continued health insurance provided by this section shall automatically terminate upon the disabled employee's death, recovery or return to full duty in any position listed in the definition of deceased in §2.1-133.6.

(Added by L.1998 ch. 712; chgd. by L.2000 ch. 616, eff. 7/1/2000.)

§2.1-133.8. Claim for payment.

Every beneficiary, disabled employee or his spouse, or dependent of a deceased or disabled employee hereunder shall present his claim to the chief officer, or his designee, of the appropriate division or department which last employed the deceased or disabled employee on forms to be provided by the State Comptroller's office. Such chief officer or his designee shall submit a request to the Superintendent of the Department of the State Police, who shall investigate and report upon the circumstances surrounding the deceased or disabled employee, calling upon the additional information and services of any other appropriate agents or agencies of the Commonwealth. The chief officer, or his designee, shall report his findings to the Comptroller within forty-five days of receipt of a claim.

(Added by L.1995 ch. 156; chgd. by L.1998 ch. 712, eff. 7/1/2000.)

§2.1-133.9. Order of Comptroller.

A. If it appears to the Comptroller that the requirements of either subsection A or B of §2.1-133.7 shall have been satisfied, he shall issue his warrant in the appropriate amount for payment out of the general fund of the state treasury to the surviving spouse or to such persons and subject to such conditions as may be proper in his administrative discretion, and in the event there is no beneficiary, the Comptroller shall issue such payment to the estate of the deceased. The Comptroller shall issue a decision, and payment, if appropriate, shall be made no later than forty-five days following receipt of the report required under §2.1-133.8.

B. If it appears to the Comptroller that the requirements of either subsection A or B of §2.1-133.7:1 have been satisfied, he shall issue his warrants in the appropriate amounts for payment from the general fund of the state treasury to ensure continued health care coverage for the persons designated under §2.1-133.7:1. The Comptroller shall issue a decision, and payments, if appropriate, shall commence no later than forty-five days following receipt of the report required under §2.1-133.8. Such payments shall be retroactive to the first date that such disability existed.

(Added by L.1995 chs. 156, 597; chgd. by L.1998 ch. 712, eff. 7/1/2000.)

§2.1-133.10. Appeal from decision of Comptroller.

Any beneficiary, disabled employee or his spouse, or dependent of a deceased or disabled employee aggrieved by the decision of the Comptroller shall present a petition to the court in which the will of the deceased is probated or in which the personal representative of the deceased is qualified or might qualify or in the jurisdiction in which the disabled employee resides. The Commonwealth shall be represented in such proceeding by the Attorney General or his designee. The court shall proceed as chancellor without a jury. If it appears to the court that the requirements of this chapter have been satisfied, the judge shall enter an order to that effect. The order shall also direct the Comptroller to issue his warrant in the appropriate amount for the payment out of the general fund of the state treasury to such persons and subject to such conditions as may be proper. If, in the case of a deceased, there is no beneficiary, the judge shall direct such payment as is due under §2.1-133.7 to the estate of the deceased.

(Added by L.1995 chs. 156, 597; chgd. by L.1998 ch. 712, eff. 7/1/2000.)

§2.1-133.11. Appeals.

Appeals from judgments entered pursuant to this chapter shall be allowed as in chancery matters generally.

(Added by L.1995 ch. 156, eff. 7/1/95.)

CHAPTER 21
VIRGINIA FREEDOM OF INFORMATION ACT
(Selected Articles)

ARTICLE 1
PUBLIC RECORDS AND MEETINGS
(Heading added to conform with L.2000 ch. 917, eff. 7/1/2000.)
(Complete Article)

Section
2.1-340. Short title.
2.1-340.1. Policy of chapter.
2.1-341. Definitions.
2.1-341.1. Notice of chapter.

§2.1-340. Short title.

This chapter may be cited as "The Virginia Freedom of Information Act."

§2.1-340.1. Policy of chapter.

By enacting this chapter, the General Assembly ensures the people of the Commonwealth ready access to records in the custody of public officials and free entry to meetings of public bodies wherein the business of the people is being conducted. The affairs of government are not intended to be conducted in an atmosphere of secrecy since at all times the public is to be the beneficiary of any action taken at any level of government. Unless a public body or public official specifically elects to exercise an exemption provided by this chapter or any other statute, every meeting shall be open to the public, and all public records shall be available for inspection and copying upon request. All public records and meetings shall be presumed open, unless an exemption is properly invoked.

The provisions of this chapter shall be liberally construed to promote an increased awareness by all persons of governmental activities and afford every opportunity to citizens to witness the operations of government. Any exemption from public access to records or meetings shall be narrowly construed, and no record shall be withheld or meeting closed to the public unless specifically made exempt pursuant to this chapter or other specific provision of law. This chapter shall not be construed to discourage the free discussion by government officials or employees of public matters with the citizens of the Commonwealth.

All public bodies and public officials shall make reasonable efforts to reach an agreement with a requester concerning the production of the records requested.

Any ordinance adopted by a local governing body which conflicts with the provisions of this chapter shall be void.
(Chgd. by L.1999 chs. 703, 726, eff. 7/1/99.)

§2.1-341. Definitions.

As used in this chapter unless the context requires a different meaning:

"Closed meeting" means a meeting from which the public is excluded.

"Emergency" means an unforeseen circumstance rendering the notice required by this chapter impossible or impracticable and which circumstance requires immediate action.

"Meeting" or "meetings" means the meetings including work sessions, when sitting physically, or through telephonic or video equipment pursuant to §2.1-343.1, as a body or entity, or as an informal assemblage of (i) as many as three members or (ii) a quorum, if less than three, of the constituent membership, wherever held, with or without minutes being taken, whether or not votes are cast, of any public body. The gathering of employees of a public body shall not be deemed a "meeting" subject to the provisions of this chapter.

"Open meeting" or "public meeting" means a meeting at which the public may be present.

"Public body" means any legislative body; any authority, board, bureau, commission, district or agency of the Commonwealth or of any political subdivision of the Commonwealth, including cities, towns and counties; municipal councils, governing bodies of counties, school boards and planning commissions; boards of visitors of public institutions of higher education; and other organizations, corporations or agencies in the Commonwealth supported wholly or principally by public funds. It shall include any committee or subcommittee of the public body created to perform delegated functions of the public body or to advise the public body. It shall not exclude any such committee or subcommittee because it has private sector or citizen members. Corporations organized by the Virginia Retirement System are "public bodies" for purposes of this chapter.

"Public records" means all writings and recordings which consist of letters, words or numbers, or their equivalent, set down by handwriting, typewriting, printing, photostatting, photography, magnetic impulse, optical or magneto-optical form, mechanical or electronic recording or other form of data compilation, however stored, and regardless of physical form or characteristics, prepared or owned by, or in the possession of a public body or its officers, employees or agents in the transaction of public business.

"Scholastic records" means those records containing information directly related to a student and maintained by a public body which is an educational agency or institution or by a person acting for such agency or institution.
(Chgd. by L.1996 ch. 609; L.1997 ch. 641; L.1999 chs. 703, 726, eff. 7/1/99.)

§2.1-341.1. Notice of chapter.

A. Any person elected, reelected, appointed or reappointed to any body not excepted from this chapter shall be furnished by the public body's administrator or legal counsel with a copy of this chapter within two weeks following election, reelection, appointment or reappointment.

B. Public officials shall read and familiarize themselves with the provisions of this chapter.
(Chgd. by L.1999 chs. 703, 726, eff. 7/1/99.)

§2.1-341.2. Public bodies and records to which chapter inapplicable; voter registration and election records.

A. The provisions of this chapter shall not apply to:

1. The Virginia Parole Board, except that (i) information from the Virginia Parole Board providing the number of inmates considered by such Board for discretionary parole, the number of inmates granted or denied parole, and the number of parolees returned to the custody of the Department of Corrections solely as a result of a determination by such Board of a violation of parole shall be open to inspection and available for release, on a monthly basis, as provided by §2.1-342, and (ii) all records concerning the finances of the Virginia Parole Board shall be public records and subject to the provisions of this chapter. The information required by clause (i) shall be furnished by offense, sex, race, age of the inmate, and the

locality in which the conviction was obtained, upon the request of the party seeking the information;

2. Petit juries and grand juries;

3. Family assessment and planning teams established pursuant to §2.1-753; and

4. The Virginia State Crime Commission.

B. Public access to voter registration and election records shall be governed by the provisions of Title 24.2 and this chapter. The provisions of Title 24.2 shall be controlling in the event of any conflict.

(Added by L.1999 chs. 703, 726, eff. 7/1/99.)

§2.1-342. Public records to be open to inspection; procedure for requesting records and responding to request; charges.

A. Except as otherwise specifically provided by law, all public records shall be open to inspection and copying by any citizens of the Commonwealth during the regular office hours of the custodian of such records. Access to such records shall not be denied to citizens of the Commonwealth, representatives of newspapers and magazines with circulation in the Commonwealth, and representatives of radio and television stations broadcasting in or into the Commonwealth. The custodian of such records shall take all necessary precautions for their preservation and safekeeping.

B. A request for public records shall identify the requested records with reasonable specificity. The request need not make reference to this chapter in order to invoke the provisions of this chapter or to impose the time limits for response by a public body. Any public body which is subject to this chapter and which is the custodian of the requested records shall promptly, but in all cases within five working days of receiving a request, make one of the following responses:

1. The requested records will be provided to the requester.

2. The requested records will be entirely withheld because their release is prohibited by law or the custodian has exercised his discretion to withhold the records in accordance with this chapter. Such response shall (i) be in writing, (ii) identify with reasonable particularity the volume and subject matter of withheld records, and (iii) cite, as to each category of withheld records, the specific Code section which authorizes the withholding of the records.

3. The requested records will be provided in part and withheld in part because the release of part of the records is prohibited by law or the custodian has exercised his discretion to withhold a portion of the records in accordance with this chapter. Such response shall (i) be in writing, (ii) identify with reasonable particularity the subject matter of withheld portions, and (iii) cite, as to each category of withheld records, the specific Code section which authorizes the withholding of the records. When a portion of a requested record is withheld, the public body may delete or excise only that portion of the record to which an exemption applies and shall release the remainder of the record.

4. It is not practically possible to provide the requested records or to determine whether they are available within the five-work-day period. Such response shall be in writing and specify the conditions which make a response impossible. If the response is made within five working days, the public body shall have an additional seven work days in which to provide one of the three preceding responses.

C. Any public body may petition the appropriate court for additional time to respond to a request for records when the request is for an extraordinary volume of records and a response by the public body within the time required by this chapter will prevent the public body from meeting its operational responsibilities. Before proceeding with the petition, however, the public body shall make reasonable efforts to reach an agreement with the requester concerning the production of the records requested.

D. Subject to the provisions of subsections G and H, no public body shall be required to create a new record if the record does not already exist. However, a public body may abstract or summarize information under such terms and conditions as agreed between the requester and the public body.

E. Failure to respond to a request for records shall be deemed a denial of the request and shall constitute a violation of this chapter.

F. A public body may make reasonable charges for its actual cost incurred in accessing, duplicating, supplying, or searching for the requested records. No public body shall impose any extraneous, intermediary or surplus fees or expenses to recoup the general costs associated with creating or maintaining records or transacting the general business of the public body. Any duplicating fee charged by a public body shall not exceed the actual cost of duplication. The public body may also make a reasonable charge for the cost incurred in supplying records produced from a geographic information system at the request of anyone other than the owner of the land that is the subject of the request. However, such charges shall not exceed the actual cost to the public body in supplying such records, except that the public body may charge, on a pro rata per acre basis, for the cost of creating topographical maps developed by the public body, for such maps or portions thereof, which encompass a contiguous area greater than fifty acres. All charges for the supplying of requested records shall be estimated in advance at the request of the citizen.

In any case where a public body determines in advance that charges for producing the requested records are likely to exceed $200, the public body may, before continuing to process the request, require the requester to agree to payment of a deposit not to exceed the amount of the advance determination. The deposit shall be credited toward the final cost of supplying the requested records. The period within which the public body shall respond under this section shall be tolled for the amount of time that elapses between notice of the advance determination and the response of the requester.

G. Public records maintained by a public body in an electronic data processing system, computer database, or any other structured collection of data shall be made available to a requester at a reasonable cost, not to exceed the actual cost in accordance with subsection F. When electronic or other databases are combined or contain exempt and nonexempt records, the public body may provide access to the exempt records if not otherwise prohibited by law, but shall provide access to the nonexempt records as provided by this chapter.

H. Every public body of state government shall compile, and annually update, an index of computer databases which contains at a minimum those databases created by them on or after July 1, 1997. "Computer database" means a structured collection of data or records residing in a computer. Such index shall be a public record and shall include, at a minimum, the following information with respect to each database listed therein: a list of data fields, a description of the format or record layout, the date last updated, a list of any data fields to which public access is restricted, a description of each format in which the database can be copied or reproduced using the public body's computer facilities, and a schedule of fees for the production of copies in each available form. The form, context, language, and guidelines for the indices and the databases to be indexed shall be developed by the Director of the Department of Information Technology in consultation with the Librarian of Virginia and the State Archivist. The public body shall not be required to disclose its software security, including passwords.

Public bodies shall produce nonexempt records maintained in an electronic database in any tangible medium identified by the requester, including, where the public body has the capability, the option of posting the records on a website or delivering the records through an electronic mail address provided by the requester, if that medium is used by the public body in the regular course of business. No public body shall be required to produce records from an electronic database in a format not regularly used by the public body. However, the public body shall make reasonable efforts to provide records in any format under such terms and conditions as agreed between the requester and public body, including the payment of reasonable costs. The excision of exempt fields of information from a database or the conversion of data from one available format to another shall not be deemed the creation, preparation or compilation of a new public record.

(Chgd. by L.1995 chs. 299, 362, 499, 562, 638, 722, 812, 837; L.1996 chs. 168, 469, 589, 599, 783, 786, 794, 855, 862, 902, 905, 1001, 1046; L.1997 chs. 198, 295, 439, 567, 636, 641, 777, 782, 785, 838, 861; L.1998 chs. 427, 891; L.1999 chs. 438, 485, 518, 703, 726, 793, 849, 852, 867, 868, 881, eff. 7/1/99.)

§2.1-342.01. Exclusions to application of chapter.

A. The following records are excluded from the provisions of this chapter but may be disclosed by the custodian in his discretion, except where such disclosure is prohibited by law:

1. Confidential records of all investigations of applications for licenses and permits, and all licensees and permittees made by or submitted to the Alcoholic Beverage Control Board, the State Lottery Department, the Virginia Racing Commission, or the Charitable Gaming Commission.

2. State income, business, and estate tax returns, personal property tax returns, scholastic and confidential records held pursuant to §58.1-3.

3. Scholastic records containing information concerning identifiable individuals, except that such access shall not be denied to the person who is the subject thereof, or the parent or legal guardian of the student. However, no student shall have access to (i) financial records of a parent or guardian or (ii) records of instructional, supervisory, and administrative personnel and educational personnel ancillary thereto, which are in the sole possession of the maker thereof and which are not accessible or revealed to any other person except a substitute.

The parent or legal guardian of a student may prohibit, by written request, the release of any individual information regarding that student until the student reaches the age of eighteen years. For scholastic records of students under the age of eighteen years, the right of access may be asserted only by his legal guardian or parent, including a noncustodial parent, unless such parent's parental rights have been terminated or a court of competent jurisdiction has restricted or denied such access. For scholastic records of students who are emancipated or attending a state-supported institution of higher education, the right of access may be asserted by the student.

Any person who is the subject of any scholastic record and who is eighteen years of age or older may waive, in writing, the protections afforded by this subdivision. If the protections are so waived, the public body shall open such records for inspection and copying.

4. Personnel records containing information concerning identifiable individuals, except that access shall not be denied to the person who is the subject thereof. Any person who is the subject of any personnel record and who is eighteen years of age or older may waive, in writing, the protections afforded by this subdivision. If the protections are so waived, the public body shall open such records for inspection and copying.

5. Medical and mental records, except that such records may be personally reviewed by the subject person or a physician of the subject person's choice. However, the subject person's mental records may not be personally reviewed by such person when the subject person's treating physician has made a part of such person's records a written statement that in his opinion a review of such records by the subject person would be injurious to the subject person's physical or mental health or well-being.

Where the person who is the subject of medical records is confined in a state or local correctional facility, the administrator or chief medical officer of such facility may assert such confined person's right of access to the medical records if the administrator or chief medical officer has reasonable cause to believe that such confined person has an infectious disease or other medical condition from which other persons so confined need to be protected. Medical records shall only be reviewed and shall not be copied by such administrator or chief medical officer. The information in the medical records of a person so confined shall continue to be confidential and shall not be disclosed by the administrator or chief medical officer of the facility to any person except the subject or except as provided by law.

For the purposes of this chapter, statistical summaries of incidents and statistical data concerning patient abuse as may be compiled by the Commissioner of the Department of Mental Health, Mental Retardation and Substance Abuse Services shall be open to inspection and copying as provided in §2.1-342. No such summaries or data shall include any patient-identifying information. Where the person who is the subject of medical and mental records is under the age of eighteen, his right of access may be asserted only by his guardian or his parent, including a noncustodial parent, unless such parent's parental rights have been terminated or a court of competent jurisdiction has restricted or denied such access. In instances where the person who is the subject thereof is an emancipated minor or a student in a public institution of higher education, the right of access may be asserted by the subject person.

6. Working papers and correspondence of the Office of the Governor; Lieutenant Governor; the Attorney General; the members of the General Assembly or the Division of Legislative Services; the mayor or chief executive officer of any political subdivision of the Commonwealth; or the president or other chief executive officer of any public institution of higher education. However, no record which is otherwise open to inspection under this chapter shall be deemed exempt by virtue of the fact that it has been attached to or incorporated within any working paper or correspondence.

As used in this subdivision:

"Working papers" means those records prepared by or for an above-named public official for his personal or deliberative use.

"Office of the Governor" means the Governor; his chief of staff, counsel, director of policy, Cabinet Secretaries, and the Director of the Virginia Liaison Office; and those individuals to whom the Governor has delegated his authority pursuant to §2.1-39.1.

7. Written advice of legal counsel to state, regional or local public bodies or public officials and any other records protected by the attorney-client privilege.

8. Legal memoranda and other work product compiled specifically for use in litigation or for use in an active administrative investigation concerning a matter which is properly the subject of a closed meeting under §2.1-344.

9. Confidential letters and statements of recommendation placed in the records of educational agencies or

institutions respecting (i) admission to any educational agency or institution, (ii) an application for employment, or (iii) receipt of an honor or honorary recognition.

10. Library records which can be used to identify both (i) any library patron who has borrowed material from a library and (ii) the material such patron borrowed.

11. Any test or examination used, administered or prepared by any public body for purposes of evaluation of (i) any student or any student's performance, (ii) any employee or employment seeker's qualifications or aptitude for employment, retention, or promotion, or (iii) qualifications for any license or certificate issued by a public body.

As used in this subdivision, "test or examination" shall include (i) any scoring key for any such test or examination and (ii) any other document which would jeopardize the security of the test or examination. Nothing contained in this subdivision shall prohibit the release of test scores or results as provided by law, or limit access to individual records as provided by law. However, the subject of such employment tests shall be entitled to review and inspect all records relative to his performance on such employment tests.

When, in the reasonable opinion of such public body, any such test or examination no longer has any potential for future use, and the security of future tests or examinations will not be jeopardized, the test or examination shall be made available to the public. However, minimum competency tests administered to public school children shall be made available to the public contemporaneously with statewide release of the scores of those taking such tests, but in no event shall such tests be made available to the public later than six months after the administration of such tests.

12. Applications for admission to examinations or for licensure and scoring records maintained by the Department of Health Professions or any board in that department on individual licensees or applicants. However, such material may be made available during normal working hours for copying, at the requester's expense, by the individual who is the subject thereof, in the offices of the Department of Health Professions or in the offices of any health regulatory board, whichever may possess the material.

13. Records of active investigations being conducted by the Department of Health Professions or by any health regulatory board in the Commonwealth.

14. Records recorded in or compiled exclusively for use in closed meetings lawfully held pursuant to §2.1-344. However, no record which is otherwise open to inspection under this chapter shall be deemed exempt by virtue of the fact that it has been reviewed or discussed in a closed meeting.

15. Reports, documentary evidence and other information as specified in §§2.1-373.2 and 63.1-55.4.

16. Proprietary information gathered by or for the Virginia Port Authority as provided in §62.1-132.4 or §62.1-134.1.

17. Contract cost estimates prepared for the confidential use of the Department of Transportation in awarding contracts for construction or the purchase of goods or services, and records and automated systems prepared for the Department's Bid Analysis and Monitoring Program.

18. Vendor proprietary information software which may be in the official records of a public body. For the purpose of this subdivision, "vendor proprietary software" means computer programs acquired from a vendor for purposes of processing data for agencies or political subdivisions of the Commonwealth.

19. Financial statements not publicly available filed with applications for industrial development financings.

20. Data, records or information of a proprietary nature produced or collected by or for faculty or staff of public institutions of higher education, other than the institutions' financial or administrative records, in the conduct of or as a result of study or research on medical, scientific, technical or scholarly issues, whether sponsored by the institution alone or in conjunction with a governmental body or a private concern, where such data, records or information has not been publicly released, published, copyrighted or patented.

21. Lists of registered owners of bonds issued by a political subdivision of the Commonwealth, whether the lists are maintained by the political subdivision itself or by a single fiduciary designated by the political subdivision.

22. Confidential proprietary records, voluntarily provided by private business pursuant to a promise of confidentiality from the Department of Business Assistance, the Virginia Economic Development Partnership, the Virginia Tourism Authority, or local or regional industrial or economic development authorities or organizations, used by the Department, the Partnership, the Authority, or such entities for business, trade and tourism development; and memoranda, working papers or other records related to businesses that are considering locating or expanding in Virginia, prepared by the Partnership, where competition or bargaining is involved and where, if such records are made public, the financial interest of the governmental unit would be adversely affected.

23. Information which was filed as confidential under the Toxic Substances Information Act (§32.1-239 et seq.), as such Act existed prior to July 1, 1992.

24. Confidential records, including victim identity, provided to or obtained by staff in a rape crisis center or a program for battered spouses.

25. Computer software developed by or for a state agency, state-supported institution of higher education or political subdivision of the Commonwealth.

26. Investigator notes, and other correspondence and information, furnished in confidence with respect to an active investigation of individual employment discrimination complaints made to the Department of Human Resource Management. However, nothing in this section shall prohibit the disclosure of information taken from inactive reports in a form which does not reveal the identity of charging parties, persons supplying the information or other individuals involved in the investigation.

27. Fisheries data which would permit identification of any person or vessel, except when required by court order as specified in §28.2-204.

28. Records of active investigations being conducted by the Department of Medical Assistance Services pursuant to Chapter 10 (§32.1-323 et seq.) of Title 32.1.

29. Records and writings furnished by a member of the General Assembly to a meeting of a standing committee, special committee or subcommittee of his house established solely for the purpose of reviewing members' annual disclosure statements and supporting materials filed under §2.1-639.40 or of formulating advisory opinions to members on standards of conduct, or both.

30. Customer account information of a public utility affiliated with a political subdivision of the Commonwealth, including the customer's name and service address, but excluding the amount of utility service provided and the amount of money paid for such utility service.

31. Investigative notes and other correspondence and information furnished in confidence with respect to an investigation or conciliation process involving an alleged unlawful discriminatory practice under the Virginia Human Rights Act (§2.1-714 et seq.) or under any local ordinance adopted in accordance with the authority specified in §2.1-724, or adopted pursuant to §15.2-965, or adopted prior to July 1, 1987, in accordance with applicable law, relating to local human rights or human relations commissions.

However, nothing in this section shall prohibit the distribution of information taken from inactive reports in a form which does not reveal the identity of the parties involved or other persons supplying information.

32. Investigative notes; proprietary information not published, copyrighted or patented; information obtained from employee personnel records; personally identifiable information regarding residents, clients or other recipients of services; and other correspondence and information furnished in confidence to the Department of Social Services in connection with an active investigation of an applicant or licensee pursuant to Chapters 9 (§63.1-172 et seq.) and 10 (§63.1-195 et seq.) of Title 63.1. However, nothing in this section shall prohibit disclosure of information from the records of completed investigations in a form that does not reveal the identity of complainants, persons supplying information, or other individuals involved in the investigation.

33. Personal information, as defined in §2.1-379, (i) filed with the Virginia Housing Development Authority concerning individuals who have applied for or received loans or other housing assistance or who have applied for occupancy of or have occupied housing financed, owned or otherwise assisted by the Virginia Housing Development Authority; (ii) concerning persons participating in or persons on the waiting list for federally funded rent-assistance programs; (iii) filed with any local redevelopment and housing authority created pursuant to §36-4 concerning persons participating in or persons on the waiting list for housing assistance programs funded by local governments or by any such authority; or (iv) filed with any local redevelopment and housing authority created pursuant to §36-4 or any other local government agency concerning persons who have applied for occupancy or who have occupied affordable dwelling units established pursuant to §15.2-2304 or §15.2-2305. However, access to one's own information shall not be denied.

34. Records regarding the siting of hazardous waste facilities, except as provided in §10.1-1441, if disclosure of them would have a detrimental effect upon the negotiating position of a governing body or on the establishment of the terms, conditions and provisions of the siting agreement.

35. Appraisals and cost estimates of real property subject to a proposed purchase, sale or lease, prior to the completion of such purchase, sale or lease.

36. Records containing information on the site specific location of rare, threatened, endangered or otherwise imperiled plant and animal species, natural communities, caves, and significant historic and archaeological sites if, in the opinion of the public body which has the responsibility for such information, disclosure of the information would jeopardize the continued existence or the integrity of the resource. This exemption shall not apply to requests from the owner of the land upon which the resource is located.

37. Records, memoranda, working papers, graphics, video or audio tapes, production models, data and information of a proprietary nature produced by or for or collected by or for the State Lottery Department relating to matters of a specific lottery game design, development, production, operation, ticket price, prize structure, manner of selecting the winning ticket, manner of payment of prizes to holders of winning tickets, frequency of drawings or selections of winning tickets, odds of winning, advertising, or marketing, where such official records have not been publicly released, published, copyrighted or patented. Whether released, published or copyrighted, all game-related information shall be subject to public disclosure under this chapter upon the first day of sales for the specific lottery game to which it pertains.

38. Records of studies and investigations by the State Lottery Department of (i) lottery agents, (ii) lottery vendors, (iii) lottery crimes under §§58.1-4014 through 58.1-4018, (iv) defects in the law or regulations which cause abuses in the administration and operation of the lottery and any evasions of such provisions, or (v) the use of the lottery as a subterfuge for organized crime and illegal gambling where such official records have not been publicly released, published or copyrighted. All studies and investigations referred to under clauses (iii), (iv) and (v) shall be open to inspection and copying upon completion of the study or investigation.

39. Those portions of engineering and construction drawings and plans submitted for the sole purpose of complying with the Building Code in obtaining a building permit which would identify specific trade secrets or other information the disclosure of which would be harmful to the competitive position of the owner or lessee. However, such information shall be exempt only until the building is completed. Information relating to the safety or environmental soundness of any building shall not be exempt from disclosure.

40. Records concerning reserves established in specific claims administered by the Department of the Treasury through its Division of Risk Management as provided in Article 2.2 (§2.1-191.5 et seq.) of Chapter 14 of this title, or by any county, city, or town.

41. Information and records collected for the designation and verification of trauma centers and other specialty care centers within the Statewide Emergency Medical Services System and Services pursuant to Article 2.1 (§32.1-111.1 et seq.) of Chapter 4 of Title 32.1.

42. Reports and court documents required to be kept confidential pursuant to §37.1-67.3.

43. Investigative notes, correspondence and information furnished in confidence, and records otherwise exempted by this chapter or any Virginia statute, provided to or produced by or for the (i) Auditor of Public Accounts; (ii) Joint Legislative Audit and Review Commission; (iii) Department of the State Internal Auditor with respect to an investigation initiated through the State Employee Fraud, Waste and Abuse Hotline; or (iv) the committee or the auditor with respect to an investigation or audit conducted pursuant to §15.2-825. Records of completed investigations shall be disclosed in a form that does not reveal the identity of the complainants or persons supplying information to investigators. Unless disclosure is prohibited by this section, the records disclosed shall include, but not be limited to, the agency involved, the identity of the person who is the subject of the complaint, the nature of the complaint, and the actions taken to resolve the complaint. If an investigation does not lead to corrective action, the identity of the person who is the subject of the complaint may be released only with the consent of the subject person.

44. Data formerly required to be submitted to the Commissioner of Health relating to the establishment of new or the expansion of existing clinical health services, acquisition of major medical equipment, or certain projects requiring capital expenditures pursuant to former §32.1-102.3:4.

45. Documentation or other information which describes the design, function, operation or access control features of any security system, whether manual or automated, which is used to control access to or use of any automated data processing or telecommunications system.

46. Confidential financial statements, balance sheets, trade secrets, and revenue and cost projections provided to the Department of Rail and Public Transportation, provided such information is exempt under the federal Freedom of Information Act or the federal Interstate Commerce Act or other laws administered by the Surface Transportation Board or the Federal Railroad Administration with respect to data

provided in confidence to the Surface Transportation Board and the Federal Railroad Administration.

47. In the case of corporations organized by the Virginia Retirement System (i) proprietary information provided by, and financial information concerning, coventurers, partners, lessors, lessees, or investors and (ii) records concerning the condition, acquisition, disposition, use, leasing, development, coventuring, or management of real estate, the disclosure of which would have a substantial adverse impact on the value of such real estate or result in a competitive disadvantage to the corporation or subsidiary.

48. Confidential proprietary records related to inventory and sales, voluntarily provided by private energy suppliers to the Department of Mines, Minerals and Energy, used by that Department for energy contingency planning purposes or for developing consolidated statistical information on energy supplies.

49. Confidential proprietary information furnished to the Board of Medical Assistance Services or the Medicaid Prior Authorization Advisory Committee pursuant to Article 4 (§32.1-331.12 et seq.) of Chapter 10 of Title 32.1.

50. Proprietary, commercial or financial information, balance sheets, trade secrets, and revenue and cost projections provided by a private transportation business to the Virginia Department of Transportation and the Department of Rail and Public Transportation for the purpose of conducting transportation studies needed to obtain grants or other financial assistance under the Transportation Equity Act for the 21st Century (P.L. 105–178) for transportation projects, provided such information is exempt under the federal Freedom of Information Act or the federal Interstate Commerce Act or other laws administered by the Surface Transportation Board or the Federal Railroad Administration with respect to data provided in confidence to the Surface Transportation Board and the Federal Railroad Administration. However, the exemption provided by this subdivision shall not apply to any wholly owned subsidiary of a public body.

51. Names and addresses of subscribers to Virginia Wildlife magazine, published by the Department of Game and Inland Fisheries, provided the individual subscriber has requested in writing that the Department not release such information.

52. Information required to be provided pursuant to §54.1-2506.1.

53. Confidential information designated as provided in subsection D of §11-52 as trade secrets or proprietary information by any person who has submitted to a public body an application for prequalification to bid on public construction projects in accordance with subsection B of §11-46.

54. All information and records acquired during a review of any child death by the State Child Fatality Review team established pursuant to §32.1-283.1, during a review of any child death by a local or regional child fatality review team established pursuant to §32.1-283.2, and all information and records acquired during a review of any death by a family violence fatality review team established pursuant to §32.1-283.3.

55. Financial, medical, rehabilitative and other personal information concerning applicants for or recipients of loan funds submitted to or maintained by the Assistive Technology Loan Fund Authority under Chapter 11 (§51.5-53 et seq.) of Title 51.5.

56. Confidential proprietary records which are voluntarily provided by a private entity pursuant to a proposal filed with a public entity under the Public-Private Transportation Act of 1995 (§56-556 et seq.), pursuant to a promise of confidentiality from the responsible public entity, used by the responsible public entity for purposes related to the development of a qualifying transportation facility; and memoranda, working papers or other records related to proposals filed under the Public-Private Transportation Act of 1995, where, if such records were made public, the financial interest of the public or private entity involved with such proposal or the process of competition or bargaining would be adversely affected. In order for confidential proprietary information to be excluded from the provisions of this chapter, the private entity shall (i) invoke such exclusion upon submission of the data or other materials for which protection from disclosure is sought, (ii) identify the data or other materials for which protection is sought, and (iii) state the reasons why protection is necessary. For the purposes of this subdivision, the terms "public entity" and "private entity" shall be defined as they are defined in the Public-Private Transportation Act of 1995.

57. Records of law-enforcement agencies, to the extent that such records contain specific tactical plans, the disclosure of which would jeopardize the safety or security of law-enforcement personnel or the general public; or records of emergency service agencies to the extent that such records contain specific tactical plans relating to antiterrorist activity.

58. All records of the University of Virginia or the University of Virginia Medical Center which contain proprietary, business-related information pertaining to the operations of the University of Virginia Medical Center, including its business development or marketing strategies and its activities with existing or future joint venturers, partners, or other parties with whom the University of Virginia Medical Center has formed, or forms, any arrangement for the delivery of health care, if disclosure of such information would be harmful to the competitive position of the Medical Center.

59. Patient level data collected by the Board of Health and not yet processed, verified, and released, pursuant to §32.1-276.9, to the Board by the nonprofit organization with which the Commissioner of Health has contracted pursuant to §32.1-276.4.

60. Records of the Virginia Commonwealth University Health System Authority pertaining to any of the following: an individual's qualifications for or continued membership on its medical or teaching staffs; proprietary information gathered by or in the possession of the Authority from third parties pursuant to a promise of confidentiality; contract cost estimates prepared for confidential use in awarding contracts for construction or the purchase of goods or services; data, records or information of a proprietary nature produced or collected by or for the Authority or members of its medical or teaching staffs; financial statements not publicly available that may be filed with the Authority from third parties; the identity, accounts or account status of any customer of the Authority; consulting or other reports paid for by the Authority to assist the Authority in connection with its strategic planning and goals; and the determination of marketing and operational strategies where disclosure of such strategies would be harmful to the competitive position of the Authority; and data, records or information of a proprietary nature produced or collected by or for employees of the Authority, other than the Authority's financial or administrative records, in the conduct of or as a result of study or research on medical, scientific, technical or scholarly issues, whether sponsored by the Authority alone or in conjunction with a governmental body or a private concern, when such data, records or information have not been publicly released, published, copyrighted or patented.

61. Confidential proprietary information or trade secrets, not publicly available, provided by a private person or entity to the Virginia Resources Authority or to a fund administered in connection with financial assistance rendered

or to be rendered by the Virginia Resources Authority where, if such information were made public, the financial interest of the private person or entity would be adversely affected, and, after June 30, 1997, where such information was provided pursuant to a promise of confidentiality.

62. Confidential proprietary records which are provided by a franchisee under §15.2-2108 to its franchising authority pursuant to a promise of confidentiality from the franchising authority which relates to the franchisee's potential provision of new services, adoption of new technologies or implementation of improvements, where such new services, technologies or improvements have not been implemented by the franchisee on a nonexperimental scale in the franchise area, and where, if such records were made public, the competitive advantage or financial interests of the franchisee would be adversely affected. In order for confidential proprietary information to be excluded from the provisions of this chapter, the franchisee shall (i) invoke such exclusion upon submission of the data or other materials for which protection from disclosure is sought, (ii) identify the data or other materials for which protection is sought, and (iii) state the reason why protection is necessary.

63. Records of the Intervention Program Committee within the Department of Health Professions, to the extent such records may identify any practitioner who may be, or who is actually, impaired to the extent disclosure is prohibited by §54.1-2517.

64. Records submitted as a grant application, or accompanying a grant application, to the Commonwealth Neurotrauma Initiative Advisory Board pursuant to Article 12 (§32.1-73.1 et seq.) of Chapter 2 of Title 32.1, to the extent such records contain (i) medical or mental records, or other data identifying individual patients or (ii) proprietary business or research-related information produced or collected by the applicant in the conduct of or as a result of study or research on medical, rehabilitative, scientific, technical or scholarly issues, when such information has not been publicly released, published, copyrighted or patented, if the disclosure of such information would be harmful to the competitive position of the applicant.

65. Information which would disclose the security aspects of a system safety program plan adopted pursuant to 49 C.F.R. Part 659 by the Commonwealth's designated Rail Fixed Guideway Systems Safety Oversight agency; and information in the possession of such agency, the release of which would jeopardize the success of an ongoing investigation of a rail accident or other incident threatening railway safety.

66. Documents and other information of a proprietary nature furnished by a supplier of charitable gaming supplies to the Charitable Gaming Commission pursuant to subsection E of §18.2-340.34.

67. Personal information, as defined in §2.1-379, provided to the Board of the Virginia College Savings Plan or its employees by or on behalf of individuals who have requested information about, applied for, or entered into prepaid tuition contracts or savings trust account agreements pursuant to Chapter 4.9 (§23-38.75 et seq.) of Title 23. Nothing in this subdivision shall be construed to prohibit disclosure or publication of information in a statistical or other form which does not identify individuals or provide personal information. Individuals shall be provided access to their own personal information.

68. Any record copied, recorded or received by the Commissioner of Health in the course of an examination, investigation or review of a managed care health insurance plan licensee pursuant to §§32.1-137.4 and 32.1-137.5, including books, records, files, accounts, papers, documents, and any or all computer or other recordings.

69. Engineering and architectural drawings, operational, procedural, tactical planning or training manuals, or staff meeting minutes or other records, the disclosure of which would reveal surveillance techniques, personnel deployments, alarm systems or technologies, or operational and transportation plans or protocols, to the extent such disclosure would jeopardize the security or employee safety of (i) the Virginia Museum of Fine Arts or any of its warehouses; (ii) any government store or warehouse controlled by the Department of Alcoholic Beverage Control; (iii) any courthouse, jail, detention or law-enforcement facility; or (iv) any correctional or juvenile facility or institution under the supervision of the Department of Corrections or the Department of Juvenile Justice.

70. Records and reports related to Virginia apple producer sales provided to the Virginia State Apple Board pursuant to §§3.1-622 and 3.1-624.

71. *(As added by L.2000 ch. 237. See other paragraphs A 71 below.)* Records of the Department of Environmental Quality, the State Water Control Board, State Air Pollution Control Board or the Virginia Waste Management Board relating to (i) active federal environmental enforcement actions that are considered confidential under federal law and (ii) enforcement strategies, including proposed sanctions for enforcement actions. Upon request, such records shall be disclosed after a proposed sanction resulting from the investigation has been proposed to the director of the agency. This subdivision shall not be construed to prohibit the disclosure of records related to inspection reports, notices of violation, and documents detailing the nature of any environmental contamination that may have occurred or similar documents.

71. *(As added by L.2000 chs. 583, 592. See other paragraphs A 71 above and below.)* As it pertains to any person, records related to the operation of toll facilities that identify an individual, vehicle, or travel itinerary including, but not limited to, vehicle identification data, vehicle enforcement system information; video or photographic images; Social Security or other identification numbers appearing on driver's licenses; credit card or bank account data; home addresses; phone numbers; or records of the date or time of toll facility use.

71. *(As added by L.2000 chs. 589, 594. See other paragraphs A 71 above and below.)* Records of the Department for the Rights of Virginians with Disabilities consisting of documentary evidence received or maintained by the Department or its agents in connection with specific complaints or investigations, and records of communications between employees and agents of the Department and its clients or prospective clients concerning specific complaints, investigations or cases. Upon the conclusion of an investigation of a complaint, this exclusion shall no longer apply, but the Department may not at any time release the identity of any complainant or person with mental illness, mental retardation, developmental disabilities or other disability, unless (i) such complainant or person or his legal representative consents in writing to such identification or (ii) such identification is required by court order.

71. *(As added by L.2000 chs. 947, 1006. See other paragraphs A 71 above and below.)* Information furnished in confidence to the Department of Employment Dispute Resolution with respect to an investigation, consultation, or mediation under Chapter 10.01 (§2.1-116.01 et seq.) of this title, and memoranda, correspondence and other records resulting from any such investigation, consultation or mediation. However, nothing in this section shall prohibit the distribution of information taken from inactive reports in a form which does not reveal the identity of the parties involved or other persons supplying information.

71. *(As added by L.2000 ch. 1064. See other paragraphs A 71 above.)* Trade secrets, as defined in the Uniform Trade Secrets Act (§59.1-336 et seq.) of Title 59.1, submitted by CMRS providers as defined in §56-484.12 to the Wireless Carrier E–911 Cost Recovery Subcommittee created pursuant to §56-484.15, relating to the provision of wireless E–911 service.

B. Neither any provision of this chapter nor any provision of Chapter 26 (§2.1-377 et seq.) of this title shall be construed as denying public access to (i) contracts between a public official and a public body, other than contracts settling public employee employment disputes held confidential as personnel records under subdivision 4 of subsection A; (ii) records of the position, job classification, official salary or rate of pay of, and records of the allowances or reimbursements for expenses paid to any officer, official or employee of a public body; or (iii) the compensation or benefits paid by any corporation organized by the Virginia Retirement System or its officers or employees. The provisions of this subsection, however, shall not require public access to records of the official salaries or rates of pay of public employees whose annual rate of pay is $10,000 or less.

C. No provision of this chapter shall be construed to afford any rights to any person incarcerated in a state, local or federal correctional facility, whether or not such facility is (i) located in the Commonwealth or (ii) operated pursuant to the Corrections Private Management Act (§53.1-261 et seq.). However, this subsection shall not be construed to prevent an incarcerated person from exercising his constitutionally protected rights, including, but not limited to, his rights to call for evidence in his favor in a criminal prosecution.

(Added by L.1999 chs. 703, 726, incorporating changes to Section 2.1-342 by L.1999 chs. 485, 518, 793, 849, 852, 867, 868, 881; chgd. by L.2000 chs. 66, 237, 382, 400, 430, 583, 589, 592, 594, 618, 657, 720, 932, 933, 947, 1006, 1064, eff. 7/1/2000.)

§2.1-342.1. *(Repealed by L.1999 chs. 703, 726, eff. 7/1/99.)*

§2.1-342.2. Disclosure of criminal records; limitations.

A. As used in this section:

"Criminal incident information" means a general description of the criminal activity reported, the date and general location the alleged crime was committed, the identity of the investigating officer, and a general description of any injuries suffered or property damaged or stolen.

"Law-enforcement official" includes the attorneys for the Commonwealth.

B. Law-enforcement officials shall make available upon request criminal incident information relating to felony offenses. However, where the release of criminal incident information is likely to jeopardize an ongoing investigation or prosecution, or the safety of an individual; cause a suspect to flee or evade detection; or result in the destruction of evidence, such information may be withheld until the above-referenced damage is no longer likely to occur from release of the information. Nothing in this subsection shall be construed to prohibit the release of those portions of such information that are not likely to cause the above-referenced damage.

C. Information in the custody of law-enforcement officials relative to the identity of any individual, other than a juvenile, who is arrested and charged, and the status of the charge or arrest shall be released.

D. The identity of any victim, witness or undercover officer, or investigative techniques or procedures need not but may be disclosed unless disclosure is prohibited or restricted under §19.2-11.2.

E. The identity of any individual providing information about a crime or criminal activity under a promise of anonymity shall not be disclosed.

F. The following records are excluded from the provisions of this chapter, but may be disclosed by the custodian, in his discretion, except where such disclosure is prohibited by law:

1. Complaints, memoranda, correspondence and evidence relating to a criminal investigation or prosecution, other than criminal incident information as defined in subsection A;

2. Adult arrestee photographs when necessary to avoid jeopardizing an investigation in felony cases until such time as the release of the photograph will no longer jeopardize the investigation;

3. Reports submitted in confidence to (i) state and local law-enforcement agencies, (ii) investigators authorized pursuant to §53.1-16 or §66-3.1, and (iii) campus police departments of public institutions of higher education established pursuant to Chapter 17 (§23-232 et seq.) of Title 23;

4. Portions of records of local government crime commissions that would identify individuals providing information about crimes or criminal activities under a promise of anonymity;

5. Records of local law-enforcement agencies relating to neighborhood watch programs that include the names, addresses, and operating schedules of individual participants in the program that are provided to such agencies under a promise of anonymity; and

6. All records of persons imprisoned in penal institutions in the Commonwealth provided such records relate to the imprisonment.

G. Records kept by law-enforcement agencies as required by §15.2-1722 shall be subject to the provisions of this chapter except:

1. Those portions of noncriminal incident or other investigative reports or materials containing identifying information of a personal, medical or financial nature provided to a law-enforcement agency where the release of such information would jeopardize the safety or privacy of any person;

2. Those portions of any records containing information related to plans for or resources dedicated to undercover operations; or

3. Records of background investigations of applicants for law-enforcement agency employment or other confidential administrative investigations conducted pursuant to law.

H. In the event of conflict between this section as it relates to requests made under this section and other provisions of law, this section shall control.

(Added by L.1999 chs. 703, 726; chgd. by L.2000 ch. 227, eff. 7/1/2000.)

§2.1-343. Meetings to be public; notice of meetings; recordings; minutes.

A. All meetings of public bodies shall be open, except as provided in §2.1-344.

B. No meeting shall be conducted through telephonic, video, electronic or other communication means where the members are not physically assembled to discuss or transact public business, except as provided in §2.1-343.1, §2.1-343.1:1, or as may be specifically provided in Title 54.1 for the summary suspension of professional licenses.

C. Every public body shall give notice of the date, time, and location of its meetings by placing the notice in a prominent public location at which notices are regularly posted and in the office of the clerk of the public body, or in the case of a public body which has no clerk, in the office of the chief administrator. Publication of meeting notices by electronic means shall be encouraged. The notice shall be posted at least three working days prior to the meeting. Notices for meetings of state public bodies on which there is at least one member appointed by the Governor shall state whether or not public comment will be received at the meeting and, if so, the approximate point during the meeting when public comment will be received.

D. Notice, reasonable under the circumstance, of special or emergency meetings shall be given contemporaneously with the notice provided members of the public body conducting the meeting.

E. Any person may annually file a written request for notification with a public body. The request shall include the requester's name, address, zip code, daytime telephone number, electronic mail address (if available), and organization, if any. The public body receiving such request shall provide notice of all meetings directly to each such person. Without objection by the person, the public body may provide electronic notice of all meetings in response to such requests.

F. At least one copy of all agenda packets and, unless exempt, all materials furnished to members of a public body for a meeting shall be made available for public inspection at the same time such documents are furnished to the members of the public body.

G. Nothing in this chapter shall be construed to prohibit the gathering or attendance of two or more members of a public body (i) at any place or function where no part of the purpose of such gathering or attendance is the discussion or transaction of any public business, and such gathering or attendance was not called or prearranged with any purpose of discussing or transacting any business of the public body or (ii) at a public forum, candidate appearance, or debate, the purpose of which is to inform the electorate and not to transact public business or to hold discussions relating to the transaction of public business, even though the performance of the members individually or collectively in the conduct of public business may be a topic of discussion or debate at such public meeting. The notice provisions of this chapter shall not apply to informal meetings or gatherings of the members of the General Assembly.

H. Any person may photograph, film, record or otherwise reproduce any portion of a meeting required to be open. The public body conducting the meeting may adopt rules governing the placement and use of equipment necessary for broadcasting, photographing, filming or recording a meeting to prevent interference with the proceedings.

I. Minutes shall be recorded at all open meetings. However, minutes shall not be required to be taken at deliberations of (i) standing and other committees of the General Assembly, (ii) legislative interim study commissions and committees, including the Virginia Code Commission, (iii) study committees or commissions appointed by the Governor, or (iv) study commissions or study committees, or any other committees or subcommittees appointed by the governing bodies or school boards of counties, cities and towns, except where the membership of any such commission, committee or subcommittee includes a majority of the governing body of the county, city or town or school board. Minutes, including draft minutes, and all other records of open meetings, including audio or audio/visual records shall be deemed public records and subject to the provisions of this chapter. Audio or audio/visual records of open meetings shall be public records which shall be produced in accordance with §2.1-342.

(Chgd. by L.1995 ch. 562; L.1999 chs. 696, 703, 726; L.2000 ch. 227, eff. 7/1/2000.)

§2.1-343.1. Electronic communication meetings.

A. It shall be a violation of this chapter for any political subdivision or any governing body, authority, board, bureau, commission, district or agency of local government or any committee thereof to conduct a meeting wherein the public business is discussed or transacted through telephonic, video, electronic or other communication means where the members are not physically assembled. Nothing in this section shall be construed to prohibit the use of interactive audio or video means to expand public participation.

B. For purposes of this section, "public body" means any public body of the Commonwealth, but excludes any political subdivision or any governing body, authority, board, bureau, commission, district or agency of local government.

State public bodies may conduct any meeting, except closed meetings held pursuant to §2.1-344, wherein the public business is discussed or transacted through telephonic or video means. Where a quorum of a public body of the Commonwealth is physically assembled at one location for the purpose of conducting a meeting authorized under this section, additional members of such public body may participate in the meeting through telephonic means provided such participation is available to the public.

C. Notice of any meetings held pursuant to this section shall be provided at least thirty days in advance of the date scheduled for the meeting. The notice shall include the date, time, place and purpose for the meeting and shall identify the locations for the meeting. All locations for the meeting shall be made accessible to the public. All persons attending the meeting at any of the meeting locations shall be afforded the same opportunity to address the public body as persons attending the primary or central location. Any interruption in the telephonic or video broadcast of the meeting shall result in the suspension of action at the meeting until repairs are made and public access restored.

Thirty-day notice shall not be required for telephonic or video meetings continued to address an emergency as provided in subsection F or to conclude the agenda of a telephonic or video meeting of the public body for which the proper notice has been given, when the date, time, place and purpose of the continued meeting are set during the meeting prior to adjournment.

The public body shall provide the Director of the Department of Information Technology with notice of all public meetings held through telephonic or video means pursuant to this section.

D. An agenda and materials which will be distributed to members of the public body and which have been made available to the staff of the public body in sufficient time for duplication and forwarding to all locations where public access will be provided shall be made available to the public at the time of the meeting. Minutes of all meetings held by telephonic or video means shall be recorded as required by §2.1-343. Votes taken during any meeting conducted through telephonic or video means shall be recorded by name in roll-call fashion and included in the minutes. In addition, the public body shall make an audio recording of the meeting, if a telephonic medium is used, or an audio/visual recording, if the meeting is held by video means. The recording shall be preserved by the public body for a period of three years following the date of the meeting and shall be available to the public.

E. No more than twenty-five percent of all meetings held annually by a public body, including meetings of any ad hoc or standing committees, may be held by telephonic or video means. Any public body which meets by telephonic or video means shall file with the Director of the Department of Information Technology by July 1 of each year a statement identifying the total number of meetings held during the preceding fiscal year, the dates on which the meetings were held and the number and purpose of those conducted through telephonic or video means.

F. Notwithstanding the limitations imposed by subsection E, a public body may meet by telephonic or video means as often as needed if an emergency exists and the public body is unable to meet in regular session. Public bodies conducting emergency meetings through telephonic or video means shall comply with the provisions of subsection D requiring minutes, recordation and preservation of the audio or audio/visual recording of the meeting. The nature of the emergency shall be stated in the minutes.

(Chgd. by L.1995 ch. 278; L.1996 ch. 289; L.1999 chs. 703, 726, eff. 7/1/99.)

§2.1-343.1:1. *(Repealed by L.1998 chs. 777, 839, eff. 7/1/2000.)*

§2.1-343.2. Transaction of public business other than by votes at meetings prohibited.

Unless otherwise specifically provided by law, no vote of any kind of the membership, or any part thereof, of any public body shall be taken to authorize the transaction of any public business, other than a vote taken at a meeting conducted in accordance with the provisions of this chapter. No public body shall vote by secret or written ballot, and unless expressly provided by this chapter, no public body shall vote by telephone or other electronic communication means.

Notwithstanding the foregoing, nothing contained herein shall be construed to prohibit (i) separately contacting the membership, or any part thereof, of any public body for the purpose of ascertaining a member's position with respect to the transaction of public business or (ii) the House of Delegates or the Senate of Virginia from adopting rules relating to the casting of votes by members of standing committees.

(Chgd. by L.1999 chs. 703, 726; L.2000 ch. 932, eff. 7/1/2000.)

§2.1-344. Closed meetings authorized for certain limited purposes.

A. Public bodies may hold closed meetings only for the following purposes:

1. Discussion, consideration or interviews of prospective candidates for employment; assignment, appointment, promotion, performance, demotion, salaries, disciplining or resignation of specific public officers, appointees or employees of any public body; and evaluation of performance of departments or schools of public institutions of higher education where such evaluation will necessarily involve discussion of the performance of specific individuals. Any teacher shall be permitted to be present during a closed meeting in which there is a discussion or consideration of a disciplinary matter which involves the teacher and some student and the student involved in the matter is present, provided the teacher makes a written request to be present to the presiding officer of the appropriate board.

2. Discussion or consideration of admission or disciplinary matters concerning any student of any public institution of higher education or any state school system. However, any such student, legal counsel and, if the student is a minor, the student's parents or legal guardians shall be permitted to be present during the taking of testimony or presentation of evidence at a closed meeting, if such student, parents or guardians so request in writing and such request is submitted to the presiding officer of the appropriate board.

3. Discussion or consideration of the acquisition of real property for a public purpose, or of the disposition of publicly held real property, where discussion in an open meeting would adversely affect the bargaining position or negotiating strategy of the public body.

4. The protection of the privacy of individuals in personal matters not related to public business.

5. Discussion concerning a prospective business or industry or the expansion of an existing business or industry where no previous announcement has been made of the business' or industry's interest in locating or expanding its facilities in the community.

6. The investing of public funds where competition or bargaining is involved, where, if made public initially, the financial interest of the governmental unit would be adversely affected.

7. Consultation with legal counsel and briefings by staff members or consultants pertaining to actual or probable litigation, where such consultation or briefing in open meeting would adversely affect the negotiating or litigating posture of the public body; and consultation with legal counsel employed or retained by a public body regarding specific legal matters requiring the provision of legal advice by such counsel. For the purposes of this subdivision, "probable litigation" means litigation which has been specifically threatened or on which the public body or its legal counsel has a reasonable basis to believe will be commenced by or against a known party. Nothing in this subdivision shall be construed to permit the closure of a meeting merely because an attorney representing the public body is in attendance or is consulted on a matter.

8. In the case of boards of visitors of public institutions of higher education, discussion or consideration of matters relating to gifts, bequests and fund-raising activities, and grants and contracts for services or work to be performed by such institution. However, the terms and conditions of any such gifts, bequests, grants and contracts made by a foreign government, a foreign legal entity or a foreign person and accepted by a public institution of higher education shall be subject to public disclosure upon written request to the appropriate board of visitors. For the purpose of this subdivision, (i) "foreign government" means any government other than the United States government or the government of a state or a political subdivision thereof; (ii) "foreign legal entity" means any legal entity created under the laws of the United States or of any state thereof if a majority of the ownership of the stock of such legal entity is owned by foreign governments or foreign persons or if a majority of the membership of any such entity is composed of foreign persons or foreign legal entities, or any legal entity created under the laws of a foreign government; and (iii) "foreign person" means any individual who is not a citizen or national of the United States or a trust territory or protectorate thereof.

9. In the case of the boards of trustees of the Virginia Museum of Fine Arts and The Science Museum of Virginia, discussion or consideration of matters relating to specific gifts, bequests, and grants.

10. Discussion or consideration of honorary degrees or special awards.

11. Discussion or consideration of tests, examinations or other records excluded from this chapter pursuant to §2.1-342.01 A 11.

12. Discussion, consideration or review by the appropriate House or Senate committees of possible disciplinary action against a member arising out of the possible inadequacy of the disclosure statement filed by the member, provided the member may request in writing that the committee meeting not be conducted in a closed meeting.

13. Discussion of strategy with respect to the negotiation of a siting agreement or to consider the terms, conditions, and provisions of a siting agreement if the governing body in open meeting finds that an open meeting will have an adverse effect upon the negotiating position of the governing body or the establishment of the terms, conditions and provisions of the siting agreement, or both. All

discussions with the applicant or its representatives may be conducted in a closed meeting.

14. Discussion by the Governor and any economic advisory board reviewing forecasts of economic activity and estimating general and nongeneral fund revenues.

15. Discussion or consideration of medical and mental records excluded from this chapter pursuant to §2.1-342.01 A 5, and those portions of disciplinary proceedings by any regulatory board within the Department of Professional and Occupational Regulation or Department of Health Professions conducted pursuant to §9-6.14:11 or §9-6.14:12 during which the board deliberates to reach a decision.

16. Discussion, consideration or review of State Lottery Department matters related to proprietary lottery game information and studies or investigations exempted from disclosure under subdivisions 37 and 38 of subsection A of §2.1-342.01.

17. Those portions of meetings by local government crime commissions where the identity of, or information tending to identify, individuals providing information about crimes or criminal activities under a promise of anonymity is discussed or disclosed.

18. Discussion, consideration, review and deliberations by local community corrections resources boards regarding the placement in community diversion programs of individuals previously sentenced to state correctional facilities.

19. Those portions of meetings in which the Board of Corrections discusses or discloses the identity of, or information tending to identify, any prisoner who (i) provides information about crimes or criminal activities, (ii) renders assistance in preventing the escape of another prisoner or in the apprehension of an escaped prisoner, or (iii) voluntarily or at the instance of a prison official renders other extraordinary services, the disclosure of which is likely to jeopardize the prisoner's life or safety.

20. Discussion of plans to protect public safety as it relates to terrorist activity.

21. In the case of corporations organized by the Virginia Retirement System, discussion or consideration of (i) proprietary information provided by, and financial information concerning, coventurers, partners, lessors, lessees, or investors and (ii) the condition, acquisition, disposition, use, leasing, development, coventuring, or management of real estate the disclosure of which would have a substantial adverse impact on the value of such real estate or result in a competitive disadvantage to the corporation or subsidiary.

22. Those portions of meetings in which individual child death cases are discussed by the State Child Fatality Review team established pursuant to §32.1-283.1, and those portions of meetings in which individual child death cases are discussed by a regional or local child fatality review team established pursuant to §32.1-283.2, and those portions of meetings in which individual death cases are discussed by family violence fatality review teams established pursuant to §32.1-283.3.

23. Those portions of meetings of the University of Virginia Board of Visitors and those portions of meetings of any persons to whom management responsibilities for the University of Virginia Medical Center have been delegated, in which there is discussed proprietary, business-related information pertaining to the operations of the University of Virginia Medical Center, including its business development or marketing strategies and its activities with existing or future joint venturers, partners, or other parties with whom the University of Virginia Medical Center has formed, or forms, any arrangement for the delivery of health care, if disclosure of such information would adversely affect the competitive position of the Medical Center.

24. In the case of the Virginia Commonwealth University Health System Authority, discussion or consideration of any of the following: the acquisition or disposition of real or personal property where disclosure would adversely affect the bargaining position or negotiating strategy of the Authority; operational plans that could affect the value of such property, real or personal, owned or desirable for ownership by the Authority; matters relating to gifts, bequests and fund-raising activities; grants and contracts for services or work to be performed by the Authority; marketing or operational strategies where disclosure of such strategies would adversely affect the competitive position of the Authority; members of its medical and teaching staffs and qualifications for appointments thereto; and qualifications or evaluations of other employees.

25. Those portions of the meetings of the Intervention Program Committee within the Department of Health Professions to the extent such discussions identify any practitioner who may be, or who actually is, impaired pursuant to Chapter 25.1 (§54.1-2515 et seq.) of Title 54.1.

26. Meetings or portions of meetings of the Board of the Virginia College Savings Plan wherein personal information, as defined in §2.1-379, which has been provided to the Board or its employees by or on behalf of individuals who have requested information about, applied for, or entered into prepaid tuition contracts or savings trust account agreements pursuant to Chapter 4.9 (§23-38.75 et seq.) of Title 23 is discussed.

27. Discussion or consideration, by the Wireless Carrier E–911 Cost Recovery Subcommittee created pursuant to §56-484.15, of trade secrets, as defined in the Uniform Trade Secrets Act (§59.1-336 et seq.) of Title 59.1, submitted by CMRS providers as defined in §56-484.12, related to the provision of wireless E–911 service.

B. No resolution, ordinance, rule, contract, regulation or motion adopted, passed or agreed to in a closed meeting shall become effective unless the public body, following the meeting, reconvenes in open meeting and takes a vote of the membership on such resolution, ordinance, rule, contract, regulation or motion which shall have its substance reasonably identified in the open meeting.

C. Public officers improperly selected due to the failure of the public body to comply with the other provisions of this section shall be de facto officers and, as such, their official actions are valid until they obtain notice of the legal defect in their election.

D. Nothing in this section shall be construed to prevent the holding of conferences between two or more public bodies, or their representatives, but these conferences shall be subject to the same procedures for holding closed meetings as are applicable to any other public body.

E. This section shall not be construed to (i) require the disclosure of any contract between the Intervention Program Committee within the Department of Health Professions and an impaired practitioner entered into pursuant to Chapter 25.1 (§54.1-2515 et seq.) of Title 54.1 or (ii) require the board of directors of any authority created pursuant to the Industrial Development and Revenue Bond Act (§15.2-4900 et seq.), or any public body empowered to issue industrial revenue bonds by general or special law, to identify a business or industry to which subdivision A 5 applies. However, such business or industry shall be identified as a matter of public record at least thirty days prior to the actual date of the board's authorization of the sale or issuance of such bonds. *(Chgd. by L.1995 ch. 499; L.1996 chs. 855, 862, 902, 905, 1046; L.1997 chs. 439, 641, 785, 861; L.1999 chs. 485, 518, 703, 726, 849, 867, 868; L.2000 chs. 382, 400, 720, 1064, eff. 7/1/2000.)*

§2.1-344.1. Closed meetings procedures; certification of proceedings.

A. No closed meeting shall be held unless the public body proposing to convene such meeting has taken an affirmative recorded vote in an open meeting approving a motion which (i) identifies the subject matter, (ii) states the purpose of the meeting and (iii) makes specific reference to the applicable exemption from open meeting requirements provided in §2.1-343 or subsection A of §2.1-344. The matters contained in such motion shall be set forth in detail in the minutes of the open meeting. A general reference to the provisions of this chapter, the authorized exemptions from open meeting requirements, or the subject matter of the closed meeting shall not be sufficient to satisfy the requirements for holding a closed meeting.

B. The notice provisions of this chapter shall not apply to closed meetings of any public body held solely for the purpose of interviewing candidates for the position of chief administrative officer. Prior to any such closed meeting for the purpose of interviewing candidates, the public body shall announce in an open meeting that such closed meeting shall be held at a disclosed or undisclosed location within fifteen days thereafter.

C. The public body holding a closed meeting shall restrict its discussion during the closed meeting only to those matters specifically exempted from the provisions of this chapter and identified in the motion required by subsection A.

D. At the conclusion of any closed meeting, the public body holding such meeting shall immediately reconvene in an open meeting and shall take a roll call or other recorded vote to be included in the minutes of that body, certifying that to the best of each member's knowledge (i) only public business matters lawfully exempted from open meeting requirements under this chapter and (ii) only such public business matters as were identified in the motion by which the closed meeting was convened were heard, discussed or considered in the meeting by the public body. Any member of the public body who believes that there was a departure from the requirements of subdivisions (i) and (ii), shall so state prior to the vote, indicating the substance of the departure that, in his judgment, has taken place. The statement shall be recorded in the minutes of the public body.

E. Failure of the certification required by subsection D to receive the affirmative vote of a majority of the members of the public body present during a meeting shall not affect the validity or confidentiality of such meeting with respect to matters considered therein in compliance with the provisions of this chapter. The recorded vote and any statement made in connection therewith, shall upon proper authentication, constitute evidence in any proceeding brought to enforce the provisions of this chapter.

F. A public body may permit nonmembers to attend a closed meeting if such persons are deemed necessary or if their presence will reasonably aid the public body in its consideration of a topic which is a subject of the meeting.

G. Except as specifically authorized by law, in no event may any public body take action on matters discussed in any closed meeting, except at an open meeting for which notice was given as required by §2.1-343.

H. Minutes may be taken during closed meetings of a public body, but shall not be required. Such minutes shall not be subject to mandatory public disclosure.
(Chgd. by L.1999 chs. 703, 726, eff. 7/1/99.)

§2.1-345. *(Repealed by L.1999 chs. 703, 726, eff. 7/1/99.)*

§2.1-346. Proceedings for enforcement of chapter.

A. Any person, including the attorney for the Commonwealth acting in his official or individual capacity, denied the rights and privileges conferred by this chapter may proceed to enforce such rights and privileges by filing a petition for mandamus or injunction, supported by an affidavit showing good cause, addressed to the general district court or the court of record of the county or city from which the public body has been elected or appointed to serve and in which such rights and privileges were so denied. Failure by any person to request and receive notice of the time and place of meetings as provided in §2.1-343 shall not preclude any person from enforcing his or her rights and privileges conferred by this chapter.

B. Any petition alleging denial of rights and privileges conferred by this chapter by a board, bureau, commission, authority, district or agency of the state government or by a standing or other committee of the General Assembly, shall be addressed to the general district court or the circuit court of the residence of the aggrieved party or of the City of Richmond. In any action brought before a general district court, a corporate petitioner may appear through its officer, director or managing agent without the assistance of counsel, notwithstanding any provision of law or Rule of the Supreme Court of Virginia to the contrary.

C. The petition for mandamus or injunction shall be heard within seven days of the date when the same is made. However, any petition made outside of the regular terms of the circuit court of a county which is included in a judicial circuit with another county or counties, the hearing on the petition shall be given precedence on the docket of such court over all cases which are not otherwise given precedence by law.

D. The petition shall allege with reasonable specificity the circumstances of the denial of the rights and privileges conferred by this chapter. A single instance of denial of the rights and privileges conferred by this chapter shall be sufficient to invoke the remedies granted herein. If the court finds the denial to be in violation of the provisions of this chapter, the petitioner shall be entitled to recover reasonable costs and attorney's fees from the public body if the petitioner substantially prevails on the merits of the case, unless special circumstances would make an award unjust. In making this determination, a court may consider, among other things, the reliance of a public body on an opinion of the Attorney General or a decision of a court that substantially supports the public body's position.

E. In any action to enforce the provisions of this chapter, the public body shall bear the burden of proof to establish an exemption by a preponderance of the evidence. Any failure by a public body to follow the procedures established by this chapter shall be presumed to be a violation of this chapter.
(Chgd. by L.1996 ch. 578; L.1999 chs. 703, 726, eff. 7/1/99.)

§2.1-346.1. Violations and penalties.

In a proceeding commenced against members of public bodies under §2.1-346 for a violation of §§2.1-342, 2.1-342.01, 2.1-342.2, 2.1-343, 2.1-343.1, 2.1-343.2, 2.1-344 or §2.1-344.1, the court, if it finds that a violation was willfully and knowingly made, shall impose upon such member in his individual capacity, whether a writ of mandamus or injunctive relief is awarded or not, a civil penalty of not less than $100 nor more than $1,000, which amount shall be paid into the State Literary Fund. For a second or subsequent violation, such civil penalty shall be not less than $500 nor more than $2,500.
(Chgd. by L.1996 ch. 578; L.1999 chs. 703, 726, eff. 7/1/99.)

CHAPTER 40.1
STATE AND LOCAL GOVERNMENT CONFLICT OF INTERESTS ACT
(Selected Articles)

ARTICLE 2
GENERALLY PROHIBITED AND UNLAWFUL CONDUCT
(Complete Article)

§2.1-639.3. Application.

This article applies to generally prohibited conduct which shall be unlawful and to state and local government officers and employees.

§2.1-639.4. Prohibited conduct.

No officer or employee of a state or local governmental or advisory agency shall:

1. Solicit or accept money or other thing of value for services performed within the scope of his official duties, except the compensation, expenses or other remuneration paid by the agency of which he is an officer or employee. This prohibition shall not apply to the acceptance of special benefits which may be authorized by law;

2. Offer or accept any money or other thing of value for or in consideration of obtaining employment, appointment, or promotion of any person with any governmental or advisory agency;

3. Offer or accept any money or other thing of value for or in consideration of the use of his public position to obtain a contract for any person or business with any governmental or advisory agency;

4. Use for his own economic benefit or that of another party confidential information which he has acquired by reason of his public position and which is not available to the public;

5. Accept any money, loan, gift, favor, service, or business or professional opportunity that reasonably tends to influence him in the performance of his official duties. This subdivision shall not apply to any political contribution actually used for political campaign or constituent service purposes and reported as required by Chapter 9 (§24.2-900 et seq.) of Title 24.2;

6. Accept any business or professional opportunity when he knows that there is a reasonable likelihood that the opportunity is being afforded him to influence him in the performance of his official duties;

7. Accept any honoraria for any appearance, speech, or article in which the officer or employee provides expertise or opinions related to the performance of his official duties. The term "honoraria" shall not include any payment for or reimbursement to such person for his actual travel, lodging, or subsistence expenses incurred in connection with such appearance, speech, or article or in the alternative a payment of money or anything of value not in excess of the per diem deduction allowable under §162 of the Internal Revenue Code, as amended from time to time. The prohibition in this subdivision shall apply only to the Governor, Lieutenant Governor, Attorney General, Governor's Secretaries, and heads of departments of state government;

8. Accept a gift from a person who has interests that may be substantially affected by the performance of the officer's or the employee's official duties under circumstances where the timing and nature of the gift would cause a reasonable person to question the officer's or employee's impartiality in the matter affecting the donor. Violations of this subdivision shall not be subject to criminal law penalties; or

9. Accept gifts from sources on a basis so frequent as to raise an appearance of the use of his public office for private gain. Violations of this subdivision shall not be subject to criminal law penalties.

§2.1-639.4:1. Prohibited conduct for certain officers and employees of the state government.

In addition to the prohibitions contained in §2.1-639.4, no state officer or employee shall, during the one year after the termination of his public employment or service, represent a client or act in a representative capacity on behalf of any person or group, for compensation, on any matter before the agency of which he was an officer or employee.

For the purposes of this section, "state officer or employee" shall mean (i) the Governor, Lieutenant Governor, Attorney General, and officers appointed by the Governor, whether confirmation by the General Assembly or by either house thereof is required or not, who are regularly employed in a full-time salaried basis; those officers and employees of executive branch agencies who report directly to the agency head; and those at the level immediately below those who report directly to the agency head and are at a salary grade of sixteen or higher and (ii) the officers and professional employees of the legislative branch designated by the joint rules committee of the General Assembly. For the purposes of this section, the General Assembly and the legislative branch agencies shall be deemed one agency.

The prohibitions of this section shall apply only to persons engaged in activities that would require registration as a lobbyist under §30-28.2.

Any person subject to the provisions of this section may apply to the Attorney General, as provided in §2.1-639.23, for an advisory opinion as to the application of the restriction imposed by this section on any post-public employment position or opportunity.

ARTICLE 3
PROHIBITED CONDUCT REGARDING CONTRACTS
(Complete Article)

§2.1-639.5. Application.

This article prescribes certain conduct relating to contracts by state and local government officers and employees.

§2.1-639.6. Prohibited contracts by officers and employees of state government.

A. No officer or employee of any governmental agency of state government shall have a personal interest in a contract with the governmental agency of which he is an officer or employee, other than his own contract of employment.

B. No officer or employee of any governmental agency of state government shall have a personal interest in a contract with any other governmental agency of state government unless such contract is (i) awarded as a result of competitive sealed bidding or competitive negotiation as defined in §11-37 or (ii) is awarded after a finding, in writing, by the administrative head of the governmental agency that competitive bidding or negotiation is contrary to the best interest of the public.

C. The provisions of this section shall not be applicable to:

1. An employee's personal interest in additional contracts of employment with his own governmental agency which accrue to him because of a member of his immediate family, provided the employee does not exercise any control over the employment or the employment activities of the member of his immediate family and the employee is not in a position to influence those activities;

2. The personal interest of an officer or employee of a state institution of higher education in additional contracts of employment with his own governmental agency which accrue to him because of a member of his immediate family, provided (i) the officer or employee and the immediate family member are engaged in teaching, research or administrative support positions at the educational institution, (ii) the governing board of the educational institution finds that it is in the best interests of the institution and the Commonwealth for such dual employment to exist, and (iii) after such finding, the board ensures that the officer or employee, or the immediate family member, does not have sole authority to supervise, evaluate or make personnel decisions regarding the other;

3. An officer's or employee's personal interest in a contract of employment with any other governmental agency of state government;

4. Contracts for the sale by a governmental agency of services or goods at uniform prices available to the general public;

5. An employee's personal interest in a contract between a state institution of higher education and a publisher or wholesaler of textbooks or other educational materials for students, which accrues to him solely because he has authored or otherwise created such textbooks or materials;

6. Subject to approval by the board of visitors, an employee's personal interest in a contract between a state institution of higher education which operates a school of medicine or dentistry and a not-for-profit nonstock corporation which operates a clinical practice within such state institution and of which such employee is a member or employee;

7. Subject to approval by the board of visitors, an employee's personal interest in a contract for research and development or commercialization of intellectual property between a state institution of higher education and a business in which the employee has a personal interest, if (i) the employee's personal interest has been disclosed to and approved by the state institution of higher education prior to the time at which the contract is entered into; (ii) the employee promptly files a disclosure statement pursuant to §2.1-639.15 and thereafter files such statement annually on or before January 15; (iii) the institution has established a formal policy regarding such contracts, approved by the State Council of Higher Education; and (iv) no later than December 31 of each year, the institution files an annual report with the Secretary of the Commonwealth disclosing each open contract entered subject to this provision, the names of the parties to each contract, the date each contract was executed and its term, the subject of each contractual arrangement, the nature of the conflict of interest, the institution's employee responsible for administering each contract, the details of the institution's commitment or investment of resources or finances for each contract, and any other information requested by the Secretary of the Commonwealth; or

8. Subject to approval by the board of visitors, an employee's personal interest in a contract between a state institution of higher education and a business in which the employee has a personal interest, if (i) the personal interest has been disclosed to the institution prior to the time the contract is entered into; (ii) the employee files a disclosure statement pursuant to §2.1-639.15 and thereafter annually on or before January 15; (iii) the employee does not participate in the institution's decision to contract; (iv) the president of the institution finds and certifies in writing that the contract is for goods and services needed for quality patient care by the institution's medical center, including the acquisition of drugs, therapies and medical technologies; and (v) no later than December 31 of each year, the institution files an annual report with the Secretary of the Commonwealth disclosing each open contract entered subject to this provision, the names of the parties to each contract, the date each contract was executed and its term, the subject of each contractual arrangement, the nature of the conflict of interest, the institution's employee responsible for administering each contract, the details of the institution's commitment or investment of resources or finances for each contract, and any other information requested by the Secretary of the Commonwealth.

(Chgd. by L.1995 ch. 403; L.1998 ch. 838, eff. 7/1/98.)

§2.1-639.7. Prohibited contracts by members of county boards of supervisors, city councils and town councils.

A. No person elected or appointed as a member of the governing body of a county, city or town shall have a personal interest in (i) any contract with his governing body, or (ii) any contract with any governmental agency which is a component part of his local government and which is subject to the ultimate control of the governing body of which he is a member, or (iii) any contract other than a contract of employment with any other governmental agency if such person's governing body appoints a majority of the members of the governing body of the second governmental agency.

B. The provisions of this section shall not be applicable to:

1. A member's personal interest in a contract of employment provided (i) the officer or employee was employed by the governmental agency prior to July 1, 1983, in accordance with the provisions of the Conflict of Interests Act, Chapter 22 (§2.1-347 et seq.) of Title 2.1 of the Code of Virginia, as it existed on June 30, 1983, or (ii) the employment first began prior to the member becoming a member of the governing body;

2. Contracts for the sale by a governmental agency of services or goods at uniform prices available to the public; or

3. A contract awarded to a member of a governing body as a result of competitive sealed bidding where the governing body has established a need for the same or substantially similar goods through purchases prior to the election or appointment of the member to serve on the governing body.

However, the member shall have no involvement in the preparation of the specifications for such contract, and the remaining members of the governing body, by written resolution, shall state that it is in the public interest for the member to bid on such contract.

§2.1-639.7:1. Prohibited contracts by members of school boards.

A. No person elected or appointed as a member of a local school board shall have a personal interest in (i) any contract with his school board or (ii) any contract with any governmental agency which is subject to the ultimate control of the school board of which he is a member.

B. The provisions of this section shall not be applicable to:

1. A member's personal interest in a contract of employment provided the employment first began prior to the member becoming a member of the school board;

2. Contracts for the sale by a governmental agency of services or goods at uniform prices available to the public; or

3. A contract awarded to a member of a school board as a result of competitive sealed bidding where the school board has established a need for the same or substantially similar goods through purchases prior to the election or appointment of the member to serve on the school board. However, the member shall have no involvement in the preparation of the specifications for such contract, and the remaining members of the school board, by written resolution, shall state that it is in the public interest for the member to bid on such contract.

(Added by L.1996 ch. 548, eff. 7/1/96.)

§2.1-639.8. Prohibited contracts by other officers and employees of local governmental agencies.

A. No other officer or employee of any governmental agency of local government shall have a personal interest in a contract with the agency of which he is an officer or employee other than his own contract of employment.

B. No officer or employee of any governmental agency of local government shall have a personal interest in a contract with any other governmental agency which is a component of the government of his county, city or town unless such contract is (i) awarded as a result of competitive sealed bidding or competitive negotiation as defined in §11-37 or is awarded as a result of a procedure embodying competitive principles as authorized by subsection D of §11-35, or (ii) is awarded after a finding, in writing, by the administrative head of the governmental agency that competitive bidding or negotiation is contrary to the best interest of the public.

C. The provisions of this section shall not be applicable to:

1. An employee's personal interest in additional contracts of employment with his own governmental agency which accrue to him because of a member of his immediate family, provided the employee does not exercise any control over the employment or the employment activities of the member of his immediate family and the employee is not in a position to influence those activities;

2. An officer's or employee's personal interest in a contract of employment with any other governmental agency which is a component part of the government of his county, city or town;

3. Contracts for the sale by a governmental agency of services or goods at uniform prices available to the general public;

4. Members of local governing bodies who are subject to §2.1-639.7; or

5. Members of local school boards who are subject to §2.1-639.7:1.

(Chgd. by L.1996 ch. 548, eff. 7/1/96.)

§2.1-639.9. Further exceptions.

A. The provisions of §§2.1-639.6 through 2.1-639.8 shall not apply to:

1. The sale, lease or exchange of real property between an officer or employee and a governmental agency, provided the officer or employee does not participate in any way as such officer or employee in such sale, lease or exchange, and this fact is set forth as a matter of public record by the governing body of the governmental agency or by the administrative head thereof;

2. The publication of official notices;

3. Contracts between the government or school board of a town or city with a population of less than 10,000 and an officer or employee of that town or city government or school board when the total of such contracts between the town or city government or school board and the officer or employee of that town or city government or school board or a business controlled by him does not exceed $10,000 per year or such amount exceeds $10,000 and is less than $25,000 but results from contracts arising from awards made on a sealed bid basis, and such officer or employee has made disclosure as provided for in §2.1-639.14;

4. An officer or employee whose sole personal interest in a contract with the governmental agency is by reason of income from the contracting firm or governmental agency in excess of $10,000 per year, provided the officer or employee or a member of his immediate family does not participate and has no authority to participate in the procurement or letting of such contract on behalf of the contracting firm and the officer or employee either does not have authority to participate in the procurement or letting of the contract on behalf of his governmental agency or he disqualifies himself as a matter of public record and does not participate on behalf of his governmental agency in negotiating the contract or in approving the contract;

5. Except when the governmental agency is the Virginia Retirement System, contracts between an officer's or employee's governmental agency and a public service corporation, financial institution, or company furnishing public utilities in which the officer or employee has a personal interest, provided the officer or employee disqualifies himself as a matter of public record and does not participate on behalf of his governmental agency in negotiating the contract or in approving the contract;

6. Contracts for the purchase of goods or services when the contract does not exceed $500;

7. Grants or other payment under any program wherein uniform rates for, or the amounts paid to, all qualified applicants are established solely by the administering governmental agency; or

8. An officer or employee whose sole personal interest in a contract with his own governmental agency is by reason of his marriage to his spouse who is employed by the same agency, if the spouse was employed by such agency for five or more years prior to marrying such officer or employee.

B. Neither the provisions of this chapter nor, unless expressly provided otherwise, any amendments thereto shall apply to those employment contracts or renewals thereof or to any other contracts entered into prior to August 1, 1987, which were in compliance with either the Virginia Conflict of Interests Act, Chapter 22 (§2.1-347 et seq.) or the Comprehensive Conflict of Interests Act, Chapter 40 (§2.1-599 et seq.) of this title at the time of their formation and thereafter. Those contracts shall continue to be governed by the provisions of the appropriate prior Act. Notwithstanding the provisions of subdivision (f)(4) of §2.1-348 of Chapter 22 of this title in effect prior to July 1, 1983, the employment by the same governmental agency of an officer or employee and spouse or any other relative residing in the same household shall not be deemed to create a material financial interest except when one of such persons is employed in a direct supervisory or administrative position, or both, with respect to such spouse or other relative residing in his household and the annual salary of such subordinate is $22,500 or more. *(Chgd. by L.1997 ch. 641, eff. 7/1/97.)*

ARTICLE 4
PROHIBITED CONDUCT REGARDING TRANSACTIONS
(Complete Article)

§2.1-639.10. Application.

This article proscribes certain conduct by state and local government officers and employees having a personal interest in a transaction.

§2.1-639.11. Prohibited conduct concerning personal interest in a transaction.

A. Each officer and employee of any state or local governmental or advisory agency who has a personal interest in a transaction:

1. Shall disqualify himself from participating in the transaction if the transaction has application solely to property or a business in which he has a personal interest or he is unable to participate pursuant to subdivision 2 or 3 of this subsection. Any disqualification under the provisions of this subdivision shall be recorded in the public records of the officer's or employee's governmental or advisory agency. The officer or employee shall disclose his personal interest as required by §2.1-639.13 C or §2.1-639.14 C and shall not vote or in any manner act on behalf of his agency in the transaction;

2. May participate in the transaction if he is a member of a business, profession, occupation, or group the members of which are affected by the transaction, and he complies with the declaration requirements of §2.1-639.13 D or §2.1-639.14 E; or

3. May participate in the transaction if it affects the public generally, even though his personal interest, as a member of the public, may also be affected by that transaction.

B. Disqualification under the provisions of this section shall not prevent any employee having a personal interest in a transaction in which his agency is involved from representing himself or a member of his immediate family in such transaction provided he does not receive compensation for such representation and provided he complies with the disqualification and relevant disclosure requirements of this chapter.

C. If disqualifications of officers or employees in accordance with this section leave less than the number required by law to act, the remaining member or members shall have authority to act for the agency by majority vote, unless a unanimous vote of all members is required by law, in which case authority to act shall require a unanimous vote of remaining members. Notwithstanding any provisions of this chapter to the contrary, members of a local governing body whose sole interest in any proposed sale, contract of sale, exchange, lease or conveyance is by virtue of their employment by a business involved in a proposed sale, contract of sale, exchange, lease or conveyance, and where such member's or members' vote is essential to a constitutional majority required pursuant to Article VII, Section 9 of the Constitution of Virginia and §15.1-307, such member or members of the local governing body may vote and participate in the deliberations of the governing body concerning whether to approve, enter into or execute such sale, contract of sale, exchange, lease or conveyance. Official action taken under circumstances which violate this section may be rescinded by the agency on such terms as the interests of the agency and innocent third parties require.

D. The provisions of subsection A of this section shall not prevent an officer or employee from participating in a transaction merely because such officer or employee is a party in a legal proceeding of a civil nature concerning such transaction.

E. The provisions of subsection A of this section shall not prevent an employee from participating in a transaction regarding textbooks or other educational material for students at state institutions of higher education, when those textbooks or materials have been authored or otherwise created by the employee.

ARTICLE 5
DISCLOSURE STATEMENTS REQUIRED TO BE FILED
(Selected Sections)

§2.1-639.12. Application.

This article requires disclosure of certain personal and financial interests by state and local government officers and employees.

§2.1-639.13. Disclosure by state officers and employees.

A. The Governor, Lieutenant Governor, Attorney General, Justices of the Supreme Court, judges of the Court of Appeals, judges of any circuit court, judges and substitute judges of any district court, members of the State Corporation Commission, members of the Virginia Workers' Compensation Commission, members of the Commonwealth Transportation Board, members of the Board of Trustees of the Virginia Retirement System, and members of the State Lottery Board and other persons occupying such offices or positions of trust or employment in state government as may be designated by the Governor or, in the case of officers or employees of the legislative branch, by the joint rules committees of the General Assembly, shall file, as a condition to assuming office or employment, a disclosure statement of their personal interests and such other information as is specified on the form set forth in §2.1-639.15 and thereafter shall file such a statement annually on or before January 15.

B. Nonsalaried citizen members of policy and supervisory boards, commissions and councils as designated in Chapter 1.4 (§9-6.25 et seq.) of Title 9, other than the Commonwealth Transportation Board, members of the Board of Trustees of the Virginia Retirement System, and the State Lottery Board, shall file, as a condition to assuming office, a disclosure form of their personal interests and such other information as is specified on the form set forth in §2.1-639.15:1 and thereafter shall file such form annually on or before January 15. Nonsalaried citizen members of other boards, commissions and councils, including advisory boards, may be required to file a disclosure form if so designated by the Governor, in which case the form shall be that set forth in §2.1-639.15:1.

C. The disclosure forms required by subsections A and B of this section shall be provided by the Secretary of the Commonwealth to each officer and employee so designated not later than November 30 of each year. Disclosure forms shall be filed and maintained as public records for five years in the Office of the Secretary of the Commonwealth.

D. Candidates for the offices of Governor, Lieutenant Governor or Attorney General shall file a disclosure statement of their personal interests as required by §24.2-502.

E. Any officer or employee of state government who has a personal interest in any transaction before the governmental or advisory agency of which he is an officer or employee and who is disqualified from participating in that transaction pursuant to §2.1-639.11 A 1, or otherwise elects to disqualify himself, shall forthwith make disclosure of the existence of his interest, and his disclosure shall be reflected in the public records of the agency for five years in the office of the administrative head of the officer's or employee's governmental agency or advisory agency or, if the agency has a clerk, in the clerk's office.

F. An officer or employee of state government who is required to declare his interest pursuant to §2.1-639.11 A 2, shall declare his interest do so by stating (i) the transaction involved, (ii) the nature of the officer's or employee's personal interest affected by the transaction, (iii) that he is a member of a business, profession, occupation, or group the members of which are affected by the transaction, and (iv) that he is able to participate in the transaction fairly, objectively, and in the public interest. The officer or employee shall either make his declaration orally to be recorded in written minutes for his agency or file a signed written declaration with the clerk or administrative head of his governmental or advisory agency, as appropriate, who shall, in either case, retain and make available for public inspection such declaration for a period of five years from the date of recording or receipt. If reasonable time is not available to comply with the provisions of this subsection prior to participation in the transaction, the officer or employee shall prepare and file the required declaration by the end of the next business day.

(Chgd. by L.1997 ch. 641, eff. 7/1/97.)

§2.1-639.14. Disclosure by officers and employees of local government and school boards.

A. The members of every governing body and school board of each county and city and of towns with populations in excess of 3,500 shall file, as a condition to assuming office or employment, a disclosure statement of their personal interests and other information as is specified on the form set forth in §2.1-639.15 and thereafter shall file such a statement annually on or before January 15.

Persons occupying such positions of trust appointed by governing bodies and persons occupying such positions of employment with governing bodies as may be designated to file by ordinance of the governing body shall file, as a condition to assuming office or employment, a disclosure statement of their personal interests and other information as is specified on the form set forth in §2.1-639.15 and thereafter shall file such a statement annually on or before January 15.

Persons occupying such positions of trust appointed by school boards and persons occupying such positions of employment with school boards as may be designated to file by an adopted policy of the school board shall file, as a condition to assuming office or employment, a disclosure statement of their personal interests and other information as is specified on the form set forth in §2.1-639.15 and thereafter shall file such a statement annually on or before January 15.

B. Nonsalaried citizen members of local boards, commissions and councils as may be designated by the governing body shall file, as a condition to assuming office, a disclosure form of their personal interests and such other information as is specified on the form set forth in §2.1-639.15:1 and thereafter shall file such form annually on or before January 15.

C. The disclosure forms required by subsections A and B of this section shall be provided by the Secretary of the Commonwealth to the clerks of the governing bodies and school boards not later than November 30 of each year, and the clerks of the governing body and school board shall distribute the forms to designated individuals no later than December 10 of each year. Forms shall be filed and maintained as public records for five years in the office of the clerk of the respective governing body or school board.

D. Candidates for membership in the governing body or school board of any county, city or town with a population of more than 3,500 persons shall file a disclosure statement of their personal interests as required by §24.2-502.

E. Any officer or employee of local government who has a personal interest in any transaction before the governmental or advisory agency of which he is an officer or employee and who is disqualified from participating in that transaction pursuant to §2.1-639.11 A 1, or otherwise elects to disqualify himself, shall forthwith make disclosure of the existence of his interest, and his disclosure shall be reflected in the public records of the agency for five years in the office of the administrative head of the officer's or employee's governmental or advisory agency.

F. In addition to any disclosure required by subsections A and B of this section, in each county and city and in towns with populations in excess of 3,500, members of planning commissions, boards of zoning appeals, real estate assessors, and all county, city and town managers or executive officers shall make annual disclosures of all their interests in real estate located in the county, city or town in which they are elected, appointed, or employed. Such disclosure shall include any business in which such persons own an interest, or from which income is received, if the primary purpose of the business is to own, develop or derive compensation through the sale, exchange or development of real estate in the county, city or town. Such disclosure shall be filed as a condition to assuming office or employment, and thereafter shall be filed annually with the clerk of the governing body of such county, city or town on or before January 15. Such disclosures shall be filed and maintained as public records for five years. Forms for the filing of such reports shall be prepared and distributed by the Secretary of the Commonwealth to the clerk of each governing body.

G. An officer or employee of local government who is required to declare his interest pursuant to §2.1-639.11 A 2 shall declare his interest by stating (i) the transaction involved, (ii) the nature of the officer's or employee's personal interest affected by the transaction, (iii) that he is a member of a business, profession, occupation, or group the members of which are affected by the transaction, and (iv) that he is able to participate in the transaction fairly, objectively, and in the public interest. The officer or employee shall either make his declaration orally to be recorded in written minutes of his agency or file a signed written declaration with the clerk or administrative head of his governmental or advisory agency, as appropriate, who shall, in either case, retain and make available for public inspection such declaration for a period of five years from the date of recording or receipt. If reasonable time is not available to comply with the provisions of this subsection prior to participation in the transaction, the officer or employee shall prepare and file the required declaration by the end of the next business day.

(Chgd. by L.1995 ch. 495; L.1996 ch. 526; L.2000 ch. 317, eff. 7/1/2000.)

§2.1-639.14:1. Disclosure by certain constitutional officers.

For the purposes of this Act, holders of the constitutional offices of treasurer, sheriff, attorney for the Commonwealth, clerk of the circuit court and commissioner of the revenue of each county and city, shall be deemed to be local officers and shall be required to file the Statement of Economic Interests set forth in §2.1-639.15. These officers shall file statements pursuant to §2.1-639.14 and candidates shall file statements as required by §24.1-167.

ARTICLE 6
SCHOOL BOARDS AND EMPLOYEES OF SCHOOL BOARDS
(Complete Article)

§2.1-639.16. Additional provisions applicable to school boards, and employees of school boards.

A. Notwithstanding any other provision of this chapter, it shall be unlawful for the school board of any county or city or of any town constituting a separate school division to employ or pay any teacher or other school board employee from the public funds, federal, state or local, or for a division superintendent to recommend to the school board the employment of any teacher or other employee, if the teacher or other employee is the father, mother, brother, sister, spouse, son, daughter, son-in-law, daughter-in-law, sister-in-law or brother-in-law of the superintendent, or of any member of the school board.

This section shall apply to any person employed by any school board in the operation of the public free school system, adult education programs or any other program maintained and operated by a local county, city or town school board.

B. This section shall not be construed to prohibit the employment, promotion, or transfer within a school division of any person within a relationship described in subsection A when such person:

1. Has been employed pursuant to a written contract with a school board or employed as a substitute teacher or teacher's aide by a school board prior to the taking of office of any member of such board or division superintendent of schools; or

2. Has been employed pursuant to a written contract with a school board or employed as a substitute teacher or teacher's aide by a school board prior to the inception of such relationship; or

3. Was employed by a school board at any time prior to June 10, 1994, and had been employed at any time as a teacher or other employee of any Virginia school board prior to the taking of office of any member of such school board or division superintendent of schools.

C. A person employed as a substitute teacher may not be employed to any greater extent than he was employed by the school board in the last full school year prior to the taking of office of such board member or division superintendent or to the inception of such relationship. The exceptions in subdivisions 1, 2, and 3 of subsection B shall apply only if the prior employment has been in the same school division where the employee and the superintendent or school board member now seek to serve simultaneously.

D. If any member of the school board or any division superintendent knowingly violates these provisions, he shall be personally liable to refund to the local treasury any amounts paid in violation of this law, and the funds shall be recovered from the individual by action or suit in the name of the Commonwealth on the petition of the attorney for the Commonwealth. Recovered funds shall be paid into the local treasury for the use of the public schools.
(Chgd. by L.1995 ch. 186; L.1997 ch. 84, eff. 7/1/97.)

ARTICLE 7
PENALTIES AND REMEDIES
(Complete Article)

§2.1-639.17. Knowing violation of chapter a misdemeanor.

Any person who knowingly violates any of the provisions of Articles 2 through 6 (§§2.1-639.3 through 2.1-639.16) of this chapter shall be guilty of a Class 1 misdemeanor, except that any member of a local governing body who knowingly violates §2.1-639.11 A or §2.1-639.14 C or E shall be guilty of a Class 3 misdemeanor. A knowing violation under this section is one in which the person engages in conduct, performs an act or refuses to perform an act when he knows that the conduct is prohibited or required by this chapter.

§2.1-639.18. Advisory opinions.

A. A state officer or employee shall not be prosecuted for a knowing violation of this chapter if the alleged violation resulted from his good faith reliance on a written opinion of the Attorney General and the opinion was made after a full disclosure of the facts.

B. A local officer or employee shall not be prosecuted for a knowing violation of this chapter if the alleged violation resulted from his good faith reliance on a written opinion of the Commonwealth's attorney and the opinion was made after a full disclosure of the facts.

C. If any officer or employee serving at the local level of government is charged with a knowing violation of this chapter, and the alleged violation resulted from his reliance upon a written opinion of his city, county or town attorney, made after a full disclosure of the facts, that such action was not in violation of this chapter, then the officer or employee shall have the right to introduce a copy of the opinion at his trial as evidence that he did not knowingly violate this chapter.

§2.1-639.19. Knowing violation of chapter constitutes malfeasance in office or employment.

Any person who knowingly violates any of the provisions of this chapter shall be guilty of malfeasance in office or employment. Upon conviction thereof, the judge or jury trying the case, in addition to any other fine or penalty provided by law, may order the forfeiture of said office or employment.

§2.1-639.20. Invalidation of contract; recision of sales.

A. Any contract made in violation of §2.1-639.4 or §2.1-639.6 through 2.1-639.8 may be declared void and may be rescinded by the governing body of the contracting or selling governmental agency within five years of the date of such contract. In cases in which the contract is invalidated, the contractor shall retain or receive only the reasonable value, with no increment for profit or commission, of the property or services furnished prior to the date of receiving notice that the contract has been voided. In cases of recision of a contract of sale, any refund or restitution shall be made to the contracting or selling governmental agency.

B. Any purchase by an officer or employee made in violation of §2.1-639.4 or §2.1-639.6 through 2.1-639.8 may be rescinded by the governing body of the contracting or selling governmental agency within five years of the date of such purchase.

§2.1-639.21. Forfeiture of money, etc., derived from violation of this chapter.

In addition to any other fine or penalty provided by law, any money or other thing of value derived by an officer or employee from a violation of §2.1-639.4 through 2.1-639.11 shall be forfeited and, in the event of a knowing violation, there may also be imposed a civil penalty in an amount equal to the amount of money or thing of value forfeited to the Commonwealth or the local government as the case may be. If the thing of value received by the officer or employee in violation of this chapter should enhance in value between the time of the violation and the time of discovery of the violation, the greater value shall determine the amount of forfeiture.

§2.1-639.22. Limitation of actions.

The statute of limitations for the criminal prosecution of a person for violation of any provision of this chapter shall be one year from the time the Attorney General, if the violation is by a state officer or employee, or the Commonwealth's attorney, if the violation is by a local officer or employee, has actual knowledge of the violation or five years from the date of the violation, whichever event occurs first. Any prosecution for malfeasance in office shall be governed by the statute of limitations provided by law.

§2.1-639.23. Enforcement.

A. The provisions of this chapter relating to an officer or employee serving at the state level of government shall be enforced by the Attorney General.

In addition to any other powers and duties prescribed by law, the Attorney General shall have the following powers and duties within the area for which he is responsible under this section:

1. He shall advise the agencies of state government and officers and employees serving at the state level of government on appropriate procedures for complying with the requirements of this chapter. He may review any disclosure statements, without notice to the affected person, for the purpose of determining satisfactory compliance, and shall investigate matters which come to his attention reflecting possible violations of the provisions of this chapter by officers and employees serving at the state level of government;

2. If he determines that there is a reasonable basis to conclude that any officer or employee serving at the state level of government has knowingly violated any provision of this chapter, he shall designate a Commonwealth's attorney who shall have complete and independent discretion in the prosecution of such officer or employee;

3. He shall render advisory opinions to any state officer or employee who seeks advice as to whether the facts in a particular case would constitute a violation of the provisions of this chapter. He shall determine which opinions or portions thereof are of general interest to the public and may, from time to time, be published.

Irrespective of whether an opinion of the Attorney General has been requested and rendered, any person has the right to seek a declaratory judgment or other judicial relief as provided by law.

B. The provisions of this chapter relating to an officer or employee serving at the local level of government shall be enforced by the Commonwealth's attorney within the political subdivision for which he is elected.

Each Commonwealth's attorney shall be responsible for prosecuting violations by an officer or employee serving at the local level of government and, if the Attorney General designates such Commonwealth's attorney, violations by an officer or employee serving at the state level of government. In the event the violation by an officer or employee serving at the local level of government involves more than one local jurisdiction, the Attorney General shall designate which of the attorneys for the Commonwealth of the involved local jurisdictions shall enforce the provisions of this chapter with regard to such violation.

Each Commonwealth's attorney shall establish an appropriate written procedure for implementing the disclosure requirements of local officers and employees of his county, city or town, and for other political subdivisions, whose principal offices are located within the jurisdiction served by such Commonwealth's attorney. The Commonwealth's attorney shall provide a copy of this act to all local officers and employees in the jurisdiction served by such attorney who are required to file a disclosure statement pursuant to Article 5 (§2.1-639.12 et seq.) of this chapter. Failure to receive a copy of the act shall not be a defense to such officers and employees if they are prosecuted for violations of the act.

Each Commonwealth's attorney shall render advisory opinions as to whether the facts in a particular case would constitute a violation of the provisions of this chapter to the governing body and any local officer or employee in his jurisdiction and to political subdivisions other than a county, city or town, including regional political subdivisions whose principal offices are located within the jurisdiction served by such Commonwealth's attorney. In case the opinion given by the Commonwealth's attorney indicates that the facts would constitute a violation, the officer or employee affected thereby may request that the Attorney General review the opinion. A conflicting opinion by the Attorney General shall act to revoke the opinion of the Commonwealth's attorney. The Attorney General shall determine which of his reviewing opinions or portions thereof are of general interest to the public and may, from time to time, be published.

Irrespective of whether an opinion of the Commonwealth's attorney or the Attorney General has been requested and rendered, any person has the right to seek a declaratory judgment or other judicial relief as provided by law.

§2.1-639.24. Venue.

Any prosecution for a violation involving an officer serving at the state level of government shall be brought in the Circuit Court of the City of Richmond. Any prosecution for a violation involving an employee serving at the state level of government shall be within the jurisdiction in which the employee has his principal place of state employment. Any proceeding provided in this chapter shall be brought in a court of competent jurisdiction within the county or city in which the violation occurs if the violation involves an officer or employee serving at the local level of government.

TITLE 3.1
AGRICULTURE, HORTICULTURE AND FOOD
(Selected Chapter)

CHAPTER 27.4
COMPREHENSIVE ANIMAL LAWS
(Complete Chapter)

ARTICLE 1
GENERAL PROVISIONS

§3.1-796.66. Definitions.

The following words as used in this chapter shall have the following meanings:

"Abandon" means to desert, forsake, or absolutely give up an animal without having secured another owner or custodian for the animal or by failing to provide the elements of basic care as set forth in §3.1-796.68 for a period of five consecutive days.

"Adequate care" or "care" means the responsible practice of good animal husbandry, handling, production, management, confinement, feeding, watering, protection, shelter, transportation, treatment, and, when necessary, euthanasia, appropriate for the age, species, condition, size and type of the animal and the provision of veterinary care when needed to prevent suffering or impairment of health.

"Adequate exercise" or "exercise" means the opportunity for the animal to move sufficiently to maintain normal muscle tone and mass for the age, species, size, and condition of the animal.

"Adequate feed" means access to and the provision of food which is of sufficient quantity and nutritive value to maintain each animal in good health; is accessible to each animal; is prepared so as to permit ease of consumption for the age, species, condition, size and type of each animal; is provided in a clean and sanitary manner; is placed so as to minimize contamination by excrement and pests; and is provided at suitable intervals for the species, age, and condition of the animal, but at least once daily, except as prescribed by a veterinarian or as dictated by naturally occurring states of hibernation or fasting normal for the species.

"Adequate shelter" means provision of and access to shelter that is suitable for the species, age, condition, size, and type of each animal; provides adequate space for each animal; is safe and protects each animal from injury, rain, sleet, snow, hail, direct sunlight, the adverse effects of heat or cold, physical suffering, and impairment of health; is properly lighted; is properly cleaned; enables each animal to be clean and dry, except when detrimental to the species; and, for dogs and cats, provides a solid surface, resting platform, pad, floormat, or similar device that is large enough for the animal to lie on in a normal manner and can be maintained in a sanitary manner. Under this chapter, shelters whose wire, grid, or slat floors (i) permit the animals' feet to pass through the openings, (ii) sag under the animals' weight, or (iii) otherwise do not protect the animals' feet or toes from injury are not adequate shelter.

"Adequate space" means sufficient space to allow each animal to (i) easily stand, sit, lie, turn about, and make all other normal body movements in a comfortable, normal position for the animal and (ii) interact safely with other animals in the enclosure. When an animal is tethered, "adequate space" means a tether that permits the above actions and is appropriate to the age and size of the animal; is attached to the animal by a properly applied collar, halter, or harness configured so as to protect the animal from injury and prevent the animal or tether from becoming entangled with other objects or animals, or from extending over an object or edge that could result in the strangulation or injury of the animal; and is at least three times the length of the animal, as measured from the tip of its nose to the base of its tail, except when the animal is being walked on a leash or is attached by a tether to a lead line. When freedom of movement would endanger the animal, temporarily and appropriately restricting movement of the animal according to professionally accepted standards for the species is considered provision of adequate space.

"Adequate water" means provision of and access to clean, fresh, potable water of a drinkable temperature which is provided in a suitable manner, in sufficient volume, and at suitable intervals, but at least once every twelve hours, to maintain normal hydration for the age, species, condition, size and type of each animal, except as prescribed by a veterinarian or as dictated by naturally occurring states of hibernation or fasting normal for the species; and is provided in clean, durable receptacles which are accessible to each animal and are placed so as to minimize contamination of the water by excrement and pests or an alternative source of hydration consistent with generally accepted husbandry practices.

"Adoption" means the transfer of ownership of a dog or cat from a releasing agency to an individual.

"Agricultural animals" means all livestock and poultry.

"Ambient temperature" means the temperature surrounding the animal.

"Animal" means any nonhuman vertebrate species except fish. For the purposes of §3.1-796.98, animal means any species susceptible to rabies. For the purposes of §3.1-796.122, animal means any nonhuman vertebrate species including fish except those fish captured and killed or disposed of in a reasonable and customary manner.

"Animal control officer" means a person appointed as an animal control officer or deputy animal control officer as provided in §3.1-796.104.

"Animal shelter" means a facility which is used to house or contain animals and which is owned, operated, or maintained by a duly incorporated humane society, animal welfare society, society for the prevention of cruelty to animals, animal rescue group, or any other organization devoted to the welfare, protection, and humane treatment of animals.

"Board" means the Board of Agriculture and Consumer Services.

"Boarding establishment" means a place or establishment other than a pound or animal shelter where companion animals not owned by the proprietor are sheltered, fed, and watered in exchange for a fee.

"Collar" means a well-fitted device, appropriate to the age and size of the animal, attached to the animal's neck in such a way as to prevent trauma or injury to the animal.

"Companion animal" means any domestic or feral dog, domestic or feral cat, non-human primate, guinea pig, hamster, rabbit not raised for human food or fiber, exotic or native animal, reptile, exotic or native bird, or any feral animal or any animal under the care, custody, or ownership of a person or any animal which is bought, sold, traded, or bartered by any person. Agricultural animals, game species, or any animals regulated under federal law as research animals shall not be considered companion animals for the purposes of this chapter.

"Consumer" means any natural person purchasing an animal from a dealer or pet shop or hiring the services of a boarding establishment. The term "consumer" shall not include a business or corporation engaged in sales or services.

"Dealer" means any person who in the regular course of business for compensation or profit buys, sells, transfers, exchanges, or barters companion animals. Any person who transports companion animals in the regular course of business as a common carrier shall not be considered a dealer.

"Direct and immediate threat" means any clear and imminent danger to an animal's health, safety or life.

"Emergency veterinary treatment" means veterinary treatment to stabilize a life-threatening condition, alleviate suffering, prevent further disease transmission, or prevent further disease progression.

"Enclosure" means a structure used to house or restrict animals from running at large.

"Euthanasia" means the humane destruction of an animal accomplished by a method that involves instantaneous unconsciousness and immediate death or by a method that involves anesthesia, produced by an agent which causes painless loss of consciousness, and death during such loss of consciousness.

"Exhibitor" means any person who has animals for or on public display, excluding an exhibitor licensed by the United States Department of Agriculture.

"Groomer" means any person who, for a fee, cleans, trims, brushes, makes neat, manicures, or treats for external parasites any animal.

"Housing facility" means any room, building, or area used to contain a primary enclosure or enclosures.

"Humane" means any action taken in consideration of and with the intent to provide for the animal's health and well-being.

"Humane investigator" means a person who has been appointed by a circuit court as a humane investigator as provided in §3.1-796.106.

"Humane society" means any chartered, nonprofit organization incorporated under the laws of this Commonwealth and organized for the purpose of preventing cruelty to animals and promoting humane care and treatment of animals.

"Kennel" means any establishment in which five or more canines, felines, or hybrids of either are kept for the purpose of breeding, hunting, training, renting, buying, boarding, selling, or showing.

"Law-enforcement officer" means any person who is a full-time or part-time employee of a police department or sheriff's office which is part of or administered by the Commonwealth or any political subdivision thereof and who is responsible for the prevention and detection of crime and the enforcement of the penal, traffic or highway laws of the Commonwealth. Part-time employees are compensated officers who are not full-time employees as defined by the employing police department or sheriff's office.

"Livestock" includes all domestic or domesticated: bovine animals; equine animals; ovine animals; porcine animals; cervidae animals; capradae animals; animals of the genus Lama; ratites; fish or shellfish in aquaculture facilities, as defined in §3.1-73.6; enclosed domesticated rabbits or hares raised for human food or fiber; or any other individual animal specifically raised for food or fiber, except companion animals.

"Local ordinance" means any law, rule, regulation, or ordinance promulgated by the governing body of any county, city, or town.

"Locality" or "local government" means a county, city, or town, as the context may require.

"New owner" means an individual who is legally competent to enter into a binding agreement pursuant to subdivision B 2 of §3.1-796.126:1, and who adopts or receives a dog or cat from a releasing agency.

"Other officer" includes all other persons employed or elected by the people of Virginia, or by any municipality, county, or incorporated town thereof, whose duty it is to preserve the peace, to make arrests, or to enforce the law.

"Owner" means any person who: (i) has a right of property in an animal, (ii) keeps or harbors an animal, (iii) has an animal in his care, or (iv) acts as a custodian of an animal.

"Person" means any individual, partnership, firm, joint-stock company, corporation, association, trust, estate, or other legal entity.

"Pet shop" means an establishment where companion animals are bought, sold, exchanged, or offered for sale or exchange to the general public.

"Poultry" includes all domestic fowl and game birds raised in captivity.

"Pound" means a facility operated by the Commonwealth, or any locality, for the purpose of impounding or harboring seized, stray, homeless, abandoned, or unwanted animals; or a facility operated for the same purpose under a contract with any county, city, town, or incorporated society for the prevention of cruelty to animals.

"Primary enclosure" means any structure used to immediately restrict an animal or animals to a limited amount of space, such as a room, pen, cage, compartment, or hutch. For tethered animals, the term includes the shelter and the area within reach of the tether.

"Properly cleaned" means that carcasses, debris, food waste and excrement are removed from the primary enclosure with sufficient frequency to minimize the animals' contact with the above-mentioned contaminants; the primary enclosure is sanitized with sufficient frequency to minimize odors and the hazards of disease; and the primary enclosure is cleaned so as to prevent the animals confined therein from being directly or indirectly sprayed with the stream of water, or directly or indirectly exposed to hazardous chemicals or disinfectants.

"Properly lighted" means sufficient illumination to permit routine inspections, maintenance, cleaning, and housekeeping of the housing facility, and observation of the animal; to provide regular diurnal lighting cycles of either natural or artificial light, uniformly diffused throughout the animal facilities; and to promote the well-being of the animals.

"Releasing agency" means a pound, animal shelter, humane society, animal welfare society, society for the prevention of cruelty to animals, or other similar entity that releases a dog or cat for adoption pursuant to Article 6.1 (§3.1-796.126:1 et seq.) of this chapter.

"Research facility" means any place, laboratory, or institution licensed by the U.S. Department of Agriculture at which scientific tests, experiments, or investigations involving the use of living animals are carried out, conducted, or attempted.

"Sanitize" means to make physically clean and to remove and destroy, to a practical minimum, agents injurious to health.

"State Veterinarian" means the veterinarian employed by the Commissioner of Agriculture and Consumer Services as provided in §3.1-723.

"State Veterinarian's representative" means an employee of the Department of Agriculture and Consumer Services who is under the direction of the State Veterinarian.

"Sterilize" or "sterilization" means a surgical or chemical procedure performed by a licensed veterinarian that renders a dog or cat permanently incapable of reproducing.

"Treasurer" includes the treasurer and his assistants of each county or city or other officer designated by law to collect taxes in such county or city.

"Treatment" or "adequate treatment" means the responsible handling or transportation of animals in the person's ownership, custody or charge, appropriate for the age, species, condition, size and type of the animal.

"Veterinary treatment" means treatment by or on the order of a duly licensed veterinarian.

"Weaned" means that an animal is capable of and physiologically accustomed to ingestion of solid food or food customary for the adult of the species, and has ingested such food, without nursing, for a period of at least five days.

(Chgd. by L.1995 ch. 610; L.1998 ch. 817, eff. 7/1/98.)

§3.1-796.67. Rules, regulations, and guidelines.

The board may promulgate rules and regulations or guidelines consistent with the objectives and intent of this chapter concerning the care and transportation of animals.

§3.1-796.67:1. Authority of the Commissioner.

The Commissioner of Agriculture and Consumer Services shall have the power to enter into agreements with local, state and federal agencies or other persons for the control of coyotes which pose a danger to agricultural animals.

§3.1-796.67:2. State Veterinarian's power to inspect premises where animals are kept.

The State Veterinarian and each State Veterinarian's representative shall have the power to conduct inspections of animal shelters and inspect any business premises where animals are housed or kept, including any boarding establishment, kennel, pet shop, pound, or the business premises of any dealer, exhibitor or groomer, at any reasonable time, for the purposes of determining if a violation of (i) this chapter; (ii) any other state law governing the care, control or protection of animals; or (iii) any other state law governing property rights in animals has occurred.

(Chgd. by L.1998 ch. 817, eff. 7/1/98.)

ARTICLE 2
ANIMAL WELFARE

§3.1-796.68. Care of animals by owner; penalty.

A. Each owner shall provide for each of his companion animals:

1. Adequate feed;
2. Adequate water;
3. Adequate shelter that is properly cleaned;
4. Adequate space in the primary enclosure for the particular type of animal depending upon its age, size, species, and weight;
5. Adequate exercise;
6. Adequate care, treatment, and transportation; and
7. Veterinary care when needed or to prevent suffering or disease transmission.

The provisions of this section shall also apply to every animal shelter, pound, dealer, pet shop, exhibitor, kennel, groomer, and boarding establishment. This section shall not require that animals used as food for other animals be euthanized.

B. Game and wildlife species shall be cared for in accordance with regulations promulgated by the Board of Game and Inland Fisheries by January 1, 1994.

C. Violation of this section is a Class 4 misdemeanor.

(Chgd. by L.1996 ch. 249; L.1998 ch. 817, eff. 7/1/98.)

§3.1-796.69. Transporting animals; requirements; penalty.

No owner, railroad or other common carrier when transporting any animal shall allow that animal to be confined in any type of conveyance more than twenty-four consecutive hours without being exercised, properly rested, fed and watered as necessary for that particular type and species of animal. A reasonable extension of this time shall be permitted when an accident, storm or other act of God causes a delay. Adequate space in the primary enclosure within any type of conveyance shall be provided each animal depending upon the particular type and species of animal. No person shall import into the Commonwealth, nor export from the Commonwealth, for the purpose of sale or offering for sale any dog or cat under the age of eight weeks without its dam. Violation of this section shall be punishable as a Class 1 misdemeanor.

§3.1-796.70. Sale, etc., of unweaned or certain immature animals prohibited; vaccinations required for dogs and cats; penalty.

A. No person shall sell, raffle, or offer for sale as pets or novelties, or offer or give as a prize, premium, or advertising device any living chicks, ducklings, or other fowl under two months old in quantities of less than six or any unweaned mammalian companion animal or any dog under the age of seven weeks without its dam, or any cat under the age of seven weeks without its queen. Dealers may offer immature fowl, unweaned mammalian companion animals, dogs or cats under the age of seven weeks for sale as pets or novelties with the requirement that prospective owners take possession of the animals only after fowl have reached two months of age, mammalian companion animals have been weaned, and dogs and cats are at least seven weeks of age. Nothing in this section shall prohibit the sale of an unweaned animal (i) as food for other animals or (ii) with the lactating dam or queen or a lactating surrogate dam or queen that has accepted the animal.

B. Dealers shall provide all dogs and cats with current vaccinations against contagious and infectious diseases, as recommended in writing and considered appropriate for the animal's age and breed by a licensed veterinarian, or pursuant to written recommendations provided by the manufacturer of such vaccines at least five days before any new owner takes possession of the animal. For dogs, the vaccinations required by this subsection shall include at a minimum canine distemper, adenovirus type II parainfluenza, and parvovirus. For cats, the vaccinations required by this subsection shall include at a minimum rhinotracheitis, calicivirus, and panleukopenia. Dealers shall provide the new owner with the dog's or cat's immunization history.

C. A violation of this section is punishable as a Class 3 misdemeanor.

(Chgd. by L.1995 ch. 625, eff. 7/1/95.)

§3.1-796.71. Failure of dealer or pet shop to provide adequate care, etc.; penalty.

Any dealer or pet shop that fails to adequately house, feed, water, exercise or care for animals in his or its possession or custody as provided for under this chapter shall be guilty of a Class 3 misdemeanor. Such animals shall be subject to seizure and impoundment, and upon conviction of such person the animals may be sold, euthanized, or disposed of as provided by §3.1-796.96 for licensed, tagged, or tattooed animals. Such failure shall also constitute grounds for revocation of a permit or certificate of registration after public hearing. Any funds that result from such sale shall be used first to pay the costs of the local jurisdiction for the impoundment and disposition of the animals, and any funds remaining shall be paid to the owner, if known. If the owner is not found, the remaining funds shall be paid into the Literary Fund.

§3.1-796.72. Misrepresentation of animal's condition; penalties.

No person shall misrepresent the physical condition of any animal at the animal's sale, trade, delivery, or other method of transfer. For the purpose of this section, misrepresentation shall include selling, trading, delivering or otherwise transferring an animal to another person with the knowledge that the animal has an infection, communicable disease, parasitic infestation, abnormality or other physical defect that is not made known to the person receiving the animal. However, sale of an agricultural animal that has external or internal parasites that are not made known to the person receiving the animal shall not be a violation of this section unless the animal is clinically ill or debilitated due to such parasites at the time of sale, trade, delivery or transfer of the animal. Violation of this section shall be punishable as a Class 3 misdemeanor.

(Chgd. by L.1998 ch. 817, eff. 7/1/98.)

§3.1-796.73. Abandonment of animal; penalty.

No person shall abandon any animal. Violation of this section is a Class 3 misdemeanor. Nothing in this section shall be construed to prohibit the release of an animal by its owner to an animal shelter, pound, or humane society establishment.

§3.1-796.74. Exceptions regarding veterinarians.

Sections 3.1-796.68 through 3.1-796.73, 3.1-796.78 through 3.1-796.83:2, 3.1-796.105 through 3.1-796.108, 3.1-796.120, and 3.1-796.126:1 through 3.1-796.126:7 shall not apply to: (i) a place or establishment which is operated under the immediate supervision of a duly licensed veterinarian as a hospital or boarding establishment where animals are harbored, boarded and cared for incident to the treatment, prevention, or alleviation of disease processes during the routine practice of the profession of veterinary medicine, or (ii) animals boarded under the immediate supervision of a duly licensed veterinarian.

§3.1-796.75. Procedure for animals left unclaimed with veterinarian or boarding establishment after public notice; lien; sale.

Any animal not claimed by its owner from a licensed veterinarian or boarding establishment within fourteen days after a letter of notice has been sent to the owner, by the veterinarian or boarding establishment, may be sold by the veterinarian or boarding establishment. The animal may be sold at public or private sale for fair compensation to a person capable of providing care consistent with this chapter. Any expense incurred by the veterinarian or boarding establishment becomes a lien on the animal and the proceeds of the sale shall first discharge this lien. Any balance of the proceeds shall be paid to the owner. If the owner cannot be found within the next ensuing thirty days, the balance shall be paid to the state treasury. If no purchaser is found, the animal may be offered for adoption or euthanized.

§3.1-796.76. Injured or sick animal; action by veterinarian.

A. If a licensed veterinarian is called or by his own action comes upon an animal that is sick or injured and the owner of such animal cannot be immediately located, then the licensed veterinarian, in his professional judgment, may treat, hospitalize or euthanize the animal without the permission of the owner. The veterinarian shall make such reports and keep such records of such sick or injured animals as may be prescribed by the Board of Veterinary Medicine, including the information required under subsection B of §3.1-796.105.

B. In no event shall a licensed veterinarian who has acted in good faith and properly exercised professional judgment regarding an animal be subject to liability for his actions in (i) acting in accordance with subsection A or (ii) reporting cases of suspected cruelty to animals.

(Chgd. by L.1999 ch. 620, eff. 7/1/99.)

§3.1-796.77. Disposal of animals by means of decompression chamber prohibited.

No animal shall be euthanized pursuant to the provisions of this chapter by means of a high altitude decompression chamber.

ARTICLE 3
SALE OF DOGS AND CATS BY DEALERS

Section

§3.1-796.78. Sale without pet dealer's animal history certificate violation of Consumer Protection Act; contents of certificate.

It shall be a violation of the Virginia Consumer Protection Act (§59.1-196 et seq.) for any pet dealer to sell a dog or cat within the Commonwealth stating, promising or representing that the animal is registered or capable of being registered with any animal pedigree registry organization, without providing the consumer with a pet dealer's animal history certificate at the time the consumer takes possession of the dog or cat. The pet dealer's animal history certificate shall be signed by the pet dealer, his agent or employee, and shall contain the following information:

1. The animal's breed, sex, age, color, and birth date;
2. The name and address of the person from whom the pet dealer purchased the animal;
3. The breeder's name and address;
4. The name and registration number of the animal's sire and dam;
5. If the animal has been so examined, the date on which the animal has been examined by a licensed veterinarian, the name and address of such veterinarian, and a brief statement of any findings made; and
6. A statement of all vaccinations administered to the animal, including the identity and quantity of the vaccine, and the name and address of the person or licensed veterinarian administering or supervising the vaccinations.

The information contained in the pet dealer's animal history certificate required herein shall be informative only, and the pet dealer shall not be responsible in any manner for the accuracy of such information unless he knows or has reason to know that such information is erroneous.

A copy of the pet dealer's animal history certificate signed by the consumer shall be maintained by the pet dealer for a period of one year following the date of sale.

§3.1-796.79. Inclusion of false or misleading statements in certificate violation of Consumer Protection Act.

It shall be a violation of the Virginia Consumer Protection Act (§59.1-196 et seq.) for a pet dealer to include in the pet dealer's animal history certificate provided for in §3.1-796.78 any false or misleading statement regarding the information to be contained therein.

§3.1-796.80. Consumer remedies for receipt of diseased animal upon certification by veterinarian.

If, at any time within ten days following receipt of an animal described as being registered or capable of being registered with any animal pedigree organization and subject to this chapter, a licensed veterinarian certifies such animal to be unfit for purchase due to illness, a congenital defect deleterious to the health of the animal or the presence of symptoms of a contagious or infectious disease, the pet dealer shall afford the consumer the right to choose one of the following options:

1. The right to return the animal and receive a refund of the purchase price including sales tax; or
2. The right to return the animal and to receive an exchange animal of equivalent value from the dealer, subject to the choice of the consumer.

The refund or reimbursement required by this section shall be made by the pet dealer not later than ten business days following receipt of a signed veterinary certification as hereinafter provided.

§3.1-796.81. Written notice of consumer remedies required to be supplied by pet dealers.

A pet dealer shall give the notice hereinafter set forth in writing to a consumer prior to the delivery of a dog or cat. Such notice shall be embodied in either a written contract, the pet dealer's animal history certificate or a separate document and shall state in ten point bold face type the following:

NOTICE

The sale of certain dogs and cats described as being registered or capable of being registered with any animal pedigree organization is subject to the provisions of the Virginia Consumer Protection Act (§59.1-196 et seq.). In the event that a licensed veterinarian certifies your animal to be unfit for purchase within ten days following receipt of your animal, you may choose: (i) to return your animal and receive a refund of the purchase price, or (ii) to return the animal and receive an exchange animal of your choice of equivalent value.

In order to exercise these rights you must present a written veterinary certification that the animal is unfit to the pet dealer within three business days after receiving such certification.

If the pet dealer has promised to register your animal or to provide the papers necessary therefor and fails to do so within 120 days following the date of contract, you are entitled to return the animal and receive a refund of the purchase price or to retain the animal and receive a refund of an amount not to exceed fifty percent of the purchase price.

§3.1-796.82. Failure of pet dealer to effect registration after promise; violation of Consumer Protection Act; remedies; veterinary certification; finding of intestinal parasites; illness subsequent to sale.

A. It shall be a violation of the Virginia Consumer Protection Act (§59.1-196 et seq.) for a pet dealer to state, promise, or represent that a dog or cat is registered or capable of being registered with any animal pedigree registry organization if the pet dealer shall then fail to either effect such registration or provide the consumer with the documents necessary therefor within 120 days following the date of sale of such animal. In the event that a pet dealer fails to effect registration or to provide the necessary documents therefor within 120 days following the date of sale, the consumer shall be entitled to choose one of the following options:

1. To return the animal and to receive a refund of the purchase price plus sales tax; or
2. To retain the animal and to receive a refund of an amount not to exceed fifty percent of the purchase price and sales tax.

B. The veterinary certification and statement required herein shall be presented to the pet dealer not later than three business days following receipt thereof by the consumer and shall contain the following information:

1. The name of the owner;
2. The date or dates of the examination;
3. The breed, color, sex, and age of the animal;
4. A description of the veterinarian's findings;
5. A statement that the veterinarian certifies the animal to be unfit for purchase; and
6. The name and address of the certifying veterinarian and the date of the certification.

C. A veterinary finding of intestinal parasites shall not be grounds for declaring the animal unfit for purchase unless the animal is clinically ill due to such condition. An animal may not be found unfit for purchase on account of an injury sustained or illness contracted subsequent to the consumer taking possession thereof.

§3.1-796.83. Remedies cumulative.

The remedies provided for pursuant to this article are cumulative and not exclusive and shall be in addition to any other remedy provided for by law.

ARTICLE 3.1
BOARDING ESTABLISHMENTS

Section

§3.1-796.83:1. Boarding establishments and groomers; veterinary care requirements; consumer notification; penalty.

A. When an animal is boarded at a boarding establishment, or under the care, custody or subject to the actions of a groomer, the boarding establishment or groomer shall be responsible for providing the animal care requirements for each animal as specified in §3.1-796.68.

B. If an animal becomes ill or injured while in the custody of the boarding establishment or groomer, the boarding establishment or groomer shall provide the animal with emergency veterinary treatment for the illness or injury. The consumer shall bear the reasonable and necessary costs of emergency veterinary treatment for any illness or injury occurring while the animal is in the custody of the boarding establishment or groomer. The boarding establishment or groomer shall pay for veterinary treatment of any injury that the animal sustains while at the establishment or under the care or custody of a groomer if the injury resulted from the establishment's or groomer's failure, whether accidental or intentional, to provide the care required by §3.1-796.68, or if the injury is a result of the actions of the boarding establishment or groomer; however, boarding establishments and groomers shall not be required to bear the cost of veterinary treatment for injuries resulting from the animal's self-mutilation.

C. If an animal is seized from a boarding establishment or groomer because of the establishment's or groomer's failure to provide adequate food, water, shelter, exercise, and care as defined in §3.1-796.66 and required by §3.1-796.68 or because of any other violation of this chapter, the animal shall be returned to the rightful owner as soon as possible or, if the owner refuses to reclaim the animal, be impounded and disposition made pursuant to §3.1-796.115.

D. Violation of this section by a boarding establishment or groomer is a Class 1 misdemeanor.

(Chgd. by L.1996 ch. 249, eff. 7/1/96.)

§3.1-796.83:2. Written notice of consumer remedies required to be supplied by boarding establishments; penalty.

A. A boarding establishment shall give the notice hereinafter set forth in writing to a consumer prior to the consumer's delivery of the animal to the boarding establishment. Such notice shall be embodied in a written document and shall state in ten-point bold-faced type the following:

NOTICE

The boarding of animals is subject to Article 3.1 (§3.1-796.83:1 et seq.) of Chapter 27.4 of Title 3.1. If your animal becomes ill or injured while in the custody of the boarding establishment, the boarding establishment shall provide the animal with emergency veterinary treatment for the illness or injury.

The consumer shall bear the reasonable and necessary costs of emergency veterinary treatment for any illness or injury occurring while the animal is in the custody of the boarding establishment. The boarding establishment shall bear the expenses of veterinary treatment for any injury the animal sustains while at the boarding establishment if the injury resulted from the establishment's failure, whether accidental or intentional, to provide the care required by §3.1-796.68; however, boarding establishments shall not be required to bear the cost of veterinary treatment for injuries resulting from the animal's self-mutilation.

B. In addition, the boarding establishment shall display the following notice, in ten-point bold-faced type, on a sign placed in a conspicuous location and manner at the boarding establishment's intake area:

PUBLIC NOTICE

THE BOARDING OF ANIMALS BY A BOARDING ESTABLISHMENT IS SUBJECT TO ARTICLE 3.1 (§3.1-796.83:1 et seq.) OF CHAPTER 27.4 OF TITLE 3.1 OF THE CODE OF VIRGINIA. YOU HAVE SPECIFIC REMEDIES WHEN BOARDING ANIMALS IN THIS OR ANY OTHER BOARDING ESTABLISHMENT IN VIRGINIA. A COPY IS AVAILABLE IMMEDIATELY UPON REQUEST AND IS TO BE PRESENTED TO YOU AT THE TIME OF INTAKE IN THE FORM OF A WRITTEN DOCUMENT. IF YOU HAVE A COMPLAINT, YOU MAY CONTACT YOUR LOCAL LAW-ENFORCEMENT OFFICER OR THE VIRGINIA DEPARTMENT OF AGRICULTURE AND CONSUMER SERVICES, RICHMOND, VIRGINIA.

C. Failure to display or provide the consumer with the written notice as required by this section is punishable as a Class 3 misdemeanor.

(Chgd. by L.1998 ch. 817, eff. 7/1/98.)

ARTICLE 4
AUTHORITY OF LOCAL GOVERNING BODIES AND LICENSING OF DOGS

Section

§3.1-796.84. Local ordinances; penalties.

The governing body of any county, city or town may, by local ordinance, require a person operating a pet shop or operating as a dealer in companion animals to obtain a permit. Such local governing body may charge no more than fifty dollars per year for such permit. The revenues derived therefrom shall be used for the administration and enforcement of such ordinance.

The aforementioned local ordinance may provide: (i) that records be kept by the permittees as are deemed necessary; (ii) for public hearing prior to issuance, renewal or revocation of any such permit; or (iii) for the denial of issuance, denial of renewal or for the revocation of such permit for fraudulent practices or inhumane treatment of the animals dealt with by the permittee.

The local ordinance may also provide penalties for violation of the ordinance not to exceed those of a Class 3 misdemeanor.

§3.1-796.85. Unlicensed dogs prohibited; local ordinances for licensing cats.

A. It shall be unlawful for any person to own a dog four months old or older in this Commonwealth unless such dog is licensed, as required by the provisions of this article.

B. The governing body of any county, city or town may, by local ordinance, prohibit any person from owning a cat four months or older within such locality unless such cat is licensed as provided by this article.

§3.1-796.86. How to obtain license.

Any person may obtain a dog license or cat license if required by an ordinance adopted pursuant to subsection B of §3.1-796.85, by making oral or written application to the treasurer of the county or city in which such person resides, accompanied by the amount of license tax and current certificate of vaccination as required by this article. The treasurer or other officer charged with the duty of issuing dog and cat licenses shall only have authority to license dogs and cats of resident owners or custodians who reside within the boundary limits of his county or city and may require information to this effect from any applicant. Upon receipt of proper application and current certificate of vaccination as required by this article, the treasurer or other officer charged with the duty of issuing dog and cat licenses shall issue a license receipt for the amount on which he shall record the name and address of the owner or custodian, the date of payment, the year for which issued, the serial number of the tag, whether dog or cat, whether male, unsexed female, female or kennel, and deliver the metal license tags or plates provided for herein. The information thus received shall be retained by the treasurer, open to public inspection, during the period for which such license is valid. The treasurer may establish substations in convenient locations in the county or city and appoint agents for the collection of the license tax and issuance of such licenses.

§3.1-796.87. Amount of license tax.

The governing body of each county or city shall impose by ordinance a license tax on the ownership of dogs within its jurisdiction. The governing body of any county, city or town which has adopted an ordinance pursuant to subsection B of §3.1-796.85 shall impose by ordinance a license tax on the ownership of cats within its jurisdiction. The governing body may establish different rates of taxation for ownership of female dogs, male dogs, spayed or neutered dogs, female cats, male cats, and spayed or neutered cats. The tax for each dog or cat shall not be less than one dollar and not more than ten dollars for each year. If the dog or cat has been spayed, the tax shall not exceed the tax provided for a male dog or cat. Any ordinance may provide for a license tax for kennels of ten, twenty, thirty, forty or fifty dogs not to exceed fifty dollars for any one such block of kennels.

No license tax shall be levied on any dog that is trained and serves as a guide dog for a blind person, that is trained and serves as a hearing dog for a deaf or hearing impaired person or that is trained and serves as a service dog for a mobility-impaired person.

As used in this section, "hearing dog" means a dog trained to alert its owner by touch to sounds of danger and sounds to which the owner should respond and "service dog" means a dog trained to accompany its owner for the purpose of carrying items, retrieving objects, pulling a wheelchair or other such activities of service or support.

§3.1-796.88. When license tax payable.

A. On January 1 and not later than January 31 of each year, the owner of any dog or cat four months old or older shall pay a license tax as prescribed in §3.1-796.87.

B. If a dog or cat becomes four months of age or comes into the possession of any person between January 1 and November 1 of any year, the license tax for the current calendar year shall be paid by the owner.

C. If a dog or cat becomes four months of age or comes into the possession of any person between October 31 and December 31 of any year, the license tax for the succeeding calendar year shall be paid by the owner and this license shall be valid from the date the license is purchased.

D. Notwithstanding subsections A, B and C above, the governing body of each county or city which requires dogs or cats to have a rabies inoculation prior to the issuance of a license may designate when the tax is payable and allow the tax to be payable for up to a three-year period thereafter, as long as this period does not exceed the period that the rabies inoculation is effective as certified by a veterinarian.

§3.1-796.89. Effect of dog or cat not wearing collar as evidence.

Any dog or cat not wearing a collar bearing a license tag of the proper calendar year shall prima facie be deemed to be unlicensed, and in any proceedings under this chapter the burden of proof of the fact that such dog or cat has been licensed, or is otherwise not required to bear a tag at the time, shall be on the owner of the dog or cat.

§3.1-796.90. What dog or cat license shall consist of.

A dog or cat license shall consist of a license receipt and a metal tag. The tag shall be stamped or otherwise permanently marked to show the jurisdiction issuing the license and the calendar year for which issued and bear a serial number. The

tag may be stamped or otherwise marked to show the sex of the dog or cat.
(Chgd. by L.1998 ch. 394, eff. 7/1/98.)

§3.1-796.91. Duplicate license tags.

If a dog or cat license tag is lost, destroyed or stolen, the owner or custodian shall at once apply to the treasurer or his agent who issued the original license for a duplicate license tag, presenting the original license receipt. Upon affidavit of the owner or custodian before the treasurer or his agent that the original license tag has been lost, destroyed or stolen, he shall issue a duplicate license tag which the owner or custodian shall immediately affix to the collar of the dog. The treasurer or his agent shall endorse the number of the duplicate and the date issued on the face of the original license receipt. The fee for a duplicate tag for any dog or cat shall be one dollar.

§3.1-796.92. Displaying receipts; dogs to wear tags.

Dog and cat license receipts shall be carefully preserved by the licensees and exhibited promptly on request for inspection by any animal control officer or other officer. Dog license tags shall be securely fastened to a substantial collar by the owner or custodian and worn by such dog. It shall be unlawful for the owner to permit any licensed dog four months old or older to run or roam at large at any time without a license tag. The owner of the dog may remove the collar and license tag required by this section when (i) the dog is engaged in lawful hunting, (ii) the dog is competing in a dog show, (iii) the dog has a skin condition which would be exacerbated by the wearing of a collar, (iv) the dog is confined, or (v) the dog is under the immediate control of its owner.
(Chgd. by L.1998 ch. 817, eff. 7/1/98.)

§3.1-796.93. Governing body of county, city or town may prohibit dogs from running at large.

The governing bodies of the counties, cities and towns of this Commonwealth are hereby authorized to prohibit the running at large of all or any category of dogs in all or any designated portion of such county, city or town during such months as they may designate. Governing bodies may also require that dogs be confined, restricted or penned up during such periods. For the purpose of this section, a dog shall be deemed to run at large while roaming, running or self-hunting off the property of its owner or custodian and not under its owner's or custodian's immediate control. Any person who permits his dog to run at large, or remain unconfined, unrestricted or not penned up shall be deemed to have violated the provisions of this section.

§3.1-796.93:1. Authority to control dangerous or vicious dogs.

A. The governing body of any county, city or town may enact an ordinance regulating dangerous dogs and vicious dogs.

B. As used in this section, "dangerous dogs" means a canine or canine crossbreed which has bitten, attacked, or inflicted injury on a person or companion animal, other than a dog, or killed a companion animal, and "vicious dog" means a canine or canine crossbreed which has (i) killed a person; (ii) inflicted serious injury to a person, including multiple bites, serious disfigurement, serious impairment of health, or serious impairment of a bodily function; or (iii) continued to exhibit the behavior which resulted in a previous finding by a court that it is a dangerous dog, provided that its owner has been given notice of that finding.

C. Any ordinance enacted pursuant to this section shall prescribe the following provisions:

1. Any animal control officer who has reason to believe that a canine or canine crossbreed within his jurisdiction is a dangerous dog or vicious dog shall apply to a magistrate of the jurisdiction for the issuance of a summons requiring the owner or custodian, if known, to appear before a general district court at a specified time. The summons shall advise the owner of the nature of the proceeding and the matters at issue. The animal control officer shall confine the animal until such time as evidence shall be heard and a verdict rendered. If the animal control officer determines that the owner or custodian can confine the animal in a manner that protects the public safety, he may permit the owner or custodian to confine the animal until such time as evidence shall be heard and a verdict rendered. The court, through its contempt powers, may compel the owner, custodian or harborer of the animal to produce the animal. If, after hearing the evidence, the court finds that the animal is a dangerous dog, the court shall order the animal's owner to comply with the provisions of the ordinance. If, after hearing the evidence, the court finds that the animal is a vicious dog, the court shall order the animal euthanized in accordance with the provisions of §3.1-796.119.

2. No canine or canine crossbreed shall be found to be a dangerous dog or vicious dog solely because it is a particular breed, nor shall the local governing body prohibit the ownership of a particular breed of canine or canine crossbreed. No animal shall be found to be a dangerous dog or vicious dog if the threat, injury or damage was sustained by a person who was (i) committing, at the time, a crime upon the premises occupied by the animal's owner or custodian, (ii) committing, at the time, a willful trespass or other tort upon the premises occupied by the animal's owner or custodian or (iii) provoking, tormenting, or physically abusing the animal, or can be shown to have repeatedly provoked, tormented, abused, or assaulted the animal at other times. No police dog which was engaged in the performance of its duties as such at the time of the acts complained of shall be found to be a dangerous dog or a vicious dog. No animal which, at the time of the acts complained of, was responding to pain or injury, or was protecting itself, its kennel, its offspring, or its owner or owner's property, shall be found to be a dangerous dog or a vicious dog.

3. The owner of any animal found to be a dangerous dog shall, within ten days of such finding, obtain a dangerous dog registration certificate from the local animal control officer for a fee of fifty dollars in addition to other fees that may be authorized by law. The local animal control officer shall also provide the owner with a uniformly designed tag which identifies the animal as a dangerous dog. The owner shall affix the tag to the animal's collar and ensure that the animal wears the collar and tag at all times. All certificates obtained pursuant to this subdivision shall be renewed annually for the same fee and in the same manner as the initial certificate was obtained.

4. All certificates or renewals thereof required to be obtained under this section shall only be issued to persons eighteen years of age or older who present satisfactory evidence (i) of the animal's current rabies vaccination, if applicable, and (ii) that the animal is and will be confined in a proper enclosure or is and will be confined inside the owner's residence or is and will be muzzled and confined in the owner's fenced-in yard until the proper enclosure is constructed. In addition, owners who apply for certificates or renewals thereof under this section shall not be issued a certificate or renewal thereof unless they present satisfactory evidence that (i) their residence is and will continue to be posted with clearly visible signs warning both minors and adults of the presence of a dangerous dog on the property and (ii) the animal has been permanently identified by means of a tattoo on the inside thigh or by electronic implantation.

5. While on the property of its owner, an animal found to be a dangerous dog shall be confined indoors or in a securely

enclosed and locked structure of sufficient height and design to prevent its escape or direct contact with or entry by minors, adults, or other animals. The structure shall be designed to provide the animal with shelter from the elements of nature. When off its owner's property, an animal found to be a dangerous dog shall be kept on a leash and muzzled in such a manner as not to cause injury to the animal or interfere with the animal's vision or respiration, but so as to prevent it from biting a person or another animal.

6. If the owner of an animal found to be a dangerous dog is a minor, the custodial parent or legal guardian shall be responsible for complying with all requirements of this section.

7. After an animal has been found to be a dangerous dog, the animal's owner shall immediately, upon learning of same, notify the local animal control authority if the animal (i) is loose or unconfined; (ii) bites a person or attacks another animal; (iii) is sold, given away, or dies; or (iv) has been moved to a different address.

8. The owner of any animal which has been found to be a dangerous dog who willfully fails to comply with the requirements of the ordinance shall be guilty of a Class 1 misdemeanor.

9. All fees collected pursuant to the ordinance, less the costs incurred by the animal control authority in producing and distributing the certificates and tags required by the ordinance, shall be paid into a special dedicated fund in the treasury of the locality for the purpose of paying the expenses of any training course required under §3.1-796.105.

D. Any ordinance enacted pursuant to this section may prescribe the following provisions:

1. All certificates or renewals thereof required to be obtained under this section shall only be issued to persons eighteen years of age or older who present satisfactory evidence that the animal has been neutered or spayed.

2. All certificates or renewals thereof required to be obtained under this section shall only be issued to persons who present satisfactory evidence that the owner has liability insurance coverage, to the value of at least $50,000, that covers animal bites.

E. Notwithstanding the provisions of subdivision C 1, any ordinance enacted pursuant to this section may provide that an animal control officer may determine, after investigation, whether a dog is a dangerous dog. If the animal control officer determines that a dog is a dangerous dog, he may order the animal's owner to comply with the provisions of the ordinance. If the animal's owner disagrees with the animal control officer's determination, he may appeal the determination to the general district court for a trial on the merits.

(Chgd. by L.1997 chs. 582, 892; L.1998 ch. 817; L.2000 chs. 11, 727, eff. 7/1/2000.)

§3.1-796.93:2. Authority to prohibit training of attack dogs.

Any county with the urban county executive form of government may enact an ordinance which prohibits persons from training dogs on residential property to attack. As used in this section, "attack" means to attack or respond aggressively, either with or without command. Any such ordinance shall exempt from its provisions the training of dogs owned by any person who resides on the property.

(Added by L.1999 ch. 848, eff. 7/1/99.)

§3.1-796.94. Governing body of county, city, or town may adopt certain ordinances.

A. The governing bodies of counties, cities, and towns of the Commonwealth are hereby authorized to adopt, in their discretion, ordinances which parallel §§3.1-796.84 through 3.1-796.93, 3.1-796.95 through 3.1-796.104, 3.1-796.115 through 3.1-796.119, 3.1-796.121, 3.1-796.122, 3.1-796.126:1 through 3.1-796.126:7, and 3.1-796.127 through 3.1-796.129 of this chapter.

Any funds collected pursuant to the enforcement of ordinances adopted pursuant to the provisions of this section may be used for the purpose of defraying the costs of local animal control, including efforts to promote sterilization of cats and dogs.

Nothing in this section shall be construed so as to prevent or restrict any local governing body from adopting local animal control ordinances which are more stringent than §§3.1-796.84 through 3.1-796.93, 3.1-796.95 through 3.1-796.104, 3.1-796.115 through 3.1-796.119, 3.1-796.121, 3.1-796.122, 3.1-796.126:1 through 3.1-796.126:7, and 3.1-796.127 through 3.1-796.129 of this chapter.

B. The governing bodies of counties, cities or towns of the Commonwealth are hereby authorized to adopt, in their discretion, ordinances establishing uniform schedules of civil penalties for violations of specific provisions of ordinances adopted pursuant to this section. However, civil penalties may not be imposed for violations of ordinances which parallel §3.1-796.122. Designation of a particular violation for a civil penalty shall be in lieu of criminal sanctions and preclude prosecution of such violation as a criminal misdemeanor. The schedule for civil penalties shall be uniform for each type of specified violation and the penalty for any one violation shall not be more than $150. Imposition of civil penalties shall not preclude an action for injunctive, declaratory or other equitable relief. Moneys raised pursuant to this subsection shall be placed in the locality's general fund.

An animal control officer or law-enforcement officer may issue a summons for a violation. Any person summoned or issued a ticket for a scheduled violation may make an appearance in person or in writing by mail to the department of finance or the treasurer of the county, city or town issuing the summons or ticket prior to the date fixed for trial in court. Any person so appearing may enter a waiver of trial, admit liability, and pay the civil penalty established for the offense charged.

(Chgd. by L.1995 ch. 832; L.1997 ch. 587; L.1998 ch. 817, eff. 7/1/98.)

§3.1-796.94:1. Regulation of keeping of animals and fowl.

A. Any county may, whenever in the judgment of the board of supervisors the same is necessary for the preservation of public health, regulate by ordinance the keeping of animals or fowl, other than dogs and cats, within a certain distance of residences or other buildings or wells, springs, streams, creeks, or brooks, and provide that all or certain of such animals shall not be kept within certain areas.

B. A municipal corporation may, by ordinance, prohibit cruelty to and abuse of animals and fowl; and may regulate or prohibit the running at large and the keeping of animals and fowl and provide for the impounding and confiscation of any such animal or fowl found at large or kept in violation of such regulations. Any such ordinance may require that owners of any exotic or poisonous animal found running at large pay a fee to cover the locality's actual cost in locating and capturing or otherwise disposing of the animal.

(Added by L.1997 ch. 587; chgd. by L.1999 ch. 663, eff. 7/1/99.)

§3.1-796.94:2. Regulation of sale of animals procured from animal shelters.

Any city, county or town which supports, in whole or in part, an animal shelter may by ordinance provide that no person who acquires an animal from such shelter shall be able to sell such animal within a period of six months from

the time the animal is acquired from the shelter. Violation of such an ordinance shall constitute a misdemeanor.
(Added by L.1997 ch. 587, eff. 12/1/97.)

§3.1-796.95. Referendum on ordinance requiring dogs to be kept on leash, etc.

The governing body of any city may adopt regulations or ordinances requiring that dogs within the confines of any such city be kept on a leash or otherwise restrained and may, by resolution directed to the circuit court of such city, request the court to order a referendum as to whether any such ordinance so adopted shall become effective in the city. Such referendum shall be held and conducted, and the results thereof ascertained and certified in accordance with §24.2-684. The court shall require the governing body to give appropriate notice of the time, place and subject matter of such referendum.

The results of the referendum shall not be binding upon the governing body of any such city but may be used in ascertaining the sense of the voters.

§3.1-796.96. County or city pounds; confinement and disposition of stray animals; penalties.

A. The governing body of each county or city shall maintain or cause to be maintained a pound [in accordance with guidelines issued by the Department of Agriculture and Consumer Services] and shall require dogs running at large without the tag required by §3.1-796.92 or in violation of an ordinance passed pursuant to §3.1-796.93 to be confined therein. The governing body of any county or city need not own the facility required by this section but may contract for its establishment with a private group or in conjunction with one or more other local governing bodies. The governing body shall require that the pound be accessible to the public at reasonable hours during the week. Nothing in this section shall be construed to prohibit confinement of other companion animals in such a pound.

B. An animal confined pursuant to this section shall be kept for a period of not less than five days, such period to commence on the day immediately following the day the animal is initially confined in the facility, unless sooner claimed by the rightful owner thereof.

The operator or custodian of the pound shall make a reasonable effort to ascertain whether the animal has a collar, tag, license, tattoo, or other form of identification. If such identification is found on the animal, the animal shall be held for an additional five days, unless sooner claimed by the rightful owner. If the rightful owner of the animal can be readily identified, the operator or custodian of the pound shall make a reasonable effort to notify the owner of the animal's confinement within the next forty-eight hours following its confinement.

If any animal confined pursuant to this section is claimed by its rightful owner, such owner shall be charged with the actual expenses incurred in keeping the animal impounded.

C. If an animal confined pursuant to this section has not been claimed upon expiration of the appropriate holding period as provided by subsection B, it shall be deemed abandoned and become the property of the pound or shelter. If such abandoned animal did not, when delivered to the pound, bear a collar, tag, license, tattoo, or other form of identification, it may be humanely destroyed or disposed of by:

1. Sale or gift to a federal agency, state-supported institution, agency of the Commonwealth, agency of another state, or a licensed federal dealer having its principal place of business located within the Commonwealth, provided that such agency, institution or dealer agrees to confine the animal for an additional period of not less than five days;
2. Delivery to any humane society or animal shelter within the Commonwealth;
3. Adoption by any person who is a resident of the county or city for which the pound is operated and who will pay the required license fee, if any, on such animal;
4. Adoption by a resident of an adjacent political subdivision of the Commonwealth;
5. Adoption by any other person, provided that no animal may be adopted by any person who is not a resident of the county or city for which the pound or animal shelter is operated, or of an adjacent political subdivision, unless the animal is first sterilized; or
6. Delivery, for the purposes of adoption or euthanasia only, to a humane society or an animal shelter located in and lawfully operating under the laws of another state, provided that such humane society or animal shelter (i) maintains records which would comply with §3.1-796.105; (ii) requires that adopted dogs and cats be sterilized; and (iii) has been approved by the State Veterinarian or his designee as a facility which maintains such records, requires adopted dogs and cats to be sterilized, and provides adequate care and euthanasia.

If such abandoned animal, when delivered to the pound, bore a collar, tag, license, tattoo, or other form of identification, it may be humanely destroyed or disposed of by the methods described in subdivision 2, 3, 4, or 5 of this subsection.

No pound or shelter shall deliver more than two animals or a family of animals during any thirty-day period to any one person under subdivision 3, 4 or 5 of this subsection.

If an animal is required to be sterilized prior to adoption pursuant to subdivision 5 of this subsection, the pound or animal shelter may require that the sterilization be done at the expense of the person adopting the animal.

D. Nothing in this section shall prohibit the immediate destruction of a critically injured, critically ill, or unweaned animal for humane purposes. Any animal destroyed pursuant to the provisions of this chapter shall be euthanized by one of the methods prescribed or approved by the State Veterinarian.

E. Nothing in this section shall prohibit the immediate destruction or disposal by the methods listed in subdivisions 2 through 6 of subsection C of an animal that has been delivered voluntarily or released to a pound, animal shelter, animal control officer, or humane society by the animal's rightful owner after the rightful owner has, in writing, surrendered all property rights in such animal and has read and signed a statement (i) certifying that no other person has a right of property in the animal and (ii) acknowledging that the animal may be immediately euthanized or disposed of by the methods listed in subdivisions 2 through 6 of subsection C.

F. Nothing in this section shall prohibit any feral dog or feral cat not bearing a collar, tag, tattoo, or other form of identification which, based on the written certification of a disinterested person, exhibits behavior that poses a risk of physical injury to any person confining the animal, from being euthanized after being kept for a period of not less than three days, at least one of which shall be a full business day, such period to commence on the day the animal is initially confined in the facility, unless sooner claimed by the rightful owner. The certification of the disinterested person shall be kept with the animal as required by §3.1-796.105. For purposes of this subsection, a disinterested person shall not include a person releasing or reporting the animal to the facility.

G. For purposes of this section:

"Animal" shall not include agricultural animals.

"Rightful owner" means a person with a right of property in the animal.

"Humane society," when referring to an organization without the Commonwealth, means any nonprofit organization organized for the purpose of preventing cruelty to animals and promoting humane care and treatment or adoption of animals.

H. The governing body shall require that the pound be operated in accordance with regulations issued by the Board. If this chapter or such regulations are violated, the locality may be assessed a civil penalty by the Board in an amount that does not exceed $1,000 per violation. Each day of the violation shall constitute a separate offense. In determining the amount of any civil penalty, the Board shall consider (i) the history of previous violations at the pound; (ii) whether the violation has caused injury to, death or suffering of, an animal; and (iii) the demonstrated good faith of the locality to achieve compliance after notification of the violation. All civil penalties assessed under this section shall be recovered in a civil action brought by the Attorney General in the name of the Commonwealth. Such civil penalties shall be paid into a special fund in the state treasury to the credit of the Department to be used in carrying out the purposes of this chapter.

(Chgd. by L.1995 ch. 496; L.1997 ch. 159; L.1998 ch. 817; L.1999 chs. 627, 672; L.2000 ch. 1010, eff. 7/1/2001. Matter in brackets eff. only until 7/1/2001. Matter in italics eff. 7/1/2001.)

§3.1-796.96:1. Disposition of animals other than those in county or city pounds.

No animal bearing a tag, license or tattooed identification shall be used or accepted by any person for the purpose of medical research or experimentation, unless the individual who owns such animal consents thereto in writing.

§3.1-796.97. Evidence showing inoculation for rabies prerequisite to obtaining dog or cat license; rabies clinics.

No license tag shall be issued for any dog or cat unless there is presented, to the treasurer or other officer of the county or city charged by law with the duty of issuing license tags for dogs and cats at the time application for license is made, evidence satisfactory to him showing that such dog or cat has been inoculated or vaccinated against rabies by a currently licensed veterinarian or currently licensed veterinary technician who was under the immediate and direct supervision of a licensed veterinarian on the premises.

Rabies clinics, approved by the appropriate health department and governing body, shall be held at least once per year in each county in which the governing body finds that the number of resident veterinarians is otherwise inadequate to meet the need.

(Chgd. by L.1996 ch. 351, eff. 7/1/96.)

§3.1-796.97:1. Rabies inoculation of dogs and domesticated cats; availability of certificate.

The owner or custodian of all dogs and domesticated cats four months of age and older shall have them currently vaccinated for rabies by a licensed veterinarian or licensed veterinary technician who is under the immediate and direct supervision of a licensed veterinarian on the premises. The supervising veterinarian on the premises shall provide the owner of the dog or the custodian of the domesticated cat with a certificate of vaccination. The owner of the dog or the custodian of the domesticated cat shall furnish within a reasonable period of time, upon the request of an animal control officer, humane investigator, law-enforcement officer, State Veterinarian's representative, or official of the Department of Health, the certificate of vaccination for such dog or cat. The vaccine used shall be licensed by the United States Department of Agriculture for use in that species.

(Chgd. by L.1996 ch. 351; L.1998 ch. 817, eff. 7/1/98.)

§3.1-796.98. Rabid animals.

When there is sufficient reason to believe that a rabid animal is at large, the governing body of any county, city or town shall have the power to pass an emergency ordinance which shall become effective immediately upon passage, requiring owners of all dogs and cats therein to keep the same confined on their premises unless leashed under restraint of the owner in such a manner that persons or animals will not be subject to the danger of being bitten by the rabid animal. Any such emergency ordinance enacted pursuant to the provisions of this section shall be operative for a period not to exceed thirty days unless renewed by the governing body of such county, city or town. The governing body of any county, city or town shall also have the power and authority to pass ordinances restricting the running at large in their respective jurisdiction of dogs and cats which have not been inoculated or vaccinated against rabies and to provide penalties for the violation thereof.

Dogs or cats showing active signs of rabies or suspected of having rabies shall be confined under competent observation for such a time as may be necessary to determine a diagnosis. If confinement is impossible or impracticable, such dog or cat shall be euthanized by one of the methods approved by the State Veterinarian as provided in §3.1-796.96.

Every person having knowledge of the existence of an animal apparently afflicted with rabies shall report immediately to the local health department the existence of such animal, the place where seen, the owner's name, if known, and the symptoms suggesting rabies.

Any dog or cat, for which no proof of current rabies vaccination is available, and which is exposed to rabies through a bite, or through saliva or central nervous system tissue, in a fresh open wound or mucous membrane, by an animal believed to be afflicted with rabies, shall be confined in a pound, kennel or enclosure approved by the health department for a period not to exceed six months at the expense of the owner; however, if this is not feasible, the dog or cat shall be euthanized by one of the methods approved by the State Veterinarian as provided in §3.1-796.96. A rabies vaccination shall be administered prior to release. Inactivated rabies vaccine may be administered at the beginning of confinement. Any dog or cat so bitten, or exposed to rabies through saliva or central nervous system tissue, in a fresh open wound or mucous membrane with proof of a valid rabies vaccination, shall be revaccinated immediately following the bite and shall be confined to the premises of the owner, or other site as may be approved by the local health department, for a period of ninety days.

At the discretion of the director of a local health department, any animal which has bitten a person shall be confined under competent observation for ten days, unless the animal develops active symptoms of rabies or expires before that time. A seriously injured or sick animal may be humanely euthanized as provided in §3.1-796.96, and its head sent to the Division of Consolidated Laboratory Services of the Department of General Services, or the local health department, for evaluation.

When any potentially rabid animal, other than a dog or cat, exposes or may have exposed a person to rabies through a bite, or through saliva or central nervous system tissue, in a fresh open wound or mucous membrane, that animal shall be confined at the discretion of a local health director in a manner approved by the health department or humanely euthanized as provided in §3.1-796.96 and its head sent to the Division of Consolidated Laboratory Services of the Department of General Services or the local health department for evaluation.

When any animal, other than a dog or cat, is exposed to rabies through a bite, or through saliva or central nervous system tissue, in a fresh open wound or mucous membrane, by an animal believed to be afflicted with rabies, that newly exposed animal shall be confined at the discretion of a local health director in a manner approved by the health department or humanely euthanized as provided in §3.1-796.96.

§3.1-796.99. Inoculation for rabies at animal shelters.

Dogs and cats being adopted from an animal shelter during the period an emergency ordinance is in force, as provided for in §3.1-796.98 may be inoculated for rabies by a certified animal technician at such shelter if the certified animal technician is under the immediate and direct supervision of a licensed veterinarian.

§3.1-796.100. Regulations to prevent spread of rabies and running at large of vicious dogs.

The governing body of any county, city or town may adopt such ordinances, regulations or other measures as may be deemed reasonably necessary to prevent the spread within its boundaries of the disease of rabies, and to regulate and control the running at large within its boundaries of vicious or destructive dogs. Penalties may be provided for the violation of any such ordinances. If the ordinance declares the existence of an emergency, then the ordinance shall be in force upon passage.

§3.1-796.101. Disposition of funds.

Unless otherwise provided by ordinance of the local governing body, the treasurer of each locality shall keep all moneys collected by him for dog and cat license taxes in a separate account from all other funds collected by him. The locality shall use the funds for the following purposes:

1. The salary and expenses of the animal control officer and necessary staff;
2. The care and maintenance of a pound;
3. The maintenance of a rabies control program;
4. Payments as a bounty to any person neutering or spaying a dog up to the amount of one year of the license tax as provided by ordinance;
5. Payments for compensation as provided in §3.1-796.118; and
6. Efforts to promote sterilization of dogs and cats.

Any part or all of any surplus remaining in such account on December 31 of any year may be transferred by the governing body of such locality into the general fund of such locality.

(Chgd. by L.1998 ch. 817, eff. 7/1/98.)

§3.1-796.102. Supplemental funds.

Localities may supplement the dog and cat license tax fund with other funds as they consider appropriate. However, localities shall supplement the dog and cat license tax fund to the extent necessary to provide for the salary and expenses of the animal control officer and staff and the care and maintenance of a pound as provided in subdivisions 1 and 2 of §3.1-796.101.

(Chgd. by L.1998 ch. 817, eff. 7/1/98.)

§3.1-796.103. Payment of license tax subsequent to summons.

Payment of the license tax subsequent to a summons to appear before a court for failure to pay the license tax within the time required shall not operate to relieve such owner from the penalties provided.

ARTICLE 5
ANIMAL CONTROL OFFICERS AND HUMANE INVESTIGATORS

§3.1-796.104. Position of animal control officer created.

The governing body of each county or city shall, or each town may, appoint an officer to be known as the animal control officer who shall have the power to enforce this chapter, all ordinances enacted pursuant to this chapter and all laws for the protection of domestic animals. The governing body may also appoint one or more deputy animal control officers to assist the animal control officer in the performance of his duties. Animal control officers and deputy animal control officers shall have a knowledge of the animal control and protection laws of Virginia which they are required to enforce. When in uniform or upon displaying a badge or other credentials of office, animal control officers and deputy animal control officers shall have the power to issue a summons to any person found in the act of violating any such law or any ordinance enacted pursuant to such law of the locality in which the control officer or deputy animal control officer is appointed. The animal control officer and the deputy animal control officers shall be paid as the governing body of each locality shall prescribe.

Any locality in which an animal control officer or deputy animal control officers have been appointed may contract with one or more additional localities for enforcement of animal protection and control laws by the animal control officers or deputy animal control officers. Any such contract may provide that the locality employing the animal control officer or deputy animal control officers shall be reimbursed a portion of the salary and expenses of the animal control officer or deputy animal control officers.

Every locality employing an animal control officer shall submit to the Department of Criminal Justice Services, on a form provided by it, information concerning the employment and training status of the animal control officers employed by the locality. The Department may require that the locality notify the Department of any change in such information.
(Chgd. by L.1998 ch. 817, eff. 7/1/98.)

§3.1-796.104:1. Training of animal control officers.

A. After April 1, 1999, every locality appointing animal control officers shall require that every animal control officer and deputy animal control officer completes the following training:

1. Within two years after appointment, a basic animal control course that has been approved by the Department of Criminal Justice Services and the State Veterinarian; and
2. Every three years, additional training approved by the Department of Criminal Justice Services and the State Veterinarian, fifteen hours of which shall be training in animal control and protection.

The Department of Criminal Justice Services and the State Veterinarian shall develop criteria to be used in approving training courses and shall provide an opportunity for public comment on proposed criteria before the final criteria are adopted.

Subdivision 1 of this subsection shall not apply to animal control officers or deputy animal control officers appointed before July 1, 1998. The State Veterinarian may grant exemptions from the requirements of subdivision 1 to animal control officers appointed on or after July 1, 1998, based on the animal control officer's previous training.

B. Upon cause shown by a locality, the State Veterinarian may grant additional time during which the training required by subsection A may be completed by an animal control officer in such locality.

C. Any animal control officer that fails to complete the training required by subsection A shall be removed from office, unless the State Veterinarian has granted additional time as provided in subsection B.
(Added by L.1998 ch. 817, eff. 7/1/98.)

§3.1-796.105. Animal control officers and humane investigators; limitations; records; penalties.

A. No animal control officer, humane investigator, humane society or custodian of any pound or animal shelter shall (i) obtain the release or transfer of an animal by the animal's owner to such animal control officer, humane investigator, humane society or custodian for personal gain or (ii) give or sell or negotiate for the gift or sale to any individual, pet shop, dealer, or research facility of any animal which may come into his custody in the course of carrying out his official assignments. No animal control officer, humane investigator or custodian of any pound or animal shelter shall be granted a dealer's license. Violation of this subsection shall be a Class 1 misdemeanor. Nothing in this section shall preclude any animal control officer or humane investigator from lawfully impounding any animal pursuant to §3.1-796.115.

B. An animal control officer, law-enforcement officer, humane investigator or custodian of any pound or animal shelter, upon taking custody of any animal in the course of his official duties, or any representative of a humane society, upon obtaining custody of any animal on behalf of the society, shall immediately make a record of the matter. Such record shall include:

1. The date on which the animal was taken into custody;
2. The date of the making of the record;
3. A description of the animal including the animal's species, color, breed, sex, approximate age and approximate weight;
4. The reason for taking custody of the animal and the location where custody was taken;
5. The name and address of the animal's owner, if known;
6. Any license or rabies tag, tattoo, collar or other identification number carried by or appearing on the animal; and
7. The disposition of the animal.

Records required by this subsection shall be maintained for at least five years, and shall be available for public inspection upon request. A summary of such records shall be submitted annually to the State Veterinarian in a format prescribed by him.

C. Any animal control officer or custodian of any pound who violates any provision of this chapter which relates to the seizure, impoundment and custody of animals by an animal control officer may be subject to suspension or dismissal from his position.

D. Custodians and animal control officers engaged in the operation of a pound shall be required to have a knowledge of the laws of Virginia governing animals, including this chapter, as well as basic animal care.
(Chgd. by L.1997 ch. 286; L.1998 ch. 817, eff. 7/1/98.)

§3.1-796.106. Humane investigators; qualifications; appointment; term; penalty.

A. The Board shall establish by regulation reasonable qualifications for humane investigators. Such qualifications shall include a knowledge of the provisions of this chapter and the regulations adopted pursuant to this chapter. The State Veterinarian shall maintain a current list of persons who have demonstrated that they meet such qualifications and shall make the list available for public inspection.

B. A circuit court may appoint any person as a humane investigator for any locality within its jurisdiction if the person:

1. Is listed by the State Veterinarian as provided in subsection A as being qualified to be a humane investigator; and
2. Has never been convicted of animal cruelty or neglect, any felony, or any crime of moral turpitude according to a criminal background check which shall be performed by the attorney for the Commonwealth at the expense of the person seeking the appointment.

A person residing outside the Commonwealth may be appointed as a humane investigator only if he is employed by a humane society located within the locality for which he is seeking appointment.

C. On July 1, 2001, the appointment of every humane investigator who was appointed before July 1, 1998, shall expire. Any humane investigator whose appointment has so expired may be reappointed if he certifies to the appointing court that he has within the preceding three years completed fifteen hours of training in animal care and protection approved by the State Veterinarian.

D. Except as provided in subsection C, appointments of humane investigators shall be for terms of three years. Each humane investigator shall, during each term for which he is appointed, complete fifteen hours of training in animal care and protection approved by the State Veterinarian. If a humane investigator is appointed to a succeeding term before or within thirty days after his current term expires, a criminal background check shall not be required. If a humane investigator's term expires and he is not appointed to a succeeding term before or within thirty days after his current term expires, the circuit court that appointed him shall notify the State Veterinarian of the expiration of his term.

E. Approval of a training course by the State Veterinarian as required by this section shall remain in effect for one year from the approval date, unless the State Veterinarian establishes an earlier date.

F. The State Veterinarian shall remove from the list required by subsection A any person:

1. Who has not been appointed as a humane investigator within three years of having been placed on the list;

2. Whose appointment as a humane investigator has been revoked as provided in §3.1-796.106:1; or

3. Whose term as a humane investigator has expired, if such person has not been appointed to a succeeding term by the circuit court before or within thirty days after the term expired.

(Chgd. by L.1998 ch. 817, eff. 7/1/98.)

§3.1-796.106:1. Revocation of appointment of humane investigators; State Veterinarian may investigate allegations.

A. Upon a motion by the attorney for the Commonwealth, the circuit court that appointed a humane investigator may revoke his appointment if he is no longer able to perform the duties of a humane investigator; has been convicted of any felony, Class 1 misdemeanor, or a violation of any provision of this chapter or any other law regarding animals; or for good cause shown. The court shall notify the State Veterinarian of each such revocation.

B. The State Veterinarian may investigate any allegation that a humane investigator has violated this chapter and report his findings and recommendations to the attorney for the Commonwealth. The State Veterinarian may authorize a State Veterinarian's representative to conduct such investigation. The report shall be held confidential except that the substance of the allegation against the humane investigator shall be disclosed to the humane investigator upon his written request.

(Added by L.1998 ch. 817; chgd. by L.1999 ch. 376, eff. 7/1/99.)

§3.1-796.106:2. Powers and duties of humane investigators.

A. Any humane investigator may, within the locality for which he has been appointed, investigate violations of laws and ordinances regarding care and treatment of animals and disposal of dead animals.

B. Each humane investigator shall carry during the performance of his powers and duties under this chapter an identification card issued by the State Veterinarian. The identification card shall include the following information regarding the humane investigator:

1. His full name;
2. The locality for which he has been appointed;
3. The name of the circuit court that appointed him;
4. The signature of the circuit court judge that appointed him;
5. A photograph of his face; and
6. The date of expiration of his appointment.

C. Each humane investigator shall record on a form approved by the State Veterinarian every investigation he performs, maintain such record for five years, and make such record available upon request to any law-enforcement officer, animal control officer or State Veterinarian's representative. Each humane investigator shall file quarterly a report summarizing such records with the State Veterinarian on a form approved by him. A humane investigator's appointment may be revoked as provided in §3.1-796.106:1 if he fails to file such report.

(Added by L.1998 ch. 817, eff. 7/1/98.)

§3.1-796.107. Complaint of suspected violation; investigation.

A. Upon receiving a complaint of a suspected violation of this chapter, any ordinance enacted pursuant to this chapter or any law for the protection of domestic animals, any animal control officer, law-enforcement officer, or State Veterinarian's representative may, for the purpose of investigating the allegations of the complaint, enter upon, during business hours, any business premises, including any place where animals or animal records are housed or kept, of any dealer, pet shop, groomer, or boarding establishment. Upon receiving a complaint of a suspected violation of any law or ordinance regarding care or treatment of animals or disposal of dead animals, any humane investigator may, for the purpose of investigating the allegations of the complaint, enter upon, during business hours, any business premises, including any place where animals or animal records are housed or kept, of any dealer, pet shop, groomer, or boarding establishment.

Upon obtaining a warrant as provided for in §3.1-796.113, the law-enforcement officer, animal control officer, State Veterinarian's representative, or humane investigator may enter upon any other premises where the animal or animals described in the complaint are housed or kept. Attorneys for the Commonwealth and law-enforcement officials shall provide such assistance as may be required in the conduct of such investigations.

B. If the investigation discloses that a violation of §3.1-796.68 has occurred, the investigating official shall notify the owner or custodian of the complaint and of what action is necessary to comply with this chapter.

(Chgd. by L.1998 ch. 817, eff. 7/1/98.)

§3.1-796.108. Impoundment; expenses; lien; disposition of animal.

When an animal control officer, humane investigator, law-enforcement officer or State Veterinarian's representative finds that an apparent violation of this chapter has rendered an animal in such a condition as to constitute a direct and immediate threat to its life, safety or health which the owner or custodian has failed or refuses to remedy, such animal control officer, humane investigator, law-enforcement officer or State Veterinarian's representative may impound the animal pursuant to §3.1-796.115 in a facility which will provide the elements of good care as set forth in §3.1-796.68 and shall then proceed to take such steps as are required to dispose of the animal pursuant to §3.1-796.115.

(Chgd. by L.1998 ch. 817, eff. 7/1/98.)

§3.1-796.109. *(Repealed by L.1998 ch. 817, eff. 7/1/98.)*

§3.1-796.110. Expenses of humane investigators.

Neither the appointment of any humane investigator, nor the performance of any service or duty by him, shall require any locality or the Commonwealth to pay any cost or expense incurred by or on behalf of a humane investigator. Any locality may reimburse any humane investigator appointed for that locality for reasonable expenses incurred as the result of a specific request for services from the locality.

(Chgd. by L.1998 ch. 817, eff. 7/1/98.)

§3.1-796.111. Preventing cruelty to animals; interference; penalty.

Each animal control officer, humane investigator or State Veterinarian's representative shall interfere to prevent the perpetration of any act of cruelty upon any animal in his presence. Any person who shall interfere with or obstruct or resist any animal control officer, humane investigator or State Veterinarian's representative in the discharge of his rights, powers, and duties as authorized and prescribed by law shall be deemed guilty of a Class 4 misdemeanor.

(Chgd. by L.1998 ch. 817, eff. 7/1/98.)

§3.1-796.112. Enforcement authority.

All law-enforcement officers in the Commonwealth of Virginia and State Veterinarian's representatives shall enforce the provisions of this chapter to the same extent other laws in the Commonwealth are enforced.
(Chgd. by L.1998 ch. 817, eff. 7/1/98.)

§3.1-796.113. Power of search for violations of statutes against cruelty to animals.

When a sworn complaint is made to any proper authority by any animal control officer, humane investigator, law-enforcement officer or State Veterinarian's representative that the complainant believes and has reasonable cause to believe that the laws in relation to cruelty to animals have been, are being, or are about to be violated in any particular building or place, such authority, if satisfied that there is reasonable cause for such belief, shall issue a warrant authorizing any sheriff, deputy sheriff or police officer, to search the building or place. No search shall be made after sunset unless specially authorized by the authority upon satisfactory cause shown.
(Chgd. by L.1998 ch. 817, eff. 7/1/98.)

§3.1-796.114. When animals to be destroyed; procedure.

Any humane investigator may lawfully cause to be destroyed any animal in his charge or found abandoned or not properly cared for when, in the judgment of the humane investigator and two reputable citizens called to view the same in his presence, and who shall give their written certificate, the animal appears to be injured, disabled or diseased, past recovery, or the injury, disease or disability is such that a reasonable owner would cause the animal to be destroyed.

Any humane investigator shall make every reasonable effort immediately to notify the owner of the animal that the humane investigator intends for the animal to be destroyed. The owner shall have a right to select one of the two reputable citizens called to view the animal and give written certificate of the animal's condition. In no event shall the determination as to disposition of the animal be delayed beyond forty-eight hours after such humane investigator first decides the animal should be destroyed. In the event that the two citizens called to give such certificate are unable to agree, they shall select a third reputable citizen and his decision shall be final.
(Chgd. by L.1998 ch. 817, eff. 7/1/98.)

§3.1-796.115. Seizure and impoundment of animals; notice and hearing; disposition of animal; disposition of proceeds upon sale.

A. Any humane investigator, law-enforcement officer or animal control officer may lawfully seize and impound any animal that has been abandoned, has been cruelly treated, or is suffering from an apparent violation of this chapter that has rendered the animal in such a condition as to constitute a direct and immediate threat to its life, safety or health. Before seizing or impounding any agricultural animal, such humane investigator, law-enforcement officer or animal control officer shall contact the State Veterinarian or a State Veterinarian's representative, who shall recommend to such person the most appropriate action for the disposition of the agricultural animal. The humane investigator, law-enforcement officer or animal control officer shall notify the owner of the agricultural animal and the local attorney for the Commonwealth of the recommendation. The humane investigator, law-enforcement officer or animal control officer may impound the agricultural animal on the land where the agricultural animal is located if:

1. The owner or tenant of the land where the agricultural animal is located gives written permission;
2. A general district court so orders; or
3. The owner or tenant of the land where the agricultural animal is located cannot be immediately located, and it is in the best interest of the agricultural animal to be impounded on the land where it is located until the written permission of the owner or tenant of the land can be obtained.

If there is a direct and immediate threat to an agricultural animal, the humane investigator, law-enforcement officer or animal control officer may seize the animal, in which case the humane investigator, law-enforcement officer or animal control officer shall file within five business days on a form approved by the State Veterinarian a report on the condition of the animal at the time of the seizure, the disposition of the animal, and any other information required by the State Veterinarian.

Upon seizing or impounding an animal, the humane investigator, law-enforcement officer or animal control officer shall petition the general district court in the city or county wherein the animal is seized for a hearing. The hearing shall be not more than ten business days from the date of the seizure of the animal. The hearing shall be to determine whether the animal has been abandoned, has been cruelly treated, or has not been provided adequate care.

B. The humane investigator, law-enforcement officer, or animal control officer shall cause to be served upon the person with a right of property in the animal or the custodian of the animal notice of the hearing. If such person or the custodian is known and residing within the jurisdiction wherein the animal is seized, written notice shall be given at least five days prior to the hearing of the time and place of the hearing. If such person or the custodian is known but residing out of the jurisdiction where such animal is seized, written notice by any method or service of process as is provided by the Code of Virginia shall be given. If such person or the custodian is not known, the humane investigator, law-enforcement officer, or animal control officer shall cause to be published in a newspaper of general circulation in the jurisdiction wherein such animal is seized notice of the hearing at least one time prior to the hearing and shall further cause notice of the hearing to be posted at least five days prior to the hearing at the place provided for public notices at the city hall or courthouse wherein such hearing shall be held.

C. The procedure for appeal and trial shall be the same as provided by law for misdemeanors. Trial by jury shall be as provided in Article 4 (§19.2-260 et seq.) of Chapter 15 of Title 19.2. The Commonwealth shall be required to prove its case beyond a reasonable doubt.

D. The humane investigator, law-enforcement officer, or animal control officer shall provide for such animal until the court has concluded the hearing. Any locality may, by ordinance, require the owner of any animal held pursuant to this subsection for more than thirty days to post a bond in surety with the locality for the amount of the cost of boarding the animal for a period of time set in the ordinance, not to exceed nine months.

If the court determines that the animal has been neither abandoned, cruelly treated, nor deprived of adequate care, the animal shall be returned to the owner. If the court determines that the animal has been abandoned, cruelly treated, or deprived of adequate care, then the court shall order that the animal be: (i) sold by a local governing body; (ii) humanely destroyed, or disposed of by sale or gift to a federal agency, state-supported institution, agency of the Commonwealth, agency of another state, or a licensed federal dealer having its principal place of business located within the Commonwealth; (iii) delivered to any local humane society or shelter, or to any person who is a resident of the county or city where the animal is seized or an adjacent county or city in the Commonwealth and who will pay the required license fee, if any, on such animal; or (iv) delivered to the person with a right of property in the animal as provided in subsection E.

E. In no case shall the owner be allowed to purchase, adopt, or otherwise obtain the animal if the court determines that the animal has been abandoned, cruelly treated, or deprived of adequate care; however, the court shall direct that the animal be delivered to the person with a right of property in the animal, upon his request, if the court finds that the abandonment, cruel treatment, or deprivation of adequate care is not attributable to the actions or inactions of such person.

F. The court shall order the owner of any animal determined to have been abandoned, cruelly treated, or deprived of adequate care to pay all reasonable expenses incurred in caring and providing for such animal from the time the animal is seized until such time that the animal is disposed of in accordance with the provisions of this section, to the provider of such care.

G. The court may prohibit the possession or ownership of other companion animals by the owner of any companion animal found to have been abandoned, cruelly treated, or deprived of adequate care. In making a determination to prohibit the possession or ownership of companion animals, the court may take into consideration the owner's past record of convictions under this chapter or other laws prohibiting cruelty to animals or pertaining to the care or treatment of animals and the owner's mental and physical condition.

H. If the court finds that an agricultural animal has been abandoned or cruelly treated, the court may prohibit the possession or ownership of any other agricultural animal by the owner of the agricultural animal if the owner has exhibited a pattern of abandoning or cruelly treating agricultural animals as evidenced by previous convictions of violating §3.1-796.73 or §3.1-796.122. In making a determination to prohibit the possession or ownership of agricultural animals, the court may take into consideration the owner's mental and physical condition.

I. Any person who is prohibited from owning or possessing animals pursuant to subsection G or H may petition the court to repeal the prohibition after two years have elapsed from the date of entry of the court's order. The court may, in its discretion, repeal the prohibition if the person can prove to the satisfaction of the court that the cause for the prohibition has ceased to exist.

J. When a sale occurs, the proceeds shall first be applied to the costs of the sale then next to the unreimbursed expenses for the care and provision of the animal, and the remaining proceeds, if any, shall be paid over to the owner of the animal. If the owner of the animal cannot be found, the proceeds remaining shall be paid into the Literary Fund of the state treasury.

K. Nothing in this section shall be construed to prohibit the humane destruction of a critically injured or ill animal for humane purposes by the impounding humane investigator, law-enforcement officer, animal control officer, or licensed veterinarian.

L. The provisions of this section which address whether an animal has been provided with or deprived of adequate care shall apply only with respect to companion animals.
(Chgd. by L.1998 ch. 817; L.1999 ch. 113, eff. 7/1/99.)

§3.1-796.116. Dogs killing, injuring or chasing livestock or poultry.

It shall be the duty of any animal control officer or other officer who may find a dog in the act of killing or injuring livestock or poultry to kill such dog forthwith whether such dog bears a tag or not. Any person finding a dog committing any of the depredations mentioned in this section shall have the right to kill such dog on sight as shall any owner of livestock or his agent finding a dog chasing livestock on land utilized by the livestock when the circumstances show that such chasing is harmful to the livestock. Any court shall have the power to order the animal control officer or other officer to kill any dog known to be a confirmed livestock or poultry killer, and any dog killing poultry for the third time shall be considered a confirmed poultry killer. The court, through its contempt powers, may compel the owner, custodian, or harborer of the dog to produce the dog.

Any animal control officer who has reason to believe that any dog is killing livestock or poultry shall be empowered to seize such dog solely for the purpose of examining such dog in order to determine whether it committed any of the depredations mentioned herein. Any animal control officer or other person who has reason to believe that any dog is killing livestock, or committing any of the depredations mentioned in this section, shall apply to a magistrate of the county, city or town wherein such dog may be, who shall issue a warrant requiring the owner or custodian, if known, to appear before a general district court at a time and place named therein, at which time evidence shall be heard. If it shall appear that the dog is a livestock killer, or has committed any of the depredations mentioned in this section, the district court shall order that the dog be (i) killed immediately by the animal control officer or other officer designated by the court or (ii) removed to another state which does not border on the Commonwealth and prohibited from returning to the Commonwealth. Any dog ordered removed from the Commonwealth which is later found in the Commonwealth shall be ordered by a court to be killed immediately.
(Chgd. by L.1998 ch. 817, eff. 7/1/98.)

§3.1-796.117. Dog killing other domestic animals other than livestock or poultry.

The governing body of any county, city or town, which has not adopted an ordinance pursuant to §3.1-796.93:1, may adopt an ordinance to provide for the confinement of dogs which kill other dogs or domestic animals other than livestock or poultry. The ordinance shall provide that any animal control officer who has reason to believe that any dog is killing other dogs or domestic animals other than livestock or poultry shall apply to a magistrate of the county, city or town wherein the dog may be located for the issuance of a warrant requiring the owner or custodian, if known, to appear before a general district court at a specified time. The animal control officer or owner shall confine the dog until such time as evidence shall be heard and a verdict rendered. If it appears from the evidence that the dog has habitually killed other dogs or domestic animals, the court may order the dog killed in accordance with the provisions of §3.1-796.119.
(Chgd. by L.1998 ch. 817, eff. 7/1/98.)

§3.1-796.118. Compensation for livestock and poultry killed by dogs.

Any person who has any livestock or poultry killed or injured by any dog not his own shall be entitled to receive as compensation the fair market value of such livestock or poultry not to exceed $400 per animal or $10 per fowl, provided that: (i) the claimant has furnished evidence within sixty days of discovery of the quantity and value of the dead or injured livestock and the reasons the claimant believes that death or injury was caused by a dog; (ii) the animal control officer or other officer shall have been notified of the incident within seventy-two hours of its discovery; and (iii) the claimant first has exhausted his legal remedies against the owner, if known, of the dog doing the damage for which compensation under this section is sought. Exhaustion shall mean a judgment against the owner of the dog upon which an execution has been returned unsatisfied.

Local jurisdictions may by ordinance waive the requirements of (ii) or (iii) or both provided that the ordinance

adopted requires that the animal control officer has conducted an investigation and that his investigation supports the claim. Upon payment under this section the local governing body shall be subrogated to the extent of compensation paid to the right of action to the owner of the livestock or poultry against the owner of the dog and may enforce the same in an appropriate action at law.
(Chgd. by L.1998 ch. 817, eff. 7/1/98.)

§3.1-796.119. Capturing, confining, and euthanizing companion animals by animal control officers; approval of drugs, etc., used.

It shall be the duty of the animal control officer or any other officer to capture and confine any companion animal of unknown ownership found running at large on which the license fee has not been paid. Following the expiration of the holding period prescribed in §3.1-796.96, the animal control officer or other officer may deliver such companion animal to any person in his jurisdiction who will pay the required license fee on such companion animal. Prior to disposition by euthanasia or otherwise, all the provisions of §3.1-796.96 shall have been complied with. For all companion animals not otherwise disposed of as provided for in this chapter, it shall be the duty of the animal control officer or any other officer to euthanize such companion animals. Any person, animal control officer, or other officer euthanizing a companion animal under this chapter shall cremate, bury, or sanitarily dispose of the same.

All drugs and drug administering equipment used by animal control officers or other officers to capture companion animals pursuant to this chapter shall have been approved by the State Veterinarian.
(Chgd. by L.1997 ch. 159; L.1998 ch. 817, eff. 7/1/98.)

§3.1-796.120. Gift, sale, or delivery of animals from pounds or animal shelters; penalties.

A. The governing body of any political subdivision shall dispose of impounded animals in accordance with the provisions of §3.1-796.96. Any proceeds deriving from the gift, sale, or delivery of such animals shall be paid directly to the treasurer of the political subdivision, and no part of such proceeds shall accrue to any individual.

B. The following shall confine and dispose of animals in their custody in accordance with the provisions of §3.1-796.96:

1. Any humane investigator who has custody of any animal pursuant to his official duties;
2. Any humane society; and
3. Any animal shelter.

Animals which have been confined at a county or city pound as required by §3.1-796.96 prior to being delivered to a local humane society or animal shelter may be immediately placed for adoption, or humanely euthanized in accordance with methods approved by the State Veterinarian. Any proceeds deriving from the gift, sale, or delivery of such animals shall be paid directly to the clerk or treasurer of the humane society for the expenses of the society and expenses incident to any agreement concerning the disposing of such animal. No part of the proceeds shall accrue to any individual except for the aforementioned purposes. Humane societies, humane investigators and animal shelters shall keep accurate records of all animals handled. Records shall include a description of the animal including color, breed, sex, approximate weight, reason for bringing in, age, owner's or finder's name, address and telephone number, license number or other identifying tags or markings, as well as disposition of the animal. Humane societies and animal shelters shall submit a summary of such records to the State Veterinarian annually in a format prescribed by him.

C. If this chapter or any laws governing the care or protection of animals are violated by an animal shelter, the operator of the shelter may be assessed a civil penalty by the Board in an amount that does not exceed $1,000 per violation. Each day of the violation shall constitute a separate offense. In determining the amount of any civil penalty, the Board shall consider (i) the history of previous violations at the shelter; (ii) whether the violation has caused injury to, death or suffering of, an animal; and (iii) the demonstrated good faith of the operator to achieve compliance after notification of the violation. All civil penalties assessed under this section shall be recovered in a civil action brought by the Attorney General in the name of the Commonwealth. Such civil penalties shall be paid into a special fund in the state treasury to the credit of the Department to be used in carrying out the purposes of this chapter.
(Chgd. by L.1996 ch. 213; L.1997 ch. 286; L.2000 ch. 1010, eff. 7/1/2001. Matter in italics eff. 7/1/2001.)

§3.1-796.121. Disposal of dead companion animals.

The owner of any companion animal which has died from disease or other cause shall forthwith cremate, bury, or sanitarily dispose of the same. If, after notice, any owner fails to do so, the animal control officer or other officer shall bury or cremate the companion animal, and he may recover on behalf of the local jurisdiction from the owner his cost for this service.
(Chgd. by L.1998 ch. 817, eff. 7/1/98.)

ARTICLE 6
CRUELTY TO ANIMALS

§3.1-796.122. Cruelty to animals; penalty.

A. Any person who (i) overrides, overdrives, overloads, tortures, ill-treats, abandons, willfully inflicts inhumane injury or pain not connected with bona fide scientific or medical experimentation, or cruelly or unnecessarily beats, maims, mutilates, or kills any animal, whether belonging to himself or another; or (ii) deprives any animal of necessary food, drink, shelter or emergency veterinary treatment; or (iii) willfully sets on foot, instigates, engages in, or in any way furthers any act of cruelty to any animal; or (iv) carries or causes to be carried in or upon any vehicle, vessel or otherwise any animal in a cruel, brutal, or inhumane manner, so as to produce torture or unnecessary suffering; or (v) causes any of the above things, or being the owner of such animal permits such acts to be done by another, shall be guilty of a Class 1 misdemeanor.

B. Any person who (i) tortures, willfully inflicts inhumane injury or pain not connected with bona fide scientific or medical experimentation, or cruelly and unnecessarily beats, maims, mutilates or kills any animal whether belonging to himself or another; or (ii) instigates, engages in, or in any way furthers any act of cruelty to any animal set forth in clause (i) of this subsection; or (iii) causes any of the actions described in subdivisions (i) and (ii) of this subsection, or being the owner of such animal permits such acts to be done by another; and has been within five years convicted of a violation of this subsection or subsection A, shall be guilty of a Class 6 felony if the current violation or any previous violation of this subsection or subsection A resulted in the death of an animal or the euthanasia of an animal based on the recommendation of a licensed veterinarian upon determination that such euthanasia was necessary due to the condition of the animal, and such condition was a direct result of a violation of this subsection or subsection A.

C. Any person who abandons any dog, cat or other domesticated animal in any public place including the right-of-way of any public highway, road or street or on the property of another shall be guilty of a Class 3 misdemeanor.

D. Nothing in this section shall be construed to prohibit the dehorning of cattle.

E. For the purposes of this section and §§3.1-796.111, 3.1-796.113, 3.1-796.114, 3.1-796.115, and 3.1-796.125, the word animal shall be construed to include birds and fowl.

F. This section shall not prohibit authorized wildlife management activities or hunting, fishing or trapping as regulated under other titles of the Code of Virginia, including, but not limited to Title 29.1, or to farming activities as provided under this title or regulations promulgated thereto.

G. In addition to the penalties provided in subsection A, the court may, in its discretion, require any person convicted of a violation of subsection A to attend an anger management or other appropriate treatment program or obtain psychiatric or psychological counseling. The court may impose the costs of such a program or counseling upon the person convicted.

H. It is unlawful for any person to kill a domestic dog or cat for the purpose of obtaining the hide, fur or pelt of the dog or cat. A violation of this subsection shall constitute a Class 1 misdemeanor. A second or subsequent violation of this subsection shall constitute a Class 6 felony.

(Chgd. by L.1998 ch. 817; L.1999 chs. 209, 620, 645, eff. 7/1/99.)

§3.1-796.123. Soring horses; penalty.

For the purposes of this section, a horse shall be considered to be sored if, for the purpose of affecting its gait, a blistering agent has been applied internally or externally to any of the legs, ankles, feet, or other parts of the horse, or if burns, cuts, or lacerations have been inflicted on the horse, or if a chemical agent, or tacks, nails, or wedges have been used on the horse, or if any other method or device has been used on the horse, including, but not limited to chains or boots, which may reasonably be expected currently (i) to result in physical pain to the horse when walking, trotting, or otherwise moving, or (ii) to cause extreme fear or distress to the horse.

It shall be unlawful for any person to deliver or receive into this Commonwealth for the purpose of showing or exhibiting, any horse which such person has reason to believe is suffering from the effects of being sored. It shall also be unlawful to show or exhibit or enter in any horse show or exhibition for the purpose of showing any horse which such person has reason to believe is sored. No one shall participate in or conduct any horse show or exhibition in which there is shown or exhibited a horse which such person has reason to believe is sored.

Any person who violates any provision of this section shall be guilty of a Class 3 misdemeanor.

§3.1-796.124. Dogfighting; penalty.

A. No person shall knowingly do any of the following:

1. Promote, engage in, or be employed in the fighting of dogs for amusement, sport or gain;

2. Wager money or anything of value on the result of such fighting;

3. Receive money or anything of value for the admission of another person to a place for dogfighting; or

4. Permit any act described in subdivisions 1 through 3 of this subsection on any premises under his charge or control, or aid or abet any such act.

B. Any animal control officer, as defined in §3.1-796.66, shall confiscate any dogs that have been, are, or are intended to be used in dogfighting and any equipment used in training such dogs or used in dogfighting.

C. Any person convicted of violating this section may be prohibited by the court from possession or ownership of other companion animals.

D. Any person who violates any provision of this section shall be guilty of a Class 6 felony.

(Chgd. by L.1998 ch. 817; L.1999 ch. 113, eff. 7/1/99.)

§3.1-796.125. Fighting cocks or other animals; attendance at fighting; penalty.

Any person engaging in the fighting of cocks or other animals, except dogs, for money, prize or anything of value, or betting or wagering money or anything of value on the result of such fight, shall be guilty of a Class 3 misdemeanor. Attendance at the fighting of cocks, dogs or other animals where an admission fee is charged, directly or indirectly, shall also constitute a Class 3 misdemeanor.

§3.1-796.126. Shooting pigeons, etc., for amusement, and renting premises for such purposes; penalty.

Live pigeons or other birds or fowl shall not be kept or used for the purpose of a target, or to be shot at either for amusement or as a test of skill in marksmanship. It shall be a Class 4 misdemeanor to shoot at a bird kept or used as aforesaid, or to be a party to such shooting. Any person who lets any building, room, field or premises, or knowingly permits the use thereof for the purpose of such shooting shall be guilty of a Class 4 misdemeanor.

Nothing contained herein shall apply to the shooting of wild game.

ARTICLE 6.1
MANDATORY STERILIZATION OF DOGS AND CATS ADOPTED FROM RELEASING AGENCIES

Section

§3.1-796.126:1. Sterilization of adopted dogs and cats; enforcement; civil penalty.

A. Every new owner of a dog or cat adopted from a releasing agency shall cause to be sterilized the dog or cat pursuant to the agreement required by subdivision 2 of subsection B of this section.

B. A dog or cat shall not be released for adoption from a releasing agency unless:

1. The animal has already been sterilized; or

2. The individual adopting the animal signs an agreement to have the animal sterilized by a licensed veterinarian (i) within thirty days of the adoption, if the animal is sexually mature, or (ii) within thirty days after the animal reaches six months of age, if the animal is not sexually mature at the time of adoption.

C. A releasing agency may extend for thirty days the date by which a dog or cat must be sterilized on presentation of a written report from a veterinarian stating that the life or health of the adopted animal may be jeopardized by sterilization. In cases involving extenuating circumstances, the veterinarian and the releasing agency may negotiate the terms of an extension of the date by which the animal must be sterilized.

D. Nothing in this section shall preclude the sterilization of a sexually immature dog or cat upon the written agreement of the veterinarian, the releasing agency, and the new owner.

E. Upon the petition of an animal control officer, humane investigator, the State Veterinarian or a State Veterinarian's representative to the district court of the county or city where a violation of this article occurs, the court may order the new owner to take any steps necessary to comply with the requirements of this article. This remedy shall be exclusive of and in addition to any civil penalty which may be imposed under this article.

F. Any person who violates subsection A or B of this section shall be subject to a civil penalty not to exceed fifty dollars.

(Chgd. by L.1998 ch. 817, eff. 7/1/98.)

§3.1-796.126:2. Sterilization agreement.

Any agreement used by a releasing agency pursuant to subsection B of §3.1-796.126:1 shall contain:

1. The date of the agreement;
2. The names, addresses, and signatures of the releasing agency and the new owner;
3. A description of the dog or cat to be adopted;
4. The date by which the dog or cat is required to be sterilized; and
5. A statement printed in conspicuous, bold print, that sterilization of the dog or cat is required under this article; that a person who violates this article is subject to a civil penalty; and that the new owner may be compelled to comply with the provisions of this article.

§3.1-796.126:3. Sterilization confirmation; civil penalty.

Each new owner who signs a sterilization agreement shall, within seven days of the sterilization, cause to be delivered or mailed to the releasing agency written confirmation signed by the veterinarian who performed the sterilization. The confirmation shall briefly describe the dog or cat; include the new owner's name and address; certify that the sterilization was performed; and specify the date of the procedure. Any person who violates this section shall be subject to a civil penalty not to exceed $150.

(Chgd. by L.1999 chs. 627, 672, eff. 7/1/99.)

§3.1-796.126:4. Notification concerning lost, stolen or dead dogs or cats; civil penalty.

If an adopted dog or cat is lost or stolen or dies before the animal is sterilized and before the date by which the dog or cat is required to be sterilized, the new owner shall, within seven days of the animal's disappearance or death, notify the releasing agency of the animal's disappearance or death. Any person who violates this section shall be subject to a civil penalty not to exceed twenty-five dollars.

§3.1-796.126:5. Exemptions.

This article shall not apply to:

1. An owner reclaiming his dog or cat from a releasing agency;
2. A releasing agency located in a county, city, or town that has adopted a more stringent mandatory sterilization ordinance; and
3. A local governing body which has disposed of an animal by sale or gift to a federal agency, state-supported institution, agency of the Commonwealth, agency of another state, or licensed federal dealer having its principal place of business located within the Commonwealth.

§3.1-796.126:6. Releasing agency; fees and deposits.

A local governing body or releasing agency may charge and collect from the new owner a fee or deposit before releasing a dog or cat for adoption to ensure sterilization.

§3.1-796.126:7. Civil penalties.

Any animal control officer, humane investigator, the State Veterinarian or State Veterinarian's representative shall be entitled to bring a civil action for any violation of this article which is subject to a civil penalty. Any civil penalty assessed pursuant to this article shall be paid into the treasury of the city or county in which such civil action is brought and used for the purpose of defraying the costs of local animal control, including efforts to promote sterilization of cats and dogs.

(Chgd. by L.1998 ch. 817, eff. 7/1/98.)

ARTICLE 6.2
HYBRID CANINES

(Added by L.1997 ch. 918, eff. 7/1/97.)

Section

§3.1-796.126:8. Definitions.

As used in this article:

"Adequate confinement" means that, while on the property of its owner and not under the direct supervision and control of the owner or custodian, a hybrid canine shall be confined in a humane manner in a securely enclosed and locked structure of sufficient height and design to (i) prevent the animal's escape; or if the hybrid canine is determined to be a dangerous dog pursuant to §3.1-796.93:1, the structure shall prevent direct contact with any person or animal not authorized by the owner to be in direct contact with the hybrid canine, and (ii) provide a minimum of 100 square feet of floor space for each adult animal. Tethering of a hybrid canine not under the direct supervision and control of the owner or custodian shall not be considered adequate confinement.

"Hybrid canine" means any animal which at any time has been or is permitted, registered, licensed, advertised or otherwise described or represented as a hybrid canine, wolf or coyote by its owner to a licensed veterinarian, law-enforcement officer, animal control officer, humane investigator, official of the Department of Health, or State Veterinarian's representative.

"Responsible ownership" means the ownership and humane care of a hybrid canine in such a manner as to comply with all laws and ordinances regarding hybrid canines and prevent endangerment by the animal to public health and safety.

(Added by L.1997 ch. 918; chgd. by L.1998 ch. 817, eff. 7/1/98.)

§3.1-796.126:9. Hybrid canine ordinance; penalty.

A. Any county, city or town may, by ordinance, establish a permit system to ensure the adequate confinement and responsible ownership of hybrid canines. Such ordinance may include requirements pertaining to: (i) the term and expiration date of the permit, (ii) the number of hybrid canines that may be owned by a permittee, (iii) identification tags or tattooing of the animal, (iv) where the animal may be kept, (v) handling of the animal while not on the property of the owner, and (vi) information required to be provided when applying for a permit, such as the sex, color, height, vaccination records, length, or identifying marks of the hybrid canine. The ordinance shall not require that hybrid canines be disposed of by the owner unless the owner fails or refuses to obtain or renew any required permit or violates a provision of the ordinance or any other law pertaining to the responsible ownership of the hybrid canine. The locality may impose a permit fee to cover the cost of the permitting system.

B. Violation of an ordinance enacted pursuant to this section shall be a Class 3 misdemeanor for the first violation and a Class 1 misdemeanor for a second or a subsequent violation. The ordinance may require a violator to surrender the hybrid canine for euthanasia in accordance with §3.1-796.119.

C. The provisions of this section shall not affect any ordinance adopted prior to the effective date of this section.
(Added by L.1997 ch. 918, eff. 7/1/97.)

§3.1-796.126:10. Hybrid canines killing, injuring or chasing livestock.

It shall be the duty of any animal control officer or other officer who may find a hybrid canine in the act of killing or injuring livestock or poultry to kill such hybrid canine forthwith, whether such hybrid canine bears a tag or not. Any person finding a hybrid canine committing any of the depredations mentioned in this section shall have the right to kill such hybrid canine on sight as shall any owner of livestock or his agent finding a hybrid canine chasing livestock on land lawfully utilized by the livestock when the circumstances show that such chasing is harmful to the livestock. Any court shall have the power to order the animal control officer or other officer to kill any hybrid canine known to be a confirmed livestock or poultry killer, and any hybrid canine killing poultry for the third time shall be considered a confirmed poultry killer. The court, through its contempt powers, may compel the owner, custodian, or harborer of the hybrid canine to produce the hybrid canine.

Any animal control officer who has reason to believe that any hybrid canine is killing livestock or poultry shall be empowered to seize such hybrid canine solely for the purpose of examining such hybrid canine in order to determine whether it committed any of the depredations mentioned herein. Any animal control officer or other person who has reason to believe that any hybrid canine is killing livestock, or committing any of the depredations mentioned in this section, shall apply to a magistrate for the county, city or town wherein such hybrid canine may be, who shall issue a warrant requiring the owner or custodian, if known, to appear before a general district court at a time and place named therein, at which time evidence shall be heard. If it appears that the hybrid canine is a livestock killer, or has committed any of the depredations mentioned in this section, the district court shall order that the hybrid canine be (i) killed immediately by the animal control officer or other officer designated by the court or (ii) removed to another state which does not border on the Commonwealth and prohibited from returning to the Commonwealth. Any hybrid canine ordered removed from the Commonwealth which is later found in the Commonwealth shall be ordered by a court to be killed immediately.
(Added by L.1997 ch. 918; chgd. by L.1998 ch. 817, eff. 7/1/98.)

§3.1-796.126:11. Compensation for livestock and poultry killed by hybrid canines.

Any person who has any livestock or poultry killed or injured by any hybrid canine not his own shall be entitled to receive as compensation the fair market value of such livestock or poultry not to exceed $400 per animal or $10 per fowl, provided that: (i) the claimant has furnished evidence within sixty days of discovery of the quantity and value of the dead or injured livestock and the reasons the claimant believes that death or injury was caused by a hybrid canine; (ii) the animal control officer or other officer shall have been notified of the incident within seventy-two hours of its discovery; and (iii) the claimant first has exhausted his legal remedies against the owner, if known, of the hybrid canine doing the damage for which compensation under this section is sought. Exhaustion shall mean a judgment against the owner of the hybrid canine upon which an execution has been returned unsatisfied.

Local jurisdictions may by ordinance waive the requirements of (ii) or (iii) or both provided that the ordinance adopted requires that the animal control officer has conducted an investigation and that his investigation supports the claim. Upon payment under this section the local governing body shall be subrogated to the extent of compensation paid to the right of action to the owner of the livestock or poultry against the owner of the hybrid canine and may enforce the same in an appropriate action at law.
(Added by L.1997 ch. 918; chgd. by L.1998 ch. 817, eff. 7/1/98.)

ARTICLE 7
MISCELLANEOUS PROVISIONS

Section

§3.1-796.127. Dogs and cats deemed personal property; rights relating thereto.

All dogs and cats shall be deemed personal property and may be the subject of larceny and malicious or unlawful trespass. Owners, as defined in §3.1-796.66, may maintain any action for the killing of any such animals, or injury thereto, or unlawful detention or use thereof as in the case of other personal property. The owner of any dog or cat which is injured or killed contrary to the provisions of this chapter by any person shall be entitled to recover the value thereof or the damage done thereto in an appropriate action at law from such person.

An animal control officer or other officer finding a stolen dog or cat, or a dog or cat held or detained contrary to law, shall have authority to seize and hold such animal pending action before a general district court or other court. If no such action is instituted within seven days, the animal control officer or other officer shall deliver the dog or cat to its owner.

The presence of a dog or cat on the premises of a person other than its legal owner shall raise no presumption of theft against the owner, and the animal control officer may take such animal in charge and notify its legal owner to remove it. The legal owner of the animal shall pay a reasonable charge as the local governing body by ordinance shall establish for the keep of such animal while in the possession of the animal control officer.
(Chgd. by L.1998 ch. 817, eff. 7/1/98.)

§3.1-796.128. Unlawful acts; penalties.

A. The following shall be unlawful acts and constitute Class 4 misdemeanors:

1. License application. – For any person to make a false statement in order to secure a dog or cat license to which he is not entitled.

2. License tax. – For any dog or cat owner to fail to pay any license tax required by this chapter before February 1 for the year in which it is due. In addition, the court may order confiscation and the proper disposition of the dog or cat.

3. Leash ordinance. – For any dog owner to allow a dog to run at large in violation of an ordinance passed pursuant to §3.1-796.95.

4. Rabies regulations. – For any person to fail to obey an ordinance passed pursuant to §§3.1-796.98 and 3.1-796.100.

5. Dead companion animals. – For any owner to fail to dispose of the body of his companion animals in accordance with §3.1-796.121.

6. Diseased dogs and cats. – For the owner of any dog or cat with a contagious or infectious disease to permit such dog or cat to stray from his premises if such disease is known to the owner.

7. Concealing a dog or cat. – For any person to conceal or harbor any dog or cat on which any required license tax has not been paid.

8. Removing collar and tag. – For any person, except the owner or custodian, to remove a legally acquired license tag from a dog or cat without the permission of the owner or custodian.

9. Other violations. – Any other violation of this chapter for which a specific penalty is not provided.

B. It shall be a Class 1 misdemeanor for any person to:

1. Present a false claim or to receive any money on a false claim under the provisions of §3.1-796.118; or

2. Impersonate a humane investigator.

(Chgd. by L.1998 ch. 817, eff. 7/1/98.)

§3.1-796.128:1. Intentional interference with a guide or leader dog; penalty.

A. It is unlawful for a person to, without just cause, willfully impede or interfere with the duties performed by a dog if the person knows or has reason to believe the dog is a guide or leader dog. A violation of this subsection is punishable as a Class 3 misdemeanor.

B. It is unlawful for a person to, without just cause, willfully injure a dog if the person knows or has reason to believe the dog is a guide or leader dog. A violation of this subsection is punishable as a Class 1 misdemeanor.

"Guide or leader dog" means a dog that (i) serves as a dog guide for a blind person as defined in §63.1-142 or for a person with a visual disability, (ii) serves as a listener for a deaf or hard-of-hearing person as defined in §63.1-85.3:1, or (iii) provides support or assistance for a physically disabled or handicapped person.

(Added by L.1995 ch. 209, eff. 7/1/95.)

§3.1-796.128:2. Selling garments containing dog or cat fur prohibited; penalty.

It is unlawful for any person to sell a garment containing the hide, fur or pelt which he knows to be that of a domestic dog or cat. A violation of this section shall be punishable by a fine of not more than $10,000.

(Added by L.1999 chs. 646, 678, eff. 7/1/99.)

§3.1-796.129. Jurisdiction of general district courts; right of appeal.

Unless otherwise provided, the provisions of this article may be enforced by any general district court in cities or counties wherein the offense is committed, or the offender or owner may be found. Every such offender shall have the right of appeal to the appropriate circuit court.

TITLE 4.1
ALCOHOLIC BEVERAGE CONTROL ACT
(Selected Chapters)

CHAPTER 1
DEFINITIONS AND GENERAL PROVISIONS
(Selected Sections)

§4.1-100. Definitions.

As used in this title unless the context requires a different meaning:

"Alcohol" means the product known as ethyl or grain alcohol obtained by distillation of any fermented liquor, rectified either once or more often, whatever the origin, and shall include synthetic ethyl alcohol, but shall not include methyl alcohol and alcohol completely denatured in accordance with formulas approved by the government of the United States.

"Alcoholic beverages" includes alcohol, spirits, wine, and beer, and any one or more of such varieties containing one-half of one percent or more of alcohol by volume, including mixed alcoholic beverages, and every liquid or solid, patented or not, containing alcohol, spirits, wine, or beer and capable of being consumed by a human being. Any liquid or solid containing more than one of the four varieties shall be considered as belonging to that variety which has the higher percentage of alcohol, however obtained, according to the order in which they are set forth in this definition.

"Barrel" means any container or vessel having a capacity of more than forty-three ounces.

"Bed and breakfast establishment" means any establishment (i) having no more than fifteen bedrooms; (ii) offering to the public, for compensation, transitory lodging or sleeping accommodations; and (iii) offering at least one meal per day, which may but need not be breakfast, to each person to whom overnight lodging is provided.

"Beer" means any alcoholic beverage obtained by the fermentation of an infusion or decoction of barley, malt, and hops or of any similar products in drinkable water and containing one-half of one percent or more of alcohol by volume.

"Board" means the Virginia Alcoholic Beverage Control Board.

"Bottle" means any vessel intended to contain liquids and having a capacity of not more than forty-three ounces.

"Club" means any private nonprofit corporation or association which is the owner, lessee, or occupant of an establishment operated solely for a national, social, patriotic, political, athletic, or other like purpose, but not for pecuniary gain, the advantages of which belong to all of the members. It also means the establishment so operated. A corporation or association shall not lose its status as a club because of the conduct of charitable gaming conducted pursuant to Article 1.1:1 (§18.2-340.15 et seq.) of Chapter 8 of Title 18.2 in which nonmembers participate frequently or in large numbers, provided that no alcoholic beverages are served or consumed in the room where such charitable gaming is being conducted while such gaming is being conducted and that no alcoholic beverages are made available upon the premises to any person who is neither a member nor a bona fide guest of a member.

Any such corporation or association which has been declared exempt from federal and state income taxes as one which is not organized and operated for pecuniary gain or profit shall be deemed a nonprofit corporation or association.

"Container" means any barrel, bottle, carton, keg, vessel or other receptacle used for holding alcoholic beverages.

"Convenience grocery store" means an establishment which (i) has an enclosed room in a permanent structure where stock is displayed and offered for sale and (ii) maintains an inventory of edible items intended for human consumption consisting of a variety of such items of the types normally sold in grocery stores.

"Designated area" means a room or area approved by the Board for on-premises licensees.

"Dining area" means a public room or area in which meals are regularly served.

"Establishment" means any place where alcoholic beverages of one or more varieties are lawfully manufactured, sold, or used.

"Farm winery" means an establishment (i) located on a farm in the Commonwealth with a producing vineyard, orchard, or similar growing area and with facilities for fermenting and bottling wine on the premises where the owner or lessee manufactures wine that contains not more than eighteen percent alcohol by volume or (ii) located in the Commonwealth with a producing vineyard, orchard, or similar growing area or agreements for purchasing grapes or other fruits from agricultural growers within the Commonwealth, and with facilities for fermenting and bottling wine on the premises where the owner or lessee manufactures wine that contains not more than eighteen percent alcohol by volume. As used in this definition, the terms "owner" and "lessee" shall include a cooperative formed by an association of individuals for the purpose of manufacturing wine. In the event such cooperative is licensed as a farm winery, the term "farm" as used in this definition includes all of the land owned or leased by the individual members of the cooperative as long as such land is located in the Commonwealth.

"Gift shop" means any bona fide retail store selling, predominantly, gifts, books, souvenirs, specialty items relating to history, original and handmade arts and products, collectibles, crafts, and floral arrangements, which is open to the public on a regular basis. Such shop shall be a permanent structure where stock is displayed and offered for sale and which has facilities to properly secure any stock of wine or beer. Such shop may be located (i) on the premises or grounds of a government registered national, state or local historic building or site or (ii) within the premises of a museum. The Board shall consider the purpose, characteristics, nature, and operation of the shop in determining whether it shall be considered a gift shop.

"Gourmet brewing shop" means an establishment which sells to persons to whom wine or beer may lawfully be sold, ingredients for making wine or brewing beer, including packaging, and rents to such persons facilities for manufacturing, fermenting and bottling such wine or beer.

"Gourmet shop" means an establishment provided with adequate inventory, shelving, and storage facilities, where, in consideration of payment, substantial amounts of domestic and imported wines and beers of various types and sizes and related products such as cheeses and gourmet foods are habitually furnished to persons.

"Government store" means a store established by the Board for the sale of alcoholic beverages.

"Hotel" means any duly licensed establishment, provided with special space and accommodation, where, in consideration of payment, food and lodging are habitually furnished to persons, and which has four or more bedrooms. It shall also mean the person who operates such hotel.

"Interdicted person" means a person to whom the sale of alcoholic beverages is prohibited by order pursuant to this title.

"Intoxicated" means a condition in which a person has drunk enough alcoholic beverages to observably affect his manner, disposition, speech, muscular movement, general appearance or behavior.

"Licensed" means the holding of a valid license issued by the Board.

"Licensee" means any person to whom a license has been granted by the Board.

"Low alcohol beverage cooler" means a drink containing one-half of one percent or more of alcohol by volume, but not more than seven and one-half percent alcohol by volume, and consisting of spirits mixed with nonalcoholic beverages or flavoring or coloring materials; it may also contain water, fruit juices, fruit adjuncts, sugar, carbon dioxide, preservatives or other similar products manufactured by fermenting fruit or fruit juices. Low alcohol beverage coolers shall be treated as wine for all purposes of this title; except that low alcohol beverage coolers shall not be sold in localities that have not approved the sale of mixed beverages pursuant to §4.1-124. In addition, low alcohol beverage coolers shall not be sold for on-premises consumption other than by mixed beverage licensees.

"Meals" means, for a mixed beverage license, an assortment of foods commonly ordered in bona fide, full-service restaurants as principal meals of the day. Such restaurants shall include establishments specializing in full course meals with a single substantial entree.

"Member of a club" means (i) a person who maintains his membership in the club by the payment of monthly, quarterly, or annual dues in the manner established by the rules and regulations thereof or (ii) a person who is a member of a bona fide auxiliary, local chapter, or squadron composed of direct lineal descendants of a bona fide member, whether alive or deceased, of a national or international organization to which an individual lodge holding a club license is an authorized member in the same locality. It shall also mean a lifetime member whose financial contribution is not less than ten times the annual dues of resident members of the club, the full amount of such contribution being paid in advance in a lump sum.

"Mixed beverage" or "mixed alcoholic beverage" means a drink composed in whole or in part of spirits.

"Mixer" means any prepackaged ingredients containing beverages or flavoring or coloring materials, and which may also contain water, fruit juices, fruit adjuncts, sugar, carbon dioxide, or preservatives which are not commonly consumed unless combined with alcoholic beverages, whether or not such ingredients contain alcohol. Such specialty beverage product shall be manufactured or distributed by a Virginia corporation.

"Place or premises" means the real estate, together with any buildings or other improvements thereon, designated in the application for a license as the place at which the manufacture, bottling, distribution, use or sale of alcoholic beverages shall be performed, except that portion of any such building or other improvement actually and exclusively used as a private residence.

"Public place" means any place, building, or conveyance to which the public has, or is permitted to have, access, including restaurants, soda fountains, hotel dining areas, lobbies, and corridors of hotels, and any highway, street, lane, park, or place of public resort or amusement.

The term shall not include (i) hotel or restaurant dining areas or ballrooms while in use for private meetings or private parties limited in attendance to members and guests of a particular group, association or organization; (ii) restaurants licensed by the Board in office buildings or industrial or similar facilities while such restaurant is closed to the public and in use for private meetings or parties limited in attendance to employees and nonpaying guests of the owner or a lessee of all or part of such building or facility; (iii) offices, office buildings or industrial facilities while closed to the public and in use for private meetings or parties limited in attendance to employees and nonpaying guests of the owner or a lessee of all or part of such building or facility; or (iv) private recreational or chartered boats which are not licensed by the Board and on which alcoholic beverages are not sold.

"Residence" means any building or part of a building or structure where a person resides, but does not include any part of a building which is not actually and exclusively used as a private residence, nor any part of a hotel or club other than a private guest room thereof.

"Resort complex" means a facility (i) with a hotel owning year-round sports and recreational facilities located contiguously on the same property or (ii) owned by a nonstock, nonprofit, taxable corporation with voluntary membership which, as its primary function, makes available golf, ski and other recreational facilities both to its members and the general public. The hotel or corporation shall have a minimum of 140 private guest rooms or dwelling units contained on not less than 50 acres. The Board may consider the purpose, characteristics, and operation of the applicant establishment in determining whether it shall be considered as a resort complex. All other pertinent qualifications established by the Board for a hotel operation shall be observed by such licensee.

"Restaurant" means, for a beer, or wine and beer license, any establishment provided with special space and accommodation, where, in consideration of payment, meals or other foods prepared on the premises are regularly sold.

"Restaurant" means, for a mixed beverage license, an established place of business (i) where meals with substantial entrees are regularly sold and (ii) which has adequate facilities and sufficient employees for cooking, preparing, and serving such meals for consumption at tables in dining areas on the premises, and includes establishments specializing in full course meals with a single substantial entree.

"Sale" and "sell" includes soliciting or receiving an order for; keeping, offering or exposing for sale; peddling, exchanging or bartering; or delivering otherwise than gratuitously, by any means, alcoholic beverages.

"Special agent" means an employee of the Department of Alcoholic Beverage Control whom the Board has designated as a law-enforcement officer pursuant to §4.1-105.

"Special event" means an event sponsored by a duly organized nonprofit corporation or association and conducted for an athletic, charitable, civic, educational, political, or religious purpose.

"Spirits" means any beverage which contains alcohol obtained by distillation mixed with drinkable water and other substances, in solution, and includes, among other things, brandy, rum, whiskey, and gin, or any one or more of the last four named ingredients; but shall not include any such liquors completely denatured in accordance with formulas approved by the United States government.

"Wine" means any alcoholic beverage obtained by the fermentation of the natural sugar content of fruits or other agricultural products containing (i) sugar, including honey and milk, either with or without additional sugar; (ii) one-half of one percent or more of alcohol by volume; and (iii) no product of distillation. The term includes any wine to which wine spirits have been added, as provided in the Internal Revenue Code, to make products commonly known as "fortified wine" which do not exceed an alcohol content of twenty-one percent by volume.

"Wine cooler" means a drink containing one-half of one percent or more of alcohol by volume, and not more than three and two-tenths percent of alcohol by weight or four percent by volume consisting of wine mixed with nonalcoholic beverages or flavoring or coloring materials, and which may also contain water, fruit juices, fruit adjuncts, sugar, carbon dioxide, or preservatives and shall include other similar products manufactured by fermenting fruit or fruit juices. Wine coolers and similar fermented fruit juice beverages shall be treated as wine for all purposes except for taxation under §4.1-236.

"With or without meals" means the selling and serving of alcoholic beverages by retail licensees for on-premises consumption whether or not accompanied by food so long as the total food-beverage ratio required by §4.1-210, or the monthly food sale requirement established by Board regulation, is met by such retail licensee.

(Chgd. by L.1995 chs. 497, 518, 661; L.1996 chs. 558, 604; L.1997 chs. 124, 425; L.1999 chs. 93, 171, 481; L.2000 chs. 786, 1037, 1052, eff. 7/1/2000.)

§4.1-103.01. Additional powers; access to certain tobacco sales records; inspections; penalty.

A. Notwithstanding the provisions of §58.1-3 or any other provision of law, the Tax Commissioner shall provide to the Board the name, address, and other identifying information within his possession of all wholesale cigarette dealers.

B. All invoices, books, papers or other memoranda and records concerning the sale of cigarettes maintained by wholesale cigarette dealers pursuant to §58.1-1007 shall be subject to inspection during normal business hours by special agents of the Board. Any person who, upon request by a special agent, unreasonably fails or refuses to allow an inspection of the records authorized by this subsection shall be guilty of a Class 2 misdemeanor.

C. The Board may use the information obtained from the Tax Commissioner or by the inspections authorized by subsection B only for the purpose of creating and maintaining a list of retail dealers to facilitate enforcement of the laws governing the sale of tobacco products to minors. Neither the Board nor any special agent shall divulge any information provided by the Tax Commissioner or obtained in the performance of the inspections authorized by subsection B to anyone other than to another special agent. Any person violating the provisions of this subsection shall be guilty of a Class 2 misdemeanor.

(Added by L.1998 chs. 189, 364, eff. 7/1/98.)

§4.1-105. Police power of members, agents and employees of Board.

Members of the Board are vested, and such agents and employees of the Board designated by it shall be vested, with like power to enforce the provisions of (i) this title and the criminal laws of the Commonwealth as is vested in the chief law-enforcement officer of a county, city, or town; (ii) §18.2-371.2; and (iii) §58.1-1037.

(Chgd. by L.1997 chs. 812, 882; L.2000 chs. 880, 901, eff. 7/1/2000.)

CHAPTER 2
ADMINISTRATION OF LICENSES
(Selected Article)

ARTICLE 1
GENERAL PROVISIONS
(Selected Sections)

§4.1-200. Exemptions from licensure.

The licensure requirements of this chapter shall not apply to:

1. A person in charge of an institution regularly conducted as a hospital or sanatorium for the care of persons in ill health, or as a home devoted exclusively to the care of aged people, who administers or causes to be administered alcoholic beverages to any bona fide patient or inmate of the institution who is in need of the same, either by way of external application or otherwise for emergency medicinal purposes. Such person may charge for the alcoholic beverages so administered, and carry such stock as may be necessary for this purpose. No charge shall be made of any patient for the alcoholic beverages so administered to him where the same have been supplied to the institution by the Board free of charge.

2. The manufacture, sale and delivery or shipment by persons authorized under existing laws to engage in such business of any medicine containing sufficient medication to prevent it from being used as a beverage.

3. The manufacture, sale and delivery or shipment by persons authorized under existing laws to engage in such business of any medicinal preparations manufactured in accordance with formulas prescribed by the United States pharmacopoeia; national formulary, patent and proprietary preparations; and other bona fide medicinal and technical preparations; which contain no more alcohol than is necessary to extract the medicinal properties of the drugs contained in such preparations, and no more alcohol than is necessary to hold the medicinal agents in solution and to preserve the same, and which are manufactured and sold to be used exclusively as medicine and not as beverages.

4. The manufacture, sale and delivery or shipment of toilet, medicinal and antiseptic preparations and solutions not intended for internal human use nor to be sold as beverages.

5. The manufacture and sale of food products known as flavoring extracts which are manufactured and sold for cooking and culinary purposes only and not sold as beverages.

6. Any person who manufactures at his residence or at a gourmet brewing shop for domestic consumption at his residence, but not to be sold, dispensed or given away, except as hereinafter provided, wine or beer or both, in an amount not to exceed the limits permitted by federal law.

Any person who manufactures beer in accordance with this subdivision may remove from his residence an amount not to exceed fifteen gallons of such beer on any one occasion for (i) personal or family use, provided such use does not violate the provisions of this title or Board regulations; (ii) giving to any person to whom beer may be lawfully sold an amount not to exceed seventy-two ounces per person per year, provided such gift is for noncommercial purposes; or (iii) giving to any person to whom beer may lawfully be sold a sample of such beer, not to exceed two ounces by volume for on-premises consumption at events organized for judging or exhibiting such beer, including events held on the premises of a retail licensee. Nothing in this paragraph shall be construed to authorize the sale of such beer.

7. Any person who keeps and possesses lawfully acquired alcoholic beverages in his residence for his personal use or that of his family. However, such alcoholic beverages may be served or given to guests in such residence by such person, his family or servants when such service or gift is in no way a shift or device to evade the provisions of this title.

8. Any person who manufactures and sells cider to distillery licensees, or any person who manufactures wine from grapes grown by such person and sells it to winery licensees.

9. The sale of wine and beer in or through canteens or post exchanges on United States reservations when permitted by the proper authority of the United States.

10. The keeping and consumption of any lawfully acquired alcoholic beverages at a private meeting or private party limited in attendance to members and guests of a particular group, association or organization at a banquet or similar affair, or at a special event, if a banquet license has been granted.

(Chgd. by L.1995 chs. 497, 518, eff. 7/1/95.)

§4.1-201. Conduct not prohibited by this chapter; limitation.

A. This chapter shall not prohibit:

1. Any club licensed under this chapter from keeping for consumption by its members any alcoholic beverages lawfully acquired by such members, provided the alcoholic beverages are not sold, dispensed or given away in violation of this title.

2. Any person from having grain, fruit or fruit products and any other substance, when grown or lawfully produced by him, distilled by any distillery licensee, and selling the distilled alcoholic beverages to the Board or selling or shipping them to any person outside of the Commonwealth in accordance with Board regulations. However, no alcoholic beverages so distilled shall be withdrawn from the place where distilled except in accordance with Board regulations.

3. Any person licensed to manufacture and sell, or either, in the Commonwealth or elsewhere, alcoholic beverages other than wine or beer, from soliciting and taking orders from the Board for such alcoholic beverages.

4. The receipt by a person operating a licensed brewery of deliveries and shipments of beer in closed containers from other breweries owned by such person or the sale, delivery or shipment of such beer, in accordance with Board regulations to (i) persons licensed to sell beer at wholesale, (ii) persons licensed to sell beer at retail for the purpose of resale only as provided in subdivision B 4 of §4.1-216, (iii) owners of boats registered under the laws of the United States sailing for ports of call of a foreign country or another state, and (iv) persons outside the Commonwealth for resale outside the Commonwealth.

5. The granting of any retail license to a brewery or winery licensee, or to an applicant for such license, or to a lessee of such person, a wholly owned subsidiary of such person, or its lessee, provided the places of business or establishments for which the retail licenses are desired are located upon the premises occupied or to be occupied by such winery or brewery, or upon property of such person contiguous to such premises, or in a development contiguous to such premises owned and operated by such person or a wholly owned subsidiary.

6. The receipt by a distillery licensee of deliveries and shipments of alcoholic beverages, other than wine and beer, in closed containers from other distilleries, or the sale, delivery or shipment of such alcoholic beverages, in accordance

with Board regulations, to the Board and to persons outside the Commonwealth for resale outside the Commonwealth.

7. The receipt by a winery licensee of deliveries and shipments of wine in closed containers from other wineries owned by such licensee or the receipt by a winery licensee or farm winery licensee of deliveries and shipments of spirits distilled from fruit or fruit juices in closed containers from distilleries to be used only for the fortification of wine produced by the licensee in accordance with Board regulations, or the sale, delivery or shipment of such wine, in accordance with Board regulations, to persons licensed to sell wine at wholesale for the purpose of resale, and to persons outside the Commonwealth for resale outside the Commonwealth.

8. The receipt by a fruit distillery licensee of deliveries and shipments of alcoholic beverages made from fruit or fruit juices in closed containers from other fruit distilleries owned by such licensee, or the sale, delivery or shipment of such alcoholic beverages, in accordance with Board regulations, to persons outside of the Commonwealth for resale outside of the Commonwealth.

9. Any farm winery licensee from shipping or delivering its wine in closed containers to another farm winery licensee for the purpose of additional bottling in accordance with Board regulations and the return of the wine so bottled to the manufacturing farm winery licensee.

B. No deliveries or shipments of alcoholic beverages to persons outside the Commonwealth for resale outside the Commonwealth shall be made into any state the laws of which prohibit the consignee from receiving or selling the same.

(Chgd. by L.1995 chs. 253, 317; L.1997 ch. 386; L.2000 ch. 786, eff. 7/1/2000.)

CHAPTER 3
PROHIBITED PRACTICES; PENALTIES; PROCEDURAL MATTERS
(Selected Articles)

ARTICLE 1
PROHIBITED PRACTICES GENERALLY
(Complete Article)

§4.1-300. Illegal manufacture and bottling; penalty.

A. Except as otherwise provided in §§4.1-200 and 4.1-201, no person shall manufacture alcoholic beverages in the Commonwealth without being licensed under this title to manufacture such alcoholic beverages. Nor shall any person, other than a brewery licensee or bottler's licensee, bottle beer for sale.

B. The presence of mash at an unlicensed distillery shall constitute manufacturing within the meaning of this section.

C. Any person convicted of a violation of this section shall be guilty of a Class 6 felony.

§4.1-301. Conspiracy to violate §4.1-300; penalty.

If two or more persons conspire together to do any act which is in violation of §4.1-300, and one or more of these persons does any act to effect the object of the conspiracy, each of the parties to such conspiracy shall be guilty of a Class 6 felony.

§4.1-302. Illegal sale of alcoholic beverages in general; penalty.

If any person who is not licensed sells any alcoholic beverages except as permitted by this title, he shall be guilty of a Class 1 misdemeanor.

In the event of a second or subsequent conviction under this section, a jail sentence of no less than thirty days shall be imposed and in no case be suspended.

§4.1-303. Purchase of alcoholic beverages from person not authorized to sell; penalty.

If any person buys alcoholic beverages from any person other than the Board, a government store or a person authorized under this title to sell alcoholic beverages, he shall be guilty of a Class 1 misdemeanor.

§4.1-304. Persons to whom alcoholic beverages may not be sold; penalty.

No person shall, except pursuant to subdivisions 1 through 5 of §4.1-200, sell any alcoholic beverages to any person when at the time of such sale he knows or has reason to believe that the person to whom the sale is made is (i) less than twenty-one years of age, (ii) interdicted, or (iii) intoxicated.

Any person convicted of a violation of this section shall be guilty of a Class 1 misdemeanor.

§4.1-305. Purchasing or possessing alcoholic beverages unlawful in certain cases; exceptions; penalty; forfeiture.

A. No person to whom an alcoholic beverage may not lawfully be sold under §4.1-304 shall purchase or possess, or attempt to purchase or possess, any alcoholic beverage, except (i) pursuant to subdivisions 1 through 7 of §4.1-200; (ii) where possession of the alcoholic beverages by a person less than twenty-one years of age is due to such person's making a delivery of alcoholic beverages in pursuance of his employment or an order of his parent; or (iii) by any state, federal, or local law-enforcement officer when possession of an alcoholic beverage is necessary in the performance of his duties.

B. No person under the age of twenty-one years shall use or attempt to use any (i) altered, fictitious, facsimile or simulated license to operate a motor vehicle, (ii) altered, fictitious, facsimile or simulated document, including, but not limited to a birth certificate or student identification card, or (iii) motor vehicle operator's license, birth certificate or student identification card of another person in order to establish a false identification or false age for himself to purchase or attempt to purchase an alcoholic beverage.

C. Any person found guilty of a violation of this section shall be guilty of a Class 1 misdemeanor; and upon conviction, (i) such person shall be ordered to pay a fine of at least $500 or ordered to perform a minimum of fifty hours of community service and (ii) such person's license to operate a motor vehicle in the Commonwealth may be suspended for a period of not more than one year. The court, in its discretion and upon a demonstration of hardship, may authorize any person convicted of a violation of this section the use of a restricted permit to operate a motor vehicle in accordance with the provisions of subsection D of §16.1-278.9 or subsection E of §18.2-271.1. The court may require a person issued a restricted permit under the provisions of this subsection to be monitored by an alcohol safety action program during the period of license suspension. The alcohol safety action program shall report to the court any violation of the terms of the restricted permit, any condition related thereto or any failure to remain alcohol-free during the suspension period. However, the sentence imposed pursuant to clause (i) of this subsection shall not be suspended.

D. Any alcoholic beverage purchased or possessed in violation of this section shall be deemed contraband and forfeited to the Commonwealth in accordance with §4.1-338.

E. Any retail licensee who in good faith promptly notifies the Board or any state or local law-enforcement agency of a violation or suspected violation of this section shall be accorded immunity from an administrative penalty for a violation of §4.1-304.

(Chgd. by L.1995 ch. 374; L.1996 chs. 626, 730; L.2000 ch. 325, eff. 7/1/2000.)

§4.1-306. Purchasing alcoholic beverages for one to whom they may not be sold; penalty; forfeiture.

A. If any person purchases alcoholic beverages for another person, and at the time of such purchase knows or has reason to believe that the person for whom the alcoholic beverage was purchased was (i) less than twenty-one years of age, (ii) interdicted, or (iii) intoxicated, he shall be guilty of a Class 1 misdemeanor.

B. Any alcoholic beverages purchased in violation of this section shall be deemed contraband and forfeited to the Commonwealth in accordance with §4.1-338.

§4.1-307. Persons by whom alcoholic beverages may not be sold or served for on-premises consumption; penalty.

No person shall permit anyone employed by him under the age of (i) eighteen years to sell, serve or dispense in any manner alcoholic beverages for on-premises consumption, except pursuant to subdivisions 1 through 5 of §4.1-200 or (ii) twenty-one years to prepare or mix alcoholic beverages in the capacity of bartender.

Any person convicted of a violation of this section shall be guilty of a Class 1 misdemeanor.

§4.1-308. Drinking alcoholic beverages, or offering to another, in public place; penalty.

A. If any person takes a drink of alcoholic beverages or offers a drink thereof to another, whether accepted or not, at or in any public place, he shall be guilty of a Class 4 misdemeanor.

B. This section shall not prevent any person from drinking alcoholic beverages or offering a drink thereof to another in any rooms or areas approved by the Board in a licensed establishment, provided such establishment or the person who operates the same is licensed to sell alcoholic beverages at retail for on-premises consumption and the alcoholic beverages drunk or offered were purchased therein.

C. This section shall not prevent any person from drinking alcoholic beverages or offering a drink thereof to another in any room or area approved by the Board at an event for which a banquet license or mixed beverage special events license has been granted. Nor shall this section prevent, upon authorization of the licensee, any person from drinking his own lawfully acquired alcoholic beverages or offering a drink thereof to another in approved areas and locations at events for which a coliseum or stadium license has been granted.

D. This section shall not prevent any person from drinking alcoholic beverages or offering a drink thereof to another on a chartered boat being used for the transportation of passengers for compensation which is not licensed by the Board and which does not sell alcoholic beverages.

§4.1-309. Drinking or possessing alcoholic beverages in or on public school grounds; penalty.

A. No person shall possess or drink any alcoholic beverage in or upon the grounds of any public elementary or secondary school during school hours or school or student activities.

B. In addition, no person shall drink and no organization shall serve any alcoholic beverage in or upon the grounds of any public elementary or secondary school after school hours or school or student activities, except for religious congregations using wine for sacramental purposes only.

C. Any person convicted of a violation of this section shall be guilty of a Class 2 misdemeanor.

D. This section shall not prohibit any person from possessing or drinking alcoholic beverages or any organization from serving alcoholic beverages in areas approved by the Board at a performing arts center owned by any city having a population between 100,000 and 105,000, provided the organization operating the performing arts center or its lessee has a license granted by the Board.

(Chgd. by L.1997 chs. 784, 837, eff. 7/1/97.)

§4.1-310. Illegal importation, shipment and transportation of alcoholic beverages; penalty; exception.

A. No alcoholic beverages, other than wine or beer, shall be imported, shipped, transported or brought into the

Commonwealth, other than to distillery licensees or winery licensees, unless consigned to the Board. However, the Board may permit such alcoholic beverages ordered by it from outside the Commonwealth for (i) persons, for industrial purposes, (ii) the manufacture of articles allowed to be manufactured under §4.1-200, or (iii) hospitals, to be shipped or transported directly to such persons. On such orders or shipments of alcohol, the Board shall charge only a reasonable permit fee.

B. No wine shall be imported, shipped, transported or brought into the Commonwealth unless it is consigned to a wholesale wine licensee.

C. No beer shall be imported, shipped, transported or brought into the Commonwealth except to persons licensed to sell it.

D. Any person convicted of a violation of this section shall be guilty of a Class 1 misdemeanor.

E. The provisions of this chapter shall not prohibit (i) any person from bringing, in his personal possession or in his accompanying baggage, into the Commonwealth not for resale, alcoholic beverages in an amount not to exceed one gallon or four liters if any part of the alcoholic beverages being transported is held in metric-sized containers, (ii) the shipment or transportation into the Commonwealth upon a permit issued by the Board of a reasonable quantity of alcoholic beverages in the personal or household effects of a person moving his residence to the Commonwealth, or (iii) the possession or storage of alcoholic beverages on passenger boats, dining cars, buffet cars and club cars, licensed under this title, or common carriers engaged in interstate or foreign commerce.

(Chgd. by L.1995 chs. 253, 317, eff. 7/1/95.)

§4.1-311. Limitations on transporting lawfully purchased alcoholic beverages; penalty.

A. The transportation of alcoholic beverages lawfully purchased in the Commonwealth in excess of the following limits is prohibited except in accordance with Board regulations:

1. Wine and beer, no limitation.
2. Alcoholic beverages other than wine and beer, three gallons, provided that not more than one gallon thereof shall be in containers holding less than one-fifth of a gallon. If any part of the alcoholic beverages being transported is held in metric-sized containers, the three-gallon limitation shall be construed to be 12 liters, and not more than 4 liters thereof shall be in containers smaller than 750 milliliters.

B. The Transportation of alcoholic beverages lawfully purchased outside the Commonwealth, within, into or through the Commonwealth, in quantities in excess of one gallon or four liters if any part of the alcohol being transported is held in metric-sized containers, is prohibited except in accordance with Board regulations adopted pursuant to this section.

C. Any person transporting alcoholic beverages in violation of this section shall be guilty of a Class 1 misdemeanor.

§4.1-312. Limitation on carrying alcoholic beverages in motor vehicle transporting passengers for hire; penalty.

The transportation of alcoholic beverages in any motor vehicle which is being used, or is licensed, for the transportation of passengers for hire is prohibited, except when carried in the possession of a passenger who is being transported for compensation at the regular rate and fare charged other passengers.

Any person convicted of a violation of this section shall be guilty of a Class 1 misdemeanor.

§4.1-313. Possessing, transporting, etc., alcoholic beverages illegally acquired; penalty.

A. No person, other than a common carrier, shall have, possess, keep, carry, ship or transport alcoholic beverages upon which the tax imposed by the laws of the United States has not been paid.

B. No person shall possess alcoholic beverages in amounts in excess of the limits provided in §4.1-311 in containers not bearing evidence that they have been purchased from the Board or a person licensed to sell them, or other evidence that the tax due to the Commonwealth or the markup required by the Board has been paid, unless it can be proved that the alcoholic beverages were lawfully acquired by the possessor.

C. Any person convicted of a violation of this section shall be guilty of a Class 1 misdemeanor.

§4.1-314. Keeping, possessing or storing still or distilling apparatus without a permit; penalty.

No person shall keep, store or have in his possession any still, or distilling apparatus, without a permit from the Board.

Any person convicted of a violation of this section shall be guilty of a Class 1 misdemeanor.

§4.1-315. Possession without license to sell alcoholic beverages upon premises of restaurant; exceptions; penalty.

A. No alcoholic beverages shall be kept or allowed to be kept upon any premises or upon the person of any proprietor or person employed upon the premises of a restaurant or other place where food or refreshments of any kind are furnished for compensation, except such alcoholic beverages as such person owning or operating such place of business is licensed to purchase and to sell at such place of business.

B. This section shall not apply to (i) any residence, (ii) alcoholic beverages in the possession of a passenger being transported for compensation as provided in subsection D of §4.1-308, (iii) dining rooms in restaurants licensed by the Board while such areas are in use for private meetings or parties limited in attendance to members and guests of a particular group, association or organization, or (iv) licensed restaurants in office buildings, industrial or similar facilities while such restaurant is closed to the public and is in use for private meetings or parties limited in attendance to employees and nonpaying guests of the owner or a lessee of all or part of such building, or facility.

C. Any person convicted of a violation of this section shall be guilty of a Class 1 misdemeanor.

§4.1-316. Keeping or drinking alcoholic beverages upon premises of club; penalty.

No person operating a club for profit or otherwise, either public or private, shall (i) keep or allow to be kept any alcoholic beverages, either by himself or any other person, upon the premises or (ii) permit the drinking of any alcoholic beverages upon the premises, unless he is licensed to sell alcoholic beverages.

Any person convicted of a violation of this section shall be guilty of a Class 1 misdemeanor.

§4.1-317. Maintaining common nuisances; penalties.

A. All houses, boathouses, buildings, club or fraternity or lodge rooms, boats, cars and places of every description where alcoholic beverages are manufactured, stored, sold, dispensed, given away or used contrary to law, by any scheme or device whatever, shall be deemed common nuisances.

No person shall maintain, aid, abet or knowingly associate with others in maintaining a common nuisance.

Any person convicted of a violation of this subsection shall be guilty of a Class 1 misdemeanor.

B. In addition, after due notice and opportunity to be heard on the part of any owner or lessor not involved in the original offense, by a proceeding analogous to that provided in §§4.1-339 through 4.1-348 and upon proof of guilty knowledge, judgment may be given that such house, building, boathouse, car or other place, or any room or part thereof, be closed up. The court may, upon the owner or lessor giving bond in the penalty of not less than $500 and with security to be approved by the court, conditioned that the premises shall not be used for unlawful purposes, or in violation of the provisions of this chapter for a period of five years, turn the same over to its owner or lessor; or proceeding may be had in equity as provided in §4.1-335.

C. In a proceeding under this section judgment shall not be entered against the owner, lessor, or lienholder of property unless it is proved he (i) knew of the unlawful use of the property and (ii) had the right, because of such unlawful use, to enter and repossess the property.

§4.1-318. Violations by armed person; penalty.

No person shall unlawfully manufacture, transport or sell any alcoholic beverages, and at the time of the unlawful manufacturing, transporting, or selling or aiding or assisting in any manner in such act, shall carry on or about his person, or have on or in any vehicle which he may be using to aid him in any such purpose, or have in his possession, actual or constructive, at or within 100 yards of any place where any such alcoholic beverages are being unlawfully manufactured, transported or sold, any dangerous weapon as described in §18.2-308.

Any person convicted of a violation of this section shall be guilty of a Class 6 felony.

§4.1-319. Disobeying subpoena; hindering conduct of hearing; penalty.

No person shall (i) fail or refuse to obey any subpoena issued by the Board, any Board member, or agent authorized by the Board to issue such subpoena or (ii) hinder the orderly conduct and decorum of any hearing held and conducted by the Board, any Board member, or agent authorized by the Board to hold and conduct such hearing.

Any person convicted of a violation of this section shall be guilty of a Class 1 misdemeanor.

§4.1-320. Illegal advertising; penalty; exception.

Except in accordance with Board regulations, no person shall advertise in or send any advertising matter into the Commonwealth about or concerning alcoholic beverages other than those which may be legally manufactured or sold without any license.

Any person convicted of a violation of this section shall be guilty of a Class 1 misdemeanor.

Neither this section nor any Board regulation shall prohibit (i) the awarding of watches of a wholesale value of less than $100 by a licensed distillery, winery or brewery, to participants in athletic contests; (ii) the exhibition or display of automobiles, boats, or aircraft regularly and normally used in racing or other competitive events and the sponsorship of an automobile, boat or aircraft racing team by a licensed distillery, winery or brewery and the display on the automobile, boat or aircraft and uniforms of the members of the racing team the trademark or brand name of an alcoholic beverage manufactured by a distillery, winery, or brewery; (iii) the sponsorship of a professional athletic event, including, but not limited to, golf, auto racing or tennis, by a licensed distillery, winery or brewery or the use of any trademark or brand name of any alcoholic beverage in connection with such sponsorship; (iv) the advertisement of beer by the display of such product's name on any airship, which advertising is paid for by the manufacturer of such product; or (v) the advertisement of beer or any alcoholic beverage by the display of such product's name on any scale model, reproduction or replica of any motor vehicle, aircraft or watercraft offered for sale.

(Chgd. by L.1995 ch. 222, eff. 7/1/95.)

§4.1-321. Delivery of alcoholic beverage to prisoners in jail prohibited; penalty.

No person shall deliver, or cause to be delivered, to any prisoner in any local correctional facility, any alcoholic beverage.

Any person convicted of a violation of this section shall be guilty of a Class 1 misdemeanor.

§4.1-322. Possession or consumption of alcoholic beverages by interdicted persons; penalty.

No person who has been interdicted pursuant to §4.1-333 or §4.1-334 shall possess any alcoholic beverages, except those acquired in accordance with subdivisions 1 through 5 of §4.1-200, nor be drunk in public in violation of §18.2-388.

Any interdicted person found to be in violation of this section shall be guilty of a Class 1 misdemeanor.

(Chgd. by L.1996 ch. 717, eff. 7/1/96.)

§4.1-323. Attempts; aiding or abetting; penalty.

No person shall attempt to do any of the things prohibited by this title or to aid or abet another in doing, or attempting to do, any of the things prohibited by this title.

On an indictment, information or warrant for the violation of this title, the jury or the court may find the defendant guilty of an attempt, or being an accessory, and the punishment shall be the same as if the defendant were solely guilty of such violation.

ARTICLE 2
PROHIBITED PRACTICES BY LICENSEES
(Selected Sections)

§4.1-324. Illegal sale or keeping of alcoholic beverages by licensees; penalty.

A. No licensee or any agent or employee of such licensee shall:

1. Sell any alcoholic beverages of a kind other than that which such license or this title authorizes him to sell;

2. Sell beer to which wine, spirits or alcohol has been added;

3. Sell wine to which spirits or alcohol, or both, have been added, otherwise than as required in the manufacture thereof under Board regulations;

4. Sell alcoholic beverages of a kind which such license or this title authorizes him to sell, but to any person other than to those to whom such license or this title authorizes him to sell;

5. Sell alcoholic beverages which such license or this title authorizes him to sell, but in any manner other than such license or this title authorizes him to sell;

6. Sell any alcoholic beverages when forbidden by this title;

7. Keep or allow to be kept, other than in his residence and for his personal use, any alcoholic beverages other than that which he is authorized to sell by such license or by this title;

8. Sell any beer to a retail licensee, except for cash, if the seller holds a brewery, bottler's or wholesale beer license;

9. Sell any beer on draft and fail to display to customers the brand of beer so sold or misrepresent the brand of any beer sold; or

10. Sell any wine for delivery within the Commonwealth to a retail licensee, except for cash, if the seller holds a wholesale wine or farm winery license.

B. Any person convicted of a violation of this section shall be guilty of a Class 1 misdemeanor.
(Chgd. by L.1998 ch. 238, eff. 7/1/98.)

§4.1-325. Prohibited acts by mixed beverage licensees; penalty.

A. In addition to §4.1-324, no mixed beverage licensee nor any agent or employee of such licensee shall:

1. Sell or serve any alcoholic beverage other than as authorized by law;

2. Sell any authorized alcoholic beverage to any person or at any place except as authorized by law;

3. Allow at the place described in his license the consumption of alcoholic beverages in violation of this title;

4. Keep at the place described in his license any alcoholic beverage other than that which he is licensed to sell;

5. Misrepresent the brand of any alcoholic beverage sold or offered for sale;

6. Keep any alcoholic beverage other than in the bottle or container in which it was purchased by him except in a frozen drink dispenser of a type approved by the Board and in the case of wine, in containers of a type approved by the Board pending automatic dispensing and sale of such wine;

7. Refill or partly refill any bottle or container of alcoholic beverage or dilute or otherwise tamper with the contents of any bottle or container of alcoholic beverage;

8. Sell or serve any brand of alcoholic beverage which is not the same as that ordered by the purchaser without first advising such purchaser of the difference;

9. Remove or obliterate any label, mark or stamp affixed to any container of alcoholic beverages offered for sale;

10. Deliver or sell the contents of any container if the label, mark or stamp has been removed or obliterated;

11. Allow any immoral, lewd, obscene, indecent or profane conduct, language, literature, pictures, performance or materials on the licensed premises;

12. Allow any striptease act, or the like on the licensed premises;

13. Allow persons connected with the licensed business to appear nude or partially nude;

14. Consume or allow the consumption by an employee of any alcoholic beverages while on duty;

15. Deliver to a consumer an original bottle of an alcoholic beverage purchased under such license whether the closure is broken or unbroken except in accordance with §4.1-210;

16. Be intoxicated while on duty or employ an intoxicated person on the licensed premises;

17. Conceal any sale or consumption of any alcoholic beverages;

18. Fail or refuse to make samples of any alcoholic beverages available to the Board upon request or obstruct special agents of the Board in the discharge of their duties;

19. Store alcoholic beverages purchased under the license in any unauthorized place or remove any such alcoholic beverages from the premises;

20. Knowingly employ in the licensed business any person who has the general reputation as a prostitute, panderer, habitual law violator, person of ill repute, user or peddler of narcotics, or person who drinks to excess or engages in illegal gambling; or

21. Keep on the licensed premises a slot machine or any prohibited gambling or gaming device, machine or apparatus.

B. Any person convicted of a violation of this section shall be guilty of a Class 1 misdemeanor.
(Chgd. by L.2000 ch. 780, eff. 7/1/2000.)

§4.1-326. Sale of; purchase for resale; wine or beer from a person without a license; penalty.

No licensee, other than a common carrier operating in interstate or foreign commerce, licensed to sell wine or beer at retail shall purchase for resale or sell any wine or beer purchased from anyone other than a wholesale wine, farm winery, brewery, bottler's or wholesale beer licensee.

Any person convicted of a violation of this section shall be guilty of a Class 1 misdemeanor.

§4.1-327. Prohibiting transfer of wine or beer by licensees; penalty.

A. No retail licensee, except (i) a retail on-premises wine and beer licensee or (ii) a retail on-premises beer licensee, shall transfer any wine or beer from one licensed place of business to another licensed place of business whether such places of business are under the same ownership or not.

B. Any person convicted of a violation of this section shall be guilty of a Class 1 misdemeanor.

§4.1-328. Prohibited trade practices; penalty.

A. No licensee shall violate, attempt to violate, solicit another person to violate or consent to any violation of §4.1-216 or regulations adopted pursuant to subdivision B 3 of §4.1-111.

B. Any person convicted of a violation of this section, §4.1-216 or of Board regulations adopted pursuant to subdivision B 3 of §4.1-111 shall be guilty of a Class 1 misdemeanor.

C. No person shall be deemed guilty of a Class 1 misdemeanor or to have admitted such guilt by virtue of the fact that administrative sanctions have been imposed pursuant to §4.1-227 either as a result of Board proceedings or the acceptance by the Board of an offer in compromise in response to the institution of such administrative proceedings.

§4.1-329. Illegal advertising materials; penalty.

No retail licensee shall induce, attempt to induce, or consent to, any manufacturer, bottler, wholesaler, or importer selling, renting, lending, buying for or giving to such retailer any advertising materials or decorations under circumstances prohibited by law.

Any person convicted of a violation of this section shall be guilty of a Class 1 misdemeanor.

ARTICLE 3
PROCEDURAL MATTERS
(Selected Sections)

§4.1-333. Interdiction of intoxicated driver or habitual drunkard.

A. When after a hearing upon due notice it appears to the satisfaction of the circuit court of any county or city that any person, residing within such county or city, has been convicted of driving any automobile, truck, motorcycle, engine or train while intoxicated or has shown himself to be an habitual drunkard, the court may enter an order of interdiction prohibiting the sale of alcoholic beverages to such person until further ordered. The court entering any such order shall file a copy of the order with the Board.

B. The court entering any order of interdiction may alter, amend or cancel such order as it deems proper. A copy of any alteration, amendment or cancellation shall be filed with the Board.

§4.1-334. Interdiction for illegal manufacture, possession, transportation or sale of alcoholic beverages.

When any person has been found guilty of the illegal manufacture, possession, transportation or sale of alcoholic beverages or maintaining a common nuisance as defined in §4.1-317, the court may without further notice or additional hearing enter an order of interdiction prohibiting the sale of alcoholic beverages to such person for one year from the date of the entry of the order, and thereafter if further ordered.

§4.1-336. Contraband beverages and other articles subject to forfeiture.

All stills and distilling apparatus and materials for the manufacture of alcoholic beverages, all alcoholic beverages and materials used in their manufacture, all containers in which alcoholic beverages nay be found, which are kept, stored, possessed, or in any manner used in violation of the provisions of this title, and any dangerous weapons as described in §18.2-308, which may be used, or which may be found upon the person or in any vehicle which such person is using, to aid such person in the unlawful manufacture, transportation or sale of alcoholic beverages, or found in the possession of such person, or any horse, mule or other beast of burden, any wagon, automobile, truck or vehicle of any nature whatsoever which are found in the immediate vicinity of any place where alcoholic beverages are being unlawfully manufactured and which such animal or vehicle is being used to aid in the unlawful manufacture, shall be deemed contraband and shall be forfeited to the Commonwealth.

Proceedings for the confiscation of the above property shall be in accordance with §4.1-338 for all such property except motor vehicles which proceedings shall be in accordance with §§4.1-339 through 4.1-348.

Such dangerous weapons seized by any officer charged with the enforcement of this title shall be forfeited to the Commonwealth upon the conviction of the person owning or possessing such weapons and shall be sold by order of court and the proceeds of such sale shall be paid into the Literary Fund.

§4.1-337. Search warrants.

A. If complaint on oath is made that alcoholic beverages are being manufactured, sold, kept, stored, or in any manner held, used or concealed in a particular house, or other place, in violation of law, the judge, magistrate or other person having authority to issue criminal warrants, to whom such complaint is made, if satisfied that there is a probable cause for such belief, shall issue a warrant to search such house or other place for alcoholic beverages. Such warrants, except as herein otherwise provided, shall be issued, directed and executed in accordance with the laws of the Commonwealth pertaining to search warrants.

B. Warrants issued under this title for the search of any automobile, boat, conveyance or vehicle, whether of like kind or not, or for the search of any article of baggage, whether of like kind or not, for alcoholic beverages, may be executed in any part of the Commonwealth where they are overtaken, and shall be made returnable before any judge within whose jurisdiction such automobile, boat, conveyance, vehicle, truck, or article of baggage, or any of them, was transported or attempted to be transported contrary to law.

§4.1-338. Confiscation proceedings; disposition of forfeited articles.

A. All proceedings for the confiscation of articles, except motor vehicles, declared contraband and forfeited to the Commonwealth under this chapter shall be as provided in this section.

B. Production of seized property. – Whenever any article declared contraband under the provisions of this title and required to be forfeited to the Commonwealth has been seized, with or without a warrant, by any officer charged with the enforcement of this title, he shall produce the contraband article and any person in whose possession it was found. In those cases where no person is found in possession of such articles the return shall so state and a copy of the warrant shall be posted on the door of the buildings or room where the articles were found, or if there is no door, then in any conspicuous place upon the premises.

In case of seizure of a still, doubler, worm, worm tub, mash tub, fermenting tub, or other distilling apparatus, for any offense involving their forfeiture, where it is impracticable to remove such distilling apparatus to a place of safe storage from the place where seized, the seizing officer may destroy the such apparatus only as necessary to prevent the use of all or any part thereof for the purpose of distilling. The destruction shall be in the presence of at least one credible witness, and such witness shall join the officer in a sworn report of the seizure and destruction, to be made to the Board. The report shall set forth the grounds of the claim of forfeiture, the reasons for seizure and destruction, an estimate of the fair cash value of the apparatus destroyed, and the materials remaining after such destruction. The report shall include a statement that, from facts within their own knowledge, the seizing officer and witness have no doubt whatever that the distilling apparatus was set up for use, or had been used in the unlawful distillation of spirits, and that it was impracticable to remove such apparatus to a place of safe storage.

In case of seizure of any quantity of mash, or of alcoholic beverages on which the tax imposed by the laws of the United States has not been paid, for any offense involving forfeiture of the same, the seizing officer may destroy them to prevent the use of all or any part thereof for the purpose of unlawful distillation of spirits or any other violation of this title. The destruction shall be in the presence of at least one credible witness, and such witness shall join the officer in a sworn report of the seizure and destruction, to be made to the Board. The report they shall set forth the grounds of the claim of forfeiture, the reasons for seizure and destruction, and a statement that, from facts within their own knowledge, the seizing officer and witness have no doubt whatever that the mash was intended for use in the unlawful distillation of spirits, or that the alcoholic beverages were intended for use in violation of this title.

C. Hearing and determination. – Upon the return of the warrant as provided in this section, the court shall fix a time not less than ten days, unless waived by the accused in writing, and not more than thirty days thereafter, for the hearing on such return to determine whether or not the articles seized, or any part thereof, were used or in any manner kept, stored or possessed in violation of this title.

At such hearing if no claimant appears, the court shall declare the articles seized forfeited to the Commonwealth and, if such articles are not necessary as evidence in any pending prosecution, shall turn them over to the Board. Any person claiming an interest in any of the articles seized may appear at the hearing and file a written claim setting forth particularly the character and extent of his interest. The court shall certify the warrant and the articles seized along with any claim filed to the circuit court to hear and determine the validity of such claim.

If the evidence warrants, the court shall enter a judgment of forfeiture and order the articles seized to be turned over to the Board. Action under this section and the forfeiture of any articles hereunder shall not be a bar to any prosecution under any other provision of this title.

D. Disposition of forfeited beverages and other articles. – Any articles forfeited to the Commonwealth and turned over to the Board in accordance with this section, shall be destroyed or sold by the Board as it deems proper. The net proceeds from such sales shall be paid into the Literary Fund. If the Board believes that any alcoholic beverages forfeited to the Commonwealth and turned over to the Board in accordance with this section cannot be sold and should not be destroyed, it may give such alcoholic beverages for medicinal purposes to any institution in the Commonwealth regularly conducted as a hospital, nursing home or sanatorium for the care of persons in ill health, or as a home devoted exclusively to the care of aged people, to supply the needs of such institution for alcoholic beverages for such purposes, provided that (i) the State Health Commissioner has issued a certificate stating that such institution has need for such alcoholic beverages, and (ii) preference is accorded by the Board to institutions supported either in whole or in part by public funds. A record shall be made showing the amount issued in each case, to whom issued and the date when issued, and shall be kept in the offices of the State Health Commissioner and the Board. No charge shall be made to any patient for the alcoholic beverages supplied to him where they have been received from the Board pursuant to this section. Such alcoholic beverages shall be administered only upon approval of the patient's physician.

If the Board believes that any foodstuffs forfeited to the Commonwealth and turned over to the Board in accordance with this section are usable, should not be destroyed and cannot be sold or whose sale would be impractical, it may give such foodstuffs to any institution in the Commonwealth and shall prefer a gift to the local jail or other local correctional facility in the jurisdiction where seizure took place. A record shall be made showing the nature of the foodstuffs and amount given, to whom given and the date when given, and shall be kept in the offices of the Board.
(Chgd. by L.1995 ch. 196, eff. 7/1/95.)

§4.1-339. Search and seizure of conveyances or vehicles used in violation of law; arrests.

A. When any officer charged with the enforcement of the alcoholic beverage control laws of the Commonwealth has reason to believe that alcoholic beverages illegally acquired, or being illegally transported, are in any conveyance or vehicle of any kind, either on land or on water (except a conveyance or vehicle owned or operated by a railroad, express, sleeping or parlor car or steamboat company, other than barges, tugs or small craft), he shall obtain a search warrant and search such conveyance or vehicle. If illegally acquired alcoholic beverages or alcoholic beverages being illegally transported in amounts in excess of one quart or one liter if in a metric-sized container are found, the officer shall seize the alcoholic beverages, seize and take possession of such conveyance or vehicle, and deliver them to the chief law-enforcement officer of the locality in which such seizure was made, taking his receipt therefor in duplicate.

B. The officer making such seizure shall also arrest all persons found in charge of such conveyance or vehicle and shall forthwith report in writing such seizure and arrest to the attorney for the Commonwealth for the county or city in which seizure and arrest were made.

§4.1-349. Punishment for violations of title or regulations; bond.

A. Any person convicted of a misdemeanor under the provisions of this title without specification as to the class of offense or penalty, or convicted of violating any other provision thereof, or convicted of violating any Board regulation, shall be guilty of a Class 1 misdemeanor.

B. In addition to the penalties imposed by this title for violations, any court before whom any person is convicted of a violation of any provision of this title may require such defendant to execute bond, with approved security, in the penalty of not more than $1,000, with the condition that the defendant will not violate any of the provisions of this title for the term of one year. If any such bond is required and is not given, the defendant shall be committed to jail until it is given, or until he is discharged by the court, provided he shall not be confined for a period longer than six months. If any such bond required by a court is not given during the term of the court by which conviction is had, it may be given before any judge or before the clerk of such court.

C. The provisions of this title shall not prevent the Board from suspending, revoking or refusing to continue the license of any person convicted of a violation of any provision of this title.

D. No court shall hear such a case unless the respective attorney for the Commonwealth or his assistant has been notified that such a case is pending.

§4.1-351. Previous convictions.

In any indictment, information or warrant charging any person with a violation of any provision of this title, it may be alleged and evidence may be introduced at the trial of such person to prove that such person has been previously convicted of a violation of this title.

TITLE 5.1
AVIATION
(Selected Chapters)

CHAPTER 1
AIRCRAFT, AIRMEN AND AIRPORTS GENERALLY

ARTICLE 1
GENERAL PROVISIONS
(Selected Sections)

§5.1-1. Definitions.

When used in this title, unless expressly stated otherwise:

"Board" means the Virginia Aviation Board.

"Person" means any individual, corporation, government, political subdivision of the Commonwealth, or governmental subdivision or agency, business trust, estate, trust, partnership, two or more of any of the foregoing having a joint or common interest, or any other legal or commercial entity.

"Aircraft" means any contrivance now known, or hereafter invented, used or designed for navigation of or flight in the air, including a balloon or other contrivance designed for maneuvering in airspace at an altitude greater than twenty-four inches above ground or water level except that any contrivance now or hereafter invented of fixed or flexible wing design, operating without the assistance of any motor, engine, or other mechanical propulsive device, which is designed to utilize the feet and legs of the operator or operators as the sole means of initiating and sustaining forward motion during the launch and of providing the point of contact with the ground upon landing, and commonly called a "hang glider" shall not be included within this definition.

"Public aircraft" means an aircraft used exclusively in the service of any state, or political subdivision thereof, or the federal government.

"Civil aircraft" means any aircraft other than a public aircraft.

"Airman" means any individual, including the person in command, and any pilot, mechanic, or member of the crew, who engages in the navigation of aircraft while under way within Virginia airspace, and any individual who is directly in charge of the inspection, maintenance, overhauling or repair of aircraft, aircraft engines, propellers or accessories; and any individual who serves in the capacity of aircraft dispatcher.

"Airport" means any area of land or water which is used, or intended for public use, for the landing and takeoff of aircraft, and any appurtenant areas which are used, or intended for use, for airport buildings or other airport facilities or rights-of-way, easements and together with all airport buildings and facilities located thereon.

"Landing area" or "landing field" means any locality, whether over land or water, including airports and intermediate landing fields, which is used or intended to be used for the landing and takeoff of aircraft, and open to the public for such use, whether or not facilities are provided for the sheltering, servicing or repair of aircraft, or for receiving or discharging passengers or cargo.

"Airspace" means all that space above the land and waters within the boundary of this Commonwealth.

"Drop zone" means any locality whether over land or water which is used, or intended for use, for the landing and recovery of sky divers, or parachutists using a parachute or other contrivance designed for sport jumping.

"Department" means the Department of Aviation.

"Commercial aircraft" means any civil aircraft used in flight activity for compensation or for hire.

"Contract carrier by aircraft" or "contract carrier" means any person, not included under §5.1-89 (c) or (d), who, under special and individual contracts or agreements, and whether directly or by a lease or any other arrangement, transports passengers or property by aircraft for compensation and in the transportation of passengers does not charge individual fares.

"Air navigation facility" means any airport ground or air navigation facility, other than one owned and operated by the United States, used in, available for use in, or designed for use in aid of air navigation, including any structures, buildings, mechanisms, lights, beacons, markers, communicating systems, or other instrumentalities, or devices, and any combination of any or all of such facilities, used or useful as an aid, or constituting any advantage or convenience, to the safe taking off, navigation, and landing of aircraft, in the safe and efficient operation or maintenance of an airport, in the safe, efficient and convenient handling or processing of aviation passengers, mail or cargo, or in the servicing or maintenance of aircraft or ground equipment.

"Airport hazard" shall mean any structure, object or natural growth, or use of land which obstructs the airspace required for the flight of aircraft in landing or taking off at an airport or is otherwise hazardous to such landing or taking off of aircraft.

§5.1-1.4. Enforcement of laws, rules and regulations.

Except for the provisions of Chapters 7 (§5.1-77 et seq.) and 9 (§5.1-89 et seq.) of this title, the Department shall have the authority to enforce any provision of this title and any rules and regulations promulgated by the Board in reference to aircraft, airfields, pilots and other similar subjects. Said rules and regulations, and enforcement actions taken in connection therewith, shall be in accordance with the substantive and procedural requirements of the Administrative Process Act, Chapter 1.1:1 (§9-6.14:1 et seq.) of Title 9.

§5.1-2.1. Virginia Aviation Commission continued as Virginia Aviation Board; membership; terms; Chairman.

A. The Virginia Aviation Commission, a public body corporate and politic, is hereby continued within the Department of Aviation as a political subdivision of the

Commonwealth and shall hereafter be known as the Virginia Aviation Board. The Board shall consist of eight members, selected so far as practicable from different geographic areas of the Commonwealth, appointed by the Governor, subject to confirmation by the General Assembly, to serve at the pleasure of the Governor. Members shall serve for four-year terms and no member shall serve for more than two full successive terms. Initial appointments to the Board shall be made as follows: one shall be for a term of one year, two shall be for terms of two years, two shall be for terms of three years, and two shall be for terms of four years each and thereafter all appointments shall be for terms of four years each. The Chairman of the Board shall be appointed by the Governor.

B. Whenever the Board shall acquire ownership or jurisdiction over an airport or airports previously operated by an agency of the United States, there may be a member appointed to the Board by the President of the United States. Such member shall have the powers and duties of other members of the Board only with respect to the airport or airports so acquired.

C. There may be a member of the Board from any county or city wherein the Board acquires or constructs an airport, to be elected by the governing body of the county or city and to serve at its pleasure. Such member shall have the powers and duties of other members of the Board only with respect to such airport. If the Board acquires an airport which was constructed by one political subdivision but is located in another, the political subdivision which constructed the airport, rather than the political subdivision in which it is located, shall be represented on the Board.

§5.1-2.2. Powers and duties of Board.

The Board shall exercise the following powers and duties:

1. Provide a means of citizen access to the Department;
2. Provide a means of publicizing the policies and programs of the Department in order to educate the public and elicit public support for Department activities;
3. Monitor the policies and activities of the Department and have the right of access to departmental information;
4. Advise the Governor and the Director on matters relating to the Commonwealth's aviation policies and programs;
5. Promulgate such rules and regulations relating to airports, landing fields and other aviation facilities, aircraft, air traffic, construction and inspection of aircraft, qualifications and licensing of airmen, stunt flying, and such other kindred matters and things as may be proper and necessary to promote and develop safe aviation practices and operations; and
6. Develop on behalf of the Department recommendations for distribution of funds to localities by the State Corporation Commission for aviation development through the end of the 1978–80 biennium, after which time the Board shall be responsible for the allocation on behalf of the Department of all such funds as provided in this act, which funds shall be distributed by the Department in accordance with such allocation.

§5.1-2.2:1. Further powers and duties of the Board.

The Board shall have all the powers necessary or convenient to carry out the purposes of this chapter including, but not limited to, the power:

1. To sue in its own name, to have a seal, and to have perpetual succession;
2. To execute such contracts and other instruments and take such other action as may be necessary or convenient to carry out the purposes of this chapter;
3. To plan, establish, develop, construct, enlarge, improve, maintain, equip, operate, regulate, and protect airports and air navigation facilities, within this Commonwealth and within any adjoining state, including the acquisition, construction, installation, equipment, maintenance, and operation at such airports of buildings and other facilities for the servicing of aircraft or for the comfort and accommodation of air travelers, and the purchase and sale of supplies, goods, and commodities as an incident to the operation of its airport properties. For such purposes the Board may, by purchase, gift, devise, lease, condemnation, or otherwise, acquire property, real or personal, or any interest therein, including easements in airport hazards or land outside the boundaries of an airport or airport site, as are necessary to permit the removal, elimination, obstruction marking or obstruction lighting of airport hazards or to prevent the establishment of airport hazards, or for the enlargement of an airport constructed or acquired under this subdivision 3; provided, however, such power of eminent domain shall not extend to the taking of any radio or television towers or installation in existence on June 27, 1958;
4. To acquire, by purchase, gift, devise, or lease, existing airports and air navigation facilities;
5. To establish or acquire and maintain airports in, over, and upon any public waters of this Commonwealth or any submerged lands under such public waters; and to construct and maintain terminal buildings, landing floats, causeways, roadways, and bridges for approaches to or connecting with any such airport, and landing floats and breakwaters for the protection thereof;
6. To construct, or permit the construction of, for sale or lease, on such terms and conditions as the Board may deem proper, industrial, commercial or recreational facilities and approaches thereto and appurtenances thereof, on any lands of the Board not acquired by eminent domain and not needed for operational use of an airport owned or operated by it; provided, that any such factory or manufacturing facility shall be so constructed as not to constitute an airport hazard. In the exercise of the powers conferred by this subdivision, the Board shall comply with any applicable zoning restrictions of the political subdivision in which any airport or facility is, or is proposed to be located.

§5.1-2.3. Meetings of Board; quorum.

The Board shall meet at least once every three months, and on the call of the Chairman, when in his opinion additional meetings are necessary. Four members of the Board shall constitute a quorum.

§5.1-4. Aircraft for use of Department; construction, etc., of aviation facilities by Department.

Within the limits of appropriations made for such purposes, the Department is authorized to purchase aircraft for the use of the Department, provided, however, that the Department shall not purchase any new or used executive aircraft unless specifically requested in the Governor's budget and approved by the General Assembly in the Appropriations Act, and to purchase land for and to construct, maintain and improve airports, landing fields and other aviation facilities within the Commonwealth for the promotion of aviation in the interest of the public; and neither the appropriations nor any part thereof may be transferred or used for any other purpose than is specified in this section.

§5.1-5. Licensing of aircraft.

(a) Every resident of this Commonwealth owning a civil aircraft, every nonresident owning a civil aircraft based in this Commonwealth over sixty days during any twelve-month period and every owner of an aerial application aircraft operating within this Commonwealth or of a civil aircraft operated in this Commonwealth as a for-hire intrastate air carrier shall, before the same is operated in this

Commonwealth, obtain from the Department an aircraft license for such aircraft.

(b) The Department shall provide for the issuance, expiration, suspension and revocation of licenses of aircraft in accordance with regulations promulgated by the Board. The Department shall furnish any necessary forms pursuant to the issuance of such licenses, and may assess a fee for such issuance not in excess of five dollars annually. The Department may in lieu of issuing aircraft licenses required by subsection (a) of this section, issue commercial aircraft licenses to air carriers and commercial dealers, and issue to noncommercial dealers noncommercial dealer fleet licenses, to cover all aircraft owned by such dealers and all aircraft for sale held by dealers on a consignment basis from an aircraft manufacturer. The Department may assess a fee not in excess of $50 annually for any such noncommercial dealer fleet licenses issued and a fee not in excess of $100 annually for any such commercial fleet licenses issued. The fee for a commercial single aircraft license shall not be in excess of ten dollars annually.

§5.1-7. Licensing of airports and landing areas.

Except as provided in §5.1-7.2, every person, before operating an airport or landing area or adding or extending a runway, shall first secure from the Department a license. The application therefor shall be made on the form prescribed and furnished by the Department and shall be accompanied by a fee not exceeding $100.

Such license shall be issued for a period not to exceed seven years, and shall be renewed every seven years. Before issuing such license, the Department shall require the holder of such license to furnish proof of financial responsibility prescribed in Chapter 8.2 of this title.

It shall be unlawful for any person to operate any airport or landing area which is open to the general public for the landing or departure of any aircraft until a license therefor shall be issued by the Department.

Before issuing such license for the establishment of a new airport, the Department shall investigate the location of such airport or landing area with the relation to its proximity to and its runway orientation in relation to any other airport or landing area and shall provide for the safety of civil aircraft alighting thereon or departing therefrom. If the proposed airport or landing area shall be so situated as to endanger aircraft using the same or any other airport or landing area in close proximity, and if proper provisions have not been made in all other respects for the safety of aircraft alighting thereon or departing therefrom, the license shall not be granted. To be licensed, an airport required to be licensed under §5.1-7.2 must meet this criterion and any applicable requirement provided for in regulation promulgated under this section, but no others.

The Board may, by regulation, adopt any other requirements for licensure that are related to the safety of civil aircraft using such airport or landing area. Any airport having a license issued prior to October 1, 1995, and not meeting one or more minimum standards as defined in Part III of the Virginia Aviation Regulations (VR 165-01-02:1), shall be exempt from having to comply with those noncomplying standards for as long as the airport remains an active public-use facility. Should such airport cease to be open to the public for one year, and subsequently reopen, it shall then be required to comply with all applicable minimum standards for licensure.

In addition to the above safety requirements, before a license is initially issued, the Department shall consider the reviews and comments of appropriate state agencies coordinated by the Department of Environmental Quality, and shall cause a public hearing to be held concerning the economic, social and environmental effects of the location or runway orientation of the airport or landing area if the facility is listed in the Virginia Air Transportation System Plan; however, such coordinated review by the Department of Environmental Quality shall not exceed ninety days after the Department has requested review by the Department of Environmental Quality. The public hearing required by this section shall be conducted by the Department of Environmental Quality in the jurisdiction in which the airport or landing area is located, after publication of notice of the hearing in a newspaper of general circulation in such jurisdiction at least ten days in advance of such hearing.

Any license issued shall describe the number of runways, the length and orientation of each runway and/or, if appropriate, the landing area.

If a runway is to be extended or new runways are to be added, a revised license shall be applied for from the Department. If the airport or landing area is listed in the Virginia Air Transportation System Plan, the Department shall consider the reviews and comments of appropriate state agencies, coordinated by the Department of Environmental Quality, and shall cause a public hearing to be held concerning the economic, social and environmental effects of such changes to the license.

Whenever a public hearing is called for herein, if there has been a public hearing associated with the development of any environmental documents to comply with the receipt of federal funds, the Department and the Department of Environmental Quality may rely on such document or hearing in carrying out their respective duties set out in this section.

If an airport or landing area cannot meet the requirements for licensure that have been adopted by the Virginia Aviation Board, or having met those requirements cannot maintain compliance, the Department may issue conditional licenses to allow time for the airport or landing areas to take steps to meet those requirements or may revoke any license issued, if requirements for licensure are not met or cannot be met.

Any party aggrieved by the granting or refusal to grant any such license shall have a right of appeal to the circuit court of the jurisdiction where the airport or landing area is to be located, which appeal shall be filed in accordance with the Administrative Process Act, Chapter 1.1:1 of Title 9 of the Code of Virginia.

All airports or landing areas that hold licenses or permits shall be issued new licenses, without charge, on or before October 1, 1995, describing the number, length and orientation of the runway or runways or, if appropriate, the landing area, which shall be valid for up to seven years. The length of the new license term may be staggered so that all licenses will not become renewable at the same time. If any airport landing area does not meet the current requirements for licensure, a new license may be issued.

(Chgd. by L.1995 chs. 682, 690; L.1996 chs. 148, 303, eff. 7/1/96.)

§5.1-7.2. Registration of private landing areas not within five miles of commercial airport.

Any person owning an area for landing any aircraft, which area is not within five miles of a commercial airport and has been constructed by such person for his private use and which is not open to the general public, shall only be required to register, upon forms furnished by the Department, such landing area with the Department and with the Federal Aviation Administration.

§5.1-9. Disposition of fees.

All fees or sums collected by the Department under the provisions of this chapter shall be paid into the special fund created by §5.1-51.

§5.1-9.1. Certain privately owned airports declared to be works of public improvement; exemption from local taxation authorized.

(a) Any public use privately owned airport in this Commonwealth, or any improvements made thereto, which is open to the public at no charge and which has been licensed by the Department is hereby declared to be a work of internal improvement.

(b) The governing body of any city, town or county in this Commonwealth is authorized to exempt from local taxation, as an inducement to their location, the runways and taxiways of any privately owned, public use airport, which is available to the public at no charge and which has been licensed by the Department.

§5.1-9.2. Contract carriers; permit and license required.

No person shall operate or engage in the business of a contract carrier by aircraft intrastate in the airspace of this Commonwealth unless such person has secured from the Department a permit authorizing him to conduct such operation or to engage in such business and has licensed under §5.1-5 all aircraft used in this Commonwealth.

§5.1-9.3. Same; application for permit; fee; action of Department.

Any person desiring a permit under this chapter shall file with the Department an application in the form prescribed by the Department with a fee of fifty dollars. Such application shall contain a promise of compliance by the applicant with the provisions of this title and with the lawful rules and regulations of the Department governing the operations of contract carriers by aircraft in the airspace of the Commonwealth. Such application may be filed with the Department by the applicant in person or transmitted by registered mail. Upon being satisfied that the provisions of this chapter and the lawful rules and regulations of the Department adopted pursuant hereto, which are prerequisite to the granting of a permit, have been complied with, the Department shall issue such permit to such applicant, subject to such terms, limitations and restrictions as the Department may deem proper, without further proceedings.

§5.1-9.5. Same; bonds, insurance or certificate of insurance required prior to issuance of license or permit; securities deposited in lieu thereof.

A. No license or permit shall be issued by the Department to any contract carrier by aircraft until and after such contract carrier has filed with the Department an insurance policy, a bond underwritten by an insurer, or certificate of insurance in lieu thereof, which certificate shall certify that such policy or bond covers the liability of such contract carrier in accordance with the provisions of this statute.

B. Such policy, bond or certificate of insurance shall be issued or underwritten only by an insurer approved or authorized to do business in Virginia, or by one who is eligible as a surplus lines insurer pursuant to Chapter 48 of Title 38.2, and shall be in amounts not less than the following minimum limits: liability for bodily injury to or death of any one person, passenger or other, aboard the aircraft; $75,000, liability for each occurrence in any one aircraft of at least an amount equal to the sum produced by multiplying $75,000 by seventy-five percent of the total number of passenger seats installed in the aircraft; and liability for loss or damage to cargo owned by others than the insured of at least $10,000 for each occurrence. However, the holder of a license or permit issued by the Department shall not be required to file any cargo insurance, bond, or bonds for cargo liability for the hauling of property transported under contract.

C. In no event shall the limits required herein for contract carriers be less than those prescribed for like carriers by the Civil Aeronautics Board or the Federal Aviation Administration or their successors.

D. In lieu of such policy, underwritten bond or certificate of insurance, a contract carrier may, with the consent of the Department, submit bonds, in an amount approved by the Department, of the United States of America, the Commonwealth of Virginia, or of any municipality of this Commonwealth as security for its bond. Such federal, state, or municipal bonds shall be deposited with the State Treasurer, and shall not be reduced in amount, pledged as security, or otherwise encumbered for any other purpose during the life of such license or permit, except with the prior written approval of the Department.

§5.1-9.6. Same; duration and custody of bonds, etc.

Insurance policies, bonds, certificates of insurance, or federal, state, or municipal bonds filed with the Department shall be kept in full force at all times. The policy, bond, or certificate of insurance shall remain in the custody of the Department six months after the insurance or bond has expired or has been cancelled for any cause. If federal, state, or municipal bonds are deposited with the State Treasurer as security, such bonds shall remain so deposited until six months after the authority for use of equipment insured has expired or is cancelled for any cause, unless otherwise ordered by the Department.

§5.1-9.7. Same; condition of bond, etc.

The insurance bond, or other security, shall obligate the insurer or surety to pay any final judgment for damages sustained by the passengers, shippers, or consignees for injury to any passenger or passengers, or for loss or damage to property entrusted to such contract carrier when a cargo policy is required, and for any and all injuries to persons and loss of, or damage to, property resulting from the negligent operation of any aircraft.

§5.1-9.8. Same; effect of failure to give or maintain adequate security.

Failure of any contract carrier holding a license or permit issued by and under the authority of the Department to comply with any of the provisions of §§5.1-9.5 through 5.1-9.7 shall be a Class 1 misdemeanor and punishable as such.

§5.1-9.9. Same; duration of permits; suspension or revocation; penalty.

A. Contract carrier permits issued pursuant to this chapter shall be effective from the date of issuance and shall remain in effect only so long as the contract carrier's insurance, underwritten bond or certificate of insurance required by §5.1-9.5 remains in full force and effect.

B. The Department may suspend or revoke such permit for violation of any of the aviation laws of this Commonwealth or of the United States of America, or for violation of any of the rules and regulations of the Virginia Aviation Board.

C. Willful misrepresentation of any material fact in obtaining a contract carrier permit shall be a Class 1 misdemeanor and punishable as such.

§5.1-11. Government-owned aircraft.

This article shall not apply to public aircraft owned by the United States but shall apply to all other public aircraft.

§5.1-12. Federally certificated airlines and interstate service.

This article shall not apply to any aircraft operated by any air carrier operating under Federal Aviation Regulation Part 121 or Part 135 if operating with an exemption from Title IV of the Federal Aviation Act to provide scheduled passenger service.

ARTICLE 2
ILLEGAL OPERATION, ETC.; PROCEDURE; PENALTIES
(Complete Article)

§5.1-13. Operation of aircraft while under influence of intoxicating liquors or drugs; reckless operation.

Any person who shall operate any aircraft within the airspace over, above or upon the lands or waters of this Commonwealth, while under the influence of intoxicating liquor or of any narcotic or any habit-forming drugs shall be guilty of a felony and shall be confined in a state correctional facility not less than one nor more than five years, or, in the discretion of the court or jury trying the case, be confined in jail not exceeding twelve months and fined not exceeding $500, or both such fine and imprisonment.

Any person who shall operate any aircraft within the airspace over, above or upon the lands or waters of this Commonwealth carelessly or heedlessly in willful or wanton disregard of the rights or safety of others, or without due caution and circumspection and in a manner so as to endanger any person or property, shall be guilty of a misdemeanor.

§5.1-14. Operation of unlicensed aircraft.

Any person who operates or causes to be operated any civil aircraft within the airspace over, above or upon the lands or waters of this Commonwealth, which aircraft has not been and is not at the time of such operation properly certificated under and in accordance with existing federal law and licensed under and in accordance with the existing laws of this Commonwealth and rules and regulations promulgated in pursuance thereof, shall be guilty of a misdemeanor.

§5.1-15. Operation of aircraft by unlicensed persons.

Any person who operates any civil aircraft within the airspace over, above, or upon the lands or waters of this Commonwealth, without being, at the time of such operation, in possession of a valid airman's certificate for such operation, issued under and in accordance with existing federal law shall be deemed to be guilty of a Class 1 misdemeanor.

§5.1-16. Tampering with, etc., airplanes or markings of airports, landing fields or other aeronautical facilities.

It shall be unlawful for any person to tamper with, alter, destroy, remove, carry away, or cause to be carried away, an airplane or other flying device or instrumentality or any objects used for the marking of airports, landing fields, drop zones or other aeronautical facilities, or in any way change their position or location, except by and under the direction of the proper authorities charged with the maintenance and operation of such facilities. Any person violating any of the provisions of this section or who shall illegally have in his possession any objects or devices used for such markings, shall be guilty of a misdemeanor.

§5.1-16.1. Misuse of licensed airports.

It shall be unlawful for any person or persons to use licensed airport runways, taxiways or ramp areas for other than aeronautical purposes without written approval of the controlling authority of such airport.

§5.1-17. Use of aircraft for hunting.

It shall be unlawful for any person to hunt, pursue or kill any wild waterfowl or other birds or animals by any means whatever during such time as such person is in flight in an aircraft in the airspace over the lands or waters of this Commonwealth. A violation of this section shall be deemed a misdemeanor.

§5.1-20. Pilot may restrain or arrest person interfering with operation of aircraft carrying passengers for hire.

The pilot of any aircraft carrying passengers for hire, or any person subject to his direction, may take such action as is reasonably necessary to restrain or arrest any person who interferes with, or threatens to interfere with, the operation of the aircraft in flight over the territory of this Commonwealth or to a destination within this Commonwealth.

§5.1-21. Powers of conservator of the peace conferred upon pilot.

The pilot of any aircraft carrying passengers for hire while actively engaged in the operation of such aircraft shall be a special policeman and have all the powers of a conservator of the peace in the enforcement of order on such aircraft and while in pursuit of persons for disorder upon such aircraft and until such persons as may be arrested by him shall have been placed in confinement or delivered to the custody of some other conservator of the peace or police officer.

§5.1-21.1. Powers of conservators of the peace conferred upon airport managers or designees.

The airport manager of any licensed Virginia airport or in his absence not more than two employees who are designated by him shall be special policemen and have all the powers of conservators of the peace in the enforcement of this title and its regulations as promulgated by the Board. Persons arrested by them shall be placed in confinement or delivered to the custody of some other conservator of the peace or police officer.

§5.1-22. Interference with operation of aircraft; penalties; venue.

Any person who interferes with or threatens to interfere with the operation of any aircraft on or over the territory of this Commonwealth shall be guilty of a Class 1 misdemeanor. Where the act or acts of interference or threatened interference are of such a nature as to endanger the life of the aircraft's operator or the life of any other person, the person interfering or threatening to interfere shall be guilty of a Class 6 felony. Venue for the issuance of a warrant for the arrest and trial of any such person is hereby conferred upon any court having criminal jurisdiction in the political subdivision in this Commonwealth where the aircraft either took off prior to such offense, or where it lands or comes to rest subsequent to such offense, or in or over which the offense occurred.

§5.1-23. Jurisdiction of local and State Police.

The local police authorities of any city, incorporated town or county shall have jurisdiction on the premises of any airport, drop zone or landing field operated hereunder, either individually or jointly and the State Police shall have jurisdiction to investigate any aircraft accident. In the exercise of such jurisdiction the State Police and officers of the department of law enforcement of any city or county with an optional form of government may enter with immunity and without a warrant upon private property for the purpose of conducting such investigations. This section shall not repeal the provisions of any city charter in conflict herewith.

§5.1-24. Penalties.

Any person violating any of the provisions of this chapter, or violating any of the rules or regulations promulgated pursuant thereto by the Board, except as otherwise specifically provided, shall be deemed guilty of a misdemeanor and upon conviction shall be punished by a fine of not more than $100 or imprisonment in jail not exceeding one month, or both, in the discretion of the judge or jury trying the case; provided, that any person (excepting any government, political subdivision of the Commonwealth, or governmental subdivision or agency) establishing or operating an airport without first obtaining a permit as provided in §5.1-8 shall, upon conviction, be fined not less than $100 nor more than $500 for each offense, and each day that the airport is operated without such permit shall be construed as a separate offense.

§5.1-25. Operation of aircraft by nonresident.

A nonresident of this Commonwealth may operate aircraft engaged in operations other than for hire or reward in accordance with regulations promulgated by the Board, provided such nonresident and the aircraft to be so operated shall have been certified under federal law and shall have complied with the laws of the state in which such nonresident resides relative to aircraft and the operation thereof. A nonresident-owned aircraft engaged in intrastate operation for hire or reward must be licensed with the Department in accordance with this title and the Board's regulations.

ARTICLE 3
STRUCTURES DANGEROUS TO AIRCRAFT
(Complete Article)

§5.1-25.1. Permit required for erection of certain structures.

It shall be unlawful for any person to erect any structure, any part of which penetrates into or through any licensed airport's or United States government or military air facility's clear zone, approach zone, imaginary surface, obstruction clearance surface, obstruction clearance zone, or surface or zone as described in regulations of the Department of Aviation or the Federal Aviation Administration, without securing a permit for its erection from the Board. This section shall not apply to any structure to be erected in a county, city or town which has an ordinance regulating the height of such structures to prevent the penetration of zones and surfaces provided for in Federal Aviation Regulation Part 77 and Rule 19 of the Department of Aviation.

For the purpose of this section, "structure" shall mean any object, including a mobile object, constructed or erected by man, including but not limited to buildings, towers, cranes, smokestacks, earth formations, overhead transmission lines, flag poles, and ship masts.

§5.1-25.2. Application for permit; notice and hearing.

Any person desiring to erect or cause to be erected any such structure shall make application to the Department for the issuance of a permit for such erection. Such application shall be forwarded immediately to the Board. The Department shall undertake an appropriate review of such application and submit its contents in writing to the Board as expeditiously as possible. The Board, after such notice to the public as it deems necessary, shall hold a public hearing not less than thirty days after the giving of such notice at which all interested parties shall be admitted to attend and state any objection which they may have to the erection of such structure.

§5.1-25.3. When permit issued or denied; conditions to issuance.

The Board, if it finds that the erection of such structure will not be dangerous to aircraft using the airways of this Commission, shall issue the permit requested; but if it shall find that the erection of such structure will create a hazard to aircraft using such airways, it shall refuse the issuance of such a permit. The Board may, as a condition to the issuance of any permit, require the installation and maintenance of warning lights and any other devices which may be reasonably required to reduce the hazard which might be presented by the erection of such structure.

§5.1-25.4. Injunctions.

If any person commences the erection of a structure of the nature described in §5.1-25.1 without securing the permit therein required, the Department shall have power to apply forthwith to the circuit court of the jurisdiction in which the structure is located or is to be located, for injunctive relief.

CHAPTER 9
AIR CARRIERS
(Selected Articles)

(For other carriers see Title 46.2, Subtitle V, Motor Carriers.)

ARTICLE 1
IN GENERAL
(Complete Article)

 Zv

§5.1-89. Definitions.

Whenever used in this chapter unless expressly stated otherwise:

(a) The term "person" means any individual, firm, copartnership, corporation, company, association or joint-stock association, and includes any trustee, receiver, assignee, or personal representative thereof.

(b) The term "aircraft" means any contrivance, except a contrivance operating twenty-four inches or less above ground or water level, now known or hereafter invented, used, or designed for navigation of, or flight in, the airspace in the transportation of passengers, property or mail.

(c) The term "common carrier by aircraft" means any person who undertakes, whether directly or by a lease or any other arrangement, to transport passengers, property for the general public, or mail by aircraft for compensation (wholly within the airspace of the Commonwealth), whether over regular or irregular routes, including such aircraft operations of carriers by rail, water or motor vehicle and of express or forwarding companies.

(d) The term "restricted common carrier by aircraft" means any person who undertakes, whether directly or by lease or other arrangement, to transport passengers or property of any restricted class or classes by aircraft for compensation whether over regular or irregular routes.

(e) *(Repealed.)*

(f) The term "air carrier" includes a common carrier by aircraft, a restricted common carrier by aircraft, and a contract carrier by aircraft.

(g) The term "broker" means any person not included in the term air carrier and not a bona fide employee or agent of any such carrier, who, as principal or agent, sells or offers for sale any transportation subject to this chapter, or negotiates for, or holds himself out by solicitation, advertisement, or otherwise as one who sells, provides, furnishes, contracts, or arranges for such transportation.

(h) The "services" and "transportation" to which this chapter applies include all aircraft operated by, for, or in the interest of, any air carrier irrespective of ownership or contract, express or implied, together with all facilities and property operated or controlled by any such carrier or carriers and used in the transportation of passengers, property or mail or in the performance of any service in connection therewith.

(i) The term "certificate" means a certificate of public convenience and necessity issued by the State Corporation Commission to common carriers by aircraft and restricted common carriers by aircraft under this chapter.

(j) *(Repealed.)*

(k) The term "airport" means a landing area used regularly by aircraft for receiving or discharging passengers or cargo, and open to the public for use.

(*l*) The term "landing area" means any locality, either of land or water, including airports and intermediate landing fields, which is used, or intended to be used, for the landing and takeoff of aircraft, whether or not facilities are provided for the shelter, servicing, or repair of aircraft, or for receiving or discharging passengers or cargo, and open to the public for such use.

(m) The term "airspace" means all airspace above the lands and waters within the boundary of this Commonwealth.

(n) For the purposes of this chapter, "Commission" means the State Corporation Commission.

§5.1-90. Exempted aircraft.

This chapter shall not be construed to cover or include aircraft used exclusively in transporting or handling United States mail, or aircraft while used exclusively in interstate commerce; provided, however, that any common carrier of passengers by airplane holding proper authority for and operating in interstate commerce on January 1, 1970, in the transportation of passengers between any licensed airport adjacent to or within three miles of the Virginia State Line on the one hand and any other licensed airport in Virginia on the other, shall, without further proceedings, be issued a certificate by the Commission authorizing such operations as a common carrier of passengers by aircraft in intrastate commerce if application is made to the Commission within 120 days after this section takes effect. Pending the determination of any such application, the continuance of such operation without a certificate shall be lawful.

§5.1-90.1. Incidental transportation of certain passengers and property by motor vehicle.

Nothing in this chapter or in Chapter 12 (§56-273 et seq.) of Title 56 shall be construed to prohibit the transportation of property or guards or other attendants of such property by motor vehicle when such transportation is incidental to transportation by aircraft, provided that such transportation shall not exceed twenty-five miles from airport to destination of such guards or other attendants or property.

§5.1-91. Air carriers to comply with chapter; subject to regulation by Commission.

No air carrier shall operate any aircraft for the transportation of passengers or property for compensation in the airspace of this Commonwealth except in accordance with the provisions of this chapter, and every such air carrier is hereby declared to be subject to control, supervision and regulation by the Commission.

§5.1-92. Regulation by Commission; reports; prevention of discrimination.

The Commission shall supervise, regulate and control all air carriers, doing business in this Commonwealth, in all matters relating to the performance of their public duties and their charges therefor, and shall correct abuses therein by such air carriers; and to that end the Commission shall, from time to time, prescribe reasonable rules, regulations, forms and reports for such air carriers in furtherance of the administration and operation of this chapter; and the Commission shall have the right at all times to require from such air carriers special reports and statements under oath, concerning their business.

The Commission shall, from time to time, make and enforce such requirements, rules and regulations as may be necessary to prevent unjust and unreasonable discriminations by any air carrier in favor of, or against, any person, locality, community or connecting carrier in the matter of service, schedule, efficiency of transportation or otherwise, in connection with the public duties of such air carriers; and the Commission shall administer and enforce all provisions of this chapter, and prescribe reasonable rules, regulations and procedure looking to that end.

§5.1-93. Regulation of brokers.

The Commission shall also regulate brokers and make and enforce reasonable requirements respecting their licenses, financial responsibility, accounts, records, reports, operations and practices.

ARTICLE 2
ISSUANCE OF CERTIFICATES OF CONVENIENCE AND RIGHTS THEREUNDER

(Complete Article)

§5.1-94. Required certificate of public convenience and necessity.

No common carrier by aircraft or restricted common carrier by aircraft (not herein exempted) shall engage in intrastate operation in the airspace of this State without first having obtained from the Commission a certificate of public convenience and necessity authorizing such operation.

§5.1-95. Application for certificate; notices, etc.

The Commission shall prescribe the form of the application for a certificate of convenience and necessity, and such reasonable requirements as to notices, publication, proof of service and information as may in its judgment be necessary.

§5.1-96. Fees in connection with certificates.

Every air carrier, upon filing with the Commission an application for a certificate, shall deposit with the Commission as a filing fee the sum of $100, and for the transfer of such certificate the sum of $100, and for the issuance of a duplicate certificate the sum of $5; provided, however, that an applicant for a certificate in lieu of an existing certificate, as provided by law, shall not be required to pay the fees prescribed in this section.

§5.1-97. Hearing on application; action of Commission.

Upon the filing of an application for a certificate of public convenience and necessity, the Commission shall, within a reasonable time, fix a time and place of hearing on such application. If the Commission shall find that the proposed operation justified it, it shall issue a certificate to the applicant, subject to such terms, limitations and restrictions as the Commission may deem proper. If the Commission shall find the proposed operation not justified, the application shall be denied.

§5.1-98. Factors to be considered by the Commission in granting certificates.

In granting certificates of public convenience and necessity pursuant to §5.1-94, the Commission shall take into consideration, among other things, the business experience of the particular passenger air carrier in the field of air operations, the financial stability of the carrier, the insurance coverage of the carrier, the type of aircraft which the carrier would employ, proposed routes and minimum schedules to be established, whether the carrier could economically give adequate service to the communities involved, the need for the service, and any other factors which may affect the public interest.

§5.1-99. Occasional deviations from authorized routes; emergency landings.

A common carrier by aircraft, or a restricted common carrier by aircraft, operating under a certificate issued by the Commission may occasionally deviate from the route over which it is authorized to operate under the certificate, under such general or special rules and regulations as the Commission may prescribe.

No air carrier shall be deemed to have violated any term, condition, or limitation of its certificate by landing or taking off during an emergency at a point not named in its certificate or by operating in an emergency, under regulations which may be prescribed by the Commission, between terminal and intermediate points other than those specified in its certificate.

§5.1-100. Transportation of baggage, mail, etc., with passengers.

A certificate for the transportation of passengers may include, when so authorized by the Commission, authority to transport, in the same aircraft with passengers, the baggage of such passengers, newspapers, express parcels, or United States mail when the transportation thereof is authorized by the government of the United States of America; provided that the total weight of the aircraft and its contents shall not exceed that weight authorized by the "Operations Record" of the individual aircraft.

§5.1-101. Chartered parties covered by common carriers.

Any common carrier by aircraft transporting passengers under a certificate issued by the Commission may operate to any place special or chartered parties, under such reasonable rules and regulations as the Commission may prescribe.

§5.1-102. Schedule changes require Commission approval.

A common carrier by aircraft or a restricted common carrier by aircraft operation under a certificate issued by the Commission shall not make any change in schedules or service without having first received the approval of the Commission for such change in schedules or service.

ARTICLE 5
REGULATION OF BROKERS
(Complete Article)

Section

§5.1-108. When broker's license required.

No person shall for compensation sell or offer for sale transportation subject to this chapter or shall make any contract, agreement, or arrangement to provide, procure, furnish, or arrange for such transportation or shall hold himself or itself out by advertisement, solicitation, or otherwise as one who sells, provides, procures, contracts, or arranges for such transportation, unless such person holds a broker's license issued by the Commission to engage in such transactions; provided that the provisions of this section shall not apply to any carrier holding a certificate or permit under the provisions of this chapter or to any bona fide employee or agent of such carrier so far as concerns transportation to be furnished wholly by such carrier or jointly with other air carriers holding like certificates or permits, or with a common carrier by railroad, motor vehicle, express or water; nor shall they apply to any air carrier not engaged in intrastate operations or to any bona fide employee of such carrier.

§5.1-109. Application for broker's license.

The Commission shall prescribe the form of application for a broker's license and such reasonable requirements and information as may in its judgment be necessary, and may assess a fee of ten dollars for filing.

§5.1-110. Hearing on such application and action thereon.

Upon the filing of an application for a broker's license the Commission may fix a time and place for the hearing of the application and require such notices, publication, or other service as may, in its judgment, be necessary. If the Commission finds the application proper and in the public interest it shall issue a license, subject to such terms, limitations and restrictions as the Commission may deem proper.

§5.1-111. Authority over brokers; bond.

The Commission shall have the same authority over persons operating under and holding a brokerage license as it has over air carriers under this chapter and shall require a broker to furnish bond or other security approved by the Commission and sufficient for the protection of travelers or shippers by aircraft.

§5.1-112. Broker's license not substitute for other certificates or permits required.

No person who holds a broker's license under this chapter shall engage in transportation subject to this chapter unless he holds a certificate or permit as provided in this chapter. In the execution of any contract, agreement, or arrangement to sell, provide, procure, furnish, or arrange for such transportation, it shall be unlawful for such person to employ any aircraft which is not the lawful holder of an effective certificate or permit issued as provided in this chapter.

ARTICLE 6
DURATION, REVOCATION, TRANSFER AND VALUE OF CERTIFICATES, ETC.; PENALTIES
(Complete Article)

§5.1-113. Duration of certificates, etc.; suspension, revocation, or amendment; penalties.

Certificates, permits and licenses issued under the provisions of this chapter shall be effective from the dates specified therein and shall remain in effect until terminated as herein provided. The Commission may at any time, by its order duly entered after hearing held after notice to the holder of any such certificate, permit or license and an opportunity to such holder to be heard at which it shall be proved that such holder has willfully made any misrepresentation of a material fact in obtaining such certificate, permit or license, or has willfully violated or refused to observe the laws of this Commonwealth touching such certificate, permit or license, or any of the terms of his certificate, permit or license, or any of the Commission's proper orders, rules or regulations, impose a penalty not exceeding $1,000, which may be collected by the process of the Commission as provided by law; or the Commission may suspend, revoke, alter or amend any such certificate, permit or license for any of the causes set forth above. But no such certificate, permit or license shall be revoked, altered or amended (except upon application of the holder thereof) unless the holder thereof shall willfully fail to comply, within a reasonable time to be fixed by the Commission, with the lawful order of the Commission or with the lawful rule or regulation of the Commission, or with the term, condition or limitation of such certificate, permit or license, found by the Commission to have been violated by such holder.

Proceedings for the imposition of any penalty provided for in this section may be commenced upon the complaint of any person or upon the Commission's own initiative.

From any order of the Commission suspending, revoking, altering or amending any certificate, permit or license, the holder thereof shall have the right of appeal to the Supreme Court of Virginia, as a matter of right, as in other cases of appeals from the Commission.

§5.1-114. Transfer or lease of certificate.

Any certificate issued under this chapter may be transferred or leased, subject to the approval of the Commission and under such reasonable rules and regulations as may be prescribed by the Commission. An application for such approval shall be made jointly by the transferor and transferee, or lessor and lessee.

No certificate shall be transferred, leased or otherwise disposed of when any consideration is paid or promised which exceeds the then value of the tangible property sold in connection with the transfer or lease of such certificate.

§5.1-115. No value allowed for certificates.

No value shall be allowed for any purpose for any certificate issued under this chapter.

ARTICLE 7
BONDS OR INSURANCE
(Complete Article)

§5.1-116. Bonds, insurance or certificate of insurance required prior to issuance of certificate or permit.

No certificate or permit shall be issued by the Commission to any air carrier until and after such air carrier shall have filed with, and the same has been approved by, the Commission, an insurance policy, bond or certificate of insurance in lieu thereof, certifying that such policy or bond covers the liability of such air carrier in accordance with the provisions of this article, issued by an insurance company or association or other insurer authorized to transact business in this Commonwealth, or bonds, to an amount approved by the Commission, of the Commonwealth of Virginia, of the United States of America, or of any municipality in this Commonwealth. Such state, federal, or municipal bonds shall be deposited with the State Treasurer, and such surety shall not be reduced during the life of such certificate or permit, except in accordance with an order of the Commission.

§5.1-117. Bonds or insurance to be kept in force.

Each holder of a certificate or permit issued by the Commission shall also keep in force at all times insurance or a bond underwritten by an insurer approved or authorized to do business in Virginia, or by one who is eligible as a surplus lines insurer in accordance with the provisions of Chapter 48 of Title 38.2 in amounts of not less than the following minimum limits: (a) liability for bodily injury to or death to any one person, passenger or other, aboard the aircraft, $75,000; and a limit for each occurrence in any one aircraft of at least an amount equal to the sum produced by multiplying $75,000 by seventy-five percent of the total number of passenger seats installed in the aircraft; and for the loss or damage to cargo owned by other than the insured, at least

$10,000 for each occurrence; provided, however, that a holder of a permit issued by the Commission shall not be required to file any cargo insurance, bond or bonds for cargo liability for the hauling of property transported under contract. However, in no event shall the limits required herein for air common carriers be less than those prescribed for like carriers by the Civil Aeronautics Board or the Federal Aviation Administration.

§5.1-118. Policies, bonds or certificates to be filed with Commission; securities deposited in lieu thereof.

Each holder of a certificate or permit issued by the Commission shall keep on file with the Commission an insurance policy, bond or certificate of insurance in lieu thereof, certifying that such policy or bond covers the liability of such air carrier in accordance with the provisions of this article, issued by an insurance company or association or other insurer authorized to transact business in this Commonwealth, and such insurance, bond or certificate of insurance filed with the Commission shall be kept in full force at all times. The policy, bond or certificate of insurance shall remain in the files of the Commission six months after the insurance or bond has expired or has been cancelled for any cause. If federal, state or municipal bonds are deposited with the State Treasurer in lieu thereof, such bonds shall remain so deposited until six months after the authority for use of equipment insured has expired or is cancelled for any cause, unless otherwise ordered by the Commission.

§5.1-119. Condition of bond, etc.

The insurance bond, or other security, shall obligate the insurer or surety to pay any final judgment for damages sustained by the passengers, shippers, or consignees for injury to any passenger or passengers, or for loss or damage to property entrusted to such air carrier when a cargo policy is required, and for any and all injuries to persons and loss of, or damage to, property resulting from the negligent operation of any aircraft.

§5.1-120. Effect of failure to give security.

Failure of any holder of a certificate or permit issued by and under the authority of the Commission to comply with any of the requirements of §§5.1-116, 5.1-117 or 5.1-118 shall be cause without further proceedings for the revocation or suspension of the certificate or permit, and upon further proceedings for the imposition of a fine not exceeding $1,000.

ARTICLE 8
THROUGH ROUTES, SERVICE, RATES, ETC.
(Selected Sections)

Section

§5.1-121. Duties of carriers of passengers as to through routes, equipment, rates, regulations, etc.

Every common carrier or restricted common carrier of passengers by aircraft shall establish reasonable through routes with other such common carriers and provide safe and adequate service, equipment, and facilities for the transportation of passengers; shall establish, observe, and enforce just and reasonable individual and joint rates, fares and charges and just and reasonable regulations and practices relating thereto, and to the issuance, form, and substance of tickets, the carrying of personal, sample, and excess baggage, the facilities for transportation, and all other matters relating to or connected with the transportation of passengers; and in case of such joint rates, fares, and charges shall establish just, reasonable and equitable divisions thereof as between the carriers participating therein which shall not unduly prefer or prejudice any of such participating carriers.

§5.1-122. Duties of carriers of property as to service, rates and regulations.

Every common carrier or restricted common carrier of property by aircraft shall provide safe and adequate service, equipment, and facilities for the transportation of property; and shall establish, observe, and enforce just and reasonable rates, charges, and classifications, and just and reasonable regulations and practices relating thereto and to the manner and method of presenting, marking, packing, and delivering property for transportation, the facilities for transportation, and all other matters relating to or connected with the transportation of property.

§5.1-123. Through routes, joint rates, etc., not required may be established.

Common carriers or restricted common carriers of property by aircraft may establish reasonable routes and joint rates, charges, and classifications with other such carriers or with common carriers by railroad, motor vehicle, express and/or water; and common carriers or restricted common carriers of passengers by aircraft may establish reasonable through routes and joint rates, fares, or charges with common carriers by railroad, motor vehicle, and/or water. In case of such joint rates, fares or charges it shall be the duty of the carriers parties thereto to establish just and reasonable regulations and practices in connection therewith, and just, reasonable and equitable divisions thereof as between the carriers participating therein which shall not unduly prefer or prejudice any of such participating carriers.

§5.1-124. Undue preference not permitted.

It shall be unlawful for any common carrier or restricted common carrier by aircraft to make, give, or cause any undue or unreasonable preference or advantage to any particular person, port, gateway, locality, or description of traffic in any respect whatsoever, or to subject any particular person, port, gateway, locality, or description of traffic to any unjust discrimination or any undue or unreasonable prejudice or disadvantage in any respect whatsoever; provided, however, that this section shall not be construed to apply to discriminations, prejudices or disadvantages to the traffic of any other carrier of whatever description.

§5.1-125. Complaints; action of Commission thereon or on own initiative.

Any person, state board, organization, or body politic may make complaint in writing to the Commission that any rate, fare, charge, classification, rule, regulation, or practice of any common carrier or restricted common carrier by aircraft, in effect or proposed to be put into effect, is or will be in violation of §§5.1-121 to 5.1-124, or §5.1-133. Whenever after hearing, upon complaint or in an investigation on its own initiative, the Commission shall be of the opinion that any individual or joint rate, fare, or charge, demanded, charged, or collected by any common carrier or restricted common carrier by aircraft or by any common or restricted common carrier by aircraft in conjunction with any common carrier by railroad, motor vehicle, express and/or water, or any classification, rule, regulation or practice whatsoever of such carrier affecting such rate, fare, or charge or the value of the service thereunder, is or will be unjust or unreasonable or unjustly discriminatory or unduly preferential or unduly prejudicial, it shall determine and prescribe the lawful rate, fare, or charge or the maximum or minimum rate, fare, or charge thereafter to be observed, or the lawful classification, rule, regulation, or practice thereafter to be made effective.

§5.1-126. Establishment of through routes, etc., by Commission.

The Commission shall, whenever deemed by it to be necessary or desirable in the public interest, after hearing, upon complaint or upon its own initiative without a complaint, establish through routes, and joint rates, fares, charges, regulations, or practices, applicable to the transportation of passengers by common or restricted common carriers by aircraft, or the maximum or minimum to be charged, and the terms and conditions under which such through routes shall be operated.

§5.1-132. Tariffs showing rates, fares and charges, etc.

Every common carrier and restricted common carrier by aircraft shall file with the Commission, and print, and keep open to public inspection, tariffs showing all the rates, fares and charges for transportation, and all services in connection therewith, of passengers or property between points on its own route and between points on its own route and points on the route of any other such carrier, or on the route of any common carrier by railroad, motor vehicle, express and/or water, when a through route and joint rate shall have been established. Such rates, fares, and charges shall be stated in terms of lawful money of the United States. The tariffs required by this section shall be published, filed, and posted in such form and manner, and shall contain such information, as the Commission by regulations shall prescribe; and the Commission is authorized to reject any tariff filed with it which is not in consonance with this section and with such regulations. Any tariff so rejected by the Commission shall be void and its use shall be unlawful.

§5.1-133. Unlawful to charge other than published tariff.

No common carrier or restricted common carrier by aircraft shall charge or demand or collect or receive a greater or less or different compensation for transportation or for any service in connection therewith between the points enumerated in such tariff than the rates, fares, and charges specified in the tariff in effect at the time; and no such carrier shall refund or remit in any manner or by any device, directly or indirectly, or through any agent or broker or otherwise, any portion of the rates, fares, or charges so specified, or extend to any person any privileges or facilities for transportation except such as specified in its tariffs.

§5.1-134. Changes in tariffs, etc.

No change shall be made in any rate, fare, charge, or classification, or any rule, regulation, or practice affecting such rate, fare, charge, or classification, or the value of the service thereunder, specified in any effective tariff of a common carrier or restricted common carrier by aircraft, except after thirty days' notice of the proposed change, filed and posted in accordance with §5.1-132. Such notice shall plainly state the change proposed to be made and the time when such change will take effect. The Commission may, in its discretion and for good cause shown, allow such change upon notice less than that herein specified or modify the requirements of this section and §5.1-132 with respect to posting and filing of tariffs either in particular instances or by general order applicable to special or peculiar circumstances or conditions.

§5.1-135. No transportation except when rates have been filed and published.

No common carrier or restricted common carrier by aircraft, unless otherwise provided by this chapter, shall engage in the transportation of passengers or property unless the rates, fares, and charges upon which the same are transported by such carrier have been filed and published in accordance with the provisions of this chapter.

§5.1-136. Free passes or reduced rates.

No air carrier subject to the provisions of this chapter shall, directly or indirectly, issue or give any free ticket, free pass or free transportation for passengers, but nothing in this section shall apply (1) to the carriage, storage or handling of property free or at reduced rates, when such rates have been authorized or prescribed by the Commission for the United States, state or municipal governments, or for charitable purposes or to or from fairs and expositions for exhibition thereat, or (2) to the free carriage of homeless and destitute persons and the necessary agents employed in such transportation, or (3) to mileage, excursion or commutation passenger tickets.

Nor shall anything in this section be construed to prohibit any air carrier from giving reduced rates or free passage to ministers of religion, or regular traveling secretaries of the Young Men's Christian Association or Young Women's Christian Association, whose duties require regular travel in supervising and directing Young Men's Christian or Young Women's Christian Association work, secretaries of duly organized religious work, or to indigent persons, or to inmates of the Confederate homes or State homes for disabled soldiers and sailors, or to disabled soldiers and sailors, including those about to enter, and those returning home after discharge; nor from giving free carriage to its own officers, employees, and members of their families, representatives of the press and members of the Department of State Police or to any other person or persons to whom the giving of such free carriage is not otherwise prohibited by the law; nor to prevent the principal officers of any air carrier from exchanging passes or tickets with other air carriers of any air, motor vehicle, steamship, or electric railway companies for their officers, employees and members of their families.

§5.1-137. Payment of rates and charges before delivery of freight.

No common carrier or restricted common carrier by aircraft shall deliver or relinquish possession at destination of any freight transported by it until all tariff rates and charges thereon have been paid, except under such rules and regulations as the Commission may from time to time prescribe to govern the settlement of all such rates and charges, including rules and regulations for weekly or monthly settlement, and to prevent unjust discrimination or undue preference or prejudice; provided, that the provisions of this section shall not be construed to prohibit any such carrier from extending credit in connection with rates and charges on freight transported for the United States, for any department, bureau, or agency thereof, or for any state or territory or political subdivision thereof, or for the District of Columbia.

ARTICLE 9
MISCELLANEOUS
(Selected Sections)

§5.1-140. Unlawful to disclose certain information.

It shall be unlawful for any air carrier or broker or any officer, receiver, trustee, lessee, agent, or employee of such carrier, broker, or person, or for any other person authorized by such carrier, broker, or person to receive information, knowingly to disclose to, or permit to be acquired by any person other than the shipper or consignee, without the consent of such shipper or consignee, any information concerning the nature, kind, quantity, destination, consignee, or routing of any property tendered or delivered to such air carrier or broker for such transportation, which information may be used to the detriment or prejudice of such shipper or consignee, or which may improperly disclose his business transactions to a competitor; and it shall also be unlawful for any person to solicit or receive knowingly any such information which may be so used.

Nothing in this chapter shall be construed to prevent the giving of such information in response to any legal process issued under the authority of any court, or to any officer or agent of the government of the United States or of any state, territory, or district thereof, in the exercise of his power, or to any officer or other duly authorized person seeking such information for the prosecution of persons charged with or suspected of crimes or to another carrier or broker, or its duly authorized agent, for the purpose of adjusting mutual traffic accounts in the ordinary course of business of such carriers or brokers.

§5.1-141. Waiting rooms and other public facilities.

All waiting rooms, rest rooms and other public facilities used by or in connection with aircraft carriers shall be kept in good and sanitary condition by the operators thereof, and the Commission shall have the right to inspect all such waiting rooms, rest rooms or other public facilities at any time, and after inspection may require such changes as the Commission may deem proper.

§5.1-143. Reports of accidents.

It shall be the duty of the manager, agent or other proper officer of every air carrier doing business or operating in this Commonwealth to make to the Commission such report or reports as may be required by it, under oath, of all accidents in this Commonwealth resulting in injury to persons, equipment, or property of any kind, under such rules and regulations as may be prescribed by the Commission.

§5.1-144. Certificate or permit holder not relieved of liability for negligence.

Nothing in this chapter shall relieve any holder of a certificate or permit by and under the authority of the Commission from any liability resulting from his negligence, whether or not he has complied with the requirements of this chapter.

§5.1-145. Enforcement under Department of State Police or Commission; concurrent jurisdiction for investigations of accidents.

The enforcement of any provision of this chapter requiring the use of police officers shall be under the Department of State Police or under the Commission; except the department of law enforcement of any city or county with an optional form of government shall have concurrent jurisdiction for the investigations of aircraft accidents occurring within such city or county.

§5.1-146. Violations and penalties.

(a) Any person knowingly and willfully violating any provision of this chapter, or any rule, regulation, requirement, or order thereunder for which a penalty is not otherwise herein provided, shall, after proper proceeding before the Commission, and upon conviction thereof, be fined not more than $100 for the first offense and not more than $500 for any subsequent offense. Each day of such violation shall constitute a separate offense.

(b) Any person, whether carrier, shipper, consignee, or broker, or any officer, employee, agent, or representative thereof, who shall knowingly offer, grant, or give, or solicit, accept, or receive any rebate, concession, or discrimination in violation of any provision of this chapter, or who, by means of any false statement or representation, or by the use of any false or fictitious bill, bill of lading, receipt, voucher, roll, account, claim, certificate, affidavit, deposition, lease, or bill of sale or by any other means or device, shall knowingly and willfully assist, suffer or permit any person, natural or artificial, to obtain transportation of passengers or property subject to this chapter for less than the applicable rate, fare, or charge, or who shall knowingly and willfully by any such means or otherwise fraudulently seek to evade or defeat regulation as in this chapter provided for air carriers or brokers, shall be deemed guilty of a misdemeanor and upon conviction thereof be fined not more than $500 for the first offense and not more than $2,000 for any subsequent offense.

(c) Any air carrier, or broker, or any officer, agent, employee, or representative thereof who shall willfully fail or refuse to make a report to the Commission as required by this chapter, or to keep accounts, records and memoranda in the form and manner approved or prescribed by the Commission, or shall knowingly and willfully falsify, destroy, mutilate, or alter any such report, account, record, or memorandum, or shall knowingly and willfully file any false report, account, record, or memorandum, shall, after proper proceeding before the Commission and upon conviction thereof, be subject for each offense to a fine of not less than $100 and not more than $5,000.

§5.1-147. Disposition of fees or sums collected.

All fees or sums collected by the Commission under the provisions of this chapter shall be deposited with the State Treasurer, and shall be set aside by him for the use of the Commission for the administration and enforcement of this chapter.

§5.1-148. Employees of Commission not to have interest in carriers.

No employee of the Commission appointed or employed in the administration of this chapter shall in any manner have any pecuniary interest in, own any securities of, or hold any position with any air carrier, motor carrier, railroad, steamboat or canal company.

§5.1-149. No property rights in airspace conferred by chapter.

Nothing in this chapter shall confer any proprietary or property rights in the use of the airspace of this Commonwealth.

§5.1-150. Licenses, taxes, etc., not affected.

Nothing in this chapter shall be construed to relieve any person from the payment of any licenses, fees, taxes or levies now or hereafter imposed by law.

§5.1-151. Right to amend, revoke, etc., rights, certificates or franchises.

The right and power of the General Assembly to amend, alter, revoke or repeal any and all rights, certificates, or franchises granted pursuant to the provisions of this chapter is hereby reserved.

TITLE 6.1
BANKING AND FINANCE
(Selected Chapters)

CHAPTER 2
BANKING ACT
(Selected Article)

ARTICLE 11
OFFENSES
(Selected Sections)

§6.1-111. Doing banking or trust business without authority; Commission may examine accounts, etc., of suspected person; penalty.

Every person, association or company who shall trade or deal as a bank or trust company, or carry on banking or do a trust business, without authority of law, and their officers and agents therein, shall be guilty of a Class 6 felony.

The Commission shall have authority to examine the accounts, books and papers of any person, copartnership or corporation who it has reason to suspect is doing a banking business, or a trust business, in order to ascertain whether such person, copartnership, or corporation has violated, or is violating, any provision of this title, and the refusal to submit such accounts, books and papers shall be prima facie evidence of such violation.

§6.1-112. Unlawful use of terms indicating that business is bank, trust company, etc.; penalty.

A. No person, entity or organization not authorized to engage in the banking business or trust business in this Commonwealth by the provisions of this title or under the laws of the United States shall (i) use any office sign having thereon any name or other words indicating that any such office is the office of a bank or trust company; (ii) use or circulate any letterheads, billheads, blank notes, blank receipts, certificates, circulars or any written or printed paper whatever, having thereon any name or word indicating that such person, entity or organization is a bank or trust company; or (iii) use the word "bank," "banking," "banker," or "trust" or the equivalent thereof in any foreign language, or the plural thereof in connection with any business other than a banking or trust business.

B. The foregoing prohibitions shall not apply to use by a bank holding company, as defined in §6.1-47, of the word "bank," "banks," "banking," "banker," "trust" or the equivalent thereof in its name, or of a name similar to that of a subsidiary bank of such bank holding company.

C. The use of the above-mentioned words in the name of, or in connection with, any other business shall not be prohibited if the context or remaining words show clearly and definitely that the business is not a bank or trust company, and is not carrying on a banking or trust business.

D. Any person, entity or organization violating the provisions of this section, either individually or as an interested party, shall be guilty of a Class 6 felony.

(Chgd. by L.2000 ch. 56, eff. 7/1/2000.)

§6.1-119. Making derogatory statements affecting banks.

Any person who willfully and maliciously makes, circulates or transmits to another, any statement, rumor or suggestion, written, printed or by word of mouth, which is directly or by reference derogatory to the financial condition or affects the solvency or financial standing of any bank or trust company doing business in this Commonwealth, or who counsels, aids, procures or induces another to start, transmit or circulate any such statement or rumor, shall be guilty of a misdemeanor and, upon conviction thereof, shall be sentenced to pay a fine of not more than $2,500 or to be confined in jail for not more than one year, or both.

§6.1-120. False certification of checks.

Whoever, being an officer, employee, agent or director of a bank, certifies a check drawn on such bank and willfully fails forthwith to charge the amount thereof against the account of the drawer thereof, or willfully certifies a check drawn on such bank when the drawer of such check has not on deposit with the bank the amount of money subject to the payment of such check and equivalent to the amount therein specified, shall be guilty of a misdemeanor.

§6.1-122. Embezzlement, fraud, false statements, etc. by officer, director, agent or employee of bank, trust company or trust subsidiary.

Any officer, director, agent or employee of any bank, trust company or trust subsidiary who embezzles, abstracts, or willfully misapplies any of the moneys, funds or credits of, or in the possession or control of such corporation, shall be guilty of larceny and punished as provided by law. Any officer, director, agent or employee of any bank, trust company or trust subsidiary who issues or puts forth any certificate of deposit, draws any order or bill of exchange, makes any acceptance, assigns any note, bond, draft, bill of exchange, mortgage, judgment, decree or other instrument in writing, or who makes any false entry in any book, report or statement of such bank, trust company or trust subsidiary with intent in any case to injure or defraud such corporation, or any other company, body politic or corporate, or any individual person, or to deceive any officer of such corporation, or the State Corporation Commission, or any agent or examiner authorized to examine the affairs of such corporation, and any person who, with like intent, aids or abets any such officer, director, agent or employee of such bank, trust company or trust subsidiary in any such violation, shall be guilty of a felony and upon conviction thereof shall be confined in a state correctional facility not less than one year or more than ten years, or be confined in jail not exceeding twelve months and fined not exceeding $5,000.

Any such officer who knowingly makes a false statement of the condition of any such bank or institution, shall be deemed guilty of a felony and upon conviction shall be fined not less than $100 nor more than $5,000, and be imprisoned in a state correctional facility not less than one nor more than ten years.

§6.1-123. Officers, directors, agents and employees violating or causing bank, trust company or trust subsidiary to violate laws; civil liability not affected.

Any officer, director, agent or employee of any bank, trust company or trust subsidiary who knowingly violates or who knowingly causes any bank, trust company or trust subsidiary to violate any provision of this chapter, or knowingly participates or knowingly acquiesces in any such violation, shall unless other punishment be provided for the offense of such officer, agent or employee, be guilty of a misdemeanor and be punished accordingly. The provisions of this section shall not affect the civil liability of any such officer, director, agent or employee.

§6.1-124. Receiving deposit knowing bank or broker to be insolvent.

Any officer or director of any bank and any private banker or broker or any employee of such bank, banker or broker, who shall take and receive, or permit to be received, a deposit from any person with the actual knowledge that the bank, banker or broker is at the time insolvent, shall be guilty of embezzlement, and shall be punished by a fine double the amount so received, and be confined in a state correctional facility not less than one nor more than three years, in the discretion of the jury, for each offense. On the trial of any indictment under this section it shall be the duty of any such bank, banker or broker, its agent or officers, to produce in court on demand of the attorney for the Commonwealth, all books and papers of such bank, banker or broker, to be read as evidence on the trial of such indictment; but in determining the question of the solvency of any bank, the capital stock thereof shall not be considered as a liability due by it.

§6.1-125. Penalties for violation of Commission's orders.

The Commission may impose, enter judgment for, and enforce by its process, a fine not in excess of $10,000 against any bank, trust company or trust subsidiary or against any of its directors, officers or employees for violating any lawful order of the Commission; and may remove from office any director or officer who a second time violates any such order; but in all cases the defendant shall have an opportunity to be heard and to introduce evidence, and the right to appeal as provided by law.

CHAPTER 3.01
VIRGINIA SAVINGS INSTITUTIONS ACT
(Selected Article)

ARTICLE 10
MISCELLANEOUS
(Selected Sections)

§6.1-194.93. False statement and similar actions prohibited.

Whoever knowingly makes or causes to be made, directly or indirectly, or through any agency whatsoever, any false statement or report, or willfully overvalues any land, property or security, for the purpose of influencing in any way the action of any savings institution upon any application, advance, discount, purchase or repurchase agreement, commitment, or loan or any change or extension of the same, by renewal, deferment of action or otherwise, or the acceptance, release or substitution of security therefor, shall be guilty of a Class 1 misdemeanor.

§6.1-194.94. Defamation of savings institutions and certain federal agencies prohibited.

Whoever willfully and knowingly makes, issues, circulates, transmits or causes or knowingly permits to be made, issued, circulated, or transmitted, any statement or rumor, written, printed, reproduced in any manner, or by word of mouth, which is untrue in fact and is (i) malicious, in that it is calculated to injure reputation or business, and (ii) derogatory to the financial condition or standing of any savings institution or Federal Home Loan Bank shall be guilty of a Class 2 misdemeanor.

CHAPTER 4.01
VIRGINIA CREDIT UNION ACT
(Selected Article)

ARTICLE 14
MISCELLANEOUS
(Selected Sections)

§6.1-225.62. Offenses.

Any officer, director, employee, receiver, or agent of a credit union who willfully does any of the following shall be guilty of a Class 6 felony:

1. With the intent to deceive, falsifies any book of account, report, statement, record, or other document of a credit union whether by alteration, false entry, omission, or otherwise;

2. Signs, issues, publishes, or transmits to a government agency any book of account, report, statement, record, or other document which he knows to be false;

3. By means of deceit, obtains a signature to a writing which is a subject of forgery;

4. With intent to deceive, destroys any credit union book of account, report, statement, record, or other document; or

5. With the intent to defraud, shares or receives directly or indirectly any money, property, or benefits through any transaction of the credit union.

§6.1-225.64. Making or circulating derogatory statements affecting credit unions.

Any person who willfully and maliciously makes, circulates, or transmits to another or others any statement or rumor, written, printed or by word of mouth, which is untrue in facts and is directly or by inference derogatory to the financial condition or affects the solvency or financial standing of any credit union doing business in this Commonwealth, or who knowingly counsels, aids, procures, or induces another to start, transmit, or circulate any such statement or rumor, shall be guilty of a Class 3 misdemeanor.

TITLE 8.01
CIVIL REMEDIES AND PROCEDURE
(Selected Chapters)

Chapter

CHAPTER 3
ACTIONS
(Selected Articles)

Article

ARTICLE 7
MOTOR VEHICLE ACCIDENTS
(Complete Article)

Section

§8.01-63. Liability for death or injury to guest in motor vehicle.

Any person transported by the owner or operator of any motor vehicle as a guest without payment for such transportation and any personal representative of any such guest so transported shall be entitled to recover damages against such owner or operator for death or injuries to the person or property of such guest resulting from the negligent operation of such motor vehicle. However, this statute does not limit any defense otherwise available to the owner or operator.

§8.01-64. Liability for negligence of minor.

Every owner of a motor vehicle causing or knowingly permitting a minor under the age of sixteen years who is not permitted under the provisions of §46.2-335 of this Code to drive such a vehicle upon a highway, and any person who gives or furnishes a motor vehicle to such minor, shall be jointly or severally liable with such minor for any damages caused by the negligence of such minor in driving such vehicle.

§8.01-65. Defense of lack of consent of owner.

It shall be a valid defense to any action brought for the negligent operation of a motor vehicle for the owner of such vehicle to prove that the same was being driven or used without his knowledge or consent, express or implied, but the burden of proof thereof shall be on such owner.

§8.01-66. Recovery of damages for loss of use of vehicle.

A. Whenever any person is entitled to recover for damage to or destruction of a motor vehicle, he shall, in addition to any other damages to which he may be legally entitled, be entitled to recover the reasonable cost which was actually incurred in hiring a comparable substitute vehicle for the period of time during which such person is deprived of the use of his motor vehicle. However, such rental period shall not exceed a reasonable period of time for such repairs to be made or if the original vehicle is a total loss, a reasonable time to purchase a new vehicle. Nothing herein contained shall relieve the claimant of the duty to mitigate damages.

B. Whenever any insurance company licensed in this Commonwealth to write insurance as defined in §38.2-124 or any self-insured company refuses or fails to provide a comparable temporary substitute vehicle to any person entitled to recover the actual cost of hiring a substitute vehicle as set forth in subsection A, and if the trial judge of a court of proper jurisdiction subsequently finds that such refusal or failure was not made in good faith, such company shall be liable to that person in the amount of $500 or double the amount of the rental cost he is entitled to recover under subsection A of this section, whichever amount is greater. If the trial court finds that an action brought against an insurance company or any self-insured company under subsection B of this section is frivolous, or not to have been brought in good faith, the court may in its discretion require the plaintiff to pay the reasonable attorney's fees, not to exceed $200, incurred by the defendant in defending the action. This section shall in no way preclude any party from seeking such additional common law remedies as might otherwise be available.

§8.01-66.1. Remedy for arbitrary refusal of motor vehicle insurance claim.

A. Whenever any insurance company licensed in this Commonwealth to write insurance as defined in §38.2-124 denies, refuses or fails to pay to its insured a claim of $2,500 or less in excess of the deductible, if any, under the provisions of a policy of motor vehicle insurance issued by such company to the insured and it is subsequently found by the judge of a court of proper jurisdiction that such denial, refusal or failure to pay was not made in good faith, the company shall be liable to the insured in an amount double the amount otherwise due and payable under the provisions of the insured's policy of motor vehicle insurance, together with reasonable attorney's fees and expenses.

The provisions of this subsection shall be construed to include an insurance company's refusal or failure to pay medical expenses to persons covered under the terms of any medical payments coverage extended under a policy of motor vehicle insurance, when the amount of the claim therefor is $2,500 or less and the refusal was not made in good faith.

B. Notwithstanding the provisions of subsection A, whenever any insurance company licensed in this Commonwealth to write insurance as defined in §38.2-124 denies, refuses or fails to pay to a third party claimant, on behalf of an insured to whom such company has issued a policy of motor vehicle liability insurance, a claim of $2,500 or less made by such third party claimant and if the judge of a court of proper jurisdiction finds that the insured is liable for the claim, the third party claimant shall have a cause of action against the insurance company. If the judge finds that such denial, refusal or failure to pay was not made in good faith, the company, in addition to the liability assumed by the company under the provisions of the insured's policy of motor vehicle liability insurance, shall be liable to the third party claimant in an amount double the amount of the judgment awarded the third party claimant, together with reasonable attorney's fees and expenses.

C. Notwithstanding the provisions of subsections A and B, whenever any person who has paid a fee to the Department of Motor Vehicles to register an uninsured motor vehicle pursuant to §46.2-706 or any person who has furnished proof of financial responsibility in lieu of obtaining a policy or policies of motor vehicle liability insurance pursuant to the provisions of Title 46.2 or any person who is required and has failed either to pay such fee or to furnish such proof pursuant to the provisions of Title 46.2 denies, refuses or fails to pay to a claimant a claim of $2,500 or less made by such claimant as a result of a motor vehicle accident; and if the trial judge of a court of proper jurisdiction finds that such denial, refusal or failure to pay was not made in good faith, such person shall be liable to the claimant in an amount double the amount otherwise due and payable together with reasonable attorney's fees and expenses.

For the purposes of this subsection C "person" shall mean and include any natural person, firm, partnership, association or corporation.

D. 1. Whenever a court of proper jurisdiction finds that an insurance company licensed in this Commonwealth to write insurance as defined in §38.2-124 denies, refuses or fails to pay to its insured a claim of more than $2,500 in excess of the deductible, if any, under the provisions of a policy of motor vehicle insurance issued by such company to the insured and it is subsequently found by the judge of a court of proper jurisdiction that such denial, refusal or failure to pay was not made in good faith, the company shall be liable to the insured in the amount otherwise due and payable under the provisions of the insured's policy of motor vehicle insurance, plus interest on the amount due at double the rate provided in §6.1-330.53 from the date that the claim was submitted to the insurer or its authorized agent, together with reasonable attorney's fees and expenses.

2. The provisions of this subsection shall be construed to include an insurance company's refusal or failure to pay medical expenses to persons covered under the terms of any medical payments coverage extended under a policy of motor vehicle insurance when the refusal was not made in good faith.

(Chgd. by L.1997 ch. 401, eff. 7/1/97.)

ARTICLE 21
MISCELLANEOUS PROVISIONS
(Selected Sections)

§8.01-225. Persons rendering emergency care, obstetrical services exempt from liability.

A. Any person who:

1. In good faith, renders emergency care or assistance, without compensation, to any ill or injured person at the scene of an accident, fire, or any life-threatening emergency, or en route therefrom to any hospital, medical clinic or doctor's office, shall not be liable for any civil damages for acts or omissions resulting from the rendering of such care or assistance.

2. In the absence of gross negligence, renders emergency obstetrical care or assistance to a female in active labor who has not previously been cared for in connection with the pregnancy by such person or by another professionally associated with such person and whose medical records are not reasonably available to such person shall not be liable for any civil damages for acts or omissions resulting from the rendering of such emergency care or assistance. The immunity herein granted shall apply only to the emergency medical care provided.

3. In good faith and without compensation, administers epinephrine to an individual for whom an insect sting treatment kit has been prescribed shall not be liable for any civil damages for ordinary negligence in acts or omissions resulting from the rendering of such treatment if he has reason to believe that the individual receiving the injection is suffering or is about to suffer a life-threatening anaphylactic reaction.

4. Provides assistance upon request of any police agency, fire department, rescue or emergency squad, or any governmental agency in the event of an accident or other emergency involving the use, handling, transportation, transmission or storage of liquefied petroleum gas, liquefied natural gas, hazardous material or hazardous waste as defined in §18.2-278.1 or regulations of the Virginia Waste Management Board shall not be liable for any civil damages resulting from any act of commission or omission on his part in the course of his rendering such assistance in good faith.

5. Is an emergency medical care attendant or technician possessing a valid certificate issued by authority of the State Board of Health who in good faith renders emergency care or assistance whether in person or by telephone or other means of communication, without compensation, to any injured or ill person, whether at the scene of an accident, fire or any other place, or while transporting such injured or ill person to, from or between any hospital, medical facility, medical clinic, doctor's office or other similar or related medical facility, shall not be liable for any civil damages for acts or omissions resulting from the rendering of such emergency care, treatment or assistance, including but in no way limited to acts or omissions which involve violations of State Department of Health regulations or any other state regulations in the rendering of such emergency care or assistance.

6. Has attended and successfully completed a course in cardiopulmonary resuscitation which has been approved by the State Board of Health who, in good faith and without compensation, renders or administers emergency cardiopulmonary resuscitation, cardiac defibrillation, including, but not limited to, the use of an automated external defibrillator, or other emergency life-sustaining or resuscitative treatments or procedures which have been approved by the State Board of Health to any sick or injured person, whether at the scene of a fire, an accident or any other place, or while transporting such person to or from any hospital, clinic, doctor's office or other medical facility, shall be deemed qualified to administer such emergency treatments and procedures, and shall not be liable for acts or omissions resulting from the rendering of such emergency resuscitative treatments or procedures.

7. In compliance with §32.1-111.14:1 registers an automated external defibrillator for use at the scene of an emergency, operates a registered automated external defibrillator at the scene of an emergency, trains individuals to be operators of registered automated external defibrillators, or orders automated external defibrillators which are subsequently registered, shall be immune from civil liability for any personal injury that results from any act or omission in the use of a registered automated external defibrillator in an emergency where the person performing the defibrillation acts as an ordinary, reasonably prudent person would have acted under the same or similar circumstances, unless such personal injury results from gross negligence or willful or wanton misconduct of the person rendering such emergency care.

8. Is a volunteer in good standing and certified to render emergency care by the National Ski Patrol System, Inc., who, in good faith and without compensation, renders emergency care or assistance to any injured or ill person, whether at the scene of a ski resort rescue, outdoor emergency rescue or any other place or while transporting such injured or ill person to a place accessible for transfer to any available emergency medical system unit, or any resort owner voluntarily providing a ski patroller employed by him to engage in rescue or recovery work at a resort not owned or operated by him, shall not be liable for any civil damages for acts or omissions resulting from the rendering of such emergency care, treatment or assistance, including but not limited to acts or omissions which involve violations of any state regulation or any standard of the National Ski Patrol System, Inc., in the rendering of such emergency care or assistance, unless such act or omission was the result of gross negligence or willful misconduct.

B. Any employee of a school board, authorized by a prescriber and trained in the administration of insulin and glucagon, who, upon the written request of the parents as defined in §22.1-1, assists with the administration of insulin or administers glucagon to a student diagnosed as having diabetes who requires insulin injections during the school day or for whom glucagon has been prescribed for the emergency treatment of hypoglycemia shall not be liable for any civil damages for ordinary negligence in acts or omissions resulting from the rendering of such treatment if the insulin is administered according to the child's medication schedule or such employee has reason to believe that the individual receiving the glucagon is suffering or is about to suffer life-threatening hypoglycemia. Whenever any employee of a school board is covered by the immunity granted herein, the school board employing him shall not be liable for any civil damages for ordinary negligence in acts or omissions resulting from the rendering of such insulin or glucagon treatment.

C. Any licensed physician serving without compensation as the operational medical director for a licensed emergency medical services agency in this Commonwealth shall not be liable for any civil damages for any act or omission resulting from the rendering of emergency medical services in good faith by the personnel of such licensed agency unless such act or omission was the result of such physician's gross negligence or willful misconduct.

Any person serving without compensation as a dispatcher for any licensed public or nonprofit emergency services agency in this Commonwealth shall not be liable for any civil damages for any act or omission resulting from the rendering of emergency services in good faith by the personnel of such licensed agency unless such act or omission was the result of such dispatcher's gross negligence or willful misconduct.

Any individual, certified by the State Office of Emergency Medical Services as an emergency medical services instructor and pursuant to a written agreement with such office, who, in good faith and in the performance of his duties, provides instruction to persons for certification or recertification as a certified basic life support or advanced life support emergency medical services technician shall not be liable for any civil damages for acts or omissions on his part directly relating to his activities on behalf of such office unless such act or omission was the result of such emergency medical services instructor's gross negligence or willful misconduct.

Any licensed physician serving without compensation as a medical advisor to an E–911 system in this Commonwealth shall not be liable for any civil damages for any act or omission resulting from rendering medical advice in good faith to establish protocols to be used by the personnel of the E–911 service, as defined in §58.1-3813.1, when answering emergency calls unless such act or omission was the result of such physician's gross negligence or willful misconduct.

Any licensed physician who directs the provision of emergency medical services, as authorized by the State Board of Health, through a communications device shall not be liable for any civil damages for any act or omission resulting from the rendering of such emergency medical services unless such act or omission was the result of such physician's gross negligence or willful misconduct.

Any licensed physician serving without compensation as a supervisor of a registered automated external defibrillator in this Commonwealth shall not be liable for any civil damages for any act or omission resulting from rendering medical advice in good faith to the registrant of the automated external defibrillator relating to personnel training, local emergency medical services coordination, protocol approval, automated external defibrillator deployment strategies, and equipment maintenance plans and records unless such act or omission was the result of such physician's gross negligence or willful misconduct.

D. Any provider of telecommunication service, as defined in §58.1-3812, including mobile service, in this Commonwealth shall not be liable for any civil damages for any act or omission resulting from rendering such service with or without charge related to emergency calls unless such act or omission was the result of such service provider's gross negligence or willful misconduct.

Any volunteer engaging in rescue or recovery work at a mine or any mine operator voluntarily providing personnel to engage in rescue or recovery work at a mine not owned or operated by such operator, shall not be liable for civil damages for acts or omissions resulting from the rendering of such rescue or recovery work in good faith unless such act or omission was the result of gross negligence or willful misconduct.

E. Nothing contained in this section shall be construed to provide immunity from liability arising out of the operation of a motor vehicle.

For the purposes of this section, the term "compensation" shall not be construed to include (i) the salaries of police, fire or other public officials or personnel who render such emergency assistance, (ii) the salaries or wages of employees of a coal producer engaging in emergency medical technician service or first aid service pursuant to the provisions of §§45.1-161.38, 45.1-161.101, 45.1-161.199 or §45.1-161.263, (iii) complimentary lift tickets, food, lodging or other gifts provided as a gratuity to volunteer members of the National Ski Patrol System, Inc., by any resort, group or agency, or (iv) the salary of any person who, in compliance with §32.1-111.14:1, (a) registers an automated external defibrillator for the use at the scene of an emergency, (b) trains individuals, in courses approved by the Board of Health, to operate registered automated external defibrillators at the scene of emergencies, (c) orders automated external defibrillators for subsequent registration and use at the scene of emergencies, or (d) operates, in accordance with the training required by §32.1-111.14:1, a registered automated external defibrillator at the scene of an emergency.

For the purposes of this section, an emergency medical care attendant or technician shall be deemed to include a person licensed or certified as such or its equivalent by any other state when he is performing services which he is licensed or certified to perform by such other state in caring for a patient in transit in this Commonwealth, which care originated in such other state.
(Chgd. by L.1996 ch. 899; L.1997 chs. 334, 809; L.1998 chs. 493, 500; L.1999 chs. 570, 1000; L.2000 chs. 928, 1064, eff. 7/1/2000.)

§8.01-225.1. Immunity for team physicians.

Any physician, surgeon or chiropractor licensed to practice by the Board of Medicine in this Commonwealth who, in the absence of gross negligence or willful misconduct, renders emergency medical care or emergency treatment to a participant in an athletic event sponsored by a public, private or parochial elementary, middle or high school while acting without compensation as a team physician, shall not be liable for civil damages resulting from any act or omission related to such care or treatment.

§8.01-225.2. Immunity for those rendering emergency care to animals.

Any person, including a person licensed to practice veterinary medicine, who in good faith and without compensation renders emergency care or treatment to an injured animal at the scene of an emergency or accident shall not be liable for any injuries to such animals resulting from the rendering of such care or treatment.
(Added by L.1998 ch. 669, eff. 7/1/98.)

§8.01-226. Duty of care to law-enforcement officers and firefighters, etc.

An owner or occupant of real property containing premises normally open to the public shall, with respect to such premises, owe to firefighters, Department of Emergency Services hazardous materials officers, nonfirefighter regional hazardous materials emergency response team members, and law-enforcement officers who in the performance of their duties come upon that portion of the premises normally open to the public the duty to maintain the same in a reasonably safe condition or to warn of dangers thereon of which he knows or has reason to know, whether or not such premises are at the time open to the public.

An owner or occupant of real property containing premises not normally open to the public shall, with respect to such premises, owe the same duty to firefighters, Department of Emergency Services hazardous materials officers, nonfirefighter regional hazardous materials emergency response team members, and law-enforcement officers who he knows or has reason to know are upon, about to come upon or imminently likely to come upon that portion of the premises not normally open to the public.

While otherwise engaged in the performance of his duties, a law-enforcement officer, Department of Emergency Services hazardous materials officer, nonfirefighter regional hazardous materials emergency response team member, or firefighter shall be owed a duty of ordinary care.

For purposes of this section, the term "law-enforcement officers" shall mean only police officers, sheriffs and deputy sheriffs and the term "firefighter" includes (i) emergency medical personnel and (ii) special forest wardens designated pursuant to §10.1-1135.
(Chgd. by L.1996 chs. 646, 660; L.2000 ch. 962, eff. 7/1/2000.)

CHAPTER 8
PROCESS
(Selected Article)

ARTICLE 4
WHO TO BE SERVED
(Selected Sections)

§8.01-307. Definition of terms "motor vehicle" and "nonresident" in motor vehicle and aircraft accident cases.

For the purpose of §§8.01-308 through 8.01-313:

1. The term "motor vehicle" shall mean every vehicle which is self-propelled or designed for self-propulsion and every vehicle drawn by or designed to be drawn by a motor vehicle and includes every device in, upon, or by which any person or property is or can be transported or drawn upon a highway, except devices moved by human or animal power and devices used exclusively upon stationary rails or tracks.

2. The term "nonresident" includes any person who, though a resident of the Commonwealth when the accident or collision specified in §8.01-308 or §8.01-309 occurred, has been continuously outside the Commonwealth for at least sixty days next preceding the date when process is left with the Commissioner of the Department of Motor Vehicles or the Secretary of the Commonwealth and includes any person against whom an order of publication may be issued under the provisions of §8.01-316.

§8.01-308. Service on Commissioner of the Department of Motor Vehicles as agent for nonresident motor vehicle operator.

Any operation in the Commonwealth of a motor vehicle by a nonresident, including those nonresidents defined in subdivision 2 of §8.01-307, either in person or by an agent or employee, shall be deemed equivalent to an appointment by such nonresident of the Commissioner of the Department of Motor Vehicles, and his successors in office, to be the attorney or statutory agent of such nonresident for the purpose of service of process in any action against him growing out of any accident or collision in which such nonresident, his agent, or his employee may be involved while operating motor vehicles in this Commonwealth. Acceptance by a nonresident of the rights and privileges conferred by Article 5 (§46.2-655 et seq.) of Chapter 6 of Title 46.2 shall have the same effect under this section as the operation of such motor vehicle, by such nonresident, his agent, or his employee.

§8.01-309. Service on Secretary of Commonwealth as agent of nonresident operator or owner of aircraft.

Any nonresident owner or operator of any aircraft that is operated over and above the land and waters of the Commonwealth or uses aviation facilities within the Commonwealth, shall by such operation and use appoint the Secretary of the Commonwealth as his statutory agent for the service of process in any action against him growing out of any accident or collision occurring within or above the Commonwealth in which such aircraft is involved.

§8.01-310. How service made on Commissioner and Secretary; appointment binding.

A. Service of process on either the Commissioner of the Department of Motor Vehicles as authorized under §8.01-308 or on the Secretary of the Commonwealth as authorized under §8.01-309, shall be made by leaving a copy of such process together with the fee for service of process on parties, in the amount prescribed in §2.1-71.2, for each party to be thus served, in the hands, or in the office, of such Commissioner or such Secretary and such service shall be sufficient upon the nonresident. All fees collected by the Commissioner pursuant to the provisions of this section shall be paid into the state treasury and shall be set aside as a special fund to be used to meet the expenses of the Department of Motor Vehicles.

B. Appointment of the Commissioner or Secretary as attorney or agent for the service of process on a nonresident under §8.01-308 or §8.01-309 shall be irrevocable and binding upon the executor or other personal representative of such nonresident:

1. Where a nonresident has died before the commencement of an action against him regarding an accident or collision under §8.01-308 or §8.01-309 shall be irrevocable and binding upon the executor or other personal representative of such nonresident; or

2. Where a nonresident dies after the commencement of an action against him regarding an accident or collision under §8.01-308 or §8.01-309, the action shall continue and shall be irrevocable and binding upon his executor, administrator, or other personal representative with such additional notice of the pendency of the action as the court deems proper.

(Chgd. by L.2000 ch. 579, eff. 7/1/2000.)

§8.01-311. Continuance of action where service made on Commissioner or Secretary.

The court, in which an action is pending against a nonresident growing out of an accident or collision as specified in §§8.01-308 and 8.01-309, may order such continuances as necessary to afford such nonresident reasonable opportunity to defend the action.

§8.01-312. Effect of service on statutory agent; duties of such agent.

A. Service of process on the statutory agent shall have the same legal force and validity as if served within the Commonwealth personally upon the person for whom it is intended.

Provided that such agent shall forthwith send by registered or certified mail, with return receipt requested, a copy of the process to the person named therein and for whom the statutory agent is receiving the process.

Provided further that the statutory agent shall file an affidavit of compliance with this section with the papers in the action; this filing shall be made in the office of the clerk of the court in which the action is pending.

B. Unless otherwise provided by §8.01-313 and subject to the provisions of §8.01-316, the address for the mailing of the process required by this section shall be that as provided by the party seeking service.

§8.01-313. Specific addresses for mailing by statutory agent.

A. For the statutory agent appointed pursuant to §§8.01-308 and 8.01-309, the address for the mailing of the process as required by §8.01-312 shall be the last known address of the nonresident or, where appropriate under subdivision 1 or 2 of §8.01-310 B, of the executor, administrator, or other personal representative of the nonresident. However, upon the filing of an affidavit by the plaintiff that he does not know and is unable with due diligence to ascertain any post-office address of such nonresident, service of process on the statutory agent shall be sufficient without the mailing otherwise required by this section. Provided further that:

1. In the case of a nonresident defendant licensed by the Commonwealth to operate a motor vehicle, the last address reported by such defendant to the Department of Motor Vehicles as his address on an application for or renewal of a driver's license shall be deemed to be the address of the defendant for the purpose of the mailing required by this section if no other address is known, and, in any case in which the affidavit provided for in §8.01-316 of this chapter is filed, such a defendant, by so notifying the Department of such an address, and by failing to notify the Department of any change therein, shall be deemed to have appointed the Commissioner of the Department of Motor Vehicles his statutory agent for service of process in an action arising out of operation of a motor vehicle by him in the Commonwealth, and to have accepted as valid service such mailing to such address; or

2. In the case of a nonresident defendant not licensed by the Commonwealth to operate a motor vehicle, the address shown on the copy of the report of accident required by §46.2-372 filed by or for him with the Department, and on file at the office of the Department, or the address reported by such a defendant to any state or local police officer, or sheriff investigating the accident sued on, if no other address is known, shall be conclusively presumed to be a valid address of such defendant for the purpose of the mailing provided for in this section, and his so reporting of an incorrect address, or his moving from the address so reported without making provision for forwarding to him of mail directed thereto, shall be deemed to be a waiver of notice and a consent to and acceptance of service of process served upon the Commissioner of the Department of Motor Vehicles as provided in this section.

B. For the statutory agent appointed pursuant to §26-59, the address for the mailing of process as required by §8.01-312 shall be the address of the fiduciary's statutory agent as contained in the written consent most recently filed with the clerk of the circuit court where in the qualification of such fiduciary was had or, in the event of the death, removal, resignation or absence form the Commonwealth of such statutory agent, or in the event that such statutory agent cannot with due diligence be found at such address, the address of the clerk of such circuit court.

CHAPTER 9
PERSONAL JURISDICTION IN CERTAIN ACTIONS
(Complete Chapter)

§8.01-328. Person defined.

As used in this chapter, "person" includes an individual, his executor, administrator, or other personal representative, or a corporation, partnership, association or any other legal or commercial entity, whether or not a citizen or domiciliary of this State and whether or not organized under the laws of this State.

§8.01-328.1. When personal jurisdiction over person may be exercised.

A. A court may exercise personal jurisdiction over a person, who acts directly or by an agent, as to a cause of action arising from the person's:

1. Transacting any business in this Commonwealth;
2. Contracting to supply services or things in this Commonwealth;
3. Causing tortious injury by an act or omission in this Commonwealth;
4. Causing tortious injury in this Commonwealth by an act or omission outside this Commonwealth if he regularly does or solicits business, or engages in any other persistent course of conduct, or derives substantial revenue from goods used or consumed or services rendered, in this Commonwealth;
5. Causing injury in this Commonwealth to any person by breach of warranty expressly or impliedly made in the sale of goods outside this Commonwealth when he might reasonably have expected such person to use, consume, or be affected by the goods in this Commonwealth, provided that he also regularly does or solicits business, or engages in any other persistent course of conduct, or derives substantial revenue from goods used or consumed or services rendered in this Commonwealth;
6. Having an interest in, using, or possessing real property in this Commonwealth;
7. Contracting to insure any person, property, or risk located within this Commonwealth at the time of contracting;
8. Having (i) executed an agreement in this Commonwealth which obligates the person to pay spousal support or child support to a domiciliary of this Commonwealth, or to a person who has satisfied the residency requirements in suits for annulments or divorce for members of the armed forces pursuant to §20-97 provided proof of service of process on a nonresident party is made by a law-enforcement officer or other person authorized to serve process in the jurisdiction where the nonresident party is located, (ii) been ordered to pay spousal support or child support pursuant to an order entered by any court of competent jurisdiction in this Commonwealth having in personam jurisdiction over such person, or (iii) shown by personal conduct in this Commonwealth, as alleged by affidavit, that the person conceived or fathered a child in this Commonwealth; or
9. Having maintained within this Commonwealth a matrimonial domicile at the time of separation of the parties upon which grounds for divorce or separate maintenance is based, or at the time a cause of action arose for divorce or separate maintenance or at the time of commencement of such suit, if the other party to the matrimonial relationship resides herein.

Jurisdiction in subdivision 9 of this subsection is valid only upon proof of service of process pursuant to §8.01-296 on the nonresident party by a person authorized under the provisions of §8.01-320. Jurisdiction under subdivision 8(iii) of this subsection is valid only upon proof of personal service on a nonresident pursuant to §8.01-320.

B. Using a computer or computer network located in the Commonwealth shall constitute an act in the Commonwealth. For purposes of this subsection, "use" and "computer network" shall have the same meanings as those contained in §18.2-152.2.

C. When jurisdiction over a person is based solely upon this section, only a cause of action arising from acts enumerated in this section may be asserted against him; however, nothing contained in this chapter shall limit, restrict or otherwise affect the jurisdiction of any court of this Commonwealth over foreign corporations which are subject to service of process pursuant to the provisions of any other statute.

(Chgd. by L.1999 chs. 886, 904, 905, eff. 7/1/99.)

§8.01-329. Service of process or notice; service on Secretary of Commonwealth.

A. When the exercise of personal jurisdiction is authorized by this chapter, service of process or notice may be made in the same manner as is provided for in Chapter 8 (§8.01-285 et seq.) of this title in any other case in which personal jurisdiction is exercised over such a party, or process or notice may be served on any agent of such person in the county or city in this Commonwealth in which that agent resides or on the Secretary of the Commonwealth of Virginia, hereinafter referred to in this section as the "Secretary," who, for this purpose, shall be deemed to be the statutory agent of such person.

B. When service is to be made on the Secretary, the party or his agent or attorney seeking service shall file an affidavit with the court, stating either (i) that the person to be served is a nonresident or (ii) that, after exercising due diligence, the party seeking service has been unable to locate the person to be served. In either case, such affidavit shall set forth the last known address of the person to be served.

When the person to be served is a resident, the signature of an attorney, party or agent of the person seeking service on such affidavit shall constitute a certificate by him that process has been delivered to the sheriff or to a disinterested person as permitted by §8.01-293 for execution and, if the sheriff or disinterested person was unable to execute such service, that the person seeking service has made a bona fide attempt to determine the actual place of abode or location of the person to be served.

C. Service of such process or notice on the Secretary shall be made by the plaintiff's, his agent's or the sheriff's leaving a copy of the process or notice, together with a copy of the affidavit called for in subsection B hereof and the fee prescribed in §2.1-71.2 in the office of the Secretary in the City of Richmond, Virginia. Service of process or notice on the Secretary may be made by mail if such service otherwise meets the requirements of this section. Such service shall be sufficient upon the person to be served, provided that notice of such service, a copy of the process or notice, and a copy of the affidavit are forthwith mailed by certified mail, return receipt requested, by the Secretary to the person or persons to be served at the last known post-office address of such person, and a certificate of compliance herewith by the Secretary or someone designated by him for that purpose and having knowledge of such compliance, shall be forthwith filed with the papers in the action. Service of process or notice on the Secretary shall be effective on the date the certificate of compliance is filed with the court in which the action is pending.

D. Service of process in actions brought on a warrant or motion for judgment pursuant to §16.1-79 or §16.1-81 shall be void and of no effect when such service of process is received by the Secretary within ten days of any return day set by the warrant. In such cases, the Secretary shall return the process or notice, the copy of the affidavit, and the prescribed fee to the plaintiff or his agent. A copy of the notice of the rejection shall be sent to the clerk of the court in which the action was filed.

E. The Secretary shall maintain a record of each notice of service sent to a person for a period of two years. The record maintained by the Secretary shall include the name of the plaintiff or the person seeking service, the name of the person to be served, the date service was received by the Secretary, the date notice of service was forwarded to the person to be served, and the date the certificate of compliance was sent by the Secretary to the appropriate court. The Secretary shall not be required to maintain any other records pursuant to this section.

(Chgd. by L.1998 ch. 259, eff. 7/1/98.)

§8.01-330. Jurisdiction on any other basis authorized.

A court of this State may exercise jurisdiction on any other basis authorized by law.

CHAPTER 11
JURIES
(Selected Articles)

ARTICLE 1
WHEN JURY TRIAL MAY BE HAD
(Complete Article)

§8.01-336. Jury trial of right; waiver of jury trial; court-ordered jury trial; trial by jury of plea in equity; issue out of chancery.

A. The right of trial by jury as declared in Article I, §11, of the Constitution of this Commonwealth and by statutes thereof shall be preserved inviolate to the parties.

B. Waiver of jury trial. In any action at law in which the recovery sought is greater than $100, exclusive of interest, unless one of the parties demand that the case or any issue thereof be tried by a jury, or in a criminal action in which trial by jury is dispensed with as provided by law, the whole matter of law and fact may be heard and judgment given by the court.

C. Court ordered jury trial. Notwithstanding any provision in this Code to the contrary, in any action at law in which there has been no demand for trial by jury by any party, a circuit court may on its own motion direct one or more issues, including an issue of damages, to be tried by a jury.

D. Trial by jury of plea in equity. In any action in which a plea has been filed to an equitable claim, and the allegations of such plea are denied by the plaintiff, either party may have the issue tried by jury.

E. Issue out of chancery. In any suit in equity, the court may, of its own motion or upon motion of any party, supported by such party's affidavit that the case will be rendered doubtful by conflicting evidence of another party, direct an issue to be tried by a jury.

ARTICLE 2
JURORS
(Complete Article)

§8.01-337. Who liable to serve as jurors.

All citizens over eighteen years of age who have been residents of the Commonwealth one year, and of the county, city or town in which they reside six months next preceding their being summoned to serve as such, and competent in other respects, except as hereinafter provided, shall be liable to serve as jurors. No person shall be deemed incompetent to serve on any jury because of blindness or partial blindness. Military personnel of the United States Army, Air Force or Navy shall not be considered residents of this Commonwealth by reason of their being stationed herein.

§8.01-338. Who disqualified.

The following persons shall be disqualified from serving as jurors:

1. Persons adjudicated incapacitated;
2. Persons convicted of treason or a felony; or
3. Any other person under a disability as defined in §8.01-2 and not included in subdivisions 1 or 2 above.

(Chgd. by L.1997 ch. 801, eff. 1/1/98.)

§8.01-339. No person eligible for whom request is made.

No person shall be eligible to serve on any jury when he, or any person for him, solicits or requests a jury commissioner to place his name in a jury box or in any way designate such person as a juror.

§8.01-340. No person to serve who has case at that term.

No person shall be admitted to serve as a juror at a term of a court during which he has any matter of controversy which has been or is expected to be tried by a jury during the same term.

§8.01-341. Who are exempt from jury service.

The following shall be exempt from serving on juries in civil and criminal cases:

1. The President and Vice-President of the United States,
2. The Governor, Lieutenant Governor and Attorney General of the Commonwealth,
3. The members of both houses of Congress,
4. The members of the General Assembly, while in session or during a period when the member would be entitled to a legislative continuance as a matter of right under §30-5,
5. Licensed practicing attorneys,
6. The judge of any court, members of the State Corporation Commission, members of the Industrial Commission of Virginia, and magistrates,
7. Sheriffs, deputy sheriffs, state police, and police in counties, cities and towns,

8. The superintendent of the penitentiary and his assistants and the persons composing the guard,

9. Superintendents and jail officers, as defined in §53.1-1, of regional jails.

(Chgd. by L.1998 ch. 83, eff. 7/1/98.)

§8.01-341.1. Exemptions from jury service upon request.

Any of the following persons may serve on juries in civil and criminal cases but shall be exempt from jury service upon his request:

1 to 3. *(Repealed.)*

4. A mariner actually employed in maritime service,

5 to 7. *(Repealed.)*

8. A person who has legal custody of and is necessarily and personally responsible for a child or children sixteen years of age or younger requiring continuous care by him during normal court hours,

9. A person who is necessarily and personally responsible for a person having a physical or mental impairment requiring continuous care by him during normal court hours,

10. Any person over seventy years of age,

11. Any person whose spouse is summoned to serve on the same jury panel,

12. Any person who is the only person performing services for a business, commercial or agricultural enterprise and whose services are so essential to the operations of the business, commercial or agricultural enterprise that such enterprise must close or cease to function if such person is required to perform jury duty.

(Chgd. by L.1997 ch. 693; L.1999 ch. 153, eff. 7/1/99.)

§8.01-341.2. Deferral or limitation of jury service for particular occupational inconvenience.

The court, on its own motion, may exempt any person from jury service for a particular term of court, or limit that person's service to particular dates of that term, if serving on a jury during that term or certain dates of that term of court would cause such person a particular occupational inconvenience. Any such person who is selected for jury service, and who is exempted under the provisions of this section, shall not be discharged from his obligation to serve on a jury, but such obligation shall only be deferred until the term of court next after such particular occupational inconvenience shall end.

§8.01-342. Restrictions on amount of jury service permitted.

A. The jury commissioners shall not include on the jury list provided for in §8.01-345 the name of any person who has been called and reported to any state court for jury duty at any time during the period of three years next preceding the date of completion of such jury list.

B. If such person has been called and reported for jury duty in the trial of any case, either civil or criminal, at any one term of a court, he shall not be permitted to serve as a juror in any civil or criminal case, at any other term of that court during the three-year period set forth in subsection A of this section, unless all the persons whose names are in the jury box have been drawn to serve during such three-year period; however, such person shall be permitted to serve on any special jury ordered pursuant to §8.01-362 and on any grand jury.

ARTICLE 4
JURY SERVICE
(Selected Section)

§8.01-356. Failure of juror to appear.

If any juror who has been given due notice to appear in court shall fail to do so without sufficient excuse, he shall be fined not less than $25 nor more than $100.

CHAPTER 17
JUDGMENTS AND DECREES GENERALLY
(Selected Article)

ARTICLE 5
KEEPING OF DOCKET BOOKS; EXECUTION THEREON; DISPOSAL OF EXHIBITS
(Selected Section)

§8.01-446.1. Keeping of docket books by clerk of court using micrographic process; form.

Whenever judgments are docketed in the judgment lien book in the office of the clerk of the circuit court and are recorded by a procedural micrographic process as provided in §17-70.1, or by any other method or process which renders impractical or impossible the subsequent entry of notations upon the docketed judgment, an appropriate certificate of assignment, release, partial release, certified copy of any order, or other separate instrument setting forth the necessary information as provided in this section shall be recorded and indexed according to law. Such instrument shall conform substantially with the following form:

ORIGINAL BOOK # ..... PAGE ....
ORIGINAL DATE DOCKETED: ....

TYPE OF FILING (Check One)
( ) Assignment
( ) Release
( ) Partial Release
( ) Credit(s)
( ) Additional Debtor(s)
( ) New Name of Debtor

Date of Judgment:
Amount of Judgment:
Plaintiff(s):

Defendant(s):

Assignee (If assignment): ....

Payments (If credits): AMOUNT ....
DATE PAID ....

(Complete below if additional debtor or change of name of debtor)

Debtor:
Social Security Number of Debtor (If known):

Given under my hand this ...... day of ...., ...

....
(Plaintiff) (Attorney for Plaintiff)
(Authorized Agent for Plaintiff)

Any judgment creditor who knowingly gives false information upon such certificate made under this section shall be guilty of a Class 1 misdemeanor.

TITLE 9
COMMISSIONS, BOARDS AND INSTITUTIONS GENERALLY
(Selected Chapter)

CHAPTER 27
DEPARTMENT OF CRIMINAL JUSTICE SERVICES; BOARD
(Selected Articles)

ARTICLE 1.6
CRIME PREVENTION CENTER
(Complete Article)

§9-173.16. Creation of Crime Prevention Center.

The Department of Criminal Justice Services shall establish a Crime Prevention Center for the purpose of providing crime prevention assistance and training, resource material, and research into methods and procedures to reduce the opportunity for crime. Any state funding for such Center shall be subject to the approval of the General Assembly.

§9-173.17. Creation of McGruff House Program; duties of Department.

The symbol of "McGruff" with the phrase "McGruff House" shall be the symbol used to designate a house in the Commonwealth where a child who is abused, neglected or otherwise emotionally or physically in danger may seek refuge and assistance.

The Department of Criminal Justice Services shall adopt a standard symbol to be used throughout the Commonwealth which is the same as or substantially similar to the McGruff House symbol in use in other states. The Department shall establish by regulation appropriate procedures governing (i) qualifications and criteria for designation as a McGruff House and participants' duties and responsibilities, such regulations to include, but not be limited to, duties regarding reporting of incidents to the local law-enforcement agency and department of social services' child-protective services program, (ii) programs to publicize the McGruff House Program, (iii) dissemination of the McGruff House symbol to day care centers, schools, and law-enforcement agencies, (iv) designation and registration of McGruff Houses with, and monitoring and periodic review of such houses by, local law-enforcement agencies, and (v) coordination of the program with the child-protective services component of the local department of social services. Nothing herein shall prohibit the use of a symbol other than "McGruff" by a locality which currently has some other safe house program in existence and operation.

§9-173.18. Designation of McGruff House; penalty.

All persons displaying the McGruff House symbol so that it is visible from the outside of their house shall first apply for designation as a McGruff House with the local law-enforcement agency. Upon receipt of an application for designation, the local law-enforcement agency shall conduct a background check of the applicant in accordance with Chapter 23 (§19.2-387 et seq.) of Title 19.2 and the regulations promulgated by the Department at no charge to the applicant. Any background checks of applicants for this program conducted by the Department of Social Services through the Child Abuse Registry shall be done at no charge. Upon finding that the applicant meets the criteria established by the Department for maintaining a McGruff House and receipt of a signed statement by the applicant agreeing to the terms and conditions of the McGruff House Program, the law-enforcement agency shall provide the applicant with the McGruff House symbol.

The McGruff House symbol remains the property of the local law-enforcement agency. Upon a determination by the issuing law-enforcement agency that a house no longer meets the established criteria for a McGruff House, the symbol shall promptly be returned to the issuing law-enforcement agency. Failure to return the symbol promptly after receipt of a written request to do so, which shall state the reason for the request, shall be subject to a civil penalty of up to $100. Subsequent to July 1, 1994, display of a McGruff House symbol by persons not designated pursuant to this section to participate in the program shall be subject to a civil penalty of up to $100.

§9-173.19. Establishment of crime prevention specialists.

The Board of Criminal Justice Services shall promulgate regulations establishing minimum standards for certification of crime prevention specialists. The duties of a crime prevention specialist shall include, but not be limited to, the following:

1. To provide citizens living within his jurisdiction information concerning personal safety and the security of property, and other matters relating to the reduction of criminal opportunity;

2. To provide business establishments within his jurisdiction information concerning business and employee security, and other matters relating to the reduction of criminal activity;

3. To provide citizens and businesses within his jurisdiction assistance in forming and maintaining neighborhood and business watch groups and other community-based crime prevention programs;

4. To provide assistance to other units of government within his jurisdiction in developing plans and procedures related to the reduction of criminal activity within government and the community; and

5. To promote the reduction and prevention of crime within his jurisdiction and the Commonwealth.

§9-173.20. Eligibility; requirements for crime prevention specialists.

A. Any employee of a local or state law-enforcement agency is eligible to be trained and certified as a crime prevention specialist.

B. The chief executive of any local or state law-enforcement agency may designate one or more employees in his department or office to be trained and certified as a crime prevention specialist.

ARTICLE 1.7
VIRGINIA CENTER FOR SCHOOL SAFETY

(Added by L.2000 ch. 519.)*
(Complete Article)

**The second enactment of L.2000 ch. 519 provides:*
"That the provisions of this act shall not become effective unless an appropriation effectuating the purposes of this act is included in the 2000 Appropriation Act, passed during the 2000 Session of the General Assembly and signed into law by the Governor."

§9-173.21. Virginia Center for School Safety created; duties.

A. From such funds as may be appropriated, the Virginia Center for School Safety is hereby established within the Department of Criminal Justice Services and shall be referred to in this section as the Center. The Center shall:

1. Provide training for Virginia public school personnel in school safety and the effective identification of students who may be at risk for violent behavior and in need of special services or assistance;
2. Serve as a resource and referral center for Virginia school divisions by conducting research, sponsoring workshops, and providing information regarding current school safety concerns, such as conflict management and peer mediation, school facility design and technology, current state and federal statutory and regulatory school safety requirements, and legal and constitutional issues regarding school safety and individual rights;
3. Maintain and disseminate information to local school divisions on effective school safety initiatives in Virginia and across the nation;
4. Collect, analyze, and disseminate various Virginia school safety data, including school safety audit information, collected by the Department;
5. Encourage the development of partnerships between the public and private sectors to promote school safety in Virginia;
6. Provide technical assistance to Virginia school divisions in the implementation of initiatives promoting school safety; and
7. Develop a memorandum of understanding between the Commissioner of the Department of Criminal Justice Services and the Superintendent of Public Instruction to ensure collaboration and coordination of roles and responsibilities in areas of mutual concern, such as school safety audits and crime prevention.

B. All agencies of the Commonwealth shall cooperate with the Center and, upon request, assist the Center in the performance of its duties and responsibilities.
(Added by L.2000 ch. 519, pending funding. See note at beginning of article.)

ARTICLE 2.1
PRIVATE SECURITY SERVICES BUSINESSES

(Complete Article)

§9-183.1. Definitions.

As used in this chapter, unless the context requires a different meaning:

"Alarm respondent" means a natural person who responds to the signal of an alarm for the purpose of detecting an intrusion of the home, business or property of the end user.

"Armed" means a private security registrant who carries or has immediate access to a firearm in the performance of his duties.

"Armed security officer" means a security officer, as defined below, who carries or has immediate access to a firearm in the performance of his duties.

"Armored car personnel" means persons who transport or offer to transport under armed security from one place to another, money, negotiable instruments or other valuables in a specially equipped motor vehicle with a high degree of security and certainty of delivery.

"Board" means the Criminal Justice Services Board or any successor board or agency.

"Business advertising material" means display advertisements in telephone directories, letterhead, business cards, local newspaper advertising and contracts.

"Central station dispatcher" means a natural person who monitors burglar alarm signal devices, burglar alarms or any other electrical, mechanical or electronic device used to prevent or detect burglary, theft, shoplifting, pilferage or similar losses; used to prevent or detect intrusion; or used primarily to summon aid for other emergencies.

"Certification" means the method of regulation indicating that qualified persons have met the minimum requirements as private security services training schools, private security services instructors, compliance agents, unarmed security officers, electronic security employees, or electronic security technician's assistants.

"Compliance agent" means a natural person who owns or is employed by a licensed private security services business to ensure the compliance of the private security services business with this title.

"Courier" means any armed person who transports or offers to transport from one place to another documents or other papers, negotiable or nonnegotiable instruments, or other small items of value that require expeditious services.

"Department" means the Department of Criminal Justice Services or any successor agency.

"Electronic security business" means any person who engages in the business of or undertakes to (i) install, service, maintain, design or consult in the design of any electronic security equipment to an end user, (ii) respond to or cause a response to electronic security equipment for an end user, or (iii) have access to confidential information concerning the design, extent, status, password, contact list, or location of an end user's electronic security equipment.

"Electronic security employee" means a natural person who is employed by an electronic security business in any capacity which may give him access to information concerning the design, extent, status, password, contact list, or location of an end user's electronic security equipment.

"Electronic security equipment" means electronic or mechanical alarm signaling devices including burglar alarms or holdup alarms or cameras used to detect intrusions, concealment or theft.

"Electronic security equipment" shall not include tags, labels, and other devices which are attached or affixed to items offered for sale, library books, and other protected articles as part of an electronic article surveillance and theft-detection and deterrence system.

"Electronic security sales representative" means a natural person who sells electronic security equipment on behalf of an electronic security business to the end user.

"Electronic security technician" means a natural person who installs, services, maintains or repairs electronic security equipment.

"Electronic security technician's assistant" means a natural person who works as a laborer under the supervision of the electronic security technician in the course of his normal duties, but who may not make connections to any electronic security equipment.

"End user" means any person who purchases or leases electronic security equipment for use in that person's home or business.

"Firearms training verification" means verification of the successful completion of either initial or retraining requirements for handgun or shotgun training, or both.

"License number" means the official number issued to a private security services business licensed by the Department.

"Person" means any individual, group of individuals, firm, company, corporation, partnership, business, trust, association, or other legal entity.

"Personal protection specialist" means any natural person who engages in the duties of providing close protection from bodily harm to any person.

"Private investigator" means any natural person who engages in the business of, or accepts employment to make, investigations to obtain information on (i) crimes or civil wrongs; (ii) the location, disposition, or recovery of stolen property; (iii) the cause of accidents, fires, damages, or injuries to persons or to property; or (iv) evidence to be used before any court, board, officer, or investigative committee.

"Private security services business" means any person engaged in the business of providing, or who undertakes to provide armored car personnel, security officers, personal protection specialists, private investigators, couriers, security canine handlers, security canine teams, alarm respondents, central station dispatchers, electronic security employees, electronic security sales representatives or electronic security technicians and their assistants to another person under contract, express or implied.

"Private security services instructor" means any natural person certified by the Department to provide mandated instruction in private security subjects for a certified private security services training school.

"Private security services registrant" means any qualified natural person who has met the requirements under this article to perform the duties of alarm respondent, armored car personnel, central station dispatcher, courier, electronic security sales representative, electronic security technician, personal protection specialist, private investigator, security canine handler, or armed security officer.

"Private security services training school" means any person certified by the Department to provide instruction in private security subjects for the training of private security services business personnel in accordance with this article.

"Registration" means a method of regulation whereby certain personnel employed by a private security services business are required to obtain a registration from the Department pursuant to this article.

"Security canine" means a dog that has attended, completed, and been certified as a security canine by a certified security canine handler instructor in accordance with approved Department procedures and certification guidelines. "Security canine" shall not include detector dogs.

"Security canine handler" means any natural person who utilizes his security canine in the performance of private security duties.

"Security canine team" means the security canine handler and his security canine performing private security duties.

"Security officer" means any natural person employed by a private security services business to (i) safeguard and protect persons and property or (ii) prevent theft, loss, or concealment of any tangible or intangible personal property on the premises contracted to protect.

"Supervisor" means any natural person who directly or indirectly supervises registered or certified private security services business personnel.

"Unarmed security officer" means a security officer who does not carry or have immediate access to a firearm in the performance of his duties.

(Chgd. by L.1995 ch. 79; L.1996 ch. 541; L.1997 ch. 80; L.1998 chs. 122, 807; L.1999 ch. 33, eff. 7/1/99.)

§9-183.2. Exceptions.

The provisions of this article shall not apply to the following:

1. An officer or employee of the United States of America, or of this Commonwealth or a political subdivision of either, while the employee or officer is performing his official duties.

2. A person engaged exclusively in the business of obtaining and furnishing information regarding an individual's financial rating or a person engaged in the business of a consumer reporting agency as defined by the Federal Fair Credit Reporting Act.

3. An attorney or certified public accountant licensed to practice in Virginia or his employees.

4. The legal owner of personal property which has been sold under any security agreement while performing acts relating to the repossession of such property.

5. A person receiving compensation for private employment as a security officer who is also a law-enforcement officer as defined by §9-169 and employed by the Commonwealth or any political subdivision thereof.

6. Any person appointed under §46.2-2003 or §56-353 while engaged in the employment contemplated thereunder, unless they have successfully completed training mandated by the Department.

7. Persons who are regularly employed to investigate accidents or to adjust claims and who do not carry weapons in the performance of their duties.

8. Regular employees of persons engaged in other than the private security services business, where the regular duties of such employees primarily consist of protecting the property of their employers. Any such employee who carries a firearm and is in direct contact with the general public in the performance of his duties shall possess a valid registration with this Department as provided in subsection B of §9-183.3. "General public" means individuals who have access to areas open to all and not restricted to any particular class of the community.

9. Persons, sometimes known as "shoppers," employed to purchase goods or services solely for the purpose of determining or assessing the efficiency, loyalty, courtesy, or honesty of the employees of a business establishment.

10. Licensed or registered private investigators from other states entering Virginia during an investigation originating in their state of licensure or registration when the other state offers similar reciprocity to private investigators licensed and registered by the Commonwealth of Virginia.

11. Unarmed regular employees of telephone public service companies where the regular duties of such employees consist of protecting the property of their employers and investigating the usage of telephone services and equipment furnished by their employers, their employers' affiliates, and other communications common carriers.

12. An end user.

13. A material supplier who renders advice concerning the use of products sold by an electronics security business and who does not provide installation, monitoring, repair or maintenance services for electronic security equipment.

14. Members of the security forces who are directly employed by electric public service companies.

15. Any professional engineer or architect licensed in accordance with Chapter 4 (§54.1-400 et seq.) of Title 54.1 to practice in the Commonwealth, or his employees.

16. Any person who only performs telemarketing or schedules appointments without access to information concerning the electronic security equipment purchased by an end user.

17. Any certified forensic scientist employed as an expert witness for the purpose of possibly testifying as an expert witness.

18. Members of the security forces who are directly employed by shipyards engaged in the construction, design, overhaul or repair of nuclear vessels for the United States Navy.

19. An out-of-state central station dispatcher employed by a private security services business licensed by the Department provided he (i) possesses and maintains a valid license, registration, or certification as a central station dispatcher issued by the regulatory authority of the state in which he performs the monitoring duties and (ii) has submitted his fingerprints to the regulatory authority for the conduct of a national criminal history records search.

(Chgd. by L.1995 ch. 79; L.1996 chs. 541, 543, 576; L.1997 chs. 80, 204; L.2000 ch. 26, eff. 7/1/2000.)

§9-183.3. Licensing and registration.

A. No person shall engage in the private security services business or solicit private security business in the Commonwealth without having obtained a license from the Department. No person shall be issued a private security services business license until a compliance agent is designated in writing on forms provided by the Department. The compliance agent shall assure the compliance of the private security services business with this article and shall meet the qualifications and perform the duties required by the regulations promulgated by the Board. A compliance agent shall have either a minimum of (i) three years of managerial or supervisory experience in a private security services business; with a federal, state or local law-enforcement agency; or in a related field or (ii) five years of experience in a private security services business; with a federal, state or local law-enforcement agency; or in a related field.

B. No person shall act as private security services training school or solicit students for private security training in the Commonwealth without being certified by the Department. No person shall be issued a private security services training school certification until a school director is designated in writing on forms provided by the Department. The school director shall ensure compliance of such school with the provisions of this article and shall meet the qualifications and perform the duties required by the regulations promulgated by the Board.

C. No person shall be employed by a licensed private security services business in the Commonwealth as armored car personnel, courier, armed security officer, security canine handler, private investigator, personal protection specialist, alarm respondent, central station dispatcher, electronic security sales representative, or electronic security technician without possessing a valid registration issued by the Department, except as provided in this article.

D. A temporary license may be issued in accordance with Board regulations for the purpose of awaiting the results of the state and national fingerprint search. However, no person shall be issued a temporary license until (i) he has designated a compliance agent who has complied with the compulsory minimum training standards established by the Board pursuant to subsection A of §9-182 for compliance agents, (ii) each principal of the business has submitted his fingerprints for a National Criminal Records search and a Virginia Criminal History Records search, and (iii) he has met all other requirements of this article and the regulations of the Board.

E. A temporary registration may be issued in accordance with Board regulations for the purpose of awaiting the results of the state and national fingerprint search. However, no person shall be issued a temporary registration until he has (i) complied with, or been exempted from the compulsory minimum training standards established by the Board, pursuant to subsection A of §9-182, for armored car personnel, couriers, armed security officers, security canine handlers, private investigators, personal protection specialist, alarm respondents, central station dispatchers, electronic security sales representatives or electronic security technicians, (ii) submitted his fingerprints to be used for the conduct of a National Criminal Records search and a Virginia Criminal History Records search, and (iii) met all other requirements of this article and the regulations of the Board.

F. A temporary certification as a private security instructor or private security training school may be issued in accordance with Board regulations for the purpose of awaiting the results of the state and national fingerprint search. However, no person shall be issued a temporary certification as a private security services instructor until he has (i) met the education, training and experience requirements established by the Board and (ii) submitted his fingerprints to be used for the conduct of a National Criminal Records search and a Virginia Criminal History Records search. No person shall be issued a temporary certification as a private security services training school until (a) he has designated a training director, (b) each principal of the training school has submitted his fingerprints to be used for the conduct of a National Criminal Records search and a Virginia Criminal History Records search, and (c) he has met all other requirements of this article and the regulations of the Board.

G. A licensed private security services business in the Commonwealth shall not employ as an unarmed security officer, electronic security technician's assistant, unarmed alarm respondent, central station dispatcher, electronic security sales representative, or electronic security technician, any person who has not complied with, or been exempted from, the compulsory minimum training standards established by the Board, pursuant to subsection A of §9-182, except that such person may be so employed for not more than ninety days while completing compulsory minimum training standards.

H. No person shall be employed as an electronic security employee, electronic security technician's assistant, unarmed alarm respondent, central station dispatcher, electronic security sales representative, electronic security technician, or supervisor until he has submitted his fingerprints to the Department to be used for the conduct of a National Criminal Records search and a Virginia Criminal History Records search. The provisions of this subsection shall not apply to an out-of-state central station dispatcher meeting the requirements of subdivision 19 of §9-183.2.

I. The compliance agent of each licensed private security services business in the Commonwealth shall maintain documentary evidence that each private security registrant and certified employee employed by his private security services business has complied with, or been exempted from, the compulsory minimum training standards required by the Board and that an investigation to determine suitability of each unarmed security officer employee has been conducted, except that any such unarmed security officer, upon initiating a request for such investigation under the provisions of subdivision 11 of subsection A of §19.2-389, may be employed for up to thirty days pending completion of such investigation.

J. No person with a criminal record of a misdemeanor involving moral turpitude or any felony shall be (i) employed as a registered or certified employee by a private security services business or training school or (ii) issued a private security services registration, certification as an unarmed security officer, electronic security employee or technician's assistant, a private security services training school or instructor certification, compliance agent certification, or a private security services business license, except that, upon written request, the Director of the Department of Criminal Justice Services may waive such prohibition.

K. The Department may grant a temporary exemption from the requirement of a license, certification, or registration for a period of not more than thirty days in a situation deemed an emergency by the Department.

L. All private security services businesses and private security services training schools in the Commonwealth shall include their license or certification number on all business advertising materials.

(Chgd. by L.1995 ch. 79; L.1996 ch. 541; L.1998 chs. 53, 122, 807; L.2000 ch. 26, eff. 7/1/2000.)

§9-183.4. Powers of Department.

In addition to the powers otherwise conferred upon it by law, the Department shall have the power to:

1. Charge each applicant for licensure, certification or registration a nonrefundable fee as established by the Board to cover the costs of the Department for processing an application for a registration, certification or license, and enforcement of these regulations, and other costs associated with the maintenance of this program of regulation.

2. Charge nonrefundable fees for private security services training as established by the Board for processing school certifications and enforcement of training standards.

3. Conduct investigations to determine the suitability of applicants for registration, licensure, or certification of compliance agents, training schools and instructors. For purposes of this investigation, the Department shall have access to criminal history record information maintained by the Central Criminal Records Exchange of the Department of State Police and shall conduct a background investigation, to include a National Criminal Records search and a Virginia Criminal History Records search.

4. The Director, or agents appointed by him, are vested with the authority to administer oaths or affirmations for the purpose of receiving complaints and conducting investigations of violations of this article, or any regulation promulgated pursuant to authority given by this article. Information concerning alleged criminal violations shall be turned over to law-enforcement officers in appropriate jurisdictions. Agents shall be vested with authority to serve such paper or process issued by the Department or the Board under regulations approved by the Board.

5. In addition to the authority granted in §9-6.14:13 to issue subpoenas, the Director or a designated subordinate shall have the right to make an ex parte application to the circuit court for the city or county wherein evidence sought is kept or wherein a licensee does business, for the issuance of a subpoena duces tecum in furtherance of the investigation of a sworn complaint within the jurisdiction of the Department or the Board to request production of any relevant records, documents and physical or other evidence of any person, partnership, association or corporation licensed or regulated by the Department pursuant to this article. The court shall be authorized to issue and compel compliance with such a subpoena upon a showing of reasonable cause. Upon determining that reasonable cause exists to believe that evidence may be destroyed or altered, the court may issue a subpoena duces tecum requiring the immediate production of evidence.

6. Recover costs of the investigation and adjudication of violations of this article or the regulations of the Board. Such costs may be recovered from the respondent when a sanction is imposed to fine or place on probation, suspend, revoke, or deny the issuance of any license, certification, or registration. Such costs shall be in addition to any monetary penalty which may be imposed. All costs recovered shall be deposited into the state treasury to the credit of the Private Security Services Regulatory Fund.

(Chgd. by L.1998 chs. 122, 807, eff. 7/1/98.)

§9-183.5. Private Security Services Advisory Board.

There shall be a Private Security Services Advisory Board which shall be composed of eleven members. Two of the members shall be private investigators; two shall be representatives of electronic security businesses; three shall be representatives of private security services businesses providing security officers, armed couriers or guard dog handlers; one shall be a representative of a private security services business providing armored car personnel; one shall be a representative of a private security services business involving personal protection specialists; one shall be a certified private security services instructor; and one shall be a representative of law enforcement. The Private Security Services Advisory Board shall be appointed by the Criminal Justice Services Board and shall advise the Criminal Justice Services Board on all issues relating to regulation of private security services businesses.

(Chgd. by L.1997 ch. 79, eff. 7/1/97.)

§9-183.6. Bond or insurance required.

A. Every person licensed as a private security services business under subsection A of §9-183.3 or certified as a private security services training school under subsection B of §9-183.3 shall, at the time of receiving the license or certification and before the license or certification shall be operative, file with the Department (i) a cash bond or evidence that the licensee or certificate holder is covered by a surety bond, executed by a surety company authorized to do business in this Commonwealth, in a reasonable amount to be fixed by the Department, conditioned upon the faithful and honest conduct of his business or employment; or (ii) evidence of a policy of liability insurance in an amount and with coverage as fixed by the Department. The bond or liability insurance shall be maintained for so long as the licensee or certificate holder is licensed or certified by the Department.

B. If any person aggrieved by the misconduct of any person licensed or certified under subsections A or B of §9-183.3 recovers judgment against the licensee or certificate holder, such person may, after the return unsatisfied, either in whole or in part, of any execution issued upon such judgment, maintain an action in his own name upon the bond of the licensee or certificate holder.

(Chgd. by L.1998 chs. 122, 807, eff. 7/1/98.)

§9-183.7. Fingerprints required.

Each applicant for registration, licensure or certification as a compliance agent, or private security services training

 Zv

school or instructor under the provisions of this article and every person employed as an electronic security employee or electronic security technician's assistant shall submit his fingerprints to the Department on a form provided by the Department.

(Chgd. by L.1995 ch. 79; L.1998 chs. 122, 807, eff. 7/1/98.)

§9-183.8. Powers of registered armed security officers; limitations.

Compliance with the provisions of this article shall not itself authorize any person to carry a concealed weapon or exercise any powers of a conservator of the peace. A registered armed security officer of a private security services business while at a location which the business is contracted to protect shall have the power to effect an arrest for an offense occurring (i) in his presence on such premises or (ii) in the presence of a merchant, agent, or employee of the merchant the private security business has contracted to protect, if the merchant, agent, or employee had probable cause to believe that the person arrested had shoplifted or committed willful concealment of goods as contemplated by §18.2-106. For the purposes of §19.2-74, a registered armed security officer of a private security services business shall be considered an arresting officer.

§9-183.9. Penalties.

A. It shall be a Class 1 misdemeanor for any person required to possess a registration under subsection C of §9-183.3 to be employed by a private security services business, except as provided in this article, as armored car personnel, courier, armed security officer, security canine handler, personal protection specialist, private investigator, alarm respondent, central station dispatcher, electronic security sales representative or electronic security technician, without possessing a valid registration.

B. It shall be a Class 1 misdemeanor for any person licensed or required to be licensed under subsection A of §9-183.3 to employ or otherwise utilize, except as provided in this article, as armored car personnel, courier, armed security officer, security canine handler, personal protection specialist, private investigator, alarm respondent, central station dispatcher, electronic security sales representative or electronic security technician, any person not possessing a valid registration.

C. It shall be a Class 1 misdemeanor for any compliance agent employed or otherwise utilized by a person licensed or required to be licensed under subsection A of §9-183.3, to employ or otherwise utilize as an unarmed security officer, except as provided in this article, any individual for whom the compliance agent does not possess documentary evidence of compliance with, or exemption from, the compulsory minimum training standards established by the Board for unarmed security officers and documentary evidence that an investigation to determine suitability has been conducted.

D. Except as provided by this article, it shall be a Class 1 misdemeanor for any compliance agent employed or otherwise utilized by a person licensed or required to be licensed under subsection A of §9-183.3 to employ or otherwise utilize as an electronic security technician's assistant any individual for whom the compliance agent does not possess documentary evidence of compliance with, or exemption from, the compulsory minimum training standards established by the Board for electronic security technician's assistants.

E. It shall be a Class 1 misdemeanor for any person required to possess an instructor certification under subsection D of §9-183.3 to provide mandated instruction, except as provided in §9-182 and regulations of the Board, without possessing a valid private security instructor certification.

F. It shall be a Class 1 misdemeanor for any person certified or required to be certified as a private security services training school under subsection B of §9-183.3 to employ or otherwise utilize, except as provided in §9-182 and the regulations of the Board, as a private security instructor, any person not possessing a valid instructor certification.

(Chgd. by L.1995 ch. 79; L.1998 chs. 122, 807, eff. 7/1/98.)

§9-183.10. Unlawful procurement of a license; penalty.

A. It shall be unlawful:

1. For any person to procure, or assist another to procure, through theft, fraud or other illegal means, a registration or license, by giving to, or receiving from, any person any information, oral, written or printed, during the administration of the examination, which is intended to, or will, assist any person taking the examination in passing the examination and obtaining the required registration or license;

2. For any person, other than a designee of the Department, to procure or have in his possession prior to the beginning of an examination, without written authority of the Department, any question intended to be used by the Department, or to receive or furnish to any person taking the examination, prior to or during the examination, any written or printed material purporting to be answers to, or aid in answering such questions;

3. For any person to attempt to procure, through theft, fraud or other illegal means, any questions intended to be used by the Department conducting the examination, or the answers to the questions; and

4. To promise or offer any valuable or other consideration to a person having access to the questions or answers as an inducement to procure for delivery to the promisor, or any other person, a copy or copies of any questions or answers.

If an examination is divided into separate parts, each of the parts shall be deemed an examination for the purposes of this section.

B. Any person violating the provisions of subsection A shall be guilty of a Class 2 misdemeanor.

§9-183.11. Unlawful conduct; powers of Department; penalty.

A. It shall be unlawful for any person, partnership, corporation or other entity to engage in any of the following acts:

1. Practicing any trade or profession licensed, certified or registered under this article without obtaining the necessary license, certification or registration required by statute or regulation;

2. Materially misrepresenting facts in an application for licensure, certification or registration;

3. Willfully refusing to furnish the Department information or records required or requested pursuant to statute or regulation; and

4. Violating any statute or regulation governing the practice of the private security services businesses or training schools regulated by this article.

Any person who willfully engages in any unlawful act enumerated in this section shall be guilty of a Class 1 misdemeanor. Any person convicted of a third or subsequent offense under this section during a thirty-six-month period shall be guilty of a Class 6 felony.

B. In addition to the provisions of subsection A of this section, the Department may institute proceedings in equity to enjoin any person, partnership, corporation or any other entity from engaging in any unlawful act enumerated in this section. Such proceedings shall be brought in the name of the

Commonwealth by the Department in the circuit court of the city or county in which the unlawful act occurred or in which the defendant resides.
(Chgd. by L.1998 chs. 122, 807, eff. 7/1/98.)

§9-183.12. Same; monetary penalty.
Any person licensed, certified or registered by the Board pursuant to this article who violates any statute or regulation pertaining to the Board who is not criminally prosecuted shall be subject to the monetary penalty provided in this section. If the Board determines that a respondent is guilty of the violation complained of, the Board shall determine the amount of the monetary penalty for the violation, which shall not exceed $2,500 for each violation. The penalty may be sued for and recovered in the name of the Commonwealth. Such monetary penalty shall be paid into the state treasury to the credit of the Literary Fund in accordance with §19.2-353.
(Chgd. by L.1998 chs. 122, 807, eff. 7/1/98.)

ARTICLE 4
DIVISION OF FORENSIC SCIENCE

(Added by L.1996 chs. 154, 952, eff. 7/1/96.)
(Selected Sections)

§9-196.8. Disposal of certain hazardous materials.
Any material which is seized in any criminal investigation and which is deemed to be hazardous to health and safety, may be disposed of upon written application of the Division of Forensic Science to the attorney for the Commonwealth in the city or county where the material is seized or where any criminal prosecution in which such material is proposed to be evidence is pending. Upon receipt thereof, the attorney for the Commonwealth shall file the application in the circuit court of such county or city. A sworn analysis report signed by a person designated by the Director of the Division of Forensic Science shall accompany the application for disposal and shall clearly identify and designate the material to be disposed of. The application shall state the nature of the hazardous materials, the quantity thereof, the location where seized, the person or persons from whom the materials were seized, and the manner whereby such materials shall be destroyed. When the ownership of the hazardous material is known, notice shall be given to the owner thereof at least three days prior to any hearing relating to the destruction, and, if any criminal charge is pending in any court as a result of such seizure, such notice shall be given to the accused if other than the owner. Upon receipt of the analysis report and the application, the court may order the destruction of all, or a part of, such material; however, a sufficient and representative quantity of such material shall be retained to permit an independent analysis when a criminal prosecution may result from such seizure. A return under oath, reporting the time, place, and manner of destruction, shall be made to the courts. Copies of the analysis report, application, order, and return shall be made a part of the record of any criminal prosecution. The sworn analysis report shall be admissible as evidence to the same extent as the disposed-of material would have been admissible.
(Added by L.1996 chs. 154, 952, eff. 7/1/96.)

§9-196.9. Disposal of certain other property.
Personal property, including drugs, not subject to be disposed of under §9-196.8, which has been submitted to the Division of Forensic Science or the former Bureau of Forensic Science for analysis or examination and which has not been reclaimed by the agency submitting such property for analysis or examination, may be disposed of by the Division in accordance with this section if, after the expiration of 120 days after the receipt by the Division of the property, the Director notifies the circuit court of the county or city from which the property was taken, in writing, that the analysis or examination has been completed, and a report submitted to the agency that the property has not been reclaimed by the agency submitting it and that the Division proposes to dispose of such property. The notice shall state the nature of the property, the quantity thereof, the location where seized, the name of the accused, if known, and the proposed method of disposing of the property. When the ownership of the property is known, a copy of such notice shall be sent simultaneously with the notice to the court to the owner, or, if any criminal charge is pending in any court relating to the property, the copy shall be sent to the accused at his last known address. Notice shall be by certified mail. The court, within thirty days after receipt of the notice, may direct that the property be disposed of by the Division, by an alternative method designed to preserve the property, at the expense of the agency submitting the property to the Division. If the court does not so direct within such thirty-day period, then the Division may dispose of the property by the method set out in the notice. Copies of the analysis report and notice shall be made a part of the record of any criminal prosecution. The report, if sworn to, shall be admissible as evidence to the same extent as the disposed-of property would have been admissible.
(Added by L.1996 chs. 154, 952, eff. 7/1/96.)

§9-196.10. Disposal of property.
Notwithstanding the provisions of §§9-196.8 and 9-196.9, the Division of Forensic Science may file an application in the Circuit Court of the City of Richmond seeking an order authorizing the disposal of all personal property, including drugs, received by the Division more than fifteen years prior to the filing of the application. The application, under oath, shall list each item of property, the date of submission to the Division, the agency or individual submitting the property, and the proposed method of disposal. The application shall also state that written notice by first-class mail was given to each agency or individual submitting property listed at least thirty days prior to the application, and that no agency or individual objected to the disposal. A return, under oath, reporting the time, place, and manner of disposal, shall be made to the court.
(Added by L.1996 chs. 154, 952, 987, eff. 7/1/96.)

§9-196.11. Rights of accused person or his attorney to results of investigation or to investigation.
Upon the request of any person accused of a crime or upon the request of an accused person's attorney, the Division of Forensic Science or the Division of Consolidated Laboratory Services shall furnish to the accused or his attorney the results of any investigation which has been conducted by it and which is related in any way to a crime for which such person is accused. In any case in which an attorney of record for a person accused of violation of any criminal law of the Commonwealth, or the accused, may desire a scientific investigation, he shall, by motion filed before the court in which the charge is pending, certify that in good faith he believes that a scientific investigation may be relevant to the criminal charge. The motion shall be heard ex parte as soon as practicable, and the court shall, after a hearing upon the motion and being satisfied as to the correctness of the certification, order that the same be performed by the Division of Forensic Science or the Division of Consolidated Laboratory Services and shall prescribe in its order the

method of custody, transfer, and return of evidence submitted for scientific investigation. Upon the request of the attorney for the Commonwealth of the jurisdiction in which the charge is pending, he shall be furnished the results of the scientific investigation.
(Added by L.1996 chs. 154, 952, eff. 7/1/96.)

TITLE 10.1
CONSERVATION
(Selected Subtitle)

SUBTITLE II
ACTIVITIES ADMINISTERED BY OTHER ENTITIES
(Selected Chapters)

CHAPTER 11
FOREST RESOURCES AND THE DEPARTMENT OF FORESTRY
(Selected Article)

ARTICLE 6
FOREST WARDENS AND FIRES
(Selected Sections)

§10.1-1139. Who may be summoned to aid forest warden.

Any forest warden to whom written instructions have been issued by the State Forester authorizing him to employ persons to assist in suppressing forest fires, shall have the authority to summon as many able-bodied persons between eighteen and fifty years of age as may, in his discretion, be reasonably necessary to assist in extinguishing any forest fire in any county or city of the Commonwealth which is organized for forest fire control under the direction of the State Forester. Any person summoned by a forest warden to fight a forest fire shall be paid at the rate of pay provided in the Department of Forestry wage scale for fire fighting in effect in the county or city, or part thereof, in which the fire is fought. Wardens shall not summon for such service any person while engaged in maintaining the rights-of-way of railroads for the safe passage of trains, nor any station agent, operator or other person while engaged in duties necessary for the safe operation of trains.

Any person summoned who fails or refuses to assist in fighting the fire, unless the failure is due to physical instability or other valid reason, shall be guilty of a Class 4 misdemeanor.

§10.1-1142. Regulating the burning of woods, brush, etc.; penalties.

A. It shall be unlawful for any owner or lessee of land to set fire to, or to procure another to set fire to, any woods, brush, logs, leaves, grass, debris, or other inflammable material upon such land unless he previously has taken all reasonable care and precaution, by having cut and piled the same or carefully cleared around the same, to prevent the spread of such fire to lands other than those owned or leased by him. It shall also be unlawful for any employee of any such owner or lessee of land to set fire to or to procure another to set fire to any woods, brush, logs, leaves, grass, debris, or other inflammable material, upon such land unless he has taken similar precautions to prevent the spread of such fire to any other land.

B. During the period February 15 through April 30 of each year, even though the precautions required by the foregoing subsection have been taken, it shall be unlawful, in any county or city or portion thereof organized for forest fire control under the direction of the State Forester, for any person to set fire to, or to procure another to set fire to, any brush, leaves, grass, debris or field containing dry grass or other inflammable material capable of spreading fire, located in or within 300 feet of any woodland, brushland, or field containing dry grass or other inflammable material, except between the hours of 4:00 p.m. and 12:00 midnight.

The provisions of this subsection shall not apply to any fires which may be set on federal lands and, between February 15 and March 1 of each year, on lands owned by the Department of Game and Inland Fisheries.

C. Any person who builds a fire in the open air, or uses a fire built by another in the open air, within 150 feet of any woodland, brushland or field containing dry grass or other inflammable material, shall totally extinguish the fire before leaving the area and shall not leave the fire unattended.

D. Any person violating any provisions of this section shall be guilty of a Class 3 misdemeanor for each separate offense. If any forest fire originates as a result of the violation by any person of any provision of this section, such person shall, in addition to the above penalty, be liable to the Commonwealth for the full amount of all expenses incurred by the Commonwealth in suppressing such fire. Such amounts shall be recoverable by action brought by the State Forester in the name of the Commonwealth on behalf of the Commonwealth and credited to the Forestry Operations Fund.
(Chgd. by L.1996 chs. 74, 1008, eff. 7/1/96.)

§10.1-1143. Throwing inflammatory objects from vehicle on highway while in or near certain lands.

It shall be unlawful for any person to throw, toss or drop from a vehicle moving or standing on a highway any lighted smoking material, lighted match, lighted material of any nature, or any bomb or device liable to set fire to inflammable material on the ground while in or near any forestland, brushland or field containing inflammable vegetation or trash.

Any person violating the provisions of this section shall be guilty of a Class 2 misdemeanor for each separate offense.

CHAPTER 14
VIRGINIA WASTE MANAGEMENT ACT
(Selected Articles)

ARTICLE 7
TRANSPORTATION OF HAZARDOUS MATERIALS
(Complete Article)

§10.1-1450. Waste Management Board to promulgate regulations regarding hazardous materials.

The Board shall promulgate regulations designating the manner and method by which hazardous materials shall be loaded, unloaded, packed, identified, marked, placarded, stored and transported. Such regulations shall be no more restrictive than any applicable federal laws or regulations.
(Chgd. by L.1997 ch. 260, eff. 7/1/97.)

§10.1-1451. Enforcement of article and regulations.

The Department of State Police and all other law-enforcement officers of the Commonwealth who have satisfactorily completed the course in Hazardous Materials Compliance and Enforcement as prescribed by the U.S. Department of Transportation, Research and Special Programs Administration, Office of Hazardous Materials Transportation, in federal safety regulations and safety inspection procedures pertaining to the transportation of hazardous materials, shall enforce the provisions of this article, and any rule or regulation promulgated hereunder. Those law-enforcement officers certified to enforce the provisions of this article and any regulation promulgated hereunder, shall annually receive in-service training in current federal safety regulations and safety inspection procedures pertaining to the transportation of hazardous materials.

§10.1-1452. Article not to preclude exercise of certain regulatory powers.

The provisions of this article shall not preclude the exercise of the statutory and regulatory powers of any agency, department or political subdivision of the Commonwealth having statutory authority to regulate hazardous materials on specified highways or portions thereof.

§10.1-1453. Exceptions.

This article shall not apply to regular military or naval forces of the United States, the duly authorized militia of any state or territory thereof, police or fire departments, or sheriff's offices and regional jails of this Commonwealth, provided the same are acting within their official capacity and in the performance of their duties, or to the transportation of hazardous radioactive materials in accordance with §44-146.30.
(Chgd. by L.1995 ch. 112, eff. 7/1/95.)

§10.1-1454. Transportation under United States regulations.

Any person transporting hazardous materials in accordance with regulations promulgated under the laws of the United States, shall be deemed to have complied with the provisions of this article, except when such transportation is excluded from regulation under the laws or regulations of the United States.

ARTICLE 7.2
TRANSPORTATION OF MUNICIPAL SOLID AND MEDICAL WASTE BY TRUCK
(Added by L.1999 chs. 584, 613, 947, eff. 7/1/99.)
(Complete Article)

§10.1-1454.3. Regulation of road transportation of waste.

A. The Board, in consultation with the appropriate agencies, shall develop regulations governing the commercial transport of nonhazardous municipal solid waste (except scrap metal and source-separated recyclables) and regulated medical waste by truck as are necessary to protect the health, safety, and welfare of the citizens of the Commonwealth, and to protect the Commonwealth's environment and natural resources from pollution, impairment, or destruction. Included in the regulations, to the extent allowable under federal law and regulation, shall be provisions:

1. Governing the transport of wastes by truck and the design and construction of the containers and trailers transporting waste by truck so that they will be designed, constructed and maintained so as to, as much as is reasonably practicable, prevent the escape of wastes and liquids and to prevent the loss or spillage of wastes to the extent possible in the event of an accident; and

2. Requiring owners of trucks transporting wastes regulated under this article to demonstrate financial responsibility sufficient to comply with the requirements of this article as a condition of operation. Regulations governing the amount of any financial responsibility required shall take into consideration (i) the risk of potential damage or injury that may result from spillage or leakage; (ii) the potential costs of containment and cleanup; and (iii) the nature and degree of injury or interference with general health, welfare and property that may result.

B. The owner or operator of a truck from which there is spillage or loss of wastes subject to regulations under this article shall immediately report such spillage or loss in accordance with the regulations of the Board and shall immediately take all such actions as may be necessary to contain and remove such wastes.

C. No person shall transport by truck wastes regulated under this article unless the containers carried thereon are designed, constructed, loaded, operated and maintained in accordance with the regulations developed pursuant to subsection A. A violation of this subsection shall be a Class 1 misdemeanor.

D. For the purposes of this section, the term "truck" means any tractor truck semitrailer combination with four or more axles.
(Added by L.1999 chs. 584, 613, 947, eff. 7/1/99; renumbered in 1999 from Section 10.1-1454.2.)

ARTICLE 8
PENALTIES, ENFORCEMENT AND JUDICIAL REVIEW
(Selected Section)

§10.1-1455. Penalties and enforcement.

A. Any person who violates any provision of this chapter, any condition of a permit or certification, or any regulation or order of the Board shall, upon such finding by an appropriate circuit court, be assessed a civil penalty of not more than $25,000 for each day of such violation. All civil penalties under this section shall be recovered in a civil action brought by the Attorney General in the name of the Commonwealth. Such civil penalties shall be paid into the state treasury and deposited by the State Treasurer into the Virginia Environmental Emergency Response Fund pursuant to Chapter 25 (§10.1-2500 et seq.) of this title.

B. In addition to the penalties provided above, any person who knowingly transports any hazardous waste to an unpermitted facility; who knowingly transports, treats, stores, or disposes of hazardous waste without a permit or in violation of a permit; or who knowingly makes any false statement or representation in any application, disclosure statement, label, manifest, record, report, permit, or other document filed, maintained, or used for purposes of hazardous waste program compliance shall be guilty of a felony punishable by a term of imprisonment of not less than one year nor more than five years and a fine of not more than $25,000 for each violation, either or both. The provisions of this subsection shall be deemed to constitute a lesser included offense of the violation set forth under subsection I.

Each day of violation of each requirement shall constitute a separate offense.

C. The Board is authorized to issue orders to require any person to comply with the provisions of any law administered by the Board, the Director or the Department, any condition of a permit or certification, or any regulations promulgated by the Board or to comply with any case decision, as defined in §9-6.14:4, of the Board or Director. Any such order shall be issued only after a hearing with at least thirty days' notice to the affected person of the time, place and purpose thereof. Such order shall become effective not less than fifteen days after mailing a copy thereof by certified mail to the last known address of such person. The provisions of this section shall not affect the authority of the Board to issue separate orders and regulations to meet any emergency as provided in §10.1-1402.

D. Any person willfully violating or refusing, failing or neglecting to comply with any regulation or order of the Board or the Director, any condition of a permit or certification or any provision of this chapter shall be guilty of a Class 1 misdemeanor unless a different penalty is specified.

Any person violating or failing, neglecting, or refusing to obey any lawful regulation or order of the Board or the Director, any condition of a permit or certification or any provision of this chapter may be compelled in a proceeding instituted in an appropriate court by the Board or the Director to obey such regulation, permit, certification, order or provision of this chapter and to comply therewith by injunction, mandamus, or other appropriate remedy.

E. Without limiting the remedies which may be obtained in this section, any person violating or failing, neglecting or refusing to obey any injunction, mandamus or other remedy obtained pursuant to this section shall be subject, in the discretion of the court, to a civil penalty not to exceed $25,000 for each violation. Such civil penalties shall be paid into the state treasury and deposited by the State Treasurer into the Virginia Environmental Emergency Response Fund pursuant to Chapter 25 of this title. Each day of violation of each requirement shall constitute a separate offense. Such civil penalties may, in the discretion of the court assessing them, be directed to be paid into the treasury of the county, city or town in which the violation occurred, to be used to abate environmental pollution in such manner as the court may, by order, direct, except that where the owner in violation is the county, city or town itself, or its agent, the court shall direct the penalty to be paid into the state treasury and deposited by the State Treasurer into the Virginia Environmental Emergency Response Fund pursuant to Chapter 25 of this title.

F. With the consent of any person who has violated or failed, neglected or refused to obey any regulation or order of the Board or the Director, any condition of a permit or any provision of this chapter, the Board may provide, in an order issued by the Board against such person, for the payment of civil charges for past violations in specific sums, not to exceed the limits specified in this section. Such civil charges shall be instead of any appropriate civil penalty which could be imposed under this section. Such civil charges shall be paid into the state treasury and deposited by the State Treasurer into the Virginia Environmental Emergency Response Fund pursuant to Chapter 25 of this title.

G. In addition to all other available remedies, the Board may issue administrative orders for the violation of (i) any law or regulation administered by the Board; (ii) any condition of a permit or certificate issued pursuant to this chapter; or (iii) any case decision or order of the Board. Issuance of an administrative order shall be a case decision as defined in §9-6.14:4. Orders issued pursuant to this subsection may include penalties of up to $25,000 per violation and may compel the taking of corrective actions or the cessation of any activity upon which the order is based. Orders issued pursuant to this subsection shall become effective five days after having been delivered to the affected persons or mailed by certified mail to the last known address of such persons. Should the Board find that any person is adversely affecting the public health, safety or welfare, or the environment, the Board shall, after a reasonable attempt to give notice, issue, without a hearing, an emergency administrative order directing the person to cease the activity immediately and undertake any needed corrective action, and shall within ten days hold a hearing, after reasonable notice as to the time and place thereof to the person, to affirm, modify, amend or cancel the emergency administrative order. If the Board finds that a person who has been issued an administrative order or an emergency administrative order is not complying with the order's terms, the Board may utilize the enforcement and penalty provisions of this article to secure compliance.

H. In addition to all other available remedies, the Department and generators of recycling residues shall have standing to seek enforcement by injunction of conditions which are specified by applicants in order to receive the priority treatment of their permit applications pursuant to §10.1-1408.1.

I. Any person who knowingly transports, treats, stores, disposes of, or exports any hazardous waste in violation of this chapter or in violation of the regulations promulgated by the Board and who knows at the time that he thereby places another person in imminent danger of death or serious bodily injury, shall, upon conviction, be guilty of a felony punishable by a term of imprisonment of not less than two years nor more than fifteen years and a fine of not more than $250,000, either or both. A defendant that is not an individual shall, upon conviction of violating this section, be subject to a fine not exceeding the greater of one million dollars or an amount that is three times the economic benefit realized by the defendant as a result of the offense. The maximum penalty shall be doubled with respect to both fine and imprisonment for any subsequent conviction of the same person.

J. Criminal prosecutions under this chapter shall be commenced within three years after discovery of the offense, notwithstanding the provisions of any other statute.

K. The Board shall be entitled to an award of reasonable attorneys' fees and costs in any action brought by the Board under this section in which it substantially prevails on the merits of the case, unless special circumstances would make an award unjust.

(Chgd. L.1998 ch. 837; L.1999 ch. 876, eff. 7/1/99.)

TITLE 14.1
COSTS, FEES, SALARIES AND ALLOWANCES

(Repealed by L.1998 ch. 872, eff. 10/1/98. See Title 17.1 for statutes effective 10/1/98.)

TITLE 15.2
COUNTIES, CITIES AND TOWNS

(Added by L.1997 ch. 587, eff. 12/1/97.)
(Selected Subtitle)

SUBTITLE II
POWERS OF LOCAL GOVERNMENT

(Selected Chapters)

CHAPTER 11
POWERS OF CITIES AND TOWNS

(Selected Article)

ARTICLE 1
UNIFORM CHARTER POWERS

(Selected Sections)

§15.2-1120. Detentive, correctional and penal institutions.

A municipal corporation may provide and operate, within or outside the municipal corporation, detentive, correctional and penal institutions; or may contract with others for supplying the services and facilities provided at such institutions.

(Added by L.1997 ch. 587, eff. 12/1/97.)

§15.2-1122. Parking or storage of vehicles.

A municipal corporation may provide and operate places for, and limited to, the parking or storage of vehicles by the public, which shall include but shall not be limited to parking lots, garages, buildings and other land, structures, equipment and facilities; provide for their management and operation by an agency of the municipality; contract with others for the operation and management thereof upon such terms and conditions as shall be prescribed by the municipal corporation; and charge or authorize the charging of compensation for the parking or storage of vehicles.

(Added by L.1997 ch. 587, eff. 12/1/97.)

§15.2-1123. Airports and facilities.

A municipal corporation may provide and operate within or outside the municipal corporation airports and lands, structures, equipment and facilities appurtenant thereto; provide for their management and operation by an agency of the municipality; contract with others for the operation and management thereof upon such terms and conditions as shall be prescribed by the municipal corporation; and charge or authorize the charging of compensation for the use of the airport or any of its appurtenances or facilities.

(Added by L.1997 ch. 587, eff. 12/1/97.)

§15.2-1124. Police jurisdiction over lands, buildings and structures; jurisdiction of offenses; appeals; jurisdiction in certain public buildings with magistrate's offices.

A. Lands, buildings or structures provided and operated by a municipality for any purpose defined in this article shall be under the police jurisdiction of the municipal corporation for the enforcement of its regulations respecting the use or occupancy thereof. All regular and special police officers of the municipal corporation shall have jurisdiction to make arrests on such land and in such buildings or structures for violations of such regulations. Such criminal case shall be prosecuted in the locality in which the offense was committed.

B. In any public building that is located in a county with a population between 56,000 and 57,000 adjoining a municipal corporation and that contains a magistrate's office which serves the municipal corporation, the sheriff, any deputy sheriff, and any police officer of the municipal corporation shall have the same powers which such sheriff, deputy sheriff or police officer would have in the municipal corporation itself. The courts of the municipal corporation and the locality in which such public building is located shall have concurrent jurisdiction of any offense committed against or any escape from any such sheriff, deputy sheriff, or police officer in such public building, provided that the sheriff, deputy sheriff, or police officer was present in the public building while in the performance of his official duties. Such police powers and concurrent jurisdiction shall also apply during travel between the municipal corporation and the public building by such sheriff, deputy sheriffs, and police officers while in the performance of their official duties. For purposes of this subsection, a "public building" shall include the surrounding grounds of such building.

(Added by L.1997 ch. 587, eff. 12/1/97, incorporating changes to former Section 15.1-887 by L.1997 ch. 739, eff. 12/1/97.)

CHAPTER 15
LOCAL GOVERNMENT PERSONNEL, QUALIFICATION FOR OFFICE, BONDS, DUAL OFFICE HOLDING AND CERTAIN LOCAL GOVERNMENT OFFICERS

(Selected Article)

ARTICLE 1
GENERAL PROVISIONS FOR CERTAIN OFFICERS AND EMPLOYEES
(Selected Section)

§15.2-1511. Allowances to injured officials and employees and their dependents.

The governing body of any locality is authorized in its discretion to make allowances by appropriation of funds, payable in monthly or semimonthly installments, for the relief of any of its officials, employees, police officers, firefighters, sheriffs or deputy sheriffs, town sergeants and town deputy sergeants, or their dependents, who suffer injury or death as defined in Title 65.2, whether such injury was suffered or death occurs before or after June 29, 1948 (which date is the effective date of the section). The allowance shall not exceed the salary or wage being paid such official, employee, police officer, firefighter, sheriff or deputy sheriff, town sergeants and town deputy sergeants, at the time of such injury or death, and the payment of the allowance shall not extend beyond the period of disability resulting from such injury. In case death results from the injury, the allowance may be made for the dependents as defined in Title 65.2. In localities which have established retirement or pension systems for injured, retired or superannuated officials, employees, members of police or fire departments, sheriffs, deputy sheriffs, town sergeants and deputy sergeants, or for the dependents of those killed in line of duty, the agencies provided for the administration of such systems shall determine the existence of such injury or cause of death before any appropriation to pay such allowance is made and shall determine the extent of and period of disability resulting from such injury and the cause in case of death. All sums paid to any such official, employee, police officer, firefighter, sheriff or deputy sheriff, town sergeants and deputy sergeants, as compensation under Title 65.2 and all sums paid to the dependents of such official, employee, police officer, firefighter, sheriff or deputy sheriff, town sergeant and deputy sergeant, if he is killed, and all sums paid under any retirement or pension system shall be deducted from the allowance made under this section in such installments as the agency determines. If the agency determines that any official, employee, police officer, firefighter, sheriff or deputy sheriff, town sergeant and deputy sergeant, who suffered injury in the line of duty is engaged or is able to engage in a gainful occupation, then the allowance shall be reduced by the agency to an amount which, together with the amount earnable by him, equals the allowance. Should the earning capacity of the official, employee, police officer, firefighter, sheriff or deputy sheriff, town sergeant and deputy sergeant, be later changed, such allowance may be further modified, up or down, provided the new allowance shall not exceed the amount of the allowance originally made nor an amount which, when added to the amount earnable by him, exceeds such allowance.

The death of, or any condition or impairment of health of, any member of a local police department, or of a sheriff or deputy sheriff, caused by hypertension or heart disease resulting in total or partial disability shall be presumed to have been suffered in the line of duty unless the contrary be shown by competent evidence; provided that prior to making any claim based upon such presumption for retirement, sickness or other benefits on account of such death or total or partial disability, such member, sheriff, or deputy sheriff, shall have been found free from hypertension or heart disease, as the case may be, by a physical examination which shall include such appropriate laboratory and other diagnostic studies as such governing body shall prescribe and which shall have been conducted by physicians whose qualifications shall have been prescribed by such governing body. In the case of a claim for disability, that any such member, sheriff, or deputy sheriff shall, if requested by such governing body or its authorized representative, submit himself to physical examination by any physician designated by such governing body, such examination to include such tests or studies as may reasonably be prescribed by the physician so designated. Such member, sheriff or deputy sheriff, or claimant shall have the right to have present at such examination, at his own expense, any qualified physician he may designate. In the case of a claim for death benefits, any person entitled to make a claim for such benefits, claiming that such person's death was suffered in the line of duty, shall submit the body of the deceased to a postmortem examination to be performed by the medical examiner for the county, city or town appointed under §32.1-282.

(Added by L.1997 ch. 587, eff. 12/1/97.)

§15.2-1512.2. Political activities of firefighters, emergency medical technicians and law-enforcement officers.

A. For the purposes of this section:

"Emergency medical technician" means any person who is employed within the fire department or public safety department of a locality whose primary responsibility is the provision of emergency medical care to the sick or injured, using either basic or advanced techniques. Emergency medical technicians may also provide fire protection services and assist in the enforcement of the fire prevention code.

"Firefighter" means any person who is employed within the fire department or public safety department of a locality whose primary responsibility is the prevention or extinguishment of fires, the protection of life and property, or the enforcement of local or state fire prevention codes or laws pertaining to the prevention or control of fires.

"Law-enforcement officer" means any person who is employed within the police department, bureau or force of any locality, including the sheriff's department of any city or county, and who is authorized by law to make arrests.

"Locality" means counties, cities, towns, authorities or special districts.

"Political campaign" means activities engaged in for the purpose of promoting a political issue, for influencing the outcome of an election for local or state office, or for influencing the outcome of a referendum or special election.

"Political candidate" means any person who has made known his or her intention to seek, or campaign for, local or state office in a general, primary or special election.

"Political party" means any party, organization or group having as its purpose the promotion of political candidates or political campaigns.

B. Notwithstanding any contrary provision of law, general or special, no locality shall prohibit firefighters, emergency medical technicians or law-enforcement officers within its employment from participating in political activities while these employees are off duty, out of uniform and not on the premises of their employment with the locality.

C. For purposes of this section, the term "political activities" includes, but is not limited to: voting; registering to vote; soliciting votes or endorsements on behalf of a political candidate or political campaign; expressing opinions, privately or publicly, on political subjects and candidates; displaying a political picture, sign, sticker, badge or button; participating in the activities of, or contributing financially to, a political party, candidate or campaign or an organization that supports a political candidate or campaign; attending or participating in a political convention, caucus, rally, or other political gathering; initiating, circulating or signing a political petition; engaging in fund-raising activities for any political party, candidate or campaign; acting as a recorder, watcher, challenger or similar officer at the polls on behalf of a political party, candidate or campaign; or becoming a political candidate.

D. Firefighters, emergency medical technicians, or law-enforcement officers are prohibited from using their official authority to coerce or attempt to coerce a subordinate employee to pay, lend or contribute anything of value to a political party, candidate or campaign, or to discriminate against any employee or applicant for employment because of that person's political affiliations or political activities, except as such affiliation or activity may be established by law as disqualification for employment.

E. Firefighters, emergency medical technicians, or law-enforcement officers are prohibited from discriminating in the provision of fire fighting, emergency medical, or law-enforcement services, or responding to requests for such services, on the basis of the political affiliations or political activities of the person or organization for which such services are provided or requested.

F. Firefighters, emergency medical technicians, or law-enforcement officers are prohibited from suggesting or implying that a locality has officially endorsed a political party, candidate or campaign.

(Added by L.2000 ch. 791, eff. 7/1/2000.)

CHAPTER 16
LOCAL CONSTITUTIONAL OFFICERS, COURTHOUSES AND SUPPLIES
(Selected Article)

ARTICLE 3
SHERIFF
(Selected Sections)

§15.2-1609. Sheriff.

The voters in every county and city shall elect a sheriff unless otherwise provided by general law or special act. The sheriff shall exercise all the powers conferred and perform all the duties imposed upon sheriffs by general law. He shall enforce the law or see that it is enforced in the locality from which he is elected; assist in the judicial process as provided by general law; and be charged with the custody, feeding and care of all prisoners confined in the county or city jail. He may perform such other duties, not inconsistent with his office, as may be requested of him by the governing body. The sheriff shall be elected as provided by general law for a term of four years.

(Added by L.1997 ch. 587, eff. 12/1/97.)

§15.2-1613. Operation of sheriff's office.

Any county or city may appropriate funds for the operation of the sheriff's office.

In addition to those items listed in §14.1-80, counties and cities shall provide at their expense in accordance with standards set forth in §15.2-1610 a reasonable number of uniforms and items of personal equipment required by the sheriff to carry out his official duties.

(Added by L.1997 ch. 587, eff. 12/1/97.)

CHAPTER 17
POLICE AND PUBLIC ORDER
(Complete Chapter)

ARTICLE 1
GENERAL PROVISIONS

§15.2-1700. Preservation of peace and good order.

Any locality may provide for the protection of its inhabitants and property and for the preservation of peace and good order therein.

(Added by L.1997 ch. 587, eff. 12/1/97.)

§15.2-1701. Organization of police forces.

Any locality may, by ordinance, provide for the organization of its authorized police forces. Such forces shall include a chief of police, and such officers and other personnel as appropriate.

When a locality provides for a police department, the chief of police shall be the chief law-enforcement officer of that locality. However, in towns, the chief law-enforcement officer may be called the town sergeant.

(Added by L.1997 ch. 587, eff. 12/1/97.)

§15.2-1702. Referendum required prior to establishment of county police force.

A. A county shall not establish a police force unless (i) such action is first approved by the voters of the county in accordance with the provisions of this section and (ii) the General Assembly enacts appropriate authorizing legislation.

B. The governing body of any county shall petition the court, by resolution, asking that a referendum be held on the question, "Shall a police force be established in the county and the sheriff's office be relieved of primary law-enforcement responsibilities?" The court, by order entered of record in accordance with Article 5 (§24.2-681 et seq.) of Chapter 6 of Title 24.2, shall require the regular election officials of the county to open the polls and take the sense of the voters on the question as herein provided.

The clerk of the circuit court for the county shall publish notice of the election in a newspaper of general circulation in the county once a week for three consecutive weeks prior to the election. The notice shall contain the ballot question and a statement of not more than 500 words on the proposed question. The explanation shall be presented in plain English, shall be limited to a neutral explanation, and shall not present arguments by either proponents or opponents of the proposal. The attorney for the county or city or, if there is no county or city attorney, the attorney for the Commonwealth shall prepare the explanation. "Plain English" means written in nontechnical, readily understandable language using words of common everyday usage and avoiding legal terms and phrases or other terms and words of art whose usage or special meaning primarily is limited to a particular field or profession.

C. The county may expend public funds to produce and distribute neutral information concerning the referendum; provided, however, public funds may not be used to promote a particular position on the question, either in the notice called for in subsection B, or in any other distribution of information to the public.

D. The regular election officers of the county shall open the polls on the date specified in such order and conduct the election in the manner provided by law. The election shall be by ballot which shall be prepared by the electoral board of the county and on which shall be printed the following:

"Shall a police force be established in the county and the sheriff's office be relieved of primary law-enforcement responsibilities?

☐ Yes

☐ No"

The ballots shall be counted, returns made and canvassed as in other elections, and the results certified by the electoral board to the court ordering the election. If a majority of the voters voting in the election vote "Yes," the court shall enter an order proclaiming the results of the election and a duly certified copy of such order shall be transmitted to the governing body of the county. The governing body shall proceed to establish a police force following the enactment of authorizing legislation by the General Assembly.

E. After a referendum has been conducted pursuant to this section, no subsequent referendum shall be conducted pursuant to this section in the same county for a period of four years from the date of the prior referendum.

(Added by L.1997 ch. 587; chgd. by L.2000 ch. 298, eff. 7/1/2000.)

§15.2-1703. Referendum to abolish county police force.

The police force in any county which established the force subsequent to July 1, 1983, may be abolished and its responsibilities assumed by the sheriff's office after a referendum held pursuant to this section.

Either (i) the voters of the county by petition signed by not less than ten percent of the registered voters therein on the January 1 preceding the filing of the petition or (ii) the governing body of the county, by resolution, may petition the circuit court for the county that a referendum be held on the question, "Shall the county police force be abolished and its responsibilities assumed by the county sheriff's office?" The court, by order entered of record in accordance with Article 5 (§24.2-681 et seq.) of Chapter 6 of Title 24.2, shall require the regular election officials of the county at the next general election held in the county to open the polls and take the sense of the voters on the question as herein provided. The clerk of the circuit court for the county shall publish notice of the election in a newspaper of general circulation in the county once a week for three consecutive weeks prior to the election.

The ballot shall be printed as follows:

"Shall the county police force be abolished and its responsibilities assumed by the county sheriff's office?

☐ Yes

☐ No"

The election shall be held and the results certified as provided in §24.2-684. If a majority of the voters voting in the election vote in favor of the question, the court shall enter an order proclaiming the results of the election, and a duly certified copy of such order shall be transmitted to the governing body of the county. The governing body shall proceed with the necessary action to abolish the police force and transfer its responsibilities to the sheriff's office, to become effective on July 1 following the referendum.

Once a referendum has been held pursuant to this section, no further referendum shall be held pursuant to this section within four years thereafter.

(Added by L.1997 ch. 587, eff. 12/1/97.)

§15.2-1704. Powers and duties of police force.

A. The police force of a locality is hereby invested with all the power and authority which formerly belonged to the office of constable at common law and is responsible for the prevention and detection of crime, the apprehension of criminals, the safeguard of life and property, the preservation of peace and the enforcement of state and local laws, regulations, and ordinances.

B. A police officer has no authority in civil matters, except (i) to execute and serve temporary detention and emergency custody orders and any other powers granted to law-enforcement officers in §37.1-67.01 or §37.1-67.1, (ii) to serve an order of protection pursuant to §§16.1-253.1, 16.1-253.4 and 16.1-279.1 or (iii) to execute all warrants or summons as may be placed in his hands by any magistrate for the locality and to make due return thereof. A town police officer, after receiving training under subdivision 8 of §9-170, may, with the concurrence of the local sheriff, also serve civil papers, and make return thereof, only when the town is the plaintiff and the defendant can be found within the corporate limits of the town.

(Added by L.1997 ch. 587; chgd. by L.1998 ch. 425; L.1999 ch. 495, eff. 7/1/99.)

§15.2-1705. Minimum qualifications; waiver.

A. The chief of police and all police officers of any locality, all deputy sheriffs and jail officers in this Commonwealth, and all law-enforcement officers as defined in §9-169 who enter upon the duties of such office after July 1, 1994, are required to meet the following minimum qualifications for office. Such person shall (i) be a citizen of the United States, (ii) be required to undergo a background investigation including fingerprint-based criminal history records inquiries to both the Central Criminal Records Exchange and the Federal Bureau of Investigation, (iii) have a high school education or have passed the General Educational Development exam, (iv) possess a valid driver's license if required by the duties of office to operate a motor vehicle, (v) undergo a physical examination, subsequent to a conditional offer of employment, conducted under the supervision of a licensed physician, (vi) be at least eighteen years of age, (vii) not have been convicted of or pleaded guilty or no contest to a felony or any offense that would be a felony if committed in Virginia, and (viii) not have produced a positive result on a pre-employment drug screening, if such screening is required by the hiring law-enforcement agency or jail, where the positive result cannot be explained to the law-enforcement agency's or jail administrator's satisfaction.

B. Upon request of a sheriff or chief of police, or the director or chief executive of any agency or department employing law-enforcement officers as defined in §9-169, or jail officers as defined in §53.1-1, the Department of Criminal Justice Services is hereby authorized to waive the requirements for qualification as set out in subsection A of this section for good cause shown.

(Added by L.1997 ch. 587, eff. 12/1/97.)

§15.2-1706. Certification through training required for all law-enforcement officers.

All law-enforcement officers as defined in §9-169 and all jail officers as defined in §53.1-1 must be certified through the successful completion of training at an approved criminal justice training academy in order to remain eligible for appointment or employment. In order to obtain such certification, all entry level law-enforcement officers seeking certification on or after July 1, 2001, shall successfully complete statewide certification examinations developed and administered by the Department of Criminal Justice Services. The Department may delegate administration of the examinations to an approved criminal justice training academy and may revoke such delegation at its discretion. The appointee's or employee's hiring agency must provide the Department of Criminal Justice Services with verification that law-enforcement or jail officers first hired after July 1, 1994, have met the minimum standards set forth in §15.2-1705.

(Added by L.1997 ch. 587; chgd. by L.1999 ch. 635, eff. 7/1/99.)

§15.2-1707. Decertification of law-enforcement officers.

Upon written notification from the sheriff, chief of police or agency administrator that any certified law-enforcement or jail officer has (i) been convicted of or pled guilty or no contest to a felony or any offense that would be a felony if committed in Virginia, (ii) failed to comply with or maintain compliance with mandated training requirements, or (iii) refused to submit to a drug screening or has produced a positive result on a drug screening reported to the employing agency, where the positive result cannot be explained to the agency administrator's satisfaction, which notification, where appropriate, shall be accompanied by a copy of the judgment of conviction, the Criminal Justice Services Board shall decertify such law-enforcement or jail officer. Such officer shall not have the right to serve as a law-enforcement officer within this Commonwealth until his certification has been reinstated by the Board.

The clerk of any court in which a conviction of a felony is made who has knowledge that a law-enforcement or jail officer has been convicted shall have a duty to report these findings promptly to the employing agency.

When a conviction has not become final, the Board may decline to decertify the officer until the conviction becomes final, after considering the likelihood of irreparable damage to the officer if such officer is decertified during the pendency of an ultimately successful appeal, the likelihood of injury or damage to the public if the officer is not decertified, and the seriousness of the offense.

(Added by L.1997 ch. 587, eff. 12/1/97.)

§15.2-1708. Notice of decertification.

A. Service of notice. The Board shall, within ten days of decertification, serve notice upon an affected officer, in person or by certified mail, and upon the law-enforcement or jail agency employing said officer, by certified mail, specifying the action taken and remedies available. The Board shall stay final action until the period for requesting a hearing expires.

B. Decertification hearing. Any law-enforcement or jail officer who has been decertified may, within thirty days of receipt of notice served by the Board, request, by certified mail, a hearing which shall be granted by the Board. Upon receipt of such request, the Board shall set a date, time, and place for the hearing within sixty days and serve notice by certified mail upon the affected officer. The Board, or a committee thereof shall conduct such hearing. The affected officer may be represented by counsel. In the absence of a request for hearing, decertification shall, without further proceedings, become final thirty days after the initial notice.

C. Standard of review. The decertification of a law-enforcement or jail officer under §15.2-1707 shall be sustained by the Board unless such law-enforcement or jail officer shows, by a preponderance of the evidence, good cause for his certification to be reinstated.

D. Final decision after request for hearing. The Board shall render a final decision within thirty days.

E. Notice of final action. The Board shall notify the officer and the law-enforcement or jail agency involved, by certified mail, of the final action regarding decertification.

F. Reinstatement after decertification. Any officer who is decertified may, after a period of not less than five years, petition the Board to be considered for reinstatement of certification.

(Added by L.1997 ch. 587, eff. 12/1/97.)

§15.2-1709. Employer immunity from liability; disclosure of information regarding former deputy sheriffs and law-enforcement officers.

Any sheriff or chief of police, the director or chief executive of any agency or department employing deputy sheriffs or law-enforcement officers as defined §9-169, or jail officers as defined in §53.1-1, and the Director of the Department of Criminal Justice Services or his designee who discloses information about a former deputy sheriff's or law-enforcement officer's or jail officer's job performance to a prospective law-enforcement or jail employer of the former appointee or employee is presumed to be acting in good faith and, unless lack of good faith is shown by clear and convincing evidence, is immune from civil liability for such disclosure or its consequences. For purposes of this section, the presumption of good faith is rebutted upon a showing that the information disclosed by the former employer was knowingly false or deliberately misleading, was

rendered with malicious purpose, or violated any civil right of the former employee or appointee.
(Added by L.1997 ch. 587, eff. 12/1/97.)

§15.2-1710. Fees and other compensation.
A police officer shall not receive any fee or other compensation out of the state treasury or the treasury of a locality for any service rendered under the provisions of this chapter other than the salary paid him by the locality and a fee as a witness in cases arising under the criminal laws of the Commonwealth. A police officer shall not receive any fee as a witness in any case arising under the ordinances of his locality, nor for attendance as a witness before any magistrate in his locality. However, if it is necessary or expedient for him to travel beyond the limits of the locality in his capacity as a police officer, he shall be entitled to his actual expenses, as provided by law for other expenses in criminal cases.

Nothing in this section shall be construed as prohibiting a police officer of a locality from claiming and receiving any reward which may be offered for the arrest and detention of any offender against the criminal laws of this or any other state or nation.
(Added by L.1997 ch. 587, eff. 12/1/97.)

§15.2-1711. Providing legal fees and expenses for law-enforcement officers; repayment to locality of two-thirds of amount by Compensation Board.
If any law-enforcement officer is investigated, arrested or indicted or otherwise prosecuted on any criminal charge arising out of any act committed in the discharge of his official duties, and no charges are brought, the charge is subsequently dismissed or upon trial he is found not guilty, the governing body of the locality wherein he is appointed may reimburse such officer for reasonable legal fees and expenses incurred by him in defense of such investigation or charge; such reimbursement shall be paid from the treasury of the locality.

When a governing body reimburses its sheriff or a law-enforcement officer in the sheriff's employment for reasonable legal fees and expenses as provided for in this section, then, upon certification of the reimbursement to the Chairman of the Compensation Board by the presiding officer of the governing body, the Compensation Board shall pay to the applicable locality two-thirds of the amount so certified.
(Added by L.1997 ch. 587, eff. 12/1/97.)

§15.2-1712. Employment of off-duty officers.
Notwithstanding the provisions of §§2.1-639.1 through 2.1-639.24, any locality may adopt an ordinance which permits law-enforcement officers and deputy sheriffs in such locality to engage in off-duty employment which may occasionally require the use of their police powers in the performance of such employment. Such ordinance may include reasonable rules to apply to such off-duty employment, or it may delegate the promulgation of such reasonable rules to the chief of the respective police departments or the sheriff of the county or city.
(Added by L.1997 ch. 587, eff. 12/1/97.)

§15.2-1713. Localities authorized to offer and pay rewards in felony and misdemeanor cases.
When any felony or misdemeanor has been committed, or there has been any attempt to commit a felony in any locality, the governing body of the locality or its duly authorized agent may offer and pay a reward for the arrest and final conviction of the person or persons who committed the felony or misdemeanor or attempted to commit the felony. The reward may be paid out of the general fund of such locality.
(Added by L.1997 ch. 587, eff. 12/1/97.)

§15.2-1714. Establishing police lines, perimeters, or barricades.
Whenever fires, accidents, wrecks, explosions, crimes, riots or other emergency situations where life, limb or property may be endangered may cause persons to collect on the public streets, alleys, highways, parking lots or other public area, the chief law-enforcement officer of any locality or that officer's authorized representative who is responsible for the security of the scene may establish such areas, zones or perimeters by the placement of police lines or barricades as are reasonably necessary to (i) preserve the integrity of evidence at such scenes, (ii) notwithstanding the provisions of §§46.2-888 through 46.2-891, facilitate the movement of vehicular and pedestrian traffic into, out of and around the scene, (iii) permit firefighters, police officers and emergency services personnel to perform necessary operations unimpeded, and (iv) protect persons and property.

Any police line or barricade erected for these purposes shall be clearly identified by wording such as "Police Line – DO NOT CROSS" or other similar wording. If material or equipment is not available for identifying the prohibited area, then a verbal warning by identifiable law-enforcement officials positioned to indicate a location of a police line or barricade shall be given to any person or persons attempting to cross police lines or barricades without proper authorization.

Such scene may be secured no longer than is reasonably necessary to effect the above-described purposes. Nothing in this section shall limit or otherwise affect the authority of or be construed to deny access to such scene by, any person charged by law with the responsibility of rendering assistance at or investigating any such fires, accidents, wrecks, explosions, crimes or riots.

Personnel from information services such as press, radio and television, when gathering news, shall be exempt from the provisions of this section except that it shall be unlawful for such persons to obstruct the police, firemen and rescue workers in the performance of their duties at such scene. Such personnel shall proceed at their own risk.
(Added by L.1997 ch. 587, eff. 12/1/97.)

§15.2-1715. Authority to declare Intensified Drug Enforcement Jurisdictions; expenditure of funds.
Whenever, in the judgment of the Governor or his designee, a locality or multi-jurisdictional area is confronted with a drug trafficking problem of such a magnitude as to warrant additional resources to supplement the efforts of local officials responsible for the apprehension and prosecution of persons engaged in drug trafficking activities, he may declare such areas Intensified Drug Enforcement Jurisdictions. Upon such declaration, the Governor, or his designee, may make available funds from the Intensified Drug Enforcement Jurisdictions Fund provided for in §14.1-133.3.
(Added by L.1997 ch. 587, eff. 12/1/97.)

§15.2-1716. Reimbursement of expenses incurred in responding to DUI incident.
Any locality may provide by ordinance that any person who is convicted of a violation of §§18.2-51.4, 18.2-266 or §29.1-738, or a similar ordinance, when his operation of a motor vehicle, engine, train or watercraft while so impaired is the proximate cause of any accident or incident resulting in an appropriate emergency response, shall be liable in a separate civil action to the locality or to any volunteer rescue squad, or both, which may provide such emergency response for the reasonable expense thereof in an amount not to exceed $1,000 in the aggregate for a particular accident or incident occurring in such locality. As used in this section, "appropriate emergency response" includes all costs of providing law-enforcement, fire-fighting, rescue, and

emergency medical services. The provisions of this section shall not preempt or limit any remedy available to the Commonwealth, to the locality or to any volunteer rescue squad to recover the reasonable expenses of an emergency response to an accident or incident not involving impaired driving or operation of a vehicle as set forth herein.
(Added by L.1997 ch. 587, eff. 12/1/97, incorporating changes to former Section 15.1-132.1 by L.1997 ch. 691, eff. 12/1/97.)

§15.2-1717. Preventing interference with pupils at schools.

Localities may adopt any reasonable ordinance necessary to prevent any improper interference with or annoyance of the pupils attending or boarding at any schools situated in such locality.
(Added by L.1997 ch. 587, eff. 12/1/97.)

§15.2-1717.1. Designation of police to enforce trespass violations.

Any locality may by ordinance establish a procedure whereby the owner of real property may designate the local law-enforcement agency as a "person lawfully in charge of the property" for the purpose of forbidding another to go or remain upon the lands, buildings or premises of the owner as specified in the designation. The ordinance shall require that any such designation be in writing and on file with the local law-enforcement agency.
(Added by L.1999 ch. 275, eff. 7/1/99.)

§15.2-1718. Receipt of missing child reports.

No police or sheriff's department shall establish or maintain any policy which requires the observance of any waiting period before accepting a missing child report as defined in §52-32. Upon receipt of a missing child report by any police or sheriff's department, the department shall immediately enter identifying and descriptive data about the child into the National Crime Information Center Computer, forward the report to the Missing Children Information Clearinghouse within the Department of State Police, notify all other law-enforcement agencies in the area, and initiate an investigation of the case.
(Added by L.1997 ch. 587, eff. 12/1/97.)

§15.2-1719. Disposal of unclaimed property in possession of sheriff or police.

Any locality may provide by ordinance for (i) the public sale in accordance with the provisions of this section or (ii) the retention for use by the law-enforcement agency of any unclaimed personal property which has been in the possession of its law-enforcement agencies and unclaimed for a period of more than sixty days. As used herein, "unclaimed personal property" shall be any personal property belonging to another which has been acquired by a law-enforcement officer pursuant to his duties, which is not needed in any criminal prosecution, which has not been claimed by its rightful owner and which the State Treasurer has indicated will be declined if remitted under the Uniform Disposition of Unclaimed Property Act (§55-210.1 et seq.). Unclaimed bicycles and mopeds may also be disposed of in accordance with §15.2-1720. Unclaimed firearms may also be disposed of in accordance with §15.2-1721.

Prior to the sale or retention for use by the law-enforcement agency of any unclaimed item, the chief of police, sheriff or their duly authorized agents shall make reasonable attempts to notify the rightful owner of the property, obtain from the attorney for the Commonwealth in writing a statement advising that the item is not needed in any criminal prosecution, and cause to be published in a newspaper of general circulation in the locality once a week for two successive weeks, notice that there will be a public display and sale of unclaimed personal property. Such property, including property selected for retention by the law-enforcement agency, shall be described generally in the notice, together with the date, time and place of the sale and shall be made available for public viewing at the sale. The chief of police, sheriff or their duly authorized agents shall pay from the proceeds of sale the costs of advertisement, removal, storage, investigation as to ownership and liens, and notice of sale. The balance of the funds shall be held by such officer for the owner and paid to the owner upon satisfactory proof of ownership. Any unclaimed item retained for use by the law-enforcement agency shall become the property of the locality served by the agency and shall be retained only if in the opinion of the chief law-enforcement officer, there is a legitimate use for the property by the agency and that retention of the item is a more economical alternative than purchase of a similar or equivalent item.

If no claim has been made by the owner for the property or proceeds of such sale within sixty days of the sale, the remaining funds shall be deposited in the general fund of the locality and the retained property may be placed into use by the law-enforcement agency. Any such owner shall be entitled to apply to the locality within three years from the date of the sale and, if timely application is made therefor and satisfactory proof of ownership of the funds or property is made, the locality shall pay the remaining proceeds of the sale or return the property to the owner without interest or other charges or compensation. No claim shall be made nor any suit, action or proceeding be instituted for the recovery of such funds or property after three years from the date of the sale.
(Added by L.1997 ch. 587, eff. 12/1/97.)

§15.2-1720. Localities authorized to license bicycles and mopeds; disposition of unclaimed bicycles and mopeds.

Any locality may, by ordinance, (i) provide for the public sale or donation to a charitable organization of any bicycle or moped which has been in the possession of the police or sheriff's department, unclaimed, for more than thirty days; (ii) require every resident owner of a bicycle or moped to obtain a license therefor and a license plate or tag, of such design and material as the ordinance may prescribe, to be substantially attached to the bicycle or moped; (iii) prescribe the license fee, the license application forms and the license form; and (iv) prescribe penalties for operating a bicycle or moped on public roads or streets within the locality without an attached license plate or tag. The ordinance shall require the license plates or tags to be provided by and at the cost of the locality. Any locality may provide that the license plates or tags shall be good for the life of the bicycles and mopeds to which they are attached or for such other period as it may prescribe and may prescribe such fee therefor as it may deem reasonable. When any town license is required as provided for herein, the license shall be in lieu of any license required by any county ordinance. Any bicycle or moped found and delivered to the police or sheriff's department by a private person which thereafter remains unclaimed for thirty days after the final date of publication as required herein may be given to the finder; however, the location and description of the bicycle or moped shall be published at least once a week for two successive weeks in a newspaper of general circulation within the locality. In addition, if there is a license tag affixed to the bicycle or moped, the record owner shall be notified directly.
(Added by L.1997 ch. 587, eff. 12/1/97.)

§15.2-1721. Disposal of unclaimed firearms or other weapons in possession of sheriff or police.

Any locality may destroy unclaimed firearms and other weapons which have been in the possession of law-enforcement agencies for a period of more than sixty days. For the purposes of this section, "unclaimed firearms and other weapons" means any firearm or other weapon belonging to another which has been acquired by a law-enforcement officer pursuant to his duties, which is not needed in any criminal prosecution, which has not been claimed by its rightful owner and which the State Treasurer has indicated will be declined if remitted under the Uniform Disposition of Unclaimed Property Act (§55-210.1 et seq.).

At the discretion of the chief of police, sheriff, or their duly authorized agents, unclaimed firearms and other weapons may be destroyed by any means which renders the firearms and other weapons permanently inoperable. Prior to the destruction of such firearms and other weapons, the chief of police, sheriff, or their duly authorized agents shall comply with the notice provision contained in §15.2-1719.

(Added by L.1997 ch. 587, eff. 12/1/97.)

§15.2-1722. Certain records to be kept by sheriffs and chiefs of police.

A. It shall be the duty of the sheriff or chief of police of every locality to insure, in addition to other records required by law, the maintenance of adequate personnel, arrest, investigative, reportable incidents, and noncriminal incidents records necessary for the efficient operation of a law-enforcement agency. Failure of a sheriff or a chief of police to maintain such records or failure to relinquish such records to his successor in office shall constitute a misdemeanor. Former sheriffs or chiefs of police shall be allowed access to such files for preparation of a defense in any suit or action arising from the performance of their official duties as sheriff or chief of police. The enforcement of this section shall be the duty of the attorney for the Commonwealth of the county or city wherein the violation occurs.

B. For purposes of this section, the following definitions shall apply:

"Arrest records" means a compilation of information, centrally maintained in law-enforcement custody, of any arrest or temporary detention of an individual, including the identity of the person arrested or detained, the nature of the arrest or detention, and the charge, if any.

"Investigative records" means the reports of any systematic inquiries or examinations into criminal or suspected criminal acts which have been committed, are being committed, or are about to be committed.

"Noncriminal incidents records" means compilations of noncriminal occurrences of general interest to law-enforcement agencies, such as missing persons, lost and found property, suicides and accidental deaths.

"Personnel records" means those records maintained on each and every individual employed by a law-enforcement agency which reflect personal data concerning the employee's age, length of service, amount of training, education, compensation level, and other pertinent personal information.

"Reportable incidents records" means a compilation of complaints received by a law-enforcement agency and action taken by the agency in response thereto.

(Added by L.1997 ch. 587; chgd. by L.1999 chs. 703, 726, eff. 7/1/99.)

§15.2-1723. Validation of certain police forces.

Any police force in existence on July 1, 1980, whose existence is authorized or was authorized by any provision of law, general or special, that was repealed by Chapter 333 of the Acts of Assembly of 1979 is hereby validated and shall continue. Any police force in existence on December 1, 1996, whose existence is authorized or was authorized by any provision of law, general or special, that is repealed by this act is hereby validated and shall continue.

(Added by L.1997 ch. 587, eff. 12/1/97.)

ARTICLE 2
INTERJURISDICTIONAL LAW-ENFORCEMENT AUTHORITY AND AGREEMENTS

§15.2-1724. Police and other officers may be sent beyond territorial limits.

Whenever the necessity arises (i) for the enforcement of laws designed to control or prohibit the use or sale of controlled drugs as defined in §54.1-3401 or laws contained in Article 3 (§18.2-344 et seq.) of Chapter 8 of Title 18.2, (ii) in response to any law-enforcement emergency involving any immediate threat to life or public safety, (iii) during the execution of the provisions of §37.1-67.01 or §37.1-67.1 relating to orders for temporary detention or emergency custody for mental health evaluation or (iv) during any emergency resulting from the existence of a state of war, internal disorder, or fire, flood, epidemic or other public disaster, the police officers and other officers, agents and employees of any locality and the police of any state-supported institution of higher learning appointed pursuant to §23-233 may, together with all necessary equipment, lawfully go or be sent beyond the territorial limits of such locality or such state-supported institution of higher learning to any point within or without the Commonwealth to assist in meeting such emergency or need, or while en route to a part of the jurisdiction which is only accessible by roads outside the jurisdiction. However, the police of any state-supported institution of higher learning may be sent only to a locality within the Commonwealth, or locality outside the Commonwealth, whose boundaries are contiguous with the locality in which such institution is located. No member of a police force of any state-supported institution of higher learning shall be sent beyond the territorial limits of the locality in which such institution is located unless such member has met the requirements established by the Department of Criminal Justice Services as provided in subdivision 2(i) of §9-170.

In such event the acts performed for such purpose by such police officers or other officers, agents or employees and the expenditures made for such purpose by such locality or a state-supported institution of higher learning shall be deemed conclusively to be for a public and governmental purpose, and all of the immunities from liability enjoyed by a locality or a state-supported institution of higher learning

 Zv

when acting through its police officers or other officers, agents or employees for a public or governmental purpose within its territorial limits shall be enjoyed by it to the same extent when such locality or a state-supported institution of higher learning within the Commonwealth is so acting, under this section or under other lawful authority, beyond its territorial limits.

The police officers and other officers, agents and employees of any locality or a state-supported institution of higher learning when acting hereunder or under other lawful authority beyond the territorial limits of such locality or such state-supported institution of higher learning shall have all of the immunities from liability and exemptions from laws, ordinances and regulations and shall have all of the pension, relief disability, workers' compensation and other benefits enjoyed by them while performing their respective duties within the territorial limits of such locality or such state-supported institution of higher learning.

(Added by L.1997 ch. 587, eff. 12/1/97.)

§15.2-1725. Extending police power of localities over lands lying beyond boundaries thereof; jurisdiction of courts.

Any locality owning and operating an airport, public hospital, sanitarium, nursing home, public water supply or watershed, public park, recreational area, sewage disposal plant or system, public landing, dock, wharf or canal, public school, public utility, public buildings and other public property located beyond the limits of the locality shall have and may exercise full police power over the property, and over persons using the property, and may, by ordinance, prescribe rules for the operation and use of the property and for the conduct of all persons using the property and may, further, provide penalties for the violation of such rules contained in an ordinance; such penalties, however, shall not exceed those provided by general law for misdemeanors. However, no ordinances in conflict with an ordinance of the jurisdiction wherein the property is located shall be enacted.

Any locality which maintains or operates in whole or in part any property enumerated in this section may lawfully send its law-enforcement officers to the property owned beyond the limits of the locality for the purpose of protecting the property, keeping order therein, or otherwise enforcing the laws of the Commonwealth and ordinances of the locality owning the property as such laws and ordinances may relate to the operation and use thereof. The law-enforcement officer shall have power to make an arrest for a violation of any law or ordinance relating to the operation and use of the property. The district court in the city or town where the offense occurs shall have jurisdiction of all cases arising therein, and the district court of the county where the offense occurs shall have jurisdiction of all cases arising therein.

It shall be the duty of the attorney for the Commonwealth for the locality wherein the offense occurs to prosecute all violators of the ordinances of the locality that pertain to the operation and use of the property enumerated in this section.

(Added by L.1997 ch. 587, eff. 12/1/97.)

§15.2-1726. Agreements for consolidation of police departments or for cooperation in furnishing police services.

Any locality may, in its discretion, enter into a reciprocal agreement with any other locality, any agency of the federal government exercising police powers, police of any state-supported institution of higher learning appointed pursuant to §23-233, or with any combination of the foregoing, for such periods and under such conditions as the contracting parties deem advisable, for cooperation in the furnishing of police services. Such localities also may enter into an agreement for the cooperation in the furnishing of police services with the Department of State Police. The governing body of any locality also may, in its discretion, enter into a reciprocal agreement with any other locality, or combination thereof, for the consolidation of police departments or divisions or departments thereof. Subject to the conditions of the agreement, all police officers, officers, agents and other employees of such consolidated or cooperating police departments shall have the same powers, rights, benefits, privileges and immunities in every jurisdiction subscribing to such agreement, including the authority to make arrests in every such jurisdiction subscribing to the agreement; however, no police officer of any locality shall have authority to enforce federal laws unless specifically empowered to do so by statute, and no federal law-enforcement officer shall have authority to enforce the laws of the Commonwealth unless specifically empowered to do so by statute.

The governing body of a county also may enter into a tripartite contract with the governing body of any town, one or more, in such county and the sheriff for such county for the purpose of having the sheriff furnish law-enforcement services in the town. The contract shall be structured as a service contract and may have such other terms and conditions as the contracting parties deem advisable. The sheriff and any deputy sheriff serving as a town law-enforcement officer shall have authority to enforce such town's ordinances. Likewise, subject to the conditions of the contract, the sheriff and deputy sheriffs while serving as a town's law-enforcement officers shall have the same powers, rights, benefits, privileges and immunities as those of regular town police officers. The sheriff under any such contract shall be the town's chief of police.

(Added by L.1997 ch. 587, eff. 12/1/97.)

§15.2-1727. Reciprocal agreements with localities outside the Commonwealth.

A locality or a state-supported institution of higher learning may, in its discretion, enter into reciprocal agreements for such periods as it deems advisable with any locality outside the Commonwealth, including the District of Columbia, in order to establish and carry into effect a plan to provide mutual aid through the furnishing of its police and other employees and agents, together with all necessary equipment, in the event of such need or emergency as provided herein. No locality or state-supported institution of higher learning shall enter into such agreement unless the agreement provides that each of the parties to such agreement shall: (i) waive any and all claims against all the other parties thereto which may arise out of their activities outside their respective jurisdictions under such agreement and (ii) indemnify and save harmless the other parties to such agreement from all claims by third parties for property damage or personal injury which may arise out of the activities of the other parties to such agreement outside their respective jurisdictions under such agreement.

The principal law-enforcement officer in any locality or of a state-supported institution of higher learning having a reciprocal agreement with a jurisdiction outside the Commonwealth for police mutual aid under the provisions hereof shall be responsible for directing the activities of all police officers and other officers and agents coming into his jurisdiction under the reciprocal agreement. While operating under the terms of the reciprocal agreement, the principal law-enforcement officer is empowered to authorize all police officers and other officers and agents from outside the Commonwealth to enforce the laws of the Commonwealth of Virginia to the same extent as if they were duly authorized law-enforcement officers of the locality or a state-supported institution of higher learning in Virginia.

The governing body of any locality or a state-supported institution of higher learning in the Commonwealth is s authorized to procure or extend the necessary public liability insurance to cover claims arising out of mutual aid agreements executed with other localities outside the Commonwealth.

The police officers, and other officers, agents and employees of a locality or a state-supported institution of higher learning serving in a jurisdiction outside the Commonwealth under a reciprocal agreement entered into pursuant hereto are authorized to carry out the duties and functions provided for in the agreement under the command and supervision of the chief law-enforcement officer of the jurisdiction outside the Commonwealth.

In counties where no police department has been established and the sheriff is the chief law-enforcement officer, the sheriff may enter into mutual aid agreements and furnish and receive such assistance as provided by this section. Sheriffs and their deputies providing assistance pursuant to such a mutual aid agreement shall enjoy all of the authority, immunities and benefits as provided herein for police officers, including full police powers.

(Added by L.1997 ch. 587, eff. 12/1/97, incorporating changes to former Section 15.1-131 by L.1997 chs. 638 and 668, eff. 12/1/97.)

§15.2-1728. Mutual aid agreements between police departments and federal authorities.

In any case where exclusive jurisdiction over any property or territory has been granted by the Commonwealth to the United States government, or to a department or agency thereof, the governing body of any contiguous locality may enter into a mutual aid agreement with the appropriate federal authorities to authorize police cooperation and assistance within such property or territory. Subject to the conditions of any such agreement, all police officers and agents of the contracting governing body shall have the same powers, rights, benefits, privileges and immunities while acting in the performance of their duties on the property or territory under federal authority as are lawfully conferred upon them within their own jurisdictions.

(Added by L.1997 ch. 587, eff. 12/1/97.)

§15.2-1729. Agreements for enforcement of state and county laws by federal officers on federal property.

A. The governing body of any county may enter into an agreement with the United States government or a department or agency thereof under the terms of which agreement law-enforcement officers employed by such government, including but not limited to members of the United States Park Police, may enforce the laws of such county and the Commonwealth on federally owned properties within such county, and on the highways located therein and other public places abutting such properties. In the event such an agreement is entered into, all of the provisions of §15.2-1724 shall be applicable, mutatis mutandis.

B. The governing body of any county governed under the provisions of Chapter 8 (§15.2-800 et seq.) may enter into an agreement with the United States government or a department or agency thereof under the terms of which agreement law-enforcement officers employed by such government, including but not limited to members of the United States Park Police, may enforce the laws of such county and the Commonwealth on federally owned properties within such county, and on the highways and other public places abutting such properties. In the event such an agreement is entered into, all of the provisions of §15.2-1724 shall be applicable, mutatis mutandis.

(Added by L.1997 ch. 587, eff. 12/1/97, incorporating changes to former Section 15.1-131.4 by L.1997 ch. 537, eff. 12/1/97.)

§15.2-1730. Calling upon law-enforcement officers of counties, cities or towns for assistance.

In case of an emergency declared by the chief law-enforcement officer of a locality, such officer may call upon the chief law-enforcement officer of towns within his county and the chief law-enforcement officer of an adjoining county or city, or towns in adjoining counties for assistance from him or his deputies or other police officers, without the necessity for deputizing such deputies or officers. Such deputies or officers shall have full police powers in such locality as are conferred upon them by law during the period of such emergency.

(Added by L.1997 ch. 587, eff. 12/1/97.)

§15.2-1730.1. Authority and immunity of sheriffs and deputies.

In counties where no police department has been established and the sheriff is the chief law-enforcement officer, the sheriff may enter into agreements with any other governmental entity providing law-enforcement services in the Commonwealth, and may furnish and receive interurisdictional law-enforcement assistance for all law-enforcement purposes, including those described in this chapter, and for purposes of Chapter 3.2 (§44-146.13 et seq.) of Title 44. Sheriffs and their deputies, providing or receiving such assistance, shall have all the authority, benefits, immunity from liability and exemptions from laws, ordinances and regulations as officers acting within their own jurisdictions.

(Added by L.1999 ch. 352, eff. 7/1/99.)

ARTICLE 3
AUXILIARY POLICE FORCES IN LOCALITIES

§15.2-1731. Establishment, etc., authorized; powers, authority and immunities generally.

A. Localities, for the further preservation of the public peace, safety and good order of the community, may establish, equip and maintain auxiliary police forces, the members of which when called into service as hereinafter provided shall have all the powers and authority and all the immunities of constables at common law.

B. Localities also may establish, equip and maintain auxiliary police forces which have all the powers and authority and all the immunities of full-time law-enforcement officers, if all such forces have met the training requirements established by the Department of Criminal Justice Services under §9-170. Any auxiliary officer employed prior to July 1, 1987, shall be exempted from any initial training requirement, except that any such officer shall not be permitted to carry or use a firearm while serving as an auxiliary police officer unless such officer has met the firearms training requirements established in accordance with in-service training standards for law-enforcement officers as prescribed by the Criminal Justice Services Board.

(Added by L.1997 ch. 587, eff. 12/1/97.)

§15.2-1732. Appropriations for equipment and maintenance.

Localities may make such appropriations as may be necessary to arm, equip, uniform and maintain such auxiliary police force.
(Added by L.1997 ch. 587, eff. 12/1/97.)

§15.2-1733. Appointment of auxiliary police officers; revocation of appointment; uniform; organization; rules and regulations.

The governing body of the locality may appoint or provide for the appointment as auxiliary police officers as many persons of good character as it deems necessary, not to exceed the number fixed by ordinance adopted by the governing body, and their appointment shall be revocable at any time by the governing body. The governing body may prescribe the uniform, organization, and such rules as it deems necessary for the operation of the auxiliary police force.
(Added by L.1997 ch. 587, eff. 12/1/97.)

§15.2-1734. Calling auxiliary police officers into service; police officers performing service to wear uniform; exception.

A. A locality may call into service or provide for calling into service such auxiliary police officers as may be deemed necessary (i) in time of public emergency, (ii) at such times as there are insufficient numbers of regular police officers to preserve the peace, safety and good order of the community, or (iii) at any time for the purpose of training such auxiliary police officers. At all times when performing such service, the members of the auxiliary police force shall wear the uniform prescribed by the governing body.

B. Members of any auxiliary police force who have been trained in accordance with the provisions of §15.2-1731 may be called into service by the chief of police of any locality to aid and assist regular police officers in the performance of their duties.

C. When the duties of an auxiliary police officer are such that the wearing of the prescribed uniform would adversely limit the effectiveness of the auxiliary police officer's ability to perform his prescribed duties, then clothing appropriate for the duties to be performed may be required by the chief of police.
(Added by L.1997 ch. 587, eff. 12/1/97.)

§15.2-1735. Acting beyond limits of jurisdiction of locality.

The members of any such auxiliary police force shall not be required to act beyond the limits of the jurisdiction of any such locality except when called upon to protect any public property belonging to the locality which may be located beyond its boundaries, or as provided in §15.2-1736.
(Added by L.1997 ch. 587, eff. 12/1/97.)

§15.2-1736. Mutual aid agreements among governing bodies of contiguous localities.

The governing bodies of localities, and state-supported institutions of higher learning having a police force appointed pursuant to §23-233, as well as sheriffs with law-enforcement authority within localities without a police force, or any combination thereof whose boundaries are contiguous, by proper resolutions, may enter in and become a party to contracts or mutual aid agreements for the use of their joint police or other law-enforcement forces, both regular and auxiliary, their equipment and materials to maintain peace and good order. Any police or other law-enforcement officer, regular or auxiliary, while performing his duty under any such contract or agreement, shall have the same authority in such locality as he has within the locality where he was appointed.

In counties where no police department has been established, the sheriff may, in his discretion, enter into mutual aid agreements as provided by this section.
(Added by L.1997 ch. 587, eff. 12/1/97, incorporating changes to former Section 15.1-159.7 by L.1997 ch. 604, eff. 12/1/97.)

ARTICLE 4
SPECIAL POLICE OFFICERS IN LOCALITIES

Section

§15.2-1737. Circuit courts may appoint special police officers.

A. The circuit court for any locality may, upon the application of, and a showing of a necessity for the security of property or the peace by, the sheriff or chief of police, appoint special police officers for a locality within its jurisdiction. The special police officers shall be suitable and discreet persons and shall serve as such for such length of time as the court may designate, but not exceeding four years under any one appointment. Such person or persons so appointed shall be conservators of the peace under the supervision of the person or agency making application for the appointment, who shall likewise be civilly liable for any wrongful action or conduct committed by the appointee while within the scope of his employment.

B. The court shall, prior to appointment, order the applicant to conduct a background investigation, in accordance with clause A(ii) of §15.2-1705 of each prospective appointee who is not a law-enforcement officer as defined in §9-169.
(Added by L.1997 ch. 587, eff. 12/1/97.)

§15.2-1738. Application for appointment as special police officer; qualifications.

Before any person is appointed as a police officer under §15.2-1737, the sheriff or chief of police shall make written application for such appointment to the circuit court. Such application shall state the necessity for the appointment and the prospective appointee's full name, age, place of residence, occupation and regular employer. A part-time deputy of the sheriff may be appointed as such police officer.
(Added by L.1997 ch. 587; chgd. by L.1999 ch. 278, eff. 7/1/99.)

§15.2-1739. Compensation of special police officer.

A locality, if deemed proper, except where the police officer is otherwise regularly employed and his duties as police officer are merely incidental to such private employment, may allow such compensation to the police officer appointed under the provisions of §15.2-1737 as, together with any expenses incurred in executing his duties, shall be deemed right and proper by the governing body to be paid out of the local levy.
(Added by L.1997 ch. 587, eff. 12/1/97.)

§15.2-1740. Certain special police officers not employees of Commonwealth or locality.

No police officer appointed under §15.2-1737 who is otherwise regularly employed and whose duties as police officer are merely incidental to such private employment shall be deemed to be an employee of the Commonwealth or locality within the meaning of the Virginia Workers' Compensation Act (§65.2-100 et seq.).
(Added by L.1997 ch. 587, eff. 12/1/97.)

§15.2-1741. Removal of special police officers; filling vacancies.

The court may, at any time, remove any or all of such police, and appoint others, and may fill any vacancy that may occur in such police force, or may add to the number previously appointed.
(Added by L.1997 ch. 587, eff. 12/1/97.)

§15.2-1742. Removal from locality creates vacancy.

The removal from the locality in which he was appointed shall vacate the office of the person appointed, or the person may resign or decline appointment.
(Added by L.1997 ch. 587, eff. 12/1/97.)

§15.2-1743. Bond of special police officers.

Before entering upon the duties of his office, any person initially appointed on or after July 1, 1996, shall give bond in the penalty of such sum as may be fixed by the court, with approved security before the circuit court clerk, with condition faithfully to discharge his official duties. No bond shall be required, however, if the person so appointed has successfully completed the minimum entry-level law-enforcement training requirements established by the Department of Criminal Justice Services under §9-170 within three years of the date of initial appointment or has been employed as a law-enforcement officer as defined by subdivision 9 of §9-169 within the preceding three years.
(Added by L.1997 ch. 587, eff. 12/1/97.)

§15.2-1744. Jurisdiction and authority of special police officers; evidence of their office.

The jurisdiction and authority of special police shall extend no further than the limits of the locality in which they are appointed, and a copy of the order of appointment made by the court, attested by the clerk of such court, shall in all cases be received as evidence of their official character. But the authority of special police shall extend throughout the Commonwealth when actually in pursuit of persons accused of crime and when acting under authority of a duly executed warrant for the arrest of persons accused of committing crime.

The jurisdiction and authority of special police upon order entered of record by the circuit court for the locality may be limited to a specific place or places in a locality; may limit or prohibit the carrying of weapons by special police; and shall prescribe the type of uniform, badge, insignia or identification to be worn or carried by special police to the extent that the uniform, badge, insignia or identification shall not resemble or be in facsimile of the uniform, badge, insignia or identification of the State Police or that of any sheriff or member of a police department in the locality or an adjoining locality. Any special police officer initially appointed on or after July 1, 1996, whose order of appointment does not prohibit the carrying of weapons while within the scope of his employment as such may be required by the court to meet the minimum entry training requirements established by the Department of Criminal Justice Services under §9-170 for law-enforcement officers within twelve months of his appointment. Such order may provide that special police shall, within the limits of their jurisdiction, have the same authority and responsibility as deputy sheriffs with regard to the service of civil and criminal process.

However, the jurisdiction and authority of special police, upon an order entered of record by the circuit court for an adjoining locality, may be extended into such adjoining locality or into such part thereof as the order may designate, provided that the special circumstances necessitating such extension of jurisdiction and authority are set forth in the order.
(Added by L.1997 ch. 587, eff. 12/1/97.)

§15.2-1745. Duties and powers of special police officers.

Special police shall apprehend and carry before a judge or magistrate to be dealt with according to law, all persons whom they may be directed by the warrant of a judge or magistrate to apprehend, shall have the authority to make arrests and issue summonses in accordance with Chapter 7 (§19.2-71 et seq.) of Title 19.2; and may execute any search warrant issued under §§19.2-52 and 19.2-53. If property that is mentioned in these sections is found, the police shall proceed as officers acting under Chapter 5 (§19.2-52 et seq.) of Title 19.2.
(Added by L.1997 ch. 587, eff. 12/1/97.)

§15.2-1746. Duty of district judge; may bind to good behavior, etc.

In all cases arising under §15.2-1745, the district judge before whom the person so arrested is brought shall examine the case and dispose of it according to law. If he thinks the person so apprehended ought to enter into a recognizance to keep the peace and be of good behavior, he shall require him to do so, and in default thereof such person may be committed to jail.
(Added by L.1997 ch. 587, eff. 12/1/97.)

ARTICLE 5
CRIMINAL JUSTICE TRAINING ACADEMIES

Section

§15.2-1747. Creation of academies.

A. The governing bodies of two or more localities or other political subdivisions or other public bodies hereinafter collectively referred to as "governmental units," may by ordinance or resolution enter into an agreement which creates a regional criminal justice training academy under an appropriate name and title containing the words "criminal justice training academy" which shall be a public body politic and corporate. Any regional criminal justice training academy created under this article shall also be subject to the requirements of §9-170.

B. The agreement shall set forth (i) the name of the academy, (ii) the governmental subdivision in which its principal office shall be situated, (iii) the effective date of the organization of the academy and the duration of the agreement, (iv) the composition of the board of directors of the academy which may include representation of each locality, political subdivision or governmental entity party to the agreement, the members of which shall be the governing body of the academy, (v) the method for selection and the terms of office of the board of directors, (vi) the voting rights of the directors which need not be equal, (vii) the procedure for amendment of the agreement [and for addition of other governmental units which are not parties to the original agreement, (viii) the procedure for withdrawal from the academy by governmental units electing to do so], and [(ix)] *(viii)* such other matters as the governmental units creating the academy deem appropriate. Sheriffs and members of the governing bodies of the governmental units as well as other public officials or employees may be members of the board of directors.

C. Any governmental unit not a party to an original agreement creating an academy under this section or §15.2-1300 may join the academy only by two-thirds vote of the board of directors of the academy. The governing body of the governmental unit seeking to join the academy shall request membership by resolution or ordinance. The board of directors shall provide for the addition of the joining governmental unit to the academy and the number, terms of office, and voting rights of members of the board of directors, if any, to be appointed by the joining governmental unit.

D. A governmental unit may withdraw from an academy created under this section or §15.2-1300 only by two-thirds vote of the board of directors of the academy. The governing body of the governmental unit seeking to withdraw from the academy shall signify its desire by resolution or ordinance. The board of directors shall consider requests to withdraw in October, 2001, and in October of every fifth year thereafter. No requests to withdraw shall be considered at any other time, unless agreed to unanimously. Any withdrawal approved by the board of directors shall be effective on June 30 of the following year. The board of directors shall provide for the conditions of withdrawal.

[C.] *E.* The chairman of the academy board shall serve as a member and as the chairman of an executive committee. The composition of the remaining membership of the executive committee, the term of office of its members and any alternate members, procedures for the conduct of its meetings, and any limitations upon the general authority of the executive committee shall be established in the bylaws of the academy. The bylaws shall also establish any other special standing committees, advisory, technical or otherwise, as the board of directors shall deem desirable for the transaction of its affairs.

(Added by L.1997 ch. 587; chgd. by L.2000 ch. 772, eff. 7/1/2001. Matter in brackets eff. only until 7/1/2001. Matter in italics eff. 7/1/2001.)

§15.2-1748. Powers of the academies.

A. Upon organization of an academy, it shall be a public body corporate and politic, the purposes of which shall be to establish and conduct training for public law-enforcement and correctional officers, those being trained to be public law-enforcement and correctional officers and other personnel who assist or support such officers. The persons trained by an academy need not be employed by a locality which has joined in the agreement creating the academy.

B. Criminal justice training academies may:

1. Adopt and have a common seal and alter that seal at the pleasure of the board of directors;

2. Sue and be sued;

3. Adopt bylaws and make rules and regulations for the conduct of its business;

4. Make and enter into all contracts or agreements, as it may determine are necessary, incidental or convenient to the performance of its duties and to the execution of the powers granted under this article;

5. Apply for and accept, disburse and administer for itself or for a member governmental unit any loans or grants of money, materials or property from any private or charitable source, the United States of America, the Commonwealth, any agency or instrumentality thereof, or from any other source;

6. Employ engineers, attorneys, planners and such other professional experts or consultants, and general and clerical employees as may be deemed necessary and prescribe such experts, consultants, and employees' powers, duties, and compensation;

7. Perform any acts authorized under this article through or by means of its own officers, agents and employees, or by contracts with any person, firm or corporation;

8. Acquire, whether by purchase, exchange, gift, lease or otherwise, any interest in real or personal property, and improve, maintain, equip and furnish academy facilities;

9. Lease, sell, exchange, donate and convey any interest in any or all of its projects, property or facilities in furtherance of the purposes of the academy as set forth in this article;

10. Accept contributions, grants and other financial assistance from the United States of America and its agencies or instrumentalities thereof, the Commonwealth, any political subdivision, agency or public instrumentality thereof or from any other source, for or in aid of the construction, acquisition, ownership, maintenance or repair of the academy facilities, for the payment of principal of, or interest on, any bond of the academy, or other costs incident thereto, or make loans in furtherance of the purposes of this article of such money, contributions, grants, and other financial assistance, and comply with such conditions and to execute such agreements, trust indentures, and other legal instruments as may be necessary, convenient or desirable and agree to such terms and conditions as may be imposed;

11. Borrow money from any source for capital purposes or to cover current expenditures in any given year in anticipation of the collection of revenues;

12. Mortgage and pledge any or all of its projects, property or facilities or parts thereof and pledge the revenues therefrom or from any part thereof as security for the payment of principal and premium, if any, and interest on any bonds, notes or other evidences of indebtedness;

13. Create an executive committee which may exercise the powers and authority of the academy under this article pursuant to authority delegated to it by the board of directors;

14. Establish fees or other charges for the training services provided;

15. Exercise the powers granted in the agreement creating the academy; and

16. Execute any and all instruments and do and perform any and all acts necessary, convenient or desirable for its purposes or to carry out the powers expressly given in this article.

(Added by L.1997 ch. 587, eff. 12/1/97.)

§15.2-1749. Revenue bonds.

A. Each academy is hereby authorized, after a resolution adopted by a majority of its board of directors, to issue, at one time or from time to time, revenue bonds of the academy on a taxable or tax-exempt basis for the purpose of acquiring, purchasing, constructing, reconstructing, or improving training facilities and acquiring necessary land or equipment therefor, and to refund any bonds issued for such purposes. The bonds of each issue shall be dated, shall mature at such time or times not exceeding forty years from their issue date or dates and shall bear interest at such fixed or variable rate or rates as may be determined by the board of directors, and may be made redeemable before maturity at the option of the board of directors at such price or prices and under such terms and conditions as may be fixed by the authority prior to the issuance of the bonds. The board of directors shall determine the form of the bonds, including any interest coupons to be attached thereto, and the manner of execution of the bonds, and shall affix the denomination or denominations of the bonds and the place or places of payment of principal and interest, which may be at any bank or trust company within or outside the Commonwealth. In case any officer whose signature or a facsimile of whose signature appears on any bonds or coupons ceases to be such officer before the delivery of such bonds, such signature or facsimile shall nevertheless be valid and sufficient for all purposes the same as if he had remained in office until such delivery. Notwithstanding any of the other provisions of this article or any recitals in any bonds issued under the provisions of this article, all such bonds shall be deemed to be negotiable instruments under the laws of this Commonwealth. The bonds may be issued in coupon or registered form or both, as the board of directors may determine, and provision may be made for the registration of any coupon bonds as to principal alone and also as to both principal and interest, and for the reconversion into coupon bonds of any bonds registered as to both principal and interest. The board of directors may sell such bonds in such manner, either at public or private sale, and for such price as it may determine to be for the best interests of the academy.

B. The resolution providing for the issuance of revenue bonds, and any trust agreement securing such bonds, may also contain such limitations upon the issuance of additional revenue bonds as the board of directors may deem proper and such additional bonds as shall be issued under such restriction and limitations as may be prescribed by such resolution or trust agreement.

C. Bonds may be issued under the provisions of this article without obtaining the consent of any commission, board, bureau, or agency of the Commonwealth or of any political subdivision and without any other proceedings or conditions as are specifically required by this article.

D. Bonds issued under the provisions of this article shall not be deemed to constitute a debt of the Commonwealth or of any political subdivision thereof or a pledge of the faith and credit of the Commonwealth or of any political subdivision thereof. The bonds shall be payable solely from revenues or other property of the academy specifically pledged for such purpose.

E. "Bonds" or "revenue bonds" as used in this article shall embrace notes, bonds and other obligations authorized to be issued pursuant to this article.

(Added by L.1997 ch. 587, eff. 12/1/97.)

§15.2-1750. Governmental units authorized to appropriate or lend funds.

The governmental units which are parties of the agreement creating the academy or which arrange to have personnel trained at the academy are authorized to appropriate or lend funds; pay fees or charges for services; convey by sale, lease or gift real or personal property, or any interest therein; provide services to the academy; or enter into such other contracts with the academy as may be appropriate to carry out any other power granted to those localities or the academy.

(Added by L.1997 ch. 587, eff. 12/1/97.)

§15.2-1751. Exemption from taxation.

Any academy created under the provisions of this article shall not be required to pay taxes or assessments upon any project or upon any property acquired or used by it or upon the income therefrom and income derived from bonds shall be exempt at all times from every kind and nature of taxation by this Commonwealth or by any of its political subdivisions, municipal corporations, or public agencies of any kind.

(Added by L.1997 ch. 587, eff. 12/1/97.)

§15.2-1752. Governmental immunity.

Any academy created pursuant to this article shall be deemed to be a governmental entity exercising essential governmental powers, and any such academy and its directors, officers and employees shall be entitled to immunity in any civil action or proceeding for damages or injury to any person or property of any person to the same extent that counties and their officers and employees are immune. Members of the board of directors of the academy shall have the same immunity as members of county boards of supervisors.

(Added by L.1997 ch. 587, eff. 12/1/97.)

§15.2-1753. Liability of board members.

No member of the board of directors of an academy shall be personally liable for any indebtedness, obligation or other liability of an academy, barring willful misconduct.

(Added by L.1997 ch. 587, eff. 12/1/97.)

CHAPTER 20
STREETS AND ALLEYS
(Selected Article)

Article

ARTICLE 5
MISCELLANEOUS
(Selected Sections)

Section

§15.2-2018. Use of certain public property without consent or franchise.

Notwithstanding the provisions of §15.2-2000 A, any person or corporation, except a public service corporation, that occupies or uses any streets, avenues, parks, bridges or any other public places or public property or any public easement of a county, in a manner not permitted to the general public, without having first obtained the consent of the governing body of such county or a franchise therefor, shall be guilty of a Class 4 misdemeanor. Each day's continuance thereof shall be a separate offense. Such occupancy or use shall be deemed a nuisance. The court trying the case may cause the nuisance to be abated and commit the offenders and all their agents and employees engaged in such offenses to jail until the order of the court is obeyed.

(Added by L.1997 ch. 587, eff. 12/1/97.)

§15.2-2028. Regulation of traffic.

Every locality may regulate and control the operation of motor and other vehicles and the movement of vehicular and pedestrian travel and traffic on streets, highways, roads, alleys, bridges, viaducts, subways, underpasses and other public rights-of-way and places, provided such regulations shall not be inconsistent with the provisions of Chapter 13 (§46.2-1300 et seq.) of Title 46.2.

(Added by L.1997 ch. 587, eff. 12/1/97.)

CHAPTER 21
FRANCHISES; SALE AND LEASE OF CERTAIN MUNICIPAL PUBLIC PROPERTY; PUBLIC UTILITIES
(Selected Article)

Article

ARTICLE 1
FRANCHISES; SALE AND LEASE OF CERTAIN PUBLIC PROPERTY
(Selected Section)

§15.2-2107. Persons occupying or using streets, etc., contrary to law.

Any person occupying or using any of the streets, avenues, parks, bridges or any other public places or public property or any public easement of any description of a city or town, in a manner not permitted to the general public, without having first legally obtained the consent of the city or town shall be guilty of a Class 4 misdemeanor. Each day's continuance thereof shall be a separate offense. Such occupancy or use shall be deemed a nuisance. The court trying the case may cause the nuisance to be abated and commit the offenders and all their agents and employees engaged in such offenses to jail until the order of the court is obeyed.
(Added by L.1997 ch. 587, eff. 12/1/97.)

CHAPTER 28
VIRGINIA INDOOR CLEAN AIR ACT
(Selected Section)

§15.2-2801. Statewide regulation of smoking.

A. The Commonwealth or any agency thereof and every locality shall provide reasonable no-smoking areas, considering the nature of the use and the size of the building, in any building owned or leased by the Commonwealth or any agency thereof or a locality. The provisions of this chapter shall not apply to office, work or other areas of the Department of Corrections which are not entered by the general public in the normal course of business or use of the premises.

B. Smoking shall be prohibited in (i) elevators, regardless of capacity, except in any open material hoist elevator, not intended for use by the public; (ii) public school buses; (iii) the interior of any public elementary, intermediate, and secondary school; however, smoking may be allowed by a local school division in a designated area which is not a common area, including but not limited to, a classroom, library, hallway, restroom, cafeteria, gymnasium, or auditorium after regular school hours so long as all student activities in the building have been concluded; (iv) hospital emergency rooms; (v) local or district health departments; (vi) polling rooms; (vii) indoor service lines and cashier lines; (viii) public restrooms in any building owned or leased by the Commonwealth or any agency thereof; (ix) the interior of a child day center licensed pursuant to §63.1-196 that is not also used for residential purposes; however, this prohibition shall not apply to any area of a building not utilized by a child day center, unless otherwise prohibited by this chapter; and (x) public restrooms of health care facilities.

C. Any restaurant having a seating capacity of fifty or more persons shall have a designated no-smoking area sufficient to meet customer demand. In determining the extent of the no-smoking area, the following shall not be included as seating capacity: (i) seats in any bar or lounge area of a restaurant and (ii) seats in any separate room or section of a restaurant which is used exclusively for private functions.

D. The proprietor or other person in charge of an educational facility, except any public elementary, intermediate, or secondary school, health care facility, or a retail establishment of 15,000 square feet or more serving the general public, including, but not limited to, department stores, grocery stores, drug stores, clothing stores, shoe stores, and recreational facilities shall designate reasonable no-smoking areas, considering the nature of the use and the size of the building.

E. The proprietor or other person in charge of a space subject to the provisions of this chapter shall post signs conspicuous to public view stating "Smoking Permitted" or "No Smoking," and in restaurants, signs conspicuous to ordinary public view at or near each public entrance stating "No-Smoking Section Available." Any person failing to post such signs may be subject to a civil penalty of not more than twenty-five dollars.

F. No person shall smoke in a designated no-smoking area and any person who continues to smoke in such area after having been asked to refrain from smoking may be subject to a civil penalty of not more than twenty-five dollars.

G. Any law-enforcement officer may issue a summons regarding a violation of this chapter.

H. The provisions of this chapter shall not be construed to regulate smoking in retail tobacco stores, tobacco warehouses or tobacco manufacturing facilities.
(Added by L.1997 ch. 587, eff. 12/1/97.)

TITLE 16.1
COURTS NOT OF RECORD
(Selected Chapter)

CHAPTER 11
JUVENILE AND DOMESTIC RELATIONS DISTRICT COURTS
(Selected Articles)

ARTICLE 1
GENERAL PROVISIONS
(Complete Article)

§16.1-226. Short title.

The short title of the statutes embraced in this chapter is "Juvenile and Domestic Relations District Court Law."
(Chgd. by L.1996 ch. 616, eff. 7/1/96.)

§16.1-227. Purpose and intent.

This law shall be construed liberally and as remedial in character, and the powers hereby conferred are intended to be general to effect the beneficial purposes herein set forth. It is the intention of this law that in all proceedings the welfare of the child and the family, the safety of the community and the protection of the rights of victims are the paramount concerns of the Commonwealth and to the end that these purposes may be attained, the judge shall possess all necessary and incidental powers and authority, whether legal or equitable in their nature.

This law shall be interpreted and construed so as to effectuate the following purposes:

1. To divert from or within the juvenile justice system, to the extent possible, consistent with the protection of the public safety, those children who can be cared for or treated through alternative programs;

2. To provide judicial procedures through which the provisions of this law are executed and enforced and in which the parties are assured a fair hearing and their constitutional and other rights are recognized and enforced;

3. To separate a child from such child's parents, guardian, legal custodian or other person standing in loco parentis only when the child's welfare is endangered or it is in the interest of public safety and then only after consideration of alternatives to out-of-home placement which afford effective protection to the child, his family, and the community; and

4. To protect the community against those acts of its citizens, both juveniles and adults, which are harmful to others and to reduce the incidence of delinquent behavior and to hold offenders accountable for their behavior.
(Chgd. by L.1996 chs. 755, 914, eff. 7/1/96.)

§16.1-228. Definitions.

When used in this chapter, unless the context otherwise requires:

"Abused or neglected child" means any child:

1. Whose parents or other person responsible for his care creates or inflicts, threatens to create or inflict, or allows to be created or inflicted upon such child a physical or mental injury by other than accidental means, or creates a substantial risk of death, disfigurement or impairment of bodily or mental functions;

2. Whose parents or other person responsible for his care neglects or refuses to provide care necessary for his health; however, no child who in good faith is under treatment solely by spiritual means through prayer in accordance with the tenets and practices of a recognized church or religious denomination shall for that reason alone be considered to be an abused or neglected child;

3. Whose parents or other person responsible for his care abandons such child;

4. Whose parents or other person responsible for his care commits or allows to be committed any sexual act upon a child in violation of the law; or

5. Who is without parental care or guardianship caused by the unreasonable absence or the mental or physical incapacity of the child's parent, guardian, legal custodian or other person standing in loco parentis.

"Adoptive home" means the place of residence of any natural person in which a child resides as a member of the household and in which he has been placed for the purposes of adoption or in which he has been legally adopted by another member of the household.

"Adult" means a person eighteen years of age or older.

"Ancillary crime" or "ancillary charge" means any delinquent act committed by a juvenile as a part of the same act or transaction as, or which constitutes a part of a common scheme or plan with, a delinquent act which would be a felony if committed by an adult.

"Boot camp" means a short term secure or nonsecure juvenile residential facility with highly structured components including, but not limited to, military style drill and ceremony, physical labor, education and rigid discipline, and no less than six months of intensive aftercare.

"Child," "juvenile" or "minor" means a person less than eighteen years of age.

"Child welfare agency" means a child-placing agency, child-caring institution or independent foster home as defined in §63.1-195.

"Child in need of services" means a child whose behavior, conduct or condition presents or results in a serious threat to the well-being and physical safety of the child; however, no child who in good faith is under treatment solely by spiritual means through prayer in accordance with the tenets and practices of a recognized church or religious denomination shall for that reason alone be considered to be a child in need of services, nor shall any child who habitually remains away from or habitually deserts or abandons his family as a result of what the court or the local child protective services unit determines to be incidents of physical, emotional or sexual abuse in the home be considered a child in need of services for that reason alone.

However, to find that a child falls within these provisions, (i) the conduct complained of must present a clear and substantial danger to the child's life or health or (ii) the child or his family is in need of treatment, rehabilitation or services not presently being received, and (iii) the intervention of the court is essential to provide the treatment, rehabilitation or services needed by the child or his family.

"Child in need of supervision" means:

1. A child who, while subject to compulsory school attendance, is habitually and without justification absent from school, and (i) the child has been offered an adequate opportunity to receive the benefit of any and all educational services and programs that are required to be provided by law and which meet the child's particular educational needs, (ii) the school system from which the child is absent or other appropriate agency has made a reasonable effort to effect the child's regular attendance without success, and (iii) the school system has provided documentation that it has complied with the provisions of §22.1-258; or

2. A child who, without reasonable cause and without the consent of his parent, lawful custodian or placement authority, remains away from or deserts or abandons his family or lawful custodian on more than one occasion or escapes or remains away without proper authority from a residential care facility in which he has been placed by the court, and (i) such conduct presents a clear and substantial danger to the child's life or health, (ii) the child or his family is in need of treatment, rehabilitation or services not presently being received, and (iii) the intervention of the court is essential to provide the treatment, rehabilitation or services needed by the child or his family.

"The court" or the "juvenile court" or the "juvenile and domestic relations court" means the juvenile and domestic relations district court of each county or city.

"Delinquent act" means (i) an act designated a crime under the law of this Commonwealth, or an ordinance of any city, county, town or service district, or under federal law, (ii) a violation of §18.2-308.7 or (iii) a violation of a court order as provided for in §16.1-292, but shall not include an act other than a violation of §18.2-308.7, which is otherwise lawful, but is designated a crime only if committed by a child. For purposes of §16.1-241 and §16.1-278.9, the term shall include a refusal to take a blood or breath test in violation of §18.2-268.2 or a similar ordinance of any county, city or town.

"Delinquent child" means a child who has committed a delinquent act or an adult who has committed a delinquent act prior to his eighteenth birthday, except where the jurisdiction of the juvenile court has been terminated under the provisions of §16.1-296.6.

"Department" means the Department of Juvenile Justice and "Director" means the administrative head in charge thereof or such of his assistants and subordinates as are designated by him to discharge the duties imposed upon him under this law.

"Family abuse" means any act involving violence, force, or threat including any forceful detention, which results in physical injury or places one in reasonable apprehension of serious bodily injury and which is committed by a person against such person's family or household member.

"Family or household member" means (i) the person's spouse, whether or not he or she resides in the same home with the person, (ii) the person's former spouse, whether or not he or she resides in the same home with the person, (iii) the person's parents, stepparents, children, stepchildren, brothers, sisters, grandparents and grandchildren, regardless of whether such persons reside in the same home with the person, (iv) the person's mother-in-law, father-in-law, sons-in-law, daughters-in-law, brothers-in-law and sisters-in-law who reside in the same home with the person, (v) any individual who has a child in common with the person, whether or not the person and that individual have been married or have resided together at any time or (vi) any individual who cohabits or who, within the previous twelve months, cohabited with the person, and any children of either of them residing in the same home with the person.

"Foster care services" means the provision of a full range of casework, treatment and community services for a planned period of time to a child who is abused or neglected as defined in §63.1-248.2 or in need of services as defined in this section and his family when the child (i) has been identified as needing services to prevent or eliminate the need for foster care placement, (ii) has been placed through an agreement between the local board of social services or a public agency designated by the community policy and management team and the parents or guardians where legal custody remains with the parents or guardians, (iii) has been committed or entrusted to a local board of social services or child welfare agency, or (iv) has been placed under the supervisory responsibility of the local board pursuant to §16.1-293.

"Intake officer" means a juvenile probation officer appointed as such pursuant to the authority of this chapter.

"Jail" or "other facility designed for the detention of adults" means a local or regional correctional facility as defined in §53.1-1, except those facilities utilized on a temporary basis as a court holding cell for a child incident to a court hearing or as a temporary lock-up room or ward incident to the transfer of a child to a juvenile facility.

"The judge" means the judge or the substitute judge of the juvenile and domestic relations district court of each county or city.

"This law" or "the law" means the Juvenile and Domestic Relations District Court Law embraced in this chapter.

"Legal custody" means (i) a legal status created by court order which vests in a custodian the right to have physical custody of the child, to determine and redetermine where and with whom he shall live, the right and duty to protect, train and discipline him and to provide him with food, shelter, education and ordinary medical care, all subject to any residual parental rights and responsibilities or (ii) the legal status created by court order of joint custody as defined in §20-107.2.

"Permanent foster care placement" means the place of residence in which a child resides and in which he has been placed pursuant to the provisions of §§63.1-56 and 63.1-206.1 with the expectation and agreement between the placing agency and the place of permanent foster care that the child shall remain in the placement until he reaches the age of majority unless modified by court order or unless removed pursuant to §16.1-251 or §63.1-248.9. A permanent foster care placement may be a place of residence of any natural person or persons deemed appropriate to meet a child's needs on a long-term basis.

"Secure facility" or "detention home" means a local, regional or state public or private locked residential facility which has construction fixtures designed to prevent escape and to restrict the movement and activities of children held in lawful custody.

"Shelter care" means the temporary care of children in physically unrestricting facilities.

"State Board" means the State Board of Juvenile Justice.

"Status offender" means a child who commits an act prohibited by law which would not be criminal if committed by an adult.

"Status offense" means an act prohibited by law which would not be an offense if committed by an adult.

"Residual parental rights and responsibilities" means all rights and responsibilities remaining with the parent after the transfer of legal custody or guardianship of the person, including but not limited to the right of visitation, consent to adoption, the right to determine religious affiliation and the responsibility for support.

"Violent juvenile felony" means any of the delinquent acts enumerated in subsection B or C of §16.1-269.1 when committed by a juvenile fourteen years of age or older.
(Chgd. by L.1996 chs. 616, 755, 914; L.1999 chs. 453, 665, 697, 721, eff. 7/1/99.)

§16.1-229. This chapter controlling in event of conflict.

Whenever any specific provision of this chapter differs from or is in conflict with any provision or requirement of any other chapters of this title relating to the same or a similar subject, then such specific provision shall be controlling with respect to such subject or requirement.

ARTICLE 2
ORGANIZATION AND PERSONNEL
(Selected Sections)

§16.1-236. Supervisory officers.

In any court where more than one probation officer or other court services staff has been appointed under the provisions of this law, one or more probation officers may be designated to serve in a supervisory position by the chief judge of the juvenile and domestic relations district court.

The transfer or demotion of supervisory officers of state court service units shall be made only for good cause shown, in accordance with Chapter 10 (§2.1-110 et seq.) of Title 2.1. The transfer or demotion of supervisory officers of local court service units shall be made only for good cause shown, after due notice and opportunity to be heard.
(Chgd. by L.1996 ch. 616, eff. 7/1/96.)

§16.1-237. Powers, duties and functions of probation officer.

In addition to any other powers and duties imposed by this law, a probation officer appointed hereunder shall:

A. Investigate all cases referred to him by the judge or any person designated so to do, and shall render reports of such investigation as required;

B. Supervise such persons as are placed under his supervision and shall keep informed concerning the conduct and condition of every person under his supervision by visiting, requiring reports and in other ways, and shall report thereon as required;

C. Under the general supervision of the director of the court service unit, investigate complaints and accept for informal supervision cases wherein such handling would best serve the interests of all concerned;

D. Use all suitable methods not inconsistent with conditions imposed by the court to aid and encourage persons on probation and to bring about improvement in their conduct and condition;

E. Furnish to each person placed on probation a written statement of the conditions of his probation and instruct him regarding the same;

F. Keep records of his work and perform such other duties as the judge or other person designated by him or the Director shall require;

G. Have the authority to administer oaths and take acknowledgements for the purposes of §§16.1-259 and 16.1-260 to facilitate the processes of intake and petition; and

H. Have the powers of arrest of a police officer and the power to carry a concealed weapon when specifically so authorized by the judge.

ARTICLE 3
JURISDICTION AND VENUE
(Selected Sections)

Section

§16.1-241. Jurisdiction.

The judges of the juvenile and domestic relations district court elected or appointed under this law shall be conservators of the peace within the corporate limits of the cities and the boundaries of the counties for which they are respectively chosen and within one mile beyond the limits of such cities and counties. Except as hereinafter provided, each juvenile and domestic relations district court shall have, within the limits of the territory for which it is created, exclusive original jurisdiction, and within one mile beyond the limits of said city or county, concurrent jurisdiction with the juvenile court or courts of the adjoining city or county over all cases, matters and proceedings involving:

A. The custody, visitation, support, control or disposition of a child:

1. Who is alleged to be abused, neglected, in need of services, in need of supervision, a status offender, or delinquent except where the jurisdiction of the juvenile court has been terminated or divested;

2. Who is abandoned by his parent or other custodian or who by reason of the absence or physical or mental incapacity of his parents is without parental care and guardianship;

2a. Who is at risk of being abused or neglected by a parent or custodian who has been adjudicated as having abused or neglected another child in the care of the parent or custodian;

3. Whose custody, visitation or support is a subject of controversy or requires determination. In such cases jurisdiction shall be concurrent with and not exclusive of courts having equity jurisdiction, except as provided in §16.1-244;

4. Who is the subject of an entrustment agreement entered into pursuant to §63.1-56 or §63.1-204 or whose parent or parents for good cause desire to be relieved of his care and custody;

5. Where the termination of residual parental rights and responsibilities is sought. In such cases jurisdiction shall be concurrent with and not exclusive of courts having equity jurisdiction, as provided in §16.1-244; and

6. Who is charged with a traffic infraction as defined in §46.2-100.

In any case in which the juvenile is alleged to have committed a violent juvenile felony enumerated in subsection B of §16.1-269.1, and for any charges ancillary thereto, the jurisdiction of the juvenile court shall be limited to conducting a preliminary hearing to determine if there is probable cause to believe that the juvenile committed the act alleged and that the juvenile was fourteen years of age or older at the time of the commission of the alleged offense, and any matters related thereto. In any case in which the juvenile is alleged to have committed a violent juvenile felony enumerated in subsection C of §16.1-269.1, and for all charges ancillary thereto, if the attorney for the Commonwealth has given notice as provided in subsection C of §16.1-269.1, the jurisdiction of the juvenile court shall be limited to conducting a preliminary hearing to determine if there is probable cause to believe that the juvenile committed the act alleged and that the juvenile was fourteen years of age or older at the time of the commission of the alleged offense, and any matters related thereto. A determination by the juvenile court following a preliminary hearing pursuant to subsection B or C of §16.1-269.1 to certify a charge to the grand jury shall divest the juvenile court of jurisdiction over the charge and any ancillary charge. In any case in which a transfer hearing is held pursuant to subsection A of §16.1-269.1, if the juvenile court determines to transfer the case, jurisdiction of the juvenile court over the case shall be divested as provided in §16.1-269.6.

In all other cases involving delinquent acts, and in cases in which an ancillary charge remains after a violent juvenile felony charge has been dismissed or a violent juvenile felony has been reduced to a lesser offense not constituting a violent juvenile felony, the jurisdiction of the juvenile court shall not be divested unless there is a transfer pursuant to subsection A of §16.1-269.1.

The authority of the juvenile court to adjudicate matters involving the custody, visitation, support, control or disposition of a child shall not be limited to the consideration of petitions filed by a mother, father or legal guardian but shall include petitions filed at any time by any party with a legitimate interest therein. A party with a legitimate interest shall be broadly construed and shall include, but not be limited to, grandparents, stepparents, former stepparents, blood relatives and family members. A party with a legitimate interest shall not include any person (i) whose parental rights have been terminated by court order, either voluntarily or involuntarily, or any other person whose interest in the child derives from or through such person whose parental rights have been so terminated, including but not limited to grandparents, stepparents, former stepparents, blood relatives and family members, if the child subsequently has been legally adopted, except where a final order of adoption is entered pursuant to

§63.1-219.48, or (ii) who has been convicted of a violation of subsection A of §18.2-61, §18.2-63 or subsection B of §18.2-366 when the child who is the subject of the petition was conceived as a result of such violation. The authority of the juvenile court to consider a petition involving the custody of a child shall not be proscribed or limited where the child has previously been awarded to the custody of a local board of social services.

B. The admission of minors for inpatient treatment in a mental health facility in accordance with the provisions of Article 16 (§16.1-335 et seq.) of this chapter and the commitment of a mentally ill person or judicial certification of eligibility for admission to a treatment facility of a mentally retarded person in accordance with the provisions of Chapters 1 (§37.1-1 et seq.) and 2 (§37.1-63 et seq.) of Title 37.1. Jurisdiction of the commitment and certification of adults shall be concurrent with the general district court.

C. Except as provided in subsections D and H hereof, judicial consent to such activities as may require parental consent may be given for a child who has been separated from his parents, guardian, legal custodian or other person standing in loco parentis and is in the custody of the court when such consent is required by law.

D. Judicial consent for emergency surgical or medical treatment for a child who is neither married nor has ever been married, when the consent of his parent, guardian, legal custodian or other person standing in loco parentis is unobtainable because such parent, guardian, legal custodian or other person standing in loco parentis (i) is not a resident of this Commonwealth, (ii) has his whereabouts unknown, (iii) cannot be consulted with promptness, reasonable under the circumstances, or (iv) fails to give such consent or provide such treatment when requested by the judge to do so.

E. Any person charged with deserting, abandoning or failing to provide support for any person in violation of law.

F. Any parent, guardian, legal custodian or other person standing in loco parentis of a child:

1. Who has been abused or neglected;

2. Who is the subject of an entrustment agreement entered into pursuant to §63.1-56 or §63.1-204 or is otherwise before the court pursuant to subdivision A 4 of this section; or

3. Who has been adjudicated in need of services, in need of supervision, or delinquent, if the court finds that such person has by overt act or omission induced, caused, encouraged or contributed to the conduct of the child complained of in the petition.

G. Petitions filed by or on behalf of a child or such child's parent, guardian, legal custodian or other person standing in loco parentis for the purpose of obtaining treatment, rehabilitation or other services which are required by law to be provided for that child or such child's parent, guardian, legal custodian or other person standing in loco parentis. Jurisdiction in such cases shall be concurrent with and not exclusive of that of courts having equity jurisdiction as provided in §16.1-244.

H. Judicial consent to apply for a work permit for a child when such child is separated from his parents, legal guardian or other person standing in loco parentis.

I. The prosecution and punishment of persons charged with ill-treatment, abuse, abandonment or neglect of children or with any violation of law which causes or tends to cause a child to come within the purview of this law, or with any other offense against the person of a child. In prosecution for felonies over which the court has jurisdiction, jurisdiction shall be limited to determining whether or not there is probable cause.

J. All offenses in which one family or household member is charged with an offense in which another family or household member is the victim and all offenses under §18.2-49.1.

In prosecution for felonies over which the court has jurisdiction, jurisdiction shall be limited to determining whether or not there is probable cause. Any objection based on jurisdiction under this subsection shall be made before a jury is impaneled and sworn in a jury trial or, in a nonjury trial, before the earlier of when the court begins to hear or receive evidence or the first witness is sworn, or it shall be conclusively waived for all purposes. Any such objection shall not affect or be grounds for challenging directly or collaterally the jurisdiction of the court in which the case is tried.

K. Petitions filed by a natural parent, whose parental rights to a child have been voluntarily relinquished pursuant to a court proceeding, to seek a reversal of the court order terminating such parental rights. No such petition shall be accepted, however, after the child has been placed in the home of adoptive parents.

L. Any person who seeks spousal support after having separated from his spouse. A decision under this subdivision shall not be res judicata in any subsequent action for spousal support in a circuit court. A circuit court shall have concurrent original jurisdiction in all causes of action under this subdivision.

M. Petitions filed for the purpose of obtaining an order of protection pursuant to §16.1-253.1 or §16.1-279.1.

N. Any person who escapes or remains away without proper authority from a residential care facility in which he had been placed by the court or as a result of his commitment to the Virginia Department of Juvenile Justice.

O. Petitions for emancipation of a minor pursuant to Article 15 (§16.1-331 et seq.) of this chapter.

P. Petitions for enforcement of administrative support orders entered pursuant to Chapter 13 (§63.1-249 et seq.) of Title 63.1, or by another state in the same manner as if the orders were entered by a juvenile and domestic relations district court upon the filing of a certified copy of such order in the juvenile and domestic relations district court.

Q. Petitions for a determination of parentage pursuant to Chapter 3.1 (§20-49.1 et seq.) of Title 20.

R. Petitions for the purpose of obtaining an emergency protective order pursuant to §16.1-253.4.

S. Petitions filed by school boards against parents pursuant to §§16.1-241.2 and 22.1-279.3.

T. Petitions to enforce any request for information or subpoena that is not complied with or to review any refusal to issue a subpoena in an administrative appeal regarding child abuse and neglect pursuant to §63.1-248.6:1.

U. Petitions filed in connection with parental placement adoption consent hearings, pursuant to §63.1-219.40. Such proceedings shall be advanced on the docket so as to be heard by the court within ten days of filing of the petition, or as soon thereafter as practicable so as to provide the earliest possible disposition.

V. Petitions filed by a juvenile seeking judicial authorization for a physician to perform an abortion if a minor elects not to allow notice to an authorized person. After a hearing, a judge may authorize a physician to perform an abortion upon finding that the minor is mature and capable of giving informed consent to the proposed abortion. If the judge determines that the minor is not mature, the judge shall, after a hearing, determine whether the performance of an abortion upon the minor without notice to an authorized person would be in the minor's best interest, and if the court finds that the abortion would be in the minor's best interest, it shall so authorize a physician.

The minor may participate in the court proceedings on her own behalf, and the court may appoint a guardian ad litem for the minor. The court shall advise the minor that she has a right to counsel and shall, upon her request, appoint counsel for her.

Court proceedings under this subsection shall be confidential and shall be given precedence over other pending matters so that the court may reach a decision promptly and without delay in order to serve the best interests of the minor. Court proceedings under this subsection shall be heard as soon as practicable but in no event later than four days after the petition is filed.

Notwithstanding any other provision of law, an expedited confidential appeal to the circuit court shall be available to any minor for whom the court denies an order authorizing an abortion without notice. Any such appeal shall be heard and decided no later than five days after the appeal is filed. An order authorizing an abortion without notification shall not be subject to appeal.

No filing fees shall be required of the minor at trial or upon appeal.

If either the original court or the circuit court fails to act within the time periods required by this subsection, the court before which the proceeding is pending shall immediately authorize a physician to perform the abortion without notice to an authorized person.

A physician shall not knowingly perform an abortion upon an unemancipated minor unless notice has been given or the minor delivers to the physician a court order entered pursuant to this section. However, neither notice nor judicial authorization shall be required if the minor declares that she is abused or neglected and the attending physician has reason to suspect that the minor may be an abused or neglected child as defined in §63.1-248.2 and reports the suspected abuse or neglect in accordance with §63.1-248.3; or if, in the attending physician's good faith medical judgment, (i) the abortion is medically necessary immediately to avert the minor's death or (ii) there is insufficient time to provide the required notice or judicial authorization because a delay would create a serious risk of substantial impairment of a major bodily function or substantial physical injury. The attending physician shall certify the facts justifying the exception in the minor's medical record.

For purposes of this subsection:

"Authorized person" means (i) a parent or duly appointed legal guardian or custodian of the minor or (ii) a person standing in loco parentis, including, but not limited to, a grandparent or adult sibling with whom the minor regularly and customarily resides and who has care and control of the minor.

"Notice" means that (i) the physician or his agent has given actual notice of his intention to perform such abortion to an authorized person, either in person or by telephone, at least twenty-four hours previous to the performance of the abortion; or (ii) the physician or his agent, after a reasonable effort to notify an authorized person, has mailed notice to an authorized person by certified mail, addressed to such person at his usual place of abode, with return receipt requested, at least seventy-two hours prior to the performance of the abortion; or (iii) at least one authorized person is present with the minor seeking the abortion; or (iv) the minor has delivered to the physician a written statement signed by an authorized person and witnessed by a competent adult that the authorized person knows of the minor's intent to have an abortion.

"Perform an abortion" means to interrupt or terminate a pregnancy by any surgical or nonsurgical procedure or to induce a miscarriage as provided in §§18.2-72, 18.2-73 or §18.2-74.

"Unemancipated minor" means a minor who has not been emancipated by (i) entry into a valid marriage, even though the marriage may have been terminated by dissolution; (ii) active duty with any of the armed forces of the United States; (iii) willingly living separate and apart from his or her parents or guardian, with the consent or acquiescence of the parents or guardian; or (iv) entry of an order of emancipation pursuant to Article 15 (§16.1-331 et seq.) of Chapter 11 of Title 16.1.

W. Petitions filed pursuant to Article 17 (§16.1-349 et seq.) of Chapter 11 of Title 16.1 relating to standby guardians for minor children.

The ages specified in this law refer to the age of the child at the time of the acts complained of in the petition.

Notwithstanding any other provision of law no fees shall be charged by a sheriff for the service of any process in a proceeding pursuant to subdivision 3 of subsection A or subsection B, D, M or R of this section.

Notwithstanding the provisions of §18.2-71, any physician who performs an abortion in violation of subsection V shall be guilty of a Class 3 misdemeanor.

(Chgd. by L.1995 chs. 7, 665, 772, 826, 852; L.1996 chs. 616, 755, 914; L.1997 chs. 690, 708; L.1998 ch. 829; L.1999 chs. 697, 721, 1028; L.2000 ch. 830, eff. 7/1/2000.)

§16.1-241.1. Jurisdiction of experimental family court; venue.

Notwithstanding the provisions of §16.1-241 and any other section of this title, those juvenile and domestic relations district courts designated as experimental family courts by the Judicial Council of Virginia pursuant to §20-96.1 shall have, in addition to jurisdiction over the matters delineated in §16.1-241, jurisdiction over suits for annulling or affirming marriage and for divorce that are referred to them by the designated circuit courts. Venue shall be as provided in §20-96.

(Chgd. by L.1996 ch. 616, eff. 7/1/96.)

§16.1-241.3. Newborn children; substance abuse.

Upon the filing of a petition, within twenty-one days of a child's birth, alleging that an investigation has been commenced in response to a report of suspected abuse or neglect of the child based upon a factor specified in subsection A1 of §63.1-248.3, the court may enter any order authorized pursuant to this chapter which the court deems necessary to protect the health and welfare of the child pending final disposition of the investigation pursuant to Chapter 12.1 (§63.1-248.1 et seq.) of Title 63.1 or other proceedings brought pursuant to this chapter. Such orders may include, but shall not be limited to, an emergency removal order pursuant to §16.1-251, a preliminary protective order pursuant to §16.1-253 or an order authorized pursuant to subdivisions 1 through 4 of subsection A of §16.1-278.2. The fact that an order was entered pursuant to this section shall not be admissible as evidence in any criminal, civil or administrative proceeding other than a proceeding to enforce the order.

The order shall be effective for a limited duration not to exceed the period of time necessary to conclude the investigation and any proceedings initiated pursuant to Chapter 12.1 (§63.1-248.1 et seq.) of Title 63.1, but shall be a final order subject to appeal.

(Added by L.1998 chs. 704, 716, eff. 7/1/98.)

§16.1-242. Retention of jurisdiction.

When jurisdiction has been obtained by the court in the case of any child, such jurisdiction may be retained by the court until such person becomes twenty-one years of age, except when the person is in the custody of the Department or when jurisdiction is divested under the provisions of §16.1-244. In any event, when such person reaches the age of twenty-one and a prosecution has not been commenced against him, he shall be proceeded against as an adult, even if he was a juvenile when the offense was committed.

(Chgd. by L.1996 ch. 616, eff. 7/1/96.)

§16.1-243. Venue.

A. Original venue:

1. Cases involving children, other than support or where protective order issued: Proceedings with respect to children under this law, except support proceedings as provided in subdivision 2 of this subsection or family abuse proceedings as provided in subdivision 3 of this subsection, shall:

a. Delinquency: If delinquency is alleged, be commenced in the city or county where the acts constituting the alleged delinquency occurred or they may, with the written consent of the child and the attorney for the Commonwealth for both jurisdictions, be commenced in the city or county where the child resides;

b. Custody or visitation: In cases involving custody or visitation, be commenced in the court of the city or county which, in order of priority, (i) is the home of the child at the time of the filing of the petition, or had been the home of the child within six months before the filing of the petition and the child is absent from the city or county because of his removal or retention by a person claiming his custody or for other reasons, and a parent or person acting as a parent continues to live in the city or county, (ii) has significant connection with the child and in which there is substantial evidence concerning the child's present or future care, protection, training and personal relationships, (iii) is where the child is physically present and the child has been abandoned or it is necessary in an emergency to protect the child because he has been subjected to or threatened with mistreatment or abuse or is otherwise neglected or dependent or (iv) it is in the best interest of the child for the court to assume jurisdiction as no other city or county is an appropriate venue under the preceding provisions of this subdivision;

c. Adoption: In parental placement adoption consent hearings pursuant to §§16.1-241, 63.1-219.40 and 63.1-219.44, be commenced (i) in the city or county where the child to be adopted was born, (ii) in the city or county where the birth parent(s) reside, or (iii) in the city or county where the prospective adoptive parent(s) reside; and

d. All other cases: In all other proceedings, be commenced in the city or county where the child resides or in the city or county where the child is present when the proceedings are commenced.

2. Support: Proceedings that involve child or spousal support or child and spousal support, exclusive of proceedings arising under Chapter 5 (§20-61 et seq.) of Title 20, shall be commenced in the city or county where either party resides or in the city or county where the respondent is present when the proceeding commences.

3. Family abuse: Proceedings in which an order of protection is sought as a result of family abuse shall be commenced where (i) either party has his or her principal residence, (ii) the abuse occurred or (iii) a protective order was issued if at the time the proceeding is commenced the order is in effect to protect the petitioner or a family or household member of the petitioner.

B. Transfer of venue:

1. Generally: Except in custody, visitation and support cases, if the child resides in a city or county of the Commonwealth and the proceeding is commenced in a court of another city or county, that court may at any time, on its own initiative or a motion of a party for good cause shown, transfer the proceeding to the city or county of the child's residence for such further action or proceedings as the court receiving the transfer may deem proper. However, such transfer may occur only after adjudication in delinquency proceedings.

2. Custody and visitation: In custody and visitation cases, if venue lies in one of several cities or counties, the court in which the motion for transfer is made shall determine which such city or county is the most appropriate venue unless the parties mutually agree to the selection of venue. In the consideration of the motion, the best interests of the child shall determine the most appropriate forum.

3. Support: In support proceedings, exclusive of proceedings arising under Chapter 5 (§20-61 et seq.) of Title 20, if the respondent resides in a city or county in the Commonwealth and the proceeding is commenced in a court of another city or county, that court may, at any time on its own motion or a motion of a party for good cause shown or by agreement of the parties, transfer the proceeding to the city or county of the respondent's residence for such further action or proceedings as the court receiving the transfer may deem proper. For the purposes of determining venue of cases involving support, the respondent's residence shall include any city or county in which the respondent has resided within the last six months prior to the commencement of the proceeding or in which the respondent is residing at the time that the motion for transfer of venue is made. If venue is transferable to one of several cities or counties, the court in which the motion for transfer is made shall determine which such city or county is the most appropriate venue unless the parties mutually agree to the selection of such venue.

When the support proceeding is a companion case to a child custody or visitation proceeding, the provisions governing venue in the proceeding involving the child's custody or visitation shall govern.

4. Subsequent transfers: Any court receiving a transferred proceeding as provided in this section may in its discretion transfer such proceeding to a court in an appropriate venue for good cause shown based either upon changes in circumstances or mistakes of fact or upon agreement of the parties. In any transfer of venue in cases involving children, the best interests of the child shall be considered in deciding if and to which court a transfer of venue would be appropriate.

5. Enforcement of orders for support, maintenance and custody: Any juvenile and domestic relations district court to which a suit is transferred for enforcement of orders pertaining to support, maintenance, care or custody pursuant to §20-79(c) may transfer the case as provided in this section.

C. Records: Originals of all legal and social records pertaining to the case shall accompany the transfer of venue. The transferor court may, in its discretion, retain such copies as it deems appropriate.

(Chgd. by L.1995 chs. 772, 826; L.1996 chs. 616, 866; L.2000 ch. 830, eff. 7/1/2000.)

§16.1-244. Concurrent jurisdiction; exceptions.

A. Nothing contained in this law shall deprive any other court of the concurrent jurisdiction to determine the custody of children upon a writ of habeas corpus under the law, or to determine the custody, guardianship, visitation or support of children when such custody, guardianship, visitation or support is incidental to the determination of causes pending in such courts, nor deprive a circuit court of jurisdiction to determine spousal support in a suit for separate maintenance. However, when a suit for divorce has been filed in a circuit court, in which the custody, guardianship, visitation or support of children of the parties or spousal support is raised by the pleadings and a hearing is set by the circuit court on any such issue for a date certain to be heard within twenty-one days of the filing, the juvenile and domestic relations district courts shall be divested of the right to enter any further decrees or orders to determine custody, guardianship, visitation or support when raised for such hearing and such matters shall be determined by the circuit court unless both parties agreed to a referral to the juvenile court. Nothing in this section shall deprive a circuit court of the authority to refer any such case to a commissioner for a hearing or shall deprive the juvenile and domestic relations district courts of the jurisdiction to enforce its valid orders prior to the entry of a conflicting order of any circuit court for any period during which the order was in effect or to temporarily place a child in the custody of any person when that child has been adjudicated abused, neglected, in need of services or delinquent subsequent to the order of any circuit court.

B. Jurisdiction of cases involving violations of federal law by a child shall be concurrent and shall be assumed only if waived by the federal court or the United States attorney.
(Chgd. by L.1996 ch. 616; L.2000 ch. 781, eff. 7/1/2000.)

ARTICLE 4
IMMEDIATE CUSTODY, ARREST, DETENTION AND SHELTER CARE
(Selected Sections)

§16.1-246. When and how child may be taken into immediate custody.

No child may be taken into immediate custody except:

A. With a detention order issued by the judge, the intake officer or the clerk, when authorized by the judge, of the juvenile and domestic relations district court in accordance with the provisions of this law or with a warrant issued by a magistrate; or

B. When a child is alleged to be in need of services or supervision and (i) there is a clear and substantial danger to the child's life or health or (ii) the assumption of custody is necessary to ensure the child's appearance before the court; or

C. When, in the presence of the officer who makes the arrest, a child has committed an act designated a crime under the law of this Commonwealth, or an ordinance of any city, county, town or service district, or under federal law and the officer believes that such is necessary for the protection of the public interest; or

C1. When a child has committed a misdemeanor offense involving (i) shoplifting in violation of §18.2-103, (ii) assault and battery or (iii) carrying a weapon on school property in violation of §18.2-308.1 and, although the offense was not committed in the presence of the officer who makes the arrest, the arrest is based on probable cause on reasonable complaint of a person who observed the alleged offense; or

D. When there is probable cause to believe that a child has committed an offense which if committed by an adult would be a felony; or

E. When a law-enforcement officer has probable cause to believe that a person committed to the Department of Juvenile Justice as a child has run away or that a child has escaped from a jail or detention home; or

F. When a law-enforcement officer has probable cause to believe a child has run away from a residential, child-caring facility or home in which he had been placed by the court, the local department of public welfare or social services or a licensed child welfare agency; or

G. When a law-enforcement officer has probable cause to believe that a child (i) has run away from home or (ii) is without adult supervision at such hours of the night and under such circumstances that the law-enforcement officer reasonably concludes that there is a clear and substantial danger to the child's welfare; or

H. When a child is believed to be in need of inpatient treatment for mental illness as provided in §16.1-340.
(Chgd. by L.1996 ch. 616, eff. 7/1/96.)

§16.1-247. Duties of person taking child into custody.

A. A person taking a child into custody pursuant to the provisions of §16.1-246 A, during such hours as the court is open, shall, with all practicable speed, and in accordance with the provisions of this law and the orders of court pursuant thereto, bring the child to the judge or intake officer of the court and the judge, intake officer or arresting officer shall, in the most expeditious manner practicable, give notice of the action taken, together with a statement of the reasons for taking the child into custody, orally or in writing to the child's parent, guardian, legal custodian or other person standing in loco parentis.

B. A person taking a child into custody pursuant to the provisions of subsection B, C or D of §16.1-246, during such hours as the court is open, shall, with all practicable speed, and in accordance with the provisions of this law and the orders of court pursuant thereto:

1. Release the child to such child's parents, guardian, custodian or other suitable person able and willing to provide supervision and care for such child and issue oral counsel and warning as may be appropriate; or

2. Release the child to such child's parents, guardian, legal custodian or other person standing in loco parentis upon their promise to bring the child before the court when requested; or

3. If not released, bring the child to the judge or intake officer of the court and, in the most expeditious manner practicable, give notice of the action taken, together with a statement of the reasons for taking the child into custody, in writing to the judge or intake officer, and the judge, intake officer or arresting officer shall give notice of the action taken orally or in writing to the child's parent, guardian, legal custodian or other person standing in loco parentis. Nothing herein shall prevent the child from being held for the purpose of administering a blood or breath test to determine the alcoholic content of his blood where the child has been taken into custody pursuant to §18.2-266.

C. A person taking a child into custody pursuant to the provisions of subsections E and F of §16.1-246, during such hours as the court is open, shall, with all practicable speed and in accordance with the provisions of this law and the orders of court pursuant thereto:

1. Release the child to the institution, facility or home from which he ran away or escaped; or

2. If not released, bring the child to the judge or intake officer of the court and, in the most expeditious manner

practicable, give notice of the action taken, together with a statement of the reasons for taking the child into custody, in writing to the judge or intake officer, and the judge, intake officer or arresting officer shall give notice of the action taken orally or in writing to the institution, facility or home in which the child had been placed and orally or in writing to the child's parent, guardian, legal custodian or other person standing in loco parentis.

D. A person taking a child into custody pursuant to the provisions of §16.1-246 A, during such hours as the court is not open, shall with all practicable speed and in accordance with the provisions of this law and the orders of court pursuant thereto:

1. Release the child taken into custody pursuant to a warrant on bail or recognizance pursuant to Chapter 9 (§19.2-119 et seq.) of Title 19.2; or

2. Place the child in a detention home or in shelter care; or

3. Place the child in a jail subject to the provisions of §16.1-249.

E. A person taking a child into custody pursuant to the provisions of subsection B, C or D of §16.1-246 during such hours as the court is not open, shall:

1. Release the child pursuant to the provisions of subsection B 1 or B 2 of this section; or

2. Release the child on bail or recognizance pursuant to Chapter 9 (§19.2-119 et seq.) of Title 19.2; or

3. Place the child taken into custody pursuant to §16.1-246 B in shelter care after the issuance of a detention order pursuant to §16.1-255; or

4. Place the child taken into custody pursuant to subsection C or D of §16.1-246 in shelter care or in a detention home after the issuance of a warrant by a magistrate; or

5. Place the child in a jail subject to the provisions of §16.1-249 after the issuance of a warrant by a magistrate; or

6. In addition to any other provisions of this subsection, detain the child for a reasonably necessary period of time in order to administer a breath or blood test to determine the alcohol content of his blood, if such child was taken into custody pursuant to §18.2-266.

F. A person taking a child into custody pursuant to the provisions of §16.1-246 E, during such hours as the court is not open, shall:

1. Release the child to the institution or facility from which he ran away or escaped; or

2. Detain the child in a detention home or in a jail subject to the provisions of §16.1-249 after the issuance of a warrant by a magistrate.

G. A person taking a child into custody pursuant to the provisions of §16.1-246 F, during such hours as the court is not open, shall:

1. Release the child to the facility or home from which he ran away; or

2. Detain the child in shelter care after the issuance of a detention order pursuant to §16.1-255 or after the issuance of a warrant by a magistrate.

H. If a parent, guardian or other custodian fails, when requested, to bring the child before the court as provided in subdivisions B 2 and E 1 hereof, the court may issue a detention order directing that the child be taken into custody and be brought before the court.

I. A law-enforcement officer taking a child into custody pursuant to the provisions of §16.1-246 G shall notify the intake officer of the juvenile court of the action taken. The intake officer shall determine if the child's conduct or situation is within the jurisdiction of the court and if a petition should be filed on behalf of the child. If the intake officer determines that a petition should not be filed, the law-enforcement officer shall as soon as practicable:

1. Return the child to his home;

2. Release the child to such child's parents, guardian, legal custodian or other person standing in loco parentis;

3. Place the child in shelter care for a period not longer than twenty-four hours after the issuance of a detention order pursuant to §16.1-255; or

4. Release the child.

During the period of detention authorized by this subsection no child shall be confined in any detention home, jail or other facility for the detention of adults.

J. If a child is taken into custody pursuant to the provisions of subsection B, F or G of §16.1-246 by a law-enforcement officer during such hours as the court is not in session and the child is not released or transferred to a facility or institution in accordance with subsection E, G, or I of this section, the child shall be held in custody only so long as is reasonably necessary to complete identification, investigation and processing. The child shall be held under visual supervision in a nonlocked, multipurpose area which is not designated for residential use. The child shall not be handcuffed or otherwise secured to a stationary object.
(Chgd. by L.1996 ch. 616, eff. 7/1/96.)

§16.1-248.1. Criteria for detention or shelter care.

A. A juvenile taken into custody whose case is considered by a judge, intake officer or magistrate pursuant to §16.1-247 shall immediately be released, upon the ascertainment of the necessary facts, to the care, custody and control of such juvenile's parent, guardian, custodian or other suitable person able and willing to provide supervision and care for such juvenile, either on bail or recognizance pursuant to Chapter 9 (§19.2-119 et seq.) of Title 19.2 or under such conditions as may be imposed or otherwise. However, a juvenile may be detained in a secure facility, pursuant to a detention order or warrant, only upon a finding by the judge, intake officer, or magistrate, that there is probable cause to believe that the juvenile committed the act alleged, and that at least one of the following conditions is met:

1. The juvenile is alleged to have committed an act which would be a felony or Class 1 misdemeanor if committed by an adult, and there is clear and convincing evidence that:

a. Considering the seriousness of the current offense or offenses and other pending charges, the seriousness of prior adjudicated offenses, the legal status of the juvenile and any aggravating and mitigating circumstances, the release of the juvenile, constitutes a clear and substantial threat to the person or property of others;

b. The release of the juvenile would present a clear and substantial threat of serious harm to such juvenile's life or health; or

c. The juvenile has threatened to abscond from the court's jurisdiction during the pendency of the instant proceedings or has a record of willful failure to appear at a court hearing within the immediately preceding twelve months.

2. The juvenile has absconded from a detention home or facility where he has been directed to remain by the lawful order of a judge or intake officer.

3. The juvenile is a fugitive from a jurisdiction outside the Commonwealth and subject to a verified petition or warrant, in which case such juvenile may be detained for a period not to exceed that provided for in §16.1-323 while arrangements are made to return the juvenile to the lawful custody of a parent, guardian or other authority in another state.

4. The juvenile has failed to appear in court after having been duly served with a summons in any case in which it is alleged that the juvenile has committed a delinquent act or that the child is in need of services or is in need of supervision; however, a child alleged to be in need of services or in

need of supervision may be detained for good cause pursuant to this subsection only until the next day upon which the court sits within the county or city in which the charge against the child is pending, and under no circumstances longer than seventy-two hours from the time he was taken into custody.

When a juvenile is placed in secure detention, the detention order shall state the offense for which the juvenile is being detained, and, to the extent practicable, other pending and previous charges.

B. Any juvenile not meeting the criteria for placement in a secure facility shall be released to a parent, guardian or other person willing and able to provide supervision and care under such conditions as the judge, intake officer or magistrate may impose. However, a juvenile may be placed in shelter care if:

1. The juvenile is eligible for placement in a secure facility;

2. The juvenile has failed to adhere to the directions of the court, intake officer or magistrate while on conditional release;

3. The juvenile's parent, guardian or other person able to provide supervision cannot be reached within a reasonable time;

4. The juvenile does not consent to return home;

5. Neither the juvenile's parent or guardian nor any other person able to provide proper supervision can arrive to assume custody within a reasonable time; or

6. The juvenile's parent or guardian refuses to permit the juvenile to return home and no relative or other person willing and able to provide proper supervision and care can be located within a reasonable time.

C. The criteria for continuing the juvenile in detention or shelter care as set forth in this section shall govern the decisions of all persons involved in determining whether the continued detention or shelter care is warranted pending court disposition. Such criteria shall be supported by clear and convincing evidence in support of the decision not to release the juvenile.

D. Nothing in this section shall be construed to deprive the court of its power to punish a juvenile summarily for contempt for acts set forth in §18.2-456, other than acts of disobedience of the court's dispositional order which are committed outside the presence of the court.

E. A detention order may be issued pursuant to subdivision 2 of subsection A by the committing court or by the court in the jurisdiction from which the juvenile fled or where he was taken into custody.

(Chgd. by L.1996 chs. 755, 914; L.2000 ch. 836, eff. 7/1/2000.)

§16.1-248.2. Mental health screening and assessment for certain juveniles.

Whenever a juvenile is placed in a secure facility pursuant to §16.1-248.1, the staff of the facility shall gather such information from the juvenile and the probation officer as is reasonably available and deemed necessary by the facility staff. As part of the intake procedures at each such facility, the staff shall ascertain the juvenile's need for a mental health assessment. If it is determined that the juvenile needs such an assessment, the assessment shall take place within twenty-four hours of such determination. The community services board serving the jurisdiction where the facility is located shall be responsible for conducting the assessments and shall be compensated from funds appropriated to the Department of Juvenile Justice for this purpose. The Department of Juvenile Justice shall develop criteria and a compensation plan for such assessments.

(Added by L.1996 chs. 755, 914; chgd. by L.1998 ch. 434, eff. 7/1/98.)

§16.1-249. Places of confinement for juveniles.

A. If it is ordered that a juvenile remain in detention or shelter care pursuant to §16.1-248.1, such juvenile may be detained, pending a court hearing, in the following places:

1. An approved foster home or a home otherwise authorized by law to provide such care;

2. A facility operated by a licensed child welfare agency;

3. If a juvenile is alleged to be delinquent, in a detention home or group home approved by the Department;

4. Any other suitable place designated by the court and approved by the Department;

5. To the extent permitted by federal law, a separate juvenile detention facility located upon the site of an adult regional jail facility established by any county, city or any combination thereof constructed after 1994, approved by the Department of Juvenile Justice and certified by the Board of Juvenile Justice for the holding and detention of juveniles.

B. No juvenile shall be detained or confined in any jail or other facility for the detention of adult offenders or persons charged with crime except as provided in subsection D, E, F or G of this section.

C. The official in charge of a jail or other facility for the detention of adult offenders or persons charged with crime shall inform the court immediately when a juvenile who is or appears to be under the age of eighteen years is received at the facility, and shall deliver him to the court upon request, or transfer him to a detention facility designated by the court.

D. When a case is transferred to the circuit court in accordance with the provisions of subsection A of §16.1-269.1 and an order is entered by the circuit court in accordance with §16.1-269.6, or in accordance with the provisions of §16.1-270 where the juvenile has waived the jurisdiction of the district court, or when the district court has certified a charge to the grand jury pursuant to subsection B or C of §16.1-269.1, the juvenile, if in confinement, may be transferred to a jail or other facility for the detention of adults and need no longer be entirely separate and removed from adults.

E. If, in the judgment of the custodian, a juvenile has demonstrated that he is a threat to the security or safety of the other juveniles detained or the staff of the home or facility, the judge shall determine whether such juvenile should be transferred to another juvenile facility or, if the child is fourteen years of age or older, a jail or other facility for the detention of adults; provided, that (i) the detention is in a room or ward entirely separate and removed from adults, (ii) adequate supervision is provided, and (iii) the facility is approved by the State Board of Corrections for detention of juveniles.

F. If, in the judgment of the custodian, it has been demonstrated that the presence of a juvenile in a facility creates a threat to the security or safety of the other juveniles detained or the staff of the home or facility, the custodian may transfer the juvenile to another juvenile facility, or, if the child is fourteen years of age or older, a jail or other facility for the detention of adults pursuant to the limitations of clauses (i), (ii) and (iii) of subsection E for a period not to exceed six hours prior to a court hearing and an additional six hours after the court hearing unless a longer period is ordered pursuant to subsection E.

G. If a juvenile fourteen years of age or older is charged with an offense which, if committed by an adult, would be a felony or Class 1 misdemeanor, and the judge or intake officer determines that secure detention is needed for the safety of the juvenile or the community, such juvenile may be detained for a period not to exceed six hours prior to a court hearing and six hours after the court hearing in a temporary lock-up room or ward for juveniles while arrangements are completed to transfer the juvenile to a juvenile facility. Such room or ward may be located in a building which also contains a jail or other facility for the detention of adults, provided (i) such room or ward is totally separate and removed from adults or juveniles transferred to the circuit court pursuant to Article 7 (§16.1-269.1 et seq.) of this chapter, (ii) constant supervision is provided, and (iii) the facility is approved by the State Board of Corrections for the detention of juveniles. The State Board of Corrections is authorized and directed to prescribe minimum standards for temporary lock-up rooms and wards based on the requirements set out in this subsection.

G1. Any juvenile who has been ordered detained in a secure detention facility pursuant to §16.1-248.1 may be held incident to a court hearing (i) in a court holding cell for a period not to exceed six hours provided the juvenile is entirely separate and removed from detained adults or (ii) in a nonsecure area provided constant supervision is provided.

H. A judge may order the predispositional detention of persons eighteen years of age or older (i) in a juvenile facility only for a violation of the terms and conditions of release from a juvenile correctional center or (ii) in an adult facility.

I. The Departments of Corrections, Juvenile Justice and Criminal Justice Services shall assist the localities or combinations thereof in implementing this section and ensuring compliance herewith.

(Chgd. by L.1995 chs. 746, 748, 798, 802; L.1996 chs. 755, 914; L.1998 ch. 576, eff. 7/1/98, ch. 830, eff. 4/22/98.)

§16.1-250. Procedure for detention hearing.

A. When a child has been taken into immediate custody and not released as provided in §16.1-247 or §16.1-248.1, such child shall appear before a judge on the next day on which the court sits within the county or city wherein the charge against the child is pending. In the event the court does not sit within the county or city on the following day, such child shall appear before a judge within a reasonable time, not to exceed seventy-two hours, after he has been taken into custody. If the seventy-two hour period expires on a Saturday, Sunday or other legal holiday, the seventy-two hours shall be extended to the next day which is not a Saturday, Sunday or legal holiday.

B. The appearance of the child may be by (i) personal appearance before the judge or (ii) use of two-way electronic video and audio communication. If two-way electronic video and audio communication is used, a judge may exercise all powers conferred by law and all communications and proceedings shall be conducted in the same manner as if the appearance were in person, and any documents filed may be transmitted by electronically transmitted facsimile process. The facsimile may be served or executed by the officer or person to whom sent, and returned in the same manner, and with the same force, effect, authority, and liability as an original document. All signatures thereon shall be treated as original signatures. Any two-way electronic video and audio communication system used for an appearance shall meet the standards set forth in §19.2-3.1 B.

C. Notice of the detention hearing, either oral or written, stating the time, place and purpose of the hearing shall be given to the parent, guardian, legal custodian or other person standing in loco parentis if he can be found, to the child if twelve years of age or over and to the attorney of the Commonwealth.

D. During the detention hearing, the judge shall advise the parties of the right to counsel pursuant to §16.1-266. The parties shall be informed of the child's right to remain silent with respect to any allegation of delinquency and of the contents of the petition. The attorney for the Commonwealth shall be given the opportunity to be heard.

E. If the judge finds that there is not probable cause to believe that the child committed the delinquent act alleged, the court shall order his release. If the judge finds that there is probable cause to believe that the child committed the delinquent act alleged but that the full-time detention of a child who is alleged to be delinquent is not required, the court shall order his release, and in so doing, the court may impose one or more of the following conditions singly or in combination:

1. Place the child in the custody of a parent, guardian, legal custodian or other person standing in loco parentis under their supervision, or under the supervision of an organization or individual agreeing to supervise him;

2. Place restrictions on the child's travel, association or place of abode during the period of his release;

3. Impose any other condition deemed reasonably necessary and consistent with the criteria for detaining children specified in §16.1-248.1; or

4. Release the child on bail or recognizance in accordance with the provisions of Chapter 9 (§19.2-119 et seq.) of Title 19.2.

F. An order releasing a child on any of the conditions specified in this section may, at any time, be amended to impose additional or different conditions of release or to return the child who is alleged to be delinquent to custody for failure to conform to the conditions previously imposed.

G. All relevant and material evidence helpful in determining probable cause under this section or the need for detention may be admitted by the court even though not competent in a hearing on the petition.

H. If the child is not released and a parent, guardian, legal custodian or other person standing in loco parentis is not notified and does not appear or does not waive appearance at the hearing, upon the request of such person, the court shall rehear the matter on the next day on which the court sits within the county or city wherein the charge against the child is pending. If the court does not sit within the county or city on the following day, such hearing shall be held before a judge within a reasonable time, not to exceed seventy-two hours, after the request.

I. In considering probable cause under this section, if the court deems it necessary to summon witnesses to assist in such determination then the hearing may be continued and the child remain in detention, but in no event longer than three consecutive days, exclusive of Saturdays, Sundays, and legal holidays.

(Chgd. by L.1995 ch. 451, eff. 7/1/95.)

§16.1-250.1. Appointment of counsel; detention review hearing.

When a child is not released after a detention hearing held pursuant to §16.1-250 and, at the time of the detention hearing, the child was not represented by legal counsel, then the child shall be afforded the opportunity to be represented by counsel prior to a detention review hearing.

The court shall, upon request of counsel, rehear the matter as soon as is practicable but in no event later than seventy-two hours after the request for the review hearing. During the hearing, the court shall evaluate the need for continued detention of the child.

Notice of the detention review hearing, either oral or written, stating the time, place and purpose of the hearing shall be given to the parent, guardian, legal custodian or other person standing in loco parentis if he can be found, to the child's attorney, to the child if twelve years of age or over, and to the attorney for the Commonwealth who shall be given an opportunity to be heard.

§16.1-251. Emergency removal order.

A. A child may be taken into immediate custody and placed in shelter care pursuant to an emergency removal order in cases in which the child is alleged to have been abused or neglected. Such order may be issued ex parte by the court upon a petition supported by an affidavit or by sworn testimony in person before the judge or intake officer which establishes that:

1. The child would be subjected to an imminent threat to life or health to the extent that severe or irremediable injury would be likely to result if the child were returned to or left in the custody of his parents, guardian, legal custodian or other person standing in loco parentis pending a final hearing on the petition.

2. Reasonable efforts have been made to prevent removal of the child from his home and there are no alternatives less drastic than removal of the child from his home which could reasonably protect the child's life or health pending a final hearing on the petition. The alternatives less drastic than removal may include but not be limited to the provision of medical, educational, psychiatric, psychological, homemaking or other similar services to the child or family or the issuance of a preliminary protective order pursuant to §16.1-253.

When a child is removed from his home and there is no reasonable opportunity to provide preventive services, reasonable efforts to prevent removal shall be deemed to have been made.

B. Whenever a child is taken into immediate custody pursuant to an emergency removal order, a hearing shall be held in accordance with §16.1-252 as soon as practicable, but in no event later than five business days after the removal of the child.

C. In the emergency removal order the court shall give consideration to temporary placement of the child with a relative or other interested individual, including grandparents, under the supervision of the local department of social services, until such time as the hearing in accordance with §16.1-252 is held.

D. The local department of social services having legal custody of a child as defined in §16.1-228(i) shall not be required to comply with the requirements of this section in order to redetermine where and with whom the child shall live, notwithstanding that the child had been placed with a natural parent.

(Chgd. by L.2000 ch. 385, eff. 7/1/2000.)

§16.1-252. Preliminary removal order; hearing.

A. A preliminary removal order in cases in which a child is alleged to have been abused or neglected may be issued by the court after a hearing wherein the court finds that reasonable efforts have been made to prevent removal of the child from his home. The hearing shall be in the nature of a preliminary hearing rather than a final determination of custody.

B. Prior to the removal hearing, notice of the hearing shall be given at least twenty-four hours in advance of the hearing to the guardian ad litem for the child, to the parents, guardian, legal custodian or other person standing in loco parentis of the child and to the child if he or she is twelve years of age or older. If notice to the parents, guardian, legal custodian or other person standing in loco parentis cannot be given despite diligent efforts to do so, the hearing shall be held nonetheless, and the parents, guardian, legal custodian or other person standing in loco parentis shall be afforded a later hearing on their motion regarding a continuation of the summary removal order. The notice provided herein shall include (i) the time, date and place for the hearing; (ii) a specific statement of the factual circumstances which allegedly necessitate removal of the child; and (iii) notice that child support will be considered if a determination is made that the child must be removed from the home.

C. All parties to the hearing shall be informed of their right to counsel pursuant to §16.1-266.

D. At the removal hearing the child and his parent, guardian, legal custodian or other person standing in loco parentis shall have the right to confront and cross-examine all adverse witnesses and evidence and to present evidence on their own behalf. If the child was fourteen years of age or under on the date of the alleged offense and is sixteen or under at the time of the hearing, the child's attorney or guardian ad litem, or if the child has been committed to the custody of the Department of Social Services, the local department of social services, may apply for an order from the court that the child's testimony be taken in a room outside the courtroom and be televised by two-way closed-circuit television. The provisions of §63.1-248.13:1 shall apply, mutatis mutandis, to the use of two-way closed-circuit television except that the person seeking the order shall apply for the order at least forty-eight hours before the hearing, unless the court for good cause shown allows the application to be made at a later time.

E. In order for a preliminary order to issue or for an existing order to be continued, the petitioning party or agency must prove:

1. The child would be subjected to an imminent threat to life or health to the extent that severe or irremediable injury would be likely to result if the child were returned to or left in the custody of his parents, guardian, legal custodian or other person standing in loco parentis pending a final hearing on the petition; and

2. Reasonable efforts have been made to prevent removal of the child from his home and there are no alternatives less drastic than removal of the child from his home which could reasonably and adequately protect the child's life or health pending a final hearing on the petition. The alternatives less drastic than removal may include but not be limited to the provision of medical, educational, psychiatric, psychological, homemaking or other similar services to the child or family or the issuance of a preliminary protective order pursuant to §16.1-253.

When a child is removed from his home and there is no reasonable opportunity to provide preventive services, reasonable efforts to prevent removal shall be deemed to have been made.

F. If the court determines that pursuant to subsection E hereof the removal of the child is proper, the court shall:

1. Order that the child be placed in the temporary care and custody of a suitable person, subject to the provisions of subsection F1 of this section and under the supervision of the local department of social services, with consideration being given to placement in the temporary care and custody of a relative or other interested individual, including grandparents, until such time as the court enters an order of disposition pursuant to §16.1-278.2, or, if such placement is not available, in the care and custody of a suitable agency;

2. Order that reasonable visitation be allowed between the child and his parents, guardian, legal custodian or other person standing in loco parentis, if such visitation would not endanger the child's life or health; and

3. Order that the parent or other legally obligated person pay child support pursuant to §16.1-290.

In addition, the court may enter a preliminary protective order pursuant to §16.1-253 imposing requirements and conditions as specified in that section which the court deems appropriate for protection of the welfare of the child.

F1. Prior to the entry of an order pursuant to subsection F of this section transferring temporary custody of the child to a relative or other interested individual, including grandparents, the court shall consider whether the relative or other interested individual is one who (i) is willing and qualified to receive and care for the child; (ii) is willing to have a positive, continuous relationship with the child; and (iii) is willing and has the ability to protect the child from abuse and neglect. The court's order transferring temporary custody to a relative or other interested individual should provide for compliance with any preliminary protective order entered on behalf of the child in accordance with the provisions of §16.1-253; initiation and completion of the investigation as directed by the court and court review of the child's placement required in accordance with the provisions of §16.1-278.2; and, as appropriate, ongoing provision of social services to the child and the temporary custodian.

G. At the conclusion of the preliminary removal order hearing, the court shall determine whether the allegations of abuse or neglect have been proven by a preponderance of the evidence. Any finding of abuse or neglect shall be stated in the court order. However, if, before such a finding is made, a person responsible for the care and custody of the child, the child's guardian ad litem or the local department of social services objects to a finding being made at the hearing, the court shall schedule an adjudicatory hearing to be held within thirty days of the date of the initial preliminary removal hearing. The adjudicatory hearing shall be held to determine whether the allegations of abuse and neglect have been proven by a preponderance of the evidence. Parties who are present at the preliminary removal order hearing shall be given notice of the date set for the adjudicatory hearing and parties who are not present shall be summoned as provided in §16.1-263. The hearing shall be held and an order may be entered, although a party to the preliminary removal order hearing fails to appear and is not represented by counsel, provided personal or substituted service was made on the person, or the court determines that such person cannot be found, after reasonable effort, or in the case of a person who is without the Commonwealth, the person cannot be found or his post office address cannot be ascertained after reasonable effort.

The preliminary removal order and any preliminary protective order issued shall remain in full force and effect pending the adjudicatory hearing.

H. If the preliminary removal order includes a finding of abuse or neglect and the child is removed from his home or a preliminary protective order is issued, a dispositional hearing shall be held pursuant to §16.1-278.2. The dispositional hearing shall be scheduled at the time of the preliminary removal order hearing and shall be held within seventy-five days of the preliminary removal order hearing. If an adjudicatory hearing is requested pursuant to subsection G, the dispositional hearing shall nonetheless be scheduled at the initial preliminary removal order hearing. All parties present at the preliminary removal order hearing shall be given notice of the date scheduled for the dispositional hearing; parties who are not present shall be summoned to appear as provided in §16.1-263.

I. The local department of social services having legal custody of a child as defined in §16.1-228(i) shall not be required to comply with the requirements of this section in order to redetermine where and with whom the child shall live, notwithstanding that the child had been placed with a natural parent.

J. Violation of any order issued pursuant to this section shall constitute contempt of court.

(Chgd. by L.1995 ch. 817; L.1997 ch. 790; L.1999 ch. 668; L.2000 ch. 385, eff. 7/1/2000.)

§16.1-253. Preliminary protective order.

A. Upon the motion of any person or upon the court's own motion, the court may issue a preliminary protective order, after a hearing, if necessary to protect a child's life, health, safety or normal development pending the final determination of any matter before the court. The order may require a child's parents, guardian, legal custodian, other person standing in loco parentis or other family or household member of the child to observe reasonable conditions of behavior for a specified length of time. These conditions shall include any one or more of the following:

1. To abstain from offensive conduct against the child, a family or household member of the child or any person to whom custody of the child is awarded;

2. To cooperate in the provision of reasonable services or programs designed to protect the child's life, health or normal development;

3. To allow persons named by the court to come into the child's home at reasonable times designated by the court to visit the child or inspect the fitness of the home and to determine the physical or emotional health of the child;

4. To allow visitation with the child by persons entitled thereto, as determined by the court;

5. To refrain from acts of commission or omission which tend to endanger the child's life, health or normal development; or

6. To refrain from such contact with the child or family or household members of the child, as the court may deem appropriate, including removal of such person from the residence of the child. However, prior to the issuance by the court of an order removing such person from the residence of the child, the petitioner must prove by a preponderance of the evidence that such person's probable future conduct would constitute a danger to the life or health of such child, and that there are no less drastic alternatives which could reasonably and adequately protect the child's life or health pending a final determination on the petition.

B. A preliminary protective order may be issued ex parte upon motion of any person or the court's own motion in any matter before the court, or upon petition. The motion or petition shall be supported by an affidavit or by sworn testimony in person before the judge or intake officer which establishes that the child would be subjected to an imminent threat to life or health to the extent that delay for the provision of an adversary hearing would be likely to result in serious or irremediable injury to the child's life or health. If an ex parte order is issued without an affidavit being presented, the court, in its order, shall state the basis upon which the order was entered, including a summary of the allegations made and the court's findings. Following the issuance of an ex parte order the court shall provide an adversary hearing to the affected parties within the shortest practicable time not to exceed five business days after the issuance of the order.

C. Prior to the hearing required by this section, notice of the hearing shall be given at least twenty-four hours in advance of the hearing to the guardian ad litem for the child, to the parents, guardian, legal custodian, or other person standing in loco parentis of the child, to any other family or household member of the child to whom the protective order may be directed and to the child if he or she is twelve years of age or older. The notice provided herein shall include (i) the time, date and place for the hearing and (ii) a specific statement of the factual circumstances which allegedly necessitate the issuance of a preliminary protective order.

D. All parties to the hearing shall be informed of their right to counsel pursuant to §16.1-266.

E. At the hearing the child, his or her parents, guardian, legal custodian or other person standing in loco parentis and any other family or household member of the child to whom notice was given shall have the right to confront and cross-examine all adverse witnesses and evidence and to present evidence on their own behalf.

F. If a petition alleging abuse or neglect of a child has been filed, at the hearing pursuant to this section the court shall determine whether the allegations of abuse or neglect have been proven by a preponderance of the evidence. Any finding of abuse or neglect shall be stated in the court order. However, if, before such a finding is made, a person responsible for the care and custody of the child, the child's guardian ad litem or the local department of social services objects to a finding being made at the hearing, the court shall schedule an adjudicatory hearing to be held within thirty days of the date of the initial preliminary protective order hearing. The adjudicatory hearing shall be held to determine whether the allegations of abuse and neglect have been proven by a preponderance of the evidence. Parties who are present at the hearing shall be given notice of the date set for the adjudicatory hearing and parties who are not present shall be summoned as provided in §16.1-263. The adjudicatory hearing shall be held and an order may be entered, although a party to the hearing fails to appear and is not represented by counsel, provided personal or substituted service was made on the person, or the court determines that such person cannot be found, after reasonable effort, or in the case of a person who is without the Commonwealth, the person cannot be found or his post office address cannot be ascertained after reasonable effort.

Any preliminary protective order issued shall remain in full force and effect pending the adjudicatory hearing.

G. If at the preliminary protective order hearing held pursuant to this section the court makes a finding of abuse or neglect and a preliminary protective order is issued, a dispositional hearing shall be held pursuant to §16.1-278.2. The dispositional hearing shall be scheduled at the time of the hearing pursuant to this section, and shall be held within seventy-five days of this hearing. If an adjudicatory hearing is requested pursuant to subsection F, the dispositional hearing shall nonetheless be scheduled at the hearing pursuant to this section. All parties present at the hearing shall be given notice of the date and time scheduled for the dispositional hearing; parties who are not present shall be summoned to appear as provided in §16.1-263.

H. Nothing in this section enables the court to remove a child from the custody of his or her parents, guardian, legal custodian or other person standing in loco parentis, except as provided in §16.1-278.2, and no order hereunder shall be entered against a person over whom the court does not have jurisdiction.

I. Violation of any order issued pursuant to this section shall constitute contempt of court.

(Chgd. by L.1996 ch. 866; L.1997 ch. 790; L.1998 ch. 550, eff. 7/1/98.)

§16.1-253.1. Preliminary protective orders in cases of family abuse; confidentiality.

A. Upon the filing of a petition alleging that the petitioner is or has been, within a reasonable period of time, subjected to family abuse, the court may issue a preliminary protective order against an allegedly abusing person in order to protect the health and safety of the petitioner or any family or household member of the petitioner. The order may be issued in an ex parte proceeding upon good cause shown when the petition is supported by an affidavit or sworn testimony before the judge or intake officer. Immediate and present danger of family abuse or evidence sufficient to establish probable cause that family abuse has recently occurred shall constitute good cause.

A preliminary protective order may include any one or more of the following conditions to be imposed on the allegedly abusing person:

1. Prohibiting acts of family abuse.
2. Prohibiting such other contacts between the parties as the court deems appropriate.
3. Prohibiting such other contacts with the allegedly abused family or household member as the court deems necessary to protect the safety of such persons.
4. Granting the petitioner possession of the premises occupied by the parties to the exclusion of the allegedly abusing person; however, no such grant of possession shall affect title to any real or personal property.
5. Granting the petitioner temporary possession or use of a motor vehicle owned by the petitioner alone or jointly owned by the parties to the exclusion of the allegedly abusing person; however, no such grant of possession or use shall affect title to the vehicle.
6. Requiring that the allegedly abusing person provide suitable alternative housing for the petitioner and any other family or household member, where appropriate.

B. As soon as practicable after receipt of the order by a local law-enforcement agency for service, the agency shall enter the name of the person subject to the order and other appropriate information required by the Department of State Police into the Virginia criminal information network system established and maintained by the Department pursuant to Chapter 2 (§52-12 et seq.) of Title 52. Where feasible and practical, the court may transfer information electronically to the Virginia criminal information network system. A copy of a preliminary protective order shall be served as soon as possible on the allegedly abusing person in person as provided in §16.1-264, and upon service, the agency making service shall enter the date and time of service into the Virginia criminal information network system. The preliminary order shall specify a date for the full hearing. The hearing shall be held within fifteen days of the issuance of the preliminary order. Upon request after the order is issued, the clerk shall provide the petitioner with a copy of the order and information regarding the date and time of service. The order shall further specify that either party may at any time file a motion with the court requesting a hearing to dissolve or modify the order. The hearing on the motion shall be given precedence on the docket of the court.

Upon receipt of the return of service or other proof of service pursuant to subsection C of §16.1-264, the clerk shall forward forthwith an attested copy of the preliminary protective order to the local police department or sheriff's office which shall, on the date of receipt, enter into the Virginia criminal information network system any other information required by the State Police which was not previously entered. If the order is later dissolved or modified, a copy of the dissolution or modification order shall also be attested, forwarded and entered in the Virginia criminal information network system as described above.

C. The preliminary order is effective upon personal service on the allegedly abusing person. Except as otherwise provided in §16.1-253.2, a violation of the order shall constitute contempt of court.

D. At a full hearing on the petition, the court may issue a protective order pursuant to §16.1-279.1 if the court finds that the petitioner has proven the allegation of family abuse by a preponderance of the evidence.

E. As used in this section, "copy" includes a facsimile copy.

(Chgd. by L.1996 ch. 866; L.1997 ch. 603; L.1998 ch. 684; L.2000 chs. 34, 654, eff. 7/1/2000.)

§16.1-253.2. Violation of provisions of protective orders; penalty.

In addition to any other penalty provided by law, any person who violates any provision of a protective order issued pursuant to §§16.1-253, 16.1-253.1, 16.1-253.4, 16.1-278.14, 16.1-279.1 or subsection B of §20-103, which prohibits such person from going or remaining upon land, buildings or premises or from further acts of family abuse, or which prohibits contacts between the respondent and the respondent's family or household member as the court deems appropriate shall be guilty of a Class 1 misdemeanor. Upon conviction, the person shall be sentenced to a term of

confinement and in no case shall the entire term imposed be suspended.
(Chgd. by L.1996 ch. 866, eff. 7/1/97.)

§16.1-253.4. Emergency protective orders authorized in certain cases; penalty.

A. Any judge of a circuit court, general district court, juvenile and domestic relations district court or magistrate may issue a written or oral ex parte emergency protective order pursuant to this section in order to protect the health or safety of any person.

B. When a law-enforcement officer or an allegedly abused person asserts under oath to a judge or magistrate, and on that assertion or other evidence the judge or magistrate finds that (i) a warrant for a violation of §18.2-57.2 has been issued and there is probable danger of further acts of family abuse against a family or household member by the respondent or (ii) reasonable grounds exist to believe that the respondent has committed family abuse and there is probable danger of a further such offense against a family or household member by the respondent, the judge or magistrate shall issue an ex parte emergency protective order, except if the respondent is a minor, an emergency protective order shall not be required, imposing one or more of the following conditions on the respondent:

1. Prohibiting acts of family abuse;

2. Prohibiting such contacts by the respondent with family or household members of the respondent as the judge or magistrate deems necessary to protect the safety of such persons; and

3. Granting the family or household member possession of the premises occupied by the parties to the exclusion of the respondent; however, no such grant of possession shall affect title to any real or personal property.

C. An emergency protective order issued pursuant to this section shall expire seventy-two hours after issuance. If the expiration of the seventy-two-hour period occurs at a time that the court is not in session, the emergency protective order shall be extended until 5 p.m. of the next business day that the juvenile and domestic relations district court is in session. The respondent may at any time file a motion with the court requesting a hearing to dissolve or modify the order. The hearing on the motion shall be given precedence on the docket of the court.

D. A law-enforcement officer may request an emergency protective order pursuant to this section and, if the person in need of protection is physically or mentally incapable of filing a petition pursuant to §16.1-253.1 or §16.1-279.1, may request the extension of an emergency protective order for an additional period of time not to exceed seventy-two hours after expiration of the original order. The request for an emergency protective order or extension of an order may be made orally, in person or by electronic means, and the judge of a circuit court, general district court, or juvenile and domestic relations district court or a magistrate may issue an oral emergency protective order. An oral emergency protective order issued pursuant to this section shall be reduced to writing, by the law-enforcement officer requesting the order or the magistrate on a preprinted form approved and provided by the Supreme Court of Virginia. The completed form shall include a statement of the grounds for the order asserted by the officer or the allegedly abused person.

E. As soon as practicable after receipt of the order by a local law-enforcement agency for service, the agency shall enter the name of the person subject to the order and other appropriate information required by the Department of State Police into the Virginia criminal information network system established and maintained by the Department pursuant to Chapter 2 (§52-12 et seq.) of Title 52. A copy of an emergency protective order issued pursuant to this section shall be served upon the respondent as soon as possible, and upon service, the agency making service shall enter the date and time of service into the Virginia criminal information network system. One copy of the order shall be given to the allegedly abused person when it is issued, and one copy shall be filed with the written report required by §19.2-81.3 C. The original copy shall be verified by the judge or magistrate who issued the order and then filed with the clerk of the juvenile and domestic relations district court within five business days of the issuance of the order. If the order is later dissolved or modified, a copy of the dissolution or modification order shall also be attested, forwarded and entered in the system as described above. Upon request, the clerk shall provide the allegedly abused person with information regarding the date and time of service.

F. The availability of an emergency protective order shall not be affected by the fact that the family or household member left the premises to avoid the danger of family abuse by the respondent.

G. The issuance of an emergency protective order shall not be considered evidence of any wrongdoing by the respondent.

H. As used in this section, a "law-enforcement officer" means (i) any full-time or part-time employee of a police department or sheriff's office which is part of or administered by the Commonwealth or any political subdivision thereof and who is responsible for the prevention and detection of crime and the enforcement of the penal, traffic or highway laws of the Commonwealth and (ii) member of an auxiliary police force established pursuant to subsection B of §15.2-1731. Part-time employees are compensated officers who are not full-time employees as defined by the employing police department or sheriff's office.

I. As used in this section, "copy" includes a facsimile copy.
(Chgd. by L.1996 chs. 616, 866; L.1997 ch. 603; L.1998 chs. 677, 684; L.1999 ch. 807, eff. 7/1/99.)

§16.1-254. Responsibility for and limitation on transportation of children.

A. The detention home having custody or responsibility for supervision of a child pursuant to §§16.1-246, 16.1-247, 16.1-248.1, 16.1-249, and 16.1-250 shall be responsible for transportation of the child to all local medical appointments, dental appointments, psychological and psychiatric evaluations. Transportation of youth to special placements pursuant to §16.1-286 shall be the responsibility of the court service unit.

B. However, the chief judge of the juvenile and domestic relations district court, on the basis of guidelines approved by the Board, shall designate the appropriate agencies in each county, city and town, other than the Department of State Police, to be responsible for (i) the transportation of violent and disruptive children and (ii) the transportation of children to destinations other than those set forth in subsection A of this section, pursuant to §§16.1-246, 16.1-247, 16.1-248.1, 16.1-249, and 16.1-250, and as otherwise ordered by the judge.

No child shall be transported with adults suspected of or charged with criminal acts.
(Chgd. by L.1996 ch. 616, eff. 7/1/96.)

§16.1-255. Limitation on issuance of detention orders for juveniles.

No detention order shall be issued for any juvenile except when authorized by the judge or intake officer of a juvenile court or by a magistrate as provided in §16.1-256.

In matters involving the issuance of detention orders, each state or local court service unit shall ensure the

capability of a prompt response by an intake officer who is either on duty or on call.
(Chgd. by L.1996 chs. 616, 755, 914; L.1997 ch. 862, eff. 7/1/97.)

§16.1-256. Limitations as to issuance of warrants for juveniles; detention orders.

No warrant of arrest shall be issued for any juvenile by a magistrate, except as follows:

1. As provided in §16.1-260 on appeal from a decision of an intake officer; or

2. Upon a finding of probable cause to believe that the child is in need of services or is a delinquent, when (i) the court is not open and (ii) the judge and the intake officer of the juvenile and domestic relations district court are not reasonably available. For purposes of this section, the phrase "not reasonably available" means that neither the judge nor the intake officer of the juvenile and domestic relations district court could be reached after the appearance by the juvenile before a magistrate or that neither could arrive within one hour after he was contacted.

When a magistrate is authorized to issue a warrant pursuant to subdivision 2, he may also issue a detention order, if the criteria for detention set forth in §16.1-248.1 have been satisfied.

Warrants issued pursuant to this section shall be delivered forthwith to the juvenile court.
(Chgd. by L.1996 chs. 616, 755, 914, eff. 7/1/96.)

§16.1-257. Interference with or obstruction of officer; concealment or removal of child.

No person shall interfere with or obstruct any officer, juvenile probation officer or other officer or employee of the court in the discharge of his duties under this law, nor remove or conceal or cause to be removed or concealed any child in order that he or she may not be brought before the court, nor interfere with or remove or attempt to remove any child who is in the custody of the court or of an officer or who has been lawfully committed under this law. Any person willfully violating any provision of this section is guilty of a Class 1 misdemeanor.

ARTICLE 5
INTAKE, PETITION AND NOTICE
(Selected Sections)

§16.1-260. Intake; petition; investigation.

A. All matters alleged to be within the jurisdiction of the court shall be commenced by the filing of a petition, except as provided in subsection H of this section and in §16.1-259. The form and content of the petition shall be as provided in §16.1-262. No individual shall be required to obtain support services from the Department of Social Services prior to filing a petition seeking support for a child. Complaints, requests and the processing of petitions to initiate a case shall be the responsibility of the intake officer. However, (i) the attorney for the Commonwealth of the city or county may file a petition on his own motion with the clerk, (ii) the Department of Social Services may file support petitions on its own motion with the clerk, and (iii) any attorney may file petitions on behalf of his client with the clerk except petitions alleging that the subject of the petition is a child alleged to be in need of services, in need of supervision or delinquent. Complaints alleging abuse or neglect of a child shall be referred initially to the local department of public welfare or social services in accordance with the provisions of Chapter 12.1 (§63.1-248.1 et seq.) of Title 63.1. Motions and other subsequent pleadings in a case shall be filed directly with the clerk. The intake officer or clerk with whom the petition or motion is filed shall inquire whether the petitioner is receiving child support services or public assistance. No individual who is receiving support services or public assistance shall be denied the right to file a petition or motion to establish, modify or enforce an order for support of a child. If the petitioner is seeking or receiving child support services or public assistance, the clerk, upon issuance of process, shall forward a copy of the petition or motion, together with notice of the court date, to the Division of Child Support Enforcement.

B. The appearance of a child before an intake officer may be by (i) personal appearance before the intake officer or (ii) use of two-way electronic video and audio communication. If two-way electronic video and audio communication is used, an intake officer may exercise all powers conferred by law. All communications and proceedings shall be conducted in the same manner as if the appearance were in person, and any documents filed may be transmitted by facsimile process. The facsimile may be served or executed by the officer or person to whom sent, and returned in the same manner, and with the same force, effect, authority, and liability as an original document. All signatures thereon shall be treated as original signatures. Any two-way electronic video and audio communication system used for an appearance shall meet the standards as set forth in subsection B of §19.2-3.1.

B1. When the court service unit of any court receives a complaint alleging facts which may be sufficient to invoke the jurisdiction of the court pursuant to §16.1-241, the unit, through an intake officer, may proceed informally to make such adjustment as is practicable without the filing of a petition or may authorize a petition to be filed by any complainant having sufficient knowledge of the matter to establish probable cause for the issuance of the petition.

An intake officer may proceed informally on a complaint alleging a child is in need of services, in need of supervision or delinquent only if the juvenile (i) is not alleged to have committed a violent juvenile felony; (ii) has not previously been proceeded against informally or adjudicated in need of supervision or delinquent; or (iii) is not the subject of a complaint filed pursuant to §22.1-258 and the attendance officer has provided documentation to the intake officer or magistrate that the relevant school division has complied with the provisions of §22.1-258. A petition alleging that a juvenile committed a violent juvenile felony shall be filed with the court. A petition alleging that a juvenile is in need of supervision or delinquent shall be filed with the court if the juvenile had previously been proceeded against informally by intake or had been adjudicated in need of supervision or delinquent.

Whenever informal action is taken as provided in this subsection on a complaint alleging that a child is in need of services, in need of supervision or delinquent, the intake officer shall (i) develop a plan for the juvenile, which may include restitution and the performance of community service, based upon community resources and the circumstances which resulted in the complaint, (ii) create an official record of the action taken by the intake officer and file such record in the juvenile's case file, and (iii) advise the juvenile and the juvenile's parent, guardian or other person standing in loco parentis and the complainant that any subsequent complaint alleging that the child is in need of supervision or delinquent based upon facts which may be sufficient to invoke the jurisdiction of the court pursuant to §16.1-241 will result in the filing of a petition with the court.

C. The intake officer shall accept and file a petition in which it is alleged that (i) the custody, visitation or support of a child is the subject of controversy or requires determination, (ii) a person has deserted, abandoned or failed to provide support for any person in violation of law, (iii) a child or such child's parent, guardian, legal custodian or other person standing in loco parentis is entitled to treatment, rehabilitation or other services which are required by law, or (iv) family abuse has occurred and a protective order is being sought pursuant to §§16.1-253.1, 16.1-253.4 or §16.1-279.1. If any such complainant does not file a petition, the intake officer may file it. In cases in which a child is alleged to be abused, neglected, in need of services, in need of supervision or delinquent, if the intake officer believes that probable cause does not exist, or that the authorization of a petition will not be in the best interest of the family or juvenile or that the matter may be effectively dealt with by some agency other than the court, he may refuse to authorize the filing of a petition.

D. Prior to the filing of any petition alleging that a child is in need of supervision, the matter shall be reviewed by an intake officer who shall determine whether the petitioner and the child alleged to be in need of supervision have utilized or attempted to utilize treatment and services available in the community and have exhausted all appropriate nonjudicial remedies which are available to them. When the intake officer determines that the parties have not attempted to utilize available treatment or services or have not exhausted all appropriate nonjudicial remedies which are available, he shall refer the petitioner and the child alleged to be in need of supervision to the appropriate agency, treatment facility or individual to receive treatment or services, and a petition shall not be filed. Only after the intake officer determines that the parties have made a reasonable effort to utilize available community treatment or services may he permit the petition to be filed.

E. If the intake officer refuses to authorize a petition relating to an offense that if committed by an adult would be punishable as a Class 1 misdemeanor or as a felony, the complainant shall be notified in writing at that time of the complainant's right to apply to a magistrate for a warrant. If a magistrate determines that probable cause exists, he shall issue a warrant returnable to the juvenile and domestic relations district court. The warrant shall be delivered forthwith to the juvenile court, and the intake officer shall accept and file a petition founded upon the warrant. If the court is closed and the magistrate finds that the criteria for detention or shelter care set forth in §16.1-248.1 have been satisfied, the juvenile may be detained pursuant to the warrant issued in accordance with this subsection. If the intake officer refuses to authorize a petition relating to a child in need of services or in need of supervision, a status offense, or a misdemeanor other than Class 1, his decision is final.

Upon delivery to the juvenile court of a warrant issued pursuant to subdivision 2 of §16.1-256, the intake officer shall accept and file a petition founded upon the warrant.

F. The intake officer shall notify the attorney for the Commonwealth of the filing of any petition which alleges facts of an offense which would be a felony if committed by an adult.

G. After a petition is filed alleging that a juvenile committed an act which would be a crime if committed by an adult, the intake officer shall, as soon as practicable, provide notice by telephone of the filing of the petition and the nature of the offense to the superintendent of the school division in which the petitioner alleges the juvenile is or should be enrolled, provided the violation involves:

1. A firearm offense pursuant to Articles 4 (§18.2-279 et seq.), 5 (§18.2-288 et seq.), 6 (§18.2-299 et seq.), or 7 (§18.2-308 et seq.), of Chapter 7 of Title 18.2;
2. Homicide, pursuant to Article 1 (§18.2-30 et seq.) of Chapter 4 of Title 18.2;
3. Felonious assault and bodily wounding, pursuant to Article 4 (§18.2-51 et seq.) of Chapter 4 of Title 18.2;
4. Criminal sexual assault, pursuant to Article 7 (§18.2-61 et seq.) of Chapter 4 of Title 18.2;
5. Manufacture, sale, gift, distribution or possession of Schedule I or II controlled substances, pursuant to Article 1 (§18.2-247 et seq.) of Chapter 7 of Title 18.2;
6. Manufacture, sale or distribution of marijuana pursuant to Article 1 (§18.2-247 et seq.) of Chapter 7 of Title 18.2;
7. Arson and related crimes, pursuant to Article 1 (§18.2-77 et seq.) of Chapter 5 of Title 18.2;
8. Burglary and related offenses, pursuant to §§18.2-89 through 18.2-93; or
9. Robbery pursuant to §18.2-58.

Promptly after filing a petition the intake officer shall also mail notice, by first-class mail, to the superintendent. The failure to provide information regarding the school in which the juvenile who is the subject of the petition may be enrolled shall not be grounds for refusing to file a petition.

The information provided to a division superintendent pursuant to this section may be disclosed only as provided in §16.1-305.2.

H. The filing of a petition shall not be necessary:

1. In the case of violations of the traffic laws, including offenses involving bicycles, hitchhiking and other pedestrian offenses, game and fish laws or a violation of the ordinance of any city regulating surfing or any ordinance establishing curfew violations or animal control violations. In such cases the court may proceed on a summons issued by the officer investigating the violation in the same manner as provided by law for adults. Additionally, an officer investigating a motor vehicle accident may, at the scene of the accident or at any other location where a juvenile who is involved in such an accident may be located, proceed on a summons in lieu of filing a petition.

2. In the case of seeking consent to apply for the issuance of a work permit pursuant to subdivision H of §16.1-241.

3. In the case of a violation of §18.2-266 or §29.1-738, or the commission of any other alcohol-related offense, provided the juvenile is released to the custody of a parent or legal guardian pending the initial court date. The officer releasing a juvenile to the custody of a parent or legal guardian shall issue a summons to the juvenile and shall also issue a summons requiring the parent or legal guardian to appear before the court with the juvenile. Disposition of the charge shall be in the manner provided in §16.1-278.8 or §16.1-278.9. If the juvenile so charged with a violation of §18.2-266 or §29.1-738 refuses to provide a sample of blood or breath or samples of both blood and breath for chemical analysis pursuant to §§18.2-268.1 through 18.2-268.12 or §29.1-738.2, the provisions of these sections shall be followed except that the magistrate shall authorize execution of the warrant as a summons. The summons shall be served on a parent or legal guardian and the juvenile, and a copy of the summons shall be forwarded to the court in which the violation of §18.2-266 or §29.1-738 is to be tried.

4. In the case of offenses which, if committed by an adult would be punishable as a Class 3 or Class 4 misdemeanor. In such cases the court may direct that an intake officer proceed as provided in §16.1-237 on a summons issued by the officer investigating the violation in the same manner as provided by law for adults provided that notice of the summons to appear is mailed by the investigating officer

within five days of the issuance of the summons to a parent or legal guardian of the juvenile.

I. Failure to comply with the procedures set forth in this section shall not divest the juvenile court of the jurisdiction granted it in §16.1-241.

(Chgd. by L.1995 chs. 347, 429; L.1996 chs. 616, 755, 914; L.1997 ch. 862; L.1999 chs. 54, 526, 952, eff. 7/1/99.)

§16.1-261. Statements made at intake or mental health screening and assessment.

Statements made by a child to the intake officer or probation officer during the intake process or during a mental health screening or assessment conducted pursuant to §16.1-248.2 and prior to a hearing on the merits of the petition filed against the child, shall not be admissible at any stage of the proceedings.

(Chgd. by L.1996 chs. 755, 914, eff. 7/1/96.)

§16.1-262. Form and content of petition.

The petition shall contain the facts below indicated:

"Commonwealth of Virginia, In re ...." a (name of child) child under eighteen years of age.

"In the Juvenile and Domestic Relations District Court of the county (or city) of ...."

1. Statement of name, age, date of birth, if known, and residence of the child.
2. Statement of names and residence of his parents, guardian, legal custodian or other person standing in loco parentis and spouse, if any.
3. Statement of names and residence of the nearest known relatives if no parent or guardian can be found.
4. Statement of the specific facts which allegedly bring the child within the purview of this law. If the petition alleges a delinquent act, it shall make reference to the applicable sections of the Code which designate the act a crime.
5. Statement as to whether the child is in custody, and if so, the place of detention or shelter care, and the time the child was taken into custody, and the time the child was placed in detention or shelter care.

If any of the facts herein required to be stated are not known by the petitioner, the petition shall so state. The petition shall be verified, except that petitions filed under §63.1-219.44 may be signed by the petitioner's counsel, and may be upon information.

In accordance with §16.1-69.32, the Supreme Court may formulate rules for the form and content of petitions in the juvenile court concerning matters related to the custody, visitation or support of a child and the protection, support or maintenance of an adult where the provisions of this section are not appropriate.

(Chgd. by L.1995 chs. 772, 826; L.1996 ch. 616; L.2000 ch. 830, eff. 7/1/2000.)

§16.1-263. Summonses.

A. After a petition has been filed, the court shall direct the issuance of summonses, one directed to the juvenile, if the juvenile is twelve or more years of age, and another to at least one parent, guardian, legal custodian or other person standing in loco parentis, and such other persons as appear to the court to be proper or necessary parties to the proceedings. The summons shall require them to appear personally before the court at the time fixed to answer or testify as to the allegations of the petition. Where the custodian is summoned and such person is not a parent of the juvenile in question, a parent shall also be served with a summons. The court may direct that other proper or necessary parties to the proceedings be notified of the pendency of the case, the charge and the time and place for the hearing.

B. The summons shall advise the parties of their right to counsel as provided in §16.1-266. A copy of the petition shall accompany each summons for the initial proceedings. The summons shall include notice that in the event that the juvenile is committed to the Department or to a secure local facility, at least one parent or other person legally obligated to care for and support the juvenile may be required to pay a reasonable sum for support and treatment of the juvenile pursuant to §16.1-290. Notice of subsequent proceedings shall be provided to all parties in interest. In all cases where a party is represented by counsel and counsel has been provided with a copy of the petition and due notice as to time, date and place of the hearing, such action shall be deemed due notice to such party, unless such counsel has notified the court that he no longer represents such party.

C. The judge may endorse upon the summons an order directing a parent or parents, guardian or other custodian having the custody or control of the juvenile to bring the juvenile to the hearing.

D. A party, other than the juvenile, may waive service of summons by written stipulation or by voluntary appearance at the hearing.

E. No such summons or notification shall be required if the judge shall certify on the record that (i) the identity of a parent or guardian is not reasonably ascertainable or (ii) in cases in which it is alleged that a juvenile has committed a delinquent act, crime, status offense or traffic infraction or is in need of services or supervision, the location, or in the case of a parent or guardian located outside of the Commonwealth the location or mailing address, of a parent or guardian is not reasonably ascertainable. An affidavit of the mother that the identity of the father is not reasonably ascertainable shall be sufficient evidence of this fact, provided there is no other evidence before the court which would refute such an affidavit. In cases referred to in clause (ii), an affidavit of a law-enforcement officer or juvenile probation officer that the location of a parent or guardian is not reasonably ascertainable shall be sufficient evidence of this fact, provided that there is no other evidence before the court which would refute the affidavit.

(Chgd. by L.1996 chs. 616, 755, 914; L.1997 ch. 441; L.1999 ch. 952, eff. 7/1/99.)

§16.1-264. Service of summons; proof of service; penalty.

A. If a party designated in §16.1-263 A to be served with a summons can be found within the Commonwealth, the summons shall be served upon him in person or by substituted service as prescribed in §8.01-296(2).

If a party designated to be served in §16.1-263 is without the Commonwealth but can be found or his address is known, or can with reasonable diligence be ascertained, service of summons may be made either by delivering a copy thereof to him personally or by mailing a copy thereof to him by certified mail return receipt requested.

If after reasonable effort a party other than the person who is the subject of the petition cannot be found or his post-office address cannot be ascertained, whether he is within or without the Commonwealth, the court may order service of the summons upon him by publication in accordance with the provisions of §§8.01-316 and 8.01-317.

B. Service of summons may be made under the direction of the court by sheriffs, their deputies and police officers in counties and cities or by any other suitable person designated by the court.

C. Proof of service may be made by the affidavit of the person other than an officer designated in subsection B hereof who delivers a copy of the summons to the person summoned, but if served by a state, county or municipal officer his return shall be sufficient without oath.

D. The summons shall be considered a mandate of the court and willful failure to obey its requirements shall subject any person guilty thereof to liability for punishment as for contempt.
(Chgd. by L.1996 ch. 616, eff. 7/1/96.)

§16.1-265. Subpoena.

Upon application of a party and pursuant to the rules of the Supreme Court of Virginia for the issuance of subpoenas, the clerk of the court shall issue, and the court on its own motion may issue, subpoenas requiring attendance and testimony of witnesses and production of records, documents or other tangible objects at any hearing.

(Paragraph expires 7/1/2001 by the second enactment of L.2000 ch. 813 unless reenacted by the 2001 General Assembly.) Subpoenas duces tecum for medical records shall be subject to the provisions of §§8.01-413 and 32.1-277.1:03 except that no separate fee shall be imposed. A subpoena may also be issued in a civil proceeding by an attorney-at-law who is an active member of the Virginia State Bar at the time of issuance, as an officer of the court. Any such subpoena shall be on a form approved by the Committee on District Courts, signed by the attorney as if a pleading and shall include the attorney's address. A copy, together with the attorney's certificate of service pursuant to Rule 1:12, shall be mailed or delivered to the clerk's office of the court in which the case is pending on the day of issuance by the attorney. The law governing subpoenas issued by a clerk shall apply mutatis mutandis, except that attorneys may not issue subpoenas in those cases in which they may not issue a summons as provided in §8.01-407 and may not issue a subpoena duces tecum less than five business days prior to the date that production of evidence is required. When an attorney-at-law transmits one or more subpoenas or subpoenas duces tecum to a sheriff to be served in his jurisdiction, the provisions in §8.01-407 regarding such transmittals shall apply.

(Paragraph expires 7/1/2001 by the second enactment of L.2000 ch. 813 unless reenacted by the 2001 General Assembly.) If the time for compliance with a subpoena issued by an attorney is less than fourteen days after service of the subpoena, the person to whom it is directed may serve upon the party issuing the subpoena a written objection setting forth any grounds therefor. If objection is made, the party on whose behalf the subpoena was issued and served shall not be entitled to compliance, except pursuant to an order of the court, but may, upon notice to the person to whom the subpoena was directed, move for an order to compel compliance. Upon such timely motion, the court may quash, modify or sustain the subpoena.
(Chgd. by L.2000 ch. 813, eff. 7/1/2000.)

ARTICLE 6
APPOINTMENT OF COUNSEL
(Complete Article)

§16.1-266. Appointment of counsel.

A. Prior to the hearing by the court of any case involving a child who is alleged to be abused or neglected or who is the subject of an entrustment agreement or a petition terminating residual parental rights or is otherwise before the court pursuant to subdivision A 4 of §16.1-241, the court shall appoint a discreet and competent attorney-at-law as guardian ad litem to represent the child pursuant to §16.1-266.1.

B. Prior to the detention review hearing or the adjudicatory or transfer hearing by the court of any case involving a child who is alleged to be in need of services, in need of supervision or delinquent, such child and his or her parent, guardian, legal custodian or other person standing in loco parentis shall be informed by a judge, clerk or probation officer of the child's right to counsel and of the liability of the parent, guardian, legal custodian or other person standing in loco parentis for the costs of such legal services pursuant to §16.1-267 and be given an opportunity to:

1. Obtain and employ counsel of the child's own choice; or

2. If the court determines that the child is indigent within the contemplation of the law pursuant to the guidelines set forth in §19.2-159 and his or her parent, guardian, legal custodian or other person standing in loco parentis does not retain an attorney for the child, a statement of indigence substantially in the form provided by §19.2-159 and a financial statement shall be executed by such child, and the court shall appoint an attorney-at-law to represent him; or

3. Waive the right to representation by an attorney, if the court finds the child and the parent, guardian, legal custodian or other person standing in loco parentis of the child consent, in writing, to such waiver and that the interests of the child and the parent, guardian, legal custodian or other person standing in loco parentis in the proceeding are not adverse. Such written waiver shall be in accordance with law and shall be filed with the court records of the case.

C. Prior to the hearing by the court of any case involving a parent, guardian or other adult charged with abuse or neglect of a child or a parent or guardian who could be subjected to the loss of residual parental rights and responsibilities, such parent, guardian or other adult shall be informed by a judge, clerk or probation officer of his right to counsel and be given an opportunity to:

1. Obtain and employ counsel of the parent's, guardian's or other adult's own choice; or

2. If the court determines that the parent, guardian or other adult is indigent within the contemplation of the law pursuant to the guidelines set forth in §19.2-159, a statement substantially in the form provided by §19.2-159 and a financial statement shall be executed by such parent, guardian or other adult and the court shall appoint an attorney-at-law to represent him; or

3. Waive the right to representation by an attorney in accordance with the provisions of §19.2-160.

D. In all other cases which in the discretion of the court require counsel or a guardian ad litem to represent the interests of the child or children or the parent or guardian, a discreet and competent attorney-at-law may be appointed by the court. However, in cases where the custody of a child or children is the subject of controversy or requires determination and each of the parents or other persons claiming a right to custody is represented by counsel, the court shall not appoint counsel or a guardian ad litem to represent the interests of the child or children unless the court finds, at any stage in the proceedings in a specific case, that the interests of the child or children are not otherwise adequately represented.

E. Any state or local agency, department, authority or institution and any school, hospital, physician or other health or mental health care provider shall permit a guardian ad litem appointed pursuant to this section to inspect and copy, without the consent of the child or his parents, any records relating to the child whom the guardian represents upon presentation by him of a copy of the court order appointing him or a court order specifically allowing him such access. Upon request therefor by the guardian ad litem made

 Zv

at least seventy-two hours in advance, a mental health care provider shall make himself available to conduct a review and interpretation of the child's treatment records which are specifically related to the investigation. Such a request may be made in lieu of or in addition to inspection and copying of the records.
(Chgd. by L.1996 ch. 616; L.1997 ch. 790, eff. 7/1/97.)

§16.1-266.1. List of qualified attorneys.

A. On or before January 1, 1995, the Judicial Council of Virginia, in conjunction with the Virginia State Bar and the Virginia Bar Association, shall adopt standards for attorneys appointed as guardians ad litem pursuant to §16.1-266. The standards shall, in so far as practicable, take into consideration the following criteria: (i) license or permission to practice law in Virginia, (ii) current training in the roles, responsibilities and duties of guardian ad litem representation, (iii) familiarity with the court system and general background in juvenile law, and (iv) demonstrated proficiency in this area of the law.

B. The Judicial Council shall maintain a list of attorneys admitted to practice law in Virginia who are qualified to serve as guardians ad litem based upon the standards and shall make the names available to the courts. If no attorney who is on the list is reasonably available, a judge in his discretion, may appoint any discreet and competent attorney who is admitted to practice law in Virginia.
(Chgd. by L.1995 ch. 273, eff. 7/1/95.)

§16.1-266.2. Appointment of pro bono counsel by judges of the First and Second Judicial District in certain cases.

The judges of the juvenile and domestic relations district court of the First and Second Judicial District are authorized to appoint pro bono counsel for alleged victims in family abuse cases in which the court is authorized to issue a preliminary protective order under §16.1-253.1, or an emergency protective order under §16.1-253.4. Such counsel shall have no prosecutorial authority except as granted in writing by the attorney for the Commonwealth for the jurisdiction in which the representation is to occur.

Any attorney appointed under the provisions of this section shall be a volunteer and serve without compensation and shall be subject to any rules adopted by the court and approved by the Virginia Supreme Court providing for the establishment and conduct of a project providing pro bono services to victims of family abuse.
(Added by L.1995 ch. 806; chgd. by L.1997 ch. 151, eff. 7/1/97.)

§16.1-267. Compensation of appointed counsel.

A. When the court appoints counsel to represent a child pursuant to §16.1-266 A and, after an investigation by the court services unit, finds that the parents are financially able to pay for the attorney and refuse to do so, the court shall assess costs against the parent for such legal services in the amount awarded the attorney by the court under the circumstances of the case, considering such factors as the ability of the parents to pay and the nature and extent of the counsel's duties in the case. Such amount shall not exceed $100 if the action is in circuit court or the maximum amount specified in subdivision (1) of §19.2-163 if the action is in district court.

When the court appoints counsel to represent a child pursuant to §16.1-266 B and, after an investigation by the court services unit, finds that the parents are financially able to pay for the attorney in whole or in part and refuse to do so, the court shall assess costs in whole or in part against the parents for such legal services in the amount awarded the attorney by the court. Such amount shall not exceed $100 if the action is in circuit court or the maximum amount specified in subdivision (1) of §19.2-163 if the action is in district court. In determining the financial ability of the parents to pay for an attorney to represent the child, the court shall utilize the financial statement required by §19.2-159.

In all other cases, except as provided in §16.1-343, counsel appointed to represent a child shall be compensated for his services pursuant to §19.2-163.

B. When the court appoints counsel to represent a parent, guardian or other adult pursuant to §16.1-266, such counsel shall be compensated for his services pursuant to §19.2-163.
(Chgd. by L.1996 ch. 616, eff. 7/1/96.)

§16.1-268. Order of appointment.

The order of appointment of counsel pursuant to §16.1-266 shall be filed with and become a part of the record of such proceeding. The attorney so appointed shall represent the child or parent, guardian or other adult at any such hearing and at all other stages of the proceeding unless relieved or replaced in the manner provided by law.

ARTICLE 7
TRANSFER AND WAIVER
(Complete Article)

§16.1-269.1. Trial in circuit court; preliminary hearing; direct indictment; remand.

A. Except as provided in subsections B and C, if a juvenile fourteen years of age or older at the time of an alleged offense is charged with an offense which would be a felony if committed by an adult, the court shall, on motion of the attorney for the Commonwealth and prior to a hearing on the merits, hold a transfer hearing and may retain jurisdiction or transfer such juvenile for proper criminal proceedings to the appropriate circuit court having criminal jurisdiction of such offenses if committed by an adult. Any transfer to the appropriate circuit court shall be subject to the following conditions:

1. Notice as prescribed in §§16.1-263 and 16.1-264 shall be given to the juvenile and his parent, guardian, legal custodian or other person standing in loco parentis; or attorney;

2. The juvenile court finds that probable cause exists to believe that the juvenile committed the delinquent act as alleged or a lesser included delinquent act which would be a felony if committed by an adult;

3. The juvenile is competent to stand trial. The juvenile is presumed to be competent and the burden is on the party alleging the juvenile is not competent to rebut the presumption by a preponderance of the evidence; and

4. The court finds by a preponderance of the evidence that the juvenile is not a proper person to remain within the jurisdiction of the juvenile court. In determining whether a juvenile is a proper person to remain within the jurisdiction

of the juvenile court, the court shall consider, but not be limited to, the following factors:

a. The juvenile's age;

b. The seriousness and number of alleged offenses, including (i) whether the alleged offense was committed in an aggressive, violent, premeditated, or willful manner; (ii) whether the alleged offense was against persons or property, with greater weight being given to offenses against persons, especially if death or bodily injury resulted; (iii) whether the maximum punishment for such an offense is greater than twenty years confinement if committed by an adult; (iv) whether the alleged offense involved the use of a firearm or other dangerous weapon by brandishing, threatening, displaying or otherwise employing such weapon; and (v) the nature of the juvenile's participation in the alleged offense;

c. Whether the juvenile can be retained in the juvenile justice system long enough for effective treatment and rehabilitation;

d. The appropriateness and availability of the services and dispositional alternatives in both the criminal justice and juvenile justice systems for dealing with the juvenile's problems;

e. The record and previous history of the juvenile in this or other jurisdictions, including (i) the number and nature of previous contacts with juvenile or circuit courts, (ii) the number and nature of prior periods of probation, (iii) the number and nature of prior commitments to juvenile correctional centers, (iv) the number and nature of previous residential and community-based treatments, (v) whether previous adjudications and commitments were for delinquent acts that involved the infliction of serious bodily injury, and (vi) whether the alleged offense is part of a repetitive pattern of similar adjudicated offenses;

f. Whether the juvenile has previously absconded from the legal custody of a juvenile correctional entity in this or any other jurisdiction;

g. The extent, if any, of the juvenile's degree of mental retardation or mental illness;

h. The juvenile's school record and education;

i. The juvenile's mental and emotional maturity; and

j. The juvenile's physical condition and physical maturity.

No transfer decision shall be precluded or reversed on the grounds that the court failed to consider any of the factors specified in subdivision A 4 of §16.1-269.1.

B. The juvenile court shall conduct a preliminary hearing whenever a juvenile fourteen years of age or older is charged with murder in violation of §§18.2-31, 18.2-32 or §18.2-40, or aggravated malicious wounding in violation of §18.2-51.2.

C. The juvenile court shall conduct a preliminary hearing whenever a juvenile fourteen years of age or older is charged with murder in violation of §18.2-33, felonious injury by mob in violation of §18.2-41, abduction in violation of §18.2-48, malicious wounding in violation of §18.2-51, malicious wounding of a law-enforcement officer in violation of §18.2-51.1, felonious poisoning in violation of §18.2-54.1, adulteration of products in violation of §18.2-54.1, robbery in violation of §18.2-58 or carjacking in violation of §18.2-58.1, rape in violation of §18.2-61, forcible sodomy in violation of §18.2-67.1 or object sexual penetration in violation of §18.2-67.2, provided the attorney for the Commonwealth gives written notice of his intent to proceed pursuant to this subsection. The notice shall be filed with the court and mailed or delivered to counsel for the juvenile or, if the juvenile is not then represented by counsel, to the juvenile and a parent, guardian or other person standing in loco parentis with respect to the juvenile at least seven days prior to the preliminary hearing. If the attorney for the Commonwealth elects not to give such notice, or if he elects to withdraw the notice prior to certification of the charge to the grand jury, he may proceed as provided in subsection A.

D. Upon a finding of probable cause pursuant to a preliminary hearing under subsection B or C, the juvenile court shall certify the charge, and all ancillary charges, to the grand jury. Such certification shall divest the juvenile court of jurisdiction as to the charge and any ancillary charges. Nothing in this subsection shall divest the juvenile court of jurisdiction over any matters unrelated to such charge and ancillary charges which may otherwise be properly within the jurisdiction of the juvenile court.

If the court does not find probable cause to believe that the juvenile has committed the violent juvenile felony as charged in the petition or warrant or if the petition or warrant is terminated by dismissal in the juvenile court, the attorney for the Commonwealth may seek a direct indictment in the circuit court. If the petition or warrant is terminated by nolle prosequi in the juvenile court, the attorney for the Commonwealth may seek an indictment only after a preliminary hearing in juvenile court.

If the court finds that the juvenile was not fourteen years of age or older at the time of the alleged commission of the offense or that the conditions specified in subdivision 1, 2, or 3 of subsection A have not been met, the case shall proceed as otherwise provided for by law.

E. An indictment in the circuit court cures any error or defect in any proceeding held in the juvenile court except with respect to the juvenile's age. If an indictment is terminated by nolle prosequi, the Commonwealth may reinstate the proceeding by seeking a subsequent indictment.

(Chgd. by L.1996 chs. 616, 755, 914; L.1997 ch. 862, eff. 7/1/97.)

§16.1-269.2. Admissibility of statement; investigation and report; bail.

A. Statements made by the juvenile at the transfer hearing provided for under §16.1-269.1 shall not be admissible against him over objection in any criminal proceedings following the transfer, except for purposes of impeachment.

B. Prior to a transfer hearing pursuant to subsection A of §16.1-269.1, a study and report to the court, in writing, relevant to the factors set out in subdivision A 4 of §16.1-269.1, as well as an assessment of any affiliation with a youth gang as defined in §16.1-299.2, shall be made by the probation services or other qualified agency designated by the court. Counsel for the juvenile and the attorney for the Commonwealth shall have full access to the study and report and any other report or data concerning the juvenile which are available to the court. The court shall not consider the report until a finding has been made concerning probable cause. If the court so orders, the study and report may be expanded to include matters provided for in §16.1-273, whereupon it may also serve as the report required by this subsection, but on the condition that it will not be submitted to the judge who will preside at any subsequent hearings except as provided for by law.

C. After the completion of the hearing, whether or not the juvenile court decides to retain jurisdiction over the juvenile or transfer such juvenile for criminal proceedings in the circuit court, the juvenile court shall set bail for the juvenile in accordance with Chapter 9 (§19.2-119 et seq.) of Title 19.2, if bail has not already been set.

(Chgd. by L.1996 ch. 616; L.1999 ch. 350, eff. 7/1/99.)

§16.1-269.3. Retention by juvenile court; appeal.

If a case is not transferred following a transfer hearing or is not certified following a probable cause hearing, the judge who conducted the hearing shall not, over the objection of any interested party, preside at the adjudicatory hearing on

the petition, but rather it shall be presided over by another judge of that court. If the attorney for the Commonwealth deems it to be in the public interest, and the juvenile is fourteen years of age or older, he may, within ten days after the juvenile court's final decision to retain the case in accordance with subsection A of §16.1-296.1, file a notice of appeal of the decision to the appropriate circuit court. A copy of such notice shall be furnished at the same time to the counsel for the juvenile.
(Chgd. by L.1996 chs. 616, 755, 914, eff. 7/1/96.)

§16.1-269.4. Transfer to circuit court; appeal by juvenile.
If the juvenile court transfers the case pursuant to subsection A of §16.1-269.1, the juvenile may, within ten days after the juvenile court's final decision, file a notice of appeal of the decision to the appropriate circuit court. A copy of the notice shall be furnished at the same time to the attorney for the Commonwealth.
(Chgd. by L.1996 chs. 616, 755, 914, eff. 7/1/96.)

§16.1-269.5. Placement of juvenile.
The juvenile court may order placement of the transferred juvenile in either a local correctional facility as approved by the State Board of Corrections pursuant to the limitations of subsection E of §16.1-249 or a juvenile detention facility.
(Chgd. by L.1996 ch. 616, eff. 7/1/96.)

§16.1-269.6. Circuit court hearing; jury; termination of juvenile court jurisdiction; objections and appeals.
A. Within seven days after receipt of notice of an appeal from the transfer decision pursuant to subsection A of §16.1-269.1, by either the attorney for the Commonwealth or the juvenile, or if an appeal to such a decision to transfer is not noted, upon expiration of the time in which to note such an appeal, the clerk of the court shall forward to the circuit court all papers connected with the case, including any report required by subsection B of §16.1-269.2, as well as a written court order setting forth the reasons for the juvenile court's decision. The clerk shall forward copies of the order to the attorney for the Commonwealth and other counsel of record.

B. The circuit court shall, within a reasonable time after receipt of the case from the juvenile court pursuant to subsection A of §16.1-269.1, (i) if either the juvenile or the attorney for the Commonwealth has appealed the transfer decision, examine all such papers, reports and orders and conduct a hearing to take further evidence on the issue of transfer, to determine if there has been substantial compliance with subsection A of §16.1-269.1, but without redetermining whether the juvenile court had sufficient evidence to find probable cause; and (ii) enter an order either remanding the case to the juvenile court or advising the attorney for the Commonwealth that he may seek an indictment. Upon advising the attorney for the Commonwealth that he may seek an indictment, the circuit court may issue an order transferring the juvenile from the juvenile detention facility to an appropriate local correctional facility where the juvenile need no longer be entirely separate and removed from adults, unless, upon motion of counsel, good cause is shown for placement of the juvenile pursuant to the limitations of subdivision E (i), (ii), and (iii) of §16.1-249. However, in cases where a charge has been certified by the juvenile court to the grand jury pursuant to subsection B or C of §16.1-269.1, the attorney for the Commonwealth may seek an indictment upon such charge and any ancillary charge without obtaining an order of the circuit court advising him that he may do so.

C. The circuit court order advising the attorney for the Commonwealth that he may seek an indictment shall divest the juvenile court of its jurisdiction over the case as well as the juvenile court's jurisdiction over any other allegations of delinquency arising from the same act, transaction or scheme giving rise to the charge for which the juvenile has been transferred. In addition, upon conviction of the juvenile following transfer or certification and trial as an adult, the circuit court shall issue an order terminating the juvenile court's jurisdiction over that juvenile with respect to any future criminal acts alleged to have been committed by such juvenile and with respect to any pending allegations of delinquency which have not been disposed of by the juvenile court at the time of the criminal conviction. Upon receipt of the order terminating the juvenile court's jurisdiction over the juvenile, the clerk of the juvenile court shall forward any pending petitions of delinquency for proceedings in the appropriate general district court.

D. The judge of the circuit court who reviewed the case after receipt from the juvenile court shall not, over the objection of any interested party, preside over the trial of such charge or charges.

E. Any objection to the jurisdiction of the circuit court pursuant to this article shall be waived if not made before arraignment.

F. The time period beginning with the filing of a notice of appeal pursuant to §16.1-269.3 or §16.1-269.4 and ending with the order of the circuit court disposing of the appeal shall not be included as applying to the provisions of §19.2-243.
(Chgd. by L.1996 chs. 616, 755, 914; L.1997 ch. 862, eff. 7/1/97.)

§16.1-270. Waiver of jurisdiction of juvenile court in certain cases.
At any time prior to commencement of the adjudicatory hearing, a juvenile fourteen years of age or older charged with an offense which if committed by an adult could be punishable by confinement in a state correctional facility, with the written consent of his counsel, may elect in writing to waive the jurisdiction of the juvenile court and have his case transferred to the appropriate circuit court, in which event his case shall thereafter be dealt with in the same manner as if he had been transferred pursuant to this article.
(Chgd. by L.1996 ch. 616, eff. 7/1/96.)

§16.1-271. Subsequent offenses by juvenile.
The trial or treatment of a juvenile as an adult pursuant to the provisions of this chapter shall preclude the juvenile court from taking jurisdiction of such juvenile for subsequent offenses committed by that juvenile.

Any juvenile who is tried and convicted in a circuit court as an adult under the provisions of this article shall be considered and treated as an adult in any criminal proceeding resulting from any alleged future criminal acts and any pending allegations of delinquency which have not been disposed of by the juvenile court at the time of the criminal conviction.

All procedures and dispositions applicable to adults charged with such a criminal offense shall apply in such cases, including, but not limited to, arrest; probable cause determination by a magistrate or grand jury; the use of a warrant, summons, or capias instead of a petition to initiate the case; adult bail; preliminary hearing and right to counsel provisions; trial in a court having jurisdiction over adults; and trial and sentencing as an adult. The provisions of this article regarding a transfer hearing shall not be applicable to such juveniles.
(Chgd. by L.1996 ch. 616, eff. 7/1/96.)

§16.1-272. Power of circuit court over juvenile offender.
A. In any case in which a juvenile is indicted, the offense for which he is indicted and all ancillary charges shall be

tried in the same manner as provided for in the trial of adults, except as otherwise provided with regard to sentencing. Upon a finding of guilty of any charge other than capital murder, the court shall fix the sentence without the intervention of a jury.

1. If a juvenile is convicted of a violent juvenile felony, the sentence for that offense and for all ancillary crimes shall be fixed by the court in the same manner as provided for adults, but the sentence may be suspended conditioned upon successful completion of such terms and conditions as may be imposed in a juvenile court upon disposition of a delinquency case including, but not limited to, commitment under subdivision 14 of §16.1-278.8 or §16.1-285.1.

2. If the juvenile is convicted of any other felony, the court may sentence or commit the juvenile offender in accordance with the criminal laws of this Commonwealth or may in its discretion deal with the juvenile in the manner prescribed in this chapter for the hearing and disposition of cases in the juvenile court, including, but not limited to, commitment under §16.1-285.1 or may in its discretion impose an adult sentence and suspend the sentence conditioned upon successful completion of such terms and conditions as may be imposed in a juvenile court upon disposition of a delinquency case.

3. If the juvenile is not convicted of a felony but is convicted of a misdemeanor, the court shall deal with the juvenile in the manner prescribed by law for the disposition of a delinquency case in the juvenile court.

B. If the circuit court decides to deal with the juvenile in the same manner as a case in the juvenile court and places the juvenile on probation, the juvenile may be supervised by a juvenile probation officer.

C. Whether the court sentences and commits the juvenile as a juvenile under this chapter or under the criminal law, in cases where the juvenile is convicted of a felony in violation of §§18.2-61, 18.2-63, 18.2-64.1, 18.2-67.1, 18.2-67.2, 18.2-67.3, 18.2-67.5, 18.2-370 or §18.2-370.1 or, where the victim is a minor or is physically helpless or mentally incapacitated as defined in §18.2-67.10, subsection B of §18.2-361 or subsection B of §18.2-366, the clerk shall make the report required by §19.2-390 to the Sex Offender Registry established pursuant to §19.2-390.1.

(Chgd. by L.1996 chs. 616, 755, 914; L.2000 ch. 793, eff. 7/1/2000.)

§16.1-272.1. Claim of error to be raised within one year.

In addition to any other curative provisions, waivers, procedural defaults, or requirements for timely objection, including but not limited to those in subsection J of §16.1-241, subsection E of §16.1-269.1 and subsection E of §16.1-269.6, any claim of error or defect under this chapter, jurisdictional or otherwise, that is not raised within one year from the date of final judgment of the circuit court or one year from the effective date of this act, whichever is later, shall not constitute a ground for relief in any judicial proceeding.

(Added by L.2000 ch. 418, eff. 7/1/2000.)

ARTICLE 8
ADJUDICATION
(Selected Sections)

§16.1-273. Court may require investigation of social history and preparation of victim impact statement.

A. When a juvenile and domestic relations district court or circuit court has adjudicated any case involving a child subject to the jurisdiction of the court hereunder, except for a traffic violation, a violation of the game and fish law or a violation of any city ordinance regulating surfing or establishing curfew violations, the court before final disposition thereof may require an investigation, which (i) shall include a drug screening and (ii) may include the physical, mental and social conditions, including an assessment of any affiliation with a youth gang as defined in §16.1-299.2, and personality of the child and the facts and circumstances surrounding the violation of law. However, in the case of a juvenile adjudicated delinquent on the basis of an act committed on or after January 1, 2000, which would be a felony if committed by an adult, or a violation under Article 1 (§18.2-247 et seq.) or Article 1.1 (§18.2-265.1 et seq.) of Chapter 7 of Title 18.2 and such offense would be punishable as a Class 1 or Class 2 misdemeanor if committed by an adult, the court shall order the juvenile to undergo a drug screening. If the drug screening indicates that the juvenile has a substance abuse or dependence problem, an assessment shall be completed by a certified substance abuse counselor as defined in §54.1-3500 employed by the Department of Juvenile Justice or by a locally operated court services unit or by an individual employed by or currently under contract to such agencies and who is specifically trained to conduct such assessments under the supervision of such counselor.

B. The court also shall, on motion of the attorney for the Commonwealth with the consent of the victim, or may in its discretion, require the preparation of a victim impact statement in accordance with the provisions of §19.2-299.1 if the court determines that the victim may have suffered significant physical, psychological or economic injury as a result of the violation of law.

(Chgd. by L.1996 ch. 616; L.1998 chs. 783, 840; L.1999 chs. 350, 891, 913; L.2000 chs. 1020, 1041, eff. 7/1/2000.)

§16.1-277.1. Time limitation.

A. When a child is held continuously in secure detention, he shall be released from confinement if there is no adjudicatory or transfer hearing conducted by the court for the matters upon which he was detained within twenty-one days from the date he was first detained.

B. If a child is not held in secure detention or is released from same after having been confined, an adjudicatory or transfer hearing on the matters charged in the petition or petitions issued against him shall be conducted within 120 days from the date the petition or petitions are filed.

C. When a child is held in secure detention after the completion of his adjudicatory hearing or is detained when the juvenile court has retained jurisdiction as a result of a transfer hearing, he shall be released from such detention if the disposition hearing is not completed within thirty days from the date of the adjudicatory or transfer hearing.

D. The time limitations provided for in this section shall be tolled during any period in which (i) the whereabouts of the child are unknown, (ii) the child has escaped from custody, or (iii) the child has failed to appear pursuant to a court order. The limitations also may be extended by the court for a reasonable period of time based upon good cause shown, provided that the basis for such extension is recorded in writing and filed among the papers of the proceedings.

(Chgd. by L.1996 ch. 616; L.1999 ch. 58, eff. 7/1/99.)

ARTICLE 9
DISPOSITION
(Selected Sections)

§16.1-278.7. Commitment to Department of Juvenile Justice.

Only a juvenile who is adjudicated as a delinquent and is eleven years of age or older may be committed to the Department of Juvenile Justice. No juvenile court or circuit court shall order the commitment of any child jointly to the Department of Juvenile Justice and to a local board of social services or transfer the custody of a child jointly to a court service unit of a juvenile court and to a local board of social services. Any person sentenced and committed to an active term of incarceration in the Department of Corrections who is, at the time of such sentencing, in the custody of the Department of Juvenile Justice, upon pronouncement of sentence, shall be immediately transferred to the Department of Corrections.

(Chgd. by L.2000 chs. 954, 981, 988, eff. 7/1/2000.)

§16.1-278.8. Delinquent juveniles.

A. If a juvenile is found to be delinquent, except where such finding involves a refusal to take a blood or breath test in violation of §18.2-268.2 or a similar ordinance, the juvenile court or the circuit court may make any of the following orders of disposition for his supervision, care and rehabilitation:

1. Enter an order pursuant to the provisions of §16.1-278;

2. Permit the juvenile to remain with his parent, subject to such conditions and limitations as the court may order with respect to the juvenile and his parent;

3. Order the parent of a juvenile living with him to participate in such programs, cooperate in such treatment or be subject to such conditions and limitations as the court may order and as are designed for the rehabilitation of the juvenile and his parent;

4. Defer disposition for a period of time not to exceed twelve months, after which time the charge may be dismissed by the judge if the juvenile exhibits good behavior during the period for which disposition is deferred;

4a. Defer disposition and place the juvenile in the temporary custody of the Department to attend a boot camp established pursuant to §66-13 provided bed space is available for confinement and the juvenile (i) has been found delinquent for an offense which would be a Class 1 misdemeanor or felony if committed by an adult, (ii) has not previously been and is not currently being adjudicated delinquent or found guilty of a violent juvenile felony, (iii) has not previously attended a boot camp, (iv) has not previously been committed to and received by the Department, and (v) has had an assessment completed by the Department or its contractor concerning the appropriateness of the candidate for a boot camp. Upon the juvenile's withdrawal, removal or refusal to comply with the terms and conditions of participation in the program, he shall be brought before the court for a hearing at which the court may impose any other disposition as authorized by this section which could have been imposed at the time the juvenile was placed in the custody of the Department;

5. Without entering a judgment of guilty and with the consent of the juvenile and his attorney, defer disposition of the delinquency charge for a period not to exceed twelve months and place the juvenile on probation under such conditions and limitations as the court may prescribe. Upon fulfillment of the terms and conditions, the court shall discharge the juvenile and dismiss the proceedings against him. Discharge and dismissal under these provisions shall be without adjudication of guilt;

6. Order the parent of a juvenile with whom the juvenile does not reside to participate in such programs, cooperate in such treatment or be subject to such conditions and limitations as the court may order and as are designed for the rehabilitation of the juvenile where the court determines this participation to be in the best interest of the juvenile and other parties concerned and where the court determines it reasonable to expect the parent to be able to comply with such order;

7. Place the juvenile on probation under such conditions and limitations as the court may prescribe;

7a. Place the juvenile on probation and order treatment for the abuse or dependence on alcohol or drugs in a program licensed by the Department of Mental Health, Mental Retardation and Substance Abuse Services for the treatment of juveniles for substance abuse provided that (i) the juvenile has received a substance abuse screening and assessment pursuant to §16.1-273 and that such assessment reasonably indicates that the commission of the offense was motivated by, or closely related to, the habitual use of alcohol or drugs and indicates that the juvenile is in need of treatment for this condition; (ii) the juvenile has not previously been and is not currently being adjudicated for a violent juvenile felony; and (iii) such facility is available. Upon the juvenile's withdrawal, removal, or refusal to comply with the conditions of participation in the program, he shall be brought before the court for a hearing at which the court may impose any other disposition authorized by this section. The court shall review such placements at thirty-day intervals;

8. Impose a fine not to exceed $500 upon such juvenile;

9. Suspend the motor vehicle and driver's license of such juvenile or impose a curfew on the juvenile as to the hours during which he may operate a motor vehicle. Any juvenile whose driver's license is suspended may be referred for an assessment and subsequent referral to appropriate services, upon such terms and conditions as the court may order. The court, in its discretion and upon a demonstration of hardship, may authorize the use of a restricted permit to operate a motor vehicle by any juvenile who enters such program for any of the purposes set forth in subsection E of §18.2-271.1 or for travel to and from school. The restricted permit shall be issued in accordance with the provisions of such subsection. However, only an abstract of the court order which identifies the juvenile and the conditions under which the restricted license is to be issued shall be sent to the Department of Motor Vehicles.

If a curfew is imposed, the juvenile shall surrender his driver's license, which shall be held in the physical custody of the court during any period of curfew restriction. The court shall send an abstract of any order issued under the provisions of this section to the Department of Motor Vehicles, which shall preserve a record thereof. Notwithstanding the provisions of Article 12 (§16.1-299 et seq.) of this chapter or the provisions of Title 46.2, this record shall be available only to all law-enforcement officers, attorneys for the Commonwealth and courts. A copy of the court order, upon which shall be noted all curfew restrictions, shall be provided to the juvenile and shall contain such information regarding the juvenile as is reasonably necessary to identify him. The juvenile may operate a motor vehicle under the court order in accordance with its terms.

Any juvenile who operates a motor vehicle in violation of any restrictions imposed pursuant to this section shall be guilty of a violation of §46.2-301.

The Department of Motor Vehicles shall refuse to issue a driver's license to any juvenile denied a driver's license until such time as is stipulated in the court order or until notification by the court of withdrawal of the order imposing the curfew;

10. Require the juvenile to make restitution or reparation to the aggrieved party or parties for actual damages or loss caused by the offense for which the juvenile was found to be delinquent;

11. Require the juvenile to participate in a public service project under such conditions as the court prescribes;

12. In case of traffic violations, impose only those penalties which are authorized to be imposed on adults for such violations. However, for those violations punishable by confinement if committed by an adult, confinement shall be imposed only as authorized by this title;

13. Transfer legal custody to any of the following:

a. A relative or other individual who, after study, is found by the court to be qualified to receive and care for the juvenile;

b. A child welfare agency, private organization or facility which is licensed or otherwise authorized by law to receive and provide care for such juvenile. The court shall not transfer legal custody of a delinquent juvenile to an agency, organization or facility outside of the Commonwealth without the approval of the Director; or

c. The local board of social services of the county or city in which the court has jurisdiction or, at the discretion of the court, to the local board of the county or city in which the juvenile has residence if other than the county or city in which the court has jurisdiction. The board shall accept the juvenile for care and custody, provided that it has been given reasonable notice of the pendency of the case and an opportunity to be heard. However, in an emergency in the county or city in which the court has jurisdiction, such local board may be required to temporarily accept a juvenile for a period not to exceed fourteen days without prior notice or an opportunity to be heard if the judge entering the placement order describes the emergency and the need for such temporary placement in the order. Nothing in this subdivision shall prohibit the commitment of a juvenile to any local board of social services in the Commonwealth when such local board consents to the commitment. The board to which the juvenile is committed shall have the final authority to determine the appropriate placement for the juvenile. Any order authorizing removal from the home and transferring legal custody of a juvenile to a local board of social services as provided in this subdivision shall be entered only upon a finding by the court that reasonable efforts have been made to prevent removal and that continued placement in the home would be contrary to the welfare of the juvenile, and the order shall so state;

14. Commit the juvenile to the Department of Juvenile Justice, but only if he is eleven years of age or older and the current offense is (i) an offense which would be a felony if committed by an adult, (ii) an offense which would be a Class 1 misdemeanor if committed by an adult and the juvenile has previously been found to be delinquent based on an offense which would be a felony if committed by an adult, or (iii) an offense which would be a Class 1 misdemeanor if committed by an adult and the juvenile has previously been adjudicated delinquent on three occasions for offenses which would be Class 1 misdemeanors if committed by an adult;

15. Impose the penalty authorized by §16.1-284;

16. Impose the penalty authorized by §16.1-284.1;

17. Impose the penalty authorized by §16.1-285.1;

18. Impose the penalty authorized by §16.1-278.9; or

19. Require the juvenile to participate in a gang-activity prevention program including, but not limited to, programs funded under the Virginia Juvenile Community Crime Control Act pursuant to §16.1-309.7, if available, when a juvenile has been found delinquent of any of the following violations: §§18.2-51, 18.2-51.1, 18.2-52, 18.2-53, 18.2-55, 18.2-56, 18.2-57, 18.2-57.2, 18.2-121, 18.2-127, 18.2-128, 18.2-137, 18.2-138, 18.2-146, or §18.2-147, or any violation of a local ordinance adopted pursuant to §18.2-138.1.

B. If the court finds a juvenile delinquent of any of the following offenses, the court shall require the juvenile to make at least partial restitution or reparation for any property damage, for loss caused by the offense, or for actual medical expenses incurred by the victim as a result of the offense: §§18.2-51, 18.2-51.1, 18.2-52, 18.2-53, 18.2-55, 18.2-56, 18.2-57, 18.2-57.2, 18.2-121, 18.2-127, 18.2-128, 18.2-137, 18.2-138, 18.2-146, or §18.2-147; or for any violation of a local ordinance adopted pursuant to §18.2-138.1. The court shall further require the juvenile to participate in a community service project under such conditions as the court prescribes.

(Chgd. by L.1996 chs. 616, 755, 914; L.1997 ch. 318; L.1999 chs. 350, 622; L.2000 chs. 954, 978, 981, 988, 1020, 1041, eff. 7/1/2000.)

§16.1-278.8:01. Juveniles found delinquent of first drug offense; screening; assessment; drug tests; costs and fees; education or treatment programs.

Whenever any juvenile who has not previously been found delinquent of any offense under Article 1 (§18.2-247 et seq.) of Chapter 7 of Title 18.2 or under any statute of the United States or of any state relating to narcotic drugs, marijuana, or stimulant, depressant or hallucinogenic drugs, or has not previously had a proceeding against him for a violation of such an offense dismissed as provided in §18.2-251, is found delinquent of any offense concerning the use, in any manner, of drugs, controlled substances, narcotics, marijuana, noxious chemical substances and like substances, the juvenile court or the circuit court shall require such juvenile to undergo a substance abuse screening pursuant to §16.1-273 and to submit to such periodic substance abuse testing, to include alcohol testing, as may be directed by the court. Such testing shall be conducted by a court services unit of the Department of Juvenile Justice, or by a locally operated court services unit or by personnel of any program or agency approved by the Department. The cost of such testing ordered by the court shall be paid by the Commonwealth from funds appropriated to the Department for this purpose. The court shall also order the juvenile to undergo such treatment or education program for substance abuse, if available, as the court deems appropriate based upon consideration of the substance abuse assessment. The treatment or education shall be provided by a program licensed by the Department

of Mental Health, Mental Retardation and Substance Abuse Services or by a similar program available through a facility or program operated by or under contract to the Department of Juvenile Justice or a locally operated court services unit or a program funded through the Virginia Juvenile Community Crime Control Act (§16.1-309.2 et seq.).
(Added by L.2000 chs. 1020, 1041, eff. 7/1/2000.)

§16.1-278.9. Delinquent children; loss of driving privileges for alcohol, firearm and drug offenses; truancy.

A. If a court has found facts which would justify a finding that a child at least thirteen years of age at the time of the offense is delinquent and such finding involves (i) a violation of §18.2-266 or of a similar ordinance of any county, city or town, (ii) a refusal to take a blood or breath test in violation of §18.2-268.2, (iii) a felony violation of §§18.2-248, 18.2-248.1 or §18.2-250, (iv) a misdemeanor violation of §§18.2-248, 18.2-248.1, or §18.2-250 or a violation of §18.2-250.1, (v) the unlawful purchase or possession of alcohol in violation of §4.1-305 or the unlawful drinking or possession of alcoholic beverages in or on public school grounds in violation of §4.1-309, (vi) public intoxication in violation of §18.2-388 or a similar ordinance of a county, city or town, or (vii) the unlawful use or possession of a handgun or possession of a "streetsweeper" as defined below, the court shall order that the child be denied a driver's license. In addition to any other penalty authorized by this section, if the offense involves a violation designated under clause (i) and the child was transporting a person seventeen years of age or younger, the court shall impose the additional fine and order community service as provided in §18.2-270. If the offense involves a violation designated under clause (i), (ii) or (iii), the denial of a driver's license shall be for a period of one year or until the juvenile reaches the age of seventeen, whichever is longer, for a first such offense or for a period of one year or until the juvenile reaches the age of eighteen, whichever is longer, for a second or subsequent such offense. If the offense involves a violation designated under clause (iv), (v) or (vi) the denial of driving privileges shall be for a period of six months unless the offense is committed by a child under the age of sixteen, in which case the child's ability to apply for a driver's license shall be delayed for a period of six months following his sixteenth birthday. If the offense involves a violation designated under clause (i), (ii), (v) or (vi), the court shall impose the license sanction without entering a judgment of guilt and shall defer disposition of the delinquency charge until such time as the court disposes of the case pursuant to subsection F of this section. If the offense involves a violation designated under clause (iii) or (iv), the court shall impose the license sanction and shall dispose of the delinquency charge pursuant to the provisions of this chapter or §18.2-251. If the offense involves a violation designated under clause (vii), the denial of driving privileges shall be for a period of not less than thirty days, except when the offense involves possession of a concealed handgun or a striker 12, commonly called a "streetsweeper," or any semi-automatic folding stock shotgun of like kind with a spring tension drum magazine capable of holding twelve shotgun shells, in which case the denial of driving privileges shall be for a period of two years unless the offense is committed by a child under the age of sixteen, in which event the child's ability to apply for a driver's license shall be delayed for a period of two years following his sixteenth birthday.

A1. If a court finds that a child at least thirteen years of age has failed to comply with school attendance and meeting requirements as provided in §22.1-258, the court shall order the denial of the child's driving privileges for a period of not less than thirty days. If such failure to comply involves a child under the age of sixteen, the child's ability to apply for a driver's license shall be delayed for a period of not less than thirty days following his sixteenth birthday.

B. Any child who has a driver's license at the time of the offense or at the time of the court's finding as provided in subsection A1 shall be ordered to surrender his driver's license, which shall be held in the physical custody of the court during any period of license denial.

C. The court shall report any order issued under this section to the Department of Motor Vehicles, which shall preserve a record thereof. The report and the record shall include a statement as to whether the child was represented by or waived counsel or whether the order was issued pursuant to subsection A1 of this section. Notwithstanding the provisions of Article 12 (§16.1-299 et seq.) of this chapter or the provisions of Title 46.2, this record shall be available only to all law-enforcement officers, attorneys for the Commonwealth and courts. No other record of the proceeding shall be forwarded to the Department of Motor Vehicles unless the proceeding results in an adjudication of guilt pursuant to subsection F.

The Department of Motor Vehicles shall refuse to issue a driver's license to any child denied a driver's license until such time as is stipulated in the court order or until notification by the court of withdrawal of the order of denial under subsection E.

D. If the finding as to the child involves a violation designated under clause (i), (ii), (iii) or (vi) of subsection A, the child may be referred to a certified alcohol safety action program in accordance with §18.2-271.1 upon such terms and conditions as the court may set forth. If the finding as to such child involves a violation designated under clause (iii), (iv), (v) or (vii) of subsection A, such child may be referred to appropriate rehabilitative or educational services upon such terms and conditions as the court may set forth.

The court, in its discretion and upon a demonstration of hardship, may authorize the use of a restricted permit to operate a motor vehicle by any child who has a driver's license at the time of the offense or at the time of the court's finding as provided in subsection A1 for any of the purposes set forth in subsection E of §18.2-271.1 or for travel to and from school, except that no restricted license shall be issued if the finding as to such child involves a violation designated under clause (iii) or (iv) of subsection A, or if it involves a second or subsequent violation of any offense designated in subsection A or a second finding by the court of failure to comply with school attendance and meeting requirements as provided in subsection A1. The issuance of the restricted permit shall be set forth within the court order, a copy of which shall be provided to the child, and shall specifically enumerate the restrictions imposed and contain such information regarding the child as is reasonably necessary to identify him. The child may operate a motor vehicle under the court order in accordance with its terms. Any child who operates a motor vehicle in violation of any restrictions imposed pursuant to this section shall be guilty of a violation of §46.2-301.

E. Upon petition made at least ninety days after issuance of the order, the court may review and withdraw any order of denial of a driver's license if for a first such offense or finding as provided in subsection A1. For a second or subsequent such offense or finding, the order may not be reviewed and withdrawn until one year after its issuance.

F. If the finding as to such child involves a violation designated under clause (i), (ii), (v), (vi) or (vii) of subsection A, upon fulfillment of the terms and conditions prescribed by the court and after the child's driver's license has been restored, the court shall or, in the event the violation resulted in the injury or death of any person, may discharge the child and dismiss the proceedings against him. Discharge and

dismissal under these provisions shall be without an adjudication of guilt but a record of the proceeding shall be retained for the purpose of applying this section in subsequent proceedings. Failure of the child to fulfill such terms and conditions shall result in an adjudication of guilt. If the finding as to such child involves a violation designated under clause (iii) or (iv) of subsection A, the charge shall not be dismissed pursuant to this subsection but shall be disposed of pursuant to the provisions of this chapter or §18.2-251.
(Chgd. by L.2000 ch. 835, eff. 7/1/2000.)

§16.1-278.10. Traffic infractions.

In cases involving a child who is charged with a traffic infraction, the court may impose only those penalties which are authorized to be imposed on adults for such infractions.

§16.1-278.14. Criminal jurisdiction; protective orders; family offenses.

In cases involving the violation of any law, regulation or ordinance for the education, protection or care of children or involving offenses committed by one family or household member against another, the juvenile court or the circuit court may impose a penalty prescribed by applicable sections of the Code and may impose conditions and limitations upon the defendant to protect the health or safety of family or household members, including, but not limited to, a protective order as provided in §16.1-279.1, treatment and counseling for the defendant and payment by the defendant for crisis shelter care for the complaining family or household member.
(Chgd. by L.1996 ch. 616, eff. 7/1/96, ch. 866, eff. 7/1/97.)

§16.1-279.1. Protective order in cases of family abuse.

A. In cases of family abuse, the court may issue a protective order to protect the health and safety of the petitioner and family or household members of the petitioner. A protective order issued under this section may include any one or more of the following conditions to be imposed on the respondent:

1. Prohibiting acts of family abuse;
2. Prohibiting such contacts by the respondent with the petitioner or family or household members of the petitioner as the court deems necessary for the health or safety of such persons;
3. Granting the petitioner possession of the residence occupied by the parties to the exclusion of the respondent; however, no such grant of possession shall affect title to any real or personal property;
4. Granting the petitioner temporary possession or use of a motor vehicle owned by the petitioner alone or jointly owned by the parties to the exclusion of the respondent; however, no such grant of possession or use shall affect title to the vehicle;
5. Requiring that the respondent provide suitable alternative housing for the petitioner and, if appropriate, any other family or household member;
6. Ordering the respondent to participate in treatment, counseling or other programs as the court deems appropriate; and
7. Any other relief necessary for the protection of the petitioner and family or household members of the petitioner, including a provision for temporary custody or visitation of a minor child.

B. The protective order may be issued for a specified period; however, unless otherwise authorized by law, a protective order may not be issued under this section for a period longer than two years. A copy of the protective order shall be served on the respondent and provided to the petitioner as soon as possible. The clerk shall forward forthwith an attested copy of the order to the local police department or sheriff's office which shall, on the date of receipt, enter the name of the person subject to the order and other appropriate information required by the Department of State Police into the Virginia criminal information network system established and maintained by the Department pursuant to Chapter 2 (§52-12 et seq.) of Title 52. Where feasible and practical, the court may transfer information electronically to the Virginia criminal information network system. If the order is later dissolved or modified, a copy of the dissolution or modification order shall also be attested, forwarded and entered in the system as described above.

C. Except as otherwise provided in §16.1-253.2, a violation of a protective order issued under this section shall constitute contempt of court.

D. The court may assess costs and attorneys' fees against either party regardless of whether an order of protection has been issued as a result of a full hearing.

E. Any judgment, order or decree, whether permanent or temporary, issued by a court of appropriate jurisdiction in another state, the United States or any of its territories, possessions or Commonwealths, the District of Columbia or by any tribal court of appropriate jurisdiction for the purpose of preventing violent or threatening acts or harassment against or contact or communication with or physical proximity to another person, including any of the conditions specified in subsection A, shall be accorded full faith and credit and enforced in the Commonwealth as if it were an order of the Commonwealth, provided reasonable notice and opportunity to be heard were given by the issuing jurisdiction to the person against whom the order is sought to be enforced sufficient to protect such person's due process rights and consistent with federal law. A person entitled to protection under such a foreign order may file the order in any juvenile and domestic relations district court or family court by filing with the court an attested or exemplified copy of the order. Upon such a filing, the clerk shall forward forthwith an attested copy of the order to the local police department or sheriff's office which shall, on the date of receipt, enter the name of the person subject to the order and other appropriate information required by the Department of State Police into the Virginia criminal information network system established and maintained by the Department pursuant to Chapter 2 (§52-12 et seq.) of Title 52. Where feasible and practical, the court may transfer information electronically to the Virginia criminal information network system.

Upon inquiry by any law-enforcement agency of the Commonwealth, the clerk shall make a copy available of any foreign order filed with that court. A law-enforcement officer may, in the performance of his duties, rely upon a copy of a foreign protective order or other suitable evidence which has been provided to him by any source and may also rely upon the statement of any person protected by the order that the order remains in effect.

F. Either party may at any time file a written motion with the court requesting a hearing to dissolve or modify the order. Proceedings to dissolve or modify a protective order shall be given precedence on the docket of the court.

G. As used in this section, "copy" includes a facsimile copy.
(Chgd. by L.1996 chs. 866, 900, 945; L.1997 ch. 603; L.1998 ch. 684; L.2000 chs. 34, 654, eff. 7/1/2000.)

§16.1-284. When adult sentenced for juvenile offense.

When the juvenile court sentences an adult who has committed, before attaining the age of eighteen, an offense which would be a crime if committed by an adult, the court may impose the penalties which are authorized to be imposed on adults for such violations, not to exceed the punishment for a

Class 1 misdemeanor for a single offense or multiple offenses.
(Chgd. by L.1996 chs. 755, 914, eff. 7/1/96.)

§16.1-284.1. Placement in secure local facility.

A. If a juvenile fourteen years of age or older is found to have committed an offense which if committed by an adult would be punishable by confinement in a state or local correctional facility as defined in §53.1-1, and the court determines (i) that the juvenile has not previously been *and is not currently adjudicated* [found guilty of a] delinquent [act within the preceding twelve months] *or found guilty of a violent juvenile felony*, (ii) that the interests of the juvenile and the community require that the juvenile be placed under legal restraint or discipline, and (iii) that other placements authorized by this title will not serve the best interests of the juvenile, then the court may order the juvenile confined in a detention home or other secure facility for juveniles for a period not to exceed [thirty calendar days] *six months* from the date the order is entered, [inclusive of time served in a detention home or other secure facility,] for a single offense or multiple offenses.

The period of confinement ordered may exceed thirty calendar days if the juvenile has had an assessment completed by the secure facility to which he is ordered concerning the appropriateness of the placement.

B. [If a juvenile fourteen years of age or older is found to have committed an offense which if committed by an adult would be punishable by confinement in a state or local correctional facility as defined in §53.1-1, and the court determines (i) after receipt of a social history compiled within the immediately preceding twelve months pursuant to §16.1-273 that the juvenile has been adjudged a delinquent within the immediately preceding twelve months and has failed to respond to past treatment efforts, (ii) that the juvenile is amenable to continued treatment efforts in the community, and (iii) the interests of the community and the juvenile require that the juvenile be placed under legal restraint or discipline, based on the nature of the present offense, the nature of the juvenile's prior delinquency record, and the nature of the past treatment efforts] *If the period of confinement in a detention home or other secure facility for juveniles is to exceed thirty calendar days*, then the court may order the juvenile committed to the Department, *if he is eligible pursuant to subdivision A 14 of §16.1-278.8*, but suspend such commitment [and order the juvenile confined in a detention home or other secure facility for juveniles for a period not to exceed six months, inclusive of time served in detention while awaiting disposition, for a single offense or for multiple offenses]. In suspending the commitment to the Department as provided for in this subsection, the court shall specify conditions for the juvenile's [participation in] *satisfactory completion of* one or more community *or facility based* treatment programs as may be appropriate for the juvenile's rehabilitation.

C. During any period of confinement *which exceeds thirty calendar days* ordered pursuant to this section, the court shall conduct a mandatory review hearing at least once during each thirty days [of the period of confinement] and at such other times upon the request of the juvenile's probation officer, for good cause shown. If it appears at such hearing that the purpose of the order of confinement has been achieved, the juvenile shall be released on probation for such period and under such conditions as the court may specify and remain subject to the order suspending commitment to the State Department of Juvenile Justice. If *the juvenile's commitment to the Department has been suspended as provided in subsection B of this section, and if* the court determines at the first or any subsequent review hearing that the juvenile is consistently failing to comply with the conditions specified by the court or the policies and program requirements of the facility, then the court shall order that the juvenile [either] be [(i) released under such conditions as the court may specify subject to the suspended commitment or (ii)] committed to the State Department of Juvenile Justice [pursuant to §16.1-291]. If the court determines at the first or any subsequent review hearing that the juvenile is not actively involved in any community *or facility based* treatment program through no fault of his own, then the court shall order that the juvenile be released under such conditions as the court may specify subject to the suspended commitment.

D. A juvenile may only be ordered confined pursuant to this section to a facility in compliance with standards established by the State Board for such placements. Standards for these facilities shall [have regard for reasonable utilization of these facilities and the requirements of §16.1-309.4] *require juveniles placed pursuant to this section for a period which exceeds thirty calendar days be provided separate services for their rehabilitation*, consistent with the intent of this section.

E. The Department of Juvenile Justice shall assist the localities or combinations thereof in implementing this section consistent with the statewide plan required by §16.1-309.4 and pursuant to standards promulgated by the State Board, in order to ensure the availability and reasonable access of each court to the facilities the use of which is authorized by this section.
(Chgd. by L.1995 chs. 330, 696, 699; L.1996 chs. 755, 914; L.2000 ch. 978, eff. 7/1/2002. Matter in brackets eff. only until 7/1/2002. Matter in italics eff. 7/1/2002.)

§16.1-285. Duration of commitments.

Except as provided in §16.1-285.1, all commitments under this chapter shall be for an indeterminate period having regard to the welfare of the juvenile and interests of the public, but no juvenile committed hereunder shall be held or detained longer than thirty-six continuous months or after such juvenile has attained the age of twenty-one years. However, the thirty-six month limitation shall not apply in cases of commitment for an act of murder or manslaughter. The Department shall have the authority to discharge any juvenile from its custody in accordance with policies and procedures established by the State Board and with other provisions of law.
(Chgd. by L.1996 chs. 755, 914; L.2000 chs. 954, 981, 988, eff. 7/1/2000.)

§16.1-285.1. Commitment of serious offenders.

A. In the case of a juvenile fourteen years of age or older who has been found guilty of an offense which would be a felony if committed by an adult, and either (i) the juvenile is on parole for an offense which would be a felony if committed by an adult, (ii) the juvenile was committed to the state for an offense which would be a felony if committed by an adult within the immediately preceding twelve months, (iii) the felony offense is punishable by a term of confinement of greater than twenty years if the felony was committed by an adult, or (iv) the juvenile has been previously adjudicated delinquent for an offense which if committed by an adult would be a felony punishable by a term of confinement of twenty years or more, and the circuit court, or the juvenile or family court, as the case may be, finds that commitment under this section is necessary to meet the rehabilitative needs of the juvenile and would serve the best interests of the community, then the court may order the juvenile committed to the Department of Juvenile Justice for placement in a juvenile correctional center for the period of time prescribed pursuant to this section.

B. Prior to committing any juvenile pursuant to this section, the court shall consider:

 Zv

1. The juvenile's age;

2. The seriousness and number of the present offenses, including (i) whether the offense was committed in an aggressive, violent, premeditated, or willful manner; (ii) whether the offense was against persons or property, with greater weight being given to offenses against persons, especially if death or injury resulted; (iii) whether the offense involved the use of a firearm or other dangerous weapon by brandishing, displaying, threatening with or otherwise employing such weapon; and (iv) the nature of the juvenile's participation in the alleged offense;

3. The record and previous history of the juvenile in this or any other jurisdiction, including (i) the number and nature of previous contacts with courts, (ii) the number and nature of prior periods of probation, (iii) the number and nature of prior commitments to juvenile correctional centers, (iv) the number and nature of previous residential and community-based treatments, (v) whether previous adjudications and commitments were for delinquent acts that involved the infliction of serious bodily injury, and (vi) whether the offense is part of a repetitive pattern of similar adjudicated offenses; and

4. The Department's estimated length of stay.

Such commitment order must be supported by a determination that the interests of the juvenile and community require that the juvenile be placed under legal restraint or discipline and that the juvenile is not a proper person to receive treatment or rehabilitation through other juvenile programs or facilities.

C. In ordering commitment pursuant to this section, the court shall specify a period of commitment not to exceed seven years or the juvenile's twenty-first birthday, whichever shall occur first. The court may also order a period of determinate or indeterminate parole supervision to follow the commitment but the total period of commitment and parole supervision shall not exceed seven years or the juvenile's twenty-first birthday, whichever occurs first.

D. Upon receipt of a juvenile committed under the provisions of this section, the Department shall evaluate the juvenile for the purpose of considering placement of the juvenile in an appropriate juvenile correctional center for the time prescribed by the committing court. Such a placement decision shall be made based on the availability of treatment programs at the facility; the level of security at the facility; the offense for which the juvenile has been committed; and the welfare, age and gender of the juvenile.

E. The court which commits the juvenile to the Department under this section shall have continuing jurisdiction over the juvenile throughout his commitment. The continuing jurisdiction of the court shall not prevent the Department from removing the juvenile from a juvenile correctional center without prior court approval for the sole purposes of routine or emergency medical treatment, routine educational services, or family emergencies.

F. Any juvenile committed under the provisions of this section shall not be released at a time earlier than that specified by the court in its dispositional order except as provided for in §16.1-285.2. The Department may petition the committing court for a hearing as provided for in §16.1-285.2 for an earlier release of the juvenile when good cause exists for an earlier release. In addition, the Department shall petition the committing court for a determination as to the continued commitment of each juvenile sentenced under this section at least sixty days prior to the second anniversary of the juvenile's date of commitment and sixty days prior to each annual anniversary thereafter.

(Chgd. by L.1996 chs. 755, 914, eff. 7/1/96.)

§16.1-285.2. Release and review hearing for serious offender.

A. Upon receipt of a petition of the Department of Juvenile Justice for a hearing concerning a juvenile committed under §16.1-285.1, the court shall schedule a hearing within thirty days and shall appoint counsel for the juvenile pursuant to §16.1-266. The court shall provide a copy of the petition, the progress report required by this section, and notice of the time and place of the hearing to (i) the juvenile, (ii) the juvenile's parent, legal guardian, or person standing in loco parentis, (iii) the juvenile's guardian ad litem, if any, (iv) the juvenile's legal counsel, and (v) the attorney for the Commonwealth who prosecuted the juvenile during the delinquency proceeding. The attorney for the Commonwealth shall provide notice of the time and place of the hearing by first-class mail to the last known address of any victim of the offense for which the juvenile was committed if such victim has submitted a written request for notification to the attorney for the Commonwealth.

B. The petition shall be filed in the committing court and shall be accompanied by a progress report from the Department. This report shall describe (i) the facility and living arrangement provided for the juvenile by the Department, (ii) the services and treatment programs afforded the juvenile, (iii) the juvenile's progress toward treatment goals and objectives, which shall include a summary of his educational progress, (iv) the juvenile's potential for danger to either himself or the community, and (v) a comprehensive aftercare plan for the juvenile.

B1. The appearance of the juvenile before the court may be by (i) personal appearance before the judge, or (ii) use of two-way electronic video and audio communication. If two-way electronic video and audio communication is used, a judge may exercise all powers conferred by law and all communications and proceedings shall be conducted in the same manner as if the appearance were in person, and any documents filed may be transmitted by facsimile process. A facsimile may be served or executed by the officer or person to whom sent, and returned in the same manner, and with the same force, effect, authority, and liability as an original document. All signatures thereon shall be treated as original signatures. Any two-way electronic video and audio communication system used for an appearance shall meet the standards as set forth in subsection B of §19.2-3.1.

C. At the hearing the court shall consider the progress report. The court may also consider additional evidence from (i) probation officers, the juvenile correctional center, treatment professionals, and the court service unit; (ii) the juvenile, his legal counsel, parent, guardian or family member; or (iii) other sources the court deems relevant. The hearing and all records relating thereto shall be governed by the confidentiality provisions of Article 12 (§16.1-299 et seq.) of this chapter.

D. At the conclusion of the hearing, the court shall order (i) continued commitment of the juvenile to the Department for completion of the original determinate period of commitment or such lesser time as the court may order or (ii) release of the juvenile under such terms and conditions as the court may prescribe. In making a determination under this section, the court shall consider (i) the experiences and character of the juvenile before and after commitment, (ii) the nature of the offenses that the juvenile was found to have committed, (iii) the manner in which the offenses were committed, (iv) the protection of the community, (v) the recommendations of the Department, and (vi) any other factors the court deems relevant. The order of the court shall be final and not subject to appeal.

(Chgd. by L.1995 ch. 536; L.1996 chs. 755, 914, eff. 7/1/96.)

ARTICLE 12
CONFIDENTIALITY AND EXPUNGEMENT
(Selected Sections)

§16.1-299. Fingerprints and photographs of juveniles.

A. All duly constituted police authorities having the power of arrest may take fingerprints and photographs of any juvenile who is taken into custody and charged with a delinquent act an arrest for which, if committed by an adult, is required to be reported to the Central Criminal Records Exchange pursuant to subsection A of §19.2-390. Whenever fingerprints are taken, they shall be maintained separately from adult records and a copy shall be filed with the juvenile court on forms provided by the Central Criminal Records Exchange. However, all duly constituted police authorities having the power of arrest shall take fingerprints and photographs of any juvenile fourteen years of age or older charged with a "violent juvenile felony" as defined in §16.1-228.

B. If a juvenile (i) of any age is adjudicated delinquent or found guilty of any offense which would be a felony if committed by an adult or any other offense for which a report to the Central Criminal Records Exchange is required by subsection C of §19.2-390 if the offense were committed by an adult or (ii) fourteen or older is charged with a "violent juvenile felony" as defined in §16.1-228, or a crime ancillary thereto, copies of his fingerprints and a report of the disposition shall be forwarded to the Central Criminal Records Exchange and to the jurisdiction making the arrest by the clerk of the court which heard the case.

C. If a petition or warrant is not filed against a juvenile whose fingerprints or photographs have been taken in connection with an alleged violation of law, the fingerprint card, all copies of the fingerprints and all photographs shall be destroyed sixty days after fingerprints were taken. If a juvenile charged with a delinquent act other than a violent juvenile felony or a crime ancillary thereto is found not guilty, or if a juvenile under fourteen is charged with a delinquent act which otherwise would be a violent juvenile felony or a crime ancillary thereto, or in any other case resulting in a disposition for which fingerprints are not required to be forwarded to the Central Criminal Records Exchange, the court shall order that the fingerprint card, all copies of the fingerprints and all photographs be destroyed within six months of the date of disposition of the case.
(Chgd. by L.1996 chs. 616, 755, 914; L.1997 ch. 657; L.2000 ch. 431, eff. 7/1/2000.)

§16.1-299.1. Blood, saliva or tissue sample required for DNA analysis upon conviction or adjudication of felony.

A juvenile convicted of a felony or adjudicated delinquent on the basis of an act which would be a felony if committed by an adult shall have a sample of his blood, saliva or tissue taken for DNA analysis provided the juvenile was fourteen years of age or older at the time of the commission of the offense.

The provisions of Article 1.1 (§19.2-310.2 et seq.) of Chapter 18 of Title 19.2 shall apply to all persons and all blood samples taken as required by this section, mutatis mutandis.
(Added by L.1996 chs. 755, 914; chgd. by L.1998 ch. 280, eff. 7/1/98.)

§16.1-299.2. Youth gangs; reporting.

When it is determined, either by admission or investigation, by a state or local law-enforcement agency or a regional multi-jurisdictional law-enforcement task force, that a juvenile who has been arrested is a member of a youth gang, the arresting officer shall enter the juvenile's name and other appropriate gang-related information required by the Department of State Police into the Youth Gang File of the Virginia Crime Information Network. The entry shall be made as soon as practicable after the determination is made.

For purposes of this section "youth gang" means an ongoing organization, association or group (i) having common characteristics, including but not limited to initiation practices, hand signals, structured style of dress, specific geographic territorial claim or identifiable leadership and (ii) consisting of three or more individuals, at least one of whom is a juvenile, who identify themselves as a group by a name or symbol and are involved in a pattern of recurrent felonious criminal conduct.
(Added by L.1997 ch. 541, eff. 7/1/97.)

§16.1-301. Confidentiality of law-enforcement records.

A. The court shall require all law-enforcement agencies to take special precautions to ensure that law-enforcement records concerning a juvenile are protected against disclosure to any unauthorized person. The police departments of the cities of the Commonwealth, and the police departments or sheriffs of the counties, as the case may be, shall keep separate records as to violations of law other than violations of motor vehicle laws committed by juveniles. Such records with respect to such juvenile shall not be open to public inspection nor their contents disclosed to the public unless a juvenile fourteen years of age or older is charged with a violent juvenile felony as specified in subsections B and C of §16.1-269.1.

B. Inspection of such records shall be permitted only by the following:

1. A court having the juvenile currently before it in any proceeding;
2. The officers of public and nongovernmental institutions or agencies to which the juvenile is currently committed, and those responsible for his supervision after release;
3. Any other person, agency, or institution, by order of the court, having a legitimate interest in the case or in the work of the law-enforcement agency;
4. Law-enforcement officers of other jurisdictions, by order of the court, when necessary for the discharge of their current official duties;
5. The probation and other professional staff of a court in which the juvenile is subsequently convicted of a criminal offense for the purpose of a presentence report or other dispositional proceedings, or by officials of penal institutions and other penal facilities to which he is committed, or by a parole board in considering his parole or discharge or in exercising supervision over him;
6. The juvenile, parent, guardian or other custodian and counsel for the juvenile by order of the court; and
7. As provided in §§19.2-389.1 and 19.2-390.

C. The police departments of the cities and towns and the police departments or sheriffs of the counties may release, upon request to one another and to state and federal law-enforcement agencies, current information on juvenile arrests. The information exchanged shall be used by the receiving agency for current investigation purposes only and shall not result in the creation of new files or records on individual juveniles on the part of the receiving agency.

D. Nothing in this section shall prohibit the exchange of other criminal investigative or intelligence information among law-enforcement agencies.

(Chgd. by L.1995 ch. 752; L.1996 chs. 755, 914; L.1997 ch. 430; L.2000 ch. 211, eff. 7/1/2000.)

§16.1-302. Dockets, indices and order books; when hearings and records private; right to public hearing; presence of juvenile in court.

A. Every juvenile court shall keep a separate docket of cases arising under this law.

B. Every circuit court shall keep a separate docket, index, and, for entry of its orders, a separate order book or file for cases on appeal from the juvenile court except: (i) cases involving support pursuant to §20-61 or subdivisions A 3, F or L of §16.1-241; (ii) cases involving criminal offenses committed by adults which are commenced on a warrant or a summons as described in Title 19.2; and (iii) cases involving civil commitments of adults pursuant to Title 37.1. Such cases shall be docketed on the appropriate docket and the orders in such cases shall be entered in the appropriate order book as used with similar cases commenced in circuit court.

C. The general public shall be excluded from all juvenile court hearings and only such persons admitted as the judge shall deem proper. However, proceedings in cases involving an adult charged with a crime and in hearings held on a petition or warrant alleging that a juvenile fourteen years of age or older committed an offense which would be a felony if committed by an adult shall be open. Subject to the provisions of subsection D for good cause shown, the court may, sua sponte or on motion of the accused or the attorney for the Commonwealth close the proceedings. If the proceedings are closed, the court shall state in writing its reasons and the statement shall be made a part of the public record.

D. In any hearing held for the purpose of adjudicating an alleged violation of any criminal law, or law defining a traffic infraction, the juvenile or adult so charged shall have a right to be present and shall have the right to a public hearing unless expressly waived by such person. The chief judge may provide by rule that any juvenile licensed to operate a motor vehicle who has been charged with a traffic infraction may waive court appearance and admit to the infraction or infractions charged if he or she and a parent, legal guardian, or person standing in loco parentis to the juvenile appear in person at the court or before a magistrate or sign and either mail or deliver to the court or magistrate a written form of appearance, plea and waiver, provided that the written form contains the notarized signature of the parent, legal guardian, or person standing in loco parentis to the juvenile. An emancipated juvenile charged with a traffic infraction shall have the opportunity to waive court appearance and admit to the infraction or infractions if he or she appears in person at the court or before a magistrate or signs and either mails or delivers to the court or magistrate a written form of appearance, plea, and waiver, provided that the written plea form containing the signature of the emancipated juvenile is accompanied by a notarized sworn statement which details the facts supporting the claim of emancipated status. Whenever the sole purpose of a proceeding is to determine the custody of a child of tender years, the presence of such juvenile in court may be waived by the judge at any stage thereof.

(Chgd. by L.1996 chs. 616; 755, 914, eff. 7/1/96.)

§16.1-302.1. Right of victim or representative to attend certain proceedings; notice of hearings.

During proceedings involving petitions or warrants alleging that a juvenile is delinquent, including proceedings on appeal, a victim may remain in the courtroom and shall not be excluded unless the court determines in its discretion that the presence of the victim would impair the conduct of a fair trial. In any such case involving a minor victim, the court may permit an adult chosen by the minor victim to be present in the courtroom during the proceedings in addition to or in lieu of the minor's parent or guardian.

The attorney for the Commonwealth shall give prior notice of any such proceedings and changes in the scheduling thereof to any known victim and to any known adult chosen in accordance with this section by a minor victim at the address or telephone number, or both, provided in writing by such persons.

(Added by L.1996 chs. 755, 914; chgd. by L.2000 ch. 339, eff. 7/1/2000.)

§16.1-308. Effect of adjudication on status of child.

Except as otherwise provided by law for a juvenile found guilty of a felony in circuit court whose case is disposed of in the same manner as an adult criminal case, a finding of guilty on a petition charging delinquency under the provisions of this law shall not operate to impose any of the civil disabilities ordinarily imposed by conviction for a crime, nor shall any such finding operate to disqualify the child for employment by any state or local governmental agency.

(Chgd. by L.1996 chs. 755, 914, eff. 7/1/96.)

§16.1-309. Penalty.

A. Except as provided in §§16.1-299, 16.1-300, 16.1-301, 16.1-305 and 16.1-307, any person who (i) files a petition, (ii) receives a petition or has access to court records in an official capacity, (iii) participates in the investigation of allegations which form the basis of a petition, (iv) is interviewed concerning such allegations and whose information is derived solely from such interview or (v) is present during any court proceeding, who discloses or makes use of or knowingly permits the use of identifying information not otherwise available to the public concerning a juvenile who is suspected of being or is the subject of a proceeding within the jurisdiction of the juvenile court pursuant to subdivisions 1 through 5 of subsection A of §16.1-241 or who is in the custody of the State Department of Juvenile Justice, which information is directly or indirectly derived from the records or files of a law-enforcement agency, court or the Department of Juvenile Justice or acquired in the course of official duties, shall be guilty of a Class 3 misdemeanor.

B. The provisions of this section shall not apply to any law-enforcement officer or school employee who discloses to school personnel identifying information concerning a juvenile who is suspected of committing or has committed a delinquent act that has met applicable criteria of §16.1-260 and is committed or alleged to have been committed on school property during a school-sponsored activity or on the way to or from such activity, if the disclosure is made solely for the purpose of enabling school personnel to take appropriate disciplinary action within the school setting against the juvenile. Further, the provisions of this section shall not apply to school personnel who disclose information obtained pursuant to §§16.1-305.1 and 22.1-288.2, if the disclosure is made solely to enable school personnel to take appropriate actions within the school setting with regard to the juvenile or another student.

(Chgd. by L.1996 chs. 616, 755, 914, eff. 7/1/96.)

§16.1-309.1. Exception as to confidentiality.

A. Notwithstanding any other provision of this article, where consideration of public interest requires, the judge shall make available to the public the name and address of a juvenile and the nature of the offense for which a juvenile has been adjudicated delinquent (i) for an act which would be a Class 1, 2 or 3 felony, forcible rape, robbery or burglary or a related offense as set out in Article 2 (§18.2-89 et seq.) of Chapter 5 of Title 18.2 if committed by an adult or (ii) in any case where a juvenile is sentenced as an adult in circuit court.

B. 1. At any time prior to disposition, if a juvenile, charged with a delinquent act which would be forcible rape, robbery, burglary or a related offense as set out in Article 2 (§18.2-89 et seq.) of Chapter 5 of Title 18.2 or a Class 1, 2 or 3 felony if committed by an adult, becomes a fugitive from justice, the attorney for the Commonwealth or, upon notice to the Commonwealth's attorney, the Department of Juvenile Justice or a locally operated court services unit may petition the court having jurisdiction of the offense to authorize public release of the juvenile's name, age, physical description and photograph, the charge for which he is sought or for which he was adjudicated and any other information which may expedite his apprehension. Upon a showing that the juvenile is a fugitive and for good cause, the court shall order release of this information to the public.

2. After final disposition, if a juvenile (i) found to have committed a delinquent act which would be forcible rape, robbery, burglary or a related offense as set out in Article 2 (§18.2-89 et seq.) of Chapter 5 of Title 18.2 or a Class 1, 2, or 3 felony if committed by an adult becomes a fugitive from justice or (ii) who has been committed to the Department of Juvenile Justice pursuant to subdivision 14 of §16.1-278.8 or §16.1-285.1 becomes a fugitive from justice by escaping from a facility operated by or under contract with the Department or from the custody of any employee of such facility, the Department may release to the public the juvenile's name, age, physical description and photograph, the charge for which he is sought or for which he was committed, and any other information which may expedite his apprehension. The Department shall promptly notify the attorney for the Commonwealth of the jurisdiction in which the juvenile was tried whenever information is released pursuant to this paragraph. If a juvenile specified in clause (i) being held after disposition in a secure facility not operated by or under contract with the Department becomes a fugitive by such escape, the attorney for the Commonwealth of the locality in which the facility is located may release the information as provided in this paragraph.

C. Whenever a juvenile fourteen years of age or older is charged with a delinquent act that would be a criminal violation of Article 2 (§18.2-38 et seq.) of Chapter 4 of Title 18.2, a felony involving a weapon, a felony violation of Article 1 (§18.2-247 et seq.) of Chapter 7 of Title 18.2, or an "act of violence" as defined in subsection A of §19.2-297.1 if committed by an adult, the judge may, where consideration of the public interest requires, make the juvenile's name and address available to the public.

D. Upon the request of a victim of a delinquent act which would be a felony if committed by an adult, the court may order that such victim be informed of the charge or charges brought, the findings of the court, and the disposition of the case. For purposes of this section, "victim" shall be defined as in §19.2-11.01.

E. Upon request, the judge or clerk may disclose if an order of emancipation of a juvenile pursuant to §16.1-333 has been entered, provided (i) the order is not being appealed, (ii) the order has not been terminated, or (iii) there has not been a judicial determination that the order is void ab initio.

F. Notwithstanding any other provision of law, a copy of any court order that imposes a curfew or other restriction on a juvenile may be provided to the chief law-enforcement officer of the county or city wherein the juvenile resides. The chief law-enforcement officer shall only disclose information contained in the court order to other law-enforcement officers in the conduct of official duties.

(Chgd. by L.1995 chs. 558, 687, 804; L.1997 chs. 434, 452; L.1999 ch. 710; L.2000 chs. 563, 603, eff. 7/1/2000.)

ARTICLE 12.1
VIRGINIA JUVENILE COMMUNITY CRIME CONTROL ACT

(Added by L.1995 chs. 698, 840, eff. 1/1/96.)
(Complete Article)

§16.1-309.2. Purpose and intent.

The General Assembly, to ensure the imposition of appropriate and just sanctions and to make the most efficient use of correctional resources for those juveniles before intake on complaints or the court on petitions alleging that the juvenile is a child in need of services, child in need of supervision, or delinquent, has determined that it is in the best interest of the Commonwealth to establish a community-based system of progressive intensive sanctions and services that correspond to the severity of offense and treatment needs. The purpose of this system shall be to deter crime by providing immediate, effective punishment that emphasizes accountability of the juvenile offender for his actions as well as reduces the pattern of repeat offending. In furtherance of this purpose, counties, cities or combinations thereof are encouraged to develop, implement, operate and evaluate programs and services responsive to their specific juvenile offender needs and juvenile crime trends.

This article shall be interpreted and construed to accomplish the following purposes:

1. Promote an adequate level of services to be available to every juvenile and domestic relations district court.

2. Ensure local autonomy and flexibility in addressing juvenile crime.

3. Encourage a public and private partnership in the design and delivery of services for juveniles who come before intake on a complaint or the court on a petition alleging a child is in need of services, in need of supervision or delinquent.

4. Emphasize parental responsibility and provide community-based services for juveniles and their families which hold them accountable for their behavior.

5. Establish a locally driven statewide planning process for the allocation of state resources.

6. Promote the development of an adequate service capacity for juveniles before intake on a complaint or the court on petitions alleging status or delinquent offenses.

(Added by L.1995 chs. 698, 840; chgd. by L.1996 chs. 671, 682, eff. 7/1/96.)

§16.1-309.3. Establishment of a community-based system of services; biennial local plan; quarterly report.

A. Any county, city or combination thereof may establish a community-based system pursuant to this article, which shall provide, or arrange to have accessible, a variety of predispositional and postdispositional services. These services may include, but are not limited to, diversion, community service, restitution, house arrest, intensive juvenile supervision, substance abuse assessment and testing, first-time offender programs, intensive individual and family treatment, structured day treatment and structured residential programs, aftercare/parole community supervision and residential and nonresidential services for juvenile offenders who are before intake on complaints or the court on petitions alleging that the juvenile is delinquent, in need of services or in need of supervision but shall not include secure detention for the purposes of this article. Such community-based systems shall be based on an annual review of court-related data and an objective assessment of the need for services and programs for juveniles before intake on complaints or the court on petitions alleging that the juvenile is a child in need of services, in need of supervision, or delinquent. The community-based system shall be developed after consultation with the judge or judges of the juvenile and domestic relations district court, the director of the court services unit, the community policy and management team established under §2.1-751, and, if applicable, the director of any program established pursuant to §66-26.

B. Community-based services instituted pursuant to this article shall be administered by a county, city or combination thereof, and may be administered through a community policy and management team established under §2.1-750 or a commission established under §16.1-315. Such programs and services may be provided by qualified public or private agencies, pursuant to appropriate contracts. Any commission established under §16.1-315 providing predispositional and postdispositional services prior to the enactment of this article which serves a member jurisdiction that is a city having a population between 135,000 and 165,000 shall directly receive the proportion of funds calculated under §16.1-309.7 on behalf of the owner localities. The funds received shall be allocated directly to the member localities. Any member locality which elects to withdraw from the commission shall be entitled to its full allocation as provided in §§16.1-309.6 and 16.1-309.7. The Department of Juvenile Justice shall provide technical assistance to localities, upon request, for establishing or expanding programs or services pursuant to this article.

C. Funds provided to implement the provisions of this article shall not be used to supplant funds established as the state pool of funds under §2.1-757.

D. Any county, city or combination thereof which establishes a community-based system pursuant to this article shall biennially submit to the State Board for approval a local plan for the development, implementation and operation of such services, programs and facilities pursuant to this article. The plan shall provide (i) the projected number of juveniles served by alternatives to secure detention and (ii) any reduction in secure detention rates and commitments to state care as a result of programs funded pursuant to this article. The State Board shall solicit written comments on the plan from the judge or judges of the juvenile and domestic relations court, the director of the court services unit, and if applicable, the director of programs established pursuant to §66-26. Prior to the initiation of any new services, the plan shall also include a cost comparison for the private operation of such services.

E. Each locality shall report quarterly to the Director the data required by the Department to measure progress on stated objectives and to evaluate programs and services within such locality's plan.

(Added by L.1995 chs. 698, 840; chgd. by L.1996 chs. 671, 682; L.1997 ch. 347; L.2000 chs. 195, 806, eff. 7/1/2000.)

§16.1-309.4. Statewide plan for juvenile services.

It shall be the duty of the Department of Juvenile Justice to devise, develop and promulgate a statewide plan for the establishment and maintenance of a range of institutional and community-based, diversion, predispositional and postdispositional services to be reasonably accessible to each court. The Department shall be responsible for the collection and dissemination of the required court data necessary for the development of the plan. The plan shall utilize the information provided by local plans submitted under §16.1-309.3. The plan shall be submitted to the Board on or before July 1 in odd-numbered years. The plan shall include a biennial forecast with appropriate annual updates as may be required of future juvenile correctional center and detention home needs.

(Added by L.1995 chs. 698, 840; chgd. by L.1996 chs. 671, 682, 755, 914, eff. 7/1/96.)

§16.1-309.5. Construction, etc., of detention homes and other facilities; reimbursement in part by Commonwealth.

A. The Commonwealth shall reimburse any county, city or any combination thereof for one-half the cost of construction, enlargement, renovation, purchase or rental of a detention home or other facilities the plans and specifications of which were approved by the Board and the Governor in accordance with the provisions of subsection C of this section.

B. The construction, renovation, purchase, rental, maintenance and operation of a detention home or other facilities established by a county, city or any combination thereof and the necessary expenses incurred in operating such facilities shall be the responsibility of the county, city or any combination thereof.

C. The Board shall promulgate regulations to include criteria to serve as guidelines in evaluating requests for such reimbursements and to ensure the geographically equitable distribution of state funds provided for such purpose. Priority funding shall be given to multijurisdictional initiatives. No such reimbursement for costs of construction shall be made, however, unless the plans and specifications, including the need for additional personnel therefor, have been submitted to the Governor and the construction has been approved by him. Such reimbursement shall be paid by the State Treasurer out of funds appropriated to the Department. In the event that a county or city requests and receives financial assistance from other public fund sources outside the provisions of this law, the total financial assistance and reimbursement shall not exceed the total construction cost of the project exclusive of land and site improvement costs, and such funds shall not be considered state funds.

(Added by L.1995 chs. 698, 840; chgd. by L.2000 chs. 562, 601, eff. 7/1/2000.)

§16.1-309.6. How state appropriations for operating costs of Juvenile Community Crime Control Act programs determined; notice of financial aid.

The Governor's proposed biennial budget shall include, for each fiscal year, an appropriation for operating costs for Juvenile Community Crime Control Act programs. The proposed appropriation shall include amounts for compensating counties, cities and combinations thereof which elect to establish a system of community-based services pursuant to this article. Upon approval pursuant to the provisions of this article, any county, city or combination thereof which utilized predispositional or postdispositional block grant services or programs in fiscal year 1995 shall contribute an amount not less than the sum of its fiscal year 1995 expenditures for child care day placements in predispositional and postdispositional block grant alternatives to secure detention for implementation of its local plan. Such amount shall not include any expenditures in fiscal year 1995 for secure detention and placements made pursuant to §2.1-757.

The Department shall review annually the costs of operating services, programs and facilities pursuant to this article and recommend adjustments to maintain the Commonwealth's proportionate share. The Department shall no later than the fifteenth day following adjournment sine die of the General Assembly provide each county and city an estimate of funds appropriated pursuant to this article.

(Added by L.1995 chs. 698, 840; chgd. by L.1996 chs. 671, 682; L.1998 ch. 54, eff. 7/1/98.)

§16.1-309.7. Determination of payment.

A. The Commonwealth shall provide financial assistance to localities whose plans have been approved pursuant to subsection D of §16.1-309.3 in quarterly payments based on the annual calculated costs which shall be determined as follows:

1. For community diversion services, one-half of the calculated costs as determined by the following factors: (i) the statewide daily average costs for predispositional nonresidential services and (ii) the total number of children in need of services and children in need of supervision complaints diverted at intake by the locality in the previous year.

2. For predispositional community-based services, three-quarters of the calculated costs as determined by the following factors: (i) the statewide daily average cost evenly divided for predispositional community-based residential and nonresidential services and (ii) the number of arrests of juveniles based on the locality's most recent year available Uniform Crime Reports for (a) one-third of all Part 1 crimes against property, (b) one-third of all drug offenses and (c) all remaining Part 2 arrests.

3. For postdispositional community-based services for adjudicated juveniles, one-half of the calculated costs as determined by the following factors: (i) the statewide average daily costs for postdispositional community-based nonresidential services and (ii) the locality's total number of juveniles, who, in the previous year, were adjudicated delinquent for the first time.

4. For postdispositional community-based services for juveniles adjudicated delinquent for a second or subsequent offense, one-half of the calculated costs as determined by the following factors: (i) the statewide average daily costs evenly divided for postdispositional community-based residential and nonresidential services and (ii) the locality's total number of court dispositions which, in the previous year, adjudicated juveniles as (a) delinquent for a second or subsequent offense, (b) children in need of services, or (c) children in need of supervision, less those juveniles receiving services under the provisions of §§16.1-285.1 and 16.1-286.

B. Any moneys distributed by the Commonwealth under this article which are unexpended at the end of each fiscal year within a biennium shall be retained by the county, city or combination thereof and subsequently expended for operating expenses of Juvenile Community Crime Control Act programs. Any surplus funds remaining at the end of a biennium shall be returned to the state treasury.

(Added by L.1995 chs. 698, 840; chgd. by L.1996 chs. 820, 970, eff. 7/1/96.)

§16.1-309.8. Costs of maintenance of juveniles in Community Crime Control Act programs.

Any county, city or combination thereof operating a Juvenile Community Crime Control Act program may collect from any locality of this Commonwealth from which a juvenile is placed in its program a daily rate calculated to allow the operating locality or localities to meet but not exceed the costs of providing services. Additionally, this rate may not be higher than the rate charged other counties, cities or combinations thereof using the same program.

(Added by L.1995 chs. 698, 840; chgd. by L.1996 chs. 671, 682; L.1998 ch. 538, eff. 7/1/98.)

§16.1-309.9. Establishment of standards; determination of compliance.

A. The State Board of Juvenile Justice shall develop, promulgate and approve standards for the development, implementation, operation and evaluation of the range of community-based programs, services and facilities authorized by this article. The State Board shall also approve minimum standards for the construction and equipment of detention homes or other facilities and for food, clothing, medical attention, and supervision of juveniles to be housed in these facilities and programs.

B. The State Board may prohibit, by its order, the placement of juveniles in any place of residence which does not comply with the minimum standards. It may limit the number of juveniles to be detained or housed in a detention home or other facility and may designate some other place of detention or housing for juveniles who would otherwise be held therein.

C. The Department shall periodically review all services established and annually review expenditures made under this article to determine compliance with the approved local plans and operating standards. If the Department determines that a program is not in substantial compliance with the approved plan or standards, the Department may suspend all or any portion of financial aid made available to the locality until there is compliance.

D. Orders of the State Board of Juvenile Justice shall be enforced by circuit courts as is provided for the enforcement of orders of the State Board of Corrections under §53.1-70.

(Added by L.1995 chs. 698, 840, eff. 1/1/96.)

§16.1-309.10. Visitation and management of detention homes; other facilities; reports of superintendent.

In the event that a detention home, group home or other residential care facility for children in need of services or delinquent or alleged delinquent youth is established by a county, city, or any combination thereof, it shall be subject to visitation, inspection and regulation by the State Board or its agents, and shall be furnished and operated so far as possible as a family home under the management of a superintendent. It shall be the duty of the superintendent to furnish the Department such reports and other statistical data relating to the operation of such detention homes, group homes or other residential care facilities for children in need of services or delinquent or alleged delinquent youth as may be required by the Director.

(Added by L.1995 chs. 698, 840, eff. 1/1/96.)

ARTICLE 18
JUVENILE COMPETENCY

(Added by L.1999 chs. 958, 997, eff. 7/1/99.)
(Complete Article)

§16.1-356. Raising question of competency to stand trial; evaluation and determination of competency.

A. If, at any time after the attorney for the juvenile has been retained or appointed pursuant to a delinquency proceeding and before the end of trial, the court finds, sua sponte or upon hearing evidence or representations of counsel for the juvenile or the attorney for the Commonwealth, that there is probable cause to believe that the juvenile lacks substantial capacity to understand the proceedings against him or to assist his attorney in his own defense, the court shall order that a competency evaluation be performed by at least one psychiatrist, clinical psychologist, licensed professional counselor, or licensed clinical social worker who is qualified by training and experience in the forensic evaluation of juveniles.

The Commissioner of Mental Health, Mental Retardation and Substance Abuse Services shall approve the training and qualifications for individuals authorized to conduct juvenile competency evaluations and provide restoration services to juveniles pursuant to this article. The Commissioner shall also provide all juvenile courts with a list of guidelines for the court to use in the determination of qualifying individuals as experts in matters relating to juvenile competency and restoration.

B. The evaluation shall be performed on an outpatient basis at a community services board or behavioral health authority, juvenile detention home or juvenile justice facility unless the court specifically finds that (i) the results of the outpatient competency evaluation indicate that hospitalization of the juvenile for evaluation of competency is necessary or (ii) the juvenile is currently hospitalized in a psychiatric hospital. If one of these findings is made, the court, under authority of this subsection, may order the juvenile sent to a hospital designated by the Commissioner of Mental Health, Mental Retardation and Substance Abuse Services as appropriate for the evaluation of juveniles against whom a delinquency petition has been filed.

C. The court shall require the attorney for the Commonwealth to provide to the evaluators appointed under subsection A any information relevant to the evaluation, including, but not limited to (i) a copy of the warrant or petition, (ii) the names and addresses of the attorney for the Commonwealth, the attorney for the juvenile, and the judge ordering the evaluation, and (iii) information about the alleged offense. The court shall require the attorney for the juvenile to provide to the evaluator only the psychiatric records and other information that is deemed relevant to the evaluation of competency. The moving party shall provide the evaluator a summary of the reasons for the evaluation request. All information required by this subsection shall be provided to the evaluator within ninety-six hours of the issuance of the court order requiring the evaluation and when applicable, shall be submitted prior to admission to the facility providing the inpatient evaluation. If the ninety-six-hour period expires on a Saturday, Sunday or other legal holiday, the ninety-six hours shall be extended to the next day which is not a Saturday, Sunday or legal holiday.

D. If the juvenile is hospitalized under the provisions of subsection B, the juvenile shall be hospitalized for such time as the director of the hospital deems necessary to perform an adequate evaluation of the juvenile's competency, but not to exceed ten days from the date of admission to the hospital. All evaluations shall be completed and the report filed with the court within fourteen days of receipt by the evaluator of all information required under subsection C.

E. Upon completion of the evaluation, the evaluator shall promptly and in no event exceeding fourteen days after receipt of all required information submit the report in writing to the court and the attorneys of record concerning (i) the juvenile's capacity to understand the proceedings against him; (ii) his ability to assist his attorney; and (iii) his need for services in the event he is found incompetent, including a description of the suggested necessary services and least restrictive setting to assist the juvenile in restoration to competency. No statements of the juvenile relating to the alleged offense shall be included in the report.

F. After receiving the report described in subsection E, the court shall promptly determine whether the juvenile is competent to stand trial for adjudication or disposition. A hearing on the juvenile's competency is not required unless one is requested by the attorney for the Commonwealth or the attorney for the juvenile or when required under §16.1-357 B. If a hearing is held, the party alleging that the juvenile is incompetent shall bear the burden of proving by a preponderance of the evidence the juvenile's incompetency. The juvenile shall have the right to notice of the hearing and the right to personally participate in and introduce evidence at the hearing.

If the juvenile is otherwise able to understand the charges against him and assist in his defense, a finding of incompetency shall not be made based solely on any or all of the following: (i) the juvenile's age or developmental factors, (ii) the juvenile's claim to be unable to remember the time period surrounding the alleged offense, or (iii) the fact that the juvenile is under the influence of medication.

(Added by L.1999 chs. 958, 997; chgd. by L.2000 ch. 337, eff. 7/1/2000.)

§16.1-357. Disposition when juvenile found incompetent.

A. Upon finding pursuant to subsection F of §16.1-356 that the juvenile is incompetent, the court shall order that the juvenile receive services to restore his competency in either a nonsecure community setting or a secure facility as defined in §16.1-228. A copy of the order shall be forwarded to the Commissioner of Mental Health, Mental Retardation and Substance Abuse Services, who shall arrange for the provision of restoration services in a manner consistent with the order. Any report submitted pursuant to subsection E of §16.1-356 shall be made available to the agent providing restoration.

B. If the court finds the juvenile incompetent but restorable to competency in the foreseeable future, it shall order restoration services for up to three months. At the end of three months from the date restoration is ordered under subsection A of this section, if the juvenile remains incompetent in the opinion of the agent providing restoration, the agent shall so notify the court and make recommendations concerning disposition of the juvenile. The court shall hold a hearing according to the procedures specified in subsection F of §16.1-356 and, if it finds the juvenile unrestorably incompetent, shall order one of the dispositions pursuant to

§16.1-358. If the court finds the juvenile incompetent but restorable to competency, it may order continued restoration services for additional three-month periods, provided a hearing pursuant to subsection F of §16.1-356 is held at the completion of each such period and the juvenile continues to be incompetent but restorable to competency in the foreseeable future.

C. If, at any time after the juvenile is ordered to undergo services under subsection A of this section, the agent providing restoration believes the juvenile's competency is restored, the agent shall immediately send a report to the court as prescribed in subsection E of §16.1-356. The court shall make a ruling on the juvenile's competency according to the procedures specified in subsection F of §16.1-356.
(Added by L.1999 chs. 958, 997, eff. 7/1/99.)

§16.1-358. Disposition of unrestorably incompetent juvenile.

If, at any time after the juvenile is ordered to undergo services pursuant to subsection A of §16.1-357, the agent providing restoration concludes that the juvenile is likely to remain incompetent for the foreseeable future, he shall send a report to the court so stating. The report shall also indicate whether, in the agent's opinion, the juvenile should be (i) committed pursuant to Article 16 (§16.1-335 et seq.) of this chapter or, if the juvenile has reached the age of eighteen years at the time of the competency determination, pursuant to §§37.1-67.01 through 37.1-70, (ii) certified pursuant to §37.1-65.1, (iii) provided other services by the court, or (iv) released. Upon receipt of the report, the court shall make a competency determination according to the procedures specified in subsection F of §16.1-356. If the court finds that the juvenile is incompetent and is likely to remain so for the foreseeable future, it shall order that the juvenile (i) be committed pursuant to Article 16 (§16.1-335 et seq.) of this chapter or, if the juvenile has reached the age of eighteen years at the time of the competency determination, pursuant to §§37.1-67.01 through 37.1-70, (ii) be certified pursuant to §37.1-65.1, (iii) have a child in need of services petition filed on his behalf pursuant to §16.1-260 D, or (iv) be released. If the court finds the juvenile incompetent but restorable to competency in the foreseeable future, it may order restoration services continued until three months have elapsed from the date of the provision of restoration ordered under subsection A of §16.1-357.

If not dismissed without prejudice at an earlier time, charges against an unrestorably incompetent juvenile shall be dismissed in compliance with the time frames as follows: in the case of a charge which would be a misdemeanor, one year from the date of the juvenile's arrest for such charge; and in the case of a charge which would be a felony, three years from the date of the juvenile's arrest for such charges.
(Added by L.1999 chs. 958, 997; chgd. by L.2000 ch. 216, eff. 7/1/2000.)

§16.1-359. Litigating certain issues when juvenile is incompetent.

A finding of incompetency does not preclude the adjudication, at any time before trial, of a motion objecting to the sufficiency of the petition, nor does it preclude the adjudication of similar legal objections which, in the court's opinion, may be undertaken without the personal participation of the juvenile.
(Added by L.1999 chs. 958, 997, eff. 7/1/99.)

§16.1-360. Disclosure by juvenile during evaluation or restoration; use at guilt phase of trial adjudication or disposition hearing.

No statement or disclosure by the juvenile concerning the alleged offense made during a competency evaluation ordered pursuant to §16.1-356, or services ordered pursuant to §16.1-357 may be used against the juvenile at the adjudication or disposition hearings as evidence or as a basis for such evidence.
(Added by L.1999 chs. 958, 997, eff. 7/1/99.)

§16.1-361. Compensation of experts.

Each psychiatrist, clinical psychologist, licensed clinical social worker, licensed professional counselor, or other expert appointed by the court to render professional service pursuant to §16.1-356, shall receive a reasonable fee for such service. With the exception of services provided by state mental health or mental retardation facilities, the fee shall be determined in each instance by the court that appointed the expert, in accordance with guidelines established by the Supreme Court after consultation with the Department of Mental Health, Mental Retardation and Substance Abuse Services. If any such expert is required to appear as a witness in any hearing held pursuant to §16.1-356, he shall receive mileage and a fee of $100 for each day during which he is required to serve. An itemized account of expenses, duly sworn to, must be presented to the court, and when allowed shall be certified to the Supreme Court for payment out of the state treasury, and be charged against the appropriations made to pay criminal charges. Allowance for the fee and for the per diem authorized shall also be made by order of the court, duly certified to the Supreme Court for payment out of the appropriation to pay criminal charges.
(Added by L.1999 chs. 958, 997; chgd. by L.2000 ch. 337, eff. 7/1/2000.)

TITLE 17
COURTS OF RECORD

(Repealed by L.1998 ch. 872, eff. 10/1/98. See Title 17.1 for statutes effective 10/1/98.)

TITLE 17.1
COURTS OF RECORD

(Added by L.1998 ch. 872, eff. 10/1/98.)
(Selected Chapters)

CHAPTER 1
GENERAL PROVISIONS

(Selected Section)

§17.1-112. Sheriff to attend court as its officer.

Neither the Supreme Court nor the Court of Appeals shall be attended by any sheriff in the City of Richmond. In all other cases, the sheriff of the county or city in which any court is held shall attend it and act as its officer.
(Added by L.1998 ch. 872, eff. 10/1/98.)

CHAPTER 3
SUPREME COURT
(Selected Article)

ARTICLE 1
COMPOSITION; JURISDICTION, ETC.
(Selected Sections)

§17.1-312. Where criminal jurisdiction exercised.

The appellate jurisdiction of the Supreme Court in any criminal case may be exercised at any place of session, no matter where the court may have been held which rendered the judgment in such case.
(Added by L.1998 ch. 872, eff. 10/1/98.)

§17.1-313. Review of death sentence.

A. A sentence of death, upon the judgment thereon becoming final in the circuit court, shall be reviewed on the record by the Supreme Court.

B. The proceeding in the circuit court shall be transcribed as expeditiously as practicable, and the transcript filed forthwith upon transcription with the clerk of the circuit court, who shall, within ten days after receipt of the transcript, compile the record as provided in Rule 5:14 and transmit it to the Supreme Court.

C. In addition to consideration of any errors in the trial enumerated by appeal, the court shall consider and determine:

1. Whether the sentence of death was imposed under the influence of passion, prejudice or any other arbitrary factor; and

2. Whether the sentence of death is excessive or disproportionate to the penalty imposed in similar cases, considering both the crime and the defendant.

D. In addition to the review and correction of errors in the trial of the case, with respect to review of the sentence of death, the court may:

1. Affirm the sentence of death;

2. Commute the sentence of death to imprisonment for life; or

3. Remand to the trial court for a new sentencing proceeding.

E. The Supreme Court may accumulate the records of all capital felony cases tried within such period of time as the court may determine. The court shall consider such records as are available as a guide in determining whether the sentence imposed in the case under review is excessive. Such records as are accumulated shall be made available to the circuit courts.

F. Sentence review shall be in addition to appeals, if taken, and review and appeal may be consolidated. The defendant and the Commonwealth shall have the right to submit briefs within time limits imposed by the court, either by rule or order, and to present oral argument.

G. The Supreme Court shall, in setting its docket, give priority to the review of cases in which the sentence of death has been imposed over other cases pending in the Court. In setting its docket, the Court shall also give priority to the consideration and disposition of petitions for writs of habeas corpus filed by prisoners held under sentence of death.
(Added by L.1998 ch. 872, eff. 10/1/98.)

CHAPTER 6
COSTS GENERALLY
(Selected Sections)

§17.1-617. Number of witnesses paid fees in criminal cases.

Not more than the maximum number of witnesses provided for herein shall be paid out of the state treasury in criminal cases.

The maximum number that may be (i) caused to be summoned by an attorney for the Commonwealth in any one case to go before a grand jury – five; (ii) used before a court not of record in the trial of any criminal case – five; and (iii) caused to be summoned by an attorney for the Commonwealth for the trial of any criminal case – ten.

Nothing herein shall be construed to limit (i) the number of witnesses that may be authorized by any court or the judge thereof to be used when the necessity for additional witnesses appears to the court or judge and the consent of the court or judge is first obtained or (ii) the number of witnesses that a grand jury may of its own motion summon.
(Added by L.1998 ch. 872, eff. 10/1/98.)

§17.1-618. Allowances for jurors; expenses of keeping jury together; fees of jury commissioners and commissioner in chancery for drawing of juries.

Every person summoned as a juror in a civil or criminal case shall be entitled to thirty dollars for each day of attendance upon the court for expenses of travel incident to jury service and other necessary and reasonable costs as the court may direct. Jurors summoned from another political subdivision pursuant to §8.01-363 may be allowed by the court, in addition to the above allowance, their actual expenses. When kept together overnight under the supervision of the court, the jurors and the sheriff or his deputies keeping the jury shall be furnished suitable board and lodging. Reimbursement for board and lodging shall be set by the judge in an amount not to exceed the amount authorized by travel regulations promulgated pursuant to §2.1-20.8. Allowances and other costs will be allowed a juror in only one case the same day.

Every person serving as a jury commissioner and every person serving as a commissioner in chancery for the drawing of juries for a circuit court of this Commonwealth may be allowed, by the court appointing him, a fee not exceeding thirty dollars per day for the time actually engaged in such work and such other necessary and reasonable costs as the court may direct.
(Added by L.1998 ch. 872, eff. 10/1/98.)

§17.1-619. How jurors paid.

A. The compensation and allowances of persons attending the court as jurors in all felony cases shall be paid by the

 Zv

Commonwealth. Jurors in misdemeanor cases shall be paid by the Commonwealth unless the charge is written on a local warrant or summons, in which case the jurors shall be paid by the political subdivision in which the summons is issued. Jurors in all civil cases shall be paid by the political subdivision in which the summons is issued. Payment in all cases shall be by negotiable check, or warrant, upon the Commonwealth, or the political subdivision, as the case may be.

When, during the same day any juror is entitled to compensation from both the Commonwealth and from the political subdivision in which he has served, the court shall divide the pay for such day between the Commonwealth and the political subdivision. It shall be the duty of the sheriff at the term of the court during which an allowance is made or has been made under this section, to furnish the clerk of the court with a statement showing the number and names of the jurors in attendance upon the court.

B. A county or city may provide by local ordinance that a juror may direct in writing that compensation due him be paid to the court service unit or to any other agency, authority or organization which is ancillary to and provides services to the courts of the county or city.
(Added by L.1998 ch. 872, eff. 10/1/98.)

§17.1-620. When juror not entitled to compensation.
No person shall be entitled to receive any compensation for service as a juror if he departs without the leave of the court, or, being summoned as a witness for the Commonwealth, charges for his attendance as such.
(Added by L.1998 ch. 872, eff. 10/1/98.)

§17.1-621. Clerk to make entry on minutes stating amount due and by whom payable.
The clerk of any court in which juries are impaneled shall, before its final adjournment at each term, and under the direction of the court, make an entry upon its minutes stating the amount to which each juror is entitled for his services or attendance during the term, and specifying how much is payable by the Commonwealth, and how much by the political subdivision.
(Added by L.1998 ch. 872, eff. 10/1/98.)

§17.1-622. Clerk to transmit orders making allowances to Supreme Court, treasurer and jurors.
Such clerk shall immediately, after the adjournment of the court, transmit to the Supreme Court a list of all orders under §17.1-621 making allowances against the Commonwealth, and to the treasurer of the political subdivision a list of all such orders making allowances against the political subdivision, with a certificate to the correctness of the list and the aggregate amount thereof annexed thereto and signed by the judge of the court and himself, and such clerk shall also deliver to each juror copies of any orders making an allowance to him, whether the same be payable by the Commonwealth or by the political subdivision.
(Added by L.1998 ch. 872, eff. 10/1/98.)

§17.1-623. Payment of allowances.
The treasurer of such political subdivision shall upon demand pay to such juror the amount allowed him by negotiable check, which shall be repaid to such treasurer out of the public treasury or out of the political subdivision levy, as the case may be, upon the production of satisfactory proof that the same has been actually paid by him. But such treasurer shall not be repaid any allowance made against the Commonwealth unless it appear on the list directed to be sent to the Supreme Court. No such allowance shall be paid unless presented within two years from the time of rendering the service.
(Added by L.1998 ch. 872, eff. 10/1/98.)

§17.1-629. No judgment for costs against Commonwealth; exception.
In no case, civil or criminal, whether in a court of record or a court not of record, except when otherwise specially provided, shall there be a judgment for costs against the Commonwealth.
(Added by L.1998 ch. 872, eff. 10/1/98.)

TITLE 20
DOMESTIC RELATIONS
(Selected Chapters)

CHAPTER 2
MARRIAGE GENERALLY
(Selected Sections)

§20-28. Penalty for celebrating marriage without a license.
If any person knowingly perform the ceremony of marriage without lawful license, or officiate in celebrating the rites of marriage without being authorized by law to do so, he shall be confined in jail not exceeding 1 year, and fined not exceeding $500.

§20-32. Penalty on clerks for neglect of duty.
If any clerk of a court or county clerk fail to perform any duty required of him under this chapter, he shall forfeit ten dollars for every such offense.

§20-33. Penalty for clerk issuing license contrary to law.
If any clerk of a court knowingly issue a marriage license contrary to law, he shall be confined in jail not exceeding 1 year, and fined not exceeding $500.

CHAPTER 3
UNLAWFUL MARRIAGES GENERALLY
(Selected Section)

§20-45.2. Marriage between persons of same sex.
A marriage between persons of the same sex is prohibited. Any marriage entered into by persons of the same sex in another state or jurisdiction shall be void in all respects in Virginia and any contractual rights created by such marriage shall be void and unenforceable.
(Chgd. by L.1997 chs. 354, 365, eff. 7/1/97.)

CHAPTER 5
DESERTION AND NONSUPPORT
(Selected Section)

§20-61. Desertion or nonsupport of wife, husband or children in necessitous circumstances.

Any spouse who without cause deserts or willfully neglects or refuses or fails to provide for the support and maintenance of his or her spouse, and any parent who deserts or willfully neglects or refuses or fails to provide for the support and maintenance of his or her child under the age of 18 years of age, or child of whatever age who is crippled or otherwise incapacitated from earning a living, the spouse, child or children being then and there in necessitous circumstances, shall be guilty of a misdemeanor and upon conviction shall be punished by a fine of not exceeding $500, or confinement in jail not exceeding 12 months, or both, or on work release employment as provided in §53.1-131 for a period of not less than 90 days nor more than 12 months; or in lieu of the fine or confinement being imposed upon conviction by the court or by verdict of a jury he or she may be required by the court to suffer a forfeiture of an amount not exceeding the sum of $1,000 and the fine or forfeiture may be directed by the court to be paid in whole or in part to the spouse, or to the guardian, curator, custodian or trustee of the minor child or children, or to some discreet person or responsible organization designated by the court to receive it. This section shall not apply to any parent of any child of whatever age, if the child qualifies for and is receiving aid under a federal or state program for aid to the permanently and totally disabled; or is an adult and meets the visual requirements for aid to the blind; and for this purpose any state agency shall use only the financial resources of the child of whatever age in determining eligibility.

TITLE 22.1
EDUCATION
(Selected Chapters)

Chapter

CHAPTER 12
PUPIL TRANSPORTATION
(Selected Article)

Article

ARTICLE 1
GENERAL PROVISIONS
(Complete Article)

Section

§22.1-176. Transportation of pupils authorized; when fee may be charged; contributions; regulations of Board of Education.

A. School boards may provide for the transportation of pupils, but nothing herein contained shall be construed as requiring such transportation except as provided in §22.1-221.

B. When a school board provides transportation to pupils for extracurricular activities, other than those covered by an activity fund, which are sponsored by the pupils' school apart from the regular instructional program and which the pupils are not required to attend or participate in, the school board may accept contributions for such transportation or charge each pupil utilizing such transportation a reasonable fee not to exceed his pro rata share of the cost of providing such transportation. A school board may waive such fees for any pupil whose parent or guardian is financially unable to pay them.

C. When a school board provides transportation to pupils for field trips which are a part of the program of the pupils' school or are sponsored by such school, the school board may accept contributions for such transportation.

D. The Board of Education shall promulgate such regulations as shall be in the public interest to effect the intent of this section.

§22.1-177. Regulations.

The Board may make regulations relating to the construction, design, operation, equipment, and color of public school buses and shall have the authority to issue an order prohibiting the operation on public streets and highways of any public school bus which does not comply with such regulations. Any such order shall be enforced by the Department of State Police.

No regulation of the Board shall unreasonably limit the authority of any local school division to purchase and use school buses using compressed natural gas or other alternative fuels or convert its school buses to use compressed natural gas or other alternative fuels.

§22.1-178. Requirements for persons employed to drive school buses.

A. No school board shall hire, employ, or enter into any agreement with any person for the purposes of operating a school bus transporting pupils unless the person proposed to so operate such school bus shall:

1. Have a physical examination of a scope prescribed by the Board of Education with the advice of the Medical Society of Virginia and furnish a form prescribed by the Board of Education showing the results of such examination.

2. Furnish a statement or copy of records from the Department of Motor Vehicles showing that the records of such Department do not disclose that the person, within the preceding five years, has been convicted upon a charge of driving under the influence of alcohol or drugs, convicted of a felony or assigned to any alcohol safety action program or driver alcohol rehabilitation program pursuant to §18.2-271.1 or, within the preceding twelve months, has been convicted of two or more moving traffic violations or required to attend a driver improvement clinic by the Commissioner of the Department of Motor Vehicles pursuant to §46.2-497.

3. Furnish a statement signed by two reputable residents of the school division that the person is of good moral character.

4. Exhibit a license showing the person has successfully undertaken the examination prescribed by §46.2-339.

5. Have reached the age of eighteen on the first day of the school year.

B. Any school board may require successful completion of the American National Red Cross first-aid course or its equivalent as a condition to employment to operate a school bus transporting pupils.

C. School boards may require persons accepting employment after July 1, 1994, as a driver of a school bus transporting pupils to agree, as a condition of employment, to submit to alcohol and controlled substance testing. Any such tests shall be conducted in compliance with Board of Education regulations.

D. The documents required pursuant to subdivisions A 1 and A 2 of this section shall be furnished annually prior to the anniversary date of the employment agreement as a condition to continuing employment to operate a school bus.

E. The documents required pursuant to this section shall be filed with, and made a part of, the records of the school board employing such person as a school bus operator.

F. The State Department of Education shall furnish to the several division superintendents the necessary forms to be used by applicants in furnishing the information required by this section. Insofar as practicable, such forms shall be designed to limit paperwork, avoid the possibility of mistake, and furnish all parties involved with a complete and accurate record of the information required.

G. The physical examination required by subsection A may be performed and the report of the results signed by a licensed nurse practitioner.

(Chgd. by L.1998 ch. 287, eff. 7/1/98.)

§22.1-180. Requirements for persons employed to transport pupils attending parochial or private schools.

No person, partnership, association or corporation operating any parochial or private school shall hire, employ or enter into any agreement with any person for the purpose of transporting pupils by motor vehicle unless such person shall present the documents and meet the qualifications required of operators of public school buses by subsection A of §22.1-178. The State Department of Education shall furnish the forms prescribed for the purposes of §22.1-178 to any person, partnership, association or corporation who shall request such forms for the purpose of compliance with this section.

§22.1-181. Training program for school bus operators.

The Board of Education shall develop a training program for persons applying for employment, and employed, to operate school buses and shall promote its implementation.

§22.1-182. Use of school buses for public purposes.

The school board of any school division may enter into agreements with the governing body of any county, city or town in the school division, any state agency or any agency established or identified pursuant to United States Public Law 89–73 or any law amendatory or supplemental thereto providing for the use of the school buses of such school division by such agency or by departments, boards, commissions or officers of such county, city or town for public purposes, including transportation for the elderly. Each such agreement shall provide for reimbursing the school board in full for the proportionate share of any and all costs, both fixed and variable, of such buses incurred by such school board attributable to the use of such buses pursuant to such agreement. The governing body, state agency or agency established or identified pursuant to United States Public Law 89–73 or any law amendatory or supplemental thereto shall indemnify and hold harmless the school board from any and all liability of the school board by virtue of use of such buses pursuant to an agreement authorized herein.

§22.1-183. When warning lights and identification to be covered.

It shall be unlawful for a school bus licensed in this Commonwealth to be operated on the public highways of this Commonwealth for the purpose of transporting persons or commodities other than school personnel, school children or elderly or mentally or physically handicapped persons unless the lettered identification and school bus traffic warning lights on the front and rear of such bus are covered with some opaque detachable material. This section shall not apply to any such bus when operated by a salesman or demonstrator in connection with a prospective sale or delivery of a bus.

§22.1-184. School bus emergency drills.

At every public school having public school buses there shall be held, at least once during the first ninety calendar days of each school session and oftener if necessary, a drill in leaving school buses under emergency circumstances.

§22.1-185. Shelters on bus routes.

The governing body of any county, city or town may expend funds for the construction and maintenance at points on school bus routes of such shelters, platforms or other structures as it may deem necessary or convenient for the protection and comfort of children of school age who go to such points to meet school buses.

§22.1-186. Payments for transportation of pupils.

The regulations of the Board of Education governing state payments for pupil transportation shall provide for payments to school divisions for pupil transportation provided by the school divisions both through systems operated by the school divisions and through contracts with public transportation facilities.

§22.1-187. Exemption from payment of tolls by certain students, etc.

It shall be unlawful to collect any toll for the use of any road, highway, bridge or ferry in this Commonwealth, except those financed under the State Revenue Bond Act (§33.1-267 et seq.) or other act authorizing the construction by the State or a political subdivision thereof of projects financed by the issuance of bonds payable solely from tolls and other revenues of the project, (i) by any student or other person using the road, highway, bridge or ferry daily for going to or from immediate attendance upon any school, college, or other educational institution in this Commonwealth, or classes in water safety training conducted under the auspices of the American Red Cross or (ii) by the vehicle carrying the student or other person.

Any such student or other person or the parent or guardian of any such student may apply for and receive from the principal of any school, college, or other educational institution in this Commonwealth a card certifying that the student or other person uses such road, highway, bridge or ferry daily for regularly attending such school, college, educational institution or classes. Such card exhibited to the person in charge of any tollgate on any road, highway, bridge or ferry in this Commonwealth shall be accepted in lieu of all charges for the passage through such tollgate of any such student, person or the vehicle carrying him when using the road, highway, bridge or ferry daily for going to or from immediate attendance upon any such school, college, other educational institution, or classes.

Any person using any such card, except for the purpose herein specified, shall be guilty of a Class 4 misdemeanor.

CHAPTER 14
PUPILS
(Selected Articles)

ARTICLE 1
COMPULSORY SCHOOL ATTENDANCE
(Selected Sections)

§22.1-254. Compulsory attendance required; excuses and waivers; alternative education program attendance; exemptions from article.

A. Except as otherwise provided in this article, every parent, guardian, or other person in the Commonwealth having control or charge of any child who will have reached the fifth birthday on or before September 30 of any school year and who has not passed the eighteenth birthday shall, during the period of each year the public schools are in session and for the same number of days and hours per day as the public schools, send such child to a public school or to a private, denominational or parochial school or have such child taught by a tutor or teacher of qualifications prescribed by the Board of Education and approved by the division superintendent or provide for home instruction of such child as described in §22.1-254.1.

As prescribed in the regulations of the Board of Education, the requirements of this section may also be satisfied by sending a child to an alternative program of study or work/study offered by a public, private, denominational or parochial school or by a public or private degree-granting institution of higher education. Further, in the case of any five-year-old child who is subject to the provisions of this subsection, the requirements of this section may be alternatively satisfied by sending the child to any public educational prekindergarten program, including a Head Start program, or in a private, denominational or parochial educational prekindergarten program.

Instruction in the home of a child or children by the parent, guardian or other person having control or charge of such child or children shall not be classified or defined as a private, denominational or parochial school.

The requirements of this section shall apply to (i) any child in the custody of the Department of Juvenile Justice or the Department of Corrections who has not passed his eighteenth birthday and (ii) any child whom the division superintendent has required to take a special program of prevention, intervention, or remediation as provided in subsection C of §22.1-253.13:1 and in §22.1-254.01. However, the requirements of this section shall not apply to any child who has obtained a high school diploma, its equivalent, or a certificate of completion or who has otherwise complied with compulsory school attendance requirements as set forth in this article.

B. A school board shall excuse from attendance at school:

1. Any pupil who, together with his parents, by reason of bona fide religious training or belief is conscientiously opposed to attendance at school. For purposes of this subdivision, "bona fide religious training or belief" does not include essentially political, sociological or philosophical views or a merely personal moral code; and

2. On the recommendation of the juvenile and domestic relations district court of the county or city in which the pupil resides and for such period of time as the court deems appropriate, any pupil who, together with his parents, is opposed to attendance at a school by reason of concern for such pupil's health, as verified by competent medical evidence, or by reason of such pupil's reasonable apprehension for personal safety when such concern or apprehension in that pupil's specific case is determined by the court, upon consideration of the recommendation of the principal and division superintendent, to be justified.

C. A school board may excuse from attendance at school:

1. On recommendation of the principal and the division superintendent and with the written consent of the parent or guardian, any pupil who the school board determines, in accordance with regulations of the Board of Education, cannot benefit from education at such school; and

2. On recommendation of the juvenile and domestic relations district court of the county or city in which the pupil resides, any pupil who, in the judgment of such court, cannot benefit from education at such school.

D. Local school boards may allow the requirements of subsection A of this section to be met under the following conditions:

For a student who is at least sixteen years of age, there shall be a meeting of the student, the student's parents, and the principal or his designee of the school in which the student is enrolled in which an individual student alternative education plan shall be developed in conformity with guidelines prescribed by the Board, which plan must include:

a. Career guidance counseling;

b. Mandatory enrollment and attendance in a general educational development preparatory program or other alternative education program approved by the local school board with attendance requirements that provide for reporting of student attendance by the chief administrator of such GED preparatory program or approved alternative education program to such principal or his designee;

c. Counseling on the economic impact of failing to complete high school; and

d. Procedures for reenrollment to comply with the requirements of subsection A of this section.

A student for whom an individual student alternative education plan has been granted pursuant to this subsection and who fails to comply with the conditions of such plan shall be in violation of the compulsory school attendance law, and the division superintendent or attendance officer of the school division in which such student was last enrolled shall seek immediate compliance with the compulsory school attendance law as set forth in this article.

Students enrolled with an individual student alternative education plan shall be counted in the average daily membership of the school division.

E. A school board may, in accordance with the procedures set forth in §22.1-277 and upon a finding that a school-age child has (i) committed an offense in violation of school board policies, (ii) been charged with an offense relating to the Commonwealth's laws, or with a violation of school board policies, on weapons, alcohol or drugs, or intentional injury to another person, or (iii) been expelled from school attendance pursuant to §22.1-277.01, require the child to attend an alternative education program as provided in §22.1-209.1:2 or §22.1-277.1.

F. Whenever a court orders any pupil into an alternative education program offered in the public schools, the local school board of the school division in which the program is offered shall determine the appropriate alternative education placement of the pupil, regardless of whether the pupil attends the public schools it supervises or resides within its school division.

The juvenile and domestic relations district court of the county or city in which a pupil resides or in which charges are pending against a pupil, or any court in which charges are pending against a pupil, may require the pupil who has been charged with (i) a crime which resulted in or could have resulted in injury to others, (ii) a violation of Article 1 (§18.2-77 et seq.) of Chapter 5 of Title 18.2, or (iii) any offense related to possession or distribution of any Schedule I, II, or III controlled substances to attend an alternative education program, including, but not limited to, night school, adult education, or any other education program designed to offer instruction to students for whom the regular program of instruction may be inappropriate.

This subsection shall not be construed to limit the authority of school boards to expel, suspend, or exclude students, as provided in §§22.1-277, 22.1-277.01, and 22.1-277.2. As used in this subsection, the term "charged" means that a petition or warrant has been filed or is pending against a pupil.

G. Within one calendar month of the opening of school, each school board shall send to the parents or guardian of each student enrolled in the division a copy of the compulsory school attendance law and the enforcement procedures and policies established by the school board.

H. The provisions of this article shall not apply to:

1. Children suffering from contagious or infectious diseases while suffering from such diseases;

2. Children whose immunizations against communicable diseases have not been completed as provided in §22.1-271.2;

3. Children under ten years of age who live more than two miles from a public school unless public transportation is provided within one mile of the place where such children live;

4. Children between the ages of ten and seventeen, inclusive, who live more than 2.5 miles from a public school unless public transportation is provided within 1.5 miles of the place where such children live; and

5. Children excused pursuant to subsections B and C of this section.

Further, any child who will not have reached his sixth birthday on or before September 30 of each school year whose parent or guardian notifies the appropriate school board that he does not wish the child to attend school until the following year because the child, in the opinion of the parent or guardian, is not mentally, physically or emotionally prepared to attend school, may delay the child's attendance for one year.

The distances specified in subdivisions 3 and 4 of this subsection shall be measured or determined from the child's residence to the entrance to the school grounds or to the school bus stop nearest the entrance to the residence of such children by the nearest practical routes which are usable for walking or riding. Disease shall be established by the certificate of a reputable practicing physician in accordance with regulations adopted by the Board of Education.

(Chgd. by L.1996 chs. 163, 916, 964; L.1997 ch. 828; L.1999 chs. 488, 552; L.2000 ch. 184, eff. 7/1/2000.)

§22.1-254.01. Certain students required to attend summer school or after-school sessions.

In the event that a student is required to take a special program of prevention, intervention, or remediation in a public summer school program or to participate in another form of remediation as provided in subsection C of §22.1-253.13:1 and in accordance with clause (ii) of subsection A of §22.1-254, and the division superintendent determines that remediation of the student's poor academic performance, passage of the [literacy passport test or of a] Standards of Learning [assessment] *Assessment* in grades three, five, or eight, or promotion is directly related to the student's attendance in such summer school program or participation in another form of remediation, and after a reasonable effort to seek the student's attendance in such session has failed, including direct notification of the parents or guardians of such student of the attendance requirement and failure of the parents or guardians to secure the student's attendance, the division superintendent may seek immediate compliance with the compulsory school attendance law as set forth in §22.1-254.

(Added by L.1996 ch. 163; chgd. by L.1997 chs. 466, 828; L.1998 ch. 902, eff. 7/1/98, chs. 602, 627, eff. 7/1/2003; L.1999 chs. 488, 552, eff. 7/1/99. Matter in brackets eff. only until 7/1/2003. Matter in italics eff. 7/1/2003.)

§22.1-255. Nonresident children.

Any person who has residing with him for a period of sixty days or more any child within the ages prescribed in §22.1-254 whose parents or guardians reside in another state or the District of Columbia shall be subject to the provisions of §22.1-254 and shall pay or cause to be paid any tuition charges for such child that may be required pursuant to §22.1-5 or shall return such child to the home of his parents or legal guardians.

§22.1-262. Complaint to court when parent fails to comply with law.

A list of persons notified pursuant to §22.1-261 shall be sent by the attendance officer to the appropriate school principal. If the parent (i) fails to comply with the provisions of §22.1-261 within the time specified in the notice; or (ii) fails to comply with the provisions of §22.1-254; or (iii) refuses to participate in the development of the plan to resolve the student's nonattendance or in the conference provided for in §22.1-258, it shall be the duty of the attendance officer, with the knowledge and approval of the division superintendent, to make complaint against the pupil's parent in the name of the Commonwealth before the juvenile and domestic relations district court. If proceedings are instituted against the parent for failure to comply with the provisions of §22.1-258, the attendance officer is to provide documentation to the court regarding the school division's compliance with §22.1-258. In addition thereto, such child may be proceeded against as a child in need of services or a child in need of supervision as provided in Chapter 11 (§16.1-226 et seq.) of Title 16.1.

(Chgd. by L.1996 chs. 616, 891, 964; L.1999 ch. 526, eff. 7/1/99.)

§22.1-263. Violation constitutes misdemeanor.

Any person violating the provisions of either §22.1-254, except for clause (ii) of subsection A, §§22.1-255, 22.1-258, or §22.1-267 shall be guilty of a Class 3 misdemeanor. Upon a finding that a person knowingly and willfully violated any provision of §22.1-254, except for clause (ii) of subsection A, or any provision of §§22.1-255, 22.1-258, or §22.1-267 and that such person has been convicted previously of a violation of any provision of §22.1-254, except for clause (ii) of subsection A, or any provision of §§22.1-255,

22.1-258, or §22.1-267, such person shall be guilty of a Class 2 misdemeanor.
(Chgd. by L.1996 chs. 891, 964; L.1999 chs. 488, 526, 552, eff. 7/1/99.)

§22.1-264. Misdemeanor to make false statements as to age.

Any person who makes a false statement concerning the age of a child between the ages set forth in §22.1-254 for the purpose of evading the provisions of this article shall be guilty of a Class 4 misdemeanor.

§22.1-265. Inducing children to absent themselves.

Any person who induces or attempts to induce any child to be absent unlawfully from school or who knowingly employs or harbors, while school is in session, any child absent unlawfully shall be guilty of a Class 3 misdemeanor and may be subject to the penalties provided by subdivision 5 a of subsection B of §16.1-278.5 or §18.2-371. Upon a finding that a person knowingly and willfully violated the provisions of this section and that such person has been convicted previously of a violation of this section, such person shall be guilty of a Class 2 misdemeanor.
(Chgd. by L.1996 chs. 891, 916, 964, eff. 7/1/96.)

§22.1-266. Law-enforcement officers and truant children.

A. Notwithstanding the provisions of §16.1-246, any law-enforcement officer as defined in §9-169 or any attendance officer may pick up any child who (i) is reported to be truant from a public school by a school principal or division superintendent or (ii) the law-enforcement officer or attendance officer reasonably determines to be a public school student and by reason of the child's age and circumstances is either truant from public school or has been expelled from school and has been required to attend an alternative education program pursuant to §22.1-277.1, and may deliver such child to the appropriate public school, alternative education program, or truancy center and personnel thereof without charging the parent or guardian of such child with a violation of any provision of law.

B. Any such law-enforcement officer or attendance officer shall not be liable for any civil damages for any acts or omissions resulting from picking up or delivering a public school child as provided in subsection A when such acts or omissions are within the scope of the employment of such law-enforcement officer or attendance officer and are taken in good faith, unless such acts or omissions were the result of gross negligence or willful misconduct. This subsection shall not be construed to limit, withdraw or overturn any defense or immunity already existing in statutory or common law or to affect any claim occurring prior to the effective date of this law.

C. For the purposes of this section, "truancy center" means a facility or site operated by a school division, sometimes jointly with the local law-enforcement agency, and designated for receiving children who have been retrieved by a law-enforcement officer or attendance officer for truancy from school.
(Chgd. by L.1999 chs. 395, 1023, eff. 7/1/99.)

§22.1-267. Proceedings against habitually absent child.

Any child permitted by any parent, guardian, or other person having control thereof to be habitually absent from school contrary to the provisions of this article may be proceeded against as a child in need of supervision as provided in Chapter 11 (§16.1-226 et seq.) of Title 16.1.

ARTICLE 5
PUPIL RECORDS
(Selected Section)

§22.1-288.1. Cooperation with local law-enforcement agencies; notation in school records of missing children.

Each school board shall develop a cooperative arrangement with the local law-enforcement agencies within its jurisdiction to receive reports of disappearances of any children living within the school division.

Upon notification by a local law-enforcement agency of a child's disappearance, the principal of any school in which the child was enrolled at the time of the disappearance shall indicate in the child's cumulative record that the child has been reported as missing.

Upon receiving a request from any school or person for copies of the cumulative records and birth certificate of any child who has been reported by a local law-enforcement agency to be missing, the school being requested to transfer the records shall immediately notify the law-enforcement agency which provided the report to the school of the child's disappearance of the location of the school or person requesting the cumulative records and birth certificate of the child.

CHAPTER 16
PRIVATE TRADE, TECHNICAL, BUSINESS AND CORRESPONDENCE SCHOOLS; SCHOOLS FOR STUDENTS WITH DISABILITIES
(Selected Sections)

§22.1-323. Licenses and certificates generally.

A. No person shall open, operate or conduct any school in this Commonwealth without a license or certificate to operate such school issued by the Board of Education. A license or certificate shall be issued for a school if it is in compliance with the regulations of the Board issued pursuant to this chapter, any fee for such license or certificate has been paid, and its facilities are approved by the Board after an inspection by the Department. No such license or certificate shall be transferable. The license or certificate shall be prominently displayed on the premises of the school in a place open for inspection by any interested person during the hours of operation.

B. Any license or certificate issued to a residential school for students with disabilities, except a provisional or conditional license or certificate issued pursuant to §22.1-323.1, which is in effect on July 1, 1992, may, upon written notification to the school, expire on a date subsequent to its stated expiration date and determined at the discretion of the Board, but in no case later than three years from the effective date. Licenses and certificates issued to residential schools for students with disabilities which are effective on or after July 1, 1992, may be issued for periods of up to three successive years. Licenses may be issued to private day special education schools for periods up to three successive years.

C. The Superintendent or his authorized agents shall make at least one unannounced inspection of each residential school for students with disabilities each year.

§22.1-331. Violations.

Any person who opens, operates or conducts any school without a certificate required by this chapter shall be guilty of a Class 2 misdemeanor. Each day such person permits the school to be open and operate without such a certificate shall constitute a separate offense.

TITLE 23
EDUCATIONAL INSTITUTIONS
(Selected Chapters)

CHAPTER 1
GENERAL PROVISIONS
(Selected Section)

§23-9.2:4. Payments to institutions of higher education for certain courses taken by law-enforcement officers.

The State Department of Criminal Justice Services is hereby authorized and directed to enter into contracts to make payments to accredited institutions of higher education within this Commonwealth for tuition, books and mandatory fees for law-enforcement officers of the Commonwealth, or its political subdivisions, departments or authorities, or of any county, city or town thereof enrolled on a full-time or part-time basis in courses included in an undergraduate or graduate program which leads to a degree or certificate in an area related to law enforcement or an area suitable for law-enforcement officers. No payments shall be made pursuant to this section to any institution of higher education operating within this Commonwealth whose primary campus is outside this Commonwealth. Assistance under this section may be granted only on behalf of an applicant who enters into an agreement to continue to serve as a law-enforcement officer in Virginia upon completion of his course of study for a period at least as long as the length of the course of study undertaken and paid for under the provisions of this section, and in the event such service is not completed, to repay the full amount of such payments on the terms and in the manner the State Department of Criminal Justice Services may prescribe.

Any person receiving the benefit of funds expended pursuant to this section shall be required to make reimbursement of such funds if he fails to satisfactorily complete the course or courses for which the funds were expended.

Any reimbursement of money advanced under the provisions of this section shall be returned to the State Department of Criminal Justice Services and used in accordance with the purposes of this section.

CHAPTER 17
CAMPUS POLICE DEPARTMENTS
(Complete Chapter)

§23-232. Establishment authorized; employment of officers.

A. The governing board of each public institution of higher learning named in §23-14, hereafter sometimes referred to in this chapter as "institution," is authorized to establish a campus police department and to employ campus police officers and auxiliary forces upon appointment as provided in §§23-233 and 23-233.1. Such employment shall be governed by the Virginia Personnel Act, as set forth in Chapter 10 (§2.1-110 et seq.) of Title 2.1.

B. The Virginia Commonwealth University Health System Authority shall be authorized to employ police officers and auxiliary forces as provided in this chapter and in §23-50.15:11, except that the employment of such officers and forces shall not be governed by the Virginia Personnel Act (§2.1-110 et seq.).

(Chgd. by L.1996 chs. 905, 1046; L.2000 ch. 720, eff. 7/1/2000.)

§23-232.1. Authorization for campus police departments in private institutions of higher education.

The governing board of each private institution of higher education is authorized to establish, in compliance with the provisions of this chapter, a campus police department and to employ campus police officers upon appointment as provided in §23-233. Except as such provisions apply exclusively to public institutions or employees, the provisions of this chapter shall apply to the appointment and employment of officers, operation, powers, duties and jurisdiction of private campus police departments, and such departments shall be subject to and enjoy the benefits of this chapter. However, to be qualified to use the word "police" to describe the department or its officers, any private college or university which establishes a campus police department shall require that each officer comply with the training or other requirements for law-enforcement officers established by the Department of Criminal Justice Services pursuant to Chapter 27 (§9-167 et seq.) of Title 9.

§23-232.2. Inspection of criminal incident information.

A. Criminal incident information, as described in subsection B, of any campus police department established pursuant to §23-232.1, shall be open to inspection and copying by any (i) citizen of the Commonwealth, (ii) currently registered student of the institution, or (iii) parent of a registered student, during the regular office hours of the custodian of such information.

B. Criminal incident information shall include (i) the date, time, and general location of the alleged crime; (ii) a general description of injuries suffered or property damaged or stolen; and (iii) the name and address of any individual arrested as a result of felonies committed against persons or property or misdemeanors involving assault, battery, or moral turpitude reported to the campus police, except where disclosure is prohibited by law; however, where the release of such information is likely to jeopardize an ongoing criminal investigation or the safety of an individual, cause a suspect to flee or evade detection, or result in the destruction of evidence, such information may be withheld until the above-referenced damage is no longer likely to occur from the release of such information.

§23-233. Appointment of officers.

Upon application of the governing board of an institution, the circuit court of the county or city wherein the institution is located, in its discretion, may, by order, appoint the persons named in the application to be campus police officers at such institution.

§23-233.1. Establishment of auxiliary police forces; power, authority and immunities generally.

The governing boards, for the further preservation of public peace, safety and good order of the campus community, shall have the power to establish, equip, and maintain auxiliary police forces. When called into service pursuant to procedures established by the governing board, members of these auxiliary forces shall have all the powers, authority, and immunities of public institutions of higher education campus police officers.

§23-234. Powers and duties; jurisdiction.

A campus police officer appointed as provided in §23-233 or appointed and activated pursuant to §23-233.1 may exercise the powers and duties conferred by law upon police officers of cities, towns, or counties, and shall be so deemed, including but not limited to the provisions of Chapters 5 (§19.2-52 et seq.), 7 (§19.2-71 et seq.), and 23 (§19.2-387 et seq.) of Title 19.2, (i) upon any property owned or controlled by the relevant public or private institution of higher education, or, upon request, any property owned or controlled by another public or private institution of higher education and upon the streets, sidewalks, and highways, immediately adjacent thereto, (ii) pursuant to a mutual aid agreement provided for in §15.2-1727 between the governing board of a public or private institution and such other institution of higher education, public or private, in the Commonwealth or adjacent political subdivisions, (iii) in close pursuit of a person as provided in §19.2-77, and (iv) upon approval by the appropriate circuit court of a petition for concurrent jurisdiction in designated areas with the police officers of the county, city, or town in which the institution, its satellite campuses, or other properties are located.

§23-234.1. Extending police power of public institutions of higher education beyond boundaries thereof; jurisdiction of courts.

A. The governing board of any public institution of higher education that leases, rents, or owns satellite campuses, public buildings, and other property located beyond the limits of such institution shall have and may exercise full police power over these properties and over persons using the same. The governing board may prescribe rules and regulations for the operation and use of these properties and for the conduct of all persons using them and may provide appropriate administrative penalties for the violation of these rules and regulations.

B. The district court for the county, city, or town where violations of law or approved regulations of the institution occurs shall have the jurisdiction of all cases arising within the county, city, or town.

It shall be the duty of the attorney for the Commonwealth for the county, city, or town where the offenses occurs to prosecute all violators of the laws pertaining to the provisions enumerated in this chapter.

§23-235. Officers to comply with requirements of Department of Criminal Justice Services.

All persons appointed and employed as campus police officers or as members of auxiliary forces pursuant to this chapter shall comply with the requirements for law-enforcement officers as established by the Department of Criminal Justice Services pursuant to Chapter 27 (§9-167 et seq.) of Title 9.

§23-236. Investigation of prospective officers; terms of employment; uniforms, etc.

A. Prior to appointment as a campus police officer or member of an auxiliary force, each person shall be investigated by the campus police department of the institution applying for the order of appointment or, if none has been established, by the police department of the county, city or town in which such institution is located. Such investigation shall determine whether the person is responsible, honest and in all ways capable of performing the duties of a campus police officer.

B. Each campus police officer and member of an auxiliary force appointed and employed pursuant to this chapter shall be a state employee of the institution named in the order of appointment. Insofar as not inconsistent with the Virginia Personnel Act (§2.1-110 et seq.), the governing board of such institution shall provide for the conditions and terms of employment and compensation and provide a distinctive uniform and badge of office.

§23-237. Termination of employment of officers.

A person appointed as a campus police officer shall exercise his powers only as long as he remains employed or activated, as the case may be, by the institution named in the order of the appointment. The appointment order entered by the circuit court shall automatically be revoked upon the termination of the officer's employment at the institution and may be revoked by the court for malfeasance, misfeasance, or nonfeasance. The institution shall notify the court upon termination of the officer's employment at the institution.

§23-238. Security departments and other security services.

Nothing in this chapter shall abridge the authority of the governing board of an institution to establish security departments, whose officers and employees shall not have the powers and duties set forth in §23-234, in place of or supplemental to campus police departments or to rely upon municipal, county or state police forces or to contract for security services from private parties.

TITLE 27
FIRE PROTECTION
(Selected Chapters)

CHAPTER 2
FIRE DEPARTMENTS AND FIRE COMPANIES
(Selected Article)

ARTICLE 1
PROVISIONS APPLICABLE TO COUNTIES, CITIES AND TOWNS
(Selected Sections)

§27-17. Entry of buildings on fire and premises adjoining.

The chief of any fire department, or company or other authorized officer in command at a fire, and his subordinates, upon his order or direction, shall have the right at any time of the day or night to enter any building or upon any premises where a fire is in progress, or any building or premises adjacent thereto for the purpose of extinguishing the same.

§27-19. Penalty for disobeying chief or other officer in command.

If any person at a fire refuse or neglect to obey any order duly given by the chief or other officer in command, he shall, upon conviction of such offense, be fined not to exceed $100.

CHAPTER 3
LOCAL FIRE MARSHALS
(Selected Sections)

§27-34. Duties and powers at fires.

Whenever any fire occurs, it shall be the duty of such fire marshal or his designated representative to be present at the same and advise and act in concert with such officers of police as may be present; and, for preserving order at and during the existence of such fire, and for the protection of property, he shall have concurrent powers with the officers of police, and the chief or other officer in charge, but shall not exercise any authority which will conflict with the powers of any chief or other officer in command of any fire department in the discharge of his special duties as such.

§27-34.2. Power to arrest, to procure and serve warrants and to issue summons; limitation on authority.

In addition to such other duties as may be prescribed by law, the local fire marshal and his assistants appointed pursuant to §27-36 shall, if authorized by the governing body of the county, city or town appointing the local fire marshal, have the authority to arrest, to procure and serve warrants of arrest and to issue summons in the manner authorized by general law for violation of fire prevention and fire safety laws and related ordinances. The authority granted in this section shall not be exercised by any local fire marshal or assistant until such person has satisfactorily completed a training course designed specifically for local fire marshals and their assistants, which course shall be approved by the Virginia Fire Services Board.

The Department of Fire Programs in cooperation with the Department of Criminal Justice Services shall have the authority to design, establish and maintain the required courses of instruction through such agencies and institutions as the Departments jointly may deem appropriate and to approve such other courses as such Departments determine appropriate.

The authority granted in this section shall not be construed to authorize a fire marshal or his assistants to wear or carry firearms.

(Chgd. by L.1997 ch. 436, eff. 7/1/97.)

§27-34.2:1. Police powers of fire marshals.

In addition to such other duties as may be prescribed by law, the local fire marshal and those assistants appointed pursuant to §27-36 designated by the fire marshal shall, if authorized by the governing body of the county, city or town appointing the local fire marshal, have the same police powers as a sheriff, police officer or law-enforcement officer. The investigation and prosecution of all offenses involving hazardous material, fires, fire bombings, bombings, attempts or threats to commit such offenses, false alarms relating to such offenses, possession and manufacture of explosive devices, substances and fire bombs shall be the responsibility of the fire marshal or his designee, if authorized by the governing body of the county, city or town appointing the local fire marshal. The police powers granted in this section shall not be exercised by any local fire marshal or assistant until such person has satisfactorily completed a course for fire marshals with police powers, designed by the Department of Fire Programs in cooperation with the Department of Criminal Justice Services, which course shall be approved by the Virginia Fire Services Board.

In addition, fire marshals with police powers shall continue to exercise those powers only upon satisfactory participation in in-service and advanced courses and programs designed by the Department of Fire Programs in cooperation with the Department of Criminal Justice Services, which courses shall be approved by the Virginia Fire Services Board.

(Chgd. by L.2000 chs. 39, 390, eff. 7/1/2000.)

CHAPTER 6
DEPARTMENT OF STATE POLICE; PUBLIC BUILDING SAFETY LAW; ARSON REPORTING IMMUNITY ACT
(Selected Article)

ARTICLE 1
GENERAL PROVISIONS
(Selected Sections)

§27-55. Department of State Police or successor agency to keep record of fires and explosions; when open to public inspection.

The Department of State Police or its successor agency shall keep in its office a record of all fires occurring in the State, investigation of which is provided for in this article, together with all facts, statistics and circumstances concerning the same, including the origin of the fires. Such records shall not be open to public inspection, except insofar as the Department shall permit otherwise. Whenever the word "Department" appears in this article it shall be deemed to mean the Department of State Police or its successor agency in the Office of Public Safety.

§27-56. Department to examine into origin of fires; appointment of arson investigators.

The Department shall examine, or cause examination to be made, into the origin and circumstances of all fires occurring in this State, which may be brought to its attention by official report, or otherwise, and for that purpose shall have authority to call for and demand of the chief or other head officer of the fire department. and the chief or other head officer of the police department, of any city or town, and the sheriff of any county, for any information or assistance it may require in making or furthering such examination.

The Department shall appoint a chief arson investigator and assistant arson investigators, who shall have the same police powers as a sheriff in the investigation and prosecution of all offenses involving fires, fire bombings, bombings, attempts, threats to commit such offense, false alarms relating to any such offense, possession and manufacture of explosive devices, substances and firebombs.

§27-58. Right to examine buildings or premises.

The Department, and such person or persons as it may appoint, shall have authority at all times of the day, in the performance of the duties imposed by the provisions of §27-56, to enter upon and examine any building or premises where any fire has occurred, and any other buildings or premises immediately adjoining the same; provided, that such adjoining building is not at the time occupied and used as a dwelling house.

§27-59. Criminal prosecutions.

If the Department shall be of opinion, after investigation as to the cause or origin of any fire, that there is sufficient evidence to charge any person with the crime of arson, or with incendiary burning of property, it shall furnish to the Commonwealth's attorney of the city or county all such evidence, together with the names of witnesses, and all information obtained by it, including a copy of all pertinent and material testimony taken by it touching such offense.

§27-60. Department to conduct investigations in certain cases; investigations may be private.

The Department may petition an appropriate judicial officer to summons and compel the attendance of witnesses to testify in relation to any matter which is, by the provisions of this chapter, a subject of inquiry and investigation. It may also administer oaths and affirmations to such witnesses, and false swearing in any such matter shall be deemed perjury, and shall be punished as such. It may in its discretion take or cause to be taken the testimony on oath of all persons supposed to be cognizant of any facts or to have means of knowledge in relation to the matters as to which any examination is, in this chapter, required to be made, and shall cause the same to be reduced to writing. Investigations in relation to such matters may, in the discretion of the Department, be private, and persons other than those required to be present by the provisions of this chapter may be excluded from that place where such examination is held, and witnesses may be kept separate and apart from each other, and not allowed to communicate with each other until they have been examined.

§27-61. When Department or fire chief may remedy inflammable or unsafe conditions.

The Department of Housing and Community Development, by its representative, or the chief or other head of the fire department of any county, city or town or district thereof, shall have the right, at all reasonable hours, for the purpose of examination, to enter into and upon any public school building or any other building or premises not at the time occupied and used as a dwelling house, within their respective jurisdictions, for examination as to combustible materials or inflammable or unsafe conditions in any such building or upon any such premises. Upon complaint of any person having an interest in any building or premises or property adjacent thereto, in his jurisdiction, an officer shall make an immediate investigation as to the presence of any combustible materials or the existence of inflammable or unsafe conditions in such buildings or upon such premises. Whenever any officer finds in any building or upon any premises combustible, inflammable or unsafe conditions, dangerous to the safety of the building or premises, or other property, he shall order the same to be removed or remedied, and the order shall, within a reasonable time to be fixed in the order, be complied with by the owner or occupant of the building or premises.

Any owner or occupant aggrieved by such order may within five days after notice of such order, appeal to the Department of Housing and Community Development, and the cause of his complaint shall be at once investigated by the Director of the Department of Housing and Community Development, and unless by its authority such order is revoked, the order shall remain in force and the owner or occupant shall comply with the order.

Any owner or occupant of any building or premises failing to comply with any final order made or given under the authority of this section, shall be deemed guilty of a misdemeanor, and punished by a fine of not less than $5 nor more than $100 for each offense.

§27-62. Penalty on local officers for violating law.

Any city, town or county officer referred to in this article who willfully neglects or refuses to comply with any of the requirements of this article shall be deemed guilty of a misdemeanor, and upon conviction thereof, be punished by a fine of not less than $5, nor more than $100.

CHAPTER 9
STATEWIDE FIRE PREVENTION CODE ACT
(Selected Sections)

§27-96. Statewide standards.

The purposes of this chapter are to provide for statewide standards for optional local enforcement to safeguard life and property from the hazards of fire or explosion arising from the improper maintenance of life safety and fire prevention and protection materials, devices, systems and structures, and the unsafe storage, handling, and use of substances, materials and devices, including explosives and blasting agents, wherever located.

§27-98.2. Issuance of warrant.

Search warrants for inspections or reinspection of buildings, structures, property, or premises subject to inspections pursuant to the Code, to determine compliance with regulations or standards set forth in the Code, shall be based upon a demonstration of probable cause and supported by affidavit. Such inspection warrants may be issued by any judge or magistrate having authority to issue criminal warrants whose territorial jurisdiction encompasses the building, structure, property or premises to be inspected or entered, if he is satisfied from the affidavit that there is probable cause for the issuance of an inspection warrant. No inspection warrant shall be issued pursuant to this chapter except upon probable cause, supported by affidavit, particularly describing the place, thing or property to be inspected, examined or tested and the purpose for which the inspection, examination, testing or collection of samples for testing is to be made. Probable cause shall be deemed to exist if such inspection, examination, testing or collection of samples for testing are necessary to ensure compliance with the Fire Prevention Code for the protection of life and property from the hazards of fire or explosion. The supporting affidavit shall contain either a statement that consent to inspect, examine, test or collect samples for testing has been sought and refused or facts or circumstances reasonably justify the failure to seek consent in order to enforce effectively the fire safety laws, regulation or standards of the Commonwealth which authorize such inspection, examination, testing or collection of samples for testing. In the case of an inspection warrant based upon legislative or administrative standards for selecting buildings, structures, property or premises for inspections, the affidavit shall contain factual allegations sufficient to justify an independent determination by the judge or magistrate that the inspection program is based on reasonable standards and that the standards are being applied to a particular place in a neutral and fair manner. The issuing judge or magistrate may examine the affiant under oath or affirmation to verify the accuracy of any matter in the affidavit.

§27-98.3. Duration of warrant.

An inspection warrant shall be effective for the time specified therein, for a period of not more than seven days, unless extended or renewed by the judicial officer who signed and issued the original warrant. The judicial officer may extend or renew the inspection warrant upon application for extension or renewal setting forth the results which have been obtained or a reasonable explanation of the failure to obtain such results. The extension or renewal period of the warrant shall not exceed seven days. The warrant shall be executed and returned to the judicial officer by whom it was issued within the time specified in the warrant or within the extended or renewed time. The return shall list any samples taken pursuant to the warrant. After the expiration of such time, the warrant, unless executed, shall be void.

§27-100. Violation a misdemeanor.

It shall be unlawful for any owner or any other person, firm, or corporation, on or after the effective date of any Code provisions, to violate any provisions of the Fire Prevention Code. Any such violation shall be deemed a Class 1 misdemeanor, and any owner, or any other person, firm, or corporation convicted of such violation shall be punished in accordance with the provisions of §18.2-11.

TITLE 28.2
FISHERIES AND HABITAT OF THE TIDAL WATERS
(Selected Subtitles)

SUBTITLE I
GENERAL PROVISIONS RELATING TO MARINE RESOURCES COMMISSION
(Selected Chapter)

CHAPTER 1
ADMINISTRATION
(Selected Articles)

ARTICLE 1
COMMISSION; COMMISSIONER
(Selected Section)

§28.2-100. Definitions.

As used in this title, unless the context requires a different meaning:

"Commission" means the Marine Resources Commission.

"Commissioner" means the Commissioner of Marine Resources.

"Fish" or "marine fish" means those finfish species which spend a major portion of their lives in marine or estuarine waters. Sunfish, crappies, and carp are not considered to be marine fish.

"Fishing", "fisheries" or "to fish" means all operations involved in (i) taking or catching, (ii) using, setting or operating apparatus employed in killing, taking or catching, or (iii) transporting or preparing for market marine fish, shellfish, and marine organisms.

"Habitat" means those state-owned bottomlands, tidal wetlands and coastal primary sand dunes which are subject to regulation under Subtitle III of this title.

"Marine organisms" means those species other than marine finfish or marine shellfish which inhabit marine or estuarine waters. Terrapin and marine mammals are considered to be marine organisms.

"Marine shellfish" or "shellfish" means such species of mollusca as oysters and clams, and such species of crustacea as crabs.

"Officer" means a member of the Virginia Marine Patrol.

"Territorial sea" means the waters within the belt, three nautical miles wide, that is adjacent to Virginia's coast and seaward of the mean low-water mark.

"Tidewater Virginia" means the following counties: Accomack, Arlington, Caroline, Charles City, Chesterfield, Essex, Fairfax, Gloucester, Hanover, Henrico, Isle of Wight, James City, King and Queen, King George, King William, Lancaster, Mathews, Middlesex, New Kent, Northampton, Northumberland, Prince George, Prince William, Richmond, Spotsylvania, Stafford, Surry, Westmoreland, and York; and the Cities of Alexandria, Chesapeake, Colonial Heights, Fairfax, Falls Church, Fredericksburg, Hampton, Hopewell, Newport News, Norfolk, Petersburg, Poquoson, Portsmouth, Richmond, Suffolk, Virginia Beach, and Williamsburg.

ARTICLE 2
SUPPORT ACTIVITIES
(Selected Section)

§28.2-106. Virginia Marine Patrol; law-enforcement responsibilities; qualifications; oath.

A. The law-enforcement division of the Commission shall be designated as the Virginia Marine Patrol. It shall exercise such powers and duties as the General Assembly may confer upon it by law and as provided in regulations adopted pursuant to law, including but not limited to:

1. Patrolling the tidal waters and shoreline of the Chesapeake Bay, its tidal tributaries, and territorial sea;
2. Enforcing marine fishery and habitat conservation laws and regulations;
3. Enforcing health laws pertaining to the harvesting of seafood from condemned areas.
4. Enforcing or assisting other agencies in enforcing laws pertaining to the removal of obstructions and abandoned vessels from the water, to boating operation and navigation, and to larceny on the water;
5. Providing for water-borne safety; and
6. Conducting search and rescue activities.

B. Officers of the Virginia Marine Patrol shall have the same powers as regular game wardens appointed pursuant to Chapter 2 (§29.1-200 et seq.) of Title 29.1.

C. A person shall be (i) at least twenty-one years old and (ii) a high school graduate or equivalent to qualify for appointment as an officer.

D. Each officer shall qualify before the clerk of the circuit court of the county or city in which he resides, or in which his district may be, by taking the oaths prescribed by law.

SUBTITLE II
TIDAL FISHERIES
(Selected Chapters)

CHAPTER 2
GENERAL PROVISIONS
(Selected Articles)

ARTICLE 1
POWERS AND DUTIES
(Selected Sections)

§28.2-200. Definitions.

As used in this subtitle, unless the context requires a different meaning:

"Cultured hard-shell clams" means hard-shell clams (Mercenaria mercenaria) that have been spawned in a hatchery or controlled setting for the purpose of producing seed clams (juveniles), and planted on leased grounds, floating structures, or other privately controlled growing areas, and covered with netting or otherwise protected from predators until harvested.

"Haul seine" means any net set from the shore or in shallow waters not exceeding eight feet in depth at mean low water. Every haul seine shall have one end stationary at all times while the seine is being used, except when closing the net, the stationary end may be changed.

"James River seed area" means that area in the James River and its tributaries above a line drawn from Cooper's Creek in Isle of Wight County on the south side of the James River to a line in a northeasterly direction across the James River to the Newport News municipal water tank located on Warwick Boulevard between 59th Street and 60th Street in the City of Newport News.

"Mouth of the Rappahannock River" means the area beginning at Stingray Point, Middlesex County, at the United States Army Corps of Engineers survey station "Bird," an aluminum disk set in the top of a concrete monument, being located at coordinates 453,785.17 North, 2,638,116.66 East, 1927 North American Datum – Virginia South Zone; thence 12° 52′ 35″ (grid azimuth) 20,846.73 feet to a point on the Eastern side of Windmill Point, Lancaster County, designated as Virginia Marine Resources Commission survey station "Windmill," a one and one half inch iron pipe driven flush with the ground, being located at coordinates 474,107.68 North, 2,642,762.29 East, 1927 North American Datum – Virginia South Zone.

"Pound net" means any net having a funnel mouth, round mouth or square mouth with the head exposed above the water.

"Resident" means any person who maintains his principal place of abode in Virginia with the intent to make Virginia his domicile.

"Shoals" means subaqueous elevations covered by water less than four feet deep at mean low water.

§28.2-201. Authority of Commission to make regulations, establish licenses, and prepare fishery management plans; enforcement; penalty for violation of regulation.

The Commission may:

1. Promulgate regulations, including those for taking seafood, necessary to promote the general welfare of the seafood industry and to conserve and promote the seafood and marine resources of the Commonwealth. The Commission may also promulgate regulations necessary for the conservation and reasonable use of surf clams.

2. Establish a license commensurate with other licenses in an amount not to exceed $100 for any device used for taking or catching seafood in the tidal waters of the Commonwealth when the device (i) is not otherwise licensed in this title and (ii) is used for commercial purposes. The Commission may specify, when issuing such a license, any restriction or control over the device or the person operating the device.

3. Prepare fishery management plans containing evaluations of regulatory management options, based upon scientific, economic, biological, and sociological information, and use them in the development of regulations. The Commissioner may appoint a fisheries advisory committee and its chairman, consisting of representatives of the various fishery user groups, to assist in the preparation and implementation of the fishery management plans. The Commission may expend funds to compensate the members of the committee pursuant to §14.1-5.2.

4. Provide for enforcement of any regulation governing surf clams by any law-enforcement officer of any agency of the Commonwealth or its political subdivisions or by any law-enforcement officer of any agency of the federal government. Enforcement agreements with other agencies or political subdivisions shall be stated in the regulation.
(Chgd. by L.1995 ch. 136, eff. 3/9/95.)

§28.2-205. Scientific collection permits; penalty.

A. Except as provided for in §28.2-1101, it is unlawful for any person to remove from the waters of the Commonwealth under the jurisdiction of the Commission any marine fish, marine shellfish, or marine organisms for technical research, scientific, educational or museum purposes without having first obtained from the Commissioner a collection permit.

A violation of this subsection is a Class 3 misdemeanor.

B. Application for a permit shall be made in writing to the Commissioner. There shall be no charge for a permit, and the permit shall not be transferable. The issuance of the permit shall be governed by applicable Commission regulations and shall be subject to any reasonable terms and conditions imposed by the Commissioner. The Commissioner may, with the approval of the Commission, require an applicant for such permit to submit to the Commissioner any data or results acquired through the use of the permit.

C. Any person who has been issued a scientific collection permit shall be exempt from any licensing provisions of this subtitle relating to the taking or catching of fish, shellfish, or marine organisms.

ARTICLE 5
LICENSING GENERALLY
(Selected Sections)

§28.2-225. Fishing license required; penalty.

It shall be unlawful to fish in the tidal waters of the Commonwealth or those waters under the joint jurisdiction of the Commonwealth without first obtaining the required license, subject to the exemptions set out in §28.2-226.

Any person who violates this section is guilty of a Class 1 misdemeanor.

§28.2-227. Special nonresident harvester's license; fee and oath; revocation; penalty.

A. Any nonresident desiring to take or catch marine fish, crabs or any other seafood, except oysters, clams or other mollusks, from the tidal waters of the Commonwealth for which a license is required shall pay to any officer or agent a fee for a nonresident harvester's license. The fee, to be established by the Commission, shall be no less than $350 or more than $1,150. Three hundred fifty dollars of each fee shall be credited to the Virginia Marine Products Fund as provided under §3.1-684.63. The remainder of the fee shall be credited to the Marine Fishing Improvement Fund, as established pursuant to §28.2-208.

B. The license shall be required of each boat used in Virginia's tidal waters and shall be in addition to any other licenses required for the activity involved.

C. The nonresident shall state under oath his true name and address, the name and number of the boat being licensed, and that he will not violate any of the laws of this Commonwealth governing the taking and catching of seafood.

D. A nonresident harvester's license shall be required prior to the purchase of any other license for the harvesting of seafood. Revocation of this license in accordance with §28.2-232 shall constitute revocation of any other license held by the nonresident under the provisions of this subtitle.

E. Any Virginia resident who enters into a partnership or other agreement with the intent to defeat the object of this section is guilty of a Class 1 misdemeanor.

§28.2-228. License for purchase of fish, shellfish, or marine organisms from the catcher; fee.

A. Any person, purchasing from the catcher, oysters or clams caught from the public grounds of the Commonwealth or the Potomac River, or crabs, fish, or other seafood caught from the waters of the Commonwealth or the Potomac River, shall pay a license fee of (i) fifty dollars for each place of business and (ii) twenty-five dollars for each boat or motor vehicle used for buying.

B. No license shall be required of any person purchasing seafood for personal consumption, any place of business which is solely a restaurant, or any person who operates a business which is subject to local license taxes under §58.1-3703 and who has in his possession no more than one bushel of peeler crabs to be sold as bait.

§28.2-228.1. Seafood landing licenses.

A. The Commission may by regulation establish licenses for the landing of seafood in Virginia, the fee for which shall not exceed $150. The regulations may limit the number of such licenses that may be issued and may establish eligibility criteria. Fees collected from the sale of seafood landing licenses shall be deposited to the Marine Fishing Improvement Fund established in §28.2-208.

 Zv

B. The Commission may grant exceptions to the license requirement established in subsection A to any person registered as a commercial fisherman under the provisions of §28.2-241.

C. The following shall be Class 3 misdemeanors: (i) landing seafood without the license that may be required under this section and (ii) failure to produce or have available for inspection the license that may be required under this section when requested by any officer. Failure to produce the license is prima facie evidence that the person is landing seafood without a license.

(Added by L.1996 ch. 214, eff. 7/1/96.)

§28.2-229. When licenses terminate; proration and refund not permitted.

A. The Commission shall issue all licenses on an annual basis. All licenses shall be valid from January 1 of each year or their later date of purchase and expire on December 31 of the year in which issued.

B. Refunds shall not be made or prorated if the fishing effort is reduced, or seasons are closed (i) in order to promote conservation of the fisheries or (ii) due to natural conditions. Refunds shall not be made for any license that is suspended or revoked.

§28.2-230. Penalty for false statements or altering a fishing license; penalty.

It shall be unlawful for any person to (i) subscribe to a materially false statement in applying to secure a license to fish or (ii) alter of change such license.

A violation of this section shall be a Class 1 misdemeanor.

§28.2-231. Exhibition of license; display to officers; penalty.

Any person engaged in fishing shall have the required license available for inspection and shall present such license when requested by an officer. Failure to present the license upon request of any officer is a Class 1 misdemeanor and prima facie evidence that the person is fishing without a license.

§28.2-232. Revocation of licenses.

The Commission may revoke and prohibit the issuance, reissuance, or renewal of any licenses if, after a hearing held after ten days' notice to the applicant or licensee, it finds that the person has violated any provision of this subtitle.

The duration of the revocation and prohibition shall be fixed by the Commission up to a maximum of two years, taking into account (i) evidence of repeated or habitual disregard for conservation, health and safety laws and regulations; (ii) abusive conduct and behavior toward officers; and (iii) the severity of any damage that has occurred, or might have occurred, to the natural resources, the public health, or the seafood industry.

An appeal from the Commission's decision may be taken to the courts as provided in Article 3 (§28.2-216 et seq.) of this chapter.

ARTICLE 6
MARKING OF BOATS, NETS AND OTHER DEVICES
(Complete Article)

Section

§28.2-233. License tags or identification generally.

The Commission shall provide metal license tags or identification numbers to licensees in a form and manner prescribed by the Commission.

§28.2-234. License tags and identification numbers to be fastened; penalty.

A. License tags or identification numbers shall be attached and displayed in the following manner:

1. License tags for fixed fishery devices, including pound nets, fyke nets, crab traps, and staked gill nets, shall be fastened to one of the offshore stakes.

2. License tags for anchored gill nets and drift gill nets shall be fastened to a flagstaff or a buoy that is visible from the surface.

3. License tags for vessels using haul seines, purse nets, trawl nets, crab pots, trotlines, and crab scrapes shall be fastened at a conspicuous place on the starboard side or the mast of the vessel.

4. License tags issued for businesses purchasing seafood shall be affixed in a conspicuous place on the business establishment, boat or motor vehicle.

5. Identification numbers when issued for particular devices shall be applied by the license holder and shall be in place at all times when the gear is deployed.

B. Any such licensee who fails to properly attach or display such a license tag or identification number is guilty of a Class 1 misdemeanor.

§28.2-235. Duty to apply for new tag in case of loss; penalty.

Should the metal tag required by §28.2-234 be removed or destroyed by accident, by the force of the sea, or in any other casual manner, the licensee shall apply for a new tag within twenty-four hours after the discovery of the destruction or loss of the original tag. Failure to do so is a Class 3 misdemeanor.

§28.2-236. Seizure of unmarked devices.

Any fishing device not marked, tagged or identified in the required manner may be seized by an officer and held for any forthcoming legal proceeding.

§28.2-237. Removal of abandoned pole or stake; revocation of licenses for failure to remove stakes.

A. Any person fishing a pound net or any other type of fishing device requiring the use of fixed poles or stakes shall remove all such abandoned poles or stakes; however, one pole or stake may be left standing at least four feet above mean high water at old stands as an identification marker.

Abandoned poles or stakes are considered to be poles or stakes which are not used for fishing.

B. The Commission may revoke any fishing licenses issued to such person, as set forth in §28.2-232, if abandoned poles or stakes are not promptly removed. Failure to remove such poles or stakes is a Class 1 misdemeanor. The most recent licensee for the fishing device is responsible for removing the poles or stakes.

§28.2-238. Concealing name or number of vessel; penalty.

Any captain or owner who covers or conceals the name, registration number, or fishing license tag of any boat licensed and engaged in the fisheries under this subtitle is guilty of a Class 1 misdemeanor.

§28.2-239. Exemption from article.

Nothing in this article applies to boats used purely for recreation, or for taking fish or shellfish by rod and line or with hand lines, for family use only.

ARTICLE 7
REGISTRATION OF COMMERCIAL FISHERMEN
(Selected Sections)

§28.2-241. Registration of commercial fishermen required; exemption; penalty.

A. On and after January 1, 1993, holders of gear licenses, except those issued pursuant of §28.2-402, issued January 1, 1992, through December 31, 1992, shall register as commercial fishermen as provided for in regulation.

B. *(Repealed.)*

C. On and after January 1, 1993, fishermen not registered as commercial fishermen but who desire to sell their catch shall apply to the Commission for registration as commercial fishermen. The effective date of status as a commercial fisherman shall be two years from the date the application is approved by the Commission. A person whose registration as a commercial fisherman is not effective shall not sell, trade or barter his catch or give his catch to another in order that it may be sold, traded or bartered.

D. For purposes of this section and §§28.2-242, 28.2-243 and 28.2-244, "commercial fisherman" means any person who fishes in tidal waters using any gear and who sells, trades or barters his catch or gives his catch to another in order that it may be sold, traded or bartered. The Commission shall provide, by regulation, for exemptions from the definition of "commercial fisherman" those persons who independently sell, trade or barter minnows and who are not part of, hired by, or engaged in a continuing business enterprise as may be defined by the Commission. Such regulation may include, but is not limited to, limits on the quantity of minnows that may be sold, traded or bartered by a person that may be exempted from the definition of commercial fisherman.

E. The cost of registration as a commercial fisherman shall be $150 annually, due no later than the effective date of registration; however, the cost of registration for a person seventy years of age or older shall be seventy-five dollars. All fees collected from the registration of commercial fishermen shall be deposited in the state treasury and credited to the Marine Fishing Improvement Fund as established in §28.2-208.

F. Registrations of commercial fishermen shall not be transferable.

G. Whenever a court finds that a defendant has violated any of the provisions of this section, the court shall assess a civil penalty of $500. All civil penalties assessed pursuant to this section shall be paid into the Marine Fishing Improvement Fund as established in §28.2-208.

H. Only commercial fishermen with valid registrations may purchase licenses pursuant to §§28.2-301, 28.2-501 and 28.2-702.

I. Persons who have obtained a recreational gear license pursuant to §28.2-226.1 or §28.2-302.1 are exempt from the provisions of this section.

(Chgd. by L.1996 ch. 277, eff. 7/1/96.)

§28.2-244. Purchase of shellfish or finfish; penalty.

A person shall not purchase shellfish or finfish from any fisherman who is known by such person to have not registered as a commercial fisherman as required by §28.2-241. Whenever a court finds that a defendant has violated the provisions of this section, the court shall assess a civil penalty of $500. All civil penalties assessed pursuant to this section shall be paid into the Marine Fishing Improvement Fund as established in §28.2-208.

CHAPTER 8
HEALTH AND SANITATION PROVISIONS
(Selected Article)

ARTICLE 2
CONTROL OF CRUSTACEA, FINFISH AND SHELLFISH; VIOLATIONS AND PENALTIES
(Selected Sections)

§28.2-810. Removal, transportation, etc., from polluted ground; penalty.

A. It is unlawful for any person to take, catch, transport, sell, offer for sale, remove, receive, keep or store shellfish from condemned areas, or relay shellfish taken from such areas, until the Commissioner of Marine Resources or his designee has issued a special permit. The permittee shall carry the permit when engaged in such operation.

B. It is unlawful for any person to take or remove shellfish from private grounds in condemned areas without written authority in his possession from the owner or lessee, in addition to the permit required by subsection A of this section.

C. It is unlawful for any person to transport, relay, or move shellfish from condemned areas after sunset or before sunrise, except by motor vehicle properly sealed as required by §28.2-812. It is unlawful to mix clean shellfish and shellfish from condemned areas in the same cargo.

§28.2-821. Violations; penalty.

A. It is unlawful for any person to have in his possession, to store, to sell, or to offer for sale any shellfish which have been removed or taken from a condemned area other than as provided in §28.2-810. Any person who violates this section or any provision of this chapter is guilty of a Class 1 misdemeanor.

B. Upon conviction of violating any provision of this chapter any boat, vessel, motor vehicle or equipment used in committing the violation may be forfeited as provided by the provisions of Chapter 9 (§19.2-369 et seq.) of Title 19.2.

§28.2-825. Importing fish, shellfish or crustacea for introduction into waters of the Commonwealth; penalty.

A. It shall be unlawful for any person to import any fish, shell fish or crustacea into the Commonwealth with the intent of placing such fish, shellfish or crustacea into the waters of the Commonwealth unless one of the following conditions exists:

1. The fish, shellfish or crustacea are coming from within the continental United States from a state or waters which are on the Marine Resources Commission's list of approved states and waters, and are species which are on the Marine Resources Commission's list of approved species; or

2. The person has notified the Commissioner of Marine Resources of such intent and has received written permission from the Commissioner of Marine Resources.

The list of approved states and waters shall be published by the Commissioner of Marine Resources, and a state or water shall be placed on or removed from such list only with the concurrence of the Director of the Virginia Institute of Marine Science. The Commissioner of Marine Resources, with the concurrence of the Director of the Virginia Institute of Marine Science, is authorized to change the list when he determines that it is necessary for the protection of the waters of the Commonwealth.

The list of approved species shall be published by the Commissioner of Marine Resources, and a species shall be placed on or removed from such list only with the concurrence of the Director of the Virginia Institute or Marine Science. The Commissioner of Marine Resources, with the concurrence of the Director of the Virginia Institute of Marine Science, is authorized to change the list when he determines that it is necessary for the protection of the waters of the Commonwealth.

B. The notification of intent to import shall be in writing and submitted to the Commissioner of Marine Resources at least thirty days prior to the date of importation. The notice shall state: (i) the specific fish, shellfish or crustacea to be imported, (ii) from what waters the fish, shellfish or crustacea are being taken, (iii) the period of time over which importation is to be accomplished, (iv) the quantities involved, and (v) into what waters the fish, shellfish or crustacea are to be placed.

A violation of this section is a Class 1 misdemeanor.

CHAPTER 9
ENFORCEMENT OF SUBTITLE II; JURISDICTION
(Complete Chapter)

§28.2-900. Arrest with or without warrant; larceny; violations of boating laws and Title 62.1.

A. Officers may, with or without warrant, (i) arrest any person violating any provision of this subtitle, (ii) seize any net, pot, or other fishing device or gear used in violating such laws and (iii) seize fish, shellfish or marine organisms taken or handled in violation of this subtitle. Each seized property shall be forfeited to the Commonwealth. The forfeiture shall be enforced as provided in Chapter 22 (§19.2-369 et seq.) of Title 19.2. The officer seizing the property to be forfeited shall immediately give notice to the attorney for the Commonwealth.

B. All officers may arrest, with or without a warrant, any person who commits in his presence (i) and larceny committed upon or adjacent to the waters of the Commonwealth, (ii) any violation of the provisions of Chapter 7 of Title 29.1, of any regulations promulgated thereunder, or (iii) any violation of the provisions of Chapter 18 (§62.1-187 et seq.) or 20 (§62.1-194 et seq.) or Title 62.1.

§28.2-901. Summons issued instead of being taken into custody; failure to appear.

A. Whenever any person is detained by or is in the custody of an arresting officer for any violation of the laws enforceable pursuant to §28.2-900, the arresting officer shall take the name and address of each person detained and issue a summons or otherwise notify him in writing to appear at a time and court to be specified in the summons or notice. When the person gives his written promise to appear at the designated time and place, the officer shall immediately release him from custody.

B. If the arresting officer (i) believes a detained person is likely to disregard a summons issued under the provisions of this section or (ii) reasonably believes a detained person is likely to harm himself or another, or if the person refuses to give his written promise to appear, the officer may take the offender, vessel and property into custody. The person shall be brought before the nearest or most accessible judicial officer or other person qualified to admit bail having jurisdiction.

C. The failure of any person to appear as required by a summons issued under the provisions of this section shall suspend all licenses issued to the person pursuant to this subtitle until such time as he appears to answer the charges against him. Failure to appear shall bar the issuance of any further license to the person until he appears.

§28.2-902. Procedure after arrest and seizure.

Any person arrested may be (i) taken before a court of competent jurisdiction for trail, (ii) committed to jail pending trial, (iii) admitted to bail or released on recognizance as provided by general law, or (iv) issued a summons requiring him to appear for trial. The time specified in the summons shall not be less than five days from the date of arrest unless such person requests an earlier hearing. Any person failing to appear as directed in the summons shall be guilty of a Class 1 misdemeanor, regardless of the disposition of, and in addition to, the charge upon which he was originally arrested. If the person fails to appear, a warrant for his arrest may be issued.

Any property seized under the provisions of subsection A of §28.2-900 may be held by the officer or other official who made the seizure, pending final outcome of the legal proceedings.

§28.2-903. Violations constitute misdemeanor.

A violation of any provisions of this subtitle or regulation promulgated thereunder, unless otherwise specifically provided, is a Class 3 misdemeanor. A second or subsequent violation of any provision of this subtitle or regulation promulgated thereunder committed by the same person within twelve months of a prior violation is a Class 1 misdemeanor.

§28.2-903.1. Impeding lawful fishing in tidal waters; penalty.

A. It is unlawful for any person to willfully and intentionally impede the lawful fishing of any species of fish or shellfish. "Fishing" means those activities defined in §28.2-100 as "fishing," "fisheries" or "to fish."

B. Notwithstanding any other provision of law, any person convicted of a violation of this section shall be guilty of a Class 3 misdemeanor.
(Added by L.1997 ch. 703, eff. 7/1/97.)

§28.2-904. Pursuit and detention across the Maryland – Virginia line.
When, in the opinion of the legally constituted authorities of the Commonwealth, there has occurred on the waters of Virginia a violation of the laws of the Commonwealth enforceable pursuant to §28.2-900, or when, in the opinion of the legally constituted authorities of Maryland, there has occurred on the waters of Maryland a violation of any provisions of the Natural Resources Article, Annotated Code of Maryland, the offender may be pursued by the legally constituted authorities of the state where the offense was committed up to and across the Maryland – Virginia boundary into the state where the offender flees. If a capture is made in continuous pursuit, the offender, vessel and property shall be dealt with as authorized by the laws of the state where the offense was committed.

The provisions of this section shall be effective as long as the State of Maryland has in force similar provisions authorizing legally constituted authorities of Virginia to make pursuit and arrests in Maryland for violations of the laws of Virginia.

§28.2-905. Resistance to officer or authorized person, etc., penalty.
Any person found guilty of resisting or impeding an officer or other person authorized to make arrests, seizures, examinations or other performances of duties under this subtitle, shall be guilty of a Class 1 misdemeanor.

§28.2-906. Failure to perform duty; penalty.
The failure of any officer or other person to perform any duty required of him by any provision of this subtitle is a Class 1 misdemeanor.

§28.2-907. Jurisdiction of courts.
Any proceeding under any section of this subtitle shall be before a court of competent jurisdiction in the county or city (i) in which the offense was committed or (ii) adjacent to the waters in which the offense was committed.

TITLE 29.1
GAME, INLAND FISHERIES AND BOATING
(Selected Chapters)

Chapter

CHAPTER 1
ADMINISTRATION OF GAME AND INLAND FISHERIES
(Selected Article)

Article

ARTICLE 1
GENERAL PROVISIONS
(Selected Section)

Section

§29.1-100. Definitions.
As used in this title, or in any of the regulations of the Board, unless the context clearly requires a different meaning:

"Bag or creel limit" means the quantity of game, fish or fur-bearing animals that may be taken, caught, or possessed during a period fixed by the Board.

"Board" means the Board of Game and Inland Fisheries.

"Closed season" means that period of time fixed by the Board during which wild animals, birds or fish may not be taken, captured, killed, pursued, hunted, trapped or possessed.

"Department" means the Department of Game and Inland Fisheries.

"Director" means the Director of the Department of Game and Inland Fisheries.

"Fishing" means taking, capturing, killing, or attempting to take, capture or kill any fish in and upon the inland waters of this Commonwealth.

"Fur-bearing animals" includes beaver, bobcat, fox, mink, muskrat, opossum, otter, raccoon, skunk, and weasel.

"Game" means wild animals and wild birds that are commonly hunted for sport or food.

"Game animals" means deer, bear, rabbit, fox, squirrel, bobcat and raccoon.

"Game fish" means trout (including all Salmonidae), all of the sunfish family (including largemouth bass, smallmouth bass and spotted bass, rock bass, bream, bluegill and crappie), walleye or pike perch, white bass, chain pickerel or jackfish, muskellunge, and northern pike, wherever such fish are found in the waters of this Commonwealth and rockfish or striped bass where found above tidewaters or in streams which are blocked from access from tidewaters by dams.

"Game warden" means supervising wardens, and regular and special game wardens.

"Hunting and trapping" includes the act of or the attempted act of taking, hunting, trapping, pursuing, chasing, shooting, snaring or netting birds or animals, and assisting any person who is hunting, trapping or attempting to do so regardless of whether birds or animals are actually taken; however, when hunting and trapping are allowed, reference is made to such acts as being conducted by lawful means and in a lawful manner. The Board of Game and Inland Fisheries may authorize by regulation the pursuing or chasing of wild birds or wild animals during any closed hunting season where persons have no intent to take such birds or animals.

"Lawful," "by law," or "law" means the statutes of this Commonwealth or regulations adopted by the Board which the Director is empowered to enforce.

"Migratory game birds" means doves, ducks, brant, geese, swan, coot, gallinules, sora and other rails, snipe, woodcock and other species of birds on which open hunting seasons are set by federal regulations.

"Nonmigratory game birds" means grouse, bobwhite quail, turkey and all species of birds introduced into the Commonwealth by the Board.

"Nuisance species" means blackbirds, crows, cowbirds, grackles, English sparrows, starlings, or those species designated as such by regulations of the Board, and those species found committing or about to commit depredation upon ornamental or shade trees, agricultural crops, wildlife, livestock or other property or when concentrated in numbers and manners as to constitute a health hazard or other nuisance. However, the term nuisance does not include (i) animals designated as endangered or threatened pursuant to §§29.1-563, 29.1-564, and 29.1-566, (ii) animals classified as game or fur-bearing animals, and (iii) those species protected by state or federal law.

"Open season" means that period of time fixed by the Board during which wild animals, wild birds and fish may be taken, captured, killed, pursued, trapped or possessed.

"Possession" means the exercise of control of any wild animal, wild bird, fish or fur-bearing animal, or any part of the carcass thereof.

"Properly licensed person" means a person who, while engaged in hunting, fishing or trapping, or in any other activity permitted under this title, in and upon the lands and inland waters of this Commonwealth, has upon his person all the licenses, permits and stamps required by law.

"Regulation" means a regulation duly adopted by the Board pursuant to the authority vested by the provisions of this title.

"Transportation" means the transportation, either upon the person or by any other means, of any wild animal or wild bird or fish.

"Wildlife" means all species of wild animals, wild birds and freshwater fish in the public waters of this Commonwealth.

CHAPTER 2
GAME WARDENS
(Selected Sections)

§29.1-202. Ex officio wardens.

All sheriffs, police officers or other peace officers of this Commonwealth shall be ex officio game wardens.

§29.1-203. Jurisdiction; power to serve process.

Game wardens shall have jurisdiction throughout the Commonwealth to enforce the hunting, trapping and inland fish laws and may serve process in all matters arising from violations of such laws.

§29.1-205. Power to make arrests.

All game wardens are vested with the authority, upon displaying a badge or other credential of office, to issue a summons or to arrest any person found in the act of violating any of the provisions of the hunting, trapping, inland fish and boating laws.

Regular game wardens are vested with the same authority as sheriffs and other law-enforcement officers to enforce all of the criminal laws of the Commonwealth.

Any special game warden shall have general police power while performing his duty on properties owned or controlled by the Board.

Any commissioned, warrant or petty officers of the United States Coast Guard and of the United States Coast Guard Reserve while engaged on active duty, in the conduct of their official duties in uniform, and any officers of the customs as defined by 19 U.S.C. §1709(b), in the conduct of their official duties in uniform, shall have the same power to make arrests under Chapter 7 of Title 29.1 as game wardens.

§29.1-207. Impeding game warden, etc., in discharge of his duty.

If any person, by threats or force, attempts to intimidate or impede any law-enforcement officer enforcing the game, inland fish and boating laws, he shall, be guilty of a Class 2 misdemeanor and shall be subject to arrest by the officer and to the procedures set forth in §29.1-210.

§29.1-208. Searches and seizures.

All game wardens are vested with the authority to search any person arrested as provided in §29.1-205 together with any box, can, package, barrel or other container, hunting bag, coat, suit, trunk, grip, satchel or fish basket carried by, in the possession of, or belonging to such person. Game wardens shall also have the authority, immediately subsequent to such arrest, to enter and search any refrigerator, building, vehicle, or other place in which the officer making the search has reasonable ground to believe that the person arrested has concealed or placed any wild bird, wild animal or fish, which will furnish evidence of a violation of the hunting, trapping and inland fish laws. Such a search may be made without a warrant, except that a dwelling may not be searched without a warrant. Should any container as described in this section reveal any wild bird, wild animal or fish, or any part thereof, which has been illegally taken, possessed, sold, purchased or transported, the game warden shall seize and hold as evidence the container, together with such wild bird, wild animal or fish, and any unlawful gun, net, or other device of any kind for taking wild birds, wild animals or fish which he may find.

§29.1-209. Inspection of game and fish without arrest.

In order to see that bag or creel limits are being observed, game wardens shall also have the power to inspect game, fur-bearing animals and fish taken by any person found hunting, trapping or fishing without arresting the person.

§29.1-210. Person arrested may be committed to jail, bailed, recognized or summoned.

Any person arrested for a violation of the game, inland fish and boating laws may be committed to jail pending trial or admitted to bail or released on recognizance as provided by general law; or the arresting officer may issue a summons requiring the person to appear for trial at a time and place specified therein before a court having jurisdiction to try such offenses if the person gives his written promise to appear at the specified time. Such time shall not, however, be less than five days from the date of arrest unless the person requests an earlier hearing.

Any person refusing to give the written promise to appear shall be taken immediately by the arresting or other police officer before the nearest or most accessible judicial officer.

Any person who willfully violates his written promise to appear, given in accordance with this section, shall be guilty of a Class 2 misdemeanor.

CHAPTER 3
LICENSES
(Selected Article)

ARTICLE 1
HUNTING, TRAPPING AND FISHING LICENSES
(Selected Sections)

§29.1-300. Unlawful to hunt, trap or fish without license.

It shall be unlawful to hunt, trap or fish in or on the lands or inland waters of this Commonwealth without first obtaining a license, subject to the exceptions set out in §29.1-301.

§29.1-301. Exemptions from license requirements.

A. No license shall be required of landowners, their spouses, or their children and minor grandchildren, resident or nonresident, to hunt, trap and fish within the boundaries of their own lands and inland waters or while within such boundaries or upon any private permanent extension therefrom, to fish in any abutting public waters.

B. No license shall be required of any stockholder owning fifty percent or more of the stock of any domestic corporation owning land in this Commonwealth, his or her spouse and children and minor grandchildren, resident or nonresident, to hunt, trap and fish within the boundaries of lands and inland waters owned by the domestic corporation.

C. No license shall be required of bona fide tenants, renters or lessees to hunt, trap or fish within the boundaries of the lands or waters on which they reside or while within such boundaries or upon any private permanent extension therefrom, to fish in any abutting public waters if such individuals have the written consent of the landlord upon their person. A guest of the owner of a private fish pond shall not be required to have a fishing license to fish in such pond.

D. No license shall be required of resident persons under sixteen years old to fish.

D1. No license shall be required of resident persons under twelve years old to hunt, provided such person is accompanied and directly supervised by an adult who has, on his person, a valid Virginia hunting license as described in subsection B of §29.1-300.1.

E. No license shall be required of a resident person sixty-five years of age or over to hunt or trap on private property in the county or city in which he resides. An annual license at a fee of one dollar shall be required of a resident person sixty-five years of age or older to fish in any inland waters of the Commonwealth which shall be in addition to a license to fish for trout as specified in subsection B of §29.1-310. A resident sixty-five years of age or older may, upon proof of age satisfactory to the Department and the payment of a one-dollar fee, apply for and receive from any authorized agent of the Department a nontransferable annual license permitting such person to hunt or an annual license permitting such person to trap in all cities and counties of the Commonwealth. Any lifetime license issued pursuant to this article prior to July 1, 1988, shall remain valid for the lifetime of the person to whom it was issued. Any license issued pursuant to this section includes any damage stamp required pursuant to Article 3 (§29.1-352 et seq.) of this chapter.

F. No license to fish, except for trout as provided in subsection B of §29.1-310, shall be required of nonresident persons under twelve years of age when accompanied by a person possessing a valid license to fish in Virginia.

G. No license shall be required to trap rabbits with box traps.

H. No license shall be required of resident persons under sixteen years of age to trap when accompanied by any person eighteen years of age or older who possesses a valid state license to trap in this Commonwealth.

I. No license to hunt, trap or fish shall be required of any Indian who habitually resides on an Indian reservation; however, such Indian must have on his person an identification card or paper signed by the chief of his reservation, setting forth that the person named is an actual resident upon such reservation. Such card or paper shall create a presumption of residence, which may be rebutted by proof of actual residence elsewhere.

J. No license to fish shall be required of legally blind persons.

K. No fishing license shall be required in any inland waters of the Commonwealth, except those stocked with trout by the Department or other public body, on free fishing days. The Board shall designate no more than three free fishing days in any calendar year.

L. No license to fish, except for trout as provided in subsection B of §29.1-310, in Laurel Lake and Beaver Pond at Breaks Interstate Park shall be required of a resident of the State of Kentucky who (i) possesses a valid license to fish in Kentucky or (ii) is exempt under Kentucky law from the requirement of possessing a valid fishing license.

M. No license to hunt shall be required of any person who is not hunting but is aiding a disabled person to hunt when such disabled person possesses a valid Virginia hunting license under §29.1-302 or §29.1-302.1.

(Chgd. by L.1996 chs. 118, 151; L.1997, ch. 267; L.2000 chs. 110, 142, eff. 3/17/2000.)

§29.1-305. Special license for hunting bear, deer and turkey.

A special license is required for hunting bear, deer and turkey in this Commonwealth, which shall be in addition to the license required to hunt other game. The fee for the special license shall be twelve dollars for a resident age sixteen or over, seven dollars and fifty cents for a resident under age sixteen and sixty dollars for a nonresident.

The license to hunt bear, deer and turkey may be obtained from the clerk or agent of any county or city whose duty it is to sell hunting licenses.

§29.1-310.1. Sportsman's hunting and fishing license established.

A. Upon implementation of an automated point-of-sale licensing system, any resident individual may apply for and receive from the Department, after payment of the appropriate fee, a sportsman's hunting and fishing license. This license shall serve in lieu of any person having to obtain hunting or fishing licenses provided for under subdivision 2 of §29.1-303 and §§29.1-305, 29.1-306, and 29.1-307, and subdivisions A 2 and B 1 of §29.1-310.

B. Applications for the license authorized by this section shall be made to the Department. The license shall be valid for the seasons as established by the Board. The form and issuance of the license shall conform to the provisions of this chapter for all licenses.

C. The Board shall establish the fee for this license, which shall not exceed the total cost of purchasing each license separately.

(Added by L.2000 ch. 12, eff. 7/1/2000.)

§29.1-335. Hunting, trapping or fishing without a license.

No person shall hunt, trap, or fish without having obtained a license when such a license is required. For the purposes of this article, the term "license" shall include any temporary license issued by a clerk or agent to a buyer and authorized to be used in a manner prescribed by the Director. Any person who violates this section shall be guilty of a Class 3 misdemeanor and shall pay to the clerk a fee equal to the cost of the required license to be paid into the state treasury and credited to the game protection fund.

The purchase of a license subsequent to an arrest or notice of summons to appear in court for hunting, trapping or fishing without a license shall not relieve the person from the penalties specified in this section.

(Chgd. by L.2000 ch. 132, eff. 7/1/2000.)

§29.1-336. Carrying licenses.

Every person who is issued a hunting, trapping or fishing license must carry the license on his person while hunting, trapping or fishing. Persons who have been issued such licenses and fail to carry them when required shall be guilty of a Class 4 misdemeanor.

§29.1-337. Displaying license upon request.

A. Every person who is issued a hunting, trapping or fishing licenses and is carrying such a license when hunting, trapping or fishing shall present it immediately upon demand of any officer whose duty it is to enforce the game and inland fish laws. Refusing to exhibit the license upon demand of any game warden or other officer shall be a Class 3 misdemeanor.

B. In accordance with §18.2-133, the hunting, trapping or fishing license shall also be shown upon the demand of any owner or lessee, or of any employee or representative of such owner or lessee, upon whose lands or waters the person may be hunting, fishing or trapping.

C. The Director may supply buttons or license holders and require the license or button to be displayed in a manner he may determine.

§29.1-337.1. Penalty for false statements; altering, borrowing or lending license.

It shall be unlawful for any person to make a false statement in order to secure a license or to alter, change, borrow, or lend or attempt to use, borrow or lend a license. Any person violating this provision shall be guilty of a Class 2 misdemeanor.

§29.1-338. Revocation of license; penalties.

If any person is found guilty of violating (i) any of the provisions of the hunting, trapping, or inland fish laws, any provisions of §§18.2-131 through 18.2-135 and §§18.2-285 through 18.2-287.1, or any regulations adopted by the Board pursuant thereto, a second time within three years of a previous conviction of violating any such law or regulation, or (ii) any provisions of law or ordinance governing the dumping of refuse, trash or other litter, while engaged in hunting, trapping or fishing, the license issued to such person shall be revoked by the court trying the case and that person shall not apply for a new license until twelve months succeeding the date of conviction. The court may also prohibit the convicted person from obtaining any license to hunt, fish, or trap in the Commonwealth for a period of one year to five years. If found hunting, trapping or fishing during this prohibited period, the person shall be guilty of a Class 2 misdemeanor. Licenses revoked shall be sent to the Director.

CHAPTER 4
PERMITS REQUIRED
(Selected Articles)

ARTICLE 1
DEALING IN FURS
(Selected Sections)

§29.1-400. Unlawful to deal in furs without a permit.

It shall be unlawful to buy, sell, barter, exchange, traffic or trade in, bargain for, solicit for purchase or possess the hides, furs or pelts of wild animals, or otherwise deal in fur as a business, without having first obtained a permit, subject to the exemptions in §29.1-401.

§29.1-406. Penalty for violations.

The violation of any of the terms of this article shall constitute a Class 3 misdemeanor. Furthermore, the trial court shall revoke the permit of the fur dealer, and he shall not have a similar permit for that season or for the succeeding season. He may, however, be eligible for a permit thereafter.

ARTICLE 2
NATIONAL FORESTS
(Selected Sections)

§29.1-408. Permit required; exceptions.

No person shall hunt, fish, or trap on any lands in the national forests in this Commonwealth without first obtaining, in addition to the regular resident or nonresident license, a special permit to hunt, fish, or trap on such areas in the national forests as the Board and the Forest Service may agree upon. However, no such permit shall be required of (i) residents under the age of sixteen to fish or trap; (ii) residents over the age of sixty-five to fish; (iii) nonresidents under the age of twelve to fish, except for trout, when accompanied by a person possessing a valid license to fish therein; (iv) residents possessing a license as provided by §29.1-301 E; and (v) persons holding a license as provided by §29.1-339.

The violation of any of the terms of this article shall constitute a Class 3 misdemeanor.

§29.1-409. From whom permits obtained; fee.

The special national forest permit may be obtained from the clerk or agent of any county or city whose duty it is to sell hunting, fishing, and trapping licenses. The fee for the special permit shall be three dollars.

CHAPTER 5
WILDLIFE AND FISH LAWS
(Complete Chapter)

ARTICLE 1
GENERAL PROVISIONS

§29.1-501. Promulgation of regulations; publication of proposed regulations or change therein; validation; evidentiary nature of publication.

A. The Board may promulgate regulations pertaining to the hunting, taking, capture, killing, possession, sale, purchase and transportation of any wild bird, wild animal, or inland water fish.

B. The full text or an informative summary of any proposed regulation or change in the regulations shall be published not less than fifteen nor more than thirty days before it may be acted upon. The publication shall name the time and place that the specified matters will be taken up, at which time any interested citizen shall be heard. If the proposed regulation or change in the regulations is of local application, the publication shall appear in a newspaper published in or within reasonable proximity to the affected locality. However, if the proposed regulation or change in the regulations is of statewide application, the publication shall be made in a sufficient number of newspapers having a general circulation throughout the entire Commonwealth.

C. A copy of proposed regulations or a change in the regulations, of either local application or statewide application, shall be published in the Virginia Register of Regulations pursuant to §9-6.14:22.

D. Prima facie evidence of any regulation may be given in all courts and proceedings by the production of a copy of the regulation, which shall be certified by the Director or his deputy.

§29.1-502. Adoption of regulations.

The Board may adopt regulations and amendments to regulations upon completion of all applicable hearing and notice requirements. The Board shall file the regulations with the Registrar of Regulations pursuant to §9-6.18.

§29.1-504. Annual publication of laws and regulations.

All laws relating to hunting, fishing and trapping, together with the regulations of the Board, of both general and local application, shall be published annually by the Department in a handbook or pamphlet. The courts of the Commonwealth shall take judicial notice of all laws and regulations contained in such publication.

§29.1-505. Penalty for violation of regulations.

It shall be a misdemeanor to violate any regulation promulgated pursuant to this title. Any person violating such a regulation shall be guilty of a Class 3 misdemeanor unless another penalty is specified.

§29.1-505.1. Conspiracy; penalty.

If any person conspires with another to commit any offense defined in Title 29.1 or any of the regulations of the Board of Game and Inland Fisheries, and one or more such persons does any act to effect the object of the conspiracy, he shall be guilty of conspiracy to commit the underlying offense and shall be subject to the same punishment prescribed for the offense the commission of which was the object of the conspiracy.

§29.1-506. Prescribing seasons and bag limits for taking fish and game.

After careful study of each species of wild bird, animal and fish within the jurisdiction of the Board in cities and counties of the Commonwealth, the Board shall have the power to prescribe the seasons and bag limits for hunting, fishing, trapping or otherwise taking such wild birds, animals and fish by regulation adopted as provided in this article.

§29.1-507. Closing or shortening open season.

The Board may close or shorten the open season in any county or city (i) whenever extreme weather threatens the welfare of wild birds, wild animals or fish; (ii) whenever such wild birds, wild animals or fish have been seriously affected by adverse weather conditions; (iii) when investigation of the Board shows that there is an unusual scarcity of any species or; (iv) when there is substantial demand from any county or city. The Board shall immediately give notice of any closing or shortening of an open season by publishing the announcement in one or more newspapers having a general circulation in the county or city affected. The notice shall be published at least three days before the action becomes effective.

§29.1-508. Board to prescribe seasons, bag limits and methods of taking and killing fish and game on lands and waters owned or controlled by Board.

The Board is hereby authorized to adopt rules and regulations to prescribe and enforce the seasons, bag limits and methods of taking fish and game on lands and waters owned by the Board and on lands owned by others but controlled by the Board.

§29.1-509. Duty of care and liability for damages of landowners to hunters, fishermen, sightseers, etc.

A. For the purpose of this section:

"Fee" means any payment or payments of money to a landowner for use of the premises or in order to engage in any activity described in subsections B and C of this section, but does not include rentals or similar fees received by a landowner from governmental sources or payments received by a landowner from incidental sales of forest products to an individual for his personal use, or any action taken by another to improve the land or access to the land for the purposes set forth in subsections B and C of this section or remedying damage caused by such uses.

"Land" or "premises" means real property, whether rural or urban, waters, boats, private ways, natural growth, trees and any building or structure which might be located on such real property, waters, boats, private ways and natural growth.

"Landowner" means the legal title holder, lessee, occupant or any other person in control of land or premises.

B. A landowner shall owe no duty of care to keep land or premises safe for entry or use by others for hunting, fishing, trapping, camping, participation in water sports, boating, hiking, rock climbing, sightseeing, hang gliding, skydiving, horseback riding, foxhunting, racing, bicycle riding or collecting, gathering, cutting or removing firewood, for any other recreational use, or for use of an easement granted to the Commonwealth or any agency thereof to permit public passage across such land for access to a public park, historic site, or other public recreational area. No landowner shall be required to give any warning of hazardous conditions or uses of, structures on, or activities on such land or premises to any person entering on the land or premises for such purposes, except as provided in subsection D.

C. Any landowner who gives permission, express or implied, to another person to hunt, fish, launch and retrieve boats, swim, ride, foxhunt, trap, camp, hike, rock climb, hang glide, skydive, sightsee, engage in races, to collect, gather, cut or remove forest products upon land or premises for the personal use of such person, or for the use of an easement as set forth in subsection B does not thereby:

1. Impliedly or expressly represent that the premises are safe for such purposes; or

2. Constitute the person to whom such permission has been granted an invitee to whom a duty of care is owed; or

3. Assume responsibility for or incur liability for any intentional or negligent acts of such person or any other person, except as provided in subsection D.

D. Nothing contained in this section, except as provided in subsection E, shall limit the liability of a landowner which may otherwise arise or exist by reason of his gross negligence or willful or malicious failure to guard or warn against a dangerous condition, use, structure, or activity. The provisions of this section shall not limit the liability of a landowner which may otherwise arise or exist when the landowner receives a fee for use of the premises or to engage in any activity described in subsections B and C of this section. Nothing contained in this section shall relieve any sponsor or operator of any sporting event or competition including but not limited to a race or triathlon of the duty to exercise ordinary care in such events.

E. For purposes of this section, whenever any person enters into an agreement with, or grants an easement to, the Commonwealth or any agency thereof, any county, city, or town, or with any local or regional authority created by law for public park, historic site or recreational purposes, concerning the use of, or access over, his land by the public for any of the purposes enumerated in subsections B and C of this section, the government, agency, county, city, town, or authority with which the agreement is made shall hold a person harmless from all liability and be responsible for providing, or for paying the cost of, all reasonable legal services required by any person entitled to the benefit of this section as the result of a claim or suit attempting to impose liability. Any action against the Commonwealth, or any agency, thereof, for negligence arising out of a use of land covered by this section shall be subject to the provisions of the Virginia Tort Claims Act (§8.01-195.1 et seq.). Any provisions in a lease or other agreement which purports to waive the benefits of this section shall be invalid, and any action against any county, city, town, or local or regional authority shall be subject to the provisions of §15.2-1809, where applicable.

ARTICLE 2
HUNTING AND TRAPPING

§29.1-510. Big game; small game.

For the purpose of the hunting and trapping laws of the Commonwealth, big game shall include bear and deer and small game shall include other game animals and all game birds.

§29.1-511. Open season on nuisance species.

There shall be a continuous open season for killing nuisance species of wild birds and wild animals as defined in §29.1-100.

§29.1-512. Closed season on other species.

There shall be a continuous closed hunting season on all birds and wild animals which are not nuisance species as defined in §29.1-100, except as provided by law.

 Zv

§29.1-513. Daily and season bag limits as promulgated by Board regulations.

It shall be lawful to hunt wild birds and wild animals specified in this article within any applicable daily and season bag limits during the open seasons as may be provided by Board regulations.

§29.1-514. Nonmigratory game birds.

A. The following nonmigratory game birds may be hunted during prescribed open seasons:

Birds introduced by the Board.
Bobwhite quail.
Grouse.
Pheasants.
Turkey.

B. The following provisions shall also be applicable to the raising and hunting of the particular nonmigratory game bird species listed:

1. The Board may issue a permit to raise or purchase pheasants which shall entitle the permittee to release pheasants raised or purchased by him on land owned or leased by him, and such pheasants may be hunted under rules and regulations promulgated by the Board.

2. The Board may open the season, including Sunday operation, on pen-raised game birds on controlled shooting areas licensed under Chapter 6 of this title under regulations as may be promulgated by the Board. However, the regulations promulgated by the Board shall not allow Sunday operation in those counties having a population of not less than 54,000, nor more than 55,000, or in any county or city which prohibits Sunday operation by ordinance.

Prior to obtaining a license from the Board to operate a commercially operated controlled shooting area, an applicant shall (i) notify adjoining landowners of the proposed use and (ii) obtain approval from the governing body of the county, city or town that such activity is permitted under existing ordinances. The requirements of clauses (i) and (ii) shall only apply to applications filed on or after July 1, 1993, for commercially operated controlled shooting area licenses issued under Chapter 6 (§29.1-600 et seq.) of this title and shall not apply to existing preserve licenses or renewals issued for the shooting of pen-raised game birds.

§29.1-515. Migratory game birds.

Migratory game birds may be hunted in accordance with regulations of the Board. Board regulations shall conform to the regulations of the United States government insofar as open seasons and bag limits are concerned.

§29.1-516. Game animals.

The following provisions shall apply to the killing and hunting of the particular game animals listed:

Black bear. Black bear may be killed by any person when (i) it is inflicting or attempting to inflict injury to a person, or (ii) when a person is in pursuit of the bear commenced immediately after the commission of such offense. Any person killing a bear under this provision shall immediately report the killing to a state game warden.

Deer. It shall be unlawful for a person to kill or attempt to kill a deer in the water of any stream, lake or pond. It shall be unlawful to hunt deer with dogs in the counties west of the Blue Ridge Mountains.

Fox. There shall be a continuous open season for hunting with dogs only. The hunting or pursuit of foxes shall mean the actual following of the dogs while in pursuit of a fox or foxes or managing the dog or dogs while the fox or foxes are being hunted or pursued. Foxes may be killed at any time by the owner or tenant of any land when such animals are doing damage to domestic stock or fowl.

Rabbits and squirrels. It shall be unlawful to kill rabbits and squirrels during the closed season; however, the following persons may kill rabbits or squirrels for their own use during the closed season:

1. A landowner and members of his immediate family;
2. Resident members of hunt clubs who own the land in fee, either jointly or through a holding company;
3. Tenants residing on the premises, with the written permission of the landowner.

When such animals are committing substantial damage to fruit trees, gardens, crops, or other property, the owner of the premises may kill the animals or have them killed under a permit obtained from the game warden.

§29.1-517. Fur-bearing animals.

A landowner may shoot fur-bearing animals except beaver, muskrats or raccoons, upon his own land during closed season. When muskrats or raccoons are damaging crops or dams, the owner of the premises may kill them or have them killed under a permit obtained from the game warden.

§29.1-518. When killing of beaver permitted.

When beaver are substantially damaging crops or lands, the owner of the premises, his agent or tenant, may kill the animals, or have them killed, under a permit obtained from the game warden.

§29.1-519. Guns, pistols, revolvers, etc., which may be used; penalty.

A. All wild birds and wild animals may be hunted with the following weapons unless shooting is expressly prohibited:

1. A shotgun not larger than ten gauge;
2. An automatic-loading or hand-operated repeating shotgun capable of holding not more than three shells the magazine of which has been cut off or plugged with a one-piece filler incapable of removal through the loading end, so as to reduce the capacity of the gun to not more than three shells at one time in the magazine and chamber combined;
3. A rifle;
4. A bow and arrow; or
5. A crossbow, which is a type of bow and arrow, used by disabled individuals. Such individuals who meet criteria established by the Department and attested to by a licensed physician on a standardized form provided by the Department, which shall be in the individual's possession while hunting, shall be allowed to participate in hunting seasons under the same rules, regulations, laws, and conditions that apply to hunters using standard archery equipment.

B. A pistol, muzzle-loading pistol or revolver may be used to hunt nuisance species of birds and animals between sunrise and sunset except over inland waters, and raccoons during the legal hunting hours for said species.

C. In the counties west of the Blue Ridge Mountains, and counties east of the Blue Ridge where rifles of a caliber larger than .22 caliber may be used for hunting wild birds and animals, game birds and animals may be hunted with pistols or revolvers firing cartridges rated in manufacturers' tables at 350 foot pounds of energy or greater and under the same restrictions and conditions as apply to rifles, provided that no cartridge shall be used with a bullet of less than .23 caliber. In no event shall pistols or revolvers firing cartridges rated in manufacturers' tables at 350 foot pounds of energy or greater be used if rifles of a caliber larger than .22 caliber are not authorized for hunting purposes.

D. The use of muzzle-loading pistols and .22 caliber rimfire handguns is permitted for hunting small game where .22 caliber rifles are permitted.

E. The hunting of wild birds and wild animals with fully automatic firearms, defined as a machine gun in §18.2-288, is prohibited.

F. The hunting of wild birds or wild animals with (i) weapons other than those authorized by this section or (ii) weapons that have been prohibited by this section shall be punishable as a Class 3 misdemeanor.

(Chgd. by L.1998 ch. 144, eff. 7/1/98.)

§29.1-520. Times for hunting.

A. Nonmigratory game birds and game animals may be hunted from one-half hour before sunrise to one-half hour after sunset.

B. Fur-bearing animals and nuisance species of birds and animals may be hunted by day or by night, except that muskrats may be hunted by day only.

C. A violation of this section shall be punishable as a Class 3 misdemeanor.

§29.1-521. Unlawful to hunt, trap, possess, sell or transport wild birds and wild animals except as permitted; penalty.

A. The following shall be unlawful:

1. To hunt or kill any wild bird or wild animal, including any nuisance species, with a gun, firearm or other weapon on Sunday, which is hereby declared a rest day for all species of wild bird and wild animal life, except raccoons, which may be hunted until 2:00 a.m. on Sunday mornings.

2. To destroy or molest the nest, eggs, dens or young of any wild bird or wild animal, except nuisance species, at any time without a permit as required by law.

3. To hunt or attempt to kill or trap any species of wild bird or wild animal after having obtained the daily bag or season limit during such day or season. However, any person who has obtained such daily bag or season limit while hunting for turkeys, ducks, geese or swans may assist others hunting such game by calling turkeys, ducks, geese or swans if the weapon in his possession is an unloaded firearm, a bow without a nocked arrow or a crossbow having an unloaded bolt. A person who has obtained such season limit prior to commencement of the hunt may assist others hunting as previously described, provided he does not have a firearm, bow, or crossbow in his possession.

4. To occupy any baited blind or other baited place for the purpose of taking or attempting to take any wild bird or wild animal or to put out bait or salt for any wild bird or wild animal for the purpose of taking or killing them. However, this shall not apply to baiting nuisance species of animals and birds, or to baiting traps for the purpose of taking fur-bearing animals that may be lawfully trapped.

5. To kill or capture any wild bird or wild animal adjacent to any area while a field or forest fire is in progress.

6. To shoot or attempt to take any wild bird or wild animal from an automobile or other vehicle, except as provided in §29.1-521.3.

7. To set a trap of any kind on the lands or waters of another without attaching to the trap the name and address of the trapper.

8. To set a trap where it would be likely to injure persons, dogs, stock or fowl.

9. To fail to visit all traps once each day and remove all animals caught, and immediately report to the landowner as to stock, dogs or fowl which are caught and the date.

10. To hunt, trap, take, capture, kill, attempt to take, capture or kill, possess, deliver for transportation, transport, cause to be transported, by any means whatever, receive for transportation or export, or import, at any time or in any manner, any wild bird or wild animal or the carcass or any part thereof, except as specifically permitted by law and only by the manner or means and within the numbers stated. However, the provisions of this section shall not be construed to prohibit the (i) use or transportation of legally taken turkey carcasses, or portions thereof, for the purposes of making or selling turkey callers or (ii) the manufacture or sale of implements, including, but not limited to, tools or utensils made from legally harvested deer skeletal parts, including antlers.

11. To offer for sale, sell, offer to purchase, or purchase, at any time or in any manner, any wild bird or wild animal or the carcass or any part thereof, except as specifically permitted by law. However, any nonprofit organization exempt from taxation under §501(c)(3) of the Internal Revenue Code, which is (i) organized to provide wild game as food to the hungry and (ii) is authorized by the Department to possess, transport and distribute donated or unclaimed meat to the hungry, may pay a processing fee in order to obtain such meat. Such fees shall not exceed the actual cost for processing the meat. A violation of this subdivision shall be punishable as provided in §29.1-553.

B. A violation of subdivisions 1 through 10 of subsection A of this section shall be punishable as a Class 3 misdemeanor.

(Chgd. by L.1997 ch. 249; L.1998 ch. 415; L.2000 ch. 13, eff. 7/1/2000.)

§29.1-521.1. Willfully impeding hunting or trapping; penalty.

A. It shall be unlawful to willfully and intentionally impede the lawful hunting or trapping of wild birds or wild animals.

B. Any person convicted of a violation of this section shall be guilty of a Class 3 misdemeanor.

§29.1-521.2. Violation of §18.2-286 while hunting; forfeiture of firearm; revocation of license.

A. Any firearm, crossbow or bow and arrow used by any person to hunt any game bird or game animal in a manner which violates §18.2-286 may, upon conviction of such person violating §18.2-286, be forfeited to the Commonwealth by order of the court trying the case. The forfeiture shall be enforced as provided in Chapter 22 (§19.2-369 et seq.) of Title 19.2. The officer or other person seizing the property shall immediately give notice to the attorney for the Commonwealth.

B. The court may revoke the current hunting license, if any, of a person hunting any game bird or game animal in a manner that constitutes a violation of §18.2-286. The court may prohibit the issuance of any hunting license to that person for a period of up to five years. If found hunting during this prohibited period, the person shall be guilty of a Class 2 misdemeanor. Notification of such revocation or prohibition shall be forwarded to the Department pursuant to subsection C of §18.2-56.1.

§29.1-521.3. Shooting wild birds and wild animals from stationary vehicles by disabled persons.

Any person, upon application to a game warden and the presentation of a medical doctor's written statement based on a physical examination that such person is permanently unable to walk due to impaired mobility, may, in the discretion of the game warden, be issued a permit to shoot wild birds and wild animals from a stationary automobile or other vehicle during established open hunting seasons and in accordance with other laws and regulations. Permits issued pursuant to this section shall (i) be issued on a form provided by the Department, (ii) not authorize shooting from a stationary vehicle less than 50 feet from nor in or across any public road or highway subject to the provisions of §29.1-526, (iii) be issued for the lifetime of the permittee and be issued only to those persons who are properly licensed to hunt, and (iv) be nontransferable. Any permit found in possession of any person not entitled to such permit shall be subject to confiscation by a game warden.

§29.1-522. Unlawful to kill male deer unless antlers visible above hair.

Unless the Board declares otherwise by regulation, it shall be unlawful to kill male deer in any county or city of the Commonwealth unless the deer has antlers visible above the hair.

§29.1-523. Killing deer by use of certain lights; acts raising presumption of attempt to kill.

Any person who kills or attempts to kill any deer between a half hour after sunset and a half hour before sunrise by use of a light attached to any vehicle or a spotlight or flashlight shall be guilty of a Class 2 misdemeanor. The flashing of a light attached to any vehicle or a spotlight or flashlight from any vehicle between a half hour after sunset and half hour before sunrise by any person or persons, then in possession of a rifle, shotgun, pistol, crossbow, or bow and arrow or speargun, without good cause, shall raise a presumption of an attempt to kill deer in violation of this section. Every person in or on any such vehicle shall be deemed a principal in the second degree and subject to the same punishment as a principal in the first degree. Every person who, in any manner, aids, abets or acts in concert with any person or persons violating this section shall be deemed a principal in the second degree and subject to the same punishment as a principal in the first degree.

In addition to the penalty prescribed herein, the court shall revoke the current hunting license, if any, of the person convicted of violating this section and prohibit the issuance of any hunting license to that person for the next license year. If found hunting during this prohibited period, the person shall be guilty of a Class 2 misdemeanor. Notification of such revocation or prohibition shall be forwarded to the Department pursuant to subsections C and D of §18.2-56.1.

This section shall not apply to persons duly authorized to kill deer according to the provisions of §29.1-529.

§29.1-524. Forfeiture of vehicles and weapons used for killing or attempt to kill.

Every vehicle, rifle, shotgun, pistol, crossbow, bow and arrow, or speargun used with the knowledge or consent of the owner or lienholder thereof, in killing or attempting to kill deer between a half hour after sunset and a half hour before sunrise in violation of §29.1-523, and every vehicle used in the transportation of the carcass, or any part thereof, of a deer so killed shall be forfeited to the Commonwealth. Upon being condemned as forfeited in proceedings under Chapter 22 (§19.2-369 et seq.) of Title 19.2, the proceeds of sale shall be disposed of according to law.

§29.1-525. Employment of lights under certain circumstances upon places used by deer.

A. Any person in any vehicle and then in possession of any rifle, shotgun, pistol, crossbow, bow and arrow or speargun who employs a light attached to the vehicle or a spotlight or flashlight to cast a light beyond the water or surface of the roadway upon any place used by deer shall be guilty of a Class 2 misdemeanor. Every person in or on any such vehicle shall be deemed prima facie a principal in the second degree and subject to the same punishment as a principal in the first degree. This subsection shall not apply to a landowner in possession of a weapon when he is on his own land and is making a bona fide effort to protect his property from damage by deer and not for the purpose of killing deer unless the landowner is in possession of a permit to do so pursuant to the provisions of §29.1-529.

B. Any person in any motor vehicle who deliberately employs a light attached to such vehicle or a spotlight or flashlight to cast a light beyond the surface of the roadway upon any place used by deer, except upon his own land or upon land on which he has an easement or permission for such purpose, shall be guilty of a Class 4 misdemeanor. Every person in or on any such vehicle shall be deemed prima facie a principal in the second degree and subject to the same punishment as a principal in the first degree.

C. In addition to the penalties prescribed in subsection A of this section, the court shall revoke the current hunting license, if any, of the person convicted of a violation of subsection A of this section and prohibit the issuance of any hunting license to that person for the next license year. In addition to the penalties prescribed in subsection B of this section, the court may revoke the current hunting license, if any, of the person convicted of a violation of subsection B of this section and prohibit the issuance of any hunting license to that person for the next license year. If a person convicted of a violation of subsection A or subsection B of this section is found hunting during the prohibited period, the person shall be guilty of a Class 2 misdemeanor. Notification of such revocation or prohibition shall be forwarded to the Department pursuant to subsections C and D of §18.2-56.1.

§29.1-526. Counties and cities may prohibit hunting or trapping near primary and secondary highways.

The governing body of any county or city may prohibit by ordinance the hunting, with a firearm, of any game bird or game animal while the hunting is on or within 100 yards of any primary or secondary highway in such county or city and may provide that any violation of the ordinance shall be a Class 3 misdemeanor. In addition, the governing body of any county or city may prohibit by ordinance the trapping of any game animal or furbearer within fifty feet of the shoulder of any primary or secondary highway in the county or city and may provide that any violation of the ordinance shall be a Class 3 misdemeanor. No such ordinance shall prohibit such trapping where the written permission of the landowner is obtained. It shall be the duty of the governing body enacting an ordinance under the provisions of this section to notify the Director by registered mail no later than May 1 of the year in which the ordinance is to take effect. If the governing body fails to make such notice, the ordinance shall be unenforceable.

For the purpose of this section, the terms "hunt" and "trap" shall not include the necessary crossing of highways for the bona fide purpose of going into or leaving a lawful hunting or trapping area.

§29.1-527. Counties, cities or towns may prohibit hunting near public schools and county, city, town or regional parks.

The governing body of any county, city or town may prohibit by ordinance, shooting or hunting with a firearm, or prohibit hunters from traversing an area while in possession of a loaded firearm, within 100 yards of any property line of a public school or a county, city, town or regional park. The governing body may, in such ordinance, provide that any violation thereof shall be a Class 4 misdemeanor. Nothing in this section shall give any county, city or town the authority to enforce such an ordinance on lands within a national or state park or forest, or wildlife management area.

§29.1-528. Counties or cities may prohibit hunting with certain firearms.

A. The governing body of any county or city may, by ordinance, prohibit hunting in such county or city with a shotgun loaded with slugs, or with a rifle of a caliber larger than .22 rimfire. However, such ordinance may permit the

 Zv

hunting of groundhogs with a rifle of a caliber larger than .22 rimfire between March 1 and August 31. Such ordinance may also permit the use of muzzle-loading rifles during the prescribed open seasons for the hunting of game species. Any such ordinance may also specify permissible type of ammunition to be used for such hunting.

B. No such ordinance shall be enforceable unless the governing body notifies the Director by registered mail prior to May 1 of the year in which the ordinance is to take effect.

C. In adopting an ordinance pursuant to the provisions of this section the governing body of any county or city may provide that any person who violates the provisions of the ordinance shall be guilty of a Class 3 misdemeanor.

§29.1-529. Killing of deer or bear damaging fruit trees, crops, livestock, or personal property or creating a hazard to aircraft or motor vehicles.

A. Whenever deer or bear are damaging fruit trees, crops, livestock or personal property utilized for commercial agricultural production in the Commonwealth, the owner or lessee of the lands on which such damage is done shall immediately report the damage to the Director or his designee for investigation. If after investigation the Director or his designee finds that deer or bear are responsible for the damage, he shall authorize in writing the owner, lessee or any other person designated by the Director or his designee to kill such deer or bear when they are found upon the land upon which the damages occurred. However, the Director, or his designee, shall have the option of authorizing the capture and relocation of such bear rather than authorizing the killing of the bear, provided that the relocation occurs within a reasonable period of time; and whenever deer cause damage on parcels of land of five acres or less, except when such acreage is used for commercial agricultural production, the Director, or his designee, shall have discretion as to whether to issue a written authorization to kill the deer. The Director or his designee may limit such authorization by specifying in writing the number of animals to be killed and the period of time for which the authorization is effective. The Director or his designees issuing these authorizations shall specify in writing that only antlerless deer shall be killed, unless the Director or his designee determines that there is clear and convincing evidence that the damage was done by deer with antlers. Deer or bear killed pursuant to such authorization shall be utilized or disposed of within twenty-four hours of being killed. Any owner or lessee of land who has been issued a written authorization shall not be issued an authorization in subsequent years unless he can demonstrate to the satisfaction of the Director, or his designee, that during the period following the prior authorization, the owner or his designee have hunted bear or deer on the land for which he received a previous authorization.

B. Whenever deer are creating a hazard to the operation of any aircraft or to the facilities connected with the operation of aircraft, the person or persons responsible for the safe operation of the aircraft or facilities shall report such fact to the Director or his designee for investigation. If after investigation the Director or his designee finds that deer are creating a hazard, he shall authorize such person or persons, or their representatives, to kill the deer when they are found to be creating such a hazard.

C. Whenever deer are creating a hazard to the operation of motor vehicle traffic within the corporate limits of any city, the operator of a motor vehicle may report such fact to the Director or his designee for investigation. If after investigation the Director or his designee finds that deer are creating a hazard within such city, he may authorize responsible persons, or their representatives, to kill the deer when they are found to be creating such a hazard. The carcass of every deer or bear so killed may be awarded to the owner or lessee by the Director or his designee, who shall give such person a certificate to that effect on forms furnished by the Department. Any person awarded a deer or bear under this section may use the carcass as if he had killed the animal during the hunting season for deer or bear.

D. Whenever deer are damaging property in a locality in which deer herd population reduction has been recommended in the current Deer Management Plan adopted by the Board, the owner or lessee of the lands on which such damage is being done may report such damage to the Director or his designee for investigation. If after investigation the Director or his designee finds that deer are responsible for the damage, he may authorize in writing the owner, lessee or any other person designated by the Director or his designee to kill such deer when they are found upon the land upon which the damages occurred. The Director or his designee also may limit such authorization by specifying in writing the number of animals to be killed and the period of time for which the authorization is effective. The carcass of every deer so killed may be awarded to the owner or lessee by the Director or his designee, who shall give such person a certificate to that effect on forms furnished by the Department. Any person awarded a deer under this section may use the carcass as if he had killed the animal during the hunting season for deer. The requirement in subsection A of this section, that an owner or lessee of land demonstrate that during the period following the prior authorization deer or bear have been hunted on his land, shall not apply to any locality that conducts a deer population control program authorized by the Department.

E. The Director or his designee may revoke or refuse to reissue any authorization granted under this section when it has been shown by a preponderance of the evidence that an abuse of the authorization has occurred. Such evidence may include a complaint filed by any person with the Department alleging that an abuse of the written authorization has occurred. Any person aggrieved by the issuance, denial or revocation of a written authorization can appeal the decision to the Department of Game and Inland Fisheries. Any person convicted of violating any provision of this title shall* receive written authorization to kill deer or bear, but shall not (i) be designated as a shooter nor (ii) carry out the authorized activity for a person who has received such written authorization.

(Chgd. by L.1996 ch. 314; L.1998 ch. 179; L.1999 ch. 563; L.2000 ch. 6, eff. 7/1/2000.)

**So in original.*

§29.1-530. Open and closed season for trapping, bag limits, etc.

A. There shall be a continuous open season for trapping nuisance species and a continuous closed trapping season on all other species of wild birds and wild animals, except as provided by Board regulations. However, a landowner or his agent may trap and dispose of, except by sale, squirrels creating a nuisance on his property at any time in any area where the use of firearms for such purpose is prohibited by law or local ordinance.

B. In addition, the following general rules shall be applicable to any person trapping in the Commonwealth:

1. The trapper shall be responsible for all damage done by an illegally set trap, and any person finding a trap set contrary to law may report it to the landowner upon whose land the trap is located or to any game warden who may destroy or otherwise make the trap inoperable.

2. A landowner may trap furbearing animals, except beaver, muskrat and raccoons, upon his own land during closed season.

3. Licensed trappers may shoot wild animals caught in traps during the open hunting season if the trapper has a license to hunt.

4. It shall be lawful to trap wild animals within the daily bag and season limits, if any, during the open season provided by Board regulations.

§29.1-530.1. Blaze orange clothing required at certain times.

During any firearms deer season, except during the special season for hunting deer with a muzzle-loading rifle only, in counties and cities designated by the Board, every hunter, or any person accompanying a hunter, shall wear a blaze orange hat or blaze orange upper body clothing that is visible from 360 degrees or display at least 100 square inches of solid blaze orange material at shoulder level within body reach visible from 360 degrees.

Any person violating the provisions of this section shall, upon conviction, pay a fine of twenty-five dollars.

Violations of this section shall not be admissible in any civil action for personal injury or death as evidence of negligence, contributory negligence or assumption of the risk.

This section shall not apply when (i) hunting waterfowl from stationary or floating blinds, (ii) hunting waterfowl over decoys, (iii) hunting waterfowl in wetlands as defined in §62.1-13.2, (iv) hunting waterfowl from a boat or other floating conveyance, (v) participating in hunting dog field trials permitted by the Board of Game and Inland Fisheries, or (vi) on horseback while hunting foxes with hounds but without firearms.

§29.1-530.2. Unlawfully killing bear; penalty.

Any person who kills or attempts to kill a bear in violation of any provision of this article or of a regulation adopted thereunder shall be guilty of a Class 1 misdemeanor.

ARTICLE 3
FISHING LAWS

§29.1-531. Unlawful to take or attempt to take, possess, sell or transport fish except as permitted.

A. Unless otherwise provided by a regulation of the Board, it shall be unlawful for any person to take or attempt to take any fish in inland waters other than shad, herring or mullet, except by fishing with a hook and line or rod and reel, held in the hand.

B. It shall be unlawful to catch, trap, take, capture, kill, or attempt to take, capture or kill, possess, deliver for transportation, transport, cause to be transported, receive for transport, export, or import at any time or in any manner any species of game fish, or the carcass or any part thereof, except as specifically permitted by law and only by the means and within the numbers stated.

C. In Mecklenburg, Pittsylvania, Prince Edward, Charlotte, Campbell, Halifax, Amelia (except between Vaughn's Pond and Meadsville Dam), Caroline and King George Counties, in the City of Danville, and in the Meherrin River in Lunenburg County, it shall be lawful to fish with fish traps, fish pots or haul seines in any streams and waters, provided that no person shall catch fish with fish traps or fish pots or haul seines for commercial purposes. However, it shall be unlawful in such localities to remove from the waters thereof any game fish caught with fish pots, fish traps or haul seines, and any person doing so shall immediately return them to the waters. The Board shall have the authority to close any streams or rivers or parts of streams or rivers in such localities when the waters are stocked with fish by the Department.

D. It shall be lawful to sell or offer to sell trout which have been lawfully acquired, provided such trout have been propagated and raised in a hatchery or by other artificial means. The Board shall by appropriate regulation establish a practical system of identification of trout so offered for sale for table or other uses as directed by the Board.

E. It shall be unlawful to offer for sale, sell, offer to purchase, or purchase at any time or in any manner any species of game fish, or the carcass or any part thereof, except as specifically permitted by law and only by the means and within the numbers stated. A violation of the provisions of this subsection shall be punishable as provided in §29.1-553.

F. A violation of the provisions of subsections A through D shall constitute a Class 2 misdemeanor.
(Chgd. by L.2000 chs. 403, 447, eff. 7/1/2000.)

§29.1-532. Dams and fishways.

Any dam or other object in a watercourse, which obstructs navigation or the passage of fish, shall be deemed a nuisance, unless it is used to work a mill, factory or other machine or engine useful to the public, and is allowed by law or order of court. Any person owning or having control of any dam or other obstruction in the streams of the Commonwealth which may interfere with the free passage of anadromous and other migratory fish, shall provide every such dam or other obstruction with a suitable fishway unless the Board considers it unnecessary. The purpose of such a fishway is for anadromous and other migratory fish to have free passage up and down the streams during March, April, May and June, and down the streams throughout the remaining months. "Suitable fishway" means a fishway which passes significant numbers of the target fishes, as determined by the Board.

Owners of such dams or other authorized obstructions shall maintain and keep fishways operational, in good repair, and restore them in case of destruction.

Owners of dams or other obstructions which are not authorized by law must have the obstacles removed at their expense when the Board determines that the obstacles interfere with the free passage of anadromous and other migratory fish within the streams of the Commonwealth.

The circuit court of the county or city in which the dam is situated, after reasonable notice to the parties or party interested and upon satisfactory proof of the failure to comply, may order any necessary construction or destruction to be initiated or put in good repair at the expense of the owner of the dam or other obstruction. All such construction or destruction must be initiated within one year of the court order and completed within three years of the court order.

Any person failing to comply with this section shall pay as a penalty a percentage of the estimated cost of construction or destruction equal to the percentage specified on the judgment rate of interest pursuant to §6.1-330.54, and the Board shall provide construction or destruction cost estimates.

Penalties collected pursuant to this section shall be directed to the Department of Game and Inland Fisheries.

This section shall not apply to the Meherrin River within the Counties of Brunswick and Greensville, nor to the Meherrin River within or between the Counties of Lunenburg and Mecklenburg, nor to the Nottoway River between the Counties of Lunenburg and Nottoway, nor to

Abram's Creek in Shawnee district, Frederick County, nor to the James River between the City of Lynchburg and the County of Amherst, nor to the James River within the City of Richmond and between the City of Richmond and Henrico County, except that the exemption for those dams west of Virginia Route 161 which are located on the James River within the City of Richmond and between the City of Richmond and Henrico County shall expire on January 1, 1990, nor any streams within the Counties of Augusta, Lunenburg, Mecklenburg, Louisa, Buckingham, Halifax, Montgomery, Pulaski, Franklin, Russell, Tazewell, Giles, Bland, Craig, Wythe, Carroll and Grayson, nor to that part of any stream that forms a part of the boundary of Halifax and Franklin Counties. Furthermore, no fish ladders shall be required on dams twenty feet or more in height. The City of Richmond shall continue to work with the Department of Game and Inland Fisheries toward implementing and funding a plan for breaching dams to provide fishways for the passage of anadromous and other migratory fish.

§29.1-533. Prohibition against use of substances injurious to fish.

It shall be unlawful to use any explosive for the destruction of fish, or knowingly cast any noxious substance or matter into any watercourse of the Commonwealth where fish or fish spawn may be destroyed, or to place or to allow to pass into the watercourses of the Commonwealth any sawdust, ashes, lime, gas, tar, or refuse of gas works, injurious to fish. Any person violating any of the provisions of this section shall be guilty of a Class 3 misdemeanor, except that any person convicted of destroying fish by means of explosives shall be guilty of a Class 1 misdemeanor.

The owner or lessee of any property on which fish are destroyed by means of explosives shall be entitled to recover liquidated damages in an amount deemed appropriate by the court from any person convicted of destroying fish by such means.

§29.1-534. Right to fish in interjurisdictional inland waters.

A Virginia resident or a resident of an adjoining jurisdiction which has inland water lying adjacent to Virginia land or water may take fish with hook and line after complying with the requirements of the laws of the jurisdiction of which he is a resident for the taking of fish in such interjurisdictional inland waters. For the purposes of this section and §29.1-535, the term "jurisdiction" shall include the District of Columbia.

§29.1-535. Reciprocal agreement as to fishing in such waters.

The Board shall have the necessary authority to enter into a reciprocal agreement with an adjoining jurisdiction having inland waters lying adjacent to Virginia land or water relating to the following:

1. A sport fishing license acquired in an adjoining jurisdiction shall be recognized when it is used by the person whose name appears on the face of such license, when such licensee is fishing in that portion of inland waters lying in either Virginia or the other jurisdiction or partly in each of the jurisdictions. Such recognition shall be contingent upon a reciprocal recognition by the adjoining jurisdiction to a licensee of Virginia who is fishing in the same waters.

2. Creel limits, open seasons for fishing and all other laws and regulations of the jurisdiction entering into the agreement shall be strictly observed, and any person failing to comply with the regulations set up under the agreement shall be guilty of a Class 2 misdemeanor and punished accordingly.

ARTICLE 4
POSSESSION, TRANSPORTATION, AND SALE OF GAME AND FISH

§29.1-536. Sale.

When taken in accordance with the provisions of law or regulation, bear, muskrat, opossum, rabbits, raccoon and squirrels may be bought and sold during the open hunting season only, but the hides, furs or pelts of fur-bearing animals legally taken and possessed, and the carcass of any fur-bearing animal may be sold at any time in accordance with §§29.1-400 through 29.1-407.

(Chgd. by L.1999 ch. 204, eff. 7/1/99.)

§29.1-537. Possession.

When taken in accordance with the provisions of this title, each species of wild bird, wild animal or fish may be possessed at any time.

§29.1-539. Keeping deer or bear struck by motor vehicle; procedure to be followed by driver.

Any person driving a motor vehicle who collides with a deer or bear may, upon compliance with the provisions of this section, keep the deer or bear for his own use as if the animal had been killed by that person during hunting season for the animal.

Any person so killing any deer or bear shall immediately report the accident to the game warden or other law-enforcement officer of the county or city where the accident occurred. The game warden or other law-enforcement officer shall view the deer or bear and if he believes that the deer or bear was killed by the collision with the motor vehicle or injured to such an extent as to require its death, he shall award the animal to the person claiming the deer or bear, and shall give the person a certificate to that effect on forms furnished by the Department.

§29.1-540. Carriage and shipment.

When taken in accordance with the provisions of this title, wild birds, wild animals or fish may be transported as follows:

1. By any person properly licensed, for lawful use in or out of the county or city where taken to another county or city in the Commonwealth or to another state during the open season in the county or city where taken.

2. By any properly licensed person via freight, express, parcel post or airplane mail, as a gift and not for market or sale, and so stating on the shipping tag. The wild bird, wild animal or fish may be transported in or out of the county or city where taken to another county or city in this Commonwealth, or to another state, during the open season in the county or city where taken. Any package in which birds, animals or fish are transported shall have the name and address of the shipper and consignee and a statement of the numbers and kinds of birds, animals or fish being transported clearly and conspicuously marked on the outside of the container.

Any such birds, animals or fish in transit during the open season may continue in transit, not to exceed five days, in order to reach their destination.

For the purposes of this section the terms "wild birds," "wild animals" and "fish" shall mean all or any part of the carcasses of any such birds, animals or fish.

§29.1-541. Storage.

It shall be unlawful for any person to store any wild birds, wild animals or fish if selling them is prohibited by law, except persons may store them in a bona fide domicile or in a licensed cold storage establishment. Any licensed cold storage establishment which receives any wild birds, wild animals or fish, where selling them is prohibited by law, shall attach a ticket to each lot of wild birds, wild animals or fish. The ticket shall show the number of each kind of wild bird, wild animal or fish, the date upon which they are brought for storage and the name and address of the person storing them. Every such licensed cold storage establishment shall keep a record of all deliveries of game and fish so stored, the dates they are delivered, the number of each species delivered and the name of each person to whom any such delivery is made. Possession of any wild birds, wild animals or fish which are prohibited by law to be sold, in any place of business, except in a licensed cold storage establishment, shall be unlawful.

Any person who violates any provision of this section shall be guilty of a Class 2 misdemeanor.

For the purposes of this section the terms "wild birds," "wild animals" and "fish" shall mean all or any part of the carcasses of any such birds, animals or fish.

§29.1-542. Importation.

Live wolves or coyotes, or birds and animals otherwise classed as predatory or undesirable, may not be imported into the Commonwealth or liberated therein, or possessed therein, except under a special permit of the Board. Nonpredatory birds, animals or fish may be imported, but upon arrival in the Commonwealth, shall be subject to the laws governing the possession of such birds, animals and fish in Virginia. Any person may bring into the Commonwealth, either in his personal possession or as his baggage, on the same conveyance with him and plainly labeled or tagged with his name and address, game and fish legally taken in another state or foreign country, but in no greater quantity than he could legally possess while in such other state or foreign country. Nothing in this section shall be construed as applying to birds, animals and fish being transported in unbroken packages from beyond the confines of Virginia through the Commonwealth to another state.

§29.1-543. Game and fish taken and packaged outside the Commonwealth.

It shall be lawful to possess, store, transport, offer for sale, sell, offer to purchase, purchase and otherwise deal in any wild animal, bird, fish or any part thereof, which has been taken and packaged in a can, tin, pot or other receptacle outside the Commonwealth by any person, company or corporation duly licensed by the state in which such cannery or processing plant is located and recognized by the Board. Such packages may be transported into the Commonwealth, so long as the original package remains unbroken, unopened and intact.

§29.1-544. Dressing, packing and selling bobwhite quail.

A. It shall be lawful for the licensee of a shooting preserve or his designated agents to dress, pack and sell bobwhite quail raised by him for use as food, under rules or regulations to be prescribed by the Board.

B. It shall be lawful to sell mounted bobwhite quail in the Commonwealth that have been legally raised captively and mounted outside of the Commonwealth.
(Chgd. by L.1998 ch. 179, eff. 7/1/98.)

§29.1-545. Possession, sale, offering for sale or liberation of live nutria.

It shall be unlawful for any person, firm, association or corporation to possess, sell, offer for sale, or liberate in the Commonwealth any live fur-bearing animal commonly referred to as nutria.

ARTICLE 5
PENALTIES IN GENERAL

Section

§29.1-546. General penalty.

Any person convicted of violating any of the provisions of this title shall, unless otherwise specified, be guilty of a Class 2 misdemeanor.

§29.1-547. Trapping, selling, purchasing, etc., migratory game birds.

Notwithstanding the provisions of §§29.1-546 and 29.1-553, any person convicted of trapping or attempting to trap any migratory game bird, as defined in §29.1-100, or convicted of possessing any such migratory game bird taken by means of a trap, shall be guilty of a Class 1 misdemeanor. Any person convicted of offering for sale, selling, offering to purchase, or purchasing any migratory game bird shall be subject to penalties as provided in §29.1-553.

§29.1-548. Killing deer illegally.

Any person killing a deer in violation of Board regulations, or who exceeds the bag limit for deer, or who kills a deer during the closed season shall be guilty of a Class 2 misdemeanor. However, any person who kills a deer illegally during the open season shall be guilty of a Class 3 misdemeanor if such person immediately delivers the complete carcass in good condition to the game warden of the county or city in which it was killed. At that time it shall be confiscated and disposed of by the game warden or as otherwise provided. Any such person delivering such carcass to the game warden shall be exempt from replacement cost as provided in §29.1-551.

§29.1-549. Hunting deer from watercraft; confiscation of watercraft and weapons used.

A. Any person who kills or attempts to kill any deer while the person is in a boat or other type watercraft shall be guilty of a Class 4 misdemeanor.

B. Every boat or other watercraft and their motors, and any rifle, shotgun, crossbow, bow and arrow, or speargun used with the knowledge or consent of the owner or lienholder thereof, in killing or attempting to kill deer in violation of this section, shall be forfeited to the Commonwealth, and upon being condemned as forfeited in proceedings under Chapter 22 (§19.2-369 et seq.) of Title 19.2 the proceeds of sale shall be disposed of according to law.

§29.1-550. Taking game or fish during closed season or exceeding bag limit.

It shall be unlawful for any person to (i) take, or attempt to take, any wild bird, wild animal or fish during the closed season, (ii) exceed the bag or creel limit for any wild bird, wild animal or fish, or (iii) possess over the daily bag or creel limit for any wild bird, wild animals or fish while in the forests, fields or waters of the Commonwealth. Any person convicted of violating any provisions of this section shall be guilty of a Class 2 misdemeanor.

§29.1-551. Assessment of value of game or fish unlawfully taken.

The judge or court, upon convicting any person of a violation of §§29.1-523, 29.1-530.2, 29.1-548, 29.1-550 or §29.1-552 shall, in addition to imposition of the punishment prescribed in those sections, ascertain the approximate replacement value of animals, birds or fish taken in violation of those sections and shall assess the value against the person convicted. The assessment shall be paid by the person so convicted within the time prescribed in the judgment of the judge or court, not exceeding sixty days, and the collecting officer shall forward such payments to the Board for payment into the state treasury. The Comptroller shall credit such payments to the game protection fund.

§29.1-552. Killing wild turkey during closed season.

Any person who kills a wild turkey during the closed season, or who kills a beardless turkey during an open hunting season prescribed by the Board for bearded turkeys only, shall be guilty of a Class 2 misdemeanor for each such turkey killed. However, if a person kills a beardless turkey when only the hunting of bearded turkeys is permitted, and immediately delivers the complete carcass in good condition to a game warden or game checking station authorized by the Board, it shall be confiscated and disposed of as otherwise provided, and the person delivering the carcass shall be exempt from replacement cost provided in §29.1-551.

§29.1-553. Selling or offering for sale; penalty.

A. Any person who offers for sale, sells, offers to purchase, or purchases any wild bird or wild animal, or any part thereof, or any freshwater fish, except as provided by law, shall be guilty of a Class 1 misdemeanor. However, when the aggregate of such sales or purchases or any combination thereof, by any person totals $200 or more during any ninety-day period, that person shall be guilty of a Class 6 felony.

B. Whether or not criminal charges have been placed, when any property is taken possession of by a game warden for the purpose of being used as evidence of a violation of this section or for confiscation, the game warden making such seizure shall immediately report the seizure to the Attorney for the Commonwealth.

C. In any prosecution for a violation of this section, photographs of the wild bird, wild animal, or any freshwater fish, or any part thereof shall be deemed competent evidence of such wild bird, wild animal, or freshwater fish, or part thereof and shall be admissible in any proceeding, hearing, or trial of the case to the same extent as if such wild bird, wild animal, or any freshwater fish, or part thereof had been introduced as evidence. Such photographs shall bear a written description of the wild bird, wild animal, or freshwater fish, or parts thereof, the name of the place where the alleged offense occurred, the date on which the alleged offense occurred, the name of the accused, the name of the arresting officer or investigating officer, the date of the photograph, and the name of the photographer. The photographs shall be identified by the signature of the photographer.
(Chgd. by L.1997 ch. 172, eff. 7/1/97.)

§29.1-554. Violation of sanctuaries, refuges, preserves and water used for propagation.

It shall be unlawful for any person, including a property owner, to commit the following acts, the violation of which shall constitute a Class 3 misdemeanor:

1. To violate any regulation of the Board concerning refuges, sanctuaries and public shooting or fishing preserves in impounded waters or in forest and watershed areas owned by the United States government;
2. To damage the boundary enclosure of or enter a game refuge owned, leased or operated by the Board for the purpose of molesting any bird or animal, or permit his dog or livestock to go thereon;
3. To fish or trespass with intent to fish upon any waters or lands being utilized for fish propagation, or damage or destroy any pond, pool, flume, dam, pipeline, property or appliance belonging to or being utilized by the Board; or
4. To interfere with, obstruct, pollute, or diminish the natural flow of water into or through a fish hatchery.

§29.1-554.1. Impeding lawful fishing in inland waters; penalty.

A. It is unlawful for any person to willfully and intentionally impede the lawful fishing of any species of fish. "Fishing" means those activities defined in §29.1-100 as "fishing."

B. Any person convicted of a violation of this section shall be guilty of a Class 3 misdemeanor.
(Added by L.1997 ch. 703, eff. 7/1/97.)

§29.1-556. Unlawful devices to be destroyed.

Any firearm, trap, net, or other device of any kind or nature for taking wild birds, wild animals, or fish, except as specifically permitted by law, shall be considered unlawful. Any person who violates the provisions of this section shall be guilty of a Class 3 misdemeanor, and the device shall be forfeited to the Commonwealth. Nets, traps or other such devices, excluding firearms, shall be destroyed by the game warden if the owner or user of the device cannot be located within thirty days. Unlawful fixed devices may be destroyed by the game warden at the place where the devices are found.

§29.1-556.1. Release of certain balloons prohibited; civil penalty.

A. It shall be unlawful for any person to knowingly release or caused to be released into the atmosphere within a one-hour period, fifty or more balloons which are (i) made of a nonbiodegradable or nonphotodegradable material or any material which requires more than five minutes' contact with air or water to degrade and (ii) inflated with a substance which is lighter than air. Any person who violates this section shall be liable for a civil penalty not to exceed five dollars per balloon released above the allowable limit, which shall be paid into the Lifetime Hunting and Fishing Endowment Fund established pursuant to §29.1-101.1.

B. The provisions of this section shall not apply to (i) balloons released by or on behalf of any agency of the Commonwealth, or the United States or pursuant to a contract with the Commonwealth, the United States, or any other state, territory, or government for the scientific or meteorological purposes or (ii) hot air balloons that are recovered after launch.

§29.1-557. Confiscation of wild birds and animals under certain circumstances; disposition.

Wild birds, wild animals and fish are the property of the Commonwealth and may be reduced to personal possession only in accordance with law. Any wild bird, wild animal or fish which is illegally taken, possessed, sold, purchased, transported or imported shall be forfeited to the Commonwealth.

§29.1-561. Self-incrimination.

No person shall be excused from testifying for the Commonwealth as to any offense committed by another under the provisions of the game, inland fish and boating laws by reason of his testimony tending to incriminate himself, but the testimony given by any such person on behalf of the Commonwealth when called as witness for the prosecution shall in no case be used against him, nor shall he be prosecuted as to the offense to which he has testified.

ARTICLE 6
ENDANGERED SPECIES

§29.1-563. Definitions.

For the purposes of this article:

"Endangered species" means any species which is in danger of extinction throughout all or a significant portion of its range;

"Fish or wildlife" means any member of the animal kingdom, vertebrate or invertebrate, except for the class Insecta, and includes any part, products, egg, or the dead body or parts thereof;

"Person" means any individual, firm, corporation, association or partnership;

"Threatened species" means any species which is likely to become an endangered species within the foreseeable future throughout all or a significant portion of its range.

§29.1-564. Taking, transportation, sale, etc., of endangered species prohibited.

The taking, transportation, processing, sale, or offer for sale within the Commonwealth of any fish or wildlife appearing on any list of threatened or endangered species published by the United States Secretary of the Interior pursuant to the provisions of the federal Endangered Species Act of 1973 (P.L. 93–205), or any modifications or amendments thereto, is prohibited except as provided in §29.1-568.

§29.1-566. Regulations.

The Board is authorized to adopt the federal list, as well as modifications and amendments thereto by regulations; to declare by regulation, after consideration of recommendations from the Director of the Department of Conservation and Historic Resources and from other reliable data sources, that species not appearing on the federal lists are endangered or threatened species in Virginia; and to prohibit by regulation the taking, transportation, processing, sale, or offer for sale within the Commonwealth of any threatened or endangered species of fish or wildlife.

§29.1-567. Penalties; authority of game wardens and police officers; disposition of property seized.

A. Any person who violates the provisions of §29.1-564 or §29.1-566, or any regulations issued pursuant to these sections, or whoever violates any regulation or permit issued under §29.1-568 shall be guilty of a Class 1 misdemeanor; however, the sale, offering for sale, purchasing or offering to purchase within the Commonwealth of any fish or wildlife appearing on a list of threatened or endangered species as prohibited by §29.1-564 shall be punishable as provided in §29.1-553.

B. Any judicial officer or other officer authorized to issue criminal warrants shall have authority to issue a warrant for the search and seizure of any goods, business records, merchandise or fish or wildlife taken, employed or used in connection with a violation of any provision of this article. All such search warrants shall be issued and executed pursuant to Chapter 5 (§19.2-52 et seq.) of Title 19.2.

C. Goods, merchandise, fish or wildlife or records seized under the provisions of subsection B of this section shall be held by an officer or agent of the Department at the direction of the judge or court pending disposition of court proceedings, and thereafter be forfeited to the Commonwealth for destruction or disposition as the Director may deem appropriate. However, prior to forfeiture, the Director may direct the transfer of fish or wildlife so seized to a qualified zoological, educational, or scientific institution for safekeeping, with costs assessable to the defendant. The Board is authorized to issue regulations to implement this section.

§29.1-568. When Board may permit taking, etc., of endangered species.

The Board may permit the taking, exportation, transportation or possession of any fish or wildlife which is listed by the provisions of this article, for zoological, educational, or scientific purposes and for propagation of such fish or wildlife in captivity for preservation purposes.

§29.1-569. Keeping of reptiles generally; penalty.

It shall be unlawful for the owner or keeper of any exotic reptile or type of reptile not native to the Commonwealth of Virginia, including but not limited to the American alligator, to keep the reptile in any manner that will permit its escape or to knowingly permit the reptile to run at large. Any violation of this section shall constitute a Class 2 misdemeanor.
(Chgd. by L.1999 ch. 85, eff. 7/1/99.)

§29.1-570. Cooperation of state agencies.

All departments, commissions, boards, authorities, agencies, offices and institutions within any branch of the state government shall cooperate with the Board in carrying out the purposes of this article.

CHAPTER 7
BOATING LAWS
(Complete Chapter)

ARTICLE 1
BOAT REGISTRATION AND IDENTIFICATION

§29.1-700. Definitions.

As used in this chapter, unless the context clearly requires a different meaning:

"Motorboat" means any vessel propelled by machinery whether or not the machinery is the principal source of propulsion.

"No wake" means operation of a motorboat at the slowest possible speed required to maintain steerage and headway.

"Operate" means to navigate or otherwise control the movement of a motorboat or a vessel.

"Owner" means a person, other than a lien holder, having the property in or title to a motorboat. The term includes a person entitled to the use or possession of a motorboat subject to an interest in another person, reserved or created by agreement and securing payment of performance of an obligation, but the term excludes a lessee under a lease not intended as security.

"Personal watercraft" means a motorboat less than sixteen feet in length which uses an inboard motor powering a jet pump as its primary motive power and which is designed to be operated by a person sitting, standing, or kneeling on, rather than in the conventional manner of sitting or standing inside, the vessel.

"Vessel" means every description of watercraft, other than a seaplane on the water, used or capable of being used as a means of transportation on water.

"Waters of the Commonwealth" means any public waters within the territorial limits of the Commonwealth, the adjacent marginal sea and the high seas when navigated as a part of a journey or ride to or from the Virginia shore.

(Chgd. by L.1998 ch. 84, eff. 7/1/98, chs. 443, 512, 514, 515, 533, 537, eff. 1/1/99, ch. 563, eff. 7/1/98.)

§29.1-701. Department to administer chapter; Motorboat Committee; funds for administration; records; rules and regulations.

A. It shall be the duty of the Department to enforce and administer the provisions of this chapter.

B. The chairman of the Board shall designate from among the members of the Board three members who shall serve as the Motorboat Committee. This committee shall place special emphasis on the administration and enforcement of this chapter.

C. All expenses required for administration and enforcement of this chapter shall be paid from the funds collected pursuant to the numbering and certificate of title provisions of this chapter. All moneys collected pursuant to the numbering and certificate of title provisions of this chapter shall be deposited into the state treasury credited to a special fund, known as the game protection fund, and accounted for as a separate part to be designated as the motorboat and water safety fund. Such moneys shall be made available to the Department solely for the administration and enforcement of this chapter, for educational activities relating to boating safety and for other activities and purposes of direct benefit to the boating public. Moneys from the motorboat and water safety fund shall not be diverted to any other state agency. The motorboat and water safety fund and moneys otherwise provided for in this chapter shall be made available to carry out the intent and purposes as set forth in this chapter in accordance with plans approved by the Board. All such funds are hereby reserved until expended for the enforcement, administration and other provisions of this chapter. However, the Board is authorized to adopt a plan or formula for the use of these moneys for employing and equipping any additional personnel necessary to carry out the provisions of this chapter and for paying a proportionate share of the salaries, expense, and operational costs of existing personnel according to the time and effort expended by them in carrying out the provisions of this chapter. Such plan or formula may be altered or amended from time to time by the Board as existing conditions may warrant. No funds derived from the sale of hunting licenses or fishing licenses shall be expended or diverted for carrying out the provisions of this chapter.

D. The Department shall maintain a record of all certificates of title it issues. The certificates of title may be located (i) under a distinctive title number assigned to each watercraft, (ii) under the hull identification number of each watercraft, (iii) under the registration number, (iv) alphabetically under the name of the owner, and (v) at the discretion of the Board by any additional methods it determines.

E. The Board shall make such rules and regulations as it deems necessary and proper for the effective administration of this chapter. The proposal and adoption of rules and regulations shall take place as prescribed in Article 1 (§29.1-500 et seq.) of Chapter 5 of this title and all rules and regulations shall be published by the Board in a convenient form. The Board shall cooperate with the Department of Taxation in issuing titles and collecting tax thereon.

§29.1-702. Registration requirements; display of numbers; cancellation of certificate; exemption.

A. 1. The owner of each motorboat requiring numbering by the Commonwealth shall file an application for a number with the Department on forms approved by it. The owner of the motorboat or the owner's agent shall sign the application and pay the following boat registration fee:

a. For a motorboat under sixteen feet, eighteen dollars;

b. For a motorboat sixteen feet to less than twenty feet, twenty-two dollars;

c. For a motorboat twenty feet to less than forty feet, twenty-eight dollars;

d. For a motorboat forty feet and over, thirty-six dollars.

2. Owners, other than manufacturers or dealers, of more than ten motorboats numbered by the Commonwealth, shall pay eighteen dollars each for the first ten such boats and twelve dollars for each additional boat.

3. Upon receipt of the application in approved form, the Department shall have the application entered upon the records of its office and issue to the applicant a certificate of number stating the identification number awarded to the motorboat and the name, address and a social security number or numbers, or federal tax identification number of the owner or owners. Any certificate issued in accordance with this chapter shall expire three years from the first day of the month in which it was issued. Upon proper application and payment of fee, and in the discretion of the Director, the certificate may be renewed.

B. The owner shall paint on or attach to each side of the bow of the motorboat the identification number in the manner prescribed by rules and regulations of the Board. The number shall be maintained in legible condition. The certificate of number shall be pocket-size and shall be available for inspection on the motorboat for which issued whenever such motorboat is in operation. However, the certificate of number for any vessel less than twenty-six feet in length, and leased or rented to another for the lessee's noncommercial use for less than twenty-four hours, may be retained on shore by the vessel's owner or his representative at the place at which the vessel departs and returns to the possession of the owner or his representative, provided the vessel is appropriately identified as to its owner while in use under such lease or rental.

C. No number other than the number awarded to a motorboat or granted reciprocity pursuant to this chapter shall be displayed on either side of the bow of the motorboat.

D. The Department is authorized to cancel and recall any certificate of number issued by the Department when it appears proper payment has not been made for the certificate of number or when the certificate has been improperly or erroneously issued.

E. Any motorboat purchased and used by a nonprofit volunteer rescue squad or volunteer fire department shall be exempt from the registration fees imposed by subsection A of this section.

§29.1-702.1. Making false affidavit or swearing falsely, perjury; penalty.

Any person who knowingly makes any false affidavit or knowingly swears to or affirms falsely any matter or thing required by Chapter 7 (§29.1-700 et seq.) or Chapter 8 (§29.1-800 et seq.) of this title or by the Director incidental to his administration of the boating laws shall, upon conviction, be guilty of perjury.

§29.1-703. Identification numbers required; decals.

Every motorboat on the waters of this Commonwealth shall be numbered except those specifically exempt in §29.1-710. No person shall operate or give permission for the operation of any motorboat on such waters unless the motorboat is numbered in accordance with this chapter, federal law, or a federally approved numbering system of another state, or has been issued a temporary registration certificate pursuant to the provisions of §29.1-703.1. In addition to the numbering requirements, (i) the certificate of number awarded or temporary registration certificate issued to the motorboat must be in effect, (ii) the identifying number set forth in the certificate of number must be displayed on each side of the bow of the motorboat, and (iii) decals signifying the last month and year during which the certificate of number is valid must be displayed on each side of the motorboat within six inches of the registration number so as to be visible while the motorboat is being operated. Decals will be furnished with each certificate of number issued or reissued by the Department. Expired decals must be removed from the vessel. Upon written request and for good cause, the Board may allow exceptions to the requirement to display decals. If a decal becomes defaced, lost or destroyed, application for replacement shall be made to the Board within fifteen days. A fee of one dollar shall be charged for each decal or set of decals replaced. Decals must be displayed upon the watercraft for which they were purchased and are not transferable.

(Chgd. by L.1995 ch. 241, eff. 7/1/95.)

§29.1-703.1. Temporary registration certificate; fee; application.

A. An owner may obtain a temporary registration certificate from the Department or an authorized agent of the Department. The fee for the temporary registration certificate shall be ten dollars. Each temporary registration certificate issued shall be valid for a period of thirty days from the date of issuance. To qualify for a temporary registration certificate, the owner shall provide his name and address (including zip code), sufficient proof of ownership as determined by the Department and a description of the motorboat to include the: present number on the boat (if any); make and model; type of propulsion; year of manufacture; length as measured along the centerline; hull identification number; state of principal use; and required fee. Application for the permanent certificate of number and certificate of title (if applicable) with applicable fees shall be submitted to the Department immediately upon receipt of a temporary registration certificate.

B. A temporary registration certificate shall not be valid as proof of ownership for any vessel.

(Added by L.1995 ch. 241, eff. 7/1/95.)

§29.1-703.2. Designation of agents; compensation to agents; deposit of temporary registration certificate moneys.

A. The Director may authorize any person to act as an agent to issue temporary registration certificates. Persons accepting such authorization may be issued temporary registration certificates which upon issuance, in conformity with this chapter and with any rules and regulations of the Board, shall be valid as if issued directly by the Director.

B. Notwithstanding the provisions of §2.1-180, the money received for temporary registration certificates issued pursuant to §29.1-703.1 shall be paid by each agent to the Department for payment into the state treasury. All moneys collected by the Department from the issuance of temporary registration certificates shall be deposited into the game protection fund and credited to the motorboat and water safety fund.

C. As compensation for such service, agents shall add and retain an amount equal to the fee provided to agents for the sale of hunting and fishing licenses as provided in §29.1-332.

D. Remittance to the Department shall be made by each agent as required by the Department.

(Added by L.1995 ch. 241, eff. 7/1/95.)

§29.1-704. Recording previously awarded numbers.

The owner of any motorboat already covered by a number in effect which has been awarded to it pursuant to then operative federal law or pursuant to a federally approved numbering system of another state shall record the number prior to operating the motorboat on the waters of this Commonwealth in excess of the ninety-day reciprocity period provided for in §29.1-710. Such recordation shall be in the manner and pursuant to the procedure required for the award of a number under §29.1-702, except that no additional or substitute number shall be issued.

§29.1-705. Change of ownership of motorboat; lost certificates.

Should the ownership of a numbered motorboat change, a new application form with the appropriate fee as provided in §29.1-702 shall be filed with the Department, and a new certificate bearing the same number shall be awarded in the manner as provided for in an original award of number. If the registration of the former owner is valid and the new owner has in his possession the dated bill of sale and the valid registration card of the former owner, the new owner may operate the vessel for thirty days from the date of purchase. If a certificate is lost, a new certificate bearing the same number shall be issued upon payment of a fee of fifty cents. Possession of the certificate shall in cases involving prosecution for violation of any provision of this chapter be prima facie evidence that the person whose name appears thereon is the owner of the boat.

§29.1-706. Agents awarding numbers.

The Director may award any certificate of number directly or may authorize any person to act as an agent to make award. Persons accepting such authorization may be assigned a block of numbers and certificates which upon award, in conformity with this chapter and with any rules and regulations of the Board, shall be valid as if awarded directly by the Director.

§29.1-707. Records.

All records of the Department made or kept pursuant to this section shall be public records and shall be open for inspection subject to conditions the Board may prescribe. The Director shall furnish, without cost, the annual lists of boat registrations, as of January 1, to the commissioners of revenue of each county or city, except that the Director shall not send the lists to any commissioner who requests that he not receive them.

§29.1-708. Transfer, destruction or abandonment of motorboat.

The owner shall furnish the Department with notice of (i) the transfer of all or any part of his interest other than the creation of a security interest in a motorboat numbered in Virginia pursuant to §29.1-702 or §29.1-704 or (ii) the destruction or abandonment of such motorboat, within fifteen days thereof. Such transfer, destruction, or abandonment shall terminate the certificate of number for the motorboat except that, in the case of a transfer of a part interest which does not affect the owner's right to operate such motorboat, the transfer shall not terminate the certificate of number.

§29.1-709. Change of address of certificate holder.

Any holder of a certificate of number shall notify the Department within fifteen days if his address appearing on the certificate changes, and he shall furnish the Department with his new address. The Board may provide in its rules and regulations for the surrender of the certificate bearing the former address and for certificate replacements or alterations bearing the new address.

§29.1-710. Exemption from numbering requirements.

A motorboat shall not be required to be numbered under this chapter if it is:

1. A motorboat which has been awarded a number pursuant to federal law or a federally approved numbering system of another state if the boat has been within the Commonwealth for less than ninety consecutive days.
2. A motorboat from a country other than the United States temporarily using the waters of the Commonwealth.
3. A motorboat which is used in a governmental function by the United States, a state or a subdivision of the state.
4. A ship's lifeboat.
5. A vessel which has a valid marine document issued by the Bureau of Customs of the United States government or any federal agency successor thereto.
6. A racing boat used during an authorized race and during a twenty-four-hour period before and after the race.
7. A motorboat belonging to a class of vessels which has been exempted from numbering by a regulation adopted by the Board after the Board has found that applicable federal law or federal regulation has exempted, or permitted the exemption of, such class of vessels.
8. A motorboat for which (i) a valid temporary registration certificate has been issued by the Department or an authorized agent of the Department, and (ii) an application has been made for a permanent registration and title (if applicable).

(Chgd. by L.1995 ch. 241, eff. 7/1/95.)

§29.1-711. Dealers and manufacturers of motorboats.

The following shall apply to dealers and manufacturers:

1. The registering and numbering requirements of this chapter shall apply to dealers and manufacturers of motorboats.
2. Applications for certificates of number shall be made on the approved application form prescribed in this chapter. Dealers and manufacturers shall certify that they are dealers or manufacturers.
3. Applications shall be accompanied by a fee of twenty-five dollars for dealers and forty dollars for manufacturers, by check or money order, and shall be forwarded to the Department.
4. Upon receipt by the Department of a properly completed application and fee, it shall issue to the applicant a dealer's or manufacturer's certificate of number, as appropriate, which may be used in connection with the operation of any motorboat in the possession of the dealer or manufacturer when the boat is being used for demonstration purposes.
5. Additional dealer's or manufacturer's certificates of number may be obtained by applying in the same manner as prescribed for the initial certificate with payment of an additional fee of twelve dollars for each additional certificate.
6. Manufacturers or dealers may have the number or numbers awarded to them printed upon or attached to a removable sign or signs to be temporarily but firmly mounted upon or attached to the boat being demonstrated, so long as the display meets the requirements of this chapter.

ARTICLE 2
WATERCRAFT TITLING CERTIFICATES

§29.1-712. Definitions.

As used in this article:

"Dealer" means any watercraft dealer as defined in §29.1-801.

"Watercraft" means any vessel, other than a seaplane, on the water, propelled by machinery whether or not the machinery is the principal source of propulsion or any sail-powered vessel longer than eighteen feet measured along the centerline. Watercraft which have a valid marine document issued by the United States Coast Guard shall not be included in this definition.

(Chgd. by L.1997 ch. 877, eff. 1/1/98.)

§29.1-713. Who must or may apply for certificate of title; authority of employees of Department.

A. Any owner, except a registered dealer, of any watercraft shall apply to the Department for a certificate of title in the name of the owner before the watercraft is operated.

B. Any owner of a vessel not required to be titled under this article and not titled elsewhere, may apply to the Department for a certificate of title. The Department shall issue the certificate upon reasonable evidence of ownership such as a bill of sale or other document satisfactory to the Department.

C. Employees of the Department are authorized to administer oaths and take acknowledgements and affidavits incidental to the administration and enforcement of this section. They shall receive no compensation for these services.

D. The issuance of a certificate of title, other than in the case of the initial issuance to a purchaser from a dealer, shall not invalidate a previously perfected security interest under the Uniform Commercial Code, other than a security interest in inventory.

§29.1-714. Form and contents of application.

A. Every application for a certificate of title shall be made by the owner or his duly authorized attorney-in-fact and shall contain the name, residence, social security number or motor vehicle driver's license number, if any, and mailing address of the owner, a statement of the applicant's title and of all liens or encumbrances upon the watercraft in the order of their priority, and the names and addresses of all persons having any interest in the watercraft and the nature of the interest.

B. Every application for a certificate of title shall contain a brief description of the watercraft to be registered, including the name of the manufacturer, state identification number, hull identification number, length, type, and principal material of construction, model year, the date of purchase, identification of the motor, including manufacturer's name and serial number, except on motors of twenty-five horsepower or less, and the name and address of the person from whom the watercraft was purchased.

The application shall be on forms prescribed and furnished by the Department and shall contain any other information required by the Director.

§29.1-715. Notice by owner of change of address.

Whenever any person, after applying for or obtaining the certificate of title of a watercraft, moves from the address shown in the application or upon the certificate of title, he shall, within thirty days, notify the Department in writing of his change of address.

A fee of seven dollars shall be imposed upon anyone failing to comply with this section within the time prescribed.

§29.1-716. Certificate of title prerequisite to issuance of certificate of number.

The Department shall neither issue nor renew a certificate of number to any watercraft required to be titled in this Commonwealth unless the Department has issued a certificate of title to the owner. However, any owner of a watercraft that was not previously required to be titled, and whose certificate of number expires after January 1, 1998, shall apply for a certificate of title at the time of renewal of his certificate of number.

(Chgd. by L.1997 ch. 877, eff. 1/1/98.)

§29.1-717. Certificate of title required; certificate as evidence; duration; transfer of title.

A. Except for amphibious vessels which have a valid title issued by the Department of Motor Vehicles, a watercraft owned by a bona fide dealer licensed as provided in §58.1-1406, or any watercraft not required to be titled pursuant to §29.1-716, no person shall operate a watercraft subject to titling under this chapter unless the owner has applied to the Department for a certificate of title for the watercraft or has been issued a valid temporary registration certificate as provided for in §29.1-703.1.

B. A certificate of title is prima facie evidence of the ownership of a watercraft. A certificate of title shall be in force for the life of the watercraft so long as the certificate is owned or held by the legal holder.

C. To sell, assign, or transfer a watercraft title in the Commonwealth, the certificate of title must be delivered to the purchaser or transferee with an assignment on the certificate showing title in the name of the purchaser or transferee. To purchase or otherwise acquire a watercraft required to be titled in the Commonwealth, any purchaser or transferee other than a licensed dealer must obtain a certificate of title for it in his name.

(Chgd. by L.1995 ch. 241; L.1997 ch. 877, eff. 1/1/98.)

§29.1-717.1. Transfer when certificate of title lost, etc.

Whenever the applicant for the numbering of a watercraft or a new certificate of title thereto is unable to present a certificate of title by reason of the same being lost or unlawfully detained by one in possession or whenever such certificate of title is otherwise not available, the Department may receive the application, inquire into the circumstances of the case and require the filing of affidavits or other information. When the Department is satisfied that the applicant is entitled, it may number and title the watercraft and issue a new certificate of number and certificate of title.

§29.1-717.2. Transfer by operation of law.

In the event of a transfer by operation of law of the title or interest of an owner in and to a watercraft numbered and titled under the provisions of this chapter, the transferee or his legal representative shall make application to the Department for a certificate of title therefor, giving the name and address of the person entitled thereto, and accompany such application with the certificate of number and certificate of title previously issued for the watercraft, if available, together with such instruments or documents of authority, or certified copies thereof, as are required by law to evidence or effect a transfer of title or interest in or to chattels in such case. The Department shall cancel the certificate of number and title of the watercraft and issue a new certificate of number and title to the person entitled thereto.

For purposes of this section, transfers by operation of law shall include transfers to anyone as legatee or distributee or as surviving joint owner or by an order in bankruptcy or insolvency, or transfers by execution sale, sales as provided for in §43-34, repossession upon default in the performing of the terms of a lease or executory sales contract or transfers pursuant to any written agreement ratified or incorporated in a decree or order of a court of record, or otherwise than by the voluntary act of the person whose title or interest is so transferred.

§29.1-717.3. Transfer of title when no qualification on estate.

If the holder of a certificate of title is dead and there has been no qualification on his estate, a transfer may be made by a legatee or distributee if there is presented to the Department a statement made by the legatee or distributee to the effect that there has not been and there is not expected to be a qualification on the estate and that the decedent's debts have been paid or that the proceeds from the sale of the watercraft will be applied against his debts. The statement shall contain the name, residence at the time of death, and date of death of the decedent, and the names of any other persons having an interest in the watercraft for which the title is sought to be transferred. If these persons are of legal age, they shall signify in writing their consent to the transfer of the title.

§29.1-718. Department's records; fees; exemption.

A. The Department shall maintain a record of any certificate of title it issues.

The Department shall charge seven dollars for issue of each certificate of title, transfer of title or for the recording of a supplemental lien.

The Department shall charge two dollars for the issuance of each duplicate title and for changes to a previously issued certificate of title which are made necessary by a change of the motor on the watercraft.

B. Any watercraft purchased and used by a nonprofit volunteer rescue squad shall be exempt from the fees imposed under this section.

§29.1-719. Acquisition of watercraft by dealer.

Any registered dealer who acquires a watercraft for resale shall be exempt from the titling requirement in this chapter.

Any dealer transferring a watercraft required to be titled under this chapter shall assign the title to the new owner or, in the case of a new watercraft, assign the certificate of origin. The dealer shall forward all fees and applications to the Department within fifteen days of sale.

§29.1-720. Transfer to or from dealer; manufacturer's or importer's certificate.

A. No dealer shall purchase or acquire a new watercraft without obtaining from the seller a manufacturer's or importer's certificate.

B. No manufacturer, importer, dealer, or other person shall sell or otherwise dispose of a new watercraft to a dealer for purposes of display and resale without delivering to the dealer a manufacturer's or importer's certificate.

C. The manufacturer's or importer's certificate shall be a uniform or standardized form prescribed by the Department and shall contain:

1. A description of the watercraft including its trade name, if any, year, series or model, body type, and manufacturer's serial number;

2. Certification of date of transfer of watercraft and name and address of transferee;

3. Certification that this was the transfer of watercraft in ordinary trade and commerce; and

4. Signature and address of a representative of the transferor.

D. On the reverse side of each manufacturer's or importer's certificate shall appear an assignment form, including the name and address of the transferee, a certification that the watercraft is new, and a warranty that the title at the time of delivery is subject only to such liens and encumbrances as set forth and described in full in the assignment.

§29.1-721. Dealer's records.

Every dealer shall maintain a record for six years of any watercraft he bought, sold, exchanged or received for sale or exchange. This record shall be available for inspection by Department representatives during reasonable business hours.

§29.1-722. Duplicate certificate of title.

The Department may issue a duplicate certificate of title plainly marked "duplicate" across its face upon application by the person entitled to hold such certificate if the Department is satisfied that the original certificate has been lost, stolen, mutilated, destroyed, or has become illegible. Mutilated or illegible certificates shall be returned to the Department with the application for a duplicate. If a duplicate certificate of title has been issued and the lost or stolen original is recovered, the original shall be promptly surrendered to the Department for cancellation.

§29.1-723. Certificate to show security interests.

The Department, upon receiving an application for a certificate of title to a watercraft showing security interests upon the watercraft, shall, upon issuing the certificate of title to the owner, show upon the face of the certificate of title all security interests in the order of their priority as shown in the application.

§29.1-724. Security interests subsequently created.

Security interests, other than a security interest in inventory held for sale to be perfected only as provided in §§8.9-301 to 8.9-408, created in watercraft by the voluntary act of the owner after the original issue of title to the owner must be shown on the certificate of title. In such cases, the owner shall file an application with the Department on a blank furnished for that purpose, setting forth the security interests and such other information as the Department requires. The Department, if satisfied that the information should be recorded and upon surrender of the certificate of title covering the watercraft, shall then issue a new certificate of title showing the security interests in the order of their priority according to the date of the filing of the application. For the purpose of recording the subsequent security interest, the Department may require any secured party to deliver the certificate of title to the Department. The newly issued certificate shall be sent or delivered to the secured party from whom the prior certificate was obtained.

§29.1-725. Certificate as notice of security interest.

The certificate of title, when issued by the Department showing a security interest, shall be deemed adequate notice to the Commonwealth, creditors, and purchasers that a security interest in the watercraft exists and the recording or filing of such creation or reservation of a security interest in the county or city wherein the purchaser or debtor resides or elsewhere shall not be required. Watercraft, other than those which are inventory held for sale, for which a certificate of title has been issued under this chapter shall be exempt from the provisions of §§8.9-302, 8.9-304, 8.9-307, 8.9-309, 8.9-312, 8.9-318, 8.9-401 to 8.9-408, and 55-96.

§29.1-726. Security interest may be filed within thirty days after purchase.

If application for the recordation of a security interest to be placed upon a watercraft is filed in the principal office of the Department within thirty days from the date of such applicant's purchase of the watercraft, it shall be valid to all persons, including the Commonwealth, as if the recordation had been done on the day the security interest was acquired.

§29.1-727. Priority of security interests shown on certificates.

The security interests, except security interests in watercraft which are inventory held for sale and which are perfected under §§8.9-401 to 8.9-408, shown upon the certificates of title issued by the Department pursuant to applications for certificates shall have priority over any other liens or security interests against the watercraft however created and recorded, except for a mechanics lien for repairs to the extent of $150 given by §43-33 if the requirements exist, provided the mechanic furnishes the holder of any such recorded lien who may request it with an itemized sworn statement of the work done and materials supplied for which the lien is claimed.

§29.1-728. Who to hold certificate of title subject to security interest.

The certificate of title of the watercraft shall be delivered to the person holding the security interest having first priority upon the watercraft and retained by that person until the entire amount of the security interest is fully paid by the owner of the watercraft. The certificate of title shall then be delivered to the secured party next in order of priority and so on, or, if none, then to the owner of the watercraft.

§29.1-729. Release of security interests shown on certificate of title.

An owner, upon securing the release of any security interest upon a watercraft shown upon the certificate of title issued for the watercraft, may exhibit the documents evidencing the release, signed by the person or persons making such release, and the certificate of title to the Department. When it is impossible to secure the release from the secured party, the owner may exhibit to the Department any available evidence showing that the debt secured has been satisfied, together with a statement by the owner under oath that the debt has been paid. When the Department is satisfied as to the genuineness and regularity of the satisfied debt, the Department shall issue to the owner either a new certificate of title in proper form or an endorsement or rider showing the release of the security interest which the Department shall attach to the outstanding certificate of title.

§29.1-730. Surrender of certificate required when security interest paid.

It shall constitute a Class 1 misdemeanor for a secured party who holds a certificate of title as provided in this chapter to refuse or fail to surrender the certificate of title to the person to whom it is legally entitled within ten days after the security interest has been paid and satisfied.

§29.1-731. Levy of execution, etc.

A levy made by virtue of an execution, fieri facias or other proper court order, upon a watercraft for which a certificate of title has been issued by the Department, shall constitute a lien, subsequent to security interests previously recorded by the Department and subsequent to security interests in inventory held for sale and perfected as otherwise permitted by law, when the officer making the levy reports to the Department at its principal office, on forms provided by the Department, that the levy has been made and that the watercraft levied upon is in the custody of the officer. Should the lien thereafter be satisfied or should the watercraft levied upon and seized thereafter be released by the officer, he shall immediately report that fact to the Department at its principal office. Any owner who, after such levy and seizure by an officer and before the report is made by the officer to the Department, fraudulently assigns or transfers his title to or interest in the watercraft, or causes the certificate of title to be assigned or transferred, or causes a security interest to be shown upon such certificate of title, shall be guilty of a Class 1 misdemeanor.

§29.1-732. Possession of certificate of title issued to another unlawful.

It shall constitute a Class 1 misdemeanor for any person in the Commonwealth to have in his possession a certificate of title issued by the Department to a person other than the lawful holder, unless the certificate of title has been duly assigned to the holder as provided in this chapter. This section shall not apply to secured parties who legally hold such certificates of title as provided in this chapter.

§29.1-733. Registration prima facie evidence of ownership; rebuttal.

Issuance of registration under the provisions of §29.1-702 shall be prima facie evidence of ownership of a watercraft and entitlement to a certificate of title under the provisions of this chapter, but such registration and certificate of title shall be subject to rebuttal.

§29.1-733.1. Acquiring title to an abandoned vessel.

A. Any vessel abandoned for a period exceeding twelve months is subject to the provisions of this section.

B. A landowner, his lessee, or his agent may acquire title to any vessel abandoned on his land or the water immediately adjacent to his land. Acquisition of title, under the provisions of this section, divests any other person of any interest in the vessel.

C. If a vessel has a registration number assigned by the Commonwealth or any other state, or if there are other means of identifying the owner, the person desiring to acquire title shall make a good faith effort to secure the owner's and lien holder's last known address. He shall notify the owner and the lien holder by registered letter that if ownership is not claimed and the vessel not removed within thirty days, he will apply for title to the vessel in his name.

D. The person desiring to acquire title also shall place a notice, to appear for three consecutive days, in a newspaper of general circulation published in the county or city where the vessel is located. The notice shall describe the vessel, its location, and any identifying number or numbers. The notice shall state that if the vessel is not claimed and removed within thirty days after the first day the notice was published, the person who has placed the notice shall apply to the Department for title to the vessel.

E. At the end of the thirty-day period the person seeking to acquire the vessel shall apply to the Department for title. The application shall be accompanied by the following: (i) an affidavit stating that to the best of the applicant's knowledge the vessel has been abandoned for a period of at least twelve months; (ii) proof that the registered letter required by the Department was mailed at least thirty days prior to application or a detailed explanation of the steps taken to identify the owner and lien holder; and (iii) proof that a notice was printed in a newspaper as required in subsection D of this section.

F. Upon receipt by the Department of all items required by subsection E of this section, and after all fees and taxes due have been paid, the Department shall then issue title to the vessel to the applicant.

G. All costs incurred in obtaining title to a vessel under this section shall be borne by the applicant.

ARTICLE 3
BOATING SAFETY

§29.1-734. Authorization for and placing of markers in waters of the Commonwealth used for public swimming areas; no motorboating, waterskiing in marked area.

A. Any owner of real estate which touches any of the waters of this Commonwealth or the agent of the owner may petition the Board to authorize the placing of markers approved by the Board around a public swimming or bathing area.

B. The Department, upon receiving the petition and sufficient proof that the water adjacent to the real estate is used in whole or in part as a public swimming or bathing area, may authorize the placement of the markers to designate the area as a swimming or bathing area.

C. The cost of the purchase and placement of the markers shall be borne by the party requesting the placement of the markers.

D. No person shall operate a motorboat or manipulate skis within the area of the waters of the Commonwealth marked under this section. Persons violating this subsection shall be guilty of a Class 4 misdemeanor.

§29.1-734.1. Skin and scuba divers.

A. No person shall engage in skin diving or scuba diving from a boat in the waters of this Commonwealth which are open to boating, or assist in such diving, without displaying a diver's flag from a mast, buoy, or other structure at the place of diving; and no person shall display such flag except when diving operations are under way or in preparation or display a diver's flag in a location which will unreasonably obstruct vessels from making legitimate navigational use of the water.

B. The diver's flag shall be square, not less than twelve inches on a side, and shall be of red background with a diagonal white stripe, of a width equal to one fifth of the flag's height, running from the upper corner adjacent to the mast downward to the opposite outside corner.

C. No operator of a vessel under way in the waters of this Commonwealth shall permit such vessel to approach closer than twenty-five yards to any structure from which a diver's flag is then being displayed.

§29.1-735. Regulations for vessel operation and equipment.

A. The Board shall adopt such regulations as it deems appropriate: (i) to provide rules for the safe and reasonable operation of vessels so as to reduce the risks of collision, personal injury and property damage as a result of such operation; and (ii) to govern the number, type, condition, performance capabilities, use, and stowage on board, of lifesaving (personal flotation) devices and other safety equipment to be carried on vessels or classes of vessels operated on waters within the territorial limits of this Commonwealth.

B. The Board is hereby authorized to make regulations to the extent necessary to keep these requirements generally in conformity with the provisions of the federal navigation laws, or with the rules promulgated by the United States Coast Guard or the United States Secretary of Transportation.

C. No person shall operate or give permission for the operation of a vessel which is not equipped as required by Board regulations.

§29.1-735.1. Board authorized to promulgate regulations for seaplanes.

The Board may promulgate regulations governing the takeoff, landing and taxi of seaplanes on impoundments located in the inland waters of the Commonwealth, so as to reduce the risks of collision, personal injury and property damage as a result of such operation. Such regulations shall not be inconsistent with regulations of the Federal Aviation Administration. Game wardens shall report any alleged violations of federal or state regulations regarding the operation of seaplanes or aircraft to the appropriate federal authorities responsible for regulating the operation of seaplanes and aircraft.

§29.1-736. Boat rentals; equipment; safety course.

A. It shall be unlawful to rent a motorboat to any person unless the provisions of this chapter have been complied with. It shall be the duty of persons renting motorboats to equip them as required by this chapter.

B. It shall be unlawful for any person to regularly offer a boat or boats, other than a motorboat, for rent for use on the public waters of the Commonwealth unless such person provides, for the use of each passenger in the boat, a life preserver of the sort prescribed by the regulations of the Board.

C. It shall be unlawful for any person, without first successfully completing a basic boating safety education course approved by the Director, to rent a personal watercraft to another person.

(Chgd. by L.1998 ch. 515, eff. 1/1/99.)

§29.1-737. Muffling devices.

The exhaust of every internal combustion engine used on any motorboat shall be effectively muffled by equipment so constructed and used as to muffle the noise of the exhaust in a reasonable manner. The muffling device shall exhaust at or below the water line or it shall be equipped with mechanical baffles. The use of cutouts is prohibited, except as approved by the Department or the U.S. Coast Guard.

(Chgd. by L.1997 ch. 108, eff. 7/1/97.)

§29.1-738. Operating boat or manipulating water skis, etc., in reckless manner or while intoxicated, etc.

A. No person shall operate any motorboat or vessel, or manipulate any skis, surfboard, or similar device, or engage in any spearfishing while skin diving or scuba diving in a reckless manner so as to endanger the life, limb, or property of any person.

B. No person shall operate any watercraft, as defined in §29.1-712, or motorboat which is underway (i) while such person has a blood alcohol concentration at or greater than the blood alcohol concentration at which it is unlawful to drive or operate a motor vehicle as provided in §18.2-266 as indicated by a chemical test administered in accordance with §29.1-738.2, (ii) while such person is under the influence of alcohol, (iii) while such person is under the influence of any narcotic drug or any other self-administered intoxicant or drug of whatsoever nature, or any combination of such drugs, to a degree which impairs his ability to operate the watercraft or motorboat safely or (iv) while such person is under the combined influence of alcohol and any drug or drugs to a degree which impairs his ability to operate the watercraft or motorboat safely.

C. For purposes of this article, the word "operate" shall include being in actual physical control of a watercraft or motorboat and "underway" shall mean that a vessel is not at anchor, or made fast to the shore, or aground.

Any person who violates any provision of this section shall be guilty of a Class 1 misdemeanor.

(Chgd. by L.1996 chs. 929, 1015; L.1997 ch. 703, eff. 7/1/97.)

§29.1-738.01. Operating boat in an improper manner; penalty.

Notwithstanding the provisions of §29.1-738, upon the trial of any person charged with reckless boating where the degree of culpability is slight, the court in its discretion may find the accused not guilty of reckless boating but guilty of improper boating. Improper boating shall be punishable as a Class 3 misdemeanor.

§29.1-738.02. Persons under age twenty-one operating watercraft after illegally consuming alcohol; penalty.

A. It shall be unlawful for any person under the age of twenty-one to operate any watercraft or motorboat upon the waters of the Commonwealth after consuming alcohol. Any such person with a blood alcohol concentration of 0.02 percent or more by weight by volume or 0.02 grams or more per 210 liters of breath but less than 0.08 by weight by volume or less than 0.08 grams per 210 liters of breath as indicated by a chemical test administered as provided in Article 2 (§18.2-266 et seq.) of Chapter 7 of Title 18.2 shall be in violation of this section.

B. A violation of this section shall be punishable by denial by the court of such person's privilege to operate a watercraft or motorboat for a period of six months from the date of conviction and by a fine of not more than $500. Any person convicted of a violation of this section shall be eligible to attend an Alcohol Safety Action Program under the provisions of §29.1-738.5.

(Added by L.1996 ch. 631, eff. 7/1/96.)

§29.1-738.03. Reckless operation of a personal watercraft.

A person shall be guilty of reckless operation of a motorboat or vessel who operates any personal watercraft recklessly or at a speed or in such a manner so as to endanger the life, limb or property of any person, which shall include, but not be limited to:

1. Weaving through vessels which are underway, stopped, moored or at anchor while exceeding a reasonable speed under the circumstances and traffic conditions existing at the time;
2. Following another vessel or person on water skis or other similar device, crossing the path of another vessel, or jumping the wake of another vessel more closely than is reasonable and prudent, having due regard to the speed of both vessels and the traffic on and the condition of the waters at the time;
3. Crossing between the towing vessel and a person on water skis or other device; or
4. Steering toward an object or person and turning sharply in close proximity to such object or person in order to spray or attempt to spray the object or person with the wash or jet spray of the personal watercraft.

A person who violates this section shall be guilty of a Class 1 misdemeanor, and for a second or subsequent offense, the court shall order the person not to operate a personal watercraft which is underway upon the waters of the Commonwealth for a period of twelve months.

(Added by L.1998 ch. 514, eff. 1/1/99.)

§29.1-738.1. Analysis of breath to determine alcohol content of blood.

Any person who is suspected of a violation of subsection B of §29.1-738 or §29.1-738.02 shall be entitled, if such equipment is available, to have a preliminary breath analysis for the purpose of obtaining an analysis of the probable alcohol content of his blood. The procedures and requirements of §18.2-267 shall apply, mutatis mutandis.

(Chgd. by L.1996 ch. 631, eff. 7/1/96.)

§29.1-738.2. Consent to blood or breath test.

A. Any person who operates a watercraft or motorboat which is underway upon waters of the Commonwealth shall be deemed thereby, as a condition of such operation, to have consented to have samples of his blood, breath, or both blood and breath taken for a chemical test to determine the alcohol, drug, or both alcohol and drug content of his blood, if such person is arrested for operating a watercraft or motorboat which is underway in violation of subsection B of §29.1-738, §29.1-738.02, or of a similar ordinance of any county, city or town, within two hours of the alleged offense. Any person so arrested for a violation of clause (i) or (ii), or both, of §29.1-738 B, §29.1-738.02, or of a similar ordinance, shall submit to a breath test. If the breath test is not available, or the person is physically unable to submit to the breath test, a blood test shall be given. The accused shall, prior to administration of the test, be advised by the person administering the test that he has the right to observe the process of analysis and to see the blood-alcohol reading on the equipment used to perform the breath test. If such equipment automatically produces a written printout of the breath test result, this written printout, or a copy thereof, shall be given to the accused in each case.

B. Any person, after having been arrested for a violation of clause (iii) or (iv) of §29.1-738 B, §29.1-738.02, or of a similar ordinance, may be required to submit to a blood test to determine the drug or both drug and alcohol content of his blood. When a person, after having been arrested for a violation of clause (i) or (ii), or both, of §29.1-738 B, submits to a breath test, in accordance with subsection A of this section, or refuses to take or is incapable of taking such a breath test, he may be required to submit to tests to determine the drug or both drug and alcohol content of his blood if the law-enforcement officer has reasonable cause to believe the person was operating a watercraft or motorboat under the influence of any drug or combination of drugs, or the combined influence of alcohol and drugs.

C. If a person, after being arrested for a violation of subsection B of §29.1-738, §29.1-738.02, or of a similar ordinance of any county, city or town and after having been advised by the arresting officer that a person who operates a watercraft or motorboat which is underway upon the waters of the Commonwealth shall be deemed thereby, as a condition of such operation, to have consented to have a sample of his blood and breath taken for a chemical test to determine the alcohol or drug content of his blood, and that the unreasonable refusal to do so constitutes grounds for a court to order him not to operate a watercraft or motorboat which is underway upon the waters of the Commonwealth, then refuses to permit the taking of a sample of his blood or breath or both blood and breath samples for such tests, the arresting officer shall take the person arrested before a committing magistrate. If he again so refuses after having been further advised by such magistrate of the law requiring a blood or breath sample to be taken and the penalty for refusal, and so declares again his refusal in writing upon a form provided by the Supreme Court of Virginia, or refuses or fails to so declare in writing and such fact is certified as prescribed in §18.2-268.3, then no blood or breath sample shall be taken even though he may thereafter request same.

D. When any person is arrested for operating a watercraft or motorboat which is underway in violation of subsection B of §29.1-738 or §29.1-738.02, the procedures and requirements of §§18.2-268.1 through 18.2-268.11 shall apply, mutatis mutandis, to this section.

E. If the court or jury finds the defendant guilty of unreasonably refusing to permit a blood or breath sample to be taken, the court shall order such person not to operate a watercraft or motorboat which is underway for a period of twelve months for a first offense and for twenty-four months for a second or subsequent offense of refusal within five years of the first or other such refusal. However, if the defendant pleads guilty to a violation of subsection B of §29.1-738, the court may dismiss the refusal warrant.

(Chgd. by L.1995 ch. 130; L.1996 ch. 631, eff. 7/1/96.)

§29.1-738.3. Presumptions from alcoholic content.

In any prosecution for operating a watercraft or motorboat which is underway in violation of clause (ii) or (iv) of subsection B of §29.1-738, or of a similar ordinance of any county, city or town, the amount of alcohol in the blood of the accused at the time of the alleged offense as indicated by a chemical analysis of a sample of the accused's blood or breath to determine the alcoholic content of his blood in accordance with the provisions of §29.1-738.2 shall give rise to the rebuttable presumptions of subdivisions (1) through (3) of subsection A of §18.2-269.

(Chgd. by L.1995 ch. 130, eff. 3/8/95.)

§29.1-738.4. Additional penalty for reckless or intoxicated operation of a watercraft or motorboat.

In addition to any other penalties authorized by law, upon conviction of any person for violation of any provision of §29.1-738, the court shall order such person not to operate a watercraft or motorboat which is underway upon the waters of the Commonwealth for a period of twelve months from the date of a first conviction or for a period of three years from the date of a second or subsequent conviction within ten years of a first conviction. The period specified in any such order prohibiting operation of a watercraft or motorboat which is underway imposed pursuant to this section shall run consecutively with any such order imposed for refusal to permit a blood or breath sample to be taken.

A first offense of violating this section shall constitute a Class 2 misdemeanor. A second or subsequent offense shall constitute a Class 1 misdemeanor. In addition, the court shall suspend the person's privilege to operate a motorboat or watercraft for the same period for which it had been suspended or revoked when such person violated this section.

The period specified in any such order prohibiting operation of a watercraft or motorboat which is underway imposed pursuant to this section may be suspended by the court only as authorized in §29.1-738.5.

(Chgd. by L.1996 chs. 929, 1015, eff. 4/17/96.)

§29.1-738.5. Participation in rehabilitation program.

A. Any person convicted of a violation of subsection B of §29.1-738, or any ordinance of a county, city or town similar to the provisions thereof, or any second offense thereunder, shall, with leave of court or upon court order, enter into an alcohol safety action program certified by the Commission on the Virginia Alcohol Safety Action Program (VASAP) in the judicial district in which the charge is brought or in any other judicial district upon such terms and conditions as the court may set forth. In the determination of the eligibility of such person to enter a program, the court shall consider his prior record of participation in any other rehabilitation program. Suspension of the penalties imposed pursuant to §29.1-738.4 shall be conditioned upon successful completion of such a program.

B. The court shall require the person entering such program under the provisions of subsection A to pay a fee of no less than $250 but no more than $300. A reasonable portion of such fee, as may be determined by the Commission on VASAP, but not to exceed ten percent, shall be forwarded quarterly to be deposited with the State Treasurer for expenditure by the Commission on VASAP, and the balance shall be held in a separate fund for local administration of alcohol rehabilitation programs. Upon a finding that the defendant is

 Zv

indigent, the court may reduce or waive the fee. In addition to the costs of the proceeding, fees as may reasonably be required of defendants referred for extended treatment under such program may be charged.

C. Upon such conviction, the court shall impose the sentence authorized. Upon a finding that a person so convicted is eligible for participation in an alcohol rehabilitation program, the court shall enter the conviction on the warrant, and shall note that the person so convicted has been referred to a program. If the court finds that a person is not eligible for a program or subsequently that the person has violated, without good cause, any of the conditions set forth by the court in entering the program, the court shall dispose of the case as if no program had been entered. Appeals from any such disposition shall be allowed as provided by law.

The court shall have jurisdiction over any person entering a program under the provisions of this section until such time as the case has been disposed of by either successful completion of the program, or final imposition of sentence upon ineligibility or violation of a condition imposed by the court, whichever occurs first.

D. The Commission on VASAP shall establish standards and criteria for the implementation and operation of water safety alcohol rehabilitation programs. The Commission on VASAP shall also establish criteria for the modalities of administration of such programs, as well as public information, accounting procedures and allocation of funds.

§29.1-738.6. When arrested person operating a vessel; how vessel removed from scene of arrest.

In any case in which a law enforcement officer arrests the operator of a vessel, and there is no legal cause for the retention of the vessel by the officer, the officer shall allow the person arrested to designate another person who is present at the scene of the arrest to operate the vessel from the scene to a place designated by the person arrested. If such a designation is not made, the officer may cause the vessel to be taken to the nearest appropriate place for safekeeping.
(Added by L.1997 ch. 152, eff. 7/1/97.)

§29.1-739. Duty of operator involved in collision, accident or other casualty; immunity from liability; report of collision, etc.; summons in lieu of arrest.

A. It shall be the duty of the operator of a vessel involved in a collision, accident, or other casualty, so far as he can do so without serious danger to his own vessel, crew, and passengers (if any), to render persons affected by the collision, accident, or other casualty such assistance as may be practicable and as may be necessary in order to minimize any danger caused by the collision, accident, or other casualty, and also give his name, address, and identification of his vessel in writing to any person injured and to the owner of any property damaged in the collision, accident, or other casualty. Any person who complies with this subsection or who gratuitously and in good faith renders assistance at the scene of a vessel collision, accident, or other casualty without objection of any person assisted, shall not be held liable for any civil damages as a result of the rendering of assistance or for any act or omission in providing or arranging salvage, towage, medical treatment or other assistance where the assisting person acts as an ordinary, reasonably prudent person would have acted under the same or similar circumstances.

B. In case of collision, accident, or other casualty involving a vessel, the operator of the vessel, if the collision, accident, or other casualty is of such a nature as to be reportable pursuant to regulations adopted by the Board, shall notify within a reasonable time a law-enforcement officer of the Commonwealth, game warden, or Marine Resources Commission inspector.

The operator shall file with the Department a full report of the collision, accident, or other casualty, as the regulations of the Board may require. The report shall be without prejudice, shall be for the information of the Department only, and shall not be open to public inspection. The fact that such a report has been made shall be admissible in evidence solely to show compliance with this section and applicable regulations, but no such report nor any statement contained in the report shall be admissible as evidence for any other purpose in any trial.

C. Any officer investigating any collision, accident or other casualty shall have authority, in lieu of arresting any person charged with violating any of the provisions of this chapter, to issue a written summons to the person (stating name, address, boat number, offense charged, etc.) to appear in court as in §46.2-936.

§29.1-739.1. Disregarding signal by law-enforcement to stop; attempts to elude; penalty.

A. Any person who, having received a visible or audible signal of a flashing light or siren from any game warden or other law-enforcement officer to bring his motorboat or other vessel, or seaplane to a stop, fails to do so promptly shall be guilty of a Class 3 misdemeanor.

B. Any person who, having received a visible or audible signal of a flashing light or siren from any game warden or other law-enforcement officer to bring his motorboat or other vessel, or seaplane to a stop, (i) operates or navigates such motorboat or other vessel, or seaplane in willful or wanton disregard of such signal so as to endanger the life of the law-enforcement officer or other persons or to interfere with the operation of a law-enforcement vessel, or (ii) increases his speed and attempts to escape or elude a law-enforcement officer shall be guilty of a Class 1 misdemeanor.

§29.1-740. Duty to stop and render assistance; penalties for violations.

It shall be the duty of every operator of a vessel involved in a collision to stop and render assistance as required by §29.1-739. If any person knowingly fails to comply with the provisions of §29.1-739 when the collision, accident or other casualty results in serious bodily injury to, or the death of, any person, he shall be guilty of a Class 6 felony. If any person knowingly fails to comply with the provisions of §29.1-739, when the collision, accident or other casualty results only in damage to property, he shall be guilty of a Class 1 misdemeanor. However, if the vessel struck is unattended and the damage is less than fifty dollars, such person shall be punished only by a fine not exceeding fifty dollars.

§29.1-741. Furnishing information to agency of United States.

In accordance with any request duly made by an authorized official or agency of the United States, any information compiled or otherwise available to the Department pursuant to §29.1-739 B shall be transmitted to the official or agency of the United States.

§29.1-742. Towing water skis, surfboards, etc.

A. No person shall operate a vessel on any waters of the Commonwealth for towing a person or persons on water skis, a surfboard, or a similar device unless there is in the vessel a person, in addition to the operator, in a position to observe the progress of the person or persons being towed or unless the skier or skiers wear life preservers.

B. No person shall operate a vessel on any water of the Commonwealth towing a person or persons on water skis, a surfboard, or a similar device, nor shall any person engage in water skiing or a similar activity at any time between the hours from one-half hour after sunset to one-half hour before sunrise. The provisions of this subsection shall not constitute a defense to any provision of §29.1-738.

C. The provisions of subsections A and B of this section do not apply to a performer engaged in a professional exhibition.

D. No person shall operate or manipulate any vessel, towrope, or other device by which the direction or location of water skis, a surfboard, or a similar device may be affected or controlled in such a way as to cause the water skis, surfboard, or similar device, or any person upon the device to collide with any object or person.
(Chgd. by L.1997 ch. 108, eff. 7/1/97.)

§29.1-743. *(Repealed by L.1997 ch. 108, eff. 7/1/97.)*

§29.1-744. Local regulation; application for placement or removal of "no wake" buoys, etc.

A. Any political subdivision of this Commonwealth may, at any time, but only after public notice, formally apply to the Board for special rules and regulations with reference to the safe and reasonable operation of vessels on any water within its territorial limits and shall specify in the application the reasons which make the special rules or regulations necessary or appropriate.

B. The Board is authorized upon application by a political subdivision or its own motion to make special or general rules and regulations with reference to the safe and reasonable operation of vessels on any waters within the territorial limits of any political subdivision of this Commonwealth. Without limiting the generality of the grant of such power, a system of regulatory or navigational markers may be adopted by the Board. Nothing in this section shall be construed to affect the application of any general law concerning the tidal waters of this Commonwealth.

C. Any county, city or town of this Commonwealth may enact ordinances which parallel general law regulating the operation of vessels on any waters within its territorial limits, including the marginal adjacent ocean, and the conduct and activity of any person using such waters. The locality may also provide for enforcement and penalties for the violation of the ordinances, provided the penalties do not exceed the penalties provided in this chapter for similar offenses.

D. After notice to the Department, any county, city or town may, by ordinance, establish "no wake" zones along the waterways within the locality in order to protect public safety and prevent erosion damage to adjacent property. The markers and buoys designating a no wake zone shall conform to the requirements established by the Board. Any marker or buoy which is not placed in conformance with the regulations of the Board or which is not properly maintained shall be removed by the locality. The locality may provide for enforcement and penalties for the violation of the ordinance.

E. Any person who desires to place or remove "no wake" buoys or other markers relating to the safe and efficient operation of vessels pursuant to any local ordinance shall apply to the local governing body. The local governing body shall approve, disapprove or approve with modifications the application and forward it to the Director, who shall approve, disapprove or approve with modifications within thirty days the placement and type of marker to be used or the removal of "no wake" buoys or other markers. The cost of the purchase and placement or the removal of buoys or markers shall be borne by the person requesting the placement or removal of the buoys or markers. Any marker or buoy which is not placed in conformance with the regulations of the Board or which is not properly maintained may be removed by the Department.
(Chgd. by L.1997 ch. 522; L.1999 ch. 489, eff. 7/1/99.)

§29.1-744.1. *(Repealed by L.1998 ch. 537, eff. 1/1/99.)*

§29.1-744.2. *(Repealed by L.1998 ch. 857, eff. 1/1/99.)*

§29.1-744.3. Slacken speed and control wakes near structures.

It shall be unlawful to operate any motorboat, except personal watercraft, at a speed greater than the slowest possible speed required to maintain steerage and headway when within fifty feet or less of docks, piers, boathouses, boat ramps, and people in the water. Nothing in this section shall prohibit a motorboat from towing a person with a rope less than fifty feet in length.
(Added by L.1998 ch. 857, eff. 1/1/99.)

§29.1-745. Enforcement of chapter; vessels displaying Coast Guard inspection decal.

Every game warden, Marine Resources Commission inspector, and every other law-enforcement officer of the Commonwealth and its subdivisions shall have the authority to enforce the provisions of this chapter and shall have authority to stop, board and inspect any vessel subject of this chapter after having identified himself in his official capacity. Except for enforcement of §29.1-738 and the requirement of having the registration certificate on board, the provisions of this section shall not apply to any vessel of twenty-six feet or more in length on which is displayed a current valid United States Coast Guard or United States Coast Guard Auxiliary inspection decal.

§29.1-746. Penalties.

Unless specified otherwise, any person who violates any provision of this chapter or any regulation adopted under this chapter shall be guilty of a Class 4 misdemeanor for each such violation.

ARTICLE 4
PERSONAL WATERCRAFT

§29.1-747. *(Repealed by L.1998 ch. 84, eff. 7/1/98, chs. 443, 512, 514, 515, 537, eff. 1/1/99, ch. 563, eff. 7/1/98.)*

§29.1-748. Restrictions on operation; penalty.

A. It shall be unlawful for any person to:

1. Operate a personal watercraft unless he is at least sixteen years of age, except any person fourteen or fifteen years of age shall be allowed to operate a personal watercraft if he (i) has successfully completed a boating safety education course approved by the Director and (ii) carries on his person, while operating a personal watercraft, proof of successful completion of such course. Upon the request of a law-enforcement officer, such person shall provide proof of having successfully completed an approved course;

2. Operate a personal watercraft unless each person riding on the personal watercraft is wearing a type I, type II, type III, or type V personal flotation device approved by the United States Coast Guard;

3. Fail to attach the lanyard to his person, clothing, or personal flotation device, if the personal watercraft is equipped with a lanyard-type engine cut-off switch;

4. Operate a personal watercraft on the waters of the Commonwealth between sunset and sunrise;

5. Operate a personal watercraft while carrying a number of passengers in excess of the number for which the craft was designed by the manufacturer;

6. Operate a personal watercraft in excess of the slowest possible speed required to maintain steerage and headway within fifty feet of docks, piers, boathouses, boat ramps, people in the water, and vessels other than personal watercraft. Nothing in this section shall prohibit a personal watercraft from towing a person with a rope less than fifty feet in length.

B. A violation of any provision of this section shall constitute a Class 4 misdemeanor.

C. A violation of this section shall not constitute negligence, be considered in mitigation of damages of whatever nature, be admissible in evidence or be the subject of comment by counsel in any action for the recovery of damages arising out of the operation, ownership, or maintenance of a personal watercraft, nor shall anything in this section change any existing law, rule, or procedure pertaining to any such civil action, nor shall this section bar any claim which otherwise exists.

(Chgd. by L.1998 chs. 443, 537, eff. 1/1/99.)

§29.1-749. Owner of personal watercraft permitting violation; penalty.

A. It shall be unlawful for the owner of or any person having control of a personal watercraft to authorize or knowingly permit a person under the age of sixteen to operate the personal watercraft, unless the person fourteen or fifteen years of age has successfully completed a boating safety education course as required under subdivision A 1 of §29.1-748.

B. A violation of any provision of this section shall constitute a Class 4 misdemeanor.

(Chgd. by L.1998 ch. 443, eff. 1/1/99.)

§29.1-749.1. Identification of personal watercraft rentals.

Every business located in a city with a population greater than 390,000 that provides personal watercraft for rent shall place the letter "R," at least eleven inches in height and eight and one-half inches in width, on both sides of each personal watercraft rental, in either red or black, whichever color represents the clearest contrast from the basic color of the rental unit.

(Added by L.1998 ch. 84, eff. 7/1/98.)

§29.1-749.2. Local regulation of personal watercraft rentals; penalty.

A. Any city with a population in excess of 390,000 may by ordinance regulate personal watercraft as provided in this section. Any ordinance enacted pursuant to this section may include any of the following provisions:

1. Any business which offers personal watercraft for rent shall (i) require any person to whom a personal watercraft is rented to present, prior to such rental, a government-issued identification card containing his photograph and (ii) retain such identification card, or a copy thereof, during the time the personal watercraft is being rented.

2. No person who rents or leases a personal watercraft shall knowingly misrepresent any material fact or falsify any information requested on the rental agreement or application.

3. Any business which offers personal watercraft for hourly short-term rental shall have at least one motorboat of at least fifty horsepower operated by an employee or agent of the business, in order to monitor and ensure the safe operation of the personal watercraft.

4. No business which offers personal watercraft for rent shall rent a personal watercraft that has an engine displacement which exceeds 800 cubic centimeters.

5. Any business which offers personal watercraft for rent shall have at least two marine VHF radios in operation during the time that a personal watercraft rental is being operated. The radios shall monitor channel 16 whenever they are not being actively used on a working channel.

B. Any locality may by ordinance establish standards for insurance coverage for any business which offers personal watercraft for rent.

C. Any ordinance adopted by a locality pursuant to this section may provide for a penalty for violation of the ordinance not to exceed the penalty applicable to a Class 3 misdemeanor.

(Added by L.1998 ch. 563; renumbered in 1998 from Section 29.1-749.1; chgd. by L.1999 ch. 536, eff. 7/1/99.)

§29.1-749.3. Personal watercraft instruction; rental agents.

Any person who is in the business of renting personal watercraft to the public shall provide to any person who rents a personal watercraft instruction on the laws of the Commonwealth governing motorboat operation, specific operating requirements of the personal watercraft being rented, motorboat safety equipment requirements, requirements in the case of a reportable accident, and such other information as the Director may require. The content and methods of instruction shall be approved by the Director.

Any attorney for the county, city or town in which an alleged violation of this section occurred may enforce this section by a civil action to recover a civil penalty not to exceed $250. The civil penalty shall be paid into the local treasury. No filing fee or other fee or cost shall be charged to the county, city or town which instituted the action.

The fact of a violation of this section shall not constitute negligence per se, be considered in mitigation of damages of whatever nature, be admissible in evidence or be the subject of comment by counsel in any action for the recovery of damages arising out of the operation, ownership or maintenance of a personal watercraft. This section shall not change any existing law, rule or procedure pertaining to any such civil action, nor shall this section bar any claim which otherwise exists.

(Added by L.1998 ch. 512, eff. 1/1/99; renumbered in 1998 from Section 29.1-749.1.)

§29.1-750. Exemptions.

The provisions of this article shall not apply to participants in regattas, races, marine parades, tournaments, or exhibitions approved by the Board or United States Coast Guard.

TITLE 30
GENERAL ASSEMBLY
(Selected Chapter)

CHAPTER 3.1
LEGISLATIVE SUPPORT COMMISSION
(Selected Section)

§30-34.2:1. Powers, duties and functions of Capitol Police.

The Capitol Police may exercise within the limits of the Capitol Square and, when assigned to any other property owned or controlled by the Commonwealth or any agency, department, institution or commission thereof, all the powers, duties and functions which are exercised by the police of the city, or the police or sheriff of the county within which said property is located. The jurisdiction of the Capitol Police shall further extend 300 feet beyond the boundary of any property they are required to protect, such jurisdiction to be concurrent with that of other law-enforcement officers of the locality in which such property is located. Additionally, the Capitol Police shall have concurrent jurisdiction with law-enforcement officers of the City of Richmond and of any county contiguous thereto in any case involving the theft or misappropriation of the personal property of any member or employee of the General Assembly. Members of the Capitol Police, when assigned to accompany the Governor, members of the Governor's family, the Lieutenant Governor, the Attorney General, members of the General Assembly, or members of the Virginia Supreme Court, shall be vested with all the powers and authority of a law-enforcement officer of any city or county in which they are required to be. All members of the Capitol Police shall be subject to the provisions of Chapter 10.1 (§2.1-116.1 et seq.) of Title 2.1 and to the provisions of Chapter 10.01 (§2.1-116.01 et seq.) of Title 2.1.

(Chgd. by L.1995 chs. 770, 818, eff. 7/1/95.)

TITLE 32.1
HEALTH
(Selected Chapters)

CHAPTER 2
DISEASE PREVENTION AND CONTROL
(Selected Article)

ARTICLE 3
DISEASE CONTROL MEASURES
(Selected Section)

§32.1-45.1. Deemed consent to testing and release of test results related to infection with human immunodeficiency virus or hepatitis B or C viruses.

A. Whenever any health care provider, or any person employed by or under the direction and control of a health care provider, is directly exposed to body fluids of a patient in a manner which may, according to the then current guidelines of the Centers for Disease Control, transmit human immunodeficiency virus or hepatitis B or C viruses, the patient whose body fluids were involved in the exposure shall be deemed to have consented to testing for infection with human immunodeficiency virus or hepatitis B or C viruses. Such patient shall also be deemed to have consented to the release of such test results to the person who was exposed. In other than emergency situations, it shall be the responsibility of the health care provider to inform patients of this provision prior to providing them with health care services which create a risk of such exposure.

B. Whenever any patient is directly exposed to body fluids of a health care provider, or of any person employed by or under the direction and control of a health care provider, in a manner which may, according to the then current guidelines of the Centers for Disease Control, transmit human immunodeficiency virus or hepatitis B or C viruses, the person whose body fluids were involved in the exposure shall be deemed to have consented to testing for infection with human immunodeficiency virus or hepatitis B or C viruses. Such person shall also be deemed to have consented to the release of such test results to the patient who was exposed.

C. For the purposes of this section, "health care provider" means any person, facility or agency licensed or certified to provide care or treatment by the Department of Health, Department of Mental Health, Mental Retardation and Substance Abuse Services, Department of Rehabilitative Services, or the Department of Social Services, any person licensed or certified by a health regulatory board within the Department of Health Professions except for the Boards of Funeral Directors and Embalmers and Veterinary Medicine or any personal care agency contracting with the Department of Medical Assistance Services.

D. "Health care provider," as defined in subsection C of this section, shall be deemed to include any person who renders emergency care or assistance, without compensation and in good faith, at the scene of an accident, fire, or any life-threatening emergency, or while en route therefrom to any hospital, medical clinic or doctor's office during the period while rendering such emergency care or assistance. The Department of Health shall provide appropriate counseling and opportunity for face-to-face disclosure of any test results to any such person.

E. Whenever any law-enforcement officer is directly exposed to body fluids of a person in a manner which may, according to the then current guidelines of the Centers for Disease Control, transmit human immunodeficiency virus or hepatitis B or C viruses, the person whose body fluids were involved in the exposure shall be deemed to have consented to testing for infection with human immunodeficiency virus or hepatitis B or C viruses. Such person shall also be deemed to have consented to the release of such test results to the law-enforcement officer who was exposed. In other than emergency situations, it shall be the responsibility of the law-enforcement officer to inform the person of this provision prior to the contact which creates a risk of such exposure.

F. Whenever a person is directly exposed to the body fluids of a law-enforcement officer in a manner which may, according to the then current guidelines of the Centers for Disease Control, transmit human immunodeficiency virus or hepatitis B or C viruses, the law-enforcement officer whose body fluids were involved in the exposure shall be deemed to have consented to testing for infection with human immunodeficiency virus or hepatitis B or C viruses. The law-enforcement officer shall also be deemed to have consented to the release of such test results to the person.

G. For the purposes of this section, "law-enforcement officer" means a person who is both (i) engaged in his public duty at the time of such exposure and (ii) employed by any sheriff's office, any adult or youth correctional facility, or any state or local law-enforcement agency, or any agency or department under the direction and control of the Commonwealth or any local governing body that employs persons who have law-enforcement authority.

H. If the person whose blood specimen is sought for testing refuses to provide such specimen, any person potentially exposed to the human immunodeficiency virus or hepatitis B or C viruses, or the employer of such person, may petition the general district court of the county or city in which the person whose specimen is sought resides or resided, or, in the case of a nonresident, the county or city where the health care provider or law-enforcement agency has its principal office, for an order requiring the person to provide a blood specimen or to submit to testing and to disclose the test results in accordance with this section. At any hearing before the court, the person whose specimen is sought or his counsel may appear. The court shall be advised by the Commissioner or his designee prior to entering any testing order. If a testing order is issued, both the petitioner and the person from whom the blood specimen is sought shall receive counseling and opportunity for face-to-face disclosure of any test results by a licensed practitioner or trained counselor.
(Chgd. by L.1997 ch. 869, eff. 7/1/97.)

CHAPTER 8
POSTMORTEM EXAMINATIONS AND SERVICES
(Selected Article)

ARTICLE 2
ANATOMICAL GIFTS
(Selected Sections)

§32.1-289.1. Sale of body parts prohibited; exceptions; penalty.

With the exception of hair, ova, blood and other self-replicating body fluids, it shall be unlawful for any person to sell, to offer to sell, to buy, to offer to buy or to procure through purchase any natural body part for any reason including but not limited to, medical and scientific uses such as transplantation, implantation, infusion or injection. Nothing in this section shall prohibit the reimbursement of expenses associated with the removal and preservation of any natural body parts for medical and scientific purposes. This section shall not apply to any transaction pursuant to Article 3 (§32.1-298 et seq.) of Chapter 8 of this title.

Any person engaging in any of these prohibited activities shall be guilty of a Class 6 felony.

§32.1-289.2. Donation or sale of blood, body fluids, organs and tissues by persons infected with human immunodeficiency virus.

Any person who donates or sells, who attempts to donate or sell, or who consents to the donation or sale of blood, other body fluids, organs and tissues, knowing that the donor is, or was, infected with human immunodeficiency virus, and who has been instructed that such blood, body fluids, organs or tissues may transmit the infection, shall be guilty, upon conviction, of a Class 6 felony.

This section shall not be construed to prohibit the donation of infected blood, other body fluids, organs and tissues for use in medical or scientific research.

CHAPTER 9
REGULATION OF MEDICAL ASSISTANCE
(Complete Chapter)

ARTICLE 1
IN GENERAL

§32.1-310. Declaration of purpose; authority to audit records.

The General Assembly finds and declares it to be in the public interest and for the protection of the health and welfare of the residents of the Commonwealth that a proper regulatory and inspection program be instituted in connection with the providing of medical, dental and other health services to recipients of medical assistance. In order to effectively accomplish such purpose and to assure that the recipient receives such services as are paid for by the Commonwealth, the acceptance by the recipient of such services and the acceptance by practitioners of reimbursement for performing such services shall authorize the Attorney General or his authorized representative to inspect and audit all records in connection with the providing of such services.

§32.1-312. Fraudulently obtaining excess or attempting to obtain excess benefits or payments; penalty.

A. No person, agency or institution, but not including an individual medical assistance recipient of health care, on behalf of himself or others, shall obtain or attempt to obtain benefits or payments pursuant to the Plan for Medical Assistance and any amendments thereto as provided for in §32.1-325, hereafter referred to as "medical assistance" in a greater amount than that to which entitled by means of:

1. A willful false statement;

2. By willful misrepresentation, or by willful concealment of any material facts; or

3. By other fraudulent scheme or device, including, but not limited to, billing for services, drugs, supplies or equipment that were unfurnished or were of a lower quality, or a substitution or misrepresentation of items billed.

B. Any person, agency or institution knowingly violating any of the provisions of subsection A of this section shall be liable for repayment of any excess benefits or payments received, plus interest on the amount of the excess benefits or payments at the rate of 1½% each month for the period from the date upon which payment was made to the date upon which repayment is made to the Commonwealth. Such person, agency or institution, in addition to any other penalties provided by law, shall be subject to civil penalties. The state Attorney General may petition the circuit court in the jurisdiction of the alleged offense, to seek an order assessing civil penalties in an amount not to exceed three times the amount of such excess benefits or payments. Such civil penalties shall not apply to any acts or omissions occurring prior to the effective date of this law.

C. A criminal action need not be brought against a person for that person to be civilly liable under this section.

D. Civil penalties shall be deposited in the general fund of the state treasury upon their receipt.

§32.1-313. Liability for excess benefits or payments obtained without intent to violate chapter.

Any person, agency or institution, but not including an individual medical assistance recipient of health care, that, without intent to violate this chapter, obtains benefits or payments under medical assistance to which such person, agency or institution is not entitled, or in a greater amount than that to which entitled, shall be liable for (i) any excess benefits or payments received, and (ii) interest on the amount of the excess benefits or payments at the judgment rate as defined in §6.1-330.54 from the date upon which such person, agency, or institution knew or reasonably should have known that it had received excess benefits or payments to the date upon which repayment is made to the Commonwealth. No person, agency or institution shall be liable for payment of interest, however, when excess benefits or payments were obtained as a result of errors made solely by the Department of Medical Assistance Services. Whenever a penalty or interest is due under this section or §32.1-312, such penalty or interest shall not be reimbursable by the Commonwealth as an allowable cost under any of the provisions of this chapter.

§32.1-314. False statement or representation in applications for payment or for use in determining rights to payment; concealment of facts; penalty.

Any person who engages in the following activities shall be guilty of a felony punishable by a term of imprisonment of not less than one nor more than twenty years, or in the discretion of the jury or the court trying the case without a jury, confinement in jail for not more than twelve months and, in addition to such imprisonment or confinement, may be fined an amount not to exceed $25,000:

1. Knowingly and willfully making or causing to be made any false statement or representation of a material fact in any application for any payment under medical assistance; or

2. At any time knowingly and willfully making or causing to be made any false statement or representation of a material fact for use in determining rights to such payment, or knowingly and willfully falsifying, concealing or covering up by any trick, scheme or device a material fact in connection with such application or payment; or

3. When having knowledge of the occurrence of any event affecting (i) the initial or continued right to any payment, or (ii) the initial or continued right to any such payment of any other individual in whose behalf he has applied for or is receiving such payments, willfully concealing or failing to disclose such event with an intent fraudulently to secure such payment either in a greater amount or quantity than is due or when no such payment is authorized.

(Chgd. by L.1995 ch. 491, eff. 7/1/95.)

§32.1-315. Solicitation or receipt of remuneration for certain services; offer or payment of remuneration for inducement of such services; penalty.

A. A person shall be guilty of a Class 6 felony and, in addition, may be fined an amount not to exceed $25,000, if he knowingly and willfully solicits or receives any remuneration, including any kickback, bribe or rebate, directly or indirectly, overtly or covertly, in cash or in-kind:

1. In return for referring an individual to a person for the furnishing or arranging for the furnishing of any item or service for which payment may be made in whole or in part under medical assistance; or

2. In return for purchasing, leasing, ordering, or arranging for or recommending purchasing, leasing or ordering any goods, facility, service or item for which payment may be made in whole or in part under medical assistance.

B. A person shall be guilty of a Class 6 felony and, in addition, may be fined an amount not to exceed $25,000, if he knowingly and willfully offers or pays any remuneration, including any kickback, bribe, or rebate, directly or indirectly, overtly or covertly, in cash or in-kind to any person to induce such person:

1. To refer an individual to a person for the furnishing or arranging for the furnishing of any item or service for which payment may be made, in whole or in part, under medical assistance; or

2. To purchase, lease, order, or arrange for or recommend purchasing, leasing or ordering any goods, facility, service or item for which payment may be made in whole or in part under medical assistance.

C. Subsections A and B of this section shall not apply to:

1. A discount or other reduction in price obtained by a provider of services or other person under medical assistance, if the reduction in price is properly disclosed and appropriately reflected in the cost claimed or charges made by the provider or other person under medical assistance;

2. Any reasonable compensation paid by an employer to an employee who has a bona fide employment relationship with such employer, for employment in the provision of covered items or services; and

3. An agreement by health care providers for the group purchase of equipment, goods, services, or supplies which results in fees paid to an agent of the providers, when such agreement has been presented to and authorized by the Department of Medical Assistance Services on the basis that the agreement will reduce the costs of providers of institutional services.

§32.1-316. False statement or representation as to conditions or operations of institution or facility; penalty.

Any person who knowingly, willfully, and fraudulently makes or causes to be made, or induces or seeks to induce the making of, any false statement or representation of a material fact with respect to the conditions or operations of any institution or facility in order that such institution or facility may qualify, either upon initial certification or upon recertification, as a hospital, skilled nursing facility, intermediate care facility, or home care organization, shall be guilty of a Class 6 felony. In addition thereto, a fine may be imposed in an amount not to exceed $5,000.

§32.1-317. Collecting excess payment for services; charging, soliciting, accepting or receiving certain consideration as precondition for admittance to facility or requirement for continued stay; penalty.

When the cost of services provided in a facility or by an individual to a patient is paid for, in whole or in part, under medical assistance, any person who knowingly and willfully:

1. Collects from a patient for any service provided under medical assistance, money or other consideration at a rate in excess of entitlements established by the Department of Medical Assistance Services; or

2. Charges, solicits, accepts or receives, in addition to any amount otherwise required to be paid under medical assistance any gift, money, donation or other consideration, other than a charitable, religious or philanthropic contribution from an organization or from a person unrelated to the patient:

a. As a precondition of admitting a patient to a hospital, skilled nursing facility or intermediate care facility; or

b. As a requirement for the patient's continued stay in such facility; shall be guilty of a Class 6 felony. In addition thereto, a fine may be imposed in an amount not to exceed $25,000.

§32.1-318. Knowing failure to deposit, transfer or maintain patient trust funds in separate account; penalty.

A. Any person having any patient trust funds in his possession, custody or control, who, knowing that he is violating any statute or regulation, deliberately fails to deposit, transfer or maintain such funds in a separate, designated, trust bank account as required by such statute or regulation shall be guilty of a Class 1 misdemeanor.

B. "Patient trust funds" are funds received by any health care facility which belong to patients and are required by any state or federal statute or regulation to be kept in a separate trust bank account for the benefit of such patients.

C. This section shall not be construed to prevent a prosecution pursuant to Chapter 5 (§18.2-77 et seq.) of Title 18.2 of this Code.

§32.1-319. Written verification of application, statement or form; penalty for false or misleading information.

The State Board of Medical Assistance Services may require in its Plan for Medical Assistance that any application, statement, or form filled out by suppliers of medical care under medical assistance shall contain or be verified by a written statement that it is made under the penalties of perjury and such declaration shall be in lieu of any oath otherwise required, and each such paper shall in such event so state. Any person who knowingly and willfully makes or subscribes any such papers or forms containing any false or misleading information shall be guilty of a Class 4 misdemeanor.

§32.1-320. Duties of Attorney General; medical services providers audit and investigation unit.

A. There shall be established within the Office of the Attorney General a unit to audit and investigate providers of services furnished under the State Medical Assistance Plan. The Department of Medical Assistance Services shall cooperate with the Office of the Attorney General in conducting such audits and investigations and shall provide such information for these purposes as may be requested by the Attorney General or his authorized representative.

B. The Attorney General or his authorized representative shall have the authority to:

1. Conduct audits and investigations of providers of medical and other services furnished under medical assistance. The relevant board within the Department of Health Professions shall serve in an advisory capacity to the Attorney General in the conduct of audits or investigations of health care providers licensed by the respective regulatory boards. In the conduct of such audits or investigations, the Attorney General may examine only those records or portions thereof, including patient records, for which services were rendered by a health care provider and reimbursed by the Department of Medical Assistance Services under the Plan for Medical Assistance, notwithstanding the provisions of Chapter 26 (§2.1-377 et seq.) of Title 2.1 or of any other statute which may make or purport to make such records privileged or confidential. No original patient records shall be removed from the premises of the health care provider, except in accordance with Rule 4:9 of the Rules of the Supreme Court of Virginia. The disclosure of any records or information by the Attorney General is prohibited, unless such disclosure is directly connected to the official purpose for which the records or information was obtained. The disclosure of patient information as required under this section shall not subject any physician or other health services provider to any liability for breach of any confidential relationship between the provider and the patient, but no evidence resulting from such disclosure may be used in any civil, administrative or criminal proceeding against the patient unless a waiver of the applicable evidentiary privilege is obtained. The Attorney General shall cause all copies of patient medical records in his possession or that of his designee to be destroyed upon completion of the audit, investigation or proceedings, including appeals;

2. Issue subpoenas, compel the attendance of witnesses, administer oaths, certify to official acts, take depositions within and without the Commonwealth as now provided by law, and compel the production of pertinent books, payrolls, accounts, papers, records, documents and testimony relevant to such investigation. If a person in attendance before the Attorney General or his authorized representative refuses, without reasonable cause, to be examined or to answer a legal and pertinent question, or to produce a book or paper or other evidence when ordered to do so by the Attorney General or his authorized representative, the Attorney General or his authorized representative may apply to the judge of the circuit court of the jurisdiction where such person is in attendance, upon affidavit, for an order returnable in not less than two nor more than five days, directing such person to show cause why he should not produce such records. Upon the hearing of such order, if the court shall determine that such person, without reasonable cause, has refused to be examined or to answer a legal or pertinent question, or to produce a book or paper which he was ordered to bring or produce, he may forthwith assess all costs and reasonable attorney's fees against such person. If the motion for an order is granted and the person thereafter fails to comply with the order, the court may make such orders as are provided for in the Rules of the Supreme Court of Virginia. Subpoenas shall be served and

witness fees and mileage paid as allowed in civil cases in the circuit courts of this Commonwealth.

§32.1-321. Prosecution of cases.

The State Attorney General shall refer cases for prosecution in accordance with the provisions of this chapter to the Commonwealth's attorney in the city or county where the offense occurred. The Commonwealth's attorney shall obtain the assistance of the office of the Attorney General in the conduct of litigation arising under this chapter and shall be considered the authorized representative of the Attorney General for the purposes of this chapter.

ARTICLE 2
REGULATION OF RECIPIENT ELIGIBILITY

§32.1-321.1. Powers and duties of Department.

The Department of Medical Assistance Services shall have the following powers and duties:

1. To investigate and refer for prosecution violations of applicable state and federal laws and regulations pertaining to the application for and receipt of services or benefits;

2. To investigate and refer for civil recovery any debts owed to the medical assistance program or funds paid for services or benefits as a result of violations of applicable state and federal laws and regulations pertaining to the application for and receipt of services or benefits; and

3. To cooperate with the federal government, other state agencies and the State Attorney General's Office in the detection and deterrence of fraud by recipients of medical assistance or their agents.

§32.1-321.2. Liability for excess benefits or payments obtained without intent to violate this article; recovery of Medical Assistance erroneously paid.

Any person who, without intent to violate this article, obtains benefits or payments under medical assistance to which he is not entitled shall be liable for any excess benefits or payments received. If the recipient knew or reasonably should have known that he was not entitled to the excess benefits, he may also be liable for interest on the amount of the excess benefits or payments at the judgment rate as defined in §6.1-330.54 from the date upon which such person knew or reasonably should have known that he had received excess benefits or payments to the date on which repayment is made to the Commonwealth. No person shall be liable for payment of interest, however, when excess benefits or payments were obtained as a result of errors made solely by the Department of Medical Assistance Services.

Any payment erroneously made on behalf of a recipient or former recipient of medical assistance may be recovered by the Department of Medical Assistance Services from the recipient or the recipient's income, assets or estate unless such property is otherwise exempted by state or federal law or regulation.

§32.1-321.3. Fraudulently obtaining benefits; liability for fraudulently issued benefits; civil action to recover; penalty.

Any person who, on behalf of himself or another, issues, obtains or attempts to obtain medical assistance benefits by means of (i) willful false statement, (ii) willful misrepresentation or concealment of a material fact, or (iii) any other fraudulent scheme or device shall be liable for repayment of the cost of all benefits issued as a result of such fraud, plus interest on the amount of the benefits issued at the rate of one and one-half percent per month for the period from the date upon which payment was made for such benefits to the date on which repayment is made to the Commonwealth.

Such matters may be referred for criminal action to the attorney for the Commonwealth having jurisdiction over the case. The Attorney General may, independent of any referral to or decision of the attorney for the Commonwealth, petition the circuit court in the jurisdiction of the alleged offense to seek an order assessing civil penalties in the amount of the benefits issued, in addition to repayment and interest and any other penalties provided by law.

All civil penalties shall be deposited in the general fund of the state treasury upon receipt.

(Chgd. by L.1996 chs. 941, 991, eff. 7/1/96.)

§32.1-321.4. False statement or representation in applications for eligibility or for use in determining rights to benefits; concealment of facts; criminal penalty.

A. Any person who engages in the following activities, on behalf of himself or another, shall be guilty of larceny and, in addition to the penalties provided in §§18.2-95 and 18.2-96 as applicable, may be fined an amount not to exceed $10,000:

1. Knowingly and willfully making or causing to be made any false statement or misrepresentation of a material fact in an application for eligibility, benefits or payments under medical assistance;

2. Knowingly and willfully falsifying, concealing or covering up by any trick, scheme, or device a material fact in connection with an application for eligibility, benefits or payments;

3. Knowingly and willfully concealing or failing to disclose any event affecting the initial or continued right of any individual to any benefits or payment with an intent to secure fraudulently such benefits or payment in a greater amount or quantity than is authorized or when no such benefit or payment is authorized;

4. Knowingly and willfully converting any benefits or payment received pursuant to an application for another person and receipt of benefits or payment on behalf of such other person to use other than for the health and welfare of the other person; or

5. Knowingly and willfully failing to notify the local department of welfare or social services, through whom medical assistance benefits were obtained, of changes in the circumstances of any recipient or applicant which could result in the reduction or termination of medical assistance services.

B. It shall be the duty of the Director of Medical Assistance Services or his designee to enforce the provisions of this section. A warrant or summons may be issued for violations of which the Director or his designee has knowledge. Trial for violation of this section shall be held in the county or city in which the application for medical assistance was made or obtained.

§32.1-322. Severability of chapter.

The several provisions of this chapter are hereby declared to be separate and severable, and if any clause, sentence, paragraph, subdivision, section or part thereof shall for any reason be adjudged invalid or unconstitutional, such invalidity or unconstitutionality shall not affect any clause, sentence, paragraph, subdivision or section.

CHAPTER 11
VIRGINIA INDIGENT HEALTH CARE TRUST FUND
(Selected Sections)

§32.1-333. Creation of Fund; administration.

A. There is hereby created the Virginia Indigent Health Care Trust Fund whose purpose is to receive moneys appropriated by the Commonwealth and contributions from certain hospitals and others for the purpose of distributing these moneys to certain hospitals subject to restrictions as provided in this chapter.

B. The Fund shall be the responsibility of the Board and Department of Medical Assistance Services and shall be maintained and administered separately from any other program or fund of the Board and Department. However, all funds voluntarily contributed or donated to the Fund for the purpose of subsidizing pilot health care projects for the uninsured, including any funds voluntarily contributed by local governments, shall be administered by the Technical Advisory Panel in accordance with Board regulations.

C. The Board may promulgate rules and regulations pursuant to the Administrative Process Act (§9-6.14:1 et seq.) for the administration of the Fund consistent with this chapter, including but not limited to:

1. Uniform eligibility criteria to define those medically indigent persons whose care shall qualify a hospital for reimbursement from the Fund. Such criteria shall define medically indigent persons as only those individuals whose gross family income is equal to or less than 100 percent of the federal nonfarm poverty level as published for the then current year in the Code of Federal Regulations.

2. Hospital inpatient and outpatient medical services qualifying for reimbursement from the Fund. Such medical services shall be limited to those categories of inpatient and outpatient hospital services covered under the Medical Assistance Program, but shall exclude any durational or newborn infant service limitations.

3. A mechanism to ensure that hospitals are compensated from the Fund only for charity care as defined in this chapter.

4. Terms, conditions and reporting requirements for hospitals participating in the Fund.

5. Terms, conditions, and reporting requirements for pilot health care projects for the uninsured.

(Chgd. by L.1995 ch. 333, eff. 7/1/95.)

§32.1-341. Failure to comply; fraudulently obtaining participation or reimbursement; criminal penalty.

A. Any person who engages in the following activities, on behalf of himself or another, shall be guilty of a Class 1 misdemeanor in addition to any other penalties provided by law:

1. Knowingly and willfully making or causing to be made any false statement or misrepresentation of a material fact in order to participate in or receive reimbursement from the Fund;

2. Knowingly and willfully failing to provide reports to the Department as required in this chapter; or

3. Knowingly and willfully failing to pay in a timely manner the contribution to the Fund by a hospital as calculated by the Department pursuant to §32.1-337.

B. Conviction of any provider or any employee or officer of such provider of any offense under this section shall also result in forfeiture of any payments due.

CHAPTER 12
STATE/LOCAL HOSPITALIZATION PROGRAM
(Selected Sections)

§32.1-344. State/Local Hospitalization Program.

There is hereby established within the Department of Medical Assistance Services the State/Local Hospitalization Program for indigent persons. With such funds as are appropriated for this purpose, the Director of the Department of Medical Assistance Services is authorized to administer this program and to expend state and local funds in accordance with the provisions of this chapter.

§32.1-350. Fraudulently obtaining benefits; criminal penalty.

A. Any person who engages in the following activities, on behalf of himself or another, shall be guilty of a Class 1 misdemeanor in addition to any other penalties provided by law:

1. Knowingly and willfully making or causing to be made any false statement or misrepresentation of a material fact in an application for eligibility under this program or in order to participate in or receive reimbursement from the program;

2. Knowingly and willfully concealing or failing to disclose any event affecting the initial or continued right of any individual to any benefits with an intent to secure fraudulently such benefits in a greater amount or quantity than is authorized or when no such benefit is authorized;

3. Knowingly and willfully failing to notify the local department of welfare or social services, through whom the benefits of this program were obtained, of changes in the circumstances of any recipient or applicant which could result in reduction or termination of the benefits;

4. Knowingly and willfully failing to provide any reports or data to the Department as required in this chapter.

B. Conviction of any provider or any employee or officer of such provider of any offense under this section shall also result in forfeiture of any payment due.

TITLE 33.1
HIGHWAYS, BRIDGES AND FERRIES
(Selected Chapters)

CHAPTER 1
COMMONWEALTH TRANSPORTATION BOARD AND HIGHWAYS GENERALLY
(Selected Articles)

ARTICLE 1
COMMONWEALTH TRANSPORTATION BOARD
(Selected Section)

§33.1-13.1. Policy of the Commonwealth regarding use of highways by motorcycles; discrimination by political subdivisions prohibited.

In formulating transportation policy; promulgating regulations; allocating funds; and planning, designing, constructing, equipping, operating and maintaining transportation facilities, no action of the Commonwealth Transportation Board, the Commonwealth Transportation Commissioner, or the Virginia Department of Transportation shall in any way have the effect of discriminating against motorcycles, motorcycle operators, or motorcycle passengers. No regulation or action of the Board, Commissioner or Department shall have the effect of enacting a prohibition or imposing a requirement that applies only to motorcycles or motorcyclists, and the principal purpose of which is to restrict or inhibit access of motorcycles and motorcyclists to any highway, bridge, tunnel, or other transportation facility.

The provisions of this section shall also apply to transportation facilities and projects undertaken or operated by counties, cities, towns, and other political subdivisions of the Commonwealth where state or federal funds have been used in whole or in part to plan, design, construct, equip, operate, or maintain the facility or project.

(Added by L.1999 chs. 332, 496, eff. 7/1/99.)

ARTICLE 2
THE STATE HIGHWAY SYSTEM
(Selected Section)

§33.1-46.2. Designation of high-occupancy vehicle lanes; use of such lanes; penalties.

A. In order to facilitate the rapid and orderly movement of traffic to and from urban areas during peak traffic periods, the Commonwealth Transportation Board may designate one or more lanes of any highway in the interstate, primary, or secondary highway systems as high-occupancy vehicle lanes, hereinafter referred to in this section as HOV lanes. When lanes have been so designated and have been appropriately marked with such signs or other markers as the Board may prescribe, they shall be reserved during periods designated by the Board for the exclusive use of buses and high-occupancy vehicles. Any local governing body may also, with respect to highways under its exclusive jurisdiction, designate HOV lanes and impose and enforce restrictions on the use of such HOV lanes. Any highway for which the local jurisdiction receives highway maintenance funds pursuant to §33.1-41.1 shall be deemed to be within the exclusive jurisdiction of the local governing body for the purposes of this section. HOV lanes shall be reserved for high-occupancy vehicles of a specified number of occupants as determined by the Board or, for HOV lanes designated by a local governing body, by that local governing body. Notwithstanding the foregoing provisions of this section, no designation of any lane or lanes of any highway as HOV lanes shall apply to the use of any such lanes by:

1. Emergency vehicles such as fire-fighting vehicles, ambulances, and rescue squad vehicles,
2. Law-enforcement vehicles,
3. Motorcycles,
4. a. Transit and commuter buses designed to transport sixteen or more passengers, including the driver,
   b. Commuter buses and motor coaches operating under irregular route passenger certificates issued under §46.2-2010 and any vehicle operating under a certificate of Public Convenience and Necessity or as a common carrier of passengers under §46.2-2004 or §46.2-2010,
5. Vehicles of public utility companies operating in response to an emergency call, or
6. Until July 1, 2004, vehicles bearing clean special fuel vehicle license plates issued pursuant to §46.2-749.3.

In the Hampton Roads Planning District, HOV restrictions may be temporarily lifted and HOV lanes opened to use by all vehicles when, because of an accident, emergency, or other exceptional circumstance, restricting use of HOV lanes becomes impossible or undesirable and the temporary lifting of HOV limitations is indicated by law-enforcement officers at the scene or by signs along or above the affected portion of highway.

The Commissioner of VDOT shall implement a one-year pilot program of the HOV facilities in the Hampton Roads Planning District beginning not later than May 1, 2000. This program shall include the temporary lifting of HOV restrictions and the opening of HOV lanes to all traffic when an incident resulting from nonrecurring causes within the general lanes occurs such that a lane of traffic is blocked or is expected to be blocked for 10 minutes or longer. The HOV restrictions for the facility will be reinstated when the general lane is no longer blocked and is available for use.

The Commissioner shall maintain necessary records to evaluate the effects of such openings on the operation of the general lanes and the HOV lanes. He shall report on the effects of this pilot. This pilot program will terminate if the Federal Highway Administration requires repayment of any federal highway construction funds because of the pilot program's impact on the HOV facilities in Hampton Roads.

B. In designating any lane or lanes of any highway as HOV lanes, the Board, or local governing body as the case may be, shall specify the hour or hours of each day of the week during which the lanes shall be so reserved, and the hour or hours shall be plainly posted at whatever intervals along the lanes the Board or local governing body deems appropriate. Any person driving a motor vehicle in a designated HOV lane in violation of this section shall be guilty of a traffic infraction which shall not be a moving violation and on conviction shall be fined fifty dollars. However, violations committed within the boundaries of Planning District Eight shall be punishable as follows:

For a first offense, by a fine of $50;

For a second offense, by a fine of $100;

For a third offense within a period of two years of the second offense, by a fine of $250; and

For a fourth or subsequent offense within a period of three years of the second offense, by a fine of $500.

Upon a conviction under this section, the court shall furnish to the Commissioner of the Department of Motor Vehicles in accordance with §46.2-383 an abstract of the record of such conviction which shall become a part of the person's driving record. Notwithstanding the provisions of §46.2-492, no driver demerit points shall be assessed for any violation of this section.

C. In the prosecution of an offense, committed in the presence of a law-enforcement officer, of failure to obey a road sign restricting a highway, or portion thereof, to the use of high-occupancy vehicles, proof that the vehicle described in the HOV violation summons was operated in violation of this section, together with proof that the defendant was at the time of such violation the registered owner of the vehicle, shall constitute in evidence a rebuttable presumption that such registered owner of the vehicle was the person who committed the violation. Such presumption shall be rebutted if the registered owner of the vehicle testifies in open court under oath that he was not the operator of the vehicle at the time of the violation. A summons for a violation of this section may be executed in accordance with §19.2-76.2. Such rebuttable presumption shall not arise when the registered owner of the vehicle is a rental or leasing company.

D. Notwithstanding the provisions of §19.2-76, whenever a summons for a violation of this section is served in any county, city, or town, it may be executed by mailing by first-class mail a copy thereof to the address of the owner of the vehicle as shown on the records of the Department of Motor Vehicles. If the summoned person fails to appear on the date of return set out in the summons mailed pursuant to this section, the summons shall be executed in the manner set out in §19.2-76.3.

No proceedings for contempt or arrest of a person summoned by mailing shall be instituted for his failure to appear on the return date of the summons.

E. Notwithstanding §33.1-252, high-occupancy vehicles having three or more occupants (HOV–3) may be permitted to use the Omer L. Hirst-Adelard L. Brault Expressway (Dulles Toll Road) without paying a toll.

F. Notwithstanding the contrary provisions of this section, the following conditions shall be met before the HOV–2 designation of Interstate Route 66 outside the Capital Beltway can be changed to HOV–3 or any more restrictive designation:

1. The Department shall publish a notice of its intent to change the existing designation and also immediately provide similar notice of its intent to all members of the General Assembly representing districts that touch or are directly impacted by traffic on Interstate Route 66.

2. The Department shall hold public hearings in the corridor to receive comments from the public.

3. The Department shall make a finding of the need for a change in such designation, based on public hearings and its internal data and present this finding to the Commonwealth Transportation Board for approval.

4. The Commonwealth Transportation Board shall make written findings and a decision based upon the following criteria:

a. Is changing the HOV–2 designation to HOV–3 in the public interest?

b. Is there quantitative and qualitative evidence that supports the argument that HOV–3 will facilitate the flow of traffic on Interstate Route 66?

c. Is changing the HOV–2 designation beneficial to comply with the federal Clean Air Act Amendments of 1990?

G. *(Subsection effective when the Department of Transportation receives notice and certification from the federal government that any and all federal funds provided for the construction of the HOV lanes shall not be required to be repaid or refunded.)* Notwithstanding any other provision of this section, no high-occupancy vehicle lanes shall be designated on any portion of Virginia Route 44, Interstate Route 64, or Interstate Route 264 located within any city having a population greater than 250,000 or within any city having a population of more than 150,000 but less than 170,000.

(Chgd. by L.1995 ch. 55; L.1996 chs. 34, 187, 191, 695, 921, 1037; L.1997 ch. 504; L.1998 ch. 321; L.1999 chs. 914, 960; L.2000 ch. 322, eff. 4/3/2000.)

ARTICLE 15
MISCELLANEOUS PROVISIONS
(Selected Sections)

§33.1-193. Closing highways for safety of public or proper completion of construction; injury to barriers, signs, etc.

If it shall appear to the Commissioner necessary for the safety of the traveling public or for proper completion of work which is being performed to close any road or highway coming under his jurisdiction to all traffic or any class of traffic, the Commissioner may close, or cause to be closed, the whole or any portion of such road or highway deemed necessary to be excluded from public travel and may exclude all or any class of traffic from such closed portion. While any such road or highway, or portion thereof, is so closed, or while any such road or highway, or portion thereof, is in process of construction or maintenance, the Commissioner or contractor, under authority from the Commissioner, may erect, or cause to be erected, suitable barriers or obstructions thereon, may post, or cause to be posted, conspicuous notices to the effect that the road or highway, or portion, is closed and may place warning signs, lights and lanterns on such road or highway, or portions thereof. When such road or highway is closed for the safety of the traveling public or in process of construction or maintenance, as provided in this section, any person who willfully breaks down, drives into new construction work, removes, injures or destroys any such barrier or barriers or obstructions, tears down, removes, or destroys any such notices or extinguishes, removes, injures or destroys any such warning lights or lanterns so erected, posted or placed shall be guilty of a misdemeanor.

§33.1-218. Rules and regulations for use of recreational waysides.

The Commonwealth Transportation Board is authorized and empowered to establish rules and regulations for the use of recreational waysides including rules and regulations relating to (a) the time, place and manner of parking of vehicles, (b) activities which may be conducted within such waysides, (c) solicitation and selling within the waysides, (d) such other matters as may be necessary or expedient in the interest of the motoring public.

The rules and regulations when adopted by the Commonwealth Transportation Board shall be posted in a conspicuous place at each wayside, along with such other signs as the Commonwealth Transportation Commissioner deems necessary to advise the public.

Any person violating any rule and regulation adopted under this section shall be guilty of a misdemeanor and upon conviction be fined not less than $5 nor more than $100 for each offense.

CHAPTER 3
FERRIES, BRIDGES AND TURNPIKES
(Selected Article)

ARTICLE 1
GENERAL PROVISIONS
(Selected Section)

§33.1-252. Free use of toll bridges, etc., by certain state officers and employees; penalties.

A. Vehicles transporting two or more persons, including the driver, may be permitted toll-free use of the Dulles Toll Road during rush hours by the Commonwealth Transportation Board; however, notwithstanding the provisions of subdivision B 1 of §56-543 said vehicles shall not be permitted toll-free use of a roadway as defined pursuant to the Virginia Highway Corporation Act of 1988 (§56-535 et seq.). Upon presentation of a toll pass issued pursuant to regulations promulgated by the Commonwealth Transportation Board, the following persons may use all toll bridges, toll ferries, toll tunnels, and toll roads in this Commonwealth without the payment of toll while in the performance of their official duties:

1. The Commonwealth Transportation Commissioner;
2. Members of the Commonwealth Transportation Board;
3. Employees of the Virginia Department of Transportation;
4. The Superintendent of the Department of State Police;
5. Officers and employees of the Department of State Police;
6. Members of the Alcoholic Beverage Control Board;
7. Employees of the regulatory and hearings divisions of the Department of Alcoholic Beverage Control and special agents of the Department of Alcoholic Beverage Control;
8. The Commissioner of the Department of Motor Vehicles;
9. Employees of the Department of Motor Vehicles;
10. Local police officers;
11. Sheriffs and their deputies;
12. Regional jail officials;
13. Animal wardens;
14. The Director and officers of the Department of Game and Inland Fisheries;
15. Persons operating fire-fighting equipment and ambulances owned by a political subdivision of the Commonwealth or a nonprofit association or corporation;
16. Operators of school buses being used to transport pupils to or from schools;
17. Operators of (i) commuter buses having a capacity of twenty or more passengers, including the driver, and used to regularly transport workers to and from their places of employment and (ii) public transit buses;
18. Employees of the Department of Rail and Public Transportation;
19. Employees of any transportation facility created pursuant to the Virginia Highway Corporation Act of 1988; and
20. Notwithstanding the foregoing provision of this subsection requiring presentation of a toll pass for toll-free use of such facilities, in cases of emergency and circumstances of concern for public safety on the highways of the Commonwealth, the Department shall, in order to alleviate an actual or potential threat or risk to the public's safety, facilitate the flow of traffic on or within the vicinity of the toll facility by permitting the temporary suspension of toll collection operations on its facilities.

a. The assessment of the threat to public safety shall be performed and the decision temporarily to suspend toll collection operations shall be made by the Commissioner or his designee.

b. Major incidents that may require the temporary suspension of toll collection operations shall include, but not necessarily be limited to (i) natural disasters such as hurricanes, tornadoes, fires, and floods; (ii) accidental releases of hazardous materials such as chemical spills; (iii) major traffic accidents such as multi-vehicle collisions; and (iv) other incidents deemed to present a risk to public safety.

c. In any judicial proceeding in which a person is found to be criminally responsible or civilly liable for any incident resulting in the suspension of toll collections as provided in this subsection, the court may assess against the person an amount equal to lost toll revenue as a part of the costs of the proceeding and order that such amount, not to exceed $2,000 for any individual incident, be paid to the Department for deposit into the toll road fund.

B. Any tollgate keeper who shall refuse to permit the persons listed in subsection A of this section to pass through such tollgate or over such toll bridge or ferry, or toll road or toll tunnel upon presentation of such a toll pass, shall be guilty of a misdemeanor and punished by a fine of not more than fifty dollars, and not less than two dollars and fifty cents. Any person other than those listed in subsection A of this section who shall exhibit any such toll pass for the purpose of using any toll bridge, toll tunnel or ferry shall be guilty of a Class 1 misdemeanor and punished accordingly.

B1. Any vehicle operated by the holder of a valid driver's license issued by Virginia or any other state shall be allowed free use of all toll bridges, toll roads, and other toll facilities in Virginia, if:

1. The vehicle is specially equipped to permit its operation by a handicapped person;
2. The driver of the vehicle has been certified, either by a physician licensed by Virginia or any other state or by the Adjudication Office of the United States Veterans Administration, as being severely physically disabled and having permanent upper limb mobility or dexterity impairments which substantially impair his ability to deposit coins in toll baskets;
3. The driver has applied for and received from the Department of Transportation a vehicle window sticker identifying him as eligible for such free passage; and
4. Such identifying window sticker is properly displayed on the vehicle.

A copy of this subsection shall be posted at all toll bridges, toll roads, and other toll facilities in Virginia. The Department of Transportation shall provide envelopes for payments of tolls by those persons exempted from tolls pursuant to this subsection and shall accept any payments made by such persons.

C. Nothing contained in this section or in §33.1-251 or §33.1-285 shall operate to affect the provisions of §22.1-187.

D. Notwithstanding the provisions of subsections A and B of this section, only the following persons may use the Chesapeake Bay Bridge–Tunnel or facilities of the Richmond Metropolitan Authority without the payment of toll when necessary and incidental to the conduct of official business:

1. The Commonwealth Transportation Commissioner;
2. Members of the Commonwealth Transportation Board;
3. Employees of the Department of Transportation;

4. The Superintendent of the Department of State Police;
5. Officers and employees of the Department of State Police;
6. The Commissioner of the Department of Motor Vehicles;
7. Employees of the Department of Motor Vehicles; and
8. Sheriffs and deputy sheriffs.

(Chgd. by L.1995 ch. 572; L.1996 ch. 138; L.1998 ch. 565, eff. 7/1/98.)

CHAPTER 6
OFFENSES CONCERNING HIGHWAYS OR TRAVELERS THEREON
(Complete Chapter)

§33.1-344. "Road" construed.

In this chapter, the word "road" shall be construed to mean any state or county road.

§33.1-345. Cutting or injuring trees near highways, injuring bridges, markers, etc.; obstructing roads, etc.

Any person shall be guilty of a Class 1 misdemeanor who shall:

(1) Cut or injure a tree within fifty feet of a road so as to render it liable to fall and leave it standing;

(2) Knowingly and willfully, without lawful authority, break down, destroy or injure any bridge or log placed across a stream for the accommodation of pedestrians;

(3) Obstruct any road or any ditch made for the purpose of draining any such road;

(4), (5) *(Repealed.)*

(6) Willfully or maliciously displace, remove, destroy or injure any highway sign or historical marker or any inscription thereon lawfully within a highway;

(7) Put or cast into any public road any glass, bottles, glassware, crockery, porcelain or pieces thereof, or any pieces of iron or hard or sharp metal, or any nails, tacks or sharp-pointed instruments of any kind, likely in their nature to cut or puncture any tire of any vehicle or injure any animal traveling thereon. This subdivision shall not apply to the use of any tire deflation device by a law-enforcement officer while in the discharge of his official duties, provided the device was approved for use by the Division of Purchase and Supply.

(Chgd. by L.1997 ch. 136, eff. 7/1/97.)

§33.1-346. Dumping trash, etc., on highway, right-of-way or private property; penalty.

A. It shall be unlawful for any person to dump or otherwise dispose of trash, garbage, refuse, litter, or other unsightly matter, on public property, including a public highway, right-of-way, property adjacent to such highway or right-of-way, or on private property without the written consent of the owner thereof or his agent. Any violation of this subsection shall constitute a misdemeanor punishable by confinement in jail for not more than twelve months and a fine of not less than $250 or more than $2,500, either or both.

B. When any person is arrested for a violation of this section, and the matter alleged to have been illegally dumped or disposed of has been ejected from a motor vehicle or transported to the disposal site in a motor vehicle, the arresting officer may comply with the provisions of §46.2-936 in making such arrest.

When a violation of the provisions of this section has been observed by any person, and the matter illegally dumped or disposed of has been ejected or removed from a motor vehicle, the owner or operator of such motor vehicle shall be presumed to be the person ejecting or disposing of such matter. However, such presumption shall be rebuttable by competent evidence.

Any person convicted of a violation of this subsection shall be guilty of a misdemeanor punishable by confinement in jail for not more than twelve months and a fine of not less than $250 or more than $2,500, either or both.

C. The governing bodies of counties, cities and towns are hereby authorized to adopt ordinances not in conflict with the provisions of this section, and may repeal, amend or modify such ordinances.

D. The provisions of this section shall not apply to the lawful disposal of such matter in landfills.

(Chgd. by L.1995 ch. 657; L.2000 ch. 20, eff. 7/1/2000.)

§33.1-346.1. Penalties for violation of §33.1-346.

Upon conviction of any person for a violation of §33.1-346, the court may suspend the imposition of any sentence on condition that the defendant volunteer his services for such period of time as the court may designate to remove litter from the highway. Any such sums collected shall be paid into the court and forwarded to the State Treasurer for the construction and maintenance of state highways.

§33.1-347. Dump creating fire hazard to public bridge.

It shall be unlawful for any person to establish or maintain a public or private dump containing inflammable articles within 500′ of any public bridge constructed wholly or partly of wood so as to create a fire hazard to such bridge. Any person violating this section shall be guilty of a misdemeanor and punished as provided by law. Each day of operation in violation hereof shall constitute a separate offense. An offense hereunder may be enjoined in the manner provided by law for the abatement of public nuisances.

§33.1-348. Junkyards.

(a) For the purpose of promoting the public safety, health, welfare, convenience and enjoyment of public travel, to protect the public investment in public highways, and to preserve and enhance the scenic beauty of lands bordering public highways, it is hereby declared to be in the public interest to regulate and restrict the establishment, operation, and maintenance of junkyards in areas adjacent to the highways within this Commonwealth.

(b) For the purpose of this section the following definitions shall apply:

(1) "Junk" shall mean old or scrap copper, brass, rope, rags, batteries, paper, trash, rubber, debris, waste, or junked, dismantled, or wrecked automobiles, or parts thereof, iron, steel, and other old or scrap ferrous or nonferrous material.

(2) "Automobile graveyard" shall mean any lot or place which is exposed to the weather and upon which more than five motor vehicles of any kind, incapable of being operated, and which it would not be economically practical to make operative, are placed, located or found.

(3) "Junkyard" shall mean an establishment or place of business which is maintained, operated, or used for storing,

keeping, buying, or selling junk, or for the maintenance or operation of an automobile graveyard, and the term shall include garbage dumps and sanitary fills.

(4) "Interstate system" shall mean the system presently defined in subsection (e) of §103 of Title 23, United States Code.

(5) "Primary highway" shall mean any highway within the State Highway System as established and maintained under Article 2 (§33.1-25 et seq.), Chapter 1, Title 33.1 of this Code, including extensions of such System within municipalities.

(6) "Federal-aid primary highway" shall mean any highway within that portion of the State Highway System as established and maintained under Article 2 (§33.1-25 et seq.), Chapter 1, Title 33.1 of this Code, including extensions of such System within municipalities, which has been approved by the Secretary of Commerce pursuant to subsection (b) of §103 of Title 23, United States Code.

(7) "Visible" shall mean capable of being seen without visual aid by a person of normal visual acuity.

(c) No junkyard shall be hereafter established, any portion of which is within 1,000′ of the nearest edge of the right-of-way of any interstate or primary highway or within 500′ of the nearest edge of the right-of-way of any other highway or city street, except the following:

(1) Junkyards which are screened by natural objects, plantings, fences, or other appropriate means so as not to be visible from the main-traveled way of the highway or city street, or otherwise removed from sight.

(2) Junkyards which are located in areas which are zoned for industrial use under authority of state law or in unzoned industrial areas as determined by the Commonwealth Transportation Board.

(3) Junkyards which are not visible from the main-traveled way of the highway or city street.

(d) Any junkyard lawfully in existence on April 4, 1968, which is within 1,000′ of the nearest edge of the right-of-way and visible from the main-traveled way of any interstate or federal-aid primary highway, and not located within an industrial area, shall be screened, if feasible, by the Commonwealth Transportation Commissioner at locations on the highway right-of-way or in areas acquired for such purposes outside the right-of-way, so as not to be visible from the main-traveled way of such highways.

Any junkyard lawfully in existence on April 4, 1968, which is within 1,000′ of the nearest edge of the right-of-way of any other primary highway or within 500′ of the nearest edge of the right-of-way of any other highway and visible from the main-traveled way of such highway, and not located within an industrial area, may be screened by the Commonwealth Transportation Commissioner in the same manner as junkyards adjacent to interstate or federal-aid primary highways.

The Commonwealth Transportation Commissioner is hereby authorized to acquire by purchase, gift or the power of eminent domain such lands or interests in lands as may be necessary to provide adequate screening of such junkyards.

(e) When the Commonwealth Transportation Commissioner determines that the topography of the land adjoining an interstate or federal-aid primary highway will not permit adequate screening of such junkyards or the screening of such junkyards would not be economically feasible, the Commonwealth Transportation Commissioner shall have the authority to acquire by gift, purchase or the power of eminent domain, such interests in lands as may be necessary to secure the relocation, removal, or disposal of the junkyards, and to pay for the costs of relocation, removal, or disposal, thereof. When the Commonwealth Transportation Commissioner determines that the topography of the land adjoining any other highway will not permit adequate screening or such would not be feasible, the Commissioner may exercise the same authority to relocate such junkyards as is vested in him in regard to interstate and federal-aid primary highways.

(f) Any junkyard which comes into existence after April 4, 1968, and which cannot be made to conform to this section, is declared to be a public and private nuisance and may be forthwith removed, obliterated or abated by the Commissioner or his representatives. The Commissioner may collect the cost of such removal, obliteration or abatement from the person owning or operating such junkyard.

(g) The Commonwealth Transportation Board is authorized to enter into agreements with the United States as provided in 23 U.S.C. §136 with respect to control of junkyards.

(h) The Commonwealth Transportation Commissioner shall not be required to expend any funds for screening or relocation under this section unless and until federal-aid matching funds are made available for this purpose.

(i) Any person violating any provision of this section shall be guilty of a misdemeanor.

CHAPTER 7
OUTDOOR ADVERTISING IN SIGHT OF PUBLIC HIGHWAYS
(Complete Chapter)

ARTICLE 1
GENERAL REGULATIONS

§33.1-351. Policy; definitions.

In order to promote the safety, convenience, and enjoyment of travel on and protection of the public investment in highways within this Commonwealth, to attract tourists and promote the prosperity, economic well-being, and general welfare of the Commonwealth, and to preserve and enhance the natural scenic beauty or aesthetic features of the highways and adjacent areas, the General Assembly declares it to be the policy of the Commonwealth that the erection and maintenance of outdoor advertising in areas adjacent to the rights-of-way of the highways within the Commonwealth shall be regulated in accordance with the terms of this article and regulations promulgated by the Commonwealth Transportation Board pursuant thereto.

The following terms, wherever used or referred to in this article, shall have the following meanings unless a different meaning clearly appears from the context:

"Advertisement" means any writing, printing, picture, painting, display, emblem, drawing, sign, or similar device which is posted or displayed outdoors on real property and is intended to invite or to draw the attention or to solicit the patronage or support of the public to any goods, merchandise, real or personal property, business, services, entertainment, or amusement manufactured, produced, bought, sold, conducted, furnished, or dealt in by any person; the term shall also include any part of an advertisement recognizable as such.

"Advertising structure" means any rigid or semirigid material, with or without any advertisement displayed thereon, situated upon or attached to real property outdoors, primarily or principally for the purpose of furnishing a background or base or support upon which an advertisement may be posted or displayed.

"Business of outdoor advertising" means the erection, use or maintenance of advertising structures or the posting or display of outdoor advertisements by any person who receives profit gained from rentals or any other compensation from any other person for the use or maintenance of such advertising structures or the posting or display of such advertisements, except reasonable compensation for materials and labor used or furnished in the actual erection of advertising structures or the actual posting of advertisements. The business of outdoor advertising shall not include the leasing or rental of advertising structures or advertisements used to advertise products, services, or entertainment sold or provided on the premises where the advertising structures or advertisement is located.

"Certification Acceptance Program" means a program which will allow any person, firm, or corporation owning five or more signs, advertisements, or outdoor advertising structures within a municipality to inspect their own signs, advertisements, or outdoor advertising structures two times during each calendar year, with inspections at least four to six months apart, and certify to the Commonwealth Transportation Commissioner that the inspections have been performed and that their outdoor advertising structures meet all applicable laws, rules, and regulations in lieu of paying an annual permit fee as required in §§33.1-360, 33.1-361, and 33.1-362. The Commonwealth Transportation Commissioner may, after a hearing, de-certify any person, firm, or corporation that fails to perform the required inspections annually or whose sign, advertisement, or outdoor advertising structures are found in violation of any federal, state or local law, rule, or regulation and shall collect all permit fees for the year the de-certification occurs and all subsequent years if the Commissioner finds that the violation has been committed.

"Highway" means every way or place of whatever nature open to the use of the public for purposes of vehicular travel in this Commonwealth.

"Municipalities" means cities and incorporated towns.

"Person" includes an individual, partnership, association or corporation.

"Post" means post, display, print, paint, burn, nail, paste or otherwise attach.

"Real property" includes any property physically attached or annexed to real property in any manner whatsoever.

"Town" means an incorporated town.

"Historic place, museum or shrine" includes only places that are maintained wholly at public expense or by a nonprofit organization.

"Information center" means an area or site established and maintained at rest areas for the purpose of informing the public of places of interest within the Commonwealth and providing such other information as the Commonwealth may consider desirable.

"Rest area" means an area or site established and maintained within or adjacent to the right-of-way or under public supervision or control, for the convenience of the traveling public.

"Centerline of the highway" means a line equidistant from the edges of the median separating the main traveled ways of a divided highway, or the centerline of the main traveled way of a nondivided highway.

"Interchange" means a grade separated intersection with one or more turning roadways for travel between intersection legs, or an intersection at grade, where two or more highways join or cross.

"Legible" means capable of being read without visual aid by a person of normal visual acuity.

"Maintain" means to allow to exist.

"Main traveled way" means the traveled way of a highway on which through traffic is carried. In the case of a divided highway, the traveled way of each of the separated roadways for traffic in opposite directions is a main traveled way. It does not include such facilities as frontage roads, turning roadways, or parking areas.

"National highway system" means the federal-aid highway system described in subsection (b) of §103 of Title 23, United States Code, and regulations adopted pursuant thereto. For the purpose of this article, outdoor advertising controls on the national highway system shall be implemented as those highways are designated and approved by congressional action and such designation and approval shall be kept on file in the central office of the Department of Transportation and placed in the minutes of the Commonwealth Transportation Board by the Commonwealth Transportation Commissioner. Prior to congressional approval, highways classified as National System of Interstate and Defense Highways, Dwight D. Eisenhower National System of Interstate and Defense Highways, Interstate System, or federal-aid primary as defined herein shall be considered as the national highway system.

"National System of Interstate and Defense Highways," "Dwight D. Eisenhower National System of Interstate and Defense Highways," and "Interstate System" means the system presently defined in subsection (e) of §103 of Title 23, United States Code.

"Federal-aid primary highway" means any highway within that portion of the State Highway System as established and maintained under Article 2 (§33.1-25 et seq.), Chapter 1, Title 33.1, including extensions of such system within municipalities, which has been approved by the Secretary of Transportation pursuant to subsection (b) of §103 of Title 23, United States Code, as that system existed on June 1, 1991.

"Scenic area" means any public park, area of particular scenic beauty or historical significance designated as a scenic area by the Commonwealth Transportation Board.

"Sign" means any outdoor sign, display, device, figure, painting, drawing, message, placard, poster, billboard, or other thing which is designed, intended, or used to advertise or inform, any part of the advertising or informative contents of which is visible from any highway.

"Trade name" shall include brand name, trademark, distinctive symbol, or other similar device or thing used to identify particular products or services.

"Traveled way" means the portion of a roadway for the movement of vehicles, exclusive of shoulders.

"Turning roadway" means a connecting roadway for traffic turning between two intersection legs of an interchange.

"Visible" means capable of being seen (whether or not legible) without visual aid by a person of normal visual acuity.

"Distance from edge of a right-of-way" shall be the horizontal distance measured along a line normal or perpendicular to the centerline of the highway.

"Urban area" means an urbanized area or, in the case of an urbanized area encompassing more than one state, that part of the "urbanized area" within the Commonwealth, or an urban place.

"Urban place" means an area so designated by the United States Bureau of the Census having a population of 5,000 or more and not within any urbanized area, within boundaries fixed by the Commonwealth Transportation Commissioner, in his discretion, in cooperation with the governing bodies of the several counties, towns or cities affected and the appropriate federal authority. Such boundaries shall, as a minimum, encompass the entire urban place designated by the United States Bureau of the Census.

"Urbanized area" means an area so designated by the United States Bureau of the Census, within boundaries fixed by the Commonwealth Transportation Commissioner, in his discretion, in cooperation with the governing bodies of the several counties, towns or cities affected and the appropriate federal authority. Such boundaries shall, as a minimum, encompass the entire urbanized area within a state as designated by the United States Bureau of the Census.

A "nonconforming sign," "nonconforming advertisement," or "nonconforming advertising structure" is one which was lawfully erected adjacent to any highway in the Commonwealth, but which does not comply with the provisions of state law, state regulations, or ordinances adopted by local governing bodies passed at a later date or which later fails to comply with state law, state regulations, or ordinances adopted by local governing bodies due to changed conditions.

"Virginia byway" and "scenic highway" means those highways designated by the Commonwealth Transportation Board pursuant to Article 5 (§33.1-62 et seq.) of Chapter 1 of this title. For the purposes of the article, a Virginia byway shall mean a scenic byway as referenced in Title 23, United States Code, §131(s).

(Chgd. by L.1996 ch. 777; L.2000 chs. 432, 449, eff. 7/1/2000.)

§33.1-352. Enforcement of provisions by Commissioner.

The Commissioner shall administer and enforce the provisions of this article. He may, in the performance of his duties hereunder, assign to division engineers and other employees in the Department of Transportation such duties other than discretional powers as he may think appropriate.

§33.1-353. Territory to which article applies.

The territory under the jurisdiction of the Commonwealth Transportation Commissioner for the purposes of this article shall include all of the Commonwealth, exclusive of that portion thereof which lies within the corporate limits of municipalities except the jurisdiction of the Commonwealth Transportation Commissioner shall apply to all the territory within municipalities on which signs, advertisements, or advertising structures are visible from the main traveled way of any interstate highway, federal-aid primary highway as that system existed on June 1, 1991, or national highway system highway.

§33.1-354. Entry upon lands; hindering Commissioner or agent.

The Commissioner and all employees under his direction may enter upon such lands as may be necessary in the performance of their functions and duties as prescribed by this article. Any person who shall hinder or obstruct the Commissioner or any assistant or agent of the Commissioner in carrying out such functions and duties shall be guilty of a misdemeanor.

§33.1-355. Excepted signs, advertisements and advertising structures.

The following signs and advertisements, if securely attached to real property or advertising structures, and the advertising structures, or parts thereof, upon which they are posted or displayed are excepted from all the provisions of this article save those enumerated in §§33.1-353, 33.1-356, 33.1-360, subdivisions (2) through (13) of §33.1-369 and §§33.1-370 and 33.1-375:

(1) Advertisements securely attached to a place of business or residence, and not to exceed ten advertising structures with combined total area, exclusive of the area occupied by the name of the business, owner or lessee, of advertisements and advertising structures not to exceed 500 square feet, erected or maintained, or caused to be erected or maintained, by the owner or lessee of such place of business or residence, within 250 feet of such place of business or residence or located on the real property of such place of business or residence and relating solely to merchandise, services or entertainment sold, produced, manufactured or furnished at such place of business or residence;

(2) Signs erected or maintained, or caused to be erected or maintained, on any farm by the owner or lessee of such farm and relating solely to farm produce, merchandise, services or entertainment sold, produced, manufactured or furnished on such farm;

(3) Signs upon real property posted or displayed by the owner, or by the authority of the owner, stating that the property, upon which the sign is located, or a part of such property, is for sale or rent or stating any data pertaining to such property and its appurtenances, and the name and address of the owner and the agent of such owner;

(4) Official notices or advertisements posted or displayed by or under the direction of any public or court officer in the performance of his official or directed duties, or by trustees under deeds of trust, deeds of assignment or other similar instruments;

(5) Danger or precautionary signs relating to the premises or signs warning of the condition of or dangers of travel on a highway, erected or authorized by the Commonwealth

Transportation Commissioner; or forest fire warning signs erected under authority of the State Forester and signs, notices or symbols erected by the United States government under the direction of the United States Forestry Service;

(6) Notices of any telephone company, telegraph company, railroad, bridges, ferries or other transportation company necessary in the discretion of the Commonwealth Transportation Commissioner for the safety of the public or for the direction of the public to such utility or to any place to be reached by it;

(7) Signs, notices or symbols for the information of aviators as to location, direction and landings and conditions affecting safety in aviation erected or authorized by the Commonwealth Transportation Commissioner;

(8) Signs containing sixteen square feet or less and bearing an announcement of any county, town, village or city, or historic place or shrine, situated in this Commonwealth, advertising itself or local industries, meetings, buildings or attractions, provided the same is maintained wholly at public expense, or at the expense of such historic place or shrine;

(9) Signs or notices containing two square feet or less, placed at a junction of two or more roads in the State Highway System denoting only the distance or direction of a church, residence or place of business, provided such signs or notices do not exceed a reasonable number in the discretion of the Commonwealth Transportation Commissioner;

(10) Signs or notices erected or maintained upon property giving the name of the owner, lessee or occupant of the premises;

(11) Advertisements and advertising structures within the corporate limits of cities and towns, except as specified in §33.1-353;

(12) Historical markers erected by duly constituted and authorized public authorities;

(13) Highway markers and signs erected, or caused to be erected, by the Commissioner or the Commonwealth Transportation Board or other authorities in accordance with law;

(14) Signs erected upon property warning the public against hunting, fishing or trespassing thereon;

(15) Signs erected by Red Cross authorities relating to Red Cross Emergency Stations. And authority is hereby expressly given for the erection and maintenance of such signs upon the right-of-way of all highways in this Commonwealth at such locations as may be approved by the Commonwealth Transportation Commissioner;

(16) Signs advertising agricultural products and horticultural products, or either, when such products are produced by the person who erects and maintains the signs; provided, however, that the location and number of such signs shall be in the sole discretion of the Commonwealth Transportation Commissioner;

(17) Signs advertising only the name, time and place of bona fide agricultural, county, district or state fairs, together with announcements of special events in connection therewith which do not consume more than fifty percent of the display area of such signs, provided the person who posts the signs or causes them to be posted will post a cash bond as may be prescribed by the Commonwealth Transportation Commissioner, adequate to reimburse the Commonwealth for the actual cost of removing such signs as are not removed within thirty days after the last day of the fair so advertised;

(18) Signs of eight square feet or less, or one sign structure containing more than one sign of eight square feet or less, which denote only the name of a civic service club or church, location and directions for reaching same, and time of meeting of such organization, provided such signs or notices do not exceed a reasonable number as determined by the Commonwealth Transportation Commissioner.

(Chgd. by L.1996 ch. 125, eff. 7/1/96.)

§33.1-356. License required of outdoor advertiser.

No person shall engage or continue in the business of outdoor advertising in this Commonwealth outside of the corporate limits of municipalities or within the corporate limits of municipalities if their off-premises sign, advertisement, or advertising structure is visible from the main traveled way of any interstate, federal-aid primary, or national highway system highway without first obtaining a license therefor from the Commonwealth Transportation Commissioner. Persons engaged in the business of outdoor advertising who own signs, advertisements, or advertising structures visible from the main traveled way of any interstate, federal-aid primary, or national highway system highway within municipalities shall have until October 1, 1993 to obtain a license form the Commonwealth Transportation Commissioner or remove such sign, advertisement, or advertising structure form the view from the main traveled way of any interstate, federal-aid primary, or national highway system highway. The Commonwealth Transportation Commissioner shall notify persons known to be engaged in the business of outdoor advertising within municipalities by August 1, 1993, of the need to obtain a license. The fee for such license, hereby imposed for revenue for the use of the Commonwealth, shall be $500 per year, payable annually in advance. Applications for licenses, or renewal of licenses, shall be made on forms furnished by the Commonwealth Transportation Commissioner, shall contain such information as the Commonwealth Transportation Commissioner may require and shall be accompanied by the annual fee. Licenses granted under this section shall expire on December 31 of each year and shall not be prorated. Applications for renewal of licenses shall be made not less than thirty days prior to the date of expiration. Nothing in this section shall be construed to require any person who advertises upon a structure or fixture on his property or a licensed advertiser's structure or other space to obtain a license.

§33.1-357. Revocation of license.

The Commissioner shall have the right, after thirty days' notice in writing to the licensee, to revoke any license granted by him upon repayment of a proportionate part of the license fee, in any case in which he shall find that any of the information required to be given in the application for the license is knowingly false or misleading or that the licensee has violated any of the provisions of this article, unless such licensee shall, before the expiration of such thirty days, correct such false or misleading information and comply with the provisions of this article.

§33.1-358. Judicial review of revocation.

Any person whose license is so revoked is entitled to judicial review of such revocation in accordance with the provisions of the Administrative Process Act (§9-6.14:1 et seq.). Any person aggrieved by the judgment of such court shall have the right of appeal to the Court of Appeals.

§33.1-359. Bond required from out-of-state licensee.

No license to engage or continue in the business of outdoor advertising shall be granted to any person having his principal place of business outside the Commonwealth or which is incorporated outside the Commonwealth for the posting or display of any advertisement or the erection, use or maintenance of any advertising structure, until such person shall have furnished and filed with the Commissioner a bond payable to the Commonwealth, with surety approved by the Commissioner and in form approved by the Attorney General, in the sum of $1,000, conditioned that such licensee shall fulfill all requirements of law and the regulations and orders of the Commissioner, relating to the display of advertisements or the erection of advertising structures. Such bond shall remain in full force and effect so long as any obligations of such licensee to the Commonwealth shall remain unsatisfied.

§33.1-360. Permits required.

Except as in this article otherwise provided, no person, whether engaged in the business of outdoor advertising or not, shall erect, use, maintain, post or display any advertisement or advertising structure in this Commonwealth, outside of municipalities, without first obtaining a permit therefor from the Commonwealth Transportation Commissioner and paying the annual fee therefor, as provided in this article. A permit shall be required for an off-premises sign, advertisement, or advertising structure authorized by §33.1-370 if it is located within a municipality and is visible from the main traveled way of any interstate, federal-aid primary, or national highway system highway unless the owner of such sign, advertisement, or advertising structure has entered in a Certification Acceptance Program as described in §33.1-351. Owners of signs, advertisements, or advertising structures within municipalities shall have until December 1, 1993, to obtain a permit from the Commissioner or to remove the sign, advertisement, or advertising structure. The Commonwealth Transportation Commissioner shall notify the owners of known signs, advertisements, or advertising structures within municipalities by August 1, 1993.

No bond or permit shall be required for the posting or display of any advertisement posted or displayed on any advertising structure or space for which a permit has been issued or renewed for the then current calendar year under the provisions of this article unless such permit has been revoked.

§33.1-361. Applications for permits; fees.

A separate application for a permit shall be made for each separate advertisement or advertising structure, on a form furnished by the Commonwealth Transportation Commissioner, which application shall be signed by the applicant or his representative duly authorized in writing to act for him and shall describe and set forth the size, shape and the nature of the advertisement or advertising structure it is proposed to post, display, erect or maintain and its actual or proposed location with sufficient accuracy to enable the Commonwealth Transportation Commissioner to identify such advertisement or advertising structure and to find its actual or proposed location.

Each application shall be accompanied by an application fee in an amount determined as follows on the basis of the area of the advertisement or advertising structure for which the permit is sought, according to the following schedule:

1. Three dollars if such area does not exceed thirty-two square feet;
2. Five dollars and fifty cents if such area exceeds thirty-two square feet but does not exceed seventy-four square feet;
3. Twenty dollars if such area exceeds seventy-four square feet but does not exceed 424 square feet;
4. Twenty-five dollars if such area exceeds 424 square feet but does not exceed 624 square feet; and
5. An additional fifteen dollars for each 200 square feet of such area in excess of 624 square feet except, within municipalities, the fifteen-dollar fee for each additional 200 square feet of such area in excess of 624 square feet shall not apply.

In the computation of fees under this section, each side of advertisement or advertising structure used or constructed to be used shall be separately considered.

The fee shall be retained by the Commonwealth Transportation Commissioner if the permit is issued. If the permit is refused, the Commonwealth Transportation Commissioner shall refund one-half the application fee to the applicant.

In addition to the above, on any original application for an advertisement or advertising structure there shall be imposed an inspection charge of fifty dollars for any advertisement or advertising structure to be located on an interstate, federal-aid primary, or national highway system highway and twenty-five dollars on any other highway. Inspection fees shall not be charged within municipalities for any such sign, advertisement, or advertising structure in existence on July 1, 1993.

Each application shall be accompanied by the written consent, or in lieu thereof a copy certified by an officer authorized to take acknowledgments to deeds in this Commonwealth, of the owner of the real property upon which such advertisement or advertising structure is to be erected, used, maintained, posted or displayed, or of such other person having the legal right to grant such consent, or of the duly authorized agent of such owner, or other person; provided, that in the marsh or meadowland owned by the Commonwealth along either side of the causeway leading from the mainland to the town of Chincoteague, the legal right to grant such consent shall be vested in the governing body of such town.

Application shall be made in like manner for a permit to use, maintain or display an existing advertisement or advertising structure.

§33.1-362. Duration and renewal of permit.

Except as provided in §33.1-365, permits issued hereunder shall run for the calendar year, and may be renewed upon application made upon forms furnished by the Commissioner and the payment of the same fee required to be paid upon application for a permit. Permits will not be extended or renewed in cases where the permittee has not exercised the privilege of erecting such advertising structure or displayed such advertisement during the period for which the permit was issued. Annual permits issued after December fifteenth will cover the following calendar year.

§33.1-363. Area of advertising structure.

The area of an advertising structure shall be determined from its outside measurements, excluding as a part thereof, the height and overall width of supports and supporting structure and any other portion or portions thereof beneath the normal area upon which an advertisement is posted or intended to be posted.

§33.1-364. Revocation of permit.

The Commissioner may, after thirty days' notice in writing to the permittee, revoke any permit issued by him under §33.1-360 upon repayment of a proportionate part of the fee in any case in which it shall appear to the Commissioner that the application for the permit contains knowingly false or misleading information, that the permittee has failed to keep in a good general condition and in a reasonable state of repair the advertisement or advertising structure for which such permit was issued or that the permittee has violated any of the provisions of this article unless such permittee shall, before the expiration of such thirty days, correct such false or misleading information, or make the necessary repairs or improvement in the general condition of such advertisement or advertising structure or comply with the provisions of this article, as the case may be. If the erection, maintenance and display of any advertisement or advertising structure for which a permit is issued by the Commissioner and the permit fee has been paid as above provided, shall be prevented by any zoning board, commission or other public agency which also has jurisdiction over the proposed advertisement or advertising structure or its site, the application fee for such advertisement or advertising structure shall be returned by the Commissioner and the permit revoked. But one-half of the application fee shall be deemed to have accrued upon the erection of an advertising structure or the display of an advertisement followed by an inspection by the Commissioner or his representative.

§33.1-365. Temporary permit.

In any case if an applicant for a permit shall certify in his application that he is unable to state the actual or proposed location of the advertisement or advertising structure or to file the written consent of the landowner or other person having the legal right to the real estate upon which the advertisement or advertising structure is to be erected, used, maintained, posted or displayed, the Commissioner shall issue to such applicant a temporary permit, together with the proper identification number to be attached to such advertisement or advertising structure, which temporary permit shall expire sixty days from the date of its issue. Applications for temporary permits must indicate the county and route on which the advertisement or advertising structure is to be located and must be accompanied by a fee of two dollars to cover the cost of issuance of the temporary permit. If within such sixty days, the applicant shall file with the Commissioner an application setting forth all of the information required in §33.1-361, together with the required fees, the Commissioner shall issue to such applicant a permit. In the event that the permit is not issued, the fees submitted shall be returned, except the two dollars for the temporary permit.

§33.1-366. Appeal from refusal or revocation of permit.

Any person aggrieved by any action of the Commissioner in refusing to grant or in revoking a permit under §33.1-361 or §33.1-364 may appeal from the decision of the Commissioner in accordance with the provisions of the Administrative Process Act (§9-6.14:1 et seq.).

§33.1-367. Transfer of licenses and permits to successor concerns.

Any license or permit issued pursuant to this article may be transferred to any person who acquires as a successor the business of the person for whom such license or permit was issued.

§33.1-368. Identification of advertising structure or advertisement.

The Commissioner shall require that each advertising structure and each advertisement not posted or displayed on an advertising structure shall bear an identification number, furnished by the Commissioner, and if erected, maintained or displayed by a licensed outdoor advertiser shall also bear his name. The Commissioner shall make suitable provisions for the details thereof.

§33.1-369. Certain advertisements or structures prohibited.

No advertisement or advertising structure shall be erected, maintained or operated:

(1) Within 660 feet of the nearest edge of the right-of-way of the Blue Ridge Parkway, the Colonial National Parkway, the Mount Vernon Boulevard, or any other parkway within this Commonwealth or within 660 feet of any public cemetery, public park reservation, public playground, national forest or state forest, outside the limits of any municipality; however, any advertisement or advertising structure which is lawfully in place on April 6, 1966, and which does not conform to the 660-foot distance requirement may be maintained for the life of such advertisement or advertising structure;

(2) Which involves motion or rotation of any part of the structure, moving reflective disks, running animation, or displays an intermittent light or lights visible from any highway. The prohibition of this subsection shall not apply to: (a) an on-premises advertisement or advertising structure with the message changed by electronic means or remote control, programmed or sequenced to change no more than once every four seconds; (b) an off-premises advertisement or off-premises advertisement structure visible only from a highway that is not a part of the interstate, federal-aid primary, or national highway system with messages changed by electronic means or remote control, programmed or sequenced to change no more than once every four seconds; or (c) an on-premises advertisement or advertising structure with messages displayed as scrolling words and/or numbers;

(3) Which uses the words "stop" or "danger" prominently displayed or presents or implies the need or requirement of stopping or the existence of danger on any highway, or which is a copy or imitation of official highway signs;

(4) *(Reserved.)*

(5) Which, within visible distance of any highway, advertises any county, city, town, village, historic place or shrine without the consent, in writing of such county, city, town or village or of the owner of such historic place or shrine;

(6) Which is mobile and is designed to and effectively does distract the attention of passing motorists on any highway by flashing lights, loud and blatant noises or movable objects;

(7) Which involve red, green or amber lights or reflectorized material and which resemble traffic signal lights or traffic control signs and are within visible distance of any highway;

(8) Within fifteen feet of the nearest edge of the pavement of any highway; however, the Commonwealth Transportation Commissioner may waive this restriction whenever the advertisement or advertising structure is actually anchored outside of the right-of-way, and, within his discretion, does not constitute a safety hazard or conflict with any other restriction contained in this section;

(9) At any public road intersection in such manner as would obstruct the clear vision in either direction between a point on the center line of the side road 20 feet from the nearest edge of the pavement of the main road and points on the main road 400 feet distant, measured along the nearest edge of the pavement of the main road;

(10) At any grade intersection of a public road and a railroad in such manner as would obstruct the clear vision in either direction within triangular areas formed by (a) a point at the center of the railroad-public road intersection, (b) a point on the public road 400 feet from the center of the railroad-public road intersection as measured along the center of the public road, and (c) a point on the railroad 500 feet from the center of the railroad-public road intersection as measured along the center of the railroad;

(11) At or near any curve in a road in such a manner as to obstruct the clear vision of traffic from any one point on such curve to any other point not more than 400 feet apart, as measured between each point from the nearest edge of the pavement;

(12) Which advertises activities which are illegal under state or federal laws or regulations in effect at the location of such sign or advertisement or at the location of such activities;

(13) Which is obsolete or inconsistent with this article or regulations adopted by the Commonwealth Transportation Board pursuant to this article; or

(14) After December 18, 1991, adjacent to any interstate, federal-aid primary, or national highway system highway in the Commonwealth which has been designated as a Virginia byway or scenic highway, except directional and official signs and notices defined in this article and regulations adopted under this article, on-premises signs, and

signs advertising the sale or lease of property upon which they are located.

(Chgd. by L.1999 ch. 290; L.2000 ch. 140, eff. 7/1/2000.)

§33.1-370. Special provisions pertaining to interstate, national highway system, and federal-aid primary highways.

A. Notwithstanding the territorial limitation set out in §33.1-353, no sign or advertisement adjacent to any interstate, national highway system, or federal-aid primary highway shall be erected, maintained, or displayed which is visible from the main traveled way within 660 feet of the nearest edge of the right-of-way, except as provided in subsections B and D of this section, and outside of an urban area no sign or advertisement beyond 660 feet of the nearest edge of the right-of-way of any interstate, national highway system, or federal-aid primary highway which is visible from the main traveled way shall be erected, maintained, or displayed with the purpose of its message being read from the main traveled way, except as set forth in subsection C.

B. The following signs, advertisements or advertising structures may be erected, maintained and displayed within 660 feet of the right-of-way of any interstate, national highway system, or federal-aid primary highway:

Class 1 – Official signs. Directional and official signs and notices, which signs and notices shall include, but not be limited to, signs and notices pertaining to the availability of food, lodging, vehicle service and tourist information, natural wonders, scenic areas, museums and historic attractions, as authorized or required by law; however, where such signs or notices pertain to facilities or attractions which are barrier free, such signs or notices shall contain the International Barrier Free Symbol. The Commonwealth Transportation Board shall determine the type, lighting, size, location, number, and other requirements of signs of this class.

Class 2 – On-premises signs. Signs not prohibited by other parts of this article which are consistent with the applicable provisions of this section and which advertise the sale or lease of, or activities being conducted upon, the real property where the signs are located; provided, that any such signs, which are located adjacent to and within 660 feet of any interstate highway and do not lie in commercial or industrial zones within the boundaries of incorporated municipalities, as such boundaries existed on September 21, 1959, wherein the use of real property adjacent to the Interstate System is subject to municipal regulation or control, or in areas where land use as of September 21, 1959, was clearly established by state law as industrial or commercial, shall comply with the following requirements:

1. Not more than one sign advertising the sale or lease of the same property may be erected or maintained in such manner as to be visible to traffic proceeding in any one direction on any one interstate highway;

2. Not more than one sign, visible to traffic proceeding in any one direction on any one interstate highway and advertising activities being conducted upon the real property where the sign is located, may be erected or maintained more than fifty feet from the advertised activity, and no such sign may be located more than 250 feet from the center of the advertised activity; and

3. No sign, except one which is not more than fifty feet from the advertised activity, that displays any trade name which refers to or identifies any service rendered or product sold, shall be erected or maintained unless the name of the advertised activity is displayed as conspicuously as such trade name.

Class 3 – Other signs. Any signs or advertisements which are located within areas adjacent to any interstate, national highway system, or federal-aid primary highway which are zoned industrial or commercial under authority of state law, or in unzoned commercial or industrial areas as determined by the Commonwealth Transportation Board from actual land uses. The Commonwealth Transportation Board shall determine the size, lighting and spacing of signs of this class, provided that such determination shall be no more restrictive than valid federal requirements on the same subject.

C. The following signs, advertisements or advertising structures may be erected, maintained and displayed beyond 660 feet of the right-of-way of any interstate, national highway system, or federal-aid primary highway outside of urban areas.

1. Class 1 and Class 2 signs, advertisements or advertising structures set forth in subsection B of this section.

2. All other signs, advertisements or advertising structures erected, maintained or displayed more than 660 feet from the nearest edge of the right-of-way of an interstate, national highway system, or federal-aid primary highway; unless said sign or advertisement is visible from the main traveled way of said highways and erected, maintained or displayed with the purpose of its message being read from the main traveled way of said highways.

In determining whether a sign, advertisement or advertising structure is "erected, maintained or displayed with the purpose of its being read" the Commissioner is not limited to, but will consider, the nature of the business or product advertised thereon, the availability of such business or product to users of the controlled highway, the visibility of the sign, advertisement or advertising structure from the main traveled way of the controlled highway (such visibility may be measured by considering the size or height of the sign, advertisement or advertising structure; the configuration, size, and height of recognizable emblems, images, and lettering thereon; the angle of the sign, advertisement or advertising structure to the main traveled way of the controlled highway; the degree to which physical obstructions hinder the view of the sign, advertisement or advertising structure from the main traveled way of the controlled highway; and the time which such sign, advertisement or advertising structure is exposed to view by travelers on the main traveled way of the controlled highway traveling at the maximum and minimum speeds posted).

D. In order to provide information in the specific interest of the traveling public, the Commonwealth Transportation Board is hereby authorized to maintain maps and to permit informational directories and advertising pamphlets to be made available at rest areas, and to establish information centers at rest areas for the purpose of informing the public of places of interest within the Commonwealth and providing such other information as may be considered desirable.

E. Notwithstanding any other provision of law, lawfully erected and maintained nonconforming signs, advertisements, and advertising structures shall not be removed under state law or local ordinances without compensation as described in subsection F of this section.

F. The Commonwealth Transportation Commissioner is authorized to acquire by purchase, gift or the power of eminent domain and to pay just compensation upon the removal of nonconforming signs, advertisements or advertising structures lawfully erected and maintained under state law or state regulations. Provided, however, subsequent to November 6, 1978, whenever any local ordinance which is more restrictive than state law requires the removal of such signs, advertisements, or advertising structures, the local governing body shall initiate the removal of such signs, advertisements, or advertising structures with the Commissioner, who shall have complete authority to administer the removal of such signs, advertisements, or advertising structures. Upon proof of payment presented to the local governing bodies, the local governing bodies shall reimburse the Commissioner the funds expended which are associated with the removal of such signs, advertisements, or advertising structures required by local ordinances, less any federal funds received for such purposes. Notwithstanding the above, nothing shall prohibit the local governing bodies from removing signs, advertisements, or advertising structures which are made nonconforming solely by local ordinances so long as those ordinances require the local governing bodies to pay 100% of the cost of removing them and just compensation upon their removal.

Such compensation is authorized to be paid only for the taking from the owner of such sign or advertisement of all right, title, leasehold and interest in such sign or advertisement, and the taking from the owner of the real property on which the sign or advertisement is located, of the right to erect and maintain such sign or advertisement thereon.

The Commonwealth Transportation Commissioner shall not be required to expend any funds under this section unless and until federal-aid matching funds are made available for this purpose.

(Chgd. by L.2000 chs. 432, 449, eff. 7/1/2000.)

§33.1-371. Regulations and agreements with United States implementing §33.1-370.

The Commonwealth Transportation Board may issue regulations, and is authorized to enter into agreements with the United States as provided in 23 United States Code §131, with respect to the regulation and control of signs, advertisements and advertising structures in conformity with §33.1-370; provided that such agreements shall not prevent the General Assembly of Virginia from amending or repealing §33.1-370 at any time, and provided further, that in the event the federal law is amended to lessen the special restrictions applicable to signs, advertisements and advertising structures adjacent to interstate or federal-aid primary highways, the Commonwealth Transportation Board is authorized to adopt regulations to conform to such change in federal law and to amend any agreement with the United States relating to such control.

§33.1-371.1. Selective pruning permits; penalty.

A. The Commonwealth Transportation Commissioner shall by permit authorize the selective pruning, within highway rights-of-way, of vegetation that obstructs motorists' view of signs displayed on outdoor advertising structures legally erected and properly maintained along the highways. Such permits shall be subject to such conditions as the Commissioner deems appropriate for the enhancement of highway safety and beautification, including but not limited to the following:

1. All work performed under the permit shall be (i) subject to the direction of the Commissioner or his designee, (ii) supervised on-site by a certified arborist approved by the Commissioner, (iii) completed to the satisfaction of the Department's Environmental Manager or his designee, and (iv) performed solely at the expense of the permittee.

2. All pruning shall be performed in a manner that (i) creates a picture frame effect around the sign and (ii) beautifies the area surrounding the advertising structure. All cutting shall be limited to vegetation with trunk base diameters of less than six inches. Pruning cuts of vegetation with diameters greater than four inches and clear cutting shall not be authorized and shall be strictly prohibited.

3. Any diseased or unsightly vegetation or any vegetation that endangers the health or retards the growth of desirable vegetation may be removed at the discretion of the certified arborist supervising the work. Any such removed vegetation shall be replaced at the permittee's expense with desirable vegetation.

B. The requirements of this section shall not apply to the owner or authorized agent of the owner of any sign, advertisement, or advertising structure exempted from the provisions of this article by §33.1-355.

C. The Commissioner shall promulgate such regulations as he deems necessary or desirable to carry out the provisions of this section. Such regulations shall include but not necessarily be limited to the following requirements:

1. Every application for a permit submitted under this section shall be accompanied by photographs of the affected site and a detailed description of work proposed to be performed.

2. A fee of $400 shall accompany every application. All such fees shall be paid by the Commissioner into the state treasury, allocated to the Commonwealth Transportation Board.

3. Every applicant shall post a bond payable to the Commonwealth, with surety approved by the Commissioner and in a form approved by the Attorney General, in the sum of $2,500, conditioned on the permittee's fulfillment of all requirements of the permit.

4. No permit shall be issued under this section in order to create a new site for an outdoor advertising structure.

D. Any person found by a court of competent jurisdiction to have violated any provision of this section, any regulation adopted pursuant to this section, or any permit issued under this section, shall, in addition to the penalties provided in §33.1-377, be prohibited by the court from applying for any other permit under this section for a period of not more than five years.

(Added by L.1998 chs. 525, 540, eff. 7/1/98.)

§33.1-372. Pasting advertisements prohibited in certain instances.

No advertisement shall be pasted or glued on any building, fence, wall, tree, rock or other similar structure or object, unless the same be an advertising structure for which a permit has been issued and is in effect.

§33.1-373. Advertising on rocks, poles, etc., within limits of highway; civil penalty.

Any person who in any manner (i) paints, prints, places, puts or affixes any advertisement upon or to any rock, stone, tree, fence, stump, pole, mile-board, milestone, danger-sign, guide-sign, guidepost, highway sign, historical marker, building or other object lawfully within the limits of any highway or (ii) erects, paints, prints, places, puts, or affixes any advertisement within the limits of any highway shall be assessed a civil penalty of $100. Each occurrence shall be subject to a separate penalty. All civil penalties collected under this section shall be paid into the Highway Maintenance and Operating Fund. Advertisements placed within the limits of the highway are hereby declared a public and private nuisance and may be forthwith removed, obliterated, or abated by the Commonwealth Transportation Commissioner or his representatives without notice. The Commonwealth Transportation Commissioner may collect the cost of such removal, obliteration, or abatement from the person erecting, painting, printing, placing, putting, affixing or using such advertisement. When no one is observed erecting, painting, printing, placing, putting, or affixing such sign or advertisement, the person, firm or corporation being advertised shall be presumed to have placed the sign or advertisement and shall be punished accordingly. Such presumption, however, shall be rebuttable by competent evidence. In addition, the Commissioner or his representative may seek to enjoin any recurring violator of this section.

The provisions of this section shall not apply to signs or other outdoor advertising regulated under Chapter 7 (§33.1-351 et seq.) of this title.

§33.1-374. Harmony of regulations.

No zoning board or commission or any other public officer or agency shall permit any sign, advertisement or advertising structure which is prohibited under the provisions of this article, nor shall the Commissioner permit any sign, advertisement or advertising structure which is prohibited by any other public board, officer or agency in the lawful exercise of its or their powers.

§33.1-375. Violation a nuisance; abatement.

Any sign, advertisement or advertising structure which is erected, used, maintained, operated, posted or displayed in violation of §§33.1-369, 33.1-370, or §33.1-372 or for which no permit has been obtained where such is required, or after revocation or more than thirty days after expiration of a permit, or which, whether or not excepted under the provisions of §33.1-355, is not kept in a good general condition and in a reasonably good state of repair and is not, after thirty days' written notice to the person erecting, using, maintaining, posting or displaying the same, put into good general condition and in a reasonably good state of repair, is hereby declared to be a public and private nuisance and may be forthwith removed, obliterated or abated by the Commissioner or his representatives. The Commissioner may collect the cost of such removal, obliteration or abatement from the person erecting, using, maintaining, operating, posting or displaying such sign, advertisement or advertising structure.

§33.1-375.1. Commissioner may enter into certain agreements; penalties.

A. The Commonwealth Transportation Commissioner may enter into agreements with the local governing body of any county having a population of at least 57,000 but no more than 57,450 authorizing local law-enforcement agencies or other local governmental entities to act as agents of the Commissioner for the purpose of (i) enforcing the provisions of §33.1-373 and (ii) collecting the penalties and costs provided for in that section. However, no local governing body shall enter into any such agreement until it has held a public hearing thereon.

B. Notwithstanding the provisions of §33.1-373, one-half of the penalties and costs collected under this section shall be paid to the affected locality, and the remainder shall be remitted to the Commissioner and paid into the Highway Maintenance and Operating Fund.

C. Notwithstanding the foregoing provisions of this section, the following signs and advertising shall not be subject to the agreements provided for in subsection A of this section:

1. Signs and advertising supporting an individual's candidacy for elected public office or other ballot issues, provided this exception shall not include signs and advertising in place more than three days after the election to which they apply.

2. Signs and advertising promoting and/or providing directions to a special event to be held at a specified date stated on the sign or advertising, provided this exception shall not include special event signs in place more than three days after the conclusion of the special event.

3. Other signs and advertising erected for no more than three days.

D. Notwithstanding the foregoing provisions of this section, the Commissioner may enter into agreements with the local governing bodies of localities to which the foregoing provisions of this section do not apply to authorize those governing bodies to act as agents of the Commissioner and the Department in enforcing the provisions of §33.1-373. The limitations applicable to agreements entered into under subsections A through C of this section shall not apply to agreements entered into under this subsection.

(Added by L.1998 ch. 835; chgd. by L.1999 ch. 195; L.2000 ch. 672, eff. 7/1/2000.)

§33.1-376. Disposition of fees.

All moneys received by the Commissioner under the provisions of this article shall be paid by him into the state treasury and allocated to the Commonwealth Transportation Board for use in the regulation and control of outdoor advertising and landscaping of highways.

§33.1-377. Penalty for violation.

Any person, firm or corporation violating any provision of this article for which violation no other penalty is prescribed by this article shall be guilty of a misdemeanor and, upon conviction thereof, shall be fined not less than ten dollars nor more than fifty dollars. Each day during which such violation is continued after conviction may be treated for all purposes as a separate offense.

§33.1-378. Construction of article.

This article shall be liberally construed with a view to the effective accomplishment of its purposes.

ARTICLE 2
FALSE AND MISLEADING SIGNS

§33.1-379. Prohibition of such signs.

It shall be unlawful for any person to erect or maintain alongside, or in plain view of, any public highway any false or misleading sign of any kind or character purporting to furnish travel information relating to place or direction. It shall be unlawful for any person to erect or maintain alongside, or in plain view of, any public highway any sign of any kind or character purporting to furnish travel information relating to merchandise or services unless the design of such sign, the information thereon, and the location thereof, be approved in writing by the Commonwealth Transportation Commissioner; provided, however, that the provisions of this section as to merchandise and service shall not:

(1) Apply to or restrict the right of any person to post, display, erect or maintain on any store, dwelling house or other building, together with so much land therewith as shall be necessary for the convenience, use and enjoyment thereof, or on any mercantile appliances, contrivances or machinery annexed or immediately adjacent thereto, any sign advertising goods, merchandise, property, real or personal, business services, entertainment or amusements actually and in good faith manufactured, produced, bought, sold, conducted, furnished or dealt in on the premises;

(2) Limit or restrict the publication of official notices by or under the direction of any public or court officer in the performance of his official or directed duties;

(3) Limit or restrict notice of sale by a trustee under a deed of trust, deed of assignment, or other similar instrument; or

(4) Apply to or restrict the right of any property owner, his agent, lessee or tenant to maintain any sign offering to the public farm products, including livestock of every kind, or board or lodging or similar entertainment, or of the sale, rental or lease of the property.

Nothing in this section shall limit the right of any person, firm or corporation to erect signs which advertise natural scenic attractions in the Commonwealth.

§33.1-380. Penalty for violation of preceding section; existing signs.

Any person who shall violate any of the provisions of §33.1-379 shall, upon conviction thereof, be punished by a fine not to exceed ten dollars for each offense, and it shall be deemed a separate offense for the same person to erect, or permit to be erected, a similar sign at each of two or more places; provided, however, as to any such sign erected before June 19, 1936, if it be satisfactorily proven that the information thereon given is correct, the person who erected the same, as well as the person who permitted the same to be erected, shall not be deemed guilty of such violation.

§33.1-381. Removal of such signs by Commissioner.

The Commonwealth Transportation Commissioner, whenever he shall ascertain that any such sign gives incorrect information, shall notify the person who erected the same, and the person on whose property it is located, in writing, to remove it forthwith, and if it be not removed within ten days after receipt of such notice, the Commissioner shall remove and destroy the same, or cause it to be removed and destroyed, without liability for damages therefor; and, if any person convicted of erecting or maintaining any such sign, or of permitting the same to be erected or maintained, as hereinabove provided, shall fail or refuse to remove the same within ten days after such judgment of conviction, the Commissioner shall remove and destroy such sign, or cause the same to be removed and destroyed, without liability for damages therefor.

TITLE 37.1
INSTITUTIONS FOR THE MENTALLY ILL; MENTAL HEALTH GENERALLY
(Selected Chapters)

CHAPTER 2
ADMISSIONS AND DISPOSITIONS IN GENERAL
(Selected Articles)

ARTICLE 1
ADMISSIONS
(Selected Sections)

§37.1-63. Applicability of chapter.

In the application of the provisions of this chapter to any person to whom the terms mentally retarded, alcoholic, or drug addict are applicable, such appropriate term or terms shall be used in any determination, certification, order or record relating to such person.

§37.1-67.01. Emergency custody; issuance and execution of order.

Based upon probable cause to believe that the person is mentally ill and in need of hospitalization and that the person presents an imminent danger to self or others as a result of mental illness, or is so seriously mentally ill as to be substantially unable to care for self, any magistrate may, upon the sworn petition of any responsible person or upon his own motion, issue an emergency custody order requiring any person within his judicial district who is incapable of volunteering or unwilling to volunteer for treatment to be taken into custody and transported to a convenient location to be evaluated by a person designated by the community services board who is skilled in the diagnosis and treatment of mental illness and who has completed a certification program approved by the Department in order to assess the need for hospitalization. A law-enforcement officer who, based upon his observation or the reliable reports of others, has probable cause to believe that a person meets the criteria for emergency custody as stated in this section may take that person into custody and transport that person to an appropriate location to assess the need for hospitalization without prior authorization. Such evaluation shall be conducted immediately. The person shall remain in custody until a temporary detention order is issued or until the person is released, but in no event shall the period of custody exceed four hours. A law-enforcement officer may lawfully go to or be sent beyond the territorial limits of the county, city or town in which he serves to any point in the Commonwealth for the purpose of executing an order for emergency custody pursuant to this section. Nothing herein shall preclude a law-enforcement officer from obtaining emergency medical treatment or further medical evaluation at any time for a person in his custody as provided in this section.

If an order of emergency custody is not executed within four hours of its issuance the order shall be void and shall be returned unexecuted to the office of the clerk of the issuing court or, if such office is not open, to any judge or magistrate thereof.

(Added by L.1995 ch. 844; chgd. by L.1996 ch. 893; L.1998 ch. 611, eff. 1/1/99.)

§37.1-67.1. Involuntary temporary detention; issuance and execution of order.

For the purposes of this section, a designee of a community services board is defined as an examiner able to provide an independent examination of the person who is not related by blood or marriage to the person, who has no financial interest in the admission or treatment of the person, who has no investment interest in the hospital detaining or admitting the person under this article and, except for employees of state hospitals and of the U.S. Department of Veterans Affairs, who is not employed by such hospital. For purposes of this section, investment interest means the ownership or holding of an equity or debt security, including, but not limited to, shares of stock in a corporation, interests or units of a partnership, bonds, debentures, notes, or other equity or debt instruments.

A magistrate may, upon the sworn petition of any responsible person or upon his own motion, and only after an in-person evaluation by an employee of the local community services board or its designee who is skilled in the assessment and treatment of mental illness and who has completed a certification program approved by the Department, issue an order of temporary detention if it appears from all evidence readily available, including any recommendation from a physician treating the person or from a clinical psychologist treating the person, that the person is mentally ill and in need of hospitalization and that the person presents an imminent danger to self or others as a result of mental illness, or is so seriously mentally ill as to be substantially unable to care for self, and the person is incapable of volunteering or unwilling to volunteer for treatment. Such order may include transportation of the person to such other medical facility as may be necessary to obtain emergency medical evaluation or treatment prior to placement.

A magistrate may issue such order of temporary detention without an emergency custody order proceeding. A magistrate may issue an order of temporary detention without a prior in-person evaluation if (i) the person has been personally examined within the previous seventy-two hours by an employee of the local community services board or its designee who is skilled in the assessment and treatment of mental illness and who has completed a certification program approved by the Department or (ii) there is a significant physical, psychological or medical risk, to the person or to others, associated with conducting such evaluation.

An employee of the local community services board or its designee shall determine the facility of temporary detention for all individuals detained pursuant to this section. The facility shall be identified on the prescreening report and indicated on the temporary detention order. The Board of Medical Assistance Services shall, by regulation, establish a reasonable rate per day of inpatient care for temporary detention. The institution or other place of detention shall be approved pursuant to regulations of the Board of Mental Health, Mental Retardation and Substance Abuse Services. The employee of the community services board or its designee who is conducting the evaluation pursuant to this section shall determine, prior to the issuance of the temporary detention order, the insurance status of the person. Except as provided herein for defendants requiring hospitalization in accordance with subdivision A 2 of §19.2-169.6, such person shall not be detained in a jail or other place of confinement for persons charged with criminal offenses.

A law-enforcement officer may lawfully go to or be sent beyond the territorial limits of the county, city, or town in which he serves to any point in the Commonwealth for the purpose of executing any order for temporary detention pursuant to this section. The duration of temporary detention shall not exceed forty-eight hours prior to a hearing. If the forty-eight-hour period herein specified terminates on a Saturday, Sunday or legal holiday, such person may be detained, as herein provided, until the next day which is not a Saturday, Sunday or legal holiday. Nothing herein shall preclude a law-enforcement officer from obtaining emergency medical treatment or further medical evaluation at any time for a person in his custody as provided in this section.

In any case in which temporary detention is ordered pursuant to this section upon petition of a person having custody of a defendant in accordance with subdivision A 2 of §19.2-169.6, the magistrate executing the order of temporary detention shall place such person in a hospital designated by §19.2-169.6 B, or if such facility is not available, the defendant shall be detained in a jail or other place of confinement for persons charged with criminal offenses and shall be transferred to such hospital as soon as possible thereafter. The hearing shall be held, upon notice to the attorney for the defendant, either (i) before the court having jurisdiction over the defendant's case, or (ii) before a judge as defined in §37.1-1 in accordance with the provisions of §37.1-67.4, in which case the defendant shall be represented by counsel as specified in §37.1-67.3. In any case in which temporary detention is ordered pursuant to this section upon petition for involuntary commitment of a minor, the petition shall be filed and the hearing scheduled in accordance with the provisions of §16.1-341.

On such petition and prior to a hearing as authorized in §37.1-67.3 or §16.1-341, the judge may release such person on his personal recognizance or bond set by the judge if it appears from all evidence readily available that such release will not pose an imminent danger to himself or others. In the case of a minor, the judge may release the minor to his parent. The director of the hospital in which the person is detained may release such person prior to a hearing as authorized in §37.1-67.3 or §16.1-341 if it appears, based on an evaluation conducted by the psychiatrist or clinical psychologist treating the person, that the person would not present an imminent danger to self or others if released.

If an order of temporary detention is not executed within twenty-four hours of its issuance, or within such shorter period as is specified in the order, the order shall be void and shall be returned unexecuted to the office of the clerk of the issuing court or if such office is not open, to any judge or magistrate thereof. Subsequent orders may be issued upon the original petition within ninety-six hours after the petition is filed. However, a magistrate must again obtain the advice of an employee of the local community services board or its designee who is skilled in the diagnosis or treatment of mental illness and who has completed a certification program approved by the Department prior to issuing a subsequent order upon the original petition. Any petition for which no order of temporary detention or other process in connection therewith is served on the subject of the petition within ninety-six hours after the petition is filed shall be void and shall be returned to the office of the clerk of the issuing court.

The chief judge of each general district court shall establish and require that a magistrate, as provided by this section, be available seven days a week, twenty-four hours a day, for the purpose of performing the duties established by this section. Each community services board shall provide to each general district court and magistrate's office within its jurisdiction a list of its employees and designees who are available to perform the evaluations required herein.

(Chgd. by L.1995 ch. 844; L.1996 chs. 343, 893; L.1998 chs. 37, 594, eff. 7/1/98, ch. 611, eff. 1/1/99.)

§37.1-67.3. Same; involuntary admission and treatment.

The commitment hearing shall be held within forty-eight hours of the execution of the temporary detention order as provided for in §37.1-67.1; however, if the forty-eight-hour period herein specified terminates on a Saturday, Sunday, or legal holiday, such person may be detained, as herein provided, until the next day which is not a Saturday, Sunday, or legal holiday, but in no event may the person be detained for a period longer than seventy-two hours or ninety-six hours when such legal holiday occurs on a Monday or Friday. A Saturday, Sunday, or legal holiday shall be deemed to include the time period up to 8:00 a.m. of the next day which is not a Saturday, Sunday, or legal holiday.

The judge, in commencing the commitment hearing, shall inform the person whose involuntary admission is being sought of his right to apply for voluntary admission and treatment as provided for in §37.1-65 and shall afford such person an opportunity for voluntary admission. The judge shall ascertain if such person is then willing and capable of seeking voluntary admission and treatment. If the person is capable and willingly accepts voluntary admission and treatment, the judge shall require him to accept voluntary admission for a minimum period of treatment and after such minimum period, not to exceed seventy-two hours, to give the hospital forty-eight hours' notice prior to leaving the hospital, during which notice period he shall not be discharged, unless sooner discharged pursuant to §37.1-98 or §37.1-99. Such person shall be subject to the transportation provisions as provided in §37.1-71 and the requirement for prescreening by a community services board or community mental health clinic as provided in §37.1-65.

If a person is incapable of accepting or unwilling to accept voluntary admission and treatment, the judge shall inform such person of his right to a commitment hearing and right to counsel. The judge shall ascertain if a person whose admission is sought is represented by counsel, and if he is not represented by counsel, the judge shall appoint an attorney-at-law to represent him. However, if such person requests an opportunity to employ counsel, the court shall give him a reasonable opportunity to employ counsel at his own expense.

A written explanation of the involuntary commitment process and the statutory protections associated with the process shall be given to the person and its contents explained by an attorney prior to the commitment hearing. The written explanation shall include, at a minimum, an explanation of the person's right to retain private counsel or be represented by a court-appointed attorney, to present any defenses including independent evaluation and expert testimony or the testimony of other witnesses, to be present during the hearing and testify, to appeal any certification for involuntary admission to the circuit court, and to have a jury trial on appeal. The judge shall ascertain whether the person whose admission is sought has been given the written explanation required herein.

To the extent possible, during or before the commitment hearing, the attorney for the person whose admission is sought shall interview his client, the petitioner, the examiner described below, the community services board staff, and any other material witnesses. He shall also examine all relevant diagnostic and other reports, present evidence and witnesses, if any, on his client's behalf, and otherwise actively represent his client in the proceedings. The role of the attorney shall be to represent the wishes of his client, to the extent possible.

The petitioner shall be given adequate notice of the place, date, and time of the commitment hearing. The petitioner shall be entitled to retain counsel at his own expense, to be present during the hearing, and to testify and present evidence. The petitioner shall be encouraged but shall not be required to testify at the hearing and the person whose admission is sought shall not be released solely on the basis of the petitioner's failure to attend or testify during the hearing.

Notwithstanding the above, the judge shall require an examination of such person by a psychiatrist or a psychologist who is licensed in Virginia by either the Board of Medicine or the Board of Psychology who is qualified in the diagnosis of mental illness or, if such a psychiatrist or psychologist is not available, any mental health professional who is (i) licensed in Virginia through the Department of Health Professions and (ii) qualified in the diagnosis of mental illness. The examiner chosen shall be able to provide an independent examination of the person. The examiner shall not be related by blood or marriage to the person, shall not be responsible for treating the person, shall have no financial interest in the admission or treatment of the person, shall have no investment interest in the hospital detaining or admitting the person under this article, and, except for employees of state hospitals and of the U.S. Department of Veterans Affairs, shall not be employed by such hospital. For purposes of this section, investment interest means the ownership or holding of an equity or debt security, including, but not limited to, shares of stock in a corporation, interests or units of a partnership, bonds, debentures, notes, or other equity or debt instruments.

All such examinations shall be conducted in private. The judge shall summons the examiner who shall certify that he has personally examined the individual and has probable cause to believe that the individual (i) is or is not so seriously mentally ill as to be substantially unable to care for himself or (ii) does or does not present an imminent danger to himself or others as a result of mental illness, and (iii) requires or does not require involuntary hospitalization or treatment. Alternatively, the judge, in his discretion, may accept written certification of the examiner's findings if the examination has been personally made within the preceding five days and if there is no objection sustained to the acceptance of such written certification by the person or his attorney. The judge shall not render any decision on the petition until such examiner has presented his report either orally or in writing.

Except as otherwise provided in this section, prior to making any adjudication that such person is mentally ill and shall be confined to an institution pursuant to this section, the judge shall require from the community services board which serves the political subdivision where the person resides a prescreening report, and the board or clinic shall provide such a report within forty-eight hours or within seventy-two hours if the forty-eight-hour period terminates on a Saturday, Sunday or legal holiday. If it is impossible or impractical to obtain a prescreening report from the community services board which serves the political subdivision where the person resides, the judge may obtain such report from the community services board of the political subdivision where the person is located. The report shall be admissible as evidence of the facts stated therein and shall state whether the person is deemed to be so seriously mentally ill that he is substantially unable to care for himself, an imminent danger to himself or others as a result of mental illness and in need of involuntary hospitalization or treatment, whether there is no less restrictive alternative to institutional confinement and what the recommendations are for that person's care and treatment. In the case of a person sentenced and committed to the Department of Corrections and who has been examined by a psychiatrist or clinical psychologist, the judge may proceed to adjudicate whether the person is mentally ill and should be confined pursuant to this section without requesting a prescreening report from the community services board.

After observing the person and obtaining the necessary positive certification and any other relevant evidence which may have been offered, if the judge finds specifically (i) that the person presents an imminent danger to himself or others as a result of mental illness or has been proven to be so seriously mentally ill as to be substantially unable to care for himself, and (ii) that alternatives to involuntary confinement and treatment have been investigated and deemed unsuitable and there is no less restrictive alternative to institutional confinement and treatment, the judge shall by written order and specific findings so certify and order that the person be placed in a hospital or other facility for a period of treatment not to exceed 180 days from the date of the court order. Such placement shall be in a hospital or other facility designated by the community services board which serves the political subdivision in which the person was examined as provided in this section. If the community services board does not provide a placement recommendation at the commitment hearing, the person shall be placed in a hospital or other facility designated by the Commissioner.

After observing the person and obtaining the necessary positive certification and any other relevant evidence which may have been offered, if the judge finds specifically (i) that the person presents an imminent danger to himself or others as a result of mental illness or has been proven to be so seriously mentally ill as to be substantially unable to care for himself, and (ii) that less restrictive alternatives to institutional confinement and treatment have been investigated and are deemed suitable, and if, moreover, the judge finds specifically that (i) the patient has the degree of competency necessary to understand the stipulations of his treatment, (ii) the patient expresses an interest in living in the community and agrees to abide by his treatment plan, (iii) the patient is deemed to have the capacity to comply with the treatment plan, (iv) the ordered treatment can be delivered on an outpatient basis, and (v) the ordered treatment can be monitored by the community services board or designated providers, the judge shall order outpatient treatment, day treatment in a hospital, night treatment in a hospital, outpatient involuntary treatment with anti-psychotic medication pursuant to §37.1-134.21, or such other appropriate course of treatment as may be necessary to meet the needs of the individual. Upon failure of the patient to adhere to the terms of the outpatient treatment, the judge may revoke the same and, upon notice to the patient and after a commitment hearing, order involuntary commitment for treatment at a hospital. The community services board which serves the political subdivision in which the person resides shall recommend a specific course of treatment and programs for provision of such treatment. The community services board shall monitor the person's compliance with such treatment as may be ordered by the court under this section, and the person's failure to comply with involuntary outpatient treatment as ordered by the court may be admitted into evidence in subsequent hearings held pursuant to the provisions of this section.

The judge shall make or cause to be made a tape or other audio recording of the hearing and shall submit such recording to the appropriate district court clerk to be retained in a confidential file. Such recordings shall only be used to document and to answer questions concerning the judge's conduct of the hearing. These recordings shall be retained for at least three years from the date of the relevant commitment hearing. The judge shall also order that copies of the relevant medical records of such person be released to the facility or program in which he is placed upon request of the treating physician or director of the facility or program. Except as provided in this section, the court shall keep its copies of relevant medical records, reports, and court documents pertaining to the hearings provided for in this section confidential if so requested by such person, or his counsel, with access provided only upon court order for good cause shown. Such records, reports, and documents shall not be subject to the Virginia Freedom of Information Act (§2.1-340 et seq.). Such person shall be released at the expiration of 180 days unless involuntarily committed by further petition and order of a court as provided herein or such person makes application for treatment on a voluntary basis as provided for in §37.1-65.

The procedures required by this section shall be followed at such commitment hearing. The judge shall render a decision on such petition after the appointed examiner has presented his report, either orally or in writing, and after the community services board which serves the political subdivision where the person resides has presented a prescreening report, either orally or in writing, with recommendations for that person's placement, care and treatment. These reports, if not contested, may constitute sufficient evidence upon which the court may base its decision.

The clerk shall certify and forward forthwith to the Central Criminal Records Exchange, on a form provided by the Exchange, a copy of any order for involuntary commitment to a hospital. The copy of the form and the order shall be kept confidential in a separate file and used only for the purpose of conducting a firearms transaction record check authorized by §18.2-308.2:2.

(Chgd. by L.1995 chs. 489, 668, 844; L.1996 chs. 343, 893; L.1997 chs. 558, 921; L.1998 ch. 446, eff. 7/1/98.)

§37.1-67.4. Same; where hearings may be held; services during temporary detention; costs.

The hearing provided for pursuant to §37.1-67.3 may be conducted by the judge at the convenient institution or other place provided for in §37.1-67.1, if he deems it advisable, even though such institution or place is located in a county or city other than his own. In conducting such hearings in a county or city other than his own, the judge shall have all of the authority and power which he would have in his own county or city. A judge, substitute judge or special justice of the county or city in which such institution or place is located may conduct the hearing provided for in §37.1-67.3.

Any such convenient institution caring for a person placed with it pursuant to a temporary order of detention is authorized to provide emergency medical and psychiatric services within its capabilities when the institution determines such services are in the best interests of the person within its care. The costs incurred as a result of such hearings and such costs incurred by the convenient institution in providing such services during such period of temporary detention shall be paid and recovered as provided in §37.1-89. The maximum costs reimbursable by the Commonwealth pursuant to this section shall be established by the State Board of Medical Assistance Services based on reasonable criteria.

Where coverage by a third-party payor exists, the institution seeking reimbursement under this section shall first seek reimbursement from the third-party payor. The Commonwealth shall reimburse the providers only for the balance of costs remaining after the allowances covered by the third-party payor have been received.

(Chgd. by L.1995 ch. 844, eff. 7/1/95.)

§37.1-67.5. Same; interpreters for deaf persons in commitment or certification proceedings.

In any proceeding pursuant to §37.1-65.1 or §§37.1-67.1 through 37.1-67.4 in which a deaf person is alleged to be mentally retarded or mentally ill, an interpreter for such deaf person shall be appointed by the justice of the court in which such proceeding is pending from a list of qualified interpreters provided by the Department for the Deaf and Hard-of-Hearing. Such interpreter shall be compensated as provided for in §37.1-89 of the Code.

§37.1-67.6. Appeal of commitment or certification order.

Any person involuntarily committed pursuant to §37.1-67.3 or certified as eligible for admission pursuant to §37.1-65.1 shall have the right to appeal such order to the circuit court in the jurisdiction wherein he was committed or certified or wherein the hospital or mental retardation facility to which he was admitted is located. Choice of venue shall rest with the party noting the appeal. The court may transfer the case upon a finding that the other forum is more convenient. Such appeal must be filed within thirty days from the date of the order and shall be given priority over all other pending matters before the court and heard as soon as possible, notwithstanding §19.2-241 providing time within which the court shall set criminal cases for trial. The clerk of the court from which an appeal is taken shall immediately transmit the record to the clerk of the appellate court. The clerk of the circuit court shall provide written notification of the appeal to the petitioner in the case in accordance with procedures set forth in §16.1-112. No appeal bond or writ tax shall be required and the appeal shall proceed without the payment of costs or other fees. Costs may be recovered as provided for in §37.1-89.

The appeal shall be heard de novo. An order continuing the commitment shall be entered only if the criteria in §37.1-67.3 are met at the time the appeal is heard. The person so committed or certified shall be entitled to trial by jury. Seven persons from a panel of thirteen shall constitute a jury in such cases.

If such person is not represented by counsel, the judge shall appoint an attorney-at-law to represent him. Counsel so appointed shall be paid a fee of seventy-five dollars and his necessary expenses. The order of the court from which the appeal is taken shall be defended by the attorney for the Commonwealth.

ARTICLE 2
TRANSPORTATION OF ADMITTED PERSONS; ESCAPE

(Selected Sections)

§37.1-71. Transportation of person certified for admission.

When a person has been certified for admission to a hospital under §§37.1-67.3, 37.1-67.4 or §37.1-67.6, a determination shall be made by the judge regarding the transportation of that person to the proper hospital. The judge may consult with the person's treating mental health professional and any involved community services board staff regarding the person's dangerousness and whether the sheriff should transport or whether transportation alternatives as provided in §37.1-72 may be utilized. If the judge determines that the person requires transportation by the sheriff, such person may be delivered to the care of the sheriff, as specified in this section, who shall transport such person to the proper hospital. In no event shall transport commence later than six hours after notification to the sheriff of such certification.

The sheriff of the jurisdiction where the person is a resident shall be responsible for transporting the person unless the sheriff's office of such jurisdiction is located more than 100 road miles from the nearest boundary of the jurisdiction in which the proceedings took place. In cases where the sheriff of the jurisdiction of which the person is a resident is more than 100 road miles from the nearest boundary of the jurisdiction in which the proceedings took place, it shall be the responsibility of the sheriff of the latter jurisdiction to transport the person. The cost of transportation of any person so applying or certified for admission pursuant to §37.1-67.3 or §37.1-67.4 shall be paid by the Commonwealth from the same funds as for care in jail.

If any state hospital has become too crowded to accommodate any such person certified for admission therein, the Commissioner shall give notice of the fact to all sheriffs and shall designate the hospital to which they shall transport such persons.

(Chgd. by L.1995 ch. 844; L.1996 ch. 184, eff. 7/1/96.)

§37.1-72. Custody of certified person for purpose of transportation.

Any judge who shall certify an admission under this chapter may order that such person be placed in the custody of any responsible person or persons, including a representative of the facility in which the individual is temporarily hospitalized during the temporary detention period, for the sole purpose of transporting such person to the proper hospital.

(Chgd. by L.1995 ch. 844, eff. 7/1/95.)

§37.1-73. Detention in jail after certification.

It shall be unlawful for any sheriff, sergeant or other officer to use any jail or other place of confinement for criminals as a place of detention for any person in his custody for transportation to a hospital, unless the detention therein of such person not to exceed a period of twenty-four hours is specifically authorized by the committing judge, except that such authority shall not be given by any judge for the Counties of Augusta, Arlington and Fairfax and the Cities of Alexandria, Fairfax, Falls Church, Waynesboro and Staunton.

§37.1-74. Mentally ill persons not to be confined in cells with criminals.

In no case shall any sheriff or jailer confine any mentally ill person in a cell or room with prisoners charged with or convicted of crime.

§37.1-75. Escape, sickness, death or discharge of certified person while in custody; warrant for person escaping.

If any person who has been certified for admission to a hospital, while in the custody of a sheriff or other person, shall escape, become too sick to travel, die, or be discharged by due process of law, the sheriff or other person shall immediately notify the Commissioner of that fact. If any person with whose custody a sheriff or other person has been charged under the provisions of this chapter shall escape, the sheriff or other person having such individual in custody shall immediately secure a warrant from any officer authorized to issue warrants charging the individual with escape from lawful custody, directing his apprehension and stating what disposition shall be made of such person upon arrest.

§37.1-76. Arrest of certain persons involuntarily confined.

If any person involuntarily confined in any hospital escape therefrom, the director may forthwith issue a warrant directed to any officer authorized to make arrests, who shall arrest such person and carry him back to the hospital or such other appropriate facility operated by the Department of Mental Health, Mental Retardation and Substance Abuse Services which is in close proximity to the jurisdictions served by the arresting officer. The officer to whom the warrant is directed may execute the same in any part of the Commonwealth.

§37.1-77. Arrest without warrant.

Any officer authorized to make arrests is authorized to make such an arrest under a warrant issued under the provisions of §37.1-75 or §37.1-76, without having such warrant in his possession, provided the same has been issued and the arresting officer has been advised of the issuance thereof by telegram, radio or teletype message containing the name of the person wanted, directing the disposition to be made of the person when apprehended, and stating the basis of the issuance of the warrant.

ARTICLE 7
TESTING LEGALITY OF DETENTION
(Complete Article)

§37.1-103. Habeas corpus as means.
Any person held in custody as mentally ill may by petition for a writ of habeas corpus have the question of the legality of his detention determined by a court of competent jurisdiction. Upon the petition, after notice to the authorities of the hospital or other institution in which such person is confined, the court shall in some courtroom of such county or city, or in some other convenient public place in such county or city determine whether such person is mentally ill and whether he should be detained.

§37.1-104. Procedure when person confined in hospital or other institution.
If the person mentioned in §37.1-103 is held in custody and actually confined in any hospital or other institution, he may file his petition in the circuit court of the county or the city in which such hospital or other institution is located or in the circuit court of the county or the city adjoining the county or city in which such hospital or other institution is located.

§37.1-104.1. Procedure when person not confined in hospital or other institution.
In all cases, other than those provided for in §37.1-104, the person may file his petition in the circuit court of the county or the city in which he resides, or in which he was certified to be mentally ill, or in which an order was entered authorizing his retention for continued hospitalization, pursuant to Chapter 2, Article 1 (§37.1-63 et seq.) of this title.

§37.1-104.2. Duty of attorney for Commonwealth.
In any case to test the legality of the detention of such person whether by habeas corpus or otherwise, the attorney for the Commonwealth of the county or city in which the hearing is had shall on request of the director of the hospital or other institution having or claiming custody of such person represent the Commonwealth in opposition to any such petition, appeal or procedure for the discharge of such person from custody.

CHAPTER 5
MISCELLANEOUS AND PENAL PROVISIONS
(Complete Chapter)

§37.1-148. Officers may be appointed conservators of the peace; regulation of traffic.
Pursuant to §19.2-13, the director, resident officers, policemen and fire fighters of any hospital may be appointed conservators of the peace on the hospital property and shall have, in addition to the powers of conservators of the peace, authority to patrol and regulate traffic on all roadways and roads through hospital property, and with power to issue summons for violations thereof.

§37.1-149. Offenses by officers.
It shall be unlawful for any clerk of a court, sheriff or other officer to fail to perform any duty required of him in this title, or offend against any prohibition contained in this title.

§37.1-150. Mistreatment of patients in hospital.
It shall be unlawful for any officer or employee or other person to maltreat or misuse any patient confined in any hospital, or one lawfully admitted to a hospital, who may be absent on convalescent leave.

§37.1-151. Aiding and abetting in escapes.
It shall be unlawful for any officer or employee of any hospital or any other person to aid or abet in the escape or secretion of any lawfully admitted patient of any hospital, either while in the hospital or on convalescent leave, bond or escapement, or who having given written obligation to return a patient on convalescent leave under his care and custody to any hospital in which he is a patient shall when directed in writing to do so by the superintendent of such hospital, willfully fail or refuse to do so.

§37.1-152. Disorderly conduct on grounds and interference with officers.
It shall be unlawful for any person to conduct himself in an insulting or disorderly manner on the grounds of any hospital, or in any way resist or interfere with any officer or employee of any hospital in discharge of his duty.

§37.1-153. Providing alcoholic beverages for patients.
It shall be unlawful for any person to sell or give to any patient at any hospital, or bring on the premises of such hospital, any alcoholic beverages or administer same to the patient or place or cause same to be placed where any such patient may receive the same, except it be prescribed by the director or physicians of such hospital.

§37.1-154. Contriving or conspiring to maliciously procure admission of person.
It shall be unlawful for any person to knowingly and maliciously contrive or conspire to procure the admission of any person to any hospital.

§37.1-155. Penalty.
Except as otherwise specified, any person who violates any provision of this chapter shall be guilty of a Class 1 misdemeanor.

CHAPTER 8
LICENSING PERSONS ESTABLISHING, OPERATING, ETC., FACILITIES AND INSTITUTIONS
(Selected Sections)

§37.1-184. Necessity for supervision by licensed persons.

It shall be unlawful for any person to maintain or operate any institution, hospital, or home for the care or treatment of mentally ill or mentally retarded persons unless such institution, hospital or home is under the direct supervision of a person duly licensed hereunder.

§37.1-189. Penalty.

Any person violating any provision of this chapter or any applicable rule or regulation made under such provisions shall be guilty of a Class 3 misdemeanor, and each day, or part thereof, of continuation of any such violation shall constitute a separate offense.

TITLE 40.1
LABOR AND EMPLOYMENT
(Selected Chapters)

CHAPTER 3
PROTECTION OF EMPLOYEES
(Selected Article)

ARTICLE 1
GENERAL PROVISIONS
(Selected Sections)

§40.1-27. Preventing employment by others of former employee.

No person doing business in this Commonwealth, or any agent or attorney of such person after having discharged any employee from the service of such person or after any employee shall have voluntarily left the service of such person shall willfully and maliciously prevent or attempt to prevent by word or writing, directly or indirectly, such discharged employee or such employee who has voluntarily left from obtaining employment with any other person. For violation of this section the offender shall be guilty of a misdemeanor and shall, on conviction thereof, be fined not less than $100 nor more than $500. But this section shall not be construed as prohibiting any person from giving on application for any other person a truthful statement of the reason for such discharge, or a truthful statement concerning the character, industry and ability of such person who has voluntarily left.

§40.1-28. Unlawful to require payment for medical examination as condition of employment.

It shall be unlawful for any employer to require any employee or applicant for employment to pay the cost of a medical examination or the cost of furnishing any medical records required by the employer as a condition of employment.

Any employer who violates the provisions of this section shall be subject to a civil penalty not to exceed $100 for each violation. A penalty determination by the Commissioner shall be final, unless within fifteen days after receipt of such notice the person charged with the violation notifies the Commissioner by certified mail that he intends to contest the proposed penalty before the appropriate general district court.

Civil penalties owed under this section shall be paid to the Commissioner for deposit into the general fund of the Treasury of the Commonwealth. The Commissioner shall prescribe procedures for the payment of proposed penalties which are not contested by employers.

§40.1-28.1. Employers to allow employees at least one day of rest in each week.

Except in an emergency, every employer shall allow each person employed by him in connection with any business or service at least twenty-four consecutive hours of rest in each calendar week in addition to the regular periods of rest normally allowed or legally required in each working day.

§40.1-28.2. Employees entitled to choose Sunday as day of rest.

Every nonmanagerial person employed by any employer shall, as a matter of right, be entitled to choose Sunday as a day of rest in accordance with §40.1-28.1 and upon the filing of written notice by the employee with the employer that such employee chooses Sunday as a day of rest, no employer shall, in any manner, discharge, discipline or penalize such employee for exercising his rights under this section and the provisions of this section may not be waived on an application for employment.

§40.1-28.3. Employees entitled to choose Saturday as day of rest.

Any nonmanagerial employee who conscientiously believes that the seventh day of the week ought to be observed as a Sabbath, and actually refrains from all secular business and labor on that day, shall be entitled to choose the seventh day of the week as his day of rest in accordance with §40.1-28.1 and upon the filing of written notice by the employee with the employer that such employee chooses the seventh day of the week as a day of rest, no employer shall, in any manner, discharge, discipline or penalize such employee for exercising his rights under this section.

§40.1-28.4. Penalties for violation of §§40.1-28.1 through 40.1-28.3; investigations.

Any employer who violates §§40.1-28.1, 40.1-28.2 or §40.1-28.3 shall be guilty of a misdemeanor and shall, upon conviction thereof, be fined not less than $250 nor more than $500 for each offense. Moreover, in the event such employer compels a nonmanagerial employee to work on his chosen day of rest in violation of the heretofore stated sections, such employer shall be liable to such employee for wages at the rate of three times the employee's regular rate of pay for all hours worked by such employee on his chosen day of rest.

Nothing contained herein shall be construed to permit any fine or penalty against any supervisory employee or agent who has been caused, directed or authorized by his employer to violate any provision of the heretofore stated sections, in which case the employer shall be subject to the sanctions prescribed by this section.

The Commissioner of Labor and Industry shall be authorized to conduct investigations of possible violations and thereafter, if compliance is not achieved, report any findings to the appropriate attorney for the Commonwealth.

§40.1-28.5. Exceptions to application of §§40.1-28.1 through 40.1-28.4.

The provisions of §§40.1-28.1 through 40.1-28.4 shall not apply to persons engaged in any of the industries or businesses enumerated in §18.2-341 A(1) through (19), except (15).

CHAPTER 4
LABOR UNIONS, STRIKES, ETC.
(Selected Articles)

ARTICLE 1
IN GENERAL
(Selected Sections)

§40.1-53. Preventing persons from pursuing lawful vocations, etc.; illegal picketing; injunction.

No person shall singly or in concert with others interfere or attempt to interfere with another in the exercise of his right to work or to enter upon the performance of any lawful vocation by the use of force, threats of violence or intimidation, or by the use of insulting or threatening language directed toward such person, to induce or attempt to induce him to quit his employment or refrain from seeking employment.

No person shall engage in picketing by force or violence, or picket alone or in concert with others in such manner as to obstruct or interfere with free ingress or egress to and from any premises, or obstruct or interfere with free use of public streets, sidewalks or other public ways.

Any person violating any of the provisions of this section shall be guilty of a misdemeanor, and punished accordingly.

Notwithstanding the punishments herein provided any court of general equity jurisdiction may enjoin picketing prohibited by this section, and in addition thereto, may enjoin any picketing or interference with lawful picketing when necessary to prevent disorder, restrain coercion, protect life or property, or promote the general welfare.

§40.1-54. Payment of certain charges by carriers or shippers to or for benefit of labor organization.

(1) As used in this section, the term "labor organization" means any organization of any kind, or any agency or employee representation committee or plan, in which employees participate and which exists for the purpose, in whole or in part, of dealing with employers concerning grievances, labor disputes, wages, rates of pay, hours of employment, or conditions of work.

(2) It shall be unlawful for any carrier or shipper of property, or any association of such carriers or shippers, to agree to pay, or to pay, to or for the benefit of a labor organization, directly or indirectly, any charge by reason of the placing upon, delivery to, or movement by rail, or by a railroad car, of a motor vehicle, trailer, or container which is also capable of being moved or propelled upon the highways, and any such agreement shall be void and unenforceable.

(3) It shall be unlawful for any labor organization to accept or receive from any carrier or shipper of property, or any association of such carriers or shippers, any payment described above.

(4) Any corporation, association, organization, firm or person who agrees to pay, or who does pay, or who agrees to receive, or who does receive, any payment described hereinabove shall be guilty of a misdemeanor and shall be fined not less than $100 nor more than $1,000 for each offense. Each act of violation, and each day during which such an agreement remains in effect, shall constitute a separate offense.

§40.1-54.1. Public policy as to strikes and work stoppages at hospitals.

It is hereby declared to be the public policy of the Commonwealth that hospitals shall be free from strikes, and work stoppages.

§40.1-54.2. Strikes and work stoppages at hospitals prohibited; penalty.

No employee of any hospital shall engage in any strike or work stoppage at such hospital which in any way interferes with the operation of such hospital.

Any person violating any of the provisions of this section shall be guilty of a misdemeanor and punished accordingly.

Notwithstanding the penalties herein provided, any court of general equity jurisdiction may enjoin conduct proscribed by this section.

ARTICLE 2
STRIKES BY GOVERNMENT EMPLOYEES
(Complete Article)

§40.1-55. Employee striking terminates, and becomes temporarily ineligible for, public employment.

Any employee of the Commonwealth, or of any county, city, town or other political subdivision thereof, or of any agency of any one of them, who, in concert with two or more other such employees, for the purpose of obstructing, impeding or suspending any activity or operation of his employing agency or any other governmental agency, strikes or willfully refuses to perform the duties of his employment shall, by such action, be deemed to have terminated his employment and shall thereafter be ineligible for employment in any position or capacity during the next twelve months by the Commonwealth, or any county, city, town or other political subdivision of the Commonwealth, or by any department or agency of any of them.

§40.1-56. Department head, etc., to notify employee of such termination, etc.

In any such case the head of any department of the state government, or the mayor of any city or town, or the chairman of the board of supervisors or other governing body of any county, or the head of any other such employing agency, in which such employee was employed, shall forthwith notify such employee of the fact of the termination of his employment and at the same time serve upon him in person or by registered mail a declaration of his ineligibility for reemployment as before provided. Such declaration shall state the fact upon which the asserted ineligibility is based.

§40.1-57. Appeal by employee from declaration of ineligibility.

In the event that any such employee feels aggrieved by such declaration of ineligibility he may within ninety days after the date thereof appeal to the circuit court of the county or the circuit court of the city in which he was employed by filing a petition therein for a review of the matters of law and fact involved in or pertinent to the declaration of ineligibility. A copy of the petition shall be served upon or sent by registered mail to the official signing the declaration, who may file an answer thereto within ten days after receiving the same. The court or the judge thereof in vacation shall, as promptly as practicable, hear the appeal de novo and notify the employee and the signer of the declaration of ineligibility of the time and place of hearing. The court shall hear such testimony as may be adduced by the respective parties and render judgment in accordance with the law and the evidence. Such judgment shall be final.

§40.1-57.1. Appeal by employer for reemployment of terminated employee.

Notwithstanding any provision of law to the contrary, in the event that the employer of an individual terminated under this article deems it necessary for the protection of the public welfare that such individual be reemployed within the twelve months following his termination, the employer may, within ninety days after the date of the declaration of ineligibility, appeal to the circuit court of the county or the circuit court of the city in which the individual was employed by filing a petition therein setting forth the reasons why the public welfare requires reemployment. A copy of the petition shall be served upon or sent by registered mail to the former employee, who may file an answer therein ten days after receiving the same. The court or the judge thereof in vacation shall notify the employer and former employee of the time and place of the hearing on the appeal, such hearing to be de novo and to be held as promptly as possible. The court shall hear such testimony as may be adduced by the respective parties and render judgment in accordance with the law and the evidence. Such judgment shall be final.

ARTICLE 2.1
COLLECTIVE BARGAINING FOR GOVERNMENTAL EMPLOYEES
(Complete Article)

§40.1-57.2. Prohibition against collective bargaining.

No state, county, municipal, or like governmental officer, agent or governing body is vested with or possesses any authority to recognize any labor union or other employee association as a bargaining agent of any public officers or employees, or to collectively bargain or enter into any collective bargaining contract with any such union or association or its agents with respect to any matter relating to them or their employment or service.

§40.1-57.3. Certain activities permitted.

Nothing in this article shall be construed to prevent employees of the Commonwealth, its political subdivisions, or of any governmental agency of any of them from forming associations for the purpose of promoting their interests before the employing agency.

ARTICLE 3
DENIAL OR ABRIDGEMENT OF RIGHT TO WORK
(Selected Sections)

§40.1-58. Policy of article.

It is hereby declared to be the public policy of Virginia that the right of persons to work shall not be denied or abridged on account of membership or nonmembership in any labor union or labor organization.

§40.1-58.1. Application of article to public employers and employees.

As used in this article, the words, "person," "persons," "employer," "employees," "union," "labor union," "association," "organization" and "corporation" shall include but not be limited to public employers, public employees and any representative of public employees in this Commonwealth. The application of this article to public employers, public employees and their representatives shall not be construed as modifying in any way the application of §40.1-55 to government employees.

§40.1-59. Agreements or combinations declared unlawful.

Any agreement or combination between any employer and any labor union or labor organization whereby persons not members of such union or organization shall be denied the right to work for the employer, or whereby such membership is made a condition of employment or continuation of employment by such employer, or whereby any such union or organization acquires an employment monopoly in any enterprise, is hereby declared to be against public policy and an illegal combination or conspiracy.

§40.1-60. Employers not to require employees to become or remain members of union.

No person shall be required by an employer to become or remain a member of any labor union or labor organization as a condition of employment or continuation of employment by such employer.

§40.1-61. Employers not to require abstention from membership in union.

No person shall be required by an employer to abstain or refrain from membership in any labor union or labor organization as a condition of employment or continuation of employment.

§40.1-62. Employer not to require payment of union dues, etc.

No employer shall require any person, as a condition of employment or continuation of employment, to pay any dues, fees or other charges of any kind to any labor union or labor organization.

§40.1-63. Recovery by individual unlawfully denied employment.

Any person who may be denied employment or be deprived of continuation of his employment in violation of §§40.1-60, 40.1-61 or §40.1-62 or of one or more of such sections, shall be entitled to recover from such employer and from any other person, firm, corporation or association acting in concert with him by appropriate action in the courts of this Commonwealth such damages as he may have sustained by reason of such denial or deprivation of employment.

§40.1-64. Application of article to contracts.

The provisions of this article shall not apply to any lawful contract in force on April 30, 1947, but they shall apply in all respects to contracts entered into thereafter and to any renewal or extension of an existing contract.

§40.1-65. Agreement or practice designed to cause employer to violate article declared illegal.

Any agreement, understanding or practice which is designated to cause or require any employer, whether or not a party thereto, to violate any provision of this article is hereby declared to be an illegal agreement, understanding or practice and contrary to public policy.

§40.1-66. Conduct causing violation of article illegal; peaceful solicitation to join union.

Any person, firm, association, corporation, or labor union or organization engaged in lockouts, layoffs, boycotts, picketing, work stoppages or other conduct, a purpose of which is to cause, force, persuade or induce any other person, firm, association, corporation or labor union or organization to violate any provision of this article shall be guilty of illegal conduct contrary to public policy; provided that nothing herein contained shall be construed to prevent or make illegal the peaceful and orderly solicitation and persuasion by union members of others to join a union, unaccompanied by any intimidation, use of force, threat of use of force, reprisal or threat of reprisal, and provided that no such solicitation or persuasion shall be conducted so as to interfere with, or interrupt the work of any employee during working hours.

§40.1-69. Violation a misdemeanor.

Any violation of any of the provisions of this article by any person, firm, association, corporation, or labor union or organization shall be a misdemeanor.

ARTICLE 4
MEDIATION AND CONCILIATION OF LABOR DISPUTES
(Selected Sections)

§40.1-70. Department designated agency to mediate disputes.

The Department is hereby designated as the state agency authorized to mediate and conciliate labor disputes.

§40.1-71. Notice of proposed termination or modification of collective bargaining contract; notice prior to work stoppage; injunctions and penalties.

Whenever there is in effect a collective bargaining contract covering employees of any utility engaged in the business of furnishing water, light, heat, gas, electric power, transportation or communication, the utility or the collective bargaining agent recognized by the utility and its employees shall not terminate or modify such contract until the party desiring such termination or modification serves written notice upon the Department of the proposed termination or modification at least thirty days prior to the expiration date thereof or, in the event such contract contains no expiration date, at least thirty days prior to the date it is proposed to make such termination or modification; provided, however, that a party having given notice of modification as provided herein shall not be required to give a notice of termination of the same contract.

Where there is no collective bargaining contract in effect, the utility or its employees shall give at least thirty days' notice to the Department prior to any work stoppage which would affect the operations of the utility engaged in the business of furnishing any of the utilities as described in this section.

If the utility or its employees, or the collective bargaining agent recognized by the utility and its employees, as the case may be, fails to give thirty days' notice as required by this section, the utility or its employees or such collective bargaining agent, as the case may be, may file a bill of complaint with the clerk of the circuit court having equity jurisdiction over the place of employment asking the court to temporarily enjoin such termination, modification or work stoppage until the proper notice has been served and the thirty-day period has been observed. The court shall have the authority to impose against any person who violates the notice provisions of this section a fine of up to $100 for each day such termination, modification or work stoppage continues until proper notice has been served and observed or against the collective bargaining agent the court shall have the authority to impose a fine of up to $1,000 for each day such termination or modification continues until proper notice has been served and observed.

§40.1-74. Right of entry.

In order to carry out the duties imposed by this article, the Commissioner or his designated agent shall have the right to enter upon the property of the utility.

§40.1-75. Article not applicable when National Railway Labor Act applies.

Nothing in this article shall apply to any utility to which the National Railway Labor Act is applicable.

TITLE 42.1
LIBRARIES
(Selected Chapter)

CHAPTER 5
OFFENSES
(Complete Chapter)

§42.1-72. Injuring or destroying books and other property of libraries.

Any person who willfully, maliciously or wantonly writes upon, injures, defaces, tears, cuts, mutilates, or destroys any book or other library property belonging to or in the custody of any public, county or regional library, The Library of Virginia, other repository of public records, museums or any library or collection belonging to or in the custody of any educational, eleemosynary, benevolent, hereditary, historical library or patriotic institution, organization or society, shall be guilty of a Class 1 misdemeanor.

§42.1-73. Concealment of book or other property while on premises of library; removal of book or other property from library.

Whoever, without authority, with the intention of converting to his own or another's use, wilfully conceals a book or other library property, while still on the premises of such library, or willfully or without authority removes any book or other property from any of the above libraries or collections shall be deemed guilty of larceny thereof, and upon conviction thereof shall be punished as provided by law. Proof of the willful concealment of such book or other library property while still on the premises of such library shall be prima facie evidence of intent to commit larceny thereof.

§42.1-73.1. Exemption from liability for arrest of suspected person; electronic article surveillance devices.

A library or agent or employee of the library causing the arrest of any person pursuant to the provisions of §42.1-73, shall not be held civilly liable for unlawful detention, slander, malicious prosecution, false imprisonment, false arrest, or assault and battery of the person so arrested, whether such arrest takes place on the premises of the library or after close pursuit from such premises by such agent or employee, if, in causing the arrest of such person, the library or agent or employee of the library had at the time of such arrest probable cause to believe that the person committed willful concealment of books or other library property.

The activation of an electronic article surveillance device as a result of a person exiting the premises or an area within the premises of a library where an electronic article surveillance device is located shall constitute probable cause for the detention of such person by such library or agent or employee of the library, provided that such person is detained only in a reasonable manner and only for such time as is necessary for an inquiry into the circumstances surrounding the activation of the device, and provided that clear and visible notice is posted at each exit and location within the premises where such device is located indicating the presence of an anti-theft device. For purposes of this section, "electronic article surveillance device" means an electronic device designed and operated for the purpose of detecting the removal from the premises or a protected area within such premises, of any specially marked or tagged book or other library property.

§42.1-74. Failure to return book or other library property.

Any person having in his possession any book or other property of any of the above libraries or collections, which he shall fail to return within thirty days after receiving notice in writing from the custodian, shall be guilty of a misdemeanor and punished according to law; provided, however, that if such book should be lost or destroyed, such person may, within thirty days after being so notified, pay to the custodian the value of such book, the value to be determined by the governing board having jurisdiction.

§42.1-74.1. "Book or other library property" defined.

The terms "book or other library property" as used in this chapter shall include any book, plate, picture, photograph, engraving, painting, drawing, map, newspaper, magazine, pamphlet, broadside, manuscript, document, letter, public record, microform, sound recording, audiovisual materials in any format, magnetic or other tapes, electronic data processing records, artifacts, or other documentary, written, or printed material, regardless of physical form or characteristics, belonging to, on loan to, or otherwise in the custody of any library, museum, repository of public or other records institution as specified in §42.1-72.

TITLE 44
MILITARY AND EMERGENCY LAWS
(Selected Chapters)

CHAPTER 3.2
EMERGENCY SERVICES AND DISASTER LAW
(Complete Chapter)

§44-146.13. Short title.

This chapter may be cited as the "Commonwealth of Virginia Emergency Services and Disaster Law of 2000."
(Chgd. by L.2000 ch. 309, eff. 7/1/2000.)

§44-146.14. Findings of General Assembly.

(a) Because of the ever present possibility of the occurrence of disasters of unprecedented size and destructiveness resulting from enemy attack, sabotage or other hostile action, resource shortage, or from fire, flood, earthquake, or other natural causes, and in order to insure that preparations of the Commonwealth and its political subdivisions will be adequate to deal with such emergencies, and generally to provide for the common defense and to protect the public peace, health, and safety, and to preserve the lives and property and economic well-being of the people of the Commonwealth, it is hereby found and declared to be necessary and to be the purpose of this chapter:

(1) To create a State Department of Emergency Management, and to authorize the creation of local organizations for emergency management in the political subdivisions of the Commonwealth;

(2) To confer upon the Governor and upon the executive heads or governing bodies of the political subdivisions of the Commonwealth emergency powers provided herein; and

(3) To provide for rendering of mutual aid among the political subdivisions of the Commonwealth and with other states and to cooperate with the federal government with respect to the carrying out of emergency service functions.

(b) It is further declared to be the purpose of this chapter and the policy of the Commonwealth that all emergency service functions of the Commonwealth be coordinated to the maximum extent possible with the comparable functions of the federal government, other states, and private agencies of every type, and that the Governor shall be empowered to provide for enforcement by the Commonwealth of national emergency services programs, to the end that the most effective preparation and use may be made of the nation's resources and facilities for dealing with any disaster that may occur.
(Chgd. by L.2000 ch. 309, eff. 7/1/2000.)

§44-146.15. Construction of chapter.

Nothing in this chapter is to be construed to:

(1) Limit, modify, or abridge the authority of the Governor to exercise any powers vested in him under other laws of this Commonwealth independent of, or in conjunction with, any provisions of this chapter;

(2) Interfere with dissemination of news or comment on public affairs; but any communications facility or organization, including, but not limited to, radio and television stations, wire services, and newspapers, may be required to transmit or print public service messages furnishing information or instructions in connection with actual or pending disaster;

(3) Affect the jurisdiction or responsibilities of police forces, fire-fighting forces, units of the armed forces of the United States or any personnel thereof, when on active duty; but state, local and interjurisdictional agencies for emergency services shall place reliance upon such forces in the event of declared disasters; or

(4) Interfere with the course of conduct of a labor dispute except that actions otherwise authorized by this chapter or other laws may be taken when necessary to forestall or mitigate imminent or existing danger to public health or safety.
(Chgd. by L.2000 ch. 309, eff. 7/1/2000.)

§44-146.16. Definitions.

As used in this chapter unless the context requires a different meaning:

(1) "Natural disaster" means any hurricane, tornado, storm, flood, high water, wind-driven water, tidal wave, earthquake, drought, fire or other natural catastrophe resulting in damage, hardship, suffering or possible loss of life;

(2) "Man-made disaster" means any condition following an attack by any enemy or foreign nation upon the United States resulting in substantial damage of property or injury to persons in the United States and may be by use of bombs, missiles, shell fire, nuclear, radiological, chemical or biological means or other weapons or by overt paramilitary actions; terrorism, foreign and domestic; also any industrial, nuclear or transportation accident, explosion, conflagration, power failure, resources shortage or other condition such as sabotage, oil spills and other injurious environmental contaminations, which threaten or cause damage to property, human suffering, hardship or loss of life;

(2a) "Emergency" means any occurrence, or threat thereof, whether natural or man-made, which results or may result in substantial injury or harm to the population or substantial damage to or loss of property or natural resources and may involve governmental action beyond that authorized or contemplated by existing law because governmental inaction for the period required to amend the law to meet the exigency would work immediate and irrevocable harm upon the citizens or the environment of the Commonwealth or some clearly defined portion or portions thereof;

(3) "Emergency services" means the preparation for and the carrying out of functions, other than functions for which military forces are primarily responsible, to prevent, minimize and repair injury and damage resulting from natural or man-made disasters, together with all other activities necessary or incidental to the preparation for and carrying out of the foregoing functions. These functions include, without limitation, fire-fighting services, police services, medical and health services, rescue, engineering, warning services, communications, radiological, chemical and other special weapons defense, evacuation of persons from stricken areas,

emergency welfare services, emergency transportation, emergency resource management, existing or properly assigned functions of plant protection, temporary restoration of public utility services, and other functions related to civilian protection. These functions also include the administration of approved state and federal disaster recovery and assistance programs;

(4) "Major disaster" means any natural catastrophe, including any: hurricane, tornado, storm, high water, wind-driven water, tidal wave, tsunami, earthquake, volcanic eruption, landslide, mudslide, snowstorm or drought, or regardless of cause, any fire, flood, or explosion, in any part of the United States, which, in the determination of the President of the United States is, or thereafter determined to be, of sufficient severity and magnitude to warrant major disaster assistance under the Strafford Act (P.L. 43–288, as amended) to supplement the efforts and available resources of states, local governments, and disaster relief organizations in alleviating the damage, loss, hardship, or suffering caused thereby and is so declared by him;

(5) "State of emergency" means the condition declared by the Governor when in his judgment, the threat or actual occurrence of an emergency or a disaster in any part of the Commonwealth is of sufficient severity and magnitude to warrant disaster assistance by the Commonwealth to supplement the efforts and available resources of the several localities, and relief organizations in preventing or alleviating the damage, loss, hardship, or suffering threatened or caused thereby and is so declared by him;

(6) "Local emergency" means the condition declared by the local governing body when in its judgment the threat or actual occurrence of an emergency or disaster is or threatens to be of sufficient severity and magnitude to warrant coordinated local government action to prevent or alleviate the damage, loss, hardship or suffering threatened or caused thereby; provided, however, that a local emergency arising wholly or substantially out of a resource shortage may be declared only by the Governor, upon petition of the local governing body, when he deems the threat or actual occurrence of such an emergency or disaster to be of sufficient severity and magnitude to warrant coordinated local government action to prevent or alleviate the damage, loss, hardship or suffering threatened or caused thereby; provided, however, nothing in this chapter shall be construed as prohibiting a local governing body from the prudent management of its water supply to prevent or manage a water shortage;

(7) "Local emergency management organization" means an organization created in accordance with the provisions of this chapter by local authority to perform local emergency service functions;

(8) "Political subdivision" means any city or county in the Commonwealth and for the purposes of this chapter, the Town of Chincoteague and any town of more than 5,000 population which chooses to have an emergency management program separate from that of the county in which such town is located;

(9) "Interjurisdictional agency for emergency management" is any organization established between contiguous political subdivisions to facilitate the cooperation and protection of the subdivisions in the work of disaster prevention, preparedness, response, and recovery;

(10) "Resource shortage" means the absence, unavailability or reduced supply of any raw or processed natural resource, or any commodities, goods or services of any kind which bear a substantial relationship to the health, safety, welfare and economic well-being of the citizens of the Commonwealth;

(11) "Discharge" means spillage, leakage, pumping, pouring, seepage, emitting, dumping, emptying, injecting, escaping, leaching, fire, explosion, or other releases;

(12) "Hazardous substances" means all materials or substances which now or hereafter are designated, defined, or characterized as hazardous by law or regulation of the Commonwealth or regulation of the United States government;

(13) "Hazard mitigation" means any action taken to reduce or eliminate the long-term risk to human life and property from natural hazards.

(Chgd. by L.2000 ch. 309, eff. 7/1/2000.)

§44-146.17. Powers and duties of Governor.

The Governor shall be Director of Emergency Management. He shall take such action from time to time as is necessary for the adequate promotion and coordination of state and local emergency services activities relating to the safety and welfare of the Commonwealth in time of natural or man-made disasters.

The Governor shall have, in addition to his powers hereinafter or elsewhere prescribed by law, the following powers and duties:

(1) To proclaim and publish such rules and regulations and to issue such orders as may, in his judgment, be necessary to accomplish the purposes of this chapter including, but not limited to such measures as are in his judgment required to control, restrict, allocate or regulate the use, sale, production and distribution of food, fuel, clothing and other commodities, materials, goods, services and resources under any state or federal emergency services programs. He may adopt and implement the Commonwealth of Virginia Emergency Operations Plan, which provides for state-level emergency operations in response to any type of disaster or large-scale emergency affecting Virginia and that provides the needed framework within which more detailed emergency plans and procedures can be developed and maintained by state agencies, local governments and other organizations. He may direct and compel evacuation of all or part of the populace from any stricken or threatened area if this action is deemed necessary for the preservation of life, implement emergency mitigation, preparedness, response or recovery actions; prescribe routes, modes of transportation and destination in connection with evacuation; and control ingress and egress at an emergency area, including the movement of persons within the area and the occupancy of premises therein. Executive orders, to include those declaring a state of emergency and directing evacuation, shall have the force and effect of law and the violation thereof shall be punishable as a Class 1 misdemeanor in every case where the executive order declares that its violation shall have such force and effect. Except as to emergency plans issued to prescribe actions to be taken in the event of disasters and emergencies, no rule, regulation, or order issued under this section shall have any effect beyond June 30 next following the next adjournment of the regular session of the General Assembly but the same or a similar rule, regulation, or order may thereafter be issued again if not contrary to law;

(2) To appoint a State Coordinator of Emergency Management and authorize the appointment or employment of other personnel as is necessary to carry out the provisions of this chapter, and to remove, in his discretion, any and all persons serving hereunder;

(3) To procure supplies and equipment, to institute training and public information programs relative to emergency management and to take other preparatory steps including the partial or full mobilization of emergency management organizations in advance of actual disaster, to insure the furnishing of adequately trained and equipped forces in time of need;

(4) To make such studies and surveys of industries, resources, and facilities in the Commonwealth as may be necessary to ascertain the capabilities of the Commonwealth and to plan for the most efficient emergency use thereof;

(5) On behalf of the Commonwealth enter into mutual aid arrangements with other states and to coordinate mutual aid plans between political subdivisions of the Commonwealth;

(6) To delegate any administrative authority vested in him under this chapter, and to provide for the further delegation of any such authority, as needed;

(7) Whenever, in the opinion of the Governor, the safety and welfare of the people of the Commonwealth require the exercise of emergency measures due to a threatened or actual disaster, he may declare a state of emergency to exist;

(8) To request a major disaster declaration from the President, thereby certifying the need for federal disaster assistance and ensuring the expenditure of a reasonable amount of funds of the Commonwealth, its local governments, or other agencies for alleviating the damage, loss, hardship, or suffering resulting from the disaster; and

(9) To provide incident command system guidelines for state agencies and local emergency response organizations.
(Chgd. by L.1997 ch. 893; L.2000 ch. 309, eff. 7/1/2000.)

§44-146.17:1. Transmittal to General Assembly of rules, regulations, and orders.

The Governor shall cause copies of any order, rule, or regulation proclaimed and published by him pursuant to §44-146.17 to be transmitted forthwith to each member of the General Assembly.

§44-146.18. Department of Emergency Services continued as Department of Emergency Management; administration and operational control; coordinator and other personnel; powers and duties.

(a) The State Office of Emergency Services is continued and shall hereafter be known as the Department of Emergency Management. Wherever the words "State Department of Emergency Services" are used in any law of this Commonwealth, they shall mean the Department of Emergency Management. During a declared emergency this Department shall revert to the operational control of the Governor. The Department shall have a coordinator who shall be appointed by and serve at the pleasure of the Governor and also serve as State Emergency Planning Director. The Department shall employ the professional, technical, secretarial, and clerical employees necessary for the performance of its functions.

(b) The State Department of Emergency Management shall in the administration of emergency services and disaster preparedness programs:

(1) Promulgate plans and programs which are conducive to adequate disaster mitigation preparedness, response and recovery programs;

(2) Prepare and maintain a State Emergency Operations Plan for disaster response and recovery operations that assigns primary and support responsibilities for basic emergency services functions to state agencies, organizations and personnel as appropriate;

(3) Coordinate and administer disaster mitigation, preparedness, response and recovery plans and programs with the proponent federal, state and local government agencies and related groups;

(4) Provide guidance and assistance to state agencies and units of local government in developing and maintaining emergency management programs, plans and systems;

(5) Make necessary recommendations to agencies of the federal, state, or local governments on preventive and preparedness measures designed to eliminate or reduce disasters and their impact;

(6) Determine requirements of the Commonwealth and its political subdivisions for those necessities needed in the event of a declared emergency which are not otherwise readily available;

(7) Assist state agencies and political subdivisions in establishing and operating training programs and programs of public information and education regarding emergency services and disaster preparedness activities;

(8) Develop standards, provide guidance and encourage the maintenance of local and state agency emergency operations plans;

(9) Prepare, maintain, coordinate or implement emergency resource management plans and programs with federal, state and local government agencies and related groups, and make such surveys of industries, resources, and facilities within the Commonwealth, both public and private, as are necessary to carry out the purposes of this chapter;

(10) Coordinate with the federal government and any public or private agency or entity in achieving any purpose of this chapter and in implementing programs for disaster prevention, mitigation, preparation, response, and recovery; and

(11) Establish guidelines pursuant to §44-146.28, and administer payments to eligible applicants as authorized by the Governor.

(c) The State Department of Emergency Management shall during a period of declared emergency be responsible for:

(1) The receipt, evaluation, and dissemination of intelligence pertaining to an impending or actual disaster;

(2) Providing facilities from which state agencies and supporting organizations may conduct emergency operations;

(3) Providing an adequate communications and warning system capable of notifying all political subdivisions in the Commonwealth of an impending disaster within a reasonable time;

(4) Establishing and maintaining liaison with affected political subdivisions;

(5) Determining requirements for disaster relief and recovery assistance;

(6) Coordinating disaster response actions of federal, state and volunteer relief agencies;

(7) Coordinating and providing guidance and assistance to affected political subdivisions to ensure orderly and timely response to and recovery from disaster effects.

(d) The State Department of Emergency Management shall be provided the necessary facilities and equipment needed to perform its normal day-to-day activities and coordinate disaster-related activities of the various federal, state, and other agencies during a state of emergency declaration by the Governor or following a major disaster declaration by the President.

(e) The State Department of Emergency Management is authorized to enter into all contracts and agreements necessary or incidental to performance of any of its duties stated in this section or otherwise assigned to it by law, including contracts with the United States, other states, agencies and government subdivisions of the Commonwealth, and other appropriate public and private entities.
(Chgd. by L.1997 ch. 893; L.2000 ch. 309, eff. 7/1/2000.)

§44-146.18:1. Virginia Disaster Response Funds disbursements; reimbursements.

There is hereby created a nonlapsing revolving fund which shall be maintained as a separate special fund account within the state treasury, and administered by the Coordinator of Emergency Management, consistent with the purposes of this chapter. All expenses, costs, and judgments recovered pursuant to this section, and all moneys received as reimbursement in accordance with applicable provisions of federal law, shall be paid into the fund. Additionally, an annual appropriation to the fund from the general fund or other unrestricted nongeneral fund, in an amount determined by the Governor, may be authorized to carry out the purposes of this chapter. All recoveries from occurrences prior to March 10, 1983, and otherwise qualifying under this section, received subsequent to March 10, 1983, shall be paid into the fund. No moneys shall be credited to the balance in the fund until they have been received by the fund. An accounting of moneys received and disbursed shall be kept and furnished to the Governor or the General Assembly upon request.

Disbursements from the fund may be made for the following purposes and no others:

1. For costs and expenses, including, but not limited to personnel, administrative, and equipment costs and expenses directly incurred by the Department of Emergency Management or by any other state agency or political subdivision or other entity, acting at the direction of the Coordinator of Emergency Management, in and for preventing or alleviating damage, loss, hardship, or suffering caused by emergencies, resource shortages, or natural or man-made disasters; and

2. For procurement, maintenance, and replenishment of materials, equipment, and supplies, in such quantities and at such location as the Coordinator of Emergency Management may deem necessary to protect the public peace, health, and safety and to preserve the lives and property and economic well-being of the people of the Commonwealth; and

3. For costs and expenses incurred by the Department of Emergency Management or by any other state agency or political subdivision or other entity, acting at the direction of the Coordinator of Emergency Management, in the recovery from the effects of a disaster or in the restoration of public property or facilities.

The Coordinator of Emergency Management shall promptly seek reimbursement from any person causing or contributing to an emergency or disaster for all sums disbursed from the fund for the protection, relief and recovery from loss or damage caused by such person. In the event a request for reimbursement is not paid within sixty days of receipt of a written demand, the claim shall be referred to the Attorney General for collection. The Coordinator of Emergency Management shall be allowed to recover all legal and court costs and other expenses incident to such actions for collection. The Coordinator is authorized to recover any sums incurred by any other state agency or political subdivision acting at the direction of the Coordinator as provided in this paragraph.

(Chgd. by L.2000 ch. 309, eff. 7/1/2000.)

§44-146.18:2. Authority of Coordinator of Emergency Management in undeclared emergency.

In an emergency which does not warrant a gubernatorial declaration of a state of emergency, the Coordinator of Emergency Management, after consultation with and approval of the Secretary of Public Safety, may enter into contracts and incur obligations necessary to prevent or alleviate damage, loss, hardship, or suffering caused by such emergency and to protect the health and safety of persons and property. In exercising the powers vested by this section, the Coordinator may proceed without regard to normal procedures pertaining to entering into contracts, incurring of obligations, rental of equipment, purchase of supplies and materials, and expenditure of public funds; however, mandatory constitutional requirements shall not be disregarded.

(Chgd. by L.2000 ch. 309, eff. 7/1/2000.)

§44-146.19. Powers and duties of political subdivisions.

A. Each political subdivision within the Commonwealth shall be within the jurisdiction of and served by the Department of Emergency Management and be responsible for local disaster mitigation, preparedness, response and recovery. Each political subdivision may maintain in accordance with state disaster preparedness plans and programs an agency of emergency management which, except as otherwise provided under this chapter, has jurisdiction over and services the entire political subdivision.

B. Each political subdivision shall have a director of emergency management who, after the term of the person presently serving in this capacity has expired and in the absence of an executive order by the Governor, shall be the following:

1. In the case of a city, the mayor or city manager, who shall have the authority to appoint a coordinator of emergency management with consent of council;

2. In the case of a county, a member of the board of supervisors selected by the board or the chief administrative officer for the county, who shall have the authority to appoint a coordinator of emergency management with the consent of the governing body;

3. A coordinator of emergency management may be appointed by the council of any town to ensure integration of its organization into the county emergency management organization;

4. In the case of the Town of Chincoteague and of towns with a population in excess of 5,000 having an emergency management organization separate from that of the county, the mayor or town manager shall have the authority to appoint a coordinator of emergency services with consent of council;

5. In Smyth County and in York County, the chief administrative officer for the county may appoint a director of emergency management, with the consent of the governing body, who shall have the authority to appoint a coordinator of emergency management with the consent of the governing body.

C. Whenever the Governor has declared a state of emergency, each political subdivision within the disaster area may, under the supervision and control of the Governor or his designated representative, control, restrict, allocate or regulate the use, sale, production and distribution of food, fuel, clothing and other commodities, materials, goods, services and resource systems which fall only within the boundaries of that jurisdiction and which do not impact systems affecting adjoining or other political subdivisions, enter into contracts and incur obligations necessary to combat such threatened or actual disaster, protect the health and safety of persons and property and provide emergency assistance to the victims of such disaster. In exercising the powers vested under this section, under the supervision and control of the Governor, the political subdivision may proceed without regard to time-consuming procedures and formalities prescribed by law (except mandatory constitutional requirements) pertaining to the performance of public work, entering into contracts, incurring of obligations, employment of temporary workers, rental of equipment, purchase of supplies and materials, levying of taxes, and appropriation and expenditure of public funds.

D. The director of each local organization for emergency management may, in collaboration with other public and private agencies within this Commonwealth or within an adjacent state, develop or cause to be developed mutual aid arrangements for reciprocal assistance in case of a disaster too great to be dealt with unassisted. Such arrangements shall be consistent with state plans and programs and it shall be the duty of each local organization for emergency management to render assistance in accordance with the provisions of such mutual aid arrangements.

E. Each local and interjurisdictional agency shall prepare and keep current a local or interjurisdictional emergency operations plan for its area. The plan shall include, but not be limited to, responsibilities of all local agencies and shall establish a chain of command. Each political subdivision having a nuclear power station or other nuclear facility within ten miles of its boundaries shall, if so directed by the Department of Emergency Management, prepare and keep current an appropriate emergency plan for its area for response to nuclear accidents at such station or facility.
(Chgd. by L.2000 ch. 309, eff. 7/1/2000.)

§44-146.20. Joint action by political subdivisions.
If two or more political subdivisions find that disaster operation plans and programs would be better served by interjurisdictional arrangements in planning for, preventing, or responding to disaster in that area, then direct steps may be taken as necessary, including creation of an interjurisdictional relationship, a joint emergency operations plan, mutual aid, or such other activities as necessary for planning and services. Any political subdivision may provide or receive assistance in the event of a disaster or emergency, pursuant to this chapter, under the provisions of any local mutual aid agreement or by the Statewide Mutual Aid program if agreed to by resolution of the governing body. The action of the governing body may include terms and conditions deemed necessary by the governing body for participation in the program. The governing body may withdraw from participation in the Statewide Mutual Aid program by adoption of a resolution or ordinance upon a finding that participation is no longer in the public interest. The locality shall immediately notify the State Coordinator of Emergency Services of the adoption of a participation or withdrawal resolution.
(Chgd. by L.2000 chs. 309, 437, eff. 7/1/2000.)

§44-146.21. Declaration of local emergency.
(a) A local emergency may be declared by the local director of emergency management with the consent of the governing body of the political subdivision. In the event the governing body cannot convene due to the disaster or other exigent circumstances, the director, or in his absence, the deputy director, or in the absence of both the director and deputy director, any member of the governing body may declare the existence of a local emergency, subject to confirmation by the governing body at its next regularly scheduled meeting or at a special meeting within fourteen days of the declaration, whichever occurs first. The governing body, when in its judgment all emergency actions have been taken, shall take appropriate action to end the declared emergency.

(b) A declaration of a local emergency as defined in §44-146.16(6) shall activate the local Emergency Operations Plan and authorize the furnishing of aid and assistance thereunder.

(c) *(Repealed.)*

(c1) Whenever a local emergency has been declared, the director of emergency management of each political subdivision or any member of the governing body in the absence of the director, if so authorized by the governing body, may control, restrict, allocate or regulate the use, sale, production and distribution of food, fuel, clothing and other commodities, materials, goods, services and resource systems which fall only within the boundaries of that jurisdiction and which do not impact systems affecting adjoining or other political subdivisions, enter into contracts and incur obligations necessary to combat such threatened or actual disaster, protect the health and safety of persons and property and provide emergency assistance to the victims of such disaster, and proceed without regard to time-consuming procedures and formalities prescribed by law (except mandatory constitutional requirements) pertaining to the performance of public work, entering into contracts, incurring of obligations, employment of temporary workers, rental of equipment, purchase of supplies and materials, and other expenditures of public funds, provided such funds in excess of appropriations in the current approved budget, unobligated, are available. Whenever the Governor has declared a state of emergency, each political subdivision affected may, under the supervision and control of the Governor or his designated representative, enter into contracts and incur obligations necessary to combat such threatened or actual disaster beyond the capabilities of local government, protect the health and safety of persons and property and provide emergency assistance to the victims of such disaster. In exercising the powers vested under this section, under the supervision and control of the Governor, the political subdivision may proceed without regard to time-consuming procedures and formalities prescribed by law pertaining to public work, entering into contracts, incurring of obligations, employment of temporary workers, rental of equipment, purchase of supplies and materials, levying of taxes, and appropriation and expenditure of public funds.

(d) No interjurisdictional agency or official thereof may declare a local emergency. However, an interjurisdictional agency of emergency management shall provide aid and services to the affected political subdivision authorizing such assistance in accordance with the agreement as a result of a local or state declaration.

(e) None of the provisions of this chapter shall apply to the Emergency Disaster Relief provided by the American Red Cross or other relief agency solely concerned with the provision of service at no cost to the citizens of the Commonwealth.
(Chgd. by L.2000 ch. 309, eff. 7/1/2000.)

§44-146.22. Development of measures to prevent or reduce harmful consequences of disasters.
In addition to disaster prevention measures included in state, local and interjurisdictional emergency operations plans, the Governor shall consider, on a continuing basis, hazard mitigation or other measures that could be taken to prevent or reduce the harmful consequences of disasters. At his direction, and pursuant to any other authority, state agencies, including, but not limited to, those charged with responsibilities in connection with floodplain management, stream encroachment and flow regulation, weather modification, fire prevention and control, air quality, public works, land use and land-use planning, and construction standards, shall make studies of disaster prevention. The Governor, from time to time, shall make recommendations to the General Assembly, local governments, and other appropriate public and private entities as may facilitate measures for prevention or reduction of the harmful consequences of disasters.
(Chgd. by L.2000 ch. 309, eff. 7/1/2000.)

§44-146.23. Immunity from liability.
(a) Neither the Commonwealth, nor any political subdivision thereof, nor federal agencies, nor other public or private agencies, nor, except in cases of willful misconduct, public or private employees, nor representatives of any of them, engaged in any emergency services activities, while complying with or attempting to comply with this chapter or any rule, regulation, or executive order promulgated pursuant to the provisions of this chapter, shall be liable for the death of, or any injury to, persons or damage to property as a result of such activities. The provisions of this section shall not affect the right of any person to receive benefits to which he would otherwise be entitled under this chapter, or under the Workers' Compensation Law (§65.2-100 et seq.), or

under any pension law, nor the right of any such person to receive any benefits or compensation under any act of Congress.

(b) Any person owning or controlling real estate or other premises who voluntarily and without compensation grants a license or privilege, or otherwise permits the designation or use of the whole or any part or parts of such real estate or premises for the purpose of sheltering persons, of emergency access or of other uses relating to emergency services shall, together with his successors in interest, if any, not be liable for negligently causing the death of, or injury to any person on or about such real estate or premises or for loss of or damage to the property of any person on or about such real estate or premises during such actual or impending disaster.

(c) If any person holds a license, certificate, or other permit issued by any state, or political subdivision thereof, evidencing the meeting of qualifications for professional, mechanical, or other skills, the person may gratuitously render aid involving that skill in this Commonwealth during a disaster, and such person shall not be liable for negligently causing the death of, or injury to, any person or for the loss of, or damage to, the property of any person resulting from such gratuitous service.

(d) No person, firm or corporation which gratuitously services or repairs any electronic devices or equipment under the provisions of this section after having been approved for the purposes by the State Coordinator shall be liable for negligently causing the death of, or injury to, any person or for the loss of, or damage to, the property of any person resulting from any defect or imperfection in any such device or equipment so gratuitously serviced or repaired.

(e) Notwithstanding any law to the contrary, no individual, partnership, corporation, association, or other legal entity shall be liable in civil damages as a result of acts taken voluntarily and without compensation in the course of rendering care, assistance, or advice with respect to an incident creating a danger to person, property, or the environment as a result of an actual or threatened discharge of a hazardous substance, or in preventing, cleaning up, treating, or disposing of or attempting to prevent, clean up, treat, or dispose of any such discharge, provided that such acts are taken under the direction of state or local authorities responding to the incident. This section shall not preclude liability for civil damages as a result of gross negligence, recklessness or willful misconduct. The provisions of this section shall not affect the right of any person to receive benefits to which he would otherwise be entitled under this chapter, or under the Workers' Compensation Law (§65.2-100 et seq.), or under any pension law, nor the right of any such person to receive any benefits or compensation under any act of Congress. The immunity provided by the provisions of this paragraph shall be in addition to, not in lieu of, any immunities provided by §8.01-225 of the Code.

§44-146.24. Cooperation of public agencies.

In carrying out the provisions of the chapter, the Governor, the heads of state agencies, the local directors and governing bodies of the political subdivisions of the Commonwealth are directed to utilize the services, equipment, supplies and facilities of existing departments, offices, and agencies of the Commonwealth and the political subdivisions thereof to the maximum extent practicable consistent with state and local emergency operation plans. The officers and personnel of all such departments, offices, and agencies are directed to cooperate with and extend such services and facilities to the Governor and to the State Department of Emergency Management upon request.
(Chgd. by L.2000 ch. 309, eff. 7/1/2000.)

§44-146.25. Certain persons not to be employed or associated in emergency services organizations; loyalty oath required.

No person shall be employed or associated in any emergency services organization established under this chapter who advocates or has advocated a change by force or violence in the constitutional form of government of the United States or in this Commonwealth or the overthrow of any government in the United States by force, or violence, or who has been convicted of, or is under indictment or information charging any subversive act against the United States. Each person who is appointed to serve in an organization for emergency services shall, before entering upon his duties, take an oath, in writing, before a person authorized to administer oaths in this Commonwealth, which shall be substantially as follows:

"I .... do solemnly swear (or affirm) that I will support and defend the Constitution of the United States and the Constitution of the Commonwealth of Virginia, against all enemies foreign and domestic; that I will bear true faith and allegiance to the same; that I take this obligation freely, without any mental reservation or purpose of evasion; and that I will well and faithfully discharge the duties upon which I am about to enter.

"And I do further swear (or affirm) that I do not advocate, nor am I a member of any political party or organization that advocates the overthrow of the Government of the United States or of this State by force or violence and that during such time as I am a member of the (name of emergency services organization), I will not advocate, nor become a member of any political party or organization that advocates the overthrow of the Government of the United States or of this State by force or violence."

§44-146.26. Duties of emergency management organizations.

It shall be the duty of every organization for emergency management established pursuant to this chapter and of the officers thereof to execute and enforce such orders, rules and regulations as may be made by the Governor under authority of this chapter. Each organization shall have available for inspection at its office all such orders, rules and regulations.
(Chgd. by L.2000 ch. 309, eff. 7/1/2000.)

§44-146.27. Supplementing federal funds; assistance of federal agencies; acceptance of gifts and services; appropriations by local governing bodies.

A. If the federal government allots funds for the payment of a portion of any disaster programs, projects, equipment, supplies or materials or other related costs, the remaining portion may be paid with a combination of state and local funds available for this purpose and consistent with state emergency management plans and program priorities.

B. Whenever the federal government or any agency or officer thereof offers to the Commonwealth, or through the Commonwealth to any political subdivision thereof, services, equipment, supplies, materials, or funds by way of gift, grant or loan for purposes of emergency services, the Commonwealth, acting through the Governor, or such political subdivision, acting with the consent of the Governor and through its local director or governing body, may accept such offer and agree to the terms of the offer and the rules and regulations, if any, of the agency making the offer, including, but not limited to, requirements to hold and save the United States free from damages and to indemnify the federal government against any claims arising from the services, equipment, supplies, materials, or funds provided. Upon such acceptance, the Governor or local director or governing body of such political subdivision may authorize any officer of the Commonwealth or of the political subdivision, as the case may be, to receive such services, equipment, supplies, materials, or funds on behalf of the Commonwealth or such political subdivision, in accordance with the terms of the agreement, and subject to the rules and regulations, if any, of the agency making the offer.

C. Whenever any person, firm or corporation offers to the Commonwealth or to any political subdivision thereof services, equipment, supplies, materials, or funds by way of gift, grant or loan, for purposes of emergency management, the Commonwealth, acting through the Governor, or such political subdivision, acting through its local director or governing body, may accept such offer and upon such acceptance the Governor or local director or governing body of such political subdivision may authorize any officer of the Commonwealth or of the political subdivision, as the case may be, to receive such services, equipment, supplies, materials, or funds on behalf of the Commonwealth or such political subdivision, and subject to the terms of the offer.

D. The governing bodies of the counties, cities and towns are hereby authorized to appropriate funds for expenditure by any local or regional organization for emergency management established pursuant to this chapter and for local or regional disaster service activities.

(Chgd. by L.1999 chs. 6, 7; L.2000 ch. 309, eff. 7/1/2000.)

§44-146.28. Authority of Governor and agencies under his control in declared state of emergency.

(a) In the case of a declaration of a state of emergency as defined in §44-146.16, the Governor is authorized to expend from all funds of the state treasury not constitutionally restricted, a sum sufficient. Allotments from such sum sufficient may be made by the Governor to any state agency or political subdivision of the Commonwealth to carry out disaster service missions and responsibilities. Allotments may also be made by the Governor from the sum sufficient to provide financial assistance to eligible applicants located in an area declared to be in a state of emergency, but not declared to be a major disaster area for which federal assistance might be forthcoming. This shall be considered as a program of last resort for those local jurisdictions that cannot meet the full cost.

The Virginia Department of Emergency Management shall establish guidelines and procedures for determining whether and to what extent financial assistance to local governments may be provided.

The guidelines and procedures shall include, but not be limited to, the following:

(1) Participants may be eligible to receive financial assistance to cover a percentage of eligible costs if they demonstrate that they are incapable of covering the full cost. The percentage may vary, based on the Commission on Local Government's fiscal stress index. The cumulative effect of recent disasters during the preceding twelve months may also be considered for eligibility purposes.

(2) Only eligible participants that have sustained an emergency or disaster as defined in §44-146.16 with total eligible costs of four dollars or more per capita may receive assistance except that (i) any town with a total population of less than 3,500 shall be eligible for disaster assistance for incurred eligible damages of $15,000 or greater and (ii) any town with a population of 3,500 or more, but less than 5,000 shall be eligible for disaster assistance for incurred eligible damages of $20,000 or greater and (iii) any town with a population of 5,000 or greater with total eligible costs of four dollars or more per capita may receive assistance. No site or facility may be included with less than $1,000 in eligible costs. However, the total cost of debris clearance may be considered as costs associated with a single site.

(3) Eligible participants shall be fully covered by all-risk property and flood insurance policies, including provisions for insuring the contents of the property and business interruptions, or shall be self-insured, in order to be eligible for this assistance. Insurance deductibles shall not be covered by this program.

(4) Eligible costs incurred by towns, public service authorities, volunteer fire departments and volunteer rescue squads may be included in a county's or city's total costs.

(5) Unless otherwise stated in guidelines and procedures, eligible costs are defined as those listed in the Public Assistance component of Public Law 93–288, as amended, excluding beach replenishment and snow removal.

(6) State agencies, as directed by the Virginia Department of Emergency Management, shall conduct an on-site survey to validate damages and to document restoration costs.

(7) Eligible participants shall maintain complete documentation of all costs in a manner approved by the Auditor of Public Accounts and shall provide copies of the documentation to the Virginia Department of Emergency Management upon request.

If a jurisdiction meets the criteria set forth in the guidelines and procedures, but is in an area that has neither been declared to be in a state of emergency nor been declared to be a major disaster area for which federal assistance might be forthcoming, the Governor is authorized, in his discretion, to make an allotment from the sum sufficient to that jurisdiction without a declaration of a state of emergency, in the same manner as if a state of emergency declaration had been made.

The Governor shall report to the Chairmen of the Senate Finance Committee, the House Appropriations Committee, and the House Finance Committee within thirty days of authorizing the sum sufficient pursuant to this section. The Virginia Department of Emergency Management shall report annually to the General Assembly on the local jurisdictions that received financial assistance and the amount each jurisdiction received.

(b) Public agencies under the supervision and control of the Governor may implement their emergency assignments without regard to normal procedures (except mandatory constitutional requirements) pertaining to the performance of public work, entering into contracts, incurring of obligations, employment of temporary workers, rental of equipment, purchase of supplies and materials and expenditures of public funds.

(Chgd. by L.1997 ch. 893; L.2000 chs. 309, 1023, eff. 7/1/2000.)

§44-146.28:1. Compact enacted into law; terms.

The Emergency Management Assistance Compact is hereby enacted into law and entered into by the Commonwealth of Virginia with all other states legally joining therein, in the form substantially as follows:

EMERGENCY MANAGEMENT ASSISTANCE COMPACT

ARTICLE I.
PURPOSE AND AUTHORITIES

This compact is made and entered into by and between the participating member states which enact this compact, hereinafter called party states. For the purposes of this compact, the term "states" is taken to mean the several states, the Commonwealth of Puerto Rico, the District of Columbia, and all U.S. territorial possessions.

The purpose of this compact is to provide for mutual assistance between the states entering into this compact in managing any emergency or disaster that is duly declared by the Governor of the affected state, whether arising from natural disaster, technological hazard, man-made disaster, civil emergency aspects of resources shortages, community disorders, insurgency, or enemy attack.

This compact shall also provide for mutual cooperation in emergency-related exercises, testing, or other training activities using equipment and personnel simulating performance of any aspect of the giving and receiving of aid by party states or subdivisions of party states during emergencies, such actions occurring outside actual declared emergency periods. Mutual assistance in this compact may include the use of the states' National Guard forces, either in accordance with the National Guard Mutual Assistance Compact or by mutual agreement between states.

ARTICLE II.
GENERAL IMPLEMENTATION

Each party state entering into this compact recognizes that many emergencies transcend political jurisdictional boundaries and that intergovernmental coordination is essential in managing these and other emergencies under this compact. Each state further recognizes that there will be emergencies which require immediate access and present procedures to apply outside resources to make a prompt and effective response to such an emergency. This is because few, if any, individual states have all the resources they may need in all types of emergencies or the capability of delivering resources to areas where emergencies exist.

The prompt, full, and effective utilization of resources of the participating states, including any resources on hand or available from the federal government or any other source, that are essential to the safety, care, and welfare of the people in the event of any emergency or disaster declared by a party state, shall be the underlying principle on which all articles of this compact shall be understood.

On behalf of the Governor of each state participating in the compact, the legally designated state official who is assigned responsibility for emergency management will be responsible for formulation of the appropriate interstate mutual aid plans and procedures necessary to implement this compact.

ARTICLE III.
PARTY STATE RESPONSIBILITIES

A. It shall be the responsibility of each party state to formulate procedural plans and programs for interstate cooperation in the performance of the responsibilities listed in this article. In formulating such plans, and in carrying them out, the party states, insofar as practical, shall:

1. Review individual state hazards analyses and, to the extent reasonably possible, determine all those potential emergencies the party states might jointly suffer, whether due to natural disaster, technological hazard, man-made disaster, emergency aspects of resources shortages, civil disorders, insurgency, or enemy attack;

2. Review party states' individual emergency plans and develop a plan which will determine the mechanism for the interstate management and provision of assistance concerning any potential emergency;

3. Develop interstate procedures to fill any identified gaps and to resolve any identified inconsistencies or overlaps in existing or developed plans;

4. Assist in warning communities adjacent to or crossing the state boundaries;

5. Protect and assure uninterrupted delivery of services, medicines, water, food, energy and fuel, search and rescue, and critical lifeline equipment, services, and resources, both human and material;

6. Inventory and set procedures for the interstate loan and delivery of human and material resources, together with procedures for reimbursement or forgiveness; and

7. Provide, to the extent authorized by law, for temporary suspension of any statutes or ordinances that restrict the implementation of the above responsibilities.

B. The authorized representative of a party state may request assistance of another party state by contacting the authorized representative of that state. The provisions of this compact shall only apply to requests for assistance made by and to authorized representatives. Requests may be verbal or in writing. If verbal, the request shall be confirmed in writing within thirty days of the verbal request. Requests shall provide the following information:

1. A description of the emergency service function for which assistance is needed, including, but not limited to, fire services, law enforcement, emergency medical, transportation, communications, public works and engineering, building inspection, planning and information assistance, mass care, resource support, health and medical services, and search and rescue;

2. The amount and type of personnel, equipment, materials and supplies needed, and a reasonable estimate of the length of time they will be needed; and

3. The specific place and time for staging of the assisting party's response and a point of contact at that location.

C. There shall be frequent consultation between state officials who have assigned emergency management responsibilities and other appropriate representatives of the party states with affected jurisdictions and the United States Government, with free exchange of information, plans, and resource records relating to emergency capabilities.

ARTICLE IV.
LIMITATIONS

Any party state requested to render mutual aid or conduct exercises and training for mutual aid shall take such action as is necessary to provide and make available the resources covered by this compact in accordance with the terms hereof; provided that it is understood that the state rendering aid may withhold resources to the extent necessary to provide reasonable protection for such state.

Each party state shall afford to the emergency forces of any party state, while operating within its state limits under the terms and conditions of this compact, the same powers, except that of arrest unless specifically authorized by the receiving state, duties, rights, and privileges as are afforded forces of the state in which they are performing emergency services. Emergency forces will continue under the command and control of their regular leaders, but the organizational units will come under the operational control of the emergency services authorities of the state receiving assistance. These conditions may be activated, as needed, only subsequent to a declaration of a state emergency or disaster by the governor of the party state that is to receive assistance or upon commencement of exercises or training for mutual aid and shall continue so long as the exercises or training for mutual aid are in progress, the state of emergency or disaster remains in effect, or loaned resources remain in the receiving state, whichever is longer.

ARTICLE V.
LICENSES AND PERMITS

Whenever any person holds a license, certificate, or other permit issued by any state party to the compact evidencing the meeting of qualifications for professional, mechanical, or other skills, and when such assistance is requested by the receiving party state, such person shall be deemed licensed, certified, or permitted by the state requesting assistance to render aid involving such skill to meet a declared emergency or disaster, subject to such limitations and conditions as the Governor of the requesting state may prescribe by executive order or otherwise.

ARTICLE VI.
LIABILITY

Officers or employees of a party state rendering aid in another state pursuant to this compact shall be considered agents of the requesting state for tort liability and immunity purposes. No party state or its officers or employees rendering aid in another state pursuant to this compact shall be liable on account of any act or omission in good faith on the part of such forces while so engaged or on account of the maintenance or use of any equipment or supplies in connection therewith. Good faith in this article shall not include willful misconduct, gross negligence, or recklessness.

ARTICLE VII.
SUPPLEMENTARY AGREEMENTS

Inasmuch as it is probable that the pattern and detail of the machinery for mutual aid among two or more states may differ from that among the states that are party hereto, this compact contains elements of a broad base common to all states, and nothing herein shall preclude any state entering into supplementary agreements with another state or affect any other agreements already in force between states. Supplementary agreements may comprehend, but shall not be limited to, provisions for evacuation and reception of injured and other persons and the exchange of medical, fire, police, public utility, reconnaissance, welfare, transportation and communications personnel, and equipment and supplies.

ARTICLE VIII.
COMPENSATION

Each party state shall provide for the payment of compensation and death benefits to injured members of the emergency forces of that state and representatives of deceased members of such forces in case such members sustain injuries or are killed while rendering aid pursuant to this compact, in the same manner and on the same terms as if the injury or death were sustained within their own state.

ARTICLE IX.
REIMBURSEMENT

Any party state rendering aid in another state pursuant to this compact shall be reimbursed by the party state receiving such aid for any loss or damage to or expense incurred in the operation of any equipment and the provision of any service in answering a request for aid and for the costs incurred in connection with such requests; provided, that any aiding party state may assume in whole or in part such loss, damage, expense, or other cost, or may loan such equipment or donate such services to the receiving party state without charge or cost; and provided further, that any two or more party states may enter into supplementary agreements establishing a different allocation of costs among those states. Article VIII expenses shall not be reimbursable under this article.

ARTICLE X.
EVACUATION

Plans for the orderly evacuation and interstate reception of portions of the civilian population as the result of any emergency or disaster of sufficient proportions to so warrant, shall be worked out and maintained between the party states and the emergency management/services directors of the various jurisdictions where any type of incident requiring evacuations might occur. Such plans shall be put into effect by request of the state from which evacuees come and shall include the manner of transporting such evacuees, the number of evacuees to be received in different areas, the manner in which food, clothing, housing, and medical care will be provided, the registration of the evacuees, the providing of facilities for the notification of relatives or friends, and the forwarding of such evacuees to other areas or the bringing in of additional materials, supplies, and all other relevant factors. Such plans shall provide that the party state receiving evacuees and the party state from which the evacuees come shall mutually agree as to reimbursement of out-of-pocket expenses incurred in receiving and caring for such evacuees, for expenditures for transportation, food, clothing, medicines and medical care, and like items. Such expenditures shall be reimbursed as agreed by the party state from which the evacuees come. After the termination of the emergency or disaster, the party state from which the evacuees come shall assume the responsibility for the ultimate support of repatriation of such evacuees.

ARTICLE XI.
IMPLEMENTATION

A. This compact shall become effective immediately upon its enactment into law by any two states. Thereafter, this compact shall become effective as to any other state upon enactment by such state.

B. Any party state may withdraw from this compact by enacting a statute repealing the same, but no such withdrawal shall take effect until thirty days after the Governor of the withdrawing state has given notice in writing of such withdrawal to the Governors of all other party states. Such action shall not relieve the withdrawing state from obligations assumed hereunder prior to the effective date of withdrawal.

C. Duly authenticated copies of this compact and of such supplementary agreements as may be entered into shall, at the time of their approval, be deposited with each of the party states and with the Federal Emergency Management Agency and other appropriate agencies of the United States Government.

ARTICLE XII.
VALIDITY

This compact shall be construed to effectuate the purposes stated in Article I. If any provision of this compact is declared unconstitutional, or the applicability thereof to any person or circumstances is held invalid, the constitutionality of the remainder of this compact and the applicability thereof to other persons and circumstances shall not be affected.

ARTICLE XIII.
ADDITIONAL PROVISIONS

Nothing in this compact shall authorize or permit the use of military force by the National Guard of a state at any place outside that state in any emergency for which the President is authorized by law to call into federal service the militia, or for any purpose for which the use of the Army or the Air Force would in the absence of express statutory authorization be prohibited under §1385 of Title 18 of the United States Code.

(Added by L.1995 ch. 280, eff. 3/16/95.)

CHAPTER 3.3
TRANSPORTATION OF HAZARDOUS RADIOACTIVE MATERIALS
(Complete Chapter)

§44-146.30. Department of Emergency Management to monitor transportation of hazardous radioactive materials.

The Coordinator of the Department of Emergency Management, pursuant to regulations promulgated by the Virginia Waste Management Board, will maintain a register of shippers of hazardous radioactive materials and monitor the transportation within the Commonwealth of those hazardous radioactive materials, as defined by the Virginia Waste Management Board, which may constitute a significant potential danger to the citizens of the Commonwealth in the event of accidental spillage or release. The regulations promulgated by the Board shall not be in conflict with federal statutes, rules, or regulations. Other agencies and commissions of the Commonwealth shall cooperate with the Virginia Waste Management Board in the formulation of regulations as herein provided.
(Chgd. by L.2000 ch. 309, eff. 7/1/2000.)

CHAPTER 4
AIR RAID PRECAUTIONS
(Complete Chapter)

§44-147. Authorization of precautions.

(a) Whenever a state of war exists between the United States and any foreign country, and whenever, in the opinion of the Governor, the Commonwealth is in grave peril, the Governor is authorized to establish air raid precautions; and pursuant thereto to order blackouts in such areas, under such conditions, at such times and for such periods as he deems advisable or upon the request of any federal military or naval authority, and also to regulate and prohibit during such blackouts the movement of vehicular traffic on public highways and streets and to make such regulations as he deems necessary to insure the success of such blackouts and the protection of life and property during the same.

(b) All political subdivisions of this Commonwealth are authorized and directed to enforce the orders and regulations of the Governor issued or made pursuant to this chapter; and they are further authorized to order blackouts in their own jurisdictions whenever they are requested by proper federal military or naval authority and to make reasonable regulations to insure the success of the same and the protection of life and property, provided that such regulations do not conflict with any regulations of the Governor.

§44-148. Nonliability for damages.

Neither the Commonwealth nor any political subdivision thereof shall be liable for any damage to persons or property caused directly or indirectly by an authorized blackout, or any other air raid precaution or anything incidental thereto.

§44-149. Appointment of special officers.

The Governor may authorize appropriate local authorities to appoint citizens of the United States as air raid wardens, fire watchers, auxiliary fire fighters, and policemen, and he shall prescribe the powers, duties, rights, privileges and immunities of persons so appointed. In the absence of an agreement therefor, such appointee shall serve without compensation.

§44-150. Violations of regulations.

Any person violating any regulation made pursuant to this chapter shall upon conviction thereof be punishable by a fine not exceeding $1,000 or imprisonment for not exceeding 30 days, or both.

§44-151. When chapter in effect.

This chapter shall be in effect only during such time as a state of war exists between the United States and a foreign country, and whenever, in the opinion of the Governor, the Commonwealth is in grave peril.

CHAPTER 5
MOBILIZATION OF FIRE FIGHTERS
(Complete Chapter)

§44-152. Outside service by fire departments.

Whenever a state of war exists between the United States and any foreign country and at the request of the chief executive of any county, city or town in this Commonwealth the head of any other fire department may, or if so ordered by the Governor shall, detail, assign and make available for duty and use in such county, town or city any part of the officers, fire fighters, forces, fire-fighting apparatus or other equipment under his command or control.

§44-153. Powers, duties, rights, privileges and immunities.

Whenever all or any part of the regular fire-fighting forces of any county, town or city in this Commonwealth are engaged in rendering services pursuant to this chapter, the officers and members of such fire-fighting forces shall have the same powers, duties, rights, privileges and immunities as if they were performing their duties in the political subdivision in which they are normally employed.

§44-154. Loss, damages, expense or cost.

The county, town or city in which any equipment is used pursuant to this chapter shall be liable for any loss or damage thereto and to the supplies therefor and shall pay any expenses incurred in the operation and maintenance thereof, including the cost of all materials and supplies therefor. No claim for any such loss, damage, expense or cost shall be allowed unless, within sixty days after the same has been sustained or incurred, a written notice of such claim, under oath and itemizing the same, is served by mail or otherwise upon the treasurer of such county, town or city where such equipment was so used.

§44-155. Liability for acts or omissions.

Neither the Commonwealth nor the political subdivision of the Commonwealth whose fire-fighting forces are engaged pursuant to this chapter shall be liable or accountable in any way for or on account of any act or omission on the part of an officer or member of such forces while engaged pursuant to this chapter or for or on account of the operation, maintenance or use of any apparatus, equipment or supplies in connection therewith, nor shall any fire commissioner, fire chief or other superior officer or head of a fire department, fire company or other fire-fighting forces, acting pursuant to this chapter, be held liable or accountable in any way for or on account of any act or omission on the part of any of his subordinates without the political subdivision of their appointment while such subordinates are under the command of an officer other than himself.

§44-156. Reimbursement for salaries and expenses.

The political subdivision in which aid or assistance is given pursuant to this chapter shall reimburse the political subdivision furnishing such aid and assistance for any moneys paid for the salaries or other compensation of employees furnished under this chapter during the time they shall not be performing their duties in the political subdivision by which they are employed or act and shall defray the actual traveling and maintenance expenses of such employees while they are rendering such aid and assistance. The provisions of this section and the term "employee" as used herein shall mean and apply with equal effect to paid and volunteer fire fighters.

§44-157. Temporary substitute fire-fighting forces.

Whenever all or any part of the regular fire-fighting forces of any county, city or town in the Commonwealth are engaged in rendering aid and assistance, pursuant to this chapter, substitute fire fighters, not exceeding the number of regular fire fighters engaged in rendering such aid and assistance, may be appointed in the same manner as provided by law for the appointment of such regular fire fighters. Except in the case of a volunteer fire company, the compensation of such substitute fire fighters shall be fixed at a sum not greater than the lowest rate of pay for a regular fire fighter in such fire department, company or fire-fighting force. Each person appointed under this section shall be vested with the same powers and charged with the same duties as if he were a regular member of such fire department, company or fire-fighting force. No appointment under this section shall continue for more than two days after the regular fire fighters for whom they are substituting have returned to duty. The compensation of any substitute fire fighter appointed pursuant to this section and any allowable expense actually and necessarily incurred by him in the performance of his duties shall be charged against the county, city or town in and for which he was appointed and shall be audited and allowed in the same manner as other charges against the county, city or town are audited and allowed.

§44-158. Rules and regulations.

The Governor is hereby authorized and empowered to prescribe all necessary and reasonable rules and regulations in order to carry out the provisions of this chapter.

§44-159. When chapter in effect.

This chapter shall be in effect only during the time a state of war exists between the United States and any foreign country.

CHAPTER 7
MISCELLANEOUS LAWS
(Complete Chapter)

Section

§44-204. Leaves of absence for employees of Commonwealth or political subdivisions.

All officers and employees of the Commonwealth, or of any political subdivision of the Commonwealth who are members of the Virginia State Defense Force or National Defense Executive Reserve shall be entitled to leaves of absence from their respective duties without loss of pay, seniority, accrued leave or efficiency rating on all days during which they shall be engaged in training approved by the Governor or his designee, not to exceed fifteen workdays per federal fiscal year. When relieved from such duty, they shall be restored to positions held by them when ordered to duty.

§44-205. Traffic regulations.

(1) Powers of Governor. Whenever a state of war exists between the United States and any foreign country, the Governor alone, or through such state departments and agencies as he shall designate, is hereby authorized to:

(a) Cooperate with the agencies of other states and of the federal government in the furtherance of national defense by the formulation and execution of plans for the rapid and safe movement over public highways and streets of troops, vehicles of a military nature, materials for national defense, and all other traffic;

(b) Coordinate the activities of the departments or agencies of this Commonwealth and its political subdivisions concerned directly or indirectly with public highways and streets in a manner which will best effectuate any plan for the rapid and safe movement over the same of troops, vehicles of a military nature, and materials for national defense;

(c) Promulgate rules and regulations and do any and all other things by him deemed necessary and desirable for the control of traffic over public highways and streets to accomplish the purposes of this section.

(2) Powers of political subdivisions. The chief executive of the governing body of each political subdivision of this Commonwealth is hereby authorized and directed upon request of the Governor to cooperate with him and any state department or agency designated by him in carrying out the purposes of this section.

(3) When section in effect. This section shall be in effect only during the time a state of war exists between the United States and any foreign country.

§44-206. Issuing agents for sale of obligations of United States.

Notwithstanding the provisions of any other laws, all individuals, partnerships, associations or corporations organized, operating or doing business under the laws of this Commonwealth are hereby authorized, during the continuance of any emergency proclaimed by the President of the United States or of a state of war between the United States and a foreign nation or nations, and for such time thereafter as may be expedient or necessary, and upon designation by and qualification with the Secretary of the Treasury of the

United States or under his authority, to act as issuing agents for the sale and issue of obligations of the United States.

§44-207. Laws continued in effect.

The following laws are continued in effect subject to such limitations as to duration as are contained therein:

(1) Health and sanitation areas. – Chapter 216 of the Acts of 1942, approved March 13, 1942, codified as §§2673(145)–2673(151) of Virginia Code 1942, relating to special emergency health and sanitation areas.

(2) Motor vehicle tires. – Chapter 319 of the Acts of 1942, approved March 30, 1942, codified as §2673(182) of Virginia Code 1942, relating to acquisition of motor vehicle tires.

(3) Powers of attorney and agency agreements. – Chapter 111 of the Acts of 1944, approved March 2, 1944, codified as §2673(184) of Virginia Suppl. 1946, relating to powers of attorney or agency agreements executed by persons in military service or absent from United States in connection with war work.

§44-208. Securing site of structural failure, fire, explosion, or industrial or transportation accident.

The official in charge of the investigation of any structural failure, fire, explosion, or industrial or transportation accident which results in the loss of human life, except when caused by a natural disaster or war, may secure for no more than twelve hours so much of the site where it occurred as, in his opinion, may be necessary to gather evidence regarding the cause of the occurrence. No owner or lessee of the site may be denied entrance except to prevent the destruction of evidence.

In cases of fire from any cause, the chief or other authorized officer of any fire department or fire company in command at the fire shall have the rights and authority granted to him and his subordinates upon his order or direction by §27-17.1 of this Code. Nothing in this section shall limit or otherwise affect the authority of, or be construed to deny access to such site by, any person charged by law with the responsibility of investigating any such accident.

TITLE 51.1
PENSIONS, BENEFITS AND RETIREMENT
(Selected Chapters)

Chapter

CHAPTER 2
STATE POLICE OFFICERS' RETIREMENT SYSTEM
(Complete Chapter)

Section

§51.1-200. State Police Officers' Retirement System continued; administration; application of provisions of Virginia Retirement System.

The State Police Officers' Retirement System is continued and shall be administered by the Board of Trustees of the Virginia Retirement System. Except as otherwise provided, the provisions of Chapter 1 (§51.1-100 et seq.) of this title shall apply to and govern the operation of the State Police Officers' Retirement System.

§51.1-201. Definitions.

As used in this chapter, unless the context requires a different meaning:

"Employee" means a state police officer.

"Member" means any person included in the membership of the retirement system as provided in this chapter.

"Normal retirement date" means a member's sixtieth birthday.

"Retirement system" means the State Police Officers' Retirement System.

§51.1-202. Membership in retirement system.

Membership in the retirement system shall be compulsory for all state police officers.

§51.1-203. Creditable service.

A. Service qualifying for credit under the provisions of the Virginia Retirement System shall be included as creditable service for the purposes of this chapter, provided the requirements set forth in Chapter 1 (§51.1-100 et seq.) of this title for crediting service have been complied with and any payment required is credited in the member's contribution account.

B. Service purchased in accordance with the provisions of §51.1-143 shall not be considered:

1. In determining the actuarial equivalent for early retirement.

2. In determining the twenty years of service requirement of subsection B of §51.1-206, except for that which had been rendered in a hazardous position and had been credited in the retirement system of a political subdivision of this Commonwealth.

3. Twice in determining any disability allowance payable under this chapter.

C. If a member ceases to be employed as a state police officer, has not received a refund of the accumulated contributions credited to his member's contribution account, and accepts employment in a position covered by the Virginia Retirement System or the Judicial Retirement System, he shall be entitled to credit for his previous creditable service under this chapter. His accumulated contributions shall be transferred and credited to his member's contribution account in the appropriate retirement system. Future retirement rights shall be as set forth under the provisions of the appropriate retirement system.

§51.1-204. Contributions by Commonwealth.

The Commonwealth shall contribute an amount equal to the sum of the normal contribution, any accrued liability contribution, and any supplementary contribution. The amount shall be determined and paid as provided in Chapter 1 (§51.1-100 et seq.) of this title.

§51.1-205. Service retirement generally.

A. Normal retirement. – Any member in service at his normal retirement date with five or more years of creditable service may retire upon written notification to the Board, setting forth the date the retirement is to become effective. Any member, except one appointed by the Governor or elected by the people, who attains seventy years of age shall be retired forthwith. Any employer, subsequent to the employee's normal retirement date, may provide for compulsory service retirement upon a determination that age is a bona fide occupational qualification reasonably necessary to the normal operation of the particular business or that the employee is incapable of performing his duties in a safe and efficient manner. Any such determination shall be made by the employer.

B. Early retirement. – Any member in service who has attained his fiftieth birthday with five or more years of creditable service may retire upon written notification to the Board setting forth the date the retirement is to become effective.

C. Deferred retirement for members terminating service. – Any member who terminates service after five or more years of creditable service, may retire under the provisions of subsection A, B, or D of this section if he has not withdrawn his accumulated contributions prior to the effective date of his retirement or if he has five or more years of creditable service, regardless of termination date, for which his employer has paid the contributions and such contributions cannot be withdrawn. For the purposes of this subsection, any requirements as to the member being in service shall not apply. No member shall be entitled to the benefits of this subsection if his employer certifies that his service was terminated because of dishonesty, malfeasance, or misfeasance in office. The certification may be appealed to the Board.

D. 50/10 retirement. – Any member in service on or after January 1, 1994, who has attained his fiftieth birthday with ten or more years of creditable service may retire prior to his normal retirement date upon written notification to the Board setting forth the date the retirement is to become effective.

E. Effective date of retirement. – The effective date of retirement shall be after the last day of service of the member, but shall not be more than ninety days prior to the filing of the notice of retirement.

F. Notification on behalf of member. – If the member is physically or mentally unable to submit written notification of his intention to retire, the member's appointing authority may submit notification on his behalf.

Chgd. by L.1995 chs. 152, 692, 811; L.1996 ch. 997; L.1999 ch. 111; L.2000 chs. 66, 657, 911, eff. 7/1/2000.)

§51.1-206. Service retirement allowance.

A. A member shall receive an annual retirement allowance, payable for life, as follows:

1. Normal retirement. – The allowance shall equal 1.70 percent of his average final compensation multiplied by the amount of creditable service.

For retirements between October 1, 1994, and December 31, 1998, any state police officer who is a member or beneficiary of a retirement system administered by the Board shall receive an additional retirement allowance equal to three percent of the service or disability retirement allowance payable under this section. Average final compensation attributable to service as Governor, Lieutenant Governor, Attorney General, or member of the General Assembly shall not be included in computing this additional retirement allowance.

2. Early retirement. – The allowance shall be determined in the same manner as for normal retirement with creditable service and average final compensation being determined as of the date of actual retirement. If the member has less than twenty-five years of service at retirement, the amount of the retirement allowance shall be reduced on an actuarial equivalent basis for the period by which the actual retirement date precedes the earlier of (i) his normal retirement date or (ii) the first date on or after his fiftieth birthday on which he would have completed a total of twenty-five years of creditable service.

3. 50/10 retirement. – The allowance shall be payable in a monthly stream of payments equal to the greater of (i) the amount the member would receive if he had taken early retirement or (ii) the actuarially calculated present value of the member's accumulated contributions, including accrued interest.

B. In addition to the allowance payable under subsection A, a member shall receive annually from the date of his retirement until his sixty-fifth birthday an allowance equal to $9,264. Beginning July 1, 2001, and biennially thereafter, such allowance shall be reviewed and adjusted by the Board to an amount recommended by the actuary of the Virginia Retirement System based upon increases in social security benefits in the interim.

This subsection shall not apply to the following: (i) any member who qualifies for retirement under subsection C of §51.1-205 and is credited with less than twenty years' service rendered in a hazardous position or (ii) any member employed initially on or after July 1, 1974, who is credited with less than twenty years' service rendered in a hazardous position.

C. If a beneficiary of a service retirement allowance under this chapter is at any time in service as an employee in a position covered for retirement purposes under the provisions of this or any chapter other than Chapter 7 (§51.1-700 et seq.) of this title, his retirement allowance shall cease while so employed.

(Chgd. by L.1995 chs. 152, 692, 811; L.1998 chs. 674, ch. 676; L.2000 ch. 911, eff. 7/1/2000.)

§51.1-207. Death before retirement.

A. Each member shall designate who is to receive a refund of accumulated contributions credited to his account in the event of the death of the member prior to retirement. The designation must be made on a form prepared by the Board, signed and acknowledged by the member before a person authorized to take acknowledgments, and filed in a manner prescribed by the Board. The designation may be changed by the member by the written designation of some other person, signed, acknowledged, and filed in a manner prescribed by the Board. If the death of the designated person occurs prior to the death of the member and another designation has not been made, payment shall be made to the executors or administrators of the estate of the member.

If no designation has been made, the proceeds shall be paid to the persons surviving at the death of the member in the following order of precedence:

First, to the spouse of the member;

Second, if no surviving spouse, to the children of the member and descendants of deceased children, per stirpes;

Third, if none of the above, to the parents of the member;

Fourth, if none of the above, to the duly appointed executor or administrator of the estate of the member;

Fifth, if none of the above, to other next of kin of the member entitled under the laws of the domicile of the member at the time of his death.

If a member dies at any time before retirement and if no benefits are payable under subsection B, the amount of his accumulated contributions shall be paid to the designated beneficiary or to the persons qualifying in the order of precedence. This amount shall be reduced by the amount of any retirement allowance previously received by the member.

B. If a member dies in service and if no benefits are payable under subsection C, a retirement allowance shall be paid to the person designated as provided in subsection A of this section if the person is the (i) surviving spouse, (ii) minor child, (iii) mother, or (iv) father of the member. If no designation has been made, a retirement allowance shall be paid in the following order of precedence to the (i) surviving spouse, (ii) minor child, (iii) mother, or (iv) father of the member. The retirement allowance shall be paid to the first person qualifying in the orders of precedence set out in this subsection. If more than one minor child survives the deceased member, the allowance shall be divided among them in a manner determined by the Board. The retirement allowance shall be continued during the lifetime of the person or in the case of a minor child until the child dies or attains the age of majority, whichever occurs first. The retirement allowance shall equal the decreased retirement allowance that would have been payable under the joint and survivor option so that the same amount would be continued to such person after the member's death. If the member dies prior to his fiftieth birthday, then, for purposes of this subsection, the member shall be presumed to be age fifty on his date of death. When determining the allowance that would have been payable to the member had the member retired on the date of his death, the provisions of subsection B of §51.1-206 shall not apply. If the person elects in writing under seal and duly acknowledged, the amount of the member's accumulated contributions shall be paid to the person exclusively, in lieu of any other benefits under this section. This amount shall be reduced by the amount of any retirement allowance previously received by the member.

C. If a member dies in service from a cause compensable under the Virginia Workers' Compensation Act (§65.2-100 et seq.), a retirement allowance shall be paid to the member's surviving spouse. If no compensation is finally awarded under the Virginia Workers' Compensation Act due to legal proceedings or otherwise resulting in settlement from the persons causing such death, the Virginia Workers' Compensation Commission shall determine whether the member's death was from a cause compensable under the Virginia Workers' Compensation Act. If the member leaves no surviving spouse, or the surviving spouse dies or remarries, any minor children of the deceased member shall be paid an allowance until the children die or attain the age of majority, whichever occurs first. If more than one minor child survives the deceased member, the allowance shall be divided in a manner determined by the Board. If the deceased member leaves neither surviving spouse nor minor child, the allowance, divided in a manner determined by the Board, shall be paid to the member's parents during their lives.

The retirement allowance, payable hereunder to a qualifying survivor, shall be the annual amount which when added to the compensation payable under the Virginia Workers' Compensation Act for the death of the member, shall equal fifty percent of the member's average final compensation if the survivor does not qualify for death benefits under the provisions of the Social Security Act in effect on the date of the death of the member. If the survivor qualifies for death benefits under the provisions of the Social Security Act in effect on the date of the death of the member, the allowance payable from the retirement system when added to the compensation payable under the Virginia Workers' Compensation Act shall equal thirty-three and one-third percent of the member's average final compensation.

Any beneficiary entitled to the entire amount of a retirement allowance under the provisions of this subsection as a result of the death of a member shall be entitled to waive his rights to the allowance by written notification to the Board within ninety days after the death of the member in order to make available a retirement allowance under the provisions of subsection B of this section.

(Chgd. by L.1998 ch. 407; L.1999 chs. 111, 510, eff. 7/1/99.)

§51.1-208. Post-retirement supplements.

In computing the amount of any post-retirement supplements, any additional allowances being paid under the provisions of subsection B of §51.1-206 shall be disregarded. Any recipient of an allowance which initially commenced on or prior to January 1, 1990, shall be entitled to post-retirement supplements effective July 1, 1991.

§51.1-209. Disability as the result of felonious misconduct of another.

Any member in service who is totally and permanently disabled while on active duty as the result of the felonious misconduct of another may retire for disability as provided in subsection B of §51.1-156 and shall be entitled to maintenance and services at or under the supervision of the Woodrow Wilson Rehabilitation Center without being liable to pay for the same.

§51.1-210. Disability benefit.

Any member in service who (i) is credited with at least twenty years of service in a hazardous duty position and (ii) meets the (a) requirements for a disability retirement allowance under §51.1-156 and (b) minimum age requirements of §51.1-205 may elect to receive the higher of the disability retirement allowance payable under Article 9 (§51.1-152 et seq.) of Chapter 1 of this title or the service retirement allowance payable under §51.1-206 less any reduction in allowance required by subsection C of §51.1-157 or §51.1-158.

(Added by L.1997 ch. 889, eff. 7/1/97.)

CHAPTER 2.1
VIRGINIA LAW OFFICERS' RETIREMENT SYSTEM

(Added by L.1999 ch. 585, eff. 10/1/99.)
(Complete Chapter)

Section

§51.1-211. Virginia Law Officers' Retirement System; application of provisions of Virginia Retirement System.

The Virginia Law Officers' Retirement System is created and shall be administered by the Board of Trustees of the Virginia Retirement System. Except as otherwise provided, the provisions of Chapter 1 (§51.1-124.1 et seq.) of this title shall apply to and govern the operation of the Virginia Law Officers' Retirement System.

(Added by L.1999 ch. 585, eff. 10/1/99.)

§51.1-212. Definitions.

As used in this chapter, unless the context requires a different meaning:

"Employee" means any (i) member of the Capitol Police Force as described in §30-34.2:1, (ii) campus police officer appointed under the provisions of Chapter 17 (§23-232 et seq.) of Title 23, (iii) game warden in the Department of Game and Inland Fisheries appointed under the provisions of Chapter 2 (§29.1-200 et seq.) of Title 29.1, (iv) special agent of the Department of Alcoholic Beverage Control appointed under the provisions of Chapter 1 (§4.1-100 et seq.), (v) law-enforcement officer employed by the Virginia Marine Resources Commission as described in §9-169, (vi) correctional officer as the term is defined in §53.1-1, and including correctional officers employed at a juvenile correction facility as the term is defined in §66-25.3, (vii) any parole officer appointed pursuant to §53.1-143, and (viii) any commercial vehicle enforcement officer employed by the Department of State Police.

"Member" means any person included in the membership of the Retirement System as provided in this chapter.

"Normal retirement date" means a member's sixtieth birthday.

"Retirement System" means the Virginia Law Officers' Retirement System.

(Added by L.1999 ch. 585, eff. 10/1/99.)

§51.1-213. Membership in Retirement System.

Membership in the Retirement System shall be compulsory for all employees.

(Added by L.1999 ch. 585, eff. 10/1/99.)

§51.1-214. Creditable service.

A. Service qualifying for credit under the provisions of the Virginia Retirement System shall be included as creditable service for the purposes of this chapter, provided the requirements set forth in Chapter 1 (§51.1-124.1 et seq.) of this title for crediting service have been complied with and any payment required is credited in the member's contribution account.

B. Service purchased in accordance with the provisions of §51.1-143 shall not be considered:

1. In determining the actuarial equivalent for early retirement.

2. In determining the twenty-years-of-service requirement of subsection B of §51.1-217, except for that which had been rendered in a hazardous position and had been credited in the retirement system of a political subdivision of this Commonwealth.

3. Twice in determining any disability allowance payable under this chapter.

C. If a member ceases to be an employee, has not received a refund of the accumulated contributions credited to his member's contribution account, and accepts employment in a position covered by the Virginia Retirement System, the Judicial Retirement System or the State Police Officers' Retirement System, he shall be entitled to credit for his previous creditable service under this chapter. His accumulated contributions shall be transferred and credited to his member's contribution account in the appropriate retirement system. Future retirement rights shall be as set forth under the provisions of the appropriate retirement system.

(Added by L.1999 ch. 585, eff. 10/1/99.)

§51.1-215. Contributions by Commonwealth.

The Commonwealth shall contribute an amount equal to the sum of the normal contribution, any accrued liability contribution, and any supplementary contribution. The amount shall be determined and paid as provided in Chapter 1 (§51.1-124.1 et seq.) of this title.

(Added by L.1999 ch. 585, eff. 10/1/99.)

§51.1-216. Service retirement generally.

A. Normal retirement. – Any member in service at his normal retirement date with five or more years of creditable service may retire upon written notification to the Board, setting forth the date the retirement is to become effective.

B. Early retirement. – Any member in service who has attained his fiftieth birthday with five or more years of creditable service may retire upon written notification to the Board setting forth the date the retirement is to become effective.

C. Deferred retirement for members terminating service. – Any member who terminates service after five or more years of creditable service may retire under the provisions of subsection A, B, or D of this section if he has not withdrawn his accumulated contributions prior to the effective date of his retirement or if he has five or more years of creditable service for which his employer has paid the contributions and such contributions cannot be withdrawn. For the purposes of this subsection, any requirements as to the member being in service shall not apply. No member shall be entitled to the benefits of this subsection if his employer certifies that his service was terminated because of dishonesty, malfeasance, or misfeasance in office. The certification may be appealed to the Board.

D. 50/10 retirement. – Any member in service on or after January 1, 1994, who has attained his fiftieth birthday with ten or more years of creditable service may retire prior to his normal retirement date upon written notification to the Board setting forth the date the retirement is to become effective.

E. Effective date of retirement. – The effective date of retirement shall be after the last day of service of the member, but shall not be more than ninety days prior to the filing of the notice of retirement.

F. Notification on behalf of member. – If the member is physically or mentally unable to submit written notification of his intention to retire, the member's appointing authority may submit notification on his behalf.

(Added by L.1999 ch. 585; chgd. by L.2000 chs. 66, 657, 911, eff. 7/1/2000.)

§51.1-217. Service retirement allowance.

A. A member shall receive an annual retirement allowance, payable for life, as follows:

1. Normal retirement. – The allowance shall equal 1.70 percent of his average final compensation multiplied by the amount of creditable service.

2. Early retirement. – The allowance shall be determined in the same manner as for normal retirement with creditable service and average final compensation being determined as of the date of actual retirement. If the member has less than twenty-five years of service at retirement, the amount of the retirement allowance shall be reduced on an actuarial equivalent basis for the period by which the actual retirement date precedes the earlier of (i) his normal retirement date or (ii) the first date on or after his fiftieth birthday on which he would have completed a total of twenty-five years of creditable service.

3. 50/10 retirement. – The allowance shall be payable in a monthly stream of payments equal to the greater of (i) the amount the member would have received if he had taken early retirement or (ii) the actuarially calculated present value of the member's accumulated contributions, including accrued interest.

B. In addition to the allowance payable under subsection A, a member shall receive annually from the date of his retirement until his sixty-fifth birthday an allowance equal to $9,264. Beginning July 1, 2001, and biennially thereafter, such allowance shall be reviewed and adjusted by the Board to an amount recommended by the actuary of the Virginia Retirement System based upon increases in Social Security benefits in the interim. This subsection shall not apply to the following: (i) any member who qualifies for retirement under subsection C of §51.1-216 and is credited with less than twenty years' service rendered in a hazardous position or (ii) any member employed initially on or after July 1, 1974, who is credited with less than twenty years' service rendered in a hazardous position.

C. If a beneficiary of a service retirement allowance under this chapter is at any time in service as an employee in a position covered for retirement purposes under the provisions of this or any chapter other than Chapter 7 (§51.1-700 et seq.) of this title, his retirement allowance shall cease while so employed.

(Added by L.1999 ch. 585; chgd. by L.2000 ch. 911, eff. 7/1/2000.)

§51.1-218. Death before retirement.

A. Each member shall designate who is to receive a refund of accumulated contributions credited to his account in the event of the death of the member prior to retirement. The designation must be made on a form prepared by the Board, signed and acknowledged by the member before a person authorized to take acknowledgments, and filed with the Board. The designation may be changed by the member by the written designation of some other person, signed, acknowledged, and filed with the Board. If the death of the designated person occurs prior to the death of the member and another designation has not been made, payment shall be made to the executors or administrators of the estate of the member.

If no designation has been made, the proceeds shall be paid to the persons surviving at the death of the member in the following order of precedence:

First, to the spouse of the member;

Second, if no surviving spouse, to the children of the member and descendants of deceased children, per stirpes;

Third, if none of the above, to the parents of the member;

Fourth, if none of the above, to the duly appointed executor or administrator of the estate of the member;

Fifth, if none of the above, to other next of kin of the member entitled under the laws of the domicile of the member at the time of his death.

If a member dies at any time before retirement and if no benefits are payable under subsection B, the amount of his accumulated contributions shall be paid to the designated beneficiary or to the persons qualifying in the order of precedence. This amount shall be reduced by the amount of any retirement allowance previously received by the member.

B. If a member dies in service and if no benefits are payable under subsection C, a retirement allowance shall be paid to the person designated as provided in subsection A of this section if the person is the (i) surviving spouse, (ii) minor child, (iii) mother, or (iv) father of the member. If no designation has been made, a retirement allowance shall be paid in the following order of precedence to the (i) surviving spouse, (ii) minor child, (iii) mother, or (iv) father of the member. The retirement allowance shall be paid to the first person qualifying in the order of precedence set out in this subsection. If more than one minor child survives the deceased member, the allowance shall be divided among them in a manner determined by the Board. The retirement allowance shall be continued during the lifetime of the person or in the case of a minor child until the child dies or attains the age of majority, whichever occurs first. The retirement allowance shall equal the decreased retirement allowance that would have been payable under the joint and survivor option so that the same amount would be continued to such person after the member's death. If the member dies prior to his fiftieth birthday, then, for purposes of this subsection, the member shall be presumed to be age fifty on his date of death. When determining the allowance that would have been payable to the member had the member retired on the date of his death, the provisions of subsection B of §51.1-217 shall not apply. If the person elects in writing under seal and duly acknowledged, the amount of the member's accumulated contributions shall be paid to the person exclusively, in lieu of any other benefits under this section. This amount shall be reduced by the amount of any retirement allowance previously received by the member.

C. If a member dies in service from a cause compensable under the Virginia Workers' Compensation Act (§65.2-100 et seq.), a retirement allowance shall be paid to the member's surviving spouse. If no compensation is finally awarded under the Virginia Workers' Compensation Act due to legal proceedings or otherwise resulting in settlement from the persons causing such death, the Virginia Workers' Compensation Commission shall determine whether the member's death was from a cause compensable under the Virginia Workers' Compensation Act. If the member leaves no surviving spouse, or the surviving spouse dies or remarries, any minor children of the deceased member shall be paid an allowance until the children die or attain the age of majority, whichever occurs first. If more than one minor child survives the deceased member, the allowance shall be divided in a manner determined by the Board. If the deceased member leaves neither surviving spouse nor minor child, the allowance shall be paid to the member's parents, divided in a manner determined by the Board, during the lives of the parents.

The retirement allowance, payable hereunder to a qualifying survivor, shall be the annual amount which, when added to the compensation payable under the Virginia Workers' Compensation Act for the death of the member, shall equal fifty percent of the member's average final compensation if the survivor does not qualify for death benefits under the provisions of the Social Security Act in effect on the date of the death of the member. If the survivor qualifies for death benefits under the provisions of the Social Security Act in effect on the date of the death of the member, the allowance payable from the Retirement System when added to the compensation payable under the Virginia Workers' Compensation Act shall equal thirty-three and one-third percent of the member's average final compensation.

Any beneficiary entitled to the entire amount of a retirement allowance under the provisions of this subsection as a result of the death of a member shall be entitled to waive his rights to the allowance by written notification to the Board within ninety days after the death of the member in order to make available a retirement allowance under the provisions of subsection B of this section.

(Added by L.1999 ch. 585; chgd. by L.2000 ch. 911, eff. 7/1/2000.)

§51.1-219. Postretirement supplements.

In computing the amount of any postretirement supplements, any additional allowances being paid under the provisions of subsection B of §51.1-217 shall be disregarded.

(Added by L.1999 ch. 585, eff. 10/1/99.)

§51.1-220. Disability benefit.

Any member in service who (i) is credited with at least twenty years of service in a hazardous duty position and (ii) meets the (a) requirements for a disability retirement allowance under §51.1-156 and (b) minimum age requirements of §51.1-216 may elect to receive the higher of the disability retirement allowance payable under Article 9 (§51.1-152 et seq.) of Chapter 1 of this title or the service retirement allowance payable under §51.1-217 less any reduction in allowance required by subsection C of §51.1-157 or by §51.1-158.

(Added by L.1999 ch. 585, eff. 10/1/99.)

CHAPTER 4
PROVISIONS COORDINATING PAST AND PRESENT RETIREMENT PLANS
(Selected Section)

§51.1-405. Special retirement guarantee.

The retirement allowance payable to any member of the State Police Officers' Retirement System who was in service on June 30, 1966, and who retires on or after his normal retirement date shall equal two percent of his average final compensation multiplied by his years of creditable service not in excess of twenty-five years. If a member retires prior to his normal retirement date, his allowance shall be determined in the same manner; however, the allowance shall be reduced on an actuarial equivalent basis for the period by which the actual retirement date precedes the normal retirement date. For the purposes of this section, the retirement allowance shall be determined on the assumption that it is payable to the member alone and that no optional retirement allowance is elected.

CHAPTER 8
LOCAL RETIREMENT SYSTEMS
(Selected Article)

ARTICLE 2
MEMBERS OF POLICE DEPARTMENTS
(Complete Article)

§51.1-807. Police officers' pension and retirement boards.

Any county, city, or town in this Commonwealth having a police department may establish, in the manner hereinafter provided, a board to be known as the "police officers' pension and retirement board." The board shall be a body corporate and consist of five members. One member shall be the treasurer of the county, city, or town and shall also be the treasurer of the board. Two members shall be elected by the majority vote of the members of the police department, one for a term of four years and one for a term of two years, and all successors in office of the one elected for two years shall be elected for terms of four years. Two members shall be appointed by the governing body for terms of four years.

When any board is established, it shall, at its first meeting and annually thereafter, elect one of its members as president and one as secretary. The board may also elect a vice president.

§51.1-808. Powers, authority, and duties of board.

The general powers, authority, and duties of any police officers' pension and retirement board shall be as follows:

1. To adopt bylaws and regulations which the board deems necessary to conduct its affairs;
2. To provide for appropriate clerical, legal, medical, and other services and to pay reasonable compensation for such services;
3. To require deductions from the salaries of active and paid members of the police department and to pay certain percentages of salaries, as hereinafter specified, into the treasury of the board to raise funds for the necessary purposes of the board in the administration of its affairs;
4. To draw warrants on the treasurer of the board, for the payment of pensions, benefits, and administrative costs. Warrants shall be signed in the name of the board and countersigned by its president; and
5. Upon request by the policemen's pension and retirement board, the governing body of the county may by ordinance amend the retirement plan and trust at any time for the purpose of defining, enlarging and improving the benefits that any member thereof may receive and shall by ordinance amend the retirement plan and trust at any time for the purpose of compliance with federal or state law.

§51.1-809. Treasurer of board.

The treasurer of the board shall be the custodian of the board's funds and securities and shall give bond, payable to the board, in such amount and with such surety as the board requires, conditioned for the faithful performance of duties and the proper accounting for all funds and securities which the treasurer receives. The cost of the bond shall be paid out of the funds of the board. The treasurer shall disburse board funds on warrants drawn on him by the board, and signed and countersigned by the board's president.

§51.1-810. Time credited to service record.

The time of service of any member of a police department having a police pension and retirement board prior to June 22, 1940, shall be computed to the credit of the member's service record; however, the pension amount payable shall be determined by that proportion of the amounts provided for by this chapter, which the time of service of such member serving in the police department at the time of his retirement or disability, bears to twenty years.

§51.1-811. Eligibility for retirement; retirement allowance.

Any member of a police department who has completed twenty years of service in the department and attained the age of fifty years may retire and receive the pension and benefits provided in this section. Upon retirement, a member shall receive a retirement allowance, payable to the member for life, equal to fifty percent of the members' annual salary, computed on the basis of the last three years of service and an additional amount equal to two percent of the member's salary for each year of service after the age of fifty and after twenty years of service in the department.

§51.1-812. Disability from natural causes not originating in performance of official duties.

Any member disabled on account of a natural cause or causes not originating in the performance of the member's official duties shall receive a minimum sum equal to ten percent of the member's salary, during such disability, if the member's disability occurs at any time during the first five years of service and an additional amount equal to two percent of the member's salary for each additional year of service exceeding five years. At no time shall the disability payment amount exceed one-half of the member's salary.

§51.1-813. Disability resulting from activities in discharge of official duties.

If any member of a police department of a county, city, or town, other than the City of Richmond, which has a pension plan becomes disabled as a result of activities in the discharge of the member's official duties, the member shall receive, as pension and benefits during such disability, the sum of not less than sixty-six and two-thirds percent of the member's salary until eligible to retire under age and service retirement. The member shall then be retired on the age and service pension as provided in §51.1-811.

Any member of a county, city, or town police department or any sheriff or deputy sheriff who dies or is totally or partially disabled as a result of hypertension or heart disease shall be presumed to have died or become disabled in the line of duty, unless the contrary is shown by a preponderance of competent evidence. To be eligible, or for a beneficiary to be eligible, for retirement, sickness, or other benefit payments based upon such presumption, a member, sheriff, or deputy sheriff shall, before the claim was filed, have had a physical examination and been found free from hypertension or heart disease. The physical examination shall have included such appropriate laboratory and other diagnostic studies as the governing body prescribed and shall have been conducted by physicians whose qualifications were prescribed by the governing body. Any member, sheriff, or deputy sheriff filing a claim for such benefits based upon disability incurred in the line of duty shall, if requested by the governing body, submit to a physical examination by any physician designated by the governing body. The examination may include such tests or studies as may reasonably be prescribed by the designated physician or, in the case of a claim for death benefits, include a postmortem examination to be performed by the medical examiner for the county, city, or town appointed under §32.1-282. The member or claimant shall have the right to have present at such examination, at his own expense, any qualified physician he may designate.

§51.1-814. Employing such presumption in determining eligibility for benefits.

The presumption established in §51.1-813 shall be employed in determining eligibility for death, retirement, sickness, and other benefits, provided pursuant to any other provision of law, the charter of any city or town, or otherwise, for any member of a county, city, or town police department or sheriff or deputy sheriff who dies or becomes totally or partially disabled.

§51.1-815. Counties, cities, and towns authorized to provide relief to surviving spouse and children.

Any county, city, or town may provide for the relief of any children and surviving spouse of any law-enforcement officer, sheriff, or deputy sheriff who dies while in the service of the county, city, or town. If any policeman loses his life while in the discharge of official duties, there shall be paid to the surviving spouse until death, or remarriage, a pension of not less than one-half of the policeman's salary at the time of death. The relief provided shall be exclusive of any payment out of the general fund of the state treasury pursuant to §15.1-136.1 et seq.

§51.1-816. Reduction of pension and benefits where income earned during disability retirement.

If any person receives a disability pension or benefit under this article and subsequently becomes employed, whether full time or part time, the pensions and benefits received shall be reduced by the amount of income received which exceeds the difference between the benefits received under this section and the amount of pay to which the member would have been entitled had the member's employment progressed in the same rank and grade with credit for the level of seniority the member would have attained had the member not been disabled. The reduction shall continue until the member would have been eligible for normal retirement, based on age and service, had the member remained uninjured and employed. For the purposes of this section, "income" means gross income received less deductions for social security taxes only.

Any person receiving pensions or benefits under the provisions of this section shall upon request, on or before May 1 of each year, provide a copy of all W–2 forms showing income received, or a statement under oath as to whether the member has received compensation for work performed in the previous calendar year, to the governing body of the jurisdiction providing this pension. Refusal to provide such documents shall be grounds for termination of benefits under this section until such documents are produced. Production of the documents shall be required until the person would have been eligible for normal retirement had the member remained uninjured.

Nothing contained in this section shall limit or restrict the right of any person to receive Worker's Compensation benefits under Title 65.2.

§51.1-817. Salary deductions payable to estate or refunded.

If any police officer dies while in active service and leaves no dependents, the member's salary deductions shall be payable to the member's estate. If any police officer separates from service before becoming eligible for a pension, seventy-five percent of salary deductions shall be refunded to the member.

§51.1-818. Funds for payment of pension and benefits.

Any and all cash assets and funds not necessary for immediate payment of pensions or benefits shall be invested in securities that are legal investments under the laws of the Commonwealth for public sinking funds. Any funds raised by any police officers' pension and retirement board for the payment of pensions and benefits shall be paid over to the treasurer of such board who shall deposit and pay the funds as provided in this section to the credit of the board.

§51.1-819. Adoption of article optional by counties, cities, and towns; appeal.

Any county, city, or town in this Commonwealth having a police department may adopt the provisions of this article and establish a police officers' pension and retirement board if the governing body of the county, city or town adopts a resolution approved by a majority of all the members thereof, by a recorded yea and nay vote.

Upon adoption of a resolution and establishment of the police officers' pension and retirement board, the board shall be vested with all the powers, authority, and duties established under this article.

A members shall be entitled to an appeal of right to the circuit court of the county or city which has jurisdiction of the board from any action on any matter in which the board has discretionary power.

§51.1-820. Police officers' pensions and retirements.

All of the provisions of this article, including all authorizations and all requirements, shall apply to all counties having the county manager plan of government, except Arlington county.

TITLE 53.1
PRISONS AND OTHER METHODS OF CORRECTION
(Selected Chapters)

CHAPTER 2
STATE CORRECTIONAL FACILITIES
(Selected Article)

ARTICLE 1
GENERAL PROVISIONS
(Selected Sections)

§53.1-20. Commitment of convicted persons to custody of Director.

A. Every person convicted of a felony committed before January 1, 1995, and sentenced to the Department for a total period of more than two years shall be committed by the court to the custody of the Director of the Department. The Director shall receive all such persons into the state corrections system within sixty days of the date on which the final sentencing order is mailed by certified letter or sent by electronic transmission to the Director by the clerk.

B. Persons convicted of felonies committed on or after January 1, 1995, and sentenced to the Department or sentenced to confinement in jail for a year or more shall be placed in the custody of the Department and received by the Director into the state corrections system within sixty days of the date on which the final sentencing order is mailed by certified letter or sent by electronic transmission to the Director by the clerk.

C. If the Governor finds that the number of prisoners in state facilities poses a threat to public safety, it shall be within the discretion of the Director to determine the priority for receiving prisoners into the state corrections system from local correctional facilities.

D. All felons sentenced to a period of incarceration and not placed in an adult state correctional facility pursuant to this section shall serve their sentences in local correctional facilities which shall not include a secure facility or detention home as defined in §16.1-228.

E. Felons committed to the custody of the Department for a new felony offense shall be received by the Director into the state corrections system in accordance with the provisions of this section without any delay for resolution of (i) issues of alleged parole violations set for hearing before the Parole Board or (ii) any other pending parole-related administrative matter.

(Chgd. by L.1997 ch. 840, eff. 7/1/97.)

§53.1-20.1. Compensation of local jails for cost of incarceration.

If the Director is unable to accommodate in a state correctional facility any convicted felon sentenced to the Department for a felony committed before January 1, 1995, whose sentence totals more than two years or who is convicted of a felony committed on or after January 1, 1995, and who is required to serve a total period of one year or more in a state correctional facility, the Department of Corrections shall compensate local jails for the cost of incarceration as provided for in the general appropriation act beginning on the sixty-first day following the date of mailing by certified letter or electronic transmittal by the clerk of the committing court to the Director of the final order.

(Chgd. by L.1997 ch. 775, eff. 7/1/97.)

§53.1-21. Transfer of prisoners into and between state and local correctional facilities.

A. Any person who (1) is accused or convicted of an offense (a) in violation of any county, city or town ordinance within the Commonwealth, (b) against the laws of the Commonwealth or (c) against the laws of any other state or country, or (2) is a witness held in any case in which the Commonwealth is a party and who is confined in a state or local correctional facility, may be transferred by the Director, subject to the provisions of §53.1-20, to any other state or local correctional facility which he may designate.

B. The following limitations shall apply to the transfer of persons into the custody of the Department:

1. No person convicted of violating §20-61 shall be committed or transferred to the custody of the Department.

2. No person who is convicted of any violation pursuant to Article 9 (§46.2-355.1 et seq.) of Chapter 3 of Title 46.2 shall be committed or transferred to the custody of the Department without the consent of the Director.

3. No person who is convicted of a misdemeanor or a felony and receives a jail sentence of twelve months or less shall be committed or transferred to the custody of the Department without the consent of the Director.

4. Beginning July 1, 1991, and subject to the provisions of §53.1-20, no person, whether convicted of a felony or misdemeanor, shall be transferred to the custody of the Department when the combined length of all sentences to be served totals two years or less, without the consent of the Director.

(Chgd. by L.1999 chs. 945, 987, eff. 7/1/99.)

CHAPTER 3
LOCAL CORRECTIONAL FACILITIES
(Selected Articles)

ARTICLE 3
FUNDING LOCAL CORRECTIONAL FACILITIES AND PROGRAMS
(Selected Sections)

§53.1-93. When sheriffs to summon or employ guards and other persons; allowances therefor.

Whenever in the discretion of the court it is necessary for the safekeeping of a prisoner under charge of or sentence for a crime, whether the prisoner be in jail, hospital, court or elsewhere, the court may order the sheriff to summon a sufficient guard. Whenever ordered by the court to do so, the sheriff shall summon or employ temporarily such persons as may be needed to preserve proper order or otherwise to aid the court in its proper operation and functioning. For such guard or other service the court may allow so much as it deems proper, not exceeding the hourly equivalent of the minimum annual salary paid a full-time deputy sheriff who performs like services in the same county or city. In addition, mileage and other expenses for rendering the services shall be paid for each such person.

§53.1-94. Same when paid by county or city; same when by Compensation Board.

The circuit court, before certifying any allowance pursuant to §53.1-93, shall inquire into the condition of the jail. If it appears that a guard was necessary because of the insecurity of the jail, it shall order the allowance to be certified to the governing body of the county or city. If otherwise, and the guard was necessary, the allowance shall be paid out of the budget of the sheriff as approved by the Compensation Board.

ARTICLE 6
DUTIES OF SHERIFFS
(Selected Sections)

§53.1-118. Courts to fine sheriffs for failure to perform duties.

If it appears to the circuit court having jurisdiction that the sheriff or jail superintendent has in any respect failed to perform his duties with respect to the operation of the jail, the court may, after summoning him to show cause against it, summarily fine him not more than fifty dollars.

§53.1-119. Court duties of sheriff.

The sheriff shall provide officers to attend the courts within his jurisdiction while such courts are in session as the respective judges may require. The sheriff, or the superintendent of a regional jail or jail farm, shall receive into the jail facility all persons committed by the order of such courts, or under process issuing therefrom, and all persons committed by any other lawful authority.
(Chgd. by L.1995 ch. 112, eff. 7/1/95.)

§53.1-120. Sheriff to provide for courthouse and courtroom security; designation of deputies for such purpose.

A. Each sheriff shall designate deputies who shall ensure that the courthouses and courtrooms within his jurisdiction are secure from violence and disruption. A list of such designations shall be forwarded to the Director of the Department of Criminal Justice Services.

B. The chief circuit court judge, the chief general district court judge and the chief juvenile and domestic relations district court judge shall be responsible by agreement with the sheriff of the jurisdiction for the designation of courtroom security deputies for their respective courts. If the respective chief judges and sheriff are unable to agree on the number, type and working schedules of courtroom security deputies for the court, the matter shall be referred to the Compensation Board for resolution in accordance with existing budgeted funds and personnel.

C. The sheriff shall have the sole responsibility for the identity of the deputies designated for courtroom security.
(Chgd. L.1996 ch. 616, eff. 7/1/96.)

§53.1-127. Who may enter interior of local correctional facilities; searches of those entering.

A. Members of the local governing bodies which participate in the funding of a local correctional facility may go into the interior of that facility. Agents of the Board may go into the interior of any local correctional facility. In addition, Department of Corrections staff and state and local health department staff shall, in the performance of their duties, have access to the interior of any local correctional facility subject to the standards promulgated pursuant to §53.1-68 A and B. Attorneys shall be permitted in the interior of a local correctional facility to confer with prisoners who are their clients and with prisoners who are witnesses in cases in which they are involved. Except for the announced or unannounced inspections authorized pursuant to §53.1-68 A and B, the sheriff, jail administrator or other person in charge of the facility shall prescribe the time and conditions under which attorneys and other persons may enter the local correctional facility for which he is responsible.

B. Any person seeking to enter the interior of any local correctional facility shall be subject to a search of his person and effects. Such search shall be performed in a manner reasonable under the circumstances and may be a condition precedent to entering a local correctional facility.
(Chgd. by L.1995 ch. 797, eff. 7/1/95.)

§53.1-127.1. Establishment of stores in local correctional facilities.

Each sheriff who operates a correctional facility is authorized to provide for the establishment and operation of a store or commissary to deal in such articles as he deems proper. The net profits from the operation of such store shall be used within the facility for educational, recreational or other purposes for the benefit of the inmates as may be prescribed by the sheriff. The sheriff shall be the purchasing agent in all matters involving the commissary and nonappropriated funds received from inmates.

ARTICLE 7
PRISONER PROGRAMS AND TREATMENT
(Complete Article)

§53.1-128. Work forces.

The local governing body of any county, city or town may establish work forces in the county, city or town under such conditions as it may prescribe. Such work forces are authorized to work on public property or works owned, leased or operated by the county, city or town, or on a privately operated national park on federal land, or any property owned by a nonprofit organization which is exempt from taxation under 26 U.S.C. §501(c)(3) or (c)(4) and which is organized and operated exclusively for charitable or social welfare purposes whether the same be located within such county, city or town, or elsewhere. Every person eighteen years of age or older who is convicted and confined for any violation of a local ordinance and who is confined as a punishment or for failure to pay a required fine, shall be liable to work in such work force. Every person eighteen years of age or older who is confined pending disposition of a nonviolent criminal offense or an offense under Chapter 5 (§20-61 et seq.) of Title 20 may work in such work force on a voluntary basis with the approval of and under the supervision of the sheriff.

(Chgd. by L.1997 chs. 123, 546, eff. 7/1/97.)

§53.1-129. Order permitting prisoners to work on state, county, city, town or nonprofit organization property or community improvement projects; bond of person in charge of prisoners.

The circuit court of any county or city may, by order entered of record, allow persons confined in the jail of such county or city who are awaiting disposition of, or serving sentences imposed for, misdemeanors or felonies to work on (i) state, county, city or town property, (ii) any property owned by a nonprofit organization which is exempt from taxation under 26 U.S.C. §501(c)(3) or (c)(4) and which is organized and operated exclusively for charitable or social welfare purposes on a voluntary basis with the consent of the county, city, town or state agency or the local public service authority or upon the request of the nonprofit organization involved, or (iii) private property which is part of a community improvement project sponsored by a locality. The district court of any county or city may allow persons confined in the jail of such county or city who are awaiting disposition of, or serving sentences imposed for, misdemeanors to work on (i) state, county, city or town property, (ii) any property owned by a nonprofit organization which is exempt from taxation under 26 U.S.C. §501(c)(3) or (c)(4) and which is organized and operated exclusively for charitable or social welfare purposes on a voluntary basis with consent of the county, city, town or state agency or the local public service authority or upon the request of the nonprofit organization involved, or (iii) private property which is part of a community improvement project sponsored by a locality. Prisoners performing work as provided in this paragraph may receive credit on their respective sentences for the work done, whether such sentences are imposed prior or subsequent to the work done, as the court orders.

The court may, by order entered of record, require a person convicted of a felony to work on state, county, city or town property, with the consent of the county, city, town or state agency or the local public service authority involved, for such credit on his sentence as the court orders.

In the event that a person other than the sheriff or jail superintendent is designated by the court to have charge of such prisoners while so working, the court shall require a bond of the person, in an amount to be fixed by the court, conditioned upon the faithful discharge of his duties. Neither the sheriff nor the jail superintendent shall be held responsible for any acts of omission or commission on the part of such person.

Any person committed to jail upon a felony offense committed on or after January 1, 1995, who receives credit on his sentence as provided in this section shall not be entitled to good conduct credit, sentence credit, earned sentence credit, other credit, or a combination of any credits in excess of that permissible under Article 4 (§53.1-202.2 et seq.) of Chapter 6 of this title. So much of an order of any court contrary to the provisions of Article 4 shall be deemed null and void.

(Chgd. by L.1997 chs. 134, 546; L.1998 ch. 311; L.1999 chs. 277, 951, 1007, eff. 7/1/99.)

§53.1-130. Sheriffs, jail superintendents, etc., not to be interested in property where work performed; penalty.

No sheriff, jail superintendent, deputy or other jail officer shall have any prisoner work on property owned by him or by his relative, or on projects in which he is interested, nor shall any such prisoner be used for the personal gain or convenience of any sheriff or of any other individual. Any person found guilty of a violation of this section shall be guilty of a Class 1 misdemeanor.

§53.1-131. Provision for release of prisoner from confinement for employment, educational or other rehabilitative programs; escape; penalty; disposition of earnings.

A. Any court having jurisdiction for the trial of a person charged with a criminal offense or charged with an offense under Chapter 5 (§20-61 et seq.) of Title 20 may, if the defendant is convicted and (i) sentenced to confinement in jail or (ii) being held in jail pending completion of a presentence report pursuant to §19.2-299, and if it appears to the court that such offender is a suitable candidate for work release, assign the offender to a work release program under the supervision of a probation officer, the office of the sheriff or the administrator of a local or regional jail or a program designated by the court. The court further may authorize the offender to participate in educational or other rehabilitative programs designed to supplement his work release employment. The court shall be notified in writing by the director or administrator of the program to which the offender is assigned of the offender's place of employment and the location of any educational or rehabilitative program in which the offender participates.

Any person who has been sentenced to confinement in jail or who has been convicted of a felony but is confined in jail pursuant to §53.1-20, in the discretion of the sheriff or the administrator of a local or regional jail, may be assigned by the sheriff or the administrator of a local or regional jail to a work release program under the supervision of the office of the sheriff or the administrator of a local or regional jail. The sheriff or the administrator of a local or regional jail may further authorize the offender to participate in educational or other rehabilitative programs as defined in this section designed to supplement his work release employment. The court that sentenced the offender shall be notified in writing by the sheriff or the administrator of a local or regional jail of any such assignment and of the offender's place of employment or other rehabilitative program. The court, in its discretion, may thereafter revoke the authority for such an offender to participate in a work release program.

The sheriff or other administrative head of a local correctional facility and the Director may enter into agreements whereby persons who are committed to the Department, whether such persons are housed in a state or local correctional facility, and who have met all standards for such release, may participate in a local work release program or in educational or other rehabilitative programs as defined in this section. All persons accepted in accordance with this section shall be governed by all regulations applying to local work release, notwithstanding the provisions of any other section of the Code. Local jails shall qualify for compensation for cost of incarceration of such persons pursuant to §53.1-20.1, less any payment for room and board collected from the inmate.

Any offender assigned to such a program by the court or sheriff or the administrator of a local or regional jail who, without proper authority or just cause, leaves the area to which he has been assigned to work or attend educational or other rehabilitative programs, or leaves the vehicle or route of travel involved in his going to or returning from such place, shall be guilty of a Class 1 misdemeanor. In the event such offender leaves the Commonwealth, the offender may be found guilty of an escape as provided in §18.2-477. An offender who is found guilty of a Class 1 misdemeanor in accordance with this section shall be ineligible for further participation in a work release program during his current term of confinement.

The Board shall prescribe regulations to govern the work release, educational and other rehabilitative programs authorized by this section.

Any wages earned pursuant to this section by an offender may, upon order of the court, be paid to the director or administrator of the program after standard payroll deductions required by law. Distribution of such wages shall be made for the following purposes:

1. To pay an amount to defray the cost of his keep;

2. To pay travel and other such expenses made necessary by his work release employment or participation in an educational or rehabilitative program;

3. To provide support and maintenance for his dependents or to make payments to the local department of welfare or social services or the Commissioner of Social Services, as appropriate, on behalf of dependents who are receiving public assistance as defined in §63.1-87; or

4. To pay any fines, restitution or costs as ordered by the court.

Any balance at the end of his sentence shall be paid to the offender upon his release.

B. For the purposes of this section:

"Work release" means full-time employment or participation in suitable vocational training programs.

"Educational program" means a program of learning recognized by the State Council of Higher Education, the State Board of Education or the State Board of Corrections.

"Rehabilitative program" includes an alcohol and drug treatment program, mental health program, family counseling, community service or other community program approved by the court having jurisdiction over the offender. *(Chgd. by L.2000 ch. 423, eff. 7/1/2000.)*

§53.1-131.1. Provision for sentencing of person to nonconsecutive days in jail; payment to defray costs; penalty.

Any court having jurisdiction for the trial of a person charged with a misdemeanor or traffic offense or charged with any offense under Chapter 5 (§20-61 et seq.) of Title 20 may, if the defendant is convicted and sentenced to confinement in jail, impose the time to be served on weekends or nonconsecutive days to permit the convicted defendant to retain gainful employment. A person sentenced pursuant to this section shall be ordered to pay an amount ordered by the court to defray the cost of his keep, which amount shall be the actual cost of incarceration but shall not exceed that amount charged to the Compensation Board for purposes of reimbursement as provided in the general appropriation act. Such amount shall be collected by the clerk of the court. If the defendant willfully fails to report at times specified by the court, the sentence imposed pursuant to this section shall be revoked and a straight jail sentence imposed.

The time served by a person sentenced for violation of state law in a local jail, regional jail, or local jail farm pursuant to this section shall be included in the count of prisoner days reported by the Department for the purpose of apportioning state funds to local correctional facilities for operating costs in accordance with §53.1-84.
(Chgd. by L.1999 ch. 9, eff. 7/1/99.)

§53.1-131.2. Assignment to a home/electronic incarceration program; payment to defray costs; escape; penalty.

A. Any court having jurisdiction for the trial of a person charged with a criminal offense, a traffic offense or an offense under Chapter 5 (§20-61 et seq.) of Title 20 may, if the defendant is convicted and sentenced to confinement in a state or local correctional facility, and if it appears to the court that such an offender is a suitable candidate for home/electronic incarceration, assign the offender to a home/electronic incarceration program as a condition of probation, if such program exists, under the supervision of the office of the sheriff, the administrator of a local or regional jail, or a Department of Corrections probation and parole district office established pursuant to §53.1-141. However, any offender who is convicted of any of the following violations of Chapter 4 (§18.2-30 et seq.) of Title 18.2 shall not be eligible for participation in the home/electronic incarceration program: (i) first and second degree murder and voluntary manslaughter under Article 1 (§18.2-30 et seq.); (ii) mob-related felonies under Article 2 (§18.2-38 et seq.); (iii) any kidnapping or abduction felony under Article 3 (§18.2-47 et seq.); (iv) any malicious felonious assault or malicious bodily wounding under Article 4 (§18.2-51 et seq.); (v) robbery under §18.2-58.1; or (vi) any criminal sexual assault punishable as a felony under Article 7 (§18.2-61 et seq.). The court may further authorize the offender's participation in work release employment or educational or other rehabilitative programs as defined in §53.1-131. The court shall be notified in writing by the director or administrator of the program to which the offender is assigned of the offender's place of home/electronic incarceration, place of employment, and the location of any educational or rehabilitative program in which the offender participates.

B. In any city or county in which a home/electronic incarceration program established pursuant to this section is available, the court, subject to approval by the sheriff or the jail superintendent of a local or regional jail, may assign the accused to such a program pending trial if it appears to the court that the accused is a suitable candidate for home/electronic incarceration.

C. Any person who has been sentenced to jail or convicted and sentenced to confinement in prison but is actually serving his sentence in jail, after notice to the attorney for the Commonwealth of the convicting jurisdiction, may be assigned by the sheriff or the administrator of a local or regional jail to a home/electronic incarceration program under the supervision of the office of the sheriff, the administrator of a local or regional jail, or a Department of Corrections probation and parole office established pursuant to §53.1-141. However, if the offender violates any provision of the terms of the home/electronic incarceration agreement, the offender may have the assignment revoked and, if revoked, shall be held in the jail facility to which he was originally sentenced. Such person shall be eligible if his term of confinement does not include a sentence for a conviction of a felony violent crime, a felony sexual offense, burglary or manufacturing, selling, giving, distributing or possessing with the intent to manufacture, sell, give or distribute a Schedule I or Schedule II controlled substance. The court shall retain authority to remove the offender from such home/electronic incarceration program. The court which sentenced the offender shall be notified in writing by the sheriff or the administrator of a local or regional jail of the offender's place of home/electronic incarceration and place of employment or other rehabilitative program.

D. The Board may prescribe regulations to govern home/ electronic incarceration programs.

E. Any offender or accused assigned to such a program by the court or sheriff or the administrator of a local or regional jail who, without proper authority or just cause, leaves his place of home/electronic incarceration, the area to which he has been assigned to work or attend educational or other rehabilitative programs, or the vehicle or route of travel involved in his going to or returning from such place, shall be guilty of a Class 1 misdemeanor. An offender or accused who is found guilty of a violation of this section shall be ineligible for further participation in a home/electronic incarceration program during his current term of confinement.

F. The director or administrator of a home/electronic incarceration program who also operates a residential program may remove an offender from a home/electronic incarceration program and place him in such residential program if the offender commits a noncriminal program violation. The court shall be notified of the violation and of the placement of the offender in the residential program.

G. The director or administrator of a home/electronic incarceration program shall charge the offender or accused a fee for participating in the program to pay for the cost of home/electronic incarceration equipment. The offender or accused shall be required to pay the program for any damage to the equipment which is in his possession or for failure to return the equipment to the program.

H. Any wages earned by an offender or accused assigned to a home/electronic incarceration program and participating in work release shall be paid to the director or administrator after standard payroll deductions required by law. Distribution of the money collected shall be made in the following order of priority to:

1. Meet the obligation of any judicial or administrative order to provide support and such funds shall be disbursed according to the terms of such order;
2. Pay any fines, restitution or costs as ordered by the court;
3. Pay travel and other such expenses made necessary by his work release employment or participation in an education or rehabilitative program, including the sums specified in §53.1-150; and
4. Defray the offender's keep.

The balance shall be credited to the offender's account or sent to his family in an amount the offender so chooses.

The Board of Corrections shall promulgate regulations governing the receipt of wages paid to persons participating in such programs, the withholding of payments and the disbursement of appropriate funds.

(Chgd. by L.2000 ch. 423, eff. 7/1/2000.)

§53.1-132. Furloughs from local work release programs; penalty for violations.

The director of any work release program authorized by §53.1-131 may, subject to rules and regulations prescribed by the Board, extend the limits of confinement of any offender participating in a work release program which is subject to the director's authority, to permit the offender a furlough for the purpose of visiting his home or family. Such furlough shall be for a period to be prescribed by the director, not to exceed three days.

Any offender who, without proper authority or without just cause, fails to remain within the limits of confinement set by the director hereunder, or fails to return within the time prescribed to the place designated by the director in granting such authority, shall be guilty of a Class 1 misdemeanor. An offender who is found guilty of a Class 1 misdemeanor in accordance with this section shall be ineligible for further participation in a work release program during his current term of confinement.

(Chgd. by L.2000 ch. 423, eff. 7/1/2000.)

§53.1-133. Treatment of prisoner with contagious disease.

Upon application of the person in charge of a local correctional facility, if that application is affirmed by the physician serving such facility, a judge of a circuit court is authorized to have removed from any correctional facility within his jurisdiction any person confined therein who has contracted any contagious or infectious disease dangerous to the public health. Such persons shall be removed to some other place designated by the judge. When any person is so removed, he shall be safely kept and receive proper care and attention including medical treatment. As soon as he recovers his health, he shall be returned to the correctional facility from which he was moved, unless the term of his imprisonment has expired, in which event he shall be discharged, but not until all danger of his spreading contagion has passed. Expenses incurred under and by reason of this section shall be paid as provided by law.

§53.1-133.01. Medical treatment for prisoners.

Any sheriff or superintendent may establish a medical treatment program for prisoners in which prisoners participate and pay towards a portion of the costs thereof. The Board of Corrections shall develop a model plan and promulgate regulations for such program, and shall provide assistance, if requested, to the sheriff or superintendent in the implementation of a program.

§53.1-133.01:1. Payment for bodily injury.

Each jail superintendent or sheriff who operates a correctional facility is authorized to establish administrative procedures according to regulations promulgated by the Board for recovering from an inmate the cost for medical treatment of a physical injury that is inflicted intentionally on any person by the inmate. Such administrative procedures shall ensure that the inmate is afforded due process.
(Added by L.1997 ch. 125, eff. 7/1/97.)

§53.1-133.02. Notice to be given upon prisoner release, escape, etc.

Prior to the release, including work release, or discharge of any prisoner, or his transfer to a prison, a different jail facility or any other correctional or detention facility, or upon his escape or the change of his name, the sheriff or superintendent who has custody of the prisoner shall give notice of any such occurrence, delivered by first-class mail or by telephone or both, to any victim of the offense as defined in §19.2-11.01 who, in writing, requests notice or to any person designated in writing by the victim. The notice shall be given at least fifteen days prior to release or transfer, or as soon as practicable following an escape or change of name. Notice shall be given using the address and telephone number provided in writing by the victim. For the purposes of this section, "prisoner" means a person sentenced to serve more than thirty days of incarceration or detention.

No civil liability shall attach for a failure to give notice as provided in this section.
(Added by L.1995 ch. 687, eff. 7/1/95.)

§53.1-133.03. Exchange of medical and mental health information and records.

Notwithstanding any other provision of law relating to disclosure and confidentiality of patient records maintained by a health care provider, medical and mental health information and records of any person committed to jail, and transferred to another correctional facility, may be exchanged among the following:

1. Administrative personnel of the correctional facilities involved and of the administrative personnel within the holding facility when there is reasonable cause to believe that such information is necessary to maintain the security and safety of the holding facility, its employees, or prisoners. The information exchanged shall continue to be confidential and disclosure shall be limited to that necessary to ensure the safety and security of the facility.
2. Members of the Parole Board or its designees, as specified in §53.1-138, in order to conduct the investigation required under §53.1-155.
3. Probation and parole officers for use in parole and probation planning, release and supervision.
4. Officials of the facilities involved and officials within the holding facility for the purpose of formulating recommendations for treatment and rehabilitative programs; classification, security and work assignments; and determining the necessity for medical, dental and mental health care, treatment and other such programs.
5. Medical and mental health hospitals and facilities, both public and private, including community service boards and health departments, for use in treatment while committed to jail or a correctional facility while under supervision of a probation or parole officer.

Substance abuse records subject to federal regulations, Confidentiality of Alcohol and Drug Abuse Patient Records, 42 C.F.R. §2.11 et seq., shall not be subject to the provisions of this section. The disclosure of results of a test for human immunodeficiency virus shall not be permitted except as provided in §§32.1-36.1 and 32.1-116.3.

The release of medical and mental health information and records to any other agency or individual shall be subject to all regulations promulgated by the Board of Corrections which govern confidentiality of such records. Medical and mental health information concerning a prisoner which has been exchanged pursuant to this section may be used only as provided herein and shall otherwise remain confidential and protected from disclosure.

Nothing contained in this section shall prohibit the release of records to the Department of Health Professions or health regulatory boards consistent with Subtitle III (§54.1-2400 et seq.) of Title 54.1 of the Code of Virginia.
(Added by L.1997 ch. 443, eff. 7/1/97.)

CHAPTER 4
PROBATION AND PAROLE
(Selected Articles)

ARTICLE 2
STATE PROBATION AND PAROLE SERVICES
(Selected Sections)

§53.1-145. Powers and duties of probation and parole officers.

In addition to other powers and duties prescribed by this article, each probation and parole officer shall:

1. Investigate and report on any case pending in any court or before any judge in his jurisdiction referred to him by the court or judge;
2. Except those persons placed in probation supervision programs established under §§53.1-181 and 53.1-182.1, supervise and assist all persons within his territory placed on probation or post-release supervision pursuant to §19.2-295.2, secure, as appropriate and when available resources permit, placement of such persons in a substance abuse treatment program which may include utilization of acupuncture and other treatment modalities, and furnish every such person with a written statement of the conditions of his probation or post-release supervision and instruct him therein;
3. Supervise and assist all persons within his territory released on parole, secure, as appropriate and when available resources permit, placement of such persons in a substance abuse treatment program which may include utilization of acupuncture and other treatment modalities, and, in his discretion, assist any person within his territory who has completed his parole or has been mandatorily released from any correctional facility in the Commonwealth and requests assistance in finding a place to live, finding employment, or in otherwise becoming adjusted to the community;
4. Arrest and recommit to the place of confinement from which he was released, or in which he would have been confined but for the suspension of his sentence or of its imposition, for violation of the terms of probation,

post-release supervision pursuant to §19.2-295.2 or parole, any probationer, person subject to post-release supervision or parolee under his supervision, or as directed by the Chairman, Board member or the court, pending a hearing by the Board or the court, as the case may be;

5. Keep such records, make such reports, and perform other duties as may be required of him by the Director or by regulations prescribed by the Board of Corrections, and the court or judge by whom he was appointed;

6. Order and conduct, in his discretion, drug and alcohol screening tests of any probationer, person subject to post-release supervision pursuant to §19.2-295.2 or parolee under his supervision who the officer has reason to believe is engaged in the illegal use of controlled substances or marijuana or the abuse of alcohol. Upon one instance of a failed drug test, such officer shall notify the local department of social services. The cost of the test may be charged to the person under supervision. Regulations governing the officer's exercise of this authority shall be promulgated by the Board; and

7. Have the power to carry a concealed weapon in accordance with regulations promulgated by the Board and upon the certification of appropriate training and specific authorization by a judge of the circuit court to which the officer is assigned.

Nothing in this article shall require probation and parole officers to investigate or supervise cases before juvenile and domestic relations district courts.
(Chgd. by L.1995 chs. 502, 574; L.1996 ch. 616; L.1997 ch. 526, eff. 7/1/97.)

§53.1-149. Arrest of probationer without warrant; written statement.

Any probation officer appointed pursuant to this chapter may arrest a probationer without a warrant, or may deputize any other officer with power to arrest to do so, by a written statement setting forth that the probationer has, in the judgment of the probation officer, violated one or more of the terms or conditions upon which the probationer was released on probation. Such a written statement by a probation officer delivered to the officer in charge of any local jail or lockup shall be sufficient warrant for the detention of the probationer.

§53.1-150. Contributions by persons on parole, probation, and work release.

A. Any person convicted of a felony, multiple felonies or a combination of felonies and misdemeanors shall be required to pay, as part of the fixed felony fee pursuant to §17.1-275.1 or the fixed fee for felony reduced to misdemeanor assessed pursuant to §17.1-275.2, a contribution towards the cost of his confinement, supervision or participation in a local community-based probation program or home/electronic incarceration program as a condition of his sentence.

Any person convicted of a misdemeanor or multiple misdemeanors and who is sentenced to incarceration in a local correctional facility, or who is granted suspension of sentence and probation by a court of competent jurisdiction, or who is participating in a local community-based probation program as provided in §53.1-181, or who is participating in a home/electronic incarceration program as provided in §53.1-131.2, shall be required to pay a fee of fifty dollars towards the cost of his confinement, supervision or participation as a condition of his sentence.

In the event of multiple convictions under any of the above provisions, the fees imposed herein shall be assessed on a pro rata basis. Such fees shall be in addition to any other costs or fees provided by law.

All fees assessed pursuant to this section for the cost of confinement, supervision or participation shall be paid to the clerk of the sentencing court. All such funds collected pursuant to this section shall be deposited in the general fund of the state treasury.

B. The sentencing court may exempt a defendant from the requirements of subsection A on the grounds of unreasonable hardship.

Any defendant who is exempted from the requirements of subsection A shall be required to perform community service as an alternative to the contribution toward the cost of his confinement, supervision or participation.

C. Any person (i) who is granted parole or (ii) who participates in a work release program pursuant to the provisions of §§53.1-60 and 53.1-131 shall be required to pay the fee required in subsection A as a condition of parole or work release.
(Chgd. by L.1999 ch. 9; L.2000 ch. 1040, eff. 7/1/2000.)

§53.1-150.1. Contribution by persons on parole.

Any person who is granted parole and who is required to receive substance abuse treatment as a condition of parole shall contribute towards the cost of such treatment based upon his ability to pay, as established pursuant to regulations promulgated by the Board of Corrections. The regulations shall provide that (i) any fees collected for such treatment shall be paid directly to the service provider and (ii) any person may be exempt from the payment of such fees on the grounds of unreasonable hardship.
(Added by L.1996 ch. 807, eff. 7/1/96.)

ARTICLE 3
PROCEDURES GOVERNING PAROLE
(Selected Sections)

§53.1-161. Arrest and return of parolee or felon serving a period of postrelease supervision; warrant; release pending adjudication of violation.

The Chairman or any member of the Board may at any time upon information or a showing of a violation or a probable violation by any parolee or felon serving a period of postrelease supervision of any of the terms or conditions upon which he was released on parole or postrelease period of supervision, issue or cause to be issued, a warrant for the arrest and return of the parolee or felon serving a period of postrelease supervision to the institution from which he was paroled, or to any other correctional facility which may be designated by the Chairman or member. However, a determination of whether a parolee or felon serving a period of postrelease supervision returned to a correctional facility pursuant to this section shall be returned to a state or local correctional facility shall be made based on the length of the parolee's original sentence as set forth in §53.1-20 or the period of postrelease supervision as set at sentencing. Each such warrant shall authorize all officers named therein to arrest and return the parolee to actual custody in the facility from which he was paroled, or to any other facility designated by the Chairman or member.

In any case in which the parolee or felon serving a period of postrelease supervision is charged with the violation of any law, the violation of which caused the issuance of such warrant, upon request of the parolee or his attorney, the

Chairman or member shall as soon as practicable consider all the circumstances surrounding the allegations of such violation, including the probability of conviction thereof, and may, after such consideration, release the parolee, pending adjudication of the violation charged.
(Chgd. by L.2000 ch. 767, eff. 7/1/2000.)

§53.1-162. Arrest of parolee or felon serving a period of postrelease supervision without warrant; written statement.

Any probation and parole officer may arrest a parolee or felon serving a period of postrelease supervision without a warrant or may deputize any other officer with power of arrest to do so by a written statement setting forth that the parolee or felon serving a period of postrelease supervision has, in the judgment of the probation and parole officer, violated one or more of the terms or conditions of his parole or postrelease period of supervision. Such a written statement by a probation and parole officer delivered to the officer in charge of any state or local correctional facility shall be sufficient warrant for the detention of the parolee or felon serving a period of postrelease supervision.
(Chgd. by L.2000 ch. 767, eff. 7/1/2000.)

§53.1-163. Parolee considered as escapee after issuance of warrant.

Any parolee for whose arrest a warrant has been issued by the Board or by the Chairman shall after the issuance of the warrant be treated as an escaped prisoner. The time from the issuing of such warrant to the date of his arrest shall not be counted as any part of the time to be served under his sentence.

CHAPTER 7
CRIMES AND CRIMINAL PROCEEDINGS INVOLVING PRISONERS
(Selected Article)

ARTICLE 1
CRIMES BY PRISONERS
(Selected Sections)

§53.1-203. Felonies by prisoners; penalties.

It shall be unlawful for a prisoner in a state, local or community correctional facility or in the custody of an employee thereof to:

1. Escape from a correctional facility or from any person in charge of such prisoner;
2. Willfully break, cut or damage any building, furniture, fixture or fastening of such facility or any part thereof for the purpose of escaping, aiding any other prisoner to escape therefrom or rendering such facility less secure as a place of confinement;
3. Make, procure, secrete or have in his possession any instrument, tool or other thing for the purpose of escaping from or aiding another to escape from a correctional facility or employee thereof;
4. Make, procure, secrete or have in his possession a knife, instrument, tool or other thing not authorized by the superintendent or sheriff which is capable of causing death or bodily injury;
5. Procure, sell, secrete or have in his possession any chemical compound which he has not lawfully received;
6. Procure, sell, secrete or have in his possession a controlled substance classified in Schedule III of the Drug Control Act (§54.1-3400 et seq.) or marijuana;
7. Introduce into a correctional facility or have in his possession firearms or ammunition for firearms;
8. Willfully burn or destroy by use of any explosive device or substance, in whole or in part, or cause to be so burned or destroyed, any personal property, within any correctional facility; or
9. Conspire with another prisoner or other prisoners to commit any of the foregoing acts.

For violation of any of the provisions of this section, except subdivision 6, the prisoner shall be guilty of a Class 6 felony. For a violation of subdivision 6, he shall be guilty of a Class 5 felony. If the violation is of subdivision 1 of this section and the escapee is a felon, he shall be sentenced to a minimum of one year's confinement, which sentence shall not be suspended, in whole or in part, nor served concurrently with any other sentence. The prisoner shall, upon conviction of escape, immediately commence to serve such escape sentence, and he shall not be eligible for parole during such period. Any prisoner sentenced to life imprisonment who escapes shall not be eligible for parole. No part of the time served for escape shall be credited for the purpose of parole toward the sentence or sentences, the service of which is interrupted for service of the escape sentence, nor shall it be credited for such purpose toward any other sentence.

§53.1-204. If prisoner commits any other felony, how punished.

If a prisoner in a state, local or community correctional facility or in the custody of an employee thereof commits any felony other than those specified in §§18.2-31, 18.2-55 and 53.1-203, which is punishable by confinement in a state correctional facility or by death, such prisoner shall be subject to the same punishment therefor as if he were not a prisoner.

CHAPTER 10
COMMITMENT OF ALIENS
(Selected Section)

§53.1-218. Duty of officer in charge to inquire as to citizenship; notice to federal immigration officer of commitment of alien.

Whenever any person is committed to a correctional facility, it shall be the duty of the director, sheriff or other officer in charge of such facility to inquire as to whether the person is a citizen of the United States, and if he is not, such director, sheriff or other officer shall inquire as to the person's alien status.

If it appears that the person is an alien, the director, sheriff or other officer in charge of the facility shall immediately notify the Central Criminal Records Exchange. However, notification need not be made if it is apparent that a report on alien status has previously been made to the Exchange pursuant to §19.2-294.2.

CHAPTER 12
EXECUTIVE CLEMENCY
(Complete Chapter)

§53.1-229. Powers vested in Governor.

In accordance with the provisions of Article V, Section 12 of the Constitution of Virginia, the power to commute capital punishment and to grant pardons or reprieves is vested in the Governor.

§53.1-230. Commutation of capital punishment.

In any case in which the Governor shall exercise the power conferred on him to commute capital punishment, he may issue his order to the Director, who shall receive and confine the person whose punishment is commuted according to such order. To carry into effect any commutation of punishment, the Governor may issue his warrant directed to any proper officer, and the same shall be obeyed and executed.

§53.1-231. Investigation of cases for executive clemency by Parole Board.

The Virginia Parole Board shall, at the request of the Governor, investigate and report to the Governor on cases in which executive clemency is sought. In any other case in which it believes action on the part of the Governor is proper or in the best interest of the Commonwealth, the Board may investigate and report to the Governor with its recommendations.

CHAPTER 13
DEATH SENTENCES
(Complete Chapter)

§53.1-232. Procedures for execution of death sentence; subsequent process.

A. Sentence of death shall not be executed sooner than thirty days after the sentence is pronounced. The court shall, in imposing such sentence, fix a day when the execution shall occur.

B. Whenever the day fixed for the execution of a sentence of death shall have passed without the execution of the sentence and it becomes necessary to fix a new date therefor, the circuit court which pronounced the sentence shall fix another day for the execution. The person to be executed need not be present but shall be represented by an attorney when such other day is fixed. A copy of the order fixing the new date of execution shall be promptly furnished by the clerk of the court making the order to the Director. The Director shall cause a copy of the order to be delivered to the person to be executed, and, if he is unable to read it, cause it to be explained to him at least ten days before the date fixed for such execution, and make return thereof to the clerk of the court which issued such order.

C. When the day fixed for the execution of a sentence of death has passed without the execution of the sentence by reason of a reprieve granted by the Governor, it shall not be necessary for the court to resentence the prisoner. The sentence of death shall be executed on the day to which the prisoner has been reprieved.

D. Should the condemned prisoner be granted a reprieve by the Governor, or obtain a writ of error from the Supreme Court of Virginia, or should the execution of the sentence be stayed by any other competent judicial proceeding, notice of such reprieve, writ of error or stay of execution shall be served upon (i) the Director, (ii) the warden or superintendent having actual custody of the prisoner, and (iii) the prisoner himself; the Director shall yield obedience to the same. In any subsequent proceeding, the mandate of the court having regard to the condemned prisoner shall be served upon the Director, the warden or superintendent having actual custody of the prisoner and upon the prisoner. Should the condemned prisoner be resentenced to death by the court, the proceedings shall be as hereinabove provided under the original sentence. Should a new trial be granted, such condemned prisoner shall be conveyed back to the place of trial by such officer or officers as the Director may direct.

§53.1-232.1. When execution dates required.

In a criminal case where a sentence of death has been imposed, the trial court shall set an execution date when it is notified in writing by the Attorney General or the attorney for the Commonwealth, and the court finds that: (i) the Supreme Court of Virginia has denied habeas corpus relief or the time for filing a timely habeas corpus petition in that Court has passed without such a petition being filed, (ii) the Supreme Court of the United States has issued a final order disposing of the case after granting a stay to review the judgment of the Supreme Court of Virginia on habeas corpus, (iii) the United States Court of Appeals has affirmed the denial of federal habeas corpus relief or the time for filing a timely appeal in that court has passed without such an appeal being filed, or (iv) the Supreme Court of the United States has issued a final order after granting a stay in order to dispose of the petition for a writ of certiorari to review the judgment of the United States Court of Appeals.

The trial court shall conduct a proceeding to set the date within ten days after receiving the written notice from the Attorney General or the attorney for the Commonwealth. The execution date shall be set by the trial court in accordance with the provisions of §§53.1-232 and 53.1-234, but in any event shall be no later than sixty days after the date of the proceeding. Nothing in this provision shall prohibit the trial court from setting an execution date under circumstances other than those specified herein. Once an execution date is scheduled, a stay of execution may be granted by the trial court or the Supreme Court of Virginia only upon a showing of substantial grounds for habeas corpus relief.
(Added by L.1995 ch. 503, eff. 7/1/95.)

§53.1-233. Death chamber; who to execute death sentence.

The Director is hereby authorized and directed to provide and maintain a permanent death chamber and necessary appurtenant facilities within the confines of a state correctional facility. The death chamber shall have all the necessary appliances for the proper execution of prisoners by electrocution or by continuous intravenous injection of a substance or combination of substances sufficient to cause death. Any such substance shall be applied until the prisoner is pronounced dead by a physician licensed in the Commonwealth. All prisoners upon whom the death penalty has been imposed shall be executed in the death chamber. Each execution shall be conducted by the Director or one or more assistants designated by him.

§53.1-234. Transfer of prisoner; how death sentence executed; who to be present.

The clerk of the circuit court in which is pronounced the sentence of death against any person shall, after such judgment becomes final in the circuit court, deliver a certified copy thereof to the Director. Such person so sentenced to death shall be confined prior to the execution of the sentence in a state correctional facility designated by the Director. Not less than four days before the time fixed in the judgment of the court for the execution of the sentence, the Director shall cause the condemned prisoner to be conveyed to the state correctional facility housing the death chamber.

The Director, or the assistants appointed by him, shall at the time named in the sentence, unless a suspension of execution is ordered, cause the prisoner under sentence of death to be electrocuted or injected with a lethal substance, until he is dead. The method of execution shall be chosen by the prisoner. In the event the prisoner refuses to make a choice at least fifteen days prior to the scheduled execution, the method of execution shall be by lethal injection. Execution by lethal injection shall be permitted in accordance with procedures developed by the Department. At the execution there shall be present the Director or an assistant, a physician employed by the Department or his assistant, such other employees of the Department as may be required by the Director and, in addition thereto, at least six citizens who shall not be employees of the Department. In addition, the counsel for the prisoner and a clergyman may be present.

(Chgd. by L.1996 ch. 679, eff. 7/1/96.)

§53.1-235. Certificate of execution of death sentence.

After execution of the death sentence as provided in this chapter, the physician in attendance shall perform an examination to determine that death has occurred. The Director shall certify the fact of the execution, appending the physician's death certificate thereto, to the clerk of the court by which such sentence was pronounced. The clerk shall file the certificate with the papers of the case and shall enter the same upon the records of the case.

§53.1-236. Disposition of remains.

Upon application of the relatives of the person executed, the remains after execution shall be returned to their address and at their cost. If no such application is made within three days of the date of execution, the provisions of §32.1-298 shall apply.

TITLE 54.1
PROFESSIONS AND OCCUPATIONS
(Selected Subtitles)

Subtitle

**See also Chapter 34, Drug Control Act, following Title 52, Police (State).*

SUBTITLE I
GENERAL PROVISIONS RELATING TO REGULATORY BOARDS
(Selected Chapter)

Chapter

CHAPTER 1
GENERAL PROVISIONS
(Selected Section)

Section

§54.1-102. Unlawful procurement of certificate, license or permit; unauthorized possession of examination or answers; penalty.

A. It shall be unlawful:

1. For any person to procure, or assist another to procure, through theft, fraud or other illegal means, a certificate, license or permit, from any state board, or other body charged by law with the responsibility of examining persons desiring to engage in a regulated business or profession, by giving to, or receiving from, any person any information, oral, written or printed, during the administration of the examination, which is intended to, or will, assist any person taking the examination in passing the examination and obtaining the required certificate, license or permit;

2. For any person, other than a member or officer of the board or body, to procure or have in his possession prior to the beginning of an examination, without written authority of a member or officer of the board or body, any question intended to be used by the board or body conducting the examination, or to receive or furnish to any person taking the examination, prior to or during the examination, any written or printed material purporting to be answers to, or aid in answering such questions;

3. For any person to attempt to procure, through theft, fraud or other illegal means, any questions intended to be used by the board or body conducting the examination, or the answers to the questions;

4. To promise or offer any valuable or other consideration to a person having access to the questions or answers as an inducement to procure for delivery to the promisor, or any other person, a copy or copies of any questions or answers.

If an examination is divided into separate parts, each of the parts shall be deemed an examination for the purposes of this section.

B. Any person violating the provisions of subsection A shall be guilty of a Class 2 misdemeanor.

SUBTITLE II
PROFESSIONS AND OCCUPATIONS REGULATED BY THE DEPARTMENT OF PROFESSIONAL AND OCCUPATIONAL REGULATION AND BOARDS WITHIN THE DEPARTMENT
(Selected Chapters)

Chapter

CHAPTER 6
AUCTIONEERS
(Selected Section)

§54.1-606. Unlawful to advertise as an auctioneer.

It shall be unlawful for any person not licensed under the provisions of this chapter to advertise that he is in the auction business or to hold himself out to the public as an auctioneer.

CHAPTER 9
BRANCH PILOTS
(Selected Article)

ARTICLE 6
OFFENSES AND PENALTIES GENERALLY
(Selected Sections)

§54.1-924. Piloting, etc., vessel without license; how offenders proceeded against.

No person shall conduct or pilot a vessel to or from sea, or to or from any port or place in Virginia unless he is licensed under this chapter.

Warrants for persons violating this section may be issued by any magistrate, upon the oath of any party complaining, and shall be returnable to the Circuit Court of the City of Norfolk. After a bond hearing held pursuant to Chapter 9 (§19.2-119 et seq.) of Tile 19.2, the bond shall be returned by the judicial officer to the circuit court of the City of Norfolk, which shall have jurisdiction for trial of such misdemeanor.

§54.1-927. Violation of chapter a misdemeanor.

Any person who violates any of the provisions of this chapter shall be guilty of a Class 1 misdemeanor.

CHAPTER 18
POLYGRAPH EXAMINERS
(Complete Chapter)

§54.1-1800. Definitions.

As used in this chapter, unless the context requires a different meaning:

"Course of instruction" means a formal course of instruction in the detection of deception in an institution approved by the Director.

"Department" means the Department of Professional and Occupational Regulation.

"Director" means the Director of the Department of Professional and Occupational Regulation.

"Person" means any natural person, partnership, association, corporation or trust.

"Polygraph" means any mechanical or electronic instrument or device used to test or question individuals for the purpose of determining truthfulness.

"Polygraph examiner" or "examiner" means any person who uses any device or instrument to test or question individuals for the purpose of determining truthfulness.

"Polygraph examiner intern" means any person engaged in the study of polygraphy and the administration of polygraph examinations under the personal supervision and control of a polygraph examiner.

§54.1-1801. Licenses.

All polygraph examiners shall be licensed pursuant to this chapter.

§54.1-1802. Regulations.

The Director shall promulgate regulations not inconsistent with the laws of Virginia necessary to carry out the provisions of this chapter and Chapter 1 (§54.1-100 et seq.).

§54.1-1803. Approval of schools to teach courses of instruction.

The Director shall promulgate regulations for the approval of schools in which courses of instruction are taught.

§54.1-1804. Submission of fingerprints.

Each applicant for licensure as a polygraph examiner and each polygraph examiner intern shall submit his fingerprints to the Department on a form provided by the Department.

§54.1-1805. Instrument to be used.

Each examiner shall use an instrument which records permanently and simultaneously the subject's cardiovascular and respiratory patterns as minimum standards, but such an instrument may record additional physiological changes pertinent to the determination of truthfulness.

§54.1-1806. Prohibition of use of certain questions on polygraph tests for employment.

No licensed polygraph operator shall, during a polygraph examination required as a condition of employment, ask any question concerning the sexual activities of the person being examined if the question violates state or federal law. A violation of this section shall constitute grounds for disciplinary action pursuant to §54.1-1802.

SUBTITLE III
PROFESSIONS AND OCCUPATIONS REGULATED BY BOARDS WITHIN THE DEPARTMENT OF HEALTH PROFESSIONS
(Selected Chapters)

CHAPTER 24
GENERAL PROVISIONS
(Selected Sections)

§54.1-2400.1. Mental health service providers; duty to protect third parties; immunity.

A. As used in this section:

"Certified substance abuse counselor" means a person certified to provide substance abuse counseling in a state-approved public or private substance abuse program or facility.

"Client" or "patient" means any person who is voluntarily or involuntarily receiving mental health services or substance abuse services from any mental health service provider.

"Clinical psychologist" means a person who practices clinical psychology as defined in §54.1-3600.

"Clinical social worker" means a person who practices social work as defined in §54.1-3700.

"Licensed practical nurse" means a person licensed to practice practical nursing as defined in §54.1-3000.

"Licensed substance abuse treatment practitioner" means any person licensed to engage in the practice of substance abuse treatment as defined in §54.1-3500.

"Marriage and family therapist" means a person licensed to engage in the practice of marriage and family therapy as defined in §54.1-3500.

"Mental health professional" means a person who by education and experience is professionally qualified and licensed in Virginia to provide counseling interventions designed to facilitate an individual's achievement of human development goals and remediate mental, emotional, or behavioral disorders and associated distresses which interfere with mental health and development.

"Mental health service provider" or "provider" refers to any of the following: (i) a person who provides professional services as a certified substance abuse counselor, clinical psychologist, clinical social worker, licensed substance abuse treatment practitioner, licensed practical nurse, marriage and family therapist, mental health professional, physician, professional counselor, psychologist, registered nurse, school psychologist, or social worker; (ii) a professional corporation, all of whose shareholders or members are so licensed; or (iii) a partnership, all of whose partners are so licensed.

"Professional counselor" means a person who practices counseling as defined in §54.1-3500.

"Psychologist" means a person who practices psychology as defined in §54.1-3600.

"Registered nurse" means a person licensed to practice professional nursing as defined in §54.1-3000.

"School psychologist" means a person who practices school psychology as defined in §54.1-3600.

"Social worker" means a person who practices social work as defined in §54.1-3700.

B. A mental health service provider has a duty to take precautions to protect third parties from violent behavior or other serious harm only when the client has orally, in writing, or via sign language, communicated to the provider a specific and immediate threat to cause serious bodily injury or death to an identified or readily identifiable person or persons, if the provider reasonably believes, or should believe according to the standards of his profession, that the client has the intent and ability to carry out that threat immediately or imminently. If the third party is a child, in addition to taking precautions to protect the child from the behaviors in the above types of threats, the provider also has a duty to take precautions to protect the child if the client threatens to engage in behaviors that would constitute physical abuse or sexual abuse as defined in §18.2-67.10. The duty to protect does not attach unless the threat has been communicated to the provider by the threatening client while the provider is engaged in his professional duties.

C. The duty set forth in subsection B is discharged by a mental health service provider who takes one or more of the following actions:

1. Seeks civil commitment of the client under Chapter 2 (§37.1-63 et seq.) of Title 37.1.

2. Makes reasonable attempts to warn the potential victims or the parent or guardian of the potential victim if the potential victim is under the age of eighteen.

3. Makes reasonable efforts to notify a law-enforcement official having jurisdiction in the client's or potential victim's place of residence or place of work, or place of work of the parent or guardian if the potential victim is under age eighteen, or both.

4. Takes steps reasonably available to the provider to prevent the client from using physical violence or other means of harm to others until the appropriate law-enforcement agency can be summoned and takes custody of the client.

5. Provides therapy or counseling to the client or patient in the session in which the threat has been communicated until the mental health service provider reasonably believes that the client no longer has the intent or the ability to carry out the threat.

D. A mental health service provider shall not be held civilly liable to any person for:

1. Breaching confidentiality with the limited purpose of protecting third parties by communicating the threats described in subsection B made by his clients to potential third party victims or law-enforcement agencies or by taking any of the actions specified in subsection C.

2. Failing to predict, in the absence of a threat described in subsection B, that the client would cause the third party serious physical harm.

3. Failing to take precautions other than those enumerated in subsection C to protect a potential third party victim from the client's violent behavior.

(Chgd. by L.1996 ch. 1036; L.1997 ch. 901, eff. 7/1/97.)

§54.1-2400.4. Mental health service providers duty to inform; immunity; civil penalty.

A. Any mental health service provider, as defined in §54.1-2400.1, shall, upon learning of evidence that indicates a reasonable probability that another mental health provider is or may be guilty of a violation of standards of conduct as defined in statute or regulation, advise his patient of his right to report such misconduct to the Department of Health Professions, hereinafter referred to as the "Department."

B. The mental health service provider shall provide relevant information to the patient, including, but not limited to, the Department's toll-free complaint hotline number for consumer complaints and written information, published by the Department of Health Professions, explaining how to file a report. The mental health service provider shall document in the patient's record the alleged misconduct, the category of licensure or certification, and approximate dates of treatment, if known, of the mental health service provider who will be the subject of the report, and the action taken by the mental health service provider to inform the patient of his right to file a complaint with the Department of Health Professions.

C. Any mental health service provider informing a patient of his right to file a complaint against a regulated person and providing the information required by this section shall be immune from any civil liability or criminal prosecution resulting therefrom unless such person acted in bad faith or with malicious intent.

D. Notwithstanding any other provision of law, any person required to inform a patient of his right to file a complaint against a regulated person pursuant to this section who

fails to do so shall be subject to a civil penalty not to exceed $100.
(Added by L.2000 ch. 578, eff. 7/1/2000.)

§54.1-2409.1. Criminal penalties for practicing certain professions and occupations without appropriate license.

Any person who, without holding a current valid license, issued by a regulatory board pursuant to this title (i) performs an invasive procedure for which a license is required; (ii) administers, prescribes, sells, distributes, or dispenses a controlled drug; or (iii) practices a profession or occupation after having his license to do so suspended or revoked shall be guilty of a Class 6 felony.

CHAPTER 29
MEDICINE AND OTHER HEALING ARTS
(Selected Articles)

ARTICLE 1
GENERAL PROVISIONS
(Selected Sections)

§54.1-2902. Unlawful to practice without license.

It shall be unlawful for any person to practice medicine, osteopathic medicine, chiropractic, podiatry, or as a physician's or podiatrist's assistant in the Commonwealth without a valid unrevoked license issued by the Board of Medicine.
(Chgd. by L.1996 chs. 937, 980; L.2000 ch. 688, eff. 7/1/2000.)

§54.1-2903. What constitutes practice.

Any person shall be regarded as practicing the healing arts who actually engages in such practice as defined in this chapter, or who opens an office for such purpose, or who advertises or announces to the public in any manner a readiness to practice or who uses in connection with his name the words or letters "Doctor," "Dr.," "M.D.," "D.O.," "D.P.M.," "D.C.," "Healer," or any other title, word, letter or designation intending to designate or imply that he is a practitioner of the healing arts or that he is able to heal, cure or relieve those suffering from any injury, deformity or disease. No person regulated under this chapter shall use the title "Doctor" or the abbreviation "Dr." in writing or in advertising in connection with his practice unless he simultaneously uses a clarifying title, initials, abbreviation or designation or language that identifies the type of practice for which he is licensed.

Signing a birth or death certificate, or signing any statement certifying that the person so signing has rendered professional service to the sick or injured, or signing or issuing a prescription for drugs or other remedial agents, shall be prima facie evidence that the person signing or issuing such writing is practicing the healing arts within the meaning of this chapter except where persons other than physicians are required to sign birth certificates.
(Chgd. by L.1996 chs. 937, 980; L.2000 ch. 688, eff. 7/1/2000.)

ARTICLE 8
HEALTH CARE DECISIONS ACT
(Selected Sections)

§54.1-2981. Short title.

The provisions of this article shall be known and may be cited as the "Health Care Decisions Act".

§54.1-2983. Procedure for making advance directive; notice to physician.

Any competent adult may, at any time, make a written advance directive authorizing the providing, withholding or withdrawal of life-prolonging procedures in the event such person should have a terminal condition. A written advance directive may also appoint an agent to make health care decisions for the declarant under the circumstances stated in the advance directive if the declarant should be determined to be incapable of making an informed decision. A written advance directive shall be signed by the declarant in the presence of two subscribing witnesses.

Further, any competent adult who has been diagnosed by his attending physician as being in a terminal condition may make an oral advance directive to authorize the providing, withholding or withdrawing of life-prolonging procedures or to appoint an agent to make health care decisions for the declarant under the circumstances stated in the advance directive if the declarant should be determined to be incapable of making an informed decision. An oral advance directive shall be made in the presence of the attending physician and two witnesses.

It shall be the responsibility of the declarant to provide for notification to his attending physician that an advance directive has been made. In the event the declarant is comatose, incapacitated or otherwise mentally or physically incapable of communication, any other person may notify the physician of the existence of an advance directive. An attending physician who is so notified shall promptly make the advance directive or a copy of the advance directive, if written, or the fact of the advance directive, if oral, a part of the declarant's medical records.
(Chgd. by L.1997 ch. 801, eff. 1/1/98.)

§54.1-2987.1. Durable Do Not Resuscitate Orders.

A. A Durable Do Not Resuscitate Order may be issued by a physician for his patient with whom he has a bona fide physician/patient relationship as defined in the guidelines of the Board of Medicine, and only with the consent of the patient or, if the patient is a minor or is otherwise incapable of making an informed decision regarding consent for such an order, upon the request of and with the consent of the person authorized to consent on the patient's behalf.

B. This section shall not authorize any health care provider or practitioner to follow a Durable Do Not Resuscitate Order for any patient who is able to, and does, express to such health care provider or practitioner the desire to be resuscitated in the event of cardiac or respiratory arrest.

If the patient is a minor or is otherwise incapable of making an informed decision, the expression of the desire that the patient be resuscitated by the person authorized to consent on the patient's behalf shall so revoke the provider's or practitioner's authority to follow a Durable Do Not Resuscitate Order.

The expression of such desire to be resuscitated prior to cardiac or respiratory arrest shall constitute revocation of the Order; however, a new Order may be issued upon consent of the patient or the person authorized to consent on the patient's behalf.

C. Durable Do Not Resuscitate Orders issued in accordance with this section shall remain valid and in effect until revoked. In accordance with this section and regulations promulgated by the Board of Health, (i) qualified emergency medical services personnel as defined in §32.1-111.1 and (ii) licensed health care practitioners in any facility, program or organization operated or licensed by the Board of Health or by the Department of Mental Health, Mental Retardation and Substance Abuse Services or operated, licensed or owned by another state agency are authorized to follow Durable Do Not Resuscitate Orders that are available to them in a form approved by the Board of Health.

D. The provisions of this section shall not authorize any qualified emergency medical services personnel or licensed health care provider or practitioner who is attending the patient at the time of cardiac or respiratory arrest to provide, continue, withhold or withdraw treatment if such provider or practitioner knows that taking such action is protested by the patient incapable of making an informed decision. No person shall authorize providing, continuing, withholding or withdrawing treatment pursuant to this section that such person knows, or upon reasonable inquiry ought to know, is contrary to the religious beliefs or basic values of a patient incapable of making an informed decision or the wishes of such patient fairly expressed when the patient was capable of making an informed decision. Further, this section shall not authorize the withholding of other medical interventions, such as intravenous fluids, oxygen or other therapies deemed necessary to provide comfort care or to alleviate pain.

E. For the purposes of this section:

"Health care provider" includes, but is not limited to, qualified emergency medical services personnel.

"Person authorized to consent on the patient's behalf" means any person authorized by law to consent on behalf of the patient incapable of making an informed decision or, in the case of a minor child, the parent or parents having custody of the child or the child's legal guardian or as otherwise provided by law.

F. This section shall not prevent, prohibit or limit a physician from issuing a written order, other than a Durable Do Not Resuscitate Order, not to resuscitate a patient in the event of cardiac or respiratory arrest in accordance with accepted medical practice.

G. Valid Do Not Resuscitate Orders or Emergency Medical Services Do Not Resuscitate Orders issued before July 1, 1999, pursuant to the then-current law, shall remain valid and shall be given effect as provided in this article.

(Chgd. by L.1998 chs. 564, 628, 630, 803, 854; L.1999 ch. 814, eff. 7/1/99.)

§54.1-2988. Immunity from liability; burden of proof; presumption.

A health care facility, physician or other person acting under the direction of a physician shall not be subject to criminal prosecution or civil liability or be deemed to have engaged in unprofessional conduct as a result of issuing a Durable Do Not Resuscitate Order or the withholding or the withdrawal of life-prolonging procedures under authorization or consent obtained in accordance with this article or as the result of the provision, withholding or withdrawal of ongoing life-sustaining care in accordance with §54.1-2990. No person or facility providing, withholding or withdrawing treatment or physician issuing a Durable Do Not Resuscitate Order under authorization or consent obtained pursuant to this article or otherwise in accordance with §54.1-2990 shall incur liability arising out of a claim to the extent the claim is based on lack of authorization or consent for such action.

A person who authorizes or consents to the providing, withholding or withdrawal of ongoing life-sustaining care in accordance with §54.1-2990 or of life-prolonging procedures in accordance with a qualified patient's advance directive or as provided in §54.1-2986 or a Durable Do Not Resuscitate Order pursuant to §54.1-2987.1 shall not be subject, solely on the basis of that authorization or consent, to (i) criminal prosecution or civil liability for such action or (ii) liability for the cost of treatment.

The provisions of this section shall apply unless it is shown by a preponderance of the evidence that the person authorizing or effectuating the withholding or withdrawal of life-prolonging procedures, or issuing, consenting to, making or following a Durable Do Not Resuscitate Order in accordance with §54.1-2987.1 did not, in good faith, comply with the provisions of this article.

The distribution to patients of written advance directives in a form meeting the requirements of §54.1-2984 and assistance to patients in the completion and execution of such forms by health care providers shall not constitute the unauthorized practice of law pursuant to Chapter 39 (§54.1-3900 et seq.) of this title.

An advance directive or Durable Do Not Resuscitate Order made, consented to or issued in accordance with this article shall be presumed to have been made, consented to, or issued voluntarily and in good faith by a competent adult, physician or person authorized to consent on the patient's behalf.

(Chgd. by L.1998 chs. 803, 854; L.1999 ch. 814; L.2000 chs. 590, 598, eff. 7/1/2000.)

§54.1-2989. Willful destruction, concealment, etc., of declaration or revocation; penalties.

Any person who willfully conceals, cancels, defaces, obliterates, or damages the advance directive or Durable Do Not Resuscitate Order of another without the declarant's or patient's consent or the consent of the person authorized to consent for the patient or who falsifies or forges a revocation of the advance directive or Durable Do Not Resuscitate Order of another, thereby causing life-prolonging procedures to be utilized in contravention of the previously expressed intent of the patient or a Durable Do Not Resuscitate Order shall be guilty of a Class 6 felony.

Any person who falsifies or forges the advance directive or Durable Do Not Resuscitate Order of another, or willfully conceals or withholds personal knowledge of the revocation of an advance directive or Durable Do Not Resuscitate Order, with the intent to cause a withholding or withdrawal of life-prolonging procedures, contrary to the wishes of the declarant or a patient, and thereby, because of such act, directly causes life-prolonging procedures to be withheld or withdrawn and death to be hastened, shall be guilty of a Class 2 felony.

(Chgd. by L.1998 chs. 803, 854; L.1999 ch. 814, eff. 7/1/99.)

§54.1-2990. Medically unnecessary treatment not required; procedure when physician refuses to comply with an advance directive or a designated person's treatment decision; mercy killing or euthanasia prohibited.

A. Nothing in this article shall be construed to require a physician to prescribe or render medical treatment to a patient that the physician determines to be medically or ethically inappropriate. However, in such a case, if the physician's determination is contrary to the terms of an advance directive of a qualified patient or the treatment decision of a person designated to make the decision under this article or a Durable Do Not Resuscitate Order, the physician shall make a reasonable effort to inform the patient or the patient's designated decision-maker of such determination and the reasons for the determination. If the conflict remains unresolved, the physician shall make a reasonable effort to transfer the patient to another physician who is willing to comply with the terms of the advance directive. The physician shall provide the patient or his authorized decision-maker a reasonable time of not less than fourteen days to effect such transfer. During this period, the physician shall continue to provide any life-sustaining care to the patient which is reasonably available to such physician, as requested by the patient or his designated decision-maker.

B. For purposes of this section, "life-sustaining care" means any ongoing medical treatment that utilizes mechanical or other artificial means to sustain, restore or supplant a spontaneous vital function, including hydration, nutrition, maintenance medication, and cardiopulmonary resuscitation.

C. Nothing in this section shall require the provision of treatment that the physician is physically or legally unable to provide, or treatment that the physician is physically or legally unable to provide without thereby denying the same treatment to another patient.

D. Nothing in this article shall be construed to condone, authorize or approve mercy killing or euthanasia, or to permit any affirmative or deliberate act or omission to end life other than to permit the natural process of dying.

(Chgd. by L.1999 ch. 814; L.2000 chs. 590, 598, eff. 7/1/2000.)

§54.1-2991. Effect of declaration; suicide; insurance; declarations executed prior to effective date.

The withholding or withdrawal of life-prolonging procedures in accordance with the provisions of this article shall not, for any purpose, constitute a suicide. Nor shall the making of an advance directive pursuant to this article affect the sale, procurement or issuance of any policy of life insurance, nor shall the making of an advance directive or the issuance of a Durable Do Not Resuscitate Order pursuant to this article be deemed to modify the terms of an existing policy of life insurance. No policy of life insurance shall be legally impaired or invalidated by the withholding or withdrawal of life-prolonging procedures from an insured patient in accordance with this article, notwithstanding any term of the policy to the contrary. A person shall not be required to make an advance directive or consent to a Durable Do Not Resuscitate order as a condition for being insured for, or receiving, health care services.

The declaration of any qualified patient made prior to July 1, 1983, an advance directive made prior to July 1, 1992, or the issuance, in accordance with the then current law, of a Do Not Resuscitate Order or an Emergency Medical Services Do Not Resuscitate Order prior to July 1, 1999, shall be given effect as provided in this article.

(Chgd. by L.1999 ch. 814, eff. 7/1/99.)

CHAPTER 33
PHARMACY
(Selected Article)

ARTICLE 1
GENERAL PROVISIONS
(Selected Section)

§54.1-3303. Prescriptions to be issued and drugs to be dispensed for medical or therapeutic purposes only.

A. A prescription for a controlled substance may be issued only by a practitioner of medicine, osteopathy, podiatry, dentistry or veterinary medicine who is authorized to prescribe controlled substances, or by a licensed nurse practitioner pursuant to §54.1-2957.01, a licensed physician assistant pursuant to §54.1-2952.1, or a TPA-certified optometrist pursuant to Article 5 (§54.1-3222 et seq.) of Chapter 32 of this title. The prescription shall be issued for a medicinal or therapeutic purpose and may be issued only to persons or animals with whom the practitioner has a bona fide practitioner-patient relationship.

For purposes of this section, a bona fide practitioner-patient-pharmacist relationship is one in which a practitioner prescribes, and a pharmacist dispenses, controlled substances in good faith to his patient for a medicinal or therapeutic purpose within the course of his professional practice. In addition, a bona fide practitioner-patient relationship means that the practitioner shall (i) ensure that a medical or drug history is obtained; (ii) provide information to the patient about the benefits and risks of the drug being prescribed; (iii) perform or have performed an appropriate examination of the patient, either physically or by the use of instrumentation and diagnostic equipment through which images and medical records may be transmitted electronically; except for medical emergencies, the examination of the patient shall have been performed by the practitioner himself, within the group in which he practices, or by a consulting practitioner prior to issuing a prescription; and (iv) initiate additional interventions and follow-up care, if necessary, especially if a prescribed drug may have serious side effects. Any practitioner who prescribes any controlled substance with the knowledge that the controlled substance will be used otherwise than medicinally or for therapeutic purposes shall be subject to the criminal penalties provided in §18.2-248 for violations of the provisions of law relating to the distribution or possession of controlled substances.

B. In order to determine whether a prescription which appears questionable to the pharmacist results from a bona fide practitioner-patient relationship, the pharmacist shall contact the prescribing practitioner or his agent and verify the identity of the patient and name and quantity of the drug prescribed. The person knowingly filling an invalid prescription shall be subject to the criminal penalties provided in §18.2-248 for violations of the provisions of law relating to the sale, distribution or possession of controlled substances.

No prescription shall be filled unless there is a bona fide practitioner-patient-pharmacist relationship. A prescription not issued in the usual course of treatment or for authorized research is not a valid prescription.

C. A pharmacist may dispense a controlled substance pursuant to a prescription of an out-of-state practitioner of medicine, osteopathy, podiatry, dentistry or veterinary medicine authorized to issue such prescription if the prescription complies with the requirements of this chapter and Chapter 34 (§54.1-3400 et seq.) of this title, known as the "Drug Control Act," except that out-of-state prescriptions are not required to comply with the provisions of subsection A of §32.1-87 and subsection C of §54.1-3408 which establish a prescription blank format accommodating the Virginia Voluntary Formulary.

D. A licensed nurse practitioner who is authorized to prescribe controlled substances pursuant to §54.1-2957.01 may issue prescriptions or provide manufacturers' professional samples for controlled substances and devices as set forth in Chapter 34 of this title in good faith to his patient for a medicinal or therapeutic purpose within the scope of his professional practice.

E. A licensed physician assistant who is authorized to prescribe controlled substances pursuant to §54.1-2952.1 may issue prescriptions or provide manufacturers' professional samples for Schedule VI controlled substances and devices as set forth in Chapter 34 of this title in good faith to his patient for a medicinal or therapeutic purpose within the scope of his professional practice.

F. A TPA-certified optometrist who is authorized to prescribe controlled substances pursuant to Article 5 (§54.1-3222 et seq.) of Chapter 32 of this title may issue prescriptions in good faith or provide manufacturers' professional samples to his patients for medicinal or therapeutic purposes within the scope of his professional practice for the drugs specified on the TPA-Formulary, established pursuant to §54.1-3223, which shall be limited to oral analgesics included in Schedules III and VI, as defined in §§54.1-3450 and 54.1-3455 of the Drug Control Act (§54.1-3400 et seq.), when appropriate to relieve ocular pain, and topically applied Schedule VI drugs, as defined in §54.1-3455 of the Drug Control Act.

(Chgd. by L.1996 chs. 152, 158, 408; L.1997 ch. 806; L.1998 ch. 101; L.1999 ch. 745; L.2000 chs. 882, 924, eff. 7/1/2000.)

SUBTITLE V
OCCUPATIONS REGULATED BY LOCAL GOVERNING BODIES
(Selected Chapters)

Chapter

CHAPTER 40
PAWNBROKERS
(Complete Chapter)

Section

§54.1-4000. Definition of pawnbroker.

"Pawnbroker" means any person who lends or advances money or other things for profit on the pledge and possession of tangible personal property, or other valuable things, other than securities or written or printed evidences of indebtedness or title, or who deals in the purchasing of personal property or other valuable things on condition of selling the same back to the seller at a stipulated price.

(Chgd. by L.1998 ch. 848, eff. 7/1/98.)

§54.1-4001. License required; license authorized by court; building designated in license; penalty.

A. No person shall engage in the business of a pawnbroker without having a valid license issued by the county, city or town in which the pawnbroker conducts such business.

B. The circuit court of any county or city may authorize any county, city or town to issue to any individual, who has not been convicted of a felony or a crime involving moral turpitude in the last ten years, a license to engage in the business of a pawnbroker in that county, city or town. No such license shall be issued by any county, city or town except with such authority. Prior to the issuance of the license, the applicant shall furnish his date of birth, a sworn statement or affirmation disclosing any criminal convictions or any pending criminal charges, whether within or without the Commonwealth, and such other information to the licensing authority as may be required by the governing body. The license shall designate the building in which the licensee shall carry on such business.

C. No person shall engage in the business of a pawnbroker in any location other than the one designated in his license, except with consent of the court which authorized the license.

D. Any person who violates the provisions of this section shall be guilty of a Class 1 misdemeanor. Each day's violation shall constitute a separate offense.

(Chgd. by L.1998 ch. 848, eff. 7/1/98.)

§54.1-4002. Local limitations as to number of pawnshops.

A. In addition to all limitations and restrictions and notwithstanding any other relevant provisions of this chapter, the governing body of any county, city or town may reasonably limit by resolution or ordinance the number of pawnshops that may be operated at any one time within its territorial limits.

B. The circuit court of any county or city which has, by resolution or ordinance, limited the number of pawnshops therein shall not authorize any license to any pawnbroker after the commissioner of the revenue or other tax assessing officer of the county, city or town over which it has jurisdiction for the issuance of such licenses has filed with the court a statement that the number of licensed pawnshops within the county, city or town has reached the maximum number of pawnshops authorized to be operated therein, unless the number has been reduced below the maximum prescribed. In the event that a properly licensed pawnbroker sells his business, the circuit court of the county or city shall authorize the county, city or town in which such business operates to issue to the purchaser a new license for the same location if the purchaser has not been convicted of a felony or a crime

involving moral turpitude in the last ten years. Prior to the issuance of the license, the purchaser shall furnish his date of birth and such other information to the licensing authority as may be required by the local governing body.
(Chgd. by L.1998 ch. 848, eff. 7/1/98.)

§54.1-4003. Bond required; private action on bond.
A. No person shall be licensed as a pawnbroker or engage in the business of a pawnbroker without having in existence a bond with surety in the minimum amount of $50,000 to secure the payment of any judgment recovered under the provisions of subsection B.
B. Any person who recovers a judgment against a licensed pawnbroker for the pawnbroker's misconduct may maintain an action in his own name upon the bond of the pawnbroker if the execution issued upon such judgment is wholly or partially unsatisfied.
(Chgd. by L.1998 ch. 848, eff. 7/1/98.)

§54.1-4004. Memorandum to be given pledgor; fee; lost ticket charge.
Every pawnbroker shall at the time of each loan deliver to the person pawning or pledging anything, a memorandum or note, signed by him, containing the information required by §54.1-4009. A lost-ticket fee of five dollars may be charged, provided that the pawner is notified of the fee on the ticket.
(Chgd. by L.1998 ch. 848, eff. 7/1/98.)

§54.1-4005. Sale of goods pawned.
No pawnbroker shall sell any pawn or pledge item until (i) it has been in his possession for the minimum term set forth in the memorandum, but not less than thirty days, plus a grace period of fifteen days and (ii) a statement of ownership is obtained from the pawner. If a motor vehicle is pawned, the owner of the motor vehicle shall comply with the requirements of §46.2-637. In the event of default by the pawner, the pawnbroker must comply with the requirements of §46.2-633. Otherwise, the pawnbroker must comply with the requirements of §46.2-636 et seq. All sales of items pursuant to this section may be made by the pawnbroker in the ordinary course of his business.
(Chgd. by L.1998 ch. 848; L.1999 ch. 327, eff. 7/1/99.)

§§54.1-4006, 54.1-4007. *(Repealed by L.1998 ch. 848, eff. 7/1/98.)*

§54.1-4008. Interest chargeable.
A. No pawnbroker shall ask, demand or receive a greater rate of interest than ten percent per month on a loan of $25 or less, or seven percent per month on a loan of more than $25 and less than $100, or five percent per month on a loan of $100 or more, secured by a pledge of tangible personal property. No loan shall be divided for the purpose of increasing the percentage to be paid the pawnbroker. Loans may be renewed based on the original loan amount. Loans may not be issued that compound the interest or storage fees from previous loans on the same item.
B. An annual percentage rate computed and disclosed under the provisions of the federal Truth-in-Lending Act shall not be deemed a violation of this section.
(Chgd. by L.1998 ch. 848; L.1999 ch. 327, eff. 7/1/99.)

§54.1-4009. Records to be kept; credentials of person pawning goods.
A. Every pawnbroker shall keep at his place of business an accurate and legible record of each loan or transaction in the course of his business. The account shall be recorded at the time of the loan or transaction and shall include:
1. A description, serial number, and a statement of ownership of the goods, article or thing pawned or pledged or received on account of money loaned thereon;
2. The time, date and place of the transaction;
3. The amount of money loaned thereon at the time of pledging the same;
4. The rate of interest to be paid on such loan;
5. The fees charged by the pawnbroker, itemizing each fee charged;
6. The full name, residence address, telephone number, and driver's license number or other form of identification of the person pawning or pledging the goods, article or thing, together with a particular description, including the height, weight, date of birth, race, gender, hair and eye color, and any other identifying marks, of such person;
7. Verification of the identification by the exhibition of a government-issued identification card such as a driver's license or military identification card. The record shall contain the type of identification exhibited, the issuing agency, and the number thereon;
8. The terms and conditions of the loan, including the period for which any such loan may be made; and
9. All other facts and circumstances respecting such loan.
B. The Superintendent of State Police shall promulgate regulations specifying the nature of the particular description for the purposes of subdivision A 6 above.
The Superintendent of State Police shall promulgate regulations specifying the nature of identifying credentials of the person pawning or pledging the goods. Such credentials shall be examined by the pawnbroker, and an appropriate record retained thereof.
(Chgd. by L.1998 ch. 848, eff. 7/1/98.)

§54.1-4010. Daily reports.
Every pawnbroker shall prepare a daily report of all goods, articles or things pawned or pledged with him that day and shall file such report by noon of the following day with the chief of police or other law-enforcement officer of the county, city or town where his business is conducted designated by the local attorney for the Commonwealth to receive it. The report shall include the pledgor's name, residence, and driver's license number or other form of identification, and a description of the goods, articles or other things pledged and shall be in writing and clearly legible to any person inspecting it.
Any person, firm or corporation violating any of the provisions of this section shall be guilty of a Class 4 misdemeanor.
(Chgd. by L.1998 ch. 848, eff. 7/1/98.)

§54.1-4011. Officers may examine records or property; warrantless search and seizure authorized.
Every pawnbroker and every employee of the pawnbroker shall admit to the pawnbroker's place of business during regular business hours, any duly authorized law-enforcement officer of the jurisdiction where the business is being conducted, or any law-enforcement official of the state or federal government. The pawnbroker or employee shall permit the officer to (i) examine all records required by this chapter and any article listed in a record which is believed by the officer to be missing or stolen and (ii) search for and take into possession any article known to him to be missing, or known or believed by him to have been stolen. However, the officer shall not take possession of any article without providing to the pawnbroker a receipt.
(Chgd. by L.1998 ch. 848, eff. 7/1/98.)

§54.1-4012. Property pawned not to be disfigured or changed.
No property received on deposit or pledge by any pawnbroker shall be disfigured or its identity destroyed or affected in any manner (i) so long as it continues in pawn or in the

possession of the pawnbroker while in pawn or (ii) in an effort to obtain a serial number or other information for identification purposes.
(Chgd. by L.1998 ch. 848; L.1999 ch. 327, eff. 7/1/99.)

§54.1-4013. Care of tangible personal property; evaluation fee.

A. Pawnbrokers shall store, care for and protect all of the tangible personal property in the pawnbroker's possession and protect the property from damage or misuse. Nothing in this chapter shall be construed to mean that pawnbrokers are insurers of pawned property in their possession.

B. A pawnbroker may charge a monthly storage fee for any items requiring storage, which fee shall not exceed five percent of the amount loaned on such item.
(Chgd. by L.1998 ch. 848, eff. 7/1/98.)

§54.1-4014. Penalties; violation of the Virginia Consumer Protection Act.

A. Except as otherwise provided in §54.1-4001, any licensed pawnbroker who violates any of the provisions of this chapter shall be guilty of a Class 4 misdemeanor. In addition, the court may revoke or suspend the pawnbroker's license for second and subsequent offenses.

B. Additionally, any violation of the provisions of the chapter shall constitute a prohibited practice in accordance with §59.1-200 and shall be subject to any and all of the enforcement provisions of the Virginia Consumer Protection Act (§59.1-196 et seq.).
(Chgd. by L.1998 ch. 848, eff. 7/1/98.)

CHAPTER 41
PRECIOUS METALS DEALERS
(Complete Chapter)

§54.1-4100. Definitions.

For the purposes of this chapter, unless the context requires a different meaning:

"Coin" means any piece of gold, silver or other metal fashioned into a prescribed shape, weight and degree of fineness, stamped by authority of a government with certain marks and devices, and having a certain fixed value as money.

"Dealer" means any person, firm, partnership, or corporation engaged in the business of (i) purchasing secondhand precious metals or gems; (ii) removing in any manner precious metals or gems from manufactured articles not then owned by the person, firm, partnership, or corporation; or (iii) buying, acquiring, or selling precious metals or gems removed from manufactured articles. "Dealer" includes all employers and principals on whose behalf a purchase is made, and any employee or agent who makes any purchase for or on behalf of his employer or principal.

The definition of "dealer" shall not include persons engaged in the following:

1. Purchases of precious metals or gems directly from other dealers, manufacturers, or wholesalers for retail or wholesale inventories, provided that the selling dealer has complied with the provisions of this chapter.

2. Purchases of precious metals or gems from a qualified fiduciary who is disposing of the assets of an estate being administered by the fiduciary.

3. Acceptance by a retail merchant of trade-in merchandise previously sold by the retail merchant to the person presenting that merchandise for trade-in.

4. Repairing, restoring or designing jewelry by a retail merchant, if such activities are within his normal course of business.

5. Purchases of precious metals or gems by industrial refiners and manufacturers, insofar as such purchases are made directly from retail merchants, wholesalers, dealers, or by mail originating outside the Commonwealth.

6. Persons regularly engaged in the business of purchasing and processing nonprecious scrap metals which incidentally may contain traces of precious metals recoverable as a by-product.

"Gems" means any item containing precious or semiprecious stones customarily used in jewelry.

"Precious metals" means any item except coins composed in whole or in part of gold, silver, platinum, or platinum alloys.

§54.1-4101. Records to be kept; copy furnished to local authorities.

A. Every dealer shall keep at his place of business an accurate and legible record of each purchase of precious metals or gems. The record of each purchase shall be retained by the dealer for at least twenty-four months and shall set forth the following:

1. A complete description of all precious metals or gems purchased from each seller. The description shall include all names, initials, serial numbers or other identifying marks or monograms on each item purchased, the true weight or carat of any gem, and the price paid for each item;

2. The date, time and place of receiving the items purchased;

3. The full name, residence address, work place, home and work telephone numbers, date of birth, sex, race, height, weight, hair and eye color, and other identifying marks;

4. Verification of the identification by the exhibition of a government-issued identification card such as a driver's license or military identification card. The record shall contain the type of identification exhibited, the issuing agency, and the number thereon; and

5. A statement of ownership from the seller.

B. The information required by subdivisions 1 through 3 of subsection A of this section shall appear on each bill of sale for all precious metals and gems purchased by a dealer, and a copy shall be mailed or delivered within twenty-four hours of the time of purchase to the chief law-enforcement officer of the locality in which the purchase was made.

§54.1-4101.1. Officers may examine records or property; warrantless search and seizure authorized.

Every dealer or his employee shall admit to his place of business during regular business hours the chief law-enforcement officer or his designee of the jurisdiction in which the dealer is located or any law-enforcement officer of the state or federal government. The dealer or his employee shall permit the officer to (i) examine all records required by this chapter and any article listed in a record which is believed by the officer to be missing or stolen and (ii) search for and take into possession any article known to him to be missing, or known or believed by him to have been stolen.

§54.1-4102. Credentials and statement of ownership required from seller.

No dealer shall purchase precious metals or gems without first (i) ascertaining the identity of the seller by requiring an identification issued by a governmental agency with a photograph of the seller thereon, and at least one other corroborating means of identification, and (ii) obtaining a statement of ownership from the seller.

The governing body of the locality wherein the dealer conducts his business may determine the contents of the statement of ownership.

§54.1-4103. Prohibited purchases.

A. No dealer shall purchase precious metals or gems from any seller who is under the age of eighteen.

B. No dealer shall purchase precious metals or gems from any seller who the dealer believes or has reason to believe is not the owner of such items, unless the seller has written and duly authenticated authorization from the owner permitting and directing such sale.

§54.1-4104. Dealer to retain purchases.

A. The dealer shall retain all precious metals or gems purchased for a minimum of ten calendar days from the date on which a copy of the bill of sale is received by the chief law-enforcement officer of the locality in which the purchase is made. Until the expiration of this period, the dealer shall not sell, alter, or dispose of a purchased item in whole or in part, or remove it from the county, city, or town in which the purchase was made.

B. If a dealer performs the service of removing precious metals or gems, he shall retain the metals or gems removed and the article from which the removal was made for a period of ten calendar days after receiving such article and precious metals or gems.

§54.1-4105. Record of disposition.

Each dealer shall maintain for at least twenty-four months an accurate and legible record of the name and address of the person, firm, or corporation to which he sells any precious metal or gem in its original form after the waiting period required by §54.1-4104. This record shall also show the name and address of the seller from whom the dealer purchased the item.

§54.1-4106. Bond or letter of credit required of dealers when permit obtained.

A. Every dealer shall secure a permit as required by §54.1-4108, and each dealer at the time of obtaining such permit shall enter into a recognizance to the Commonwealth secured by a corporate surety authorized to do business in this Commonwealth, in the penal sum of $10,000, conditioned upon due observance of the terms of this chapter. In lieu of a bond, a dealer may cause to be issued by a bank authorized to do business in the Commonwealth a letter of credit in favor of the Commonwealth for $10,000.

B. If any county, city, or town has an ordinance which regulates the purchase and sale of precious metals and gems pursuant to §54.1-4111, such bond or letter of credit shall be executed in favor of the local governing body.

C. A single bond upon an employer or principal may be written or a single letter of credit issued to cover all employees and all transactions occurring at a single location.

§54.1-4107. Private action on bond or letter of credit.

Any person aggrieved by the misconduct of any dealer which violated the provisions of this chapter may maintain an action for recovery in any court of proper jurisdiction against the dealer and his surety. Recovery against the surety shall be only for that amount of the judgment which is unsatisfied by the dealer.

§54.1-4108. Permit required; method of obtaining permit; no convictions of certain crimes; approval of weighing devices; renewal; permanent location required.

A. No person shall engage in the activities of a dealer as defined in §54.1-4100 without first obtaining a permit from the chief law-enforcement officer of each county, city, or town in which he proposes to engage in business.

B. To obtain a permit, the dealer shall file with the proper chief law-enforcement officer an application form which includes the dealer's full name, any aliases, address, age, date of birth, sex, and fingerprints; the name, address, and telephone number of the applicant's employer, if any; and the location of the dealer's place of business. Upon filing this application and the payment of a $200 application fee, the dealer shall be issued a permit by the chief law-enforcement officer or his designee, provided that the applicant has not been convicted of a felony or crime of moral turpitude within seven years prior to the date of application. The permit shall be denied if the applicant has been denied a permit or has had a permit revoked under any ordinance similar in substance to the provisions of this chapter.

C. Before a permit may be issued, the dealer must have all weighing devices used in his business inspected and approved by local or state weights and measures officials and present written evidence of such approval to the proper chief law-enforcement officer.

D. This permit shall be valid for one year from the date issued and may be renewed in the same manner as such permit was initially obtained with an annual permit fee of $200. No permit shall be transferable.

E. If the business of the dealer is not operated without interruption, with Saturdays, Sundays, and recognized holidays excepted, the dealer shall notify the proper chief law-enforcement officer of all closings and reopenings of such business. The business of a dealer shall be conducted only from the fixed and permanent location specified in his application for a permit.

§54.1-4109. Exemptions from chapter.

A. The chief law-enforcement officer of a county, city or town, or his designee, may waive by written notice implementation of any one or more of the provisions of this chapter, except §54.1-4103, for particular numismatic, gem, or antique exhibitions or craft shows sponsored by nonprofit organizations, provided that the purpose of the exhibitions is nonprofit in nature, notwithstanding the fact that there may be casual purchases and trades made at such exhibitions.

B. Neither the provisions of this chapter nor any local ordinances dealing with the subject matter of this chapter shall apply to the sale or purchase of coins.

C. Neither the provisions of this chapter nor any local ordinance dealing with the subject matter of this chapter shall apply to any bank, branch thereof, trust company or bank holding company, or any wholly owned subsidiary thereof, engaged in buying and selling gold and silver bullion.

§54.1-4110. Penalties; first and subsequent offenses.

A. Any person convicted of violating any of the provisions of this chapter shall be guilty of a Class 2 misdemeanor for the first offense. Upon conviction of any subsequent offense he shall be guilty of a Class 1 misdemeanor.

B. Upon the first conviction of a dealer for violation of any provision of this chapter, the chief law-enforcement officer may revoke the dealer's permit for one full year from the date the conviction becomes final. Such revocation shall be mandatory upon a second conviction.

§54.1-4111. Local ordinances.

Nothing in this chapter shall prevent any county, city, or town in this Commonwealth from enacting an ordinance regulating dealers in precious metals and gems which parallels this chapter, or which imposes terms, conditions, and fees that are stricter, more comprehensive, or larger than those imposed by this chapter. In any event, the terms, conditions, and fees imposed by this chapter shall constitute minimum requirements in any local ordinance. Any fee in excess of the one specified in §54.1-4108 shall be reasonably related to the cost of enforcement of such local ordinance.

CHAPTER 42
DEALERS IN FIREARMS
(Complete Chapter)

§54.1-4200. Definitions.

For the purpose of this chapter, unless the context requires a different meaning:

"Dealer in firearms" means (i) any person, firm, partnership, or corporation engaged in the business of selling, trading or transferring firearms at wholesale or retail; (ii) any person, firm, partnership, or corporation engaged in the business of making or fitting special barrels, stocks, or trigger mechanisms to firearms; or (iii) any person, firm, partnership, or corporation that is a pawnbroker.

"Engaged in business" means as applied to a dealer in firearms a person, firm, partnership, or corporation that devotes time, attention, and labor to dealing in firearms as a regular course of trade or business with the principal objective of livelihood and profit through repetitive purchase or resale of firearms, but such term shall not involve a person who makes occasional sales, exchanges, or purchases of firearms for the enhancement of a personal collection or for a hobby, or who sells all or part of his personal collection of firearms.

"Firearms show" means any gathering or exhibition, open to the public, not occurring on the permanent premises of a dealer in firearms, conducted principally for the purposes of exchanging, selling or trading firearms as defined in §18.2-308.2:2.

§54.1-4201. Records to be kept; inspection of records.

A. Every dealer in firearms shall keep at his place of business, for not less than a period of two years, the original consent form required to be completed by §18.2-308.2:2 for each firearm sale.

B. Every dealer in firearms shall admit to his place of business during regular business hours the chief law-enforcement officer, or his designee, of the jurisdiction in which the dealer is located, or any law-enforcement official of the Commonwealth, and shall permit such law-enforcement officer, in the course of a bona fide criminal investigation, to examine and copy those records related to the acquisition or disposition of a particular firearm required by this section. This section shall not be construed to authorize the seizure of any records.

§54.1-4201.1. Notification by sponsor of firearms show to State Police and local law-enforcement authorities required; records; penalty.

A. No promoter of a firearms show shall hold such show without giving notice at least thirty days prior to the show to the State Police and the sheriff or chief of police of the locality in which the firearms show will be held. The notice shall be given on a form provided by the State Police. A separate notice shall be required for each firearms show.

"Promoter" means every person, firm, corporation, club, association, or organization holding a firearms show in the Commonwealth.

The promoter shall, not later than seventy-two hours prior to the opening of the show, by mail, by hand, or by fax, transmit to the authorities to which prior notice is required, a list of vendors or exhibitors who have registered to sell or exhibit in the show.

The promoter shall maintain for the duration of the show a list of all vendors or exhibitors in the show and a copy of the prior notice for immediate inspection by any law-enforcement authorities, and within seventy-two hours after the conclusion of the show, by nail, by hand or by fax, transmit a copy of the complete vendor or exhibitor list to the law-enforcement authorities to which prior notice was required. The vendor or exhibitor list shall contain the full name and residence address and the business name and address, if any, of the vendors or exhibitors.

B. A wilful violation of this section shall be a Class 3 misdemeanor.

C. The provisions of this section shall not apply to firearms shows held in any town with a population of not less than 1,995 and not more than 2,010, according to the 1990 United States census.

§54.1-4202. Penalties for violation of the provisions of this chapter.

Any person convicted of a first offense for willfully violating the provisions of this chapter shall be guilty of a Class 2 misdemeanor. Any person convicted of a second or subsequent offense under the provisions of this chapter shall be guilty of a Class 1 misdemeanor.

TITLE 56
PUBLIC SERVICE COMPANIES
(Selected Chapter)

(For air carriers see Title 5.1, Chapter 9, Air Carriers.)

CHAPTER 13
RAILROAD CORPORATIONS
(Selected Articles)

ARTICLE 2
POWERS
(Selected Section)

§56-353. Railroad company may appoint police agents.

The president or any other executive officer of any railroad company incorporated by this Commonwealth may, with the approval of the circuit court of any county or the corporation court of any city through which the road passes or has its chief office, appoint one or more police agents, who shall have authority in all cases in which the rights of such railroad company are involved to exercise within the Commonwealth all powers which can be lawfully exercised by any police officer for the preservation of the peace, the arrest of offenders and disorderly persons, and for the enforcement of laws against crimes; and such president or other executive officer may remove any such agent at his pleasure; but, any court giving such consent may at any time revoke it.

ARTICLE 6
HIGHWAY CROSSINGS
(Complete Article)

§56-405. Railroad companies to maintain grade crossings of public highways and approaches; repair by Commonwealth Transportation Commissioner or public road authority; recovery of cost from railroad company.

At every crossing, now existing or hereafter established, of a public road by a railroad or of a railroad by a public highway at grade, it shall be the duty of the railroad company to keep such crossing in good repair to the full width of the public highway, and to maintain such crossing in a smooth condition so as to admit of reasonable and safe travel over the same, and it shall also be the duty of the railroad company to maintain and keep in good repair that portion of the highway located between points two feet on either side of the extreme rails. A railroad may request that a public highway be closed for grade crossing maintenance activities and the representative of the Commonwealth Transportation Commissioner or the representative of the appropriate public road authority may approve such closing where a reasonable detour is available. Any railroad company violating the provisions of this section shall be deemed guilty of a misdemeanor, and upon conviction, shall be fined not less than $10 nor more than $500.

The Commonwealth Transportation Commissioner or the representative of the public road authority, whenever he or it shall ascertain that any such crossing is not being properly maintained shall notify the railroad company involved in writing to repair the crossing forthwith; the railroad company upon receipt of notice may request a conference on the condition of the crossing and the need, if any, for the repair of such crossing and such conference shall be held within thirty days after receipt of the Commissioner's or the public road authority's notice. After the conference if the Commissioner or the public road authority is of the opinion that such repairs are required and the railroad is not willing to proceed promptly with such repairs, he or the public road authority may repair the same or cause it to be repaired and recover from the railroad company the actual cost of such work including any administration and engineering cost.

If no conference is requested by the railroad company within the thirty-day period, the Commissioner or the public road authority with advance notice may repair the crossing or cause it to be repaired and recover from the railroad company the actual cost of such work including any administration and engineering cost.

In any action under this section to recover the cost of the repair of any such crossing, the need for, and reasonableness of, the repairs may be put in issue.

Nothing herein shall be construed as placing a duty on the railroad company to construct or reconstruct any such crossing in the event any such crossing is relocated or the highway approaches thereto are widened or reconstructed.
(Chgd. by L.1996 chs. 114, 157, eff. 7/1/96.)

§56-405.02. Railroads to adjust certain public highways at grade crossings.

When adjustments are made to railway trackage grade which crosses public rights-of-way in use as a public highway or street in any locality, the railway company making such adjustments to their trackage shall also make initial adjustments to those public highways or streets so affected thereby to maintain a safe vertical relationship between trackage and street surfaces and to insure positive storm drainage such as existed prior to such repairs. After making such initial adjustments the responsibility for the continuing maintenance of the areas within such public highways and streets so adjusted shall be controlled by §56-405.

The cost of all such initial street improvements necessitated by railway trackage adjustments shall be the responsibility of the railway company making such initial adjustments irrespective of whether or not the street improvements extended beyond railway right-of-way.
(Chgd. by L.1996 chs. 114, 157, eff. 7/1/96.)

§56-405.1. Agreements with Commonwealth Transportation Commissioner or public road authority representative for maintenance and repair of public grade crossings.

Whenever the Commonwealth Transportation Commissioner or representative of the appropriate public road authority determines that it is in the best interest of the public to assist a railroad in their grade crossing maintenance and repair activities, he is authorized to enter into an agreement with any railroad company for the repair or maintenance of any crossing of a railroad and a public highway or for the sale

of materials to the railroad company for the repair and maintenance of any such crossing. Any such agreement shall provide for the railroad company to bear the cost of the repair or maintenance or material furnished and such other conditions as the Commonwealth Transportation Commissioner or representative of the appropriate public road authority deems necessary or advisable to protect the interest of the public.
(Chgd. by L.1996 chs. 114, 157, eff. 7/1/96.)

§56-405.2. Construction and maintenance of crossbucks.

Every railroad company shall cause signal boards, hereinafter referred to as crossbucks, well supported by posts or otherwise and approved by the Department of Transportation at such heights as to be easily seen by travelers from both directions of the public highway, and not obstructing travel, containing in capital letters, at least five inches high, the inscription "railroad crossing," to be placed, and constantly maintained, at each public highway at or near and, on both sides of, each place where it is crossed by the railroad at the same level; provided that the requirements of this section in localities that maintain their own streets may be waived at specific crossings on the petition of any such company to both the Commonwealth Transportation Commissioner and the public road authority if both the Commissioner and the public road authority determine that any such crossing has or will have other adequate warning devices or that the placement of new crossbucks will not enhance the safety of the traveling public. Neither official action nor failure to act as hereinabove provided shall impair the power of the Commissioner or the public road authority to require crossbucks at specific public crossings should a subsequent determination of their need be made.

The cost of erecting crossbucks placed at a public highway for the first time or whenever the Commissioner or the public road authority determines an upgrade of the standards is required may be paid or supplemented from federal funds when available to the Department of Transportation for such purpose at the sole discretion of the Commonwealth Transportation Commissioner. But the election of the Commissioner not to participate in such cost shall not relieve any company from the obligation of this section.

This section shall apply as to cities and towns in the case of new crossbucks beginning July 1, 1977.
(Chgd. by L.1996 chs. 114, 157, eff. 7/1/96.)

§56-406.1. Proceedings for installation and maintenance of automatically operated gates, signals and other automatic crossing warning devices.

Railroads shall cooperate with the Virginia Department of Transportation and the Department of Rail and Public Transportation in furnishing information and technical assistance to enable the Commonwealth to develop plans and project priorities for the elimination of hazardous conditions at any crossing of a public highway which crosses at grade including, but not limited to grade crossing elimination, reconstruction of existing grade crossings, and grade crossing improvements. The Commonwealth shall provide each locality a listing of their grade crossing safety needs for their consideration. Information collected and analyses undertaken by the designated state agencies are subject to 23 U.S.C. §409. A railroad shall not unilaterally select or determine the type of grade crossing warning system to be installed at any crossing of a public highway and railroad at grade. The railroad shall only install or upgrade a grade crossing warning system at any crossing of a public highway and railroad at grade pursuant to an agreement with the Virginia Department of Transportation or representative of the appropriate public road authority authorized to enter into such agreements. A railroad is not required but is permitted to upgrade, at its own expense, components of any public highway at grade warning system when such upgrade is incidental to a railroad improvement project relating to track, structures or train control systems.

When required by the Commonwealth Transportation Commissioner or representative of the appropriate public road authority, every railroad company shall cause a grade crossing warning device including flashing lights approved by the Department of Transportation at such heights as to be easily seen by travelers, and not obstructing travel, to be placed, and maintained at each public highway at or near each place where it is crossed by the railroad at the same level. Such warning device shall be automatically activated by the approaching train so as to be clearly discernible to travelers approaching the railroad crossing from each direction at a distance of two-hundred feet. Such warning devices shall be erected at the initiative of the appropriate public road authority only when required by ordinance or resolution adopted by the Commissioner or the appropriate public road authority thereof stating that such political subdivision will pay the full initial installation cost of such warning devices and that maintenance costs will be fixed as provided in §56-406.2. A certified copy of such ordinance or resolution shall be delivered to such railroad company, and such railroad company shall forthwith install such warning devices at the full initial cost of such public road authority. The cost of such installation and maintenance of such warning devices may be shared by agreement between such railroad company and the Commonwealth Transportation Commissioner or the appropriate public road authority, when initiating such installation. The railroad shall be responsible for the continuing maintenance of the warning devices.

In the event that such Commissioner or representative of the appropriate public road authority and the railroad company or companies involved are unable to agree (1) on the necessity for such grade crossing warning device, or (2) the plans and specifications for and the method and manner of construction or operation thereof, or (3) the share of the cost of construction, if any, to be borne by the railroad company or companies involved, then the Commonwealth Transportation Commissioner or representative of the appropriate public road authority, as the case may be, shall petition the State Corporation Commission setting forth the grade crossing warning devices desired and the plans and specifications for and the method and manner of construction and operation of the devices desired and the facts which, in the opinion of the petitioner, justify the requiring of the same. Copies of the petition and plans and specifications shall be forthwith served by the State Corporation Commission on the railroad company or companies involved. Within twenty days after service on it of such petition and plans and specifications, each such railroad company shall file an answer with the State Corporation Commission setting out its objections to the proposed project and the Commission shall hear and determine the matter as other matters are heard and determined by that body. The Commission shall consider all the facts and circumstances surrounding the case and shall determine (1) whether public necessity justifies or requires the proposed warning devices, (2) whether the plans and specifications or the method and manner of construction and operation be proper and appropriate, and (3) what share of the cost of the project, if any, to be borne by any railroad company involved is fair and reasonable, having regard to the benefits, if any, accruing to such railroad company from providing such grade crossing warning devices, and either dismiss the proceeding as against such railroad company or enter an order deciding and disposing of all of the matters hereinbefore submitted to its jurisdiction.
(Chgd. by L.1996 ch. 114, 157, eff. 7/1/96.)

§56-406.2. Proceeding for fixing cost of maintaining such warning devices at public grade crossings.

Whenever any automatically operated gate, signal or other automatic crossing warning device has been or may hereafter be installed at any highway, road or street grade crossing by any railroad company, the Commonwealth Transportation Commissioner or the public road authority may agree with the railroad company involved as to the division of the cost of the future maintenance of any such device or devices. The basis for the division of costs will be determined by the Department of Rail and Public Transportation utilizing the calculated average maintenance cost of all previous warning device maintenance performed and documented by all railroads operating in Virginia. In the event that the Commissioner or the public road authority and the railroad company involved are unable to agree upon the share of the cost of maintenance of any such device or devices to be borne by the railroad company, if any, then such railroad company may file a petition with the State Corporation Commission setting forth the crossing protection provided at such crossing, the terms of the contract and/or the conditions of the order of said Commission or the public road authority under which it was constructed and installed and the estimated future annual cost of maintaining the same. Copies of such petition shall forthwith be served by the State Corporation Commission upon the Commonwealth Transportation Commissioner or the public road authority who shall, within twenty days after service of such petition, file an answer thereto setting out reasons for declining to participate in the future cost of maintaining such warning device or devices as requested by the railroad company and the Commission shall thereupon hear and determine the matter as other matters are heard and determined by that body. The Commission shall consider all the facts and circumstances surrounding the case and shall determine what share of the cost of the future maintenance of such warning device or devices, if any, shall be borne by the railroad company and/or the Commonwealth Transportation Board or the public road authority, having regard to the benefits, if any, accruing to such railroad company from the continued maintenance of such protection of said public highway, road or street grade crossing, and either dismiss the proceeding or enter an order deciding and disposing of the matters therein submitted to its jurisdiction.

(Chgd. by L.1996 chs. 114, 157, eff. 7/1/96.)

§56-408. Signs similar to crossing signs prohibited.

No device or sign which is in the form of a railroad crossing signboard shall be erected or permitted to remain on or near any of the public roads of this Commonwealth, except as required by §56-405.2.

Any person who shall erect such a device or sign, as aforesaid, and every sign owner who shall permit such a device or sign to remain on or near the public roads of this Commonwealth, and every landowner or tenant in possession who shall knowingly permit such a sign to remain on his land in view of any public road, shall be guilty of a misdemeanor, and upon conviction shall be fined not less than $5 nor more than $100.

§56-411. Removal of brush and trees from right-of-way.

Every railway company operating in this Commonwealth shall be required to clear from its right-of-way trees and brush for 100′ on each side of public road crossings at grade when such trees or brush would otherwise obstruct the view of approaching trains.

Every railway company violating the provisions of this section shall be fined not more than $500 for each offense, to be imposed by the State Corporation Commission after due notice and hearing upon the company or the employee so offending.

(Chgd. by L.1996 chs. 114, 157, eff. 7/1/96.)

§56-412. When trains shall be stopped before getting to railroad crossing.

Whenever railroads cross each other on the same grade in this Commonwealth, the trains shall be brought to a full stop at least fifty feet before getting to the crossing.

The provisions of this section shall not be applicable where the crossings of such roads are regulated by derailing switches, or other safety appliances, which prevent collision at crossings, nor where a flagman or watchman is stationed, or signal tower is located, and signals that the trains may cross in safety.

§56-412.1. Railroad cars obstructing street or road; standing vehicle on railroad track.

It shall be unlawful for any railroad company, or any receiver or trustee operating a railroad, to obstruct for a longer period than five minutes the free passage on any street or road by standing cars or trains across the same, except a passenger train while receiving or discharging passengers, but a passway shall be kept open to allow normal flow of traffic; nor shall it be lawful to stand any wagon or other vehicle on the track of any railroad which will hinder or endanger a moving train; provided that when a train has been uncoupled, so as to make a passway, the time necessarily required, not exceeding three minutes, to pump up the air after the train has been recoupled shall not be included in considering the time such cars or trains were standing across such street or road. Any such railroad company, receiver or trustee, violating any of the provisions of this section shall be fined not less than $100 nor more than $500; provided that the fine may be $100 for each minute beyond the permitted time but the total fine shall not exceed $500.

This section shall not apply when the train is stopped due to breakdown, mechanical failure or emergency.

§56-412.2. Ordinances conflicting with §56-412.1.

No city, town or county shall adopt any ordinance, order or resolution in conflict with the provisions of §56-412.1 and all ordinances, orders or resolutions of any city, town or county heretofore adopted in conflict with such section are hereby repealed to the extent of such conflict.

ARTICLE 7
SAFETY PROVISIONS
(Complete Article)

§56-413.01. Locomotive and rail car standards.

All locomotives and rail cars operating over the tracks of a railroad company are subject to Federal Railroad Administration jurisdiction and shall be maintained in accordance with federal standards. Locomotives designed with spark arrestors shall be cleaned and maintained on a regularly scheduled basis.

(Added by L.1996 chs. 114, 157, eff. 7/1/96.)

§56-414. Bell and whistle or horn; when sounded.

Every railroad company shall provide each locomotive passing upon its road with a bell of ordinary size and steam whistle or horn, and such whistle or horn shall be sharply sounded outside cities and towns at least twice at a distance of not less than 300 yards nor more 600 yards from the place where the railroad crosses upon the same level any public highway or crossing, and such bell shall be rung or whistle or horn sounded continuously or alternately until the locomotive has reached such highway crossing, and shall give such signals in cities and towns as their local governing bodies may require.

The governing body of any county, city, or town may by ordinance require locomotives to sound their whistle upon approaching designated railroad trestles or bridges having lengths of 100 feet or more. Notice of any such requirement shall be given by registered mail to the registered agent of the railroad operating in the affected county, city, or town. Affected railroads shall comply with any such ordinance within thirty days of receiving the notice.

§56-415. Penalty for violation of §56-414.

Every officer or employee of any railway company, whose duty it shall be to carry out any of the provisions of §56-414 and shall fail to do so, shall be punished by a fine not exceeding ten dollars for each offense.

§56-416. Effect of failure to give statutory signals.

If the employees in charge of any railroad engine or train fail to give the signals required by law on approaching a grade crossing of a public a highway not protected with an automatically operating gate, operating wigwag signal or other operating electrical or operating automatic crossing protection device, the fact that a traveler on such highway failed to exercise due care in approaching such crossing shall not bar recovery for an injury to or death of such traveler, nor for an injury to or the destruction of property in his charge, where such injury, death, or destruction results from a collision on such crossing between such engine or train and such traveler or the property in his charge, respectively; but the failure of the traveler to exercise such care may be considered in mitigation of damages.

§56-417.1. Clearance to provided in construction, etc. of railroad structures.

No railroad, nor any person, firm or corporation operating any railroad shall hereafter construct or erect any track, building, sign, guidepost, switch stand or structure of any kind unless there is sufficient clearance provided for the safety of any employee or servant in the normal and customary operations of such railroad or any part thereof. The State Corporation Commission may inspect any such track or structure of any railroad in this Commonwealth, and upon complaint, or on its own motion and after timely notice to the railroad company affected and a hearing thereon, by proper order or orders, may require any railroad to make such changes as may be found necessary to safeguard and preserve the safety of its employees, servants and the general public. Provided, however, that this section shall not apply to any track, building, sign, guidepost, switch stand or structure of any kind in existence prior to January 1, 1953, nor to any private or industrial siding; provided, further, however, that any private or industrial siding constructed after January 1, 1953 shall, as far as practical, conform to the foregoing provisions.

§56-419. Duplicate switch keys of railroads; unlawful making, etc.; punishment.

It shall be unlawful for any person to make, buy, sell, or give away to any other person any duplicate key to any lock belonging to, or in use by any railroad company in this Commonwealth on its switches or switch tracks, except upon the written order of that officer of the railroad company whose duty it is to distribute and issue switch lock keys to the employees of such railroad company. Any person violating the provisions of this section shall be deemed guilty of a misdemeanor.

§56-419.2. Safety requirements applicable to vehicles transporting railroad employees.

A. As used in this section "motor vehicle" shall mean any motor vehicle designed for highway use, owned or operated by a railroad, whether or not it is used on the highways of this Commonwealth.

B. No motor vehicle shall be used for transporting one or more railroad employees three miles or more to or from a work situs unless such motor vehicle is constructed and maintained so as to provide safe transportation for such employees.

C. The requirement of safe transportation as set out hereinabove shall include, but not be limited to, the construction and maintenance of motor vehicles so as:

1. To provide an enclosure providing full cover from the elements for all railroad employees being so transported. Such enclosure shall be heated.
2. To provide within said enclosure fixed seats with backs for all railroad employees being so transported.
3. To provide a means to effectively communicate to the driver of the motor vehicle the emergency needs of the railroad employees being so transported.

D. The provisions of this section shall not apply to any motor vehicle when an emergency arises and such vehicle must be used to meet such an emergency.

E. The failure of any railroad company to correct any violation of this section within seven days from receipt of written notice thereof shall subject said company to the penalty provided by §56-449; provided, however, any unsafe vehicle shall be removed immediately from service until repaired.

TITLE 58.1
TAXATION
(Selected Subtitles)

Subtitle	
I.	Taxes Administered by the Department of Taxation. (Chaps. 10, 10.1)
II.	Taxes Administered by Other Agencies. (Chaps. 22, 27)
IV.	Other Sources of State Revenue. (Chap. 40)

SUBTITLE I
TAXES ADMINISTERED BY THE DEPARTMENT OF TAXATION
(Selected Chapters)

Chapter	
10.	Cigarette Tax. (Secs. 58.1-1005 to 58.1-1017)
10.1.	Enforcement of Illegal Sale or Distribution of Cigarettes Act. (Secs. 58.1-1032 to 58.1-1037)

CHAPTER 10
CIGARETTE TAX
(Selected Article)

Article	
1.	Excise Tax. (Secs. 58.1-1005 to 58.1-1017)

ARTICLE 1
EXCISE TAX
(Selected Sections)

§58.1-1005. Duties of carriers, etc., transporting cigarettes.

All common carriers, contract carriers, buses, and trucks transporting cigarettes shall maintain a statement or record of all consignments or deliveries of cigarettes, showing date, point of origin, point of delivery and to whom delivered, and time of delivery, and may be required under regulations to be prescribed by the Department to transmit to the Department a periodic statement of such consignments or deliveries. Any person who fails to maintain the statement or record required by this section or who refuses to transmit to the Department the statement herein above provided for shall be guilty of a Class 2 misdemeanor.

§58.1-1015. Removal, reuse, unauthorized sale, etc., of stamps; counterfeit stamps.

Whoever removes or otherwise prepares any Virginia revenue stamp with intent to use, or cause the same to be used, after it has already been used, or buys, sells, offers for sale, or gives away any such washed or removed or restored stamps to any person for using or who used the same, or has in his possession any washed or restored or removed or altered stamp which has been removed from the article to which it has been previously affixed, or whoever for the purpose of indicating the payment of any tax hereunder reuses any stamp which has heretofore been used for the purpose of paying any tax provided in this article, or whoever manufactures, buys, sells, offers for sale, or has in his possession any reproduction or counterfeit of the Virginia revenue stamps provided for in this article, or whoever sells any Virginia revenue stamps not affixed to taxable cigarettes shall be guilty of a Class 5 felony.

§58.1-1017. Sale, purchase, possession, etc., of cigarettes for purpose of evading tax.

It shall be unlawful for any person, except as otherwise provided by law, to sell, purchase, transport, receive or possess cigarettes unless the same have been stamped in the manner required by law, for the purpose of evading the payment of the taxes on such products, Any person violating the provisions of this section shall be guilty of a Class 2 misdemeanor.

If a person who is not a regularly licensed dealer as provided in §58.1-1011 has in his possession within the Commonwealth more than thirty packages of unstamped cigarettes, such possession shall be presumed to be for the purpose of evading the payment of the taxes due thereon.

CHAPTER 10.1
ENFORCEMENT OF ILLEGAL SALE OR DISTRIBUTION OF CIGARETTES ACT

(Added by L.2000 chs. 880, 901, eff. 7/1/2000.)
(Selected Sections)

§58.1-1032. Applicability.

The provisions of this chapter shall not apply to (i) cigarettes allowed to be imported or brought into the United States for personal use or (ii) cigarettes sold or intended to be sold as duty-free merchandise by a duty-free sales enterprise in accordance with the provisions of 19 U.S.C. §1555(b) and any implementing regulations. This section, however, shall apply to cigarettes described in clause (ii) that are brought back into the customs territory for resale within the customs territory.
(Added by L.2000 chs. 880, 901, eff. 7/1/2000.)

§58.1-1033. Prohibited acts.

It shall be unlawful for any person to:

1. Sell or distribute in the Commonwealth, acquire, hold, own, possess, or transport, for sale or distribution in the Commonwealth, or import, or cause to be imported, into the Commonwealth for sale or distribution in the Commonwealth (i) any cigarettes the package of which bears any statement, label, stamp, sticker, or notice indicating that the manufacturer did not intend the cigarettes to be sold, distributed, or used in the United States, including but not limited to labels stating "For Export Only," "U.S. Tax-Exempt," "For Use Outside U.S.," or similar wording; (ii) any cigarettes the package of which does not comply with (a) all requirements imposed by or pursuant to federal law regarding warnings and other information on packages of cigarettes manufactured, packaged, or imported for sale, distribution, or use in the United States, including but not limited to the precise warning labels specified in the Federal Cigarette Labeling and Advertising Act, 15 U.S.C. §1333, or (b) all federal trademark and copyright laws; (iii) any cigarettes imported into the United States in violation of 26 U.S.C. §5754 or any other federal law or regulations; (iv) any cigarettes that such person otherwise knows or has reason to know the manufacturer did not intend to be sold, distributed, or used in the United States; or (v) any cigarettes for which there has not been submitted to the Secretary of the U.S. Department of Health and Human Services the list or lists of the ingredients added to tobacco in the manufacture of such cigarettes required by the Federal Cigarette Labeling and Advertising Act, 15 U.S.C. §1335a;

2. Alter the package of any cigarettes, prior to sale or distribution to the ultimate consumer, so as to remove, conceal or obscure (i) any statement, label, stamp, sticker, or notice described in clause (i) of subdivision 1 or (ii) any health warning that is not specified in, or does not conform with the requirements of, the Federal Cigarette Labeling and Advertising Act, 15 U.S.C. §1333; or

3. Affix any stamp required pursuant to Chapter 10 (§58.1-1000 et seq.) of this title to the package of any cigarettes described in subdivision 1 of this section or altered in violation of subdivision 2 of this section.
(Added by L.2000 chs. 880, 901, eff. 7/1/2000.)

§58.1-1037. Seizure.

Cigarettes that are acquired, held, owned, possessed, transported in, imported into, or sold or distributed in the Commonwealth in violation of this chapter shall be deemed contraband and shall be subject to seizure, forfeiture and destruction. Such cigarettes shall be deemed contraband whether or not the violation of this chapter is with knowledge.
(Added by L.2000 chs. 880, 901, eff. 7/1/2000.)

SUBTITLE II
TAXES ADMINISTERED BY OTHER AGENCIES
(Selected Chapters)

CHAPTER 22
VIRGINIA FUELS TAX ACT
(Added by L.2000 chs. 729, 758, eff. 1/1/2001.)
(Selected Articles)

ARTICLE 9
DISPOSITION OF TAX REVENUES
(Complete Article)

§58.1-2289. Disposition of tax revenue generally.
(Section effective 1/1/2001.)

A. Unless otherwise provided in this section, all taxes and fees, including civil penalties, collected by the Commissioner pursuant to this chapter, less a reasonable amount to be allocated for refunds, shall be promptly paid into the state treasury and shall constitute special funds within the Commonwealth Transportation Fund. Any balances remaining in these funds at the end of the year shall be available for use in subsequent years for the purposes set forth in this chapter, and any interest income on such funds shall accrue to these funds. Except as provided in §33.1-23.03:1, no portion of the revenue derived from taxes collected pursuant to §§58.1-2217, 58.1-2249 or §58.1-2701, and remaining after authorized refunds for nonhighway use of fuel, shall be used for any purpose other than the construction, reconstruction or maintenance of the roads and projects comprising the State Highway System, the Interstate System and the secondary system of state highways and expenditures directly and necessarily required for such purposes, including the retirement of revenue bonds.

Revenues collected under this chapter may be also used for (i) contributions toward the construction, reconstruction or maintenance of streets in cities and towns of such sums as may be provided by law and (ii) expenditures for the operation and maintenance of the Department of Transportation, the Department of Rail and Public Transportation, the Department of Aviation, the Virginia Port Authority, and the Department of Motor Vehicles as may be provided by law.

The Governor is hereby authorized to transfer out of such fund an amount necessary for the inspection of gasoline and motor grease measuring and distributing equipment, and for the inspection and analysis of gasoline for purity.

B. The tax collected on each gallon of aviation fuel sold and delivered or used in this Commonwealth, less refunds, shall be paid into a special fund of the state treasury. Proceeds of this special fund within the Commonwealth Transportation Fund shall be disbursed upon order of the Department of Aviation, on warrants of the Comptroller, to defray the cost of the administration of the laws of this Commonwealth relating to aviation, for the construction, maintenance and improvement of airports and landing fields to which the public now has or which it is proposed shall have access, and for the promotion of aviation in the interest of operators and the public generally.

C. One-half cent of the tax collected on each gallon of fuel on which the refund has been paid at the rate of seventeen cents per gallon, or in the case of diesel fuel, fifteen and one-half cents per gallon, for fuel consumed in tractors and unlicensed equipment used for agricultural purposes shall be paid into a special fund of the state treasury, known as the Virginia Agricultural Foundation Fund, to be disbursed to make certain refunds and defray the costs of the research and educational phases of the agricultural program, including supplemental salary payments to certain employees at Virginia Polytechnic Institute and State University, the Department of Agriculture and Consumer Services and the Virginia Truck and Ornamentals Research Station, including reasonable expenses of the Virginia Agricultural Council.

D. One and one-half cents of the tax collected on each gallon of fuel used to propel a commercial watercraft upon which a refund has been paid shall be paid to the credit of the Game Protection Fund of the state treasury to be made available to the Board of Game and Inland Fisheries until expended for the purposes provided generally in subsection C of §29.1-701, including acquisition, construction, improvement and maintenance of public boating access areas on the public waters of this Commonwealth and for other activities and purposes of direct benefit and interest to the boating public and for no other purpose. However, one and one-half cents per gallon on fuel used by commercial fishing, oystering, clamming, and crabbing boats shall be paid to the Department of Transportation to be used for the construction, repair, improvement and maintenance of the public docks of this Commonwealth used by said commercial watercraft. Any expenditures for the acquisition, construction, improvement and maintenance of the public docks shall be made according to a plan developed by the Virginia Marine Resources Commission.

From the tax collected pursuant to the provisions of this chapter from the sales of gasoline used for the propelling of watercraft, after deduction for lawful refunds, there shall be paid into the state treasury for use by the Marine Resources Commission, the Virginia Soil and Water Conservation Board, the State Water Control Board, and the Commonwealth Transportation Board to (i) improve the public docks as specified in this section, (ii) improve commercial and sports fisheries in Virginia's tidal waters, (iii) make environmental improvements including, without limitation, fisheries management and habitat enhancement in the Chesapeake and its tributaries, and (iv) further the purposes set forth in §33.1-223, a sum as established by the General Assembly.

E. Notwithstanding other provisions of this section, there shall be transferred from moneys collected pursuant to this section to a special fund within the Commonwealth Transportation Fund in the state treasury, to be used to meet the necessary expenses of the Department of Motor Vehicles, an amount equal to one percent of a sum to be calculated as follows: the tax revenues collected pursuant to this chapter, at the tax rates in effect on December 31, 1986, less refunds authorized by this chapter and less taxes collected for aviation fuels.

(Added by L.2000 chs. 729, 758, eff. 1/1/2001.)

ARTICLE 10
FLOORSTOCKS TAX
(Complete Article)

§58.1-2290. Floorstocks tax.
(Section effective 1/1/2001.)

A. There is hereby levied a floorstocks tax on taxable motor fuel and alternative fuel held in storage as of the close of the business day preceding January 1, 2001. For the purposes of this section, "close of the business day" means the time at which the last transaction has occurred for that day. The floorstocks tax shall be payable by the person in possession of the fuel on January 1, 2001. The amount of the floorstocks tax on motor fuel shall be equal to the sum of (i) the tax rate specified by §58.1-2217 for the type of fuel and (ii) the storage tank fee rate specified under §62.1-44.34:13, multiplied by the gallons in storage as of the close of the business day preceding January 1, 2001. The amount of the floorstocks tax on alternative fuel shall be equal to the tax rate specified by subsection A of §58.1-2249, multiplied by the gallons in storage as of the close of the business day preceding January 1, 2001.

B. Persons in possession of taxable fuel in storage as of the close of the business day preceding January 1, 2001, shall:

1. Take an inventory at the close of the business day preceding January 1, 2001, to determine the gallons in storage for purposes of determining the floorstocks tax;

2. Report the gallons listed in subsection A, on forms provided by the Commissioner, not later than February 1, 2001; and

3. Remit the tax levied under this section no later than July 1, 2001.

In the event the tax due is paid to the Department on or before February 1, 2001, the person remitting the tax may deduct from their submission ten percent of the tax liability due.

C. In determining the amount of floorstocks tax due under this section, the person may exclude the amount of taxable motor fuel in dead storage. "Dead storage" means the amount of taxable motor fuel that will not be pumped out of a storage tank because the fuel is below the mouth of the draw pipe. Such person may assume that the amount of motor fuel in dead storage is 200 gallons for a tank with a capacity of less than 10,000 gallons and 400 gallons for a tank with a capacity of 10,000 gallons or more. Alternatively, the amount of motor fuel in dead storage in a tank may be computed by using the manufacturer's conversion table for the tank and number of inches between the bottom of the tank and the mouth of the draw pipe. If the conversion table method is used to compute the amount of motor fuel in dead storage, the distance between the bottom of the tank and the mouth of the draw pipe will be assumed to be six inches, unless otherwise established.

(Added by L.2000 chs. 729, 758, eff. 1/1/2001.)

CHAPTER 27
ROAD TAX ON MOTOR CARRIERS
(Complete Chapter)

§58.1-2700. Definitions.

Whenever used in this chapter, the term:

"Carrier" means a person who operates or causes to be operated a commercial highway vehicle on any highway in the Commonwealth.

"Department" means the Department of Motor Vehicles, acting through its officers and agents.

"Identification marker" means a decal issued by the Department to show that a vehicle operated by a carrier is properly registered with the Department for the payment of the road tax.

"IFTA" means the International Fuel Tax Agreement, as entered into by the Department, and as amended by the International Fuel Tax Association, Inc.

"Licensee" means a carrier who holds an uncancelled IFTA license issued by the Commonwealth.

"Motor carrier" means every person, firm or corporation who owns or operates or causes to be operated on any highway in this Commonwealth any qualified highway vehicle.

"Operations" means the physical activities of all such vehicles, whether loaded or empty, whether for compensation or not for compensation, and whether owned by or leased to the motor carrier who operates them or causes them to be operated.

"Qualified highway vehicle" means a highway vehicle used, designed, or maintained for transportation of persons or property that (i) has two axles and a gross vehicle weight or registered gross vehicle weight exceeding 26,000 pounds or 11,797 kilograms, (ii) has three or more axles regardless of weight, or (iii) is used in combination, when the weight of such combination exceeds 26,000 pounds or 11,797 kilograms gross vehicle or registered gross vehicle weight. "Qualified highway vehicle" does not include recreational vehicles.

"Tractor truck" means every motor vehicle designed and used primarily for drawing other vehicles and not so constructed as to carry a load other than a part of the load and weight of the vehicle attached thereto.

"Truck" means every motor vehicle designed to transport property on its own structure independent of any other vehicle and having a registered gross weight in excess of 7,500 pounds.

(Chgd. by L.1995 chs. 744, 803; L.1996 ch. 575; L.1997 ch. 283, eff. 7/1/97.)

§58.1-2700.1. Interstate motor carrier road tax.

In accordance with the provisions of IFTA, as amended, the Department shall issue a license and vehicle identification markers to each carrier that operates qualified highway vehicles in the Commonwealth and at least one other jurisdiction participating in IFTA so as to report its road tax liabilities. The Department shall issue vehicle identification markers to carriers that operate qualified highway vehicles in the Commonwealth solely, or in the Commonwealth and at least one other jurisdiction not participating in IFTA. Each application shall contain the name and address of the carrier, and such other information as may be required by the Department.

The Department shall issue to the motor carrier identification markers for each vehicle in the carrier's fleet that will be operated within the Commonwealth.

The identification markers issued to the vehicles of the IFTA-licensed carriers shall expire on December 31 of each year. All other identification markers issued to carriers shall expire on June 30 of each year. The identification markers may be renewed prior to expiration provided (i) the carrier's privilege to operate vehicles in the Commonwealth has not been revoked or canceled, (ii) all required tax reports have been filed, and (iii) all road taxes, penalties, and interest due have been paid.

The cost of the identification markers issued to each vehicle in the carrier's fleet shall be ten dollars per vehicle.

In an emergency, the Department may, by letter, telegram, or other electronic means, authorize a vehicle to be operated without identification markers for not more than ten days. Before sending such authorization, the Department shall collect from the carrier a fee of twenty dollars for each vehicle so operated.

(Added by L.1995 chs. 744, 803; chgd. by L.1996 ch. 575, eff. 4/4/96.)

§58.1-2700.2. Placement of identification markers.

All carriers licensed by the Department shall place the identification markers issued by the Department on each vehicle in the carrier's fleet in the place prescribed by the Department.

(Added by L.1995 chs. 744, 803, eff. 7/1/95.)

§58.1-2700.3. Waiver in emergency situations.

The Department shall have the authority to waive the requirements of this title for vehicles under emergency conditions.

(Added by L.1995 chs. 744, 803, eff. 7/1/95.)

§58.1-2701. Amount of tax.

Every motor carrier [of property] shall pay a road tax equivalent to nineteen and one-half cents per gallon calculated on the amount of motor fuel, diesel fuel or liquefied gases (which would not exist as liquids at a temperature of sixty degrees [F.] *Fahrenheit* and a pressure of 14.7 pounds per square inch absolute), used in its operations within the Commonwealth.

The tax imposed by this chapter shall be in addition to all other taxes of whatever character imposed on a motor carrier by any other provision of law.

All taxes and fees paid under the provisions of this chapter shall be credited to the Highway Maintenance and Operating Fund, a special fund within the Commonwealth Transportation Fund.

(Chgd. by L.1996 ch. 575; L.1997 ch. 423; L.2000 chs. 729, 758, eff. 1/1/2001. Matter in brackets eff. only until 1/1/2001. Matter in italics eff. 1/1/2001.)

§58.1-2702. Exemptions and exceptions.

The provisions of this chapter shall not apply to a person, firm or corporation owning or operating:

1. [A single recreational vehicle] *Recreational vehicles, as defined in the provisions of the International Fuel Tax Agreement (IFTA)*;
2. The first two Virginia-licensed trucks and tractor trucks, if used exclusively for farm use as defined in §46.2-698 and if not licensed in any other state;
3. Qualified highway vehicles of a licensed highway vehicle dealer when operated without compensation for purposes incident to a sale or for demonstration; or
4. Any highway vehicle owned and operated by the United States, the District of Columbia, the Commonwealth of Virginia or any municipality or any other political subdivision of the Commonwealth, or any other state.

(Chgd. by L.1995 chs. 744, 803; L.1996 ch. 575; L.1997 ch. 283; L.2000 chs. 729, 758, eff. 1/1/2001. Matter in brackets eff. only until 1/1/2001. Matter in italics eff. 1/1/2001.)

§58.1-2703. Payment of tax.

The tax imposed under §58.1-2701 shall be paid by each motor carrier quarterly to the State Treasurer on or before the last day of April, July, October and January of each year and calculated upon the amount of gasoline or other motor fuel used in its operations within the Commonwealth by each such carrier during the quarter ending with the last day of the preceding month.

§58.1-2704. How amount of fuel used in the Commonwealth ascertained.

On or after October 1, 1992, the amount of gasoline or other motor fuel used in the operations of any motor carrier in the Commonwealth shall be determined by dividing the total number of miles traveled within the Commonwealth by such carrier's vehicles during a calendar quarter by a consumption factor, such factor being comprised of the total number of miles traveled by all vehicles of the motor carrier during the quarter divided by the total amount of gasoline or other motor fuel used in its entire operations during such quarter.

§58.1-2705. Reports of carriers.

Every motor carrier subject to the tax imposed by this chapter or filing under the terms of the International Fuel Tax Agreement shall, on or before the last day of April, July, October and January of every year, make to the Department or proper agency pursuant to the International Fuel Tax Agreement such reports of its operations during the quarter ending the last day of the preceding month as the Department may require and such other reports from time to time as the Department may deem necessary.

(Chgd. by L.1995 chs. 744, 803, eff. 1/1/96.)

§58.1-2706. Credit for payment of motor fuel, diesel fuel or liquefied gases tax.

A. Every motor carrier subject to the road tax shall be entitled to a credit on such tax equivalent to sixteen cents per gallon on all motor fuel, diesel fuel and liquefied gases purchased by such carrier within the Commonwealth for use in its operations either within or without the Commonwealth and upon which the motor fuel, diesel fuel or liquefied gases tax imposed by the laws of the Commonwealth has been paid by such carrier. Evidence of the payment of such tax in such form as may be required by, or is satisfactory to, the Department shall be furnished by each carrier claiming the credit herein allowed.

B. When the amount of the credit to which any motor carrier is entitled for any quarter exceeds the amount of the tax for which such carrier is liable for the same quarter, the excess may: (i) be allowed as a credit on the tax for which such carrier would be otherwise liable for any of the eight succeeding quarters or (ii) be refunded, upon application, duly verified and presented and supported by such evidence as may be satisfactory to the Department.

C. The Department may allow a refund upon receipt of proper application and review. It shall be at the discretion of the Department to determine whether an audit is required.

D. The refund may be allowed without a formal hearing if the amount of refund is agreed to by the applicant. Otherwise, a formal hearing on the application shall be held by the Department after notice of not less than ten days to the applicant and the Attorney General.

E. Whenever any refund is ordered it shall be paid out of the Highway Maintenance and Construction Fund.

F. Whenever a person operating under lease to a motor carrier to perform transport services on behalf of the carrier purchases motor fuel, diesel fuel or liquefied gases relating to such services, such payments or purchases may, at the discretion of the Department, be considered payment or purchases by the carrier.
(Chgd. by L.1995 chs. 744, 803; L.1996 ch. 575; L.1999 ch. 94, eff. 7/1/99.)

§58.1-2707. Refunds to motor carriers who give bond.

A motor carrier not operating as an IFTA licensee may be required to give a surety company bond in the amount of not less than $2,000, as shall appear sufficient in the discretion of the Department, payable to the Commonwealth and conditioned that the carrier will pay all taxes due and to become due under this chapter from the date of the bond to the date when either the carrier or the bonding company notifies the Department that the bond has been canceled. The surety shall be a corporation authorized to write surety bonds in Virginia. So long as the bond remains in force the Department may order refunds to the motor carrier in the amounts appearing to be due on applications duly filed by the carrier under this chapter (§58.1-2700 et seq.) without first auditing the records of the carrier. The surety shall be liable for all omitted taxes assessed pursuant to §58.1-2025 against the carrier, including the penalties and interest provided in such section, even though the assessment is made after cancellation of the bond, but only for taxes due and payable while the bond was in force and penalties and interest on the taxes.
(Chgd. by L.1995 chs. 744, 803, eff. 7/1/95.)

§58.1-2708. Inspection of books and records.

The Department and its authorized agents and representatives shall have the right at any reasonable time to inspect the books and records of any motor carrier subject to the tax imposed by this chapter.
(Chgd. by L.1995 chs. 744, 803, eff. 7/1/95.)

§58.1-2709. Penalties.

The Department may, after a hearing had upon notice, duly served not less than ten days prior to the date set for such hearing, impose a penalty, which shall be in addition to any other penalty imposed by this chapter, not exceeding $2,500, upon any non-IFTA-licensed motor carrier violating any provision of this chapter, or failing to comply with any regulation of the Department promulgated pursuant to this chapter. Each such failure or violation shall constitute a separate offense. The penalty shall be collectible by the process of the Department as provided by law. Any person against whom an order or decision of the Commissioner has been adversely rendered relating to the tax imposed by this chapter may, within fifteen days of such order or decision, appeal from such an order or decision to the Circuit Court of the City of Richmond. In addition to imposing such penalty, or without imposing any penalty, the Department may suspend or revoke any certificate, permit or other evidence of right issued by the Department which the motor carrier holds.
(Chgd. by L.1995 chs. 744, 803, eff. 7/1/95.)

§58.1-2710. Penalty for false statements.

Any person who willfully and knowingly makes a false statement orally, or in writing, or in the form of a receipt for the sale of motor fuel, for the purpose of obtaining or attempting to obtain or to assist any other person, partnership or corporation to obtain or attempt to obtain a credit or refund or reduction of liability for taxes under this chapter shall be guilty of a Class 1 misdemeanor.

§58.1-2711. Assistance of Department of Taxation.

At the request of the Department, the Department of Taxation shall furnish the Department the amount of deduction from income taken by any person conducting business as a motor carrier as defined in §58.1-2700 on account of the purchase of motor fuel, diesel fuel or liquefied gases.
(Chgd. by L.1995 chs. 744, 803; L.1996 ch. 575, eff. 4/4/96.)

§58.1-2712.1. International Fuel Tax Agreement.

The Department may, with the approval of the Governor, enter into the International Fuel Tax Agreement for interstate motor carriers and abide by the requirements set forth in the Agreement. All requirements of the Agreement shall also apply to motor carriers operating in intrastate commerce unless specific requirements are determined by the Department to be not in the best interest of the motor carrier industry.
(Added by L.1995 chs. 744, 803, eff. 7/1/95.)

SUBTITLE IV
OTHER SOURCES OF STATE REVENUE
(Selected Chapter)

CHAPTER 40
STATE LOTTERY LAW
(Selected Sections)

§58.1-4003. State Lottery Department established.

Notwithstanding the provisions of Article 1 (§18.2-325 et seq.) of Chapter 8 of Title 18.2 or any other provision of law, there is hereby established as an independent agency of the Commonwealth, exclusive of the legislative, executive or judicial branches of government, a State Lottery Department, which shall include a Director and a State Lottery Board for the purpose of operating a state lottery.

§58.1-4008. Employees of the Department; background investigations of employees.

All persons employed by the Department shall be fingerprinted before, and as a condition of, employment. These fingerprints shall be submitted to the Federal Bureau of Investigation for a National Criminal Records search and to the Department of State Police for a Virginia Criminal History Records search. All board members, officers and employees of any vendor to the State Lottery Department of lottery on-line or instant ticket goods or services working directly on a contract with the Lottery Department for such goods or services shall be subject to a National Criminal Records search conducted by the chief security officer of the State Lottery Department. A background investigation shall be conducted by the chief security officer of the State Lottery Department

 Zv

on every applicant prior to employment by the Department. However, all division directors of the State Lottery Department and employees of the State Lottery Department performing duties primarily related to security matters shall be subject to a background investigation report conducted by the Department of State Police prior to employment by the Department. The Department of State Police shall be reimbursed by the State Lottery Department for the cost of investigations conducted pursuant to this section or §58.1-4005. No person who has been convicted of a felony, bookmaking or other forms of illegal gambling, or of a crime involving moral turpitude shall be employed by the Department or on contracts with vendors described in this section.

§58.1-4009. Licensing of lottery sales agents; penalty.

A. No license as an agent to sell lottery tickets or shares shall be issued to any person to engage in business primarily as a lottery sales agent. Before issuing such license the Director shall consider such factors as (i) the financial responsibility and security of the person and his business or activity; (ii) the accessibility of his place of business or activity to the public; (iii) the sufficiency of existing licensees to serve the public convenience; and (iv) the volume of expected sales.

B. For the purposes of this section, the term "person" means an individual, association, partnership, corporation, club, trust, estate, society, company, joint stock company, receiver, trustee, assignee, referee, or any other person acting in a fiduciary or representative capacity, whether appointed by a court or otherwise, and any combination of individuals. "Person" also means all departments, commissions, agencies and instrumentalities of the Commonwealth, including counties, cities, municipalities, agencies and instrumentalities thereof.

C. The chief security officer of the State Lottery Department shall conduct a background investigation, to include a National Criminal Records search and a Virginia Criminal History Records search, on applicants for licensure as lottery sales agents. The Director may refuse to issue a license to operate as an agent to sell lottery tickets or shares to any person who has been (i) convicted of a crime involving moral turpitude, (ii) convicted of bookmaking or other forms of illegal gambling, (iii) found guilty of any fraud or misrepresentation in any connection, or (iv) convicted of a felony. The Director may refuse to grant a license or may suspend, revoke or refuse to renew a license issued pursuant to this chapter to a partnership or corporation, if he determines that any general or limited partner, or officer or director of such partnership or corporation has been (i) convicted of a crime involving moral turpitude, (ii) convicted of bookmaking or other forms of illegal gambling, (iii) found guilty of any fraud or misrepresentation in any connection or (iv) convicted of a felony. Whoever knowingly and willfully falsifies, conceals or misrepresents a material fact or knowingly and willfully makes a false, fictitious or fraudulent statement or representation in any application for licensure to the State Lottery Department for lottery sales agent, shall be guilty of a Class 1 misdemeanor.

D. Prior to issuance of a license, every lottery sales agent shall be bonded by a surety company entitled to do business in this Commonwealth in such amount and penalty as may be prescribed by the regulations of the Department, payable to the State Lottery Department and conditioned upon the faithful performance of his duties.

E. Every licensed agent shall prominently display his license, or a copy thereof, as provided in the regulations of the Department.

§58.1-4014. Price of tickets or shares; who may sell; penalty.

A. No person shall sell a ticket or share at any price or at any location other than that fixed by rules and regulations of the Department. No person other than a licensed lottery sales agent or his employee shall sell lottery tickets or shares, except that nothing in this section shall be construed to prevent any person from giving lottery tickets or shares to another person over the age of eighteen years as a gift.

B. Any person convicted of violating this section shall be guilty of a Class 1 misdemeanor.

§58.1-4015. Sale of ticket or share to person under eighteen prohibited; penalty.

No ticket or share shall be sold to or redeemed from any person under the age of eighteen years. Any licensee who knowingly sells or offers to sell or redeem a lottery ticket or share to or from any person under the age of eighteen years is guilty of a Class 1 misdemeanor.

§58.1-4016. Gift to minor prohibited.

No ticket or share shall be given as a gift or otherwise to any person under the age of eighteen years. Any person who knowingly gives a lottery ticket or share to any person under the age of eighteen years is guilty of a Class 3 misdemeanor.

§58.1-4017. Alteration and forgery; presentation of counterfeit or altered ticket or share; penalty.

Any person who forges, alters or fraudulently makes any lottery ticket or share with intent to present for payment or to transfer to another person to be presented for payment or knowingly presents for payment or transfers to another person to be presented for payment such forged, altered or fraudulently made counterfeit lottery ticket or share sold pursuant to this chapter is guilty of a Class 6 felony.

§58.1-4018. Prohibited actions; penalty.

Any person who wrongfully and fraudulently uses, disposes of, conceals or embezzles any public money or funds associated with the operation of the lottery shall be guilty of a Class 2 felony. Any person who wrongfully and fraudulently tampers with any equipment or machinery used in the operation of the lottery shall be guilty of a Class 2 felony. Any person who makes inaccurate entries regarding a financial accounting of the lottery in order to conceal the truth, defraud the Commonwealth and obtain money to which he is not entitled shall be guilty of a Class 2 felony.

§58.1-4019. Certain persons ineligible to purchase tickets or shares or receive prizes.

A. No ticket or share shall be purchased by, and no prize shall be paid on a ticket purchased by or transferred to, any Board member, officer or employee of the lottery, or any board member, officer or employee of any vendor to the lottery of lottery on-line or instant ticket goods or services working directly on a contract with the Department for such goods or services, or any person residing in the same household of such member, officer or employee or any person under the age of eighteen years, or transferee of any such persons.

B. Only natural persons may purchase lottery tickets and claim prize winnings. In all cases, the identity and social security number of all natural persons who receive a prize greater than $100 from a winning ticket redeemed at any Department office shall be provided in order to comply with this section and §§58.1-4015, 58.1-4016 and 58.1-4026, and Chapter 13 (§63.1-249 et seq.) of Title 63.1.
(Chgd. by L.1999 ch. 34, eff. 7/1/99.)

 Zv

§58.1-4019.1. License required for "instant ticket" games or contests.

No person who owns or is employed by any retail establishment in the Commonwealth shall use any "instant ticket" game or contest for the purpose of promoting or furthering the sale of any product without first obtaining a license to do so from the Director. For the purposes of this section, an "instant ticket" game or contest means a game of chance played on a paper ticket or card where (i) a person may receive gifts, prizes, or gratuities and (ii) winners are determined by preprinted concealed letters, numbers, or symbols which, when exposed, reveal immediately whether the player has won a prize or entry into a prize drawing, but shall not include any "instant ticket" game or contest licensed by the Charitable Gaming Commission pursuant to Article 1.1:1 (§18.2-340.15 et seq.) of Title 18.2. The fact that no purchase is required in order to participate shall not exclude such game or contest from the provisions of this section; however, nothing in this section shall prohibit any retail establishment from using a Virginia lottery ticket to promote or further the sale of any products except those having both a federal and state excise tax placed on them. Any person convicted of a violation of this section shall be guilty of a Class 3 misdemeanor.

(Added by L.1996 chs. 462, 505, eff. 4/1/96.)

TITLE 59.1
TRADE AND COMMERCE
(Selected Chapters)

Chapter
4.1. Remedies for Violations of Preceding Chapters and Chapter 6, Article 8, of Title 18.2. (Secs. 59.1-68.2 to 59.1-68.5)
4.2. Conspiracy to Rig Bids to Government. (Secs. 59.1-68.6 to 59.1-68.8)
5. Transacting Business Under Assumed Name. (Secs. 59.1-69 to 59.1-75)
10. Explosives. (Secs. 59.1-137 to 59.1-141)
11. Fireworks. (Secs. 59.1-142 to 59.1-148)
11.1. Firearms. (Sec. 59.1-148.1 to 59.1-148.4)

CHAPTER 4.1
REMEDIES FOR VIOLATIONS OF PRECEDING CHAPTERS AND CHAPTER 6, ARTICLE 8, OF TITLE 18.2
(Complete Chapter)

Section
59.1-68.2. Authority of Attorney General.
59.1-68.3. Action for damages or penalty for violation of Article 8, Chapter 6 of Title 18.2 or Chapter 2.1 of Title 59.1; attorney's fees.
59.1-68.4. Suits by Commonwealth's attorneys and city and county attorneys.
59.1-68.5. Further provisions as to actions for violation of Article 8, Chapter 6 of Title 18.2.

§59.1-68.2. Authority of Attorney General.

Notwithstanding any other provisions of the law to the contrary, the Attorney General may investigate and bring an action in the name of the Commonwealth to enjoin any violation of Chapters 2.1 (§59.1-21.1 et seq.) through 3.1 (§59.1-41.1 et seq.) and of Article 8 (§18.2-214 et seq.), Chapter 6 of Title 18.2 of this Code.

§59.1-68.3. Action for damages or penalty for violation of Article 8, Chapter 6 of Title 18.2 or Chapter 2.1 of Title 59.1; attorney's fees.

Any person who suffers loss as the result of a violation of Article 8 (§18.2-214 et seq.), Chapter 6 of Title 18.2 or Chapter 2.1 (§59.1-21.1 et seq.) of Title 59.1 of this Code shall be entitled to bring an individual action to recover damages, or $100, whichever is greater. Certified copies of the transcript and exhibits in evidence in any final proceeding in which the Attorney General has obtained a permanent injunction for a violation of Article 8, Chapter 6 of Title 18.2 or Chapter 2.1 of Title 59.1 shall be admissible in evidence in any action brought pursuant to this section by any person claiming damage as a result of the enjoined conduct. Notwithstanding any other provision of law to the contrary, in addition to the damages recovered by the aggrieved party, such person may be awarded reasonable attorney's fees.

§59.1-68.4. Suits by Commonwealth's attorneys and city and county attorneys.

Notwithstanding any other provisions of the law to the contrary, any Commonwealth's attorney, or the attorney for any city or county, may investigate and cause to be brought suit in the name of the Commonwealth, or of the county or city, to enjoin any violation of Chapter 2.1 (§59.1-21.1 et seq.) of this title and of Article 8 (§18.2-214 et seq.), Chapter 6 of Title 18.2 of this Code. The court having jurisdiction may enjoin such violations notwithstanding the existence of an adequate remedy at law. In any action under this section, it shall not be necessary that damages be alleged or proved.

§59.1-68.5. Further provisions as to actions for violation of Article 8, Chapter 6 of Title 18.2.

Any person who suffers loss as the result of a violation of Article 8 (§18.2-214 et seq.), Chapter 6 of Title 18.2 of this Code shall be entitled to bring an individual action to recover damages, or $100, whichever is greater. Certified copies of the transcript and exhibits in evidence in any final proceeding in which the Commonwealth, or a county or city has obtained a permanent injunction for a violation of Article 8, Chapter 6 of Title 18.2 shall be admissible in evidence in any action brought pursuant to this section by any person claiming damage as a result of the enjoined conduct. Notwithstanding any other provision of law to the contrary, in addition to the damages recovered by the aggrieved party, such person may be awarded reasonable attorney's fees.

CHAPTER 4.2
CONSPIRACY TO RIG BIDS TO GOVERNMENT
(Complete Chapter)

Section
59.1-68.6. Definitions.
59.1-68.7. Combinations to rig bids.
59.1-68.8. Enforcement.

§59.1-68.6. Definitions.

As used in this chapter, unless the text indicates otherwise:

1. "Person" means any individual, firm, partnership or corporation;

2. "Governmental units" means all state agencies and all political subdivisions or agencies thereof;

3. "Bid" means any submission of a price, whether written or oral, for any goods, services or construction to be provided.

§59.1-68.7. Combinations to rig bids.

A. Any combination, conspiracy or agreement to intentionally rig, alter or otherwise manipulate, or to cause to be rigged, altered or otherwise manipulated any bid submitted to the Commonwealth of Virginia or any governmental unit for the purpose of allocating purchases or sales to or among persons, raising or otherwise fixing the prices of the goods or services, or excluding other persons from dealing with the Commonwealth or any other governmental unit shall be unlawful.

B. Any person violating this section shall be guilty of a Class 6 felony.

§59.1-68.8. Enforcement.

The Attorney General of Virginia, with respect to state agencies only, shall have concurrent power and authority to investigate and prosecute any violation of §59.1-68.7. In addition, the Commonwealth's attorneys of the several counties and cities shall retain the power and authority to prosecute any and all violations of §59.1-68.7 occurring within their jurisdiction.

CHAPTER 5
TRANSACTING BUSINESS UNDER ASSUMED NAME
(Selected Sections)

§59.1-69. Certificate required of person, partnership, limited liability company or corporation transacting business under assumed name.

A. No person, partnership, limited liability company or corporation shall conduct or transact business in this Commonwealth under any assumed or fictitious name unless such person, partnership, limited liability company or corporation shall sign and acknowledge a certificate setting forth the name under which such business is to be conducted or transacted, and the names of each person, partnership, limited liability company or corporation owning the same, with their respective post-office and residence addresses (and, when (i) the partnership or limited liability company is a foreign limited partnership or limited liability company, the date of the certificate of registration to transact business in this Commonwealth issued to it by the State Corporation Commission, or (ii) when the corporation is a foreign corporation, the date of the certificate of authority to transact business in this Commonwealth issued to it by the State Corporation Commission), and file the same in the office of the clerk of the court in which deeds are recorded in the county or corporation wherein the business is to be conducted.

B. No person, partnership, limited liability company or corporation shall use an assumed or fictitious name in the conduct of its business to intentionally misrepresent the geographic origin or location of any such person or entity.
(Chgd. by L.1995 ch. 168; L.1996 ch. 904, eff. 7/1/96.)

§59.1-70. Limited partnership, limited liability company or corporation to file copy of certificate with State Corporation Commission; fee; release certificate.

A. When business is conducted in this Commonwealth under an assumed or fictitious name by a limited partnership filing a certificate under §50-73.11, by a foreign limited partnership required to register with the Commission under §50-73.54, or by a limited liability company or corporation, such domestic or foreign limited partnership, limited liability company or corporation shall file in the office of the clerk of the State Corporation Commission a copy of the certificate described in §59.1-69, duly attested by the clerk of the court in which the original is on file. The State Corporation Commission shall charge a ten-dollar fee for the filing of a fictitious or an assumed name.

B. When business is no longer conducted in this Commonwealth under an assumed or fictitious name by a limited partnership filing a certificate under §50-73.11, by a foreign limited partnership required to register with the Commission under §50-73.54, or by a limited liability company or corporation, the domestic or foreign limited partnership, limited liability company or corporation may file with the clerk of the State Corporation Commission a copy of a release certificate, duly attested by the clerk of the court in which the certificate is on file. The Commission shall charge a ten-dollar fee for the filing of such certificate.
(Chgd. by L.1995 ch. 168, eff. 7/1/95.)

§59.1-71. Filing power of attorney for service of process.

Persons owning and transacting business as set out in this chapter who do not reside in the county or city in which a place of business is operated, shall, before commencing to do business in such city or county, by written power of attorney, appoint some practicing attorney-at-law residing in the Commonwealth as its attorney or agent, upon whom all legal processes against the owner may be served and who shall be authorized to enter an appearance in its own behalf. The power of attorney, together with an acknowledgment of acceptance of the power by the attorney, shall be recorded in the clerk's office in which deeds are recorded, of the county or city wherein the place of business is located. Such power of attorney shall remain effective until lawfully revoked. When lawfully revoked, a new power of attorney to the same or some other attorney, acknowledged by that attorney, shall be immediately executed and recorded. Written notice of the resignation of the attorney, or of the voluntary revocation of such power of attorney by the owner, shall be forthwith filed in the clerk's office where it is recorded. The power of attorney shall remain effective until such time as notice of revocation is recorded with the clerk. For such services rendered, the clerk shall receive the same fee as prescribed in §14.1-112.

§59.1-72. Service of process upon clerk of court.

If there be no such attorney in fact residing in such county or city, or if for any reason such attorney in fact be not subject to personal service,. then all legal processes against such owner may be served upon the clerk of the court of such county or city wherein such place of business is located having jurisdiction of the suit, action or proceeding. When process or notice is so served under the provisions of this chapter, upon the clerk of the court of the county or city wherein is located the place of business, such clerk upon whom such process or notice is served shall forthwith mail a copy of such process or notice to the defendant or defendants therein named at such address, if any, as may have been filed, of the owner, with such clerk. And such clerk shall certify in such papers in the cause the fact of mailing such process or notice, and the address to which it was mailed, or that no such address is on file.

Such process or notice when so served and certified to have been so mailed, or if no such address has been filed, the services as herein provided alone shall constitute personal service, and authorize a judgment or decree in personam against such owner.

§59.1-74. Recordation of certificate and registration of names.

The clerk with whom the certificate provided for in §59.1-69 is filed shall keep a book in which all such certificates shall be recorded, with their date of record, and shall keep a register in which shall be entered in alphabetical order the name under which every such business is conducted, the name of the statutory agent, and the names of every person owning the same. The clerk shall be entitled to a fee of ten dollars for filing and recording such certificate and entering such names. No license shall be issued by the Commissioner of the Revenue until the certificate has been made and filed in the clerk's office and evidence of same produced before him.

§59.1-75. Penalty for violation.

Any person violating any of the provisions of this chapter shall be guilty of a misdemeanor and, upon conviction, shall be punished by a fine not exceeding $2,500 or by confinement in jail for not more than one year, or both.

CHAPTER 10
EXPLOSIVES
(Complete Chapter)

§59.1-137. Definition.

Whenever used in this chapter:

"Explosives" means any chemical compound, mechanical mixture or device the primary or common purpose of which is to function by explosion, The term includes, but is not limited to dynamite and other high explosives, black blasting powder, pellet powder, initiating explosives, blasting caps, electric blasting caps, detonators, safety fuse, fuse igniters, fuse lighters, squibs, cordeau detonant fuse, instantaneous fuse, detonating cord, igniter cord, igniters and those materials included in the list published annually in the Federal Register by the Department of the Treasury pursuant to the Organized Crime Control Act of 1970 (18 U.S.C. §841 et seq.)

§59.1-138. Record of sales required; signing by purchasers; sales to persons under eighteen prohibited.

(a) Any person selling any explosive covered by this chapter shall keep a record of all such explosives sold, showing the kind and quantity sold, the name and address of the purchaser, and the date of each sale. The person selling such explosives shall also require any person purchasing such explosives to sign such record at the time of such purchase.

(b) No person shall sell, deliver, give away, or otherwise dispose of any explosives to any individual under eighteen years of age, whether such individual is acting for himself, herself, or for any other person.

§59.1-139. Persons possessing explosives to give notice of theft.

Any person having in his possession any explosives covered by this chapter shall immediately notify the sheriff of the county or the police officials of the city in which any such explosives are being stored or used in the event that any such explosives are stolen.

§59.1-140. Effect of chapter upon municipal regulation.

Nothing contained in this chapter shall:

Affect any existing ordinance, rule or regulation of any city or municipality in this Commonwealth that is not less restrictive than this chapter; or affect, modify or limit the power of such cities or municipalities to make ordinances, rules or regulations not less restrictive than this chapter, governing the storage, possession, sale and use of explosives within their respective corporate limits.

§59.1-141. Penalty.

Any person who violates any provision of this chapter shall be guilty of a misdemeanor and, upon conviction thereof, be punished accordingly.

CHAPTER 11
FIREWORKS
(Complete Chapter)

§59.1-142. When manufacture, transportation, sale, etc., of fireworks unlawful.

A. Except as otherwise provided in this chapter, it shall be unlawful for any person, firm or corporation to transport, manufacture, store, sell, offer for sale, expose for sale, or to buy, use, ignite or explode any firecracker, torpedo, skyrocket, or other substance or thing, of whatever form or construction, that contains any explosive or inflammable compound or substance, and is intended, or commonly known, as fireworks and which explodes, rises into the air or travels laterally, or fires projectiles into the air, other than sparks or those fireworks excepted under the provisions of subsection (a) of §59.1-147.

B. Unless prohibited pursuant to §59.1-148, the provisions of subsection A shall not be applicable to any person, firm or corporation that manufactures, stores, markets and distributes fireworks for the sole purpose of fireworks displays permitted under §59.1-144 or the laws of other states.

§59.1-143. Seizure and destruction of certain fireworks.

Any law-enforcement officer arresting any person for a violation of this chapter shall seize any article mentioned in §59.1-142 in the possession or under the control of the person so arrested and shall hold the same until final disposition of any criminal proceedings against such person. If a judgment of conviction be entered against such person, the court shall order destruction of such articles upon expiration of the time allowed for appeal of such judgment of conviction.

§59.1-144. Permits for display of fireworks; sales for use thereunder.

The governing bodies of the several counties, cities and towns shall have the power to provide for the issuance of permits, upon application in writing, for the display of fireworks by fair associations, amusement parks, or by any organization or group of individuals, under such terms and conditions as they may prescribe. After such permit has been issued sales of fireworks may be made for use under such permit, and the association, organization or group to which it is issued may make use of such fireworks under the terms and conditions of such permit.

§59.1-145. Penalty for violation.

Any person who violates any provision of this chapter shall be guilty of a misdemeanor and, upon conviction thereof, be punished by confinement in jail not to exceed twelve months, or by a fine not exceeding $1,000, or both such fine and imprisonment.

§59.1-146. Exemptions generally.

This chapter shall have no application to any officer or member of the armed forces of this Commonwealth, or of the United States, while acting within the scope of his authority and duties as such, nor to any offer of sale or sale of fireworks to any authorized agent of such armed forces; nor shall it be applicable to the sale or use of materials or equipment, otherwise prohibited by this chapter, when such materials or equipment is used or to be used by any person for signaling or other emergency use in the operation of any boat, railroad train or other vehicle for the transportation of persons or property.

§59.1-147. Chapter inapplicable to certain fireworks; such fireworks to be used only on private property.

(a) This chapter shall not apply to the use or the sale of sparklers, fountains, Pharaoh's serpents, caps for pistols, or to pinwheels commonly known as whirligigs or spinning jennies;

(b) Provided, however, the fireworks listed in subsection (a) may only be used, ignited or exploded on private property with the consent of the owner of such property.

§59.1-148. Local ordinances not affected.

Nothing contained in this chapter shall apply to any ordinance prohibiting the sale, storage, use, possession or manufacture of fireworks heretofore or hereafter adopted by any county, city or town.

CHAPTER 11.1
FIREARMS
(Complete Chapter)

§59.1-148.1. Purchase of firearms in contiguous state.

Any resident of the Commonwealth of Virginia, including a corporation or other business entity maintaining a place of business in this Commonwealth, who may lawfully purchase and receive delivery of a rifle or shotgun in this Commonwealth, may purchase a rifle or shotgun in a contiguous state and transport or receive the same into the Commonwealth of Virginia provided the sale meets the lawful requirements of each such state, meets all lawful requirements of any federal statute, and is made by a licensed importer, licensed manufacturer, licensed dealer, or licensed collector.

§59.1-148.2. Sale of firearms to resident of contiguous state.

Any importer, manufacturer, dealer or collector licensed to sell rifles or shotguns in this Commonwealth may sell such firearms to a resident of a contiguous state provided the sale meets the lawful requirements of each state as well as the requirements of any federal statute pertaining thereto.

§59.1-148.3. Purchase of handguns of certain officers.

A. The Department of State Police, the Department of Game and Inland Fisheries, the Department of Alcoholic Beverage Control, the Marine Resources Commission, the Capitol Police, any sheriff, and any local police department may allow any full-time sworn law-enforcement officer, deputy, or any former Superintendent of the Department of State Police who leaves service after a minimum of five years, a local fire department may allow any full-time sworn fire marshal, the Department of Motor Vehicles may allow any law-enforcement officer, and any institution of higher learning named in §23-14 may allow any campus police officer appointed pursuant to Chapter 17 (§23-232 et seq.) of Title 23, retiring on or after July 1, 1991, who retires after at least twenty years of service or as a result of a service-incurred disability to purchase the service handgun issued to him by the agency or institution at a price of one dollar. Other weapons issued by the Department of State Police for personal duty use of an officer, may, with approval of the Superintendent be sold to the officer subject to the qualifications of this section at a fair market price determined as in subsection B, so long as the weapon is a type and configuration that can be purchased at a regular hardware or sporting goods store by a private citizen without restrictions other than the instant background check.

B. The agencies listed above may allow any full-time sworn law-enforcement officer who retires with ten or more years of service, but less than twenty, to purchase the service handgun issued to him by the agency at a price equivalent to the weapon's fair market value on the date of the officer's retirement. Any full-time sworn law-enforcement officer employed by any of the agencies listed above who is retired for disability as a result of a nonservice-incurred disability may purchase the service handgun issued to him by the agency at a price equivalent to the weapon's fair market value on the date of the officer's retirement. Determinations of fair market value may be made by reference to a recognized pricing guide.

C. The agencies listed above may allow the immediate survivor of any full-time sworn law-enforcement officer (i) who is killed in the line of duty or (ii) who dies in service and has at least twenty years of service to purchase the service handgun issued to the officer by the agency at a price of one dollar.

D. The governing board of any institution of higher learning named in §23-14 may allow any campus police officer appointed pursuant to Chapter 17 (§23-232 et seq.) of Title 23 who retires on or after July 1, 1991, to purchase the service handgun issued to him at a price equivalent to the weapon's fair market value on the date of the officer's retirement. Determinations of fair market value may be made by reference to a recognized pricing guide.

E. The Department of State Police may allow any full-time sworn state police law-enforcement officer who retires as a result of a service-incurred disability and who was on disability leave at the time the Department issued 10-mm semiautomatic handguns to its officers to purchase one of the 10-mm semiautomatic handguns used by the Department of State Police at a price of one dollar.

F. The Department of State Police may allow any officer who at the time of his retirement was a full-time sworn law-enforcement officer and who retires after twenty years of state service, even if a portion of his service was with another state agency, to purchase the service handgun issued to him by the Department at a price of one dollar.

G. The sheriff of any county with a population between 63,000 and 65,000 may allow any auxiliary or volunteer deputy sheriff with a minimum of fifteen years of service, upon leaving office, to purchase for one dollar the service handgun issued to him.

(Chgd. by L.1996 ch. 50; L.1998 ch. 173; L.1999 ch. 312; L.2000 ch. 391, eff. 7/1/2000.)

§59.1-148.4. Sale of firearms by law-enforcement agencies prohibited; exception.

A law-enforcement agency of this Commonwealth shall not sell or trade any firearm owned and used or otherwise lawfully in its possession except (i) to another law-enforcement agency of the Commonwealth, (ii) to a licensed firearms dealer, (iii) to the persons as provided in §59.1-148.3 or (iv) as authorized by a court in accordance with §18.2-310.

TITLE 60.2
UNEMPLOYMENT COMPENSATION
(Selected Chapters)

CHAPTER 5
TAXATION
(Selected Article)

ARTICLE 2
EMPLOYER REPORTING REQUIREMENTS
(Selected Section)

§60.2-518. False statements, etc., by employing units; failure to furnish reports, etc.

A. Any employing unit or any officer or agent of an employing unit or any other person shall be guilty of a Class 1 misdemeanor if it or he:

1. Makes a false statement or representation knowing it to be false, or who knowingly fails to disclose a material fact (i) to prevent or reduce the payment of benefits to any individual entitled thereto, (ii) to avoid becoming or remaining subject to this title or (iii) to avoid or reduce any tax or other payment required from an employing unit under this title; or

2. Willfully fails or refuses (i) to furnish any reports required by this title or (ii) to produce or permit the inspection or copying of records as required hereunder.

B. Each such false statement, representation or failure to disclose a material fact listed in this section, and each day of such failure or refusal shall constitute a separate offense.

CHAPTER 6
BENEFITS
(Selected Article)

ARTICLE 6
VIOLATIONS, PENALTIES, AND LIABILITIES
(Complete Article)

§60.2-632. False statements, etc., to obtain or increase benefits.

Whoever makes a false statement or representation knowing it to be false or knowingly fails to disclose a material fact, with intent to obtain or increase any benefit or other payment under this title, the unemployment compensation act of any other state, or any program of the federal government which is administered in any way under this title, either for himself or for any other person, shall be guilty of a Class 1 misdemeanor. Each such false statement or representation or failure to disclose a material fact shall constitute a separate offense.

§60.2-633. Receiving benefits to which not entitled.

A. Any person who has received any sum as benefits under this title to which he was not entitled shall be liable to repay such sum to the Commission. In the event the claimant does not refund the overpayment, the Commission shall deduct from any future benefits such sum payable to him under this title unless overpayment occurred due to administrative error, in which case the Commission shall deduct only fifty percent of the payable amount for any future week of benefits claimed, rounded down to the next lowest dollar until the overpayment is satisfied. Administrative error shall not include decisions reversed in the appeals process. In addition, the overpayment may be collectible by civil action in the name of the Commission. Amounts collected in this manner may be subject to an interest charge as prescribed in §58.1-15 from the date of judgment and may be subject to fees and costs. Collection activities for any benefit overpayment established of five dollars or less may be suspended. The Commission may, for good cause, determine as uncollectible and discharge from its records any benefit overpayment which remains unpaid after the expiration of seven years from the date such overpayment was determined, or immediately upon the death of such person or upon his discharge in bankruptcy occurring subsequently to the determination of overpayment. Any existing overpayment balance not equal to an even dollar amount shall be rounded to the next lowest even dollar amount.

B. The Commission is authorized to accept repayment of benefit overpayments by use of a credit card. The Virginia Employment Commission shall add to such payment a service charge for the acceptance of such card. Such service charge shall not exceed the percentage charged to the Virginia Employment Commission for use of such card.

(Chgd. by L.1996 ch. 95, eff. 7/1/96.)

§60.2-634. Receiving back pay after reinstatement.
Whenever the Commission finds that a discharged employee has received back pay at his customary wage rate from his employer after reinstatement such employee shall be liable to repay any benefits paid to such person during the time he was unemployed. When such an employee is liable to repay benefits to the Commission, such sum shall be collectible without interest by civil action in the name of the Commission.

§60.2-635. Deprivation of further benefits.
Any person who has been finally convicted under this chapter shall be deprived of any further benefits for the one-year period next ensuing after the date of conviction.

TITLE 61.1
WAREHOUSES, COLD STORAGE AND REFRIGERATED LOCKER PLANTS
(Selected Chapters)

CHAPTER 4
TOBACCO WAREHOUSES AND REGULATIONS IN GENERAL
(Selected Sections)

§61.1-44. Manufactured tobacco; false branding.
If any person use, or permit to be used, on any cask, box or keg of manufactured tobacco, any brand or mark indicating a place or a manufacturer different from the place in which, or the manufacturer by whom, it was really manufactured, he shall be guilty of a misdemeanor and shall be punished as provided in §18.2-12.

None of the provisions of this chapter, other than this section, shall be construed to apply to manufactured tobacco.

§61.1-45. Nesting punished.
If any person nest a basket or parcel of tobacco with inferior tobacco, or other things, with intent to defraud the purchaser, he shall be guilty of a misdemeanor and shall be punished as provided in §18.2-12.

CHAPTER 5
PREVENTION OF FRAUDS IN SALE OF LEAF TOBACCO
(Selected Sections)

§61.1-51. Violations constituting misdemeanors.
Any person who shall give a fictitious or false name to the warehouseman or cooperative marketing association hereinbefore referred to, or who shall fail to give to such warehouseman or cooperative marketing association the true name of the owner of such leaf tobacco or the person from whom the tobacco was obtained, or the grower and the landlord, upon delivering the same as aforesaid, shall be guilty of a misdemeanor. Any warehouseman or cooperative marketing association who shall fail to comply with any of the provisions of this chapter, or who shall deny to any such representative the privilege of inspection or access as provided in §61.1-50, shall be guilty of a misdemeanor. Any warehouseman or cooperative marketing association who shall buy or sell leaf tobacco as above set forth, knowing that the name in which the tobacco is sold or any name given pursuant to the provisions hereof, is false or fictitious, shall be guilty of a misdemeanor.

§61.1-52. Punishment for a misdemeanor.
Any person guilty of a misdemeanor under the provisions of this chapter shall be punished as provided in §18.2-12.

CHAPTER 7
HANDLING AND SALE OF BURLEY TOBACCO
(Selected Sections)

§61.1-58. Commingling burley and other tobacco; moving tobacco before sale.
It shall be unlawful for any person to commingle, mix, place in same basket with other tobacco or in any other manner or means to handle tobacco so as to lose its identity, for the purpose of sale at auction, loose-leaf tobacco grown by one producer with loose-leaf burley tobacco grown by any other producer, or of the same producer after being placed on the loose-leaf floor.

After tobacco is weighed and set upon the warehouse floor for sale no basket of tobacco shall be moved, without the consent of the owner, from its place on the floor until sale is confirmed by the owner of same. This shall not apply to official inspectors of the Department of Agriculture and Consumer Services, who in the course of their duties find it necessary to move piles of tobacco.

§61.1-61. Penalty for violation.
The violation of any provision of this law or valid rules and regulations promulgated hereunder shall constitute a misdemeanor and shall be punishable by fine of not less than $50 for the first offense and for each subsequent offense shall be punished by a fine of not less than $500 or imprisonment in jail not less than thirty days, or both such fine and imprisonment in the discretion of the court or jury.

TITLE 63.1
WELFARE (SOCIAL SERVICES)
(Selected Chapters)

CHAPTER 3
LOCAL BOARDS OF PUBLIC WELFARE
(Selected Article)

ARTICLE 2
FUNCTIONS, POWERS AND DUTIES
(Selected Section)

§63.1-55.3. Protection of aged or incapacitated adults; physicians, nurses, etc., to report abuse, neglect or exploitation of adults; complaint by others; penalty for failure to report.

A. Any person licensed to practice medicine or any of the healing arts, any hospital resident or intern, any person employed in the nursing profession, any person employed by a public or private agency or facility and working with adults, any person providing full-time or part-time care to adults for pay on a regularly scheduled basis, any person employed as a social worker, any mental health professional and any law-enforcement officer, in his professional or official capacity, who has reason to suspect that an adult is an abused, neglected or exploited adult, shall report the matter immediately to the local department of the county or city wherein the adult resides or wherein the abuse, neglect or exploitation is believed to have occurred. If neither locality is known, then the report shall be made to the local department of the county or city where the abuse, neglect, or exploitation was discovered. If the information is received by a staff member, resident, intern or nurse in the course of professional services in a hospital or similar institution, such person may, in place of the report, immediately notify the person in charge of the institution or department, or his designee, who shall make such report forthwith. Any person required to make the report or notification required by this subsection shall do so either orally or in writing and shall disclose all information which is the basis for the suspicion of abuse, neglect or exploitation of the adult. Upon request, any person required to make the report shall make available to the adult protective services worker and the local department investigating the reported case of abuse, neglect or exploitation any information, records or reports which document the basis for the report. All persons required to report suspected abuse, neglect or exploitation who maintain a record of a person who is the subject of such a report shall cooperate with the investigating adult protective services worker of a local department and shall make information, records and reports which are relevant to the investigation available to such worker to the extent permitted by state and federal law.

B. The report required by subsection A shall be reduced to writing within seventy-two hours by the director of the local department on a form prescribed by the State Board of Social Services.

C. Any person required to make a report pursuant to subsection A who has reason to suspect that an adult has been sexually abused as that term is defined in §18.2-67.10, and any person in charge of a hospital or similar institution, or a department thereof, who receives such information from a staff member, resident, intern or nurse, also shall immediately report the matter, either orally or in writing, to the local law-enforcement agency where the adult resides or the sexual abuse is believed to have occurred, or if neither locality is known, then where the abuse was discovered. The person making the report shall disclose and, upon request, make available to the law-enforcement agency all information forming the basis of the report.

D. Any person other than those specified in subsection A who suspects that an adult is an abused, neglected or exploited adult may report the matter to the local department of the county or city wherein the adult resides or wherein the abuse, neglect or exploitation is believed to have occurred. Such a complaint may be oral or in writing.

E. Any person who makes a report or provides records or information pursuant to subsection A or D of this section or who testifies in any judicial proceeding arising from such report, records or information shall be immune from any civil or criminal liability on account of such report, records, information or testimony, unless such person acted in bad faith or with a malicious purpose.

F. All law-enforcement departments and other state and local departments, agencies, authorities and institutions shall cooperate with each adult protective services worker of a local department in the detection and prevention of abuse, neglect or exploitation of adults.

G. Any person who is found guilty of failing to make a required report or notification pursuant to subsection A or C of this section, within 24 hours of having the reason to suspect abuse shall be fined not more than $500 for the first failure and not less than $100 nor more than $1,000 for any subsequent failures.

(Chgd. by L.1997 ch. 687; L.1999 ch. 749, eff. 7/1/99.)

CHAPTER 6
PUBLIC AID AND ASSISTANCE
(Selected Article)

ARTICLE 2
GRANTS OF ASSISTANCE
(Selected Sections)

§63.1-112. Notification of change in circumstances.

If at any time during the continuance of assistance there shall occur any change, including but not limited to, the possession of any property or the receipt of regular income by the recipient, in the circumstances upon which current eligibility or amount of assistance were determined, which would materially affect such determination, it shall be the duty of such recipient immediately to notify the local department of such change, and thereupon the local board may either cancel the assistance, or alter the amount thereof.

For purposes of this section, any receipt of property or income by any person who is included within a recipient's grant or for whom money is being paid under a recipient's grant shall be reported immediately by the recipient to the local department for the purpose of determining whether the recipient's grant is affected thereby.

Any recipient who knows or reasonably should know that such change in circumstances will materially affect his eligibility for assistance or the amount thereof and willfully

 Zv

fails to comply with the provisions of this section, shall be guilty of a violation of §63.1-124.

§63.1-124. False statements, representations, impersonations and fraudulent devices.

Whoever obtains, or attempts to obtain, or aids or abets any person in obtaining, by means of a willful false statement or representation, or by impersonation, or other fraudulent device, assistance or benefits from other programs designated under rules and regulations of the State Board of Social Services or State Board of Health or the Board of Medical Assistance Services to which he is not entitled or who fails to comply with the provisions of §63.1-112 shall be deemed guilty of larceny, and upon conviction, shall be punished as specified in Article 3 (§18.2-95 et seq.) of Chapter 5 of Title 18.2. It shall be the duty of the local director, the Commissioner of Health or the Director of the Department of Medical Assistance Services to investigate alleged violations and enforce the provisions of this section. A warrant or summons may be issued for each violation of which the local director, the Commissioner of Health or the Director of the Department of Medical Assistance Services has knowledge. The local director, the Commissioner or the Director shall ensure that the attorney for the Commonwealth is notified of any investigation or alleged violation under this section. Trial for violations of this section shall be in the county or city from whose department of public welfare or social services assistance was sought or obtained.

In any prosecution under the provisions of this section, it shall be lawful and sufficient in the same indictment or accusation to charge and therein to proceed against the accused for any number of distinct acts of such false statements, representations, impersonations or fraudulent devices which may have been committed by him within six months from the first to the last of the acts charged in the indictment or accusation.

(Chgd. by L.1995 ch. 294, eff. 7/1/95.)

§63.1-124.1. Unauthorized use of food stamps, electronic benefit transfer cards, and fuel assistance prohibited; penalties.

Whoever knowingly and with intent to defraud transfers, acquires, alters, traffics in or uses, or aids and abets another person in transferring, acquiring, altering, trafficking in, using or possessing food stamps, electronic benefit transfer cards or other devices subject to federal reserve system regulations regarding Electronic Fund Transfers 12 CFR §205.1 et seq. or benefits from fuel assistance programs, or possesses food coupons, authorization to purchase cards, electronic benefit transfer cards or other devices subject to federal reserve system regulations regarding Electronic Fund Transfers 12 CFR §205.1 et seq., or benefits from fuel assistance programs in any manner not authorized by law shall be deemed guilty of larceny and, upon conviction thereof, be punished accordingly.

A violation of this section may be prosecuted either in the county or city where the public assistance was granted or in the county or city where the violation occurred.

CHAPTER 8
BUSINESS ENTERPRISES FOR AND SALE OF GOODS MADE BY THE BLIND; RIGHTS OF BLIND, DEAF AND PHYSICALLY DISABLED PERSONS
(Selected Article)

ARTICLE 3
RIGHTS OF BLIND, DEAF AND PHYSICALLY DISABLED PERSONS
(Selected Section)

§63.1-171.3. Duty of driver approaching blind pedestrian; effect of failure of blind person to carry white cane or use dog guide.

The driver of a vehicle approaching a totally or partially blind pedestrian who is carrying a cane predominantly white or metallic in color (with or without a red tip) or using a dog guide shall take all necessary precautions to avoid injury to such blind pedestrian and dog guide, and any driver who fails to take such precautions shall be liable in damages for any injury caused such pedestrian and dog guide; provided that a totally or partially blind pedestrian not carrying such a cane or using a dog guide in any of the places, accommodations or conveyances listed in §51.5-44, shall have all of the rights and privileges conferred by law upon other persons, and the failure of a totally or partially blind pedestrian to carry such a cane or to use a dog guide in any such places, accommodations or conveyances shall not be held to constitute nor be evidence of contributory negligence; provided, that nothing in this section shall be construed to limit the application of §46.2-933 or §46.2-934.

CHAPTER 10
CHILD WELFARE, HOMES, AGENCIES AND INSTITUTIONS
(Selected Sections)

§63.1-198.3. Allowing sex offender or child abuser to operate or reside in family day home.

It shall be unlawful for any person to operate a family day home if he, or if he knows that any other person who resides in the home, has been convicted of a felony in violation of §§18.2-48, 18.2-61, 18.2-63, 18.2-64.1, 18.2-67.1, 18.2-67.2, 18.2-67.3, 18.2-67.5, 18.2-355, 18.2-361, 18.2-366, 18.2-369, 18.2-370, 18.2-370.1, 18.2-371.1, or §18.2-374.1 or is the subject of a founded complaint of child abuse or neglect within or outside the Commonwealth. A violation of this section shall be punishable as a Class 1 misdemeanor.

(Chgd. by L.1998 chs. 551, 581, eff. 7/1/98.)

§63.1-198.5. Records checks of unregulated child day centers or family day homes and their employees and volunteers receiving state and local funds; penalty.

Whenever any unlicensed or unregistered child day center or family day home applies to enter into a contract with a local department of social services to provide child care services to clients of the local department of social services, the local department of social services shall require a criminal records check pursuant to subdivision A 11 of §19.2-389, as well as a search of the central registry maintained pursuant to §63.1-248.8 on any child abuse or neglect investigation, of the applicant, any employee, prospective

employee, volunteers, agents involved in the day-to-day operation, all agents who are alone with, in control of, or supervising one or more of the children, and any other adult living in a family day home. The applicant shall provide the local department of social services with copies of these records checks. The child day center or family day home shall refuse employment or work to any person who has been (i) the subject of a founded complaint of child abuse or neglect or (ii) convicted of any offense specified in §63.1-198.1. The child day center or family day home shall also require the above individuals to provide a sworn statement or affirmation disclosing whether or not the person has ever been (i) the subject of a founded case of child abuse or neglect or (ii) convicted of or is the subject of any pending charges for any offense specified in this section within the Commonwealth or any equivalent offense outside the Commonwealth. Any person making a materially false statement regarding any such offense shall be guilty of a Class 1 misdemeanor. If a person is denied employment or work because of information from the central registry or convictions appearing on his criminal history record, the child day center or family day program shall provide a copy of such information obtained from the central registry or Central Criminal Records Exchange to the person. Further dissemination of the information provided to the facility, beyond dissemination to the local department of social services, is prohibited.
(Added by L.1999 ch. 727, eff. 7/1/99.)

§63.1-215. Penalty for operation without license.
Any person who operates or engages in the activities of a child welfare agency without first obtaining a license as required by this chapter, or after such license has been revoked or has expired and not been renewed, and each officer and each member of the governing board of any association or corporation which operates a child welfare agency without obtaining such license or after such revocation or expiration shall be guilty of a misdemeanor and, upon conviction thereof, shall be punished by a fine of not more than $100, or by imprisonment for not more than twelve months, or by both such fine and imprisonment. Every day's violation of this section shall constitute a separate offense.

CHAPTER 12.1
CHILD ABUSE AND NEGLECT
(Complete Chapter)

§63.1-248.1. Policy of the State.
The General Assembly declares that it is the policy of this Commonwealth to require reports of suspected child abuse and neglect for the purpose of identifying children who are being abused or neglected, of assuring that protective services will be made available to an abused or neglected child in order to protect such a child and his siblings and to prevent further abuse or neglect, and of preserving the family life of the parents and children, where possible, by enhancing parental capacity for adequate child care.

§63.1-248.2. Definitions.
As used in this chapter unless the context requires a different meaning:
"Abused or neglected child" means any child less than eighteen years of age:
1. Whose parents or other person responsible for his care creates or inflicts, threatens to create or inflict, or allows to be created or inflicted upon such child a physical or mental injury by other than accidental means, or creates a substantial risk of death, disfigurement, or impairment of bodily or mental functions;
2. Whose parents or other person responsible for his care neglects or refuses to provide care necessary for his health. However, no child who in good faith is under treatment solely by spiritual means through prayer in accordance with the tenets and practices of a recognized church or religious denomination shall for that reason alone be considered to be an abused or neglected child;
3. Whose parents or other person responsible for his care abandons such child;
4. Whose parents or other person responsible for his care commits or allows to be committed any act of sexual exploitation or any sexual act upon a child in violation of the law; or
5. Who is without parental care or guardianship caused by the unreasonable absence or the mental or physical incapacity of the child's parent, guardian, legal custodian or other person standing in loco parentis.

"Complaint" means any information or allegation of abuse or neglect made orally or in writing other than the reports referred to below.

"Department" means the State Department of Social Services.

"Family assessment" means the collection of information necessary to determine:

1. The immediate safety needs of the child;
2. The protective and rehabilitative services needs of the child and family that will deter abuse or neglect;
3. Risk of future harm to the child; and
4. Alternative plans for the child's safety if protective and rehabilitative services are indicated and the family is unable or unwilling to participate in services.

"Investigation" means the collection of information necessary to determine:

1. The immediate safety needs of the child;
2. The protective and rehabilitative services needs of the child and family that will deter abuse or neglect;
3. Risk of future harm to the child;
4. Alternative plans for the child's safety if protective and rehabilitative services are indicated and the family is unable or unwilling to participate in services;
5. Whether or not abuse or neglect has occurred;
6. If abuse or neglect has occurred, who abused or neglected the child; and
7. A finding of either founded or unfounded based on the facts collected during the investigation.

"Local department" means the department of public welfare or social services of any county or city in this Commonwealth.

"Prevention" means efforts that (i) promote health and competence in people and (ii) create, promote and strengthen environments that nurture people in their development.

"Report" means an official document on which information is given concerning abuse and neglect and which is required to be made by persons designated herein and by local departments in those situations in which a complaint from the general public reveals suspected abuse or neglect.

"The court" means the juvenile and domestic relations district court of the county or city.

"Valid report or complaint" means the local department of social services has evaluated the information and allegations of the report or complaint and determined that the local department shall conduct an investigation or family assessment because the following elements are present:

1. The alleged victim child or children are under the age of eighteen at the time of the complaint or report;
2. The alleged abuser is the alleged victim child's parent or other caretaker;
3. The local department receiving the complaint or report is a local department of jurisdiction; and
4. The circumstances described allege suspected child abuse or neglect.

Nothing in this section shall relieve any person specified in §63.1-248.3 from making reports required in that section, regardless of the identity of the person suspected to have caused such abuse or neglect.
(Chgd. by L.1995 ch. 520; L.1996 ch. 616; L.2000 ch. 500, eff. 7/1/2000.)

§63.1-248.2:1. Child protective services differential response system.

The Department shall implement a child protective services differential response system in all local departments of social services. The differential response system allows local departments of social services to respond to valid reports or complaints of child abuse or neglect by conducting either an investigation or a family assessment. The Department shall publish a plan to implement the child protective services differential response system in local departments of social services by July 1, 2000, and complete implementation in all local departments of social services by July 1, 2003. The Department shall develop a training program for all staff persons involved in the differential response system, and all such staff shall receive this training.
(Added by L.2000 ch. 500, eff. 7/1/2000.)

§63.1-248.3. Physicians, nurses, teachers, etc., to report certain injuries to children; penalty for failure to report.

A. The following persons who, in their professional or official capacity, have reason to suspect that a child is an abused or neglected child, shall report the matter immediately, except as hereinafter provided, to the local department of the county or city wherein the child resides or wherein the abuse or neglect is believed to have occurred or to the Department of Social Services' toll-free child abuse and neglect hotline:

1. Any person licensed to practice medicine or any of the healing arts;
2. Any hospital resident or intern, and any person employed in the nursing profession;
3. Any person employed as a social worker;
4. Any probation officer;
5. Any teacher or other person employed in a public or private school, kindergarten or nursery school;
6. Any person providing full-time or part-time child care for pay on a regularly planned basis;
7. Any duly accredited Christian Science practitioner;
8. Any mental health professional;
9. Any law-enforcement officer;
10. Any mediator eligible to receive court referrals pursuant to §8.01-576.8;
11. Any professional staff person, not previously enumerated, employed by a private or state-operated hospital, institution or facility to which children have been committed or where children have been placed for care and treatment;
12. Any person associated with or employed by any private organization responsible for the care, custody or control of children; and
13. Any person who is designated a court-appointed special advocate pursuant to Article 1.4 (§9-173.6 et seq.) of Chapter 27 of Title 9.

If neither the locality in which the child resides or where the abuse or neglect is believed to have occurred is known, then such report shall be made to the local department of the county or city where the abuse or neglect was discovered or to the Department of Social Services' toll-free child abuse and neglect hotline.

If an employee of the local department is suspected of abusing or neglecting a child, the report shall be made to the juvenile and domestic relations district court of the county or city where the abuse or neglect was discovered. Upon receipt of such a report by the court, the judge of the juvenile and domestic relations district court shall assign the report to a local department of social services that is not the employer of the suspected employee for investigation or family assessment; or, if the judge believes that no local department of social services within a reasonable geographic distance can be impartial in responding to the reported case, the judge shall assign the report to the court service unit of his court for evaluation. The judge may consult with the State Department of Social Services in selecting a local department to respond to the report or the complaint.

If the information is received by a teacher, staff member, resident, intern or nurse in the course of professional services in a hospital, school or similar institution, such person may, in place of said report, immediately notify the person in charge of the institution or department, or his designee, who shall make such report forthwith.

The initial report may be an oral report but such report shall be reduced to writing by the child abuse coordinator of the local department on a form prescribed by the State Board of Social Services. The person required to make the report shall disclose all information which is the basis for his suspicion of abuse or neglect of the child and, upon request, shall make available to the child-protective services coordinator and the local department of social services, which is the agency of jurisdiction, any records or reports which document the basis for the report.

A1. For purposes of subsection A, "reason to suspect that a child is abused or neglected" shall include (i) a finding made by an attending physician within seven days of a child's birth that the results of a blood or urine test conducted within forty-eight hours of the birth of the child indicate the presence of a controlled substance not prescribed for the mother by a physician; (ii) a finding by an attending physician made within forty-eight hours of a child's birth that the child was born dependent on a controlled substance which was not prescribed by a physician for the mother and has demonstrated withdrawal symptoms; (iii) a diagnosis by an attending physician made within seven days of a child's birth that the child has an illness, disease or condition which, to a reasonable degree of medical certainty, is attributable to in utero exposure to a controlled substance which was not prescribed by a physician for the mother or the child; or (iv) a diagnosis by an attending physician made within seven days of a child's birth that the child has fetal alcohol syndrome attributable to in utero exposure to alcohol. When "reason to suspect" is based upon this subsection, such fact shall be included in the report along with the facts relied upon by the person making the report.

B. Any person required to file a report pursuant to this section who fails to do so within seventy-two hours of his first suspicion of child abuse or neglect shall be fined not more than $500 for the first failure and for any subsequent failures not less than $100 nor more than $1,000.

(Chgd. by L.1995 ch. 810; L.1996 ch. 616; L.1998 chs. 704, 716; L.1999 ch. 606; L.2000 ch. 500, eff. 7/1/2000.)

§63.1-248.4. Complaints by others of certain injuries to children.

Any person who suspects that a child is an abused or neglected child may make a complaint concerning such child, except as hereinafter provided, to the local department of the county or city wherein the child resides or wherein the abuse or neglect is believed to have occurred or to the Department of Social Services' toll-free child abuse and neglect hotline. If an employee of the local department is suspected of abusing or neglecting a child, the complaint shall be made to the juvenile and domestic relations district court of the county or city where the abuse or neglect was discovered. Upon receipt of such a report by the court, the judge of the juvenile and domestic relations district court shall assign the report to a local department of social services that is not the employer of the suspected employee for investigation or family assessment; or, if the judge believes that no local department of social services in a reasonable geographic distance can be impartial in responding to the reported case, the judge shall assign the report to the court service unit of his court for evaluation. The judge may consult with the State Department of Social Services in selecting a local department to respond to the report or complaint. Such a complaint may be oral or in writing and shall disclose all information which is the basis for the suspicion of abuse or neglect of the child.

(Chgd. by L.1996 ch. 616; L.2000 ch. 500, eff. 7/1/2000.)

§63.1-248.5. Immunity of person making report, etc., from liability.

Any person making a report pursuant to §63.1-248.3, a complaint pursuant to §63.1-248.4, or who takes a child into custody pursuant to §63.1-248.9, or who participates in a judicial proceeding resulting therefrom shall be immune from any civil or criminal liability in connection therewith, unless it is proven that such person acted in bad faith or with malicious intent.

§63.1-248.5:1. Retention of records in all reports; procedures regarding unfounded reports alleged to be made in bad faith or with malicious intent.

A. The local department shall retain the records of all reports or complaints made pursuant to this chapter, in accordance with rules and regulations approved by the Board.

B. The Department shall maintain a Child Abuse and Neglect Information System that includes a central registry of founded complaints, pursuant to §63.1-248.8. The Department shall maintain all (i) unfounded investigations, (ii) family assessments, and (iii) reports or complaints determined to be not valid in a record which is separate from the central registry and accessible only to the Department and to local departments for child protective services. The purpose of retaining these complaints or reports is to provide local departments with information regarding prior complaints or reports. In no event shall the mere existence of a prior complaint or report be used to determine that a subsequent complaint or report is founded. The subject of the complaint or report is the person who is alleged to have committed abuse or neglect. The subject of the complaint or report shall have access to his own record. The record of unfounded investigations, family assessments, and complaints and reports determined to be not valid shall be purged one year after the date of the complaint or report if there are no subsequent complaints or reports regarding the same child or the person who is the subject of the complaint or report in that one year. The department shall retain the records for an additional period of up to two years if requested in writing by the person who is the subject of such complaint or report. The child protective services records regarding the petitioner which result from such complaint or report shall be purged immediately by any custodian of such records upon presentation to the custodian of a certified copy of a court order that there has been a civil action which determined that the complaint or report was made in bad faith or with malicious intent. After purging the records, the custodian shall notify the petitioner in writing that the records have been purged.

C. At the time the local department notifies a person who is the subject of a complaint or report made pursuant to this chapter that such complaint or report is either an unfounded investigation or a completed family assessment, it shall notify him that the record will be retained for one year and of the availability of the procedures set out in this section regarding reports or complaints alleged to be made in bad faith or with malicious intent.

D. Any person who is the subject of an unfounded report or complaint made pursuant to this chapter who believes that such report or complaint was made in bad faith or with malicious intent may petition the circuit court in the jurisdiction in which the report or complaint was made for the release to such person of the records of the investigation or family assessment. Such petition shall specifically set forth the reasons such person believes that such report or complaint was made in bad faith or with malicious intent. Upon the filing of such petition, the court shall request and the department shall provide to the court its records of the investigation or family assessment for the court's in camera review. The petitioner shall be entitled to present evidence to support his petition. If the court determines that there is a reasonable question of fact as to whether the report or complaint was made in bad faith or with malicious intent and that disclosure of the identity of the complainant would not be likely to endanger the life or safety of the complainant, it shall provide to the petitioner a copy of the records of the investigation or family assessment. The original records shall be subject to discovery in any subsequent civil action regarding the making of a complaint or report in bad faith or with malicious intent.

(Chgd. by L.1996 chs. 616, 780, 791; L.2000 ch. 500, eff. 7/1/2000.)

§63.1-248.5:1.01. Knowingly making false reports; penalties.

A. Any person fourteen years of age or older who makes or causes to be made a report of child abuse or neglect pursuant to this chapter which he knows to be false shall be guilty of a Class 1 misdemeanor. Any person fourteen years of age or older who has been previously convicted under this subsection and who is subsequently convicted under this subsection shall be guilty of a Class 6 felony.

B. The child protective services records regarding the person who was alleged to have committed abuse or neglect which result from a report for which a conviction is obtained under this section shall be purged immediately by any custodian of such records upon presentation to the custodian of a certified copy of such conviction. After purging the records, the custodian shall notify the person in writing that such records have been purged.

(Added by L.1996 chs. 813, 836; chgd. by L.1999 ch. 828, eff. 7/1/99.)

§63.1-248.6. Local departments to establish child-protective services; duties.

A. Each local department shall establish child-protective services under a departmental coordinator within such department or with one or more adjacent local departments which shall be staffed with qualified personnel pursuant to regulations promulgated by the State Board of Social Services. The local department shall be the public agency responsible for receiving and responding to complaints and reports, except that (i) in cases where the reports or complaints are to be made to the juvenile and domestic relations district court and the judge determines that no local department of social services within a reasonable geographic distance can impartially respond to the report, the court shall assign the report to the court services unit of his court for evaluation; and (ii) in cases where an employee at a private or state-operated hospital, institution or other facility, or an employee of a school board is suspected of abusing or neglecting a child in such hospital, institution or other facility, or public school, the local department shall request the Department and the relevant private or state-operated hospital, institution or other facility, or school board to assist in conducting a joint investigation in accordance with rules and regulations approved by the State Board, in consultation with the Departments of Education, Health, Medical Assistance Services, Mental Health, Mental Retardation and Substance Abuse Services, Juvenile Justice and Corrections.

B. The local department shall ensure, through its own personnel or through cooperative arrangements with other local agencies, that personnel who respond to reports or complaints that an employee of a private or state-operated hospital, institution or other facility, or an employee of a school board, abused or neglected a child in such hospital, institution or other facility, or public school, are qualified and assisted by the Department and the relevant private or state-operated hospital, institution or other facility, or school board in accordance with State Board regulations.

C. The local department shall ensure, through its own personnel or through cooperative arrangements with other local agencies, the capability of receiving reports or complaints and responding to them promptly on a twenty-four-hours-a-day, seven-days-per-week basis.

D. The local department shall widely publicize a telephone number for receiving complaints and reports.

E. The local department shall upon receipt of a complaint report immediately to the attorney for the Commonwealth and the local law-enforcement agency and make available to them the records of the local department when abuse or neglect is suspected in any case involving (i) death of a child; (ii) injury or threatened injury to the child in which a felony or Class 1 misdemeanor is also suspected; (iii) any sexual abuse, suspected sexual abuse or other sexual offense involving a child, including but not limited to the use or display of the child in sexually explicit visual material, as defined in §18.2-374.1; (iv) any abduction of a child; (v) any felony or Class 1 misdemeanor drug offense involving a child; or (vi) contributing to the delinquency of a minor in violation of §18.2-371, and provide the attorneys for the Commonwealth and the local law-enforcement agency with records of any complaints of abuse or neglect involving the victim or the alleged perpetrator. The local department shall not allow reports of the death of the victim from other local agencies to substitute for direct reports to the attorney for the Commonwealth and the local law-enforcement agency.

F. When abuse or neglect is suspected in any case involving the death of a child, the local department shall report the case immediately to the regional medical examiner and the local law-enforcement agency.

G. The local department shall use reasonable diligence to locate (i) any child for whom a report of suspected abuse or neglect has been received and is under investigation, receiving family assessment, or for whom a founded determination of abuse and neglect has been made and a child protective services case opened and (ii) persons who are the subject of a report that is under investigation or receiving family assessment, if the whereabouts of the child or such persons are unknown to the local department.

H. When an abused or neglected child and the persons who are the subject of an open child protective services case have relocated out of the jurisdiction of the local department, the local department shall notify the child protective services agency in the jurisdiction to which such persons have relocated, whether inside or outside of the Commonwealth, and forward to such agency relevant portions of the case record. The receiving local department shall arrange protective and rehabilitative services as required by this section.

I. When a child for whom a report of suspected abuse or neglect has been received and is under investigation or receiving family assessment and the child and/or the child's parents or other persons responsible for the child's care who are the subject of the report that is under investigation or family assessment have relocated out of the jurisdiction of the local department, the local department shall notify the child protective services agency in the jurisdiction to which the child and/or such persons have relocated, whether inside or outside of the Commonwealth, and complete such investigation or family assessment by requesting such agency's assistance in completing the investigation or family assessment. The local department that completes the investigation or family assessment shall forward to the receiving agency relevant portions of the case record in order for the receiving agency to arrange protective and rehabilitative services as required by this section.

J. Upon receipt of a report of child abuse or neglect, the local department shall determine the validity of such report and shall make a determination to conduct an investigation pursuant to §63.1-248.6:01 or, if designated as a child protective services differential response agency by the Department according to §63.1-248.2:1, a family assessment pursuant to §63.1-248.6:02.

K. The local department shall foster, when practicable, the creation, maintenance and coordination of hospital and community-based multi-disciplinary teams which shall include where possible, but not be limited to, members of the medical, mental health, social work, nursing, education, legal and law-enforcement professions. Such teams shall assist the local departments in identifying abused and neglected children; coordinating medical, social, and legal services for the children and their families; developing innovative programs for detection and prevention of child abuse; promoting community concern and action in the area of child abuse and neglect; and disseminating information to the general public with respect to the problem of child abuse and neglect and the facilities and prevention and treatment methods available to combat child abuse and neglect. These teams may be the family assessment and planning teams established pursuant to §2.1-753. Multi-disciplinary teams may develop agreements regarding the exchange of information among the parties for the purposes of the investigation and disposition of complaints of child abuse and neglect, delivery of services, and child protection. Any information exchanged in accordance with the agreement shall not be considered to be a violation of the provisions of §63.1-53 or §63.1-209.

The local department shall also coordinate its efforts in the provision of these services for abused and neglected children with the judge and staff of the court.

L. The local department shall develop, where practical, memoranda of understanding for responding to reports of child abuse and neglect with local law enforcement and the local office of the Commonwealth's Attorney.

M. The local department shall report annually on its activities concerning abused and neglected children to the court and to the Child-Protective Services Unit in the Department on forms provided by the Department.

N. Statements, or any evidence derived therefrom, made to local department child-protective services personnel, or to any person performing the duties of such personnel, by any person accused of the abuse, injury, neglect or death of a child after the arrest of such person, shall not be used in evidence in the case in chief against such person in the criminal proceeding on the question of guilt or innocence over the objection of the accused, unless the statement was made after such person was fully advised (i) of his right to remain silent, (ii) that anything he says may be used against him in a court of law, (iii) that he has a right to the presence of an attorney during any interviews, and (iv) that if he cannot afford an attorney, one will be appointed for him prior to any questioning.

O. Notwithstanding any other provision of law, the local department, in accordance with Board regulations, shall transmit information regarding founded complaints or family assessments and may transmit other information regarding reports, complaints, family assessments and investigations involving active duty military personnel or members of their household to family advocacy representatives of the United States Armed Forces.

(Chgd. by L.1996 chs. 616, 858, 863; L.1998 chs. 704, 716; L.2000 chs. 500, 854, eff. 7/1/2000.)

§63.1-248.6:01. Investigations by local departments.

If the local department responds to the report or complaint by conducting an investigation, the local department shall:

1. Make immediate investigation and, if the report or complaint was based upon one of the factors specified in subsection A1 of §63.1-248.3, the department may file a petition pursuant to §16.1-241.3;

2. Complete a report and transmit it forthwith to the Department, except that no such report shall be transmitted in cases in which the cause to suspect abuse or neglect is one of the factors specified in subsection A1 of §63.1-248.3 and the mother sought substance abuse counseling or treatment prior to the child's birth;

3. Consult with the family to arrange for necessary protective and rehabilitative services to be provided to the child and his family;

4. Petition the court for services deemed necessary including, but not limited to, removal of the child or his siblings from their home;

5. Determine within forty-five days if a report of abuse or neglect is founded or unfounded and transmit a report to such effect to the Department and to the person who is the subject of the investigation. However, upon written justification by the local department, such determination may be extended, not to exceed a total of sixty days. If through the exercise of reasonable diligence the department is unable to find the child who is the subject of the report, the time the child cannot be found shall not be computed as part of the forty-five-day or sixty-day period and documentation of such reasonable diligence shall be placed in the record; and

6. If a report of abuse or neglect is unfounded, transmit a report to such effect to the complainant and parent or guardian and the person responsible for the care of the child in those cases where such person was suspected of abuse or neglect.

(Added by L.2000 ch. 500, eff. 7/1/2000.)

§63.1-248.6:02. Family assessments by local departments.

A. When a local department has been designated as a child protective services differential response system participant by the Department pursuant to §63.1-248.2:1 and responds to the report or complaint by conducting a family assessment, the local department shall:

1. Conduct an immediate family assessment and, if the report or complaint was based upon one of the factors specified in subsection A1 of §63.1-248.3, the department may file a petition pursuant to §16.1-241.3;

2. Immediately contact the subject of the report and the family of the child alleged to have been abused or neglected and give each a written explanation of the family assessment procedure. The family assessment shall be in writing and shall be completed in accordance with Board regulation;

3. Complete the family assessment within forty-five days and transmit a report to such effect to the Department and to the person who is the subject of the family assessment. However, upon written justification by the local department, the family assessment may be extended, not to exceed a total of sixty days;

4. Consult with the family to arrange for necessary protective and rehabilitative services to be provided to the child and his family;

5. Petition the court for services deemed necessary including, but not limited to, removal of the child or his siblings from their home;

6. Make no disposition of founded or unfounded for reports in which a family assessment is completed; and

7. Commence an immediate investigation, if at any time during the completion of the family assessment, the local department determines that an investigation is required.

B. When a local department of social services has been designated as a child protective services differential response agency by the Department, the local department may investigate any report of child abuse or neglect, but the following valid reports of child abuse or neglect shall be investigated: (i) sexual abuse, (ii) child fatality, (iii) abuse or neglect resulting in serious injury as defined in §18.2-371.1, (iv) child has been taken into the custody of the local department of social services, or (v) cases involving a caretaker at a state-licensed child day center, religiously exempt child day center, regulated family day home, private or public school, or hospital or any institution.

(Added by L.2000 ch. 500, eff. 7/1/2000.)

§63.1-248.6:1. Appeals of certain actions of local departments.

A. A person who is suspected of or is found to have committed abuse or neglect may, within thirty days of being notified of that determination, request the local department rendering such determination to amend the determination and the local department's related records. Upon written request, the local department shall provide the appellant all information used in making its determination. Disclosure of the reporter's name or information which may endanger the well-being of a child shall not be released. The identity of collateral witnesses or any other person shall not be released if disclosure may endanger their life or safety. Information prohibited from being disclosed by state or federal law or regulation shall not be released. The local department shall hold an informal conference or consultation where such person, who may be represented by counsel, shall be entitled to informally present testimony of witnesses, documents, factual data, arguments or other submissions of proof to the local department. With the exception of the director of the local department, no person whose regular duties include substantial involvement with child abuse and neglect cases shall preside over the informal conference. If the local department refuses the request for amendment or fails to act within forty-five days after receiving such request, the person may, within thirty days thereafter, petition the Commissioner, who shall grant a hearing to determine whether it appears, by a preponderance of the evidence, that the determination or record contains information which is irrelevant or inaccurate regarding the commission of abuse or neglect by the person who is the subject of the determination or record and therefore shall be amended. A person who is the subject of a report who requests an amendment to the record, as provided above, has the right to obtain an extension for an additional specified period of up to sixty days by requesting in writing that the forty-five days in which the local department must act be extended. The extension period, which may be up to sixty days, shall begin at the end of the forty-five days in which the local department must act. When there is an extension period, the thirty-day period to request an administrative hearing shall begin on the termination of the extension period.

B. The Commissioner shall designate and authorize one or more members of his staff to conduct such hearings. The decision of any staff member so designated and authorized shall have the same force and effect as if the Commissioner had made the decision. The hearing officer shall have the authority to issue subpoenas for the production of documents and the appearance of witnesses. The hearing officer is authorized to determine the number of depositions that will be allowed and to administer oaths or affirmations to all parties and witnesses who plan to testify at the hearing. The State Board of Social Services shall promulgate regulations necessary for the conduct of such hearings. Such regulations shall include provisions stating that the person who is the subject of the report has the right: (i) to submit oral or written testimony or documents in support of himself, and (ii) to be informed of the procedure by which information will be made available or withheld from him. In case of any information withheld, such person shall be advised of the general nature of such information and the reasons, for reasons of privacy or otherwise, that it is being withheld. Upon giving reasonable notice, either party at his own expense may depose a nonparty and submit such deposition at the hearing pursuant to State Board regulation. Upon good cause shown, after a party's written motion, the hearing officer may issue subpoenas for the production of documents or to compel the attendance of witnesses at the hearing, except that alleged child victims of the person and their siblings shall not be subpoenaed, deposed or required to testify. The person who is the subject of the report may be represented by counsel at the hearing. Upon petition, the juvenile and domestic relations court or family court, as the case may be, shall have the power to enforce any subpoena that is not complied with or to review any refusal to issue a subpoena. Such decisions may not be further appealed except as part of a final decision that is subject to judicial review. Such hearing officers are empowered to order the amendment of such determination or records as is required to make them accurate and consistent with the requirements of this chapter or the regulations promulgated hereunder. If, after hearing the facts of the case, the hearing officer determines that the person who is the subject of the report has presented information that was not available to the local department at the time of the local conference and which if available may have resulted in a different determination by the local department, he may remand the case to the local department for reconsideration. The local department shall have fourteen days in which to reconsider the case. If, at the expiration of fourteen days, the local department fails to act or fails to amend the record to the satisfaction of the appellant, the case shall be returned to the hearing officer for a determination. If aggrieved by the decision of the hearing officer, such person may obtain further review of the decision in accordance with Article 4 (§9-6.14:15 et seq.) of the Administrative Process Act.

C. Whenever an appeal of the local department's finding is made and a criminal charge is also filed against the appellant for the same conduct involving the same victim as investigated by the local department, the appeal process shall automatically be stayed until the criminal prosecution in circuit court is completed. During such stay, the appellant's right of access to the records of the local department regarding the matter being appealed shall also be stayed. Once the criminal prosecution in circuit court has been completed, the local department shall advise the appellant in writing of his right to resume his appeal within the time frames provided by law and regulation.

(Chgd. by L.1995 ch. 7, eff. 7/1/95.)

§63.1-248.6:2. Tape recording child abuse investigations.

Any person who is suspected of abuse or neglect of a child and who is the subject of an investigation or family assessment pursuant to this chapter may tape record any communications between him and child protective services personnel which take place during the course of such investigation or family assessment, provided all parties to the conversation are aware the conversation is to be recorded. The parties' knowledge of the recording shall be demonstrated by a declaration at the beginning of the recorded portion of the conversation that the recording is to be made. If a person who is suspected of abuse or neglect of a child and who is the subject of an investigation or family assessment

pursuant to this chapter elects to make a tape recording as provided in this section, the child protective services personnel may also make such a recording.
(Chgd. by L.2000 ch. 500, eff. 7/1/2000.)

§63.1-248.7. Establishment of Child-Protective Services Unit; duties.

There is created a Child-Protective Services Unit in the Department of Social Services which shall have the following powers and duties:

1. To evaluate and strengthen all local, regional and state programs dealing with child abuse and neglect.
2. To assume primary responsibility for directing the planning and funding of child-protective services. This shall include reviewing and approving the annual proposed plans and budgets for protective services submitted by the local departments.
3. To assist in developing programs aimed at discovering and preventing the many factors causing child abuse and neglect.
4. To prepare and disseminate, including the presentation of, educational programs and materials on child abuse and neglect.
5. To provide educational programs for professionals required by law to make reports under this chapter.
6. To establish standards of training and provide educational programs to qualify workers in the field of child-protective services.
7. To establish standards of training and educational programs to qualify workers to determine whether complaints of abuse or neglect of a child in a private or state-operated hospital, institution or other facility, or public school, are founded.
8. To maintain staff qualified pursuant to State Board regulations to assist local department personnel in determining whether an employee of a private or state-operated hospital, institution or other facility or an employee of a school board, abused or neglected a child in such hospital, institution, or other facility, or public school.
9. To monitor the processing and determination of cases where an employee of a private or state-operated hospital, institution or other facility, or an employee of a school board, is suspected of abusing or neglecting a child in such hospital, institution, or other facility, or public school.
10. To help coordinate child-protective services at the state, regional, and local levels with the efforts of other state and voluntary social, medical and legal agencies.
11. To maintain a Child Abuse and Neglect Information System that includes all cases of child abuse and neglect within the Commonwealth.
12. To provide for methods to preserve the confidentiality of all records in order to protect the rights of the child, his parents or guardians.

(Chgd. by L.2000 ch. 500, eff. 7/1/2000.)

§63.1-248.7:1. State Board of Social Services oversight duties.

The State Board shall be responsible for establishing standards for out-of-family investigations and family assessments. The State Board shall establish an advisory committee including, but not limited to, representatives of the following types of organizations or groups: public school employees, a hospital for children, a licensed child care center, a juvenile detention home, a public or private residential facility for children, a family day care home, a local department of social services, a religious organization with a program for children, and Virginians for Child Abuse Prevention. The Chairman of the State Board shall appoint such persons for terms established by the Board. The committee shall advise the State Board on the effectiveness of the policies and standards governing out-of-family investigations and family assessments.
(Chgd. by L.2000 ch. 500, eff. 7/1/2000.)

§63.1-248.7:2. Background check required; residential facilities for juveniles.

A. As a condition of employment, volunteering or providing services on a regular basis, every residential facility for juveniles which is regulated or operated by the Department of Social Services, the Department of Education, or the Department of Mental Health, Mental Retardation and Substance Abuse Services shall require any individual who (i) accepts a position of employment at such a facility who was not employed by that facility prior to July 1, 1994, (ii) volunteers for such a facility on a regular basis and will be alone with a juvenile in the performance of his duties who was not a volunteer at such facility prior to July 1, 1994, or (iii) provides contractual services directly to a juvenile for such facility on a regular basis and will be alone with a juvenile in the performance of his duties who did not provide such services prior to July 1, 1994; to submit to fingerprinting and to provide personal descriptive information, to be forwarded along with the applicant's fingerprints through the Central Criminal Records Exchange to the Federal Bureau of Investigation for the purpose of obtaining criminal history record information regarding such applicant. The residential facility shall inform the applicant that he is entitled to obtain a copy of any background check report and to challenge the accuracy and completeness of any such report and obtain a prompt resolution before a final determination is made of the applicant's fitness to have responsibility for the safety and well-being of children. The applicant shall provide the residential facility with a written statement or affirmation disclosing whether he has ever been convicted of or is the subject of pending charges for any offense within or outside the Commonwealth. Prior to permitting an applicant to begin his duties, the residential facility shall obtain the statement or affirmation from the applicant and shall submit the applicant's fingerprints and personal descriptive information to the Central Criminal Records Exchange.

The Central Criminal Records Exchange, upon receipt of an individual's record or notification that no record exists, shall forward it to the state agency which operates or regulates the facility with which the applicant is affiliated. The state agency shall, upon receipt of an applicant's record lacking disposition data, conduct research in whatever state and local record-keeping systems are available in order to obtain complete data. The state agency shall report to the facility whether the applicant meets the criteria to have responsibility for the safety and well-being of children based on whether or not the applicant has ever been convicted of or is the subject of pending charges for the following crimes: murder as set out in Article 1 (§18.2-30 et seq.) of Chapter 4 of Title 18.2, abduction for immoral purposes as set out in §18.2-48, assault and bodily wounding as set out in Article 4 (§18.2-51 et seq.)of Chapter 4 of Title 18.2, robbery as set out in §18.2-58, extortion by threat as set out in §18.2-60, sexual assault as set out in Article 7 (§18.2-61 et seq.) of Chapter 4 of Title 18.2, arson as set out in Article 1 (§18.2-77 et seq.) of Chapter 5 of Title 18.2, burglary as set out in Article 2 (§18.2-89 et seq.) of Chapter 5 of Title 18.2, possession or distribution of drugs as set out in Article 1 (§18.2-247 et seq.) of Chapter 7 of Title 18.2, pandering as set out in §18.2-355, crimes against nature involving children as set out §18.2-361, taking indecent liberties with children as set out in §18.2-370 or §18.2-370.1, abuse and neglect of children as set out in §18.2-371.1, failure to secure medical attention for an injured child as set out in §18.2-314, obscenity offenses as set out in §18.2-374.1, abuse and neglect of incapacitated adults as set out in §18.2-369, employing or permitting a minor to assist in an act constituting an offense under Article 5 of Chapter 8 of Title 18.2, as set out in §18.2-379, or an equivalent offense in another state. If the applicant is denied employment, or the opportunity to volunteer or provide services at a facility because of information appearing on his criminal history record, and the applicant disputes the information upon which the denial was based, upon written request of the applicant the state agency shall furnish the applicant the procedures for obtaining his criminal history record from the Federal Bureau of Investigation. If the applicant has been permitted to provide services pending receipt of the report, the residential facility is not precluded from suspending the applicant from his position or denying the applicant unsupervised access to clients pending a final determination of the applicant's fitness to have responsibility for the safety and well-being of children. The information provided to the facility shall not be disseminated except as provided in this section.

B. Those individuals listed in clauses (i), (ii) and (iii) of subsection A shall also authorize the facility to obtain a copy of information from the central registry maintained pursuant to §63.1-248.8 on any investigation of child abuse or neglect undertaken on him. The applicant shall provide the residential facility with a written statement or affirmation disclosing whether he has ever been the subject of a founded case of child abuse or neglect within or outside the Commonwealth. The facility shall submit the request for information to the central registry prior to permitting an applicant to begin his duties. The facility shall obtain a copy of the information from the central registry within twenty-one days of the applicant beginning his duties. The provisions of this subsection also shall apply to every residential facility for juveniles which is regulated or operated by the Department of Juvenile Justice.

C. The Boards of Social Services, Education, Juvenile Justice and Mental Health, Mental Retardation and Substance Abuse Services may promulgate regulations to comply with the provisions of this section. Copies of any information received by a facility pursuant to this section shall be available to the agency that regulates or operates the facility but shall not be disseminated further. The cost of obtaining the criminal history record and the central registry information shall be borne by the employee or volunteer unless the juvenile facility, at its option, decides to pay the cost.

(Chgd. by L.1996 ch. 747, eff. 7/1/96.)

§63.1-248.8. Central registry; disclosure of information.

The central registry shall contain such information as shall be prescribed by State Board regulation; however, when the founded case of abuse or neglect does not name the parents or guardians of the child as the abuser or neglector, and the abuse or neglect occurred in a licensed or unlicensed child day center, a regulated family day home, a private or public school, a child-caring institution or a residential facility for juveniles, the child's name shall not be entered on the registry without consultation with and permission of the parents or guardians. If a child's name currently appears on the registry without consultation with and permission of the parents or guardians for a founded case of abuse and neglect that does not name the parents or guardians of the child as the abuser or neglector, such parents or guardians may have the child's name removed by written request to the Department. The information contained in the central registry shall not be open to inspection by the public. However, appropriate disclosure may be made in accordance with State Board regulations.

The Department shall respond to requests made by local school boards, pursuant to §22.1-296.4, in cases where there is no match within the central registry regarding applicants for employment within ten business days of receipt of such requests. In cases where there is a match within the central registry regarding applicants for employment, the Department of Social Services shall respond to requests made by local school boards within thirty business days of receipt of such requests. The response may be by first-class mail or facsimile transmission.

Any central registry check of a person who has applied to be a volunteer with a Virginia affiliate of Big Brothers/Big Sisters of America, volunteer fire company or volunteer rescue squad, or with a court-appointed special advocate program pursuant to §9-173.8 shall be conducted at no charge.

(Chgd. by L.2000 chs. 95, 734, 805, eff. 7/1/2000.)

§63.1-248.9. Authority to take child into custody.

A. A physician or protective service worker of a local department or law-enforcement official investigating a report or complaint of abuse and neglect may take a child into custody for up to seventy-two hours without prior approval of parents or guardians provided:

1. The circumstances of the child are such that continuing in his place of residence or in the care or custody of the parent, guardian, custodian or other person responsible for the child's care, presents an imminent danger to the child's life or health to the extent that severe or irremediable injury would be likely to result or if evidence of abuse is perishable or subject to deterioration before a hearing can be held; and
2. A court order is not immediately obtainable; and
3. The court has set up procedures for placing such children; and
4. Following taking the child into custody, the parents or guardians are notified as soon as practicable that he is in custody; and
5. A report is made to the local department; and
6. The court is notified and the person or agency taking custody of such child obtains, as soon as possible, but in no event later than seventy-two hours, an emergency removal order pursuant to §16.1-251; however, if a preliminary removal order is issued after a hearing held in accordance with §16.1-252 within seventy-two hours of the removal of the child, an emergency removal order shall not be necessary.

B. If the seventy-two-hour period for holding a child in custody and for obtaining a preliminary or emergency removal order expires on a Saturday, Sunday, or other legal holiday, the seventy-two hours shall be extended to the next day that is not a Saturday, Sunday, or other legal holiday, but in no event shall either such period exceed ninety-six hours.

(Chgd. by L.1998 ch. 760, eff. 7/1/98.)

§63.1-248.10. Authority to talk to child or sibling.

Any person required to make a report or conduct an investigation or family assessment, pursuant to this chapter may talk to any child suspected of being abused or neglected or to any of his siblings without consent of and outside the presence of his parent, guardian, legal custodian, or other person standing in loco parentis, or school personnel.

(Chgd. by L.2000 ch. 500, eff. 7/1/2000.)

§63.1-248.11. Physician-patient and husband-wife privileges inapplicable.

In any legal proceeding resulting from the filing of any report or complaint pursuant to this chapter, the physician-patient and husband-wife privileges shall not apply.

§63.1-248.13. Photographs and X–rays of child; use as evidence.

In any case of suspected child abuse, photographs and X–rays of said child may be taken without the consent of the parent or other person responsible for such child as a part of the medical evaluation. Photographs of said child may also be taken without the consent of the parent or other person responsible for such child as a part of the investigation or family assessment of the case by the local department or the juvenile and domestic relations district court; provided, however, that such photographs shall not be used in lieu of medical evaluation. Such photographs and X–rays may be introduced into evidence in any subsequent proceeding.

The court receiving such evidence may impose such restrictions as to the confidentiality of photographs of any minor as it deems appropriate.

(Chgd. by L.1996 ch. 616; L.2000 ch. 500, eff. 7/1/2000.)

§63.1-248.13:1. Testimony by child using two-way closed-circuit television.

A. In any civil proceeding involving alleged abuse or neglect of a child pursuant to this chapter or pursuant to §§16.1-241, 16.1-251, 16.1-252, 16.1-253, 16.1-283 or §20-107.2, the child's attorney or guardian ad litem or, if the child has been committed to the custody of the Department of Social Services, the attorney for the local Department of Social Services may apply for an order from the court that the testimony of the alleged victim or of a child witness be taken in a room outside the courtroom and be televised by two-way closed-circuit television. The person seeking such order shall apply for the order at least seven days before the trial date.

A1. The provisions of this section shall apply to the following:

1. An alleged victim who was fourteen years of age or under on the date of the alleged offense and is sixteen or under at the time of the trial; and

2. Any child witness who is fourteen years of age or under at the time of the trial.

B. The court may order that the testimony of the child be taken by closed-circuit television as provided in subsections A and A1 if it finds that the child is unavailable to testify in open court in the presence of the defendant, the jury, the judge, and the public, for any of the following reasons:

1. The child's persistent refusal to testify despite judicial requests to do so;

2. The child's substantial inability to communicate about the offense; or

3. The substantial likelihood, based upon expert opinion testimony, that the child will suffer severe emotional trauma from so testifying.

Any ruling on the child's unavailability under this subsection shall be supported by the court with findings on the record or with written findings in a court not of record.

C. In any proceeding in which closed-circuit television is used to receive testimony, the attorney for the child and the defendant's attorney and, if the child has been committed to the custody of the Department of Social Services, the attorney for the local Department of Social Services shall be present in the room with the child, and the child shall be subject to direct and cross-examination. The only other persons allowed to be present in the room with the child during his testimony shall be the guardian ad litem, those persons necessary to operate the closed-circuit equipment, and any other person whose presence is determined by the court to be necessary to the welfare and well-being of the child.

D. The child's testimony shall be transmitted by closed-circuit television into the courtroom for the defendant, jury, judge and public to view. The defendant shall be provided with a means of private, contemporaneous communication with his attorney during the testimony.

(Chgd. by L.1999 ch. 668, eff. 7/1/99.)

§63.1-248.13:2. Admission of evidence of sexual acts with children.

A. In any civil proceeding involving alleged abuse or neglect of a child pursuant to this chapter or pursuant to §§16.1-241, 16.1-251, 16.1-252, 16.1-253, 16.1-283 or §20-107.2, an out-of-court statement made by a child the age of twelve or under at the time the statement is offered into evidence, describing any act of a sexual nature performed with or on the child by another, not otherwise admissible by statute or rule, may be admissible in evidence if the requirements of subsection B are met.

B. An out-of-court statement may be admitted into evidence as provided in subsection A if:

1. The child testifies at the proceeding, or testifies by means of a videotaped deposition or closed-circuit television, and at the time of such testimony is subject to cross-examination concerning the out-of-court statement or the child is found by the court to be unavailable to testify on any of these grounds:

(a) The child's death;

(b) The child's absence from the jurisdiction, provided such absence is not for the purpose of preventing the availability of the child to testify;

(c) The child's total failure of memory;

(d) The child's physical or mental disability;

(e) The existence of a privilege involving the child;

(f) The child's incompetency, including the child's inability to communicate about the offense because of fear or a similar reason; and

(g) The substantial likelihood, based upon expert opinion testimony, that the child would suffer severe emotional trauma from testifying at the proceeding or by means of a videotaped deposition or closed-circuit television.

2. The child's out-of-court statement is shown to possess particularized guarantees of trustworthiness and reliability.

C. A statement may not be admitted under this section unless the proponent of the statement notifies the adverse party of his intention to offer the statement and the substance of the statement sufficiently in advance of the proceedings to provide the adverse party with a reasonable opportunity to prepare to meet the statement, including the opportunity to subpoena witnesses.

D. In determining whether a statement possesses particularized guarantees of trustworthiness and reliability under subdivision B 2, the court shall consider, but is not limited to, the following factors:

1. The child's personal knowledge of the event;

2. The age and maturity of the child;

3. Certainty that the statement was made, including the credibility of the person testifying about the statement and any apparent motive such person may have to falsify or distort the event including bias, corruption or coercion;

4. Any apparent motive the child may have to falsify or distort the event, including bias, corruption, or coercion;

5. The timing of the child's statement;

6. Whether more than one person heard the statement;

7. Whether the child was suffering pain or distress when making the statement;

8. Whether the child's age makes it unlikely that the child fabricated a statement that represents a graphic, detailed account beyond the child's knowledge and experience;

9. Whether the statement has internal consistency or coherence, and uses terminology appropriate to the child's age;

10. Whether the statement is spontaneous or directly responsive to questions;

11. Whether the statement is responsive to suggestive or leading questions; and

12. Whether extrinsic evidence exists to show the defendant's opportunity to commit the act complained of in the child's statement.

E. The court shall support with findings on the record, or with written findings in a court not of record, any rulings pertaining to the child's unavailability and the trustworthiness and reliability of the out-of-court statement.

§63.1-248.13:3. Use of videotaped statements of complaining witnesses as evidence.

A. In any civil proceeding involving alleged abuse or neglect of a child pursuant to this chapter or pursuant to §§16.1-241, 16.1-251, 16.1-252, 16.1-253, 16.1-283 or §20-107.2, a recording of a statement of the alleged victim of the offense, made prior to the proceeding, may be admissible as evidence if the requirements of subsection B are met and the court determines that:

1. The alleged victim is the age of twelve or under at the time the statement is offered into evidence;

2. The recording is both visual and oral, and every person appearing in, and every voice recorded on, the tape is identified;

3. The recording is on videotape or was recorded by other electronic means capable of making an accurate recording;

4. The recording has not been altered;

5. No attorney for any party to the proceeding was present when the statement was made;

6. The person conducting the interview of the alleged victim was authorized to do so by the child-protective services coordinator of the local department of welfare or social services;

7. All persons present at the time the statement was taken, including the alleged victim, are present and available to testify or be cross-examined at the proceeding when the recording is offered; and

8. The parties or their attorneys were provided with a list of all persons present at the recording and were afforded an opportunity to view the recording at least ten days prior to the scheduled proceedings.

B. A recorded statement may be admitted into evidence as provided in subsection A if:

1. The child testifies at the proceeding, or testifies by means of closed-circuit television, and at the time of such testimony is subject to cross-examination concerning the recorded statement or the child is found by the court to be unavailable to testify on any of these grounds:

(a) The child's death;

(b) The child's absence from the jurisdiction, provided such absence is not for the purpose of preventing the availability of the child to testify;

(c) The child's total failure of memory;

(d) The child's physical or mental disability;

(e) The existence of a privilege involving the child;

(f) The child's incompetency, including the child's inability to communicate about the offense because of fear or a similar reason;

(g) The substantial likelihood, based upon expert opinion testimony, that the child would suffer severe emotional trauma from testifying at the proceeding or by means of closed-circuit television; and

2. The child's recorded statement is shown to possess particularized guarantees of trustworthiness and reliability.

C. A recorded statement may not be admitted under this section unless the proponent of the statement notifies the adverse party of his intention to offer the statement and the substance of the statement sufficiently in advance of the proceedings to provide the adverse party with a reasonable opportunity to prepare to meet the statement, including the opportunity to subpoena witnesses.

D. In determining whether a recorded statement possesses particularized guarantees of trustworthiness and reliability under subdivision B 2, the court shall consider, but is not limited to, the following factors:

1. The child's personal knowledge of the event;

2. The age and maturity of the child;

3. Any apparent motive the child may have to falsify or distort the event, including bias, corruption, or coercion;

4. The timing of the child's statement;

5. Whether the child was suffering pain or distress when making the statement;

6. Whether the child's age makes it unlikely that the child fabricated a statement that represents a graphic, detailed account beyond the child's knowledge and experience;

7. Whether the statement has a "ring of verity," has internal consistency or coherence, and uses terminology appropriate to the child's age;

8. Whether the statement is spontaneous or directly responsive to questions;

9. Whether the statement is responsive to suggestive or leading questions; and

10. Whether extrinsic evidence exists to show the defendant's opportunity to commit the act complained of in the child's statement.

E. The court shall support with findings on the record, or with written findings in a court not of record, any rulings pertaining to the child's unavailability and the trustworthiness and reliability of the recorded statement.

§63.1-248.14. Court may order certain examinations.

The court may order psychological, psychiatric and physical examinations of the child alleged to be abused or neglected and of the parents, guardians, caretakers or siblings of a child suspected of being neglected or abused.

§63.1-248.15. Prima facie evidence for removal of child custody.

In the case of a petition in the court for removal of custody of a child alleged to have been abused or neglected, competent evidence by a physician that a child is abused or neglected shall constitute prima facie evidence to support such petition.

§63.1-248.16. Advisory Committee continued as Advisory Board.

The Advisory Committee on Child Abuse and Neglect is continued and shall hereafter be known as the Advisory Board on Child Abuse and Neglect. The Advisory Board shall be composed of nine persons appointed by the Governor for three-year staggered terms, and permanent members including the Superintendent of Public Instruction, the Commissioner of the Department of Health, the Commissioner of the Department of Mental Health, Mental Retardation and Substance Abuse Services, the Commissioner of the Department of Social Services, the Director of the Department of Juvenile Justice, the Director of the Department of Corrections, the Director of the Department of Criminal Justice Services, and the Attorney General of Virginia, or their designees. The Advisory Board shall meet quarterly and as the need may arise, to advise the Department, Board of Social Services and Governor on matters concerning programs for the prevention and treatment of abused and neglected children and their families.

§63.1-248.17. Cooperation by state entities.

All law-enforcement departments and other state and local departments, agencies, authorities and institutions shall cooperate with each child-protective services coordinator of a local department and any multi-discipline teams in the detection and prevention of child abuse.

§63.1-248.18. *(Chgd. by L.2000 ch. 482, eff. 7/1/2000. Repealed by L.2000 ch. 500, eff. 7/1/2000.)*

§63.1-248.19. Evaluation of the child protective services differential response system.

The Department shall evaluate and report on the impact and effectiveness of the implementation of the child protective services differential response system in meeting the purposes set forth in this chapter. The evaluation shall include, but is not limited to, the following information: changes in the number of investigations, the number of families receiving services, the number of families rejecting services, the impact on out-of-home placements, the availability of needed services, community cooperation, successes and problems encountered, the overall operation of the child protective services differential response system and recommendations for improvement. The Department shall submit annual reports to the House Committee on Health, Welfare and Institutions and the Senate Committee on Rehabilitation and Social Services.

(Added by L.2000 ch. 500, eff. 7/1/2000.)

VIRGINIA CRIMINAL LAW AND MOTOR VEHICLE HANDBOOK – INDEX

(Unless otherwise noted, all references are to sections of the Code of Virginia.)

Zv

 Zv

 Zv

 Zv

 Zv

 Zv

 Zv

 Zv

 Zv

 Zv

 Zv

 Zv

 Zv

 Zv

 Zv

 Zv

 Zv

 Zv

 Zv

 Zv

NOTES

NOTES

NOTES

NOTES

GOULD'S QUICK FIND LOCATOR™

HOW TO USE: Bend the edge and follow the arrow to the corresponding black mark.